Reader's Guide to the

SOCIAL SCIENCES

Volume 1

EDITORIAL ADVISORY COMMITTEE

Reader's Guide to the

SOCIAL SCIENCES

Volume 1

Editor

JONATHAN MICHIE

FITZROY DEARBORN PUBLISHERS
LONDON · CHICAGO

**British Library and Library of Congress Cataloguing in Publication Data
are available**

ISBN 1-57958-091-2

First published in the USA and UK 2001

Typeset by Florence Production Ltd, Stoodleigh, Devon

Cover design by Hybert Design

Cover image: from Sigmund Freud's manuscript of *Das Ich und das Es*
(1923; *The Ego and the Id,* 1927)

CONTENTS

EDITOR'S NOTE

Aims, Scope, and Selection of Entries

The aim of the *Reader's Guide the Social Sciences* is to do exactly what its title promises — to guide the reader towards the key texts on specific topics. The individual entries present and critically review the literature on a range of topics from the social sciences. In almost all cases the references given will themselves cite a huge number of additional references, so what is provided here will serve as a useful springboard for any literature search. This is not, then, an encyclopedia. The entries do not attempt to describe and discuss the actual topics in any great depth; rather, they aim to point the reader to the publications where this is done, including in some cases to encyclopedia entries or to more substantive literature surveys on the topics. Indeed, there are many topics that one would expect to find included in an encyclopedia but on which there is not actually a distinct literature, and so these were not included in this *Reader's Guide*. This is a *Reader's Guide* to the literature.

The term "Social Sciences" encompasses a huge range of academic disciplines and subject areas. This *Reader's Guide* concentrates on economics; political economy; politics; sociology; law; management and business; psychology and organizational psychology; organizational behaviour; human geography; international relations; and research and analysis methods in the social sciences. A few topics are included from other subject areas where these overlap with the major disciplines chosen, for example philosophy and social anthropology.

The authors were asked to select the texts and devise their entries so as to be useful to students or researchers beginning a literature search, and to teachers and lecturers constructing reading lists. The volume of secondary material now available is often overwhelming, and these entries provide expert guidance to and critical analysis of selected texts, to assist in the selection of the most appropriate books for research and study.

In addition to the standard length entries, we commissioned major "survey" entries on each of the subject areas that the *Reader's Guide* covers, and an additional survey of the history and development of the social sciences. These surveys act as large-scale maps enabling readers to put the standard length entries into context, to understand the historical development of the discipline, and to appreciate key controversies and points of departure between different schools of thought.

The literature on many of the subjects covered will overlap, for example on the European Union and on European Monetary Union. We have therefore included *see also* notes at the end of many of the entries, to related entries whose selected texts will also be of relevance. The relationships among the entries may also be examined in the Thematic List.

Arrangement of Entries

Entries appear in alphabetical order. A complete list of these can be found in the Alphabetical List of Entries (p. xvii). Where there are entries sharing the same general heading (e.g. Politics), the order does not normally proceed alphabetically. Where there is a "General" entry in such a group, it is always placed first. In cases where these principles offer no guidance, alphabetical order is followed.

Thus although the overall arrangement of entries is alphabetical, the *Reader's Guide* contains various aides to facilitate access to its contents. These are:

1. Thematic List (p. xxix). This list should be consulted to see the full range of entries that relate to a particular subject area. The list is more detailed than simply the subject areas listed above, such as "economics", and instead groups the entries further by theme, such as macroeconomics and labour economics.
2. Booklist Index (p. 1781 in volume 2). This lists, in alphabetical order, the authors of all books and articles discussed in the entries and can be used to locate discussions of the work of particular scholars.
3. General Index (p. 1943 in volume 2). This lists individuals, topics, and particular works mentioned in the entries. The index will be particularly useful for locating references to individuals or topics that have no entry of their own.
4. *See also* notes. These appear at the end of many of the entries and refer the reader to entries on related topics.

Format within Entries

Each entry begins with a list of the books or articles to be discussed in the essay. Complete publication details are provided, including dates of the first publication and, where appropriate, the most recent revised edition. Reprints and paperback editions are normally omitted unless the original publication is more than 50 years old. Most entries begin with a short introduction that either gives an overview of the subject or discusses the issues on which scholars have focused. In the text of each essay, the first significant mention of each publication is indicated by the appearance of the author's name in capital letters. In cases where more than one book by the same author is discussed in the same entry, dates in parentheses are used to distinguish the publications. Although the list of books in each entry proceeds in alphabetical order, the books are not normally discussed in that order in the text. It was left to the judgement of contributors to decide whether to discuss books in order of publication or, more often, according to the subject matter and emphasis of each book.

Acknowledgements

I am extremely grateful to a number of friends and colleagues for assisting with this project. The main thanks must go to Carol Jones. First she was an outstanding student at Cambridge University. Next she was an excellent Research Officer at the Judge Institute of Management Studies at Cambridge, working with me on the Economic and Social Research Council's "Contracts & Competition" programme, as well as on an EU-funded series of Euroconferences. She was unflappable, even when it came to pay for the conference dinner on a boat in Rome when we discovered they did not take credit cards and I had inadvertently spent the conference dinner money the previous evening. When Carol moved from Cambridge to London she resigned her Judge Institute post to work as a Commissioning Editor at Fitzroy Dearborn, from where she persuaded me to work with her on this *Reader's Guide*. I doubt that there is anyone else who would have succeeded in persuading me to take it on; in the case of Carol I knew that she would do the bulk of the work and do it faultlessly. This she did, before then moving on to found and run an internet gardening business. It would be bordering on the perfunctory simply to include Carol amongst the acknowledgements, and so I would like also to dedicate the *Reader's Guide* to her. This is particularly appropriate since a large number of the Advisers and authors have also enjoyed working with Carol on this as well as other projects, from my Judge Institute colleague Dr Jane Collier who recommended Carol to me for the Research Officer post, to Professor Daniele Archibugi, sometime visitor at the Judge Institute and saviour regarding the unpayable bill on the boat in Rome.

I was fortunate that all the Fitzroy Dearborn staff did an excellent job on the *Reader's Guide* from start to finish, from Daniel Kirkpatrick through to Gillian Lindsey who took over from Carol in the final year of the project, organizing and stewarding it through to completion.

I am grateful to all the Advisers for their work in suggesting topics and authors, and for stepping in when necessary to write entries themselves. Particular thanks in this regard are due to Professor Ilene Grabel, Dr Sarah Kay McDonald and Professor Vishnu Padayachee.

I am also grateful to all the authors and in particular those who stepped into the breach, either to write the entries that no one else would, or to cover for people who said they would but did not deliver.

I am especially grateful to colleagues at Birkbeck College, including Professor David Guest and Dr Jenny Kidd for advice on Organizational Psychology, Elaine Macdonald for providing an entry at the same time as doing a more than full-time Research Officer's job, lecturing, assisting with conference organizing and researching for a PhD over the weekends, Professor Ron Smith for assisting with an entry that had failed to materialize on the deadline, and Steve Warby. Particular thanks for just making Birkbeck such an efficient and enjoyable place to work are due to Sally Bland, Jenny Cook, Sally Pierson and Lee Shailer.

Finally I would like as always to thank my wife Carolyn Downs and sons Alex and Duncan Michie for all their love and support.

JONATHAN MICHIE
September 2000

ADVISERS AND CONTRIBUTORS

Lina Abirafeh
Peter Alldridge
Scott Allen
Jonathan E. Alltimes
Morris Altman
Dibyesh Anand
Paul Anand
John Anchor
Steve Anderman
Birgitte Andersen
David Andress
Neil Andrews
Svetlana Andrianova
Helmut Anheier
Nicholas Apergis
Daniele Archibugi
Philip Arestis
Nick Armstrong
Mak Arvin
Bjørn Asheim
Adam Atherly
Mary Welek Atwell
Robert Ausch
Roger E. Backhouse
Jeff Baenziger
Bruce C. Bain
Matt Baird
Suzanne Baker
Terence Ball
Paul F. Ballantyne
Kimberley Balsam
Armando Barrientos
John Barry
Dean Bartlett
Will Bartlett
Peter E. Bastian
Athina Nicolaides Bastien
William J. Baumol
Philip Bean
Arjun Singh Bedi
Bernard C. Beins
Robert Bennett III

Thomas W. Bennett
Kenneth R. Benoit
Joy K. Benson
Kristina Bentley
Manfred Max Bergman
Michael Berheide
Michael Beverland
Colin Bird
Terry G. Birtles
Brian Bix
David Black
Robert A. Black
Richard Bloom
Herbert H. Blumberg
Martin Boddy
Klaus Bosselmann
Frank Boyd
Simon Boyes
D. Brent Smith
David L. Brunsma
Peter Buckley
Kurt Bumby
Brendan Burchell
Ross Burkhart
Judith Burnett
John Callaghan
Fiona K. Campbell
Kevin Campbell
Andrew Cardow
Andrew P. Carlin
Garry D. Carnegie
Patricia Carr
Adrian N. Carr
Lysiane Cartelier
Bob Carter
Michael Carter
Shani D. Carter
Peter Casson
Susan Turnbull Caton
Martin Cave
Adrian Chan
Elizabeth Chapman

H. Lee Cheek Jr
Pei-Yao Chen
Mary Childs
George Cho
George A. Christodoulakis
Victor V. Claar
Graham Clarke
Harry Clarke
Kate Clegg
David Coates
Jane Collier
Antony Colombo
Thomas M. Conroy
Alexandra Cook
Elizabeth Cooke
John Corcoran
Philip J. Corr
Thomas Coskeran
Anna Coveney
Helen Cowie
Marco Crocco
Charles Crothers
David Crowther
Philip L. Culbertson
Parviz Dabir-Alai
Richard Dagger
Wendy A. Darr
Joyce Davidson
Huw T.O. Davies
Scott Alan Davies
Colin Dawson
Sandra Dawson
Michael P. Dean
Sally Dear
Frédéric Declerck
Chantal Deines
Panicos O. Demetriades
Sanjit Dhami
Julie Dickinson
Robert Dimand
Brian Dirck
Andrew Dobson
Lynn Dobson
Klaus Dodds
Brian Doherty
John P. Donnelly
Peter E. Doolittle
Mohammed Dore
Peter Dorey
Pamela Downe
Michael Drake
Ciaran Driver
Windy Dryden
L.A. Duhs
Bethany K. Dumas
Nigel Dunnett
Jillian Dutton
Gary A. Dymski
Alexander Ebner
Robert J. Edelmann

Peter W. Edge
Steve Edgell
Charles Edquist
Richard Ekins
Howard Elcock
Mary Ann Elston
Paul Englert
Leona M. English
Prescott C. Ensign
Stephen Evans
Stephen Farrall
Bassam Fattouh
Dietrich K. Fausten
Patty Ferguson
Dyanne J. Ferk
Paul Finkelman
Frank Fisher
Tony Fitzpatrick
V.G. Fitzsimons
Gregory L. Flanagan
Robert L. Flood
David Floyd
Simon Folkard
Liz Forbat
Evelyn Forget
Laura Foster
Vojmir Franičević
Mark Franklin
Fay Fransella
David W. Frantz
Bill Freund
Jeff Freyman
Steve Fuller
Libon Fung
Jonathan Gabe
Kathleen Gabelmann
Jean-Luc Gaffard
Christopher Gale
Daniel J. Gallagher
Thomas P. Gallanis
Chris Game
Mike Gane
Penny Gardiner
Mark Garner
Virginia C. Mueller Gathercole
Alan James Geare
Christian Gehrke
M. Anne George
Donald A.R. George
Alan Gilbert
Evan Gilbert
David E.A. Giles
Richard William Girling
Andrew Glyn
Jerold R. Gold
Raymond E. Goodman
Phil Goodwin
John Goodwin
Barry Goss
Ilene Grabel

Norman Graves
Ellen Gredley
Michael Green
Richard Green
Stuart P. Green
Edwin Greenlee
Dylan Griffiths
Nigel Grimwade
Michael Grojean
Edward Gross
Francesco Guala
Nigel Guenole
Cherif Guermat
David Guest
Baogang Guo
Carol Guthrie
Frederick Guy
Adam Habib
Kaddour Hadri
Ralph Hall
Douglas Hamilton
James Hampshire
Kathy A. Hanisch
Jalna Hanmer
G.C. Harcourt
Jane Hardy
Vivienne Harpwood
Mark Harrison
Jeffrey Harrop
Andrew S. Harvey
Bernd Hayo
Daniel Heggs
Gert Hekma
Frank Heller
David Hess
Anthony Heyes
Clive E. Hill
Mils Hills
Andrew Hinde
Colin Hines
Geoffrey Hodgson
M.H. Hoeflich
Karla Hoff
Rosalie Holian
Barbara E. Holler
Georgia Holmes
Susan Horton
Branko Horvat
Brett E. House
Mike Howe
Geraint Howells
Phil Hubbard
Ian Hudson
Maria Hudson
Jane Humphries
Petros Iosifides
Patrick James
Annabelle James
Andrew Jenkins
Shane R. Jimerson

Helen Johnson
Lucy Johnston
Ron Johnston
Therese A. Joiner
Lieven Jonckheere
Carolyn Jones
Fiona Jones
Kenneth Jones
Bruno Jossa
Robert Jupe
George Kadmos
Christopher Kam
Maria Kambouri
Ismo Kantola
Jeffrey Kaplan
Sohbet Karbuz
Nixon Kariithi
Carolyn Kaufman
Nitasha Kaul
Ashraf Kazi
William Keegan
Thomas Keenan
Mike Kennerley
Brian Kenny
Dianna T. Kenny
Gérard Kester
Jennifer M. Kidd
Geoffrey Kiel
Dave King
John E. King
Michael Kitson
Alfred Kleinknecht
George Klosko
George Knysh
Tim Koechlin
Mathias Koenig-Archibugi
Kevin R. Kosar
Kyriakos Kouveliotis
Richard Kramer
Cordula Kropp
Vanya Kumar
Heinz D. Kurz
Christian Lager
Louise Lamontagne
Richard Lampard
Dorothy Lander
David A. Lane
Kim Langfield-Smith
Philip Larkin
Sabina W. Lautensach
Kostas A. Lavdas
Gary Lea
Frederick S. Lee
Martha F. Lee
Simon Lee
Charles Lees
Loretta Lees
Richard A. Leo
Kathryn Levit
Katrien Libbrecht

Jo Lindsay
A. Elizabeth Lindsey
Irwin Lipnowski
Marjorie Lister
Catherine Liston-Heyes
Mary Little
Eric Longley
Francisco Louçã
P. Eric Louw
George Lucki
Ron Lukens-Bull
Bengt-Åke Lundvall
Carmela Lutmar
Robert Lynch
Willem Maas
Kevin Magill
Ann Mahon
Russell Mannion
Donna Marino
Bérengère Marques-Pereira
James Martin
Ron Martin
A.R. Maryanski
Peter Mason
Paul Mastrangelo
Alan Matthews
R.O. Matthews
Suzanne Maurer
Kenneth Mayer
Kevin McCauley
Ray McChesney
Aileen McColgan
John S.L. McCombie
Arthur E. McCullough
Sarah-Kathryn McDonald
Elaine McDonald
Paul McDevitt
Seamus McErlean
Andrew McGee
W.M. McInnes
Marcia J. McKinley-Pace
Robert Mears
Carol Ann Medlicott
Stephen K. Medvic
Geoff Meeks
Fernando Merino
Stan Metcalfe
Laura Methot
Melvina Metochi
Jonathan Michie
Ken Millen-Penn
Edgar Miller
Robert L. Miller
Clare Mills
Seumas Milne
Byung S. Min
Dale Mineshima
Lisle S. Mitchell
H. Lyle Mitchell
William F. Mitchell

Andrew Monk
Beverley M. Moodie
Janet Morrison
Pamela Moss
Tracy Mott
David Lee Muggleton
Mark Mullenbach
Ann Mumford
Lyle Munro
Robin F. Neill
Yew-Kwang Ng
Siang Ng
Trien T. Nguyen
David J. Nightingale
Gavin Nicholson
Nicola Nixon
Dany Nobus
Peter Nolan
Randy Norsworthy
R.D. Norton
Dan O'Donoghue
Lawrence H. Officer
Roderick Ogley
Ayodele Ogundipe
Frances Oldale
Michael J. Oliver
Lutfun N. Khan Osmani
David Oswell
Keith F. Otterbein
Eben Otuteye
R.G. Owens
Vishnu Padayachee
Paul Pagliano
Minu Palani
Glen Palmer
John C. Palmer
Mića Panić
Vassilis Papadakis
Brian Parkinson
Patrick N. Parkinson
Nick Perdikis
Gregory Peter
George A. Petrochilos
Timothy Phillips
Jason L. Pierce
Jennifer Piesse
Christos Pitelis
Vincent Kelly Pollard
Robert Pollin
Leslie Pollock
Pitman Potter
Dominic Power
Marcus Power
Kenneth Prandy
Renée Prendergast
Katherine Presnell
Jeffrey L. Prewitt
Mark Priestley
Anastasia N. Pseiridis
Douglas J. Puffert

Frances Ann Pyne
Allan Quigley
Dave Radlett
Enrique S. Rajchenberg
Luis Moura Ramos
Nigel J. Rapport
John David Rausch Jr
Angelo Reati
Brad Reid
Gerda Reith
Carl W. Roberts
Peri Roberts
Joanne Roberts
Andrew Robinson
Ana Laura Rodriguez-Gusta
Terry Royed
Elisabetta Ruspini
Gerard F. Rutan
Adam Rutland
Thomas K. Rymes
Mike Saks
Neri Salvadori
Stephan M. Salzberg
Roberta Sassatelli
Malcolm Sawyer
Gian Carlo Scarsi
Roberto Scazzieri
William Schabas
Christopher M. Schnaubelt
Ingrid Schoon
Maria Schoonraad
Markus Schulte
Andrea Schuman
Jacqueline L. Scott
Clive Seale
Sunanda Sen
Željko Šević
Hamel Shah
Bhavani Shankar
Steven Sherman
Heling Shi
Arthur B. Shostak
Stephen Shute
Steven D. Silver
Shao-Chee Sim
Avital Simhony
Alan Simon
Ajit Singh
Ajit Sinha
Suzanne Skevington
Catherine Skinner
Roger S. Slack
Denis Smith
Greg Smith
Martin J. Smith
Peter K. Smith
Ron Smith
Kimberlee Snyder
Maureen Spencer
Christina Stanway

John Stapleford
James Steeley
Catherine J. Stevens
Nick Stevenson
David Storey
Charles R. Stowe
Carl Stychin
Cristina Suárez Gálvez
Mangala Subramaniam
Gerald Sullivan
Peter Sutch
Siddharth Swaminathan
G.M. Peter Swann
Michael Tadman
Leigh Tesfatsion
Phyllis Tharenou
Colin Thirtle
Ray Thomas
Grahame F. Thompson
Stuart C. Thomson
Mark Thornton
John J. Tilley
Christis G. Tombazos
Simon Tormey
Keith Trace
Peter Trim
Gordon Tullock
Geoff Turner
Jonathan H. Turner
Denis C.E. Ugwuegbu
Jennifer A. Vadeboncoeur
Romesh Vaitilingam
Michalis Vafopoulos
Cees van Beers
Johan Veldeman
Max Velmans
Paul Verhaeghe
G.N. von Tunzelmann
D. Stephen Voss
Vera Vratusa(-Zunjic)
Faye Linda Wachs
Daniel B. Waggoner
David S. Wall
Greg Wallace
Andrew D. Walsh
Tony Walter
Barbara R. Walters
Steven Warby
Chris Warhurst
Malcolm Warner
Jon Warren
Peter A. Watt
Martin J. Watts
Bruce Wearne
Bart Weathington
Justin Weinberg
W. Michael Weis
Cindy E. Weisbart
Bruce A. Weisse
Gary L. Wells

Robert M. Whaples
Stephen Whittle
Rorden Wilkinson
Alan Williams
Colin Williams
Gareth Williams
Nathan L. Williams
Richard Williams
Lawrence A. Winans
Gorm Winther
Barry Witcher
Elizabeth M.H. Withey-Vandiver
Thomas Wolf
Joel Wolfe
Jennifer Wood
Victor Douglas Wooddell
Myrna Wooders

Robert Woodfield
Adrian Woods
Helen Woolley
David Worland
Danaya C. Wright
Robert E. Wright
Dominic Wring
Helen Xanthaki
Xiaokia Yang
Sung-Kyung Yoo
Paul Zarembka
Harry Zarenda
Steve Zavestoski
Zehava Zevit
Xing Quan Zhang
Yimin Zhao

ALPHABETICAL
LIST OF ENTRIES

THEMATIC LIST

Entries by Category

ECONOMICS
Business and accounting
Economics: general
Economic geography
Economic history
Finance and financial economics
Globalization and international economics
History of economic thought
Industrial economics
Industrial sectors and studies
Innovation studies
Labour economics
Macroeconomic theory and policy
Microeconomic theory and policy
Monetary economics
Political economy
Public economics
Regional economies
Regulation and regulatory economics
Social economics
Statistics, econometrics and methodology

HUMAN GEOGRAPHY
Business and economic geography
Cultural geography
Political and global geography
Regional geography
Urban geography

LAW
Administrative and constitutional law
Business and commercial law
Criminal law
European Union law
History of law
Judicial process
Law and society
Legal theory
National systems of law
Private law
Property law

MANAGEMENT AND BUSINESS
Change management
Financial management
Human resource management
Innovation and entrepreneurship
International business environment
Management and business: general
Marketing management
Operations research and management
Strategic management

ORGANIZATIONAL BEHAVIOUR

PHILOSOPHY

POLITICS AND INTERNATIONAL RELATIONS
Civil rights and liberties
Elections
European politics and policy
Forms and systems of government
History of political thought
International relations
Political history
Political parties and movements
Political philosophy
Political theory
Politics: general
Public administration and public policy

PSYCHOLOGY
Clinical psychology, psychotherapy, psychoanalysis
Cognitive and neuropsychology
Developmental and educational psychology
Forensic psychology
Occupational and organizational psychology
Personality and social psychology
Psychology of sex relations

RESEARCH AND ANALYSIS METHODS IN THE SOCIAL SCIENCES

SOCIOLOGY

Aging and ageism
Community and society
Criminology and sociology of law
Global change and modern societies
Family sociology
Gender studies
History of sociological thought
Politics and power
Race and ethnicity

Slavery, colonialism and imperialism
Social anthropology
Social behaviour
Social organization and stratification
Sociology and medicine
Sociology of culture
Sociology of language
Sociology of religion
Sociology and the environment / and moral protests
Sociological theory
Urban sociology
Work and economic life

Economics

Business and accounting
Accounting, balance sheet
Accounting concepts
Accounting history
Accounting policies
Creative accounting
Financial accounting
Management accounting

Economics: general
Aggregate production function
Anti-trust economics
Business cycles
Catastrophe theory
Competitive strategy
Complexity
Contestable markets
Contracts and competition
Corruption
Decision theory
Deconstruction
Development economics
Diminishing returns
Division of labour, economics
Economic psychology
Economics and biology
Efficient markets hypothesis
Emerging markets
Endogenous growth theory
Expectations
Experimental economics
Externalities
Female employment, developing countries
Feminist economics
Flexible specialization
Growth accounting
Income
Increasing returns
Input-output economics
Instability
Investment

Investments, business
Law and economics
Market failure
Markets
Mesoeconomics
Network externalities
Nonlinear dynamics
Path dependence
Political economy survey
Real business cycles
Savings
Service sector
Shareholder value management
Short termism
Staple theory of economic growth
Thatcher governments' economic record
Total factor productivity
Transaction costs economics
Transport economics
Uncertainty in economics
Venture capital
Wealth, economic

Economic geography
Cities, economics
Demography, economic
Economic geography
Industrial districts
Natural resources
Optimum currency areas and currency unions
Regional development (US)
Regional policy
Third World, economics
Urban economics
Urban entrepreneurialism
Urban petty trading

Economic history
Bretton Woods
Economic history

Economic thought, history of
Economics and history
Gold standard
Golden age of capitalism
Great Depression
Industrial revolution
Long swings in economic activity
Magna Carta

Finance and financial economics
Arbitrage
Arbitrage pricing theory
Banking law, economic
Banks and banking
Capital asset pricing models
Corporate finance
Debt markets
Discounting
Financial deregulation
Financial economics
Financial fragility
Financial globalization and financial integration
Financial services
Futures markets
Insurance
Insurance, economics
Interest rates
Leverage, leveraged buy-outs
Microfinance (Grameen Bank)
Options
Short termism in financial markets
Speculation
Speculative bubbles
Stock markets

Globalization and international economics
Balance of payments
Balance-of-payments constrained growth
Comparative advantage

Competitiveness
Dependency theory
European Monetary System (EMS),
    Exchange Rate Mechanism (ERM)
    and European Monetary Integration
    (EMI)
European Union, economics
European single currency
Exchange rates
Exports and export-led growth
Foreign aid
Foreign direct investment
Free trade
General Agreement on Tariffs and
    Trade (GATT), and World Trade
    Organisation (WTO)
Globalization, economic
Globalization: critiques and
    alternatives
Globalization of technology
Imperialism, economic
Import substitution
International debt crisis
International economics
International Monetary Fund
International trade policy, political
    economy
Multinational corporations
Purchasing power parity
Third World, economics
Tobin tax
Trade and the environment
Trade theory, development of
World systems theory
World Trade Organisation

History of economic thought
Arrow, Kenneth J.
Austrian School
Cambridge controversy
Cambridge School
Capital theory controversy
Chandler, Alfred
Chicago School
Classical economics
Coase, R.H.
Economic methodology
Economic thought, history of
Galbraith, J.K.
Greece (ancient), political economy
Hayek, F.A.
Hicks, John R.
Historical school (German and British)
Kaldor, Nicholas
Kaldor's laws
Kalecki, Michal
Keynes, John Maynard
Keynes' General Theory
Keynesian economics
Kondratiev cycles

Labour theory of value
Malthus, Thomas
Marshall, Alfred
Marx and Marxism
Marxist economics
Materialism
Mathematization of economics
Macroeconomics, post-Keynesian
    microeconomic foundations
Myrdal, Gunnar
Neo-Ricardian economics
Neoclassical economics
Neoclassical-Keynesian synthesis
New classical economics
New industrial economics
New institutionalism, economics
New Keynesian economics
New trade theory
Penrose, Edith
Post-Keynesian economics
Radical economics
Rhetoric of economics
Ricardo, David
Robinson, Joan
Samuelson, Paul A.
Say, J.B.
Say's law
Schumpeter, Joseph
Simon / Shaikh Critique of the
    aggregate production function
Sraffa, Piero
Sraffian economics
Transformation problem
Value
Veblen, Thorstein, economics
Utilitarianism, economic
Wealth of Nations
Weber, Max

Industrial economics
Barriers to entry
Capacity
Industrial districts
Industrial dynamics
Industrial organization
Industrial policy
Industrialism
Mergers and acquisitions
Monopoly
Monopoly capitalism
Monopoly pricing
Networks
Networks of firms
Oligopoly and vertical integration
Ownership and control, divorce
    between
Privatization
Producer cooperatives
Production functions
Rate-of-return regulation

Small and medium-sized enterprises
Theory of production
Theory of the firm

Industrial sectors and studies
Aerospace industry
Agricultural economics
Biotechnology industry
Communications and new media:
    economics, policy and regulation
Computer industry
Defence economics
Electricity industry
Health economics
Information and communication
    technologies
Local government finance
Local government management
Science and technology, economics
Technological capabilities
Technology transfer

Innovation studies
Innovation, economic
Innovation, diffusion of
Learning economy
National systems of innovation
Patents
Research and development (R&D)
Systems of innovation
Technology, economics
Technology transfer

Labour economics
Bargaining, economic
Employee share-ownership plans
Full employment
High performance work systems
Household as an economic agent
Human capital
Labour economics
Labour-managed and participatory
    firms, economics of
Labour market
Labour market flexibility
Labour process
Migration, economic
Minimum wage
Minimum wage (US)
Natural rate of unemployment and
    NAIRU
Part-time employment
Pensions
Phillips curve
Profit sharing
Self-employment
Trade unions, economics
Unemployment, historical experience
Unemployment, international
    experience

Unemployment statistics
Unemployment theories
Unemployment, Keynesian
Unemployment, technological
Wages
Work

Macroeconomic theory and policy
Convergence
Deindustrialization
Demand and supply
Distribution of income
Growth
Macroeconomics
Macroeconomics, post-Keynesian
   microeconomic foundations
Profits
Rent seeking

Microeconomic theory and policy
Adverse selection, incentives
Agency theory, economic
Agent-based computational economics
Auctions
Competition, economic
Consumer behaviour
Contracts, implicit
Cost functions
Economics of information
Economies of scale and scope
Efficiency analysis
Game theory
General equilibrium theory
Individualism and economics
Inflation
Mark-up, post-Keynesian literature
Microeconomics
Microeconomics, post-Keynesian
Moral hazard
Prices and pricing
Profit maximization
Rent
Risk
Stakeholder analysis
X-efficiency

Monetary economics
Monetarism
Monetary policy
Money and finance

Political economy
Accumulation of capital
Capitalism
Political economy survey
Classical economics
Corporate economy
Economic crises
Economics and politics
Hierarchies, economic

Evolution, economic
Fordism
Institutional economics
International trade policy, political
   economy
Market socialism
Planned economy
Post-Fordism
Regimes of accumulation
Resource-based economics
Social ownership
Stakeholder
Trust, economics

Public economics
Central banks
Civil service, economics
Club goods
Coase theorem
Property rights, economic
Public enterprise
Public finance
Public goods
Public ownership
Public sector
Public spending, optimal size
Public choice theory and rational
   expectations
Quasi-markets
Second and third best theories
Supply side economics
Taxation
Third sector economy
Welfare state, economic

Regional economies
Africa, Northern, economy and
   economic record
Asian crisis, 1997–98
Asian developmental state
Asian model of capitalism
Australian economy and economic
   record
Chinese economy and economic record
Developing economies
East Asian economies
Eastern and Central European
   economies in transformation
European Union, economics
French economy and economic record
German economy and economic
   record
Greece (ancient), political economy
Greek economy and economic record
Irish economy and record, Northern
   Ireland
Irish economy and record, Republic of
   Ireland
Islamic economics
Italian economy and economic record

Japanese economy and economic
   record
Latin America, economy and economic
   record
Middle Eastern economies
Newly industrializing countries,
   economics
North American Free Trade Area
   (NAFTA)
Organisation for Economic
   Cooperation and Development
   (OECD)
Organization of Petroleum Exporting
   Countries (OPEC)
Polish economy and economic record
Postcommunist economies
Russian and Soviet economy and
   economic record
Scandinavian economies and economic
   record
Single European market
South Africa, economic transition from
   apartheid
South Africa, progressive economists in
   the transition to democracy
South African economy and economic
   record
Southern Africa Development
   Community
South Asian and Southeast Asian
   economies and economic record
South Korean economy and economic
   record
Spanish economy and economic record
Tiger economies
Transition economies
United Kingdom relative economic
   decline
United States relative economic decline

Regulation and regulatory economics
Anti-trust economics
Economic analysis of regulation change
French regulation school
Regulation and competition
Regulatory economics
Standards, technical
Tradeable pollution permits
Utility regulation

Social economics
Apartheid, economics
Behavioural economics
Civil economy
Cooperation
Democracy in the workplace
Democratic consolidation
Dependency theory
Discrimination, economic
Economic analysis of law

Economic democracy
Economic psychology
Economic sociology
Economics and sociology
Economics of the arts
Employee share ownership plans
Environmental audit
Environmental economics
Equity
Equity vs efficiency
Famine

Foreign aid
Hidden economy
Institutions
Keiretsu
Natural resources
Property rights, economic
Social corporatism
Social economics
Soccer, economics of
Sports economics
Trust, economics

Statistics, econometrics and methodology
Causation, economic
Econometrics methods, textbooks
Econometrics software packages
Economics and mathematics
Linear programming
Time in economics

Human Geography

Business and economic geography
Business geography
Cities, economics
Clusters
Economic geography
Geography of money
Geographical information systems
Industrial districts
Location theory
Natural resources
Retail geography

Cultural geography
Colonialism
Cultural landscape
Feminist geographies
Geographical education
Geography of money
Globalization
Human geography survey
Imperialism

Locale
Nationalism
Place
Recreation geography
Residential segregation and urban
    social geography
Social geography
Spaces of consumption
Tourism
Urbanism

Political and global geography
Common heritage of mankind
Electoral geography
Environmental ethics
Famine
Geopolitics
Globalization, human geography
Governance and human geography
Natural resources
Political geography

Regional geography
Areal differentiation
Region and regional geography
Regional convergence
Regional development (US)
Regional policy
Regional restructuring
Scale in geography

Urban geography
Cities, economics
City system
Location theory
Metropolis
Residential segregation and urban
    social geography
Suburbs
Urban geography
Urban entrepreneurialism
Urbanization, human geography

Law

Administrative and constitutional law
    See also European Union law,
    Forms and systems of government
Act of Parliament
Administrative law
Bill of rights
Civil liberties
Civil rights (non-US)
Civil rights (US)
Constitutional law
Environmental law
Human rights (law)
Rule of law
State liability

Business and commercial law
Banking law
Bankruptcy law
Commercial law
Company law

Consumer law
Corporate manslaughter
Financial services, law
Insolvency
Intellectual property law
Warnings

Criminal law
    See also Criminology and sociology
    of law
Accessories
Blackmail
Corporate manslaughter
Criminal law
Criminal sentencing
Criminology
Cybercrimes, computer crimes, internet
    crimes
Cyberlaw and internet law
Deception

Drugs
Libel and slander
Pornography
Prostitution, law
Rape

European Union law
Council of Ministers
Direct effect
Directives
European Community and European
    Union, development of
European Convention on Human
    Rights
European Court of Justice
European Union law
Factortame
Regulations (EU law)
Treaty on European Union
    (Maastricht)

History of law
Ancient law
Aquinas, Thomas
Canon law
Habeas corpus
Law survey
Law and history
Law and history through textbooks
Lawyers and the legal profession,
    history of
Magna Carta
Roman law
Slavery, law

Judicial process
Appeal, Court of Appeal
Capital punishment
Confessions
Contempt of court
Criminal sentencing
Cross examination
Estoppel
Evidence
Eyewitness testimony
Forensic linguistics
High Court
House of Lords as a judicial body
Jury instructions
Legal aid
Legislative drafting
Trial
Witnesses

Law and society
Economic analysis of law
Law survey
Law and anthropology
Law and economics
Law and geography
Law and multiculturalism
Law and society
Women and the law

Legal theory
Queer theory in law
Legal positivism
Legal realism
Natural law theory
Natural rights

National systems of law
Africa, Northern, law and legal
    system
Africa, Southern, law and legal system
Africa, Central, law and legal system
Chinese contract law
Chinese dispute resolution
Chinese law and legal system
Chinese intellectual property law
Civil law
Customary law
Indian law and legal system
International law
Islamic law

Japanese law and legal systems
Middle Eastern law and legal
    systems
Russian and Soviet law and legal
    systems
United States law and legal systems

Private law
AIDS law
Child law
Common law
Confidential information
Custody
Guardianship
Homosexuality, law
Medical law and clinical negligence
Prejudice at work
Self-defence
Sports law
Tort
Transgender, law
Trust law
Women and the law

Property law
Copyright
Exhaustion of rights
Chinese intellectual property law
Intellectual property rights
Ownership
Property rights, economic
Search order

Management and Business

Change management
Change management
Force field analysis
Learning organization
Organizational culture

Financial management
Corporate governance
Intellectual capital
Investments, business
Financial accounting
Management accounting
Mergers and acquisitions
Multinational corporations
Pensions

Human resource management
Absenteeism
Appraisal, performance appraisal
Burnout
Career, concept
Career guidance
Codetermination, works councils
Employee relations

Feedback
Goals, goal setting
Hawthorne effect
Health and safety at work
Human resource management
Hours of work, working hours
Industrial relations
Interviewing, the selection interview
Job satisfaction
Labour market flexibility
Performance evaluation
Prejudice at work
Profit sharing
Redundancy, job loss, downsizing
Retirement
Stress at work
Training
Workload
Work–leisure interaction

Innovation and entrepreneurship
Creativity
Enterprise culture
Entrepreneur

Innovation, diffusion of
Innovation, organizational
Intrapreneurship
Lateral thinking
Leadership
Systems thinking

International business environment
Competitive strategy
Competitiveness
Environment, external
Globalization, management and
    business
Multinational corporations

Management and business: general
Benchmarking
Business ethics
Business research methods
Corporate governance
Corporate social performance
Crisis management
Empowerment
Environmental audit

Equal opportunity, equal pay
Ergonomics
Fordism
Glass ceiling
Health services research
High performance work systems
Hoshin kanri
Keiretsu
Management and business survey
Management and business studies,
    history of
Management and business textbooks
Management by objectives
Management consulting
Management control systems
Management textbooks
Management theories
Performance measurement, business
Performance measurement, public
    sector

Project management
Self-employment
Stakeholder
Stakeholder analysis
Women in management

Marketing management
Consumer behaviour
Management and business textbooks
Market research
Organizational buyer and buying
    behaviour
Strategic marketing management

Operations research and management
Benchmarking
Japanese management
Just-in-time production
Linear programming
Operations management

Operations research
Project management
Systems thinking
Total quality management

Strategic management
Business plans
Business strategy
Change management
Competitive strategy
Corporate strategy
Decision making
Decision theory
Environment, external
Hoshin hanri
Management by objectives
Performance measurement,
    business
Quality circles
Strategic marketing management

Organizational Behaviour

Adaptation
Communication in organizations
Competencies
Control, need for control
Democracy in the workplace
Employee ownership and cooperative
    societies: comparative performance
    studies
Employee share ownership plans
Empowerment
Enterprise culture
Expectancy theory
Fairness

Hawthorne effect
Hawthorne research
Hierarchies, organizational
Industrial democracy
Innovation, diffusion of
Innovation, organizational
Job design
Job enrichment
Learning organization
Motivation
Organizational behaviour survey
Organizational buyer and buying
    behaviour

Organizational climate
Organizational culture
Organizational learning
Organizational participation
Organizational structure
Participatory democracy
Participatory democracy in
    organizations
Quality circles
Teamwork
Women in management, organizational
    determinants of
Workplace participation

Philosophy

Aristotle
Comte, Auguste
Cultural relativism
Equality

Foucault, Michel
Free will and moral responsibility
Kant, Immanuel
Natural law theory

Natural rights
Philosophy and sociology
Politics and philosophy

Politics and International Relations

Civil rights and liberties
Bill of Rights
Civil liberties
Civil rights (non-US)
Civil rights (US)
Freedom
Gay and lesbian politics
Human rights, politics
Liberty
Natural rights
Race and politics (US)

Elections
Campaign, electoral
Class and politics
Elections
Electoral geography
Electoral law
Manifesto
Media and politics
Political geography
Political participation
Proportional representation

Public opinion polls
Suffrage

European politics and policy
European Community, politics
European integration
European Union, politics
European Union development
    policy
Globalization
Multilateralism

Treaty on European Union
  (Maastricht)

Forms and systems of government
Accountability
Authoritarianism
Cabinet
Church and state
Coalition
Congress (US)
Decentralization
Democracy
Dictatorship and despotism
Electoral college
Federalism
Federal Government
Governance
Military dictatorship
Monarchy
Multiparty system
Nation state
One-party state
Parliament
Parliamentary socialism
Presidency, US
Prime minister
Political leadership
Republicanism
Social democracy
Socialism
Totalitarianism

History of political thought
  See also Political history
Bentham, Jeremy
Brezhnev, Leonid
Collectivism
Collectivization
Communism
Engels, Friedrich
Fordism
Gramsci, Antonio
Gramsci and Fordism
Green, Thomas Hill
Johnson, Lyndon Baines
Kennedy, John F.
Khruschev, Nikita
King, Martin Luther, Jr
Lenin, V.I.
Lincoln, Abraham
Locke, John
Mandela, Nelson
Marx and Marxism
Nixon, Richard
Political thought, history of
Politics and history
Rousseau, Jean-Jacques
Thatcher, Margaret
William of Ockham

International relations
Arms race
Balance of power
Civil wars
Cold War
Common heritage of mankind
Constructivism in international
  relations theory
Detente
Deterrence
Devolution (UK and Europe)
Devolution (US)
Diplomacy
Globalization, politics
Globalization: critiques and
  alternatives
Independence
Institutionalism in international
  relations theory
International Monetary Fund
International regimes
International relations theory
International trade policy, political
  economy
League of Nations
Liberalism in international relations
  theory
Lomé Convention
Multilateralism
Nation
National identity
National interest
National security
Nationalism
New world order
Newly industrializing countries,
  politics
Non-governmental organizations
North Atlantic Treaty Organisation
  (NATO)
Peace psychology
Realism in international relations
  theory
Sovereignty
State
State apparatus
State capitalism
State sovereignty
Terrorism
United Nations (UN)
War
World systems theory

Political history
Apartheid, politics
Civil wars
Cold War
Colonialism
Democratic consolidation
Democratic transition

European Community and European
  Union, development of
French revolution
Genocide, politics
Imperialism
Independence
New Deal
Political leadership
Politics and history
Postcolonialism
South Africa, political transition from
  apartheid
Thatcher governments
Treaty on European Union
  (Maastricht)

Political parties and movements
Centre-left
Christian democracy
Catch-all parties
Communist party (US and UK)
Conservative Party (UK)
Eurocommunism
Labour parties
Labour Party (UK)
Moral Majority
Nation of Islam
New Labour
New Right
Party politics
Political parties
Populism
Third Way
Trade unions, politics

Political philosophy
Anarchism
Aristotle
Autonomy
Bentham, Jeremy
Bolshevism
Communism
Communitarianism
Conservatism
Democracy
Equality
Environmental politics
Fabianism
Facism
Feminism, politics
General will
Governmentality
Humanism and world politics
Idealism
Legitimacy
Leninism
Liberal democracy
Liberalism
Libertarianism
Locke, John

Marx and Marxism
Nazism
Politics and philosophy
Revisionism
Rousseau, Jean-Jacques
Thatcherism
Trotskyism
Utilitarianism
Utopias

Political theory
Chinese political theories
Division of labour, political
Hegemony, politics
Ideology, political

Justice
Modernity
New institutionalism, political
Postmodernism and politics
Rationality
Political development
Political leadership
Political obligation
Political theory
Power, politics
Public choice theory, political

Politics: general
Economics and politics
Media and politics

Politics survey
Politics and philosophy
Politics and sociology
Politics textbooks

Public administration and public policy
Accountability
Corruption
Decentralization
Local government finance
Local government management

Psychology

Clinical psychology, psychotherapy, psychoanalysis
Agoraphobia
Anorexia
Antipsychiatry
Anxiety
Archetype
Arson
Behaviour, behaviour therapy
Bulimia
Counselling children
Counselling psychology
Depression
Double bind
Dreams, dreaming
False memory syndrome
Family therapy
Fear
Feminism and psychoanalysis
Freud, Sigmund
Group therapy
Health and illness
Hypnosis
Hysteria
Impulsivity
Manic-depressive psychosis
Marital therapy
Mass hysteria
Mental illness
Multiple personality syndrome
Neurolingustic programming
Neurosis
Obesity
Obsessive-compulsive disorder
Oedipus complex
Pain, psychology of
Paranoia
Paraphilia
Projective testing
Psychoanalysis
Psychodrama

Psychology survey
Psychopathy
Rational emotive behaviour therapy
Risk assessment in psychology
Schizophrenia
Separation-individuation
Shame
Shyness
Suicide
Token economy
Transference
Unconscious

Cognitive and neuropsychology
Aphasia and related disorders
Attention
Bilingualism in early childhood
Cognitive dissonance
Cognitive developmental theory
Computational theory of mind
Consciousness
Dementia
Frontal lobe impairments
Information processing
Intelligence
Locus of control
Memory
Neural networks
Neuropsychology
Psychology survey
Semantic differential
Talent
Theory of mind
Whorf hypothesis

Developmental and educational psychology
Adolescence
Adulthood
Attachment theory in infancy
Behaviourism

Bullying in schools
Childhood
Cognitive developmental theory
Habituation effect
Intelligence
Imitation
Learning
Nature vs nurture
Peer support
Play
Psychology survey

Forensic psychology
Eyewitness testimony
False memory syndrome
Forensic linguistics
Forensic psychology
Jury instructions
Suggestibility

Occupational and organizational psychology
   See also Organizational behaviour
Absenteeism
Ability testing
Achievement
Aggressive behaviour in the workplace
Appraisal, performance appraisal
Assertiveness training
Assessment
Assessment centres
Attribution theory
Boredom at work
Burnout
Career counselling
Counselling at work
Emotional labour
Hawthorne effect
Hawthorne research
Interviewing, the selection interview
Performance evaluation

Psychology survey
Psychological testing, psychometrics
Stress at work
Vigilance
Workload

Personality and social psychology
Affect regulation
Aggression
Anger
Attribution theory
Behaviourism
Bias
Big five personality factors
Body projects
Bullying in schools
Cognitive dissonance
Conflict
Constructionism
Counterfactual thinking
Critical psychology
Discrimination, social
Dramaturgical analysis
Economic psychology
Emotion
Emotional labour

Essentialism
Fairness and socialization
Group socialization theory
Guilt
Human–computer interaction
Identification
Identity
Imitation
Impulsivity
Ingroup and outgroup
Locus of control
Looking-glass self
Love
Mass hysteria
Motivation
Obedience
Personal construct theory
Psychology survey
Self
Shame
Shyness
Small group conflict theory
Social competence
Social interaction
Stereotype
Stigma

Suggestibility
Temperament

Psychology of sex relations
Child abuse
Exhibitionism
Fantasy
Gender schema
Gender, constructions of
Incest
Infantile sexuality
Lesbianism, psychology
Masochism
Oedipus complex
Paedophilia
Prostitution, psychology
Paraphilia
Perversion
Psychology survey
Rape
Sadism
Safe sex
Sexuality
Sexual offenders
Transgender, medical
Transgender, psychology

Research and Analysis Methods in the Social Sciences

Applied social research
Business research methods
Causal relationship
Causation, sociology
Construct
Construct validity
Conversation analysis
Correlation
Correlation analysis
Descriptive statistics
Discourse analysis
Dramaturgical analysis
Empiricism
Ethics in research
Evaluation
Evaluation research
Factor analysis
Generalizability theory
Grounded theory

Inferential statistics
Informed consent
Interview
Life history
Likert scale
Linear programming
Longitudinal research in psychology
Longitudinal research with offenders
Meta-analysis
Multiple regression analysis
Objectivity
Observational research
Personal construct research
Placebo effect
Psychological testing, psychometrics
Qualitative research
Quantitative research
Quantitative text analysis
Questionnaire design

Questionnaire research
Questionnaires
Regression analysis
Reliability
Research methods, psychology and
    education
Research methods, social
Sample, sampling
Scale in geography
Scales of measurement
Self-reports
Semantic differential
Significance
Single-case research
Spatial analysis
Survey
Time-series design
Validity
Validity of tests

Sociology

Aging and ageism
Age stratification
Ageism
Disengagement theory
Gerontology
Human longevity
Mourning
Retirement

Community and society
Alternative communities and
    lifestyles
Civil society
Communitarianism
Gemeinschaft and Gesellschaft
Law and society
Traditional society

Criminology and sociology of law
    See also Criminal law
Arson
Capital punishment
Criminal law
Criminal sentencing
Criminology
Deception
Drugs
Fear of crime
Gambling
Labelling theory
Longitudinal research with offenders
Offenders, desistance from crime
Policing
Pornography
Prostitution, sociology
Probation and reducing reoffending
Rape
Rehabilitation
Sexual offenders

Global change and modern societies
Cyberspace revolution
Demography, sociology
Dependency theory
Futurism
Globalization, sociology
Information society
Modernization theory
Newly industrializing countries
Social change
Third World, sociology
World systems theory

Family sociology
Cohabitation
Domestic violence
Family
Homogamy

Incest
Love
Marriage
Sociology of childhood

Gender studies
Body projects
Citizenship and gender
Clitoridectomy
Domestic violence
Epistemology, feminist
Female employment, developing
    countries
Femininity
Feminism, political
Feminism, sociology
Feminism, Eastern European
Feminist anthropology
Feminism and psychoanalysis
Feminist economics
Feminist geographies
Feminization of poverty
Gay and lesbian politics
Gender, constructions of
Gender and social relations
Gender ideology
Gender roles
Gender schema
Homosexuality, law
Household as an economic agent
Imperialism and feminism
Informal and feminist organizations
Lesbianism, psychology
Patriarchy
Pornography
Postcolonial feminism
Queer theory in law
Rape
Transgender
Women and the law
Women in management
Women in management, organizational
    determinants of

History of sociological thought
Ariès, Philippe
Durkheim, Emile
Comte, Auguste
Marx and Marxism
Merton, Robert K.
Rousseau, Jean-Jacques
Social sciences, history and
    development
Sociology, history of
Sociology survey
Sociology textbooks
Veblen, Thorstein
Weber, Max

Politics and power
Authoritarianism
Citizenship
Citizenship and gender
Democracy
Genocide
Hegemony, sociology
Liberal democracy
Nationalism
Nation state
Participatory democracy
Political participation
Politics and sociology
Power, politics
Power, sociology
Rebellion
State, sociology
War

Race and ethnicity
Afrocentrism, Afrocentric movement
Antisemitism
Discrimination, social
Ethnic cleansing, the debate on
    Yugoslavia
Ethnicity
Ethnicity, sociology
Ethnocentrism
National identity
Race
Race and politics (US)
Racism
Slavery and racism
Stereotype

Slavery, colonialism and imperialism
Colonialism
Decolonization
Imperialism
Imperialism and feminism
Postcolonial feminism
Postcolonialism, sociology
Slave resistance
Slavery, economics
Slavery, law
Slavery and racism

Social anthropology
Animism
Beliefs
Clans
Commonsense beliefs
Descent
Economic anthropology
Ethnography
Feminist anthropology
Folklore
Hunting and gathering

Law and anthropology
Magic
Ritual
Stateless (acephalous) societies
Superstition
Tradition
Traditional society

Social behaviour
See also Social psychology
Attribution theory
Dramaturgical analysis
Ethnomethodology
Fashion
Group socialization theory
Humour
Human–computer interaction
Mass hysteria
Motivation, sociology
Realistic conflict theory
Role
Small group conflict theory
Social interaction
Social learning
Sociobiology
Sociology of emotions
Symbolic interactionism
Sexuality
Time use, time budgets, time
    allocation

Social organization and stratification
Bureaucracy
Feminization of poverty
Homelessness
Inequality
Informal and feminist organizations
Master status
Role
Slavery and racism
Slavery, economics
Slavery, law
Social indicators
Social stratification
Social structure
Social mobility
Status
Structural social mobility
Poverty, absolute
Poverty, relative
Trade unionism
Underclass, sociology
Underclass and social policy
Unemployment, experience of
Wealth, sociology
Welfare state, sociology

Sociology and medicine
Abortion
AIDS, sociology

Circumcision
Clitoridectomy
Death and dying
Depression
Disability
Euthanasia
Health and illness
Health services research
Human longevity
Infertility
Medicalization
Mental health, policy and practice
Mental illness: asylum
Mourning
Reproductive technology
Safe sex
Smoking
Vegetarianism

Sociology of culture
Civic culture
Cultural capital
Cultural integration
Cultural landscape
Cultural reproduction
Culture
Cultural relativism
Counterculture
Ethnocentrism
High culture
Mass media
Material culture
Media texts
Multiculturalism
Non-material culture
Popular culture
Sociocultural evolution
Sociology of science
Sports sociology
Subculture
Traditional society

Sociology of language
Conversation analysis
Discourse analysis
Epistemology, feminist
Hate speech
Literacy
Neurolingustic programming
Semantic differential
Sociolinguistics

Sociology of religion
Beliefs
Church
Church and state
Civil religion
Islamic fundamentalism
Magic
Monotheism

Sociology and the environment / and moral protests
Animal rights
Energy politics
Energy supply systems
Environmental ethics
Environmental science as a social
    science
Risk society

Sociological theory
Civil society
Critical realism
End of ideology
Ethnomethodology
Functionalism in sociology
Human nature
Ideology, sociology
Modernity, sociological
Modernization theory
Nature vs nurture
Positivist research
Postmodernism
Poststructuralism
Pragmatism
Public
Risk society
Social Darwinism
Social exchange theory
Sociobiology
Sociological theory
Structuralism
Structuration theory
Symbolic interactionism

Urban sociology
Cities, sociology
Gardens, urban use and value
Metropolis
Suburbs
Urbanism
Urbanization, sociology
Urban environment and youth

Work and economic life
Consumer behaviour
Economics and sociology
Economic sociology
Household as an economic agent
Institutions
Profession
Self-employment
Social economics
Unemployment, experience of
Trade unionism
Wealth, sociology
Welfare state, sociology
Work
Work–leisure interaction

A

Ability testing

Carroll, John B., *Human Cognitive Abilities: A Survey of Factor-analytic Studies*, New York and Cambridge: Cambridge University Press, 1993

Cronbach, Lee J., *Essentials of Psychological Testing*, 5th edition, New York and London: Harper and Row, 1990

Drasgow, Fritz and Julie Olson-Buchanan (editors), *Innovations in Computerized Assessment*, Mahwah, New Jersey: Erlbaum, 1999

Fleishman, Edwin A. and Maureen E. Reilly (editors), *Handbook of Human Abilities: Definitions, Measurements, and Job Task Requirements*, Palo Alto, California: Consulting Psychologists Press, 1992

Gottfredson, Linda, "Why G Matters: The Complexity of Everyday Life", *Intelligence*, 24/1 (1997): 79–132

Guion, Robert M., *Assessment, Measurement, and Prediction for Personnel Decisions*, Mahwah, New Jersey: Erlbaum, 1998

Hunter, John and Ronda Hunter, "Validity and Utility of Alternative Predictors of Job Performance", *Psychological Bulletin*, 96/1 (1984): 72–98

Mackenzie, Brian, "Explaining Race Differences in IQ: The Logic, the Methodology, and the Evidence", *American Psychologist*, 39/11 (1984): 1214–33

Sternberg, Robert J., *Beyond IQ: A Triarchic Theory of Human Intelligence*, Cambridge and New York: Cambridge University Press, 1985

Wagner, Richard, "Intelligence, Training, and Employment", *American Psychologist*, 52/10 (1997): 1059–69

In order adequately to comprehend the present state of ability testing, the contributions, debates, and setbacks of the past must first be reviewed. The history of the testing of human abilities is presented in CARROLL, who reviews the bulk of the literature on individual differences in cognitive abilities. This book is a valuable source of information concerning the background of our present notions of the structure, function, and measurement of human abilities. It is useful to researchers, teachers, and students of cognitive abilities as both a reference work and as an advanced course textbook.

A primary debate within the field of ability testing has focused on the efficacy of testing a single general cognitive ability (g) as opposed to testing several more specific abilities. In GOTTFREDSON, evidence is provided for the utility of g,

particularly when predicting performance on complex tasks. Although differences across social settings exist, the probability of a given individual's success on normal life skills is significantly enhanced by higher levels of g. The author supports her arguments with findings from personnel selection research and research done in connection with the National Adult Literacy Survey.

Perhaps the most cited research on the validity of ability testing is HUNTER & HUNTER. In a meta-analysis of studies that measured various predictors of job performance, they found that no single predictor equalled or excelled the validity of ability testing (0.53 corrected) for predicting success in entry-level jobs. In addition to the meta-analytic evidence, the estimated costs of changing predictors in organizations currently using ability testing add to the argument for retaining this method of predicting work performance. A negative consequence associated with ability testing is also presented in this article: adverse impact on minority groups. Possible solutions, such as using additional predictors in combination with ability testing, are suggested.

WAGNER explores the possibility of supplementing general ability testing with additional predictors. Three related issues are presented: (a) maximizing the validity and utility of ability testing for work selection while maintaining fairness across groups, (b) training as a viable option to selection, and (c) an agenda for future ability testing research and application. The validity statements made in meta-analytic studies are questioned and the lack of hypothesized and tested causal models is pointed out. Also discussed is the economic utility of using ability testing as a selection device and the adverse impact associated with ability testing. Wagner suggests several factors to supplement selection by ability testing: measures of prior work experience, practical intelligence, personality, personal interests, motivation, and training.

In order fully to understand ability testing, a reading of a text on psychological testing is necessary. CRONBACH does a thorough job of presenting not only the fundamentals of psychological assessment, but also provides the reader with insights on general cognitive ability, test selection, and test administration. As an introductory undergraduate text, teachers and students alike will find useful the big picture of how to think about psychometrics, as well as the in-depth presentations of ability testing and personality testing. The section on ability testing includes coverage of the definition of cognitive ability, development of cognitive ability, appraisal methods, multiple abilities, and personnel selection. In addition to its value as a classroom text, Cronbach serves as a valuable testing reference for all social scientists.

FLEISHMAN & REILLY provide a comprehensive guide to tests that measure the range of human abilities. A taxonomy of human tasks, categorized into cognitive, psychomotor, physical, and sensory-perceptual domains, was used in framing the contents of the book. Each ability domain is divided into its subdivisions (for example, twenty-one subdivisions are included under the general heading of cognitive ability), with definitions of each subdivision, tasks related to each, jobs requiring the specific ability, and examples of tests of the specific ability. The name and address of the publisher of each test is also provided. Obviously, this handbook is an essential resource for a wide range of practitioners from business, industrial, and educational settings seeking means to measure various human abilities.

Ability testing has been found to predict a variety of criteria, but the use of testing has remained primarily in the fields of educational and vocational assessment. Addressing the latter, GUION presents the theory and application of ability testing in vocational assessment from a psychometric viewpoint. The first section of the book covers the rationale for making personnel decisions, the second part covers the evaluation of assessment procedures, and the last section concentrates on the various methods used in personnel assessment. The book is intended as a text for a graduate-level readership, as well as a technical reference for consultants, researchers, and litigators. Excellent reference sections are included in each chapter, providing sources for additional reading on this topic.

Another ongoing debate in the ability testing literature centres on the between-group differences in test and criterion scores. That these differences are primarily due to genetics is questioned by MACKENZIE, who disagrees with the existing arguments for this claim. The author points out that evidence for a genetic basis follows from a heritability bias in existing research. Mackenzie reviews studies that have attempted to explain between-group differences with environmental, genetic, and joint models. Support is found for environmental causes of IQ; however, insufficient research has been conducted treating environmentality and heritability as equally important. In order to meet this challenge, Mackenzie suggests a research agenda from a joint perspective with emphasis on developing causal models including both environmental and genetic factors.

Since the 1970s, improvements in computer technology have had an appreciable influence on ability testing. Two of the biggest challenges to social scientists interested in computerizing ability tests have been: (a) keeping up with the rapidly changing available technology and (b) finding the best fit between their testing needs and existing technology. In their edited book, DRASGOW & OLSON-BUCHANAN provide one of the most current publications addressing both of these challenges. The authors, representing a variety of disciplines, present the challenges each have found when developing computerized assessments for an array of target populations. Additionally, the advantages of computerization in ability testing are given for both vocational and educational contexts.

STERNBERG is one of several authors presenting arguments against ability testing as a primary source of information for making selection decisions. In his book, human ability is theor-

ized as having three parts – a triarchic theory of intelligence. The first part, contextual, is associated with one's ability to select, adapt, and shape their environment. A second part emphasizes the experiential component of ability formation and the third part emphasizes the cognitive processes involved in ability processing. The book contains five parts, with the first section placing the triarchic theory into the history of human ability research. The second section fully describes the triarchic theory of intelligence and the third section presents tests of the theory. The fourth and fifth sections focus on implications and integrations of the theory. This book is an excellent source for an alternative view of how human ability should be conceptualized and tested.

SCOTT ALAN DAVIES

See also Psychological testing, psychometrics

Abortion

Costa, Marie, *Abortion: A Reference Handbook*, 2nd edition, Santa Barbara, California: ABC Clio, 1996

Githens, Marianne and Dorothy McBride Stetson (editors), *Abortion Politics: Public Policy in Cross-Cultural Perspective*, New York and London: Routledge, 1996

Gorney, Cynthia, *Articles of Faith: A Frontline History of the Abortion Wars*, New York: Simon and Schuster, 1998

Hadley, Janet, *Abortion: Between Freedom and Necessity*, Philadelphia: Temple University Press, and London: Virago, 1996

Jacoby, Kerry N., *Souls, Bodies, Spirits: The Drive to Abolish Abortion since 1973*, Westport, Connecticut, and London: Praeger, 1998

Kulczycki, Andrzej, *The Abortion Debate in the World Arena*, New York: Routledge, and Basingstoke: Macmillan, 1999

Simon, Rita J., *Abortion: Statutes, Policies, and Public Attitudes the World Over*, Westport, Connecticut: Praeger, 1998

Steffen, Lloyd (editor), *Abortion: A Reader*, Cleveland: Pilgrim Press, 1996

Tribe, Laurence H., *Abortion: The Clash of Absolutes*, 2nd edition, New York: Norton, 1992

COSTA's reference book begins with the classical Greek origins of abortion and navigates the reader through the biographical sketches of abortion leaders and into landmark court cases and statistics. The author's directory of organizations, annotated bibliographies, and glossary are a worthwhile resource to any reader who journeys into the abortion debate. Despite its lack of depth, the handbook's value is in its objectivity and comprehensiveness.

SIMON provides a comprehensive comparative summary of abortion statutes in 189 countries ranging from Western Europe to the Middle East and Central America. Devoid of in-depth analysis, the author presents the history, social regulation, government funding, and demographics surrounding abortion in each country. The most valuable contribution of this book is its compilation of public opinion on abortion according to age, educational level, and other demographic characteristics.

TRIBE expertly re-enacts the political and legal battles of the abortion debate. The author examines constitutional legal decisions and two centuries of abortion history in the US. Arguing for a common ground among warring factions, the author imports abortion policies from communities outside the US and explores complex legal questions such as privacy and personhood. Expanding the abortion debate, the author highlights how the issue of abortion effects other political issues such as the right to die and foetal endangerment. This book's strength is its insightful and intelligent discussion of the legal complexities surrounding the abortion debate.

Positioning abortion as a multidimensional contemporary issue, KULCZYCKI explores the political, legal, religious, and health aspects of abortion within Kenya, Mexico, and Poland. The author delves into the distinctive concerns of abortion in developing countries and addresses the influence of Western ideology. Each case study begins with empirical data and includes comprehensive cross sections of key actors. Focusing primarily on religious influences, the author skilfully contextualizes the multiplicatous nature of the abortion debate and develops a transferable methodology.

HADLEY presents a comparative crosscultural analysis of the abortion debate while strongly advocating a prochoice political alignment. Beginning with a brief introduction to the US's presidential influences, the author expertly explores the political controversy surrounding abortion in Ireland and Germany and additionally examines foetal personhood and feminism. The cacophony of the abortion debate, as illustrated by the crosscultural analysis of a woman's right to refuse, is brilliantly exposed through the intersections of law, policy, and morality. The author also presents an excellent discussion of the link between abortion and contraception within the contrasting communities of Russia, Holland, and Britain. Despite the author's overemphasis on the dangers of back-alley abortions, she does set forth arguments for and against abortion. This book's strongest asset is its categorical methodology and supportive crosscultural analysis.

GORNEY presents a riveting historical account of the abortion wars in the state of Missouri in the US. The author describes the US abortion controversy from 1968 to 1997, based on 500 personal interviews. This narrative history of abortion transports the reader into the frontlines of the controversy and exposes all opposing sides of the abortion war.

JACOBY, in examining US abortion abolitionists, contextualizes the act of abortion as a focal point on which US ideals and belief systems converge. While tracing the history of abortion abolitionists, the author composes a useful methodological framework to examine abortion activists in the future and within varying contexts. The author, in describing the historical reality and belief systems of radical right-wing abortion activists, demonstrates how the act of abortion complicates questions of life, death, political rights, and technology. This book's strength is its sensitivity and optimistic search for open-minded understanding of all sides of the abortion controversy.

Assembling a superb collection of authors, GITHENS & STETSON examine the role of political institutions in determining and implementing abortion policy. The collection, taking a global comparative perspective, addresses the rhetoric of abortion and the legal struggle to define reproductive rights. The essays reveal that abortion policy, when implemented, restricts availability and access to abortion services. Discussing public opinion, the collection explores the intersection of domestic and regional influence on abortion policy within the European community. The work also examines how new reproductive technologies alter abortion rhetoric and policy.

STEFFEN provides a comprehensive collection of essays that discuss the moral complexity of abortion. Focusing on religion and theology, the collection shows how the meaning of abortion is influenced by ethical concerns that are not easily extracted from religion. The essays' diverse range of religious influences, including Christian and non-Christian, disclose the intricate relationship between abortion and morality. Questioning the language of abortion, the collection distinguishes between beliefs in abortion based on religion and faith. The essays go beyond the single issue of morality and expose the relationship of abortion with the interconnectedness of morality, law, and policy.

LAURA FOSTER

Absenteeism

Bycio, Peter, "Job Performance and Absenteeism: A Review and Meta-Analysis", *Human Relations*, 45/2 (1992): 193–220

Drago, Robert and Mark Wooden, "The Determinants of Labor Absence: Economic Factors and Workgroup Norms across Countries", *Industrial and Labor Relations Review*, 45/4 (1992): 764–78

Edwards, Paul and Colin Whitston, *Attending to Work: The Management of Attendance and Shopfloor Order*, Oxford and Cambridge, Massachusetts: Blackwell, 1993

Frayne, Colette A., *Reducing Employee Absenteeism through Self-Management Training: A Research-Based Analysis and Guide*, New York: Quorum, 1991

Hanisch, Kathy A., "Behavioral Families and Multiple Causes: Matching the Complexity of Responses to the Complexity of Antecedents", *Current Directions in Psychological Science*, 4 (1995): 156–62

Harrison, David A. and Joseph J. Martocchio, "Time for Absenteeism: A 20-Year Review of Origins, Offshoots, and Outcomes", *Journal of Management*, 24/3 (1998): 305–50

Hulin, Charles L., "Adaptation, Persistence, and Commitment in Organizations" in *Handbook of Industrial and Organizational Psychology*, 2nd edition, edited by Marvin D. Dunnette and Leaetta M. Hough, Palo Alto, California: Consulting Psychologists Press, 1991

Johns, Gary, "Contemporary Research on Absence from Work: Correlates, Causes and Consequences" in *International Review of Industrial and Organizational Psychology 1997*, edited by C.L. Cooper and I.T. Robertson, Chichester and New York: Wiley, 1997

Absenteeism has been and continues to be a concern for those who manage employees due to its significant costs to organizations, industries, and society in general. There can also be significant costs to employees. This selection primarily examines summary articles published since the 1990s to obtain a picture of the current state of research knowledge on employee absenteeism. Two books published in the 1990s are also included as they provide a unique perspective on controlling absenteeism. Although many articles are published on absenteeism every year, most examine very specific variables that are not interrelated to other important facets of absenteeism, resulting in a knowledge base that lacks depth. In the next decades we must begin to see studies that empirically evaluate absenteeism within a connected framework that brings together many of the piecemeal designed studies, in order to obtain a comprehensive understanding of employee absenteeism, its causes, and outcomes.

HARRISON & MARTOCCHIO present a 20-year summary (1977–96) of absenteeism research. They divide work on absenteeism into short-term (1 day to 3 months), mid-term (4–12 months), and long-term (greater than 12 months), and discuss how these different time periods suggest different absenteeism outcomes and consequences for employees, social environments, and organizations. This comprehensive review of absenteeism provides a significant amount of useful information for those wanting a summary of prior work on absenteeism as well as good suggestions for future research.

The review by JOHNS covers published research from approximately 1980 to 1995 and attempts to offer a fairly complete review of employee absenteeism. Topics briefly reviewed include models of absenteeism that he labels as process, decision-making, withdrawal, demographic, medical, stress, social and cultural, conflict, deviance, and economic. A short description of each model is presented and within some of the models more details are offered. For example, the relations between absenteeism and job satisfaction, organizational commitment, and the relations among other forms of withdrawal (e.g. turnover, lateness) are discussed under the withdrawal model. The most important contribution from this article is a discussion of studying absenteeism within the organizational context, something that has been lacking in the absenteeism literature. Edwards & Whitston (see below) also make this point forcibly.

The statistical review by BYCIO provides one example of several meta-analyses that have been carried out, which include employee absenteeism. Bycio's meta-analysis examines the relationship between employee performance and absenteeism using data from 46 articles. Although the credibility intervals were wide, his general findings indicate that there is a significant tendency that those employees who were frequently absent were poor job performers. Several other meta-analyses involving absenteeism have been completed; the following are examples: Mitra, Jenkins & Gupta ("A meta-analytic review of the relationship between absence and turnover", *Journal of Applied Psychology*, 1992), Hackett ("Age, tenure, and employee absenteeism", *Human Relations*, 1990), and Hackett & Guion ("A reevaluation of the absenteeism-job satisfaction relationship", *Organizational Behavior and Human Decision Processes*, 1985). Meta-analyses are very useful when individuals desire a statistical summary of research on a topic and typically prove more beneficial than single, empirical studies if the meta-analyses are detailed, complete, and include several studies.

DRAGO & WOODEN is useful primarily because it includes an economic perspective on absence taking that had been neglected for several years. Specifically, the authors describe three explanations of voluntary absence behavior including (a) the labour-leisure choice framework, (b) the work discipline version of efficiency wage theory, and (c) workgroup norms. They use a cross-national data set with several industries represented. Although their primary analyses provide results consistent with all three explanations, they offer some additional information that is supportive of workgroup norms. They also note how their data support the importance of human resource activities and policies regarding job satisfaction.

HANISCH presents a unique attitude-behaviour model that focuses on behavioural families of withdrawal. In previous empirical work, Hanisch and her colleagues identified two behavioural families of withdrawal: work and job withdrawal. Absenteeism is one component of work withdrawal as it is a behaviour that removes an employee from the work itself but not from the organization. These two behavioural families have been empirically linked to job dissatisfactions (such as work dissatisfaction, supervisor dissatisfaction), work stress, and organizational commitment, as well as health problems and dissatisfactions. This article argues that absenteeism needs to be studied within the context of other withdrawal behaviours, as it is extremely unlikely that employees only choose absenteeism when reacting to the myriad variables impinging on them. Hanisch and others (e.g. Johns above, Hulin, see below) also argue for an evaluation of the relations among withdrawal behaviors, including absenteeism, in an effort to better understand the interdependencies or effects one withdrawal behavior may have on another. Hanisch, Hulin & Roznowski ("The importance of individuals' repertoires of behaviors: The scientific appropriateness of studying multiple behaviors and general attitudes", *Journal of Organizational Behavior*, 1998) expands upon Hanisch's work and provide further details on studying absenteeism as one form of withdrawal behaviour.

HULIN provides an integration of attitude-behaviour models and organizational adaptation of which absenteeism is one component. He presents a thorough review of work attitudes that have been linked with absenteeism as well as other withdrawal behaviours (for example lateness, turnover) and provides a good discussion of the problems with studying withdrawal behaviours (e.g. low base rates, skewed distributions). Hulin also describes absenteeism as one component of a syndrome or behavioural family and suggests studying absenteeism within that framework as opposed to individually much the same as Hanisch does in her article; their prior empirical work supports this view.

FRAYNE provides empirical support for self-management training in the reduction of employee absenteeism. Self-management training, a product of social learning theory, teaches employees to be in control over their circumstances and consists of goal setting, setting a contract, self-monitoring, and applying reinforcement and punishment based on self-evaluation. This book provides a useful application for managers on how to use self-management training to increase employee attendance. It is a welcome addition to the literature on absenteeism as it provides a blend of academic theory and research and applies it to the organizational world. In the context of absenteeism, the author's main emphasis is on self-efficacy and how individuals can overcome obstacles to attending work with a focus on the production of favorable and unfavorable outcomes. Recommendations for administering self-management training programs and incorporating the research results into future managerial endeavors are also provided.

EDWARDS & WHITSTON, although not exclusively about absenteeism, focuses on human resource management, which is an integral part of dealing with employee attendance issues. The authors emphasize managers' definitions of acceptable attendance polices, how these are managed, how integrated attendance policies are with other employment policies, and the consequences to workers' behavior. As Edwards & Whitson note, there is often no connection between the research literature on absenteeism and the control of attendance, a problem alluded to by Frayne as well. This book presents several case studies that are interesting and useful to read as a means to obtain an understanding of how employees and managers interact in the control of attendance.

KATHY A. HANISCH

Accessories

Alldridge, Peter, "The Doctrine of Innocent Agency", *Criminal Law Forum*, 2 (1990): 45–83

Dressler, Joshua, "Reassessing the Theoretical Underpinnings of Accomplice Liability: New Solutions to an Old Problem", *Hastings Law Journal*, 37 (1985): 91–140

Fletcher, George P., *Rethinking Criminal Law*, Boston: Little Brown, 1978

Gillies, Peter, *The Law of Criminal Complicity*, Sydney: Law Book Company, 1980

Herlitz, Carl Erik, *Parties to a Crime and the Notion of a Complicity Object: A Comparative Study of the Alternatives Provided by the Model Penal Code, Swedish Law and Claus Roxin*, Uppsala: Iustus, 1992

Kadish, Sanford, "Complicity, Cause and Blame: A Study in the Interpretation of Doctrine", *California Law Review*, 73 (1985): 323

Law Commission, *Assisting and Encouraging Crime*, London: HMSO, 1993

Smith, K.J.M., *A Modern Treatise on the Law of Criminal Complicity*, Oxford: Clarendon Press, and New York: Oxford University Press, 1991

Accessories are participants in crime other than the perpetrator. In English law one who aids and abets is liable to the same sentence as the perpetrator. For a comprehensive account of the law the most helpful modern work is SMITH, and a helpful comparator from a cognate jurisdiction is GILLIES. Both are now slightly dated, but this is not an area in which the issues of principle change significantly. The conceptual issues that arise include the relationship between the liability of various forms of accessory liability and that of the principal, the mental state required for the principal, and whether instigators should be regarded differently from other accessories.

Much writing has dealt with the question of whether the liability of the accessory is original or derivative from the liability of the principal. The consequence is that there may be limits to the accessory's liability. A distinction that followed from the English law insistence upon the primary liability of the perpetrator was that between presence and absence: there was some support for the view that persons absent from the offence could not be convicted of a more serious offence than

those who were present. The focus has been upon the case of *Richards* (1974: QB 776), in which a woman was only convicted of maliciously inflicting grievous bodily harm (rather than wounding with intent to cause grievous bodily harm) because she was not present at the event and the perpetrators were only convicted of the less serious offence. The English writers have generally taken the view that Richards was incorrectly decided. ALLDRIDGE (1990) takes the contrary view, explaining the cases in which heavier liability can be justified upon causal grounds and arguing that the apparent reversal of Richards in *Howe & Bannister* (1987: AC 416) was erroneous.

The continental view, which also prevailed in the US (DRESSLER, KADISH) was that instigation could not only command a heavier sentence but could also be classified as more serious offence than perpetration, notwithstanding the absence of the accomplice. FLETCHER's enormous significance for the development of criminal law theory in the Anglo-American world is his knowledge of the continental systems, and his willingness to set the conceptual systems one against another. Writing from Sweden, HERLITZ gives a more detailed consideration.

The other major doctrinal issue is the mental state that would give rise to a conviction as an accessory. The alternative views were a wider or a narrower one – either (wider) mere contemplation or intention that the crime should take place or (at least) something nearer to intention that the consequences take place. The idea that mere contemplation would be sufficient existed for a long time. The obvious objection was always that this made it easier under English law to convict accessories than perpetrators, and that if the perpetrator is to remain the focus of liability, that is unjustifiable. This is Smith's position.

In its review, the LAW COMMISSION leaned towards giving instigation a special role, to confining the required *mens rea*, and to dispense with many of the anomalies arising from the cases of "accessories without principals". Increasingly, however, what seems to be happening is that criminal legislation is directed against "organized crime" and will allocate responsibility according to some other rules than the old rules of accessorial liability. This is most clearly the case in respect of such offences as money laundering.

PETER ALLDRIDGE

Accountability

Calvert, Randall L., Mathew D. McCubbins and Barry R. Weingast, "A Theory of Political Control and Agency Discretion", *American Journal of Political Science*, 33/3 (1989): 588–611

Finer, S.E., "The Individual Responsibility of Ministers", *Public Administration*, 34 (Summer 1956): 377–96

McCubbins, Mathew D. and Thomas Schwartz, "Congressional Oversight Overlooked: Police Patrols versus Fire Alarms", *American Journal of Political Science*, 28/1 (1984): 165–79

McCubbins, Mathew D., Roger G. Noll and Barry R. Weingast, "Structure and Process, Politics and Policy: Administrative Arrangements and the Political Control of Agencies", *Virginia Law Review*, 75/2 (1989): 431–82

Marshall, Geoffrey (editor), *Ministerial Responsibility*,
    Oxford and New York: Oxford University Press, 1989

Palmer, Michael, "The Economics of Ministerial
    Responsibility", *Journal of Law Economics, and
    Organization*, 11/1 (1995): 164–88

Powell, G. Bingham Jr, "Constitutional Design and Citizen
    Electoral Control", *Journal of Theoretical Politics*, 1/2
    (1989): 107–30

Wood, B. Dan and Richard W. Waterman, "The Dynamics of
    Political Control of the Bureaucracy", *American Political
    Science Review*, 85/3 (1991): 801–28

Woodhouse, Diana, *Ministers and Parliament: Accountability
    in Theory and Practice*, Oxford: Clarendon Press, and
    New York: Oxford University Press, 1994

Woodhouse, Diana, *In Pursuit of Good Administration:
    Ministers, Civil Servants, and Judges*, Oxford: Clarendon
    Press, and New York: Oxford University Press, 1997

This entry deals with the political accountability of the bureaucracy rather than the electoral accountability of politicians. Readers interested in the latter topic will want to read POWELL who evaluates how well different electoral systems deliver representation, responsiveness, and accountability.

The British and American literatures on accountability are quite distinct. The British literature concentrates on the efficacy of the constitutional convention of ministerial responsibility. The research strategy is overwhelmingly inductive, examining historical data to determine if the doctrine can be said to constrain ministerial and bureaucratic behaviour effectively. The American literature is more concerned with explaining why politicians control the bureaucracy in ostensibly suboptimal ways. This literature is dominated by deductive theories predicated on rational choice assumptions; some familiarity with game theory or organizational economics is therefore helpful to the reader.

FINER's examination of ministerial resignations and non-resignations between 1855 and 1955 marks a break with older works that described the constitutional theory rather than the political practice of ministerial responsibility. The irregularity of the conditions under which ministers resigned led Finer to conclude that one could not speak sensibly of a convention of ministerial responsibility.

MARSHALL's edited volume brings together academic analyses and parliamentary reports and speeches on the application of ministerial responsibility to politicians and civil servants. The introduction highlights the divergence between constitutional theory and political practice and the inconsistencies in constitutional interpretations of the doctrine of ministerial responsibility. These themes are revisited in the readings: the parliamentary reports and speeches highlight politicians' struggles to interpret the doctrine of ministerial responsibility in everyday political life, the academic commentaries reveal how these practical interpretations are often internally inconsistent and developed with an eye to political expediency rather than constitutional probity.

The first half of WOODHOUSE (1994) reads like an updated version of Finer. The introductory chapters fill out the constitutional content of the doctrine of ministerial responsibility and examine the ministerial crises of the Thatcher and Major governments. Woodhouse argues that accountability is lost in the gap between the constitutional requirements and the political practice of ministerial responsibility. The second half of the book examines how the devolution of departmental activities to arms-length ("Next Steps") agencies may affect ministerial responsibility and political accountability. Woodhouse argues that the Next Steps agencies may make bureaucrats more responsive to ministers, but she is unconvinced that they will make ministers correspondingly more responsive to Parliament. The concluding chapter examines the effects of similar reforms on accountability in New Zealand and Australia.

WOODHOUSE (1997) examines how the new public management (of which the Next Steps reforms are an important part) and an increasingly interventionist judiciary have challenged Whitehall's traditional conception of good administration. Woodhouse (1994) is agnostic about the effects of new public management on political accountability, but in Woodhouse (1997) she argues that the movement has undermined accountability by allowing ministers to pronounce themselves responsible only for policy and not administration. Woodhouse also finds the new public management to be hostile to judicial interpretations of accountability because the latter give more weight to concerns of due process and fairness than to economic efficiency.

McCUBBINS & SCHWARZ is an accessible introduction to the American literature. The paper uses a deductive argument to show that congressional oversight of the bureaucracy is more efficient (in political terms at least) than it first appears. The authors begin their argument by making two common assumptions: (a) that members of Congress are chiefly interested in re-election, and (b) that this interest leads members to take as much credit as possible for the benefits enjoyed by potential supporters while expending as little effort as possible. From these assumptions the authors deduce that members of Congress prefer decentralized and indirect forms of oversight that can be triggered by concerned constituents (fire alarms) to centralized, direct, and more costly forms of oversight such as committee hearings (police patrols).

Bureaucracies often operate under layers of onerous procedural requirements. This "red tape" is manifestly inefficient – and yet politicians choose not to remove it. McCUBBINS, NOLL & WEINGAST use principal-agent theory to advance one solution to this puzzle. The authors demonstrate that the existence of multiple political principals allows an agent to act contrary to the principals' wishes. This result is important because it suggests that legislative bargains reached jointly by the Senate, House, and President may not effectively constrain bureaucratic behaviour. The model also reveals that the political principals are unlikely to agree on corrective legislation because at least one principal stands to benefit from the bureaucratic agent's actions. Consequently, political principals place onerous procedural requirements in the enacting legislation in an attempt to limit *ex post* bureaucratic noncompliance.

CALVERT, McCUBBINS & WEINGAST examine the extent to which political appointments can be relied upon to limit bureaucratic noncompliance. The authors argue that as long as legislative and executive actors are sure of an appointee's policy preferences, they can effectively dictate policy outcomes simply by making judicious appointments. Moreover, uncertainty over appointees' preferences diminishes political control of policy outcomes only slightly. Thus judicious political appointments are more likely to secure bureaucratic compliance than additional layers of procedural requirements. Empirical work by WOOD & WATERMAN confirms that political appointments control bureaucratic behaviour more effectively than legislation or budget changes.

PALMER is important because it is one of a small number of papers that attempt to deal with ministerial responsibility in the economic and deductive fashion of the American literature. Palmer likens Westminster parliamentary government to a hierarchical monopoly preserved intact but subject to franchise bidding (the electoral competition between political parties). Ministerial responsibility controls the abuses of power that accompany the Westminster monopoly of government by sharpening the electoral competition between the political parties.

CHRISTOPHER KAM

Accounting concepts

Accounting Standards Committee, *Statement of Standard Accounting Practice*, no. 2: *Disclosure of Accounting Policies*, London: Accounting Standards Committee, 1971

Chambers, Raymond J., "The Moonitz and Sprouse Studies on Postulates and Principles", *Proceedings* of January Conference of the Australian Association of University Teachers of Accounting, Canberra (1964): 34–54; reprinted in *Chambers on Accounting*, vol. 3: *Accounting Theory and Research*, edited by Raymond J. Chambers and Graeme W. Dean, New York and London: Garland, 1986

Macve, Richard, *A Conceptual Framework for Financial Accounting and Reporting: The Possibilities for an Agreed Structure*, London: Institute of Chartered Accountants in England and Wales, 1981

Moonitz, Maurice, *The Basic Postulates of Accounting*, New York: American Institute of Certified Public Accountants, 1961

Paton, William A., *Accounting Theory*, New York: Ronald Press, 1922; reprinted Lawrence, Kansas: Scholars Book Company, 1973

Paton, William A. and Ananias C. Littleton, *An Introduction to Corporate Accounting Standards*, Sarasota, Florida: American Accounting Association, 1940

Sanders, Thomas H., Henry R. Hatfield and Underhill Moore, *A Statement of Accounting Principles*, New York: American Institute of Certified Public Accountants, 1938; reprinted Sarasota, Florida: American Accounting Association, 1959

Sprouse, Robert T. and Maurice Moonitz, *A Tentative Set of Broad Accounting Principles for Business Enterprises*, New York: American Institute of Certified Public Accountants, 1962

Walton, Peter, "Introduction to Special Section: A European True and Fair View?", *European Accounting Review*, 2/1 (1993): 49–104

Zeff, Stephen, *Forging Accounting Principles in Five Countries: A History and an Analysis of Trends*, Champaign, Illinois: Stipes, 1972

Accounting concepts are the broad principles that underlie the preparation of financial statements by accountants. The term "concepts" is often regarded as nearly synonymous with other terms such as assumptions, conventions, and postulates. Much work has been done, particularly in the US, to develop a range of generally acceptable accounting concepts or principles. Early work by individual researchers focused on the development of key accounting concepts, whereas later efforts, sponsored by both professional and standard-setting bodies, have attempted a more broadly based conceptual framework incorporating interrelated concepts.

Pioneering work in the derivation of accounting concepts was carried out in the US in the 1920s by PATON, who identified 11 accounting postulates. These included items that would appear in many later compilations (such as the "entity", "going concern", and "accrual postulates") along with more individualistic postulates (such as the assumption that stock valuation follows the first-in-first-out method). Paton can be criticized for focusing on the income statement at the expense of the balance sheet in his development of postulates, but his ideas provided the foundation for subsequent accounting scholarship.

Paton's early work was later refined by PATON & LITTLETON, who attempted to generalize six basic concepts, or assumptions, from US accounting practice. These included the "entity", "continuity", "matching", and "verifiable evidence" concepts. The aim, as stated in their preface, was "to weave together the fundamental ideas of accounting ... to build a framework". Their monograph was widely read in both academic and professional circles, and influenced subsequent accounting research.

Another substantial work that followed the inductive approach was that of SANDERS, HATFIELD & MOORE. They developed 25 accounting principles through research that included interviewing users and preparers of accounts, and studying corporate practices. Their broad analysis of principles was subdivided into several key areas, including general principles, income-statement principles, and balance-sheet principles. Key principles included the concept that information should be provided relating to both the financial condition and income of a business; that capital and revenue items must be separated; and that income statements should show all relevant information. This broad perspective attempted an integrated approach to the principles underlying financial statements, and so may be seen as a precursor to subsequent efforts to construct a conceptual framework.

A later attempt to develop a coherent framework based on accounting concepts was supported by the American Institute of Certified Public Accountants. In two of the research studies it sponsored, the focus was on accounting postulates (MOONITZ) and accounting principles (SPROUSE & MOONITZ). These researchers used deductive reasoning to produce 14 postulates and eight principles, the aim being to develop postulates that underlie key accounting principles. A very useful critique of this ambitious project was provided by CHAMBERS, who found problems with the methodology employed but nevertheless argued that the work would be seen as being in the vanguard of progress in accounting as this was first time that a deductive approach had been applied in a major study of accounting concepts.

ZEFF provides an excellent comparative analysis of the development of accounting principles across five countries. His very well-documented study surveys the US, Mexico, and Canada, along with England and Scotland. It demonstrates the major influence that the accounting profession has had in the development of the accounting principles underlying accounting practice, and so puts into perspective the contributions of various academic researchers.

Some of the concepts discussed by academic researchers were eventually included in the guidelines issued by professional accountancy bodies and, ultimately, in accounting standards. In the UK, for example, the ACCOUNTING STANDARDS COMMITTEE incorporated four fundamental accounting concepts into its second Statement of Standard Accounting Practice. Two of these concepts ("going concern" and "accruals") can be traced back to Paton, the remainder ("consistency" and "prudence") appearing in later studies. In the absence of a statement to the contrary, the presumption was that companies would observe these concepts when preparing their accounts. These four concepts assumed greater importance when they were included in the UK Companies Act 1981, as a result of the European Fourth Directive.

Another important concept implemented through the European Fourth Directive was the requirement that corporate accounts should show a true and fair view of the financial affairs of a company. This concept, which did not appear in early studies but was developed by the accounting profession, is a very nebulous one, as it is possible for more than one set of financial statements to show a true and fair view of a company's financial position. WALTON provides a stimulating introduction to a useful series of articles that discuss the problems of harmonizing this concept, which is subject to different interpretations across various European countries. He emphasizes the bizarre British notion of "true and fair view". This concept has the characteristic that

> no one knows what it means ... it is a legal term in origin and yet the Companies Acts have never defined it ... There is no definition of it in accounting standards, auditing standards or other professional pronouncements (p.49).

A useful attempt to harmonize accounting concepts would involve the development of a generally applicable conceptual framework. There is no agreement as to the precise content of such a framework, but any model would need to include accounting concepts in its structure. The most ambitious attempt to construct a conceptual framework was that of the US Financial Accounting Standards Board in the 1970s and 1980s. This proved to be very difficult, and so the project was abandoned in 1985. MACVE provides an excellent analysis of the problems involved in, and the potential benefits of, developing a conceptual framework. His analysis draws upon the US project, along with work done in the UK and Canada, and includes many useful references and appendices. He concludes that it is not feasible to hope for a conceptual framework that will give explicit guidance for the preparation of financial statements. However, Macve argues that the quest for such a framework is very important, as it obliges researchers to ask important questions about the nature of accounting.

ROBERT JUPE

Accounting history

Carnegie, Garry D. and Christopher J. Napier, "Critical and Interpretive Histories: Insights into Accounting's Present and Future through Its Past", *Accounting, Auditing & Accountability Journal*, 9/3 (1996): 7–39

Chambers, R.J. (editor), *An Accounting Thesaurus: 500 Years of Accounting*, Oxford:: Pergamon Press, 1995

Chatfield, Michael and Richard Vangermeersch (editors), *The History of Accounting: An International Encyclopedia*, New York: Garland, 1996

Edwards, J.R., *A History of Financial Accounting*, London and New York: Routledge, 1989

Edwards, John Richard (editor), *Twentieth Century Accounting Thinkers*, London and New York: Routledge, 1994

Hopwood, Anthony G. and Peter Miller (editors), *Accounting as Social and Institutional Practice*, Cambridge and New York: Cambridge University Press, 1994

Johnson, Thomas H. and Robert S. Kaplan, *Relevance Lost: The Rise and Fall of Management Accounting*, Boston: Harvard Business School Press, 1987; 2nd edition 1991

Kirkham, Linda M. and Anne Loft, "Gender and the Construction of the Professional Accountant", *Accounting, Organizations and Society*, 18/6 (1993): 507–58

Littleton, A.C. and B.S. Yamey (editors), *Studies in the History of Accounting*, London: Sweet and Maxwell, 1956

Matthews, Derek, Malcolm Anderson and J.R. Edwards, *The Priesthood of Industry: The Rise of the Professional Accountant in Business Management*, Oxford: Oxford University Press, 1998

Parker, Robert H. (editor), *Accounting in Australia: Historical Essays*, New: Garland, 1990

Parker, R.H. and B.S. Yamey (editors), *Accounting History: Some British Contributions*, Oxford: Clarendon Press, and New York: Oxford University Press, 1994

Previts, Gary John and Barbara Dubis Merino, *A History of Accountancy in the United States: The Cultural Significance of Accounting*, Columbus: Ohio State University Press, 1998

Zeff, Stephen A., *Forging Accounting Principles in Five Countries: A History and an Analysis of Trends*, Champaign, Illinois: Stipes, 1972

LITTLETON & YAMEY's edited collection of 22 essays on the history of accounting and especially on the origins of double entry bookkeeping is generally acknowledged as a classic. Illuminating the long history of double entry was one of the purposes of this collection. While the history of double entry bookkeeping tended to preoccupy early accounting historians, an increasing number of present scholars in the field are more prone to view accounting as a social and institutional practice with implications for organizational and social functioning, rather than as a neutral, if not benign, technical practice. Certain essays in this collection – such as those by de Roover, de Ste Croix, Edey & Panitpakdi, and Jackson – are still widely read or consulted.

CARNEGIE & NAPIER explore the different roles played by the study of accounting history. They examine the appeals to accounting's past as a status symbol, attempts to use accounting's past to understand its dynamic nature and to provide a database for solutions to present problems, and recent efforts to understand accounting's present and past through the use of theoretical perspectives drawn from relevant disciplines such as economics, sociology, and political theory. The authors also propose certain research directions in accounting history, including prosopography and comparative international accounting history, and some innovative research methods, particularly oral and quantitative history.

Today's accounting history scholars have also expanded their interests beyond the procedural aspects of accounting. MATTHEWS, ANDERSON & EDWARDS, for instance, examine the rise of the accounting profession and, in particular, the key roles played by accountants in British management. The authors point to the remarkable success of the profession in establishing accounting as the leading management qualification in Britain. EDWARDS (1994) presents an edited collection of 19 essays on accounting thinkers of the 20th century. Subjects are selected from a range of countries, and include Blough, Chambers, Dicksee, Kurosawa, Limperg Jr, MacNeal, Mattessich, Schmalenbach, Stamp, and Zappa. The biographical essays address the contributions of the subjects to the development of accounting theory, and attempt to assess their influence on contemporary practice.

The two main forms of accounting, financial accounting or financial reporting, and management accounting, have often been the subject of separate historical analysis. EDWARDS (1989) examines the development of financial accounting practices in Britain. The 21 chapters are grouped under the following section headings: introduction; from ancient times to the Industrial Revolution; corporate financial reporting practices; rules and regulations; and the development of a profession. The author seeks to identify the various sources of accounting practices adopted in Britain at the time of writing, and to identify key changes in practice and the timing of, and reasons for, those changes.

In a provocative work, JOHNSON & KAPLAN traced the development of US management accounting practices from the early 1800s through to the mid-1980s. The authors point to the stagnation in the innovation of management accounting practices from 1925 onwards. They attribute this stagnation to the dominance of external financial reporting systems during the 20th century. Their volume sparked a series of rebuttals, but stimulated a renewed focus on management accounting practices within corporations.

Histories of accounting development in specific countries are common. PREVITS & MERINO present a chronicle of accounting development in the US from the colonial period to the late 1990s. Based on an earlier work of a similar title published in 1979, this revised work of eight chapters attempts to place the development of accounting in its major institutional domains, including public practice, financial reporting, business management, government, and education. PARKER's edited collection of articles and some previously unpublished works describes the history of accounting in Australia. The 27 contributions are grouped under the following headings: early accounting records; the financial year; corporate financial reporting; audit; professional accountancy; accounting literature; and biographies and bibliographies. ZEFF examines the experiences of five countries comprising Canada, Mexico,

England, Scotland, and the US in the development of accounting principles. Separate chapters address the historical evolution of accounting pronouncements in each country, and a critical review of trends is given in the final chapter.

In an enlightening study of the professionalisation of accounting, based on an analysis of British census records from 1870–1930, KIRKHAM & LOFT examine how the professional accountant came to be constituted as neither a bookkeeper nor a clerk, and also not as a woman. The authors thus categorize the professionalisation project in accounting as fundamentally gendered, and elucidate its success as linked to maintaining a masculine identity for the professional accountant. Works of a similar genre appear in HOPWOOD & MILLER's edited collection of 12 essays. Regarded as the first major collection of critical and sociohistorical analyses of accounting, the collection challenges conventional views of accounting as a technical practice, and portrays accounting as social and institutional practice. The essays are concerned with accounting in various contexts, and thus with its relevance beyond the discipline itself.

Two key reference books in the field of accounting history scholarship are the edited international encyclopedia of CHATFIELD & VANGERMEERSCH, and an illuminating thesaurus on accounting by CHAMBERS. The former volume presents more than 400 entries on such subjects as publications, institutional bodies, accounting and economic concepts, accounting issues, accounting authors, leaders in the profession, and historical researchers. Comprising over 6000 quotations drawn from 500 years of English-language accounting literature, especially from the past 150 years, the thesaurus contains entries on a variety of matters, including accounting rules, practices and standards, professional and academic opinions, and the social and logical foundations of accounting.

PARKER & YAMEY present important published work of leading British scholars. The 23 articles comprising this volume are grouped under the following headings: the ancient world; before double entry; double entry; corporate accounting; local government accounting; cost and management accounting; accounting theory; and accounting in context. Together, these articles elucidate an understanding from a general perspective of the development of accounting, especially in the UK.

GARRY D. CARNEGIE

Accounting policies

Dechow, Patricia M., Richard G. Sloan and Amy P. Sweeney, "Detecting Earnings Management", *Accounting Review*, 70/2 (1995): 193–225

Healy, Paul M., "The Effect of Bonus Schemes on Accounting Decisions", *Journal of Accounting and Economics*, 7/1–3 (April 1985): 85–107

International Accounting Standards Committee, *Presentation of Financial Statements*, International Accounting Standard, IAS 1, London: International Accounting Standards Committee, 1997

Jones, Jennifer J., "Earnings Management During Import Relief Investigations", *Journal of Accounting Research*, 29/2 (1991): 193–228

McInnes, W.M., "A Longitudinal Study of Accounting Changes: The UK Gas Industry 1969–1974", *Accounting and Business Research*, 20/80 (1990): 315–27

Ronen, Joshua and Simcha Sadan, *Smoothing Income Numbers: Objectives, Means and Implications*, Reading, Massachusetts and London: Addison Wesley, 1981

Watts, Ross L., "Corporate Financial Statements, A Product of the Market and Political Processes", *Australian Journal of Management*, 2 (April 1977): 53–75

Watts, Ross L. and Jerold L. Zimmerman, "Towards a Positive Theory of the Determination of Accounting Standards", *Accounting Review*, 53/1 (1978): 112–34

Watts, Ross L. and Jerold L. Zimmerman, *Positive Accounting Theory*, Englewood Cliffs, New Jersey and London: Prentice Hall, 1986

Zmijewski Mark E. and Robert L. Hagerman, "An Income Strategy Approach to the Positive Theory of Accounting Standard Setting/Choice", *Journal of Accounting and Economics*, 3/2 (August 1981): 129–49

Accounting policies are defined by the INTERNATIONAL ACCOUNTING STANDARDS COMMITTEE as "the specific principles, bases, conventions, rules and practices adopted by an enterprise in preparing and presenting financial statements". Examples of matters for which different accounting policies are recognized and that may have a material effect on reported results and financial position include: depreciation of fixed assets; amortization of intangible assets; stocks and work in progress; long-term contracts; and deferred taxation. The main purpose of accounting standards is to reduce managers' discretion in their choices of accounting policies. Nevertheless, managers still have some discretion in these choices.

It has been argued that this discretion provides management with the opportunity to use accounting policies to manage earnings. The first attempts to investigate accounting policy choices focused on the hypothesis that managers' accounting choices are aimed at smoothing reported income. RONEN & SADAN provide a useful review of the income smoothing literature. Income smoothing research has subsequently been criticized because it is based implicitly on the assumption that managers believe that investors cannot, or will not, adjust fully for managers' accounting choices. Subsequent empirical work (reviewed in WATTS & ZIMMERMAN, 1986, chapter four) suggests that accounting choices with no known cashflow consequences do not affect security prices (investors do adjust for managers' accounting choices).

The above investigations into the relationship between accounting choices and movements in stock prices identified apparently systematic accounting choices that could not be explained. A more recent strand of empirical accounting research has adopted a different approach to explain such choices. This research assumes that contracting and information costs in both the contracting and political processes are nonzero and then tests simple hypotheses that are based on the further assumption that accounting choices have the potential to affect the firm's or the managers' future cashflows. The arguments from which these simple hypotheses are derived were explored originally by WATTS (1977) and WATTS & ZIMMERMAN (1978) and these papers should provide useful background reading for a newcomer to this literature.

These arguments are refined in WATTS & ZIMMERMAN (1986, chapters eight, nine and ten). The three main hypotheses that have been tested to date are the bonus plan hypothesis, the debt\equity hypothesis, and the political-cost hypothesis. The arguments underpinning the first two hypotheses are drawn from the literature on the contracting process. It is argued that if a firm operates a management compensation plan its managers have incentives to adopt income-increasing accounting choices to increase their bonus payments. The argument underpinning the second hypothesis is that the higher the proportion of debt to equity the more likely it is that managers will adopt income-increasing accounting choices to reduce the probability of violating restrictive covenants in debt contracts. The third hypothesis is drawn from the literature on the political process. It is based on the argument that if a firm is politically sensitive its managers have incentives to adopt income-decreasing accounting choices to reduce its political sensitivity and hence the probability of suffering negative wealth transfers or political costs that would increase the firm's cash outflows.

Watts & Zimmerman (1986, chapter 11) also provide a comprehensive review of the tests of these hypotheses up to 1985. Most of the early studies focus on a single accounting choice (for example, depreciation). According to the theoretical framework that underpins these studies, most firms probably face conflicting pressures from the contracting and political processes. They therefore probably do not opt for extreme income-increasing or income-decreasing accounting choices. Thus a single accounting choice may not be representative of a firm's other accounting choices. Furthermore, focusing on a single accounting choice reduces the power of the tests as managers are concerned with how the combination of accounting policies affects reported earnings instead of the effect of just one accounting choice.

The first study to investigate more than one accounting choice was ZMIJEWSKI & HAGERMAN who treat a firm's set of accounting choices as a single comprehensive decision, which they term the firm's "income strategy". They include four accounting choices in their study but still achieve only low explanatory power. In a UK context McINNES (1990) investigates all the accounting changes made by one organization, the British Gas Corporation, over a five-year period. He finds ten income-decreasing accounting changes during the three years when there are incentives to decease earnings. This finding is consistent with the argument in Zmijewski & Hagerman that a firm's accounting choices are not made independently.

An even more comprehensive approach is adopted by HEALY who focuses on total accruals, which include not only the effects of accounting policy choices but also the effects of accounting estimates. Total accruals are defined as the difference between operating earnings and net cashflow from operations and are generally calculated as the change in noncash working capital accruals less total depreciation expense. The main weakness of Healy's research is that he did not attempt to estimate what total accruals would have been in the absence of manipulation. Nevertheless, Healy's total accruals approach is innovative and is still one of the most heavily cited papers in the earnings management literature.

JONES is also innovative, heavily cited, and important as her total accruals model (or a modification thereof) has been adopted by many subsequent researchers in the earnings management area. She attempts to improve on Healy's approach by partitioning total accruals into nondiscretionary and discretionary components. The former are estimated by regressing total accruals on changes in revenues and on the fixed asset balance at the beginning of the year. Discretionary accruals are the difference between total accruals and the estimate of the nondiscretionary component.

DECHOW, SLOAN & SWEENEY test the ability of five total accruals models, including those of Healy and of Jones to detect earnings management. They also include a Modified Jones model. This is the original Jones model, which Dechow, Sloan & Sweeney modify by adjusting the change in revenues for the change in receivables. They find that all of the models lack power in detecting earning management but that the Modified Jones model works best. As a result several recent studies have used the Modified Jones model.

W.M. McINNES

Accounting, balance sheet

Accounting Standards Board, *Draft Statement of Principles for Financial Reporting*, London: Accounting Standards Board, 1995

Archer, Simon, "The ASB's Exposure Draft Statement of Principles: A Comment", *Accounting and Business Research*, 27/3 (1997): 229–41

Belkaoui, Ahmed R., *Accounting Theory*, 3rd edition, Cambridge and New York: Cambridge University Press, 1992

Chambers, Raymond J., "The Function of the Balance Sheet", *Chartered Accountant in Australia*, April (1957): 565–70; reprinted in *Chambers on Accounting*, vol. 3: *Accounting Theory and Research*, edited by Raymond J. Chambers and Graeme W. Dean, New York: Garland, 1986

Holmes, Geoffrey and Alan Sugden, *Interpreting Company Reports and Accounts*, 6th edition, New York and Hemel Hempstead, Hertfordshire: Prentice Hall, 1997

Lee, Tom A., *Company Financial Reporting*, 2nd edition, Wokingham, Berkshire: Van Nostrand Reinhold, 1982

Nobes, Christopher and Robert H. Parker, *Comparative International Accounting*, 5th edition, Hemel Hempstead, Hertfordshire: Prentice Hall, 1998

Parker, Robert H., *Understanding Company Financial Statements*, 4th edition, London: Penguin, 1994

Solomons, David, *Guidelines for Financial Reporting Standards*, London: Institute of Chartered Accountants in England and Wales, 1989; New York: Garland, 1997

Whittington, Geoffrey, *Inflation Accounting: An Introduction to the Debate*, Cambridge and New York: Cambridge University Press, 1983

The balance sheet is one of the primary financial statements prepared by an enterprise. It summarizes an enterprise's assets, liabilities, and equity at a point in time. All balance sheets conform to the accounting identity (assets equal liabilities plus equity), which shows how the assets of an enterprise have been financed. PARKER provides a very good introductory treatment of the accounting identity and the balance sheet. He shows how to understand, analyse, and interpret the elements in a balance sheet. The study includes many useful definitions of key terms, along with further reading on particular aspects of the balance sheet.

LEE contains a more specialized treatment of the balance sheet. He covers a large amount of material, set in a context that includes the legislative development of company financial reporting. Lee analyses the content of balance sheets in detail, examines problems involved in their construction, and discusses the difficulties in providing comprehensible balance-sheet data for users.

Another more specialized analysis of the balance sheet is provided by HOLMES & SUGDEN. They have produced a very useful practical guide to the analysis of financial statements, including balance sheets, in company accounts. Frequent reference is made to recent UK legal and accounting requirements that underlie the preparation of balance sheets. They use many extracts from actual company accounts to illustrate the analysis of balance-sheet items, such as fixed and current assets and liabilities.

All balance sheets conform to the accounting identity, but there are substantial differences between balance sheets prepared by enterprises in different countries. NOBES & PARKER provide very valuable international comparisons of both the format and content of balance sheets across different countries and continents. The treatment of assets, for instance, varies considerably between countries. In the US and Japan, balance sheets are structured to show assets in decreasing order of liquidity, whereas in European countries such as France they appear in increasing order of liquidity. Valuation also varies between countries, with asset revaluation banned in Japan, for example, but allowed in the UK.

The balance sheet's content is determined at a conceptual level by the perspective taken on how company earnings are identified. BELKAOUI provides a valuable discussion of the three broad perspectives that may be adopted: the balance-sheet view, the income-statement view, and the nonarticulated view. The first perspective holds that revenue and expenses result from changes in assets and liabilities; the second emphasizes income measurement and views assets and liabilities as residual by-products of revenues and expenses. Both these views are articulated, in the sense that they assume the balance sheet and the income statement to be linked by the same measurement process. The nonarticulated approach is the most radical, as it views the two financial statements as being quite independent of each other.

Before the 1920s, accounting was dominated by the balance-sheet view. In the 1930s and 1940s, however, income statements came to dominate financial reporting. CHAMBERS provides a concise early critique of the postulated primacy of the income statement and the subsequent relegation of the balance sheet to an inferior position. He focuses on the importance of the balance sheet for analysing the return on capital of a business, together with the misleading nature of traditional balance sheets based on outdated asset valuations.

Work by both academic researchers and standard-setting bodies has meant that in more recent years, the balance sheet has been accorded a greater significance. SOLOMONS provides a detailed case in favour of the primacy of the balance sheet approach. He argues that assets and liabilities are the essential elements of financial statements and that other items, or sub-elements, are derived from changes in these elements. Solomons argues that this approach is based on a logical set of principles, is more closely related to wealth creation, and discourages artificial methods of income smoothing. He advocates measuring balance-sheet items according to their value to the business.

WHITTINGTON provides an extremely valuable and well-written survey of the issues involved in inflation accounting. The debate over how financial statements, particularly balance sheets, could reflect the impact of inflation was prominent in the 1960s and 1970s as inflation rates rose. Whittington examines the debate in detail, covering the contributions of many academics and analysing various models that have been proposed to improve the information content of balance sheets. He concludes that there is no universally correct model that will serve all users in all circumstances.

A radical attempt to change UK company balance sheets by introducing current cost accounting was abandoned in the 1980s, after opposition from companies and the accounting profession. However, the principle of incorporating some current values into balance sheets has recently been advocated by the ACCOUNTING STANDARDS BOARD (ASB). The ASB argues that current values are already used to an extent in balance sheets as, for example, some companies revalue their fixed assets rather than leaving them at historical cost. More controversially, however, it argues (paragraph 5.38) that "practice should develop by evolving in the direction of greater use of current values to the extent that this is consistent with the constraints of reliability and cost".

ARCHER has produced a detailed critique of the ASB's attempt to develop current value reporting in balance sheets. He argues that there are several problems with the ASB's approach. Archer criticizes the proposal to incorporate current values into balance sheets on the grounds of cost-effectiveness, the lack of relevance to users, and the opportunities that would be offered to companies for creative accounting. He concludes that the ASB needs to establish a broader framework for the standard-setting process before it can consider specific details such as the valuation principle to be adopted for balance sheets.

ROBERT JUPE

Accumulation of capital

Bukharin, Nikolai I., *Imperialism and the Accumulation of Capital* (with *The Accumulation of Capital: An Anti-Critique* by Rosa Luxemburg), edited by Kenneth J. Tarbuck, London: Allen Lane, 1972; New York: Monthly Review Press, 1973 (Russian edition 1924)

Frank, Andre Gunder, *World Accumulation, 1492–1789*, New York: Monthly Review Press, 1978

Lenin, V.I., "A Characterization of Economic Romanticism (Sismondi and Our Native Sismondists)" in his *Collected Works*, vol. 2, Moscow: Progress, 1963 (published in Russian 1897)

Lenin, V.I., *The Development of Capitalism in Russia*, Moscow: Foreign Languages Publishing House, 1956 (published in Russian 1899)

Lenin, V.I., "Karl Marx: A Brief Biographical Sketch with an Exposition of Marxism" in his *Collected Works*, vol. 21, Moscow: Progress, 1964 (published in Russian 1915)

Luxemburg, Rosa, *The Accumulation of Capital*, London: Routledge and Kegan Paul, and New Haven, Connecticut: Yale University Press, 1951 (German edition 1913)

Luxemburg, Rosa, *The Accumulation of Capital: An AntiCritique* (with *Imperialism and the Accumulation of Capital* by Nikolai Bukharin), edited by Kenneth J. Tarbuck, London: Allen Lane, 1972; New York: Monthly Review Press, 1973 (German edition 1921)

Marx, Karl, *Capital*, vol. 1: *A Critical Analysis of Capitalist Production*, London and New York: Penguin, 1976 (German edition 1867)

Ricardo, David, *On the Principles of Political Economy and Taxation*, 3rd edition, London: John Murray, 1821; in *The Works and Correspondence of David Ricardo*, edited by Piero Sraffa and M.H. Dobb, vol. 1, Cambridge: Cambridge University Press, 1951

Robinson, Joan, *The Accumulation of Capital*, 3rd edition, London: Macmillan, 1969

Smith, Adam, *An Inquiry into the Nature and Causes of the Wealth of Nations*, edited by Kathryn Sutherland, Oxford and New York: Oxford University Press, 1993 (first published 1776)

SMITH and RICARDO, although having forerunners, are considered to be the founders of political economy. Smith considered capital to be the "stock" possessed by individuals which will yield a revenue or profit over time. This capital can be circulating capital, as in the case of raising livestock, manufacturing, or purchasing and reselling goods; or fixed capital, as in the case of land improvements, machinery, and equipment. Accumulation of capital is simply the increase in this stock over time. However, Smith does not analyse how capital accumulates, or the effects of its accumulation.

Ricardo is a genuine economic theorist, and in a famous chapter "On Machinery" introduced into the 3rd edition of his *Principles*, he considered whether the introduction of new machinery would necessarily raise the wages of workers. He came to the conclusion that new machinery need not raise wages, because machinery could substitute for the labour of workers, thereby reducing the demand for workers and leading to a cut in worker income. ROBINSON continued concerns Ricardo raised and addressed new issues.

MARX broke theoretically with the basic principles of classical political economy, but did not decisively break on the issue of accumulation of capital. While he does address accumulation in other parts of his work, the main discussion is found in Part VII of *Capital* towards the end of the book. Marx uses the word "capital" mainly in connection with the relationship between the capitalist class and the class of wage labourers: *Capital*, his main work, is subtitled *A Critique of Political Economy*, and implies a critique of the whole structure of the bourgeois political economy. If he indeed has redefined "capital" to refer to a class relation, surely his redefinition applies to the accumulation of capital. Indeed, he writes that "reproduction on a progressive scale, i.e., accumulation, reproduces the capital relation on a progressive scale, more capitalists or larger capitalists at this pole, more wage workers at that" so that "accumulation of capital is, therefore, increase of the proletariat" (pp.575–6). Furthermore, this discussion is nothing more than a logical conclusion of preceding chapters on "Simple Reproduction" and "Conversion of Surplus Value into Capital".

Just as Marx introduced "labour power" only late in his theoretical development, in order to distinguish his theoretical concept from "labour" in classical political economy and from common usage, so too he might have reconsidered "accumulation of capital", perhaps referring to accumulation of "capitalist relations". The theoretical space left somewhat ambiguous by Marx has been refilled with the concepts of classical economics by many authors writing in the Marxist tradition.

LENIN's (1915) biographical sketch on Marx states that:

new and important in the highest degree is Marx's analysis of the *accumulation of capital*, i.e. the transformation of a part of surplus value into capital, and its use, not for satisfying the personal needs or whims of the capitalist, but for new production (p.64, italics in original).

Note the absence of any reference to the exploitation of wage-labourers. Similar references can be found earlier in Lenin's theoretical work. For example, LENIN (1897, p.155 in Collected Works) agrees with David Ricardo that "accumulation is indeed the excess of production over revenue (articles of consumption)". LENIN (1899) contains very little explicit reference to accumulation of capital. It is an impressive work in its own right and one which could have connected the concept when writing "what is important is that capitalism cannot exist and develop without constantly expanding the sphere of its domination, without colonising new countries and drawing old noncapitalist countries into the whirlpool of world economy" (p.600 of 1956 edition).

No Marxist has written more about the accumulation of capital as a concept than LUXEMBURG (1913, 1921), who devoted a long book and a long pamphlet (published two years after her murder) to the topic, summarizing her position and replying to critics. Many of Luxemburg's critics switched political sides and supported Germany at the advent of World War I: thus what appear initially to be purely theoretical positions, are in fact related to political positions. Luxemburg's position can be summarized as follows. Although in *Capital*, Marx described an economy in which the only significant classes are capitalists and workers (and to a lesser extent, landlords), this was only a simplifying theoretical assumption, and he was quite aware of the existence of other classes. However, this theoretical simplification got Marx into trouble when analysing the accumulation of capital. Luxemburg proceeds by logical deduction to consider the potential uses of surplus value in such an economy. A capitalist must market products produced, yet there are only two basic classes, capitalists and workers. Capitalists must sell to workers the workers' basic subsistence goods, but nothing more than that. They can sell to themselves both subsistence and luxury goods, but there are only so many luxury goods they can consume, and the drive within capitalism is quite distinctly for accumulation, not merely for luxury consumption. So their only other outlet is marketing more means of production. Marketing more and more means of production can be sustained in the shortrun, but with no other outlet (such as civil servants, the military, academics, the clergy, etc. – who are viewed simply as hangers-on to capitalists), the system would eventually reach an impasse. Consequently, there is a need, says Luxemburg, to create a home market, or for imperialist expansion, or both.

In 1913 Lenin began a critique of Luxemburg, which he never completed. He did say, as late as 1922, that "she was mistaken on the theory of the accumulation of capital". BUKHARIN undertook a detailed analysis of Luxemburg's position, published in the same year as his alignment with Stalin in the postLenin power struggles. The work has all the marks of theoretical hatchet work. He, along with Stalinists in general, seems to have effectively buried much interest in Luxemburg's *Accumulation*.

"Primitive" accumulation is discussed extensively by FRANK (particularly his chapter 7). Marx had introduced the concept, referring to the transition from feudalism to capitalism in Europe, an accumulation not the result of the capitalist mode of production, but its starting point ... The socalled primitive accumulation, therefore, is nothing else than the historical process of divorcing the producer from the means of production. It appears as primitive, because it forms the prehistoric stage of capital and of the mode of production corresponding with it (Marx, p.667–68).

Frank's discussion corresponds to a common perception that any separation of persons from noncapitalist modes of production, and their conversion into wagelabourers working for capitalists, represents primitive accumulation, even in today's world. However, he distinguishes "primary" from primitive, in that "primary" refers to the modern world, and can refer to subsistence agricultural plots which sustain wageworkers, or to housewives sustaining families through domestic work. Primitive accumulation itself thus retains Marx's usage. Yet little is resolved in Frank's work, since overall accumulation of capital remains a somewhat ambiguous concept. Luxemburg's view is summarized in exactly one sentence (p.249), but not addressed.

PAUL ZAREMBKA

See also Marxist economics

Achievement

Ashton, Patricia T. and Rodman B. Webb, *Making a Difference: Teachers' Sense of Efficacy and Student Achievement*, New York: Longman, 1986

Bandura, Albert, Claudio Barbaranelli, Gian Vittorio Caprara and Concetta Pastorelli, "Multifaceted Impact of Self-efficacy Beliefs on Academic Functioning", *Child Development*, 67 (1996): 1206–22

Bandura, Albert, *Self-efficacy: The Exercise of Control*, New York: Freeman, 1997

Childs, T. Stephen and Carol Shakeshaft, "A Meta-Analysis of Research on the Relationship between Educational Expenditures and Student Achievement", *Journal of Education Finance*, 12/2 (1986): 249–63

Conoley, Jane and James Impara (editors), *The Twelfth Mental Measurements Yearbook*, Lincoln: University of Nebraska Press, 1995

Elliott, Elaine and Carol Dweck, "Goals: An Approach to Motivation and Achievement", *Journal of Personality and Social Psychology*, 54/1 (1988): 5–12

Fyans, Leslie (editor), *Achievement Motivation: Recent Trends in Theory and Research*, New York and London: Plenum, 1980

Glasgow, Kristan, Sanford Dornbusch, Lisa Troyer, Laurence Steinberg, and Phil Ritter, "Parenting Styles, Adolescents' Attributions, and Educational Outcomes in Nine Heterogeneous High Schools", *Child Development*, 68/3 (1997): 507–29

Gronlund, Norman E., *Assessment of Student Achievement*, 6th edition, Boston: Allyn and Bacon, 1998

Hanushek, Eric A., "The Economics of Schooling: Production and Efficiency in Public Schools", *Journal of Economic Literature*, 24 (September 1986): 1141–47

Horner, Matina, "Toward an Understanding of Achievement-Related Conflicts in Women", *Journal of Social Issues*, 28/2 (1972): 157–76

Jenkins, Sharon J., "Need for Achievement and Women's Careers over 14 Years: Evidence for Occupational Structure Effects", *Journal of Personality and Social Psychology*, 53/5 (1987): 922–32

Jussim, Lee and Jacquelynne Eccles, "Teacher Expectations II: Construction and Reflection of Student Achievement", *Journal of Personality and Social Psychology*, 63/6 (1992): 947–61

Klinger, Eric, "Fantasy Need Achievement as a Motivational Construct", *Psychological Bulletin*, 66/4 (1966): 291–308

Lea, Stephen E.G., Roger M. Tarpley, and Paul Webley, *The Individual in the Economy: A Textbook of Economic Psychology*, Cambridge and New York: Cambridge University Press, 1987

Loeb, Susanna and John Bound, "The Effect of Measured School Inputs on Academic Achievement: Evidence from the 1920s, 1930s and 1940s Birth Cohorts", *Review of Economics and Statistics*, 78/4 (1996): 653–64

McClelland, David C., *The Achieving Society: With a New Introduction*, New York: Irvington, 1976 (first published 1961)

Rueda, R. and M.H. Dembo, "Motivational Processes in Learning: A Comparative Analysis of Cognitive and Sociocultural Frameworks", *Advances in Motivation and Achievement*, 9 (1995): 255–89

Schlesinger, I.M. and Louis Guttman, "Smallest Space Analysis of Intelligence and Achievement Tests", *Psychological Bulletin*, 71/2 (1969): 95–100

Spangler, William, "Validity of Questionnaire and TAT Measures of Need for Achievement: Two Meta-Analyses", *Psychological Bulletin*, 112/1 (1992): 140–54

Triandis, H.C., "Motivation and Achievement in Collectivist and Individualist Cultures", *Advances in Motivation and Achievement*, 9 (1995): 1–30

Urdan, T.C., L. Kneisel, and V. Mason, "Interpreting Messages about Motivation in the Classroom, Examining the Effects of Achievement Goal Structures", *Advances in Motivation and Achievement*, 11 (1999): 123–58

Wentzel, Kathryn, "Parents' Aspirations for Children's Educational Attainments: Relations to Parental Beliefs and Social Address Variables", *Merrill-Palmer Quarterly*, 44/1 (1998): 20–37

As studied in the social sciences, the construct of achievement unites several different literatures. First, achievement has long been studied as educational attainment, especially in relation to intelligence and other ability and background variables. The paradigmatic approach which endures to the present time relates achievement as a state or level of accomplishment (measured, for example, by standardized test scores, grades or actual educational and career attainment) to intelligence and other ability measures, and to background variables such as family interaction, social class, and school quality. Both cognitive mediating variables (such as self-efficacy beliefs) and social interaction patterns in the family, at school, and in peer relationships are being increasingly integrated into accounts of academic achievement.

Over the lengthy consideration of these relationships, cognitive mediating variables such as social motives, control beliefs, and values have become increasingly important. Second, the study of achievement as a social motive has developed into a line of inquiry of its own and been related to such diverse topics as the maintenance of social class, economic inequality, entrepreneurship, and economic growth, as well as to academic achievement. At the present time, studies of achievement have been extended to include effects of differences in goal structures and consequences of performance feedback for subsequent achievement.

SCHLESINGER & GUTTMAN exemplifies psychometric studies of the structure of intelligence and achievement relationships in the absence of mediating variables. The authors use the statistical technique of smallest space analysis to relate rule-inferring and rule-applying abilities of intelligence to achievement across verbal, digital, and figural modalities. Reviews of a sample of currently used tests of academic achievement and evidence for their reliability and validity can be found in CONOLEY & IMPARA. GRONLUND is the current edition of a widely referenced text on the construction and assessment of achievement tests.

Early studies of the relationship between family background, school quality and academic achievement have reported significant effects of background variables such as parental education and occupation, but have not found significant effects of school quality. The frequently cited 1966 Coleman report, also known as the Equality of Educational Opportunity Report, studied a representative national sample of schools, and showed slight effects of school quality once differences in family background were controlled. HANUSHEK's research review was unable to define a measurable characteristic of schools that consistently related to school achievement. In their meta-analysis, CHILDS & SHAKESHAFT also reported a minimal relationship between educational expenditure and student achievement except for direct instructional expenditure as in teacher salaries and supplies. Recently, LOEB & BOUND have indicated that previous results for school quality may reflect whether aggregate or micro data were used in the analysis. Using aggregate historical data on school inputs to predict the scholastic achievement of individuals in three cohorts, their results showed highly significant effects of school inputs on achievement.

WENTZEL, and GLASGOW et al, relate background variables to achievement and family interaction in the home. Results of these studies show that in addition to the parents' race, sex, and age; parental beliefs and aspirations, amount and style of parental involvement, and the communities in which individuals reside have consistently important effects on children's educational attainment. Other inquiries focusing upon teacher variables have also shown strong and significant effects of teacher sense of efficacy (ASHTON & WEBB) and teacher expectations (JUSSIM & ECCLES) on student achievement measures.

KLINGER provides both a useful review of the history of achievement as a motivational construct and a critique of the early measurement procedures for the construct and its relationship to performance measures. His study is among the early indicators of the importance of cognitive, situational, and developmental variables to relationships between achievement motivation and performance measures. This discussion is updated and extended by SPANGLER who uses meta-analysis to cumulate the evidence relating the strength of the measured motive to outcomes and differences between projective and questionnaire measures of the motive in these relationships.

McCLELLAND initiated broad application of the achievement motive in societal contexts outside of education. The most well-known of these is his application of the achievement motive to economic growth in a Weberian framework. Although subsequent empirical evidence has not supported his empirics relating the achievement motive to growth (for example, see LEA, TARPLEY & WEBLEY, pp.436–41), the originality of McClelland's analysis and the scope of evidence he assembled across decades of study continues to influence thinking on the achievement motive and its applications.

Implications of early studies of sex differences in achievement motivation and related cognitive processing are discussed in HORNER. More recently, JENKINS has studied achievement motivation and women's careers. Her longitudinal study reports that achievement motivation predicts career outcomes when work situations and sex-differentiated occupational structures are considered, and that occupational structure also has effects on achievement motivation over time.

The chapters in FYANS remain of interest as early background statements of the directions that have been taken in studying the achievement motive by investigators who have been prominent in subsequent development of the construct. These include the relationship of this motive to causal attributions of success or failure, implications of sex differences in the motive, teacher expectations as they interact with the motive, and achievement motivation across the life span.

TRIANDIS provides a useful review of cultural differences in defining achievement and the relationship of the achievement motive to self, family, and to other motives across cultures. The organizing dimension of his review is in individualistic-collectivistic differences between cultures.

Recent study of motivation and achievement has greatly strengthened conceptual and empirical relationships suggested in earlier studies. Goals theory as it follows from earlier forms by investigators such as Weiner and Ames is detailed in ELLIOT & DWECK. The authors show that learning goals of mastery-oriented children result in responses to non-success feedback which are different from the responses of children without these goals. Their study of interactions of "learning" vs. "performance" goals and high vs. low perceived ability show conditions that correspond to patterns of failure attribution and negative affect found in naturally occurring "learned helplessness". The cognitive perspective on achievement that these studies presage is discussed at length in RUEDA & DEMBO and URDAN, KNEISEL & MASON.

Bandura's integration of the construct of self-efficacy in a comprehensive account of academic achievement is an important recent contribution to cognitive frameworks. BANDURA et al. details the cognitive and motivational effects of self-efficacy as they operate within social relations in the family and school on academic functioning. BANDURA provides a comprehensive statement on self-efficacy and its wide ranging effects on the exercise of agency including academic achievement.

STEVEN D. SILVER

See also Goals, Intelligence, Motivation

Act of Parliament

Allan, T.R.S., "Parliamentary Sovereignty: Law, Politics and Revolution", *Law Quarterly Review*, 113 (July 1997): 443–52

Bell, John and George Engle, *Statutory Interpretation*, 3rd edition, London: Butterworths, 1995 (original edition 1976, by Rupert Cross)

Bennion, F.A.R., *Statutory Interpretation: A Code*, 3rd edition, London: Butterworths, and Charlottesville, Virginia: Michie, 1997

Burrows, Noreen, "Unfinished Business: The Scotland Act 1998", *Modern Law Review*, 62/2 (1999): 241–60

Evershed, Francis Raymond, *The Impact of Statute on the Law of England*, London: Oxford University Press, 1957

Freeman, Michael (editor), *Legislation and the Courts*, Aldershot, Hampshire: Dartmouth, 1997

Greer, Steven, " A Guide to the Human Rights Act 1998", *European Law Review*, 24/1 (1999): 3–21

Law Commission, *Statute Law Revision: Sixteenth Report: Draft Statute Law (Repeals) Bill*, London: HMSO, 1998

Lyell, Nicholas, "Pepper v. Hart: The Government's Perspective", *Statute Law Review*, 15/1 (1994): 1–9

McMurtie, Sheena N., "The Constitutionality of the War Crimes Act 1991", *Statute Law Review*, 13/2 (1992): 128–49

Miers, David R., "Barking Up the Wrong Tree: Determining the Intention of Parliament", *Statute Law Review*, 13/1 (1992): 50–62

Thomas, E.W., "Parliamentary Supremacy and the Judicial Function", *Law Quarterly Review*, 112 (April 1996): 177–82

An Act of Parliament is an instrument that results from the highest expression of the legislative function of a parliamentary body. Traditionally, the UK Parliament has been treated by the courts as a sovereign body, capable of passing Acts without let or hindrance as to content and effect. A classic exposition of the development of this view and a more general history of the role of Acts of Parliament can be found in Lord EVERSHED's 1956 Maccabaean lecture in jurisprudence before the British Academy.

More recently, however, the interaction with European Community law (cf. European Communities Act 1972) and the recent incorporation of the European Convention on Human Rights has rendered the proposition that Parliament's sovereignty is absolute a dubious one. The procedures for passing an Act of Parliament and the rules of recognition that determine what are a valid Act belong in the more general category of constitutional law (q.v. and note the relevant passages on Acts of Parliament in De Smith & de Brazier (*Constitutional and Administrative Law*, 8th edition, 1998) but one interesting issue that arises in the present context is the extent to which an Act passed under the Parliament Acts (which purport to lay down procedures for bypassing the House of Lords) should be regarded as Acts at all, an issue considered by McMURTIE in relation to the War Crimes Act 1991.

To lawyers, the most important questions to ask about any Act are: "what does it mean?" and "what does it do?" In order to answer the first question, the key issue is the proper mode of statutory interpretation to be applied by the courts, tribunals, and other official bodies that have to execute the law or adjudicate on disputes arising under it. BELL & ENGLE sets out to examine statutory interpretation in a traditional manner: it looks at the history of treatment of Acts and considers the view of English jurists such as Coke and, starting from this point, looks at the various (sometimes conflicting) presumptions and rules of statutory interpretation.

BENNION, by contrast, takes a more purposive approach in that it tries to codify and weight the various factors that determine how the wording of an Act is construed. The book includes a full review of the important case of *Pepper v. Hart* ([1993] AC 593, a House of Lords decision that conditionally permitted use of Hansard in determining the meaning of an Act), a section reviewing the effect of EU legal rules and principles on British legislation, and a section on principles of statutory interpretation in the area of tax avoidance.

The articles by MIERS and by LYELL pick up the question of statutory interpretation: the former, written before *Pepper v. Hart*, is still of interest because it shows that the notion of hunting for the intention of Parliament is a somewhat illusory exercise and that, albeit within bounds, judges still have considerable discretion in shaping statutory law in practice (the worked example given is s1, Guard Dogs Act 1975). The article by Lyell goes on to look at the practical implications of the *Pepper v Hart* decision from an unusual angle: to what extent would members of the UK Government have to restrain themselves in making statements to Parliament for fear of having their words used against them?

The essays edited by FREEMAN look at the changing nature of the relationship between courts and Parliament and, consequently, the courts' abilities to constrain or override Acts of Parliament. Starting with the decision in the *Factortame* case that a statute could be abrogated by a court by virtue of the overriding effect of Community law (examined and criticised by ALLAN), there has been a recent expansion of the ability of the courts to deal with legislative invalidity under the new Human Rights Act 1998, examined in detail by GREER.

To finish with, there are two more specific articles and one reference work: THOMAS considers the interaction not just between the courts and Parliament but also relations with the Crown; the curtailment of Royal prerogative powers in favour of legislative schemes for criminal injuries compensation ties these subject areas together.

BURROWS examines the use of Acts of Parliament as a mechanism for redistributing power within the UK's constitutional framework by reference to the Scotland Act 1998; this put in place the arrangements for devolution such as the powers and functions of the new Scottish Parliament, its legislative competence, and its control over taxation.

The LAW COMMISSION report shows the sort of work that is put before that body for changes and working drafts to be prepared: recent proposals have included the criminalization of taking of trade secrets.

GARY LEA

Adaptation

Baum, Joel A.C. and Jitendra V. Singh (editors), *Evolutionary Dynamics of Organizations*, Oxford and New York: Oxford University Press, 1994

Burgelman, Robert A., "Intraorganizational Ecology of Strategy Making and Organizational Adaptation: Theory and Field Research", *Organization Science*, 2/3 (1991): 239–62

Dorf, Richard C. (editor), *The Technology Management Handbook*, Boca Raton, Florida: CRC Press, 1999

Hannan, Michael T. and John Freeman, "The Population Ecology of Organizations", *American Journal of Sociology*, 82/5 (1977): 929–64

Hrebiniak, Lawrence G. and William F. Joyce, "Organizational Adaptation: Strategic Choice and Environmental Determinism", *Administrative Science Quarterly*, 30 (1985): 336–49

Jantsch, Erich, *The Self-organizing Universe: Scientific and Human Implications of the Emerging Paradigm of Evolution*, Oxford and New York: Pergamon Press, 1980

Meyer, Alan D., Geoffrey R. Brooks and James B. Goes, "Environmental Jolts and Industry Revolutions: Organizational Responses to Discontinuous Change", *Strategic Management Journal*, 11 (1990): 93–110

Singh, Jitendra V. (editor), *Organizational Evolution: New Directions*, Newbury Park, California and London: Sage, 1990

Tushman, Michael L. and Philip Anderson (editors), *Managing Strategic Innovation and Change: A Collection of Readings*, Oxford and New York: Oxford University Press, 1997

Van de Ven, Andrew H. and Marshall Scott Poole, "Explaining Development and Change in Organizations", *Academy of Management Review*, 20/3 (1990): 510–40

"Adaptation" is used here to describe the process by which organizations respond to their environments. As a term, adaptation was first borrowed from the field of evolution. Organizational theorists and practitioners have gone on to expand and extend the concept, applying what was first a biological concept to the social environment. JANTSCH provides a good overview of many of the scientific concepts behind the theory of evolution and the concept of adaptation. The work is important because evolutionary concepts are defined at various levels: physical, chemical, biological, socio-biological, ecological, and sociocultural.

HANNAN & FREEMAN apply a population ecology model specifically to organizations. This is done in part as a challenge to the adaptation concept. The emphasis here is placed on the determinative role of the environment as opposed to the voluntary choices made by organizations. Although many theorists since Hannan & Freeman have questioned their model, this is a classic reference point in the field. BAUM & SINGH provide a more general view of the application of evolutionary concepts to the development of organizations. The reader will find chapters one, five and seven to be of particular interest. These chapters lay out the concepts of the variation-selection-retention model, trace the evolutionary processes of selected businesses, and introduce the notion of intentional adaptation.

As various theoretical orientations to adaptation developed, several efforts to classify these have been made. VAN DE VEN & POOLE present a more philosophically oriented typology of change theories: life cycle, teleology, dialectics, and evolution. This is useful in placing adaptation in perspective. An excellent taxonomy of various change theoretical orientations also appears in this resource. HREBINIAK & JOYCE focus more specifically on variations of evolutionary theory related to organizations. Hrebiniak & Joyce present a very helpful matrix of the approaches by outlining possible combinations between strategic choice positions and environmental determinism positions – a useful way to present the historical debate around the concept of adaptation. Four main types are identified: natural selection, differentiation, strategic choice, and undifferentiated choice. The authors skilfully link various organizational theorists to each of these four types.

As it has developed, the concept of adaptation has been used to explain how organizations and firms have adapted to and influenced their environmental surroundings. Three edited works provide excellent readings on these topics. All three have extensive bibliographies and additional resources. SINGH, following his earlier work, focuses on the survival of firms and the competitive processes affecting organizations. Chapters nine and ten, entitled "Organizational adaptation, environmental selection, and random walks", and "Evolution in communities of voluntary organizations", by Daniel Levinthal and J. Miller McPherson, respectively, are of particular interest. TUSHMAN & ANDERSON present a compendium of articles directed at understanding organizational processes for managing innovation and strategic change. The entire volume is worth reading, but the sections on technology cycles, technological change, and implementing new designs are especially related to the concept of adaptation. DORF represents a more limited, but equally comprehensive handbook, focused on how technology is managed. It was not specifically written on the subject of adaptation, but one of the major sections of the handbook is on innovation and change. This section includes readings on the evolution of innovation, discontinuous innovation, technology life cycles, and the diffusion of innovations. All three of these edited works have numerous references to organizational case studies.

Finally, two articles are noted that have taken the concepts and applied them to real life organizations. BURGELMAN takes the concept of adaptation and relates it to Intel Corporation's strategy choices between 1972 and 1988. Although this article is somewhat dated, it is of particular value because it clearly illustrates how the concepts of retention, selection, and variation can be used to illuminate an actual organizational situation. It also serves as a good recapitulation of the various theoretical options, outlining four different forms of adaptation: relative inertia, adjustment, reorientation, and strategic renewal (proposed as a new type by the author). Likewise, MEYER, BROOKS & GOES look at a specific industry, healthcare, to determine how adaptation occurs. Like some of the previous works, the authors present their own matrix of change models, which distinguishes adaptation from metamorphosis, evolution, and revolution. This is probably a suitable concluding point because the authors implicitly suggest that the concept of adaptation itself should be adapted and needs to be updated in the face of rapid and discontinuous change in the environment. Perhaps more modestly, they explicitly contend that there has been a gap in the theory and research around how organizations respond to discontinuous change.

DAVID W. FRANTZ

See also Organizational learning

Administrative law

Allen, Michael J., Brian Thompson and Bernadette Walsh, *Cases and Materials on Constitutional and Administrative Law*, London: Blackstone Press, 1990

Cann, Steven J., *Administrative Law*, London and Thousand Oaks, California: Sage, 1995

Douglas, Roger and Melinda Jones, *Administrative Law: Commentary and Materials*, 2nd edition, Sydney: Federation Press, 1996

Evans, J.M., *De Smith's Judicial Review of Administrative Action*, 4th edition, London: Stevens, 1980

Foulkes, David, *Administrative Law*, 8th edition, London: Butterworths, 1995

Hotop, Stanley D., *Cases and Materials on Review of Administrative Action*, 2nd edition, Sydney: Law Book Company, 1983

Jain, M.P. and S.N. Jain, *Principles of Administrative Law*, 4th edition, Bombay: Tripathi, 1986

Schwartz, Bernard, *Administrative Law*, 3rd edition, Boston and London: Little Brown, 1991

Streets, Susan, *Administrative Law: Butterworths Casebook Companions*, Melbourne: Butterworths, 1997

Wade, William, *Administrative Law*, 6th edition, Oxford: Clarendon Press, and New York: Oxford University Press, 1988

Wade, William and Christopher Forsyth, *Administrative Law*, Oxford: Clarendon Press, and New York: Oxford University Press, 1994

Yardley, D.C.M., *Principles of Administrative Law*, 2nd edition, London: Butterworths, 1986

ALLEN, THOMPSON & WALSH's analysis of administrative law includes a discussion of the procedure of judicial review and the Treaty on European Union. The rule of law as a broad political doctrine, and the rule of law and discretionary powers and individual rights are elaborated. The operation of the parliamentary style of government and the accountability of government are also examined. The rationale for tribunals and the characteristics of tribunals are included.

CANN concentrates on the working of bureaucracy but focuses on administrative law. His work is organized around a conceptual framework and a study of significant policy making by technocrats and bureaucrats. Case studies illustrate the theme of each chapter. This work contains helpful legal principles and summaries of administrative law doctrines.

DOUGLAS & JONES begins with the rise and problems of administrative law. It discusses judicial activism and selects several old favourites like *Roberts v. Hopwood* for analysis. Recent cases, which are more appropriate, are also discussed, and the importance of new administrative law is highlighted. The role of the ombudsman is discussed in connection with the investigation of administrative decisions. Negotiations through Members of Parliament and negotiations with civil servants are examined in the chapter on the merits of administrative review. Other topics of importance are delegated legislation, judicial review, discretionary powers, duty to act in good faith, procedural fairness, the rule against bias, and judicial remedies.

De Smith's Judicial Review of Administrative Action (see EVANS) has established itself as the most authoritative and comprehensive exposition of the role played by English courts in administrative law. It is considered a uniquely valuable work of scholarship. Smith concentrates on the role of courts in administrative law. Decisions of statutory tribunals and the scope for challenging these decisions, errors of law and fact, fair hearing, duty to give reasons, and legal standards to be maintained while exercising administrative discretion, form the basis of the book. The book begins with judicial review in administrative law and it continues by examining the scope of judicial review and judicial remedies. Developments in law since 1973 are also included.

FOULKES provides a brief historical and constitutional setting of administrative law. He also accounts for some of the wide range of administrative authorities. His discussion on legislation and administration deals with delegated legislation. It also includes codes of practice, inquiries with an emphasis on the administrative schemes, administrative arrangements including consultation, public participation, and licensing procedures. This book should be of use to practitioners as it raises constitutional issues. It also considers grounds on which the courts exercise common law powers and will strike down a decision on grounds of misuse of power. Natural justice and judicial reviews of administrative action are also highlighted.

HOTTOP concentrates upon the importance of administrative law. His book is a comprehensive collection of cases and other source materials dealing with the principles governing the review of administrative action. Although it appears to satisfy the needs of teaching administrative law, it also aims to serve the needs of legal practitioners. There are useful, brief introductory comments at the beginning of most of the chapters. The book emphasizes substantive common-law principles governing the grounds of judicial review of administrative action and deals in detail with delegated legislation, judicial review, classification of governmental powers, denial of natural justice, the contents and breach of natural justice, *ultra vires*, judicial remedies, and extrajudicial review of administrative action. There is an interesting note on the liability of the Crown and statutory authorities in contract and tort.

JAIN & JAIN was first published in 1971. Since then, several editions and reprints have appeared, and the book is very popular with students and practitioners. According to the authors, judges were slow in responding to the challenging problems generated by the modern administrative process. Judicial conservatism and traditional and inbuilt restraints within the legal process were seen as hindrances. The courts are now evolving new principles of administrative behaviour and controlling administrative process. This book deals with Indian administrative law along with English principles of administrative law. Some of the topics include the nature and scope of administrative law, delegated legislation, administrative adjudication, writs, and judicial remedies.

SCHWARTZ begins by explaining administrative law and highlights the importance of administrative agencies. The book results from thirty years experience of teaching in administrative law. Fundamental concepts, basic principles, and doctrines are elaborated. A discussion of the delegation of powers, due process, and separation of functions, along with an explanation of cases, make this book very useful. It is highly appreciated by students, practitioners, and judges. It has also been cited in hundreds of federal and state cases.

STREETS focusses on an overview of administrative structure and discusses important cases in detail. Topics like access to information, alternatives to judicial review, judicial review and its limitations, the merits, role, and importance of the ombudsman, constitutional frameworks in relation to administrative law, the nature of administrative power, sources of power, and reviews of administrative action are also dealt with extensively.

WADE contains a discussion of withholding of remedies in judicial discretion and judicial review, public law, and private law. Administrative justice and the need for independent Administrative Review Commission are also examined. Sir Robin Cooke's comments on judicial review have also been incorporated. The constitutional foundations of the powers of the courts, public corporations, government, natural justice, and administrative legislation are also discussed in detail.

WADE & FORSYTH analyses the standards of administrative justice in administrative law. According to the authors, administrative law must work within the framework of constitutional law. The dichotomy between public and private law effected by *O'Reilly v. Mackman* is examined along with procedural complexity and problems faced by litigants. Starting with a discussion of administrative law, government, law, and justice, they conclude that the judges appear to be under severe pressure from the surging tides of judicial review.

YARDLEY is an overall view of administrative law. It is a collection of essays presented in simple language examining doctrinally significant aspects of administrative law, the purposes of administrative law, and topics such as delegated legislation, ultra vires, natural justice, and ombudsmen. It enables the reader to able to cut through the tangle of confused case law.

ASHRAF U. KAZI

Adolescence

Bakan, David, "Adolescence in America: From Idea to Social Fact" in *Twelve to Sixteen: Early Adolescence*, edited by Jerome Kagan and Robert Coles, New York: Norton, 1972

Bandura, Albert and Richard H. Walters, *Adolescent Aggression: A Study of the Influence of Child-training Practices and Family Interrelationships*, New York: Ronald Press, 1959

Benedict, Ruth, *Patterns of Culture*, Boston: Houghton Mifflin, 1934; London: Routledge, 1935

Blos, Peter, *The Adolescent Passage: Developmental Issues*, New York: International Universities Press, 1979

Bronfenbrenner, Urie, *The Ecology of Human Development: Experiments by Nature and Design*, Cambridge, Massachusetts: Harvard University Press, 1979

Coleman, James S., *The Adolescent Society*, New York: Free Press, 1961; London: Collier Macmillan, 1971

Dornbusch, Sanford M., Anne C. Petersen and E. Mavis Hetherington, "Projecting the Future of Research on Adolescence", *Journal of Research on Adolescence*, 1 (1991): 7–17

Elder, Glen, "Adolescence in Historical Perspective" in *Handbook of Adolescent Psychology*, edited by Joseph Adelson, New York and Chichester: Wiley, 1980

Erikson, Erik H., *Identity: Youth and Crisis*, New York: Norton, and London: Faber, 1968

Freud, Anna, "Adolescence", *Psychoanalytic Study of the Child*, 13 (1958): 255–78

Friedenberg, Edgar Z., *The Vanishing Adolescent*, Boston: Beacon Press, 1959

Hall, G. Stanley, *Adolescence*, 2 vols, New York: Appleton, 1904

Hoffman, Lois Wladis, "Progress and Problems in the Study of Adolescence", *Developmental Psychology*, 32/4 (1996): 777–80

Inhelder, Bärbel and Jean Piaget, *The Growth of Logical Thinking from Childhood to Adolescence: An Essay on the Construction of Formal Operational Structures*, London: Routledge, and New York: Basic Books, 1958 (French edition 1955)

Kett, Joseph, *Rites of Passage: Adolescence in America, 1790 to the Present*, New York: Basic Books, 1977

Lewin, Kurt, *Field Theory in Social Science: Selected Theoretical Papers*, New York: Harper and Row, 1951; London: Tavistock, 1952

Mannheim, Karl, *Essays on the Sociology of Knowledge*, London: Routledge and Kegan Paul, and New York: Oxford University Press, 1952

Mead, Margaret, *Coming of Age in Samoa: A Psychological Study of Primitive Youth for Western Civilization*, New York: Morrow, 1928; London: Cape, 1929

Rice, F. Philip F., *The Adolescent: Development, Relationships, and Culture*, 8th edition, Boston: Allyn and Bacon, 1996

Rutter, Michael, *Changing Youth in a Changing Society: Patterns of Adolescent Development and Disorder*, London: Nuffield Provincial Hospital Trust, 1979; Cambridge, Massachusetts: Harvard University Press, 1980

Santrock, John W., *Adolescence*, 7th edition, Boston: McGraw Hill, 1998

Simmons, Roberta G. and Dale A. Blyth, *Moving into Adolescence: The Impact of Pubertal Change and School Context*, New York: Aldine de Gruyter, 1987

Sprinthall, Norman A. and W. Andrew Collins, *Adolescent Psychology: A Developmental View*, 3rd edition, New York and London: McGraw Hill, 1995

Historians often recognize HALL as the "father" of the scientific study of adolescence. His two-volume set on adolescence during the first decade of the 1900s was influenced by the work of Charles Darwin. From a biosocial theoretical perspective Hall emphasized the hormonal, biological, and physical changes of puberty as the driving forces of the storm and stress experienced during adolescence. Hall proposed that adolescence was naturally and inevitably a period of storm and stress that would cause challenges for both the individual and those around the adolescent. Hall's early writings include systematic study and theory which was amongst the first regarding the period of adolescence. Although contemporary developmental scientists no longer contend that adolescence is an inherently stressful period, the importance of biological factors is recognized. Contemporary research continues to explore sociobiological bases of adolescent behaviour.

Anna FREUD provides a more organismic perspective incorporating the biological changes of adolescence with the contextual influences. She extended much of her father's psychoanalytic ideas to the study of adolescence elaborating on the process and changes in the psychic structure of adolescents during puberty. Numerous neo-Freudians such as ERIKSON and BLOS have also addressed development during adolescence. Blos writes about adolescent's developing a sense of individuation and proposes that this process begins early in infancy and develops through adolescence as one develops the differentiation of behaviours, feelings, and judgements from one's parents, moving towards autonomy and perceiving one's self as competent.

Erikson emphasized psychosocial development during adolescence. He proposed that the crisis during adolescence revolves around establishing an ego identity versus identity diffusion, which is influenced by changes during puberty and by the society or culture adolescents live in. Erikson outlined seven major components of identity development during adolescence (temporal perspective versus time confusion, self-certainty versus self-consciousness, role experimentation versus role fixation, apprenticeship versus work paralysis, sexual polarization versus bisexual confusion, leadership and followership versus authority confusion, and ideological commitment versus confusion of values).

While Freud, Blos, and Erikson emphasized emotional development, Piaget focused on cognitive development during adolescence. As with the above organismic theorists, INHELDER & PIAGET also emphasized the interplay between biological and contextual factors influencing development. Inhelder & Piaget proposed that adolescence is a time of transition from concrete to abstract thought, wherein the individual is able to engage in propositional logic, inductive, and hypothetical and deductive reasoning in solving problems and establishing conclusions. Adolescence is proposed to be a period when greater introspection occurs and youth can think about the future and plan for it. Inhelder & Piaget provide a discussion of changes in adolescent behaviour that may be associated with changes in cognitive abilities.

BANDURA & WALTERS are social learning theorists who suggest ways in which adolescents learn how to behave. They emphasize the processes of modelling and observational learning, which both occur within the context of the family and with peers. The major contribution of learning theorists is that they have helped us to understand how the specific context or environment may influence an adolescent's behaviour.

LEWIN and FRIEDENBERG have each contributed sociological theories of adolescence focusing on relations between generations, and how adolescents come of age in society. During the mid 1900s adolescents were viewed as "second-class citizens". Their work emphasized the power difference that exists between the adolescent and adult generations and the idea of marginality (being in transition from childhood to adulthood). Other sociological theorists such as MANNHEIM and COLEMAN both address concerns of intergenerational conflict commonly referred to as the generation gap. The basic idea is that growing up during different social circumstances the individuals develop different sets of attitudes, beliefs, and values.

ELDER and KETT emphasize a historical perspective that points to the importance of the historical era during which one experiences adolescence. This is because, the issues adolescents face during development depend largely on the social, political, and economic forces of a given time. Thus, the degree to which adolescence is stressful or a time of identity crisis is greatly influenced by the context and circumstance during the historical period. BAKAN has been referred to as an inventionist theorist given his argument that adolescence is a social invention.

Bakan presents the idea that drawing a boundary between childhood and adolescence or adolescence and adulthood is no more than a reflection of the political, economic, and social circumstances in which we live. For instance, sociohistorical conditions contributed to the period 1890–1920 being referred to as the "age of adolescence", as this was the time when compulsory legislation aimed at youth was enacted (for example, prohibiting most employment and requiring secondary school).

BENEDICT and MEAD each provide an anthropological and sociocultural view of adolescence. Both emphasized that societies vary considerably in the ways they view adolescence and that various cultures influence adolescent development in different ways. For instance, from her observations of adolescents on the island of Samoa, Mead suggests that some societies perceive adolescence as difficult and stressful whereas others see it as calm and peaceful.

It should be noted that there is some controversy over Mead's reports of adolescence on Samoa. Benedict distinguished between continuous and discontinuous societies. In continuous societies the transition through adolescence is usually gradual and peaceful, whereas, in discontinuous societies (industrialized and rapidly changing), the transition may be more abrupt and challenging as development is characterized as distinct stages in the lifespan.

BRONFENBRENNER provides an ecological view of adolescence, emphasizing that development occurs within multiple contexts, including families, communities, and countries. His ecological model includes: the self (for example, biological disposition); microsystem, which are influences with whom the adolescent has immediate contact (such as family, friends); mesosystem, which encompasses reciprocal relationships among microsystem settings; exosystem, which is those settings in which the adolescent does not play an active role (for example, neighbours, mass media, community organizations); and the macrosystem, which includes attitudes, customs, laws, and ideologies of a particular culture. Bronfenbrenner's ecological systems theory has recently been characterized as a bioecological model as it incorporates both environmental forces and biological disposition.

SIMMONS & BLYTH discuss many important aspects of the transition into adolescence and an overview of salient developmental tasks of adolescence. In particular, they contributed additional information regarding early and late-maturing girls. RUTTER provides an informative review in his discussion of both normative and disordered developmental patterns, emphasizing the contextual influences in adolescent development. His book illustrates how understanding pathological or disordered patterns of development informs our understanding of normative development. There are many current texts on adolescence that provide invaluable information regarding this period of the lifespan. Recent texts by SPRINTHALL & COLLINS, by SANTROCK, and by RICE include a historical perspective, sociobiological information, discuss cognitive, social, and personality development, and review the range of contexts important to adolescent development (such as families, peers, schools, culture).

Contemporary research has emphasized the complexity of adolescent development. Recent research has focused on the contexts of adolescent development, giving special attention to the sociocultural contexts of culture, ethnicity, and gender. During the past two decades there has been an increase in research examining the multitude of changes that take place between childhood and adulthood. DORNBUSCH, PETERSEN & HETHERINGTON wrote a seminal paper discussing the past, present, and future of developmental research, examining issues relevant to adolescence. HOFFMAN discusses the progress and problems in the study of adolescence in her overview of a special journal issue devoted to the period of adolescence.

Hoffman highlights a wealth of current literature exploring the transitions through adolescence. Three of the articles in the special issue address adolescent development from a behaviour genetics approach, several articles examined the continuity of transitions from childhood to adolescence and adolescence to adulthood, while most of the articles focus on changes that occur during adolescence.

SHANE R. JIMERSON

Adulthood

Beck, Clive, *Learning to Live the Good Life: Values in Adulthood*, Toronto: OISE Press, 1993

Erikson, Erik H. (editor), *Adulthood: Essays*, New York: Norton, 1978

Gerstein, Martin, *Understanding Adulthood: A Review and Analysis of Three Leading Authorities on the Stages and Crises in Adult Development*, Fullerton: California Personnel and Guidance Association, 1981

Kegan, Robert, *In over Our Heads: The Mental Demands of Modern Life*, Cambridge, Massachusetts: Harvard University Press, 1994

Lander, Dorothy, "Telling Transgression: A Bridge between Contract and Carnival in Making Student Services Policy", *Journal of Education Policy*, 14(6), 587–603, 1999

McClusky, Howard Y., "Course of the Adult Life Span" in *Psychology of Adults*, edited by Wilbur C. Hallenbeck, Chicago: Adult Education Association of the USA, 1963

Merriam, Sharan B. and M. Carolyn Clark, *LifeLines: Patterns of Work, Love, and Learning in Adulthood*, San Francisco: Jossey Bass, 1991

Rose, Nikolas S., *Inventing Our Selves: Psychology, Power, and Personhood*, Cambridge and New York: Cambridge University Press, 1998

Sinnott, Jan D. (editor), *Interdisciplinary Handbook of Adult Lifespan Learning*, Westport, Connecticut: Greenwood Press, 1994

McCLUSKY introduces the concept of power load margin (PLM) for studying and understanding adulthood. Power is the combination of interacting factors that the adult exercises to sustain the load imposed by self and society. McClusky's analysis of the exercise of power presages postmodern writings on disciplinary power (for example Rose, see below). The load-power ratio determines margin and is based on the dimensions and value of load and the capacity of an adult to carry the load. His formula breaks with the stereotypes of age and stage approaches to adulthood. To exemplify the operational usefulness of margin for meeting the emergencies of life, McClusky draws on 1950s America. In this way, he places PLM in context, validating it as a conceptual tool that crosses time and culture.

The monograph by GERSTEIN serves as a navigational aid to the writings of the leading authorities on age-linked developmental *stages* of adulthood, particularly Erikson, Levinson, and Sheehy. The scholarly influences and assumptions underlying these life-stage theories offer readers a critical lens for approaching the original writings. Erikson's work on childhood development in the 1960s introduced eight life stages, the last three occurring in the adult years. Sheehy's (1976) *Passages* and Levinson's (1978) *The Seasons of a Man's Life* rework Erikson's concepts of transition and predictable crises at each stage. With particular reference to the mid-life crisis, the authors challenge these assumptions, arguing that adult social roles trigger transitions and create stability and order.

In ERIKSON's edited book *Adulthood*, his introductory essay entitled "Reflections on Dr Borg's life cycle" offers one of the few explicit applications of Erikson's theory. Dr Borg's life history, based on Bergman's motion picture *Wild Strawberries*, becomes the tool Erikson uses to tease out crises at each age-linked stage and to document the need to resolve successfully the conflicts in one stage before proceeding to the next, higher stage. This narrative juxtaposed to a chart that depicts the "interplay of successive stages" lends coherence to Erikson's theory although such immaculate order may invite reader incredulity. The other chapters span a variety of disciplines and professions, such as medicine, Islam, Japanese spiritualism, American literature, and secular law. To his credit, Erikson includes authors who do not adopt his theory uncritically. The wide range of cultural perspectives on adulthood problematizes the tendency to universalize the process of becoming adult.

BECK encourages a values approach to change and struggle in adulthood. This approach brings helpful context and rationale to his critique of age, stage, and phase approaches. He argues convincingly that the stage theorists' claim (for example Erikson) that higher (and older) is better is not borne out in life experience. Sheehy's passages and Levinson's seasons are examples of phase theory; both claim that each period is different, not better. Beck also seeks to understand adult values in terms of life phases but he critiques existing phase theory that distorts and stereotypes the values of adults in various age groups. Beck integrates the theory and practice of the values approach in his readily adaptable sample study units. He poses goal-oriented activities for learning and teaching values as they apply to adult problems relating to transitions in health, family life, and work.

MERRIAM & CLARK invite the reader to trace a research process that begins with their hunch that adulthood is a continually evolving process at the intersection of work, love, and learning. The reader can readily follow the procedures of this comprehensive research methodology and engage with the particulars of working, loving, and learning. The patterns of adulthood emerge from the life stories and dialogue of the adult research participants. The research findings create the authors' theory that the essence of adulthood is learning to make meaning from life experience.

"Interdisciplinary" and "learning" are the key ideas that SINNOTT, the editor, deliberately connects to adulthood. The various authors accomplish the editor's purpose of considering adult lifespan learning from multiple perspectives. Sinnott's expectation of counterbalancing earlier work on lifespan *decline* by emphasizing lifespan *learning* is met in chapters in which the authors focus on adult learning related to spirituality, chaos theory, psychotherapy, health behaviour change, and the workplace. It is more difficult for the reader to stay connected with the thread of lifespan learning in the chapters on brain injury and Alzheimer's disease.

KEGAN invites readers to trace the evolutionary complexity of the adult mind, which he conceptualizes as organizing meaning and experience. The tensions between modernism and postmodernism subtend Kegan's analytic tool for studying the structures of adult consciousness. This tool conceptualizes complexity as the relationship between the psychological phenomenon of evolving consciousness and the cultural phenomenon of creating demands on the minds of adults in their private and public lives. Kegan applies the evolving order of complexity to parenting, partnering, work, diversity, adult learning, and psychotherapy. This analysis has the effect of rehearsing the reader in holding the contradictions of complexity and relating the evolving order of complexity to the postmodern.

LANDER documents the interplay of the social categories of contract and carnival insofar as they constitute the ambiguity of young adulthood. The historical basis of these adult categories can be traced to Rousseau's "social contract" and Bakhtin's analysis of medieval carnival. The author applies contract and carnival to the organizational stories of drinking experiences among traditionally aged first year students in contemporary Western universities. Readers, researchers, and policymakers who connect adulthood to citizenship and participatory democracy will be attracted to this analysis.

Selfhood and personhood are favoured terms in much critical, postmodern writing as they suggest more fluid categories than adulthood. ROSE, inspired by the work of Foucault, Deleuze, and feminist writers, holds that psychological discourses and practices are an array of technologies and systems of judgement that assemble and inscribe a multiplicity of selves. By extension, selves enact the emancipatory projects of adulthood. Rose provides a useful and provocative alternative to Merriam & Clark (1991) and Kegan (1994) who tie psychological conceptions of adulthood to meaning making. Rose theorizes that it is not what psychological discourses *mean* to the individual but what they *do* that capacitates adults and that embodies power. This distinction renders psychology a social science. The implication is that adults need to expose the multiple authorities beyond self that are acting upon us in order to invent our selves differently.

DOROTHY LANDER

Adverse selection, incentives

Akerlof, George A., "The Market for 'Lemons': Quality, Uncertainty and the Market Mechanism", *Quarterly Journal of Economics*, 84/3 (1970): 488–500

Browne, Mark J. and Helen I. Doerpinghaus, "Information Asymmetries and Adverse Selection in the Market for Individual Medical Expense Insurance", *Journal of Risk and Insurance*, 60/2 (1993): 300–12

Rothschild, Michael and Joseph E. Stiglitz, "Equilibrium in Competitive Insurance Markets: An Essay on the Economics of Imperfect Information", *Quarterly Journal of Economics*, 90/4 (1976): 629–49

Shapiro, Carl and Joseph E. Stiglitz, "Equilibrium Unemployment as a Worker Discipline Device», *American Economic Review*, 74/3 (1984): 433–44

Spence, Michael, *Market Signaling: Informational Transfer in Hiring and Related Screening Processes*, Cambridge, Massachusetts: Harvard University Press, 1974

Stiglitz, Joseph E. and Andrew Weiss, "Credit Rationing in Markets with Imperfect Information", *American Economic Review*, 71/3 (1985): 393–410

Wilson, Charles, "The Nature of Equilibrium in Markets with Adverse Selection", *Bell Journal of Economics*, 11/1 (1980): 108–30

AKERLOF demonstrates adverse selection in his famous article on the second-hand car market. While there are good quality cars to be found in this market, there are also many "lemons". Although dealers are fully aware of the condition of the vehicles they offer, the buyers, for the most part, are not. All they can see is the distribution of quality, here into two categories (good and bad cars), and not the quality itself (referred to as q). Cars are traded at a single price, p, which does not allow buyers to consider the price as a signal of quality. For any car of quality q, Akerlof assumes that the reservation value is 3/2q for a buyer, whereas it is q for the seller. In a situation of complete information and if the number of buyers is greater than the number of sellers, transactions take place at an equilibrium price equal to 3/2q. In a situation of asymmetric information, on the other hand, where dealers may offer good cars and "lemons" at the same price, buyers (aware of this risk) associate with any price p offered to them an average quality equal to q/2. Given this relation between price and average quality, buyers will therefore value any car for sale at only 3/4p. At such price only the sellers of bad cars will agree to sell and the good cars are gradually withdrawn from the market until only "lemons" are left. There is thus indeed adverse selection, as the bad cars drive out the good ones, and Akerlof shows that there is ultimately no exchange at all, the equilibrium situation corresponding to an absence of transactions. This is obviously a dire finding for standard economic theory. He shows that when agents have private information on an exogenous variable, that is to say one which they do not choose, adverse selection prevents them from finding mutually beneficial arrangements.

WILSON widens the breach by generalizing Akerlof's result and showing that in certain circumstances multiple equilibria are possible. When buyers' preferences are heterogeneous, and the average quality of the item sold increases sufficiently with the price, some buyers prefer to buy at higher prices, which is reflected in an atypical shape in the demand curve, which is upward-sloping over some price ranges. As the demand curve may intersect the supply curve at several points, the result is (a) that several equilibria are possible and (b) that higher equilibrium prices are matched by higher demand. Wilson shows that in certain situations (constant marginal rate of substitution between the purchase of a quality car and the consumption of other goods) each buyer prefers a higher to a lower equilibrium price. As this preference is also that of any seller, higher equilibrium prices thus appear Pareto-superior to lower equilibrium prices.

Wilson also showed that equilibrium may be marked by supply rationing, an idea taken up by STIGLITZ & WEISS to explain how adverse selection results in rationing in the credit market, which, like the insurance market, is especially vulnerable to the principal-agent problem of adverse selection.

Bankers are unable to differentiate between borrowers (here Akerlof's informed sellers), despite the fact that they belong to different risk categories, which is far from irrelevant to the bankers. Borrowers know the class of risk (π_i) to which they belong, that is to say the probability of making a success of their particular project and of repaying the banker. The banker (here Akerlof's uninformed buyer) cannot adjust the interest rate according to the quality of the borrower. The probability of success and loan repayment by the borrower is therefore π_i and that of defaulting $(1 - \pi_i)$. For a project-expected return, called R, the borrower's net gain is $(R - (1 + r) \pi_i k)$, where r is the interest rate and k the amount of the project being financed. It can thus be seen that the lower π_i (i.e. the more uncertain the project), the greater the borrower's acceptance of a high interest rate r, as he or she will not repay. In raising r, the banker therefore selects increasingly risky borrowers. As for banks, they lend so long as it is in their interest to do so, i.e. so long as their expected rate of return is greater than the interest rate. The two rates go together only up to a certain point r*, which is the bank optimal rate. However, owing to adverse selection, if at r* there is excess demand for loans, banks will refuse to satisfy it. Even if borrowers agree to pay a rate higher than r*, it is more risky for banks to lend in such conditions. Equilibrium is therefore characterized by credit rationing, for the same reason that in the SHAPIRO & STIGLITZ model the efficiency wage as a means of limiting adverse selection is characterized by a rationing of the labour supply (unemployment) in equilibrium.

According to Akerlof, the assumption up to this point is that sellers have no means of signalling their quality or that of their products to buyers. The significance of SPENCE's work is precisely to have introduced the idea of signalling. Sellers may agree to incur expenditure in order to signal the quality of their products. The signal studied by Spence is education. Hence, it may be beneficial for an economic agent to invest in education, even if this is costly. However, the signal needs to be credible, which means that its cost must be lower for "good" agents than for "bad" agents. Spence assumes that either intelligent individuals obtain their qualifications more easily, therefore at less cost, or, being more convinced of their abilities and therefore of the future profitability of their investment, they invest more than others in education. In both cases, their qualifications are a signal to an employer that they are more productive than other suppliers of labour. Here, therefore, the role of education is not so much to train individuals so as to make them more efficient, but to allow them to be selected by displaying their quality.

Adverse selection has important consequences on the nature of equilibria. They have been highlighted by ROTHSCHILD & STIGLITZ, who distinguish between pooling and separating equilibria. In a pooling equilibrium, the two types of sellers send the same signal (or send no signal, which amounts to the same thing). The goods are thus sold for the same price irrespective of their quality. In a separating equilibrium, only sellers of good quality goods send a costly signal and, correspondingly, obtain a better price, whereas those who do not send a signal sell at a lower price. The "good" sellers are therefore less penalised than with Akerlof, even if they bear the cost of the signal.

The consequences of adverse selection have been studied in the insurance market in particular, where insurers soon saw it was in their interest to offer separating contracts, where possible. Particular mention should be made of BROWNE &

DOERPINGHAUS among the abundant literature in the wake of Rothschild & Stiglitz's pioneering article. Browne & Doerpinghaus study the individual medical insurance market and, using empirical tests, show the risk of adverse selection when both kinds of agents take out a pooling contract and how low-risk agents in fact subsidize high-risk agents.

LYSIANE CARTELIER

See also Agency theory, Economics of information, Moral hazard

Aerospace industry

Adams, A.R., *Good Company: The Story of the Guided Weapons Division of British Aircraft Corporation*, Stevenage: British Aircraft Corporation, 1976

Bright, Charles D., *The Jet Makers: The Aerospace Industry from 1945 to 1972*, Lawrence: Regents Press of Kansas, 1978

Ford, Terry, "Matra Marconi Space", *Aircraft Engineering and Aerospace Technology*, 70/5 (1998): 356–59

Georgiades, Diane and Brian H. Kleiner, "What Defence Companies Have Done to be More Commercially Successful", *Aircraft Engineering and Aerospace Technology*, 69/3 (1997): 282–86

Levine, Alan J., *The Missile and Space Race*, Westport, Connecticut: Praeger, 1994

Lloyd, Ian, *Rolls-Royce: The Years of Endeavour*, London: Macmillan, 1978

Papin, Mike W. and Brian H. Kleiner, "Effective Strategic Management in the Aerospace Industry", *Aircraft Engineering and Aerospace Technology*, 70/1 (1998): 38–44

Rae, John B., *Climb to Greatness: The American Aircraft Industry, 1920–1960*, Cambridge, Massachusetts: MIT Press, 1968

Reed, Arthur, *Britain's Aircraft Industry: What Went Right? What Went Wrong?*, London: Dent, 1973

Serling, Robert J., *Legend and Legacy: The Story of Boeing and Its People*, New York: St Martin's Press, 1992

Simonson, G.R. (editor), *The History of the American Aircraft Industry: An Anthology*, Cambridge, Massachusetts: MIT Press, 1968

Smith, David J., "Strategic Alliances in the Aerospace Industry: A Case of Europe Emerging or Converging", *European Business Review*, 97/4 (1997): 171–78

From its beginnings with one man in an aircraft, the aerospace industry has taken less than 65 years to become one of the world's largest manufacturing employers, a crucial element in the economy, and a military necessity. In his anthology of the US aircraft industry, SIMONSON reviews five strands of aviation history, each corresponding to a different period. The first strand covers the invention of the aircraft in 1903, through World War I, to the beginning of the great depression in 1930. The second, covering the following decade, examines the consolidation of the remaining successful manufacturers and the exporting of aeronautical equipment. The third addresses the industry's expansion during World War II. The fourth reflects on the immediate postwar contraction, and the subsequent expansion as a result of the Korean War. The fifth examines the new industrial opportunities created after 1955 by the space and missile programmes.

RAE describes and explains the phenomenal growth of the industry from shoestring beginnings in the 1920s to a US$17 billion plus industry in the 1960s, when 80 per cent of the world's aircraft were US-built. He discusses specific characteristics of the US aircraft industry – rapid rates of technological growth, dependence on a considerable amount of scientific research, and on the US government market – and relates these characteristics to the industry's business and financial organization, and overall growth. The author observes that, although the government has been its largest customer, the industry has not been dominated by government procurement agencies. Instead, these agencies have served to maintain competition in the production of airframes, engines, and other components. Focusing on the problems of manufacturing aircraft, he describes developments in design from "wood-and-wire puddle jumpers" with in-line piston engines to all-metal, cantilevered-wing aircraft powered by giant turbine engines, and jet-propelled aircraft moving through the stratosphere at supersonic speeds. He also elaborates on the mid-1950s when the practical operation of helicopters and jet aircraft, and the development of missiles and space vehicles, marked the transformation of the industry from "aircraft" to "aerospace".

In a complementary volume, BRIGHT presents the history of the US jet aircraft manufacturing industry from World War II to 1972, documenting the evolution of its technology, and examining the intricacies of its management, economics, and relations with government. This volume provides a valuable contribution to general aviation history and a unique insight into the dynamics of a major industry. Bright traces the momentous revolution of the aerospace era using the jet aircraft industry as a base, and investigates all significant aspects: the coming-of-age of aviation during World War II, the development of jets and missiles from the Truman era to the Vietnam war, the controlling influence of national military strategy, the US air force and other government markets, the prevailing "design or die" philosophy in ordering technology, and different systems of production through the years. The author also reflects on the overall economic pattern from the first demand for aerospace machines for military, space, and commercial uses to the failures as the industry encountered recession and peacetime equilibrium. Probing an industry which has shown incredible resilience, and which has responded to often unreasonable customer demands, the author details the reasons for the leadership of the US in the jet age – enterprising business managers, scientists, and engineers – and discusses the pressure of economics and the manifold competition brought on by the Cold War.

LEVINE recounts the events that led up to and accompanied President Kennedy's 1961 decision to land a man on the moon and return him safely to Earth. He discusses the interplay between the development of space travel, the missile race, and the international politics of the quarter of a century following World War II. The author examines the development of space travel and the technology behind it. This includes the development of vehicles, with reference to the contribution from intercontinental ballistic missiles? and rocket research aircraft, and the development of engines and fuels, including the abortive attempt to develop nuclear propulsion.

The US was not the only country with a developing aircraft industry. REED examines the history of the British industry, from its promising position at the end of World War II. Crisis points that are analysed include the failure of the first Comets, the cancellation of the TSR2 bomber, the controversial development of the Concorde, and the Rolls-Royce bankruptcy. Reed also discusses the crucial matters of the industry's dependence on government finance, the role played by government research establishments such as Farnborough, international collaboration, and the effect of pressure from the environmental lobby. The volume includes a series of interviews with key people in the industry who were central to many of the events described. Finally, the author reflects on the future of aircraft construction, and considers measures for the industry's survival against foreign competition.

In the light of US dominance and British concern about foreign competition, SMITH provides a timely article on the strategic alliances that are now widely used in the aerospace industry. Reflecting on Europe's Airbus Industrie, and the Rolls-Royce, Daimler-Benz, and BMW engine consortium, he considers how these collaborative ventures have played an important part in helping the individual organizations build market share within this highly competitive global market. He reviews the changes that have taken place within both the airframe and the engine sectors of the aerospace industry in recent years and critically evaluates the part that strategic alliances have played in the increasing commercial success of the European Union in both sectors. He also highlights differences in the nature and role of such alliances, as well as their impact on the structure of each sector.

As a result of the end of the Cold War, government expenditure in the aerospace industry has decreased markedly. PAPIN & KLEINER examines the various long-term management strategies employed by US aerospace companies, in order to determine which are most effective in this period of decline.

GEORGIADES & KLEINER looks at how those aerospace companies previously reliant on defence spending have managed the transition to commercial products. The authors review the commercially successful strategies of Lockheed Martin, Hughes Electronics, and Rockwell. The strategies discussed include management change, consolidation, derived products, partnerships, mergers, and acquisitions. The authors also examine the negative side-effects of the transition, including downsizing and less investment in technology research.

No reading guide on the aerospace industry would be complete without reference to some of the many volumes that have been written about specific companies. ADAMS writes about the people and the activities of the Guided Weapons Division of the British Aircraft Corporation. FORD contributes an independent account of the Matra Marconi Space Company's range of activities. LLOYD provides an insight into the mistakes, the failures, and the outstanding successes of Rolls-Royce. Finally, SERLING looks at Boeing, arguably the largest aerospace company in the world, and its involvement in aircraft, rockets, missiles, and the future international space station.

GEOFF TURNER

Affect regulation

Clark, Margaret S. and Alice M. Isen, "Toward
    Understanding the Relationship between Feeling States and
    Social Behavior" in *Cognitive Social Psychology*, edited by
    Albert H. Hastorf and Alice M. Isen, New York: Elsevier,
    1982

Eisenberg, Nancy and Richard A. Fabes, *Emotion and its
    Regulation in Early Development*, San Francisco: Jossey
    Bass, 1992

Gross, James J., "The Emerging Field of Emotion Regulation:
    An Integrative Review", *Review of General Psychology*,
    2/3 (1998): 271–99

Lazarus, Richard S., "The Self-Regulation of Emotion" in
    Emotions: Their Parameters and Measurement, edited by
    Lennart Levi, New York: Raven Press, 1975

Morris, William N. and Nora P. Reilly, "Toward the Self-
    Regulation of Mood: Theory and Research", *Motivation
    and Emotion*, 11/3 (1987): 215–49

Nolen-Hoeksema, Susan, "Responses to Depression and Their
    Effects on the Duration of Depressive Episodes", *Journal
    of Abnormal Psychology*, 100/4 (1991): 569–82

Parkinson, Brian *et al.*, *Changing Moods: The Psychology of
    Mood and Mood Regulation*, London and New York:
    Addison Wesley Longman, 1996

Parrott, W. Gerrod, "Beyond Hedonism: Motives for
    Inhibiting Good Moods and for Maintaining Bad Moods"
    in *Handbook of Mental Control*, edited by Daniel M.
    Wegner and James W. Pennebaker, Englewood Cliffs, New
    Jersey: Prentice Hall, 1993

Salovey, Peter, Christopher K. Hsee and John D. Mayer,
    "Emotional Intelligence and the Self-Regulation of Affect"
    in *Handbook of Mental Control*, edited by Daniel M.
    Wegner and James W. Pennebaker, Englewood Cliffs, New
    Jersey: Prentice Hall, 1993

Thayer, Robert E., *The Origin of Everyday Moods: Managing
    Energy, Tension, and Stress*, New York: Oxford University
    Press, 1996

Wegner, Daniel M., "Ironic Processes of Mental Control",
    Psychological Review, 101/1 (1994): 34–52

Affect regulation refers to the range of control processes that modify or maintain moods and emotions. These may include some forms of *coping* with unpleasant feelings as well as homeostatic operations that preserve a dynamic equilibrium in experience. LAZARUS prefigured much of the subsequent psychological interest in this topic by discussing anticipatory coping, in which threat is short circuited before it is manifested in emotional response, and intrapsychic regulation techniques such as denial and distancing. His eclectic analysis presents anecdotal as well as empirically grounded examples of emotion regulation, some of which imply a dampening rather than an intensification of positive affect (such as modulation of feelings of love depending on the other party's reciprocation) in contrast with the subsequent near-exclusive emphasis on hedonistically oriented regulation (see also PARROTT). In general, this reading provides an underused source of insightful observations for researchers in this area.

CLARK & ISEN's influential chapter suggests that people's responses to feeling states not only depend on automatic processes, but also might be based on controlled strategies motivated by a desire to maximize happiness. In particular, when in a bad mood, we often want it to end as soon as possible and deliberately engage in what later became known as *mood-repair* strategies (such as focusing on something positive or performing some pleasantly distracting activity) to counteract its effects. On the other hand, we usually prefer our good moods to continue and therefore deploy mood-maintenance strategies to keep them going. Although the discussion of affect regulation occupies only a short section of this chapter, the concept was quick to take hold of researchers' imaginations.

MORRIS & REILLY's early review article surveys and integrates research relevant to the developing concept of mood regulation. Adapting classifications derived from the literature on coping, they distinguish three basic varieties: *direct action* on the situation provoking or sustaining the mood, *cognitive redefinition* of the situation's meaning, and mood management, which deals with the affective experience itself. Their paper represents a largely successful attempt to stimulate and orient further research into an understudied area.

THAYER's book presents his own theory of mood as based on feelings of energy and tension, then discusses its implications for regulation. Studies exploring the variety of available mood-regulation strategies and their relative effectiveness are described in a no-nonsense, down-to-earth style. The volume concludes with practical advice about improving moods on a daily basis using exercise (to increase energy) and relaxation (to reduce tension) in particular. If the book's attempt to resolve the competing requirements of an academic monograph and a self-help guide is not always successful and results in some inconsistency of tone, together with occasional simplification and repetition of material, its sustained development of a coherent biopsychological approach to mood remains impressive.

PARKINSON *et al.* also endeavour to summarize the mood-regulation literature in an accessible way. Their book focuses in turn on the structure of mood, its causes and effects, how it changes over time, and how it is regulated. Finally, applications to clinical disorders of affect, and implications for future research are considered. The book puts less emphasis than Thayer's on the physiological aspects of mood, preferring to concentrate instead on social and cognitive factors.

GROSS provides an up-to-date integrative review and describes his model of processes potentially involved in emotion regulation. He specifically distinguishes between two varieties of regulatory attempt, one directed at the situation provoking the emotion, and the other concerned with the experiences, expressions, behaviours, or physiological reactions resulting from emotional events. "Antecedent-focused" regulation of the former kind is described as involving situation selection, situation modification, attention deployment, and/or cognitive change, whereas "response-focused regulation" involves direct operations on aspects of the emotional reaction using drugs, exercise, relaxation and so on. The article represents a welcomed step towards systematization of regulation-related concepts.

Despite the abundance of classificatory schemes, the literature contains relatively few attempts to explain precisely how affect regulation is achieved, perhaps because such a wide variety of mechanisms are involved. An important exception is WEGNER's paper, which develops an "ironic theory of mental control" and applies it specifically to the management of mood as well as other forms of self-regulation. The model proposes that regulation requires two basic processes: an operating process, which makes the appropriate changes by generating distracting thoughts, and a monitoring process, which checks whether the operating process is working. As the monitor functions by bringing failures of regulation such as unwanted negative thoughts to conscious attention, any interference with the operating process may lead to effects that are opposite to those intended, making people less cheerful instead of more so. Wegner spells out some of this account's implications for the control of depression and draws some interesting conclusions. His analysis is clearly and compellingly presented although its cybernetic flavour will not appeal to all readers.

NOLEN-HOEKSEMA demonstrates that people sometimes ruminate about unpleasant events despite the negative consequences for affect, partly because they believe that this process will help them better understand what has happened in preparation for future contingencies. She contrasts this style of coping with the use of distraction, which typically has more immediate positive consequences. According to her analysis, women are more likely than men to adopt a ruminative response style, an observation that goes some way to explaining why they suffer a higher risk of depression. Apart from its obvious clinical implications, this account is also important because it emphasizes that not all possible reactions to affect are provoked solely by a desire for instant gratification.

PARROTT also questions whether affect regulation is always hedonistically motivated listing 12 reasons why people might want to attenuate their pleasant moods and another 12 why they might want to maintain unpleasant affect. For example, individuals may attempt to bring their feelings into line with those of others with whom they are interacting (whether or not these feelings are pleasant), or to postpone their happiness so that it can be enjoyed more fully at some more appropriate time in the future. The chapter provides a challenging corrective to prevailing assumptions in this research area.

SALOVEY, HSEE & MAYER apply their pioneering formulation of "emotional intelligence", conceptualized as the capacity for the monitoring and use of feelings to guide future thinking and actions, to the topic of affect regulation. Three domains of emotional intelligence are considered: accurate appraisal and expression of emotion, adaptive regulation, and utilization of emotion-based knowledge. The chapter reviews some of the personal dispositions potentially underlying emotional intelligence and makes a case for understanding affect in process terms as a temporally dynamic phenomenon. As originators and active researchers in this area, the authors are able to give an informed and enlightening account of the relevant work.

The preceding commentary has focused mainly on theory and research in personality and social psychology. A largely independent but relevant literature concerning emotion regulation is also available from the perspective of developmental psychology, and EISENBERG & FABES' edited book provides a range of useful sources in this regard, including reports of a number of studies emphasizing the social basis of affect regulation over the course of development. Clearly, many areas of psychoanalytic work are also pertinent to this topic.

Taking a more interdisciplinary approach by exploring the developmental origins, motivational bases, and cultural background of affect regulation seems likely to yield synergistic benefits.

BRIAN PARKINSON

See also Emotion, Emotional labour

Africa, Central, law and legal system

Center for Reproductive Law and Policy (editors), *Women of the World: Laws and Policies Affecting their Reproductive Lives*, New York: Center for Reproductive Law and Policy, 1997

L'Encyclopédie juridique de l'Afrique, 10 vols, Abidjan: Nouvelles Editions Africaines, 1982

International Bureau of Fiscal Documentation (editors), *African Tax Systems*, Amsterdam: International Bureau of Fiscal Documentation, 1999

Katende, John and M.R. Chesterman, *The Law and Business Organisations in East and Central Africa*, Nairobi: East African Literature Bureau, 1976

Maugenest, Denis and Paul-Gérard Pougoué, *Droits de l'homme en Afrique centrale*, Yaounde, Cameroun: UCAC, and Paris: Karthala, 1996

Ojwang, J.B. and Janet W. Kabeberi, *Law and the Public Interest*, Nairobi: Institute of Development Studies, University of Nairobi, 1988

Shivji, Issa G., *Law, State and the Working Class in Tanzania c.1920–1964*, London: Currey, 1986

Vasdev, Krishna, *The Law of Evidence in the Sudan*, London: Butterworths, 1981

Any bibliographical entry concerning African legal systems would be very poor without reference to the exquisite and rarely analytical ENCYCLOPEDIE JURIDIQUE DE L'AFRIQUE. This multi-volume work provides an in-depth comparative analysis of the legal systems of Africa on areas such as philosophy of law and specific legal fields. Thus, the constitutional law volume includes a chapter on the constitutions of Africa, the political institutions, executive power, the political parties' administrative jurisdiction, and new techniques for the introduction of new legislation. Of profound importance to any comparative lawyer seeking a full review of the legal systems in Africa, with exceptional work on their similarities and differences, this work was unfortunately last updated in 1983. Even so, it is still essential for Francophone legal researchers and analysts.

The issue of human rights in Central Africa is expertly presented by MAUGENEST & POUGOUE in an edited collection of article presented in a 1994 colloquium in Yaoundé. The book includes critical analysis of the universality and relativity of human rights with particular reference to an in-depth comparison between European and African models of human rights, an introduction to concepts of human rights among the black Africans, an analysis of traditional social policy in Africa, and a presentation of the judicial mechanisms that enforce human rights in Africa.

Lack of familiarity with the legal systems of the countries of East and Central Africa does not seem to inhibit the impressive volume of trade between these African states and the West. Having said that, the more familiar practitioners and traders are with the legal framework governing their transactions, the more encouraged they are to exploit the diverse opportunities on offer. The work of KATENDE & CHESTERMAN aims to fill this gap. In their detailed work on the law of business organizations in East and Central Africa, the authors present cases and materials on this field of law in an impressively huge volume of more than 1200 pages. It includes commentaries linking the various materials, excerpts from legal and non-legal books, and problems of a practical nature. Although this is clearly a textbook intended to educate students on their national law, it provides an invaluable aid to foreign practitioners and researchers in need of further knowledge on this issue. The chapters on cooperative societies and public corporations take a particularly analytical approach, whereas the appendices provide a wealth of information on the practical side of the paperwork necessary for the creation, dissolution, and functioning of a company in East and Central Africa.

The publication of the INTERNATIONAL BUREAU OF FISCAL DOCUMENTATION on tax law in Africa is a multi-volume looseleaf work, which covers all African countries. It presents all relevant legislation, is frequently updated, and includes a full list of all relevant bilateral agreements, as well as an invaluable complete bibliographical review of all relevant publications in each country.

The human rights of women are one of the more important human rights issues in Africa, and indeed in the whole world. CENTER FOR REPRODUCTIVE LAW AND POLICY presents in some detail, but clearly and precisely, the legal and policy issues in this field of legislation in African countries such as Ethiopia, Ghana, Kenya, Nigeria, Tanzania, and Zimbabwe. Each chapter focuses on the sources of relevant legislation, and provides a comparative and detailed analysis of the general legal and political framework on health and reproductive rights for women, together with an analysis of women's rights in marriage and a presentation of the relevant legislation concerning adolescents. Although it would be unfair to focus on just one of the chapters of this book, the last chapter – on the trends in the human rights of women in Africa – is a revelation for those who feel that nowadays women can find equality in areas of policy that have been the focus of research over the last decade, such as HIV/AIDS, abortion, contraception, mutilation and circumcision, and enforcement in the field of sexual offences.

OJWANG & KABEBERI provide a valuable insight into Kenyan law and public interest. The book includes edited chapters on issues of particular theoretical and practical value, such as agrarian reform, the role of the law in commercial and industrial expansion, natural resources and taxation, fiscal aspects of petroleum exploration, environmental management, and public health and the law. Although these chapters are all of high quality and useful as individual essays, they appear to be unconnected. Equally disappointing is the lack of a concluding chapter, which would enable the reader to understand the aim of this edited collection.

There is a profound lack of English-speaking material analysing specific fields of law in individual African countries.

VASDEV's work on the law of evidence in Sudan is an exception. It includes a concise but adequately complete reference to all aspects of the law of evidence. Unfortunately, it dates from 1981, and therefore the accuracy of its information for the researcher or practitioner interested in material of legal value today is doubtful.

An excellent presentation of the working class in Tanzania is offered in the work of SHIVJI, who explores the law, state and society, capital and the semiproletariat, and trade unions. This fascinating but obviously Marxist book clarifies the role of capitalism in the formulation of the legal system in Tanzania, although it is somewhat repetitive and simplistic.

HELEN XANTHAKI

Africa, Northern, economy and economic record

Allan, J.A. (editor), *Libya since Independence: Economic and Political Development*, London: Croom Helm, and New York: St Martin's Press, 1982

Bellin, Eva, "The Politics of Profit in Tunisia: Utility of the Rentier Paradigm?", *World Development*, 22/3 (1994): 427–36

Bennoune, Mahfoud, *The Making of Contemporary Algeria, 1830–1987: Colonial Upheavals and Post-Independence Development*, Cambridge and New York: Cambridge University Press, 1988

Nellis, John R., "A Comparative Assessment of the Development Performances of Algeria and Tunisia", *Middle East Journal*, 37/3 (1983): 370–93

Pfeifer, Karen, *Agrarian Reform under State Capitalism in Algeria*, Boulder, Colorado: Westview Press, 1985

Richards, Alan and John Waterbury, *A Political Economy of the Middle East*, 2nd edition, Boulder, Colorado: Westview Press, 1996

Swearingen, Will D., *Moroccan Mirages: Agrarian Dreams and Deceptions, 1912–1986*, London: Tauris, 1988; Princeton, New Jersey: Princeton University Press, 1987

Zartman, I. William (editor), *The Political Economy of Morocco*, New York: Praeger, 1987

Zartman, I. William (editor), *Tunisia: The Political Economy of Reform*, Boulder, Colorado: Rienner, 1991

RICHARDS & WATERBURY make a seminal contribution to the study of the political economy of the Middle East, which they define rather more loosely than is customary, to encompass the North African countries as well. The authors provide insightful discussions, scattered throughout the text, on a wide range of issues pertaining to the North African economies, from education and agriculture to the public sector and population growth. The encyclopedic nature of the study makes it easier to view the North African economies both in relation to each other and in relation to the broader context of the Arab world, Turkey, and Iran. The authors adopt an instrumentalist view of the state that emphasizes the state's capacity to create social actors and to define their interests. They utilize a complex institutional analysis of the patterns of economic growth and of the evolving relationships between the state and the public and private sectors. By offering a broad systemic view of the region's economies, the study provides an ideal starting point for research. The book is a landmark of the literature, accessibile to the nonspecialist, while offering new insights to the specialist.

BENNOUNE provides a detailed analysis of the broad sweep of Algerian political economy, from the period before the arrival of French colonialism in 1830, until 1987. The methodology that Bennoune employs is both historical and Marxian in that it examines not only the complex evolution of the Algerian economy, but the power structures that underpinned it. The study includes a penetrating analysis of the conditions in Algeria after the war of independence in 1962, and of the economic and political exigencies that drove the regime to pursue both extensive state-led industrialisation and large-scale intervention in the agricultural sector. Bennoune is deeply pessimistic about the liberalizing directions the Algerian state was taking in the 1980s, viewing it as increasingly guided by reactionary interests that favoured closer ties with foreign multinationals in preference to domestic industrial development. His analysis is complex but rewarding, especially in its coverage of the industrialization drive of the 1960s and 1970s.

PFEIFER provides a very detailed analysis of Algerian agricultural policy in the 1960s and 1970s. She argues that under a strategy of state capitalism, the agricultural sector was seen as an appendage to urban accumulation, and was consequently starved of resources. The use of oil revenues to subsidize food imports, along with extensive price controls, encouraged farmers to reduce investment in basic food production and to switch to more profitable crops destined for export or urban domestic markets. Furthermore, for agricultural workers and landless peasants, the agrarian reforms did not significantly reduce unemployment or the inequalities between the different rural classes. While the reforms achieved increased production and did away with absentee ownership, Pfeifer argues that they ultimately led to widespread disenchantment among the rural classes. The study, which is based on meticulous studies of the effects of the reforms in the various regions of the country, is thorough, and full of insights into the rural political economy of Algeria.

NELLIS presents a comparative analysis of Algerian and Tunisian development from the 1960s to the early 1980s. While there have been important developments in both economies since this period, the article effectively highlights the similarities and differences in the developmental strategies pursued by the two countries after independence. Nellis examines both countries along three dimensions: economic growth, income distribution, and sociopolitical participation. The first dimension, economic growth, is the best developed in the analysis. Nellis prefers Tunisia's market-orientated system to that of Algeria, which adheres more rigidly to socialist planning and dependence on oil exports. However, he also points out that the differences between their respective economic systems are not as stark as some accounts suggest. For example, during the period under consideration, both had heavily regulated agricultural sectors. The article remains a good general introduction to the comparative study of the political economies of the two countries.

BELLIN provides a concise and lucid examination of the position of industrialists within the Tunisian political economy.

The study is embedded within a critical discussion of the "rentier paradigm" (analytically identical to the rent-seeking approach) which argues that state intervention creates "crony capitalists", allied to bureaucrats who engage in non-productive competition for government-created rents, instead of generating productive activity. Bellin argues that the negative consequences of this behaviour depend on the state structure and the political coalitions underpinning the regime. Thus, despite the fact that Tunisia's industrialists form a rentier class whose profits are mediated by the state, Bellin argues that this has not had a notable detrimental effect on welfare, the political autonomy of the entrepreneurial class, or the developmental capacity of the state. Bellin contends that a key reason for this more benign result is the fact that industrialists have never been part of the regime's coalition, thus permitting industrialists more political latitude and the state more autonomy from the industrial capitalist class. Bellin's study is by no means comprehensive, but it does effectively clarify an important aspect of Tunisian political economy.

ZARTMAN (1991) assembles a collection of essays on the political, economic, and social aspects of reform in Tunisia in the late 1980s and early 1990s. The essays addressing the economic aspects of the reforms include discussions on the relationship between industrialists and the state; on state enterprises and privatization; on rural development; on private sector development; and even one on the hazards of desert locusts. The essays are in general supportive of the movement towards economic liberalization in Tunisia. As in Zartman's earlier volume on Morocco (discussed below), the economic articles are not exhaustive or analytical, but rather descriptive and easily accessible. The collection as a whole provides a sound discussion of the Tunisian political economy and a useful starting point for examining the literature.

SWEARINGEN presents a historical analysis of Moroccan agricultural policy, from the beginning of the French protectorate in 1912, until 1986. He describes the evolution of French agricultural policy in Morocco, from an ill-fated attempt to establish wheat as the primary crop, to the subsequent policy of developing fruit and vegetable-based agriculture, inspired by the example of California. Both policies aimed to create a dominant French presence in the countryside and to aid modern agricultural development by concentrating productive land in the hands of French settlers. This evolution of agricultural policy was joined in the 1930s with an ambitious attempt to harness the surface waters of the country through vast irrigation projects. Swearingen argues that independent Morocco has continued to pursue the agricultural vision of the colonial administration (with the substitution of a Moroccan landholding elite for the French settlers), leading to pervasive income inequality, persistent deficits in agricultural trade, high levels of foreign borrowing to finance dam and irrigation projects, and the neglect of traditional small-scale agriculture, which has encouraged a rural exodus to the cities. The study presents a framework in which to view Moroccan agriculture that is both insightful and well written.

ZARTMAN (1987) brings together a group of fine essays that discuss the political economy of Morocco. Will Swearingen, in a precis of his book discussed above, describes the problems besetting agriculture, while Richard Pomfret provides a good discussion of Morocco's external economic relations. An article by Ahmed Rhazaoui describing economic developments in Morocco is clearly dated, but nevertheless provides a good discussion of economic trends in Morocco up to the mid-1980s. The articles are far from exhaustive, and a discussion of the macroeconomic environment confronting Morocco is neglected. Nevertheless, the collection can be regarded as a seminal contribution, in that it has brought together fine discussions of disparate elements of Morocco's political economy. The articles are not technical, and are thus easily accessible to non-specialists in the field.

ALLAN assembles a collection of essays on Libyan development from independence in 1951 until the early 1980s. The articles address issues ranging from agricultural development and oil policy to industrialization and natural resource use. The second part of the book discusses political developments that are of more historical interest. The historical, climatic, and social constraints that Libya has had to confront in its quest for development are well described in this collection. These clear and accessible articles form a good introduction to Libyan political economy.

BRUCE A. WEISSE

Africa, Northern, law and legal system

Azziman, Omar, *La Traditionalisation du droit: Tradition juridique Islamique et droit privé marocain*, Rome: Centro di studi e ricerche di diritto comparato e straniero, 1993

Blaustein, A.P. and G.H. Flanz (editors), *Constitutions of the Countries of the World*, 20 vols with supplements, Dobbs Ferry, New York: Oceana, 1971–

Center for Reproductive Law and Policy (editor), *Women of the World: Laws and Policies Affecting Their Reproductive Lives*, New York: Center for Reproductive Law and Policy, 1997

Davies, Michael H., *Business Law in Egypt*, Boston: Kluwer, 1984

L'Encyclopédie juridique de l'Afrique, 10 vols, Abidjan: Nouvelles Editions Africaines, 1982

Hill, Enid, *Mahkama! Studies in the Egyptian Legal System: Courts and Crimes, Law and Society*, London: Ithaca Press, 1979

International Bureau of Fiscal Documentation (editors), *African Tax Systems*, Amsterdam: International Bureau of Fiscal Documentation, 1999

Karam, Nicola and Michael Davies, *Business Laws of Egypt*, London: Graham and Trotman, 1999

Revue Tunisienne de Droit

Salacuse, Jeswald W., *An Introduction to Law in French-speaking Africa*, vol. 1: *Africa South of the Sahara*, Charlottesville, Virginia: Michie, 1969; vol.2: *North Africa*, Charlottesville, Virginia: Michie, 1975

The main source for constitutional law in any part of modern world is without doubt BLAUSTEIN & FLANZ. The editors have undertaken the burdensome task of updating the collection of constitutional law instruments. Thus, the multi-volume loose-leaf edition constitutes the safest reference to constitutional law texts in the world today. Morocco, Algeria, Egypt and Tunisia have separate chapters, which – however – suffer from the main pitfall of the work, namely the lack of commentary or even annotation.

Any bibliographical entry concerning African legal systems would be very poor without reference to the exquisite and rarely analytical ENCYCLOPEDIE JURIDIQUE DE L'AFRIQUE. This multi-volume work provides an in-depth comparative analysis of the legal systems of Africa on areas such as philosophy of law to specific legal fields. Thus, the constitutional law volume includes a chapter on the constitutions of Africa, the political institutions, executive power, the political parties, administrative jurisdiction and new techniques for the introduction of new legislation. Of profound importance to any comparative lawyer seeking a full review of the legal systems in Africa with an exceptional work on their similarities and differences, this work was unfortunately last updated in 1983. Even so, it is still essential for Francophone legal researchers and analysts.

Of equal value to the same readership is the publication of the INTERNATIONAL BUREAU OF FISCAL DOCUMENTATION on tax law in Africa. All African countries are included in this multi-volume loose-leaf work, which benefits from a presentation of all relevant legislation, frequently updated, including a full list of all relevant bilateral agreements, as well as an invaluable complete bibliographical review of all relevant publications per country.

One of the more important human rights issues in Africa, as indeed in the whole world, is the human rights of women. The book of the CENTER FOR REPRODUCTIVE LAW AND POLICY presents in some detail, but with great clarity and precision, the legal and policy issues in this field of legislation in countries of northern and central Africa. Each chapter focuses on the sources of relevant legislation, a comparative and detailed analysis of the general legal and political framework on health and reproductive rights for women, an analysis of women's rights in marriage and a presentation of the relevant legislation concerning adolescents. Although it would be unfair to focus on just one of the chapters of this book, the last chapter on trends is a revelation for those who feel that nowadays women can find equality in areas of policy that have been the focus of research over the last decade, such as HIV/AIDS, abortion, contraception, mutilation and circumcision and enforcement in the field of sexual offences.

One of the fullest presentations of the law in northern African countries ever published is the classic work of SALA-CUSE. The book analyses the land and the people, the constitution, the sources of law, and all aspects of the judicial system in Algeria, Morocco and Tunisia. Although it is highly informative on the law of a bibliographically neglected area of the world (at least in European bibliography), the book is out of date and excludes one of the major northern African countries, Egypt.

The gap in the pursuit of material on Egyptian law is filled by the work of HILL, who has published a concise and brief, even somewhat simplistic, but still extremely valuable presentation of the Egyptian legal system. Particular reference is made to the courts, the legal profession, divorce, possession, and crime and punishment in Egypt. It provides a brief introduction to certain aspects of Egyptian law, which unfortunately suffers from lack of depth, bibliographical references and old age.

The recognition that Egyptian law needs further research is reflected in the multi-volume looseleaf work of KARAM & DAVIES on business laws in Egypt. An extremely rich source of legislation, this publication is essential for those interested in the field. However, the publication would have benefited from further commentary along the lines of the excellent introductory chapter, reference to case law and doctrine, and a lengthier glossary of terms, although in the same style. Such commentary and analysis can be found in DAVIES, which is best read in conjunction with Karam & Davies.

Moroccan law seems to be the second most neglected national system of North Africa (Libya's being the first). AZZIMAN's brief presentation of the traditionalization of the law in Moroccan private international law seems to be one of the few relevant publications available in Europe. The author looks at tradition as a reflection of Islamic values, and suggests that there is an Islamization of modern private international law in Morocco.

Tunisian law is expertly analysed, albeit by reference to articles analysing specific issues of Tunisian law in the REVUE TUNISIENNE DU DROIT. The journal, published in French, seems to be the only main source of information on Tunisian law available in Europe.

HELEN XANTHAKI

Africa, Southern, law and legal system

Abel, Richard L., *Politics by Other Means: Law in the Struggle against Apartheid, 1980–1994*, New York and London: Routledge, 1995

Asimov, Michael, "Administrative Law under South Africa's Final Constitution: The Need for an Administrative Justice Act", 113 (1996): 613–31

Corder, Hugh (editor), *Essays on Law and Social Practice in South Africa*, Cape Town: Juta, 1988

Hosten, W.J. *et al.*, *Introduction to South African Law and Legal Theory*, 3rd edition, Durban: Butterworths, 1999

Klaaren, Jonathan, "Structures of Government in the 1996 South African Constitution: Putting Democracy Back into Human Rights, *South African Journal of Human Rights*, 13 (1997): 3–43

Klug, Heinz, "Constitutional Law", *Annual Survey of South African Law*, (1995): 1–24

Mahomed, The Hon. Mr Justice, "The Independence of the Judiciary", *South African Law Journal*, 115 (1999): 658–67

Neethling, J., J.M. Potgieter and P.J. Visser, *Law of Delict*, 2nd edition, Durban: Butterworths, 1994

CORDER is an excellent introduction to the general philosophy behind the legal system of South Africa. The book attempts to develop a responsive awareness of the nature and function of law in South African society by focusing on questions such as the role of the legal system in the maintenance

of the political order, the means that lawyers have to seek justice more effectively, the role of trade unions in legal processes, the importance of rights, and the relationship between the South African legal system and the theories of philosophers (such as Calvin, Marx, Kelsen, Fuller, Hart, and Dworkin). The book reflects the crisis in South African legal culture at the time of its writing (in 1988), when jurisprudence was considered to be an innovative legal field, the almost total absence of which from the South African legal system was considered to be a sign of health, rather than a shortcoming.

The development of the recent jurisprudence of the South African Constitutional Court is one of the treasures included in the recent work of KLUG on the constitution in South Africa. The article focuses on the unfolding constitutional process by considering both the continued implementation of the interim Constitution of 1993 and the formulation of the working draft of the new constitution presented to the South African public in 1995. The author provides a valuable insight into the theory and practice of constitutional law in South Africa by reference to a large number of important works in this field. The critical analysis of the existing constitutional regime and the evaluation of its future is important reading for those interested in newly formed legal systems.

The effect of the new constitution on administrative law in South Africa is expertly analysed by ASIMOV, who explains that although administrative law will undoubtedly play an essential role in South Africa's imminent future, it has so far been neglected by the South African regimes both pre- and post-apartheid. The author supports the view that the need to introduce clear and complete administrative law provisions, capable of meeting the need for redistributive programmes such as land restitution and affirmative action, can only be met through executive branch administrative bodies empowered by statute. Administrative procedure must seem and be democratic, fully accountable, effective, and accessible. The author then proceeds to propose such bodies by stating that the Bill of Rights must be limited by statutes enacted by the electorally accountable Parliament, rather than by the courts. Moreover, the administrative-justice provisions of section 33 of the new constitution must be appropriately limited by legislation.

The importance of the division of powers, a so-far neglected constitutional issue, is brought to light by KLAAREN's excellent analysis of the issue. The author points out that, in the introduction and maintenance of a democratic regime in South Africa, constitutional lawyers and government officials tend to look to the separation of powers in the levels of local, regional and central government, rather to the more traditional separation in executive, legislative, and judicial. The author accepts that the demarcation of national, provincial, and local spheres can promote accountable, responsive, open and democratic government, and that the effective protection of human rights is part and parcel of democracy. However, the author argues that the relations between the institutions of central government, within the framework of the separation of powers, are crucially significant to the achievement of democracy, and warrant close attention. They also provide an important approach to interpreting the constitution itself. The article argues that a normative perspective that privileges neither democracy nor human rights and is contextual and critical is the way forward for South Africa, and describes the prominent institutions of the 1996 constitution with particular reference to the Constitutional Court.

Another article on the same field, written by the Hon. Mr Justice MAHOMED, refers to the independence of the judiciary, which is viewed by the author as the ultimate shield against the incremental and invisible corruption of universal morality. The author examines the legal basis of the independence of the judiciary in the legal system of South Africa and presents the right and duty of judges to demand that any new legislation respects and endorses this fundamental guarantee of democracy.

An overview of the law of delict in South African law can be found in the concise, yet in-depth analysis by NEETHLING, POTGIETER & VISSER The authors clarify the general principles of the law of delict, define fault, discuss causation, and present the concept of damage and the delictual remedies. Specific forms of delict, such as *damnum iniuria datum* and liability without fault are expertly presented by reference to South African doctrine and case law.

Any bibliographical entry on South African law would be incomplete without reference to the complete and detailed work of HOSTEN *et al.*. The authors provide an excellent in-depth presentation and critical evaluation of most fields of South African law. Chapters on the idea of law, the history of the South African legal system, the sources of law, family law, obligations, constitutional law, mercantile law, the law of persons, criminal law, formal law, and private and public international law would constitute a superb source of reference and understanding of the logic and practice in each legal field.

ABEL raises the interesting issue of the role of the law in the struggle of South Africans against apartheid. The book documents the diverse fight against this irrational regime in areas of legalized discriminatory policy and practice, such as state terrorism, police torture, and censorship.

HELEN XANTHAKI

Afrocentrism, Afrocentric movement

Appiah, Kwame Anthony, "Europe Upside Down: Fallacies of the New Afrocentrism", *Times Literary Supplement*, 4689 (1993): 24–25

Asante, Molefi Kete, *The Afrocentric Idea*, Philadelphia: Temple University Press, 1987; revised edition 1998

Ben-Jochannan, Yosef, *Black Man of the Nile*, New York: Alkebu-Lan, 1970; revised edition as *Black Man of the Nile and His Family*, 1972, reprinted Baltimore: Black Classic Press, 1989

Bernal, Martin, *Black Athena: The Afroasiatic Roots of Classical Civilization*, vol. 1: *The Fabrication of Ancient Greece, 1785–1985*, New Brunswick, New Jersey: Rutgers University Press, and London: Free Association Press, 1987

Diop, Cheikh Anta, *Civilization or Barbarism: An Authentic Anthropology*, New York: Lawrence Hill, 1991

Lips, Julius E., *The Savage Hits Back*, New Haven, Connecticut: Yale University Press, 1937

Mudimbe, V.Y., *The Invention of Africa: Gnosis, Philosophy, and the Order of Knowledge*, Bloomington: Indiana University Press, 1988

Onyewuenyi, Innocent C., *The African Origin of Greek Philosophy: An Exercise in Afrocentrism*, Nsukka, Nigeria: University of Nsukka Press, 1994

Owusu, Maxwell, "Ethnography of Africa: The Usefulness of the Useless", *American Anthropologist*, 80/1 (1978): 310–34

Williams, Chancellor, *The Destruction of Black Civilization: Great Issues of a Race from 4500 bc to 2000 ad*, 3rd edition, Chicago: Third World Press, 1987

LIPS was far ahead of his time in attempting to present the white world through genuine non-Western eyes. His study unveils the hypocrisy of the ethnographic canon of seeing ourselves as others see us when in fact it is most often the Western other who describes, analysis, and theorizes on the non-Western other. Although he uses materials from other non-Western societies besides Africa, his work meets the Afrocentric credo and continues to find relevance in today's discourse concerning the presentation of African societies in Western scholarship.

BEN-JOCHANNAN helped sow the seed of modern Afrocentrism in the heydays of black studies programmes in the US in the early 1970s. His thesis that black ancient Egypt, therefore Africa, is mother of Western civilization was so revolutionary back then that his work acquired cult status among African Americans. His work is important in its challenge of the arbitrary received dichotomy of Africa into white north Africa and black subsaharan Africa, excluding South Africa, by African studies programmes popular in the 1960s in the US. His work continues to stimulate the search for origins in black history, athletics, arts, and philosophy. It is essential to read this work for an understanding of the Afrocentric movement.

WILLIAMS produced a seminal work on the destruction of black civilization based on 16 years of historical research in 26 countries and 105 societies in Africa. His continent-wide survey is a painstaking examination of Africa over seven time periods from prehistoric times though the colonial period of the 19th century. His research establishes blacks as original dwellers and the very earliest builders of a great civilization in ancient Egypt. His clarion call for continued research into black history is being answered by new generation of black scholars. His work is a pioneer text for understanding modern Afrocentrism.

ASANTE, a prime mover of the Afrocentric movement in the US is prolific on Afrocentric themes. This work is selected because it provides a comprehensive treatment of the idea of putting Africa at the centre of world civilization, in contrast to seeing Africa as backward and unproductive through Eurocentric eyes. He calls for a rise to action to set the records straight by rediscovery and re-establishing whatever has been stolen, suppressed, distorted, omitted in black heritage, whether scientific, cultural, economic, or philosophical. Tracing the roots of African-American frustration and alienation to miseducation and an overdose of Western ideology, he advocates a reconstruction and rewriting of human history to reflect Africa as origin of man in more ways than one.

BERNAL is claimed by Afrocentrists for refuting the modern view that classical Greece owed nothing to Egypt. He provides a scholarly history of the rise and disappearance of the ascendancy of black ancient Egypt in the history of world civilizations. He posits that, beginning from Herodotus, European scholars earlier accepted Greek colonization by Egypt but with 18th century and 19th century historians succumbing to racism and chauvinism, the later model was devised which signalled the beginning of the degradation of African societies. His work is a compelling resource for Afrocentrism.

DIOP argues that it was Europe that was dependent on her exploitation of Africa, not Africa that was supported by Europe. Although his thesis was considered preposterous, he collected evidence that black African culture was transmitted to Greece across the Mediterranean, giving rise to a European civilization. His work is an important resource in the rise of the Afrocentric movement and his views are enthusiastically shared by Afrocentrists. He holds that that many European writings on Africa are biased and Eurocentric, that the achievements of other cultures are subordinated to Europe, that the belief that the achievements of ancient Egypt have been accomplished by a black civilization are based on racial assumptions, and that Europe should henceforth be judged by African standards.

ONYEWUENYI practicalizes the tenets of Afrocentrism by engaging in a meticulous research into the history of classical philosophy in order to provide documentary evidence of the existence of Egyptian origins for Greek philosophy, the silence of Western philosophers, and their active suppression of African contribution to the discipline of philosophy. His findings lead to Egyptian prototypes of Greek philosophy from the early Ionian school through the Pythagoreans to Plato and Aristotle. The text addresses scholars and professors of philosophy, white European and American students, and black African and African American students. It is a remarkable exercise in Afrocentrism with familiarity with important texts and arguments.

OWUSU's essay is a brilliant example of the necessary kind of critique that African scholars should apply to existing works on African studies to ascertain how scientific and reliable the work of Africanists is by applying a rigorous examination of methodology, communication, and interpretative skills in their field work. He successfully points out flawed conclusions resulting from a methodology that largely ignores the importance of language and communication in some of the major received ethnographies of Africa. He asserts correctly that the realities and complexities of a foreign culture cannot begin to be realized without possessing adequate language skills in indigenous languages.

APPIAH sees Afrocentrism as "a composite of truth and error, insight and illusion, moral generosity and meanness". He does not think the savage should strike back because that could be committing the same errors as Eurocentrics. He is scathing in his observation that Afrocentrics, in their fixation with Egypt, overlook the rest of Africa and seem to be unaware of the many contributions to epistemology by modern-day African scholars. He also chastises the idea of African unanimism, which does not seem to him to recognise the diversity of African cultures.

MUDIMBE's erudite examination of Africa and Africanisms through the basic issues of African anthropology, history, and philosophy, is a seminal work on the study of African people and cultures. Intellectual, original, and provocative, his work applies a successful methodology to the transformation of

different types of knowledge. The various strands of knowledge of otherness are woven together skilfully to form an unforgettable pattern. It is an important landmark in the continuing discourse on the presentation of Africa in intellectual discourse.

AYODOLE OGUNDIPE

Age stratification

Borgatta, Edgar F. and Neil G. McCluskey (editors), *Aging and Society: Current Research and Policy Perspectives*, Beverly Hills, California: Sage, 1980

Burbank, Victoria Katherine, *Aboriginal Adolescence: Maidenhood in an Australian Community*, New Brunswick, New Jersey: Rutgers University Press, 1988

Cole, Thomas R., *The Journey of Life: A Cultural History of Aging in America*, Cambridge and New York: Cambridge University Press, 1992

Formanek, Susanne and Sepp Linhart, *Aging: Asian Concepts and Experiences, Past and Present*, Vienna: Österreichischen Akademie der Wissenschaften, 1997

Heath, Shirley Brice and Milbrey McLaughlin, *Identity and Inner-city Youth: Beyond Ethnicity and Gender*, New York: Teacher's College Press, 1993

Kertzer, David I. and Jennie Keith (editors), *Age and Anthropological Theory*, Ithaca, New York: Cornell University Press, 1984

Kurimoto, Eisei and Simon Simonse (editors), *Conflict, Age and Power in North East Africa: Age Systems in Transition*, Oxford: Currey, and Athens: Ohio University Press, 1998

Taylor, Ronald, *African-American Youth: Their Social and Economic Status in the United States*, Westport, Connecticut: Praeger, 1995

Van Tassel, David and Peter N. Stearns (editors), *Old Age in a Bureaucratic Society: The Elderly, the Experts, and the State in American History*, Westport, Connecticut: Greenwood Press, 1986

Yelland, Nicola (editor), *Gender in Early Childhood*, London and New York: Routledge, 1998

A primary challenge to social scientists is how to deepen one's disciplinary knowledge while broadening it through new ways of thinking that develop in other areas of knowledge. Crosscultural studies show that the concept of "age" shifts between and within societies, defining what is meant by "child", "adolescent", and "adult". Further, age stratification emphasizes societal-level elements rather than individuals. BORGATTA & McCLUSKEY use the paradigm of age stratification to focus upon the elderly as a demographic phenomenon, and as a social problem. The collection of brief and selective essays stimulate thought about the economic, psychological health, welfare, and sociopolitical issues that an ageing population generates, thereby providing a broad introduction to the problems of stratifying societies through a category termed "age".

BURBANK's work surveys the difficulties of executing a sociocultural definition of adolescence, because different societies use different strategies for identifying and managing adolescence. Nonetheless her work uses age-stratification analysis in its concentration on age strata, where individuals are associated with roles and statuses in a cohort that passes into a new status at a different point in historical time. Her study of a group of young Australian-Aboriginal women focuses on adolescent sexual behaviour, marriage, and the conflict between adult expectations and adolescent behaviour. It portrays the potential conflicts that can arise between fundamental ideas about Aboriginal social organization and social transformations wrought by an imposed culture.

In his desire to understand how "chronological age becomes a tool for regulating the life course" COLE presents a study of ageing in Western societies, a history of ageing in America, and a discussion of the ways that science has (re)created notions of normal ageing. His animated and stimulating voice creates an intelligent, detailed portrait of American views of ageing and deepens the understanding of people's experience in the past.

Exploring the interest of the West in the cultural construction of old age in previous centuries and in other societies, FORMANEK & LINHART have collated 17 papers that study old age in Asian societies. Their "consciousness of the social plasticity of human old age" deconstructs rigid notions of age stratification. The authors question the imagined utopian past in which respect for and valuation of the elderly was better evolved in preliterate and Asian societies. Rather, they argue for a connection between ancestor worship and seniority in social hierarchies. The work is important in providing both flexible perceptions of "old age" and crosscultural complexity to Western notions of age stratification.

HEATH & McLAUGHLIN, a linguistic anthropologist and policy analyst respectively, have collated a selection of essays that address issues generated by five years of research with inner city youth organizations in the US. McLaughlin focuses upon the ways that institutions conceptualised "youth" and formulated programmes to assist them. Heath concentrates on how youth organizations empowered youngsters within their sphere of influence in order to understand how young people construct a sense of self. The book is useful in its exemplification of how youngsters make choices to create their daily existence.

KERTZER & KEITH's edited collection considers how age is a major variable in terms of social structure, the life course of individuals, and perceptions of culture. Divided into three parts, the work addresses age, evolution, and biology in the first; emphasizes kinship, domestic groups, economics, and power relations in the second; and assesses the links between age and culture and how it is incorporated in symbolism and ritual in the third. The introduction, in particular, offers a cogent elucidation of age stratification and analysis of cohort relationships over time.

Working from the standpoint that age systems function as military and political organizations in most societies, the essays compiled by KURIMOTO & SIMONSE, contest functionalist African research that promotes the aspects of social integration enjoyed by age-set members. The 11 essays trace the ritualized violence and politicized confrontation practised by members of many age systems, coterminously argue for the notion of "society" as an accurate unit of analysis for North

East African age systems, and place age systems into regional and historical contexts. The work offers a broad-based cross-cultural understanding of age stratification that necessarily complicates analyses of "age" and accepted social behaviour.

TAYLOR's overview introduces his edited collection of 13 authors. They examine social differences between black and white adolescents through various indicators of wellbeing, as well as the growing polarization by socioeconomic status within black communities. The authors move from theoretical contextualization, through analyses of family socialization, and understandings of areas where black youth are at risk, to considerations of effective social intervention. This is an important work that provides clear considerations of a range of issues affecting black youngsters.

In a work separated into five parts, VAN TASSEL & STEARNS have collected assorted essays that advance knowledge about the elderly by placing them in a broad temporal context. They elucidate changes in the modern experience of the elderly that can be shaped by contemporary social policy in industrialized societies, and survey the social history of and relationships between: demography and family structure, culture, and institutions and policies. Disagreements amongst the contributors create a lively text that reflects the diversity of interpretations generated by different research topics. The work is an excellent stimulus to debate around issues of what constitutes the social strata termed "the elderly".

In a study conducted within a range of Western societies a recent text, edited by YELLAND, considers the ways that gender is socially constructed according to the sex of the infant, and how the construction and maintenance of gender categories pervades all aspects of daily life. The essays examine how young children interpret their sense of self in relation to notions of gender, how children negotiate different gender positions for strategic value, and the ways that people, practices, and policies influence the lives of youngsters to shape their interactions with others and with their culture's commodities.

HELEN JOHNSON

See also Ageism, Demography

Ageism

Albert, Steven M. and Maria G. Cattell, *Old Age in Global Perspective: Cross-Cultural and Cross-National Views*, New York: G.K. Hall, 1994

Amoss, Pamela T. and Stevan Harrell (editors), *Other Ways of Growing Old: Anthropological Perspectives*, Stanford, California: Stanford University Press, 1981

Furlong, Andy and Fred Cartmel, *Young People and Social Change: Individualization and Risk in Late Modernity*, Buckingham: Open University Press, 1997

Hooyman, Nancy R. and H. Asuman Kiyak, *Social Gerontology: A Multidisciplinary Perspective*, 4th edition, Boston: Allyn and Bacon, 1996

Jerrome, Dorothy (editor), *Ageing in Modern Society: Contemporary Approaches*, London: Croom Helm, and New York: St Martin's Press, 1983

Kiesler, Sara B., James N. Morgan and Valerie Kincade

Oppenheimer (editors), *Aging: Social Change*, New York and London: Academic Press, 1981

Lesnoff-Caravaglia, Gari (editor), *The World of the Older Woman: Conflicts and Resolutions*, New York: Human Sciences Press, 1984

Minichiello, Victor, Neena Chappell, Hal Kendig and Alan Walker (editors), *Sociology of Aging: International Perspectives*, Melbourne: Venereology, 1996

Pipher, Mary, *Reviving Ophelia: Saving the Selves of Adolescent Girls*, New York: Putnam, 1994; London: Vermilion, 1996

Sokolovsky, Jay (editor), *The Cultural Context of Aging: Worldwide Perspectives*, 2nd edition, Westport, Connecticut: Bergin and Garvey, 1997

Social perceptions of other people change at different times in the viewers' own lives. Ageism encapsulates the prejudices and demeaning attitudes that are produced by the difficulties in understanding the experiences of people in generations other than one's own. Equally, it can be as difficult to understand that "age" may mean different things to people in non-Western cultures. Melding qualitative orientations and quantitative sociological paradigms, ALBERT & CATTELL compile knowledge about ageing across the globe. They offer alternative approaches to the temporal element of ageing, suggesting that biological, chronological, and social dimensions form part of the process. They describe intergenerational and intragenerational relationships, conflicts over succession, and culturally different living arrangements that combine notions of social benefit and individual autonomy, to assert that variation in experiences of ageing, and conflicts that are generated around the elderly, are wider than Western experience suggests.

AMOSS & HARRELL have designed a collection that brings a crosscultural perspective to the study of social ageing. They assert that in order to combat ageism it is important to distinguish between those aspects of ageing that are general across and within societies, and those that are shaped by the particularities of a sociocultural system and, therefore, may be more easily transformed. In challenging the notion that the elderly are valued more highly in "primitive" societies, the authors argue that the social rank of the old is determined by the balance between their maintenance costs and their contribution, but also that family and kinship networks can act to protect the elderly in all societies. Their approach provides suggestions about the ways in which Western societies may increase the social utility and value of the aged.

FURLONG & CARTMEL set social prejudice against youth within the context of social change that results from labour market restructuring, an increased demand for educated workers, specialization in the workplace, and social policies that force young people to be dependent on family support. In arguing that such dramatic transformations produce perceptions that the social world is both risky and unpredictable, and must therefore be negotiated as an individual, they propose that change increases the potential for feelings of separation from society and failure as a result of individual shortcomings. Covering issues relating to education, health, the labour market, crime and politics, the authors clearly articulate their theoretical framework and provide lucid statistical support to substantiate their arguments.

HOOYMAN & KIYAK's work focuses entirely on the elderly. Their statistically and theoretically detailed contribution undermines prejudice against elderly people that arises from misconceptions and myths about them. The work focuses on how the elderly are studied, contemporary social theories of ageing, and the physiological, psychological and social contexts of ageing. The text is useful in courses that work to develop the connection between learning about ageing and understanding one's own behaviour and that of others. It presents the diversity of the ageing experience within US culture, using a multidisciplinary perspective.

JERROME collates an eclectic mix of essays derived from conference papers. The first part provides a thoughtful assessment of the changing social circumstances in which ageing occurs, focusing on subjectivity, care and provision, and theoretical concerns. The contributions work towards a position that contemporary experiences of ageing need to be considered within the context of social change and cultural diversity. The second part focuses on changing perspectives on ageing, both official and popular, to acknowledge the positive aspects of ageing, the validation of continuity of experience, and the importance of treating older people with dignity and respect.

In a welcome exploration of ageing and women, LESNOFF-CARAVAGLIA has fashioned a hard-hitting, radical, and invigorating range of essays into a collection that is compelling and broad-based. Launching from the "double stigmata" of being female and old, the varied authors examine abuse and rape of older women, legal issues, institutionalization, widowhood, and policies and programmes targeting elderly women. Examining the culturally-ascribed roles that expect women to give birth and act as primary caregivers to children, the authors explore the particular kind of female anguish that can accompany the ageing process in Western societies. They explore the discrimination of ageism, asserting that it is not always deliberate and malicious, but appears in acts of omission, producing a society in which women suffer low self-image, poverty, and minimal independence. This work is a necessary corrective to many researchers who mass together a diverse population as "the elderly" with minimal consideration of gender difference.

One of three volumes that examine social and behavioural science research perspectives on ageing, KIESLER, MORGAN & OPPENHEIMER's work concentrates on the elderly and offers a token chapter about women. They address, in particular, the need for both psychological and institutional social support when elderly people experience life crises. The need for elderly people to express their difficulties in a potentially contracting social world requires the transcendence of ageist preconceptions. They explore ageism through the plight of elderly people's self-perceptions of redundancy and their acceptance of Western society's stereotyped and limiting labels, the labels themselves being a reinforcement of society's dominant view of the elderly.

MINICHIELLO *et al.* have edited a collection of conference papers that question accepted assumptions behind many public discourses about the successes and problems of ageing. The contributors alert the reader to controversial issues involving caregiving and family support, healthcare, work and retirement, government policy, and gender. They show how social institutions and human agency create both privilege and disadvantage in later life. The text is helpful in its review of early theories about ageing, and the way in which it works with and builds on the need to socially contextualize the ageing process. The contributors examine the ageism in the social and political processes that exclude older people – their legally-imposed withdrawal from paid employment, their representational absence in popular culture such as fashion and the media, the low status of care for the aged, their labelling as a social burden by statisticians and policy makers, the devaluation of the aged body, and caregivers' invisibility as workers. This is an exemplary text for second and third year university courses.

PIPHER addresses the issue of ageism through her overt concern for young women. She considers the often-unnamed social difficulties that face adolescent girls within the context of broader cultural forces. She documents the physical, emotional, intellectual, academic, social, and spiritual changes that occur during the development of young women in their teenage years. The author articulates the specific difficulties that young women in the United States encounter, and the ways that culture can be changed to emphasize the importance of sustaining innate values and building a more nurturing, less violent and sexualized environment that sustains young women's personal growth. This text should be made available to young women in secondary school and university years.

SOKOLOVSKY reinforces the need to analyse ageing within specific cultural contexts so that images of the catastrophic loss of youth can be reconstructed to promote the crucial roles that elders maintain in kin and community groups throughout human societies. This edited collection combats the limited conceptions and perceptions that promote ageism by describing and interpreting the "wondrous array of social responses to the physical imperatives of growing old". The 18 essays examine how older adults function as socially active agents in diverse societies and how their cultural context creates a varied reality of what ageing can signify. This work is important to broaden students' understanding of ageing, and to enable them to imagine the social potential for ageing with grace, dignity, and serenity.

HELEN JOHNSON

Agency theory, economic

Baron, David P. and Roger B. Myerson, "Regulating a Monopolist with Unknown Costs", *Econometrica*, 50/4 (1982): 911–30

Grossman, Sanford J. and Oliver D. Hart, "An Analysis of the Principal–Agent Problem", *Econometrica*, 51/1 (1983): 7–45

Laffont, Jean-Jacques and Jean Tirole, *A Theory of Incentives in Procurement and Regulation*, Cambridge, Massachusetts: MIT Press, 993

Macho-Stadler, Ines and J. David Perez-Castrillo, *An Introduction to the Economics of Information: Incentives and Contracts*, Oxford and New York: Oxford University Press, 1997

Molho, Ian, *The Economics of Information: Lying and Cheating in Markets and Organizations*, Oxford and Malden, Massachusetts: Blackwell, 1997

Ross, Stephen A., "The Economic Theory of Agency: The Principal's Problem", *American Economic Review*, 63/2 (1973): 134–39

Rothschild, Michael and Joseph E. Stiglitz, "Equilibrium in Competitive Insurance Markets: An Essay on the Economics of Imperfect Information", *Quarterly Journal of Economics*, 90/4 (1976): 629–49

Shapiro, Carl and Joseph E. Stiglitz, "Equilibrium Unemployment as a Worker Discipline Device", *American Economic Review*, 74/3 (1984): 433–44

Stiglitz, Joseph E. and Andrew Weiss, "Credit Rationing in Markets with Imperfect Information", *American Economic Review*, 71/3 (1981): 393–410

Stiglitz, Joseph E., Principal and Agent entry in *The New Palgrave: Allocation, Information and Markets*, edited by John Eatwell, Murray Milgate and Peter Newman, London: Macmillan, 1989

Agency theory deals with the hierarchical relations between two individuals where the utility of one is affected by the actions of the other. When information is unequally distributed between them, this interdependence is a source of problems referred to as principal–agent problems (risk sharing, moral hazard, adverse selection).

Agency theory is now split into two main trends, normative and positive. Normative agency theory is a branch of economic theory relating to imperfect information. Positive agency theory, which is concerned with the contractual arrangements actually implemented by the parties to limit agency costs, belongs to management. The selected bibliography refers only to normative agency theory.

It was ROSS who first expressed agency relations in principal–agent terms. The principal (an employer or the state) enlists the services of a paid agent (an employee or a civil servant) to carry out duties on the former's behalf. As information is asymmetrically distributed to the agent's advantage, and as everyone tries to maximize his or her own utility, there may be a loss of utility for the principal, who is in part dependent on the information held by the agent, whose interest may lie in not revealing it. In asking how an agent may be made to choose the action which best matches the principal's interests, Ross highlights the fact that a principal–agent problem is above all one of incentive – to reveal hidden information or choose one course of action rather than another, in short, to cooperate. He thus sets out the microeconomic basis for dealing with a very common situation, as there is an agency relationship between lenders and borrowers, insurers and insured, landlords and tenants, etc.

GROSSMAN & HART look at the agency problem in mathematical terms. According to their model, the agent's action cannot be observed by the principal (shareholder), but the outcome of such action can, as it is the firm's profit. The agent (a manager or a firm when the principal is a bank) has a choice between several courses of action (or effort levels), such choice being dependent on a comparison between the effort required and the salary received, since some courses of action are more costly for the agent than others in terms of effort required. It is necessary, therefore, to devise a programme of incentives in which each (verifiable) result of the agent's actions is linked to a certain level of pay from the principal. After setting out the benefits and costs for the principal, depending on the action taken by the agent, Grossman & Hart give optimal solutions for such a system of incentives.

Agency theory is applicable to any market in which there is an agency relationship at work. Consideration is given in particular to three markets where, as pointed out by STIGLITZ, the essentially intertemporal nature of relations between individuals make principal-agent problems especially common.

SHAPIRO & STIGLITZ's model relates to the labour market. The employer suffers a moral hazard because of the private information relating to on-the-job effort held by the agent. How can the employer incite the agent to work efficiently, bearing in mind that the effort level is a rational choice by the agent, that is to say one which takes account of the risk of being seen as "shirking" and therefore of being fired. If it is impossible or too expensive to monitor workers directly, the other answer is to increase the cost of dismissal for them. When there is high unemployment or other firms offer unattractive salaries, an efficiency wage, that is to say higher than the going rate, is an incentive, discouraging the agent from adopting opportunistic behaviour, by making such behaviour unprofitable for him or her. However, the authors show that if all firms adopt such an approach, the wage differential between one firm and its competitors is no longer a sufficient incentive. As this situation leads to involuntary unemployment in equilibrium, it is the market equilibrium unemployment rate which acts as a worker-discipline device.

In the life-insurance market, where there is a great risk of adverse selection, two kinds of equilibria (pooling and separating equilibria), and hence two corresponding kinds of contract, are highlighted by ROTHSCHILD & STIGLITZ. The insurer has only imperfect knowledge of the class of risk to which each potential insured person belongs, whereas this should be an essential factor in the price adjustments it may offer. This uncertainty over the agent's "quality" means that if the insurer proposes contracts with 100% compensation, high-risk agents (those who are ill) have a greater interest in insuring themselves than low-risk agents (those in good health). It is in the insurer's interest, therefore, to differentiate between these two classes of agents. One way of differentiating is by means of the franchise. There is reason for thinking that a contract with a high franchise and a low premium will be chosen by low-risk agents, whereas a contract with a low franchise and a high premium will be preferred by high-risk agents. In choosing one or other type of contract the agents reveal their private information (here, the class of risk to which they belong, or their "quality").

Applying the same reasoning to the bank loans market, STIGLITZ & WEISS show that in equilibrium this market may be characterized by credit rationing, which again illustrates the idea that the law of supply and demand is valid only where there is complete information and the information is equally distributed.

A thorough overview of principal-agent problems and recent developments in signalling theory (job-market signalling, screening as a self-selection mechanism, and further literature on signalling theory) is to be found in MOLHO. For undergraduate teaching, MACHO-STADLER & PEREZ-CASTRILLO give several examples from the fields of finance, technology transfers, public subsidies and the regulation of public firms.

Normative agency theory also applies to organizations. BARON & MYERSON's model concerns relations between a regulatory body and a public utility. The authors assume that the firm has better information on its costs than the regulatory body when put under the latter's control. Such private information allows it to obtain an information rent. The greater the firm's efficiency in relation to the terms of the contract with the regulatory body, the higher the rent. This model is a good illustration of the idea that when information is asymmetrical, the agent's strategic behaviour leads to new constraints upon the allocation of resources. The regulatory body must therefore arbitrate between the search for efficiency and information rents which it abandons to firms. LAFFONT & TIROLE apply this approach more generally by studying situations where both adverse selection (hidden information) and moral hazard (hidden action) are present. The question addressed is that of maximizing a social welfare function, defined as the sum of the surpluses of firm and consumers. They thereby define the characteristics of optimal regulation. After comparing traditional forms of regulation, they describe various kinds of optimal and intermediate incentive contracts.

LYSIANE CARTELIER

See also Adverse selection, Economics of information, Moral hazard

Agent-based computational economics

Arthur, W. Brian, John H. Holland, Blake LeBaron, Richard Palmer and Paul Taylor, "Asset Pricing under Endogenous Expectations in an Artificial Stock Market" in *The Economy as an Evolving Complex System*, vol. 2, edited by W. Brian Arthur, Steven N. Durlauf and David A. Lane, Reading, Massachusetts: Addison Wesley, 1997

Axelrod, Robert M., *The Complexity of Cooperation: Agent-Based Models of Competition and Collaboration*, Princeton, New Jersey: Princeton University Press, 1997

Epstein, Joshua and Robert Axtell, *Growing Artificial Societies: Social Science from the Bottom Up*, Cambridge, Massachusetts: MIT Press, 1996

Kirman, Alan, "The Economy as an Interactive System" in *The Economy as an Evolving Complex System*, vol. 2, edited by W. Brian Arthur, Steven N. Durlauf and David A. Lane, Reading, Massachusetts: Addison Wesley, 1997

Kollman, Ken, John H. Miller and Scott E. Page, "Computational Political Economy" in *The Economy as an Evolving Complex System*, vol. 2, edited by W. Brian Arthur, Steven N. Durlauf and David A. Lane, Reading, Massachusetts: Addison Wesley, 1997

Nelson, Richard, "Recent Evolutionary Theorizing about Economic Change", *Journal of Economic Literature*, 33 (1995): 48–90

Samuelson, Larry, *Evolutionary Games and Equilibrium Selection*, Cambridge, Massachusetts: MIT Press, 1997

Tesfatsion, Leigh, "A Trade Network Game with Endogenous Partner Selection" in *Computational Approaches to*

Economic Problems, edited by Hans Amman, Berc Rustem, and Andrew Whinston, Dordrecht and Boston: Kluwer, 1997

Vriend, Nicolaas, "Self-Organization of Markets: An Example of a Computational Approach", *Computational Economics*, 8 (1995): 205–31

Young, H. Peyton, *Individual Strategy and Social Structure: An Evolutionary Theory of Institutions*, Princeton, New Jersey: Princeton University Press, 1998

The newly developing field of agent-based computational economics (ACE) is roughly defined by its practitioners as the computational study of economies modelled as evolving decentralized systems of autonomous interacting agents. A principal concern of ACE researchers is to understand the apparently spontaneous formation of global regularities in economic processes, such as the unplanned coordination of trading activities in decentralized market economies that economists associate with Adam Smith's "invisible hand". The challenge is to explain how these global regularities arise through the repeated local interactions of autonomous agents channelled through socioeconomic institutions, rather than relying on fictitious coordination mechanisms such as imposed market-clearing constraints or an assumption of single representative agents.

The study of evolutionary economics is by no means new. Even before Darwin, attempts were made to apply evolutionary ideas to socioeconomic behaviour. Although economists now largely ignore this early work, economic textbooks still typically include at least some mention of the ideas of Joseph Schumpeter regarding the evolution of economic institutions. Moreover, Schumpeter's work, together with the seminal work by A.A. Alchian on uncertainty and evolution in economic systems, appears to have strongly influenced the subsequent well-known work by R. Nelson, S. Winter, and various of their collaborators, on evolutionary theories of economic change. There is also the work of W.B. Arthur on economies incorporating positive feedback, the work by Richard Day on dynamic economies characterized by complex phase transitions, the work by J. Foster on an evolutionary approach to macroeconomics, R. Heiner's work on the origins of predictable behaviour, J. Hirshleifer's work on evolutionary models in economics and law, and U. Witt's work on economic natural selection. NELSON reviews these and numerous other interesting studies on evolutionary economics.

More recently, as discussed in SAMUELSON, a number of researchers have been focusing on the potential economic applicability of evolutionary game theory with replicator dynamics. In these studies, game strategies are distributed over a fixed number of strategy types, and the strategies reproduce over time in direct proportion to their relative fitness.

Exploiting the recent advent of more powerful computational tools such as object-oriented programming, the work of ACE researchers such as ARTHUR *et al.*, AXELROD, EPSTEIN & AXTELL, KIRMAN, KOLLMAN, MILLER & PAGE, TESFATSION, VRIEND, and YOUNG has extended this earlier work on evolutionary economics in four key ways.

First, agents in ACE frameworks are typically modelled as heterogeneous entities that determine their interactions with other agents and with their environment on the basis of internalized data and behavioural rules. These agents thus tend to have a great deal more internal cognitive structure and autonomy than conventionally modelled economic agents. Second, a broader range of agent interactions is typically permitted in ACE frameworks, with predatory and cooperative associations taking centre stage along with price and quantity relationships. Third, the evolutionary process is generally represented as natural selection pressures acting directly on agent characteristics rather than as population-level laws of motion. These natural selection pressures result in the continual creation of new modes of agent behaviour and an ever-changing network of agent interactions. Fourth, ACE frameworks are implemented by computers, as virtual economic worlds that grow themselves along a real timeline, much like a culture dish develops in a laboratory. In principle, once initial conditions are set, all subsequent events in these virtual economic worlds are initiated and driven by agent–agent and agent–environment interactions; no further outside interventions by the modeller (such as off-line fixed-point calculations) are permitted.

ACE represents a methodological approach that may ultimately permit two important developments: first, the rigorous testing, refinement, and extension of theories developed in the earlier literature on evolutionary economics that were found to be analytically intractable; and second, the rigorous formulation and testing of conceptually integrated socioeconomic theories compatible with theory and data from many different relevant fields currently separated by artificial disciplinary boundaries.

To illustrate the ACE approach in more concrete terms, Tesfatsion has developed the Trade Network Game (TNG) for studying the formation and evolution of trade networks. The TNG consists of successive generations of traders who choose and refuse trade partners on the basis of continually updated expected payoffs, engage in risky trades modelled as two-person games, and evolve their trade strategies over time.

The TNG framework facilitates the computational study of markets from an agent-based perspective in three key ways. First, each agent is instantiated as an autonomous, endogenously interacting software agent with internally stored state information and with internal behavioural rules. The agents can therefore engage in anticipatory behaviour. Moreover, using stored agent addresses together with internalized communication protocols, they can communicate with each other at event-triggered times, a feature not present in standard economic models. Second, the TNG framework is modular in design. This means that experimentation with alternative specifications for market structure, search and matching among traders, trade site interactions, expectation formation and updating, and evolution of trade site strategies, can easily be undertaken – much like changing a light bulb in a multi-bulb lamp – as long as the interfaces (inputs and outputs) for the modules implementing these specifications remain unchanged. Moreover, each module can potentially be grounded in trader-initiated action, in the sense that it is implemented via behavioural rules internal to the traders. Third, the transitory and longer run implications of each alternative module specification can be studied at three different levels: individual characteristics of traders; interactions among traders (network formation); and social welfare, as measured by descriptive statistics such as average trader welfare.

For extensive on-line ACE resources, including surveys, an annotated syllabus of readings, software, and pointers to other ACE-related Web sites, see the ACE Web site at http://www. econ.iastate.edu/tesfatsi/ace.htm.

LEIGH TESFATSION

Aggregate production function

Brown, Murray, Kazuo Sato and Paul Zarembka, *Essays in Modern Capital Theory*, Amsterdam: North Holland, 1976

Clark, John Bates, *The Distribution of Wealth: A Theory of Wages, Interest and Profit*, New York: Macmillan, 1899; reprinted New York: Kelley, 1965

Hicks, John, *Capital and Growth*, Oxford: Clarendon Press, and New York: Oxford University Press, 1965

Levhari, David, "A Nonsubstitution Theorem and Switching of Techniques", *Quarterly Journal of Economics*, 79 (1965): 98–105

Pasinetti, Luigi L. *et al.*, "Paradoxes in Capital Theory: A Symposium", *Quarterly Journal of Economics*, 80 (1966): 503–83

Robinson, Joan, "The Production Function and the Theory of Capital", *Review of Economic Studies*, 21 (1953): 81–106

Solow, Robert M., "The Production Function and the Theory of Capital", *Review of Economic Studies*, 23 (1955): 101–08

Solow, Robert M., "Discussion" in *Essays in Modern Capital Theory*, edited by Murray Brown, Kazuo Sato and Paul Zarembka, Amsterdam: North Holland, 1976

Zarembka, Paul, "Capital Heterogeneity, Aggregation and the Two-sector Model", *Quarterly Journal of Economics*, 89 (1975): 103–14

A production function in economic theory purports to relate well-defined outputs – bushels of wheat grain, steel pipes of specific dimensions – to well-defined inputs – labour hours of unskilled labour, hectares of land of certain fertility, and so on. It is an outcome of the marginalist, or "neoclassical" revolution in economic theory that began in the 1870s, and is based upon microeconomics, the economics of individual firm, and consumer behaviour.

Macroeconomics is the economics of an economy as a whole, with the aggregate production function beginning to develop a quarter century after the marginalist revolution. CLARK (particularly chapter IX) took an initial step when, in addition to inputs of labour time, he contrasted "capital" from "capital goods". "Capital" is the instruments of production considered in a mutable form, and so is "perfectly mobile"; "capital goods" are the actual physical objects, which may have important production roles in one industry but are totally useless to other production processes. For Clark, capital (not capital goods) lives "by transmigration, taking itself out of one set of bodies and putting itself into another, again and again" (p.120) – those bodies being the specific instruments of production, the capital goods. This may sound tidy enough and did lead Clark to be able to ascribe a marginal productivity to labor in connection with an employed "capital". But it also led eventually to major disputes.

Instruments of production are "reproducible" – can be produced anew, unlike land (ignoring improvements), which is irreproducible. In other words, instruments are produced in factories and can be produced repeatedly in factories, or they can be changed. Therefore, any quick analogy to a marginal productivity of land may be completely misplaced. ZAREMBKA, however, attempted a theoretical description of technology that could tie the physically distinct instruments of production into a larger concept of "capital" in Clark's sense. The assumptions behind the attempt are quite restrictive. Rather than making Clark's approach more acceptable, perhaps they make it less so.

ROBINSON had rolled out a theoretical time bomb into the discussion, which took more than a decade to penetrate the profession. With an acknowledgment to Ruth Cohen, she noted a curious possibility in the very last page of an article: using a very abstract model, she stated that higher wage rates could be associated with *lower*, not higher, mechanization for certain intervals of the potential wage rates. This seemed to fly in the face of the neoclassical tradition. Following a conjecture of Samuelson, LEVHARI claimed to deny the possibility more than a decade later. He was wrong. Both he and Samuelson admitted it after PASINETTI *et al.* (and in particular Garegnani) demonstrated Levhari's error and affirmed the possibility of "reswitching".

Most accessible conceptually in HICKS (1965), reswitching is the theoretical possibility that, at one wage rate, one fixed-input technology is used in an economy (a very simple one in fact – only one consumption good and one piece of machinery being used throughout the economy), that at a higher wage rate a new completely different (albiet still simple) technology is used, while at an even higher wage rate the economy reverts to the initial technology. The implication is that the very concept of "capital" (see above discussion on Clark) has broken down. Therefore, the concept of a marginal productivity of labour also seemed to break down. Any macroeconomic, marginal productivity theory of income distribution to labour and "capital", at least in the simple version which Clark was attempting, also failed.

SOLOW (1955), a leading representative of neoclassical macroeconomics, had described the aggregate production function as kind of a theoretical exercise without claiming a lot of rigour for the concept. Later, SOLOW (1976, pp.138–9) goes further:

> I invoked the formal conditions for rigorous aggregation not in the hope that they would be applicable . . . but rather to suggest the hopelessness of any formal justification of an aggregate production function in capital and labor. The only way to find out whether aggregation works, and if so how much, is actual empirical experimentation.

Such empirical support has not been forthcoming and the aggregate production function is little used with serious intent as a characterization of economic reality. Attempts to sustain a neoclassical capital theory remain, however (for illustration, see some of the articles in BROWN, SATO & ZAREMBKA).

PAUL ZAREMBKA

See also Production functions

Aggressive behaviour in the workplace

Adams, Andrea, *Bullying at Work: How to Confront and Overcome It*, London: Virago, 1992

Björkqvist, Kaj, Karin Österman and Kirsti Lagerspetz, "Sex Differences in Covert Aggression in Adults", *Aggressive Behavior*, 20 (1994): 27–33

Brodsky, Carroll, *The Harassed Worker*, Lexington, Massachusetts: Lexington Books, 1976

Cooper, Cary and Roy Payne, *Causes, Coping and Consequences of Stress at Work*, Chichester and New York: Wiley, 1988

Crawford, Neil, "Bullying at Work: A Psychoanalytic Perspective", *Journal of Community and Applied Social Psychology*, 7/3 (1997): 219–26

Einarsen, Ståle and B. Raknes, *Mobbing I arbeitslivet: En unsokerelse av forekomst og helsemessige konsekvenser av mobbing på norske arbeidsplasses*, Bergen: FASH Universitetet I Bergen, 1991

Einarsen, Ståle and Anders Skogstad, "Bullying at Work: Epidemiological Findings in Public and Private Organisations", *European Journal of Work and Organisational Psychology*, 5 (1996): 185–201

Leymann, Hans, "Mobbing and Psychological Terror at Workplaces", *Violence and Victims*, 5 (1990): 119–26

Niedl, K., *Mobbing / bullying am Arbeitsplatz*, Munich: Hampp, 1995

Rayner, Charlotte and Helge Hoel, "A Summary Review of Literature Relating to Workplace Bullying", *Journal of Community and Applied Social Psychology*, 7/3 (1997): 181–91

Smith, Peter K., "Bullying in Life-span Perspective: What Can Studies of School Bullying and Workplace Bullying Learn from Each Other?", *Journal of Community and Applied Social Psychology*, 7/3 (1997): 249–55

Trades Union Congress, *Beat Bullying at Work: A Guide for Trade Union Representatives and Personnel Managers*, London: TUC Publications, 1998

The TRADES UNION CONGRESS (TUC) describes bullying as

> a serious workplace issue which too often people think is just an occasional problem between individuals. But bullying is more than an occasional bout of anger or the odd tiff. It is regular and persistent intimidation which undermines the integrity and confidence of the bully's victim, and it is often accepted or even encouraged as part of the culture of the organization.

A survey of 1002 adults in the UK carried out by the TUC in 1998 found that 11 per cent of respondents were either currently bullied or had been bullied, and 27 per cent were aware that colleagues had been bullied. According to the survey, men and women were equally likely to be the victims of bullying (11 per cent of men and 11 per cent of women). A study of union members by the public sector union UNISON in 1997 showed that 66 per cent had either witnessed or experienced bullying at work. Seventy-five per cent of those in the

Unison study who had witnessed or experienced bullying reported that it had affected them physically or mentally. Stress, depression, and lowered self-esteem were the most common complaints.

COOPER & PAYNE argued that bullying is a significant factor in stress at work accounting for over one-third of employment-related sickness absence due to stress.

RAYNER & HOEL, in a useful review, addressed the difficulties in defining adult bullying. They grouped bullying behaviours into the following categories: threat to professional status (for example by belittling opinion, public professional humiliation, accusing the victim of lack of effort); threat to personal standing (for example by name calling, insults, intimidation, devaluing with reference to age); isolation (for example by preventing access to opportunities, physical or social isolation, withholding of information); overwork (for example undue pressure, impossible deadlines, unnecessary disruptions); destabilization (for example failure to give credit when due, meaningless tasks, removal of responsibility, repeated reminders of blunders, setting up to fail).

Rayner & Hoel also pointed out that the areas of racial or sexual harassment are linked. For individuals to be bullied they must feel harassed, their work must be affected, and there must be some repetition of the action.

In a pioneering study of workplace harassment in the US, BRODSKY, the doctor on the Californian Workers' Compensation Appeals Board, identified the phenomenon as "repeated and persistent attempts by one person to torment, wear down, frustrate or get a reaction from another" and distinguished between subjective (as experienced by the victim) and objective (behaviour that breached agreed criteria of acceptable behaviour) forms of harassment. The two aspects of the phenomenon were, in his view, linked. He concluded that harassment is a "basic mechanism in human interaction" if unchecked, and recommended that companies build into the social structure of the workplace changes that could encourage productive, rather than destructive, interaction.

More recently, adult bullying in the workplace has been extensively studied in Scandinavia (BJORKQVIST, ÖSTERMAN & LAGERSPETZ; LEYMANN; EINARSEN & SKOGSTAD), and in the UK (ADAMS; CRAWFORD; RAYNER & HOEL; TUC).

LEYMANN, another pioneer in the field, included in his definition the concepts of persistency and continuity of actions that have negative effect on the victim, and suggested the criterion with regard to frequency as being around one incident per week over a period of at least six months. Leymann considered bullying to affect the victim's communication skills, social contact, respect from others, work, and health; at its most extreme, he argued, aggression in the workplace was responsible for a substantial proportion of suicides each year.

Einarsen and his colleagues (for example EINARSEN & RAKNES; EINARSEN & SKOGSTAD) viewed the culture of the workplace as a form of filter through which behaviours are interpreted and through which a range of behaviours are accepted or tolerated. Einarsen & Raknes found that aggression and harassment were significant problems in their sample of 460 industrial workers in a Norwegian marine engineering industrial context. Seven per cent of the men in their sample reported being subjected on a weekly basis to ridicule, insulting behaviour, verbal abuse, rumours, hostility, social exclusion or derogation of work. This behaviour indicated a focus on "male masculinity and continuous testing of one's ability to tolerate teasing and ridicule". Although these acts were common, they nevertheless appeared to have adverse effects on wellbeing and health as well as overall job satisfaction. In fact, the bystanders were also affected. Employees who were not the victims of bullying experienced a high degree of role conflict when they observed aggressive behaviour and reported a poor quality of environment in these circumstances.

Einarsen & Skogstad analysed data from 14 different Norwegian surveys, with a total sample size of 7986. They found that large organizations, in particular those that were male-dominated, had the highest rates of bullying. Bullies were as frequently superiors as colleagues. More men were reported as bullies than women; men were also more likely to bully in groups. They also found that men harass men, and women harass women. Björkqvist, Östermann & Lagerspetz proposed that this apparent gender difference might be explained by the gender imbalance in workplace hierarchies, in that men are more often in superior positions than women. As leaders/managers they experience less risk associated with aggression.

ADAMS and CRAWFORD documented useful case studies of workplace bullying. Adams stressed the high cost of bullying and aggression in the workplace. She documented high rates of sickness and absenteeism, low morale, reduced productivity, high turnover of staff, damage to mental and physical health, and a poor company ethos. She emphasized the need to train staff in identifying bullying in their workplace, and highlighted the need for companies to have a well-publicized anti-bullying policy to protect staff, and consistent action to deal with complaints, and recommended that aggressive managers should be given training in how to deal with anger and stress. Crawford, a psychotherapist working with bullies, victims, and organizations, identified personality aspects of the problem. He linked the presence of bullying behaviour to unresolved childhood conflicts in the individual. These manifest themselves through difficulty in dealing with frustration and stress at work. Like Adams, he advised that companies should be not only legally liable for acts of aggression in the workplace, but that they should also take moral responsibility for it. He emphasized the importance of working collectively towards greater sensitivity to the interpersonal needs of colleagues working together.

A number of companies in the UK now recognize the need to change the culture of the workplace in order to tackle bullying in the organization as a whole and have developed clear company policies to offer appropriate protection for employees. For example, "dignity at work" policies emphasize the importance of a positive working environment characterized by clear communication and consultation, respectful relationships among employees and between management and workforce, and sanctions against unacceptable behaviour. Currently there is an initiative by trade unionists to draft a Dignity at Work Bill for Parliament. To date, the proposed Bill has been debated in the House of Lords and is on the political agenda.

HELEN COWIE

See also Bullying in schools

Agoraphobia

Baker, Roger (editor), *Panic Disorder: Theory, Research, and Therapy*, Chichester and New York: Wiley, 1992

Bordo, Susan, Binnie Klein and Marilyn K. Silverman, "Missing Kitchens" in *Places Through the Body*, edited by Heidi J. Nast and Steve Pile, London and New York: Routledge, 1998

Capps, Lisa and Elinor Ochs, *Constructing Panic: The Discourse of Agoraphobia*, Cambridge, Massachusetts: Harvard University Press, 1995

Fodor, Iris G., "The Phobic Syndrome in Women" in *Women in Therapy: New Psychotherapies for a Changing Society*, edited by Violet Franks and Vasanti Burtle, New York: Bruner Mazel, 1974

Gournay, Kevin, "Agoraphobia: A Woman's Problem? The Sex-role Perspective" in *Agoraphobia: Current Perspectives on Theory and Treatment*, edited by Kevin Gournay, London and New York: Routledge, 1989

Hallam, Richard, *Counselling for Anxiety Problems*, London: Sage, 1992

Marks, Isaac M., *Fears, Phobias, and Rituals: Panic, Anxiety, and Their Disorders*, Oxford and New York: Oxford University Press, 1987

Mathews, Andrew M., Michael G. Gelder and Derek W. Johnston, *Agoraphobia: Nature and Treatment*, London: Tavistock, and New York: Guilford Press, 1981

Vines, Robyn, *Agoraphobia: The Fear of Panic*, London: Fontana, 1987

MARKS has published prolifically on the subject of agoraphobia over the past three decades and his 1987 book provides an extensive and useful overview of its relation to anxiety disorders in general. He offers a helpful definition of agoraphobia that encompasses both the term's origin and immediate environmental aetiology; "the Greek *agora* refers not to open spaces but to public places of assembly, as befits the frequency of fears of streets and crowded places found in this condition" (p.323). Marks characterizes agoraphobia as a subset of "simple", or "pure" panic disorder. He believes that, for agoraphobics, the experience and fear of panic attacks may lead sufferers to doubt their ability to cope with the outside world to the extent that they become completely housebound.

Marks' chapter in BAKER provides a less comprehensive, though more concise, introductory account. Baker draws together a number of contributors from psychiatric and clinical psychology backgrounds who offer varying perspectives on aspects of agoraphobia and panic in sections relating to phenomenology, aetiology, treatment, and classification. The chapters in the phenomenology section are particularly strong and provide the reader with essential accounts of the symptoms of panic attacks. Baker's own contribution to this section is an informative and insightful recital of "personal accounts of panic". Such experiential accounts serve to enrich a largely detached volume aimed particularly at healthcare professionals.

Self-help resources, including audio and video cassettes, as well as books and pamphlets, are an important aspect of treatment and a source of information for many agoraphobia sufferers. VINES' contribution is an interesting and popular example of the genre. Written in an accessible and often conversational style, it nonetheless offers the reader a wealth of information about the disorder, and often condenses some less-accessible but relevant passages from clinical literature. It is primarily geared towards reassuring the sufferer as to the commonality and "harmlessness" of their agoraphobic symptoms, and to foster the belief that these can be managed, and even overcome. The inclusion of details of case histories and tales of improvement will be encouraging in this respect.

An extensive overview of the range of treatments available for sufferers from agoraphobia constitutes a substantial part of the work of MATHEWS, GELDER & JOHNSTON. Perhaps of greater interest for the social science researcher, however, would be the sections concerned with theoretical perspectives on agoraphobia, and discussions about the nature of the disorder more generally. In addition to biological factors, the authors consider the possible role of, for example, personality dimensions, family environment, and life events and stress in the development and exacerbation of agoraphobic symptoms. They review the existing research and literature pertaining to these models, and attempt to develop their own explanation of, and approach to, agoraphobia by integrating aspects of neurological and sociological theories.

The tension between psychological and sociological approaches to agoraphobia is exemplified in HALLAM who provides a well-informed and informative manual for those involved in counselling sufferers from anxiety problems, including agoraphobia. His characterization of the symptoms of panic and anxiety is sympathetic, and he encourages a sensitive approach to sufferers' difficulties. He makes helpful recommendations for further reading for the lay as well as professional reader, and includes references to texts dealing with related problems such as depression. However, Hallam argues that the counsellor's approach needs to be grounded in a strong sociotheoretical framework, and devotes a substantial part of his first chapter to an engaging discussion of the way anxiety is *socially constructed* in everyday life.

FODOR's paper is concerned with the fact that *at least* two-thirds of sufferers from agoraphobia are women. She reviews literature that has dealt with this aspect of the disorder's distribution, and explores the issue of whether agoraphobic symptoms are related to what she terms "sex-role conflict". She writes "[s]tereotypically, women are viewed as emotional, submissive, excitable, passive, house-oriented, not at all adventurous and showing a strong need for security and dependency" (p.133). Her contention is that these characteristics are clearly congruent with those associated with agoraphobia, and that the *socialization* of women thus contributes to their increased susceptibility to anxiety and agoraphobic avoidance.

In a chapter included in his own edited collection, GOURNAY disputes Fodor's account. He draws attention to research that suggests the actual percentage of male sufferers may be disguised by factors such as unwillingness to seek treatment, and by alcohol abuse in response to agoraphobic fears. Gournay's contribution is a welcome addition to this debate. However, his discussion leaves the impression that much more substantive research would be required to counter the overwhelming evidence that the majority of agoraphobia sufferers are women or to disrupt the implications of the fact that agoraphobic behaviour tends to correspond with that considered to be stereotypically *feminine*.

Studies of agoraphobia outside clinical contexts are few and far between, but CAPPS & OCHS' discourse analysis of an agoraphobic life-story provides a notable exception. Drawing on literature from a range of academic disciplines, the authors develop an interpretation of agoraphobia as a *communicative disorder*, that is to say, as being connected with the sufferers' inability to communicate emotions, and especially how this *reserve* might constrain one's response to others. The focus on the role of language in constructing agoraphobic world-views is highly unusual and fascinating, and often demonstrates considerable depth while providing a valuable alternative account of the nature of agoraphobia. It is inevitable, given the authors' over-dependence on a single case study, that their interpretation and conclusions seem simplistic at times but their approach opens a new avenue for research on agoraphobia that may produce valuable findings in the future.

The chapter contributed by BORDO, a theorist better known for her work on eating disorders, was written collaboratively with her two sisters, and focuses on their recollections of childhood in their parents' home. Bordo's emphasis on the *embodied* experience of agoraphobia perhaps comes closest to overcoming the divide between psychological naturalism and social constructivism. Although the piece does not deal exclusively with agoraphobia, it deserves to be consulted for Bordo's beautifully written and insightful account of her own and her mother's experience of the disorder. She usefully outlines the circumstances surrounding what seems to have been, for her, a discrete episode of agoraphobia, and explores the nature of what are termed "panic-making places". This account demonstrates powerfully how debilitating agoraphobia can be, and is set against Bordo's rediscovery of the world as an exciting, as opposed to terrifying, place.

JOYCE DAVIDSON

See also Anxiety

Agricultural economics

Alston, Julian, George W. Norton and Philip G. Pardey, *Science under Scarcity: Principles and Practice for Agricultural Research Evaluation and Priority Setting*, Ithaca, New York: Cornell University Press, 1995; Wallingford, Oxfordshire: CAB International, 1998

Colman, David and Trevor Young, *Principles of Agricultural Economics: Markets and Prices in Less Developed Countries*, Cambridge and New York: Cambridge University Press, 1989

Gardner, Bruce L., "Changing Economic Perspectives on the Farm Problem", *Journal of Economic Literature*, 30/1 (March 1992): 62–101

Hallberg, M.C., *Policy for American Agriculture: Choices and Consequences*, Ames: Iowa State University Press, 1992

Hobbs, Jill E., William A. Kerr and James D. Gaisford, *The Transformation of the Agrifood System in Central and Eastern Europe and the New Independent States*, Wallingford, Oxfordshire: CAB International, 1997

Ingersent, Ken A. and A.J. Rayner, *Agricultural Policy in Western Europe and the United States*, Cheltenham, Gloucestershire: Elgar, 1999

Peters, George H., *Agricultural Economics*, Aldersho, Hampshire: Elgar, 1995

Rabinowicz, Ewa, "Redesigning the CAP to Meet the Challenges of EU Enlargement and the WTO: What Can Agricultural Economic Research Contribute?", *European Review of Agricultural Economics*, 26/3 (August 1999): 265–81

Agricultural economics is concerned with understanding the performance of, and evaluating policy affecting, the food and fibre system. Food and fibre is produced on farms and sold through commodity markets. Thus the central core of the discipline has consisted of the analysis of farmer decision making and behaviour (agricultural production economics), the behaviour of commodity markets (agricultural market analysis), and the impact of government intervention in agricultural markets (agricultural policy analysis). From these initial interests, the focus and work of agricultural economists has broadened and diversified in response both to changes in the way food is produced and marketed and changing public concerns about the food system. Agricultural economists work increasingly on issues to do with structure, conduct, and performance of the food industry, on the interactions between agriculture and the environment, on the role of agriculture in the rural economy (rural development), and on the problems of agriculture in transition and developing economies.

Agricultural economics texts often assume no prior knowledge of economics and in many cases are microeconomic principles texts, with case studies and examples drawn from agriculture. COLMAN & YOUNG provides an accessible introduction to the subject matter of agricultural economics. This textbook is subtitled *Markets And Prices In Less Developed Countries* but in fact contains an overview of the mainstream neoclassical model with little institutional context. The developing country focus is reflected in the choice of examples throughout the text, but does not detract from its general relevance as an overall introduction. The book moves rapidly from production through demand theory, equilibrium and exchange, the analysis of agricultural markets, and some basic welfare economics, before concluding with two chapters on the economics of trade and food and agricultural policy.

PETERS illustrates the scope of agricultural economics but with a bias towards agricultural policy. It is a collection of key journal articles and is thus intended for a more advanced reader. The selected material is arranged into five sections entitled "Dominant issues in agricultural economics", "Agricultural policy analysis", "Agricultural policy studies – national setting", "Agricultural policy studies – international setting", and "Issues relating to the developing countries". A short introduction sets the selected articles into their scientific context.

INGERSENT & RAYNER provides a good starting point to the concerns of agricultural policy economists. An introductory chapter discusses the rationale for government intervention in agricultural markets. The following six chapters cover agricultural policy developments in both the US and Western Europe in the period up to 1930; the 1930s; 1940–73; 1973–1980s; international policy adjustment in the Uruguay Round Agriculture Agreement; and policy reforms in the 1990s, respectively. Each chapter first discusses the European

and then the US experience, followed by a short summary comparing policy responses in the two regions in that period. The policy discussion is comprehensive without getting bogged down into too much detail – no mean feat given the complexity and inventiveness of agricultural support legislation. Many chapters usefully include a discussion of the main developments in farm policy analysis. This allows the reader to see how agricultural economics both reflected and stimulated policy concerns in each period.

HALLBERG provides a more analytical account of agricultural policy analysis from a US perspective. After an introductory section dealing with the rationale for government intervention in agricultural markets and a summary of past US farm policy, the second section of the book examines the benefits and costs of price and income support for agriculture. The final section deals in detail with the merits and demerits of agricultural policies that focus on expanding domestic demand, providing price support to farmers, controlling farm output, providing various forms of market control, restricting or expanding international trade, conserving farm resources, and stabilizing farm prices and/or quantities. The book can be read without a significant economics background and, although its publication date of 1992 means that it does not cover the significant farm policy changes in the 1990s in the US, its blend of history and theory make it an appealing introduction to policy analysis.

Underlying much farm policy legislation in both the US and the EU in the postwar period was a model of structural adjustment in agriculture which resulted in farm incomes lagging behind the growth of non-farm incomes. The economic assumptions behind this model are carefully disentangled by GARDNER, confronted with historical evidence, and found wanting. This article also contains a useful discussion of commodity policy from a US perspective.

Governments play an important role in promoting agricultural growth through the provision of infrastructure and the supply of public goods. Agricultural research has been a prime example of an agricultural public good provided by the public sector. ALSTON, NORTON & PARDEY reviews, synthesizes and assesses research evaluation and priority-setting procedures. The particular strength of this book is its comprehensive and detailed examination of ways to measure and evaluate the impact of research. The second half of the book addresses implementation issues: formal programming methods are contrasted with more informal scoring models in terms of their ability to analyse the tradeoffs involved in allocating scarce resources across competing programmes.

The transformation of the former centrally-planned economies in Central and Eastern Europe and the former Soviet Union into market economies raised a whole new set of questions for agricultural economics. Much of this literature is emphemeral and descriptive, but the HOBBS, KERR & GAISFORD volume provides a thoughtful overview of the issues raised for the agrifood sector in making the transition to a market economy. Their book goes beyond the debate on the process of transforming former collective and state farms to include the other elements in the agrifood system. They apply a transactions cost approach in addressing policy issues such as privatization and monopolization, the development of marketing channels, appropriate farm size, and foreign investment. They also focus on the market institutions which need to be developed in order to reduce transactions costs.

Despite its European focus, RABINOWICZ provides a good review of some current research issues in agricultural economics. It reviews the case for domestic policy support to agriculture for food security, environmental, and rural development reasons and finds it wanting. It also examines the case for trade measures to protect food safety and the implications of direct payments to farmers for WTO negotiations and EU enlargement. It highlights the fact that the research agenda identified focuses more on consumer and taxpayer behaviour than on the traditional agricultural economics concern with farmer behaviour, and points to increasing competition from other applied economists in addressing these issues.

ALAN MATTHEWS

AIDS law

Burris, Scott, Harlon L. Dalton and Judith Leonie Miller (editors), *AIDS Law Today: A New Guide for the Public*, 2nd edition, New Haven, Connecticut: Yale University Press, 1993

Gostin, Lawrence O. and Lane Porter (editors), *International Law and AIDS: International Response, Current Issues, and Future Directions*, Chicago: American Bar Association, 1992

Haigh, Richard and Dai Harris (editors), *AIDS: A Guide to the Law*, 2nd edition, London and New York: Routledge, 1995

Hermann, Donald H.J. and William P. Schurgin, *Legal Aspects of AIDS*, Deerfield, Illinois: Callaghan, 1991

Hunter, Nan D. and William B. Rubenstein, *AIDS Agenda: Emerging Issues in Civil Rights*, New York: New Press, 1992

Jarvis, Robert M. *et al.*, *AIDS Law in a Nutshell*, St Paul, Minnesota: West, 1996

Rubenstein, William B., Ruth Eisenberg and Lawrence O. Gostin, *The Rights of People Who Are HIV Positive: The Authoritative ACLU Guide to the Rights of People Living with HIV Disease and AIDS*, Carbondale: Southern Illinois University Press, 1996

Webber, David W. (editor), *AIDS and the Law*, 3rd edition, New York and Chichester: Wiley, 1997

The classic volume edited by BURRIS, DALTON & MILLER offers a good general overview of the key issues in AIDS and the law. The chapters in this text cover major topics such as torts, criminal law, and discrimination in employment and housing in the context of HIV and AIDS. Basic legal terminology is introduced for lay readers and the historical and public health context in which AIDS developed is presented. The chapters cover a number of issues including detailed analyses of HIV testing and its relationship to privacy law; the conflict between the need for health care providers to offer their services to patients who are HIV positive, and the fear and bias about contracting the virus in the health care setting; and the special difficulties which HIV positive prisoners face, including housing segregation and discrimination in programs

offered in the prison setting. Each of the chapters contains a detailed bibliography which would be useful for conducting further research on any of the areas that the book covers.

JARVIS *et al.* offers a good, non-technical introduction to the legal issues surrounding AIDS and HIV as well as an overview of the many areas of the law which are impacted by HIV. Major topics discussed include employment, education , and family law. The legal aspects of HIV in the areas of insurance and health care law are also included along with a discussion of tort and criminal law. The book also looks at the impact of AIDS on public health law, discussing the important areas of HIV testing and the confidentiality of testing and other HIV-related records. In addition, there are brief discussions of international legal dimensions of the AIDS crisis such as the impact on immigration law, as well as short reviews of the medical and political backgrounds of the spread of HIV.

RUBENSTEIN, EISENBERG & GOSTIN presents a popular introduction to AIDS and the law. The essays cover many of the same legal areas as Jarvis *et al.* does, but with a stress on issues of particular interest to HIV positive individuals such as health care decision making, conflicts surrounding private insurance and public benefits, and discrimination in a variety of areas including access to health care, housing, and employment. Other topics covered include legal issues surrounding HIV-infected individuals in schools and prisons, and injection drug use.

The essays collected in HUNTER & RUBENSTEIN look at a number of special contexts for HIV and the law. These include: women and HIV; adolescents and HIV; the duty of health care providers to offer HIV positive individuals appropriate care; the role of the state in providing for the care of patients with HIV- and AIDS-related diseases; and the use of federal antidiscrimination statutes such as the Americans with Disabilities Act to address HIV discrimination in the workplace.

Drawing on legal experience in England and Wales, HAIGH & HARRIS presents an overview of the major areas of AIDS law, including criminal law and HIV infection; HIV and the rights of prisoners; the legal issues which face HIV positive individuals in the area of housing and employment; and insurance issues facing individuals infected with HIV. In addition, this volume examines estate planning, powers of attorney, and the issues which children who are HIV positive, and their parents, face. The family law section also deals with the appointment of guardians, parental disputes over children, and the education of children infected with HIV.

The essays collected in GOSTIN & PORTER go well beyond the basic HIV- related legal issues. Focusing on international law, Gostin & Porter discuss a number of topics including HIV screening of international travelers and restrictions on travel for HIV- infected individuals , and legal aspects of public health programs in various countries to combat HIV infection. They also discuss human rights and the AIDS crisis.

HERMANN & SCHURGIN offers a comprehensive, systematic treatise on AIDS and the law which is updated annually by supplements. After providing a good medical and historical background on HIV infection and AIDS, a number of other topics are covered. These include several issues relating to medical care, such as access to care; HIV testing and the confidentiality of testing-related medical information; informed consent and HIV testing; the reporting of HIV test results to governmental agencies; and warning third parties. Other topics discussed include the rights and duties of health care professionals with regard to the care of HIV positive patients, and access to mental health care. The authors also provide a detailed discussion of tort issues, including liability related to the provision of blood and blood products; liability in the context of sexual transmission of HIV; liability related to drug use; and liability for transmission of HIV in the context of childbirth. A number of family law issues are covered in this volume, including premarital testing for HIV, the duty to disclose HIV status to a sexual partner, and children and HIV. Family planning topics are also included, for example: discussions of wills, living wills, powers of attorney, and guardianship. A number of criminal law issues are reviewed including criminal prosecution of conduct which is likely to transmit HIV; public health offences; and HIV-specific criminal offences. There is also a large section on state schools, covering issues such as the exclusion of HIV positive children from the classroom and students' privacy rights *vis a vis* HIV-related information. This volume is regularly supplemented with the latest case and statutory law in the areas of AIDS and HIV and it contains an extensive bibliography on AIDS law.

The essays collected in WEBBER offer overviews of all of the major areas of AIDS law. Some of the unique contributions in this volume include a discussion of AIDS education and the issues of censorship of this educational material both in the school curriculum and on the internet. Webber also provides excellent analyses of HIV and AIDS-related legal issues in the workplace including a discussion of several relevant US federal statutes including the Americans with Disabilities Act, the Rehabilitation Act of 1973, and Family Medical Leave Act. Webber also discusses AIDS and the armed forces, HIV as a workplace hazard and the interaction of this hazard with the relevant Occupational Health and Safety Administration regulations, and HIV testing in the workplace. Another essay looks at the various public benefits in the US which are available to persons with HIV including Social Security disability, veterans' disability benefits, Medicaid, and Medicare. Additional chapters address international human rights issues and HIV infection, and immigration law and HIV. Lastly, the volume contains an appendix which presents a state-by-state summary of HIV-specific statues and regulations. Like Hermann & Schurgin, Webber is kept up to date by annual supplements.

EDWIN GREENLEE

AIDS, sociology

Beyrer, Chris, *War in the Blood: Sex, Politics, and AIDS in Southeast Asia*, Bangkok: White Lotus, and London: Zed, 1998

Bloor, Michael, *The Sociology of HIV Transmission*, London and Thousand Oaks, California: Sage, 1995

Brummelhuis, Han ten and Gilbert Herdt (editors), *Culture and Sexual Risk: Anthropological Perspectives on AIDS*, New York: Gordon and Breach, 1995

Goldstein, Nancy and Jennifer L. Manlowe (editors), *The Gender Politics of HIV/AIDS in Women: Perspectives on*

the Pandemic in the United States, New York: New York University Press, 1997

Myrick, Roger, *AIDS, Communication, and Empowerment: Gay Male Identity and the Politics of Public Health Messages*, New York: Harrington Park Press, 1996

Patton, Cindy, *Inventing AIDS*, London and New York: Routledge, 1990

Patton, Cindy, *Last Served? Gendering the HIV Pandemic*, London: Taylor and Francis, 1994

Roberts, Dorothy E., *Killing the Black Body: Race, Reproduction, and the Meaning of Liberty*, New York: Pantheon, 1997

Tulloch, John and Deborah Lupton, *Television, AIDS, and Risk: A Cultural Studies Approach to Health Communication*, Sydney: Allen and Unwin, 1997

The AIDS pandemic has produced social, political, and economic change around the globe since it was first diagnosed. Fear, ignorance, accusations and gender politics have fused in a lethal combination to create a very destructive phenomenon. BEYRER approaches AIDS in Southeast Asia as a war, documenting the rapid and pervasive diffusion of the HIV virus among the peoples of the region. He uncovers the diversities and similarities of seven countries, some with expanding economies, others dominated by the subsistence poor. The author's compassionate voice and use of interviewees' stories add complexity to the dry statistics that document the suffering, devastation, and death. He examines the ways in which lack of democratic freedom can inhibit health and social programmes, and suggests the formulation of public policies that support development linked to a nation state's commitment to HIV prevention.

BLOOR's clear and accessible work contests popular and media images of the AIDS epidemic by providing sociological evidence of the complexities of risk behaviour. The work also investigates the development of the epidemic in Third World countries. Bloor focuses on the differing social epidemiology of the HIV epidemic, and analyses sociological reports of risk behaviour when associated with intimacy and trust, or with strategic power relations. Concentrating on the presentation of practical and empirical evidence, the author also addresses issues of interpretation.

GOLDSTEIN & MANLOWE's decision to include gendered perspectives not only contests the supremacy of biological over sociocultural standpoints, but also brings into the debate numerous peoples marginalized by biological and masculinist approaches. The authors criticize the reliance of biomedical approaches on individualistic models that assume the agency and free will of subjects, but that fail to consider the subjects' social context. They argue that HIV and AIDS are best understood as socially, culturally, ideologically, and biologically determined phenomena, and that gender and race, class, and sexuality all play significant roles in how women are infected and affected.

MYRICK's treatment of the AIDS debate focuses on the institutional power created through the process of labelling people, specifically with gay identities. He analyses government discourse through the lens of power relations rather than biological concepts. Using a Foucauldian perspective, he asserts that discourse about AIDS is frequently represented as educational, informative, and scientific, but he believes that it remains politically marked. Myrick's historical and contemporary analyses describe how health education stigmatizes marginal groups through social constructions of "otherness", and associations with disease.

In PATTON (1990), ideas about public policies and the "factual" programmes designed to service AIDS patients are questioned and critiqued. Patton criticizes the cultural and administrative discourses that have invented and described AIDS, in order to propose new ways of conceptualizing the disease. Her analysis of the historical relations of power that mark contemporary biomedical discourse and institutional processes describe systems of power that inhibit and enable community organization, and decide who is allowed to speak and who is not. The author examines the social construction of scientific knowledge and its relation to AIDS policies.

In PATTON (1994) the author takes a gendered perspective on the treatment of women and AIDS and connects with Myrick's work about gay identity. She describes how particular ideas about gender have influenced contemporary views on policy for women in the HIV epidemic. Using recent gender studies theory and analysis of documents representative of popular, research, and policy discourses, the author argues that ignorance of women's needs is systematic, anchored in a complex array of media representations, cultural beliefs, and research and policy paradigms that are gender biased and not easily transformed.

ROBERTS examines the oppressive social and political tyrannies that target poor black women in particular, concludes these to be the cause of the spread of AIDS and of social problems that are seen to corrupt the wider American community. She analyses the politics of blame and its role in diminishing black women's capacities to make decisions concerning their reproduction and protecting themselves from AIDS.

It is impossible to address the issue of AIDS without considering the interaction of global forces with local societal characteristics. Consequently, BRUMMELHUIS & HERDT's compilation of 16 conference papers addresses the ways in which the character of a culture can influence perception of the risks of sexual HIV transmission and can thereby act as a barrier to effective combat of the epidemic. The collection's reliance on intensely subjective perspectives provides a different theoretical challenge from Bloor's conceptualization of "risk behaviour". The work's initial focus is on culture, and the need to socially contextualize risk behaviour, and it draws information from a wide range of countries to argue that AIDS is primarily an illness of the disadvantaged. The editors then compare these standpoints with Western practices and perceptions to offer critical comment on the relationship between perception and culture.

The international scope of the AIDS crisis is examined in Australia by TULLOCH & LUPTON, who discuss the ways that AIDS awareness television programmes in many countries have missed their target audience and/or failed to communicate the desired message. The authors examine the different ways of knowing that are articulated in television productions, both in informative messages and popular drama productions. They propose that the complexity of the target community's day-to-day experience should be understood so that messages aim to increase understanding by working on the real needs

and understandings of the audience, rather than the top-down approach using the authority of government and expert knowledge.

HELEN JOHNSON

Alternative communities and lifestyles

Bell, Michael Maverfeld, "The Ghosts of Place," *Theory and Society*, 26/6 (December 1997): 813–36

Elgin, Duane, *Voluntary Simplicity: Toward a Way of Life That Is Outwardly Simple, Inwardly Rich*, revised edition, New York: Quill, 1993

Gamson, Joshua, *Freaks Talk Back: Tabloid Talk Shows and Sexual Nonconformity*, Chicago: University of Chicago Press, 1998

Hardy, Dennis, *Alternative Communities in Nineteenth Century England*, London and New York: Longman, 1979

Kanter, Rosabeth Moss, *Commitment and Community: Communes and Utopias in Sociological Perspective*, Cambridge, Massachusetts: Harvard University Press, 1972

Leviatan, Uriel, Hugh Oliver and Jack Quarter (editors), *Crisis in the Israeli Kibbutz: Meeting the Challenge of Changing Times*, Westport, Connecticut: Praeger, 1998

Mills, Richard, *Young Outsiders: A Study of Alternative Communities*, New York: Pantheon, and London: Routledge and Kegan Paul, 1973

Pitzer, Donald E. (editor), *America's Communal Utopias*, Chapel Hill: University of North Carolina Press, 1997

Schor, Juliet, B., *The Overspent American: Upscaling, Downshifting, and the New Consumer*, New York: Basic Books, 1998

Schumacher, E.F., *Small Is Beautiful: A Study of Economics as if People Mattered*, London: Blond and Biggs, and New York: Harper and Row, 1973

Selth, Jefferson, P., *Alternative Lifestyles: A Guide to Research Collections on Intentional Communities, Nudism, and Sexual Freedom*, Westport, Connecticut: Greenwood Press, 1985

Smith, Dorothy, E., *The Everyday World as Problematic: A Feminist Sociology*, Boston: Northeastern University Press, 1987; Milton Keynes: Open University Press, 1988

Zicklin, Gilbert, *Countercultural Communes: A Sociological Perspective*, Westport, Connecticut: Greenwood Press, 1983

The works listed here interconnect alternative notions of social organization, culture, power, ethnicity, gender, sexual orientation, spirituality, environment, and economics. MILLS is an important and often-cited classic work on alternative communities in England in the early 1970s. This monograph focuses on how values and ideology shape the social organization of lifestyles. Specifically, Mills uses the framework of space and time utilization to examine individual lifestyles and their impact on social change. He argues that English hippies created their own diverse culture that became a force and direction for a change in society. HARDY provides a more historical account of alternative communities in 19th-century England. Hardy explains that alternative communities form as a reaction to the dominant culture, but rarely end up changing the structure of society. Although it is often difficult to generalize from case studies beyond their own context, Mills and Hardy provide rich historical analysis and important theoretical frameworks for studying the changing social order.

KANTER enlightens her readers with an account of utopian communities from the other side of the Atlantic. Kanter first traces the origins of utopian communities in the US and then proceeds with a theoretical explanation. She argues that the utopian values of human perfectibility, order, brotherhood, harmony of body and mind, spirit of experimentation, and group coherence provide ideals to live by but need to be balanced with the material realities of life. She also presents a critical look at the processes that lead to commitment to communal groups. ZICKLIN, building on Kanter's work, studied communes in the San Francisco Bay Area. Zicklin's theoretical framework provides a sociological explanation of communal lifestyles using several themes: increased environmental and social connections, spirituality, expression of sentiments/feelings, and social movements. For a more recent update on the progress of "communal utopias" in the US, PITZER's edited volume weaves diverse lifestyle accounts together and adds holistic analyses of ethnicity. Pitzer gathered anthropologists, sociologists, historians, and geographers to provide a collection of interrelated chapters on the Shakers, Mormons, Brook Farm, the Amana Colonies, Oneida Perfectionists, Icarian Communities, Hutterites, and many more communal groups. The appendix has a wonderful compilation of all communal utopias founded in the US by 1965 as well as a bibliographic essay on the historical research of communal lifestyles. Another cultural perspective is offered by LEVI-ATAN, OLIVER & QUARTER, on the widely studied Israeli Kibbutzim. Eleven of the 13 authors are kibbutz members and all are social scientists, researchers, and teachers. The individual chapters are interrelated by the argument that kibbutz ideology is a powerful and "moving force" created and maintained by its members. The authors argue that kibbutzim will continue to meet the challenges of the future as long as they are able to balance individualism with collectivism while still retaining their basic values and principles.

Moving from the community level of analysis to individual lifestyle, SMITH's classic feminist research reminds us that our lifestyle experiences operate within seemingly dualistic but actually interconnected consciousness. She argues that we reorganize (and ultimately try to balance) our actual everyday experiences in the US against the dominant constructions of hegemonic male culture. By problematizing the everyday world, social scientists include gender and power implications as well as hegemonic cultural influences on the social organization of lifestyle.

SELTH is a humanities and arts bibliographer who has collected and annotated research on intentional communities, nudism, and sexual freedom in the US. In the process of compiling this information, he conducted personal interviews and visited many of the 36 collections described. GAMSON analyses the production, narrative, and reception of the culture of sexual nonconformity in the context of TV talk shows in the US. He takes an activist stance arguing that "talk shows, even if they aren't good for you, are at least good for us – especially those of us with an investment in social change" (p.17). Research for Gamson's well-written book included interviews with production staff and guests, as well as participant observation at taped shows, a content analysis of transcripts, and focus groups with viewers of different sexual orientations. For more discussion along similar lines of research, *Sociological Theory*, 12(2), 1994, devoted 82 pages for a symposium on queer theory in sociology.

Perhaps no other author in this entry could claim the same influence on social organization and lifestyle change as SCHU-MACHER. Schumacher shakes the seemingly solid foundations of capitalism with an analysis of the fundamental concepts of production, consumption, and what he calls "human scale". In a prescient 1973 statement he declared "To say the least – which is already very much – we must thoroughly understand the problem and begin to see the possibility of evolving a new life-style, with new methods of production and new patterns of consumption: a lifestyle designed for permanence" (p.17). Schumacher argues for an alternative world where technology has a "human face".

Another element that is integral to our lifestyle choice as well as personal identity is the importance of place. BELL provocatively argues that place as a social construct has largely been ignored in the social sciences, particularly in sociology. He suggests that the social meaning we give to a place consists of the "aura of social life" in that place, also known as the "ghosts of place". Bell's work temporally and spatially weaves our social world with our physical environment. Further along the lines of recognizing our connection to the Earth is ELGIN. Elgin speaks of lifestyle movements that try to rebalance the materialistic, unsustainable, and unequal values of the dominant culture with more aesthetic, more sustainable, and more equitable values of voluntary simplicity. With homage to Elgin, SCHOR provides a contemporary, theoretically grounded, and empirically robust study of lifestyle changes in the US. She traces the "downshifters" – people who work less, consume less, and strive for a better cultural lifestyle.

The above dialogue with different authors is just the beginning of the cultural conversations about alternative communities and lifestyles. These conversations will continue whether we collectively decide to participate in creating our communities or sit back and poke fun at *those* that are not like *us*. Schumacher ever so gently reminds us: "But if we now realize that the modern lifestyle is putting us into mortal danger, we may find it in our hearts to support and even join these pioneers rather than to ignore or ridicule them" (p.148).

GREGORY PETER

See also Communitarianism, Counterculture, Subculture, Utopias

Anarchism

Bookchin, Murray, *Post-Scarcity Anarchism*, Berkeley, California: Ramparts, 1971; 2nd edition, Montreal and Buffalo, New York: Black Rose, 1986

Carter, April, *The Political Theory of Anarchism*, London: Routledge and Kegan Paul, and New York: Harper and Row, 1971

Guerin, Daniel, *Anarchism: From Theory to Practice*, New York: Monthly Review Press, 1970

Joll, James, *The Anarchists*, 2nd edition, London: Methuen, 1979; Cambridge, Massachusetts: Harvard University Press, 1980

Marshall, Peter, *Demanding the Impossible: A History of Anarchism*, London: Fontana, 1993

Miller, David, *Anarchism*, London: Dent, 1984

Nettlau, Max, *A Short History of Anarchism*, London: Freedom Press, 1996 (originally published 1934)

Ritter, Alan, *Anarchism: A Theoretical Analysis*, Cambridge and New York: Cambridge University Press, 1980

Wolff, Robert Paul, *In Defence of Anarchism*, New York: Harper and Row, 1976

Woodcock, George, *Anarchism: A History of Libertarian Ideas and Movements*, Harmondsworth: Penguin, and New York: Meridian, 1962; 2nd edition, Penguin, 1986

The academic study of anarchism began with Nettlau's monumental nine-volume study (*Geschichte der Anarchie*, 1890) of anarchists and anarchisms from the earliest proto-libertarians to the Spanish Civil War. Fortunately for less committed scholars, NETTLAU produced a "short history" of anarchism that summarizes the findings of the major works. Nettlau was himself a passionate and convinced anarchist, and his motivation to write was in part inspired by a desire to counteract the anti-anarchist propaganda of both mainstream political thought and orthodox revolutionary socialism. None the less, the *Short History* is a reliable and scholarly work that has stood the test of time.

Less daunting, though equally committed to the anarchist cause, is WOODCOCK's celebrated survey. Like Nettlau, his account is intended to give the reader an overview of the entire anarchist tradition of thought and practice. His work differs, however, in clearly separating theorists and movements thereby allowing the reader to use the book as a work of reference. Woodcock is a fluent essayist and his accounts of the various strands and tendencies are entertaining and lucid taken as a whole or in parts.

GUERIN, on the other hand, attempts a systematic exposition of anarchist doctrine by threading together the persistent elements in 19th- and 20th-century anarchist thought, in particular that of Proudhon, Bakunin, and Kropotkin. The result is a remarkably homogenous whole, though those interested in the contrasts between anarchists on central problems of organization and distribution will be wary of his tendency to suppress such differences in his quest for a workable doctrine. Some later reprints, e.g. 1971, also include a valuable and original introductory essay by Noam Chomsky, arguably the most influential libertarian writer of the late 20th century.

Interest in anarchist theory and practice received a significant boost as a result of the 1968 unrests in France and the US. This is reflected in the publication of both original contributions to anarchist discourse and of further useful surveys that bring the study of anarchism up to date. The most important of the original works are WOLFF's development of "philosophical anarchism" and BOOKCHIN's attempt to marry anarchist theory with newly emergent ecological concerns. Wolff's book can be read as a continuation of the individualist critique of the state associated with American 19-century anarchists such as Benjamin Tucker, Lysander Spooner, and Josiah Warren. His vision is of autonomous individuals freed from the constraint of taxation and enforced obligations. He thus shares the neoliberal distaste for the welfare state that was to be such a feature of American and European politics from the mid-1970s onwards. By contrast, Bookchin's work reconnects with the collectivist tradition associated with 19th-century European anarchist thought. It also brought to anarchism many of the themes to have emerged in 1968 with the rise of the New Left, principally the power of imagination, the necessity for "realistic" utopias, and the Tolstoyan theme of the importance of self-transformation as a prelude to social transformation. Bookchin was also one of the earliest thinkers to state in unequivocal terms the necessary connection between ecological sustainability and anarchism, seeing in the latter the key to organizing society in a manner that would guarantee the survival of the planet.

Anarchism's re-emergence as a serious object of study was signalled by the respectful treatment afforded anarchist ideas by CARTER and by RITTER, both of whom produced useful analyses of the relevance of anarchist ideas for contemporary political thought and practice. Carter is a much more sympathetic critic than Ritter, seeking as she does to utilize anarchist ideas for the purpose of reinvigorating radical critique. Ritter's work, on the other hand, is notable for being the first really sustained examination of the relevance of anarchist ideas for the analysis of advanced industrial societies.

Despite the lack of success enjoyed by anarchists over the course of the century in advancing their ideals, interest in anarchist ideas has rarely been greater. This is manifested by the appearance of a number of updated surveys of the anarchist tradition, taking account of recent developments in anarchist theory and practice. MILLER and JOLL, for example, both provide serious treatments of the classical anarchist tradition together with an appraisal of the relevance of anarchist ideas. Miller's work is more schematic and analytical, and aims at providing an assessment of the successes and failures of anarchism considered as a political philosophy competing for influence and support with other political philosophies. Joll on the other hand, follows Woodcock's lead in attempting an assessment of individual thinkers and traditions of thought, and can therefore be more readily used as a work of reference.

It is probably MARSHALL, however, who has produced the most significant recent contribution to the understanding of anarchism. An elephantine digest of virtually every thinker and movement with any association to anarchism at all, Marshall's study shows the astonishing variety of anarchist concerns and approaches. What also impresses in reading his work is the timeless nature of anarchist fears and hopes. For those seeking a comprehensive overview of anarchist concerns, together with a crisp assessment of every contending vision, Marshall's work must now be considered the logical place to begin.

SIMON TORMEY

Ancient law

Carmichael, Calum M., *The Origins of Biblical Law: The Decalogues and the Book of the Covenant*, Ithaca, New York: Cornell University Press, 1992a

Carmichael, Calum M. (editor), *Collected Works of David Daube*, vol. 1: *Talmudic Law*, Berkeley, California: Robbins Collection, 1992b

Daube, David, *Studies in Biblical Law*, Cambridge: Cambridge University Press, 1947

Diamond, Alan (editor), *The Victorian Achievement of Sir Henry Maine: A Centennial Reappraisal*, Cambridge and New York: Cambridge University Press, 1991

Johns, C.H.W., *Babylonian and Assyrian Laws, Contracts and Letters*, Edinburgh: Clark, 1904

Maine, Henry Sumner, *Ancient Law*, edited by Frederick Pollock, New York: Holt, and London: John Murray, 1906

Pollock, Frederick, *Introduction and Notes to Sir Henry Maine's "Ancient Law"*, London: John Murray, and New York: Holt, 1906

Taubenschlag, Raphael, *The Law of Greco-Roman Egypt in the Light of the Papyri*, 332BC–640AD, New York: Herald Square Press, 1944

CARMICHAEL (1992a) provides an overview of biblical law from the perspective of modern, secular scholarship. He brings to this study not only expertise in biblical law itself, but also a thorough grounding in biblical literature and in the laws and literary traditions of the ancient Near East. This is not a book for beginners but it is an excellent introduction to modern thinking on the subject.

CARMICHAEL (1992b) is a collection of the most important essays of the greatest modern scholar of ancient Jewish and biblical law: David Daube. The essays look at a wide variety of crucial issues in Talmudic law, including the legal regulation of sin, duress, corruption, dissent, tyranny, and marriage. They also include path-breaking studies of the relationship between Jewish law and Hellenistic law and the legal rights of women in ancient law.

DAUBE presents a series of his own essays relating specifically to biblical law and its setting in ancient Near Eastern, Hellenistic, and Roman law. The essays are thoroughly grounded in the study of the Bible, as well as presenting the issues within a modern, secular, and comparative perspective.

DIAMOND collects the essays of a number of leading modern scholars centred around the seminal study by Sir Henry MAINE, entitled *Ancient Law*. In addition to specific studies of Maine's masterpiece there is a series of essays written in the light of modern scholarship on subjects discussed by Maine. Particularly important are Raymond Cocks' essay on the concept of progress in Maine's work and in ancient law; D.E.C. Yale's essay on historical jurisprudence; and the editor's essay on legal fictions. This volume of essays is a necessary adjunct to Maine's own work.

JOHNS is the classic introductory study of Babylonian and Assyrian law. It provides a useful narrative outlining the key points of these ancient legal systems as well as useful translations from the original Assyrian and Babylonian legal documents. Although somewhat old, it is still the classic treatment

of these legal systems and the starting point for serious research as well as an excellent introduction for the general reader.

Maine's book that introduced the English-speaking world to the study of ancient law from a comparative perspective. Although very much situated in the Victorian intellectual tradition, Maine transcends his era and provides a lasting analysis of fundamental legal ideas shared by several ancient civilizations including Greece, Rome, the biblical world, and ancient India. Maine's work was the first serious attempt to look at ancient law from a sociological perspective, and his insights into the origins and functions of law in the ancient world continue to be of prime importance. Although more modern, specialized scholarship has made some of the details outdated, the book as a whole remains the starting point for any reader interested in a broad view of ancient law. Reprinted countless times, the best edition remains that edited by Sir Frederick Pollock. Maine should be read in conjunction with Diamond and Pollock.

POLLOCK provides a detailed introduction to Maine as well as a series of learned narrative excurses on specific subjects discussed by Maine. Pollock was an influential late 19th-century judge and jurist who enriches Maine with the perspective of a working lawyer as well as that of a legal theorist.

TAUBENSCHLAG provides a scholarly introduction to the study of ancient law through one of its most important sources – papyri. Many of the most important advances in ancient scholarship in the 20th century, including the discovery of the Genizah archives, have involved the detailed study of papyri found in the Middle East. Taubenschlag provides an introduction to papyrological scholarship as well as a discussion of the substantive law of Graeco-Roman Egypt found in the papyri. Taubenschlag is an excellent first book for the English-speaking reader with an interest in Hellenistic law and papyrological studies.

M.H. HOEFLICH

See also Law and history, Law and history through textbooks, Roman law

Anger

Averill, James R. (editor), *Anger and Aggression: An Essay on Emotion*, New York: Springer, 1982

Beck, Robert and Ephrem Fernandez, "Cognitive-Behavioral Therapy in the Treatment of Anger: A Meta-Analysis", *Cognitive Therapy and Research*, 22 (1998): 63–74

Canary, Daniel J., Brian H. Spitzberg and Beth A. Semic, "The Experience and Expression of Anger in Interpersonal Settings" in *Handbook of Communication and Emotion: Research, Theory, Applications, Contexts*, edited by Peter A. Andersen and Laura K. Guerrero, San Diego: Academic Press, 1998

DiGiuseppe, Raymond, Raymond Tafrate and Christopher Eckhardt, "Critical Issues in the Treatment of Anger", *Cognitive and Behavioral Practice*, 1 (1994): 111–32

Edmondson, Christine B. and Judith C. Conger, "A Review of Treatment Efficacy for Individuals with Anger Problems: Conceptual, Assessment, and Methodological Issues", *Clinical Psychology Review*, 16 (1996): 251–75

Journal of Clinical Psychology, special issue on Anger in Psychotherapy, 55/3 (1999): 275–379

Journal of Counseling Psychology, special section on Anger, 43/2 (1996): 131–69

Kassinove, Howard (editor), *Anger Disorders: Definition, Diagnosis, and Treatment*, Washington, DC: Taylor and Francis, 1995

Unlike most traditional theories of emotion, AVERILL characterizes anger as a socially constructed syndrome. This book, although dated, is a valuable resource for its analysis of the norms and functions of anger within social systems. Averill examines anger from three basic levels of analysis: biological, psychological, and sociocultural. His description of the historical underpinnings of anger establish it as a highly complex, interpersonal emotion, and justify its interpretation as a passive rather than active occurrence. This text uses anger as a paradigm for outlining a social constructivist approach to the study of emotion in general, and is most useful on a broad theoretical level.

The construct of anger has proven difficult to define, and scholars continue to disagree about its nature and fundamental features. Drawing upon Averill's work, CANARY, SPITZBERG & SEMIC attempt to clarify this issue by providing an interpersonal account of anger with an emphasis on its types and causes. As a social phenomenon, anger entails not only its experience but also its expression. Accordingly, this text considers several proposed links between anger and aggression and challenges the common conception that anger is a necessary predecessor to aggression. In a deviation from the predominant view of anger expression as a negative occurrence, the authors frame anger as an integral part of human emotion and discriminate adaptive from maladaptive ways in which anger is expressed.

Currently, the fourth edition of the *Diagnostic and Statistical Manual* (DSM-IV) does not include a classification for anger disorders. KASSINOVE outlines problems that have resulted from this omission in an account that is intended to appeal to both scientists and laypersons. He goes on to propose a comprehensive classification system for anger disorders. This work touches upon a range of pertinent topics, such as the role of pathological anger in the commission of crimes, and crosscultural considerations in anger. However, the bulk of this text is devoted to treatment issues, including chapters addressing ideal treatment packages for both adults and children.

A special section of the JOURNAL OF COUNSELING PSYCHOLOGY addresses gaps in various aspects of the anger literature and exemplifies the trend towards developing more clearly articulated theories of anger through empirical validation. The first article establishes the validity of the state-trait anger theory and the utility of the trait anger scale (TAS) through a series of eight studies. A second article demonstrates the efficacy of two cognitive-behavioural treatments for anger reduction with early adolescents. Despite methodological limitations, this study allows a broader evaluation of treatment impact because it assesses treatment outcome on a number of anger-related variables. The next article explores the role of gender, gender role socialization, depression, and mental health functioning in the experience and expression of anger. It suggests that gender role socialization may be a more important factor in anger expression than gender per se, and identifies anger suppression as a potential risk factor for a variety of mental health problems. A final article puts into perspective the contributions and limitations of the studies presented in this section, noting in particular a neglect of the sociocultural aspects of anger. While these articles address vastly different issues, they each succeed in making substantial inroads to clarifying unresolved questions in the anger literature.

Over the past decade, a number of studies have examined the efficacy of anger interventions while a separate body of literature has focused on the theoretical construct of anger. EDMONDSON & CONGER convincingly argue for the integration of these ostensibly distinct enterprises. Their approach represents a movement towards the development of theory-driven and empirically validated anger interventions. The major contributions of this work are its comprehensive analysis of recent research using effect-size comparisons, and its review and critique of theories underlying treatment wherein fundamental assumptions of popular theories of anger are challenged. In addition, the authors offer a dense but thorough analysis of the multidimensional-associationistic model of anger, compare and contrast it with a social constructivist model, and draw clear implications for treatment.

A special issue of the JOURNAL OF CLINICAL PSYCHOLOGY on anger examines the conceptualization and treatment of anger from a variety of approaches, including self psychology, cognitive-behavioural and experiential systems, and Buddhist perspectives. Collectively, these articles expose the reader to a broad overview of multiple theoretical accounts of anger, and provide an excellent introduction to the conceptualization and treatment of anger. One strength of this approach is that each account addresses the same two case studies, enabling direct comparisons among the different treatment models. A review of clinically relevant research on anger in psychotherapy also gives the reader a practical look at evidence for the theories presented. The final article of this issue demonstrates the convergence of the multiple approaches and presents ideal components for anger treatments based on the extant literature. This journal issue is an excellent resource for individuals who are interested in gaining an understanding of anger from multiple perspectives.

DiGUISEPPE, TAFRATE & ECKHARDT look at major issues in the treatment of anger. After reviewing a number of self-administered anger inventories, the authors recommend two that are considerable improvements over previous measures. They also identify potential difficulties in establishing a therapeutic relationship, agreeing on treatment goals, and achieving therapeutic change. The practical value of this work, though, arises from the inclusion of concrete strategies for overcoming these obstacles. Taking a step back, the authors situate anger treatment theory within the context of broader psychological theories, offering insight into the current state of anger interventions. That insight is then used to provide new directions for advancing therapy.

BECK & FERNANDEZ conduct a meta-analytic review of 50 studies completed over 20 years examining the efficacy of cognitive-behavioural interventions for the treatment of anger. The authors improve upon previous work by reviewing more studies, including many that were unpublished, and by using more rigorous statistical techniques. For those unfamiliar with meta-analytic procedures, the authors also provide a clear and concise overview of the theory behind this technique and the merits of its application to psychological research. This review is the most comprehensive examination of the efficacy of cognitive-behavioural anger interventions to date.

DAVID BLACK AND KATHERINE PRESNELL

Animal rights

Arluke, Arnold and Clinton Sanders, *Regarding Animals*, Philadelphia: Temple University Press, 1996

Cartmill, Matt, *A View to a Death in the Morning: Hunting and Nature through History*, Cambridge, Massachusetts: Harvard University Press, 1993

Dizard, Jan E., *Going Wild: Hunting, Animal Rights, and the Contested Meaning of Nature*, Amherst: University of Massachusetts Press, 1994

Finsen, Lawrence and Susan Finsen, *The Animal Rights Movement in America: From Compassion to Respect*, New York: Twayne, 1994

Garner, Robert, *Political Animals: Animal Protection Politics in Britain and the United States*, London: Macmillan, and New York: St Martin's Press, 1998

Jasper, James M. and Dorothy Nelkin, *The Animal Rights Crusade: The Growth of a Moral Protest*, New York: Free Press, 1992

Ritvo, Harriet, *The Animal Estate: The English and Other Creatures in the Victorian Age*, Cambridge, Massachusetts: Harvard University Press, 1987

Tester, Keith, *Animals and Society: The Humanity of Animal Rights*, London and New York: Routledge, 1991

Thomas, Keith, *Man and the Natural World: Changing Attitudes in England, 1500–1800*, Harmondsworth: Penguin, 1984

Wolfe, Alan, *The Human Difference: Animals, Computers, and the Necessity of Social Science*, Berkeley: University of California Press, 1993

There is no better place to start reading about animal rights than THOMAS's history of our changing attitudes towards nonhuman animals between 1500 and 1800. In this fascinating account Thomas describes the origins of anthropocentrism and the gradual development of compassion for animals. By 1700, pet keeping in England had become an obsession and had "created the psychological foundation for the view that some animals at least were entitled to moral consideration". The book observes that the subjugation of nature in the early modern period was characterized by a contradiction that underpins modern civilization: a conflict between compassion and our dependence on creature comforts.

RITVO's excellent history focuses on the English and their social relations with animals in the Victorian age. The book is richly illustrated with over 50 graphics that reveal a wide range of human attitudes and practices involving both wild and domesticated animals. Focusing on the contexts of animal husbandry, vivisection, menageries, hunting, and natural history studies, Ritvo describes the Victorian Age's relentless pursuit of mastery over the brute creation as well as the emergence of the first humane and anti-cruelty organizations, which became the forerunners of today's animal rights/welfare movement.

The sociology of our relations with other animals is the subject of seven papers by ARLUKE & SANDERS who document the tensions between our caring for animals and our complicity in their exploitation. The authors seek an explanation for this ambivalence in the social forces at work in veterinary clinics, dog training classes, animal shelters, and primate labs. Arluke & Sanders claim that humans use a sociozoologic scale to rank animals as either good or bad. In the most disturbing illustration of this "boundary work", they show how the moral elevation of certain nonhuman animals was promoted in Nazi Germany while certain humans whom the Nazis believed to be inferior were simultaneously animalized.

Much has been written about the rights and wrongs of vivisection, intensive farming, the killing of animals for fur, and the ethics of zoos and circuses, but comparatively little attention has been given to sport hunting, although it is one of the main targets of animal liberationists. CARTMILL's comprehensive account of hunting throughout human history goes a long way toward filling this gap. His definition of hunting as "the deliberate, direct, violent killing of unrestrained wild animals" suggests that killing animals for sport cannot be conceived as an authentic confrontation between humans and the wild. Sport hunting, to Cartmill, is closer to butchery than to authentic hunting. The sociologist and hunter DIZARD is much more sympathetic to the hunt in his detailed study of the conflicting values of hunters, animal rights advocates, and the managers of the Quabbin reservoir from which the city of Boston draws its water. In the later 1980s, when the forest that purified the water was threatened by an unusually large herd of ravenous deer, the rights of oak saplings versus the rights of the deer to eat them were contested by various interest groups. In extensive interviews with 35 of the protagonists, the case study explores the meaning that nature has for these groups. Although the analysis is biased against animal rightists, DIZARD's data successfully demonstrates how people construct nature according to their values.

JASPER & NELKIN were the first American sociologists to analyse animal rights as a social movement. They argue that a tradition of sentimental anthropomorphism and a modernist critique of instrumentalism characterize today's animal rights movement. Their categorization of animal protectionists as welfarists, pragmatists, and fundamentalists would be improved by distinguishing the ideological and programmatic differences between these groups. The label of "abolitionist" is more accurate than fundamentalist as the latter implies an extremism that does not typify the tactics of mainstream animal protectionists. Jasper & Nelkin's discussion of five seminal animal rights campaigns is rich in descriptive detail and accurately reflects their characterization of the movement as a moral crusade. A less analytical, albeit useful complement to their study, is provided by FINSEN & FINSEN who describe animal rights as a movement of ideas. The strengths and weaknesses in the arguments of the movement's principal philosophers are clearly and competently outlined by the authors, who are both professional philosophers. Their deep knowledge of the US movement is reflected in the profiles of the organizations and campaigns and the descriptions of some of the movement's opponents as well as its potential allies in other movements.

GARNER's study reports on the progress made by the animal protection movement in Britain and the United States. The author's exhaustive examination of animal welfare policies in the two countries provides a useful comparative analysis of the movement's relationship with the state. The focus on policy networks roughly corresponds to social movement organizations studied by sociologists. More than 50 such organizations (balanced evenly between animal users and their defenders) are mentioned, providing the reader with an excellent reference on the politics of animal protection. What is missing in this meticulously researched study is a sense of what the animal movement means to its grass roots supporters. It is this that ultimately underwrites the movement's capacity to mobilize public opinion, a fact that Garner seems tacitly to acknowledge.

TESTER's analysis of animal rights was the first book length study of the movement by a British sociologist. Although innovative in its approach, the author's thesis – that animal rights is not about animal welfare but about humans who want to assert their superiority as moral beings – is not convincing. The book offers a refreshingly different perspective on animal rights – that it is a bourgeois project to classify and define humanity – but it is an example of strict constructionism in which animals are intellectualized away as "useful for humans to be able to think human".

WOLFE's book vigorously defends anthropocentrism against the threats posed by a number of recent developments, including animal rights and an environmental impulse that puts the rights of nature above human wants and needs. According to Wolfe, humans are meaning-producing creatures who need to exploit animals in order to live a life of fantasy, excitement, and creativity. He claims, for instance, that it is singularly human for hunters to seek "the sensual pleasures of violent sport", whereas children develop imagination and fantasy by visiting zoos. Although animal liberationists will be disturbed by Wolfe's speciesism, the book is none the less a clear and forthright statement about what makes us different from most other species.

Lyle Munro

Animism

Durkheim, Emile, *The Elementary Forms of the Religious Life*, London: Allen and Unwin, 1915; new translation as *The Elementary Forms of Religious Life*, New York: Free Press, 1995 (French edition 1912)

Evans-Pritchard, E.E., *Theories of Primitive Religion*, Oxford: Clarendon Press, and New York: Oxford University Press, 1965

Frazer, J.G., *The Golden Bough: A Study in Magic and Religion*, London: Macmillan, 12 vols, 1911–15, New York: Macmillan, 1935; abridged edition, London and New York: Macmillan, 1 vol. 1922; many reprints

Lang, Andrew, *The Origins of Religion, and Other Essays*, London: Watts, 1908

Spencer, Herbert, *Descriptive Sociology*, vol. 3: *Types of Lowest Races, Negritto Races, and Malayo-Polynesian Races*, London: Williams and Norgate, and New York: Appleton, 1874

Tylor, Edward Burnett, *Primitive Culture: Researches into the Development of Mythology, Philosophy, Religion, Language, Art, and Custom*, London: John Murray, 1871; 5th edition, 2 vols, 1913

The notion of animism is not now widely used in anthropology and tends to be referred to more as a historical curiosity for what it can tell us about anthropological thought in the 19th century than for what it can say about the beliefs of people in the modern world.

SPENCER laid the foundations for the notion of animism in his discussion of primitive beliefs in his *Descriptive Sociology*. He located the origin of all religious thought in the experiences of dreaming, death, and states of semi-consciousness, where it appeared as if a part of the individual was released from the confines of the physical body and allowed to roam freely in the supernatural realm. This was the source of the universal belief in the dual nature of man – the spiritual and the material. It also gave rise to the belief in the existence of the spirit after death, represented by ghosts, from which developed the notion of gods – the ghosts of remote ancestors – and the practice of ancestor worship. This, for Spencer, was the root of all religion that gradually evolved, in a succession of stages, into more "advanced" and complex forms.

Similar ideas were used by TYLOR, and although his *Primitive Culture* was published before Spencer's work, the ideas of the latter had already been developed before the former appeared. Tylor introduced the term "animism" into anthropology in the late 19th century, describing it as "the theory which endows the phenomena of nature with personal life". In other words, the belief that natural phenomena, such as climatic phenomena, or rocks and stones, could possess some kind of "spirit" or life force so that the apparently lifeless material world was actually animated by a host of unseen and supernatural forces. Unlike Spencer, Tylor emphasized the belief in the soul, rather than in ghosts and ancestor worship, and the concept of animism was used to refer to inanimate objects that not only had life and personality, but also possessed such souls. He accounted for this phenomenon with an appeal to a kind of "psychological universalism" – the common human experiences of dreaming, visions, trances, and death. "Primitive" peoples explained these experiences with reference to the existence of an immaterial entity – the soul – the idea of which was then transferred to all the material phenomena around them. Tylor argued that animism was universal and pervasive, occurring in the earliest stages of every society in the world. He regarded it as the first and most basic stage of a tripartite model of social-religious evolution, after which societies moved on to polytheistic beliefs, and then finally, to the highest form of all – monotheism – the belief in a Supreme Being or Creator.

This model was adopted by FRAZER in his evolutionary argument that all societies move through the same stages of development – from magic to religion to science – which is unilinear and necessarily progressive. His massive 12-volume tome, *The Golden Bough*, was essentially an analysis of the importance of totemism in the development of world religion and mythology. Animistic beliefs were an important aspect of this, existing among many peoples as the idea that vegetation, and especially trees, were conscious beings, possessing spirits and sometimes even the souls of dead ancestors. These animated beings were credited with various powers over nature, such as the ability to make the sun shine and the rain fall, and as such they were revered and worshipped, with strict rules protecting them from harm. The arguments advanced by Frazer, like those of Spencer and Tylor, were based on the assumption that in the most primitive beliefs can be found, as if somehow suspended or "frozen" in time, the same beliefs that more advanced societies held at an earlier stage in their development. Although highly ethnocentric and evolutionist in their premise, they ultimately aimed to show the rationality of primitive customs. According to Frazer, such customs may appear "ridiculous" but, viewed in evolutionary perspective, they actually made sense and could be subject to scientific investigation. These arguments were highly influential in classical, literary, and scholarly as well as anthropological circles at the time, and remained more or less unchallenged until the 20th century.

One detractor was LANG, who rejected the evolutionary perspective and questioned the tendency of European anthropologists to range religious beliefs in hierarchical order. Although allowing that the source of religious ideas of the soul may derive from the experiences of semi-conscious states, he pointed out, crucially, that monotheistic ideas were to be found in the most apparently "primitive" cultures, as well as animistic ones in the more "advanced" cultures. Lang's alternative hypothesis had a chronological aspect, however. He postulated the existence of general monotheistic beliefs in a "high god" along with animistic and polytheistic ones in ancestral ghosts. Because of their more immediate presence, the latter came to assume greater significance in religious life, resulting in a kind of "merging" of the two beliefs with the originally transcendental "high god" assuming human characteristics. Although not tinged with the evolutionism of his contemporaries, Lang's theory suffered from a similar reliance on untestable assumptions and an attribution of universal forms and stages of belief to all societies.

DURKHEIM mounted a convincing attack on the basic tenets of animism, which he found antithetical to the argument for the fundamental rationality of religious belief. He began by considering the assumption of both Spencer and Tylor that the origin of animism was to be found in ideas of the soul or spirit, which in turn had their source in the "vague and inconsistent" images of dreams and other unconscious and semiconscious states. He considered this argument for the origin of the dual nature of man to be problematic, largely because it took for granted the assumption that the mental representations experienced by individuals when awake were accorded the same value and reality as those experienced when asleep. This led him to another criticism of the theory, namely the extension of the idea of spirit or soul to inanimate objects. Tylor explained the extension with reference to the particular mentality of "primitives", which, he argued, fundamentally did not distinguish between animate and inanimate and endowed objects with human qualities. The possession of such a mentality, Durkheim countered, attributed a "blind credulity" to such individuals, depriving them of any claim to rationality.

Finally, and most damning of all, he rejected animism because of its implications for the ontological status of religion in general. It was regarded as the most basic form of religious life, and it rested on a tangle of confused and mistaken ideas, so it therefore reduced the very idea of religion itself to "nothing more than a system of hallucination". As a writer who regarded religion as a phenomenon that represented fundamental realities in the social world in much the same way that physics and chemistry represented the natural world, Durkheim's positivism could not allow him to accept any theory that denied the basic rationality of a social fact.

The notion of animism has been criticized by EVANS-PRITCHARD in his series of published lectures, *Theories of Primitive Religion*. Although primarily concerned with the relationship between religion and magic, he also considers the role of the notion of animism in such debates, providing a succinct summary of its main shortcomings and also contextualizing its place in anthropological theory in general. He pointed to the evolutionary bias in such ideas, typical of nineteenth century thought in general, which held that there was a universal tendency for societies to develop from simple, homogenous forms to complex, heterogeneous ones. What he called the "intellectualist theorizing" of Spencer, Tylor, and Frazer was compounded by the further shortcomings of inadequate observations, faulty inferences, and mistaken conclusions. These writers based the notion of animism on unreliable second-hand accounts of primitive beliefs brought back by European explorers and never on empirical fieldwork. He argued that such "armchair anthropology" was speculative and, although often amassing a huge volume of comparative material, by using it to attempt to explain the universal foundations of human belief, it was often just plain wrong.

GERDA REITH

Anorexia

Bryant-Waugh, Rachel Lask and Bryan Lask, "Annotation: Eating Disorders in Children", *Journal of Child Psychology and Psychiatry*, 36 (1995): 431–37

Golder, Elliot and Laird Birmingham, "Anorexia Nervosa: Methods of Treatment" in *Understanding Eating Disorders: Anorexia Nervosa, Bulimia Nervosa, and Obesity*, edited by LeeAnn Alexander-Mott and D. Barry Lumsden, Washington, DC: Taylor and Francis, 1994

Keel, Pamela, Jayne Fulkerson and Gloria Leon, "Disordered Eating Precursors in Pre- and Early Adolescent Girls and Boys", *Journal of Youth and Adolescence*, 26/2 (1997): 203–16

Lucas, Alexander, Mary Beard, Michael O'Fallon and Leonard Kurland, "50-Year Trends in the Incidence of Anorexia Nervosa in Rochester, Minnesota: A Population-based Study", *American Journal of Psychiatry*, 148/7 (1991): 917–22

Robin, Arthur, Marcia Gilroy and Amy Dennis, "Treatment of Eating Disorders in Children and Adolescents", *Clinical Psychology Review*, 18/4 (1998): 421–46

Smolak, Linda, Michael P. Levine and Ruth Striegel-Moore (editors), *The Developmental Psychopathology of Eating Disorders: Implications for Research, Prevention, and Treatment*, Mahwah, New Jersey: Erlbaum, 1996

Steiner, Hans and James Lock, "Anorexia Nervosa and Bulimia Nervosa in Children and Adolescents: A Review of the Past 10 Years", *Journal of the American Academy of Child and Adolescent Psychiatry*, 37/4 (1998): 352–59

Szmukler, George, Chris Dare and Janet Treasure (editors), *Handbook of Eating Disorders: Theory, Treatment and Research*, Chichester and New York: Wiley, 1995

STEINER & LOCK provide an overview of eating disorders from 1988 to 1998. Their work highlights contemporary diagnosis, prevention, and treatment of anorexia nervosa and bulimia nervosa. The authors review the changes in the *Diagnostic and Statistical Manual of Mental Disorder*, provide recent epidemiological data, discuss psychiatric comorbidity, present studies of risk factors, and review treatment effectiveness studies. They conclude that most of the literature focuses on risk, whereas there is less of a focus on protective factors. This article points to several persistent methodological problems in the current literature: most studies involve mixed samples of adults and juveniles, age at onset of illness and duration of illness are rarely controlled for, and thus may confound treatment results. They assert that further research is needed addressing normative data on the development of eating behaviour and specific risk and resilience factors for pathology during specific developmental periods. Steiner & Lock identify that studies regarding the continuities and discontinuities of eating disturbances across the lifespan are important but rare. This article states that to establish risks and causal models, any developmental model of eating disorders must account for the normal development of complex factors in multiple domains and their interactions. Finally, the authors point to the need for longitudinal data to yield further insights regarding the etiology and optimal treatment of eating disorders. Most of the literature in this review focuses on adolescents. This article provides many recent citations.

BRYANT-WAUGH & LASK provide a ten-year review (1985–95) of literature that includes an emphasis on children's eating disorders. Their discussion focuses specifically on the early-onset age group. A range of etiological factors is discussed including biological and familial correlates. The authors emphasize that there are unique characteristics of children with eating disorders and those who experience early-onset of anorexia. There are specific assessments for younger children and their recent work includes a discussion of these instruments. The Steiner & Lock and Bryant-Waugh & Lask reviews each provide a wealth of resources for both practitioners and scientists, considering their relative emphasis on different developmental periods it is important to consider each.

LUCAS *et al.* provide a comprehensive incidence and prevalence study of anorexia nervosa by studying all persons residing in Rochester, Minnesota, from 1935–1984. For girls aged 10–19, the incidence fell from 16.6 per 100,000 person-years during the 1935–9 period to a low of 7.0 in 1950–4. However, in recent years (1980–4), this figure has increased to 26.3. The authors concluded that the rate of anorexia nervosa is more common than previously recognized; in particular, for girls

aged 15–19, it is very common. The incidence of anorexia nervosa in their broad sample increased among females aged 15–24, but not among older women or among males. Lucas *et al.* also discuss other international studies on the incidence and prevalence rates of anorexia nervosa.

KEEL, FULKERSON & LEON provide an important empirical study of precursors of anorexia nervosa including both males and females. The article begins with a clear discussion of numerous factors associated with eating disorders (for example, puberty, depression, self-esteem, body image). The methods section includes a discussion of multiple measures that may be used to assess eating disorders. The researchers assessed fifth- and sixth-grade boys and girls, depression, body image, self-esteem, eating behaviours and attitudes, weight, height, and pubertal development in year one and again in year two. For girls, year-one body mass index and pubertal development predicted year-two disordered eating, while for boys, year-two disordered eating was predicted by poor body image in year one. This article also provides a good background as well as a discussion of the implications of the study.

ROBIN, GILROY & DENNIS present a cogent discussion of treating individuals with eating disorders. They review Dare and Szmukler's (1991) approach to family therapy for adolescents with anorexia nervosa, which emphasizes the family as a resource that has to be mobilized to help the starving person. In this approach, the therapist refrains from expressing views about the etiology of the condition, but suggests that the family is presented with a problem of unknown origin which is not their fault, but that will require all of their resources to overcome. When this therapy was compared to a supportive individual therapy, family therapy had a more favourable outcome for the early-onset (before age 18), short-duration (less than three years) type of anorexia (similar to the results found in the Eisler, 1997 article). They discuss research that supports the effectiveness of family-oriented treatments. Robin, Gilroy & Dennis also review the cognitive-behavioural approach to the treatment of anorexia nervosa. In this approach the therapist focuses on using cognitive restructuring to modify distorted beliefs and attitudes about the meaning of weight, shape, and appearance, which are believed to underlie dieting and fear of weight gain. The authors state that limited empirical work is available to support the cognitive-behavioural approaches to the treatment of anorexia nervosa. Issues are raised about the minimum age and level of cognitive development necessary for implementing this type of treatment.

GOLDER & BIRMINGHAM focus on a set of primary treatment components (for example, medical stabilization, establishment of a therapeutic alliance, weight restoration) in working with anorexic clients. The authors allude to different types of treatment, such as cognitive behavioural, family, and psychodynamic therapies. The emphasis of this chapter is on the need to focus on key components of treatment. This chapter contains important information for both practitioners and researchers in considering key issues related to treatment of anorexics.

Several recent edited books provide many useful chapters about important aspects of anorexia. SMOLAK, LEVINE & STRIEGEL-MOORE edited a book exploring the developmental psychopathology of eating disorders. This book begins with an introduction to the field of developmental psychopathology, which offers a framework for better understanding etiological aspects of anorexia and has implications for treatment as well. Developmental research is presented throughout and the principals of developmental process and context are highlighted, including transitions during adolescence, media influences, and developmental vulnerabilities. The implications of developmental models for prevention programs are also discussed.

SZMUKLER, DARE & TREASURE edited a recent handbook on eating disorders, which includes a discussion of theory, treatment, and research. This volume provides a relatively comprehensive review of anorexia nervosa. The focus is on salient ideas, models, and hypotheses that have dominated the field of eating disorders since the 1970s. These ideas and models are critically examined for their value to both academicians and clinicians.

SHANE R. JIMERSON

See also Bulimia

Antipsychiatry

Foucault, Michel, *Madness and Civilization: A History of Insanity in the Age of Reason*, New York: Pantheon, 1965; London: Tavistock, 1967

Goffman, Erving, *Asylums: Essays on the Social Situation of Mental Patients and Other Inmates*, New York: Doubleday, 1961; Harmondsworth: Penguin, 1968

Ingleby, David (editor), *Critical Psychiatry: The Politics of Mental Health*, New York: Pantheon, 1980; Harmondsworth: Penguin, 1981

Laing, R.D., *The Divided Self: An Existential Study in Sanity and Madness*, London: Tavistock, and Chicago: Quadrangle, 1960

Laing, R.D., *The Politics of Experience*, Harmondsworth: Penguin, and New York: Pantheon, 1967

Rosenhan, David, L., "On Being Sane in Insane Places", *Science*, 179 (1973): 250–58

Sedgwick, Peter, *Psycho Politics: Laing, Foucault, Goffman and the Future of Mass Psychiatry*, London: Pluto Press, and New York: Harper and Row, 1982

Szasz, Thomas S., *Ideology and Insanity: Essays on the Psychiatric Dehumanization of Man*, Harmondsworth and Baltimore: Penguin, 1974

"Antipsychiatry" generically refers to all those who oppose traditional psychiatric attempts to conceptualize the problem of mental illness primarily through a medical-organic perspective. This umbrella term does not presume, however, that everyone opposing the medical model is united in defining exactly what mental illness represents. In fact, as this review will show, among antipsychiatrists everyone tends to disagree with everyone else.

LAING (1967, 1960), a psychiatrist, was the first to reject the notion that mental disorder qualifies as "illness". Throughout both books he develops the argument that the strange behaviour and odd excited outbursts of talk from psychotic patients – which are often defined by psychiatrists as either inconsequential or symptomatic of an organic disease process

– can, from a more sophisticated vantagepoint, be interpreted as a sane response by the patient to an insane environment. Once we acknowledge this, Laing goes on to provide an indepth analysis of how demanding families bombard adolescents with incompatible messages, which, for some, provoke a coping strategy involving the specific symptoms that psychiatrists associate with schizophrenia. What is it that the person is experiencing in their mental illness? One possible answer given is the *divided-self* generated by the need to resolve the conflict between the expectations of the family for one's *self*, and the actual needs of the *self*. Both texts should be read in order to grasp Laing's ideas, the issues are complex but his vivid, clear style certainly makes it worthwhile taking some time over.

Another psychiatrist who has campaigned most vociferously as an antipsychiatrist is Thomas Szasz. Since the 1960s, a voluminous literature on his theoretical ideas has appeared, scattered across a variety of different books and journals. However, the key elements of his antipsychiatric approach are broadly drawn together by a collection of 14 essays published in 1974. Essentially, SZASZ rejects the notion that mental illness qualifies as an "illness" just like any other. He argues that as mental symptoms have no proven link to objective physical lesions, they can only exist as purely subjective judgements and so are dependent upon sociocultural norms. Hence, mental disorders result not from diseases but from problems in living – it is not something one has but is something one does or is. Szasz then goes on to show how defining mental disorder as a medical problem susceptible to professional solutions can devalue sufferers' experiences, control socially unacceptable behaviour, and mask life's moral and ethical dilemmas. Theoretically, the arguments presented by Szasz are interesting and persuasive, yet at the same time they appear disjointed and lacking in structure. As a consequence, the reader will get the impression that Szasz is promoting a crusade rather than developing a useful and coherent theory that is likely to have relevance within the context of modern psychiatric practice.

Erving Goffman began his influence in antipsychiatry at the same time as Szasz but is better known as an ethnographic sociologists than a theoretician of mental health issues. Throughout the four major essays presented in *Asylums* GOFFMAN develops his counterpsychiatric views from observing "the moral carer of the mental patient" as they cope with life inside psychiatric hospitals. Essentially, he argues that the bizarre forms of behaviour displayed by patients are not indications of some underlying mental disease process but instead represent a deliberate strategy employed by patients in order to survive the harsh, imprisoning environments of such "total institutions" that are trying to destroy them. Goffman offers a great deal of insight into the interactive experiences of patients, however, the reader should be aware that this purely micro sociological approach has been viewed as his work's weakness as well as its strength.

FOUCAULT, a French philosopher and historian, attempts to define the problem of mental illness through studying insanity from the Middle Ages to the time when the "mad" started to be isolated from the rest of society during the late 18th century. His approach, however, may be regarded as an antihistory of psychiatry. Thus, he does not follow a liberal evolutionist perspective, which views our past barbaric and cruel treatment of the insane as merely stages on a slope tending inevitably towards an "enlightened" medical present. Instead, he argues that the rise of the medical model simply reflected the need for greater political control, to remove dangerous deviants from society, rather than as a response by science to help through legitimate medical means. Furthermore, he asserts that those involved are not aware that this is going on, and that in this respect both patients and psychiatrists become no more than puppets on a wider social stage. Foucault's work is quite detailed-even the shortened English translation of his original text-however, his views are clearly organized and colourfully presented.

A further approach within antipsychiatry starts from the assertion that the symptoms of mental disorder arise not from the disorder itself, but from the impact on the individual of being labelled as "mentally disordered". A dramatic illustration of the potential power of such labels was described by ROSENHAN's experimental research of voluntary mental hospital admissions. Rosenhan organized a group of "normal" people to present themselves for admission through falsifying symptoms of schizophrenia. Once admitted to hospital they reverted to their usual "normal" behaviour, yet the hospital staff never detected the pseudopatients as "fakes". In fact, nothing they could say or do could convince the staff that they were sane – even openly writing research notes was labelled "obsessive writing behaviour". This paper is entertaining and persuasive, and has become a classic in its field; however, the significance of labelling per se in shaping/defining mental illness is now generally accepted as oversimplistic and too extreme.

INGLEBY's edited work attempts to inject new life into the antipsychiatric approaches that gained so much prominence during the 1960s. Written during the early 1980s, the contributors to this book surveyed the state of psychiatry, and the movements critical of its practice, across various Western capitalist countries – the US, Britain, France, Italy, and Norway – with the aim of trying to develop a cogent critique of psychiatry by drawing upon the similarities in the circumstances appropriate to each society. The book draws heavily upon theoretical questions, particularly in the first chapter, which deals in part with political interpretations of mental illness, and so can make for hard reading. Each chapter can, however, be read independently and so the theoretical chapter may be attempted at another time.

SEDGWICK provides an excellent critical overview of the ideas put forward by the principal antipsychiatrists – Laing, Szasz, Goffman, and Foucault. Essentially, the first part of this book places their arguments within a broader political perspective, whereas the second evaluates attempts by various mental health movements to transform psychiatric practice away from institutionalized management towards community-based methods of treatment and care. The book is thought provoking and will be of most benefit to those who have already gained some knowledge of the key antipsychiatric approaches mentioned above.

ANTONY COLOMBO

See also Mental illness

Antisemitism

Avineri, Shlomo, "Dreyfus Was Not the Reason", *Midstream*, (May/June 1998): 16–17

Berlin, Naphtali Zvi Yehuda, *Why Antisemitism? A Translation of the Remnant of Israel*, edited and translated by Howard S. Joseph, London and Northvale, New Jersey: Aronson, 1996

Gilman, Sander L., *The Visibility of the Jew in the Diaspora: Body Imagery and Its Cultural Context*, Syracuse, New York: Syracuse University, 1992

Lewis, Bernard, *Semites and Anti-Semites: An Enquiry into Conflict and Prejudice*, New York: Norton, and London: Weidenfeld and Nicolson, 1986

MacDonald, Kevin, *Separation and Its Discontents: Toward an Evolutionary Theory of Anti-Semitism*, Westport, Connecticut: Praeger, 1998

Reinharz, Jehuda (editor), *Living with Antisemitism: Modern Jewish Responses*, Hanover, New Hampshire: University Press of New England, 1987

Sartre, Jean Paul, *Anti-Semite and Jew*, New York: Schocken, 1948; as *Portrait of an Anti-Semite*, London: Secker and Warburg, 1948 (French edition 1946)

Wistrich, Robert S., *Antisemitism: The Longest Hatred*, New York: Pantheon, and London: Thames Methuen, 1991

AVINERI's brief article, originally published in Hebrew in the Israeli newspaper *Ha'Aretz*, challenges a famous myth about the history of antisemitism. According to the myth, the writer Theodor Herzl, founder of Zionism, was inspired to advocate a Jewish state by witnessing in France the public humiliation of Alfred Dreyfus, a Jewish military officer falsely accused of treason and whose case was tinged with antisemitism. Avineri denies that it was the Dreyfus affair that prompted Herzl's conversion to Zionism. Citing Herzl's journals and other sources, Avineri argues that the Dreyfus matter did not particularly stir Herzl's heart as a Jew. In contrast, claims Avineri, Herzl was much more influenced to become a Zionist by the rise of antisemitism in Herzl's native Austria-Hungary.

WISTRICH explores the history of antisemitism from its origins to the present day. The persecution of Jews in lands governed by Christians or Muslims is attributed, in large part, to popular impulses derived from these two religions. In other words, antisemites in the Christian and Muslim communities are said to have taken their language of justification from their respective religions. At the same time, Wistrich points to antisemites, at least in the Christian world, whose antisemitism stems from anti-Christian attitudes. Such antisemites, argues Wistrich, were attempting to undermine the Jewish foundations of Christianity with their doctrines. Also covered in Wistrich's survey of antisemitism worldwide are the economic and social conditions, both among Jews and gentiles, which provided the context for, and sometimes the cause of, antisemitism. Economic jealousy of the Jews is one factor mentioned as contributing to antisemitism. Wistrich provides a good survey of the topic, examining the history of antisemitism in different parts of the world.

LEWIS' work is more dated than Wistrich's, but it takes the same historical approach to antisemitism. Like Wistrich, Lewis distinguishes between the antisemitism which stems from a distorted Christianity and the antisemitism fostered by anti-Christians who wish to undermine the Jewish foundations of the Christian Church. Lewis gives more attention than does Wistrich to the issue of the modern state of Israel, and how hostility toward the latter, or toward Israel's founding philosophy of Zionism, is sometimes associated with antisemitism.

BERLIN was a 19th-century Russian rabbi. His work is based on the dilemma of assimilation, as exacerbated by antisemitism. The author does not want the Jewish people to lose their distinctive character in the middle of the changes of the modern era; he prescribes a return to God

MACDONALD's work is controversial; the author himself predicts that his book will be labelled antisemitic, a label that the author deems false. The book claims Judaism is a form of evolutionary adaptation to the gentile environment, and that antisemitism is an adaptation by gentiles to the presence of Jews among them. Historical instances of antisemitism, which allegedly prove this thesis, are examined.

SARTRE wrote about French Jews at the end of World War II, but his analysis can be applied to antisemitism throughout the world. The great existentialist writer analyses the antisemite in a manner reminiscent of Eric Hoffer's analysis of true believers in *The True Believer* (first published 1951). Sartre also discusses his theory that Jews are defined (at least in the gentile world) with respect to the persecutions that gentiles laid upon them.

The historical essays that REINHARZ compiles from a variety of authors are highly informative and deserve study. There are case studies on Jewish reaction to antisemitism in a wide variety of times and places, from England and the United States to Argentina, Germany, central Europe, and the Arab world. Thematic essays discuss the Zionist movement as a response to antisemitism, the Holocaust, and the tendency of some Jews to "convert" to Christianity as a response to persecution on the part of nominal Christians.

GILMAN's brief piece gives attention to the physical characteristics possessed by, or attributed by antisemites to, Jewish people and how these supposed physical characteristics played into the whole dynamic of outsider status and self-image. Half of the essay is devoted to the nose stereotype.

ERIC LONGLEY

Anti-trust economics

Amato, Giuliano, *Antitrust and the Bounds of Power: The Dilemma of Liberal Democracy in the History of the Market*, Oxford: Hart, 1997

Areeda, P. and D. Turner, "Predatory Pricing and Related Practices under Section Two of the Sherman Act", *Harvard Law Review*, 88 (February 1975): 697–733

Bork, Robert H., *The Antitrust Paradox: A Policy at War with Itself*, New York: Basic Books, 1978

Mason, Edward Sagendorph, *Economic Concentration and the Monopoly Problem*, Cambridge, Massachusetts: Harvard University Press, 1957

US Department of Justice, *Merger Guidelines*, prepared by Antitrust Division, Washington. DC: US Department of Justice, reprinted in *Antitrust Bulletin*, 27 (1982): 633–65

Competition law and policy have always operated across the boundaries of economics, law, and politics, with different forces in the ascendancy at different times. The passage of the founding US legislation, the Sherman Act of 1890 and the Clayton Act of 1914, occurred at a time of popular trust-busting crusades. By the time initial UK legislation was passed in 1948, and the competition articles of the Treaty of Rome were adopted in 1957, more orthodox economic analysis had taken over in the US. MASON is an example of the so-called Harvard School of competition economics, which applied recently developed principles of industrial economics to identify particular practices, such as tying, that were held to be potentially anti-competitive.

Analysis also focused extensively on alternative forms of barriers to entry, such as economies of scale, brand advantages, and technological knowhow. These laid whole industries open, if not to monopolization, then to small-numbers competition, which was detrimental to consumers. This analytical approach tended to encourage interventionist policies based on discrete pieces of economic analysis. These often operated within the so-called S-C-P framework, in which the Structure of an industry determined the Conduct of firms and hence industrial Performance.

The sharpest riposte to the Harvard approach, and to decisions taken in the US courts between 1940 and 1960, was provided by the Chicago School, best exemplified by BORK (1978). Reverting to a more classical style of economic analysis, Bork argues that many practices that were viewed with suspicion, and sometimes regarded as *per se* illegal, were in fact innocent or even beneficial. One example is vertical restraint, where a manufacturer sells through exclusive outlets or imposes a minimum retail price. Bork argues that vertical restraint is unlikely to enhance the benefit to the manufacturer of any monopoly power it might possess, as "a monopoly profit can only be made once". Instead, it is likely to be introduced to benefit consumers by, for example, ensuring that they have access to such benefits as after-sales service; benefits which, in the absence of exclusive distribution, might be eliminated from the market by free riding. Bork exposes interventionist doctrine and legal decisions to an unremitting attack. He also argues that attempts to deal with the relatively rare cases of market failure whose existence he allows might also be contaminated with government or legal failure.

The rather simplistic certainties of the Chicago School had a huge impact upon the practice of competition law. But a new stage has been reached in which economists and lawyers seek to deploy increasingly sophisticated arguments to identify circumstances in which particular practices (or mergers) are likely to have detrimental effects. For example, AREEDA & TURNER – the work of two Harvard law professors – addresses the question of the appropriate test for predatory conduct. Conduct of this kind was one of the charges laid against the trusts, such as Standard Oil, at the time of the Sherman Act. The trick is to find a means of separating out price cuts that are the results of the proper operation of the competitive process from those that are intended to drive competitors from the market, allowing the predator subsequently to reestablish its monopoly. (Note it is one of the tenets of the Chicago School that such predation is a rare or non-existent phenomenon.) The test must be both theoretically robust and capable of being argued before a court, using generally available management accounting data. The Areeda-Turner proposal, that prices below average variable cost should be viewed as suspect, was subsequently considered and adopted by the European Court of Justice when it addressed the question in the AKZO case.

A further major advance in recent decades has been the acceptance throughout the world of a criterion for defining the market within which firms compete. This was achieved in the US DEPARTMENT OF JUSTICE *Merger Guidelines*, which define markets in a way that naturally leads on to considerations of whether dominance and abuse of dominance are also exhibited. According to the definition, a market comprises the smallest set of goods and services that would allow any "hypothetical monopolist" gaining control of it to raise prices above the competitive level by a small but significant amount for a non-transitory period. Once a market has been defined in this way, it is natural then to ask: first, whether any firm is dominant (i.e. can act independently of customers and competitors) and secondly, whether it does in fact abuse dominance by acting in that way. This approach, now accepted by competition authorities throughout the world, imparts significant rigour (and standardization) to investigations.

Finally, AMATO recalls the crucial social and political role in anti-trust activity. A former head of the Italian Anti-trust Authority and Prime Minister of Italy, he summarises the development of anti-trust in both the US and the EU, but couples this with a broader argument relating to economic and political freedom. At the end of the 19th century, the trusts were seen as threats to political freedom as well as instruments of economic domination. Competition law thus had a variety of goals, including the protection of certain types of competitor (for example, small producers) as well as the competitive process. Throughout the 20th century, a variety of countervailing forces – labour unions, industrial customers, consumers' organisations – came into operation to make up the democratic deficit. As a result, competition policy has become more focussed on economic efficiency, but obliged increasingly to adapt to take account of globalization. There is thus a need to consider supranational institutions for competition policy. Although Amato does not mention it, the World Trade Organisation has sometimes been proposed for this role.

MARTIN CAVE

See also Contracts and competition, Mergers and acquisitions, Regulation and competition

Anton Piller order, *see* Search order

Anxiety

Barlow, David H., *Anxiety and its Disorders: The Nature and Treatment of Anxiety and Panic*, New York: Guildford Press, 1988

Beck, Aaron T. and Gary Emery, *Anxiety Disorders and Phobias: A Cognitive Perspective*, New York: Basic Books, 1985

Edelmann, Robert J., *Anxiety: Theory, Research and Intervention in Clinical and Health Psychology*, Chichester and New York: Wiley, 1992

Eysenck, Michael N., *Anxiety: The Cognitive Perspective*, Hillsdale, New Jersey: Erlbaum, 1992

Freud, Sigmund, "Inhibitions, Symptoms, and Anxiety" in *An Autobiographical Study; Inhibitions, Symptoms and Anxiety; The Question of Lay Analysis; and Other Works*, edited by James Strachey, London: Hogarth Press, 1959 (*The Standard Edition of the Complete Psychological Works*, vol. 20)

Gray, Jeffrey A., *The Neuropsychology of Anxiety: An Enquiry into the Functions of the Sept-Hippocampal System*, Oxford: Clarendon Press, and New York: Oxford University Press, 1982

Lang, Peter J., "Fear Reduction and Fear Behavior: Problems in Treating a Construct" in *Research in Psychotherapy: Proceedings of the Third Conference*, edited by J.M. Schlien, Washington DC: American Psychological Association, 1966

Spielberger, Charles D., "Anxiety as an Emotional State" in *Anxiety: Current Trends in Theory and Research*, vol. 1, edited by Charles D. Spielberger, New York: Academic Press, 1972

Wells, Adrian, *Cognitive Therapy of Anxiety Disorders: A Practice Manual and Conceptual Guide*, Chichester and New York: Wiley, 1997

Williams, Mark G., Fraser N. Watts, Colin MacLeod and Andrew Mathews, *Cognitive Psychology and Emotional Disorders*, 2nd edition, Chichester and New York: Wiley, 1997

Anxiety is a widely used concept within the psychological literature yet it is often used uncritically and to reflect diverse meanings. Anxiety is not only presumed to underlie "anxiety disorders" such as social phobia, panic disorder, and post-traumatic stress disorder, but is also considered an important factor in relation to a range of physical health complaints. The term anxiety has been used both to describe an emotional state and a relatively stable personality characteristic. The references selected illustrate these points.

Ever since FREUD's pioneering work a number of theories of anxiety have been proposed. Freud's own views on anxiety underwent a number of revisions leading to his publication of *Inhibitions, Symptoms and Anxiety* in which he differentiated "primary anxiety", which could be traced to somatic sources (often the birth process), and later "subsequent anxiety", resulting from separation from either mother, or other significant object, or castration fears, or other crises of psychosexual development. Within Freud's familiar tripartite model anxiety could be separated into realistic, moral, or neurotic forms. Realistic anxiety was a direct response to external threat; moral anxiety was associated with shame and guilt; while neurotic anxiety referred to phobic and free-floating anxiety and panic sensations. Many subsequent writers have questioned the validity of Freudian theories, and subsequent theoretical developments concerning anxiety have trodden a path heavily rooted in experimental psychology and the individual's learning history.

Although a number of researchers and theoreticians had advanced the view that anxiety was more than just a unitary construct it was not until LANG's seminal work that the three-systems analysis of anxiety was popularized. Lang proposed that human emotion in general, and anxiety in particular, involves responses in three main behavioural systems consisting of largely independent components of (a) motor behaviour, (b) linguistic expressions, and (c) physiological states. Numerous subsequent studies have found that when all three systems are assessed there is a low non-significant relationship between them both at any point in time and over time in relation to anxiety reduction procedures. This has implications both for assessment and therapy.

Theorists of all persuasions acknowledge the role of neurobiology in anxiety, but some consider it primary and causal. Jeffrey Gray is one of the best known of such theorists. GRAY presents his neuropsychological theory of anxiety which he has continued to work on in the two decades since its publication. Gray argued that anxiety consists of activity on the behavioural inhibition system (BIS) which comprises the septohippocampal system, its monoaminergic afferents from the brain stem, and its neocortical projections in the frontal lobe. Within Gray's model, the major function of the BIS is to monitor ongoing behaviour, checking continuously that it coincides with expectations.

A number of theorists have considered the role of cognition in anxiety. SPIELBERGER is one of the few theorists who, as evidenced in his state-trait conception, considers anxiety as a personality trait. He viewed state anxiety as a transitory emotional state and the disposition to experience state anxiety frequently, or to be "anxiety-prone", as a personality trait. The extent to which both external stressors and internal sensations are appraised as anxiety provoking is, in part, a function of the individual's level of trait anxiety.

A cognitive approach with a different emphasis is advocated in the pioneering work of BECK & EMERY. The key relationship with anxiety revolves around cognitive schemas and automatic thoughts. Information about one's self, the world and the future is continuously processed in a distorted way as dangerous. Consequently, states of anxiety are associated with automatic thoughts and images relevant to danger. For Beck, these automatic thoughts and images, resulting from distorted information processing, trigger inappropriate motor, physiological, and affective components of the anxiety response. The theory is really a theory of anxiety disorders rather than of anxiety *per se*.

Cognitive theories of anxiety have developed in recent years and the empirical validity of the theory tested empirically in numerous studies. The idea that people vary in the degree to which they are vulnerable to anxiety has been a generally accepted proposition within the literature. However, EYSENCK summarizes the growing evidence of a vulnerability that is largely cognitive in nature. He regards anxious hypervigilance as both a reaction to potential threat and as a cognitive vulnerability to anxiety. He argues that people who are predisposed to anxiety manifest hypervigilance in four ways: environmental scanning, selective attention to threat-related stimuli, a broadening of attention prior to the detection of such stimuli, and a narrowing of attention when a salient stimulus is being processed.

A further excellent analysis of empirical foundations of cognitive aspects of anxiety is presented by WILLIAMS *et al.*

The authors overview the large and increasing body of empirical research providing evidence for an attentional bias in relation to anxiety with only weak and contradictory evidence for a memory bias. The authors are leading authorities in the field and the book has been described as essential reading for anyone wishing to become conversant with cutting-edge theory and research on the cognitive aspects of anxiety.

BARLOW represents a key contribution, summarizing a vast body of knowledge pertaining to anxiety and the anxiety disorders. The first two chapters overview various conceptualizations and theories of anxiety, discussing anxiety in relation to emotions in general. In the following fourteen chapters Barlow discusses empirical research and therapy in relation to each of the recognized anxiety disorders. He discusses the strengths and weaknesses of diverse approaches ranging from the phenomenological to biochemical and presents an integration of emerging concepts regarding anxiety disorder.

Although not as ambitious as Barlow's text, EDELMANN presents an accessible overview of anxiety in relation to mental health, but in addition goes beyond this in discussing anxiety in relation to physical health concerns. The first two chapters discuss conceptual and theoretical issues with the ensuing five chapters discussing anxiety disorders. The final four chapters discuss anxiety in relation to sexual dysfunction, health and disease, and preparation for surgery. Edelmann provides a consistent framework throughout the book with each chapter organized to reflect theory, assessment, and therapy outcome.

The timely book by WELLS reflects theoretical developments in relation to anxiety and the anxiety disorders which have occurred within the past three decades. The first chapter presents an overview of cognitive theory and models of anxiety with the second chapter presenting an overview of assessment issues. The third and fourth chapters present basic characteristics and techniques of cognitive therapy which are then applied in relation to the anxiety disorders. The book is both empirically based and practical in intent, providing questionnaires and outcome measures for professional use.

ROBERT J. EDELMANN

Apartheid, economics

Hindson, Doug, *Pass Controls and the Urban African Proletariat in South Africa*, Johannesburg: Ravan Press, 1987

Horwitz, Ralph, *The Political Economy of South Africa*, London: Weidenfeld and Nicolson, 1967

Johnstone, Frederick, "White Prosperity and White Supremacy in South Africa Today", *African Affairs*, 275 (1970): 125–40

Lacey, Marian, *Working for Boroko: The Origins of a Coercive Labour System in South Africa*, Johannesburg: Ravan Press, 1981

Legassick, Martin, "Legislation, Ideology and Economy in post-1948 South Africa", *Journal of Southern African Studies*, 1/1 (1974): 5–34

Lipton, Merle, *Capitalism and Apartheid: South Africa, 1910–84*, Aldershot: Gower, and Totowa, New Jersey: Rowman and Allanhed, 1985

Moll, Terence, "Did the 'Apartheid Economy' Fail?", *Journal of Southern African Studies*, 17/2 (1991): 271–91

Nattrass, Nicoli, "Post-War Profitability in South Africa: A Critique of Regulation Analysis in South Africa", *Transformation*, 9 (1989): 66–80

O'Meara, Dan, *Forty Lost Years: The Apartheid State and the Politics of the National Party, 1948–1994*, Athens: Ohio University Press, 1996

Posel, Deborah, *The Making of Apartheid: Conflict and Compromise*, Oxford: Clarendon Press, and New York: Oxford University Press, 1991

Saul, John S. and Stephen Gelb, *The Crisis in South Africa*, New York: Monthly Review Press, 1981

Van der Horst, Sheila T., "The Effect of Industrialization on Labour Relations in South Africa" in *Industrialization and Race Relations*, edited by Guy Hunter, London and New York: Oxford University Press, 1965

Wolpe, Harold, "Capitalism and Cheap Labour-Power in South Africa: From Segregation to Apartheid" in *Segregation and Apartheid in Twentieth-Century South Africa*, edited by William Beinart and Saul Dubow, London and New York: Routledge, 1995

Apartheid was a political slogan that became fashionable in the 1940s in South Africa and, according to O'MEARA, won the election for the Purified Afrikaner National Party in 1948. Although it was too vague a term to allow for a precise definition, it can be said to refer to a system of political governance and social policy in which the rights and obligations of the population were determined according to membership of race groups. The four important groups were white, Indian, black (the majority – earlier called the "native" or "Bantu" group), and coloured (a mixed-race and residual category). Classification was determined by custom and by arbitrary official decisions rather than by the application of scientific criteria. For its defenders, the economics of apartheid were about propping up the "civilized standards of whites" in general and the promotion of Afrikaners in particular, largely through institutionalizing the official status of the Afrikaans language as a legal requirement in many circumstances, and as a language for educational purposes.

It was really the opponents of apartheid who fought over its economic implications. One type of opponent was usually defined as "liberal". Liberal opponents such as VAN DER HORST and HORWITZ have emphasized the economic irrationality of apartheid and the constraints that the legal barriers linked to racial categories placed on the free operations of business to hire whomever, wherever, and whenever it wanted. The other type of opponent – the "radicals" – emphasized the complicity of South African capitalism in forging the racial system, and called for its downfall using classic hypotheses put forth by LEGASSICK and WOLPE. The revival of the African National Congress from the late 1970s, the influence of its allies, the South African Communist Party, the emergence of "independent" trade unionism among black workers, and the simultaneous growth in the 1980s of mass protest in poor black communities, especially amongst the youth, all increased the salience and appeal of the latter interpretation enormously.

Was apartheid good or bad for South African capitalism? The difficulty in defining what is meant by "apartheid" tends to make this a difficult question to answer in simple terms. For instance, NATTRASS has recorded the very high profit rates experienced by South African capitalism during and after World War II and their decline thereafter by stages, ascribing the decline to the onset and application of apartheid. At best, as she says, it may be difficult to assert that the general rate of profitability in the economy benefited from apartheid in its heyday. In fact, however, it is quite unclear to what extent South Africa was simply following secular trends that were operative globally. Her assumption that one can equate "apartheid" with everything done by the National Party in power after 1948 is questionable. On the one hand, many aspects of the South African racial system in the first third of the 20th century represent much earlier precursors of apartheid, usually referred to as "segregation", as covered by scholars such as LACEY. On the other, the National Party in power can be understood in terms of a number of distinct phases where different policies prevailed, as revealed in the careful assessment by POSEL.

Moreover, there are numerous race-linked aspects of the economic system that were distinctive in South Africa. One can emphasize the constraints of hiring, the nature of the education system, the impact of the Bantustans and their financing, the Group Areas Act of 1950 and the forced resettlements that peaked during the 1960s and 1970s, the rise of the security state, and the economic pressures associated with sanctions. These factors did not occur at the same time.

There is some consensus that the 1950s were a decade of significant but declining economic growth, followed by the boom years of the following decade, the most expansive known in South African history. This boom period inspired persuasive contributions that emphasized the advantages apartheid was posing to capitalist development in South Africa. Classic radical analyses were put forward at the close of this phase by JOHNSTONE, by LEGASSICK, and by WOLPE. In particular, reliance on cheap, unfree labour was fundamental to the management of accumulation in South Africa. The structure of the labour market was modulated over time to meet the changing dictates of capital so as to offset the rigidities imposed by some aspects of apartheid legislation, as noted by HINDSON and POSEL.

By contrast, South Africa experienced a very much more uneven economic pattern after 1973. Slow growth was mitigated by the favourable impact of two huge increases in the gold price. The decade of international "stagflation" was, however, problematic after the golden era of postwar capitalism as in many other countries. In its final decade, from about 1983, the South African economy under apartheid experienced considerable difficulties, a very slow growth rate, and declining profit and investment rates in a period when some developing economies grew rapidly. South Africa was affected by lack of investor confidence and growing international isolation, but also suffered from problems common to countries that had built up industry on an import-substitution basis and were dependent on sales of primary products to international markets. It was also spending huge sums on building up its armed forces and on the expansion of a multi-racial bureaucracy, that the budget could not afford.

LIPTON posed a characteristic liberal riposte to the radical charge linking capitalism to apartheid. She absorbed what the radicals said about the historic circumstances of capital accumulation in agriculture and mining in South Africa, but continued to emphasize the growing salience of industry, which had to oppose apartheid in order to advance, and which, over time, became more important in influencing capital as a whole. By contrast, a new generation of radicals such as SAUL & GELB were obliged to assess apartheid in crisis, an *organic crisis* of capital that could not really be pinned down in purely economic terms.

With the end of apartheid (non-racial democratic elections were held in 1994), the debate about capitalism and apartheid began to drift into history and became less heated. A late contributor, MOLL, has tried to shift the argument away from profit and growth rates to the qualitative issues and the lost opportunities that lay behind the adoption of apartheid policies. South Africa at the end of the 20th century remained a country with low indicators in human capital resources and one of the highest Gini coefficients in the world, and thus where economic growth, even when positive, tended to benefit the majority of the population relatively little. The poorest half of the population had few skills and little capital. The security state and its multiple bureaucracies implied wastage that would take a long time to efface. It might be hoped that future contributions will focus more on the way in which South African racial politics formed and moulded the economy and its legacy rather than on the heated debate about the relation between capitalism and apartheid during the years of struggle.

BILL FREUND

See also South Africa, economic and political transition from apartheid

Apartheid, politics

Adam, Heribert and Hermann Giliomee, *Ethnic Power Mobilized: Can South Africa Change?* New Haven, Connecticut: Yale University Press, 1979

Adam, Heribert and Kogila Moodley, *South Africa without Apartheid: Dismantling Racial Domination*, Berkeley: University of California Press, 1986

Davenport, T.R.H., *South Africa: A Modern History*, 4th edition, London: Macmillan, and Toronto: University of Toronto Press, 1991

De Klerk, Willem A., *The Puritans in Africa: A Story of Afrikanerdom*, London: Collings, 1975

De Villiers, Rene, "Afrikaner Nationalism" in *The Oxford History of South Africa*, edited by Monica Wilson and Leonard Thompson, vol. 2, Oxford and New York: Oxford University Press, 1971

Jaarsveld, F.A. van, *Die evolusie van apartheid* (The Evolution of Apartheid), Cape Town: Tafelberg, 1979

Lipton, Merle, *Capitalism and Apartheid: South Africa, 1910–84*, Aldershot, Hampshire: Gower, and Totowa, New Jersey: Rowman and Allanheld, 1985

Louw, P. Eric, "Shifting Patterns of Political Discourse in the New South Africa", *Critical Studies in Mass Communication*, 11/1 (1994): 22–53

O'Meara, Dan, *Volkskapitalisme: Class, Capital and Ideology in the Development of Afrikaner Nationalism, 1934–1948*, Cambridge and New York: Cambridge University Press, 1983

Truth and Reconciliation Commission, *Truth and Reconciliation Commission of South Africa Report*, 5 vols, Cape Town: The Commission, 1999

ADAM & GILIOMEE have arguably produced the classic analysis of Afrikaner nationalism and the growth of the apartheid system. They unravel the history, economics, sociology, and politics of the struggle for Afrikaner political power and describe the sociopolitical mechanics of apartheid governance. Their book was published just after apartheid entered its crisis phase and so is useful for understanding both the emergence of apartheid and the period when the apartheid system was ascendant and seemingly unchallengeable. Giliomee's position as an academic at the most prestigious of Afrikaner universities gave this work a certain "access" to an insider's (albeit a critical insider's) knowledge about the apartheid system.

ADAM & MOODLEY effectively serves as a follow-up text to Adam & Giliomee, but Adam & Moodley examine the apartheid system in crisis and decline. This book tries to explain the crisis of apartheid. More importantly, it examines the series of sophisticated attempts that were made to save apartheid by reforming the system. When writing the book, Adam & Moodley were "exiled" from South Africa because their mixed-race marriage was outlawed.

DAVENPORT's history of South Africa contains a number of chapters (chapters 14 to 19) that are very useful for understanding the apartheid phenomenon. It is also a useful source for understanding apartheid as an unfolding policy process or sequence of events. Davenport's basic argument is that apartheid was the outcome of a struggle between black and white over the possession of land. The apartheid government briefly banned this book when it was first published.

DE KLERK is an important work for anyone studying apartheid. It argues that the roots of apartheid are located in a particular strand of Western thinking, namely Calvinism. Calvinism, when exported to the hostile environment of Africa, necessarily generated mutations of the original Calvinist project. De Klerk (an Afrikaner opposed to apartheid) argues that apartheid needs to be understood as an attempt by a small, beleaguered people to try to remake their world according to a rational plan from the radical right.

DE VILLIERS's chapter on Afrikaner nationalism provides the explanation of apartheid that became the dominant view among liberals in the Anglo-Saxon world. For DeVilliers, apartheid was at its heart a race-based conflict motivated by an Afrikaner desire for racial domination.

LIPTON has provided the most thorough unravelling of the relationship between apartheid and the capitalist system. She argues, with empirical support, that apartheid was not some aberrant Afrikaner racist ideology artificially grafted onto an unwilling Anglo-capitalist system (a position that was widely propagated by South Africa's Anglo business sector). Instead, Lipton shows how apartheid's roots lay squarely *within* the capitalist system built up by Anglo capitalists. Within the South African context she argues that apartheid was functional for, and served, capital's needs.

LOUW looks at apartheid as a discourse with its roots in Lord Milner's post-Boer War restructuring of South Africa. He explores the path by which racist discourse was born as an Anglo-colonial discourse in the early 20th century, mutated into Afrikaner nationalism in the middle of the century, and later mutated into black nationalism at the end of the century. This article also looks at the death throes of apartheid, when the National Party abandoned its own ideology.

O'MEARA produced a seminal political economic analysis of the origins of apartheid. He undertook an examination of the economic reasons for Afrikaner nationalism, which were found to be the creation of an affirmative action programme to upgrade Afrikaners who had been impoverished by British colonialism. This affirmative action programme was called "Volkskapitalisme" ("the people's capitalism"). For those seeking to understand why apartheid happened, this is arguably the most important book to read. It explains apartheid's particular vision of capitalism; its anticommunism; its relationship with the Dutch Reformed Church; and why apartheid's social engineers built the social infrastructures that they did.

THE TRUTH AND RECONCILIATION COMMISSION, in the wake of the apartheid era, undertook to confront the legacy of apartheid. For this purpose, the Truth and Reconciliation Commission was appointed under the chairmanship of Archbishop Desmond Tutu. Tutu presented the Final Report of this Commission to President Mandela on 29 October 1998. The five volumes of this report provide a useful history of apartheid as viewed by the new post-apartheid order. Especially useful are volume one, chapter 13, which provides a chronology of all apartheid legislation; volume two, which looks at the apartheid state's machinery and its activities inside and outside South Africa, the liberation movement's struggle against apartheid, and the black homeland governments; and volume 4, which explores the relationship between the apartheid state and various sectors of society (such as the press, the legal profession, the church, business, and so on).

VAN JAARSVELD produced a very useful periodization of the development of apartheid thinking. Unfortunately, his 23-page essay "The Evolution of Apartheid" (chapter one in his book of the same name) is only available in Afrikaans but those who can read Dutch, Flemish, or German should be able to understand this essay. The key value of the essay lies in the fact that Van Jaarsveld, a prominent Afrikaner nationalist academic, provides a look at apartheid from "within".

P. Eric Louw

See also Apartheid (economic), South Africa, economic transition from apartheid, South Africa, political transition from apartheid

Aphasia and related disorders

Benson, D. Frank and Alfredo Ardila, *Aphasia: A Clinical Perspective*, New York: Oxford University Press, 1996

Code, Chris and Dave J. Muller, *Aphasia Therapy*, 2nd edition, London: Cole and Whurr, 1989

Ellis, Andrew W. and Andrew W. Young, *Human Cognitive Neuropsychology: A Textbook with Readings*, revised edition, Hove, Sussex: Psychology Press, 1996

Feinberg, Todd E. and Martha Farah (editors), *Behavioral Neurology and Neuropsychology*, New York: McGraw Hill, 1997

McCarthy, Rosaleen A. and Elizabeth K. Warrington, *Cognitive Neuropsychology: A Clinical Introduction*, San Diego: Academic Press, 1990

Riddoch, M. Jane and Glyn W. Humphreys (editors), *Cognitive Neuropsychology and Cognitive Rehabilitation*, Hove, Sussex: Erlbaum, 1994

Sarno, Martha T. (editor), *Acquired Aphasia*, 3rd edition, San Diego: Academic Press, 1998

Springer, Sally P. and Georg Deutsch, *Left Brain, Right Brain*, 4th edition, New York: Freeman, 1993

Aphasia can be defined as a disturbance in language as a result of damage to, or disease of, the brain. The core ability to appreciate and use language is impaired. It can be distinguished from the ability to perceive and analyse sounds or incoming sensory information, on the one hand, and impairments in the ability to form speech sounds or the movements involved in writing, on the other. FEINBERG & FARAH include a number of chapters dealing with aspects of aphasia or related language disorders, such as disturbances in writing (agraphia) or reading (acquired dyslexia). SARNO provides a much more detailed text solely devoted to aphasia and related issues including a discussion of such things as the psychosocial consequences.

Language impairments can be examined at a number of levels. Aphasia presents what is probably the strongest and most consistent evidence of functional asymmetry in the brain. This is because aphasia and related language disturbances are most commonly associated with lesions in the left hemisphere of the brain and indicate a strong tendency for the left hemisphere to play a dominant role in language. BENSON & ARDILA take up this issue and relate laterality of the lesion producing aphasia to handedness. A small proportion of those with aphasia have right-sided lesions and these are usually people with strong left-handed tendencies where the usual pattern of lateralization of function within the brain may be partly or wholly reversed.

SPRINGER & DEUTSCH deal with the lateralization of language in much greater detail and sets this in the context of different ways of studying lateralization as well as setting speech lateralization in the context of other functions carried out by the brain. In particular they set out the evidence indicating that lateralization of function is not something that is confined to language. For example, some impairments in the appreciation of spatial relationships are more commonly found after right-hemisphere lesions.

Considering only those with left hemisphere dominance for language, there is considerable variation in the pattern of language impairment or aphasia associated with left-sided brain lesions. This variation has been described or modelled in many different ways but Benson & Ardila, as well as a chapter in Sarno, give an outline of one of the most satisfactory of these. A fundamental distinction is made between "fluent" and "nonfluent" aphasias. Nonfluent aphasias are associated with lesions in the more anterior parts of the areas involved in speech. They are characterized by, among other things, a low rate of verbal output, effortful production of speech, short phrase length, and a predominance of substantive or semantically rich words (nouns, action verbs and descriptive adjectives). The fluent aphasias associated with more posterior lesions in the speech areas of the brain, are the opposite. Verbal output is normal and there is a normal rhythm and flow to speech that does not demand undue effort from the speaker. Where words are lost, these tend to be of the more substantive kind and the fluent aphasic tends to fill the gap with circumlocutions, which are phrases introduced to obviate the need to use a word that is unavailable. Speech may often contain a lot of meaningless or near-meaningless phrases such as "that's right isn't it?" and "just as you say". Some more detailed subdivisions then follow, with both fluent and non fluent aphasias being further subdivided. What both these general forms of aphasia have in common is that they both involve at least some difficulty in naming objects or pictures of objects.

It is possible to examine more specific language functions such as naming, reading or the comprehension of spoken speech. Such analyses have been very much the domain of the cognitive neuropsychologists and examples are provided by ELLIS & YOUNG and McCARTHY & WARRINGTON. To outline but one instance, there has been considerable interest in acquired dyslexia. Acquired dyslexia is impaired reading ability following a stroke or other brain lesion in people who once were able to read fluently and who learned to read with normal facility. It therefore has to be distinguished from the more commonly encountered developmental dyslexia, where there is a difficulty in learning to read in the first place.

Some patients with acquired dyslexia may make errors suggesting a difficulty in converting the written symbols to sounds, and may be unable to pronounce a written non-word like "ding". However, they will recognize and pronounce a word like "cite". Others may show the reverse, and read "cite" as "kite" (using a hard "c") yet be able to read non-words like "ding" which are readily pronounceable by following the basic spelling rules for written English. Yet other acquired dyslexics may show reading errors in which they see a word like "bird" and read it as a semantically related but ortho-graphically dissimilar word such as "robin".

It is suggested, on the basis of evidence like this, that word recognition and reading depend upon two input routes to the brain. One is based on converting graphical representations to sounds and the other being based on some direct access to an internal semantic representation of the word without involving any conversion of graphical features to sounds.

CODE & MULLER offer a collection of chapters that outline different approaches to the very important practical problem of the treatment of aphasia. Many varied forms of therapy have been advocated but there is an increasing tendency to base therapeutic interventions on the work of the cognitive neuropsychologists as described by RIDDOCH & HUMPHREYS. Determining what really works and why remains a particular area of difficulty for aphasia therapy.

EDGAR MILLER

See also Neuropsychology

Appeal, Court of Appeal

Bailey, S.H. and M.J. Gunn, *Smith and Bailey on the Modern English Legal System*, 3rd edition, London: Sweet and Maxwell, 1996

Ingman, Terence, *The English Legal Process*, 7th edition, London: Blackstone Press, 1998
Lord Chancellor's Department, *Review of the Court of Appeal (Civil Division): Report to the Lord Chancellor, September 1997*, London: Court of Appeal (Civil Division) Review, 1997
Mansfield, Michael and Nicholas Taylor, "Post-Conviction Procedures" in *Justice in Error*, edited by Clive Walker and Keir Starmer, London: Blackstone Press, 1993
Pattenden, Rosemary, *English Criminal Appeals, 1844–1994: Appeals against Conviction and Sentence in England and Wales*, Oxford: Clarendon Press, and New York: Oxford University Press, 1996
Royal Commission on Criminal Justice, *Report*, London: HMSO, 1993 (Cm 2263)
Walker, Clive P. and Keir Starmer (editors), *Introduction to Justice in Error*, London: Blackstone Press, 1993
Walker, Clive P. and Keir Starmer, *Miscarriages of Justice: A Review of Justice in Error*, London: Blackstone Press, 1999
Zander, Michael, *Cases and Materials on the English Legal System*, 7th edition, London: Butterworths, 1996

Widely recognized as the leading text on the English legal system and aimed primarily at undergraduates, the third edition of BAILEY & GUNN takes account of developments to the end of January 1996. This text provides a clear, comprehensive account of the English legal system, dealing *inter alia* with both divisions of the Court of Appeal, civil, and criminal appeals. It is accompanied by flowcharts illustrating the court structure and the workload of the criminal and civil divisions.

This edition consolidates the previous editions work on the history of the Court of Appeal, leading to the Judicature Acts. Tables are provided showing statistics of numbers dealt with from 1938 to 1995. The work also takes account of recent developments in the area of criminal appeals caused by the enactment of the Criminal Appeal Act 1995, looking at the changes in the grounds of appeal, the contribution of the Criminal Cases Review Commission in the post-appeal procedure, and has a section on the reception of fresh evidence, including all relevant case law. The area of civil appeals is comprehensively covered, detailing the statutory provisions for appeal, conditions for grant of leave, and procedures. The book gives details of decision making and associated case law. In addition, it details extensively appeals on tribunal decisions and judicial review.

In the most up-to-date and wide-ranging text on the English legal system stating the law as at the end of March 1998, INGMAN expands on the many previous editions of this text, taking account of all relevant developments in the areas of both divisions of the Court of Appeal, civil, and criminal appeals.

Ingman looks into the history of the appeal courts, dating back to the creation of the Court of Appeal, Civil Division by the Judicature Act 1873, and the 1966 Criminal Appeal Act which established the Criminal Division. He then examines the composition of the court, giving details of appeal court judges over the years and then extensively analyses both divisions' jurisdictions, their governing statutes, procedures, and practices. He includes analysis of recent reports on the appeals and the working of the courts, most notably the Royal Commission on Criminal Justice in 1993 and the Review of the Court of Appeal Civil Division in 1997 and subsequent statutory changes and procedural developments in the system. Ingman also includes an extensive examination of the criminal postappeal system, detailing the notorious miscarriage of justice cases and the previous and present mechanisms for their correction.

Ingman also provides a section on appeals against the decisions of public bodies, including recent developments in case law on areas such as judicial review and private law proceedings. Overall, this text would be suitable for the teaching of undergraduate students on both civil and criminal appeals, both divisions of the Court of Appeal, appeals in the administrative law system, and postappeal remedies in criminal cases.

As a comprehensive overview of the Court of Appeal Civil Division, the report by the LORD CHANCELLOR'S DEPARTMENT provides examination of its rules, procedures, and working methods, covering the scope of its jurisdiction, analysis of the appropriate constitution of the Court for different types of cases, and comments on required legal and administrative support. Although not a text designed mainly with students and academics in mind, this report clearly sets out relevant issues regarding the Civil Division of the Court of Appeal, and comes to important conclusions as to the way its efficiency and productivity can be maximized. It also examines the aims of this division of the court, both in public and private aspects relating to the maintenance of standards, and the development of clarification in its practices and procedures. As an extensive yet thorough examination of the Court of Appeal Civil Division, all relevant issues are taken into account.

PATTENDEN takes account of recent developments following the Royal Commission on Criminal Justice Report in 1993, examining all provisions for appeal against conviction and sentence in the criminal courts. These are assessed in the light of their historical origins, development, and statistics. This text is a detailed study in a league of its own, and while it may be too detailed for an undergraduate English legal system course, it provides invaluable information for those wishing more in-depth material.

Although this book only takes into account developments up to 12 October 1994 in its main text, the vital changes as a result of the 1995 Criminal Appeal Act are detailed in the appendix. What this text lacks in recent case law is more than made up for by Pattenden's detailed and systematic analysis of case law and practices, dealing with all types of criminal appeals at all levels throughout the court structure.

A fundamental report, providing the foundations for the recent developments in the Criminal Appeal process, the REPORT OF THE ROYAL COMMISSION ON CRIMINAL JUSTICE provides a comprehensive review of the pre-1997 criminal appeal procedures and informative criticism and suggestions for future reform. These reforms formed the basis of the Criminal Appeal Act 1995 and the establishment of the Criminal Cases Review Commission to investigate and refer cases of alleged miscarriages of justice.

This report was written following many submissions to the Royal Commission, and is the accumulation of legal opinions of academics and practitioners alike. The text provides a good overview of many aspects of the criminal justice process and suggestions for reform and would make a good research text for anyone researching the background to the new criminal appeal system.

WALKER & STARMER's first book (1993) came out just before the publication of the 1993 Royal Commission on Criminal Justice report. It looks at the English legal system in the light of the recent revelations of miscarriages of justice, showing the possible factors contributing to these, and noting suggested solutions. This is a valuable text, which although now out of date on the criminal appeals context, contains valid background information. For the postappeal system, many case details and statistics are relevant for the effective examination of the period in question. Two chapters are particularly pertinent to the subject of criminal appeals. First, the introduction by Clive Walker is more than just a brief introduction. In this chapter Walker provides an insight into the nature of miscarriages of justice, having regard to the terms of reference of the Royal Commission on Criminal Justice. He describes the various factors leading to miscarriage of justice cases and chronologizes the notorious cases and their appeals and then goes on to look at the common forms of miscarriages of justice in practice. In their chapter on post-conviction procedures, MANSFIELD & TAYLOR look in detail at the role of the Home Secretary, his powers and his practices in dealing with applications for appeal after all normal appeal rights had been exhausted. They go on to examine the role of the Court of Appeal in dealing with allegations of miscarriage of justice and the admission of fresh evidence, and the still-relevant case law on this issue. They then suggest several reforms to make the appeal and post-appeal system fairer. As an appendix, the relevant sections of the Criminal Appeal Act 1968 are included.

In an update on their 1993 text, WALKER & STARMER (1999) provide a systematic analysis of changes in the criminal justice system since their last edition. Since then there has been much official response to the problems existing in the criminal justice system, first by the report of the Royal Commission on Criminal Justice, and then in legislative implementation and other reforms. This book examines whether there has been any notable improvement in the criminal justice system as a result of these reforms. Drawing on the research and experience of the contributors from the academic and practitioner fields, this text provides essential reading as both a source book and for critical analysis of the subject. This text would be suitable for students studying criminology, criminal justice, and legal systems.

ZANDER's text compiles material on the English legal system, including criminal and civil appeals and the corresponding divisions of the Court of Appeal, from a wide variety of sources. It looks at the court structure and statutory provisions governing the powers used in criminal and civil appeals and is up to date on developments such as the Royal Commission on Criminal Justice report, the establishment of the Criminal Cases Review Commission, and the Woolf report on civil justice, and has supporting statistics and case law. The *New Law Journal* has stated that the scope of this text's material is "wide and deep, critical and constructive", and indeed this is the case for all material up until May 1996.

ANNABELLE JAMES

Applied social research

Argyris, Chris, Robert Putnam and Diana McLain Smith, *Action Science: Concepts, Methods and Skills for Research and Intervention*, San Francisco: Jossey Bass, 1985

Bickman, Leonard and Debra J. Rog (editors), *Handbook of Applied Social Research Methods*, Thousand Oaks, California and London: Sage, 1998

Galster, George (editor), *Reality and Research: Social Science and US Urban Policy since 1960*, Washington, DC: Urban Institute Press, and Aldershot, Hampshire: Avebury, 1996

Haas, Peter J. and J. Fred Springer, *Applied Policy Research: Concepts and Cases*, New York: Garland, 1998

Hedrick, Terry E., Leonard Bickman and Debra J. Rog, *Applied Research Design: A Practical Guide*. Newbury Park, California and London: Sage, 1993

Kimmel, Allan J., *Ethics and Values in Applied Social Research*, Newbury Park, California and London: Sage, 1988

Research in Social Problems and Public Policy, 1979–

Ristock, Janice L. and Joan Pennell, *Community Research as Empowerment: Feminist Links, Postmodern Interruptions*, Oxford and New York: Oxford University Press, 1996

Robson, Colin, *Real World Research: A Resource for Social Scientists and Practitioner-Researchers*, Oxford and Cambridge, Massachusetts: Blackwell, 1993

Vaughan, Roger J. and Terry F. Buss, *Communicating Social Science Research to Policymakers*, Thousand Oaks, California and London: Sage, 1998

Wenger, G. Clare (editor), *The Research Relationship: Practice and Politics in Social Policy Research*, London and Boston: Allen and Unwin, 1987

Yin, Robert K., *Applications of Case Study Research*, Newbury Park, California and London: Sage, 1993

Increasingly, social scientists are being called upon to conduct research that is considered useful in informing policy. Such research is referred to as applied social research, and is distinguished from basic research in a number of ways including its purpose, context, and methods used. HEDRICK, BICKMAN & ROG document these differences and set out the main features of and issues involved in applied research design, although predominantly from a quantitative perspective. This book is one of a series of applied social research methods books published by Sage, each of which deals with a special topic.

Despite these differences, applied social research draws on the methods used in basic research, and the many similarities between these types of research have led to challenges to the usefulness of the distinction. These challenges are discussed in KIMMEL, who addresses the broad ethical issues and dilemmas involved in undertaking applied social research. These issues include rights to confidentiality and privacy by research participants, as well as the need to obtain informed consent. Other ethical concerns are also discussed and it is argued that clarification of these problems is an important feature of applied research.

While research methods are mostly common to both basic and applied research, the ways in which they are used can differ. Texts devoted specifically to outlining research methods in an applied context are useful to supplement the wide range of texts on research methods and design. ROBSON includes descriptions of the most commonly used research methods and how these are adapted to the specific demands of applied research. BICKMAN & ROG includes a collection of articles covering the major topics and issues in applied social research contributed by leading experts in the field.

The case study is a research design that is particularly appropriate to applied research, where inclusion of context is a major aspect of a study. Developments of case study methodology and its application to a variety of research problems including education, management information systems, and evaluation of social programs are outlined by YIN, building on his earlier work in this field.

Since much applied social research is conducted in business, government, or community settings and involves interaction and cooperation with government agencies, community groups, and other stakeholders, many applied researchers have seen their role as active participants, working with the stakeholders, as distinct from detached, neutral observers. ARGYRIS, PUTNAM & McLAIN SMITH outlines the principles of action research appropriate for working with stakeholders.

Ways of involving stakeholders in research can range from consultation, where control of the research is firmly in the hands of the researchers, to empowerment, where stakeholders take control of the research project. RISTOCK & PENNELL argues for empowerment in community research and provides examples and guidelines for how this can be achieved.

The outcomes of much applied social research impact directly or indirectly on policy. HAAS & SPRINGER describes the features of policy research, provides guidelines for the design and conduct of policy research, and gives examples of case studies on the application of policy research in the US. GALSTER provides many additional examples of the application of social research to urban policy in the US. The case studies included in this collection find mixed results: sometimes the research was implemented as intended, sometimes the studies were excellent but ignored, and sometimes the studies were conducted merely to support policy adopted for other reasons.

The problem of communicating research to policy makers with a view to getting better implementation of findings is taken up by VAUGHAN & BUSS, which provides a guide for researchers who want their ideas and research to have influence on policy makers. There is often a gap, however, between research findings and their implementation in the policy arena. Communicating research findings to policy makers does not of itself guarantee implementation, as many other factors intervene between the research outcomes and the policy decision. These factors are dealt with by WENGER who examines the political and other factors which hinder the implementation of social policy research.

While the references included here give many examples of applied social research, many more examples and discussions of methods and design can be found in applied journals in the various disciplines that make up the social sciences. An example is RESEARCH IN SOCIAL PROBLEMS AND PUBLIC POLICY, which includes articles dealing with these issues.

RALPH HALL

See also Research methods, social

Appraisal, performance appraisal

Arvey, R.D. and K.R. Murphy, "Performance Evaluation in Work Settings", *Annual Review of Psychology*, 49 (1998): 141–68

Bernardin, H. John, Jeffrey S. Kane, Susan Ross, James D. Spina and Dennis L. Johnson, "Performance Appraisal Design, Development, and Implementation" in *Handbook of Human Resource Management*, edited by Gerald R. Ferris, Sherman D. Rosen and Darold T. Barnum, Cambridge, Massachusetts: Blackwell, 1995

Cardy, Robert L. and Gregory H. Dobbins, *Performance Appraisal: Alternative Perspectives*, Cincinnati: South-Western, 1994

Drenth, Pieter J.D., "Personnel Appraisal" in *Handbook of Work and Organizational Psychology*, 2nd edition, vol. 3: *Personnel Psychology*, edited by Pieter J.D. Drenth, Henk Thierry and Charles J. De Wolff, Hove, Sussex: Psychology Press, 1998

Fletcher, Clive, *Appraisal: Routes to Improved Performance*, 2nd edition, London: Institute of Personnel and Development, 1997

Folger, Robert, Mary A. Konovsky and Russell Cropanzano, "A Due Process Metaphor for Performance Appraisal", *Research in Organizational Behaviour*, 14 (1992): 129–77

Heneman, Robert L. and Courtney Von Hippel, "The Assessment of Job Performance: Focusing Attention on Context, Process, and Group Issues" in *The Human Resource Management Handbook*, part 3, edited by David Lewin, Daniel J.B. Mitchell and Mahmood A. Zaidi, Greenwich, Connecticut: Jai Press, 1997

Murphy, Kevin R. and Jeanette N. Cleveland, *Understanding Performance Appraisal: Social, Organizational, and Goal-Based Perspectives*, Thousand Oaks, California: Sage, 1995

Smither, James W. (editor), *Performance Appraisal: State of the Art in Practice*, San Francisco: Jossey Bass, 1998

Williams, Richard S., *Performance Management: Perspectives on Employee Performance*, London and Boston: International Thomson Business Press, 1998

Performance appraisal or performance management? If nothing else we are seeing a change in terminology. Whereas an organization once would have referred to "performance appraisal", today the likelihood is that that term will have been replaced by the label "performance management" in the same way that the term "human resource management" has come to replace "personnel management" (but without necessarily any real change in philosophy or practice). This, though, may be too simplistic a view of the change that we are seeing in the latter part of the 1990s. As WILLIAMS notes, the term "performance management" has several meanings, and much turns on the level of analysis that we adopt – individual, organizational, or something in between. Williams reviews contemporary perspectives on performance management, and ranges over such issues as the nature of performance (organizational and individual), feedback, reward, and the design, implementation, and evaluation of systems.

"Performance management" and "performance appraisal" might be seen as interchangeable labels for the same practice (or set of practices) but there also is the view that performance appraisal is one component of the latter. FLETCHER includes a chapter that illustrates this perspective. Fletcher also considers contemporary issues such as the use of multi-source, multi-level appraisal/feedback.

Fletcher's book is aimed firmly at a practitioner audience (including students on vocational courses, such as courses in personnel management). The volume edited by SMITHER takes a similar approach. This has three parts. The first part, on the performance-appraisal environment, includes chapters that reflect political, customer, and quality perspectives on performance appraisal. One chapter considers international aspects and there is another that deals with legal issues. The latter concentrates on the situation in the US. Part two is about methods and it deals with a range of issues: fairness in performance management, team appraisal, multi-source appraisal, self-assessment, the evaluation of executive performance, and appraisal training. Part three examines linkages to other human resource management systems such as training and development and performance-related pay.

Taken together, these three volumes provide substantial coverage of the field of performance appraisal, especially from the perspective of the practitioner. A great many other textbooks exist. Of particular interest are those by CARDY & DOBBINS and MURPHY & CLEVELAND. Although relevant to practitioners, these are much more academic in their tenor than either Fletcher or Smither. They are similar to each other to the extent that they both provide wide-ranging overviews of the performance-appraisal literature and they include the sort of topics that one would expect to see in any appraisal text, such as consideration of different methods of appraisal and rating formats. They also bring their own particular perspectives to bear. For example, Cardy & Dobbins devote a chapter to laboratory studies versus field studies. They also provide one of the relatively few treatments of the contribution of person and system factors to performance.

A distinguishing feature of Murphy & Cleveland is that they put forward a goal-orientated model of appraisal. They are referring here not to work goals (see entry on Goals, goal setting) but rather the goals that those involved in appraisal (such as appraisers, appraisees, or human resource managers) might wish to accomplish. They view appraisal as more of a social-psychological and communication process than as measurement and contend that appraisal systems should be designed so as to try to meet the goals of the several interested parties who have a stake. This stands in contrast to the traditional perspective that tends to see organizational goals for appraisal as supreme. Although overlapping, these two volumes should be regarded as essential reading because of their distinctiveness.

As well as the several textbooks there is an enormous number of papers in journals, chapters in books, and review essays. The following represents an illustrative selection. It draws on material published in the past five years for the most part. FOLGER, KONOVSKY & CROPANZANO is of particular interest because it offers a different perspective from the traditional emphasis on measurement that has characterized so much of the performance-appraisal literature. The authors provide a critique of the measurement perspective by challenging three underlying assumptions. They are also critical of the political perspective that arose, in their view, because of inadequacies in the traditional model (considered also in Cardy & Dobbins). Instead, they offer a "due process" model that they see as overcoming deficiencies in the measurement and political models. Although not the first treatment of performance appraisal from an organizational justice perspective this essay is especially noteworthy because the comparative assessment they present.

BERNARDIN *et al.* is of interest because the authors convey a view of individual performance that might be seen as being at odds with the behavioural view that has come to feature in much of the social sciences literature (see also Cardy & Dobbins and Williams). They define performance in terms of outcomes, a view that is more commonly found in practitioner orientated "how-to-do-it" volumes. They also refer to situational constraints that may inhibit performance. In most other respects, however, they offer a general overview of the field.

HENEMAN & VON HIPPEL is another example of an overview of performance appraisal. What sets it apart from many is the concentration on certain aspects of appraisal (as indicated by the subtitle). They claim that one of the changes in practice that has taken place is that greater emphasis is afforded to the appraisal of team performance, although this is not to say that this shift has been at the expense of the assessment of individual performance. They also pay some attention to the context within which performance appraisal operates. Again, this is not a new theme in the literature (see also Murphy & Cleveland), but their treatment is helpful as it points the reader in the direction of further material. They are also consistent with the general body of contemporary literature that views performance appraisal in broad process terms, not simply as a measurement activity.

ARVEY & MURPHY provide a rapid introduction to literature that has appeared from 1993. They organize their work according to a number of themes, one of which is the definition of job performance; this has emerged as an especially important theme during the 1990s. Arvey & Murphy summarize the literature that takes a predominantly behavioural approach to defining performance. They also examine measurement issues. Although other perspectives on performance appraisal have been developed, the interest in measurement has far from disappeared. They consider such psychometric issues as validity and rater accuracy as well as fairness and sources of appraisals. They also explore utility analysis, which, although not much taken up by practitioners, continues to attract some academic interest: Arvey & Murphy direct the reader to relevant literature.

By far the bulk of the literature and research on performance appraisal has US origins. Some UK sources have been suggested above but their coverage none the less reflects the US dominance. This is true also of DRENTH but his chapter also has the merit of drawing on European literature.

RICHARD WILLIAMS

See also Feedback, Goals, goal setting, Performance evaluation

Aquinas, Thomas *c.*1225–1274

Italian theologian

Aquinas, Thomas, *Opera Omnia iussu impensaque Leonis XIII P.M.* [The Whole Works Printed at the Order of Pope Leo XIII], Rome: De Propaganda Fide, 1882–

Aquinas, Thomas, *Selected Political Writings*, edited by A.P. D'Entrèves, Oxford: Blackwell, 1948

Aquinas, Thomas, *On Kingship, to the King of Cyprus*, edited by I.T. Eschmann, Toronto: Pontifical Institute for Medieval Studies, 1949

Boyle, Leonard E., "The De Regno and the Two Powers" in *Essays in Honour of Anton Charles Pegis*, edited by J. Reginald O'Donnell, Toronto: Pontifical Institute of Medieval Studies, 1974

Chenu, Marie Dominique, *Toward Understanding St Thomas*, Chicago: Regnery, 1964

Copleston, F.C., *Aquinas*, Harmondsworth: Penguin, 1955

Finnis, John, *Aquinas: Moral, Political, and Legal Theory*, Oxford and New York: Oxford University Press, 1998

Gilson, Etienne, *Autour de Saint Thomas*, Paris: Vrin, 1983

Thomas Aquinas was one of the most influential scholars and theologians of the Middle Ages. His various works, including his great treatise, *Summa Theologica*, had an immense influence on the development of political theory, philosophy, and law. In many respects, he must be given a place next to Aristotle and Plato in the pantheon of great philosophers. Aquinas has been the subject of countless biographies and his works have been published and republished both in the original Latin and in translations for centuries.

AQUINAS (1882–) is the great modern edition of Aquinas' work commissioned by Pope Leo XIII in 1879 and which began publication in 1882. Volumes continue to appear. It is the standard scholarly edition for those works published so far.

D'Entreves was one of the great historians of political philosophy of the first half of the 20th century. His collection of selections in English from Aquinas' works on political philosophy, AQUINAS (1948), are expertly chosen to represent the essence of Aquinas' thought and are the standard collection in English.

One of the most important political works in the canon is Aquinas' advice treatise on government written for the King of Cyprus. AQUINAS (1949) is an English translation that presents an excellent text of the work for the reader who cannot use the Latin original.

BOYLE's work presents a learned study of Aquinas' thought on one of the key political and philosophical issues of the Middle Ages: the proper relationship between church and state. Father Boyle is an expert on medieval political philosophy as well as papal government in the Middle Ages.

CHENU presents an introduction and general overview of Thomas Aquinas' works in all fields for the general reader in English. The author is one of the most respected of modern historians of medieval philosophy.

COPLESTON is an excellent introductory biography and study of Aquinas and his works in English. It is written for the general reader and beginner student. The author is a prominent historian of philosophy.

FINNIS is the most recent study of Aquinas' political philosophy by the foremost exponent of the importance of natural law theory writing in English today. The volume begins with a brief biography and then moves on to a critical analysis of Aquinas' thought. The volume treats Aquinas by subject rather than by individual work. This volume is not for the beginner but, rather, is aimed at the advanced student or scholar.

The GILSON volume is the leading study of Aquinas by one of the most prominent French-speaking historians of philosophy. As such it presents a somewhat different perspective on Aquinas from studies by English-speaking authors.

M.H. HOEFLICH

Arbitrage

Black, Fischer and Myron Scholes, "The Pricing of Options and Corporate Liabilities", *Journal of Political Economy*, 81 (1975): 637–54

Cox, John and Stephen Ross, "A Survey of Some New Results in Financial Option Pricing Theory", *Journal of Finance*, 31/1 (1976): 383–402

Cox, John, Stephen Ross and Mark Rubinstein, "Option Pricing: A Simplified Approach", *Journal of Financial Economics*, 7/3 (1979): 229–63

Dybvig, Philip and Stephen Ross, Arbitrage entry in *The New Palgrave: A Dictionary of Economics*, edited by John Eatwell, Murray Milgate and Peter Newman, 4 vols, London: Macmillan, and New York: Stockton Press, 1987

Jensen, Michael, Arbitrage, Information Theft and Insider Trading entry in *The New Palgrave: A Dictionary of Economics*, edited by John Eatwell, Murray Milgate and Peter Newman, 4 vols, London: Macmillan, and New York: Stockton Press, 1987

Keynes, John Maynard, *A Tract on Monetary Reform*, London: Macmillan, 1923, New York: Harcourt Brace, 1924; in *The Collected Writings of John Maynard Keynes*, vol. 4, London: Macmillan, and New York: Cambridge University Press, 1971

Merton, Robert, "The Theory of Rational Option Pricing", *Bell Journal of Economics and Management Science*, 4/1 (1973): 141–83

Modigliani, Franco and Merton Miller, "The Cost of Capital, Corporate Finance, and the Theory of Investment", *American Economic Review*, 48 (1958): 261–97

Ross, Stephen, "Risk, Return, and Arbitrage" in *Risk and Return in Finance*, edited by Irwin Friend and James L. Bicksler, Cambridge, Massachusetts: Ballinger, 1977

Varian, Hal, "The Arbitrage Principle in Financial Economics", *Journal of Economic Perspectives*, 1/2 (1987): 55–72

A situation in which it is possible for an investor to earn a positive rate of return without investing any funds nor taking any risk is known as an arbitrage opportunity. Hence, arbitrage relates to an investment strategy in which a certain return is guaranteed without any investment. The study of arbitrage in financial economics is principally the study of the implications of no arbitrage. One consequence of no arbitrage in financial markets is the law of one price. The law of one price states that identical assets will sell at the same price in different markets apart from transportation costs. While arbitrage is recognized as a pervading principle in economics, especially financial economics, it has been used mainly in securities and option pricing, from the original BLACK & SCHOLES derivation of option prices to the pricing of new exotic options. This entry reflects that bias.

KEYNES was the first to enunciate the parity theory of the forward exchange based on the law of one price. This theory essentially states that there is a fixed relationship between the spot exchange rate, the forward exchange rate, the domestic interest rate, and the foreign interest rate if there is no arbitrage. While modern discussions of the no arbitrage condition take place mainly in the context of pricing of risky financial assets, Keynes' original work is still worth reading for its ingenious approach to the topic.

ROSS has contributed to the formulation and development of modern no-arbitrage analysis through the study of underlying and derivative securities pricing. His elegant but intuitive exposition provides an excellent introduction to the concept and its applications. Other financial economists had earlier made significant contributions in the application of the no-arbitrage condition to the pricing of derivatives, but Ross is primarily responsible for the use of this principle in the derivation of an equilibrium asset pricing model. Ross presented the first statement and proof that the absence of arbitrage implied the existence of non-negative-state-space prices and, more generally, of a positive linear operator that could be used to value risky assets. The asset pricing model arising from this observation is the arbitrage pricing theory.

The work of Black and Scholes has had a big impact on the pricing of derivatives. Their original derivation of the pricing of call options is founded on no-arbitrage arguments. In particular, they relied on the fact that a riskless portfolio made up of the underlying stock and a call option on the stock must yield the risk-free rate of return, otherwise an arbitrage situation will result. This is a demonstration of the law of one price – a riskless portfolio will yield the same return as the riskless asset even though the two entities are structurally different.

DYBVIG & ROSS, present a detailed exposition of several financial applications of the no-arbitrage condition. They begin with the definition of arbitrage and the corresponding no-arbitrage condition. They show that the absence of arbitrage is implied by the existence of an optimum for any agent who prefers more or less. They also give the first statement and proof of the fundamental theorem of asset pricing. The major implication of this theorem is that the no-arbitrage condition necessarily leads to a linear asset pricing function. The rest of the paper is devoted to examples of applications of the no-arbitrage condition in option pricing, corporate finance, asset pricing, and efficient markets.

MERTON and COX & ROSS applied the no-arbitrage principle to derive bounds to option prices, the relationship between call and put prices, and between American and European options. They also derived necessary and sufficient conditions on option prices for arbitrage to be impossible. The significance of using the arbitrage approach is that it is not necessary to specify any utility preferences or asset price distribution functions. Using the no-arbitrage argument, Cox & Ross derived what they termed a "complete set of qualitative properties of any given collection of options".

COX, ROSS & RUBINSTEIN derive the binomial option-pricing model based purely on arbitrage arguments. They show that creating a hedge portfolio using a combination of options and primitive securities when there is no arbitrage will lead to a unique equilibrium for the option. As is common with most of these papers the arbitrage approach usually implies one can do away with complex mathematics and still derive very fundamental and robust results.

MODIGLIANI & MILLER use no-arbitrage arguments to derive a number of fundamental corporate finance propositions. Their capital structure and dividend irrelevance propositions state that, in a perfect capital market, the capital structure or the dividend policy of a firm is irrelevant in valuing the firm. This implies that firms that are identical in all respects apart from their capital structure will be priced equally. Similarly, firms that are identical in all respects apart from their dividend policy will be priced equally. If equality in valuation does not hold then there will be opportunity for arbitrage. While this is one of the earliest uses of (no) arbitrage in deriving equilibrium conditions, the power of the argument was not realized until much later mainly through the works of Ross.

VARIAN makes a cogent case that the no-arbitrage hypothesis is one of the most basic unifying concepts for the study of financial markets. He starts by showing that if a complete set of markets for all Arrow–Debreu securities exists, and the price of an asset ever deviated from the price of a portfolio of Arrow–Debreu securities that generates the same pattern of payoffs, then there would be a sure way of making money; in other words there would be an arbitrage opportunity. If no arbitrage possibilities exist and a complete set of Arrow–Debreu securities are marketed, then any asset can be valued in terms of prices of the Arrow–Debreu assets. The arbitrage argument has been used to derive several results in the theory of financial markets including the value additivity theorem and option pricing.

JENSEN approaches the topic of arbitrage from a slightly different angle. He focuses on the activities of arbitrageurs. He argues that arbitrageurs provide important productive services to investors. According to Jensen, much of the opposition to arbitrage and the attempt to identify it with insider trading fails to recognize that target shareholder interests are served by a legal rule that allows the producer of privately created information to share that information with others, including arbitrageurs. He contends that a distinction should be made between insider trading, which is economically damaging, and trading based on information that is obtained legally albeit in private. He illustrates with several examples. In this context, the activities of arbitrageurs to take advantage of arbitrage opportunities leads to efficient price discovery and efficient allocation of resources.

EBEN OTUTEYE

Arbitrage pricing theory

Bansal, Ravi, David A. Hsieh and S. Viswanathan, "A New Approach to International Arbitrage Pricing", *Journal of Finance*, 48/5 (1993): 1719–47

Chan, Louis K.C., J. Karceski and Josef Lakonishok, "The Risk and Returns from Factors", *Journal of Financial and Quantitative Analysis*, 33/2 (1998): 159–88

Chen, Nai-fu, Richard Roll and Stephen A. Ross, "Economic Forces and the Stock Market", *Journal of Business*, 59/3 (1986): 383–403

Connor, Gregory and Robert A. Korajczyk, "The Arbitrage Pricing Theory and Multifactor Models of Asset Returns", *LSE Discussion Paper*, 149 (September 1992): 1–94

Connor, G., "The Three Types of Factor Models: A Comparison of Their Explanatory Power", *Financial Analysts Journal* (May/June 1995): 42–46

Ferson, Wayne E. and Robert A. Korajczyk, "Do Arbitrage Pricing Models Explain the Predictability of Stock Returns?", *Journal of Business*, 68/3 (1995): 309–49

Geweke, John and Guofu Zhou, "Measuring the Pricing Error of the Arbitrage Pricing Theory", *Review of Financial Studies*, 9/2 (1996): 557–87

Handa, Puneet and Scott C. Linn, "Arbitrage Pricing with Estimation Risk", *Journal of Financial and Quantitative Analysis*, 28/1 (1993): 81–100

MacKinlay, A. Craig, "Multifactor Models Do Not Explain Deviations from the CAPM", *Journal of Financial Economics*, 38/1 (1995): 3–28

Roll, Richard, "R^2", *Journal of Finance*, 43/3 (1988): 541–66

Ross, S., "Risk, Return and Arbitrage" in *Risk and Return in Finance*, edited by Irwin Friend and James L. Bicksler, 2 vols, Cambridge, Massachusetts: Ballinger, 1977

Shanken, Jay, "On the Estimation of Beta-Pricing Models", *Review of Financial Studies*, 5/1 (1992): 1–33

The arbitrage pricing theory (APT) by ROSS, and its extensions, constitute an important branch of asset pricing theory and are regarded as a primary alternative to the capital asset pricing model (CAPM). Ross's basic insight is intuitive. Suppose that stock and bond returns are governed by a set of unobservable sources. It follows that such a system lends itself naturally to factor modelling. The random return of each security can then be decomposed into a small number of common, or pervasive, factors, plus an asset-specific random variable.

The relative performance between the CAPM and the APT is often examined. ROLL compares the explanatory power of the two models using both the monthly and daily returns on stocks traded on the New York and American Stock Exchanges. He finds that, even with hindsight, the ability to explain stock price changes by either model is modest. Empirically, there is only a weak relation between the explanatory power and either the firm's size or its industry. There is little improvement in the explanatory power (R^2) from eliminating all dates surrounding news reports in the financial press.

One of the most cited contributions to the literature on macroeconomic variable models is CHEN, ROLL & ROSS. They observe that exogenous forces drive asset prices as daily experience seems to support the view that prices react to unexpected news. If these forces are not diversifiable, the market will compensate investors for bearing those risks. They find that the most significant forces are industrial production, changes in the risk premium, twists in the yield curve, and somewhat more weakly, measures of unanticipated inflation and changes in expected inflation during periods when these variables were highly volatile. Contrary to previous belief, they find that market return is not priced despite its high content of explanatory power.

CONNOR & KORAJCZYK provide a detailed survey on the development of APT theory and its extensions. They provide a theoretical foundation for the strict, approximate, and conditional factor models. The pricing restrictions under different assumptions are also discussed. A large number of empirical papers on APT are reviewed. This paper contains over 300 references and serves as an excellent starting point for a literature search.

Multifactor models can be divided into three types: macroeconomic, fundamental, and statistical factor models. Macroeconomic factor models use observable economic time series, such as inflation and interest rates, as measures of the pervasive shocks to security returns (see Chen, Roll & Ross). Fundamental factor models use the returns on portfolios associated with observed security attributes such as dividends yield, the book-to-market ratio, and industry identifiers. Statistical factor models derive their pervasive factors from factor analysis of the panel data set of security returns. CONNOR examines the explanatory power of each model using US equity returns. He finds that, under a particular specification of each model, the statistical and fundamental factor models substantially outperform the macroeconomic factor model. The fundamental factor model slightly outperforms the statistical factor model.

One of the issues in testing the APT is the appropriate number of factors. Connor & Korajczyk provide a summary of the empirical consideration of the appropriate number of factors in both the strict and approximate factor models.

Another issue is the errors-in-variable (EIV) problem associated with the traditional two-pass regression technique used in most empirical tests on the APT and the CAPM. As SHANKEN points out, the estimates from the first-pass time-series regression usually contain estimation errors. The traditional statistical inference often overstates the precision of price of risk estimates in the second-pass cross-sectional regression. He derives an asymptotically consistent correction for the EIV problem. Modifications to accommodate serial correlation in market-wide factors are also discussed.

Besides the EIV problem, HANDA & LINN point out that, in reality, investors do not usually have complete information to estimate the parameters of the asset pricing models. This adds an extra element of risk to the already uncertain prospect of holding financial securities. This estimation risk may not be diversified away and, therefore, influences both the factor betas and asset returns. Intuitively, investors attributed higher systematic risk to assets with low information than to assets with high information and, hence, this extra estimation risk effects not only the off-diagonal elements of the covariance matrix of returns, but does so differentially for high and low information assets. This implies that a time-series regression of historic returns on the returns of a set of factors mimicking portfolios yields estimates of the complete information betas and not the betas used by investors.

GEWEKE & ZHOU provide an exact Bayesian framework for analysing the APT. Their approach involves measuring the APT pricing restriction by obtaining its exact posterior distribution. The advantage of this procedure is that there is no need to estimate separately either the factors or the factor loadings to infer the validity of the APT, and hence it can avoid the EIV problem. Using monthly portfolio returns ranked by industries and market capitalization, they find little evidence for more than one factor.

BANSAL, HSIEH & VISWANATHAN provide a new approach to model the APT. They derive a nonlinear arbitrage-pricing model that requires no restrictions on the payoff space. On comparison with a conditional linear factor model and an unconditional linear factor model, they find that only the nonlinear arbitrage-pricing model performs well in explaining the time series behaviour of a cross-section of international returns.

CHAN, KARCESKI & LAKONISHOK examine the performance of several factors in capturing return comovements. They find that factors associated with the market, firm size, past return, book-to-market, and dividend yield help explain return co-movement on an out-of-sample basis. Like Connor, Chan, Karceski & Lakonishok find little support for the macroeconomic factor model.

FERSON & KORAJCZYK is the first study to compare the prespecified economic factor model and the asymptotic principal component on conditional asset returns. They examine the predictability in US stock returns for monthly, quarterly, and annual investment horizons. Their analysis shows that performance of the principal components and the prespecified factor models are broadly the same.

LIBON FUNG

See also Capital asset pricing models

Archetype

Campbell, Joseph, *The Hero with a Thousand Faces*, New York: Pantheon, 1949; 2nd edition Princeton, New Jersey: Princeton University Press, 1968, London: Abacus, 1975

Culbertson, Philip, "Men Dreaming of Men: Using Mitch Walker's 'Double Animus' in Pastoral Care", *Harvard Theological Review*, 86/2 (1993): 219–32

Franz, Marie-Louise von, *Archetypal Patterns in Fairy Tales*, Toronto: Inner City, 1997

Jacobi, Jolande, *Complex, Archetype, Symbol in the Psychology of C.G. Jung*, New York: Pantheon, and London: Routledge, 1959

Jaffé, Aniela, *The Myth of Meaning in the Work of C.G. Jung*, London: Hodder and Stoughton, 1970; as *The Myth of Meaning*, New York: Putnam, 1971

Jung, C.G., "Archetypes of the Collective Unconscious" in *The Archetypes and the Collective Unconscious*, vol. 9, part 1 of *Collected Works*, New York: Pantheon, 1959; 2nd edition Princeton, New Jersey: Princeton University Press, 1968

Jung, C.G., *Aion: Researches into the Phenomenology of the Self*, vol. 9, part 2 of *Collected Works*, New York:

Pantheon, 1959; 2nd edition, Princeton, New Jersey: Princeton University Press, 1968

Jung, C.G., Marie-Louise von Franz, Joseph Henderson, Jolande Jacobi and Aniela Jaffé, *Man and His Symbols*, London: Aldus, and New York: Doubleday, 1964

Monick, Eugene, *Phallos: Sacred Image of the Masculine*, Toronto: Inner City, 1987

Palmer, Michael, *Freud and Jung on Religion*, London and New York: Routledge, 1997

Segal, Robert A. (editor), *Encountering Jung on Mythology*, Princeton, New Jersey: Princeton University Press, 1998; as *Jung on Mythology*, London: Routledge, 1998

Walker, Steven F., *Jung and the Jungians on Myth*, New York: Garland, 1995

The theory of archetypes is usually attributed to the great Swiss psychologist C.G. Jung. JUNG (1959a) discussed archetypes and their interpretation in many places throughout his extensive writings, but the primary location is his essay, "Archetypes of the collective unconscious". Jung parted ways with his mentor Freud over several issues, one being Jung's insistence that there was a collective unconscious as well as a personal unconscious. The primary content of the collective unconscious is the archetypes: psychic instincts and their associated behavioural patterns. These archetypal images are among the highest treasures of the psyche, and give rise to the great mythologies of every society. The archetypes do not have specific content: Jung likened them to dry riverbeds that give form and direction to rain that falls. There are many archetypes, such as King, Saviour, Bride, Mother, Trickster, Puer, and so on. The embodiment of the archetypes is culture specific. For example, in Greek culture the Trickster may appear as Pan; in Polynesian culture as Maui. In addition to mythological expression, archetypes may also appear as cherished religious symbols, as JUNG (1964) explored in his posthumously published *Man and His Symbols*.

Even Jung's basic concepts such as anima and animus are described as archetypes. In his book *Aion*, JUNG (1959b), who was the son of a Protestant minister, addressed traditional Christian images such as God and Christ, again understanding them as archetypes whose expression is culture-specific. PALMER artfully summarizes Jung's thinking on God as archetype. For a complete list of Jung's references to archetype, see the index volume to the Bollingen series, or see the comprehensive studies of the role of myth in Jungian thought by SEGAL and by WALKER.

JACOBI, a student of Jung, took his thought on archetypes a step further. She connects individual "emotional complexes" -such as the inferiority complex, the anxiety complex, and the martyr complex -with the larger Jungian conceptions of archetype and symbol. Contrary to Freudian thought, which saw dreams as "the royal road to the unconscious", Jung and Jacobi see complexes as that royal road. Yet dreams are not to be ignored, for this is where the complexes find their most vivid expression through archetypal themes and individual and collective symbols. The second half of Jacobi's book is an exploration of the symbol system at work in a "big dream" by an eight-year-old child.

JAFFÉ, also a student of Jung's, extends the archetypes into the realm of spirituality. Jung had observed that one-third of his clients did not suffer from any definable neurosis, but rather from the senselessness and aimlessness of their lives. The meaning of life is to be found in the awareness of the ways in which we human beings live out the archetypal motifs, for their manifestations carry the luminous. In the constant "giving form" to archetypal God-images, human beings become co-creators with God of both inner and outer reality. Jaffe calls this "the miracle of the second theogony".

VON FRANZ takes up Jung's challenge, that studying fairy tales is a good way to study the comparative anatomy of the collective unconscious. She emphasizes the conservative nature of archetypes, noting that when they become tainted with individualistic neuroses, listeners reject the fairy tales that otherwise so vividly capture the healing interplay of archetypal dramatics. She has repeatedly studied fairy tales from a variety of cultures, and her analysis of them makes archetypal thinking particularly vivid.

Second and third generations, training at the C.G. Jung Institute in Zurich, have spun-out further extensions of Jungian thought on archetypes. MONICK is an interesting example of this sort of amplification, straddling both Freudian and Jungian interests. He explores the archetypal phallos and its incarnation in masculinity, both personal and communal. Among the manifestations of the phallos are the logos tree of philosophy and wisdom and the quadrilateral mandala, both emphasizing sexuality as a cosmological experience. On the appearance of archetypes in dreams, see CULBERTSON.

Yet another example of archetypal amplification is CAMPBELL's *Hero*. Focusing specifically on mythology, symbol, and rite of passage, Campbell presents a composite of the journey of the archetypal Hero. The journey is a series of tasks to be accomplished, to transcend tragedy and to achieve the goal of mature manhood. Campbell illustrates this journey with wide-ranging examples from Christianity, Judaism, Islam, Buddhism, and a variety of classical mythologies. On more popular uses of archetypal theory, such as that of Robert Bly, see mythopoesis in the entry on Gender.

PHILIP L. CULBERTSON

Areal differentiation

Bowen, Margarita, *Empiricism and Geographical Thought: From Francis Bacon to Alexander von Humboldt*, Cambridge and New York: Cambridge University Press, 1981

Bunge, William, *Theoretical Geography*, Lund: Gleerup, 1962; 2nd edition 1966

Cormack, Lesley B., *Charting an Empire: Geography at the English Universities, 1580–1620*, Chicago: University of Chicago Press, 1997

Entrikin, J. Nicholas and Stanley D. Brunn (editors), *Reflections on Richard Hartshorne's "The Nature of Geography"*, Washington, DC: Association of American Geographers, 1989

Hartshorne, Richard, *The Nature of Geography: A Critical Survey of Current Thought in the Light of the Past*, Lancaster, Pennsylvania: Association of American Geographers, 1939

Hartshorne, Richard, *Perspective on the Nature of Geography*, Chicago: Rand McNally, 1959

Livingstone, David N., *The Geographical Tradition: Episodes in the History of a Contested Enterprise*, Oxford: Blackwell, 1992

McDowell, L. "Understanding Diversity: The Problem of / for Theory" in *Geographies of Global Change: Remapping the World in the Late Twentieth Century*, edited by R.J. Johnston, Peter J. Taylor and Michael J. Watts, Oxford: Blackwell, 1995

Paassen, Christiaan van, *The Classical Tradition of Geography*, Gröningen: Wolters, 1957

Schaefer, F.K., "Exceptionalism in Geography: A Methodological Examination", *Annals of the Association of American Geographers*, 43 (1953): 226–49

Geography as the study of areal differentiation was the major theme of statements regarding the discipline's *raison d'être* throughout most of the 20th century. The most detailed argument was by HARTSHORNE (1939). In the light of contemporary American debates and unable to undertake his proposed fieldwork on political boundaries, he spent much of 1938 reading in German libraries about the nature and philosophy of geography. The result was a detailed exegesis of a large literature leading to a definition of the discipline as "concerned to provide accurate, orderly, and rational description and interpretation of the variable character of the Earth surface". Hartshorne viewed geography, with history, as an "exceptionalist" discipline (as did Kant, although Hartshorne apparently wrote in ignorance of his writings): whilst most disciplines focus on a particular systematic specialism, history and geography synthesize the findings from other studies – historians by time periods and geographers by regional divisions of the Earth's surface.

This exceptionalist view had a long history, even though it was not recognized as such, as represented in the books by BOWEN and VAN PAASSEN. It was attacked strongly in the early 1950s, however, notably in a posthumously published paper by SCHAEFER, who argued that geography should be a nomothetic discipline "concerned with the formulation of the laws governing the spatial distribution of certain features on the earth's surface". Hartshorne rejected such apparent "scientific determinism", arguing that geographers should focus on appreciating individual cases, although this did not involve ignoring generic concepts where they were relevant to such understanding, and in a 1959 book-length response (HARTSHORNE 1959) he presented a very similar definition to that of 20 years earlier (geography is "that discipline that seeks to describe and to interpret the variable character from place to place of the earth as the world of man [*sic*]") and then set out a detailed formulation of the discipline's method:

Geography seeks (1) on the basis of empirical observation as independent as possible of the person of the observer, to describe phenomena with the maximum degree of accuracy and certainty; (2) on this basis, to classify the phenomena, as far as reality permits, in terms of generic concepts or universals; (3) through rational consideration of the facts thus secured and by logical processes of analysis and synthesis, including the construction and use wherever possible of general principles or laws of generic relationships, to attain the maximum comprehension of the scientific interrelationships of phenomena; and (4) to arrange these findings in orderly systems so that what is known leads directly to the margin of the unknown.

Such an orientation for geographical study – also known as *chorology* – had been undertaken in British universities for several centuries, although it had not been known as geography (as described by CORMACK). It was the focus of much debate in the 1960s as protagonists of Schaefer's cause (such as BUNGE) sought to establish geography as a spatial science searching for spatial order rather than describing the unique characteristics of individual places. During this debate, Hartshorne's position was frequently misrepresented, as stressed in the volume edited by ENTRIKIN & BRUNN to mark the fiftieth anniversary of the publication of Hartshorne's "*Nature*". The author of this work's preface claims that Hartshorne's approach "continues to provide us with an effective framework for understanding . . . [the discipline's] growth and for explaining that growth to fellow professionals" and Entrikin argues that it "offers modern geographers insights into the issues associated with the logic of the study of the particular, and that such insights are of use in the renewed concern with specific place, region and landscape". For Stoddart, Hartshorne's book is "one of the most remarkable contributions to geographical scholarship" for four reasons: it "brought maturity to American geography"; it "internationalized American geography"; it "had a remarkable effect overseas . . . it stimulated the emerging coherence of world geography as an intellectual discipline, at least in the English-speaking realms"; and it encouraged considerations of "questions of philosophy, history, epistemology, contextuality, and their mutual and reciprocal relations".

The importance of particular places soon became a major subject of interest again within geographical scholarship, although this was promoted in very different philosophical contexts. Hence McDOWELL's 1995 definition of geography has many resonances with Hartshorne's: "a discipline . . . whose *raison d'être* is the explanation of difference and diversity". In the "new regional geography" places are not given and are not simply the objects of study: they are produced and continually reproduced through human agency, and are the arenas within which much socialization takes place and where social behaviour patterns are learned. Areal differentiation is both the product of human action and the producer of human difference.

RON JOHNSTON

See also Human geography survey, Region and regional geography, Social geography

Ariès, Philippe 1914–1984

French social historian

Archard, David, *Children: Rights and Childhood*, London and New York: Routledge, 1993

Ariès, Philippe, *Centuries of Childhood: A Social History of Family Life*, London: Cape, and New York: Knopf, 1962 (French edition 1960)

Ariès, Philippe, *Western Attitudes toward Death: From the Middle Ages to the Present*, Baltimore: John Hopkins University Press, 1974

Ariès, Philippe, *The Hour of Our Death*, London: Allen Lane, and New York: Knopf, 1981 (French edition 1977)

Ariès, Philippe and André Béjin (editors), *Western Sexuality: Practice and Precept in Past and Present Times*, Oxford and New York: Blackwell, 1985 (French edition 1982)

deMause, Lloyd (editor), *The History of Childhood*, New York: Psychohistory Press, 1974; London: Souvenir Press, 1976

Pilcher, Jane and Stephen Wagg (editors), *Thatcher's Children? Politics, Childhood and Society in the 1980s and 1990s*, London: Falmer Press, 1996

Pollock, Linda A., *Forgotten Children: Parent–Child Relations from 1500 to 1900*, Cambridge and New York: Cambridge University Press, 1983

Postman, Neil, *The Disappearance of Childhood*, New York: Delacorte Press, 1982; London: W.H. Allen, 1983

Stone, Lawrence, *The Family, Sex and Marriage in England, 1500–1800*, London: Weidenfeld and Nicolson, and New York: Harper, 1977

Toward the later stages of his life, the French historian Philippe Ariès wrote on the great themes of sex and death. In ARIES (1974) and ARIES (1981) he opens the topic of death to careful social historical investigation. He shows how, in the 11th century, death became centred on the self, rather than seen in terms of its impact on the community. In the 16th century the concern about death became a concern about one's family. In the 19th century it was seen as a point on the path to the world hereafter and, in the 20th century, death is presented as something hidden from our everyday lives. In writing such a history Ariès puts into discourse that which is often silent.

In contrast, in 1982 he co-edited a series of articles for a book on Western sexuality – a topic that has been endlessly discussed. ARIES & BEJIN contains an impressive list of historians, of one form or another, including the historian of thought, Michel Foucault, and the historian of the ancient world, Paul Veyne. The book was based on a series of seminars that the editors organized and the collection of essays (which include four by Ariès – on chastity, marriage, and homosexuality) have provided an important contribution to our understanding of the persistence of the dominant thematics of sexuality.

Despite the importance of his later writings, Ariès is best known in the English-speaking world for his earlier historical research on the emergence of the "concept of childhood". In ARIES (1962), he argues that in mediaeval society the idea of childhood did not exist. As soon as infants could speak and walk, they were integrated into the world of adults. Ariès draws on evidence from art and from the diary of the French royal doctor, Heroard, who details the early life of Louis XIII. Ariès finds that children and adults dressed the same, played the same games and occupied the same social and cultural spaces. From the 16th century onward, children begin to be recognized as different from adults. Through the institutions of religion, education, and the family, children came to be treated as "innocent", in need of care, and fundamentally different from adults. As such, children came to live in different social and cultural worlds from those of adults.

Ariès' research on the invention of childhood has had a profound impact on the study of childhood, not simply in the discipline of history, but also, for example, in sociology, literary studies, philosophy, and media studies. PILCHER & WAGG, for instance, state that "sociologists around the world have, from time to time and with varying degrees of conviction, endorsed the book's central tenet, namely that childhood is socially constructed and is, thus, specific to certain times and places in human history". The contributions in this volume then proceed to detail the contemporary relations between New Right thinking (caught in the contradiction of economic liberalism and moral authoritarianism), children, and the social construction of childhood.

In his work on media technologies and childhood, POSTMAN uses Ariès' thesis concerning the lack of a concept of childhood in the mediaeval period in order to make the claim that childhood emerges in the 16th century with the development of the printing press. He makes a series of technologically deterministic claims concerning the way in which print technology brings about a new conception of adulthood (with regard to individualism and consciousness) that excludes children. Children are thus separated from the world of adulthood and a whole set of educational, social, and cultural apparatuses develop to construct the distinct world of childhood. He also argues that the development of television, which he sees as a "total disclosure medium" requiring no prior literacy skills, effectively dissolves the boundary between the worlds of childhood and adulthood.

In philosophy, ARCHARD provides a detailed discussion of Ariès' thesis in order to set the conceptual framework for an analysis of children's rights. Archard argues that Ariès is guilty of a form of "presentism", namely that the past is interpreted in the light of contemporary attitudes and dispositions toward children. Archard argues that, at best, we can state that the past lacked "*our* concept of childhood". Moreover, there is nothing to suggest that the Mediaeval period did not hold different conceptions of childhood or that affective relations toward children were any less in the past than now.

Ariès' research has been most debated within the discipline of history. For example, his work on childhood has been conflated with other research by leading scholars who argue that the history of childhood is the history of increasing care toward children. DEMAUSE adopts a psychohistorical model in order to make the claim, not simply that a modern conception of childhood emerged from the 16th century onward, but that adults have become increasingly kinder and less distant toward children. For deMause, the history of childhood is a history of cruelty. Similarly, STONE has argued that, as a consequence of high infant mortality, parents could not emotionally afford to invest in their children *qua* children. Only with advances in medical technologies could parents learn how to care for their children, how to protect them and, correspondingly, how to construct them as innocent. It should be noted that although Ariès is often placed alongside such traditional teleological histories, he himself makes no such claims.

POLLOCK, however, in her highly influential work on parent-child relations from 1500 to 1900, argues that history does not show that parents have increasingly become more caring toward their children. On the contrary, she argues that parents have always been concerned about the welfare of their children and brutality was the exception, not the rule. She draws upon a range of primary sources, such as letters, diaries, and journals, to show how parents have always been attached to their offspring. For Pollock the relation between parent and child is not historically and socially contingent; rather, it is constituted through deeply felt biological mechanisms that make possible the continuation of one's family and the human species.

DAVID OSWELL

See also Childhood, Death and dying

Aristotle 384–322 BC

Greek philosopher

Aquinas, Thomas, *Summa Theologica*, 5 vols, translated and edited by the English Dominican Province, Westminster, Maryland: Christian Classics, 1981 (written 13th century)

Barnes, Jonathan, Malcolm Schofield and Richard Sorabji (editors), *Articles on Aristotle*, vols 1–4, London: Duckworth, 1975–79

Barnes, Jonathan, *Aristotle*, Oxford and New York: Oxford University Press, 1982

Jaeger, Werner, *Aristotle: Fundamentals of the History of His Development*, Oxford: Clarendon Press, 1934; 2nd edition 1948

Lear, Jonathan, *Aristotle: The Desire to Understand*, Cambridge and New York: Cambridge University Press, 1988

Rorty, Amelie Oksenberg, *Essays on Aristotle's Ethics*, Berkeley: University of California Press, 1980

Ross, W.D., *Aristotle*, 5th edition, London: Methuen, 1956

Taylor, A.E., *Aristotle*, revised edition, New York: Dover, and London: Constable, 1955

Veatch, Henry B., *Aristotle: A Contemporary Appreciation*, Bloomington: Indiana University Press, 1974

Voegelin, Eric, *Order and History*, vol. 3: *Plato and Aristotle*, Baton Rouge: Louisiana State University Press, 1957

AQUINAS' *Summa* remains the most comprehensive and influential, albeit turgid, exposition of Aristotle's thought. As the most significant medieval theologian, Aquinas attempted to synthesize the recently rediscovered works of Aristotle with Christianity in the *Summa*. The work is a model of the scholastical mode of disputation, with the proposing of questions followed by answers. In the *Summa*, Aquinas accepts and extends Aristotle's formal logic; he also uses Aristotle's categories of thought: theoretical, practical, and productive.

BARNES' volume provides a brief and accessible introduction to the breadth of Aristotle's achievements as a thinker, authored by one of the most distinguished contemporary students of Greek philosophy. Aristotle is analysed succinctly, in his many facets: as a public figure, scientist, teacher, and philosopher. Barnes' attempt to unify Aristotle's scientific work with his philosophical labours encourages an appreciation of the thinker as systematic, although Barnes also judiciously raises questions that will cause the reader to reconsider such generalizations. Perhaps the most important attribute of Barnes' approach can be found in his presentation throughout the work of Aristotle's goal for all of his theoretical labours: the advancement of truth and knowledge.

One of the most expansive assessments of Aristotle's multifaceted impartment to learning can be found in the four volumes edited by BARNES, SCHOFIELD & SORABJI. All dimensions of Aristotle's thought are critiqued, including his ethical theory, his views of social and political life, and his contributions to metaphysics, and science, among many others.

JAEGER's treatise is one of the most influential works on Aristotle published in the 20th century. The study is a comprehensive survey of the stages of Aristotle's life and work. Jaeger presents the accomplishments of Aristotle within the context of ancient Greece, noting his development of logical inquiry and an "analytical habit of mind", and his contributions to metaphysics, science, ethics, and the universality of philosophy.

LEAR's readable, yet erudite, introduction to Aristotle concentrates upon achieving a greater appreciation of the thinker's suggestion that all persons possess a desire to know. The author assumes a twofold approach: assessing Aristotle's thesis that all humans naturally desire to know reality more completely, as well as the importance of such a quest for Aristotle's worldview. Lear begins with a survey of Aristotle's view of human nature and the soul. He proceeds to a discussion of Aristotle's views of the ethical life and political society.

While RORTY's volume is a compilation of the best available scholarship on Aristotle's ethics, the collection is more than a commentary on a classic text; the work is a significant explication of many central Aristotelian themes. The tome contains essays by some of the most insightful contemporary students of Aristotle, including M.F. Burnyeat, T.H. Irwin, John M. Cooper, and Martha Craven Nussbaum. A wide variety of scholarly concerns are addressed in the book that are of interest to the general reader and specialist.

As a time-honoured work on Aristotle by one of the century's most prominent classical scholars, ROSS' book remains a worthwhile guide to Aristotle. The primary limitation of the study is its brevity. Some aspects of Aristotle's life and work deserve greater elucidation than these concerns receive in Ross' classic study.

Originally published as a revised edition in 1919, TAYLOR's short survey of Aristotle's life and contribution is a useful work. Taylor's essay attempts to identify Aristotle's divergences from Plato's teachings, especially in regard to science. For Aristotle, Taylor argues, science is "knowledge that certain truths follow from still simpler truths". Although less sympathetic to the contribution of Aristotle than most studies, Taylor nevertheless views Aristotle as working within the Socratic-Platonic worldview. Taylor's treatment of Aristotle's "practical philosophy" is a useful summary for the general reader.

VEATCH's readable and insightful tome is an attempt at recovering the importance of Aristotle's thought for the present day; according to the author, the modern world needs Aristotle's wisdom so that he might "anchor us once again to those everyday realities to which sombre judgement and common sense of all mankind would appear to bear indefensible testimony." Veatch presents the Aristotelian account of change, premised upon principles and causes as the supreme example of "common sense" thinking that deserves the continued attention of students and scholars alike. This work also provides a lively account of Aristotle's notion of the soul. For humankind to live the good life – based on the existence of wisdom and intelligence – reason and understanding must be regularly employed. The book concludes with a discussion of Aristotle's theories of metaphysics and logic.

With Aristotle, as in the case of Plato, VOEGELIN attempted to explicate and clarify the philosophic search for order, or meaning. Aristotle is interpreted as a thinker more interested in the analysis of existing phenomena than the proposing of a philosophical system. To appreciate Aristotle's social and political theory, Voegelin suggested one must first understand his view of human nature. For Voegelin, Aristotle's great contribution lies in his experiential understanding of how humanity acquires knowledge. Voegelin provides an important comparison between Aristotle and his teacher, Plato.

H. LEE CHEEK JR

Arms race

Ayoob, Mohammed, *The Third World Security Predicament: State Making, Regional Conflict, and the International System*, Boulder, Colorado: Rienner, 1995

Gjelstad, Jørn and Olav Njølstad (editors), *Nuclear Rivalry and International Order*, London and Thousand Oaks, California: Sage, 1996

Glad, Betty (editor), *Psychological Dimensions of War*, Newbury Park, California: Sage, 1990; London: Sage, 1991

Gleditsch, Nils Petter and Olav Njølstad (editors), *Arms Races: Technological and Political Dynamics*, London: Sage, 1989; Newbury Park, California: Sage, 1990

Kolodziej, Edward A., *Making and Marketing Arms: The French Experience and Its Implications for the International System*, Princeton, New Jersey: Princeton University Press, 1987

Lasswell, Harold, *Essays on the Garrison State*, edited by Jay Stanley, New Brunswick, New Jersey: Transaction, 1997

Luxemburg, Rosa, *The Accumulation of Capital*, London: Routledge and Kegan Paul, 1951 (original German edition 1923)

Richardson, Lewis Fry, *Arms and Insecurity: A Mathematical Study of the Causes and Origins of War*, Pittsburgh: Boxwood, 1960

Stockholm International Peace Research Institute (SIPRI), *SIPRI Yearbook 1998: Armaments, Disarmaments and International Security*, Oxford: Oxford University Press, 1998

The literature on the arms race needs to be seen in the context of political relations, which also incorporate military industrial complexes, state and corporate power, international conflict, and the balance of powers.

LUXEMBURG is the starting point for a long line of Marxist writings on arms and imperialism. Her book, written in 1923, explains intrinsic connections between capitalism, nationalism, and militarism up to World War I. In the last chapter on "militarism as a province of accumulation", she proposes that military spending forms a structural part of the reproduction strategy of capitalism. Later Marxist accounts similarly view Cold War military spending, including two regional wars in Asia, as countervailing factors in *monopoly capital's stagnationist* tendencies in the US. Many writers, Marxist and otherwise, linked arms more or less directly into their critiques of capitalism, socialism, and bureaucracy. The list includes Ernst Mandel, Paul Baran, Seymour Melman, Paul Sweezy, and C. Wright Mills.

LASSWELL originally introduced the concept of the garrison state in an analysis of the Sino-Japanese War, warning of a world in which the specialists on violence are the most powerful group in society. The introduction by Jay Stanley, former editor of the journal *Armed Forces and Society*, traces Lasswell's themes in sociological thought, and appraises their continuing relevance.

RICHARDSON's posthumously published study shows that defensive arming could develop into arms races along the lines of mechanical or ecological models. From the 1960s the conditions for such escalations and reactions became important to social science analysts of strategies, games, fights and debates. They propagate dynamic and strategic models using economic constraints, decision lags, deception, and many other institutional and psychological factors. Much of the literature from the 1970s relates to the arms race in nuclear weapons.

GJELSTAD & NJØLSTAD show the role of nuclear arms in interstate rivalry, examines their contribution to the "long peace" between superpowers during the Cold War, and discusses subsequent proliferations as well as opportunities for disarmament. Part 1, containing seven articles, discusses nuclear weapons and peace among the great powers. Part 2 contains six articles that deal with proliferation, nuclear rivalry and international order after the Cold War, including specific articles on nonproliferation, nuclear export controls, and nuclear developments in India and Pakistan.

AYOOB has written a very comprehensive text that begins by addressing the concepts of "Third World" and "security". The major cause of conflict is seen in terms of the early stage of statemaking in postcolonialism, rather than dependency or development. The analyses are particularly related to the dynamics of interstate conflict and the role of Third World countries in the international system. This provides a useful entry to world systems analyses of conflict that can be read in the Fernand Braudel Centre's journal, *Review*.

KOLODZIEJ provides a definitive case study of international competition for the supply of arms and military technology in the contexts of NATO, military nuclear technology, defence industry and arms manufacturers, corporate networks, state investment, foreign diplomacy, and the French position in the international system. He considers the significance of the complex and multiple payoffs that exist between the defence industries and political parties, emphasizing the intricate dependencies that preclude definite control by any one group. From the point of view of the Fifth Republic the arms business, at times, seemed like a highly impressive bureaucratized runaway train, but it is hampered by technological rivalries, competition for client states, debt crises, and global instability.

GLEDITSCH & NJØLSTAD include the most comprehensive theoretical and empirical work on the arms race since the 1960s. Many of the writers are experts related to the International Peace Research Institute (Oslo), and the Norwegian Institute for Defence Studies. The book takes up the internal factors of arms dynamics, such as bureaucratic politics and the military industrial complex, as well as external factors such as interactive arms dynamics between the major powers. It also deals with the question of technological determinations, long economic waves, and power transitions.

One of the STOCKHOLM INTERNATIONAL PEACE RESEARCH INSTITUTE's (SIPRI) stated objectives for its *Yearbooks* is to discuss total resources devoted to military purposes. It thus contrasts with the International Institute for Strategic Studies' annual publication *Military Balance*, which aims to measure the relative military power of different nations. The international nature of SIPRI enables it to correct some western biases in arms studies, and to explicate the methodologies used. The 1998 edition focuses on a common, institutionalized system of standards and shared values rather than on concepts based on the balance of power. Its highlights are: of the 25 major armed conflicts in 1997, only one, between India and Pakistan, was between states – all the others were internal conflicts; world military expenditure declined by around one-third between 1988 and 1997, due mainly to the cut in Russian spending in 1992; the most significant restructuring in 1997 was in the form of mergers and acquisitions in the US arms industry. The 13 chapters cover security and conflicts, military spending and armaments, nonproliferation, arms control and disarmament.

GLAD's 20 essays include Anatol Rapoport's "The Problems With Gains-Maximizing Strategies"; Leonard Berkowitz's "Biological Roots: Are Humans Inherently Violent?"; and Betty Glad and Charles Taber's "The Domino Theory of the United States". This work is an original contribution to the literature on how psychological factors influence the origins, processes and consequences of the arms race.

ARTHUR E. McCULLOUGH

See also Cold War, Deterrence

Arrow, Kenneth J. 1921–

US economist

Arrow, Kenneth J., "An Extension of the Basic Theorems of Classical Welfare Economics" in *Proceedings of the Second Berkeley Symposium on Mathematical Statistics and Probability*, edited by Jerzy Neyman, Berkeley: University of California Press, 1951

Arrow, Kenneth J., *Social Choice and Individual Values*, New York: Wiley, 1951, 2nd edition 1963

Arrow, Kenneth J. and Gerard Debreu, "Existence of an Equilibrium for a Competitive Economy", *Econometrica*, 22 (1954): 256–90

Arrow, Kenneth J., H.D. Block and L. Hurwicz, "On the Stability of the Competitive Equilibrium, 2", *Econometrica*, 27 (1959): 82–109

Arrow, Kenneth J., *Essays in the Theory of Risk Bearing*, Amsterdam: North Holland, 1970; Chicago: Markham, 1971

Arrow, Kenneth J. and F.H. Hahn, *General Competitive Analysis*, San Francisco: Holden Day, and Edinburgh: Oliver and Boyd, 1971

Arrow, Kenneth J., *Collected Papers*, 6 vols, Cambridge, Massachusetts: Harvard University Press, and Oxford: Blackwell, 1983–85

Arrow, Kenneth J., Yew-Kwang Ng and Xiaokai Yang (editors), *Increasing Returns and Economic Analysis*, London: Macmillan, and New York: St Martin's Press, 1998

Feiwel, George R. (editor), *Arrow and the Foundations of the Theory of Economic Policy*, London: Macmillan, and New York: New York University Press, 1987

Kemp, Murray C. and Yew-Kwang Ng, "On the Existence of Social Welfare Functions, Social Orderings, and Social Decisions Functions", *Economica*, 45 (1976): 59–66

Little, Ian M.D., "Social Choice and Individual Values", *Journal of Political Economy*, 60 (1952): 422–32

Parks, Robert P., "An Impossibility Theorem for Fixed Preferences: A Dictatorial Bergson-Samuelson Welfare Function", *Review of Economic Studies*, 43 (1976): 447–50

Roberts, Kevin W.S., "Social Choice Theory: The Single-Profile and Multi-Profile Approaches", *Review of Economic Studies*, 47 (1980): 441–50

Samuelson, Paul A., "Arrow's Mathematical Politics" in *Human Values and Economic Policy: A Symposium*, edited by Sidney Hook, New York: New York University Press, 1967

Sen, Amartya K., "Quasi-Transitivity, Rational Choice, and Collective Decisions", *Review of Economic Studies*, 36 (1969): 381–93

Weizsacker, C.C. von, "Kenneth Arrow's Contributions to Economists", *Scandinavian Journal of Economics*, 74/4 (December 1972); reprinted in *Contemporary Economists in Perspective*, edited by Henry W. Spiegel and Warren J. Samuels, Greenwich, Connecticut: Jai Press, 1984

Kenneth Arrow has made so many important contributions to his field that the early (1972) award of the Nobel Prize in economics was within expectation. Apart from the pathbreaking contributions discussed below, Arrow has numerous significant publications on discrimination, education, the environment, game theory, information, invaluables, innovation, inventory, justice, learning by doing, nonlinear programming, production function, public investment, rationality, regulation, resource allocation processes, technical progress, transition; you name it. Moreover, now in his late 70s, he is still prolific.

Born on 23 August 1921 in New York to a family of Romanian-Jewish origin, Arrow's intellectual gift showed early. Witnessing the misery of the Great Depression as a child, the young Arrow was leftwing-inclined, with his "dramatic, even traumatic turning point" occurring with the publicity of the Moscow trials of 1935–36. After his PhD in 1951 (delayed by 3 years of war service), Arrow spent most of his academic life at Stanford (1953–68, 1979–) and Harvard (1968–79) universities. Arrow spoke at such a lightning speed and was so knowledgeable in so many areas that his colleagues decided to play a friendly trick on him. Before a party, they read up on the breeding habits of whales from an old issue of the *National Geographic*. However, Arrow had no difficulty in joining in the conversation, citing more original references than the *National Geographic*. (One does not only find such interesting episodes in FEIWEL, but many papers on issues related to Arrow's contributions including social choice, welfare, organization, resource utilization, as well as interviews with Arrow. For a survey of Arrow's contributions, *See also* VON WEIZSACKER. The two volumes of Arrow's collected papers contain his important papers in social choice and justice and in general equilibrium.)

Arrow is probably most well known for his impossibility theorem (ARROW 1951/1963). While the paradox of voting (possible cyclicity of collective or social preference based on individual orderings of the alternatives in accordance to the majority rule) was known earlier, Arrow's impossibility theorem states a much more general negative result. A rule of constitution from which the collective orderings of the relevant alternatives (including social states for the case of social choice) based on individual orderings of these alternatives, satisfying some compelling conditions, does not exist. The conditions are: (a) Free orderings: Individuals may order the alternatives in any logically consistent way; (b) The weak Pareto principle: if all individuals prefer *x* to *y*, the collective should prefer *x* to *y*; (c) Independence of irrelevant alternatives. The collective ordering of any subset (including a pair) of the alternatives depends only on the individual orderings of alternatives in this subset (not on those on some other irrelevant alternatives); (d) Nondictatorship. No single individual should be able to dictate the collective choice in the sense that his or her preference implies collective preference.

Due to the complete specification of all relevant aspects of the alternatives and their mutual exclusiveness (the choice of any alternative excludes the others), condition (c) is compelling in the context despite some misunderstanding and some ambiguity in Arrow's presentation (his formal statement, mathematical formulation, and example differ slightly, although all capture some essential aspect).

Most attempts to bypass Arrow's theorem fail one way or other. For example, the relaxation of collective rationality from a collective ordering into a collective decision (picking only the top alternative) does not work, as SEN shows that the impossibility result is resurrected by imposing an additional reasonable condition. LITTLE and SAMUELSON attempt to reject Arrow's result as not applicable to economics by adopting a new rule as individual orderings change. However, KEMP & NG, PARKS, and ROBERTS establish impossibility results even holding individual orderings unchanged.

Arrow's impossibility theorem implies that, at least when information permits, collective choice cannot be reasonably based on individual *ordinal* preferences only, but must be based on interpersonal comparison of individual *intensity* of preferences or cardinal welfare indices, as may be obtained through commonsense judgements, happiness surveys, willingness to pay, log-rolling, and so on. However, ARROW (1963: p.109) rejects the log-rolling argument, "a social state is a whole bundle of issues That this included log-rolling seemed to me so obvious as not to be worth spelling out." This ignores the point that, with log-rolling and other means of revealing the intensities of preferences, we may no longer wish to observe the ordering aspect of the third condition. Nevertheless, the difficulty of obtaining interpersonal comparable cardinal utilities makes Arrow's impossibility still significant.

Arrow is also well-known for the Arrow–Debreu model of general equilibrium analysis (ARROW & DEBREU), which proves the existence of general competitive equilibrium in a satisfactory way, after benefiting from the use of such mathematical tools as the fixed-point theorems. ARROW & HAHN provide simpler proofs and extensions, including those on externalities, an intertemporal model, and monopolistic competition (although the proof of the last is still not very satisfactory as some contrived condition, "visibility", has to be assumed). Apart from proving existence, Arrow also contributes to the analysis of the stability (ARROW, BLOCK & HURWICZ 1959) and Pareto optimality (ARROW 1951) of a competitive equilibrium.

A main limitation of general equilibrium analysis is the unrealistic assumptions of perfect competition and non-increasing returns. However, Arrow has recently been involved in the analysis of increasing returns. ARROW, NG & YANG (1998) contains papers extending the inframarginal analysis of division of labour and the micro-macro analysis of non-perfect competition (see separate entry Mesoeconomics).

The economics of uncertainty is another area in which Arrow has made major contributions. ARROW (1971) is a revision of his book six years earlier, which surveys and advances aspects of the theory of uncertainty on which he wrote (in French) as early as 1953, including the concept of contingent commodity and the corresponding general equilibrium analysis, a new proof of the expected utility theorem, and the measure of the degree of risk aversion and its application, and insurance.

YEW-KWANG NG

See also Division of labour, Mesoeconomics

Arson

Barnett, W. and M. Spitzer, "Pathological Firesetting, 1951–1991: A Review", *Medicine Science and Law*, 34/1 (1994): 4–20

Clare, I.C.H., G.H. Murphy, D. Cox and E.H. Chaplin, "Assessment and Treatment of Fire Setting: A Single Case Investigation Using a Cognitive Behavioural Model", *Criminal Behaviour and Mental Health*, 2 (1992): 253–68

Fineman, K., "A Model for the Qualitative Analysis of Child and Adult Fire Deviant Behavior", *American Journal of Forensic Psychology*, 13/1 (1995): 31–60

Geller, J., "Arson in Review: From Profit to Pathology", *Clinical Forensic Psychiatry*, 15/3 (1992): 623–45

Jackson, H.F., C. Glass and S. Hope, "A Functional Analysis of Recidivistic Arson", *British Journal of Clinical Psychology*, 26 (1987): 175–85

Lewis, Nolan D.C. and Helen Yarnell, *Pathological Firesetting (Pyromania)*, New York: Nervous and Mental Disease Monographs, 1951

McKerracher, D.W. and A.J.I. Dacre, "A Study of Arsonists in a Special Security Hospital", *British Journal of Psychiatry*, (1966): 1151–1154

Stewart, L.A. "Profile of Female Firesetters: Implications for Treatment", *British Journal of Psychiatry*, 163 (1993): 248–56

BARNETT & SPITZER provides an excellent review of 40 years of published research on arson. The paper takes a psychiatric approach and reviews findings from the US, Europe and Asia, providing a useful global feel to the developing understanding of arson. The authors draw on psychiatric diagnostic labels and biology to identify explanations for firesetting behaviour. The review goes on to look at psychoanalytic understandings and child-development theory. Therapy and prevention are discussed, and the authors conclude that only a limited amount of work has addressed this problem. Cursory glances are directed toward the literature on female firesetters and recidivism, two areas that provide good summaries, although the authors fail to document the variety of academic and therapeutic debates current within these complex areas. The authors also draw the reader's attention to the lack of understanding of arson without apparent motive.

McKERRACHER & DACRE describes an experimental design study based on psychological assessments of a group of people convicted of arson. This study has been quoted widely by subsequent authors in the field. The results of the study are broken down into nine comments focusing on offender characteristics, and a tabulated summary comparing arsonists with non-arsonists on dimensions of "conditionability", "symptomotology", "offences" and "sex offences". This paper is the first to debunk theories of latent homosexuality whilst beginning to link self-injurious behaviour to arson.

CLARE *et al.* documents a single case study, picking out points relevant to the treatment of offenders. The authors draw heavily on the model of cognitive behavioural therapy, encouraging the development of adaptive coping strategies to cope with the feelings of wanting to start fires. Self-esteem is flagged up as an integral part of the treatment programme.

JACKSON, GLASS & HOPE draw on their experiences within a maximum-security hospital to understand recidivism. The authors look to antecedent conditions and consequences in the maintenance of firesetting behaviour, within the framework of functional analysis. Recidivism itself is well addressed (including concepts of dangerousness and risk assessment), but implications for therapeutic interventions are not tackled.

FINEMAN reviews three assessment instruments to identify and understand the thoughts, behaviours and affect that accompany arson. The rationale for the development of the assessments is covered and locates understanding within the dynamic behavioural model of firesetting. The author helpfully provides vignettes to lead the reader through the use of the tools and includes assessment forms within the body of the text. Fineman makes use only of the male pronoun throughout

the paper, though clearly identifying his finding that around 10 per cent of arsonists are female.

GELLER reviews findings from the US and Canada, documenting interesting findings of incidence of firesetting, deaths, and financial costs. The author also plots the history of arson and its repercussions from ancient Rome through the 1800s and 1900s, looking at diagnoses of mental disorder as explanatory frameworks. Geller points to Freud as last century's most influential thinker in conceiving psychological factors associated with firesetting. The author considers the understanding of arson as a communicative tool, and examines the implications that this has for therapeutic work. Helpfully, suggestions for future work are documented, focusing on collaborations between child and adult work, outcome measures of interventions, and follow-up studies of child arson offenders. More work is indicated in assessing the frequency of firesetting in people with mental health problems.

STEWART identifies that women constitute a small but significant proportion of arsonists. The author begins with a summary of different characteristics that set female arsonists aside from their male counterparts; the findings showed higher incidence of psychosis, learning disability, and self-injurious behaviour. The study looks specifically at the psychological and situational antecedents to firesetting among a group of 28 female arsonists. Measures used within the study looked at cognitive functioning, depression, and self-esteem. Psychiatric diagnoses were also tabulated. Specific behavioural and psychological antecedents were identified that could be targeted in treatment programmes, and personal histories were documented illustrating a pattern of family deprivation and disruption, often with physical and sexual abuse.

LEWIS & YARNELL has become the seminal text on arson as the first systematic study of firesetting. The work includes a history of firesetting, and the author's own study and findings. Case histories of firesetters are drawn from the 1500 reviewed in their study collected from The National Board of Fire Underwriters. Chapters are presented in an accessible, discursive style, addressing topics such as volunteer firefighers who set fires, firesetting related to sexual activity, and children who set fires. This text concludes with a lengthy theoretical discussion drawing together the threads of the book.

The reader should be made aware that although this text is widely quoted and provides an excellently written guide to the literature – there is only one copy in the UK – held at the Institute of Psychiatry, London.

LIZ FORBAT

Asian crisis, 1997–98

Boyle, Peter, "Crisis in the Asia-Pacific", paper presented at the Asia Pacific Solidarity Conference, Asia Pacific Institute for Democratisation and Development, Sydney, April 1998, http://www.peg.apc.org/~apiaustralia/

Brookings Review, special issue on Asia's financial crisis, 16/3 (Summer 1998), available at http://www.brookings.org/press/review/oldtoc.htm

Bustelo, Pablo, "The East Asian Financial Crisis: An Analytical Survey", ICEI Working Paper, Complutense

University of Madrid, October 1998, available at
http://www.ucm.es/info/icei/asia/Bustweb1.htm

Chang, H-J, G. Palma and D.H. Whittaker (editors), special
issue on the Asian crisis, *Cambridge Journal of
Economics*, 23/3 (1988): 649–808

Corsetti, Giancarlo, Paolo Pesenti and Nouriel Roubini,
"What Caused the Asian Currency and Financial Crisis?"
part 1: "A Macroeconomic Overview"; part 2: "The
Policy Debate", Cambridge, Massachusetts: National
Bureau of Economic Research, 1998 (NBER Working
Papers 6833 and 6834)

Goldstein, Morris, "The Asian Financial Crisis: Causes,
Cures, and Systemic Implications", *Policy Analyses in
International Economics*, 55, (1998), available at
http://www.iie.com/CATALOG/EASTASIA/catasia.htm

Griffith-Jones, Stephany, Jacques Cailloux and Stephan
Pfaffenzeller, "The East Asian Financial Crisis: A
Reflection on Its Causes, Consequences and Policy
Implications", Brighton: Institute of Development Studies,
University of Sussex, 1998, available at
http://www.ids.ac.uk/ids (Discussion Paper 367)

International Monetary Fund, *IMF-Supported Programs in
Indonesia, Korea and Thailand: A Preliminary Assessment*,
Washington, DC: IMF, 1999, available at
http://www.imf.org/external/pubind.htm

Krugman, Paul, "The Myth of Asia's Miracle", *Foreign
Affairs*, 73/6 (1994): 62–78

Radelet, Steven and Jeffrey Sachs, "What Have We Learned,
So Far, from the Asian Financial Crisis" (mimeo),
Cambridge, Massachusetts: Harvard Institute for
International Development, Harvard University, January
1999, available at http://www.hiid.harvard.edu/pub/

Sen, Surya, "Analysis of Financial Crisis in Asia", Chicago:
Federal Reserve Bank of Chicago, December 1998,
available at http://www.frbchi.org/pubs-
speech/publications/periodicals/chilet/welcome.html

World Bank, *East Asia: The Road to Recovery*, Washington,
DC: World Bank, 1998, also available at
http://www.worldbank.org/html/extdr/offrep/eap/eap.htm

The global economic crisis, which began in Thailand in July 1997, spread rapidly throughout East Asia and has affected almost every country to some degree. What happened, why the Asian miracle became an Asian 'flu, and how the contagion spread have been the basic questions asked. However, even before the crisis, there were already some people like KRUGMAN stating that the Asian miracle was merely a myth. According to him, the rapid Asian economic growth was primarily the result of extraordinary growth in inputs whereas total factor productivity showed little or no growth. Although his claim has been attacked from an empirical point of view, his provocative papers (at http://web.mit.edu/krugman/www) are one of the main references on the causes of the Asian crisis.

The WORLD BANK report first discusses whether the so-called Asian miracle was real and then observes that East Asia's crisis is unique in that it has fused a currency and banking crisis and a regional panic into a particularly virulent strand of economic malady. It describes the emergence of the region's structural vulnerability to external shocks and financial panic.

The Bank claims that East Asia's crisis is best seen as a story of rapid growth built on an incomplete foundation. After discussing the social impacts and environmental dimension of the crisis, it speaks to the region's strategy for recovery and the economic forces shaping its prospects. The report argues that reforms in the financial and corporate sectors, together with sound macroeconomic policies and a supportive international community, can put Asia on the road to recovery.

GRIFFITH-JONES, CAILLOUX & PFAFFENZELLER give an analytical overview of the issues raised at a conference held at the Institute of Development Studies in July 1998 on the East Asian crisis. They group the causes of the crisis into two parts: domestic factors and external factors. After giving views on the social and economic costs of the crisis, they discuss various approaches to policy design for crisis prevention and better crisis management.

GOLDSTEIN explains how the Asian crisis arose and spread. He traces the crisis through its interrelated origins: financial sector weakness; moral hazard; large external deficits; and widespread contagion. He then outlines a multi-pronged strategy, and also offers specific prospects for improving the international financial architecture. Goldstein claims that the IMF's prescriptions are counterproductive. He concludes that recovery will only take place when the crisis economies have made enough progress in implementing structural reforms to regain confidence, and when there has been enough rescheduling of private debt to make creditors comfortable enough to provide new lending.

Fourteen short papers in the BROOKINGS REVIEW bring together a wide range of views on the causes, implications, and possible cures for Asia's problems. The papers say that the fundamental issue was liquidity, not solvency. Losing global competitiveness, rapid inflow of foreign funds, a financial intermediation system concentrated in bank operations, and poor governance are given as signs. The special issue analyses the investment boom and financial bust in Korea; discusses Japan's distressing long-term malaise; explores the economic and political effects of the crisis on the US; questions whether foreign direct investment is the key to Asia's future economic growth; and examines the security issues in the region. It claims that the IMF is not perfect, but essential, and that its role should be redefined. A final remark states that there is still a future in Asia.

RADELET & SACHS expand their views on the Asian crisis based on their two previous influential papers. They claim that a sudden reversal of capital flows was the origin of the crisis, and also discuss the reasons. After presenting policy implications in some detail they argue that the world simply still does not understand financial crisis very well.

CORSETTI, PESENTI & ROUBINI explore the view that the currency and financial crises in Asia reflected structural and policy distortions in the region's economies. The first part provides an overview of economic fundamentals in Asia. The second part presents a reconstruction of the crisis from the period leading to the crisis to the developments in mid-1998 in parallel with a survey of the debate on the strategies to recover from the crisis, the role of international intervention, and the costs and benefits of capital controls. A very detailed chronology of the events in Asia can be found at Roubini's

Asia home page (http://www.stern.nyu.edu/~nroubini/asia/Asia Homepage.htmlge.html), which also contains many links and papers.

BUSTELO starts with the review of East Asia's economic background with a discussion on the onset and developments of the crisis. He classifies the competing explanations based on financial bubbles and declining returns to investment, bad banking, misguided macro management, unsound fundamentals and international capital markets, self-fulfilling panics in external financial markets, financial underregulation, and speculative attacks. He then presents a combined alternative explanation based on common factors as well as on some specific features. He assesses the IMF's approach to the crisis and extracts some theoretical conclusions. The paper contains a rich bibliography.

SEN summarizes the discussions of the FRB Chicago and IMF cosponsored conference held in October 1998 on the Asian crisis. He brings together different views on the financial turmoil in Asia, clarifying the issues and recommendations to minimize the impacts. He first discusses the origins of the crisis based on economic fundamentals and financial panic, and argues that various theories had many elements in common. He mentions that there appears to be a growing belief that the IMF must redefine its purpose and policies to remain effective under contemporary economic conditions. However, he claims that policy decisions other than the ones suggested by the IMF would have damaged the Asian economies in their fragile state. He also agrees on the need for alternative strategies to protect against the volatility of free capital markets while fostering economic growth. He concludes that the turmoil in Asia in ongoing, and its impacts are more severe than originally thought.

The IMF assessment mostly extends the views of a series of articles published in the June 1998 issue of its journal *Finance and Development* by focusing on Indonesia, Korea and Thailand. The report is intended to increase public understanding of the IMF's role in the crisis, and widen discussions on how to prevent future crises and handle those that may erupt. It looks at the causes of the crises and the Fund's role, and tries to assess the experience. It says that the policies that the Fund recommended were broadly appropriate. There is also a discussion of social safety nets. However, it only covers the experience with IMF-supported programmes as they evolved up to October 1998. More recent developments are covered in the IMF *World Economic Outlook and International Capital Markets* report (1998). Response to some criticism of the programs are given in a paper entitled *The IMF's Response to the Asian crisis*, published by the IMF in January 1999 (see http://www.imf.org/External/np/exr/facts/asia.htm).

BOYLE takes a rather different stance from the other references given above and focuses on the political significance of the crisis and its broader context. He claims that the crisis arose because even the partial industrialization of a few nations from the Third World has produced more than world markets can absorb. Hence, the Asian crisis is the last expression of a protracted world capitalist crisis of overproduction. His and the other papers presented at the conference mostly argue that the crisis occurred due to financial liberalization, globalization (argued to be neocolonialism) and IMF-supervised robbery.

The special issue of the *Cambridge Journal of Economics* collects 12 articles with a useful introductory survey by the editors CHANG, PALMA & WHITTAKER. The four opening general articles are followed by entries concentrating on individual countries.

SOHBET KARBUZ

See also East Asian economies, Tiger economies

Asian developmental state

Aoki, Masahiko, Hyung-Ki Kim and Masahiro Okuno-Fujiwara (editors), *The Role of Government in East Asian Economic Development: Comparative Institutional Analysis*, Oxford: Clarendon Press, and New York: Oxford University Press, 1997

Chang, Ha-Joon, Gabriel Palma and Hugh Whittaker (editors), special issue on "The Asian Crisis", *Cambridge Journal of Economics*, 22/6 (1998): 649–808

Deyo, Frederic C. (editor), *The Political Economy of New Asian Industrialism*, Ithaca, New York: Cornell University Press, 1987

Evans, Peter, Dietrich Rueschemeyer and Theda Skocpol (editors), *Bringing the State Back In*, Cambridge and New York: Cambridge University Press, 1985

Evans, Peter, *Embedded Autonomy: States and Industrial Transformation*, Princeton, New Jersey: Princeton University Press, 1995

Johnson, Chalmers A., *MITI and the Japanese Miracle: The Growth of Industrial Policy, 1925–1975*, Stanford: Stanford University Press, 1982

Kohli, Atul, "Where Do High Growth Political Economies Come From? The Japanese Lineage of Korea's 'Developmental State'", *World Development*, 22/9 (1994): 1269–93

Singh, Ajit, "'Asian Capitalism' and the Financial Crisis", in *Global Instability: The Political Economy of World Economic Governance*, edited by J. Michie and J. Smith, London and New York: Routledge, 1999

Wade, Robert, *Governing the Market: Economic Theory and the Role of Government in East Asian Industrialization*, Princeton, New Jersey: Princeton University Press, 1990

World Bank, *The East Asian Miracle: Economic Growth and Public Policy*, New York: Oxford University Press, 1993

A wide array of competing explanations have been offered to explain the rapid economic growth experienced in Asia (particularly East Asia) since World War II. An influential strand of analysis reacts against the more narrowly-conceived economic approaches by looking at the Asian state's capacity to create incentives, force compliance, and direct resources towards development goals. The rich literature on the Asian developmental state thus spans both political science and economics. Two more recent contributions (SINGH and CHANG, PALMA & WHITTAKER) discuss the Asian financial crisis and the role of the state.

JOHNSON represents a classic early contribution to the understanding of the Japanese developmental state (which served as the model for other Asian states) and its economic pilot agency, the Ministry of International Trade and Industry

(MITI). The book presents a detailed view of the workings and objectives of MITI and the political dispensation that, at least in the early postwar years, allowed it wide latitude in its dealings with industry. The Japanese state, Johnson argues, was characterized by "bureaucratic dominance" in policy formation, which served to insulate industrial policy from political demands. The book carefully details the evolution of MITI and Japanese industrial policy in the 1925–75 period and the various factors, both designed and providential, that contributed to its success. Despite being dense in the administrative details of MITI, the book is accessible to a wide audience and continues to be a necessary starting point for the study of the developmental state in Asia.

EVANS, RUESCHEMEYER & SKOCPOL present an early and influential collection of essays that views states across the boundaries of history, sociology, and economics. Various aspects of state action are addressed, but the first section, "States as Promoters of Economic Development and Social Redistribution", is the most relevant to the analysis of the Asian developmental state. Rueschemeyer and Evans argue along Weberian lines that developmental states must, over the long term, build elite effective bureaucracies to intervene in the economy, and they must attain at least some autonomy from dominant social groups to promote accumulation and redistribution. The relevance of this analysis can be found in Alice Amsden's chapter on the Taiwanese developmental state. While not providing a detailed view of the development of state bureaucratic capacity in Taiwan (for this analysis, see Wade), Amsden highlights the important fact that the political dominance of the Kuomintang in Taiwan, in contrast to its more tenuous position in pre-1949 China, allowed it to reach deeply into the economy and society and aided the implementation of industrial policy. The essays are accessible to nonspecialists and provide a good introduction to the concepts underlying analyses of developmental states.

DEYO provides a collection of papers that analyse many facets of the developmental state in Asia, and is both accessible and detailed. Chalmers Johnson presents an article that discusses the developmental state in South Korea and Taiwan in addition to Japan. Bruce Cumings highlights the historical dynamics (both political and economic) that created the particular political economy of northeast Asia. Further articles address the questions of the lessons of the Asian developmental state for Latin Americanists, the status of labour in Asian development, and the relationship between the state and foreign capital in Asia. The articles seek to embed the Asian developmental state in its wider historical, social, and economic context, and to extract from this analysis the reasons behind its capacity to intervene extensively in both the society and economy to shape private actions.

EVANS advances his influential framework of "embedded autonomy" in a readable and comprehensive study of state-led industrialization. "Embedded autonomy" refers to two things: (a) the relative independence of developmental states from powerful social forces that can obstruct industrial transformation; (b) a bureaucratic state that is embedded in complex alliances with business and dominant classes that further its capacity to direct industrial policy. It is a complex concept and one that Evans elucidates in this study with case studies of Korea, Brazil, and India. The study is extremely useful as a

close-up view of the interaction of state structures and their capacity to lead industrial transformation. It thus highlights the distinctive political economy of Korea that led to rapid state-led growth.

WADE presents a detailed and accessible study of the Taiwanese developmental state and the various policy tools through which it influenced and guided economic transformation. The study includes discussions of the historical origins of the developmental state in Taiwan, details of the government agencies that spearheaded state involvement, and the industrial and economic policies pursued by the state. In his analysis of the state itself, Wade's analysis is in the tradition of Johnson, Amsden (in Evans, Rueschmeyer & Skocpol), and Kohli, in that it stresses the political alignments underlying bureaucratic power and the reasons behind the state's ability to deeply intervene in the economy. Wade contrasts three interpretations of Taiwan's success: the "free market" and the "simulated free market" views; more liberal neoclassical views, close to the World Bank approach; and the "governed market" perspective, which stresses the developmental state. The study is rich and detailed and provides extensive institutional analysis of the policy and administrative workings of a developmental state.

KOHLI provides a fascinating historical analysis of Japanese colonial government in Korea and its decisive influence on the postwar developmental state of South Korea. As such, it complements Johnson as a study in the institutional and political foundations of a strong interventionist bureaucratic state. Kohli notes that three elements of the Korean model were instilled in the Japanese colonial period: a highly bureaucratized state; a state-dominated alliance of state and property owners; and repressive social control of the working classes. Kohli argues that the divergent development paths taken by countries are very dependent on historical factors (such as differing colonial legacies) and that this fact should make us careful not to overestimate their replicability in other contexts. The article is accessible and provides an insightful and concise view of the historical origins of a developmental state.

WORLD BANK presents an interpretation of the East Asian developmental state that conforms more to a liberal economic perspective. The report argues that while the Asian state did intervene in many sectors, the intervention had only marginal effects on the industrial structure and that productivity growth was not higher in promoted sectors. Thus, while acknowledging the role of the state in many areas (for example, education) and the importance of institutions, the report shifts the balance of the explanation for Asia's success towards the market and away from a developmental state. The Asian state, the report argues, was essentially a neoclassical developmental state in which state interventions sought to conform to and augment the operation of the market. Thus, while the report does move some way towards accomodating analyses that emphasize state intervention, its approach still diverges markedly from that of writers like Wade and Johnson who place more of an emphasis on the role of an interventionist developmental state in transforming and guiding market outcomes through activist industrial policies.

AOKI, KIM & OKUNO-FUJIWARA gather together a rich collection of essays on the mechanisms of state involvement in industrial transformation in East Asia. The editors view their contribution as defining a third interpretation of the role of the Asian state in late development. Instead of the "market-friendly" view (expressed in the World Bank study) or the developmental state view (held by Johnson, Deyo, Wade, and Kohli), they argue for a "market-enhancing" view that stresses the role of government policy in complementing private sector coordination. The essays vary in terms of their emphasis and methodology, but generally they are geared towards an audience of professional economists. The essays address many diverse issues, including coordination problems in late development, state policy towards finance, the structure of government institutions in Japan, and state industrial and redistributive policies in Malaysia.

SINGH provides a clear and robust defense of the Asian developmental state in response to critics who argued that it was a primary cause of the Asian financial crisis of 1997. Singh argues that the Asian state had produced not only rapid rates of growth and industrial transformation but also beneficial social effects such as relatively equal income distributions and poverty reduction. While critics contend that the crisis was caused by extensive state intervention that led to inefficient industries, corruption, and moral hazard, Singh argues that the main causes of the crisis were ill-considered liberalizations of financial markets and the capital account. Thus, the crisis was caused not by the activities of the traditional Asian developmental state but rather by the dismantling of its capacity to guide economic development.

CHANG, PALMA & WHITTAKER provides a collection of fine articles on various facets of the Asian financial crisis and case studies of several countries. The articles generally support the non-orthodox position that the cause of the crisis was not the Asian developmental state (in its various forms across East and South East Asia), but rather market failures arising from under-regulated and over-liquid international financial markets. Ronald Dore and Whittaker and Kurosawa discuss the evolution of the 'Japanese model' and the role of the state in the 1990s. Chang, Park, and Yoo analyse the Korean crisis of 1997 and its relation to the development model pursued, with modifications, by the state since the 1960s. They conclude that the hasty and poorly planned financial liberalisation carried out by the Kim Young Sam administration in the early 1990s was the primary cause of the explosive growth of short-term indebtedness that sparked the crisis of 1997. K.S. Jomo and Pincus and Ramli discuss the contexts of the Malaysian and Indonesian crises, respectively. The volume is notable in that its contributors acknowledge the key, if varying, role of the state in promoting industrial development in East and South East Asia and present an alternative to the orthodox interpretation of the crisis as arising from the policies and workings of the developmental state.

BRUCE A. WEISSE

Asian model of capitalism

Akyuz, Yilmaz (editor), "East Asian Development: New Perspectives", special issue of *Journal of Development Studies*, 34/1 (1998)
Amsden, Alice H., *Asia's Next Giant: South Korea and Late Industrialization*, New York: Oxford University Press, 1989
Aoki, Masahiko, Hyung-Ki Kim and Masahiro Okuno-Fujiwara (editors), *The Role of Government in East Asian Economic Development: Comparative Institutional Analysis*, Oxford: Clarendon Press, and New York: Oxford University Press, 1997
Chang, Ha-Joon (editor), *The Political Economy of Industrial Policy*, London: Macmillan, and New York: St Martin's Press, 1994
Deyo, Frederic C. (editor), *The Political Economy of the New Asian Industrialism*, Ithaca, New York: Cornell University Press, 1987
Ito, Takatoshi and Anne Krueger (editors), "Growth Theories in Light of the East Asian Experience", *NBER East Asian Seminar on Economics*, vol. 4, Chicago: University of Chicago Press, 1995
Johnson, Chalmers A., *MITI and the Japanese Miracle: The Growth of Industrial Policy, 1925–1975*, Stanford, California: Stanford University Press, 1982
Singh, Ajit, "Causes of Fast Economic Growth in East Asia" in *UNCTAD Review*, New York: United Nations, 1995
Wade, Robert, *Governing the Market: Economic Theory and the Role of Government in East Asian Industrialization*, Princeton, New Jersey: Princeton University Press, 1990
World Bank, *The East Asian Miracle: Economic Growth and Public Policy*, Oxford and New York: Oxford University Press, 1993

The rapid industrialization of East Asia in the five decades after World War II has been the most successful episode of sustained high growth rates in human history. Not surprisingly, this success has led to a vigorous debate in academic and policy circles about the causes of this rapid growth and the true components of the "Asian model" of capitalism. More orthodox, neoclassical economists tend to see the model as composed of the relatively free operation of market forces and "market-friendly" state interventions. Another group of economists, influenced by non-neoclassical theories and institutionalist perspectives, view active government industrial and commercial policies as central to the process of accumulation and technological progress in East Asia.

SINGH presents a comprehensive and accessible overview of the debate on the Asian model. His article discusses the main theses in the debate, the efficacy of industrial policy, the nature of Asian trade regimes, competition in domestic markets, and the determinants of high savings and investment rates in East Asia. He argues that nonorthodox perspectives provide a more coherent view of the East Asian experience than the neoclassical paradigm.

JOHNSON provides the classic account of Japanese industrial policy in the postwar years. The book analyses in depth the institutional structure and politics of the Ministry of International Trade and Industry. The functions of industrial policy and its effects on Japanese industry during the era of rapid growth are also analysed. A concluding chapter outlines the various institutional elements that comprise the "Japanese model" of capitalism. The book remains a standard study of state-led industrialization and, as such, remains an important source for both political scientists and economists.

AMSDEN presents a very accessible account of South Korean industrialization. The analysis is in terms of non-neoclassical economic theory, which emphasizes the role of the state in guiding the economy towards the production of higher value-added products that could succeed in international markets. Amsden presents a comprehensive view of the problems of late industrialization and the unique role of the state in these contexts. The book analyses the inadequacies of neoclassical economic theory in explaining the South Korean experience. Various chapters also provide detailed accounts of labour markets, education policy, and case studies of the ship-building, steel, and textile industries.

CHANG analyses the industrial policy of the South Korean state in the postwar period. The presentation is more theoretical than Amsden's, and provides a useful review of the literature on state intervention. The study is both lucid and clear in its presentation but uses more complex economic concepts in its arguments. Problems of information, coordination, and rent-seeking are all explored, and the study provides a coherent and useful framework for viewing industrial policy. The study's conclusions about the efficacy of industrial policy are broadly consonant with those of Amsden and Wade.

WADE provides a comprehensive and clear account of Taiwanese economic and industrial policy in the postwar period. Like Amsden, Wade emphasizes the role of the state in guiding the market and creating the conditions for sustained industrial growth. The study ranges from discussions of the theoretical debate surrounding Taiwanese success to detailed accounts of the workings of bureaucratic controls in the economy. The relationship between economic and industrial policy on one hand and politics on the other is also examined. Two concluding chapters provide very useful overviews of the nonorthodox account of Asian economic success.

ITO & KRUEGER contains articles that elucidate the East Asian experience in the light of neoclassical endogenous growth theory. Essentially, this view supports the contention that a complex of policies, from education policy to "outward-orientation" in trade, led to unprecedented growth rates in the East Asian economies. The book contains articles on specific countries as well as overviews of the Asian growth experience. A concluding section analyses how well endogenous growth theory can explain the East Asian growth experience. The articles are in general technical and not readily accessible to readers without a background in economics.

The WORLD BANK report provides a comprehensive presentation of the orthodox view of Asian economic success. The analysis acknowledges that government policy did help in fuelling the industrialization drive in Asia, but argues that this role was clearly subsidiary to market forces emanating from correct microeconomic and macroeconomic fundamentals. The study focuses on human capital formation, high investment and savings rates, and the efficient use of resources as the major engines of economic growth. The study is both clearly written and easily accessible to noneconomists.

AOKI, KIM & OKUNO-FUJIWARA contains a wide-ranging and sophisticated overview of the role of the government in East Asian development. The editors explicitly present the collected essays as a rebuttal of the World Bank view that state policy was only supplementary to market processes in creating sustained economic growth. Instead, they favour a "market-enhancing" perspective that views the East Asian experience as evidence that the government can facilitate and complement private sector agents in their efforts to overcome coordination problems and other market imperfections. The essays include analyses of the role of the government in overcoming market failure, the evolution of institutional structures, and the political economy of state–business interactions. The articles vary in the extent to which they are easily accessible, but in general they provide clear summaries of the main points. The introductory chapter provides a clear introduction to the "market-enhancing" view of Asian development.

DEYO contains a collection of articles on the political underpinnings of rapid industrialization in East Asia. The authors broadly argue that the political alignments within Asian countries in the postwar period allowed the state greater latitude in formulating economic and industrial policies by removing the constraints that powerful landed, business, or labour interests could place on policymakers. Chalmers Johnson compares government–business interactions in Japan, South Korea, and Taiwan whereas other authors examine the issues of foreign capital, state–labour relations, and class structures in East Asia. The book provides a lucid and comprehensive overview of the political economy issues surrounding Asian industrialization.

AKYUZ contains a recent overview of nonorthodox economic analyses of Asian development. Peter Evans analyses the degree to which East Asian institutional structures can be replicated in other developing countries; Jong-Il You presents a study of income distribution in East Asia; and Ajit Singh analyses savings and investment behaviour in East Asian corporations. The articles present sophisticated analyses but are accessible to noneconomists.

AJIT SINGH AND BRUCE A. WEISSE

See also Asian crisis, East Asian economies

Assertiveness training

Carlisle, Jane and Kathleen M. Donald, "The Use of Art Exercises in Assertiveness Training", *Journal of Counseling and Development*, 64 (1985): 149–50

Ernst, John M. and Martin Heesacker, "Application of the Elaboration Likelihood Model of Attitude Change to Assertion Training", *Journal of Counseling Psychology*, 40/1 (1993): 37–45

Giesen, Carol B., "Becoming and Remaining Assertive: A Longitudinal Study", *Psychological Reports*, 63 (1988): 595–605

Jakubowski, Patricia and Arthur J. Lange, *The Assertive Option: Your Rights and Responsibilities*, Champaign, Illinois: Research Press, 1978

Pentz, Mary Ann Wood, "Assertion Training and Trainer Effects on Unassertive and Aggressive Adolescents", *Journal of Counseling Psychology*, 27/1 (1980): 76–83

Pfost, Karen S., Michael J. Stevens, Jerry C. Parker and John F. McGowan, "The Influence of Assertion Training on Three Aspects of Assertiveness in Alcoholics", *Journal of Clinical Psychology*, 48/2 (1992): 262–68

Tanner, Vicki L. and W.B. Holliman, "Effectiveness of Assertiveness Training in Modifying Aggressive Behaviors of Young Children", *Psychological Reports*, 62 (1988): 39–46

Thompson, Kathryn L., Kaarre A. Bundy and Wende R. Wolfe, "Social Skills Training for Young Adolescents: Cognitive and Performance Components", *Adolescence*, 31/123 (1996): 505–21

Wood, Peggy S. and Brent Mallincrodt, "Culturally Sensitive Assertiveness Training for Ethnic Minority Clients", *Professional Psychology: Research and Practice*, 21/1 (1990): 5–11

Assertive behaviour has been defined in a variety of ways. JAKUBOWSKI defined assertiveness as a situation-specific behaviour, not a pervasive personality trait. She classified communication behaviour into three categories: nonassertive, assertive, and aggressive. According to her, assertiveness is defined as standing up for one's rights and expressing what one believes, feels, and wants in direct, appropriate ways that respect the rights of the other person.

Several cognitive-behavioural techniques, including variations of modelling, frequent rehearsal, and feedback were reported as effective in enhancing assertiveness. These behavioural techniques were often combined to improve assertiveness training effects. For example, PENTZ examined the effectiveness of structured learning training (SLT) to improve assertive behaviours. Structured learning training is a combination training approach, modelling with guided rehearsal and feedback. It was found to produce more assertive behaviours. In addition to changing overt behaviour, most assertiveness training aims to change cognitions related to assertiveness. For instance, Jakubowski provided a four-stage training process to improve assertiveness: (a) identifying one's personal rights and the rights of others in specific situations; (b) discriminating between nonassertive, assertive, and aggressive responses; (c) identifying and changing the thoughts which are barriers to assertive behaviour; (d) practising specific, new, more assertive behaviour.

In addition to cognitive-behavioural techniques, other techniques are combined to enhance the assertiveness training effect. CARLISLE & DONALD added art exercise in traditional assertiveness training curriculum. Although they did not empirically examine the effect of the art exercises in assertiveness training, they suggested the usefulness of art exercises to activate imagination and to provide nonverbal methods of practice in assertiveness training.

Despite the reported effectiveness of assertiveness training, issues have been raised pertaining to the generalizability of training effects. Related to the generalizability issue, GIESEN indicated that many studies examined the effectiveness of assertiveness training, but few studies have examined the duration of the effect of assertiveness training. She said that when training is completed, group members may no longer be in contact with one another and this important source of practice and social reinforcement may be lost, and the maintenance of the newly learned assertive behaviours may not be guaranteed. If the new assertive behaviour is ineffective as a means of coping with situational demands, she stated that the pre-existing behaviours are likely to return. Discussing factors that influence the maintenance of newly learned assertive behaviours, she argued that both extrinsic and intrinsic are important to maintaining assertive training effects. ERNST & HEESACKER also raised the generalizability issue. Reporting that only ten per cent of assertiveness training is actually effective, they suggested that new concepts need to be investigated in assertiveness training to improve the transfer of skill from training to real-life situations. They emphasized the attitudinal commitment to behave assertively to enhance assertive behaviour in real-life situations. The elaboration likelihood model (ELM) of attitude change was applied to the structured group training of assertiveness. The ELM-based group was significantly better at producing favourable assertive behaviours than a typical assertion group, which confirms the important role of attitude to maintain assertiveness training effects. In their relatively recent study on social skills training for young adolescents, THOMPSON, BUNDY & WOLFE argued that group participants' motivation to behave assertively influences their performance of assertiveness. And, therefore, it was suggested that group participants' motivation should be considered when planning interventions to enhance assertiveness.

As to the issue of relative effectiveness of assertiveness training on different clients, WOOD & MALLINCRODT discussed the different cultural values regarding assertive behaviours in different ethnic groups. They indicated that assertive interpersonal skills are a basic necessity for effective functioning in many aspects of life in the US, but members of many ethnic minority groups have values about assertive responding that differ markedly from those of the dominant culture. They suggested that therapists providing crosscultural assertiveness training be sensitive to cultural values regarding assertiveness in the client's culture. They said that therapists must be certain that learning assertive skills is a goal of the client, not just therapist. The following strategies were recommended for culturally sensitive assertiveness: determining the etiology of non-assertiveness; using self-report inventories that avoid words, slang, or situations that may not be meaningful to the client; developing norms for the cultural groups for which the inventory will be used. They also discussed specific assertiveness training strategies that are relevant to the cultural values of four ethnic minority groups-Blacks, Latinos, Asian Americans, and Native Americans.

The effectiveness of assertiveness training has been examined mostly with adults and adolescents. However, the training target group has been expanded. For example, TANNER & HOLLIMAN examined the effectiveness of assertiveness training in modifying aggressive behaviours of young children. They found that children given assertiveness training exhibited an increase in cooperative interaction and a decrease in physical aggression. PFOST *et al.* investigated the influence of assertion training on treating alcoholics. The alcoholics showed some behavioural competencies after assertion training, although such training did not differentially reduce discomfort in negative situations that call for assertive behaviour, or the discrepancy between perceptions of assertiveness in sober versus intoxicated states.

Sᴜɴɢ-Kʏᴜɴɢ Yᴏᴏ

Assessment

Berk, Ronald A. (editor), *Performance Assessment: Methods and Applications*, Baltimore: Johns Hopkins University Press, 1986

Campbell, Donald T. and Julian C. Stanley, *Experimental and Quasi-experimental Designs for Research*, Boston: Houghton Mifflin, 1963

Cardy, Robert L. and Gregory H. Dobbins, *Performance Appraisal: Alternative Perspectives*, Cincinnati: South-Western, 1994

Carmines, Edward G. and Richard A. Zeller, *Reliability and Validity Assessment*, Beverly Hills and London: Sage, 1979

Cook, Thomas D. and Donald T. Campbell, *Quasi-Experimentation: Design and Analysis for Field Settings*, Boston: Houghton Mifflin, 1979

DeVellis, Robert F., *Scale Development: Theory and Applications*, Newbury Park, California, California and London: Sage, 1991

Impara, James C. and Barbara S. Plake (editors), *The Thirteenth Mental Measurements Yearbook*, Lincoln, Nebraska: Buros Institute, 1998; supplements in alternate years (first Yearbook published in 1938); text of 10th–Yearbooks available on CD-ROM

Landy, Frank J. and James L. Farr, *The Measurement of Work Performance: Methods, Theory, and Applications*, New York and London: Academic Press, 1983

Murphy, Linda L., Jane Close Conoley and James C. Impara (editors), *Tests in Print 4: An Index to Tests, Test Reviews, and the Literature on Specific Tests*, Lincoln, Nebraska: Buros Institute, 1994

Nunnally, Jum C., *Psychometric Theory*, 3rd edition, New York and London: McGraw Hill, 1994

BERK contains nineteen essays by leading researchers in the field of performance assessment. The essays review research findings to date, suggest areas of future research, and provide recommendations for the assessment of employee and student performance. The volume effectively combines methodological issues with practical applications. The methodological essays discuss job analysis, rating scales, performance tests, appraisal interviews, utility analysis, and performance distribution assessment. The applications-related essays discuss job evaluation and methods to assess performance of technical, mechanical, and clinical employees, teachers, and students. The essays also present methods that raters can use to assess writing, listening, and speaking skills. The volume contains numerous tables, charts, and graphics that effectively support concepts presented in the text. Researchers and practitioners will find the volume to be a useful tool.

CARDY & DOBBINS focus on practical issues of performance assessment. They begin with a discussion of the relationships between appraisals, management, human resource management, and organizational politics. For example, they accurately state that raters give ratings that are more lenient when those ratings are used for administrative purposes than the ratings that are given when used for experimental purposes. They give a brilliant discussion of rating errors, rating formats, and the effects of cognition and affect on appraisal accuracy.

They also provide an in-depth discussion of types of raters (for example, self, peer, supervisor) and the effects of rater type on the accuracy of ratings. The book is written in an exceptionally lucid manner and is a useful tool for practitioners designing performance assessment systems and for faculty teaching an undergraduate course in assessment. The book would also be an effective reference for trainers who will teach managers how to rate the performance of their subordinates accurately.

LANDY & FARR have written an advanced volume of the theories of performance assessment, which would be a useful tool for faculty, researchers, and graduate students. The volume would also be suitable for practitioners who have advanced knowledge of, or extensive experience with, performance assessment. The volume begins with a discussion of technological and measurement aspects of performance assessment such as reliability, validity, accuracy, and types of performance measures. The authors then give a detailed discussion of sources of systematic and random error in assessment. They describe in detail the process of the appraisal including the observation of performance, recall, judgement, data analysis, and administrative outcome of the rating. The authors make effective use of tables and diagrams to elaborate on these themes. There is also an excellent discussion of administrative, research, and counselling uses of performance data. The final third of the volume is devoted to a discussion of utility analysis, and emerging theories in social and cognitive psychology on which future research should focus.

CARMINES & ZELLER complements Landy & Farr by presenting a clear discussion of the aspects of measurement theory that are related to determining the usefulness of an instrument. They begin by defining and discussing the different forms of validity, including construct, content, and criterion-related validity. They also discuss the most widely used forms of reliability including test-retest, parallel forms, split halves, and internal consistency. They demonstrate how correlation and factor analyses can be used to measure these different forms of reliability and validity. The concepts presented are applicable to the evaluation of all types of multi-item instruments, including ability tests, personality surveys, and performance appraisals. The material is presented in a discerning and meaningful way, such that the volume is an effective primer for graduate students and practitioners who are beginning the study of measurement methods and is also a useful refresher volume for researchers who have advanced measurement knowledge.

DeVELLIS is an excellent resource for readers who plan to design instruments to collect data such as attitudes, opinions, or perceived performance. The volume begins with a brief but relevant history of measurement in the social sciences, and follows with an in-depth discussion of the phenomenon of latent variables. DeVellis gives clearly written, systematic instructions regarding writing questions, choosing a scale (for example Likert, or semantic differential), pretesting an instrument, and optimizing instrument length. Factor analytic strategies for evaluating an instrument are expertly discussed, although readers will want to rely more heavily on Carmines & Zeller for methods to evaluate instrument reliability and validity. DeVellis closes with an excellent discussion of administrative issues such as the implications of using a written or interview format for collecting data.

The Buros Institute ("Buros", see IMPARA & PLAKE) and MURPHY, CONOLEY & IMPARA have produced companion reference works. Each reference is updated periodically. Murphy, Conoley & Impara list the great majority of psychometric instruments that are sold in the US, their publishers, and their prices. Measurable phenomena that are listed include personality, motivation, career choice, psychological health, and many others. The volume also gives references to peer-reviewed studies of the tests contained in Buros. These studies of the tests in Buros contain discussions of test reliability and validity, developmental history, and cost, but readers should understand the concepts in DeVellis and Carmines & Zeller before reading the test reviews in Buros. Buros and Murphy, Conoley & Imara are invaluable resources for researchers or practitioners who are planning to use commercially available measurement instruments. They are also useful for faculty members who wish to teach the practical implications of measurement theory.

COOK & CAMPBELL is the definitive volume regarding quasi-experimentation. Their volume gives a rich description of methods researchers can use to gather data to maximize the possibility of showing causation between a predictor and criterion. There is an in-depth discussion of internal and external validity issues (such as history and selection), and there are instructions for using experimental groups, control groups, treatments, and randomization to increase internal and external validity. There is also an effective discussion of the use of analysis of variance, correlation, regression, and path models for data analysis. Overall, the book is an excellent resource for graduate students and researchers who will use random or non-random assignment as measurement tools. CAMPBELL & STANLEY's volume is essentially a concise version of Cook & Campbell, and is written in a manner that is more accessible for practitioners.

Like Cook & Campbell's volume, NUNNALLY also is definitive in the field of psychometric measurement. Nunnally, however, takes a significantly more conceptual approach to the field, and readers should therefore have a full understanding of basic statistics (for example, correlation, regression, factor analysis) before using this volume. Nunnally brilliantly discusses the intricate details of measurement, scaling, validity, covariance, factor analysis, and multidimensional scaling. Lastly, Nunnally gives an excellent discussion of measurement of abilities, personality, and sentiments, and the effects of speed, guessing, and participant bias on data collection.

SHANI D. CARTER

See also Appraisal, Performance evaluation

Assessment centres

Ahmed, Yasmin, Tim Payne and Steve Whiddett, "A Process for Assessment Exercise Design: A Model of Best Practice", *International Journal of Selection and Assessment*, 5/1 (1997): 62–68
Ballantyne, Iain and Nigel Povah, *Assessment and Development Centres*, Aldershot, Hampshire: Gower, 1995
Baron, Helen and Karen Janman, "Fairness in the Assessment Centre" in *International Review of Industrial and*

Organizational Psychology, vol. 11, edited by Cary L. Cooper and Ivan T. Robertson, Chichester and New York: Wiley, 1996
Carrick, Peter and Richard Williams, "Development Centres: A Review of Assumptions", *Human Resource Management Journal*, 9/2 (1999): 77–92
Gaugler, B.B., D.B. Rosenthal, G.C. Thornton and C. Bentson, "Meta-analysis of Assessment Center Validity", *Journal of Applied Psychology*, 72/3 (1987): 493–511
Guion, Robert M., *Assessment, Measurement, and Prediction for Personnel Decisions*, Mahwah, New Jersey: Erlbaum, 1998
Jansen, Paul and Ferry de Jongh, *Assessment Centres: A Practical Handbook*, Chichester and New York: Wiley, 1997
Klimoski, R. and M. Brickner, "Why Do Assessment Centers Work? The Puzzle of Assessment Center Validity", *Personnel Psychology*, 40 (1987): 243–60
Lee, Geoff and David Beard, *Development Centres: Realizing the Potential of Your Employee through Assessment and Development*, London and New York: McGraw Hill, 1994
Lievens, Filip, "Factors Which Improve the Construct Validity of Assessment Centers: A Review", *International Journal of Selection and Assessment*, 6/3 (1998): 141–52
Sackett, Paul R. and George F. Dreher, "Constructs and Assessment Center Dimensions: Some Troubling Empirical Findings", *Journal of Applied Psychology*, 67/4 (1982): 401–10
Salgado, Jésus F., "Personnel Selection Methods" in *International Review of Industrial and Organizational Psychology*, vol. 14, edited by Cary L. Cooper and Ivan T. Robertson, Chichester and New York: Wiley, 1999
Thornton, George C. III and William C. Byham, *Assessment Centers and Managerial Performance*, New York and London: Academic Press, 1982
Thornton, George C. III, *Assessment Centers in Human Resource Management*, Reading, Massachusetts: Addison Wesley, 1992
Woodruffe, Charles, *Assessment Centres: Identifying and Developing Competence*, 2nd edition, London: Institute of Personnel and Development, 1993
Zaal, Jac N., "Assessment Centre Methods" in *Handbook of Work and Organizational Psychology*, 2nd edition, vol. 3, *Personnel Psychology*, edited by P.J.D. Drenth, Henk Thierry and Charles J. de Wolff, Hove, Sussex: Psychology Press, 1998

As there is an enormous literature on assessment centres, this entry will concentrate on textbooks and review papers, although one or two other key articles also will be mentioned. The entry will also touch on development centres, that is the application of the assessment centre method for development rather than selection purposes.

Surveys of practice show that there has been a substantial increase in the use of assessment and development centres, and it is not surprising therefore that a considerable proportion of the literature is orientated towards practitioners. Books of particular interest include BALLANTYNE & POVAH, JANSEN & DE JONGH, LEE & BEARD, and WOODRUFFE.

There's little to choose amongst them; they all cover similar sort of ground and draw to some extent on relevant research. Though clearly intended to be practically helpful, this sort of "how to do it" guide tends not to cover everything that the practitioner might need to know, either because some issues are not touched on at all or because they are dealt with only sketchily. For example, AHMED, PAYNE & WHIDDETT point to the relative absence of practical guidance on how to design the content of assessment centre exercises: they offer advice intended to try to fill this gap. Another issue on which practitioner-orientated literature is relatively silent is the vexed question of assessment centre construct validity, a matter that will be returned to shortly. In other words, the "how to do it" literature is helpful only up to a point, and practitioners sensibly ought to delve into the more academic sources.

As a starting point THORNTON & BYHAM can hardly be bettered. This is an important source for the early research on assessment centres; it also gives an account of their history. Judged by today's standards the text's focus on managerial performance might be seen as rather narrow, but this in large part is a reflection of the predominant application of the assessment centre method in the earlier days. There is no more recent text comparable to Thornton & Byham, although a later work by THORNTON serves as an update. This has more of a practitioner orientation to it, and is soundly based in research. Thornton also deals more fully with matters that were only touched on in Thornton & Byham, such as the provision of feedback to participants (and others).

For more recent reviews it is necessary to turn to other sources, particularly journals and edited volumes. GUION and ZAAL provide overviews of assessment centres, as well as reviewing key research findings. Guion helpfully examines a number of continuing problems and issues with assessment centres, and Zaal has the merit of drawing on European literature. SALGADO provides a brief summary of research published during the 1990s. BARON & JANMAN pursue a more specific theme, namely fairness in the assessment centre. Although they adopt a narrower view of fairness than is found in much of the contemporary literature (see the entry on fairness), their review is helpful as it indicates where hazards to fairness may intrude; they also consider separately the fairness of the various components that may make up an assessment centre, and to this extent they provide an overview of selection methods more generally.

The growth in popularity of assessment centres almost certainly stemmed in part from their apparent effectiveness in predicting future performance. The important meta-analysis by GAUGLER et al. brought together the early evidence on this. But, as is clear from the reviews cited above, though evidence for the criterion-related validity of assessment centres has continued to accumulate, considerable doubt remains as to construct validity. Warning bells were sounded quite early on in assessment centre history (SACKETT & DREHER) and since then studies generally have confirmed their suspect construct validity: in short, it remains unclear that assessment centres measure the constructs, dimensions, or competencies that they are designed to assess. This has led to the question, "why do assessment centres work?" (see KLIMOSKI & BRICKNER). There is no clear answer to this question, and on the face of it the construct validity problem seems to be pretty much intractable. However, evidence-based advice for practitioners is offered by LIEVENS who has reviewed key studies bearing on construct validity.

There is a view in the literature that the apparent absence of construct validity is not necessarily a problem. This view is sometimes articulated where assessment centres are used wholly for selection purposes, the argument being along the lines that it is sufficient to know that assessment centres predict future performance/potential-it doesn't matter that we do not know why. This is not a particularly strong argument, whether viewed from a theoretical or practical perspective. Moreover, assessment centres commonly are used for development purposes; indeed, they often serve both selection and developmental ends. For the latter, demonstrable construct validity is of heightened importance. Issues to do with the use of the assessment centre method for development are examined by Thornton. A more recent review, by CARRICK & WILLIAMS, which also serves to direct the reader to relevant research, questions the assumptions that underlie the developmental use of assessment centres. This review also introduces the reader to the literature on the impact of assessment and development centres.

RICHARD WILLIAMS

See also Human resource management

Attachment theory in infancy

Ainsworth, Mary et al., *Patterns of Attachment: A Psychological Study of the Strange Situation*, Hillsdale, New Jersey: Erlbaum, 1978

Ainsworth, Mary, "Patterns of Infant-mother Attachments: Antecedents and Effects on Development", *Bulletin of New York Academy of Medicine*, 66 (1985): 771–91

Bowlby, John, *Child Care and the Growth of Love*, edited by Margery Fry, Harmondsworth and Baltimore: Penguin, 1953

Bowlby, John, *Attachment and Loss: Attachment*, New York: Basic Books, and London: Hogarth Press, 1969

Bowlby, John, *Attachment and Loss: Separation, Anxiety and Anger*, New York: Basic Books, and London: Hogarth Press, 1973

Bowlby, John, *Attachment and Loss: Loss, Sadness and Depression*, New York: Basic Books, and London: Hogarth Press, 1980

Clarke, Alan and Ann Clarke, *Early Experience: Myth and Evidence*, London: Open Books, and New York: Free Press, 1976

Dunn, Judy, *Young Children's Close Relationships: Beyond Attachment*, London and Newbury Park, California: Sage, 1993

Fonagy, Peter, Howard Steele, Miriam Steele and Juliet Holder, "Attachment and Theory of Mind: Overlapping Constructs?" in *Bonding and Attachment: Current Issues in Research and Practice*, edited by Gillian Forrest, Association for Child Psychology and Psychiatry, 1997

Holmes, Jeremy, *John Bowlby and Attachment Theory*, London and New York: Routledge, 1993

Ijzendoorn, Marinus van and P.M. Kroonenberg, "Cross-cultural Patterns of Attachment: A Meta-analysis of the Strange Situation", *Child Development*, 59 (1988): 147–56

Rutter, Michael and the English and Romanian Adoptees (ERA) team, "Developmental Catch-up, and Deficit, Following Adoption after Severe Global Early Privation", *Journal of Child Psychology and Psychiatry and Allied Disciplines*, 39/4 (1998a): 465–76

Rutter, Michael, "Practitioner Review: Routes from Research to Clinical Practice in Child Psychiatry: Retrospect and Prospect", *Journal of Child Psychology and Psychiatry and Allied Disciplines*, 39/6 (1998b): 805–16

Singer, Elisabeth, *Child-care and the Psychology of Development*, London and New York: Routledge, 1992

Theories of childcare have evolved over the years and across cultures to guide and inform the practice of parenting. In Western cultures, in the 20th century, the process of child rearing has been influenced by the work of child psychologists whose research has addressed such questions as: What is the nature of the caring relationship between children and their parents (and other caregivers)? How do these relationships work to promote normal psychological development? What are the effects on the child when these relationships are damaged or break down?

Attachment theory, originating in the work of BOWLBY (1953), has had an important influence on Western thinking about childcare. The model suggests that effective caregivers are sensitive and responsive to their children and give them a secure base from which to venture forth into the world. (For a useful review, see HOLMES).

BOWLBY (1969, 1973, 1980) argued that the propensity to form strong emotional bonds with particular individuals was a fundamental characteristic of human young; it had survival value by bringing nurturance, protection, and security to the infant. In an early formulation of this perspective, he was influenced by psychodynamic thinking and by ethology. This led him to create a theory about the bonding relationship that develops between parents and their children, and the disruption to that relationship that can occur when parents and children are separated, or where there is bereavement or some form of emotional deprivation.

Bowlby (1969, 1973, 1980) considered attachment in the early years of life as a behavioural system with a set goal – that of proximity to the primary caregiver, usually the mother. Separations from the caregiver, he proposed, would activate the attachment system in order to restore proximity. When the attachment system had achieved its goal – being close to the caregiver – then attachment behaviours, such as crying and clinging, would subside. The infant's need for proximity to the caregiver was balanced, according to Bowlby (1969, 1973, 1980), by the predisposition to explore the world around. This need to explore took the child away from the caregiver and counteracted the need for proximity. All children needed to find a balance between these two opposing tendencies. In a situation of threat, for example being separated from the parent, when the child is ill, or when the child is in an unfamiliar place, the attachment behaviours were activated.

One of Bowlby's (1953) early ideas was the now-discredited maternal deprivation hypothesis. He suggested that there was a critical period between six months and three years when the child needed continuous care from the caregiver. Significant separations at this stage would have a damaging effect on the child's social and emotional development. He drew on research from diverse sources to support his hypothesis, including studies of primates reared in isolation, of children reared in orphanages, and of children separated from parents through bereavement or illness. He concluded that the absent mother could not be a sensitive mother since, by her absence, she was not available to meet her child's needs. The maternal deprivation hypothesis was very influential when it was first proposed in the 1950s in a report to the World Health Organization (WHO), and it made many mothers anxious and guilty about leaving their young children in the care of other adults.

One important extension of Bowlby's early work was the focus on the nature of the attachment relationship. Foremost in this research was AINSWORTH who studied patterns of attachment shown by young children in different contexts and over time, emphasizing the quality of the caregiver-child relationship. She suggested that the behaviour of the primary caregiver, usually the mother, in the early years of a child's life could predict the type of relationship that the mother and child would have later on. She extended Bowlby's concept of the secure base and proposed that mothers who are responsive, sensitive, accessible, and co-operative during the child's first year will have children who develop a secure attachment. This in turn forms the basis for feelings within the child of self-worth and self-confidence.

AINSWORTH *et al.* studied separations and reunions between mothers and young children in an experiment known as the "strange situation" in which one-year old children were left briefly in the presence of a person unfamiliar to them. As a result, she distinguished between secure (known as type B) and insecure (known as types A and C) attachment patterns. Type B children cried when separated from their mothers but were easily soothed on their return. Any distress shown during separation was clearly related to the mother's absence. They preferred their mother to the stranger. Type A children shunned contact with the mother on her return, mingling welcome with responses such as turning away, moving past her or averting gaze. The mother and the stranger were treated in a similar way. Type C children were very upset when the mother left but were not easily comforted on her return. They resisted contact with her but combined this behaviour with attempts to get close to her – an ambivalent response. They also resisted comfort from the stranger.

The concept of sensitive mothering remains controversial (for a review see SINGER). The obligation to aspire to the ideal of the sensitive, available, responsive caregiver can be overwhelming to parents, especially to mothers. Some women do not find that the role of sensitive, available caregiver as a satisfying one. Cross-cultural comparisons (such as IJZENDOORN & KROONENBERG) also indicate that there are wide differences in the patterns of interaction that lead to secure and insecure attachment between parents and their children.

CLARKE & CLARKE revisited the evidence that Bowlby had provided and reviewed a range of studies to identify the factors that caused young primates or children reared apart from their parents to suffer. Monkeys isolated from their mothers showed signs of being depressed and withdrawn but, when normally reared three month old monkeys were introduced into the cages, the isolates presented fewer stereotypical responses and after six months were scarcely presenting any social deficits. Studies of human infants revealed that one to two year olds can form good social relationships with adults other than their parents and with older children, and that these relationships can be strong and enduring. The effects of short separations, for example through hospitalization, can be greatly alleviated by regular visits from important attachment figures. The disruption to the capacity of children reared in institutions to form close, lasting relationships was probably caused by unstimulating conditions and by the large turnover of staff rather than by the separation from parents in itself.

Research has not confirmed a straightforward link between early experiences of separation from the mother and disordered behaviour in adolescence. RUTTER (1998b) indicated that different constellations of early experience are associated with different outcomes. He made a distinction between *privation* of affectional bonds, where, for example, children growing up in institutions may be denied the opportunity of establishing such bonds, and *disruption* of affectional bonds where established maternal care is lost.

More recently, RUTTER (1998b) argued that there has been a revolution in medical research and medical practice over the past 40 years. Interventions and treatments differ in that they are now (in comparison to the 1950s) more focussed and time limited; interventions relate to current real life challenges and problems, to cognitive processing of experiences, to active coping-problem-solving strategies, and to behavioural contingencies and consequences. It is now acknowledged that children affect parents and other adults just as they are influenced by the ways in which they are dealt with. Research into risk and protective factors has provided clinically relevant findings that go far beyond attachment issues. Rutter (1998b) highlights the following issues:

There is evidence forcing a movement away from a view of children as passive recipients of experience to one that recognizes their active role in influencing the behaviour of other people, shaping and selecting their experiences, and actively processing their experiences, and so imposing a meaning on them. Even family-wide experiences impact differently on each child in the family. The effect of these research findings has been to shift emphasis to children's coping strategies and to their processing of their experiences.

There is growing recognition of the individual differences in children's responses to stress and adversity. There are protective mechanisms both in the child and in the interplay between the child and the environment. Changes for the better can occur even in adult life provided that the right "turning point" experiences occur.

Research evidence shows the importance of influences outside the parent-child relationship, including peers, siblings, the community and school. There are great opportunities for prevention and treatment that are only just beginning to be taken up.

Rutter's ongoing research (RUTTER, 1998a) on children adopted into UK families from Romanian orphanages provides contemporary evidence. Conditions in the Romanian orphanages varied from poor to appalling. The children were confined to cots, had few toys, little talk from caregivers, no personalized care giving, they were fed gruel from propped bottles, and the physical environments were often harsh. Washing, for example, involved being hosed down with cold water. These children suffered emotional privation, were undernourished, and may well have been physically abused in some cases. However, the research has shown that, for those who were adopted before six months, there has been almost complete cognitive and physical catch-up by the age of four years; for those adopted after six months, the mean was one standard deviation below that of adopted UK children. Rutter has also found that there was a high degree of resilience among the children, and concludes that the remaining cognitive deficit was likely to be a consequence of the early privation, with psychological privation more important than nutritional privation.

FONAGY *et al.* have made important links between attachment and the capacity to understand mental states in self and others – a concept known as *theory of mind*. He argues (p.36) that

the caregiver's perception of the child as an intentional being lies at the root of sensitive caregiving, which is viewed by attachment theorists to be the cornerstone of secure attachment ... Secure attachment in its turn provides the psychosocial basis for acquiring an understanding of mind.

This idea is confirmed by the work of DUNN who proposes that the process of engaging in conversations about feelings and the reasons behind other people's actions are linked to the development of the capacity to understand others' mental states. Dunn also notes the importance of relationships with same-age peers and with siblings in predicting social and cognitive competence.

Although Bowlby's predictions were not completely upheld by the evidence, he made an enormous contribution to the ways in which young children are treated, for example in residential or day care, or in hospital, and to research in the early years. There is now much greater awareness of the importance of children's intimate social relationships as they develop over time. Attachment theory is only one of a number of influential developmental theories in psychology and it remains controversial.

HELEN COWIE

Attention

Allport, D.A., "Attention and Control: Have We Been Asking the Wrong Questions? A Critical Review of Twenty-Five Years" in *Attention and Performance 14: Synergies in Experimental Psychology, Artificial Intelligence, and Cognitive Neuroscience*, edited by David Meyer and Sylvan Kornblum, Cambridge, Massachusetts: MIT Press, 1993

Broadbent, D.E., *Perception and Communication*, New York and London: Pergamon Press, 1958

Kramer, Arthur F., Michael G.H. Coles and Gordon D. Logan (editors), *Converging Operations in the Study of Visual Selective Attention*, Washington, DC: American Psychological Association, 1996

Lavie, N. and Y. Tsal, "Perceptual Load as a Major Determinant of the Locus of Selection in Visual Attention", *Perception and Psychophysics*, 56/2 (1994): 183–97

Neuman, O., " Automatic Processing: A Review of Recent Findings and a Plea for an Old Theory" in *Cognition and Motor Processes*, edited by W. Prinz and A.F. Sanders, Berlin and New York: Springer, 1984

Norman, D.A. and T. Shallice, "Attention to Action: Willed and Automatic Control of Behavior" in *Consciousness and Self Regulation: Advances in Research and Theory*, edited by Gary Schwartz and David Shapiro, New York: Plenum, 1986

Posner, M.I. and S.E. Petersen, "The Attentional System of the Human Brain", *Annual Review of Neuroscience*, 13 (1990): 25–42

Reason, James, *Human Error*, Cambridge and New York: Cambridge University Press, 1990

Styles, Elizabeth A., *The Psychology of Attention*, Hove, Sussex: Psychology Press, 1997

Treisman, A., "The Perception of Features and Objects" in *Attention: Selection, Awareness and Control: A Tribute to Donald Broadbent*, edited by Alan Baddeley and Lawrence Weiskrantz, Oxford and New York: Clarendon Press, 1993

Wright, R.D. and L.M. Ward, "Shifts of Visual Attention: An Historical and Methodological Overview", *Canadian Journal of Experimental Psychology*, 48/2 (1994): 151–66

Attention was a worthy topic for experimental investigation by Hermann von Helmholtz and for insightful discussion by William James around the turn of the 19th century, but was neglected under the behaviourist tradition that dominated the early and mid 20th century as representing perhaps the most intangible of mental constructs. BROADBENT, in his work on auditory attention, introduced many of the concepts that are currently employed in the field – terms borrowed from engineering, such as "filters", "buffers" and "bottlenecks" in the flow of information. Broadbent's book can be seen as one of the most important starting points for information processing approaches to studying cognition.

The conception of attention as the selection of a subset of perceptually analysed information for further processing has sparked major issues in attention research: the extent to which unattended information is processed, and particularly whether such information is processed for meaning and whether it can exert an influence on behaviour. LAVIE & TSAL provide a review and attempt to reconcile data and theory in this "early versus late selection" debate.

Much research has progressed by exploiting and understanding a small number of experimental paradigms to the full. The review paper by WRIGHT & WARD is brief but introduces much of the recent work concerning shifts of visual atten-

tion, particularly research concerning the benefits and costs to perception of cueing visual locations, independent of eye-movements to those locations. A significant figure in this area of research for several decades has been Michael Posner. POSNER & PETERSEN describe the brain systems that are thought to underlie various aspects of attention, with particular emphasis on their own account of the disengagement, shifting, and engagement of attention as separate processes. The chapter by TREISMAN provides a summary of her feature integration theory, a very influential account of the role of attention in the binding of separately processed attributes (such as colour and form) to give perceptual objects. This theory is based to a large extent upon results gleaned from another experimental paradigm, that of visual search.

The view that visual attention operates by the selection of spatial locations (leading to metaphors such as spotlights and zoom lenses) has been challenged recently. There is evidence that selection may operate at the level of objects, organized by pre-attentive perceptual processes. A number of the chapters in the book edited by KRAMER, COLES & LOGAN are concerned with the evidence to support their view. The book also provides papers on a number of topics such as negative priming, mathematical models, neurology, and disorders of attention following brain injury. These papers make few concessions to those requiring an introduction to the subject, but rather give state-of-the-art research at an advanced level – with the advantage of being collected in a single volume.

Although definitions are somewhat hazy and perhaps even circular, an important distinction has been made between automatic and controlled processes; the distinction is made in almost every domain of cognition. Automatic processes are those that operate without attention whereas controlled processes demand attention and cannot be, to some extent at least, simultaneously performed. The relationship between the two has to do with skill acquisition and expertise. A good starting point is NEUMAN who summarizes, and heavily critiques, the earlier and less accessible research.

NORMAN & SHALLICE propose an influential cognitive model of the systems underlying the control of behaviour. The model addresses some difficult issues such as the distinction between automatic and supervised or willed control of actions, and the planning of behaviour, and has something (constructive) to say about the role of consciousness in cognition. The model draws in part upon evidence from people with damage to the frontal lobes of the brain in support for its architecture and operation. REASON's book gives evidence for the importance of understanding selection for action in everyday life, detailing the repercussions of slips and lapses of attention in producing both minor absentmindedness and significant blunder.

Given the complexities and vagaries of attention research, a very useful accompaniment to any reading is ALLPORT's review paper, which usefully challenges many of the basic assumptions of the research programme and provides much food for thought. For example, he stresses that we should consider the role that attention plays in cognition – what it is actually for – before attempting to tackle it experimentally. It is certainly the case that attention is not one thing. Finally, STYLES provides a clearly written text. Unlike sections on attention in more general psychology textbooks, it goes beyond earlier research, which defined the area and is surprisingly comprehensive in its coverage of more recent issues. It is therefore one of the best single introductions available.

MICHAEL P. DEAN

Attribution theory

Augoustinos, Martha and Iain Walker, *Social Cognition: An Integrated Introduction*, London and Thousand Oaks, California: Sage, 1995

Heider, Fritz, *The Psychology of Interpersonal Relations*, New York: Wiley, 1958

Hewstone, Miles, *Causal Attribution: From Cognitive Processes to Collective Beliefs*, Oxford and Cambridge, Massachusetts: Blackwell, 1989

Hilton, Denis J., "Conversational Processes and Causal Explanation" in *Psychological Bulletin*, 107/1 (1990): 65–81

Jones, Edward E. and Keith E. Davis, "From Acts to Dispositions: The Attribution Process in Person Perception" in *Advances in Experimental Social Psychology*, vol. 2, edited by Leonard Berkowitz, New York: Academic Press, 1965

Kelley, Howard H., "The Processes of Causal Attribution", *American Psychologist*, 28 (1973): 107–28

Schneider, David J., Albert H. Hastorf and Phoebe C. Ellsworth, *Person Perception*, 2nd edition, Reading, Massachusetts: Addison Wesley, 1979

Weary, Gifford, Melinda A. Stanley and John H. Harvey, *Attribution*, New York: Springer, 1989

Weiner, Bernard, *An Attributional Theory of Motivation and Emotion*, New York: Springer, 1986

The origin of what has come to be known as attribution theory is usually traced to Fritz HEIDER. He argued that individuals are predisposed to see cause–effect relationships in their own and other individuals' actions, and that they are concerned to attribute actions to internal (dispositional) or external (situational) causes. He described for the first time a number of important psychological effects, such as the tendency to underestimate situational causes and overestimate dispositional causes (*the fundamental attribution error*). The 1958 text is the most full and detailed exposition of his ideas. It is wide ranging and discursive but useful for the information it provides on the roots of attribution theory in the cognitive and social psychology of the time.

JONES & DAVIS are accredited with the next major step in attribution theory. They developed Heider's ideas into a coherent theoretical framework and proposed the theory of correspondent inferences, which addresses how people decide which particular actions correspond to internal or dispositional causes. The 1965 paper is a detailed exposition of correspondent inference theory and an evaluation of the empirical support for the theory. It also provides some of the earliest evidence that attributions may be subject to motivational biases.

The third of the three classic authors of attribution theory is KELLEY. There are many accounts of his work to choose from but the 1973 paper has the advantage of being succinct as well as covering all important aspects of his covariation, and configuration principles. The covariation principle describes the way that people determine the cause of an action when they have information from multiple observations. It is a rational model of decision making. The configuration principle describes how people use past experience to reach a plausible explanation when they do not have enough information to employ the rational calculus of the covariation principle. The paper goes on to speculate about the cause of errors or bias in attributions and to argue that attributions are important because they provide a basis for future action.

The effects of attributions on subsequent behaviour are the focus of WEINER's work. He addresses how decisions about the cause of an event affect the emotional reaction to that event and future motivation. For instance, if a man attributes his failure in an examination to lack of ability, he may experience low self esteem and a lack of motivation to study for future exams. Weiner's book discusses two decades of empirical research on attribution and motivation. It covers his influential work on how attributions are more likely to be made in response to unexpected outcomes or failure, but its main focus is the very specific model of the cognitive steps from an event to its behavioural consequences. The book perhaps represents the apotheosis of purely cognitive approaches to attribution.

For a fluent and thoughtful introduction to attribution theory in the context of person perception, SCHNEIDER, HASTORF & ELLSWORTH is hard to beat. The authors describe the three main approaches of Heider, Jones & Davis, and Kelley and directly compare the correspondent inference, covariation, and configuration models. They also cover research on attributional bias and the implications of attribution theory for behaviour, including Weiner's research. The book is well paced and full of examples. Although it was written in 1979 it is still an excellent text for use with undergraduates.

WEARY, STANLEY & HARVEY provides a good review of the foundations of attribution theory and more recent advances in, and applications of, attribution theory. The chapters on applications look at how individual attributions affect behaviour in close relationships, health behaviours, dysfunctional behaviours such as depression, and motivation and achievement. They also discuss how attribution theory has been applied to therapeutic interventions.

Research on attribution theory was most active in the 1970s and 1980s. More recently this research has been criticized for too much of a focus on individual reasoning removed from social context. HILTON points out that causal explanations are provided in conversation and that appropriate answers to *why* questions depend on the participants' understanding of the drift of the conversation. In this paper he argues that a recognition of the interpersonal, interactional nature of normal causal attribution can make a different sense of attributional processes and biases.

HEWSTONE attempts to rebuff the criticism that attribution theory is divorced from social aspects of behaviour by examining attribution theory and research from four different levels of analysis: the intrapersonal, interpersonal, intergroup, and societal levels. The latter two levels in particular are concerned with how group membership and culture influence the attributions we make.

The text by AUGOUSTINOS & WALKER is a useful account of attribution theory in several respects. First, they provide a short but clear introduction to the founding theories of attribution theory followed by a more detailed account of attributional biases. This is one of the most accessible accounts of attribution research. Then, like Hewstone, they attempt to integrate attribution theory with the more social perspectives on explanation provided by theories of intergroup behaviour and social representations, but in doing so they provide their own critique of individualistic approaches in attribution theory and social cognition generally. Finally, they address the extent to which attributions are ideological. For instance, they argue that the fundamental attribution error reflects the dominant ideology of individualism within Western culture.

JULIE DICKINSON

Auctions

Cassady, Ralph Jr, *Auctions and Auctioneering*, Berkeley: University of California Press, 1967

Kagel, John H., "Auctions: A Survey of Experimental Research" in *The Handbook of Experimental Economics*, edited by John H. Kagel and Alvin E. Roth, Princeton, New Jersey: Princeton University Press, 1995

Klemperer, Paul D., "Auction Theory: A Guide to the Literature", *Journal of Economic Surveys*, 13/3 (1999): 227–86; reprinted as chapter 1 of *The Economic Theory of Auctions*, edited by Paul D. Klemperer, Cheltenham: Elgar, 2000

Laffont, Jean-Jacques, "Game Theory and Empirical Economics: The Case of Auction Data", *European Economic Review*, 41/1 (1997): 1–35

McAfee, R. and John McMillan, "Auctions and Bidding", *Journal of Economic Literature*, 25/2 (1987): 699–738

McMillan, John, "Selling Spectrum Rights", *Journal of Economic Perspectives*, 8/3 (1994): 145–62

Milgrom, Paul and Robert Weber, "A Theory of Auctions and Competitive Bidding", *Econometrica*, 50/5 (1982): 1089–1122

Milgrom, Paul, "Auctions and Bidding: A Primer", *Journal of Economic Perspectives*, 3/3 (1989): 3–22

Myerson, Roger B., "Optimal Auction Design", *Mathematics of Operations Research*, 6/1 (1981): 58–73

Riley, John G. and William F. Samuelson, "Optimal Auctions", *American Economic Review*, 71/3 (1981): 381–92

Vickrey, William, "Counterspeculation, Auctions, and Competitive Sealed Tenders", *Journal of Finance*, 16/1 (1961): 8–37

Wolfstetter, Elmer, "Auctions: An Introduction", *Journal of Economic Surveys*, 10/4 (1995): 367–420

Auctions are commonly used to trade art and antiques, cars, commodities and livestock, houses, mineral exploration rights, and Treasury securities. In AD 193, the Praetorian Guards auctioned the Roman Empire. More recently, governments have conducted auctions to sell public enterprises and licences to use electronic spectrum. CASSADY provides a comprehensive account of the history and practice of auctions, together with advice of how to conduct and participate in them.

The modern study of auctions originated with the seminal paper by VICKREY, who was the first scholar to approach auctions from a game theory perspective. Vickrey sought to address the problem of achieving efficient allocations in situations of imperfect competition. He compares the properties of common auction forms, the ordinary open ascending ("English") auction, the descending ("Dutch") auction, and the sealed bid auction. He proves the fundamental revenue equivalence theorem, which asserts that the choice of auction form was immaterial in equilibrium with homogeneous bidders. He also recognizes that, where bidders are inhomogeneous or insufficiently sophisticated to compute the equilibrium strategies, the Dutch or first price sealed bid auction may lead to inefficient outcomes. Consequently, he proposes the second price sealed bid ("Vickrey") auction mechanism as a means of achieving efficient outcomes with minimum transactions costs. In such a game, it is a dominant strategy for each bidder to bid his true value. The good is automatically assigned to the bidder who values it most highly, and the bidders do not have to worry about predicting the behaviour of their rivals.

The stimulus provided by Vickrey culminated in the path-breaking contributions of Milgrom, Weber, and Myerson. In a remarkable synthesis, MILGROM & WEBER formulate a general theoretical framework for the analysis of auctions and competitive bidding, establishing 21 theorems detailing the relative merits of various auction forms in different circumstances. MILGROM provides a concise and readable overview of the key insights of his work with Weber, drawing conclusions for the prevalence of different institutional arrangements in practice.

MYERSON addresses the related question of optimal auctions. Among the host of conceivable auction forms, which will maximise the expected revenue of the seller? Myerson approaches the problem as one of mechanism design, invoking his *revelation principle* to show that it suffices to restrict analysis to incentive compatible direct auctions. Though less general, RILEY & SAMUELSON is a more readable account of optimal auction theory, with many insightful illustrations. They show that the revenue equivalence theorem applies much more generally to a broad class of auction mechanisms, provided that the bidders are risk neutral and their valuations are independent.

Auction theory has developed special techniques of analysis. Consequently, in their full generality, the key results of auction theory can appear less than convincing to the first-time reader. WOLFSTETTER avoids this problem by explicitly deriving optimal strategies in a very simple model in which it is easy to demonstrate the revenue equivalence theorem. He then outlines the modifications and extensions required as the basic framework is modified to allow for risk aversion, multi-unit and repeated auctions, and the possibility of collusion. He ends with applications to oligopoly and the selling of rights to natural monopoly.

McAFEE & McMILLAN is an excellent survey article aimed at the general reader. As a literature survey, it is now a little dated and not exhaustive. As an exposition, their contribution is notable for its insight and readability. After some introductory comments on the role of auctions, they present an elegant exposition of the revenue equivalence theorem in the standard private values model. They then discuss the implications of relaxing each of the assumptions in turn.

The valuable collection edited by KLEMPERER contains the most important original papers in the field, including all but two of the articles cited in this essay. His introductory chapter is a comprehensive, well-organized, and up-to-date survey of the literature on auctions. In addition to a comprehensive bibliography, key papers are listed by section, providing an invaluable guide to the literature for individual study. Four appendices elaborate technical details and provide numerical examples.

Auction theory would seem readily amenable to empirical testing, since the models make sharp predictions and the practice generates voluminous data. LAFFONT surveys the empirical evidence based on auction data, finding limited validation of the theoretical predictions. Experiments avoid some of difficulties identified by Laffont, enabling the researcher to control characteristics such as the distribution of values. KAGEL surveys the experimental evidence, also finding violations of the theoretical predictions. The fundamental difficulty in both real auction and experimental data is that it is virtually impossible to distinguish between a violation of the assumptions of the model and a contravention of the predictions.

Thirty years after Vickrey's paper, the New Zealand government was persuaded to use the Vickrey mechanism in their pioneering auction of spectrum licences for radio, television, and cellular telephone frequencies. Unfortunately, the design was flawed and the results disappointing. However, this negative experience was influential in the care and effort taken to design "the greatest auction in history", the very successful spectrum auctions conducted in the United States in 1994 and 1995. McMILLAN tells the fascinating story of this triumph of economic theory in the design of practical economic policy.

MICHAEL CARTER

Australian economy and economic record

Bell, Stephen, *Ungoverning the Economy: The Political Economy of Australian Economic Policy*, Melbourne, Oxford and New York: Oxford University Press, 1997

Corden, Max W., *The Road to Reform: Essays on Australian Economic Policy*, Melbourne: Addison Wesley, 1997

Fahrer, Jerome and John Simon, "Capital Constraints and Employment", *Australian Economic Review*, 109 (January 1995): 23–34

Hunter, Boyd, "The Social Structure of the Australian Urban Labour Market, 1976–1991", *Australian Economic Review*, 110 (April 1995): 65–79

Kriesler, Peter (editor), *The Australian Economy* 2, Sydney: Allen and Unwin, 1997

Lewis, William, Karen McCann, Robert J. McLean and Eric W. Zitzewitz, "What Ails Australia?", *McKinsey Quarterly*, 1 (1996): 90–102

Pinkstone, Brian, *Global Connections: A History of Exports and the Australian Economy*, Canberra: Australian Government Publishing Service Press, 1992

Saunders, Peter, "Poverty in the 1990s: A Challenge to Work and Welfare" in *Dialogues on Australia's Future: In Honour of the Late Professor Ronald Henderson*, edited by Peter Sheehan, Bhajan Grewal and Margarita Kumnick, Melbourne: Centre for Strategic Economic Studies, Victoria University, 1996

Tonts, Matthew, "Some Recent Trends in Australian Regional Economic Development Policy", *Regional Studies*, 33/6 (1999): 581–86

The Australian economy experienced strong growth during the 1990s after emerging from the deep recession of 1990–91. The fact that the economy continued to expand despite the Asian crisis, in which many of Australia's trading partners suffered deep contractions, was quite remarkable. However despite strong economic growth, unemployment (6.8 per cent in mid-2000) remains a complex issue: only recently has the rate fallen to pre-recession levels.

PINKSTONE provides an excellent account of Australia's economic history over the past two centuries by separating Australian economic development into three stages. The creation of the Australian economy as a "functional component" of the 19th-century British Empire is discussed in stage one. The local economy was supported by vast sums of infrastructure investment from Britain. The absolute advantage Australia enjoyed over Europe with respect to agriculture continued largely unimpeded until the outbreak of World War I. Stage two examines the dislocation in Australia's economic development that lasted from the commencement of hostilities in 1914 to the early 1950s. It is argued that the two world wars provided an impetus to local industries while disrupting Australia's export sector. The isolationist attitude prevalent between the wars encouraged the creation of domestic manufacturing industries founded on the principle of "self-reliance" and fed on new protectionist policies. The so-called "long boom" between 1950 and 1972 is discussed in stage three. The rapid development of Australia's resource sector was ignited with the emergence of the Japanese economy.

KRIESLER provides an account of Australia's economic development over the past 25 years. Falling world prices during the 1970s began a long decline in the importance of the farming sector to the Australian economy. Since the early 1980s these changes have been exacerbated by a gradual removal of the protective barriers that manufacturers had enjoyed in previous decades. It is argued that Australia's protectionist policies never encouraged the economy to compete in a global environment. In conclusion, the book maintains that the economy was led by an inward-looking, protectionist attitude that fell well short of international standards of quality and productivity.

The process of economic rationalism in Australian is reviewed by CORDEN. The author believes that the change in Australian economic policy has been rather remarkable, the period after 1988 being of special note. The article compares Australian economic development with several other economies that started with higher protection levels than those in Australia.

LEWIS *et al.* provides a more critical analysis of Australia's economy by emphasizing that despite the progress of economic reform since the mid-1980s, Australia's relative economic prosperity has not improved since the 1970s. Australian GDP per capita is still 30 per cent behind the United States. Both poor labour productivity and low employment per capita are raised as the main causes for the prosperity gap. The authors compare Australia's economic performance with the US in five industries: processed foods, construction, retail, banking, and aviation. Australia appears to be as competitive as the US in only two areas: construction and aviation. In retail, Australia is seen as being 15–20 years behind the US in best-practice methods. A contributing factor is Australia's hesitation to adopt innovative new processes developed overseas. Australian firms need to develop a culture that encourages innovation as well as improving the effectiveness of middle managers.

BELL provides a sustained critique of economic rationalism that has dominated Australian economic policy over the past 20 years. The author aims to explain the transformation of Australian political economy since the 1970s and how it has been influenced by wider global economic change. In conclusion, the book maintains that Australia has unique problems of her own stemming largely from the fact that Australia's export earnings are too heavily reliant on value-added commodities. An over-dependence on imported capital and consumption goods limits economic expansion in Australia because every time the economy expands, increases in imports choke economic expansion resulting in boom-bust economic cycles. The resulting hypothesis is that economic growth is limited in Australia because of an inappropriate mix of industries. The main thrust of the book is to emphasize that economic rationalism has benefited key business and financial interests while damaging the wider economic society.

The changing social structure of the Australian labour market and its distributional and efficiency implications on Australian society is discussed in HUNTER. The article investigates the increase in employment inequality among Australian urban neighbourhoods. The author discusses possible causes for the differential in employment and decomposes the changes in the employment rate into its demand and supply components. It is concluded that the structural shift in the Australian economy has been a major explanation of the difference in the employment rate within Australian cities. The article raises questions as to Australia's ability to adjust to the structural changes necessary to compete in a global market.

The study by FAHRER & SIMON considers whether the lack of capital investment is a restraint on employment growth in Australia. The authors calculate the level of capital constraint employment in seven sectors in the Australian economy. A model using linear programming techniques and historical data is used to generate their projections. The results of their study suggest that in manufacturing, transport, communication, recreation, and personal services there is sufficient capital to accommodate substantially higher employment and output. In mining and wholesale and retail trade the level of capital is under-utilized. However the level of labour is greater than necessary, suggesting that employment growth in these sectors is limited. In the other sectors of the economy, such as electricity, gas, and water, investment has been virtually nil and there is a need for an increase.

TONTS discusses recent trends in Australia's regional economic development, arguing that Federal governments are only recently becoming more interested in regional economic development after an absence spanning nearly two decades. Since the early 1970s, governments had increasingly neglected regional issues in favour of more densely populated areas. A backlash from the bush in recent years has been successful in getting the economic and social development of non-metropolitan Australia back on the political agenda. Governments are now acutely aware of encouraging a regional development framework that alleviates the damage inflicted from the withdrawal and rationalization of basic public services from rural areas. This has undermined the economic and social sustainability of communities.

In an article that endeavours to provide some future direction in Australian economic policy, SAUNDERS stresses one of the major challenges facing Australia is to ensure that the pain of reform is shared evenly among socioeconomic groups. Evidence suggests that microeconomic reform has disproportionately hit low socioeconomic groups. These people now find themselves less likely to obtain reasonable employment, let alone improve their overall economic status. The key for Australian authorities is to ensure that economic reform is implemented in conjunction with social objectives, thus ensuring that both can coexist together. Governments, businesses, unions, and individuals need to coordinate future economic policy in order to achieve continuous improvement in product quality, productivity, profitability, and job creation.

GEORGE KADMOS

Austrian school of economics

Böhm-Bawerk, Eugen von, *Capital and Interest*, 4th edition, 3 vols, South Holland, Illinois: Libertarian Press, 1959 (German edition, 1884–89)

Hayek, F.A., *The Road to Serfdom*, Chicago: University of Chicago Press, and London: Routledge and Kegan Paul, 1944

Holcombe, Randall G. (editor), *15 Great Austrian Economists*, Auburn, Alabama: Ludwig von Mises Institute, 1999

Menger, Carl, *Principles of Economics*, Grove City, Pennsylvania: Libertarian Press, 1994 (German edition 1871)

Mises, Ludwig von, *The Theory of Money and Credit*, Indianapolis: Liberty Classics, 1980 (German edition 1912)

Mises, Ludwig von, *Socialism: An Economic and Sociological Analysis*, Indianapolis: Liberty Classics, 1981 (German edition 1922)

Mises, Ludwig von, *Human Action: A Treatise on Economics*, New Haven, Connecticut: Yale University Press, and London: Hodge, 1949; as *Human Action*, Auburn, Alabama: Ludwig von Mises Institute, 1999

Mises, Ludwig von, *Theory and History: An Interpretation of Social and Economic Evolution*, New Haven, Connecticut: Yale University Press, 1957; reprinted Auburn, Alabama: Ludwig von Mises Institute, 1985

Rothbard, Murray Newton, *Man, Economy, and State: A Treatise on Economic Principles*, 2 vols, Los Angeles: Nash, 1971

Rothbard, Murray Newton, *America's Great Depression*, 4th edition, New York: Richardson and Snyder, 1983

MENGER marks the beginnings of a marginalist revolution in economics and its foundation on the concept of utility. He established with this work a deductive economic theory that was based on a methodology of subjectivism and individualism. Value is based on individual subjective valuation, utility is an ordering of values, and price is determined by marginal utilities in the process of exchange. He thus established an economic theory of the price of goods, including labour and capital, based solely on value, not on the cost of production.

In addition to his path-breaking general contributions to economics, Menger also established the characteristic features of the Austrian school of economics. Following him, Austrian economists do not use mathematics or empirical testing. Rather, theory is used as a guide to empirical studies. The methodology allows economists to study the development and characteristics of social institutions such as law and money, and to extend theory to the study of non-commercial activities, such as war, politics, and the family. Austrians see human action as rational, purposeful behaviour and that private property, entrepreneurship, and the price system are the best means for achieving ends and economic prosperity. While remaining value-free scientists, Austrians are generally advocates of a free-market economy because they have consistently found government intervention to be disruptive for the achievement of individual ends and counterproductive for achieving "social" ends.

The school expanded and grew in influence in the late 19th century, most notably through the work of BÖHM-BAWERK who was both an important public official in Austria and the leading academic economist of the time. Central to his writings was a thorough and devastating critique of existing theories of interest and the system of Marxist economics, which held that interest was the source of capitalist exploitation. On the positive side, he showed that interest is based on time preference ("now" is preferred to "later") and his concept has come to form the foundation of both Austrian and mainstream views of the interest rate. Given that more "roundabout" production processes are more productive, the interest rate becomes the key factor in determining the roundaboutness and thus productivity of production processes in the economy.

VON MISES's (1912) contributions to monetary economics and business cycle mark the beginnings of modern, micro-based, macroeconomics. He solved the classical dichotomy between value theory and monetary theory with his regression theorem, showing that the value of money was based on the same principles as the value of goods. He also developed what is now known as the Austrian theory of the business cycle, based on the foundations provided by Menger and Böhm-Bawerk.

VON MISES (1922) is also noteworthy in the history of economic thought for starting the socialist calculation debate – a debate that he is now considered to have won. He demonstrated that society must be based on private property, monetary exchange, and market prices, that pure socialism was impossible and that socialist-orientated policies were inefficient.

Furthermore, VON MISES (1957) rebuilt the entire methodological foundations of the school on the concept of praxeology. Here human action is seen as purposeful, and economic theory is universally applicable across time and place and is the organizing principle for the social sciences. *Human Action* (VON MISES 1949) is the first complete treatise of the Austrian school covering methodology, theory, policy analysis, and subjects generally considered outside of economics.

HAYEK developed many of von Mises's theoretical and policy contributions, most notably the instability of the mixed economy and its inherent tendency to drift towards (or away from) socialism. He became famous for warning nations during World War II that they were moving towards socialism, a prediction that was no doubt one of the reasons he was given the Nobel Prize in economics.

Murray Newton Rothbard further refined the praxeological method by unifying all economic theory, policy analysis, and ethics on the basis of property rights. *Man, Economy, and State* (ROTHBARD 1971) is the modern treatise on the economics of the Austrian school. ROTHBARD (1983) also provided the best illustration of the Austrian business cycle theory as applied to the Great Depression. He showed that monetary inflation by the Federal Reserve System during the 1920s caused the Depression of the 1930s and that the New Deal policies of Herbert Hoover and Franklin Roosevelt made it "Great".

The great names of the Austrian school include precursors such as Frédéric Bastiat, Jean-Baptiste Say, Richard Cantillon, A.R.J. Turgot, and the Spanish scholastics. Friedrick von Wieser, Philip Wicksteed, Frank Fetter, Benjamin Anderson, Henry Hazlitt, William Hutt, and Wilhelm Röpke were all important members of the school. The school remains small and outside the mainstream of economic thought, but it is one of the oldest surviving schools and is considered to be one of the fastest growing.

MARK THORNTON

See also F.A. Hayek

Authoritarianism

Collier, David (editor), *The New Authoritarianism in Latin America*, Princeton, New Jersey: Princeton University Press, 1979

Friedrich, Carl J. and Zbigniew K. Brzezinski, *Totalitarian Dictatorship and Autocracy*, 2nd edition, Cambridge, Massachusetts: Harvard University Press, 1965

Huntington, Samuel P. and Clement H. Moore (editors), *Authoritarian Politics in Modern Society: The Dynamics of Established One-Party Systems*, New York: Basic Books, 1970

Jackson, Robert H. and Carl G. Rosberg, *Personal Rule in Black Africa: Prince, Autocrat, Prophet, Tyrant*, Berkeley: University of California Press, 1982

Linz, Juan, "Totalitarianism and Authoritarian Regimes" in *Handbook of Political Science*, vol. 3, edited by Fred I. Greenstein and Nelson W. Polsby, Reading, Massachusetts: Addison Wesley, 1975

Linz, Juan J. and Alfred Stepan (editors), *The Breakdown of Democratic Regimes*, Baltimore: Johns Hopkins University Press, 1978

O'Donnell, Guillermo A., *Modernization and Bureaucratic-Authoritarianism: Studies in South American Politics*, Berkeley: Institute of International Studies, University of California, 1973

O'Donnell, Guillermo, Philippe C. Schmitter and Laurence Whitehead (editors), *Transitions from Authoritarian Rule; Prospects for Democracy*, Baltimore: Johns Hopkins University Press, 1986

Perlmutter, Amos, *Modern Authoritarianism: A Comparative Institutional Analysis*, New Haven, Connecticut: Yale University Press, 1981

LINZ's essay provides perhaps the best starting point for understanding authoritarianism as a concept in political science. This literally encyclopaedic 237-page analysis of nondemocratic regimes presents a sweepingly comprehensive theoretical understanding of both authoritarian and totalitarian regimes. According to Linz, there are three basic regime categories: democracy, totalitarianism, and authoritarianism. Authoritarian regimes are

> political systems with limited, not responsible, political pluralism, without elaborate and guiding ideology, but with distinctive mentalities, without extensive nor intensive political mobilization, except at some points in their development, and in which a leader or occasionally a small group exercises power within formally ill-defined limits but actually quite predictable ones.

Linz develops a sevenfold typology of authoritarian regimes according to the degree and type of participation, the degree of limited pluralism permitted, and the commitment to ideology that Linz refers to as the mentality of the regime. The types of regimes include bureaucratic-authoritarianism (see O'DONNELL), organic statism, mobilizational, postindependence mobilizational, exclusionary racial and ethnic "democracies", "defective and pretotalitarian" regimes, and posttotalitarian regimes. By contrasting authoritarianism with totalitarianism, the work also clarifies differences in kind between these two regime types along such dimensions as ideology and participation. Although now dated, because of its analysis and its thorough survey of other writers before him, Linz's essay remains a key work in understanding authoritarianism.

The collection of essays in HUNTINGTON & MOORE focuses on the character of established one-party authoritarian systems, after somewhat vaguely categorizing all nondemocratic governments as "authoritarian". Huntington's introductory chapter provides a tightly reasoned and thoroughly comprehensive typology of every conceivable type of one-party system, focusing on the processes of transformation that can bring about an established one-party system and outlining what he considers to be the key characteristics of such systems for effective modernization and development. Moore's chapter further clarifies the array of one-party system types by distinguishing among their various uses of ideology. The volume is rounded out by a set of illuminating case studies including one-party state systems in the US, in Africa, southern Europe, Eastern Europe, the Soviet Union, and China, as well as three chapters contrasting interesting unlike pairs of countries and regions.

PERLMUTTER emphasizes the differences between modern authoritarianism and earlier forms of authoritarian rule, examining the political institutions of Nazi Germany, Fascist Italy, the Soviet Union, and a variety of other communist, corporatist and praetorian regimes. Modern authoritarian regimes depend on specialized political institutions and organization, rather than ideology, for their stability and continued existence. While stressing that modern authoritarian regimes have as their major objective the establishment of political monopoly over all forces, interests, and institutions within the system, Perlmutter also emphasizes the dependence of modern authoritarianism on skilful exploitation of the relationships between elite support, the state, party, parallel and auxiliary structures, and even mass society. Another characteristic for successful party-state authoritarian regimes is subordination of professional and revolutionary military interests to civilian rule. Perlmutter also devotes considerable attention to the role of ideology in authoritarianism. Authoritarian regimes may or may not exploit ideology as a means of sustaining their institutional control, but in any case ideology is an instrument and not an ultimate objective. Ideology may be a useful means of maintaining power but only when wedded to political organization. Perlmutter includes many regimes that others might classify as "totalitarian", such as in the more dated usage by FRIEDRICH & BRZEZINSKI of the mixed category of "totalitarian dictatorship." Perlmutter considers instead that the term "totalitarianism" is ideologically motivated and analytically not useful.

O'Donnell's work examining the linkages between political change and economic modernization introduced the concept of "bureaucratic authoritarianism" (B-A), regimes, distinguished from other forms of authoritarianism by the growth of organizational strength of social sectors, governmental attempts at control by "encapsulation", the career patterns and power bases of technocrats, and the central role played by large bureaucracies. The main theme concerns the linkages between modernization and political regimes. O'Donnell's examination of Argentina and Brazil leads him to conclude that social differentiation is determined by the size of domestic markets and a system's productive structure, and that variations in economically-driven social pressures explain the rise of B-A regimes. Specifically, B-A regimes result from the failure of import substitution, the failure to extend and deepen industry, the failure of populism, and the increasing need for political stability as social and economic conditions deteriorate. The work raised issues of great normative and analytic importance, and has received considerable attention in the work of other scholars, albeit often highly critical (see COLLIER).

The chapters in Collier provide a critique of the B-A model from both theoretical and empirical perspectives. The authors present sufficient evidence in this 456-page collection to raise serious questions about many of the central assumptions of O'Donnell's model. Most important, the close relationship between economic problems related to industrialization and the emergence of B-A regimes is questioned by several of the papers. Excellent theoretical essays are included by Henrique Cordoso and by Albert O. Hirschmann, in addition to several empirical chapters looking at not just the southern cone of Latin America but also drawing on European cases.

The comprehensive collection of essays in the four volumes

edited by O'DONNELL, SCHMITTER & WHITEHEAD form a major addition to the literature on modern authoritarianism and the process by which such regimes either perish or persist. The collection includes seven theoretical essays, 13 country studies including a separate volume on Latin America and one on southern Europe, and a substantial concluding essay on the work as a whole. The authors share a common perspective focusing on the dynamic interaction of structural, superstructural, and conjectural factors in the context of changes in authoritarian rule. For example, changes in the degree of institutionalization of an authoritarian regime determine the character and extent of its transition to democracy; accordingly, the authors draw distinctions between liberalization and full-fledged democratization. The essays emphasize the strategic interaction between elements in both the opposition and the authoritarian regime itself in explaining regime change. For both its theoretical depth and empirical scope this four-volume set is an extremely important addition to the understanding of authoritarian regimes especially in a dynamic context.

Taking the converse side of democratic regimes as a starting point, LINZ & STEPAN's four-volume set examines how authoritarian regimes result from the breakdown of democratic regimes. This collection of 12 national case studies from Latin American and Europe, plus theoretical essays introducing the 700-page work.

JACKSON & ROSBERG examines authoritarian regimes based on personal rulership, distinguishing princely, autocratic, prophetic, and tyrannical (referred to by Linz as "sultanism"). Their analysis of postcolonial regimes in Africa fills in a category of non-democratic and non-totalitarian regimes often overlooked in analyses based on Latin American and European contexts.

KENNETH R. BENOIT

Autonomy

Benn, Stanley I., *A Theory of Freedom*, Cambridge and New York: Cambridge University Press, 1988

Berlin, Isaiah, "Two Concepts of Liberty" in *Four Essays on Liberty*, London and New York: Oxford University Press, 1969

Christman, John (editor), *The Inner Citadel: Essays on Individual Autonomy*, Oxford and New York: Oxford University Press, 1989

Dworkin, Gerald, *The Theory and Practice of Autonomy*, Cambridge and New York: Cambridge University Press, 1988

Hannum, Hurst, *Autonomy, Sovereignty, and Self-Determination: The Accommodation of Conflicting Rights*, revised edition, Philadelphia: University of Pennsylvania Press, 1996

Haworth, Lawrence, *Autonomy: An Essay in Philosophical Psychology and Ethics*, New Haven, Connecticut: Yale University Press, 1986

Lindley, Richard, *Autonomy*, Basingstoke: Macmillan, and Atlantic Highlands, New Jersey: Humanities Press, 1986

Nedelsky, Jennifer, "Reconceiving Autonomy: Sources, Thoughts, and Possibilities", *Yale Journal of Law and Feminism*, 1/1 (1989): 7–36

Pohlmann, R., Autonomie entry in *Historisches Wörterbuch der Philosophie*, edited by Joachim Ritter, Basel: Schwabe, 1971

Schneewind, J.B., *The Invention of Autonomy: A History of Modern Moral Philosophy*, Cambridge and New York: Cambridge University Press, 1998

Young, Robert, *Personal Autonomy: Beyond Negative and Positive Liberty*, London: Croon Helm, and New York: St Martin's Press, 1986

"Autonomy" derives from the Greek *autonomia*, which combined the Greek words for "self" and "law". To be autonomous, then, is to be self-governing. When the Greeks used the word, according to POHLMANN, they were typically referring to a self-governing political unit, notably the city-state. He points out, however, that Sophocles also used the term in the Chorus's description of the character of Antigone (*Antigone*, line 821). The term is still used to characterize both persons and political units, although analyses of the concept now tend to focus on personal autonomy.

Pohlmann's essay seems to be the only attempt to trace the history of the concept of autonomy. After brief accounts of how ancient Greeks and Romans employed the word, and following the observation that the Middle Ages did not know the concept of autonomy, Pohlmann devotes the bulk of the essay to the period from the Reformation to the mid-20th century, with sections on autonomy in jurisprudence, philosophy, theology, psychology and pedagogy, and sociology. The emphasis throughout, but especially in the sections on jurisprudence, philosophy, and theology, is on German scholars.

Current discussions of the autonomy of *political units* tend to concentrate on the relations of regions, subunits, or peoples, such as Quebec or the Kurds, to the overarching state (or states) in which they find themselves. As HANNUM puts it, "An autonomous region should enjoy effective control over matters that are primarily of local concern, within the overall framework of the fundamental norms of the state" (p.468). In addition to nine case studies from Asia, Central America, and Europe, his book includes numerous examples of "autonomous arrangements".

SCHNEEWIND and the writers discussed below are concerned with *personal* or *individual* autonomy. Schneewind's particular concern is to show how the conception of "morality as obedience" came to be challenged in the 17th and 18th centuries by the conception of "morality as self-governance" – a challenge that made possible Immanuel Kant's invention of "morality as autonomy". Schneewind has little to say about the concept of autonomy itself, but his lucid analysis of shifts in modern moral philosophy clarifies not only Kant's appeal to autonomy but also current debates about autonomy's meaning and value.

The point of departure for many recent discussions of personal or individual autonomy is BERLIN's celebrated essay on negative and positive liberty. In Part III of the essay Berlin connects the desire for autonomy to the "retreat to the inner citadel" (p.135) – that is, the desire for self-mastery, even at the expense of withdrawal into isolation and self denial. This treatment of autonomy has sparked many debates and furnished the title for CHRISTMAN's valuable collection of philosophically sophisticated essays. The collection includes

Harry Frankfurt's influential "Freedom of the Will and the Concept of a Person" (originally published in 1971), which introduces the distinction between first-order desires – such as the desire for alcohol – and second-order desires – such as the desire *not* to desire alcohol – that has been at issue in many subsequent arguments about personal autonomy.

LINDLEY begins by accepting Berlin's claim that "the underlying idea of the concept of autonomy is self-mastery" (p.6), but he gives self mastery a more benign interpretation than does Berlin. After chapters on Kant's, David Hume's, and J.S. Mill's conceptions of autonomy, Lindley develops his own "liberal" synthesis. YOUNG, as the subtitle of his book indicates, sees autonomy as a concept that promises a chance to move beyond futile debates about negative and positive liberty. Freedom is a necessary condition for autonomy, he argues, but autonomy is more than being free: "self-determination is hardly displayed in . . . freely but mindlessly mimicking the tastes, opinions, ideals, goals, principles, or values of others" (p.8). HAWORTH also distinguishes "liberty *simpliciter*" from "liberty autonomously exercised" (p.139), with particular attention to the ways in which individual preferences are formed. Someone who makes it a rule to drink a certain brand of coffee or tea will be acting autonomously only if his or her preference for that brand is not the result of some induced preference, brought about by brainwashing, perhaps, or by deceit or manipulation, but of his or her own initiative. Similar issues arise in DWORKIN, whose book brings together ten of his widely discussed essays. The first part contains essays on "theory", or problems in the definition and analysis of autonomy, with the essays on "practice" in the second part taking up practical issues, such as paternalism, informed consent, and entrapment, that raise concerns about protecting or promoting personal autonomy.

The richest of all recent works on autonomy may be BENN's, which gives an acute analysis of the concept a central place in a fully developed theory of freedom. This analysis relies on a distinction between "autarchy", or the capacity to direct one's life, and autonomy, which he takes to be a character ideal, requiring a consistent and coherent set of beliefs that one continually adjusts in light of critical reflection.

Some feminists and other critics of liberalism have complained that autonomy is an individualistic concept that deflects attention from the importance of community and social relations. NEDELSKY offers a clear and sensitive statement of this position. Rather than abandoning the concept of autonomy, however, she proposes to reconceive it. Instead of thinking of autonomy as a kind of personal property that protects our independence, she argues, we would do better to think of it in terms of childrearing and interdependence, for no individual can *be* autonomous unless others help him or her to *become* autonomous.

RICHARD DAGGER

B

Balance of payments

Fausten, Dietrich K. and Robert D. Brooks, "The Balancing Item in Australia's Balance of Payments: An Impressionistic View", *Applied Economics*, 28 (1996): 1303–11

Feldstein, Martin and Charles Horioka, "Domestic Saving and International Capital Flows", *Economic Journal*, 90 (June 1980): 314–29

Frankel, Jeffrey A., "Monetary and Portfolio-Balance Models of Exchange Rate Determination" in *Economic Interdependence and Flexible Exchange Rates*, edited by Jagdeep S. Bhandari and Bluford H. Putnam, Cambridge, Massachusetts: MIT Press, 1983

International Monetary Fund, *Report on the World Current Account Discrepancy*, Washington, DC: IMF, 1987

International Monetary Fund, *Report on the Measurement of International Capital Flows*, Washington, DC: IMF, 1992

Johnson, Harry G., "Towards a General Theory of the Balance of Payments" in his *International Trade and Economic Growth*, Cambridge, Massachusetts: Harvard University Press, 1967

Johnson, Harry G., "The Monetary Approach to Balance-of-Payments Theory", *Journal of Financial and Quantitative Analysis*, (March 1972): 1555–72

Maldonado, R.M., "Recording and Classifying Transactions in the Balance of Payments", *International Journal of Accounting*, 15 (Fall 1979): 105–33

Meade, J.E., *The Theory of International Economic Policy*, vol. 1: *The Balance of Payments*, London and New York: Oxford University Press, 1951

Niehans, Jürg, *International Monetary Economics*, Oxford: Philip Allan, and Baltimore: Johns Hopkins University Press, 1984

The balance of payments records all crossborder transactions undertaken by residents of a given country during a specified period of time. As a retrospective transactions record, balance of payments accounts provide information about crossborder resource flows and their financing. To the extent that financing flows affect a country's international indebtedness they change that country's net national wealth. Accordingly, as national economies open up with the progress of international integration, the accuracy of balance of payments records becomes increasingly important for the formation and monitoring of economic policies. At the same time, the balance of payments is a core element of the macroeconomy. Crossborder resource transfers reflect configurations of national productivity and thrift. As such, they are the means for the forward-looking pursuit of optimal resource allocation globally, and their financing influences price determination in currency and asset markets. Hence, the determination and behaviour of the balance of payments are of major analytical concern in understanding and guiding the macroeconomic adjustment process. It is useful to address the accounting and economic perspectives in turn.

MALDONADO presents systematically and comprehensively the principles and application of the conventions of double entry bookkeeping to crossborder transactions. Strict adherence to these conventions should ensure systemic consistency; the global economy is a closed system that must satisfy relevant adding-up constraints. In a two-country setting, this is illustrated by the fact that one country's external deficit is the flipside of the surplus of the other country. This formal adding-up requirement stands in marked contrast to the empirical record. The consolidated current account balance of all trading nations has been showing aggregate deficits for the world as a whole, exceeding US$100 billion in 1982.

In their investigations of the glaring deficiencies of global balance of payments statistics, INTERNATIONAL MONETARY FUND (IMF) working parties (1987 & 1992) have identified severe inadequacies in data reporting and processing. On current account, the reporting of crossborder investment income was the major source for discrepancies. Specific areas of misrepresentation include the excessive reporting of reinvested direct investment income and the underreporting of portfolio investment income from cross-border positions with banks. On capital account, the statistical deficiencies were found to pervade all major transactions categories. To alleviate this "state of crisis", the working parties recommended extensive reappraisal and extensions of methodologies for data collection as well as improved cooperation, under the leadership of the IMF, between the various statistical agencies at national and international levels. Specifically, they suggest that more general adoption of standard survey techniques would help to improve data collection on direct investment income. Fuller use of stock data of crossborder assets and liabilities would complement the inadequate information that is contained in the assembled data on transactions flows.

Aside from the problems of global consistency, statistical practices generate implementation problems at the national level. FAUSTEN & BROOKS investigate the "balancing item" in the balance of payments. Accounting conventions ensure that national balance of payments accounts also satisfy the adding-up constraint: the balances on current, capital, and money accounts necessarily sum to zero. However, many transactions are recorded incorrectly (known as "errors"), and some transactions are not recorded at all (known as "omissions"). Unavoidable imperfections in the compilation, collection, and processing of domestic data of crossborder transactions provide the rationale for the emergence of the "balancing item". This residual entry has displayed secular growth and increasing volatility that transcend the generally agreed and IMF-sanctioned bounds of acceptability. Fausten & Brooks document for some countries the quantitative and policy significance of the inaccuracies revealed by the published statistics. Conventionally attributed to "leads and lags in international trade", postwar financial deregulation and innovation have shifted attention to so-called "hot money" flows and "off-balance sheet" items as the source of misrepresentations of capital account transactions. The lack of progress in the reliable diagnosis of the defects of statistical systems and data collection techniques hampers the alleviation of the system-wide reporting deficiencies. At the same time, it exacerbates the potential for destabilizing national policies that are motivated by the release of balance-of-payments outcomes known to be severely flawed statistically.

The behavioural perspective focuses on the determination and adjustment of the balance of payments, and on their implications for the conduct of national economic policy. Its modern evolution can be illustrated in terms of shifts in the analytical focus among the component balances of the external accounts. MEADE's systematic analysis of the balance of payments from a general equilibrium perspective helped to explode the "policy dilemma" myth that had emerged with the recognition of the external balance as a distinct target for economic policy. The attempt to control both domestic activity and the external balance by the single policy instrument of generalized demand management contributed to the "stop–go" pattern of output and employment during the early postwar era. Distinguishing between the level of aggregate demand and its composition in terms of domestic and foreign goods, Meade was able to focus on a second instrument of economic policies that could be used to manage the latter. With two instruments, the policy problem of pursuing two independent targets was solvable.

This "goods markets view" was preoccupied with the determination of equilibrium flows in goods markets. With the exception of foreign direct investments, international capital and reserve flows were regarded as "accommodating", determined by the residual financing requirements of crossborder resource flows. This perception seemed quite apposite for an environment of pervasive exchange controls and regulation of capital flows, but the unidirectional view of causation became increasingly suspect. With the progress of financial liberalization and deregulation, the conventional wisdom was joined by alternative hypotheses that acknowledged autonomy of financial transactions. This "asset market view" focused on the behaviour of the financial accounts of the balance of payments and their relation to domestic (and global) asset markets (FRANKEL). Harry JOHNSON (1967) attempted to sketch a unifying theory of the balance of payments by focusing on the payments side of voluntary market transactions. By treating all

payments symmetrically, this approach embraced an agnostic position regarding the autonomy or otherwise of current and capital account transactions. Its emphasis on net crossborder flows of payments and receipts positioned balance of payments analysis firmly in the general equilibrium stock-flow context.

JOHNSON (1972) developed a specific implementation of that perspective for monetized exchange systems, as distinct from barter systems, in the form of the monetary approach to the balance of payments. Using the defining characteristic of monetized economies that "money" is the *quid pro quo* in exchange, that is to say that widgets like bonds have to be paid for with the legally accepted medium of exchange, Johnson focused on the flows of money payments and receipts. Accordingly, the analytically relevant measure of the balance of payments is the net crossborder flow of internationally accepted money – international reserves or, more formally, net official monetary movements. In this view the balance of payments was firmly embedded in national money markets, determined by the interaction between the demand and supply of money. The balance of payments provided the means to enable transactors to adjust existing stocks of money balances to their desired level. It follows that inappropriate national money supply policies are the main culprit for external balance "problems". As this diagnosis was crucially based on the inherent stability of the demand for money, the monetary approach has lost some policy relevance in the face of mounting evidence of shifts in money demand associated with secular changes in monetary institutions. Johnson's work has, however, provided a major impetus towards understanding the general equilibrium nature of the balance of payments and its component balances. In the process, it has helped to clarify the nature of stock-flow interactions that drive the adjustment process. However, the preoccupation with money markets as the fundamental driving force for adjustment restricts its scope of analysis and, hence, its general validity.

NIEHANS (especially chapter 6) provides a forceful statement of the general principle that the balance of payments and its component accounts cannot meaningfully be treated in isolation. A particularly important application of this principle is in the area of international capital flows. During the post-World War II era, capital movements were increasingly regarded as determined principally in financial markets. This narrow perspective nourished the complacent view that globalization of financial markets would render capital perfectly mobile internationally. Yet substantial crosscountry disparities in capital endowments continue to exist, notwithstanding the wholesale dismantling of exchange controls. The puzzling coexistence of manifestly imperfect capital mobility in an environment of globally integrated financial markets bears testimony of the complacency of narrow, segmented interpretations of general equilibrium phenomena.

This coexistence ceases to be puzzling with the recognition that financial arbitrage is not the sole determinant of resource movements. Ultimately, crossborder flows of real capital are determined by international configurations of productivity and thrift.

FELDSTEIN & HORIOKA (1980) have put this "real" dimension of international capital movements to the test by investigating the behaviour of national saving and investment rates. Insofar as *ex ante* saving-investment discrepancies change yield patterns, they influence the direction of internationally mobile capital. With perfect mobility such yield changes would attract sufficient capital flows to offset any discrepancy between planned national savings and investment. Hence, perfect capital mobility should be reflected in independent movement of those two variables. Instead, Feldstein & Horioka observe robust co-movements between national saving and investment that indicate the persistence of barriers to capital flows. Despite financial globalization, individual countries appear to continue to rely systematically on national savings to fund national investment. Conversely, empirical evidence that financial arbitrage conditions are not violated is no guarantee of pervasive real sector adjustments.

The capital mobility debate once again illustrates the potential pitfalls that lie in the path of narrowly confined partial analysis of the external balance. The balance of payments is the quintessential general equilibrium phenomenon: its component accounts are linked to the various national markets, which in turn are subject to budget constraints as well as to the dictates of optimizing behaviour by groups of transactors in all the countries that interact in the internationalized markets.

DIETRICH K. FAUSTEN

Balance-of-payments constrained growth

(Thirlwall's law)

Cornwall, John, *Modern Capitalism: Its Growth and Transformation*, London: Martin Robertson, and New York: St Martin's Press, 1977

Davidson, P., "Minisymposium on Thirlwall's Law and Economic Growth in an Open-Economy Context", *Journal of Post Keynesian Economics*, 19/3 (1997): 311–85

Krugman, Paul, "Differences in Income Elasticities and Trends in Real Exchange Rates", *European Economic Review*, 33/5 (1989) 1031–46

McCombie, John S.L., "Economic Growth, the Harrod Foreign Trade Multiplier and the Hicks Super-Multiplier" in *Applied Economics*, 17/1 (1985): 55–72

McCombie, John S.L., "Economic Growth, Trade Interlinkages and the Balance-of-Payments Constraint", *Journal of Post Keynesian Economics*, 15/4 (1993): 471–505

McCombie, John S.L. and Anthony P. Thirlwall, *Economic Growth and the Balance-of-Payments Constraint*, Basingstoke: Macmillan, and New York: St Martin's Press, 1994

McCombie, John S.L. and Anthony P. Thirlwall, "Economic Growth and the Balance-of-Payments Constraint Revisited" in *Markets, Unemployment, and Economic Policies: Essays in Honour of G.C. Harcourt*, vol. 2, edited by Philip Arestis, Gabriel Palma and Malcolm Sawyer, London and New York: Routledge, 1997a

McCombie, John S.L. and Anthony P. Thirlwall, "The Dynamic Harrod Foreign Trade Multiplier and the Demand Orientated Approach to Economic Growth: An Evaluation", *International Review of Applied Economics*, 11/1 (1997b): 5–26

Thirlwall, Anthony P., "The Balance of Payments Constraint as an Explanation of International Growth Rate Differences", *Banca del Lavoro Quarterly Review*, 32/128 (1979): 145–53

Thirlwall, Anthony P., " Regional Problems are 'Balance-of-Payments' Problems", *Regional Studies*, 14/4 (1980): 419–25

Thirlwall, Anthony P., "Professor Krugman's 45-Degree Rule", *Journal of Post Keynesian Economics*, 14/1 (1991–92): 23–28

Thirlwall, Anthony P, "Reflections on the Concept of Balance-of-Payments Constrained Growth", *Journal of Post Keynesian Economics*, 19/3 (1997): 377–85

The orthodox neoclassical approach to economic growth, whether it be the Solow model or the later endogenous growth models, is very much a supply-orientated approach. All factors are fully employed and investment adjusts to saving. Demand does not explicitly enter the picture. However, CORNWALL has documented how, even in the Golden Age (1950–73) of economic growth of the advanced countries, labour was never an exogenous determinant of growth. If the demand was there, greater labour supplies could be found from immigration, increased participation rates and, especially in continental Europe, the transfer of labour from agriculture to the other sectors. Technical change is enhanced through the Verdoorn effect and is a function of the growth of the demand for industrial output. There is little doubt that many developing countries could effectively increase their utilization of resources if the growth of demand was there. Thus, what may be termed a Keynesian approach sees long-run growth being determined by the growth of demand factors. This raises the question of "what determines the growth of demand and why does it vary between countries?"

An answer has been provided by THIRLWALL (1979) who developed a demand-orientated Keynesian approach to economic growth, where the growth of exports and the balance of payments play a key role. (A comprehensive discussion of this approach and the empirical evidence is found in McCOMBIE & THIRLWALL, 1994.) Thirlwall demonstrated that, in the long run, growth must be such that the basic balance (the current account plus long-term capital flows) is in equilibrium, or possibly a surplus. Although a deficit can be financed in the short run by capital inflows, this will merely lead to a growth in the international-debt-to-GDP ratio, eventually leading to a collapse in the exchange rate and the danger of a resulting inflation/depreciation spiral.

The growth rate consistent with balance-of-payments equilibrium is termed the "balance-of-payments equilibrium growth rate" (y_B) and, if this is below the maximum growth rate consistent with productive potential, the growth of a country is said to be balance-of-payments constrained.

Thirlwall constructed a model whereby the balance-of-payments equilibrium growth rate is a function of the growth of world income, the rate of change of relative prices, and the growth of capital inflows. If the last two flows are quantitatively insignificant, then the equilibrium growth rate may be approximated by the rule $y_B = \varepsilon z/\pi$ where ε, z, and π are respectively the income elasticity of demand for the country's exports, the growth of world income, and the income elasticity of demand for imports. If prices have no significant effect on the growth of exports (x), then an alternative equation is $y_B = x/\pi$. These expressions have become known as alternative specifications of "Thirlwall's law".

There are significant differences between countries in their values of π and, especially, ε. These differences reflect disparities between countries in their non-price competitiveness, such as delivery dates, after-sales service, quality, the effectiveness of distribution networks, and so on. Thus, the supply side is important to the extent that these supply characteristics play a crucial role in explaining the differences in the growth of exports and hence output. However, this stands in marked contrast to the way the neoclassical approach emphasizes the supply side.

A necessary condition for the balance-of-payments constraint to be binding, and for Thirlwall's law to hold, is that exchange rate changes are relatively unimportant in determining the growth of exports and imports. This may be true for a number of reasons (McCombie & Thirlwall, 1994). First, real-wage resistance may make it difficult for a nominal devaluation to be translated into a sustained real devaluation. Secondly, oligopolistic pricing and pricing to market may mean that imports and exports are unresponsive to a depreciation of the currency. Finally, with the growing importance of non-price competition, the price elasticity of demand for imports and exports may be so low that, even if the Marshall–Lerner conditions are satisfied, the quantitative effect on the value of imports and exports of a depreciation may be small. Moreover, if the prices are to be effective in relaxing the balance-of-payments constraint so that the rate of growth may be increased, any depreciation must be continuous over time. McCOMBIE & THIRLWALL (1997a) show that an increase in the rate of growth of capital inflows is unlikely to be sufficient to raise the balance-of-payments equilibrium growth rate to any significant degree.

Thirlwall found that his law was none other than the dynamic Harrod multiplier and that Kaldor had also been working along similar lines at the same time. (See THIRL-WALL (1997) for a discussion of the history of the development of the law.) McCOMBIE (1985) showed that the law could be regarded more generally as reflecting the workings of the Hicks supermultiplier.

There have been several papers that have attempted to test Thirlwall's law, some of which are reviewed in McCombie & Thirlwall (1994). Estimates of ε and π are obtained from the estimation of export and import demand functions (which include a relative price term) using time-series data. It is found that estimates of y_B, which are calculated over periods of about a decade or longer, give a very close approximation to the observed growth rates for many countries. For more recent contributions, see the minisymposium (DAVIDSON) in the 1997 edition of the *Journal of Post Keynesian Economics* and the papers there by Atesoglu, Bairam, Hieke, and McCombie, together with the references they contain. The use of more fashionable econometric techniques, such as testing for the order of integration of the data has not undermined the earlier results.

Recognizing that not all countries can be simultaneously balance-of-payments constrained, McCOMBIE (1993) produced a theoretical model that provides a generalization to two trading blocs, one with a resource- or policy-constrained growth rate, and the other with a balance-of-payments constrained growth rate. The model shows how one group of countries, pursuing, say, monetarist policies in an attempt to reduce inflation can, by reducing their own growth rates through deflationary policies, limit the growth of another group. This is even if the latter group does not have the same concern about inflation, but values a faster economic growth rate more highly.

The approach is not just applicable to countries, as THIRL-WALL (1980) has shown in a paper modelling regional balance of payments. The implication of his model is that a common currency, such as that introduced by some of the European Union countries, although it will remove the problems of a currency crisis, will not prevent the underlying balance-of-payments constraint from operating.

Thirlwall's law has had its critics. McCombie & Thirlwall (1994) contains lively discussions between the authors and McGregor & Swales, which first appeared on the pages of *Applied Economics*. KRUGMAN also rediscovered the law, which he termed the 45-degree rule. (This is because the ratio of two countries' growth rates is found to be equal to the ratio of the two countries' (ε/π.) Krugman interprets the law in a very neoclassical manner and assumes that the income elasticities change endogenously so the balance of payments can be brought automatically into equilibrium at the growth rate of productive potential. In other words, there can be no balance-of-payments constraint. However, THIRLWALL (1991–92) has criticized the assumptions necessary for this conclusion. See also McCOMBIE & THIRLWALL (1997b), which contains a further discussion, including a criticism of the law raised by Crafts, and a response to that criticism. It also reviews the more recent literature.

JOHN S.L. McCOMBIE

See also Kaldor's laws

Balance of power

Bueno de Mesquita, Bruce, *The War Trap*, New Haven, Connecticut: Yale University Press, 1981

Bull, Hedley, *The Anarchical Society: A Study of Order in World Politics*, London: Macmillan, and New York: Columbia University Press, 1977

Claude, Inis L., Jr, *Power and International Relations*, New York: Random House, 1962

Cusack, Thomas R. and Richard J. Stoll, *Exploring Realpolitik: Probing International Relations Theory with Computer Simulation*, Boulder, Colorado: Lynne Rienner, 1990

Diehl, Paul F. and Frank Wayman, "Realpolitik: Dead End, Detour, or Road Map?" in *Reconstructing Realpolitik*, edited by Frank W. Wayman and Paul F. Diehl, Ann Arbor: University of Michigan Press, 1994

James, Patrick, *Crisis and War*, Montreal: McGill–Queen's University Press, 1988

Midlarsky, Manus I., *The Onset of World War*, Boston: Unwin Hyman, 1988

Morgenthau, Hans J., *Politics among Nations: The Struggle for Power and Peace*, revised by Kenneth W. Thompson, New York: McGraw Hill, 1993 (originally published 1948)

Niou, Emerson M.S., Peter C. Ordeshook and Gregory F. Rose, *The Balance of Power: Stability in International Systems*, Cambridge and New York: Cambridge University Press, 1989

Balance of power politics in the modern era begins with MORGENTHAU's classic text, which established principles that continue to shape the field of international relations half a century later. Morgenthau's basic principles of power politics are as follows: an assumption of rationality, with leaders defining their interests in terms of power, an objective (but changing) basis for power, context-dependent morality, and an autonomous sphere for interstate relations. Given these assumptions about human behaviour, balance-of-power politics – referring to shifting alliances and alignments as a function of how national interests are perceived by leaders at a given time – become inevitable and serve as a stabilizing factor for the system of sovereign states. Alliances become essential to the pursuit of common interests, with the understanding that these arrangements may be altered as situations change. It would be fair to say that the general public's understanding of international relations and a significant element within the academic community continues to reflect the ideas about balance of power put forward by Morgenthau.

CLAUDE isolated four general usages of the concept of balance of power. It could mean (a) a situation where power is distributed in a manner that promotes stability; (b) a policy option; (c) a system of international relations with a unique set of rules; or (d) a symbol or guide to conduct. This set of categories is important because it clarifies the bifurcated nature of balance of power as a concept: The list identifies normative and empirical elements. Thus research in terms of balance-of-power politics could move forward more effectively in two ways as a result of Claude's analysis: in terms of explaining interstate relations and providing policy recommendations with greater clarity.

With an emphasis on anarchy, international order and society, the exposition by BULL represents a further step forward in the analysis of balance-of-power politics. Bull refined the idea of a system of states, or international system, which is formed when states interact on a regular basis and create, at some level, a society. Balance-of-power politics within modern international society, according to Bull, includes sovereign states who pay some minimal respect to basic rules of coexistence while existing in what can be described best as an anarchical society. Bull's analysis remains important because it draws attention to the effects that the international system and its member states have on each other.

BUENO DE MESQUITA uses microeconomic theory to put forward an expected utility theory of war. This theory, which uses precise measurements of the interests and capabilities of states, is more successful than balance-of-power theory in predicting which states will go to war with each other. Bueno de Mesquita's principal contributions are to point out that balance of power theory would benefit from refinement to place it in more exact terms and that a rival power-oriented theory could explain more, at least with regard to which combinations of states in the system are most likely to fight with each other.

JAMES responds to the need for more precision in stating propositions derived from balance of power theory. He explores aspects ranging from the static versus dynamic nature of the balance to its geographic domain. James finds that propositions from the balance of power about the escalation of crisis to war can help to explain outcomes but also confirms the greater explanatory power of expected utility theory.

MIDLARSKY moves the analysis of balance of power forward with the introduction of a unifying concept: the hierarchical equilibrium. His analysis includes alliances, conflict relationships, dyadic commitments, historical influences, and disparities in capabilities, which makes it the most comprehensive treatment of balance-of-power politics attempted to date. Midlarsky concludes that the hierarchical equilibrium, a structural condition that inhibits the accumulation of conflicts leading to systemic war, is achieved when two major powers and their respective allies form blocs that compete within mutually intelligible boundaries. Midlarsky's contribution continues to be important because it points to the multiple components of balance-of-power politics at the system level.

NIOU, ORDESHOOK & ROSE produce a formal model that explores implications from balance-of-power theory for systems of different sizes. One important finding is that a system with a smaller number of members may be at an advantage regarding stability. The reason is that transaction costs in forming and maintaining alliances increase as more actors are involved; system-preserving negotiations therefore may become more complex, with greater potential for miscalculation, as the size of the system increases. Niou, Ordeshook & Rose conclude by reinforcing one of the basic insights from balance-of-power politics: Although the pace of economic, technological, political, and social change has been accelerating over several centuries, the underlying character of the international system – the behaviour of self-interested states intent on maximizing their viability – has remained constant.

CUSACK & STOLL introduce computer simulation into the study of balance-of-power politics. The basic question for leaders, represented within this simulation, is this: how many resources should be allocated to external purposes versus those within the state? Essential characteristics of the simulation model include the size of the state system, geopolitical characteristics of its members, and the assumption that leaders can observe the system and decide upon and implement courses of action. With a complex design that includes variation in factors ranging from the initial distribution of capabilities and types of leaders, it turns out that, under certain conditions, balance-of-power systems can survive without conscious efforts by their members to ensure that outcome. The study by Cusack and Stoll continues to be relevant for its attempt to build in a vast range of interacting factors that are relevant to balance-of-power politics in order to test for the relative viability and durability of systems based on such principles.

DIEHL & WAYMAN sum up the current view of balance of power, and the perspective of power politics in general, by calling for more comprehensive research designs. In particular, there is a need for the statement of logically consistent and falsifiable propositions derived from balance-of-power theory.

PATRICK JAMES

Balance sheet, *see* Accounting, balance sheet

Banking law

Birks, Peter (editor), *Laundering and Tracing*, Oxford: Clarendon Press, and New York: Oxford University Press, 1995

Cranston, Ross, *Principles of Banking Law*, Oxford: Clarendon Press, and New York: Oxford University Press, 1997

Cunningham, Lawrence A., "Capital Market Theory, Mandatory Disclosure, and Price Discovery", *Washington and Lee Law Review*, 51 (1994): 843–76

Fehlberg, Belinda, *Sexually Transmitted Debt: Surety Experience and English Law*, Oxford: Clarendon Press, and New York: Oxford University Press, 1997

Goebel, Roger J., "Legal Framework: European Economic and Monetary Union: Will the EMU Ever Fly?", *Columbia Journal of European Law*, 4 (1998): 249–320

Hazen, Thomas Lee, "Symposium on Securities Market Regulation", *Catholic University Law Review*, 36 (1987): 987–96

Laifer, Daniel M., "Putting the Super Back in the Supervision of International Banking, Post- BCCI", *Fordham Law Review*, 60 (1992): 467–99

Pinto, Arthur R., "Corporate Governance: Monitoring the Board of Directors in American Corporations", *American Journal of Comparative Law*, 46 (1998): 317–46

Taylor, Celia R., "Capital Market Development in the Emerging Markets: Time to Teach an Old Dog Some New Tricks", *American Journal of Comparative Law*, 45 (1997): 71–106

Wegen, Gerhard, "Congratulations from Your Continental Cousins, 10b-5: Securities Fraud Regulation from the European Perspective", *Fordham Law Review*, 61 (1993): 57–98

Banking law was very much in a state of flux at the end of 1999. What was once primarily the law of cheques has evolved into a much more catholic topic. CRANSTON is the best primary source for this new approach, embracing banking organizations, interbank networks, banking regulation, the internationalization of banking law, as well as the primary relationship between bank and customer.

FEHLBERG provides a theoretical analysis of the famous O'Brien case, as well as many more difficult issues surrounding the relationship between "husband", "wife", and bank.

BIRKS is notable as one of the early, strong texts addressing the sorely underwritten area of money laundering. Of particular note are Birks' own offering, at pp.289–348, providing a solid overview of the problems, and Gleeson's explanation, at pp.115–34, of the potential liability of bankers for depositing the proceeds of crime.

GOEBEL analyses the goals, benefits, and drawbacks of European Monetary Union, while WEGEN provides a good analysis of how the European Union acts only by way of directive and subsequent national implementation. HAZEN addresses the internationalization of the securities markets, and the linkages that have tied markets together in different countries.

LAIFER explains the BCCI scandal clearly, outlining what happened, why it happened, and the international legal structures that were in place when it happened. PINTO explains the workings of efficient capital market hypothesis, an economic theory on which a stock market functions as a monitoring mechanism. CUNNINGHAM clarifies what is wrong with the efficient capital market hypothesis, and elaborates other theories crucial to internationalization of capital markets.

TAYLOR discusses efforts to implement regulatory structure in emerging European economies that would enable the maximum amount of trading and the most economically efficient allocation of capital in the shortest time.

ANN MUMFORD

Banking law, economic

Barth, James, Daniel Nolle and Tara Rice, *Commercial Banking Structure, Regulation, and Performance: An International Comparison*, Washington, DC: Office of the Comptroller of the Currency, 1997

Coggins, Bruce, *Does Financial Deregulation Work? A Critique of Free Market Approaches*, Cheltenham, Gloucestershire: Elgar, 1998

Dale, Richard, *International Banking Deregulation: The Great Banking Experiment*, Oxford and Cambridge, Massachusetts: Blackwell, 1992

D'Arista, Jane, *The Evolution of U.S. Finance*, 2 vols, Armonk, New York: Sharpe, 1994

Dermine, Jean (editor), *European Banking in the 1990s*, 2nd edition, Oxford and Cambridge, Massachusetts: Blackwell, 1993

International Monetary Fund, *Annual Report*, Washington, DC: International Monetary Fund, 1998

Lindgren, Carl-Johan, Gillian Garcia and Matthew I. Saal, *Bank Soundness and Macroeconomic Policy*, Washington, DC: International Monetary Fund, 1996

Litan, Robert, *What Should Banks Do?*, Washington, DC: Brookings Institution, 1986

Selgin, George, *Bank Deregulation and Monetary Order*, London and New York: Routledge, 1996

Story, Jonathan and Ingo Walter, *Political Economy of Financial Integration in Europe: The Battle of the Systems*, Cambridge, Massachusetts: MIT Press, 1997

Banking law and regulation have undergone a global transformation since 1980. Many nations have increased the scope of permissible activities for their banking firms, deregulating credit markets to allow entry into markets previously reserved for depository institutions, and harmonizing banking laws and rules to conform with those of other nations. Whereas laws, regulations, and conventions at the national and even state or provincial level once regulated bank behaviour, banks are now increasingly governed by rules established by supranational authorities. That these governing rules lack the force of national law does not diminish their authority.

No one volume has told the story of this revolution in banking law. LITAN provides a vigorous overview of product-line, interest-rate, branching, and anti-monopoly laws in US banking from the Depression to the Deregulation Acts of the 1980s. He then summarizes the case for deregulation. While the branching and anti-monopoly laws are idiosyncratic to the US, product-line restrictions and price ceilings characterized most advanced nations' banking laws after World War II.

DERMINE describes prudential and regulatory restrictions in six European countries prior to the 1980s period of deregulation. BARTH, NOLLE & RICE provides a detailed examination of commercial-banking powers and regulations in 19 advanced economies. The insightful volume by DALE explores in greater depth than Dermine or Barth, Nolle & Rice the most important of the advanced nations' banking restrictions: the firewall between commercial and investment banking activities. Dale shows that the removal or maintenance of these firewalls is fundamentally important, because they are associated with different institutional mechanisms for organizing investment-savings linkages. What banks should do in an economic system depends on the role they play in linking savings to investment.

D'ARISTA's invaluable two-volume work supplements these intra national analyses of banking law by describing the evolution of US cross-border capital flows and regulations in the post war period. She illustrates the evolution of international financial flows from an instrument of US policy to a destabilizing threat. In so doing, D'Arista focuses on the Achilles' heel of the dollar-based Bretton Woods system.

Monetary economists have throughout history debated how much to regulate banking systems. From the 1960s to the early 1980s, the dimming memories of Great Depression banking failures and the maturation of efficient-markets financial theory encouraged the free-market view that binding restrictions on prices in banking markets result in efficiency losses and allocative distortions. National commissions in many nations recommended the dismantling of banking regulations. These commission findings were amplified by groups of market-oriented economists advocating deregulation in each country. Among the most influential of these groups were the members of the Shadow Financial Regulatory Committee in the US. COGGINS gives a thorough review of these members' individual and collective activities and publications; his volume also contains extensive references to the works of those opposed to deregulation, and challenges the claim that deregulation leads to more efficient outcomes. The chief point at issue between the deregulationists and critics such as Coggins is whether the financial markets should be regarded as invariably efficient or as prone to periodic bouts of speculative excess.

The most extreme deregulationist position is taken not by the economists analysed by Coggins, but by proponents of the free banking hypothesis. SELGIN, a proponent of this view, summarizes the extensive theoretical literature on how banking and money markets would work in the absence of government oversight, and the historical research on the operation of free banking systems. In this viewpoint, government regulation is itself the principal cause of banking instability.

The macroeconomic turbulence and high nominal interest rates of the early 1980s forced literally every nation to deregulate its banking system. Dermine and Litan describe details

of this transformation in Europe and the US, respectively. During this same period, the Latin American debt crisis put great pressure on the large banks in Europe, Japan, and the US, which had lent heavily to Latin American borrowers. Ironically, the debt crisis led the Bank for International Settlements to develop the Basle accords: the criterion that all banks worldwide, especially those involved in cross-border lending, should meet capital-asset adequacy standards; and that in particular, every banks' equity capital should total eight per cent of its assets.

National banking regulations in the 1980s and 1990s were reorganized to simultaneously free banks to pursue new activities while putting new prudential safeguards in place. Dale emphasizes that the elimination of most firewalls between commercial and investment banking activities creates new and largely untested risks.

While banking was being deregulated in industrialized countries, many banking systems in the developing world were being liberalized. This liberalization has often occurred under the guidance or mandate of the International Monetary Fund (IMF). The principles of banking system design preferred by the IMF as an accompaniment to economic openness are spelled out in LINDGREN, GARCIA & SAAL. This volume argues that banking-system soundness requires: adequate supervision and transparency; government abdication of any role in credit allocation; and the adoption of macroeconomic policies emphasizing fiscal balance and the free flow of goods, services, and capital across national borders. The global financial crisis of 1997 has put this approach under scrutiny, as many of the countries adversely affected had been following these guidelines prior to the crisis.

The INTERNATIONAL MONETARY FUND report re-examines the problem of banking-system design in open developing economies in the light of this financial crisis. It emphasizes microeconomic aspects of banking systems, especially the need for prudential supervision, adequate banking capital (per the Basle accords), and transparent and timely information about borrowers and lenders.

The current testing ground for the limits to national authority in regulating banking activities is the creation of European monetary and economic union. STORY & WALTER offer a detailed guide to the political and economic struggles that have accompanied these efforts to hammer out a unified banking framework. This volume includes an authoritative treatment of the UK, French, and German banking systems, which examines their unique systemic features prior to harmonization, their step-by-step shifts toward convergence, and the political and economic ramifications of harmonization and convergence in the three nations concerned.

GARY A. DYMSKI

Bankruptcy law

Berry, Christopher and Edward Bailey, *Bankruptcy Law and Practice*, London: Butterworth, 1987
Boyce, Wendy (editor), *Debt and Insolvency on Family Breakdown*, Bristol: Family Law, 1994

Grenville, Clive, *Bankruptcy: The Law and Practice*, London: Fourmat, 1987

Grier, Ian S. and Richard E. Floyd, *Personal Insolvency: A Practical Guide*, London: Sweet & Maxwell, 1993

Pond, Keith, "The IVA Experience", *Journal of Business Law*, (1995): 118

Williams, Roland L. Vaughan, Muir Hunter and David Graham, *The Law and Practice of Bankruptcy*, 19th edition, London: Stevens, 1979

The major difficulty in giving guidance on suitable reading materials in this area is that it has been somewhat neglected for many years. Within English legal terminology "bankruptcy" refers only to the position of individuals. Where companies are concerned, the term "insolvency" (q.v.) is used. This section follows that practice by containing only references to works on the position of individuals.

Bankruptcy is a subject that may be viewed in isolation as a corpus of legal rules and procedures, but also has implications for other areas of law, including business law and family law. The subject is sometimes therefore dealt with as an appendage to more detailed treatment of those other areas

WILLIAMS, HUNTER & GRAHAM is without doubt established as the leading practitioner work in this area. It deals at great length with the relevant case law and with the complex mass of regulations and procedures governing bankruptcy. Like most practitioner works, it does not concern itself with underlying theories or with the broader aspects of the subject.

GRENVILLE is a response to the wholesale reform of the law of bankruptcy in 1985–6. The author traces some of the history of the law of bankruptcy, emphasizing the shift away from bankruptcy procedures as a kind of penalty on the debtor towards a view of the system as a reasonably humane and effective way of clearing up the mess caused by bankruptcy and rehabilitating the debtor to become a useful member of society to the benefit of his creditors, himself, and his family. He highlights the moves made in the 1985–6 reforms to simplify the procedures, to encourage appropriate use of informal rescue mechanisms, and at the same time to professionalize the administration of bankruptcy procedures through the introduction of licensed insolvency practitioners. He shows himself somewhat sceptical about the probable effectiveness of what remains a complex mass of rules in achieving any major simplification.

The edition of GRIER & FLOYD's book cited here comes from a slightly later date, by which time it had become possible to review with more confidence the workings of the new legislation. The authors make the point that the new legislation had its first practical trials at a time when a protracted economic recession pushed bankruptcies to record levels. One unintended effect of this coincidence of circumstances was an increase in the use, during this period, of the new individual voluntary arrangement (IVA) scheme that was provided by the 1986 Act. The authors look at the evidence arising from the use of that procedure and predict, rightly as it has turned out, a continuing growth in IVAs as an alternative to completed bankruptcy proceedings.

BOYCE has edited one of the few pieces of work in this area to devote an entire book to spin-off effects of bankruptcy

– in this case the effect of bankruptcy on families. The book shows that, in practice, it is often the family of the bankrupt that is the major loser as a result of existing bankruptcy rules and procedures. Thus, it highlights one of the great unreconciled dilemmas of insolvency, namely the need to protect creditors and discourage irresponsible behaviour by debtors while at the same time not imposing unjustified penalties on innocent third parties caught up in the process.

BERRY & BAILEY provide a useful guide to the current legislation in the form of an annotated copy of the Act and the rules. As is usual with this format, the strength of the book lies in the detailed attention it is able to give to individual pieces of statutory drafting.

POND looks at the IVA. Drawing on his own empirical work, he is able to show that this has proved to be a valuable addition to the range of options in cases of individual financial difficulty, providing a significant number of debtors with an escape that does not involve the stigma of actual bankruptcy – although some problems remain, especially in relation to identifying accurately those cases where the IVA is a proper solution.

ANDREW MCGEE

See also Banking law, Insolvency

Banks and banking

Baltensperger, Ernst, "Alternative Approaches to the Theory of the Banking Firm", *Journal of Monetary Economics*, 6/1 (1980): 1–37

Berger, Allen N., Rebecca S. Demsetz and Philip E. Strahan, "The Consolidation of the Financial Services Industry: Causes, Consequences, and Implications for the Future", *Journal of Banking and Finance*, 23/2 (1999): 135–94

Dymski, Gary, *The Bank Merger Wave: The Economic Causes and Social Consequences of Financial Consolidation*, Armonk, New York: Sharpe, 1999

Fama, Eugene, "Banking in the Theory of Finance", *Journal of Monetary Economics*, 6/1 (1980): 39–57

Freixas, Xavier and Jean-Charles Rochet, *Microeconomics of Banking*, Cambridge, Massachusetts: MIT Press, 1997

Gertler, Mark, "Financial Structure and Aggregate Economic Activity: An Overview", *Journal of Money, Credit, and Banking*, 20/3, part 2 (1988): 559–87

Hill, R.L. St., "A Post Keynesian Perspective on Commercial Bank Behavior and Regulation", *Metroeconomica*, 46/1 (1995): 35–62

Litan, Robert, *American Finance for the 21st Century*, Washington, DC: Brookings Institution, 1998

Minsky, Hyman, *Can "It" Happen Again?*, Armonk, New York: Sharpe, 1982

Moore, Basil, *Horizontalists versus Verticalists: The Macroeconomics of Credit Money*, Cambridge and New York: Cambridge University Press, 1988

The fundamental economic questions about banking are "why do banks exist?" and "how do they affect real economic outcomes?" Economists have developed several conflicting answers. FREIXAS & ROCHET summarize the vast literature that explains banks as institutions that permit agents to overcome coordination problems involving borrower–lender contracts, usually under asymmetric information. This volume efficiently summarizes the entire agency-theoretic literature: Diamond's costly monitoring approach, which views banks as solving a moral-hazard problem of inducing borrowers to avoid risk; Bernanke and Gertler's models of collateral-based lending; and the Diamond and Dybvig model of banks as optimal insurance contracts in the presence of exogenous liquidity risk.

Freixas & Rochet's book contains exhaustive references to the new Keynesian microfoundational literature, but its coverage is otherwise selective. It provides an abbreviated treatment of the huge industrial-organization literature on banking, which predates the information-theoretic approach. This approach explains why banks exist by emphasizing their efficiency in processing deposits and making loans; the nuances of principal–agent interaction in the loan market under asymmetric information recede from view, and attention centres instead on the behaviour of banks as profit-maximizing firms. The reader interested in industrial-organization models of banking behaviour must turn to the analytical review article of BALTENSPERGER, which remains unsurpassed, despite being dated.

Freixas & Rochet also contains no coverage of the post-Keynesian literature on banking, which has focused on the endogenous creation of money by banks and other firms, and on the endogenous generation of financial fragility in economies with speculative asset markets. The themes of endogenous money and fragility receive some attention in the asymmetric-information literature reviewed in Freixas & Rochet, but they have been explored far more richly by post-Keynesians, who emphasize fundamental uncertainty about the future and not asymmetric information. Much of the post-Keynesian scholarship on endogenous money has involved an extended debate with the thesis elaborated in MOORE.

Moore argues, contrary to the monetarist view, that the money supply is infinitely elastic at the interest rate established by the central bank. Banks, he asserts, will invariably accommodate demands for credit, especially from larger firms. The debate about whether Moore has become "too vertical", in Goodhart's phrase, turns on two questions: whether the role of banks in credit creation is passive, and whether credit finance is constrained by savings. The article by HILL provides references to this debate and formulates a sophisticated post-Keynesian model of the banking firm, incorporating endogenous money creation.

The theoretical industrial-organization approach to banking atrophied after the choice-theoretic asymmetric-information literature emerged, but the empirical industrial-organization literature on banking has grown steadily in size and sophistication. No one source could summarize this vast literature, which is largely fed by the empirical studies conducted by economists at the Federal Reserve Board and at the regional Federal Reserve Banks. BERGER, DEMSETZ & STRAHAN provide references to much of this empirical work, and convey the prevailing wisdom of many Federal Reserve economists: that the systematic dismantling of the Great Depression era regulations and ongoing banking consolidation will yield efficiency gains and reduce distortions in credit flows. DYMSKI reviews

this same empirical literature and reaches a different conclusion: that banking consolidation is not driven by operational efficiency considerations, but by the high equity-market prices of banks.

Yet another answer to the question of what banks do is the "new view" portfolio-theoretic macroeconomic approach. The history of this approach is recounted in some detail, if not with complete sympathy, by GERTLER. The "new view" was initiated by Gurley and Shaw, and developed further by Tobin and Brainard, and others. These authors showed how a financial structure that becomes "deeper" – in the sense of possessing more financial intermediaries offering more financial assets – can enhance economic growth: the law of large numbers permits banks and other financial intermediaries to provide more liquidity to wealth-holders, and more long-term and specialized loans to borrowers, than would otherwise be possible. Proponents of the "new view" initially used it to show the limitations of monetarism. However, theorists such as MacKinnon and Shaw repackaged it as the financial deepening hypothesis, which argued that financial liberalization in developing economies would yield palpable gains in economic growth. FAMA took this view of banking to its logical conclusion when he showed that, in efficient financial markets, banks have no effect on the equilibrium allocation of credit and capital.

Gertler is interested in showing how the Gurley-Shaw approach matured into the asymmetric-information approach, to which he himself has contributed. He gives no attention to the financial system crises that have accompanied banking liberalization. This is not surprising: the asymmetric-information literature explores how banks solve agents' problems, not how they worsen them. This leaves unanswered the question of how profit-seeking banks can fall prey to recurrent crises. However, answering this question is a central aim of MINSKY's financial-fragility model. In Minsky's view, the uncertain (not merely risky) environment in which banks and borrowers operate leads both to systematically underassess lending risk in upswings and to systematically overassess lending risk in downturns. In consequence, lending is prone to boom–bust cycles that are fed sometimes by euphoric expectations and sometimes by desperate runs to liquidity.

A recurring problem in much of the theoretical literature on banks is that the instruments and practices described only dimly resemble the behaviour of banks in the real world. LITAN is one of several of his books with the singular virtue of summarizing, in accessible prose, the state of banking practices in view of theoretical insights and recent historical experience. Litan's work has consistently characterized banks as being pushed into risky new markets, consolidation, and occasional crises, by non-banks' capture of large portions of their former market niches. Litan advocates banking deregulation and tracks the transformation of banks into financial-service providers. At the same time he surpasses his previous works by acknowledging, if timidly, the problems of banks in managing risk and ensuring access to opportunity. Dymski provides a fuller discussion of – and references to the literature on – the problems of racial discrimination and of limited lower-income access to financial services; he shows that these problems have persisted even as banking consolidation has proceeded apace.

GARY A. DYMSKI

Bargaining, economic

Aumann, Robert J. and Michael Maschler, "The Bargaining Set for Cooperative Games" in *Advances in Game Theory*, edited by M. Dresher, L.S. Shapley and A.W. Tucker, Princeton, New Jersey: Princeton University Press, 1964

Binmore, K.G., "Nash Bargaining 2" in *The Economics of Bargaining*, edited by Ken Binmore and Partha Dasgupta, Oxford: Blackwell, 1987

Edgeworth, F.Y., *Mathmatical Psychics: An Essay on the Application of Mathematics to the Moral Sciences*, London: Kegan Paul, 1881; reprinted New York: Kelley, 1967

Foldes, Lucien, "A Determinate Model of Bilateral Monopoly", *Economica*, New Series, 31/122 (1964): 117–31

Harsanyi, John, "Approaches to Bargaining before and after the Theory of Games: A Critical Discussion of Zeuthen's, Hicks', and Nash's Theories", *Econometrica*, 26/2 (1956): 144–47

Kalai, Ehud and Meir Smorodinsky, "Other Solutions to Nash's Bargaining Problem", *Econometrica*, 43/3 (May 1975): 513–18

Kalai, E., "Solutions to the Bargaining Problem" in *Social Goals and Social Organization*, edited by Leonid Hurwicz, David Schmeidler and Hugo Sonnenschein, Cambridge and New York: Cambridge University Press, 1985

Khilstrom, R.E., A.E. Roth and D. Schmeidler, "Risk Aversion and Solutions to Nash's Bargaining Problem" in *Social Goals and Social Organization*, edited by Leonid Hurwicz, David Schmeidler and Hugo Sonnenschein, Cambridge and New York: Cambridge University Press, 1985

Maschler, Michael and Micha A. Perles, "The Present Status of the Super-additive Solution" in *Essays in Game Theory and Mathematical Economics, in Honor of Oskar Morgenstern*, edited by Robert J. Aumann *et al.*, Mannheim: Bibliographisches Institut, 1981

Nash, John, "The Bargaining Problem", *Econometrica*, 18/2 (1950): 155–62

Nash, John, "Two-Person Cooperative Games", *Econometrica*, 21/1 (1953): 128–40

Osborne, Martin J. and Ariel Rubinstein, *Bargaining and Markets*, San Diego and London: Academic Press, 1990

Roth, Alvin E., *Axiomatic Models of Bargaining*, Berlin and New York: Springer, 1979

Roth, Alvin E. (editor), *Game-theoretic Models of Bargaining*, Cambridge: Cambridge University Press, 1985

Rubinstein, Ariel, "Perfect Equilibrium in a Bargaining Model", *Econometrica*, 50/1 (1982): 97–109

Rubinstein, Ariel, "A Bargaining Model with Incomplete Information about Time Preferences", *Econometrica*, 53/5 (September 1985): 1151–72

Schelling, T.C., "An Essay on Bargaining", *American Economic Review*, 46/3 (1956): 281–306

Young, Oran R., *Bargaining: Formal Theories of Negotiation*, Urbana: University of Illinois Press, 1975

Zeuthen, Frederik, *Problems of Monopoly and Economic Warfare*, London and New York: Routledge, 1930

EDGEWORTH initiated the pioneering formal analysis of bargaining, in the setting of bilateral monopoly. With two parties whose preferences and initial endowments are given exogenously, Edgeworth's task was to determine the quantities exchanged, subject to the condition that such exchange be mutually beneficial. He delimited the set of "efficient" potential trades, in the sense that there could be no further mutually beneficial exchange between the parties, denoting this set the "contract curve," and concluded that the outcome was indeterminate. The quest for a determinate solution to the bargaining problem has been a central issue addressed by successive theorists. In the analytical framework of Edgeworth, a determinate outcome for the bilateral monopoly exchange problem was developed by FOLDES, whose model incorporated costs from delay in reaching an agreement.

ZEUTHEN formulated a solution to the problem of a union and a group of employers bargaining over the wage rate. Zeuthen envisaged a sequential process in which the parties begin with incompatible demands and then weigh the alternatives of accepting the other side's position ("conceding") and standing firm. If neither side concedes when the demands are incompatible, no agreement occurs – a possibility considered to be a fixed threat to both parties. Each party thus compares the relative payoff expected from conceding with that from holding out. Holding out may induce the other party to concede – to which possibility each party assigns a subjective probability – or may result in no agreement. Recasting Zeuthen's approach in terms of von Neumann–Morgenstern utility, optimal behavior is guided by expected utility maximization. The certain gain from conceding is compared to the potentially larger but riskier gain from holding out in the hope that the other party will concede.

NASH (1950) achieved a *unique* solution to the bargaining problem by means of an axiomatic approach. Beginning with two agents who can reach an agreement in the set A of feasible agreements or failing that, realize the disagreement event D, Nash assumes that all agents have transitive preferences with respect to A∪D. Their attitude to risk is critical, because there is an inherent risk of no agreement being reached. The preference relation of each party $\geq_i$ is with respect to lotteries over A∪D, expressed as a von Neumann–Morgenstern utility function u_i, with each agent seeking to maximize expected utility. Denoting by S the set of pairs $(u_1(a), u_2(a))$ for a∈A, and by d the point $(u_1(D), u_2(D))$, the set of utility pairs that can be the outcome of bargaining is S∪d, the primitive of Nash's bargaining problem. Nash axiomatically specified four properties for the solution to the bargaining problem: (1) invariance to the particular utility function expressing the agents' underlying preferences; (2) that S∪d fully captures any asymmetry between the agents, and that if the players are symmetric, the solution should assign the same utility to each; (3) independence with respect to irrelevant alternatives; and (4) Pareto efficiency. Nash proved that the unique solution would be the pair of feasible utilities s_1 and s_2 that maximize the product of the utility gain from agreement to each party, i.e., $(s_1 - d_1)(s_2 - d_2)$.

NASH (1953) later extended the bargaining model in two respects: by allowing more than two parties to be engaged in bargaining, and by allowing each party to become committed to taking a particular action (which is a mixed strategy that can be interpreted as carrying out a threat in case no agreement is reached). When all have chosen their respective mixed strategies, the disagreement point is the utility vector that would result if all the threats were carried out. The set of optimal threats constitutes a Nash equilibrium (from the theory of non-cooperative games), and so the Nash solution can be applied to the resulting bargaining game.

HARSANYI (1956) recasts Zeuthen's analysis in a game-theoretic framework that assigns von Neumann–Morgenstern utility functions to both parties. He defines party i's "risk limit" as the maximum subjective probability of the "no agreement" event that i is prepared to tolerate without itself conceding. Harsanyi then demonstrates a remarkable result: that if the parties behave according to the Zeuthen principle – namely, that the next concession is made by the player having the lower risk limit – they will tend to reach the Nash solution as their agreement point.

The article by SCHELLING is an important precursor of the literature on strategic bargaining. Although his analysis is informal, many of his profound ideas – on strategic pre-commitment, and on the paradoxical notion that perceived weakness can be a source of bargaining power – laid the groundwork for subsequent formal game-theoretic developments in bargaining theory.

OSBORNE & RUBINSTEIN provide a thorough and rigorous analysis of Nash's bargaining solution, proving that none of Nash's four axioms is superfluous. They show that if any one of Nash's four axioms is removed, the remaining three imply a solution that differs from Nash's solution.

ROTH (1979) provides a very comprehensive survey of the state of axiomatic models of bargaining as of 1979, including some results on the effect on the Nash solution of the bargainers' respective attitudes to risk, subsequently published in KHILSTROM, ROTH & SCHMEIDLER.

A concise and highly authoritative survey of axiomatic bargaining theory, with greater emphasis on post-Nash solutions than in Roth's survey, appears in KALAI. Among the alternative axiomatic solutions surveyed is that described in the work of KALAI & SMORODINSKY. The Kalai–Smorodinsky axiomatization replaces the "independence of irrelevant alternatives" by an axiom of "individual monotonicity" – while maintaining Nash's other three axioms – and determines a unique solution. The KS solution entails that "the players choose the best outcome subject to getting the same proportions of their ideal gains".

MASCHLER and PERLES provide an alternative axiomatization of the bargaining problem that replaces the "independence of irrelevant alternatives" by two axioms – a technical "continuity" condition and an axiom of "superadditivity". The latter condition is motivated by the fact that any pair of utilities in S, the set of feasible agreements, may represent expectations about uncertain events. The Nash solution entails reaching a solution before such uncertainty is necessarily resolved. The superadditivity axiom induces all parties to avoid delaying agreement, in order to resolve such uncertainties.

A very useful collection of earlier articles – some path-breaking, others providing a synthesis or a critical survey of the literature, can be found in YOUNG.

In an entirely different stream of literature, on coalitional bargaining in the theory of cooperative games, AUMANN & MASCHLER invented a solution concept – the "bargaining set" – and proved its existence. The bargaining set addresses the issue of how the members of a coalition would divide that coalition's joint payoff if the coalition is to be immune to initiatives by any of its members to improve his or her payoff at the expense of some other member. In the setting of a strictly superadditive game, in which Pareto efficiency requires the formation of a grand coalition, but in which the core is empty (i.e. there is no division of the joint payoff amongst the players which can simultaneously satisfy all of the stability conditions of the core), the bargaining set provides a blueprint for a "stable" (in the AM sense of the bargaining set) Pareto efficient outcome.

The most recent breakthrough in modelling the bargaining problem as a strategic non-cooperative game is due to RUBINSTEIN (1982). His seminal paper models two-player bargaining as a non-cooperative infinite horizon game of alternating offers under complete information, with discounting of future payoffs. The solution concept used is subgame perfect equilibrium. A unique agreement is determined by backward inductive reasoning: with a common discount factor δ, in the first period, player 1 offers player 2 the settlement ($s^* = 1/(1 + \delta)$, $1 - s^* = \delta/(1 + \delta)$), and player 2 accepts. (If the players' discount rates differ, the unique subgame perfect equilibrium is only slightly more complicated: in that case as well, player 1 proposes a unique subgame perfect equilibrium settlement in period 1, which player 2 immediately accepts). RUBINSTEIN (1985) also models the case of incomplete information about time preferences. A very useful guide to the precursors of Rubinstein's (1982) model and to the extensive literature spawned by that model and his 1985 model, is provided in Osborne and Rubinstein's notes to their chapter three and chapter five. They survey the literature on a striking result first noted by BINMORE – the intimate connection between Nash's solution and the subgame perfect equilibrium solution to a non-cooperative sequential bargaining game that assumes an exogenous probability of breakdown in each period if no agreement has been reached, and that also assumes no time preference.

ROTH (1985) is a collection of seventeen papers which are representative of the diverse directions and fruitful developments in the recent game-theoretic modelling of bargaining, including developments in the areas of games of incomplete information and reputation effects.

IRWIN LIPNOWSKI

See also Game theory

Barriers to entry

Bain, Joe S., *Barriers to New Competitions: Their Character and Consequences in Manufacturing Industries*, Cambridge, Massachusetts: Harvard University Press, 1956

Baumol, W.J., J.C. Panzar and R.D. Willig, "Contestable Markets: An Uprising in the Theory of Industry Structure", *American Economic Review*, 72 (1982): 1–15

Baumol, W.J. and R.D. Willig, "Contestability: Developments since the Book", *Oxford Economic Papers*, 38 (1986): 9–36

Demsetz, H., "Why Regulate Utilities", *Journal of Law and Economics*, 11 (1968): 55–65

The Economist, "The Economics of Antitrust", 2 May 1998, 66–68

Goldschmid, Harvey J., H. Michael Mann and J. Fred Weston (editors), *Industrial Concentration: The New Learning*, Boston: Little Brown, 1974

Harbord, D. and T. Hoehn, "Barriers to Entry and Exit in European Competition Policy", *International Review of Law and Economics*, 14/4 (1994): 411–35

Norman, George and Manfredi La Manna (editors), *The New Industrial Economics: Recent Developments in Industrial Organization, Oligopoly and Game Theory*, Aldershot, Hampshire: Elgar, 1992

Schmalensee, Richard, "Inter-industry Studies of Structure and Performance" in *Handbook of Industrial Organization*, edited by R. Schmalensee and Robert D. Willig, Amsterdam: North Holland, 1989

Schmalensee, Richard and Robert D. Willig (editors), *Handbook of Industrial Organization*, Amsterdam: North Holland, 1989

Schwartz, M., "The Nature and Scope of Contestability Theory", *Oxford Economic Papers*, 38 (1986): 37–57

Shepherd, William G., *The Economics of Industrial Organization*, 4th edition, Upper Saddle River, New Jersey: Prentice Hall, 1997

Tirole, Jean, *The Theory of Industrial Organization*, Cambridge, Massachusetts: MIT Press, 1988

The term "barriers to entry" was first coined by BAIN. In general, the concept refers to any situation that prevents or limits competition within an industry. It arises within the broader microeconomic topic of industrial organization, which examines industry structure, the reasons for the prevailing structure, and its economic implications. These, in turn, are influential in competition, regulatory and antitrust policies, and legislation.

A vital issue in the functioning of markets is whether those markets are competitive. This comes from the standard neoclassical assumption that competitive markets lead to optimal outcomes. The only acceptable reason for monopoly may be where there are significant economies of scale, as in the case of a "natural monopoly". In other cases, the cost of uncompetitive markets may include misallocation of resources, excess monopoly profits, X-inefficiency, loss of choice in the market, and less invention and innovation.

Literature on barriers to entry is intimately linked with the theory of the firm and the theory of oligopoly. SHEPHERD reviews the basic theories and gives a comprehensive introduction to the major theoretical developments and debates that have occurred within the area of industrial organization. He also provides a historical sweep, noting that the consequences of lack of competition were referred to as far back as in Aristotle's writings, in 347 BC. Theoretical and empirical research findings are found throughout, as well as a number of case studies. The different schools of thought, as outlined below, are referred to "structuralist", "antistructuralist", "potential competition", and "behaviourist".

The major distinctions among the schools of thought include the existence, type, and height of perceived or actual barriers, and the linkages and the direction of causation among industry structure, conduct, and performance. These range from a relatively linear process, where structure is the main determinant of performance, or vice versa, to emphasizing the primary role of conduct.

The structuralist or mainstream view is exemplified by Bain. Also referred to as the "Harvard tradition", it embodies the structure-conduct-performance paradigm and concludes that monopoly is harmful. Market structure (the number and relative sizes of firms in the industry) is the primary determinant of conduct (pricing, output, innovation, and investment decisions), which, in turn, leads to performance (quality, efficiency, and volume). Any entry barriers form an element of market structure and so will influence performance. Barriers may occur due to economies of scale, absolute cost advantages, product differentiation, or capital requirements. A strong empirical stance is embodied within this school and market power is typically deduced from the results of studies using methodological tools such as the "Herfindahl index" or the "Lerner index". Further developments led to limit-pricing models, where incumbent firms deliberately charge low prices in order to dissuade entry or to induce exit.

Theories collectively known as "new industrial organization" challenged the mainstream approach on two fundamental grounds – firstly, the interpretation of empirical descriptions of the relationship between structure and performance, and secondly, on its less-than-rigorous theoretical underpinnings.

The Chicago-UCLA school, which developed in the 1970s, turns the structure-conduct-performance direction of causation around, and placed greater weight on theoretical rigour. Shepherd calls this the "antistructuralist view", and it derives from earlier Chicago school economists, notably George Stigler, who theorized that the norm was competitive markets, with monopoly being "limited, transient, and weak", a reversal of the orthodoxy of the time (p.8).

DEMSETZ questioned the assumption "stated explicitly or suggested implicitly" (p.55) that the number of firms and degree of competition are always positively related. The "Demsetz critique" disputes the basic monopoly model from which such conclusions are derived on the grounds that the models simply *assume* market power, without giving an adequate explanation of how such power is acquired and maintained. In his analysis, a concentrated market structure comes about as a result of some firms being more efficient than others, therefore only the more efficient survive in the market. Monopolies, rather than exemplifying all that can go wrong with unfettered markets, in fact reflect efficiency. Barriers either do not exist or are irrelevant.

Implicit in the debate over the interpretation of empirical results is whether market dominance has emerged through competitive or anti-competitive means. A series of essays on the "concentration debate" is found in GOLDSCHMID *et al.* SCHMALENSEE gives a critical survey of empirical results from interindustry studies, and a broad range of research findings on the effects of market power on variables such as prices and efficiency are cited in Shepherd.

The theory of "contestable markets", developed by BAUMOL, PANZAR & WILLIG focuses on the role of potential competition. Even if a monopoly does exist, so long as it faces the *possibility* of competition then its behaviour will be modified and outcomes will tend towards the competitive model. The policy implication – that government intervention runs the risk of worsening rather than rectifying the situation – proved persuasive for governments following free-market approaches with respect to public utilities and regulatory policies in the 1980s.

Contestability theory led to a prolific amount of research. One source of contention has been the restrictive conditions, such as the assumption of zero sunk costs. In general, although contestability theory is considered to have some merit, the conditions are too restrictive for it to serve as a real disciplinary device for monopolies. SCHWARTZ synthesizes a range of research looking at the issues from a variety of perspectives. BAUMOL & WILLIG update and address some of the issues and state that the concept of "perfect contestability" is meant to be a benchmark.

Other theoretical developments have involved the use of game theory, and examine entry deterrence by the use of strategic behaviour by firms in situations of duopoly or oligopoly. TIROLE gives a comprehensive theoretical treatment of different types of strategic behaviour. In these models, there is no straight linear connection between structure-conduct-performance. Rather, it is a dynamic process, with the focus on the conduct of firms. Unlike the models of perfect competition or monopoly, under oligopoly barriers to entry may be endogenously imposed through the strategic behaviour of the firms themselves, rather than being exogenously or structurally imposed. A criticism of these theories is that behavioural variations lead to so many permutations and possible outcomes that they have little practical use. A series of papers in NORMAN & LA MANNA include theoretical constructs of the effects of diversification, patents, and the role of entrepreneurship.

Competing theories offer different explanations about how and why market structure matters and have different policy implications. Intrinsic to each are definitions and concepts of what "competition" actually implies and this is where the economics profession and the legal profession become enjoined. See HARBORD & HOEHN for a recent study of European legal approaches to assessing entry barriers.

SCHMALENSEE & WILLIG edit a series of surveys by specialists, providing a comprehensive overview of applications of industrial organization and the role of barriers in microeconomic and macroeconomic contexts.

Current and future research will be increasingly directed towards the role and implications of technology. Two perspectives, in particular, are relevant – the potential for technology to act as a barrier to entry, and its role in empirical research methods used to test the validity and predictive power of theoretical models. In a brief article, THE ECONOMIST outlines the current state of thinking in the area and how technological developments are enhancing econometric models.

BEVERLEY M. MOODIE

See also Competition, economic, Contestable markets, Monopoly

Behaviour, behaviour therapy

Alberto, Paul A. and Anne C. Troutman, *Applied Behavior Analysis for Teachers*, 5th edition, Englewood Cliffs, New Jersey: Prentice Hall, 1999

Canter, Lee and Marlene Canter, *Succeeding with Difficult Students: New Strategies for Reaching Your Most Challenging Students*, Santa Monica, California: Canter, 1993

Douglas, Jo, *Behaviour Problems in Young Children: Assessment and Management*, London and New York: Tavistock/Routledge, 1989

Glasser, William, *Control Theory in the Classroom*, New York: Harper and Row, 1986

Goldstein, Arnold P., R. Sprafkin, N. Gershaw and P. Klein, *Skill-streaming the Adolescent: A Structured Learning Approach to Teaching Prosocial Skills*, Champaign, Illinois: Research Press, 1980

Graham, Philip (editor), *Cognitive-Behaviour Therapy for Children and Families*, Cambridge and New York: Cambridge University Press, 1998

Kaplan, Joseph S., *Beyond Behavior Modification: A Cognitive-Behavioral Approach to Behavior Management in the School*, 3rd edition, Austin, Texas: Pro-Ed, 1995

Kauffman, James M., Mark Mostert, Stanley Trent and Daniel Hallahan, *Managing Classroom Behavior: A Reflective Case-Based Approach*, 2nd edition, Boston: Allyn and Bacon, 1998

McAuley, Roger and Patricia McAuley, *Child Behaviour Problems: An Empirical Approach to Management*, London: Macmillan, 1977; New York: Free Press, 1978

Walker, Hill M., Geoff Colvin and Elizabeth Ramsey, *Antisocial Behavior in School: Strategies and Best Practices*, Pacific Grove, California: Brookes/Cole, 1995

Watson, T. Steuart and Frank M. Gresham (editors), *Handbook of Child Behavior Therapy*, New York: Plenum, 1998

ALBERTO & TROUTMAN recently revised their text of the principles, constructs, and applications of applied behaviour analysis (ABA) within a classroom context. From this behaviourist perspective of behavioural management, Alberto & Troutman offer the novice behaviourist the language of the model, the assessment procedures, research designs, and reinforcement theory to implement these approaches within a classroom context. Specific case studies are included, as well as excellent descriptions of vocabulary associated with these approaches, within text and glossary format. Various single-subject designs and interventions, as well as reinforcers, are detailed within chapters. Numerous school- and classroom-based examples enhance and deepen understanding of the specific behavioural concepts discussed in a format organized according to the actual process of applying behavioural analysis.

The central focus of CANTER & CANTER's "assertive discipline" is to establish a classroom in which student and teacher needs are met, where behaviour is managed in a humane way, and learning occurs as intended. These goals are accomplished by establishing class rules of behaviour, teaching students to behave properly, and talking to students who misbehave. The foundation of assertive discipline lies on the teacher providing the students with positive attention, establishing a climate of mutual trust and respect, and attending closely to student needs. The logic behind the work is, first of all, that teachers have the right to teach without disruption occurring. The students have a right to learn in a safe and calm environment, with the full support of the teacher. They feel that these ends are best met by teachers who are in charge, but who do not violate students' best interests. Finally, they believe that trust, respect, and perseverance on the part of the teacher earn student cooperation. The Canters have contributed a classroom control strategy that places teachers humanely in charge in the classroom, as well as a behavioural system that allows teachers to invoke positive and negative consequences in a calm and fair manner. The assertive discipline model has also contributed specific techniques for teaching students how to behave and techniques for dealing with challenging students. This text describes numerous strategies to control behaviour and reduce behaviour problems within the classroom of children and adolescents.

DOUGLAS provides a comprehensive account of emotional and behavioural problems in pre-school children in the areas of both assessment and treatment. This text serves as a practical guide for parents and health professionals working with young families, as well as clinicians who advise parents on how to manage their children through daily practice. Drawing on vast practical experiences, Douglas discusses the causes of the behavioural problems, advises on their assessment, and gives details on a range of treatment options. The specific difficulties include eating and feeding, sleep problems, aggression, toilet training, and emotional problems. Case studies are used to illustrate issues discussed. Current research is referenced, but the format is appropriate for various audiences.

The central focus of GLASSER's "non-coercive discipline" is that children and adolescents have control of their own behaviour; that is, they choose to behave as they do. Parents, educators, and other professionals, therefore, have the power and the obligation to help children and adolescents make better choices. Educators who learn to function as leaders of quality classrooms, by providing a stimulating learning environment, encouraging students, and helping them as much as possible, promote quality learning and therefore reduce discipline problems. Focus is also placed on increasing student satisfaction through meeting their basic needs for belonging, freedom, fun, and power. Glasser emphasizes quality in curriculum, teaching, and learning. Glasser has contributed the concept and the practice of classroom meetings as a regular part of the curriculum. He has also contributed the idea that focus should be placed on meeting students' basic needs, which he feels is the key element in good discipline and behaviour therapy. Glasser has given educators the concepts and practices of quality curriculum, quality teaching, and quality learning in this text and based upon the research and earlier writing contained within *Reality Therapy: A New Approach to Psychiatry*.

According to GOLDSTEIN *et al.*, a behaviour-management problem is any behaviour that prevents a group (students in a classroom) from working towards the goal. Therefore, this text focuses on the purpose of structured learning; that is, to teach useful, purposeful, prosocial skills. Behaviour management

problems fall into two categories: behavioural excesses and behavioural deficiencies. Behavioural excesses actively interfere with or intrude upon the desired behaviour, such as hyperactivity, aggressive or impulsive behaviour, disruption, temper tantrums, and dependency. Behavioural deficiencies are an absence or weakness of the prosocial or developmentally appropriate behaviours, such as isolation, negativism, apathy, anxiety, and a lack of self-concept. Goldstein *et al.* explore, define, and explicitly detail specific behaviour-modification techniques, social skills techniques (instruction), and relationship-based techniques to address the behaviour problems identified. Goldstein *et al.* also offer a companion text for elementary-aged children.

The 15 essays contained within GRAHAM focus on the relatively new treatment approach of cognitive-behaviour therapy, which now has a firm theoretical base and has been subject to empirical validation. Cognitive-behaviour therapy has been demonstrated to be an effective form of treatment for the estimated ten per cent of children and young people who suffer from developmental, emotional, or behavioural problems. This volume uniquely provides a comprehensive account of cognitive-behavioural approaches to psychological problems in children, adolescents, and their families, including topics such as attention-deficit hyperactivity disorder, clinical depression, conduct and anxiety disorders, post-traumatic stress disorders, and obsessive-compulsive disorders. The text is structured developmentally, from preschool through adolescence. An introductory chapter outlines general principles of cognitive-behaviour therapy, while the last chapter highlights the vision for the future. The authors of each essay first describe the rationale for treatment and then proceed to describe the assessment and therapy, including case studies. This very recent addition to the area of behaviour therapy is a very practical handbook and resource for a wide range of individuals, which specifically address therapeutic and service issues.

KAPLAN offers the various models of behaviour management within a format for practitioners that links the theoretical frameworks, conceptual models, and specific treatments with classroom and home applications and assessments. At the outset, the five conceptual models of behaviour management (psychoeducational, biophysical, behavioural, social learning theory, and ecological) are described. By using case studies, chapter reviews, and numerous examples, Kaplan illustrates the major concepts of behaviour modification, from identifying and specifying the behaviours to self-management strategies. Excellent information on measuring change through data collection, display, and analysis is included. Various cognitive strategies and techniques for treatment of behavioural problems, as well as social skills development as replacement behaviours, complete the topical discussions of this cognitive approach to behaviour modification. This source offers excellent instructional tools for the comprehension and application of the major constructs of these behavioural approaches.

KAUFFMAN *et al.* not only provide excellent descriptions of the constructs and research of behaviour theories, but also relate to specific case studies and resultant discussions to enhance the specific constructs. This two-text series offers discussion topics and researched, validated practices for consideration within each issue-related chapter. In Part I, an overview of basic concepts of behaviour management for school-aged children and adolescents is given through vignettes, research, and questions for reflection. Part II offers case studies for analysis. This approach reflects the real-life complexities of behaviour management that do not ordinarily occur, through brief vignettes, hypothetical examples, and the straightforward exposition of principles.

McAULEY & McAULEY draw from their clinical experiences as a child psychiatrist and social worker to present a text that is responsive to the techniques of applied behaviour analysis (ABA) and reinforcement theory. The ABA strategy argues that deviant behaviour is developed and maintained by its short-term stimulus associations. The discovery of these associations, by parents and health care providers, should detail a systematic plan to shift how this cycle operates. Macauley & Macauley, through research, cases studies, and numerous specific interventions for each of the problem areas identified, offer the process and the complexities inherent with applied behaviour analysis. Specific and applied programming and therapies based upon accurate assessment of the behaviour is detailed in three sections: assessment, planning, and intervention. References include textbooks, journals, and glossary of behavioural terms.

WALKER, COLVIN and RAMSEY produced a comprehensive text based upon the principles of social learning that govern how diverse forms of behaviour are acquired, maintained, and reduced or eliminated. These principles have been derived from a solid empirical knowledge base developed through objective, rigorous, scientific methods. Understanding social contingencies and their influence on the behaviour of individuals and their interactions is extremely important to the approaches and techniques described by the authors. The 13 chapters in this text address the issues of antisocial behaviour at school and its prevention and remediation. Traditionally, schools have used strategies such as control, containment, exclusion, and punishment for students who exhibit behaviour problems. Walker, Colvin & Ramsey designed this text to enhance the educator's understanding of the nature, origins, and causes of antisocial behaviour, while also providing information on the most current research-based interventions, practices, and model programmes for preventing and remediating behaviour problems in school-aged children and adolescents.

WATSON & GRESHAM believe that effective treatment of problem behaviour arises from the effective diagnosis of the function of the behaviour through a problem-solving approach. While offering this perspective and realizing the departure from radical behaviourists and applied behaviour analysts, Watson & Gresham suggest that this "cognitive" approach may offer a new perspective for treatment. Therefore, this edited book reflects the relationship between assessment and treatment, more specifically functional assessment and analysis, and describes the process that a clinician uses when treating particular behaviour problems from a cognitive perspective. Watson & Gresham stress functional assessment to provide the methodology by which the variables related to each of the specific problems can be explored to greatly enhance the likelihood of effective treatment. The second theme for each chapter is behavioural consultation, which provides the process that one uses when working with parents, teachers, or other professionals providing services. After an overview of the foundations of child behaviour therapy, current reviews of problems

associated with school, home, and more chronic conditions are included. Specific, researched assessment procedures and references are offered with each problem, as well as therapeutic approaches from various models (for example, ecobehavioral, behavioural, or social). Current issues and research in behaviour and behaviour therapy are discussed within the context described.

MARY LITTLE

See also Rational emotive behaviour therapy

Behavioural economics

Akerlof, George A. and Janet L. Yellen (editors), *Efficiency Wage Models of the Labor Market*, Cambridge and New York: Cambridge University Press, 1986

Altman, Morris, *Human Agency and Material Welfare: Revisions in Microeconomics and Their Implications for Public Policy*, Boston: Kluwer, 1996

Becker, Gary S., *Accounting for Tastes*, Cambridge, Massachusetts: Harvard University Press, 1996

Cyert, Richard M. and James G. March, *A Behavioral Theory of the Firm*, 2nd edition, Cambridge, Massachusetts: Blackwell, 1992

Frantz, Roger S., *X-Efficiency: Theory, Evidence and Applications*, Boston: Kluwer, 1997

Kagel, John H. and Alvin E. Roth (editors), *The Handbook of Experimental Economics*, Princeton, New Jersey: Princeton University Press, 1995

Kahneman, D. and A. Tversky, "Prospect Theory: An Analysis of Decision under Risk", *Econometrica*, 47 (1979): 263–91

Kahneman, D., J.L. Knetsch and R.H. Thaler, "Fairness and the Assumptions of Economists" in *Rational Choice: The Contrast between Economics and Psychology*, edited by Robin M. Hogarth and Melvin W. Reder, Chicago: University of Chicago Press, 1987: 101–16

Leibenstein, Harvey, "Allocative Efficiency vs X-Efficiency", *American Economic Review*, 56 (1966): 392–415

Leibenstein, Harvey, *Collected Essays*, vol. 2: *X-Efficiency and Micro-Micro Theory*, edited by Kenneth Button, Aldershot, Hampshire: Elgar, 1989

Maital, Shlomo and Sharone L. Maital (editors), *Economics and Psychology*, Aldershot, Hampshire: Elgar, 1993

Shiller Robert J., *Market Volatility*, Cambridge, Massachusetts: MIT Press, 1993

Simon, Herbert A., "Rational Choice and the Structure of the Environment", *Psychological Review*, 63 (1956): 129–38

Simon, Herbert A., "Theories of Decision Making in Economics and Behavioral Science", *American Economic Review*, 49 (1959): 252–83

Simon, Herbert A., "Rationality as a Process and as a Product of Thought", *American Economic Review*, 70 (1978): 1–16

Simon, Herbert A., Behavioural Economics entry in *The New Palgrave: A Dictionary of Economics*, edited by John Eatwell, Murray Milgate and Peter Newman, 4 vols, London: Macmillan, and New York: Stockton Press, 1987

Stiglitz, Joseph E., "The Causes and Consequences of the Dependence of Quantity on Price", *Journal of Economic Literature*, 25 (1987): 1–48

Thaler, Richard H., *The Winner's Curse: Paradoxes and Anomalies of Economic Life*, New York: Free Press, 1992

Tversky, Amos and Daniel Kahneman, "The Framing of Decisions and the Psychology of Choice", *Science*, 211 (1981): 453–58

Williamson, Oliver E., *Markets and Hierarchies: Analysis and Antitrust Implications*, 2nd edition, New York: Free Press, and London: Collier Macmillan, 1983

Behavioural economics, as a defining concept for a particular methodological approach in economics, appears in the first instance to be an oxymoron as economics is a discipline that explicitly deals with the economic aspects of human behaviour. This point is clearly exemplified in the work of BECKER, whose research spans the gamut from the economics of discrimination and the family to the economics of drug addiction. However, as SIMON (1987) notes in his brief survey of behavioural economics, behavioural economics must be contrasted with and defined relative to the now conventional neoclassical approach to economic questions within which Becker's work clearly fits. In contrast with neoclassical economics, which assumes that the realism of behavioural assumptions is of no analytical consequence, and in which only the accuracy of a theory's analytical predictions are of any significance, behavioural economics assumes that the realism of behavioural assumptions can be of fundamental analytical importance. Behavioural economics is therefore distinguished by its efforts to test for the empirical validity of a theory's behavioural assumptions and to determine the analytical and policy-related significance of introducing more realistic assumptions into standard theories. Moreover, it is concerned with the social and institutional constraints that influence individual behaviour.

The end game of the behavioural assumptions of neoclassical theory is that, given their goals and motivation, individuals make consistent choices from among all relevant available alternatives and that these choices are rational in the sense that they are consistent with individuals maximizing their expected utility. Such optimizing behaviour is assumed to be forced upon individuals by dint of circumstance or, more specifically, by the pressure of the market place. Herbert Simon has played an important role in the development of behavioural economics, introducing the concepts of bounded rationality and satisficing into the economic profession's theoretical toolbox. SIMON (1956, 1959) integrates into economic theory the fact that the computational ability and knowledge of individuals is limited. Once these limitations are recognized, one can no longer assume that individuals know all available alternatives and know all of the consequences of their choices. The acquisition of such knowledge comes at a high cost, so individuals adopt behavioural procedures designed to limit such costs. Rational behaviour therefore takes places within the bounds or cognitive limitations of the individual and, therefore, individuals tend to work with incomplete or imperfect information. Mainstream theory has integrated this important insight.

SIMON (1956) introduces the concept of "satisficing" as a direct logical follow up to bounded rationality. "Satisficing" is seen as an alternative to optimizing where individuals who control the firm attempt to maximize profits and thereby utility and, in so doing, maximize output per unit of input and thereby minimize costs. A satisficer will maximize but only given the constraints of bounded rationality. In this case, the firm's output and profit are less than they would be in world with no limits to human cognitive abilities. Conventional wisdom has integrated this concept in the sense that it is now often assumed that optimization takes place within the constraints of positive search costs associated with the process of optimization. Individuals are still doing the best possible job for the economy as predicted by the theory, but not as well as could have been done in a world with unlimited cognitive abilities. Of fundamental importance to Simon is that his findings speak to the importance of understanding the process of developing mechanisms and searching and acquiring information to achieve goals and targets set by individuals and organizations. CYERT & MARCH employ SIMON's (1959) behavioural assumptions to develop a behavioural theory of the firm that focuses on the process of decision making within the context of bounded rationality. Simon's work has also given rise to the transactions cost theory of the firm, pioneered by WILLIAMSON.

LEIBENSTEIN (1966), whose critical papers are collected in LEIBENSTEIN (1989), rejects the neoclassical view – even in the form that incorporates Simon's (1956, 1959) contributions – that individuals optimize in the sense of maximizing output per unit of input. He argues that individual behaviour, in terms of how hard and how well people work, is affected by their pay and by the overall motivational structure within the firm, by their own psychological worldview towards work, by peer relationships, and by agent–principal relationships within the firm. Leibenstein pioneered the concepts of efficiency wages and x-inefficiency to incorporate this understanding into a theory of the firm. Conventional wisdom assumes that effort per unit of time is at a maximum and is invariable.

Efficiency wages refer to a situation whereby effort per unit of time is a positive function of wages; wages affect the physical capacity of individuals to work. The concept of efficiency wages has been extended and applied to relatively higher income societies where wages affect effort input through the perceptual filter of fairness. Efficiency wage theory typically assumes that there exists a unique wage, known to the firm, which maximizes effort per unit of time and thereby minimizes unit production costs. If this assumption does not hold, no unique wage will be efficient. AKERLOF & YELLEN present a collection of some of the classic theoretical papers in this area, whereas STIGLITZ, who has contributed to efficiency wage theory, provides one of the best interpretative surveys of the theory.

X-inefficiency theory states that effort per unit of time is affected by an array of variables inside the firm such that the firm ends up being less productive than under an ideal organizational setup within the firm. The deviation of productivity from the ideal is referred to as x-inefficiency. X-inefficient firms, because they are less productive, are relatively high unit-cost producers. They can survive only when protected by imperfect product markets and subsidies. Such potential inefficiencies are assumed away by conventional wisdom, which maintains that, in the long haul, market forces will force individuals to optimize or perish. ALTMAN extends both the efficiency wage and x-inefficiency behavioural frameworks to deal with how utility-maximizing or goal-oriented individuals can produce x-inefficiently or sub-optimally and survive even in a competitive market. X-efficient behaviour comes at a psychological and economic cost that varies across individuals. There is also no predetermined and known efficiency wage. Under these conditions, inefficient firms can survive when protected by a low-wage environment and high-wage firms can survive and prosper if they are x-efficient. Market forces, by themselves, cannot force individuals to optimize. This denies a basic premise of neoclassical theory. Whether or not optimization takes place, then, becomes a function of psychological, social, institutional, and cultural variables, with important public policy implications. FRANTZ provides an elaborate survey of the empirical and theoretical x-efficiency literature that is most closely related to Leibenstein's contributions.

Behavioural economics and psychology are often closely intertwined as the former borrows heavily from the insights on human behaviour discovered by the latter. MAITAL & MAITAL present an important collection of papers that deal with the interplay between the two fields. Experimental economics plays an important but more peripheral role in behavioural economics. Laboratory experiments provide important insights on how individuals might behave in the real world and provide us with suggestions on how better to design the behavioural assumptions underlying economic theory. Nevertheless, economists of various genres remain unconvinced that experiments can provide us with the fundamentals of how individuals actually behave in the real world as the incentive structures in the real economy differ markedly from those in the best-designed laboratory experiments. KAGEL & ROTH provide an informative review of the main currents in experimental economics by some its leading players.

Of particular importance to the interplay between economic psychology, experimental economics and behavioural economics are the findings of cognitive psychologists KAHNEMAN & TVERSKY on decisions made under conditions of uncertainty – decisions that require the exploitation by individuals of their limited and varied computational capacities. Many of these choices are inconsistent with the analytical predictions of the standard neoclassical model of "rational choice", where the latter prescribes choice behaviour that will yield the greatest wealth to the decision maker. Kahneman & Tversky's descriptions of experimentally based behaviour speak to the importance of the framing or context of problems for the type and direction of decision making. They have also developed the influential certainty principle and the Kahneman & Tversky value function. These have all given rise to much experimental research. All told, their research, and related research, as exemplified in THALER, suggest that, at a minimum, individuals consistently err and are inconsistent with regards to purely wealth-maximizing decisions. However, many of these decisions are not subject to market pressures and may very well be consistent with rational utility maximizing behaviour in a world of imperfect information. Moreover, many of these errant decisions are correctable through learning.

Finally, a domain where behavioural economics has played an increasingly important role is in the study of financial markets. Behavioural research has challenged the longstanding efficient market hypothesis, which asserts that financial prices reflect, at all points in time, the true value of investments and, therefore, incorporate all relevant public and private information related to such investments. This assumes that individuals have the capacity to know and process all relevant information at all points in time and to act on such information, maximizing their wealth over time. Evidence is mounting that there are many cases where short- and even medium-term prices deviate from their efficient representations because, for example, bounded rationality, psychological, and cultural variables, which are ignored in the efficient market literature, can affect individual decision making. Contemporary research in behavioural finance is well illustrated in SHILLER.

MORRIS ALTMAN

See also Economic psychology, Experimental economics

Behaviourism

Bruch, Michael and Frank W. Bond, *Beyond Diagnosis: Case Formulation Approaches in CBT*, Chichester and New York: Wiley, 1998

Eysenck, Hans J. and Irene Martin, *Theoretical Foundations of Behaviour Therapy*, London and New York: Plenum, 1987

Goldstein, Arnold P., *Psychological Skill Training: The Structured Learning Technique*, New York: Pergamon Press, 1981

Graziano, Anthony M., *Behaviour Therapy with Children*, Chicago: Aldine Atherton, 1975

Herbert, Martin, *ABC of Behavioural Methods*, Leicester: British Psychological Society, 1996

Krasner, Leonard, *Environmental Design and Human Behavior: A Psychology of the Individual in Society*, New York: Pergamon Press, 1980

McKenna, Eugene, *Business Psychology and Organisational Behaviour*, London: Erlbaum, 1994

O'Donohue, William and Richard Kitchener, *Handbook of Behaviorism*, San Diego: Academic Press, 1999

Rachlin, Howard, *Introduction to Modern Behaviurism*, 3rd edition, New York: Freeman, 1991

Roche, B. (guest editor), "Special Feature on New Wave Analysis", *The Psychologist*, 12/10 (October 1999)

Skinner, B.F., *About Behaviorism*, New York: Knopf, and London: Cape, 1974

Todd, James T. and Edward K. Morris (editors), *Modern Perspectives on John B. Watson and Classical Behaviorism*, Westport, Connecticut: Greenwood Press, 1994

Todd, James T. and Edward K. Morris (editors), *Modern Perspectives on B.F. Skinner and Contemporary Behaviorism*, Westport, Connecticut: Greenwood Press, 1995

Ullmann, Leonard P. and Leonard Krasner, *A Psychological Approach to Abnormal Behavior*, Englewood Cliffs, New Jersey and London: Prentice Hall, 1975

Watson, J.B., "Psychology as a Behaviourist Views It", *Psychological Review*, 20 (1913): 159–77

Wolpe, Joseph, *The Practice of Behaviour Therapy*, 4th
    edition, Oxford and New York: Pergamon Press, 1973
Zuriff, G.E., *Behaviorism: A Conceptual Reconstruction*,
    New York: Columbia University Press, 1985

Behaviourism changed the way we look at ourselves. As
RACHLIN remarks, in his presentation of the history of behaviourism, to understand its impact we have to look at what
came before. Psyche is the symbol used to depict psychology
and it is fitting for a branch of knowledge that deals with the
human spirit, soul, or mind. The link between reason and faith
was central to thinking from the Middle Ages onward. René
Descartes, mathematician and philosopher took the view that
there are two classes of human behaviour: involuntary and
voluntary. The former are purely mechanical and originate as
simple responses to objects in the physical world, but the latter
were seen to originate in the mind. As a result, the study of
the mind through behaviour was held to be impossible: you
could only study the mind by looking inwards – introspection.
This Cartesian dualism, in various forms, influenced many who
contributed to psychological thought and the later development of intra-psychic models.

John Broadus WATSON declared that introspection should
be banished from psychology and that all observations should,
as in any other scientific study, be concentrated on that which
could be reliably observed, namely behaviour. Behaviourism
was born with this assertion and came to be a dominant force
in psychology. Watson was concerned with understanding how
we learn. As someone committed to the concept of biological
continuity between species he believed that we could study
animal and human behaviour using the same principles, and
that learning served an adaptive function. He followed Pavlov
and demonstrated the relationship between stimulus and
response in behaviour. His classical example showed how a
fearful response to a neutral object could become established
(conditioned) by pairing the neutral object with a feared
stimulus.

Rachlin presents an overview of these arguments and traces
the development of behaviourism, its main contributors, and
its impact on our understanding of the way we learn. While
behaviourism is primarily associated with Watson, and later
SKINNER, it builds on the important contributions of Pavlov
and Guthrie, and subsequent efforts of Wolpe, Eysenck, and
many others. Its impact is felt in fields as diverse as behaviour
therapy, education, management, study of clinical behaviour,
environmental management, and community change. Its many
critics point to the initial views of Watson, promulgated in the
1920s, and act as if nothing has changed since. Modern behaviourism, as Rachlin's book demonstrates, is rather different.
The extent of the debate on the influence of behaviourism can
be seen in modern perspectives on the classic work of Watson
and Skinner by TODD & MORRIS (1994, 1995), on attempts
at reconceptualizations of behaviourism by ZURIFF, and on
the various forms of behaviourism by O'DONOHUE &
KITCHENER. WOLPE, one of behaviour therapy's leading
pioneers, has pointed to the consistent misreporting of behavioural ideas by other professionals.

Hans Eysenck, himself a major contributor to the development of behaviour therapy, outlines the criticisms levelled at
behaviourism, from within and outside the discipline in

EYSENCK & MARTIN. He challenges the view that modern
behaviourism (a) does not concern itself with subjective experience, attitudes, beliefs, and thoughts; (b) is mechanistic; and
(c) is solely concerned with reward and punishment. He
presents the work of leading practitioners contributing to our
understanding of behaviour therapy, knowledge and control,
language, anxiety, depression, motivation, emotion, heredity,
and neurohormones.

ULLMANN & KRASNER similarly demonstrated, in an
influential text, that modern behaviourism has much to
contribute to generating a psychological approach to understanding abnormal behaviour. Their work, which was widely
used by an early generation of clinical psychologists, demonstrated that much of the complexity associated with abnormal
behaviours could be illuminated by simpler theories based on
learning models. They reformulate much of traditional psychiatry and psychoanalysis in behavioural terms. KRASNER also
made a major contribution to applying these ideas to the design
of environments.

However, the application of behaviourism was not uncontroversial, as GRAZIANO pointed out in work on behaviour
therapy with children. Behaviourism became associated in the
public mind with a "clockwork orange" society, causing
the American Vice President Spiro Agnew to call it a threat to
American values. Many of the criticisms were unwarranted,
but it was the spread of behavioural applications in prisons
and mental health that caused the greatest concern. In marked
contrast to alternative methods, behaviourism worked – hence
it needed to be taken seriously. Graziano carefully explores this
debate, confronting a century of tradition and the social
contexts that led to the re-emergence of behaviourism in the
1950s after a generation of neglect following Watson. The
arguments are worth revisiting even after the lapse of a quarter
of a century. His book covers a critical period in the history
of behaviourism and the excitement and challenge of the period
is reflected.

The influence of behavioural approaches is now so pervasive
that many people use the ideas without realising it. Extensive
programmes in education, covering programmed learning,
work with children with learning difficulties and social skills
training schemes (see GOLDSTEIN) all owed a fundamental
debt to behaviourism. Introductory texts such as HERBERT
are widely used, not just by psychologists but also by other
professionals and parents. Popular texts on management theory
(such as McKENNA) contain large sections demonstrating the
contribution that behaviourism has made.

The criticism persists that the legacy of behaviourism is a
standardized, mechanical approach to human behaviour. It is
not, but it does rest on the fundamental tenet that behaviour
must be understood in its environmental context as argued in
a recent edited review by ROCHE. The behavioural literature
itself actively features the debate on the role of a standardized
"diagnostic" approach as opposed to models that reflect the
particular circumstances of one individual. In the clinical
setting the idea that you can formulate an understanding on
the basis of individualized assessment has been promulgated
for more than thirty years. The proponents of an individual
case formulation approach argue that it is more effective than
an approach that focuses on matching techniques to symptoms. BRUCH & BOND present this approach in a book that

they claim goes beyond diagnosis. Some would argue that it goes beyond behaviourism, but its roots can be firmly traced to pioneers such as Watson, Raynor and Jones, Pavlov, Guthrie, Skinner, and Shapiro. As a method of scientific enquiry it embraces Watson's concern with observable verifiable phenomena, but adopts an ethical approach to resolving individual dilemmas by concerning itself with both means (process) and ends (outcomes). Modern behaviourism remains controversial, but it is certainly not mechanistic and perhaps even reflects some part of the human spirit.

DAVID A. LANE

Beliefs

Bateson, Gregory, *Steps to an Ecology of Mind*, New York: Ballantine, and London: Intertext, 1972

Bateson, Mary Catherine, *Peripheral Visions: Learning along the Way*, New York: HarperCollins, 1994

Cameron, Mary M., *On the Edge of the Auspicious: Gender and Caste in Nepal*, Urbana: University of Illinois Press, 1998

Chidester, David, *Patterns of Power: Religion and Politics in American Culture*, Englewood Cliffs, New Jersey: Prentice Hall, 1988

Hill, Carole E. (editor), *Symbols and Society: Essays on Belief Systems in Action*, Athens: University of Georgia Press, 1975

Kratz, Corinne A., *Affecting Performance: Meaning, Movement, and Experience in Okiek Women's Initiation*, Washington, DC: Smithsonian Institution Press, 1994

Little, Richard and Steve Smith (editors), *Belief Systems and International Relations*, Oxford and New York: Blackwell, 1988

Szalay, Lorand, Jean B. Strohl, Liu Fu and Pen-Shui Lao, *American and Chinese Perceptions and Belief Systems: A People's Republic of China–Taiwanese Comparison*, New York: Plenum Press, 1994

Tambiah, Stanley Jeyaraja, *Magic, Science, Religion, and the Scope of Rationality*, Cambridge and New York: Cambridge University Press, 1990

As the assumptions of individuals and groups, beliefs can be interpolated from observations of behaviour patterns. Indeed, like the authors who have contributed to HILL's edited collection, most authors begin their study with an analysis of culturally specific beliefs and behaviour. In addition to essays addressing ideology as a cultural belief system, these authors provide a range of case studies from different societies.

BATESON (1972) has a special place in belief system studies as he provides useful conceptual tools for challenging established epistemological assumptions, and this enables the reader to consider radically different concepts and perceptions. The essays contained were written by the author over 35 years, and propose new ways of thinking about ideas and the aggregate of ideas that he calls the "mind". The work is intellectually beneficial for students engaging in research either within a society, or between societies.

BATESON's (1994) proposal of new ways to be human takes readers on an intellectual voyage across and within a number of societies, examining and elucidating how people change their beliefs in order to negotiate social and psychic transformation. A theme of this text is that contemporary survival depends on humanity's willingness to move away from familiar patterns and to seek new ways of interrelating through gracious and harmonious modes of being. Narratives enrich her argument that humanity requires a new way of learning, appreciating, and living.

Adding cross-cultural detail to discussions of beliefs and beliefs systems, CAMERON focuses on the lower-caste women of Nepal to investigate how gender and caste are negotiated through both social position and cultural practice. Linking religious systems, ideologies, and relations of power, Cameron proposes that although low-caste women live in a society that frames them as inferior, they neither completely agree, nor apply its dominant patriarchal codes to their interrelations.

From personal experience while teaching in a South African university during apartheid, CHIDESTER was compelled to change the focus of his work from the meaning of belief systems toward the ways in which their constituent categories were used in relations of power. Historical, social, and symbolic dimensions of religious and political authority initiate his reflections on patterns of power in America. His work offers a framework for discussing how people's identities are negotiated within the powerful dynamics of inclusion and exclusion that drive many belief systems.

LITTLE & SMITH's edited collection extends the scope of belief system analysis to the international arena, specifically by investigating the effect of beliefs on international behaviour. They examine the link between political ideologies, normative beliefs, and the ways that disagreement between belief systems can be expressed, particularly through aspirations for and relations of power. The authors survey belief systems in the social sciences, then focus on beliefs in academic studies and political practices, concluding with analyses of individuals' belief systems.

Sociocultural analysis involves separating and distilling generalities in order to consider significant details, as well as reassembling them for a comprehensive view of cultural processes informed by particularities. KRATZ does this in her work about initiation beliefs and practices amongst rural Okiek women in Kenya. Her multiple understandings of initiation through different people and different sources expand knowledge of social relations, ways of thinking, and lived experience among a remarkable community.

SZALAY *et al.* present findings from comparable college student samples in order to analyse the students' belief systems and subjective worldview. The work focuses on the postmodern industrial society of the United States, the planned socialist environment of the People's Republic of China, and the free market environment of Taiwan to explicate cultural similarities and differences in views of self and world.

From the standpoint of a social anthropologist who has studied religious and social phenomena in the field and is concomitantly interested in the intellectual origins of religion, magic, and science in Western thought, TAMBIAH presents a collection of epistemological and sociological issues that try to understand other cultures in their own terms, and then map such ideas and practices onto Western modes of thinking and analysis. The author argues that the issue of rationality and the limits of Western scientism as a paradigm of knowledge must be considered.

HELEN JOHNSON

Benchmarking

Andersen Consulting, *The World-Wide Manufacturing Competitiveness Survey: The Second Lean Enterprise Benchmarking Project Report*, London: Andersen Consulting, 1994

Arthur Andersen, *Global Best Practices*, http://www.arthurandersen.com/GBP/index.asp

Bendell, Tony, Louise Boulter and Paul Goodstadt, *Benchmarking for Competitive Advantage*, 2nd edition, London: Pitman, 1998

Bogan, Christopher E. and Michael J. English, *Benchmarking for Best Practices: Winning Through Innovative Adaptation*, New York: McGraw Hill, 1994

Boxwell, Robert J., *Benchmarking for Competitive Advantage*, New York: McGraw Hill, 1994

Camp, Robert C., *Benchmarking: The Search for Industry Best Practices That Lead to Superior Performance*, Milwaukee: Quality Press, 1989

Camp, Robert C., *Business Process Benchmarking: Finding and Implementing Best Practices*, Milwaukee: Quality Press, 1995

Flynn, Barbara B., Roger G. Schroeder, E. James Flynn, Sadao Sakakibara and Kimberly A. Bates, "World Class Manufacturing Project: Overview and Selected Results", *International Journal of Operations and Production Management*, 17/7 (1997): 671–85

International Benchmarking Clearinghouse, http://www.apqc.org/

International Quality Study, *Best Practices Report: An Analysis of Management Practices That Impact Performance*, New York: American Quality Foundationn / Ernst & Young, 1993

Miller, Jeffrey G., Arnoud De Meyer and Jinichiro Nakane, *Benchmarking Global Manufacturing: Understanding International Suppliers, Customers, and Competitors*, Homewood, Illinois: Irwin, 1992

Office of Naval Research, *Best Manufacturing Practices Centre of Excellence*, http://www.bmpcoe.org/

Voss, Christopher A., P. Ahlstrom and Kate Blackmon, "Benchmarking and Operational Performance: Some Empirical Results", *International Journal of Operations and Production Management*, 17/10 (1997): 1046–58

Watson, Gregory H., *Strategic Benchmarking: How to Rate Your Company's Performance Against the World's Best*, New York: Wiley, 1993

Wheatley, Malcolm, Marek Szwejczewski and Colin New, *The Making of Britain's Best Factories*, London: Business Intelligence, 1996

Whybark, D. Clay, "GMRG Survey Research in Operations Management", *International Journal of Operations and Production Management*, 17/7–8, (1997): 686–96

Womack, James P., Daniel T. Jones and Daniel Roos, *The Machine That Changed the World*, New York: Rawson, 1990

Although similar techniques have been used in Japan for some time, it was CAMP (1989) who initiated the considerable recent interest in benchmarking. He reports the pioneering work undertaken by the Xerox Corporation and defines benchmarking as "the search for industry best practices that lead to superior performance". The work reflects the need to compare against others in order to improve. Comparison of performance measures identifies performance gaps. Benchmarking also reflects the need to identify and implement practices that will close these gaps and achieve superior performance. Camp uses individual cases to illustrate the process of benchmarking, and provides a seminal text on what has become a popular management tool. Moreover, Camp defines a ten-step benchmarking process from planning to action, including adoption of benchmarking on an organization-wide scale.

The precise process used for benchmarking can vary from company to company. Authors such as BENDELL, BOULTER & GOODSTADT explain that successful implementation of benchmarking is made more likely by the adoption of a simple approach. The numbers of steps in the process can range widely, but BOGAN & ENGLISH outline that the key phases to benchmarking generally include: (1) the commitment and launch phase; (2) the organization and planning phase; (3) the "reach-out" phase; (4) the assimilation and analysis phase; and (5) the act/implementation phase.

CAMP (1995) offers additional insights into the benchmarking process, and provides greater focus on such issues as leadership and strategic management. He includes refined definitions that distinguish four types of benchmarking: internal benchmarking (comparing branches or divisions within an organization); competitor benchmarking (comparing with best-performing competitors); functional benchmarking (looking at how organizations in other industries perform the same or similar functions); and generic benchmarking (looking for the best innovative and exemplar practices, wherever they may be).

Again, based on experiences at Xerox, WATSON goes beyond the simple "how to" of the process to show how benchmarking fits into long-term strategic planning. He uses examples to explain the theory and practice of benchmarking a company against others, using inter-business cooperation as part of overall strategic planning to increase competitiveness.

As indicated by BOXWELL, benchmarking is not an end in itself but only one of many inputs to planning. He points out that benchmarking is most applicable to organizational practices that can readily be copied from one firm or organization to another. However, managers who uncritically adopt the practices prevailing in other organizations run the risk of copying practices that do not currently contribute to enhanced performance and business excellence – and may actually hinder overall organizational success. Furthermore, only organizations that have a high capacity and readiness for change and can undertake sustained implementation programmes are likely to succeed in introducing major benchmarking results.

Camp (1995) reflects the movement of attention away from benchmarking the performance of other companies to a quest to identify, manage, and transfer best practices. This approach is believed to be more useful for revolutionizing performance. Much of the literature in the area of best practices has been descriptive, describing practices that successful companies have in place. However, there are relatively few studies that empirically link practices with performance.

Various benchmarking surveys have been carried out in the area of manufacturing. One of the first extensive benchmarking surveys of the manufacturing sector was that of the International Motor Vehicle Program (IMVP), reported by WOMACK, JONES & ROOS. Their book provides useful insights into practices that were being used by Toyota, and draws general conclusions regarding sets of practices that help explain how Toyota achieved a 2:1 differential in performance over its competitors, in terms of both quality and productivity. However, the book represents more of an interesting insight into how Toyota functions, rather than a comprehensive examination of how specified practices affect organizational performance.

ANDERSEN CONSULTING's report aimed to test the lean production model, as proposed by studies such as the IMVP, investigating the link between high performance and the use of lean production practices. It revealed a 2:1 differential in productivity, and a 100:1 differential in quality. In addition, the study discussed general links with performance, and concluded that Europe as a whole lagged behind Japan, although there were large variations between European countries in terms of performance.

The Global Manufacturing Practices Project, reported by WHYBARK, aimed to understand differences in manufacturing practices between various countries in different regions of the world. The study found a degree of consistency in practices between countries, rather than between industries worldwide, thus indicating that national context does influence the choice of practices within a company. It also provided a database containing information on differences in practices, which could be used to confirm or eliminate relationships between certain variables and measures of performance. The survey is useful in confirming variables relating to production planning and control and establishing that certain relationships hold between them; however, it does not expressly indicate which practices are best in terms of improving performance.

Through the "Best Factories Award", WHEATLEY, SZWEJCZEWSKI & NEW benchmark companies according to set performance criteria, and make general observations regarding best practices in particular areas. They provide information to companies on how their performance relates to that of other companies in the same industry, and to that of other companies in general. They encourage the development of best practices that can be used to improve a particular area of performance. However, they do not discuss the transferability of these practices, or the extent to which each practice impacts on specific areas of performance.

One of the objectives of the "Made in Britain" and "Made in Europe" studies, reported by VOSS, AHLSTROM & BLACKMON, was to test the relationship between practice and performance, and to investigate whether companies that implement perceived "best" practices perform better. They found that the most successful companies were those that adopted best practices to improve operational performance in every area of manufacturing. They suggest that, in many instances, the relationships between best practices and

improved performance are assumed to be self-evident. Thus there is a need to investigate which practices actually do improve which areas of performance, so that companies can be given the means to improve specific areas of performance.

The "Global Manufacturing Futures Survey", reported by MILLER, DE MEYER & NAKANE, benchmarks organizations' rates of improvement in certain competitive priorities. The study focuses on levels of performance, and how they have been achieved, by asking companies to list overall improvement programmes and key improvement initiatives, but no link is made between particular improvement programmes and measures of performance or strategic priorities. It provides a database from which trends in manufacturing strategy and competitive priorities can be highlighted.

The "World Class Manufacturing Project" (FLYNN et al.) investigated the relationship between just-in-time management (JIT) and total quality management (TQM), in terms of both practices and performance and the impact of specific quality practices on quality performance. An important theme of this study is the importance of a supporting infrastructure of practices for the improvement of quality performance. The authors categorized practices into core practices (those expected to lead directly to improved quality performance) and infrastructure practices (which must be in place for core practices to be fully effective). They also argued that practices implemented for a specific purpose can have beneficial effects on other areas of performance.

The INTERNATIONAL QUALITY STUDY (IQS) set out to test the hypothesis of the quality movement – that implementation of "universally beneficial" quality practices will improve performance. The study was predicated on the assumption that many organizations were experiencing mixed results from implementing such quality practices, giving rise to a need to investigate the actual relationship between such practices and performance, and the circumstances under which they bring about the desired result. The findings did not support the hypothesis of universally beneficial practices. Practices that were shown to be of value at one level of organizational performance showed little positive correlation, or in some instances negative correlation, with performance at other levels. A conclusion of the study was that companies can adopt a set of best practices and thereby move to higher levels of performance and gain competitive advantage. However, this is an incremental process with no "shortcuts that are the secret to heightened performance". The study found correlation between practices that collectively appeared to help each of the categories – lower-, middle- and higher-performing companies – to improve performance. It also found that unless companies understood their starting position, they could not adopt and utilize the practices that would yield them the highest performance benefits. Very few practices were found to be beneficial and constant in their impact, regardless of industry, country, or starting position. It was concluded that, in order to progress from one performance level to the next, organizations need to extend their range of practices.

The growth of the World Wide Web is encouraging information regarding best practices to be more readily available. The OFFICE OF NAVAL RESEARCH's "Best Manufacturing Practices Programme" contains information on best manufacturing practices among over 95 companies in the United States, many of which can be found online. However, the basis for determining how practices are classified as "best" is not stated. At ARTHUR ANDERSEN's "Global Best Practices" site, companies can find out about best practices in a specified area, answer a questionnaire about how they relate to these practices themselves, and generate a report on their performance. The INTERNATIONAL BENCHMARKING CLEARING-HOUSE is dedicated to helping companies find and adopt best practices. The site includes a code of conduct for benchmarkers, a good list of quality-related web sites, and full-text articles on benchmarking. These tools are important in creating awareness of performance gaps and disseminating best practice; however they do not provide information on prerequisites for the implementation of these practices and do not specify the basis of their superiority.

MIKE KENNERLEY

See also Performance measurement, business

Bentham, Jeremy 1748–1832

British philosopher and social reformer

Bahmueller, Charles F., *The National Charity Company: Jeremy Bentham's Silent Revolution*, Berkeley: University of California Press, 1981

Boralevi, Lea Campos, *Bentham and the Oppressed*, Berlin and New York: de Gruyter, 1984

Bowring, John (editor), *The Works of Jeremy Bentham*, 11 vols, 1838–43; reprinted New York: Russell, 1962

Burns, J.H., John R. Dinwiddy and Fred Rosen (editors), *The Collected Works of Jeremy Bentham*, London: Athlone Press, and Oxford: Oxford University Press, 1968–

Dinwiddy, John, *Bentham*, Oxford and New York: Oxford University Press, 1989

Halévy, Elie, *The Growth of Philosophic Radicalism*, London: Faber, and New York: Macmillan, 1928; reprinted Boston: Beacon Press, 1955, London: Faber, 1972 (French edition 1900)

Harrison, Ross, *Bentham*, London and Boston: Routledge and Kegan Paul, 1983

Long, Douglas G., *Bentham on Liberty: Jeremy Bentham's Idea of Liberty in Relation to His Utilitarianism*, Toronto: University of Toronto Press, 1977

Mack, Mary Peter, *Jeremy Bentham: An Odyssey of Ideas*, London: Heinemann, and New York: Columbia University Press, 1963

Mack, Mary Peter (editor), *A Bentham Reader*, New York: Pegasus Press, 1969

Parekh, Bhikhu (editor), *Jeremy Bentham: Critical Assessments*, 4 vols, London: Routledge, 1993

Plamenatz, John, *The English Utilitarians*, 2nd edition, Oxford: Blackwell, 1966

Semple, Janet, *Bentham's Prison: A Study of the Panopticon Penitentiary*, Oxford and New York: Oxford University Press, 1993

Stephen, Leslie, *The English Utilitarians*, 3 vols, London: Duckworth, and New York: Putnam, 1900; reprinted London: London School of Economics and Political Science, and New York: P. Smith, 1950

Thomas, William, *The Philosophic Radicals: Nine Studies in Theory and Practice, 1817–1841*, Oxford: Clarendon Press, 1979

The English political philosopher and legal reformer Jeremy Bentham is generally regarded as the originator of utilitarianism (although David Hume and William Paley can claim the title as well). As a utilitarian, Bentham believed that "the greatest happiness of the greatest number" supplied the standard according to which all laws, practices, and policies should be judged.

BOWRING was the first collection of Bentham's voluminous and wide-ranging writings. Although there are numerous lapses and lacunae in Bowring's edition, it remains the most complete collection of Bentham's wide-ranging works on law, economics, penology, and political theory.

It will one day be replaced by BURNS, DINWIDDY & ROSEN, which aims to publish a complete and definitive edition of Bentham's works. This massive undertaking by the Bentham Project at University College London has so far resulted in the publication of several of Bentham's major works – including his *Constitutional Code* and the *Introduction to the Principles of Morals and Legislation* – with the promise of more to come.

Of the shorter and more selective collections of Bentham's work MACK (1969) provides a very useful and accessible compendium of Bentham's writings, including his *Pannomial Fragments, Book of Fallacies*, and other shorter works, and preceded by a very useful introduction.

There is as yet no entirely satisfactory biography of Bentham. But MACK (1963) includes a good deal of biographical information in her ambitious and comprehensive study of the origins and development of Bentham's thought. Among its attractions are the many pictures and illustrations, including the "auto-icon" – Bentham's name for his embalmed and seated corpse on display in a glass case at University College London.

The secondary literature on Bentham, his philosophy, and his followers is large and still growing. STEPHEN was among the first systematic studies of the philosophical sources of and themes within Bentham's philosophy. It is also among the most caustic and critical early studies, but is witty, opinionated, and readable. Volume I deals with Bentham and volumes II and III with James and John Stuart Mill, respectively.

HALÉVY has attained the status of a classic. It is a wide-ranging and synoptic survey of the thinkers who preceded and influenced Bentham's "philosophic radicalism", followed by a careful explication of the views of Bentham and his followers. Halévy, however, overemphasizes the intellectual dimension and largely overlooks the political context within and against which Bentham formulated his philosophy.

THOMAS does a much better job of situating Bentham and his disciples – James and John Stuart Mill most especially – in the political context of their time. His masterful study shows how deeply Bentham and his small circle were involved in debates about public education, extending the franchise, reforming penal practices, and other politically controversial questions.

DINWIDDY provides a brief but informative introduction to Bentham's overall outlook, and his political philosophy in particular. He begins with a biographical sketch, discusses Bentham's "greatest happiness principle", his critique of English law, his constitutional theory, and his practical proposals for legal and penal reform. For the reader who knows nothing about Bentham, this is the best introduction to his ideas.

HARRISON provides a minute and meticulous examination of Bentham's philosophical arguments of and justifications for his theoretical claims and practical proposals. He explicates and criticizes Bentham's conception of "happiness", of "interest", the "greatest happiness" principle, and other key concepts.

Although brief, PLAMENATZ offers a readable and insightful overview of Utilitarianism, beginning with Bentham's predecessor Hume, followed by an account of the development of Bentham's own views, and concluding with an overall assessment of Bentham and his school, including James and John Stuart Mill.

Scholarly studies in professional journals are too numerous to list in detail. PAREKH reprints a wide-ranging collection of modern scholarly essays by many hands. The essays in volume I deal with Bentham's life and the development of his thought; those in volume II with his work on philosophy, psychology, and religion; volume III with law and politics; and volume IV with economics and a variety of other topics, including, among many others, debates over whether Bentham was in fact a "feminist" (pp.23–57).

Bentham's views regarding women, slaves, and other oppressed groups are analysed in BORALEVI. She views Bentham as "the father of feminism" and as a paragon without parallel. Unfortunately her view of Bentham tends to be uncritical and even hagiographic.

Much more critical is BAHMUELLER, who examines in great detail Bentham's plan for and justification of his programme for alleviating poverty in England. Responding to the obvious inadequacies of the Poor Law, Bentham proposed a semipublic joint-stock company that he called the National Charity Company whose purpose was to administer a more humane version of the workhouse to which the poor could be consigned against their will and presumably for their own good. Modelled on his plan for a Panopticon prison (see Semple), these workhouses were supposed to cure the poor of the vice that made them poor in the first place: idleness.

Bentham's understanding of liberty is analysed insightfully by LONG, who shows in great detail how Bentham's views were formed and how they changed over time. On one key point Bentham's views remained constant: his conviction that liberty is (in his word) a "negative" concept in that its presence requires the absence of something else, namely some impediment or other. Thus Bentham can quite rightly be viewed as an early exponent of "negative liberty" in the sense later made famous by Isaiah Berlin. But Bentham emerges as a less-than-liberal thinker who came to value security over liberty. In this respect Bentham rather resembles B.F. Skinner, who proposed that modern society move "beyond freedom and dignity" and toward a scientifically designed and administered utopia.

Among Bentham's passions was prison reform. He even went so far as to design his own "humane" prison. SEMPLE offers a meticulous account of the origin, design, and ultimate failure of Bentham's project to build a "panopticon" prison (from the Greek *pan optes*, "all-seeing"). The British Parliament's failure to fund his scheme left Bentham bitter and lastingly distrustful of politicians.

TERENCE BALL

See also Utilitarianism

Bias

Aboud, Frances, *Children and Prejudice*, Oxford and Cambridge, Massachusetts: Blackwell, 1988

Allport, G.W., *The Nature of Prejudice*, Cambridge, Massachusetts: Addison Wesley, 1954

Brewer, Marilynn B. and Norman Miller, *Intergroup Relations*, Milton Keynes, Buckinghamshire: Open University Press, and Pacific Grove, California: Brooks Cole, 1996

Brown, R.J., *Group Processes: Dynamics within and between Groups*, Oxford and New York: Blackwell, 1988

Brown, R.J., *Prejudice: Its Social Psychology*, Oxford and Cambridge, Massachusetts: Blackwell, 1995

Hogg, Michael A. and Dominic Abrams, *Social Identifications: A Social Psychology of Intergroup Relations and Group Processes*, London and New York: Routledge, 1988

Oakes, Penelope J., S. Alexander Haslam and John C. Turner, *Stereotyping and Social Reality*, Oxford and Cambridge, Massachusetts: Blackwell, 1994

Rutland, Adam, "The Development of National Prejudice, In-Group Favouritism and Self-Stereotypes in British Children", *British Journal of Social Psychology*, 38 (1999): 55–70

Spears, Russell *et al.* (editors), *The Social Psychology of Stereotyping and Group Life*, Oxford and Cambridge, Massachusetts: Blackwell, 1997

ALLPORT's *The Nature of Prejudice* has become recognized as the beginning of modern investigations into biases within people's social perception. This book not only provides an insight into the origins of intergroup bias, anticipating some of the discoveries of modern-day social psychology, but also provides a collection of policy recommendations for its elimination. Indeed, many of the most practical attempts to improve ethnic relations in the US, especially in schools over the last 40 years, have been based on Allport's ideas. Allport defined prejudice as "an antipathy based upon a faulty and inflexible generalization" directed towards groups or individuals because of their group membership. This definition continues to influence numerous modern understandings of prejudice. Contemporary social psychologists often follow Allport's example and also emphasize such features as "incorrectness" or "inaccuracy" in their attempts to define prejudice. Allport was the first to convey that prejudice is essentially a social orientation towards whole groups of people or towards individuals because of their particular group membership and that it clearly involves a negative evaluation and affect.

The most up-to-date alternative to Allport's classic text is BROWN (1995). This is a comprehensive, clear and accessible analysis of prejudice as a central social psychological phenomenon. Brown takes us through a well-structured description of the literature on social categorization, prejudiced individuals, stereotyping, "old" and "new" racism, development of prejudice in childhood, intergroup relations, and the question of how to reduce prejudice. Throughout the book Brown includes many well-chosen examples from contemporary life and different kinds of prejudice. Brown takes a slightly different perspective on prejudice from Allport. He emphasizes the social nature of prejudice, viewing it as a primarily intergroup phenomenon and one rooted in the societal setting of group life. Acknowledgement of this creates conceptual difficulties because it is often difficult to ascertain whether social judgements are "faulty" or "at variance with reality". Brown does not perceive prejudice as necessarily a "false" or "irrational" set of beliefs held by people with individual pathologies. Rather, Brown sees prejudice as essentially rooted in group processes, as it is both orientated to whole groups of people rather than individuals and it is most frequently socially shared among group members. Consequently Brown chooses a simpler and more inclusive definition of prejudice that avoids any specific reference to the idea that prejudice is always due to false information processing. To Brown, prejudice is simply a negative attitude, emotion, or behaviour towards members of a group on account of their membership of that group.

BROWN (1988) provides a very readable introduction to the whole field of group processes and intergroup relations, including prejudice and intergroup bias. He takes a particular European rather than a US perspective, with a critique of more individualistic accounts of prejudice and intergroup bias in chapter six. He argues that we can simultaneously study prejudice as a group-based phenomenon and also at the level of individual cognition, emotion, and behaviour. In chapter seven Brown presents an alternative non individualistic account of intergroup bias, which stresses the importance of goal relationships between groups. When goal relationships are conflictual, biased intergroup attitudes are more likely because they are functional to the group and social identity maintenance.

BREWER & MILLER presents a readable but scholarly introduction to intergroup bias with a focus on the cognitive and motivational processes that give rise to intergroup conflict and discrimination. The book starts with a discussion of the psychological needs and motives associated with individuals' attachment and loyalty to their own group. It then turns attention to biased attitudes and emotions directed towards other groups. Finally, it examines how comparisons between one's own group and other groups lead to intergroup bias and discrimination. The basic thesis is that social comparison between salient groups enhances social competition, relative deprivation, and social instability, and all these factors contribute to the generation of intergroup bias.

HOGG & ABRAMS provide detailed coverage of theory and research in group process and intergroup relations, and the book is probably still the most comprehensive overview of social identity theory. This theory has been particularly influential in various social psychological accounts of intergroup bias and discrimination (see Brown for example). The fundamental premise of this theory is that the social categorization may be the only precondition for being a group and engaging in intergroup bias, provided that people identify with the category. Chapters three and four focus specifically on intergroup bias and attitudes towards other groups, with chapter four extending the analysis of intergroup relations with an examination of stereotyping (the way groups are perceived).

OAKES, HASLAM & TURNER provides a detailed and technical discussion, mainly from a social identity theory/self-categorization theory perspective, of stereotyping as it relates to social cognition and intergroup bias. Stereotyping is often presented as a psychological process that is closely tied to intergroup bias and discrimination. In the same way that prejudice is often viewed as resulting from false information processing, stereotyping has predominately been represented as involving perceptual or cognitive distortion of social reality. Oakes and colleagues challenge this view, and in doing so, they present a significant theoretical analysis of stereotyping based upon research that the authors have been conducting over the recent years.

SPEARS et al. provides an up-to-date and comprehensive account of stereotyping from an intergroup perspective. The book includes contributions from many researchers who have been central to the profound reassessment of stereotyping in recent years (such as Oakes, Yzerbyt, Worchel, Reicher, Haslam, McGarty, Ellemers, Doosje, and Turner). The contributors debate and challenge more cognitive approaches that regard stereotyping primarily as a bias produced by the limits of individual information processing. They contend that, in order to understand the nature and function of stereotyping, it is essential to understand its role in, and relationship to, the activities of social groups. In short, the book examines how stereotypes and biased thinking are structured by social identities and the relations between groups.

ABOUD is a rare example of a text that examines the under researched field of prejudice in childhood. Aboud presents an account of intergroup bias and stereotyping based upon cognitive-developmental theory and in opposition to social reflection theory and inner state theory. This approach perceives childhood prejudice as information processing errors due to young children's insufficient cognitive ability to perceive people in individual terms. Therefore Aboud argues that cognitively immature young children are prone to intergroup bias and prejudice because they are unable to decentre. The book contains various examples of research into ethnic prejudice among children, primarily in North America, to support Aboud's argument.

RUTLAND presents a study of national prejudice development in British children. This tested the prediction, derived from self-categorization theory and in opposition to Aboud's cognitive-developmental theory, that the supposed limited cognitive ability of young children to engage in individuated perception will not necessarily result in intergroup bias and stereotyping. He found that national prejudice, in-group bias or stereotyping developed only in children aged over ten years and was not evident in young children. These findings question the validity of the cognitive-developmental approach. Rutland discusses the apparent contradiction between the findings of this study and previous research on ethnic prejudice development in terms of the potential importance of group norms in determining the willingness of people to express national prejudice and in-group bias.

ADAM RUTLAND

See also Identification

Big five personality factors

Barrick, Murray R. and Michael K. Mount, "The Big Five Personality Dimensions and Job Performance: A Meta-Analysis", *Personnel Psychology*, 44/1 (1991): 1–26

Barrick, Murray R. and Michael K. Mount, "Autonomy as a Moderator of the Relationship between the Big Five Personality Dimensions and Job Performance", *Journal of Applied Psychology*, 78/1 (1993): 111–18

Digman, John M., "Personality Structure: Emergence of the Five Factor Model", *Annual Review of Psychology*, 41 (1990): 417–40

Goldberg, Lewis R., "Language and Individual Differences: The Search for Universals in Personality Lexicons" in *Review of Personality and Social Psychology* (1981)

Goldberg, Lewis R., "An Alternative 'Description of Personality': The Big-Five Factor Structure", *Journal of Personality and Social Psychology*, 59/6 (1990): 1216–29

John, Oliver P., "The 'Big Five' Factor Taxonomy: Dimensions of Personality in the Natural Language and in Questionnaires" in *Handbook of Personality: Theory and Research*, edited by Lawrence A. Pervin, New York: Guilford Press, 1990

McCrae, Robert R. and Oliver P. John, "An Introduction to the Five Factor Model and Its Applications", *Journal of Personality*, 60/2 (1992): 175–215

Pervin, Lawrence A., *The Science of Personality*, New York and Chichester: Wiley, 1996

Watson, David, "Strangers' Ratings of the Five Robust Personality Factors: Evidence of a Surprising Convergence with Self-Report", *Journal of Personality and Social Psychology*, 1/57 (1989): 120–28

Wiggins, Jerry S. and Aaron L. Pincus, "Personality: Structure and Assessment", *Annual Review of Psychology*, 43 (1992): 473–504

Yang, Kuo-Shu and Michael Harris Bond, "Exploring Implicit Personality Theories with Indigenous or Imported Constructs: The Chinese Case", *Journal of Personality and Social Psychology*, 6/58 (1990): 1087–95

PERVIN offers an overview of the different approaches to understanding and researching personality for the uninitiated reader or researcher in this field. He emphasizes the controversies and complexities that challenge personality psychologists, rather than merely presenting the "grand theories" of personality. Thus, the book provides a contextual backdrop for the study of the "big five" personality factors (or the five-factor model of personality). Chapter two specifically covers the trait approaches to studying personality leading to the development of the five-factor model. Evidence that validates the model is also discussed. The chapter concludes with a critical overview of trait theory and factor analysis, the statistical technique most commonly used in trait research.

McCRAE & JOHN provide a thorough introduction to the five-factor model. Their article is an introductory article to a special issue devoted to the five-factor model in the *Journal of Personality* (60/2, 1992). The article begins with a brief history of the model covering the lexical and the personality questionnaire approaches. The authors label the five factors as extroversion, agreeableness, conscientiousness, neuroticism, and openness, although they emphasize that there is variation among researchers over the factor names. Table 1 (p.178) is useful in presenting examples of respective natural language trait terms (the lexical approach) and respective questionnaire items for the five factors. Table 2 (p.182) shows the assignment of standard personality scales to the "big five" factors. As noted by McCrae & John, tables of this type not only demonstrate the pervasiveness of the five-factor model, but also provide a basis for meta-analytic research in this area. The authors raise some key empirical and conceptual issues relating to the model, including whether there are too few or too many factors, observer ratings versus self-reports, cognitive artefacts versus realistic description, and the exact naming and concomitant conceptualization of the five factors. McCrae & John conclude that "its long history, cross-cultural replication, and empirical validation across many methods and instruments make the five-factor model a basic discovery of personality psychology" (p.207). The other articles in the special issue of the *Journal of Personality* cover the history of the model, address methodological issues, and consider the application of the model.

JOHN provides a comprehensive history of the research leading to the discovery of the "big five" personality factors. John reviews the two main historical routes that led to the five-factor model: the lexical approach and the personality questionnaire approach. The lexical approach examines the basic units of personality by selecting, and subsequently analysing, natural language trait terms. The questionnaire approach analyses questionnaire items, usually presented in the form of a sentence rather than the trait-descriptive adjectives used in the lexical approach. John concludes by emphasizing some of the critical methodological and theoretical issues surrounding the five-factor model. Areas of furthers research are also suggested, including the crosscultural generalizability of the model and the predictive utility of the model in important areas of people's lives.

WATSON is a good example of research attempting to validate the five-factor model, as well as to extend previous findings in this area. The comparison of self-ratings versus peer-ratings of the personality traits represents one avenue of validation research for the model. Earlier research reported significant self–peer agreement correlations; however, well-acquainted peers tended to produce more reliable ratings compared with stranger peers. Watson's study confirms this finding and further finds that self-peer agreement correlations tend to increase as the number of peer raters increase. The study also finds, consistent with previous research, that the more observable traits, extraversion and conscientiousness and to a lesser extent culture (otherwise labelled openness or intelligence), produce higher convergent correlations than the less observable traits of agreeableness and emotional stability (otherwise labelled neuroticism). The final section of the paper explores possible explanations for self–stranger convergence.

YANG & BOND's research represent one of a number of studies examining the crosscultural generalizability of the five-factor model. The authors are concerned that psychological instruments developed in Anglo-American cultures may be inferior to the development of indigenous instruments. As such, Chinese personality descriptors were used by Chinese subjects to rate others. The same Chinese subjects rated the target others using translated American personality descriptors. Yang & Bond confirm a five-factor model for the Chinese language descriptors. They also find that the imported (translated) dimensions do a reasonable job of identifying four of the five indigenous factors; however, a one-to-one mapping of the imported to the indigenous factors was limited.

Research on the big five personality factors predominantly focuses on validating the model, but research is emerging on how the model can be used in an organizational setting. In their meta-analytic review, BARRICK & MOUNT (1991) provide evidence that demonstrates that certain personality dimensions are consistently predictive of key job-related criteria. BARRICK & MOUNT (1993) examine the moderating effect of autonomy on the relationship between the "big five" personality factors and superior-rated job performance. They find that the more conscientious, extroverted managers perform better in jobs characterized by high autonomy compared with those managers working in low autonomy jobs. Unexpectedly, Barrick & Mount's (1993) results also reveal that managers with lower scores on "agreeableness" perform better in high autonomy jobs compared with those managers working in low autonomy jobs. Their results have performance implications for matching the personality characteristics of managers to particular organizational situations. Future research could (a) examine the generalizability of the results to different jobs; (b) examine different moderating variables, such as job difficulty; and/or (c) use other job-related outcome variables, such as job satisfaction.

Relevant recent articles in the *Annual Review of Psychology* include DIGMAN and WIGGINS & PINCUS. Digman's entry provides an enthusiastic overview of the "big five" personality model, including the historical roots of the model along with theoretical and methodological issues surrounding the model at the time. It serves as an excellent introduction to the topic. Wiggins & Pincus's article updates the reservations and controversies surrounding the model. The article is more complex than the Digman entry and assumes a solid understanding of personality psychology.

A number of authors have noted that GOLDBERG (1981) was probably the first to coin the phrase "big five" and is thus worthy of mention. However his latter work (GOLDBERG, 1990) is significant in providing evidence in support of a five-factor model extracted from a comprehensive set of non-Cattellian English trait adjectives. It is also noteworthy that Goldberg's (1990) five-factor structure was also virtually invariant under different methods of factor analysis.

THERESE A. JOINER

Bilingualism in early childhood

Arnberg, Lenore, *Raising Children Bilingually: The Pre-school Years*, Clevedon, Avon and Philadelphia: Multilingual Matters, 1987

Bain, Bruce and Agnes Yu, "Vygotsky, Luria and Slama-Cazacu: Raising Children Bilingually According to Grammont's Principle in the Alsace, Alberta and Hong Kong" in *Dynamic Contexts of Language Use: Papers in Honor of Tatiana Slama-Cazacu*, edited by Giuseppe Mininni and Stefania Stame, Bologna: Clueb, 1994

Bain, Bruce, *Pathways to the Peak of Mount Piaget and Vygotsky: Speaking and Cognizing Monolingually and Bilingually*, Rome: Bulzoni, 1996

De Houwer, Annick, *The Acquisition of Two Languages from Birth: A Case Study*, Cambridge and New York: Cambridge University Press, 1990

Dopke, Susanne, "One Parent One Language: An Interactional Approach" in *Studies in Bilingualism*, vol. 3, edited by Kees De Brot and Thom Huebner, Amsterdam: Benjamins, 1992

Imedadze, Natela, "On the Psychological Nature of Child Speech Formation under Conditions of Exposure to Two Languages", *International Journal of Psychology*, 2/2 (1967): 129–32

Leopold, Werner F., *Speech Development of a Bilingual Child: A Linguist's Record*, Evanston, Illinois: Northwestern University Press
  1 *Vocabulary Growth in the First Two Years*, 1939
  2 *Sound-learning in the First Two Years*, 1947
  3 *Grammar and General Problems*, 1949a
  4 *Diary from Age 2*, 1949b

Ronjat, Jules, *Le Développement du langage observé chez un enfant bilingue*, Paris: Champion, 1913

Titone, Renzo, "Some Personality Dimensions in Bilingual Children" in *On the Bilingual Person*, edited by Renzo Titone, Ottawa: Legas, 1989

Everyday beliefs about childrearing are liberally laced with totems and taboos of diverse vintages and credibility, but no aspect of childrearing is more endowed with prejudices and inanities than bilingual childrearing. A few documented examples will suffice. A well-educated expatriate English businessman and parent in Hong Kong told me in all sincerity that "it is undesirable to raise children in two languages because they will become psychologically devious and culturally tortured". An intense Canadian schoolteacher and parent in Vancouver told me that "a second language should be taught only after the mother-tongue has been mastered otherwise the child will suffer from linguistic, intellectual, and moral confusion". Research presented below argues that rearing a child bilingually is not for the uninformed or the faint of heart. There are numerous practical problems in the initial stages, about which parents must be clear. However, if parents consistently stick to Grammont's principle of "one parent, one language" between the ages of six months and four years, the results are highly desirable, linguistically and cognitively.

The French pedagogue and linguist, RONJAT, was the first linguist formally to describe the speech development of a child reared bilingually. In 1908, the French-speaking Ronjat and his German-speaking wife wished to raise their child, Louis, as a French-German bilingual speaker. An observant colleague, Maurice Grammont, told Monsieur and Frau Ronjat:

> There is nothing for the child to be taught. It is sufficient to speak to him … in one of the languages he is to learn. But here is the crux: *each language must be embodied in a different person.* You should always talk French to him, and his mother, German only. *Never switch roles.* (p.3)

The "one parent, one language" principle was strictly enforced by the Ronjats, and the results were as Grammont predicted. By one year and ten months, Louis could distinguish between the two languages. Louis initially tended to favour German because he spent more time with his mother. This imbalance was short lived: by three years and eight months Louis was seeking and using words in both languages; by three years and ten months he was functionally bilingual. Ronjat's research methods would not be acceptable by today's standards, but his findings of a) an initially mixed stage, b) followed by an imbalance of one language predominant over the other stage, c) followed by separation of the two languages and functional bilingualism have not been seriously challenged to this day.

LEOPOLD supports the general picture presented by Ronjat in a four-volume work of 859 printed pages. Although not theoretically profound, Leopold's is a descriptively thorough and empirically solid single case study; in this instance, of his daughter, Hildegard, being reared simultaneously in German and English, from birth to 14 years. This detailed work on the evolution of vocabulary, syntax, and phonetics in a bilingually reared child is classic. Leopold speculates but does not empirically substantiate the belief that a child reared bilingually acquires a unique form of consciousness.

Another meticulously descriptive linguist, DE HOUWER, studied the Dutch and English speech development of Kate, from two years seven months to three years four months. De Houwer also addressed an important theoretical question, namely, the validity of the "separate development hypothesis", which proposes that each language of a bilingual child's morphosyntactic development proceeds in a language-specific manner. De Houwer concluded that each of the bilingual child's languages follows a language-specific course of development.

In a short but influential article, the Georgian psychologist IMEDADZE argued that, over the course of their development, bilingually reared children focus increasingly on the meaning of the message and less on the syntactic and lexical aspects of the message vehicles. Based on a claim that meaning is not a linguistic given but a cognitive construction, Imedadze concluded that bilingually reared children develop an intrinsic fascination with language play for its own sake, as well as for purposes of achieving other cognitive goals.

DOPKE found that, a) if both parents interacted with an equivalent level of child-centredness, then the child learned to actively use both languages; but, b) if one parent displayed less child-centred behaviour, then the child acquired only passive understandings of that parent's language regardless of specific linguistic features, and ended up actively using and understanding the language of the more child-centred parent. Dopke's research effectively centres the problem of childhood

bilingualism in the modern psychological claim that "language is a social means of thinking".

ARNBERG described Dopke-type findings in very readable prose, and wisely argues the importance of parent-child dynamics and social context. Arnberg's is probably and justly the most widely read general text on early childhood bilingualism.

BAIN & YU refined Grammont's principle with their finding that it is not simply a matter of each parent consistently using his or her own language until the child makes a functional separation of the two languages. It is also the case that each parent should maintain a clearly defined communicative context. This is to say, each parent should maintain a set of behavioural routines, consisting of parent, place, objects, activities, and specific language. To do otherwise is to prolong the stages of mixed and imbalanced usage.

BAIN reviews and analyses the highlights of the history of childhood bilingualism as an introduction to a major multinational, multilanguage comparative study of the development of monolingual and bilingual speaking and thinking. The core of Bain's research is a developmental analysis of the evolution of childhood egocentrism and childhood voluntary control of cognitive processes of monolingually and bilingually reared children in China and Canada. Bain concludes that being reared bilingually empowers more, restricts less, and challenges the mind more fully than does being reared monolingually. The empirical finding that monolingualism insufficiently challenges the mind substantiates a claim of Vygotsky (*Thought and Language*, 1962) that speech is a tool, the structural characteristics of which – whether monolingual or bilingual – shape the mind of the user.

TITONE's research concerned the nature of the developmental dynamics between speaking, thinking, and personality. Titone's insight that all dimensions of mind and social context must be studied holistically contains the seeds of a new paradigm for psychology and linguistics.

BRUCE C. BAIN

Bill of Rights

Amar, Akhil Reed, *The Bill of Rights: Creation and Reconstruction*, New Haven, Connecticut: Yale University Press, 1998

Brant, Irving, *The Bill of Rights: Its Origin and Meaning*, Indianapolis: Bobbs Merrill, 1965

Bryner, Gary C. and A.D. Sorenson (editors), *The Bill of Rights: A Bicentennial Assessment*, Provo, Utah: Brigham Young University, 1993

Dworkin, Ronald, *Taking Rights Seriously*, Cambridge, Massachusetts: Harvard University Press, and London: Duckworth, 1977

Glendon, Mary Ann, *Rights Talk: The Impoverishment of Political Discourse*, New York: Free Press, 1991

Hand, Learned, *The Bill of Rights*, Cambridge, Massachusetts: Harvard University Press, 1958

Hickok, Eugene W. Jr (editor), *The Bill of Rights: Original Meaning and Current Understanding*, Charlottesville: University Press of Virginia, 1991

Lacey, Michael J. and Knud Haakonssen (editors), *A Culture of Rights: The Bill of Rights in Philosophy, Politics, and*

Law, 1791 and 1991, Cambridge and New York: Cambridge University Press, 1991

Murphy, Paul L., *The Meaning of Freedom of Speech: First Amendment Freedoms from Wilson to FDR*, Westport, Connecticut: Greenwood Press, 1972

Rutland, Robert Allen, *The Birth of the Bill of Rights, 1776–1791*, revised edition, Boston: Northeastern University Press, 1983

Stone, Geoffrey R., Richard A. Epstein and Cass R. Sunstein (editors), *The Bill of Rights in the Modern State*, Chicago: University of Chicago Press, 1992

The Bill of Rights comprises the first ten Amendments to the US Constitution. These include the rights of free speech and assembly, a free press, the right to trial by jury, and other freedoms that Americans have come to take for granted.

BRANT offers a synoptic survey of the history of the Bill of Rights. Part I traces its background in English and American law and politics, and Part II its "foreground" since its adoption in 1791. He shows how hard-fought and controversial was the idea that individual citizens had rights against the state, and how successive court cases have expanded the scope and range of the rights enumerated in the Bill of Rights. For example, freedom of speech and the freedom of the press have come to mean freedom of expression of various sorts, including artistic and other nonverbal forms of expression. Good as it is, however, Part II of Brant's book is now somewhat dated, as some "implied" or "unenumerated" rights, such as the right to privacy, have been greatly expanded by the Supreme Court's decision regarding abortion in *Roe v. Wade* (1973) and other controversial cases.

RUTLAND traces the growing popularity of and calls for a "bill of rights" in the period between the commencement of the American Revolution and the adoption of the Bill of Rights in 1791. He offers a minute analysis of the Ratification Debate of 1787–88 and the growing pressure to add a bill of rights. Several states refused to ratify the proposed Constitution unless a bill of rights were included, but finally did so on condition that one be added and adopted later. Rutland examines the arguments for and against, and the political pressures that led James Madison to draft the Bill of Rights.

The book by HAND presents the reflections of a distinguished legal scholar and jurist's reflections on the role and significance of the Bill of Rights in American law and life. Interestingly, Hand regards the "real" Bill of Rights as Amendments 1–8 and 14. This small book is rich in references to illustrative cases and decisions that have expanded the scope of the Bill of Rights – often in ways that Hand clearly disapproves of because he believes them to be damaging or dangerous to the continuation of balanced constitutional government.

HICKOK provides a wide-ranging anthology consisting of thirty-one essays by judges, lawyers, legal scholars, and political scientists. Written to celebrate the bicentennial of the Bill of Rights, each of these stock-taking essays examines both the original (or intended) meanings of free speech, due process, "takings", and a host of other rights, and how their meanings have been modified in the course of American legal and political history. Happily, no single outlook or orthodoxy dominates this useful collection.

Another valuable bicentennial volume is STONE, EPSTEIN & SUNSTEIN. The editors asked their contributors to analyse the role of the Bill of Rights, not as originally intended by Madison and others, but in the late 20th-century US. The result is a collection of essays by jurists and legal scholars on a variety of topics ranging from free speech to social welfare. Especially valuable are the paired "pro and con" essays on religious freedom and free speech.

BRYNER & SORENSON, another important examination and celebration of the bicentennial of the Bill of Rights, is divided into three parts. The first examines different theories of rights and of legal interpretation. The second consists of assessments of the current status of rights, especially as regards women, racial minorities, and religious groups. The two concluding essays in the third part examines the future of rights: will they expand or contract and, if so, in what directions?

Many studies of the Bill of Rights analyse the specific rights enumerated therein. The most studied of these is the First Amendment guaranteeing freedoms of speech, press, assembly, and religion. MURPHY is an especially valuable history of the First Amendment in the period between World War I and World War II. He looks at landmark court cases involving communists, anarchists, and other unpopular political groups and how the resulting decisions expanded the scope of the First Amendment, which had previously been much more narrowly interpreted, especially as regards freedom of speech.

AMAR offers a controversial reinterpretation of the meaning and significance of the Bill of Rights. Taking a "holistic" or "structural" approach, he argues that the Bill of Rights is not a series of different and discrete individual rights, but was originally intended to recognize and protect the authority of local and state governments. The post-Civil War Reconstruction-era amendments (especially the Fourteenth) transformed the original meaning of the Bill of Rights almost beyond recognition. The Bill of Rights became a bulwark of individual rights against state and local government, and thereby greatly expanded the scope and power of the national (or federal) government to interfere in or override rights that were originally reserved to the several states.

As LACEY & HAAKONSSEN observe, Americans inhabit "a culture of rights". It is a culture that has been a long time in the making, arguably going back as far as Magna Carta, and further fuelled by natural rights theory. As Alan Ryan notes (chapter 7), in no other nation – not even in the UK – is the idea of individual rights so deeply inscribed in the national psyche as in the US. Scholars are divided as to whether this is an achievement to be celebrated and further augmented, or whether Americans have gone too far in the direction of individual rights at the risk of downplaying correlative duties to the wider community. Two examples will illustrate the debate.

In liberal individualist discourse, as DWORKIN notes, "rights are trumps" – that is, if you have a constitutionally guaranteed right to something, then that right overrides all other considerations. Rights are thus understood as absolute immunities from state interference in the affairs of an individual, subject only, of course, to the proviso that the rights-bearing individual does not infringe the rights of other individuals.

GLENDON, by contrast, claims that such "rights talk" has unduly elevated the importance of individual rights, and has eclipsed the duties that once went along with those rights. By detaching duties from rights and favouring the latter over the former, American legislators and courts have done a disservice to society at large. They have set citizen against citizen, group against group, and have thereby weakened the social bond and devalued the importance of compromise and conciliation, and the sense of community. This divisive view of individual (and, more recently, group) rights is far from what Madison and others had in mind in framing the Bill of Rights.

TERENCE BALL

Biotechnology industry

Acharya, Rohini, *The Emergence and Growth of Biotechnology: Experiences in Industrialised and Developing Countries*, Cheltenham, Gloucestershire: Elgar, 1999

Ballantine, B., L.J.F. Burke and S.M. Thomas, *Benchmarking the Competitiveness of Biotechnology in Europe*, Brussels: Europa, 1997

Bud, Robert, *The Uses of Life: A History of Biotechnology*, Cambridge and New York: Cambridge University Press, 1993

Fransman, Martin and Shoko Tanaka, "Government, Globalisation, and Universities in Japanese Biotechnology", *Research Policy*, 24/1 (1995): 13–49

Galambos, Louis and Jane Eliot Sewell, *Networks of Innovation: Vaccine Development at Merck, Sharp and Dohme, and Mulford, 1895–1995*, Cambridge and New York: Cambridge University Press, 1995

Hacking, Andrew J., *Economic Aspects of Biotechnology*, Cambridge and New York: Cambridge University Press, 1986

Office of Technology Assessment, *Biotechnology in a Global Economy*, Washington, DC: US Government Printing Office, 1991

Orsenigo, Luigi, *The Emergence of Biotechnology: Institutions and Markets in Industrial Revolution*, New York: St Martin's Press, and London: Pinter, 1989

Pisano, Gary P., *The Development Factory: Unlocking the Potential of Process Innovation*, Boston, Massachusetts: Harvard Business School Press, 1997

Senker, Jacqueline (editor), *Biotechnology and Competitive Advantage: Europe's Firms and the US Challenge*, Cheltenham, Gloucestershire: Elgar, 1998

Wheale, Peter R. and Ruth M. McNally, *Genetic Engineering: Catastrophe or Utopia?*, Hemel Hempstead, Hertfordshire: Harvester Wheatsheaf, and New York: St Martin's Press, 1988

Biotechnology is a difficult industry to appraise, not only because of its comparative newness, which means that the historical statistics are not well developed, but even more importantly because it is a process rather than an industry in the usual product-oriented sense. Like information technology, it is in reality one of the oldest of all industries, an early example being the use of yeast for brewing and baking, but modern concerns date from the mid-1970s, with the emergence of recombinant DNA (gene splitting) and cell fusion (hybridomas). Ethical questions have always been high on the agenda. The industry has progressed more slowly than expected, partly for ethical reasons but also because cost-effective applications require lengthy development.

BUD offers a chronological history of the biotech industry, with most emphasis on its early manifestations. A final chapter surveys the 1980s. The history is written in a very accessible style, with many illustrations.

ORSENIGO gives a general account of the emergence of the biotech industry. The approach adopted is that of evolutionary economics coupled with innovation studies. The span of the book is rather wider than the subtitle suggests. In addition to institutions and markets, the book has much to say about technological "regimes", and also covers such issues as the role of government. The study can be recommended to readers lacking a detailed scientific background in biotechnology.

The study by HACKING was an early effort to examine economic aspects of the industry. In a fast-moving industry its findings are seriously out of date, but the concepts introduced still have relevance for present-day studies. However the author is a commercial scientist, not a social scientist, and his primary intention is to provide insights into the commercial world for other scientists, rather than the opposite.

The survey by WHEALE & McNALLY is a rather technical account of biotechnology, which only occasionally ventures into the apocalyptic areas implied by the subtitle. It should not be confused with other collections edited by these authors, which are more unashamedly propagandist. However readers need to be aware that the authors possess ulterior motives, with which they are at liberty to agree or disagree.

The book by ACHARYA covers much territory in its rather short span. As a result some elements are skipped over fairly summarily, for example the development of the technology and the state of competitiveness of a range of developed nations. The less orthodox contributions of the book are the focus on developing as well as developed countries, including the key issue of trade, and also on biodiversity. Little is said about the controversial field of intellectual property rights, however. Instead, the emphasis lies primarily on building technological capabilities for biotech in developing countries.

The short monograph by BALLANTINE, BURKE & THOMAS was produced as a report by Business Decisions and the Science Policy Research Unit at the University of Sussex for EuropaBio. It draws on confidential data supplied to the authors and their research assistants by firms and organizations. The study is important for its attempt to construct an overall estimate of total European output of biotechnology, a difficult task in view of the specific character of this "industry". The authors find that, despite significant progress in recent years, Europe still lies well behind the US in biotech by nearly every measure, although it is ahead of Japan. The most important factor underlying competitiveness is seen as the external business environment, together with the importance of the science base for smaller firms. The study investigates a wide range of areas of application of biotechnology.

The volume edited by SENKER brings together work prepared by a variety of authors, mostly under the aegis of the EC biotechnology programme. The focus lies primarily on the question posed by the subtitle, namely the extent of European catch up in biotech. There is no attempt to construct a full-scale study of the industry, but the chapters nevertheless manage to cover most of the relevant ground, for example, regulation, new entry, applications, gene therapy. The main finding is a call for a better integrated research-and-development effort, if catch-up is to succeed.

By contrast, the study by the OFFICE OF TECHNOLOGY ASSESSMENT of the US Congress looks at competitiveness from a US standpoint. Unusually for a US publication, the survey is low on American triumphalism (which is arguably justified in this arena), and high on international comparisons. Interesting appendices assess the strengths and weaknesses of potential competitor nations. There is substantial emphasis on applications of biotechnology – the downstream end of the business. Specific topics such as finance, intellectual property, regulation are also well covered.

The paper by FRANSMAN & TANAKA places its main emphasis on the role of government and universities in the rather neglected Japanese biotech industry. Implicitly, they consider what has become known nowadays as the "triple helix" model: the intertwining of government, universities, and industry. The main issue covered is the impact of the "opening" of Japan to global competition and influences. However the authors somewhat overlook the peculiar aspects of Japanese biotechnology, which include its strong industrial orientation.

The monograph by GALAMBOS & SEWELL is one of the finest business histories available. Its focus is very narrow, on just one aspect of technology in one particular firm, but it brings in very broad repercussions, including the interdependence between private and public sectors in biotech development.

Similarly broad issues arise out of the study by PISANO, which, however, goes beyond biotechnology and considers it in relation to other developments in the pharmaceutical industry. The author unveils the objectives of firms in combining biotech with advances in chemistry, and points to many problems that remain. The author's main objective is to assert the underappreciated importance of process innovation in the chemicals industry.

G.N. VON TUNZELMANN

Blackmail

Alldridge, Peter, "Attempted Murder of a Soul: Blackmail, Privacy and Secrets", *Oxford Journal of Legal Studies*, 13 (1993): 368–87

Berman, Mitchell N., "The Evidentiary Theory of Blackmail: Taking Motives Seriously", *University of Chicago Law Review*, 65/3 (1998): 795–878

Bourne, Kenneth (editor), *The Blackmailing of the Chancellor: Some Intimate and Hitherto Unpublished Letters from Harriette Wilson to Her Friend Henry Brougham, Lord Chancellor of England*, London: Lemon Tree Press, 1975

Coase, R.H., "Blackmail", *Virginia Law Review*, 74 (1988): 655–76

Epstein, Richard A., "Blackmail, Inc.", *University of Chicago Law Review*, 50/5 (1983): 553–66

Fletcher, George P., "Blackmail: The Paradigmatic Crime", *University of Pennsylvania Law Review*, 141 (1993): 1617–38

Ginsburg, Douglas H. and Paul Shechtman, "Blackmail: An Economic Analysis of the Law", *University of Pennsylvania Law Review*, 141 (1993): 1849–76

Hepworth, Mike, *Blackmail: Publicity and Secrecy in Everyday Life*, London and Boston: Routledge and Kegan Paul, 1975

Katz, Leo, "Blackmail and Other Forms of Arm-Twisting", *University of Pennsylvania Law Review*, 141 (1993): 1567–1615

Lindgren, James, "Unraveling the Paradox of Blackmail", *Columbia Law Review*, 84 (1984): 670–717

Posner, Richard A., "Blackmail, Privacy, and Freedom of Contract", *University of Pennsylvania Law Review*, 141 (1993): 1817–47

Thompson, E.P., "The Crime of Anonymity" in *Albion's Fatal Tree: Crime and Society in Eighteenth-Century England*, edited by Douglas Hay *et al.*, London: Allen Lane, and New York: Pantheon, 1975

Literature on blackmail falls into three major areas: historical and sociological accounts of the crime, attempt to justify or discredit blackmail regulation through moral reasoning, and economic accounts. The history of the crime of blackmail dates from Scottish borders protection rackets in Elizabethan times. Among the many capital offences created by the Black Act (1723) were some to do with the uttering of threats. THOMPSON's essay deals with the use of anonymous threatening letters as part of civil – frequently industrial – unrest. BOURNE provides a glimpse of a particular episode of 19th century blackmail. ALLDRIDGE considers the development of the crime of blackmail in its relationship to the exposure of the sexual persona. He argues that although stereotypes of the Victorian era would suggest that sexual blackmail reached its apogee then, and that concentration upon the exposure of the sexual persona as constituting blackmail would, on that account, have declined throughout the 20th century. The 20th century has been one of increased concentration upon the threat of exposure of sexual behaviour as being the central and most serious forms of blackmail, commanding sentences equivalent to those for rape. Alldridge draws upon Foucault's account of the developing relationship between sexuality and personhood during the century to account for this.

Amongst the criminological writers, the fullest British account is HEPWORTH's. A full consideration would have to deal with the connected phenomena of computer hacking and blackmail of supermarkets and other food outlets with threats to poison food.

The major analytical issue is the justification of the existence of the crime at all. Many authors have struggled to construct a response to the "paradox" that it may be lawful to make information public, lawful to threaten to make it public, but not lawful to take money for keeping it secret. The starting point for the modern discussion is LINDGREN, who analysed and found wanting the then-existing explanations. Since then a very large literature has developed. The 1993 symposium held by the University of Pennsylvania Law Review was central.

Of course, keeping secrets is not the only form of conduct

that is lawful unless remunerated. Many forms of corruption fall under the same head, as do offences concerned with organ donation and surrogacy. The fundamental question in all these cases is whether the law should countenance the operation of a market. This is why the area has been important to economic theorists, who had largely neglected "serious" crime. EPSTEIN, perhaps tongue in cheek, makes the argument for legalisation. Blackmail is simply the operation of markets. Subsequent economic theorists (POSNER, GINSBURG) have rendered further variant analyses. Of particular interest is COASE.

The alternative approach is to concentrate upon the moral status of the act of blackmail. On that basis FLETCHER argued that, far from being some aberrance that requires to be explained somewhere at the periphery of "proper" crime is the paradigmatic crime because of the relationship of domination and subordination that it constructs. KATZ, similarly rooted in the moral sustainability of the enterprise, wittily adds various twists.

The traditional approach to motive in criminal law has been to dismiss it as being irrelevant to liability, but to take it into account in identifying suspects and in assessing sentence. BERMAN is useful both as an account of the way in which the blackmail debates have progressed since Lindgren and Epstein's seminal pieces and in advancing the idea that motive is central.

PETER ALLDRIDGE

Body projects

Bordo, Susan, *Unbearable Weight: Feminism, Western Culture, and the Body*, Berkeley: University of California Press, 1993

Davis, Kathy, *Reshaping the Female Body: The Dilemma of Cosmetic Surgery*, London and New York: Routledge, 1995

Favazza, Armando R., *Bodies under Siege: Self-Mutilation and Body Modification in Culture and Psychiatry*, 2nd edition, Baltimore: Johns Hopkins University Press, 1996

Featherstone, Mike, "The Body in Consumer Culture", *Theory, Culture and Society*, 1/2 (1982): 18–33

Foucault, Michel, *The History of Sexuality*, vol. 1: *An Introduction*, New York: Pantheon, 1978; London: Allen Lane, 1979

Garfinkel, Harold, "Passing and the Managed Achievement of Sex Status in an 'Intersexed' Person" in *Studies in Ethnomethodology*, edited by Harold Garfinkel, Englewood Cliffs, New Jersey: Prentice Hall, 1967

Goffman, Erving, *Stigma: Notes on the Management of Spoiled Identity*, Englewood Cliffs, New Jersey: Prentice Hall, 1963; Harmondsworth: Penguin, 1968

Klein, Alan M., *Little Big Men: Bodybuilding Subculture and Gender Construction*, Albany: State University of New York Press, 1993

Shilling, Chris, *The Body and Social Theory*, London and Newbury Park, California: Sage, 1993

Turner, Bryan S., *The Body and Society: Explorations in Social Theory*, 2nd edition, London and Thousand Oaks, California: Sage, 1996

A variety of voluntary physical transformations and body projects have recently become objects for sociological reflection in their own right. This may well be traced back to GARFINKEL's classical study. Garfinkel analyses how Agnes, an intersexed person, tries to secure her rights to live in the elected sex status, learning to be a woman while presenting herself as a natural one. Agnes' struggle for a sex-change operation, which would satisfy her male boyfriend too, shows the potency of the male/female duality. Although criticized for underplaying the influence of doctors on the one hand and on the other the erotic dimension, this essay remains crucial for understanding the performative nature of femininity, and for observing how agency and embodiment may be implicated in both resistance and normalization.

Direct attempts to correct perceived bodily defects are discussed in GOFFMAN, where they are placed among the coping strategies available to the stigmatized. Goffman is well known for having indicated body presentation as crucial to individual identity. Both character, i.e. the actor's conception of himself or herself, and social position may be derived from one's own appearance and demeanour. If normal and stigmatized people alike struggle to present themselves as adequate, body language can only to a degree be spoken strategically. Persons with physical blemishes appear thus as forever engaged in a work of disguise, impression management, and confrontation. Despite criticism from within the field of disability studies for an alleged unsympathetic and pessimistic view, Goffman has paved the way for the study of the implications of embodiment in the construction of deviance and normality.

The notions of deviance and normality are crucial for FOUCAULT's first volume of *The History of Sexuality*. He addresses the practices by which, in modernity, individuals were led to acknowledge themselves as subjects of desire, where desire located in the body contains the truth of their being. The development of psychoanalysis epitomizes the fact that the truth of individuals is no longer linked to the position they occupy in the universal order of things, but is constructed around a normalizing notion of inner responsibility, requiring an endless hermeneutics of the self. Despite a number of criticisms – for attributing primacy to the discursive over the non-discursive realm; for overstretching the notion of power; for reducing the subject to the body and the body to a passive text; or for bestowing a somewhat essentialist quality of resistance to subjugated forms of embodiment – Foucault's work has been pivotal in recognizing that the body is directly implicated in a political field. While power takes on a productive character, shaping subjectivity and bodies, sexuality becomes a project for the modern individual, and is deeply implicated in the legitimization of the bourgeois elite.

While Foucault concentrates on the political, much of the contemporary literature has associated the rise of reflexive body projects with the development of consumer culture. According to FEATHERSTONE, in contemporary culture the reward for ascetic fitness and health regimes ceases to be spiritual salvation, and becomes an enhanced appearance and a more marketable self. Consumer culture latches onto the prevalent self-preservationist conception of the body – which encourages the individual to adopt instrumental strategies to combat decay – and combines it with the notion that the body is a vehicle of pleasure and self-expression. Despite its disputable view of reflexivity and the actor, Featherstone's analysis of the body in consumer culture has influenced TURNER's fundamental contribution to the sociology of the body. Turner's work is worth mentioning, because in spite of its functionalist and dualistic tones, it represents the first attempt to provide a coherent theory of the body in society by reconceptualizing the classical Hobbesian problem of order as the problem of the government of the body.

The gendered nature of the way in which bodies are governed and shaped in contemporary commercial culture is analysed by BORDO. Like most feminist thinkers, Bordo takes a critical view of the way women are associated with the body via a number of minute and mundane practices which confine them to a life centred on physical appearance. In particular, she maintains that a postmodern paradigm of plasticity, assimilating plastic surgery to make-up, lies behind women's projects of beauty and perfection, and that these projects should be considered as patriarchal domination by other means. Bordo has been criticized both within feminism – for failing to address women's diversity – and without it – for reducing women to cultural dupes.

Plastic surgery is apparently becoming more and more accepted in western societies. DAVIS addresses this issue going beyond standard feminist views based on critical readings of the way women are represented in popular images and discourses. Through ethnographic and qualitative sources, she looks at how women account for their decisions to have plastic surgery, providing a far more articulated picture of the phenomenon, and showing that women are active manipulators of the beauty system as much as they appear to be its victims. Although, with greater emphasis on the situated element of action, the rich ethnographic material could have been used to construct a theoretical paradigm alternative to choice, the book remains one of the best recent endeavours to capture the complexity of contemporary body projects.

The amount of emotional work which accompanies physical transformation is matched by actual material labour in the case of bodybuilding. Bodybuilding has been interpreted by KLEIN as a form of therapeutic narcissism, whereby men negotiate their masculinity. His ethnographic work shows that the harder a man exercises, the more he may be trying to overcome his feelings of inadequacy and helplessness. Although weak on the historical development and specificity of bodybuilding, this is another work which addresses body projects as concrete practices of identity negotiation, thereby grasping their ambivalence in relation to rationality and freedom.

Body projects may entail not only the growth of the body or the achievement of an improved natural look. If piercing and tattooing are prominent features of contemporary commercial culture, scarification and self-mutilation on the verge of "neo-primitivism" thrive in subcultural contexts. FAVAZZA shows how these phenomena are treated in culture and psychiatry. His book integrates sociological insights into a psychological perspective, to the detriment of a coherent social-theoretical and historical analysis. However, it illustrates to what extent these bodily practices are a potential site of resistance to standardization, and yet may be de-politicized as private symptoms of disquiet, or incorporated into the mainstream as exotic.

Developing a Giddensian perspective on reflexivity in high modernity, SHILLING has brought body projects to bear on social theory. Bodily conducts always occur within the constraints provided by an individual's social location, but in the conditions of high modernity, individuals are invited to adopt reflexive body regimes in order to sustain their self-identities. The body becomes a never-ending project: it appears as the last retreat from which to face ontological insecurity, while disappearing as a given, natural basis for legitimatizing one's own lifestyle. Although unfinished in its overstressed anti-dualistic stance, Shilling's work provides a useful social-theoretical overview of the way the body – as nature and discourse – is implicated in identity production and reproduction.

ROBERTA SASSATELLI

See also Transgender

Bolshevism

Beilharz, Peter, *Labour's Utopias: Bolshevism, Fabianism, Social Democracy*, London and New York: Routledge, 1992
Cohen, Stephen F., *Bukharin and the Bolshevik Revolution: A Political Biography, 1888–1938*, London: Wildwood House, 1974; New York: Vintage, 1975
Haimson, Leopold H., *The Russian Marxists and the Origins of Bolshevism*, Cambridge, Massachusetts: Harvard University Press, 1955
Harding, Neil, *Lenin's Political Thought: Theory and Practice in the Democratic and Socialist Revolutions*, London: Macmillan, 1983
Kołakowski, Leszek, *Main Currents of Marxism: Its Rise, Growth, and Dissolution*, 3 vols, Oxford: Clarendon Press, and New York: Oxford University Press, 1978
Kotkin, Stephen, *Magnetic Mountain: Stalinism as a Civilization*, Berkeley: University of California Press, 1995
Liebman, Marcel, *Leninism under Lenin*, London: Cape, 1975
Mills, C. Wright, *The Marxists*, New York: Dell, 1962; Harmondsworth: Penguin, 1963
Ulam, Adam B., *Lenin and the Bolsheviks: The Intellectual and Political History of the Triumph of Communism in Russia*, London: Secker and Warburg, 1965
Wilson, Edmund, *To the Finland Station: A Study in the Writing and Acting of History*, New York: Harcourt Brace, and London: Secker and Warburg, 1940
Wolfe, Bertram D., *Three Who Made a Revolution: A Biographical History*, 4th edition, New York: Dell, 1964

"Bolshevism" is by no means an easy term to define. At one level Bolshevism refers to the theory and practice of the Bolshevik Party (later Communist Party) of the Soviet Union, or of Bolshevik or communist parties more generally. Others argue that it represents a specific ideological offshoot of Marxism, complete with its own assumptions about the nature of the historical process and political action. Both approaches have their difficulties, and because of this the conclusion has been drawn that the term lacks utility for analytical purposes, or that, like the term "totalitarianism", it is an invention of

Cold Warriors keen to provide simplistic labels for dividing up the world. What is offered here, therefore, is a selection of the most influential works in which the term "Bolshevism" is explored or repudiated.

For those interested in the development of Bolshevism as a distinct interpretation of Marxism, KOŁAKOWSKI is still the obvious starting point. His three-volume history of Marxism is the most comprehensive, intelligent, and well-written account of the doctrine in all its many guises. The reader should be aware, however, that Kołakowski is a deeply unsympathetic critic of Russian Marxism in general and of Lenin – the "inventor" of Bolshevism – in particular. Given that at least part of Kołakowski's aim is to seek the origins of "communist totalitarianism", this is hardly surprising; but nonetheless readers should be aware that Kołakowski's reading of the origins of Bolshevism is controversial.

An alternative to Kołakowski might still be MILLS, which, although written in the early 1960s, is still a useful short guide to the development of Marxism. Mills is a much more sympathetic chronicler of Marxism than Kołakowski, and unlike the latter, regards Bolshevism as an orthodox interpretation of Marxism. Again, readers need to be aware that Mills's views on the relationship between Marxism and Bolshevism are tendentious and coloured by his own political sympathies.

Beyond these broad surveys of the Marxist tradition there are also a number of classic studies of the "origins of Bolshevism" which still repay study. Both HAIMSON and WILSON, for example, focus not just on the origins of Bolshevism as a doctrine emerging out of Marxism, but as a broader cultural and social phenomenon with roots in Russian populism, Jacobinism, and Slavic romanticism. The tendency of these studies is teleological. They start from the assumption that Bolshevism is a single, homogenous entity whose appearance needs to be "explained". As will be apparent, this view has its critics.

Other classic studies of Bolshevism, which set the tone for much of the debate about the relationship between Bolshevism and Marxism, include ULAM and WOLFE. Both writers are representative of the views associated with the "totalitarian school" of interpretation that emerged in the 1940s and 1950s. They both see the development of the Soviet Union into a totalitarian state as being the logical end product of the attempt to realise the "Bolshevik project". A feature of both works is the tendency to suppress the differences between members of the Bolshevik Party for the sake of highlighting the perceived continuity between doctrine and outcome. None the less, as scholarly and well-written contributions to the literature on the evolution of Russian Marxism and Soviet political practice, they are still worth consulting.

Important correctives to the analysis associated with the commentators above include HARDING and LIEBMAN. Both offer a reappraisal of Lenin's political thought and attempt to challenge the idea that Lenin generated a new doctrine for Russian conditions or that he drew inspiration either from the Jacobin example or from Russian authoritarian populism. Both studies attempt to show how orthodox Lenin's Marxism was and thus how difficult it is to regard Bolshevism as a separate doctrine or philosophy. For them, Bolshevism was the adumbration of Marxists confronted by conditions that necessitated a large degree of flexibility of thought and practice.

Similarly, COHEN argues that it is questionable whether there ever was a Bolshevik ideology to which all members of the Bolshevik Party adhered. As he shows in his study of Bukharin, a key figure in the Bolshevik Party until the late 1920s, the principal characteristic of debates within the Bolshevik Party was the remarkable lack of consensus over how the regime was to proceed on all key issues. If it can be termed an ideology, Bolshevism was clearly a highly flexible one that permitted myriad interpretation and readings. The idea that Stalinism can be explained as the logical unfolding of Bolshevik ideology is thus highly questionable. Bolshevism is, in Cohen's view, more accurately regarded as an approach to politics rather than a tightly defined set of goals.

As regards Bolshevism as a mode of practice rather than an ideology, one of the most interesting (and provocative) of recent studies is KOTKIN. Deploying a Foucaultian method that favours genealogical explanation over the structural or intentional, Kotkin argues that what Bolshevism means can only be assessed by reference to the practice of the Soviet state. Given the way in which the Soviet state single-mindedly set itself the task of industrializing and proletarianizing the country, Bolshevism should not be regarded as a deviation from the Marxist model of rationality (or indeed that of the Enlightenment more generally), but rather as its most extreme representation. Bolshevism, in this sense, can be equated with that cluster of shared understandings and aspirations produced in the course of the creation of a new society, not with any distinct doctrine or philosophy.

Finally, BEILHARZ is useful for situating Bolshevism within the socialist tradition more broadly. He sees Bolshevism as one of the rival visions of socialism competing with those of social democrats and Fabians. In short, Beilharz seeks to overcome the view of Bolshevism as a specifically Russian phenomenon or as a doctrine of relevance only to radicals in the developing world. Rather, it should be seen as one model of socialism competing with others for the support of those seeking to transcend, rather than merely reform, liberal capitalism.

SIMON TORMEY

See also Communism, V.I. Lenin, Marx and Marxism

Boredom at work

Csikszentmihalyi, Mihaly, *Beyond Boredom and Anxiety*, San Francisco: Jossey Bass, 1975

Dyer-Smith, Martyn B.A. and David A. Wesson, "Resource Allocation Efficiency as an Indicator of Boredom, Work Performance and Absence", *Ergonomics*, 40/5 (1997): 515–21

Farmer, Richard and Norman D. Sundberg, "Boredom Proneness: The Development and Correlates of a New Scale", *Journal of Personality Assessment*, 50/1 (1986): 4–17

Fisher, Cynthia D., "Boredom at Work: A Neglected Concept", *Human Relations*, 46/3 (1993): 395–417

Gemmill, Gary and Judith Oakley, "The Meaning of Boredom in Organizational Life", *Group & Organizational Management*, 17/4 (1992): 358–69

Klapp, Orrin E., *Overload and Boredom: Essays on the Quality of Life in the Information Society*, New York: Greenwood Press, 1986

Smith, Richard P., "Boredom: A Review", *Human Factors*, 23/3 (1981): 329–40

Vodanovich, Stephen J., Chris Weddle and Chris Piotrowski, "The Relationship between Boredom Proneness and Internal and External Work Values", *Social Behavior and Personality*, 25/3 (1997): 259–64

SMITH provides an effective review of the early, though sparse, literature on boredom written in Europe and North America from the period 1926 to 1980. Early interest in the topic of boredom and monotony in the industrial sector originated because of the relationship between boredom, fatigue, and depression on the job. Many of these early writings focused on the person as the source and cause of boredom. Drug therapy was used successfully in some early studies to increase a person's state of arousal on the job. As a result drugs were thought by some to lessen the degree of boredom and provide at least a partial solution to the problem of boredom on the job.

A useful modern review of the boredom construct is provided by FISHER, who proposes "main effects" and "person main effects" of boredom. Main effects are the objective task and environmental conditions external to the person. The person main effects are those individual differences within each person that influence how a given situation is experienced. Such factors include personality, intelligence, and mental health. Fisher goes on to propose that appropriate fit between person and situation is the key to minimizing boredom. Workplace consequences of boredom discussed in this article include: lapses in attention, emotional upset and hostility, absenteeism, taking longer to notice and correct errors, falling asleep on the job as in the case of the pilot who fell asleep and overflew a destination by 100 miles, increasing drug and alcohol consumption and abuse, and greater levels of stress-related problems such heart attacks. Fisher also discusses recognition of boredom in the workplace and appropriate responses by managers and organizations to boredom in the workplace.

GEMMILL & OAKLEY suggests that boredom is the state that occurs when organizational members no longer experience emotional and intellectual meaning in what they are doing in their work processes. In this written work, emphasis is on the perception of the person as opposed to what is occurring externally. The authors go on later to acknowledge that the level of stimulation in one's work is not the sole influencing factor for determining whether or not one's work is boring. Either a high-level or low-level stimulation environment may be boring.

Gemmill and Oakley indicate that Western societies tend to socialize children to believe that boredom is a personal failing as opposed to a failing or defect of the social system. Children are taught to sit in their seats and listen to a teacher and not question authority. As a result, workers enter the workplace ready and willing to accept authority and the boredom of the workplace . To admit that one is bored in a social or work situation may be compared to admitting that one is "inadequate" or "sick".

The authors also discuss an inverse relationship between boredom and creativity. A bored individual cannot be creative.

Interventions for organizational change and issues for a change agent seeking to lead organizational members suffering from chronic boredom through a change journey are explored. They posit that an organization is suffering from chronic boredom when members are unable to identify, accept, or create meaning in their work life and existence together. The first step for an organization seeking change is issue identification. Specific intervention strategies for an organization wanting to deal with boredom are discussed.

A collection of essays by KLAPP explores the effect of boredom caused by information overload. He asserts that boredom is just as likely to come from an overload of stimulation as an underload of stimulation. The broader issues of quality of life as well as the narrower issue of work life are discussed. One chapter discusses boredom as related to several work and social groups including high school students, stay-at-home mothers, those employed by the military, upper-middle-class professional workers, organized religious groups, and political groups, as well as assembly line workers. He also links certain French, British, Japanese, and Swiss national incidents to boredom.

One of the most frequently used instruments to assess boredom is the Boredom Proneness (BP) Scale, developed by FARMER & SUNDBERG in 1986. This instrument is a 28-item self-report instrument that demonstrates the respondent's tendency toward experiencing boredom. Farmer & Sundberg provide full-text for the instrument and discussion regarding its use and psychometric properties.

VODANOVICH, WEDDLE & PIOTROWSKI used the Boredom Proneness Scale and Survey of Work Values Scale to find that subjects high in boredom proneness possessed significantly higher extrinsic work value scores. Subjects with low boredom proneness scores possessed significantly higher intrinsic work value scores. These results have implications for job placement and motivation strategies. Perhaps those high in boredom proneness would benefit from occupations that offer clear external, tangible rewards. On the other hand, low boredom-prone individuals may benefit from situations that offer intrinsic reward strategies.

DYER-SMITH & WESSON use the inertial resource allocation model to explain boredom in terms of mismatches between task demands and resource allocations in an inertial system. Subjects were clerical personnel working for a government agency. Individual performance factors found to be related to boredom included accuracy of output and days absent from work.

CSIKSZENTMIHALYI contrasts the low-satisfaction, and low-performance state of boredom with the high-satisfaction, high-performance state of what he designates as "flow". If one's skills are greater than the opportunity to use them, then boredom will be felt. When an opportunity for action is evenly matched by one's capabilities, then flow may be experienced. Along with flow may come the feelings of zest, involvement, joy in action, and total immersion, whether the activity is work or play. Such feelings are the antithesis of the boredom experienced by many in workplaces resulting in one being "in the flow". Csikszentmihalyi profiles individuals at work and at play in his attempts to develop and illustrate his theory of flow and its contrast with boredom.

As we begin the new millennium, boredom is clearly an issue

in the workplace, though it is as elusive as ever to measure and deal with. The future will bring changes in the workplace that will probably include what work will be done, how work will be accomplished, and the characteristics and qualifications required for successful job performance. As information becomes a more important part of each and every job, and as knowledge becomes more abundant and more rapidly available, information overload also becomes a potential problem. KLAPP recognized the relationship between information overload and boredom in 1980s and might caution today's organizational manager that the bombardment and pace of new information being generated today leaves workers susceptible to overload, boredom, and other types of unproductive responses. One major challenge for successful organizations will be early recognition and diagnosis of boredom and the implementation of effective intervention strategies.

DYANNE J. FERK

Bretton Woods

Bretton Woods Commission, *Bretton Woods: Looking to the Future*, Washington, DC: Bretton Woods Commission, 1994

Gardner, Richard N., *Sterling–Dollar Diplomacy in Current Perspective: The Origins and Prospects of Our International Economic Order*, revised edition, New York: Columbia University Press, 1980

James, Harold, *International Monetary Cooperation since Bretton Woods*, Washington, DC: International Monetary Fund, and Oxford: Oxford University Press, 1996

MacDougall, Donald, *The World Dollar Problem: A Study in International Economics*, London: Macmillan, and New York: St Martin's Press, 1957

Panić, Mića, "The Bretton Woods System: Concept and Practice" in *Managing the Global Economy*, edited by Jonathan Michie and John Grieve Smith, Oxford and New York: Oxford University Press, 1995

Payer, Cheryl, *The Debt Trap: The International Monetary Fund and the Third World*, New York: Monthly Review Press, and Harmondsworth: Penguin, 1974

Payer, Cheryl, *The World Bank: A Critical Analysis*, New York and London: Monthly Review Press, 1982

Solomon, Robert, *The International Monetary System, 1945-81*, revised edition, New York: Harper and Row, 1982

Triffin, Robert, *Gold and the Dollar Crisis: The Future of Convertibility*, New Haven, Connecticut: Yale University Press, 1960

US Department of State, *Proceedings and Documents of United Nations Monetary and Financial Conference: Bretton Woods, New Hampshire July 1–22, 1944*, 2 vols, Washington, DC: United States Government Printing Office, 1948

PANIĆ gives a succinct overview and analysis of the most important aspects of the Bretton Woods system, from its origins in the disintegration of the international economic order in the 1930s to its successful functioning for a time after World War II, followed by growing instability and collapse in the early 1970s. Particular attention is paid to the postwar realities that, first, made the principles agreed at Bretton Woods inapplicable and, quarter of a century later, the whole system, as it operated in practice, unworkable. This explains why there was such an important difference between the international order planned at the Bretton Woods conference and the international financial regime that evolved after the war. The final section considers the possibility of creating a "New Bretton Woods" – often debated by economists, bankers, and politicians – and the reasons why such a system would be, at least in the foreseeable future, even more difficult to set up and operate successfully than the one that collapsed at the beginning of the 1970s.

GARDNER acquired the status of a "classic" almost as soon as it was first published in the 1950s. It is both a history and a careful assessment of the Anglo-American attitudes in the early 1940s towards a new global economic order, including plans for its creation after the war produced by governments of Britain and the US. Equally important, the book gives what is still the best account of negotiations between British and US experts and governments that led, eventually, to the formation of supranational economic organizations such as the International Monetary Fund (IMF), the World Bank, and the General Agreement on Trade and Tariffs (GATT). The book is also important as a study of problems that are likely to arise in any attempt to create effective supranational organizations. This explains why, as the author shows, it became clear as soon as the two Bretton Woods institutions (the IMF and the World Bank) began their operations in the second half of the 1940s that they would be unable to perform the tasks for which they were created.

The conference held at Bretton Woods in July 1944 is unique historically. It was the first and, so far, the only successful attempt by a large number of countries to create a supranational global financial and trading system. With the disastrous experience of the 1930s still fresh in everybody's mind, all the participants agreed that this was essential if they were to achieve their national economic objectives after the war. The two volumes published by the US DEPARTMENT OF STATE are, therefore, of considerable historical interest. They bring together various proposals for creating a postwar international financial system tabled at the conference, verbatim accounts of some of the debates that followed, and the Articles of Agreement, approved by the participating countries, which specified duties and responsibilities of the IMF and the World Bank and the way that they were to function after the war.

SOLOMON, for many years a senior official at the US Federal Reserve Board, provides in this book a highly readable insider's account of how the international monetary system operated from 1945 until the beginning of the 1980s. Combining history, analysis, and reminiscences, the author charts important developments during the period: from the effects of the Marshall Plan to the mounting difficulties in the 1960s and several unsuccessful attempts at the beginning of the 1970s to save the Bretton Woods system. The final chapters deal with monetary consequences of a number of events, all with major global financial consequences, that occurred soon after the demise of the system: the impact of OPEC, international stagflation, and the effect of floating exchange rates.

JAMES' book is a substantial, detailed, and (at the end of the 1990s) the most up-to-date history of international monetary developments since World War II. With much more prominence given to events during the last thirty years of the 20th century, only about a third of the book is devoted to the period during which the Bretton Woods system operated. The history was written on the initiative of, and with full cooperation of, the IMF, whose senior members of staff selected the author for the task. It is hardly surprising, therefore, that his view of the world does not differ significantly from theirs. Nevertheless, the book contains a wealth of valuable information, often provided or elucidated by some of the key participants in the events that have shaped the international economic order in the second half of the 20th century.

One of the most important aims of the Bretton Woods conference was to create a supranational global system that would be independent of economic policies and performance of any one country. Yet the system that operated from the late 1940s until the early 1970s was, like the classical gold standard, heavily dependent on and, consequently, managed by the dominant economy at the time, in this case the US. One of the unavoidable and, in the long run, fatal weaknesses of such a system is analysed in TRIFFIN. The "Triffin Dilemma", as the problem became known, shows how dependence of the international community on the currency of one country imposes major policy constraints on the country concerned and the risk of serious, unsustainable instability on the international system as a whole.

The book by MACDOUGALL achieved some international notoriety for predicting long-term shortage of dollars in the world economy precisely at the moment when the shortage began to turn into a glut. Yet the book deserves to be read for much more than the fact that even eminent and widely respected economists (and MacDougall was by no means the only one to be concerned at the time about "the dollar problem") may fail to notice powerful trends that are at work in a dynamic world economy. The real relevance of this important study of the relationship between the US and the rest of the world in the first ten years after the end of World War II lies in its analysis of the risks inherent in an international economy dependent on the policies of a single country. The risks are particularly great when the country happens to be as large and self-sufficient as the US – exactly the kind of problem that the Bretton Woods conference was trying, unsuccessfully as it turned out, to avoid.

Although the Bretton Woods system collapsed in the early 1970s, the two institutions created with the task of running it, the IMF and the World Bank, have survived. What is more, with no country in the position to manage the international financial system they are far more influential now than they were during the Bretton Woods period. The report prepared by a group of experts for the BRETTON WOODS COMMISSION, an independent private organization in Washington, to mark the fiftieth anniversary of the Bretton Woods conference, looks to the future by reviewing past performance of the two organizations. The authors then propose a number of reforms that would make both institutions more effective in a rapidly changing international economic and political environment. The report deserves to be studied carefully because it reflects the views of those with considerable influence in the world of international finance. The reasons why they would like to give the two institutions an even more central role in the world

economy are also instructive, not least because they happen to be rather different from those that Keynes, White, and other architects of the Bretton Woods system had in mind.

By contrast, PAYER's two books, written from a Third World perspective, are highly critical of the role played by the IMF and the World Bank. In this, they anticipate many of the criticisms of the two organizations that have become common at the end of the 1990s. The main argument in both books is that the two Bretton Woods institutions have, through their lending policies, forced developing countries to pursue completely unsuitable policies. The policies have exacerbated their economic problems and have contributed to social divisions and political instability, leading in many cases to military dictatorships. The book on the IMF illustrates the central thesis with case studies from a number of heavily indebted Third World countries. The Fund is criticized for imposing on each of them policies that were highly inappropriate to their long-term needs, or even to the immediate problems that they were trying to solve. Specific examples are also used in the book on the World Bank Group to show that the institutions comprising it have been primarily concerned with promoting the interests of powerful corporations from industrial countries, mainly the US. The importance of the two books is that they reflect the views widely held in developing countries. As these views are rarely given much prominence in the mainstream literature on international finance, the books ought to be read in order to acquire a balanced view of the problems that can arise in the way that supranational organizations operate. Whatever the original intentions, there is no guarantee that "universal" institutions will promote "universal" interests!

MIĆA PANIĆ

See also International Monetary Fund

Brezhnev, Leonid 1906–1982
Soviet political leader

Bessinger, Mark, "The Age of the Soviet Oligarchs", *Current History*, 83/495 (1983): 305–08, 339–42

Breslauer, George W., *Khrushchev and Brezhnev as Leaders: Building Authority in Soviet Politics*, London and Boston: Allen and Unwin, 1982

Brezhneva, Luba, *The World I Left Behind: Pieces of a Past*, New York: Random House, 1995

Dornberg, John, *Brezhnev: The Masks of Power*, New York: Basic Books, and London: Deutsch, 1974

Goldman, Marshall I., *USSR in Crisis: The Failure of an Economic System*, New York: Norton, 1983

Medvedev, Roy, "Brezhnev: A Bureaucrat's Profile", *Dissent* (Spring 1983): 224–33

Millar, James R. (editor), *Cracks in the Monolith: Party Power in the Brezhnev Era*, Armonk, New York: Sharpe, 1992

Murphy, Paul J., *Brezhnev, Soviet Politician*, Jefferson, North Carolina: McFarland, 1981

Simis, Konstantin M., *USSR – The Corrupt Society: The Secret World of Soviet Capitalism*, New York: Simon and Schuster, and London: Dent, 1982

Valenta, Jiri, *Soviet Intervention in Czechoslovakia, 1968:
Anatomy of a Decision*, Baltimore: Johns Hopkins
University Press, 1979; revised edition 1991

Under the leadership of Leonid Brezhnev the Soviet Union
acquired American recognition of its superpower status, while
internally, the stability of the Communist Party was maintained. In 1964, Brezhnev emerged as the head of the
Communist Party of the Soviet Union, in a triumvirate that
also included Aleksei Kosygin and Nikolai Podgorny. During
his eighteen years in power Brezhnev gradually acquired dominance in the Soviet Union. He was responsible for pursuing
detente with the West – concluding the first strategic armaments agreements to be conducted with the US – as well as
reining in Soviet allies and clients, including Czechoslovakia
in 1968, Afghanistan in 1979, and Poland in 1980. At the
same time, Brezhnev's idea of "respect for cadres" condemned
the communist regime to destruction, given its failure to undertake rapid modernization of agriculture and industry. At the
end of his rule Brezhnev symbolized the gerontocracy that ruled
the Soviet Union and failed to respond with needed reforms.

The rising age of the members of the Brezhnev Politburo
between 1966 and 1982 is the focus of BESSINGER. Brezhnev's
approach gave top policy makers job security. Bessinger sees the
failure to transfer or remove officials as resulting in political
and economic stagnation, which presented major problems for
the Andropov and Chernenko administrations.

How power was consolidated by Khrushchev and Brezhnev
is the focus of BRESLAUER's study. Each of these two Soviet
leaders sought to build legitimate authority but by different
means: Khrushchev sought to decentralize the state apparatus,
empowering local leaders; whereas Brezhnev sought to
centralize authority. Crucial to the success of each strategy was
the climate of opinion, as well as the leader's personality and
knowledge about the political system. This is a study that
should be read by those who seek a systemic understanding
of how authority was consolidated in the USSR.

BREZHNEVA, a niece of the former Soviet leader, offers
insights into the family life and background of the Brezhnev
family, especially during the years of Leonid Brezhnev's rule.
The hypocrisy exhibited by the former Soviet leader is interesting in this account of his public versus private statements,
and the importance he attached to bringing privileges to his
family in the form of apartments, jobs, and virtual immunity
from prosecution. Brezhneva's volume is loaded with information about the party elite and foreign communist leaders as
well as reactions to major foreign policy events. Readers must
be cautioned, however, that there is virtually no documentation to verify many of her claims, thus one is dependent on
the accuracy of her thoughts and motives in writing this
volume.

Never was a study more aptly named than DORNBERG's,
given its focus on the many connections that Brezhnev used in
establishing his rule, as symbolized in the citation "Brezhnev
is different things to different people" (p.284). He examines
Brezhnev's early life, from this youth as an ethnic Russian in
the Ukraine, through the signing of the first SALT Treaties, to
the emergence of the Brezhnev cult of personality. Dornberg
is insightful in his recognition of emerging trends, such as the
rounding up of dissidents, and Brezhnev's desire for a formal

position in the Soviet state. This book is interesting and worth
reading in that it offers a mid-term evaluation of Brezhnev and
his government during the first years of their rule, rather than
after the stagnation that set in during the late 1970s.

Reform of the Stalinist economic model is the focus of
GOLDMAN. The Stalinist model "lacks the ability to adapt.
Once in place, the Stalinist model builds up strong vested interests. Not only economic surgery, but even economic tinkering
sets off disruption and distrust among all levels of Soviet
society" (p.47). Lacking the *will* to use terror again, the Soviet
leadership was unable to reform the economic and political
structures. Under Brezhnev this system reached crisis proportions, and the leadership lacked the ability to deal with the
situation, given the disruption that effective action promised
to bring.

MEDVEDEV examines Brezhnev's personality and explains
how his bureaucratic mentality enabled him to gain power.
Brezhnev's loyalty to his friends, vanity in desiring ceremonial
power, and refusal to discipline corrupt Party personnel are
recognized by Medvedev as having determining roles in this
regard, as was the creation of the Secretariat as an independent source of support. Believing that, from 1971, a concern
for international affairs dominated Brezhnev's rule, Medvedev
questions why Brezhnev concentrated more on foreign affairs
than domestic matters during his last years in power. These
are interesting and under-examined issues.

Social, political, ideological, and economic life in Brezhnev's
Soviet Union is the subject of MILLAR's edited collection of
eight essays, based on the Soviet Interview Project of Soviet
citizens arriving in the US between 1979 and 1988. In each
case the question was: "What was the party's role, influence,
and actual contribution in its integration with some other
bureaucracy – the legal system, enterprise management, and so
forth?" While uniting the Soviet system under a ruling force,
interference by the Communist Party's *nomenklatura* was
generally weak, as they were often dependent on other structures, particularly economic ones, for their wellbeing. The
Communist Party was viewed as a parasite among the respondents because it contributed little to the nation, and more
people sought membership for the material rewards it brought
them than for ideological reasons. This is a solid work that
challenges many of the conventional beliefs about the power
of the Communist Party in the Soviet Union, and suggests new
reasons for the stagnation of the late Brezhnev period.

The skills and manoeuvering that made Leonid Brezhnev a
great political leader are discussed by MURPHY. Brezhnev is
seen as a man who came from a poor background and who,
through his skill, was able to climb the Party hierarchy by being
on the winning side of policy debates. Murphy contends that
the key to Brezhnev's success, particularly at the Politburo level,
was that he sought the creation of a consensus on issues in order
to avoid total responsibility should a policy initiative fail, or
should someone have to be removed from power. According to
the standard view of the politics of the "Kremlin", the position
of power – and the strength of one's supporters in power –
determine one's ability to develop consensus and to protect oneself from removal.

Power and economics are the focus of SIMIS. "True power
in the Soviet Union belongs to the apparat of the Community
Party, and it is the members of that apparat who are the true

leaders of the country" (p.24). Those at the centre of power had special privileges (dining halls, medical facilities, and so on) and the further one went from the centre, the more dependent one was on corruption. Such corruption, according to Simis, allowed illegal enterprises to operate. This is an important study for those seeking to understand the consequences of Brezhnev's policy of "respect for cadres".

VALENTA, in a study of the Soviet decision to intervene militarily in Czechoslovakia, emphasizes a bureaucratic political paradigm. This study is based on interviews with Czechoslovak officials and other prominent persons. The author develops an understanding of the course of events that led up to the intervention and that motivated the Brezhnev regime to reverse the public appearance of agreement between the two sides in the aftermath of the Cierna and Bratislava agreements. The significance of Valenta's study is that it demonstrates the importance of pulling and hauling within Soviet decision-making bodies. It cites those who feared that intervention would damage the Soviet position internationally, and those who supported intervention, fearing that Czech reforms, which had produced "socialism with a human face", would weaken Soviet socialism and their own positions of power inside the Soviet Union.

JEFFREY L. PREWITT

See also Cold War, Collectivization, Nikita Khrushchev

Bulimia

Agras, W. Stewart, "Pharmacotherapy of Bulimia Nervosa and Binge Eating Disorder: Longer-term Outcomes", *Psychopharmacology Bulletin*, 33 (1997): 433–36

Kutlesic, Vesna, Donald Williamson, David Gleaves, Jane Barbin and Kathleen Murphy-Eberenz, "The Interview for the Diagnosis of Eating Disorders-IV: Application to DSM-IV Diagnostic Criteria", *Psychological Assessment*, 10 (1998): 41–48

Lewandowski, Lisa, Tracy Gebing, Jennifer Anthony and William O'Brien, "Meta-analysis of Cognitive-Behavioral Treatment Studies for Bulimia", *Clinical Psychology Review*, 17 (1997): 703–18

Lowe, Michael, David Gleaves and Kathleen Murphy-Eberenz, "On the Relation of Dieting and Bingeing in Bulimia Nervosa", *Journal of Abnormal Psychology*, 107 (1998): 263–71

Mintz, Laurie, M. Sean O'Halloran, Amy Mulholland and Paxton Schneider, "Questionnaire for Eating Disorder Diagnosis: Reliability and Validity of Operationalizing DSM-IV Criteria into a Self-report Format", *Journal of Counseling Psychology*, 44 (1997): 63–79

Robin, Arthur, Marcia Gilroy and Amy Baker-Dennis, "Treatment of Eating Disorders in Children and Adolescents", *Clinical Psychology Review*, 18 (1998): 421–46

Smolak, Linda, Michael P. Levine and Ruth Striegel-Moore (editors), *The Developmental Psychopathology of Eating Disorders: Implications for Research, Prevention, and Treatment*, Mahwah, New Jersey: Erlbaum, 1996

Sullivan, Patrick, Cynthia Bulik and Kenneth Kendler, "Genetic Epidemiology of Bingeing and Vomiting", *British Journal of Psychiatry*, 173 (1998): 75–79

Tantillo, Mary, "A Relational Approach to Group Therapy for Women with Bulimia Nervosa: Moving from Understanding to Action", *International Journal of Group Psychotherapy*, 48 (1998): 477–98

Turnbull, Sue, Anne Ward, Janet Treasure, Hershel Jick and Laura Derby, "The Demand for Eating Disorder Care: An Epidemiological Study Using the General Practice Research Database", *British Journal of Psychiatry*, 169 (1996): 705–12

Walsh, B. Timothy and Michael Devlin, "Eating Disorders: Progress and Problems", *Science*, 280 (1998): 1387–90

Wilfley, Denise and Lisa Cohen, "Psychological Treatment of Bulimia Nervosa and Binge Eating Disorder", *Psychopharmacology Bulletin*, 33 (1997): 437–54

TURNBULL *et al.* identify that bulimia nervosa is an important psychological disorder that has been the subject of less research than the other major eating disorder, anorexia nervosa. Their epidemiological study of eating disorders in the UK included both bulimia and anorexia. They suggest that over a six-year period, incidence rates indicate that bulimia is more common than anorexia and, indeed, is probably underreported, as individuals suffering from the disorder tend to be secretive about its existence and do not necessarily exhibit symptoms such as dramatically reduced body weight. Based on the results of their study, the authors conclude that the incidence of bulimia is increasing. It is also acknowledged that there is some controversy about whether the incidence of bulimia is increasing. Bulimia does seem to be diagnosed increasingly frequently, but it remains to be seen whether this reflects an increasing prevalence of the disease or a wider recognition of the symptoms of the disorder and therefore a higher rate of diagnosis.

SULLIVAN, BULIK & KENDLER present recent information regarding the relative genetic and environmental influences on bulimia nervosa. In addition, they examine the validity of the DSM-IV diagnostic criteria for the disorder. Based on their study of nearly 2000 twins, the authors suggest genetic factors and individual-specific environmental factors both partially influence bingeing and vomiting behaviours of bulimics. They also interpret their results as indicating that the DSM-IV criteria for bulimia nervosa are valid. This study is an important step forward in understanding the genetic and environmental etiology of bulimia nervosa, an issue that has recently received much attention and remains unresolved (see commentary by Curtis and also Morgan in the same volume, for additional discussion of genetic and environmental influences).

The etiology of bulimia remains unresolved, however, biological, psychological, and sociocultural influences have each been investigated. As discussed above Sullivan, Bulik & Kendler explored the relative contributions of genetic and environmental influences. LOWE, GLEAVES & MURPHY-EBERENZ provide a good overview of the psychological model that is proposed to underlie the dieting-bingeing-purging cycle. The researchers hypothesize that the psychological stress associated with dieting increases the likelihood of binge eating, which can then lead to purging behaviour. The authors provide both a critique and modification of this model, suggesting that dieting plays an important part only in the initial instigation of the cycle. TANTILLO provides a discussion of relational theory as related to the etiology of bulimia nervosa. According to relational theory, the bingeing and purging behaviour seen in bulimia nervosa is a strategy women use to take control and express themselves in the absence of any mutual relationships with other individuals. From a sociocultural perspective, the female "thin ideal" seen in some cultures has been proposed as another influence on bulimia. It is hypothesized that some women have internalized these sociocultural bodyshape standards to such a high degree that they use extreme measures (dieting, bingeing, and purging) to control their weight and figure. WALSH & DEVLIN provide a brief overview of the current knowledge regarding bulimia. Biological, psychological, and cultural theories of the etiology are reviewed and treatments are also discussed. Directions for future research are also presented.

MINTZ *et al.* present an overview of multiple questionnaires used in the assessment of bulimia. This review includes the most popular questionnaires; the Eating Attitudes Test-26 (EAT-26), the Eating Disorder Inventory-2 (EDI-2), and the Bulimia Test-Revised (BULIT-R). Mintz *et al.* discuss the development of the Questionnaire for Eating Disorder Diagnosis (Q-EDD) which is one of the few questionnaires aligned with the current diagnostic criteria in the DSM-IV. This is a new eating-disorder assessment tool and the article presents promising reliability and validity. In addition, the authors discuss possible uses and limitations of the Q-EDD.

Another popular bulimia assessment technique is the use of a structured or semistructured interview. Two such interviews are the Eating Disorders Examination (EDE; Fairburn & Cooper) and the Interview for the Diagnosis of Eating Disorders-IV (IDED-IV; KUTLESIC *et al.*). The EDE is the older of the two interviews and like some of the above questionnaires, was not based on current DSM-IV diagnostic criteria. KUTLESIC *et al.* discuss the development of the IDED-IV, present reliability and validity results, and explore how it differs from other structured interviews used to assess eating disorders. It is important to note that the assessment tools are often redesigned to incorporate current theories and understanding of eating disorders.

Numerous treatments for bulimia nervosa exist, but two strategies predominate (cognitive-behavioural and pharmacological). WILFLEY & COHEN provide a comprehensive review of the psychological treatments of bulimia. The authors focus mainly on cognitive-behavioural therapy and provide evidence from various studies supporting its effectiveness. They compare cognitive-behavioural therapy to alternative treatments for bulimia including medication, behavioural therapy, nondirective psychotherapy, psychodynamic therapy, interpersonal psychotherapy, and self-help treatments. Wilfley & Cohen also discuss directions for future research. LEWANDOWSKI *et al.* provide a literature review and meta-analysis of cognitive-behavioural treatment studies for bulimia and conclude that this treatment strategy appears to result in substantial reduction of unhealthy thoughts and behaviours related to bulimia. The other major technique used in the treatment of bulimia is medication. Psychopharmeceuticals were initially used in treating bulimia nervosa because of its high comorbidity with depressive disorders. AGRAS provides a brief but comprehensive review of the literature on the pharmacological treatments of bulimia. He presents information regarding its effectiveness, length of treatment, side effects, cost effectiveness, and use in conjunction with psychotherapy.

ROBIN, GILROY & BAKER-DENNIS provide a review of the literature on eating disorders which focuses on children and adolescents and emphasizes a developmental perspective. Diagnostic criteria and treatment strategies are reviewed and specific recommendations are made in regard to treatment. SMOLAK, LEVINE & STRIEGEL-MOORE edited a book exploring the developmental psychopathology of eating disorders. Included in this book is an introduction to the field of developmental psychopathology, which offers a framework for better understanding etiological aspects of bulimia and also has implications for treatment. Developmental research is presented throughout and the principles of developmental process and context are highlighted, including; transitions during adolescence, media influences, and developmental vulnerabilities. Implications of developmental models for prevention programmes are also presented in this edited volume.

SHANE R. JIMERSON

See also Anorexia

Bullying in schools

Björkqvist, K., K.M.J. Lagerspetz and A. Kaukiainen, "Do Girls Manipulate and Boys Fight? Developmental Trends in Regard to Direct and Indirect Aggression", *Aggressive Behavior*, 18/2 (1992): 117–27

Crick, N.R. and J.K. Grotpeter, "Children's Treatment by Peers: Victims of Relational and Overt Aggression", *Development and Psychopathology*, 8/2 (1996): 367–80

Olweus, Dan, *Aggression in the Schools: Bullies and Whipping Boys*, Washington, DC: Hemisphere Press, 1978

Olweus, Dan, *Bullying at School: What We Know and What We Can Do*, Oxford and Cambridge, Massachusetts: Blackwell, 1993

Rigby, Ken, *Bullying in Schools, and What to Do About It*, Melbourne: Australian Council for Educational Research, 1996; London: Kingsley, 1997

Ross, D.M., *Childhood Bullying and Teasing: What School Personnel, Other Professionals, and Parents Can Do*, Alexandria, Virginia: American Counseling Association, 1996

Salmivalli, C. *et al.*, "Bullying as a Group Process: Participant Roles and Their Relations to Social Status within the Group", *Aggressive Behavior*, 22/1 (1996): 1–15

Sharp, Sonia and Helen Cowie, *Counselling and Supporting Children in Distress*, London: Sage, 1998

Smith, Peter K. and Sonia Sharp (editors), *School Bullying: Insights and Perspectives*, London and New York: Routledge, 1994

Smith, Peter K. *et al.* (editors), *The Nature of School Bullying: A Cross-National Perspective*, London: Routledge, 1999

Although bullying can occur in any institution (see the entry on Aggression in the workplace), the term originates historically in descriptions of children's bullying in schools. Despite the probable antiquity of the phenomenon, serious research on the issue only dates from the 1970s. Since then it has expanded rapidly.

Modern research on school bullying first started in Scandinavia. Dan Olweus is generally credited as being the founding father of the field, and his first book (OLWEUS 1978) set out the nature of the phenomenon, including age and sex differences, and characteristics of bullies and of victims (called then "whipping boys"). OLWEUS (1993) not only provided a synopsis of the findings from several large scale surveys in Norway and Sweden that he had carried out, but also demonstrated the success (under certain conditions) of the nationwide intervention campaign in schools that took place in Norway in the 1980s. This was a school-based intervention, supported by materials for teachers and parents and a videotape for use with pupils.

Research on school bullying was also being carried out independently in Japan in the 1980s; as in Norway and later in the UK, research and intervention has been fuelled by concerns over adolescent suicides due to bullying. Olweus' work had more immediate impact in other European countries. In England, a school intervention project was strongly influenced by the Norwegian experience. The edited book by SMITH & SHARP describes the design of this project and the outcomes obtained. In this work, intervention focused on whole school policy development, together with classroom work, playground improvements, and work with pupils particularly involved either as victims or bullies. Reductions in bullying were obtained, though not to the same extent as in Olweus' work. However, a very thorough description of the various interventions used, and the relative success of different schools in applying them, is provided in the Smith & Sharp account.

Other research has revealed more about the different forms which bullying can take. BJÖRKQVIST, LAGERSPETZ & KAUKIAINEN, working in Finland, showed that whereas male bullying was often physical in nature, and both sexes often used direct verbal bullying and teasing, girls often used indirect forms of bullying such as rumour mongering and social exclusion. The authors also delineated age trends (for both sexes) from physical to more indirect forms. Indirect bullying is less obvious to the outsider and the authors consider that female bullying and aggression may have been underestimated in the research of the 1970s and 1980s as a consequence.

CRICK & GROTPETER pursued parallel work in the US, but using the term "relational" rather than "indirect" aggression. Besides confirming the sex differences, these authors have indicated that the consequences of indirect bullying can be more severe than the consequences of direct bullying. This and other research suggests that prolonged bullying can have marked negative effects on self-esteem and mental well-being, and they provide a strong rationale for intervention work.

To be successful, interventions should take account of the social structural context in which bullying occurs. SALMIVALLI et al. have delineated the different roles in bullying episodes in more detail; in particular, they distinguish ringleader bullies, reinforcers (who encourage the bullies), assistants (who join in with the ringleaders), and defenders (who help the victim). Other studies (see Olweus, Smith & Sharp and RIGBY) have distinguished between passive victims and provocative victims.

Knowledge of social structure and dynamics in peer groups is important in evaluating the opportunities and difficulties facing peer support schemes for tackling bullying. These aim to counteract bystander apathy and encourage peers to take a more proactive stance in challenging bullying. SHARP & COWIE discuss the different forms that peer support can take (such as befriending, mediation, mentoring, and a counselling approach), and the successes as well as the difficulties experienced in implementation.

Both ROSS, in the US, and Rigby, in Australia, have written excellent overviews of the last two decades of research on school bullying. They cover additional areas such as ways of studying bullying; attitudes to bullying; parental and family influences on bullying; and the importance of school climate, organization, and ethos.

The last decade has seen interest in many countries come together with increasing international cooperation on the topic. The book edited by SMITH et al. brings together contributors from 21 countries and the developing world, each providing an overview of the research and intervention carried out in their own country on school bullying.

PETER K. SMITH

See also Aggressive behaviour in the workplace

Bureaucracy

Beetham, David, *Bureaucracy*, Milton Keynes: Open University Press, and Minneapolis: University of Minnesota Press, 1987

Blau, Peter M., *Bureaucracy in Modern Society*, New York: Random House, 1956; 3rd edition with Marshal W. Meyer, 1987

Fredrickson, H.G. and F. Marini, "Bureaucracy and Democracy: Essays in Honor of Dwight Waldo", *Public Administration Review*, 57/3 (1997): 190–220

Gouldner, Alvin W., *Patterns of Industrial Bureaucracy*, Glencoe, Illinois: Free Press, 1954; London: Routledge and Kegan Paul, 1955

Merton, Robert K. *et al.* (editors), *Reader in Bureaucracy*, Glencoe, Illinois: Free Press, 1952

Rourke, Francis E., *Bureaucracy, Politics and Public Policy*, 2nd edition, Boston: Little Brown, 1976; 3rd edition 1984

Shaw, C.K.Y., "Hegel's Theory of Modern Bureaucracy", *American Political Science Review*, 86/2 (1992): 381–89

Weber, Max, "Bureaucracy" in *From Max Weber: Essays in Sociology*, edited and translated by H.H. Gerth and C. Wright Mills, New York: Oxford University Press, 1946; London: Kegan Paul and Trench Trubner, 1948

Wilson, James Q., *Bureaucracy: What Government Agencies Do and Why They Do It*, New York: Basic Books, 1989

Bureaucracy is commonly understood as an epithet for inefficiency and red tape (see BLAU). At the same time, the concept is central to understanding the organization of modern society, government, and business. The engagement with the concept of bureaucracy within social thought is prevalent, and the following texts serve only as a scant introduction to the theoretical basis for the concept of bureaucracy, the expansion and modification of this thesis, and finally, contemporary applications. The texts have been chosen on the basis that they go beyond superficially blaming bureaucracy for the failings of modern society, and engage with both its strengths and weaknesses.

WEBER's writing on bureaucracy and the rationalization of modern life is the seminal text that underpins virtually all subsequent theory and writing about bureaucracy. Weber sees bureaucracy as central to comprehending modern society and Weberian theory serves as a keystone to subsequent considerations of bureaucracy. Gerth and Mills's collection of Weber's work includes a substantial chapter in which the conditions of an ideal-type bureaucracy are outlined. The style and content are, however, complex, and perhaps not the best introduction to bureaucratic concepts. One could gain more from starting with a summary of the theoretical points (such as BEETHAM or Blau) and returning to Weber in examination of the arguments put forward by others.

MERTON et al.'s collection of writings on bureaucracy is a comprehensive aggregation of the writing on the subject prior to 1952. It is still very valuable in terms of illustrating the theoretical underpinnings of almost all contemporary writings on the topic. This edited volume contains excerpts from some of the most influential thinkers (Weber, Simon, Friedrich, Mannheim, and Gouldner) as well as some who are lesser known (or remembered). The collection consists of both empirical and theoretical contributions and is organized into groups of papers addressing topics such as "the structure of bureaucracy", "conflicts of authority", and "field methods for the study of bureaucracy". The comprehensibility obviously depends largely on the original authors but, overall, this reader provides an introduction to many different schools of thought in relation to bureaucracy.

GOULDNER sets out to empirically test Weber's theory of bureaucracy within an industrial setting. He proposes that most previous considerations of bureaucracy relied on documentary or anecdotal evidence. Gouldner's book presents the results of an in-depth case study of a single factory, and is interesting both in terms of the description of setting, methods, and findings, as well as the resulting reflections about the relevance of bureaucratic theory to an understanding of everyday life. The study seeks to uncover the reasons for increasing or decreasing levels of bureaucracy, as well as the problems for which bureaucracy can be seen as a solution. Gouldner provides a comprehensive conclusion in which he clearly sets out the study's working hypotheses, and the way that these are addressed by the data.

Blau's consideration of bureaucracy would be an appropriate place from which to begin to examine this topic. Blau's book effectively serves as a concise introductory text covering basic theoretical premises and going on to consider bureaucratic authority, bureaucracy, and democracy, and the role of bureaucracy in social change in greater detail. Blau successfully presents an overview of the concepts underpinning this increasingly pertinent subject.

Although ROURKE's book falls somewhere between a classic and contemporary selection, I feel that it is worth including within a consideration of writing in this area. Rourke seeks to examine the role and significance of bureaucratic organizations to public policy. Bureaucracy is increasingly the focus of investigations into policy failures. When policy goals are not met, the obvious scapegoat is the organization charged with their attainment. Moreover, the association of bureaucratic organizations with political agents does not abate concern.

Rourke points to responsiveness and effectiveness as the cornerstones upon which bureaucratic policy systems rest, and suggests that such criteria frequently pull in opposite directions. This relatively concise book considers the ways in which bureaucratic organizations influence policy and why some organizations are more influential than others. The analysis is supported by illustrations from US policy that may not interest readers who are unfamiliar with (or uninterested in) such a setting.

Beetham identifies bureaucratic power and efficiency as recurring themes within the literature. He examines the meaning of bureaucracy by considering the relationship between competing perspectives and the possible reasons why different social groups might be interested in bureaucracy. The main body of the text is divided into three sections dealing with different applications of bureaucratic principles, sociological theories of bureaucracy (primarily Weberian and Marxist approaches), and finally the role of bureaucracy within a democratic system.

According to its author, this book's main claim to distinction is that it is "the shortest one to date on the subject". This may be accurate, but it underestimates its value as both an introduction to, and summary of, different considerations of bureaucracy. The book is clear and provides a good bibliography and suggestions for further reading.

WILSON's analysis is based on comparisons of more and less successful examples of three typical bureaucracies: armies, prisons, and schools. Wilson emphasizes the complexity and variation in and between bureaucratic organizations. Additionally, unlike many other writers, he focuses on the way that bureaucracies work behind (or below) the official structural level. In effect, Wilson adds the human element into his consideration of bureaucracy. The book looks at the importance of organizing systems, collective goals, as well as a sense of mission, autonomy, and organizational culture. The choice of illustrations, as well as the fluid style of writing, make this both a relevant and stimulating text.

SHAW's article compares neglected Hegelian bureaucratic theory with Weber's ideal type. He concludes that not only is Hegel's theory of bureaucracy as comprehensive as Weber's on several levels, but that it is also more applicable to modern political reality. For Hegel, bureaucracy is indispensable to the contemporary constitutional state. Shaw's article is important as it provides an alternative interpretation of bureaucracy to that of Weber: one in which a bureaucratic structure need not threaten modern democracy. Familiarity with Weberian concepts of bureaucracy is essential background to this text.

Finally, FREDRICKSON & MARINI present five articles that address the role played by bureaucracy in a modern democracy. This collection provides a stimulating consideration of relevant issues, and is structured as an active academic dialogue. The articles give careful consideration to the complexity of the relationship between bureaucracy and democracy, challenging simplistic attributions of blame for failing policies and institutions on failures of a bureaucratic structure.

KATE CLEGG

Burnout

Golembiewski, Robert T. and Robert F. Munzenrider, *Phases of Burnout: Developments in Concepts and Applications*, New York: Praeger, 1988

Maslach, Christina and Michael P. Leiter, *The Truth about Burnout: How Organizations Cause Personal Stress and What to Do About It*, San Francisco: Jossey Bass, 1997

Schaufeli, Wilmar B., Christina Maslach and Tadeusz Marek (editors), *Professional Burnout: Recent Developments in Theory and Research*, Washington, DC: Taylor and Francis, 1993

Schaufeli, Wilmar and Dirk Enzmann, *The Burnout Companion to Study and Practice: A Critical Analysis*, London and Philadelphia: Taylor and Francis, 1998

Burnout is a contemporary social research construct. Since the 1970s, the definition for burnout has identified three primary components: emotional exhaustion, depersonalization, and diminished personal accomplishment. Two perspectives have emerged over the past three decades. The first view is based on conflicts in interpersonal/social relationships. The second distinguishes burnout as a result of job-specific mismatches with the individual. This is more specifically distinguished as job or occupational burnout.

SCHAUFELI, MASLACH & MAREK is the most extensive historical outline of burnout to date. After the 1990 European Conference of Professional Burnout, 14 authors were asked to write essays outlining their different views of burnout. This conference was the catalyst for the convergence of ideas regarding burnout as a social phenomenon. In the context of collaboration, each author expressed their academic perspectives, which moulded the concept of burnout. The book outlines a succinct history of the development of the concept, including the primary tools of measurement (e.g. Maslach Burnout Inventory and Tedian Measure) and the influential academic models.

SHAUFELI & ENZMANN is the most comprehensive review of burnout in the field. It is written systematically, so that applications or interventions to address burnout are directed by research. A common criticism of many books is that practical application is disconnected from its roots in academic research. This book makes considerable strides in linking practice with the theory and models of burnout.

GOLEMBIEWSKI & MUNZENRIDER looks at burnout from a strict research perspective. The authors outline a model identifying different phases of burnout. The scope of this book is precise, since it outlines the details of the phases of burnout by using statistical justification to substantiate the authors' model. The strength of this book is that the authors take a strict approach to studying the subject. They add to the general understanding of burnout by proposing a micro-analysis, or a step-by-step developmental model. However, there is neither a definite time when burnout is critical to target, nor specific symptoms outlined in the model. Nevertheless, approaching burnout from a developmental approach has merit.

MASLACH & LEITER indicates that causes for burnout can be found by focusing on the social components of the organization and the effects they have on the employee. Although written by academics, this text focuses on six practical ways to address the mismatches between the nature of the job, the organization, and the employee. There is also a broad overview of different themes common to the burnout experience. Their approach to the treatment of burnout, if put in the proper context, might be influential in addressing strategic planning or organizational development issues. However, there is little indication of how the authors propose to do this. The book's main contribution is its emphasis on integrating the two views of burnout in an organizational setting.

SCOTT ALLEN

See also Stress at work

Business cycles

Benhabib, Jess (editor), *Cycles and Chaos in Economic Equilibrium*, Princeton, New Jersey: Princeton University Press, 1992

Dore, Mohammed H.I., *The Macrodynamics of Business Cycles: A Comparative Evolution*, Cambridge, Massachusetts: Blackwell, 1993

Frisch, Ragnar, "Propagation Problems and Impulse Problems in Dynamic Economics" in *Economic Essays in Honour of Gustav Cassel*, edited by K. Koch, London: Allen and Unwin, 1933; reprinted London: Cass, and New York: Kelley, 1967

Hicks, J.R., *A Contribution to the Theory of the Trade Cycle*, Oxford: Oxford University Press, 1950

Kaldor, Nicholas, "A Model of the Trade Cycle", *Economic Journal*, 50 (1940): 78–92

Kalecki, Michal, "A Macrodynamic Theory of Business Cycles", *Econometrica*, 3 (1935): 327–44

Louçã, Francisco, "Intriguing Pendula", *Cambridge Journal of Economics*, forthcoming 2000

Maddison, Angus, *Dynamic Forces in Capitalist Development: A Long Run Comparative View*, Oxford: Oxford University Press, 1991

Mitchell, Wesley Clair, *Business Cycles: The Problem and Its Setting*, New York: National Bureau of Economic Research, 1927

Mullineux, Andy, David Dickinson and Wensheng Peng, *Business Cycles: Theory and Evidence*, Oxford: Blackwell, 1993

Nelson, C. and C. Plosser, "Trends and Random Walks in Macroeconomic Time Series", *Journal of Monetary Economics*, 10 (1982): 139–62

Schumpeter, Joseph A., *Business Cycles: A Theoretical, Historical, and Statistical Analysis of the Capitalist Process*, 2 vols, New York: McGraw Hill, 1939

Slutskii, Eugen, "The Summation of Random Causes as the Source of Cyclical Processes", *Econometrica*, 5 (1937): 105–46

Yule, G.U., "On a Method of Investigating Periodicities in Disturbed Series", *Philosophical Transactions*, 226A (1927): 267–98

YULE's 1927 paper on how to measure business cycles, and in particular on how to detect true causal relations, is certainly not the first important contribution to the field: Yule himself, and many others, had already made significant progress in understanding the persistent fluctuations in macroeconomic variables. Given the impact of this paper, however, the importance of the author in statistical analysis of time series, and the rigour of his discussion of spurious correlation, the paper is taken as a point of departure for this reading list.

On the other hand, 1927 was also a decisive moment for the analyses of cycles. By that time many mathematical economists had dedicated a large part of their efforts to this topic, because the impressive recurrence of periods of depression and expansion was becoming very obvious. The following years, with the world depression of 1929–30 and its dramatic consequences, reminded economists that crises, protectionism, and conflict over colonial resources were still on the agenda and could lead to war. SLUTSKII, working at the Conjuncture Institute in Moscow, and quite isolated from his Western colleagues, provided a second building block for the analysis of cycles, proving that the averaging of random variables could be one of the causes for the appearance of cycles. His paper, as well as Yule's, played a decisive role in the introduction of the probabilistic approach in economics.

FRISCH, the founder of econometrics, was at that time working on a similar problem, and took notice of both Yule's and Slutskii's contributions. His paper was published six years later, and addressed a larger issue: he suggested a mixed system of difference and differential equations in order to represent capital accumulation, preference for liquidity, and investment lags – the dynamics of modern industrial economies – and added some stochastic perturbations in order to generate experimental series closely following the business cycle schedule. In this framework, he reinterpreted Slutskii's results as not disproving the existence of the business cycle but as providing the description of the stimuli to the propagation mechanism to be explained by dynamic economic theory.

For decades this remained the paradigm for the explanation of the business cycle, based on the superimposition of shocks to the deterministic model tending to equilibrium. Yet LOUÇÃ proved that, because Frisch and his colleagues could not at the time formally represent the model of oscillation they had in mind, and just used simple metaphors for it (the rocking horse, the pendulum), they missed the implications of these models. They did not even recognize their nonlinear structure and possible chaotic outcomes, which challenge the conclusions from the simplistic propagation *cum* shocks, or equilibrium and cycle scheme.

MITCHELL also wrote on cycles in 1927, and in fact dedicated most of his scientific career to this topic. He founded the National Bureau of Economic Research (NBER), which was and remains one of the top centres of research on economic conjunctures. Unlike the previous authors, he developed a thorough empirical study and new descriptive methods, and the 1927 book is a compilation of this work.

SCHUMPETER was one of the more influential economists of the first half of the 20th century. He consistently argued for a new vision of the economic process, because he was convinced that the peculiar characteristic of capitalist development was the permanent process of "creative destruction", of generation of innovations challenging the previous capital accumulation. *Business Cycles* is his *magnum opus* and provides a detailed historical account of major economic changes and fluctuations as well as a theoretical discussion of causes of cycles. In particular, Schumpeter distinguished between three types of cycle: (a) the traditional business cycle of seven to 11 years, which he named after Clément Juglar, the French physicist who published one of the first accounts of economic fluctuations in the 1860s; (b) he named a longer cycle of 40 to 60 years the Kondratiev cycle (see entry on Long swings in economic activity) and (c) a shorter oscillation, the Kitchin cycle, of some 40 months. His book is the first thorough discussion of the entrainment of different modes of oscillation in economics.

KALECKI, KALDOR and then HICKS published in the 1930s, 1940s and 1950s several seminal pieces on business cycles. These examples indicate some of their preliminary work and original models representing the mechanics of the "trade cycle". As part of the broad Keynesian movement (indeed, Kalecki even preceded Keynes in major topic of his "general theory", but Hicks was instrumental in the dissolution of Keynes's agenda and in the truce with neoclassical economics), these models reflect the Cambridge approach to economic cycles and the first tentative attempt to encapsulate theories in formal models whose solution should provide both the path to equilibrium and the specific details of the behaviour of the main explanatory variables.

NELSON & PLOSSER's paper represents a recent contribution as part of the general movement known as the real business cycles (RBC) approach. Although in a Frischian tradition, RBC authors presented a much more sophisticated framework for analysis, considering that most macroeconomic series are not stationary fluctuations around a deterministic trend but instead non-stationary stochastic processes. They suggested the decomposition of the series as the sum of a permanent and a cyclical component. Stochastic shocks were considered to both components, and were generally explained as technological innovations impinging on the economic system, with permanent effects.

Another modern approach is represented in the book edited by BENHABIB, which includes a collection of essays on chaotic models of cycles. Some of these just redefine the original assumptions of well-known models in economics, adding nonlinearity, and then proceed to study the emergent chaotic properties. Others discuss empirical evidence and tests of the existence of low-dimensional chaos in economic series. Although the results are inconclusive and not at all coincident, the book illustrates the state of the art in the nonlinear models of cycles in the 1980s and early 1990s.

MADDISON has been, for some time now, one of the researchers on macroeconomic evolution who closely followed Mitchell's concern with empirical data. Considering, rightly, that theories without verification are as pernicious as data without interpretation, Maddison developed a large-scale programme for compilation of relevant information and published historical series which are some of the best available. Furthermore, his book discusses, compares and evaluates some of the alternative theories of cycles.

MULLINEUX *et al.*'s book, as well as DORE's, are general overviews of the field, detailed and useful since they provide both a mathematical treatment of the available models of cycles and a discussion of their theoretical underpinnings. Both use empirical data and "stylized facts" as a guideline for the evaluation of models, and discuss some of the more advanced techniques, solutions and puzzles that dominate the field these days.

FRANCISCO LOUÇÃ

See also Kondratiev cycles, Long swings in economic activity, Real business cycles

Business ethics

De George, Richard T., *Competing with Integrity in International Business*, Oxford and New York: Oxford University Press, 1993

Donaldson, Thomas and Thomas W. Dunfee, "Toward a Unified Conception of Business Ethics: Integrative Social Contracts Theory", *Academy of Management Review*, 19/2 (1994): 252–84

Gray, Rob, Dave Owen and Carol Adams, *Accounting and Accountability: Changes and Challenges in Corporate Social and Environmental Reporting*, London and New York: Prentice Hall, 1996

Jones, Thomas M., "Instrumental Stakeholder Theory: A Synthesis of Ethics and Economics", *Academy of Management Review*, 20/2 (1995): 404–37

Kanungo, Rabindra N. and Manuel Mendonca, *Ethical Dimensions of Leadership*, London and Thousand Oaks, California: Sage, 1996

Nielsen, Richard P., *The Politics of Ethics: Methods for Acting, Learning and Sometimes Fighting with Others in Addressing Ethics Problem in Organizational Life*, Oxford and New York: Oxford University Press, 1996

Paine, Lynn Sharp, "Managing for Organizational Integrity", *Harvard Business Review*, 72/2 (March/April 1994): 106–17

Werhane, Patricia H., *Persons, Rights and Corporations*, Englewood Cliffs, New Jersey: Prentice Hall, 1985

Ethics is the quest for an understanding of what is good or right for human individuals and an evaluation of the kind of action and states of affairs that can foster the "good" and the "right". Business ethics sets these questions within the context of organizations in general and business organizations in particular. In terms of ethical theorizing, business ethics reflect the variety of normative perspectives to be found in pluralistic societies such as rights, responsibilities, duties, interests, and virtues, and much of the business ethics literature addresses the decisions and actions of individual organizational members in these terms. However, the unique perspective of business ethics centres on questions of collective moral agency and on the issues that arise from this in terms of what it might mean to talk about "ethical" organizations. Corporations are moral agents in the sense that they act intentionally, but not all corporate action is redescribable in terms of individual actions. WERHANE develops a view of corporate action as collective "secondary" action: she argues that although "primary" (individual) actions within corporations happen as a result of corporate decision taking and policy making, the corporate "act" is neither redescribable in terms of the aggregate of individual actions nor is it reattributable in every instance to any person or persons. The implication is that, because corporations are moral agents, in the sense that collective "secondary" actions are attributable to their agency, they are morally responsible for their outcomes and thus can be held accountable for them.

"Good" business therefore demands an organizational culture that combines a degree of ethical sensitivity with organizational systems that are effective in handling ethical issues. However, there is a distinction to be made between organizational approaches that codify ethical requirements, and those that attempt to "build ethics in". Compliance with legal and regulatory frameworks will not alter perceptions and behaviours: corporate moral self-governance requires an approach that reaches beyond compliance. PAINE demonstrates the value to organizations of adopting an "integrity" strategy as opposed to a "compliance" strategy. In an organization that competes with integrity ethical values become the frame of reference for choice of direction, the drivers of decision taking, and the unifying force that identifies and strengthens corporate purpose. Paine's article is representative of a business ethics literature that takes an "agent-centred", as opposed to an "act-centred", approach to ethics in business. This perspective emphasizes that if businesses can *be* ethical in a cultural and systemic sense they are more likely to *do* the morally right thing when it comes to business decisions. It also holds the possibility that ethically "good" business decisions are likely to result in "good" business in the sense of value creation and effectiveness.

The notion of responsibility is central to the concept of corporate moral agency. Two questions present themselves: "what is the nature of that responsibility?" and "to whom is the corporation responsible?" Responsibility is first of all social. Society sanctions the operations of corporations, so there is an implicit social contract that requires corporations to fulfil social expectations. DONALDSON & DUNFEE see contractarian theory as providing a source and a justification for organizational ethical obligations that transcend the particularities of company, of industry, and, above all, of culture. Universalistic western ethical theory is of little relevance outside its own context, they argue, whereas contractarian approaches can take into account varieties of institutional and cultural norms and practices. However, the significance, and thus the usefulness, of the contractarian view of responsibility is tempered by the fact that responsibility is not only social. As moral agents corporations are also morally responsible for their actions. Social responsibility is different from, and does not necessarily entail, moral responsibility, so that a full account of corporate responsibility needs to include both "agency" and "contract" perspectives.

The second question, "to whom is the corporation responsible?" has given rise to a variety of arguments which revolve round the extent to which responsibility to stockholders should take precedence over responsibility to stakeholders (employees, customers, suppliers, banks, the community). Companies have a fiduciary duty to stockholders, but this does not imply that their only or even their primary responsibility should be defined in this way. There is an extensive literature on "stakeholder theory", not all of which rates as foundational theory building. Many contributions are descriptive; others take a normative approach. However, an instrumental focus is the most useful in terms of analysing ways in which stakeholder relationships work. JONES advances an instrumental theory of stakeholder management based on trust and cooperation. He contrasts this view of stakeholder relationships with that implied by trans-action cost economics, where "contracting" in the context of asymmetric information generates opportunistic behaviour. There are significant costs associated with reducing or pre-venting opportunism, so firms that develop stakeholder rela-tionships based on mutual trust, respect, cooperative, and even altruistic behaviour will gain a competitive advantage. The value of Jones's contribution is that it builds firm links between stakeholder theory on the one hand and alternative views of the way in which organizational relationships work.

Business has become global and corporate, moral, and social responsibility has to be exercised in crosscultural contexts where legal and regulatory structures are inadequate to provide guidance. In tackling this issue DE GEORGE identifies the need for background institutional frameworks that would regulate the power of multinational corporations to exploit weaker market participants. In the absence of such frameworks, however, guidelines are needed, and De George develops seven "guideline" principles that should govern international busi-ness decisions. Corporate ethicality is a question of "bottom-up" practice as well as "top-down" principles, and here De George's approach exactly mirrors current corporate practice. Personal integrity, moral imagination, and moral courage are required in all business dealings. However, when ethical dilemmas present themselves, organization members need to use a technique of "ethical displacement" – in other words, they need to seek the solution to the problem on a level other than the one on which the problem appears. For example, is it ethical to bribe in a culture where such payments are part of business practice when the payment will ensure a large order? The answer depends on the company policy. Similarly, how should the company formulate its policies? According to the principle of transparency and responsibility to stakeholders. If the bribe appears in the accounts as legitimate business expenditure then the payment can be made, otherwise not. If the company has difficulties in establishing its policy in this respect then it should seek guidance at the next level, within the relevant industry and within national confederations.

This implies that leadership has a central role to play in enabling the realization of organizational responsibilities, and indeed De George makes this point forcefully. The leader-ship of ethical organizations must itself be ethical, however, it must be transformational rather than transactional, altruistic rather than self seeking, and a leadership of service rather than a leadership of power. The significance of KANUNGO & MENDONCA's contribution to the literature on leadership lies in their emphasis on the need for leaders to develop their own spiritual and moral resources so that, in their mode of lead-ership, they demonstrate the values that inform the organiza-tion's ethicality.

Ethical leadership will facilitate, but it will not create respon-sible organizations. Some account is needed of the organiza-tional processes that can generate and maintain corporate responsibility. NIELSEN explores the problems of thinking and acting ethically in large organizations by setting them in the context of the literature on organizational learning, and illu-minating the whole with reference to archetypes drawn from literature and philosophy. His book provides important insights for both theoreticians and practitioners on the dynamics of intra-organizational debates and decisions on normative issues.

Responsibility requires accountability, and for organizations to be accountable to stakeholders there must be effective moni-toring and reporting, not merely of corporate actions, but of the ways in which past experience holds lessons for future deci-sions. The issue of monitoring and reporting has become partic-ularly sensitive due to the growing awareness of the effects of corporate actions on the natural environment. GRAY, OWEN & ADAMS adopt a systems perspective in order to examine the roots of corporate accountability, and review the current state of the theory and practice of corporate social and envi-ronmental accounting and disclosure, as well as the require-ments for its implementation in terms of adequate management information systems and social auditing procedures. Inevitably, perhaps, this implies that conventional accounting practices and bodies should concern themselves to a greater extent with the issue of corporate social reporting, as it is they who have the skills and experience to take its development forward.

JANE COLLIER

Business geography

Birkin, Mark, Graham Clarke, Martin Clarke and Alan Wilson, *Intelligent GIS: Location Decisions and Strategic Planning*, Cambridge: GeoInformation, and New York: Wiley, 1996
Castle, Gilbert H. III (editor), *Profiting from a Geographic Information System*, Fort Collins, Colorado: GIS World, 1993
Clarke, Graham and Moss Madden (editors), *Regional Science in Business*, Berlin: Springer, 2000
GeoInformation International, *GIS for Business: Discovering the Missing Piece in Your Business Strategy*, Cambridge: GeoInformation International 1995
Grimshaw, David, *Bringing Geographical Information Systems into Business*, Harlow, Essex: Longman and New York: Wiley, 1994
Longley, Paul and Graham Clarke (editors), *GIS for Business and Service Planning*, Cambridge: GeoInformation, and New York: Wiley 1995
Pacione, Michael (editor), *Applied Geography*, London, Routledge, 1999

Within human geography there has been a major resurgence in the question of relevance and a renewed interest in applying different methodologies to business problems. This resurgence has been driven to a great extent by the emergence of desktop geographical information systems (GIS). GIS vendors developed largely outside academic geography departments and have been very influential in increasing the levels of awareness of what GIS packages can do for a range of different types of business environment. However, outside the GIS community there is little that is directly concerned with business applications.

CASTLE provides a very good introduction to GIS and its capabilities within the US business world. Having defined what GIS is, the book examines the contribution of GIS in areas as diverse as banking, insurance, real estate, retailing, manufacturing, healthcare, transport, and telecommunications. The detailed steps involved in many of these applications are, however, similar: entering customer data into a computer database (geocoding), mapping the addresses of these customers; analysing how far customers travel (thus defining buffers or zones of influence); identifying the characteristics of these travel-defined zones (that is, overlaying the population disaggregated by age, social class, and so forth); and then looking for similar catchment areas elsewhere for new developments (a process called "buffer and overlay"). Following the discussion of the various applications, there is a discussion of data sources and possible future developments.

GRIMSHAW's book is a useful addition to that of Castle. Although he, too, defines and explains the principles of GIS, he recognizes the importance of managing information within large organizations. He describes the "organizational challenge" of how to introduce this new form of management system and how to implement a successful project within GIS. This is followed by many case studies that explore the use of GIS in business in the US and Europe. He also recognizes the different levels of use that GIS has occupied, from operational levels (most likely to involve the computerization of previously manual tasks) to more tactical and strategic levels.

The GEOINFORMATION INTERNATIONAL text is a collection of short articles exploring the use of GIS in a wide variety of business environments. Although some of these are written by vendors (and are therefore very much glossy marketing articles), the majority are written by business users of GIS. The collection is therefore useful in the sense that it is possible to glean some of the operational issues of introducing GIS and the business benefits of so doing. In addition to the applications described, there are interesting sections relating to legal issues, and to the use of the Internet for GIS services.

LONGLEY & CLARKE provide a more UK-focused examination of GIS for business. Part one discusses data sources and the problems of using Census of Population data in business applications. Part two concentrates on geodemographics, which are especially important to many business organizations. Geodemographics are systems designed to label geographical areas according to the characteristics of the majority of the population that resides in those areas. The labels used thus cover the range from "very affluent" (typified by green, leafy suburbs) to "very poor" (typified in the UK by inner-city locations). Such labels give organizations a simple and immediate portrait of the nature of different locations (to be used for target marketing or, in retailing, for new store locations). The latest form of geodemographics – those concerned with lifestyles – are also discussed. Part three looks at various applications of both proprietary systems and customized systems. The advantages and disadvantages of each are elaborated in some detail.

A number of authors have become more critical of the use of GIS for business. BIRKIN *et al.* argue that GIS are more appropriate for operational than for strategic or tactical applications, and that analysis of a more sophisticated kind is required in such systems. They argue for the marriage of GIS to spatial modelling techniques, which have long been used (often in isolation) as tools for location analysis. In particular, they explore the relevance and benefits of spatial interaction modelling in a wide range of business environments. They build on their own consultancy company, called GMAP, which by late 1996 employed well over 100 geography graduates and enjoyed a turnover of some $8 million, with application areas including retailing, financial services, the car industry, healthcare, and the water industry.

Outside the literature directly concerned with GIS, business applications are much harder to find (although there are some links to the literature on operational research). However, PACIONE has recently put together a very interesting collection of papers on applied geography. Although many chapters cover aspects of the physical environment, there are none the less some papers that describe very interesting applications of human geography. Readers interested in business geography will generally find useful background material in the chapters on retailing, healthcare, transport, and rural/agriculture (and the up-to-date bibliographies will also be useful).

The principal aim of CLARKE & MADDEN is to review the usefulness and appropriateness of a range of regional science methodologies for applied analysis. Their book considers applications in both business (private sector) and government (public sector) research. Regional science is a discipline that unites economists, geographers, and other social scientists who deal with the spatial outcomes of particular theories. It has to be said that many of the methodologies of regional science are complex and have rarely been used in real-world business applications. The aim of this book is to show that these methodologies can be of interest to non-academic organizations. Each contribution follows a set pattern: summary of methods/models; client's requirements; data issues; development of methods and models to meet the client's requirements and the data available; and examples of results and policy simulations.

GRAHAM CLARKE

See also Geographical information systems

Business plans

Barrow, Colin, Paul Barrow and Robert Brown, *The Business Plan Workbook*, 3rd edition, London: Kogan Page, 1998

Finch, Brian, *30 Minutes . . . To Write a Business Plan*, London: Kogan Page, 1997

Johnson, Ron, *The 24 Hour Business Plan: A Step-by-step Guide to Producing a Tailor-made Business Plan in 24 Working Hours*, revised edition, London: Century, 1997

Maitland, Iain, *Successful Business Plans in a Week*, 2nd edition, London: Hodder and Stoughton, 1998

Record, Matthew, *Preparing a Business Plan*, 2nd edition, Plymouth: How To Books, 1997

Stutely, Richard, *The Definitive Business Plan*, London: Financial Times Prentice Hall, 1999

West, Alan, *A Business Plan: Build a Great Plan for the Growing Business*, 3rd edition, London: Financial Times Management, 1998

A business plan is a tool for helping to make the correct decisions today on the basis of what might happen in the future. Furthermore, it is a communication tool for influencing key people such as financiers, prospective business partners, and staff. Of the many books available on business planning, the following have been selected to illustrate the variety available. In practice, the appropriate choice of book will depend on the reader's previous business experience, needs, and timeframe.

FINCH is a pocket book that provides the reader with a quick idea of what a business plan encompasses. It is appropriate for those with little prior business experience or as a first read while developing an initial business idea. Despite being a pocket book it is reasonably comprehensive and covers most important areas. It is jargon free and provides much practical advice, yet on its own would be insufficiently sophisticated to produce more than the most basic of business plans.

MAITLAND provides a step-by-step guide to developing a business plan with a different set of tasks being assigned to different days of the week. Although more detailed than the pocket book above it is also appropriate for those with little prior business experience or as a first read. "Presenting the business plan" is an important area covered in addition to areas covered by the pocket book. Despite being easy to read its style can be slightly wordy and it lacks the excitement contained in some of the other books.

JOHNSON, despite its title, is far more detailed than the first two books. It is well structured, taking the reader through the major areas step by step. The examples, tables to fill in, and checklists are very useful. Furthermore, a business plan grid is included for the reader to copy and complete. The implications of the Internet are also considered in a very basic manner. Depth in certain areas, however, seems to have been sacrificed in order to maintain the book's fluidity. Its presentation and layout are attractive and well thought out.

RECORD is part of the "How To" series. It begins by explaining the reasons for writing a business plan and takes the reader through to "presenting your plan" and "running your business to plan". The other areas covered are "your business idea", "the market", "your marketing plan", "your operational plan", "your sales forecast", "your financial analysis", and "your appendices". Hence all the important areas are covered and a sample business plan is included at the end. Each chapter contains a checklist, (brief) case studies, and points for discussion. At the end of the book there are handy sections containing useful addresses and further reading. Overall the book is practical and informative yet slightly dull in style and presentation.

BARROW, BARROW & BROWN is based on the enterprise programme at Cranfield School of Management. The workbook contains 20 assignments, which, once completed, should ensure that readers have the information they need to write and present a successful business plan. It shows how subjects such as marketing, finance, and law relate to the

formulation of a good business plan. The book is separated into seven sections: history and position to date, market research, competitive business strategy, operations, forecasting results, business controls, writing up and presenting your business plan. It is littered with questions and useful examples from actual business plans to ensure that the reader covers all the important areas. It is extremely practical and provides useful contact addresses (for UK businesses) as well as suggesting suitable further reading in each section.

WEST is aimed at small-to-medium sized enterprises already operating, rather than startups. It attempts to help the reader make planning integral to the organization so that it becomes a continuous monitoring and control process. Implementation is heavily emphasized, as is building up an understanding of the business through checklists and charts. Case-study material is also used. The book covers current company position; building an information system; short-term, corrective action; strategic drivers in the medium and long term; developing strategy; implementing and monitoring the new plan.

STUTELY has been developed for "competent business people – executives and entrepreneurs". The author achieves an extremely high level of acuity. It manages to be pragmatically detailed yet readable for the target audience. It is attractively presented and contains thought-provoking anecdotes throughout. Handy "fast track" boxes can be found in each chapter giving the reader the ability rapidly to construct a business plan if required. Despite lacking case-study material, coverage is comprehensive. It contains relevant information on how to perform the analysis, strategic thought, and planning, as well as outlining the business planning process itself.

HAMEL SHAH

Business research methods

Bryman, Alan, *Quantity and Quality in Social Research*, London and Boston: Unwin Hyman, 1988

Cooper, Donald R. and C. William Emory, *Business Research Methods*, 5th edition, Chicago: Irwin, 1995

Denzin, Norman K., *The Research Act: A Theoretical Introduction to Sociological Methods*, 3rd edition, Englewood Cliffs, New Jersey: Prentice Hall, 1989

Gay, L.R. and P.L. Diehl, *Research Methods for Business and Management*, New York: Macmillan, and Oxford: Maxwell Macmillan International, 1992

Hussey, Jill and Roger Hussey, *Business Research: A Practical Guide for Undergraduate and Postgraduate Students*, London: Macmillan, 1997

Remenyi, Dan, Brian Williams, Arthur Money and Ethné Swartz, *Doing Research in Business and Management: An Introduction to Process and Method*, London and Thousand Oaks, California: Sage, 1998

Saunders, Mark N.K., Philip Lewis and Adrian Thornhill, *Research Methods for Business Students*, London: Pitman, 1997

Sekaran, Uma, *Research Methods for Business: A Skill Building Approach*, 2nd edition, New York: Wiley, 1992

Simon, Alan, Amrik Sohal and Alan Brown, "Generative and Case Study Research in Quality Management", *International Journal of Quality & Reliability Management*, 13/1 (1996): 32–42

Yin, Robert K., *Case Study Research: Design and Methods*, 2nd edition, London and Thousand Oaks, California: Sage, 1994

Zikmund, William G., *Business Research Methods*, 4th edition, Fort Worth, Texas: Dryden Press, 1994

Towards the end of the 19th century, the business environment began to change and develop rapidly. Mass-production factories were being established on a large scale, competition increased, and businesses moved from being largely family concerns to professionally managed organizations. In order to understand how to run businesses more effectively in the light of these changes, research into business practices began to be undertaken.

Business is an amalgam of art, pure science, and social science, so a variety of research methodologies have been used to analyse and understand it. The two main streams of research methods that emerged were quantitative and qualitative. BRYMAN's discussion on the "quantitative versus qualitative research methods" debate is comprehensive and objective. The discussion is not aimed solely at business researchers, but it is nonetheless very useful in illustrating why both methodologies are important. Bryman concludes by proposing that quantitative and qualitative research methods should be combined to achieve the fullest understanding of the phenomenon/problem under investigation; he states (p.127):

> [t]he rather partisan, either/or tenor of the debate about quantitative and qualitative research may appear somewhat bizarre to an outsider, for whom the obvious way forward is likely to be fusion of the two approaches so that their respective strengths might be reaped.

DENZIN, while addressing social sciences in a broad context, presents an in-depth look into the theoretical underpinnings of research. His work espouses a view that research is a sociological enterprise that is based on three interconnected, inseparable elements: theory, research, and substantive interest. Denzin also emphasizes the need for the researcher to be methodologically imaginative by using multiple data collection methods/procedures (referred to, by Denzin, as triangulation) in order to gain the broadest possible view of the area being studied. Reading this text will lead to a thorough understanding of the research act.

The SEKARAN text is an introduction to business research, using examples, diagrams, and graphs to illustrate and clarify points. The highlight of this book is the thorough, quite meticulous, yet accessible discussion of the research process itself. Sekaran also explains measurement of variables, sampling, data collection/interpretation techniques, and the writing of the research report. It should be noted, however, that this text does not undertake more than a very basic discussion of statistical methods. ZIKMUND covers research methods, statistics, data management, and report writing for business students. Technical information is interspersed with numerous examples, samples, tables, schematics, and case studies, making it easier

to understand the ideas presented. Although there are occasional shortfalls in the depth of information, this is a useful treatise on business research.

COOPER & EMORY present a systematic and interesting discussion of business research methods for those commencing research. The text is divided into four parts: introduction to business research; the design of the research; the sources and collection of data; and analysis and presentation of data. Although enlivened by memorable, topic-related scenarios at the start of every chapter, it covers much of the same ground, in a similar format and length as ZIKMUND and SEKARAN. GAY & DIEHL is another work covering the basics of conducting business research. The tone and approach of this book is a little more serious than Cooper & Emory's text however. The explanations are very methodical and well organized.

SAUNDERS, LEWIS & THORNHILL and HUSSEY & HUSSEY's texts are written specifically for undergraduate and postgraduate students undertaking business research. Therefore, although similar topics to other business research texts are covered, they also include practical advice on issues that arise while undertaking research. They may be likened to manuals on business research. REMENYI *et al.* is a text/manual intended for postgraduate students. Despite covering similar territory to Saunders, Lewis & Thornhill and Hussey & Hussey, it delves deeply into the theoretical underpinnings of the various aspects of the research process, enabling a deeper understanding of the issues involved.

YIN's text is not only a defence of the case study as a research strategy, but also a guide to undertaking effective case studies. The variations, rationales, and approaches to case-study-based research designs are discussed at length. As a point of interest, each chapter includes famous examples of case studies that illustrate effectively the use of this method in research. This is not written solely for business researchers, but it is, nevertheless, a worthwhile book for those intending to use this research strategy.

SIMON, SOHAL & BROWN's article is significant for its discussion of the generative research design. This three-phase approach to business research combines both quantitative and qualitative data collection techniques (thus enabling triangulation) while allowing sufficient flexibility for the researcher to choose which techniques are most appropriate for the topic at hand. Another major benefit of the generative research design is that the main research themes are generated from the target population itself.

The references mentioned above show that there is no one correct way to undertake business research. There are, however, ways to make the research more reliable and valid. The methods selected are contingent upon the nature of the business research being conducted and where possible both quantitative and qualitative techniques should be used to collect the data. Most of the texts and authors mentioned in this list have some experience in undertaking research and their writings have flowed from this. While the above list is not exhaustive, it certainly is comprehensive, covering the major controversies, issues, and techniques associated with business research methods.

ALAN SIMON AND VANYA KUMAR

Business strategy

Faulkner, David and Cliff Bowman, *The Essence of Competitive Strategy*, New York and London: Prentice Hall, 1995

Grant, Robert M., *Contemporary Strategy Analysis: Concepts, Techniques, Applications*, 3rd edition, Oxford and Malden, Massachusetts: Blackwell, 1998

Hamel, Gary and C.K. Prahalad, *Competing for the Future*, Boston: Harvard Business School Press, 1994

Mintzberg, Henry and James Brian Quinn, *The Strategy Process*, 2nd edition, Englewood Cliffs, New Jersey and London: Prentice Hall, 1991; 3rd edition 1996

Mintzberg, Henry, *The Rise and Fall of Strategic Planning: Reconceiving Roles for Planning, Plans, Planners*, New York: Free Press, and London: Prentice Hall, 1994

Mintzberg, Henry, Bruce Ahlstrand and Joseph Lampel, *Strategy Safari: A Guided Tour through the Wilds of Strategic Management*, New York and London: Prentice Hall, 1998

Ohmae, Kenichi, *The Mind of the Strategist*, New York and London: McGraw Hill, 1982

Porter, Michael E., *On Competition*, Boston: Harvard Business School Press, 1998

Schwartz, Peter, *The Art of the Long View*, New York: Doubleday, 1991; London: Century, 1992

A firm favourite with lecturers and consultants alike, GRANT's concise and practical guide to the theory and practice of strategy analysis gives a thorough grounding in all the key areas of business strategy. Starting right at the beginning with the concept of strategy, Grant covers such staples as industry analysis, competitive advantage, and corporate level strategy. He does include topics such as strategy-as-process and the resource-based theory of the firm, but the analytical nature of the book means that it is weighted towards the external, market-orientated school of strategy. Grant's great strengths are his practical approach and his concern to keep the book up to date with new developments in strategic thinking. The third edition is packed with illuminating examples from Madonna to Shell, Disney to the African National Congress, and includes a closing chapter that seeks to identify emerging trends in strategy in both business and academia.

MINTZBERG & QUINN take a different approach in their wide-ranging text by introducing a series of original articles by themselves and other leading writers. "The Strategy Process" is organized into three sections covering the concept of strategy, the impact organizations have on strategy, and the context in which strategies are developed and implemented. If there is a single message to be drawn from the collection it is that there is no one best way to create strategy and no one best form of organization. While Porter and other market-based strategy writers do get an airing, they are far from dominant with the editors selecting a range of eclectic, and occasionally contradictory, articles. The "human" side of strategy formation and implementation, by its nature resistant to codification (and so often ignored), receives worthy attention, as does the actual process of strategy development – a theme that Mintzberg first brought to prominence in the 1980s. A useful addition, too, is

the inclusion of case studies at the end of each section on which to apply the theories proposed.

MINTZBERG, AHLSTRAND & LAMPEL embark on a whirlwind tour of almost every major theory of business strategy that has ever been developed. Organised into ten "schools of thought" the authors cover everything from strategy as a position in the market place to strategy as a process of negotiation. By putting the theories into their historical context the authors draw a contrast between the older, more prescriptive theories, which were based on economics or planning, and the newer, descriptive theories that tend to be founded on the culture of organizations and the process of strategy development. The book makes a welcome break from the market-based/resource-based dichotomy of much strategy writing and opens up the strategist's eyes to the equally important disciplines of psychology and sociology.

Ever since the publication of his groundbreaking article "How Competitive Forces Shape Strategy" in 1979, PORTER has dominated strategy writing. Credited with bridging the worlds of business and economics, he has revolutionized the way companies analyse the markets they compete in through such tools as the five forces framework and the value chain. A key proponent of the market-based view of strategy, he has written prolifically on competitive strategy, the importance of location in competition, and, more recently, on the use of competition theory to solve problems in society as a whole. It is a sign of his influence and longevity that Porter has attracted a number of critics over the years (not least from the resource-based school of strategy) but his work has stood the test of time and is a fundamental component of any course on strategy. "On Competition" is a collection of his seminal articles and provides an excellent introduction to his work.

HAMEL & PRAHALAD first came to prominence in 1990 when they introduced the concept of core competencies. As proponents of a theory coming from the resource-based school of strategy, they were the first to seriously challenge the market-based orthodoxy of Porter that been dominant during the 1980s. Using the core competence framework they exhort business leaders to develop an independent view of the future and to use the competencies a company already has (or can build) to compete by changing "the rules of the game" as opposed to just following the herd by benchmarking the current competition. Competing to shape the future and to establish competence leadership then becomes more important to a firm's strategy than simply analysing today's competitive environment. The success of the core competence creed has been in its recognition that where product markets are changing rapidly a firm's strategy needs to be rooted in something more substantial than its position in a transient market place. Widespread acceptance of the core competence framework and their popularity amongst both business leaders and academics have made Hamel and Prahalad the dominant force in strategic thinking in the 1990s.

FAULKNER & BOWMAN, in the space of just 131 pages, cover the key concepts of competitive strategy and introduce several new concepts of their own. Of key interest is their model for looking at competitive markets in terms of customer and producer matrices. This framework allows the dynamic element of competition to be assessed – an aspect often missing from writings on competitive strategy – and identifies gaps in the producer's core competencies that need to be filled. By extending Ansoff's work on new product/new market development the authors then show how the options open to the producer to close the core competence gap (internal development, alliances, or acquisition) can be viewed as a "risk cube". They close by suggesting how a company might pursue each of these options. A valuable book (that deserves wider recognition), Faulkner and Bowman should be read for the fresh theoretical insights it gives into the world of competitive strategy.

SCHWARTZ's book on scenario planning has its origins in the successful navigation of Royal Dutch/Shell through the oil crises of the 1970s and Schwartz's own work as a futurist. Following Shell's success, scenario planning has become a key tool in the strategy development and decision making processes of many companies around the world. As Schwartz stresses, scenario planning does not enable you to predict the future but is used to generate a range of possible futures against which potential strategies and decisions can be tested. Although largely a practical guide on how to carry out scenario planning, the insights and case histories that Schwartz interweaves throughout the text, and the increasing importance of scenario planning to business, makes this book a worthwhile read for any student of strategy.

As relevant now as when the original version was first published in Japan in 1975, OHMAE's insightful text has become a strategy classic. His central thesis is that "successful business strategies result not from rigorous analysis but from a particular state of mind". To this end he draws on his experience as a strategy consultant to many of the world's most successful companies to describe a range of tools and techniques that can be used to generate creative strategic solutions for even the worst cases of competitive stalemate. Always practical, Ohmae offers fresh ways to look at existing business problems and illustrates his ideas with case histories drawn from Japan and elsewhere. Many of these ideas can be seen as precursors of later, better popularized, theories and, although Ohmae is often seen as a market-orientated strategist, his chapters on "Focusing on Key Factors" and "Exploiting Strategic Degrees of Freedom" have much in common with the (subsequent) core competence school of strategic thinking.

MINTZBERG has long been a critic of the notion of "strategic planning" arguing that planning concerns analysis whereas strategy should be about the very different process of synthesis. In charting the rise and fall of strategic planning he demonstrates how most strategy is actually "emergent" rather than deliberate or intended and that the process of strategic planning is itself often harmful to an organization. Full of historical evidence, this key text can almost be taken as a study into how a management theory can gain common acceptance and be put into practice across the commercial world only to be discredited a decade or two later. A powerful lesson for students of strategy everywhere.

MATT BAIRD

C

Cabinet

Blondel, Jean and Ferdinand Müller-Rommel (editors), *Cabinets in Western Europe*, 2nd edition, Basingstoke: Macmillan, and New York: St Martin's Press, 1997

Burch, Martin and Ian Holliday, *The British Cabinet System*, London and New York: Prentice Hall, 1996

Hennessy, Peter, *Cabinet*, Oxford and New York: Blackwell, 1986

Herman, Valentine and James E. Alt (editors), *Cabinet Studies: A Reader*, London: Macmillan, and New York: St Martin's Press, 1975

James, Simon, *British Cabinet Government*, 2nd edition, London and New York: Routledge, 1999

Jennings, Ivor, *Cabinet Government*, 3rd edition, London and New York: Cambridge University Press, 1969

Mackintosh, John P., *The British Cabinet*, 3rd edition, London: Stevens, 1977

Madgwick, P.J., *British Government: The Central Executive Territory*, Hemel Hempstead, Hertfordshire: Philip Allan, 1991

Rhodes, R.A.W. and Patrick Dunleavy, *Prime Minister, Cabinet, and Core Executive*, Basingstoke: Macmillan, and New York: St Martin's Press, 1995

Walker, Patrick Gordon, *The Cabinet*, revised edition, London: Heinemann, 1972

Texts on the Cabinet have proliferated during the last two decades, partly due to the intensification of a long-standing debate concerning the alleged trend towards "prime ministerial government" and the consequent demise of Cabinet government. Margaret Thatcher's style of leadership, and her lengthy tenure, undeniably served to fuel this debate, and provided the context for a plethora of new books on the Cabinet.

What has also prompted the recent spate of literature in this field is the concomitant development of a rather different perspective, which emphasizes the countervailing trend towards fragmentation and greater complexity within the "core executive", of which the Cabinet is but one element. This more contemporary approach focuses not on the power of the Prime Minister or the Cabinet, but on the constraints and conflicts that are characteristic of modern government and policy making.

Such a perspective is far removed from the decidedly historico-constitutional approach of JENNINGS. He provided the first major study of the Cabinet, and while it has subsequently been bestowed with such epithets as "seminal" and "classic", it is now mainly of historical interest. Indeed, the bulk of his analysis is located in 19th- and early 20th-century developments and events, as evinced by the copious examples and anecdotes involving Queen Victoria, George V, William Gladstone, and Stanley Baldwin. His mastery of empirical detail cannot be disputed, but the overriding emphasis on traditional constitutional principles and history effectively limit the contemporary salience of this text

Also widely hailed as a classic, but again somewhat dated, is the lengthy text by MACKINTOSH. He too provides a rich and detailed historical account of the Cabinet, in this case up until 1945, but then provides only an overview of postwar developments. Crucial topics such as the role of Cabinet committees, individual and collective responsibility, and the power of the Prime Minister *vis-à-vis* ministerial colleagues, are only addressed in a cursory manner, although there is a useful chapter on the influence of the governing party's backbenchers. It is disappointing, though, that a book of over 600 pages should end with a conclusion of less than four.

A much more contemporary and comprehensive overview is provided by MADGWICK, who draws upon the relatively recent tranche of ministerial diaries and autobiographies to paint a highly illuminating picture of the modern Cabinet. He highlights the increased role of Cabinet committees since 1945, which is attributable primarily to the increased volume and complexity of government business. These Cabinet committees also reflect a paradox at the heart of British government, namely the dialectic between greater centralization and increasing fragmentation within the core executive. This, in turn, can be cited as evidence both for and against the Prime Ministerial government thesis, which has been commonly expounded since the 1960s.

The collection of essays in RHODES & DUNLEAVY illustrate the extent to which the modern Cabinet can only be adequately comprehended in the context of what is now widely known as the core executive. As such, there is careful consideration not merely of the Cabinet and its plethora of committees, but also on the Prime Minister, Cabinet Office, the relationships within and between government departments, and the dynamics of policy making in contemporary British government. Focusing primarily on events and developments during the 1980s and 1990s, a number of the essays provide excellent empirical case studies to illustrate the theoretical and conceptual approaches. Particularly informative is the study of the fateful decision to join the exchange rate mechanism, for this not only illustrates the interaction between institutions and individuals within the core executive, but also how "policy disasters" can occur.

Also providing a judicious combination of conceptual analysis and empirical case studies are BURCH & HOLLIDAY. Their sophisticated account pays particular attention to the manner in which government business and public policy are processed within the Cabinet system, along with the contribution of various institutional and policy networks. There is a highly informative account of the budgetary process and the manner in which public expenditure is determined, along with 14 case studies. These include the 1976 IMF crisis, the Falklands invasion, the poll tax, civil service reform, National Health Service reform, and the 1992 coal mine closures. All of the case studies trace the trajectory of the policy in question from entry into the Cabinet system through to "exit", thereby highlighting the interplay between individuals, institutional actors, and circumstances whose interaction shapes public policy in Britain.

A former journalist covering Whitehall for *The Times*, HENNESSY provides an erratic and somewhat idiosyncratic examination of the Cabinet. Some chapters provide a wonderful insight into this key institution of British government, particularly those analysing "the Cabinet machine" and the "conviction Cabinets" of the first two Thatcher governments. His journalistic background ensures that there is a wealth of "insider" material and illustrative anecdotes not usually available to more conventional academic writers. Yet the chapter on postwar Cabinets up to 1979 is often extremely dense, and the excessive number of footnotes and references suggests that he is trying unnecessarily hard to prove his scholarly credentials. As such, he produces a text that is scintillating in parts, turgid in others, and therefore lacks overall coherence or consistency.

WALKER's semi-autobiographical book, drawing on his own observations as a Cabinet minister in the Attlee and Wilson governments, provides a basic introductory overview and offers some useful insights, but is obviously dated. Much the same can be said of the essays garnered by HERMAN & ALT, although a few are of interest by virtue of having been written by former Cabinet ministers themselves.

The collection of essays in BLONDEL & MÜLLER-ROMMEL is one of the few comparative texts on this topic, exploring the organization and operation of Cabinets in 13 West European countries. With each of the chapters adopting the same format, namely outlining the origins and constitutional context of the Cabinet, its structure and composition, relationship with the legislature, and the decision-making process, the book reveals both the similarities and the contrasts between the Cabinets of Western Europe.

One of the most lucid and informative accounts is provided by JAMES. Making judicious use of Ministerial memoirs and published recollections of other Whitehall "insiders", he explains the manner in which various aspects of the Cabinet have developed and changed since 1945. It becomes clear that the role and character of the Cabinet as a collective decision-making body have altered significantly, as the increasing volume and complexity of government business has resulted in the greater delegation of policy formulation to a plethora

of committees and bilateral negotiations. This "government overload" has also reinforced the trend towards departmentalism, with ministers becoming immersed in the work of their own particular departments. One consequence of such fragmentation is that the Prime Minister's power is simultaneously enhanced and undermined; they have greater scope for providing strategic leadership and co-ordination while their ministerial colleagues are preoccupied with departmental policies, yet at the same time, they are more reliant on the expertise and cooperation of their ministers. If, however, the Prime Minister turns to outside advisers in order to reduce this dependency, then the result tends to be increasing isolation and suspicion from their Cabinet colleagues, thereby further weakening the Cabinet as a whole. This then increases the likelihood of policy conflicts and failures, and ultimately threatens the political survival of the government itself.

PETER DOREY

See also Prime Minister

Cambridge controversy

Ahmad, Syed, *Capital in Economic Theory: Neo-classical, Cambridge, and Chaos*, Aldershot, Hampshire: Elgar, 1991

Bliss, C.J., *Capital Theory and the Distribution of Income*, Amsterdam: North Holland, and New York: Elsevier, 1975

Burmeister, Edwin, *Capital Theory and Dynamics*, Cambridge and New York: Cambridge University Press, 1980

Eatwell, John, Murray Milgate and Peter Newman (editors), *The New Palgrave: Capital Theory*, London: Macmillan, 1990

Garegnani, P., "Heterogeneous Capital, the Production Function and the Theory of Distribution", *Review of Economic Studies*, 37 (1970): 407–36

Harcourt, G.C. and N.F. Laing (editors), *Capital and Growth: Selected Readings*, Harmondsworth: Penguin, 1971

Harcourt, G.C., *Some Cambridge Controversies in the Theory of Capital*, Cambridge: Cambridge University Press, 1972

Kurz, Heinz D. and Neri Salvadori, *Theory of Production: A Long-Period Analysis*, Cambridge and New York: Cambridge University Press, 1995

Quarterly Journal of Economics, special issue, 80 (1966): 503–83

Robinson, J.V., "The Production Function and the Theory of Capital", *Review of Economic Studies*, 21 (1953): 81–106

The controversy was triggered by ROBINSON (Cambridge, UK). She attacked the conventional value measure of heterogeneous capital goods for representing the "quantity of capital" in the aggregate production function. That quantity, she argued, cannot be ascertained independently of relative prices, which in turn depend on the rate of profit. To conceive of the latter in terms of the marginal product of "capital" involves arguing in a circle. Joan Robinson illustrated her argument, and the possibility of reswitching, in terms of "productivity curves", which, however, did not become a widely used tool.

AHMAD provides a useful overall account of the controversy. He starts from Joan Robinson's criticism of the aggregate production function and the concept of capital used in it. A good deal of attention is devoted to the phenomena of reswitching and capital reversing and other so-called "paradoxes" in the theory of capital. There is also a brief introduction to chaotic dynamics.

HARCOURT's book is based on his highly influential survey article published three years earlier in the *Journal of Economic Literature*. He also gave the controversy its name, which refers to Cambridge University (UK) on one side and Cambridge, Massachusetts (US), where Harvard and MIT are located, on the other. The book contains a detailed account of the early rounds of the controversy, focusing attention on the problem of the measurement of capital raised by Joan Robinson, the reswitching of techniques, the possibility of reverse capital deepening, Solow's concept of the social rate of return and Pasinetti's criticism of it, and Kaldor's observation that in neoclassical theory it is impossible to distinguish between a movement along a production function and a shift of the function.

BLISS argues that the criticism put forward against neoclassical long-period theory cannot be refuted. This does not mean, however, that the scarcity approach to the theory of value and distribution has been shown to be untenable, it only shows that a particular variant of it cannot be sustained. The criticism is said not to apply to the more sophisticated versions of that approach – that is, intertemporal and temporary equilibrium theory. Bliss is not impressed by perfect foresight intertemporal models, but he is nevertheless of the opinion that the general equilibrium models are both useful and logically impeccable.

BURMEISTER looks at the capital controversy from the point of view of dynamic economic theory. He admits that reswitching and reverse capital deepening cannot be excluded *a priori*, but he expresses the belief that empirically these possibilities are not that important. He feels justified to rule out these possibilities in terms of sufficiently bold assumptions concerning the technical alternatives available to cost-minimizing producers and speaks of a "regular economy" if it displays the usual properties of neoclassical long-period models. In particular, he thus assumes that the capital-labour ratio and the rate of profit-wage ratio are inversely related.

The volume edited by EATWELL, MILGATE & NEWMAN contains a reprint of those entries in *The New Palgrave: A Dictionary of Economics*, edited by the same people, devoted to the theory of capital, plus a long essay by Piero Garegnani on "Quantity of capital". The latter deals with the problem of capital in major neoclassical authors concerned with establishing a sound long-period theory of income distribution, most notably W.S. Jevons, L. Walras, E. von Böhm-Bawerk, A. Marshall, K. Wicksell, and J.B. Clark.

Amongst the contributions to the debate, GAREGNANI's paper stands out as a particularly insightful one. He shows that the difference between the classical theories on the one hand and the neoclassical theories on the other is essentially a difference in the underlying views of the problem of distribution. Whereas the classical economists treated the distributive variables asymmetrically, taking the real wage rate as given

(or independently variable) and determining the rate of profit in terms of the remaining "surplus product", the marginalist authors attempted to treat both wages and the rate of profit in terms of supply and demand of the respective "factors of production", labour, and "capital".

HARCOURT & LAING contains a set of some of the most prominent earlier contributions to the controversy, including papers and excerpts from books by Piero Garegnani, Luigi Pasinetti, Joan Robinson, Paul Samuelson, Robert Solow, and Piero Sraffa. The editors' introduction provides a summary account of the controversy, with Harcourt advocating the position of the critics of neoclassical theory and Laing that of its followers.

KURZ & SALVADORI provide a detailed account of the classical approach to the theory of value and distribution, as it was revived by Piero Sraffa and as it is implied also, for example, in John von Neumann's growth model. The analytical work is complemented by substantial discussions of the historical geneses of the theories dealt with and the concepts used. Chapter 14 is concerned with the problem of capital in neoclassical theories and presents a modern treatment of the controversy.

The 1966 special issue of the QUARTERLY JOURNAL OF ECONOMICS was dedicated to a discussion of the possibility of the reswitching of techniques and the implications of this finding for economic theory. In a paper published one year earlier, D. Levhari had put forward a nonswitching theorem, which was proved false by several of the contributors. We speak of "reswitching" if a technique, or system of production, is cost minimizing at two disconnected ranges of the rate of profit and not so in between these ranges. The conventional neoclassical idea that alternative techniques can be monotonically ordered in terms of capital intensity (or "degree of mechanization") with the rate of interest is not generally true. The implication of this is that the "demand function" of capital need not be monotonically decreasing with the interest rate.

HEINZ D. KURZ AND NERI SALVADORI

See also Capital theory controversy

Cambridge School

Groenewegen, Peter, *A Soaring Eagle: Alfred Marshall, 1842–1924*, Aldershot, Hampshire: Elgar, 1995

Harcourt, G.C., *Some Cambridge Controversies in the Theory of Capital*, Cambridge: Cambridge University Press, 1972

Harcourt, Geoffrey C., "The Cambridge Contribution to Economics" in *Cambridge Contributions*, edited by Sarah J. Ormrod, Cambridge and New York: Cambridge University Press, 1998

Hutchison, T.W., *A Review of Economic Doctrines, 1870–1929*, Oxford: Clarendon Press, 1953

Kurz, Heinz D., Capital Theory: Debates entry in *The New Palgrave: A Dictionary of Economics*, edited by John Eatwell, Murray Milgate and Peter Newman, 4 vols, London: Macmillan, and New York: Stockton Press, 1987

Kurz, Heinz D. and Neri Salvadori, *Theory of Production: A Long-period Analysis*, Cambridge and New York: Cambridge University Press, 1995

Robinson, Austin, "John Maynard Keynes, 1883–1946", *Economic Journal*, 57 (1947): 1–68

Shackle, G.L.S., *The Years of High Theory: Invention and Tradition in Economic Thought, 1926–1939*, Cambridge: Cambridge University Press, 1967

Sraffa, Piero, *Production of Commodities by Means of Commodities: Prelude to a Critique of Economic Theory*, Cambridge: Cambridge University Press, 1960

The term "Cambridge School" is somewhat ambiguous, because it is sometimes used to refer to the particular version of neoclassical economics that was developed around the turn of the century by Alfred Marshall and his associates – in particular Arthur Cecil Pigou – and sometimes as a label for a group of Cambridge-based economists who provided a fundamental critique of the neoclassical theory of capital in the 1950s and 1960s, including Piero Sraffa, Joan Robinson, Nicholas Kaldor, Luigi Pasinetti, and Pierangelo Garegnani. In this entry the notion will be understood to cover both meanings and, indeed, to refer even more broadly to the contributions of Cambridge-based economists.

HARCOURT (1998) provides a good survey of the Cambridge contributions to economics that is also easily accessible to non-specialized readers. Harcourt's article introduces the reader to the main ideas of all the major Cambridge-based economists, including Thomas Robert Malthus, Henry Sidgwick, Alfred Marshall, Arthur Cecil Pigou, John Maynard Keynes, Joan Robinson, Nicholas Kaldor, and Piero Sraffa.

HUTCHISON's review of economic doctrines covers the period from around 1870 to the late 1920s. His chapter on the Cambridge School, apart from appraising the contributions of Sidgwick, Marshall, and Pigou, also supplies some biographical information. GROENEWEGEN has written a comprehensive biography of Alfred Marshall, which is extremely rich in biographical detail but less helpful for an appraisal of Marshall's contributions to economics.

The contributions that were made by the Cambridge economists during the 1920s and 1930s are masterfully reconstructed by SHACKLE, who gives an excellent account of the debate over Marshall's theory of returns that was triggered by Piero Sraffa's seminal article "The laws of returns under competitive conditions" of 1926. In addition, Shackle also provides an appraisal of Joan Robinson's *The Theory of Imperfect Competition* of 1931, and of the genesis and significance of John Maynard Keynes' *The General Theory of Employment, Interest and Money* of 1936. The secondary literature on Keynes is abundant; however, for an appraisal of the man and his contributions ROBINSON's obituary article of 1947 is still worth reading.

HARCOURT (1972) is the classic source for an account of the so-called "Cambridge controversies in the theory of capital", with contributions on the Cambridge (UK) side by Joan Robinson, Piero Sraffa, Pierangelo Garegnani, and Luigi Pasinetti. A short and non-technical overview of the debates in capital theory is provided by KURZ. The basis of the critique of the neoclassical theory of capital was laid by Piero SRAFFA in his book *Production of Commodities by Means of Com-*

modities (1960). The most up-to-date appraisal of Sraffa's contribution to the revival of classical political economy and its modern reformulation is contained in KURZ & SALVADORI (1995).

CHRISTIAN GEHRKE

See also Cambridge controversy, Nicholas Kaldor, Alfred Marshall, Joan Robinson, Piero Sraffa

Campaign, electoral

Alexander, Herbert E. (editor), *Comparative Political Finance in the 1980s*, Cambridge and New York: Cambridge University Press, 1989

Ansolabehere, Stephen and Shanto Iyengar, *Going Negative: How Political Advertisements Shrink and Polarize the Electorate*, New York: Free Press, 1995

Budge, Ian and Dennis J. Farlie, *Explaining and Predicting Elections: Issue Effects and Party Strategies in Twenty-Three Democracies*, London and Boston: Allen and Unwin, 1983

Budge, Ian, David Robertson and Derek Hearl (editors), *Ideology, Strategy, and Party Change: Spatial Analyses of Post-War Election Programmes in 19 Democracies*, Cambridge and New York: Cambridge University Press, 1987

Downs, Anthony, *An Economic Theory of Democracy*, New York: Harper and Row, 1957

Kaid, Lynda Lee and Christina Holtz-Bacha (editors), *Political Advertising in Western Democracies: Parties and Candidates on Television*, Thousand Oaks, California: Sage, 1995

LeDuc, Lawrence, Richard G. Niemi and Pippa Norris (editors), *Comparing Democracies: Elections and Voting in Global Perspectives*, Thousand Oaks, California: Sage, 1996

Robertson, David, *A Theory of Party Competition*, London and New York: Wiley, 1976

Swanson, David L. and Paolo Mancini (editors), *Politics, Media, and Modern Democracy: An International Study of Innovations in Electoral Campaigning and Their Consequences*, Westport, Connecticut: Praeger, 1996

West, Darrell M., *Air Wars: Television Advertising in Election Campaigns, 1952–1996*, 2nd edition, Washington, DC: Congressional Quarterly, 1997

Two factors make analysis of research on campaigns difficult. First, the majority of work on electoral politics has focused on elections themselves, and particularly the behaviour of voters, rather than campaigning. Second, campaigns vary greatly according to the nature of specific electoral systems. The latter point means that any list of essential research on campaigning must consist primarily of comparative studies.

There is a body of theoretical literature that applies to campaigns in multiple settings. DOWNS's *An Economic Theory of Democracy* is a key study that has served as the foundation for much research on party campaigning. The Downsian tradition, often referred to as the "spatial theory" of campaigning, posits a one-dimensional, left/right continuum along which potential issue positions can be arranged. Parties and voters place themselves at some point on that continuum. Voters choose parties closest to their positions, so parties have incentive to locate themselves near the median voter, thereby maximizing votes. Critics maintain that parties are not as flexible as the spatial theory of campaigning suggests. Indeed, parties are constrained by a number of factors (including history) that do not allow them to simply adjust their positions to appeal to the median voter.

"Saliency theory," as put forward by ROBERTSON and by BUDGE & FARLIE, argues that parties selectively emphasize those issues that work to their advantage and ignore those that are beneficial to their opponents. Parties come to be identified with certain issues by voters and, thus, the parties are thought to "own" those issues. In the United States, for example, Democrats are believed to be better able to handle education, unemployment, and the environment while Republicans are thought superior at foreign policy, battling inflation, and cutting taxes. The result is that parties do not directly debate one another on common issues and that parties are not free to move great distances along an ideological continuum. Nevertheless, as the collective research in BUDGE, ROBERTSON & HEARL found, parties in a given system can converge toward a rough consensus on policy positions even as they emphasize different issues during campaigns. Thus, saliency theory can hold in a (qualified) spatial context (see Budge, Robertson & Hearl, pp.26–8).

As noted above, only comparative examinations account for the variation that exists among electoral systems. LEDUC, NIEMI & NORRIS bring together a number of authors to deal with various aspects of elections and voting around the world. Of particular relevance to campaigns are Katz's essay on "party organizations and finance", Farrell's on "campaign strategies and tactics", and Semetko's on "the media". These chapters, and indeed the entire book, are thorough introductions to the literature on campaigns and elections.

Perhaps the most widely studied aspect of campaigning is the role of campaign media. A wonderful general introduction can be found in SWANSON & MANCINI. This edited volume is comparative but seeks to explain the common environment in which campaigns are now conducted. In particular, the editors' introduction and concluding chapter provide excellent discussions of modern campaigning and its elements, which include personalized politics, the "scientificization" of politics, a loosening of party identification, a centralization of an autonomous mass media, and a shift in political participation from citizenship to spectatorship (pp.14–16).

Studies of campaign media often focus, more narrowly, on political advertising. Much of this research concerns American campaigns, but KAID & HOLTZ-BACHA have edited a volume on "political advertising in western democracies". Based on the country specific research in their book and on their own research, the editors summarize the trends in political advertising as such: most advertisements focus on issues rather than image and most are positive rather than negative. Despite the positive emphasis on issues, most candidates and parties appeal to emotion rather than logic. Regardless of country, candidates of the same status (challengers or incumbents) employ similar strategies and, to a lesser extent, message content. Production style, which is often dictated by govern-ment regulation of format, is perhaps the biggest difference between countries. Finally, advertising effects are particularly evident in terms of candidate images (p.223). In the end, this book proves invaluable to those seeking to understand the role played by political advertising in various media and electoral systems.

For those solely interested in advertising in the American system, two books are particularly noteworthy. WEST's *Air Wars* is a comprehensive examination of political advertising from 1952–96. Among the important conclusions that emerge from his analysis are the findings that political advertisements help voters learn about candidates and prioritize issues. In addition, advertisements alter the criteria that voters use to evaluate candidates and assist them in placing blame for problems. Not surprisingly, campaign commercials are found to work best in low-information contexts. The content of the advertisements themselves (as well as the timing of their use) is also influential.

ANSOLABEHERE & IYENGAR's work on negative political advertising has been controversial. They have argued, from a series of extensive experiments, that negative advertising depresses voter turnout (whereas positive advertising increases it), particularly among nonpartisan voters. Furthermore, advertising reinforces partisan attachments, especially among those with low levels of information. The result is a smaller, more polarized electorate. Although they recognize the positive contributions of advertising (for example, its informing function), the authors are clearly more concerned with its negative aspects. Some have argued, however, that the use of experiments in their study overstates the negative effects of "attack" advertising.

Finally, scholars are increasingly paying attention to the way campaigns are financed. Although there has been little comparative work on the topic, ALEXANDER's edited volume is an invaluable resource for understanding the issues involved in campaign finance and its reform. His introduction sets the context for the book and argues that the impact of public financing on political systems has yet to be sufficiently studied. Alexander is particularly concerned with the potential for public funding plans to limit the equality of opportunity of certain (especially small) parties. The remaining chapters do a good job of outlining the historical trends and current (as of the late 1980s) status of campaign finance legislation in eleven, mostly West European, countries.

STEPHEN K. MEDVIC

Canon law

Brundage, James, *Medieval Canon Law*, London and New York: Longman, 1995

Clarence Smith, J.A., *Medieval Law Teachers and Writers, Civilian and Canonist*, Ottawa: University of Ottawa Press, 1975

Donahue, Charles (editor), *The Records of the Medieval Ecclesiastical Courts*, part 2: *England*, Berlin: Duncker & Humblot, 1994

Fournier, Paul and Gabriel Le Bras, *Histoire des collections canoniques en Occident*, 2 vols, Paris: Sirey, 1931–32

Helmholz, R.H., *Roman Canon Law in Reformation
   England*, Cambridge and New York: Cambridge University
   Press, 1990
Helmholz, R.H. (editor), *Canon Law in Protestant Lands*,
   Berlin: Duncker and Humblot, 1992
Helmholz, R.H., *The Spirit of Classical Canon Law*, Athens:
   University of Georgia Press, 1996
Kuttner, Stephan, *Repertorium der Kanonistik (1140–1234)*,
   Vatican City: Biblioteca Apostolica Vaticana, 1937
Owen, Dorothy, *The Medieval Canon Law: Teaching
   Literature and Transmission*, Cambridge and New York:
   Cambridge University Press, 1990
Schulte, Johann Friedrich von, *Die Geschichte der Quellen
   und Literatur des canonischen Rechts*, 2 vols, Stuttgart:
   Enke, 1875–80; reprinted Graz: Akademische Druck- und
   Verlagsanstalt, 1956

BRUNDAGE provides a superb introduction to the history and sources of canon law from the early church to the end of the Middle Ages. He provides a full account of both the law itself and the context within which it was created and in which it functioned. He is particularly strong on the development of the profession of canon law and provides helpful biographical information on many canonists. He also provides two extremely useful appendices. The first is an explanation of the "Romano-canonical citation system", which will be particularly helpful to beginners in the field. The second contains short biographical paragraphs on all of the major canonical writers of the Middle Ages, arranged in alphabetical order. His "select bibliography" is a good guide to further reading.

CLARENCE SMITH is a biographical dictionary of canon law and Roman law writers and teachers of the Middle Ages. It is extremely useful for beginners and gives basic bibliographical as well as biographical material for each author entry.

DONAHUE provides an introduction to the sources for the ecclesiastical courts of Canterbury and York in England. He and Jane Sayers provide introductory essays and a detailed catalogue of documents from the Canterbury and York archives.

FOURNIER & LE BRAS provide the fundamental study of the law of the early church. Although some of the details of the development of canon law in the early Middle Ages are outdated due to recent manuscript discoveries, their general account of this development remains the best available. They are particularly strong in describing the historical development of canonical doctrine during the Carolingian period.

HELMHOLTZ (1996) provides an excellent overview of the classical period of canon law between the 12th and the 14th centuries. It begins with a short analysis of the sources of canon law and then moves on to a series of chapters in which he deals with specific topics including church governance, clergy, property rights, criminal law, and the papacy. Each chapter presents a detailed analysis of the legal issues involved, with many citations to canonical sources. At the end of the volume, there is a useful bibliography of early printed canon-law texts.

HELMHOLZ (1992) is a collection of essays written by leading canon-law scholars concerned with canon law in the post medieval period. The essays discuss the development of canon law in a number of European countries, including Germany, the Netherlands, Switzerland, Ireland, and England, as well as in the United States. They are particularly useful for the history of canon-law studies in the various countries. The essay by Lloyd Bonfield on the history of canon law in early American courts has an especially interesting discussion of canonical holdings in early American libraries.

HELMHOLZ (1990) is the finest history of canon law and ecclesiastical jurisdiction ever written. It provides a detailed study of the development both of doctrine and of canonical courts in Reformation England. Its history of these subjects is based on a remarkable study of English canonical manuscripts, many of which were unknown prior to this volume's publication.

KUTTNER is a one-volume catalogue of canon-law manuscripts held in European libraries, accompanied by detailed analyses of their contents. As the majority of canonical works are not available in print, they must be consulted in manuscript. This is the starting point for any serious investigation of these manuscripts. It is also a good introduction to Stephan Kuttner's voluminous scholarship, which is particularly important for the study of canon-law manuscripts.

OWEN is a set of brief lectures on several aspects of canon law. The third and fourth lectures are particularly useful. The third explains the importance of formularies in medieval canon law. The fourth is one of the few discussions available of post-Reformation canon-law studies and the collection of medieval canon-law manuscripts by scholars of this later period.

VON SCHULTE is the classic 19th-century work on the history of canon law. Voluminous in scope and obsessive in detail, much of what it contains has now been superseded. Nevertheless, it is a necessary starting point for any serious canon-law research, and is also a valuable resource for understanding the nature of 19th-century canon-law scholarship.

M.H. HOEFLICH

See also Church and state, Law and history, Law and history through textbooks

Capacity

Anxo, Dominique, Gerhard Bosch, Derek Bosworth, Gilbert
   Cette, Thomas Sterner and Dominique Taddei (editors),
   *Work Patterns and Capital Utilisation: An International
   Comparative Study*, Dordrecht: Kluwer, 1995
Coutts, Kenneth, Wynne Godley and William Nordhaus,
   Industrial Pricing in the United Kingdom, Cambridge and
   New York: Cambridge University Press, 1978
Dutt, Amitava Krishna (editor), *New Directions in Analytical
   Political Economy*, Aldershot, Hampshire: Elgar, 1994
Michie, Jonathan and John Grieve Smith (editors), *Creating
   Industrial Capacity: Towards Full Employment*, Oxford:
   Oxford University Press, 1996
Oughton, Christine, "Competitiveness Policy in the 1990s",
   Economic Journal, 107 (September 1997): 1486–1503

The term "capacity" in economics refers to the output capacity of firms, whether individually or in aggregate. An important economic indicator is "capacity utilization", which reports how fully firms are using their existing capacity. Capacity utilization is therefore an indicator of the business cycle. Capacity in this sense tends to refer to the physical capacity in the sense of buildings, machinery, and so on. Other aspects tend to be referred to explicitly, such as "managerial capacity", which relates to the ability and training of managers rather than simply numbers available. Likewise labour supply and skills shortages are not usually included in the terms capacity and capacity utilization but are rather referred to explicitly. If there is unemployment in the economy this will therefore be due either to capacity utilization being at too low a level or else the overall capacity in the economy may be inadequate – or possibly both.

The various authors in the volume edited by MICHIE & GRIEVE SMITH deal in detail with the issue of capacity. In his foreword, Professor Brian Reddaway, previously Director of the Department of Applied Economics at the University of Cambridge, asks why so much importance should be attached to trying to expand industrial capacity. His own answer is that the real capital stock in Britain is – or at least was at the time he wrote – inadequate to employ the available labour force in a satisfactory way. Over long periods the stock of capital in the UK has grown at about the same average rate as has gross domestic product, namely at around 2.5 per cent a year. However, since around 1980, this growth of the capital stock has been subnormal and this has been reflected in a relatively high level of unemployment. In addition to this general reason for being concerned at a low growth rate of the capital stock, Reddaway warns that the problem of an inadequate manufacturing capital stock is of particular concern given the importance of manufacturing in international trade, and hence the danger that balance-of-payments constraints might inhibit economic growth in the future (see the separate entry on Exports and export-led growth). Thus in his introductory overview to the book Michie argues that the key to sustainable growth and a return to full employment is to ensure both a continuous expansion of demand, and for this to be matched by increased output rather than by inflation or, in the case of individual countries, trade imbalances. Genuine supply side policies – by which Michie means policies that will lead to an increased and more efficient supply of goods and services, rather than the deflationary and deregulatory policies which are usually referred to as "supply side economics" simply because they are being promoted in the context of a disregard for demand conditions (on which, see the separate entry on Supply side economics) – require an expansion of industrial capacity, and of economic capacity more generally.

The issue of capital utilization is analysed in detail in ANXO et al. The book reports international comparative work on the decision-making processes that lead to the adoption of particular work patterns, and considers the economic consequences of these decisions for capital utilization, productivity growth, and employment. Alternative measures of capital utilization are discussed and detailed international data are provided on the post-World War II patterns of work and capital utilization.

Several of the contributors to DUTT discuss issues of capacity and capacity utilization. Malcolm Sawyer discusses the role of capacity utilization not only in determining employment levels but also in relation to pricing decisions. He makes the point that the importance of capacity utilization is missed by neoclassical economics which tends not to appreciate the way in which prices are set by a mark-up over costs.

This issue is analysed in detail in COUTTS, GODLEY & NORDHAUS, whose authors find that these costs are generally "normal" costs taken over the course of the business cycle, but this in turn means that the fluctuation in profits caused by variations in the rate of capacity utilization will be much greater than if the mark-up itself altered to take account of changes in the rate of capacity utilization.

OUGHTON reports on the policies of the UK government and the European Commission regarding capacity. The author reports that both the UK and European policies recognize a clear link between investment in capacity and economic growth, but that in contrast to the EU, the UK Government's policy at that time (1995) was based on an assessment that there was no significant under-performance in investment in fixed and intangible assets with which to be concerned – in contrast to the concerns raised by Reddaway reported above. Oughton reports that international comparisons of investment per employee indicate that since 1970 the UK had experienced one of the worst performances of all the OECD economies. Six broad approaches are discussed to tackle this problem of inadequate investment in capacity: investment grants and support; changes in the tax treatment of corporate profits, dividends, and capital allowances; changing the relative tax on savings and consumption; increased public investment in infrastructure – education, training, R&D, transport, and communication; reducing macroeconomic instability; and institutional change in the relationship between industry and the financial sector.

JONATHAN MICHIE

See also Exports and export-led growth, Supply side economics

Capital asset pricing models

Black, Fischer, "Capital Market Equilibrium with Restricted Borrowing", *Journal of Business*, 45/3 (1972): 444–55

De Santis, Giorgio and Bruno Gerard, "International Asset Pricing and Portfolio Diversification with Time-varying Risk", *Journal of Finance*, 52/5 (1997): 1881–1912

Fama, Eugene F. and James D. MacBeth, "Risk, Return, and Equilibrium: Empirical Tests", *Journal of Political Economy*, 81/3 (1973): 607–36

Fama, Eugene F. and Kenneth R. French, "The Cross-section of Expected Stock Returns", *Journal of Finance*, 47/2 (1992): 427–65

Fama, Eugene F., and Kenneth R. French, "Multifactor Explanations of Asset Pricing Anomalies", *Journal of Finance*, 51/1 (1996): 55–84

Ferson, Wayne E., *Theory and Empirical Testing of Asset Pricing Models*, Chicago: Center of Security Prices, University of Chicago, 1992 (Working Paper 352)

Huang, Chi-fu and Robert H. Litzenberger, *Foundations for Financial Economics*, Englewood Cliffs, New Jersey: Prentice Hall, 1993

Jagannathan, Ravi and Zhenyu Wang, "The Conditional CAPM and the Cross-section of Expected Returns", *Journal of Finance*, 51/1 (1996): 3–53

Kandel, Shmuel and Robert F. Stambaugh, "Portfolio Inefficiency and the Cross-section of Expected Returns", *Journal of Finance*, 50/1 (1995): 157–84

Kim, Dongcheol, "The Errors in the Variables Problem in the Cross-section of Expected Stock Returns", *Journal of Finance*, 50/5 (1995): 1605–34

Kothari, S.P., Jay Shanken and Richard G. Sloan, "Another Look at the Cross-section of Expected Stock Returns", *Journal of Finance*, 50/1 (1995): 185–224

Lintner, John, "The Valuation of Risky Assets and the Selection of Risky Investments in Stock Portfolios and Capital Budgets", *Review of Economics and Statistics*, 47 (1965): 13–37

Roll, Richard, "A Critique of the Asset Pricing Theory's Tests Part 1: On Past and Potential Testability of the Theory", *Journal of Financial Economics*, 4/2 (1977): 129–76

Sharpe, William F., "Capital Asset Pricing: A Theory of Market Equilibrium under Conditions of Risk", *Journal of Finance*, 19 (1964): 425–42

One of the most popular cross-sectional asset pricing models in contemporary finance is the capital asset pricing model (CAPM). Using the two-fund separation theorem and under a set of restrictive assumptions, SHARPE, LINTNER, and BLACK show that the expected return on each asset in the market is proportional to its market risk, beta. This relation provides a foundation to value risky assets and capital projects in corporate finance.

HUANG & LITZENBERGER is an excellent textbook that covers econometric issues in testing the CAPM. They argue that whether the CAPM fulfils itself as a positive asset pricing model should not be judged by the realism of its assumptions. It may be impossible to model a long and detailed list of realistic assumptions, and this would at best be a mere institutional description that may not have any predictive value in itself. Consequently, the early tests on the CAPM focus on the predictive content of betas. They also highlight three conceptual problems associated with testing the CAPM. First, the CAPM implies relationships between *ex ante* risk premia and betas that are not directly observable. Second, these premia and betas are unlikely to be stationary over time. Third, many assets are not marketable and tests of the CAPM are invariably based on proxies for the market portfolio that excluded major classes of assets such as human capital, private businesses, and private real estates.

The paper by FAMA & MACBETH is one of the early empirical tests of the CAPM. They overcome the first conceptual problem by assuming that the realized rates of return on assets in a given time period are drawn from the *ex ante* probability distributions of returns on those assets. They partition assets into portfolios ranked by their betas. Time series regressions are carried out between the excess returns on each portfolio and the excess returns on the market over the first four years of the sample period, implicitly assuming that the risk premia and betas are stationary over that period. The excess returns on each portfolio in the following year are then regressed on to these estimated betas. This procedure is repeated by moving the time series window one year forward each time. The cross-sectional regression results appear to suggest that there is a linear relation between the excess returns on each portfolio and their estimated betas.

ROLL points out that, regardless of the return-generating process, there will always be an infinite number of *ex post* mean-variance efficient portfolios in any sample of observations on individual returns. If betas on individual assets are measured relative to an *ex post* frontier portfolio, it follows from the mathematics of the portfolio frontier that the average realized returns on these assets would have an exact linear relation to these betas. He argues that the only testable hypothesis associated with the CAPM is whether the true market portfolio is mean-variance efficient. When a proxy for the true market portfolio is used, either the proxy itself might be mean-variance efficient when the true market portfolio is not, or the chosen proxy may turn out to be inefficient; but this alone implies nothing about the true market portfolio's efficiency. The theory is, therefore, not testable unless the exact composition of the true market portfolio is known and used in the tests.

KANDEL & STAMBAUGH show that the cross-sectional mean-beta relation fitted in an ordinary least-square regression bears essentially no relation to the mean-variance location of an inefficient index portfolio. By randomizing the returns and variances of ten size-based portfolios using stocks from the New York Stock Exchange, they produce a near-perfect linear relation between the portfolio betas and their returns when the original index portfolio is grossly inefficient (lying below and within the efficient frontier). They show that the explanatory power (R^2) of a general least-square regression between portfolio betas and their returns approximates a relative measure of the portfolio efficiency.

An extensive body of empirical research has recently provided evidence contradicting the prediction of the CAPM. This research documents that deviations from the linear CAPM risk-return tradeoff are related to, among other variables, firm size, earnings yield, leverage, and the book-to-market ratio. FERSON provides an extensive summary of these empirical tests on the CAPM and its anomalies up to 1991.

FAMA & FRENCH (1992) show that by employing a new approach for portfolio grouping, there is only a weak positive relation between average monthly stock returns and market betas over the period 1941–90. This relation virtually disappears over a shorter period 1963–90. However, firm size and the book-to-market equity ratio have considerable power. The findings in this paper cast serious doubt over the validity of the CAPM as the true cross-sectional asset pricing model and have caused a new wave of empirical attention to be focused on the CAPM.

KOTHARI *et al.* re-examine the findings of Fama & French (1992). They find that when annual returns are used in the estimation of beta, there is substantial *ex post* compensation for the beta risk over the period 1941–90 and even more over the longer 1927–90 period. They also point out that the results of Fama & French (1992) are subject to a combination of survivorship bias in the COMPUSTAT database, which affects the high book-to-market stocks' performance and the period-specific performance of both low book-to-market, past "winner" stocks, and high book-to-market, past "loser" stocks. Using an alternative data source, they find that the book-to-market ratio is only weakly related to average stock returns.

Another problem related to Fama & French's (1992) approach is that the betas estimated in the first-pass time series regression are inevitably subject to measurement errors. This errors-in-variable (EIV) problem is well documented. A recent paper by KIM reviews this subject matter and proposes a new approach to correct for the EIV problem. He finds that after correcting for the EIV problem, market beta has economically and statistically significant explanatory power for average monthly stock returns both in the presence and in the absence of the firm-size variable in the regression, and the firm size factor, while still significant, becomes much less important.

FAMA & FRENCH (1996) argue that many of the CAPM anomalies are related, and they are captured by a three-factor model incorporating (a) the excess return of a broad market portfolio; (b) the difference between the return on a portfolio of small stocks and the return on a portfolio of large stocks (SMB); and (c) the difference between the return on a portfolio of high book-to-market stocks and the return on a portfolio of low book-to-market stocks (HML), proposed in their earlier work. They show that this model is a good description of returns on portfolios formed on size, book-to-market ratio, earning-to-price ratio, and sales growth. They also suggest that this three-factor model is an equilibrium-pricing model, a version of the intertemporal CAPM or the arbitrage pricing theory. In their view, the SMB and HML factors mimic combinations of two underlying risk factors or state variables of special hedging concern to investors.

JAGANNATHAN & WANG challenge the assumption made in most empirical studies of the static CAPM that betas remain constant over time and that the return on the value-weighted portfolio of all stocks is a proxy for the return on aggregate wealth. They assume that the CAPM holds in a conditional sense. They use the yield spread between BAA- and AAA-rated bonds as a proxy for the conditional market risk premium and include the return on human capital when measuring the return on aggregate wealth. They find substantial improvement in explaining the cross-section of average returns.

The dynamics of the conditional moments in stock returns have received considerable attention in recent years. The family of autoregressive conditional heteroskedasticity (ARCH) models generally captures these dynamics. DE SANTIS & GERARD review the previous work on the conditional CAPM with correction for autoregressive conditional heteroskedasticity. They test the conditional CAPM for the world's eight largest equity markets using a parsimonious generalized ARCH parameterization and find evidence to support most of the pricing restrictions of the model.

LIBON FUNG

See also Arbitrage pricing theory

Capital punishment

Acker, James R., Robert M. Bohm and Charles S. Lanier (editors), *America's Experiment with Capital Punishment: Reflections of the Past, Present, and Future of the Ultimate Penal Sanction*, Durham, North Carolina: Carolina Academy Press, 1998

Black, Charles L. Jr, *Capital Punishment: The Inevitability of Caprice and Mistake*, 2nd edition, New York: Norton, 1981
Bowers, William J., *Legal Homicide: Death as Punishment in America, 1864–1982*, Boston: Northeastern University Press, 1984
Haines, Herbert H., *Against Capital Punishment: The Anti-Death Penalty Movement in America, 1972–1994*, New York and Oxford: Oxford University Press, 1996
Mello, Michael, *Against the Death Penalty: The Relentless Dissents of Justices Brennan and Marshall*, Boston: Northeastern University Press, 1996
Potter, Harry, *Hanging in Judgment: Religion and the Death Penalty in England from the Bloody Code to Abolition*, New York: Continuum, and London: SCM Press, 1993
Radelet, Michael L., Hugo Adam Bedau and Constance E. Putnam, *In Spite of Innocence: Erroneous Convictions in Capital Cases*, Boston: Northeastern University Press, 1992
Sarat, Austin (editor), *The Killing State: Capital Punishment in Law, Politics, and Culture*, New York and Oxford: Oxford University Press, 1998
Schabas, William A., *The Abolition of the Death Penalty in International Law*, 2nd edition, Cambridge and New York: Cambridge University Press, 1997
Sheleff, Leon Shaskolsky, *Ultimate Penalties: Capital Punishment, Life Imprisonment, Physical Torture*, Columbus: Ohio State University Press, 1987

ACKER, BOHM & LANIER edited the most comprehensive reader extant on the death penalty. If one were to read only one book on the subject, it would be wise to choose this one. The volume provides a collection of both empirical and theoretical articles that assess the state of capital punishment in the US at the beginning of the 20th century. Divided into sections that deal with public opinion and legislation, justice issues, the administration of the death penalty, and a section on the final stages of a death sentence, the work includes the most notable scholarship on the topic. It includes some pro-death penalty work, but the overwhelmingly critical slant of the articles suggests that the empirical research does not support the positive claims made by death-penalty supporters. Recent studies continue to find racial bias in the administration of the death penalty, no reliable evidence for a deterrent effect, and numerous due process defects in the way the laws are applied. A curious reader who studies this volume would put it down with serious doubts about the wisdom of capital punishment.

The collection edited by SARAT is more concerned with the symbolic politics of the death penalty, its effect on the total legal system, and its role in contemporary "culture wars". The anthology includes work by scholars who study the law of capital punishment, such as Hugo Bedau who makes an argument based on substantive due process, and an essay that examines various states' definitions of aggravating factors. It also includes several postmodernist essays, one of which deals with popular films featuring executions. The overall thrust of the works provides a description of a policy fraught with impossible moral and constitutional contradictions.

BLACK, a professor of law at Yale University, opposes the death penalty for reasons similar to those invoked by the

Supreme Court when they declared capital punishment unconstitutional in *Furman v Georgia* (1972). He maintains that execution is unacceptable because, despite attempted reforms after *Furman*, the process of selecting candidates for death is full of error and lacking in standards. Many offenders are eligible for death under the law, but only a few, arbitrarily selected, are actually killed. Black also argues that the potential for a mistake in conviction or sentencing makes the punishment unacceptable by the standards of 20th-century civilization.

MELLO approaches the dissents of Justice William Brennan and Justice Thurgood Marshall in the Supreme Court's death penalty cases with great admiration. The two jurists were "relentless" dissenters in every case that upheld capital punishment after the Court reinstated it in 1976. As opposed to the view that their opinions were essentially meaningless reiterations of a contrarian viewpoint, Mello argues that they wrote with compassion for the accused and with a sense that the law should be an instrument for advancing the common good. He found their opinions in dissent were theoretically and historically legitimate. Besides expressing opposition to the death penalty on moral grounds, the two justices also provided arguments for defence lawyers to use in the lower courts. Mello's discussion of the dissents is original in its organization and intellectually rigorous.

RADELET, BEDAU & PUTNAM examined 416 cases in the US during the 20th century. In each, the wrong person was convicted and sentenced to death. Over one hundred of these innocent persons were actually executed. The standards for inclusion in the collection of true stories are quite high. The authors consider only those who were factually innocent (no cases based only on a denial of due process were included). The most common errors that convicted suspects erroneously were perjury by prosecution witnesses and mistaken eyewitness identifications. Others were wrongly sentenced based on racial prejudice, community hysteria, or the failure of police work. By citing so many stories of wrongful convictions, Radelet, Bedau & Putnam provide powerful ammunition against the death penalty.

HAINES addresses the question of why the US, virtually alone among democratic societies, retains and expands the use of capital punishment. He focuses especially on the reasons why the anti-death-penalty movement has not been successful. Since the 1970s, it appears that challenges to capital punishment in the courts will not be successful and that attacks on the sentence on constitutional grounds will fail. Instead, the issue will be fought out in state legislatures, where public opinion exerts strong influence. Haines recommends that opponents collaborate with other reform interests and that they shift the argument from one based on moral objections to execution to one based on the cost to taxpayers of the death penalty.

BOWERS, in a volume considered indispensable for students of the death penalty, brings an empirical treatment to the issue of whether the procedure is acceptable in modern American society. Working from criteria stated in Supreme Court opinions, Bowers argues that to meet the not "cruel and unusual punishment" test, capital punishment must: be applied fairly, serve as a deterrent, and be compatible with contemporary values. The author provides both historical and modern data, American and crossnational statistics. He cites research showing that the death penalty has been used as a "repressive response" to perceived rising crime rates, that it is used most frequently against members of oppressed and minority groups, and that it fails as a deterrent but instead has a brutalizing effect. The study concludes that it is impossible to separate discrimination and brutalization from the death penalty, and that therefore the procedure is beyond legal reform.

SHELEFF shifts the debate about capital punishment from its interest in the condemned person and/or the victim to a focus on the role of the state. He postulates that the argument over execution is inseparable from discussions of the place of the other two ultimate penalties, torture and life imprisonment, in the life of a society. If deterrence and retribution are major purposes of the death penalty, why should a community eschew torture and opt for the least painful method? How does the state know what the accused believes to be the worst penalty? What role do politically motivated executions play in the life of the modern state? Sheleff's concluding recommendations try to approach an "enlightened penology". They include less reliance on the ultimate penalties and more confidence in penultimate penalties. He also proposes mechanisms for international judicial review before death or life imprisonment can be carried out.

SCHABAS considers the death penalty in international law and the process of its abolition, particularly since the adoption of the Universal Declaration of Human Rights in 1948. That document and many subsequent international conventions contained mention of the "right to life" or the "right to live". Abolition of the death penalty was considered a goal flowing from those rights, rather than a binding norm. The book examines the evolution of two systems for the protection of human rights, one embodied in the European Convention on Human Rights and the other in the American Convention on Human Rights of the Organization of American States. Since 1948, the conventions have been modified to either abolish the death penalty in peacetime or, as in the Americas, to provide for procedural safeguards. Schabas argues that universal abolition of the death penalty is unlikely in the near future given the practices of the Islamic states. However, international law has served to create norms that have influenced death penalty law in most other nations.

POTTER examines the history of capital punishment in England from its extensive use in the early modern period to its abolition in 1965. Of particular interest is Potter's treatment of the interaction between the Church of England and the political environment in which capital punishment existed. He faults the Church for coming late to the abolitionist viewpoint and leaving the moral high ground to the more marginal religious groups. He argues that, had the Church opposed the death penalty earlier, the sentence would have lost public and political support sooner. The British example, with the influence of the established Church, stands in marked contrast to the US where the anti-capital punishment position of many Churches has had little influence on the public debate.

MARY WELEK ATWELL

Capital theory controversy

Bharadwaj, K., "Value through Exogenous Distribution", *Economic Weekly*, 15 (1963) 14504; reprinted in Harcourt and Laing, 1971

Bliss, C.J., *Capital Theory and the Distribution of Income*, Amsterdam: North Holland, 1975

Burmeister, Edwin, *Capital Theory and Dynamics*, Cambridge and New York: Cambridge University Press, 1980

Cohen, Avi J., "Prices, Capital and the OneCommodity Model in Neoclassical and Classical 'Theories'", *History of Political Economy*, 21 (1989): 23151

Dixit, Avinash, "The Accumulation of Capital Theory", *Oxford Economic Papers*, 29 (1977): 1–29

Garegnani, Pierangelo, "Heterogeneous Capital, the Production Function and the Theory of Distribution", *Review of Economic Studies*, 37 (1970): 407–36

Garegnani, Pierangelo, Quantity of Capital entry in *The New Palgrave: Capital Theory*, edited by John Eatwell, Murray Milgate and Peter Newman, London: Macmillan, and New York: Norton, 1990

Harcourt, G.C., "Some Cambridge Controversies in the Theory of Capital", *Journal of Economic Literature*, 7 (1969): 369–405

Harcourt, G.C. and N.F. Laing, *Capital and Growth: Selected Readings*, Harmondsworth: Penguin, 1971

Harcourt, G.C., *Some Cambridge Controversies in the Theory of Capital*, Cambridge: Cambridge University Press, 1972

Harcourt, G.C., "The Capital Theory Controversies" in *The Elgar Companion to Radical Political Economy*, edited by Philip Arestis and Malcolm Sawyer, Aldershot, ampshire: Elgar, 1994; reprinted in *Capitalism, Socialism and PostKeynesianism: Selected Essays of G.C. Harcourt*, G.C. Harcourt, Aldershot: Elgar, 1995

Levhari, D., "A Nonsubstitution Theorem and Switching of Techniques", *Quarterly Journal of Economics*, 79 (1965): 98–105

Metcalfe, J.S. and I. Steedman, "Heterogeneous Capital and the HeckscherOhlinSamuelson Theory of Trade" in *Essays in Modern Economics*, edited by Michael Parkin, London: Longman, and New York: Barnes and Noble, 1973

Pasinetti, L.L., "Changes in the Rate of Profit and Switches of Techniques", *Quarterly Journal of Economics*, 80 (1966): 503–17

Pasinetti, L.L., "Switches of Technique and the 'Rate of Return' in Capital Theory", *Economic Journal*, 79 (1969): 508–31

Robinson, Joan, "The Production Function and the Theory of Capital", *Review of Economic Studies*, 21 (1953–54): 81–106

Rogers, Colin, *Money, Interest and Capital: A Study in the Foundations of Monetary Theory*, Cambridge and New York: Cambridge University Press, 1989

Samuelson, Paul A., "Parable and Realism in Capital Theory: The Surrogate Production Function", *Review of Economic Studies*, 29 (1962): 193–206

Samuelson, Paul A., "A Summing Up", *Quarterly Journal of Economics*, 80 (1966): 56883

Sen, A.K., "On Some Debates in Capital Theory", *Economica*, 41 (1974): 328–35

Solow, R.M., "A Contribution to the Theory of Economic Growth", *Quarterly Journal of Economics*, 70 (1956): 65–94

Solow, R.M., "Technical Change and the Aggregate Production Function", *Review of Economics and Statistics*, 39 (1957): 312–20

Solow, Robert M., *Capital Theory and the Rate of Return*, Amsterdam: North Holland, 1963, and Chicago: Rand McNally, 1964

Sraffa, Piero, *Production of Commodities by Means of Commodities: Prelude to a Critique of Economic Theory*, Cambridge: Cambridge University Press, 1960

Stiglitz, Joseph E., "The CambridgeCambridge Controversy in the Theory of Capital: A View from New Haven: A Review Article", *Journal of Political Economy*, 82 (1974): 893–903

Swan, T.W., "Economic Growth and Capital Accumulation", *Economic Record*, 32 (1956): 334–61

The most recent bout of controversy in capital theory starts with ROBINSON, which asked at least three fundamental questions: What do we mean by capital in traditional (neoclassical) theory? How do we measure it? That is to say, is there a technical unit corresponding to hours for labour and acres for land that (a) is independent of distribution and prices, so that all the arguments of the aggregate production function are coherent; (b) may be precisely defined; and (c) may legitimately be regarded as one of the determinants of distribution? (This was a rhetorical question.) What sense can be made of the notion of an economy getting into equilibrium? Either it is *in* equilibrium (all plans and expectations are fulfilled) and has always been so, or it is in a particular state and past happenings, current events, especially those which were not expected, and future expectations determine what happens next. Moreover, there is no guarantee (or even sense in the notion) of convergence on, or fluctuations around, an equilibrium position.

These questions and her answers spawned a huge literature, the contents of which sometimes overlapped but, more often, were akin to ships passing in a dark night. Many papers concentrated on the more secondary question of the measurement as opposed to the meaning of capital. The latter made it necessary to ask what sort of society is being analysed and what vision of it has been translated into the approach taken.

SRAFFA's classic provides crucial insights into both these issues. He shows that, in the supply and demand approach, it is impossible to find a unit that is independent of distribution and prices with which to measure capital (implicitly outside the confines of a one, allpurpose commodity model). He argues that the approach of the classical political economists and Marx, the crucial organizing concept of which was the surplus (its creation, extraction, distribution, and use), was a more fruitful way to view economic processes. Krishna BHARADWAJ wrote a remarkable review article of Sraffa's book, emphasizing these points and Avi COHEN has shown that both approaches run into incoherence outside the confines of the one commodity model.

Those who concentrated most on measurement, but who were never the less far too astute not to understand meaning, include Trevor SWAN (see especially the appendix to his article), Robert SOLOW (1956) and the most influential of them all, Paul SAMUELSON's (1962) surrogate production function article. There, he attempted to show that the results of the one commodity model, which exhibited all the agreeable propositions concerning the workings of competitive capitalism and which reflected the central insight that price is an index of scarcity, carried over to the rigorous general equilibrium heterogeneous commodities models of the Massachusetts Institute of Technology and elsewhere. Not content with this, in 1965 his pupil David LEVHARI claimed to have shown that Sraffa's refutation of the agreeable results, especially his demonstration of capital-reversing and reswitching, were not true of a model of an economy but only of a model of an industry. This precipitated a symposium in the *Quarterly Journal of Economics* refuting Levhari's claim. (PASINETTI (1966) was the first to have done so.) It included a handsome summing up article by SAMUELSON (1966). He accepted the refutation, used an Austrian model to explain why the so-called paradoxes – nondownward sloping demand curves for capital, no watertight guarantee that abstinence and accumulation would result in higher living standards for all – could occur, and why he had missed this point first time around. In fact, he had sense the reasons in his 1962 article, in which he cited a fundamental paper by Pierangelo GAREGNANI that was only later published in 1970. In it he alerted Samuelson as to how special his results were. GAREGNANI (1990) is his most full and authoritative account of these issues.

SOLOW (1963), following arguments with Joan Robinson over "capital" and "its" marginal product, argued that it would be better to handle capital theory and the process of accumulation by concentrating on the rate of return on investment derived from Irving Fisher and Knut Wicksell rather than on the former concepts, which the critics argued were incoherent. Solow developed both the theory and the application of the latter concept in his 1963 book. PASINETTI (1969) returned to Fisher's writings in the light of Joan Robinson's and especially Piero Sraffa's critique in order to argue that Solow's approach (and Fisher's theory) were as vulnerable to the new results as were the foundations of the aggregate production function. The latter was used in neoclassical growth theory, Swan, Solow (1956), and in the applied work on technical progress and productivity growth, SOLOW (1957).

Two books that critically survey these issues are HARCOURT (1972, which grew out of HARCOURT 1969), and BLISS 1975). The first is partial (to say the least) to the Cambridge UK critique; Bliss is more partial to the neoclassical MIT approach but is also fundamentally independent, criticizing both approaches whenever it was deemed necessary. Bliss's book was lauded in a review article by DIXIT. STIGLITZ's review article of Harcourt (1972) was not laudatory. An amusing, insightful but slightly fence-sitting article is SEN. The principal papers in the debate are collected in HARCOURT & LAING. Finally, BURMEISTER is a technically competent but conceptually naive survey. In the 1970s the results were used to criticise mainstream international trade theory, see METCALFE & STEEDMAN), and, in the 1980s, mainstream monetary theory – see ROGERS.

Harcourt's last say – to date – is HARCOURT (1994), where he concludes that "the current position is an uneasy state of rest, under the foundations of which a time bomb is ticking away, planted by a small, powerless group of economists who are either ageing or dead"(p.45).

G.C. HARCOURT

See also Cambridge controversy

Capitalism

Friedman, Milton, *Capitalism and Freedom*, Chicago: University of Chicago Press, 1962

Galbraith, John Kenneth, *The New Industrial State*, 4th edition, Boston: Houghton Mifflin, 1985

Hayek, F.A., *The Road to Serfdom*, Chicago: University of Chicago Press, 1944, new edition 1994

Heilbroner, Robert L., *The Worldly Philosophers: The Lives, Times and Ideas of Great Economic Thinkers*, 6th edition, New York: Simon and Schuster, 1986

Hume, David, *Writings on Economics*, edited by Eugene Rotwein, Madison: University of Wisconsin Press, 1970

Marshall, Alfred, *Principles of Economics*, 9th edition, edited by C.W. Guillebaud, 2 vols, London and New York: Macmillan, 1961 (1st edition 1890)

Marx, Karl, *Capital*, vol. 1: *A Critical Analysis of Capitalist Production*, London and New York: Penguin, 1976 (German edition 1867)

Novak, Michael, *The Spirit of Democratic Capitalism*, New York: Simon and Schuster, 1982

Schumpeter, Joseph A., *Capitalism, Socialism, and Democracy*, New York: Harper, 1941, London: Allen and Unwin, 1943; 6th edition London and Boston: Unwin, 1987

Smith, Adam, *An Inquiry into the Nature and Causes of the Wealth of Nations*, edited by Kathryn Sutherland, Oxford and New York: Oxford University Press, 1993 (first published 1776)

Veblen, Thorstein, *The Theory of the Leisure Class*, New York: Macmillan, 1899; with an introduction by Robert Lekachman, London and New York: Penguin, 1994

In his exploration of the causes of the disparities of wealth among nations SMITH identified the accumulation of capital – goods designed to be used in production – as a key determinant of economic growth. Capital accumulation through the institution of private property rights facilitates the division of labour that in turn raises productivity and expands trade. Almost a century later MARX assigned the term "capitalists" to producers (manufacturers) and the system where the majority of the means of production and economic activity falls to private individuals and organizations has become termed "capitalism". Smith's vision of government limited to preservation of law and order, protection of citizens, enforcement of contracts, erection of large public works, and maintenance of the conditions of competition is the widely accepted view of what constitutes the system of capitalism. Socialism, by way of contrast, shifts the locus of the ownership of the means of production from private hands to government, replacing the allocation of resources through market forces by central planning through the public sector.

HUME, writing during the decline of the guilds, the ascendancy of mercantilism, and the dawn of the industrial revolution, first broke with the entrenched belief that pursuit of self-interest was contrary to social interest. Rejecting the mercantilist fixation on the nation state's accumulation of specie, Hume's analysis of human behaviour formed a basis for his "hands off" approach to the balance of trade and a general reliance on self-interest as a basis for economic progress. Building on – but well beyond – Hume, Smith's *Wealth of Nations* was the foundation for more than a century of classical economic analysis and still represents the intellectual framework for capitalism throughout the world.

During the first half of the 19th century the ascendancy of capitalism help to usher in the industrial revolution with rapid urbanization (congestion, pollution, disease) and a working class generally characterized by low wages, long hours, and poor working conditions. Springing from the Hegelian dialectic (thesis, antithesis, synthesis), Marx envisioned capitalism evolving into socialism as the tension between the capitalists and labour resulted in the ownership of the means of production being transferred into the hands of labour, the true source of value in production. The resulting communism represents "the complete return of man to himself as a social being".

Despite Marx's predictions, capitalism continued to flourish in the Western democracies. The conceptual underpinnings of capitalist practices were given a significant boost around the end of the 19th century by the publication of the first edition of MARSHALL's *Principles*. Marshall's work ushered in the neoclassical period of economics, providing a conceptual framework that is still used in the principal textbooks to this day. His concern was with the happiness of all classes of society, equal gains in material resources, and the material progress of the human race. Among other things, his conceptual work demonstrated that in a competitive market system all factors of production, including labour, would receive a return equal to their contribution to output, and inputs and outputs would be allocated according to the preferences of individual consumers.

After fleeing from the Nazis in Austria, HAYEK ultimately shocked his host country, England, by claiming in his 1944 publication that British socialism was taking the nation down the same road trod by Hilter and his regime. Building on the traditions of Adam Smith, Hayek rejects central planning and the use of coercion in economic affairs and argues there cannot be political freedom without economic freedom. One of the best safeguards against totalitarian oppression and tyranny is the private ownership of the means of production. FRIEDMAN, in *Capitalism and Freedom*, picks up Hayek's torch, citing the free market as the only mechanism ever discovered for achieving participatory democracy. In a collection of brilliant essays he outlines the proper role for government in maintaining a system of competitive capitalism, based upon explicit summary principles. Hayek's and Friedman's books still stand as the classic intellectual defences of capitalism.

SCHUMPETER, like Marx, prophesized the collapse of capitalism, although for different reasons. For Schumpeter the key to economic growth over the long haul is the introduction of economic innovations by entrepreneurs. Clusters of innovations cause a structural shift in an economy, moving it to a new and higher growth path. With the seemly irreversible evolution of capitalism toward larger and larger industrial giants, Schumpeter saw entrepreneurship being crushed by takeovers and smothered by bureaucracy. The simultaneous shift following the Great Depression toward higher progressive taxes, rising government spending and income redistribution, the politicization of labour relations, and increased public regulation of business spelled the inevitable end of real capitalism.

VEBLEN, a founding father of the institutionalist school of economic thought, claimed that capitalism fostered a predatory leisure class engaged in such nonproductive activities as government, war, sports, and devout occupations. In order to impress others and maintain their status the leisure class engages in wasteful conspicuous consumption. Institutions, as a result of social inertia and conservatism, help to prop up the leisure class and delay social progress. Without government intervention, economic man will not evolve into social man and conspicuous consumption will continue. GALBRAITH, the most prominent current institutionalist, sees the market and consumer sovereignty being superseded by the rise of the industrial state.

Conservative rhetoric aside, a system of planning, including state control of aggregate demand, military, space and related procurement, the modern education establishment, and mature corporations with control over prices and consumer behaviour together with indifferent stockholders, has replaced the market apparatus. The time is at hand to accept this reality and ensure that the goals of the planning system are responsive to the larger purposes of society.

It is widely accepted today that market economies are more successful than centrally owned and planned economies at creating economic growth, but capitalism's apparent emphasis on individual self-interest over community, on hedonism over charity, and on meritocracy over equality remains a bitter pill for many to swallow. NOVAK, once a Jesuit candidate for the priesthood, was converted from socialism to capitalism by the reality of economic conditions in the Third World. A proponent of democratic capitalism, Novak sees extreme danger in any centralization of power and supports competition within and among the political, economic, and moral-cultural systems. Man is sinful and democratic capitalism is a differentiation of systems designed to squeeze some good from sinful tendencies. Socialism, by contrast, concentrates unconstrained power in the hands of imperfect and perhaps even evil persons. Democratic capitalism is "a system designed to be constantly reformed and transformed, and it alone of all known systems has within it the resources for transformation through peaceful means".

Finally, HEILBRONER provides for the lay person a comprehensive yet succinct review of the evolution of both capitalism and socialism. He frames the current debate, which will survive as long as our society survives, with the informed voices of the past 250 years.

JOHN STAPLEFORD

Career, concept

Arnold, John, "The Psychology of Careers in Organizations", *International Review of Industrial and Organizational Psychology*, 12 (1997): 1–37

Arthur, Michael B., Douglas T. Hall and Barbara S. Lawrence (editors), *Handbook of Career Theory*, Cambridge and New York: Cambridge University Press, 1989

Arthur, Michael B. and Denise M. Rousseau (editors), *The Boundaryless Career: A New Employment Principle for a New Organizational Era*, New York and Oxford: Oxford University Press, 1996

Gallos, Joan V., "Exploring Women's Development: Implications for Career Theory, Practice, and Research" in *Handbook of Career Theory*, 1989

Hall, Douglas T., *Careers in Organizations*, Pacific Palisades, California: Goodyear, 1976

Herriot, Peter and Carole Pemberton, "Contracting Careers", *Human Relations*, 49/6 (1996): 757–90

Kanter, Rosabeth M., "Careers and the Wealth of Nations: A Macro-Perspective on the Structure and Implications of Career Forms" in *Handbook of Career Theory*, 1989

Nicholson, N. and M. West, "Transitions, Work Histories and Careers" in *Handbook of Career Theory*, edited by Michael B. Arthur, Douglas T. Hall and Barbara S. Lawrence, Cambridge and New York: Cambridge University Press, 1989

Savickas, Mark L. and Robert W. Lent (editors), *Convergence in Career Development Theories: Implications for Science and Practice*, Palo Alto, California: CPP, 1994

Super, Donald E., "A Life-Span, Life-Space Approach to Career Development", *Journal of Vocational Behavior*, 16 (1980): 282–98

The concept of "career" has become increasingly important in the field of organizational behaviour. It encourages the study of individuals and institutions and the changing relationship between them. The current climate of industrial and organizational change has led writers to adopt definitions of "career" that are broader than the popular idea of hierarchical progress within an occupation or organization, but even recent definitions vary considerably.

ARNOLD provides a useful overview of some influential definitions of "career" and reviews some of the diverse psychological literature in the field. He suggests that a common feature of all definitions of career is that they refer to sequences of roles and positions over time.

In general, two rather separate bodies of knowledge have informed our understanding of careers: vocational psychology and organizational behaviour. The vocational psychology literature tends to focus on early career decision making, and many theories in this tradition have direct implications for career counselling. In contrast, the organizational literature on careers is more concerned with later career development and how organizational practices and processes affect this.

SAVICKAS & LENT, in the former tradition, provide a useful resource on the main theories of career choice and development. The book arose from a conference organized to explore the possibilities for convergence between disparate theories, and each of the most well-known theorists

describes the basic concepts of his or her own theories and then discusses the possibility of developing more unifying approaches. The chapters by Krumboltz, Dawis, Holland, Bordin and Super provide general summaries of the theories, as well as thoughts about innovative career constructs and frameworks that could help to link the various approaches. Not surprisingly, some authors are reluctant to see any approach other than their own as the source of these frameworks, but the book contains useful analyses and commentaries on the central theories in the field.

Within the organizational behaviour literature, ARTHUR, HALL & LAWRENCE is a key text on career theory, and several chapters are worthy of mention in this review. In the editor's introduction ("Generating New Directions in Career Theory: The Case for a Transdisciplinary Approach"), they discuss the diverse social science perspectives that can potentially contribute to the study of individuals, organizations, and their interaction, and argue that although psychology and sociology are the most common disciplines employed, others, for example economics and politics, could equally play a role in theory development. GALLOS, in her chapter on women's career development, asks how far current concepts of career encompass the unique experiences of women, and this analysis also raises questions about the models of career success implicit in notions of career development more generally. In the final chapter of the book KANTER argues for broader notions of career that take account of the fact that for many individuals career development takes place independently from employing organizations. Her outline of the main features of professional, entrepreneurial and bureaucratic careers also leads to a discussion of some of the societal consequences of different career patterns and forms.

A distinction is commonly made between objective and subjective careers, and this distinction is discussed and elaborated in several chapters of ARTHUR, HALL & LAWRENCE. Objectively, it is possible to observe and describe the positions individuals have held, both within and between employing organizations, and plot changes over time. However, this is only part of the picture. The subjective sense people make of their careers has long been a theme in this field. For example, in an influential article, SUPER uses the image of a rainbow to describe individuals' "life space" and their experiences of the various roles within it. This model provides a view of career that is contextualized within adult development generally, but it is more descriptive than explanatory. Little attention is given to how careers are experienced within organizations.

Other writers take a more interactive view of careers, and focus more on the process of career development, rather than attributes of the individual or the organizational context. NICHOLSON & WEST, for example, view careers as sequences of transitions, and describe the reciprocal influence of individuals and organizations on the preparation for, and adjustment to, changes in work roles. This model draws attention to the dynamic nature of careers and it can be applied equally to minor role changes within an employing organization or to more significant changes of occupation or industrial sector. Unlike many other approaches to career development, this framework pays some attention to emotional states and reactions, although the emphasis is more on negative rather than positive emotions.

A common theme in the literature is the need to exercise self-direction over one's career development. HALL first coined the term "Protean career" in 1976 to refer to the "interminable series of experiments and explorations" that describe the greater personal responsibility that, arguably, is needed to cope with career-related tasks. HERRIOT & PEMBERTON take that view that employees should proactively negotiate and renegotiate their "psychological contract" (defined as what they expect to offer their employer and what they expect their employer to provide). A model of organizational careers is presented that builds upon their definition of careers as "the repeated renegotiation of the psychological contract", and sets out the likely consequences when contracts are either honoured or violated. It is argued that these negotiations can be implicit, but the model does rather suggest that individuals who for whatever reason are unable to discuss their needs and expectations with their employer do not have careers, in this sense of the term. For this reason it may be more appropriate to describe careers as repeated "understandings" rather than "negotiations" of expectations.

ARTHUR & ROUSSEAU introduce the term "boundaryless career" to emphasize how individuals need to take responsibility for their own futures as their careers become more independent of organizational structures. The term "boundaryless" is used to refer to a range of different types of "postcorporate" careers, including professional careers as well as those characterized by greater inter- and intra-organizational mobility. The book lacks cohesion and would have benefited by more intervention from the editors to integrate ideas. It is also debatable whether the term "boundaryless" is precise enough to be useful. However, it contains several stimulating chapters on ideas about the changing nature of careers.

JENNIFER M. KIDD

Career counselling

Handy, Charles, *The Hungry Spirit: Beyond Capitalism: A Quest for Purpose in the Modern World*, London: Hutchinson, 1997; New York: Broadway Books, 1998

Herr, Edwin L. and Stanley H. Cramer, *Career Guidance and Counseling Through the Life Span: Systematic Approaches*, 5th edition, New York: HarperCollins, 1996

Herr, Edwin L., "A Personal View – Career Counselling: A Process in Process", *British Journal of Guidance and Counselling*, 25 (1997): 81–93

Holland, John L., Barbara A. Fritzsche and Amy B. Powell, *Self-Directed Search (SDS): Technical Manual*, Odessa, Florida: Psychological Assessment Resources, 1994

Holland, John L., "New and Old Perspectives", *British Journal of Guidance and Counselling*, 26 (1998): 555–58

Isaacson, Lee E. and Duane Brown, *Career Information, Career Counseling, and Career Development*, 7th edition, Needham Heights, Massachusetts: Allyn and Bacon, 2000

Nelson-Jones, Richard, *Lifeskills Helping: Helping Others Through a Systematic People-Centered Approach*, Pacific Grove, California: Brooks/Cole Publishing, 1993

Parmenter, Trevor R., "Quality of Life of People with Developmental Disabilities", *International Review of Research in Mental Retardation*, 18 (1992): 247–87

Patton, Wendy and Mary McMahon (editors), *Career Development in Practice: A Systems Theory Perspective*, North Sydney, Australia: New Hobsons Press, 1997

Watts, A.G., Ruth Hawthorne, John Killeen, Bill Law, Jenny Kidd and Jennifer M. Kidd, *Rethinking Careers Education and Guidance: Theory, Policy and Practice*, London and New York: Routledge, 1997

HERR & CRAMER's comprehensive text examines a wide range of aspects relating to career guidance, career counselling, and career education for children, adolescents, and adults in educational institutions (primary, secondary, tertiary), business, industry, and community agencies. The authors trace the evolution of career counselling, with particular emphasis on the North American perspective, from meagre beginnings in the 1800s to its current prominence as an essential design feature of the interdependent global economy. The book provides detailed information on the use of developmental approaches, the identification of particular techniques, assessment devices, materials and resources, relevant research, and social issues.

ISAACSON & BROWN give prominence to both theory and practice. Key historical and contemporary developments lead into an outline of future trends. Most information relates particularly to the American context, however the book has relevance for career counselling services worldwide. Career information sources are listed and details of advantages, disadvantages, and storage methods provided. Organization and delivery demands of primary, secondary, tertiary, and adult programs are presented with strong links drawn between career development assessment and career counselling. The process of finding a job in the electronic era is described, as is the introduction of several new theories.

Theory, policy, and practice are examined from a United Kingdom perspective in WATTS *et al.* An extensive review of career theories is provided and some new career learning theories are introduced. The development of career provision in schools, colleges, higher education, work, and other organizations is examined and the main aspects of practice are highlighted including the use of computer technology. Particular strengths are the exploration of ways of supporting development and evaluation, the analysis of the role of public policy and the review of development of guidance systems from other parts of the world.

HOLLAND is "the author of a traditional career theory and several related inventories and scales, . . . white and upper-middle-class, . . . trained in the heyday of logical positivism . . . [and is] sceptical about strategies that have a tenuous relation to evidence" (Holland, 1998, p. 555). In his theory, occupational choice is viewed as an expression of personality. A typology of six different personal orientations to life has been proposed: Realistic (R), Investigative (I), Artistic (A), Social (S), Enterprising (E), and Conventional (C). A hexagonal model assists defining relations among these personality types and environments and their interactions. This trait-factor theory has been extensively researched and the principal tenets supported. HOLLAND, FRITZSCHE & POWELL's self directed search, which is based on Holland's theory, continues to be highly regarded as both efficient and capable of achieving consistency and differentiation across a diverse array of social and cultural settings.

HANDY provides a vision of work in the 21st century. He argues that purpose in life better comes from philosophy than from economics. "Proper selfishness" (p.9) is the realization that the process of making the world a better place begins with our own actions. A redesigned education system, promoting the feeling that life and society is ours to shape, prepares individuals to develop increased levels of personal responsibility and begins the process. In a future where 20 per cent are overworked and overpaid, with 80 per cent unemployed or underemployed, expanded work definitions including both paid (wage work, fee work) and free work (homework, gift work, and study work) will be required.

HERR identifies three significant factors fuelling the constant expansion and redefinition of career guidance, counselling, and intervention as: one, the emergence of new theories to provide improved insights into possible benefits; two, social equality legislation; and three, increased demands for greater efficiency. Career counselling has taken on both macro (international, national) and micro characteristics (personal, local). The process has become both a national instrument of human capital development, influenced by changing economic, social and political dynamics, and more chooser-focussed. This expansion into the personal involves the integration of work roles with the total person, heightened awareness of lifestyle options/choices, and a fusion of career and personal counselling.

Individuals often encounter problems because they have inadequate lifeskills. Some lifeskill counselling fails to provide sufficient assistance to ensure new skills are learnt, maintained over time, and internalized for use within a wide range of different individual future life circumstances. Good lifeskills enable individuals to live more effective lives, both within and outside their work roles. NELSON-JONES offers a five-stage model to assist individuals acquire lifeskills for them to assume increased responsibility for their own feelings, thoughts, and actions. Clients become their own best helpers through problem confrontation and clarification, problem assessment and skill redefinition, setting goals and self-help interventions, plan implementation and evaluation of consequences.

PATTON and McMAHON's edited book was written by ten specialists who argue that systems theory facilitates a more holistic approach to career development than those currently used thereby extending the traditional reliance on trait and factor analysis. The approach offers a convergence of career theory with practice by providing a framework to acknowledge and respond to the rapid changes and increasing complexity of the individual's world. Furthermore the approach fits in with increased pressure within society for institutions to prepare individuals for careers that match the individual's interpersonal life. Practical applications, where a systems theory approach to career development is examined include women, Australian Aborigines, poverty, rural isolation, multiculturalism, multiple disadvantage, and use within changing organizations.

Career development for individuals with disabilities is mostly debated under the disability banner with the topic focus expanding to include work, leisure, and lifeskills. Particular attention in the literature is given to supporting the individual's transition from the comparative safety and security of school

to the relative uncertainty of independent adult life in the community. Quality of life has emerged as a possible measure of disability service success in the career development area. PARMENTER provides an extensive review of the quality of life literature. He describes a three component model consisting of the individual's perception of self (cognitive, affective, personal life style), functional behaviours (social interactions, material well being, accommodation, and access), and social influences (attitudes, values).

PAUL PAGLIANO

Career guidance

Cochran, Larry, *Career Counseling: A Narrative Approach*, London: Sage, 1997

Holland, John, *Making Vocational Choices: A Theory of Vocational Personalities and Work Environments*, 2nd edition, Englewood Cliffs, New Jersey: Prentice Hall, 1985

Kidd, Jennifer M. and John Killeen, "Are the Effects of Careers Guidance Worth Having? Changes in Practice and Outcomes", *Journal of Occupational and Organizational Psychology*, 65/3 (1992): 219–34

Killeen, John, Michael White and A.G. Watts, *The Economic Value of Careers Guidance*, London: Policy Studies Institute / National Institute for Careers Education and Counselling, 1992

Roberts, Ken, "The Social Conditions, Consequences and Limitations of Careers Guidance", *British Journal of Guidance and Counselling*, 5/1 (1977): 1–9

Savickas, Mark L. and W. Bruce Walsh (editors), *Handbook of Career Counseling Theory and Practice*, Palo Alto, California: Davies Black, 1996

Super, Donald E., *The Psychology of Careers*, New York: Harper and Row, 1957

Walsh, W. Bruce and Samuel H. Osipow (editors), *Career Counseling: Contemporary Topics in Vocational Psychology*, Hillsdale, New Jersey: Erlbaum, 1990

Watts, A.G. *et al.*, *Rethinking Careers Education and Guidance: Theory, Policy and Practice*, London: Routledge, 1996

In the UK, the term "career guidance" has come to be used as an umbrella term to describe a range of activities employed to help individuals with career decisions. These include group work, provision of information, assessment of individual differences, and in-depth career counselling. A range of public and private sector agencies provide guidance services, and there is considerable diversity in the type of service offered – from one short interview to a series of counselling sessions spanning several months.

Until recently, theory and research in career guidance was dominated by the American vocational psychology literature. Among the theories with greatest impact were those of Super and Holland. SUPER, in his most well-known book, proposed that career development proceeds through stages as individuals seek to "implement a self-concept" in their choice of occupation. He identified five career stages – growth, exploration, establishment, maintenance, and decline – and set out key developmental tasks within each stage. Super's work had far-reaching effects on the practice of career education and guidance; schools began to introduce career education at an earlier stage as they recognized that young people needed to reach a stage of "vocational maturity" before being able to make wise decisions about their future. However, this work has been criticized for cultural bias and for failing to deal adequately with adult career development and with the experiences of women. Furthermore, it is largely a descriptive model of career development that lacks explanatory propositions.

Developmental theories of careers can be contrasted with differential theories, which view career choices as largely determined by individual differences (such as interests, personality traits, values, and aptitudes). The most widely researched theory of this type is that of HOLLAND, who proposes that individuals seek occupations that are congruent with their interests, defined as preferences for particular work activities. Holland argues that people and occupational environments can be categorized into six interest types – realistic, investigative, artistic, social, enterprising, and conventional – and that these types form a hexagon. Adjacent types on the hexagon (such as "social/enterprising") tend to be more strongly related than opposite types (such as "artistic/conventional"). Furthermore, occupational choice is the result of attempts to achieve congruence between interests and occupational environments, and the greater the congruence the more likely the individual will achieve job satisfaction and a stable career. Holland's theory suggests that the assessment of occupational interests should be a central activity in career guidance. The theory still stimulates a vast amount of research, but it takes a predominantly static approach to choice and lacks attention to adult career development. In addition, recent changes in the world of work call the structure of the hexagon itself into question.

A useful overview of contemporary approaches to career counselling is WALSH & OSIPOW. This book discusses six models: trait factor, person centred, psychodynamic, developmental, social learning, and social psychological. Computer-assisted career counselling is also presented as a separate approach, but, arguably, computer technology can be used within any of the other approaches covered. The final chapter of this book attempts to summarize and integrate the approaches and to make more explicit the career counselling techniques suggested by each. Similarly the book by SAVICKAS & WALSH offers a comprehensive review, mainly based on the American literature. However, it provides a more sophisticated exploration of the interface between theory and practice. Several chapters, for example, discuss how the disparate cultures of researchers and practitioners limit the ways in which theory and practice inform each other.

Writers in the UK have tended to pay more attention to the social and economic context of guidance than to the psychological processes of career development. Here, in contrast with other countries, educationalists, psychologists, sociologists and, more recently, economists have all contributed to theory and research in career guidance. ROBERTS's influential paper, for example, castigates psychologists for not taking account of the roles of social background and the structure of opportunities in the entry into work, and questioned how far career guidance could make any difference to the work trajectories of most young people. The debate that ensued after the publication of this paper highlighted the sterility of purely psychological or purely sociological theories of career guidance and development and demonstrated the need for a multidisciplinary approach.

WATTS et al. discusses theory, policy, and practice in all sectors of provision in the UK. The chapters on theory cover career theories as well as guidance theories, and issues concerning relationships between theory and practice are debated throughout. In the current context of greater career uncertainty and discontinuity lifelong career guidance is receiving more attention from policymakers, and three chapters deal with policy-related matters. Guidance is presented here as a sociopolitical intervention: it can be a tool of social reform, but it can also act to preserve the status quo. Five areas of practice are examined: the career counselling interview, career education, experience-based learning, recording achievement and action planning, and the use of computers in guidance.

A number of writers have identified a trend away from positivist methodologies in this field. Constructivist approaches, which emphasize the individual's personal narrative and construction of meaning, are becoming more popular with researchers and practitioners alike (though there has been little informed or balanced debate about the relative merits of positivism and constructivism as applied to guidance). Guidance practitioners using methods based on this approach aim to help clients identify themes across different elements of their "life story", re-author their story, and encourage a greater sense of agency in the narrative. COCHRAN's book is one of the first attempts to offer practical guidance on how to use narrative methods in career counselling. Although it succeeds in incorporating diverse theories and approaches into the narrative framework, it pays little attention to the difficulties individuals may have in making sense of discontinuity and fragmentation in their working lives.

There has been longstanding interest in evaluating the effectiveness of guidance interventions. KIDD & KILLEEN review research into the outcomes of career guidance, tracking how changes in practice over the years have led to the use of different types of outcome criteria in studies of its effectiveness. Early studies focused on job satisfaction and success, but as guidance became more client centred developmental evaluators shifted their attention to "learning outcomes" (such as self-awareness, knowledge of opportunities, and decision-making skills). The authors also argue for extending the range of outcomes to include the planning, monitoring, and negotiating skills needed for effective career management. KILLEEN, WHITE & WATTS take a broader perspective, with a convincing analysis of the potential contribution of career guidance to a range of economic outcomes for individuals and for society. They also review studies that bear upon these outcomes, identifying gaps in present knowledge. Their conclusion, which should be of interest to policy makers, is that guidance has the potential to make a substantial contribution to the workings of the labour market.

JENNIFER M. KIDD

See also Careers: career concept, Career counselling

Catastrophe theory

Bonanno, G., "Monopoly Equilibria and Catastrophe
Theory", *Australian Economic Papers*, 26/49 (1987):
197–215

Fischer, E.O. and W. Jammernegg, "Empirical Investigation of
a Catastrophe Theory Extension of the Phillips Curve",
Review of Economics and Statistics, 68/1 (1986): 9–17

Gregory-Allen, Russell B. and Glenn V. Henderson Jr, "A
Brief Review of Catastrophe Theory and a Test in a
Corporate Failure Context", *Financial Review*, 26/2
(1991): 127–55

Ho, Thomas S.Y. and Anthony Saunders, "A Catastrophe
Model of Bank Failure", *Journal of Finance*, 35/5 (1980):
1189–1207

Pol, Eduardo, "Theoretical Economics and Catastrophe
Theory: An Appraisal", *Australian Economic Papers*,
32/61 (1993): 258–71

Rand, David, "Thresholds in Pareto Sets", *Journal of
Mathematical Economics*, 3/2 (1976): 139–54

Varian, Hal R., "Catastrophe Theory and the Business
Cycle", *Economic Enquiry*, 17/1 (1979): 14–28

Vendrik, Maarten C.M., "Habits, Hystereses and
Catastrophes in Labor Supply", *Journal of Economic
Behaviour and Organization*, 20/3 (1993): 353–72

Catastrophe theory is a branch of mathematics developed by, among others, the French mathematician René Thom, with a view to application in biology. It is particularly useful in modelling situations involving a discontinuous relationship between variables and their underlying causes. In such a situation, a small change in one variable can give rise to a jump in another. Economists have used catastrophe theory as a modelling tool because some economic variables (such as exchange rates and share prices) are actually observed to jump.

Economic models frequently involve multiple equilibria and have the property that small parameter perturbations can cause equilibria to vanish or reappear. A variable whose level is determined by an equilibrium that suddenly vanishes, will jump to a neighbouring equilibrium. Many of the economic applications of catastrophe theory rely on a theorem (due to Thom) which provides a topological classification of these singularities in terms of the "elementary catastrophes".

RAND examines a pure exchange economy, focusing attention on the set of Pareto-efficient allocations (the "Pareto set"). He follows a procedure common in catastrophe models, namely to distinguish a fast from a slow dynamic. In his model, the former represents trading that moves the economy towards the Pareto set, whereas the latter reflects changes in traders' endowments. Threshold points, where stability is lost, occur when the Hessian matrix is singular. Rand argues that such singularities may arise if at least one trader has nonconvex preferences and that, under certain conditions, the structurally stable singularities of the model could be classified by appeal to Thom's theorem.

BONANNO develops a simple model in which a monopolist can sell to a large number of consumers with different reservation prices. He characterizes monopoly equilibrium by means of the hazard rate function associated with the distribution of reservation prices. Thom's classification theorem is then invoked to provide a description of the way in which equilibrium price and output depend on cost and demand conditions. The paper contains an interesting example in which the firm's response to changes in demand is discontinuous and apparently perverse.

An interesting way to apply catastrophe theory is to treat a catastrophe manifold as a description of the equilibria of a differential equation (or system of differential equations). That part of the manifold consisting of the stable equilibria will act as an attractor for the differential equations, whereas that part consisting of the unstable equilibria will act as a repellor. Movements near the attractor correspond to a "slow dynamic", and movements ("jumps") between sections of the attractor correspond to a "fast dynamic". This approach is adopted by VARIAN, who provides a model of the business cycle. Following Kaldor, he assumes an investment function that is nonlinear in the level of GNP, and combines this with a standard consumption function. In such a model, multiple macroeconomic equilibria arise. The fast dynamic is provided by the usual multiplier mechanism that moves the economy towards equilibrium, for a given level of the capital stock. The slow dynamic corresponds to changes in the capital stock determined by the (net) investment function. Applying catastrophe theory, Varian shows that the model implies business cycles involving discontinous leaps and drops in GNP and investment. Varian's model has been criticized on the grounds that it is not explicitly based on maximizing behaviour, and does not incorporate rational expectations. These are not fatal criticisms, however, as the ultimate test of an economic model must be empirical. Moreover, Varian's model is interesting in that it illustrates how catastrophe theory can be used in conjunction with differential equations.

Catastrophe models often display the property of hysteresis (where the level of a variable may depend not only on the levels of the variables determining it, but also on their recent timepaths). VENDRIK develops a model of locally unstable habit formation involving consumption, household time, and corporate time. The model has multiple equilibria and exhibits both catastrophic jumps and hysteresis. Vendrik argues that his model explains some dramatic, and actually observed, changes in labour-supply preferences and behaviour. Examples include the low motivation on the part of the long-term unemployed to obtain employment, and the strong orientation towards paid employment of women who had formerly worked only in the home.

POL provides a critical appraisal of catastrophe theory as a tool in economic theory. He starts by contrasting "classical" and "modern" analytical procedures. The former are typified by Samuelson's famous formulation of comparative statics and dynamics (see Samuelson, *Foundations of Economic Analysis*, 1983), whereas the latter involve the application of differential topology to analyse singularities and bifurcations. Pol then discusses the "fast/slow" approach to dynamics, which figures in many economic applications of catastrophe theory, and he provides a useful and concise discussion of Thom's classification theorem. This is followed by an illustrative example, involving the application of catastrophe theory to analyse balance-of-payments crises. An important feature of Pol's article is that he discusses the limitations of catastrophe theory as an economic modelling device, as well as its advantages. In particular he points out that: (a) Thom's theorem does not specify that singularities *must* occur in any particular model, but merely classifies any singularities that do occur; (b) even though Thom's theorem does not require restrictions on the dimensionality of the behaviour space, it does require that the parameter space must not be more than five-dimensional; and (c) as applied to dynamic models, catastrophe theory can only deal with "gradient-like" dynamics. Pol concludes by arguing that there are relatively few situations in theoretical economics that satisfy the restrictions necessary to apply the mathematics of catastrophe theory.

FISCHER & JAMMERNEGG investigate inflationary hysteresis using a modified catastrophe theory approach. An important modification is the analysis of stochastic rather than deterministic differential equations. Using the Livingston survey data set on inflationary expectations in the US, they apply a modified least-squares regression technique capable of estimating a multi modal density function. The article is an important example of an empirical test of a catastrophe model. It illustrates a fundamental difficulty with catastrophe theory, namely that Thom's theorem provides a *qualitative* (topological) classification of singularities – i.e. that, under certain conditions, a singularity must be topologically equivalent (diffeomorphic) to one of the "elementary catastrophes". A huge variety of relationships will satisfy this equivalence, and thus catastrophe theory provides little guidance on the specification of equations for estimation purposes.

HO & SAUNDERS apply catastrophe theory to an important policy issue – the regulation of banks. They note that most models of bank failure assume that the path towards bankruptcy or insolvency is a smooth one, not involving sudden change. This approach has led banking regulators to adopt a variety of early-warning indicators to help them identify potential problem banks. The authors argue that this approach is unlikely to be useful if bank failures are sudden and catastrophic jumps. Accordingly, they develop a catastrophe model in which, under reasonable behavioural assumptions, the probability of bank failure can jump suddenly, even with a continuous source of lender-of-last-resort loans. This model shows that, even if regulators intervene to aid banks with high perceived probabilities of failure, this will not be sufficient to prevent catastrophic jumps in the probability of failure. They go on to discuss which banks are most likely to fail, and the circumstances under which several banks might fail simultaneously.

GREGORY-ALLEN & HENDERSON also deal with the question of corporate bankruptcy. They review catastrophe theory and then provide an empirical test of a catastrophe model of bankruptcy. They construct a time series of stock returns for companies that have filed under the chapter 11 bankruptcy procedure. Under certain common conditions, the model predicts a structural shift in stock returns as the date of filing is approached. The authors' results confirm that such a shift does occur in a way that supports the catastrophe model, which they feel raises questions about some of the techniques commonly used in the analysis of bankruptcies.

DONALD A.R. GEORGE

Catch-all parties

Burin, Frederic S. and Kurt L. Shell (editors), *Politics, Law and Social Change: Selected Essays of Otto Kirchheimer*, New York: Columbia University Press, 1969

Downs, Anthony, *An Economic Theory of Democracy*, New York: Harper and Row, 1957

Katz, Richard S. and Peter Mair, "Changing Models of Party Organization and Party Democracy: The Emergence of the Cartel Party", *Party Politics*, 1/1 (1995): 5–28

Kirchheimer, Otto, "The Transformation of the Western European Party System" in *Political Parties and Political Development*, edited by Joseph LaPalombara and Myron Weiner, Princeton, New Jersey: Princeton University Press, 1966

Koole, Ruud, "Cadre, Catch-all or Cartel? A Comment on the Notion of the Cartel Party", *Party Politics*, 2/4 (1996): 507–23

Mair, Peter (editor), *The West European Party System*, Oxford and New York: Oxford University Press, 1990

Mendilow, Jonathan, "Israel's Labor Alignment in the 1984 Elections: Catch-all Tactics in a Divided Society", *Comparative Politics*, 20 (1988): 443–60

Roper, Steven D., "The Romanian Party System and the Catch-all Party Phenomenon", *East European Quarterly*, 28/4 (1994): 519–32

Wolinetz, Steven B., "The Transformation of Western European Party Systems Revisited", *West European Politics*, 2 (1979): 4–28

KIRCHHEIMER originated the term "catch-all" for political parties, and remains influential as a touchstone. Focusing first on the historical development of different types of political organization, Kirchheimer observed that political parties were attempting to exchange effectiveness in depth for a wider audience and more immediate electoral success. By sketching out a number of claims about the changing functions performed by political parties, Kirchheimer sparked much subsequent debate. The article is strongest in identifying specific characteristics of catch-all parties, such as reduced ideological baggage, strengthened top leadership, downgraded role for individual party members, movement toward wider recruitment (instead of focusing on appeals to a core constituency), and secured access to a range of specific interest groups.

DOWNS helped provide the theoretical underpinnings for the concept of catch-all parties by positing that political parties attempt to maximize the number of votes they receive. By drawing an analogy between political organizations and economically rational entrepreneurs, Downs suggested that parties would change their platforms in order to attract voters.

The articles compiled in BURIN & SHELL further elaborate Kircheimer's thinking about the concept of catch-all parties. In particular, the essays in Part two of the volume – concerned with the transformation of democratic politics – consider party change and development. The same preoccupation caused WOLINETZ to usefully reconsider Kirchheimer's contribution in the light of further changes in party alignments in Western Europe.

MENDILOW and ROPER are two more recent examples of works that apply the concept of catch-all parties. Exploring the operation of such parties in Israel, Mendilow posits that, in Western multiparty systems, they will suffer electoral losses unless they retrieve their ideological cargo. The article examines the decision taken by Israel's two largest parties (Alignment and Likud) to adopt catch-all tactics, and the consequences of that decision in the period leading up to the parliamentary elections of 1981 and some years beyond. ROPER, by contrast, focuses on the Romanian case to examine whether broad-based political organizations in Eastern Europe can be described as catch-all parties. In addition to explicating the theoretical relationship between transformations in the party system and the process of nation-building, the article elaborates on earlier work to suggest that catch-all parties have indeed emerged in Eastern Europe.

KATZ & MAIR represents perhaps the most important recent theoretical reconsideration of catch-all parties. The authors challenge the notion (based on the precipitous decline in party membership and related observations) that political parties are waning in influence. Instead, they argue, social scientists should conceive of various models of how parties relate to civil society and to the state. Within this typology, a new model has recently emerged: the cartel party. Cartel parties become agents of the state and collude with each other in employing state resources to ensure their own survival. The article argues that catch-all parties and other forms of political organization have been transformed into cartel parties. Rather than declining, political parties have simply changed form.

KOOLE responds to KATZ & MAIR by arguing that, instead of attempting to discern which kind of party (cadre, catch-all, or cartel) is dominant, it makes more sense to develop a typology that allows for different types to coexist, without assuming that a single model reigns supreme. The author questions both the conceptual clarity and the empirical validity of the notion of cartel parties. The relationship between civil society and the state that the cartel party model assumes may be too static, while at the same time the evidence is mixed about the extent to which parties collude to maintain their dominance.

Finally, MAIR usefully compiles abbreviated versions of the Kirchheimer and Wolinetz articles discussed above, along with other seminal works that analyse political parties and party systems.

WILLEM MAAS

See also Party politics

Causal relationship

Baumrind, Diana, "Specious Causal Attributions in the Social Sciences: The Reformulated Stepping-Stone Theory of Heroin Use as Exemplar", *Journal of Personality and Social Psychology*, 45/6 (1983): 1289–98
Blalock, H.M. Jr (editor), *Causal Models in Panel and Experimental Designs*, New York: Aldine, 1985
Cliff, Norman, "Some Cautions Concerning the Application of Causal Modeling Methods", *Multivariate Behavioral Research*, 18/1 (1983): 115–26
Finkel, Steven E., *Causal Analysis with Panel Data*, Thousand Oaks, California and London: Sage, 1995
Luecke, Daniel F. and Noel F. McGinn, "Regression Analyses and Education Production Functions: Can They Be Trusted?", *Harvard Educational Review*, 45/3 (1975): 325–50
Reichardt, Charles S. and Harry F. Gollob, "Satisfying the Constraints of Causal Modeling" in *Advances in Quasi-Experimental Design and Analysis*, edited by William M.K. Trochim, San Francisco: Jossey Bass, 1986
Sobel, Michael E., "Effect Analysis and Causation in Linear Structural Equation Models", *Psychometrika*, 55/3 (1990): 495–515

The standard for determining causal relations between variables is the controlled experiment in which an independent variable is manipulated to see the effect on a measured, dependent variable. In essence, when a researcher manipulates an independent variable and holds all other variables constant, any changes in the dependent variable can be causally attributed to the effects of the independent variable. BLALOCK has edited a very useful volume that deals with using causal models in experimental designs. Although researchers may habitually assume that causal interpretations emerge without ambiguity from experimental designs, Blalock's edited volume contains some useful caveats regarding interpretation. The creation of variables and the nature of the research design are discussed as important considerations. Further, Blalock's work includes a discussion of causal determination in panel designs involving repeated measurements over time. For this consideration, measurement issues and reliability predominate. This book is not overly technical and should be accessible to those with a modest background in research design and notation and in data analysis.

In recent years, researchers have begun to use statistical controls rather than experimental controls in an attempt to determine causal relations. Although researchers can use these statistical approaches to assess causation, CLIFF points out that they should do so with caution. He points out some of the limitations associated with these approaches. He makes four main points regarding drawing causal inferences based on statistical models. First, data do not confirm a statistical model; rather they merely fail to disconfirm it. This idea comes from Popper's philosophical analysis of the scientific method. A corollary idea is that, even if a proposed model is supported by research, there is an infinite number of others that will also do so. One's initial model may not be the most nearly veridical approach. Second, correlational data are fundamentally unsuitable for assessing causation. Unknown variables may actually influence the measured variables, the so-called third variable problem. Cliff states that one's confidence in causal statements can be enhanced through converging lines of evidence. The third main point that Cliff makes involves the fact that, simply because we develop a hypothetical construct, it does mean that our measurement of that construct is useful. The manifest variable and the construct will not be isomorphic; further, measurement of the manifest variable is subject to random error. Finally, when researchers use statistical models, they can test multiple models until they hit upon one that fits the data. The resulting *ex post facto* explanations may be due entirely to chance. Subsequently, if such conclusions are applied to social policies, the results may be problematic. In a very readable article, Cliff reviews the principles of causal inference and the limitations of using statistics to replace experimental manipulation.

One of the limitations of using correlational data to determine causation is that, although variables may be related and causation might be present, it may be difficult to determine which of two variables is the cause and which is the effect. This is the so-called directionality problem. FINKEL discusses potential solutions to this problem through the use of cross-lagged panel correlations. He discusses the three widely cited conditions required for concluding that variable X exerts a causal effect on variable Y: (a) X must covary with Y; (b) X must precede Y; and (c) X must be the most likely factor to cause Y. Finkel's slim volume especially focuses on the temporal question. He discusses relevant concerns in collecting data over time and in imputing causality. These concerns include the possibility of reciprocal causality, in which X and Y may affect one another, leading to potentially poor models of causality. Further, problems with reliability of measurement can lead to statistical models suggesting a poorer fit to the data than actually exists. Finally, the presence of unmeasured variables that affect both X and Y may lead to spurious determination of causality. In some cases, based on theoretical or logical grounds, one could rule out this third variable problem, but it may pose significant concerns in others. Finkel presents potential solutions to this difficult problem. Finkel's presentation is accessible and relatively nontechnical, although it is easier to comprehend if one is familiar with the basics of the notation commonly used in statistical modelling.

Discussions of causation regarding complex, social behaviours, especially those associated with high visibility issues, provide continued controversy in the social sciences. BAUMRIND discusses replacement of experimental controls with statistical controls in experimentation; she uses the notion of factors leading to heroin use to illustrate her points. An obvious tradeoff is present here: experimental controls artificially constrain social situations so that the experimental findings may not be generalizable beyond the immediate setting. At the same time, those experimental controls let researchers examine potentially causal variables specifically. Statistical controls show a reversed strength and weakness. One underlying problem in asserting causal relationships is that social behaviour is malleable and may change precisely because a supposed causal relationship has been spotted. Further, human behaviour is so plastic that, in the social sciences, the associations between a potential causal variable and its effect are often weak. As such, it is critical for social scientists to recognize the possibility that other, intervening variables provide the causal link between behaviours. Baumrind presents an interesting example of the dilemmas facing researchers regarding causation.

When researchers study events in natural settings, random assignment of participants to conditions is generally impossible. Consequently, attempts to identify causal relations among variables are made only with great caution. REICHARDT & GOLLOB describe a method for generating tentative, causal statements with data using nonrandom assignment. This approach is structural equation modelling. The authors provide a generally nontechnical description of structural modelling, which involves creating a variable that is a weighted, additive combination of a number of independent or predictor variables. Reichardt & Gollob discuss some of the pitfalls of this technique, specifically bias in estimating the parameters of the structural equation, the omission of relevant causal variables in the equation, the imperfect measurement of the variables, and ignoring the fact that in many cases it is imprudent to assume that effects follow causes without delay. The authors discuss how one can deal with, but probably not eliminate, these problems. In the end, they note, researchers should employ designs with random assignment in addition to nonequivalent designs.

In a very technical presentation, SOBEL analyses the use of structural equation models for assessing causation. He asserts that researchers using this approach to modelling sometimes impute causal relations when they are not logically or mathematically justified. He discusses measurement of the effects of an independent variable on a dependent variable and of intervening variables on the dependent variables. A major point is that, in some cases, the presence of intervening variables may render a causal analysis inappropriate. This article presents a sophisticated discussion about the limitations of using structural equation modelling to determine causation; it requires background in both philosophy and causal modelling for full appreciation.

LUECKE & McGINN provide a simulation that models several factors that are associated with educational achievement among students. Using causal relations programmed into the data, they examine both longitudinal and cross-sectional models that characterize academic progress. A number of earlier studies using cross-sectional designs had revealed that factors like school quality and teacher quality are less predictive of student achievement than is family background. Luecke & McGinn argue that the lack of importance of school and teacher quality arise from the choice of cross-sectional designs. Longitudinal research would reveal a different pattern of importance among variables. In short, the choice of research design and statistical analysis has a profound impact on the conclusions drawn. On a more general level, one can conclude that assessing causation in a dynamic, time-dependent environment is laden with methodological problems. This article provides a useful discussion of some of those methodological issues and the tradeoffs that researchers must make in their decisions about research design.

BERNARD C. BEINS

See also Causation, economic, Causation, sociology

Causation, economic

Cartwright, Nancy, *Nature's Capacities and Their Measurement*, Oxford: Clarendon Press, and New York: Oxford University Press, 1989

Cartwright, Nancy, *The Dappled World: A Study of the Boundaries of Science*, Cambridge and New York: Cambridge University Press, 1999

Engle, Robert F., David F. Hendry and Jean-François Richard, "Exogeneity", *Econometrica*, 51/2 (March 1983): 277–304

Granger, C.W.J., "Testing for Causality: A Personal Viewpoint", *Journal of Economic Dynamics and Control*, 2/4 (November 1980): 329–52

Hausman, Daniel M., *Essays on Philosophy and Economic Methodology*, Cambridge and New York: Cambridge University Press, 1992

Hoover, Kevin D., "The Logic of Causal Inference: Econometrics and the Conditional Analysis of Causation", *Economics and Philosophy*, 6/2 (October 1990): 207–34

Hoover, Kevin D., *Causality in Macroeconomics*, Cambridge: Cambridge University Press, 2000

Simon, Herbert Alexander, "Causal Ordering and Identifiability" in *Models of Man – Social and Rational; Mathematical Essays on Rational Human Behavior in a Social Setting*, New York: Wiley, 1957

Woodward, James, "Causation and Explanation in Econometrics" in *On the Reliability of Economic Models: Essays in the Philosophy of Economics*, edited by Daniel Little, Dordrecht: Kluwer, 1995

The debate on causation in economics has traditionally revolved around three questions: Is economics about causal relations (an interpretative problem)? If yes, what sort of relations are these (a conceptual-ontological problem)? And how can we know about them (an epistemological problem)? The first issue is particularly puzzling due to the prominence of equilibrium modelling in neoclassical economic theory. HAUSMAN provides a good introduction to the problems of economic causation and argues that static analysis is causal in character, using standard supply-demand models as an example. He also shows how the concept of causal relation is strictly related to the idea of *ceteris paribus* law.

The "probabilistic" approach to causal analysis is one of the most popular research programmes in philosophy and in the social sciences. In its original version, it attempts to solve both the conceptual and the epistemological problems by providing a definition of the notion of cause as well as a set of inferential techniques to tell causes from statistical data. GRANGER is the main proponent of this approach in economics. In its simplest formulation, the probabilistic approach requires that "C causes E if Prob(E|C)>Prob(E)." This version, however, seems to be inadequate as a solution both to the conceptual and the epistemological problems of causation.

CARTWRIGHT (1989) shows why the above statement fails to provide a non-circular definition of causation. Her point can be synthesized in the following dilemma: *either* the probabilistic approach cannot distinguish between causal and spurious relations (consider, to take a stock example, the actual high correlation between coffee-drinking and lung cancer); *or* it must introduce qualifications featuring causal notions, thus failing to provide an independent definition of causation (for example, "C causes E if Prob(E|C)>Prob(E) in all populations which are homogenous with respect to other contributing and counteracting factors"). This dilemma has damaging implications on the epistemological front too, as it suggests that no purely statistical information is sufficient to identify causal links. As Cartwright puts it: "No causes in, no causes out".

Today's common wisdom is that attempts to reduce causation to other independent and more fundamental notions are bound to fail. Most contemporary research takes the idea of

a causal relation as primitive, and tries to characterize it in a way that helps to solve specific problems arising from the practice of science. Cartwright's own theory of "capacities" incorporates some ideas belonging to the so-called "structural approach" to causation. SIMON provides a classic brief statement of this approach, whose origins go back to the birth of econometrics itself (in the work of Frisch, Koopmans, Haavelmo and Tinbergen).

Relationships between economic entities are customarily represented in the form of simultaneous equations. From a mathematical viewpoint, there exist a number of equivalent combinations of the variables and coefficients appearing in these equations. Moreover, given a set of data, the possible combinations will also be *observationally equivalent*: for different values assigned to the parameters of the theory, there is no way to discriminate between the arrangement representing genuine causal relations and those that are spurious. The structural approach solves this problem by stating that it is characteristic of a causal relation that its form is *invariant* to changes in the value of its independent variables. WOODWARD provides an accessible philosophical defence of this conception of causation, to conclude that invariance comes in degrees and that economic relationships are invariant only to changes in a certain range of typical circumstances.

The idea of "partially invariant" relations introduces a problematic element in the structural approach. *How much* invariant should a causal relation be? HOOVER (1990, 2000) builds on Simon to propose a test for causal claims that can account for the use of correlation and regression analysis in econometrics: for C to cause E it must be that a change in Prob(C) is reflected in a change in Prob(E) and of course in Prob(C|E), but *not* in Prob(E|C). The "strength" of the effect of C on E must remain invariant across (natural or human) interventions on the exogenous factors.

At the origins of the structural approach, econometric techniques for causal inference were explicitly shaped on the idea of a "natural controlled experiment". The requirement that Prob(E|C) remains fixed may indeed be justified in experiments, but appears shakier in natural conditions. Whereas in the laboratory an intervention on C is supposed to leave everything else untouched, uncontrolled systems are characterized by simultaneous changes at different levels. In these environments, tests like the one above cannot work. This suggests that the structural approach conflates two concepts that are aptly distinguished by ENGLE, HENDRY & RICHARD: that of a causal (or "exogenous") relationship (internal to a given stable system) and that of a ("super-exogenous") relationship, invariant to more drastic changes in circumstances.

CARTWRIGHT's (1999) most recent work builds on this distinction to argue that the correct application of statistical techniques in the non-experimental sciences requires the satisfaction of a set of rather stringent conditions, both at the ontological and the epistemic level. First, the statistical data must be produced by a "nomological machine" – a stable system repeatedly operated in the absence of external interference. Secondly, we must know this, which requires the independent collection of detailed information on the data generating process before we engage in a statistical analysis of the data themselves.

FRANCESCO GUALA

Causation, sociology

Asher, Herbert B., *Causal Modeling*, 2nd edition, Beverly Hills, California: Sage, 1983

Berry, William D., *Nonrecursive Causal Models*, Beverly Hills, California: Sage, 1984

Blalock, Hubert M. Jr, *Causal Inferences in Nonexperimental Research*, Chapel Hill: University of North Carolina Press, 1964

Blalock, Hubert M. Jr, (editor), *Causal Models in the Social Sciences*, Chicago: Aldine-Atherton, 1971; 2nd edition 1985

Blossfeld, Hans-Peter and Götz Rohwer, *Techniques of Event History Modeling: New Approaches to Causal Analysis*, Mahwah, New Jersey: Erlbaum, 1995

Davis, James A., *The Logic of Causal Order*, Beverly Hills, California: Sage, 1985

Finkel, Steven E., *Causal Analysis with Panel Data*, Thousand Oaks, California: Sage, 1995

Godwin, Deborah D., "Causal Modeling in Family Research", *Journal of Marriage and the Family*, 50 (1988): 917–27

Simon, Herbert A. (editor), *Models of Man: Social and Rational: Mathematical Essays on Rational Human Behavior in a Social Setting*, New York: Wiley, 1957

Vogt, Paul W., *Dictionary of Statistics and Methodology: A Nontechnical Guide for the Social Sciences*, 2nd edition, Thousand Oaks, California: Sage, 1999

Causal modelling is a strategy through which researchers enhance their ability to draw causal inferences from their empirical research. Following VOGT, causal relations may be simple or multiple. In simple causation, whenever the first event (the cause) happens, the second (the effect) always happens too. Multiple causation is much more common in the social and behavioural sciences. Multiple causes may be such that any one of several causes can produce the same effect. They also may be such that no one of them will necessarily produce the effect, but several of them in combination make it more likely.

DAVIS' comprehensive textbook is an introductory approach to causal modelling in the social sciences. Researchers are introduced to the reasoning behind "causal order" in a set of variables, that is, the assumptions about which is the "cause" and which is the "effect" when one looks at the relationship between two variables. The monograph begins with the notion of causal direction and the principles to use when the researcher decides that X is the cause of Y instead of the other way round. Then the author explains how the collection of variables may be viewed as a causal system and discusses the issue of when to introduce variables as controls. The book ends with the discussion of a set of analysis strategies ranging from the very simple idea of "elaboration" to the complex and sophisticated technique called "path analysis". The idea is to explain the reasoning behind "elaboration", "effect analysis", and "path analysis".

A second introductory textbook, which deals practically with causal modelling is the one by ASHER. The author analyses in detail the fundamental characteristics of causal analysis and its relative advantages and disadvantages. The volume presents the basic concepts behind causal modelling, including a discussion of path analysis and multiple indicators, and an explanation of spurious correlation. The volume also describes a number of techniques of causal modelling, beginning with the works of BLALOCK, and of SIMON (particularly interesting, in that they are directly linked to developments in causal analysis in sociology), and moving on to recursive and nonrecursive path estimation. Special attention is given to a number of problems in the causal analysis of data. The book includes a wide range of examples from studies in political socialization and voting behaviour.

The issue of nonrecursive causal models is the focus of the interesting book by BERRY. Causal modelling has most commonly been carried out with a recursive model that specifies unidirectional causal effects among the continuous endogenous variables and where the errors in equations are assumed to be uncorrelated. Where an assumption of unidirectionality in causal effects is "unrealistic", recursive (unidirectional) models cannot be used, and more complex nonrecursive models are necessary. Unfortunately, many nonrecursive models are "unidentified", that is, there are too many unknowns in the causal model for a meaningful parameter estimation to be possible. Even when they are identified, it would be inappropriate to use ordinary least squares regression techniques (appropriate for recursive models) for the purpose of estimation. Within this context, the book discusses the concept of identification, and the factors that lead to it. Moreover, various tests for determination are provided. Illustrations from a variety of social science disciplines are used throughout the book.

The issue of causal modelling in family studies is examined closely in GODWIN. The author first discusses the uses of, and critics' views of, causal modelling in order to explain the reasons for its controversial position in the social sciences. She then reviews the requirements for effectively implementing a causal modelling strategy and comments on some attempts by family researchers to use it. The article includes suggestions that should enhance applications of causal modelling in future research on families.

Panel data are commonly used in the social sciences to test theories of individual and social change. A panel data set is one that follows a given sample of individuals or households over time, and thus provides multiple observations on each individual/household in the sample. The book by FINKEL provides a useful overview of models appropriate for the analysis of panel data: particularly, it focuses on the area where panels offer major advantages over cross-sectional research designs: the analysis of causal interrelationships among variables. The author demonstrates how panel data offer multiple ways of strengthening the causal inference process. He also explores how to estimate models with reciprocal causation and models of spurious association, and discusses the measurement of error models.

The book by BLOSSFELD & ROHWER gives a comprehensive introduction of event history modelling techniques and their usefulness for causal analysis in the social sciences. Event history data records all the changes in qualitative variables and their timing. For many processes within the social sciences, continuous measurement of qualitative variables seems to be the only suitable method of empirically assessing social change.

When the data are recorded in a continuous time, the number and sequence of events and the duration between them can all be calculated. Such information is very powerful when one is concerned with understanding life-course processes and how they interrelate. The main aim of the book is to demonstrate that event history models are an extremely useful approach to uncover causal relationships or to map out a system of causal relations. Event history models are linked to a causal understanding of social processes because they relate change in future outcomes to conditions in the past. The book includes a wide range of practical examples that the authors draw from their own teaching experience: the strengths and weaknesses of event history modelling techniques are emphasized in each example.

ELISABETTA RUSPINI

See also Causation, economic, Causal relationship

Central banks

Bagehot, Walter, *Lombard Street: A Description of the Money Market*, London: King, 1873

Cukierman, Alex, *Central Bank Strategy, Credibility, and Independence: Theory and Evidence*, Cambridge, Massachusetts: MIT Press, 1992

Fry, Maxwell J., C.A.E. Goodhart and Alvaro Almeida, *Central Banking in Developing Countries: Objectives, Activities and Independence*, London and New York: Routledge, 1996

Goodhart, C.A.E., *The Evolution of Central Banks*, Cambridge, Massachusetts: MIT Press, 1988

Goodhart, C.A.E., *The Central Bank and the Financial System*, London: Macmillan, and Cambridge, Massachusetts: MIT Press, 1995

Hawtrey, R.G., *The Art of Central Banking*, London and New York: Longman, 1932

Lastra, Rosa Maria, *Central Banking and Banking Regulation*, London: Financial Markets Group, London School of Economics, 1996

Šević, Željko, entry on Central Bank in *Elgar Companion to Law and Economics*, edited by Jürgen Backhaus, Cheltenham, Gloucestershire: Elgar, 1999

Smith, Vera C., *The Rationale of Central Banking*, London: King, 1936; reprinted Indianapolis: Liberty Press, 1990

It is almost impossible to begin a study of central banks and central banking without mentioning the seminal book by BAGEHOT, which has had many reprints in this century alone. Despite its main aim, which is to analyse the achievements of the Bank of England, and see how it can be educated and persuaded to perform its functions more effectively, the book concludes that the banking system would perform even better without a central bank. The banking system is seen as a hypothetical, imaginary but natural system of entirely independent banks, which can operate on its own. This is a very useful account of the banking system and social situation of late 19th-century England. The contributions by HAWTREY and SMITH, written around the time of the Great Depression, further support the concept of "free banking", giving historical examples showing how large commercial banks can

perform some of the functions of a central bank. Hawtrey and Smith draw special attention to the experience of the early national banking system in the US.

GOODHART (1988) gives a very good account of the development of the central bank as a social institution, and the idea of central banking. Although a strong supporter of central banking, he discusses alternative schools of thought, including free banking. With a mixture of analytical and descriptive styles, his book enables the reader to gain a good grasp of the history of central banks, especially in continental Europe and Japan. The central bank is analysed primarily as an institution, but the author also considers, to a certain extent, the development of central bank functions over time. In contrast with this historical book, GOODHART (1995) is a carefully chosen selection of previously published and unpublished papers, giving a state-of-the-art description of central banking theory. The author is known as a strong proponent of the separation of the supervisory and monetary policy functions of the central bank. The central bank is subjected to a positive and normative analysis, and most of the papers offer policy advice, or open debate about possible policy implications.

CUKIERMAN provides a positive and normative analysis of the central bank, especially its monetary functions, using a game-theoretic approach. Parts of the positive analysis can be easily understood by a person with a basic knowledge of economics, but other parts, especially those focused on monetary policy formulation and implementation, require quite a sound knowledge of game theory and of contemporary concepts of monetary economics. This book provides a fine account of what was, until recently, a very popular issue: the accountability and independence of the central bank. In contrast with most other works on central bank independence, which look at the relationship between the degree of independence of a central bank from government and from inflation, Cukierman analyses the issue using a game-theoretic approach, and moves from a positive to a normative analysis.

In a unique way, LASTRA analyses the interrelationship between the central bank and banking regulations. The main prerequisite for the successful central bank is its independence from the government of the day. In order to provide a framework for the independent central bank, it is necessary to establish a system of legal norms that will safeguard independence. A central bank should be "accountably independent", as various political and economic reasons argue for independence, whereas democratic legitimacy, reasons of consistent economic policy, the system of incentives, and bureaucratic behaviour argue against independence. It is argued that the central bank should perform supervisory functions, including the regulation of the national banking system. The reader will find an entire chapter on international banking regulation, which is somewhat excessive, and does not fit well into the book's overall format. However, this is an important read for those interested in regulatory and supervisory issues, and the role of the central bank in such issues. This comprehensive survey also gives a non-exhaustive list of the functions of the central bank, and describes the emerging European central banking network, but does not predict future developments in this domain.

SEVIC provides a survey of works on central banking from a legal and economic perspective. It begins with the German authors of the late 19th century, followed by the developments of the early 20th century, and ends by analysing the social and legal position of the central bank, and its functions in a modern society. Seeing the central bank as being at the core of the national banking system, the survey follows the development of the former alongside that of the latter. National laws regulating central banking are analysed from positive and normative points of view. Many of the references mentioned are long forgotten: this text gives an overview of economic thought on central banking at the end of the 19th century, when economics and law were still inseparably linked in continental Europe, particularly in the field of education.

FRY, GOODHART & ALMEIDA gives an account of central banking theory and practice in 44 developing countries, mainly those that were formerly in the "sterling area". Central bank activities are examined from the wider perspective of the overall macroeconomy. Central banks are seen to play a very important role in the financial system – much bigger than that of market forces. The conclusions of this book are largely based on statistical analysis resulting from questionnaires sent to the targeted central banks. Technical material is presented in such a way as not to interrupt the flow of the text. This book is very strong in explaining how reserve requirements and liquidity ratios can sometimes be governmental revenue measures masquerading as prudential controls. The issues of financial repression are also tackled. Regarding the objectives of central banks, the authors found that price stability is the primary objective. However, the book lacks proofs to substantiate these claims.

An important feature of all the works mentioned here is that each of them offers a long list of references which are useful for anyone interested in deepening his or her research on central banking.

Željko Šević

Centre-left

Addison, Paul, *The Road to 1945: British Politics and the Second World War*, London: Cape, 1975

Durbin, Elizabeth, *New Jerusalems: The Labour Party and the Economics of Democratic Socialism*, London and Boston: Routledge and Kegan Paul, 1985

Haseler, Steven, *The Gaitskellites: Revisionism in the British Labour Party, 1951–1964*, London: Macmillan, 1969

McBriar, A.M., *Fabian Socialism and English Politics, 1884–1918*, Cambridge: Cambridge University Press, 1962

Minkin, Lewis, *The Labour Party Conference: A Study in the Politics of Intra-Party Democracy*, London: Allen Lane, 1978

Pimlott, Ben, *Labour and the Left in the 1930s*, Cambridge and New York: Cambridge University Press, 1977

Ponting, Clive, *Breach of Promise: Labour in Power, 1964–1970*, London: Hamish Hamilton, 1989

Shaw, Eric, *The Labour Party since 1979: Crisis and Transformation*, London and New York: Routledge, 1994

Skidelsky, Robert, *Politicians and the Slump: The Labour Government of 1929–1931*, London: Macmillan, 1967

Centre-left is an imprecise term that identifies a position, more accurately a relationship, on the political spectrum – one that is subject to change over time. McBRIAR's study of Fabianism is one of the fullest accounts of the politics of the Fabian Society in the period when it was dominated by the gradualist philosophy of Sidney Webb, Beatrice Webb, and George Bernard Shaw. This English variety of parliamentary reformism was grounded in an evolutionary determinism that conceptualized the rise of socialism (or collectivism) as the inevitable consequence of industrialism and democracy. As such it provided a sophisticated rationale for the practice of the British Labour Party. Both McBriar and SKIDELSKY show, albeit in different ways, what the limitations of Fabian influence upon the Labour Party actually were, and the latter makes clear that as late as the second minority Labour government of 1929–31 the Party was led by men who were still liberals in matters of economics. Skidelsky's stimulating book has, nevertheless, to be handled with care – the argumentative eloquence of its critique of parliamentary socialism sometimes rising well above the historical evidence.

A more balanced account of Labour's economic thinking, and its relationship to socialism, taking the story through the 1930s, is provided by DURBIN who has written an extremely detailed account of the work of the National Executive Committee subcommittees under Hugh Dalton's supervision in the period when the party began a serious search for feasible economic reforms (after the 1931 political crisis). Durbin investigates the party's encounter with Keynesianism and the liberal economics of Friedrich von Hayek, through the medium of Dalton's proteges, and shows how more radical forms of economic interventionism were marginalized as Labour recovered its faith in cautious reform. Though the 1930s is often thought of as a "red decade" PIMLOTT argues that the left was rarely weaker. There were continuing signs of the Labour Party's deepening roots, but the extra-parliamentary left had little effect on policy as the Labour MPs were hugely outnumbered in Parliament. The centre-left was thus not as weakened by this turbulent period as is often supposed.

The war revived Labour's fortunes and, according to ADDISON, the radicalism it generated was accurately reflected in the Beveridge report and the sort of centre-left policies pursued by the Attlee governments after 1945, and largely adhered to by their political opponents after 1951. Addison's rich narrative is full of evidence to support the contention that the war inaugurated an era of consensus. The Labour Party itself entered upon something of an identity crisis in the aftermath of the Attlee reforms and this eventually gave rise to a new statement of its centre-left strategy in the form of revisionism. HASELER, who makes no secret of his sympathies with this dominant strand of Labour thinking in the 1950s, takes the story as far as the formation of the first of Harold Wilson's Labour governments. PONTING has written the best account of these governments (prior to the release of the relevant public documents). Making use of documentary sources lodged in the US, he shows that Wilson's particular version of the revisionist agenda was largely undermined by a determination to maintain Britain's overseas role and the sterling area in the context of a chronic balance of payments crisis and recurring speculation against the pound.

The experience of the Wilson governments inaugurated a period of change in Labour politics during which the centre-left of the party was forced into retreat. MINKIN's impressive study of the party's annual conference is probably the best analysis of Labour's intra-party politics in the years leading to this breakdown. It goes a long way to explain the sources of policy making in the organization; the balance of power between the different centres of authority within the party; its factions, and the nature of the relationship between its centre-left parliamentary leadership and the rest of the Party. SHAW, a student of Minkin, has written the best account of how the centre-left reasserted the dominance of the parliamentary leadership in the years of successive electoral defeats, 1979–92. In the process the centre-left reinvented itself by casting off the ideology with which the party leadership had been associated since 1951. By the end of the century it was widely supposed that mainstream Labour politics anticipated a formal realignment with the Liberals; this is not quite where they both began as each party has changed profoundly since 1900.

JOHN CALLAGHAN

See also Labour parties, Parliamentary socialism, Revisionism

Chandler, Alfred D. Jr 1918–

US business historian

Amatori, Franco, Alfred D. Chandler Jr and Takashi Hikino (editors), *Big Business and the Wealth of Nations*, Cambridge and New York: Cambridge University Press, 1997

Chandler, Alfred D. Jr, *Strategy and Structure: Chapters in the History of the Industrial Enterprise*, Cambridge, Massachusetts: MIT Press, 1962

Chandler, Alfred D. Jr, *The Visible Hand: The Managerial Revolution in American Business*, Cambridge, Massachusetts: Harvard University Press, 1977

Chandler, Alfred D. Jr, *Scale and Scope: The Dynamics of Industrial Capitalism*, Cambridge, Massachusetts: Harvard University Press, 1990

John, Richard R., "Elaborations, Revisions, Dissents: Alfred D. Chandler, Jr's *The Visible Hand* after Twenty Years", *Business History Review*, 71 (1997): 151–200

Ingham, John N., *Making Iron and Steel: Independent Mills in Pittsburgh, 1820–1920*, Columbus: Ohio State University Press, 1991

Lazonick, William, *Business Organization and the Myth of the Market Economy*, Cambridge and New York: Cambridge University Press, 1991

McCraw, Thomas K. (editor), *The Essential Alfred Chandler: Essays Toward a Historical Theory of Big Business*, Boston: Harvard Business School Press, 1988

Piore, Michael J. and Charles F. Sabel, *The Second Industrial Divide: Possibilities for Prosperity*, New York: Basic Books, 1984

Teece, David J., "The Dynamics of Industrial Capitalism: Perspectives on Alfred Chandler's *Scale and Scope*", *Journal of Economic Literature*, 31 (1993): 199–225

Williamson, Oliver E., "The Modern Corporation: Origins, Evolutions, Attributes", *Journal of Economic Literature*, 19 (1981): 1537–68

Alfred Dupont Chandler, Jr is arguably one of the most influential contemporary American historians. Over the last half century his work has not only revolutionized the study of business history, but the concepts and analytical framework he has developed have gained currency in numerous other disciplines. Consequently, his work has generated an ongoing dialogue throughout much of the social sciences. Chandler, throughout his career, has had a singular focus on the evolution of the large-scale business enterprise. Using a comparative historical approach, he has been able to generate broad-based generalizations as to the nature and growth of the large modern enterprise wherein the modern American corporation has come to serve as an ideal type. The explanatory power of his thesis has been subject to much criticism, but his studies nevertheless have produced the best accounts to date of the rise of big business and its organizational development.

Chandler has been very prolific. Four major works, however, offer the best overview of his research agenda. CHANDLER (1962) offers a copiously detailed narrative of how four major American enterprises responded to technologically induced shifts in their markets by changing their long-term goals, their strategy, and how they went about achieving their ends. They did so by altering their organizational design or structure. Chandler traces these changes from a centralized, functionally departmentalized body, the U form, to a multi-divisional or M form, with its corporate office and various product and geographical divisions. The popular legacy of this work, that strategy defines structure, is a slightly simplistic rendering of the author's intentions, but nevertheless it has held tremendous influence in America's boardrooms and business schools.

CHANDLER (1977) is a study that many consider to be his seminal work. He details how technology prompted organizational changes within America's largest enterprises and spurred a managerial revolution in America between 1840 and 1920. Technological advances in production and distribution created a need for an administrative structure with which to coordinate the flows of goods and services to producers and consumers. Thus, the modern business enterprise, with its team of managers, the visible hand of management, evolved and came to take the place of market mechanisms – Smith's "invisible hand" of the market – in coordinating the activities of the market and in allocating its resources. For Chandler, therefore, technology best explains organizational innovation, and the new form of organization that technology produced, the large vertically integrated enterprise, became the central force in American economic growth at the turn of the 20th century.

CHANDLER (1990) moves beyond the American case and offers an impressive look at how industrial enterprises in America, Germany, and Great Britain sought to restructure internally in order to better capture the economies of scale and scope afforded by technological advances. The adoption of capital-intensive techniques of production by large industrial enterprises drove down the unit costs of production and distribution, and produced economies of scale on one hand, while, on the other, diversifying output and producing for different markets produced economies of scope. Some systems and structures did this better than others. Chandler maintains that the American model of the large-scale enterprise, with its complex hierarchy and widely dispersed ownership, did so best. Germany followed the American model, although its enterprises were tempered by a different set of historical, institutional and organizational dynamics. Furthest removed from the American model, British firms favoured smaller-scale operations with less hierarchical and more personal management. These developments, he argues, weakened Britain's industrial sector and the British economy. Chandler held that the large industrial enterprise was the underlying force in the development of modern industrial capitalism. Chandler, it should be noted, has been criticized for exaggerating both the extent to which the German case parallels the American model, and the extent to which the British case differs from it.

The comparative evolution of big business in over a dozen different countries is the subject of Chandler's edited volume, *Big Business and the Wealth of Nations* (AMATORI *et al.*). Various authors examine the development of large enterprises in different settings, including advanced, emerging, and centrally planned economies, over the last century. Chandler again makes the case that the large corporation is clearly the engine of economic growth, and holds up the American model of managerial capitalism as the standard against which the performance of other nations is to be measured. Many of the other authors in the book, however, disagree, and question how useful the American model is in explaining developments elsewhere. They highlight some of the problems inherent in the Chandler thesis and discuss the role that other factors, be they government, labour, or the system of property rights, may have had on economic growth and development.

The collection of excerpts in McCRAW provides a useful overview of Chandler's prodigious output. Especially enlightening is McCraw's introductory essay in which he details the forces, both personal and intellectual, that have shaped Chandler's work and prompted him to go beyond the simple narrative in business history to produce a historical theory of the firm. JOHN provides a valuable discussion of Chandler's thesis along with a good summary of the views of Chandler's critics. The objections raised to the Chandler thesis are many and varied, and range from charges of technological or structural determinism and excessive rationalism, to detailed questions about his narrative. Still others worry about the larger effects Chandler's research agenda and its unrivalled dominance are having on the study of business history. INGHAM believes that the preoccupation with big business that has resulted from Chandler's thesis has created a skewed picture of American industry in the 19th and early 20th century. His study of small iron and blister steel producers in Pittsburgh and of the efficiencies they achieved in specialized markets is meant to serve as an initial corrective, since small producers were more characteristic of American manufacturing at that time.

PIORE & SABEL effectively challenge the Chandler thesis by showing that the development of the large modern enterprise was not, as they believe Chandler and others would have it, the inevitable product of technological progress in the late 19th century. Rather, they point to the persistence of the small firm as evidence of an alternative form of industrial organization. Much like Ingham's blister steel mills, these small firms met more specialized demand using flexible, as opposed to

single purpose, technologies. As champions of flexible production, Piore & Sabel are essential reading. They see the large American corporation with its high-volume standardized products as being a historically and geographically specific response to a very particular set of circumstances.

The implications that flow from Chandler's work for the theory of the firm in economics and industrial organization are explored in TEECE who links the Chandlerian view of the firm to a growing heterodox literature in organizational economics. Teece correctly points out that Chandler has a novel view of scale and scope. Chandler's interpretation emphasizes organizational factors, how firms managed the opportunities made available to them by new technology since technology was largely available to all firms. This view, Teece believes, unlike the conventional wisdom that still views scale and scope as being almost exclusively a function of technology-driven economies of production and distribution, can have a transforming influence in economics.

Other economists, like WILLIAMSON, believe that Chandler does not pay enough attention to the market. Williamson provides a revisionist economic perspective on the rise of the large corporation. He argues that the size of the firm is largely a product of the efforts of firms to minimize transaction costs, the costs of developing, signing, enforcing, and adjusting contracts, between individuals. In this fashion, transaction costs economizing helps to explain the allocation of economic activities between the market and the visible hand of the firm, where the invisible hand of the market remains the vital determinant of economic activity. LAZONICK is well worth reading for his critical examination of the views of a number of economists, including Williamson, and for his analysis of how most practitioners still fail to confront what he calls the myth of the market, or how firms go about altering their environments and forming markets.

LOUISE LAMONTAGNE

Change management

Bolman, Lee G. and Terence E. Deal, *Reframing Organizations: Artistry, Choice, and Leadership*, San Francisco: Jossey Bass, 1991

Carnall, Colin A., *Managing Change in Organisations*, London and New York: Prentice Hall, 1995

Cummings, Thomas G. and Christopher G. Worley, *Organization Development and Change*, 6th edition, Cincinnati: South-Western, 1997

D'Aprix, Roger, *Communicating for Change: Connecting the Workplace with the Marketplace*, San Francisco: Jossey Bass, 1996

Eccles, Tony, *Succeeding with Change: Implementing Action-driven Strategies*, London and New York: McGraw Hill, 1994

Kotter, John P., *Leading Change*, Boston, Massachusetts: Harvard Business School Press, 1996

Robey, Daniel, *Designing Organisations*, 4th edition, Homewood, Illinois: Irwin, 1994

Change management is a generic process applicable to all kinds of organizations, which uses knowledge and skills to bring about substantial organizational change to improve effectiveness and efficiency. Change may be required due to an outdated organizational structure, poor responsiveness to clients, technological change, a merger, or an inappropriate organizational culture. In most cases, a combination of several factors is involved.

While change now concerns most managers, it is only in the last decade that change management has become a distinct subfield of general management, joining project management, operations management, and services management. It now has its own research and theoretical literature, professional bodies, and record of successes and failures.

Being an applied activity, the theoretical and practical dimensions of change management are inextricably linked. Published literature covers (a) overviews of the field of organizational change and development; and (b) conceptual models of organizations and the change process derived largely from consulting experiences.

CUMMINGS & WORLEY provide an overview of approaches, issues, and problems in change management within the wider field of organization development. Adopting the perspective of the external consultant, they outline an open-system model for diagnosing organizations to locate key problems at organizational, group, and individual levels. Common problems at the organizational level centre on an organization's strategy (mission, goals and objectives, intent, policies), structure (linkages between subunits and the allocation of authority), and processes (measurement and human resource systems). Ideally, strategy, structure, and processes should be sychronized but, in practice, such fit is seldom attained. A key task of many change managers is to improve the level of synchronization. Cummings & Worley also provide models for assessing how groups and individual roles are functioning in existing organizations. Groups can be assessed in terms of design features like the clarity of their goals, the composition of their membership, and their performance norms – all of which affect their cohesiveness, the quality of their decisions, and their productivity. Individual jobs can be diagnosed in terms of skill variety, autonomy, and feedback about performance. Central to Cummings & Worley's model is that the design features at the organizational, group, and individual levels should be congruent. They also provide a comprehensive evaluation of techniques and approaches to improve organizations based on diagnostic data. Many examples are provided to show the relevance of change management theory to practical problems.

CARNALL's perspective on change management is from the practising manager's viewpoint rather than the external consultant's. He uses research, consulting, and related material to take us through issues in the change process including: choices of structure; blocks to attaining and sustaining effectiveness; techniques for assessing organisations; leadership and managerial skills for change; and how employees cope with organizational change. Many case studies, mainly British, are provided.

Change management proceeds on the basis of a set of assumptions about "how organizations work and what might make them work better" (BOLMAN & DEAL). Bolman & Deal develop a set of "frames" by which to picture organizational realities: "Frames help us order experience and decide what action to take" (p.11). The structural frame highlights goals, organizational structure, and formal roles and relationships. The human resource frame accesses individuals and groups in organizations and the interrelationships between them. The political frame "views organizations as arenas in which different interest groups compete for power and scarce resources" (p.15). The symbolic frame draws out the rituals, ceremonies, stories, heroes, and other cultural features of organizations – organizational life as analogous to live theatre with organizational members as actors. No one frame is more important or more representative of reality than another; change managers need an appreciation of all four.

Academic texts often describe change management as a huge uphill battle, complicated, and difficult to accomplish. ECCLES' approach is almost the opposite. Basing his success model on a set of core propositions (for example "implementation can take place quickly," "concentrated power is an aid to rapid implementation"), he places himself in the change manager's role to elaborate on six different kinds of change (takeover, injection, succession, renovation, partnership, catalytic) each requiring a different approach to change management, particularly in the use of power. Fourteen factors of change, derived from his and other's experiences and extensive interview data, are also detailed. Each addresses the concerns of change managers head on: for example the illusion of unity (you cannot expect everyone to be behind the change) and how open to be (there are risks in being too candid). Eccles makes a solid contribution to change management by integrating experience and research data to create models and principles for practitioners. As a result, he avoids the ideological bias of some change management gurus.

D'APRIX believes that what is said and how it is said is axiomatic to success with organizational change. "Too often" he says "communication failures undermine leadership attempts at change, leaving employees without the crucial knowledge to understand what is happening and why" (p.3). But even when communication is used, it is often used poorly or thoughtlessly. As a result, many employees end up confused, angry, sceptical, and cynical. But what should be communicated and how? D'Aprix gives a clear, reader-friendly response based on his central thesis derived from 35 years consulting experience: "The only argument powerful enough to encourage people to embrace change is one that is rooted in the marketplace" (p.3).

To be successful, managers involved in wide-ranging organizational change need to be "transformational leaders" with particular characteristics: lifelong learners, driven by values, visionaries with a capacity to deal with complexity, ambiguity, uncertainty, and high levels of risk (ROBEY). Several authors have developed these leadership requirements into a set of prescriptions for change managers.

KOTTER, for example, provides an eight-stage leadership model that takes us through establishing a sense of urgency, creating teamwork based on trust and a common goal, developing a vision and strategy, empowering employees, and consolidating gains, and producing more change.

STUART C. THOMSON

See also Learning organization, Organizational learning

Chicago School

Argy, Fred, *Australia at the Crossroads: Radical Free Market or a Progressive Liberalism?*, Sydney: Allen and Unwin, 1998

Becker, Gary S., *The Economic Approach to Human Behavior*, Chicago: University of Chicago Press, 1976

Becker, Gary, "Nobel Lecture: The Economic Way of Looking at Behavior", *Journal of Political Economy*, 101/3 (1993): 385–409

Coase, R.H., "Law and Economics at Chicago", *Journal of Law and Economics*, 36 (April 1993): 239–254

Colander, David and Arjo Klamer, "The Making of an Economist", *Economic Perspectives*, 1/2 (Fall 1987): 95–111

Friedman, Milton and Rose Friedman, *Free to Choose: A Personal Statement*, New York: Harcourt Brace, 1980

Krugman, Paul, *Peddling Prosperity: Economic Sense and Nonsense in the Age of Diminished Expectations*, New York: Norton, 1994

McKenzie, Richard B. and Gordon Tullock, *The New World of Economics*, 5th edition, New York: McGraw Hill, 1994

Posner, Richard, "Utilitarianism, Economics and Legal Theory", *Journal of Legal Studies*, 8/1 (January 1979): 103–140

Samuels, Warren J. (editor), *The Chicago School of Political Economy*, University Park, Pennsylvania: Association for Evolutionary Economics, 1976

Stigler, George J., *The Citizen and the State: Essays on Regulation*, Chicago: University of Chicago Press, 1975

COLANDER & KLAMER surveyed graduate students in US Ivy League universities and concluded that "there definitely seems to be a Chicago School of Economics". Chicago students evidenced a higher degree of confidence in the market, a readier acceptance that there is a sharp line between positive and normative economics, more conviction that inflation is primarily a monetary phenomenon, and more commitment to the view that the Federal Reserve should maintain a constant growth of the money supply. Students at other schools (such as Stanford and MIT) demonstrated more interest in assumptions of price rigidity, imperfect competition, and mark-up pricing.

Milton FRIEDMAN is the celebrated father of the Chicago School and has long argued that capitalist economies need to eliminate the many forms of government intervention that presently distort market signals. Friedman's creed – now increasingly influential throughout the world, including the formerly communist world of Eastern Europe – is that government failure is commonly worse than market failure. Friedman's argument is that government intervention – in the form of minimum wage laws, housing rent controls, fixed exchange rates, tariff protection, and suchlike – actually yields three significant disadvantages in terms of its impact on economic efficiency, equity, and destruction of the social fabric. Minimum wage laws are intended to help the poor but actually lead to unemployment – particularly of young Blacks in the US, thus contributing to heightened racial tension. Despite significant deregulation of Western (and Eastern) economies in the last two decades, he continues to argue that reducing the scope of government is our most important single objective. He rails against drug laws, state schools, and licensing arrangements, for example. Friedman does not fear drugs, just what governments do about drugs. Since anti-drug laws lead to illicit drug trafficking, Friedman is adamant that it is the government that is responsible for the murder of many innocent drug victims. In the case of subsidized university education he contends that our hypocrisy reaches new heights because we know it is the relatively rich who attend, whereas – in the name of "equity" – it is the relatively poor taxpayer who foots the bill.

BECKER (1976) defines economics by its method, rather than by its subject matter, and accordingly came "to the position that the economic approach is a comprehensive one that is applicable to all human behaviour". Under Becker's influence, economics proclaimed itself "an imperialist science" and set about injecting itself into sociology, politics, and psychology. Chicago School writers thus produced analyses of the economics of suicide, of church attendance, of extramarital affairs, and, importantly, of the economics of law. BECKER (1993) concludes that "the rational choice model provides the most promising basis presently available for a unified approach to the analysis of the social world by scholars from different social sciences".

McKENZIE & TULLOCK highlight crime and punishment as one policy area in which the gulf between Chicago and traditional approaches is still wide. Chicago treats crime as just one more human activity and accordingly stresses the potential for increased punishment costs to reduce the supply of crime. Criminologists often still object to this approach, however, arguing that punishment is both expensive and ineffective and that rehabilitation is what is needed.

COASE revolutionized the way that economists treat externalities, with consequent impact upon the law. He argued that in a regime of zero transaction costs the kind of government action that economists previously thought to be required was completely unnecessary, because negotiations between the parties would always lead to a solution that maximized wealth. In a regime of positive transaction costs, however, consideration must be given to how the parties actually handle the problem of harmful external effects, and the property rights established by law become one of the main factors determining the performance of the economy. Coase concluded that the Pigovian approach to externalities was empty and that economists had overestimated the benefits of government regulation. The efficient solution is to look not for one-sided "blame" so much as for the least costly of two potential hurts when it is recognized that there is a reciprocal arrangement in which either A hurts B or B hurts A. Accordingly, major law schools now commonly employ an economist to advise on matters of the economic efficiency of law – a theme that POSNER has developed in the *Journal of Legal Studies*. Posner advocates wealth maximization as a normative principle and concludes that a free market for babies, for example, would be far preferable to the present allocative system for adoptions, because the supply of babies would expand and society would be wealthier. Posner enjoins the courts to reach decisions by mimicking the market, giving rise to the criticism that under Chicago School influence jurisprudence has been redefined as economic efficiency.

STIGLER investigated government regulation of industry and demonstrated that, in practice, regulations designed to protect consumers often end up benefiting producers. He concluded that regulation is a response to interest group pressures and "as a rule, regulation is acquired by the industry and is designed and operated primarily for its benefit".

KRUGMAN provides a critique of conservative macroeconomic theory and concludes that, by the 1990s, it had been exposed as inadequate in all its variants, leaving New Keynesianism as the only game left in town. Krugman concludes that Friedman's monetarist argument – that discretionary control of the money supply does more harm than good – is fundamentally unconvincing and that by mid-1982 even the pretence of monetarism was abandoned by the Federal Reserve System, never to be resumed. Lucas's rational expectations approach went further but Krugman also dismisses it as wrong because it does not represent the way in which firms actually make their decisions. By 1992 Krugman concludes that monetarist and rational expectations theories had lost virtually all credibility and influence.

SAMUELS provides an early collection of papers that offer an overview of Chicago claims and critiques. He concludes that paradoxically – by endogenizing everything and "piercing the veil of important institutions . . . the Chicago School may be even more revolutionary, albeit in a more subtle way, than Karl Marx . . . although this is no part of their intention." A contemporary critique is provided by ARGY, who concludes that there is no clear evidence that the Chicago or "hard liberal" agenda performs better even in terms of narrow economic criteria, although it nonetheless performs worse than moderate liberalism in terms of social issues.

L.A. DUHS

Child abuse

Behrman, Richard E. (editor), "Protecting Children from Abuse and Neglect", special issue of *The Future of Children*, 8/1 (Spring 1998)

Briere, John, Lucy Berliner, Josephine A. Bulkley, Carole Jenny and Theresa Reid (editors), *The APSAC Handbook on Child Maltreatment*, Thousand Oaks, California: Sage, 1996

Child Welfare League of America, *Standards of Excellence*, revised edition, Washington, DC: CWLA Press, 1999

Gelles, Richard J., *Intimate Violence in Families*, 3rd edition, Thousand Oaks, California and London: Sage, 1997

Kraizer, Sherryll, *Recovery: A Therapeutic Prevention Program*, Tulsa, Oklahoma: National Resource Center for Youth Services, 1992

Monteleone, James A., *Recognition of Child Abuse for the Mandated Reporter*, 2nd edition, St Louis: G.W. Medical Publishing, 1996

Rycus, Judith S. and Ronald C. Hughes, *Field Guide to Child Welfare*, vol. 1: *Foundations of Child Protective Services*, vol. 2: *Case Planning and Family-Centered Casework*, vol. 3: *Child Development and Child Welfare*, vol. 4: *Placement and Permanence*, Washington, DC: CWLA Press, 1998

BEHRMAN is part of *The Future of Children*, published three times a year as a controlled-circulation publication distributed free of charge. The series is intended to complement the kind of technical analysis found in academic journals. The purpose of this collection is to translate existing knowledge in the field of child abuse and neglect into multidisciplinary programs, policies, and constructive institutional change. The target audience is policy makers, professionals in the public and private sector, legislators, executives, and practitioners within the field of child protective services. Each article covers a different area of child abuse and neglect, and is especially useful both for disseminating timely information on major issues, but also for providing concrete practical recommendations on how to solve, or at least alleviate, some of the issues surrounding children's wellbeing.

BRIERE *et al.*'s work is one of the most significant resources within the field of child abuse. The American Professional Society on the Abuse of Children (APSAC) provides this handbook as a resource for alleviating the causes and consequences of child abuse and neglect. This handbook is invaluable for its comprehensive coverage of physical and sexual abuse, all forms of neglect, and psychological maltreatment. All topics are covered by the experts in their respective specialized areas. Each chapter is designed to convey the most current empirical research and literature available, as well as strategies for assessment, treatment, intervention, and prevention of child maltreatment. This handbook has an intended audience of professionals in mental health, law, medicine, law enforcement, and child protective services.

Since its formation in 1920, the CHILD WELFARE LEAGUE OF AMERICA (CWLA) has been committed to setting standards and improving practice in all child welfare services. This handbook is a series of standards based upon current knowledge, the developmental needs of children, and tested ways of meeting those needs effectively. The preparation of these standards results from an examination of current practices, a survey of professional literature, and a study of the most recent experiences of social work and the related fields of child development, child care, education, mental health, psychology, medicine, psychiatry, and sociology. In the shift from issue identification to issue resolution, this handbook sets the criteria essential to consistently raise the standard of care to children and the services provided to their families.

It seems both prudent and necessary to include a study of familial violence in any discussion of child abuse. GELLES breaks new ground by dismantling many commonly held myths concerning physical, emotional, psychological, and sexual abuse within the much broader spectrum of familial abuse. His work is groundbreaking in that it views the issue of child abuse in the larger context of the family with emphasis placed upon hidden victims of familial violence such as siblings, parents, and the elderly. Gelles then takes the next step to examining the effectiveness of intervention and treatment programmes, concentrating upon intensive family preservation programs and men's treatment programmes.

KRAIZER takes the lead in the discovery of life beyond the pain of the abuse. She has developed the "recovery programme" to introduce specific life skills that will maximize recovery from child abuse and assist in the prevention of further abuse. Her training programme is a unique combination of conceptual and experiential learning designed to assist participants in enhancing personal competency and raising self-esteem. Although very therapeutic as a training programme, "recovery" is not the same as therapy, when therapy is defined as the treatment of an illness or disability. The distinction is that "recovery" is an educational curriculum with planned discussion, activities, and follow-up designed to be used as a learning tool in support of the therapeutic process.

MONTELEONE provides one of the few resources available for mandated child abuse reporters such as teachers, nurses, social workers, daycare workers, and law enforcement officers. Whether a person is mandated to report suspected child abuse legally or morally, they still need to feel comfortable and secure when making the report, and this resource goes a long way towards raising that comfort level. Monteleone examines how to recognize physical, psychological, and sexual abuse, as well as, identification of suspicious indicators of possible abuse. He also takes a unique stance attempting to balance the protection of children without unjustly accusing caregivers.

RYCUS & HUGHES developed this field guide to child welfare as a four-volume set. They designed the set to be used as a college textbook, an in-service training tool, a tool to transfer knowledge, and a reference text for practitioners and administrators. The field guides help providers organize, integrate, and apply current information on child welfare practice. Volume I explores the values of child welfare programmes and introduces a family-centred approach to child protection through the identification of abuse and neglect, dynamics of child maltreatment, risk assessment techniques, and comprehensive family assessment. Volume II applies the family-centred philosophy to case planning. Special emphasis is placed on integrating casework and protective authority, developing a casework relationship, developing the case plan, case closure, and recidivism. Volume III analyses the effects of abuse and neglect at the various developmental stages of a child's transition into adulthood. There is also a close examination of child welfare services for children with developmental disabilities. Volume IV explores the various options available for placement and permanency planning with an emphasis on attachment issues, working with the families of children in placement, and the foster care and adoption systems. This series is invaluable within the context of the US child protective system, yet it may need some modifications to be fully utilized in other countries with their varying philosophies and approaches to child protection and family services.

JEFF BAENZIGER

See also Counselling children, Incest

Child law

Alston, Philip, Stephen Parker and John Seymour (editors), *Children, Rights and the Law*, Oxford: Clarendon Press, and New York: Oxford University Press, 1992

Bainham, Andrew, *Children: Tthe Modern Law*, Bristol: Family Law, 1998

Chambers, David, "Rethinking the Substantive Rules for Custody Disputes in Divorce", *Michigan Law Review*, 83 (1984): 477–569

Elster, Jon, *Solomonic Judgements: Studies in the Limitations of Rationality*, Cambridge and New York: Cambridge University Press, 1989

Fineman, Martha A., *The Neutered Mother, The Sexual Family and Other Twentieth Century Tragedies*, New York: Routledge, 1995

King, Michael and Christine Piper, *How the Law Thinks about Children*, 2nd edition, Aldershot, Hampshire: Arena, 1995

Krause, Harry (editor), *Child Law: Parent, Child and State*, Aldershot, Hampshire: Dartmouth, 1992

Mnookin, Robert, "Child Custody Adjudication: Judicial Functions in the Face of Indeterminacy", *Law and Contemporary Problems*, 39 (1975): 226–93

Smart, Carol and Selma Sevenhuijsen (editors), *Child Custody and the Politics of Gender*, London and New York: Routledge, 1989

Ziff, Bruce, "The Primary Caretaker Presumption: Canadian Perspectives on an American Development", *International Journal of Law and the Family*, 4 (1990): 186–213

Children have contact with the legal system or are the subjects of legal processes, in a variety of ways, and also may have a variety of different legal rights. Even when they are in the womb, they may be entitled to inherit property provided that they are born subsequently. Injury to them in the womb may also give them an entitlement to sue tortfeasors for damages. Newborns (and indeed older children) may be the subject of an adoption application. The courts may be concerned about the welfare of children in the context of child protection proceedings or where parent-child conflicts are so serious that the child or young person is considered to be "beyond parental control". Children may also be witnesses in criminal proceedings and special provisions govern the admissibility and reception of their evidence.

The areas of the law with which children are most likely to be involved are in relation to family law proceedings and the juvenile justice system. Custody and access decisions, or "residence" and "contact" decisions as they are now known in England and Australia, are determined on the basis that the best interests of the child is the paramount consideration. When children and young people commit offences, concern for their welfare is also a motivating factor. The focus of the juvenile justice system is not only on punishment but also on rehabilitation.

Few books cover the whole scope of child law. The most comprehensive treatment in Britain is BAINHAM, which includes chapters on all the topics one might find in a family law course such as residence and contact decisions, child support, and child protection. It also has chapters on juvenile justice, education and children in international law. KRAUSE is an edited collection of readings that have been selected as seminal contributions to child law.

KING & PIPER, applying Luhmann's theory of autopoiesis, argue that child law has an autonomous existence. The law "thinks" about children, independently of the way in which individual lawyers and judges may think about them by selecting and interpreting those matters which the law is able to "know" and "understand" for the purposes of legal decision-making. This, they argue, makes it difficult for the law to take cognisance of the insights of other disciplines because it reconstructs those insights for the purposes of legal decision making.

Children's rights are an important theme within child law. The concept of children's rights is given an international dimension by the United Nations Convention on the Rights of the Child, 1989. ALSTON, PARKER & SEYMOUR is an important edited collection of essays on children's rights from different philosophical perspectives. It provides a variety of different interpretations of what it means for children to have "rights" and also includes essays which are sceptical of the utility of talking about children's rights.

There are many controversies about how courts should make decisions concerning children's welfare following parental separation and divorce. SMART & SEVENHUIJSEN's collection of essays provides a valuable introduction to feminist theory on child custody and access with contributors from a variety of countries. FINEMAN offers a perspective based on a feminism of difference and examines how motherhood is constructed in law. She argues that in promoting law reform, feminists should focus not on grand theory but on the material and emotional circumstances that arise from women's greater connection with their children.

The notion that courts are able to determine objectively where the best interests of the child lie has been subjected to sustained challenge. MNOOKIN's article is a classic critique of the best interests principle. He argues that the principle is inherently indeterminate because it requires the courts to make predictions about the future and the court's own decision is part of the future the court is endeavouring to predict. He argues also that the test involves value judgments about life itself. ELSTER (chapter 3) builds upon Mnookin's arguments about the indeterminacy of the test. He also argues that the "best interests of the child" test may be theoretically optimal in focusing on the needs of the individual child but this disregards the harm to the child from the decision-making process itself. He argues that the best interests of children will be promoted by a rule which minimises the costs of litigation, rather than one which requires an individualised assessment in each case.

CHAMBERS offers a review of alternatives to the "best interests" test, which he examines in the light of psychological knowledge about the effects of marriage breakdown on children. The alternative which is most commonly discussed is the primary caretaker presumption, which provides that custody should be awarded to the parent who has had the primary role in day to day care as long as she (or he) is a fit parent. ZIFF offers a critical analysis of this approach, pointing out that the primary caretaker presumption focuses on physical caring rather than capacity for wise judgment in parenting and that children's needs change over time so that a retrospective test is not a sure guide for determining the best interests of the child in the future.

PATRICK N. PARKINSON

See also Custody

Childhood

Ariès, Phillipe, *Centuries of Childhood: A Social History of Family Life*, New York: Knopf, and London: Jonathan Cape, 1962

Bowlby, John, *Attachment and Loss*, 3 vols, New York: Basic Books, and London: Hogarth Press, 1969–80; 2nd edition 1982

Bruner, Jerome and Helen Haste, *Making Sense: The Child's Construction of the World*, London and New York: Methuen, 1987

deMause, Lloyd (editor), *The History of Childhood*, New York: Psychohistory Press, 1974

Erikson, Erik H., *Childhood and Society*, New York: Norton, 1950; enlarged edition 1963, London: Penguin, 1965

Gesell, Arnold, *The Mental Growth of the Preschool Child*, New York: Macmillan, 1925

Mead, Margaret and Martha Wolfenstein (editors), *Childhood in Contemporary Cultures*, Chicago: University of Chicago Press, 1955

Moen, Phyllis, Glen H. Elder Jr and Kurt Lüscher (editors), *Examining Lives in Context: Perspectives on the Ecology of Human Development*, Washington, DC: American Psychological Association, 1995

Piaget, Jean, *The Origins of Intelligence in Children*, New York: International Universities Press, 1952; as *The Origin of Intelligence in the Child*, London: Kegan Paul, 1953 (French edition 1936)

Rutter, Michael and Marjorie Rutter, *Developing Minds: Challenge and Continuity across the Life Span*, London: Penguin, 1992; New York: Basic Books, 1993

Sargent, Carolyn and Nancy Scheper-Hughes (editors), *Small Wars: The Cultural Politics of Childhood*, Berkeley: University of California Press, 1998

Vygotsky, L.S., *Thought and Language*, Cambridge, Massachusetts: MIT Press, 1962

Werner, Emmy E. and Ruth S. Smith, *Overcoming the Odds: High Risk Children from Birth to Adulthood*, Ithaca, New York: Cornell University Press, 1992

Whiting, Beatrice Blyth and Carolyn Pope Edwards, *Children of Different Worlds: The Formation of Social Behavior*, Cambridge, Massachusetts: Harvard University Press, 1988

Scholarly writings on childhood in the 20th century can be broadly grouped by focus into those with an educational, historical, developmental, psychological, or sociological bent. Several lines of debate can be traced to earlier centuries, however, including the ever-controversial one between those who favour the centrality of inborn factors as determinants of developmental outcome and those who emphasize the contribution of the environment and experience of the growing child. This "nature versus nurture" dispute, as it has come to be known, is foreshadowed on the "nature" side, for instance, as early as St Augustine's view that children's misconduct is rooted in original sin, and somewhat later on the "nurture" side by Locke's epistemology. The "nature versus nurture" conflict has had practical consequences for children in the educational sphere, and the approach taken to child training and discipline throughout the centuries.

ARIES provides an interesting social history of the concept of childhood, which he contends did not really exist prior to the 13th century. Previously, children entered into almost all spheres of adult life as soon as they progressed beyond the totally dependent state of infancy. The 17th century saw a further shift in emphasizing the importance both of the family and of formal schooling to the child's healthy development, while the 19th century begins a turn toward valuing the child for narcissistic ends that continues to this day. Ariès sees the move away from collectivistic lifestyles as a negative event for social and cultural life and for children's position within it.

The growth of psychoanalysis influenced writers in many disciplines concerned with childhood. DEMAUSE's edited collection of papers in psychohistory clearly illustrates this influence. Unlike Ariès, deMause sees continual progress in the treatment of children, and adopts a view of historical change with parent/child relations at its centre. As each generation of parents becomes more empathetic to the special conditions of childhood, social relations are gradually improved. DeMause's contribution to this volume frames papers by nine other historians considering issues in the psychohistory of Euro-American childhood from Roman times through to the 19th century.

ERIKSON extends the psychoanalytic approach from a purely individualistic one focused on the ego to consideration of the individual's growth within the social context. His is a stage theory, in which mastery of key conflicts at different levels of maturity leads to ego growth. MOEN, ELDER & LUSCHER's edited volume provides a good overview of the implications of Bronfenbrenner's seminal work on the ecology of human development, focusing again on the importance of social factors. This collection of papers by a distinguished interdisciplinary group of researchers locates development in the interplay between context, time, individual biology, and experience, thereby affirming the importance of both nature and nurture.

The sociological/anthropological approach to childhood has been concerned primarily with socialization. Both MEAD & WOLFENSTEIN's edited collection and WHITING & EDWARDS provide good examples of a different emphasis on the role of environmental factors in development, in seeking to elaborate the influence of culture on personality. Reacting against the contemporary emphasis of child psychology on standardized testing and observation of behaviour in controlled settings, these investigators turned instead to naturalistic observation and interpretative method to elicit a picture of the "real child", rejecting backward extrapolation from adult psychoanalysis. Whiting & Edwards represents one of several analytical works constructed from data gathered in follow up to the massive "six culture project", which focuses on cultural variation in experience and the reciprocal effects of biological and cognitive factors.

GESELL's maturationist views led him to focus on the minute description of the unfolding of children's abilities, providing the basis for much of the developmental testing and assessment of young children widely practised today. He believed that the emergence of particular abilities is "encoded" in the growing organism, which passes through defined and observable stages, and assigned little importance to environmental factors. PIAGET may also be considered a stage theorist whose work remains highly influential. Concerned primarily with cognitive development, Piaget conceived of the child as an active participant in the acquisition of knowledge through the manipulation of objects in the environment. Both Gessell and Piaget have been criticized for inadequately explaining the dynamics of movement from one stage to the increasingly complex next stage. BRUNER & HASTE characterize Piaget's child as the "little scientist" (p.2), and appeal to the work of VYGOTSKY in underlining the importance of seeing the child as an active actor in the sociocultural sphere. Vygotsky offers a corrective to Piaget's atomistic views, contending that thought and action are inextricably bound within a particular social context, and that thinking is a collective process based in interaction. In this he may be seen as a forerunner of social constructionist thinking.

Risk and resilience, or those factors that may jeopardize healthy development and those that may cushion the impact of negative events, is an important area of investigation currently. BOWLBY's attachment theory remains influential, with its focus on the emotional needs of infants and young children. "Secure attachment" is the desired state to be achieved between the child and the primary caregiver (mother) during the second half of the first year of life, characterized by non-stressful, reliable, and unambiguous communication. Bowlby's view of family life and appropriate interaction patterns may be criticized for its middle-class Eurocentric aspects. His theories have also been used to locate blame with mothers in cases of childhood emotional disturbance.

WERNER & SMITH report on a longitudinal study of children on the island of Kauai who had experienced perinatal stress. In seeking to identify factors that support better outcomes for children, they draw attention to favourable social and physical aspects of the environment in mitigating the effects of early biological stress.

RUTTER & RUTTER take a bioenvironmental, lifespan approach to human development, emphasizing that early negative events do not always herald later difficulties, and that both continuities and discontinuities in the individual developmental course are the norm. Theirs is a strong presentation of the issues in contemporary developmental theory, focusing on risk and protective factors affecting individuals across the life course.

SARGENT & SCHEPER-HUGHES' edited volume of 18 contributions locates children squarely within the global economy of the end of the 20th century, highlighting the many forms of disregard to which they are subject. International financial policy, violence, poverty, and neglect are all examined with regard to their effects on the healthy survivability of childhood. The authors report that the news is not good, and that the disempowered status of children serves to keep them invisible in the policy context.

ANDREA SCHUMAN

Chinese contract law

Cohen, Jerome Alan, "The New Foreign Contract Law," including translation of "Law of the PRC on Economic Contracts Involving Foreign Interests", in *China Business Review* (July-August 1985)

Feinerman, James V., "Legal Institution, Administrative Device, or Foreign Import: The Roles of Contract in the People's Republic of China" in *Domestic Law Reforms in Post-Mao China*, edited by Pitman B. Potter, Armonk, New York: Sharpe, 1994

Jones, William C. (editor), *Basic Principles of Civil Law in China*, Armonk, New York: Sharpe, 1989

Lee, Tahirih V. (editor), *Contract, Guanxi, and Dispute Resolution in China*, New York: Garland, 1997

Potter, Pitman B., *The Economic Contract Law of China: Legitimation and Contract Autonomy in the PRC*, Seattle: University of Washington Press, 1992

Scogin, Hugh, "Between Heaven and Man: Contract and the State in Han Dynasty China" in *Southern California Law Review*, 63 (1990): 1325ff

Vout, Paul T., Ye Jing-sheng and Gong Bai-hua, *China Contracts Handbook*, Hong Kong: Sweet and Maxwell, 1997

Zheng, Henry R., *China's Civil and Commercial Law*, London: Butterworths, 1988

SCOGIN presents an analysis of contract relations in Han dynasty China. Challenging the conventional wisdom that private commercial law meant little in traditional China, Scogin suggests that commerce was indeed subject to legal requirements, and that commercial actors were prepared to rely on legal means to pursue their interests. Scogin also offers useful insights into the study of Chinese law and comparative law more generally.

The historical context for contract law in China is provided not only by Scogin, but also by POTTER. Potter examines the 1981 Economic Contract Law (ECL) in the light of its purpose to build legitimacy and its historical antecedents of contract regulation in the 1950s and the early 1960s. Potter suggests that, despite its conflicting roles, contract law may gain a degree of practical legitimacy as a potentially useful tool in furthering commercial advantage in business relations.

FEINERMAN analyses the role of contracts in China, which highlights the conflicts inherent in the use of a liberal legal institution in a socialist planned economy. As with much Chinese legal reform effort after 1978, legal institutions such as contracts have been based largely on imported foreign norms. As Feinerman points out, this borrowing process is hampered substantially when attendant principles such as freedom of contract are not recognized and enforced. Feinerman's article provides a most useful contextual analysis of the tensions facing contract law in the Peoples' Republic of China (PRC) – tensions that remain even as the contract law system undergoes its current reform process.

COHEN provides a useful and succinct overview of the 1985 Foreign Economic Contract Law of the PRC. This statute embraced limited notions of party autonomy, and permitted foreign interests significantly wider latitude in negotiating contracts than was accorded to domestic companies under the ECL. The Foreign Economic Contract Law, along with the ECL and the Technology Contracts Law, were incorporated into a unified contract statute from the beginning of spring 1999.

VOUT provides a descriptive overview of the various forms of contract and contract law in the PRC, along with a practitioner's perspective on contract negotiations and enforcement.

This practical study is useful particularly in conjunction with the contextual analysis provided by Feinerman and Potter.

Among the many past debates on contract law in the PRC, was the issue of whether contracts were part of "economic law" or "civil law". The former denoted a heavier degree of state control, and the latter recognized the broader autonomy of civil parties in using contracts to arrange their relationships. ZHENG addresses the role of contract under China's General Principles of Civil Law (GPCL). The GPCL expressed the recognition that contracts, even those concerning business relations, were in effect civil law relations, and should be accorded a higher degree of autonomy. This was a sensitive political and policy issue, though, and hence Zheng's treatment should be read in context. The civil law context for contract law in China is expanded in JONES's edited translation of the GPCL, which contains important references to contract relations.

LEE's edited volume offers a useful series of scholarly articles on contracts and other aspects of China's emerging legal system.

PITMAN POTTER

See also Chinese law and legal system

Chinese dispute resolution

Alford, William P., "Tasselled Loafers for Barefoot Lawyers: Transformation and Tension in the World of Chinese Legal Workers", special issue on "China's Legal Reforms", *China Quarterly*, 141 (1995): 22–38

Clarke, Donald C., "The Execution of Civil Judgments in China", special issue on "China's Legal Reforms", *China Quarterly*, 141 (1995): 65–81

Crawford, Alastair and Christian Salbaing, "Resolving International Commercial Disputes in China" in *Doing Business in China*, edited by William Streng and Allen Wilcox, New York: Bende, 1990

Dicks, Anthony R., "Compartmentalized Law and Judicial Restraint: An Inductive View of Some Jurisdictional Barriers to Reform", special issue on "China's Legal Reforms", *China Quarterly*, 141 (1995): 82–109

Hunter, Chris (managing editor), *Dispute Resolution in the PRC: A Practical Guide to Litigation and Arbitration in China*, Hong Kong: Asia Law and Practice, 1995

Lee, Tahirih V. (editor), *Contract, Guanxi, and Dispute Resolution in China*, New York: Garland, 1997

Wang, Sheng-chang, *Resolving Disputes in the PRC: A Practical Guide to Arbitration and Conciliation in China*, Hong Kong: FT Law and Tax Asia Pacific, 1996

An increase in the number of commercial disputes has accompanied the development of China's legal system, with a resulting expansion of the institutional systems for resolving these disputes. As with other aspects of the legal system in China, however, due appreciation of the historical and policy context is essential. DICKS provides an insightful analysis of the attitudinal and institutional limits on reform in the Chinese judicial system. ALFORD provides a penetrating critique of the contradictions between the form and the reality in China's professional bar. Each of these experienced observers of

Chinese law notes the significant achievements in developing a dispute resolution system in the People's Republic of China (PRC), but each is also realistic about the limits of that system.

The limits of the dispute resolution system in China extend beyond jurisdictional and lawyering issues, to the question of the execution of civil judgements. CLARKE has built a significant reputation based on several publications addressing this issue. His superb research and writing on the enforcement of civil judgements has significantly expanded scholarly understanding of this important aspect of dispute resolution.

HUNTER provides a useful overview of the content of laws and regulations in the PRC, and an operational analysis of their practical effects. Combining a series of case studies with discussions of statutory provisions, the ALP volume is a useful practical overview.

Knowledge of the statutes and institutions pertaining to dispute resolution in the PRC remains important. WANG, and CRAWFORD & SALBAING provide such treatment. These practical studies are invaluable, but must be read in conjunction with the contextual nuances provided in other works.

LEE offers further discussion of the interplay between cultural and commercial interests and of the role of the courts in China.

PITMAN POTTER

See also Chinese contract law, Chinese law and legal system

Chinese economy and economic record

Hu, Zuliu and Mohsin S. Khan, *Why Is China Growing So Fast?*, Washington, DC: International Monetary Fund, 1997

Jin, Hehui and Yingyi Qian, "Public versus Private Ownership of Firms: Evidence from Rural China", *Quarterly Journal of Economics*, 112/3 (1997): 773–808

Li, Wei, "The Impact of Economic Reform on the Performance of Chinese State Enterprises, 1980–1989", *Journal of Political Economy*, 105/5 (1997): 1080–1106

Lin, Justin Yifu, Richard Burcroff and Gershon Feder, *Agricultural Reform in a Socialist Economy: The Experience of China*, Washington, DC: World Bank, 1993

Lin, Justin Yifu, Fang Cai and Zhou Li, *The China Miracle: Development Strategy and Economic Reform*, Hong Kong: Chinese University Press, 1996

Lin, Justin Yifu, Fang Cai and Zhou Li, "Competition, Policy Burdens, and State-Owned Enterprise Reform", *Americna Economic Association Papers and Proceedings*, 88/2 (1998): 422–27

Naughton, Barry, *Growing Out of the Plan: Chinese Economic Reform, 1978–1993*, Cambridge and New York: Cambridge University Press, 1995

Ng, Siang and Yew-Kwang Ng, "The Recent Economic Performance and Prospect" in *Economic Growth and Transition*, edited by Clement A. Tisdel and Joseph C.H. Chai, New York: Nova Science, 1997

Ng, Siang and Yew-Kwang Ng, "Income Disparities in the Transition of China: Reducing Negative Efforts by Dispelling Misconceptions", *Journal of International Trade and Economic Development*, 9/1 (2000)

Olson, Mancur, *The Rise and Decline of Nations: Economic Growth, Stagflation, and Social Rigidities*, New Haven, Connecticut: Yale University Press, 1982

Qian, Yingyi and Chenggang Xu, "Why China's Economic Reforms Differ: The M-form Hierarchy and Entry/ Expansion of the Non-State Sector", *Economics of Transition*, 1/2 (1993): 135–70

Xiao, G., "Managerial Autonomy, Fringe Benefits, and Ownership Structure: A Comparative Study of Chinese State and Collective Enterprises", *China Economic Review*, 2/1 (1991): 47–73

Yang, Xiaokai, Jianquang Wang and Ian Wills, "Economic Growth, Commercialization, and Institutional Changes in Rural China, 1979–1987", *China Economic Review*, 3/1 (1992): 1–37

China was almost a self-reliant economy until the economic reforms in December 1978. The scope of international trade was very limited: imports were confined to capital equipment and industrial inputs whereas exports were used as means of paying for imports. Decentralization, marketization and the "open-door" policy introduced in 1978 dramatically increased China's external trade. The volume of foreign trade in 1998 was 15 times that in 1978 and China is currently the world's tenth largest exporter. Liberalization has reduced trade barriers and transaction costs, thus contributing to greater efficiency and growth. HU & KHAN show that, between 1979 and 1994, the annual average growth rate of China's total factor productivity was about 4 per cent and LI explains that much of the productivity increase can be attributed to the reform process.

Since 1978, China's real GNP has been growing at an average rate of 9.5 per cent per annum (it was 4.6 per cent between 1960 and 1977). Real GNP in 1998 was almost six times that of 1978. The stated objective of quadrupling GNP by the year 2000 was achieved six years before that date. Rapid growth (9 per cent in 1995, 9.8 per cent in 1996, 8.5 per cent in 1997, and 7.8 per cent in 1998) can be attributed to many factors associated with the reform process, but China also enjoyed many conditions favourable to growth at the beginning of the reforms. When reforms were introduced in December 1978, the country had just emerged from the decade of the Cultural Revolution (1966–75), the death of Mao (1976), the downfall of the Gang of Four (1976), and the transition of power from Hua (Mao's designated successor) to Deng (1978). With the effects and memories of the three disasters (Anti-Right Movement in the mid-1950s, the infamous "Great Leap Forward" from 1958 to 1961, and the "Great Proletariat Cultural Revolution" 1966–1975) still fresh in their minds, people were eagerly looking for a change. Thus, the overwhelming majority of the people supported the pragmatic and economically oriented policies of Deng. Though much weakened by the disillusionment associated with the three disasters, the Communist Party was still firmly in control.

QIAN & XU explain the relative ease of the Chinese transition by its more decentralized, multi-layer, multi-regional form of organizing the economy, which has more in common with a market economy than the Soviet system. JIN & QIAN attributed the success of the town and village enterprises (TVEs) to the fiscal decentralization system. Moreover, by the time of the reforms in 1978, China had not quite completed its third decade under communism (since 1949), and some businessmen in China had pre-communist experience. Thus, the entrepreneurial spirit and talents required for the market system emerged easily. Overseas Chinese also provided significant amounts of capital, entrepreneurial, technical, and professional skills that were important for the development of China.

The different lengths of time after the communist revolution may however be a significant factor affecting communist growth according to OLSON's institutional theory of sectional coalitions. A major devastating event like a revolution or being conquered in a major war eliminates most of the interest groups of a country. These groups fight for their sectional interests and hence are usually counterproductive to economic efficiency and growth. The theory may be used to partly explain the spectacular growth in China as it suffered the communist takeover in 1949 and underwent eight years of Japanese invasion (1937–44), experiencing decades of civil wars before and after this invasion.

Early success in the easier task of agricultural reform made further reforms more politically acceptable. In 1978, China was still mainly a peasant society with more than 70 per cent of employment being in the agricultural sector. Pre-reform rural China had very little division of labour, making the creation of a market-based division of labour much easier. Within three years (1979–82), in the initial period of the reform, the household responsibility system led to immediate leaps in output. LIN, BURCROFF & FEDER estimated that almost half of the 42.2 per cent growth in output in the cropping sector between 1978 and 1984 was accounted for by an increase in productivity due to reforms. YANG, WANG & WILLS show that the contribution that reforms to property rights in rural China from 1979 to 1987 made to economic growth (through their effects on organizational efficiency) accounts for 48 per cent of total growth. The contribution of the reforms through their effects on allocative efficiency accounts for 52 per cent of growth. However, after the mid-1980s, the rate of increase in agricultural output decreased to a low level. This may be due to the lack in outright ownership rights in land that inhibits long-term investment.

An advantage of China being at a lower stage of development and commercialization is its greater scope for non-inflationary expansion in money supply as the economy becomes more commercialized as suggested by NG & NG (1997). When reforms were introduced, both inflation and the balance of payments had been kept under very tight control. Before 1978, the majority of people in China held very little cash and had only small bank deposits due to the small amount of exchanges using cash. Since then, cash holdings and bank deposits have increased dramatically. This increased willingness to hold cash allows the central government to fund budget deficits by monetary expansion without adding to inflationary pressure. Moreover, with virtually no external debt, this allowed China to benefit from a substantial inflow of external resources without alarming either the external lenders, or investors, or the Chinese policymakers.

The decentralization of foreign trade and a new contract responsibility system for enterprises expanded in the 1980s. Following the success of the special economic zones – Shenzhen, Zhuhai, Shantou in Guangdong province, Xiamen in Fujian province, and Hainan province, 14 major coastal cities – Dalian, Qinhuangdao, Tianjin, Yantai, Qingdao, Lianyungang, Nantong, Shanghai, Ningbo, Wenzhou, Fuzhou, Guangzhou, Zhanjing, and Beihai – were opened up to facilitate trade and investment. Further open areas were established in Shanghai Pudong Area and in major cities along the Yangtze River and on the border with neighbouring countries. The coastal open areas were expanded to include the Yangtze River Delta, the Pearl River Delta, the Xiamen-Zhangzhou-Quanzhou Triangle in south Fujian, the Shandong Peninsula, the Liaodong Peninsula, and the Hebei and Guangxi open coastal economic zones in 1985. These open areas are given autonomy to make economic decisions outside the state plan and are able to undertake independent investment, infrastructure construction, production, trade, and marketing decisions, although they are liable to pay tax to the state. Foreign investors in these zones are given preferential taxation treatment.

The trade liberalization policy moved forward in the early 1990s due to China's intention of joining the World Trade Organization (WTO). The Chinese yuan was made partially convertible in 1996, however full convertibility will probably be delayed due to financial turbulence in Asia. All the open areas continued to develop and the acceleration in economic growth of these areas raised China's income per capita and standard of living.

China has enjoyed spectacular growth in output, low inflation, galloping exports, and increased foreign reserves (US$145 billion in 1998, excluding Hong Kong), but it still has some serious problems. As per capita income increases, demand for agricultural products increases but less than proportionately (Engels' law). There is thus pressure to transfer resources from primary to secondary and tertiary production, which concentrate in urban areas. Hence, rural–urban migration is a natural consequence of economic growth. Existing large rural–urban disparities in living standards mean that a sudden and complete dismantling of rural–urban segregation is not feasible. In terms of the ratio of urban to rural consumption, the figure of 3.13 in 1997 is higher than that of 2.93 in 1978. A policy of gradually narrowing the disparity is imperative and success or otherwise in the implementation of this significantly affects the future political stability of China. NG & NG discuss the problem of large disparities in per capita income between coastal and inland provinces. There are also problems of widespread corruption, disparities between private proprietors, high officials, and those with lucrative sources of income in addition to their formal salaries on the one hand, and others who have to rely mainly on their low salaries on the other.

In contrast with the agricultural sector, state-owned enterprises (SOEs) have seen only gradual reform and this is the least satisfactory sector in the economy. In 1998 the total losses of SOEs amount to 102.3 billion yuan, an increase of 21.9 per cent compare with 1997. Although the real growth rate of individual-owned enterprises has been very much higher than that of collectively owned enterprises, the latter's performance has been better than the SOEs. The share of industrial production due to the SOEs fell from 77.64 per cent in 1978 to 25.5

per cent in 1997. The contribution of the collective-owned, the individual-owned and joint venture/foreign-owned enterprises increased from 22.37 per cent, 0 per cent and 0 per cent in 1978 to 38.1 per cent, 17.9 per cent and 18.5 per cent respectively. This phenomenon of lagging state enterprises in contrast to the fast-growing, more efficient collective, and private enterprises has been discussed in XIAO, and LIN, FANG, & ZHOU (1996). NAUGHTON argues that the rapid and sustained growth of the non-state sector, in particular TVEs, introduced a competitive market environment in China.

LIN, FANG & ZHOU (1998) argue for the need to improve the efficiency of SOEs by removing the burden of the state, and imposing hard budget constraints. The need for better macroeconomic management of the economy is obvious following the growth in financial activities, the restructuring of the banking and financial sectors, and the opening up of the economy. The new economic environment enhances the important role of monetary and fiscal instruments in maintaining macroeconomic stability. The real growth rate of 1998 was just below the stated target (8 per cent), the other two of the stated three major objectives (capping inflation below 3 per cent and stabilizing RMB (the Chinese currency) have been achieved. Premier Zhu Rongji stressed the commitment to deepen the reform and increase openness, promoting growth by boosting domestic demand, stabilize the rural sector, and to improve the performance of SOEs. Thus, despite Asian financial turbulence, continued fast growth is expected but at a lower rate.

SIANG NG

Chinese intellectual property law

Alford, William P., *To Steal a Book is an Elegant Offense: Intellectual Property Law in Chinese Civilization*, Stanford, California: Stanford University Press, 1995

Alford, William P., "Making the World Safe for What? Intellectual Property Rights, Human Rights and Foreign Economic Policy in the Post-European Cold War World", *New York University Journal of International Law and Politics*, 29 (Fall 1996/Winter 1997): 135–52

Feng, Peter, *Intellectual Property in China*, Hong Kong: Sweet and Maxwell Asia, 1997

Floum, J.R., "Counterfeiting in the People's Republic of China: The Perspective of the 'Foreign' Intellectual Property Holder", *Journal of World Trade*, 28/5 (1994): 35–59

Matthews, Katrina, *Intellectual Property in China*, 2 vols, Hong Kong: Asia Law and Practice, 1996

Oksenberg, Michel, Pitman B. Potter and William B. Abnett, *Advancing Intellectual Property Rights: Information Technologies and the Course of Economic Development in China*, Seattle: National Bureau of Asian Research, 1996

Pendleton, Michael D., *Intellectual Property Law in the People's Republic of China: A Guide to Patents, Trade Marks and Technology Transfer*, Singapore: Butterworths, 1986

Potter, Pitman B., "Prospects for Improved Protection of Intellectual Property Rights", *China Business Review*, (1989)

Shannon, David and Tan Loke Khoon, "Intellectual Property Developments and Enforcement Challenges in Hong Kong and the PRC", *California International Practitioner*, 8 (Spring/Summer 1997): 13–27

Simone, Joseph T. Jr, "Improving Protection of Intellectual Property", *China Business Review*, (March-April 1992): 9–11

State Science and Technology Commission, *China's Intellectual Property System*, Beijing: State Science and Technology Commission of the People's Republic of China, 1992

Thurston, R.L., "Country Risk Management: China and Intellectual Property Protection" in *International Lawyer*, 57/27 (1993): 51–64

Zheng, Chengsi, with Michael Pendleton, *Chinese Intellectual Property and Technology Transfer Law*, London: Sweet and Maxwell, 1987

As with many other issues of law in the People's Republic of China (PRC), statutes must be read and understood in historical and policy context. ALFORD (1995, 1997) offers the definitive work on the historical antecedents for intellectual property law in China today. The historical ambivalence toward protection of individual rights in intellectual property goes far to explain the dilemma of IPR (intellectual property rights) violations in contemporary China. Other factors are undoubtedly relevant, but Alford's is the most important analysis of the historical elements.

The tension between the ideals of law and regulation and the practical reality of enforcement is implicitly recognized by the two-volume set edited by MATTHEWS. The first volume is devoted to discussion of law and regulation, and contains reprints of most of the relevant enactments. The second volume deals with practical strategies for IPR protection, suggesting that these strategies are made necessary by the ineffectiveness of formal law and legal institutions.

Despite uncertainties as to their effectiveness, formal laws and legal institutions on intellectual property remain important. FENG, ZHENG and PENDLETON all provide useful surveys of statutory language. These contain essential knowledge for those who wish to understand intellectual property protection in China, although they must be read with a due appreciation of the limits of the PRC legal system. THURSTON, FLOUM, and SHANNON & TAN provide useful analyses of the dilemmas of protection and enforcement. Although each recognizes that the content of formal law and regulation in the PRC is generally in accord with international requirements, these analysts give cautionary accounts of the dilemmas of enforcement.

The development of intellectual property law in China is in part a story about China's foreign economic relations – particularly its relations with the United States and the resulting pressures to improve China's intellectual property system. POTTER and SIMONE examine two important memoranda of understanding between China and the United States on intellectual property protection, each of which furthered development of the system in significant ways. OKSENBERG,

POTTER & ABNETT provide an overview of this process with suggestions on future developments.

STATE SCIENCE AND TECHNOLOGY COMMISSION has provided a useful overview of the content and ideals of intellectual property laws and regulations in China at the conclusion of the Sino–US negotiating process.

PITMAN POTTER

See also Intellectual property rights

Chinese law and legal system

Cohen, J.A., "Chinese Mediation on the Eve of Modernisation", *California Law Review*, 54 (1966): 1201–26

David, René and John E.C. Brierley, *Major Legal Systems in the World Today: An Introduction to the Comparative Study of the Law*, 2nd edition, London: Stevens, and New York: Free Press, 1978

Folsom, Ralph H. and John H. Minan, *Law in the People's Republic of China: Commentary, Readings, and Materials*, Dordrecht and Boston: Nijhoff, 1989

Legislative Affairs Commission of the Standing Committee of the National People's Congress of the People's Republic of China (editors), *Arbitration Laws of China*, Hong Kong: Sweet and Maxwell, 1997

Lin Feng, *Administrative Law Procedures and Remedies in China*, Hong Kong: Sweet and Maxwell, 1996

Liu Nanping, *Judicial Interpretation in China: Opinions of the Supreme People's Court*, Hong Kong: Sweet and Maxwell, 1997

Lubman, Stanley (editor), *China's Legal Reforms*, Oxford and New York: Oxford University Press, 1996

Tsien, Tche Hao, "La Responsabilité Civile Délictuelle en Chine Populaire", Paris: Presses universitaires de France, 1973

The classical comparative work of DAVID & BRIERLEY is a prime example of the manner in which exceptional legal minds of the West viewed Chinese law in the 1970s. Although the book is admittedly out of date in the legal details and examples used to make a point, the excellent analysis of the philosophy and religion affecting the law, as reflected even in modern Chinese legal texts, albeit to a limited extent, is a still valid interpretative approach of outstanding quality. The authors trace the main differences between Chinese and Western laws to their different approaches to the concept of social order itself. Thus, the traditional Chinese concept reflects the deep belief, separate from religion, that there is a cosmic order of things involving a reciprocal interaction between heaven, earth, and men. This leads to the evaluation of the Western concept of law by the Chinese as inherently abstract and strict.

An excellent reflection of this belief can be found in TSIEN, where the author explains that man must not assert his rights since his duty is to cooperate in the work of reconciliation and, if need be, to renounce his position in the interest of the common good. Thus, any solution must, above all and apart from legal considerations, comply with the general feeling of equity and humanity. Consequently, the aim of awarding compensation in civil law is to ensure that those who have suffered a wrong, or their families, are not reduced to a state of misery.

Another similar example in the area of mediation is provided by COHEN who emphasizes the traditional Chinese distrust in the law on the basis that it is applicable in those unfortunate cases in which equity cannot be achieved among the parties themselves. This seems to discourage the Chinese people from seeking recourse in the judicial system, thus encouraging the use of extrajudicial techniques for the settlement of disputes. The book would be better appreciated and understood if read in conjunction with the recent work of the LEGISLATIVE AFFAIRS COMMISSION OF THE STANDING COMMITTEE OF THE NATIONAL PEOPLE'S CONGRESS OF THE PEOPLE'S REPUBLIC OF CHINA. Not only is this work a recent update of Chinese law in the area of arbitration, but it provides precious insights into the work and vision of this institution.

Further understanding of the arguments put forward by Cohen can be achieved by reference to another article of similar content written by LUBMAN. The author makes clear that the settlement of disputes, the dissipation of litigation and repentance remain of the highest importance within the framework of the Chinese legal system. However, this is mainly in the formal and technical sense, as a number of deeply traditional legal values, such as the concept of social order, are undergoing major changes. First, the traditional idea of equity as the substance of social legal order seems to have been replaced by the doctrinal teachings of Marxism as interpreted by Maoism. Second, the mediation system has acquired a very obvious quasi-legal nature through the replacement of the traditional family mediation of the past by mediation conducted by the quasi-official people's mediation committees, unions, social organizations, street committees, Party cells, and police. Third, the principle of sacrifice of personal interests for the achievement of equity seems to have been superseded by the principle of the primacy of the success of state policy.

Modern Chinese law is expertly and fully presented in one of the most valuable books in this area written by FOLSOM & MINAN. The main advantage of this work lies with the detailed analysis of all aspects of Chinese law, described in depth by the authors. Each field of law is handled in a complete and global manner by reference to texts, materials, and a bibliography. The book includes an introductory chapter on the Chinese legal tradition; an analysis of the constitutional law and the Chinese Communist Party; a section on dispute settlement covering mediation and conciliation, arbitration, and the people's courts; a section on the legal profession including a presentation of the institution of the people's lawyers, the people's procuracy, and notaries; a section on procedural law, both civil and criminal; and an excellent concise reference to the substantive law of China ranging from the traditional areas of criminal and civil law to the more innovative fields of regulatory law, foreign investment and trade regulations. As if this were not enough, the authors provide a special chapter on the laws of Hong Kong and Macao.

The main Western popular belief concerning Chinese law is that it changes with time very rarely, if at all. This cliché is demolished by Lubman who attempts to present and evaluate the legal reforms of the Chinese legal system since the 1980s. The book supports the view that China has been building legal institutions in areas where no meaningful ones (at least in the Western perception) ever existed. This collection of essays attempts to demonstrate the accomplishments of Chinese law reform, and to assess the problems faced by the People's Republic in its struggle to introduce the economic reforms that led to the current economic growth. The essays included in this book refer to the changing concepts and perceptions in the fields of family law, courts and civil litigation, the operation of criminal process, judicial decision making, the evolution of the legislative process, the legal framework of foreign investments in China, and Chinese participation in the international community. Equally valuable are the editor's overview of the modernization of the Chinese legal system and his evaluation of the interrelation between changes in Chinese society and Chinese law.

A closer insight into administrative law in China is expertly presented by LIN. In this recent work, which is very probably the first book written in English on Chinese administrative law, the author analyses the structure of this field of law, administrative law theory, the structure and scope of administrative reconsideration, administrative procedures and litigation, the scope and grounds of judicial review and state compensation law. Even though this monograph refers to only one field of Chinese law, the work is still valuable. The author provides an in-depth analysis of this field in a manner common to textbooks covering local or national legislation. It is therefore an excellent addition to the library of those who claim expertise, rather than general knowledge, in the field of Chinese legislation.

Similar quality and quantity of analysis can be found in LIU. The author refers to the complex issue of judicial interpretation in China in a book covering the legal status of the Supreme Court, the *Gazette* and the documents published in it, the rule of law and its adaptability in China and the recent changes in the People's Supreme Court.

HELEN XANTHAKI

See also Chinese contract law, Chinese dispute resolution, Chinese intellectual property law

Chinese political theories

Berger, Peter L., *In Search of an East Asian Development Model*, New Brunswick, New Jersey: Transition, 1988

Brugger, Bill, *China: Liberation and Transformation, 1942–62*, London: Croom Helm, and Totowa, New Jersey: Barnes and Noble, 1981a

Brugger, Bill, *China: Radicalism to Revisionism, 1962–79*, London: Croom Helm, and Totowa, New Jersey: Barnes and Noble, 1981b

Brugger, Bill and K. Hannan (editors), *Chinese Marxism in Flux, 1978–84: Essays on Epistemology, Ideology, and Political Economy*, London: Croom Helm, and Armonk, New York: Sharpe, 1985

Chan, Adrian, "Confucianism and Development in East Asia", *Journal of Contemporary Asia*, 26/1 (1996): 28–45

Chan, Adrian, "In Search of a Civil Society in China", *Journal of Contemporary Asia*, 27/2 (1997): 242–251

Chan, Adrian, *Marxism in China: A History*, London: International Continuum, 2000

Dirlik, Arif, *The Origins of Chinese Communism*, Oxford and New York: Oxford University Press, 1989

Evans, Paul M., *John Fairbank and the American Understanding of Modern China*, Oxford and New York: Blackwell, 1988

Itoh, Fumio (editor), *China in the Twenty-first Century: Politics, Economy, and Society*, Tokyo, New York and Paris: United Nations University Press, 1997

Lieberthal, Kenneth G. and David M. Lampton (editors), *Bureaucracy, Politics, and Decision Making in Post-Mao China*, Berkeley: University of California Press, 1992

Meisner, Maurice, *Li Ta-chao and the Origins of Chinese Marxism*, Cambridge, Massachusetts: Harvard University Press, 1967

Modern China, special issue, 19/2 (1993)

Nagel, Stuart C. and Miriam K. Mills (editors), *Public Policy in China*, Westport, Connecticut: Greenwood Press, 1993

Nolan, Peter and Qimiao Fan (editors), *China's Economic Reform: The Costs and Benefits of Incrementation*, Basingstoke: Macmillan, and New York: St Martin's Press, 1994

Schram, Stuart, *The Thought of Mao Tse-tung*, Cambridge and New York: Cambridge University Press, 1989

Schwartz, Benjamin I., *Chinese Communism and the Rise of Mao*, Cambridge, Massachusetts: Harvard University Press, 1951; 2nd edition 1958

Solinger, Dorothy J., *China's Transients and the State: A Form of Civil Society?*, Shatin, Northwest Territories: Hong Kong Institute of Asia-Pacific Studies, 1991

Starr, John Bryan, *Continuing the Revolution: The Political Thought of Mao*, Princeton, New Jersey: Princeton University Press, 1979

Teiwes, Frederick C. and Warren Sun, *China's Road to Disaster: Mao, Central Politicians and Provincial Leaders in the Unfolding of the Great Leap Forward, 1955–1959*, Armonk, New York: Sharpe, 1999

Tisdell, Clement A. and Joseph C.H. Chai (editors), *China's Economic Growth and Transition: Macroeconomic, Environmental and Social-Regional Dimensions*, Commack, New York: Nova, 1997

Trauzettel, Rolf and Silke Krieger (editors), *Confucianism and the Modernization of China*, Mainz: Hase & Koehler, 1991

This survey is limited to works on the modern period. It is not an exaggeration to say the spectre of communism Marx and Engels identified as haunting Europe some 150 years ago is still haunting this branch of scholarship.

SCHWARTZ's influential book is the most successful product of the Cold War and still sets the parameters of Chinese Communism. It denies the relevance of Marxism for Asia and insists the Chinese were ignorant of Marx but were seduced by the Communist International. Its use of sources is unreliable but it is easy reading and has a copious bibliography.

MEISNER is just as "authoritative" as Schwartz (his mentor). Together they form the Cold War version of the origins of

Marxism in China and are still on reading lists for students worldwide. It also reads easily and has a good bibliography.

Though DIRLIK confessed Schwartz and Meisner were "reactions to the Cold War portrait of China", they were in reality the Cold War view of China. Dirlick also suffers from a creative treatment of sources but has a useful bibliography.

SCHRAM is also a prolific writer on Mao in the mode of Schwartz, Meisner, and Dirlik. They deserve to be read as they form the received scholarship on Chinese Marxism. EVANS, although not a study of Chinese political theory, revealed why the Cold War version of Chinese Marxism has endured in the academe of the free world.

STARR shows how Mao's ideas departed from the Chinese philosophical tradition and developed from his Marxist predecessors. The writing is more technical but deserves careful reading. It, too, has a good bibliography.

CHAN (2000) is the first systematic study of the development of the concept of Marxism in China, from the beginning to Deng Xiaoping. As it challenges received scholarship, it is, of necessity, polemical but not in trade jargon. It emphasizes the contributions of two neglected leaders, Chen Duxiu and Qu Qiubaty and Mao's indebtedness to them. This is yet another book with a good bibliography.

TEIWES & SUN is the latest of a series by these prolific writers. Their works are fact-filled studies, covering almost the entire period of the People's Republic since 1949. They are blow-by-blow accounts of the power struggles but treat ideological/policy issues as irrelevant or at least unimportant. Their books are useful factual references, not overwhelmed by trade jargons. Once again, they have useful bibliographies. Other titles by these authors include *The Tragedy of Lin Biao* (1996); *Leadership, Legitimacy and Conflict in China: from the Charismatic Mao to the Politics of Succession* (1994); *Politics and Purges in China: Rectification and the Decline of Party Norms, 1950-85* (1979).

TISDELL & CHAI provide a coherent analysis by many newer hands who take ideas seriously on a timely topic: the ninth five-year plan, 1996–2000. They do a better job than most in this genre. It is a well-argued and jargon-free analysis of the policies and their effects, giving a useful understanding of China's reformed communism and postcentralized economy. It complements the works of Teiwes & Sun, although readers may think they are looking at different countries.

ITOH is a useful factual description – a good background to Tisdell & Chai and a good counter to Teiwes & Sun.

BRUGGER is arguably still the most readable explanation of what motivated Mao to do the things he did. Brugger's works (1981a, 1981b) are the antithesis of Teiwes & Sun and most others for he treats seriously Mao's policies and ideas on social, cultural, and economic issues.

The articles in BRUGGER & HANNAN try to make sense of post-Mao Chinese communism. As the issue is incoherent, the analyses, like most similar ones, compound the problem by using a bourgeois framework to evaluate a discourse retreating from its Marxist anchor.

LIEBERTHAL & LAMPTON contains essays by scholars who assume that China is a "centralized all powerful authoritarian model" and so surprised by fragmentation even in Mao's time. It makes Teiwes & Sun seem moderate by comparison.

NOLAN & FAN is a very well researched analysis of the topic and discusses theoretical issues in post-Mao Chinese communism.

From late 1980s to the mid-1990s, there were worldwide attempts to use an ancient social theory, Confucianism, to explain the economic development in China and Asia. The work of Habermas' *Structural Transformation* (1989) on the Civil Society was also misused to explain China's social developments. CHAN (1997) rebuked those sinologists who have misread Habermas (who insisted the validity of his conclusions was historically specific to societies in 17th-century England and 18th-century France).

TRAUZETTEL is a collection of leading writers on the field from Asia, Europe, and North America. They share similar ideas and agree that Confucianism is instrumental in the rapid economic development in China.

NAGEL & MILLS is a collection of essays by senior academics in China, Hong Kong and the US. The essays share a faith in economic determinism commonly known as Thatcherism. BERGER also shares their conclusion that the future well-being of China and the Chinese depends on the adoption of a *dry* free market economy and its mode of labour management.

CHAN (1996) points out that Confucius regarded the pursuit of wealth as a morally negative pursuit. Though scholars in China have shared such arguments, they must have forgotten that Confucianism was blamed for China's backwardness and anti-Confucianism was a plank on the platform of the Chinese Communist Party until the rise of Deng Xiaoping. This fatuous abuse of Confucianism has receded from academic thought though some still try to perpetuate it.

SOLINGER suggests China's migratory workers may be considered as the beginning of a form of Civil Society, but decides that the evidence is incomplete. A special issue of MODERN CHINA was devoted to locating China's civil society. Among the contributors were historians who have published books claiming to have found evidences of civil society in late 19th-century China. Chan (1997) says, "To search for civil society in China by misusing the ideas of Habermas is like investigating the Enlightenment in Europe from a Buddhist perspective".

ADRIAN CHAN

Christian democracy

Cary, Noel D., *The Path to Christian Democracy: German Catholics and the Party System from Windthorst to Adenauer*, Cambridge, Massachusetts: Harvard University Press, 1996

Codevilla, Angelo M., "A European Wave of the Past", *Commentary*, 96/5 (November, 1993): 51–53

Fogarty, Michael P., *Christian Democracy in Western Europe, 1820–1953*, Westport, Connecticut: Greenwood Press, 1974

Hanley, David (editor), *Christian Democracy in Europe: A Comparative Perspective*, New York: St Martin's Press, 1994; London: Pinter, 1996

Kalyvas, Stathis N., *The Rise of Christian Democracy in Europe*, Ithaca, New York: Cornell University Press, 1996

Karatnycky, Adrian, "Christian Democracy Resurgent: Raising the Banner of Faith in Eastern Europe", *Foreign Affairs*, 77/1 (January/February, 1998): 13–20

Lynch, Edward A., *Latin America's Christian Democratic Parties: A Political Economy*, Westport, Connecticut: Praeger, 1993

Papini, Roberto D., *The Christian Democrat International*, Lanham, Maryland: Rowman and Littlefield, 1997

Rutan, Gerard F., "Christian Democracy in Western Europe: An Idea Whose Time has Passed?", *International Journal of Social Economics*, 24/10 (Fall, 1997)

Williams, Oliver F. and John W. Houck (editors), *Catholic Social Thought and the New World Order: Building on One Hundred Years*, Notre Dame, Indiana: University of Notre Dame Press, 1993

CARY has constructed a work that is primarily historical in its methodology and centred on the German experience in focus, but within these parameters it offers a clear analysis of the turning points from mid 19th-century German history to the present time. Cary documents the efforts of reform-minded members of the old Catholic Centre Party to break the constraints of longstanding minority mentality politics in order to form a democratic party ready to strike for political power, but always within the perimeters of parliamentary democracy. The failure of the movement to withstand the Nazi assault in the 1930s, and the rapid achievement of power in the Federal Republic under Adenauer in the 1940s, are analysed in tandem. Importantly, Cary examines the origins, founding, and work of the interdenominational Christian Democratic Union (CDU), which both gentled denominational conflict – primarily between Evangelical Lutherans and Catholics – and allowed the emergence of the most stable force for democracy in German history. This integration of conservative and liberal, Catholic and Protestant, into a single durable and progressive order is the great achievement of Christian democracy in contemporary Germany. This book is a thorough and literate history of that achievement.

CODEVILLA presents a hard-hitting, even harsh evaluation of Christian democracy in the 1990s in Europe generally, and Italy in particular. The thesis is simple: Christian democracy has failed the test. It became old, corrupt, and bankrupt of ideas and policies. It left Christianity by the roadside long ago on the way to power, and ended up with neither. In the new millennium it is "a European wave of the past". The fall of Christian democracy, says Codevilla, was long overdue. So long as communism was a threat, Christian democrats could claim that they were its most tested and trustworthy opponents. Now, however, they have no firm self-definition. Neither principled defenders of neoliberal free enterprise nor socialists, neither champions of the values of the past nor of the "new age", they decline into defenders of an increasingly meaningless status quo dedicated to the protection of self-perpetuating bureaucracies. Their ideology has been enervated to the point that it is non existent, and their programmes are little more than a pale reflection of those advanced by the moderate left. They are a movement without movement, an ideology without ideas.

Although now dated, FOGARTY still stands as one of the basic works examining and explaining the phenomenon of the resurgence and rise of Christian democracy in postwar Western Europe. The historical delineation is clear and well organized, and the ideological and philosophical presentations are complete, erudite and referenced. Fogarty is careful to balance the claims by, and charges against, Christian democracy: thus, he offers one of the best examinations of the anti-democratic tendencies of earlier movement leaders merging into the fascist period, the resistance, and the ultimate establishment of Christian democracy in Italy, Germany, the low countries, and France, as the single viable alternative to a left dominated by the communists and subverted by socialists who cooperated with them. This is one of the few works that also offer a wide focus examination of the period before World War I. The period 1820–1914 is generally ignored in the study of European Christian democracy, but Fogarty examines and explains this history with detailed exactness. This work is a necessary and serviceable source for research into the deep origins and long development of Christian democracy in the Western European experience.

HANLEY presents a comparative perspective focused on contemporary Christian democracy in Europe. The work offers not as much analysis as structural and organizational detail, but is invaluable in that regard. Here, in one volume, are the anatomy and morphology of Christian democracy in the Netherlands, Belgium, Italy, Austria, Germany, the Scandinavian countries, France, the United Kingdom, and Ireland, and valuable references to yet other Christian democratic parties or movements. The exposition of the European People's Party (the Christian democrat party group in the European Parliament) is current and factual, asking the question "is this transnational entity a new party form?" The final section entitled "the future of Christian democracy in Europe" argues for a strong, if differentiated, future for the movement throughout Europe. The references and notes are outstanding, offering nuggets of data to the inquisitive and the scholarly. This is a necessary work in any study of contemporary Christian democracy.

KALYVAS is one of the 20 separate publications in the Wilder House series in politics, history, and culture. It focuses on Christian democracy in Europe. The study grows out of the study of the political right in Europe, most of which has tended to be Christian democratic. Kalyvas found this puzzling: the odd religious connotation of the movement seemed at variance with the commitment to secular democracy. Religious integralism is now widely viewed as an enemy – even one of the major enemies – of the ideology and practice of democracy. Yet the very origins and continuing foundations for this powerful transnational political movement are at base religious, calling for an indispensable integration of Christian (meaning Catholic) social and economic thought with the practice of democratic political life and governance. Can this really be achieved? The answer is "yes", and the author demonstrates how the parties are formed, their interactions with society and polity, the intended and unintended outcomes, and the generation and implementation of policy in contemporary secularized states. The book is factual and contemporary.

KARATNYCKY maintains that a number of Central and Eastern European countries that have either majorities or sizeable minorities of Catholics are witnessing a resurgence in Christian democratic thought and organization. The 1997 electoral victories of Poland's Solidarity Electoral Action bloc

(AWS), based upon an explicit appeal to voters' Catholic religious identity and ideology, is seen to have been mirrored in later elections in Romania, Hungary, Slovakia, and Lithuania. This is a "new" Christian democracy in Eastern Europe: it struggles to be politically moderate, to become more inclusive, and more closely to link itself to Catholic social and economic thought and cultural values. At the same time it is reaching out to the electorates' spiritual needs and the widespread desire for stability in the challenge of far-reaching political and economic change. Although comparatively short, the article offers a worthwhile and up-to-date analysis of the resurgence of Catholicism as a political and ideological force in contemporary Eastern Europe.

LYNCH argues that Christian democracy has essentially failed in Latin America, even in those states that saw democracy restored in the 1980s and 1990s. The book attempts to answer the question of how and why this decline took place. The hypothesis is that Christian democracy has failed to reach its potential because it has forgotten its ideological roots in Christian thought and morality. This has caused Christian democratic parties to swerve erratically to both the political right and left in a vain attempt to emulate their more positioned rivals. Thus, Christian democracy has failed to advance a coherent ideology, let alone policy alternatives, to rival forces of both left and right throughout the continent. There is a noteworthy section on the roots of Christian democratic thought in both Catholic social theory and European Christian democracy. The analysis of Christian democracy and Latin America under the influence of American engendered neoliberalism is both current and analytic.

PAPINI presents among the most recent and probably one of the best examinations of the international aspects of Christian democracy, particularly in Western Europe but including most areas of the world. In particular, the affiliation of European Christian democratic parties is shown to be both effective and stable. The success of Christian democracy in the European Parliament as the major opposition force to the socialist – social democratic majority is scrutinized and proffered as evidence of this success. The 20th-century history of Christian democracy is presented with particular attention to the mechanics of party building and organization. The historical section on the Christian democratic parties is detailed, accurate, and thus valuable. It leads into an examination of the cooperative efforts of Christian democratic parties to reach out to each other, the so-called "Christian Democrat International", and evaluate the methods, successes and failures of those efforts. Papini is observably favourable toward Christian democracy yet his analyses are both factual and fair. This work offers the reader a rare contemporary overview of Christian democracy as an international phenomenon, an aspect not sufficiently studied by scholars, who are usually more interested in their own domestic polities and thus their own local Christian democratic party.

RUTAN offers the rejoinder to Codevilla's position that Christian democracy is a remnant of the past. He argues that Christian democracy is in a transitory period of retrenchment and reorganization, especially in Europe. Out of this is emerging a renewed vigour and influence for Christian democratic ideology and organization on the European scene, not least in the form of one of the two major party groups in the European Parliament. Rutan argues that the international aspect of Christian democracy gives it a valuable advantage over other such ideology party groups in that – as with the socialists – it is able to appeal across national/state identities to the wider European context, one with a singular base in European history and values. This transnational appeal, it is explained, is the reason why the Christian democrats (the European People's Party) and the socialists are the two major forces in the European parliament, and Christian democracy a strong force for democratic vitality in that parliament's continuing contests with the European Commission in Brussels. It is concluded that because of its wide ideological appeal, its historical religious base, and abiding talent among the Christian democratic elite, Christian democracy is not a "wave of the past" but rather an idea whose time is yet to fully dawn across Europe.

WILLIAMS & HOUCK contains edited papers presented at a symposium at Notre Dame University, 1991. The 18 papers are focused upon Christian/Catholic social and political thought, with several of them addressing Christian democracy and/or the general issues of politics and governance originating in, and based upon, Christian religious values. Of particular importance are the papers by Richard T. de George, "Neither the Hammer and Sickle Nor the Eye of the Needle: One Hundred Years of Catholic Social Thought on Economic Systems", and Paul E. Sigmund "Catholicism and Liberal Democracy". These papers summarize well current thought and scholarship on the economic and political thrusts of Christian democracy today. Several other papers (Henriot, McGrath, Paris, and Hesburgh) take the analysis of Christian democratic thinking to Africa and Latin America. Dennis McCann's paper "Toward a Theology of the Corporation: A Second Chance for Catholic Social Teaching" is both prescient and challenging. This book is a valuable, well presented anthology. It will be useful for the researcher focusing on the thought and ideology of Christian democracy.

GERARD F. RUTAN

Church

Bainbridge, William Sims and Rodney Stark, "Cult Formation: Three Compatible Models", *Sociological Analysis*, 40 (1979): 283–95

Becker, Howard, *Systematic Sociology on the Basis of the Beziehungslehre and Gebildelehre of Leopold von Wiese*, New York: Wiley, and London: Chapman and Hall, 1932

Johnson, Benton, "Church-Sect Revisited", *Journal for the Scientific Study of Religion*, 10 (1971): 124–37

Niebuhr, H. Richard, *The Social Sources of Denominationalism*, New York: Holt, 1929

Troeltsch, Ernst, *The Social Teaching of the Christian Churches*, 2 vols, New York: Macmillan, and London: Allen and Unwin, 1931 (German edition 1912)

Weber, Max, "'Churches' and 'Sects' in North America: An Ecclesiastical Socio-Political Sketch", *Sociological Theory*, 3 (1985): 1–13 (published in German, 1906)

Weber, Max, *The Sociology of Religion*, Boston: Beacon Press, 1963; London: Methuen, 1965 (German edition 1922)

Yinger, J. Milton, *The Scientific Study of Religion*, New York: Macmillan, 1970

TROELTSCH provides the mandatory starting point for 20th-century theorizing about the church type and sect type of religious organization. His discussion follows directly from his long and erudite treatise on medieval Catholicism. One of the oft-repeated limitations of his categories in fact stems from their deep-rooted association with this specific historical configuration. For Troeltsch, the church type of organization is universal and overwhelmingly conservative. It exists in harmony with the secular order, uses the state and ruling classes, and exercises domination over the masses. It develops a sacerdotal hierarchy alongside sacramental doctrine and has an objective institutional character. Membership in a church is involuntary. The church incorporates extreme asceticism and religious virtuosi through ecclesiastical monasticism thereby safeguarding itself from the sectarian movements that may accompany widespread individual and internal religiosity. The sect type of organization, by contrast, pertains to groups that are comparatively small and self-selected. Sect members are referred directly to the supernatural without intervention from the sacerdotal hierarchy. Hence, spiritual progress, or salvation, results from individual effort rather than sacraments, which are largely distrusted. Sect members aspire toward personal inward perfection and direct individual union with God, often through renunciation of the world and asceticism. Sect members, in contrast to the church, have largely renounced the idea of dominating the masses; in fact, Troeltsch associates sect membership with the lower classes, themselves the subject of domination. The attitudes of sect members toward the state may be hostile, indifferent, or tolerant.

WEBER in *Religionssoziologie* (1922) makes the distinction between prophet and priest as part of his organizational analysis. The prophet responds to a personal call based on revelation and charisma. As the bearer of a personal charisma, he can revive an existing religion or found a new religion. Prophets do not normally emerge from the class of priests, but rather exert power through personal gifts. The priest, by contrast, does not respond to a personal call, but rather functions through the authority of his office and his service within an existing sacred tradition. Weber adds congregation to the church-sect terminology. The early 1906 article (WEBER 1906) was written after his trip to America and observation of secular derivatives of sects in the form of voluntary associations.

NIEBUHR, a theologian rather than a sociologist, nonetheless adds to the occidental ecclesiastic terminology the concept of denomination, in reference to sects that have accommodated to the exigencies of the social order. The book is worth reading for its theological perspective and more sociological analysis of the way in which "the church", meaning an ideal, universal, Christian church, has yielded to the very social and class distinctions that it originally sought to transcend, thereby losing touch with its originating ethos.

BECKER employs the term "church" in reference to its function in uniting religious needs with collectives and more specifically in reference to the collectivities surrounding the five major world religions – Judaism, Buddhism, Brahamanism, Islam, and Christianity. These are distinguished from "supernaturalistic congregations" or the "social structures of pre-

literates". His analysis, nonetheless, applies almost wholly to Christianity. He deals with the vast diversity of phenomena characterized as church after the breakup of the medieval Catholic Church by refining the original church-sect distinction of Troeltsch and Weber through additional categories. These include: (a) the ecclesia, which is ascribed at birth, and closely allied with the dominant classes, national and economic interests; (b) the sect, a relatively small elective body; (c) the denomination, or sects in an advanced stage; and (d) the cult, or the extreme form available for expression of private and personal religious sentiments.

YINGER attempts to develop a system of classification for religious groups in order to describe relationships between religion and society. He refines and develops the fourfold typology of Becker based on three criteria: (a) degree of inclusiveness of members of society, (b) the extent of alienation from secular values, and (c) the degree and extent of organizational differentiation and complexity. Yinger provides needed discussion of the typology in application to religions other than Christianity. Yinger's most important contribution comes from his description and analysis of the way in which some sects develop into denominations whereas others become established sects. He then applies concepts from the social movement literature to develop a typology for sects based on the way in which sectarian groups relate to the secular world. His threefold classification of sects includes: (a) acceptance sects, which accept broader social goals but have new and esoteric means of finding them; (b) aggressive sects, which seek to change the world; and (c) avoidance sects, which devalue the significance of this life. Yinger provides an excellent bibliography for publications prior to his related to the church-sect dichotomy and the subsequent classification categories.

JOHNSON recaps problems in the church-sect literature and reiterates general concern regarding the lack of a generally accepted definition based on analytic properties applicable to all religious groups and independent of historical cases. He focuses on how sects develop and the two-way process whereby the external world may compromise sects, but likewise may itself be altered by the impact of sect behaviour.

BAINBRIDGE & STARK address the two-step process whereby new religious ideas are invented and then gain social acceptance. They define religion as a social enterprise operant in the creation, maintenance, and exchange of supernatural compensators that substitute for more prosaic and immediate rewards. They position cults within this framework as a special class operant in the development of new and exotic compensators. Three compatible models of cult formation are developed. The psychopathology model describes cult formation as the outcome of an individual psychopathology that is able to find social support for a new solution to intractable human problems. The entrepreneur model describes cult founders as individuals who consciously develop new compensatory beliefs and practices in situations that provide opportunities for profit from favourable market responses. The subcultural-evolution model describes cult formation as part of group processes through which individuals progressively commit to compensators through social interaction. Bainbridge & Stark view the models as complementary.

BARBARA R. WALTERS

Church and state

Brown, Richard, *Church and State in Modern Britain, 1700–1850*, London and New York: Routledge, 1991

Eastland, Terry (editor), *Religious Liberty in the Supreme Court: The Cases That Define the Debate over Church and State*, Lanham, Maryland: University Press of America, 1993

Fowler, Robert Booth, Allen D. Hertzke and Laura R. Olson, *Religion and Politics in America: Faith, Culture and Strategic Choices*, 2nd edition, Boulder, Colorado: Westview Press, 1999

Gedicks, Frederick Mark, *The Rhetoric of Church and State: A Critical Analysis of Religion Clause Jurisprudence*, Durham, North Carolina: Duke University Press, 1995

Jelen, Ted G. and Clyde Wilcox, *Public Attitudes toward Church and State*, Armonk, New York: Sharpe, 1995

Liskofsky, Sidney, "The UN Declaration on the Elimination of Religious Intolerance and Discrimination: Historical and Legal Perspectives", *Religion and the State: Essays in Honor of Leo Pfeffer*, edited by James E. Wood Jr, Waco, Texas: Baylor University Press, 1985

Lugo, Luis E. (editor), *Religion, Public Life, and the American Polity*, Knoxville: University of Tennessee Press, 1994

Maclear, J.F. (editor), *Church and State in the Modern Age: A Documentary History*, Oxford and New York: Oxford University Press, 1995

Robbins, Thomas and Roland Robertson (editors), *Church–State Relations: Tensions and Transitions*, New Brunswick, New Jersey: Transaction, 1987

Semonche, John E. (editor), *Religion and Constitutional Government in the United States: A Historical Overview with Sources*, Carrboro, North Carolina: Signal, 1986

Wilson, John F. (editor), *Church and State in America: A Bibliographical Guide*, New York: Greenwood Press, 1986

FOWLER, HERTZKE & OLSON provides a broad introduction to church and state in the US. Beginning with a balanced historical reconstruction of the multiple motivations behind America's separation of church and state, they map the religious landscape in the contemporary US in relation to politics. They explore the role of religious lobbies that seek to influence public policy, identify theories about how religion influences the politics of elected officials, and provide a concise overview of US Supreme Court cases involving church and state. In describing the legal system, they provide a useful typology of separationist, neutrality, accommodationist, and equal access (multiple establishment) approaches. Fowler, Hertzke & Olson provides an excellent starting point for those who seek to understand church and state in the US.

After a 72-page analysis of the structure of religious freedom in the United States, SEMONCHE provides a collection of the most often quoted sources on the issue of church and state from the writings of Roger Williams, Thomas Jefferson, James Madison, Thomas Paine, Alexis de Tocqueville, and others. Anyone who is serious about church and state should read some of these primary sources such as Madison's "A Memorial and Remonstrance on the Religious Rights of Man" (1784).

LUGO provides a collection of essays on church–state relationships with competing views regarding the visions of the Founders, the interpretations of the establishment and free-exercise clauses by the Supreme Court, and the proper relationship between religion and American political culture. Lugo begins with a helpful typology of church–state relations: strict separation, free-will separation, institutional separation, structural plurality, nonpreferentialism, and restorationism. Another chapter worthy of note is Neal Riemer's analysis of James Madison (pp.37–50).

For those who would like to engage in a more thorough study of church and state in the US, WILSON provides an annotated bibliography identifying thousands of sources. Wilson's guide begins by organizing the church and state debate chronologically within the original colonies, New England, and the Colonial South before discussing the American Revolution. It then points the reader to a multitude of resources available regarding that critical moment when the establishment and free-exercise clauses became part of the First Amendment to the US Constitution. Wilson includes chapters on issues such as communitarian experiments, new religions, education, and women.

For those who wish to focus upon the Supreme Court's role in shaping church and state, EASTLAND provides an invaluable resource. He identifies 25 of the most significant Supreme Court cases involving church and state between 1940 and 1992. After summarizing the facts of each case, Eastland presents the official "opinions" (Eastland uses the word "opinions" to identify the rulings of the Supreme Court, the dissenting opinions of the justices, and (in some cases) the responses of interested organizations) of the Supreme Court justices. For example, *Cantwell v. Connecticut* (310 U.S. 296 (1940)) appealed to the Fourteenth Amendment to claim that state legislatures were as bound to the free-exercise clause as the federal government. *Lemon v. Kurtzman* (403 U.S. 602 (1971)) provided the "Lemon test" insisting that "First, the statute must have a secular legislative purpose; second, its principal or primary effect must be one that neither advances nor inhibits religion ... finally, the statute must not foster 'an excessive government entanglement with religion'" (p.215). Such Supreme Court decisions play a central role in the contemporary American debates about church and state.

GEDICKS provides a powerful critique of Supreme Court jurisprudence on the matter of church and state. He summarizes the arguments of Richard John Neuhaus, Andrew Greeley, and others who suggest that the Supreme Court has confused hostility towards religion with neutrality towards religion. He also echoes the arguments of Stephen Carter and others who have claimed that the Supreme Court has defined religion as such a private and other-worldly matter that it has no relevance to public policy. These arguments may not be compelling to most social scientists, but they are too popular to be completely ignored.

JELEN & WILCOX provides an analysis of public attitudes in the United States to issues of church and state. The organization of this book is not always clear, but the authors identify the attitudes of various religious communities to such issues as support for a moment of prayer in public schools, support for crèches on government properties, and support for chaplains in the military. They show how factors such as race, class, gender, age, and region also affect individual's attitudes toward the separation of church and state. They demonstrate significant attitudinal gaps between elites (in academia, the media, and government) and popular opinion regarding the separation of church and state.

MACLEAR provides a collection of primary sources that address church–state relations in Europe and America since the 18th century. Maclear presents many of the most commonly quoted documents on church and state from the US, France, England, Russia, Austria, Prussia, Belgium, Scotland, Switzerland, Canada, Mexico, Germany, Hungary, Romania, Czechoslovakia, and Poland.

BROWN provides a detailed account of church and state in Great Britain. (Those who prefer a more concise analysis of the relationship between Great Britain and the Church of England could simply read Brown's fourteenth chapter, "Church and Chapel: Religion Under Pressure". Brown provides a history of the Church of England and provides insights into the relationships between Britain and Presbyterianism, Methodism, and Roman Catholicism. He identifies the forces leading to the repeal in 1828 of the Test and Corporation Acts that had enforced the spiritual monopoly of Anglicanism.

ROBBINS & ROBERTSON provides comparative perspectives on church and state that look beyond the US and Europe. One chapter looks at how the constitutions of various nation-states address the issue of church and state. Other chapters focus upon Islamic understandings of church and state and Latin American Liberation theology. Poland, Australia, and Ireland are also noted as case studies for exploring issues of church and state.

LISKOFSKY provides historical background for the "UN Declaration on the Elimination of Religious Intolerance and Discrimination" adopted in 1981. He points to the origins of this declaration, the responses of various nations and religious communities, and its likely (and unlikely) consequences for church–state relations throughout the world.

ANDREW D. WALSH

Circumcision

Derrida, Jacques, "Circumfession: Fifty-nine Periods and Paraphrases Written in a Sort of Internal Margin, between Geoffrey Bennington's Book and Work in Preparation (January 1989-April 1990)" in *Jacques Derrida*, by Geoffrey Bennington and Jacques Derrida, Chicago: University of Chicago Press, 1993

Docker, John, "Mr Bloom's Penis" in *Adventures of Identity*, New York and London: Cassell, forthcoming

Dorkenoo, Efua and Scilla Ellworthy, *Female Genital Mutilation: Proposals for Change*, London: Minority Rights Group, 1992

Gilman, Sander L., *Freud, Race, and Gender*, Princeton, New Jersey: Princeton University Press, 1993

Glenn, Jules, "Circumcision and Anti-Semitism", *Psychoanalytic Quarterly*, 29 (1960): 395–99

Goldman, Ronald and Ashley Montagu, *Circumcision, the Hidden Trauma: How an American Cultural Practice Affects Infants and Ultimately Us All*, Boston: Vanguard, 1997

Hall, Robert G., Circumcision entry in *The Anchor Bible Dictionary*, edited by David Noel Freedman, New York: Doubleday, 1992

Hoffman, Lawrence A., *Covenant of Blood: Circumcision and Gender in Rabbinic Judaism*, Chicago: University of Chicago Press, 1996

Laumann, Edward O., "The Circumcision Dilemma", *Scientific American Presents*, 10/2 (Summer 1999): 68–73

Morgenstern, Julian, "The 'Bloody Husband' (?) (Exod. 4:24–26) Once Again", *Hebrew Union College Annual*, 34 (1963): 35–70

Snowman, Leonard V., Circumcision entry in *Encyclopedia Judaica*, vol. 5, Jerusalem: Keter, 1972

Walker, Alice, *Possessing the Secret of Joy*, New York: Harcourt Brace, 1992; London: Vintage, 1993

Circumcision (the removal or alteration of the foreskin) of the male sexual organ has been practised by human beings for 7000 years, and in a variety of cultures. The practice has been explained variously as a wedding ritual, a rite of passage from boyhood to manhood, a mark of covenant relationship, a sign of national or cultural identity, for the warding off of evil spirits, as a medical or hygienic prophylactic, and as a cosmetic or aesthetic procedure. HALL surveys the history of circumcision in the ancient Near East, amongst Jews, in the Roman period, and in the early Church. Jews and Christians argued over the propriety of ritual circumcision up until the 4th century CE.

In the minds of most people, circumcision is connected with Judaism. MORGENSTERN explores in depth some of the Scriptural expectations around circumcision, concentrating on a particularly troublesome passage in the book of Exodus. As SNOWMAN points out, circumcision is often used in Jewish literature as a metaphor to describe things that are undisciplined or unresponsive to God, such as the ear, the lips, the mind, the heart, and the eyes. HOFFMAN is a comprehensive treatment of the circumcision of male Jews throughout the Biblical, Rabbinical, and Medieval periods.

Sigmund Freud (q.v.), while not a practising Jew, was himself circumcised, and struggled with his understanding of circumcision as a symbolic castration. In his famous case study of "Little Hans", Freud argued that Jewish circumcision raised castration anxiety among non-Jews, and thus was the primary psychological source of anti-Semitism. He also theorized that circumcision produces psychic trauma, which, if overcome, makes some men stronger. GLENN offers two further case studies to complement "Little Hans". The 19th and 20th century history of male circumcision as both a disease preventative and a disease spreader, as a cure for masturbation and epilepsy, and as signifying both the weakness and superiority of male Jews, is explored fully in GILMAN.

The ambiguous nature of male circumcision as ritual or castration, as weakness or strength, features prominently in several works of literature, including George Eliot's *Daniel Deronda* and James Joyce's *Ulysses*. In the latter, Bloom's combined Jewish and Irish Catholic heritage leaves him uncircumcised and confused, as explored by DOCKER. Contemporary French philosopher Jacques DERRIDA has written a rambling meditation based on *The Confessions* by St Augustine. Derrida has entitled this work *Circumfession*, a play on words between circumcision and confession. In this work Derrida muses upon his own circumcision and that of others: its meaning, its symbolism, its numinosity.

Recently, particularly in America, the issue of the routine circumcision of male babies has become a heated debate, even amongst the medical community. About 60 per cent of American boys are circumcised at or near birth, but the medical studies of its benefits are often contradictory. Some within the contemporary men's movement argue that circumcision is an act of involuntary cruelty to vulnerable children, and should be delayed until each young man can make his own decision. LAUMANN argues the case on either side. GOLDMAN & MONTAGU make a strongly argued case for the cessation of routine circumcision. Overall, the practice of male circumcision is declining, although it is still routine as a rite of passage amongst many ethnic groups, including Polynesians and Melanesians.

The issue of female circumcision, or female genital mutilation (FGM), has received much more attention in the recent decade. The practice is an ancient one in some African and Islamic countries, involving circumcising a young girl's labia and then usually sewing shut her vagina. DORKENOO & ELLWORTHY document the extensiveness of this practice, and describe its cultural role, its preservation of gender stereotypes, and its barbarity. WALKER has captured the horrors of FGM in her powerful novel, and is a leader in the international campaign to ban the practice.

PHILIP L. CULBERTSON

See also Clitoridectomy

Cities, economics

Benabou, Roland, "Workings of a City: Location, Education, and Production", *Quarterly Journal of Economics*, 58/3 (August 1993): 619–52

Boston, Thomas D. and Catherine L. Ross (editors), *The Inner City: Urban Poverty and Economic Development in the Next Century*, New Brunswick, New Jersey: Transaction, 1997

Castells, Manuel, *The Informational City: Information Technology, Economic Restructuring, and the Urban-Regional Process*, Oxford and Cambridge, Massachusetts: Blackwell, 1989

Greenhut, Melvin L., and George Norman (editors), *The Economics of Location*, Aldershot, Hampshire: Elgar, 1996

Harvey, David, *The Urban Experience*, Baltimore: Johns Hopkins University Press, and Oxford: Blackwell, 1989

Krugman, Paul R., *Development, Geography, and Economic Theory*, Cambridge, Massachusetts: MIT Press, 1995

Martin, Ron, and Peter Sunley, "Paul Krugman's Geographical Economics and Its Implications for Regional Development Theory: A Critical Assessment", *Economic Geography*, 72/3 (1996): 259–92

Richardson, Harry W., Kenneth J. Button, and Peter Nijkamp (editors), with Heonsoo Park, *Analytical Urban Economics*, Cheltenham: Elgar, 1996

Scott, Allen J., *Technopolis: High-Technology Industry and Regional Development in Southern California*, Berkeley: University of California Press, 1993

Scott, Allen J. and Edward W. Soja (editors), *The City: Los Angeles and Urban Theory at the End of the Twentieth Century*, Berkeley: University of California Press, 1996

Analyses of cities by economists have always included three distinct but intertwined components: abstract models of spatial equilibria; applied analyses drawing on insights from sociology, geography, anthropology, and political science; and policy-oriented work. This broad conceptual terrain means that research in this area is remarkably diverse.

One strand of economic research on cities develops abstract answers to questions about urban form *per se*: why do cities exist, why do cities exist where they do, and why do some cities become bigger than others? Spatial equilibrium theory investigates the achievement of stable market and residential configurations, under the assumptions that agents and firms are distributed in space, and that spatial movement involves real costs. Many of the classic contributions to this literature have been collected in two volumes. GREENHUT & NORMAN collect contributions to this tradition dating back to Von Thünen in the 1920s. RICHARDSON, BUTTON & NIJKAMP cover the spatial equilibrium of the firm and the household, central place theory, and spatial general equilibrium. Greenhut's own essays emphasize the implications of oligopolistic firms in spatial settings.

The results collected in these volumes are well known, but they have ceased to guide the development of many strands of urban economics, due in large part to increasingly deep interactions with noneconomists. Substantial controversy over the line between geographic economics and economic geography has arisen due to the interventions of Paul Krugman, the *enfant terrible* of economic theory. Krugman's initial work on spatial relations in the early 1990s drew on non-mainstream contributions to spatial theory. Since the mid-1990s, he has adopted ever more formal models, and traced their lineage exclusively to abstract theorists of spatial relations. KRUGMAN embodies this shift, arguing forcefully that economic geography will lack rigour and testable hypotheses unless it adopts models explicitly specifying rational choice and equilibrium conditions.

As MARTIN & SUNLEY point out, Krugman's characteristic method is to specify an empirical puzzle (for example, the size distribution of cities) and to develop an economic model that accounts for it. This style is familiar in non-spatial economic theory, and indeed has served Krugman well in the "new trade theory" with which he is associated: it has been so controversial in urban theory precisely because so many economic geographers have turned away from the puzzle/model approach. As Martin & Sunley explain, many economic geographers now adopt an approach in which "broad master-concepts (like 'flexible specialization' and 'post-Fordism') are mingled with anecdotal spatial stereotypes ('industrial spaces' and 'industrial districts')."

Despite Krugman's admonitions that only preference-based theory matters, much contemporary urban theory draws heavily on Marx, due in large measure to David Harvey's lucid applications of Marx's work, many of which are conveniently collected in HARVEY. Harvey's sensitivity to the importance of time and space in socioeconomic theory allows him to draw out some of Marx's most profound insights.

Perhaps the key urban theoretical schema built on Marxian ideas is the notion of a spatial regime of accumulation, adapted from French regulationist theory. This approach argues that a Fordist regime – of high working-class wages, welfare-state protection, and limited international competition – has given way to a post-Fordist regime of extensive global competition and limited state action. Urban growth patterns have correspondingly changed in the post-Fordist era (the mid-1970s to the present). SCOTT shows how urban growth in Southern California differs from the concentric-circle pattern anticipated in spatial equilibrium theory and the sociological urban-succession model: instead, he finds an extensive matrix of dispersed residential settlements, with industrial "technopoles" emerging in decentralized clusters.

CASTELLS goes further, suggesting that the ongoing information revolution is transforming the urban form and, indeed, human social organization. Castells' protean work on the urban question over the past three decades has been as extensive and influential as that of Harvey. Castells' work has gone through the same transformation as has Marx-inspired urban theory: his dense earlier works focused on theoretical structures, but his latter work has grown increasingly empirical and institutional, pursuing specific themes (recently, the implications of emerging information technology) more than grand ones.

The adoption of a postmodern sensibility by economic geographers such as Storper, Martin, Sunley, and others has led to extensive interactions with humanists and other social scientists. In the ongoing rethinking of how cities come to be as they are, Los Angeles has attracted special attention because of its status as the definitive decentred (and hence postmodern) city. The volume by SCOTT & SOJA, two leaders of the "Los Angeles" school of urban geography, is the most penetrating of several edited books that present multidisciplinary explorations of this city as both an economic and social object of study.

Krugman argues for modernist methods and against post-modern ones, but the mathematics he deploys is broadly consistent with at least the spirit of postmodern inquiry. Krugman develops models of increasing returns with what he terms "pecuniary spillovers" to explain urban agglomeration. This approach is one instance of a particular branch of nonlinear mathematics, sometimes termed complexity theory, to urban problems. Urban analysis has figured prominently in investigations of complexity theory at the Santa Fe Institute. Complexity theory is consistent with postmodernism in turn, in that it emphasizes multiple equilibria, path dependence, interaction effects, and unanticipated outcomes.

In effect, Krugman's model is just one option within the terrain of complexity theory, which permits the development of models embodying spillovers and neighbourhood effects, chaos, fractal geometry, and so on. One promising alternative to Krugman's approach is that of BENABOU, who develops a neighbourhood-effects model in which spatially separated agents decide between becoming low-skill workers, obtaining education and becoming high-skill workers, or not working. Benabou shows that when local increasing returns to education arise, some neighbourhoods will have little educational

investment and low-skill workers, whereas others will have high educational attainment and high-skill workers.

Debates over urban policy in recent years have focused on a range of topics, including the spatial mismatch hypothesis, neighbourhood redlining in credit markets, and deindustrialization. Among the more provocative proposals of recent years is management theorist Michael Porter's idea that inner-city prosperity can be restored by the use of incentives to nurture industrial and commercial clusters in these areas. This idea is summarized and debated vigorously in the edited volume of BOSTON & ROSS: the criticisms of Porter advanced here focus on his lack of attention to the multidimensional character of racial inequality in US cities.

GARY A. DYMSKI

Cities, sociology

Castells, Manuel, *The Urban Question: A Marxist Approach*, Cambridge, Massachusetts: MIT Press, and London: Arnold, 1977

Davis, Mike, *City of Quartz: Excavating the Future in Los Angeles*, London: Verso, 1990

Fincher, Ruth and Jane M. Jacobs (editors), *Cities of Difference*, New York: Guilford Press, 1998

Harvey, David, *The Condition of Postmodernity: An Enquiry into the Origins of Cultural Change*, Oxford and Cambridge, Massachusetts: Blackwell, 1989

King, Anthony D. (editor), *Re-presenting the City: Ethnicity, Capital and Culture in the 21st-Century Metropolis*, Basingstoke: Macmillan, and New York: New York University Press, 1996

Lefebvre, Henri, *Writings on Cities*, Oxford and Cambridge, Massachusetts: Blackwell, 1996

LeGates, Richard T. and Frederic Stout (editors), *The City Reader*, London and New York: Routledge, 1996

Lynch, Kevin, *The Image of the City*, Cambridge, Massachusetts: MIT Press, 1960

Mumford, Lewis, *The City in History: Its Origins, Its Transformations, and Its Prospects*, New York: Harcourt Brace, and London: Secker and Warburg, 1961

Park, Robert E., Ernest W. Burgess and Roderick D. McKenzie, *The City*, Chicago: University of Chicago Press, 1925

Scott, Allen J. and Edward W. Soja (editors), *The City: Los Angeles and Urban Theory at the End of the Century*, Berkeley: University of California, 1996

Short, John Rennie, *The Urban Order: An Introduction to Cities, Culture, and Power*, Oxford and Cambridge, Massachusetts: Blackwell, 1996

Watson, Sophie and Katherine Gibson (editors), *Postmodern Cities and Spaces*, Oxford and Cambridge, Massachusetts: Blackwell, 1995

Westwood, Sallie and John Williams (editors), *Imagining Cities: Scripts, Signs, Memory*, London and New York: Routledge, 1997

Wilson, Elizabeth, *The Sphinx in the City: Urban Life, the Control of Disorder, and Women*, London: Virago, 1991; Berkeley: University of California, 1992

Cities have received extensive and unremitting attention across a great spread of intellectual disciplines, and urban studies are currently in a flourishing and innovative state. Selection from a huge number of publications of the highest interest must therefore inevitably be to some extent arbitrary and has been designed to show the strengths of different kinds of work.

A major, indeed monumental, study was written by MUMFORD in the course of a lifetime's attention to cities as human dwelling places embodying, at their best, democratic and humanist ideals. Mumford traces through architecture and social history the cities of different ages and societies, suggesting an evolution of city types in each of which there are distinctive forms of social and spatial organization. Mumford's work is the most thorough overview of the city over time and has been influential in particular for architects and planners. The breadth, optimism, and nobility of his writing is suggested by his conclusion that a "magnification of all the dimensions of life, through emotional communion, rational communication, technological mastery, and above all, dramatic representation, has been the supreme office of the city in history".

Very different but also excellent starting-points for the study of cities are provided in the reader by LeGATES & STOUT, and by SHORT's introductory textbook which is perhaps the best of a great many, including several good examples of its kind. LeGates & Stout assemble a wide range of essays and selections over most of this century, intelligently grouped in sections including the evolution of cities; classic texts; perspectives upon the city; society, culture, politics, planning; and the city's future. They also provide concise contextual introductions and useful links to related and further reading. Short describes his book as a "guide to the latest scholarship in urban studies" and while it does this (though publications proliferate ever more rapidly) his real value is in offering a lucid overview of many kinds of debates about cities, and the changes affecting cities, in modern thought. Again there are extensive and helpful links to other reading.

The city has been studied in a variety of ways in particular historical contexts and moments. One benchmark has been the series of books exploring Chicago in the 1920s by Robert PARK and associated writers and reformers in what is known as the "Chicago school". Ethnography and life histories were used to investigate the informal networks of the varied social groups of a large city, from the poor to the wealthy, including its unattached and "gangs". Though the use of ecological metaphors for urban form has since been criticized, the systematic empirical attempt to map a city's life, set out in this programmatic text and subsequent books, has remained a point of reference for others, even if later work on the city has proceeded in extremely disparate directions.

Another, later American writer, from an architectural and planning background, is LYNCH whose short book was in its 25th printing by 1997. Lynch's approach, illustrated by drawings, rests on urban inhabitants' senses of place and its characteristics and boundaries. He is concerned with what he calls the "imageability" of a pleasing city. While highly regarded by architects and urban planners, his book also shows the "cultural turn" from urban groups (Chicago) and built form (Mumford) towards urban consciousness and representation which has gained ground in recent years.

Three writers have written significantly on urban issues from a variety of engagements with Marxist thought. Of these LEFEBVRE is the least known and most elusive for English speakers. This stems in part from the abstract and unfamiliar mode of his writing (though often shot through by particular urban observations) and partly also from the uneven, belated, and partial translations of his work (including for instance his major *The Production of Space*) which is still hard to grasp as a whole though very well selected and introduced here. The body of Lefebvre's thought concerns the contestation of urban space, but he also produces other suggestive and innovative ideas, such as his "rhythm analysis" of urban movement during times of day.

Another, more structuralist Marxism is found in the writing of CASTELLS who studies urban issues within uneven capitalist development while paying increasing attention to new urban social movements seeking justice less in places of residence and consumption rather than the workplace. The book cited is an attempt at a systematic Marxist programme for the study of the urban as a particular site within capitalism, but later books and essays develop other themes such as the rise of "the informational city". HARVEY, writing as an English Marxist geographer, also studies the production and contestation of urban space as a capitalist commodity in an important sequence of books (including *Social Justice and the City* and *Consciousness and the Urban Experience*) of which that cited may be the most accessible. Here he examines and evaluates changes being made to cities in the wake of industrial decline and situates them within a general theory of "space-time compression".

Harvey's book is an important contribution to debates about social justice in contemporary cities and the extent to which their "postmodernity" involves a significant break with the urban past or a continuation involving features of new capitalist accumulation strategies. The apparent features of the postmodern city are further and excellently investigated in the diverse essays found in WATSON & GIBSON's collection. Meanwhile Los Angeles has come to be written about extensively (to the neglect of many other cities) as a type, for better and worse, of the postmodern late century city. Here SCOTT & SOJA's anthology and its title are highly indicative. Soja is a geographer writing prolifically about Los Angeles, drawing on various theoretical models including Lefebvre, while DAVIS, by contrast, offers a haunted, merciless, and brilliantly written study of the city at its bleakest, which is also in many ways a model of writing about a city without straining to generalize it as a type of all cities.

WILSON provides a stimulating feminist perspective on cities in her spirited short polemic. It combines snapshot treatments of various types of cities with a consistent and often personal argument about the treatment of women as dangerous to patriarchal control of the urban order. While some of her examples are more convincing than others and there tends to be an essentialism in her treatment of gender difference, the book raises issues forcefully in a distinctive voice that forms part of the new diversity of writing on urban issues.

In the last few years new ways of analysing cities (involving new languages) have begun to cross-fertilize across sociology, geography, planning, and cultural studies, with strong influences from political concerns about class, gender, ethnicity, and sexuality. The diversity of this work and its range of themes is well seen in very many good collections, such as that edited by WESTWOOD & WILLIAMS. In KING's collection, stimulating essays register the shift towards the city as produced in text, as metaphor and in discourse. The analytical force of the concept of "difference" and its meaning for the simultaneous production and articulation of many urban identities is extremely well shown by the range of work in FINCHER & JACOBS' outstanding collection.

MICHAEL GREEN

See also Metropolis, Suburbs, Urbanism

Citizenship

Aron, Raymond, "Is Multinational Citizenship Possible?", *Social Research*, 41/4 (1974): 638–56

Beiner, Ronald (editor), *Theorizing Citizenship*, Albany: State University of New York Press, 1995

Clarke, Paul Barry, *Citizenship*, London: Pluto Press, 1994

Conover, Pamela Johnston, Ivor M. Crewe and Donald D. Searing, "The Nature of Citizenship in the United States and Great Britain: Empirical Comments on Theoretical Themes", *Journal of Politics*, 53/3 (1991): 800–32

Gardner, J.P. (editor), *Hallmarks of Citizenship: A Green Paper*, London: Institute for Citizenship Studies, 1994

Habermas, Jürgen, "Citizenship and National Identity: Some Reflections on the Future of Europe", *Praxis International*, 12/1 (April 1992): 1–19

Heater, Derek, *Citizenship: The Civic Ideal in World History, Politics and Education*, London and New York, Longman, 1990

Kymlicka, Will and Wayne Norman, "Return of the Citizen: A Survey of Recent Work on Citizenship Theory", *Ethics*, 104/2 (January 1994): 352–81

Marshall, T.H., "Citizenship and Social Class" in his *Citizenship and Social Class and Other Essays*, Cambridge: Cambridge University Press, 1950, edited by T.H. Marshall and Tom Bottomore, London: Pluto Press, 1992

Meehan, Elizabeth, *Citizenship and the European Community*, London and Newbury Park, California, Sage, 1993

Riesenberg, Peter, *Citizenship in the Western Tradition: Plato to Rousseau*, Chapel Hill: University of North Carolina Press, 1992

Turner, Bryan S. and Peter Hamilton, *Citizenship: Critical Concepts*, London and New York: Routledge, 1994

MARSHALL's celebrated essay, first delivered as a lecture in 1949 (and reprinted many times in his own essay collections), has been seminal in the large literature that has amassed since the mid-1980s and is still the most frequently cited work on citizenship. Marshall's area of interest is the ambivalent force of citizenship as a means of social integration within a capitalist system, but it is his schematic quasi-evolutionary analysis of modern citizenship as a status incorporating three clusters of rights – civil, political, and socioeconomic – critical

development of which occurred in the 18th, 19th, and 20th centuries respectively, which informs much of the succeeding literature.

A reliable and accessible general introduction, particularly useful for non-specialists across disciplines, is provided by HEATER. Part one presents a potted history weighted toward the modern period, part two analyses the political, social, and legal components of citizenship as status and practice, and part three depicts a multidimensional "pattern" of citizenship yoking together educational, territorial, and sociopolitical elements.

CLARKE's judicious selection of 60 readings is taken from the works of political theorists and actors over the last 2500 years. His introductory discussion posits citizenship as a continuing emancipatory project, and the readings – beginning with Solon and ending with the Maastricht Treaty – situate citizenship's subversive potential through its unfolding sociohistorical contexts: from Greek and Roman origins, through Christianity, the Renaissance, and early state formation, on to the modern nation state and world order.

KYMLICKA & NORMAN (also reproduced in BEINER) is a concise survey and contextualization of the postwar literature up to the mid-1990s and essential reading for a speedy basic grasp of the range and relationships of the major theoretical positions and debates and the trajectories of their development. The discussion traverses the breakdown of the Marshallian postwar orthodoxy, and the increasing stress on the responsibilities of citizenship as a result of (a) New Right critiques, (b) the rearticulation of citizenship's connection with societal membership, and (c) renewed focus on the idea of civic virtue by the left and radical democrats, civic republicans, civil society theorists, and liberals. It delivers the reader to the threshold of emerging debates on institutional design and identity politics in culturally pluralist, nonunitary political systems.

Two collections of note are those edited by BEINER and by TURNER & HAMILTON. Taken together they supply a comprehensive overview of the terrain, with Turner & Hamilton's broad coverage of citizenship-related topics well complemented by the depth of Beiner's focus on its core. Three entries (Habermas, Kelly, and Young) are common to both. Beiner's ten articles plus introduction is an excellent selection of some of the most thoughtful recent contributions from political theorists. As a set, the works point up the insecure status of concepts and theories of citizenship in the contemporary world and the need for their rethinking to meet the challenges of political community and action in current political and social environments. Volume one of Turner & Hamilton addresses theoretical debates, the "classics" (Mill to Rousseau) and historical origins, and volume two treats welfare (UK), ethnicity (US), the state (Europe), and contemporary criticisms. The collection's strong sociological orientation throughout entails some variability in quality: it is strong where playing to disciplinary strengths (for example, on welfare, ethnicity, and "identity" critiques), but readers trained in politics or history may find the sections on theoretical debates and historical origins unsatisfying.

RIESENBERG is an illuminating history of citizenship grounded in meticulous historical scholarship. While eschewing overschematization the work is organized around the general theme of an historical shift from one kind of citizenship, via subjecthood, to a qualitatively different "modern" citizenship, and tight thematic control coupled with the general nature of his claims make this interpretation of aid and interest to the social scientist. The account avoids sentimentalizing citizenship as an unalloyed good: on the contrary, its depiction of citizenship's (a) contingent and fitful relation to democracy, (b) theoretical and empirical compatibility with various (and varyingly desirable) political arrangements, (c) conceptual status and practical employment as discriminator and (d) ambiguous relation to the twin imperatives of public interest and private interest, supplies a corrective to some unexamined pieties common in the literature.

Empirical research into conceptions of citizenship held by citizens themselves remains scant. CONOVER, CREWE & SEARING's comparative UK–US study, which examines citizens' concepts of rights, duties, and citizen identities in the light of the theoretical axes liberal/communitarian and contractual/communal, begins to fill that gap. The study concludes that citizens' conceptual constructions of citizenship are complex, conjoining liberal and communitarian elements in unexpected ways. Interesting cross-national differences, particularly with respect to social rights, are found.

Social scientists in want of accurate systematic surveys of the legal standing and content of citizenship risk proceeding with anachronistic and distorting assumptions about its (positive) rights and duties, how citizenship relates to other rights-generating statuses, and – with the continuing growth of international law and international institutions – the range and nature of their guarantors. GARDNER provides a comparative survey across 11 European Community jurisdictions, together with informative and stimulating commentaries. His edited follow-up *White Paper* (1998) extends and deepens the analysis of British citizenship in the light of the 1994 *Green Paper*'s conclusions.

Citizenship of systems of governance other than the nation state is an increasingly pertinent and prominent field, an early foray into which is ARON's essay (also reproduced in Turner & Hamilton). Taking the EC as his example he answers the question posed in its title with a resounding "no", on the grounds that the citizens of the diverse member states share neither the same totality of political, social, and civil rights, nor the affective social precondition for citizenship (feeling they have a common destiny); further, no federal tier of authority to enforce citizens' rights has been established – and were it to be established, a transfer of citizenship across levels of authority, rather than the constitution of a multinational citizenship, would result.

However, continuing integration and the juridical creation of citizenship of the EU for the citizens of its member states in 1992 has stimulated fresh approaches to the question. The classic texts of this "new wave" are those of MEEHAN and HABERMAS. Meehan, a political scientist, draws on analysis of EC social policy in her pioneering thesis that 1990s Europe has seen a new, multidimensional, kind of citizenship, articulated with a complex configuration of EU supranational, national, subnational, and transnational institutions, beginning to take shape. Early chapters discuss national *vis-à-vis* European citizenship and civil society generally, whereas later chapters scrutinize Community law and practice across relevant policy areas in detail.

Habermas' article (also reproduced in Beiner and in Turner & Hamilton) is an influential contribution to the debate on Europe by one of its most distinguished social scientists and philosophers. His diagnosis: Europe's task is to develop a nonimperialistic political self-confidence for the 21st century in a context, after recent upheavals, of exacerbating conflict between ethical universalism and political/cultural particularism(s). His prescription: a common political culture – forged of an overlapping consensus between the electorates of Europe – as the bedrock of a "constitutional patriotism" (p.7), focused on common European political institutions, to coexist alongside the divergent national orientations and traditions in sociocultural life.

LYNN DOBSON

Citizenship and gender

Bussemaker, Jet and Rian Voet, "Citizenship and Gender: Theoretical Approaches and Historical Legacies", *Critical Social Policy*, 18/3 (1998): 277–307

Culpitt, Ian, *Welfare and Citizenship: Beyond the Crisis of the Welfare State?*, London and Newbury Park, California: Sage, 1992

Dietz, Mary, "Context Is All: Feminism and Theories of Citizenship" in *Feminism and Politics*, edited by Anne Phillips, Oxford and New York: Oxford University Press, 1998

Jelin, Elizabeth, "Citizenship Revisited: Solidarity, Responsibility and Rights" in *Constructing Democracy: Human Rights, Citizenship and Society*, edited by Elizabeth Jelin and Eric Hershberg, Oxford and Boulder, Colorado: Westview Press, 1997

Jones, Kathleen, "Citizenship in a Women-friendly Polity", *Signs*, 15/4 (1990): 781–812

Lister, Ruth, *Citizenship: Feminist Perspectives*, London: Macmillan and New York: New York University Press, 1997

Marshall, T.H., "Citizenship and Social Class" in *Sociology at the Crossroads*, London: Heinemann, 1963, as *Class Citizenship and Social Development: Essays*, New York: Doubleday, 1964

Turner, Bryan S. (editor), *Citizenship and Social Theory*, London and Newbury Park, California: Sage, 1993

MARSHALL, pioneering the current debate on citizenship, can be considered a classic work. It contains three essential theses. The first regards citizenship as a status conferred on a community's full members. The second is that civil and political rights can only be exercised when social rights are enforced. The third considers that the status of citizenship grants the right to receive social support without impairing those rights of citizenship. Marshall's theoretical understanding of the difference between the 19th century – when the poor receiving support lost their rights of citizenship – and the 20th century's welfare state, paved the way to research the depth of postwar political and state mutations. If civil and political rights are rights – freedoms which the individual enjoys with regard to the state which sees its sovereign authority limited, social rights are rights – claims of the individual on the state, which force the latter into acting through the extension of its social functions. If the main institutions that guarantee civil and political rights are, respectively, the courts and the assemblies of representatives, the institution primarily related to social rights is the welfare state and its various agencies for social protection (social insurance and assistance).

Among the many criticisms of Marshall, fault has been found with his optimism regarding the compatibility between capitalism and citizenship. It should be noted, however, that his text dates from 1950, when welfare state programmes had reached their highest level and had hardly been dulled by the Saint-Pélerin society, a forum for postwar conservative thought.

TURNER is a collection of texts responding to three different levels of reflection. The first level involves a critical review of Marshall's concept of citizenship. The controversy around Marshall focuses on: (a) his methodological approach to citizenship, which does not take into account the social struggles preceding the enforcement of each new set of rights, nor the various ways rights are *acquired* by different social groups (such as women); (b) his omission of the historical process leading to the acquisition of citizenship rights, when it is of primary importance to the understanding of subsequent forms of citizen participation (are rights gained from the top or from the bottom, in public or private spaces, and so on?); (c) his definition of citizenship, which is restricted to a juridical perspective – a series of rights and duties. A sociological perspective of citizenship must understand it as a collection of practices defining individuals as competent members of society. Turner then refers to the relationship between capitalism and citizenship. Underlying this relationship is the theoretical issue constituted by political sociology's classical question regarding the way in which market primacy may or may not encourage societal cohesion. Citizenship may play an important role in achieving this function. Lastly, Turner conceptualizes the concept of citizenship in the age of the nation state. According to Turner, in the current globalized age, the claim for human rights is more universal than the claim for citizenship rights because the former are based on a feature shared by all human existence: humankind's frailness.

The boom of conservatism in recent years has changed the foundations of the discourse and practice related to state legitimacy. Instead of stressing citizens' needs, conservative thought has placed an emphasis on state adjustment to economic needs. CULPITT exhaustively reviews both left- and right-wing arguments regarding the new reality of welfare policies and particularly privatization policies. By breaking the myth of both the assumed axiom that private enterprises are more efficient than the public sector and the also assumed neutrality of welfare state workers in determining citizen needs, Culpitt finds a way out of a vicious controversy, thus enabling an exploration of both state and societal possibilities of welfare in the contemporary world. His method of analysis and epistemological focus, underlying his definition of citizen needs and welfare policies, are contributions of great importance.

JONES offers a survey of theories on citizenship and gender during the 1980s. Her starting point is to support the androcentric nature of the concept of citizenship. If, for her, the discourse of citizenship is gendered, women cannot appear publicly as women citizens. The western political discourse does not recognize that citizenship can change its meaning through women's political practices and does not raise the problem of how the citizen identity is described. From this perspective, the author makes a state-of-the-art analysis of the different ways of building the concept of citizenship (with, for example, Pateman, Elshtain, Dietz, Young) from a gender point of view. This review considers the following themes: body politics, plurality of the political roles of women, changing political space, and political behaviour.

DIETZ reviews the major characteristics of the liberal concept of citizenship, then considers two challenges that marked feminist thought in the 1970s and 1980s: Marxist feminism and maternalistic feminism. Stressing the pitfalls of the former, the author focuses on an incisive and convincing criticism of the latter, emphasizing its essentialist, nonpolitical, and nondemocratic nature. Finally, she develops an approach to citizenship that avoids any womanism, and that is centred on democratic participation.

BUSSEMAKER & VOET consider the reasons why citizenship has become a major concept in political and social language and in academic language. The authors uphold the idea that citizenship is a gendered concept, because it concerns the separation between private and public, and the tension between equality and difference. For these authors, citizenship is clearly gendered because it is connected with maleness, the citizen being defined in one way or another as someone assuming a traditionally masculine role (for example, a soldier, an economically independent being, a bread winner). For that reason women have been denied the full status of citizenship by most theories, or allowed this status only as citizen-mothers. In this context, three major political arguments are examined: civic republicanism, liberalism, and communitarianism. Through their contextualization, the authors show their characteristics, their potential, and their limits from the perspective of gender. The purpose of the article is to enable the reader to identify the elements of these arguments in the debates on citizenship and gendering in Northern Europe in the 1990s.

JELIN is concerned with the "bottom-up" construction of citizenship in the context of democratic transitions in Latin America. By examining two dynamics – the learning of rights and obligations, and the development of a democratic institutional framework – the author is able to define the links between human rights and citizenship and the dilemmas that punctuate the construction of citizenship. In this respect, the practices of solidarity and public responsibility at both the interpersonal and macrosocial level are extremely important.

LISTER recasts traditional thinking about citizenship as an important issue to explore women's politics and political implications in all their diversity. The author emphasizes themes like inclusion and exclusion, rights and participation, inequality and differences, from a feminist point of view.

ENRIQUE S. RAJCHENBERG AND
BÉRENGÈRE MARQUES-PEREIRA

City system

Berry, Brian J.L. and Frank E. Horton, *Geographic Perspectives on Urban Systems with Integrated Readings*, Englewood Cliffs, New Jersey: Prentice Hall, 1970

Borchert, J.G., L.S. Bourne and R. Sinclair (editors), *Urban Systems in Transition*, Utrecht: Geografisch Instituut, Rijksuniversiteit Utrecht, and Amsterdam: Koninklijk Nederlands Aardrijkskundig Genootschap, 1986

Kasaba, Resat (editor), *Cities in the World-System*, New York: Greenwood Press, 1991

Knox, Paul L. and Peter J. Taylor (editors), *World Cities in a World-System*, Cambridge and New York: Cambridge University Press, 1995

Pred, Allan, *City-Systems in Advanced Economies: Past Growth, Present Processes and Future Development Options*, London: Hutchinson, 1977

Ross, Christopher (editor), *The Urban System and Networks of Corporate Control*, Greenwich, Connecticut: Jai Press, 1992

Timberlake, Michael (editor), *Urbanization in the World-Economy*, Orlando: Academic Press, 1985

PRED begins with the definition of "city system" and explores the basic concepts around this notion. He interprets the two most important attributes of the city system as the extent and structural composition of its internal interdependencies, and its degree of openness or closure. The focus of his book is on the growth and development process of city systems, which is mainly seen as the accumulation of decisions that affect the location and size of job-providing activities in the private and public sectors. However, the book is mainly an historical account of the growth and development process of city systems in the advanced economies, with particular reference to the roles of information and multilocational organizations in shaping the growth process of the city system.

BERRY & HORTON approach urban systems from a geographic perspective based on the premises of location theory. The book first reviews the various analytical frameworks of urban systems and then examines their evolution, emphasizing the interrelationships of city location, size, and shape. Migration and changes in technology are regarded as the two major factors shaping the patterns of urban systems. It then studies different elements of urban systems such as the sizes, types, hierarchical relationships, and spatial arrangement illustrated with case studies across different countries. The final parts of the book describe internal forces, changes, and structures within cities. These sections are concerned with issues like the population density, social space, and intra-urban population movement.

TIMBERLAKE's collection applies world-system theory to the interpretation of the processes of urbanisation and city system. It identifies uneven development and a hierarchical division of labour in the Fordist regime of accumulation as two important factors that shape urban processes and urban structures. The essays about urban systems focus on the size distribution of cities or the study of urban hierarchies. The specialization and differentiation of economic activities among different cities determine the different roles of cities within city systems, in which some cities function as "central places" or places of urban primacy in the hierarchical relationship in terms of economic importance. The characteristics of urban systems (urban primacy and the size distribution of cities) are measured in terms of population rather than the economic roles of cities in the city-system. Readers may find approaches or methods incoherent in some essays. The main concepts build on the notion of urban hierarchy. However this book includes good essays on the world system and pioneer work on the world city system. It is worth reading.

KASABA's collection offers an historical account of the cities at the core that have played hegemonic roles in the world system over many centuries. The essays demonstrate that urban primacy in the world system is determined not only by economic and political factors but also by cultural activities.

BORCHERT, BOURNE & SINCLAIR view urban systems as a framework for research. The key elements of such a framework are: the urban nodes and their attributes; a matrix of interactions and transactions which constitute the linkages between these nodes; and a matrix of change variables describing the relationship in the behaviour of the system over time and space. After a discussion of theoretical approaches to the analysis of urban systems the book provides case studies of changing urban systems in selected nation states, with particular emphasis on the evolution of the Dutch urban system. This book also draws considerable attention to the roles of the service sector in the development of urban systems.

ROSS studies the urban system from a network perspective. He examines organizational relationships within a city and the pattern of relations among the cities in the urban system by examining the division of labour and corporate control patterns. He argues that organizations have much more control over their internal structure and their allocation of resources than cities. Therefore, corporations exercise important power in determining a city's system position in the network. He classifies American cities into different levels of a hierarchical urban system/structure and devotes much attention to measuring their quantified interrelations based on their organizational linkages across structurally equivalent positions.

The 17 essays in KNOX & TAYLOR explore the interrelationships between the globalization of the world economy and the global urban system. The book focuses on the examination of the roles of world cities as control points and nodes of exchanges in the world system from various conceptual perspectives and at different spatial scales. A few essays also assess what characteristics or forces make cities become world cities. In general, most of the literature ignores the roles of urban regimes, the state, and culture in determining a city's position in the world system. There are few analyses on the impact of world city status on urban regimes, local politics, cultures, and social processes at local levels, and there is a lack of research on the rapid evolution of world cities and the change of their positions and functions in the post-Fordist era. The coming of the information age increases the placeless exchanges and communications that help to dehierarchicalize the world city system.

XING QUAN ZHANG

See also Urban geography, World systems theory

Civic culture

Almond, Gabriel A. and Sidney Verba (editors), *The Civic Culture Revisited: An Analytical Study*, Boston: Little Brown, 1980

Almond, Gabriel A. and Sidney Verba, *The Civic Culture: Political Attitudes and Democracy in Five Nations*, new edition, Newbury Park, California and London: Sage, 1989

Aristotle, *The Politics*, edited by Stephen Everson, Cambridge and New York: Cambridge University Press, 1988 (written 4th century BC)

Berlin, Sir Isaiah, *Four Essays on Liberty*, London and New York: Oxford University Press, 1969

Bruni, Leonardo, "Laudatio Florentinae urbis", edited by V. Zaccaria, *Studi Medievali*, series 3, 8 (1967): 529–54 (manuscript *c*.1400–03)

Burt, Ronald S., *Structural Holes: The Social Structure of Competition*, Cambridge, Massachusetts: Harvard University Press, 1992

Coleman, James S., "Social Capital in the Creation of Human Capital" in *Organizations and Institutions: Sociological and Economic Approaches to the Analysis of Social Structure*, edited by Christopher Winship and Sherwin Rosen, Chicago: University of Chicago Press, 1988

Constant, Benjamin, *Political Writings*, translated and edited by Biancamaria Fontana, Cambridge and New York: Cambridge University Press, 1988

Doria, Paolo Mattia, *La vita civile*, Naples: Vocola, 1729

Fénelon, François de Salignac de la Mothe- , *Ecrits et lettres politiques*, Geneve: Slatkine, 1981 (1st edition 1920 from manuscripts of the late 17th–early 18th centuries)

Genovesi, Antonio, *Delle lezioni di commercio o sia di economia civile*, 2 vols, Naples, 1765–67

Granovetter, Mark, "The Strength of Weak Ties", *American Journal of Sociology*, 78/6 (1973): 1360–80

Hamilton, Alexander, John Jay and James Madison, *The Federalist, or The New Constitution*, introduced by William R. Brock, London: Dent, and Rutland: Tuttle, 1992 (originally published 1787–1788)

Harrington, James, *The Commonwealth of Oceana, and A System of Politics*, edited by John G.A. Pocock, Cambridge and New York: Cambridge University Press, 1992

Locke, John, *Two Treatises on Government*, edited by Peter Laslett, 2nd edition, Cambridge: Cambridge University Press, 1967 (originally published 1690)

Matteucci, Nicola, *Alla ricerca dell'ordine politico: da Machiavelli a Tocqueville*, Bologna: Mulino, 1984

Montesquieu, Charles-Louis de Secondat, Baron de, *The Spirit of the Laws*, translated and edited by Anne M. Cohler, Basia Carolyn Miller and Harold Samuel Stone, Cambridge and New York: Cambridge University Press, 1989 (English edition of *De l'esprit des lois*, originally published 1748)

Oakeshott, Michael, *On Human Conduct*, Oxford: Clarendon Press, 1975; New York: Oxford University Press, 1990

Palmieri, Matteo, *Della vita civile*, edited by Felice Battaglia, Bologna: Zanichelli, 1944 (manuscript *c*.1439)

Putnam, Robert David, Robert Leonardi and Raffaella Y. Nanetti, *Making Democracy Work: Civic Traditions in Modern Italy*, Princeton, New Jersey: Princeton University Press, 1993

Sidney, Algernon, *Discourses Concerning Government*, edited by Thomas G. West, Indianapolis: Liberty Classics, 1990 (originally published 1698)

Tocqueville, Alexis de, *Democracy in America*, London: David Campbell, 1994 (translation of *De la démocratie en Amérique*, originally published 1835)

Witt, Jan de, *Political Maxims of the State of Holland*, London: Nourse, 1743

The political philosophy of ARISTOTLE may be considered to be at the root of the modern conception of civic culture. In particular, Aristotle called attention to the role of shared beliefs and practices (such as common meals, clubs, and education) in establishing a common cultural framework, in terms of which relationships of kinship and personal friendship could give way to common membership of a political body.

The Aristotelian conception is also an important source in the treatment of "civil life" (*vita civile*) by writers and politicians of Florentine humanism such as BRUNI and also PALMIERI. A remarkable, distinctive feature of the humanist conception of civil life is the attention paid to the economic dimension of citizenship. In this connection, both Bruni and Palmieri considered private accumulation of wealth as an important contribution to the wealth and welfare of the whole community.

WITT, writing in 17th-century Holland, further examined (in a work subsequently attributed to Pieter de la Court) the relationship between civic culture and economic interests, and expressed the view that economic interests may be an important source of social cohesion provided individual enrichment is achieved by means of economic expansion.

Subsequent literature considered the roots of civic culture by following a variety of research lines. HARRINGTON examined the relationship between property rights and the political constitution of a commonwealth, and argued that the "horizontal" division of land between medium and small proprietors is an essential condition of freedom. SIDNEY further considered the constitution of a free commonwealth and maintained that freedom can only be satisfactorily guaranteed in a republican polity, in which political influence may be directly associated with the "virtues of the persons, by which they were rendered more able than others to perform their duty, for the good of society" (p.84). FENELON and also MONTESQUIEU suggested the existence of a connection between civic culture and decentralized government and emphasized the need for constitutional defence from central political authority. The authors of the *Federalist Papers* (HAMILTON, JAY & MADISON) called attention to the role of federal governance as a political and administrative structure consistent with freedom and partnership according to a horizontal relational pattern. In particular, Madison stressed that a federal structure of government preserves the constitution of a commonwealth from "legislative usurpation" as well as from "executive usurpation".

LOCKE had addressed a characteristic feature of civic culture by maintaining that "men live upon trust" and that political authority dependent upon fear undermines the very foundations of civil life. The analysis of trust was also a central theme in the literature of the Neapolitan Enlightenment. In particular, DORIA maintained that the existence of civic culture based upon an implicit assumption of trustworthiness is likely to be conducive to an expanding web of trade and production linkages and to economic growth; on the other hand, mistrust makes economic interaction more difficult and ultimately thwarts the growth of social wealth. GENOVESI considered the implications of trust and mistrust for economic growth by examining in particular the role of "public faith" in the enforcement of contracts and other economic commitments.

CONSTANT introduced a distinction between ancient and modern liberty that has some interesting implications for the way in which civic culture may be conceived. For civic culture in the modern sense comes to be associated with a negative conception of liberty – that is, with liberty as freedom from constraints rather than as positive inducement to act (see also BERLIN).

TOCQUEVILLE, in his analysis of democratic government in the US, stressed the role of negative freedom but also noted the extent to which civic culture conducive to economic enterprise is associated with the practice of "direct" government within a federal structure.

More recently, the conception of civic culture has been explicitly associated with the informal structure of beliefs and commitments at the root of formal political arrangements in a free polity. Both OAKESHOTT and MATTEUCCI considered the political implications of horizontal social arrangements (Oakeshott's "civil associations") and called attention to the role of rational but not contractual bonds in establishing the foundations of formal social arrangements (political, economic, and otherwise). ALMOND & VERBA (1980 and 1989) considered the nature of social bonds and commitments by which civic culture could be identified, and attached special importance to the role of reciprocal trust in the pursuit of a collective purpose as a fundamental cognitive device by which civic culture may be empirically measured.

COLEMAN has recently proposed an interesting development of the theory of civic culture by introducing the concept of "social capital". The latter is meant to denote the set of informal and formal cognitive devices that are ordinarily available in a certain community and that represent the means by which such a community is capable of processing information and producing new knowledge, both at the level of formal science or technology and at the level of informal technical practices and social arrangements. GRANOVETTER has proposed a fundamental conceptual tool for the analysis of civic culture by means of the distinction between strong and weak ties. The former are shown to prevail under circumstances in which social bonds are hierarchical and rooted in mistrust; the latter, on the contrary, characterize social linkages based upon an assumption of general trust and the possibility of social exploration within an open space of social opportunities. BURT has subsequently noted a close correspondence between weak ties and the existence of "structural holes" within the relevant social network. In other words, weak ties are more likely to emerge when the opportunity space for

social connections is only partially occupied by existing linkages, so that serendipity is possible and novel encounters may be conducive to new and unexpected linkages.

Under these circumstances, new linkages may be formed more easily when a general assumption of trustworthiness makes new encounters acceptable. For this reason, Burt emphasizes the role of both a "loose" possibility space and social trust as necessary conditions for the emergence of social and economic innovation.

PUTNAM examines the issue of civic culture within a comparative framework, by analysing the roots of civic bonds and commitments across the cultural divide between northern and southern Italy. In particular, Putnam emphasizes the relationship between civic culture and political culture, and maintains that a high degree of civic culture is conducive to effective government and a social propensity to collective action. In this way, the concept of civic culture is once again associated with its original roots in the tradition of a "localized" polity, even if civic culture comes to be related to the existence of a thick web of interpersonal linkages prior to direct participation in government.

ROBERTO SCAZZIERI

Civil economy

Accarias de Sérionne, Jacques, *Les Intérêts des nations de l'Europe, dévelopés relativement au commerce*, Paris: Desain, 1766

Althusius, Johannes, *The Politics*, London: Eyre and Spottiswoode, and Boston: Beacon Press, 1964 (originally published 1603)

Bielfeld, Jacob Friedrich, *Institutions politiques*, 3 vols, The Hague: Gosse, 1760–72

Dasgupta, Partha, "The Economics of Poverty in Poor Countries", *Scandinavian Journal of Economics*, 100/1 (1998): 41–68

Doria, Paolo Mattia, *La vita civile*, Napoli: Vocola, 1729

Etzioni, Amitai, *The Moral Dimension: Toward a New Economics*, New York: Free Press, and London: Collier Macmillan, 1988

Genovesi, Antonio, *Delle lezioni di commercio o sia d'economia civile*, 2 vols, Naples, 1765–67

Greif, Avner, "Cultural Beliefs as a Common Resource in an Integrated World" in *The Economics of Transnational Commons*, edited by Partha Dasgupta, Karl-Göran Mäler and Alessandro Vercelli, Oxford: Clarendon Press, and New York: Oxford University Press, 1997

Hayek, F.A., *The Constitution of Liberty*, Chicago: University of Chicago Press, and London: Routledge, 1960

Hayek, F.A., *Law, Legislation and Liberty: A New Statement of the Liberal Principles of Justice and Political Economy*, 3 vols, London: Routledge and Kegan Paul, and Chicago: University of Chicago Press, 1973–79

Keynes, John Maynard, *A Treatise on Probability*, London: Macmillan, 1921; New York: Harper, 1962

Lipsius, Justus, *Six Bookes of Politickes or Civil Doctrine*, Amsterdam: Theatrum Orbis Terrarum, and New York: Da Capo Press, 1970 (English translation first published 1594; Latin version 1589)

Marshall, Alfred, *The Pure Theory of Domestic Values*, privately printed, 1879; reprinted in his *The Pure Theory of Foreign Trade: The Pure Theory of Domestic Values*, London: London School of Economics and Political Science, 1930; Clifton, New Jersey: Kelley, 1974

North, Douglass C., *Institutions, Institutional Change and Economic Performance*, Cambridge and New York: Cambridge University Press, 1990

Poni, Carlo, "Fashion as Flexible Production: The Strategies of the Lyons Silk Merchants in the Eighteenth Century" in *A World of Possibilities: Flexibility and Mass Production in Western Industrialization*, edited by Charles F. Sabel and Jonathan Zeitlin, Cambridge: Cambridge University Press, 1997

Porta, Pier Luigi and Roberto Scazzieri, "Towards an Economic Theory of International Civil Society: Trust, Trade and Open Government", *Structural Change and Economic Dynamics*, 8/1 (1997): 5–28

Rose, Richard, "Eastern Europe's Need for a Civil Economy", *Finance and the International Economy*, 6 (1992): 5–16

Sacco, Pier Luigi and Stefano Zamagni, "An Evolutionary Dynamic Approach to Altruism" in *Ethics, Rationality, and Economic Behaviour*, edited by Francesco Farina, Frank Hahn and Stefano Vannucci, Oxford: Clarendon Press, 1996

Scazzieri, Roberto, "Economic Beliefs, Economic Theory and Rational Reconstruction" in *Incommensurability and Translation: Kuhnian Perspectives on Scientific Communication and Theory Change*, edited by Rema Rossini Favretti, Giorgio Sandri and Roberto Scazzieri, Cheltenham, Gloucestershire: Elgar, 1999

Sen, Amartya, "Capability and Well-Being" in *The Quality of Life*, edited by Martha Nussbaum and Amartya Sen, Oxford: Clarendon Press, 1993

Smith, Adam, *The Theory of Moral Sentiments*, edited by D.D. Raphael and A.L. Macfie, Oxford: Clarendon Press, and New York: Oxford University Press, 1976 (first published 1759)

Stephen, Leslie, *The Science of Ethics*, Bristol: Thoemmes, 1991 (1st edition 1882)

Sugden, Robert, "Rational Co-ordination" in *Ethics, Rationality and Economic Behaviour*, edited by Francesco Farina, Frank Hahn and Stefano Vannucci, Oxford: Clarendon Press, 1996

Vattel, Emmerich de, *Le Droit des gens; ou, principes de loi naturelle, appliquée á la conduite et aux affaires des nations et des souverains* [The Law of Nations; or, Principles of the Law of Nature Applied to the Conduct and Affairs of Nations and Sovereigns], Washington, DC: Carnegie Institute of Washington, 1916 (originally published 1758)

Witt, Jan de, *Political Maxims of the State of Holland*, London: Nourse, 1743

Zamagni, Stefano (editor), "Introduction" in *The Economics of Altruism*, Aldershot, Hampshire: Elgar, 1995

LIPSIUS suggested an early formulation of the concept of civil economy, which he defined as the set of private arrangements and commitments among individuals in which the criterion of "reciprocal advantage or utility" (*mutua commoda sive usum*) is followed.

By examining the characteristics of federal governance, ALTHUSIUS proposed a connection between the non political concept of civil economy, and the formal political setup of a collective body. WITT (in a work subsequently attributed to Peter de la Court) suggested a definition of civil economy in terms of a shared interest in promoting variety and freedom, and highlighted the fact that a flexible arrangement of economic linkages may enhance the wealth and competitiveness of an economic system.

DORIA and GENOVESI examined the relationship between civil economy and social trust and pointed out that market exchange may lead either to mutual advantage or to a "zero sum game", depending on whether social interactions reflect trust or mistrust. They considered commercial trust and civil economy as necessary conditions for the growth of wealth within the institutional establishment of a market economy.

An interesting application of the concept of civil economy to the international sphere was suggested by BIELFELD, ACCARIAS DE SERIONNE and VATTEL. They emphasized that international trade, if carried out between partners of similar bargaining power, could be a source of horizontal linkages across political boundaries, and could contribute to the formation of an international civil society, in which economic equilibrium across national boundaries becomes a substitute for the "balance of power" associated with political and military strength.

SMITH outlined a sophisticated analysis of the formation of human beliefs, which he associated with social interaction (moral sentiments), and maintained that a particular category of beliefs (those born from the "human propensity to truck, barter and exchange one thing for another") is at the root of the special relationship between civil economy and commercial society.

STEPHEN introduced the concept of "social tissue", defined as "the general material or all-pervading substance from which the subordinate associations are constrained" (p.136), and examined how it may influence the specific form taken by social and economic interaction. MARSHALL investigated the connection between the prevailing social atmosphere, the pattern of industrial organization, and the working of markets under particular historical conditions. Marshall's conception of the "industrial district" is a remarkable product of this approach, and suggests that the existence of clusters of producers sharing a common background of skills and cognitive practices may be a critical factor in inducing the formation of a decentralized structure of small and interrelated units of production.

Subsequently, the classical and preclassical conceptions of civil economy were revived by following a variety of research lines. KEYNES called attention to the cognitive, institutional, and political prerequisites of a social setup in which market interaction could be consistent with a set of more general objectives of a social or ethical character. In particular, Keynes emphasized the role of an enlightened, informed, and "focused" social policy as a means of reducing the distance between market outcomes and moral objectives.

The conception of a civil economy has taken a different route in the writings of authors more directly involved in the analysis of the cognitive and transactional structure of a market economy. In particular, HAYEK (1960 and 1973) examines the processes by which information is elaborated and knowledge acquired within the framework of competitive market exchange. In his treatment, competitive markets are a paradigm case for a wider range of social setups, to which the concept of "catallaxy" applies. The essential features of catallaxy are decentralized access to information, the adoption of impersonal social codes and rational decision making. Catallaxy is thus the cognitive and institutional matrix from which market economies are born.

A distinct but complementary perspective was suggested by NORTH in his analysis of the ways in which the course of economic history may be influenced by "humanly devised constraints that shape human interaction" (p.3). North examined the role of the institutional heritage in determining the general form of current and future choices. In particular, he drew attention to the distinction between formal (often legal) constraints and informal constraints rooted in culture and tradition, and argued that "the tension between altered formal rules and the persisting informal constraints produces outcomes that have important implications for the way economies change" (p.45). Such an approach took North to an implicit definition of a civil economy as one in which there is broad consistency between the formal constraints guaranteeing freedom and security of contract, on the one hand, and the informal constraints used to enforce laws and rules, on the other hand. ROSE has recently proposed the explicit use of the concept of "civil economy" to denote an economic system characterized by the enforcement of laws concerning "private property, contracts, profit and loss accounts, and joint stock companies" (p.7). North's approach has recently been developed by GREIF in his analysis of "behavioural beliefs", that is, of expectations about other people's behaviour under different contingencies. Such beliefs are considered to be critical elements in explaining the emergence of particular social arrangements and formal institutions under different historical conditions. More specifically, Greif compares "collectivist" and "individualist" belief structures, and maintains that the former are often associated with "segregated" social setups (in which most economic transactions are conducted within "closed" groups), whereas the latter facilitate the emergence of more "integrated" social setups, in which "many transactions occur among individuals from different groups and individuals shift from one group to another frequently" (p.240).

Recent literature has reflected considerable interest in how economic processes may be conducive to, or consistent with, a broader range of human achievements. In particular, SEN has introduced the analysis of "functionings" and "capabilities". The former "represent parts of the state of a person – in particular the various things that he or she manages to do or be in leading a life" (p.31). The latter are "alternative combinations of functionings the person can achieve, and from which he or she can choose one collection" (p.31). Such a perspective leads Sen to estimate the quality of life in terms "of the capability to achieve valuable functionings", and to assess economic institutions and processes in terms of the likelihood for human beings to achieve valuable functionings.

The analytical framework based upon the consideration of capabilities and functionings is remarkably general, and suggests a continuum in the range of functionings, which vary "from such elementary matters as being well nourished and disease-free to more complex doings or beings, such as having self-respect, preserving human dignity, taking part in the life of the community, and so on" (p.3).

Recent literature has emphasized that economic interaction can bring about socially and morally acceptable outcomes on condition that economic actions are "embedded" within an encompassing social structure, in which self-interested behaviour is complemented by an institutional safety net, or by economic and noneconomic actions driven by reciprocity, altruism, and ethical commitments. In this connection, DASGUPTA has investigated the role of common-property resources (global and local commons) in preserving the natural and social prerequisites for active participation in economic life. In particular, Dasgupta argues that, in the absence of an adequate asset base, the nutritional status required for conversion of potential labour into actual labour may be impossible to achieve. Such a possibility highlights the critical role of communal ownership of resources such as irrigation water, threshing grounds, grazing fields, and so on – for local commons may be "the single source of vital complementary and insurance goods for poor people" (p.52), and can be instrumental in preventing them from falling into the poverty trap.

A different approach is followed by ETZIONI, who has argued that economic interaction is to a large extent "socially constructed", and that it cannot be properly understood unless encompassing social factors (such as social definitions, language, religion, and social norms) are also considered. In particular, Etzioni has drawn attention to the role of values in shaping economic actions, and has maintained that alternative sets of values could lead to a variety of viable economic arrangements. Such a perspective is at the root of Etzioni's interest in the dependence of economic arrangements upon active personal commitment, emotions, and altruistic behaviour.

Other authors have maintained that an adequate analytical reconstruction of economic behaviour requires the explicit consideration of a more comprehensive social framework, in which self-interest is not a primitive concept. In particular, SUGDEN has emphasized the critical role of the ability to identify common interests, while acknowledging that such an ability seems to require a conception of interaction "foreign to the conventional theory of rational choice" (p.261). A closely related theme is explored by ZAMAGNI, who maintains that "altruism is, basically, antecedent to self-interest in the sense that it constitutes a rational requirement for human conduct. Before becoming a possible means for individual ends, the interaction with others appears as an end in itself" (p.xviii). A remarkable implication of such a point of view is that existing social networks cannot be considered as a mere constraint upon individual behaviour: indeed, such relational frameworks should be considered as primary elements in shaping the objectives of individuals and in prompting their actions, as argued by SACCO & ZAMAGNI.

A different but complementary perspective is followed by PORTA & SCAZZIERI , who draw attention to the classical concept of "civil society", and maintain that the apparent duality between self-interest and other objectives may be solved in terms of an open social space, in which opportunities for individual betterment and excellence are considered to be a collective asset, the preservation of which belongs to the sphere of common interest. Such an approach highlights "the embedding nature of civil society with respect to the economy" (p.9), and points to the critical position of belief structures in supporting trust as a primitive concept (see also SCAZZIERI). In this connection, PONI stresses the possible co-existence of conflict and "creative cooperation" under historical circumstances in which a social capital presupposing variety is actively preserved and promoted.

ROBERTO SCAZZIERI

Civil law

Cairns, Walter and Robert McKeon, *Introduction to French Law*, London: Cavendish, 1995

Dadomo, Christian and Susan Farran, *The French Legal System*, 2nd edition, London: Sweet and Maxwell, 1996

David, René and John Brierley, *Major Legal Systems in the World Today*, 2nd edition, London: Stevens, and New York: Free Press, 1978

Dickson, Brice, *Introduction to French Law*, London and Washington, DC: Pitman, 1994

Foster, Nigel, *German Legal System and Laws*, London: Blackstone Press, 1996

Robinson, O.F., T.D. Fergus and W.M. Gordon, *European Legal History: Sources and Institutions*, 2nd edition, London: Butterworths, 1994

Vranken, Martin, *Fundamentals of European Civil Law*, London: Blackstone Press, 1997

Watkin, Thomas Glyn, *The Italian Legal Tradition*, Aldershot, Hampshire: Ashgate, 1997

Youngs, Raymond, *Sourcebook on German Law*, London: Cavendish, 1994

DAVID & BRIERLEY have written the best-known book, now considered to be a classic, on the families of contemporary law. The authors divide contemporary legal systems into the Romano-Germanic family, socialist law, the common law, Muslim law, the law of India, the laws of the Far East, and African laws. The aim of the book is to supply a guide, a first approach to legal systems, most of which are inevitably foreign to the reader. The classification of legal systems is undertaken on the basis of the fundamental elements through which the applicable rules are discovered, interpreted, and evaluated, such as the methods of reasoning, the classification of legal rules, and the techniques of their enunciation. With specific reference to civil law, the authors attribute the roots of the Romano-Germanic family to the Roman *ius civile*, originating in Europe on the basis of the compilations of the Emperor Justinian. The authors present civil law with admirable detail, covering topics that range from the history to structure and sources. In the first, historical part, civil law is described throughout its development from the customary period to the *ius commune* of the universities, the national or regional law period, and the legislative law period. The authors observe that civil law has now expanded beyond Europe into certain parts of America, Asia, and Africa. Legal rule and its certainty are chosen as the main basic civil law concepts, thus smashing the barriers of the cliché attitude of most common lawyers that civil law is really all about codes. The binding legal value of custom, case law, unwritten general principles of law, and legal writing, as sources of law, is also analysed, in a way which seems to explain adequately that, in civil law, the interpretation of legal provisions can only be done efficiently if these sources are taken into account.

ROBINSON, FERGUS & GORDON assess the reasons for the birth of civil law and its parallel existence with common law. In order to achieve this aim the authors undertake a detailed historical evaluation of Roman, feudal, canon, and common law within Europe, with specific reference to England, Scotland, Germany, and France. They argue that European legal history does not consist of the mere compilation of the legal histories of modern European states, although the very existence of a European legal history may be proven from these individual histories. The common influences and common backgrounds of the civil and common legal systems are particularly emphasized. This leads to the conclusion that Europe is again moving towards a single system where code and case law work together.

This point is examined by VRANKEN who, in his analysis of theories of convergence and divergence, concludes that a European civil law already exists and can be found in the communitarized and standardized law of the European Union. In order to prove this point the author examines the law of contract, the law of tort, labour law, commercial and company law, and procedural law. It is argued that even a superficial glance at the civil/common law divide can reveal a number of similarities, such as their shared fundamental concern to avoid contractual freedom, which seems to be more pronounced in the area of labour law. Moreover, commercial law seems to have undergone a period of intense convergence within the framework of the European Union. Having said that, there is a crucial difference between common and civil legal systems to which change seems impossible, namely the perception of the concept of law itself. For civilians, legal study continues to be an intellectual pursuit first and foremost, whereas for commoners the practical application of the law is what is really important. Does this difference signify the end of any hope for a unified legal system within Europe? The author is adamant in his answer. This difference of approach is far from a hindrance in an environment of European legal integration, as it nourishes the very substance of European civil law.

DADOMO & FARRAN aim to provide the reader with an introduction to the fundamental concepts and structures of French civil law. The sources of law, the structure of the courts and professions and the characteristics of the legal process are presented under the prism of common law and with the clear scope to draw attention to the main differences between civil and common law. Although the French terminology is retained, the structure and methodology of the legal analysis is definitely influenced by the structure and methods of common law. At least the French terminology tends to simplify things in cases where there is not a common law equivalent to the French institution described in the book, such as in the case of the division between ordinary and administrative courts. The authors give particular emphasis to the powerful role of the *Conseil d'État*, the task of the *Tribunal des Conflits* in ruling in jurisdictional disputes, and the rulings on the constitution-ality of legislation undertaken by the *Conseil Constitutionnel*. Particularly interesting is the analysis of the role of the judges and their obligation to use custom, case law (especially of the higher courts), and doctrine as a means of interpretation of written legal provisions in cases where the legislator has, inten-tionally or unintentionally, left a gap in the regulation.

DICKSON provides a basic introduction to a wide variety of French legal topics, including the history and sources of French law, the courts and lawyers, constitutional law, admin-istrative law, criminal law and procedures, civil procedures, contract law, torts, commercial and company law, labour, prop-erty law, family and succession law, and private international law. The author avoids the use of French terminology and in true common-law style chooses to present specific institutions within each aspect of law rather than to generalize on the legal theory and the true fundamental elements of French legal thought. The same uninspiring but pragmatic approach is followed by CAIRNS & McKEON, whose chapter on legal translation is particularly original.

FOSTER points out that the value of the German legal system can only be assessed if one takes into account its influence on the laws of Japan, Greece, Turkey, Austria, Switzerland, and several countries in Central and South America. In his detailed, in-depth analysis of the German legal system the author reviews the legal history and development of German law, its practice in Germany by the judiciary and the legal profession, and the operation of justice via legal representation, legal advice, and legal aid. Substantive German law is divided into public (constitutional, administrative, social, criminal, environmental law and the law of economic administration) and private (the civil code, com-mercial, company, competition and labour law). The presenta-tion of each aspect of law is achieved through reference to the main sources of each topic and interpretation of these sources by the use of case law and doctrine. The use of German terminol-ogy is another reflection of the truly knowledgeable manner in which the fundamental principles of each field of law and the main institutions are presented by reference to both legal theory and practice. The source book by YOUNGS is of particular use as a supplement to Foster.

WATKIN offers a unique analysis of Italian law, which is one of the lesser known civil-law systems. The author presents the essence of Italian legal thought by reference to the main fields of law, such as legal history, sources of law, constitu-tional law, criminal, administrative, property, family law, oblig-ations, contracts, delicts, and quasi-contracts. Each area of law is described through an examination of the main relevant legal provisions, as interpreted in legal theory and applied in judi-cial practice. Reference to comparative legal concepts aids the reader to comprehend the Italian terminology, which is reli-giously used by the author as another reflection of an attempt to view Italian law using the tools and the critical legal eye of Italian legal scientists.

HELEN XANTHAKI

Civil liberties

Dicey, A.V., *Introduction to the Study of the Law of the Constitution*, 10th edition, Basingstoke: Macmillan, and New York: St Martin's Press, 1959

Dworkin, Ronald, *A Bill of Rights for Britain*, London: Chatto and Windus, 1990

Klug, Francesca, Keir Starmer and Stuart Weir, *The Three Pillars of Liberty: Political Rights and Freedoms in the United Kingdom*, London and New York: Routledge, 1996

Lester, Anthony, *Democracy and Individual Rights*, London: Fabian Society, 1969

Locke, John, "Second Treatise of Civil Government" in *Two Treatises of Government*, edited by Peter Laslett, 2nd edition, London: Cambridge University Press, 1967 (originally published 1690)

Montesquieu, Charles-Louis de Secondat, Baron de, *The Spirit of the Laws*, edited and translated by Anne M. Cohler, Basia Carolun Miller and Harold Samuel Stone, Cambridge and New York: Cambridge University Press, 1989 (French edition as *De l'Esprit des Lois*, 1748; English translation 1750)

Rishworth, Paul, "The Birth and Rebirth of the Bill of Rights" in *Rights and Freedoms: The New Zealand Bill of Rights Act 1990 and the Human Rights Act 1993*, edited by Grant Huscroft and Paul Rishworth, Wellington,: Brooker's Legal Information, 1995

Robertson, Geoffrey, *Freedom, the Individual and the Law*, 7th edition, London: Penguin, 1993

Rousseau, Jean-Jacques, *The Social Contract*, translated by Maurice Cranston, London and Baltimore: Penguin, 1968 (French edition 1762)

Zander, Michael, *A Bill of Rights?*, 4th edition, London: Sweet and Maxwell, 1997

ROUSSEAU stressed the connection between liberty and law, freedom, and justice. Arguing that the ruler is the people's agent, not their master, he claimed that laws, and thus liberties, derived from the people's general will. However, in preaching subservience to the impersonal state for apparently libertarian purposes, he came close to defining freedom and liberty as the recognition of necessity.

In his exposition on the separation of powers and how it helps secure democracy and liberty, LOCKE identified the danger arising – particularly to civil liberties – from the posses-sion of more than one of the powers to make law, administer law, and adjudicate on the law. His work influenced those who drafted the US Declaration of Independence and Constitution.

MONTESQUIEU developed Locke's ideas into a somewhat idealized view, which did not really reflect the political reality in England at the time. His views became even more influen-tial as a means of securing individual rights inside a state in the 18th century and he was probably more influential than Locke in the development of constitutional theory adopted by revolutionaries in the 1700s and 1800s. He is possibly respon-sible for the widespread idea of a written supreme constitu-tion embodying at least some notion of individual civil liberties.

DICEY aimed to introduce readers to two or three guiding principles of the UK constitution that he clearly felt would be transferable to anywhere there was stable, elected government. Of particular relevance to civil liberties is his argument that the rights and liberties of individuals were secured not by guarantees set down in a formal document but by the ordinary remedies of private law available against those who unlawfully interfered with his liberty, whether they were private citizens or officials of the state. It seems a peculiarly naive view, although it held great sway in its day and is still part of virtually all UK public law courses.

ROBERTSON develops on probably the first comprehensive survey (produced by Harry Street) of the way in which English law deals with the many aspects of civil liberty. After an introductory description of the powers of the police, he addressed himself in detail to the main areas of freedom of expression, freedom of association, and freedom of movement. Protection against private power, the right to work, freedom of religion, freedom and security, and freedom of movement and against racial discrimination are all considered in the perspective of their time.

LESTER drew attention to the threats to the individual from a variety of sources in the UK including Parliament, the civil service, local government, and other power clusters that he regarded as being able to compete with the government in significance and scale. Other jurisdictions can see the relevant threat to liberty in their country and identify whether the bulwarks of their constitutions would be more or less likely to see off such threats. He argued that Parliament had, on occasion, reacted to popular prejudice or mass hysteria against a minority. At the start of the 1900s, the sudden influx of mainly Jewish refugees from the pogroms of Eastern Europe had driven a timid government to pass the Aliens Act 1905. Xenophobia and war hysteria had led to the Aliens Act 1914, which passed all its parliamentary stages in a single day. Both were emergency statutes, but both were still in force in the late 1960s. This incursion into the civil liberties of some groups could to some extent be safeguarded against by a Bill of Rights and this discussion is developed by Lester, informed by the reality in states where such legislation is already in force.

DWORKIN, a major voice in political and legal philosophy, discussed the practicalities and difficulties of what was then hypothetical incorporation of a Bill of Rights into a common law jurisdiction with no supreme written constitution and no theory of "superior law" apart, perhaps, from the common law itself.

RISHWORTH discusses the New Zealand Bill of Rights Act 1990 and the practicalities of applying new civil rights legislation in a common law jurisdiction.

KLUG, STARMER & WEIR carried out an audit on political freedom (and thus civil liberties) in the UK and their conclusions have international echoes. They used as their measure the rights enshrined in two international instruments to which the UK is a signatory – the European Convention on Human Rights and the United Nations International Covenant on Civil and Political Rights. The authors highlight systematic weaknesses and failings in the UK approach to protecting rights.

ZANDER discussed the controversial issues arising out of the effective incorporation of the European Convention on Human Rights into UK law by what is now the Human Rights Act 1998 (to be brought fully into force in October 2000). It considers in detail the arguments for and against a Bill of Rights and discusses its content. The recent experience of other nations, particularly of Canada under its Charter of Rights and Freedoms is drawn upon to illustrate and illuminate the debate.

CHRISTOPHER GALE

See also Bill of Rights, Civil rights, European Convention on Human Rights, Freedom

Civil religion

Bellah, Robert N., *Beyond Belief: Essays on Religion in a Post-traditional World*, New York: Harper and Row, 1970

Bellah, Robert N. *et al.* (editors), *The Good Society*, New York: Knopf, 1991

Bryant, Christopher G.A., "Civic Nation, Civil Society, Civil Religion" in *Civil Society: Theory, History, Comparison*, edited by John A. Hall, Cambridge: Polity Press, 1995

Elshtain, Jean Bethke, "In Common Together: Unity, Diversity and Civic Virtue" in *Toward a Global Civil Society*, edited by Michael Walzer, Providence, Rhode Island: Berghahn, 1995

Fogarty, Michael P., *Christian Democracy in Western Europe, 1820–1953*, London: Routledge and Kegan Paul, and Notre Dame, Indiana: University of Notre Dame Press, 1957

Martin, David, "When the Archiepiscopal Trumpet Sounds" in his *A General Theory of Secularization*, Oxford: Blackwell, and New York: Harper and Row, 1978

Marty, Martin E., "Civil Religion: Two Kinds of Two Kinds" in his *Religion and Republic: The American Circumstance*, Boston: Beacon Press, 1987

Rudolph, Susanne Hoeber, "Dehomogenizing Religious Formations" in *Transnational Religion and Fading States*, edited by Susanne Hoeber Rudolph and James Piscatori, Boulder, Colorado: Westview Press, 1997

Skillen, James W., *Recharging the American Experiment: Principled Pluralism for Genuine Civic Community*, Grand Rapids, Michigan: Eerdmans, 1994

Stackhouse, Max L., *Creeds, Society, and Human Rights: A Study in Three Cultures*, Grand Rapids, Michigan: Eerdmans, 1984

Turner, Bryan S., *Orientalism, Postmodernism, and Globalism*, London and New York: Routledge, 1994

Wilson, Bryan, *Religion in Sociological Perspective*, Oxford and New York: Oxford University Press, 1982

Wuthnow, Robert, *The Restructuring of American Religion: Society and Faith since World War II*, Princeton, New Jersey: Princeton University Press, 1988

An entry on the ancient and modern works that are important for understanding "civil religion" could start with Aristotle's "virtue" (e.g. Aristotle *Nicomachean Ethics VI* where practical and theoretical wisdom are united in the formation of intellectual virtue), move to Constantine, the Romanization of Christianity, the Reformation, Hooker and tolerance, and close with religion in America and the Islam problematic for the global politics of the 21st century. However, this entry starts with a discussion of American work because it remains very formative for most discussion in other locales. This entry then considers the issue in a British/European context, with some references relating to civil religion in other parts of the globe.

BRYANT observes that the term "civil religion" originated with Rousseau's distinction between the private religion of the devotee and the "religion of the citizenry", which is integral to any citizen's relation to society and government. Such fixed social sentiments are necessary for good citizenry. Such a communitarian view, mediated through Durkheim, has been the framework for Robert N. Bellah in his various contributions. The latest is found in BELLAH *et al.*, in which the communitarian critique of individualistic liberalism – consigning all religion to the private devotional realm where it cannot interfere with the rational pursuit of our common self-interest in the public sphere – is brought up to date. The communitarian interpretation of the US constitution assumes a prohibition upon the US Congress from making *any* law concerning the establishment of religion. The communitarian interpretation sees the constitution as promoting free exercise of religion. The famous Amendment is read so that (a) the US shall not establish any religion or religions; and (b) the US as polity shall allow for the freedom of the citizenry in its fullest extent. The communitarian interpretation thus makes a "distinction between two distinctions", as MARTY indicates – that is between church and state on the one hand (about which the State can and must make and enforce laws), and religion and politics on the other (about which the constitution support for non-establishment and free exercise provides clear guidelines for the form which any proposed "religious" law must take).

BELLAH (p.174) notes the views of George Washington who assumed that the US, in all of its affairs, public and private, was reliant upon an invisible hand, a providential agency that cannot be denied.

ELSHTAIN continues the communitarian critique of individualism, noting the religious impact of individualism upon the fraying social fabric. Woodrow Wilson attempted to unite the country by "yanking the hyphen". This earlier 20th-century popularism, driven, in effect, by a civil religious impulse, may have united the US in a nationalistic sense, but the consequences of accepting such an implicit religious self-definition have been devastating. WUTHNOW views the US in terms of a battle between two dominant civil religions. The conservatives maintain their belief in a divine sanction given to the American experiment. The liberals see themselves acting on behalf of all humanity. SKILLEN, on the other hand, sees conservative and liberal "religions" united in an underlying "undifferentiated moral discourse". The discourse is characterized by a "winner takes all" mentality in the electoral process and by other problems that the liberal-conservative world-view cannot tackle. Discussion of the place of religion in the American polity is characterized by an ongoing failure to confront complex differentiated society with a principled pluralism that lawfully respects the diversity of religious visions driving citizens who are always more than just citizens. Marty's contribution aims to restore the contribution which genuine biblical faith could make to American public affairs. What kind of religion is it, he asks rhetorically, in which one's God needs

worshippers so He can ensure His rule over the nation or the earth? As with other American argument about civil religion, this argument indicates an "upfront" desire for a renewal in Christian understanding of the relation of faith to politics. Marty's distinction between civic religion and civil religion also appears in BRYANT's attempt to develop a comparative view of how religion is related to the civil order across the globe. Thus he locates the "civil religion" option within a comparative analysis of the various combinations and permutations found in recent and not-so-recent history. Bryant's theoretical reflections are very important because they are formulated historically and with a global focus. Unlike the liberal debaters in the US who, as Wuthnow points out, tend to assume that the resolution of American problems will shape the entire world's destiny, Bryant's contribution opens the way to critical and comparative theoretical analysis of the various normative and historical resolutions of this issue.

FOGARTY remains a landmark, particularly now in the context of the European Union and the fall of communism. Various Christian political responses embodying the Roman Catholic and Reformed critiques of modernism were initiated in the final decades of the 19th century and they still have an enduring, if not muted, impact in Europe. Christian democracy is now also emerging in Central and Eastern Europe, and in lands that once were European colonies. The term "civil religion" is no longer used exclusively by the liberal or neo-liberal critique of all religion that will not consign itself to the private realm. STACKHOUSE's comparative analysis of how religious creeds are woven into the warp and weft of human rights legislation likewise shows that religion, even when ideologically banished from the public realm, seems always to be active and reactive, if not always proactive.

MARTIN's appendix is particularly pertinent to understanding how the Constantinian entrenchment of Roman notions of patriarchy, hierarchy, precedent, and privilege still has an ongoing function within Anglicanism. The Archbishop becomes a political activist in certain extreme conditions, and presumably if he (or she) has not spoken there really is no possibility of developing a Christian political viewpoint. Martin's approach also helps to identify why England particularly, with its established Church, does not, and maybe cannot, follow the European Christian democratic pattern.

For TURNER the comparative sociological viewpoint is extended even further. The issue of "civil religion" is now embedded in the processes of modernization, internationalism, and cosmopolitanism. Kant's universal morality, formulated at a time when Europe's next phase of colonial expansion was just beginning, may have led in time to a global ethic, but it implied a philosophy of history in which imperial Christianity had stamped its importance upon European civilization, which, defined as civilization, led to a wholly negative assessment of the contributions of other world religions, particularly Islam, to the international order. WILSON had already noticed this with his threefold comparing and contrasting of Christian church/state relations with the inextricable interwovenness of religious and political institutions in Islam and with the separation of religion and state in Buddhism. RUDOLPH's contribution is to point to the question of whether and how religion is a part of the civil sphere. This is a burning issue in those parts of the world that have now entered a postcommunist era. But it is also relevant, even in places where centralized communist regimes are still maintained.

Transnational agreements and global markets, let alone military alliances formed to protect ethnic and religious minorities in other countries, reinforce the fact that in the global society people are joined together in all kinds of ways that cross state and national boundaries. When people form homogenized groups they not only become a source of concern for others but they may also become a worry to themselves, because they then become visible in new ways, targets for possible attack from other homogenized groups. The question about "civil religion" is indeed the question of public justice as Skillen points out, not only in a complex and differentiated civil society in one nation, but also for a historically differentiated, complex, and changing globe that has many religious and civil conflicts.

BRUCE WEARNE

See also Christian democracy, Church and state

Civil rights (non-US)

Boxill, Bernard R., entry on Civil Rights and Civic Duties in *Encyclopedia of Ethics*, edited by Lawrence C. Becker and Charlotte B. Becker, 2 vols, New York: Garland, and London: St James Press, 1992

Brownlie, Ian (editor), *Basic Documents on Human Rights*, 3rd edition, Oxford: Clarendon Press, and New York: Oxford University Press, 1992

Cranston, Maurice, *What Are Human Rights?*, New York: Basic Books, 1962; London: Bodley Head, 1973

Gewirth, Alan, "Moral Foundations of Civil Rights Law", *Modern Schoolman*, 64 (May 1987): 235–55

Hohfeld, Wesley Newcomb, *Fundamental Legal Conceptions: As Applied in Judicial Reasoning, and Other Legal Essays*, edited by Walter Wheeler Cook, New Haven, Connecticut: Yale University Press, 1923

Kamenka, Eugene and Alice Erh-Soon Tay (editors), *Human Rights*, London: Arnold, and New York: St Martin's Press, 1978

Martin, Rex, "Human Rights and Civil Rights", *Philosophical Studies*, 37 (1980): 391–403

Mill, John Stuart, *On Liberty*, edited by Gertrude Himmelfarb, Harmondsworth and Baltimore: Penguin, 1974 (originally published 1859)

Shorts, Edwin and Claire de Than, *Civil Liberties*, London: Sweet and Maxwell, 1998

Stone, Richard, *Textbook on Civil Liberties*, 2nd edition, London: Blackstone Press, 1997

BOXILL's account of civil rights and civic duties provides a concise introduction to civil rights and identifies the distinction between civil rights in their legal, domestic sense, and in their international sense as human rights. The entry includes a brief historical account of the development of civil and political rights as universal human rights after World War II. It also refers to the distinction that is often made between civil and political rights as a class of rights that generate negative duties of enforcement, and social and economic rights that are regarded as generating positive obligations, and are sometimes excluded from accounts of human rights for this reason. It then goes on to discuss the civil rights movement in the US as a specific instance of civil rights in the domestic sense of the term.

BROWNLIE is useful because it includes the international treaties, conventions, and covenants on civil rights as human rights in international law, as well as a brief historical introduction to each. Most important among those included are the 1966 International Covenant on Civil and Political Rights and the Optional Protocol to the covenant, as the articles included in each of these form an essential part of the material for a study of civil rights in their universal, human rights sense.

MILL's classic *On Liberty* is a core text for the study of civil rights in political philosophy. The argument for the maximization of individual freedom and rights held against the state is still of great contemporary interest and relevance, and provides the basis for further study of civil rights in their moral, theoretical sense.

HOHFELD's (1919) seminal contribution to the understanding of rights in their domestic, legal sense is essential reading on the subject as it provides an analysis of four different classes of rights that may be held by citizens against the state as well as against other citizens. It also establishes the position that such legal rights, properly defined, consist of claims to the fulfilment of the object of the right, and thus in identifying and analysing the different kinds of rights and their correlatives, this provides a starting point for a study of rights in their domestic, legal sense at least. However, the date of this work must be noted as there have been significant developments in the theory and understanding of the concept of civil rights since this analysis was written.

CRANSTON is a key text examining the status of civil rights in their international sense, as this work seeks to defend the exclusive status of civil and political rights as universal human rights. The first chapter of the book gives a thorough account of human rights as moral, rather than legal, rights and provides a good basis for a study of human rights in this context.

The first chapter of SHORTS & DE THAN is of particular interest from an historical perspective as it deals with the evolution of civil rights in their international and domestic forms. It addresses the notion of civil rights in different jurisdictions and how these have come about, and then continues to consider particular civil liberties in Britain in the rest of the book. This text is useful both as a legal reference, as well as an introductory source.

STONE is a useful text as chapter one provides an accessible introduction to civil rights and distinguishes the different contexts in which the term is used. He then examines the protection of civil rights in the British and the European contexts and so for those considering civil rights and liberties in these jurisdictions this source will be particularly relevant. Chapters two to eleven deal with particular civil rights and liberties specifically within the context of English law, although the discussion can also be taken to apply to these rights generally. Specific civil rights covered include the freedom of the person, property rights, the freedom of expression, freedom of movement and assembly, freedom from discrimination, and the protection of reputation and privacy. Chapter 12 concludes the book by addressing the question of a Bill of Rights for Britain as a legal instrument to protect civil rights. An additional feature of the book is that it includes cases, statutes, EC legislation, a table of international conventions, and a copy of the European Convention on Human Rights, which contributes to its weight as a comprehensive legal text on civil rights in Europe.

Three of the articles in KAMENKA & TAY make a valuable contribution to the understanding of civil rights from an historical and a theoretical perspective. Kamenka ("The Anatomy of an Idea") gives a brief account of the development of the concept of civil rights out of the natural rights tradition and emphasizes the nature of civil rights as rights held by individuals against the state. Kleinig ("Human Rights, Legal Rights and Social Change") also casts his argument in an historical mould, arguing for a more contracted notion of civil rights as enforceable legal rights distinct from moral rights in their international sense. Starke's article ("Human Rights and International Law") article considers the position of such rights in international law in so far as they are declared and enforced, and this source is thus useful for students of civil rights in their international law sense, as well as those interested in questions of intervention to uphold such rights.

GEWIRTH's article deals with a number of key issues. He begins by arguing that civil rights in their domestic legal formulation require moral foundations for their validity and then goes on to make the connection between this argument and the notion of civil rights as human rights. Furthermore, this article presents the view that economic and social rights constitute a category of civil rights as universal human rights, and develops this to establish a philosophical argument based on rational human agency to support this position. The final section of the article applies the philosophical argument for rights to the question of affirmative action as it relates to civil rights in the US and the preferential treatment of minorities generally as a moral problem of justice.

MARTIN's article examines the relationship between human rights as universal moral rights and civil rights as the legal manifestation of these rights. He considers the position that rights as claims rely on this legal enforcement for their existence, and presents the argument that civil rights in their domestic sense are vital to the existence of human rights in their international sense.

KRISTINA BENTLEY

See also Civil liberties, Civil rights (US), Human rights

Civil rights (US)

Carson, Clayborne, *In Struggle: SNCC and the Black Awakening of the 1960s*, Cambridge, Massachusetts: Harvard University Press, 1981

Graham, Hugh Davis, *The Civil Rights Era: Origins and Development of National Policy, 1960–1972*, New York and Oxford: Oxford University Press, 1990

Key, V.O. Jr, *Southern Politics in State and Nation*, New York: Knopf, 1949

Kousser, J. Morgan, *The Shaping of Southern Politics: Suffrage Restriction and the Establishment of the One-Party South, 1880–1910*, New Haven, Connecticut: Yale University Press, 1974

Loury, Glenn C., *One by One from the Inside Out: Essays and Reviews on Race and Responsibility in America*, New York: Free Press, 1995

Lublin, David, *The Paradox of Representation: Racial Gerrymandering and Minority Interests in Congress*, Princeton, New Jersey: Princeton University Press, 1997

McAdam, Doug, *Political Process and the Development of Black Insurgency, 1930–1970*, Chicago: University of Chicago Press, 1982

Rosenberg, Gerald N., *The Hollow Hope: Can Courts Bring about Social Change?*, Chicago: University of Chicago, 1991

Stern, Mark, *Calculating Visions: Kennedy, Johnson, and Civil Rights*, New Brunswick, New Jersey: Rutgers University Press, 1992

Thernstrom, Abigail M., *Whose Votes Count? Affirmative Action and Minority Voting Rights*, Cambridge, Massachusetts: Harvard University Press, 1987

Woodward, C. Vann, *The Strange Career of Jim Crow*, New York and Oxford: Oxford University Press, 1955; 3rd edition 1974

Broadly speaking, the term "civil rights" refers to those prerogatives that the state grants a given category of individual. Privileges need not include the benefits of full citizenship, nor do they necessarily convey generous liberties. Take, for example, African slavery in the francophone New World. Conditions of bondage were regulated by a Black Code that, while clearly intended to buffer an oppressive system, nonetheless conveyed civil rights that slaves lacked in the Anglo-American context (for example, to live within recognized families, to own property, and to earn freedom).

Civil rights in the United States are conceived much more narrowly, however-at least outside the realm of political theory. The fourteenth Amendment to the US Constitution, ratified soon after the country's Civil War, promises everyone within a political jurisdiction "equal protection of the laws". Civil rights in the US context therefore mean equivalent treatment. Furthermore, although other policies sometimes fall under a rights rubric, American civil rights have evolved for the most part with respect to the position of African-American citizens, especially in the US South where slavery had been most firmly rooted. Civil Rights, conventionally understood, is the specific set of social forces moving the US toward racial equality.

The end of slavery granted blacks wide civil rights, including the right to vote, which lasted for a generation. Only in the late 1880s and afterward, as ethnocentrism gripped the entire US, did the southern states reduce blacks to clear and fairly widespread serfdom. WOODWARD provides what is still the classic narrative of how this "Jim Crow" system rose up, and how it collapsed after World War II thanks to the "Second Reconstruction" of the US South.

The early Civil Rights Movement, which lasted through the mid-1960s, was built on consensual American values (such as equal opportunity) and enjoyed widespread (although hardly universal) sympathy among non-southern whites. The period's defining activist was Martin Luther King, Jr. However, as GRAHAM documents through a detailed exploration of archival evidence, activists quickly changed their priorities from attaining equality of opportunity to attaining equality of results. His discussion centres on employment policy, with additional attention to housing and voting.

The Civil Rights Movement became increasingly radical. Black militants no longer valued participation by friendly whites, and sometimes endorsed social disorder such as riots and guerrilla resistance. Furthermore, by turning their attention to countrywide racial discrimination, activists frightened mainstream Americans who were happy to endorse civil-rights reform as long as it did not appear in their backyard. CARSON offers a classic treatment of the later period. Although primarily exploring one organization, perhaps the most radical of those battling for black rights, his volume manages to provide an excellent picture of the forces that have shaped rights discourse (for blacks, as well as more generally) since the 1960s.

Publishers have released a multitude of other historical works, treading much the same ground. The social science literature on Civil Rights has been more limited. A handful of fine books stand out as worthy of attention.

The Jim Crow South was built in part upon white supremacy in local political institutions (such as county governments, police departments, voter registration boards). Blacks constituted such a large portion of the population in some regions, however, that they threatened this control. Several prominent works have explored the arsenal of institutional mechanisms used to stave off black electoral power. KEY's seminal treatise, which was based upon both statistical analysis and an extensive body of interviews, argues that unresponsive, one-party politics developed in southern states as a means of holding down black power. KOUSSER, a quantitative historian, applies innovative techniques of aggregate data analysis to the question. He estimates the specific effects of disenfranchisement tools, such as poll taxes and literacy requirements, on both potential black voters and the political south as a whole.

National political institutions were important in breaking the southern caste system, because whites within the region feared reform. This does not mean that national leadership imposed progress upon an unwilling nation, however. Grass-roots change tracked policy change, and sometimes drove it. For example, STERN's analysis shows how shifting electoral considerations played heavily into the positions of two American presidents – John F. Kennedy and Lyndon Baines Johnson – on the racial issue. Similarly, ROSENBERG rebuts a widespread perception that federal courts drove the expansion of civil rights. Courts are inherently weak because of institutional limitations, implementation problems, and the inherent drawbacks of using a blunt instrument like rights discourse to change policy. The courts championed civil rights when the nation was ready for it.

Sociologist Doug McADAM has performed some of the most impressive and influential work on Civil Rights as a social phenomenon. He outlines a "political process" model in which elites try to protect their privileged position but sometimes cannot suppress outsiders, and applies it to the Civil Rights Movement. Outsiders succeed, he argues, when events cue them to their potential power, when they possess sufficient resources to pursue goals, and when political institutions are structured in a way conducive to outside influence. McAdam sees all three

conditions in place during the early Civil Rights Movement, but notes that the early successes eventually undermined those conditions.

Jim Crow segregation is, in retrospect, so uniformly reviled that the Civil Rights Movement enjoys great moral authority. However, it is worth noting that the heirs to this rights tradition have not gone unscathed by criticism. The largest body of dissenters, naturally, consists of individualists who oppose group-based activism. The quality of this "conservative" scholarship varies widely, but one book in the tradition that has attracted continuing attention is THERNSTROM's on voting rights. She argues that judges and bureaucrats, when interpreting statutory rights, have strayed far beyond what US political institutions originally endorsed. Rather than merely equalize voting strength, policy makers have taken affirmative steps to enhance black representation, causing undesirable political developments.

One undesirable development, from the apparent point of view of most black voters, is the declining fortunes of the Democratic Party. The rise of successful black politicians, protected in part by legislative districts designed to collect minority voters, has not produced a concomitant improvement in black representation. In fact, with the Republican Party in control of the Congress, black leaders may possess less influence than they have in decades. The reason, as LUBLIN illustrates in a growing body of research, is that majority–minority districts segregate black voters (and, therefore, Democratic voters) far more than is necessary. The paradox of representation is that putting more African-Americans in office reduces their policy influence; civil-rights strategies are counterproductive. (See Swain's book, listed under Race and politics, for a similar argument.)

LOURY, perhaps most intriguing of the supposed "black conservatives", also criticizes civil-rights strategies for their lack of productivity. His book cited here is a collection of previously published essays, in which he combines moral conviction and economic reasoning into a cogent analysis of America's racial difficulties. He argues that few persistent problems of the black underclass are created directly by a failure to ensure equal treatment. Furthermore, because the civil-rights activists are addicted to a political strategy of blaming whites, they remove from individual blacks the incentive to take responsibility for their own actions, whether successes or failures.

D. STEPHEN VOSS

See also Martin Luther King, Race and politics

Civil service, economics

Dunleavy, Patrick, *Democracy, Bureaucracy and Public Choice: Economic Explanations in Political Sciences*, London and New York: Harvester Wheatsheaf, 1991

Harris, Geoff, "Allocative Inefficiency, X-inefficiency, Bureaucracy and Corruption in Developing Countries", *Journal of Interdisciplinary Economics*, 6 (1995): 55–79

Johnson, Ronald N. and Gary D. Libecap, *The Federal Civil Service System and the Problem of Bureaucracy: The Economics and Politics of Institutional Change*, Chicago: University of Chicago Press, 1994

Lee, Dwight B. and Richard B. McKenzie, *Regulating Government: A Preface to Constitutional Economics*, Lexington, Massachusetts: Lexington Books, 1987

McGuire, Thomas, "Budget-maximizing Government Agencies: An Empirical Test", *Public Choice*, 36/2 (1981): 313–22

Niskanen, William A. Jr, *Bureaucracy and Representative Government*, Chicago: Aldine Atherton, 1971

Niskanen, William A. Jr, *Bureaucracy and Public Economics*, Aldershot, Hampshire: Elgar, 1994

DUNLEAVY provides a good account of applied institutional public choice. It was intended as a textbook that could be used for a wide range of courses in public administration and political science, and is written clearly and plainly. The second part of the book is devoted to the economic (or political economy) analysis of bureaucracy. The author presents two widely adopted models of bureaucratic behaviour (the pluralist and "new right" models), and then builds his own model, named the "bureau-shaping model".

The pluralist model sees bureaucrats as officials working permanently for large organizations in circumstances where their own contribution to organizational effectiveness cannot be directly evaluated. Bureaucrats play the same supply-side role as entrepreneurs and managers in the theory of the firm, with their own preferences and values. They are consequently rational utility-maximizers, optimizing benefits net of costs. They are driven by self-interest motives, such as power, money, prestige, convenience, and security, and broader motivations such as identification with a specific programme of action, pride in proficient performance of work, desire to serve "the public interest", and personal loyalty to the immediate work group, bureau, the wider government, or the nation.

The economic, political economy and public choice literature largely regards the civil service as a bureaucratic structure; consisting of political appointees and the holders of public office as opposed to the democratically elected government. The bureau-shaping model assumes rational bureaucrats, who have few incentives to pursue budget-maximizing strategies. They maximize self-regarding and hard-edged utilities in making official decisions. A bureau's overall policy is set by a combination of individual decisions made by its officials, and by interactions with a sponsor body. Dunleavy establishes four reasons why rational bureaucrats should not maximize budgets. First, collective action problems exist within bureaucracies and have an important influence on the overall behaviour. Second, the extent to which bureaucrats' utilities are associated with budget increases varies greatly across different components of the overall budget and across distinct types of agencies. Third, even if it is rational for some officials to maximise budgets, they will do so only up to an internal optimum level. Fourth, senior officials are much more likely to pursue work-related rather than pecuniary utilities, and consequently collective strategies of reshaping their bureaux into different agency types can best advance senior officials' interests. Therefore, senior officials can follow both bureau-shaping and budget-maximizing strategies, depending on the type of agency.

HARRIS like many economists was concerned with allocative efficiency – that is, how to make sure that the various factors of production are allocated so that the cost of any given level of output is minimized. He analyses the relative importance, in less-developed countries, of allocative inefficiency, X-inefficiency, bureaucracy, and corruption. He finds that X-inefficiencies in developed countries are more important than allocative inefficiencies. Changes in organization, incentives, and information flows, have been shown to be cost-effective. The push for privatization has embodied the desire to make economic activity more responsive to market forces, leaving less room for bureaucracy, corruption, and X-inefficiency.

JOHNSON & LIBECAP deals with a fairly complicated issue in public administration: the rise of the national Civil Service (bureaucracy). Their book analyses the institutional environment and its influence on the growth of the Civil Service in the US. They see the enlargement of the Civil Service as resulting from competitive games between presidential and congressional interests, between two main political parties (Democrats and Republicans), and between "lame-duck legislators and their replacements". They point out that what began as a system of hiring government workers by competitive examination grew into guarantees of job security and independence from political activity. Through a thorough analysis of the different phases of development of the American Civil Service, the authors analyse the reasons for and behind the rise of national bureaucracy. Their book is indispensable for all those interested in American public administration and the analysis of bureaucracy.

LEE & McKENZIE are among the main proponents of so-called "limited government". Their book is nontechnical, and seems to be targetted at a nonprofessional audience. The models that they present or develop throughout the book are oversimplified, with a *homo politicus* unduly narrow, a government too benevolent, and so on. The authors do not develop the central assumptions of constitutional analysis (that people choose rules without knowledge or concern about the distribution of the effects of these rules) and dismiss a full cost-benefit analysis as being of limited use. They present the US constitution in a rather simplified way. Their book lacks the necessary rigour for an academic study, but will be endorsed by proponents of extreme liberal ideas. This is a reading that does not require particular knowledge of political science, but it does not give a clear picture of the politico-administrative process.

NISKANEN (1971 and 1994) is certainly a leading name in the economic analysis of bureaucracy. He launched his model of the "new right" in the early 1970s, and it remains one of the dominant models. First, he assumes that the objectives of individuals are a necessary element in any theory of social behaviour, and the "purposive behaviour" of individuals is the essence of social behaviour. Bureaucracies are "non-profit organizations financed, at least in part, from a periodic appropriation or grant". Being rational, bureaucrats maximize the budgets of their respective bureaucratic organizations. The maximization of budgets is critical for an agency's survival. The organization's budget is allocated to it by a sponsor, be it a government, minister, chief executive, or a committee of the legislature. Sponsors expect to be presented with proposals for enlarged funding. During the scrutiny process, attention will focus overwhelmingly on the marginal increases being sought. Senior officials also seek budgetary expansion as a lubricant

Modelski (in Eckstein) argues that external factors play an important role in the initiation, course, and settlement of civil wars, while Deutsch (in Rosenau) maintains that in most civil wars internal and external elements are intermingled. Almond and Verba (in Eckstein) explore how to re-establish legitimate authority within a country after it has been rent by civil strife, while Falk (in Rosenau) examines the status of international law in the context of intrastate violence. These two volumes constitute a useful point of departure in the analysis of civil wars.

VAN CREVELD was one of the first to realize that Clausewitz's view of war as armed violence between sovereign states is misguided. By far the most important form of warfare since 1945 has been "low-intensity conflicts". These have involved conflicts between ethnic and religious groups, usually in the Third World, the engagement on one side at least of irregular forces, reliance on such low-tech weapons as listening devices and car-bombs, and high casualty rates as the distinction between combatants and civilians is blurred. Instead of being fought to realize policy goals or defend state interests, most contemporary wars are wages to maintain or create a community. As the French discovered in Algeria, the Americans in Vietnam, and the Soviets in Afghanistan, in the face of such wars classical strategy and modern weaponry are irrelevant.

Of the 164 wars that have occurred since 1945, HOLSTI found that 77 percent were internal, what he calls "wars of the third kind", while pure interstate wars accounted for only 18 percent. The discipline of international politics is ill-prepared to explain or to offer solutions for these kinds of war. Their origins are not to be found in the quality of relations between states or in the actions and forces at work at the regional and global level, but in the states themselves, in how they were created and how successful they have been in building both vertical and horizontal legitimacy. The failure to build "strong" states in much of the Third World and in many of the former Soviet republics has led to civil war. Although the United Nations has been pressed into service, it is ill equipped constitutionally to provide a solution for these weak or collapsed states, as its experience in Bosnia illustrates.

Focusing on the post Cold War era, BROWN and 14 contributors examine instances of internal conflict in eight regions of the world, the manner in which they spill over into neighboring states, and the history of international efforts to deal with them, focusing on such policy instruments as negotiations and sanctions and such key actors as the US, the United Nations and nongovernmental organizations. From this record of internal conflicts and international involvement, Brown draws some interesting conclusions: the proximate causes of most civil wars are internal and elite-driven; and while not caused by external factors, internal conflicts invariably have an impact on the region. Finally, he recommends steps that the international community can and should take to prevent, manage, and resolve internal conflicts.

Drawing on an analysis of seven civil wars (Ethiopia, Liberia, Mozambique, Liberia, Somalia, Sudan, and Uganda) ALI & MATTHEWS seek to explain the roots of civil war in contemporary Africa, their differing outcomes, and the prospects for long-term peace. They locate the causes of such wars within the state, attributing them to poor governance. A parallel study of how Tanzanian and Zimbabwean leaders averted civil war

thus provides a striking contrast to this history of elite mismanagement. In the search for a negotiated end to these civil wars, attention is given to assessing the role played by the United Nations, the Organization of African Unity, and subregional organizations. Finally, sufficient time had elapsed in three of the cases to allow for comments on the problems associated with peacebuilding.

The character of a war determines the nature of its peaceful settlement. Starting with this proposition RANDLE then classifies wars according to the number of actors involved (simple or complex) and whether they take place within or between states (internal or external). Focusing first on wars involving only two parties, he leads the reader through the stages of peace negotiations, identifying the factors that influence the course of those negotiations, and describing the range of plausible outcomes. If other states support either of the factions or states, the war and its settlement become necessarily more complex. Not only does the analysis have to focus on the objectives of the belligerents and their changing relations, but it must also incorporate the aims of other "war-oriented" actors. Basing his analysis on a survey of wars occurring between 1700 and 1971, and detailed histories of their peace settlement, summaries of which are placed strategically throughout the book, Randle demonstrates that all wars have elements in common and develops a very useful framework and set of tools for the analysis of wars and their settlement.

By their very nature civil wars are difficult to end through negotiation; most are ended through military victory. ZARTMAN lists several reasons for this: the asymmetrical structure of most civil wars, the inevitable internationalization of internal conflict, the lack of cohesion on both sides of the conflict, and the difficulty of finding appropriate compromises in a rapidly changing context. Drawing on case studies of four "regional" conflicts (Ethiopia, Spain, Sri Lanka, and, Sudan), and seven "centralist" struggles (Afghanistan, Angola, Colombia, Lebanon, the Philippines, South Africa, and Mozambique), Zartman finds several interesting conclusions: stalemate is best conceived as a dynamic concept combining power and legitimacy, transforming stalemate into reconciliation requires both recognition and dialogue, negotiations are most difficult when leadership struggles are ongoing, and progress in negotiations usually requires an external mediator. We are reminded that even with a negotiated settlement, the conflict does not disappear – it is merely absorbed by "normal politics".

R.O. MATTHEWS

See also Class system, *see* Social stratification

Clans

Beals, Ralph L., Harry Hoijer and Alan R. Beals, *An Introduction to Anthropology*, 5th edition, New York: Macmillan, 1977 (1st edition 1953)

Evans-Pritchard, E.E., *The Nuer: A Description of the Modes of Livelihood and Political Institutions of a Nilotic People*, Oxford: Clarendon Press, 1940

Firth, Raymond, *We, the Tikopia: A Sociological Study of Kinship in Primitive Polynesia*, 2nd edition, London: Allen and Unwin, 1957

Fortes, Meyer, *The Dynamics of Clanship among the Tallensi, Being the First Part of an Analysis of the Social Structure of a Trans-Volta Tribe*, London: Oxford University Press, 1945

Goodenough, Ward H., *Description and Comparison in Cultural Anthropology*, Chicago: Aldine, 1970; Cambridge: Cambridge University Press, 1980

Lowie, Robert H., *Social Organization*, New York: Rinehart, 1948; London: Routledge, Kegan and Paul, 1950

Mandelbaum, David G., "Social Groupings" in *Man, Culture and Society*, edited by Harry L. Shapiro, New York: Oxford University Press, 1956

Murdock, George Peter, *Social Structure*, New York: Macmillan, 1949

Ottenberg, Simon and Phoebe Ottenberg, "Introduction" in *Cultures and Societies of Africa*, by Simon Ottenberg, New York: Random House, 1960

Radcliffe-Brown, A.R. and Daryll Forde (editors), *African Systems of Kinship and Marriage*, London and New York: Oxford University Press, 1950

BEALS, HOIJER & BEALS' often-recommended standard American introductory textbook to anthropology has an excellent chapter on clans. It starts off with the problem of distinguishing between "sib", "gens", and clan. It offers its own clear definition of clan and provides a rich and detailed typology of clans using American Indian and Inuit (Eskimo) examples. The chapter is very useful as a good exposition on clans cross-culturally. The chapter also provides a summary as well as collateral reading with ethnographic references.

EVANS-PRITCHARD's rich and wide-ranging ethnography of the Nuer, a pastoralist agriculturalist people from the Nilotic Sudan, though dated in parts, is a classic study of social structure, clanship, segmentary lineage organization, and environment. This work, over the years, influenced the sociology of knowledge and made a deep impact on the discipline of anthropology as a classic exposition of a segmentary system of an acephalous lineage. The depiction of lineage framework in terms of values and concepts of time and space and fusion and fission is noteworthy. It provided theoretical insights and innovation and redirected anthropology from the search for knowledge by observation to structural and theoretical principles such as highlighting the problems of behaviour versus culture as a central problem in the study of segmented, uncentralized societies.

The study of the Tikopia by FIRTH is an ethnographic study of a central clan system in a self-contained, integral community in Polynesia. The study is noteworthy for its examination of Tikopia society as a patrilineal patrilocal patriclan representative of a social structure based on clan and kinship divisions. The importance of lineage alignment as a basis for authority, values, economics and social control is clearly depicted. The monograph is exceptional for its clear grasp of social structure and social organization.

FORTES is probably the foremost expert on kinship and descent. His classic monograph on the dynamics of clanship among the Tallensi of Ghana is recommended for its ethnographic thoroughness. The study is also valuable for the distinctions made between segments of the maximal lineage genealogically, ritually, and jurally. His work is considered as having made contributions to the social sciences and to political philosophy. It also calls attention to the relationship between the political system and social control.

The superbly edited collection by the OTTENBERG & OTTENBERG is of case studies of cultures and societies of Africa by people and environment, social groupings, authority and government, values, religion aesthetics, culture contact, and change. The quality of the essays is very high coming from various experts from their various areas of specialization. But really superb is the introduction by the editors which presents lucidly and simply a coherent state-of-knowledge introduction to African peoples, including a discussion of lineages and clans as basic unilineal descent groups. There is a very useful extensive bibliography.

GOODENOUGH attempts to illustrate successfully the difficulties underlying describing and comparing social organization cross-culturally. In this work, the author examines, among other topics, marriage and family, kindred and clan, sibling and cousin in relation to social structure. The chapter based on kindred and clan provides a well-thoughtout discussion of some recurring problems and positions in kinship analysis.

LOWIE's update of his 1920 work is a classic chapter-by-chapter attempt to negate Morgan. It rejects Morgan's evolutionary scheme of social organization and emphasizes diffusion. The work addresses issues of clan organization and of age- and sex-based groups, descent, marriage and kinship terminology. It remains an original attempt at a systematic analysis of the principles of social structure in so-called primitive societies and dominated the field of anthropology for a long time. It remains a classic of kinship terms and classification of kinship terminologies.

The chapter by MANDELBAUM on social groupings as established units of society is a good introduction to human groupings in society. Its simple language makes for easy reading and clarity on various definitions of anthropological terms. The section on clan is particularly interesting because it attempts to trace the origins of clans, and provides explanations for membership, functions and other services rendered by clans. The deft though rudimentary handling of social organization provides a discussion of considerable theoretical and practical importance and leads the way to further inquiries into other elements of social organization in the local and larger society.

MURDOCK's most important book provides an erudite analysis of kin groups and terminologies. His influential work not only demonstrates the determinants of terminologies but also expresses the problems of change of terminologies in response to changes in social relations. His work is unique, particularly for his use of statistical methods and behaviourist psychology to attempt a cross-cultural comparison and systematic classification of kinship systems the world over. Most relevant here is his influential statistical examination of kinship, marriage, and descent including well-known typology of systems, of classification of kinspeople on ego's own generation.

Radcliffe-Brown's important introduction to RADCLIFFE-BROWN & FORDE's collection of essays on African systems of kinship and marriage shows concern with general comparative and theoretical study of kinship organizations as arrangements that enable people to cooperate with one another in an orderly social life. The essay is useful for its excellent section on clans. Here he attempts to solve the issue of ambiguity in the use of the term by propounding his own definition and usage. The essay is also valuable for its review of the general principles underlying kinship systems and arriving at the most important generalizations in the study of social structure.

AYODELE OGUNDIPE

Class and politics

Butler, David and Donald Stokes, *Political Change in Britain: The Evolution of Electoral Choice*, 2nd edition, London: Macmillan, and New York: St Martin's Press, 1974

Duverger, Maurice, *Political Parties: Their Organization and Activity in the Modern State*, 2nd edition, London: Methuen, and New York: Wiley, 1959

Evans, Geoffrey (editor), *The End of Class Politics? Class Voting in Comparative Context*, Oxford and New York: Oxford University Press, 1999

Evans, Geoffrey and Pippa Norris (editors), *A Critical Election? British Voters and Parties in Long-term Perspective*, London: Sage, 1999

Franklin, Mark N., *The Decline of Class Voting in Britain: Changes in the Basis of Electoral Choice, 1964–1983*, Oxford: Clarendon Press, and New York: Oxford University Press, 1985

Franklin, Mark N. *et al.*, *Electoral Change: Responses to Evolving Social and Attitudinal Structures in Western Countries*, Cambridge and New York: Cambridge University Press, 1992

Heath, Anthony *et al.*, *Understanding Political Change: The British Voter, 1964–1987*, Oxford and New York: Pergamon Press, 1991

Lipset, Seymour Martin and Stein Rokkan (editors), *Party Systems and Voter Alignments: Cross-national Perspectives*, New York: Free Press, 1967

Norris, Pippa, *Electoral Change in Britain since 1945*, Oxford and Cambridge, Massachusetts: Blackwell, 1997

Rose, Richard and Ian McAllister, *Voters Begin to Choose: From Closed Class to Open Elections in Britain*, Beverly Hills, California and London: Sage, 1986

LIPSET & ROKKAN's seminal introductory essay suggests that the party systems of established democracies owed their origins to violent conflicts that predated (often by centuries) the coming of democracy – conflicts between Protestants and Catholics, church and state, centre and periphery, town and country, workers and factory owners. These conflicts generated enduring divisions, or "cleavages", between the social groups that stood opposed in each conflict. Indeed, Lipset and Rokkan argue that these social cleavages were so enduring that the party systems that they spawned proved resilient in the face of challenges from such newer forces as communism and National Socialism. This resilience led other contributors to this volume to characterize the party systems of the 1960s as "frozen". This "freezing hypothesis" is generally attributed to Lipset & Rokkan.

Casting some doubt on the hypothesis, DUVERGER had already described how, in some established democracies, multi-party systems rested on class and other social cleavages, whereas in other countries by the 1950s class had become the predominant cleavage. Duverger attributed the difference to the mechanical effect of electoral systems that were apparently able to give preeminence to one social cleavage in countries with first-past-the-post elections. Among these countries Britain was archetypal.

The classic work that lays out the manner in which social class gained and retained its dominance in British politics (and presumably elsewhere) is BUTLER & STOKES. This book was the first to document the mechanisms of socialization and reinforcement that enable a party based on a social cleavage to gain support and perpetuate itself. It is the first such work to be based on questionnaires administered to probability samples of the entire British electorate in surveys designed and fielded uniquely for academic purposes. The book not only explains the basis of British voting choice at the end of the 1960s, but also supplies documentation for the first three of the election studies that now constitute a series extending over 35 years and ten general elections and which provide the basis for much of the research conducted since that time.

Butler & Stokes also suggested that no sooner had class-based politics in Britain reached its peak (in 1966) than the forces maintaining the linkage between class and politics began to wane, opening the way to increasing electoral volatility and even to the rise of new parties. The apparent weakening of the link between class and politics (along with the effects of social cleavages generally) has given rise to far more controversy among scholars than did the coming of the class alignment.

FRANKLIN was the first to elaborate these ideas so as to document the changing relationship between class and politics, which he characterized as *The Decline of Class Voting in Britain*, and to speculate on the implications of this decline for the future of British politics. Focusing on the difference between class characteristics that are hard to change during adulthood (those relating to upbringing) and those that are easier to change (those relating to social location), he shows how the greatest part of the decline in class voting could be attributed to changes in upbringing. He suggests that these changes could have far-reaching political consequences in the light of social mobility and the rise of new issues – a conclusion with which ROSE & McALLISTER agree, as do others, although for somewhat different reasons. NORRIS provides the fullest account of how issues have affected contemporary voting choice.

The controversy between these authors, on the one hand, and HEATH *et al.*, on the other, rests primarily on the question of how class voting should be measured. Sociologists such as Heath are mainly interested in differences in the political behaviour of different social classes, and from this perspective class voting can legitimately be characterized in terms of "trendless fluctuations" (although Heath agrees with Franklin that these fluctuations included a clear drop in 1970). This approach ignores the changing class profile of the electorate, however, and particularly changes in the number of people who are difficult to classify in class terms. If one is interested in the overall effects of class on voting choice (as most political scientists are), then the changing class profile of the electorate must be taken into account, yielding the pattern discovered by Franklin and by others. Partly because of their different approach, Heath *et al.* do flesh out the relationship between class and voting in important ways, but they cannot explain the large changes in British politics (and particularly the rise of new parties) that began in the 1970s and continues to this day.

A comprehensive survey of the theories put forward to explain the declining connection between class and voting, as one example of the widespread decline of cleavage politics since the late 1960s, is provided by FRANKLIN *et al.* On the basis of a standard analysis that is not without critics (see below), the authors of this volume establish that the decline had been ubiquitous in all countries where voting choice was structured by social cleavages at the start of their period. In other countries (Canada and the US) the authors assume that similar early structuring had already declined before the 1960s, making this a general phenomenon to which all established democracies are subject. The book concludes that none of the existing theories (including theories relating to oil price shocks, postmaterialism, the gender gap, and consumption cleavages) satisfactorily account for these developments, and puts forward its own theory to the effect that electoral change of this kind is perhaps an inevitable concomitant of the successful working of democracy. Democratic government is supposed to resolve or defuse conflict, and the declining importance of class and other cleavages can readily be understood in such terms.

Unsurprisingly, these conclusions are contested in a new book edited by EVANS, which takes the same approach as Heath *et al.* in measuring class in such a way as to take no account of changes in class profile (referred to as "compositional effects"). They also take sophisticated issue with the methods employed by Franklin *et al.* so as to cast doubt on the findings of the earlier study. These differences parallel in the comparative sphere the differences between the sociological and political science approaches to studying class and voting in Britain.

Contributors to the volume edited by EVANS & NORRIS provide the most comprehensive and up-to-date analysis of current patterns in British voting, as well as an in-depth investigation of the 1997 election landslide and its implications for the future of British politics. Contributors represent almost all the different approaches, past and present, to understanding British voters, and they provide compelling evidence that the Labour victory of 1997 should not be regarded as a realignment of political forces yielding a new set of linkages between class and politics, but as an example of the sort of result that has become possible even in "normal" elections now that the decline of class voting has removed a straightjacket that used to limit the extent of electoral volatility (although a sociologist might characterize their findings differently).

MARK FRANKLIN

Classical economics

Bharadwaj, Krishna, *Classical Political Economy and Rise to Dominance of Supply and Demand Theories*, New Delhi: Orient Longman, 1978

Cannan, Edwin, *A History of the Theories of Production and Distribution in English Political Economy from 1776–1848*, 3rd edition, London: King, 1920 (1st edition 1893)

Eltis, Walter, *The Classical Theory of Economic Growth*, London: Macmillan, and New York: St Martin's Press, 1984

Garegnani, P., "Value and Distribution in the Classical Economists and Marx", *Oxford Economic Papers*, 36 (1984): 291–325

Hollander, Samuel, *Classical Economics*, Oxford and New York: Blackwell, 1987

Kurz, Heinz Dieter and Neri Salvadori, *Understanding "Classical" Economics: Studies in Long-Period Theory*, London and New York: Routledge, 1998

Kurz, Heinz Dieter and Neri Salvadori (editors), *Elgar Companion to Classical Economics*, Aldershot, Hampshire: Elgar, 1998

Sraffa, Piero, *Production of Commodities by Means of Commodities: Prelude to a Critique of Economic Theory*, Cambridge: Cambridge University Press, 1960

Walsh, Vivian and Harvey Gram, *Classical and Neoclassical Theories of General Equilibrium: Historical Origins and Mathematical Structure*, New York and Oxford: Oxford University Press, 1980

BHARADWAJ is mainly concerned with the reasons for the gradual submergence of classical economics and the rise to dominance of marginalist or neoclassical economics during the 19th century. The emphasis is *inter alia* on the fact that neoclassical theory can be shown to derive from a generalization of the theory of rent in terms of land of uniform quality and "intensive" margins to all factors of production, including "capital".

CANNAN contains a critical assessment of the contributions of major classical authors, especially Smith and Ricardo. This book has the advantage of being organized not on the basis of authors but on the basis of questions, with respect to each of which Cannan compares the different authors. Cannan scrutinizes the relevant texts in some detail, points out errors and omissions, but he does not see that the analysis of the classical economists differed in crucial respects from that of the marginalist economists. His discussion is very rich in terms of the problems and difficulties the classical economists encountered, but the origin of these difficulties is not made clear. Because of Cannan's intimate knowledge of the classical economists his text is still worth reading nowadays.

ELTIS deals with a main concern of the classical economists, that is, capital accumulation and economic growth. He distinguishes between several views of the problem. In Adam Smith's work the emphasis is on capital accumulation, the ensuing expansion of the extent of markets, and the implied potential for a deeper social division of labour, which tends to increase labour productivity. In David Ricardo's work economic growth is limited by diminishing returns in agriculture, which are responsible for a falling rate of profit. This tendency of the profit rate can only be thwarted by technical progress in those industries that produce wage goods or means of production used directly or indirectly in the production of wage goods. According to Thomas Robert Malthus, economic growth is demand constrained: with too great a savings rate the growth of productive capacity will be larger than the growth of effective demand, with the consequence of mass unemployment and idle plant and equipment.

GAREGNANI provides a thorough account of the classical approach to the theory of income distribution and relative prices, the difficulties encountered, and the solutions provided by the earlier authors. Explaining all shares of income other than wages in terms of the "surplus product" that remains after all used-up means of production and the means of subsistence in the support of workers have been deducted from total annual output, the classical economists were confronted with the problem of value. Setting aside the rent of land, physically the general rate of profit expresses the ratio between the surplus product and the social capital (means of production and means of subsistence), that is, the ratio between two vectors of commodities. In order to make these commensurable, a theory of value is needed. Ricardo tried to solve the problem in terms of the labour theory of value. Marx elaborated on Ricardo's procedure in terms of the so-called problem of the "transformation" of labour values in "prices of production". However, none of these authors managed to provide a correct solution. This was finally given by Piero Sraffa.

HOLLANDER provides a summary account of his extensive writings on classical authors. He has been waging a campaign in favour of a reinterpretation of the classical authors essentially following Marshallian lines. Accordingly, Smith and Ricardo ought to be understood as early contributors to the demand and supply paradigm, culminating in modern mainstream economics. This interpretation was designed as an alternative to Piero Sraffa's historical reconstruction of the classical authors. According to Sraffa the classical authors explained all shares of distribution other than wages in terms of the social "surplus product", which stands in striking contrast to the neoclassical symmetric explanation of all distributive variables in terms of the opposing forces of demand and supply.

KURZ & SALVADORI (1998a) brings together eleven of their previously published papers (written individually, jointly, and with others) and two further previously unpublished papers. The emphasis is on the long-period method as a characteristic feature of much of classical economics, old and modern. This method was designed as an approach to a highly complex system characterized by a dense network of interdependencies and feedbacks, and involves hypothesizing natural or normal values as distinct from market or actual values of relevant economic variables.

The two volumes edited by KURZ & SALVADORI (1998b) contain just under 200 entries and cover a wide range of problems and issues in classical economics. They present an analytical and historical treatment of both old and modern classical economics. One set of entries contains portraits of major classical authors. Another set deals with the reception of classical economics in various countries. Then there is a set of entries devoted to the major interpreters and critics of classical economics. Finally there is a large number of entries dedicated to important analytical concepts and doctrines. The problems dealt with include the gravitation of market prices to prices of production, extensive and intensive rent, renewable and exhaustible resources, capital accumulation and growth, the division of labour and increasing returns, wages and profits, foreign trade, money and banking, and public debt.

SRAFFA's volume contains a reformulation and generalization of the classical economists approach to the theory of value and distribution. As Sraffa stresses in his preface, this approach has been "submerged and forgotten since the advent of the marginal theory of value and distribution". Sraffa is to be credited with having expounded the different analytical structure of classical theory and demonstrated its fecundity. Taking as given (a) the technical alternatives from which cost-minimizing producers can choose, (b) the overall levels of output of the different commodities produced, and (c) one of the distributive variables (the wage rate or, alternatively, the rate of profits), Sraffa shows that the remaining distributive variables (the rate of profits or the wage rate, and the rent rates) and relative prices can be determined in a consistent way. The analytical power of the classical approach is demonstrated with regard to such intricate problems as fixed capital, joint production proper, land, and the problem of the choice of technique.

The book by WALSH & GRAM confronts classical and neoclassical theories of general economic equilibrium. Their concept of "classical theory" is essentially informed by Sraffa's 1960 work. The workhorse of the analytical work performed in the main parts of the book is a model in which two commodities are produced in single-products processes of production. The analytical work is complemented by substantial historical discussions covering the writings of the classical economists to contemporary authors.

HEINZ D. KURZ AND NERI SALVADORI

See also Neoclassical economics, David Ricardo

Clitoridectomy

Daly, Mary, *Gyn/Ecology: The Metaethics of Radical Feminism*, Boston: Beacon Press, 1990

Dorkenoo, Efua and Scilla Elworthy, *Female Genital Mutilation: Proposals for Change*, revised edition, London: Minority Rights Group, 1992

El Saadawi, Nawal, *The Hidden Face of Eve: Women in the Arab World*, London: Zed Press, 1980

Hosken, Fran P., *The Hosken Report: Genital and Sexual Mutilation of Females*, 4th edition, Lexington, Massachusetts: Women's International Network News, 1994

Kassindja, Fauziya and Layli Miller Bashir, *Do They Hear You When You Cry?*, New York: Delacorte Press: 1998

Koso-Thomas, Olayinka, *The Circumcision of Women: A Strategy for Eradication*, London: Zed, 1987

Lightfoot-Klein, Hanny, *Prisoners of Ritual: An Odyssey into Female Genital Circumcision in Africa*, New York: Harrington Park Press, 1989

Rosenthal, Sara M., *The Gynecological Sourcebook*, Los Angeles: Lowell House, 1994

Toubia, Nahid, *Female Genital Mutilation: A Call for Global Action*, New York: Women, Ink., 1993

Walker, Alice, *Possessing the Secret of Joy*, New York: Harcourt Brace, and London: Cape, 1992

Walker, Alice and Pratibha Parmar, *Warrior Marks: Female Genital Mutilation and the Sexual Blinding of Women*, New York: Harcourt Brace, 1993

Kassindja's personal account of her escape from genital mutilation in KASSINDJA & BASHIR offers useful insight for those interested in asylum law, US immigration policy, and refugees. The co-author, Bashir, is an attorney who specialized in international women's human rights abuses. This narrative is valuable for its depiction of the struggle to achieve recognition of female genital mutilation as a form of gender-based persecution under American immigration law. In addition, the rich cultural insights and intimate details give immigration a human face. The novel spans Kassindja's experience in Togo (the personal and local background, the rationale behind the practice, and the escape) and America (the imprisonment and the struggle for eventual freedom). This case serves as a landmark decision for those seeking asylum on the grounds of gender persecution and as a binding precedent on US immigration judges.

WALKER also uses the form of a novel to illustrate the social influence that pressures women into undergoing procedures of mutilation and perpetuating the custom. The novel's value also comes from the lucid account of the psychological complications that stem from clitoridectomy and similar procedures. Tashi, the protagonist, has herself made the decision to undergo the procedure, but not without excessive social influence. Her psychiatric counselling throughout the novel is an emotionally exhausting struggle to come to terms with the tradition. *Possessing the Secret of Joy* addresses the intersection of gender, sexuality, and culture through one woman's experience of mutilation.

Walker's dedication to the campaign against female genital mutilation (FGM) manifests itself in the commitment she demonstrates through her various works. WALKER & PARMAR is an informal and candid text that stems from the film by the same name. This work is written in journal form and details the process of making the film. Its particular interest lies in the emotional and spiritual journey that both women undergo in witnessing portraying such a highly charged topic. Walker & Parmar include interviews with activists, authorities, victims, and circumcisers. In its raw form, this book is not an academic or scholarly text.

HOSKEN is renowned for her work on FGM, both through *The Hosken Report* and through her organization – Women's International Network – and its newsletters (*WIN News*). Crammed with detailed information, this resource guide details the practice in its different forms in addition to the historic background and health consequences. The bulk of the work proceeds to discuss particular country cases in over a dozen countries, including the experiences of FGM in the Western world. This 1993 edition is often difficult to read, but nonetheless serves its purpose as a very thorough guide to FGM practices. The report is regionally thorough, but limited in other respects. This text may not be useful to those seeking a concise explanation of the procedure. However, Hosken continues to influence the campaign against FGM and is at the forefront of the international arena to abolish the practice.

A medical doctor and women's health activist, TOUBIA is credited with producing the most reader-accessible work on FGM. She covers the procedure itself (illustrations and photographs included) as well as the health, sexual, and psychological effects. In addition, statistics and notes on the extent to which the practice exists are country specific. Toubia clears the myriad misconceptions about the origin of the practice and negates any religious link genital mutilations may have had. Further, the cultural significance of female genital mutilation is demystified. This publication is the best factual text on the practice of mutilation as it not only educates but also inspires the reader to join the alliance to combat FGM.

Another work by a medical doctor is that of KOSO-THOMAS. Her innovative 20-year programme to eradicate mutilation could serve as a helpful model for practitioners struggling to abolish the practice without deviating from cultural norms and traditions. Offering a wealth of statistical material based on her years of work in Sierra-Leone, this guide is both concise and thorough.

Produced under the auspices of the British-based Minority Rights Group, this report is concise and practical in its approach. DORKENOO & ELWORTHY, both long-time campaigners against FGM, have taken a non-sensationalist approach to this delicate issue. Their primary focus consists of African activists and governments, whose actions determine the extent to which this custom is perpetuated. This publication is also especially useful for Western health practitioners and others who may encounter mutilations in women of African immigrant or refugee communities.

The Egyptian doctor EL SAADAWI is known as the first woman to speak openly about her own mutilation. Her work is focused on the Arab and Islamic World. Although 20 years have passed since it first appeared, this book is still relevant to the lives of women in the Middle East and covers clitoridectomy as well as a broad range of topics. El-Saadawi courageously writes of her own clitoridectomy at age six. Her expertise as a medical doctor brings a technical perspective into an emotional discussion.

The product of a six-year study in Sudan, Kenya, and Egypt, this authoritative text by LIGHTFOOT-KLEIN is deemed a primary source of information on mutilations. Focusing on her research in Sudan in particular, Lightfoot-Klein includes interviews in her anthropological work to demonstrate the tenacity with which practitioners cling to the tradition. Through her methodology, one begins to understand the cultural conditions that lead both men and women to support this practice. Further, she devotes a crucial chapter to genital mutilations in the Western world – the often-occurring yet well-kept secret of the 1800s. This helps to demystify the practice, removing it from its stereotypically barbaric context into our own history.

ROSENTHAL dedicates several pages to FGM both from the general and medical/health perspective. She also points the finger at Western society, in her section *FGM American-Style*, where she lays the blame on Freud for perpetuating the practice of clitoridectomy as a "necessary precondition for the development of femininity". Rosenthal also takes a clear stance on the debate between human rights and cultural relativism *vis-à-vis* mutilations of women.

DALY's harsh and upfront manner forces us out of complacency and into action. She bluntly reminds us all that we are guilty of our own mutilations of varying forms. Her work covers other harmful rituals imposed on women in the name of culture and tradition. Her comparison of genital mutilation to sattee and footbinding give us hope that mutilations can eventually be a practice of the past. Daly's radical feminist approach is intimidating to some and enticing to others. Irrespective, the reader finds it hard to remain neutral. This text is of use to those who are aware of the issues and are capable of formulating their own opinions.

Lina Abirafeh

See also Circumcision

Club goods

Bewley, Truman, "A Critique of Tiebout's Theory of Local Public Expenditure", *Econometrica*, 49 (1982), 713–40

Buchanan, James M., "An Economic Theory of Clubs", *Economica*, 32 (1965): 1–14

Casella, Alessandra, "The Role of Market Size in the Formation of Jurisdictions", *Review of Economic Studies*, (forthcoming)

Demange, Gabrielle, "Intermediate Preferences and Stable Coalition Structures", *Journal of Mathematical Economics*, 23/1 (1994): 45–58

Fraser, Clive and Abraham Hollander, *Revisiting The Club: Second-best Provision of Congestible and Excludable Goods*, Leicester: University of Leicester, 1997 (University of Leicester Discussion Paper No 97/2)

Greenberg, Joseph and Shlomo Weber, "Strong Tiebout Equilibrium with Restricted Preference Domain", *Journal of Economic Theory*, 38 (1986): 101–17

Greenberg, Joseph, "Coalition Structures" in *Handbook of Game Theory with Economic Applications*, vol. 2, edited by Robert J. Aumann and Sergiu Hart, Amsterdam: Elsevier, 1994

Hamilton, Bruce W., Tiebout Hypothesis entry in *The New Palgrave: A Dictionary of Economics*, edited by John Eatwell, Murray Milgate, Peter Newman, London: Macmillan, 1987

Kelso, Alexander S. Jr and Vincent P. Crawford, "Job Matching, Coalition Formation, and Gross Substitutes", *Econometrica*, 50/6 (1982): 1483–1504

Konishi, Hideo, Michel Le Breton and Shlomo Weber, "Equilibrium in a Finite Local Public Goods Economy", *Journal of Economic Theory*, 79/2 (1998): 224–44

Kurz, Mordecai, "Game Theory and Public Economics", *Handbook of Game Theory with Economic Applications*, vol. 2, edited by Robert J. Aumann and Sergiu Hart, Amsterdam: Elsevier, 1994

Ray, Debraj and Rajiv Vohra, "A Theory of Endogenous Coalition Structures", *Games and Economic Behavior*, 26/2 (1999): 286–336

Tiebout, Charles, "A Pure Theory of Local Expenditures", *Journal of Political Economy*, 64 (1956): 416–24; reprinted in *Modern Public Finance*, vol. 1, edited by A.B. Atkinson, Aldershot: Elgar, 1991

Vasil'ev, Valery, Shlomo Weber and Hans Wiesmeth, "Core Equivalence with Congested Public Goods", *Economic Theory*, 6/3 (1995): 373–87

Wooders, Myrna H., "Multijurisdictional Economies, the Tiebout Hypothesis, and Sorting", *Proceedings of the National Academy of Sciences*, 96/19 (1999): 10585–87

The notion of a "club", a group of people organized for some common purpose, appears in many different forms in the literature. BUCHANAN, a text sometimes viewed as introducing club theory into the economics literature, uses the example of a swimming pool club. Nevertheless, Buchanan stresses the need for a general theory, "a theory of clubs, a theory of cooperative membership", including such extreme cases as both purely private and purely public goods. Buchanan discusses a model in which individuals might be crowded by the numbers of other individuals in the clubs to which they belong (now called anonymous or "non-differentiated" crowding). Depending on their numbers, the crowding effects of individuals may be positive or negative. That is, if there are few club members, then an additional member may increase the well being of all members of that club, while if there are many club members, then an additional member may decrease the wellbeing of all club members.

TIEBOUT, predating Buchanan, is also important in the literature on club theory. Tiebout conjectured that when public goods are "local", in the sense that individuals can be excluded from consuming the public goods and it is optimal to have many small jurisdictions (i.e. clubs) offering diverse packages of public goods and taxes, then competition between jurisdictions will lead to an optimal "market-like" outcome. Individuals, in choosing the jurisdiction that best suits their wants, would reveal their preferences and the free-rider problem of pure public goods would not arise. These conjectures are known as "the Tiebout Hypothesis". Tiebout developed his hypothesis by discussing a model with many small jurisdictions (a continuum), constant returns to population size within each jurisdiction, and taxes within each jurisdiction equal to the average costs of public goods provided. In such circumstances Tiebout's conjecture is quite intuitive. Since individuals get only what they pay for, they would not have any incentive to conceal their preferences by making sub-optimal choices of jurisdictions.

According to Gareth Myles, researcher and author of a widely used text in public economics (*Public Economics*, 1995), there are now more than 1400 articles that cite Buchanan and more than 1000 that cite Tiebout. Thus, this entry will provide an account of several surveys marking the progress of research on club theory, as initiated by Buchanan and inspired by Tiebout, and conclude by noting some recent contributions.

Early literature on Tiebout's conjecture excited a great amount of interest. It was argued that in models with anonymous crowding, lump sum taxes paid by members of a jurisdiction together with zoning constitute, in effect, a price system with anonymous admission prices for jurisdiction membership. When the lump sum tax paid by each member of a jurisdiction equals the per capita costs of providing public goods to the jurisdiction membership, then the movement of individuals to the jurisdictions where their wants are best satisfied will lead to a voluntary sorting of individuals into communities of optimal sizes for their memberships. Moreover, communities would consist of individuals with the same tastes for public goods. References to this earlier literature treating anonymous crowding and a survey appears in HAMILTON. We note that some of the early literature was quite informal.

BEWLEY provides a number of examples illustrating some theoretical difficulties with the Tiebout Hypothesis. For economies with many agents, however, and where relatively small jurisdictions or clubs are effective for the realization of all or almost all gains to collective activities (small group effectiveness), these problems become negligible; see WOODERS for a survey.

A concept that has become very important in club theory is the "core"; the set of outcomes of economic activity with the property that no group of individuals, using only their own resources, can improve upon their part of the outcome. One approach to showing that economies with many small jurisdictions are market-like is to demonstrate that the core is equivalent to the set of outcomes of price-taking equilibrium. The first results of this nature were for economies with anonymous crowding. See again Hamilton for a discussion and also KURZ for a more detailed, rigorous treatment compared to the Tiebout/club literature which is set in a wider perspective of public goods economies in general.

The assumptions of the early literature surveyed in Hamilton and Kurz have been greatly relaxed. An important step was the introduction of differentiated crowding – that is, the preferences of members of a club and production possibilities for the club membership may depend on the characteristics of other members of the same club or jurisdiction rather than only on their numbers. In fact, the price of admission to a club or jurisdiction paid by an individual is determined by their "crowding type", those attributes of an individual that determine his or her external effects on others, such as gender, profession, skill level, charm and wit, and so on. If the crowding type of an individual is observable, and thus not private information, then the free rider problem of public goods disappears. Another important step was allowing individuals to belong to multiple clubs. See Wooders for a further discussion and additional references.

In almost all the literature noted above, if an economic outcome is in the core, then the clubs appearing in that outcome are small, and in fact bounded in size. (Exceptions in the literature are some un-referenced papers due to this author, published in *Mathematical Social Sciences* in 1988 and 1989 and in *Economic Theory* in 1997.) An alternative model of a large economy with clubs is provided in VASIL'EV, WEBER & WEISMETH. In this model, participants are crowded only by other similar participants and there are constant returns to club size. Thus, the total population is an optimal club and the only club considered. It seems possible that the model could be extended to allow the possibility of multiple clubs but this has not been done.

All the models described above treat specific and detailed economic structures, and within the context of the models considered, support the Tiebout Hypothesis. All these models also have the feature that individual preferences and/or production possibilities for goods provided by a club depend on the composition of the club. They do not, however, provide a theory that spans the set of possibilities ranging from private to public good economies. For the set of club goods permitted – those amenities or commodities offered by clubs, whatever they are – does not include pure public goods and pure private goods. More general approaches are provided by games.

A cooperative game provides an abstract model of an economy. Instead of details about economic structures, commodities, and production possibilities, for example, a cooperative game simply assigns a payoff/utility set to each coalition of agents. Thus, cooperative games can represent diverse economies, including economies with private goods, public goods, and clubs where each agent may belong to one or several clubs. GREENBERG provides an introduction to a large number of papers treating cooperative games and coalition (i.e. club) formation.

Another literature treats large cooperative games – those with many players – as models of large economies with clubs. For games with sufficiently many players, approximate cores – sets of outcomes with the property that no group of individuals can significantly improve upon their part of the outcome – are nonempty and under reasonable conditions have the equal treatment property: there can be no discrimination against individuals who have the same physical characteristic.

These results can be applied to an economy with clubs where participants may belong to multiple clubs and optimal clubs may be large, even consisting of the entire population. The major condition required is again that "small groups are effective" (SGE) – all or almost all gains to collective activities can be realized by relatively small groups of individuals. With more restrictions on the model, SGE is equivalent to the apparently mild property that per capita (or, in other words, average) gains to coalition formation are bounded. Thus, SGE allows ever-increasing per capita returns to club size. This literature is also surveyed in Wooders. Similar properties hold in economies with a fixed number of participants, provided that effective group sizes are bounded. See, for example, KELSO and CRAWFORD, who show that for two-sided matching models (models with buyers and sellers, or firms and workers for example) if there is an increase in the abundance of a group of similar players, then core payoffs to members of that group will not strictly increase and may decrease.

Other recent literature addresses cooperative/club formation without making any assumptions about the size of the total player set. A particularly interesting result is that if players can be ordered by a subset of the integers and if the "strongest" coalitions consist of sets of individuals who are conservatively numbered, then there are outcomes in the core. Moreover, coalitions that appear in outcomes in the core consist of consecutively numbered individuals. This result is due to GREENBERG & WEBER, and has been nicely extended in a number of papers; see Greenberg for additional references and DEMANGE for some of the most recent results. Such results can be applied, for example, to situations where individuals can be ordered by wealth and wealthier individuals are willing to spend more on public goods.

The theory of the core and price-taking equilibrium has been very successful in terms of yielding numerous results that hold in broad classes of economies. The theory needs a non-cooperative foundation – compelling models in which individuals behave strategically in their own self-interest and with resulting equilibrium outcomes that are in the core, that is, that cannot be improved upon by any cooperating group of individuals.

There are significant problems in achieving this objective: see KONISHI, LE BRETON & WEBER for a treatment of some of the problems of existence of a non-cooperative equilibrium in economies with clubs/jurisdictions.

The research referenced above, including that using the framework and tools of cooperative game theory, all furthers our understanding of the concept of perfect competition. In the view of this author, the conclusion to be drawn – and which will still probably be further strengthened in ongoing research – is that Tiebout was right far beyond the confines of the models he originally sketched. Roughly, it seems that whenever SGE holds then large economies resemble competitive private goods exchange economies – there is some set of commodities and a price system for those commodities that yields a Pareto-optimal equilibrium outcome.

The current literature treats situations where SGE does not hold. Certainly the case of an economy with few clubs, which allmay be smaller than the entire population, is important. A recent paper treating this case is FRASER & HOLLANDER. Some recent, quite original and innovative work in club theory (or the theory of multijurisdictional economies) is due to Cassella and her co-authors; see for example CASSELLA. This paper studies a non-cooperative model of the formation of jurisdictions/clubs for the purpose of facilitating trade in private goods. In the game-theoretic literature, new research on coalition formation in the presence of externalities promises numerous fruitful applications, e.g. RAY & VOHRA and references therein. This paper and other recent works treat situations where what a coalition (club) can achieve depends on what other clubs form – a realistic feature.

MYRNA WOODERS

Clusters

Arthur, W. Brian, "Silicon Valley Locational Clusters: When Do Increasing Returns Imply Monopoly?", *Mathematical Social Sciences*, 19/3 (1990): 235–51

Baptista, Rui, "Clusters, Innovation and Growth: A Survey of the Literature" in *The Dynamics of Industrial Clustering: International Comparisons in Computing and Biotechnology*, edited by G.M. Peter Swann, Martha Prevezer and David K. Stout, Oxford and New York: Oxford University Press, 1998

Beckmann, Martin J. and Jacques-François Thisse, "The Location of Production Activities" in *Handbook of Regional and Urban Economics*, vol. 1, edited by Peter Nijkamp, Amsterdam and New York: North Holland, 1986

David, Paul A. and Joshua L. Rosenbloom, "Marshallian Factor Market Externalities and the Dynamics of Industrial Localisation", *Journal of Urban Economics*, 28/3 (1990): 349–70

Greenhut, Melvyn L. and George Norman (editors), *The Economics of Location*, vol. 1, Aldershot, Hampshire: Elgar, 1995

Hall, Peter and Ann Markusen (editors), *Silicon Landscapes*, Boston: Allen and Unwin, 1985

Isard, Walter, *Location and Space-Economy*, Cambridge, Massachusetts: MIT Press, 1956

Jacobs, Jane, *The Economy of Cities*, London: Penguin, and New York: Random House, 1969

Jaffe, Adam, Manuel Trajtenberg and Rebecca Henderson, "Geographic Localisation of Knowledge Spillovers as Evidenced by Patent Citations", *Quarterly Journal of Economics*, 108/3 (1993): 577–98

Krugman, Paul, *Geography and Trade*, Cambridge, Massachusetts: MIT Press, 1991

Lösch, August, *The Economics of Location*, New Haven, Connecticut: Yale University Press, 1954

Perroux, François, "Economic Space: Theory and Applications", *Quarterly Journal of Economics*, 64/1 (1950): 89–104

Piore, Michael J. and Charles F. Sabel, *The Second Industrial Divide: Possibilities for Prosperity*, New York: Basic Books, 1984

Porter, Michael E., *The Competitive Advantage of Nations*, London: Macmillan, and New York: Free Press, 1990

Saxenian, AnnaLee, *Regional Advantage: Culture and Competition in Silicon Valley and Route 128*, Cambridge, Massachusetts: Harvard University Press, 1994

Stahl, Konrad, "Theories of Urban Business Location" in *Handbook of Regional and Urban Economics*, vol. 2, edited by Edwin S. Mills, Amsterdam and New York: North Holland, 1987

The analysis of clusters of businesses has attracted renewed interest among social scientists in the last ten years, but the field of regional and urban studies has a long and distinguished history. At the start of the 20th century, Marshall and Weber made telling contributions that have shaped subsequent thinking. These and other classic studies are still worthy of attention today. LÖSCH and, later, ISARD describe a theory of location in which a firm's location is determined by its output markets and resources. In the simplest form of the theory, the minimum-cost location is either at the source of supply for inputs, or in the marketplace. The analysis can be refined to take account of multiple markets, multiple sources of inputs, and more complex transport arrangements. Agglomeration economies play a central role in location theory, and both authors discuss these at length. Isard makes an important distinction between location externalities that result from agglomeration in the same industry, and more general urbanization externalities that result when companies from different industries are co-located. Lösch's work was also the first general equilibrium analysis for networks of producers and consumers.

PERROUX developed a theory of economic space in which "growth poles" play a central role. Each firm located at a "pole" generates forces that interact with others located at the same pole. In turn, each pole has a sphere of influence which interacts with the spheres around other poles. From this Perroux generates a network of markets that will frequently transcend national boundaries.

Industrial geographers have made some very important contributions to this field. Some of the most interesting studies relate to Santa Clara (or "Silicon") Valley in California and Route 128 in Massachusetts. The ten essays in HALL & MARKUSEN give a useful overview of the genesis of high-technology clusters, how they work, and their implications for growth, employment, and policy. The book offers a transatlantic perspective, describing both the US and UK experience. Part of the debate focuses on the role of universities in promoting the growth of science-based clusters: the conclusion is that proximity of universities was less important in the UK than in California. SAXENIAN provides a detailed comparison of the character of the clusters in Silicon Valley and Route 128. She shows that there are many similarities, but also some very important differences. Silicon Valley managed to survive the challenges of the 1970s and move successfully into new semiconductor technologies, but Route 128 started to decline. Saxenian argues that Silicon Valley companies were better at exploiting the rich network of social, professional, and commercial relationships, whereas companies in the Boston-Cambridge cluster were still too dependent on a self-contained, vertically integrated approach.

JACOBS is one of several of her influential books about the economy of the city. She pays particular attention to urbanization economies, believing that cities are not just larger versions of towns, but that the city grows by a gradual process of industrial diversification and differentiation. This perspective stresses that diversity in clusters plays an important role in ensuring their longevity, and has been influential in subsequent work.

The two North Holland *Handbooks of Regional and Urban Economics* give a very comprehensive survey of regional and urban economics, and two essays in particular are relevant to clusters. BECKMANN & THISSE review the literature on regional location. Their survey examines: short-term issues concerning models of location, and models of spatial pricing and output; medium-term issues concerning locational choice, focusing on minimization of transport costs, and the price–location problem in spatial monopoly and oligopoly; and long-term issues of entry, exit, new plant formation, and spatial equilibria. STAHL is a companion survey of the literature on *urban* business location. Another valuable handbook, GREENHUT & NORMAN, brings together 36 classic original papers on the economics of location.

PORTER's study has been exceptionally influential in reviving interests in clusters. It is a study of what makes a nation's firms and industries competitive in world markets, with particular reference to ten countries and 100 industries. The centrepiece of Porter's analysis is the so-called "Porter Diamond", which shows how four factors which make up a nation's economic strength are all mutually dependent: factor conditions; demand conditions; related and supporting industries; and firm strategy, structure, and rivalry. Building on his theory of competitive national advantage and clustering, Porter describes the rise and decline of particular national economies. PIORE & SABEL argue that market volatility, shorter product lifecycles and growing consumer sophistication make it essential for companies to achieve greater flexibility in production. They argue that vertically integrated companies using mass production and hierarchical control find it hard to achieve such flexibility. By contrast, if production is decentralized, and labour is divided between linked networks of producers, then flexibility can be achieved. They argue that such an arrangement is most likely to flourish in a re-emerging Marshallian industrial district, where companies can maximize benefits from co-location. The resulting industrial districts would be flexible but also specialized.

Alongside Porter, KRUGMAN has also been very influential in reminding us of the central economic importance of clusters. His book summarizes, in a non-technical way, some of his (and others') more technical research findings. Krugman argues that one of the most striking features about economic activity is its geographical concentration. He argues that this should be interpreted as evidence of certain types of increasing returns, and that the fact of increasing returns means that history and accident continue to leave their mark on the pattern of geographical location of industry. A wider literature following Krugman has emphasized the importance of path-dependence in explaining the creation, character, and survival of clusters (including ARTHUR, and DAVID & ROSENBLOOM).

An important development in the last ten years or so has been the growth of econometric studies of clustering. JAFFE, TRAJTENBERG & HENDERSON present a particularly influential study of the importance of knowledge spillovers in clusters, by examining the patterns of US patent citation. They find that patent applicants are more likely to cite patents originating from the same locality than from elsewhere in the same state, and in turn more likely to cite patents originating from the same state than from other parts of the US. They interpret this as evidence that knowledge is locally bound, and that knowledge spillovers work best when innovators are co-located.

BAPTISTA offers a valuable recent survey of some of the literature on clustering. While this survey focuses most strongly on the recent literature from economics, it also gives due credit to influential studies in regional studies, urban studies, economic geography, economic history, and to some important industry studies that have paid particular attention to the phenomenon of clustering.

G.M. PETER SWANN

See also Economic geography, Industrial districts

Coalition

Axelrod, Robert, *Conflict of Interest: A Theory of Divergent Goals with Applications to Politics*, Chicago: Markham, 1970

Bacharach, Michael, *Economics and the Theory of Games*, London: Macmillan, 1976

Browne, Eric C., *Coalition Theories: A Logical and Empirical Critique*, London and Beverly Hills, California: Sage, 1973

Budge, Ian and Hans Keman, *Parties and Democracy: Coalition Formation and Government Functioning in Twenty States*, Oxford and New York: Oxford University Press, 1990

Gamson, William, "A Theory of Coalition Formation", *American Sociological Review*, 26 (1961): 373–82

Grofman, Bernard, "A Dynamic Model of Protocoalition Formation in Ideological n-Space" in *Behavioral Science*, 27/1 (1982): 77–90

Krehbiel, Keith, "Spatial Models of Legislative Choice", *Legislative Studies Quarterly*, 13/3 (1988): 259–319

Laver, Michael and Kenneth A. Shepsle, "Coalitions and Cabinet Government", *American Political Science Review*, 84/3 (1990): 873–90

Laver, Michael and Norman Schofield, *Multiparty Government: The Politics of Coalition in Europe*, Oxford and New York: Oxford University Press, 1990

Lees, Charles, "The Red-Green Coalition" in *Bundestagswahl '98: The End of an Era?*, edited by Stephen Padgett and Thomas Saalfeld, London: Cass, 2000

Riker, William H., *The Theory of Political Coalitions*, New Haven, Connecticut: Yale University Press, 1962

Saalfeld, Thomas, "Coalition Politics and Management in the Kohl Era" in *Bundestagswahl '98: The End of an Era?*, edited by Stephen Padgett and Thomas Saalfeld, London: Cass, 2000

Shepsle, Kenneth, "Institutional Arrangements and Equilibrium in Multidimensional Voting Models", *American Journal of Political Science*, 23 (1979): 27–60

Swaan, Abram de, *Coalition Theories and Cabinet Formation: A Study of Formal Theories of Coalition Formation Applied to Nine European Parliaments after 1918*, Amsterdam and London: Elsevier, and San Francisco: Jossey Bass, 1973

A coalition is any combination of separate players – such as political parties – that cooperate in order to win a voting game, or secure some other strategic goal. Coalitions are found within nearly all social and political groups. Coalition government is common in political systems where no one party is strong enough to win a given legislative game. This is most common in those states with a "proportional" system of representation (such as Germany and Israel). As a rule, the more proportional the system, the less likely it is that any party is decisive and the more complex are the coalition arrangements needed to win the game. A large and heterogeneous literature exists relating to coalition behaviour, with game-theoretical models dominating the field. Theorists have emphasized different types of "structural attribute" and, as a result, a clear divide between "office-seeking" and "policy-seeking" models has emerged. In recent years attempts have been made to posit "unified" theories that bridge this gap and are more applicable to empirical research.

RIKER is associated with the office-seeking strand of coalition theory. He focuses on the strategies adopted by parties (assumed to be rational actors) as they attempt to gain admission to any coalition that may form. This process takes place within a game-theoretical environment that is both "constant sum" (limited in size and scope) and "zero-sum" (one player's gain diminishes the potential utility of all other players). Riker predicts that players will try to create coalitions that are only as large as they believe will ensure winning, in order to maximize the payoffs to each coalition member. In its pure theoretical form, this will result in a "minimum winning" coalition of 50 per cent plus one vote. In reality, however, exogenous constraints (such as formal party structures) mean that slightly larger "minimal winning" coalitions are more likely. It is also worth looking at the work of GAMSON, who argues that parties are intent on entering the "cheapest winning" coalition. Gamson assumes that parties would rather be a relatively large party in a small coalition than a junior partner in a bigger coalition, even when the benefits of doing so are broadly comparable. Riker and Gamson's models have a modest record in predicting real outcomes to processes of coalition bargaining and have attracted much criticism on epistemological grounds.

AXELROD builds upon office-seeking models and introduces a policy dimension, albeit as secondary formation criterion. His model assumes that office-seeking remains the central strategic goal of all players, but members of the successful coalition will ideally be adjacent to one another along a single Downsian Left–Right ideological continuum. Such "ideological adjacency" will serve to minimize conflicts of interest. Axelrod's "minimal connected winning" model performs better that pure minimal winning models in predicting actual outcomes of cabinet formation, but the underlying assumption that minimal connected winning coalitions have lower levels of conflicts of interest has been empirically challenged. Moreover, although Axelrod's model assumes ideological adjacency, it has no conception of the ideological distance between parties and cannot pick up the nuances of ideological conflict.

DE SWAAN sets out to do just this by constructing what he calls the "closed minimum range" of cabinet formation. De Swaan's theory predicts that the winning set will comprise the minimal connected winning coalition with the smallest ideological range. The policy dimension remains a single Downsian Left–Right axis, running from progressivism to conservatism, and all parties are assumed to have preference orderings of all potential coalitions, based upon their relative proximity to the median or "Mparty". De Swaan's theory is often referred to as the "median legislator" or "median party" model because it is based on the assumption that the party that controls the median legislator in any potential coalition is decisive because it blocks the axis along which any connected winning coalition must form. The median legislator model is intuitively more satisfying than pure office-seeking accounts and has more predictive power. However, the size principle is retained and one is confronted with a tradeoff between coalition size and ideological range.

Formal policy-seeking models of coalition behaviour tend to be spatial in their conceptualisation and posit the idea of a multidimensional policy space. Given the potential for disequilibrium in such a space, formal policy-driven models of coalition behaviour have focused upon conceptualising the processes that impose order upon voting games. This often involves some variation upon the game-theoretical concept of the "core" or "barycenter". Core theory is generally highly mathematical in nature and has been more popular with political theorists than empiricists. Nevertheless, KREHBIEL provides a good introduction to its application to practical politics. BROWNE suggests that core theory could be used to augment De Swaan's median legislator model. He considers the process of calculating the mean of points in multidimensional space to be analogous to De Swaan's measurement of the distance of potential coalition partners from the median of that potential coalition. The predicted coalition will be that which is winning and minimizes the policy distance of members from the core. The core is bound to exist in one-dimensional space, and finds an analogue in the Downs' "median voter" or de Swaan's "median legislator". However, as BACHARACH points out, in multidimensional space the potential for disequilibrium increases because alternative coalition packages can block any potential winning coalition. Nevertheless, although the phenomenon of constantly shifting coalitions and allegiances is not unknown in practical politics, most Western democracies are characterized by coalitions which manage to maintain themselves over time. So how does one explain the persistence of such stable institutions?

SHEPSLE addresses this problem by factoring in the institutional context while retaining a formal deductive approach. He concentrates upon the role of committees and their ability to deliver what he calls a "structure imposed equilibrium", maintained by control of the legislative agenda and a tendency towards specialisation. This effectively re-imposes a one-dimensional policy environment upon the legislative game. Key decisions are taken on one dimension at a time and dimensions cannot be linked to one another through tradeoffs. The overall package of policies agreed by the legislature will be the aggregate of the policy position of the median legislator on each separate dimension. This idea of a "dimension by dimension median" (DDM) has been developed more recently by LAVER & SHEPSLE. It is theoretically elegant and has proved a useful tool in related empirical work (see LEES; SAALFELD).

Other formal models of use empirically include those developed by LAVER & SCHOFIELD and BUDGE & KEMAN. Laver & Schofield builds upon GROFMAN's "proto-coalition" model and argues that, when forming a coalition, parties initially attempt to form a proto-coalition with the party nearest them ideologically. Proto-coalitions are assumed to then try and grow sufficiently to ensure a winning position within the legislature. This "bargaining approach" can be hierarchical (as Grofman originally suggested), or take place in a more rapacious and non-hierarchical manner. Stability is imposed by three structural attributes, relating to the nature of the regime, the coalition itself and the bargaining environment. Budge & Keman takes a more formal deductive approach, but also takes into account institutional contexts. The authors develop a small set of empirically testable assumptions that are assumed to sustain successful coalition formation and maintenance.

CHARLES LEES

Coase, R.H. 1910–

US (British-born) economist

Coase, R.H., "The Nature of the Firm", *Economica*, 4 (November 1937): 386–405

Coase, R.H., "The Marginal Cost Controversy", *Economica*, 13 (August 1946): 169–82

Coase, R.H., "The Problem of Social Cost", *Journal of Law and Economics*, 3 (October 1960): 1–44

Coase, R.H., "The Lighthouse in Economics", *Journal of Law and Economics*, 17/2 (October 1974): 357–76

Coase, R.H., *The Firm, the Market and the Law*, Chicago: University of Chicago Press, 1988

Medema, Steven G., *The Legacy of Ronald Coase in Economic Analysis*, vol. 1, Aldershot, Hampshire: Elgar, 1995

Williamson, Oliver E., "The Governance of Contractual Relations", *Journal of Law and Economics*, 22/2 (1979): 233–61

Ronald Harry Coase was born in Willesden, London in 1910. His period of study at the London School of Economics (LSE), 1929–32, coincided with the appointment in 1930 of Arnold Plant as Professor of Commerce. He taught at Dundee University (1932–34), Liverpool University (1934–35), and the LSE (1935–51). During World War II he served as a statistician, first at the Forestry Commission and then at the Central Statistical Office. Coase crossed the Atlantic for appointments at the Universities of Buffalo (1951–58), Stanford (1959), and Virginia (1959–64), and at the Chicago Law School (1964–81), where he assumed the editorship of the *Journal of Law and Economics*. Even after retirement he continued to write prolifically. In 1991 he was awarded the Alfred Nobel Memorial Prize in Economic Sciences for his work on institutional arrangements within markets (1937), and on externalities (1960), from which the ideas known as "the Coase theorem" emerged.

In his autobiographical mimeo for the Nobel Foundation in 1991, Coase credits Plant with introducing him to Adam Smith's invisible hand. "He made me aware of how a competitive economic system could be coordinated by the pricing system. But he did not merely influence my ideas. My encountering him changed my life." The independent detachment that Coase has brought throughout his career to his insights into economic problems, and his desire to relate these to the real world, have been attributed to a combination of mentor influence, and the fact that his LSE undergraduate career did not feature a single economics course. The University of London awarded him a travelling scholarship to the US in 1931–2, on which he considered why organizational structures differ across industries. Thus while still an undergraduate, the foundations were laid for his first seminal work, COASE (1937).

Its purpose was to provide a rationale for the existence of a firm and to indicate what determines the range of activities it undertakes. The firm and the market could be seen as alternative ways of organizing production:

> a firm will tend to expand until the costs of organizing an extra transaction within the firm becomes equal to the costs of carrying out the transaction by means of an exchange in the open market or the costs of organizing in another firm.

Coase's fundamental insight is that market transactions, and specifically discovering prices, are not costless activities and vary for different firms. Thus Coase interpreted the firm's decision as selecting the form of organization that minimizes the costs of an economic transaction. Like much of Coase's original work, the term "transaction costs" was not coined and built upon until much later in the 1960s and the full-scale investigation of the determinants of industrial structure and organization, and of the associated contracting processes, presaged in Coase's early work, did not begin until the 1970s.

The consequences of marginal cost pricing in a decreasing-cost "natural monopoly" industry was the next subject for Coase's scrutiny, in COASE (1946). Conventionally the loss incurred should be covered by government subsidy along with some regulation or the involvement of government itself in the production. Coase brought into the analysis the costs of administering marginal cost pricing and the costs of determining the value of the output to customers. He advocated a multi-part pricing system, but this depends on all costs being attributable to individual consumers, and currently incurred. Reflecting on this, COASE (1988) rejected the idea of marginal cost pricing, other than in a world of "blackboard economics" where the teacher, with all the information available, manipulates prices, taxes, and subsidies to bring about economic welfare. Inefficiencies will be the inevitable consequence, he argued, of disparate government agencies attempting to mimic this.

One of the most cited economic publications followed – COASE (1960). The Coase theorem, which developed from this paper, is dealt with in a separate entry. His analysis of social cost considers the problem of harmful effects (externalities) from the perspective of both their recipient and their originator, and it legitimizes the role of the market in arriving at a least-cost solution to such problems.

In COASE (1974), Coase switched his attack on Pigou's work to the market-failure example of the lighthouse, represented in economics as the classic public good. In a fastidiously researched sketch of the 19th-century British lighthouse system, he chides economists for supposing that a private system would be necessarily worse than one funded by public taxation.

MEDEMA, in an extensive and authoritative collection, identifies several themes running throughout Coase's work. The desire to construct analysis that both fits and draws from the real world is an early hallmark of Coase. Coase appears to eschew the use of mathematical or quantitative analysis, preferring to structure his arguments in an intuitive way. Central to his philosophy is the importance of an understanding of the impact and activities of the economic institutions – the market, the firm, and the law – that underpin the workings of the economic system. Related to this is his wish for a careful assessment of the worth of alternative institutional structures.

Finally, the part played by transaction costs in economic activity is crucial to his work, and is an important part of his legacy. Thus WILLIAMSON's opening words are as follows:

The new institutional economics is preoccupied with the origins, incidence and ramifications of transaction costs. Indeed, if transaction costs are negligible, the organization of economic activity is irrelevant, since any advantages one mode of organization appears to hold over another will simply be eliminated by costless contracting.

ROBERT WOODFIELD

See also Coase theorem

Coase theorem

Coase, R.H., "The Federal Communications Commission", *Journal of Law and Economics*, 2 (October 1959): 1–40
Coase, R.H., "The Problem of Social Cost", *Journal of Law and Economics*, 3 (October 1960): 1–44
Coase, R.H., *The Firm, the Market and the Law*, Chicago: University of Chicago Press, 1988
Cooter, Robert, "The Cost of Coase", *Journal of Legal Studies*, 11/1 (January 1982): 1–33
Hoffman, Elizabeth and Matthew L. Spitzer, "Experimental Tests of the Coase Theorem with Large Bargaining Groups", *Journal of Legal Studies*, 15/1 (January 1986): 149–71
Medema, Steven G., *The Legacy of Ronald Coase in Economic Analysis*, vols 1–2, Aldershot, Hampshire: Elgar, 1995
Stigler, George J., *The Theory of Price*, 3rd edition, New York: Macmillan, 1966
Zerbe, Richard O. Jr, "The Problem of Social Cost in Retrospect", *Research in Law and Economics*, 2 (1980): 83–102

The term "Coase theorem" did not originate with the man himself nor ultimately did its precise formulation. Rather it resulted from the development of ideas initially expressed in COASE (1959) and (1960) and later set out by STIGLER: "the Coase Theorem thus asserts that under perfect competition private and social costs will be equal."

When applied to environmental considerations, pollution-cost problems are argued to be non-pervasive, and can be dealt with by redefining the existing structure of property rights. Hence the Pigouvian approach – where the polluter or creator of the social cost (externality) should be liable for the damage caused to those who suffer from it, should be taxed by an amount equivalent to the damage caused, or should otherwise be banned from operating in the areas where the damage is caused – is rejected. Specifically Coase (1959) argued, in the context of a doctor disturbed by noise and vibration from a neighbouring confectioner's machinery, that whether or not the confectioner had the right to create the nuisance, that right would be acquired by the party to whom it was most valuable. Namely, "the delimitation of rights is an essential prelude to market transactions, the ultimate result (which maximizes the value of production) is independent of the legal decision". Coase (1960) put forward the proposition that the problem of an externality resides with both parties. Rather than just identifying the polluter as the cause of the damage and attributing a cost to it, the harm to the polluter of preventing his action should also be investigated in order to judge which party incurs the more serious harm. Secondly, and in the face of Pigouvian tradition, Coase declared a central role for the market in the search for solutions to such problems.

More generally, the Coase theorem can be set out as follows. Assuming perfect competition and disregarding transaction costs and income effects, voluntary agreements among the different affected parties result in a socially optimal output, even where externalities exist. Further, this result holds irrespective of which party is assigned the property rights to the resource(s) in question.

MEDEMA points to the variety in the literature of statements of the Coase theorem, which appear to have identical implications but contain important subtle differences of interpretation, and which are a source of controversy and debate. ZERBE surveys this interpretative literature and provides a set of criteria by which to judge the debate. In particular he focuses on an efficiency claim (that the outcome of the bargaining process will be efficient) and an invariance claim (that the final outcome in terms of the pattern of resource allocation will not change under alternative assignments of rights). The efficiency claim hinges on the definition of efficiency used, whether strategic bargaining is allowed for, and how the nature of the world of zero transaction costs is construed. As to the invariance claim, Medema isolates two possible interpretations. The first is that the same efficient outcome will be reached irrespective of how rights are assigned. The inclusion of income effects is agreed to render this version of the invariance claim void. The second is that alternative specifications of rights and liabilities do not lead to the same efficient outcome, but rather equally efficient outcomes. So bargaining between the different groups, given the opening structure of rights, will yield an efficient outcome. The outcomes are unlikely to be the same, however, (in resource allocation terms) under different initial assignments of rights, because of their impact on wealth, income, and tastes. However they will be equally efficient in the Pareto sense that no welfare improvement from exchange will be possible.

Coase (1960) set out what he meant by the term "transaction costs":

> In order to carry out a market transaction it is necessary to discover who it is that one wishes to deal with, to inform people that one wishes to deal and on what terms, to conduct negotiations leading up to a bargain, to draw up the contract, to undertake the inspection needed to make sure that the terms of the contract are being observed, and so on.

Discussion of the Coase theorem is usually set in a situation where these transaction costs are explicitly or implicitly assumed to be zero. In COASE (1988), Coase was keen to incorporate positive transaction costs into the analysis "so that we can study the world that exists". To do so, he maintained, would require that "we first discard the approach at present used by most economists".

If the Coase theorem can be said to hold given the full list of original assumptions associated with it, what of its wider applicability? Might the assumption that cooperation always occurs when bargaining is costless be upset when one or more greedy persons intent on settling only after gleaning more than their fair share, effectively blocks otherwise mutually advantageous trade between the parties? COOTER dubs this extreme position "Hobbes theorem", which he says is "based upon the belief that people will exercise their worst threats against each other unless there is a third party to coerce both of them". Hobbes's third party exercises coercive force to divide the surplus, implying dictatorial government with unlimited powers relative to the bargainers. In the 1980s, the Coase theorem was tested by determining the game-theoretic conditions under which bargaining in small groups reaches an efficient conclusion. HOFFMAN & SPITZER extended that experimental work to suggest that the Coase theorem is a valid tool for analysing decisions of groups of 20 persons or fewer, provided that bargaining, coordination, and enforcement costs are low, and information problems few.

ROBERT WOODFIELD

See also Ronald Coase

Codetermination, works councils

Addison, John T. and W. Stanley Siebert, "The Social Charter of the European Community: Evolution and Controversies", *Industrial and Labor Relations Review*, 44/4 (1991): 597–625

Addison, John T., Claus Schnabel and Joachim Wagner, "German Industrial Relations: An Elusive Exemplar", *Industrielle Beziehungen: Zeitschrift für Arbeit, Organisation und Management*, 2/1 (1995): 25–45

Blanpain, Roger and Paul Windey, *European Works Councils: Information and Consultation of Employees in Multinational Enterprises in Europe*, Leuven: Peeters, 1994

Gold, Michael and Mark Hall, "*Report on European-level Information and Consultation in Multinational Companies: An Evaluation of Practice*", Luxembourg: Office for Official Publications of the European Communities/European Foundation for the Improvement of Living and Working Conditions, 1992

Hyman, Richard, "Is There a Case for Statutory Works Councils in Britain?" in *The Future of Labour Law*, edited by Aileen McColgan, London: Cassell, 1996

Kaufman, Bruce E. and Morris M. Kleiner (editors), *Employee Representation: Alternatives and Future Directions*, Madison, Wisconsin: Industrial Relations Research Association, 1993

Kelly, John, "Works Councils: Union Advance or Marginalization?" in *The Future of Labour Law*, edited by Aileen McColgan, London: Cassell, 1996

Lorenz, Edward, "Promoting Workplace Participation: Lessons from Germany and France", *Industrielle Beziehungen: Zeitschrift für Arbeit, Organisation und Management*, 2/1 (1995): 46–63

Rogers, Joel and Wolfgang Streeck (editors), *Works Councils: Consultation, Representation, and Cooperation in Industrial Relations*, Chicago: University of Chicago Press, 1995

Streeck, Wolfgang, "Codetermination: The Fourth Decade" in *International Perspectives on Organizational Democracy*, vol. 2, edited by Bernhard Wilpert and Arndt Sorge, Chichester and New York: Wiley, 1984 (International Yearbook of Organizational Democracy)

Thelen, Kathleen A., "Union of Parts: Labor Politics in Postwar Germany", Ithaca, New York: Cornell University Press, 1991

In the 1990s, the German system of codetermination, and especially *one* of its elements – works councils – commanded increasing interest both within the European Union, and in other developed countries including the US, as an alternative form of institutionalised representation at the workplace. The debate is an ongoing one, with contributions from an array of disciplines, such as industrial relations, political economy, economics, and sociology. The objective in selecting key texts here was therefore to represent the debates and issues that emerge both from within the different disciplines and at the different levels of analysis (national, European, and enterprise level).

THELEN's excellent book is an invaluable addition to the literature on German industrial relations. Her thesis originates from the increasing interest, among both scholars and practitioners, in the stability and resilience characterising Germany's (former West Germany) "dual" industrial relations system, especially in the context of the economic and political crises of the 1970s and 1980s. For Thelen, Germany constitutes a special case of neocorporatism: she argues that the mutually reinforcing nature of the relationship between national bargaining and codetermination at plant and firm levels has resulted in a system with a unique capacity for what she calls "negotiated adjustment". The author masterfully synthesises a wealth of historical data and in-depth qualitative research, including some interviews with leading figures from the metalworkers' union IG Metall, which were not easy to come by. Her institutional, historical, and policy analysis of the dynamics of the German "dual" system make her book a major contribution to the analysis and understanding of the German system of industrial relations.

STREECK provides a fascinating account and assessment of the system of codetermination from the 1951 Codetermination Act through to the changes it underwent as a result of new legislation in the 1970s. His essay reveals how the relationship between capital and labour was gradually transformed alongside the developments in legislation over the three decades covered. In evaluating the impact of codetermination, Streeck argues that it has significantly changed the relations between capital and labour, by improving the status of labour at the enterprise level, forcing management to respond. At the same time, he highlights the ambivalence of both parties towards the system, and concludes warning of the dangers of the gradual replacement of industrial by enterprise unionism.

ROGERS & STREECK extends the emphasis from a narrow examinination of the German system of codetermination to an exploration of alternative modes of workplace representation in other European countries and in North America and Canada. The nine chapters devoted to the history, structure, and functions of works councils in Germany, the Netherlands, France, Spain, Sweden, Italy, Poland, Canada, and the USA are highly descriptive. However, this allows one to appreciate the diversity of experiences within different national settings, and how the resulting institutions are very much influenced by the specific conditions within and idiosyncrasies of national industrial relations systems. This idea is taken up by Streeck (chapter 11) in a valuable comparative analysis of the various arrangements found in the six Western European countries considered. He argues that in fact, behind this apparent diversity lie commonalities in the development of works councils and the related structures, throughout postwar Western Europe. Aside from the conceptual chapter by Rogers and Streeck, the theoretical analysis by Freeman and Lazear is of great value, especially to economists. Their thorough analysis of the productivity effects of works councils concludes by advocating that works councils should be mandatory, because although they have the potential to increase the joint surplus of the enterprise, neither employers nor employees have adequate incentives to implement them voluntarily. Overall, despite the descriptive character of most of the chapters in this book, it is an important text, for two main reasons: (i) the emphasis on the wider economic and political context in which institutional arrangements are formulated, which is an essential element for further research, especially regarding the debate on the transferability of institutions, and also regarding the debate at the European level which has resulted from the directives on European Works Councils (EWCs); and (ii) the identification of debates at different levels (enterprise, national, and European) and the valuable conclusions for further analysis and research, arrived at through a detailed examination of the relevant issues in the conceptual chapters.

LORENZ's comparative analysis of French and German works councils shows that legislative support may be a necessary condition for the effective operation of works councils, but that it is definitely not a sufficient condition. French legislation accords works councils many of the guarantees that legislation gives to those in Germany, yet in France they do not function in a way that the North American literature argues they should. There is no obvious payoff in cooperative industrial relations, and generally, works councils have not been a vehicle for higher firm performance, partly because of competition among the unions, and partly because of employer opposition. Lorenz's analysis therefore highlights that an "undeserved faith in the efficacy of legislative solutions" may not be altogether justifiable.

In the context of the transferability of works councils to the UK, the two excellent chapters by KELLY and HYMAN in the book edited by Aileen McColgan, which should be read in conjunction with one another, focus on the potential benefits to trade unions of instituting works councils of some form. Kelly's article is a refreshing critique of works councils, concerned principally with whether works councils in some guise or another would help or hinder the recovery of union membership and influence. This contrasts with a large body of work that primarily focuses on the impact of works councils on firm performance. Kelly arrives at a rather pessimistic conclusion about any positive impact on union recovery, given the absence of employer support and legalized union security, and is at best doubtful about the ability of works councils to function as an effective voice for employees. Hyman, on the other hand, is more concerned with identifying the *conditions* under which works councils might form part of a strategy for trade union recovery and renewal, with an emphasis on institutions, and on the wider industrial relations context. He concludes on a more optimistic note that, given the contemporary economic and political context (before the election of a Labour government in 1997), works councils constitute the best available strategic option for trade union recovery, although he acknowledges the necessity for accompanying any form of works council representation with a series of institutional and legislative reforms.

ADDISON, SCHNABEL & WAGNER provide a useful and interesting examination of the evidence (or absence of it, as appears to be the case) for the positive effects of unionization and works councils on firm performance. Their analysis demonstrates that in fact, the evidence for any such effects is inconsistent at best, which in essence undermines the case for a wider application of works councils outside Germany. Addison, Schnabel & Wagner's position directly contradicts that of other researchers such as Freeman and Lazear, who, at least in theory, are convinced of the positive effects of works councils.

The edited collection by KAUFMAN & KLEINER reflects the increasing popularity of German works councils among

American scholars, putting the whole US debate into perspective. The emphasis is on exploring various forms of employee representation, such as "employee involvement", "joint governance", "co-management", and "partnership", given the decline of trade unionism and collective bargaining, which has left many employees without an adequate form of representation at the workplace. Almost all of the contributors believe that this "representation gap" should be filled.

The large body of sociological work on German works councils should also be mentioned, with the work of Hermann Kotthoff being a notable example (see *Betriebsräte und Bürgerstatus*, 1994). Also, the work on works councils in former East Germany by Carola Frege, especially "Institutional Transfer and Effectiveness of Employee Representation: Comparing Works Councils in East and West Germany", *Economic and Industrial Democracy*, September (1999), where she has taken the unorthodox line that workers are learning how to use works councils effectively. This was also a popular argument among a number of German writers in the early 1990s.

ADDISON & SIEBERT provide an overview of the Social Charter of the European Community, examining the implications of adopting the mandated benefits proposed, and concluding that, contrary to the Community's objective, these will cause less rather than more equality. This is worthwhile reading, especially for its more critical interpretation of the legislative efforts at the level of the European Community (now Union). However, the authors' analysis does not adequately emphasise the effect, particularly by employers' resistance to some of the proposed measures, in diluting the substance and scope of legislation. This becomes more evident from the closer look at the status, progress, and content of the EWCs legislation, found in the article by Wolfgang Streeck ("From Market Making to State Building? Reflections on the Political Economy of European Social Policy" in *European Social Policy: Between Fragmentation and Integration*, 1995).

Instead of normatively prescribing a uniform mechanism of workforce participation, the drafts offer firms and countries a menu of alternative models, any of which they might adopt to satisfy legal requirements. Which alternative is chosen is determined by national traditions; the preferences of management and, perhaps, of workers and unions; and the relative strength of management and labour in a given institutional or economic environment.

GOLD & HALL provide useful evidence for the practice of works councils arrangements at European level, from interviews with both management and employee representatives. Despite the small sample of companies, the evidence reveals the slow and uneven growth of *voluntary* works councils in European multinational companies. BLANPAIN & WINDEY focus more on analysing the 1994/95 EWCs directive and examining its implications for the social partners, while at the same time providing a useful practical guide to implementing the legislation.

MELVINA METOCHI

See also Industrial relations

Cognitive developmental theory

Brainerd, C.J. (section editor), "Psychological Science Celebrates the Centennial of Jean Piaget", *Psychological Science*, 7/4 (1996): 191–225

DeLoache, Judy S., "Early Understanding and Use of Symbols: The Model Model", *Current Directions*, 4/4 (1995): 109–13

Flavell, John H., "Cognitive Development: Past, Present and Future", *Developmental Psychology*, 28 (1993): 998–1005

Flavell, John H., "Cognitive Development: Children's Knowledge about the Mind", *Annual Review of Psychology*, 50 (1999): 21–45

Halford, Graeme S., *Children's Understanding: The Development of Mental Models*, Hillsdale, New Jersey: Erlbaum, 1993

Piaget, Jean and Bärbel Inhelder, *The Psychology of the Child*, London: Routledge and Kegan Paul, and New York: Basic Books, 1969 (French edition 1966)

Siegler, Robert S., "Cognitive Variability: A Key to Understanding Cognitive Development", *Current Directions*, 3/1 (1994): 1–5

Siegler, Robert S., *Emerging Minds: The Process of Change in Children's Thinking*, New York and Oxford: Oxford University Press, 1996

Thomas, R. Murray, *Comparing Theories of Child Development*, 4th edition, Pacific Grove, California: Brooks Cole, 1996

The terms cognitive developmental theory and Jean Piaget have been synonymous for most of this century. No bibliography would be complete without a listing of some, if not all, of Piaget's prolific output. Accordingly, I have chosen as my first reference a tribute to Jean Piaget published in *Psychological Science* (1996). As part of the tribute, a bibliography of Piaget's books is included, to which the serious student of cognitive developmental theory is referred (see p.192). I have also selected one modest tome by PIAGET & INHELDER, because of its brevity and clarity, to given the student a taste of the original writing (in translation). Piaget was committed to the development of a biological theory of knowledge, which eventually assumed the title of genetic epistemology.

BRAINERD succinctly summarizes the essence of Piagetian theory thus: Piaget concluded

> that logic is inherent in action and that the roots of logic are therefore to be found in the organization of action. It was this conclusion that formed the basis for Piaget's hypothesis that even the most sophisticated forms of human reasoning are motor activities carried out on a symbolic plane (p.192).

This conviction resulted in Piaget's intensive study of the nonverbal expressions of intelligence in infants, research paradigms based on the manipulation of concrete materials, and an analysis of children's explanations of incorrect answers, methods that have subsequently formed the basis for thousands of studies in cognitive development.

A number of key developmental theorists, including Flavell, Siegler & Ellis, and Elkind, contribute to this special edition of *Psychological Science* in which the major achievements of Piagetian theory (for example, the concepts of schemas, assimilation-accommodation, equilibration, constructivism, structuralism, essentialism, and dynamism) as well as its controversies/omissions (for example, whether cognitive development proceeds in stages, the question of domain-specific development, quantitative versus qualitative developmental changes in cognition, the effects of practice, experience and expertise, the existence of natural domains and constraints, the mechanisms of development, and sociocultural influences) are discussed. One of the major criticisms of Piaget is that he consistently underestimated the capacities of very young children. A number of researchers have demonstrated, for example, that children as young as three years old understand that thinking is different from talking, an understanding that Piaget believed was not possible in even six and seven year old children, whom he claimed construed thinking as synonymous with speech. Cognitive experiments in the post-Piaget era have consistently identified cognitive skills, such as mental representation, metacognition, and empathy, in children at ages much earlier than previously believed. Gopnik (in Brainerd) points the field of cognitive developmental theory in intriguing new directions. She describes the most influential contemporary constructivist theory – " 'theory theory', the idea that cognitive development is the result of the same mechanisms that lead to theory change in science" (p.221). There are many excellent references for the interested reader to pursue.

THOMAS is a good starting point for an introductory overview of theories of child development. He describes and compares the theories of Piaget, Vygotsky, Skinner, Bandura, information processing, and sociobiological approaches among others, as well as alerting students to the standards of "good" theories.

Robert Siegler is concerned with one of the major weaknesses of many of the stage theories of cognitive development – specifying how change occurs, and the variability in the process of change. SIEGLER (1994) summarizes the major issues, which he elaborates in his book, *Emerging Minds* (SIEGLER 1996). Siegler argues that evolutionary theory is an analogy for cognitive development – "evolution is the product of interactions among mechanisms that produce variability . . . that select among varying entities . . . and that preserve the lessons of the past" (p.17). He conceptualizes cognitive development as changes in the distribution of ways of thinking (strategies) rather than as sudden shifts from one way of thinking to another. He posits five fundamental phenomena of strategy choice – variability, adaptiveness, change, individual differences, and generalization – against which he assesses formal models of strategy choice.

HALFORD is concerned with " . . . defining and explaining children's mental models, skills, and strategies" (p.237). He characterizes mental models as "representations that are active while solving a problem and that provide the workspace for inference and mental operations" (p.23). Like Siegler, Halford is interested in process and change in cognition, but their approaches are different, making for interesting comparisons. In the first five chapters, Halford describes the basic building blocks necessary for his cognitive-developmental theory, which he elaborates in chapter six. The essential element in this theory is not the development of strategies, but the development of

understanding, which he defines as " . . . a mental model that represent the structure of the concept or phenomenon" (p.238). As knowledge is necessary for understanding, the process through which knowledge is acquired (namely learning) is an essential part of the theory. Halford identifies two type of learning: basic learning and induction and acquisition of mechanisms for building cognitive skills and strategies.

Symbolic development figures prominently in many theories of cognitive development. DELOACHE's research focuses on how very young children make the symbol-referent connection and how they begin to use symbols as sources of information and as the basis for reasoning and problem solving. In this paper, she reports on a series of experiments that resulted in the development of a theory of symbolic development, the "model model". Representational insight is the core element. The age at which, and degree to which children develop representational insight varies according to the characteristics of the symbol (salience), the symbol-referent relationship (iconicity), the symbol user (experience), and the social context (instruction). The development of symbolic sensitivity is posited as the process underlying symbolic development.

FLAVELL (1999), in a state-of-the-art review in *Annual Review of Psychology*, provides an excellent overview of the "third wave" of cognitive developmental research, which includes theory theory, modular theory and simulation theory, as well as a discussion of cognitive competences developed during infancy. This, together with the earlier paper (FLAVELL 1993), is essential reading for students of development psychology.

DIANNA T. KENNY

Cognitive dissonance

Beauvois, Jean-Leon and Robert-Vincent Joule, *A Radical Dissonance Theory*, London: Taylor and Francis, 1996

Berkowitz, Leonard, "Social Motivation" in *The Handbook of Social Psychology*, 2nd edition, vol. 3, edited by Gardner Lindzey and Elliot Aronson, Reading, Massachusetts: Addison Wesley, 1969

Chapanis, Alphonse and Natalia P. Chapanis, "Cognitive Dissonance: Five Years Later", *Psychological Bulletin*, 61/1 (1964): 1–22

Cooper, Joel and Robert T. Croyle, "Attitudes and Attitude Change", *Annual Review of Psychology*, 35 (1984): 395–426

Cooper, Joel and Russell H. Fazio, "A New Look at Dissonance Theory" in *Advances in Experimental Social Psychology: Theorizing in Social Pyschology: Special Topics*, edited by Leonard Berkowitz, vol. 17, New York: Academic Press, 1984

Festinger, Leon, *A Theory of Cognitive Dissonance*, Evanston, Illinois: Row Peterson, 1957

Festinger, Leon (editor), *Conflict, Decision and Dissonance*, Stanford, California: Stanford University Press, 1964

Festinger, Leon and James M. Carlsmith, "Cognitive Consequences of Forced Compliance", *Journal of Abnormal and Social Psychology*, 58 (1959): 203–10

Heider, F., "Attitudes and Cognitive Organization", *Journal of Psychology*, 21 (1946): 107–12

Osgood, Charles E. and Percy H. Tannenbaum, "The Principle of Congruity in the Prediction of Attitude Change", *Psychological Review*, 62 (1955): 42–55

Zajonc, Robert B., "Cognitive Theories in Social Psychology" in *Handbook of Social Psychology*, 2nd edition, edited by Gardner Lindzey and Elliot Aronson, vol. 1, Reading, Massachusetts: Addison Wesley, 1968

FESTINGER (1957) is a classic in social psychology and an excellent starting point for the interested reader. It outlines a theoretical formulation of cognitive dissonance that stimulated a significant level of research activity, and also prompted the development of a range of alternative theoretical formulations based upon cognitive consistency. It was also through Festinger's work that the concept of cognitive dissonance entered popular culture. In this work he proposes that the logical inconsistency or dissonance between two or more relevant beliefs creates an unpleasant emotional state, and that the individual feels motivated to deal with this by altering one or more beliefs.

Festinger's theory is elegant in its simplicity and the predictions generated by the theory of cognitive dissonance are often startlingly counterintuitive; suggesting for example that people paid less to do an unpleasant task may actually experience more satisfaction. FESTINGER & CARLSMITH presents a compelling study in which subjects undertook a boring task and then received a small or large monetary reward for lying to others that it was enjoyable. Subjects who received the small reward subsequently believed the task to have been truly more enjoyable.

FESTINGER (1964) represents a mature view of cognitive dissonance in the context of the numerous studies that had already been undertaken. As the influence of the theory expanded so did controversy. That same year CHAPANIS & CHAPANIS (1964) provided a critical review of the theory and research findings. The authors saw the theory as vague and simplistic, and argued that since there were alternative plausible explanations for numerous findings, the theory was not supported. In fairness, alternative explanations for specific predicted outcomes are possible when one examines many theories. Research continued and COOPER & CROYLE (published 1984) indicated over 1000 published articles.

Despite reasonable criticisms, Festinger's work has certainly had tremendous heuristic value and numerous researchers have refined, revised, or extended the theory to focus on different psychological dimensions or aspects of social situations. ZAJONC is an excellent review of these developments that will guide the reader through the multiple variants of dissonance theory that arose over the first decade. For the reader interested in the further evolution of work on cognitive dissonance, COOPER & FAZIO provides one thorough and significant revision of Festinger's theory, reformulating it by utilizing elements of attribution theory.

It is also interesting to place Festinger's work in its historical context. Social psychology in the first decades after World War II was heavily influenced by a rational and cognitive view of man and thus took great interest in attitude formation and change. Historically Festinger's theory drew upon Kurt Lewin's earlier work. It was one of a number of theories that focused on the psychological motivation of achieving a state of internal cognitive consistency as central in maintaining or changing beliefs or attitudes. BERKOWITZ provides a clear overview of social motivation theory, and sets out the place of Festinger's theory within other cognitive consistency models. OSGOOD & TANNENBAUM's work on cognitive congruence or HEIDER's theory of balance are examples of related theoretical perspectives of that time.

Finally, cognitive dissonance has maintained a unique position among related concepts of its day and continues to inspire contemporary efforts, including attempts to return to Festinger's original formulation in modern reinterpretations. For example BEAUVOIS & JOULE attempts to redefine dissonance in terms of the psychological rationalization of problematic behaviour rather than a motivation toward cognitive consistency.

GEORGE LUCKI

Cohabitation

Blossfeld, Hans-Peter (editor), *The New Role of Women: Family Formation in Modern Societies*, Boulder, Colorado: Westview Press, 1995

Blumstein, Philip and Pepper Schwartz, *American Couples: Money, Work and Sex*, New York: Morrow, 1983

Cunningham, John D. and John K. Antill, "Current Trends in Nonmarital Cohabitation: In Search of the POSSLQ" in *Under-Studied Relationships: Off the Beaten Track*, edited by Julia T. Wood and Steve Duck, Thousand Oaks, California and London: Sage, 1995

Macklin, Eleanor D., "Nonmarital Heterosexual Cohabitation: An Overview" in *Contemporary Families and Alternative Lifestyles: Handbook on Research and Theory*, edited by Eleanor D. Macklin and Roger H. Rubin, Beverly Hills, California: Sage, 1983

McRae, Susan, *Cohabiting Mothers: Changing Marriage and Motherhood?*, London: Policy Studies Institute, 1993

Stephen, Parker, *Informal Marriage: Cohabitation and the Law, 1750–1989*, Basingstoke: Macmillan, and New York: St Martin's Press, 1990

The literature on unmarried heterosexual cohabitation is underdeveloped. In many sociological texts cohabiting couples are assumed to be similar to married couples. Little research on unmarried cohabitation has been conducted with the exception of demographic analysis of large-scale quantitative data sets. The major problems with most of this research are that cohabiters have been treated as a homogenous group, the research is highly descriptive, and it fails to engage with social theory. There is a need for more theoretical work on the rise of cohabitation in Western societies and research that captures social process and cohabiters' experiences in detail.

There are few reviews of the available literature on cohabitation. CUNNINGHAM & ANTILL's review covers the incidence of cohabitation, who is likely to cohabit, the changing attitudes toward cohabitation, childrearing, and the relationship between cohabitation and marriage. They argue for psychological rather than sociological research in their conclusion. MACKLIN's chapter offers a better overview of earlier research on cohabitation, mainly from the US. It covers incidence of cohabitation, the characteristics of cohabiters, some information on the nature of cohabiting relationships, and the social implications of cohabitation.

The volume edited by BLOSSFELD is primarily about family formation from a demographic perspective. However, each of the chapters has a section on the rise of cohabitation and its role in family formation in nine countries. There is information on the UK, US, Sweden, West Germany, France, The Netherlands, Italy, Spain, and Hungary. In all of the countries where cohabitation is practised in significant numbers, cohabitation is different from marriage. Although this book is not a particularly lively read, it is a useful collection of demographic information in one volume.

Although somewhat dated, BLUMSTEIN & SCHWARTZ provide the most comprehensive study of cohabitation available. Based on a large voluntary sample of couples in the US, cohabiting couples are compared with married and same-sex couples. The survey findings are illustrated with quotes from in-depth interviews. The three major topic areas are money (including income differentials and money management), work (both paid and unpaid work and the impact on relationships) and sex (including power and non-monogamy). The themes of power and relationship stability run throughout the study. This book is an accessible and interesting read.

McRAE's study of cohabiting mothers in Britain is recommended reading. The introduction provides a useful review of some historical and cross-cultural material on cohabitation. This study recognizes diversity and social process in the lives of cohabiters. Long-term cohabiting mothers are compared with mothers who had never cohabited and women who went on to marry before or after having children. The themes covered include reasons for cohabiting or marriage and aspects of family life, including surnames, the domestic division of labour, and happiness. Long-term cohabiting mothers did not have markedly different family lives from the married mothers. The legal and policy implications of cohabiting motherhood are discussed.

PARKER's historical study of British law is a detailed account of the relationship between the state and cohabiting couples. He argues that the law is best understood as an arm of the state, pursuing both its own interests and those of the state. Parker shows that family law continually reconstructs and adjusts the perceived boundaries between the state and the family. The law works in the financial interests of the state by operating to confine support obligations within the private sphere. This is a sophisticated analysis of social change, the state, and the increasing regulation of cohabitation.

JO LINDSAY

See also Marriage

Cold War

Alperovitz, Gar, *The Decision to Use the Atomic Bomb and the Architecture of an American Myth*, New York: Knopf, 1995

Ball, S.J., *The Cold War: An International History, 1947–1991*, London and New York: Arnold, 1998

Beschloss, Michael R. and Strobe Talbott, *At the Highest Levels: The Inside Story of the End of the Cold War*, Boston and London: Little Brown, 1993

Gaddis, John Lewis, *We Now Know: Rethinking Cold War History*, Oxford: Clarendon Press, and New York: Oxford University Press, 1997

Gardner, Lloyd C., *Architects of Illusion: Men and Ideas in American Foreign Policy*, Chicago: Quadrangle, 1970

Garthoff, Raymond, "Cuban Missile Crisis: The Soviet Story", *Foreign Policy*, 72 (1988): 61–80

Holloway, David, *The Soviet Union and the Arms Race*, 2nd edition, New Haven, Connecticut: Yale University Press, 1984

Kennan, George, "The Sources of Soviet Conduct", *Foreign Affairs*, 35/4 (1947): 566–82

McLellan, David S., *Dean Acheson: The State Department Years*, New York: Dodd Mead, 1976

Prewitt, Jeffery L., "Expansion of the Permanent Seats on the Security Council", *Political Crossroads*, 6/1–2 (1998): 25–55

Schlesinger, Arthur Jr, "Origins of the Cold War", *Foreign Affairs*, 46/1 (1967): 22–52

Yergin, Daniel, *Shattered Peace: The Origins of the Cold War and the National Security State*, Boston: Houghton Mifflin, 1977

Zubok, Vladislav and Constantine Pleshakov, *Inside the Cold War: From Stalin to Khrushchev*, Cambridge, Massachusetts: Harvard University Press, 1996

Scholars disagree on the causes of the Cold War, as well as the years when it began and ended, but there is general agreement that it dominated international politics in the post-World War II period. The Cold War was a political, ideological, and economic struggle in which the United States and Soviet Union, their allies and client states sought supremacy.

ALPEROVITZ remains the classic revisionist study of the origins of the Cold War. The central thesis is that in 1945 Japan was exhausted from World War II, but the United States used the atomic bomb in order to signal its willingness to engage in atomic blackmail of the Soviet Union. Interesting are the profiles of prominent American leaders and their attitudes for using atomic weapons. Readers are warned of the limited discussion of Soviet motives as Alperowitz sees US military policy as responsible for the Cold War.

Unlike most studies of the Cold War, which focus on American or Soviet personalities and national policies, BALL examines the Cold War from the international level of analysis. It presents a unique discussion of how ideology, domestic politics, and military policy interacted to produce selected Cold War policies. By examining those variables in terms of the superpowers, the major powers (Britain, China, and France) and the battleground nations (Germany, Korea, Cuba, and Vietnam) he is able to show the interaction that shaped the major events of the Cold War.

BESCHLOSS & TALBOTT provide a comprehensive examination of the interaction of American and Soviet leaders and the confidential politics that emerged during the waning years of the Cold War and the collapse of the Soviet Union. They highlight the leaders' perceptions of one another and how they led to the resolution of crises as well as the cooling of relations. This provides a useful context for examining a variety of issues of the final years of the Cold War, including the Gulf Crisis War, collapse of Soviet control in Eastern Europe, and the Soviet coup.

American interpretations of Soviet behaviour in 1946 relied heavily on KENNAN's Long Telegram of which this is the publicized version. Starting from the belief that ideology has a paramount importance in the conduct of Soviet foreign policy, Kennan argued the US must be wary of Soviet intentions. Specifically the US must contain the spread of Soviet communism, while pursuing the moral and political high ground, until such time as the Soviet government abandons its expansionist policy.

GARDNER's study represents revisionist scholarship that sought to explain the Cold War as the result of the United States' efforts to control international politics and economics. His work includes ten case studies of prominent American leaders and how their failure to offer economic aid to the USSR, a deal on atomic energy, as well as guarantees regarding German rearmament soured relations among the superpowers. Gardner is particularly critical of US efforts in the creation of the Bretton Woods system as leading to animosity between the US and USSR. The reader is left with the curious question of how international politics would have been different in the post World War II period if these "errors" had been avoided.

The long-accepted tradition of explaining the Cuban missile crisis through the application of Graham Allison's rational actor and bureaucratic politics models is challenged by GARTHOFF. His study is based on a 1987 Harvard conference of Soviet and American scholars and information later released in the Soviet Union. It specifically challenges tendencies to view the superpower crisis as under the control of Soviet and American national leaderships and the negotiation of a solution as the product of Kennedy and Khrushchev's reasonableness. Garthoff's study is essential reading for those seeking a critical evaluation of the long-accepted decision-making paradigm.

The idea of the Cold War as a competition between democratic and totalitarian empires is the focus of GADDIS' interpretation of international politics from the 1940s into the 1980s. Perhaps the most impressive feature of this study is a 36-page bibliography of American and Soviet materials on the Cold War, most of the Soviet documents being unavailable only a few years ago. In the context of Gaddis' thesis the Cold War is reviewed with emphasis on the division of the planet into respective alliances, the role of nuclear weapons, and major events like the Cuban missile crisis. The study is limited by the absence of any examination of key personalities, like Mikhail Gorbachev and Ronald Reagan, or events, like the shooting down of Korean Airline 007, the deployment of the Euromissiles, or the reunification of Germany, which occurred after 1980.

Despite its age, HOLLOWAY remains the authority on the Soviet decision-making process regarding weapon production. It specifically examines the historical experiences, policy objectives, and production institutions that guided decisions to create and produce selected weapons from the founding of the Soviet state into the 1980s. The book highlights interrelationship of Soviet governmental, military and industrial organizations in creating the nuclear bomb as well as interpretations

of American activities. Attention is also devoted to Soviet thinking on fighting a nuclear war in Europe between the superpowers, as well as the influence of nuclear weapons in conducting foreign policy. Although dated by the limited availability of Soviet materials, this book remains useful in terms of demystifying the arms creation process.

By examining the role of personality in the decision-making process, in this case that of Dean Acheson, McLELLAN offers insight into American foreign policy during the early Cold War. His study is particularly useful for the account given of the origin of the Truman Doctrine, Marshall Plan, the defeat of the Nationalist Chinese on the mainland, the Korean War, and European rearmament in the 1950s. McLellan's identification of Acheson's arrogance and realism, and his views of their influence on American foreign policy as well as their conflict with Congressional and public opinion are noteworthy.

The international geographic, economic, and military changes that occurred since 1945 are the focus of PREWITT. It notes that the Cold War circumvented the UN Security Council by substituting American and Soviet commitments to their alliances and client states as the means of maintaining security. Thus conflicts were restrained by the superpowers in order to preserve their status in this zero-sum game. In so doing, the Cold War masked changes in the international system. Once ended, these changes became apparent as regional and national conflicts previously suppressed by the superpowers erupted. This book is recommended for those who view strengthening the Security Council as a necessity for the postwar order.

SCHLESINGER's 1967 article remains a classic example of the orthodox interpretation of the Cold War, ascribing its creation to the conflict between Soviet and American values and desires. The conflict is judged by Schlesinger to have been inevitable due to the contrast between American universalism and the Soviet desire for spheres of influence. The reader is thus left with the strong sense that until one nation succumbed to the power of the other, there was no meaningful way to resolve the Cold War short of a thermonuclear exchange.

YERGIN is a useful account of the organization of the American Government to fight the Cold War. The nation-state level of analysis is used to examine the ideological, political, and economical conflicts between the US and USSR and how they motivated American leaders to engage in creating the national security state. Documents like NSC-68 are examined for their interpretations of Soviet motives and how they influenced American decision makers. Although primarily concerned with the years 1945–50, Yergin offers an excellent explanation of the establishment of the CIA and the American military buildup.

Soviet scholarship on the Cold War had been constrained by ideological and state considerations until ZUBOK & PLESHAKOV published their groundbreaking work based on a combination of Soviet and American materials, including interviews with former Soviet officials. It argues that Marxist ideology and traditional Russian messianism alternated to energize Kremlin leaders who saw the Soviet mission as one designed to save the world from American imperialism. In this idealistic struggle the authors show members of the Soviet leadership like Stalin and Khrushchev, as well as Molotov, Zhdanov, Beria, and Malenkov, whose actions suggest a degree of intellectual if not moral depravity in forging a response to the perceived American encirclement of their nation. Although this study is fascinating, it is limited by its conclusion in 1962 due to the replacement of the bipolar Cold War world with a multipolar one. Valuable information on the Brezhnev period and the eventual Soviet collapse is not examined.

JEFFREY L. PREWITT

See also Leonid Brezhnev, Nikita Khrushchev

Collectivism

Buchanan, Allen, *Ethics, Efficiency, and the Market*, Totowa, New Jersey: Rowman and Allanheld, and Oxford: Clarendon Press, 1985

Gilbert, Margaret, *On Social Facts*, Princeton, New Jersey: Princeton University Press, 1989

Hayek, F.A., *The Road to Serfdom*, Chicago: University of Chicago Press, and London: Routledge, 1944

Hayek, F.A. (editor), *Collectivist Economic Planning: Critical Studies on the Possibility of Socialism*, London: Routledge, 1935; reprinted New York: Kelley, 1975

O'Neill, John, *Modes of Individualism and Collectivism*, London: Heinemann, and New York: St Martin's Press, 1973

Pennock, J. Roland, *Democratic Political Theory*, Princeton, New Jersey: Princeton University Press, 1979

Roemer, John E., *Egalitarian Perspectives: Essays in Philosophical Economics*, Cambridge and New York: Cambridge University Press, 1994

Skidelsky, Robert, *The Road from Serfdom: The Economic and Political Consequences of the End of Communism*, London and New York: Penguin, 1996

Taylor, Charles, *Philosophical Arguments*, Cambridge, Massachusetts: Harvard University Press, 1995

Taylor, Fred M., and Oskar Lange, *On the Economic Theory of Socialism*, edited by Benjamin E. Lippincott, Minneapolis: University of Minnesota Press, 1938

"Collectivism" carries political, economic, and methodological connotations. In politics, collectivism refers to regimes in which the state directs social life in the name of a "common good" that is construed as partly or fully independent of the interests of individuals, who are viewed apart from the community they comprise. Within economics, collectivism asserts the efficiency and desirability of centralized economic planning. Collectivism in either or both of these first two senses is normally assumed to require active and extensive state intervention in social and economic life. As a methodological view, collectivism refers to the general assumption that collectivities may, for the purposes of social analysis, be regarded as entities or agents in their own right – in other words, "methodological collectivists" (sometimes called "holists") reject the view that all claims about social phenomena are reducible to claims about individuals. These three views overlap at many points, but they should be kept distinct. All of the works listed here focus on at least one of these views, but not all of them address all three.

In all of its forms, collectivism has always aroused opposition and it must be stressed that more often than not the word appears in the literature as a term of abuse. HAYEK (1944) is a good example of this. This work is the classic statement of the argument that any concession to collectivism, whether in politics or economics, must ultimately undermine the institutions of a free society. Hayek (1944) argues that collectivism involves at least three errors: first, that economic planners are able to determine efficient economic distributions better than the free market; second, that it is possible to specify a determinate social goal for the sake of which the resources of society are to be "consciously directed" by a collectivist state; third, a failure to recognize that extensive coercion and repression is required to fulfil any collectivist programme.

As its title suggests, SKIDELSKY is a recent contribution to this debate from a strongly Hayekian perspective. Skidelsky claims that the struggle between liberalism and collectivism has been the defining controversy of 20th-century history, and the book sets out to show how recent events (the collapse of the Soviet Union, the revival of neoliberal political economy in the West) vindicate the predictions of Hayek (1944). These claims remain extremely controversial, but as long as one keeps the Hayekian background in mind Skidelsky is none the less a reliable resource for those seeking to grasp the issues raised by collectivism. Chapter 2, in particular, is a valuable discussion of the nature of collectivism, albeit from a strongly critical point of view.

The arguments of Hayek (1944) and Skidelsky address the political implications of collectivism most directly, but both also allude to the economic and methodological aspects of collectivism. On the economic front, the relevant arguments are helpfully collected in HAYEK (1935), a collection of essays discussing the serious problems of calculation confronting central economic planning. Hayek (1935) includes an introduction and concluding chapter by Hayek himself. The latter is particularly important for its emphasis on the practical (as opposed to purely mathematical) difficulties involved in making reliable economic calculations for the purposes of central planning. Hayek also includes Ludwig von Mises's "Economic Calculation in the Socialist Commonwealth", a brief but important statement of his argument that collectivism precludes "rational economic activity".

TAYLOR & LANGE is a useful source for the "collectivist' or "socialist" side of the economic debate in which Hayek (1935) is engaged. In a helpful (sympathetic) introduction to Taylor & Lange, Benjamin Lippincott surveys the relevant issues and sketches some of the background and context to the socialist calculation debate.

Recent writers who remain sympathetic to collectivism as an economic project tend to focus on the notion of market socialism. In this sort of account, the market is understood as an instrument of economic planning rather than its replacement. The last chapter of BUCHANAN relates market socialism to the socialist calculation debate. In the body of the book, Buchanan lucidly explores some of the moral and political issues that surround assessments of economic efficiency. Buchanan's discussion is particularly valuable in the light of the tendency among economists to ignore or downplay issues of morality and distributive justice.

ROEMER provides a more detailed and technical discussion

of the theory of market socialism. Although Roemer's discussions are technically sophisticated, the main points of the final three chapters (on public ownership, market socialism, and the future of the socialist ideal) are accessible to those without a background in economic methodology. Roemer also includes a large bibliography containing helpful references to the expanding literature dealing with market socialism.

Hayek and Von Mises were not only concerned about collectivism as an economic issue – they also published strong criticisms of collectivism as a method of analysis. This methodological debate has tended to die down in recent years, but the essays collected in O'NEILL indicate the scope of the relevant issues. The collection includes pieces by Hayek and his fellow methodological individualist (and friend) Karl Popper, whose *Open Society and its Enemies* (1945) argued (among other things) that methodological collectivism blinded philosophers like Plato and Hegel to the dangers of totalitarianism. However, the other essays in O'Neill deal mainly with the philosophical rather than the political implications of methodological collectivism.

Although she might well reject the description, GILBERT defends a view that could reasonably be regarded as a form of methodological collectivism. In a rewarding discussion, Gilbert claims that in order to make sense of collective or social phenomena, we need the notion of a "plural subject". A social group exists, on this view, to the extent that it can be a "we" with its own will, goals, and even beliefs. Gilbert rejects the view that such collective phenomena can be regarded as merely the sum or "resultants" of individual wills, goals, or beliefs. Her final chapter serves as a useful summary of, and guide, to the rich discussion contained in the body of the book.

As Skidelsky points out, democracy seems to strongly imply collectivism, at least to the extent that democratic government is regarded as the instrument of a "collective will" disclosed by voting. It is unsurprising, then, that the third chapter of PENNOCK – a work on democratic theory – should provide one of the most helpful discussions of the methodological and political aspects of the distinction between individualism and collectivism.

Chapters 7 and 10 of TAYLOR attack methodological and political individualism from a holist and communitarian point of view (see the discussion in this volume under liberalism). These chapters offer a sensitive and careful account of the relations between what Taylor calls (in the second of the two essays) questions of social "ontology" and questions of political "advocacy". They also help us to see how the current debate between liberals and communitarians relates to the broader, older, and more enduring, divide between individualism and collectivism.

COLIN BIRD

See also Communitarianism, Liberalism, Market socialism

Collectivization

Conquest, Robert, *The Harvest of Sorrow: Soviet Collectivization and the Terror-Famine*, London: Hutchinson, and New York: Oxford University Press, 1986

Erlich, Alexander, *The Soviet Industrialization Debate, 1924–1928*, Cambridge, Massachusetts: Harvard University Press, 1960

Fainsod, Merle, *Smolensk under Soviet Rule*, Cambridge, Massachusetts: Harvard University Press, 1958

Hindus, Maurice, *Red Bread*, New York: Cape and Smith, 1931; reprinted as *Red Bread: Collectivization in a Russian Village*, Bloomington: Indiana University Press, 1988

Kopelev, Lev, *The Education of a True Believer*, New York: Harper and Row, 1980

Livi-Bacci, Massimo, "On the Human Costs of Collectivization in the Soviet Union", *Population and Development Review*, 19/4 (1993): 743–66

Nove, Alec, *The Soviet Economic System*, 3rd edition, London and Boston: Allen and Unwin, 1986

Pospielovsky, Dimitry, "The 'Link System' in Soviet Agriculture", *Soviet Studies*, 21/4 (1970): 411–35

Simonov, N.S., "'Strengthen the Defence of the Land of the Soviets': The 1927 'War Alarm' and its Consequences", *Europe–Asia Studies*, 48/8 (1996): 1355–64

Viola, Lynne, *The Best Sons of the Fatherland: Workers in the Vanguard of Soviet Collectivization*, New York: Oxford University Press, 1987

Wegren, Stephen K., "Dilemmas of Agrarian Reform in the Soviet Union", *Soviet Studies*, 44/1 (1992): 3–36

Yanov, Alexander, *The Drama of the Soviet 1960's: A Lost Reform*, Berkeley: Institute of International Studies, University of California, 1984

The quest for economic development has been a common theme under Russia's tsars, the communists, and now the democrats. Collectivization offered the communists the means to mobilize the peasants in the countryside to meet the agricultural targets set in Moscow, to establish a link between production in the countryside and cities, and to ensure the political reliability of rural areas. In the process of doing this, however, the ability to produce crop yields comparable with those of the West was eliminated. As a result, the private plot of land became the mainstay of Soviet agricultural production. Soviet leaders did not abandon collectivization and, beginning with Brezhnev, they sought to stabilize the relationship between rural and urban environments by increasing state investments to collective farms without changing their nature. Not until Mikhail Gorbachev were efforts renewed to force reform in collective farms by making them more sensitive to the needs of the Soviet population.

The value of CONQUEST's book emanates from the thesis that collectivization was the product of a lack of consensus over economic policy and a struggle for power within the Communist Party after Lenin. His study is packed with statistics detailing the human cost of collectivization in the Ukraine. He concludes that kulaks and nationalists were targeted due to their ability to resist the Soviet regime, and takes the view that such political and ideological blunders forced the Soviet Union to rely upon the small plots of land allocated to Soviet citizens as the means for making up the agricultural shortfall.

A contextual analysis of Soviet debate economic debates in the 1920s is provided by ERLICH. The positions taken by members of the Soviet leadership over how to develop the

Soviet economy in the aftermath of Lenin's death are clearly delineated, as is the failure of Marx to provide a blueprint for transforming a backward economy. A central focus is given to the role played by the failure of the revolution to materialize in the West and the bureaucratic infighting that saw the eventual triumph of Stalin's doctrine of "socialism in one country". This is an essential book for those seeking to understand the origins of collectivization in the leadership crisis.

Prior to the collapse of the Soviet Union, FAINSOD was the premier scholarly analysis on Soviet collectivization, based on Soviet documents captured by American forces from the Germans. These files, which covered the period 1917–39, revealed the central role of the *obkom* and *raion* secretaries in establishing Soviet authority in the countryside, their management of agricultural production, and the conditions under which they were promoted or purged. As Fainsod wrote:

> Through the kolkhozes it (the Party) reshaped the production pattern of the Smolensk countryside to serve state needs rather than the peasant's convenience, and siphoned off the output of the peasants to meet the rapidly growing demands of the new industrial centers. (p.279)

His work is important because for decades it was the sole Western study based on Soviet economic data.

According to HINDUS' study, based on eyewitness accounts of village life in Russia under the tsars and the communists, collectivization established Soviet power. The writings in this book are rich in anecdotal material that breathes life into an overall picture of official Soviet state policy for restructuring the countryside. Among the changes that resulted from the strengthening of the Communist Party's control over the countryside were the decline of the Orthodox Church and improvements in the lives of women. The reader should be prepared for some self-serving commentary, like that which holds that the high cost of collectivization was necessary in order for the USSR to industrialize and to defeat Nazi Germany. Likewise, as an émigré returning to the Soviet Union after the overthrow of the tsars, Hindus offers limited information on communist tactics in collectivizing the countryside.

A useful primary account of the rise of the Bolsheviks and collectivization is provided by KOPELEV, who as a member of the intelligentsia was one of those responsible for implementing agricultural policies prior to the World War II. Nowhere was this more intense than when the forces of collectivization, of which Kopelev was a member, met resistance from the kulaks. His account is especially interesting, given the anecdotal accounts of popular reactions to collectivization, Stalin's article on "Dizziness from Success", and the grain confiscation of 1933. Reading this eyewitness account, one is left with a strong sense of the progress and change brought about by the Bolsheviks and of how it appealed to those striving for a more egalitarian state.

The human costs of collectivization are addressed by LIVI-BACCI in his 1993 article, which utilizes population statistics from Soviet census reports of the 1920s and 1930s. By controlling for the normal number of deaths and births, Livi-Bacci is able to project deaths of between six to thirteen million for

the period 1926 through 1937 as the result of forced grain procurements and collectivization, greater emphasis on heavy industrialization, and a weakening of state programmes to provide for the hungry and destitute.

NOVE, who was one of the early pioneers in the study of Soviet economic policy, remains a useful source for exploring the central role of Stalin in the effort to industrialize and collectivize the USSR. Chapter five is particularly relevant, as the agricultural focus is on the *kolkhozy* (collective farm), *sovkhozy* (state farms), and private plots, and their significance in terms of state planning and support, production, and adherence to communist ideology. The problems of measurement encountered by scholars in their study of Soviet agriculture, due to differences in political systems and inadequacies of statistical measurement, are explored.

The conflict between economic need and political control is the focus of POSPIELOVSKY, who examines the rise of the "link system" in the aftermath of the poor harvest of 1963. Although private ownership of land remained prohibited, the goal of this Khrushchev era reform was to personalize the "link" between the land and the peasant so as to encourage the production of food. However by 1970 official policy was to de-emphasize the link system in favour of the traditional collective farm and increased state subsidies.

SIMONOV holds that collectivization was justified by the Soviet leadership as being necessary to motivate and organize the Soviet people in light of the war scare of the late 1920s. Collectivization ensured the political and economic reliability of the peasantry, and thus provided the means for strengthening the armed forces. His study thus offers another focus point to the economic debates of the 1920s and how they were influenced by foreign affairs.

VIOLA exemplifies the new generation of Western research based on Soviet archival sources. Her work fills a gap in Western studies of collectivization, as the focus is on the skilled urban workers, veterans, and party activists who entered the Soviet countryside during the First Five-Year Plan:

> . . . to represent the interests of Moscow against rural officialdom perceived to be incompetent, socially alien, and politically suspect (and, in so doing, to transform that officialdom by way of purge and recruitment of new cadres), and to reorganize peasant agriculture by bringing the industrial revolution to the countryside. (pp.3–4)

Serious attention needs to be given to Viola's discussion on conducting research in Russia and on the original sources available relating to collectivization.

WEGREN is a policy analysis of Soviet agriculture, from Khrushchev to Gorbachev. Its thesis is that "patterns of (agricultural) intervention (by the government) reflect leadership values *vis-à-vis* the peasantry, elite considerations of political stability, and the ability to build bases of support for a set of given policies"(p.3). Once Khrushchev had removed terror, a socialist market system emerged in which the need to produce more food for the urban areas was counterbalanced by a need to motivate the peasantry. The prospects of political and social instability produced by attempts to overhaul production outweighed any benefits. Wegren is an important source for those seeking to move beyond the role of personalities in Soviet collectivization.

YANOV provides a useful account of attempts to reform Soviet agriculture in the 1960s through the adoption of the link system. The fundamental idea is that "the function of the artel is economic; the function of the kolkhoz is political. One is oriented toward production; the other, toward control" (p.21). (The *artel* was a communitarian form of peasant self-organization, or producers' collective.) This study focuses on experimentation with the link system during the early Brezhnev period, and its subsequent rejection in favour of the collective farm system. An excellent discussion is provided of Ivan Khudenko's role in establishing the link system, and of the decline in Soviet agricultural production despite expansion of the cultivated area.

JEFFREY L. PREWITT

See also Nikita Krushchev, Leonid Brezhnev

Colonialism

Adas, Michael, *Machines as the Measure of Men: Science, Technology, and Ideologies of Western Dominance*, Ithaca, New York: Cornell University Press, 1989

Arneil, Barbara, *John Locke and America: The Defense of English Colonialism*, Oxford: Clarendon Press, and New York: Oxford University Press, 1996

Asad, Talal (editor), *Anthropology and the Colonial Encounter*, New York: Humanities Press, and London: Ithaca Press, 1973

Bremen, Jan van and Akitoshi Shimizu, editors, *Anthropology and Colonialism in Asia and Oceania*, Richmond, Surrey: Curzon, 1999

Brockway, Lucile H., *Science and Colonial Expansion: The Role of the British Royal Botanical Gardens*, New York: Academic Press, 1979

Comaroff, John and Jean Comaroff, *Ethnography and the Historical Imagination*, Boulder, Colorado: Westview Press, 1992

Dirks, Nicholas B. (editor), *Colonialism and Culture*, Ann Arbor: University of Michigan Press, 1992

Fanon, Frantz, *The Wretched of the Earth*, New York: Grove Press, and London: MacGibbon and Kee, 1965 (French edition 1961)

Ferro, Marc, *Colonization: A Global History*, London and New York: Routledge, 1997

Gouda, Frances, *Dutch Culture Overseas: Colonial Practice in the Netherlands Indies, 1900–1942*, Amsterdam: Amsterdam University Press, 1995

Graham, A.J., *Colony and Mother City in Ancient Greece*, Manchester: Manchester University Press, and New York: Barnes and Noble, 1964; 2nd edition, Chicago: Ares, 1983

Hobbes, Thomas, *Leviathan*, edited by C. B. Macpherson, Harmondsworth: Penguin, 1968 (originally published 1651)

Kat Angelino, A.D.A. de, *Colonial Policy*, 2 vols, The Hague: Martinus Nijhoff, and Chicago: University of Chicago Press, 1931

Lach, Donald F. and Edwin J. Van Kley, *Asia in the Making of Europe*, 3 vols, Chicago: University of Chicago Press, 1965–93, 3 vols

Locke, John, *Second Treatise of Government*, edited by C.B. Macpherson, Indianapolis: Hackett, 1980 (originally published 1690)

Majumdar, R.C., *Hindu Colonies in the Far East*, 2nd edition, Calcutta: Mukhopadhyay, 1963

Money, J.W.B., *Java, or, How to Manage a Colony*, 2 vols, Singapore, Oxford and New York: Oxford University Press, 1985 (originally published 1861)

Prakash, Gyan (editor), *After Colonialism: Imperial Histories and Postcolonial Displacements*, Princeton, New Jersey: Princeton University Press, 1995

Said, Edward W., *Orientalism*, New York: Pantheon, and London: Routledge, 1978; with new afterword, New York: Vintage, 1994, Harmondsworth: Penguin, 1995

Stoler, Ann Laura, *Race and the Education of Desire: Foucault's History of Sexuality and the Colonial Order of Things*, Durham, North Carolina: Duke University Press, 1995

Wallerstein, Immanuel, *The Modern World-System*, vol. 1: *Capitalist Agriculture and the Origins of the European World-Economy in the Sixteenth Century*, New York and London: Academic Press, 1974

Wallerstein, Immanuel, *The Modern World-System*, vol. 2: *Mercantilism and the Consolidation of the European World-Economy, 1600–1750*, New York and London: Academic Press, 1980

Wolf, Eric R., *Europe and the People without History*, Berkeley: University of California, 1982

Colonialism is not a single or unified phenomenon. Its instigators have not always been modern Westerners. Colonialism has sometimes, but not always, involved the transplantation of large numbers of people, either in accordance with or against their wills, from one place to another somewhat distant location. In some cases, the indigenes remained the majority of the colony's population; in others, they rapidly became minorities in their own home lands; in some places, they remain minorities in a country now deemed independent and no longer a colony. Nor has colonialism always implied direct administrative control.

GRAHAM remains the best account of ancient Greek colonialism, especially relations between mother cities and their offspring: cities in their own right. "The foundation of a city was a sacred act, sacred enough to be performed by a god" (p.26). Colonists consulted the Delphic oracle, took fire from the sacred fire of the mother city to the hearth of the new city and worship their founder god. The new city was not an administrative extension of the mother city nor were its populace and land part of the mother city. Relations were not always good; Thucydides traces the origins of the Peloponnesian Wars to a dispute between a mother city, Corinth, and one of its colonies, Corcyra. Still, "Thucydides was not alone in regarding colonies and mother cities as natural allies and unnatural enemies" (p.86).

MAJUMDAR contends that large numbers of Hindus began moving to Southeast Asia in the first centuries of the common era, drawn by the prospect of wealth and spices. There can be little doubt of Indian influence upon Southeast Asia or the interconnectedness of various Southeast Asian polities over long periods of time; whether Majumdar (p.37ff) is correct in asserting that the Chola of South India invaded Southeast Asia during the 11th century, destroying the Sailendra, is less clear. As an assertion of India's national greatness, originally put together during India's colonial and nationalist period, Majumdar's work is both interesting history and an historically interesting event. He originally planned five volumes, but only published the first three; the second edition shortens and reorganizes those three volumes.

Many would not include the ancient Greek or so-called "Hindu" examples under the rubric of colonialism.

FERRO purports to provide a global history, but takes up neither of the examples above. He also largely ignores the Dutch. He does discuss Russian, Arab, Turkish, and Japanese expansion during the last 500 years, although too briefly. Colonized people(s) do appear as agents in their own right.

Ferro supplements the generally superior accounts of WOLF and WALLERSTEIN (1974 and 1980). They seek to place colonialism within the expansion of the European capitalist world system. BROCKWAY shows the importance of botanical study centrally administered from Kew Gardens to the transplantation of cinchona (the source of quinine), rubber, and sisal and, thereby, the expansion of British imperial endeavour.

For SAID, orientalism was and is at once (a) an academic discipline or confluence of academic disciplines, (b) "a style of thought based on an ontological and epistemological distinction between 'the Orient' and (most of the time) 'the Occident'" (p.2) which feeds the general intellectual life, and (c) from the 18th century on, the corporate institution for Occidental dealings with the Orient. Orientalism was and remains an idea, a created and enduring body of theory, with consequences more than a tissue of lies. It also has specifiable cultural locations: British and French engagement with India and the Levant. Said, thus, ignores the Dutch, their Indies, and their deliberate application of ethnology to colonial administration.

FANON brings us to the nub of the recent experiences; colonialism joins the colonized and the colonizers in a violence which creates them both and in which they know each other. As a part of this violence, "The native is declared insensible to ethics; he represents not only the absence of values, but the negation of values" (pp.33–4). This Manichean division (colonizers as good, colonized as evil and, presumably vice versa) justifies the violence while giving rise to various sorts of mental disorder. Practically, Fanon advises the colonized neither to blame nor to envy Europe, for the colonized "must work out new concepts, and try to set afoot a new man" (p.255) once they undertake "the abolition of one zone [the white settlers town], its burial in the depths of the earth or its expulsion from the country" (p.33) or decolonization.

Colonialism, as described by Fanon, differs markedly from that described by Graham. Early liberals, HOBBES for example, were well aware of two possible models. Both involved numbers of men:

> sent out from the Common-wealth, under a Conductor or Governour, to inhabit a Forraign Country, either formerly voyd of Inhabitants, or made voyd then, by warre. And when a Colony is setled, they are either a Common-wealth of themselves, discharged of their subjection to their Soveraign that sent them . . . in which case the Common-wealth from which they went was called their Metropolis . . . , and requires no more of them . . . ; or else they remain united to their Metropolis, as were the Colonies of the people of *Rome*; and then they are no more Common-wealths themselves, but Provinces, and parts of the Common-wealth that sent them. (pp.301–2)

Liberal colonialism, while seeking those commodities necessary for the sustenance of the commonwealth yet foreign to the metropolis, follows the Roman administrative model. Once a territory and people were incorporated into the administratively unified commonwealth – "a constitution of *Mine*, and *Thine*, and *His*; that is to say, in one word Propriety" – p.296), all resistance to the sovereign would legitimately, according to Hobbes, be understood as civil war.

LOCKE reconstitutes the void by transmogrifying of the locus of the commodity's value to human labour from nature (Hobbes's "two breasts of our common Mother: Land and Sea" – p.295). Locke contends "in the beginning all the world was *America*" (p.29, §49), that is a vast waste given by God "to men in common" (p.18, §26). Men were also given "reason to make use of it [i.e. the world] to the best advantage of life, and convenience" (p.18, §26). "[I]t cannot be supposed he [God] meant it [the world] should always remain common and uncultivated. He gave it to the use of the industrious and rational"(p.21, §34). Portions of this common world become the property of individuals (part of these same individuals and separate from the common) through their labour. That Amerindians lived in the woods of North America was not an impediment to America being colonized as, Locke contended, they had left the woods an uncultivated waste. Note that Locke's argument about property does not justify colonial control on the grounds of conquest.

Locke is often read against the background of English politics. ARNEIL begins with an account of Locke's knowledge of North America gleaned from the travel books in his library, arguing that, for Locke, the state of nature was not an artificial construct necessary for polemical reasons but America and natural man Amerindians. She breaks new ground by drawing "links between the colonial debates [in the current US] over property, Locke's involvement in such debates [as polemicist and as member of the Commission on Trade and Plantations], the development of his theory of property . . . and the ultimate implications of his thought for the aboriginal peoples of America" (Arneil, pp.15–16).

She stresses Jefferson's affinity to and knowledge of Locke as well as Jefferson's conclusion that "natural man must eventually succumb to civil society and the hunter's life to that of the farmer" (p.20). "Both [man in civil society and natural man, for Locke] have the capacity for reason, the latter has simply chosen not to exercise his" (p.202). In a Lockean world, this purported choice not to exercise reason assumes moral dimensions.

ADAS has made two noteworthy contributions. The first illuminates a series of consequences of this purported choice not exercising the capacity for reason. Adas examines how influential achievements in material culture "ha[ve] become, especially those relating to technology and science, in shaping European perceptions of non-Western peoples" (p.3).

He traces discussions by Europeans of other people's science and technology during the 15th century, in the 18th century when these forms of practical knowledge began to play significant roles in policy formation towards China and India, again in the 19th century when scientific and technical capability became a pervasive measure of human worth, and finally during the 20th century as marked by an American ideology of development. His study focuses on sub-Saharan Africa, India, and China as seen by the British and the French, "the foremost imperial powers in the nineteenth century" (p.10); he ignores the Dutch and their colonies.

Adas' second contribution, his notion of the contest state and the fate of the political styles of resistance associated therewith in the face of militarily efficient colonial administrations, appears in a significant volume edited by DIRKS, which also includes essays by Mitchell, Stoler, and Prakash.

Dutch colonialism and the Dutch East Indies, in particular, have not always been neglected. MONEY journeyed from Calcutta to Java in the years immediately following the mutiny, and was surprised by what he found: "Our [the British] experiment has failed, the Dutch one has succeeded" (volume 2, p.258). The Dutch colony was more profitable, more stable, more peaceful than British India, despite India's larger area, and larger, more tractable and more civilized population. "The painful conviction, therefore, arises, that the difference is due more to the respective systems of administration than to any natural equality" (volume 2, p.250). Dutch administration maintained the old nobles in power, making "government by an equally turbulent, tyrannical, and extortionate aristocracy, under European supervision, a blessing instead of a curse to their country" (volume 2, p.256) while providing commoners with their own hereditary lords. Money thinks to provide an analysis of this profitable administration of colonies to his colleagues in India. Alfred Russel Wallace recommended Money's quickly translated book in *The Malay Archipelago*. The consequences of Dutch colonialism for Javanese were the subject of the first great colonial novel: Multatuli's *Max Havelaar*. KAT ANGELINO, a Dutch colonial official, provides an extensive history and description of as well as a justification for colonial policy.

Fanon argued that Europe was a creation of the colonies. LACH & VAN KLEY's survey of Asia's role in the development of European arts and sciences, especially during the 17th century, can only be termed monumental. GOUDA, in a series of interrelated essays, has shown much of how Dutch culture was reformed in colonial milieus and, so reformed, brought back to the Netherlands by the ex-colonials. Her account begins and ends with a discussion of a nostalgia for the Indies found among strata of Dutch society, among whom she counts her parents. Gouda's essay on the education of Javanese and Balinese girls also contributes to understanding how Europe entered the consciousness of some indigenes as a matter to be emulated, or what COMAROFF & COMAROFF, writing about missionary education and the Southern Tswana, tellingly call "the colonization of consciousness and the consciousness of colonization" (p.236).

STOLER has produced perhaps the most significant recent body of work on the liberal colonial interface. She reads Foucault's *The History of Sexuality: An Introduction* critically, taking full notice of his elision of the imperial context of "the normalizing bourgeois project in which racisms have developed" (Stoler p.92) and that context's relation to "those who were 'white but not quite'-mixed blood children, European-educated colonized elites, and even déclassé European colonials themselves" (p.93) understood as interior enemies of the state. Not content with critique, she seeks ways to use Foucault's thinking without replicating either Foucault's elision of the colonies or colonial discourse. She observes French Indochina and the Netherlands Indies, contending that "[c]olonial agents of the state and quasi-state institutions . . . debated issues of milieu, habitus and the shaping of sentiment with studied care" (p.207). This studied care allows us to understand better "why children's sensibilities and adult's sentiments" were crucial "to [the] making of race" (p.207).

PRAKASH notes that "the tenuousness of colonial power bears testimony to the pressure exercised silently by the subordinated" and hence to "sources of knowledge and agency simmering beneath the calm surface of colonial history and historiography" (p.4). The contributions in this volume, including Bhabha and Said, continue the analysis of liberal colonialism while looking towards both the continuing effects of empire and a decolonized world.

The preceding works ignore Japanese colonialism almost entirely and treat ethnography, understood here as the study of the colonized, sporadically at best. BREMEN & SHIMIZU's volume, following ASAD's influence, provides a comparison of Japanese and Dutch colonialism and of the ethnographic traditions which developed within and contributed to these respective colonial milieus. Several essays will repay repeated close reading, among them Bremen and Shimizu's introduction and Ben-Ari's afterword. The bibliographies are extensive.

GERALD SULLIVAN

Commercial law

Arden, Mary, "Time for an English Commercial Code?", *Cambridge Law Journal*, 56 (1997): 516

Cranston, Ross (editor), *Making Commercial Law: Essays in Honour of Roy Goode*, Oxford: Clarendon Press, and New York: Oxford University Press, 1997

Goode, R.M., *Commercial Law*, 2nd edition, Harmondsworth: Penguin, 1995

Howells, Geraint G. (editor), *European Business Law*, Aldershot, Hampshire: Dartmouth, 1996

Sealy, L.S. and R.J.A. Hooley (editors), *Text and Materials in Commercial Law*, London: Butterworths, 1994

Worthington, Sarah, *Proprietary Interests in Commercial Transactions*, Oxford: Clarendon Press, 1996

The first difficulty in identifying a suitable bibliography for commercial law is to decide where the parameters of the subject are to be drawn, for there are many different works purporting to deal with some or even all of the field, but the scope that they attribute to the subject differs widely. For present purposes commercial law is taken as being the branch of law that deals with the contractual and tortious rights and duties arising out of situations in which the involvement of at least one party is business-related. Regulatory aspects of the more broadly based subject of business law are therefore excluded.

Within that definition, GOODE is recognized, at the present time, as the leading text on commercial law as a whole. The major problems of scholarship in this area are to decide what falls within the scope of the subject and then to relate in a coherent way the various aspects of the topic. Goode takes a broad view of material to be included, covering the standard topics of sale, together with financing, as well as including some interesting material on the very important topic of dispute resolution – he rightly sees that the acid test of a legal system is not in the merit of its legal rules but in the efficiency and effectiveness of its dispute-resolution procedures. The book is notable for the lucidity and rigour of the analysis at a technical level, although there is very little attempt to produce any integrated theory that would link together the apparently disparate topics covered.

WORTHINGTON declares the influence of Goode, but represents a more modern approach to the topic in that it accepts expressly the need to confront the relationship between proprietary and contractual rights, something acknowledged elsewhere in Goode's work, but not fully developed in his textbook. Worthington takes this relationship (and at times conflict) as the starting point for an attempt to identify more broadly based principles that can be seen as linking together the strands of commercial law.

CRANSTON's edited collection of essays is valuable because it represents a relatively recent survey of the field of commercial law as a whole. Perhaps the strongest point to emerge from a perusal of these essays is the essentially international nature of commercial law at the present time. The subject is one which has European aspects, which is the subject of numerous international conventions, and which, even in the absence of formal transjurisdictional recognition, inevitably involves the law and practice of more than one country. The emphasis of the collection is towards the international trade aspects of the subject, to a degree that perhaps overemphasizes its importance within the subject of commercial law as a whole. The relationship between what might be called "pure" commercial law, and the linked subjects of corporate law and the law of insolvency, can also be observed in some of the essays.

SEALY & HOOLEY follow a well-established tradition in legal scholarship by collecting together relevant cases, statutes, and other materials into a single volume linked by a commentary. The value of such products depends essentially on the merit of the choice (and editing) of material and the interest and insight shown in the commentary. Sealy & Hooley follow a fairly traditional path in the selection of their material, giving pride of place to sale of goods (domestic and international) before giving a nod in the direction of financing techniques, insurance, and insolvency. The commentary reflects their concern both with a rigorous analysis of underlying property concepts, and with the application of the subject in a practical way.

The collection of essays edited by HOWELLS is perhaps the most interesting and most closely integrated exploration to date of the vital importance of Europe in the development of commercial law in the period since 1985. The focus of the book is specifically on the role of the EC as a promoter of developments in this area, both through formal harmonization programmes, notably in employment, insurance, and banking, and through the gradual convergence of legal systems and cultures within the member states. The various contributors demonstrate the ways in which, in their respective fields, Europe is now at the centre of the emergence of the commercial law of the 21st century.

ARDEN, who is both a High Court judge and the former Chair of the English Law Commission, writes about the arguments for and against the codification of English commercial law, a scheme in which the Law Commission has taken an active part. She describes the unhappy history of attempts at codification of branches of English law, to which successive governments have retained a rather surprising hostility. Although she recognizes the dangers of inaccurate codification and of fossilization by codification, on balance she supports the idea as bringing to the law a clarity and simplification that ought to be welcomed by all interested parties.

ANDREW MCGEE

Common heritage of mankind

Buzan, Barry, *Seabed Politics*, New York: Praeger, 1976

Grolin, Jesper, "The Deep Seabed: A North–South Perspective" in *Toward a New International Marine Order*, edited by Finn Laursen, The Hague: Nijhoff, 1982

Luard, Evan, *The Control of the Sea-Bed: A New International Issue*, London: Heinemann, and New York: Taplinger, 1974

Ogley, Roderick, *Internationalizing the Seabed*, Aldershot, Hampshire: Gower, 1984

Ogley, Roderick, "The UN and the Global Commons", *IDS Bulletin*, 26/4 (October 1995): 74–83

Pardo, Arvid, "Ocean Space, Seabed, Common Heritage of Mankind" (statement to the First Committee of the United Nations General Assembly, November 1st 1967), reproduced in his *The Common Heritage: Selected Papers on Oceans and World Order, 1967–1974*, Malta: Malta University Press, 1975

Sanger, Clyde, *Ordering the Oceans: The Making of the Law of the Sea*, London: Zed, 1986; Toronto: University of Toronto Press, 1987

Schmidt, Markus G., *Common Heritage or Common Burden? The United States Position on the Development of a Regime for Deep Sea-bed Mining in the Law of the Sea Convention*, Oxford: Clarendon Press, and New York: Oxford University Press, 1989

Vogler, John, *The Global Commons: A Regime Analysis*, Chichester and New York: Wiley, 1995

In 1967, PARDO, then Malta's delegate to the United Nations General Assembly, first launched the concept of the common heritage of mankind into the international arena. Malta proposed that it should apply to the resources on or below the ocean floor, beyond the limits of national jurisdiction, whose value and potential exploitability were then just beginning to be recognized, and that, as such, they should be managed globally. Pardo's three-hour speech of 1 November 1967, in introducing this item to the Assembly's First Committee, was a masterly and visionary survey of potential future developments in ocean use, covering military activities, drilling for oil and gas, fish farming, and "ocean parks", as well as the mining of the polymetallic nodules of the deep sea bed.

LUARD, a politician as well as a scholar, was one of those who participated in the immediate follow-up to Pardo's initiative, serving first as a UK delegate to the Assembly, and later as Minister of State at the UK Foreign and Commonwealth Office responsible for Law of the Sea matters. His book shows both an unwavering enthusiasm for the "common heritage" principle and a subtle awareness of the complications involved in trying to put it into practice. He focuses on the Sea-Bed Committee which the General Assembly set up to handle the Maltese proposal, and describes how the Assembly went on to pass three significant resolutions, one, in 1969, calling for a moratorium on all mining of the international area, the second, in 1970, committing itself to the "common heritage" principle and the necessity for a "regime and machinery" to manage it, and the third, coinciding with the second, envisaging a comprehensive conference to rewrite the Law of the Sea generally. This conference was to become the Third United Nations Conference on the Law of the Sea, or UNCLOS III. Luard wrote before UNCLOS III had met, but manages to convey some of the hopes and excitement that were to fuel it.

BUZAN also covers the Sea-Bed Committee years, but takes the story rather further, with extensive analysis of the first three sessions of UNCLOS III and a brief postscript summarizing the fourth (in New York in 1976). His more detached account is rich in detail, and well stocked with tables, categorizing the states, for instance, according to their positions on different issues, and also speculating thoughtfully about such questions as why the negotiations went the way they did, and what aspects of the process made for delay, and what, if any, for acceleration.

GROLIN, writing just before UNCLOS III finally adopted its Law of the Sea Convention in 1982, gives an excellent brief account of its handling of the common heritage theme, and its significance for relations between the industrialized "North" and the developing "South". Grolin shows how both sides tended to see the issue as setting precedents for other North–South negotiations.

OGLEY (1984) was one of the first to produce a comprehensive account of the handling of the "common heritage" issue at UNCLOS III, and its embodiment in the convention discussed above. Starting with the technological, economic, and environmental background to the negotiations, he describes the various categories of participants, the processes of decision making, and six broad and relevant areas of contention: the geographical limits to national jurisdiction (and thus the extent of the "international area"); the system of exploitation; the issue of production control (to prevent land-based exporters of the metals concerned from being swamped by sea-bed production); the structure of the proposed International Seabed Authority; the provisions for dispute settlement; and treatment of "pioneer investors", whose investments, in spite of the moratorium resolution referred to earlier, would predate the convention's coming into force.

Much of the business of UNCLOS III, as of other international conferences, was done behind the scenes, in informal, private, and even secret meetings. SANGER, writing a little later, was able to elicit many of the details of this secret diplomacy from interviews with those who participated in it and were now ready to talk. He was thus able to give a fuller, and generally better-informed, account of the negotiations than was possible before, although as a Canadian, and one who is justly proud of his country's generally constructive approach to the "common heritage", he is inclined to view it in an excessively uncritical light. It is difficult, for instance, to see any altruism in the hard bargain Canada drove with its southern neighbour on production policy, where the severe limit then agreed on sea-bed production was to the direct advantage of a major exporter of copper, cobalt, and nickel.

SCHMIDT's admirably thorough study of the US position on the "common heritage" is an updated version of a doctoral thesis, but it does not read like one. The role of the US in UNCLOS III would in any case have been vital to its success, and in 1981 the change of administration produced the most dramatic turning point in the conference's history. A compromise in the form of the Draft Convention, hammered out in August 1980, had the support of the Democratic President, Jimmy Carter, and his (Republican) Head of Delegation to UNCLOS, Elliot Richardson, but was repudiated in March 1981 by the now much-changed US delegation, serving the Reagan administration. The latter announced a total review of its policy in this field, and although concessions were made to it, the result was that in 1982 a text quite similar to the Draft Convention was adopted overwhelmingly, but against the opposition of the US. There is thus much for Schmidt to analyse, and he makes excellent use of a wealth of interviews with conference participants and other policy makers; but whether he is right to assume that, even with Carter's enthusiastic backing, the Senate would never have ratified a convention based on the 1980 draft, is more doubtful.

As both OGLEY (1995) and VOGLER show, other major sea-bed mining states were reluctant to commit themselves to the convention's common heritage regime in the face of American opposition. In the 1990s, informal North–South "consultations" by the UN Secretary-General brokered an agreement that in effect drastically amended that regime. Both Ogley and Vogler also compare the attempt to regulate sea-bed mining with the process of negotiating regimes to deal with other problems falling outside the jurisdictions of states; Ogley with ozone depletion and global warming, Vogler, with Antarctica, whaling, and outer space. Vogler's is the more theoretical treatment, subjecting each regime to sustained analysis in terms of regime theory. His verdict is that the persistent problems such "issue areas" generate, and the inability of a world divided into separate states to address them effectively, may stimulate radical change and the emergence of a centralized authority – that is world government.

RODERICK OGLEY

Common law

Baker, J.H., *An Introduction to English Legal History*, London: Butterworths, 3rd edition, 1990

Beatson, Jack, *Has the Common Law a Future?*, Cambridge: Cambridge University Press, 1997

Caenegem, R.C. van, *An Historical Introduction to Private Law*, Cambridge and New York: Cambridge University Press, 1992

Calabresi, Guido, *A Common Law for the Age of Statutes*, Cambridge, Massachusetts: Harvard University Press, 1982

Holdsworth, W.S., *A History of English Law*, 16 vols, London: Methuen, and Boston: Little Brown, 1903–66 (5 revised editions)

Levi, Edward, *An Introduction to Legal Reasoning*, Chicago: University of Chicago Press, 1948

Martínez-Torrón, Javier, *Anglo-American Law and Canon Law: Canonical Roots of the Common Law Tradition*, Berlin: Duncker & Humblot, 1998

Stein, Peter, *Legal Institutions: The Development of Dispute Settlement*, London: Butterworths, 1984

Williams, Glanville, *Learning the Law*, 11th edition, London: Stevens, 1982

Zweigert, Konrad and Hein Kötz, *An Introduction to Comparative Law*, 3rd edition, Oxford: Clarendon Press, and New York: Oxford University Press, 1998

For the history of the common law, the starting point must be BAKER's introduction to the subject. His book covers the emergence of the common-law courts and their rivals, the evolution of procedural law, the rise of the legal profession, and the evolution of the rules governing property, contract, tort, and crime. The book is learned yet accessible, incorporating a wealth of recent scholarship. In addition, each chapter contains its own bibliography, directing the reader to the leading books and articles on the particular topic.

HOLDSWORTH's multi-volume treatise is well known. In many respects, the treatise is extremely useful, because its coverage is broader and deeper than Baker's one-volume survey. However, on many points Holdsworth's work has been superseded by newer scholarship, and readers should remain alert to this possibility.

For an introduction to the common law as a system of reasoning from one judicial opinion to another, the best introductions are those of LEVI (for American readers) and WILLIAMS (for readers in the UK). Both books are short and easy to understand. Levi's treatment is a bit more scholarly, dealing strictly with the process of legal reasoning. Williams's book, in contrast, has a lighter touch, offering guidance to the would-be student of law. But notwithstanding these differences in style, both books are classics in their respective countries.

The relationship between common law and statute law is beautifully examined in the works by BEATSON and by CALABRESI. Writing in England, Beatson concentrates on the growing body of statutes generated by Parliament and the European Union. Writing in the US, Calabresi focuses on the explosion of Congressional enactments since the beginning of the New Deal. Despite their different contexts, both works

elegantly analyse the role of common-law reasoning in the modern era of frequent legislation.

Much scholarship has been directed at the relationship between the common law of England and the civil law of Continental Europe. Here, the best historical introductions are those of STEIN and of VAN CAENEGEM. Stein provides an overview of the principal features of the Roman, French, German, and English legal systems. With respect to each system, he examines both the development of substantive law and the changing procedures used for resolving disputes. Van Caenegem covers similar ground but concentrates more on the lawgivers, jurists, and judges who shaped the evolution of English and European law.

For modern comparative studies, the starting point must be the seminal treatment by ZWEIGERT & KÖTZ. This masterful volume is the ideal guidebook for comparing common law with the principal legal systems of continental Europe: French law, German law, socialist law, and Scandinavian law.

Finally, it is worth noticing that scholarship has also been directed at the relationship between English common law and the canon law of the Christian church. Here, the best survey is the recently published book by MARTÍNEZ-TORRÓN. It treats the subject systematically and demonstrates a thorough familiarity with existing scholarship.

THOMAS P. GALLANIS

See also Canon law, Civil law

Commonsense beliefs

Berger, Peter L., *The Social Reality of Religion*, London: Faber, 1969

Evans-Pritchard, E.E., *Witchcraft, Oracles, and Magic among the Azande*, Oxford: Clarendon Press, 1937; revised edition 1958

Garfinkel, Harold, "Common Sense Knowledge of Social Structures: The Documentary Method of Interpretation in Lay and Professional Fact Finding" in his *Studies in Ethnomethodology*, Englewood Cliffs: Prentice Hall, 1967; Cambridge: Polity Press, 1984

Geertz, Clifford, *Islam Observed: Religious Development in Morocco and Indonesia*, New Haven, Connecticut: University of Yale Press, 1968

Geertz, Clifford, "Common Sense as a Cultural System" in his *Local Knowledge: Further Essays in Interpretive Anthropology*, New York: Basic Books, 1983; London: Fontana, 1993

Horton, Robin, "African Traditional Thought and Western Science" in *Rationality*, edited by Bryan R. Wilson, Oxford: Blackwell, and Evanston, Illinois: Harper and Row, 1970

Latour, Bruno and Steve Woolgar, *Laboratory Life: The Construction of Scientific Facts*, London and Beverly Hills, California: Sage, 1979

Schuetz, Alfred, "Common Sense and Scientific Interpretation of Human Action" in *Collected Papers 1: The Problem of Social Reality*, edited by Maurice Natanson, The Hague: Nijhoff, 1962

Schuetz, Alfred, "The Problem of Rationality in the Social World" in his *Collected Papers 2: Studies in Social Theory*, edited by Arvid Brodersen, The Hague: Nijhoff, 1964

The foundation for much social science thinking on the everyday realities which people construct for themselves, and on the sense of naturalness with which these realities come to be invested, has been laid by the work of Alfred Scheutz. In a famous formulation (which is itself built on the phenomenological insights of Edmund Husserl) SCHUETZ (1964) posits that individuals regularly and habitually apprehend the world around them courtesy of a set of "background expectancies", which typify their experience and make it comprehensible. However concrete, obvious, and natural the facts of an individual's everyday life seem, these facts are already constructs. All thought, Schuetz claims, involves such constructs, along with rules concerning how thinking with those constructs should properly proceed: abstractions, idealizations, generalizations, and formalizations thus always intercede between human beings and the world, pre-selecting and pre-interpreting it for us. These background expectancies are taught and learnt from birth, thereby also becoming intersubjective norms shared by members of a sociocultural milieu: not only socially derived, they are also socially approved, controlled, maintained, and institutionalized. Indeed, Schuetz suggests that group membership should be analytically conceived of in terms of its members' sharing of a set of common background expectancies by which the world is properly to be typified and known.

As SCHUETZ theorizes in his work of 1962, background expectancies come in different types, perhaps the most important being that which typifies the behaviour, motivations, and goals which are deemed sensible, reasonable, and rational on an everyday basis. These expectancies might be called "commonsensical", and Schuetz claims that they point to a type of cognition, a set of constructs, which most people employ most of the time: "the paramount reality of human experience is an everyday world of commonsensical objects and practical acts". Of the many different kinds of socially imposed rules and recipes for typical sensemaking, it is common sense which provides human beings with their fundamental grounding in the world, and which makes the everyday world an obvious "natural" and "concrete" reality. "[C]ommonsense knowledge of the world", Schuetz concludes, "is a system of constructs of its typification". Schuetz's insights have been provocatively developed in a school of social analysis – ethnomethodology – associated with the work of Harold Garfinkel, Aaron Cicourel, Harvey Sacks, and others (see separate entry on Ethnomenthodology). GARFINKEL, for instance, focuses on the "methodical" and shared character which people everywhere continue to give to their lives through everyday, collaborative conversational "work". If our lives in society are structured, then this is less a feature of the *sui generis* or objective nature of social reality, Garfinkel argues, than a matter of common systems of reasoning, comprehending, and accounting, with which individuals have been socialized, and which lead them to interpret the strictures of their sociocultural milieux in routine ways. The project of social understanding involves building models of the background knowledge and methods of interpretation which actors ordinarily bring to bear in interactive

situations, and by means of which social structures are continually reconstituted. As Garfinkel puts it, this consists of "the investigation of the rational properties of indexical expressions and other practical actions as contingent ongoing accomplishments of organized artful practices of everyday life".

The constructed nature of commonsensical apprehensions of the world has also been elucidated by Clifford Geertz. GEERTZ (1983) begins by saying that common sense claims to treat reality matter-of-factly – it is but the immediate deliverances of experience, what "anyone in their right mind could see". However, crosscultural comparison of what is "matter-of-fact" and taken for granted quickly reveals that here is a specific cultural system – an ordered body of considered thought, a set of symbols and messages taught and learnt, the practice of which is as much an accomplishment as reciting a theological covenant or following a logical proof. Common sense is as dogmatic as religious knowledge, and as ambitious as scientific knowledge, Geertz argues, affording a totalizing frame of thought with which to access the ways of the world. Although the content of common sense varies greatly between sociocultural milieux, there are certain stylistic, attitudinal, and tonal features which make people's commonsensical constructions of everyday reality everywhere comparable. There is, Geertz explains, a "commonsensical voice", possessed of five distinctive features. First, common sense claims to identify things which are "natural", inevitable, and intrinsic to the world. Second, common sense claims to be a superlatively practical wisdom for getting things done. The forms it takes are anecdotes, jokes, maxims, and proverbs: together, these may amount to a disparate, heterogeneous, even contradictory potpourri, but they also provide practical advice for engaging with life in all its multifariousness. Third, common sense claims that the truths of the world which it enunciates are obvious, patent, and plain: it is what anybody who is sober can see. Fourth, common sense provides immediate wisdom that fits the moment. Finally, common sense promises wisdom which is accessible to all, needing no expertise or special powers, only maturity and some degree of worldliness. These features, to repeat, demarcate a mode of everyday knowing and being-in-the-world which Geertz regards as universal, however it may locally be dubbed (the term "common sense", and its distinction from "religion", "science", or "sociology", is merely a Western framing, he argues).

In a specific comparison of Islamic modes of thought in North Africa and South-east Asia, GEERTZ (1971) adds a further distinctive feature to commonsensical knowledge – its limited nature. Common sense, he elaborates, may be handy and economical, but it is also insufficient to deal with all of human experience and to make sense of it: in every culture and epoch it needs to be supplemented and sometimes superseded by other more theoretical, more specialized, forms of knowledge, often within the provenance of experts. Religion, science, sociology, art, law, and medicine might all be described as provinces of specialized knowledge which grow out of common sense and go beyond it – transcending, completing, or transforming it. Most of the time and for most purposes, common sense might be sufficient, but sometimes answers are needed which common sense fails to supply.

BERGER concurs with Geertz. Mundane routines, he argues, are inevitably disrupted by the advent of random, marginal, chaotic, and otherwise disorderly happenstance. At such times, the paramount reality of everyday life is left behind, and an explanation for the commonsensically inexplicable (disaster, miracle, dream, dispute, disease, death) is sought elsewhere, most usually in religion. The substantive content of what is inexplicable is wholly socioculturally contingent, Berger is keen to emphasize (as is Geertz): only the cognitive move from common sense to specialist knowledge is universal. Even here, a note of caution is required: it may be that some milieux are more dominated by a nonspecialist "colloquial" culture than others; and it may be that only some cultures square off areas of particularly systematized, "studied" expertise. Nonetheless, whatever the extent of the specialization of knowledge, it will always be true to say that the deficiencies of common sense are episodically made up for by cognitively resorting to the religious expertise of shamans, witchdoctors, and priests, the medical expertise of doctors, the legal expertise of adjudicators, the scientific expertise of chemists, and so on. An excellent ethnographic example of the way in which commonsensical knowledge is episodically superseded by the specialism of witchcraft is provided by EVANS-PRITCHARD for the Azande tribe of Sudan.

The relationship between forms of knowledge, and in particular, the ways and extents to which common sense is complemented by religious and scientific specialisms, is also the focus of important work by HORTON. Although religion and science alike provide a wider causal understanding than common sense can – breaking common sense down into componential aspects, relating these to a wider universe of forces, and so extending its limited causal vision – nonetheless, Horton argues, common sense provides the foundations from which both religion and science grow. Another way of saying this is that, whatever their ideology and mystique, bodies of specialist knowledge are not worlds apart, for it is the particular substantive qualities of common sense, in any one time and place, which give rise to the particular substantive qualities of expertise. Religion, science, sociology, art, for example, have a history which shows them not only to have been developed from the mundane world of common sense, but also to have been designed in specific ways to supersede that world.

Geertz (1983) suggested that comparative description of the ways and extents by which common sense is periodically replaced by other modes of thought provides perhaps better ways of representing the differences between sociocultural milieux than to consider one as being more "traditional", "rational", "modern", or "postmodern" than another. LATOUR & WOOLGAR, as part of an ethnographic study of a chemical laboratory in California, question indeed the extent to which specialist knowledge is able to overcome what Schuetz originally described as the "irrationalities" of common sense. Even the so-called scientific method entails a folk methodology, they assert, and it is a moot point whether or not decision-making processes in social life can ever be said to become more logical – and less grounded in commonsense beliefs.

NIGEL J. RAPPORT

See also Ethnomethodology

Communication in organizations

Cushman, Donald Peter and Sarah Sanderson King, "Communicating Change: A High-speed Management Perspective" in Communicating Organizational Change: A Management Perspective, edited by Sarah Sanderson King and Donald Peter Cushman, Albany: State University of New York Press, 1995

Davis, Keith and John W. Newstrom, "Managing Communications" in *Human Behavior at Work: Organizational Behavior*, 8th edition, New York and London: McGraw Hill, 1989

Hattersley, Michael E. and Linda Micheli McJannet, *Management Communication: Principles and Practice*, New York: McGraw Hill, 1997

Kaye, Michael, *Communication Management*, Sydney: Prentice Hall, 1994

King, Sara Sanderson and Donald Peter Cushman, "The Role of Communication in High Technology Organizations: The Emergence of High-Speed Management" in *Human Communication as a Field of Study*, edited by S.S. King, Albany: State University of New York Press, 1989

King, Sara Sanderson and Donald Peter Cushman (editors), *High-Speed Management and Organizational Communication in the 1990s: A Reader*, Albany: State University of New York Press, 1994

Miller, Katherine, *Organizational Communication: Approaches and Processes*, 2nd edition, Belmont, California: Wadsworth, 1999

Sigband, Norman B., *Communication for Management*, Glenview, Illinois: Scott Foresman, 1969

Sigband, Norman B. and Arthur H. Bell, *Communication for Management and Business*, 5th edition, Glenview, Illinois: Scott Foresman, 1989

Treece, Malra and Betty A. Kleen, *Successful Communication for Business and Management*, Upper Saddle River, New Jersey: Prentice Hall, 1998

The material on organizational communication selected here represents the multiplicity of views on communication in organizations and has been selected with a varied audience in mind. Some texts (SIGBAND and SIGBAND & BELL) have been selected as characteristic of traditional teaching materials, and highlight the developments in communication for management instruction since its introduction in business school curricula. The work by HATTERSLEY & McJANNET has been included as a valuable pedagogic text which follows a prescriptive and structured approach. Additional texts have been selected as comprehensive business communication textbooks, extensively used in undergraduate teaching of communication (TREECE & KLEEN), and as broader approaches to communication within the wider area of organizational behaviour (DAVIS & NEWSTROM).

Not all the texts presented in this section require a background in, or prior knowledge of, management or organizational behaviour theory; in some cases, comprehensive accounts of the relevant theoretical viewpoints are presented (MILLER) and in others the issue of communication arises in other social sciences (KAYE). Finally, recently introduced theories of organizational communication have been reviewed (CUSHMAN &

KING) not only because of their substantial academic value but also due to their wide applicability in the modern business environment.

Sigband presents the overall communication process, from the mechanics to oral and written communication as well as the factors promoting or inhibiting interpretation of messages. It was initially written as a source book and reference for both professionals and students in the field of communication management. It is mentioned here as it is the first edition of a successful and widely used text that was considered a typical textbook of its era and was the predecessor of Sigband & Bell (see below). The comparison of this work with modern texts gives the reader an appreciation of the changes and developments that have taken place during the last three decades in the field of communication in organizations.

Of particular interest is the first section of the book, presenting an overview of the theories associated with communication and its processes within organizations, containing references to mathematical and behavioural theories. This is still of particular use to those interested in the historical perspective and development of the construct of communication. Among the selected readings to be found in the last section of the book, is the classic paper by Rogers & Roethlisberger, "Barriers and gateways to communication", first published in the *Harvard Business Review* (July–August 1952), presenting an analysis of communication in industrial contexts.

Sigband & Bell's work has developed from Sigband and is a textbook for students of communication in a management context as well as a reference for the business community. There are supplements and teaching aids especially designed for instructors (including a resource guide, test bank, videotapes, films, and transparencies) as part of a classroom-management programme.

The text considers electronic communication and a variety of examples of written communication (reports, letters, and so on), differentiating among them on the basis of their purpose and use in contemporary business situations. There are also case studies and assignment questions that can be used in the classroom to introduce and cover current topics of communication within a multicultural business community. A new section of this book deals with career planning, offering a practical insight into communication associated with jobseeking (job applications, application letters, resumes).

Hattersley & McJannet is a traditional book in this field, employing a well-structured, prescriptive approach and presenting the "principles of effective communication", followed by applications and technique. In addition to other texts, it makes reference to the ethics of the communication process on a personal and organizational level. It is intended as a teaching text, aimed at advanced undergraduate and MBA students and includes cases to be studied and prepared by students, and references to additional reading material. The text is also accompanied by a teacher's manual. It is a useful text for a strictly structured curriculum and provides students from a wide range of backgrounds with a good grounding on ways of managing communication in a variety of organisations.

Treece & Kleen have presented the seventh edition of a highly structured textbook suitable for undergraduate teaching. It presents a very detailed account of the communication process, covering the main theoretical viewpoints and their implications for the business environment. The concise summaries of the central themes of each chapter and the clear objectives will be particularly useful to students. The book highlights throughout the interrelations among the elements and processes of communication and assumes a multidisciplinary approach to the study of the concept. The main emphases of this book include the changing nature of technology, the legal and ethical considerations, and the multicultural and diverse character of the environments in which communication takes place.

A differentiating factor between this text and other traditional textbooks is the consideration given here to the notion of collaboration and teamworking. Cases and assignments following each chapter are aimed at groups instead of individual students and, hence, reflect the diversity and complexity of the communication processes within organizations.

The chapter on "managing communications" in Davis & Newstrom presents organizational communication and its management within the general framework of organizational behaviour. The importance of communication is stressed, and communication methods are presented together with their effects on organizations. This book takes a somewhat prescriptive approach, defining eight steps for successful two-way communication, paying particular attention to factors inhibiting and encouraging effective communication. It is suitable for teaching at an advanced undergraduate level.

This chapter is followed by relevant questions for students, highlighting the main issues and theories presented in the text, and supported by an "experimental exercise" aimed at contrasting one-way and two-way communication. Further material for additional reading is recommended and this should provide undergraduate or MBA students with relevant sources to explore specific areas and themes.

Miller employs a refreshing, non-prescriptive approach in presenting a very detailed and thorough account of the key theoretical and practical issues in organizational communication. This comprehensive text objectively presents the developmental stages of organizational communication and the corresponding academic approaches and theoretical views. Written in a clear and concise way, it covers the main management theories and can be easily read and understood even by those with no prior background in management or organizational behaviour theory. The author reviews approaches to the study of organizational communication in the first part of the book and, considers research and theory concerned with particular organizational communication processes in the second part. The processes of organizational communication are considered together with corresponding models (socialization; decision making; stress and social support; external environments). The main difference from other textbooks in the field is its appreciation of the coexistence of a variety of organizational levels and situations in which communication takes place. As a result, the organizational communication processes and their effects on organizations are examined in relation to cultural and gender diversity, stress and burnout in the workplace, and new communication technologies.

Kaye is written in a pragmatic and comprehensible way. It has its foundation in academic theory, and it offers opportunities for business organizations to explore and adopt its scholarly approach. This book is a valuable resource for students and professionals from a variety of business sectors and is of particular use to human resource training specialists and those involved in adult and vocational education. The title *Communication Management* reflects the field of study developed in Australia at the beginning of the 1980s, according to which people construct meanings about their relationships with others in a variety of contexts, and, hence, become managers of their own communication processes. The theme of "competence" is interwoven throughout the book and its use, in terms of "developing communication competence", stresses the applied communication approach of this book. Unlike traditional texts in the field, the focus of this text is the "adult communication management" model through which the author presents the theoretical and practical issues concerning communication, its management and relevant developments in the field of adult communication management.

Cushman & King explore the ways in which the need for and the direction of organizational change can be communicated to the stakeholders of organizations. The communication of change is examined and proposed using the concept of "high-speed management", a relatively recent theory of organizational communication comprising a system of theoretical and practical principles for responding to rapidly changing business environments (for example, reducing the time to market in manufacturing organisations). Although this work is presented as appropriate for scholars and practitioners in the field of communication, and despite the numerous examples of large organizations that have adopted the principles of "high-speed management", it is written in a technical way that may make it difficult to read.

Other closely related references concerned with the new organisational communication theory of "high-speed management" and its practical application in the business environment include KING & CUSHMAN (1989) and KING & CUSHMAN (1994).

ATHINA NICOLAIDES BASTIEN

See also Organizational behaviour survey

Communications and new media: economics, policy and regulation

Hutchison, David, *Media Policy: An Introduction*, Oxford and Malden, Massachusetts: Blackwell, 1999

McChesney, Robert W., Ellen Meiksins Wood and John Bellamy Foster (editors), *Capitalism and the Information Age: The Political Economy of the Global Communication Revolution*, New York: Monthly Review Press, 1998

Sreberny-Mohammadi, Annabelle *et al.* (editors), *Media in Global Context: A Reader*, London and New York: Arnold, 1997

Steemers, Jeanette (editor), *Changing Channels: The Prospects for Television in a Digital World*, Luton: University of Luton Press, 1998

McCHESNEY, WOOD & FOSTER's valuable collection of 14 articles addresses a large number of political, economic and sociocultural issues arising from recent developments in the communications field, mainly from a political economy perspective. The development of the political economy of communication has been greatly influenced by the transformation of information technology, broadcasting, and telecommunications from small or medium-sized firms into huge conglomerates. The introduction and availability of new communications technology, and the trends towards globalization and liberalization, along with the growing integration of communications businesses across traditional industry and technology divisions, have resulted in a new reality characterized by a change in labour force, social, and market relations. As a consequence, research has been undertaken on the economic and political motives for such trends, their effects on the economy and polity, and the need for continuing regulation. This welcome book takes a hard look at existing trends and policies related to the new reality, by uncovering the factors that underpin them, namely, markets, profits, and class domination. Not only does it provide an informed critique of current issues, but the authors often come up with their own recommendations for policy agendas in the areas they investigate. All the contributions are characterized by a certain degree of scepticism about the introduction of market mechanisms, both with regard to its potential economic efficiency and its ability to lead to a democratic polity. An underlying theme in many of the contributions is that recent developments in global communication are not an inevitable process that cannot be altered by organized political activity.

The major weakness of the book is – inevitably, given the North American origins of the three editors – the focus on the US environment, although the situation of specific communications sectors in Britain and Canada is reviewed briefly in a couple of essays. Thus reference is made only to corporate strategies and diversification trends followed by US-based transnational enterprises. Although it is indisputable that US-based firms dominate in the global communication scene, the understanding of the emerging global system should not be only realized from the American perspective.

The book includes interesting and provocative ideas and messages; for instance, the idea that media systems are in the hands of private tyrannies and the consequences for democracy; the idea that international economic agreements favour primarily multinationals; the message that without democratic media, there can be no democracy; and the suggestion that organised political force – to demand rights and resources – would provide a positive answer to the new global order stimulated by recent technological and other developments in global communication. These evaluations of the current situation and future trends are, perhaps, one of the book's main strengths as they are bound to initiate discussion about the process of globalization and its impact on social relations, and the present and the future role of the mass media and telecommunications in reshaping the labour force and market relations.

The application of digital technologies is radically changing the content, economics and politics of the global information and communications businesses. At the same time, it finalizes convergence between three key industries involved in communications – computing, telecommunications, and broadcasting. The outcome will be the formation of new industrial alliances, mergers, and takeovers that may considerably raise levels of media market concentration. This, in turn, may eliminate competition and stifle pluralism in the market. This adds new complexity to regulation and policy, as issues like ownership and control, media access, influence and effects, and issues of representation and identity now more than ever need to be resolved.

STEEMERS's valuable anthology of six original articles crosses some of these boundaries and addresses the potential impact of digital delivery on the regulation, policy, economics and strategies adopted for television. This influential work is highly recommended. Each chapter concludes with extensive notes, while the book ends with a rich bibliography and a good index. The common denominator in all the contributions is that the potential of digital technology to alter the communications environment will not be realized as quickly as some have observed due to the uncertainty in consumer demand.

The book is both descriptive and analytical. The descriptive style allows for revealing insights to be drawn about issues of access, media ownership and control, sociocultural effects of new communications technologies, and consumer demand. The economic analysis sheds light on the value chain in television and the factors affecting it, on the economics of new distribution systems, and on demands for new services and constraints on supply. By drawing a distinction between economic and pluralistic objectives, the media policy analysis contributes to the development of an appropriate regulatory framework that will have a dual objective: to promote industry growth and maintain fair competition, and to safeguard pluralism. The contributors often come up with their own, sometimes radical, proposals (for example, (p.27)), which may stimulate discussion.

The emphasis is on economic objectives and, in particular, on the examination of the relationship between media policy and economic imperatives. The decisive emphasis on the UK media scene is a weakness, although some of the essays review briefly the situation in other EU countries. The most recent references are to mid-1997. Meanwhile, major technological, political, economic, and regulatory changes have occurred that may not affect the results of the economic analysis undertaken, but they surely make the given mapping of European present state of digital television look out of date.

SREBERNY-MOHAMMADI *et al.* have compiled 27 previously published and new articles that focus on the analysis of communication institutions and processes of media production, distribution, and consumption globally. This volume is one of a series of five readers that intend to provide the necessary resources for media studies courses (other volumes address approaches to media; media industries and professions; audiences and reception; and media texts). The essays are well written and accessible (jargon-free), with comprehensive appendices and references at the end of each essay. The work is divided into six sections. Section one investigates the concept of globalization and presents the theoretical framework surrounding the notion, whereas section two offers a variety of perspectives on the nature, degree and significance of the connection between globalization and the media. Section three is concerned with particular media actors such as the international print and television news agencies as well as the Hollywood film industry. Section four stresses the importance of regulating the means of global communication and explores the attempts by national (US), regional (EU) and

global institutions (ITU, GATT, INTELSAT, and so forth) to regulate transnational media flows. Section five addresses ethnic, gender, cultural and political concerns that emerge from the analysis of the vast transformations influencing the nature of communication, and discusses the dynamics and potential of the small, alternative media. Section six focuses on media texts and audiences. Here, there is an attempt to analyse the meaning of technological, political, economic and sociocultural changes for the way people use, interpret, and are affected by the media. Some of the authors (Negus, Straubhaar, Abu-Lughod), in a critique of the globalization notion, question the idea of a "one-way flow" of media products and services from the few to the many and from industrialized to non-industrialized countries and stress the increasing complex relations between local, national, regional and international production, distribution and consumption of media texts in a global context.

This interdisciplinary compilation of articles positions communication at the heart of global affairs. Globalization in the media is constantly discussed, but the forms and perspectives that discussions take vary considerably. The contributors provide different conceptual frameworks for thinking about globalization and take a hard look at the increasing connections between communication and the processes and experiences of globalization. Thus this volume will be of great benefit to undergraduate and MA students and lecturers in sociology and politics, and is also recommended to course organizers in media studies, journalism and broadcasting, communications, and cultural and literary studies.

The growing complexities of media policy have come to the fore recently due to technological, economic and political developments, which have reshaped the media landscape. HUTCHISON's influential work introduces the reader to the issues of media policy, familiarizes him/her with the decision-making process, and encourages argumentation and questioning. The author is a senior lecturer in media studies at Glasgow Caledonian University; for many years he was also a member of the BBC General Advisory Council and of the Scottish Film Council. The combination of both academic and practical experience in media sectors makes him more than suitable to explore the basic issues of principle, discuss the process of implementation, and give insights into actual practical consequences.

Hutchison adopts a cross-media approach to policy discussion, ranging across the press, film, television and radio and examines the links between policy in the media as a whole. Throughout the work there is a constant attempt to establish the link between the general and the specific in media discourses. The book is divided into three sections. The first provides the intellectual, political, economic, sociocultural and technological context within which media policy is shaped and exercised. Section two undertakes a historical analysis of the basis of media policy and investigates the fundamental principles that have driven it. Areas under consideration are citizenship policy, censorship versus freedom of expression, and government intervention and privacy. Section three is concerned with the ways in which policy has been conducted and applied in practice, through a series of case studies. This section offers a thorough investigation of the roles of the policy makers, such as elected politicians, civil servants and regulatory authorities in developing and implementing media policy for the benefits of both the industry and the consumer-citizen. The focus is mostly on the press and broadcasting sectors in Britain and decisive emphasis is given to the role of the Press Complaints Commission and to the role of the BBC in the third millennium. Finally, the author looks critically at the cultural imperialism term, and attempts to include the European dimension and the experience of other countries like US and Canada (very briefly indeed) in order to show useful contrasts and comparisons.

A weakness is the limited discussion of the new media and the ways by which they affect media market structure, performance, and regulation. Technological convergence and its potential impact on media policy is rarely raised. However, crucial and ambiguous issues are considered in an objective manner. A stylistic advantage is the provision of a number of examples and data to support the author's views. In addition, the book offers summaries and questions for discussion at the end of each chapter throughout sections one and two, and is well referenced throughout.

PETROS IOSIFIDES

See also Information and communication technologies

Communism

Burns, Emile (editor), *The Marxist Reader: The Most Significant and Enduring Works of Marxism*, New York: Avenel, 1982

Crossman, R.H.S. (editor), *The God That Failed: Six Studies in Communism*, London: Hamish Hamilton, and New York: Harper, 1950

Figes, Orlando, *A People's Tragedy: A History of the Russian Revolution*, London: Cape, 1996; New York: Viking, 1997

Johnson, Paul, "Karl Marx: 'Howling Gigantic Curses'" in *Intellectuals*, London: Weidenfeld and Nicolson, 1988; New York: Harper and Row, 1990

Klehr, Harvey, John Haynes and Fridrikh Firsov (editors), *The Secret World of American Communism*, New Haven, Connecticut: Yale University Press, 1995

Onate, Andres D., *Chairman Mao and the Chinese Communist Party*, Chicago: Nelson Hall, 1979

Radzinskii, Edvard, *Stalin*, New York: Doubleday, 1996; London: Sceptre, 1997

Reed, John, *Ten Days that Shook the World*, New York: Boni and Liveright, 1919; London: Modern Books, 1928

Schrecker, Ellen, *Many Are the Crimes: McCarthyism in America*, Boston: Little Brown, 1998

JOHNSON profiles Karl Marx, the founding father of communism. As described by Johnson, Marx was a shoddy and dishonest scholar, a man of violence, a sponger, an exploiter of his own domestic help, a racist, and a sexist, but otherwise was a nice guy. Johnson is out to portray Marx and other intellectuals as morally unequipped to preach new philosophies to the world, so the biographical information in this essay ought to be regarded in light of the author's goal.

BURNS provides representative works by Marx, Engels, Lenin, and Stalin. Except for the inclusion of Stalin, Burns' book is a collection of canonical communist classics.

FIGES gives a detailed account of the Russian Revolution, beginning in the 19th century. His focus is on conditions in Russia and how they led to, and were affected by, the Revolution. Communism as a doctrine is given second place to the day-to-day struggles of Russians in the Revolution. However, students of communism will of course find much of value in this narrative, which, in exploring the early years of the Revolution, gives information about how communist theory was translated into practice.

RADZINSKII had access to Soviet archives in writing his book, which contains material on the rise of the Soviet Union as the first Communist superpower under the leadership of Joseph Stalin. Radzinskii seems interested in resolving various historical controversies, not hesitating to come to his own conclusions on issues where scholars will disagree among themselves. For example, Radzinskii seizes on a Soviet military document from World War II as proof that Stalin was planning an attack on Germany at the time the USSR was attacked in 1941. Radzinskii also claims that, on the eve of his death, Stalin was planning a world war.

ONATE describes the origins of the largest communist party in the World, namely, the Chinese Communist Party. His history covers the Chinese Communist Party and Mao Tse-Tung. Onate's account describes the origins of the Chinese Communist Party, Mao's joining the party, and the turbulent history of China as Mao and his army fought the Japanese and the Chinese Nationalists for control of the country. The history of Mao's China is followed by a description of the effect of Mao on Communist theory, also known as "The Sinification of Marxism". This work is good for those who want historical background on the Chinese Communist Party.

REED provides us with a work that is part history, part communist apologetic, and part insight into the mindset of the author, one of numerous foreigners who saw hope in the Russian Revolution.

CROSSMAN provides us with accounts by intellectuals – Arthur Koestler, Ignazio Silone, Richard Wright, Louis Fischer, and Stephen Spender (there is also an account of Andre Gide presented by Enid Starkie) – who share the appellation "ex-Communist". The essays explain how the authors were attracted to communism and then left the movement. Although very dated, this work is still useful insofar as it describes what induced thoughtful and humane people to join the international communist movement. Since the authors are themselves talented writers, there is no lack of passionate discussion of these questions.

KLEHR, HAYNES & FIRSOV show us numerous documents from the Soviet archives, indicating something of the nature of the relationship between Moscow and the American Communist Party, especially in the 1920s and 1930s. The documents indicate that the American Communist Party was used as an espionage channel by the Soviets, but even today, the extent of Soviet penetration will be a matter of disagreement in a country where some veterans of the Cold War bring warm passions to the discussion.

SCHRECKER also discusses communism in America, but from a different angle than that of Klehr and his colleagues.

While acknowledging communist penetration into many areas of American life, Schrecker advances the thesis that the great danger during the Cold War came not from Communism, but from anti-Communism. Anti-Communism, in Schrecker's view, was a weapon that right-wingers and anti-communist leftists wielded to attack united-front-style coalitions, mute criticism of America's hardline foreign policy, and persecute groups that had been linked with communism, including political groups such as those in the civil rights movement.

ERIC LONGLEY

See also Communist party, Eurocommunism, Marx and Marxism

Communist party (US & UK)

Branson, Noreen, *History of the Communist Party in Britain, 1941–1951*, London: Lawrence and Wishart, 1997

Brown, Michael E. *et al.* (editors), *New Studies in the Politics and Culture of U. S. Communism*, New York: Monthly Review Press, 1993

Klehr, Harvey, *Communist Cadre: The Social Background of the American Communist Party Elite*, Stanford, California: Hoover Institution Press, 1978

Klehr, Harvey and John Earl Haynes, *The American Communist Movement: Storming Heaven Itself*, New York: Maxwell Macmillan, 1992

Modin, Yuri, *My Five Cambridge Friends: Burgess, Maclean, Philby, Blunt and Cairncross, by Their KGB Controller*, New York: Farrar Straus, and London: Headline, 1994

Radosh, Ronald and Joyce Milton, *The Rosenberg File: With a New Introduction Containing Revelations from National Security Agency and Soviet Sources*, New Haven, Connecticut: Yale University Press, 1997

Schrecker, Ellen, *Many Are the Crimes: McCarthyism in America*, Boston: Little Brown, 1998

Tanenhaus, Sam, *Whittaker Chambers: A Biography*, New York: Random House, 1997

KLEHR & HAYNES, in their history of the Communist Party in the US, do not ignore the party's persecution at the hands of the US government, but they also point to other factors in the party's decline in political influence. Why did an organization that had acquired a fair amount of influence and respectability during the Popular Front period of the 1930s and the World War II years, lose that influence and become politically marginal? The answer can be found largely in the party's myopic political tactics, say Klehr & Haynes. Supporting the Progressive Party in 1948, and seeking to go underground in the 1950s are both examples of the party's inflicting political injury on itself.

BROWN *et al.* compile a series of essays on American communism, which ought to be read by those preparing a history of the subject. The Popular Front, the party's role in the labour movement, and anti-communist persecution are among the subjects covered. There is also an essay by Ellen Schrecker that presumably forms the germ of her 1998 study, *Many are the Crimes*.

SCHRECKER argues that the issue of anticommunism provided a means by which several elements in American political life were able to come together and hurt the leftist, progressive movement in the US. Schrecker's thesis is that a wide variety of people–anticommunists, opportunists, racists–were able to enhance their own position by waging anticommunist campaigns. Schrecker's perspective is not pro-communist but anti-anticommunist. The book is well worth reading for its detail.

KLEHR's work is one of the better studies of the leadership of the American Communist Party. Giving biographical information on American party leaders, as well as background information on what led them to the party, Klehr contributes much to an understanding of what impelled people to take up the communist cause.

RADOSH & MILTON reissue their 1983 classic history of the Rosenberg spy case. The US executed the Rosenbergs in 1953 for stealing atomic secrets on behalf of the Soviet Union. Radosh & Milton maintain that Julius Rosenberg, at least, was guilty, and that he was part of a Soviet espionage ring within the US.

TANENHAUS revisits the Hiss–Chambers case from the late 1940s in America – a case in which an ex-communist named Whittaker Chambers accused a former State Department official, Alger Hiss, of spying for the Soviets. Hiss was ultimately convicted of perjuring himself about his espionage activities, but the ultimate truth behind the case continues to be debated. Tanenhaus believes that Chambers was, as he said, part of an espionage ring that included Hiss.

BRANSON gives history of the British Communist Party during World War II and the early Cold War years. The party's activities in a variety of areas (colonial policy, and so on) are examined.

MODIN gives his account of handling, on behalf of the KGB, the five men who are arguably Britain's most notorious spies: John Cairncross, Anthony Blunt, Kim Philby, Donald Maclean, and Guy Burgess. These five, who knew each other at university, passed secrets to Soviet intelligence for varying periods, beginning in the 1930s. So long as this book is approached with the scepticism warranted in the case of memoirs by ex-spies, then it could yield valuable information.

ERIC LONGLEY

See also Eurocommunism

Communitarianism

Bell, Daniel, *Communitarianism and Its Critics*, Oxford: Clarendon Press, 1993

Bellah, Robert N. *et al.*, *Habits of the Heart: Individualism and Commitment in American Life*, Berkeley: University of California Press, 1985

Etzioni, Amitai, *The New Golden Rule: Community and Morality in a Democratic Society*, New York: Basic Books, 1996

MacIntyre, Alasdair, *After Virtue: A Study in Moral Theory*, Notre Dame, Indiana: University of Notre Dame Press, and London: Duckworth, 1981; 2nd edition 1984

Moon, J. Donald, Communitarianism entry in *The Encyclopedia of Applied Ethics*, edited by Ruth Chadwick, San Diego: Academic Press, 1998

Mulhall, Stephen and Adam Swift, *Liberals and Communitarians*, Oxford and Cambridge, Massachusetts: Blackwell, 1992; 2nd edition 1996

Nisbet, Robert A., *The Quest for Community*, London and New York: Oxford University Press, 1953; reissued as *Community and Power*, 1962; reissued under original title, 1969

Sandel, Michael J., *Liberalism and the Limits of Justice*, Cambridge and New York: Cambridge University Press, 1982; 2nd edition, 1998

Taylor, Charles, *Philosophical Papers*, 2 vols, Cambridge and New York: Cambridge University Press, 1985

Tönnies, Ferdinand, *Community and Association*, translated and edited by Charles P. Loomis, London: Routledge and Paul, 1955; as *Community and Society*, East Lansing: Michigan State University Press, 1957 (German edition as *Gemeinschaft und Gesellschaft*, 1887)

Walzer, Michael, *Spheres of Justice: A Defense of Pluralism and Equality*, New York: Basic Books, and Oxford: Robinson, 1983

Communitarianism has both a general sense, with a long history in social and political thought, and a specific connection to the "liberal–communitarian debate" of the 1980s and 1990s. In the general sense, anyone who believes that community is somehow vital to a worthwhile life – and is therefore a good to be protected against various threats – is a communitarian. Such a person may be either left-wing or right-wing politically. Communitarianism, in this sense, began to take shape as a self-conscious way of thinking about society and politics in the late 19th century. According to one line of thought that developed at the time, the primary threat to community is the movement from the settled, family-focused life of villages and small towns to the unsettled, individualistic life of commerce and cities, which may lead to greater affluence and personal freedom, but at the cost of alienation, isolation, and rootlessness. TÖNNIES, with his distinction between *Gemeinschaft* (community) and *Gesellschaft* (association or society), has been especially influential in this regard. *Gemeinschaft*, as he defines it, is an intimate, organic, and traditional form of human association; *Gesellschaft* is impersonal, mechanical, and rational. To exchange the former for the latter, then, is to trade warmth and support for coldness and calculation.

A second line of communitarian thought sees the principal threat to community in the centripetal force of the modern state. NISBET provides an especially clear statement of this position, which draws more on Alexis de Tocqueville's insistence on the importance of voluntary associations of citizens than on a longing for *Gemeinschaft*. Community, in Nisbet's account, is a form of association in which people more-or-less spontaneously work together to solve common problems and live under codes of authority that they have generated themselves. However, the free and healthy life of community is under constant pressure from the modern state, with its impulses toward centralized power and bureaucratic regulation.

These two themes persist in the writings of the communitarian political theorists of recent years, whose main concern has been to protect community against liberal individualism. BELLAH *et al.* combines political theory with a sociological analysis of American life that draws on intensive interviews with more than 200, predominantly white and middle-class, Americans. The authors' conclusion is that the United States is a society in which the ideal of the "autonomous individual" leads to an estrangement from public concerns and a troubling lack of social commitment. In MACINTYRE, the worry is that conflict between the advocates of incommensurable moral positions has so riven modern societies that "[m]odern politics is civil war carried on by other means" (p.253). The turn toward reason that MacIntyre calls "the Enlightenment project" has proven doubly disastrous: first, because reason alone cannot provide a foundation for morality; and second, because the turn to reason has deflected attention from the importance of character and virtue. The best that people can do in such circumstances is to agree to disagree when that is possible, to engage in "civil war . . . by other means" when it is not, and to try to construct "local forms of community within which civility and the intellectual and moral life can be sustained through the new dark ages which are already upon us" (p.263).

SANDEL highlights the communitarian complaint against liberal individualism. With John Rawls' *A Theory of Justice* (1971) as his main target, Sandel objects that contemporary liberals often conceive of the individual as an "unencumbered self" that is, completely free to choose its goals and attachments. Such a conception is both false and pernicious, he argues, for individual selves are largely constituted by the communities that nurture and sustain them. When liberals teach individuals to think of themselves as somehow prior to and apart from these communities, then they are engaged quite literally in a *self*-defeating enterprise.

Similar claims appear in the essays collected in TAYLOR, especially the second volume, but he aims his criticisms not so much at Rawls or liberalism in general as at the "atomistic" liberalism of libertarians such as Robert Nozick. WALZER argues that attempts to devise a single theory of justice that will govern the distribution of all kinds of goods – a theory such as Rawls' – must fail because different principles of justice apply to different kinds of goods. To discover these principles requires an appreciation of how "all these differences derive from different understandings of the social goods themselves – the inevitable product of historical and cultural particularism" (p.6). Thus Walzer's emphasis on "particularism" has led many commentators to place him on the communitarian side of the liberal–communitarian debate.

None of these theorists clearly and unequivocally considers himself a communitarian, however. Indeed, MacIntyre and Sandel have tried to shake off that label in subsequent writings. But others have been happy to take it up. One of them, Amitai Etzioni, is the founder of a journal, *The Responsive Community*, that is the organ of a self-styled communitarian movement. ETZIONI is a clear statement of his attempt to accommodate individual rights within a theory that stresses the importance of communal ties and social responsibility. BELL offers a defence of communitarianism, in the form of a dialogue between a communitarian and a liberal, which is entertaining as well as enlightening. It has the added virtue of including an appendix, again in dialogical form, by a noted critic of communitarianism, Will Kymlicka.

Useful introductions to the liberal–communitarian dispute are available in MULHALL & SWIFT, which includes a helpful account of Rawls' views, and MOON, which sets out the key issues in admirably lucid fashion.

RICHARD DAGGER

See also Gemeinschaft and Gesellschaft

Company law

Cheffins, Brian R., *Company Law: Theory, Structure and Operation*, Oxford: Clarendon Press, and New York: Oxford University Press, 1997

Davies, Paul Lyndon (editor), *Gower's Principles of Modern Company Law*, 6th edition, London: Sweet and Maxwell, 1997

Farrar, John H., Nigel E. Furey and B.M. Hannigan (editors), *Farrar's Company Law*, 4th edition, London: Butterworths, 1998

Hadden, Tom, *Company Law in Context*, 2nd edition, London: Weidenfeld and Nicolson, 1990

Hoey, Amanda, "Disqualifying Delinquent Directors", *Company Lawyer*, 18 (1997): 130

McGee, Andrew and Christina Williams, *The Business of Company Law: An Introduction for Students*, Oxford and New York: Oxford University Press, 1995

Sullivan, G.R., "The Attribution of Culpability to Limited Companies", *Cambridge Law Journal*, 55 (1996): 515

This selection of works reflects the differing strands of company-law scholarship to be found at the present day. Traditionally, lawyers have regarded company law as involving the technical exposition of a mass of rules. As that body of rules has grown, traditional company-law scholarship has struggled to cope with the task of analysis. Two developments may be identified as emerging from this. The first is the trend towards looking for themes within the subject that may be used to present the material in more enlightening and accessible ways. The second is a growing dissatisfaction with mere technical analysis. Company law has thus been opened up to examination from economic and social (including sociolegal) perspectives. More recently, a trend has emerged of looking more empirically at the ways in which companies are used in practice as vehicles for the effective conduct of business activity. An important consequence of these strands is that any text in the area is forced to narrow its emphasis to a particular field of the subject and to adopt a particular perspective upon that field.

Company lawyers have long regarded *Gower's Company Law* (DAVIES) as the best academic exposition of a notoriously technical subject. His achievement has been to take the technical rules and reduce them to coherent principles, while also making a rudimentary attempt to relate those principles to the broader functions of company law. However, in the end it is the technical rules that always prevail.

FARRAR & HANNIGAN is another example of a fairly traditional approach. It views company law as a whole, rather than distinguishing between different types of company, and is therefore able to provide something of a panorama of the subject. It recognizes the role of institutional regulation, especially of public companies, and also gives some emphasis to the process of integration and harmonization of company law within the European context.

HADDEN was one of the first exponents of a more contextual approach to company law, at a time when the "Law in Context" movement was relatively new and was making some inroads into the study of many areas of law. Although the book was originally published in 1977, the ideas contained within it have stood the passage of time very successfully, and it remains a lucid and readable introduction to the contextual study of company law for students who already have some knowledge of substantive legal rules. Hadden views the company as an entity functioning within a broader societal context, and is able to see that the interest groups within the company need not be limited to the traditional list of shareholders, directors, and creditors.

CHEFFINS represents probably the most interesting and lucid example of the attempt to move the emphasis away from technical rules to the point where the broader functions of company law are allowed to lead the direction of the discussion, rather than merely forming a background to it. It differs from Hadden's work in that it aims to integrate contextual issues into the framework of the subject to a much greater extent. It also benefits from a more up-to-date engagement with the literature on corporate governance and with managerial aspects of the subject.

McGEE & WILLIAMS approach company law from the point of view of the business within which it operates. Although they cover many of the traditional topics of company law, their concern is less with a technical analysis of the rules than with the application of those rules, especially within small private companies. They also seek to relate the company law rules to other areas of law, such as that governing the activities of banks as the primary financiers of small companies, and the property law rules relating to charges and title retention. To that extent the book may be regarded as one of the few that explore the linkages between company law and commercial law.

SULLIVAN looks at a vexed topic that has attracted considerable attention among both company and criminal lawyers in recent years: the extent to which a company can properly be held to be guilty of offences that involve a particular intention or state of mind. He reiterates the obvious point that a company as such cannot form an intention. In the light of the differing theories of corporate personality and the Law Commission's proposals on the subject, he suggests that the focus should move away from highly artificial attributions of culpability in the direction of recognizing the problem as being one of the failure of the company through its agents to maintain appropriate standards.

HOEY looks at one of the strongest trends of recent years in company law – the increasing use of disqualification orders against directors of failed companies. She shows the ways in which the courts have struggled to interpret the 1986 legislation so as to produce results that appear fair in the individual case.

ANDREW McGEE

See also Corporate manslaughter

Comparative advantage

Deardorff, Alan V., "Testing Trade Theories and Predicting Trade Flows" in *Handbook of International Economics*, vol. 1, edited by Ronald W. Jones and Peter B. Kenen, Amsterdam: North Holland, 1984

Ethier, Wilfred J., "Higher Dimensional Issues in Trade Theory" in *Handbook of International Economics*, vol. 1, edited by Ronald W. Jones and Peter B. Kenen, Amsterdam: North Holland, 1984

Findlay, Ronald, "Growth and Development in Trade Models" in *Handbook of International Economics*, vol. 1, edited by Ronald W. Jones and Peter B. Kenen, Amsterdam: North Holland, 1984

Grossman, Gene M. and Elhanan Helpman, *Innovation and Growth in the Global Economy*, Cambridge, Massachusetts: MIT Press, 1991

Heckscher, Eli F., "The Effect of Foreign Trade on the Distribution of Income" in *Heckscher–Ohlin Trade Theory*, by Eli F. Heckscher and Bertil Ohlin, edited by Harry Flam and M. June Flanders, Cambridge, Massachusetts: MIT Press, 1991

Helpman, Elhanan and Paul R. Krugman, *Market Structure and Foreign Trade: Increasing Returns, Imperfect Competition, and the International Economy*, Cambridge, Massachusetts: MIT Press, 1985

Irwin, Douglas A., *Against the Tide: An Intellectual History of Free Trade*, Princeton, New Jersey: Princeton University Press, 1996

Jones, Ronald W., "The Structure of Simple General Equilibrium Models", *Journal of Political Economy*, 73/6 (1965): 557–72

Jones, Ronald W. and J. Peter Neary, "The Positive Theory of International Trade" in *Handbook of International Economics*, edited by Ronald W. Jones and Peter B. Kenen, vol. 1, Amsterdam: North Holland, 1984

Krugman, Paul R., "The Narrow Moving Band, the Dutch Disease, and the Competitive Consequences of Mrs Thatcher: Notes on Trade in the Presence of Dynamic Scale Economies", *Journal of Development Economics*, 27 (1987): 41–55

Leamer, Edward E. and James Levinsohn, "International Trade Theory: The Evidence" in *Handbook of International Economics*, vol. 3, edited by Gene M. Grossman and Kenneth Rogoff, Amsterdam: North Holland, 1995

Lucas, Robert E., "On the Mechanics of Economic Development", *Journal of Monetary Economics*, 22 (1988): 3–22

Ohlin, Bertil, "A Theory of Trade" in *Heckscher–Ohlin Trade Theory*, by Eli F. Heckscher and Bertil Ohlin, edited by Harry Flam and M. June Flanders, Cambridge, Massachusetts: MIT Press, 1991

Oniki, Hajime and Hirofumi Uzawa, "Patterns of Trade and Investment in a Dynamic Model of International Trade", *Review of Economic Studies*, 32 (1965): 15–38

Redding, Stephen, "Dynamic Comparative Advantage and the Welfare Effects of Trade", *Oxford Economic Papers*, 51 (1999): 15–39

Ricardo, David, "On the Principles of Political Economy and Taxation" in *The Works and Correspondence of David Ricardo*, edited by Piero Sraffa and M.H. Dobb, vol. 1, Cambridge: Cambridge University Press, 1951 (1st edition 1817; 3rd edition 1821)

Ridley, Matt, "The Gains from Trade" in his *The Origins of Virtue: Human Instincts and the Evolution of Cooperation*, London and New York: Viking, 1996

Samuelson, Paul A., "The Gains from International Trade", *Canadian Journal of Economics and Political Science*, 5 (1939): 195–205

Samuelson, Paul A., "The Gains from International Trade Once Again", *Economic Journal*, 72 (1962): 820–29

Smith, Adam, "Of the Causes of Improvement in the Productive Powers of Labour, and of the Order According to Which Its Produce Is Naturally Distributed among the Different Ranks of the People" and "Of Systems of Political Economy" in *An Inquiry into the Nature and Causes of the Wealth of Nations*, edited by Kathryn Sutherland, Oxford and New York: Oxford University Press, 1993 (first published 1776)

Although many non-economists are sceptical of the axiomatic qualities ascribed to the theory of comparative advantage, RIDLEY cites the existence of inter-group trade in several pre-industrial societies as suggestive evidence that humans have exploited the logic of comparative advantage for thousands of years. Ridley also points out that inter-group trade affords us a unique edge over all other animals: while many species divide tasks between individuals to increase efficiency, only humans make use of the law of comparative advantage between groups.

Despite the perennial benefits humans derive from inter-group trade, it took centuries for the concept of comparative advantage to be formalized. IRWIN surveys the arguments that underpinned pre-classical support for restrictions on trade, beginning with the views of ancient Greek and Roman philosophers and culminating with those of the 18th-century mercantilists. He then describes the emergence of free-trade thought in mediaeval scholastic and mercantilist writing, and explains its sharply analytical re-expression by the classical economists. In the second half of his book, Irwin examines some of the major theoretical qualifications of the theory of comparative advantage that have been proposed from Ricardo's time to the present. In each case Irwin outlines the economic argument against free trade and describes the debate that took place over its validity and generality. He then assesses the extent to which it was either accepted as a legitimate caveat to the theory of comparative advantage or dismissed due to illogicality or economic irrelevance.

Although most of the ideas contained in *The Wealth of Nations* were posited in disparate forms by earlier writers, SMITH wove them around an explicit social welfare criterion to create the first systematic approach to economic analysis. He used this framework to argue that the static and dynamic gains that may be realized in a single enterprise from the division of labour along lines of absolute advantage may also obtain as the result of international specialisation and trade. While Smith probably understood the essence of comparative advantage, *The Wealth of Nations* does not provide an explanation of how a country lacking in any absolute advantages can gain from trade. Nevertheless, Smith's treatise should be included in any study of comparative advantage: it provides the analytical structure in which the logic of comparative advantage was later explained, and it anticipates many of our current views on competition, growth, and trade.

While Smith provided the first cogent argument for free trade, RICARDO explained the theory of comparative advantage on which the modern case for free trade is based. In chapter seven of his "Principles", Ricardo described a now-famous hypothetical situation in which Portugal and England trade cloth and wine. Although Portugal has an absolute advantage in the production of both goods, England has a comparative advantage in the production of clothing. Both countries can, therefore, benefit from specialization and trade. Strangely, Ricardo did not again invoke the idea of comparative advantage to support his arguments for free trade, which has resulted in debate over his fundamental understanding of the concept.

The positive predictions that Ricardo's theory makes about the direction and terms of trade were arguably accepted more readily than its normative implications about the gains from trade. Paul A. Samuelson provides the first rigorous demonstration of the benefits of trading along the lines of comparative advantage. Using a general model with multiple factors and goods, SAMUELSON (1939) shows that a small country gains from trade, even if this trade is not completely free, whenever world prices differ from the country's autarkic prices. SAMUELSON (1962) induces the same gains for a large country by showing that a large country's post-trade utility-possibility frontier dominates its autarkic counterpart; hence, lump-sum taxes and compensatory transfers can be used to ensure that no one is made worse off by trade while the lot of some is unequivocally improved.

While Ricardian trade theory identifies differences in technological efficiency as the source of comparative advantage, HECKSCHER and OHLIN demonstrate that cross-country variations in relative factor endowments can also shape the pattern of trade. Following their pioneering work, JONES provides the benchmark algebraic exposition of the now-familiar two-good, two-factor general equilibrium model in which differences in technologies, factor endowments, or, alternatively, consumer preferences may produce comparative cost advantages. Jones' paper notably identifies the dual relationships that exist among many of the model's variables, and highlights the similarities between the static analysis of trade and the dynamic analysis of economic growth.

A large portion of the trade literature is concerned with extending the Ricardian and Heckscher–Ohlin models to general cases with any number of factors, tradable goods, and trading countries. ETHIER's detailed mathematical survey demonstrates the challenges posed by higher dimensionality and identifies those properties that do, and as importantly, those properties that do not generalize to higher-dimensional variants of these models. Standard trade theory has also been extended to show the ways in which the law of comparative advantage is transformed by the existence of inter-sectoral factor immobility, the presence of non-traded goods, and the exchange of factors of production, intermediate goods, or technical knowledge. JONES & NEARY concisely survey these extensions, sacrificing depth on some issues in order to provide

a coherent analytical review. Both surveys provide comprehensive bibliographies that are useful for further research.

Although the principle of comparative advantage provides a basic explanation of trade patterns based on cross-country differences, it does not account for how these differences arise in the first place. ONIKI & UZAWA present the first rigorous model in which comparative advantage evolves over time by employing a two-country Heckscher-Ohlin framework where labour and capital grow at exogenously determined rates. FINDLAY surveys a variety of similar exogenous growth models in which factor accumulation and technological change can affect the pattern of comparative costs. The salient point of both papers is that comparative advantage is not fixed, but responds to changes in cross-country endowments.

DEARDORFF reviews the many problems that bedevil attempts to test simple trade models against complex empirical data. Although he argues that no conclusive test of any trade theory has been formulated and applied, he also notes that efforts to refine our econometric techniques and to make trade theory more empirically relevant have moved us closer to achieving this goal. Deardorff identifies three major empirical regularities that are not well explained by the theory of comparative advantage: substantial intra-industry trade, high volumes of trade between relatively similar countries, and insignificant resource reallocation during episodes of substantial trade liberalization.

Taking note of these explanatory gaps in traditional trade theory, HELPMAN & KRUGMAN argue that cross-country differences in tastes, technology, and factor endowments are not the only reasons for trade. Using insights from the industrial organization literature, they propose a series of models in which economies of scale and imperfect competition provide not only additional incentives for international trade, but also account for the empirical regularities noted by Deardorff. Comparative advantage remains an important predictor of trade patterns in these models, but Helpman & Krugman contend that its explanatory monopoly has been compromised by their work. This book remains one of the definitive references on trade and imperfect competition.

Helpman and Krugman's monograph ends with a call for a dynamic version of their theories. KRUGMAN, LUCAS, and GROSSMAN & HELPMAN respond with models of endogenous growth and trade in which the changing pattern of comparative advantage is itself determined by the growth process. In the models developed by Krugman and Lucas, learning-by-doing produces growth and may also entrench patterns of specialization over time. In contrast, profit-seeking investments in research and development drive the growth process in Grossman & Helpman's models. Both approaches allow for the possibility that temporary protection can permanently alter the pattern of comparative advantage, but only Grossman & Helpman show that such protection can improve welfare. REDDING builds on these studies by refining the distinction between the standard static notion of comparative advantage and its heretofore loosely defined dynamic complement. This allows Redding to add further precision to the conditions under which temporary trade and industrial policies may be permanently welfare-improving.

LEAMER & LEVINSOHN build on Deardorff's work by reviewing recent tests of the Heckscher-Ohlin model and evaluating the emerging empirical support for models of trade that incorporate economies of scale and imperfectly competitive markets. They suggest that the existing trade data may be best explained by models in which differences in factor endowments and imperfect competition both motivate trade.

BRETT E. HOUSE

See also International trade policy, Trade theory, development of

Competencies

Boam, Rosemary and Paul Sparrow, *Designing and Achieving Competency*, Maidenhead, Berkshire: McGraw Hill, 1992

Cockerill, A.P., "Competencies" in *The Blackwell Encyclopedic Dictionary of Organizational Behaviour*, edited by Nigel Nicholson, Oxford and Cambridge, Massachusetts: Blackwell, 1995

Finegold, David, Edward L. Lawler III and Gerald E. Ledford Jr, "Organizing for Competencies and Capabilities: Bridging from Strategy to Effectiveness" in *Tomorrow's Organization: Crafting Winning Capabilities in a Dynamic World*, edited by Susan Albers Mohrman *et al.*, San Francisco: Jossey Bass, 1998

Hagan, Christine M., "The Core Competence Organization: Implications for Human Resource Practices", *Human Resource Management Review*, 6/2 (1996): 147–64

Sparrow, Paul R., "Organizational Competencies: Creating a Strategic Behavioural Framework for Selection and Assessment" in *International Handbook of Selection and Assessment*, edited by Neil Anderson and Peter Herriot, Chichester and New York: Wiley, 1997

Spencer, Lyle M. and Signe M. Spencer, *Competence at Work*, New York: Wiley, 1993

Strebler, Marie, Dilys Robinson and Paul Heron, *Getting the Best Out of Your Competencies*, Falmer, Sussex: Institute for Employment Studies, 1997

Warr, P. and Conner, M., "Job Competence and Cognition" in *Research in Organizational Behavior*, 14 (1996): 91–127

Williams, Richard S., *Performance Management: Perspectives on Employee Performance*, London and Boston: International Thomson Business Press, 1998

Wood, Robert and Tim Payne, *Competency-Based Recruitment and Selection*, Chichester and New York: Wiley, 1998

Much conceptual confusion surrounds the term "competencies" and there is little serious academic writing that helps to clear it up. The term consequently remains unclear and continues to be used to refer to properties of jobholders, jobs, and of organizations. The variety of meanings is well illustrated by the short piece by COCKERILL. Rather longer explorations are found in SPARROW and in FINEGOLD *et al.* The latter briefly considers competencies as distinctive features of the organization and as individual characteristics before going on to consider practical implications for such matters as organizational design and human resource management. Sparrow draws distinctions among "management competences", "behavioural competencies", and "organizational competences". That we have the terms "competences" as well as "competencies" does not help our understanding, of course, especially as the two sometimes are used synonymously and sometimes with different meanings. WILLIAMS has also reviewed the terms and has considered the place of competencies within a framework of theories of job performance. This analysis reveals that competencies could be seen as either antecedents or determinants of performance or, indeed, as performance itself if one adopts a behavioural definition of "performance". One further conceptual treatment is to be found in WARR & CONNER. Their work is of particular interest for two reasons. First, they seek to bring together several models of competencies and put forward a three-dimensional framework to do so. Second, they seek to integrate competencies with theories of cognitive performance.

Readers seeking reviews of the variety of meaning attaching to the term "competencies" should therefore consult the above sources. Those in search of more practical guidance also have a selection of material available. Although it is now a few years old probably still the most useful British book is that by BOAM & SPARROW. This contains chapters on how to identify and assess competencies and various accounts of the use of competencies. Another British source is STREBLER *et al.*, which draws on case-study work in a small number of UK organizations. They describe, among other things, how organizations use competencies and how competencies are assessed and measured. The investigators also were able to undertake some survey work into the reactions of users (line managers and their staff) – an issue that is relatively underexplored.

SPENCER & SPENCER is similarly wide ranging. This gives the orthodoxy of the Mcber model of competencies. It sets out a competency dictionary (or catalogue of competencies) derived from the many Mcber studies. It also describes how to identify competencies using the Mcber method of behavioural event interviewing. Five chapters present generic competency models for a range of jobs, for example salespeople and managers.

Taken together these three sources describe a range of approaches to the identification of competencies and they give numerous illustrations of competencies in use. All three are important sources and are essential reading for anyone wanting practical advice. They include several chapters on practical applications such as performance management, pay, succession planning, career development, integrated human resource management information systems, and recruitment and selection.

One specific treatment of the use of competencies in recruitment and selection is found in WOOD & PAYNE. In essence this is a how-to-do-it volume on recruitment and selection but its core theme of competencies sets it apart from many. For example, there are chapters on interviewing based on competencies, advice on designing application forms to assess competencies, and so forth.

All of the above sources are primarily about competencies as characteristics that individuals possess or as requirements of jobs. There also is the view that competencies are distinctive features of the organization. Cockerill alludes to this. For a slightly fuller treatment of this notion see HAGAN. As well as setting out the basic tenets of the core competence model she considers implications for human resource management activities.

RICHARD WILLIAMS

Competition, economic

Arrow, Kenneth J. and Gerard Debreu, "Existence of Equilibrium for a Competitive Economy", *Econometrica*, 22 (1954): 265–90

Arrow, Kenneth J., "Towards a Theory of Price Adjustment" in *The Allocation of Economic Resources*, by Moses Abramovitz *et al.*, Stanford, California: Stanford University Press, 1959

Arrow, Kenneth J. and F.H. Hahn, *General Competitive Analysis*, San Francisco: Holden Day, 1971

Davis, D.G., "A Note on Marshallian vs Walrasian Equilibrium Conditions", *Canadian Journal of Economics and Political Science*, 29 (1963)

Deaton, Angus and John Muellbauer, *Economics and Consumer Behaviour*, Cambridge and New York: Cambridge University Press, 1980

Debreu, Gerard, *Theory of Value*, New York: Wiley, 1959

Grossman, S. and O. Hart, "The Costs and Benefits of Ownership: A Theory of Vertical and Lateral Integration", *Journal of Political Economy*, 94 (1986): 691–719

Mas-Colell, Andreu, *The Theory of General Economic Equilibrium: A Differentiable Approach*, Cambridge and New York: Cambridge University Press, 1985

Porter, Michael E., *Cases in Competitive Strategy*, New York: Free Press, and London: Collier Macmillan, 1983

Samuelson, Paul A., *Foundations of Economic Analysis*, Cambridge, Massachusetts: Harvard University Press, 1947

ARROW & DEBREU is the seminal book on the concept of (general) equilibrium, perfectly competitive or price-taking behaviour, the basic assumptions underlying perfect competition, such as the absence of increasing returns to scale, and the irrelevance of strategic interaction in the presence of n identical firms producing n identical goods at a minimum efficient scale which approaches zero. The authors also describe price adjustments in a perfectly competitive set of markets, which is what general equilibrium economists refer to as Walrasian *tâtonnement*.

Price adjustment issues are also tackled by ARROW and by DEBREU separately. They familiarize the reader with such concepts as Walrasian equilibrium, Walras's law, relative prices, willingness to pay, individual rationality, and price-taking behaviour. Individual rationality leads economic agents to behave in such a way that, abstracting from space and time, price is sought according to a randomizing trial-and-error process, which eventually leads to equilibrium relative prices. Such a process is due to Leon Walras, who termed it *tâtonnement* because it bears some resemblance to the searching blindly for something in the dark.

ARROW & HAHN also analyse competition and equilibrium issues. They expound the standard assumptions behind perfect competition, such as well-behaved preferences, strong and weak axioms for regular preferences, and individual rationality of firms (profit maximization) and consumers (utility maximization). Walrasian topics are discussed, including the practical relevance of Walras' law, and its implications for the economic science as a whole. In many respects, this book on general competition theory (perfect competition) builds on

the authors' previous research and should be intended as a reference guide for students in competition and equilibrium theory.

The economic equilibrium conditions that are most frequently encountered in microeconomics are derived from the "primal" (or Marshallian) demand function, which depends upon relative prices and incomes. The Marshallian demand function – which is directly observable – can be shown to be equivalent to Hicksian demand (a function of price and utility) at equilibrium (market clearing) prices. Once supply is introduced into the picture, Marshallian equilibrium conditions in a particular market (also known as "partial equilibrium" conditions) can be compared with Walrasian equilibrium conditions in each of n markets ("general equilibrium" conditions). One can show that general equilibrium does not necessarily imply partial equilibrium, whereas partial equilibrium in $n-1$ markets necessarily implies partial equilibrium in the $n-th$ market, and thus general equilibrium (Walras's law). Marshallian and Walrasian equilibrium conditions are analysed and compared by DAVIS.

DEATON & MUELLBAUER investigate traditional issues of consumer theory. Their approach is rigorous and mathematically demanding. Axioms about preferences are analysed, and possible econometric applications (estimation of demand functions, studies on equilibrium stability) are put forward. Production theory is also compared with consumer theory – in fact, it can be said that both production and demand theories stem from the same microeconomic rationality assumptions (neoclassical hypotheses). This is a very technical book, which will suit the experienced reader.

GROSSMAN & HART is the "counterfactual" book on competition. Starting from the failure of perfect competition in the presence of increasing returns to scale (when perfectly competitive firms would incur losses because of marginal cost pricing not making up for fixed costs), the authors advance a theory of vertical and lateral (horizontal) integration. In the presence of fixed – and possibly sunk – costs, perfectly competitive firms are unlikely to survive. Therefore, firms in many markets tend to merge in order to give rise to larger structures, which realize both economies of scale and scope replacing external transactions ("buy") by internal ones ("make"). "Scale" is then reached via horizontal integration, whereas "scope" is obtained as a result of both horizontal and vertical integration. This book is relevant to competition theory, as it expounds some of the observable alternatives to well-functioning competitive markets (which are seldom found in reality).

MAS-COLELL proposes a very technical approach to general equilibrium. Starting from the seminal ideas of Arrow & Debreu, the author chooses a high-profile, mathematical treatment of preferences and production schedules. Equilibrium outcomes for n markets are analysed, with some innovative conclusions. This is the modern equivalent of Arrow & Debreu, for readers with experience in this field.

PORTER advances a completely different view of the economics of competition. A business approach is taken, where "competition" is intended as strategic interaction among several firms (with n being not particularly large) in terms of both price and non-price strategies. Competition as a series of reactions is typical of business theory. From an economic standpoint, what business theorists call "competition" is actually a form of oligopoly where firms "play" against each other, and a limited form of price-making behaviour replaces the ideal price-taking assumption of perfect competition theory.

SAMUELSON takes a general approach in his classic economics book. Part II in particular, is about microeconomics. Without unduly complicating his analysis with advanced mathematics, the author introduces inexperienced readers to perfect competition and general equilibrium theory with an elegant and light touch.

GIAN CARLO SCARSI

See also General equilibrium theory

Competition policy, *see* Anti-trust economics

Competitive strategy

Buzzell, Robert B. and Bradley T. Gale, *The PIMS Principles: Linking Strategy to Performance*, New York: Free Press and London: Collier Macmillan, 1987

de Kare-Silver, Michael, *Strategy in Crisis: Why Business Urgently Needs a Completely New Approach*, London: Macmillan, 1997; New York: New York University Press, 1998

Dess, G.G., A. Gupta, J.F. Hennart and C.W.L. Hill, "Conducting and Integrating Strategy Research at the International, Corporate, and Business Levels: Issues and Directions", *Journal of Management*, 21/3 (1995): 357–93

Faulkner, David and Cliff Bowman, *The Essence of Competitive Strategy*, New York: Prentice Hall, 1995

Hitt, Michael A., R. Duane Ireland and Robert E. Hoskisson, *Strategic Management: Competitiveness and Globalization*, 3rd edition, Cincinnati: South-Western, 1999

Miller, D., "The Generic Strategy Trap", *Journal of Business Strategy*, 13/1 (1992): 37–42

Porter, Michael E., *Competitive Strategy: Techniques for Analyzing Industries and Competitors*, New York: Free Press, 1980

Porter, Michael E., *Competitive Advantage: Creating and Sustaining Superior Performance*, New York: Free Press, and London: Macmillan, 1985

Segev, Eli, *Business Unit Strategy*, Chichester and New York: Wiley, 1997

Treacy, Michael and Fred Wiersema, *The Discipline of Market Leaders*, Reading, Massachusetts: Addison Wesley, 1995

DESS *et al.* present and discuss the major streams of thought concerning strategy. They focus on business-level or competitive strategy and consider it to be an integrated and coordinated set of commitments and actions designed to provide value to customers and gain a competitive advantage by exploiting core competencies in specific, individual product markets.

The approach to competitive strategy that has dominated strategic management theory and practice over the last two decades was developed by Michael Porter at the beginning of the 1980s. According to PORTER (1980), competitive strategy is concerned with a firm's position in an industry, relative to various competitive forces. These include established competitors, buyers/customers, suppliers, the threat of substitute products, and the threat of entry to the industry by new competitors. The goal of every company should be to position itself in its industry in such a way as to minimize the bargaining power of these five forces over the company.

To position itself effectively in its industry a company must decide on the competitive strategy to follow. PORTER (1985), in his second influential book, argues that there are three generic strategies companies must follow to establish a lead in their market: differentiation, cost leadership, and focus strategy. The differentiation strategy means that value is provided to customers through the unique features and characteristics of a firm's products or services. Products or services can be differentiated in a number of ways including: superior quality, unique features, higher customer responsiveness, rapid product innovation, advanced technological characteristics, and so on. The cost leadership strategy means that the company offers relatively standardized products with features or characteristics that are acceptable to customers at the lowest competitive price. This could be achieved by building efficient-scale facilities, establishing tight control of production, minimizing the costs of sales, production, research and development, service, and finally, investing in state-of-the-art manufacturing technologies. By implementing a differentiation or a cost-leadership strategy, the company might chose to compete on an industry-wide basis and adopt a broad competitive scope, or choose to focus so as to serve the needs of a particular customer group in an industry. Thus, a company might choose to focus on a specific segment (or niche) of the market and in this segment follow a differentiation or a cost leadership strategy.

Porter's book on competitive strategy proved invaluable in highlighting the importance and relevance of a specific strategic position. However, several authors have criticized his three generic competitive strategies. For example, DE KARE-SILVER, considered them to be superficial and claimed that generic competitive strategies lacked specificity, were not measurable, did not have enough focus on the customer, and did not reflect the business realities of the 1990s.

SEGEV cautions researchers and managers against Porter's main assumption that there are only a limited number of possible strategies. Some industries may offer more than four strategic alternatives; others offer less. Moreover, the generic strategy approach may not relate to the lifecycle concept. Porter assumes that generic strategies are successful in every stage. This may not be true as a business unit may switch strategies during various stages of its lifecycle.

Among the main critics of Porter is MILLER, who argues that cost-based strategies are not necessarily incompatible with differentiation. Porter argues that companies trying to achieve both cost leadership and differentiation become "stuck in the middle", and the outcome is poor performance. Miller bases his arguments on the work of BUZZELL & GALE, who argue for the benefits of a "virtuous circle" in strategy. This means that the search for low cost provides surpluses to reinvest in differentiation and product advantages. Thus, in certain cases, companies can follow an integrated cost leadership and differentiation strategy and be successful.

Among the few who have tried to add to the theory on competitive strategies are TREACY & WIERSEMA. They have identified three competitive strategies (value disciplines as they call them) that lead to success. The first is called "operational excellence" and is based on providing customers with reliable and easily available products or services, at competitive prices. The second is called "customer intimacy" and implies knowing customers intimately and being able to respond quickly to their specific and special needs. Finally, product leadership implies offering customers innovative products and services. Treacy & Wiersema argue that companies should try to focus on one of the value disciplines and stake their reputation on it.

HITT, IRELAND & HOSKISSON have also dealt with the definition of competitive strategy. They argue that competitive strategy concerns itself with the questions of: (a) how the company is going to compete in a specific area; (b) what sort of market opportunities the company should develop; (c) what sort of new products and services the company should/can offer; (d) how resources are going to be allocated within the company; and (e) what structure and control systems will the company adopt.

FAULKNER & BOWMAN moved further and produced a more detailed typology of competitive strategies, which they call the "strategy clock". Adopting the dimensions of perceived added value and price, the authors produce eight competitive strategies. They range from low price, low perceived-value strategies to focused differentiation strategy, to high price, low perceived-value. The strategy clock is, then, a market-based model of competitive strategy options. It does not deny that the cost base of an organization is of crucial importance, but it sees this as a means of developing strategic options and not as a basis for competitive advantage in itself.

Given the arguments against Porter's generic competitive strategies, it might be concluded that the concept has no merit. On the contrary, it is a useful tool for generating basic options in strategic analysis. However, it should be considered as the starting point in the development of such options.

Vassilis Papadakis

Competitiveness

Best, Michael, *The New Competition: Institutions of Industrial Restructuring*, Cambridge, Massachusetts: Harvard University Press, and Cambridge: Polity Press, 1990

Boltho, A. (editor), "International Competitiveness", special issue, *Oxford Review of Economic Policy*, 12/3 (1996)

Dunning, John, Edward Bannerman and Sarianna M. Lundan, *Competitiveness and Industrial Policy in Northern Ireland*, Belfast: Northern Ireland Economic Council, 1998

Francis, Arthur, "The Process of National Industrial Regeneration and Competitiveness", *Strategic Management Journal*, 13 (1992): 61–78

Group of Lisbon, *Limits to Competition*, Cambridge, Massachusetts: MIT Press, 1995

Krugman, Paul, "Competitiveness: A Dangerous Obsession", *Foreign Affairs*, 73/2 (1994): 28–44

O'Donnell, Rory, "The Competitive Advantage of Peripheral Regions: Conceptual Issues and Research Approaches" in *Competing from the Periphery: Core Issues in International Business*, edited by Brian Fynes and Seán Ennis, Dublin: Oak Tree Press, and London: Dryden, 1997

Porter, Michael E., *The Competitive Advantage of Nations*, New York: Free Press, and Basingstoke: Macmillan, 1990

Reich, Robert, *The Work of Nations*, New York: Knopf, 1991

The issue of competitiveness has come to dominate much economic thinking, especially in the context of industrial development and policy. In recent years, few topics in economics have generated as much discussion and controversy as this. The related work has been extensive and has examined the different levels of the economy at which competitiveness should be applied – nation, region, firm, and industry. There has also been an extensive debate about what exactly is meant by "competitiveness". Finally, an important distinction has been made, viewing competitiveness both as an input in terms of policy measures, and as an output in terms of performance measures. These are key issues for a full understanding of competitiveness and for the effective design and implementation of government policy.

Perhaps the best-known and most influential book on competitiveness is that by PORTER, who argues that it is the competitiveness of firms and industries that determines what he refers to as the competitive advantage of an economy, whether it be at the national or regional level. In particular, he argues that it is important to build national champions in an economy through his "diamond" of the key determinants of competitive advantage. This diamond is constructed of the following: (a) *factor conditions* – the availability and quality of the factors of production, such as skilled labour, infrastructure, and so on; (b) *demand conditions* – the nature of local and external demand for the industry's product or service, where local demand can play a vital role in encouraging product innovation and improvement; (c) *related and supporting industries* – the presence or absence of supplier industries and related industries that are also internationally competitive; and (d) *firm strategy, structure, and rivalry* – the national conditions governing how companies are created, organized, and managed. A further key issue in his analytical framework is the concept of industrial clusters, which are created from the successful interaction of the four factors in the competitiveness diamond, and which tend to be geographically concentrated. World-class buyers, suppliers, and related industries in an economy trigger self-reinforcing benefits in upgrading competitive advantage across related industries. Finally, two other factors that influence the competitiveness diamond are the role of government, and chance.

In contrast to Porter, REICH argues that because of the internationalization of domestic economies, as a result of the growing importance of multinational corporations (MNCs), the nationality of a company has become increasingly irrelevant. Consequently, because of the footloose nature of MNCs, he argues that national policies towards industry are highly restricted in scope, and government policy should, therefore, concentrate on more general issues. In particular, he sees the creation of a highly skilled workforce as the main factor in determining competitiveness.

KRUGMAN argues forcibly that the emphasis that has been placed on competitiveness is misplaced, if not harmful, at least when applied at the level of the national or regional economy. He states that "competitiveness" is a meaningless word when applied to national economies, and the obsession with competitiveness is both wrong and dangerous. This can be seen in the context of international trade, which should not be viewed as a zero-sum game, where one country wins at the expense of the other, but rather as an exchange from which both benefit through the principle of comparative advantage.

The GROUP OF LISBON also argue that being competitive has ceased to be a means to an end, and instead, competitiveness has acquired the status of a universal credo or ideology. According to this view, the excessive concentration and emphasis placed on competitiveness in a world of increasing globalization is leading to increased socioeconomic inequalities and unacceptable levels of unaccountable power in MNCs.

FRANCIS provides a good summary of many of the various views surrounding the debate around competitiveness. He suggests that work on the topic has covered the application of competitiveness at two broad levels in an economy. The first is the analysis and explanation of competitiveness at the level of the firm or industry. The second is more concerned with the link between competitiveness and national or regional economic performance.

O'DONNELL, in a useful overview of many of the issues around competitiveness, suggests that there are three dimensions to competitiveness – performance, potential, and process. Competitive performance refers to such measures as export market share; competitive potential refers to the most orthodox measures, such as productivity and price competitiveness; and competitive process refers to aspects of management within firms and governance in the wider context of an economy. Importantly, these three dimensions are interrelated and can be applied at the level of the nation, region, industry, firm, and product.

BEST provides an important and innovative contribution to the debate around competitiveness with his argument that successful industrial development is the result of a "new competition", based on new production and organizational concepts within firms, industries, and regions. The improvement of competitiveness in this framework results from a production-based strategy that leads to continuous improvement and innovation in methods, procedures, and processes. Moreover, in contrast with orthodox models of competitive processes, a key concept is collaboration and cooperation between firms operating within an environment made conducive to development by the actions of government.

In a useful application of much of this literature and analysis on competitiveness, DUNNING, BANNERMAN & LUNDAN critically discuss much of the debate around competitiveness and, by placing productivity at the heart of competitiveness, they develop what they refer to as a competitiveness pyramid, which distinguishes between competitiveness as a policy framework (input) and competitiveness as performance benchmarking (output). Drawing on case studies of competitiveness from around the world, they usefully apply their conclusions to the specific conditions of the regional economy of Northern Ireland.

BOLTHO acts as a good reference point and includes a wide-ranging series of articles on international competitiveness by many of the leading experts, including articles that examine competitiveness from the point of view of exchange rates, technology, the localization of industry, trade performance, and stabilization and adjustment policies.

DOUGLAS HAMILTON

Complexity

Anderson, Philip W., Kenneth J. Arrow and David Pines (editors), *The Economy as an Evolving Complex System*, Redwood City, California: Addison Wesley, 1988

Arthur, W. Brian, *Increasing Returns and Path Dependence in the Economy*, Ann Arbor: University of Michigan Press, 1994

Arthur, W. Brian, Steven N. Durlauf and David A. Lane (editors), *The Economy as an Evolving Complex System 2*, Reading, Massachusetts: Addison Wesley, 1997

Bak, Per, *How Nature Works: The Science of Self-Organized Criticality*, New York: Springer, 1996; Oxford: Oxford University Press, 1997

Brock, William A., David A. Hsieh and Blake LeBaron, *Nonlinear Dynamics, Chaos and Instability: Statistical Theory and Economic Evidence*, Cambridge, Massachusetts: MIT Press, 1991

Cohen, Jack and Ian Stewart, *The Collapse of Chaos: Discovering Simplicity in a Complex World*, New York and London: Viking, 1994

Cowan, George, David Pines and David Meltzer (editors), *Complexity: Metaphors, Models and Reality*, Reading, Massachusetts: Addison Wesley, 1994

Gleick, James, *Chaos: Making a New Science*, New York: Viking, and London: Heinemann, 1987

Grandmont, Jean-Michel, "On Endogenous Competitive Business Cycles", *Econometrica*, 53 (1985): 995–1045

Kauffman, Stuart A., *The Origins of Order: Self-Organization and Selection in Evolution*, New York and Oxford: Oxford University Press, 1993

Louçã, Francisco, *Turbulence in Economics: An Evolutionary Appraisal of Cycles and Complexity in Historical Processes*, Cheltenham, Gloucestershire: Elgar, 1997

Mandelbrot, Benoit, "Towards a Second Stage of Indeterminism in Science", *Interdisciplinary Science Review*, 12 (1987): 117–27

Mandelbrot, Benoit, *The Fractal Geometry of Nature*, New York: Freeman, 1988

Peters, Edgar E., *Fractal Market Analysis: Applying Chaos Theory to Investment and Economics*, New York and Chichester: Wiley, 1994

Stewart, Ian, *Does God Play Dice? The New Mathematics of Chaos*, 2nd edition, London and New York: Penguin, 1997

Waldrop, Mitchell M., *Complexity: The Emerging Science at the Edge of Order and Chaos*, New York: Simon and Schuster, 1992; London: Viking, 1993

Although some regard Poincaré as the originator of a scientific approach to apparently unpredictable systems, it was only recently that his work was discovered and interpreted and his important insights finally understood. Benoit Mandelbrot, a French mathematician working in the US for IBM, has played a crucial part in developing complexity theory, a theory which has opened a new era for science. Vindicating Poincaré against the formalist concept of mathematics generated by the Bourbaki school, MANDELBROT (1987, 1988) used his intuition to describe a new geometry of nature, suggesting self-similarity and the fractal structure of many objects as the basis for a new understanding of the world. Mandelbrot's 1988 introduction stakes out his "manifesto" – that "there is a fractal face to the geometry of nature". His work provides a simple and straightforward, but powerful argument: that after the dominance of deterministic concepts in science, later combined with the first generation of indeterminism (the traditional probabilistic theory), it is now time to move to the second generation of indeterminism, considering nonlinearities as generating change and mutation in nature.

GLEICK was a bestseller. In nontechnical language, he linked these forerunners to modern developments and, using examples, pictures and figures, addressed a set of themes – the butterfly effect, strange attractors, the geometry of nature, the origin of life – that opened the door for the first contact with chaos. It is still a good introduction, although some scientists fear that the book simplifies their endeavour.

WALDROP's book on complexity was published five years later: it is complementary to the works above and was also a bestseller. The book is focused on a new institution that represents the new scientific approach in its own conception: the Santa Fe Institute (SFI). This was created just after Gleick's book was published, and reunited a group of biologists, physicists, and economists in a new setting. Their collaboration arose from curiosity and shared challenge, and Waldrop's interviews highlight both this creativity and competition in the common pursuit of an emerging science. The SFI has been criticized more recently for too much theorizing and too little experimental science, and for publicizing results not yet grounded on scientific discussions and peer review. Waldrop points out one of the reasons, but not the only one, for this mistrust: the SFI was a place for orthodox and heterodox Darwinian biologists or neoclassical and evolutionary economists to discuss their views.

This plurality, not to say tolerance, is not so common in established academic centres, and the SFI set an example. Furthermore, the stated purpose of some of its staff members – to redefine the constitutive metaphor illuminating the methods of social sciences – led to important discussions that are still ongoing in the profession today.

ANDERSON, ARROW & PINES edited the proceedings from the first SFI conference, in 1987, when ten natural scientists and ten economists met for a challenging exchange of views. The book reproduces the fascinating discussions held after each paper, highlighting the differences between the two groups in their understanding of the same concept. One discussion was about equilibrium. According to Philip Anderson – one of the editors and a Nobel Prize winner in physics – physicists generally consider that a system whose motion suffers random fluctuations impinging to its deterministic dynamics is a disequilibrium system, whereas economists call it equilibrium. "A liberal education on the various meanings of the word 'equilibrium' was a bracing experience for all", concludes Anderson. Considering that Arrow, another of the editors of the same volume, is an influential economist who won the Nobel Prize for his work on general equilibrium, one may infer what a bracing experience it was indeed. The reader has the privilege of sharing it.

COWAN, PINES & MELTZER edited a collection of essays representing some of the viewpoints at the SFI. The notion of a "complex adaptive system" is introduced by the Nobel Prize winner Murray Gell-Man, and many examples are discussed: from cultural transmission, brain circuits, molecular biology, and ecological evolution to self-organization in dynamic processes. As with the SFI proceedings above, this work also includes the transcription of useful informal debates on the major topics addressed in the essays.

KAUFFMAN's book is representative of the "SFI approach". It challenges the traditional neo-Darwinist synthesis, suggesting that self-organization is part of – and the expression of – an adaptive process that creates spontaneous order. In its general overview of the field and of the available analytical techniques, and its discussion of new conjectures about the origin of life and the evolutionary process, this book is unique.

BAK addresses another interesting and related problem: how does nature work? The author proves that there is something in common between sandpiles, landscape formation, earthquakes, solar flares, traffic jams, black holes, pulsars, and sediment deposition – and that is "self-organized criticality (SOC)". This book presents the argument and makes a strong case for SOC as a good candidate for a general paradigm of the organization of nature. Some concepts are introduced in simple language and with abundant examples: $1/f$ noise, chaos, complexity, critical state, and catastrophes. In this sense, Bak provides a useful introduction to some of the conjectures dominating recent scientific efforts. Although the discussion of social sciences, and economics in particular, is very scant and based only on a simple toy model and the metaphor of the traffic jam, social scientists may learn from this book that what is discussed nowadays in the "hard sciences" matches perfectly with their own preoccupations.

ARTHUR, DURLAUF & LANE results from the second SFI conference, "Economy as a Complex Evolving System", held in 1996. As with the first SFO proceedings volume, this maintains the effort to bring together highly rated physicists, biologists and social scientists, in order to discuss economic evolution from different points of view. The editor's introduction is a brilliant piece, pointing out the main difficulties, paradigmatic challenges, and the agenda for the future of the research on complexity in economics. It is a daring task: to replace such traditional concepts as the representative agent, the postulate of rationality and the assumption of either perfect information or maximizing behaviour, the atomistic techniques and reversibility of time, with the consideration of heterogeneous populations, selection and variation, bounded rationality, the role of institutional forms of control, the irreversibility of time and consequently evolution.

ARTHUR's collection of papers focuses around an important topic: the role of increasing returns and path dependence in economics. Competing technologies, historical trajectories, urban systems, human learning, industry location patterns and a wide variety of themes are discussed in this inspiring book. Arthur challenges one of the more resilient traditions in economics – that of decreasing returns and negative feedback – an important building block of the concept of equilibrium, and emphasizes that new metaphors, new theories, and new tools are badly needed in economics in order to assess the real evolution of real economic systems in real time. Despite the rigour of the mathematical treatment, which does not ease the way for the uninitiated, the reader of this book may feel that a new door is being opened.

GRANDMONT's article is an example of a model of the endogenous generation of cycles, creating a bridge between cycle theory and complexity science. In his overlapping generations model, with perfect foresight and under general intertemporal Walrasian equilibrium, aperiodic and consequently unpredictable outcomes emerge. Nonlinear dynamics allows for a variety of different types of system behaviour, which are explored in this path-breaking paper, one of the first contemporary examples marking the emergence of a new generation of models in economics.

LOUÇÃ discusses complexity from yet another point of view. This historical overview of the evolution of economics is based on the contribution of some of the authors of the "years of high theory", in particular Keynes, Schumpeter, Mitchell, Frisch and others who addressed the problem of economic change throughout history. The book shows that in this period there was widespread intuition of the existence of nonequilibrium processes, structural mutation, endogenously generated change, and nonlinear and complex relations in economics. The emergence of a paradigmatic discipline around neoclassical theory and econometric confirmationism is explained, although a lively picture of the rugged theoretical landscape of economics contributes to understand some of the missing links and the lost opportunities – parts of which are revived in the framework of complexity science some decades later on.

BROCK, HSIEH & LeBARON develop a statistical test based on the measure of the correlation dimension for stationary series, in order to discriminate between low dimensional nonlinear processes and linear systems affected by random shocks. The null hypothesis asserts the existence of independent and identically distributed random variables as the residuals of the stationarized series, whereas the alternative hypothesis includes either nonlinear or non-Gaussian processes. This test is used for a variety of examples of exchange rates and stock price series, and its statistical characteristics and asymptotic distribution are thoroughly discussed. This kind of non-parametrical statistical tests has been used ever since, although the lack of an authoritative test for the detection of chaos restricts the conclusions from empirical work.

PETERS is not an academic but a senior manager in an asset management firm, and his book is based on experience in speculative markets. It builds on a critique of the random-walk hypothesis of efficient markets, and uses fractal analysis for the detection of periodicities and structure within the series, providing some very simple software versions in order to apply these tools. This accessible account witnesses the extension and potential of complexity theories, models, and statistics in order to uncover the evolutionary changes of economic variables.

STEWART's well-documented and well-written book addresses Einstein's *motum*: "I cannot believe that God plays dice with the cosmos." Stewart challenges the prevailing scientific tradition, which is positivistic and based on the presumption that the existence of universal laws, and their identification, exhaustively describes the mechanistic universe. No mathematical expertise is needed to read and understand this plea for a new science.

COHEN & STEWART examine chaos and complexity, arguing that their interaction exhibits a surprising feature: simplicity. Back to Newton? Not necessarily, as the authors emphasize that regularity in some phenomena and in prevailing structures are consequences of developmental and constrained processes – DNA, the organization of the brain, the formation of patterns in nature. "The collapse of chaos" in the title refers, therefore, to the emergence of modes of organization that were impossible in the simplistic framework of linear models and atomistic or reductionist science. Yet the results are also, in some cases, simple structures.

FRANCISCO LOUÇÃ

See also Nonlinear dynamics

Computational theory of mind

Churchland, Patricia S. and Terrence J. Sejnowski, *The Computational Brain*, Cambridge, Massachusetts: MIT Press, 1992

Crane, Tim, *The Mechanical Mind: A Philosophical Introduction to Minds, Machines, and Mental Representation*, London and New York: Penguin, 1995

Marr, David, *Vision: A Computational Investigation into the Human Representation and Processing of Visual Information*, San Francisco: Freeman, 1982

Port, Robert F. and Timothy van Gelder (editors), *Mind as Motion: Explorations in the Dynamics of Cognition*, Cambridge, Massachusetts: MIT Press, 1995

Pylyshyn, Zenon W., *Computation and Cognition: Toward a Foundation for Cognitive Science*, Cambridge, Massachusetts: MIT Press, 1986

Rumelhart, David E. and James L. McClelland (editors), *Parallel Distributed Processing: Explorations in the Microstructure of Cognition*, 2 vols, Cambridge, Massachusetts: MIT Press, 1986

Smolensky, Paul, "On the Proper Treatment of Connectionism", *Behavioral and Brain Sciences*, 11/1 (1988): 1–23

Stillings, Neil A. *et al.*, *Cognitive Science: An Introduction*, 2nd edition, Cambridge, Massachusetts: MIT Press, 1995

During the last few decades, cognitive science has emerged from a general breaking down of disciplinary boundaries between cognitive psychology, linguistics, artificial intelligence, philosophy, and neuroscience. These studies are unified by the computational theory of mind, a philosophical approach that conceives cognitive phenomena as essentially computational or information-processing in nature.

A useful overview of the relevant studies within the computational perspective is provided by STILLINGS *et al*. This is an introductory textbook, covering the different theories and empirical results of cognitive science, including recent developments.

CRANE offers an exceptionally clear introduction to the computational theory of mind, embedded in a stimulating treatment of the philosophical problem of intentionality. He defends the computational view against its prominent critics, and he confronts it with the contemporary philosophical debate concerning the nature of representation. The book will be of particular interest to the non-specialist, but anyone searching for some philosophical background to the topic should find it worth reading.

MARR's computational theory of vision focuses on the abstract aspects of visual information processing. He develops a theory of visual perception that employs three distinct levels of description. He labels these three levels the computational, the algorithmic, and the implementational level. The first level describes the function carried out by the visual system, whereas the second level describes how the system computes it. The third level describes how the function is physically realized. Marr's three-level model is now widely accepted by cognitive scientists. Theories of cognition concern themselves mainly with the first two of Marr's three levels. According to Marr, it is the top level, the level of the computational theory, that is critically important from an information-processing point of view. Marr describes an overall framework that divides the derivation of shape information from images into three representational stages: the primal sketch, the 2½-D sketch, and the 3-D model representation.

PYLYSHYN provides an illuminating account of the assumptions underlying the symbolic theory of computation, which is now called the classical view. He adopts an utterly realistic stance towards computation. The mind is viewed as operating upon symbolic representations, of which the semantic content corresponds to the content of our thoughts. Pylyshyn conceives the content of the representations postulated by cognitive psychology as roughly similar to the contents of the mental states, like beliefs and desires, that are postulated by folk psychology. The book concentrates mostly on how the higher, semantic level of explanation should be taken to be related to the lower, functional level of explanation. A computational process is conceived as depending primarily on the representational or semantic content of its states. This occurs by virtue of there being a symbolic level. Functionally relevant semantic features must be syntactically encoded at the level of a formal symbol structure.

RUMELHART & McCLELLAND is a classic in the parallel distributed processing approach, currently known as connectionism. This approach challenges the idea of symbolic computation. An alternative framework is introduced for modelling cognitive processes that seems closer to the style of computation as it might be done by the brain. Information processing is conceived as taking place through the interactions of a large number of single units. The connectionist approach emphasizes the parallel nature of processing, and the use of distributed representations. The book provides a set of tools for developing models of the neurophysiological basis of human information processing. The first volume concerns the foundations of connectionist computation, and the second volume concentrates on specific issues in psychology and biology. The results and methods of the book are still highly influential.

SMOLENSKY proposes the author's so-called subsymbolic paradigm, in which connectionism need not refute the idea that human cognition is a matter of hosting internal representations such as beliefs and desires. He argues that connectionism is entirely compatible with the symbolic view. Connectionist models are seen as providing a more detailed, accurate account of cognitive performance than symbolic models. Smolensky contrasts symbolic and subsymbolic models, and he distinguishes between conscious application of rules and intuitive processing, which he assigns to, respectively, the symbolic and the subsymbolic level. Symbolic models can give an exact account of conscious rule application but a subsymbolic account is required to obtain an exact account of intuitive processing. The intuitive processor is a connectionistic dynamic system that allows no complete, formal and precise description on the cognitive level.

CHURCHLAND & SEJNOWSKI draws on both neurobiological data and computational ideas to investigate how neural networks can produce complex cognitive tasks. With two introductory chapters on neuroscience and the science of computation, the book makes the foundational ideas of cognitive neuroscience highly accessible. The discussion is concentrated on network models, which can be more highly constrained by neurobiology than high-level psychological models. Relatively abstract computational models of visual functions are introduced, as well as more neurobiologically realistic models of plasticy and sensorimotor integration. The authors aim for a biological realism in computational models, in which the micro-level constraints are of central importance.

PORT & VAN GELDER offers an overview of the dynamical approach, according to which time is essential to cognition. An organism's evolution over time is taken to constitute temporal properties that require description by differential equations. Cognitive systems are seen, essentially, as continually evolving and mutually influencing complexes that include the body, environment, and nervous system. The core of the dynamical approach is the application of the mathematical tools of dynamics to the study of cognition. The book introduces this exciting new approach to the general reader. Each of the 18 chapters, written by different authors, is supplemented by an editor's introduction. The book covers mainly research in neural networks and psychology, and contains no investigation into neuroscience. Although the dynamical approach is completely compatible with the connectionist approach, it is here envisioned as a radical new research programme that challenges the dominance of the computational paradigm.

JOHAN VELDEMAN

See also Information processing, Neural networks, Theory of mind

Computer industry

Cringely, Robert X., *Accidental Empires: How the Boys of Silicon Valley Make Their Millions, Battle Foreign Competition, and Still Can't Get a Date*, 2nd edition, New York: Harper, and Harmondsworth: Penguin, 1996

Flamm, Kenneth, *Targeting the Computer*, Washington, DC: Brookings Institution, 1987

Flamm, Kenneth, *Creating the Computer*, Washington, DC: Brookings Institution, 1988

Freeman, Christopher, Margaret Sharp and William Walker (editors), *Technology and the Future of Europe: Global Competition and the Environment in the 1990s*, London: Pinter, 1991

Frumau, Coen C.F., "Choices in R&D and Business Portfolio in the Electronics Industry: What te Bibliometric Data Show", *Research Policy*, 21/2 (1992): 97–124

Kenney, Martin and Urs von Burg, "Technology, Entrepreneurship and Path Dependence: Industrial Clustering in Silicon Valley and Route 128", *Industrial and Corporate Change*, 8/1 (1999): 67–110

Malerba, Franco, Richard Nelson, Luigi Orsenigo and Sidney Winter, "'History-friendly' Models of Industry Evolution: The Computer Industry", *Industrial and Corporate Change*, 8/1 (1999): 3–40

Mowery, David C. (editor), *The International Computer Software Industry: A Comparative Study of Industrial Evolution and Structure*, New York and Oxford: Oxford University Press, 1996

Tijssen, Robert J.W. and Erik van Wijk, "In Search of the European Paradox: An International Comparison of Europe's Scientific Performance and Knowledge Flows in Information and Communication Technologies Research", *Research Policy*, 28/5 (1999): 519–43

Yoffie, David B. (editor), *Competing in the Age of Digital Convergence*, Boston: Harvard Business School Press, 1997

The bounds of the computer industry can be drawn widely to include its components especially the semiconductor ("chip"), which is now an essential component of many other items of equipment, and sometimes its intercommunications. At times the electronics industry at large has appeared to be converging into a homogeneous entity, based on the chip (this is often called "convergence"); at other times it has broken up into segments. Here a narrower definition is generally adopted.

The two books by FLAMM (1987, 1988) need to be read as one. They supply a convincing but at the same time heterodox view of the factors underlying the rise of the computer industry. The emphasis is on the crucial role of government – a concept that has subsequently been accepted in the literature but gathers particular strength as issuing from the Brookings Institution, which is often seen as a bastion of capitalist thinking. The main focus is on the US, but there is considerable cross-comparison, especially with Japan. Students of the computer industry should begin here.

The volume edited by YOFFIE appears under the imprint of the Harvard Business School, and reflects its general approach to industry studies. The volume begins with a long essay by the celebrated business historian, Alfred D. Chandler Jr., entitled, "The computer industry: the first half-century", implying its corporate rather than scientific basis. The role of government is played down in comparison with the studies of Flamm, on which the book is partly based. Other chapters deal with more specific subjects, including the "convergence" issue.

The paper by MALERBA *et al.* is an interesting departure from standard modelling in that the authors intentionally aim to model as closely as possible to the history of the computer industry. The paper sets out stylized facts for the industry, which can be read as a potted summary of its actual course of development. They capture these in the model through what they brand as "appreciative theorizing". The model then allows them to produce counterfactual outcomes, such as what might have happened had not IBM emerged as the dominant producer in the industry's middle period. The article is well worth reading for its methodological innovativeness as well as for its concise historical survey of the industry.

In the same journal issue as the paper by Malerba *et al.*, the paper by KENNEY & VON BURG is an attempt to reject cultural and organizational explanations for the divergent histories of Silicon Valley and Route 128 (Massachusetts), the two best-known industrial clusters in the history of microelectronics. They replace such ideas with the view that the different fortunes represented the outcomes of choosing different technological trajectories. In an acerbic comment, AnnaLee Saxenian, author of a well-received though controversial study comparing these two regions, argues that the authors do not clarify why the different technological choices were made. Whatever one's views about who gets the better of the argument, the Kenney and Von Burg paper is well worth reading for its account of the development of the two districts.

CRINGELY, written for the mass market, portrays Silicon Valley from a very different viewpoint, generally highly critical and disparaging. However the jocular tone and anecdotage mask a quite comprehensive account of the key stages in the evolution of the high-tech end of the computer business, together with a more serious purpose than first appears. It is a lighthearted way into understanding how the industry segment has developed.

The computer industry these days is driven more by the software branch than by the hardware, but studies of the latter are much more numerous than of the former. The essays edited by MOWERY therefore fill a large gap in the literature. The approach of the contributors lies mainly in the "national systems of innovation" tradition, with separate studies of the US, Japan, Western Europe, and Russia. Some, however, tackle cross-country issues such as intellectual property rights or standards. The relative difficulty of collecting material has meant that a number of the essays are more specific in scope than would ideally be desired, but the volume as a whole provides a more-than-adequate launchpad for further study of this neglected field.

The paper by FRUMAU is not limited to the computer industry, since it portrays the electronics industry more widely. Its important contribution is linking data on technology (both publications and patents) with that on research and development expenditures (seen as inputs), together with product portfolios. Most studies deploy one such indicator rather than all of them. This is undertaken for the world's top 30 electronics firms. The author is an employee of Philips but his judgement is dispassionate.

TIJSSEN & VAN WIJK use bibliometric indicators to reassess the performance of the European electronics industry, and why it has performed below par. They conclude that the science base is strong enough but perhaps there has been a lack of its strong involvement in European industry – in other words, there has been an "exploitation gap" in Europe. The former point is more satisfactorily treated than the latter in the paper.

The collection of papers edited by FREEMAN, SHARP & WALKER are the outcome of a structured investigation of European competitiveness, undertaken for the 21st anniversary of the Science Policy Research Unit at the University of Sussex. Part II deals specifically with information and communication technologies in a European setting, and on the whole makes for rather dispiriting reading in relation to European competitiveness, especially in connection with the computer industry. Arguably there has been some recovery in the software industry and semiconductors in subsequent years.

G.N. VON TUNZELMANN

Computer law, *see* Cyberlaw

Comte, Auguste 1798–1857

French sociologist

Aldridge, Alan, "Prediction in Sociology: Prospects for a Devalued Activity", *Sociological Research Online*, 4/3 (1999) <http://www.socresonline.org.uk/socresonline/4/3/aldridge.html>

Andreski, Stanislav (editor), *The Essential Comte: Selected from Cours de philosophie positive*, London: Croom Helm, and New York: Barnes and Noble, 1974

Aron, Raymond, *Main Currents in Sociological Thought*, vol. 2, London: Weidenfeld and Nicolson, and New York: Basic Books, 1965

Bottomore, Tom and Robert Nisbet (editors), *History of Sociological Analysis*, New York: Basic Books, 1978; London: Heinemann, 1979

Elias, Norbert, *What is Sociology?*, London: Hutchinson, 1978 (German edition 1970)

Gould, Julius, "Auguste Comte" in *The Founding Fathers of Social Science*, revised edition, edited by Timothy Raison, London: Scolar Press, 1979

Nisbet, Robert A., *The Sociological Tradition*, New York: Basic Books, and London: Heinemann, 1966

Simpson, George (editor), *Auguste Comte: Sire of Sociology*, New York: Crowell, 1969

Swingewood, Alan, *A Short History of Sociological Thought*, 2nd edition, Basingstoke: Macmillan, and New York: St Martin's Press, 1991

Thompson, Kenneth, *Auguste Comte: The Foundation of Sociology*, New York: Wiley, 1975; London: Nelson, 1976

Comte's principal works are: *The Positive Philosophy* in six volumes (1830–42); *A Discourse on the Positive Spirit* (1844); *A General View of Positivism* (1848); and *System of Positive Polity* in four volumes (1851–54). Edited versions of the most relevant writings for today can be found in SIMPSON, and in THOMPSON. ANDRESKI provides an abridged translation of the original standard English version of Comte's magnum opus, *The Positive Philosophy*, translated and abridged by Harriet Martineau in two volumes in London in 1853. Comte's writings would have reached an English-speaking audience far later if it had not been for the labours of Harriet Martineau. She was the first person to translate and condense *The Positive Philosophy* into English. Although there have been recent efforts to re-establish her role as the premier "Comtean" of the 19th century, feminists have claimed that her contribution to the development of sociology has been underestimated, especially in the English-speaking world. In 1874, when *Positive Philosophy* was in danger of going out of print, Martineau wrote, "They must feel sure that a book will live for which they will do and risk so much. And so it will. It will be in demand for generations to come" (in *Harriet Martineau Selected Letters*, edited by Valerie Saunders, 1990).

Comte's work is rarely part of the syllabus of the contemporary sociology student. Most only know him as the man who coined the term "sociology". He is unfashionable because his work is seen as conservative, positivistic, naive, and burdened by the weight of 19th-century evolutionary and developmental thinking. His reputation has also suffered because of the madness that plagued him in the last ten years of his life. Born of deeply conservative Catholic parents, he trained as a philosopher and became one of the most respected French intellectuals of his day. Comte, along with Durkheim, articulated the foundations for an objective "science of society" in opposition to both religious mythology and the metaphysics of philosophical speculation.

Whatever criticisms may be levelled at Comte's work, SWINGEWOOD maintains that his place within the history of sociology is guaranteed by his attempts to explain the origin and growth of industrial society and his analysis of the social effects of the division of labour, increasing wealth and development of individualism and his rejection of metaphysics in favour of positive empirical methods in the study of social facts. (p.41)

Comte's lasting contribution to the social sciences is his ambitious attempt to connect socio-structural changes to changing belief systems. His "law of the three stages" draws attention to systematic transformations in thought. He distinguishes between the theological, the metaphysical, and the positive corresponding with different stages in human evolution. He argues that the new discipline of sociology must be firmly based on "positive methods". In more recent years this has come to mean a crude empiricism. For Comte it meant the abandonment of a fruitless search for absolute knowledge to be replaced by the search for laws which connect different facts through the methods of observation and experiment. For Comte, "positive" forms of thought rely more on systematic observation, guided by theory and less and less on the search for immutable essences or abstract schema. Growing rationality of human thought is a central theme of Comte's work.

For analytic purposes societies must be studied as if they are integrated wholes. For Thompson this is an appeal for the inter-relatedness and interdependence of phenomena and for a holistic approach to social analysis. Human history has a dynamic character because it passes through successive and distinct stages. These are governed by laws which can only be revealed to us by scholars and it is their work which provides the only rational basis of human action.

The neglect of Comtean sociology is partly explained by the association of his work with various forms of positivism and a critical opposition to any form of evolutionism or developmentalism. ARON takes the view that the 19th-century evolutionism inherent in Comte's philosophy makes him unsuitable for contemporary sociology. Comte's many critics charge him with everything from naivety to totalitarianism. According to J.S. Mill, Comte had devised, "the most complete system of spiritual and temporal despotism that ever issued from the brain of any human being except perhaps Ignatius Loyola". His overarching concern with consensus and social integration was frequently interpreted as the legacy of his conservative Catholicism. In themes that are echoed in Durkheim, Comte feared the crumbling of tradition and, "the anarchy which day by day envelops society" (NISBET, p.57).

Marxists were hostile because they saw Comte's ideas as deeply conservative with regard to social classes, hierarchies, and economic inequalities. Including Comte as part of the conservative tradition in sociology, Nisbet writes, "we find in his early writings sharp criticism of the egalitarian doctrines of Enlightenment and Revolution and, in his *Positive Philosophy*, rigorous prescription for the organization of the Positivist utopia in terms of distinct social classes" (Nisbet p.182). Comte was the propagandist of social unity and he abhorred negative attacks on the values of traditional authority, morality, the family, and on religious institutions.

For Swingewood, Comte's reworking of Saint-Simon's concepts of industrialism, production, class formation, and class conflict, "were stripped of their contradictory and negative aspects and integrated into an organismic, consensual, model of society" (p.59). Others argued that Comtean sociology meant, in reality, an uncritical acceptance of social inequality. Aron notes that in debates with 19th-century socialists Comte espoused a form of "Catholic socialism" in which those who command wealth are constrained by notions of social duty. Swingewood describes Comte's concerns about the unequal distribution of wealth as limited to the opportunities they provided for "agitators and dreamers". The rhetoric of "duties" has a much higher priority than the concept of "rights" (Swingewood, p.48)

According to BOTTOMORE & NISBET, his consuming hostility was to individualism in any form. What Comte refers to pejoratively as metaphysical thinking is the atomistic individualism of the Age of Reason and the Enlightenment. "His entire sociology was built around the priority of relationships to individuals" (Bottomore and Nisbet, p.558). They attribute the dominance of contemporary structuralism to the influence of Comte via Durkheim, and they claim that, "it would be grossly unjust to deprive Comte of his position as the first systematic structural thinker in French sociology" (Bottomore and Nesbit, p.560).

Aron (p.65) regards Comte's science as a bold attempt to "resolve the crisis of the modern world, to provide a system of scientific ideas which will preside over the reorganization of society". Aron asks why Comte's ideas remain outside the mainstream of modern social thought. His answer is that historical events proved Comte to be wrong in one crucial respect. In his schema industrial society was essentially a rational scientific order in which warfare was a thing of the past. Who, therefore, "pays much deference to the man who underestimated the ideological conflicts by which the European societies have lived and for which so many have died" (p.75).

The founders of sociology were in no doubt that sociology was a predictive discipline. Comte's belief in the close link between knowledge, prediction, and action captures this belief about the potential of the sociological enterprise at its foundation. Nowadays social scientists are reluctant to engage in prediction fearful not just of getting it wrong but aware that it lays them open to charges of vulgar positivism. ALDRIDGE, making explicit reference to Comte, argues that current concerns about prediction are misplaced because if sociology is to enjoy enhanced public regard then it should be prepared to make prediction a central feature of the discipline. Aldridge is harsh in his judgement of Comte's legacy, regarding much of it as dated and irrelevant despite its impact on his contemporaries:

> Comte's vision of sociology has not fared well. His works are seldom consulted by contemporary sociologists or taught with conviction to our students, who learn that 'positivist' is one of the gravest professional insults we can utter. His law of three stages serves as a paradigm case of the futile attempt to write a meta-narrative of history. His religion of humanity and positivist catechism, [is] so embarrassing that few of us can bear to read about them . . . His positivism, far from being scientific, is discredited as misconceived and dogmatic. (Aldridge 1.1,1.2)

GOULD claims that for all his scientific claims Comte was above all a social prophet concerned about the "moral anarchy" of a rapidly industrializing society. What is undoubtedly sociological about Comte's work, and one of the ways in which he anticipates Emile Durkheim, is his insistence that humans can only exist within a social context – we are a product of our social roles. Nisbet also supports this view: "Comte makes everything human above the level of the purely physiological derive from society" (Nisbet, p.59).

ELIAS claims that the questions posed by Comte are still valid:

> He was anything but a positivist in the sense of present-day usage . . . For centuries deductionists and inductionists, rationalists and empiricists, apriorists and positivists, or whatever they called themselves, had argued against each other with unabated obstinacy. It is a *leitmotiv* of Comte's theory of science that scientific work rests upon an indivisible combination of interpretation and observation, of theoretical and empirical work. (p.35)

Elias approves of the way in which Comte, like Marx, tried to undermine the myths of classical European philosophy. In contrast to the way in which Comte is usually treated by contemporary sociologists, Elias wrote, "the way he defined problems emerges from his work still fresh, still fruitful" (p.35). For Elias, Comte together with Darwin and Marx was one of the three great pioneers of process theories and deserves recognition because of the fundamental questions he asks about the nature of sociology and its relationship between the physical, biological, and social sciences.

ROBERT MEARS

See also Positivist research, Sociology survey

Confessions

Gudjonsson, Gisli H., *The Psychology of Interrogations, Confessions, and Testimony*, Chichester and New York: Wiley, 1992

Kamisar, Yale, *Police Interrogation and Confessions: Essays in Law and Policy*, Ann Arbor, Michigan: University of Michigan Press, 1980

Kassin, Saul M. and Lawrence S. Wrightsman, "Confession Evidence" in *The Psychology of Evidence and Trial Procedure*, edited by Saul M. Kassin and Lawrence S. Wrightsman, London and Beverly Hills, California: Sage, 1985

Kassin, Saul and Katherine Kiechel, "The Social Psychology of False Confessions: Compliance, Internalization, and Confabulation", *Psychological Science*, 7/3 (1996): 125–28

Leo, Richard A. and Richard J. Ofshe, "The Consequences of False Confessions: Deprivations of Liberty and Miscarriages of Justice in the Age of Psychological Interrogation", *Journal of Criminal Law and Criminology*, 88/2 (1998): 429–96

Moston, Stephen, Geoffrey Stephenson and Thomas Williamson, "The Effects of Case Characteristics on Suspect Behavior during Police Questioning", *British Journal of Criminology*, 32/1 (1992): 23–40

Ofshe, Richard J. and Richard A. Leo, "The Decision to Confess Falsely: Rational Choice and Irrational Action", *Denver University Law Review*, 74/4 (1997): 979–1122

White, Welsh S., "False Confessions and the Constitution: Safeguards against Untrustworthy Confessions", *Harvard Civil Rights–Civil Liberties Law Review*, 32/1 (1997): 105–57

Beginning with Hugo Munsterberg's now classic 1908 study, *On the Witness Stand*, criminologists, psychologists, sociologists, sociolegal scholars, and others have researched and written hundreds of peer-reviewed articles, books, case studies, treatises, and other publications about (true and false) confessions, police interrogation practices, coercive influence techniques, and related topics. This entry will briefly review the leading social science and sociolegal scholarship on these subjects.

GUDJONSSON is the most comprehensive and detailed examination of the theory and practice of interrogation, interviewing, and confession to date. A clinical psychologist (and former police officer) by training, Gudjonsson draws on ten years of experience as a clinician and numerous cases in which suspects have made both true and false confessions during police interrogation. Gudjonsson thoroughly reviews the research literature on all the important topics bearing on interrogation and confession, including police interviewing and interrogation methods; the psychological mechanisms and processes that lead to confession; individual suggestibility under conditions of interrogation (otherwise known as "interrogative suggestibility"); the role of perception and memory in witness testimony; and the psychology of false confession. Gudjonsson's emphasis is on the theory and measurement of interrogative suggestibility, an area of study and practical application that he has pioneered by developing assessment techniques for clinicians. Gudjonsson's text is notable for its wide-ranging coverage of the psychological aspects, mechanisms, and processes of confession, especially those involving interrogative suggestibility and false confession, as well as numerous case illustrations.

Yale Kamisar is widely regarded as the leading legal scholar on the subject of interrogation and confession. In the 1960s and 1970s, Kamisar wrote numerous law review articles on interrogation and confession that significantly influenced not only the direction of legal scholarship, but also the direction that the US Supreme Court, particularly the Warren Court, would take in deciding the cases involving these issues. KAMISAR is an edited volume that collects Kamisar's most well-known and influential law review articles to 1980. Covering a number of central constitutional and policy issues, Kamisar's essays explore, among other things, the meaning of an involuntary confession under established legal doctrine, the contradictory legal norms that underlie custodial interrogation, and the doctrinal foundations and policy implications of the several well-known US Supreme Court cases, including the 1966 case of *Miranda v. Arizona* which spawned the now famous *Miranda* warnings into the American lexicon. Kamisar's collection of essays is notable for its incisive legal analysis, lucid writing, and passionate normative argumentation.

KASSIN & WRIGHTSMAN ushered in the modern era of social scientific research on the psychology of interrogation and confession. For this reason, it is arguably the seminal paper in the contemporary psychology of confession literature. Kassin & Wrightsman thoroughly review the social psychological research literature and legal rules of evidence and procedure on interrogation and confession to 1985, and go on to frame the issues that psychologists and criminologists who study interrogation and confession have been grappling with ever since (the methods of modern interrogation, the voluntariness and reliability of confession evidence, the psychology of interrogation and confessions, perceptions of confession evidence on triers of fact). Kassin & Wrightsman's most significant contribution may be the threefold typology that they generate regarding types of false confession.

KASSIN & KIECHEL is an experimental study that induced false confessions about causing a computer to crash in the laboratory. Prior to the session, research subjects were told that they were taking part in a reaction time study and were instructed not to press the ALT key of a personal computer or else the computer would malfunction and important data would be lost. During the session, the computer crashed and the experimenter accused the subject of hitting the ALT key, and, in half of the cases, a confederate said she saw the participant hit the ALT key. Sixty-nine per cent of the subjects signed a false confession to hitting the forbidden key. Kassin & Kiechel's experimental induction of a false confession is consistent with a long line of psychological research on conformity under conditions of uncertainty, the malleability of eyewitness testimony, and, more recently, the ability to plant false childhood memories.

In their 1998 article, LEO & OFSHE report on a study of 60 cases of police-induced false confessions in the post-*Miranda* era of American criminal justice (after 1966). This study authoritatively establishes that police-induced false confessions occur with troubling frequency in the American criminal justice system, that they invariably lead to unjust deprivations of liberty, and that they often lead to the wrongful prosecution, conviction, and incarceration of the innocent. The authors demonstrate that a confession – even if it was obtained under psychologically coercive interrogation and fails to be supported by any significant or credible case evidence – strongly prejudices the perceptions, reasoning, and decision making of triers of fact and lay jurors, effectively eliminating any presumption of innocence the accused might have been accorded. In this study, 73 per cent of the false confessors who took their case to a jury trial were convicted – despite the absence of any supporting evidence and often considerable evidence of innocence – only to be subsequently exonerated, usually many years later.

MOSTON, STEPHENSON & WILLIAMSON examine a random sample of more than 1,000 taped interrogations in nine police departments. Moston and his colleagues analysed the behaviour of suspects during questioning, why suspects confess, and police interrogation styles. Moston, Stephenson & Williamson's study is notable for the amount of data collected, the complex portrait of interrogation methods and suspect behaviour that emerges, and what it reveals about the variables that are primarily associated with the decision to admit an allegation during interrogation.

OFSHE & LEO put forth, and extensively illustrate with excerpts from actual interrogation transcripts, a two-step social psychological decision-making model that explains how and why modern police interrogation techniques and strategies lead to the decision to confess, both from the guilty as well as the innocent. Grounded in rational choice theory, Ofshe & Leo synthesize, modify, and extend existing research on the psychology of influence and decision-making during interrogation. Ofshe & Leo also modify and extend Kassin & Wrightsman's typology of false confessions into a fivefold classification system that more adequately describes the underlying social psychological processes at work and more fully captures the observed variance in suspects' behavioural responses to interrogation. "The Decision to Confess" is the most comprehensive and authoritative analysis of the social psychology of police interrogation, suspect decision making, and (true and false) confessions in the Anglo-American literature.

Legal scholar WHITE analyses the constitutional safeguards against the admission of untrustworthy confessions into evidence at trial. White reviews the historical evolution of the constitutional rule excluding involuntary confessions, the development of recent case law, the empirical data on interrogation techniques that lead to false confessions, and the constitutional basis for various safeguards against the admission of false confessions. White proposes several policy reforms (such as restricting police interrogation of especially vulnerable suspects, limiting the length of police interrogation, and videotaping interrogation of suspects) that, if adopted, would prevent miscarriages of justice resulting from the introduction of false confessions.

There has been considerable research on confessions and related topics (such as the social psychology of interrogation and decision making, the causes and consequences of false confessions, the law of interrogation and confession, the impact of law on police behaviour) since 1910. Because of the centrality of confession evidence in the criminal justice system, as well as the well-documented problem of false confessions leading to the wrongful conviction of the innocent, the social scientific study of confessions is enormously important for both academic and policy reasons. It is therefore imperative that psychologists, criminologists, sociologists, and legal scholars continue to expand our understanding of these issues in the 21st century.

RICHARD A. LEO

Confidential information

Coleman, Allison, *The Legal Protection of Trade Secrets*, London: Sweet and Maxwell, 1992

Coleman, Allison, "Protecting Confidential Information" in *Computer Law*, 3rd edition, edited by Chris Reed, London: Blackstone Press, 1996

Cripps, Yvonne, *The Legal Implications of Disclosure in the Public Interest: An Analysis of Prohibitions and Protections with Particular Reference to Employers and Employees*, 2nd edition, London: Sweet and Maxwell, 1994

Gurry, Francis, *Breach of Confidence*, Oxford and New York: Oxford University Press, 1984

Harrold, Todd and Michael Michalyshyn, "Confidential Information and Technical Know-how: What Leaves with Your Employees?", *Intellectual Property Journal*, 13/1 (1998): 1–24

Hull, John, *Commercial Secrecy: Law and Practice*, London: Sweet and Maxwell, 1998

Law Commission, *Breach of Confidence: Report*, London: HMSO, 1981 (Cmnd.8388)

Law Commission, *Legislating the Criminal Code: Misuse of Trade Secrets: A Consultation Paper*, London: Stationery Office, 1997 (Law Commission Consultation Paper 150)

Lesser, Harry and Zelda Pickup, "Law, Ethics and Confidentiality", *Journal of Law and Society*, 17/1 (1990): 17–28

Toulson, R.G. and C.M. Phipps, *Confidentiality*, London: Sweet and Maxwell, 1996

The law regards information as confidential so long as, as a body, it is substantial, secret, and identified. The information may be commercial, professional, personal, or governmental (official secrets). All types may be protected when there is actual or threatened disclosure or misuse and there is considerable debate about when and in what circumstances the courts ought to intervene. GURRY remains a seminal text on the nature of confidential information and the development of the action for breach of confidence. Published three years after the English

LAW COMMISSION's (1981) report on the state of the law relating to breach of confidence, it explores the concept of confidence as a distinct obligation enforceable in law and analyses the variety of information that may be regarded as confidential.

The Law Commission's recommendation that the action for breach of confidence should be replaced by a new statutory tort was not adopted. In the light of experience gained in the ensuing 15 years, TOULSON & PHIPPS examine the principles underlying the action and its further development in the absence of a statutory framework, which has permitted considerable flexibility, but has left many issues still in doubt, including the defence of "public interest". The work highlights particular relationships where a duty of confidence may arise, including medical, banking, broadcasting, counselling, teaching, spiritual, and lawyer/client. Focusing primarily on English law, the work also touches on the position in countries such as Australia, New Zealand, and Canada, and includes a brief discussion of the European Convention on Human Rights, now incorporated into UK law by the Human Rights Act 1998.

COLEMAN (1992) is an eminently readable account of the extent to which the law protects the special category of confidential information known as trade secrets. The book is written from an intellectual property rights perspective, but is equally accessible to the nonlawyer and emphasizes the commercial nature of trade secrets, which are valuable business assets. Although Coleman focuses mainly on English law, there is also information on trade secrets in other jurisdictions, including the US, Canada, and Japan. COLEMAN (1996) offers a succinct overview of the relevant civil and criminal law, with special reference to confidential information stored on computers.

At the present time deliberate misuse of trade secrets does not constitute theft under English law, although the position is different elsewhere. The LAW COMMISSION's (1997) Consultation Paper considers whether such misuse should give rise to criminal liability. Although this is a consultative document only, the work is of interest in that it explores in detail the arguments for and against criminalization and summarizes relevant law of other jurisdictions.

HULL offers a practical guide to the problem of commercial confidences and the employer/employee relationship, while devoting some attention to the issue of individual privacy. In the absence of any statutory right of privacy under English law, breach of confidence remains the best available action to protect personal confidences.

CRIPPS focuses on the diverse and uncertain areas of law relating to disclosure by employees of information which they believe to be in the public interest (popularly known as "whistleblowing") and the legal problems faced by employers and employees in attempting to institute or defend proceedings. Issues of national security and official secrets, including the "Spycatcher" case, are also discussed.

HARROLD & MICHALYSHYN highlights the problem of trade secrets in the context of "hi-tech" industries. Although the article is written from a Canadian perspective, the issues raised are of general interest and guidance is given on the types of information that may be regarded as protectable from disclosure.

Confidentiality is often regarded as a fundamental principle of medical ethics and patients mistakenly assume that all medical confidences are sacrosanct. LESSER & PICKUP examine the ethical basis of the principle of confidentiality, arguing that both the principle itself and the exceptions frequently made in practice are justified on utilitarian grounds.

ELLEN GREDLEY

Conflict

Archibald, Kathleen (editor), *Strategic Interaction and Conflict: Original Papers and Discussion*, Berkeley, California: Institute of International Studies, 1966

Brett, Jeanne M., Stephen B. Goldberg and William L. Ury, "Designing Systems for Disputes in Organizations", *American Psychologist*, 45 (1990): 162–70

Deutsch, Morton, *The Resolution of Conflict: Constructive and Destructive Processes*, New Haven, Connecticut: Yale University Press, 1973

Deutsch, Morton, "Fifty Years of Conflict" in *Retrospections on Social Psychology*, edited by Leon Festinger, New York and Oxford: Oxford University Press, 1980

Goldberg, Stephen B., Eric D. Green and Frank E.A. Sander, *Dispute Resolution*, Boston: Little Brown, 1985; 2nd edition 1992

Schelling, Thomas C., *The Strategy of Conflict*, Cambridge, Massachusetts: Harvard University Press, 1960; revised edition 1980

Ugwuegbu, Denis C., *The Psychology of Management in African Organizations*, Westport, Connecticut: Quorum Books, 2000

Walton, Richard E. and John M. Dutton, "The Management of Interdepartmental Conflict: A Model and Review", *Administrative Science Quarterly*, 14/1 (1969): 73–84

ARCHIBALD is the culmination of efforts to grapple with the irksome area of bargaining. The four lead papers from John Harsanyi, Morton Deutsch, Harold Kelley, and T.C. Schelling provide an excellent overview of available game theories. They are interesting and thought-provoking. The comments from the participants on each paper and the author's response give an adequate assessment of the contributions of each presentation. The work is suitable for graduate students.

BRETT, GOLDBERG & URY demonstrate in a practical manner what it takes to make managers and workers in organizations resolve disputes and avoid costly procedures for the resolution of grievances. A model was proposed for designing systems for resolving disputes, emphasizing that grievance resolution in organizations should focus on the costs and benefits of conflicts and should always form the criterion for evaluating any effective systems design. A second aspect of this model was that resolving conflicts on the basis of interests rather than rights or power results in lower costs and greater benefits for all. Finally, according to this model, the designer should involve the parties concerned in order to make the dispute-resolution system's design viable. Dispute-resolution system design for resolving conflicts is in its infancy but the proposal will probably produce more effective ways of resolving disputes than the old arbitration system.

DEUTSCH (1973) presents a compilation of previously published work plus fresh theoretical essays. The theories deal with a wide range of subject matter with a common denominator, namely: how does one understand the conditions in a conflict-resolution situation that leads to the constructive resolution of conflict. The collection presents several theories over seven chapters of the book and gives another five chapters of experimental studies to back up the theories.

DEUTSCH (1980) discusses earlier studies of conflict, such as those on cooperation and competition, field theory, games, and game theory, to launch this major contribution. The conditions that give rise to constructive or destructive process of conflict resolution are well treated.

GOLDBERG, GREEN & SANDER is a book written by lawyers without the usual legal jargon. The contribution emphasizes the practical aspects of dispute-resolution processes, particularly the advantages and disadvantages associated with processes such as negotiation, mediation, and adjudication. These processes are considered in detail, and are applied to conflicts such as family disputes, neighbourhood justice centres, intra-institutional disputes, consumer disputes, environmental disputes, inter-governmental disputes, and international disputes, to see how each process handles each episode. There are series of further problems that test the student's ability to apply what has been learned about the various processes. The contribution makes an interesting reading and provides practical examples of the important concepts of negotiation, mediation, and adjudication.

SCHELLING presents a series of closely interrelated essays in the theory of bargaining, the theory of conflict, and the theory of strategy. The Cold War between the East and West is presented as a bargaining situation. It was a situation in which the ability of one participant to gain its ends was dependent to a large extent on the choices or decisions that the other participant made. As a collection of essays the work does not cohere. This makes it somewhat difficult to read.

UGWUEGBU provides a useful overall account of conflict and bargaining processes, especially in the developing nations of Africa. The work distinguished between conflict and conflict-resolution phases and provided a new insight into how power and authority are played out, with examples from a real conflict situation. Graphic illustrations of costs and benefits of conflict show how difficult these are to calculate. The author deals with the issue of the institutionalization of the bargaining process, which is a fact of labour-management relationships that is often not discussed in other works.

WALTON & DUTTON present a general model for the management of interdepartmental conflict, together with a review of the relevant literature. The model successfully integrates the contextual determinants of organizational conflict, and the dynamics of conflict relationships. The adaptive and maladaptive reactions of higher executives to conflict, and the consequences of conflict between organizational units or departments, provide the feedback linkage in the model. The author maintains that in order to manage conflict successfully one must understand the phases of conflict. It has not been demonstrated that this is sufficient for effective management of conflicts.

DENIS C.E. UGWUEGBU

Congress

Arnold, R. Douglas, *The Logic of Congressional Action*, New Haven, Connecticut: Yale University Press, 1990

Brady, David W. and Craig Volden, *Revolving Gridlock: Politics and Policy from Carter to Clinton*, Boulder, Colorado: Westview Press, 1998

Fenno, Richard F., Jr, *Congressmen in Committees*, Boston: Little Brown, 1973

Fiorina, Morris, *Congress: Keystone of the Washington Establishment*, New Haven, Connecticut: Yale University Press, 1977

Hibbing, John R. and Elizabeth Theiss-Morse, *Congress as Public Enemy: Public Attitudes toward American Political Institutions*, New York and Cambridge: Cambridge University Press, 1995

Mayhew, David R., *Congress: The Electoral Connection*, New Haven, Connecticut: Yale University Press, 1974

Mayhew, David R., *Divided We Govern: Party Control, Lawmaking, and Investigations, 1946–1990*, New Haven, Connecticut: Yale University Press, 1991

Polsby, Nelson W., "The Institutionalization of the US House of Representatives", *American Political Science Review*, 62/1 (1968): 144–68

Smith, Steven S., *Call to Order: Floor Politics in the House and Senate*, Washington, DC: Brookings Institution, 1989

Sundquist, James L., *The Decline and Resurgence of Congress*, Washington, DC: Brookings Institution, 1981

A central tenet of the "American creed" that emerged during the nation's revolutionary era was suspicion of executive authority, personified not only by the British crown but also by colonial governors who often exercised remarkable local power. As a result, the US constitutional system was built to ensure (relative) legislative dominance. American presidents initially tried to exercise influence on legislative operations, as POLSBY explains, but they lacked leverage to maintain power from the outside. Congress quickly established its primacy, especially outside the realm of foreign policy, and built up institutional capacity to meet its responsibilities gradually over the course of the 19th and early 20th centuries.

The dominance of Congress within American politics naturally results in a voluminous literature on the institution, from stale textbooks intended for low-level college undergraduates to loose collections of readings updated almost yearly, to highly technical scholarly articles holding little interest outside academic political science. The potential reader's challenge is to find the gems that manage to combine both analytical depth and accessibility.

Two classic volumes from the early 1970s, by FENNO and by MAYHEW (1974), stand out for their abiding interest and usefulness. Both authors were writing at a time of growing frustration with Congress – a time when socioeconomic problems (such as crime and inflation) multiplied while government stood paralysed. The burden was to explain puzzling behaviour patterns exhibited by the complex and rule-governed congressional branch, but to do so in terms of the individuals who composed it. Both authors use a method inspired by economic rationality: stating a few first principles about how individuals should behave given their incentives, and extrapolating from these the particular attributes of the institution as a whole.

Fenno attempts to explain why particular committees within the US House of Representatives (the lower chamber) vary significantly in character. His main answer is that members typically are assigned to committees based upon their legislative priorities. This selection bias guides how each committee forms, so their personalities vary systematically. Fenno's delightful treatment of the characters who dominated postwar US politics helps explain his work's enduring popularity.

Mayhew (1974) is more focused. His goal was to explain why American legislators tend to be immune both from partisan trends against them and widespread dissatisfaction with the institution that they manage. The electorate, after all, had just returned Republican President Richard Nixon to the White House with overwhelming support, yet had also restored a legislative leadership from the opposition Democratic Party. Mayhew ultimately points at the district-based electoral system found in the US, which forces members of Congress to pander to localized constituencies. The inefficiency of Congress as a whole is a direct result of the pressures for individuals to be responsive to their electoral districts. The norms and rules of the entire institution, in fact, are shaped to help its membership please those back home – with power decentralized so that each member can pursue individual interests.

FIORINA, one of the finest writers in empirical political science, picks up where the previous two volumes left off. When he wrote, congressional incumbents appeared more entrenched than ever: their behaviour was even less concerned with the public good, and socioeconomic problems were escalating even more furiously. The volume is framed as a mystery novel, casting the author as a detective seeking out the culprit for entrenched representatives and an institution seemingly incapable of meeting expectations. Fiorina's answer, as indicated by the sinister term "establishment", owes an intellectual debt to the 1960s revolt against corporate liberalism. Congressional insiders have built up a complex and unresponsive government bureaucracy, and have positioned themselves as the ombudsmen necessary to put that machinery in motion. Politicians are judged by their effectiveness at serving constituents, not according to their ability to shape beneficial legislation.

Congressional power went into decline, starting around the turn of the 20th century. Suspicion of legislatures ran high during the Progressive era, and presidents during the 1910s toyed with more assertive roles than those filled by their predecessors. The big break with tradition, however, came with the Great Depression of the 1930s and the extended reign of Franklin Delano Roosevelt. Roosevelt and his immediate successors built up the modern presidency in part with the acquiescence of legislators, as the executive seemed more capable of grappling with complexities of industrialized society. However, SUNDQUIST makes clear that this alteration in the power balance resulted more from convention than from fundamental change. Once the country became concerned with an "imperial presidency", especially after Nixon's Watergate scandal, congressional authority, in large part, was restored.

An important component of restoring congressional influence was bringing power back to the two legislative chambers, the House and the Senate, and away from small committees.

SMITH tracks the growing importance of centralized decision making in both branches (although how badly the committees went into eclipse is a matter of debate), and along the way offers an interesting and detailed description of the Reagan-era Congress. ARNOLD also provides a wonderful and intellectually challenging picture of congressional operations in the decade before the branch would fall to Republican control. His question is a simple, but seemingly more cynical, one than those asked previously: Why does Congress sometimes free itself from particularized interests and promote the public good? The narrative builds around the complex incentives legislators face, and therefore resembles prior work, but sees some hope in legislators' dependence upon the constant electoral connection to constituents. Members of Congress are not only concerned with the short-term demands of their districts, but also with the dormant preferences that might create an electoral backlash if ignored. If a programme is likely to have beneficial impact on the country or on a district over the long term, a member of Congress often will vote for it, especially if there is a way to conceal the costs or if groups are trying to convince constituents that favourable votes for the programme are important.

The legislative branch may be restored to its influential position in the American system, but it is less clear whether the institution is up to the responsibilities. One particular barrier looms large: divided government (when voters turn control of the executive and legislative branches to opposing political parties). MAYHEW (1991) dismisses such concerns. He carefully identifies major postwar legislation, and finds that divided government is as productive as unified partisan control. Similarly, acrimonious congressional investigations of the executive branch are no more likely during divided government. However, this focus on partisan control may not make sense in a system so clearly geared toward legislative individualism. BRADY & VOLDEN argue that the inherited constitutional system, with its fractured legislative powers, is doomed to gridlock-especially when the agenda is dominated by budgetary politics. Members of Congress are growing increasingly polarized ideologically, so the best hope for significant change in American public policy is for a massive shift in voter opinion toward some sort of consensus.

HIBBING & THEISS-MORSE is a recent addition to the literature, but also worth attention. The authors wish to understand public cynicism regarding Congress, but to do so without relying on quick, close-ended survey questions, so they also used detailed focus-group sessions. The most interesting finding is that citizens generally care about the *process* through which their governmental decisions are made, not just the results. Sometimes policy details are hard to grasp, but citizens usually can distinguish whether a procedure is fair or unseemly. Americans are upset with the power of interest groups, and distrust professionalized decision makers, so Congress should reform the decision-making process to attract public trust.

D. STEPHEN VOSS

Consciousness

Baars, Bernard, *A Cognitive Theory of Consciousness*, Cambridge and New York: Cambridge University Press, 1988

Block, Ned, Owen Flanagan and Güven Güzeldere (editors), *The Nature of Consciousness*, Cambridge, Massachusetts: MIT Press, 1997

Chalmers, David, *The Conscious Mind*, New York and Oxford: Oxford University Press, 1996

Ciba Foundation Symposium 174, *Experimental and Theoretical Studies of Consciousness*, Chichester and New York: Wiley, 1993

Cohen, Jonathan D. and Jonathan W. Schooler (editors), *Scientific Approaches to Consciousness*, Mahwah, New Jersey: Erlbaum, 1997

Dennett, Daniel, *Consciousness Explained*, London: Allen Lane, and Boston: Little Brown, 1991

Farthing, G. William, *The Psychology of Consciousness*, Englewood Cliffs, New Jersey: Prentice Hall, 1992

Guttenplan, Samuel (editor), *A Companion to the Philosophy of Mind*, Oxford and Cambridge, Massachusetts: Blackwell, 1994

Hameroff, Stuart R., Alfred W. Kaszniak and Alwyn C. Scott (editors), *Toward a Science of Consciousness 2: The Second Tucson Discussions and Debates*, Cambridge, Massachusetts: The MIT Press, 1998

James, William, *The Principles of Psychology*, 2 vols, New York: Holt, and London: Macmillan, 1890; reprinted New York: Dover, 1950

Metzinger, Thomas (editor), *Conscious Experience*, Exeter: Shöningh / Imprint Academic, 1995

Searle, John R., *The Rediscovery of the Mind*, Cambridge, Massachusetts: MIT Press, 1992

Velmans, Max (editor), *The Science of Consciousness: Psychological, Neuropsychological, and Clinical Reviews*, London and New York: Routledge, 1996

Velmans, Max, *Understanding Consciousness*, London and New York: Routledge, 2000a

Velmans, Max (editor), *Investigating Phenomenal Consciousness: New Methodologies and Maps*, Amsterdam and Philadelphia: Benjamins, 2000b

JAMES, whose "radical empiricism" included all the things that one can experience and excluded all the things that one cannot experience, planted the seeds of modern psychological studies of consciousness at the turn of the twentieth century. He developed a phenomenal description of the stream of consciousness and suggested links between consciousness and aspects of mental functioning such as attention and primary memory, which, 100 years later, are still major topics of research. Creatively rich, this early text remains a classic.

Marginalized by behaviourism for over 50 years, the study of consciousness only re-emerged as a major focus of research over the last few decades. BAARS provided the first synthesis of more recent cognitive psychological work. To determine the role of consciousness in the economy of the mind he tried to specify what is different about conscious and unconscious processing in a wide range of psychological functions, including attention, goal setting, voluntary control, monitoring action,

and developing a concept of self. He then integrated these differences into an explanatory model in which consciousness plays the part of a "global workspace", access to which enables information to be broadcast throughout the central nervous system. On these grounds, he suggests no less than 18 different, adaptive functions for consciousness. Baars writes well and integrates a large body of experimental findings in a relatively simple fashion. This is a major, integrative book, although more fundamental questions surrounding the mind/body problem and the nature and function of consciousness are ignored.

FARTHING is the first general textbook in the modern era on consciousness studies with a useful introduction to the problems of definition and some philosophical background. The book focuses particularly on the uses and limitations of introspection, neuropsychological dissociations of consciousness, daydreaming and the stream of consciousness, sleep and dreaming, hypnosis, meditation, and the use of psychedelic drugs.

Designed as a core text for a "Psychology of Consciousness" course at the University of London, VELMANS (1996) is a collection of specially commissioned tutorial reviews by leading researchers in the field. These summarize the state of the art in consciousness studies within mainstream psychology, neuropsychology, and the study of mind/body interactions in a selection of clinical settings. Contributing authors Kihlstrom, Gardiner, and Baars focus on the role of consciousness in perception, learning, memory, and other aspects of cognition. Libet and Young deal with the neurophysiological conditions for consciousness and the theoretical implications of clinical dissociations of consciousness. Sheikh *et al.* and Wall focus on mind/body interactions produced by imagery, biofeedback, hypnosis and meditation, and on the placebo effect. Velmans introduces the collection with an overview of the field and ends with some suggestions about how consciousness studies relate to natural science. Simply and clearly written, the tutorial reviews provide an engaging introduction to mainstream scientific investigations in this field.

COHEN & SCHOOLER's edited collection is based on the proceedings of the 25th Carnegie Mellon Symposium on Cognition. Its 28 chapters also survey current scientific investigations of consciousness, covering attention and automaticity, subliminal perception, implicit learning and memory, metacognitive processes, neuropsychological and neurobiological approaches, and some broad theories of consciousness. Its distinguished authors include Shiffrin, Merikle, Reber, Kinsbourne, Hobson, Flanagan, Galin, Rumelhart, Mandler, and Simon. As one would expect from chapters based on conference presentations, most individual chapters are focused on particular topics rather than being broad surveys. Many of the contributions are excellent. Overall, this collection provides a good source of supplementary readings to more teaching-oriented texts (such as Farthing and Velmans (1996) above).

Scientific investigations of consciousness within cognitive psychology, neuropsychology and related fields are now well established, but the field of consciousness studies as a whole is far broader with contributions ranging from anthropology to physics. In this the role of philosophy has been of particular importance, with philosophers becoming increasingly mindful of advances in science and scientists becoming more aware of some of the philosophical problems posed by consciousness in their work. CIBA FOUNDATION SYMPOSIUM 174 provides a particularly fine example of this dialogue between philosophers and scientists. Based on a three-day international symposium hosted by the Ciba Foundation in London, this volume presents 14 chapters dealing with philosophical, neuropsychological, cognitive, and some clinical aspects of consciousness. A special feature of this book is the carefully edited discussion and debate following each chapter, which gives some insight into the heat as well as the light generated by debates in this area. Again, many of the chapters and discussions are excellent. The 25 participants include many already mentioned in the collections above along with distinguished philosophers and scientists such as Searle, Nagel, Dennett, Shoemaker, Van Gulick, Gazzaniga, Gray, Singer, Marcel, Harnad, Fenwick, Underwood, Humphrey, and Shevrin.

This guide was not intended to deal with the extensive philosophical literature in this area. However, given its importance one cannot ignore it. GUTTENPLAN provides a useful single-source handbook for one's reference shelf. With 64 contributing authors, it is organized rather like an encyclopaedia explaining the meaning, history, and use of basic terms and concepts in philosophy of mind. It also has summaries of many widely discussed philosophical positions, often written by the protagonists themselves, with a good introduction by Guttenplan. To gain a sense of the current ferment in philosophical discussions of consciousness, however, one has to delve into the literature itself. As there is less reliance on evidence, philosophical monographs tend to argue for the intuitive plausibility of a given position while highlighting the weaknesses of competing positions. A balanced picture therefore requires one to sample from a wide range of views. Useful collections of current work are BLOCK, FLANAGAN & GÜZELDERE, and METZINGER. Current, widely discussed, approachable monographs include SEARLE which argues for a form of physicalism, and DENNETT, which tries to "explain" consciousness by explaining it away – arguing that it is nothing more than a form of system functioning. CHALMERS provides a useful critique of currently dominant reductionist philosophies, and favours a form of "naturalistic dualism". VELMANS (2000a) provides an overview of the strengths and weaknesses of current reductionist and dualist positions and argues for a synthesis of science, philosophy, and common sense that is neither dualist nor reductionist.

Beyond "mainstream" studies of consciousness in psychology, neuroscience, and Western philosophy the field as a whole is truly interdisciplinary with contributions from areas as diverse as anthropology, physics, parapsychology, and Eastern philosophy. This diversity is well illustrated in the entertaining collection edited by HAMEROFF, KASZNIAK & SCOTT. This consists of 64 chapters selected from around 140 papers and 500 posters presented at the largest conference to date on consciousness, held at the University of Arizona, Tucson in 1996.

A good source of additional developments in the field is provided by the interdisciplinary *Journal of Consciousness Studies*, the more mainstream *Consciousness and Cognition*, and *Psyche* (an electronic journal). Excellent "target" articles on specific aspects of consciousness also appear periodically in the *Behavioral and Brain Sciences*, accompanied by an extensive peer commentary and an author's reply, which together provide a state-of-the-art coverage. Online papers, electronic seminars and other resources in this area are also increasingly becoming available on the World Wide Web.

The collection of 15 invited chapters in VELMANS (2000b) attempts to provide some integration in this rapidly proliferating, diverse field. It is based on an international symposium on "Methodologies for the Study of Consciousness: A New Synthesis" hosted by the Fetzer Institute (US) in 1996. Part one of the collection focuses on the potential of, and the problems associated with, studying consciousness as such, ranging from methods that combine first and third-person investigations in neuroscience to more introspective, subjective methods. Part two presents a number of alternative first "maps" of the entire consciousness studies terrain.

MAX VELMANS

Conservatism

Bloom, Allan, *The Closing of the American Mind: How Higher Education Has Failed Democracy and Impoverished the Souls of Today's Students*, New York: Simon and Schuster, 1987; Harmondsworth: Penguin, 1988

Bork, Robert H., *The Tempting of America: The Political Seduction of the Law*, New York: Free Press, and London: Collier Macmillan, 1990

Genovese, Eugene D., *The Southern Tradition: The Achievement and Limitations of American Conservatism*, Cambridge, Massachusetts: Harvard University Press, 1994

Himmelfarb, Gertrude, *On Looking into the Abyss: Untimely Thoughts on Culture and Society*, New York: Knopf, 1994

Kirk, Russell, *The Conservative Mind: From Burke to Eliot*, 7th edition, Washington, DC: Regnery, 1985

Krauthammer, Charles, "The New Assault on Bourgeois Life: Defining Deviancy Up", *New Republic*, 209/21 (1993): 20–25

Kristol, Irving, *Neoconservativism: The Autobiography of an Idea*, New York and London: Free Press, 1995

Moynihan, Daniel Patrick, "Defining Deviancy Down", *American Scholar*, 62/1, (1993): 17–30

Russell Kirk is perhaps the leading intellectual figure of modern conservativism, and KIRK is the best starting point for understanding conservative thought. The introduction presents the author's particular take on the nature of conservative ideas, which he grounds in a belief in transcendent truths, suspicion of sudden, sweeping reforms, and a distrust of "narrow rationality". He then takes the reader on a whirlwind tour of the lives of major conservative thinkers, from Edmund Burke to George Santayana, in the sweeping intellectual-biography style of Plutarch's *Lives*. The book is very much a polemic, written in a grand literary style that might alienate those looking for a more precise, analytical model. Kirk also has a precisely delimited set of ideas concerning what is and what is not "conservative", which to some readers might seem rather limited. Nevertheless, his book is required reading for anyone who wishes to undertake a serious exploration of conservative thought, and it a lively read.

Kirk wrote about what he considered to be a classic conservativism, rooted in the tradition of John Adams and Edmund Burke. KRISTOL is the work of a leading figure in an intellectual movement which took root in the 1960s known as neoconservativism. Neoconservatives accepted certain 20th-century developments, such as the advent of a welfare state and some form of government economic intervention, but they wanted strict limits placed on these activities. Neoconservatives have also been leading critics of liberal social policies such as affirmative action. Kristol's book is a collection of his essays, and provides a useful primer for neoconservative ideas.

Much of modern conservativism originated in a searching critique of postmodernism and its effects on the Western intellectual tradition. HIMMELFARB is a collection of essays by an historian who is deeply critical of postmodern thought. She excoriates modern academe for abandoning the search for objective truth and reality in the name of pursuing a fashionable cognitive and moral relativism.

In the same vein as Himmelfarb, BLOOM is the foremost critic of postmodernism's effect on the academy. Written during the 1980s, when American universities were engaged in a deeply critical re-examination of the fundamental texts of Western thought as being excessively Eurocentric, Bloom's book was a ringing reaffirmation of the value of the Western canon. At times Bloom sounds rather shrill – for example, he blames much of the downfall of modern public life on Mick Jagger – but his defence of Western philosophy and the great texts of the Western tradition is learned and well-argued.

BORK offered a searching critique of liberalism's effects on American constitutional and political institutions. He argues for a judicial philosophy that remains true to the original intent of the Constitution's framers, and avoids substituting the personal views of judges for the legitimate processes of democracy. His notoriety as the failed Reagan nominee for the Supreme Court in 1986 – an episode that he discusses at length in the last chapter of his book – should not obscure his standing as a first-rate intellect.

GENOVESE is an analysis of an important but sometimes forgotten strand of Western conservative thought: the critique of capitalism and bourgois society offered by 19th-century American Southerners like John C. Calhoun. A leading scholar of American slavery, Genovese is fully aware of the racist taint associated with some of these arguments, but he argues for the propriety of divorcing Southern conservatism from its more racist elements to take advantage of Southerners' searching critique of modern capitalism. Genovese's work reminds us that conservative thinkers have not always been enthusiastic about capitalism and big business.

MOYNIHAN is a leading New York Democrat and hence might object to the characterization of his ideas as "conservative". Nevertheless, his essay has become something of an instant classic among conservative thinkers. Moynihan criticizes what he sees as a prevailing American tendency to address declining social and moral standards by continually lowering the bar of normalcy so that what was once unacceptable behavior – for example violence, drug abuse, family disintegration – becomes acceptable. The result, he argues, is a

continual erosion of standards of behavior, with predictably deleterious effects on the community.

KRAUTHAMMER's essay is an extension of Moynihan's essay. A journalist and conservative columnist for the *Washington Post*, Krauthammer points out that Moynihan neglected the other half of the process of moral erosion. "It is not enough for the deviant to be normalized", Krauthammer writes, "The normal must be found to be deviant". Krauthammer points to trends in modern culture that suggest that middle class values of family, work, and childrearing that were once accepted have been increasingly portrayed as shot through with hypocrisy and deviance.

BRIAN DIRCK

Conservative Party, UK

Blake, Robert, *The Conservative Party from Peel to Major*, 3rd edition, London: Heinemann, 1997
Charmley, John, *A History of Conservative Politics, 1900–1996*, London: Macmillan, and New York: St Martin's Press, 1996
Clark, Alan, *The Tories: Conservatives and the Nation State, 1922–1997*, London: Weidenfeld and Nicolson, 1998
Clark, J.C.D., "A General Theory of Party, Opposition, and Government, 1688–1832", *Historical Journal*, 23/2 (1980): 295–325
Coleman, Bruce, *Conservatism and the Conservative Party in Nineteenth Century Britain*, London: Arnold, 1988
Gash, Norman, *Pillars of Government, and Other Essays on State and Society, c.1770–c.1880*, London: Arnold, 1986
Gray, John and David Willetts, *Is Conservatism Dead?*, London: Profile, 1997
Greenleaf, W.H., *The British Political Tradition*, vol. 2: *The Ideological Heritage*, London and New York: Methuen, 1983
McKenzie, Robert and Allan Silver, *Angels in Marble: Working Class Conservatives in Urban England*, London: Heinemann, and Chicago: University of Chicago Press, 1968
Nordlinger, Eric A., *The Working-Class Tories: Authority, Deference and Stable Democracy*, London: MacGibbon and Kee, and Berkeley: University of California Press, 1967
Ramsden, John, *An Appetite for Power: A History of the Conservative Party since 1830*, London: HarperCollins, 1998
Seldon, Anthony and Stuart Ball (editors), *Conservative Century: The Conservative Party since 1900*, Oxford and New York: Oxford University Press, 1994

CLARK (1980) suggested that it was meaningless to talk about the existence of the Conservative Party before the 1830s. Its birth was bound up with the emergence of the modern party system in the crisis years 1827–32. The outcome was that, for the first time, government and opposition roles became associated with distinct political groupings. GASH argued that Sir Robert Peel was the founder of modern conservatism. The Tamworth Manifesto (1834) combined an aversion to radical reform and a commitment to moderate change. This appeal gave the infant Conservative Party a wider social base at a time of rapid urban and industrial growth. A party that projected itself as a government in waiting dedicated itself to governing in the national interest.

GREENLEAF provided a useful account of the character of Conservative politics. He contended that it is more profitable to evaluate the character of a political movement than to isolate its core values. This approach was particularly apt in the case of conservatism because its proponents denied that it is an ideology at all. The growth of state power since the 19th century has brought the role of the state to the forefront of politics. The consequent struggle between the forces of collectivism and libertarianism has been particularly marked in the world of Conservative politics. Advocates of paternalism have long vied for dominance with proponents of free market economics. This "twin inheritance" proved that Thatcherism was the most recent manifestation of a much older tradition of Conservative politics.

The best single volume history of the Party remains that written by BLAKE. It was first published in 1970 when he took the story from Peel to Churchill, a second edition published in 1985 moved things on from Churchill to Thatcher, and the third edition published in 1997 concluded with the Major years. The text does not provide "a connected history" of the Conservative Party but rather "a commentary upon the history of the party". The great traditions of the Conservative Party, as exemplified by its leaders, provide the framework for a wider discussion of beliefs, support, and organization. Lord Salisbury, uncharismatic and grey, emerges as the quintessential Conservative leader. He brilliantly exploited the circumstances of his time to give the Conservative Party twenty years of power after 1885.

A more detailed history of 19th-century Conservative politics has been provided by COLEMAN. His organizing theme is that the Conservative Party has always been part of a wider conservative dispensation in British politics. The forces of conservatism have included, at various times, Tories, Conservatives, Whigs, and Liberal Unionists. An alliance of "rank, property, and privilege" first began to form at the time of the French Revolution. Peel's decision to repeal the Corn Laws in 1846 split his coalition of antiradical forces. The death of Palmerston in 1865 made a realignment of the right possible, but Disraeli demurred. Not until Gladstone introduced Irish Home Rule in 1886 was a viable conservative coalition reconstructed The Unionist Alliance remained electorally dominant until tariff reform destroyed its unity in 1903–06.

This should be supplemented, for the 20th century, by CHARMLEY. As the defenders of the status quo, Conservatives have sought to resist change, but as members of a political party they knew that they had to accommodate themselves to change in order to survive. Its "pragmatic opportunism" has been the secret of the Conservative Party's success since 1900. It explained why the party supported the postwar consensus to begin with and then abandoned it when it began to break down. Thatcher may have abandoned the consensual paternalism of Butler and Macmillan, which originated with Baldwin, but she was basically no different from previous Conservative leaders. Her radicalism "enabled the Conservative Party to adapt to a world in which the old ideas of consensus were no longer working".

Its ingrained power complex has been a recurring theme in the literature on the Conservative Party. The most recent historian to concentrate upon this appetite for power is RAMSDEN. He argued that the "most fundamental characteristic" of Conservative politics was its "drive to power". He substantiated this claim with the oftmade point that the Conservative Party has achieved a remarkable degree of electoral success throughout its history. The departure in the text is its contention that this success has been most marked when the party has pursued a consensual rather than an ideological brand of Conservatism. Thatcher may have achieved larger working majorities than Disraeli, Salisbury, Baldwin, and Macmillan, but they came closer to winning the support of half the electorate than she ever did.

Two studies deal with a vital source of electoral support: working-class conservatism. For NORDLINGER the Conservative Party has been uniquely placed to exploit the prevailing contours of British political culture. In its structures and ethos the Party has always embodied notions of hierarchy and deference. Such attributes have been particularly potent where the working class were concerned. McKENZIE & SILVER emphasized the interaction between two powerful motivating forces. The first, as above, related to the innate deference of the working class. The second related to the way in which the Conservative Party has deployed the Disraeli-inspired tradition of social reform to appeal to the material interests of the working class. This twintrack appeal has enabled the Conservative Party to continue to attract working-class support in less deferential times.

In political terms the 20th century has been the Conservative century. The collection of essays edited by SELDON & BALL provide an authoritative review of the various aspects of this unprecedented dominance. Chapter one offered a chronological survey of the Conservative Party's history since 1900. The party's success was attributed to its remarkable ability to track public opinion over time. Thereafter the approach was thematic with chapters highlighting key features and relationships. Sometimes the conclusions reinforced existing interpretations; the chapter on Conservative MPs, for example, confirmed the rise of the career politician. On other occasions the conclusions broke new ground; the chapter on the annual Party conference, for example, detailed numerous examples of rank and file assertiveness. The final chapter provided a valuable bibliographical essay on the Conservative Party.

CLARK (1998) offered a more critical account of the history of the Conservative Party in the 20th century. The Party existed to nurture, protect, and advance the interests of the "British nation state" for the benefit of everyone "within its borders". Yet this it has all too often failed to do in the years since 1922. Through a series of mistakes, beginning with Baldwin's elevation to the leadership in 1923, the Party has frequently acted in ways contrary to its own and the national interest. These mistakes have also been fuelled by personality clashes on occasion (Chamberlain, Churchill, and appeasement for instance). The Conservative Party's commitment to the "British nation state", for so long its strength, became a weakness in the 1990s, as it caused divisions over Europe.

For the debate about the future of the Conservative Party after its defeat at the polls in 1997 see GRAY & WILLETTS. For Gray the outlook was bleak as free-market Thatcherism had undermined the core values of Conservatism. Thatcher's love of the market had destroyed respect for the past and had created a society in which no one could be sure of his or her place. Conservatism could not hope to survive under such conditions; it was certainly no good trying to revive One Nation Conservatism. Willetts, however, believed that civic conservatism offered a way forward. The encroaching power of government since 1945 had undermined the vitality of those civic institutions that nourished community life. The only way to revive them was through the promotion of limited government in a free market economy.

STEPHEN EVANS

Constitutional law

Bagehot, Walter, *The English Constitution*, introduction by R.H.S. Crossman, London: Collins, 1963 (originally published 1867)

Barendt, Eric, *An Introduction to Constitutional Law*, Oxford and New York: Oxford University Press, 1998

Brazier, Rodney, *Constitutional Reform: Reshaping the British Political System*, 2nd edition, Oxford and New York: Oxford University Press, 1998

Brazier, Rodney, *Constitutional Practice: The Foundations of British Government*, 3rd edition, Oxford and New York: Oxford University Press, 1999

Dicey, A.V., *An Introduction to the Study of the Law of the Constitution*, 10th edition, London: Macmillan, 1964 (1st edition 1885)

Jennings, Ivor, *The Law and the Constitution*, 5th edition, London: University of London Press, 1959

Jowell, Jeffrey and Dawn Oliver (editors), *The Changing Constitution*, 3rd edition, Oxford: Clarendon Press, and New York: Oxford University Press, 1994

Munro, Colin R., *Studies in Constitutional Law*, 2nd edition, London: Butterworths, 1999

Wheare, Kenneth Clinton, *Modern Constitutions*, 2nd edition, Oxford and New York: Oxford University Press, 1966

The unwritten and fluid nature of the English constitution makes it ripe for discussion and argument. The area is one that is constantly developing and being reshaped. However, much useful commentary on the nature of the English constitution is to be found in a number of older texts. A.V. Dicey is regarded as perhaps the most influential writer in the area, and DICEY, first published in 1885, is the first full and detailed exposition of the English constitution. It sets out many of the fundamental principles around which the British legal and political systems have developed, and which continue to be of central importance. The text is focused upon three central principles: the sovereignty of Parliament, the Rule of Law, and the role of constitutional conventions. Dicey utilizes examples from the US and from French *Droit Administratif* in order to illustrate the fundamental principles that he outlines. This is not a text that describes the contemporary development of constitutional law; the bulk of the text has remained unchanged since its seventh incarnation in 1914. However, the text is essential

reading for anyone wishing to acquire a good understanding of the fundamentals of the area.

JENNINGS is a similar exposition of the principles that inform the operation of the English constitution through the law. However, this text not only outlines the principles but also, to a certain extent, demonstrates their practical application. Although, like Dicey, this is not a contemporary account it will be of immense use to students of the area in establishing the key concepts.

Both Jennings and Dicey owe much to BAGEHOT, another historical account. Bagehot is not descriptive of the current position but is instead a survey of the nature of the constitution as at 1867. Once again, though, students of the subject will be able to reap much of value from this text as it provides a valuable insight into the principles, and more importantly, practice of the institutions that conduct the business of the constitution. Another key text in this regard is BRAZIER (1999), which considers the nuts and bolts of the constitution. Informative and commendably current, Brazier deals concisely and stimulatingly with the constituent parts of the constitution; a useful modern comparator for the more elderly texts of Dicey and Bagehot.

Another relatively elderly, though extremely useful text is WHEARE. This seeks to explain the nature of constitutions more generally, through the adoption of a comparative approach. The text endeavours to discover what makes up a constitution, what it may contain, and the ways in which it may be interpreted and amended. The comparative approach is useful in allowing the student to consider alternative mechanisms to those utilized in an English context in order to achieve broader constitutional objectives. The purpose of Wheare is not to explain or to justify the operation of any one constitution, but to take a broad analytical approach in order to illustrate important issues and problems. Thus Wheare is again useful as part of a programme of basic reading pursued as a background to any study of modern constitutional law.

A useful and recent summary of all the principles and issues raised in the historical texts is to be found in BARENDT. This offers a succinct and concise summary of the historical material, combined with an examination and analysis of the nature of the constitutional law of the UK as it currently stands. It includes an account of the impact of the UK's membership of the European Union, an event that has proved continually problematic for those seeking to uphold the fundamental principles of the constitution elucidated by, in particular, Dicey and Jennings. Relatively recent publication means that Barendt is sufficiently current to take account of a number of recent constitutionally significant events, i.e. the enaction of the Human Rights Act 1998 and moves towards devolution in Scotland, Wales, and Northern Ireland. MUNRO offers a similar scope in terms of the subject area covered and is recent enough to be able to consider those recent developments. However, as its title suggests, Barendt is more introductory in its nature and Munro indulges in a more in-depth critical analysis of the subject matter. Both texts are accessible and authoritative.

The collection of essays to be found in JOWELL & OLIVER is significantly less contemporary than either Barendt or Munro, being published prior to the devolution and human rights reforms. However, the material found therein is still extremely useful. The stated objective of Jowell & Oliver is to consider the fundamental constitutional norms outlined primarily by Dicey, in the context of the constitution of the UK as it stood in 1994. The text seeks to do this in a number of ways. As well as analysing the position of the UK *vis-a-vis* the EU, it contains a discussion of the UK's treatment of the European Convention on Human Rights prior to its incorporation into UK law by the Human Rights Act 1998. This is likely to prove useful to those interested in the development of human rights as a part of the UK constitution. Jowell & Oliver also explicitly consider the contemporary position of the fundamental constitutional principles elucidated by Dicey before considering these together in various, narrower contexts. Jowell & Oliver is an extremely useful text, bringing together expertise from both professional and academic circles and focuses their energies with the aim of understanding the contemporary constitution. The result is an insightful, persuasive, and authoritative text.

This critical approach is taken up with vigour by BRAZIER (1998), which focuses upon the constitutional reforms initiated by the Labour government elected in 1997. However, the book is not just a critical analysis of current reforms, but also highlights the continuing shortcomings of the British constitution. It is not a policy document, nor does it seek to propose fantastical reform programmes. Instead, the author's ideas and arguments are grittily pragmatic, and the book should be considered essential reading for those interested in the "here and now" – as well as the future – of the British constitution.

SIMON BOYES

See also Law survey

Construct

Adams-Webber, Jack R., "Assimilation and Contrast in Personal Judgment: The Dichotomy Corollary" in *The Construing Person*, edited by James C. Mancuso and Jack R. Adam-Webber, New York: Praeger, 1982

Bannister, D., "The Logic of Passion" in *New Perspectives in Personal Construct Theory*, edited by D. Bannister, London: Academic Press, 1977

Fransella, Fay, "What Is a Construct?" in *Attributions, Beliefs and Constructs in Counselling Psychology*, edited by David A. Lane, Leicester: British Psychological Society, Counselling Psychology Section, 1989

Husain, Martha, "To What Can One Apply a Construct?" in *Applications of Personal Construct Theory*, edited by Jack R. Adams-Webber and James C. Mancuso, New York: Academic Press, 1983

Kelly, George A., "The Nature of Personal Constructs" (chapter 3) in his *The Psychology of Personal Constructs*, vol. 1, New York: Norton, 1955; London: Routledge, 1991

Kelly, George, A., "The Psychology of the Unknown" in *New Perspectives in Personal Construct Theory*, edited by D. Bannister, London: Academic Press, 1977

Mischel, T., "Personal Constructs, Rules, and the Logic of Clinical Activity", *Psychological Review*, 71 (1964): 180–92

Nystedt, Lars and David Magnusson, "Construction of Experience: The Construction Corollary" in *The Construing Person*, edited by James C. Mancuso and Jack R. Adam-Webber, New York: Praeger, 1982

Rychlak, Joseph, "George Kelly and the Concept of Construction", *International Journal of Personal Construct Psychology*, 3/1 (1990): 7–20

Tschudi, Finn, "Constructs are Hypotheses" in *Applications of Personal Construct Theory*, edited by Jack R. Adams-Webber and James C. Mancuso, New York: Academic Press, 1983

The term "construct" comes from George Kelly's theory of personal constructs. Constructs are the psychological building blocks of the theory. Anyone needing more general accounts of the whole theory is referred to the entry on Personal construct theory. The selection here is of interest to those who want to know something of the nature of these building blocks. There is no one book devoted to the "construct", so edited books and journal papers have been included here as well as Kelly's original text.

FRANSELLA gives a general overview of Kelly's concept of the "construct", spelling out precisely what it is and what it is not. It provides the lecturer and student with specific answers to the question "what is a construct?"

Those who want to go well beyond Fransella's general account of the construct will need to go to the source. That is chapter three in KELLY (1995). The style in his original two volumes is not easy and his 80-page chapter on the nature of personal constructs requires some dedication on the part of the reader, but those who accept the challenge will be well rewarded.

RYCHLAK is intended for the academic who is interested in the more philosophical aspects of Kelly's formulation of "the construct" and "construing" generally. Rychlak compares Kelly with Piaget, arguing that they are the only theorists to use such concepts. It is difficult reading but there is no other comparable discussion.

Kelly's theory of personal constructs is formulated as a fundamental postulate, which is elaborated by 11 corollaries, one of which is the construction corollary. NYSTEDT & MAGNUSSON deal with that corollary by giving a brief account of what Kelly describes, but they fail to discuss one of the central features of "the construct": its role in enabling anticipation or prediction of events. Those anticipations and predictions may be wrong, but they determine our behaviour. The chapter is, however, useful for those academics who want to know where the idea stands in relation to other psychological and philosophical ideas, both past and present.

In 1964, MISCHEL argued that Kelly's constructs were nothing more than a set of rules that people follow and so have nothing to do with prediction. Many journal papers resulted from that article, but it was not until 1983 that a serious refutation was put forward by TSCHUDI. He argued that Kelly's theory does mean that each human being makes sense of the world by construing it and thereby predicting the outcomes of certain behaviours. It is in that sense that Kelly referred to each person as "a scientist". The problem is that we are not all very good scientists. As with most references in this section, these discussions are very academic. The argument between Mischel and Tschudi is important in questioning the meaning of the very building blocks of Kelly's theory.

Those who feel they would like to know more about what Kelly means by the idea that prediction leads to behaviour should read KELLY (1977) describing personal construct theory as a psychology of the unknown. That is, we make a prediction stemming from our understanding of an event and that launches us into behaving in relation to that event. We will not know whether our prediction is correct or not until we have behaved. This was a very radical notion indeed against a background of the prevailing behaviourism. Kelly's account in that paper is, like all his essays, very easy to read and covers many topics from the perspective of prediction, such as that of freedom versus determinism and the nature of truth.

HUSAIN, like Nystedt & Magnusson, relates the concept of the construct to ideas outside Kelly's system. His chapter is useful for academic study in that sense. However, he mistakenly takes a "construct" to be only cognitive, ignoring the fact that Kelly was at pains to say that construing was as much to do with our experiencing of events as our conscious understanding of them.

BANNISTER takes up this cognitive versus emotion debate. The debate concerns whether "a construct" is something that is always known to us or whether it can be active outside of our conscious awareness. Bannister supports Kelly's argument that his personal construct theory is not a cognitive theory but a theory of human experiencing. Bannister cites Kelly's formulation of such feelings as guilt and anxiety in personal construct theory terms and argues that constructs may have words attached to them but, equally, they may not. They may, for instance, have been created before a child has developed language. This chapter is tightly argued, but it is easy to read and could be of interest to anyone interested in theories of "what makes people tick."

Another corollary that is central to the understanding of Kelly's formulation of "the construct" concerns its bipolar or dichotomous nature. One cannot know what "good" means if one does not have some idea of what "bad" entails. ADAMS-WEBBER describes that in some detail. He looks at the concept particularly from his own "golden section hypothesis". Research suggests that people do not apply the construct equally for both its poles. The pole a person sees as the more positive (for example "good") is used about two-thirds more often than its more negative opposite(for example "bad"). This is an important chapter, but its subject matter is complicated. It is therefore mainly valuable for those who want to have a deeper insight into Kelly's central theoretical unit, but not for those who want an easy read.

FAY FRANSELLA

See also Personal construct theory

Construct validity

Collins, Linda M., "The Measurement of Dynamic Latent Variables in Longitudinal Aging Research: Quantifying Adult Development", *Experimental Aging Research*, 17/1 (1991): 13–20

Dixon, Danny R. and Bruce A. Thyer, "Double Depression in Men: Does It Exist?", *Journal of Psychopathology and Behavioral Assessment*, 20/2 (1998): 187–97

Endler, Norman S., Eilenna Denisoff and Alexandra Rutherford, "Anxiety and Depression: Evidence for the Differentiation of Commonly Co-occuring Constructs", *Journal of Psychopathology and Behavioral Assessment*, 20/2 (1998): 149–71

Mueller, Reed M., Michael J. Lambert and Gary M. Burlingame, "Construct Validity of the Outcome Questionnaire: A Confirmatory Factor Analysis", *Journal of Personality Assessment*, 7/2 (1998): 248–62

Pitts, Steven C., Stephen G. West and Jenn-Yun Tein, "Longitudinal Measurement Models in Evaluation Research: Examining Stability and Change", *Evaluation and Program Planning*, 19/4 (1996): 333–50

Revicki, D.A., K. Chan and F. Gevirtz, "Discriminant Validity of the Medical Outcomes Study Cognitive Function Scale in HIV Disease Patients", *Quality of Life Research*, 7/6 (1998): 551–59

Construct validity relates to the question of whether psychological measurements actually assess an underlying hypothetical construct. If the measurements do not reflect the construct, then inferences based on those measurements will be suspect. PITTS, WEST & JENN-YUN TEIN discuss the use of confirmatory factor analysis (CFA) as a means of assessing construct validity in longitudinal research. This is a sophisticated methodology that provides estimates of the relationships between measured variables and underlying constructs. This methodology can be based either on theory or on empirical findings, and can lead to further modelling of constructs using structural equation modelling techniques. Confirmatory factor analysis, in this context, requires researchers to assess the internal consistency of the construct using cross-sectional analyses. Subsequently, CFA investigates whether the same construct is being measured over time, then how stable it is across individuals. The researchers examine CFA in the assessment of single or multiple constructs, multiple waves, and comparison of pre- and post-test designs using experimental and control groups. They point out that measurement invariance (measuring a construct whose nature does not change over time) is critical for the useful interpretation of data. They note the conditions in which measurement invariance is unlikely to occur, such as with long delays between measurement waves, in periods of rapid developmental change, or in nonequivalent groups or subgroups. This article provides a good, relatively non-technical description of the use of CFA in establishing construct validity.

Developmental psychologists have documented different aspects of change in latent (psychological) variables during adulthood. COLLINS argues that some of the standard research methodologies that are appropriate for static (not age- or time-dependent) variables are inappropriate for studying dynamic latent variables. The result is a poor assessment of the nature of change, hence lower levels of construct validity in conceptualizing latent variables (such as self-esteem). For example, a cross-sectional design that assesses groups of different ages may not capture the nature of change that is not strictly time dependent. Collins identifies the longitudinal

Guttman simplex and the latent transition analysis as two useful methodologies that will enhance the validity of constructs when intra-individual development is cumulative and irreversible, but heterogeneous across individuals. She stresses that a clearly articulated theoretical basis is needed for adequate measurement of dynamic latent variables. The limitations of these approaches include the fact that a thorough theoretical grounding is needed for their implementation.

Sometimes the assessment of construct validity aids the development of theory, but sometimes it has clear practical implications. For instance, MUELLER, LAMBERT & BURLINGAME use CFA to assess whether a particular instrument, the "outcome questionnaire" (OQ), is useful in identifying the success of therapy in terms of relief from (a) symptomatic distress, (b) interpersonal problems, or (c) social role dysfunction. They report that the OQ shows little construct validity with respect to the three domains in question. Although their research fails to support some uses of the OQ, it is informative in revealing that, whereas the OQ shows adequate levels of reliability and concurrent validity, such strengths are not enough because its level of construct validity is low in so far as it does not adequately differentiate between the three types of relief being addressed. They also point out some of the limitations associated with the use of CFA.

Researchers can assess construct validity using more traditional statistical approaches. REVICKI, CHAN & GEVIRTZ investigated the cognitive functioning of HIV-positive patients. Adequate measurement of cognitive functioning can be extremely time-consuming, requiring from one to seven hours, so it would be desirable to construct a brief yet valid set of measurements that would assess cognitive functioning. The researchers developed a brief six-item Likert-type questionnaire for such use; it was embedded in their HIV Health Survey. They also administered a test for depression and a well-known performance-based cognitive functioning test, the Reitan trail-making test (TMT). Using logistic regression, t-tests and analyses of variance (ANOVAs), the researchers documented that their brief six-item questionnaire, and an even shorter four-item questionnaire, proved to be good indicators of cognitive functioning as revealed by the Reitan TMT. The questionnaires may be appropriate for research on new therapies and to track changes in functioning because they require less than two minutes to complete and because they show adequate levels of construct validity regarding cognitive functioning. One caution associated with this study is that depression and cognitive functioning are confounded, so it is necessary to understand the relationship between these two phenomena in order to understand more fully the cognitive decline associated with HIV infection.

Depression has been documented as one of the most widespread psychological or psychiatric disturbances. Among its variations are major depressive disorder (MDD) and dysthymia, chronic low-grade depression. DIXON & THYER note that research has revealed that patients with a double diagnosis of MDD and dysthymia cope less well in daily life and are prone to relapses in their depression. One question that arises, however, regards the validity of this double diagnosis across genders. Published research with dual diagnosis of depression has included a predominance of women. The results of these researchers call into question the validity of the construct of double depression in men. They suggest that decisions about the existence, diagnosis, and treatment of double depression require more information about patient samples and about validated assessment instruments for dysthymia and double depression. This research is limited in that it uses a small, relatively homogeneous sample; its strength arises from the questions it poses for future researchers.

Accuracy in the identification and treatment of depression is critical for clinicians because it is so widespread in patient populations. At the same time, anxiety frequently occurs with depression. ENDLER, DENISOFF & RUTHERFORD discuss whether current diagnostic instruments reliably differentiate between anxiety and depression. These researchers report that when they administered the Beck Depression Inventory (BDI) and the Endler Multidimensional Anxiety Scales (EMAS) for state and for trait, they found significant correlations between the measures of depression and anxiety. Others have used such patterns of data to suggest that the construct of "general distress" subsumes both anxiety and depression. When scores on the BDI and on the subtests of the EMAS were analysed, the researchers noted that the BDI and the EMAS state measurement scores were related to one another, but differed from the EMAS trait measurement. Further, factor analysis revealed that subtests of the neuroticism scale loaded on distinct factors, suggesting good construct validity in discriminating between anxiety and depression, which they concluded are separately identifiable constructs. Caveats regarding this research involve the fact that the authors studied college students rather than clinically depressed or anxious individuals.

BERNARD C. BEINS

See also Validity

Constructionism

Armon-Jones, Claire, "Prescription, Explication and the Social Construction of Emotion", *Journal for the Theory of Human Behaviour*, 15/1 (1985): 1–22

Berger, Peter L. and Thomas Luckmann, *The Social Construction of Reality: A Treatise in the Sociology of Knowledge*, New York: Doubleday, and Harmondsworth: Penguin, 1966

Burr, Vivien, *An Introduction to Social Constructionism*, London and New York: Routledge, 1995

Danziger, Kurt, "The Varieties of Social Construction", *Theory and Psychology*, 7/3 (1997): 399–416

Edwards, Derek, Malcolm Ashmore and Jonathan Potter, "Death and Furniture: The Rhetoric, Politics and Theology of Bottom Line Arguments against Relativism", *History of the Human Sciences*, 8/2 (1995): 25–49

Gergen, Kenneth J., "The Social Constructionist Movement in Modern Psychology", *American Psychologist*, 40/3 (1985): 266–75

Nightingale, David J. and John Cromby (editors), *Social Constructionist Psychology: A Critical Analysis of Theory and Practice*, Buckingham: Open University Press, 1999

Parker, Ian (editor), *Social Constructionism, Discourse, and Realism*, London and Thousand Oaks, California: Sage, 1998

Searle, John R., *The Construction of Social Reality*, New
York: Free Press, 1995; London: Penguin, 1996
Shotter, John and Kenneth J. Gergen (editors), *Texts of
Identity*, London and Newbury Park, California: Sage,
1989

BERGER & LUCKMANN's seminal text paved the way for
much contemporary work in (social) constructionism within
many of the human and social sciences. Their major aim was
to demonstrate that our knowledge of reality is socially
constructed (and not a natural, objective, and discoverable
"property" of such a reality) through an analysis of the nature
of reality (in particular, an analysis of phenomena that appear
to exist independently of our volition) and an examination of
the status and scope of our knowledge regarding such a reality.
However, and as they explicitly state, they are not concerned
with the ultimate (philosophical or theoretical) validity or invalidity of our "knowledge"; rather, their analysis explores particular agglomerations of "knowledge" and "reality"" as they
pertain to particular social contexts or particular periods in
history.

Berger and Luckmann provide an analysis of constructionism
in terms of the sociology of knowledge but GERGEN offers
an account of the development and nature of constructionist
ideas within psychology. He begins by defining what he terms
the "social constructionist orientation", goes on to locate
constructionist ideas within their historical context, and
concludes with an analysis of the implications of constructionism both for psychology (in terms of the ways in which
constructionism undermines dominant conceptions regarding
the scientific and objective nature of psychology), and for
science more generally (by providing a critique of the Western
conception of knowledge, as an "objective, individualistic and
ahistoric" enterprise).

DANZIGER, in a review essay of 11 volumes in the Sage
series, *Inquiries in Social Constructionism*, explores the
commonalities and differences that inform current constructionist inquiries in the human sciences. He demonstrates that,
although many writers share certain key assumptions regarding
the socially constructed nature of both reality and knowledge,
there are important differences both in terms of the assumptions that inform their inquiries and the particular form and
scope of those inquiries. He distinguishes two broad forms or
versions of constructionism, which he terms "light constructionism" and "dark constructionism". Light constructionism
sees human life as embedded in language and discourse. This
form of constructionism is largely influenced by the "linguistic
turn" of the social sciences and emphasizes the ongoing
construction of meaning in dialogue, conversation, and joint
activity. Dark constructionism on the other hand, drawing
primarily upon the philosophy of French poststructuralist
Michel Foucault, sees language and discourse as embedded
within relations of power that both regulate and constrain
social activity.

For those who are new to this area, BURR provides a lucid
and accessible introduction to contemporary social constructionism within psychology. She begins by offering a broad definition of constructionism (both in terms of its defining
characteristics and in terms of the specific ways in which it
differs from mainstream psychology) and goes on to elucidate

key themes within current constructionist perspectives. In
particular, she considers the notion of personhood (personality,
the self, the individual) and demonstrates the various ways in
which constructionists explain personhood; from the notion
of "person as discourse-user" (similar to Danziger's light
constructionism), through "the self as constructed in language"
(akin to Danziger's dark constructionism), to "subject positions
in discourse".

The 14 chapters in SHOTTER & GERGEN explicitly focus
upon the role of language and textuality in the construction
of identity. The contributors explore the various ways in which
people are positioned within particular discursive frameworks
and how these frameworks provide their "inhabitants" with
resources that both enable and constrain the construction
of identity. For those who are unfamiliar with the critiques
of Western notions of the individual that inform many
constructionist perspectives, chapter one by Edward Sampson
provides a clear and concise summary of some of the theoretical and philosophical critiques that have been brought to
bear upon this notion.

ARMON-JONES provides a further example of the ways in
which what we commonly take to be the objective properties
of the individual are, in fact, better explained within a social
constructionist framework. She demonstrates that emotion,
normally seen as an internal and "natural" state of the individual, should be reconceptualized as "socially determined
patterns of ritual action". In other words, that what we take
ourselves to be and how we understand ourselves and others
cannot be explained in terms of objective and enduring properties or essences of the individual (for example, our personality, biology, or neurology), but should instead be seen as a
consequence of particular cultural and historical forms of
knowledge and practice.

The above texts are primarily concerned with the explanation and application of constructionist perspectives within the
human sciences but those that follow are concerned with the
realism–relativism debate – a debate with which many contemporary constructionist accounts are either explicitly or implicitly engaged. Briefly, relativism is the belief that all knowledge
is historically and culturally specific. Within many forms of
constructionism this is further articulated to suggest that all
knowledge is linguistic, discursive, or textual in origin. Realism,
on the other hand, is the belief that the external world exists
independently of our representations of it and that, in some
senses at least, our (linguistic, discursive, or textual) knowledge is always already mediated in and through, for example,
our embodied nature and the materiality of the world.

PARKER's collection provides a comprehensive introduction
to the realism–relativism debate. The contributors to this
volume present a range of positions, from relativism to realism,
that explore such notions as language, social constructionism,
discourse, practice, materiality, and revolutionary socialism in
terms of this debate. Part two of the collection provides a series
of commentaries on earlier chapters that further serve to
contextualize and explore these issues.

EDWARDS, ASHMORE & POTTER provides an eloquent
defence of relativism as "the quintessentially academic position, where all truths are to-be-established". Their defence of
relativism centres on an analysis of the ways in which "claims"
regarding realism, such as table-thumping and invoking the

Holocaust, are, by their very invocation, inevitably social, discursive, and representational acts. In other words, they claim that talk regarding external reality can never be evidence for such an external reality because such talk is always already embedded within relativized frameworks of social and discursive knowledge.

NIGHTINGALE & CROMBY takes issue with the all-encompassing relativism advocated by Edwards *et al.* and argue that language and discourse are fundamentally intertwined with extra-discursive aspects of our reality that can neither be explained nor explored within a purely relativist framework. Although accepting that both the world and ourselves are fundamentally social in origin, they take issue with relativist claims regarding the centrality of language and discourse, and argue instead that constructionism must now address issues of materiality, embodiment, and power within which such discourses are always already located.

SEARLE explores those aspects of our world that we might wish to term objective by human agreement, such as money, property, and marriage, those aspects of our world that Searle terms "objective social reality" or "institutional facts". While not denying that these aspects of our world cannot be considered to exist outside of human activity, neither can they be conceptualized as a function of individual preference, evaluation, or moral stance. Searle explores the nature of these "facts" in terms of their structure, development, creation, and maintenance. He concludes by offering a critique of attacks on realism, a discussion of the proof of external realism, and an analysis of truth and correspondence – the extent to which our knowledge may be said to correspond to external facts or reality.

DAVID J. NIGHTINGALE

See also Critical psychology, Discourse analysis, Essentialism

Constructivism in international relations theory

Haas, Peter M., *Saving the Mediterranean: The Politics of International Environmental Cooperation*, New York: Columbia University Press, 1990

Johnston, Alastair Iain, *Cultural Realism: Strategic Culture and Grand Strategy in Chinese History*, Princeton, New Jersey: Princeton University Press, 1995

Katzenstein, Peter J. (editor), *The Culture of National Security: Norms and Identity in World Politics*, New York: Columbia University Press, 1996

Keohane, Robert O., "International Institutions: Two Approaches", *International Studies Quarterly*, 32 (1988): 379–96

Kier, Elizabeth, *Imagining War: French and British Military Doctrine between the Wars*, Princeton, New Jersey: Princeton University Press, 1997

Lumsdaine, David Halloran, *Moral Vision in International Politics: The Foreign Aid Regime, 1949–1989*, Princeton, New Jersey: Princeton University Press, 1993

Ruggie, John Gerard, *Constructing the World Polity: Essays on International Institutionalization*, London and New York: Routledge, 1998

Wendt, Alexander, "Anarchy Is what States Make of It: The Social Construction of Power Politics", *International Organization*, 46/2 (1992): 391–425

In international relations theory, constructivism is the theoretical perspective that stresses the importance of identity formation, culture, and norms, as independent determinants of the behaviour of the actors in the international arena. In the past, scholars in international studies have generally paid attention to the role of values and belief systems in their research. But the predominance, in past decades, of rationalist approaches – stressing the distribution of material capabilities and the instrumental rationality of actors – has recently stimulated a reaction aiming to demonstrate that international politics is unintelligible if cultural and ideational factors are considered as simply epiphenomenal and derivative. The most recent literature aims at providing a coherent theoretical, and sometimes epistemological, alternative to the existing approaches.

KEOHANE, a prominent scholar working within the rationalist framework, has offered an early and concise comparison of the rationalist and the constructivist (or "reflectivist") approach to the study of international institutions. He argues that the former views institutions as affecting patterns of cost – they facilitate mutually beneficial exchanges by reducing uncertainty and transaction costs – whereas the latter emphasizes the cultural foundations of institutional change as well as learning processes.

RUGGIE's introduction to his collected essays from a period of 25 years provides a useful account of the reasons for adopting a constructivist approach. In his words, social constructivism "attributes to ideational factors, including culture, norms, and ideas, social efficacy over and above any functional utility they may have, including a role in shaping the way in which actors define their identity and interest in the first place". Ruggie spells out the core assumptions of this research programme, and contrasts it with the predominant theoretical stances in contemporary international relational theory, "neorealism" and "neoliberal institutionalism", which treat the actors' identities and interests as given and adopt a utilitarian framework of analysis. Ruggie argues that constructivism, as it focuses both on regulative and constitutive rules, is superior to these alternative perspectives, which account only for the former kind of rules. Constructivism can account for systemic transformations, the others cannot. He hints at the fact that constructivism's epistemology is nonpositivist or postpositivist, but this point is not elaborated in detail.

WENDT presents an influential systemic version of constructivism. Drawing on structurationist and symbolic interactionist sociology, he argues that identities and attitudes of states are constructed through interaction in the international system. Specifically, self-help and power politics do not follow necessarily from the anarchical character of the international system, as is held by structural realists, but rather from specific processes of interaction among states in which anarchy plays only a permissive role, and through which states constitute their identities and interests.

KATZENSTEIN's edited collection includes some of the most interesting work written so far within the constructivist perspective. Essays by Jepperson, Wendt, and Katzenstein, and Kowert and Legro, present theoretical reflections on the origins and impact of norms and identity in international security. Eyre and Suchman explore the role of status and norms in conventional weapons proliferation. Price and Tannenwald explain the non-use of nuclear and chemical weapons by means of the cultural and normative meanings that become attached to those kinds of weapons. Finnemore examines cases of humanitarian military intervention in the past 150 years and finds that the decision to intervene was strongly affected by the evolution of humanitarian norms. Kier relies upon the case of French military doctrine before World War II in order to show that cultural factors have an independent effect on changes in military doctrine. Johnston reconstructs Mao's strategic thought and argues that the attitude towards the use of force in Maoist China is an expression of a "hard realpolitik" strategic culture, which is not simply derivative of objective structural constraints. Herman shows that the "new thinking" accompanying Gorbachev's accession to power in the USSR was a genuine redefinition of interests grounded in new understandings about the nature of world politics, rather than simply an adjustment to changed international or domestic constraints. Berger examines the cultural context of German and Japanese defence policies, and argues that their features and endurance are best explained by constructivism rather than by structural accounts such as realism or liberalism. Risse-Kappen examines four moments of NATO's history (its origin, the Suez crisis, the Cuban missile crisis, and the post-Cold War situation) and explains them through a social constructivist interpretation of "republican liberalism", which stresses collective identity formation and norms of appropriate behaviour. Barnett examines various episodes of inter-Arab and US-Israeli relations, and finds that state identity is an important factor in threat identification and in the choice of alliance partners.

LUMSDAINE provides a powerful case for the contention that morals matter in international politics. He examines the foreign aid policies of 18 developed democracies from 1949 to 1989, employing a large quantity of historical and statistical data. By showing how aid changed over time, which donors contributed most, where the money was spent, and which groups supported aid in the donor states, Lumsdaine demonstrates that aid was given less according to the political and economic interests of the donor states than on moral convictions about humanitarian obligations and distributive justice. The differences among the aid programmes of different states and among the reasons why aid was given are best explained by differences in domestic ethical principles, among leaders and the public. And once aid was started, the dynamics of international society strengthened the norms of appropriate behaviour, imposing humanitarian goals on states.

HAAS analyses forms of international cooperation for treating marine pollution, focusing on the successful Mediterranean Action Plan, developed under the auspices of the United Nations Environment Programme. He confronts the actual evolution of cooperation in this field with three theoretical perspectives on world politics: neorealism, historical materialism, and his own "epistemic community" approach. Haas shows how the improved understanding of the causal interconnections between environment and economic activities achieved by a transnational network of experts, and the penetration of this ecological epistemic community into national and international decision making, changed the way governments formulated and implemented environmental policy, and concludes that these learning processes contributed to a substantial improvement of environmental conditions.

KIER's carefully designed and empirically rich study argues that the change or stability of military doctrine (offensive versus defensive) in the French and British armies between the World Wars cannot be explained by changes in the systemic balance of power nor by the military's preferences for offensive doctrines, as other authors have suggested. She shows that doctrinal change resulted from changes in the organizational cultures of both militaries, which involved three sets of beliefs and norms: about the nature of international politics; about the place of the military in state and society; and about the internal organization of the armed forces. This political-military culture interacts with the preferences of civilian actors, who are concerned about the effects of military organization on the domestic balance of power.

JOHNSTON has written a fascinating account of the formation of Chinese strategic culture during the Ming period (1368–1644) and of the ways in which this culture affected China's use of force against external threats. He reconstructs the Chinese "parabellum" or hard realpolitik strategic culture, and argues that it was this culture, rather than just the anarchic character of China's strategic environment, which caused strong self-help impulses and a predisposition towards the use of violence against threats.

MATHIAS KOENIG-ARCHIBUGI

See also International relations theory

Consumer behaviour

Becker, Gary S., *A Treatise on the Family*, enlarged edition, Cambridge, Massachusetts: Harvard University Press, 1991

Becker, Gary S., *Accounting for Tastes*, Cambridge, Massachusetts: Harvard University Press, 1996

Bianchi, Marina (editor), *The Active Consumer: Novelty and Surprise in Consumer Choice*, London and New York: Routledge, 1998

Deaton, Angus S. and John Muellbauer, *Economic Theory and Consumer Behaviour*, Cambridge: Cambridge University Press, 1980

Deaton, Angus S., Consumers' expenditure entry in *The New Palgrave: A Dictionary of Economics*, edited by John Eatwell, Murray Milgate and Peter Newman, 4 vols, London: Macmillan, and New York: Stockton Press, 1987

Duesenberry, James S., *Income, Saving and the Theory of Consumer Behaviour*, Cambridge, Massachusetts: Harvard University Press, 1949

Earl, Peter E., *Lifestyle Economics: Consumer Behaviour in a Turbulent World*, Brighton: Wheatsheaf, and New York: St Martin's Press, 1986

Fine, Ben and Ellen Leopold, *The World of Consumption*, London and New York: Routledge, 1993

Friedman, Milton, *A Theory of the Consumption Function*, Princeton, New Jersey: Princeton University Press, 1957

Gorman, W.M. (Terence), "A Possible Procedure for Analysing Quality Differentials in the Egg Market", *Review of Economic Studies*, 47/5 (1980): 843–56

Houthakker, Hendrik S. and Lester D. Taylor, *Consumer Demand in the United States: Analysis and Projections*, 2nd edition, Cambridge, Massachusetts: Harvard University Press, 1970

Ironmonger, Duncan S., *New Commodities and Consumer Behaviour*, Cambridge: Cambridge University Press, 1972

Lancaster, Kelvin J., *A New Theory of Consumer Demand*, New York: Columbia University Press, 1971

Mason, Roger S., *Conspicuous Consumption: A Study of Exceptional Consumer Behaviour*, Farnborough, Hampshire: Gower, and New York: St Martin's Press, 1981

Modigliani, Franco, "Life Cycle, Individual Thrift and the Wealth of Nations", *American Economic Review*, 76/3 (1986): 297–313

Stone, J. Richard N., *The Measurement of Consumers' Expenditure and Behaviour in the United Kingdom, 1920–1938*, Cambridge: Cambridge University Press, 1954

The distinctive economic approach to the analysis of consumer behaviour rests on the assumption that consumers have a significant degree of choice. This is in contrast with the perspective of other social sciences, especially sociology, which argues that consumers often have very little choice. Recent developments in economics have absorbed some of the thinking of other disciplines, and greater attention is given to the way in which social and group norms and imperatives constrain choice.

In the neoclassical theory of consumption, stemming from Marshall and surveyed most comprehensively in DEATON & MUELLBAUER, the consumer is an isolated optimiser. Choice is constrained maximization, and, although the constraints always bite, the consumer nevertheless has a large degree of discretion. After a compact statement of the basic economic theory of consumer behaviour, Deaton & Muellbauer show how the theory can be extended to human capital and labour supply, durable goods, choice under uncertainty, consumer index numbers, household characteristics and household welfare comparisons, and social welfare and inequality. Throughout the book, there is a strong emphasis on how theory can be deployed to improve applied econometric analysis. The main focus of the book is concerned with choice in situations where consumers have a lot of choice, but later chapters examine consumer behaviour under familial or life-cycle constraints. A later encyclopaedia entry by DEATON gives a summary of other more recent work in this tradition.

Two classics of the econometric study of consumer demand are still worthy of attention. STONE's study of consumer behaviour in the UK is one of the great works of applied econometrics. Stone consistently uses economic theory to guide his applied econometric method. Subsequent studies have had access to better and more voluminous data and have refined the econometric techniques used, but Stone's study makes major advances in estimating price and income elasticities for a wide variety of consumer goods. He uses income elasticities derived from cross-sectional budget studies to sharpen the estimates of own-price and cross-price elasticities obtained from time series data. HOUTHAKKER & TAYLOR's work is another major benchmark as an empirical study of demand.

Three major works, dating from the later 1940s and 1950s also shape much current thinking about consumption. They each represent an advance on the basic Keynesian consumption function in which current consumption is a simple linear function of current income. The first is the lifecycle hypothesis, dating back to work of Fisher and Ramsey, but usually associated with MODIGLIANI. The lifecycle hypothesis argues that the relationship between income in any year and consumption in that year is unlikely to be a simple linear one. At certain stages of their working lives, consumers save to accumulate wealth; later on they will stop accumulating and indeed start to run down assets. Modigliani argues that the rational utility maximizing consumers will optimize the allocation of their resources to consumption over their lifetime. Consumption at any time, therefore depends on average lifetime resources rather than current income, and the difference between these two shows up as (dis)saving. The second is the permanent income hypothesis of FRIEDMAN. Again, the concept of income that influences consumption is not current income but the expected annual level of income. In years where current income exceeds permanent income, there will be saving. In some respects, the permanent income hypothesis can be seen as a special case of the lifecycle hypothesis: where consumers live indefinitely, permanent income replaces average lifetime resources. The third is the relative income hypothesis of DUESENBERRY. This puts greatest weight on the influence of past levels of consumption to which the consumer has become accustomed. When households experience a loss of income, they nevertheless seek to maintain consumption as far as possible by running down accumulated savings. Hence, in the relative income hypothesis, current consumption depends on current income and the highest consumption standard achieved to date.

In much of this early analysis of consumer behaviour, the goods or services examined are taken to be fixed. However, a prevalent feature of the postwar economy was the increasing rate of product innovation. What did economics have to say about the demand for new goods? A key development was the "characteristics" approach to demand, most usually associated with the work of LANCASTER, but also developed independently by GORMAN, and by IRONMONGER. In the characteristics approach, the underlying demand is for product characteristics themselves, and goods and services are purchased to the extent that they supply bundles of characteristics. New goods that offer more efficient (and cheaper) ways of accumulating the desired mix of characteristics will enjoy increased demand. Although this approach has many uses throughout economic analysis, it has proven harder to implement empirically, at least with the same degree of rigour pursued in the mainstream of demand analysis.

A theme stressed by some of the classical writers, and later by Marshall, was that the economic analysis of consumption should have much to learn from the economic analysis of production. Indeed, as Deaton & Muellbauer show, the modern neoclassical theory of demand has a very close formal similarity to that of production. This similarity is further exploited in household production theory, first developed by BECKER (1991), and also by Stigler. This is sometimes bracketed together with the characteristics approach to demand, but it is in reality distinct. In household production theory, the household manager(s) combine purchased goods and services together with household labour to provide services to members of the household. Becker's work on the family shows how this approach can be applied to a variety of household decisions (including the division of labour in households, use of human capital, fertility, and altruism), as well as to areas that had previously been thought to lie outside the domain of economics, including marriage and divorce.

In the estimation of some economists, the most interesting new developments in the economics of consumer behaviour have come from the cross-fertilization of economics with other social and management sciences, notably sociology and marketing. These have shifted attention away from the conception of demand as making a privately optimum choice with given tastes, and focused instead on consumption as a lifestyle routine, as a deeply social activity, and indeed on the way in which consumer tastes evolve with experience. For example, EARL provides a compelling account of the economics of lifestyle. MASON, following in the tradition of Veblen, provides a comprehensive overview of the many varied forms of conspicuous consumption. FINE & LEOPOLD develop a broader theory of consumption, based on "systems of provision", which emphasizes the essential continuity between production, distribution, marketing, advertising, sales, and consumption.

Half of the papers by BECKER (1996) collected in his volume *Accounting for Tastes*, are concerned with personal consumption capital or routine and habit; the rest are concerned with social capital, or consumption as a social activity. The former describe a theory of rational addiction, and an analysis of the effect of price on consumption when there is rational addiction. The latter provide an economic theory of social interactions, of social influences on price, and of how social norms shape preferences.

Finally, the papers in the booked edited by BIANCHI explore the active consumer; this is really the counterpart in consumption to the innovator in production. The active consumer does not rely on the producer to create new products and services to satisfy his/her desire for variety and novelty. Rather, the active consumer plays an important part in creating his or her own innovations, whether by "journeys into the unknown" or by creating valuable collections from items of low individual value.

G.M. PETER SWANN

See also Spaces of consumption

Consumer law

Bourgoignie, Thierry and David Trubek, *Consumer Law, Common Markets and Federalism in Europe and the United States*, Berlin and New York: de Gruyter, 1987
Consumer Law Journal, 1993–
Cranston, Ross, *Consumers and the Law*, 2nd edition, London: Weidenfeld and Nicolson, 1984
Goldring, John, Lawrence Maher and Jill McKeough, *Consumer Protection Law*, 5th edition, Sydney: Federation Press, 1998

Howells, Geraint and Stephen Weatherill, *Consumer Protection Law*, Dartmouth, 1995
Howells, Geraint and Thomas Wilhelmsson, *EC Consumer Law*, Aldershot: Ashgate, 1997
Journal of Consumer Policy: Consumer Issues in Law, Economics and Behavioral Sciences, 1978–
Ramsay, Iain, *Consumer Protection: Text and Materials*, London: Weidenfeld and Nicolson, 1989
Ramsay, Iain (editor), *Consumer Law*, New York: New York University Press, 1992
Reich, Norbert, *Europäisches Verbraucherrecht*, 4th edition, Baden-Baden: Nomos, 1999
Spanogle, John A. and Ralph J. Rohner, *Consumer Law Cases and Materials*, 2nd edition, St. Paul, Minnesota: West, 1991
Weatherill, Stephen, *EC Consumer Law and Policy*, London and New York: Longman, 1997

Consumer law has developed into a discipline in its own right during the last four decades. The purpose of this review is to introduce the reader to some of the key reference points for the literature in this area. The subject can be broken down into subcategories, which experts can develop into subjects in their own right, e.g. sale of goods, product liability, consumer credit, financial services etc. However, the references listed here concern consumer law in general. My British origins are revealed by my choice of some UK works, although I have tried to select those that take a broad approach. Consumer law in Europe has been heavily influenced by EC law and so it is necessary to include EC material. And since this is a subject that lends itself to comparative research, some US and Commonwealth materials are also included.

Journals are an important source of contemporary and specialized contributions. In the consumer law field there are two main journals that seek to have an international appeal. CONSUMER LAW JOURNAL tends towards the more traditional style of legal analysis and has a well-received current survey section. It also has special issues themed on contemporary topics. For instance, issue 4 of 1999 deals with access to justice. JOURNAL OF CONSUMER POLICY, as its name suggests, tends more towards policy, social science, and theoretical contributions. It does however have some traditional legal articles and has a strong book review section.

WEATHERILL provides a succinct overview of the development of EC Consumer Law, placing it within a broader context. HOWELLS & WILHELMSSON takes a more detailed look at the substantive provisions of EC law affecting consumers, and provides a theoretical framework for its analysis. For those who read German, REICH provides an excellent treatment of the development of EC consumer law. An interesting, but somewhat dated, comparison of the problems on consumer protection and integration on both sides of the Atlantic is provided by BOURGOIGNIE & TRUBEK.

For a treatment of UK consumer law that also tries to draw upon European and comparative experiences, one might be directed to HOWELLS & WEATHERILL. CRANSTON is an excellent book which adopts the "law in context" approach and also includes comparative material. It is now rather dated, but it is understood a new edition is in preparation. In the same *Law and Context* series, RAMSAY (1989) is a useful text and materials book. This also has the benefit of including comparative material, but again is now rather dated.

RAMSAY (1992) brings together many of the most important theoretical writings on consumer law. For instance, it includes examples of Trebilcock's writing, which challenges the view that consumers benefit from protectionism, Pitofsky's views on advertising, Whitford's analysis of disclosure rules, Priest's theory on warranties, and Ramsay's own work on consumer redress.

The US was innovative in the field of consumer law in the 1970s and remains an important source of comparison. SPANOGLE & ROHNER provides a useful introduction. For analysis of Australian law see GOLDRING, MAHER & McKEOUGH.

GERAINT HOWELLS

See also European Community law

Contempt of court

Arlidge, Anthony J., David Eady and A.T.H. Smith, *The Law of Contempt*, London: Sweet and Maxwell, 1982; as *Arlidge, Eady and Smith on Contempt*, London: Sweet and Maxwell, 1999

Borrie, Gordon and Nigel V. Lowe, *The Law of Contempt*, London: Butterworths, 1973; 3rd edition by Nigel Lowe and Brenda Sufrin, London: Butterworths, and Charlottesville, Virginia: Michie, 1996

Courtney, Catherine, David Newell and Santha Rasaiah, *The Law of Journalism*, London: Butterworths, 1995

Fox, John, *The History of Contempt of Court: The Form of Trial and the Mode of Punishment*, Oxford: Clarendon Press, 1927; reprinted London: Professional Books, 1972

Miller, C.J., *Contempt of Court*, 3rd edition, Oxford: Clarendon Press, and New York: Oxford University Press, 2000

Nicol, Andrew and Heather Rogers, *Changing Contempt of Court*, London: National Council for Civil Liberties/Campaign for Press Freedom, 1981

Robertson, Geoffrey and Andrew G.L. Nicol, *Media Law: The Rights of Journalists and Broadcasters*, 3rd edition, London: Longman, 1992

ARLIDGE, EADY & SMITH, first published in 1982, has established itself as the most authoritative and comprehensive practitioners' manual on this vast and diffuse topic. Contempt can arise in wide variety of settings, ranging for example from matrimonial disputes to the reporting of criminal court cases, and the merit of this book is its largely successful effort to draw out general principles from the cases. It is only fairly recently that a body of authority has been built up. Prior to 1960 there was no right of appeal in cases of criminal contempt. The common underlying theme detected by the authors is the insistence in the cases that the power of summary punishment of contempt should be exercised only when necessary for the protection of, or to vindicate, the fair administration of justice. Another important theme is the careful consideration given in the book to the extent to which a guilty intention (*mens rea*) is a prerequisite of contempt. The authors

draw out in detail the conflicting considerations of public policy, which are involved in many of the areas touched by contempt law, including the protection of journalists' sources, the granting of injunctions against publication, and so on. The authors place emphasis on the constitutional aspects of the law relating to contempt of court: aspects which are certain to acquire even more importance when the full effect of the Human Rights Act begins to be felt.

BORRIE & LOWE is another well-known and authoritative manual, although closer in style to a textbook than to a practitioner's manual. It includes valuable discussion of the position of publications interfering with the course of justice both at common law and under the Contempt of Court Act 1981. Written in clear, straightforward language, this is a book for the inquiring layperson as well as for members of the legal profession. Both books discuss Commonwealth and Scottish law in this area in addition to the law of England and Wales.

MILLER starts with the distinction between civil and criminal contempt, then analyses procedure and jurisdiction in criminal cases, both in England and in the US, going on to deal with contempt in the face of the court, interference with legal proceedings, and contempt in relation to both criminal and civil proceedings. There are interesting chapters on open justice and on civil contempt of court, with particular reference to contempt in labour disputes. To some extent these reflect the preoccupations of the 1980s.

ROBERTSON & NICOL has a substantial chapter on contempt of court, reviewing the major recent cases in a discursive way from the standpoint of newspapers and television. They categorize contempt into five types: strict-liability contempt, for which liability can be incurred without any intention to prejudice legal proceedings; deliberate contempt; scandalous attacks on the judiciary; publishing accounts of jury deliberations; and disobedience of a court order. The book is aimed at a wider audience than the legal profession alone, and it is written, for the most part, in plain English rather than legal jargon. A fourth edition is promised at the end of 2000.

COURTNEY, NEWELL & RASAIAH is a comprehensive review of the rapidly changing area of law relating to journalism. Perhaps not as racy and partisan as Robertson & Nicol, it has a reasonably comprehensive account of the intersection of the law relating to contempt with the practice of journalism.

NICOL & ROGERS is a short campaign pamphlet directed, as its title suggests, to the reform of contempt law. It is now rather out of date and of largely historical interest.

In a scholarly analysis of the origins of the summary procedure for dealing with contempt of court, FOX demonstrates that although contempt "in the face of the court" (in full view of the tribunal) was summarily punished, the offence of contempt committed out of court was originally tried by a jury in the ordinary course of law, and that the practice of dealing summarily with such contempts was an 18th-century innovation. The book covers US as well as English history of contempt.

MAUREEN SPENCER

Contestable markets

Bailey, Elizabeth E. and Ann F. Friedlaender, "Market Structure and Multiproduct Industries", *Journal of Economic Literature*, 20/3 (September 1982): 1024–48

Baumol, William J. and Dietrich Fischer, "Cost-minimizing Number of Firms and Determination of Industry Structure", *Quarterly Journal of Economics*, 92/3 (August 1978): 439–67

Baumol, William J., "Contestable Markets: An Uprising in the Theory of Industry Structure", *American Economic Review*, 72/1 (March 1982): 1–15

Baumol, William J., John C. Panzar and Robert D. Willig, *Contestable Markets and the Theory of Industry Structure*, revised edition, San Diego: Harcourt Brace, 1988

Grossman, Sanford J., "Nash Equilibrium and the Industrial Organization of Markets with Large Fixed Costs", *Econometrica*, 49/5 (September 1981): 1149–72

Raa, Thijs ten, "Resolution of Conjectures on the Sustainability of Natural Monopoly", *Rand Journal of Economics*, 15/1 (Spring 1984): 135–41

Reed, Randall L. and Don E. Waldman, "Mergers and Air Fares: 'Contestable Markets' in the Airline Industry", *Antitrust Law and Economics Review*, 20/3 (1988): 15–20

Schwartz, Marius and Robert J. Reynolds, "Contestable Markets: An Uprising in the Theory of Industry Structure: Comment", *American Economic Review*, 73/3 (June 1983): 488–90

Stefanidis, Christodoulos, "Selective Contracts, Foreclosure, and the Chicago School View", *Journal of Law and Economics*, 41/2 (1998): 429–50

Willig, Robert D., "Contestable Market Theory and Regulatory Reform" (chapter 3, including a commentary by Lee L. Selwyn) in *Telecommunications Deregulation: Market Power and Cost Allocation Issues*, edited by John R. Allison and Dennis L. Thomas, New York: Quorum, 1990

The theory of contestable markets first appeared in the 1980s with the work of BAUMOL and of BAUMOL, PANZAR & WILLIG, with other important contributions by Elizabeth Bailey (BAILEY & FRIEDLAENDER), Dietrich Fischer (BAUMOL & FISCHER) and RAA. It has since been applied by regulations in a number of countries. For example, the theory explicitly underlies government rules on the freight rates charged by railroads in the US, and on the access charges levied by any one telephone company for use of its facilities by a rival telephone company in New Zealand.

Perfectly contestable markets are a theoretical market form that may, perhaps, rarely be approximated by industries in reality, although recent analysis suggests that it may be somewhat more widespread than is sometimes suspected (see for example REED & WALDMAN). Roughly speaking, an industry is defined as perfectly contestable if entry into and exit from its markets is quick and costless. As shown by STEFANIDIS, the same results can also be achieved indirectly if unambiguous contracts are easy and inexpensive to arrange, whether or not such contracts are actually entered into.

Contestable markets analysis has proved useful for practice as well as for theory. It has had two main applications. First,

as shown by Baumol, in a perfectly contestable market even a pure monopolist is deprived of the power to charge monopoly prices or earn monopoly profits. Consequently, the concept has appeared in a number of anti-trust cases, with the defendants claiming that they could not possibly have behaved anticompetitively because their markets are contestable. Unfortunately, there is good reason to conclude that many such claims were exaggerations, and that they did not rest on the necessary empirical evidence (see, for example WILLIG).

More important has been the use of the analysis as a guide to the regulation of firms suspected of possessing monopoly power, most recently in the case of newly-privatized firms throughout the world. That is, the theory has proved most useful as a guide to the regulation of firms that are emphatically *not* contestable. The point is that if, as is widely asserted, the regulator's task is to ensure that firms with monopoly power behave as they would *if, contrary to fact, they operated in competitive markets*, then contestable markets analysis arguably provides the appropriate guidelines. The perfect competition model cannot do the job because perfect competition requires firms to be minuscule and precludes scale economies, whereas firms with market power are generally large and often enjoy scale economies. Thus, for example, we know that a firm with scale economies cannot be expected to price its products at marginal cost, as is done by a perfectly competitive firm, because with such prices it would be condemned to insolvency.

Theory has also had at least two uses for contestable markets analysis. First, in a perfectly contestable market prices are fixed by the competitive pressures stemming from the threat of entry and so those prices cannot be manipulated by the firm. Such parametric prices greatly facilitate theoretical analysis. The concept has therefore been useful in models involving markets that are not perfectly competitive. Second, because in a perfectly contestable market a firm or group of firms cannot survive if its operation is inefficient, the number of firms that do survive in such a market will be the number that can produce the industry output most efficiently. This is, therefore, an analysis that permits study of the determination of industry structure – whether market forces will make the industry a monopoly or a duopoly or give it some other market form. This is in contrast with most of the literature on market forms that simply ignores the determination process as though it were not influenced by economic forces.

All of this can be shown to result from three welfare properties of a perfectly contestable market: no firm can earn more than competitive profits or prices because otherwise an entrant can open for business with lower but still-profitable prices and take the overcharged customers away. For the same reason, no firm or group of firms can be wasteful or inefficient. For somewhat more complicated reasons, in a perfectly contestable market with at least two firms, equilibrium prices must be set at perfectly competitive levels – that is, the levels necessary for economic efficiency.

Contestability has been equated with the absence of sunk costs, because if entry does not require the new firm to sink investments, by definition it will be able to leave without having lost any money in the process. Thus, in this case entry and exit will indeed be costless. A number of observers (such as

SCHWARTZ & REYNOLDS) have concluded that this severely limits the applicability of the analysis, because there are probably no industries with zero sunk costs, and very few in which those costs are close to zero. This observation overlooks the fact that most widespread application of contestable markets theory has been to the regulation of firms that patently are *not* even in approximately contestable markets.

More important, it overlooks the role of contracts, originally noted by GROSSMAN and more recently analysed by Stefanidis. The point is that where contracting is neither difficult not expensive an entrant can forestall a predatory countermove by an incumbent by entering into a long-term contract with customers. This, in effect, ensures for a long time the splitting of the incumbent's former ill-gotten gains between the customer and the entrant, to their mutual benefit. Stefanadis has noted that where the mere threat of such contracts is real, the incumbent may be forced to act competitively even though no such contracts are ever actually entered into.

WILLIAM J. BAUMOL

See also Anti-trust economics, Contracts and competition, Regulation and competition

Contracts and competition

Buckley, Peter J. and Jonathan Michie (editors), *Firms, Organizations and Contracts: A Reader in Industrial Organization*, Oxford and New York: Oxford University Press, 1996

Cambridge Journal of Economics, special issue on "Contracts and Competition", 21/2 (March 1997): 121–302

Campbell, David and Peter Vincent-Jones (editors), *Contract and Economic Organization: Socio-Legal Initiatives*, Aldershot and Brookfield, Vermont: Dartmouth, 1996

Deakin, Simon and Jonathan Michie (editors), *Contracts, Co-operation, and Competition: Studies in Economics, Management and Law*, Oxford and New York: Oxford University Press, 1997

Flynn, Rob and Gareth Williams (editors), *Contracting for Health: Quasi-Markets and the National Health Service*, Oxford and New York: Oxford University Press, 1997

Milne, Seamus, *Making Markets Work: Contracts, Competition and Co-operation*, 1997 (available free of charge from j.michie@bbk.ac.uk)

New Economy, special issue on "Contracts and Competition", 4/3 (Autumn 1997): 137–72

Oxford Review of Economic Policy, special issue on "Contracts and Competition", 12/4 (Winter 1996): 1–121

Salanié, Bernard, *The Economics of Contracts: A Primer*, Cambridge, Massachusetts: MIT Press, 1997

Walsh, Kieron *et al.*, *Contracting for Change: Contracts in Health, Social Care, and Other Local Government Services*, Oxford and New York: Oxford University Press, 1997

Werin, Lars and Hans Wijkander (editors), *Contract Economics*, Oxford and Cambridge, Massachusetts: Blackwell, 1992

The relationship between contracting on the one hand, and competition versus cooperation on the other was researched in depth through a major, five-year research programme funded by the UK's Economic and Social Research Council (ESRC), from 1992 to 1997. Many of the above readings emerged from the work of the 20 project teams as well as from other academics who participated in the work of the programme. Although funded by the ESRC, the programme, and many of the above publications, include contributions from international authors, particularly from the US and Australia. Some of the case study work was also international in character, including research in Germany and Italy.

The work of the 1992–97 "Contracts & Competition" programme is discussed in MILNE, a pamphlet written by the *Guardian*'s Labour Editor. This not only discusses the theoretical issues and much of the empirical work, but also represents an admirable guide to the literature, not only from the ESRC programme but much more widely. While the discussion in the pamphlet is insightful and rigorous, it is also relatively accessible, and is thus the obvious entry point to what is an immense literature.

Three journals devoted entire special issues to "Contracts & Competition": NEW ECONOMY, the CAMBRIDGE JOURNAL OF ECONOMICS and the OXFORD REVIEW OF ECONOMIC POLICY.

New Economy is a quarterly journal of economic policy, published by the London-based think-tank, the Institute for Public Policy Research. The papers in this special issue therefore focus on the policy implications of the research. Sue Richards discusses the "Lessons from the Tory experiment" and argues that if the reform processes had involved a more interdisciplinary approach to the thinking that underlay them, the results would have been the better for it. Simon Deakin and Frank Wilkinson consider "What makes markets work?" and report from surveying private sector firms in Britain, Germany, and Italy that factors such as cooperation and trust may be as important to business relationships as they are to personal ones and that cooperation within contractual relations is an important basis for dynamic efficiency. Thus, what are portrayed as "market" reforms may be undermining the very institutional and cultural bedrock on which those markets depend. Indeed, Peter Nolan, Richard Saundry, and Malcolm Sawyer report that the "freeing up" of the labour market in the docks led to orders being lost when shippers preferred not to entrust their cargoes to casual hands ("Choppy waves on air and sea").

The *Cambridge Journal of Economics* is the leading international journal for non-orthodox economics, encouraging as it does interdisciplinary and critical work. The papers in this special issue therefore reflect research and thinking not just from a variety of perspectives from within economics but also from law, sociology, management, social anthropology, and accounting. Peter J. Buckley and Malcolm Chapman discuss "The perception and measurement of transaction costs" and argue that what matters for corporate practice is not actually computed transactions costs but rather managerial perceptions of what these transactions costs are. These perceptions are not expressed in numbers, but in language. Maria H. Maher also considers "Transaction cost economics and contractual relations", reporting case study work from four industries, arguing that a critical dimension omitted from Oliver Williamson's work is market structure. Alessandro Arrighetti, Reinhard Bachmann and Simon Deakin consider "Contract law, social norms and inter-firm cooperation" and find that contract law can play an important role in underpinning long-term, cooperative relationships and in fostering trust. Christel Lane analyses "The social regulation of inter-firm relations in Britain and Germany: market rules, legal norms and technical standards" and finds that the higher degree of stability and consistency in systems of social regulation in Germany, as compared with Britain, leads to more predictable and consensual relations between firms and that the resulting development of greater mutual trust encourages more long-term and closer technological collaboration. Brendan Burchell and Frank Wilkinson discuss "Trust, business relationships and the contractual environment", reporting from empirical work that while there is some evidence of differences in the basis of trust between Britain, Germany and Italy, these were differences of degree rather than kind. Bruce Lyons and Judith Mehta report on "Contracts, opportunism and trust: self-interest and social orientation", distinguishing between the self-interested trust which is the only source of trust recognised in the mainstream economics literature, and socially oriented trust which draws on sociology. David Hughes, Lesley Griffiths and Jean V. McHale ask "Do quasi-markets evolve? Institutional analysis and the NHS", arguing that the attempt to create a market in the health service in Britain in the 1980s failed to create a market that could evolve and so in fact had to rely on periodic strategic and administrative shifts. Jane Broadbent and Richard Laughlin discuss "Contracts and competition? A reflection on the nature and effects of recent legislation on modes of control in schools", arguing that the attempt to introduce "the market" into education through the 1980s reforms in Britain failed to do so, resulting instead in a strong centralising tendency, seeking to restrict the autonomy of professionals. Finally, Colin Mayer asks, "The City and corporate performance: condemned or exonerated?", arguing that many of the conventional wisdoms concerning differences between financial systems do not stand up to scrutiny and that the main differences actually concern the concentration and nature of ownership, with more concentrated ownership having some benefits but also costs.

The *Oxford Review of Economic Policy* publishes articles on current issues in economic policy; it includes discussion of economic theory, but always with a view to the policy implications. Thus John Vickers discusses "Market Power and Inefficiency: A Contracts Perspective"; Oliver Hart and John Moore analyse "The Governance of Exchanges: Members' Cooperatives versus Outside Ownership"; and Bruce R. Lyons discusses "Market Power and Inefficiency: A Contracts Perspective". The other three articles in this Special Issue (as well as the introductory "Assessment" by Tim Jenkinson and Colin Mayer) analyse specific industries. Gianni De Fraja and Keith Hartley consider "Defence Procurement: Theory and UK Policy". Martin Chalkley and James M. Malcomson discuss "Competition in NHS Quasi-Markets". Martin Cave and Peter Williamson analyse "Entry, Competition, and Regulation in UK Telecommunications".

The "classic" literature on contracts and competition are brought together in the first of Oxford University Press'

"Oxford Management Readers" (BUCKLEY & MICHIE). The book also includes some contemporary contributions to the literature, and the Editors discuss the various contributions to the literature in their "Introduction and Overview".

Oxford University Press also produced three edited collections on contracts and competition, reporting the work from the ESRC Programme. WALSH *et al.* reports the results of their research project on health, social care, and other local government services. A number of the 20 research teams analysed the use of contracts and competition within the UK's National Health Service, and FLYNN & WILLIAMS includes reports from all these. The socio-legal aspects of contracts and competition are analysed by the various authors in the volume edited by DEAKIN & MICHIE. The socio-legal aspects are also discussed in the edited volume CAMPBELL & VINCENT-JONES.

Finally, the economics of contracts are analysed by SALANIÉ and by the various authors of the collection edited by WERIN & WIJKANDER. All the above references themselves refer extensively to what is a large and growing literature.

JONATHAN MICHIE

Contracts, implicit

Arnott, Richard J. and Joseph E. Stiglitz, "Labor Turnover, Wage Structures, and Moral Hazard: The Inefficiency of Competitive Markets", *Journal of Labor Economics*, 3/4 (1985): 434–62

Arnott, Richard J., Arthur J. Hosios and Joseph E. Stiglitz, "Implicit Contracts, Labor Mobility, and Unemployment", *American Economic Review*, 78/5 (1988): 1046–66

Azariadis, Costas, "Implicit Contracts and Underemployment Equilibria", *Journal of Political Economy*, 83/6 (1975): 1183–1202

Azariadis, Costas and Joseph E. Stiglitz, "Implicit Contracts and Fixed Price Equilibria", *Quarterly Journal of Economics*, 98/Supplement (1983): 1–22; reprinted in *New Keynesian Economics*, vol. 2, edited by N. Gregory Mankiw and David Romer, Cambridge, Massachusetts: MIT Press, 1991

Baily, Martin N., "Wages and Employment under Uncertain Demand", *Review of Economic Studies*, 41/1 (1974): 37–50

Beaudry, Paul and John DiNardo, "The Effect of Implicit Contracts on the Movement of Wages over the Business Cycle: Evidence from Micro Data", *Journal of Political Economy*, 99/4 (1991): 665–88

Bull, Clive, "The Existence of Self-Enforcing Implicit Contracts", *Quarterly Journal of Economics*, 102/1 (1987): 147–59

Campbell, Carl M. III and Kunal S. Kamlani, "The Reasons for Wage Rigidity: Evidence from a Survey of Firms", *Quarterly Journal of Economics*, 112/3 (1997): 759–89

Hart, Oliver D., "Optimal Labour Contracts under Asymmetric Information: An Introduction", *Review of Economic Studies*, 50/1 (1983): 3–35

MacLeod, W. Bentley and James M. Malcomson, "Implicit Contracts, Incentive Compatibility, and Involuntary Unemployment", *Econometrica*, 57/2 (1989): 447–80

Rosen, Sherwin, "Implicit Contracts: A Survey", *Journal of Economic Literature*, 23/3 (1985): 1144–75

Sargent, Thomas J., "Implicit Labor Contracts and Sticky Wages" in his *Macroeconomic Theory*, 2nd edition, Boston: Academic Press, 1987

Schmidt, Klaus M. and Monika Schnitzer, "The Interaction of Explicit and Implicit Contracts", *Economics Letters*, 48/2 (1995): 193–99

Taylor, Mark P., "The Simple Analytics of Implicit Labour Contracts", *Bulletin of Economic Research*, 39/1 (1987): 1–27

Implicit contract theory is a useful micro approach for analysing wages, employment, and other aspects of the labour market. The phrase "implicit contracts" was coined by AZARIADIS who together with BAILY fostered the development of the literature on this topic. Early models allow uncertainty over the value of future labour productivity or output price, take information to be symmetric, and assume workers to be immobile once they have "agreed" on a labour contract. The equilibrium contract entails risk-neutral firms guaranteeing risk-averse workers a constant real wage, implying full insurance against an otherwise uncertain income stream. Thus the basic theory can explain why wages vary little during the business cycle. Unfortunately, these contracts generally can neither account for layoffs during economic downturns, nor can they explain why fewer workers are being laid off than would occur in a spot (competitive) market when layoffs are optimal. The most basic account of the theory is TAYLOR, which provides a nontechnical and easily accessible overview using only elementary mathematics and diagrams. SARGENT contributes a more analytical treatment of the model, while ROSEN supplies an exhaustive literature survey and critical assessment of the developments up to the mid-1980s. Given the abundant literature on this topic, most of which was written during the 1980s, it is surprising that no book has ever been published exclusively on this subject.

The most common extensions involve asymmetric information (workers and firms having different sets of information about the economic environment) and *ex post* labour mobility (allowing for turnover). HART provides a useful account of a model where firms have private information with respect to workers' productivity or the state of nature. In his model, risk-averse firms would want to pay lower wages in bad states so as to share the risk with their employees. However, wages cannot be tied to economic conditions since this would give an incentive to firms to understate the state of the world to reduce their wage payments. Instead, wages are tied to a variable like hours of work, which is observable by both firms and workers. Hence, asymmetric information leads firms to reduce employment beyond what is efficient because this is the only way they can reduce wages. In other words, moral hazard leads to underemployment (fewer hours worked). This result is intuitive, but the rationale for wage rigidity, present in earlier models, is lost. Furthermore, underemployment is not an explanation of unemployment, because workers are never laid off completely. AZARIADIS & STIGLITZ provide a detailed discussion of how different models generate overemployment or underemployment compared with a first best contract (where no informational problem exists) depending on the preference structure that is assumed. (Other papers in the supplement of the *Quarterly Journal of Economics* 1983 – a symposium devoted to the theory of implicit contracts – provide the necessary background to Azariadis & Stiglitz's discussion.)

Some papers allow workers to have private information with respect to various facets of their jobs. These papers follow traditional implicit contract theory in assuming that workers are more risk averse than firms. In ARNOTT & STIGLITZ workers discover their job satisfaction, which is unobservable to firms, only after some time on the job. Firms provide implicit insurance against job dissatisfaction by paying workers more than the value of their product early on and less later. Over time the probabilities of the employees leaving are affected by the amount of such insurance, so there is moral hazard and the wage insurance is only partial. The asymmetry of information may instead concern outside job offers or search intensity. In these cases, too, the implicit contract provides insurance that is only partial because of moral hazard. But now it is the lucky workers who quit, so the "insurance premium" is paid by junior workers rather than by those who remain. ARNOTT, HOSIOS & STIGLITZ is the best example of this class of model. They show that costly search coupled with firms' inability to monitor workers' search activities can explain not only partial wage insurance but also a number of other phenomena including layoffs by low-productivity firms, which will lay off some but not all of their employees. In none of these papers, however, is there a discussion of the possibility of bilateral asymmetric information–information that is in part private to workers, and in part private to firms.

BULL provides an answer to why *implicit* contracts may be used in the labour market even though such agreements appear unenforceable and therefore, at a first glance, worthless. According to him, the answer lies in the informational asymmetry between the firm and workers on one hand and third parties who would enforce the contract. It is shown that when third parties cannot, unlike the firm and its workers, observe some aspects of the employment relationship, explicit contracts break down, thus giving rise to the phenomenon of implicit contracts, with intrafirm reputations supporting such agreements. Bull does not, however, consider another possible reason why contracts may be implicit: not all contingencies may be conceived and written into a formal contract.

MACLEOD & MALCOMSON also tackle the issue of the enforcement problem in these contracts. They develop incentive constraints for the firm and workers to ensure it is in the interest of both sides to honour the terms under all conditions. Should a worker shirk or quit, or should a firm not pay adequate compensation, separation will be inevitable, thus harming the side that has not honoured its part of the implicit agreement. The damage will be a loss in future possible rents. The interaction of these self-enforcing implicit with explicit contracts is the subject of SCHMIDT & SCHNITZER. They consider a model where some aspects of the job (such as the number of hours worked) can be written into an explicit contract, and other dimensions (such as the quality of labour supplied) cannot. The main point addressed in their paper is how the set of implicit contracts is affected if some aspects of the job can be contracted upon explicitly.

BEAUDRY & DINARDO investigate whether the labour market functions in a manner more consistent with an implicit contract or a spot market model using the Panel Study of Income Dynamics and Current Population Survey. They find that an implicit contract model with costless mobility describes the link between wages and past labour market conditions better than a spot model. However, they do not provide evidence about how the implicit contract model performs relative to other new theories of the labour market. These theories include efficiency wage setting and insider-outsider theory, which, together with implicit contracts, represent departures from the competitive textbook model of the labour market.

CAMPBELL & KAMLANI survey firms in order to investigate why they do not adjust wages in response to economic conditions. Among several competing theories of wage rigidity, they find that implicit contracts are a reasonable explanation for blue-collar and less skilled workers. Specifically, many respondents indicated that an implicit understanding with workers to keep wages stable over the business cycle was essential for not cutting compensation during a recession. Furthermore, results from this study show that respondents' greatest incentive for treating agreements as if they were binding was not a concern over a loss of their reputation, but rather the fear that workers would provide less effort in their jobs. Overall, the general failure on the part of the implicit contract theory to develop a satisfactory theory of unemployment consistent with wage rigidity may explain why the theory has been virtually abandoned since the late 1980s.

MAK ARVIN

See also Wages

Control, need for control

Alterman, Toni, Richard B. Shekelle, Sally W. Vernon and Keith D. Burau, "Decision Latitude, Psychologic Demand, Job Strain, and Coronary Heart Disease in the Western Electric Study", *American Journal of Epidemiology*, 139/6 (1994): 620–27

Fletcher, Ben C. and Fiona Jones, "A Refutation of Karasek's Demand: Discretion Model of Occupational Stress with a Range of Dependent Measures", *Journal of Organizational Behavior*, 14/4 (1993): 319–30

Ganster, Daniel C. and Marcelline R. Fusilier, "Control in the Workplace" in *International Review of Industrial and Organizational Psychology*, edited by Cary L. Cooper and Ivan Robertson, Chichester: Wiley, 1986

Karasek, Robert A., "Job Demands, Job Decision Latitude and Mental Strain: Implications for Job Redesign", *Administrative Science Quarterly*, 24 (1979): 285–307

Karasek, Robert A. and T. Theorell, *Healthy Work: Stress, Productivity and the Reconstruction of Working Life*, New York: Basic Books, 1990

Jackson, Paul R., Toby D. Wall, Robin Martin and Keith Davids, "New Measures of Job Control, Cognitive Demand, and Production Responsibility", *Journal of Applied Psychology*, 78/5 (1993): 753–62

Marmot, M.G., H. Bosma, H. Hemingway, E. Brunner and S. Stansfeld, "Contribution of Job Control and Other Risk Factors to Social Variations in Coronary Heart Disease Incidence", *The Lancet*, 350/9073 (1997): 235–39

Parker, Sharon and Toby Wall, *Job and Work Design: Organizing Work to Promote Well-Being and Effectiveness*, London and Thousand Oaks, California: Sage, 1998

Wall, Toby, J. Martin Corbett, Robin Martin, Chris W. Clegg and Paul Jackson, "Advanced Manufacturing Technology, Work Design and Performance: A Change Study", *Journal of Applied Psychology*, 75/6 (1990): 691–97

GANSTER & FUSILIER provide a wide-ranging introduction to the concept of control in the workplace. They review literature on the basic human need for control and mastery over the environment and the relationship between lack of control and stress, before moving on to discuss theories of control related more explicitly to the workplace. They trace the centrality of the notion of control to a range of theoretical perspectives. For example, it is a crucial factor in research on employee participation in decision making and in theories of job design and stress. In such theories a range of variables such as discretion, decision latitude, and autonomy are used to describe aspects of perceptions of control. Ganster & Fusilier also introduce the importance of individual differences such as locus of control – a personality variable that describes the extent to which individuals generally feel that what happens to them is within their own control or is controlled by external factors.

KARASEK focused attention explicitly on the variable of decision latitude in his "job strain" model (also known as the "demand-control" model). This model predicts that it is the interaction between a high level of job demands and a low level of decision latitude that leads to psychological and physical strain. This paper is difficult to understand and the statistical analysis has been criticized, but it remains a classic paper in this field and has stimulated a huge amount of research in the area of control in the workplace. A much less academic and more recent account can be found in KARASEK & THEORELL, which also extends the model by adding more variables. There is a wide range of studies based on the model and providing conflicting evidence. Many studies are based on epidemiological data. ALTERMAN *et al.* is a good example of such a study. In a 25-year follow-up of over 1,600 men, they found that low levels of control predicted coronary heart disease risk, though there was no effect for demand or the interaction of demand and control. This is consistent with a number of other studies that confirm the importance of control for health but cast doubt on the full model.

Many conceptual and methodological criticisms of Karasek's model exist – the key areas for criticism are covered by Ganster and Fusilier (see above). Criticisms are also discussed by FLETCHER & JONES, who report a large study that found little support for Karasek's model and suggested the amount of variance explained by control may be quite small compared to other psychosocial variables.

The concept of control has also been a focus of attention in a large study of the British Civil Service. In one of the most recent of a number of reports of their long running study MARMOT *et al.* conclude that low job control is related to higher incidence of coronary heart disease. This study has consistently shown an inverse gradient in mortality from heart disease – the lower the employment grade the higher the incidence. The authors argue that this is unlikely to be solely the effect of socioeconomic status and that much of the gradient in heart disease can be attributed to low control at work.

One criticism of much of the research on control is that the concept is very broad. A number of writers suggest that it is important to distinguish between various types of control. JACKSON *et al.* have developed measures of timing control, method control, and boundary control. These are particularly appropriate to manufacturing industry where the growth of new technology has raised new concerns about simplification of work, deskilling of workers, and an associated reduction in control that may have negative effects on wellbeing and motivation. WALL *et al.* present an interesting study that demonstrates that advanced manufacturing technology can be used in ways that increase operator control, bringing benefits in terms of increased performance, as well as increased job satisfaction, and reduced pressure. However, performance benefits were only really significant where there was a high degree of production uncertainty (for example, where the process is complex because of changes in product design or small batches). The issues related to job control are further discussed by PARKER & WALL in their recent and highly accessible account of job redesign, which discusses the concept of autonomy or control in the context of a wide range of other work characteristics. The book includes discussion of autonomous work groups – a popular way of increasing job control. They consider both theoretical and practical issues involved in increasing control at work as well as calling for a move away from a focus on a narrow range of job characteristics of which control has undoubtedly received the most attention.

Fiona Jones

See also Job design

Convergence

Abramovitz, Moses, "Catching Up, Forging Ahead, and Falling Behind", *Journal of Economic History*, 46 (1986): 385–406

Altman, Morris, "High and Low Wage Paths to Economic Growth: A Behavioral Model of Endogenous Economic Growth" in *Human Agency and Material Welfare: Revisions in Microeconomics and Their Implications for Public Policy*, Boston: Kluwer, 1996

Bairoch, Paul, "The Main Trends in National Economic Disparities since the Industrial Revolution" in *Disparities in Economic Development since the Industrial Revolution*, edited by P. Bairoch and Maurice Levy-Leboyer, London: Macmillan, and New York: St Martin's Press, 1981

Bairoch, Paul, "Was There a Large Income Differential before Modern Development" in his *Economics and World History: Myths and Paradoxes*, Chicago: University of Chicago Press, 1993

Barro, Robert J. and Xavier Sala-i-Martin, "Convergence", *Journal of Political Economy*, 100 (1992): 223–51

Baumol, William J., "Productivity Growth, Convergence, and Welfare: What the Long-Run Data Show", *American Economic Review*, 76 (1986): 1072–85

Baumol, William J. and Edward N. Wolff, "Productivity Growth, Convergence, and Welfare: Reply", *American Economic Review*, 78 (1988): 1155–59

DeLong, Bradford J., "Productivity Growth, Convergence, and Welfare: Comment", *American Economic Review*, 78 (1988): 1138–54

Maddison, Angus, *Phases of Capitalist Development*, Oxford and New York: Oxford University Press, 1982

Maddison, Angus, *Monitoring the World Economy, 1820–1992*, Paris: OECD, 1995

Pritchett, Lant, "Divergence, Big Time", *Journal of Economic Perspectives*, 11 (1997): 3–17

Samuelson, Paul A., "International Trade and Equalization of Factor Prices", *Economic Journal*, 59 (1948): 163–84

The conventional economic wisdom on economic convergence, built upon the theoretical foundations set by SAMUELSON in the late 1940s, predicts that over the long run factor prices, such as wages and interest rates, should tend towards equality through the dynamic pressures of international trade, even if factors of production are not mobile. More generally, the market, to the extent that it is reasonably free and competitive, will generate the pressures that serve to produce the convergence of nations in terms of labour productivity and, thereby, in terms of per capita income or gross domestic product (GDP). Samuelson's classic work, in turn, represented an elaboration and extension of Bertil Ohlin's *Interregional and International Trade*, published in 1933.

The notion that economies should tend to converge with respect to per capita output is referred to as the "convergence hypothesis". To determine whether or not the economies of the world at least tend towards convergence is an empirical question whose testing had to await constant dollar historical time series data for a reasonable set of countries, where these data were reduced to a common denominator. Such a data set was produced by Angus Maddison for the 1870–1979 period, in work examining the process of capitalist development among today's more economically developed economies. More recently he developed a more comprehensive data set spanning the 1870–1992 timeframe (MADDISON 1995) and incorporated both current developed economies and less developed economies. A retinue of interested scholars has exploited his data set since its first publication.

BAUMOL was the first to systematically employ Maddison's data, focusing on the 1870-1973 period for his 16 developed economies. Baumol finds that among these countries convergence took place from 1870 to 1973 in terms of labour productivity. There was a strong and negative relationship between the labour productivity growth rate of a country and its initial level of labour productivity: the lower the initial level of labour productivity, the higher the subsequent growth rate. As a result, countries that ranked low in 1870 converged to the labour productivity levels of the high-ranking countries by 1973. All countries in the sample experienced a large increase in productivity and per capita output. The key to convergence was the capacity of the low-productivity countries to adopt the best-practice technologies, seen as a public good, in place in the high-income countries. MADDISON (1982) makes a similar point in an analysis of his own data. Baumol, however, finds no evidence for convergence among all of the nations (72 in number) for which data were available for the 1950–80 period.

DELONG points out that the data set upon which Baumol bases his findings in favour of convergence predetermines his results. Baumol's data are for currently and already converged developed countries. By definition, these must have converged from 1870 to 1973. De Long argues that to test for convergence one must expand the sample of countries to include those economies that, as of 1870, appeared to hold some promise of economic development. De Long extends the Baumol sample to include Argentina, Chile, East Germany, Ireland, New Zealand, Portugal, and Spain. This expanded sample does not allow one to conclude in favour of the convergence hypothesis, because many of the countries in the larger sample failed to converge. De Long concludes that this demonstrates that the transfer of technology between economies is not automatic and, therefore, convergence is not inevitable even for countries that might be deemed to be the best candidates for convergence. In a detailed response to De Long, BAUMOL & WOLFF concur with the essence of his basic empirical finding.

PRITCHETT applies various methods and expanded data sets, including those used by Baumol & Wolff and De Long, to test for convergence in per capita income. He finds that there is no evidence whatsoever in favour of convergence in the international economy, apart from what has transpired among today's already developed economies. Growth rates have simply been much too slow among the currently less developed countries, including India and China, which, at about 2 billion people, today account for over 33 per cent of the world's population. For convergence to take place, the growth rates among the poorer nations must exceed those of the richer economies by a considerable margin. The opposite has occurred. Moreover, among many of the less developed economies growth rates show no sign of increasing and for many such countries the growth rates are all but stagnant. According to Pritchett's estimates, this has resulted in the divergence in per capita income and output between these two groups of countries such that per capita income among the poorer economies equalled 42 per cent of that of their richer counterparts in 1870 and only 18 per cent by 1990. As a result, although most economies grew over the past 100 or so years, the absolute income gap between the poorer and richer economies increased by over eight times.

BAIROCH also finds strong evidence for divergence and presents estimates suggesting that divergence took place between today's developed and less developed economies from a historical base that was very different from that previously thought to have occurred. Indeed, his estimates have been challenged. He argues that, contrary to conventional wisdom, today's less developed countries were, on average, not far behind today's developed economies in terms of per capita income in 1750, when the Industrial Revolution began in earnest. More specifically, Bairoch concludes that, in 1870, the per capita income of the poor nations of today, including China and India, probably either equalled the average per capita income of the developed economies of today or was no less than 75 to 90 per cent of their 1750 average. According to Bairoch's estimates, and even according to the estimates of his most contemporary critics, divergence in the international economy began in a big way only with the advent of the Industrial Revolution, when the rate of technical change increased at a historically unprecedented pace.

ABRAMOVITZ places the convergence literature in a social and institutional context. He, like Baumol, finds overwhelming evidence for convergence for Maddison's 16 advanced economies. But Abramovitz argues that a precondition for convergence is the existence of the necessary "social capacity", inclusive of educational and overall institutional infrastructure, which allows follower countries to adopt and adapt the best-practice technologies of the leading economies. Ceteris paribus, given the appropriate social capacity, there is a high probability that catch-up will take. Even among the now advanced economies divergences in the process of catch-up can be largely explained, according to Abramovitz, by deviations from best-practice social capacities. However, social capacity can be changed only slowly, as it is rooted in the social and cultural milieu of a society. BARRO & XAVIER SALA-I-MARTIN make a similar point for a wider array of countries and using more elaborate statistical technique to assess the relevant data.

According to ALTMAN, apart from inadequate social capacity, convergence is impeded by institutional and labour market environments that facilitate, accommodate, and maintain low-wage regimes. Moreover, low-wage regimes contribute to the persistence of inferior social capacities. Low wages contribute to low levels of productivity and productivity growth and serve to protect low-productivity firms from competitive pressure. On the other hand, high wages pressure firms into becoming more productive and pressure society into developing social capacities most conducive to higher levels of productivity. High-wage economies cannot survive on the market place if high levels of productivity do not match the high wages. In a world where wages, the work environment, and productivity are causally related, market pressures need not cause convergence unless there is a convergence in wages and work environments. Such convergence is yet to transpire in the world economy.

MORRIS ALTMAN

Conversation analysis

Anderson, Robert J. and Wesley W. Sharrock, "Analytic Work: Aspects of the Organisation of Conversational Data", *Journal for the Theory of Social Behaviour*, 14/1 (1984): 103–24

Atkinson, J. Maxwell and John Heritage (editors), *Structures of Social Action: Studies in Conversation Analysis*, Cambridge and New York: Cambridge University Press, 1984

Atkinson, Mick A., "Some Practical Uses of 'a Natural Lifetime'", *Human Studies*, 3/1 (1980): 33–46

Baker, Carolyn D., "The 'Search for Adultness': Membership Work in Adolescent–Adult Talk", *Human Studies*, 7/3–4 (1984): 301–23

Button, Graham and John R.E. Lee (editors), *Talk and Social Organization*, Clevedon and Philadelphia: Multilingual Matters, 1987

Drew, Paul and John Heritage (editors), *Talk at Work: Interaction in Institutional Settings*, Cambridge and New York: Cambridge University Press, 1992

Garfinkel, Harold and Harvey Sacks, "On Formal Structures of Practical Actions" in *Theoretical Sociology: Perspectives and Developments*, edited by John C. McKinney and Edward A. Tiryakian, New York: Appleton Century Crofts, 1970

Goodwin, Charles, "Professional Vision", *American Anthropologist*, 96/3 (1994): 606–33

Hester, Stephen and Peter Eglin (editors), *Culture in Action: Studies in Membership Categorization Analysis*, Washington, DC: University Press of America, 1997

Jayyusi, Lena, *Categorization and the Moral Order*, Boston and London: Routledge and Kegan Paul, 1984

Lee, John R.E., "Innocent Victims and Evil-doers", *Women's Studies International Forum*, 7/1 (1984): 69–73

Lee, John R.E., "Language and Culture: The Linguistic Analysis of Culture" in *Ethnomethodology and the Human Sciences*, edited by Graham Button, Cambridge and New York: Cambridge University Press, 1991

Pomerantz, Anita M. (editor), special section on "The Dan Rather / George Bush Episode on CBS News", *Research on Language and Social Interaction*, 22 (1988/89): 213–326

Psathas, George (editor), *Everyday Language: Studies in Ethnomethodology*, New York: Irvington, and London: Wiley, 1979

Psathas, George (editor), *Interaction Competence*, Washington, DC: University Press of America, and London: International Institute for Ethnomethodology and Conversation Analysis, 1990

Sacks, H., E.A. Schegloff and G. Jefferson, "A Simplest Systematics for the Organization of Turn-Taking in Conversation" in *Studies in the Organization of Conversational Interaction*, New York: Academic Press, 1978

Sacks, Harvey, *Lectures on Conversation*, edited by Gail Jefferson, 2 vols, Oxford and Cambridge, Massachusetts: Blackwell, 1992

Schegloff, Emanuel A., "Sequencing in Conversational Openings", *American Anthropologist*, 70/6 (1968): 1075–95

Schenkein, J.N. (editor), *Studies in the Organization of Conversational Interaction*, New York: Academic Press, 1978a

Schenkein, J.N., "Sketch of an Analytic Mentality for the Study of Conversational Interaction" in *Studies in the Organization of Conversational Interaction*, New York: Academic Press, 1978b

Sociology, special issue on "Language and Practical Reasoning", 12/1 (1978): 1–139

Sudnow, David (editor), *Studies in Social Interaction*, New York: Free Press, and London: Collier Macmillan, 1972

Turner, Roy (editor), *Ethnomethodology: Selected Readings*, Harmondsworth: Penguin, 1974

Conversation analysis is an offshoot of ethnomethodology, invented by the late Harvey Sacks, with the assistance of his colleagues Emanuel Schegloff and Gail Jefferson. There are no single all-encompassing texts; major contributions are located in journals and edited collections. SACKS's pioneering lectures were originally circulated in mimeo form; they were collected together for publication by Jefferson. They provide a comprehensive overview of Sacks's concerns as he developed the program of conversation analysis. These insights were elaborated by the authors discussed below, but the lectures are central to conversation analysis and repay careful reading.

The central concern of conversation analysis is the production of orderliness in social interaction. Sacks attempted to find a site where social order was visible – he chose conversation because of its accessibility, and the potential for audio recording and repeated analysis by researchers. Jefferson devised notation for the transcription of naturally occurring talk; a comprehensive summary of transcript conventions can be found in ATKINSON & HERITAGE. There has been a rapid expansion of studies using video-recorded data, whereby conversation analysts attempt to preserve as much of the setting as possible for fine-grained analysis (see GOODWIN).

The conversation analysis programme proposes a distinct "analytic mentality" (SCHENKEIN 1978b) towards the study of conversation. Its sociological focus on talk-in-interaction distinguishes it from other disciplines that use transcripts of talk, including forms of linguistics, pragmatics, and discourse analysis. In the prologue to the collection by BUTTON & LEE, Lee points out that although the discipline ostensibly resembles linguistics, notably in terms of the data used, the manner in which data are treated by conversation analysis is overwhelmingly sociological. In the same volume, Watson's interdisciplinary consideration of pronoun usage secures this foundation, arguing that pronoun choice and use is a profoundly situated matter with consequences for the unfolding interaction. The sociological focus of conversation analysis also militates against the incipient mentalism to be found in linguistics and discourse analysis (LEE, 1991).

Conversation analysis explicates the production of social order manifested in talk-in-interaction. Among the classic articles, SACKS, SCHEGLOFF & JEFFERSON report that naturally occurring conversations are organized on a turn-by-turn basis, a "turn-taking system", which is an intersubjective organization oriented to by interlocutors in the selection of current and subsequent speakers. Speakers' turns at talk are organized on an utterance-by-utterance basis, where the production of an utterance determines what happens next; that is, each utterance is "conditionally relevant" (SCHEGLOFF) upon its previous utterance. This organization is known as "adjacency pairing" (Schegloff and Sacks, in TURNER). For example, an answer accountably follows a question, a greetings-return follows a greeting, and so on. When the conditionally relevant utterance or adjacency pair part does not occur, it is "officially absent". As well as discussing the preference organization of conversations, for example, consistency and economy rules, Sacks and Schegloff (in PSATHAS 1979) introduce the notion of "recipient design", whereby each utterance is tailored to the knowledge that the hearer is presumed to possess.

Important collections of the analysis of ordinary, everyday conversations are Psathas (1979), PSATHAS (1990), SCHENKEIN (1978a), SOCIOLOGY and SUDNOW, which include discussions on cross-cultural interactions, therapeutic discourse, responding to compliments, accusations and blaming, story-telling and identity negotiations, and the methodological underpinnings of conversation analysis. The programmatic paper by Schegloff (in Psathas, 1979) elucidates how the seemingly trivial act of answering a telephone involves a complex set of achievements. The logic and method of conversation analysis, as evident through Schegloff's study of telephone conversation openings, are scrutinized by ANDERSON & SHARROCK. The pivotal piece by Heritage & Watson (in Psathas, 1979) clearly shows the influence of ethnomethodology upon conversation analysis, especially from GARFINKEL & SACKS, through empirical demonstrations of how conversations "fold back" on themselves as they are described by interlocutors.

Some analysts have examined departures from the turn-taking system of ordinary conversation in institutional settings, where the interlocutors may be of differing institutional affiliations – for example, doctor and patient, lawyer and witness. There are a number of substantial collections on this topic, for example DREW & HERITAGE. Frankel (in Psathas, 1990) examines how doctors ask the majority of questions, patient-initiated questions not being preferred. The following chapter in that collection, by Watson, examines the organization of utterances (knowledge claims, question-and-answer sequences, stories) in murder interrogations; Watson's chapter highlights the "conversational turn" of conversation analysis, which constitutes the reflexive relationship between membership categories and turn taking. Thus conversation analysis has input into substantive sociological fields of study, such as interactions in classroom, judicial, and medical settings. Notable illustrations of talk in organizational settings are to be found in POMERANTZ, where a number of analysts consider a transcript of a televised interview between President George Bush and Dan Rather. The analyses show how the news interview organizes turns in a way that highlights, *inter alia*, engendering scepticism, topic shift, confrontation, and the role of interviewers as proper recipients of answers. Conversation analysis also influences the analysis of human–computer interaction.

Another direction in conversation analysis is the explication of membership categories – ordinary descriptions of persons and formulations of place (see Schegloff, in Sudnow) used in talk. Although Schegloff departs from accepted methodological protocol by using invented sequences of talk, it remains a powerful contribution to the corpus of conversation-analytic research. Watson (in HESTER & EGLIN) shows how a shortcoming of analyses of institutional talk is the stress on the sequencing of utterances over the explication of membership categories. Sacks's seminal paper (in Turner) on children's stories shows how hearers and observers collect social types together – for example mother and baby – using membership categorization devices, including "family" and "stage of life" (ATKINSON; BAKER). Membership categorization analysis (MCA) is an extension of the arguments made in the groundbreaking papers by Sacks and Schegloff mentioned above, which until comparatively recently has received less attention than the sequential analysis of turns or utterances in conversation. Membership categorization analysis provides analytic purchase on how interlocutors organize the social world. In an excellent introduction to a collection of papers, Hester & Eglin outline the ways in which authors have investigated person categorization, through both textual and conversational analyses (JAYYUSI, LEE 1984). Their edited collection contains exemplary studies on the breadth and detail of MCA, and its application to a variety of settings. The contributions highlight the pervasiveness of membership categories in professional domains of expertise (newspaper editors, teachers and educationalists, doctors, lawyers, and sociologists). In maintaining contact with the ethnomethodological heritage of conversation analysis, the books by Jayyusi, and Hester & Eglin fill the lacuna of person-identifications in the analysis of talk in institutional settings.

ANDREW P. CARLIN AND ROGER S. SLACK

See also Discourse analysis, Ethnomethodology

Cooperation

Barnard, Chester, *The Functions of the Executive*, Cambridge, Massachusetts: Harvard University Press, 1938

Boulding, Kenneth, E., *A Preface to Grants Economics: The Economy of Love and Fear*, New York, Praeger, 1981

Cole, G.D.H., *A Century of Co-operation*, London: Allen and Unwin, 1944

Marx, Karl, *Capital: A Critique of Political Economy*, 3 vols, Harmondsworth and New York: Penguin, 1976–81 (German edition 1867–94)

Smith, Adam, *An Inquiry into the Nature and Causes of the Wealth of Nations*, edited by Kathryn Sutherland, Oxford and New York: Oxford University Press, 1993 (first published 1776)

Sober, Elliot and David S. Wilson, *Unto Others: The Evolution and Psychology of Unselfish Behaviour*, Cambridge, Massachusetts: Harvard University Press, 1998

Trivers, Robert, *Social Evolution*, Menlo Park, California: Cummings, 1985

Vanek, Jaroslav, *The General Theory of Labour Managed Economies*, Ithaca, New York: Cornell University Press, 1970

There is a long history of speculation on the nature of cooperation. The ancient philosophers of China, Confucius and Lao-tzu, the prophets of the Old Testament, and the Greek philosophers Plato and Aristotle all recognized the importance of cooperation in their philosophies. The 17th-century political philosopher Thomas Hobbes conjectured that in the state of nature anarchy ruled; this conflict could only be overcome through relinquishing personal rights to a sovereign being. Jean-Jacques Rousseau countered that primitive people were cooperative and compassionate, primarily concerned with satisfying basic needs; for Rousseau, society emerged from a social contract, an agreement by those in the state of nature to constitute a collective being, formed to develop the moral potential of people.

The Industrial Revolution of the 19th century led to a fundamental change in the ways that work was traditionally organized. Political economists observed and theorized about these changes. SMITH emphasized the productive advantages of the division of labour in bringing workers together to cooperate in commodity production, suggesting that specialized traders emerged from these advantages. The division of labour encouraged increased productivity arising from workers developing skills in particular tasks, a reduction in the time taken to move between tasks, and the promotion of invention and mechanization.

Arguably, MARX presents the most thorough analysis of cooperation in his critique of capitalism. Like Smith, he recognized the great possibilities arising from simple cooperation. Surpluses available from cooperative productive activities and military conquests had been responsible for the many architectural feats throughout history. The cooperation of workers in factory commodity production was the result of a concentration of the means of production by capitalists and their command over the workers' means of subsistence. The extent of cooperation depended on this concentration. A dynamic was created through the cooperation of wage labour creating a further demand for capital and productive activity. The capitalist, motivated to accumulate surplus value and thus exploit labour power through capital, with its directing, superintending, and adaptive functions, controlled cooperative labour. As the numbers of cooperating workers grew, a conflict became inevitable between capital and labour.

The origins and development of a specific form of cooperation is meticulously outlined by COLE. This book is a tribute to the original pioneers of what is now a worldwide dynamic: the cooperative movement. In response to the poverty and hardships suffered by working people after the Napoleonic wars in the 19th century and exacerbated by industrial capitalism and free trade, images of a new social order, promoted by the radicals Robert Owen and Charles Fourier, penetrated working-class consciousness. Owen's plan for a new moral world, to be known as "cooperation" and equivalent to socialism, was to be realized through the setting up of villages of cooperation. Owen bought land and cotton mills in New Lanark, Scotland, in order to provide a suitable work environment for distressed workers and argued that the state and church should divert their relief interventions to investment in villages of cooperation. Underlying this form of cooperation were important principles: workplace democracy, the limited return on invested capital, the reinvestment of surpluses, provision of education, and provision of unadulterated foods. This book is a *tour de force* in intellectual history and full of detail about the origins and early development of a practical type of cooperation.

The ambitious task VANEK sets himself is to construct a general theory of an economic system characterized by the democratic labour management of firms. In this economy income and surpluses are to be shared equitably between the workers, decision making is decentralized, labour is fully mobile, and the market mechanism is reliable. The key operating principle is not the maximization of profits but of net income per worker. The tools of neoclassical economics are applied in moving from a microeconomic analysis to a macroeconomic analysis. The third section of the book considers specific aspects of this type of economic system: income distribution and firm equilibrium, incentives and efficiency, intangible income, training and education, externalities, problems of entry, and capital expansion and investment decisions. The final section assesses issues of policy, pointing out that a labour-managed economy does not necessarily have to be socialist. In a mixed economy, though, the two sectors must be treated equally – legally, institutionally, and politically. This would require the formation of a national labour-management agency.

BARNARD attempted to outline a general theory of cooperative behaviour in formal organizations, similar to that of Marx, but more conservative. This book cannot be read fruitfully in one sitting and requires rereading and close scrutiny because of its abstract and wordy style. The origins of cooperation are seen to stem from the individual's biological nature and incapability of achieving purposeful behaviour alone. Human actions are determined and directed through interactions with organizations. Formal organization is conscious, deliberate, and cooperation purposeful. Successful cooperation is found to be unusual and failure is the norm. Survival of an organization depends upon the maintenance of equilibrium in a complex dynamic environment. It is an organization's process of adjustment to environmental factors that is the main focus of this important book.

BOULDING argues that the failure of economists to integrate the grant, a one-way exchange transfer, and reciprocity, the unconditional two-way exchange transfer, into modern economic theory encouraged a radical economics. This small essay is an interesting and neglected contribution to economic theory. The grant is an important measure of relationships in integrative systems. By looking at who gives what to whom, important insights into culture could, he suggests, be gained. Two types of occasionally interdependent grants are specified: the gift, arising from the motivation of love, and the tribute, arising from the motivation of fear. Expanding the intellectual framework of economics to incorporate a microeconomic theory of grants and granting behaviour enabled the development of new concepts, useful in economic analysis, to be developed. In exchange relationships an individual's image of the world is important. This image changes in response to messages that are transmitted through exchange relationships.

Dissatisfied with explanations of social behaviour arising from the disciplines of history, politics, economics, and psychology, TRIVERS finds answers to important social science questions in the study of animal behaviour. Observations of living organisms provide abundant evidence that cooperation is the result of the need of organisms to engage in activities to achieve purposes. The writer emphasizes the discovery by Charles Darwin of the evolutionary mechanism of natural selection that provided an explanation for individual characteristics, but is dismissive of those who argue that natural selection acts on groups or species. The outcome of human interaction is, from this perspective, a costs and benefits analysis, measurable in terms of reproductive success. Four types of social acts are empirically deducible: altruistic, selfish, cooperative, and spiteful. These are defined in terms of the effects on the actor and recipient. Altruistic characteristics are those that benefit the recipient at a cost to the actor. The converse is true for selfish characteristics. Cooperative traits benefit both but often contain selfish components, whereas spitefulness inflicts costs on both parties. In evolutionary theory cooperation is explainable because selection favours cooperative exchange.

In SOBER & WILSON the evidence from evolutionary biology is scrutinized. Psychological egoism, the theory that if people care about others it is because they are interested in their own welfare, is found to be unproveable and an alternative evolutionary approach to egoism and altruism is explored. The discredited idea of group selection is reassessed and a case for evolutionary and psychological altruism is put forward. The main message of the book is that groups can be functional units with individuals behaving like organs not organisms. The writers argue for an interdisciplinary approach suggesting that a multilevel selection theory provides the starting point for a unified theory within which a wide variety of perspectives can be accommodated. The psychological motives behind unselfish behaviour are discussed and a theory of the evolutionary mechanisms that motivate adaptive helping behaviour is outlined. The authors provide an explanation for how our capacity to care for others has evolved.

H. LYLE MITCHELL

Copyright

Bergh, Roger van den, "The Role and Social Justification of Copyright: A 'Law and Economics' Approach", *Intellectual Property Quarterly* (1998):17–34

Cornish, W.R., "Recent Changes in British Copyright Law", *Revue Internationale du Droit d'Auteur*, 172 (1997): 151–90

Ficsor, Mihály, "The Spring 1997 Horace S. Manges Lecture: Copyright for the Digital Era: The WIPO 'Internet' Treaties", *Columbia: VLA Journal of Law and the Arts*, 21/3–4 (1997): 197–224

Flint, Michael F., *A User's Guide to Copyright*, 4th edition, London: Butterworths, 1997

Garnett, Kevin, Jonathan Rayner James and Gillian Davies, *Copinger and Skone James on Copyright*, 14th edition, 2 vols, London: Sweet and Maxwell, 1999

Ginsburg, Jane C., "Authors and Users in Copyright", *Journal of the Copyright Society of the USA*, 45/1 (1997): 1–20

Laddie, Hugh, "Copyright: Over-Strength, Over-Regulated, Over-Rated", *European Intellectual Property Review*, 18/5 (1996): 253–60

Laddie, Hugh, Peter Prescott and Mary Vitoria, *The Modern Law of Copyright and Designs*, 2nd edition, 2 vols, London: Butterworths, 1995–98

Quaedvlieg, Antoon, "Copyright's Orbit Round Private, Commercial and Economic Law: The Copyright System and the Place of the User", *International Review of Industrial Property and Copyright Law*, 29/4 (1998): 420–38

Reichman, J.H. and Pamela Samuelson, "Intellectual Property Rights in Data", *Vanderbilt Law Review*, 50 (1997): 51–166

Ricketson, Sam, *The Berne Convention for the Protection of Literary and Artistic Works, 1886–1986*, London: Centre for Commercial Law Studies, Queen Mary College, University of London / Kluwer, 1987

Sterling, J.A.L., *World Copyright Law: Protection of Authors' Works, Performances, Phonograms, Films, Video, Broadcasts and Published Editions in National, International and Regional Law*, London: Sweet and Maxwell, 1999

This selection is designed to illustrate the various branches of the subject of copyright and the interplay between copyright and the developing information society. The works range from easy introductions for the copyright user, through comprehensive scholarly texts for the student and academic, to articles dealing with specific copyright issues and controversies.

FLINT is a concise and unintimidating introduction written for the non-specialist. It explains the basic areas of UK copyright law and addresses particular issues of interest to those working in industry and the professions, including publishing, librarianship, education, the arts, and advertising.

The needs of readers requiring a more comprehensive treatment of UK copyright law are well served by two detailed and authoritative works. LADDIE, PRESCOTT & VITORIA is regarded by many as the definitive work in its field, covering not only copyright in its narrowest sense but also rights in performances, moral rights, public lending rights, and design right. The more recent GARNETT, JAMES & DAVIES edition of *Copinger* covers similar ground. Both examine the effect on UK copyright law of European Community legislation, as well as the obligations imposed on the UK by virtue of its adherence to international conventions and treaties.

CORNISH discusses the effect on UK copyright law of the rapid developments of information technology and the various directives emanating from the European Commission. Among the topics considered are software protection, rental, lending and related rights, satellite and cable broadcasting, and duration or term of right. The article highlights the difficulties of harmonization by means of directives. A more detailed account and analysis of UK copyright law may be found in the chapters on copyright in Cornish's textbook *Intellectual Property* (4th edition, 1999).

There is a large volume of literature on the challenges to copyright presented by rapidly developing technology, including the Internet. FICSOR describes the work of the World Intellectual Property Organization (WIPO) in developing two new treaties designed to respond to these challenges: the WIPO Copyright Treaty and the WIPO Performances and Phonograms Treaty. He explains the nature and scope of the treaties and their relationship with the Berne and Rome Conventions. WIPO has arranged a series of international symposia on the impact of digital technology on copyright and neighbouring rights and the most recent of these – WIPO *International Forum on the Exercise and Management of Copyright and Neighbouring Rights in the Face of the Challenges of Digital Technology* (Geneva: WIPO, 1998) – is also worth consulting.

RICKETSON's monumental treatise is the definitive work on the history, development, and operation of the Berne Convention for the Protection of Literary and Artistic Works, which established common rules for the protection of authors and their works. Written to commemorate the centenary of Berne, it is essential reading for those with a serious interest in international copyright protection.

STERLING overviews the state of copyright and related rights at national, regional, and international level. His analysis is based on 15 reference points that provide a cohesive framework for the examination of different systems. The work includes many illustrations drawn from civil and common law jurisdictions and is essential reading for those with an interest in comparative studies and the harmonization of copyright laws. The work has a substantial section of reference materials and there is a comprehensive glossary that clarifies terminology and assists in dispelling any confusion arising from differences in usage between common law and civil systems.

Growing economic and political pressure for stronger copyright protection from business and other interest groups has raised fresh concerns about the purpose of the copyright system. LADDIE assesses the scope of copyright and asks whether it has become too powerful and all-embracing and whether the potential disadvantages of widening the scope of the monopoly have seriously been considered.

BERGH examines the different types of economic analyses and their application to copyright by legal economists such as Posner, Landes, and Breyer. Finding a balance between the production of information and the dissemination of information is the central problem in copyright, and economic analysis can provide the guidelines for delimiting copyright protection. The usefulness of an economic perspective is demonstrated by analysis of computer software and moral rights.

GINSBURG focuses on the author *versus* user debate, which has been fuelled by the increased capacity created by technology for the storage, transmission, and copying of works of authorship. She argues that copyright is not a law of "users' rights"; that users benefit from copyright law because it fosters authorship and that compulsory and unpaid dissemination of works of authorship will not in the long term encourage creativity.

QUAEDVLIEG also takes as his theme the question whether copyright adequately accommodates the interests of users and consumers. Arguing that copyright is composed as a legal balance of different interest spheres, he maintains that this delicate balance is threatened by the changing role of publishers and producers and the increasing emphasis on economic law policies in favour of stronger protection.

REICHMAN & SAMUELSON focus on the difficult and complex problem of databases. Agreeing that traditional intellectual property regimes have not adequately protected databases, they nevertheless argue that the current European and US initiatives on database protection will confer unduly broad and powerful monopolies on database developers. Instead they propose either the use of unfair competition principles to protect database contents or a regime based on more refined liability principles, rather than exclusive proprietary rights. The article thoroughly reviews the history of the drive for protection of databases in Europe and the US.

ELLEN GREDLEY

See also Intellectual property rights

Corporate economy

Ackoff, Russell L., *Management in Small Doses*, New York: Wiley, 1986

Casson, Mark, *Entrepreneurship and Business Culture*, Aldershot, Hampshire: Elgar, 1995

Herendeen, James B., *The Economics of the Corporate Economy*, New York: Dunellen, 1975

Lazonick, William, Ronald Dore and Henk W. de Jong, *The Corporate Triangle: The Structure and Performance of Corporate Systems in a Global Economy*, Oxford and Malden, Massachusetts: Blackwell, 1997

Marris, Robin and Adrian Wood (editors), *The Corporate Economy: Growth, Competition, and Innovative Potential*, London: Macmillan, 1971

Marris, Robin, *The Theory and Future of the Corporate Economy and Society*, Amsterdam: North Holland, 1979

Maynard, Herman Bryant Jr and Susan E. Mehrtens, *The Fourth Wave: Business in the 21st Century*, San Francisco: Berrett Koehler, 1993

Odagiri, Hiroyuki, *The Theory of Growth in a Corporate Economy: Management Preference Research and Development, and Economic Growth*, Cambridge and New York: Cambridge University Press, 1981

Toffler, Alvin, *The Third Wave*, New York: Morrow, 1980; London: Pan, 1981

ODAGIRI assumes that the readers of his book have an understanding of macroeconomics and microeconomics at the graduate level, and it is therefore best suited to professional economists and graduate students. The author begins with the precept that every theory of economic growth mirrors the author's view of the economy in which he or she lives. He posits that the modern capitalist economy is a mirror of the corporate economy of large corporations, whose managements possess strong, although not unlimited, power to pursue their own objectives, even against the owners' interests. In this book, the author attempts to analyse, mainly theoretically, the dynamic properties of such a corporate economy. There are five parts to the book. Parts 1 and 2 present the basic model of growth of a corporate economy, constituting the core of the study. Part 3 discusses the relevance of the model, and the remaining two parts attempt to extend the basic model.

A similar position is adopted by HERENDEEN, who acknowledges that economic policy discussions reflect the underlying political power structure. His volume draws together a comprehensive analysis of the economics of the corporate economy, and discusses its welfare and policy implications. The early chapters establish the setting by depicting the organizational, institutional, and motivational characteristics of a large corporation in the modern capitalist economy. The author then proceeds to integrate finance into the theory of the corporate enterprise, and develops growth and value models for a corporation. The growth model proposed by the author shows that the rate of growth is limited by constraints such as the escalating cost of maintaining the profitability of the organization's assets as it grows, and the rising implicit rate of debt cost as a result of increasing leverage. Furthermore, he suggests that through the manipulation of discretionary expenditure, management seeks to hide profit from owners and government, thereby increasing the organization's potential rate of growth. In his development of a political economy of corporate capitalism, the author concludes by discussing issues such as consumer information and protection, social responsibility of managers, wage-price policy and inflation, and the behaviour of corporate profits and their effect on stabilization policy.

The anthology edited by MARRIS & WOOD is designed to improve the understanding of the workings of an economy dominated by large corporations. This volume is concerned with the theory of the growth of the organization, with competition between divisions of corporations, and with relationships between the corporation and the stock market. The volume focuses on the large-scale corporate sector of the economy on the one hand, and the public economic sector on the other hand. The various contributors examine the strengths and weaknesses of each sector, and their capacity, individually and in combination, to support the development of a "good society". From proscription to prescription, the volume reviews the contemporary position that the present economic system fails to counter adverse effects of technology, fails to meet major social needs, is far less competitive than is traditionally claimed, is biased against the development of demand and production in "public" goods, is dominated by advertising, creates unnecessary wants and excessive product diversity, stimulates bellicosity, and fails to deliver on other theoretical benefits of a market economy.

In a later volume, MARRIS delineates the theory of the growth of the organization. The core of his exposition is a new theoretical model of aggregate or business concentration, which yields the conclusion that, through a stochastic process, concentration will generally increase in the course of time. Further, in the broad context of contemporary economic problems, the author discusses policy measures that may counteract this trend.

An interesting contribution to this topic is a trilogy, by LAZONICK, DORE & JONG seeking answers to the question: what is a corporation? Each contributor finds difficulty in applying standard theoretical concepts in search of their answer – so much so, that they believe more attention should be paid to the value-creating function of the organization and to the related question of how the corporation is embedded in society. Lazonick seeks the answer in the environment of the Anglo-Saxon corporate system. Dore contrasts the Japanese corporation with its counterpart in the West. De Jong examines the development and diversity of the continental European corporation. This is an international examination of a question fundamental to the future of the economic and social order.

It is not difficult to appreciate that culture plays an important role in any examination of the corporate economy. The themes raised by CASSON include cultural perspectives on economic issues, entrepreneurship in a cultural context, and the political economy of national culture. He presents a contemporary analysis of entrepreneurship and the social structures in which it is embedded, and examines how the entrepreneurial organization succeeds by synthesizing information from different sources. He posits that the quality of this information is just as important as the quantity, and that the cheapest way to ensure quality is through a moral obligation to tell the truth, which is the obligatory precursor to trust. This volume provides a definitive analysis of the importance of trust in economic life, as well as of the related concepts of networking, consultation, and empowerment.

ACKOFF has written a volume of sparkling and provocative short essays on management topics. He is highly irreverent, and a destroyer of accepted wisdom, yet not irrelevant. In chapter 9, Ackoff postulates that Western society is a curious contradiction, in that the ways we run our national macroeconomy and the microeconomics of organizations within it appear to be at opposite ends of the spectrum. He explains that we live within a macroeconomy that is regulated as little as is compatible with the national interest, yet the economies of our corporations are run much like the national economy of the former Soviet Union. This is a wonderful short essay, appealing to organizations to practise the same type of economy as they preach to the nation.

There will always be critics of the economies of our corporations. Many are challenging organizations to recognize and accept a new role on the global scene. TOFFLER is prominent in asking organizations to recognize their function as shapers of the future. He believes that, in the future, corporations will be smaller, prizing diversity and differentiation, and will become more responsible and more multipurpose institutions. Further, he acknowledges that corporations will need to continue to generate profits through the production and distribution of goods and services to survive, but they will also be the producers of moral effects – the creators of much more than a financial bottom line. The author sees the corporation becoming a creator of value; an organization that serves the customer, employee, and community; a business where strategic thinking is reoriented to anticipate future needs beyond the immediate context of the corporation.

Applying the concept of historical waves, MAYNARD & MEHRTENS look toward the next century, and foresee an era of integration and responsibility far beyond Toffler's revolutionary description of postindustrial society. The authors describe the ways in which corporations must change in the future. Their proposals concern the basics: how an institution is organized; how it defines wealth; how it relates to surrounding communities; how it responds to environmental needs; and how it takes part in the political process. The authors demonstrate the need for a new kind of leadership: managers who embrace an attitude of global stewardship; who define their assets as ideas, information, creativity, and vision; and who strive for seamless boundaries between work and private lives for all employees.

GEOFF TURNER

Corporate finance

Berens, James L. and Charles J. Cuny, "The Capital Puzzle Revisited", *Review of Financial Studies*, 8/4 (1995): 1185–1208

Bhattacharya, Sudipto, "Corporate Finance and the Legacy of Miller and Modigliani", *Journal of Economic Perspectives*, 2/4 (1988): 135–47

Brennan, Michael J. (editor), *The Theory of Corporate Finance*, 2 vols, Cheltenham, Gloucestershire: Elgar, 1996

Glen, Jack D. and Brian Pinto, "Emerging Capital Markets and Corporate Finance", *Columbia Journal of World Business*, 29/2 (1994): 30–43

Hubbard, R. Glenn, *Asymmetric Information, Corporate Finance, and Investment*, Chicago: University of Chicago Press, 1990

Hutchinson, Robert W., *Corporate Finance: Principles of Investment, Financing and Valuation*, Cheltenham: Stanley Thornes, 1995

Modigliani, Franco and Merton H. Miller, "The Cost of Capital, Corporation Finance, and the Theory of Investment", *American Economic Review*, 48/3 (1958): 267–97

Modigliani, Franco and Merton H. Miller, "Corporate Income Taxes and the Cost of Capital: A Correction", *American Economic Review*, 53/3 (1963): 433–43

Roe, Mark J., *Strong Managers, Weak Owners: The Political Roots of American Corporate Finance*, Princeton, New Jersey: Princeton University Press, 1994

BHATTACHARYA provides a good account of two seminal papers written by MODIGLIANI & MILLER (1958, 1963), which influenced the way in which corporate finance would develop. He focuses mainly on the Modigliani and Miller (MM) contribution to the theory of corporate finance and dividend policy, covering most of their papers. The innovations made by Modigliani and Miller include the notion of a risk class (a set of payoff patterns mutually replicable through trading), the consideration of investor arbitrage (home-made leverage) in the pricing of securities, the initiation of integrated after-tax analysis of the dividend and debt supply policies of firms, the consideration of empirical evidence and the introduction of "respectable" econometric methods into corporate finance, and the first steps towards the development of the economic modelling of unexplained phenomena, such as the "informal content" of dividend stock prices. Bhattacharya's paper is a sound introduction to the basics of MM thought and financial concepts.

BERENS & CUNY provides a good account of capital structure, an issue that has attracted a great deal of attention in corporate finance theory. Although they start with an analysis of the MM approach, it does not constitute a significant part of the paper. They mainly focus on the tradeoff theory of capital structure, which argues that value-maximizing firms attain an optimal capital structure by balancing the corporate tax benefits of debt against the costs associated with debt, such as personal tax, bankruptcy, agency costs, and so on. They list all the critics of tradeoff theory, but show that, once nominal growth is recognized in firm valuation, the debt ratio becomes a badly distorted measure of tax shielding. Furthermore, when a firm issues debt with fixed interest payments, growing cash-flows generated by the firm are not matched by the interest payments on current debt. The impact of nominal growth on debt ratios is largely independent of the extent to which interest is used to shield income from taxes. Consequently, since the tradeoff theory of capital structure is primarily driven by the corporate tax benefits of debt financing, it is important to recognize when testing this theory that the debt ratio provides a distorted measure of corporate tax shielding. This paper introduces the reader to what is certainly one of the main issues in corporate finance. Some prior knowledge of the MM contribution to corporate finance will be helpful.

The two-volume work edited by BRENNAN is a selection of very influential papers that have shaped the development of corporate finance. It covers all important aspects of corporate finance, with particularly strong papers analysing corporate financial structure and corporate restructuring (mergers and takeovers). Although this is a selection of very different papers, the only common denominator of which is that they are in the field of corporate finance, it is a valuable read for anyone who wants to know the state-of-the-art literature without being dragged into endless polemics about recent controversial research ideas and directions. The book looks beyond the classical frontiers of corporate finance, and offers some insight into investment and asset pricing theory.

GLEN & PINTO assesses the issues of changing corporate finance in the emerging capital markets. Using data sets from international financial (public) organizations (particularly the IFC, where the authors worked at the when time the paper was written), they discovered that the recent pattern of foreign finance emphasizes the direct funding of firms in developing countries, rather than the sovereign borrowing that had been dominant for many years in the past. There has also been a shift from bank finance to the use of capital market instruments, due to financial liberalization and privatization in developing countries. The authors conclude the paper by linking "pecking order" with the level of financial development and the degree of financial liberalization in the various countries considered.

HUBBARD edited a book of high quality papers presented at the NBER conference held under the same name. The articles study the interactions between corporate finance and the investment behaviour of firms, relying mainly on the implications of models based on asymmetric information. Some of the articles are, however, more concerned with macroeconomic aspects of corporate finance. Their authors state that the traditional approach to firms' capital structure has focused on the optimal composition of debt and equity, and find that financing patterns have changed since World War II. Internal financing is the dominant source of capital, and shows no long-term trend. Companies are also moving from public sources of funds (bonds and new equity offerings) towards private sources, such as privately placed debt, bank loans, and retained earnings. This book also provides a fairly interesting international comparison between different developed countries. It is a very good source for those readers who are interested in relating corporate finance to other branches of economics, particularly macroeconomics, in order to understand the policy implications of different approaches to corporate finance.

While the previous book is written primarily for researchers, HUTCHINSON is suitable for the beginner who requires technical rigour, but does not wish to be overwhelmed by complicated mathematical expressions. This is one of the British textbooks on corporate finance that can compete with its more widely accepted American counterparts. It covers many issues of corporate finance, such as different valuation models, the time value of money, debt valuation, corporate financial structure, and corporate financial restructuring. The presentation is sometimes rather dry, but this will not deter the well-motivated reader.

ROE provides a clear account of the political economy of historical developments in American corporate finance. The governance of American corporations is usually described as many shareholders having little power, and boards of directors having power shared with the chief executive officer. The author explains this in terms of the need for large amounts of capital to be raised from individuals unskilled in management, and looks further into the political environment that was established around that practice. The main advantage of this book is the masterful interplay of economics, politics, history, and law, which make it relevant to each of these disciplines. The author also stresses the importance of separating ownership and control. The book is, however, finished in a rather quasi-institutionalist manner recognizing the existence of informal norms – which are then unjustifiably neglected. Nevertheless, this is a book that should be read. It provides a good historical account of US developments, and does not require any prior knowledge or mathematical proficiency.

ŽELJKO ŠEVIĆ

Corporate governance

Andrews, Kenneth R., "Directors Responsibility for Corporate Strategy", *Harvard Business Review*, 58/6 (November–December 1980): 30–41

Arthur, E. Eugene, "The Ethics of Corporate Governance", *Journal of Business Ethics*, 6/1 (January 1987): 59–70

Berle, Adolf A. and Gardiner C. Means, *The Modern Corporation and Private Property*, New York: Macmillan, 1932

Breeden, Richard C., Joseph Hinsey IV, Charles Wohlstetter, Dale M. Hanson, Deborah J. Cornwall, J.W. Lorsch, Martin Lipton, Adrian Cadbury, Ram Charan, Lawrence Perlman, Louis M. Thompson Jr, Ronald J. Gilson, Reinier Kraakman and John Pound, "The Fight for Good Governance", *Harvard Business Review*, 71/1 (January–February 1993): 76–83

Cadbury, Adrian, *The Company Chairman*, Cambridge: Director Books, 1990

Coulson-Thomas, Colin, *Developing Directors: Building an Effective Boardroom Team*, London and New York: McGraw Hill, 1993

Jensen, Michael and William Meckling, "Theory of the Firm: Managerial Behavior, Agency Costs and Ownership Structure", *Journal of Financial Economics*, 3 (1976): 305–60

Johnson, Jonathon L., Catherine M. Daily and Alan E. Ellstrand, "Boards of Directors: A Review and Research Agenda", *Journal of Management*, 22/3 (Fall 1996): 409–38

Pound, John, "The Promise of the Governed Corporation", *Harvard Business Review*, 73/2 (March–April 1995): 89–98

Tricker, Robert I., *International Corporate Governance: Text, Readings, and Cases*, New York and London: Prentice Hall, 1994

Williamson, Oliver E., *The Mechanisms of Governance*, New York: Oxford University Press, 1996

Corporate governance refers to the role of the relationships between the owners and the managers of the corporation in defining the purpose of the corporation, setting the direction of the corporation, and controlling the actions of the managers. This definition of corporate governance necessarily includes the role of the corporation within society. Corporate governance has been analysed using paradigms from law, economics, management, psychology, sociology, and finance. Much of the corporate governance literature focuses on the board of directors. The area covers topics such as the composition, role, and performance of the board, the board's relationship with owners, the board's relationship with managers, and the legal framework within which the board operates. Governance varies markedly between countries and cultures, so the field lends itself to international comparative study. Essentially, major works can be classified as either theoretical development, explaining the evolution of the corporate governance mechanism, or practical works intended to improve the performance of the board itself. This entry discusses both areas.

BERLE & MEANS is a pioneering work on corporate governance, which remains relevant. Despite its somewhat dated style and US flavour, the detailed historical account and statistical background of the changing nature of ownership and control in modern corporations in the early 20th century is a central starting point for understanding the nature of corporate governance. The authors' insights into the separation of ownership and control and the consequent impact on economic theory were pivotal in the development of the area.

JENSEN & MECKLING developed the impact of this separation further in their detailed account of agency costs. They operationalized the corporation as an artificial nexus of contracts in order to develop a formal exposition of agency costs, with economic proofs that detail the impact of the rise of a managerial profession and its effect on the financial constitution of the modern corporation. They provided the formal theoretical basis of the concept of agency costs as those costs incurred by both owners and managers due to the separation of ownership and control.

WILLIAMSON views the firm as a bundle of contracts and builds on the work of Coase in establishing the role that transaction costs play in the overall governance structure of organizations. Williamson takes a different approach to governance, stating that "the study of governance is concerned with the identification, explication and mitigation of all forms of contractual hazards" (p.5). He moves the emphasis away from the actors (owners, directors, and managers) to the allocation of risk and the behaviour of economic entities in the conduct of transactions. The bibliography contains a recent collection of Williamson's writings in the area. Although it is an excellent introduction to a current economic paradigm, addressing the issue of why we have firms and the limits of their boundaries, the heavy economic focus and the concentration on a single paradigm ignore the contribution of other approaches to the area.

In contrast to the view of the firm as a legal fiction, ARTHUR adopts the German jurists' organic view of the firm as an independent entity with its own distinctive will and capacity to act. By highlighting the role of the board in developing the mission and policies of the organization, he argues for the acceptance of an ethical framework for the board that goes beyond the current focus on shareholder interests. He fails to elaborate on the ways in which this will affect organizational performance, but he does advance possible difficulties and oversights in instituting such a code.

The major works discussed so far have been concerned with the positive theoretical basis of governance. The other major literature adopts a normative approach – how to provide "better" governance for practising directors. ANDREWS examines this role of the board in determining corporate strategy (or will) from a traditional monitoring perspective. Despite his exhortation for the implementation of a strategy committee as part of the governance mechanism, he advocates boards being principally involved in the reviewing of corporate strategy, as opposed to its formulation. Such an approach is definitely dated.

In contrast, POUND outlines a view of the future of governance that embraces a broader role for the board by arguing that corporate governance is not about power but about decision-making processes. By shifting focus away from the form of governance and onto the processes used in making decisions, he details how issues such as organizational politics, personality clashes, and human heuristics all contribute to poor corporate decision making, governance, and performance. The shift in emphasis for the board, from a monitoring role to one of increasing activism, may well signal the beginning of a new emphasis in the subject development.

BREEDEN et al. provide a concise and practically focused summary of the often ideologically opposed views about current corporate governance controversies. Issues such as government regulation and intervention in governance, potential conflicts between the short-term and long-term interests of the organization in governance decisions, as well as the role of institutional investors, are all raised in a brief "letter to the editor" style. Despite the lack of depth in the arguments offered, it is a useful reference point in defining the current areas of interest in the field.

An academic perspective on current issues can be found in the work of JOHNSON, DAILY & ELLSTRAND, who review the research on boards of directors since 1989, and propose a research agenda centred on three roles of a director: monitoring (of senior executives); service (i.e. provision of advice to management); and resource dependability (i.e. ability to provide resources to the organization). Their article may be criticized for its traditional view of corporate governance, but none the less provides an excellent summary of empirical research to date.

Overall, TRICKER provides an excellent introduction to the area as well as a bridge between theory and practice. He furnishes a short but useful account of the development of corporate governance, with a particularly international flavour. His broad approach allows insights into the functions of the board and how they change with different organizational structures. The readings and case studies supplementing each chapter allow key topics to be developed in depth, and illustrate the theory with practical examples. However, the broad coverage and practical focus lead to a lack of academic rigour in many areas.

On a practical level, COULSON-THOMAS outlines how to analyse the composition of boards, and details the essential steps required to develop individual directors as well as the entire board team. The treatment of the separation of responsibilities between directors and managers is especially helpful.

Similarly, CADBURY looks at the role of the board and the chairman in particular. His pragmatic viewpoint and personal practical examples emphasize the importance of the chairman to the governance process. Although the theoretical underpin-

nings of his advice may be thin, the role of the chairman in overcoming situations critical to a corporation's future is well handled.

GEOFFREY KIEL AND GAVIN NICHOLSON

See also Corporate strategy

Corporate manslaughter

Childs, Mary, "Medical Manslaughter and Corporate Liability", *Legal Studies*, 19/3 (1999): 316–38
Field, Stewart and Nico Jorg, "Corporate Liability and Manslaughter: Should We be Going Dutch?", *Criminal Law Review*, (March 1991): 156–71
French, Peter A., *Collective and Corporate Responsibility*, New York: Columbia University Press, 1984
McColgan, Aileen, "The Law Commission Consultation Document on Involuntary Manslaughter: Heralding Corporate Liability?", *Criminal Law Review*, (August 1994): 547–57
Wells, Celia, "Cry in the Dark: Corporate Manslaughter and Cultural Meaning" in *Frontiers of Criminality*, edited by Ian Loveland, London: Sweet and Maxwell, 1995
Wells, Celia, "The Law Commission Report on Involuntary Manslaughter: The Corporate Manslaughter Proposals: Pragmatism, Paradox and Peninsularity", *Criminal Law Review*, (August 1996): 545–53

Although there is a great deal of literature addressing questions of corporate criminality in general, relatively few writings focus specifically on the question of corporate manslaughter.

WELLS raises complex questions about the cultural attitudes to blame, risk and causation that are intimately connected to the social construction of corporate criminality. She argues that these attitudes and beliefs are bound up with the prevailing social and political climate in a symbiotic relationship. Increased awareness of the potentially harmful power of large corporate organizations is associated with a cultural shift in blame. Social constructions of risk and risk acceptability are central to the criminal law's blaming process. As we become more aware of the power of corporations and as we develop increasing sophisticated technological and communications systems, so we become more likely to attribute responsibility, and therefore blame, to the corporation rather than the individual employee.

FRENCH is a philosopher who addresses the question of how and why corporations can be held responsible for wrongdoing, including homicide. He offers a metaphysical account of corporate "personhood", arguing that corporations have an existence, and a moral status, which is more than simply the total of those individuals within the corporate structure at any given time. He draws upon arguments associated with the work of other philosophers concerned with questions of moral responsibility, and shows how his approach might be applied to a range of practical examples. His work is not centrally a work on law, but he does address the legal aspects of corporate responsibility and suggests how his approach might be applied to the ascription of legal liability for manslaughter attributable to corporate fault.

FIELD & JORG consider the problems of attributing liability for negligent manslaughter caused by system failure rather than the wrongdoing of a single individual. In this article they recommend serious consideration be given to the model adopted in the criminal law of the Netherlands. This approach looks at two key factors: *power* on the part of the corporation to control what happened, and *acceptance* of these acts as in the normal course of business relations.

McCOLGAN discusses the implications of the proposals advanced in the 1993 consultation document issued by the Law Commission for England and Wales. She argues that the Law Commission's move in this document away from its usual subjectivist approach to criminal liability appears to be driven by its concern about corporate killings. She argues that the Commission should have considered the possibility of retaining a subjectivist approach to manslaughter committed by individuals, while adopting an objectivist approach to killings attributable to corporations. She further argues that it would be preferable to reform the laws of corporate criminality generally, rather than creating a special rule for manslaughter alone.

The proposals discussed by McColgan were followed in 1996 by a report addressing the reform of the law of manslaughter, half of which was devoted to a discussion of corporate killings. In the end, the Law Commission advocated the adoption of a new approach involving the enactment of a new offence using a "corporate fault" model to attribute responsibility to corporate bodies. WELLS (1996) examines these proposals, concluding that they provide the basis for a shift in the legal form of corporate liability in England and Wales. She sounds a note of caution, however, when she speculates that adoption of the proposed model, with its introduction of a special offence of corporate killing, might lead to greater marginalization of corporate manslaughter.

CHILDS examines the application of different models of corporate criminality to the phenomenon of deaths caused by medical negligence. It is argued that the approach of prosecuting individual medical professionals is usually unsatisfactory as most hospital deaths due to negligence are not simply attributable to the fault of one or two people. Rather, they tend to be the results of broader patterns of failings which all contribute to the death. Current models of corporate criminality in English law are discussed and rejected as unsuitable for dealing with hospital deaths; instead, the preferred approach is the "corporate fault" model advocated in the reform proposals advanced by the Law Commission. The article examines related issues including sentencing, consequences for civil litigation, and the use of public inquiries as an alternative to prosecution.

MARY CHILDS

Corporate social performance

Ackerman, Robert W. and Raymond A. Bauer, *Corporate Social Responsiveness: The Modern Dilemma*, Reston, Virginia: Reston Publishing, 1976

Anshen, Melvin, *Corporate Strategies for Social Performance*, New York: Macmillan, and London: Collier Macmillan, 1980

Bauer, Raymond A., "The Corporate Response Process" in *Research in Corporate Social Performance and Policy*, edited by Lee E. Preston, vol. 1, 1978

Bowen, Howard R., *Social Responsibilities of the Businessman*, New York: Harper, 1953

Buono, Anthony F. and Larry Nichols, *Corporate Policy, Values, and Social Responsibility*, New York: Praeger, 1985

Carroll, Archie B., "Corporate Social Responsibility: Evolution of a Definitional Construct", *Business and Society*, 38/3 (September 1999): 268–95

Clarkson, Max B.E., "A Stakeholder Framework for Analyzing and Evaluating Corporate Social Performance", *Academy of Management Review*, 20/1 (January 1995): 92–117

Davis, Keith, "The Case for and against Business Assumption of Social Responsibilities", *Academy of Management Journal*, 16/2 (June 1973): 312–22

Epstein, Edwin M., "The Corporate Social Policy Process: Beyond Business Ethics, Corporate Social Responsibility, and Corporate Social Responsiveness", *California Management Review*, 29/3 (Spring 1987): 99–114

Frederick, William C., "From CSR_1 to CSR_2: The Maturing of Business-and-Society Thought", *Business and Society*, 33/2 (August 1994): 150–64

Freeman, R. Edward, *Strategic Management: A Stakeholder Approach*, Boston: Pitman, 1984

Harrison, Jeffrey S. and R. Edward Freeman, "Stakeholders, Social Responsibility, and Performance: Empirical Evidence and Theoretical Perspectives", *Academy of Management Journal*, 42/5 (October 1999): 479–85

Hopkins, Michael, *The Planetary Bargain: Corporate Social Responsibility Comes of Age*, Basingstoke: Macmillan, and New York: St Martin's Press, 1999

Miles, Robert H., *Managing the Corporate Social Environment: A Grounded Theory*, Englewood Cliffs, New Jersey and London: Prentice Hall, 1987

Post, James E., Anne T. Lawrence and James Weber, *Business and Society: Corporate Strategy, Public Policy, Ethics*, 9th edition, Boston: Irwin McGraw Hill, 1999

Preston, Lee E. (editor), *Research in Corporate Social Performance and Policy*, vol. 1, Greenwich, Connecticut: Jai Press, 1978a

Preston, Lee E., "Analyzing Corporate Social Performance: Methods and Results", *Journal of Contemporary Business*, 7/1 (Winter 1978b): 135–50

Reich, Robert B., "The New Meaning of Corporate Social Responsibility", *California Management Review*, 40/2 (Winter 1998): 8–17

Sethi, S. Prakash, "Models of Business and Society Interaction" in *Business and Society: Dimensions of Conflict and Cooperation*, edited by S. Prakash Sethi and Cecilia M. Falbe, Lexington, Massachusetts: Lexington Books, 1987

Simerly, Roy L., "Measuring Corporate Social Performance: An Assessment of Techniques", *International Journal of Management*, 16/2 (June 1999): 253–57

Solomons, David, "Corporate Social Performance: A New Dimension in Accounting Reports?" in *Debits, Credits,*

Finance and Profits, edited by Harold Edey and B.S. Yamey, London: Sweet and Maxwell, 1974

Spicer, Barry H., "Accounting for Corporate Social Performance: Some Problems and Issues", *Journal of Contemporary Business*, 7/1 (Winter 1978): 151–70

Steiner, George A., *Business and Society*, 2nd edition, New York: Random House, 1975

Swanson, Diane L., "Toward an Integrated Theory of Business and Society: A Research Strategy for Corporate Social Performance", *Academy of Management Review*, 24/3 (July 1999): 506–21

Wartick, Steven L. and Philip L. Cochran, "The Evolution of the Corporate Social Performance Model", *Academy of Management Review*, 10/4 (October 1985): 758–69

Wartick, Steven L. and Donna J. Wood, *International Business and Society*, Oxford: Blackwell, 1998

Wokutch, Richard E. and Elizabeth W. McKinney, "Behavioral and Perceptual Measures of Corporate Social Performance" in *Research in Corporate Social Performance and Policy*, vol. 12, edited by James E. Post, Greenwich, Connecticut: JAI Press, 1991

Wood, Donna J., "Corporate Social Performance Revisited", *Academy of Management Review*, 16/4 (October 1991): 691–718

Wood, Donna J. and Raymond E. Jones, "Research in Corporate Social Performance: What Have We Learned" in *Corporate Philanthropy at the Crossroads*, edited by Dwight F. Burlingame and Dennis R. Young, Bloomington: Indiana University Press, 1996

As an integral part of organizational analysis, the social performance of corporations has garnered considerable attention from scholars and industry observers alike. Such focus has helped raise awareness among those in the business community that a firm is dependent upon the goodwill of society – which can either sustain or impair a company's existence.

HARRISON & FREEMAN observe in their introduction to a special research forum of the *Academy of Management Journal*, that over recent years there has been a proliferation of ideas surrounding the proper role of business organizations in society. The insightful essay by REICH confirms that an important contemporary sentiment is not whether companies should be responsible in some way to society, but rather how they should be responsible.

In the 1953 landmark text, *Social Responsibilities of the Businessman*, BOWEN argues that corporate management has an obligation to pursue those policies, to make those decisions, and to follow those courses of action which are desirable in terms of the objectives and values of the community at large. With this straightforward proposition, Bowen touched off what is frequently referred to as the "modern debate" regarding corporate social performance (CSP). Further, the pioneering work of STEINER helped set the stage for differentiating among various facets of public responsibility and corporate citizenship, while the 1978 inaugural publication of *Research in Corporate Social Performance and Policy* (PRESTON 1978a) elevated the degree of scholarly discourse devoted to the CSP construct.

Interestingly, corporate social performance has been defined in various ways. Some writers view CSP as the extent to which an organization meets the needs, expectations, and demands of certain constituencies beyond those directly linked to the firm's products and markets. The influential contribution of WARTICK & COCHRAN describes corporate social performance as the integration of principles of social responsibility, the processes of social responsiveness, and those company policies developed to adequately address social issues. WOOD's forward-thinking treatise reformulates and expands upon Wartick & Cochran's framework by offering a definition of CSP that comprises a business organization's configuration of principles of social responsibility (e.g. the consequences of business activities, with the implicit involvement of economic activity in social development), processes of social responsiveness (e.g. the action phase of management responding in the social sphere), and policies, programs, and observable outcomes of corporate behavior as they relate to an organization's internal and external constituencies and societal relationships.

As articulated in a 1977 study, *The Measurement of Corporate Social Performance: Determining the Impact of Business Actions on Areas of Social Concern*, from the American Institute of Certified Public Accountants, companies have an implicit contractual relationship with society (e.g. a "social contract"), under which society grants the firm a "license to operate" in return for a generally positive contribution to society as a whole. Following on from this idea, POST, LAWRENCE & WEBER explains that two broad principles emerged. First, the "charity principle", the idea that wealthier members of society should be charitable toward those less fortunate. Second, the "stewardship principle", whereby corporate management has an obligation to see that everyone – particularly those in need – benefit from a company's actions, and the profit-seeking enterprise deploys its resources in ways that are good not just for stockholders alone but for society generally.

WOOD & JONES, along with SWANSON, helps discern that current scholarship in the area of CSP tends to distinguish between two major aspects of performance: (a) internal social performance, which is centred around the response to social considerations within an organization, such as worker occupational health and safety, personnel development and equal employment opportunity practices, waste reduction, and resource conservation; and (b) external social performance, which focuses upon a company's relations with the outside environment, such as efforts to help strengthen local community services and foster economic revitalization, pollution control initiatives, customer care and protection, and ethical sourcing. Furthermore, two fundamental components of the firm's social performance have been identified – namely "corporate social responsibility" (CSR_1) and "corporate social responsiveness" (CSR_2).

As FREDERICK points out, the tenet of corporate social responsibility occupies a long and varied history, taking recognizable shape around the turn of the 20th century. Although first acknowledged in 1916 by J. Maurice Clark, in an article appearing in the *Journal of Political Economy*, CSR_1 as a function of firm self-interest has its formal roots in the 1932 edition of *The Modern Corporation and Private Property*, by Adolph A. Berle and Gardiner C. Means.

The American-based Committee for Economic Development (CED) in its 1971 report, *Social Responsibilities of Business Corporations*, articulated a three concentric circles model of CSR_1. The CED conceptual framework depicts an inner circle (including clear-cut basic responsibilities for efficient execution of the firm's economic function – products, jobs, and maximizing shareholder wealth), an intermediate circle (encompassing responsibility to exercise the firm's economic function with a sensitive awareness of changing social values and priorities), and an outer circle (identifying newly emerging and still amorphous responsibilities that a business enterprise should prepare to take on board for the betterment of society).

Prominent scholars such as DAVIS and EPSTEIN also offer an explanation that corporate social responsibility generally refers to an organization's consideration of, and outcomes associated with, issues transcending the narrow economic, technical, and legal requirements of the firm. Other authors like ACKERMAN & BAUER view CSR_1 as the obligation of companies to undertake proper legal, moral, ethical, and charitable steps that will help protect and enhance the welfare of both society and business as a whole. Additionally, Frederick's prodigious work portrays corporate social responsibility as a firm's obligation to deliver benefits to society – beyond producing goods and services with the objective of maximizing return on invested capital – while operating in compliance with all applicable laws and government regulations.

While corporate social responsibility leans more toward philosophical discourse and the importance attached to moral reflection (i.e. a macro emphasis), both CARROLL and Wood stress that the notion of corporate social responsiveness moves away from principled reflection and philosophical precepts and provides an action counterpoint, or "managerial phase", in responding to developments in the corporate social environment (i.e. a micro emphasis). Swanson agrees with this line of thinking and goes on to explain that CSR_2 entails the management of an organization's processes and activities through which public expectations are anticipated and identified, placed within the context of other corporate concerns and, in some fashion, woven into the ways of doing business. That is, CSR_2 tends to be anticipatory and preventative in nature with a systems orientation.

Several writers have developed thoughtful explanations regarding the features that characterize socially responsive firms. Combining concepts from organization theory and strategic management, MILES observes that companies can differ in how they relate to agents of the public interest, including legislators, government regulators, and special interest groups. He emphasizes that some firms adopt a "proactive" or "problem-solving" approach to the management of their relations with various external constituencies, whereas other companies adopt a "defensive" or "adversarial" approach to relationships and activities outside the firm. Similarly, other writers have developed "life cycle" schema and "stage models" that attempt to describe a corporate responsiveness continuum. For instance, BAUER takes seriously the thinking that social responsiveness can range on a continuum from no response (do nothing) to a proactive response (do much).

In addition to employing a social issue life cycle approach when assessing CSP, a favored perspective toward examining the social performance of the firm is to consider those affected by business decisions, referred to frequently as "stakeholder management". Popularized from the seminal work of FREEMAN, stakeholder management embodies social or societal responsibilities and responsiveness by delineating the specific groups or constituencies an organization should consider in carrying out its mission and day-to-day operations.

However, neoclassical economist and Nobel laureate, Milton Friedman, contends in his 1962 book *Capitalism and Freedom*, that a business enterprise should not deviate from its strict profit orientation and efforts to maximize shareholder wealth; the firm should be concerned only with its financial performance and increasing shareholder value. Thus, according to Friedman's provocative pronouncement, the sole constituency of corporate management is the stockholders (i.e. owners of the firm), and the sole concern of stockholders is economic return – and not social welfare considerations and stakeholder concessions.

Such a narrow view has been countered by the pathfinding work of Wartick & Cochran who assert a CSP model that recognizes and accepts the importance of a firm's economic responsibility. Yet, instead of arguing that financial and social performance are mutually exclusive, economic responsibility is identified as a subset of corporate social performance. Such a perspective has been referred to by BUONO & NICHOLS and SPICER as an "enlightened self-interest perspective".

Under the rubric of the Social Issues in Management Division of the Academy of Management, a wide range of subjects and issues pertaining to CSP have been discussed and written about. For instance, attention has been drawn toward efforts at empirically testing conceptual models about how individuals perceive and interpret CSP, the validity of CSP conceptual frameworks in cross-cultural and multinational settings, as well as critiques of existing CSP theory. In addition, considerable intellectual capital has been spent determining an association between social performance and financial performance, as well as on developing screening criteria for social investment purposes. HOPKINS points out in his informative text that such entities as the New York-based Council on Economic Priorities rates a large number of American companies behind some 1800 products in such CSP areas as charitable giving, community outreach, information disclosure, environmental impact, and family benefit initiatives.

Similarly, *Fortune* magazine publishes its annual "Corporate Reputation Survey of America's Most Admired Companies". Appearing first in January 1983, this popular source of information is generated from the opinions of senior executives, outside directors, and business analysts who are asked to rate companies by industry on several different attributes of reputation, one of which is responsibility to the community and the environment. Further, in 1990 the investment research firm of Kinder, Lydenberg, Domini & Company (KLD) launched the *Domini 400 Social Index*, a market capitalization-weighted common stock index of numerous American-based companies. The index is derived from multiple applications of KLD "social performance screens", or assessment areas, related to various dimensions of CSP.

The widely acclaimed work of SETHI suggests that contemporary approaches to analysing corporate social performance can be grouped under two broad categories: (a) a "window-in" approach, which assumes that it is primarily the external environment which is dominant in affecting changes in corporate behavior and responses; and (b) a "window-out" approach, which is internally focused and emphasizes the effects of structural design, leadership style, and organizational culture on corporate performance in response to externally defined constraints on corporate behaviour. Importantly, Wood & Jones's in-depth review of the research literature reveals that prior empirical investigations of CSP have been characterized by numerous perspectives and measurement techniques, various performance indicators, and differing strategies of operationalization and research design. For example, researchers have attempted to measure CSP utilizing forced choice survey instruments, content analyses of annual corporate reports, expert evaluations, observed activities such as efforts to control pollution, and analysis of fines imposed by regulatory agencies. Subsequently, a clear division can be identified between those who emphasize an analysis of social response processes, based on detailed examinations of organizational experience and decision making, and those who emphasize the development of formal reporting systems (e.g. corporate social and environmental auditing) containing largely quantitative data.

Swanson observes that a large portion of published CSP research has assumed the existence of some set of criteria or performance indicators against which corporate behaviour might be evaluated, rated, and assigned praise or blame. As addressed by Spicer, a thorny issue lies in achieving reasonable agreement about what performance indicators to include or exclude and on what grounds. SOLOMONS contributes to the debate by observing that before one can seriously confront the challenge of measuring CSP, a crucial question is what is the key criterion of social performance?

WOKUTCH & McKINNEY reminds the reader that while several dimensions and measures of CSP have been used in the research stream, neither perceptual nor behavioural measures alone can fully capture the multidimensionality of corporate social performance. Moreover, conventional managerial accounting, coupled with lagging financial information, has limitations as well in terms of the aspects of organizational performance excellence that can be illuminated, and in how well accompanying data serve key stakeholders' information needs. Consequently, several authors have concluded that a "balanced set" of financial and non-financial measures is necessary to adequately capture both the subjective and objective nature of the CSP construct, and communicate important decision-relevant information within the firm.

Wood goes on to add that whatever indicators of CSP are specified through identification of significant social effects of corporate activities, it is desirable to classify them in a way that facilitates greater utility of measurement and inter-firm comparisons. Concomitantly, PRESTON (1978b) and Spicer subscribe to the view that a comparable, reliable, consistent, and robust set of CSP parameters and performance metrics are necessary to highlight fundamental considerations common to the analysis of almost every business enterprise.

As discussed in the insightful critique by SIMERLY, the corporate social performance construct has proven to be one of the more difficult constructs to investigate in business research, resulting in inconsistent empirical findings. Consequently, it is not yet completely clear whether operating according to prescribed principles and criteria of CSP will place a company at a competitive advantage or disadvantage. There is evidence for both results, depending on the type of firm, industrial setting, and the social issue or problem being addressed. Furthermore, such variables as the quality of personnel involved, the degree of their commitment to various social issues, the firm's ability to secure employee input and support for policy changes, and the company's capacity to follow through on implementing CSP initiatives and activities can greatly impact the social performance achievements of an organization.

None the less, there are several indications, drawn from both the popular press and academic literature, that a growing number of firms are stepping up efforts at measuring their social and environmental performance. Important developments that seem to be responsible for stimulating such activity include: (a) intensified pressure on senior-level management to deal with social responsibility issues; (b) corporate managers adopting new attitudes about the kinds of activities their companies should undertake; and (c) many of the arguments against some form of corporate social involvement have, for the most part, been dispelled or refuted by persuasive counterarguments. While WARTICK & WOOD explain that the salience of social issues affecting particular business policies and practices may vary over time, across industries, nations, and cultures, the work of ANSHEN and CLARKSON offers several incisive arguments favouring a firm's interest in CSP, such as: enhanced public image and credibility within the community, and being viewed as a "neighbor of choice"; increased employee loyalty, commitment, and morale; the avoidance of burdensome government regulation; and strengthening the competitive position and continued viability of the organization.

DANIEL B. WAGGONER

See also Business ethics, Corporate governance, High performance work systems, Management accounting, Stakeholder, Stakeholder analysis

Corporate strategy

Buzzell, Robert D. and Bradley T. Gale, *The PIMS Principles: Linking Strategy to Performance*, New York: Free Press, and London: Collier Macmillan, 1987

Collins, James C. and Jerry I. Porras, *Built to Last: Successful Habits of Visionary Companies*, New York: Harper, 1994; London: Century, 1995

Doz, Yves L. and Gary Hamel, *Alliance Advantage: The Art of Creating Value through Partnering*, Boston: Harvard Business School Press, 1998

Goold, Michael, Andrew Campbell and Marcus Alexander, *Corporate-Level Strategy*, New York: Wiley, 1994

Hamel, Gary and C.K. Prahalad, *Competing for the Future*, Boston: Harvard Business School Press, 1994

Haspeslagh, Philippe C. and David B. Jemison, *Managing Acquisitions: Creating Value through Corporate Renewal*, New York: Free Press, 1991

Hitt, Michael A., R. Duane Ireland and Robert E. Hoskisson, *Strategic Management: Competitiveness and Globalization*, 3rd edition, Cincinati: South-Western, 1999

Markides, C. and V. Papadakis, "What Constitutes an Effective Mission Statement: An Empirical Investigation" in *New Managerial Mindsets: Organizational Transformation and Strategy Implementation*, edited by Michael A. Hitt *et al.*, London and New York: Wiley, 1998

Pearce, J.A. and F. David, "Corporate Mission Statements: The Bottom Line", *Academy of Management Executive*, 1/2 (1987): 109–16

Rumelt, Richard P., *Strategy, Structure and Economic Performance*, Boston: Harvard Business School, 1974

Sirower, Mark L., *The Synergy Trap: How Companies Lose the Acquisition Game*, New York: Free Press, 1997

According to HITT, IRELAND & HOSKISSON, corporate strategy comprises the actions taken to gain a competitive advantage through the selection and management of a mix of businesses competing in several industries or product markets. This definition broadly depicts the primary concerns of a multi-business corporation when designing its corporate strategy. These are:

(a) commitment to a long-term vision and mission that aims to guide the company into the future;

(b) decisions concerning the businesses in which the company aims to build presence in the future;

(c) decisions on how to enter these businesses, or how to exit from businesses that are not in line with the long-term vision of the company;

(d) the creation of a structure capable of helping the corporate office to manage its group of businesses;

(e) the allocation of resources among the various businesses; and

(f) the creation of a corporation that, as a whole, adds up to more than the sum of its business parts.

The first element of any successful corporate strategy is the creation of the overall mission or vision of the company. There is general agreement in both the academic literature and managerial circles that any good company needs to have a clear sense of direction, preferably articulated in a mission or vision statement. However, disagreements have arisen as to what constitutes a good or effective mission.

PEARCE & DAVID have argued that most company objectives (as articulated in company mission and vision statements) tend to be useless primarily because they: (a) state the obvious; (b) are too generic and thus fail to give guidance in making decisions and tradeoffs; (c) are too fantastical or unrealistic; and/or (d) are not shared by the employees.

COLLINS & PORRAS argue that developing an effective mission is a difficult task because, to be effective, the objective has to find the correct balance on many parameters. For example, it needs to be specific enough but not too constraining; it needs to be flexible and adaptable but should not be changed every year; it needs to be challenging and inspirational but not too unrealistic; and it needs to be measurable but, again, not constraining.

MARKIDES & PAPADAKIS argue that five broad characteristics of the mission determine its effectiveness. These are: (a) the actual content and characteristics of the mission state-ment; (b) the process used to develop it; (c) the process used to "sell" it to the rest of the organization; (d) the credibility of the seller (top management); and (e) the conditions under which it was developed and communicated.

The second question that any effective corporate strategy has to address is what businesses the firm should be in (or, in other words, into which areas should the firm diversify in the future). According to RUMELT, diversified firms vary according to two factors: (a) the level of diversification and (b) the connection or linkages between and among business units. They define as low levels of diversification the cases where firms focus on a single business or a dominant business; moderate to high levels of diversification, where firms focus on related, constrained diversification or unrelated diversification.

An excellent analysis of corporate strategy is provided by GOOLD, CAMPBELL & ALEXANDER. They examine not only the issue of corporate parenting but also how diversification strategy is supported by an assumption that managers of diversified firms possess unique management skills that can effectively be used to craft multi-business strategies and improve a firm's competitiveness. They also show why this is not always the case.

HAMEL & PRAHALAD, in one of the most influential books on strategy, focus on value creation and argue that a company, in attempting to create value, should consider its core competencies as the central theme of interest. Thus, managers should determine the unique resources and competencies that their firm possesses, and then leverage these competencies by diversifying into different businesses and product markets.

The third question that corporate strategists should answer is how is their company going to enter the targeted lines of businesses. Broadly, there exist three types of entry method: (a) internal development; (b) merger/acquisition (or disposal); and (c) joint development/strategic alliances. Internal development is where strategies are developed by building up the organization's own resource base and competencies. HASPESLAGH & JEMISON provide an excellent overview of acquisition strategy, according to which an organization develops its resources and competencies by taking over another organization.

A joint development or strategic alliance is where two or more organizations share resources and activities to pursue a strategy. DOZ & HAMEL discuss the art of creating value through partnering, an approach that, together with mergers and acquisitions, has been among the most preferred methods during the 1990s.

The fourth question concerns the way in which companies should allocate resources among various lines of business. This has been dealt by a number of techniques (usually called portfolio matrices). Probably the most important of them is the Boston Consulting Group (BCG) four-box matrix, discussed in BUZZELL & GALE. This matrix is divided into two dimensions: (a) relative industry growth, suggesting the future attractiveness of the business; and (b) relative market share, measuring the current attractiveness of the market and the power of the firm in this market. Relative industry growth appears on the vertical axis, and relative market share on the horizontal. The various businesses of a diversified firm depicted in this matrix require different amounts of cash, and have different future prospects. The company crafts its corporate strategy according to the present and future prospects of each business in the portfolio of businesses.

Finally, among the main objectives of a corporate strategy should be the creation of synergies among the various businesses. Synergy exists when the value created by business units working together exceeds the value those same units create when working independently. SIROWER also defines synergy as the specific increases in performance beyond those expected for companies to achieve independently. These synergies may include the sharing of tangible or physical resources (such as facilities and equipment) or intangible resources (such as sales force or know-how). However, according to Sirower, synergy is very difficult to achieve, and most mergers and acquisitions destroy, rather than create, shareholder value.

To summarize, there are multiple aspects to crafting a corporate strategy, and the most profound measure of the value of a firm's corporate strategy is that the businesses in its portfolio are worth more under current management than they would be under different ownership or management.

VASSILIS PAPADAKIS

See also Corporate governance

Corporatism, *see* Social corporatism

Correlation

Brigham, Thomas A., "On the Importance of Recognizing the Difference between Experiments and Correlational Studies", *American Psychologist*, 44/7 (1989): 1077–78

Cliff, Norman, "Some Cautions Concerning the Application of Causal Modeling Methods", *Multivariate Behavioral Research*, 18/1 (1983): 115–26

Cronbach, Lee J., "The Two Disciplines of Scientific Psychology", *American Psychologist*, 12/11 (1957): 671–84

Finkel, Steven E., *Causal Analysis with Panel Data*, Thousand Oaks, California and London: Sage, 1995

Gibbons, Jean Dickinson, *Nonparametric Measures of Association*, Thousand Oaks, California and London: Sage, 1993

Liebetrau, Albert M., *Measures of Association*, Beverly Hills, California and London: Sage, 1983

Reichardt, Charles S. and Harry F. Gollob, "Satisfying the Constraints of Causal Modeling" in *Advances in Quasi-Experimental Design and Analysis*, edited by William M.K. Trochim, San Francisco: Jossey Bass, 1986

Correlational studies form one of the two fundaments of behavioural research, the other being controlled experimental research. In essence, correlational research does not involve active manipulation of independent variables, only measurement of existing variables. The strength of correlational approaches is that they can examine behaviour in its fullness; the main limitation is the inability to infer causal relations among variables. A vintage article by CRONBACH highlights some of the differences between correlational and experimental approaches in behavioural research. He notes that correlational research studies differences across individuals; at the same time, experimental research considers such difference as measurement error. Further, correlational research is associated with the study of complex phenomena in their natural settings, not with the study of simplified phenomena in an artificial, laboratory setting. Cronbach states that "the correlational method . . . can study what man has not learned to control or can never hope to control" (p.672). The author notes that correlational and experimental researchers have come together to recognize the strengths and limitations of each approach. In fact, since Cronbach's optimistic suggestion of rapprochement between the two schools of thought, the appearance of new methodological and statistical approaches has reduced the schism between different camps. Cronbach's writing presents a prescient depiction of the course of psychology; this is useful in understanding the historical underpinnings of correlational approaches to the study of behaviour.

Just as the methodologies of correlational and experimental research differ, so do the conclusions that one can logically draw from them. In a brief and readable article, BRIGHAM discusses some of the basic issues about the importance of differentiating between the two approaches and the limitations of correlational research. In essence, a correlational study does not lend itself to causal statements; the author outlines some concerns regarding interpretations arising from correlational studies.

One of the limitations of using correlational data to determine causation is that, although variables may be related and causation might be present, it may be difficult to determine which of two variables is the cause and which is the effect. This is the so-called directionality problem. Such a dilemma may be problematic because researchers, especially in applied areas, are likely to be interested in assessing causation. FINKEL discusses potential solutions to this directionality problem through the use of cross-lagged panel correlations. He discusses the three widely cited conditions required for concluding that Variable X exerts a causal effect on Variable Y: (a) X must covary with Y; (b) X must precede Y; and (c) X must be the most likely factor to cause Y. Finkel's slim volume especially focuses on the temporal question. As Finkel points out, interpretations of causation may be difficult because of the possibility of reciprocal causality, in which X and Y may affect one another. Further, the presence of unmeasured variables that affect both X and Y may lead to spurious determination of causality; this is known as the third-variable problem. In some cases, based on theoretical or logical grounds, one could eliminate this third variable problem and conclude with some confidence that a causal relation exists. Finkel presents potential solutions to this difficult problem. The presentation is accessible and relatively nontechnical, although it is easier to comprehend if one is familiar with the basics of the notation commonly used in statistical modelling.

Some research projects do not lend themselves to active manipulation of an independent variable. So researchers sometimes use statistical controls rather than experimental controls in an attempt to determine causal relations. CLIFF points out the potential drawbacks associated with this practice. Fundamentally, correlational data are unsuitable for assessing causation because unknown variables may influence the measured variables; this is the so-called third variable problem. Cliff states that one's confidence in causal statements can be enhanced through converging lines of evidence. In a very readable article, Cliff reviews the principles of causal inference and the limitations of using statistics to replace experimental manipulation.

When researchers study events in natural settings, random assignment of participants to conditions is generally impossible. Research with such constraints is essentially correlational in nature, even though a design appears to have clearly separated independent and dependent variables. Consequently, in these *ex post facto* or quasi-experimental designs, attempts to identify causal relations among variables are made only with great caution. REICHARDT & GOLLOB describe a method for generating tentative, causal statements with data using nonrandom assignment. This approach is structural equation modelling. The authors provide a generally nontechnical description of structural modelling, which involves creating a variable that is a weighted, additive combination of a number of independent or predictor variables. Reichardt and Gollob discuss some of the pitfalls of this technique, specifically bias in estimating the parameters of the structural equation, the omission of relevant causal variables in the equation, the imperfect measurement of the variables, and ignoring the fact that in many cases it is imprudent to assume that effects follow causes without delay. The authors discuss how one can deal with, but probably not eliminate, these problems. In the end, they note, researchers should employ designs with random assignment in addition to nonequivalent designs.

Finally, LIEBETRAU presents an overview of measures of association (correlation) for nominal, ordinal, and metric scales of measurement and GIBBONS reviews such measures for nominal and ordinal data. These two slim volumes are fairly technical, illustrating some of the theoretical components of the statistics presented. The authors describe the commonly used correlational techniques and the circumstances in which they are appropriate. These tests include Pearson's chi-square, the Pearson product-moment correlation, Spearman's correlation for ranks, Kendall's coefficient of concordance, and Kendall's tau, as well as less well-known tests.

BERNARD C. BEINS

See also Causal relationship, Scales of measurement

Correlation analysis

Archdeacon, Thomas J., *Correlation and Regression Analysis: A Historian's Guide*, Madison: University of Wisconsin Press, 1994

Bobko, Philip, *Correlation and Regression: Principles and Applications for Industrial/Organizational Psychology and Management*, New York: McGraw Hill, 1995

Cohen, Jacob and Patricia Cohen, *Applied Multiple Regression/Correlation Analysis for the Behavioral Sciences*, 2nd edition, Hillsdale, New Jersey: Erlbaum, 1983

Kenny, David A., *Correlation and Causality*, New York and Chichester: Wiley, 1979

Liebetrau, Albert M., *Measures of Association*, Beverly Hills, California, and London: Sage, 1983

Wherry, Robert J. Sr, *Contributions to Correlational Analysis*, Orlando, Florida: Academic Press, 1984

To put it simply, correlation is a measure of the linear relationship between two variables. A description of correlation analysis is provided in virtually every statistics textbook and a basic understanding of correlation is assumed in advanced reading in many areas of the social sciences. Correlation is one of the oldest and most commonly used measures of association; however, it is important to recognize that it is only one of many techniques used to assess the relationship between variables. Due to this fact, correlation is rarely discussed in isolation. Other techniques, such as regression and factor analysis, are often discussed synonymously with correlation.

For individuals without a strong mathematical background or those who plan to rely on a computer program to perform most statistical calculations, ARCHDEACON provides a nontechnical account of correlation analysis that is targeted towards an audience that has little statistical training. His discussion specifically targets historians and those doing research involving historical data; however, his discussion and examples are easily understood by non-historians. Archdeacon begins with the assumption that the reader has little or no previous experience with statistics and provides a detailed, yet nontechnical, discussion of many of the basic concepts necessary to understand and properly interpret correlational data. He points out that an understanding of how a statistical procedure is calculated is necessary in order to understand the theory behind the statistic and to determine when it is appropriate to use a technique such as correlation. Archdeacon points out that computer-based statistical packages are an excellent tool that has made correlation analysis readily available, but understanding how a statistical procedure is calculated is "essential to understanding the theory behind it and to recognizing the sets of conditions under which use of the technique is appropriate". This book is an excellent source for beginners wishing to gain a basic understanding of correlation and statistics as well as for more advanced readers wishing a refresher course on correlation and basic statistical theory.

BOBKO provides an overview of statistical theory in the context of the applied use of correlation and regression. He recognizes that in the real world the use of correlation is not always a straightforward process. Numerous examples are provided detailing the variety of purposes for which correlation can be used and discussing the problems that can, and probably will, be encountered when attempting to use correlation in both research and practice. The first half of his book deals strictly with correlation and the second half extends the discussion to include regression analysis.

KENNY extends the discussion of correlation into the realm of causality and causal inference. His discussion goes beyond correlation and includes techniques such as path analysis and regression. The discussion of causality is well organized and provides essential information for the proper use and interpretation of correlational data. He points out that correlation, and for that matter any other statistical technique, is not in and of itself a measure of inference or causality. Correlation only indicates the extent of relationship between two variables;

it does not determine which, if either, variable causes the other. It is important to recognize that certain conditions must be met before causality can be assessed, and Kenny discusses these conditions in a straightforward and easy-to-understand manner.

WHERRY provides a discussion of the importance of correlational analysis within the broader context of statistics in general. While his discussion is not easy reading for those without a mathematical inclination his presentation of the importance of correlation and its place in statistical analysis is well thought out. Variations such as part, multiple, and composite correlation are introduced and the underlying basis as well as the use for these statistics is discussed in detail.

One of the best known and most well respected texts dealing with correlation is COHEN & COHEN. Until relatively recently the statistical techniques of analysis of variance and multiple regression and correlation were considered to be unique and unrelated processes. Cohen & Cohen address the relationships underlying these techniques and present evidence that, far from being distinct, analysis of variance is in fact a special case of the multiple regression/correlation model. Like Kenny one of the underlying themes of this book is the relationship between correlation and causality. Cohen & Cohen is written at a fairly advanced level and assumes that the reader already has a basic understanding of the multiple regression/correlation process. The focus of this book, however, is not on the mathematical aspects of correlation and regression. Instead it emphasizes the application of multiple regression/correlation in understanding the relationships between variables.

A discussion of correlation would not be complete without considering correlation in the context of other measures of association. LIEBETRAU provides a detailed discussion of multiple measures of association, including correlation. Without focusing exclusively on correlational analysis Liebetrau discusses when it is appropriate to use correlation and when other measures provide additional useful information.

BART WEATHINGTON

See also Multiple regression analysis, Regression analysis

Corruption

Acemoglu, Daron and Thierry Verdier, "Property Rights, Corruption and the Allocation of Talent: A General Equilibrium Approach", *Economic Journal*, 108/450 (September 1998): 1381–1403

Banerjee, Abhijit, "A Theory of Misgovernance", *Quarterly Journal of Economics*, 112/4 (November 1997): 1289–1332

Bardhan, Pranab, "Corruption and Development: A Review of Issues", *Journal of Economic Literature*, 35/3 (September 1997): 1320–46

Besley, Timothy and John McLaren, "Taxes and Bribery: The Role of Wage Incentives", *Economic Journal*, 103/416 (January 1993): 119–41

Bliss, Christopher and Rafael di Tella, "Does Competition Kill Corruption?", *Journal of Political Economy*, 105/5 (October 1997): 1001–23

Elliott, Kimberly Ann (editor), *Corruption and the Global Economy*, Washington, DC: Institute for International Economics, 1996

Klitgaard, Robert, *Controlling Corruption*, Berkeley: University of California Press, 1988

Rose-Ackerman, Susan, *Corruption: A Study in Political Economy*, New York and London: Academic Press, 1978

Rose-Ackerman, Susan, *Corruption and Government: Causes, Consequences, and Reform*, Cambridge and New York: Cambridge University Press, 1999

Shleifer, Andrei and Robert Vishny, "Corruption", *Quarterly Journal of Economics*, 108/3 (August 1993): 599–617

Tirole, Jean, "A Theory of Collective Reputations (with Applications to the Persistence of Corruption and to Firm Quality)", *Review of Economic Studies*, 63/1 (January 1996): 1–22

ROSE-ACKERMAN (1978) is a classic reference in the economics literature of corruption. The book represents the first systematic attempt to combine insights of political science with economic tools of analysis in studying the causes and consequences of corruption. Well written and with a crisp style of exposition, it remains essential reading for all major issues related to this topic. The book has two parts, which focus separately on high-level corruption by legislature and low-level corruption by bureaucratic administration. A unifying conclusion from these analyses is twofold. Firstly, corruption is never more than a second-best solution to the incentive problems within a public office. This may be due to inefficiencies resulting from secrecy of illegal payments, or because a supposedly benign form of corruption (for example "speed money") is potent at spreading throughout the governance structure and erodes the entire fabric of the government. Alternatively, it is the distributional considerations of public goods provision that command non-tolerance of corrupt practices: a public service is designed to reach the most needy rather than those who could pay for it. Secondly, in order to limit the extent of corruption it is necessary to decrease the scope for corruption by reducing officials' discretion and/or by lowering payoff from being corrupt. ROSE-ACKERMAN (1999) is an updated and extended analysis along the same lines. The analysis of conflict between self interest and public interest is enhanced by balanced and sophisticated discussion of reform strategies and their potential for success in developing and post-socialist countries. A strong emphasis is laid upon the interplay between economics and politics of corruption and the special role of international donors in facilitating public sector reform.

KLITGAARD is a useful study of the experience of reforms to combat endemic corruption in developing countries. Written in a lively and engaging style, the book provides an account of practical issues that the policy-makers face in changing both perceptions of corruptibility of public officials and attitudes towards acceptability of public office abuse. The case studies include instances of corruption (in the form of bribery, extortion, speed money, kickbacks, or fraud) in tax administration, police, customs offices, and procurement. Although the practical usefulness of these experiences to policy-makers in countries with dissimilar cultural, economic, and political environment may be limited, the value of the contribution by Klitgaard in documenting the details of design, implementation, and outcomes of specific anti-corruption measures in specific countries cannot be underestimated. For example, a part of the success of anti-corruption reform in the Philippines was a systematic attempt by the reformers to change the ethical climate of acceptability of corruption. This provides an invaluable insight for the policy debate on anti-corruption strategies in countries with historically high levels of corruption. It is also noteworthy that this classic reading gave rise to the most widely accepted definition of corruption as "abuse of public office for private gain".

The volume edited by ELLIOTT reflects the growing international determination to combat corruption and gives an overview of the most recent international initiatives in this area as put forward in recent years by individual countries and international non-governmental organizations. As the contributors to this volume take a global perspective on the problem of corruption, the impact of corruption on economic development, institutions, and economic performance in terms of trade, investment, and growth is extensively evaluated. A contributed empirical study suggests that there is a negative correlation between corruption indices and indicators of investment and economic growth. A particular strength of the volume is its discussion of "influence peddling" activities that encompass important non-bribery forms of corruption.

BARDHAN is a condensed overview of the issues involved in evaluating causes, costs, and consequences of corruption. The overview is particularly useful for up-to-date discussion summaries of various facets of corruption: efficiency costs of corruption, links to economic growth as well as rent-seeking, critical evaluation of benign forms of bribery, and policy issues. It also contains a highly accessible discussion of theoretical models of corruption that try to explain the differential incidence and the persistence of corruption throughout the world.

Most of the analysis of incentives to become corrupt is undertaken in an agency setting and SHLEIFER & VISHNY provide a simple model of this kind. The principal (the benevolent government) delegates a task (administration of a particular regulation) to an agent (a bureaucrat) whose actions are not observed (specifically, he has the discretion over the provision of a public good). The simplicity of the model and the focus on consequences of corruption for resource allocation delivers a strong result that weak institutions (or weak governments) are conducive to corruption, and thus may explain its persistence. However, the assumption that the power of the bureaucrat to extract bribes is exogenous to the model does not allow predicting how alternative institutional structures affect this result.

The study of corruption in tax administration by BESLEY & McLAREN is another useful contribution to an understanding of incentives for bribery, public officials' remuneration, and distributive aspects of the government. As their motivation, Besley & McLarren make extensive links to the documented evidence of malfeasance in tax collection in some developing countries, and derive conclusions about effectiveness of three different wage regimes for tax collectors in the presence of widespread corruption.

A suggestion from some earlier research (for example, in Rose-Ackerman) that one route to eliminate corruption, or limit its extent, may be to open a corrupt market to competitive pressures is examined by BLISS & DI TELLA. In this model, the bureaucrat demands a bribe from a firm that either pays or exits in a free market equilibrium. Although the analysis does not lead to unambiguous conclusions regarding the effect of the considered parameters of competition (transport costs, overhead costs, and uncertainty of cost distribution) on the corruption level, it is an important first step in formal modelling of the relationship between corruption and competition that invites further lines of inquiry.

A very interesting study of persistence of corruption is found in TIROLE who suggests that unobservable behaviour of past generations may contribute to lack of trust for younger generations. In his model, a collective reputation for honesty is likely to keep corruption levels low (in the absence of economy-wide structural changes). However, bad collective reputation is difficult to eradicate when information transmission between economic agents is limited or absent, and an economy with a historically high level of corruption may be permanently locked in the suboptimal equilibrium.

An important recent work by BANERJEE identifies underlying factors that make government bureaucracies prone to corruption. He suggests that the mere function of the government, namely equitable allocation of a scarce resource (or a public good), together with the conflict of interest between a benevolent government and a self-interested public official gives rise to corruption and red tape. This explanation of corruption may be of particular relevance for understanding endemic corruption in less-developed countries, because the problems created by market failures and asymmetry of information are likely to be exacerbated by poverty and scarcity of resources.

ACEMOGLU & VERDIER provide a general equilibrium framework for analysing the effect corruption may have on growth, property rights enforcement, investment, and the allocation of talent within an economy. In this model, misallocation of talent arises because possibilities of bribes attract economic agents to take up jobs in the public sector even when their comparative advantage may lie in private sector activities. The common argument for reducing corruption by means of higher wages in the public sector is given a new perspective by Acemoglu & Verdier, because (under certain conditions) higher wages may lead to increased investment due to better enforcement of property rights. An increased expected return to entrepreneurship also makes it attractive for more agents to choose private-sector jobs.

Svetlana Andrianova

Cost functions

Diewert, W. Erwin, "Applications of Duality Theory" in *Frontiers of Quantitative Economics*, edited by Michael Intriligator and David Kendrick, Amsterdam: North Holland, 1971

Diewert, W. Erwin, "An Application of the Shephard Duality Theorem: A Generalized Leontief Production Function", *Journal of Political Economy*, 79 (1971): 481–507

Fuss, Melvyn, Daniel McFadden and Yair Mundlak, "A Survey of Functional Forms in the Economic Analysis of Production" in *Production Economics: A Dual Approach to Theory and Applications*, vol. 1, edited by Melvyn Fuss and Daniel McFadden, Amsterdam: North Holland, 1978

Shephard, Ronald, *Cost and Production Functions*, Princeton, New Jersey: Princeton University Press, 1953

Shephard, Ronald, *Theory of Cost and Production Functions*, Princeton, New Jersey: Princeton University Press, 1970

Heathfield, David and Soren Wibe, *An Introduction to Cost and Production Functions*, London: Macmillan, 1987

Jorgenson, Dale, "Econometric Methods for Modeling Producer Behavior" in *Handbook of Econometrics*, vol. 3, edited by Zvi Griliches and Michael Intriligator, Amsterdam: North Holland, 1983

McFadden, Daniel, "Cost, Revenue and Profit Functions" in *Production Economics: A Dual Approach to Theory and Applications*, vol. 1, edited by Melvyn Fuss and Daniel McFadden, Amsterdam: North Holland, 1978

Cost functions describe the minimum cost of producing a given output at a particular set of factor prices. Early work on cost functions focused on their theoretical properties, comparative statics, and their value as dual representations of technology. The later literature on empirical implementation has dealt with finding and applying appropriate functional forms that satisfy a range of desirable properties.

Several authors developed the notion of a cost function and its properties, but the authoritative theoretical work on the subject is SHEPHARD (1953), updated in SHEPHARD (1970). Shephard's exposition charts a rigorous and path-breaking course through the theory of cost functions. At least three critical developments in the theory of cost functions originate in this work. First, the dual relationship between production and cost functions, and the demonstration that all information regarding technology can be discerned from knowledge of the cost function. Second, the original derivation and presentation of what later came to be known as "Shephard's lemma" (the derivative property of the cost function), which shows that the demand function for a particular input is given by the partial derivative of the cost function with respect to the price of that input. Third, the notion of cost functions for "homothetic" production structures, which provide the considerable convenience of multiplicative separability between the input price and output components.

Shephard also provided a valuable examination of two important issues : (a) the aggregation of inputs and input prices in the theory of cost (and production) functions; and (b) the theory of cost functions for joint production of multiple outputs.

The material in Shephard's books predominantly comprised either new, original work, or extensions and syntheses of his own prior research on the theory of cost functions. A more general survey, with historical notes on the literature, is presented by DIEWERT (1974). His treatment of cost functions is couched within a comprehensive discussion of duality theory. An intuitive explanation of the dual relationship between cost and production functions is the essay's greatest strength. Diewert also discusses the properties of cost and input demand functions, with reference to the parametric restrictions that they imply on specific functional forms such as the generalized Leontief and the translog, and hence this article serves as a good bridge between the theory and the empirical implementation of cost functions.

Another classic synthesis of cost function theory is by McFADDEN, who combines terse mathematical proofs with illuminating diagrams in his presentation of material similar in coverage to that of Diewert (1974).

An important part of the literature on cost functions consists of the search for alternative functional forms that are *linear in parameters* (for ease in econometric implementation), *flexible* (possessing sufficient parameters to enable the linear form to be interpretable as a second-order approximation to an arbitrary function), *parsimonious* (to avoid problems related to collinearity and a lack of degrees of freedom), and that satisfy the theoretical properties of cost functions. Among the first efforts in this direction is DIEWERT (1971), where the issue is raised and the generalized Leontief cost function is introduced and shown to possess the requisite features. These considerations also apply to functional forms for production and profit functions besides cost functions, and FUSS, McFADDEN & MUNDLAK provide an overview. Particularly useful in this essay is a table that presents common linear-in-parameters functional forms and their characteristics as approximations of arbitrary functions.

A survey of the major empirical applications of the new generation of functional forms can be found in JORGENSON's article. It starts with a simple introduction to the major elements of the theory of cost functions, discusses parameterization and the restrictions implied by theory, and details the econometric methods and findings of the major applied models at the date of the survey. The article's discussion of empirical applications of cost functions in multiple output production is particularly helpful.

HEATHFIELD & WIBE provide a non-technical introduction to the theory and estimation of cost functions. The theory is condensed and presented with the aid of simple diagrams and basic calculus. Novice practitioners may find the individual chapters devoted to the major functional forms useful. The authors also discuss common problems encountered in empirical implementation, and potential solutions to such problems.

BHAVANI SHANKAR

Council of Ministers

Bainbridge, Timothy and Anthony Teasdale, *The Penguin Companion to European Union*, London and New York: Penguin, 1995

Chalmers, Damien, *European Union Law*, vol. 1, Aldershot, Hampshire: Ashgate Dartmouth, 1998

Craig, Paul and Gráinne De Búrca, *EU Law: Text, Cases, and Materials*, 2nd edition, Oxford: Clarendon Press, and New York: Oxford University Press, 1998

Dinan, Desmond, *Ever Closer Union? An Introduction to the European Community*, Basingstoke: Macmillan, and Boulder, Colorado: Rienner, 1994

Ellis, Evelyn and Takis Tridimas, *Public Law of the European Community: Texts, Materials and Commentary*, London: Sweet and Maxwell, 1995

Evans, Andrew, *A Textbook on European Union Law*, Oxford: Hart, 1998

Hanlon, James, *European Community Law*, London: Sweet and Maxwell, 1998

Nugent, Neill, *The Government and Politics of the European Union*, 3rd edition, Basingstoke: Macmillan, and Durham, North Carolina: Duke University Press, 1994

The Council of Ministers of the European Union (EU), as one of the main EU institutions within the European Union, has been analysed by numerous authors in a vast number of publications dealing with the legal and political dimension of the Union. BAINBRIDGE & TEASDALE provide one of the classic presentations of the Council. The authors refer to the Council as the principal decision-making body within the EU with both executive and legislative powers. In an inspired insight into the method of functioning and time-schedule of meetings the authors attempt the first analysis of the work of the Council from within, putting particular emphasis on the secrecy still surrounding the work of this clearly significant institution of the EU.

This point is taken on by DINAN, who draws the contrast between the work of the Council, which has always been conducted in some degree of secrecy, and the work of the European Council (the institution comprising of all EU heads of state or government) whose deliberations were disclosed to the public. The author supports the view that pressure from the public and other institutions for transparency in the decision-making process appalled the Committee of Permanent Representatives (Coreper), the council secretariat and the ministers. Although, after the recent transparency policy of the Council, this argument is no longer valid, what is still applicable is the use of transparency and majority voting as reflections of the democratic deficit problem within the Council, which weakens the already tenuous ties between national governments and the EU.

In fact, as CHALMERS point out, the Council of Ministers is traditionally viewed as the representor of national interests, perhaps the only legitimate one within the EU. The author refers to the Luxembourg Accords, as amended by the Ioannina Compromise, which he estimates as being based in the reassertion of a culture that suggests that there will still be resort to informal instruments where the qualified majority vote is not thought to protect national interests adequately. The amendments to this process resulting from the Amsterdam Treaty is also briefly clarified, albeit in a rather vague and concise manner. The analysis of this process and of the role of the Council in the legislative process in general seems much more detailed and, therefore, easier to comprehend in ELLIS & TRIDIMAS, whose work benefits from their reference to materials and texts dealing with the particular issues of each step of changes separately.

HANLON analyses the composition of the Council giving particular emphasis to its fluidity based on the fact that its members change according to the issues to be discussed in each particular session. The author presents the number of votes in the disposition of each country based on the qualified-majority scheme and addresses the concern of smaller countries that this may lead to domination by the four big countries.

The issue of qualified majority is addressed by EVANS, who notes that this scheme does not guarantee strict mathematical proportionality. However, it does secure a greater degree of proportionality between voting strength and population size than would result from rigid adherence to the principle of sovereign equality of states. At the same time, the minimum number of votes introduced by the Treaties allows for the protection of smaller states against domination. The presentation of the Council by the author benefits from the author's reference to the relationship between the Council and third states within the framework of the common foreign and security policy.

CRAIG & DE BÚRCA refer to the relationship between the Council and the Commission. The authors trace the intent of the signatories at the time of the passing of the original Treaty, who envisaged that the Council would be an aid and collaborator of the Commission. In fact, the authors suggest that Treaty signatories clearly hoped that, with time, the role of the Commission as a representor of the Union interest would become far more important in comparison with the role of the Council, as national interests would subside before the common good of all member states. The authors point out that, although it would be wrong to consider that the Council and the Commission are in constant conflict with each other, it would be equally wrong to assume that the two institutions are in perfect harmony. There is a real clash between the federal, pro-integration position of the Commission and the more cautious inter-governmental perspective of the Council, which seems to be intensified by the additional powers awarded to the European Parliament by the Single European Act and the recent Inter-Governmental Conference.

Last but not least, an excellent critique of the structure and functioning of the Council is provided by NUGENT, who refers to the general recognition that these two aspects of the institution in question are unsatisfactory in a number of respects. In particular, the Council's power is judged as too dispersed, there is insufficient cohesion between, or sometimes even within, the sectoral Councils, and decision-making process are still often too cumbersome and slow. These serious problems can only be completely erased by major structural alterations, such as the introduction of a new super-council favoured by some authors. However, even though such major changes seem unlikely, the Council has still undergone less obvious but equally important changes, ranging from the increased use of majority voting to the enhancement of the role of the presidency and the increased co-operation that occurs between presidencies, of which the development of rolling policy programmes is equally important.

HELEN XANTHAKI

See also European Community and European Union, development of

Counselling children

Bateson, Gregory, *Steps to an Ecology of Mind: Collected Essays in Anthropology, Psychiatry, Evolution and Epistemology*, San Francisco: Chandler, and London: Intertext, 1972

Bettelheim, Bruno, *The Uses of Enchantment: The Meaning and Importance of Fairy Tales*, New York: Knopf, and London: Thames and Hudson, 1976

Cattanach, Ann, *Children's Stories in Play Therapy*, London: Kingsley, 1997

Cowie, Helen and Andrea Pecherek, *Counselling: Approaches and Issues in Education*, London: David Fulton, 1994

Dryden, Windy, *Rational-Emotive Counselling in Action*, London and Newbury Park, California: Sage, 1990

Freud, Anna, *The Ego and the Mechanisms of Defence*, New York: International Universities Press, 1966 (*The Writings of Anna Freud*, vol. 2; German edition 1936)

Guggenbhul, A., "Tales and Fiction", *School Psychology International*, 12 (1991): 7–16

Mental Health Foundation, *Mental Illness: The Fundamental Facts*, London: Mental Health Foundation, 1993

Rutter, M., "Developmental Catch-up, and Deficit Following Adoption after Severe Global Early Privation", *Journal of Child Psychology and Psychiatry*, 39/4 (1998): 465–76

Sharp, Sonia and Helen Cowie, *Counselling and Supporting Children in Distress*, London: Sage, 1998

White, Michael and David Epston, *Narrative Means to Therapeutic Ends*, New York and London: Norton, 1990

Wilson, P., *Mental Health in Your School: A Guide for Teachers and Others Working in Schools*, London: Kingsley, 1996

Winslade, John and Gerald Monk, *Narrative Counseling in Schools: Powerful and Brief*, Thousand Oaks, California: Corwin Press, and London: Sage, 1999

The majority of children and young people cope reasonably well with the emotional setbacks that they encounter in their lives, such as quarrels with friends or in the family, not always getting their own way, losing face in front of peers. They may be sad, angry, or disappointed, but they are not overwhelmed by such everyday events. In fact, as WILSON (p.19) suggests, children are able to learn from such experiences to develop strategies of resilience and coping.

However, it is estimated that two million children in the UK have some form of mental health problem, including eating disorders, anxiety, and depression. There is a rising level of suicide, and emotional and conduct disorders are found in ten per cent of children and 20 per cent of adolescents. In a primary school with about 400 children on roll in an inner-city area, about eight children will be seriously depressed and twice that number will be significantly distressed. Other children will have problems such as disruptive behaviour and learning difficulties (MENTAL HEALTH FOUNDATION).

Furthermore, there are events or experiences that can throw the young person's life into turmoil. Being bullied over a long period of time, experiencing emotional, physical or sexual abuse, being neglected, suffering lengthy or permanent loss and separation from loved ones, incurring illness, or having an accident, lie at this end of the spectrum. As the statistics tell us, a substantial minority of children and adolescents are unable to cope, and can be overwhelmed by these kinds of events or experiences. Children and adolescents in these circumstances would benefit from some form of counselling intervention.

Anna FREUD pioneered child analysis, and applied psychoanalytic principles to the treatment of children with mental health difficulties. She devoted her life and work to applying the conceptual framework developed by her father, Sigmund Freud, to the analysis of children, and she also studied the emotional impact on young children of separation from parents, and of substitute caregiving. Her starting point was a focus on the child's ego and its defence mechanisms, balanced by her systematic observations of children outside the analytic setting.

Later therapists in the psychodynamic tradition worked with the symbolic images of fantasy to help children to distance themselves from the fears and anxieties that formed an inevitable part of their lives. BETTELHEIM claimed that the underlying themes of fairy stories and folktales had an important therapeutic function in helping the child to explore disturbing experiences from the inner world, and to achieve some form of resolution of emotional conflicts. GUGGENBHUL encouraged children to link thoughts about common problems to their own fantasies by creating new episodes, or enacting new scenes in role-play. Through the ensuing discussion, the children were able to move from the imaginary to the real, and could apply the lessons learned from fiction to their own lives.

Play therapists (for example, CATTANACH) worked on the assumption that, by processing disturbing experiences in conversation and joint play, children are helped to regulate their emotions. The relationship between therapist and child gives meaning to the stories, through which the child can negotiate a shared interpretation of events. Play is a space in which the child can explore meanings, even difficult ones. The child can reconstruct fearful scenarios in narrative form in such a way that they can be reframed and be made less fearful.

WHITE & EPSTON have developed an approach to therapy using narrative that is derived from the writings of BATESON, who argued that people can redefine their relationships by expanding their participant roles through a "restorying" process. The stories, they argue, express selected aspects of their lived experience. But they also contain constraints that prevent them from noticing new information. This approach is particularly suitable for children. WINSLADE & MONK practise narrative counselling in school settings. They argue that many of the dominant stories that govern children's lives were generated in early experiences. Often these stories create problems because the children are defined by others as "stupid", "a victim", or "bad". They are then likely to live their lives according to the structure of a problem story laid out for them leaving them with few options about how to live with a sense of value and pride.

The narrative counsellor engages in externalizing conversation, and so separates the problem from the child, and gives the problem a name. The effect of this shift is that children begin to experience the problem as being external to them. This opens up space for a perspective where blame and shame become less significant. For example, the problem might be named 'Trouble' and the child encouraged to describe the effects that Trouble has on him. The counsellor asks questions that map the influence of the problem, gauge the relative strength of the child and the problem, and identify the influence of the child on the problem. The counsellor also takes note of any experience, however small, that stands apart from the problem story. With these fragments, a new story is woven. The child is also consulted on whether it is appropriate to continue to live by the problem story or whether it is time to move on.

Cognitive and behavioural approaches (DRYDEN) have also been found to be effective in the treatment of depression, anxieties and fears, and in the management of anger and aggression. (For a review, see COWIE & PECHEREK.) Methods include social skills training, the modelling of different behaviours, and the development of more positive cognitions about self in relation to others.

RUTTER argues that the promotion of resilience lies in the child's capacity to face up to problems rather than avoid them. We must not forget the resources that many children have (see SHARP & COWIE). Some children are better able to cope than others, but research and clinical practice indicate that the majority of children come through a crisis. Factors of resilience include the child's temperament, the cohesiveness of the family, and the network of supportive agencies in the community.

HELEN COWIE

See also Childhood

Counselling psychology

Barkham, Michael, "Quantitative Research on Psychotherapeutic Interventions" in *Handbook of Counselling Psychology*, edited by Ray Woolfe and Windy Dryden, 1996

Carroll, Michael, *Workplace Counselling: A Systematic Approach to Employee Care*, London: Sage, 1996

Clarkson, Petrúska and Michael Pokorny, *Handbook of Psychotherapy*, London and New York: Routledge, 1994

Clarkson, Petrúska, *The Therapeutic Relationship: In Psychoanalysis, Counselling Psychology, and Psychotherapy*, London: Whurr, 1995

Clarkson, Petrúska, *Counselling Psychology: Integrating Theory, Research, and Supervised Practice*, London: Routledge, 1998

Cowie, Helen and Annemarie Salm, "Doing Research in Counselling Psychology" in *Handbook of Psychotherapy*, edited by Petrúska Clarkson and Michael Pokorny, 1994

Cowie, Helen, "Bystanding or Standing By: Gender Issues in Coping with Bullying", *Aggressive Behavior*, 26/1 (2000): 85–97

Dryden, Windy (editor), *Handbook of Individual Therapy*, London and Thousand Oaks, California: Sage, 1996

Elton Wilson, Jenifer, *Time-Conscious Psychological Therapy*, London and New York: Routledge, 1996

McLeod, John, *Doing Counselling Research*, London and Thousand Oaks, California: Sage, 1994

McLeod, John, *An Introduction to Counselling*, 2nd edition, Buckingham: Open University Press, 1998

Nelson-Jones, Richard, *Practical Counselling and Helping Skills: Text and Exercises for the Lifeskills Counselling Model*, 4th edition, London: Cassell, 1997

Palmer, Stephen, Sheila Dainow and Pat Milner, *Counselling: The BAC Counselling Reader*, London: Sage, 1996

Rogers, Carl R., *Counseling and Psychotherapy: Newer Concepts in Practice*, Boston: Houghton Mifflin, 1942

Shapiro, D.A., Michael Barkham, G.E. Hardy and L.A. Morrison, "The Second Sheffield Psychotherapy Project: Rationale, Design and Preliminary Outcome Data", *British Journal of Medical Psychology*, 63 (1990): 97–108

Shapiro, D.A., Michael Barkham, G.E. Hardy, L.A. Morrison, S. Reynolds, M. Startup and H. Harper, "University of Sheffield Psychotherapy Research Program: Medical Research Council / Economic and Social Research Council Social and Applied Psychology Unit" in *Psychotherapy Research: An International Review of Programmatic Studies*, edited by Larry E. Beutler and Marjorie Crago, Washington, DC: American Psychological Association, 1991

Sharp, Sonia and Helen Cowie, *Counselling and Supporting Children in Distress*, London: Sage, 1998

Woolfe, Ray and Windy Dryden, *Handbook of Counselling Psychology*, London and Thousand Oaks, California: Sage, 1996

Counselling psychology, a relatively new discipline in the UK, has been defined as "the application of psychological knowledge to the practice of counselling" (WOOLFE & DRYDEN). It has grown out of, and in parallel with, the rapid growth of counselling and psychotherapy as professions in the UK since the 1980s.

Counselling psychology was established as a discipline in the 1940s in the US, but it was not until 1982 that the British Psychological Society (BPS) established a counselling psychology section; it became a "special group" in 1989. In 1992 the BPS established the diploma in counselling psychology, which gave psychologists whose professional training and experience lay in the field of counselling a route to chartered status. In 1994, a division of counselling psychology was established. Psychologists who had achieved the diploma (or a statement of equivalence) were now entitled to describe themselves as chartered counselling psychologists, and there were over 600 in the UK in 1999. The BPS also established a scheme for recognizing courses of training. Training in counselling psychology can take place *part time* by the independent route to the BPS diploma in counselling psychology under the guidance of a training co-ordinator, or *full-time* at a university-based course accredited by the BPS. The new generation has a clear path from graduation in psychology that confers the "graduate basis for registration", through the minimum of three years of postgraduate training in counselling psychology to chartered counselling psychologist status.

The origins of counselling lie in psychology, with a long-standing emphasis on the relationship between the helping professional and the client – a relationship that is characterized by qualities of empathy, acceptance, and congruence – the qualities that were identified and disseminated by ROGERS in the 1940s. These qualities can be operationalized by calling them "interpersonal skills", but a deeper understanding comes from considering the nature of the psychological processes that occur in the client-counsellor relationship. Counselling psychologists themselves do not engage in one therapeutic model of practice but rather employ a whole range of methods – including humanistic, psychodynamic, cognitive-behavioural, transpersonal, existentialist, and integrative. Not surprisingly, there are dialogues and debates within the discipline about the appropriateness of different orientations.

One thread that holds these different approaches together is a belief in the relationship, an emphasis on the experience of the client, a concern to understand the perspective of the client, and a willingness to further the quality of life or the personal development of that client. By sharing the client's inner world, the counsellor, the counselling psychologist, and the psychotherapist, whatever his or her theoretical orientation, forms a strong and intimate relationship based on trust (CLARKSON 1995).

Recent textbooks on *counselling* (McLEOD (1998); McLEOD (1994); NELSON-JONES; PALMER, DAINOW & MILNER), *psychotherapy* (CLARKSON & POKORNY; DRYDEN), and *counselling psychology* (CLARKSON (1998); Woolfe & Dryden) have also emerged to chart history and outline debates in theory, practice, and research.

Counselling psychologists have a distinctive role to play in refuting unjust and inaccurate criticisms, in documenting the fundamentally psychological quality of the help that practitioners have to offer (ELTON WILSON), and in evaluating outcomes and processes through well-documented evidence (COWIE & SALM). In a useful overview of psychotherapy research, BARKHAM describes three overlapping "generations" of psychological research in the field, looking in turn at outcome research, at the impact of therapist orientation, and at the nature of the therapeutic relationship.

The counselling psychologist as scientist-practitioner can address the need to research the inside perspective of both client and therapist in dialogue one with the other and in reflection on the changes, if any, which take place (SHAPIRO *et al.* 1990, 1991). There is also a critical role for the counselling psychologist as many practitioners find themselves making a shift from the boundaries of the relationship established in the consulting room to the everyday world of the workplace (CARROLL) and the school (SHARP & COWIE). Counselling psychology can also play a significant role in counteracting interpersonal problems, such as bullying or social exclusion in school and workplace. Counselling psychologists have a part to play in working with organisations and in collaboration with other practitioners and researchers to develop systems that facilitate adults and young people as sources of practical help and emotional support towards one another (COWIE).

The counselling psychologist's distinctive role can be summarized as follows:
(a) Counselling psychologists are in a position to implement well-designed research studies of counselling and psychotherapy outcomes and processes and the therapeutic relationship by making good use of innovative research methods.
(b) Counselling psychologists integrate psychological knowledge with counselling practice in a wide range of social situations, for example in the workplace or in the school, where there is a need to adapt existing methods and work creatively in partnership with other professionals.
(c) Counselling psychologists stimulate healthy debate and controversy that challenges orthodoxies, fixed beliefs, and rigid boundaries in a changing field.

HELEN COWIE

See also Counselling children, Rational emotive behaviour therapy

Counterculture

Beal, Becky, "Disqualifying the Official: An Exploration of Social Resistance through the Subculture of Skateboarding", *Sociology of Sport Journal*, 12/3 (1995): 252–67

Berger, Peter L. and Richard J. Neuhaus, *Movement and Revolution*, New York: Doubleday, 1970

Cagle, Van M., *Reconstructing Pop/Subculture: Art, Rock, and Andy Warhol*, Thousand Oaks, California and London: Sage, 1995

Campbell, Colin, *The Romantic Ethic and the Spirit of Modern Consumerism*, Oxford and New York: Blackwell, 1987

Clarke, John *et al.*, "Subcultures, Cultures and Class" in *Resistance through Rituals: Youth Subcultures in Post-War Britain*, edited by Stuart Hall and Tony Jefferson, London: Hutchinson, 1976

Fox, Kathryn Joan, "Real Punks and Pretenders: The Social Organisation of a Counterculture", *Journal of Contemporary Ethnography*, 16/3 (1987): 344–70

Gottschalk, Simon, "Uncomfortably Numb: Countercultural Impulses in the Postmodern Era", *Symbolic Interaction*, 16/4 (1993): 351–78

Martin, Bernice, *A Sociology of Contemporary Cultural Change*, Oxford: Blackwell, and New York: St Martin's Press, 1981

Roszak, Theodore, *The Making of a Counter Culture: Reflections on the Technocratic Society and Its Youthful Opposition*, New York: Doubleday, 1969; London: Faber, 1970

Seago, Alex, *Burning the Box of Beautiful Things: The Development of a Postmodern Sensibility*, Oxford: Clarendon Press, and New York: Oxford University Press, 1995

Willis, Paul E., *Profane Culture*, London and Boston: Routledge and Kegan Paul, 1978

The works by BERGER & NEUHAUS, and ROSZAK are still worth consulting as they are among the most sociologically perceptive of those that first tried to explain the various forms of social protest and gestures of disaffection by sections of Western middle-class youth in the 1960s. Both raise the issue of opposition between an increasingly bureaucratic or rationalist society and the humanistic ethos of a particular section of youth socialized into modern, permissive values. A Marxist analysis of the student and hippie counterculture is provided by CLARKE *et al.* in which the ideological and generational conflict between traditional bourgeois puritanism and the new hedonism is seen to have its basis in the post World War II shift from producer-based to consumer-based capitalism.

CAMPBELL's scholarly and detailed investigation suggests that such a conflict is not new, having been apparent throughout the development of modern capitalism since the 18th century. His thesis, Weberian in its accordance of causality to cultural belief systems, is that modern consumerism has its origin in a particular strain of Protestantism that developed into sentimentalism and romanticism. The 1960s counterculturalists can therefore be understood as inheritors of such a romantic ethic, and a relatively contemporary manifestation of bohemianism that periodically emerges to challenge a traditional puritan morality.

Another work that links the expressive ethic of the 1960s counterculture to the cultural values of romanticism is that by MARTIN. It has an additional dimension in drawing upon Douglas's classificatory schema of group and grid to theorize shifts in the collective composition of working-class youth subcultures. Focusing on structural and cultural change since the 1950s, Martin demonstrates how the countercultural ethos of "anti-structure" began to seep into and erode the traditional, ritualistic patterns of working-class life. Such an analysis informs her view of the relatively loose-knit "mod" subculture as a temporal and structural midpoint between the tightly bounded, territorial group identity of the "teddy boys" and the fully-fledged "liminality" of the "hippie" counterculture.

It is a matter of some regret that there are very few first-hand ethnographic studies of countercultures. Although each of the three mentioned below reflects the very specific social and academic context of its time, a sequential reading helps to draw out a number of common conceptual concerns. WILLIS, a member of the Centre for Contemporary Cultural Studies (CCCS) at the University of Birmingham, began his fieldwork on the "hippie" counterculture and "biker" subculture at the end of the 1960s. His portrayal of two rebellious groups from opposite ends of the class spectrum is now a sociological classic. Although his commitment to an ethnographic method makes him the prime representative of the "culturalist" paradigm in British cultural studies, there remains a suspicion that his Marxist framework and use of homological analysis has structurally overdetermined his observations and diverted him from the internal complexities of the groups and the cultural correspondences that may have existed between them.

FOX, by way of contrast, explicitly highlights the social differentiation within an anti-establishment countercultural movement, claiming to have found differing levels of commitment and authenticity within a group of American punks in the 1980s. She can, however, be accused of constructing an objective model of stratification from an ossification of the subjective perceptions of only certain members. By focusing on her respondents' attitudes towards ephemerality and image, Fox's study has the additional interest of investigating themes that are now commonly regarded as indicators of the postmodern. The whole article could, in fact, be reinterpreted and reassessed as a flawed empirical examination of postmodern countercultural characteristics.

GOTTSCHALK's agenda is the investigation of postmodern characteristics. The fragmented identities of his contemporary group of countercultural "Freaks" and their cynicism towards the metanarratives of politics and science, can, he suggests, be interpreted as aspects of a developing postmodern self. Questions can, however, be raised concerning the benchmark against which such social and cultural changes are measured. If, as other studies would seem to suggest, cultural individualism and liminality are core components of middle-class bohemian lifestyles, then it is likely that previous generations of counterculturalists would also have been found to express a fragmented and diffuse self-identity.

A different strand of research in this field has been to trace the influence of artistic movements and institutions upon the wider popular culture of the time. SEAGO uses archive material and interviews to show how the postmodern concern with image and consumerism had its genesis in a 1951–63 Royal College of Art subculture that embraced both "cool" modernist abstraction and "pop", and provided the artistic inspiration for elements that fed into the 1960s counterculture and 1970s punk. Such a detailed empirical history of discontinuities and complexities in a peculiarly British context provides a useful correction to much of the rather abstract sociological theorizing that sees postmodernism as simply a reaction to an exhausted and elitist modernism.

Relocating Hebdige's work (Subculture, the Meaning of Style, 1979) on stylistic subversion and resistance to an American context, CAGLE examines how the ideas of Andy Warhol and the "Factory" were to have a profound impact upon the "glitter" and "punk rock" subcultures. Although this is perhaps the most comprehensive account of glitter and its lineage so far attempted in either sociology or cultural studies, aspects of the analysis sometimes fail to convince. The comparison made between the "individualized" acts of bricolage engaged in by the "Factory" personnel and the "collective" actions of subcultures such as the "mods", fails to account for the way in which CCCS subcultural theory has produced an over-homogenized version of pre-"punk" youth styles. Given also the varied class backgrounds of the assorted artists and movement intellectuals associated with the "Factory", it seems more plausible to assert the explanatory role of cultural values than to hold on to a materialist account (subcultures as a response to economic contradictions) as the author wishes to do here.

BEAL defines skateboarding as a subculture and employs a hegemonic framework. Yet the anticompetitive and anticommercial practices of her respondents, along with their efforts to escape the bureaucratic and rationalized patterns of participation established by the sport's governing body, can also be classed as countercultural strategies, and this is an interesting application of the concept to the study of sport.

DAVID LEE MUGGLETON

See also Subculture

Counterfactual thinking

Gleicher, Faith *et al.*, "The Role of Counterfactual Thinking in Judgments of Affect", *Personality and Social Psychology Bulletin*, 16/2 (1990): 284–95
Kahneman, Daniel and Amos Tversky, "The Simulation Heuristic" in *Judgment under Uncertainty: Heuristics and Biases*, edited by Daniel Kahneman, Paul Slovic and Amos Tversky, Cambridge and New York: Cambridge University Press, 1982
Kahneman, Daniel and Dale T. Miller, "Norm Theory: Comparing Reality to Its Alternatives", *Psychological Review*, 93/2 (1986): 136–53
Kahneman, Daniel and Carol A. Varey, "Propensities and Counterfactuals: The Loser That Almost Won", *Journal of Personality and Social Psychology*, 59/6 (1990): 1101–10

Markman, Keith D., Igor Gavanski, Steven J. Sherman and Matthew N. McMullen, "The Mental Simulation of Better and Worse Possible Worlds", *Journal of Experimental Social Psychology*, 29/1 (1993): 87–109

Miller, Dale T., William Turnbull and Cathy McFarland, "Counterfactual Thinking and Social Perception: Thinking about What Might have Been", *Advances in Experimental Social Psychology*, 23 (1990): 305–31

Roese, Neal J., "The Functional Basis of Counterfactual Thinking", *Journal of Personality and Social Psychology*, 66/5 (1994): 805–18

Roese, Neal J. and James M. Olson (editors), *What Might have Been: The Social Psychology of Counterfactual Thinking*, Mahwah, New Jersey: Erlbaum, 1995

Roese, Neal J. and James M. Olson, "Counterfactual Thinking: The Intersection of Affect and Function", *Advances in Experimental Social Psychology*, 29 (1997): 1–59

Wells, Gary L. and Igor Gavanski, "Mental Simulation of Causality", *Journal of Personality and Social Psychology*, 56/2 (1989): 161–69

Psychological research into counterfactual thinking developed in response to a short but highly influential chapter by KAHNEMAN & TVERSKY concerning the "simulation heuristic". Their central idea was that people often estimate an event's probability on the basis of how readily it can be simulated mentally, but that this procedure does not always produce accurate results. In particular, an experienced outcome may seem unlikely because it is easy to imagine things having worked out otherwise. This imagining of alternatives to reality – what might have been as opposed to what is – is what psychologists mean by counterfactual thinking.

According to Kahneman & Tversky imagination follows a number of rules that determine the outcome of the simulation process. Their classic example involves two male travellers who take the same taxi to the airport but are delayed by heavy traffic and arrive 30 minutes after their respective flights' scheduled departure times. One traveller finds that his flight was actually delayed by 25 minutes and took off only 5 minutes ago whereas the other traveller discovers that his flight left on time. Almost everyone hearing this story believes that the first traveller feels more upset about missing the plane, despite the fact that he had the same prior expectations and experienced the same practical outcome as the second traveller. The difference arises, according to Kahneman & Tversky, because greater temporal proximity of the flight's departure makes it easier to imagine not having missed the plane, and retrospective disappointment arises as a consequence. Other kinds of perceived proximity also have similar effects, such as when a lottery ticket is only one number different from the winning one, or when school or academic work misses a higher grade by a single mark. KAHNEMAN & VAREY provide a more extended analysis of this kind of "close counterfactual", when something seems to have almost but not quite happened. Part of the attraction of the authors' analysis is that it identifies, demarcates, and provides a theoretical framework for a common, compelling, and consistent phenomenon previously neglected by researchers.

Kahneman & Tversky also suggest that psychological proximity is partly determined by *normality*, so that it is easier to imagine an unusual event being replaced by what usually happens (a "downhill change") than to imagine what usually happens being replaced by something unusual (an "uphill change"). Thus, a car accident occurring during a person's usual routine is perceived as less upsetting than one that happens when taking a diversion or after oversleeping. The unmistakable tendency in both cases is to think "if only I had done what I usually do", mentally undoing the unwanted outcome and thereby returning it to its "default" value. KAHNEMAN & MILLER extend this basic account in their proposal of "norm theory". In this difficult yet revealing paper they not only articulate the cognitive basis of retrospective norm generation but also propose additional rules governing the availability of counterfactual alternatives to reality. For example, they argue that imagination is more likely to substitute non-ideal events with ideal ones than vice versa, and that effects are more mutable (easier to undo mentally) than causes. Further, they develop the "emotional amplification" hypothesis, which states that "the affective response to an event is enhanced if its causes are abnormal" (p.145), thus explaining why negative events that happen as a consequence of breaks in routine seem more distressing. This hypothesis has been the focus of much of the subsequent research in this area.

GLEICHER *et al.* report experiments showing that emotional amplification occurs more strongly and consistently when an outcome is unpleasant rather than pleasant. For example, a financial loss suffered after changing one's investment is generally judged to be worse than a similar loss arising from an unchanged investment, but profits accruing from comparable contingencies are not so obviously evaluated in a different way from each other. The investigators' explanation is that people are motivated to pay more attention to unpleasant outcomes in order to avoid them in future, which leads to a greater tendency towards counterfactual thinking about failures. Their article provides a clear description of a reasonably representative vignette-based questionnaire study.

In addition to pioneering a new methodology for the investigation of on-line counterfactual thinking, MARKMAN *et al.* advance theory by proposing different functions for comparing what actually happened with a better or a worse possible alternative. Their specific argument is that upward comparisons are more likely when they might help people to prepare for similar events in future. In other words, we often take the opportunity to learn from our mistakes by considering how things could have been better had we acted differently, even if this makes us feel worse in the short term. On the other hand, if an outcome is uncontrollable and nonrepeatable we may be more inclined to make downward comparisons that serve a comforting function by reminding us that things could have been worse.

ROESE clarifies and develops this important analysis by pointing out that counterfactual thoughts can differ in structure as well as direction ("upward" versus "downward"). In particular, he contrasts additive counterfactuals, which insert extra imagined events, with subtractive counterfactuals, which delete something that actually happened from the simulation. Evidence is presented that upward additive counterfactuals serve preparatory functions best, because they help to generate positive intentions that facilitate subsequent avoidance of similar negative outcomes.

WELLS & GAVANSKI extend the application of counterfactual concepts into the area of causal judgement. In particular, they suggest that if mentally undoing an event leads to non-occurrence of the imagined outcome, then this event is perceived as causally influential. This account bears some resemblance to previous general models of the attribution process (for example Hilton & Slugoski's *Psychological Review* article on "Knowledge-Based Causal Attribution", 1986).

MILLER, TURNBULL & McFARLAND's and ROESE & OLSON's (1997) contributions to *Advances in Experimental Social Psychology* both provide valuable general reviews of psychological research into counterfactual thinking, and ROESE & OLSON's (1995) edited book contains a comprehensive collection of theoretical and empirical chapters written by many of the most active researchers in the field. As these last three readings show, the study of counterfactual thinking is being applied to an increasingly wide range of issues including prediction, causation, blame, emotion, and coping. Further progress will depend on integrating the developing conceptual understanding of the counterfactual process with established theory in related areas of social psychology and cognition-emotion research.

BRIAN PARKINSON

See also Attribution theory

Creative accounting

Breton G. and R.J. Taffler, "Creative Accounting and Investment Analyst Response", *Accounting and Business Research*, 25 (1995): 81–92

Griffiths, Ian, *Creative Accounting: How to Make Your Profits What You Want Them to be*, London: Sidgwick and Jackson, 1986

Naser, Kamal H.M., *Creative Financial Accounting: Its Nature and Use*, New York and London: Prentice Hall, 1993

Shah, A.K., "Creative Compliance in Financial Reporting", *Accounting, Organizations and Society*, 21 (1996): 23–39

Smith, Terry, *Accounting for Growth: Stripping the Camouflage from Company Accounts*, London: Century, 1992

Tweedie, D. and G. Whittington, "Financial Reporting: Current Problems and Their Implications for Systematic Reform", *Accounting and Business Research*, 21 (1990): 87–102

Watts, Ross L. and Jerold L. Zimmerman, *Positive Accounting Theory*, Englewood Cliffs, New Jersey: Prentice Hall, 1986

GRIFFITHS (1986) uses the term "creative accounting" to describe the techniques that managers use to manipulate the figures reported in company financial statements. Creative accounting is made possible by the flexibility and vagueness of accounting rules and of company law. Among the techniques of creative accounting described by Griffiths are those relating to income recognition, cost recognition, the use of pension funds, classification into extraordinary and exceptional items, use of taxation, and foreign currency translation. While some techniques of creative accounting are reasonably transparent, the use of others, such as off-balance-sheet financing, is difficult to detect.

Managers are seen as increasingly being required to tailor company results to meet the demands of the capital markets. Income smoothing techniques are used to produce a steady growth in profits demanded by investors, and earnings are manipulated to meet the expectations of analysts. In takeovers, creative accounting is used by both predator and target companies to flatter their results and financial positions.

SMITH suggests that much of the growth in reported company profits that occurred in the UK during the 1980s resulted from the use of accounting techniques rather than from genuine economic growth. He identifies, and describes, the main techniques that a company may use to flatter its results and financial position, and provides examples of each technique. The book also contains an "accounting health check", showing for each of over 200 major UK listed companies, whether the company uses one or more of 12 classes of creative accounting technique identified by the author. A company using five or more of these techniques is likely, according to Smith, to have poor relative share price performance.

TWEEDIE & WHITTINGTON describe, and attempt to identify the common characteristics of, a number of problems of financial reporting related to the use of creative accounting. They propose that the problems are of two main types: one having to do with issues of recognition and the other with measurement. Recognition problems relate either to determining the boundary of the reporting entity or to defining the elements of financial statements – assets, liabilities, equity, revenue, and expenses. On the other hand, measurement problems are concerned with issues of valuation or capital maintenance.

Possible methods for restricting the use of creative accounting are also discussed by Tweedie & Whittington. These include two alternative approaches that may be taken by accounting regulators. One, a fire-fighting approach, is to deal with each new problem as and when it is identified. Alternatively, accounting regulators may design accounting standards that deal the *deeper* accounting issues. Instead of relying solely on accounting standards, auditors and users of financial statements can be encouraged to act to constrain company managers to adopt the highest standards.

NASER defines creative accounting as

> (1) the process of manipulating accounting figures by taking advantage of the loopholes in accounting rules and the choices of measurement and disclosure practices in them to transform financial statements from what they should be, to what preparers would prefer to see reported, and (2) the process by which transactions are structured so as to produce the required accounting results rather than reporting transactions in a neutral and consistent way. [p. 59]

As well as describing the main techniques used in creative accounting, Naser discusses the factors that lead company managers to use such techniques. These include: (a) misinformation, signalling, and financial motives; (b) agency and political cost incentives; (c) poor management; (d) reducing uncertainty and risk; (e) weakness of current accounting concepts; and (f) pressure from large institutional investors.

WATTS & ZIMMERMAN set out to predict and explain the accounting choices made by companies rather than to deal specifically with issues of creative accounting. Accounting numbers may be incorporated into contracts in an attempt to align the interests of the contracting parties. Such contracts, however, may not be effective in aligning interests if company managers have discretion over the way in which the accounting numbers are constructed. Watts & Zimmerman, who assume that managers will generally be opportunistic in exercising discretion, look specifically to three areas in explaining accounting choice: compensation contracts, debt covenants, and political costs.

The incorporation of accounting numbers into managerial compensation contracts is seen in some cases to encourage managers to choose accounting policies that shift income from later into earlier periods. However, managers may wish to shift income into a later period where the contract specifies upper and lower profit limits within which compensation in related to profit. Second, loan agreements may include covenants based on accounting numbers. It is suggested that where a company is constrained by debt covenants it may choose accounting policies that ensure that breach of the covenant is avoided. Finally, it is assumed that a company acts to minimize political costs. As a consequence it is proposed that a large company, because of its greater visibility, is more likely that a small company to select accounting policies that reduce reported profits. Watts & Zimmerman review the empirical literature dealing with these propositions.

BRETON & TAFFLER identify two competing hypotheses relating to information processing by participants in capital markets. One, the *mechanistic* or *naive investor* hypothesis, suggests that market participants are fixated on accounting numbers and so do not make adjustments for the use by companies of creative accounting. The alternative, the *efficient market* hypothesis, is that only information relating to cash-flows is price sensitive. Breton & Taffler use a laboratory experiment to examine the extent to which investment analysts, seen as key participants in capital markets, make corrections for creative accounting in calculating accounting ratios. They find that, while more experienced analysts tend to make more corrections than less experienced ones, investment analysts generally make few corrections.

SHAH examines *creative compliance*, the manipulation of rules in order to turn them to the serve personal interests and avoid unwanted control, in accounting. Using complex convertible financial instruments as an example, he demonstrates how accounting and tax rules are circumvented in order to achieve a desired effect in a company's financial statements. A related concept, that of the *dialectic of creativity*, is illustrated by the example of legal and accounting professionals designing financial instruments to circumvent accounting rules in order to achieve desired accounting treatments, to be followed by accounting regulators formulating new rules, and then the cycle repeating itself.

PETER CASSON

Creativity

Henry, Jane (editor), *Creative Management*, London and Newbury Park, California: Sage, 1991

Hicks, Michael J., *Problem Solving in Business and Management: Hard, Soft and Creative Approaches*, London and New York: Chapman and Hall, 1991

Kirton, Michael (editor), *Adaptors and Innovators: Styles of Creativity and Problem-Solving*, London and New York: Routledge, 1989

Leonard, Dorothy and Susan Straus, "Putting Your Company's Whole Brain to Work", *Harvard Business Review*, 75/4 (July–August 1997): 110–21

Majaro, Simon, *The Creative Gap: Managing Ideas for Profit*, London: Longman, 1988

Morgan, Gareth, *Imaginization: The Art of Creative Management*, Newbury Park, California: Sage, 1993

Proctor, Tony, *The Essence of Management Creativity*, London and New York: Prentice Hall, 1995

Stacey, Ralph D., *Complexity and Creativity in Organizations*, San Francisco: Berrett Koehler, 1996

Vedin, Bengt-Arne, *Corporate Culture and Creativity Management*, Bromley, Kent: Chartwell Bratt, 1985

Most businesses now accept the need for creativity in organizations in order to generate the innovative outcomes needed to sustain competitive advantage. MORGAN presents a very readable set of ideas on managing creativity, which invites the reader to "develop new ways of thinking about organization and management" through a series of images and metaphors. His spider plant model of organizational design provides a particularly useful means of rethinking organizational structure. There are a number of other descriptions that use visual imaging to design powerful and often radical transformations. Morgan explains how organizations can become trapped in patterns of behaviour that merely reinforce the status quo. Although essentially an ideas book, later chapters explain how creative ideas can help practically, to rethink products or services or reorganize the ways in which we use time or space.

An older, but nevertheless valuable account is provided by VEDIN. The second part of this book focuses on nurturing and managing creativity, both in individuals and organizations, using media industries as a model. The author claims that, because the media are considered inherently creative, unlike many other business sectors, their cultures actively promote and reward creativity and centre on developing individual potential. Media industries are used as an example throughout, to illustrate how creativity underpins all aspects of the organization from recruitment of employees to the acceptance of failure.

HICKS provides a simple and essentially practical introduction to creative problem solving in organizations. Three approaches to problem solving and decision making are examined: creative, logical, and systemic. It is claimed that there is a place for creativity in each of the three. The author contends that the application of creativity to business is in the development of new products, processes or services, and in overcoming obstacles to desired goals and objectives. A number of blocks to creativity that frequently occur are suggested, together with some methods of dealing with these. Hicks stresses the importance of a culture that fosters creativity and insists that the starting point for a new focus on flexibility or creativity must be through modification or transformation of the existing organizational culture.

LEONARD & STRAUS present a US view of the role of creativity in organizations. This interesting but aspirational paper advocates the establishment of *creative abrasion* through recruitment of individuals with diverse thinking styles and different cognitive preferences. The authors suggest the use of two diagnostic instruments to measure employees' cognitive style and the formulation of teams comprising both left-brained (analytical, logical, and sequential) and right-brained (intuitive and non-linear) thinkers. Leaders also need to recognize their own thinking styles and to learn to appreciate and understand employees who may have differing cognitive preferences. Effective management of diversity can integrate the expertise of individuals and use abrasion between different ways of working to produce creative outputs. The incorporation of diverse cognitive styles should result in organizations with a variety of approaches to problem solving.

Different styles of thinking and problem solving are also discussed by KIRTON. He proposes two main types of personalities in organizations, based on their dominant cognitive style: *adaptors*, who accept and modify existing theories or viewpoints, and *innovators*, who reject accepted ideas and reconstruct problems in order to design new solutions. Organizations clearly need to adopt an innovative approach in certain circumstances in order to survive, but most organizations, particularly older established companies, also need to be adaptable to changing situations. Kirton takes a limited perspective and his definitions tend to be mutually exclusive, however he admits that people do not always behave according to their preferred style and that organizations need a mix of personalities and styles of behaviour.

In scientific studies, new efforts are being made to understand patterns of life in nature, based on theories of chaos and complexity. STACEY uses these theories to provide a framework for making sense of organizational systems. He examines creativity in relation to the complexity and uncertainty of today's business climate and suggests that the repression of anxiety that is a result of this turbulence leads to the impairment of creativity, both in individuals and organizations. Organizational creativity is said to occur when individuals share their creative ideas and learning, and group anxiety can be sufficiently limited through conformity of behaviour or through the establishment of a climate of empathy and trust. Stacey underlines the need to perceive organizations as complex adaptive systems and to allow space for creative working to take place.

Perhaps the most comprehensive account of creativity is provided by HENRY. A number of respected authors have contributed to wide-ranging discussions on original thinking, creative development, and the management of these processes, and include descriptions of vertical and lateral thinking, the development of creative ideas through play, and creativity in relation to scientific knowledge. It is stressed however, that truly creative ideas must be useful as well as original. This book argues for the greater use of intuitive thinking and a whole-brained approach to management and decision making. Like Kirton, authors in this book recommend a diversity of

cognitive styles in the composition of management teams. They emphasize the importance of education for the management of complexity, and advocate holistic, integrative learning rather than training in specific competencies.

Another helpful source of reference is PROCTOR, who explores the importance of creativity in management – not only the management of creative processes in others, but also practical advice for managers themselves on employing various techniques for creative problem solving, including the use of specific computer software. He maintains that the possession of creative ability is essential for any leader in dealing with new challenges or unorthodox situations, and describes six stages in creative problem solving. The author considers ways of redefining problems to provide new insights and discusses how resistance to the implementation of new ideas might be overcome.

MAJARO also addresses the management of creativity, proposing firstly a definition of creativity and a means of evaluating the level of creative activity present in an organization. A useful distinction is provided between creativity and innovation and it is pointed out that either may exist in the organization without the presence of the other. This account includes a discussion of individual creativity and some well-known exercises to encourage different types of creative thinking in individuals; it could be criticized, however, for failing to indicate the links between individual and organizational creativity. The author proposes a practical approach to managing innovation that is illustrated by case studies of two companies.

PENNY GARDINER

See also Innovation, Organizational culture

Criminal law

Ashworth, Andrew, *Principles of Criminal Law*, 3rd edition, Oxford and New York: Oxford University Press, 1999

Duff, Antony (editor), *Philosophy and the Criminal Law: Principle and Critique*, Cambridge and New York: Cambridge University Press, 1998

Fletcher, George P., *Rethinking Criminal Law*, Boston: Little Brown, 1978

Gardner, John and Stephen Shute, "The Wrongness of Rape" in *Oxford Essays in Jurisprudence: Fourth Series*, edited by Jeremy Horder, Oxford and New York: Oxford University Press, 2000

Moore, Michael S., *Placing Blame: A General Theory of the Criminal Law*, Oxford: Clarendon Press, and New York: Oxford University Press, 1997

Robinson, Paul H., *Structure and Function in Criminal Law*, Oxford: Clarendon Press, and New York: Oxford University Press, 1997

Shute, Stephen C., John Gardner and Jeremy Horder (editors), *Action and Value in Criminal Law*, Oxford: Clarendon Press, and New York: Oxford University Press, 1993

Smith, John C. and Brian Hogan, *Criminal Law*, 9th edition, London: Butterworths, 1999

Williams, Glanville, *Textbook of Criminal Law*, 2nd edition, London: Stevens, 1983

ASHWORTH is a highly innovative textbook, which aims to identify and analyse the principles and policies that ground much of the reasoning presented by courts and commentators when discussing English criminal law. Written in elegant, accessible prose, it concentrates on "middle order" principles that are designed to link criminal law rules with arguments about the criminal law's function, composition, and scope; its underlying value structure; the proper classification of offences; and the appropriate division of authority between the judiciary and the legislature. The book offers a fascinating account of the twists and turns of criminal liability.

DUFF presents five new essays on criminal law written by leading scholars in the field. The essays, which are written from different theoretical perspectives, concentrate on the extent to which the criminal law can be conceived as a body of rationale and coherent principles and on what, if anything, can be said about the logical structure of crimes in general. The result is a cutting-edge exploration of the topic in which insights abound.

FLETCHER is a groundbreaking work that brings a keen comparative eye to the task of understanding Anglo-American criminal law. Drawing on continental – particularly German – theory, the book seeks to expose the general propositions that shape and structure criminal law. Its main thesis is that the criminal law is centred on three patterns of liability: *manifest liability* (which states that behaviour must manifest its criminality on its face if it is to warrant criminal liability; in other words a neutral third-party observer must be able to recognise the activity as criminal); *subjective criminality* (which claims that the key component of criminal liability is the intention to violate a legally protected interest); and *harmful consequences*. The book also claims that an analytical distinction can helpfully be drawn between *wrongdoing* (the violation of a prohibitory rule without justification) and *attribution* of that wrongdoing to an individual.

GARDNER & SHUTE offers an account of the wrongfulness of rape. The authors argue that although rapes typically cause harm, a rape is nonetheless wrongful even when, atypically, it causes no harm. The wrongfulness of rape cannot therefore lie in its harmfulness. The authors canvass an alternative theory based on the claim that the victim of a rape has a proprietary interest in her own body, which derives from a proprietary right over it. The authors show, however, that tying the wrongfulness of rape to ownership of one's own body inverts the basic element of rape's wrongfulness, because it identifies the basic value of the body with its use value, and so concedes to the rapist that in principle the body of a person is there to be used. It thus overlooks that, in the pure case, rape's wrongfulness lies in the sheer use of a person, in the treatment of that person merely as a means, in that person's objectification

MOORE is an attempt to provide a systematic theory of criminal law. Rooted in retributivist theory, which is both explained and defended, it offers a closely-reasoned analysis (spanning more than 800 pages) of the function of the criminal law, of criminal responsibility (which the book casts in terms of wrongdoing, culpability, and personhood), of legislation, and of wrongful action.

ROBINSON centres on issues of classification and function, and represents the culmination of fifteen years of investigation.

It provides, among other things, a stimulating and insightful account of the interrelationships among the rules and doctrines of criminal law and how these might be fitted into an overarching conceptual framework.

SHUTE, GARDNER & HORDER is a collection of highly original essays on the philosophical foundations of the criminal law. Ranging across such central issues as the size and shape of the general part, the relationship between "real crimes" and "mere regulatory offences", the nature of criminal wrongs, harms, responsibility, and the doctrine of causation, the issues of moral luck and mistake, and the problem of mental illness, the book seeks to explore the logic of the criminal law from the inside.

SMITH & HOGAN provides the most authoritative and comprehensive source of doctrinal analysis of English criminal law currently available. The first edition was published in 1965. Since then the encyclopaedic and scholarly approach adopted by the authors has won them an army of readers. The book is much used by both practitioners and law students. Appellate courts also frequently refer to it.

Though dated as a primary textbook, WILLIAMS still has much to offer to the student of criminal law. Written by one of the great figures in the field, the book reflects with admirable clarity and much good humour on an often complex and obscure subject. The format is unusual in that the book adopts a conversational style with the deliberate intention of mirroring the cut and thrust of argument.

STEPHEN SHUTE

See also Law survey

Criminal sentencing

Ashworth, Andrew, *Sentencing and Criminal Justice*, 2nd edition, London: Butterworths, 1995

Ashworth, Andrew and Martin Wasik (editors), *Fundamentals of Sentencing Theory: Essays in Honour of Andrew von Hirsch*, Oxford and New York: Oxford University Press, 1998

Hood, Roger, *Race and Sentencing: A Study in the Crown Court*, Oxford: Clarendon Press, and New York: Oxford University Press, 1992

Shute, Stephen, "The Place of Public Opinion in Sentencing Law", *Criminal Law Review* (1998): 465–77

von Hirsch, Andrew, *Censure and Sanctions*, Oxford: Clarendon Press, and New York: Oxford University Press, 1993

Walker, Nigel and Nicola Padfield, *Sentencing: Theory, Law and Practice*, 2nd edition, London: Butterworths, 1996

Wasik, Martin, *Emmins on Sentencing*, 3rd edition, London: Blackstone Press, 1998

Penned by one of the most authoritative scholars in the area, ASHWORTH provides a masterly account of the law and practice of sentencing. It is a beautifully written book that makes accessible even the most obscure aspects of English sentencing law. True to the style of the "law in context" movement, it links its discussion to the wider criminal justice system, dealing with the findings of empirical researchers and the arguments of legal theorists.

ASHWORTH & WASIK is a collection of eleven stimulating essays on sentencing theory. The essays fall under three headings: (a) the foundation of the power to punish; (b) troublesome issues in sentencing theory; and (c) relating theory to contemporary punishment practice. Although designed for those who wish to delve deeply into the subject, it is nonetheless a highly readable book that repays with interest the effort taken to digest its contents.

VON HIRSCH, written by the leading light behind the "just deserts" movement, explores proportionality in sentencing. It is a full-length defence of desert theory but always with a humane edge.

HOOD provides a rare insight into the little researched area of Crown Court sentencing. The book presents the findings of the first major study conducted into whether race influences sentencing. It examines sentences passed on 3,317 defendants at five different Crown Court centres in the West Midlands and controls for the expected custody score. Among its conclusions is that "a black male committed to the Dudley Crown Court in 1989 had a greater probability of receiving a custodial sentence than if he had been committed to Birmingham Crown Court".

SHUTE examines the extent to which English law permits or requires judges to consider public opinion when determining an appropriate sentence. It draws a distinction between *mandatory inclusion* (where the law requires sentencers to factor public opinion into every decision they make); *partial permission* (where the law requires sentencers to consider the relevance of public opinion whenever they pass a sentence but permits them to deny it any influence on the outcome of a particular case if that seems appropriate in the circumstances); *full permission* (where the law gives sentencers a free hand whether they consider the relevance of public opinion or not); and *mandatory exclusion* (where the law prohibits sentencers from taking any account of public opinion). After examining the relevant legal authorities the author concludes that sentencers are at the very least duty bound to consider the relevance of public opinion (*partial permission*) and may even be required to factor public opinion into every sentence they pass (*mandatory inclusion*).

WALKER & PADFIELD is a well-respected textbook on sentencing law. The first edition was published in 1985 and the second edition remains true to the original brief, which was to describe the law governing English sentencing, to illuminate the underlying theory, and, finally, to explain how the system operates in practice.

WASIK provides an admirably clear and thoughtful guide to English sentencing law. Its straightforward and readable approach will endear it to undergraduates and practitioners alike.

STEPHEN SHUTE

See also Criminal law

Criminology

Bean, Philip, *Punishment: A Philosophical and Criminological Inquiry*, Oxford: Martin Robertson, 1981

Cohen, Stanley, *Visions of Social Control: Crime, Punishment, and Classification*, Cambridge: Polity Press, and New York: Blackwell, 1985

Erikson, K., "Notes on the Sociology of Deviance", *Social Problems*, 9 (1962): 307–14

Mannheim, Hermann (editor), *Pioneers in Criminology*, 2nd edition, Montclair, New Jersey: Patterson Smith, 1972

Vold, George B., Thomas J. Bernard and Jeffrey B. Snipes, *Theoretical Criminology*, 4th edition, New York and Oxford: Oxford University Press, 1998

Winch, Peter, *The Idea of a Social Science and Its Relation to Philosophy*, London: Routledge and Kegan Paul, and Atlantic Highlands, New Jersey: Humanities Press, 1958

Wootton, Barbara, *Social Science and Social Pathology*, London: Allen and Unwin, 1959

Criminology means, literally, the study (Greek *logi*) of crime, but nowadays it is likely to include the criminal justice system, i.e. police, prisons, probation, etc. It is becoming increasingly popular as an academic subject, and the expertise of criminologists is sought at the highest level. Traditionally, emphasis has been on studying the causes of crime, alongside the theory and practice of the penal system – although terms like "causes" have largely fallen into disuse. Developing criminological theories, however, still dominate much criminological debate.

MANNHEIM is the definitive work on the major figures and founding fathers of criminology, covering the main schools and the main academic disciplines. Criminology is still heavily dependent on the academic disciplines from which it developed, for example sociology and psychology. Philosophers such as Plato, Kant, or Bentham, who wrote extensively on crime, law, and punishment, have not been included. (See BEAN for a discussion on punishment.) The term criminology is a 19th/20th-century term and, as Mannheim shows, those who wanted to make criminology a science, in the same way that physics was a science, dominated this period ("criminal science" was also a popular term at the time). The methodology was to be scientific, or positivist as it is sometimes called, with the emphasis on the criminal, and on the facts relating to the criminal. Mannheim discusses the influence of both Cesare Lombroso and Enrico Ferri. Lombroso, one of the great pioneers of modem criminology, described himself as "a slave to facts. Facts emerge from theories" while Ferri insisted that the proper subject of crime was the offender, his or her psychological disposition, family, and social background.

The dispute between the positivists and the legalists is well documented by Mannheim. Basically, it centres on a definition of crime. Legalists define crime in terms of the criminal law – criminal behaviour is that which breaks the law. Their interests centre on legal and jurisprudential questions such as the justification for punishment and the basis of law. They have not included questions about the characteristics of the offender. They regard the positivists as imposing a scientific framework on an academic discipline that can never be a science in the sense in which physics is a science. Moreover, they say a study of the behaviour of criminals is not a study of crime.

In contrast, positivists regard the criminal law as an uncertain basis for a scientific study: laws, they say, change over time. They add that the epistemology of law is based on moral maxims, operating on the presumption of "will", "rational choice", and "intent". Nor are positivists prepared to allow others (i.e. lawyers) to determine the nature and boundary of their discipline. So, with no settled or agreed definition of crime, the discipline lacks a firm intellectual foundation, although C.R. Jeffrey (in Mannheim) has tried to seek a compromise between the two disputing parties. Criminology, however, is not the only academic discipline to suffer in this way; others are similarly placed. For example, as WINCH shows, there is no agreement about what is the foundation or basis of sociology, political science, or psychiatry; nor, one might add, is there any agreement about how a mental illness, psychosis, or neurosis are defined. This need not hold back the development of the discipline, though it might leave it open to scepticism amongst those critics who will not want to take its conclusions seriously. Winch has an important examination of the nature of social science, where he sets out in detail the arguments surrounding the basis for a science and a social science.

Attempts to resolve this dispute have rarely been successful. Labelling theorists such as Kai Erikson have shown how it is possible to extend the boundaries of criminology to include "deviant behaviour". ERIKSON gives the clearest statement on the links between crime and deviance, and the relationship between the two. This does not meet the legalists' criticisms, even though "deviant behaviour" is a logical extension of the subject matter. Yet the advantages are clear. The use of this term allows mental disorder to be included, alongside studies of those whose deviance is less obvious, e.g. those who do not break the rules when all others around them do. It also allows for a study of social and legal rules, as shown in COHEN. This seminal study looks at the organized way in which society responds to behaviour, and to the types of people it regards as deviant. This book, above all others, has pointed to new and important directions for criminology.

VOLD, BERNARD & SNIPES has shown how the dominant theoretical development in modern criminology has come from sociology, but psychologists have always shown great interest and some of the major studies have been in that discipline. It is difficult to be certain about which areas of criminology are of greatest interest to criminologists. One indicator is the biennial conference of the British Society of Criminology. Studies of the police, prisons, the media, drugs, women, ethnicity and crime, as well as crime reduction programmes, are well represented, while studies of mentally disordered offenders, sentencing, and probation are less so.

An influential criminologist such as Barbara WOOTTON may not see herself as a positivist in the formal sense, but she nonetheless insisted on the importance of an evidence-based criminology. Her standard theme was always a plea for rigour and evidence. In so doing she draws attention to an older debate left over from the positivist/legalist era. For, whilst some criminologists want the subject to return to its positivist roots (i.e. in a social science framework, evidence-based, and empirical), others want a more ideological approach. The latter

would not seem a tenable position, for without an empirical foundation it is hard to see how criminology can survive, or differ from law, jurisprudence, or philosophy.

PHILIP BEAN

Crisis management

Bignall, Victor and Joyce Fortune, *Understanding Systems Failures*, Manchester: Manchester University Press, 1984

Fortune, Joyce and Geoff Peters, *Learning from Failure: The Systems Approach*, Chichester and New York: Wiley, 1995

Kets de Vries, Manfred F.R. and Danny Miller, *The Neurotic Organization*, San Francisco: Jossey Bass, 1984

Lagadec, Patrick, *Preventing Chaos in a Crisis: Strategies for Prevention, Control, and Damage Limitation*, London and New York: McGraw Hill, 1993

Pauchant, Thierry C. and Ian I. Mitroff, *Transforming the Crisis-Prone Organization: Preventing Individual, Organizational, and Environmental Tragedies*, San Francisco: Jossey Bass, 1992

Perrow, Charles, *Normal Accidents: Living with High-Risk Technologies*, New York: Basic Books, 1984

Reason, James, *Human Error*, Cambridge and New York: Cambridge University Press, 1990

Reason, James, *Managing the Risk of Organizational Accidents*, Aldershot, Hampshire: Ashgate, 1997

Rosenthal, Uriel *et al.*, *Complexity in Urban Crisis Management: Amsterdam's Response to the Bijlmer Air Disaster*, London: James and James, 1994

Shrivastava, Paul, *Bhopal: Anatomy of a Crisis*, 2nd edition, London: Paul Chapman, 1992

Slatter, Stuart and David Lovett, *Corporate Turnaround: Managing Companies in Distress*, Harmondsworth: Penguin, 1999

Smart, C. and I. Vertinsky, "Designs for Crisis Decision Units", *Administrative Science Quarterly*, 22 (1977): 640–57

Smith, D., "Beyond Contingency Planning: Towards a Model of Crisis Management", *Industrial Crisis Quarterly*, 4/4 (1990): 263–75

Toft, Brian and Simon Reynolds, *Learning from Disasters*, London: Butterworths, 1994

Tombs, S. and D. Smith, "Corporate Responsibility and Crisis Management: Some Insights From Political and Social Theory", *Journal of Contingencies and Crisis Management*, 3/3 (1995): 135–48

Turner, Barry A., *Man-Made Disasters*, London: Wykeham, 1978; 2nd edition, with Nick F. Pidgeon, Oxford: Butterworth Heinemann, 1997

Vaughan, D., *The Challenger Launch Decision: Risky Technology, Culture, and Deviance At NASA*, Chicago: University of Chicago Press, 1996

Weick, K.E., "Enacted Sensemaking in Crisis Situations", *Journal of Management Studies*, 25 (1988): 305–17

Weick, K.E., "The Collapse of Sensemaking in Organizations: The Mann Gulch Disaster", *Administrative Science Quarterly*, 38 (1993): 628–52

For the purposes of this discussion, the term "crisis" is grounded in the management literature and is mainly concerned with crises that occur within organizations, rather than those that form a subset of international relations or disaster management. We can define a crisis as an event which exceeds, or comes close to exceeding, an organization's abilities to cope with the task demands imposed upon it. The event and its aftermath can usually cause damage or disruption to the organization's activities, reputation, or resources, or has the potential for considerable loss of life.

A crisis in an organization can be conceptualized as occurring in three broad phases, as described in SMITH. They are: the "crisis of management" (when incubation of crisis potential takes place); "operational crisis" (when the demands of an event begin to exceed the organization's abilities to cope); and "crisis of legitimation" (after the active phase of the event, when the organization seeks to recover its legitimacy with both stakeholders and regulators).

The crisis of management

Research into the initial phase of a crisis can be considered to be grouped around three areas: the process of crisis incubation; the processes of systems emergence and failure; and the nature of organizational resilience, in particular the manner in which organizational culture can develop to allow an organization to become more crisis-prepared. This area of work is also concerned with the development of dysfunctional organizational forms and their contribution to crisis generation.

TURNER is considered by many to be the seminal text in the area of crisis management. There is little doubt that the author has proved to be an enduring influence on the field, and this text is one of the most widely cited within the literature. The book makes a number of important theoretical contributions to the debates on crisis management. The first of these is the notion that crises, or disasters, can incubate within organizations and remain unnoticed by management (a concept developed further by J. Reason as resident pathogens. On the basis of his empirical research, Turner argued that it was possible to embed the potential for failure within an organization and that this could be represented as a function of the core beliefs and values held by decision makers. These would, in turn, affect the precautionary norms that management puts into place to control organizational activities. Consequently, management's inability to recognize and anticipate the range of likely failure modes results in the development of a set of precautionary norms that fail to provide sufficient resilience within the system. These inherent weaknesses then incubate until an incident exposes them and allows for their catastrophic potential to become realised. Turner develops his thesis through a number of in-depth case studies, which provide the reader with important insights into the process of incubation and the lack of foresight on the part of those charged with the management of potentially hazardous systems. Turner's conceptual model also raises the issue of organizational learning (termed "full cultural readjustment") and this early work on learning has been developed further by others (see Toft & Reynolds, below).

Turner's influence is extensive and many of the texts cited here owe a debt to his foresight in bringing these important issues to the attention of subsequent generations of scholars.

The first edition of Turner's book has been revised by Nick Pidgeon (TURNER & PIDGEON). One of the important additional contributions is Pidgeon's attempt to link Turner's work with more recent research into high reliability organizations. This in itself is a valuable contribution to the literature and the second edition deserves to be widely read.

REASON (1990) represents a major review of the psychology of error, and he provides the reader with a firm grasp of the cognitive processes that underpin slips, lapses, mistakes, and violations. Reason's work builds upon the notion of incubation developed by Turner, and grounds it within the psychological literature on human error. Reason makes the distinction between active and latent error within systems failure, with the latter proving to be much harder to identify and manage. Like Turner, Reason uses a medical metaphor, and argues that latent error potential sits within an organization or system like "resident pathogens". These pathogens remain largely undetected until a series of trigger events expose the latent error pathways and allow incidents to escalate into catastrophic accidents. Reason makes the argument that these latent errors both create the workplace conditions in which active errors and violations occur and also embed pathways through organizational defences. It is these pathways that allow for the rapid escalation of incidents into accidents, and beguile attempts at mitigation. Reason provides a number of points of intervention for management to deal with the problems of both error and violations. These intervention strategies have been developed further in his more recent work (REASON 1997), which seeks to provide insights into the management implications of both latent and active error.

The research on systems failure emphasizes the problems associated with a reductionist approach, in which the sheer complexity of the issues becomes part of the problem for management. It is in the nature of these emergent properties that they exceed the organization's abilities to predict, and therefore control, non-design emergencies. The work of J. Fortune and colleagues represents an interesting and important synthesis of the soft systems approach with the organizational studies of disaster, typified by the work of Turner and Reason. The benefit of this approach is that it takes a holistic view on the nature of the problem and, therefore, elevates the importance of latent organizational conditions. BIGNALL & FORTUNE works through a number of case studies. These are useful as a means of providing insights into the various causal factors of disaster. These case examples are then analysed within the framework of the systems approach, and some important lessons are drawn out of this analysis.

FORTUNE & PETERS takes the analysis of such events to a higher level. In particular, the authors provide a means of analysing accidents through a formal systems model for failure, and they also deal with the important notion of systems emergence in accident generation. Such emergence creates problems for operators and managers alike, as it moves the system into a degraded mode and creates problems of interpretation and sensemaking for the event. It is this process of emergence that confuses and beguiles those who try to manage crises. These emergent properties invariably challenge the core assumptions about the nature of a system, and makes it difficult for operators and managers to make sense of the event. The inherent difficulty for organizations relates to the prediction of such emergence and the development of procedures to deal with it as a consequence. While not providing a predictive diagnostic (and there are some who would argue that this is not possible in any event), the application of the formal systems model does help to frame the discussion surrounding emergent properties and allows for the development of insights into the processes that occur.

Like Reason and Turner, PERROW deals with the manner in which catastrophic failures occur within systems. In many respects, Perrow's work has much in common with Turner's earlier work, in that he deals with the issues of incubation and embedded failure potential. What makes Perrow's study important is his attempt to apply the concept of a "normal accident" – that which occurs as a function of the system's emergent properties – to a wide range of industrial and commercial settings. Like the work of Fortune and colleagues, this study includes a range of case study examples.

Perrow's discussion of the important concepts of tight coupling and interactive complexity also mark the text out from other research. The notion of interactive complexity equates in broad terms to the emergent properties within the system. Perrow provides us with an important critique of reductionism, as he challenges the core orthodoxy of management – namely, the perceived ability to control the system. Tight coupling, on the other hand, refers to the speed of interaction between the failures of the various elements within a system, and between the initiating event and the catastrophic failure (or top event). The resultant failure pathway – which is both tightly coupled and interactively complex – is ultimately a function of the embedded latent error potential associated with strategic and design-related decision making in the organization. Perrow also provides us with a warning about building layers of redundancy into a system, as this too can contribute to making the system opaque and therefore difficult to manage. As such, the book provides a useful counterargument to the rational, prescriptive approaches that often prevail within both risk and crisis management.

Research in the area of organizational resilience is generally concerned with the issues of crisis prevention. The first main area of work is concerned with the development of a crisis-prepared culture, and the majority of this work deals with the development of cultural types and pathologies within organizations. The second strand is concerned with the ethical aspects of corporate behaviour, and the creation of resilience as a consequence of suspect ethical behaviour.

KETS DE VRIES & MILLER represents an important contribution to the literature despite the authors' assertion that the book is speculative in its approach. The focus of the book is on the processes by which organizational dysfunctionality are created, and the authors identify a set of "common" neuroses which are often found in crisis-prone organizations These neurotic organizations are seen as "... troubled firms whose symptoms and dysfunctions combine to form an integrated 'syndrome' of pathology ... [in which] ... similar patterns of strategic and structural defects often point to an integrated organizational pathology" (p.17).

The emphasis upon a psychoanalytic approach to organizational failure provides the book with a unique perspective on crisis management. The authors identify five dominant organizational styles (paranoid, compulsive, dramatic, depressive,

and schizoid) from the research literature and analyse these styles against the organization's strategy, culture, structure, and behaviour. It is the focus on the "inner world" created by this complex interaction between organizational and psychoanalytic elements that gives the book its strength. Having identified the dominant characteristics of these five types, the book moves on to consider the possible strategies for intervention that are available. The book is rich in empirical case study evidence, which is used to support the main theoretical arguments, and the emphasis on typologies has proved to be an enduring focus for research within the literature.

The psychoanalytic tradition is continued in PAUCHANT & MITROFF. In common with earlier work, the authors seek to explore organizational types within the context of strategy, structure, assumptions, and core beliefs/values. They examine the notion of crisis-proneness within organizations, and present the results of considerable empirical survey data in support of their arguments. The authors argue that it is possible to conceptualize an organization as involving multiple layers that interact together to create an overall "type", and that this will exist on a continuum from crisis-prone to crisis-prepared. Their notion of an onion model, with strategy and structure as the outer layers and assumptions, and core beliefs closer to the centre, is critical of the view that there are certain aspects of the organization that are more transparent, and therefore easier to manage and change. Indeed, many organizations will seek to develop strategies to cope with crisis and possibly develop associated structural responses, but will fail to address the central issues of beliefs, assumptions, and values. Such a contingency approach, while it has some important benefits, will only have limited impact unless the organization addresses the problems associated with the assumptions and core beliefs of senior managers. The logic of this argument is well established within the literature and it was Turner that first pointed to the important relationship between such values and assumptions, and the precautionary norms that were developed as a consequence. Pauchant & Mitroff provides further empirical evidence in support of that relationship. Unless these assumptions, core beliefs, and values are addressed, any strategic and structural changes may be built upon fragile foundations. Ultimately, effective crisis prevention works from the centre of the onion outwards and is based upon a socially responsive approach to management (see Tombs & Smith, below).

It is clear from research to date that an organization's ethical stance will be an important element in its ability to prevent latent error from incubating and in shaping its actions after a crisis event. Organizations that seek to encourage dialogue, whistle-blowing and open communication are more likely to expose any latent error potential than those organizations that are more guarded and closed in their approach. TOMBS & SMITH explores the relationship between the incubation of crisis potential and an organization's approach to corporate responsibility. In essence, the main argument articulated centres around the notion that organizations that seek to move beyond the existing regulatory frameworks, and comply with wider societal demands, will become more crisis-prepared than those that slavishly seek to conform to the letter of the law. The paper draws upon the wider social science literature in order to both inform management theory and to critique existing practice. Ultimately, the ethical dynamics of crises have been severely neglected by the academic literature and it can be seen to occupy a central role across the three broad phases of the crisis process. The difficulty facing research in this area is that notions of corporate social responsibility and business ethics are seen by many managers as being too abstract to be implementable. Tombs & Smith recognizes this difficulty, but argues that these issues sit at the heart of an organization's culture and are therefore at the centre of organizational decision making for hazardous issues. The paper argues that an "ethical" approach is the most important way of ensuring crisis prevention, and will help to move organizations away from the technocratic mindset that prevents effective dialogue with those who might have to bear the costs of corporate actions. This notion of the ethical aspects of management in crisis incubation is emerging as an important area for research, although there are some considerable barriers to undertaking empirical work in this area.

The operational crisis

While there is a considerable amount of published work dealing with the "operational crisis" or active phase, much of it is aimed at the practitioner market and is prescriptive in its approach. While this work has some merits, it fails to deal with the complex issues of emergence, latent error, and coupling/complexity. The papers identified here, however, are concerned with the academic issues associated with operational crises and represent the best work in this area.

LAGADEC also takes a holistic view on the nature of crises, and attempts to provide the reader with a set of tools for both preventing and containing such events. The author argues that the book "is not a first-aid kit, but the means of sharpening the decision maker's judgment . . . in order to go beyond simply being aware of the problems involved. Then and only then is it possible to think about strategic responses to the outbreak of a crisis" (p.xi).

Lagadec's work is important in that it raises the central issues of knowledge in preventing crises and the manner in which organizations learn from such events. Lagadec frames a crisis as a major disturbance to the organization, which results in the associated loss of a managerial decision-making rubric during the event. It is this process that creates problems for managers in the operational phase of a crisis when effective decision making is required to deal with the constantly changing demands of the event.

Following on from an extensive discussion of the nature of crisis, Lagadec moves on to consider the issues involved in managing the event itself. An important contribution here is the question of the management style required to deal with the task demands of the crisis. Finally, the book concludes by examining the issues surrounding learning from crises, and Lagadec makes the point that such learning has to be managed effectively if organizations are going to develop the critical skills needed to work towards crisis prevention.

ROSENTHAL et al. investigated the 1992 Bijlmer air disaster in Amsterdam and the book represents an excellent account of the crash, as well as the manner in which the various public sector agencies dealt with its aftermath. This research represents one of the few thorough large-scale studies into public sector disaster response at the local level. The book is also important in that it provides insights into the manner by which a disaster can expose organizational failings and trigger other forms of crisis for those involved in the event. As the authors put it: "the Bijlmer case shows that a disaster may unleash forces which indeed may result in crises of a totally different nature – going all the way from an air crash in an urban district to a multi-ethnic turmoil in urban society at large" (p.131). For these insights alone the book should be considered an important contribution to the literature.

The investigating team provides detailed coverage of the various intervention strategies that were employed to deal with the event and the manner in which the various agencies coped with the demands imposed upon them. The authors draw important lessons from the disaster in terms of the various policy-level and operational decisions taken at Bijlmer, and they deal with the important supply and demand issues inherent within disaster relief in some detail. The book also provides valuable insights into the workings of a crisis management team (CMT). The empirical importance of this contribution should not be underestimated. There have been few cases where a research group has been given access to such a team, and this book provides unique perspectives on the problems faced by CMT members across the areas of decision making, psychological problems, communications issues, and the role of expertise.

The book concludes with a series of insights and lessons emerging from the Bijlmer disaster that have a wider applicability. These issues include: the problems associated with the scale of the accident and the task demands that they impose upon crisis workers; the issue of leadership in crisis; the social dimensions of large-scale technological accidents set within an urban environment; and issues surrounding risk communication, public information, and media response strategies. Perhaps the most important insights provided by the team centre around the manner in which urban crisis managers have to cope with a disaster that affects a multiethnic community, and the manner in which this impacts upon the effectiveness of their intervention strategies.

SMART & VERTINSKY is a seminal paper concerned with the manner in which decision making takes place within crisis management teams. It represents one of the earliest attempts to deal with the issues. The authors make an important point concerning the relationship between the pre-crisis stage and the operational phase of the event in their observation that: "Designs for preventing crises should be complemented by developments of capabilities for coping with crises" (p.640). Effective crisis management, therefore, requires organizations to deal with both prevention and recovery in an integrated manner. In essence, there is a significant risk that those pathologies that created the potential for the crisis may well subsequently inhibit the organization's capabilities for coping with the event. Smart & Vertinsky identify five "classes of pathologies" that are specific to crisis events and impact upon both decision making and the implementation process. These pathologies centre around cognitive narrowing, information distortion, groupthink, rigidities around decision programming (rules and procedures), and a lack of decision readiness (in terms of decision capabilities and faulty implementation techniques). These issues remain central to the process of crisis prevention and control. The paper moves beyond an identification of these pathologies towards a consideration of the possible intervention strategies available to organizations to overcome them.

The crisis of legitimation

In the final stage, the managerial requirements of disaster recovery, organizational turnaround, sensemaking and learning have attracted considerable attention within the literature and they remain, along with the issue of incubation, the most important areas for future research.

SLATTER & LOVETT (a revised edition of Slatter's *Corporate Recovery*, 1984) represents a significant contribution to the general literature on crisis management. The focus of the book is very much on the final operational and legitimation phases of crises and the approach taken will appeal to the practitioner market as well as an academic audience. The importance of the text lies in its focus on the practical aspects of turnaround and the strategies available to managers faced with a crisis. The book is both accessible and informative, and it provides the reader with some insights into the causes of crises before going on to develop likely intervention strategies for companies in trouble. The book's merits lie in its business coverage of crises, in contrast to the emphasis on technological disasters commonly found in other texts.

WEICK (1988 and 1993) has made a major contribution to the literature on crisis management through refining the "sensemaking" concept and applying it to complex failure events. While the author has carried out a considerable amount of work in this area, the papers identified here relate specifically to crises. Weick identifies a number of aspects of the sensemaking process which are held to be of importance in affecting the manner in which both managers and operators make sense of complex and rapidly evolving events. In particular, he argues that there are seven key elements involved in the sensemaking process. In the first instance, sensemaking is grounded in our notions of self. Our interpretation of events will be, in part, a function of our own values, beliefs, and experience, and will be shaped by our notion of self. By definition, sensemaking is seen as an ongoing activity and this provides us with the second main dynamic of the process. As more information becomes available, then individuals refine their interpretation and representation of events. Thirdly, sensemaking is deemed to be a retrospective process – we can only make sense of something after it has occurred and we have been able to reflect upon the nature of the events. The fourth element of sensemaking is that it is a social and interactive process. In discussing the sensemaking process involved in the Mann Gulch fire, Weick elaborates on the role of "organization" in sensemaking, arguing that we can see a "recipe for disorganization" that reads: "Thrust people into unfamiliar roles, leave some key roles unfilled, make the task more ambiguous, discredit the role system, and make all of these changes in a context in which small events can combine into something monstrous" (Weick 1993, p.638).

The social dynamic of sensemaking is also seen as an important factor in explaining the manner in which cues are interpreted, communication is shaped, and behaviours are affected. Weick has also observed that both role structures and interacting routines can be seen as important factors in framing the nature of organizations and providing insights into their behaviour. These routines and role structures are important, because when they break down they can erode organizational resilience by inhibiting effective responses from those charged with controlling events. This may, in turn, impact upon the likelihood and significance of human error as organizational members find themselves in situations for which they have not been trained, and for which there are no effective protocols. The fifth aspect of the process is that sensemaking is deemed to be focused on and extracted by cues. We extract elements of a situation and break them down in order to understand them. However, in so doing we may lose sight of the holistic nature of the problem, and oversimplify the rich mosaic of causality that is present in many events. In a related manner, sensemaking is also seen as an enacted process. We also operate in an enacted environment where our actions become embedded in the problem that we are trying to make sense of, thus creating problems of interpretation. This is the sixth element of the process. Finally, sensemaking is driven by plausibility rather than accuracy – an issue that creates immense problems under crisis conditions. If our interpretation of an event is plausible, then it is unlikely that we will be able to accept significant challenges to that event scenario. Given that crises invariably result from the emergent properties associated with a system and are therefore often unforeseen, such challenges to the conventional worldview might prove to be of immense importance, as the UK's BSE crisis so dramatically illustrates. If an event scenario remains plausible and fits our worldview then we will vigorously seek to defend that interpretation in the face of less accepted (but possibly more accurate) scenarios.

The process of sensemaking for crisis events is an important precursor to learning. Unless we can make sense of the events in an effective manner then we will be unable to learn. Sensemaking remains one of the key areas for further research within the field of crisis management.

TOFT & REYNOLDS represents a major empirical investigation into the process of organizational learning following disasters and crises. The book builds upon many of the issues raised in Turner's early work concerning the failure of foresight, with Toft's emphasis being largely on the failure of hindsight. Toft & Reynolds seeks to bring together research findings from systems thinking, organizational learning, and disaster management and apply these theoretical perspectives to the lack of learning that has taken place following public inquiries into disaster. The book develops Toft's earlier research on isomorphism within learning and grounds this in the tradition established by Turner. Toft & Reynolds defines the notion of organizational isomorphism as occurring on those "occasions on which organizations or their subunits, whether engaged in disparate enterprises or not, exhibit similar patterns of behaviour" (p.57). They develop this discussion to outline four forms of isomorphism. The first is event isomorphism, in which "two separate incidents take place and manifest themselves in two completely different ways but lead to the creation of identical hazardous situations" (p.61). They cite the examples of train crashes within the same organization to illustrate this phenomenon. In the first instance a train crashes because a driver passes a signal at danger and in the second a train crashes because the signals fail due to a maintenance problem. The end result is the same – a train collision – but the causes might be considered to be different by management, with the result that learning from one of the events might be ignored in favour of the other. In both cases, latent management error or a poor safety culture might be responsible for the accidents, but these factors could be overlooked if management do not actively seek to explore the boundaries between events. The second form that they identify is cross-organizational isomorphism. Here the issue is framed in terms of the "ownership" of the accident with organizational boundaries proving to be significant barriers to learning. Such barriers are typified by the "it could not happen here" mentality which has proved to be a significant defence mechanism employed by organizations and is typical of a dysfunctional culture. The third form is identified as "common mode isomorphism". In this case, learning is inhibited because the organizations, while employing common modes of managing and operating, are working in differing sectors and producing different products. The final group is "self isomorphism" which occurs when an organization is sufficiently large to be incapable of seeing patterns of failure that can occur across its various subunits.

The notion of isomorphism, identified by Toft & Reynolds, provides an important contribution to the crisis management literature and it helps to further refine Turner's notion of "full cultural readjustment" as an effective means of crisis prevention. Furthermore, it combines well with the process of sensemaking to provide a firm basis for a discussion of crisis-related learning.

SHRIVASTAVA provides us with what is probably the best account of the Bhopal accident. As a former resident of Bhopal and a major contributor to the crisis management literature, the author gives an analysis that is enriched by his sensitivity to both the cultural and corporate dynamics of the disaster. This study is based upon considerable empirical work carried out by Shrivastava. The text systematically works through the issues, from causal events through to the responses made by both the government and industry after the accident. Shrivastava's account examines the event from the perspective of the main stakeholders, and provides insights into the accident through the application of a range of theoretical perspectives. The book's contribution is made all the more significant because of its meticulous and rigorous nature and the strong analytical framework employed by the author. Shrivastava's account of events allows him to provide a robust theoretical platform for analysis, and to show how crises result from the complex interaction of human, organizational, and technological factors. The approach of the analysis stems from work in organizational behaviour and management, although it also deals with the important interactions that take place between elements of the state and corporate groups. This is articulated in terms of the incubation of crisis potential as well as the response of these organizations to crisis.

VAUGHAN is a well-researched analysis of the *Challenger* accident that has received considerable acclaim. The book stands as perhaps the most detailed and complete analysis of the build-up to the loss of the space shuttle *Challenger* and the subsequent investigation into its causes. Vaughan's account has become an important contribution to the literature on both crisis management and organizational behaviour, and seems destined to become a benchmark for case analyses of this nature. Perhaps the most important contribution lies in Vaughan's account of the decision-making processes that took place within NASA, and the manner in which warnings about a specific technical problem were ignored by senior managers. The book provides important insights into the processes of

technocracy within organizations, and the manner in which technological elites can create and incubate the preconditions for failure. A second important contribution lies in the book's analysis of organizational cultures and the manner in which they might become dysfunctional. As such, the book adds further weight to the evidence provided by Shrivastava and allows the reader to develop a greater understanding of the processes of incubation and latent error discussed earlier. Finally, Vaughan's account of the accident provides important insights into the manner in which managers incorporate risk taking into their decision-making process and the processes by which they make sense of complex ill-structured events.

DENIS SMITH

See also Decision making, Organizational learning, Systems thinking

Critical psychology

Burman, Erica (editor), *Deconstructing Feminist Psychology*, London and Thousand Oaks, California: Sage, 1998

Chamberlin, Judi, "The Ex-Patients' Movement: Where We've Been and Where We're Going", *Journal of Mind and Behaviour*, 11/2 (1990): 323–36

Fox, Dennis and Isaac Prilleltensky (editors), *Critical Psychology: An Introduction*, London and Thousand Oaks, California: Sage, 1997

Henriques, Julian, Wendy Hollway, Cathy Urwin, Couze Venn and Valerie Walkerdine, *Changing the Subject: Psychology, Social Regulation, and Subjectivity*, London and New York: Methuen, 1984; reprinted London and New York: Routledge, 1998

Holzkamp, Klaus, "On Doing Psychology Critically", *Theory and Psychology*, 2/2 (1992): 193–204

Ibáñez, Tomás and Lupicinio Iñiguez (editors), *Critical Social Psychology*, London and Thousand Oaks, California: Sage, 1997

Lawthom, Rebecca, "Using the 'F' Word in Organizational Psychology: Foundations for Feminist Research", *Annual Review of Critical Psychology*, 1 (1999): 65–78

Martin-Bar, Ignacio, "Toward a Liberation Psychology" in *Writings for a Liberation Psychology*, edited by Adrianne Aron and Shawn Corne, Cambridge, Massachusetts: Harvard University Press, 1994

Parker, Ian and John Shotter (editors), *Deconstructing Social Psychology*, London and New York: Routledge, 1990

Tolman, Charles W., *Psychology, Society, and Subjectivity: An Introduction to German Critical Psychology*, London and New York: Routledge, 1994

FOX & PRILLELTENSKY provide a comprehensive, accessible, and wide-ranging introduction to critical psychology. The first five chapters of the book give an overview of critical psychology, defining its scope and exploring its key theoretical, methodological, and practical assumptions. The ten chapters in part two are concerned with specific applications of critical psychology in areas such as personality theory, abnormal psychology, developmental psychology, lesbian and gay psychology, and political psychology. These chapters share a commitment to a critical psychology that seeks to (a) challenge and undermine the positivist and objectivist assumptions of mainstream psychological theory and practice, and (b) demonstrate the ways in which such mainstream practices serve to implicitly (or explicitly) maintain and uphold society's unsatisfactory *status quo*. Part three summarizes various theoretical perspectives that offer an alternative to mainstream accounts, and the final chapter reflects critically upon the book as a whole.

The seventeen chapters in IBÁÑEZ & ÍÑIGUEZ provide a detailed discussion of the historical development, theoretical commonalities (and differences), practical arenas of involvement, and methodological tools and resources that both constitute and inform critical (social) psychological approaches. Unlike Fox & Prilleltensky, who present a broadly consensual view of critical psychology, Ibáñez & Íñiguez's collection offers a more heterogeneous and fragmentary account – not in terms of their critique of mainstream psychology (which they share) – but in terms of highlighting the theoretical and methodological debates and tensions that exist within contemporary critical psychological approaches.

Originally published in 1984, HENRIQUES *et al.* is now recognized as a classic critique of mainstream psychology that paved the way for much contemporary work in critical psychology, particularly in terms of its reconceptualization of the subject (individual, person, self, and so on). Through their discussions and analyses of assessment in organizations, racism, the subject, developmental psychology, gender, and power, the authors demonstrate the ways in which critical psychology can provide "new ways of being and new ways of making sense of existence" (p.xviii).

The aim of PARKER & SHOTTER's influential book, as the title suggests, is to "deconstruct" social psychology – that is, to analyse the discourses, rhetoric, and texts that constitute it, and to demonstrate the ways in which these operate. The book focuses on the "crisis" in social psychology, and takes a critical look at the assumptions underlying not only psychology (research, therapy, and feminism) but much of Western thought. It provides an excellent introduction to the issues of power, science, and knowledge that underpin much recent work within critical psychology.

In this often difficult paper, HOLZKAMP aims to develop a rigorous method for the identification of what he terms the "psycho-phylogenesis" of psychological categories wherein "the specifically human individual psyche is reflected as a partial aspect of more comprehensive historical, societal structures" (p.193). It is important to note that, elsewhere, Holzkamp makes a great distinction between "societal" (*gesellschaftlich*) and "social" (*sozial*); the term "social" refers to general processes of social behaviour (whether human or animal), whereas "societal" indicates the uniquely human forms of interaction that can only be understood in terms of culture and history. The paper represents an attempt to move beyond the purely linguistic to locate psychological phenomena (as "real" categories) firmly within a historical and cultural framework.

TOLMAN offers an account of German Critical Psychology that arose during the late 1960s in Berlin as a consequence of the intellectual ferment associated with the student movement. Through an in-depth analysis of the work of Klaus Holzkamp (among others), he demonstrates the "synthetic" nature of

a form of critical psychology that has attempted to develop a scientific account that combines an analysis of "subjectivity" with the evolutionary history of the human species. In this sense, German critical psychology can be seen as both scientific and humanistic. Although much contemporary critical psychology is vehemently opposed to all forms of scientific psychological investigation, German critical psychology attempts a reconciliation of these seemingly incompatible modes of inquiry.

If critical psychologists are to meet the needs of oppressed members of society, it is necessary for them to go beyond the arenas of academia and research. Using liberation theology as inspiration, MARTIN-BAR ambitiously sets out a vision of a critical and praxis-orientated (Latin American) psychology that is concerned less with scientific credibility and more with providing an effective service to the majority of the population; less with an epistemology of the oppressor and more with an epistemology of the oppressed; less with distant observation and more with participation. In this sense, he is concerned with the ways in which ideas may be turned into action, theory into practice.

Like Martin-Bar, CHAMBERLIN seeks to locate critical psychology within real-world practices, in this instance the "Ex-patients' Liberation Movement" – a political liberation movement formed by people who have been diagnosed as "mentally ill" and subsequently institutionalized. This paper raises some important themes of relevance to the development of critical psychology. First, only when a group begins to emerge from subjugation can it begin to reclaim its history (p.323). Second, political liberation movements often advocate the exclusion of professionals from their ranks. The role of the critical psychologist in these movements is therefore a questionable one. Third, ex-patients advocate the right of people with "mental illness" not to be made patients. Such demands undermine dominant ideologies of "mental illness" and break down categories of "normal" and "abnormal" – questioning the whole notion of what we understand as "human".

BURMAN demonstrates the centrality of feminist theory and practice to critical psychology through an analysis of feminist struggles within and around psychology, feminism, and feminist psychology. Through a deconstruction of such notions as standpoint, the relationship between popular psychology and feminism, academic feminist psychology, and feminist psychology more generally, the contributors to this volume develop not only new ways of theorizing women's positions but also ways of acting on them. They stress the need for feminists in psychology to transcend academic boundaries, "to organize with those outside the discipline, and to work across traditional professional boundaries in order to counter psychology's injustices to all women" (p.25).

LAWTHOM offers a cogent analysis of the relationship and tensions between organizational psychology, critical psychology, and feminist theory. Her expressed aim is to offer a means whereby critical feminist work can intervene and challenge the often oppressive, subordinating, and disempowering nature of traditional organizational psychology. Through an analysis of this approach, notions of gender and women in organizational psychology, and a discussion of feminist critiques of organizational psychology, she concludes that critical feminist research is an essential component of a critical psychology that seeks to destabilize, intervene in, and/or change societal contexts (in this instance organizations) wherein traditional psychology is often drawn upon to explain, regulate, and delimit the experiences of those it purportedly describes.

DAVID J. NIGHTINGALE

See also Constructionism, Discourse analysis

Critical realism

Benton, Ted, "Realism and Social Science: Some Comments on Roy Bhaskar's 'The Possibility of Naturalism'", *Radical Philosophy*, 27 (1981): 13–21

Bhaskar, Roy, *A Realist Theory of Science*, Hassocks, Sussex: Harvester Press, and Atlantic Highlands, New Jersey: Humanities Press, 1978

Bhaskar, Roy, *The Possibility of Naturalism: A Philosophical Critique of the Contemporary Human Sciences*, Hassocks, Sussex: Harvester Press, 1979

Collier, Andrew, *Critical Realism: An Introduction to Roy Bhaskar's Philosophy*, London: Verso, 1994

Gunn, Richard, "Marxism and Philosophy: A Critique of Critical Realism", *Capital and Class*, 37 (1989): 86–114

Layder, Derek, *The Realist Image in Social Science*, Basingstoke: Macmillan, and New York: St Martin's Press, 1990

Lovering, John, "Neither Fundamentalism nor 'New Realism': A Critical Realist Perspective on Current Divisions in Socialist Theory", *Capital and Class*, 42 (1990): 30–52

Magill, Kevin, "Against Critical Realism", *Capital and Class*, 54 (1994): 113–36

Porter, Sam, "Critical Realist Ethnography: The Case of Racism and Professionalism in a Medical Setting", *Journal of Sociology*, 27/4 (1993): 591–609

Critical realism is the adopted label of a group of theorists who see the ontological claims of Roy Bhaskar as offering an alternative to both postmodernist and positivist models of social inquiry. According to its adherents, the critical realist ontology of *generative mechanisms* (deep structures operating below the level of events and appearances, which are held to be the basis of natural and societal laws) provides a basis for steering a path between various "false dichotomies" that have bedevilled debates about social scientific method, such as collectivism and individualism, fundamentalism and revisionism, and the fact/value distinction. Whether commitment to critical realism makes a difference to social research is moot: the output of the critical realist "research programme" has largely been about methodology and, arguably, the results of the few putative critical realist empirical studies would have been little affected by subtracting the methodological and ontological claims contained in them.

The main claims and commitments of critical realism were first set out by BHASKAR (1978), who argues that the objects of science – generative mechanisms – exist independently of scientific theory and of any pattern of events by means of which they are detected. His principal targets are idealist accounts of science, which – impressed by the sometimes sharply discontinuous changes in scientific accounts of the world – take scientific models as constructs of the imagination and nothing more, and empiricist accounts that treat scientific laws as consisting of constant conjunctions of events. Against the constant conjunctions model of scientific laws, he argues that the intelligibility of experimental activity presupposes that the laws it identifies are continuing to operate outside of the experimental situation and that laws must be ontologically distinct from events. Although largely ignored by philosophers of science, his work has secured a following among some social scientists.

Turning his attention to the social sciences, BHASKAR (1979) argues that society can be studied scientifically, although the social world has distinctive ontological characteristics not shared with the natural world, which have implications for the character and scope of social sciences. Specifically, the social world is dependent on human activity, which both replicates and transforms it, with the consequence that its structures, although enduring, are "less intransitive" than those of the natural world. He argues that experimental control (what he describes as "closure") is not possible for the social sciences and this, taken together with the claim that there are no regularities outside of experimental situations, entails that prediction is inappropriate for social sciences: their goal should instead be that of explanation, the purpose of which is emancipatory change (a model that has proved attractive to some socialist and radical social scientists).

LOVERING examines "Marxist fundamentalism" and "new realism" (the self-characterization of Labour party policy under Neil Kinnock) from a critical realist perspective, whose insights, he argues, provide an alternative basis for a non-monolithic body of socialist thought and research that can transcend the false dichotomies implicit in the argument between fundamentalist and new realist economics.

One of the few attempts to apply critical realist commitments to the results of empirical study is provided by PORTER, who reports on an ethnographic investigation of how racism affects working relationships between nurses and doctors. According to Porter the ethos of professionalism among those he interviewed tended to exclude open expressions of racist attitudes. This can be understood, he argues, by adopting a critical realist framework in which racism is understood as a hidden structure whose effects can be countered by interaction with other structures. Porter does not provide an account of the nature of racism as an ontological structure with causal powers, however, and it is unclear why his explanation of racist attitudes being overridden by a professionalist ethos stands in need of the critical realist ontological framework.

Notable criticisms of Bhaskar's (1979) account of the possibility of naturalism in social science have been made by realist social scientists. BENTON argues that Bhaskar perpetuates a radical dualism with respect to natural and social scientific knowledge, which repeats familiar and mistaken antinaturalist themes and which fails to offer a plausible model for social scientific investigation. The ontological (and consequently epistemological) distinctions drawn by Bhaskar between the nature of natural and social structures are, according to Benton, either false or ignore important similarities and overlaps between specific natural and social sciences. Whereas it is true, for example, that social structures cannot exist without the activities of human beings, Bhaskar's claim that social structures do not exist independently of the activities they *govern* is false. The existence of the coercive power of the state, for instance, does not depend on the actual exercise of that power. Bhaskar's claim that experiment and prediction are only possible for the natural sciences is rejected on the grounds that probabilistic prediction may be possible for the social sciences and that several natural sciences (such as geology and evolutionary biology) also lack the possibility of experimental "closure". LAYDER provides a sophisticated examination of a range of realist issues and positions in social science. He argues that Bhaskar's claim that ontological features of the world constrain knowledge – "it is the nature of objects that determines their cognitive possibilities for us" (Bhaskar 1979, p.31) – lacks the generality that Bhaskar assumes for it and ignores the importance of levels and types of discursive practice in the construction of social scientific knowledge. Bhaskar's belief that the ontological features of both natural and social reality provide determinate sources of knowledge is a variant of the empiricist idea that observation and experiment are guarantors of knowledge. This leads him to a mistaken empiricist conception of social structure as activity- and concept-dependent.

A more basic challenge to Bhaskar's (1979, p.3) claim that critical realism can serve as a guide to social inquiry is made by MAGILL, who argues that neither critical realism nor any overarching philosophical ontology can provide workable guiding principles for social scientific research and that such principles are, in any case, unnecessary. Several of Bhaskar's key arguments are rejected: prediction-licensing regularities, for example, far from being restricted to experimental situations, are a ubiquitous feature of the natural and social worlds. After criticizing Lovering's advocacy of critical realism in economics, Magill concludes by arguing that social scientists who are committed to the distinction between truth and illusion, or between science and ideology, can retain their commitments without any help from critical realism. Critical realism's claims to be able to provide a philosophical underpinning for Marxism or a philosophy for the left is also challenged by GUNN, who argues that Bhaskar's "depth ontology", involving a causal-explanatory relationship between the levels of events and appearances on the one hand and the hidden mechanisms of reality on the other, contrasts unfavourably with Marx's and Hegel's method, in which appearance and reality are understood as an internally related unity.

Notwithstanding some fanciful assessments of Bhaskar's importance ("the most exciting development in Anglophone philosophy in this half-century"), COLLIER provides a lucid and accessible introduction to the main claims and arguments of critical realism. As the book's primary purpose is exposition and popularization, it is perhaps unsurprising that there is little detailed engagement with Bhaskar's critics. Criticisms (especially of Bhaskar's account of the possibility of social scientific knowledge) are developed in the final chapter, but none that are seriously challenging to critical realism as such.

KEVIN MAGILL

Cross examination

Bentham, Jeremy, *Rationale of Judicial Evidence, Specially Applied to English Practice*, 5 vols, edited by John Stuart Mill, London: Hunt and Clarke, 1827; reprinted Littleton, Colorado: Rothman, 1995

Best, W.M., *A Treatise on the Principles of Evidence and Practice as to Proofs in Courts of Common Law, with Elementary Rules for Conducting the Examination and Cross-Examination of Witnesses*, London: Sweet, and Philadelphia: Johnson, 1849

Choo, Andrew L.-T., *Hearsay and Confrontation in Criminal Trials*, Oxford: Clarendon Press, and New York: Oxford University Press, 1996

Hastings Law Journal, "Symposium on Truth and Its Rivals: Evidence Law Reform and the Goals of Evidence Law", 2–4 (1998): 289–1189

Inbau, Fred E. and John E. Reid, *Criminal Interrogation and Confessions*, Baltimore: Williams and Wilkins, 1962

Stephens, James Fitzjames, *A Digest of the Law of Evidence*, London: Macmillan, 1876

Wellborn, Olin Guy, "Demeanor", *Cornell Law Review*, 3 (1991): 1075–1105

Wigmore, John Henry, *The Science of Judicial Proof: As Given by Logic, Psychology, and General Experience, and Illustrated in Judicial Trials*, revised edition, Boston: Little Brown, 1937

Wigmore, John Henry, *Evidence in Trials at Common Law*, 4th edition, 13 vols, Boston: Little Brown, 1961–88 (plus yearly supplement)

Cross examination has a particularly significant role in common law adversarial trials in which witnesses testify orally. The works considered relate primarily to this.

BENTHAM gives "interrogation", which he prefers to "cross-examination", a privileged position in his rationalist system of evidence – the application of true laws to true facts. In Book two, Chapter nine, "Of interrogation, considered as a security for the trustworthiness of testimony", vol.1, pp.445–510, he argues that interrogation is more effective than oaths or penalties for perjury in assessing the reliability and truthfulness of witnesses. Every witness should be subject to it with inconvenience, delay, or expense as the only exceptions. Every party with an interest should be able to cross examine a witness called by other parties, subject to the control of the judge, for example where a number of parties have identical interests. Consistent with his "natural system of proof" based on family disputes, where family members give their account and are questioned in the presence of other members, he approves of the *confrontation* in French law. The accused and the accuser interrogate each another before a judge:

> Both were present (suppose) at the same transaction: how prompt and lively in such a case is the interchange of questions and replies on both sides! How instantaneously the points of agreement and disagreement are brought to view! How instructive is the *deportment* exhibited on both sides on the occasion of such a conference. (Vol.1, pp.469–70.)

Bentham's brilliance may be concealed from some by his general crankiness and belief in his own opinions.

BEST, relying on the model of civil or Roman law treatises, extracts principles from the common law cases and fits cross examination into its procedural trial context. Chapter one of Part four, "Forensic practice respecting evidence", pp.471–89, illustrates leading questions, which are permitted in cross examination but not in examination in chief, with examples, see §436, pp.478–81. Chapter two, of the same part, "Elementary rules for conducting the examination and cross-examination of witnesses", pp.490–502 illustrate the high status of cross examination as a skill. It is padded with advice from the Roman writer Quintilian, which, understandably in 1849, is not translated.

STEPHENS is a clear and concise exposition of common-law rules as they stood in the 1870s. The book follows the structure of his abandoned *Code of Evidence*, which has been influential in subsequent restatements and codifications. Chapter 16, "Of the examination of witnesses", pp.120–9, and Article 129, "Questions lawful in cross examination" and the accompanying Note 47, pp.123–4 and pp.174–5, show the broad scope of cross examination going to the credibility of witnesses. Article 132, "Cross examination as to previous statements in writing", pp.125–6, deals with the technical rules reducing the effect of documents which were not directly introduced into evidence.

WIGMORE, *Evidence in Trials at Common Law*, is an encyclopaedic restatement of legal doctrine on evidence, including cross examination. It analyses cases, provides orthodox statements of the law and distinctions between legal rules. It evaluates the policies that the rules reflect. It shows their historic development. Cross examination is divided between many topics. Chapter 46 opens with a comprehensive account of cross examination in the context of the exclusionary hearsay rule and, in §1367, its distinctive place in the common law trial: "It may be that in more than one sense it takes the place in our system which torture occupied in the medieval system of the civilians. Nevertheless, it is the greatest legal engine ever invented for the discovery of the truth" (vol.6, p.32). In §1368 the theory and legal art of cross-examination are illustrated. The considerable freedom given in seeking to impeach or discredit a witness are considered in §878 and §§990–96, with the limitation on impeaching a party's own witness dealt with in §§909–18. Cross examination in the context of the presentation of evidence is considered in §1885, and of leading questions in §§768–88. Tribunals where it may not be available are considered in §783. Wigmore's strengths are its detailed coverage and its focus on North American common law. These, for some readers, will also be its weaknesses.

CHOO justifies the exclusionary hearsay rule and the limit imposed by the right to cross examine in criminal trials by recovering the underlying principles. He proposes substantial changes to reflect them more accurately. The need for these reforms detracts from his argument that the law is principled. The right of defendants to confront witnesses against them, included in the sixth amendment to the US Constitution, is a separate rule that also touches on cross examination. He concludes that the sixth amendment has not enlarged any exceptions to the exclusionary hearsay rule.

WIGMORE, *The Science of Judicial Proof*, attempts to integrate law with science. In Part three, Title four, "Methods of detecting testimonial error", Subtitle A, "Methods of forensic practice", Wigmore provides examples of cross examination. Subtitle B, "Methods of experimental psychology", covers scientific techniques and, in the third and last edition in 1937, blood pressure, lie detectors, and word association. This last technique measures the reaction to an idea by the repetition or repression of a word. It was Muestenberg's attack on law's naivety in ignoring it that motivated Wigmore to articulate his "science of proof", see John H. Wigmore, "Professor Muenstenberg and the psychology of testimony", *Illinois Law Review*, 1904/3, pp.399–445.

WELLBORN indirectly demonstrates Wigmore's failure by showing law's continuing autonomy from scientific knowledge. The belief that demeanour is important in assessing credibility of witnesses, used to justify cross examination, is contradicted by experiments that show no difference whether or not their demeanour is seen. He does recognize that there are other justifications for cross examination. The difficulty in court-room based research, unlike laboratory experiments, is knowing who is telling the truth.

HASTINGS LAW JOURNAL, in "Panel 6: Character evidence revisited", pp.663–894, considers character as another justification for cross examination. The exposure of witnesses' character is used to assess their credibility. While character is discussed in the context of propensity to show guilt, the material discussed also shows the uncertainty of relying on character in assessing witness credibility. The most relevant discussion is by Roger Park, "Character at the crossroads", pp.717–79, and a commentary on it and other papers by Miguel A. Méndez, "Character evidence reconsidered: 'People do not seem to be predictable characters'", pp.871–94.

INBAU & REID outline interrogation strategies for law enforcement officers. Judges may not permit deception in cross examination but the law may admit confessional evidence obtained by trick outside the court room. Techniques that might lead to false confessions, such as the use, or threat, of force and promises of leniency will generally provide strong reasons for excluding any confession. Deceit is argued to be permissible as the innocent cannot be tricked. Deceptions include false confessions by accomplices, false eyewitness identifications, and the fabrication of physical evidence, for example fingerprints purported to be taken at the scene or urine samples contaminated with gun powder. Widely influential, the first edition was used by the US Supreme Court in *Miranda v. US* 384 US 436 (1966), establishing a right to counsel, to illustrate techniques of police interrogation. The law in the third and latest edition is dated but the tricks remain similar.

NEIL ANDREWS

See also Evidence, Witnesses

Cultural capital

Alexander, Jeffrey C., *Fin de Siècle Social Theory: Reletivism, Reduction and the Problem of Reason*, London: Verso, 1995

Bourdieu, Pierre and Jean-Claude Passeron, *Les Etudiants et leurs études*, Paris: Mouton, 1964

Bourdieu, Pierre and Jean-Claude Passeron, *Reproduction in Education, Society, and Culture*, revised edition London and Newbury Park, California: Sage, 1990

Calhoun, Craig, Edward LiPuma and Moishe Postone (editors), *Bourdieu: Critical Perspectives*, Cambridge: Polity Press, and Chicago: University of Chicago Press, 1993

Calhoun, Craig, *Critical Social Theory: Culture, History, and the Challenge of Difference*, Oxford and Cambridge, Massachusetts: Blackwell, 1995

Featherstone, Mike, *Consumer Culture and Postmodernism*, London and Newbury Park, California: Sage, 1991

Garnham, Richard and Raymond Williams, "Pierre Bourdieu and the Sociology of Culture: An Introduction" in *Media, Culture, and Society: A Critical Reader*, edited by Richard Collins *et al.*, London and Beverly Hills, California: Sage, 1986

Lamont, Michele and Annette Lareau, "Cultural Capital: Allusions, Gaps and Glissandos in Recent Theoretical Development", *Sociological Theory*, 6/2 (Fall 1988): 153–68

May, Tim, *Situating Social Theory*, Buckingham: Open University Press, 1996

Robbins, Derek, *The Work of Pierre Bourdieu: Recognising Society*, Milton Keynes: Open University Press, and Boulder, Colorado: Westview Press, 1991

Sayer, Andrew, "Bourdieu, Smith and Disinterested Judgement", *Sociological Review*, 47/3 (1999): 403–31

BOURDIEU & PASSERON (1964) first introduced the concept of "cultural capital" in France to refer to high-status cultural signs used in cultural and social selection. They were concerned with seeing how culture influenced the class system and the relationship between action and social structure. They contended that the school system reflected the experiences of the "dominant class" and children from that class entering the system did so with key social and cultural cues.

The essentially economic view of culture was applied, in both the UK and the US, to a diverse number of fields including educational inequality and the sociology of consumption. BOURDIEU & PASSERON (1977) also talks about other forms of capital, namely social, symbolic, and economic. Many scholars have developed the theory of social reproduction especially in the area of the sociology of education, and applied it to ability grouping, the implementation of the curriculum and authority, and power in the classroom.

ALEXANDER attacks Bourdieu for his perceived sociological reductionism, which reduces ideas to their social origins. In addition Bourdieu's commitment to a cultural form of Marxist thought, together with elements of the two traditions he attacks, namely structuralist semiotics and rationalistic behaviourism, bring into question his critique of cultural theory. Alexander offers 88 pages of critique on Bourdieu's theoretical position, claiming that we cannot ignore his Marxist alignments, and arguing that Bourdieu has moved well beyond Marx. Alexander claims that Bourdieu's theory is basically flawed, in theoretical and empirical terms, and "ultimately in ideological and moral terms as well."

CALHOUN, LIPUMA & POSTONE have edited discussions and readings on Bourdieu's work, held at the University of Chicago in the late 1980s (including two in which Bourdieu himself participated) which bring together critical perspectives on Bourdieu's social theory. The collection is valuable because it consists of a critical debate written by distinguished scholars on Bourdieu's theoretical contributions including a reply to some criticisms by himself.

CALHOUN places Bourdieu alongside Derrida, Habermas, and Foucault in the critical social theory approach. Bourdieu's analysis of capital is heavily influenced by Marx but, unlike Marx, he treats capital simply as wealth or power thus losing sight of its historical variability. Whereas Marx laid the foundations for a theory of capital rooted in an historical specificity, Bourdieu sees it as a resource or form of wealth.

ROBBINS was the first English commentary on Bourdieu and it traces the development of his intellectual thought from 1958 to 1989. It is quite clear that we must try to understand him within the context of European thinkers such as Panofsky, Cassirer, and Bachelard. Robbins carefully traces the development of Bourdieu's ideas on social capital and how these have influenced such sociologists as A.H. Halsey, M.F.D. Young, and Basil Bernstein in the field of education.

FEATHERSTONE offers a useful analysis of cultural capital. Cultural capital exists in three forms: embodied state (style of presentation, mode of speech, looks); objectified state (cultural goods like pictures, books, buildings); and institutionalized state (educational qualifications). Within the context of postmodernism the concept of cultural capital undergoes a major shift in which existing symbolic hierarchies "are deconstructed and a more playful, popular democratic impulse becomes manifest." New cultural capital and a multiplicity of symbolic experiences are on offer in an increasingly globalized world.

The richness of Bourdieu's notion of cultural capital is demonstrated in its application to a wide range of aesthetic theory in terms of "taste" and the power and processes of capital accumulation. Various mappings of cultural capital are also feasible, such as the construction of a symbolic hierarchy of cities.

GARNHAM & WILLIAMS argued that "while Bourdieu has concentrated his attention upon the mode of domination, upon what he calls the exercise of Symbolic Power, his theory is cast in resolutely materialist terms." Their contribution is still of value because it links the theoretical contribution of Bourdieu to media and cultural studies, especially in their discussion of symbolic power. They argue that the educational system, as a historical system of certification, has created a market in cultural capital "within which certificates act as money both in terms of a common, abstract socially guaranteed medium of exchange between cultural capitals and, crucially, between cultural capital and the labour market and thus access to economic capital".

LAMONT & LAREAU is still excellent in the manner in which it traces the concept of cultural capital from its origins. They disentangle the many interpretations of cultural capital, the methodological issue, the way that exclusion and power are linked to cultural capital, and a critique of cultural capital in the US. They define cultural capital as "widely shared, legitimate culture made up of high status cultural signals (attitudes, preferences, behaviors, and goods) used in direct or indirect cultural exclusion".

MAY is of interest because he places Bourdieu contextually within the developments of social theory. He shows how Bourdieu's thought engages with other traditions and has developed from such engagement. He also discusses issues in Bourdieu's work that need resolving.

SAYER is useful for its sympathetic critique of Bourdieu's work. Accused of reductionism Bourdieu nevertheless refutes such an accusation. However, there is evidence that his "empirical studies tend to reduce actors' putative disinterested judgements to functions of their *habitus* in relation to the social field and to unconscious strategies of distinction".

KENNETH JONES

See also Human capital

Cultural integration

Archer, Margaret S., *Culture and Agency: The Place of Culture in Social Theory*, revised edition, Cambridge and New York: Cambridge University Press, 1996
Benedict, Ruth, *Patterns of Culture*, Boston: Houghton Mifflin, 1934; London: Routledge, 1935
Bidney, David, "Modes of Cultural Integration" in *Theoretical Anthropology*, New York: Columbia University Press, 1953; 2nd edition, with introduction by Martin Bidney, New Brunswick, New Jersey: Transaction, 1996
Kroeber, Alfred L., *Anthropology: Culture Patterns and Processes*, New York: Harcourt Brace, 1963
Linton, Ralph, *The Study of Man: An Introduction*, New York: Appleton Century, 1936
Malinowski, Bronisław, *A Scientific Theory of Culture and Other Essays*, Chapel Hill, University of North Carolina Press, 1944
Parsons, Talcott, *The Social System*, Glencoe, Illinois: Free Press, 1951; London: Tavistock, 1952
Radcliffe-Brown, A.R., *Structure and Function in Primitive Society*, Glencoe, Illinois: Free Press, and London: Cohen and West, 1952
Sorokin, Pitirim A., *Social and Cultural Dynamics: A Study of Change in Major Systems of Art, Truth, Ethics, Law, and Social Relationships*, 4 vols, New York: American Book Company, and London: Allen and Unwin, 1937–41; 1-vol. abridgement, London: Peter Owen, 1957, New Brunswick, New Jersey: Transaction, 1985

ARCHER is one of the latest sociological approaches to the issue of functionalist cultural integration as propagated by cultural anthropologists and redefined by sociologists. Identifying structure and culture, structure and agency as crucial technical problems in the study of society, she re-evaluates as myth the concept of cultural integration that sees culture as coherent and uniform in a symbolically consistent universe. A brilliantly crafted opening chapter on cultural integration takes on the whole idea of "parts" versus "people" in a rigorous theoretically sustained presentation. Her five theses and her position that sociocultural interaction is a source of cultural altogether form important contributions to social theory discourse.

BENEDICT, although dated and misinterpreted, is historically relevant as one of the earliest pioneers in ethnology who speaks directly to the issue of the integration of culture. A popularizer of the term "patterns", she influenced many others with her idea of cultural configurations as cultural wholes within each culture. Her advocacy by example of the diligent application of scientific techniques to anthropological analysis makes her timeless. She is also historically significant for her Nietzschean application of Apollonian and Dionysian culture types to Zuni and Plain Indian culture types in a search for comparative culturally integrative patterns.

BIDNEY provides a definitive chapter on cultural integration as a basic problem in social theory in an altogether erudite work on anthropological theories. He provides a survey of several modes of cultural integration and in doing so reviews major contributions both in anthropological and sociological literature. His critical review with an undercurrent of the importance of the reality of form and content, pattern and process, structure and events are interestingly echoed by Archer writing almost 40 years later.

KROEBER refines Malinowski's arguments by examining integration within culture growth. In this most influential work he demonstrates his primary concern with the nature of culture and the understanding of its process for instance when applied to cultural integration. His contribution to integration of culture can be found in his classificatory patterns of culture on the one hand and his configuration of culture growth on the other. By the former, his universal, systemic, whole-culture, and style types have endured, and by the latter, he has bridged anthropologists and sociologists with his observation that each culture or civilization is consistent and coheres in its own logical and creative way.

LINTON's classic on the study of man is still pertinent today, most especially for his once novel stance on society and the individual. His most enduring contribution is in defining status and role in the integrative function of the individual in society. He is also useful for an understanding of cultural integration or synchronically as an orderly societal diachronically process. His emphasis on the application of functionalism to the interrelationship of individuals and patterned interest marks the early beginnings of studies in personality and culture. His work is also memorable for supporting the idea of configurations and that any culture cohered through a whole range of pattered interests, orientations, and values of groups.

MALINOWSKI's pioneer work brought functionalism to the forefront against a background of the idea of cultural phenomena as interrelated wholes functionally integrated with elements serving as means to satisfy a whole range of basic psychosocial needs. It also marks a departure from earlier diffusionist and evolutionist theories of culture. Although criticized for not recognizing the conflict dysfunctional aspects of culture and for failure to provide a principle of integration, his work remains ground breaking and his place is assured in anthropological studies.

PARSONS is important among other things for his development of sociological approaches from anthropological functionalism and psychodynamics. In seeking a systematic and theoretically integrative approach to social action theory he proposes four functional paradigms of which one is integration. His work emphasizes the integration of social systems. His contribution strengthened the ties between social behavioural sciences. As a dominant sociologist of his time his work inspired numerous studies and theories.

RADCLIFFE-BROWN is a pathfinder in anthropological and sociological theorizing. The structuralist-functionalist approach for which he is noted is based on the concept of cultural integration. Running through the twelve essays written by him at various times is the position that cultural instructions are related to one another and all contribute to the integration of the social structure. Influenced by Durkheim, he posits that social activity contributed to the maintenance of social relations, thus providing social integration. He continues to be a benchmark in comparative ethnology and sociology and his work would influence later sociologists like Sorokin and Parsons.

SOROKIN's work is worth consulting for his most comprehensive analysis of the problem of cultural integration in contemporary sociological literature. His main contribution is his theory of the logico-meaningful integration of culture following the idealistic tradition of Hegel. He refines the anthropological holistic argument of culture while accepting that a culture must be logically consistent to be integrated. Most fascinating are his three categories of cultural mentality adduced with historical statistical evidence.

AYODELE OGUNDIPE

Cultural landscape

Atkins, Peter, "A Seance with the Living: The Intelligibility of the North Korean Landscape" in *North Korea in the New World Order*, edited by Hazel Smith *et al.*, New York: St Martin's Press, 1996

Cosgrove, Denis and Stephen Daniels (editors), *The Iconography of Landscape: Essays on the Symbolic Representation, Design, and Use of Past Environments*, Cambridge: Cambridge University Press, 1988

Cosgrove, Denis, *The Palladian Landscape: Geographical Change and Its Cultural Representations in Sixteenth-Century Italy*, Leicester: Leicester University Press, and University Park: Pennsylvania State University Press, 1993

Daniels, Stephen, *Fields of Vision: Landscape Imagery and National Identity in England and the United States*, Cambridge: Polity Press, and Princeton, New Jersey: Princeton University Press, 1993

Duncan, James S., *The City as Text: The Politics of Landscape Interpretation in the Kandyan Kingdom*, Cambridge and New York: Cambridge University Press, 1990

Duncan, James, "The Superorganic in American Cultural Geography," *Annals of the Association of American Geographers*, 70/2 (1980): 181–98

Kroeber, A.L., "The Superorganic", *American Anthropologist*, 19/2 (1917): 163–213

Olwig, Kenneth R., "Recovering the Substantive Nature of Landscape", *Annals of the Association of American Geographers*, 86/4 (1996): 630–53

Sauer, Carl O., "The Morphology of Landscape" in *Land and Life: A Selection from the Writings of Carl Ortwin Sauer*, edited by John Leighly, Berkeley: University of California Press, 1974

The most enduring influence upon the concept of cultural landscape has come from American geographer Carl Orwin Sauer. For SAUER, nature is central to the particular forms and patterns that cultures take. Nature is a stage on which humankind enacts its cultural activity, but a stage that is itself affected by that cultural activity, with the result being *cultural* landscapes that take the place of *natural* landscapes. Writing in 1925, Sauer declared that, "Culture is the agent, the natural area is the medium, the cultural landscape is the result." Sauer promoted the notion of "culture groups", which he saw as preindustrialized rural peoples whose cultural practices shaped the natural landscape itself and through whose material artefacts it is possible to infer and interpret cultural characteristics. Positioning themselves against the prevailing theory of environmental determinism, Sauer and his associates at the University of California at Berkeley advanced the notion that, instead of the environment controlling cultural and human outcomes, culture influences the way the landscape itself evolves, and landscape is the palette containing the materials for cultural expression. Observation and examination of material artefacts, along with examination of the landscape as shaped by human practices, are the windows into human societies. This approach came to be referred to as the Berkeley school.

A.L. Kroeber, an anthropologist, was a colleague of Sauer's and influential in the Berkeley school. KROEBER's "superorganic" theory sees culture as consisting of patterns of meanings, historically transmitted through various symbols, artefacts, and other material expressions. As widely critiqued as it is still studied, the superorganic was Kroeber's response to environmental determinism. Like Sauer, Kroeber rejected race and environment as explanatory tools for why cultural variation exists, and advanced the superorganic as an alternate explanation for the imparting of skills and beliefs to successive generations.

DUNCAN's (1980) critique of the superorganic is among the most widely cited works that attempts to sum up late 20th-century cultural geographers' criticisms of their predecessors' approach to interpreting culture and cultural landscape. There are three emphases in this critique: first, the Sauerian approach to cultural landscape was theoretically shallow; second, that Sauer and the Berkeley school were preoccupied with rural preindustrial culture groups, to which they attributed homogeneity and willing cultural conformity; and third, Sauer and Kroeber concentrated upon cultural manifestations, which were visible, material, and extant. However, Duncan also asserts that the superorganic is a culture of consensus, implying a view of man that is passive and impotent. He argues that, for the Berkeley School, the individual is invisible, deviance is absent or ignored, and there is no conflict within communities over cultural expression. In short, the superorganic promotes a culture of consensus, arguably unrealistic for any culture group, even in the most idyllic of rural and preindustrial circumstances.

Duncan's critique of the Berkeley school was an indicator of the emergence of a "new cultural geography", an approach to cultural landscape influenced by postmodern thinking. A 1988 collection of essays edited by COSGROVE & DANIELS is often cited as an example of the shift to cultural landscape scholarship by the "new" cultural geographers. Drawing heavily upon art and architectural history, these essays point to many concrete examples of political and cultural attitudes being constructed and reproduced through both landscape depictions and manipulation of the built environment. Additionally, they show how representation of a landscape is a political and even a radical act.

OLWIG contributes to this literature in his analysis of the term "landscape" as a concept with a particular history. Appearing well after the move to the new cultural geography was under way, Olwig's article reminds students of this literature that the term landscape is itself not unproblematic. Often casually used to refer simply to "scenery" or to aesthetic appreciation of a particular setting or of a represented setting, landscape has a substantial social history. Moreover, it developed slightly different emphases in meaning in British/American and in German social thought, respectively. Olwig argues that greater attention to the intellectual history of the term will highlight past precedents for connecting landscape with the more substantive concepts of law and social justice. For Olwig, focusing more on the substantive nature of the landscape concept would ease the task of new cultural geographers, who wish to show how cultural landscapes are not only to be examined aesthetically, but are also highly politicized texts.

Both COSGROVE and DANIELS make individual contributions to the postmodern study of cultural landscape. Cosgrove notes that the new cultural geography brings dimensions to the discipline traditionally found outside social science in the humanities – philosophy, religion, the arts, which tend to be the vehicles for direct cultural expression about nature and about the natural settings in which humans dwell. Cosgrove chooses to concentrate upon the social order of a particular period, Palladian Venice, and he presents an interpretation of how the cosmology of social and political elites was reflected in the built landscape. Also drawing upon an art history literature, but with an inverted approach, Daniels studies landscape representation and how exhibited depictions of landscape can reinscribe a particular national culture. Using English and American landscape artists, from Cole and Constable to Francis Palmer who painted for Currier and Ives, Daniels argues that such works participated in the construction and reinforcement of national identities, as the images contained in them reaffirmed cultural expectations and took on mythic and iconographic qualities. He also suggests that artistic depictions of landscapes, of both city and rural subject elements, contribute to the construction of a national culture by helping people to incorporate into their cultural lexicon landscapes they would never otherwise experience.

A widely cited 1990 work by DUNCAN presents the concept of a landscape as texts, "communicative devices that transmit information". He claims, however, that reading the landscape must be more than just a contemplative exercise, because the landscape has a role in how social power relations "are constituted, reproduced, and contested". Like the other voices in this literature, Duncan believes that the analysis of cultural landscape is best conducted through a specific historical example rather than in the abstract, and his particular study is of a 19th-century Sri Lankan kingdom.

Duncan argues that rituals enacted upon the landscape, as well as the landscape itself following its manipulation through myriad cultural practices, "were concretizations of the narratives within the political discourses". ATKINS echoes this argument with uncanny precision in his treatment of the contemporary urban, industrial, and tourist landscapes of North Korea. Somewhat obscurely located in a volume on North Korea in the post-Cold War period that may draw little readership outside of political science circles, this essay deserves to be highlighted nevertheless. The new cultural geographers tend to use specific historical examples for their analysis, but the technique of seeing a cultural landscape as a text to be interpreted can be applied anywhere and at any time, and Atkins applies the postmodern methodology for cultural landscape analysis to a little-studied contemporary setting. As a consequence of self-imposed political and social isolation, North Korea presents a landscape that can be read as a unified text reflecting the often bizarre trademark political culture in a scope of settings, from sterile and expansive urbanscapes, to showpiece industrial projects, to national parks where political slogans are carved so deeply into granite cliff faces that it seems that nature itself must be politicized.

CAROL ANN MEDLICOTT

Cultural relativism

Benedict, Ruth, *Patterns of Culture*, Boston: Houghton Mifflin, 1934; London: Routledge, 1935

Geertz, Clifford, "Anti Anti-Relativism" in *Relativism: Interpretation and Confrontation*, edited by Michael Krausz, Notre Dame, Indiana: University of Notre Dame Press, 1989

Hatch, Elvin, *Culture and Morality: The Relativity of Values in Anthropology*, New York: Columbia University Press, 1983

Herskovits, Melville J., *Cultural Relativism: Perspectives in Cultural Pluralism*, edited by Frances Herskovits, New York: Random House, 1972

Howard, Rhoda E., "Cultural Absolutism and the Nostalgia for Community", *Human Rights Quarterly*, 15/2 (1993): 315–38

Ladd, John (editor), *Ethical Relativism*, Belmont, California: Wadsworth, 1973

Nagengast, Carole and Terence Turner (guest editors), special issue on human rights and cultural relativism, *Journal of Anthropological Research*, 53/3 (1997)

Renteln, Alison Dundes, *International Human Rights: Universalism versus Relativism*, London and Newbury Park, California: Sage, 1990

Schmidt, Paul F., "Some Criticisms of Cultural Relativism", *Journal of Philosophy*, 52/25 (1955): 780–91

Shweder, Richard A., "Ethical Relativism: Is There a
    Defensible Version?", *Ethos*, 18/2 (1990): 205–18
Sumner, William Graham, *Folkways*, Boston: Ginn, 1906;
    edited by Edward Sagarin, New York: Schocken, 1979
Tilley, John J., "Cultural Relativism, Universalism, and the
    Burden of Proof", *Millennium*, 27/2 (1998): 275–97
Westermarck, Edward, *The Origin and Development of the
    Moral Ideas*, 2nd edition, 2 vols, London: Macmillan,
    1912–17
Williams, Elgin, "Anthropology for the Common Man",
    American Anthropologist, 49/1 (1947): 84–90

The term "cultural relativism" is used for a variety of theses which, unfortunately, are seldom clearly distinguished. Among them are: (a) the *moral* theory of cultural relativism, which asserts that no moral judgement is universally valid, that every moral judgement is culturally relative; (b) the *methodological* theory of cultural relativism, which asserts that every custom, belief, or action must be studied in the context of the culture in which it occurs; and (c) *descriptive* cultural relativism, which asserts that moral beliefs and customs differ fundamentally from one culture to the next. These distinctions, and several others, are discussed in the paper by TILLEY. The above bibliography focuses on thesis (a), although many of the listed works are also relevant to (b) and (c).

Those unfamiliar with cultural relativism would do well to begin with HATCH. This book is both a history and a critical study of 20th-century cultural relativism. It is brief, balanced, accessible, and informative – altogether a very edifying monograph, and no doubt the best introduction to the topic. Chapters two, three, and four include useful guides to further reading.

Following a reading of Hatch, LADD's anthology is valuable both for the importance and for the variety of its contents. Its 11 essays include classic defences of relativism by William Graham Sumner and Melville Herskovits, and some equally classic criticisms of relativism by anthropologists Clyde Kluckhohn and Robert Redfield (which focus on descriptive cultural relativism), and by *gestalt* psychologist Karl Duncker.

After studying Hatch and Ladd, the reader can proceed either to the classic sources for cultural relativism or to the debates of the 1980s and 1990s. The first option leads to the works of SUMNER, BENEDICT, WESTERMARCK and HERSKOVITS. Not one of these works is solely, or even primarily, a defence of cultural relativism. For example, Sumner's work covers enormous territory, being (as its subtitle says) "a study of the sociological importance of usages, manners, customs, mores, and morals". Also, despite initial appearances, Westermarck's moral theory is best classified as a form of subjectivism, not of cultural relativism. All the same, these four books are the chief sources for modern cultural relativism, and as such they are essential reading. Of particular importance are the first seven chapters in Westermarck; the first eight essays in Herskovits; the first three and final two chapters in Benedict; and chapters 1, 2, 11, and 15 of Sumner.

Philosophical critiques of cultural relativism are found in Tilley, SCHMIDT, and WILLIAMS. Schmidt's essay is an analysis and a forceful criticism both of cultural relativism and of the grounds on which relativism rests. It is representative of the philosophical objections that have accumulated against

cultural relativism. Williams's paper is a review of Benedict's *Patterns of Culture*. Although short, it is most illuminating, as it brings out both the strengths and weaknesses, and the many tensions, not only in Benedict's position but in cultural relativism in general. Writing in 1947, Williams does not hesitate to refer to the atrocities of World War II when considering the plausibility of the relativist's moral theory.

After reading these critical essays, one might suspect that cultural relativism has little going for it. Hence it would be wise at this point to read the sympathetic pieces by GEERTZ, RENTELN, and SHWEDER; also Elvin Hatch's "The Good Side of Relativism" in NAGENGAST & TURNER. These authors are aware of the many objections that have accumulated against cultural relativism. Yet they remain sympathetic to the relativist's thesis. Each author defends, reformulates, or looks for the "good side" of relativism. These works are important for gaining a balanced perspective on cultural relativism.

For the past two decades, much of the debate over relativism has occurred in the context of debates over international human rights, and it is not hard to see why. It is arguable that the notion of human rights (or, at the very least, the *list* of human rights in the United Nations Universal Declaration of Human Rights) is relative to Western culture, that it has no validity or relevance beyond that culture. A good source on this topic is Terence Turner's "Human Rights, Human Difference: Anthropology's Contribution to an Emancipatory Cultural Politics" in Nagengast & Turner. Renteln is an especially good source, with a useful introduction to the topic, a comprehensive bibliography, and, in its third chapter, an important defence of cultural relativism. For the anti-relativist's perspective HOWARD is first rate; so too is Elizabeth M. Zechenter's "In the Name of Culture: Cultural Relativism and the Abuse of the Individual" in Nagengast & Turner. The latter anthology contains, in addition to the pieces by Hatch, Turner, and Zechenter, two other papers: Ellen Messer's "Pluralist Approaches to Human Rights" and Carole Nagengast's "Women, Minorities, and Indigenous Peoples: Universalism and Cultural Relativity". Messer tries to steer between a relativistic approach to human rights on the one hand, and a narrowly Western approach on the other, by defending a form of cultural pluralism. Nagengast tries to combine the strengths, and avoid the weaknesses, of universalism and relativism (particularly as those views relate to the treatment of women, minorities, and indigenous groups) by arguing for "a mediated and partial universalism". Valuable bibliographies are found in the essays by Messer, Nagengast, and Zechenter.

JOHN J. TILLEY

Cultural reproduction

Bourdieu, Pierre, *Outline of a Theory of Practice*, Cambridge
    and New York: Cambridge University Press, 1977
Bourdieu, Pierre, *Distinction: A Social Critique of the
    Judgement of Taste*, London: Routledge, and Cambridge,
    Massachusetts: Harvard University Press, 1984
Bourdieu, Pierre and Jean-Claude Passeron, *Reproduction in
    Education, Society, and Culture*, 2nd edition, London and
    Newbury Park, California: Sage, 1990

Jenks, Chris, *Culture*, London and New York: Routledge, 1993a

Jenks, Chris (editor), *Cultural Reproduction*, London and New York: Routledge, 1993b

Reay, D., "Engendering Social Reproduction: Mothers in the Educational Marketplace", *British Journal of the Sociology of Education*, 19/2 (1998): 195–209

Wallace, Claire, *For Richer, for Poorer: Growing Up in and out of Work*, London and New York: Tavistock, 1987

Wallace, Claire, "Between the Family and the State: Young People in Transition", *Youth and Policy*, 25 (1988): 25–36

Willis, Paul E., *Learning to Labour: How Working Class Kids Get Working Class Jobs*, Farnborough, Hampshire: Saxon House, 1977

The concept of cultural reproduction emanates from the work of the French sociologist and cultural theorist, Pierre Bourdieu. The key concepts and assumptions of Bourdieu's theoretical framework are to be found in BOURDIEU (1977). The central concept of Bourdieu's theoretical scheme, is the notion of "habitus". The habitus is a set of "dispositions" that impel individuals to act and react in certain ways. These dispositions are inculcated, particularly during childhood, through the process of socialization. Through these dispositions, the habitus shapes perception, thought, taste, appreciation, and action. The habitus will therefore reflect the social conditions of the background in which the individual was brought up. For example, an individual from a working-class background will have acquired dispositions and values that are different from those of an individual from a middle-class background. In this way, social class differences are socially and culturally reproduced.

The concepts of social and cultural reproduction are integral to Bourdieu's work in the field of education. Bourdieu sees the education system as a complex set of institutions and practices that serve to reproduce, symbolically and culturally, the relations of power in a given society. This is achieved through "symbolic violence". The theory of symbolic violence is introduced by BOURDIEU & PASSERON in *Reproduction in Education, Society, and Culture*, first published in France in 1970. Symbolic violence, according to Bourdieu, is the imposition of systems of symbolism and meaning (culture) upon groups or classes in such a way that they are experienced as legitimate. Bourdieu argues that, because what is being inculcated through the education system is the dominant middle-class culture, educational achievement will naturally be defined in those terms. Thus, Bourdieu argues that the habitus of the subordinate working-class children does not provide them with the cultural capital required to be successful in education. Middle class children, on the other hand, through the habitus, have acquired considerable cultural capital, which enables them to do well in an essentially middle-class education system. In this way, the education system serves to ensure that class divisions are socially and culturally reproduced.

The concept of cultural reproduction is further developed by BOURDIEU (1984). In this book Bourdieu investigates the relationship between occupational position, and taste in cultural goods, arguing that taste in cultural goods can be understood as an indicator of social position. He presents an empirical analysis of occupational position in French society, claiming that the tastes, interests, and products associated with particular class fractions are dependent upon their possession of economic and cultural capital.

The concept of cultural reproduction provided the framework for WILLIS's seminal study, *Learning to Labour*. Willis set out to investigate how cultural reproduction occurs in the labour market; in other words, to discover how working-class kids get working-class jobs, and working-class thoughts, and lifestyles. Willis studied the transition from school to work of a group of working-class "lads". He found that the lads had a clear understanding of the school's authority, but used this understanding to subvert it, rather than to conform. The school was seen as an alien environment, resulting in strong anti-authoritarianism, and rejection of the prevailing middle-class norms. They derived pleasure from causing disruption to lessons, and challenging the authority of the teachers.

Willis studied these "lads" during their transition from school to work. He argues that working-class youngsters are not in competition for middle-class jobs, because they simply do not want them. The "lads", for example, saw office jobs as soft and effeminate. Their working-class backgrounds provided them with an orientation towards manual labour. Thus, the rejection of middle-class norms, along with a disrespect for authority, and the high status attached to manual labour, served to reinforce the "lads'" cultural identification as working class. The lads looked forward to going to work. As Willis points out, working in blue-collar workplaces very often involves similar features to those the lads had employed in their counter-school culture – banter, quick wit, and the ability to subvert the demands of their superiors. *Learning to Labour* therefore provides some empirical evidence of the way in which social and cultural reproduction takes place through the transition from school to work.

However, in an empirical study of the transition to adulthood, WALLACE (1987) argues against the implication that young people are merely socially and culturally reproduced as workers. Wallace argues that this is only one aspect in the transition to adulthood. WALLACE (1988) argues that the transition to adulthood can be seen as part of a process of social and cultural reproduction that takes place on three levels. Firstly, through the labour market, in the transition from school to work. Secondly, through the housing market, in the transition from the parental home to an independent residential unit. Thirdly, through the family, in the transition from family of origin, to a family of one's own.

In a more general discussion, JENKS (1993a) provides a useful and succinct chapter on cultural reproduction. He argues that the concept allows us to contemplate the necessity and complementarity of continuity and change in social experience. Jenks considers the concept of cultural reproduction from a variety of sociological approaches, such as the Marxist perspective, the Durkheimian perspective, ethnomethodology, and structuralism.

JENKS (1993b) suggests that the concept of cultural reproduction, although currently not fashionable, is still a particularly fertile area for social theory. It can be used in a variety of analytic ways, to provide insights into a number of cultural formations, including gender roles, fine art, film, journalism, style, language, and sociology itself. Jenks presents a collection of papers oriented towards the explanation of how culture is produced and reproduced. The papers draw on a number of perspectives, including poststructuralism, postmodernism, politics, and feminism, to provide a contemporary analysis of cultural reproduction in a variety of fields.

REAY highlights the centrality of women to social and cultural reproduction, through a focus on the social and cultural processes embedded in parental involvement in education. The paper argues that, in the context of a flexible labour market, middle class reproduction increasingly has to be worked for. It describes some of the gendered class processes that all the mothers in the research were at times actively engaged in. Although all the mothers helped children with schoolwork, and talked to teachers, it was only the middle-class mothers who had the power and resources to act effectively to shape the curriculum offered to their children. Reay concludes that a market system of education provides the middle classes with a competitive edge, of which they will increasingly take advantage.

COLIN DAWSON

Culture

Barthes, Roland, *Mythologies*, edited and translated by Annette Lavers, London: Jonathan Cape, 1972; New York: Hill and Wang, 1973 (French edition 1957)

Bennett, Tony, "Putting Policy into Cultural Studies" in *Cultural Studies*, edited by Lawrence Grossberg, Cary Nelson and Paula A. Treichler, London and New York: Routledge, 1992

Bhabha, Homi K. (editor), *Nation and Narration*, London and New York: Routledge, 1990

Bourdieu, Pierre, *Distinction: A Social Critique of the Judgement of Taste*, London: Routledge and Kegan Paul, and Cambridge, Massachusetts: Harvard University Press, 1984 (French edition 1979)

Ferguson, Marjorie and Peter Golding (editors), *Cultural Studies in Question*, London and Thousand Oaks, California: Sage, 1997

Hall, Stuart, "The Toad in the Garden: Thatcherism among the Theorists" in *Marxism and the Interpretation of Culture*, edited by Cary Nelson and Lawrence Grossberg, Basingstoke: Macmillan, and Urbana: University of Illinois Press, 1988

Hebdige, Dick, *Subculture: The Meaning of Style*, London: Methuen, 1979

Hoggart, Richard, *The Uses of Literacy*, London: Chatto and Windus, 1957; New Brunswick, New Jersey: Transaction, 1998

Jenks, Chris, *Culture*, London and New York: Routledge, 1993

Williams, Raymond, *Culture and Society, 1780–1950*, London: Chatto and Windus, and New York: Columbia University Press, 1958

Intellectual discussion of "culture" in the post-World War II period has been framed within the context of the emergence and proliferation of the field of cultural studies. According to one of the founding fathers of this tradition of thinking,

WILLIAMS, the term culture is intimately tied to the development of a related series of key terms, such as industrialism, democracy, class, and art, which are anchored in social change from the 19th century to the present. Williams makes his argument through an engagement with some of the key literary figures of the period covered, such as Edmund Burke, Thomas Carlyle, Matthew Arnold, and F.R. Leavis. He traces the notion of culture from its conception as a "habit of mind" to a state of intellectual development (in the sense of civilization), to a set of aesthetic practices to "a whole way of life, material, intellectual and spiritual". In doing so, he presents a clear shift from an aesthetic notion of culture to a more anthropological one.

Working closely with Williams, HOGGART in the 1950s attempted to retrieve the notion of culture from its entrenchment within an aesthetic lexicon and to locate it firmly within the field of lived experience. His discussion of UK working class cultures is played against a critique of an ensuing Americanism. He details the "authenticity" of working class trips to the seaside in opposition to the "shiny barbarism" of the new imported cultures of "milk bars", pop music, and US television "westerns". Although his analysis is dated, the rich texture of his writing has survived the travails of time and provides readers with an immediately recognizable set of oppositions that still circulate today in popular discourse.

Despite this early research by Hoggart, Williams, and also E. P. Thompson, the introduction of a sustained analysis of culture and establishment of what is known as cultural studies is greatly indebted to the work of HALL. Among other things, Hall and others at the Centre for Contemporary Cultural Studies, Birmingham, UK, engaged with the work of the Italian Marxist, Antonio Gramsci. In a more recent essay, Hall discusses the phenomenon of "Thatcherism" in order to provide an analysis of the way in which a set of political right-wing ideologies become hegemonic: namely, the way in which these ideologies become deep rooted in everyday culture. Hall articulates the notion of hegemony within a wider context of structuralist and poststructuralist arguments concerning the nature of discourse and ideology.

Hall and others at the Centre were also keen to develop an analysis of the semiotics of culture. The work of BARTHES is of prime importance in this respect. In a collection of essays entitled *Mythologies*, he detailed quotidian existence from wrestling to fashion to children's toys. The final essay in the collection provides a theoretical model for the study of meaning production and ideology. Although now surpassed by more recent writings, *Mythologies* has become a standard introduction to a semiotic analysis of culture. Writers such as HEBDIGE have used this framework to analyse how particular subcultures can be understood as the symbolic contestation of a wider hegemonic culture. He details the styles and articulation of meanings of subcultural forms, such as punks, skinheads, and Rastafarians, in terms of how they provide evidence of political struggle by another means.

The French sociologist BOURDIEU has been a central figure in discussion of culture. His work has been quickly and enthusiastically received within an Anglo-American context, and provides a provocative framework for understanding the sociology of taste. The cultural distinctions between, for example, opera and football, are discussed through the lens of a particular habitus: namely the socially and structurally constituted (and constituting) classificatory schemes, competencies, and dispositions of social agents. In this sense, Bourdieu's work provides further evidence that taste is not a universal phenomenon, but socially embedded.

The social study of culture has been deeply enhanced by work within postcolonial theory. BHABHA in his writings on nationhood has been a central figure in the debates. He provides a detailed and difficult argument in which he makes the case that "nationhood" is not the starting-point of cultural identity, but its outcome. Nationhood is enunciated through discourse. Bhabha further argues that national identity is never unitary, but necessarily hybrid.

The cultural studies approach to the study of culture has been critiqued by two notable pieces of work. Firstly, from within the heartland of cultural studies, BENNETT argues that the aesthetic, anthropological, and semiotic notions of culture need to be understood theoretically and historically within the purview of a "governmental" notion of culture. He draws on Michel Foucault's work on governmentality (a neologism for rationalities of government) to show how culture is always construed within regimes of power/knowledge and that, for example, notions of high and popular culture need to be understood as mechanisms that both make the object visible and provide its means of government. Bennett is critical of the Gramscian framework of cultural studies and argues that we cannot, *a priori*, read culture as either "progressive" or "reactionary". On the contrary, the politics of culture is always specific to particular institutional and discursive arrangements. Bennett is important because he turns the study of culture away from a radical left critique of power to a more liberal-democratic engagement with cultural policy.

Similarly, FERGUSON & GOLDING, in their edited collection, provide a critique of this earlier Gramscian moment in the study of culture and they attempt to redraw the map of cultural studies so that, on the one hand, the study of texts and audiences can be realigned with an understanding of the political economy of cultural institutions, and, on the other hand, the master narrative of the sociology of culture can provide the ground for such a realignment. The collection contains a number of writers from the heartland of cultural studies to media political economists to social psychologists. In doing so, some of the key policy questions concerning the study of culture are rethought. In this respect, JENKS' short book on the subject tries to provide a longer sociological context to the study of culture. He quickly trawls through sociologists from Durkheim and Parsons, to Garfinkel and anthropologists, from Radcliffe-Brown and Malinowski, to Geertz.

DAVID OSWELL

Currency unions, *see* Optimum currency areas and currency unions

Custody

Chesler, Phyllis, *Mothers on Trial: The Battle for Children and Custody*, New York: McGraw Hill, 1986

Fineman, Martha and Anne Opie, "The Uses of Social Science Data in Legal Policymaking: Custody Determinations at Divorce", *Wisconsin Law Review*, (1987): 107–58

Goldstein, Joseph, Anna Freud, Albert J. Solnit and Sonja Goldstein, *In the Best Interests of the Child: Professional Boundaries*, New York: Free Press, and London: Collier Macmillan, 1986

Grossberg, Michael, *Governing the Hearth: Law and the Family in Nineteenth-Century America*, Chapel Hill: University of North Carolina Press, 1985

Grossberg, Michael, *A Judgment for Solomon: The d'Hauteville Case and Legal Experience in Antebellum America*, Cambridge and New York: Cambridge University Press, 1996

Maidment, Susan, *Child Custody and Divorce: The Law in Social Context*, London: Croom Helm, 1984

Mason, Mary Ann, *From Father's Property to Children's Rights: The History of Child Custody in the United States*, New York: Columbia University Press, 1994

Smart, Carol and Selma Sevenhuijsen (editors), *Child Custody and the Politics of Gender*, London and New York: Routledge, 1989

Stone, Lawrence, *Road to Divorce: England, 1530–1987*, Oxford and New York: Oxford University Press, 1990

Wright, Danaya, "DeManneville v. DeManneville: Rethinking the Birth of Custody Law under Patriarchy", *Law and History Review*, 17 (1999): 247–307

The issue of child custody has been relatively neglected until fairly recently, when a number of studies of the family and family law have included chapters on guardianship and child custody. Until the middle of the 19th century, fathers in England and the US had virtually absolute rights to the custody of their legitimate children despite their neglect or manifest unfitness for the charge. Two things occurred to begin the transition toward a maternal preference in custody: divorce and separation became more frequent causes for the termination of marriages rather than death, which thus forced courts to consider the claims of mothers to access or custody of their children, and social attitudes toward child-rearing began to look at childhood as a period of nurturance and innocence, a period when maternal care was deemed necessary to the development of moral and responsible citizens. The literature, therefore, can be divided into two categories: histories of the rise of the best interests test and the "tender years" doctrines that gave mothers preferences over fathers when the family separated, and contemporary studies of how custody determinations are made, the effects of custodial decision making on broken families and society at large, and theories about how to resolve women's demands for greater social freedom and empowerment with their overwhelming childcare responsibilities.

On the historical side, GROSSBERG's two books are the most thorough treatment to date of the US law of child custody in the 19th century. *Governing the Hearth* looks at a wide array of family issues, from the law of courtship to contraception, bastard rights, and custody rights. Grossberg analyses the tension inherent in middle-class women going into the public world of men and courts to demand interference in the private domestic realm in what was deemed to be a growing epidemic of marital separations and divorces. He also recounts the tension between judges and legislators who were faced with different constituencies and different goals in the search for domestic justice. *Judgment for Solomon* is a lengthy analysis of a single-child custody case in Pennsylvania that captured the public imagination over a riveting battle of the rhetoric of maternal love and nurturance and the law of patriarchal rights. Grossberg's two books are of great value for placing the battle for custody within the context of the women's rights movement and for understanding the complex interplay between the institutional constraints of the legal system and the compelling demands for protection of the maternal role.

MASON brings custody law into the 20th century as she details how the idealization of mothers and the "tender years" doctrine led the judiciary toward a mother-centred jurisprudence. Mason gives a good review of the growing importance of social science literature in judicial decision making and discusses the principal arguments in favour of single-parent custody, joint custody, protecting the role of the primary caretaker, and other theories underlying the best interests standard. She takes pains to point out that until children have adult advocates, the best interests standard is likely to continue to be a forum for parents and grandparents to try to protect their legal rights by portraying everyone else as unfit for, or unworthy of, this important charge.

FINEMAN is a leading scholar of the contemporary law of child custody in the US and all of her work is important. She critiques the role of social science data in judicial decision making and concludes that, more often than not, the data will be deployed in a way that depicts either one parent or the family unit as a whole as pathological or adopts models of parental behaviour that are not adequately protected by the institutional constraints of legal categories and decision making. Fineman ultimately advocates a rule of law that protects the primary caretaker because the goal of parental equality is impossible to achieve.

The English law of child custody is most thoroughly treated in STONE and in WRIGHT's article. Stone only devotes a short chapter to the issue of child custody but, like Grossberg, places the law of custody within the larger context of family law issues of the marital contract, separation, and divorce. Wright's work is the only detailed study of the English history of child custody law and it attempts to sketch the history of custody from early feudal times to the late 19th century, showing the complex interplay between the needs of a feudal aristocracy to ensure that land is kept productive and the changes in popular opinion with regard to maternal rights and responsibilities. Wright argues that the rise in custody disputes created such a crisis in the equity courts in the early 19th century that a unified family law court was necessary to bring together the diverse jurisdictions over marital validity and divorce, marital property, and child custody and that the unified court prompted the creation of an interdependent family law that would premise custody not on child welfare but on marital fault.

The year 1925 was a turning point in English custody law, for that is the year when Parliament codified the best interests of the child as the sole test (the child's welfare) for making custody determinations. MAIDMENT is by far the most thorough treatment of how the welfare standard has been interpreted and applied in the modern courts. She analyses such diverse issues as the considerations of siblings, grandparents, and step-parents in custody determinations, the rights of homosexual parents, and even the surname of children in the custody of one or another parent. Although the law is constantly evolving to better incorporate the values of a changing society, Maidment continues to be relevant for spelling out the legal issues and identifying the institutional concerns of judges who feel constrained to follow precedent or who impose their own model of family life on the parties before them.

From the social sciences, GOLDSTEIN *et al.* is essential for professionals in the field – lawyers, child psychologists, or social workers – who have to deal with custody disputes every day. Although their preference for single parenting may not find as many supporters today as it did in the mid 1980s, the theoretical questions they raise about the ability of child professionals to cross disciplinary lines or to avoid bringing their own cultural biases into their decision-making process are important for anyone entering this field.

The two most important studies of the social effects of custody decisions, written with an eye to gender disparities and feminist methodologies, are those of CHESLER and SMART & SEVENHUIJSEN. Chesler's work is on the uneven treatment given mothers and fathers in custody decisions, especially the way in which the legal system continues to impose on mothers the burden of proving both their own fitness and the father's unfitness. More importantly, however, she depicts the pervasive biases against non-traditional forms of motherhood inherent in custody decisions and the ways in which deviation from the traditional norm by mothers results in harsher custody judgements than deviation by fathers.

Smart & Sevenhuijsen's book is an important starting place for feminist research on custody law in Canada, Australia, and Ireland and takes a decidedly feminist approach to analysing how the best interest of the child standard embodies a whole host of patriarchal assumptions and cultural biases. This book is an important critique of the traditional model of the middle-class family and contemporary efforts to sensitize men in their childrearing role through the father's rights movement. The authors criticize the illusions of neutrality that are created by a legal system that does not tackle the debilitating effects of the one-sided custody arrangements on women while continuing to depict custody issues in the rhetoric of legal rights.

DANAYA C. WRIGHT

Customary law

Allott, Antony N. and Gordon R. Woodman (editors),
    People's Law and State Law: The Bellagio Papers,
    Dordrecht: Foris, 1985
Bekker, J.C., *Seymour's Customary Law in Southern Africa*,
    5th edition, Cape Town: Juta, 1989
Bennett, T.W., *A Sourcebook of African Customary Law for
    Southern Africa*, Cape Town: Juta, 1991

Bennett, T.W., *Human Rights and African Customary Law under the South African Constitution*, Cape Town: Juta, 1995

Gluckman, Max, *The Ideas in Barotse Jurisprudence*, New Haven, Connecticut: Yale University Press, 1965; Manchester: Manchester University Press, 1972

Griffiths, Anne M.O., *In the Shadow of Marriage: Gender and Justice in an African Community*, Chicago: University of Chicago Press, 1997

Holleman, J.F., *Shona Customary Law, with Reference to Kinship, Marriage, the Family and the Estate*, Cape Town and New York: Oxford University Press, 1952

Schapera, Isaac, *A Handbook of Tswana Law and Custom*, 2nd edition, London and New York: Oxford University Press, 1955

Simons, H.J., *African Women: Their Legal Status in South Africa*, London: Hurst, and Evanston, Illinois: Northwestern University Press, 1968

Customary law is the term most commonly used to describe the largely unwritten indigenous laws recognized by European powers in their colonial territories. The basis of validity for these laws, which are similar to the "custom" of Western legal systems, lies in social practices accepted as obligatory.

When lawyers write about customary law, they have a professional concern to reduce the typically undifferentiated repertoire of principles, adages, maxims, and folk proverbs of an oral tradition to a systematic code of rules. This type of approach is exemplified by BEKKER. He draws on a variety of sources – court precedents, statutes, ethnographies, and colonial commissions of inquiry – to produce a work amenable to the requirements of courts and legal practitioners. As a result, his work has all the order and conceptual precision of a legal treatise, and, not surprisingly, it is the most frequently cited text in South African courts. Such an approach suffers certain obvious defects: because rules are abstracted from social context and are frozen in precedents and other formal legal sources, their function is obscured, as is their standing in relation to the reality of current social practice.

From an early date, however, the task of writing about customary law fell mainly to anthropologists. By taking care to situate the law in its social context, they developed a separate scholarly tradition. SCHAPERA's account of the customary laws of the various peoples of the Bechuanaland Protectorate (now Botswana) is considered a model of this genre. Tswana law is described against a background of Tswana social and political institutions and the tensions between tradition and the influences of the modern world.

Partly because Schapera's work had been commissioned for use in the colonial courts, he cast customary law in terms of Western legal categories. HOLLEMAN, although also written with a professional audience in mind, seeks to avoid this pitfall. True to the discipline of anthropology, Holleman explains the institutions of marriage and succession of a Shona people in Southern Rhodesia (now Zimbabwe) primarily with reference to their system of kinship. Both Holleman and Schapera's texts are now dated. The law and societies they describe have long since succumbed to the forces of capitalism, underdevelopment, and urbanization, not to mention such postcolonial concerns as national unity and gender equality. Their works are best considered as representative of a high point in functionalist anthropology.

SIMONS represents a third strand in the writing about customary law: that of a legal historian. The author seeks to show how social, economic, and political policies regulated the status of women in South Africa. He therefore places the law, whether customary, statute, or precedent, in the historical framework of South African politics. For instance, initially, when colonial authorities were highly conscious of their "civilizing mission", they sought to suppress bridewealth and polygyny on the ground that these practices degraded the position of women. Later, when policies of segregation and apartheid came into force, the courts and government revived African culture and with it the tradition of patriarchy.

GLUCKMAN stands in a class on his own. A leading anthropologist of the 1950s and 1960s, he acquired a reputation as "the father of African jurisprudence". Unlike the previous authors, his interest was primarily to reveal the universality of legal concepts, such as ownership, contract, delict, and crime. Although Gluckman bases his argument on a study of the Lozi in Zambia, he makes frequent comparisons with early English and Roman law. Many have criticized Gluckman for imposing English terms and concepts on his material, but his book is still a fruitful source of ideas about the effect of social structure on legal institutions.

Since the early 1980s, deliberate efforts have been made to transcend the disciplinary boundaries of law and the social sciences. A number of scholars – probably the majority now working on customary law – have adopted the methodological standpoint of "legal pluralism" in opposition to "legal centralism" (which loosely corresponds with the philosophy of legal positivism). Pluralism contends that law should be seen to be derived from social practice, not state authority. Once it is recognized that the state has no monopoly over the creation or enforcement of law, it becomes valid to study at least three different versions of customary law: an official version (one used by the legal profession), an academic variety (found in scholarly texts on the subject), and the "living" law (rules actually observed in social practice).

The collection of papers in ALLOTT & WOODMAN deals with the general theory of legal pluralism and with its application to disparate communities, ranging from Peru to Zambia to the US. Two introductory chapters define "folk" (or living) law, its regulation of semiautonomous social fields and its relationship with official systems of law. Leading writers in the field consider matters such as the interplay between official and folk procedures, the implications of applying a common-law doctrine of *stare decisis*, and the tensions between secular and Islamic law.

The book by GRIFFITHS is a sophisticated analysis in the pluralist manner of state law and the various manifestations of customary law. The author confines her inquiry to disputes arising out of women's claims to property in a small village in Botswana and how these claims are pursued through the forums of traditional rulers, the local magistrate's court, and the High Court. This work is as much about the theory of legal pluralism as about revealing new social practices. Griffiths stresses the dynamics of process and exposes the fallacy of certain conceptual distinctions, such as that between living and official law and that between recognized courts and unofficial forums. Her other concern, a dominant theme in customary law today, is about the gendered world in which individuals live. She explores the ways in which gender affects women's access to law, how women exploit rules (and contradictions between rules), and how they shop for sympathetic forums.

A different type of text is BENNETT's (1991) *Sourcebook*. Although this work concedes the tenets of legal pluralism, it is aimed at the law student and practitioner rather than the social scientist. Bennett gathers together all the major legal and anthropological sources of customary law in South Africa and provides extensive commentaries upon them. Topics include the various tribunals applying customary law, choice of law rules governing application of customary and common law, marriage, divorce, the status of women and children, and succession. A subtext on the current debates about legal and cultural theory, comparative family law reform, and human rights runs through each topic.

BENNETT's (1995) *Human Rights*, another work aimed at lawyers, addresses the growing interest in contradictions between systems of customary law and human rights. While this book examines problems of conflict and reconciliation in terms of South Africa's Bill of Rights, it has wider relevance to all constitutional and international instruments guaranteeing fundamental rights. Important preliminary questions are the right to pursue a culture of choice (suggesting that the state is obliged to recognize systems of customary law), whether culture may limit individual rights, how local culture may influence the interpretation of bills of rights, and whether such rights are applicable in personal relationships (as opposed to relations between the citizen and state). Thereafter, specific issues are considered, notably, the patriarchal tradition of customary law versus the principle of equal treatment and the inherited authority of traditional rulers versus the principle of democratic accountability.

THOMAS W. BENNETT

See also Law and anthropology

Cybercrimes, computer crimes, internet crimes

Akdeniz, Yaman, "Governance of Pornography and Child Pornography on the Global Internet: A Multi-Layered Approach" in *Law and the Internet: Regulating Cyberspace*, edited by Lilian Edwards and Charlotte Waelde, Oxford: Hart, 1997

Barlow, John Perry, "The Economy of Ideas: A Framework for Rethinking Patents and Copyrights in the Digital Age (Everything You Know about Intellectual Property Is Wrong)", *Wired*, 2/3 (1994): 84

Chandler, Amanda, "The Changing Definition and Image of Hackers in Popular Discourse", *International Journal of the Sociology of Law*, 24/2 (June 1996): 229–51

Ellison, Louise and Yaman Akdeniz, "Cyber-stalking: The Regulation of Harassment on the Internet, in special issue on "Crime, Criminal Justice and the Internet", *Criminal Law Review*, (December 1998): 29–47

Grabosky, P.N. and Russell G. Smith, *Crime in the Digital Age: Controlling Telecommunications and Cyberspace Illegalities*, Leichhardt, New South Wales: Federation Press, and New Brunswick, New Jersey: Transaction, 1998

Mann, David and Mike Sutton, "Netcrime: More Change in the Organization of Thieving", *British Journal of Criminology*, 38/2 (1998): 201–29

Sterling, Bruce, *The Hacker Crackdown: Law and Disorder on the Electronic Frontier*, New York: Bantam, 1992; London: Penguin, 1994

Taylor, Paul A., *Hackers: Crime and the Digital Sublime*, London: Routledge, 1999

Walker, Clive P. and Yaman Akdeniz, "The Governance of the Internet in Europe with Special Reference to Illegal and Harmful Content", in special issue on "Crime, Criminal Justice and the Internet", *Criminal Law Review*, (December 1998): 5–18

Walker, Clive P., "The Courts and Citizen Involvement by the Internet" in *British Politics and the Internet*, edited by S. Ward and R. Gibson, Aldershot, Hampshire: Ashgate, 2000

Wall, David S., "Catching Cybercriminals: Policing the Internet", *International Review of Law Computers and Technology*, 12/2 (1998): 201–18

Wall, David S., "Cybercrimes: New Wine, No Bottles?" in *Invisible Crimes: Their Victims and Their Regulation*, edited by Pamela Davies, Peter Francis and Victor Jupp, Basingstoke: Macmillan, and New York: St Martin's Press, 1999

Wallace, Jonathan and Mark Mangan, *Sex, Laws, and Cyberspace: Freedom and Censorship on the Frontiers of the Online Revolution*, New York: Holt, 1996

The study of cybercrime is a new and developing area. At the time of writing this entry a number of texts covering various emerging aspects of the subject were in the process of being written. As a consequence, the currently existing literature tends to be dominated by academic journal articles.

Of the more substantive published work, perhaps the most comprehensive text is GRABOSKY & SMITH, which covers the breadth of the terrain with a high level of detail. Although this book does usefully cover some of the policy issues, it tends to concentrate upon the more technical aspects of cybercrime at the expense of a more theoretical treatment. However, not only does this book contain a wealth of information, but it also proves to be a most valuable course text and it is currently without equal.

There are two main fields of focus in the literature on cybercrime. The first field relates to the use of networked computers in order to facilitate crime. MANN & SUTTON refer to this field as "netcrime". In their article of the same name they provide a very interesting and useful account of the use of Internet newsgroups for criminal recruitment and the dissemination of criminal techniques. Grabosky & Smith also illustrate the various technologies of "netcrime".

The second field of focus relates to the harmful behaviours that mostly take place within the virtual cyberspace environment. WALL (1999) maps out the cybercrime terrain by categorizing them according to their architecture. He identifies four main areas of cybercrime, Trespass (ranging from ethical hacking through to information warfare), theft (ranging from fraud through to the piracy of intellectual property), obscenity (ranging from consumer/consensual adult pornography through to child pornography), violence (ranging from hate speech through to stalking). Within these four areas the following authors provide some leadership.

STERLING provides a very interesting general analysis of the demonization of the hacker and he outlines the accompanying issues and debates. In a treatment aimed at a more academic audience, CHANDLER contextualizes the discussion over the demonization of the hacker by introducing a much broader range of literature. If Sterling and Chandler provide a good analysis of the position of the hacker in society, then TAYLOR tells us who they are. His sociology of hackers identifies them as a fairly small but cohesive virtual community that both defines itself internally and reproduces itself culturally. Grabosky & Smith, chapter three, illustrates some useful examples of hacking and its accompanying technologies.

Cybertheft is very much in its infancy. In chapters seven to nine, Grabosky & Smith usefully outline the various types of cyberfrauds and money laundering that can take place over the Internet. Another emerging form of cybertheft is the piracy of intellectual properties. BARLOW illustrates the main conceptual issues here, whereas Wall (1999) illustrates and discusses some of the more interesting contextual examples. *See also* the separate entry on Intellectual property rights.

The issue of obscenity over the Internet has long dominated the cybercrime debates. WALLACE & MANGAN's very readable text overviews the mid-1990s debate over the US Communications Decency Act and its subsequent partial repeal. WALKER & AKDENIZ complement the US-based literature by exploring the governance of pornography over the internet in Europe. Towards the end of the 20th century the "moral panic" over pornography largely subsided as a result of the "pay-for-view" access technologies. These technologies changed the architecture of the delivery of pornography over the Internet and drastically reduced the availability of (free) "one-click" access. Consequently, the main debate has shifted towards the regulation of child pornography. In his 1997 essay AKDENIZ provides a useful overview of the child pornography debate.

The subject of cyberviolence is ever present. At one end of the spectrum lies the spectre of race and hate speech. Wallace & Mangan discuss hate speech using the "Jane Doe" case as an example. At the other end of the spectrum lies cyberviolence. ELLISON & AKDENIZ describe the nature and characteristics of cyberstalking and outline the legal challenge that it poses for both the victim and also the law enforcers.

Closely tied up with the study of cybercrimes is the issue of law enforcement. WALL (1998) explores enforcement of Internet law. On the one hand he demonstrates the presence of various levels of policing that already exist to regulate behaviour over the Internet; of which the public police are but one level. On the other hand, he also suggests that it is likely that the explosion in the public use of the Internet will cause more demands to be made of the public police. He argues that the public police model is not currently equipped to respond to such demands because the politics of law and order tend to focus the resources for law enforcement upon the more traditional areas of crime.

The final issue is the resolution through the criminal justice processes of the disputes that cybercrimes generate. WALKER explores the impact of the Internet and also cybercrimes on the court process.

In addition to the above literature, which appears set to expand quickly, there are a number of academic journals that have either devoted special issues to the subject of cybercrimes or have included relevant articles. Most notable are the *International Review of Law, Computers and Technology*, which, from 1998 to 2000 featured relevant special issues and also many stand-alone cybercrime/criminal justice related articles. In addition, the 1998 special issue of the *Criminal Law Review* was solely devoted to the topic of "Crime, criminal justice and the Internet".

DAVID S. WALL

See also Cyberlaw, Cyberspace revolution

Cyberlaw and Internet law

Agre, Philip E. and Marc Rotenberg (editors), *Technology and Privacy: The New Landscape*, Cambridge, Massachusetts: MIT Press, 1997
Akdeniz, Yaman, Clive Walker and David Wall (editors), *The Internet, Law and Society*, London: Longman, 2000
Boyle, James, *Shamans, Software and Spleens: Law and the Construction of the Information Society*, Cambridge, Massachusetts: Harvard University Press, 1996
Edwards, Lillian and Charlotte Wealde (editors), *Law and the Internet: Regulating Cyberspace*, Oxford: Hart, 1997
Kahin, Brian and Brian Nesson (editors), *Borders in Cyberspace: Information Policy and the Global Information Infrastructure*, Cambridge, Massachusetts: MIT Press, 1997
Katsh, Ethan, *Law in a Digital World*, Oxford and New York: Oxford University Press, 1995
Lessig, Lawrence, *Code and Other Laws of Cyberspace*, New York: Basic Books, 1999
Rosenoer, Jonathan, *Cyberlaw: The Law of the Internet*, New York: Springer, 1997
Stefik, Mark, *The Internet Edge: Social, Legal, and Technological Challenges for a Networked World*, Cambridge, Massachusetts: MIT Press, 1999
Susskind, Richard, *The Future of Law: Facing the Challenges of Information Technology*, Oxford and New York: Oxford University Press, 1998
Walker, Clive (editor), special issue on "Crime, Criminal Justice and the Internet", *Criminal Law Review*, (December 1998): 5–18
Wallace, Jonathan and Mark Mangan, *Sex, Laws, and Cyberspace*, New York: M and T Books, 1996

Cyberlaw is an emerging legal topic that will continue to grow in importance as we ascend into the information age. Closely allied with Internet law, cyberlaw focuses upon the interaction of law with information communications technologies and computer-mediated communications systems in the area that is increasingly becoming known as "cyberspace". Cyberlaw has forged a separate identity and agenda to computer law, which tends to observe the laws that relate to the computer as a whole. Consequently, cyberlaw is found at the cutting edge of law, where the ability of law to achieve its goals is challenged. Thus, the "law" in cyberlaw tends to takes as its subject, not only the law that applies to the internet, but also the wider range of regulatory responses and strategies of governance that subsequently arise. It is as much about the "law in action" as the "law in books".

Understandably, with such a new subject area, the portfolio of cyberlaw literature is expanding and as this entry is published a number of substantive texts covering various emerging aspects of the subject are in the process of being written. The main body of current literature on cyberlaw tends to consist of US and UK edited collections, which are of an overall high quality, but individual chapters can vary in quality, as tends often to be the case with edited texts.

Two interesting, thematic discussions of the challenges that information technology poses for law and lawyers are found in SUSSKIND and in KATSH. Both have been fairly influential in developing thinking in the area. The paperback (1998) version of Susskind contains an interesting additional chapter in which he reflects upon his original (1996) arguments.

STEFIK offers a broad "eagle's eye" overview of the Internet. Stefik identifies the trends in technology that will further shape the Internet during the forthcoming decades. One of those trends is the regulatability of the Internet and the development of law. This is also a theme that greatly concerns LESSIG in his 1999 book. Lessig challenges the popular notion that "cyberspace is a wild frontier that can't be regulated". Rather he argues that the "coded architecture" of the Internet facilitates regulation, but also enforces freedoms. But Lessig also argues that a hard decision has to be made as to whether societies wish to protect intellectual property or privacy. This view reflects BOYLE's earlier (1996) arguments where he observes that a political economy of information capital is developing and that fewer intellectual property laws, rather than more, are required in order to facilitate future freedoms of expression.

A well-written work on some of the main cyberlaw issues is WALLACE & MANGAN's *Sex, Laws and Cyberspace.* While journalistic in style, which is forgivable as Wallace is a journalist, the essays in the book nevertheless penetrate challenging issues such as pornography, intellectual property, and privacy. This latter matter is the subject of AGRE & ROTENBERG, which is not only a very useful collection but also has a broader readership than the title suggests.

KAHIN & NESSON comprises a sophisticated analysis of legal issues arising from the fragmentary and globalizing tendencies of cyberspace. Although interesting, the perspectives in this collection are rather limited for a student text.

ROSENOER is aimed more at the business person than the student, and specifically at those business people who have a responsibility to consider the legal implications of on-line actions. However, it is a useful text in that it covers, in practical detail, a range of legal issues such as criminal liability.

Two edited collections that provide a fairly broad coverage of cyberlaw issues are EDWARDS & WEALDE and AKDENIZ, WALKER & WALL. Both collections contain chapters by established writers in the field and provide depth as well as breadth.

One of the key debates within cyberlaw is the rather delicate distinction between harmful and criminal behaviour. This issue is covered in a number of the articles in WALKER's special issue of the *Criminal Law Review* called "Crime, Criminal Justice and the Internet" (see the entry on cybercrimes).

There are a number of useful academic journals in addition to the above literature, which regularly publish relevant cyberlaw articles. Two examples are the *International Review of Law, Computers and Technology* (Carfax/Taylor Francis) and the *International Journal of Law and Information Technology* (Oxford University Press). Both have developed a very good reputation for publishing Internet law-related articles, but they are two of a number of law journals that now cover issues relating to law and information technology.

Alongside the printed academic journals are a growing number of on-line law journals. Two examples of such journals are the *Journal of Information, Law and Technology* (JILT) which is devoted to the subject of law and information technology, but includes a broad range of interesting issues such as legal education and artificial intelligence. A different type of on-line journal is the *Web Journal of Current Legal Issues*, which provides a web platform for publishing a broader range of legal issues.

An extremely useful feature of cyberlaw is that it has grown with the Internet, and consequently there is a wealth of useful materials available on the web to which students can gain access. Some of this material is lodged in journals, some on personal WWW sites, and others on the growing legion of on-line law libraries. These sources are too numerous to mention, but a search of the WWW using the keyword "cyberlaw" will generate much useful information. Of course, students will have to learn to be able to discern the useful information from the less useful – a key transferable skill for the information age.

DAVID S. WALL

See also Cybercrimes, Information and communication technologies, Intellectual property rights

Cyberspace revolution

Baudrillard, Jean, *Simulations*, New York: Semiotext(e),1983

Bell, Daniel, *The Coming of Post-Industrial Society: A Venture in Social Forecasting*, New York: Basic Books, 1973; London: Heinemann, 1974

Cubitt, Sean, *Digital Aesthetics*, London and Thousand Oaks, California: Sage, 1998

Holmes, David (editor), *Virtual Politics: Identity and Community in Cyberspace*, London and Thousand Oaks, California: Sage, 1997

Jones, Steven G. (editor), *Virtual Culture: Identity and Communication in Cybersociety*, London and Thousand Oaks, California: Sage, 1997

Levinson, Paul, *The Soft Edge: A Natural History and Future of the Information Revolution*, London and New York: Routledge, 1997

Loader, Brian D. (editor), *The Governance of Cyberspace: Politics, Technology, and Global Restructuring*, London and New York: Routledge, 1997

Lyon, David, *The Electronic Eye: The Rise of Surveillance Society*, Cambridge: Polity Press, and Minneapolis: University of Minnesota Press, 1994

Negroponte, Nicholas, *Being Digital*, London: Hodder and Stoughton, and New York: Knopf, 1995

Poster, Mark, *The Mode of Information, Poststructuralism and Social Context*, Cambridge: Polity Press, and Chicago: University of Chicago Press, 1990

Shields, Rob (editor), *Cultures of Internet: Virtual Spaces, Real Histories, Living Bodies*, London and Thousand Oaks, California: Sage, 1996

Stone, Allucquère Rosanne, *The War of Desire and Technology at the Close of the Mechanical Age*, Cambridge, Massachusetts: MIT Press, 1995

Toffler, Alvin, *Future Shock*, New York: Random House, and London: Bodley Head, 1970

The idea of cyberspace has become popular in recent years, and has increasingly drawn the attention of social scientists. In its loosest sense the term relates to new communications technology. However to attain any sense of how this concept operates much closer examination is required. Cyberspace is presented in spatial terms, a place where things happen, the digital realm if you like. Cyberspace can be argued to be a complex heuristic construction, necessarily constructed in geographical terms as digital communications and "time space compression" have destroyed the significance of real space. However although widely used, the notion of what cyberspace is and its meaning is vigorously debated.

The novelist William Gibson first used the term "cyberspace" in his 1984 work, *Neuromancer*. He described it as "A consensual hallucination experienced daily by billions . . . Unthinkable complexity. Lines of light ranged in the nonspace of the mind, clusters and constellations of data. Like city lights receding."

In essence the notion of cyberspace is used to describe, locate, and allow the exploration of a "digital universe". Cyberspace became necessary as computer networks and databases grew rapidly from the end of the 1960s, in order to try to situate where information existed after it entered this network. There are multiple discourses and lines of enquiry for the social scientist to follow.

The work of post-industrialists such as BELL and TOFFLER, with its stress on the importance of information technology's transforming power and the growing importance of information rather than material goods is a useful starting point. Bell offers a useful grounding in the importance of knowledge as a social commodity and is of interest as it shows how social science began to respond to the electronic revolution spawned largely by the US space program. Similarly, Toffler, in 1973, prophesized an electronic revolution. These visions of a post-industrial landscape offer the Social Scientist not only an interesting insight into the optimistic futurology of the 1970s, but also the grand narrative approach to technological development and its perceived social consequences.

However texts on "cyberspace" in the 1980s and 1990s have emerged from a myriad of disciplines. As previously mentioned, Gibson's *Neuromancer* provided a starting point for the discussion of cyberspace, and spawned the literary genre of "cyberpunk". Cyberspace has been conceived as a place where other forms of being are possible; thus its internal dynamics as well

as its external consequences have become an important part of cyberspace studies.

Arguably there are four broad perspectives from which cyberspace has been approached. These are firstly, communication, technological development, and their consequences; secondly, attempts to assess and integrate cyberspace within a broad framework of social theory; thirdly, the question of the cultural landscape of cyberspace and its effect on identity; and lastly the problems of order, regulation, and surveillance within cyber society.

The development and meaning of digital communication is outlined in clear and unambiguous terms by NEGROPONTE, the former director of the MIT research labs. This offers the reader an insight into the technological differences that differentiate digital media from its forebears. The author offers the reader his vision of the digital future and its economy. This "insider" view is a practical introduction to digital communications technology; his predictions are intriguing and their style reminiscent of Bell's optimistic futurology. However Negroponte is at pains to distance himself from previous theorists of communication, such as Marshall McLuhan. In Negroponte's own phrase: "The medium is no longer the message".

LEVINSON traces the history of communications technology. It inverts the traditional question, "what impact does communications technology have on human society?" Instead it views the evolution of technologies as increasingly shaped by human demands. This is where the "soft edge" is located. Towards the end of the book Levinson turns his gaze to cyberspace and the question of virtuality. These themes are also taken up by STONE, who sees the digital revolution and the development of cyberspace as qualitatively different to previous developments in communication. She too makes much of the interface between humans and machines; she develops the idea of prosthetic technology, which in turn leads us to the question of "cyborgs". Stone's book is wide ranging, spanning the four broad trends outlined above and could be described as a collection of stories that pose questions. The chapter entitled "the cross-dressing psychiatrist" should be of interest to anyone concerned with questions of cyberspace identity and regulation.

Social theorists have also explored the development of cyberspace. BAUDRILLARD is a central text. Although concentrating heavily upon television as a realm of "hyperreality" his argument is applicable and arguably strengthened by the subsequent development of cyberspace. Baudrillard is amongst the authors examined along with Derrida, Foucault, and Lyotard in POSTER. Poster attempts to assess and synthesize questions arising from electronic communication systems. He offers the notion of a "mode of information" as an attempt to fuse such diverse themes as the future of written media, differential access to information and the state's use of surveillance. Poster's attempt at fusion however, fails to give the reader a coherent picture of what the "mode of information" constitutes.

Cyberspace's very diversity and its continued technological and cultural expansion mean that many texts dealing with issues of cyber culture and cyber identity have appeared in the form of edited collections. SHIELDS consists of twelve articles covering a very wide range of questions, encompassing amongst other themes the body, politics, community, feminism, and psychoanalysis in cyberspace. The Internet is arguably cyberspace's most glamorous and accessible territory, and this reader provides a wide and lively tour of key themes. JONES follows a similar format, however the essays are focused around the themes of communication, community, and relationships. HOLMES offers a similar collection on virtual politics.

CUBITT raises the question of digital aesthetics in his text of the same name. He attempts to map and assess both the ethical and aesthetic properties of digital media – a truly massive task. This text's advantage is its approach, which manages to see beyond the technology.

The enhanced possibilities for surveillance that exist due to digital technology have long been discussed, LYON provides a comprehensive overview of key theorists and their work from Bentham to Foucault. Technological advance provides the backdrop, with the importance of cyberspace as a potential "digital panopticon" as a key theme.

LOADER's edited collection attempts to tackle the problems of regulation, authority, and policing the digital universe. The essays take the classic issues of state theory and rehearse them in relation to cyberspace. The result should be of interest to those interested in state theory, power, and enforcement.

Cyberspace is an area that will continue to draw the attentions of social scientists, as new technology and digital media become even more commonplace. Its situation as an area where many of the themes of the discourses on postmodernity and globalization meet ensure that it will remain worthy of critical enquiry.

JON WARREN

See also Cyberlaw, Information and communication technologies, Information society

D

Death and dying

Ariès, Philippe, *The Hour of Our Death*, London: Allen Lane, and New York: Random House, 1981

Becker, Ernest, *The Denial of Death*, New York: Free Press, 1973

Blauner, R., "Death and Social Structure", *Psychiatry*, 29 (1966): 378–94

Hertz, Robert, *Death and the Right Hand: A Contribution to the Study of the Collective Representation of Death*, 2nd edition, Glencoe, Illinois: Free Press, 1960

Kübler-Ross, Elisabeth, *On Death and Dying*, New York: Macmillan, 1969

Metcalf, Peter and Richard Huntington, *Celebrations of Death: The Anthropology of Mortuary Ritual*, 2nd edition, Cambridge and New York: Cambridge University Press, 1991

Nuland, Sherwin B., *How We Die*, London: Chatto and Windus, and New York: Random House, 1994

Prior, Lindsay, *The Social Organization of Death*, Basingstoke: Macmillan, and New York: St Martin's Press, 1989

Seale, Clive, *Constructing Death: The Sociology of Dying and Bereavement*, Cambridge and New York: Cambridge University Press, 1998

Sudnow, David, *Passing On: The Social Organization of Dying*, Englewood Cliffs, New Jersey: Prentice Hall, 1967

HERTZ, a follower of Durkheim, outlined a sociological scheme for understanding death, based on his fieldwork amongst the Dayak in Borneo at the turn of the century. He argued that mortuary rituals enable people to address the problems that arise from the death of another, both at the individual psychological level and at the level of social order. The Dayak regarded the corpse as a dangerous pollutant, a status shared to an extent by close mourners. Mortuary rites symbolized this, and ensured the eventual reintegration of mourners into the life of the community. This theory sets the parameters for much subsequent sociological and anthropological work on funerals and associated rites of disposal.

METCALF & HUNTINGTON, for example, offer a comprehensive review of anthropological work in this area, much of which has also influenced sociologists seeking to understand the experience of death in contemporary societies. The authors' own argument derived from their work on the burial of kings and other persons of importance in the community. Funeral monuments are markers of social status in many societies, indicating a desire to remember and be remembered after death. The Egyptian pyramids, for example, are understood to perform an integrative, nation-building effect, ensuring continuity and order in the face of the potentially disruptive effects of a leader's death.

To use these ideas to understand contemporary experience it is necessary to distinguish the different experiences of mortality that occur in different types of society. By far the best outline of this is BLAUNER who effectively raises our awareness of just how different is the contemporary Western experience of mortality from past times. Underlying this is demographic change, itself influenced by changing patterns of disease, resulting in increased longevity. This is coupled with the social organization of mass, industrialized societies, which places the elderly and the dying at the margins of social affairs, through mechanisms like retirement policies and specialized, sometimes institutionalized, treatment for the sick and the elderly. The disruption to the social fabric caused by a death is therefore minimized, and funeral rites focus on personal grief rather than restoring a disrupted social order.

The French historian, ARIÈS, extended this argument in a detailed account of changing European attitudes towards death. He claimed that in the distant past death was "tame", most people having experienced the death of someone they were close to; they saw their deaths and they tended their bodies after death. Now, however, death is "forbidden" or "wild", the lack of familiarity having bred fear. Dying, he says, is an alienating, brutal experience, involving excessive institutionalization. Ariès' analysis is frequently cited by those who argue that contemporary Western society is "death denying" or that its people regard death as a "taboo topic". This has been a popular theme for some sociologists of death, as well as many journalists whose announcements of "taboo" are in fact incitements to speak about the topic, but it is probably more accurate to say that in contemporary Western society death is "sequestrated", that is to say, it is somewhat hidden from view. It is not "denied", because this hiding away requires a sophisticated social organization for death, which itself constitutes an acknowledgement of the routine inevitability of deaths of society members. In addition, professional care of the dying has become significantly "humanized" since Ariès wrote.

The role of modern medicine in the social organization of death was analysed by PRIOR in a book that also showed how medical ideas about death (or medical "discourse") influence our thinking about where death comes from (from disease rather than witchcraft or bad luck, for example). Practices such as death certification, post-mortem inquiry and the construction of mortality statistics are related by Prior to a social theory derived from the work of Michel Foucault. SUDNOW's study is also about the social organization of death, but it derives from a different theoretical tradition, namely ethnomethodology – a subdiscipline of sociology that involves detailed analysis of particular interactions. Through observation of care in American hospitals, Sudnow shows how dying is managed so that social death can at times precede biological death. He reports a poignant example of social death where a nurse closed the eyes of a comatose patient near death because, as she explained, it can be hard to do this after death once the muscles have become stiff.

An example of medical discourse, which has proved a popular best seller, is NULAND's *How We Die*, in which he (as a medical doctor) outlines the bodily processes involved in death from a variety of major conditions, including heart disease, cancer, AIDS, and so on. The book satisfies curiosity about what it might be like to die at the physical and psychological levels. KÜBLER-ROSS, on the other hand, in her bestselling book on dying, is largely concerned with psychological processes as death approaches. In this book she outlines her famous "stage theory" of dying, whereby people who learn of their terminal illness pass though a series of responses to this, involving an initial numbness or shock, and then stages of depression, denial and/or bargaining, until some reach final acceptance. This depiction of dying exerted enormous influence over health care practitioners who were concerned to humanize the experience, but has been criticized on several grounds, not least of which is the view that "denial" may be regarded by some as a positive way to approach death. The ideas of Kübler-Ross are somewhat culture-bound in this respect.

BECKER presents an account of human life as being premised on a "denial" of death. Although one can say that he, too, suffers from culture-boundedness in so far as his psychological model is one of American individualism, his analysis is rooted in a more profound scholarly analysis than that of Kübler-Ross. He draws on psychoanalytic theory to understand social life as a series of self-defining, heroic struggles in the face of an inevitable mortality.

SEALE attempts to integrate all the above, arguing, on the basis of his own studies of the experience of dying and bereavement, that people in this situation in contemporary society are often able to assert membership of an imagined community, through the narrative reconstruction of personal biography, drawing on a variety of cultural scripts emanating from medicine, psychology, the media, and other sources. He argues that the maintenance of the human social bond in the face of death is a continual "resurrective practice", which permeates everyday life. In presenting this argument, Seale demonstrates the centrality of the problem of death for social theory, which increasingly seeks to acknowledge the importance of the body in human social affairs.

CLIVE SEALE

See also Mourning

Debt markets

Andersen, Torben Juul, *Euromarket Instruments: A Guide to the World's Largest Debt Market*, New York: New York Institute of Finance, 1990

Fabozzi, Frank J. and Franco Modigliani, *Capital Markets: Institutions and Instruments*, 2nd edition, Upper Saddle River, New Jersey: Prentice Hall, 1996

Fabozzi, Frank J. and T. Dessa Fabozzi, *Bond Markets: Analysis and Strategies*, 3rd edition, Englewood Cliffs, New Jersey: Prentice Hall, 1996

Freixas, Xavier and Jean-Charles Rochet, *Microeconomics of Banking*, Cambridge, Massachusetts: MIT Press, 1997

Joehnk, Michael D., "An Introduction to Fixed Income Securities" in *The Handbook of Fixed Income Securities*, 5th edition, edited by Frank J. Fabozzi, Chicago: Irwin, 1997

Stigum, Marcia, *The Money Market*, 3rd edition, Homewood, Illinois: Dow Jones Irwin, 1990

Valdez, Stephen, *An Introduction to Global Financial Markets*, London: Macmillan, 1997

ANDERSEN defines debt markets as the temporary transfer of purchasing power from savers and investors to entities in need of funds, against compensation in the form of accumulated interest. There are two principal ways of creating debt. One is through the banking system (commercial banks), and the other is through the issuance of debt instruments (securities) that are placed directly with end investors.

FREIXAS & ROCHET offer a full book focusing on the banking aspects. The presence that arises when the lender does not know enough about the borrower to make accurate decisions is called as asymmetric information, and it justifies, in part, the role of financial intermediaries. Commercial banks, as financial intermediaries, raise funds by issuing deposits and use these funds to make loans. The transformation involves various functions: providing maturity intermediation, risk reduction through diversification, reducing the cost of contracting and information processing, and providing a payment mechanism. Activities permitted under the regulation of commercial banks differ between the US and Europe. In the US, the Glass–Steagall Act of 1933 forbade commercial banks from holding corporate equity, leaving the underwriting of securities to investment banks. In Europe, commercial banks are universal and are therefore allowed to hold demand deposits while dealing with corporate equity.

FABOZZI & MODIGLIANI provide useful classifications of the securities market. One way to classify the securities market is by the maturity of the claims. There is one for short term, called the money market, and one for longer maturity, called the capital market. The traditional cutoff between short and long term is one year. A second way to classify the securities market is to determine whether or not the financial claims are newly issued. The market for newly issued financial assets is called the "primary market". The market where the asset is bought and sold among investors after a period of time is referred to as the "secondary market".

With respect to the maturity of the claim classification, STIGUM defines a money market as a wholesale market for low-risk, highly liquid short-term debt instruments or "IOUs".

It is a market for various sorts of debt securities and accomplishes various functions. One is shifting sums of money between banks, because many banks need more funds than they can obtain in deposits, and others have more money deposited with them than they can profitably use internally. Another is providing the surplus of cash-rich corporations and other institutions to banks, corporations, and other institutions that need short-term money. The Treasury can also fund quantities of debt and central banks can carry out open markets operations destined to influence interest rates and the growth of the money supply.

The money market is a collection of markets for several different instruments with a varied cast of participants. Money-market instruments include Treasury bills, commercial paper, certificates of deposit, and bankers' acceptances and repurchase agreements, among others. The market participants are diverse and include banks, the Treasury, corporations of all types, brokers and dealers, and other financial institutions.

In contrast to the money market, the capital markets, as JOEHNK points out, involve financial claims with certain degrees of price risk, and include debt securities with maturity greater than one year. Investors in those markets are exposed to a variety of sources of risk. The risks included are: the interest rate risk, which measures the variability of prices caused by changes in the level of the interest rate; the purchasing power risk, which is linked to inflation and the loss of purchasing power over time; the market risk, which is the effect of the market upon the price behaviour of securities; the liquidity risk, which has to do with the liquidity of an obligation and the ease with which the issue can be sold at or near prevailing market prices; the risk of default, which is reflected by the financial and operating risks of the issuer; and the issue-specific risk.

The different types of instruments in capital markets, as VALDEZ mentions, are: government bonds, local authority/public utility bonds, mortgage and other asset-backed, corporate bonds (debentures or convertibles), junk bonds, and Eurobonds. FABOZZI & FABOZZI provide the latest techniques for evaluating them and portfolio strategies for using them.

Fabozzi & Modigliani, who focus on whether the financial claims are newly issued or not, study primary and secondary markets. Primary markets involve a regulation of newly issued securities. The investment bank is an important financial institution that assists in the initial sale of securities. It does this by underwriting securities, which guarantee a price for corporation securities, and then selling them to the public. Secondary markets have two important functions. First, they make the instruments more liquid; second, they determine the price of the security that the issuing firm sells on the primary market, which is higher than the security's price on the secondary market.

CRISTINA SUÁREZ GÁLVEZ

Decentralization

Bennett, Robert J., *Decentralization, Local Governments, and Markets: Towards a Post-welfare Agenda*, Oxford and New York: Oxford University Press, 1990

Cheema, G. Shabbir and Dennis A. Rondinelli (editors), *Decentralization and Development: Policy Implementation in Developing Countries*, London and Beverly Hills, California: Sage, 1983

Oates, Wallace E., *Fiscal Federalism*, New York: Harcourt Brace, 1972

Prud'homme, Rémy, "The Dangers of Decentralization", *World Bank Research Observer*, 10 (1995): 201–20

Smith, B.C., *Decentralization: The Territorial Dimension of the State*, London and Boston: Allen and Unwin, 1985

Tiebout, Charles M., "A Pure Theory of Local Expenditures", *Journal of Political Economy*, 64 (1956): 412–24

Tullock, Gordon, "Some Problems of Majority Voting", *Journal of Political Economy*, 67 (1959): 571–79

Willis, Eliza, Christopher D. Garman and Stephan Haggard, "The Politics of Decentralization in Latin America", *Latin American Research Review*, 34/1 (1999): 7–56

TIEBOUT's benchmark work examines the governmental structures under which public goods can be efficiently allocated. He argues that in decentralized governments subnational governmental units "compete" for self-interested individuals, who in turn choose the community that best satisfies their preferences. Citizens, then, can not only register their preferences at the ballot box, but can also express themselves by leaving communities that do not supply their preferred public goods (the classic "voice" and "exit" options). Tiebout's "mobility model" underlies a wealth of research that explores the economic efficiency, structure, and welfare effects of decentralization.

As one of the founders of the public choice school, TULLOCK concentrates less on the economic efficiency of decentralization than on its effects on democratic governance. If provincial and municipal governments are responsible for providing public goods to their citizens, then the elected officials of those governments can be held more closely accountable for their policy choices: citizens can express their preferences directly via elections that reward the advocates of popular policies, while punishing those who choose policies inconsistent with the collective good.

OATES provides a fully elaborated model of decentralization in his study of fiscal federalism, which concentrates on the economics and organization of a decentralized public sector. His argument begins with the "decentralization theorem," which simply states that government resources are most efficiently allocated at the local level. He further argues that decentralization can create positive externalities, such as public policy entrepreneurship and innovation, which are much more likely to arise among subnational than among national government officials. Oates also considers some of the issues raised by Tiebout's work, particularly the tendency for mobile citizens to segregate themselves into income-based communities. His findings have significant public policy implications for decentralization efforts in both developed and developing countries.

An interesting counter to the fiscal federalism literature is PRUD'HOMME's essay, which outlines some of the challenges and potential pitfalls of decentralization. Prud'homme notes that decentralization is rarely a dichotomous choice, but rather a complicated process of deciding which services and functions should be devolved to sub-national governments. He also asserts that decentralization often requires the central government to manage the provision of a public good jointly with provincial or local governments: hence, he argues that a country's administrative capacity – at national and subnational levels – is a crucial factor in determining the success or failure of its decentralization programmes.

SMITH provides a solid overview of the political economy of decentralization. Particularly useful is his review of decentralization as an analytical concept, which ties together definitions from a wide-ranging literature. The primary emphasis in this volume is on the political choices involved when governments embark on decentralization, and the inevitable conflicts that arise from such choices, given the competing demands of administrative needs and fiscal efficiency. Empirically, the volume focuses primarily on countries in Western Europe, but includes occasional examples from the developing world.

BENNETT presents an impressive array of essays, contributed by economists, political scientists, geographers, and policy makers. The contributors focus on two aspects of the debate over decentralization in industrialized countries – the devolution of political power from the centre to subnational governments and the decentralization of power from central governments to market forces or nongovernmental organizations. Bennett argues that changes in the international political economy have increasingly diminished the importance of national governments and increased the importance of local and provincial governments. The theoretical chapter of Bennett's volume provides an excellent review of the public choice perspective on decentralization, which complements the work of Smith.

Much of the empirical research on decentralization – like that of Bennett and Smith – concentrates on industrialized countries. However, there is also a growing literature on decentralization in developing countries. CHEEMA & RONDINELLI's edited volume provides an empirically rich overview of political and economic decentralization in Africa, Asia, and Latin America. The contributors examine a wide variety of decentralization programmes, and the political, social, and economic requisites for their effective implementation. Moreover, Cheema and Rondinelli discuss how nonstate actors such as nongovernmental organizations, can provide technical and administrative support for decentralization. They also emphasize the importance for successful decentralization of a country's administrative capacity.

WILLIS, GARMAN & HAGGARD concentrate on the political factors that precipitate decentralization. The empirical focus of their article is Latin America, but their theoretical findings address the most general questions regarding decentralization, and have much wider implications. In their view, decentralization is not employed solely for the purpose of economic efficiency, as argued by the fiscal federalists, but is instead a complex political exchange between national and subnational political actors. Their research shows that when central governments are more sensitive to subnational political outcomes, the degree of decentralization is likely to be greater. According to this model of decentralization, which stands in sharp contrast to that of the fiscal federalists, economic efficiency gains are by no means guaranteed, because of the potentially negative effects on efficiency of the political transactions involved. Decentralization, then, may in some cases yield suboptimal economic outcomes, while maximizing the political interests of national and subnational governmental actors.

FRANK BOYD

Deception

Barnes, J.A., *A Pack of Lies: Towards a Sociology of Lying*, Cambridge and New York: Cambridge University Press, 1994

Bok, Sissela, *Lying: Moral Choice in Public and Private Life*, New York: Pantheon, 1978; London: Quartet, 1980

Ekman, Paul, *Telling Lies: Clues to Deceit in the Marketplace, Politics, and Marriage*, New York: Norton, 1985

Fried, Charles, *Right and Wrong*, Cambridge, Massachusetts: Harvard University Press, 1978

Kerr, Philip, *The Penguin Book of Lies*, New York and London: Viking Penguin, 1990

Lewis, Michael and Carolyn Saarni (editors), *Lying and Deception in Everyday Life*, New York: Guilford Press 1993

Mitchell, Robert W. and Nicholas S. Thompson (editors), *Deception: Perspectives on Human and Non-Human Deceit*, Albany: State University of New York Press, 1986

Nyberg, David, *The Varnished Truth: Truth Telling and Deceiving in Ordinary Life*, Chicago: University of Chicago Press, 1993

Deception has proven to be a subject of interest to scholars in a wide range of disciplines, including philosophy, psychology, sociology, anthropology, linguistics, political economy, and law. Much of this work has been eclectic and interdisciplinary. Questions commonly dealt with have been: what is deception, why is it morally wrong, when is it morally justified, why and how do people deceive, what role does deception play in human interaction in various societies, how can deception be detected, and what normative and legal controls are, or should be, used to address the problem of deception?

BARNES offers a well-informed and insightful consideration of the literature on deception and lying. Drawing on a broad collection of works of sociology, anthropology, psychology, philosophy, political science, fiction, and drama, he considers issues such as how the permissibility and frequency of deception varies from society to society. Barnes also deals with the dynamics of self-deception, the function of lying in social life, lying in politics and the media, and "benign" lies (such as lies that occur in fiction and the arts). A list of references at the end of the book is particularly useful and comprehensive.

BOK is perhaps the single most influential recent work on deception. Her approach is one of applied ethics rather than systematic philosophy. Focusing on lying (rather than the broader concept of deception) in the realm of medicine, law, government, academia, journalism, the family, and between friends, the book is particularly strong in treating the supposed justifications for lies – including white lies, lies to the sick and dying, lies to protect clients, and lies told by parents to children. One of Bok's major concerns is with the deleterious effect of lying on trust and social cooperation. Especially astute is the discussion of lies told by doctors to their patients. A useful appendix, containing excerpts on lying from works by Augustine, Aquinas, Bacon, Grotius, Kant, Sidgwick, and others reflects Bok's attempt to ground her discussion of contemporary moral issues in a rich tradition of Western philosophical thought.

EKMAN contains an authoritative and accessible account of how to detect deception in words, tone of voice, bodily movements, and facial expressions. His extensive frame-by-frame analysis of interview videotapes reveals what Ekman calls "leakage" – clues that lying is taking place. Ekman shows that, just as some people teach themselves to become particularly good liars, others – such as long time secret service agents and properly trained mental health professionals – become especially adept at detecting lies. The book also offers a good discussion of standard polygraph testing, which is described as seriously flawed. In two chapters added for the 1992 edition, Ekman attempts to use his methodology to determine who was lying during Congressional testimony given by controversial political figures such as Clarence Thomas, Anita Hill, Oliver North, and John Poindexter.

FRIED follows Kant and Augustine in pursuing a deontological approach to truth telling. In chapter three, he argues that lying is categorically wrong, subject only to a very small number of exceptions. To be lied to, he contends, is to have one's rights as a rational agent violated, just as plainly as one's rights are violated by an assault or murder. Like Bok, Fried acknowledges that lying can have many bad consequences, but this is not the focus of his analysis. Rather, he believes that lying is inherently wrong, and that even good consequences cannot therefore typically justify it.

NYBERG, in direct contrast to Fried, offers what might be called the "pro lie" position. Drawing on a prolific collection of literary examples, social science studies, court cases, and anecdotal evidence, Nyberg argues that "truth telling is morally overrated" and that deception is a "normal . . . attribute of practical intelligence", one that is an essential component of our notions of civility, friendship, social stability, mental health, privacy, and family life. By suggesting that intentional deceit can offer a creative and compassionate alternative to harsh truth telling, Nyberg does much to further our appreciation of the many subtle nuances surrounding lying and deception. His argument ultimately rests, however, on a rather idiosyncratic view of moral life and social relations.

The ten articles contained in LEWIS & SAARNI focus on the emotional aspects of deception – how people use deception to feel better about themselves, maintain a sense of self-continuity and comfort, and provide emotional well-being to others. Of particular interest is the discussion of how approaches and attitudes to deception vary from culture to culture and between the sexes (according to one essay, women tend "not to see" lies communicated by others, whereas men are more likely to confront deception, or at least pay closer attention to its clues). Perhaps the strongest part of the collection focuses on the kinds of deception that occur in malingering (pretending to be sick, overtired, or depressed to avoid obligation or blame) and excessive emotional dissembling (using deception to adopt an emotional mask).

MITCHELL & THOMPSON cast a wide, interdisciplinary net over the concept of deception, with a collection of twenty articles dealing with zoology, biology, developmental psychology, anthropology, and evolutionary theory. Of particular interest is the discussion of "deceptive" behaviour in the animal kingdom – such as misleading signalling by fireflies, false-alarm calling by birds and foxes, insects that are mistaken for flowers, harmless snakes that mimic the behaviour and appearance of poisonous ones, and egrets that are fooled by fish that look like stones. Despite Mitchell's ambitious framework for distinguishing among various levels of deception (contained in the book's first chapter), it is ultimately doubtful that the study of "deception" among animals has much to tell us about the uses of deception among human beings. The final chapters on deception in sports and the military, moreover, add little of value to what comes before.

KERR contains an erudite and varied anthology of excerpts and anecdotes concerning deception. The diverse collection of sources includes Plato (on "the noble lie" – the lie that may be told to the people to convince them of the case for class distinction, and thereby preserve social harmony), the Talmud (on the three circumstances in which a Jew may lie – out of modesty for his Torah learning, regarding his marital relations, and to make a guest feel comfortable), St Augustine (on the eight kinds of lies, ranging from "deadly" lies that are uttered in the teaching of religion, to lies that are harmful to no one and protect someone from physical defilement), Freud (on truth suppression and slips of the tongue), Pepys (on lying to his wife after having had sexual contact with a maid), Disraeli (on the utility of false political reports in governing), Kim Philby (on lying to British intelligence interrogators about his espionage activities), and Shere Hite (on faking orgasms). Kerr's charming introductory essay does much to illuminate the attraction and seductiveness of lies.

STUART P. GREEN

Decision making

Allison, G.T., "Conceptual Models and the Cuban Missile Crisis", *American Political Science Review*, 63/3 (1969): 689–718

Chaffee, E.E., "Three Models of Strategy", *Academy of Management Review*, 10/1 (1985): 89–98

Cyert, Richard M. and James G. March, *A Behavioral Theory of the Firm*, Englewood Cliffs, New Jersey: Prentice Hall, 1963

Hart, S.L., "An Integrative Framework for Strategy-Making Processes", *Academy of Management Review*, 17/2 (1992): 327–51

Janis, Irving L. and Leon Mann, *Decision-Making: A Psychological Analysis of Conflict, Choice, and Commitment*, New York: Free Press, 1977

Lindblom, C., "The Science of Muddling Through", *Public Administration Review*, 2/1 (1959): 79–88

Lyles, M.A. and H. Thomas, "Strategic Problem Formulation: Biases and Assumptions Embedded in Alternative Decision-Making Models", *Journal of Management Studies*, 25/2 (1988): 131–45

Papadakis, Vassilis and Patrick Barwise (editors), *Strategic Decisions*, Dordrecht, Kluwer, 1998

Pettigrew, Andrew M., *The Politics of Organizational Decision-Making*, London: Tavistock, 1973

Quinn, James Brian, *Strategies for Change: Logical Incrementalism*, Homewood, Illinois: Irwin, 1980

Simon, Herbert A., *Administrative Behavior: A Study of Decision-making Processes in Administrative Organization*, New York: Free Press, 1947; 4th edition, 1997

The literature on decision making includes a number of models that attempt to describe the making of decisions from many different disciplines, including economics, business policy, organizational behaviour, political science, and psychology.

The rational-analytic-comprehensive model is the one, according to which, decision making is a purposeful, consistent, sequential, and deliberate process. JANIS & MANN consider rationality as the ideal to be achieved during decision making. They take the view that, in rational decision making: (a) the goals and objectives of decision makers are clear and known in advance; (b) the decision maker chooses the best alternative among all possible courses of action; (c) full information about the consequences of possible courses of action is available; and (d) there is no uncertainty involved.

Conceptual elegance and rigour are the two most significant characteristics of the rational model. However, it has come under attack, because obvious problems arise in trying to meet these requirements. One of the first to shed doubt on the assumptions behind the rational model was Herbert SIMON. He argued that decision makers are not "infallible machines" that make decisions in the most rational and analytic way. On the contrary, they are "satisficers" showing little resemblance to the "economic man" presented by most economists. In fact, decision makers act with bounded rationality. Moreover, values and goals are not always clear. Most of the time, means and ends are closely interrelated. Furthermore, it is utopian to believe that full information can be achieved, or that there is an abundance of resources to be disposed. These are but some of the many limitations of the rational actor model.

In one of the landmarks in the area of decision making, CYERT & MARCH introduced the concept of "problemistic search" in their endeavour to describe the way in which decision makers act. According to them, three major terms can reliably describe the way decision makers behave: (a) they are single-minded; (b) most of the time they are biased; and (c) they are also motivated by certain specific goals. Moreover, Cyert & March introduced four major concepts that influence organizational goals, expectations, and choices: (a) quasi-resolution of conflict among several subunits that constitute the different coalitions of members within the same organization; (b) uncertainty avoidance (there is always a tendency to maintain the status quo, and if problems are ignored they will eventually go away); (c) problemistic search (decision makers tend to look to the neighbourhood of current alternatives to choose the preferred one); and (d) organizational learning (the decision making process is a learning process for any organization at any given time).

LINDBLOM is probably the most well-known proponent of "disjointed incrementalism" in decision making. Studying decision making in the public sector, Lindblom conceptualized decision making as an incremental process of "muddling through".

Decision makers take into account only those alternatives that marginally differ from the existing state of things. During the decision making process one cannot set definitive objectives to achieve: instead, objectives are reconsidered, and sometimes reformulated as the process evolves.

QUINN significantly contributed to the pool of existing theory in decision making. He took the view that fragmentation, constant evolution, and significant intuition characterize the process. The foundations of Quinn's model are built around the assertions that: (a) in today's rapidly changing competitive situations, decision makers operate in complex, demanding environments; (b) decision makers, as human beings, suffer from profound mental limitations which preclude them from acting in a completely rational-analytical manner; and (c) decision making is a fragmented process, and the major participants often differ in their values, attitudes, and interests. Despite this, one can trace areas (subunits) where rational analysis takes place. The final outcome is a mixture of both incremental and rational elements. Effective managers succeed in blending the widely recognized formal-analytical techniques with the more behavioural elements of strategic decision making, and they produce cohesive step-by-step movements toward an end. Initially, these are broadly conceived, but they are then constantly refined and reshaped as new information appears. This "logical incrementalism" school of thought advocates the use of both rational-analytical and power-behavioural aspects in decision making, and extends the previously mentioned models.

ALLISON is one of the proponents of the political model of decision making. He views decisions as the outcome of a political bargaining process. In any decision process, power is shared among several actors or groups of actors, each having different personal goals, and interpreting organizational goals in various ways. In many instances, the outcome of the decision-making process is a mixture of various competing preferences, and involves bargaining and compromise between coalitions. In several instances, constellations of interests are formulated with the aim of supporting certain views of the world. Especially in cases where adoption of a certain course of action implies a reshuffling of the future allocation of resources and power, political activity is more visible.

PETTIGREW also introduces the concept of political behaviour as a central element in the decision-making process. He sees power shared among actors as more a significant explanator of the actual choice among alternative courses of action than the notion of "satisficing" behaviour present in decision making, and suggests that organizations should be viewed as complicated political systems.

Each of the above works is based on different assumptions, advocates its own style of decision making, utilizes varied criteria, and experiences different processes. LYLES & THOMAS contend that any decision model might be in the repertoire of any decision maker, and that successful firms might be expected to utilize all of the available decision models as conceptual frameworks. Indeed, each of them represents a "pure" typology, which can be invoked under the appropriate circumstances.

CHAFFEE went one step further to suggest that there is a hierarchy of strategic typologies, some of which are more comprehensive and incorporate other, less complex ones. Moreover, firms may have the capacity to blend various decision models sequentially, or simultaneously. Each of the models seems to be more suitable for specific environmental categories and for enterprises of specific sizes. For example, in situations of low environmental uncertainty, external stimuli tend to be clear and unconfusing, and are thus interpreted in the same way by decision makers at various levels in the hierarchy. This implies that a consensus among participants is the probable outcome, and that all the available resources will be unanimously utilized in solving the problem. In such low-uncertainty, high-consensus environments, one might expect the rational model to be used.

However, HART argues that the political and incremental models might be suitable in high uncertainty situations, where debate, questioning of assumptions, and negotiation might be helpful in resolving the issues faced.

The 18 essays in PAPADAKIS & BARWISE together provide an overview of research in strategic decision making. The essays reveal that, because decision makers suffer from profound biases and cognitive limitations, issues may receive completely different interpretations from various participants. The process of making decisions is influenced by the context in which decisions take place. Moreover, the process itself influences the outcomes of decisions (in terms of economic performance, satisfaction with the outcome of the decision, effectiveness of the decision, and so on).

To summarize, decision makers do not always act rationally. Instead, they are usually highly political entities. Multiple, sometimes conflicting, organizational goals are typically present, and decision makers at various levels in the hierarchy are actors in a political process.

VASSILIS PAPADAKIS

Decision theory

Anand, Paul, *Foundations of Rational Choice under Risk*, Oxford: Clarendon Press, and New York: Oxford University Press, 1993
Arkes, Hal R. and Kenneth R. Hammond, *Judgement and Decision Making: An Interdisciplinary Reader*, Cambridge and New York: Cambridge University Press, 1986
Fishburn, Peter C., *Nonlinear Preference and Utility Theory*, Baltimore: Johns Hopkins University Press, 1988
Gardenfors, Peter and Nils-Eric Sahlin, *Decision, Probability and Utility: Selected Readings*, Cambridge and New York: Cambridge University Press, 1988
Howson, Colin and Peter Urbach, *Scientific Reasoning: The Bayesian Approach*, 2nd edition, Chicago: Open Court, 1993
Raiffa, Howard, *Decision Analysis: Introductory Lectures on Choices Under Uncertainty*, Reading, Massachusetts: Addison Wesley, 1968
Ramsey, F.P., *The Foundations of Mathematics and Other Logical Essays*, London: Routledge, 1931
Savage, Leonard J., *The Foundations of Statistics*, New York: Wiley, 1954
Von Neumann, John and Oskar Morgenstern, *Theory of Games and Economic Behavior*, Princeton, New Jersey: Princeton University Press, 1944; 3rd edition 1953

Frank Ramsey was a Cambridge academic who died at the age of 26 having made substantial contributions to mathematics, philosophy, and economics. RAMSEY's main contribution to decision theory was to provide a method for inferring subjective probabilities from human subjects. Subsequently interest shifted from the method towards the underlying assumptions or axioms that underpinned the method. Until the end of the 1960s, there appeared to be a consensus that these axioms were correct for rational agents. However, evidence of consistent violations has led researchers to develop mathematical generalizations of the subjective expected utility theory developed by Ramsey.

VON NEUMANN & MORGENSTERN is a book about game theory though it is the material at the beginning, in this case about utility theory, that has helped interest economists in the analysis of decision making under risk. John von Neumann was a brilliant mathematician who, in this collaboration with the economist Oskar Morgenstern, offers an axiomatization of expected utility theory. Their theory takes probabilities as given and shows that risk-taking behaviour can be given an axiomatic description, in a manner analogous to that used in geometry.

Lionel Savage was a mathematical statistician who gave particular attention to the technical issues underlying subjective probability, which had not been discussed by Ramsey. SAVAGE has been very influential in developing support for the subjective probability approach in economics, more so, perhaps, than it was in statistics. Savage is particularly thoughtful about the way in which axioms and normative considerations might fit together.

Howard Raiffa was a mathematician based at Harvard Business School where he pioneered the teaching of decision theory for practical decision making. RAIFFA very much reflects the context in which it was written, and is an elegant illustration of how some of the technical ideas about decision making under risk can be put across in a practical setting.

ARKES & HAMMOND's collection of papers provides an extensive collection of research primarily by psychologists. One of the key papers reprinted here is on heuristics and biases by Daniel Kahneman and Amos Tversky, originally published in *Science*. Much of this work suggests lines of research that are now regarded as complementary to that which is mathematically driven.

FISHBURN made a particularly invaluable contribution to the development of the mathematics of decision theory. He was probably one of the first to see that transitivity would not be necessary for utility maximization and this book collects some of the key results from non-expected decision theory.

GARDENFORS & SAHLIN is an important reader and contains a number of key articles in the subject. Two that are particularly worth mentioning here relate to violations of an independence axiom, or what Savage called the "sure-thing principle". The 1961 article by Daniel Ellsberg shows that people who are concerned about ambiguity (a state where events do not have point defined probabilities), as opposed to risk, may violate independence and have no coherent subjective probabilities. The paper which most closely follows Ellsberg's article was given by the philosopher Ned McClennen at a conference in Oslo in 1992 where he argued that there were no logical reasons why a rational agent should keep to independence.

HOWSON & URBACH is a rare book that, unusually, offers an excellent philosophical account of reasons for Bayesian statistics in preference to classical statistics. Written with considerable wit, this is an attractive resource for anyone interested in the foundations either of decision theory or statistics.

ANAND reviews the normative status of the rational choice model embedded in the expected utility theory of Ramsey, Von Neumann & Morgenstern, and Savage. The main contribution of the book is to show that decision theories that drop transitivity need not be regarded as theories of irrational choice. The book also contains discussions of the interpretation of the axioms of classical decision theory, an introductory account, and an overview of the empirical evidence relating to how people actually choose.

PAUL ANAND

See also Game theory, Risk, Utilitarianism

Decolonization

Cain, P.J. and A.G. Hopkins, *British Imperialism: Crisis and Deconstruction, 1914–1990*, London and New York: Longman, 1993

Chamberlain, M.E., *Decolonization: The Fall of the European Empires*, Oxford and Cambridge, Massachusetts: Blackwell, 1985

Darwin, John, "Imperialism in Decline? Tendencies in British Imperial Policy between the Wars", *Historical Journal*, 23/3 (1980): 657–79

French, Patrick, *Liberty or Death: India's Journey to Independence and Division*, London: HarperCollins, 1997

Hemming, Philip E., "Macmillan and the End of the British Empire in Africa" in *Harold Macmillan and Britain's World Role*, edited by Richard Aldous and Sabine Lee, London: Macmillan, and New York: St Martin's Press, 1996

James, Lawrence, *The Rise and Fall of the British Empire*, London: Little Brown, 1994; New York: St Martin's Press, 1996

Judd, Denis, *Empire: The British Imperial Experience from 1765 to the Present*, London: HarperCollins, 1996; New York: Basic Books, 1997

Louis, Roger, *Imperialism at Bay, 1941–1945: The United States and the Decolonization of the British Empire*, Oxford: Clarendon Press, 1977; New York: Oxford University Press, 1978

Louis, Roger, *The British Empire in the Middle East, 1945–1951: Arab Nationalism, the United States and Postwar Imperialism*, Oxford: Clarendon Press, and New York: Oxford University Press, 1984

Owen, Nicholas, "'Responsibility without Power': The Attlee Governments and the End of British Rule in India" in *The Attlee Years*, edited by Nick Tiratsoo, London and New York: Pinter, 1991

Porter, Bernard, *The Lion's Share: A Short History of British Imperialism, 1850–1995*, 3rd edition, London and New York: Longman, 1996

This review relates the main texts on decolonization that have been published since the mid-1970s to the key debates that have surrounded the end of the British empire since 1945. The review focuses upon the two main phases of decolonization, 1946–48 and 1960–64, for illustrative purposes but some reference to other key episodes will also be made.

PORTER argued that the empire sowed the seeds of its own destruction. There was a debilitating contradiction between Britain's aspirations towards capitalist growth and the anti-capitalist behaviour which British imperialism generated. The empire gave Britain a false sense of economic security by masking the reality of its uncompetitiveness in world markets. After World War II Britain was not strong enough to defend the empire (it cost too much). The British empire came to an end on 12 January 1968 when the decision to withdraw British troops from east of Suez, the Persian Gulf, and Singapore, by 1971, was taken. With the end of empire Britain was forced to come to terms with the reality of its decline since the late 19th century (which had triggered British imperialism in the first place).

Some historians have argued that Britain was forced to relinquish control of its empire after 1945. The loss of Singapore in February 1942 gave renewed impetus to colonial nationalism. Its growth in the postwar period undermined the foundations of the Britain empire. To have retained the empire after 1945 would have required a military presence on a scale that Britain could not afford. FRENCH argued that Britain's decision to quit India in August 1947 must be seen in this context. Using previously classified Foreign Office intelligence files he showed how Britain effectively lost control of India in the early 1940s. Its crucial surveillance and intelligence network, a scion of MI5, could no longer cope with the weight of such nationalist-inspired subversion as the "Quit India" movement (1942).

LOUIS (1977) showed how the US also put pressure upon Britain to decolonize after 1945. There was a strong anti-imperial dimension to American foreign policy long before the Suez crisis of 1956. America regarded the empires of all the European powers as dangerous anachronisms, but the British empire was viewed as the major threat to postwar peace. As a counter to imperialism America advanced the idea of "trusteeship", under the auspices of the United Nations, during World War II. The crisis in India in 1942 clarified American attitudes towards empire, particularly the British empire, and convinced them that all the imperial powers should prepare to dismantle their empires. The influence of American anti-colonialism on postwar British imperial strategy was clearly evident in the decision to withdraw British troops from Palestine in May 1948.

JAMES presented the "Britain jumped before she was pushed" view of decolonization. Britain achieved "an orderly and cordial withdrawal" rather than "a helterskelter retreat" from its empire. This withdrawal was not preplanned but, once it started, it gained a momentum of its own. Macmillan was "a pragmatic realist" who, along with Attlee, acted "with considerable political adroitness". The example of southern Ireland after 1918, when Britain held on for too long, served as a potent warning against the enforced retention of empire after 1945 (as did the later attempts to do so by France and Portugal). The Irish example was also important because there came a point in Ireland when armed coercion alienated public opinion in Britain (an important consideration as, until 1960, national servicemen defended the empire).

CAIN & HOPKINS emphasized the underlying metropolitan imperative to decolonization: Britain, to some extent at least, determined the timing of its departure from empire. The key player was the City of London and the central consideration was the continued international role of sterling. For the purveyors of gentlemanly capitalism the empire ceased to serve a purpose in the late 1950s. This was because the power of the sterling area declined after the convertibility of sterling was restored in 1958. By divesting itself of what was now a burden, the City hoped to take advantage of the global opportunities that existed in the postimperial world. What prevented it from doing so was the series of sterling crises that culminated in the devaluation of the pound in 1967.

CHAMBERLAIN remarked that once Britain had granted India its independence the fate of the British empire was sealed. The transfer of power in India was the first example of a victorious power in World War II relinquishing control of its overseas territorial possessions. The defining role of India in the British imperial experience was such that once it was gone the empire itself lost its purpose. The example of the Indian National Congress and the charismatic figure of Mahatma Gandhi certainly inspired later nationalist movements in Africa in their struggles against British rule. They often deployed Gandhian tactics of non-cooperation and even used the word "Congress" when they established political parties.

According to JUDD, however, the Attlee government never intended to engage in a wider process of imperial disengagement than developments in the interwar period had rendered inevitable. This meant that decolonization would be confined to the Indian subcontinent. Labour remained committed to the empire because trade between Britain and its colonies was crucial to postwar reconstruction. The role of the sterling area was important here (its dollar pool also enabled Britain to begin repaying its wartime loans from America). Development rather than devolution rapidly came to characterize the Labour government's imperial policy. American-inspired fears of communist penetration of Britain's African colonies was the prime reason for this (it also explained why Britain sent troops to Malaya in 1948). The policy of colonial development was, however, geared towards British rather than colonial needs.

Chamberlain also explained why decolonization proved to be a relatively painless experience for Britain. Britain adhered to a fundamentally different conception of empire from the other European colonial powers. After the loss of its American colonies in the late 18th century Britain viewed its possession of empire in terms of preparation for self rule. The French and Portuguese, however, did not share this improving philosophy of empire. They regarded their colonial possessions as conquered territories, which then become integral parts of France and Portugal. This difference in perception meant that decolonization was bound to be a far more traumatic experience for them. For France and Portugal it was akin to amputation whereas for Britain it resembled children leaving the nest. This was why Britain experienced none of the agonies that the French did in Algeria.

This is not to suggest, however, that everything went according to plan. OWEN refuted the argument that the transfer of power in India was an orderly process, of which the Attlee government was completely in control. Britain left India before any agreement between Hindu and Muslim had been reached and left earlier than intended in order to secure Congress' support for partition (the outcome which Britain had hoped to avoid). HEMMING argued that the Macmillan government failed to achieve one of its core objectives in Africa. Britain's decision to grant its African colonies their independence failed to improve its standing in Europe and across the Atlantic. The US was angered by Britain's inability to control the Commonwealth and Macmillan's attempt to enter the EEC foundered upon the Commonwealth link.

Decolonization has been viewed as an attempt to maintain the substance of empire under the cloak of territorial independence. Britain would continue to reap the strategic and economic benefits of empire but without the burdens of direct rule. DARWIN located the origins of this strategy in the interwar years: Britain began to think in terms of influence rather than control. New techniques of imperial rule were developed in order to enhance British power in the Middle East (the Anglo-Egyptian Treaty of 1936). LOUIS (1984) showed how the Middle East also served as the testing ground for British experiments in indirect rule after 1945. The Attlee government supported development schemes in order to retain influence in Egypt after Palestine had been evacuated. This objective foundered on Egyptian opposition to Britain's military presence in the Canal Zone.

STEPHEN EVANS

See also Colonialism, Postcolonialism

Defence economics

Chalmers, Malcolm, "Military Spending and the British Economy" in *UK Economic Decline: Key Texts*, edited by David Coates and John Hillard, London and New York: Prentice Hall/Harvester Wheatsheaf, 1995

de Fraja, Gianni and Keith Hartley, "Defence Procurement: Theory and UK Policy", *Oxford Review of Economic Policy*, 12/4 (Winter 1996): 70–88

de Soysa, Indra, Naima Mouhleb and Nils Petter Gleditsch (editors), *Armament, Disarmament and Conversion: A Bibliography*, Claremont, California: Regina Press, 2000

Dunne, Paul and Ron Smith, "Thatcherism and the UK Defence Industry" in *1979–1992: The Economic Legacy*, edited by Jonathan Michie, London: Academic Press, 1992

Gleditsch, Nils P. *et al.* (editors), *The Peace Dividend*, Amsterdam and New York: Elsevier, 1996

Hooper, Nick and Digby Waller, "The Defence Industries" in *European Industries: Structure, Conduct and Performance*, edited by Peter Johnson, Aldershot, Hampshire: Elgar, 1993

Lovering, John, "Comment: Conversion and Economic Restructuring" in *1979–1992: The Economic Legacy*, edited by Jonathan Michie, London: Academic Press, 1992

Sandler, Todd and Keith Hartley, *The Economics of Defense*, Cambridge and New York: Cambridge University Press, 1995a

Sandler, Todd and Keith Hartley (editors), *The Handbook of Defense Economics*, Amsterdam and New York: Elsevier, 1995b

Sandler, Todd and Keith Hartley, *The Political Economy of NATO: Past, Present and into the 21st Century*, Cambridge and New York: Cambridge University Press, 1999

Stockholm International Peace Research Institute, *SIPRI Annual Yearbook: Armaments, Disarmament and International Security*, Oxford: Oxford University Press, most recently 1999

Economists have analysed a vast array of topics related to military activities. These include the causes and economic consequences of military expenditures, the efficient ways to structure armed forces and procure weapons, burden sharing in alliances, and the incentives that shape the choice between acquiring wealth by peaceful production and exchange or by coercive exploitation. This work overlaps with that of security specialists, political scientists, and peace researchers. As with much of modern economics a great deal of defence economics work uses highly technical mathematical and econometric models. The standard textbook, SANDLER & HARTLEY (1995a) is quite technical. A less technical account of many of the issues can be found in SANDLER & HARTLEY (1999). The best single source is the *Handbook of Defense Economics*, SANDLER & HARTLEY (1995b), which contains articles on most aspects of defence economics.

The economic effects of the end of the Cold War in a large number of countries are investigated in GLEDITSCH *et al.* This literature is also reviewed in DE SOYSA, MOUHLEB & GLEDITSCH.

The main journal in the field is *Defence and Peace Economics*. A special anniversary issue (11/1, 2000) celebrates ten years of publication reviews developments in the field. A special "Defence Economics" issue of the *Journal of Conflict Resolution*, which also often has many defence economics papers, was published in October 2000. Other journals that publish defence economics work are *The Journal of Peace Research*, the *Cambridge Journal of Economics* (including a special issue, see below, on the political economy of military expenditure), *The American Journal of Political Science*, and occasionally some mainstream economics journals. For example, *Oxford Economics Papers* recently (October 1998: 563–73, January 1999: 168–83) published papers on the effects of civil wars and the arms trade (April 2000: 357–80).

The 1990 special issue of the *Cambridge Journal of Economics* (14/4, December) contains eight articles including an introduction from the guest editor, Professor Paul Dunne, in which he discusses the role that military spending plays in the economy, the more specific industrial effects, and also the likely impact of changes in military spending in the future. An article from David E. Kaun investigates "War and Wall Street: The Impact of Military Conflict on Investor Attitudes". An article on conversion policy by Susan Willett assesses the likely size and nature of defence cuts and the possible effects of these on employment and industry, and then discusses the differing views in the literature on the idea of pursuing an active public policy of conversion from military to civil use.

The idea that over the decades, Britain's relatively high level of military spending has contributed to relative economic decline is discussed by CHALMERS. He sets out three interrelated ways in which this has occurred. First it has squeezed out other investment and has thus resulted in civilian industrial capacity expanding more slowly than it otherwise might. Second, it has used a disproportionate amount of scarce high-technology inputs. And third it has harmed the UK balance of payments, both through diversion of resources from other industries and by the high level of overseas military expenditure.

DUNNE & SMITH look more specifically at the UK defence industry post-1979, under successive Thatcher Governments. Perhaps surprisingly given Mrs Thatcher's image, they argue that the military-industrial complex came under sustained attack during her Governments. This was not because of any ideological hostility to the military from the Government but was rather the result of the free market economic policies that were applied across the board – including to military procurement. In a comment on Dunne & Smith, LOVERING argues that it is dangerous to rely on the idea that free market forces are sufficient to deal with a bloated military sector, as active conversion policies are needed to ensure that the local communities and workforces that have in the past become reliant on military orders are able to develop sustainable alternative activities.

The European defence industries are surveyed and discussed by HOOPER & WALLER. They discuss how the "defence industries" can most usefully be defined. Given this, the size of defence production in Europe is analysed. The role of international collaboration in defence production is considered through a case study of the EH 101 helicopter, and the trend toward the internationalization of production is discussed in the context of the EC and the Single European Market.

The STOCKHOLM INTERNATIONAL PEACE RESEARCH INSTITUTE's *Annual Yearbook* is a standard source for data on conflicts, military expenditure, the arms trade, and arms production.

The main group for economists in this area is ECAAR (Economists Allied for Arms Reduction, previously Economists Against the Arms Race) at http://www.ECAAR.org, which organizes sessions at the US Allied Social Sciences Association (ASSA) meetings, and elsewhere.

Both the theory and practice of defence procurement were analysed within the UK's Economic & Social Research Council (ESRC) "Contracts & Competition" programme (1992–97). DE FRAJA & HARTLEY reports on this work. The authors discuss the economic theory of procurement, contracting, regulation, and competition. They also assess some of the resulting policy issues.

JONATHAN MICHIE AND RON SMITH

See also Aerospace industry

Deindustrialization

Bagchi, Amiya, "De-industrialisation in India in the Nineteenth Century: Some Theoretical Implications", *Journal of Development Studies*, 12/2 (1976):135–64

Blackaby, Frank (editor), *De-industrialisation*, London: Heinemann, 1979

Bluestone, Barry and Bennett Harrison, *The Deindustrialization of America: Plant Closings, Community Abandonment, and the Dismantling of Basic Industry*, New York: Basic Books, 1982

Clark, Colin, *The Conditions of Economic Progress*, 3rd edition, London: Macmillan, and New York: St Martin's Press, 1957

Fuchs, Victor R., *The Service Economy*, New York: National Bureau of Economic Research, 1968

Lawrence, Robert Z., *Can America Compete?*, Washington, DC: Brookings Institution, 1984

Lawrence, Robert Z. and Matthew Slaughter, "International Trade and American Wages in the 1980s: Giant Sucking Sound or Small Hiccup?", *Brookings Papers on Economic Activity: Microeconomics*, 2 (1993): 161–211

Rowthorn, Robert and John R. Wells, *De-Industrialization and Foreign Trade*, Cambridge and New York: Cambridge University Press, 1987

Rowthorn, Robert and Ramana Ramaswamy, *Growth, Trade, and Deindustrialization*, Washington, DC: International Monetary Fund, 1998

Singh, Ajit, "UK Industry and the World Economy: A Case of Deindustrialization?", *Cambridge Journal of Economics*, 1/2 (1977): 113–36

Wood, Adrian, *North–South Trade, Employment, and Inequality: Changing Fortunes in a Skill-Driven World*, Oxford: Clarendon Press, and New York: Oxford University Press, 1994

Deindustrialization, usually identified with the contraction of output or employment in the manufacturing sector as a whole, was a particular source of policy concern in the 1970s and 1980s. It has spawned a large academic literature, particularly in the UK, which was among the first industrial countries to manifest symptoms of deindustrialization. Analytically, deindustrialization raises two central issues. First, why should the manufacturing sector as a whole decline absolutely, or in terms of its share of national output and employment? Second, does deindustrialization matter? There has also been considerable loss of employment from agriculture, but deruralization was never a controversial issue among economists. In analysing particular cases it must be determined whether deindustrialization can be regarded as a normal response to changing technology and tastes, or rather as a structural disequilibrium in the economy as a whole with malignant consequences.

Deindustrialization has long been a subject of great interest in developing countries. BAGCHI argues in a seminal and controversial study that India suffered deindustrialization as a consequence of British colonial policies during the 19th century. The study focuses on Bihar and concludes that traditional Indian manufacturing declined during the 19th century, without being replaced by modern industry on a sufficient scale, or by expansion of other sectors of the economy. The study remains a important and accessible contribution to deindustrialization in an historical conrtext.

CLARK puts forward a influential hypothesis that the changes in employment structure during economic development are a result of major shifts in the composition of demand. The hypothesis essentially expanded Engel's law to manufacturing. While the share of income spent on food declines in the early stages of economic development, in later stages demand shifts towards services as the share of income spent on manufactures levels off and subsequently falls. In more recent work, this hypothesis has met with severe criticism. Clark's work dates from before the debate on deindustrialization intensified and is both dense and technical, but it remains a pioneering study of productivity and employment in different sectors.

FUCHS provides the best early example of work by theorists of the post-industrial, or "service", economy, who view deindustrialization, in much the same way as Clark, as essentially the natural outcome of economic development. Contrary to Clark, Fuchs finds that growth in income and the consequent shift in demand have not been a major cause of the relative growth of services employment. Instead, Fuchs argues that the reason lies in the slower growth of productivity in services relative to industry and agriculture. His book remains a detailed and important contribution to the study of productivity differentials in economic sectors, and of the transition to a service economy.

SINGH presents a new framework for analysing deindustrialization and argues that the question of whether deindustrialization can be regarded as a manifestation of structural disequilibrium in the economy must be viewed in the context of the open economy, i.e. in terms of a country's overall trading and balance-of-payments position in the world economy. Singh proposes an alternative definition of deindustrialization using the concept of an "efficient manufacturing sector" and its ability to satisfy domestic demand and pay for the nation's import requirements. In his case study of the UK, Singh concludes that an inefficient manufacturing sector has led to a structural disequilibrium in the economy that generates a cumulative process of low growth, worsening balance-of-payments position, and increased unemployment. The study provides a accessible and thorough presentation of the "Cambridge school" position, which argues that deindustrialization in the UK can be viewed as a structural problem that requires both a coherent industrial policy and reformed external economic relations to remedy.

BLACKABY compiles an important collection of articles concerning the British deindustrialization debate of the 1970s. The articles are generally accessible, but some require more familiarity with economic theory than others. A paper by Alec Cairncross and a discussion of it by Nicholas Kaldor provide a good overview of the debate. Cairncross concludes that the only sensible conceptualization of deindustrialization is provided by the "Cambridge school". Ajit Singh presents a careful exposition of the "Cambridge school" view of the UK experience which is in turn critically discussed by Walter Eltis. In sum, the papers provides a good review of the early deindustrialization debate.

ROWTHORN & WELLS argue that while deindustrialization can be pathological, it also can be the natural result of industrial maturity in advanced economies. Their study is therefore of central importance in examining the differences between what Rowthorn and Wells term "positive" deindustrialization (in which industry remains competitive, per capita income rises and the economy remains close to full employment), "negative" deindustrialization (in which in which unemployment rises and real incomes are stagnant; this is close to Singh's concept of long-term structural disequilibrium), and deindustrialization caused by changes in the structure of foreign trade. In a detailed case study of Britain, the authors conclude that it has suffered from "negative" deindustrialization compounded by changes in trade specialization. The book includes a lucid and sophisticated analysis of the economic forces underlying structural change in economic development.

ROWTHORN & RAMASWAMY follow the analysis laid out by Rowthorn and Wells but extend it to the advanced economies collectively. They conclude that deindustrialization in these economies is not a negative phenomenon but rather caused by productivity growth in manufacturing. Their study is concise and accessible to non-economists. It is also noteworthy in that it succinctly discusses the implications of deindustrialization for economic growth and industrial relations in the advanced countries.

BLUESTONE & HARRISON present a radical critique of deindustrialization in the US which they link to the need of corporations to maintain profit levels after being exposed to greater foreign competition in the 1970s. They argue that instead of looking for new markets, increasing research and raising investment, US corporations took the "low-road", abandoning highly competitive sectors, reducing investment, slashing labour costs, moving production overseas and laying off workers. Their book presents a discussion of the effects of deindustrialization on workers and their families, and proposes a comprehensive industrial policy and increased worker control as aspects of an overall policy to reverse deindustrialization.

LAWRENCE follows a more orthodox economic approach and argues that in the period 1950–80 there was no deindustrialization in the US as both employment and output grew. The shares of expenditure, employment, capital stock, and research devoted to the manufacturing sector all declined, but Lawrence argues that this can be explained by the increasing demand for services as income rises, and by the more rapid growth of productivity in manufacturing. Lawrence also argues that the deterioration of the balance of US manufacturing trade (caused he contends by US macroeconomic policy) can be rectified by a relatively small depreciation in the real exchange rate. In keeping with his mainstream analysis, Lawrence rejects selective industrial policy and instead calls for more market-based solutions and macroeconomic adjustments. His study is both comprehensive and accessible to non-economists.

LAWRENCE & SLAUGHTER analyses the decline in unskilled wages and the growing inequality of earnings between skilled and unskilled labour in the US. They argue that it has little to do with the growing trade links with the developing countries but rather is the result of stagnant productivity growth in service sector productivity. The discussion is technical and is more suited to those with a background in economics, but it provides a good exposition of the more orthodox position on deindustrialization, wages and international trade.

WOOD presents the most detailed and controversial recent study of the effects of trade with developing countries on deindustrialization in the advanced economies. In contrast to many other writers, Wood argues that trade with the developing countries has been the main cause of deindustrialization in the advanced countries. Despite the fact that trade with the developing countries accounts for a small percentage of advanced country imports, Wood contends that the effect on employment and labour-intensive industry has been disproportionate. The study does not advocate protectionism, but rather suggests improvements in education and training, boosting the demand for unskilled workers, and schemes for some income redistribution. His book provides a good review of work in the field. Although the presentation is detailed and technical, Wood provides clear summaries of his findings and thus the book is a good introduction to the debate.

AJIT SINGH AND BRUCE A. WEISSE

Demand and supply

Blaug, Mark, *Economic Theory in Retrospect*, 5th edition, Cambridge and New York: Cambridge University Press, 1997

Commons, John R., *Legal Foundations of Capitalism*, New York: Macmillan, 1924; reprinted New Brunswick, New Jersey: Transaction, 1995 (originally published 1924)

Cournot, Augustin, *Researches into the Mathematical Principles of the Theory of Wealth*, New York: Kelley, 1960 (originally published 1838)

Friedman, Milton, *Price Theory*, Chicago: Aldine, 1962

Keynes, John Maynard, *The General Theory of Employment, Interest and Money*, New York: Harcourt Brace, 1935; London: Macmillan, 1936

Marshall, Alfred, *Principles of Economics*, 9th edition, London: Macmillan, 1961 (1st edition 1890)

Nerlove, M., "Adaptive Expectations and the Cobweb Phenomena", *Quarterly Journal of Economics*, 72 (1958): 227–40

Oser, Jacob and Stanley L. Brue, *The Evolution of Economic Thought*, 4th edition, San Diego: Harcourt Brace, 1988

Samuelson, Paul A. and William D. Nordhaus, *Economics*, 16th edition, Boston: Irwin / McGraw Hill, 1998

Smith, Adam, *An Inquiry into the Nature and Causes of the Wealth of Nations* (first published 1776), edited by R.H. Campbell and A.S. Skinner, 2 vols, Oxford: Clarendon Press, and New York: Oxford University Press, 1976, reprinted Indianapolis: Liberty Classics, 1981 (*Glasgow Edition of the Works and Correspondence of Adam Smith*, vol. 2)

Walras, Leon, *Elements of Pure Economics; or, The Theory of Social Wealth*, Homewood, Illinois: Irwin, and London: Allen and Unwin, 1954 (originally published 1874)

Demand and supply is an economic theory of exchange value (or price and output determination). A theory of the demand and supply for money is implied in Jean Bodin's statement of the quantity theory in 1568. Broader statements of a theory of exchange value, using the concepts of demand and supply, are explicit in the writings of John Locke (1692), John Law (1705), and Richard Cantillon (1755). Nevertheless, SMITH receives most attention for an early explanation of how the price of a product – its value in exchange – is determined by the forces of demand and supply. His language is archaic to most ears, but his thoughts are straightforward and appropriate for all readers. Book I, chapter five of *Wealth of Nations* contains his statement of a labour theory of value. Chapter six, however, relegates the labour theory to "an early and rude state of society", and chapters six and seven go on to describe a rudimentary theory of value in which demand and supply both play a role in determining price. *Wealth of Nations* contains nothing like Alfred Marshall's mathematical demand-and-supply functions, the model contained in contemporary principles of economics texts. Smith does, however, anticipate Marshall's distinction among market-period, short-run, and long-run equilibrium prices. Smith had only two classifications, however, called "market price" and "natural price". He explains that a natural price is composed of the natural rates of wages, profits, rent on land, and interest price (chapter seven, paragraphs 1–8). He also explains how economic shocks to supply or demand for commodities can create disequilibrium where market price differs from natural price (chapter seven, paragraphs 9–12). Anticipating contemporary explanations of the entry and exit of firms in competitive markets, Smith explains how markets adjust as employers shift labour and other resources among different possible employments (chapter seven, paragraphs 13–16). His example of the effects of a period of public mourning on the price of black cloth and related goods and resources is particularly instructive (chapter seven, paragraph 19).

COURNOT drew the first negatively sloped market demand curve, using it to describe an empirical relation between actual prices and actual quantities demanded. Marshall's demand curve, on the other hand, although it followed from Cournot's work, specified a hypothetical relation between what buyers would be willing to buy at various prices, other things held constant. Cournot used market demand in the case of monopoly supply to explain the theory of profit maximization. He derived a marginal revenue curve from the demand curve, a contribution that Marshall later ignored in his theory of competitive firms. Cournot also applied demand and supply to the case of duopoly (two suppliers of a product).

WALRAS developed a general equilibrium system of the marginal analysis of demand and exchange value. His contribution was to show that, in theory, the price of anything depended on the prices of everything else. His method was more explicitly mathematical than Marshall's and therefore slower to gain acceptance. He constructed a system of simultaneous equations summarizing the demands and supplies for all products and resources. In his system, each price is functionally dependent on all other prices. Parts of Walras are very mathematical and therefore not accessible to all readers. Other passages are very readable. For example, "Lesson 38: Exposition and Refutation of the English Theory of the Price of Products" explains the interdependence of economic variables and the limited value of theories that hold things constant when they actually vary. "Lesson 16: Exposition and Refutation of Adam Smith's and J.B. Say's Doctrines of the Origin of Value in Exchange" is rather mathematical but never-

theless a good summary of Walras' own understanding of his contribution. Critics later explained that his system could determine relative prices but not the absolute level of prices. Blaug warns that Walras is difficult to understand without reading it in sequence and without the able notes of translator Jaffé.

MARSHALL outlined demand and supply theory in its contemporary form. He corrected the "marginalists" by noting that demand and marginal utility alone did not determine price, and he corrected the classical economists by noting that cost of production is not the sole determinant of price either. Demand and supply have been called "Marshall's scissors" because of his criticism by analogy of this debate over price determination: "We might as reasonably dispute whether it is the upper or the under blade of a pair of scissors that cuts a piece of paper, as whether value is governed by utility or cost of production" (book V, chapter three). As the quotation illustrates, Marshall's writing uses illustrations effectively, and it also pushes mathematics to the background. Marshall used demand and supply, along with concepts of consumer and producer surplus, to analyse the welfare effects of, for example, government policies such as a per-unit tax on a good. As opposed to Walras, Marshall analysed one market at a time, using what is called partial equilibrium analysis. Marshall's analysis of supply under competition in the market (immediate) period, short run, and long run still stands. The introduction of imperfect competition into economic analysis, however, made his supply function for the firm interdependent with the demand function. Marshall's model was less suitable for analysing the firm in imperfect competition compared to the marginal-revenue, marginal-cost approach of the theory of the firm. As to whether exchange value is determined subjectively by utility, objectively by cost, or interactively by the two as in Marshall's scissors, Marshall's method is more secure than the interpretation of his conclusion that price depends on both subjective and objective factors. The supposedly objective costs of production behind the firm's supply curve are merely the expression of the subjective value of other uses to which the productive resources could be put. Demand and supply still determine competitive price, but the objective basis of supply is in doubt. Like Walras, Marshall develops his theory throughout his text, rather than in a few short chapters like Smith. This makes a summary in a history of economic thought text a valuable guide to Walras and Marshall.

COMMONS formulated a "volitional" theory of value emphasizing legal transactions, in opposition to the competitive demand-and-supply model of exchange value of Smith, Walras, and Marshall. Commons considered the standard theory of exchange value to be "mechanistic" and based on an unreasonable assumption that most economic activity consists of exchanges conducted in atomistic competition. Instead, Commons emphasized the importance of legal transactions made between one buyer and one seller, each having only one or two possible alternate buyers or sellers. Commons' volitional theory stresses the wilful exercise or restraint of power in negotiating contract prices and wages, rather than the mechanistic determination of an equilibrium price in an auction market. Commons provides an important legal and institutional alternative to demand-and-supply mechanism as a theory of value.

KEYNES, a student of Marshall, introduced to modern macroeconomics the ideas of "aggregate demand" and "aggregate supply" but did not develop them as precisely as do current texts in macroeconomics.

NERLOVE introduced dynamics into the analysis of demand and supply with his "cobweb" model, applicable to an agricultural market. Demand for an agricultural commodity such as corn or wheat can respond immediately to a change in price, but supply decisions depend, in a world with no buffer stocks (grain reserves), on price in the previous year. This is because grain is sold at the harvest and then not planted until the next spring. Nerlove modelled the supply decision with what mathematicians call a difference equation, where quantity supplied this year depended in some way on last year's price. The particular contribution of the cobweb model is that it could explain cyclical variations in price without relying on external shocks to demand or supply. The general contribution was to further the dynamic analysis of market price by applying appropriate mathematical techniques. Economists now routinely use difference equations in advanced econometric analysis to model dynamic changes in economic variables.

Those wishing to become familiar with contemporary economic analysis should read a chapter on demand and supply in any recent principles text. Excellent texts written at various levels of complexity abound. Since 1948, the model for texts used in college courses in the US has been SAMUELSON, now in its 16th edition. A glance at the index of his text, or any similar one, will show that the model of demand and supply is used often. The demand-and-supply model explains the level of prices in competitive markets, the rates of interest in financial markets, the levels of wages in labour markets, and so on. In the aggregate, the model explains the determinants of national output, employment, and the general level of prices, and the causes of recession and inflation.

FRIEDMAN provides a higher level of modern analysis of demand and supply and its derivation and application. As with principles texts, other upper-level treatments are plentiful, from the "intermediate" undergraduate level to graduate level microeconomics. As a member of the Chicago school of economic liberalism, however, Friedman is important because of his sympathetic treatment not only of the model of demand and supply but also of the methodological individualism that it represents – building from individual decisions to buy and sell into market determination of price and output. Moreover, Friedman is sympathetic to the rationing functions of the interactions of individual decisions in actual markets, which demand and supply models.

BLAUG is a very useful history of economic thought which provides excellent chapter-by-chapter reviews of foundational economic texts. The interested reader will especially want to consult the relevant chapters on demand and supply in the texts by Smith and Marshall.

OSER & BRUE contains helpful surveys of Smith, Marshall, and the other 19th-century writers. It quotes liberally from each, has fairly simple graphs, and is more accessible to the beginner than is Blaug.

ROBERT A. BLACK

See also Labour theory of value, Prices and pricing

Dementia

Oxman, Thomas and Kathleen Baynes, "Boundaries between Normal Aging and Dementia" in *Dementia: Presentations, Differential Diagnosis, and Nosology*, edited by V. Olga B. Emery and Thomas E. Oxman, Baltimore: Johns Hopkins University Press, 1994

Weiner, Myron, John Debus and K. Goodkin, "Pharmacological Management and Treatment of Dementia and Secondary Symptoms" in *The Dementias: Diagnosis and Management*, edited by Myron Weiner, Washington, DC: American Psychiatric Press, 1991

Weiner, Myron, Ron Tintner and Kark Goodkin, "Differential Diagnosis" in *The Dementias: Diagnosis and Management*, edited by Myron Weiner, Washington, DC: American Psychiatric Press, 1991

Yeo, Gwen and Dolores Gallagher-Thompson (editors), *Ethnicity and the Dementias*, Washington, DC: Taylor and Francis, 1996

The term dementia encompasses several disorders characterized by multiple cognitive deficits such as memory impairment, aphasia (problems with reading, writing, or speaking), apraxia (problems making purposeful movements), agnosia (difficulty recognizing familiar objects), and disturbance in executive functioning (such as making plans or decisions) (American Psychiatric Association's Diagnostic and Statistical Manual (DSM-IV), fourth edition, 1994). According to the DSM-IV, the cognitive deficits must be severe enough to cause problems in occupational and/or social functioning. Dementia can be the result of the physiological effects of a general medical condition, the lasting effects of substance use, or a combination of these factors. Diagnosis and treatment vary depending upon etiology, resources available, and the sociocultural environment from which a person comes (YEO & GALLAGHER-THOMPSON). OXMAN & BAYNES note that, compared with the normal ageing processes, people with dementia show greater impairment in the following cognitive areas: memory, language, visuospatial ability, and attention. These categories roughly correspond to the criteria that form the criteria of the DSM-IV, which are discussed below. The first criterion for dementia is memory impairment and is exhibited by individuals with dementia through their difficulty in learning new material and/or forgetting previously learned material.

Particularly in advanced stages of the illness (although it also occurs in earlier stages), a person's memory for historical and personal information can be impaired. The type of cognitive impairment is considered to be one of the most useful tools for differentiating between dementia disorders. Aphasia is defined by deterioration in language functioning, both receptive and expressive. Individuals who are experiencing difficulties understanding written and spoken language (receptive language) may exhibit this in severe cases by becoming mute. Persons with difficulties in expressive language functioning may have problems finding words to express what they want to say and may use repetitive or vague language. Apraxia involves an impaired ability to perform motor functions in actions that are considered part of a person's ability to care for him or herself and function in life. For example, difficulties with the use of everyday objects such as a comb or a pencil can be noted. In addition, individuals with apraxia are observed to have deficits in everyday functioning such as cooking and dressing (DSM-IV). These deficits occur in the absence of a problem in motor ability and are the result, instead, of difficulties actually executing these functions. Agnosia involves a deficit in the ability to recognize objects and/or people. According to the DSM-IV, despite intact visual functioning, these individuals are unable to recognize or identify familiar objects such as a chair or a piece of fruit.

Problems in executive functioning are revealed by inability to plan, initiate, and halt complex behaviour (DSM-IV). An affected person might also have difficulty learning new behaviours. Also associated with dementia are anxiety, mood, and sleep dysfunctions The overall level of cognitive impairment and its effects on the functioning of a person with dementia vary depending upon a number of factors including etiology of the disorder, age, availability of social support, and ethnic identity. The following causes of dementia are outlined in the DSM-IV (p.136) in order of frequency: Alzheimer's disease, vascular disease, Pick's disease, normal-pressure hydrocephalus, Parkinson's disease, Huntingdon's disease, traumatic brain injury, brain tumours, anoxia, infectious disorders (such as the human immunodeficiency virus (HIV) or syphilis), prion diseases (such as Creutzfeldt-Jakob disease), endocrine conditions (such as hypothyroidism, hypercalcaemia, hypoglycemia), vitamin deficiencies (such as thiamine, niacin, vitamin B12), immune disorders, hepatic conditions, metabolic conditions, and other neurological conditions (such as multiple sclerosis).

Dementia tends to occur in older persons; the highest prevalence rate is at age 85 or older but the condition can occur in all age categories. Dementia of the Alzheimer's type is estimated as occurring in two to four per cent of the population over age 65; other diseases with dementia occur at a less frequent rate (DSM-IV).

The treatment for dementia varies according to the prognosis given to the progression of the disorder with which it is associated. WEINER, TINTNER & GOODKIN differentiate between three possible prognoses: reversible, fixed, and progressive. Some forms of dementia are at least partially reversible, according to Weiner, Tintner & Goodkin and, therefore, the focus of treatment is on challenging the individual to actively practise skills in the aim of restoring lost functioning.

Dementias that are somewhat reversible are those that occur as a result of psychiatric disorder, toxic ingestion of a substance (alcohol, drug, chemical poisoning, and so on), and as a result of metabolic disorders (such as anaemia or AIDS).

Fixed dementias are the result of strokes or other physiological change (such as head trauma) that do not lead to progressive degeneration of functioning. In this case, strategies may be taught to the individual to help him/her cope with lost functions.

With progressive dementias, such as Alzheimer's disease, treatment is focused on offering a supportive and simplified environment. According to WEINER, DEBUS & GOODKIN, medications are used with dementia in the treatment of symptoms related to depression, anxiety, problems with sleep, hallucinations, and so on. There are also some medications that are used to enhance cognitive functioning and improve efficiency of learning.

Finally, according to Yeo & Gallagher-Thompson, it is important to note that the symptoms experienced by people suffering from dementia can vary from person to person, depending on age, etiology of the disorder, and functioning level prior to the onset of the dementia. Social support is also very important to the person suffering from dementia, in particular for individuals with progressive illness as they become increasingly impaired in self-care. How an affected person's family or social network responds to his/her illness is related to the ethnic and cultural identity of the person and his/her family and is an important issue to consider when treatment decisions are made.

CINDY E. WEISBART

See also Aphasia

Democracy

Dahl, Robert A., *Democracy and Its Critics*, New Haven, Connecticut: Yale University Press, 1989

Di Palma, Giuseppe, *To Craft Democracies: An Essay on Democratic Transitions*, Berkeley: University of California Press, 1990

Held, David, *Democracy and the Global Order: From the Modern State to Cosmopolitan Governance*, Stanford, California: Stanford University Press, 1995

Lakoff, Sanford, *Democracy: History, Theory, Practice*, Boulder, Colorado: Westview Press, 1996

Lijphart, Arend, *Democracies: Patterns of Majoritarian and Consensus Government in Twenty-One Countries*, New Haven, Connecticut: Yale University Press, 1984

Lipset, Seymour Martin, "Some Social Requisites of Democracy", *American Political Science Review*, 53 (1959): 69–105

March, James G. and Johan P. Olsen, *Democratic Governance*, New York: Free Press, 1995

Moore, Barrington, Jr, *Social Origins of Dictatorship and Democracy: Lord and Peasant in the Making of the Modern World*, Boston: Beacon Press, 1966; London: Allen Lane, 1967

Schumpeter, Joseph A., *Capitalism, Socialism, and Democracy*, New York: Harper, 1941, London: Allen and Unwin, 1943; 6th edition London and Boston: Unwin, 1987

Stromberg, Ronald N., *Democracy: A Short, Analytical History*, Armonk, New York: Sharpe, 1996

Defining democracy requires some craft. Modern theorists tend to separate along two main fault lines: procedural and substantive considerations. Procedural considerations include free, competitive, and fair elections as a means of holding the government to account, along with the protection by the state (through an enforced constitution) of certain rights and liberties. Among substantive considerations are socially based value judgements such as equitable income distribution. This definitional separation is controversial. DAHL's excellent book seeks out common ground among the disparate camps, and in the process furthers our thinking about just what democracy means in a modern world. Although his definitional sentiments are in the procedural camp, he recognizes there is strength in the argument from the substantivists, who maintain that democracy cannot exist unless "desirable results" emanate from collective decision making (p.5).

Democracy's presence or absence in countries around the world can be attributed to several broad factors: economic, social, political, cultural, and elite/masses decision making. DI PALMA's work is decidedly in the elite/masses decision-making camp. He skilfully demonstrates the evolution of democracy through elite bargaining and negotiated agreements between ideologically opposed elites, who decide to give democracy a chance to succeed.

HELD asks whether democracy on the national level can be "understood" and can survive in a globalized world where many of the decisions shaping the international order are made by organizations beyond the control of the citizenry. Country-level democracy is also under threat from the changing nature of the nation state, which now must account for the rising importance of nonstate actors on the world stage, dividing sovereignty. These issues defy easy resolution, but the author points toward a way to do so by creating a "cosmopolitan" theory of democracy.

LAKOFF lays out, in a historical journey examining democratic practice, static and dynamic descriptions of democracy. The statics of democracy are the root conditions: normative justifications of autonomy, proper institutional expression of personal political preferences, and maintenance of fair electoral procedures. The dynamics of democracy describe how it occurs: through such mechanisms as socioeconomic development and worldwide diffusion of democratic values. Neglect of one or the other makes for an incomplete understanding of democracy.

LIJPHART's study of 22 long-established (1945–80) democracies (the French Fourth and Fifth Republics are counted as separate regimes) probes further into the issue of their institutional composition. At opposite poles are the majoritarian and consensus models of institutional composition. The majoritarian model is likely to arise under conditions of sociocultural homogeneity, as in the United Kingdom and New Zealand. Majoritarianism consists of such dimensions as plurality/majority electoral systems, executive dominance, a two-party system, and Cabinet dominance. The consensual model is likely to arise under conditions of sociocultural heterogeneity, as in Switzerland and Belgium. Consensualism consists of such dimensions as a proportional representation electoral system, a plural executive, a multiparty system, and separation of powers. The need for the consensus model arises because, with many cleavages within a heterogeneous country, there is a desire for representation of the myriad of groups. The consensus model can best provide this. Although his classificatory scheme struggles to fit the 22 regimes into it (particularly some such as the United States, which displays several majoritarian and consensus dimensions), it serves as a useful starting point for pondering the democratic institutions most appropriate for a society's sociocultural composition.

LIPSET, in his pathbreaking article, leaves space for elite guidance of democratic institutional development, but is mainly concerned with describing the economic development thesis of democracy. Due to an enlargement of the middle class and the acculturating effects of its education (a phenomenon noted by Aristotle and J.S. Mill), higher levels of economic development in countries regularly are associated with higher levels of democracy. Exceptions to this rule exist, however, making a close examination of elite, historical, and socioeconomic conditions crucial for more complete explanations of global democratic development.

MARCH & OLSEN's book should be read in tandem with Di Palma's. They lay out the behavioural patterns of the political actors creating a democratic polis. They elaborate two behavioural perspectives: rational choice and institutional, which help to explain just how "[d]emocratic institutions are temples of talk" (p.62). Neither perspective is sufficient as an explanation, but the institutional perspective seems more necessary than does the rational choice perspective.

MOORE's opus, illustrating how the resolution of economic demands that arise from increased commercial activity leads to political development, can be boiled down to "[n]o bourgeois, no democracy" (p.418). He traces the economic confrontations experienced within the English, French, American, Chinese, Japanese, and Indian societies, and to a lesser extent the Germans and the Russians, in great historical detail, with an eye to how they led to political outcomes. Where the bourgeois succeeds in creating a capitalist economic environment without hindrance from the political rulers, democracy takes place (UK, France, the US). Where the bourgeois is suppressed by a royal absolutist regime, fascist dictatorship arises (Germany, Japan). Where the bourgeois is overshadowed by an agrarian revolution, a communist dictatorship forms (China, Russia). Without the secure economic footing found across classes in more modernized countries, the author claims, Indian democracy will remain fragile. Nearly 35 years after publication, the claim remains as controversial and thought-provoking as the entire book.

SCHUMPETER presents a 1930s vision of capitalism's doom, and thus of democracy's changing condition, with a rising tide of global socialism swamping capitalism and giving new meaning to democracy. The fact that none of these predictions came to pass does not detract from the wisdom of the book, which lies in a discussion of capitalism's success creating its destruction through the greed of the entrepreneurial geniuses, the subsequent ossification of capitalism's creative engines of economic innovation, and the intellectual class's hostility toward "unheroic" capitalism (p.160). The reaction against capitalism's excesses paves the way for democratic countries to display a strong commitment to social welfare policy.

STROMBERG can be read in tandem with Lakoff. He provides a succinct introduction to the historical underpinnings of the current "third wave" of democracy. Reaching back to the 18th century for evidence, he posits two overarching themes in democratic history: that democracy is perpetually attractive as a form of political organization and that its achievement leaves one unsatisfied. The first theme is self-evident in the use of democracy, defined in a number of ways, by elites both as a talisman (the solution to all ills) and as a call to arms (to defend or attack in the name of democracy). The second theme arises from a continued debate between two different historic types of democracy, the direct form practised in ancient Greece and in many less modern societies as a small community-based exercise, and the representative form invented in parliamentary England and elaborated on in the US. These tensions leave democracy in a perpetual crisis. That democracy still tries to be perfected by civilization despite its evident contradictions and shortcomings is testimony to its remarkable historical hold on civilization.

ROSS BURKHART

Democracy in the workplace

Baddon, Lesley et al., People's Capitalism? A Critical Analysis of Profit-Sharing and Employee Share Ownership, London and New York: Routledge, 1989

Cornforth, Chris, Alan Thomas and Roger Spear, Developing Successful Worker Co-operatives, London and Newbury Park, California: Sage, 1988

Gunn, Christopher E., Workers' Self-Management in the United States, Ithaca, New York: Cornell University Press, 1984

Horvat, Branko, The Political Economy of Socialism, Armonk, New York: Sharpe, 1982

Jones, Derek C. and Jan Svejnar (editors), Advances in the Economic Analysis of Participatory and Labor-Managed Firms, 6 vols, Greenwich, Connecticut and London: JAI Press, 1985–98

Uvalić, Milića and Daniel Vaughan-Whitehead (editors), Privatization Surprises in Transition Economies: Employee-Ownership in Central and Eastern Europe, Cheltenham: Elgar, 1997

Vanek, Jan, The Economics of Workers' Management: A Yugoslav Case Study, London, Allen and Unwin, 1972

Vanek, Jaroslav, The General Theory of Labor-Managed Market Economies, Ithaca, New York: Cornell University Press, 1970

Vaughan-Whitehead, Daniel (editor), Workers' Financial Participation: East-West Experiences, Geneva, International Labour Office, 1995

Whyte, William Foot and Kathleen King Whyte, Making Mondragon: The Growth and Dynamics of the Worker Cooperative Complex, Ithaca, New York: Cornell University Press, 1988

The political economy of democracy in the workplace has been debated since the beginnings of industrialization, and HORVAT provides an excellent overview of its history and philosophy. He develops a theory of self-managed firms and a self-managed economy with special reference to Yugoslavia. Among the many rich contributions are his concept of social ownership, his consistent distinction between professional management and political control of that management so as to combine maximum democracy with maximum efficiency, and his paradoxical thesis that, although the market is the most efficient planning device, it must be balanced by a social plan similar to Rousseau's social contract. Horvat convincingly shows that worker self-management is incompatible with state socialism.

Horvat shares the intellectual leadership of comprehensive microeconomic and macroeconomic theory formation of labour management with VANEK (1970). Vanek holds that capital ownership should not be "social": it should be fully divorced from control. Under self-management, labour pays the shadow user cost of capital but retains complete usufruct and control. The function of a self-managed firm, Vanek argues, is not the maximization of profit but the maximization of income per worker. Vanek's book (followed by many subsequent publications) offers a formal theory of a labour-managed market economy, including issues of economic planning and a macroeconomic theory of national income determination.

In the second half of the 20th century Yugoslavia became a unique terrain of study of the practice of self-management. VANEK (1972) has made a most remarkable evaluation of the first 20 years of experience, which were probably, retrospectively, Yugoslavia's "best" years. Vanek concentrates on the study of the economic behaviour of the worker-managed enterprise. He demonstrates that capital accumulation and use are linked to the needs of the workers of the firm and the wider social community, without impeding technological innovation, sound investment, and high rates of economic growth. He shows that an economic firm based on work (and not on ownership) and under control of its workers, can be a viable proposition. The Yugoslav system eventually failed, but Vanek's book remains an important research-based contribution to the general theory of the behaviour of labour-managed firms.

For the analysis of labour managed firms in a capitalist environment GUNN's book on the United States stands out. He presents a description and evaluation of major American worker-controlled firms, including several private firms taken over by workers. A major contribution is that Gunn derived a set of facilitating conditions from the general theory of self management, tested these against the US experience, and thus strengthened general theory which had until then been based almost exclusively on testing grounds in Yugoslavia or other socialist environments.

The JONES & SVEJNAR volumes elaborate, test, and modify both Vanek's and Horvat's theories, and those of others, and can be regarded as the periodic monitoring of progress of the theories of the labour managed firm and of labour managed economies, as well as the broader area of participatory practice. The volumes are full of high quality and original theoretical and empirical research, providing a worldwide scope, and a wide range of topics, ranging from algebraic and econometric models to treatises on worker alienation. Special attention may be given to a long chapter by Vanek in the second volume, where he combines macroeconomic skills with insights in sociology, political science, and philosophy, in his chapter on "a just, efficient and fully democratic society".

Producer cooperatives have been a specific target of theory formation on economic democracy of the workplace. CORNFORTH, THOMAS & SPEAR provide an excellent overview of the rich literature (the introductory chapter offers an outstanding overview of the theoretical and political debate) and apply the theoretical insights obtained so far to fresh research of cooperatives and to secondary analysis of earlier empirical studies. Of particular importance is their critical review of the often asserted degeneration thesis and their research-based propositions on how to avoid constitutional and organizational disintegration of cooperatives. In general, the solution-oriented approach of this book, carefully applying scientific research and theory, makes it important reading.

The Mondragon cooperative complex (in the Basque country in Spain) has been, and still is, a model case. Among the many books on this success story of economic democracy the study of WHYTE & WHYTE stands out as it attempts a multidimensional appreciation of this most significant experience. It presents the institutional history and aptly summarizes the principle findings of major economic studies of Mondragon (including the essential role of banking, planning and marketing, education and training, research, technological development, management consultancy, the need for economic viability, and so on), and describes the essential role of professional management. The additional benefit of this book is that it deals with community values and cultural norms as well, analysing how the human condition is affected by the cooperative system, as a reminder that, in the end, the economy should be at the service of people. The Whytes' much reputed craftsmanship has produced a magnificent study.

Economic democracy in the wider sense of the word denotes a variety of forms of employee participation in the ownership of enterprises in which they are employed and in the distribution of economic rewards. The accelerated change to a neoliberal economy shifted the emphasis to employer and government initiated/encouraged profit sharing and employee share-ownership schemes. In the 1980s the British Conservative government introduced "people's capitalism" schemes widely. BADDON et al. showed that these schemes have tended to reduce the influence of workers in decision making and to start to erode collective bargaining, dividing different groups of workers in a "thirst for gold".

In the 1990s Central, and Eastern Europe became a surprising laboratory of economic democracy. The privatization wave that characterized this area was first expected to respond to classical capitalist paradigms, but a much wider range of ownership and management schemes appeared. The book edited by Vaughan-Whitehead provides a comprehensive assessment of workers' financial participation practices (workers' share ownership and profit sharing) in Western, Central, and Eastern European countries, in terms of legislation, forms and scope of financial participation arrangements, and the attitudes of the social partners as well as of the economic impact of these schemes. It provides direct empirical evidence on the necessary conditions for financial participation schemes to lead to positive effects on the motivation and productivity of workers, as well as on organizational performance and innovation. Particular attention is given to their combination with forms of workers` involvement in the decision-making process.

The book edited by UVALIĆ & VAUGHAN-WHITEHEAD provides a wide-ranging survey that considers employee ownership within privatization legislation and its diffusion and implementation problems in 14 transitional economies. Using empirical evidence (enterprise surveys and case studies) on the impact of the privatization method, the authors address issues such as enterprise restructuring, employment, wages, productivity, and investment policies. In particular, the advantages and risks of employee ownership, as these have been debated by the "Vanek school", are systematically assessed. The book concludes that many of these theoretical assumptions did not hold for Central and Eastern Europe and that the fears expressed by many policy advisors at the beginning of the transition regarding the negative implications of employee ownership were largely exaggerated.

GÉRARD KESTER

See also Employee ownership and cooperative societies, Industrial democracy, Organizational participation, Participatory democracy in organizations

Democratic consolidation

Elster, Jon, Claus Offe and Ulrich K. Preuss, *Institutional Design in Post-Communist Societies: Rebuilding the Ship at Sea*, Cambridge and New York: Cambridge University Press, 1998

Gunther, Richard, P. Nikiforos Diamandouros and Hans-Jürgen Puhle (editors), *The Politics of Democratic Consolidation: Southern Europe in Comparative Perspective*, Baltimore: Johns Hopkins University Press, 1995

Linz, Juan J. and Alfred Stepan, *Problems of Democratic Transition and Consolidation: Southern Europe, South America, and Post-Communist Europe*, Baltimore: Johns Hopkins University Press, 1996

Mainwaring, Scott, Guillermo O'Donnell and J. Samuel Valenzuela (editors), *Issues in Democratic Consolidation: The New South American Democracies in Comparative Perspective*, Notre Dame, Indiana: University of Notre Dame Press, 1992

Morlino, Leonardo, *Democracy between Consolidation and Crisis: Parties, Groups, and Citizens in Southern Europe*, Oxford and New York: Oxford University Press, 1998

Przeworski, Adam, Michael Alvarez, José Antonio Cheibub and Fernando Limongi, "What Makes Democracies Endure?", *Journal of Democracy*, 7/1 (1996): 39–55

LINZ & STEPAN is the most significant work that systematically and comprehensively compares the process of democratic consolidation in Southern Europe, South America, and postcommunist Europe. It assembles a huge amount of information, ordered according to careful interpretative categories, and offers insightful comparative analyses. The authors argue that consolidation is composed of three layers – behavioural, attitudinal, and constitutional – and in order for these to be combined five "arenas" must reinforce one another: civil society, political society, rule of law, state apparatus, and economic society. The authors develop a broad theoretical framework that informs detailed narratives of the paths of consolidation in 15 cases located in the three areas considered.

Another synthesis is that of PRZEWORSKI et al., who analyse consolidation taking a very different perspective from Linz & Stepan. The question they address is: "If a country, any randomly selected country, is to have a democratic regime *next* year, what conditions should be present in that country and around the world *this* year?" The authors count instances of survival and death of political regimes in 135 countries observed annually between 1950 (or the year of independence) and 1990, for a total of 4,318 country-years. They find that a high probability of democratic survival is associated primarily with a high level of affluence, sustained economic growth with moderate inflation, declining inequality, a favourable international climate, and a parliamentary political system. An interesting result of their calculations is that there is no evidence of "consolidation": for a given level of economic development, the likelihood that democracies will die is independent of their age.

MORLINO is considered the core work on the process of democratic consolidation in the four Southern European countries – Portugal, Spain, Greece, and Italy – but his analysis has important implications for the study of consolidation in general. He pays particular attention to definitional issues and conceptual precision and provides a helpful inventory and systematization of the sometimes-confusing theoretical vocabulary of "transitology" and "consolidology". Another strength of his work is that it goes beyond general theoretical statements, and directly tackles the difficult question of the operationalization and measurement of legitimacy and consensus – a necessary step in order to benefit fully from the extensive survey data discussed in the book. As the emphasis is on processes rather than merely on outcomes, the focus is on *actors*, both at elite and at mass level. While Morlino studies several aspects of the institutional and the electoral domain, his protagonists are the political parties and the way they are linked to civil society. On this linkage – a fundamental variable affecting consolidation and crisis – he presents a complex and innovative set of hypotheses. The relationship between parties and civil society is also one element of a new framework for identifying models of democracy, together with institutional structures and party systems. The international context is explicitly excluded from his analysis.

The book by ELSTER, OFFE & PREUSS is the most impressive work on the democratization of Eastern Europe that has appeared to date. They analyse the democratic consolidation in four countries – the Czech Republic, Slovakia, Hungary, and Bulgaria – by means of a complex theoretical framework connecting constraints inherited from the past, contingent constellations of actors and opportunities, and the institutionalization of new political rules and agency patterns. This covers constitutional provisions on basic rights and institutional structures, the choice and the consequences of electoral rules, the nature of the party system, the political cleavages, the various aspects of economic reform, and the restructuring of social policy in the four countries considered. Particularly useful are the sophisticated discussions about the constitution-making process and the discussion on the implications for consolidation of the peculiar cleavage structure that emerged in post communist societies, especially the question of ethnic mobilization and the cleavage between supporters and opponents of the previous regime. The international context is one of the few aspects of consolidation not considered in this remarkable book.

MAINWARING, O'DONNELL & VALENZUELA's collection, even though now outdated in certain respects, is still a very good overview of the problems of consolidation in South America. Among the many aspects considered are the effects of the mode of transition (in the narrow sense) on subsequent consolidation, the difficulties of integrating the military into the democratic regime, the continuing influence of traditional political elites that survived the transition, the problem of inadequate channels for representation of societal interests, and the problematic attitude of the economic elites towards democracy. These questions are explored both from a theoretical perspective (one chapter employs game theory to analyse the conditions of democratization) and by means of detailed narratives relating to specific issues and national contexts.

GUNTHER, DIAMANDOUROS & PUHLE offer a comprehensive and very helpful survey of most aspects of consolidation in Greece, Italy, Portugal, and Spain, including an argument that Southern Europe should be seen as one region consisting of these four countries. An overview chapter stresses the path-dependent character of consolidation, which is conditioned by the trajectories of transition. Other comparative chapters discuss the influence of the international context, the importance of executive stability, the character of interest intermediation, the role of the military, and the role of social movements. An extensive chapter is devoted to the complex linkages between the party system, electoral stabilization, legitimation, and consolidation.

MATHIAS KOENIG-ARCHIBUGI

Democratic transition

Haggard, Stephan and Robert R. Kaufmann, *The Political Economy of Democratic Transitions*, Princeton, New Jersey: Princeton University Press, 1995

Huntington, Samuel P., *The Third Wave: Democratization in the Late Twentieth Century*, Norman: University of Oklahoma Press, 1991

Karl, Terry Lynn and Philippe C. Schmitter, "Modes of Transition in Latin America, Southern and Eastern Europe", *International Social Science Journal*, 43/2 (1991): 269–84

Lipset, Seymour Martin, Kyoung-Ryung Seong and John C. Torres, "A Comparative Analysis of the Social Requisites of Democracy", *International Social Science Journal*, 45/2 (1993): 154–75

Moore, Barrington Jr, *Social Origins of Dictatorship and Democracy: Lord and Peasant in the Making of the Modern World*, Boston: Beacon Press, 1966; London: Allen Lane, 1967

Przeworski, Adam, *Democracy and the Market: Political and Economic Reforms in Eastern Europe and Latin America*, Cambridge and New York: Cambridge University Press, 1991

Rueschemeyer, Dietrich, Eveline Huber Stephens and John C. Stephens, *Capitalist Development and Democracy*, Cambridge: Polity Press, and Chicago: University of Chicago Press, 1992

Whitehead, Laurence (editor), *The International Dimension of Democratization: Europe and the Americas*, Oxford and New York: Oxford University Press, 1996

The main focus of this entry is countries that have been democratizing or redemocratizing during the last few decades, but it is also useful to keep in mind the literature on the historical origins of modern democracy in Western Europe and North America.

MOORE is a classic on this topic: he traces the path of democratization in the US, Britain and France, showing the differences in political development among them and between those countries and China, Japan, and India. Moore's arguments are very influential and have been discussed extensively during the last three decades by RUESCHEMEYER, STEPHENS & STEPHENS, among others. Like Moore, these authors consider the problem of democratization in connection with capitalist development, but they revise some important elements of his theses and notably emphasize the crucial role of the industrial working class, rather than the bourgeoisie, as the agent of democratization throughout the modern world.

A different approach to the question of the socioeconomic prerequisites of democratic transition is chosen by LIPSET, SEONG & TORRES. They examine 104 countries in 1960, 1965, 1975, 1980, and 1985, employing statistical techniques, and conclude that economic development is a prerequisite of political democracy. They also emphasize that other factors influence democratization, for instance the positive effect of having been a British colony instead of a colony of other powers.

KARL & SCHMITTER provide an interesting framework for classifying transitions, and draw inferences about their success. They reject the search for a set of "prerequisites" of democratization and emphasize instead the strategic choices of actors, and more contingent patterns of alliance and conflict. In this framework the specific combination of the decisive actors (on the continuum of elites/masses), and their strategies (on the continuum of compromise/force), defines the type of transition that has occurred. The ideal types are pact, reform, imposition, and revolution. The authors rank 37 recent and historical cases according to type of transition, and explore which forms of transition are most likely to lead to consolidation.

It is still very worthwhile to read HUNTINGTON's much-noted book. This is remarkable in the literature on this topic in that it deals with virtually all dimensions of democratization: the domestic and the international, the ideological and the economic, the role of the military, and so on, and that in order to underpin his arguments, it relies on examples drawn from every area of the world that was to some extent involved in the "third wave" of democratization that began in 1974. Moreover, it offers detailed recipes for democratizers and for reform-oriented representatives of the old regime. Huntington argues that, as democratization in each country is the result of a combination of causes, and as the combination of causes producing democracy varies from country to country, his goal is not to build a theory of democratization, but to provide an explanation of the complex processes that occurred in about 30 countries. However he does not forsake generalization: indeed he identifies some factors that, more than others, are able to account for why democratization occurred in some countries rather than in others, and why it occurred at a particular moment. These factors are the global decline of the ideological underpinnings of authoritarianism as compared to democracy, economic development in the long term and economic crisis in the short term, the Catholic Church's adoption of pro-democratic attitudes, more supportive external actors, and the snowballing effect of the spread of democracy.

Huntington also looks for the causes of absence of democratization in some large areas of the world (sub-Saharan Africa, Islamic countries, East Asian countries) and finds the answers either in poverty, or in specific *Weltanschauungen* (such as Confucianism and Islam), which he believes provide a bad environment for the development of the democratic ethos.

PRZEWORSKI develops a path-breaking rational choice perspective on democratic transition and consolidation. He explores how the major political forces must perceive their situation under democratic rules of the game in order for these rules to be durable, and shows how profound economic transformations can undermine the conditions of democratic stability. He distinguishes basic forms of transition from authoritarian rule to democracy (where a transition is understood as a series of strategic interactions between incumbent authoritarian rulers and oppositions, as well as among factions within both camps), and demonstrates their implications for institutional design. He shows how the social costs associated with the economic transition in new democracies induce the reformers to vacillate between a technocratic style suited to market-oriented programmes and a participatory style necessary for the legitimacy of the reforms. While Przeworski's approach has been criticized as too formal and disconnected from actual economic and institutional structures, the use of game theory and abstract reasoning makes his arguments admirably clear and compelling.

HAGGARD & KAUFMANN explore three questions: how economic conditions affect the capacity of authoritarian ruling elites to determine the timing and nature of their withdrawal; how economic and institutional legacies of the transition affect economic policy making in new democratic regimes; and under what conditions market-oriented reform and democracy can be reconciled and consolidated. The authors assume that socioeconomic structures determine, to a large extent, the identity and preferences of relevant political groups, as well as the nature of political alignments and conflicts. As a result they choose a different approach from those analytical perspectives on transitions that focus more on choice, strategic interactions, and contingent constellations of interests. They argue that the fall and survival of regimes, authoritarian or democratic, depends crucially on their perceived capacity to provide economic prosperity, and this capacity, in turn, depends, in both kind of regimes, on the nature of political institutions, and notably, on the organization of the executive authority and the structure of the party system. The authors move back and forth between theoretical construction and rich empirical description of the paths followed by the various countries they consider – seven Latin American countries and five Asian countries, of which all but one are middle-income capitalist states.

The volume edited by WHITEHEAD offers a useful overall account of the international factors influencing democratization. Although the case studies concentrate on Latin America and Southern Europe (with only one chapter on Eastern Europe), the chapters by the editor and by Philippe Schmitter provide a comprehensive theoretical framework. Whitehead draws attention to the main perspectives employed for enquiring into the topic, and Schmitter offers a complex set of propositions and hypotheses and presents them in a clear scheme. Schmitter's inventory is probably the best starting point available to date for reflecting on the impact of the international context on contemporary democratization. Unfortunately a work that coherently tests these propositions and hypotheses has not yet appeared.

MATHIAS KOENIG-ARCHIBUGI

Demography, economic

Becker, Gary S., *A Treatise on the Family*, Cambridge, Massachusetts: Harvard University Press, 1981

Cigno, Allessandro, *Economics of the Family*, Oxford: Clarendon Press, and New York: Oxford University Press, 1991

Malthus, Thomas, *An Essay on the Principle of Population*, edited by Patricia James, 2 vols, Cambridge and New York: Cambridge University Press, 1989

Pyle, Andrew (editor), *Population: Contemporary Responses to Malthus*, Bristol: Thoemmes Press, 1994

Razin, Assaf and Efraim Sadka, *Population Economics*, Cambridge, Massachusetts: MIT Press, 1995

Rosenzweig, Mark R. and Oded Stark (editors), *Handbook of Population and Family Economics*, vols 1a and 1b, Amsterdam and New York: Elsevier, 1997

Simon, Julian L. (editor), *The Economics of Population: Key Modern Writings*, vols 1–2, Cheltenham, Gloucestershire: Elgar, 1997

Economic demography, or population economics, is the examination of the economic (demographic) causes and consequences of demographic (economic) change. The Reverend Thomas MALTHUS's *An Essay on the Principle of Population*, published in 1798, was the first serious scholarly work that formulated clear relationships between economic and demographic variables. He argued that population growth follows a geometric progression whereas the growth in natural resources (and more specifically the food supply) follows an arithmetic progression. Without restraints, the growth in the food supply over time would therefore not keep pace with the growth in population, and per capita income – or more generally the average standard of living – would fall. In the longer run this would lead to a population equilibrium characterized by an average standard of living near the subsistence level. He believed that the only way to avoid this situation of chronic poverty was for individuals to engage in "moral restraint" and purposefully limit family size. Although his religious convictions would not allow him to advocate family planning methods publicly, he is often viewed as the father of the modern birth control movement.

The "Malthusian population trap" model provides a simple and appealing theory of the interaction between population growth and economic development that seemed to describe with considerable accuracy the conditions that were prevailing at the time when Malthus was writing. Over the years that followed, his pessimistic forecasts of mankind's future did not materialize, mainly because he did not anticipate the role and impact of technological change, which, for example, drastically increased the efficiency of food production. However, over the past few decades, there has been a renewed interest in Malthus, due in large part to the somewhat frightening

demographic and economic trends in some developing countries where the Malthusian trap may be re-emerging (most notably the low-income countries of Africa and Asia). The essays in PYLE provide an excellent overview of the relevance of Malthus to modern times.

The 55 previously published essays in SIMON are concerned with a variety of relationships between economic and demographic variables. They include most of the "classic" papers in economic demography and provide an excellent overview of the intellectual history of the subject. Some are concerned with causes and consequences of (mainly rapid) population growth. Others wrestle with the question of whether population growth is "good" or "bad" for economic growth and development. The link between population growth (and density) and food production and agricultural practices is well covered. The pioneering economics of fertility papers of Becker, Easterlin, Willis and others are included.

BECKER was one of the first to systematically apply rigorous microeconomic theory to a variety of seemingly "non-market" behaviours, including demographic processes such as marriage, divorce, fertility, household formation, and migration. A more recent treatment and summary can be found in CIGNO, who not only presents the main theoretical results of much of the recent literature relating to the so-called "economics of the family", but also explores some additional topics. RAZIN & SADKA consider the implications of endogenous fertility coupled with parental altruism towards children for consumption, labour supply, savings, investments in human capital, economic growth, migration, and inter- and intra-generational income redistribution. These three works demonstrate that much can be learned by applying an integrated microeconomic framework to the understanding of demographic change and are excellent surveys of the core theory that underlies much of the research carried out in population economics.

The 22 essays included in ROSENZWEIG & STARK represent a state-of-the-art summary and critical review of theoretical and empirical population economics. This "handbook" is organized around six broad themes. Part 1 surveys economic theories of the family, examines the causes and consequences of family formation and dissolution, explores how resources are distributed within families and households, and investigates inter-generational and inter-household issues. Part 2 is concerned with the costs of children and the economics of fertility in both developed and developing countries. In Part 3, the link between nutrition and mortality is surveyed and the determinants and consequences of mortality, morbidity, and health are examined. Migration is the topic of Part 4, with contributions on the determinants and consequences of internal migration in developed and developing countries. The economic impact of migration in both sending and receiving nations is considered in detail. There is also an essay concerned with outlining the links between international migration and trade. Part 5 focuses on the economics of individual ageing, the economics of population ageing, and the relationships between demographic variables and income inequality. Part 6 begins with an exploration of long-term economic-demographic equilibriums and the consequences of short-term economic and demographic shocks. This is followed by a discussion of growth models with endogenous fertility. The volume concludes with a consideration of the long-term consequences of population growth by examining the relationships between technological change, natural resources, and the environment.

For many years, population economics was a fringe subject, not really part of core economics, yet seriously researched by a dedicated groups of economists (and by demographers with an interest in economics). However, with the publication of its own "handbook", population economics has indisputably joined the ranks of mainstream economics.

ROBERT E. WRIGHT

Demography, sociology

Bongaarts, John and Robert G. Potter, *Fertility, Biology, and Behavior: An Analysis of the Proximate Determinants*, London and New York: Academic Press, 1983

Chesnais, Jean-Claude, *The Demographic Transition: Stages, Patterns, and Economic Implications: A Longitudinal Study of Sixty-Seven Countries Covering the Period 1720–1984*, Oxford: Clarendon Press, and New York: Oxford University Press, 1992 (French edition 1986)

Cleland, John, Chris Scott and David Whitelegge (editors), *The World Fertility Survey: An Assessment*, Oxford and New York: Oxford University Press, 1987

Coleman, David and John Salt, *The British Population: Patterns, Trends, and Processes*, Oxford and New York: Oxford University Press, 1992

Coleman, David (editor), *Europe's Population in the 1990s*, Oxford and New York: Oxford University Press, 1996

Hajnal, John, "Two Kinds of Preindustrial Household Formation System", *Population and Development Review*, 8/3 (1982): 449–94; reprinted in *Family Forms in Historic Europe*, edited by Richard Wall, Jean Robin and Peter Laslett, Cambridge and New York: Cambridge University Press, 1983

Kammeyer, Kenneth C.W. and Helen L. Ginn, *An Introduction to Population*, Chicago: Dorsey Press, 1986; 2nd edition by Helen Ginn Daugherty and Kenneth C.W. Kammeyer, New York: Guilford Press, 1995

Population Studies, special issue on "Population Studies", 50/3 (1996): 297–565

Shryock, Henry S., Jacob S. Siegel and associates, *The Methods and Materials of Demography*, 2 vols, Washington, DC: US Government Printing Office, 1971; revised edition, 1975; condensed edition edited by Edward G. Stockwell, London and New York: Academic Press, 1976

Wrigley, E.A. and Roger S. Schofield, *The Population History of England, 1541–1871: A Reconstruction*, London: Arnold, and Cambridge, Masachusetts: Harvard University Press, 1981; revised edition, Cambridge and New York: Cambridge University Press, 1989

Demography is the scientific study of the size and structure of human populations, and how these change over time. At its core is the quantitative description of population change. The size of a population changes for three reasons: birth, death,

and migration. Hence the three key processes that demographers study are fertility, mortality, and migration. In addition, all human populations have "structure" in that their members can be classified according to their sex, age, marital status, ethnic origin, educational attainment, occupation, etc. For the demographer, gender, age, and marital status are the most important of these characteristics. The study of changes in a population's structure therefore involves the analysis of other processes, for example marriage and divorce.

SHRYOCK & SIEGEL is a comprehensive and readable treatment of quantitative, or formal, demography. It deals with all these processes and includes valuable material on population projection (the forecasting of population size and structure), which is one of the practical skills demographers are expected to possess.

While still at the discipline's core, formal demography is nowadays only a small part of what demographers do. Much of their work involves the study of how social, economic, and cultural factors influence population change, and the social and economic impact of changes in the size and structure of populations. This project draws on and links together several social-scientific disciplines; it is sometimes referred to as "population studies" or "population sciences". KAMMEYER & GINN is a good introduction to population studies for non-specialists. Though many of their examples are drawn from US data, the book will be of interest to readers throughout the world. As with the best introductory texts, it still manages to break new ground, notably in the discussion of world population growth and population policies in the final two chapters.

If demography can be said to have any central paradigm, it is demographic transition. For most of human history, population growth rates have been very slow, with birth and death rates being approximately in balance. During the last two and a half centuries, however, almost all populations have experienced a phase of rapid growth. This growth is part of a process known as the demographic transition, by which birth and death rates move from a state of balance at high levels to a state of balance at low levels. Rapid growth occurs because death rates normally fall before birth rates. In Europe and North America, the demographic transition was associated with industrialization (though the association was not simple). Of the many studies of the demographic transition, CHESNAIS is one of the most recent, and certainly one of the most impressive.

Earlier work on the demographic transition focused on European countries. One of the motivations for this work was the hope that a study of historical trends in European countries would provide lessons for the developing world, in which rapid population growth rates were threatening continued development. In fact, one of the most important (arguably *the* most important) conclusions of this work was that in much of historical Europe, fertility and mortality prior to the transition were considerably lower than they were in developing countries. HAJNAL is a brilliant article that shows how this lower fertility and mortality was intimately bound up with European patterns of late and non-universal marriage for women and nuclear (or stem) family systems. This contrasted with the practice of early and universal marriage commonly found in Africa and Asia. WRIGLEY & SCHOFIELD is a monumental work of demographic reconstruction based on the Church of England parish registers. It shows clearly how the European household formation system, which operated *par excellence* in England during the 17th and 18th centuries, enabled population growth to be kept in check.

Largely because of their different household formation systems, rates of population growth in developing countries in recent years have far exceeded any observed in historical Europe, even at the height of the demographic transition. This has led to a burgeoning of interest in fertility and the prospects for fertility decline. One of the most influential of the many studies of the determinants of fertility is BONGAARTS & POTTER. In this book, the authors describe and elaborate a simple model by which various influences on fertility outcomes in any population can be measured. These influences include marriage patterns, the use of contraception and induced abortion, and the spacing of births (which is closely related to the average duration of breastfeeding) Because of its simplicity and conceptual appeal, this model has been applied in many subsequent empirical analyses.

Two important recent texts dealing respectively with contemporary British and European demography are COLEMAN & SALT and COLEMAN. The former is an excellent study of the demography of a single country, clearly delineating the main contemporary trends in fertility, mortality, and migration, and in such subprocesses as marriage and household formation. In the case of the latter, the contributors are keen to emphasise the rapid (and in some cases unprecedented) changes that are currently under way in Britain and other Western European countries; changes that have been described as a "second demographic transition". For example, the last three decades of the 20th century saw a large rise in the proportion of men and women "cohabiting" (living together in informal unions). One result of this has been that the proportion of children born outside legal marriages increased very greatly during this period, such that by the mid-1990s more than one in three children were born to parents who were not legally married (though a large proportion were living together). Because of these changes, demography has developed a particular focus on marriage and family life, including the study of the transitions into cohabitation and married life; childbearing; separation, divorce and widowhood; and remarriage.

In recent years there have been new developments in formal demography. The papers in CLELAND, SCOTT & WHITE-LEGGE describe one of the most significant of these, the World Fertility Survey. This comprised a series of retrospective sample surveys of fertility in both developed and developing countries, conducted largely in the 1970s. Not only was much learned about fertility levels and trends, but a range of new techniques for the analysis of retrospective birth history data was developed and applied. Subsequent surveys, notably the Demographic and Health Surveys in developing countries, which began in 1985, have benefited from many of the lessons learned in the World Fertility Survey.

Demography is a wide-ranging subject that has expanded its purview greatly during the last few decades. The papers collected in POPULATION STUDIES constitute probably the best available single-volume introduction to developments in demographic research during the last 50 years. Each is written by a leading international figure, and though they are rigorous (and some will be quite demanding for those who are not quantitatively-minded), all are accessible to the nonspecialist.

ANDREW HINDE

Dependency theory

Amin, Samir, *Unequal Development: An Essay on the Social Formations of Peripheral Capitalism*, New York: Monthly Press Review, and Brighton: Harvester Press, 1976

Baran, Paul A., *The Political Economy of Growth*, 2nd edition, New York: Monthly Review Press, 1962

Cardoso, Fernando Henrique and Enzo Falleto, *Dependency and Development in Latin America*, Berkeley: University of California Press, 1979

Emmanuel, Arghiri, *Unequal Exchange: A Study of the Imperialism of Trade*, New York: Monthly Review Press, 1972

Frank, Andre Gunder, *Capitalism and Underdevelopment in Latin America: Historical Studies of Chile and Brazil*, revised edition, New York: Monthly Press Review, 1969

Furtado, Celso, *Development and Underdevelopment*, Berkeley: University of California Press, 1964

Palma, Gabriel, "Dependency and Development: A Critical Overview" in *Dependency Theory: A Critical Reassessment*, edited by Dudley Seers, London: Pinter, 1981

Prebisch, Raúl, *The Economic Development of Latin America and Its Principal Problems*, New York: United Nations, 1950

Santos, T. dos, "The Crisis of Development Theory and the Problem of Dependence in Latin America" in *Underdevelopment and Development: The Third World Today: Selected Readings*, edited by Henry Bernstein, Harmondsworth: Penguin, 1973

Sunkel, Osvaldo, "Big Business and Dependencia", *Foreign Affairs*, 50 (April 1972): 517–31

Wallerstein, Immanuel, "Dependence in an Interdependent World: The Limited Possibilities of Transformation within the Capitalist World-Economy" in his *The Capitalist World-Economy*, Cambridge and New York: Cambridge University Press, 1979

Dependency theory began as a critique of modernization theories of development in the 1950s at the Economic Commission for Latin America (ECLA), a regional body of the United Nations. Initially, dependency theory was more an eclectic idea than a formal theory. A comprehensive definition of dependence is provided by SANTOS:

Dependence is a *continuing situation* in which the economies of one group of countries are conditioned by the development and expansion of others. A relationship of interdependence between one or more economies or between such economies and the world trading system becomes a dependent relationship when some countries can expand through self-impulsion while others, being in a dependent position, can only expand as a reflection of the expansion of the dominant countries, which may have positive or negative effects on their immediate development.

PREBISCH developed the concept of "centre-periphery" world market system which favours the centre (developed) rather than the periphery (developing) economies. In this report to the United Nations Commission for Latin America he questions the idea of universal benefits from free international trade and argues that the industrialized economies monopolized the benefits of technical progress, instead of transferring these benefits to developing countries by lowering the prices of industrial products that were exported to the periphery. Moreover, producers and labour unions at the centre were organized and interested in defending the rate of profit and higher wage levels, so the real sharing of technical progress occurred within the industrialized centre and not between the centre and periphery. In contrast, labour in the periphery was weak and badly organized. Hence, wages were lower in the periphery. Finally, the terms of trade were adverse for the periphery because of decreasing prices of raw materials and increasing prices and demand for the industrial goods produced in the centre. Prebisch concludes that those countries that specialized in the production of industrial goods had an advantage over those that specialized in the production of raw materials. Hence, he advocated the policy of autonomous industrialization of the periphery in order to alleviate its dependence on the centre and underdevelopment.

BARAN, although not directly associated with dependency literature, nonetheless has made a significant contribution in demonstrating the processes of dependency. He does not consider backwardness to be the result of precapitalist structures; on the contrary, backwardness is a product of capitalism. Capitalism is seen as a heterogeneous and hierarchical international system within which some nations, the metropolises, exploit, and subordinate others, the dependent nations. Dependent nations, in turn, exploit other weaker nations. The exploitation of dependent nations involves the transfer of surplus value to the metropolis. Backward local oligarchies are also seen to finance luxury consumption with a portion of the surplus generated domestically. Hence, capitalism does not foster economic development in the dependent nations.

FRANK advanced Baran's underdevelopment thesis and applies it to the Latin American situation. He conceptualizes the world system as being composed of "metropolis" and "satellite" nations. In this world system the countries in the metropolis appropriate the surplus value generated in the satellite nations. The world system approach suggests two dynamics: (a) capitalist expansion generates the continuous development of the metropolis and the continuous underdevelopment of the satellites: (b) development and underdevelopment are dialectically related to one another. Frank, in his analysis of Chile and Brazil, shows that underdevelopment of satellite nations does not eventually lead to their development. On the contrary, the perpetual underdevelopment of satellite nations is an enduring feature of capitalist development.

WALLERSTEIN divided the world economy into core, semiperipheral, and peripheral nations. The relationship between core, semiperipheral, and peripheral countries is that of exploitation, whereby the core appropriates the surplus produced in the periphery. The extraction of surplus is secured both by the international division of labour and political power. The semiperipheral nations serve as a middle sector that reduces the potentials for rebellion against the core, which perpetuates the unequal world system.

EMMANUEL analyses the precise mechanisms whereby surplus is transferred from the periphery to the core of the world economy. Recall that Frank and Wallerstein treat these mechanisms only generally. Emmanuel argues that an increasing international wage differential, which results from labour immobility and capital mobility, is the root cause of an unequal exchange mechanism that entails the transfer of surplus from the periphery to the core. The resilience of the unequal exchange mechanism ensures the continued underdevelopment of the periphery.

AMIN builds on Emmanuel's analysis but argues that there is a fundamental difference between the capitalist mode of surplus accumulation in the centre and in the periphery. At the centre, the level of productive forces determines the rate of surplus value, which in turn determines the distribution of national income between wages and profits. In the periphery, by contrast, surplus accumulation is initiated by the centre via the establishment of export production zones (EPZs). Export production zones ensure that capitalists in the centre maintain access to cheap raw materials and a low-wage workforce. Hence, in the periphery there is no relation between the level of productive forces and wages. Export production zones do not promote rising wages or development in the periphery because production there is independent of domestic demand conditions.

For SUNKEL, the processes of development and underdevelopment represent two faces of the historical evolution of capitalism. He demonstrates this proposition by analysing the operations of multinational corporations (MNCs) in Brazil, Chile, and Peru. Multinational corporations, according to Sunkel, always engage in capital-intensive technology production. They do not address underdevelopment in the periphery and they undermine domestic entrepreneurship. These dynamics undermine the possibilities for autonomous domestic development.

FURTADO demonstrates that it is possible for the industrial sector to grow in an underdeveloped economy, however, the proportion of population that benefits from the process of development remains small and the occupational structure of the periphery remains largely precapitalist despite industrialization. Furtado's work has some interesting parallels to the recent globalization literature. This new literature explains that industrialization in the periphery has emerged as a new vehicle of dependence via direct investment and control over resources by MNC's.

CARDOSO & FALLETO build on the shortcomings of previous works in dependency theory. Unlike most other dependency theorists, they do not deny the possibility of dependent capitalist development in the periphery. They developed the concept of "associated dependent development" (ADD). Associated dependent development is sustained by foreign investment in association with domestic capital in the periphery. The relationship between domestic and foreign capital allows for a disproportional concentration of wealth and productive capacities in the periphery.

PALMA presents a useful conceptual overview of different approaches within dependency theory. He presents a three-tiered classification of dependency approaches. First, the works of Frank and of T. dos Santos among others are classified as underdevelopment theories. These theories explain underdevelopment as directly being caused by dependence on centre (industrialized) economies and claim that capitalism in the periphery is unable to bring about a process of development. The second tier represented by Sunkel and Furtado reformulates the analysis of the first tier and emphasizes that although the obstacles to national development are due to external factors, it is possible to change those conditions through reformist government initiatives. Lastly, the works of Cardoso & Faletto seek to analyse concrete situations of dependency and emphasize the internal processes of class struggle, which necessarily mediate the influence of external factors. They reject the formal and abstract attempts to develop a general theory of underdevelopment. It is an internal as well as an external conditioning that leads to dependency of the periphery. The book also has an extensive list of references.

MINU PALANI

See also Development economics

Depression

Costello, Charles G. (editor), *Symptoms of Depression*, New York: Wiley, 1993

Elmer-Dewitt, Philip, "Depression: The Growing Role of Drug Therapies", *Time*, 7/27 (6 July 1992): 73–75

Freud, Sigmund, "Mourning and Melancholia" (published in German 1917) in *On the History of the Psycho-analytic Movement, Papers on Metapsychology, and Other Works*, London: Hogarth Press, 1957 (*The Standard Edition of the Complete Psychological Works*, vol. 14); reprinted in *On Metapsychology*, Harmondsworth: Penguin, 1984 (Pelican Freud Library, vol. 11)

LaBier, Douglas, *Modern Madness: The Emotional Fallout of Success*, Reading, Massachusetts: Addison Wesley, 1986

Lasch, Christopher, *The Minimal Self: Psychic Survival in Troubled Times*, London: Picador, 1985

Marano, Hara, "Depression: Beyond Serotonin", *Psychology Today*, 32/2 (1999): 30–36 and 72–76

Seligman, Martin, "Boomer Blues", *Psychology Today*, 22/10 (1988): 50–55

Weber, Zita, *Back from the Blues: Getting to the Other Side of Reactive Depression*, Sydney: Millennium Books, 1997

The fact that human beings are prone to depression is something that has been acknowledged since recorded history. This present century continues that acknowledgement albeit that the sources of depression may have changed and our understanding of the condition itself may have improved. For historians, and those involved in psychological health, the poem in 1947 by W.H. Auden, "The Age of Anxiety", seemed to capture the mood of a period in this present century in which Western societies appeared apprehensive about the future. An apprehension, perhaps in part, was a fear that the nuclear age was upon us and had given our species the means for self destruc-

tion. It was also widely thought that the population was apprehensive as to whether their aspirations for the future could be met after the turmoil and destruction of World War II. In the late 1960s there was an increasing number of leading figures in psychology who thought Western societies had moved into a new age, that of the "Age of Melancholy". Ontologically this made sense to some schools of psychology, for a person's failure to adequately deal with a feeling of impeding doom can lead to a state of helplessness after the "disaster" has occurred. This state of helplessness is called depression. As to whether these two Ages are indeed connected in such a way is open to speculation. Certainly the diagnosis of depression was on the increase, with almost a tenfold increase over two generations, and today it is considered the second most disabling ailment (after heart disease) in Western societies.

LASCH was one of the first to suggest that the reason for the significant increase in cases of depression was the rise of a culture in which the self has been exalted, and, at the same time, there has been a weakening of commitment to larger institutions. He argued that our sense of moral and aesthetic self-judgement, our superego strength, has declined and confidence in the future has been lost. Although in some ways it is now a somewhat dated commentary, Lasch provided an incisive analysis of the contemporary cultural debates of the day. He suggested that the traditional left and right distinctions that were made in politics were giving way to new political configurations. The emerging political landscape was such that the various parties seemed to be aligned with a specific view as to the origins and nature of the crisis of contemporary culture. These crises, Lasch argued, were best conceived as a form of ideal typology in which psychoanalytic terminology was a more accurate guide to describing this landscape than the traditional left and right distinctions. The conservative tradition seemed to view the contemporary crisis as a crisis of the super-ego – the disorder and sense of hopelessness was due to moral decay and a decline in authority. If widespread melancholy was to be overcome there was a need for stronger parental authority and moral development. The more liberal view was that the ego, or rational faculty, was what needed strengthening to make more discriminating judgements. For a third group, the new left, what is advocated is not the installation of a repressive apparatus of laws and moral dogma, nor the strengthening of the ego to cope with or adjust to a society that itself is repressive and based upon exploitation and alienating labour, but instead a cultural revolution in which technological domination is abandoned in favour of a reformulation of human relations on a more emancipatory footing. Lasch views this third position as an "ideological assault on the ego". Clearly, for Lasch, the realm of solving the crisis of widespread melancholy resides in institutional and societal reform and not within the realm of individual therapy. The residue of this can be detected as assumptions that underpin social and political commentary today. The strength of this book is its sociohistorical commentary. Its weakness is the lack of clinical evidence presented by Lasch to support his own position and conclusions.

COSTELLO is an edited volume in the Wiley series on personality processes. The collection of 14 papers in this volume presents the reader with both an understanding of the variety of symptoms of depression and also an appreciation of the methodological problems that seem to plague research literature in the area of depression. The areas of stress, anxiety, and depression, as a collective, are amongst the most researched topics in the social sciences. For all this attention, the yield has been disappointing in as much as the information gathered sometimes appears contradictory. Significant flaws in the methodology, problems in defining terminology, and a lack of an explicit theoretical framework are some of the reasons for this. This particular volume discusses some of these issues and collectively suggests that the focus of research should be upon symptoms of depression. This is not an introductory volume to the area of depression. Readers who are less familiar with the terminology of psychiatry are best advised to consult this volume having read the other publications listed in this entry.

FREUD views depression (a condition of melancholia) as a pathological form of mourning in which an "object" has been lost. The object to which Freud refers is not a person but an internal object in the form of an ideal or vision, the achievement of which leads to narcissistic gratification. This paper is an important one in terms of Freud linking psychopathology to narcissism and the ego ideal, which were to figure significantly in his second theory of the mind. It is also an important paper in the context of the "talking cure" that psychoanalytic therapy seeks to offer those with a variety of psychopathologies.

The paper by SELIGMAN is a useful one. It is representative of a number of eminent writers in the later 1980s who noted the instance of depression had increased dramatically and canvassed a number of reasons to explain this state of affairs. In the context of the increased emphasis in society upon self and individualism, Seligman believes failure and frustration to achieve personal ambitions and goals was being read as a personal failure and this ultimately resulted in depressive disorders. This is a variation on the narcissism argument raised by Lasch. Again, the weakness in making such a judgement is both a lack of reliable comparative data with other cultures as well as a reflexive appreciation of whether social attitudinal changes and health education programs had been responsible for more widespread reporting and acknowledgement of a level of depression among a population. Thus, this level of depression within the population may have always existed but may have gone unreported because of attitudes to reporting and a lack of awareness of the condition itself. Could it have been, for example, that in the past people in society subscribed more to the "sock school of psychiatry" – when feeling low all that is required is for the person to pull up their socks – thus depression was significantly under reported? Whatever the explanation, the work of Lasch, Seligman, and others led to a perception that rates of depression were on the increase, and it said something about the current society that had to be addressed at a societal, rather than an individual, level.

LABIER also makes a diagnosis that the current state of society is responsible for an increasing level of depression. Unlike Lasch, Seligman, and many others, LaBier locates depression as the legacy of working "successfully" in work organizations. He acknowledges the widespread view that a percentage (estimates of which range from six to ten per cent) of the population "naturally" suffers from biological or endogenous depression – a chemical imbalance in the body that is capable of being treated through drugs. However, LaBier argues that the larger kind of depression, exogenous/reactive/situational depression, requires that we go beyond the simple use of antidepressant drugs and an ideology of individualism and look at the world of work and the psychostructure (character type) that it promotes. This volume reports upon a study of a new generation of careerists, which reveals that some organizations are encouraging psychostructures that skew human development and result in employees experiencing feelings of emptiness and self-betrayal due to constant compromise that is demanded. LaBier criticizes the mainstream mental health establishment for failing to realize that the inner conflicts that are at the heart of depression are not so much those arising from childhood but arise from the world of work. Increasingly being cited in the literature of organization psychology and organization behaviour, this volume by LaBier calls for therapists to adopt a different orientation to the treatment of depression.

MARANO provides an excellent summary of recent research findings that have employed imaging techniques in exploring the neurobiology of depression. These research findings call into question the simple concept that by solely raising serotonin levels and enhancing the action of neurotransmitters through drugs such as Prozac, Paxil, and so on, a restorative and arresting solution to depression is at hand. Instead, the emerging evidence from these studies is that depression is a much more complex neurodegenerative disorder and the manner in which these antidepressants "work" has been misunderstood. This article notes that stressful events early in life appear to make one more prone to depressive episodes in later years as the actual nerve circuitry that controls emotions seems to be altered by stress. Stress appears to change the size, shape, and number of neurones in parts of the brain. Marano, at one point, notes that "the deeper researchers probe the brain, the more they validate the psychoanalytic view that early adverse life events can create adult psychopathology" (p.32). The research results also reveal that depression adversely effects other systems in the body including, for example, the vulnerability to heart disease and changes in bone mass. The promise of new treatments for depression is discussed and the underlying assumptions of how treatments have worked in the past is placed within a new theoretical framework. A well-written and good summary of where the field is heading, this paper is best understood if the reader has some background as to the supposed revolution in the late 1980s in the treating of depressive illness, and the "discovery" of Prozac in particular. This context can be gleaned from the article by ELMER-DEWITT, which, although written for a magazine, succinctly and clearly explains how Prozac and other antidepressant drugs work. There are well over 100 books written about Prozac, perhaps the best known being Peter Kramer's *Listening to Prozac* (Viking, 1993), however, the current state of the field reflects an interest that is much broader than one antidepressant drug. The article by Elmer-Dewitt nicely places Prozac in context and is an early example of a cautionary and critical note about reducing explanations of depression to the influence of serotonin levels.

WEBER is a recent volume that provides first-person accounts of ten people who have had exogenous/reactive/situational depression. These ten narratives were drawn by Weber as representative of a larger sample of 100 cases. Through these personal experiences, one gains a very keen sense of the causes, symptoms, and challenges associated with depression. This is a well-written book that gives the reader an insider's view of depression and possible positive outcomes from the processes of recovery.

ADRIAN N. CARR

See also Stress at work

Derivative markets, *see* Markets

Descent

Forde, Daryll, "Double Descent among the Yako" in *African Systems of Kinship and Marriage*, edited by A.R. Radcliffe-Brown and Daryll Forde, 1950

Fortes, M., "The Structure of Unilineal Descent Groups", *American Anthropologist*, 55 (1953): 17–41

Fox, Robin, *Kinship and Marriage: An Anthropological Perspective*, Harmondsworth and Baltimore: Penguin, 1967

Goody, Jack (editor), *The Character of Kinship*, Cambridge: Cambridge University Press, 1973

Mair, Lucy, *African Societies*, London and New York: Cambridge University Press, 1974

Murdock, George Peter, *Social Structure*, New York: Macmillan, 1949

Parkin, Robert, *Kinship: An Introduction to Basic Concepts*, Oxford and Malden, Massachusetts: Blackwell, 1997

Radcliffe-Brown, A.R. and Daryll Forde (editors), *African Systems of Kinship and Marriage*, London and New York: Oxford University Press, 1950

Radcliffe-Brown, A.R. "The Study of Kinship" in *Structure and Function in Primitive Society*, Glencoe, Illinois: Free Press, and London: Cohen and West, 1952

Schneider, David M. and Kathleen Gough (editors), *Matrilineal Kinship*, Berkeley: University of California Press, 1961

Schusky, Ernest L., *Manual for Kinship Analysis*, 2nd edition, New York: Holt Rinehart, 1972

Schusky, Ernest L., *Variation in Kinship*, New York: Holt Rinehart, 1974

FORDE's classic article on double descent among the Yako is listed here from a classic collection of essays on kinship and marriage in Africa. The article can also be found in a later collection of the author's various articles on the Yako called *Yako Studies*. This essay is very useful for its detailed description and clear distinction of compact patrilineal lineages from dispersed systemic matrilineal lineages forming clans.

FORTES is a foremost authority on kinship. This is probably the best-known paper on descent, being often quoted, cited, and included in many edited readings. This is so because the articles summarize knowledge of descent in Africa. Therefore the work has become most influential in broadening and modifying concepts of descent. It forms a basis on which to pit structure against particular social context. It has also constituted the grounds for later research on kinship and

descent around the globe. It is an excellent exposition of the application of the unilineal principle of kinship.

FOX has written an excellent general work on the basic concept underlying kinship and marriage. His chatty style does not hinder the import of his excellent review of the theoretical issues relevant to the study of society as determined by kinship factors. He improves earlier works by extending the exploration of kinship with his alliance theme. Also noteworthy is his analysis of the various types of kinship organization.

A revisitation of kinship and descent, family and official roles is the collection of essays edited by GOODY. The first four are the most relevant ones here. Barth pays attention to how native concepts and social groups are shaped by interaction and experience, using Middle Eastern systems. Strathern attempts the definition of kinship by looking at kinship, descent, and locality in New Guinea, and Leach treats complementary filiation and bilateral kinship in a way to prove the importance of ideology as well as empirical facts.

MAIR gives a crisp, abridged ethnography of almost 20 African societies from the Nuer in the Upper Nile to the Tonga in Southern Africa. Her method is structuralist-functionalist, concerned with the important aspects of social systems. She is relevant for her treatment of each society by descent, covering agnatic, matrilineal, double, unilineal, and cognatic descent. Her book is of significance as a collection of ethnographies in which descent categories are applied.

MURDOCK's most important book provides an erudite analysis of kin groups and terminologies. His influential work not only demonstrates the determinants of terminologies but also expresses the problems of change of terminologies in response to changes in social relations. His work is one of a kind especially with his use of statistical methods and behaviourist psychology to attempt a cross-cultural comparison and systematic classification of known kinship systems the world over. Most relevant here is his influential statistical examination of kinship, marriage, and descent including well-known typology of systems, of classification of kinspeople on ego's own generation.

PARKIN is a recent introduction to the social anthropology of kinship. It covers descent, inheritance, succession, family, residence, marriage, and kinship. The book meets its aim to provide adequate introductory account of basic concepts in a concise and clear manner. Its unpolemical and uncontroversial tone lowers the tension between formation and description. It is a very useful new text on the essential nature of kinship and descent. It applies and illustrates concepts, sometimes employing contrasting case studies. Most welcome are the references supplied on a chapter-by-chapter basis and ethnographic examples from masters in the field.

Two works by Radcliffe-Brown are cited here. RADCLIFFE-BROWN is a well-written paper distinguished by style and thought on methodology in kinship studies. RADCLIFFE-BROWN & FORDE is a much-cited classic introducing the importance, definition, and structural principles of kinship systems. The excellent introduction to kinship and classification systems treats structural, unilineal, generational, and lineage principles compellingly. The introduction is noteworthy for its grasp of general comparative and theoretical issues concerning the significance of unilineal descent. His four types of kin classification were used by social anthropologists for a long, long time.

SCHNEIDER & GOUGH is the classic on matrilineal kinship and descent. Six anthropologists put together their research findings in an impressive crosscultural examination of different societies with stunning results. Three of the writeups are particularly outstanding: Schneider's hypothetical characteristics of matrilineal systems; Gough's interpretation of the ethnographic data; and Aberle's crossclassified surveys by types of subsistence techniques, and types of descent system, complete with tables.

Two manuals by SCHUSKY (1972, 1974) are noted here. The 1972 book is a do-it-yourself manual about kinship with a direct and clear-cut approach. The 1974 primer discusses elements of kinship, diagramming, systems, classification, descent, and lineages with examples from Crow and Omaha American Indian societies. It is therefore a useful tool for diagramming and describing kin groups and technological systems. The other manual is the application of generalizations on descent and affinity to various case studies on kinship. The two books are useful companions and the bibliographies are useful sources of case studies.

AYODELE OGUNDIPE

Descriptive statistics

Appleton, David R., Joyce M. French and Mark P.J. Vanderpump, "Ignoring a Covariate: An Example of Simpson's Paradox", *American Statistician*, 50/4 (1996): 340–41

Diaconis, Persi, "Theories of Data Analysis: From Magical Thinking through Classical Statistics" in *Exploring Data Tables, Trends, and Shapes*, edited by David C. Hoaglin, Frederick Mosteller and John W. Tukey, New York and Chichester: Wiley, 1985

Hoaglin, David C., Frederick Mosteller and John W. Tukey (editors), *Understanding Robust and Exploratory Data Analysis*, New York and Chichester: Wiley, 1983

Huff, Darrell, *How to Lie with Statistics*, New York: Norton, 1954

Tufte, Edward R., *The Visual Display of Quantitative Information*, Cheshire, Connecticut: Graphics Press, 1983

Tufte, Edward R., *Visual Explanations: Images and Quantities, Evidence and Narrative*, Cheshire, Connecticut: Graphics Press, 1997

Tukey, John W., *Exploratory Data Analysis*, Reading, Massachusetts: Addison Wesley, 1977

Wainer, Howard, "Depicting Error", *American Statistician*, 50/2 (1996): 101–11

Wardrop, Robert L., "Simpson's Paradox and the Hot Hand in Basketball", *American Statistician*, 49/1 (1995): 24–28

Wiseman, Frederick and Sangrit Chatterjee, "Major League Baseball Player Salaries: Bringing Realism into Introductory Statistics Courses", *American Statistician*, 51/4 (1997): 350–52

In a delightful, classic presentation of the uses and misuses of descriptive statistics, HUFF offers the reader an extremely accessible but very useful book. He outlines many of the ways in which statistics can mislead when used improperly, and gives readers a good feel for the kinds of precautions needed before accepting supposedly objective data. Although a few of his examples are dated, the points he makes are sound. Readers with no background in statistics will find this book very understandable and enjoyable.

One of the most common ways of presenting statistical information is by visual means. In two different volumes, TUFTE (1983, 1997) does a cogent job of describing how the different elements of a visual display contribute to the information conveyed by graphs, tables, and pictures. Most of the presentation is nontechnical, although both books deal with data based on technical research. The visual presentation, as one might expect, is compelling: fortunately for the reader, so is the text. Tufte's 1983 book is more directed towards the effective presentation of research results; but his 1997 book, with a less technical orientation, also contains some material relating to empirical data. Both books provide a useful understanding of how to present data effectively in a visual manner, and of how to avoid some of the pitfalls involved.

Contrary to common knowledge, the use of descriptive statistics has proceeded beyond simple measures of central tendency (such as the arithmetic, geometric, and harmonic means, the median, and the mode) and measures of variability (such as variance and range). One relatively new approach, pioneered by TUKEY, is exploratory data analysis (EDA). In addition, HOAGLIN, MOSTELLER & TUKEY present an updated, moderately technical presentation of EDA and of robust statistical methods (i.e. those not requiring normally distributed data). Their edited volume is most fully appreciated by attending to the technical aspects of the statistical methods considered, but an interested reader can comprehend most of the main points without following some of the more difficult statistical presentations. The book explains several useful statistical techniques, including stem-and-leaf displays, boxplots, trimmed statistics, and confidence intervals.

DIACONIS describes the use of EDA and some of the ways in which initial descriptions of data can mislead a user into believing that patterns exist in randomly generated data. He uses the term "magical thinking" to refer to the tendency to persist in erroneous beliefs associated with deceptive data. His chapter begins with a clear presentation of the intuitive aspects of correcting erroneous perceptions, and ends with a more technical presentation of theories and approaches to data analysis.

Sometimes, understanding statistics requires users to appreciate what they do not know, as much as what they do know. WAINER points out that the degree of uncertainty in measurement is an important component of statistical presentation. He provides useful tabular and graphic examples of the presentation of errors when comparing different groups. His specific examples relate to the US National Assessment of Educational Proficiency. He makes the important point that, when comparing measurements, such as means, across groups, the degree of measurement error is critical as regards confidence in the reliability of the apparent differences. Wainer's three most important points about the effective display of data are that: (a) uncertainty is a reality of measurement; (b) the degree of uncertainty can itself be measured; and (c) without a clear assessment of the magnitude of the errors in data, erroneous conclusions may be drawn.

WISEMAN & CHATTERJEE, who note that many people regard statistics as boring, irrelevant, and difficult to understand, use salaries of baseball players to enhance their students' interest in statistical applications. They use salary data set to demonstrate the different measures of central tendency, variability, and location, and the graphical representations associated with descriptive statistics. Their students simulate being reporters who write about the players' salary. The salary dataset is useful in illustrating that the choice of measures of central tendency and variability greatly influences the conclusions that might be drawn. The authors also indicate how misinterpretations and distortions of their data may arise. Their article explains the effects of different types of distribution and of extreme data values on the results of statistical analysis. It also makes the point that clear operational definitions of terms are critical to clear analysis.

Averages (usually means) and proportions are frequently reported descriptive statistics. When the data involve multiple individuals, different descriptive values may emerge for individual versus aggregate data. This phenomenon is known as Simpson's Paradox. The articles by APPLETON, FRENCH & VANDERPUMP and by WARDROP provide interesting examples of Simpson's Paradox. Appleton, French & Vanderpump present data on the relationship between smoking habits of women over a 20-year period and survival rates. When the data are presented using only smoking habits and survival rates, it appears that smoking exerts a significant protective effect: proportionally fewer smokers die. The authors note that when age is factored into the evaluation, the negative effects of smoking are manifest. Using less bleak research, Wardrop presents data on free-throw shooting among basketball players. When the data are presented for individuals, there is little evidence for streak shooting, that is, the "hot hand". However, when data are pooled, evidence appears that could be construed as supporting the hot hand hypothesis. In both articles, the authors make an important point about the appropriate presentation of statistics and about how the framing of a research question may strongly affect the apparent answer.

BERNARD C. BEINS

See also Correlation, Inferential statistics, Likert scale, Reliability, Scales of measurement, Significance, Validity

Detente

Beyme, Klaus von, "Detente and East-West Economic Relations", *Journal of Politics*, 43/4 (1981): 1192–206
Froman, Michael B., *The Development of the Idea of Detente: Coming to Terms*, Basingstoke: Macmillan, 1991; New York: St Martin's Press, 1992
Garthoff, Raymond L., *Detente and Confrontation: American–Soviet Relations from Nixon to Reagan*, 2nd edition, Washington, DC: Brookings Institution, 1994
Goldmann, Kjeil, "Change and Stability in Foreign Policy: Detente as a Problem of Stabilization", *World Politics*, 34/2 (1982): 230–66
Goldmann, Kjeil, *Change and Stability in Foreign Policy: The Problems and Possibilities of Détente*, Princeton, New Jersey: Princeton University Press, and Brighton: Wheatsheaf, 1988
Gray, Colin, "Detente, Arms Control, and Strategy: Perspectives on SALT", *American Political Science Review*, 70/4 (1976): 1242–56
Korbonski, Andrzej, "Detente, East–West Trade, and the Future of Economic Integration in Eastern Europe", *World Politics*, 28/4 (1976): 568–89
Van Oudenaren, John, *Detente in Europe: The Soviet Union and the West since 1953*, Durham, North Carolina: Duke University Press, 1991
Weber, Steve, "Realism, Detente, and Nuclear Weapons", *International Organization*, 44/1 (1990): 55–92

This entry addresses a possible relationship between peace, as attainable with political detente, and international trade. The entry presents several perspectives on peace and trade, by tracing the practice of East–West trade, and by assessing the extent to which peace actually is contingent on mutually beneficial trade linkages.

BEYME addresses the plausibility of a causal relationship between international trade as a precondition of peace in the modern world, as attainable hopefully with political detente. The author analyses this question by presenting several perspectives, including a socialist one, on peace and trade, by tracing the practice of East–West trade and by assessing the extent to which peace is actually contingent on mutually beneficial trade linkages. This paper is interesting in light of the renewed scholarly attention to the possible linkages between trade and conflict, and how these two affect each other.

FROMAN describes how the leading Cold War policy makers in the US thought about relations with the Soviet Union, and how they attempted to persuade the Congress, the American people, and the world that their policies were sound. Froman presents a chronological review of detente in the Eisenhower, Kennedy, and Johnson years, its high point under Nixon and Ford, its decline during the Carter presidency, and its renaissance in the second half of the Reagan administration. Froman provides a solid, detailed overview of the different concepts of detente that informed US foreign policy from Eisenhower to Reagan. The book's key contribution is to demonstrate how conflicting aims of transforming and coexisting with the Soviet Union prevented detente from gaining a solid base of support and made it vulnerable to external shocks. Froman does not explore the possibility that the need to gain domestic support from different groups may have caused the tensions to begin with. Finally, the brief conclusions the author draws for policy recommendations at the end of the book are no longer valid since they are rooted in the assumption that US–Soviet competition will remain the central concern in US foreign policy in the future.

GARTHOFF's highly acclaimed book was first published in 1985. This new edition incorporates newly declassified Russian, as well as American, official documents. The author re-examines the historical development of American–Soviet relations from 1969 to 1980. The book takes into account both the broader context of world politics and internal political considerations and developments. Garthoff examines these developments as experienced by both sides, analysing Soviet as well as American policy, with the benefit of a new perspective on this period from the post-Soviet, post-Cold War vantage point. Despite a long history as rivals and adversaries, the US and the Soviet Union reached a detente in relations in 1972. From 1975 to 1079 however, this detente gradually eroded until it collapsed in the wake of the Soviet occupation of Afghanistan. Garthoff recounts how differences in ideology, perceptions, aims, and interests were key determinants of both American and Soviet policies. This is an essential book for any student or scholar interested in the one of the most interesting periods during the Cold War. The book will be helpful for political scientists as well as historians.

GOLDMANN (1982) deals with a very interesting question that has not been fully addressed in the international relations literature: what determines the occurrence, the scope, and the timing of major changes in foreign policy? In approaching this question, the author focuses on the "stabilizers" of foreign policy – that is, on the factors blocking, reducing the scope of, or delaying adaptation to new conditions, learning from negative feedback, or change in response to other disturbances. Goldmann offers a framework for the analysis of stability in foreign policy. He then discusses several hypothetical stabilizers of foreign policies, which are grouped into administrative, political, cognitive, and international categories. Finally, the framework is applied to the problem of East–West detente. The article offers an original approach to the analysis of change in foreign policy, and the application to the East–West detente as a case study is an interesting choice.

Assume that a nation is pursuing a given foreign policy and that we are concerned with the way in which it will act in the future. We may want to make a forecast – but then to what extent is the present policy of a nation a valid guide to its future behaviour? Or we may want to influence the nation to change its course – can we succeed? In other words, will the policy change or persist in the face of new conditions or negative feedback? GOLDMANN (1988) identifies the factors that may have an impact on whether a specific foreign policy is likely to endure or to change and develops them into a theory of foreign policy stability. He then uses this theory to explore the reasons why West German–Soviet detente during the 1970s proved to be more enduring than the improvement in relations between the US and the Soviet Union. Finally, he outlines a hypothetical scenario for a fully successful process of detente stabilization, and examines the extent to which this scenario is realistic. The book ends with some thoughts about how to conduct a policy aimed at stable detente with an adversary.

GRAY reviews six books that deal with the SALT agreements. The review summarizes the books, and presents a clear overview of the agreements as well as an interpretation of the implications of those for detente and US–Soviet relations. It serves as an invaluable source for the period, and as an excellent survey and analysis of the SALT agreements.

KORBONSKI attempts to examine the impact of East–West trade on the process of economic integration in Eastern Europe carried out under the auspices of the Council for Mutual Economic Assistance (CMEA). The discussion was focused on the proposition that, other things being equal, the continued growth of East–West trade would be incompatible with an increase in the level of economic integration in Eastern Europe.

The problem is analysed in the context of several factors: the process of regional economic integration; the attitude of the Soviet Union and of the East European political and economic elites toward both integration and East–West trade before and after detente; the influence of economic reforms in Eastern Europe; and the impact of the energy crisis and of the developing global shortage of raw materials. The conclusion emerges that, on balance, the chances of economic cooperation if not integration in the region were better then than before, but only at the expense of closer economic relations between Eastern Europe and the West.

VAN OUDENAREN examines relations between the Soviet Union and Western Europe since the death of Stalin. The author focuses on various arenas in which Soviet–Western diplomatic interaction occurred – through the Four Power process, summits and other high level meetings, parliamentary visits, arms control forums, economic institutions, cultural contacts, and pan-European institutions such as the Conference on Security and Cooperation in Europe. Although purporting to cover the entire period to the end of the Cold War in Europe, in fact only fourteen pages of the concluding chapter (and a few scattered elsewhere) deal with the Mikhail Gorbachev years from 1985 on. The book is structured in functional subject, rather than chronological, chapters. This helps draw attention to changes and continuities of, for example, economic relations, use of cultural and parliamentary exchanges, and arms control. But this advantage is purchased at the cost of doubling back in ways that cannot help but overlap. Despite the broader subtitle, the author has chosen to deal with Soviet–West European relations. In all, this is a useful, well-grounded review of many facets of Soviet relations with Western Europe. An appendix of summits and a thorough index enhance its utility.

WEBER claims that recent developments in US–Soviet relations have prompted reassessments of the effects that nuclear weapons may have had on world politics. Moreover, if there has been a "nuclear revolution", both the meaning of that term and its precise implications for the behaviour of states remain unclear. This article agrees with the realist argument that the discovery of nuclear weapons did not by itself fundamentally change the structure of the international system. However, it argues that the subsequent condition of nuclear deterrence, resulting from the widespread deployment of nuclear weapons and sophisticated delivery systems during the 1960s, does constitute a source of structural change. Under nuclear deterrence, the superpowers have acquired a new function – Weber calls it "joint custodianship" of the system – which differentiates their role from that of other states. This suggests that the international system has a new organizing principle that varies from the standard realist conception of anarchy. The argument offered by the author is as follows: structural change led to the rise of detente in the 1970s; but because the processes by which leaders in Washington and Moscow adjusted to structural change were not always parallel, this detente was limited in scope and could not be sustained. Weber's modified structural approach predicts that, as processes of adjustment begin to converge, superpower cooperation in a new detente of the 1990s will go beyond what was achieved in the 1970s, and also beyond what would be consistent with standard realist arguments.

CARMELA LUTMAR

Deterrence

Brams, Steven J. and D. Marc Kilgour, "Threat Escalation and Crisis Stability: A Game Theoretic Analysis", *American Political Science Review*, 81/3 (1987): 833–50

Downs, George W., "The Rational Deterrence Debate", *World Politics*, 41/2 (1989): 225–37

George, Alexander and Richard Smoke, *Deterrence in American Foreign Policy: Theory and Practice*, New York: Columbia University Press, 1974

Harvey, Frank P. and Patrick James, "Nuclear Deterrence Theory: The Record of Aggregate Testing and an Alternative Research Agenda", *Conflict Management and Peace Science*, 12 (1992): 17–45

Harvey, Frank P., "Rigor Mortis or Rigor, More Tests: Necessity, Sufficiency, and Deterrence Logic", *International Studies Quarterly*, 42/4 (1998): 675–707

Jervis, Robert, "Deterrence Theory Revisited", *World Politics*, 31 (1979): 289–324

Lebow, Richard Ned and Janice Gross Stein, "Rational Deterrence Theory: I Think, Therefore, I Deter", *World Politics*, 41/2 (1989): 208–24

Oneal, John R., *Foreign Policy Making in Times of Crisis*, Columbus: Ohio State University Press, 1982

Russett, Bruce M., "The Calculus of Deterrence", *Journal of Conflict Resolution*, 7 (1963): 97–109

RUSSETT's analysis of 17 crises between 1935 and 1961 appears to be the first systematic study of deterrence. Each crisis in his data set conforms to the necessary and sufficient conditions for "extended deterrence". "Extended deterrence" refers to cases where a major power attacker overtly threatened a pawn with military force, and where the defender had given (prior to the crisis) some indication that it would protect the pawn or where the defender made a commitment in time to prevent the threatened attack. "Successful deterrence" is defined as the prevention of an attack on the pawn without the defender's use of military force. The most interesting results of this study are that deterrence fails in 11 out of 17 cases and, where successful, economic ties between the defender and pawn – not the balance of military forces – appear to be most important. Russett's study is significant in setting the agenda for future work, which has focused on a wider range of variables than those connected with the standard framework of power politics.

GEORGE & SMOKE, developing a typology of deterrence failure, identified 11 major cases involving the US between 1948 and 1962. These cases begin with the Berlin blockade and end with the Cuban missile crisis. George & Smoke found at least one of three types of deterrence failure – *fait accompli*, limited probe and controlled pressure – to be present in each instance, which suggests that deterrence is likely to succeed or fail through time and stages. The study is noteworthy for identifying two central determinants of successful deterrence: the extent of the defender's commitment and the attacker's subsequent perception of that commitment. George and Smoke also indirectly point toward the need for a comparison class in making causal inferences, because an exclusive focus on deterrence failure is not sufficient for that purpose.

JERVIS draws attention to the potential for psychological factors to stand in the way of deterrence. Deterrence may be planned and implemented, but what if actions are misperceived? The role of communication is crucial and cannot simply be assumed away. In other words, deterrence may fail because of subjective factors that are at least somewhat beyond the control of participants in a conflict. What seems like a clear threat with serious consequences may be perceived very differently by the intended recipient of the message, depending on how the latter is transmitted. The study by Jervis is important for moving the analysis of deterrence toward incorporation of psychological factors.

ONEAL focuses on how foreign policy is made in times of crisis, and he makes an important contribution in terms of identifying feasible conditions for deterrence to work. Research on decision making in a series of crises indicates that the role of stress in impairing decision making may have been overrated in some previous studies. This suggests that deterrence has the potential to work in a wide range of circumstances without being impaired by stress-induced misperceptions.

BRAMS & KILGOUR extended the research programme on deterrence to include a formal, game-theory model of crisis escalation. Their model is innovative for several reasons; to cite just two examples, it includes continuous outcomes rather than just victory or defeat and it assigns precise magnitudes to the threats made by players against each other. The model shows that the properties of deterrence as a game of strategic interaction can be rigorously modelled and that optimal responses will vary with the level of the threat that is encountered.

LEBOW & STEIN focus on issues ranging from case selection to coding in order to stem the growing consensus in favour of rational deterrence theory. Their study is useful in bringing out the value of in-depth case studies, the need for context-dependent measurement in aggregate research on deterrence, and the potential relevance of psychological factors such as biased information processing in some kinds of cases.

DOWNS reasserts the value of rational deterrence theory, emphasizing the role of deductive theory building. He points out that a stronger model of deterrence would need to be more complex than those available at present, including costs and benefits, the shape of utility functions for the actors involved, the size of the stochastic component associated with assessments of the cost of war and the probability of winning, and the extent of problems of misperception and control, among other things. The study by Downs is also important for its observation that the rational and psychological schools on deterrence need to learn more from each other.

HARVEY & JAMES review the literature on deterrence with special attention to the role of nuclear weapons. They summarize models, data, and testing procedures. The basic conclusion reached by Harvey and James is that the debate over rational deterrence – especially at the nuclear level – cannot move forward without an authoritative body of evidence. This will require more attention to issues of validity and reliability in assembling data sets that are well matched with the propositions generated by deterrence theory.

HARVEY generates a breakthrough in the existing programme of research by focusing in great depth on the logic of necessary and sufficient conditions for deterrence. He describes precisely the hypothesis of necessary conditions that is cited, tested, and rejected most frequently by critics of deterrence theory. He also identifies a range of auxiliary hypotheses that have been tested and found wanting. When carefully restated propositions are evaluated, with the cases that are most relevant in terms of the presence or absence of presumably key conditions, rational deterrence theory is seen in a much more positive light. The study concludes by urging a more nuanced approach to measuring the key ingredients of deterrence and combining them into more comprehensive models.

PATRICK JAMES

Developing economies

Arnold, Guy, *The End of the Third World*, Basingstoke: Macmillan, and New York: St Martin's Press, 1993

Escobar, Arturo, *Encountering Development: The Making and Unmaking of the Third World*, Princeton, New Jersey: Princeton University Press, 1995

Frank, Andre Gunder, *Capitalism and Underdevelopment in Latin America: Historical Studies of Chile and Brazil*, New York: Monthly Review Press, 1966

Harris, Nigel, *The End of the Third World: Newly Industrializing Countries and the Decline of an Ideology*, Harmondsworth: Penguin, and New York: Viking Penguin, 1986

ILO (International Labour Office), *World Employment 1995: An ILO Report*, Geneva: International Labour Office, 1995

Independent Commission on International Development Issues, *North–South, A Programme for Survival: Report of the Independent Commission on International Development Issues*, Cambridge, Massachusetts: MIT Press, and London: Pan, 1980 (known as the Brandt report)

Kay, Cristóbal, *Latin American Theories of Development and Underdevelopment*, London and New York: Routledge, 1989

Mittelman, James H., "The Globalisation Challenge: Surviving at the Margins", *Third World Quarterly*, 15 (1994): 427–43

Munslow, Barry, "Africa: Problems of a Rebirth", *Third World Quarterly*, 15 (1994): 337–50

Myrdal, Gunnar, *Economic Theory and Under-Developed Regions*, London: Duckworth, 1957; as *Rich Lands and Poor: The Road to World Prosperity*, New York: Harper, 1958

Roxborough, Ian, *Theories of Underdevelopment*, London: Macmillan, and Atlantic Highlands, New Jersey: Humanities Press, 1979

Sachs, Wolfgang, *Nature, Justice and the End of Development*, London: Zed, 1999

Simon, David, *Cities, Capital and Development: African Cities in the World Economy*, London: Belhaven, and New York: Halstead, 1992

UNRISD (United Nations Research Institute on Social Development), *States of Disarray: The Social Effects of Globalization*, Geneva: United Nations Research Institute for Social Development, 1995

World Bank, *World Development Report*, New York: World Bank, annual

The developing economies is a term of the 1950s and 1960s, one reserved for the majority of nations from Africa, Asia, and Latin America that had emerged from colonial status and were on their way to industrialization and to higher levels of economic and social development. It was a term that replaced the phrase "undeveloped" or "underdeveloped" (MYRDAL) countries, the adjective being thought to be far too uncomplimentary of countries such as China, Egypt, India, Iran, and Turkey, which had very ancient civilisations. The term "developing" fitted the times, it was a period of optimism and most economists believed that the future would see all of these countries rapidly improving their living standards. By the 1960s, the term was becoming increasingly unfashionable because it was viewed as being too optimistic in a world where some at least of these countries showed all too little sign of developing. For this reason many started to call this group of countries the less-developed world. Others, particularly those on the political left like FRANK, KAY, and ROXBOROUGH began to call these countries "underdeveloped" because they wished to stress the fact that these economies had been underdeveloped by their relationship with the world economy (see entries on imperialism, Latin American economy). Soon another term was being used: the Third World. This term originally referred to non-aligned countries that wanted to be seen as following an independent path from the two superpowers, the US and the USSR. When the Brandt report (INDEPENDENT COMMISSION ON INTERNATIONAL DEVELOPMENT ISSUES) was published in 1980, all of these terms had acquired some kind of unfortunate political nuance and a new phrase was required. So, the term "South" was invented even though much of the area covered was not in the Southern Hemisphere and most was a long way north of certain countries of the "North" such as Australia and New Zealand. Clearly, all such grand terms are inappropriate in some way or another.

Another problem with all terms such as "developing countries" is that most observers now admit that these countries have little in common. The more developed countries of Asia and Latin America have far more in common with those of southern Europe than with the majority of African countries or those of the Indian subcontinent. For this reason, the titles of books by authors such as ARNOLD and HARRIS registered the end of the Third World. Others reacted to the increasing differentiation within poorer countries by dividing them into different categories. The WORLD BANK now classified poorer countries into low-income and middle-income. For a time the term "Fourth World" came into fashion to describe those countries in Africa and the Indian subcontinent, which are now frequently termed the least-developed nations.

From the problems of definition it is clear that it is difficult to generalize what is actually happening to the countries of Africa, Asia, and Latin America in terms of development. It is broadly true that most have seen an improvement in basic living conditions as measured by infant mortality rates, life expectancy, and nutrition levels. At the same time, many countries now have larger numbers of poor people and many countries have a higher relative incidence of poverty.

Conditions in Latin America as a whole worsened during the "lost decade" of the 1980s and few countries in sub-Saharan Africa have seen any real improvement in living conditions since the 1970s.

Even if economic growth prospects improve authorities on globalization like ILO, MITTELMAN, and UNRISD, worry that new technologies bring about a worsening distribution of income by rewarding those with skills and reducing the demand for those with few or limited skills. Even if poverty does not necessarily increase, inequality will.

But there are many who fear that there is little prospect for improvement in the new global economy. For authors such as SIMON and Mittelman Africa stands little chance of being integrated successfully into the world economy. As Mittelman puts it: (1994: p. 441):

Truncated globalisation debars the bulk of Africa from gaining access to world society's productive processes . . . The foremost contradiction of our time is the conflict between the zones of humanity integrated in the global division of labour and the ones which are excluded from it.

For such authors the only real alternative is to cut off from development and to rely on traditional or newly created means of survival. As MUNSLOW (p.337) puts it: "the most remarkable fact of life in Africa is that in spite of the awful macroeconomic and social statistics, most people not only survive but some even seem to thrive. People's survival strategies are endlessly innovative and ingenious."

African realities and the way that large areas are excluded from the benefits of development lead authors such as ESCOBAR and SACHS to question the whole rhetoric and practice of development. For most people development is a myth and, increasingly, poverty and inequality are worldwide. Today, there are poor people living in the richest cities of developed countries and the poorest parts of the developing world. The notion underlying the term developing economies is a misnomer because the inevitability of development for most people is untenable under current orthodoxies.

ALAN GILBERT

See also Imperialism, Latin America, economy and economic record, Third World, economic

Development economics

Adelman, I. and C. Morris, "Editorial: Development History and Its Implications for Development Theory", *World Development*, 25/6 (1997): 831–40

Bardhan, Pranab, "Corruption and Development: A Review of Issues", *Journal of Economic Literature*, 35 (September 1997): 1320–46

Bauer, P.T., *Dissent on Development*, London: Weidenfeld and Nicolson, 1971; revised edition, Cambridge, Massachusetts: Harvard University Press, 1976

Binswanger, H.P. and K. Deininger, "Exploring Agrarian Policies in LDCs", *Journal of Economic Literature*, 35 (December 1997): 1958–2005

Fischer, Stanley, "IMF Perspectives on Origins and Implications of the Asian Crisis", *IMF Survey*, 27/2 (January 1998): 21–22

Krugman, Paul, "Towards a Counter-counter Revolution in Development Theory" in *Proceedings of the World Bank Annual Conference on Development Economics*, Washington, DC: World Bank, 1992

Lal, Deepak, *The Poverty of "Development Economics"*, 2nd edition, London: Institute of Economic Affairs, 1997

Mosley, P., T. Subasat and J. Weeks, "Assessing Adjustment in Africa", *World Development*, 23/9 (1995): 1459–73

Stiglitz, Joseph E., "Some Lessons from the East Asian Miracle", *World Bank Research Observer*, 11/2 (August 1996): 151–75

Taylor, Lance, "The Revival of the Liberal Creed: The IMF and the World Bank in a Globalised Economy", *World Development*, 25/2 (1997): 145–52

UNDP, *Human Development Report 1998*, New York and Oxford: Oxford University Press, 1998

World Bank, *World Development Report*, New York and Oxford: Oxford University Press, 1999

The United Nations Development Programme (UNDP) *Human Development Report 1998* notes that of 4.4 billion people in developing countries nearly 60 per cent lack basic sanitation; almost one third have no access to clean water; 20 per cent have no access to modern health services and 20 per cent of children do not reach the fifth school grade. The wealthiest 20 per cent of the world's population account for 86 per cent of total private consumption expenditure, while the poorest 20 per cent account for only 1.3 per cent. While consumption per capita has increased in the last 25 years at 2.3 per cent per annum in industrial countries, at 6.1 per cent per annum in East Asia, and at 2 per cent in South Asia, the average African household has gone backwards and today consumes 20 per cent less than it did 25 years ago. "Under five" mortality rates still exceed 200 per 1000 live births in at least 10 developing countries – mostly African – and life expectancy at birth in 1995 ranged from 28 in Rwanda and 35 in Sierra Leone to 79 in Hong Kong. Life expectancy grew 34 per cent in Indonesia from 1970 to 1995, but it dropped 12 per cent in Uganda in the same period. Adult literacy in 1995 likewise ranged from 14 per cent in Niger to 98 per cent in Bahamas and in Korea.

The WORLD BANK observes in its 1998/99 *World Development Report* that wide divergences in growth rates – for example, between Ghana and Korea 1958–90 – are not explained by differences in capital accumulation alone. Education, openness to trade, and the availability of communications infrastructure all have a significant impact on economic growth. Foreign direct investment in developing economies has increased several times in the 1990s, but remains concentrated in a few markets, notably including East Asia. Large gaps in literacy, including male/female gaps, persist both within and between countries. Child mortality falls as the educational attainment level of the mother rises but the benefits of public education spending are often skewed towards the rich.

ADELMAN & MORRIS review postwar development history and conclude that the process of economic development contradicts the notion that all countries have undergone similar patterns and sequences. They conclude that institutions matter, and that for countries with similar institutional development, the critical economic policies have been those related to trade, agriculture, international factor movements and investment. They object that development theories have suffered from misplaced universality, and that situational relativism must become more commonly accepted. For the least developed 40 per cent of countries, they argue that the Lewis model is the most appropriate; at the semi-industrial stage what is required is emphasis on human capital, modernization of agriculture, and a shift in trade policy from import substitution to export promotion; while the purely neoclassical Washington Consensus theory comes into its own only for the handful of developing countries approaching OECD status.

BAUER helped spark a Chicago school counterrevolution in development economics, rejecting the Keynesian-style interventionist policies that had become orthodox in the early postwar years. Bauer forcibly rejected the need for development planning, marketing boards, and paternalistic policies, and insisted that peasant farmers would respond to personal incentives and the market mechanism. LAL extended this argument and concluded that "development economics", which had grown out of the conviction that orthodox neoclassical theory had little validity in the Third World, was actually harmful and "the demise of development economics" would be a good thing. For Bauer and Lal, government-induced distortions in developing economies have been more costly than the supposed market imperfections they were meant to cure.

KRUGMAN argued in response, however, that the Chicago counterrevolution went too far and that a counter-counterrevolution is called for in which renewed attention is given to the prospects of market failure and of remedial, selective intervention, by government.

BINSWANGER & DEININGER review agricultural policies and ask why so many developing countries adopted growth-reducing agricultural policies. They note that agriculture inclines itself to problems of information asymmetry – in credit, insurance, and labour markets – and that farmers are often forced to resort to second best strategies because of government policies. The combination of policy distortions, imperfect or missing markets, and unequal wealth distribution can cause decreased efficiency. For rural economies characterized by highly incomplete markets, fully privatized land rights may not be the most efficient arrangement.

BARDHAN considers the link between corruption and development. Where there is slow economic growth the returns to rent seeking rise relative to the returns to entrepreneurship. A significant negative correlation has been found between a country's corruption index and its rates of investment or growth.

STIGLITZ looks for the lessons to be gained from the extraordinarily successful development in pre-1997 South East Asia. That "Asian miracle" reflected no single policy but the interaction of several factors, including the interaction of a high savings rate and a high rate of human capital accumulation in a stable, market-oriented economy – but one with active government intervention.

TAYLOR argues that many Washington Consensus policies – which emphasize orthodox neoclassical requirements of reducing government intervention and facilitating freer trade –

are intellectually ill-founded and counterproductive. World Bank structural adjustment programs and International Monetary Fund (IMF) conditionality have been significant and controversial issues in recent years. Taylor's argument is that exchange rate adjustments often lead to inflationary or contractionary side effects rarely mentioned in IMF studies, just as wage cuts supposedly lead to output increases but often do not, and just as full deregulation may lead to such instability that controls have to be reimposed.

MOSLEY, SUBASAT & WEEKS similarly conclude that World Bank structural adjustment programs have not facilitated recovery in Africa. They reject the Washington Consensus view that it is always appropriate to reduce fiscal deficits, public investment, tariff protection, and agricultural subsidies. Echoing Adelman & Morris's concern about misplaced universalism, they object that "in World Bank adjustment programs subsidies both to inputs and credit are uneconomic distortions to be eliminated unconditionally", whereas in the real world of imperfect credit markets input subsidies might in fact facilitate acceptance of new technology and be efficiency creating.

FISCHER presents the IMF view that despite some problems, countries experiencing trouble are better off if they take the IMF medicine. The problems that caused the 1997 Asian crisis were "mostly homegrown", including pegged exchange rates, large external deficits, stock and property market bubbles, and lax prudential supervision. International Monetary Fund calls for interest rate hikes were necessary to halt the exchange rate collapse.

L.A. DUHS

Devolution, UK and Europe

Bogdanor, Vernon, *Devolution in the United Kingdom*, 2nd edition, Oxford and New York: Oxford University Press, 1999

Bradbury, Jonathan and John Mawson (editors), *British Regionalism and Devolution: The Challenges of State Reform and European Integration*, London: Kingsley, 1997

Bulpitt, Jim, *Territory and Power in the United Kingdom: An Interpretation*, Manchester: Manchester University Press, 1983

Hechter, Michael, *Internal Colonialism: The Celtic Fringe in British National Development, 1536–1966*, London: Routledge and Kegan Paul, and Berkeley: University of California Press, 1975

Keating, Michael and Barry Jones (editors), *The European Union and the Regions*, Oxford: Clarendon Press, and New York: Oxford University Press, 1995

Keating, Michael and Howard Elcock (editors), *Remaking the Union: Devolution and British Politics in the 1990s*, London: Frank Cass, 1998

Keating, Michael, *The New Regionalism in Western Europe: Territorial Restructuring and Political Change*, Cheltenham, Gloucestershire: Elgar, 1998

Nairn, Tom, *The Break-up of Britain: Crisis and Neo-nationalism*, London: New Left Books, 1977; 2nd edition 1981

Rokkan, Stein, and Derek W. Urwin (editors), *The Politics of Territorial Identity: Studies in European Regionalism*, London and Beverly Hills, California: Sage, 1982
Rose, Richard, *Understanding the United Kingdom: The Territorial Dimension in Government*, London: Longman, 1982

BOGDANOR provides a comprehensive account of devolution in the UK and its constituent nations. His analysis is historical and legal-institutional. History begins with Gladstone's attempts to grant Irish home rule in 1886 and the home rule movements, devolution debates, proposals and measures for Northern Ireland, Wales and Scotland are discussed in separate chapters. Bogdanor rightly realizes that devolution's effects are not restricted to Scotland, Wales, or Northern Ireland and the English dimension and Europe's role are discussed. He provides a detailed and perceptive analysis of the devolution Acts passed in 1998 and offers several insightful personal interpretations of the consequences of devolution for the British constitution.

BRADBURY & MAWSON locate the renewed vigour of the devolution debate in Britain in the 1990s in the response of peripheral elites to the economic reforms of successive Conservative governments after 1979 and the functional necessity to develop coherent structures at the regional level to compete in the single European market and benefit from the European Structural Funds. Devolution is thus regarded as a functional necessity and not solely an expression of cultural or social particularism in Scotland, Wales, or some of the English regions. Conservative governments addressed these needs and engaged in executive regionalization, most notably with the creation of the Government Offices of the Regions in England in 1994, but did not create democratically accountable bodies. The chief proponents of (democratic, accountable) devolution are within the Labour Party in Scotland, Wales and the English regions, and more cautiously, the Labour Party nationally. The editors express some scepticism as to whether mainly functional justifications for devolution will be sufficient to carry a devolution project to conclusion.

For KEATING & ELCOCK the renewed impulse for devolution in the 1990s is again described as a response to external forces, in this case Europe, globalization and a wider demand to democratize the institutions of the state. Several authors discuss devolution in terms of its implications for the British state. Other contributors discuss the attitudes and involvement of groups in civil society such as Scottish business, the Welsh home rule movement, and English local government in the devolution debate.

ROSE offers a scholarly reflection on the UK and what the devolution debates of the 1970s revealed about it. For him, the UK was a union without uniformity, a multinational state with strong religious, linguistic, and cultural differences between the component nations. These differences were accommodated to some extent within the institutions of UK government and the Crown itself was multinational. These territorial differences could support separatist political demands but there were also forces for integration within the UK including party competition, UK-wide institutions such as Parliament and the Crown, public policy and expenditure, which accommodated territorial differences and continuing support for the union

within the majority of the Crown's subjects throughout the UK. Continuing consent, Rose warned however, was contingent and the integrity of the UK could not be assumed.

BULPITT offers an original perspective on devolution and the nature of the British constitution. Whereas most authors concentrate on nationalist movements in the periphery, he views territorial management from the centre's perspective. In this view, the centre wishes to concern itself with "high politics" (such as diplomacy and defence) and leave low politics to compliant local elites. Such a separation of functions existed from about 1920 to the 1960s in his view and the UK was then characterized as a dual polity. However, from the 1960s onwards, economic problems and the decline of the imperial "external support mechanism" led to the breakdown of the dual polity and the resurgence of peripheral territorial demands.

NAIRN and HECHTER both locate the origin of Scottish, Welsh and Irish nationalism in the economic sphere. Nairn argues that the "uneven development" of capitalism across the British Isles accounts for separatist demands in the constituent nations of the UK. Hechter claims that a "cultural division of labour" emerged within the British Isles, discriminating against the Welsh, Scots, and Irish. For him, Scottish, Welsh or Irish nationalisms are a reaction against such discrimination. Like Bulpitt they, too, identify Britain's economic difficulties from the 1960s onwards as the proximate cause of the resurgence in nationalist demands in the UK.

ROKKAN & URWIN discuss the evolution of centres and peripheries across Europe over a long historical perspective. For them, the key features of peripherality are physical distance, cultural difference, and economic and political dependence. Although these have been perennial (if evolving) features of European states for several centuries, they argue that they have been politicized since the 1960s due to rising demands from the peripheries in terms of welfare and regional policy and the declining capacities of state centres to meet those demands. A series of chapters on several European states by experts on those states develop these themes and provide a rich source of comparative detail.

KEATING & JONES focus on how the institutions and the policies of the European Union provide new opportunities and new arenas for regional governments and actors to operate within and encourage the development of strategies and institutions focused on the European level. The EU challenges the historically dominant role of states over their regions. However, the editors doubt that a "Europe of the Regions" is the inevitable conclusion of the process of European integration. The chapters on regions within the different EU member states reinforce this view, showing the continuing importance of member states in mediating the regions' relationships with the EU.

KEATING argues that the "new regionalism" that emerged in Europe from the late 1980s onwards emphasizes the role of regions as autonomous actors in the competitive global economy. New regionalism is not contained within the structures of the state and unlike old regionalism, does not focus on cultural or social particularities, and is a modernizing force instead of a defence of traditional ways of life. Old regionalism continues to exist (often alongside new regionalism) and may provide resources for modernizing regional elites to mobilize regional electorates. Regions, in this perspective emerge from the shadow of states as key locations for policy innovation and experimentation.

DYLAN GRIFFITHS

See also Nationalism

Devolution, US

DiIulio, John J. and Donald F. Kettl, *Fine Print: The Contract with America, Devolution, and the Administrative Realities of American Federalism*, Washington, DC: Brookings Institution, 1995

Donahue, John D., *Disunited States*, New York: Basic Books, 1997

Goldberg, Lenny, "Come the Devolution," *American Prospect*, 24 (Winter 1995): 66–71

Kincaid, John, "The Devolution Tortoise and the Centralization Hare", special issue on "Devolution: The New Federalism", *New England Economic Review*, (May/June 1998)

Liner, E. Blaine, "Sorting Out State–Local Relations" in *A Decade of Devolution: Perspectives on State–Local Relations*, edited by E. Blaine Liner, Washington, DC: Urban Institute Press, 1989

Peterson, Paul E., *The Price of Federalism*, Washington, DC: Brookings Institution, 1995

Rivlin, Alice M., *Reviving the American Dream: The Economy, the States, and the Federal Government*, Washington, DC: Brookings Institution, 1992

Seay, Douglas and Robert E. Moffit, "Transferring Functions to the States" in *Mandate for Leadership 4: Turning Ideas into Actions*, edited by Stuart M. Butler and Kim R. Holmes, Washington, DC: The Heritage Foundation, 1997

Watson, Keith and Steven D. Gold, *The Other Side of Devolution: Shifting Relationships between State and Local Governments*, Washington, DC: Urban Institute Press, 1997 (Occasional Paper 2)

KINCAID provides a thorough contextual discussion of the devolution movement's fundamental beliefs, its philosophical, political, social and economic origins, and its progress to date in achieving its goals. He defines devolution as a transfer of specific powers or functions from a superior government to a subordinate government that should be complete, permanent, and of constitutional magnitude. He also offers a series of objectives relating to devolution, such as efficiency, competitiveness, responsiveness, and accountability. In addition to discussing the implications of the Republican Congressional majority, his paper traces devolution to the earlier suburbanization movement; migration to the Sunbelt; spreading disillusionment with the federal government; increasing credibility for states and localities; and the global trend towards decentralization, deregulation, and free enterprise as major factors that inspired the devolution movement. Finally, he concludes that the movement's progress has been limited. He finds that actions taken by the federal government have reflected both a desire to devolve federal responsibility in certain policy areas and an inclination to preempt the states in other areas.

LINER summarizes the major influences that buttress the devolutionary philosophy and outlines the setting within which the devolutionary actions of the 1980s took place. Due to the withdrawal of federal financial assistance and the growing federal mandates, states and localities have to make tough choices in their service delivery. The essay provides a thorough overview of the important milestones of devolution since the 1960s, tracing the evolution of block grants and various New Federalism initiatives to the late 1980s. It also suggests that one must sort out service provision, control, and financing, and that one must consider each separately when analysing responsibilities between states and localities. He stresses the concepts of efficiency and equity as they affect decision making in the realignment of state–local systems.

WATSON & GOLD characterize devolution as the passing of policy responsibilities from the federal government to state and local governments. Specifically, they explain that the process of devolution may include any combination of block grants to states, reduced grants-in-aid from the federal government, and increased flexibility for states in complying with federal requirements. Their paper, which focuses on the state–local relationship, describes some of the state legislation proposed or enacted in 1995 and 1996 that had the explicit intent of sharing programme funding or administrative responsibilities between state and local governments. Their essay reveals that 11 states are known to have either enacted or proposed a shift in funding or administrative responsibilities in the areas of social services, public assistance, or workforce development. They further suggest that the 1996 federal welfare reform legislation is likely to be a catalyst for further state–local devolution.

SEAY & MOFFIT frame the devolution discussion from the conservative perspective. They lament how the trend towards centralizing decision making in Washington over the past 60 years has resulted in a wide variety of problems and declining public confidence. They argue for a need to devolve federal power in restoring federalism as it is embodied in the Constitution. They maintain that only the states, which serve as the backbone of the federalism framework, have the institutional resources, the interests, and the political potential necessary to impose limits on the federal government. In turning the devolution philosophy into action, they offer a series of proposals advocating an increased role for the states, localities, and the private sector, and curtailing the size of federal bureaucracy. Their essay offers a blueprint of actions for conservative policymakers.

DONAHUE takes a critical look at devolution. It serves as a counterpoint to the emergence of devolution theory as the conventional wisdom in public policy making. Its criticism rests on a fear of the consequences of a heightened level of interstate competition. Using economic development as a prime example, the author suggests that it would lead to a race to the bottom, in which competing states might offer the most attractive tax incentive package in order to attract business investment. He also warns that the disadvantaged will be left behind under the current political climate. The book places the American debate over centralization in a contemporary global context. It effectively links state public policy deficiencies to potential dangers to the American middle class in an increasingly globalized market economy. The conclusion heavily favours an enhanced role for the federal government.

Unlike Donahue, PETERSON and RIVLIN explain the advantages in devolving federal power. Both also distinguish between developmental and redistributive public policies and favour handling redistributive functions at the national level while relegating responsibility for developmental policies to state and local governments.

GOLDBERG refutes the conventional wisdom that portrays conservatives as devolution advocates and liberals as centralists. He asserts that the current devolution debate has been misplaced, as there is no consistent concept of devolution either from the theorists or in the actions of the Republican Congress. In turn, his essay traces the devolution movement back to the 1960s, when community activists sought to empower local groups and individuals in opposition to a centralized warfare-welfare state. He reminds readers that much of the thrust of recent progressive movements was anti-bureaucratic, anti-centralist, and focused on empowerment of community and individuals. Finally, he suggests that efforts to decentralize decision making and promote local participation should be an integral part of restoring public connection to the political process.

DIIULIO & KETTL remind readers of the administrative realities of devolving power from the federal government to states and localities. They maintain that the current devolution will not succeed, as it ignores the administrative details in contemporary American federalism. They point out the federal power has always been devolved as Washington bureaucrats share their functions with state and local government employees, and vast networks of private contractors and non-profit organizations. Their essay also features an analysis on the recent history of federal–state relations, especially the history of block grants and federal mandates in relation to the devolution movement. They also assess the likely course and consequences of devolution in three areas of domestic policy: welfare, healthcare, and crime. Finally, they suggest that before translating devolution rhetoric into actions, we need to investigate how thoroughly decentralized most such programmes already are, how diverse state governments are in terms of their fiscal and administrative capacities, and how much the programme's real problems lie in the complexity of managing it.

SHAO-CHEE SIM

Dictatorship and despotism

Arendt, Hannah, *The Origins of Totalitarianism*, New York: Harcourt Brace, 1951, new edition 1973; as *The Burden of Our Time*, London: Secker and Warburg, 1951

Djilas, Milovan, *The New Class: An Analysis of the Communist System*, New York: Praeger, and London: Thames and Hudson, 1957

Hobbes, Thomas, *Leviathan*, edited by Michael Oakeshott, Oxford: Blackwell, 1946; New York: Collier, 1962 (originally published 1651)

Hoffer, Eric, *The True Believer: Thoughts on the Nature of Mass Movements*, New York: Harper, 1951; London: Secker and Warburg, 1952

Locke, John, *Two Treatises of Government*, edited by Peter Laslett, 2nd edition, London: Cambridge University Press, 1967 (originally published 1690)

Mayer, Milton, *On Liberty: Man v. The State*, Santa Barbara: Center for the Study of Democratic Institutions, 1969

Plato, *The Republic*, translated and edited by F.M. Cornford, London and New York: Oxford University Press, 1945 (written c.360 bc)

PLATO, an early theorist in favour of a despotic form of government, wanted a government that runs the mental, spiritual, and physical life of the people. The ruling class was to be separate from other social classes, and myths were to be invented to keep the other classes content with their status. Education was to be the state's responsibility so that children from each class grow up to assume their proper places in society. This work is where we get the idea of philosopher kings.

HOBBES, a 17th-century English philosopher, makes the case for a despotic form of government. Moreover, Hobbes makes his case by relying on the social compact theory, which is more often invoked in favour of limited government and the right of revolution. Unlike those (like Locke, another 17th-century philosopher) who argue for the existence of an agreement between the rulers and the ruled. Hobbes says that the social compact exists among the ruled, but not between the ruler and the ruled. The government must be unitary and near absolute in its powers, and revolt against an oppressive government is not justified, according to Hobbes.

LOCKE's work is in two parts. The first part argues against the idea of the divine right of kings, which had been defended in a book by Robert Filmer. After finishing off Filmer, Locke proceeds in the second part of his work to give his own account of the origin and nature of government. Property is the foundation of rights, and the right to property does not come from government. Governments are set up to secure property, personal security, and other rights against infringements. The people agree with their rulers to give the latter sufficient power to carry out their jobs. If a ruler tyrannizes over the people, the ruler has broken his side of the agreement, making revolution justifiable. The anti-despotism nature of the work can been seen both in the first part (in its attack on the concept of divinely ordained monarchs) and in the second part (in its outline of a limited government).

MAYER looks at the despotic tendencies seen to be inherent in any exercise of governmental power.

ARENDT looks at the factors that contribute to the growth of totalitarianism, using as her main example the Weimar Republic, which preceded Hitler's coming to power.

DJILAS looks at the class of communist operatives who came to the fore in the Yugoslavian dictatorship. Djilas spent some time in prison, so his analysis must have hit close to home.

HOFFER looks at the totalitarian mindset – the kind of people who join totalitarian movements and their motivations for so doing. The true believer, finds Hoffer, is trying to find transcendent meaning in his own life by merging himself with a broader movement.

ERIC LONGLEY

See also Military dictatorship, Totalitarianism

Diminishing returns

Anderson, James, *An Enquiry into the Nature of the Corn-laws: With a View to the New Corn-bill Proposed for Scotland*, Edinburgh: printed by and for Mrs Mundell, 1777

Bharadwaj, Krishna, *Classical Political Economy and Rise to Dominance of Supply and Demand Theories*, Calcutta: Orient Longman, 1978; 2nd edition, London: Sangam, and Madras: Universities Press, 1986

Färe, Rolf, "Strong Limitationality of Essential Proper Subsets of Factors of Production", *Zeitschrift für Nationalökonomie*, 32/4 (1972): 417–24

Färe, Rolf, *Fundamentals of Production Theory*, Berlin and New York: Springer, 1988

Gossen, Hermann-Heinrich, *The Laws of Human Relations and the Rules of Human Action Derived Therefrom*, Cambridge, Massachusetts: MIT Press, 1983 (German edition 1854)

Malthus, Thomas, *An Inquiry into the Nature and Progress of Rent and the Principles by Which It Is Regulated*, London: John Murray, 1815

Marshall, Alfred, *Principles of Economics*, 9th edition, edited by C.W. Guillebaud, 2 vols, London and New York: Macmillan, 1961 (1st edition 1890)

Menger, Karl, "The Logic of the Laws of Return: A Study in Metaeconomics" in *Economic Activity Analysis*, edited by Oskar Morgenstern, New York: Wiley, and London: Chapman and Hall, 1954

Mill, John Stuart, *Principles of Political Economy with Some of Their Applications to Social Philosophy*, edited by J.M. Robson, Toronto: University of Toronto Press, and London: Routledge and Kegan Paul, 1965 (originally published 1848)

Quadrio Curzio, Alberto, "Rent, Income Distribution and Orders of Efficiency and Rentability" in *Essays on the Theory of Joint Production*, edited by Luigi L. Pasinetti, London and New York, Macmillan, 1980

Quadrio Curzio, Alberto, "Technological Scarcity: An Essay on Production and Structural Change" in *Foundations of Economics: Structures of Inquiry and Economic Theory*, edited by Mauro Baranzini and Roberto Scazzieri, Oxford and New York: Blackwell, 1986

Ricardo, David, "On the Principles of Political Economy and Taxation" in *The Works and Correspondence of David Ricardo*, edited by Piero Sraffa and M.H. Dobb, vol. 1, Cambridge: Cambridge University Press, 1951 (1st edition 1817; 3rd edition 1821)

Scazzieri, Roberto, "Scale and Efficiency in Models of Production" in *Advances in Economic Theory*, edited by Mauro Baranzini, Oxford: Blackwell, and New York: St Martin's Press, 1982

Scazzieri, Roberto, *A Theory of Production: Tasks, Processes and Technical Practices*, Oxford: Clarendon Press, and New York: Oxford University Press, 1993

Schneider, Erich, *Theorie der Produktion*, Vienna: Springer, 1934

Senior, Nassau William, *An Outline of the Science of Political Economy*, New York: Kelley, 1965 (1st edition 1836)

Serra, Antonio, *Breve trattato delle cause che possono far abbondare li regni d'oro e d'argento, dove non sono miniere*, Calabria: Mediocredito regionale della Calabria, 1985 (originally published 1613)

Shephard, Ronald W., "Proof of the Law of Diminishing Returns", *Zeitschrift für Nationalökonomie*, 30/1–2 (1970): 7–34

Sraffa, Piero, "On the Relations between Cost and Quantity Produced" in *Italian Economic Papers*, vol. 3, edited by Luigi L. Pasinetti, New York: Oxford University Press, 1998 (originally published in Italian 1925)

Turgot, Anne Robert Jacques, *Observations sur le mémoire de M. de Saint-Peravy en faveur de l'impôt indirect*, in *Oeuvres de Mr Turgot*, 9 vols, Paris: Delance, 1808–11: vol. 4 (manuscript 1768)

Wicksteed, Philip Henry, "The Scope and Method of Political Economy in the Light of the Marginal Theory of Value and Distribution", *Economic Journal*, 24/1 (1914): 1–23

The economic analysis of diminishing returns originates with the discovery by SERRA that agricultural and manufacturing processes are associated with a different proportionality relationship between the levels of factor/inputs and the level of output. According to Serra, agricultural output increases less than proportionately with respect to the levels of factor/inputs, whereas manufacturing output often increases more than proportionately.

ANDERSON and TURGOT examined, respectively, extensive and intensive diminishing returns. Anderson noted that diminishing returns obtain when any given process can only be scaled up by switching to inferior methods of production (such as land plots of decreasing fertility). Herbert Foxwell considered Anderson's essay as "the first English statement of the Ricardian theory of rent". Turgot discussed a case in which diminishing returns are generated by increasing the quantities of capital and labour applied to a fixed area of land.

The extensive formulation of diminishing returns was central to classical economic theory (as expounded by MALTHUS and RICARDO) and provided the analytical background to the classical theory of rent (see also the work of QUADRIO CURZIO, 1980). The intensive formulation was initially considered a special case of the extensive theory, but subsequently SENIOR and MILL initiated a process by which diminishing returns of the intensive type came to be considered the standard case. In this form, diminishing returns were taken to be a general property to be detected (in a given range of input variation) whenever inputs of a certain subset are proportionately varied and the remaining inputs are fixed (law of variable proportions).

As described by BHARADWAJ, the generalization of diminishing returns was a characteristic feature of the transition from classical to postclassical economic theory which took place through a series of connected analytical steps. First, it was argued that intensive diminishing returns are immune from the analytical difficulties of the extensive case, such as the possibility of a reversal in the fertility ranking of lands (Mill). Second, diminishing returns in production were associated with the general law of diminishing yield to increasing effort, of which the psychological law of diminishing marginal utility was another example, discussed by GOSSEN. Third, the distinction between limitationality and nonlimitationality of productive inputs came to be associated with the distinction between different time horizons: more input factors are constant over a short time period than over a long time period. According to MARSHALL, the law of diminishing returns may be formulated in general terms, and is characteristic of all the cases of "excessive application of resources or of energy in any given direction".

WICKSTEED maintained that the introduction of a general law of diminishing returns is associated with a methodological shift from a "descriptive" to a "functional" approach. In the former case, qualitatively different categories of a given input (such as land) are first distinguished and then ranked. In the latter case, homogeneous doses of a given input are associated with a different incremental contribution to total output if the total number of doses is changed.

SRAFFA and SCHNEIDER criticized the generalized law of diminishing returns. Sraffa maintained that the assumption of a fixed input is seldom realized, even in agricultural processes, if production of individual crops is considered. Schneider noted that diminishing returns can seldom be observed in industrial activities.

MENGER undertook a comprehensive logical reconstruction of the law of diminishing returns, and identified conditions ensuring the invariance of the efficiency ranking of methods of production as process scale is changed.

Recent theoretical work has re-examined both the classical and postclassical approaches to diminishing returns. QUADRIO CURZIO (1986) has proposed a new formulation of classical theory, in which alternative conceptions of efficiency ranking are distinguished, and diminishing returns are derived from the invariant ranking of methods of production in terms of their physical net output rates. FARE (1972, 1988) has developed the activity analysis approach to diminishing returns, initiated by Menger and SHEPHARD, and has discussed a number of cases associated with alternative assumptions concerning the characteristics of essential inputs.

SCAZZIERI has outlined a conceptual framework in which diminishing returns are associated with the existence of upper bounds upon the scale of certain production processes, independent of the characteristics of individual inputs. This contribution shows that the scale-efficiency relation generally associated with diminishing returns is a special case requiring: (a) the contraction in the set of techniques available for any given scale; (b) producer's ranking over techniques tat is strict, transitive, and scale-neutral (c) a sequence of scrutiny of individual techniques that matches the producer's ranking of techniques.

ROBERTO SCAZZIERI

Diplomacy

Anderson, M.S., *The Rise of Modern Diplomacy, 1450–1919*, London and New York: Longman, 1993

Barston, R.P., *Modern Diplomacy*, London and New York: Longman, 1988; 2nd edition 1997

Cohen, Raymond, *Negotiating across Cultures: Communication Obstacles in International Diplomacy*, Washington, DC: United States Institute of Peace Press, 1991; revised 1997

Holland, Harrison M., *Managing Diplomacy: The United States and Japan*, Stanford, California: Hoover Institution Press, 1984

Jackson, Geoffrey, *Concorde Diplomacy: The Ambassador's Role in the World Today*, London: Hamish Hamilton, 1981

Moore, Robert J., *Third-World Diplomats in Dialogue with the First World*, London: Macmillan, 1985

Nicholson, Harold, *Diplomacy*, 3rd edition, London and New York: Oxford University Press, 1963

Plischke, Elmer (editor), *Modern Diplomacy: The Art and the Artisans*, Washington, DC: American Enterprise Institute for Public Policy Research, 1979

Susskind, Lawrence E., *Environmental Diplomacy: Negotiating More Effective Global Agreements*, New York and Oxford: Oxford University Press, 1994

ANDERSON's monograph starts with an outline of the "new diplomacy". The 15th and 16th centuries gave rise to the nation state and the notion of sovereignty. As a consequence, the development of international law required representatives from the newly established countries to attend international meetings, where important affairs of government and state were discussed. These new diplomats not only came to be seen as representatives of the sovereign country, but as Anderson points out, also performed the role of modern international political institutions. A description of the decline of Cabinet diplomacy follows ending with a thorough treatment of the quest for international peace at the 1919 treaty negotiations at Versailles. As is the case with the majority of books on diplomacy, this book fails to take into account the expressions of diplomatic discourse in non-Western societies.

Less descriptive than Anderson, and largely concerned with organizational changes in diplomacy, BARSTON takes a good long look at the practice of diplomacy since the 1960s. His analysis identifies factors influencing foreign policy assessments, financial relations, international trade and security, and overall changes in diplomatic style. The section on negotiation is especially interesting; this is an area of diplomatic activity that is most often impersonated in the role of the ambassador. Barston's account might at first glance appear to be overly concerned with the more mundane aspects of diplomacy, however, his analysis of the political powers that diplomats exert during the implementation phase of foreign policy is sharp and insightful.

It took too many years for COHEN's book to appear, but it was worth the long wait. His monograph marries the art of diplomacy to the functions of culture to form a relationship of conflict and harmony. His analysis of cultural factors concludes that these can and have affected the conduct and outcome of many international negotiations. Such miscommunication is most often a product of ignorance on the part of the negotiators rather than maliciousness. The theoretical framework he develops leads to the conclusion that there is no single, universal model for diplomatic negotiation. Instead, he presents a model of low context and high context negotiation styles based on preferences of different styles of communication that many cultures employ in international diplomacy.

This is the first book from the Jennings Randolph fellows programme published by the United States Institute of Peace. This choice reflects the quality of Cohen's book.

HOLLAND manages to write about diplomacy in such a way that it reads like a spy novel. The main antagonists are Japan and US and the setting is the proposed visit to Japan of the first nuclear powered US submarine, *Sea Dragon*. The reader will appreciate a lengthy historical overview of the two countries' diplomatic relationship that provides the basis for an introduction to Japan's style of bureaucracy. Holland pays attention to the cultural differences that exist between the two countries and shows how this difference is expressed in the implementation of Japanese diplomacy. The example of the US negotiations with Japan to gain permission to allow a nuclear-powered submarine to enter a Japanese harbour is a very good choice for it allows Holland to demonstrate the historical, as well as the political and cultural attributes of diplomatic negotiations. His informed analysis of the Japanese Ministry of Foreign Affairs (*Gaimusho*) and the detailed account of Japanese bureaucracy make this a valuable read for those interested in Japanese administration as well as US–Japan diplomatic relations.

The catchy title of JACKSON's book sets the tone. His account of his years as a diplomat is witty and easy to read with a gossipy tone. He was the youngest career diplomat and British Ambassador the UK ever had, and it quickly becomes apparent that his youth had much to do with how he approached his appointments. To make the most of Jackson's preference for namedropping it helps to be familiar with British and European politics. He takes a close look at the phenomenon of Eurodiplomats and does not hide his distaste for the American system of selecting diplomats. The author provides a stimulating discussion of life as a diplomat that is both humorous and educational. This book does not pretend to engage in an academic analysis of the diplomatic corps but rather should be considered for providing a rare glance behind the curtain of diplomatic politicking, including a clever account of the role of spies in diplomatic circles.

Not enough literature addresses the problems and difficulties that diplomats from smaller countries or developing countries face. MOORE's description of his life as a diplomat from an underdeveloped country begins with an eloquent treatment of Western diplomatic tradition ranging from selection and training to a diplomat's ambitions and expectations. By contrast, Third World diplomats must do without many of the amenities taken for granted by diplomats representing richer and larger countries. Moore puts diplomacy and the role diplomats play into a global context and argues that developing countries must not be ignored because they have an important role to play in world politics. He calls for a reexamination of traditional diplomatic concepts and suggests that diplomacy must reflect reality. This monograph provides an excellent and very honest view of diplomacy as seen through the eyes of a non-Western diplomat.

NICHOLSON is the classic text in diplomatic writing, published first in 1939. Since then it has gone through many editions. Nicholson's writings form the most widely accepted introduction to the study of diplomacy. Much of the content of the book describes the ideal diplomat, beginning with the selection process. The examinations with the British Foreign Office, later called British Service, were important, as was the training in diplomatic language. Even later editions focused primarily on the techniques that one was to acquire to practise diplomacy. This text provides a good read for students of diplomatic history, but it has outlived its present-day usefulness.

It is difficult to imagine that the writings of diplomats such as Henry Kissinger, George F. Kennan, Dag Hammarskjöld, Dean Rusk, Charles Thayer, or Warren Christopher will soon become outdated. PLISCHKE put together a remarkable collection of essays on modern diplomacy that covers every imaginable aspect of the art of diplomacy. The above writers address, in seven chapters, the functions of chiefs of diplomatic missions, the convention of diplomatic relations, and the nature and development of diplomacy, to name a few. The reader will find extensive references, a copy of the Vienna Convention on Diplomatic Relations, an extensive bibliography, and suggestions for additional readings. Although each individual essay warrants merit, presented in one collection one can appreciate the influence of diplomacy on many facets of the political arena.

SUSSKIND has become a prominent academic writer on the subject of environmental issues. Expanding on the existing literature on the art of diplomacy, this book's focus on environmental treaties provides a new viewpoint. Instead of employing the traditional analysis of the role of the diplomat, Susskind gives priority to the topic of negotiation and shows effectively how the area of environmental protection demands a new approach from those in the position to compose international treaties. He sees a need for a better balance between science and politics in order to eliminate the weaknesses of the existing treaty-making system. The extensive appendices provide a selection of global environmental treaties and declarations pertaining to nature conservation. Suggestions for further readings are included. Susskind was one of the first writers to tackle the problems of international environmental diplomacy and his contribution to the field cannot be ignored.

SABINA W. LAUTENSACH

Direct effect

Bebr, Gerhard, "Agreements Concluded by the Community and Their Possible Direct Effect: From International Fruit Company to Kupferberg", *Common Market Law Review*, 20/1 (1983): 35–73

Craig, Paul, "Once upon a Time in the West: Direct Effect and the Federalization of EEC Law", *Oxford Journal of Legal Studies*, 12 (1992): 453–73

Craig, Paul and Gráinne de Búrca, *EU Law: Text, Cases and Materials*, 2nd edition, Oxford and New York: Oxford University Press, 1998

de Búrca, Graìnne, "Giving Effect to European Community Directives", *Modern Law Review*, 55 (1992): 215–40

Eleftheriadis, Pavlos, "The Direct Effect of Community Law: Conceptual Issues", *Yearbook of European Law*, 16 (1996): 205–21

Pescatore, Pierre, "The Doctrine of 'Direct Effect': An Infant Disease of Community Law", *European Law Review*, 8 (1983): 155–77

Petersmann, Ernst Ulrich, "Proposals for a New Constitution for the European Union: Building Blocks for a Constitutional Theory and a Constitutional Law of the EU", *Common Market Law Review*, 32/5 (1995): 1123–75

Steiner, Josephine and Lorna Woods, *Textbook on EC Law*, 6th edition, London: Blackstone Press, 1998

Steiner, Josephine, "From Direct Effects to *Francovich*: Shifting Means of Enforcement of Community Law", *European Law Review*, 18 (1993): 3–22

Tridimas, Takis, "Horizontal Effect of Directives: A Missed Opportunity?", *European Law Review*, 19 (1994): 621ff.

STEINER & WOODS offer a detailed analysis of the case law of the European Court of Justice on direct and indirect effects. In order to clarify this complicated issue, the authors choose to present each judgement separately, giving particular emphasis to the additional interpretative comments on direct and indirect effect introduced by each case. Through this chronological reference to the relevant case law the reader is guided around the complicated streams of thought of the European judges, and assisted to comprehend not only the actual doctrine of each judgement but also the aim that it set out to achieve. The authors then proceed to an excellent clarification of the relationship between direct effects and state liability within the framework of the effective judicial protection of the individual.

A similar attempt to present the doctrine of direct effects is provided in CRAIG & DE BÚRCA. The authors of this book, however, choose a theoretical analysis of the underlying doctrines and their limits rather than a presentation of the case law. Thus, although the analysis of this book is rather more complicated than that of Steiner & Woods, the authors tend to analyse in depth the problems of direct effects, such as the repeated denial of horizontal direct effect in *Dori*, the lack of clarity over the boundaries of vertical direct effect in *Foster*, the uncertain scope of indirect effect after *Luciano Arcaro*, and the ambiguous new concept of indirect effect in *CIA Security*. In their relevant conclusions the authors stress the relative decrease in the value of the principle of direct effect in view of the state liability doctrine.

CRAIG examines the political implications of the principle of direct effect, with specific reference to the federalization of EU law. The principle of direct effect, as a mechanism of public enforcement, tends to be inefficient and ineffective. Moreover, it constitutes evidence of the federalization of EU law, as it calls upon the European Court of Justice to take a legislative role, thus acting as a surrogate legislature when the real legislature is unable to perform its tasks.

PESCATORE expressly states that direct effect is the ordinary state of the law for the vast majority of Community legal rules. The legal basis of the principle of direct effects is to be traced in the aim of the Treaty signatories to create a Community not only for the member states but also for its peoples and persons. It would be against this aim to deny the awarding of rights to these peoples and persons, rights that must be enforceable before the national courts, to which these peoples and persons have unlimited access. Thus, direct effect becomes a highly political idea, drawn from the perception of the constitutional system of the Community.

BEBR focuses on the issue of the direct effect of international agreements and refers to the arguments put forward by many member states that the principle of reciprocity applicable to most international agreements would be breached if member states were required to enforce such agreements before the national courts when the other party to the agreement need not do so. This argument is valid and signifies that direct effect, albeit the norm in the EU legal order, could not possibly apply to international agreements whose regulation is influenced by the principles of international law to which direct effect is more or less unknown. This view – which is also shared by the judges of the European Courts – is not supported by PETERSMANN, who, in an article mainly dealing with the issue of a Constitution for the EU, uses the General Agreement on Tariffs and Trade (GATT) as an example of an international agreement that should produce direct effects if it is to have any practical legal value.

DE BÚRCA presents the case law of the European Court of Justice on indirect effect in some detail, focusing specifically on the extreme confusion as to the legal rights and responsibilities of individuals in cases where there is a clear difference between the terms of the national measure and the Directive. Particular emphasis is given to the issue of the breach of the principle of legitimate expectations in *Marleasing*. The non-acknowledgement of such a breach can only be justified on the grounds that, in this case, the expectations are not legitimate, as they are not based on an updated knowledge of the recent development in EU law.

TRIDIMAS analyses the principle of direct and indirect effects in the light of the state liability doctrine and argues that the protection offered to the individual within the framework of state liability is not of a level that would render direct and indirect effects superfluous. In fact, direct and indirect effect allows the individual to use a provision of EU law as a sword, rather than as a shield as would be the case with state liability. The author assesses the lack of effectiveness of both the principle laid down in *Marleasing* and in state liability and calls for the final protection of the individual through the express introduction of horizontal direct effect for Directives.

The same point is made by STEINER, who examines the value of direct effects in view of the protection offered to the individual under the state liability scenario. The author observes that the principles of direct and indirect effects are of little use to the individual in cases of horizontal relationships whereas neither rectifies the primary failure of member states to implement EU law. Having said that, where the violations of member states are not clear and the conferral of rights for the benefit of individuals as a condition for the establishment of state liability is not met, individuals may still rely on direct effects for the enforcement of EU rules before the national courts.

ELEFTHERIADIS discusses the difference between direct effects and direct applicability and suggests that the distinction between the two terms should be abolished because it is quite important to be clear about the distinction between the formal and the substantive dimensions of Community rules and their application. Thus, the author suggests, direct effect and direct applicability should be taken to signify the formal validity of a Community rule in the domestic legal order.

HELEN XANTHAKI

See also European Community law

Directives

Chalmers, Damien and Erica Szyszczak, *European Union Law*, vol. 2, Aldershot, Hampshire: Ashgate Dartmouth, 1998

Evans, Andrew, *The Law of the European Community*, Deventer: Kluwer, 1994

Hartley, T.C., *The Foundations of European Community Law*, 3rd edition, Oxford: Clarendon Press, and New York: Oxford University Press, 1994

Lasok, D. and K.P.E. Lasok, *Law and Institutions of the European Union*, 6th edition, London: Butterworths, 1994

Pollard, David and Malcolm Ross, *European Community Law: Texts and Materials*, London: Butterworths, 1994

Steiner, Josephine, *Enforcing EC Law*, London: Blackstone Press, 1995

Steiner, Josephine, "The Limits of State Liability for Breach of EC Law", *European Public Law*, 4/1 (1998): 69–90

Steiner, Josephine and Lorna Woods, *Textbook on EC Law*, 6th edition, London: Blackstone Press, 1998

EVANS describes directives as European Union (EU) legislative texts that are binding, as to the result to be achieved, upon each member state to which they are addressed, but which leave the choice of the method under which the goal is to be achieved to the national legislative and administrative authorities of the member states to which the directives in question are addressed.

POLLARD & ROSS identify directives as the legislative measure used by the EU in occasions where the content of secondary legislation cannot be directly translated into the legal systems of the member states in a uniform manner because the latter may have different legislative and administrative mechanisms for dealing with the subject matter of the proposed measure (such as delegated legislation, royal or presidential decree, or statute).

As STEINER (1995) points out, directives are used to achieve approximation with a view to harmonization. They are therefore the main legal instruments employed in the creation of the internal market.

CHALMERS & SZYSZCZAK determine the difference between directives and regulations in that directives entail some degree of discretion for member states. Moreover, while the directive is similar to a regulation in that it will come into force 20 days after the publication or on the date stipulated in the directive, a directive will typically provide an express deadline by which member states must transpose it into national law. A distinction is therefore made between the ends and means with member states having discretion as to the latter but not to the former.

LASOK & LASOK point out that directives vary considerably in their scope and the precision of their text, especially where they are used as a means of achieving harmonization of national laws. Thus, directives often reflect the political compromises necessary for the achievement of a legislative text, which in the process of its agreement had to encompass the inbuilt resistance of well-entrenched national measures. It is for this reason that directives often demonstrate the lowest common denominator in the subject matter that they regulate. The second interpreting element of the authors' reference to directive refers to their excellent analysis on the interpretation of directives, where the authors suggests that the interpretation of directives involves not only the construction of the EU legislative text but also of the national implementing measure and the residual national legislation. The implementing national legislative texts must be interpreted in such a way as to give full effect to the intention of the EU legislator and any derogation must be interpreted in the narrowest possible manner.

HARTLEY analyses in some depth the complicated issue of the direct effect of directives. The author follows the evolution and development of the precedents of the European Court of Justice (ECJ) in a historical manner. It is pointed out that the principle of direct effects cannot possibly be considered to be included in the text of the treaties signed by most member states in their accession. The principle was introduced by the European Court of Justice in the 1970 *Grad* and *SACE* cases where the Court decided that, although directives opened the way to concrete legislative or administrative measures at the national level, they were still capable of producing direct effects. Despite the seeming application of the principle in the extreme and limited cases brought before the Court in *Grad* and *SACE*, in *Van Duyn*, the ECJ held that as a matter of general principle all directives may have direct effects. In *Van Duyn* the deadline for the implementation of the directive had expired. Thus, the Court gave little emphasis to the time-limit factor. However, it was in *Ratti* that the importance of the deadline was acknowledged.

This signified the beginning of a series of ECJ judgements that determined the issue of direct effects in directives in a complex and often opposing manner. The issue is expertly followed by STEINER & WOODS. The authors distinguish between horizontal and vertical direct effects and follow in as much of a rational manner as humanly possible the case law of the ECJ from *Van Duyn* to *Francovich*, *Ratti*, *Marleasing*, *Marshall*, *Foster*, *El Corte Ingles*, *Arcaro*, *von Colson*, *Litster*, *Duke*, and *Miret* are only few of the judgements of the ECJ used by the authors in this brilliantly clear and full account of the development of the principle from vertical to horizontal and from direct to indirect effects. The excellent analysis of the state liability scenario as an answer to the problems and gaps created by the principle of direct effects ends the authors' reference to one of the most crucial, complex, and still ongoing issues in EU law.

The issue of the gaps in the effective protection of the individual created by the principle of direct effects, and still remaining after the development of the state liability doctrine, are expertly identified, presented, and analysed by STEINER (1998).

HELEN XANTHAKI

See also European Community law

Disability

Abberley, Paul, "The Concept of Oppression and the Development of a Social Theory of Disability", *Disability, Handicap and Society*, 2/1 (1987): 5–19

Barnes, Colin, Geof Mercer and Tom Shakespeare, *Exploring Disability: A Sociological Introduction*, Cambridge: Polity Press, and Malden, Massachusetts: Blackwell, 1999

Barton, Len and Mike Oliver (editors), *Disability Studies: Past, Present and Future*, Leeds: Disability Press, 1997

Brechin, Ann, Penny Liddiard and John Swain (editors), *Handicap in a Social World: A Reader*, London: Hodder and Stoughton, 1981

Finkelstein, Victor, *Attitudes and Disabled People: Issues for Discussion*, New York: World Rehabilitation Fund, 1980

Lonsdale, Susan, *Women and Disability: The Experience of Physical Disability among Women*, Basingstoke: Macmillan, and New York: St Martin's Press, 1990

Morris, Jenny, *Pride against Prejudice: Transforming Attitudes to Disability*, Philadelphia: New Society, and London: Women's Press, 1991

Oliver, Michael, *The Politics of Disablement*, Basingstoke: Macmillan, 1990

Oliver, Michael, *Understanding Disability: From Theory to Practice*, Basingstoke: Macmillan, and New York: St Martin's Press, 1996

Priestley, Mark, "Constructions and Creations: Idealism, Materialism and Disability Theory", *Disability and Society*, 13/1 (1998): 25–94

Swain, John *et al.* (editors), *Disabling Barriers: Enabling Environments*, Milton Keynes: Open University Press, and Newbury Park, California: Sage, 1993

Disability studies are a rapidly expanding international field that draws on a variety of academic disciplines in the social sciences and humanities. It has gained much of its influence from the application of new sociological ideas to practical contexts (particularly in the area of social policy). More recently, disability scholars have sought to address issues of cultural representation and identity. From a sociological perspective, the most significant contribution has been the development of a "social model" approach to disability. The small sample of work selected here provides the reader with a means to trace the evolution of these ideas as they relate to contemporary thinking about the sociology of disability.

FINKELSTEIN's monograph, written for the World Rehabilitation Fund, sets out a radical agenda for thinking about disability in the modern world. It challenged much of the existing scholarship by refuting many of the assumptions held by rehabilitation professionals and medical sociologists. Drawing directly on the ideas and representations of the international disabled people's movement, the monograph identified institutional discrimination and segregation, rather than individual impairment, as the basis for disabled people's social exclusion in contemporary society. In this early work, Finkelstein encapsulates many of the core themes and concepts that were to influence the subsequent development of disability studies and the social model approach that underpins it.

The social model of disability has its origins in the political struggles of disabled people for self-empowerment, and in academic attempts to reconstruct the sociology of disability. The collection edited by BRECHIN, LIDDIARD & SWAIN provides a flavour of these influences, drawing on work by a range of disabled and nondisabled authors. Produced as an Open University reader during the United Nations International Year of Disabled People, the book provides ready access to some important early texts in the field. These include short extracts from the writings of influential figures in the disabled people's movement such as Vic Finkelstein, Gerbon De Yong and Ken Davis. Although dated, this is an important collection that highlights many of the enduring themes in the contemporary sociology of disability. There are contributions dealing with disabled people's self-definition, self-help and self-organization, as well as important critiques of traditional approaches to institutional welfare.

ABBERLEY's paper (included in BARTON & OLIVER's edited collection) brings together some of these diverse strands, by advancing the prospect of a "social theory" of disability. In this paper he analyses the concept of oppression, as a prelude to thinking about the common features of social disadvantage (comparing disability with race and gender for example). In this sense, Abberley's paper made a significant contribution to the development of social model thinking. Although it might be possible to criticize him in retrospect for failing to make a clear enough distinction between impairment and disability, he does significantly pre-empt a number of "new" sociological debates about the relationship between disability, oppression, individual experience, and the body.

The two books by OLIVER have had a seminal influence on the development of disability studies, both in Britain and around the world. Oliver is widely credited with having coined the term "social model" and his work is generally regarded as exemplifying this approach. Oliver sets out to substantiate the view, developed within the disabled people's movement, that disability is a social, rather than an individual, phenomenon. Oliver argues that disability is both culturally produced and socially created. Using an historical materialist analysis, he emphasizes the role of industrial capitalism as a driving force in the development of contemporary disabling social relations. In this context, he highlights the ideological construction of disability and its negative influence on disability identity. However, this is balanced by an equally strong emphasis on disabled people's self-empowerment. Using the concept of new social movements, Oliver examines the role of the disabled people's movement as an agent of social change.

The international journal *Disability and Society* has provided a central forum for the development of social model thinking since its inception in 1986. BARTON & OLIVER's edited collection includes 20 contributions, many previously published in the journal. These include important papers from leading writers in the field (including Colin Barnes, Paul

Abberley, Jane Campbell, and Tom Shakespeare). The book is divided into three sections. Part one examines some of the central themes from the journal's development, including issues of culture, theory, collective action, and identity politics. Part two includes a sample of six papers previously published in the journal. These have been selected on the basis of their impact on disability studies and their enduring popularity among students of the discipline. Although they deal with diverse issues (social policy, social theory, politics, and cultural representation) the papers all seek to apply social model concepts to their chosen subject matter. Part three of the book is devoted to a selection of seven shorter papers, originally published in the journal's current issues section. These provide a flavour of ongoing debates in the field. The examples seek to problematize the role of researchers, the nature of oppression and the applicability of a social model approach to personal experience.

The latter debate has been developed primarily by disabled women, seeking to apply feminist scholarship to the new sociology of disability. There are many examples but the two books by LONSDALE and MORRIS were certainly influential in this respect. Both draw directly on the personal experiences of disabled women, while retaining commitment to a social model analysis of those experiences. Importantly, they highlight the uneasy relationship between the corporeality of impairment and the social reality of disability (discrimination and social exclusion). The examples and stories paint a picture of the complexity of disability as a lived experience in both the public and the private domain.

Like the earlier Open University collection (Brechin, Liddiard & Swain), the volume edited by SWAIN et al. covers a wide variety of topics focusing on the twin themes of "disabling barriers" and "enabling environments". Here, the editors respond clearly to the emerging influence of social model thinking and to the diversity of disabled people's lived experience. There are powerful contributions on the development of the disabled people's movement (particularly in the UK) and significant contributions from leading theorists. There are also a number of papers that address aspects of commonality and difference (including race, gender, and sexuality). The impairment/disability debate begins to emerge more clearly in this volume. Other chapters deal with cultural representation and policy analysis. Disabled writers are well represented and the collection includes papers on a wide range of relevant topics. This is an excellent source book for students, which provides access to most of the major debates and issues of concern to scholars in the field.

PRIESTLEY offers an attempt to categorize the core themes of contemporary disability theory. Using a fourfold typology, the paper clarifies the ontological basis for distinguishing between individual and social model approaches in the literature. The paper identifies a number of key theoretical debates in the field and provides a guide to understanding their significance. In particular, it deals with the ability of social model theory to adequately address issues of commonality and difference among and between disabled people. A distinction is offered between materialist and idealist approaches to social model writing, and the paper concludes with an appraisal of their relative merits in developing academic thought within the discipline.

Finally, BARNES, MERCER & SHAKESPEARE provides an excellent introduction to the sociology of disability. Their textbook seeks to fill a gap in mainstream sociology, by exploring the significance of disability issues. The book charts both traditional and contemporary approaches, focusing on the social model of disability. The various chapters deal with a wide range of sociological writing, including medical sociology, disability studies, social policy, politics, culture and research methodology. The authors incorporate both European and North American traditions, framed within an historical overview of disability studies as a developing discipline. As an introduction to the subject, this would be a good place to start.

MARK PRIESTLEY

Disaster management, *see* Crisis management

Discounting

Bernstein, Peter L., *Capital Ideas: The Improbable Origins of Modern Wall Street*, New York: Free Press, 1992

Bierman, Harold Jr and Seymour Smidt, *The Capital Budgeting Decision: Economic Analysis of Investment Projects*, 7th edition, New York: Macmillan, and London: Collier Macmillan, 1988

Bromwich, Michael, *The Economics of Capital Budgeting*, Harmondsworth and New York: Penguin, 1976

Copeland, Thomas E. and J. Fred Weston, *Financial Theory and Corporate Policy*, 3rd edition, Reading, Massachusetts: Addison Wesley, 1988

Dixit, Avinash K. and Robert S. Pindyck, *Investment under Uncertainty*, Princeton, New Jersey: Princeton University Press, 1994

Fisher, Irving, *The Theory of Interest as Determined by Impatience to Spend Income and Opportunity to Invest It*, New York: Macmillan, 1930; reprinted Fairfield, New Jersey: Kelley, 1986

Hirschleifer, Jack, "On the Theory of Optimal Investment Decisions", *Journal of Political Economy*, 66/4 (1958): 329–52

Ingersoll, Jonathan and Stephen Ross, "Waiting to Invest: Investment and Uncertainty", *Journal of Business*, 65/1 (1992): 1–29

Lorie, James and Leonard Savage, "Three Problems in Rationing Capital", *Journal of Business*, 28/4 (1955): 56–66

Pointon, John, "UK Taxation and Financial Decision Making" in *Issues in Finance*, edited by Michael Firth and Simon Keane, Oxford: Philip Allan, 1986

Ross, Stephen, Chester Spatt and Philip Dybvig, "Present Values and Internal Rates of Return", *Journal of Economic Theory*, 23/1 (1980): 66–81

Wilkes, F.M., *Capital Budgeting Techniques*, 2nd edition, Chichester and New York: Wiley, 1983

Williams, John Burr, *The Theory of Investment Value*, Cambridge, Massachusetts: Harvard University Press, 1938

FISHER is the classic reference on the foundations of discounting techniques; the procedures for making precise allowance for the distance from the present of the receipts and payments associated with productive or financial investments. An example illustrates the problem for which discounting is the solution. Suppose an individual were offered the choice between receiving £1 today or £1.05 in one year's time. If the market rate of interest is 5 per cent, then these two alternatives would be identical, it being assumed that there is no possibility of default. As the £1 could be invested at 5 per cent, both alternatives are worth £1.05 in one year's time. Alternatively, both alternatives must also be worth £1 today; and we say that the discounted value of £1.05 in one year's time is £1 today. Discounting techniques are thus used more generally for all valuation problems that involve future receipts and payments – for example, the capital investment projects of companies and the financial investments made by individuals or companies.

Both Fisher and HIRSCHLEIFER demonstrate that the valuation of capital investments can be separated from the decision on how to finance them. They demonstrate that, under certainty and with equal interest rates for borrowing and lending, the optimal investment decision is to invest while the return from productive investments exceeds the market interest rate. This outcome should be chosen regardless of whether the investor needs to finance the investment or when the investor wishes to spend the proceeds of the investment.

Hirschleifer and also LORIE & SAVAGE consider extensions of these results to multi-period investments, to situations where borrowing and lending rates are no longer equal, and where the finance for the projects is rationed. In particular, they highlight situations where the choice of discounting technique may inadvertently influence the choice of investments undertaken.

BROMWICH is a largely non-technical guide to discounting techniques and their application in capital investment appraisal. It provides a guide to the different discounting techniques applying to equal (annuity) and unequal sequences of payments or receipts, and between fixed and continuing (perpetual) sequences of payments or receipts. It also considers the alternative (non-discounting) techniques that can be used to evaluate capital investment projects.

Covering much of the same ground, but at a slightly more technical level, is BIERMAN & SMIDT. This text has the advantage of including a number of case study examples involving the application of discounting techniques. More technical still is WILKES, which is particularly strong on the application of the programming methods used in the operational research field to investment appraisal problems.

COPELAND & WESTON present a comprehensive treatment of how discounting calculations should be modified to account for the influence of inflation and the term structure of interest rates. In the former case, they demonstrate how inflation can bias the investment decision if cashflows or rates of return are not all entirely in real or entirely in nominal terms. In the latter, they review the arguments about why interest rates for longer term investments may be higher than those for short-term investments, for example if investors require an inducement to lend for the longer term. Then they show how discounting calculations can be adapted to take account of the appropriate opportunity cost of each of the cashflows being appraised.

Copeland & Weston also provide a thorough introduction to the treatment of uncertainty in discounting calculations, that is when the future receipts and payments are not known with certainty. They show how both the capital asset pricing model and the arbitrage pricing theory, which are models of required rates of return on equity securities, can be used to adjust discounting calculations for the risk in capital investment appraisal. Both of these models recognize that a company may be investing in a portfolio of projects and that these projects may have offsetting attributes for the company.

By contrast, the pioneering work of BURR WILLIAMS on valuing financial securities using discounting techniques did not have the benefit of the techniques of portfolio theory developed in the 1950s and so considered financial investments as single entities. The development of portfolio theory, which recognizes the interrelationships that do occur between financial investments, and many other areas of financial economic theory are narrated in BERNSTEIN, which is designed for the non-specialist reader.

POINTON reviews the adjustments that are necessary to include corporate tax and tax allowances into capital investment appraisal and other financial decisions.

ROSS, SPATT & DYBVIG determine the general conditions under which the present value of a payment stream decreases as the interest rate, which is being used to discount the payments, rises. This builds on earlier work that had shown that this depended on whether or not the project could be costlessly abandoned.

The option to abandon a project is one of several option features that capital investments may contain and that can be included in a discounting calculation. Perhaps the most significant of these is the option to delay the start of the project. INGERSOLL & ROSS demonstrate that if interest rates are stochastic and expected to fall in the future, then it may be worthwhile delaying the start of an investment as the opportunity cost of funds is less in the future, and so the value of the investment will be greater when commenced later.

DIXIT & PINDYCK, building on foundations provided by Ingersoll & Ross and Copeland & Weston, provide a comprehensive treatment of all of the option features of investment decision making and discounting calculations. Using the techniques of stochastic calculus and dynamic programming they explore uncertainties in the initial cost of the investment, in the future payments and receipts, among the interest rates used for the discounting, and in the scale of the investment.

JAMES STEELEY

See also Interest rates, Investments

Discourse analysis

Billig, Michael, *Ideology and Opinions: Studies in Rhetorical Psychology*, London and Newbury Park, California: Sage, 1991
Burman, Erica and Ian Parker (editors), *Discourse Analytic Research: Repertoires and Readings of Texts in Action*, London and New York: Routledge, 1993

Fairclough, Norman, *Critical Discourse Analysis: The Critical Study of Language*, London and New York: Longman, 1995

Foucault, Michel, *Power/Knowledge: Selected Interviews and Other Writings, 1972–1977*, edited by Colin Gordon, Brighton: Harvester Press, and New York: Pantheon, 1980

Kendall, Gavin and Gary Wickham, *Using Foucault's Methods*, London: Sage, 1999

Parker, Ian, "Discursive Psychology" in *Critical Psychology: An Introduction*, edited by Dennis R. Fox and Isaac Prilleltensky, London and Thousand Oaks, California: Sage, 1997

Parker, Ian and the Bolton Discourse Network, *Critical Textwork: An Introduction to Varieties of Discourse and Analysis*, Buckingham: Open University Press, 1999

Potter, Jonathan and Margaret Wetherell, *Discourse and Social Psychology: Beyond Attitudes and Behaviour*, London and Newbury Park, California: Sage, 1987

Wilkinson, Sue and Celia Kitzinger (editors), *Feminism and Discourse: Psychological Perspectives*, London and Thousand Oaks, California: Sage, 1995

Willig, Carla (editor), *Applied Discourse Analysis: Social and Psychological Interventions*, Buckingham: Open University Press, 1999

The terms "discourse" and "discourse analysis" can often seem problematic and ambiguous to those coming across them for the first time. PARKER suggests that these difficulties arise as a consequence of disagreements amongst discourse theorists/analysts regarding what is meant by the term "discourse" and a subsequent disagreement regarding how discourse should be studied. He provides a useful general definition of discourse and moves on to discuss two of the main traditions of research within this area. First, he discusses Foucauldian approaches to discourse, which develop the work of French historian and philosopher Michel Foucault. Second, he considers a form of discourse analysis that arose within social psychology (derived from work on the sociology of scientific knowledge) that concerns itself with an analysis of "interpretative repertoires" (contrasting ways of explaining phenomena).

POTTER & WETHERELL provides a straightforward account of discourse analysis within the "interpretative repertoires" tradition. The book outlines some of the background to discourse analysis, showing the disciplines and traditions it draws on, and uses examples from a number of contexts that provide the reader with a working understanding of this form of analysis. In particular, they criticize the concept of "attitudes" and demonstrate the ways in which discourse analysis undermines both our everyday and traditional psychological understandings of this term. They also include a useful section that contains practical guidelines on how to carry out this form of research.

For those wishing to develop an understanding of Foucauldian discourse analysis (in terms of its historical development and theoretical orientation), FOUCAULT provides a collection of selected interviews and other writings by Michel Foucault that present a straightforward and informal account of Foucault's concerns and the major issues that inform his work. The writings include reference to the prison, the body and the flesh, geography, truth, power, health, and sexuality.

KENDALL & WICKHAM provides an accessible introduction to Foucauldian discourse analysis and organize their book around two main themes. The first of these, "history, archaeology, genealogy and discourse", explores the theoretical basis of Foucault's method of analysis, while the second, "science and culture as important objects of analysis", explores the application of such methods in particular fields. The book contains a number of extremely helpful practical exercises that allow the reader to work through both the theoretical and methodological issues pertinent to this form of analysis. The book concludes with a short but useful guide to further reading that includes a brief summary of most of the texts they recommend.

BILLIG cannot be easily categorized in terms of the two forms of discourse analysis outlined above, but his work on rhetoric, argumentation, and ideology has influenced numerous discourse analytic studies. In this book, he argues that processes of everyday thinking are ideological in that they reflect common sense maxims, values, and opinions that are products of social and historical arrangements that relate to particular patterns of domination and power. From this he concludes that psychology should study "how wider patterns of society and history are being reflected in the thinking of the individuals" (p.2). Chapters two, three, and nine expand and contextualize Billig's theoretical concerns while chapters four to eight demonstrate the empirical applications of this approach.

FAIRCLOUGH brings together his work on critical discourse analysis written between 1983 and 1992 and structures his book in terms of four main sections. The first of these is concerned with the author's attempt to develop critical discourse analysis as a framework for the analysis of language in relation to power and ideology; specifically, the development of a resource with which to challenge linguistic domination and oppression. The second explores discourse and discourse analysis in relation to notions of cultural and social change. The third discusses the necessity for the inclusion of textual analysis within discourse analysis (textual analysis considers the ways in which genres and discourses are drawn upon and combine in specific texts). The final section, "critical language awareness" is concerned with educational applications of discourse analysis within schools and other educational arenas.

The majority of chapters in BURMAN & PARKER's collection provide accessible examples of discourse analytic work. Together, they demonstrate that the typical objects of psychological inquiry – notions such as emotion, prejudice, and attitudes – do not reside within the individual (as mainstream psychology would have us believe) but are created by the language within which they both operate and are described. In this sense, discourse analysis is conceptualized as a means whereby we might explore the social/collective origin of psychological "reality". They conclude their collection with a useful chapter that explores what they see as the problems with both discourse theory and analysis.

Part one of WILKINSON & KITZINGER provides examples of discourse analytic work within a feminist perspective. From studies of menstruation, sexual harassment, gender, and anorexia nervosa, the authors demonstrate the ways in which discourse analysis uncovers the social and political origins of these supposedly "individual" phenomena. In so doing, they demonstrate the ways in which discourse analysis can serve to reveal the social and political origins of the self and subjectivity. Part two moves beyond the practical application of discourse analysis to reflect upon the utility of discourse analysis for feminism. Three central concerns guide these chapters. First, to explore the nature (or lack of it) of extra-discursive reality – a reality beyond the text. Second, to document the various forms of discourse analysis and to discuss their usefulness for feminism. Third, to explore the implications of discourse analysis for feminist theory and politics.

WILLIG's collection moves beyond a purely analytic consideration of discourse to explore the practical utility of discourse analysis within applied psychology. Using a number of examples, it assesses the extent to which discourse analytic research can be utilized for practical purposes. The chapters discuss three ways in which discourse analysis can inform social and psychological practice: first, discourse analysis as a tool to challenge; second, discourse analysis as a basis for training programmes; and third, discourse analysis as empowerment. The chapters discuss ethical, political, and epistemological problems associated with an attempt to "apply" discourse analysis and go on to differentiate between "application" and "intervention". The book concludes that discourse analysis as a method of intervention has a greater radical potential than more analytic applications of this approach.

PARKER & THE BOLTON DISCOURSE NETWORK seeks to move beyond the scope of much contemporary discourse analytic work, to progressively extend the compass of discourse research and to explore methodological issues of reading and representation applied to symbolic systems that are not usually thought of as textual. Analyses include; advertising, bodies, comics, film, letters, organizations, sign languages, and other language systems, and illustrate the ways in which discourses may be studied wherever there is meaning. There is a common structure to each chapter that greatly facilitates the reader's understanding of the ways in which discourse analysis may be applied to these apparently non-textual realms.

DAVID J. NIGHTINGALE

See also Constructionism and Critical psychology

Discrimination, economic

Aigner, Dennis J. and Glen C. Cain, "Statistical Theories of Discrimination in Labor Markets", *Industrial and Labor Relations Review*, 30/2 (1977): 175–87

Ayres, Ian, and Siegelman, Peter, "Race and Gender Discrimination in Bargaining for a New Car", *American Economic Review*, 85/3 (1995): 304–21

Becker, Gary S., *The Economics of Discrimination*, 2nd edition, Chicago: University of Chicago Press, 1971

Blau, Francine D., Marianne A. Ferber and Anne E. Winkler, *The Economics of Women, Men, and Work*, 3rd edition, Upper Saddle River, New Jersey: Prentice Hall, 1998

Buffum, David and Robert Whaples, "Fear and Lathing in the Michigan Furniture Industry: Employee-Based Discrimination a Century Ago", *Economic Inquiry*, 33/2 (1995): 234–52

Darity, William A., Jr and Patrick L. Mason, "Evidence on Discrimination in Employment: Codes of Color, Codes of Gender", *Journal of Economic Perspectives*, 12/2 (1998): 63–90

Fuchs, Victor, "Women's Quest for Economic Equality", *Journal of Economic Perspectives*, 3/1 (1989): 25–41

Goldberg, Pinelopi Koujianou, "Dealer Price Discrimination in New Car Purchases: Evidence from the Consumer Expenditures Survey", *Journal of Political Economy*, 104/3 (1996): 622–54

Heckman, James J., "Detecting Discrimination", *Journal of Economic Perspectives*, 12/2 (1998): 101–16

Ladd, Helen F., "Evidence on Discrimination in Mortgage Lending", *Journal of Economic Perspectives*, 12/2 (1998): 41–62

Neal, Derek A. and William R. Johnson, "The Role of Premarket Factors in Black–White Wage Differences", *Journal of Political Economy*, 104/5 (1996): 869–95

O'Neill, June, "The Role of Human Capital in Earnings Differences Between Black and White Men", *Journal of Economic Perspectives*, 4/4 (1990): 25–45

Roback, Jennifer, "The Political Economy of Segregation: The Case of Segregated Streetcars", *Journal of Economic History*, 46/4 (1986): 893–917

Yinger, John, "Evidence on Discrimination in Consumer Markets", *Journal of Economic Perspectives*, 12/2 (1998): 23–40

BECKER (originally published in 1957) is the seminal work on the economics of discrimination. Prior to Becker's study self-interest was seen as the cause of market discrimination. Most assumed that the majority raised their incomes by discriminating against minorities. Becker analyses discriminatory behaviour arising from prejudice or a "taste for discrimination" and shows that such discrimination hurts both groups because both forego gains from trade. He defines employer discrimination as cases in which the employer refuses to hire someone with a marginal value to production greater than the marginal cost, and he shows that employers who practise discrimination will generally end up losing profits. In a competitive market, this will make it difficult for discriminating employers to survive in the long run. Discrimination by employees generally implies that workers with a taste for discrimination must settle for lower pay when they choose to avoid working with members of the group they dislike. In a competitive market this will lead to segregation of workers by group. If customers are the source of discrimination, they will generally need to pay more, and the disliked group will be crowded into jobs with little customer contact. Becker's analysis suggests that competition is a powerful force in reducing discrimination, because one must pay for the right to discriminate. Becker tests many of the implications of his models, but the empirical sections will be of less interest because they are somewhat dated and use fairly rudimentary techniques. Becker's theoretical work is straightforward but fairly technical, so it may be inaccessible to those without formal training in economics.

Economic discrimination has been a powerful force throughout history, despite Becker's models' predictions that competition will moderate its impact. This has led economists to consider models in which discrimination is consistent with profit-maximization. These models focus on problems that risk-averse employers face in measuring the individual ability or productivity of potential workers. In this case employers may find it profitable to use group characteristics as a signal for the individual's abilities. AIGNER & CAIN carefully surveyed a range of these models of "statistical" discrimination, first simplifying and clarifying, and then adding complexity. Their article is a good overview, but may be inaccessible to those without formal training in economics.

Empirical work on the economics of discrimination is very wide-ranging. The largest strand has examined evidence of labour market discrimination facing blacks in the US. O'NEILL's article is an excellent place to enter this literature. O'Neill explains the standard technique used to gauge the impact of labour market discrimination against blacks (or any other group). This method examines individual-level data from some large sample of the population and uses ordinary least-squares regressions to estimate the determinants of wages. The regression coefficients show the payoffs to each group for a wide variety of human capital characteristics (such as age, years of schooling, and experience). Then, following the standard procedure, O'Neill takes the mean characteristics of whites and substitutes them into the blacks' regression. This result predicts what blacks' wages would be, on average, if blacks had the same characteristics as whites, but were still treated as blacks are treated in the labour market. In many studies the predicted wage of blacks falls below that of whites by about 10 percent and this gap is often identified as "labour market discrimination". O'Neill's study used the National Longitudinal Survey of Youth, and attracted considerable attention because it found virtually no evidence for discrimination against black males. Her results depend crucially on the inclusion of a previously unused measure of ability – the Armed Forces Qualifying Test (AFQT) score. Blacks perform much worse on this test than do whites with the same number of years of schooling and O'Neill argues that AFQT scores are a useful measure of educational outcomes.

NEAL & JOHNSON expand O'Neill's study, showing that the AFQT score of high-school-aged individuals can explain all or most of the racial wage gaps for these same individuals when they are about thirty years old. This ability measure explains the entire gap between black and white women's wages, all of the gap between Hispanic and white men's wages, and about three-quarters of the gap between the wages of black and white men. Neal & Johnson review evidence from studies by the National Academy of Sciences, which find no racial bias in the AFQT, and find that AFQT scores are equally good at predicting carefully measured job performance indicators for white and black members of the military. Finally, Neal & Johnson estimate the determinants of AFQT scores, finding that school environment and family background account for much of the black–white skills gap, but concluding that blacks are less likely to gain skills than similarly situated whites. Neal & Johnson's is, perhaps, the most convincing evidence that market discrimination causes insubstantial harm to minorities in the US.

DARITY & MASON reach the conclusion that labour market discrimination against American blacks is still substantial. They review a wide range of regression studies, argue that studies based on AFQT scores yield a number of anomalies and conclude that "evidence based on the AFQT should be treated with extreme caution". They review findings that wages among minorities are linked to skin colour, and survey court cases providing evidence of recent employment discrimination in the private sector. Finally, they examine findings from employment "audits" in which pairs of whites and minorities with equal credentials apply for entry-level jobs at businesses advertising openings. These generally show that whites are much more likely to receive job offers.

HECKMAN critiques Darity & Mason's article. He argues that audits provide little evidence of discriminatory behaviour, critiques the implicit assumptions of the audit model, and bemoans the fact that audit studies have primarily been conducted using overqualified college students applying for jobs in low-skill occupations. In addition, he argues that individual acts of discrimination can occur without harming minorities, because it is at the margin that economic values are set. The articles by Neal & Johnson, Darity & Mason, and Heckman give the reader a good sense of the strengths and weaknesses of evidence for and against the importance of labour market discrimination against minorities in the contemporary American labour market. The articles are written for the intelligent lay reader and include references to a vast body of research.

Modern discrimination is very mild by historical standards, so historical studies can be very useful in understanding the economics of discrimination. In addition, the nature of modern nationally representative data sets means that almost none of the empirical work on labour market discrimination attempts to detect its sources. BUFFUM & WHAPLES use historical data to show how employee-based discrimination can be detected, and estimate the compensating wage differentials received about a century ago (during a period of rampant nativism) when manufacturing employees worked with members of other ethnic groups. They find substantial evidence of employee-based discrimination and scant evidence of employer-based discrimination. This article is important in showing the historical importance of fellow-workers as the primary source of discrimination.

Another historical study of importance, by ROBACK, carefully examines discrimination in the product market. Roback shows that in an era of intense racism, streetcar companies were not the initiators of segregation, but were forced to segregate in most cities in the southern US because of Jim Crow laws, which they often actively resisted. The political process generated this form of discrimination, not the market.

The large literature on current discrimination in product markets is surveyed by YINGER, who focuses on the markets for housing and automobiles, and LADD, who focuses on mortgage lending. Both examine a wide range of regression and audit studies, providing up-to-date, accessible, and even-handed coverage of recent research methodologies and findings. (The articles by Yinger, Ladd, Darity & Mason, and Heckman are all part of a symposium on "Discrimination in Product, Credit, and Labor Markets", which is aimed at undergraduate economics majors.)

Two studies of discrimination in the auto market deserve additional attention. AYRES & SIEGELMAN use an audit study of the Chicago auto market, assigning identical bargaining strategies to matched black and white, and male and female buyers. They find that dealers' initial offers and final offers to white males are the lowest, with white females, black females, and black males paying progressively more for new cars when they are randomly assigned to dealerships. This study is uniquely informative, because it examines the race and gender of the sales agents and dealership owners, and finds that these factors are not of much importance. Thus, personal prejudice is not the source of discrimination, but sales agents seem to practice statistical discrimination, using race and gender as proxies for the customer's reservation price.

GOLDBERG examines the final sales price of autos, using national evidence from the Consumer Expenditure Survey. She finds that minorities and women do not pay more than white males. Those who may face statistical discrimination at some dealerships seem to be able to avoid these dealerships. As in the case of labour market discrimination, there is no consensus in this literature because one camp focuses on individual (average) cases of discrimination and the other focuses on the impact of discrimination at the margin. One school finds evidence of individual acts of discrimination, whereas the other finds little evidence that these acts of discrimination cause economic harm.

Economists have not ignored gender-based discrimination. Chapter 7 of BLAU, FERBER & WINKLER's textbook provides a clear overview of discrimination theories, and makes a fairly even-handed examination of the magnitude of discrimination faced by women. In addition, it briefly discusses the "glass ceiling", subtle barriers faced by women, and comparable-worth policies. FUCHS (based on an earlier book) focuses on the fairly wide occupational differences between men and women, providing considerable evidence that occupational differences reflect differing choices and attitudes between women and men. Fuchs argues that discrimination by employers may contribute to women's economic disadvantage, "but the conflict between career and family appears to be more important and pervasive". As in the case of race-based discrimination, there is no consensus about the magnitude of discrimination faced by women in the labour market, or if women are harmed by discrimination at all.

ROBERT M. WHAPLES

Discrimination, social

Allport, Gordon W., *The Nature of Prejudice*, Cambridge, Massachusetts: Addison Wesley, 1954

Brigham, John C., "Ethnic Stereotypes", *Psychological Bulletin*, 76 (1971): 15–33

Crosby, Faye, Stephanie Bromley and Leonard Saxe, "Recent Unobtrusive Studies of Black and White Discrimination and Prejudice: A Literature Review", *Psychological Bulletin*, 87/3 (1980): 546–63

Dovidio, John F., John C. Brigham, Blair T. Johnson and Samuel L. Gaertner, "Stereotyping, Prejudice and Discrimination: Another Look" in *Stereotypes and Stereotyping*, edited by C. Neil Macrae, Charles Stangor and Miles Hewstone, New York: Guilford Press, 1996

Fiske, Susan T., "Stereotyping, Prejudice and Discrimination" in *The Handbook of Social Psychology*, 4th edition, edited by Daniel T. Gilbert, Susan T. Fiske and Gardner Lindzey, Boston: McGraw Hill, 1998

La Piere, Richard T., "Attitudes vs. Actions", *Social Forces*, 13 (1934): 230–37

Mackie, Diane M. and Eliot R. Smith, "Intergroup Relations: Insights from a Theoretically Integrative Approach", *Psychological Review*, 105/3 (1998): 499–529

Tajfel, Henri, "Experiments in Intergroup Discrimination", *Scientific American*, 223/2 (1970): 96–102

Discrimination is more than simply distinguishing between social groups; it involves the inappropriate treatment of individuals due solely to their group membership. Accordingly discrimination has a pejorative meaning. Discrimination has been documented in many domains such as educational and employment settings although intergroup research, such as that conducted by TAJFEL, has demonstrated that merely categorizing individuals into arbitrary groups is sufficient to produce discrimination against outgroups.

ALLPORT provided an early discussion of the nature of prejudice. Importantly, he drew a distinction between antilocution and actual discrimination. LA PIERE's study has become a classic example of the separation of verbal and actual discriminatory behaviour. He travelled the US with a Chinese couple at a time when anti-Chinese sentiment was high. They visited over 200 establishments and were refused service only once, yet in a questionnaire survey of the proprietors of these establishments 92 per cent said they would refuse service. The lasting contribution of La Piere's study is its demonstration that the verbal situations evoked more hostility than the actual situation. People who threaten to discriminate may not actually do so.

CROSBY, BROMLEY & SAXE reviewed unobtrusive studies of anti-black racism, focusing on experiments on helping behaviour, aggression and nonverbal behaviour. They concluded that anti-black prejudice and discrimination is far more prevalent than survey data would lead one to expect. This review suggested that individuals may discriminate against others even when they claim that they would not do so. Crosby, Bromley & Saxe also attempted to reconcile the empirical findings reviewed with models of social attitudes and behaviour.

FISKE provides a recent review of research on stereotyping, prejudice, and discrimination. The focus of the chapter is to argue that stereotyping, prejudice, and discrimination are partly automatic and socially pragmatic, yet at the same time individually controllable and responsive to social structure. Fiske provides a brief review of historical approaches to explaining stereotyping, prejudice, and discrimination before moving on to the main thesis of her chapter in which she reviews recent research on both the automaticity and the control of stereotypes. Only a relatively small section of the chapter is devoted exclusively to a discussion of discrimination but, as Fiske notes, the documentation of discrimination has not received much attention in social psychological research. She does, however, argue that it is important that such research takes place. Some attention has been paid to the processes underlying discrimination, such as the self-fulfilling prophecy, and these are considered in this chapter. Fiske draws a distinction between two types of discrimination that deserve further research attention – "hot discrimination" which is based on disgust, resentment, hostility and anger, and "cold discrimination", which is based on stereotypes, knowledge, and motivations.

Discrimination is closely related to the concepts of stereotyping and prejudice. The general assumption in both the social cognition and the social identity literature has been that cognitions (stereotypes) and evaluations (prejudice) influence behaviour (discrimination). In his review of research on ethnic stereotypes BRIGHAM challenged the assumption that there is a simple relationship between the expression of stereotypes and their use in discriminatory behaviour. He argued that further research on the intrapersonal and situational conditions under which discrimination occurs was necessary in order to understand better the relationship between stereotypes and discrimination.

DOVIDIO et al. updated Brigham's analysis. Using meta-analytic techniques they considered how different aspects of stereotypes and prejudice relate to different types of interracial behaviours. Overall only modest, but consistent, relationships between racial stereotypes, prejudice, and discrimination were reported. Dovidio et al. suggested that it might be productive to consider how different aspects of stereotypes and prejudice relate to one another and predict discrimination. Accordingly they considered the moderating role of two dimensions on the interrelationships between stereotypes and behaviours. Greater correspondence of stereotypes, attitudes, and behaviours on the spontaneous-deliberative dimension produced stronger relationships among those phenomena. The affective-cognitive dimension was less influential. The usefulness of individual differences in stereotyping as a predictor of interracial behaviours is also questioned.

MACKIE & SMITH advocated an integrated theoretical approach to understanding the dissociation between stereotyping, prejudice, and discrimination. The relations among cognitions about, evaluations of, and behaviours toward social objects are a recurrent theme across a number of domains in social psychology. Accordingly, Mackie & Smith considered what the study of intergroup relations, and hence discrimination, can learn from the conceptualization of these relationships in other domains. They considered attitude–behaviour relations, impression formation research, approaches to self-knowledge, self-evaluation and self-expression, close relationships research, and norms and normative processes. Bringing together the implications from these domains Mackie & Smith suggested a number of applied and theoretical implications for intergroup relations, which await research. This is an important paper not only for research on discrimination but for social psychology more generally. Mackie & Smith did not argue that they have developed a complete and coherent social psychological theory of intergroup relations. Rather they argued that their approach is more general, and that an adequate theory of intergroup relations would essentially have to be an adequate theory of all aspects of social psychology. Such a theory is not in sight but the integrative approach taken by Mackie & Smith offers suggestions for the kinds of underlying principles and processes that may be central to such a theory.

LUCY JOHNSTON

See also Prejudice at work, Stereotype

Disengagement theory

Bengston, Vern L. and K. Warner Schaie (editors), *Handbook of Theories of Aging*, New York: Springer, 1998

Cavan, Ruth R. *et al.*, *Personal Adjustment in Old Age*, Chicago: Science Research Associates, 1949

Cavan, Ruth S., "Self and Role in Adjustment during Old Age" in *Human Behavior and Social Processes*, edited by Arnold Marshall Rose, Boston: Houghton Mifflin, 1962

Cumming, Elaine and William E. Henry, *Growing Old: The Process of Disengagement*, New York: Basic Books, 1961

Diamond, Timothy, *Making Gray Gold: Narratives of Nursing Home Care*, Chicago: University of Chicago Press, 1992

Havighurst, Robert J. and Ruth Albrecht, *Older People*, New York: Longman, 1953

Hochschild, Arlie Russell, *The Unexpected Community: Portrait of an Old Age Subculture*, revised edition, Berkeley: University of California Press, 1978

Lemon, Bruce W., Vern L. Bengston and James A. Peterson, "An Exploration of the Activity Theory of Aging: Activity Types and Life Satisfaction Among In-movers to a Retirement Community", *Journal of Gerontology*, 27/4 (1972): 511–23

Pearsall, Marilyn (editor), *The Other within Us: Feminist Explorations of Women and Aging*, Boulder, Colorado: Westview Press, 1997

Riley, Matilda White, Robert L. Kahn and Anne Foner (editors), *Age and Structural Lag: Society's Failure to Provide Meaningful Opportunities in Work, Family, and Leisure*, New York: Wiley, 1994

Thompson, Edward H. Jr (editor), *Older Men's Lives*, Thousand Oaks, California: Sage, 1994

It is difficult to conceive of a discussion of disengagement that does not begin by considering the work of CUMMING & HENRY. Pioneers in the field of gerontology, as well as the original proponents of disengagement theory, Cumming & Henry argued that a decline in social involvement plays an integral role in the process of ageing. According to disengagement theory, older individuals not only withdraw from others but also become inured to the prevailing norms. These companion tendencies are inevitable and natural. Disengagement consequently serves the needs of society and the individual alike. The odds that intergenerational tensions will grow and multiply are sharply reduced through the isolation of the elderly; the individual prepares for his or her own death by eliminating or reducing ties to others.

Disengagement theory has sometimes been described as an inaugural effort to develop a formal theory of ageing. Earlier attempts to derive a systematic explanation for the behaviour of the elderly generally reflected the "common-sense theory" that was promulgated by CAVAN et al. and HAVIGHURST & ALBRECHT. In direct opposition to disengagement, common-sense theory holds that isolation among the aged is both unnecessary and avoidable. Older individuals stand fully capable of remaining active, albeit in roles that are different from the ones that dominated their lives during early adulthood and the middle years.

Just as the proponents of disengagement critiqued the ideas of their common-sense predecessors and contemporaries, so a number of analysts responded to Cumming & Henry throughout the 1960s and 1970s. CAVAN and LEMON, BENGSTON & PETERSON, for example, carried forward the major propositions of common-sense theory in their work on activity and life satisfaction among the elderly. From the activity perspective, disengagement is a condition that is imposed upon senior citizens. It is the younger members of society who choose to distance themselves from their elders rather than vice versa. Far from being mutually beneficial to society and the individual, disengagement has negative effects on the lives of the elderly.

The qualitative research that HOCHSCHILD carried out among residents of Merrill Court, a housing project for working-class senior citizens, also sought to refute the premises of disengagement. Given the opportunity to socialize and interact with others in meaningful ways, Hochschild argued, the subjects of her study were eminently capable of remaining deeply engaged in the subculture that they had helped to create and maintain. Work, although voluntary and unpaid, nevertheless served as an important source of social identity for the individuals who lived in Merrill Court.

More recently, DIAMOND has provided a thoughtful account of the daily rituals that attend life and work in a nursing home. His book, based upon field research that he conducted while employed as a nursing assistant in several different facilities in the Chicago area, captures the personal side of one of the major growth industries in the US. Healthcare for the institutionalized elderly constitutes the "gold" to be mined in an ageing capitalistic society. Diamond alternately focuses on the residents and staff in these homes. Generally less able to initiate action and behave with autonomy than the individuals studied by Lemon and his colleagues or Hochschild, many of the residents with whom Diamond interacted were quick to convey dissatisfaction with their lives. The theoretical framework to which Diamond most often refers is ethnographic rather than gerontological in its orientation. Even so, his descriptions of enforced passivity among the residents of the homes, and the extent to which they were expected to relinquish control over the most fundamental of decisions, contradicts the assumption that disengagement occurs on a joint basis.

A volume of essays edited by THOMPSON explores the links between gender and ageing. The chief focus in each one of the essays is upon the challenges that elderly men face in their daily lives. Religious beliefs, ties to siblings or friends, and the division of labour are but a few of the topics that the authors of the essays scrutinize. Descriptive information and inferential statistics are used to develop an empirical foundation for the view that members of the male gender have remained largely "invisible" in the field of gerontology

Of greatest concern to PEARSALL, on the other hand, is the topic of women and ageing. Each one of the essays in Pearsall's book addresses a unique set of concerns, but a common thread is their emphasis on a feminist viewpoint. Like Diamond, the authors of the essays frequently rely on an experiential approach to their topic and pay minimal attention to the formal theories that have helped to shape the field of gerontology. And like Diamond, a number of the authors implicitly reject the notion that disengagement ought to be regarded as a mutual process. The essays by Agosin and Greer will hold special interest for readers who wish to learn more about cross-cultural perspectives on women and ageing.

RILEY, KAHN & FONER ponder the ramifications of two types of social changes that have affected the elderly in industrial and postindustrial societies. One consists of technological advances, including those found in the field of medicine, that have yielded a longer and more active life for many senior citizens. The other, clearly related to the first, is the increase in the number and proportion of old people in the population. The "lag" to which the three authors refer denotes the period of time between the point at which changes become apparent and the point at which social mechanisms for dealing with change begin to operate effectively. The thesis that Kahn, Foner & Riley advance rests on the assumption that social structures ought to be brought in line with the expectations and talents of older individuals rather than the other way around. Tacitly rejected is the idea that the elderly can and should withdraw from society.

Last but far from least, BENGSTON & SCHAIE review the assumptions and implications of the key theories that have emerged in gerontology during recent decades. Newcomers to the field of gerontology will find this source a boon to their efforts to place disengagement theory in the appropriate intellectual and historical context. Though not totally jargon free, the book is notable for its accessibility. Written in a down-to-earth style, it should mitigate the initial challenge of mastering the substantive aspects of the various theoretical perspectives.

SUZANNE MAURER

See also Age stratification, Ageism, Gerontology

Distribution of income

Atkinson, A.B., "On the Measurement of Inequality" in *Wealth, Income and Inequality: Selected Readings*, edited by Atkinson, Harmondsworth: Penguin, 1973

Atkinson, A.B., "Seeking to Explain the Distribution of Income" in *New Inequalities: The Changing Distribution of Income and Wealth in the United Kingdom*, edited by John Hills, Cambridge and New York: Cambridge University Press, 1996

Fields, Gary S., *Poverty, Inequality, and Development*, Cambridge and New York: Cambridge University Press, 1980

Gottschalk, P. and T. Smeeding, "Cross-National Comparisons of Earnings and Income Inequality", *Journal of Economic Literature*, 35/2 (1997): 633–88

Gregg, P. and J. Wadsworth, "More Work in Fewer Households?" in *New Inequalities: The Changing Distribution of Income and Wealth in the United Kingdom*, edited by John Hills, Cambridge and New York: Cambridge University Press, 1996

Johnson, P. and S. Webb, "Explaining the Growth in UK Income Inequality 1979–1988", *Economic Journal*, 103/417 (1993): 429–35

Klausen, S., "Growth and Well-being: Introducing Distribution-weighted Growth Rates to Reevaluate US

Postwar Economic Economic Performance", *Review of Income and Wealth*, series 40 (1994): 251–72

Kuznets, S., "Economic Growth and Income Inequality", *American Economic Review*, 45 (1955): 1–28

Levy, F. and R. Murnane, "US Earnings Levels and Earnings Inequality: A Review of Recent Trends and Proposed Explanations", *Journal of Economic Literature*, 30/3 (1992): 1333–81

Mookherjee, D. and A. Shorrocks, "A Decomposition Analysis of the Trend in UK Income Inequality", *Economic Journal*, 92 (1982): 886–902

Pen, J., *Income Distribution*, London: Allen Lane, 1971; extract reprinted as "A Parade of Dwarfs (and a Few Giants)" in *Wealth, Income and Inequality: Selected Readings*, edited by A.B. Atkinson, Harmondsworth: Penguin, 1973

A long established view of income distribution was proposed by KUZNETS. This related the pattern of income inequality to levels of industrialization. Using a two-sector model, Kuznets suggested that the proportion of labour employed in each of the sectors, the mean income, and the level of inequality between the sectors, accounted for overall inequality of income in the economy. Thus, with a higher proportion of labour employed in the industrial sector inequality increased, but as the economy matured the overall inequality of income would begin to fall. This move from an increasing to a gradually decreasing level of inequality is known as the Kuznets curve.

However, it is now clear that this did not occur and a number of authors have measured the extent to which incomes are highly unequal, some of which are in the papers following. A classic presentation of income inequality is provided by PEN. This requires the reader to imagine an hour-long parade where everyone marches by with their height proportional to their income. Those in debt march upside down and then begin to rise, but very slowly, such that after half an hour the marchers are about four feet tall. Not until 57 minutes have passed do the marchers begin to be seriously tall and the last to go by are so tall "their heads disappear into the clouds and probably they themselves do not know how tall they are" (p.53, Pen, 1971).

More quantitative approaches to the measurement of income distribution are used to compare the degree of inequality, either of distributions based on different definitions of income or between groups, perhaps countries. ATKINSON (1973) is an adaptation of an earlier paper and includes a non-mathematical summary. This paper discusses the importance of ranking distributions and challenges the simplistic metrics such as variance and Gini coefficient. The analysis is presented in terms of the familiar Lorenz curve and notes that in some cases there is no ambiguity, such as if the Lorenz curves for two distributions do not intersect. However, if this is not the case, the degree of inequality cannot be compared without introducing values about the distributions. This introduces the concept of an equally distributed equivalent level of income – that is, the level of income per head which if equally distributed would give the same level of social welfare as the actual distribution. Clearly, this requires decisions about the weight attached by society to inequality in the distribution of income.

GREGG & WADSWORTH investigate the changes in income distribution in the UK, finding a steady long-term rise in inequality, not necessarily related to unemployment levels. The particular emphasis is on the change in the distribution of work across households. Change in the composition of households due to more transitional family units is a partial explanation. But more importantly, the increase in employment opportunities has been predominantly in part-time employment, favouring a second income earner rather than full-time jobs for those in nonworking households.

The need to recognize distributional corrections to the UK growth rate is addressed and the relationship between growth and income distribution as noted by Kuznets recurs throughout this literature. KLAUSEN integrates two equal weights indices and two poverty weights indices to integrate distributional correction into measures of economic growth and performance, suggesting that this may alter policy priorities. These indices more accurately reflect changes in welfare than the standard income growth measures and rely on generally available data in many countries. The results of this adjustment significantly revise downwards the growth performance in the US during the 1980s while showing improvement in wellbeing in the 1960s.

Another of the stylized facts in the field of income distribution now being disputed is that increases or decreases in inequality follow a trend. Rather, the evidence is of events that cause a change in their direction, which then revert back to previous levels. MOOKHERJEE & SHORROCKS consider the structural influences on income distribution. They find a number of individual factors that contribute to a change in inequality, although these often contradict each other. Therefore the overall effect on aggregate inequality is hard to quantify, particularly when the single factors are working in opposite directions.

FIELDS is a comprehensive text on the methods of measuring income inequality. The central theme is to explore the distributional aspects of economic development in poor countries. The text includes a number of case studies to illustrate empirical applications for a number of developing countries. A comparison of different approaches to the decomposition of income inequality provides details of techniques and a discussion of the appropriateness of each, with examples of specific papers in the area.

The essay by ATKINSON (1996) discusses the theory of income distribution, although one laments the lack of an overall framework. The link between production economics and the theory of factor prices with the distribution of individual and household incomes is still incomplete. However, the essay does explain the recent patterns of income distribution, specifically addressing the role of the major sources of increasing inequality. This includes the effects of earnings differences but also the effect of levels of capital income, the role of the corporate sector and of financial institutions, and the distributional impact of the state.

Two very valuable surveys cover the US and the OECD countries. LEVY & MURNANE outline the changes in earnings in the US over a 40-year period, showing increasing inequality in wage income, largely attributable to differences in educational level. The disparity between skilled and nonskilled wages was the major determinant of aggregate inequality. GOTTSCHALK & SMEEDING focus on household income rather than individual wages in their cross-country comparison and note the equalizing effect of central wage setting and union power in Europe.

Further evidence of the impact of government policy on the distribution of household income in the UK is examined by JOHNSON & WEBB using a simulation model. Changes to the personal tax and benefits system are found to have a significant effect, providing a further explanation for the rise in levels of income inequality.

JENNIFER PIESSE

Division of labour, economic

Babbage, Charles, *On the Economy of Machinery and Manufactures*, London: Knight, and Philadelphia: Carey and Lea, 1832; 4th edition London: John Murray, 1846, reprinted New York: Kelley, 1963

Baumgardner, J. R., "The Division of Labor, Local Markets, and Worker Organization", *Journal of Political Economy*, 96/3 (1988): 509–27

Becker, Gary S., *A Treatise on the Family*, Cambridge, Massachusetts: Harvard University Press, 1981

Becker, Gary S. and K.M. Murphy, "The Division of Labor, Coordination Costs, and Knowledge", *Quarterly Journal of Economics*, 107/4 (1992): 1137–60

Houthakker, M., "Economics and Biology: Specialization and Speciation", *Kyklos*, 9 (1956): 181–89

Kim, S., "Labor Specialization and the Extent of the Market", *Journal of Political Economy*, 97 (1989): 692–705

Locay, L., "Economic Development and the Division of Production between Households and Markets", *Journal of Political Economy*, 98/5, part 1 (1990): 965–82

Marshall, Alfred, *Principles of Economics*, 9th edition, edited by C.W. Guillebaud, 2 vols, London and New York: Macmillan, 1961 (1st edition 1890)

Ricardo, David, *Principles of Political Economy and Taxation*, introduction by Donald Winch, London: Dent, and New York: Dutton, 1973 (1st edition 1817; 3rd edition 1821)

Rosen, S., "Substitution and the Division of Labor," *Economica*, 45 (1978): 235–50

Rosen, S., "Specialization and Human Capital," *Journal of Labor Economics*, 1/1 (1983): 43–49

Smith, Adam, *An Inquiry into the Nature and Causes of the Wealth of Nations*, edited by Kathryn Sutherland, Oxford and New York: Oxford University Press, 1993 (first published 1776)

Stigler, George, "The Division of Labor Is Limited by the Extent of the Market", *Journal of Political Economy*, 59/3 (1951): 185–93

Stigler, George, "The Successes and Failures of Professor Smith", *Journal of Political Economy*, 84 (1976): 1199–1213

Yang, Xiaokai and Yew-Kwang Ng, *Specialization and Economic Organization*, Amsterdam: North Holland, 1993

Yang, Xiaokai and Siang Ng, "Specialization and Division of Labour: A Survey" in *Increasing Return and Economic Analysis*, edited by Kenneth J. Arrow, Yew-Kwang Ng and Xiaokai Yang, London: Macmillan, 1997

Young, Allyn, "Increasing Returns and Economic Progress", *Economic Journal*, 38 (1928): 527–42

The growing literature on specialization and the division of labour is classified here in three parts. First, the classical works on specialization and division of labour are reviewed. Second, several papers are included that resist the Marshallian neoclassical mainstream of marginal analysis and try to keep the classical mainstream thinking on division of labour alive. The third part consists of papers based on marginal analysis and inframarginal analysis of division of labour.

SMITH proposed the Smith theorem: the mainspring of economic progress is the development of the division of labour; division of labour is limited by the extent of the market, which is determined by transportation conditions. RICARDO proposed the concept of exogenous comparative advantage. BABBAGE argued that the division of labour can save on learning and training costs by avoiding duplicated learning. Chapters 8–12 of MARSHALL tries to distinguish external economies of scale that are generated by the social division of labour from internal economies of scale for a firm.

Young is "the zenith of the analysis of the connection between specialization and economic development" (ROSEN 1983). YOUNG drew the distinction between economies of scale and network effects of the division of labour and proposed the Young theorem: "not only division of labor is dependent on the extent of the market, but also the extent of the market is determined by the level of division of labor." He proposed a research agenda to analyse individuals' decisions in choosing their patterns of specialization, which determine the level of division of labour for society as a whole. STIGLER (1951, 1976) tried to get mainstream economics back to Smith's track. He complained:

> almost no one used or now uses the theory of division of labor, for the excellent reason that there is scarcely such a theory ... there is no standard, operable theory to describe what Smith argued to be the mainspring of economic progress. Yet there is no evidence, so far as I know, of any serious advance in the theory of the subject since his [Smith] time, and specialization is not an integral part of the modern theory of production. (Stigler 1976)

HOUTHAKKER drew a parallel between evolution of division of labour and evolution of species, and stated "there is hardly any part of economics that would not be advanced by a further analysis of specialization".

BECKER, BECKER & MURPHY, and ROSEN (1978 and 1983) developed formal decision models of endogenous specialization, using inframarginal analysis (linear and nonlinear programming) to investigate individuals' decisions in choosing their patterns of specialization. BAUMGARDNER, KIM and LOCAY developed general equilibrium models of endogenous specialization, using marginal analysis to investigate the trade-offs that determine the equilibrium level of specialization. YANG & S. NG have surveyed the inframarginal analysis of network of division of labour. YANG & Y.-K. NG used many general equilibrium models to resurrect the spirit of classical mainstream economics in a modern body of inframarginal analysis. Inframarginal analysis is a total cost-benefit analysis across corner solutions in addition to marginal analysis of each corner solution.

XIAOKIA YANG

See also Division of labour, political

Division of labour, political

Alchian, Armen A. and Harold Demsetz, "Production, Informations Costs, and Economic Organization", *American Economic Review*, 62/5 (1972): 777–95

Ames, Edward and Nathan Rosenberg, "The Progressive Division and Specialization of Industries", *Journal of Development Studies*, 1/4 (1964–65): 363–83

Aquinas, Thomas (with portions attributed to Ptolemy of Lucca), *On the Government of Rulers: De Regimine Principum*, translated by James M. Blythe, Philadelphia: University of Pennsylvania Press, 1997 (written 13th–14th centuries)

Aristotle, *The Politics*, translated by H. Rackham, London: Heinemann, and Cambridge, Massachusetts: Harvard University Press, 1932 (Loeb edition; many reprints [written 4th century BC])

Arrow, Kenneth J., "The Economic Implications of Learning by Doing", *Review of Economic Studies*, 29/3 (1962): 155–73

Babbage, Charles, *On the Economy of Machinery and Manufactures*, 4th edition, London: Routledge / Thoemmes, 1993 (originally published 1835)

Becattini, Giacomo, *Mercato e forze locali: il distretto industriale*, Bologna: Mulino, 1987

Becker, Gary S. and Kevin M. Murphy, "The Division of Labour, Coordination Costs, and Knowledge", *Quarterly Journal of Economics*, 107/4 (1992): 1137–60

Cattaneo, Carlo, "Del pensiero come principio d'economia pubblica", [On thought as a principle of Political Economy] in *Scritti economici*, edited by Alberto Bertolino, Florence: Le Monnier, 1956 (originally published 1861)

Coase, R.H., "The Nature of the Firm", *Economica*, 4/5 (1937): 386–405

Dunoyer, Charles, *De la liberté du travail, ou simple exposé des conditions dans lesquelles les forces humaines s'exercent avec le plus de puissance*, Paris: Guillaumin, 1845

Durkheim, Emile, *The Division of Labor in Society*, New York: Free Press, 1933; new translation Free Press, 1984 (French edition 1893)

Ferguson, Adam, *An Essay on the History of Civil Society*, edited by Duncan Forbes, Edinburgh: Edinburgh University Press, 1966 (originally published 1767)

Gioja, Melchiorre, *Nuovo prospetto delle scienze economiche*, 6 vols, Milan: Gio Pirotta, 1815–17

Groenewegen, Peter, Division of Labour entry in *The New Palgrave: A Dictionary of Economics*, edited by John Eatwell, Murray Milgate and Peter Newman, vol. 1, London: Macmillan, and New York: Stockton Press, 1987

Groenewegen, Peter, "Division of Labour" in *The Elgar Companion to Classical Economics*, edited by Heinz D. Kurz and Neri Salvadori, vol. 1, Cheltenham, Gloucestershire: Elgar, 1998

Hermann, Friedrich, *Staatswirthschaftliche Untersuchungen*, Munich: Fleischmann, 1870 (1st edition 1832)

Landesmann, Michael and Roberto Scazzieri, "The Production Process: Description and Analysis" in their *Production and Economic Dynamics*, Cambridge and New York: Cambridge University Press, 1996

Lauderdale, James Maitland, *An Inquiry into the Nature and Origin of Public Wealth and into the Means and Causes of Its Increase*, Edinburgh: Constable, 1804; reprinted New York: Kelley, 1966

Lazerson, Mark and Gianni Lorenzoni, "The Firms That Feed Industrial Districts: A Return to the Italian Source", *Industrial and Corporate Change*, 8/2 (1999): 235–66

Marx, Karl, *Capital*, vol. 1: *A Critical Analysis of Capitalist Production*, London and New York: Penguin, 1976 (German edition 1867)

North, Douglass C., *Institutions, Institutional Change and Economic Performance*, Cambridge and New York: Cambridge University Press, 1990

Pasinetti, Luigi L., *Structural Economic Dynamics: A Theory of the Economic Consequences of Human Learning*, Cambridge and New York: Cambridge University Press, 1993

Petty, William, "Another Essay in Political Arithmetick Concerning the City of London" in *The Economic Writings of Sir William Petty*, edited by Charles Henry Hull, London: Routledge / Thoemmes, 1997 (written 1683)

Plato, *The Republic*, translated by Paul Shorey, 2 vols, London: Heinemann, and Cambridge, Massachusetts: Harvard University Press, 1930–35 (Loeb edition; several reprints [written 4th century BC])

Poni, Carlo, "Flexible Production: The Strategies of the Lyons Silk Merchants in the Eighteenth Century" in *A World of Possibilities*, edited by Charles F. Sabel and Jonathan Zeitlin, 1997

Rae, John, *Statement of Some New Principles on the Subject of Political Economy*, New York: Kelley, 1964 (originally published 1834)

Rosenberg, Nathan, *"Adam Smith on the Division of Labour: Two Views or One?"*, Economica, *new series*, 32/2 (1965): 127–39

Sabel, Charles F. and Jonathan Zeitlin (editors), *A World of Possibilities: Flexibility and Mass Production in Western Industrialization*, Cambridge and New York: Cambridge University Press, 1997

Say, Jean-Baptiste, *A Treatise on Political Economy; or, The Production, Distribution, and Consumption of Wealth*, New York: Kelley, 1971 (French edition 1803)

Scazzieri, Roberto, *A Theory of Production: Tasks, Processes, and Technical Practices*, Oxford: Clarendon Press, and New York: Oxford University Press, 1993

Scazzieri, Roberto, "A Theory of Resilient Flow-Fund Linkages" in *Bioeconomics and Sustainability: Essays in*

Honour of Nicholas Georgescu-Roegen, edited by Kozo Mayumi and John M. Gowdy, Cheltenham, Gloucestershire: Elgar, 1999

Sen, Amartya, *Commodities and Capabilities*, Amsterdam: North Holland, 1985

Serra, Antonio, *Breve trattato delle cause che possono far abbondare li regni d'oro e d'argento dove non sono miniere*, Calabria: Mediocredito regionale della Calabria, 1985 (originally published 1613)

Smith, Adam, *An Inquiry into the Nature and Causes of the Wealth of Nations*, edited by Edwin Cannan, Chicago: University of Chicago Press, 1976 (first published 1776)

Stigler, George, "The Division of Labour Is Limited by the Extent of the Market", *Journal of Political Economy*, 59/3 (1951): 85–93

Storch, Henri, *Cours d'économie politique; ou, exposition des principes que déterminent la prospérité des nations*, Paris: Aillaud, 1823

Turgot, Anne Robert Jacques, *Observations sur le mémoire de M. de Saint-Peravy en faveur de l'impôt indirect*, in *Oeuvres de Mr Turgot*, 9 vols, Paris: Delance, 1808–11: vol. 4 (manuscript 1768)

Valeriani, Luigi, *Discorso apologetico*, Bologna: Marsigli, 1817

Wakefield, Edward Gibbon, "Commentary" in Adam Smith's *An Inquiry into the Nature and Causes of the Wealth of Nations*, 4 vols, edited by Edward Gibbon Wakefield, London: Knight, 1843

Xenophon, *Cyropaedia*, translated by Walter Miller *et al.*, London: Heinemann, and New York: Macmillan, 1941: vol. 2 (Loeb edition; several reprints [written 4th century BC])

Yang, Xiaokai and Yew-Kwang Ng, *Specialization and Economic Organization: A New Classical Microeconomic Framework*, Amsterdam: North Holland, 1993

Young, Allyn, "Increasing Returns and Economic Progress", *Economic Journal*, 38 (1928): 527–42

PLATO, ARISTOTLE, and XENOPHON are among the originators of the intellectual tradition according to which the (social) division of labour is seen as essential to any socioeconomic setup based upon the effective use of human capabilities. In particular, Plato considered the division of labour in terms of a political and economic constitution in which social functions are distributed in accordance with the human virtues, thus conforming to the different possibilities disclosed to individuals by the education process to which they have been exposed. Such a perspective led Plato to argue that "more things are produced, and better and more easily when one man performs one task according to his nature, at the right moment, and at leisure from other occupations" (p.153). Aristotle took a different view, and considered the division of labour as a necessary consequence of the morphological variety of production processes, while acknowledging that the practice of "virtue" in a productive activity may require a teleological rather than an instrumentalist approach to human work. For example, Aristotle maintains that "wellbeing" resulting from "actions done in relation to external objects" (production) is primarily associated with "the master craftsmen who direct the action by their thoughts" (p.551). Xenophon considered, in

particular, the relationship between division of labour and the decomposition of the production process into specialized stages (technical division of labour). In this connection, he maintained that "he who devotes himself to a very highly specialized line of work is bound to do it in the best possible manner" (p.333). AQUINAS, writing at the close of the 13th century, called attention to the division of labour as an effective means of increasing the detailed knowledge of the "necessities of life", which is best obtained when different people "might be occupied in finding out different things" (p.61).

SERRA and PETTY (both writing in the 17th century) followed up the idea that the subdivision of tasks within a workshop makes the internal organization of production more effective. The contribution of TURGOT is noteworthy for its emphasis on division of labour as a coordination device by which a variety of individual preferences may lead to a coherent socioeconomic setup based upon exchange and market institutions.

SMITH provides a comprehensive analytical framework in which heterogeneous capabilities and differentiated needs are coordinated by means of division of labour, and exchange. Distinctive features of Smith's contribution are: (a) the idea that division of labour arises from a natural propensity to communicate and exchange, rather than from the natural inequality of human capabilities; (b) the consideration of the process by which specialization leads to acquired talents, and of how these may in turn be conducive to further advantages arising from division of labour; (c) the analysis of the mutual dependence between specialization of productive activities and evolution of needs, which leads to the association between an increasing division of labour and an increasing size of the market. In particular, Smith maintained that the advantages of division of labour in increasing productivity are due to the interaction of "three different circumstances":

> the increase of dexterity in every particular workman; [. . .] the saving of the time which is commonly lost in passing from one species of work to another; [. . .] the invention of a great number of machines which facilitate and abridge labour, and enable one man to do the work of many (p.17).

(*See also* GROENEWEGEN 1987, 1998.)

Smith also expressed some concern as to the ultimate consequences of technical division of labour upon the inventive ability of human beings. This issue was taken up by LAUDERDALE, who stressed that division of labour could make invention and innovation more difficult, by diminishing the human capability to make comparisons and to generalize.

A related but distinct strand of literature has focused upon the social division of labour and its implications for the emergence of social order. FERGUSON called attention to the possibility of cognitive and moral degradation associated with the narrowing of human tasks in modern civil society. DURKHEIM subsequently took up this issue in his analysis of the mutual influence of social differentiation and social coordination. More recently, ROSENBERG has considered the relationship between the technical and social division of labour, from the standpoint of the processes by which social and technological knowledge may be accumulated. In particular, Rosenberg has shown the variety of inventive activities, and the degree to which different inventions require "differing amounts of technical competence, analytical sophistication and creative and synthesizing intellect" (p.131).

The above conceptual background has been developed along a number of distinct avenues. First, SAY's consideration of the division of labour in intellectual activities led to the analysis of so-called "immaterial production" by STORCH and DUNOYER, and to an explicit distinction between the cognitive and the material factors by which labour productivity may be increased, as discussed by RAE and CATTANEO.

Second, certain authors, such as GIOJA and WAKEFIELD, considered division of labour to be a special case of the more general principle (called "association of works" or "simple cooperation") according to which cooperation may be an advantage when simultaneous efforts are required to achieve a given goal, or when capabilities and tools would otherwise be underutilized.

Third, the analysis of technical division of labour led to the discovery that an effective subdivision of tasks requires a certain minimum size of the technical unit, and is only compatible with scale variations by discrete jumps – an aspect considered by Gioja, BABBAGE, HERMANN and MARX. Contrary to this view, VALERIANI maintained, in a discussion with Gioja, that scale is conceptually independent of size, and that extensive division of labour may be introduced even within a set of interrelated and small production units.

Fourth, Alfred Marshall laid emphasis on division of labour achieved within networks of producers in the same location (industrial districts) and introduced the concept of external economies (cost-reducing processes derived from feedback interaction).

Subsequent literature has led to a concentration of attention on the following set of interrelated issues: (a) the connection between increasing effectiveness of economic interaction (increasing returns) and accumulation of knowledge (learning) associated with division of labour and specialization (considered by ARROW); (b) the division and specialization of industries deriving from decomposition of existing technical processes and emergence of new combinations (discussed by YOUNG, STIGLER, and AMES & ROSENBERG); and (c) the relationship between technical division of labour (splitting of tasks and fabrication stages) and the relational framework governing economic interaction in localized social networks (analysed by BECATTINI, and by SABEL & ZEITLIN).

Recent literature has highlighted the connection between division of labour, human capabilities, and transaction costs.

The relationship between capabilities and division of labour has been considered by examining in particular: (a) the allocation of rights and entitlements as a condition influencing the use of human capabilities (the subject of SEN); (b) the association between the coordination pattern of capabilities and that of tasks and materials-in-process within any given form of productive organization (covered by LANDESMANN & SCAZZIERI); and (c) the characteristics of technical knowledge, which has been described as a virtual space, encompassing both the technical practices of which producers have direct knowledge, and technical practices yet to be discovered (but compatible with the existing cognitive structure) (SCAZZIERI 1993 and 1999).

Other contributions have examined the relationship between division of labour and transaction costs. In particular, NORTH has developed the analytical framework introduced by COASE, by considering alternative legal and institutional arrangements by which transaction costs may be reduced and division of labour increased. ALCHIAN & DEMSETZ have argued that "partitioning and specialization" of private property rights are at the root of effective coordination, both across markets, and within individual firms. YANG & NG have examined alternative patterns of division of labour, and have discussed in particular the distinct hierarchies of productive activities that division of labour may bring about under different historical and organizational conditions.

An interest in the dynamics of human capabilities resulting from social and economic interaction has led certain authors to highlight the relationship between division of labour and the learning process. In particular, the early discussion concerning the influence of division of labour upon human capabilities (see above) has been given a new turn by authors who have argued that, under favourable conditions, specialization of tasks and subdivision of materials-in-process, far from tending to lead to a degradation of capabilities, may in fact encourage "creative cooperation" and the growth of social knowledge (an aspect discussed by PONI, and by LAZERSON & LORENZONI).

In this connection, BECKER & MURPHY have revisited Smith's analysis of the division of labour and have maintained that: (a) specialization is likely to increase until "the higher productivity from a greater division of labor is just balanced by the greater costs of coordinating a larger number of more specialized workers" (p.1157); (b) optimal division of labour increases as greater knowledge is available; and (c) division of labour induces a partition of the economic system into a certain number of "lineages", each lineage being "a 'team' of teachers, students, and workers in different periods who combine to produce consumer goods" (p.1154). It is then shown that, in each lineage, teaching associated with a lower teacher/student ratio (less intensive teaching) is "closer" to the training of workers who are directly involved in the production of consumer goods. In this case, a remarkable relationship is discovered between the internal structure of the education process within any given lineage and the relative position of that lineage in the social division of labour.

The relationship between division of labour and economic coordination is also analysed by PASINETTI, who maintains that the simplified model of a "pure labour economy" (an economic system in which goods are produced by means of direct labour to the exclusion of capital) is sufficient for the identification of necessary conditions for the internal coherence of a set of interrelated economic activities. In particular, Pasinetti examines a situation in which "[e]ach individual is so specialized that he or she contributes to produce only one type of good or even only a fraction of a good. But his or her demand concerns all, or most of, the goods produced" (p.25). Under such circumstances, the prerequisites for economic coordination can be expressed in terms of a "fundamental macroeconomic condition" linking labour coefficients and consumption coefficients, quite independently of an explicit consideration of the internal complexity (and "roundaboutness") of each production process. Such a discovery suggests a modern analytical formulation of Smith's conceptual framework, by introducing a distinction between: (a) conditions for an effective division of labour in terms of the "extent of the market" for consumer goods; and (b) prerequisites for the division of labour in terms of the available stocks of commodities and tools.

ROBERTO SCAZZIERI

Domestic violence

Cobbe, F.P., "Wife Torture in England", *Contemporary Review*, 32 (1878): 55–87

Dobash, R. Emerson and Russell Dobash, *Violence against Wives*, New York: Free Press, 1979; London: Open Books, 1980

Hanmer, Jalna, Sue Griffiths and David Jerwood, *Arresting Evidence: Domestic Violence and Repeat Victimisation*, London: Policing and Reducing Crime Unit, Home Office, 1999

Hearn, Jeff, *The Violences of Men*, London and Thousand Oaks, California: Sage, 1998

Hester, Marianne and Lorraine Radford, *Domestic Violence and Child Contact Arrangements in England and Denmark*, Bristol: Policy Press, 1996

Kelly, Liz, *Surviving Sexual Violence*, Cambridge: Polity Press, and Minneapolis: University of Minnesota Press, 1988

Mama, Amina, *The Hidden Struggle: Statutory and Voluntary Sector Responses to Violence against Black Women in the Home*, London: London Race and Housing Research Unit, 1989; Concord, Massachusetts: Paul, 1996

Mullender, Audrey, *Rethinking Domestic Violence: The Social Work and Probation Response*, London and New York: Routledge, 1996

Sheppard, Melanie and Ellen Pence (editors), *Coordinating Community Responses to Domestic Violence: Lessons from Duluth and Beyond*, Thousand Oaks, California: Sage, 1999

Stark, Evan and Anne Flitcraft, *Women at Risk: Domestic Violence and Women's Health*, Thousand Oaks, California: Sage, 1996

DOBASH & DOBASH were the first to publish in a new wave of scholarship on violence against women in the home by known men. Based on 109 interviews with women in Women's Aid refuges in Scotland, the book introduces the rediscovery of violence against wives in the 1970s, and describes theoretical approaches to violence in the home, criminological findings, the historical legacy of wives as appropriate victims, law and criminal justice. The experiential data is divided into themes that remain current today: becoming a wife; the violent event and marriage; staying, leaving, and returning; relatives, friends, and neighbours; the helping professions; the police and judicial responses; refuges; and other alternatives.

While the initial focus was on physical violence, KELLY interviewed women in depth who had and did not have experiences of rape, incest, and domestic violence. She explores current feminist debates and develops the idea of a continuum of sexual violence. The aim is to explore the connection between sexuality and male violence, to demonstrate the definitions, resistance, and coping strategies of women, and to suggest ways to end violence. This popular book explains issues of method and methodology in feminist research.

HEARN further develops the connection between heterosexuality and violence through an examination of the violence of men against women in domestic settings. This is an empirical study of 60 men and the 256 agencies with which they had contact – primarily criminal justice, but also legal, physical, and mental health; housing, social, and welfare; and voluntary agencies offering men's programmes. Themes are how men talk about and account for their violence; the contexts in which this occurs, particularly the heterosexual context; the responses of agencies and their organizational dynamics; how men move away from violence; and how change in men may be reconceptualized. This text has both depth and breath and it concludes with key issues for theory, politics, policy, and practice.

MAMA explores the domestic violence experiences of African, Asian, and Afro-Caribbean women. The aim of her in-depth study is to examine the difference that being black makes to experiences of domestic violence and the receipt of statutory and voluntary services. She concludes that the experience for black women of violence in the home is compounded by the societal racism, state repression, and economic marginalization, forcing many women to tolerate high levels of abuse. Statutory agency responses are inadequate, if not hostile, to the needs of black women. Housing receives greatest attention, but also policing, civil and criminal law, immigration, and social services. The poorly resourced refuge or shelter movement, Women's Aid, is the primary source of effective support.

The belief that no previous generation had examined violence against women by men known to them was shattered as historical work, and particularly that of COBBE was rediscovered. Cobbe provides a 19th-century explanation of wife beating that remains relevant today. Beginning with a shocking title for her influential article, "Wife torture in England", she argues that wife torture continues because women are believed to be the property of men. In this economic and political analysis she identifies perpetrators as working class and calls on men of higher social classes in Parliament to legislate on behalf of women. Cobbe understood that all men benefit from the social subordination of women and feared that only the worst forms of abuse to women would be punished. State intervention in wife torture would find new ways to continue to support gendered social inequality.

At the end of the 20th century demands for change in institutional state practices are intensifying. MULLENDER provides a professionally oriented text for social work and probation practitioners with the aim of improving practice in response to domestic violence to women by men. The book begins with a discussion of terms, common prejudices, and misunderstandings; research evidence of incidence; theories of the causation of domestic violence and evidence of social work as part of the problem. Everyday and improved practice is presented for individual agencies with ways forward to include interagency initiatives. The basic thesis is that men should take responsibility for their abusive behaviour and that women should be listened to, believed, and empowered in order to develop appropriate professional intervention.

HANMER, GRIFFITHS & JERWOOD evaluate a new approach to policing domestic violence based on increasing interventions with each additional attendance to a call for assistance. The model does not depend upon arrest, although this is always possible provided a criminal offence or a breach of the peace occurs. Letters explaining policy and giving information are sent from the first attendance while follow-up visits and police car patrols are added to later call outs. This initiative, aimed at both the victimized woman and the abusing man, reduced repeat attendance while increasing the number of women seeking assistance and providing a consistent policing service. This conceptual model, with different interventions, could be applied to any statutory service.

HESTER & RADFORD examine the response to battered women in contested child custody civil court cases. The role of court mediation and judicial decisions in further endangering women is exposed through empirical research. This timely study demonstrates the connection between child and woman abuse and the difficulty that courts have in responding to male violence in ways that protect women and children from men when they have the joint status of husband/cohabitee and father. Best practice remains illusive.

STARK & FLITCRAFT present a comprehensive analysis of domestic violence and women's health, including child abuse. This, their latest book, offers both a thorough theoretical analysis and practical advice on how to achieve best practice. It begins with historical issues of the construction of psychological and social concepts and their unhelpful application to battered women. It draws on their own research studies and those of numerous others to explain health consequences and the dual trauma of coercive control and inappropriate mental health clinical interventions with battered women. They argue for a reformulation of trauma theory and for the adoption of advocacy and empowerment strategies.

SHEPPARD & PENCE edit a collection of 13 chapters on the Duluth model of community intervention in domestic violence. The eight key components of this influential approach are described in the first nine chapters. These are understanding power and control; developing policies, protocols, and networking among service providers; building monitoring and tracking systems; an advocacy programme for battered women; and a reeducation programme for battering men. The remaining chapters either explore developments and adaptations in jurisdictions outside the US – Australia, New Zealand, and the UK – or the difficult issues of responding to violence committed by women and to marital rape.

JALNA HANMER

See also Child abuse, Rape

Double bind

Bateson, Gregory, *Steps to an Ecology of Mind*, New York: Ballantine, and London: Intertext, 1972
Birdwhistell, Ray L., *Kinesics and Context: Essays on Body Motion Communication*, Philadelphia: University of Pennsylvania Press, 1970
Goldstein, Michael J. and Angus M. Strachan, "The Family and Schizophrenia" in *Family Interaction and Psychopathology: Theories, Methods, and Findings*, edited by Theodore Jacob, New York: Plenum, 1987
Helmersen, Per, *Family Interaction and Communication in Psychopathology: An Evaluation of Recent Perspectives*, New York: Academic Press, 1983
Jacob, Theodore and Steven Lessin, "Inconsistent Communication in Family Interaction", *Clinical Psychology Review*, 2 (1982): 295–309
Mehrabian, Albert, *Nonverbal Communication*, Chicago: Aldine Atherton, 1972
Scheflen, Albert E. and Alice Scheflen, *Body Language and Social Order: Communication as Behavioral Control*, Englewood Cliffs, New Jersey: Prentice Hall, 1972
Watzlawick, Paul, Janet Helmick Beavin and Don D. Jackson, *Pragmatics of Human Communication: A Study of Interactional Patterns, Pathologies, and Paradoxes*, New York: Norton, 1967

The most significant works on the concept of the double bind were published from the early 1960s to the late 1970s, and were theoretical rather than empirical in nature. BATESON, generally recognized as one of the strongest and earliest contributors to the concepts of systems theory and the double bind, was the first to coin the term "double bind" in a paper written with D.D. Jackson, J. Haley, and J.H. Weakland in 1956. *Steps to an Ecology of Mind*, a collection of presentations and essays written by Bateson, includes not only the 1956 "Toward a Theory of Schizophrenia", but a number of works that together provide an essential and comprehensive overview of Bateson's conceptual definitions and explanations for the double bind, alcohol abuse, and general systems theory. Bateson's theoretical approach is ethological, drawing primarily from the fields of genetics and biology rather than anthropology, and many of the examples used to illustrate his concepts in this book are drawn from animal and insect physiology/behaviour.

Bateson's work was the conceptual foundation for the research conducted by a number of scholars known as the Palo Alto group. Probably the most renowned work from that group is that of WATZLAWICK, BEAVIN & JACKSON. Their book is one of the definitive works pertaining to general systems theory and pragmatic communication, and contains a chapter specifically on paradoxical communication, including paradoxical injunctions (double bind), illustrated with several case studies. A chapter on paradox in psychotherapy suggests ways in which paradoxical injunctions can be used to treat schizophrenia (therapeutic double binds).

The notion that a double bind involves specifically a contradiction between verbal and nonverbal behaviours prompted a group of scholars from the Palo Alto perspective to focus particularly on nonverbal behaviour. These scholars are generally credited with the first systematic exploration of nonverbal behaviours. BIRDWHISTELL'S explorations of nonverbal behaviour used a frame-by-frame analysis of filmed interactions to construct his "linguistic-kinesic" approach to nonverbal behaviour, based on the microcultural analysis of Margaret Mead. Birdwhistell suggests that a family's public performance can be found in verbal communication, with the more private (and controlling) messages contained in nonverbal communication. He provides chapters on behaviour during family meals and a case study detailing tactile communication between a mother and her schizophrenic son to present extended examples of this idea. Other chapters offer a guide for how to collect and analyse nonverbal data. This book is probably the most significant of Birdwhistell's published works.

SCHEFLEN, a professor of psychiatry and a close colleague of Birdwhistell, also held an ethological view of the functions of nonverbal behaviour and was primarily interested in kinesics. In this book, Scheflen proposes that kinesics function to create not only social order among human groups, but also social deviancy. One such human group is, of course, the family, and the final chapters of the book address the double bind and its origins in family communication. This particular publication presents perhaps one of the clearest definitions of double bind and the conditions essential to create one. Scheflen uses a number of provocative (and sometimes graphic) anecdotal examples to illustrate the progress of social deviancy in various individuals, all the way from binding, to a double bind, to the point of psychotic and violent reactions to a double-bind situation.

The significance of MEHRABIAN's research lies primarily in his conception of a category of nonverbal behaviours labelled as "immediacy behaviours," and in his tests of communication conditions producing double binds. *Nonverbal Communication* reports some of the first empirical tests of the double bind, and from these studies, Mehrabian first concludes that contradictions in verbal and nonverbal communication are commonplace as an everyday form of communication (for example, sarcasm). Second, he suggests that only contradictory messages producing negative meaning, rather than positive meaning, are likely to lead to schizophrenia.

Following the work of Mehrabian, most of the empirical research of the double bind and its role in the creation of schizophrenia was conducted during the 1970s. Unfortunately, the majority of studies provided little support for the double bind, and the concept waned in popularity although it remains to this day a historically and heuristically significant theoretical contribution to areas such as family counselling and nonverbal communication. The empirical discreditation of the double bind is best summarized in the early to late 1980s overviews of research regarding both the double bind and deviant family communication in general, by Jacob & Lessin, Helmersen, and Goldstein & Strachan.

JACOB & LESSIN review a number of communication studies involving the encoding and decoding of nonverbal messages, and conclude that studies offer little support for the double bind, for both conceptual and methodological reasons. HELMERSEN reviews substantive findings as well as methodological and theoretical issues and concludes, similarly, that there are few if any specific studies of the double bind that support the concept. GOLDSTEIN & STRACHAN also dismiss the double bind by concluding that inconsistencies in verbal and nonverbal behaviour are not specific to schizophrenia, nor are there any studies showing that the double bind precedes schizophrenia. They do, however, suggest that other family communication variables such as deficits in communicating meaning accurately, perspective taking, and sharing a focus of attention can be consistently associated with schizophrenia, providing a number of family communication

symptoms alternative to the double bind that the reader might find useful.

A. ELIZABETH LINDSEY

See also Schizophrenia

Dramaturgical analysis

Brissett, Dennis and Charles Edgley (editors), *Life as Theater: A Dramaturgical Sourcebook*, 2nd edition, New York: de Gruyter, 1990

Burke, Kenneth, *A Grammar of Motives*, New York: Prentice Hall, 1945; London: Dobson, 1947

Burke, Kenneth, Dramatism entry in *International Encyclopedia of the Social Sciences*, edited by David L. Sills, 17 vols, New York: Macmillan, 1968

Burns, Elizabeth, *Theatricality: A Study of Convention in the Theatre and Social Life*, London: Longman, 1972

Goffman, Erving, *The Presentation of Self in Everyday Life*, Edinburgh: University of Edinburgh, Social Sciences Research Centre, 1956; revised edition, New York: Doubleday, 1959, London: Allen Lane, 1969

Harré, Rom, *Social Being: A Theory for Social Psychology*, Oxford: Blackwell, 1979; Totowa, New Jersey: Rowman and Littlefield, 1980

Hochschild, Arlie Russell, *The Managed Heart: Commercialization of Human Feeling*, Berkeley: University of California Press, 1983

Leary, Mark R. and Robin M. Kowalski, "Impression Management: A Literature Review and Two-Component Model", *Psychological Bulletin*, 107/1 (1990): 34–47

Lyman, Stanford M. and Marvin B. Scott, *A Sociology of the Absurd*, New York: Appleton Century Crofts, 1970; 2nd edition, Dix Hills, New York: General Hall, 1989

Manning, Philip, "Goffman's Changing Use of the Dramaturgical Metaphor", *Sociological Theory*, 9/1 (1991): 70–86

Messinger, Sheldon L., Harold Sampson and Robert D. Towne, "Life as Theater: Some Notes on the Dramaturgic Approach to Social Reality", *Sociometry*, 25/1 (1962): 98–110

Meyerowitz, Joshua, *No Sense of Place: The Impact of Electronic Media on Social Behavior*, New York and Oxford: Oxford University Press, 1985

Miller, Thomas G., "Goffman, Social Acting and Moral Behavior", *Journal for the Theory of Social Behaviour*, 14/2 (1984): 141–63

Tseëlon, Efrat, "Is the Presented Self Sincere? Goffman, Impression Management and the Postmodern Self", *Theory, Culture and Society*, 9/2 (1992): 115–28

Wilshire, Bruce, *Role Playing and Identity: The Limits of Theatre as Metaphor*, Bloomington: Indiana University Press, 1982

The old similitude between life and the theatre, noted by Erasmus and immortalized by Jacques' famous speech in Shakespeare's *As You Like It* (1600), lies at the heart of dramaturgical analysis. Its modern form is most closely associated with GOFFMAN's pioneering first book, which shows how dramaturgy can furnish a consistently sociological analysis of the organization of face-to-face interaction. The embodied expressions that interactants "give" (through talk) and "give off" (through accent, intonation, and nonverbal conduct) present others with an impression of the interactant's self. Interactants, whatever their particular motives, will attempt to control the impression that others have of them; this is the "impression management" thesis. Human expressivity, treated as practices of impression management, is sociologically explicated by Goffman through a dramaturgical metaphor (in current usage the terms dramaturgy and impression management tend to be interchangeable). The conduct of an interactant is understood as a "performance", composed of components such as "personal front", "appearance", "manner", and so forth. Often interactants must collaborate with others for the performance to come off: "teamwork" is required. Everyday interactional performances usually take place in "front regions" designed for the task (living rooms, offices, conference rooms); there is also a backstage or "back region" where the interactant will prepare for the performance. Goffman concludes that for interactants to successfully stage the performances of everyday life they must have a consummate grasp of the dramaturgical "arts of impression management".

With its consistent focus on the interaction order, the realm of social life brought into being by physical copresence, Goffman's dramaturgical perspective differs from the earlier dramatism of the literary critic and cultural theorist Kenneth Burke (BURKE 1945, 1968). This presents a dramatistic pentad (act, scene, agent, agency, purpose) as a general explanatory model of human conduct. "Any complete statement about motives" writes Burke (1945, p.xv) "will offer *some kind* of answers to these five questions: what was done (act), when or where it was done (scene), who did it (agent), how he did it (agency), and why (purpose)". While Burke's dramatism has been influential in literary fields it is Goffman's dramaturgy, with its persistent bias towards the behavioural rather than the motivational, which has been taken up most extensively in the social sciences. That influence was achieved by the potency of Goffman's application of the metaphor, for "dramaturgical analysis" does not clearly demarcate an area of inquiry, nor is it an adequate characterization of the entirety of Goffman's sociological contribution (see entries on Social interaction, Symbolic interactionism).

Ever since Goffman's first formulation, there have been general questions about the scope and adequacy of dramaturgical analysis. BURNS presents a rare discussion sympathetic to Goffman's objectives. She notes that dramaturgical analysis is an "intermediate category" between symbolic interactionism and ethnomethodology that "stresses the 'compositional' aspects of behaviour, particularly the strategies involved in claiming a particular status and the expressive behaviour which more or less successfully maintains the claim" (Burns, p.139). Her systematic investigation of the conventions that frame the practices of theatre is married to a careful examination of their carryover into everyday life. Burns concludes that "without the ability to compose and to recognise the composition of our own actions and those of others" (Burns p.232), social and personal life as we know it would be likely to disintegrate.

Other commentators have been more forthrightly critical. MESSINGER, SAMPSON & TOWNE suggest that Goffman's dramaturgy is a simile not a homology and thus must not be taken as the way in which people generally understand the world in their ordinary lives. This then problematicizes the relation of two types of understanding, the analyst's to the actor's model of the world. Importantly, Messinger's mental patients want to *be* normal, not just *appear* normal – Goffman is accused of neglecting a real self. From a phenomenological baseline, WILSHIRE argues that Goffman's dramaturgy is flawed because it blurs distinctions between on and offstage life, ignoring the fictionality of the former. There is a different time sense on stage (years can pass in seconds); the actor stands in a different relation of responsibility to his/her acts (there is no prospect of a prosecution for the murder of Macbeth). Goffman's analytic failure to appreciate these differences produces an impoverished, "devitalized" (Wilshire p.280) conception of the self. MILLER offers a comparable critique, suggesting that dramaturgy gives a predatory cast to human motivation and elides critical features of truly moral conduct. MANNING defends dramaturgy, pointing to its important methodological function in Goffman's writings as a logic of discovery and noting Goffman's own reservations set out in later writings. While it aids sociological exploration of out-of-awareness features of social interaction, it is not helpful for "analyzing how rules in everyday life can be simultaneously constraints, resources, and indeterminate guides to conduct" (Manning p.85).

Many studies have shown the empirical utility of dramaturgical analysis. LYMAN & SCOTT provide broad evidence of the fertility of dramaturgical analysis for sociological investigation, in particular through their dramaturgical treatment of motives as social acts (excuses, justifications, and the like). They also forge connections between dramaturgy and the concerns of existentialist philosophy. HOCHSCHILD provides a telling analysis of the management of emotion by flight attendants and debt collectors. Her ideas of "emotional labour" and "feeling rules" suggest that some occupations call for kinds of impression management that require "deep" rather than "surface" acting. This study is an important landmark in the sociology of emotion. MEYEROWITZ applies dramaturgy to electronic media (particularly television) to propose that the traditional shaping of identity by class, gender, place, is dissolving. Electronic media are breaking down the "situational geography" of social life, collapsing physical and social distances and thus severing the links normally sustained between physical place and social place. The information made available by electronic media undermines established distinctions of age, gender, and authority. Developments like the Internet are presumably accelerating the changes Meyerowitz first ascribed to television.

A good guide to the sociological reach of dramaturgical analysis is BRISSETT & EDGLEY. They include studies of a range of social phenomena, including the management of medical definitions of the gynaecological examination, the work of mediators in workplace disputes, prisoners' self-presentations as they press for release, US Presidential practices of impression management, and mystification practices in national politics. While dramaturgical ideas may extend sociological knowledge of social relationships, self, motivation, and organizational and political settings, these studies have not yet led to cumulative theoretical development (an aim that is often at odds with the ethnographic sensibilities of many dramaturgical analysts). Brissett & Edgley usefully distinguish the dramaturgical principle (the expressive-impressive feature of interaction) from dramaturgical awareness (people's recognition of the practical consequentiality of the principle). Brissett & Edgley also review critiques of dramaturgy (as an unsystematic mode of inquiry; as trivializing social structural constraints; the ontological status of the metaphor), showing the complexity of the issues and their resistance to simple resolution.

Psychologists have used impression management to investigate aggression, attitude change, attributions, social facilitation, and kindred phenomena (see the overview in LEARY & KOWALSKI). According to TSEËLON, a significant transmutation of dramaturgy has occurred in traversing disciplinary boundaries from sociology to psychology. What Goffman construes as a panhuman potential, the *possibility* inhering in face-to-face interaction that impressions *may* be controlled to the actor's advantage, is transformed into a psychology of deception. Others who have sought to integrate dramaturgy into more broadly grounded sociological and psychological syntheses, such as the "ethogenic" perspective (HARRÉ), have tried to preserve Goffman's more semiotic conception.

The productivity of dramaturgical analysis stems from the potency of drama to typify and crystallize actual social processes and relationships. Perhaps Burke (1968) best summed this up when he claimed that drama was the form that could most powerfully assist an understanding of the real implications of those contested terms, "act" and "person".

GREG SMITH

See also Ethnomethodology, Social interaction, Symbolic interactionism

Dreams, dreaming

Carr, Adrian, "Identity, Compliance and Dissent in Organizations: A Psychoanalytic Perspective", *Organization*, 5/1 (1998): 81–99
Faraday, Ann, "The Midnight Feast: Help Yourself", *Psychology Today*, 1 (1975): 58–65, 80
Flanders, Sara (editor), *The Dream Discourse Today*, London and New York: Routledge, 1993
Freud, Sigmund, *The Interpretation of Dreams*, London: Hogarth Press, 1953 (*The Standard Edition of the Complete Psychological Works*, vols 4–5; German edition 1900)
Freud, Sigmund, "Lecture 29: Revision of the Theory of Dreams" (published in German 1933) in his *New Introductory Lectures on Psychoanalysis and Other Works*, London: Hogarth Press, 1964 (*The Standard Edition of the Complete Psychological Works*, vol. 22)
Freud, Sigmund, "On Dreams" in *The Essentials of Psychoanalysis*, edited by Anna Freud, London: Hogarth Press, 1986 (German edition 1901)
Hobson, J. Allan, *The Dreaming Brain*, New York: Basic Books, 1988
Inglis, Brian, *The Power of Dreams*, London: Grafton, 1987
MacKenzie, Norman, *Dreams and Dreaming*, London: Aldus, and New York: Vanguard Press, 1965
Miller, Laurence, "In Search of the Unconscious", *Psychology Today*, 20/12 (1986): 60–64
van den Daele, Leland, "Direct Interpretation of Dreams: Neuropsychology", *American Journal of Psychoanalysis*, 56/3 (1996): 253–68

Human beings have long been fascinated by dreams and the possibility that dreaming was an activity during which meaningful information was being conveyed, albeit in a disguised form and/or from an unknown supernatural source. CARR, in keeping with Sigmund Freud, argues that dreams contain meaningful information about the dreamer. In particular, Carr assumes that dreams contain hidden thoughts and links to experiences in life that the dreamer would, more often than not, choose to forget. Psychodynamic defence mechanisms that are at work during the day to keep certain thoughts and anxieties repressed and away from our consciousness seem to relax during sleep and the unconscious material gains expression, albeit in a distorted and disguised manner. Carr believes that dreams, once deciphered, reveal authentic information about the dreamer and, in particular, the source of anxiety that prompted psychodynamic defence mechanisms being engaged in the first place.

In the context of conflicting research results as to the sources of stress among education workers, this paper challenges the assumption that respondents are consciously aware of what causes their anxiety, and instead employs dream analysis to reveal such sources. This paper reports on a study undertaken in 1990 and is one of the first, if not the first, to employ dream analysis in a large study in the area of occupational stress. It is also noteworthy because specimen dreams are discussed, and some are linked to what Carr calls the individual's "parallel life theme", that is, the residue that is peculiar to an individual's experiential history but which is impacting upon that individual now. In encouraging and working with the respondents in his study to make associations with the manifest content of their dreams, Carr suggested associations that, in some cases, revealed information only known to the respondent that the respondent themselves wished to forget or not reveal. However, while on the one hand, this suggests what a powerful "tool" dream analysis can be, on the other hand, revealing the latent content of a dreams can be emotionally disturbing for the person concerned and, in a sense, revives the anxiety associated with the original experience.

The work of FARADAY is a very common-sense and compelling account of trying to understand the activity of dreaming and what dreams reveal about the dreamer. Sympathetic to the work of Freud, the approach taken in this paper emphasizes that in moving from manifest to latent content of a dream the symbolism needs to prompt associations for the dreamer and cannot be assumed to have some universal meaning that should be superimposed in the process of interpretation. For Faraday, a dream must first be considered in terms of its manifest meaning. She gives an example of a dream about falling from the balcony of her apartment and upon inspecting the guard rail found it to be rickety. Thus the dream represented a warning of something that she had subconsciously registered days before. Faraday suggests that if the manifest content of the dream does not prove to be a literal warning, then the content should be considered for its more symbolic meaning. Here the meaning of falling is discussed in terms of the current life circumstances of the dreamer, the same symbol having quite different meaning for different individuals. A number of common dream themes are discussed and revealed to have different associations for different dreamers due to their specific life experiences. A well-written work, this paper gives advice as to how to keep a dream diary and a list of "rules" for dream interpretation. A useful list of references is provided (p.80), even though in some ways they are now dated.

The 13 essays in the edited volume by FLANDERS provide a valuable resource to those wishing to comprehend emergent perspectives in the psychoanalytic community on dreams and dreaming. The essays represent some of the most significant papers written in the area since the mid 1970s from within the broad church of analytical schools in Europe and America. Although aimed at clinicians, the introduction to the volume is of such quality that those not familiar with psychoanalysis will be able to understand the context and the fundamental underpinning to the focus of each paper. This volume is thoroughly recommended.

Dreams and dreaming, for Freud, are the fundamental road to the subconscious activity and influences on our everyday life. In *The Interpretation of Dreams* FREUD (1900) describes dreams as the "royal road to a knowledge of the unconscious" (p.768) and this particular work, although written almost a century ago, is considered by many to be the classic work on dreams and dreaming – it was certainly considered by Freud to be his most important work. According to Freud, dreams "are disguised fulfilments of repressed wishes" (FREUD 1901, p.115 also 1900, p.244) that are prompted by conscious activities of the previous day. Freud suggested that dreams that had manifest content, which seemed unintelligible, disconnected, confused, fragmented, and/or meaningless, appeared this way because of unconscious processes which he dubbed "dream work". He argued that condensation, displacement, and representation were unconscious processes that needed to be reversed if one was to unmask the latent content. He also observed that another process acted to mask the real content of a dream when we awoke from our dreaming. This was called secondary revision, and is the waking mind's attempt to put the manifest content into some semblance of order and coherence which it did not originally posses. These processes are at the heart of Freud's understanding of dreams and are elaborately described in the three references to his work.

The 1901 work is a succinct summary of many of the central aspects of his view on dreams, but in this particular volume there is also an introduction by his daughter Anna Freud, who draws attention to the contemporary relevance of the original tome. FREUD (1933) contains some refinements of his views on dreams. These were necessary after he posited his second theory of the mind in which he hypothesized the now familiar three realms of the mind: id, ego, and super-ego. The revisions to the original theory about dreams were significant, as dreams with anxiety content were no longer viewed as exclusively

sexual, but a pairing of the residue of the preconscious activity of the waking life of the day with a traumatic situation that had been repressed. One theme common to all the three works of Freud that have been referenced here is that dream-symbolism cannot be universally interpreted as though there was some kind of dictionary of dream symbols that could be relied upon for dream interpretation. Some symbols did seem to appear in dreams and hold similar meanings, but Freud insisted that the emphasis should be upon the dreamer making associations with dream content instead of any externally imposed interpretation. He noted that some symbols had a completely different meaning for some dreamers. This is a crucial issue to keep in mind when reading Freud's work on dreams and dreaming because some of his colleagues, particularly Wilhelm Stekel (and to a lesser extent Carl Jung), were suggesting that there was indeed a universal dictionary of dream symbolism. Freud's resistance to such a view led to sufficient animosity that some of his colleagues left "Freud's" Vienna Psychoanalytic Society. One feels, in his later work, that Freud emphasized some aspects of his theory on dreams in a manner that was to distinguish it from the views of others, and dream symbolism was a major point of departure.

The books by INGLIS and MACKENZIE both discuss how dreams have been regarded through the ages and the influence/inspiration they have had upon people in power, the arts, and sciences. Both books are very readable and do reflect on the veracity of the historical record.

VAN DEN DAELE reflects upon the degree of congruence of Freud's views on dreaming and dreams with the collective wisdom emerging from neurophysiology. This paper provides an overview of modern physiological based theories of dreams and is a useful paper to set against other influential authors and publications that present different evidence and come to different conclusions. In the latter context the publications of MILLER and of HOBSON present an instructive contrast. Hobson addresses Freud's work but also discusses other competing/contrasting perspectives within the psychoanalytic community, and particularly that of Carl Jung.

ADRIAN N. CARR

Drugs

Bean, Philip, *The Social Control of Drugs*, London: Martin Robertson, and New York: Wiley, 1974

Bean, P.T., "America's Drug Courts: A New Development in Criminal Justice", *Criminal Law Review*, (October 1996): 718–21

Chaiken, J. and M. Chaiken, "Drugs and Predatory Crime" in *Drugs and Crime*, edited by Michael Tonry and James Q. Wilson, Chicago: University of Chicago Press, 1990

Goldstein, P.J., "The Drugs/Violence Nexus: A Tripartite Conceptual Framework", *Journal of Drug Issues*, 15/4 (1985): 493–506

Hough, Michael, *Drugs Misuse and the Criminal Justice System: A Review of the Literature*, London: Central Drugs Prevention Unit, 1996

Inciardi, James A., *The Drug Legalization Debate*, Newbury Park, California and London: Sage, 1991; 2nd edition 1999

Mirrlees-Black, Catriona, Tracey Budd, Sarah Partridge and Pat Mayhew, *The 1998 British Crime Survey: England and Wales*, London: Home Office, 1998

Nadelmann, E.A., "The Case for Legalization" in *The Drug Legalization Debate*, edited by James A. Inciardi, 1991

Regier, D.A. *et al.*, "Comorbidity of Mental Disorder with Alcohol and Other Drug Abuse: Results from ECA", *Journal of the American Medical Association*, 1264/19 (1980): 2511–18

The original meaning of the word "drugs" was any substance used in medicine. But more recently, it has come to mean those illicit substances controlled by legislation, e.g. in Britain, the 1971 Misuse of Drugs Act. The British Crime Survey (MIRRLEES-BLACK *et al.*) shows how drug use has increased exponentially over the last two decades. Lifetime prevalence figures show that about one-third of the general population under the age of 17 years have taken drugs at some time, with a high although decreasing number in the other age groups. The use (or abuse) of illicit drugs runs parallel with consumption of licit (prescribed) drugs used in medicine. BEAN (1974) shows that illicit drug use in Britain is a recent phenomenon, being almost unheard of up to about 1960. It increased steadily to its present levels, with the largest increase from 1990 onwards. Many explanations have been offered to account for this, but none are wholly satisfactory. Drug use has become a worldwide phenomenon, with Britain experiencing no greater problem than elsewhere.

There remains a debate about whether substances whose possession and sale are currently prohibited – such as heroin, cocaine, cannabis, and ecstasy – should be controlled by the criminal law. Ethan NADELMANN in the US has argued forcefully that legalization should be regarded as a serious alternative to the current policy of drug control. He asserts that controls cannot solve the drug problem, that young people are criminalized for what is after all a private and personal matter, and that the cost of current policies is prohibitive. Those in favour of controls see legalization as an elitist and racist policy that would increase levels of drug dependence in the ghettos, and serve to legitimate the chemical destruction of an urban generation and culture (see INCIARDI).

There have been few studies in Britain looking at the manner in which users are criminalized. The substances themselves are classified according to severity, with the most dangerous carrying the most severe penalties. Few, it seems, would argue that heroin or cocaine be completely free of legal controls (and so, for example, available to children). Most proposals concentrate on legalizing cannabis.

A central feature of the modern debate concerns drug misuse within the criminal justice system. HOUGH has reviewed the literature identifying two key areas, namely the links between drugs and crime and the treatment programmes, whether before or after sentence.

In the first case, Hough finds that, in spite of numerous claims that drug use and crime are inextricably linked, the link is actually quite tentative. Many drug users are not criminals, and many criminals are not drug users. Moreover (and to complicate matters further), many of the crimes committed by drug users would have been committed anyway. To establish a link with crime it is necessary to show that certain offences occur only as a result of drug use and not otherwise. In this respect, the research evidence by CHAIKEN & CHAIKEN shows the clearest link in the case of "street junkies" i.e. homeless heroin users who commit high levels of crime during high levels of heroin use, presumably in order to sustain their habit. Once in treatment their levels of criminality fall dramatically. Crime rates for other drugs such as cannabis, ecstasy, or LSD seem less affected.

GOLDSTEIN has provided a useful framework for analysing the link between drugs and crime. He identifies three areas. First, there is the psychopharmacological – drugs alter behaviour by reducing inhibitions or instigating aggression. Second, what he calls economically orientated crime, which occurs when drug users commit crimes to purchase drugs to pay for their habit (defined by Goldstein as occurring less frequently than often supposed). And, thirdly, what he calls systemic crime, which involves trafficking, protecting illegal drug markets, collecting debts, enforcing discipline, and so on. This framework was designed to deal specifically with violent offences, but can be used for all types of crime.

Treating drug users in the criminal justice system has led to a great deal of interest recently, prompted by the view that "treatment works". Accordingly, Hough (see above) describes new programmes that have developed, whether inside prisons, within the community (mainly through the Probation Service), or as arrest referral schemes. BEAN (1996) describes one of the most interesting new developments, that of Drug Courts. These were introduced into the US in 1989 and are now being used in other countries, including Britain. Drug Courts are likely to have an important influence far beyond the treatment of drug abuse; they have already had an impact on traditional notions of justice. They are best defined as slow track court-directed treatment programmes where control is centred in the court, unlike other court programmes where treatment is handed over to agencies such as the probation service.

Increasingly, it is recognized that substance abuse is but one of a number of morbidities that drug users present to treatment agencies. Mental disorder and AIDS/HIV are others. The problem of Dual Diagnosis, as it is often called, has been examined in the US by REGIER *et al.* This article show that almost half of schizophrenic patients were substance abusers, with a much higher percentage among those diagnosed as personality disordered. Over half of all drug abusers had a lifetime prevalence of mental disorder. To what extent these morbidities were causally linked remains an important research question.

PHILIP BEAN

Downsizing, *see* Job loss

Durkheim, Emile 1858–1917

French sociologist

Alexander, Jeffrey C. (editor), *Durkheimian Sociology: Cultural Studies*, Cambridge and New York: Cambridge University Press, 1988

Bellah, Robert N. (editor), *On Morality and Society*, by Emile Durkheim, Chicago: University of Chicago Press, 1973

Bresnard, Phillipe (editor), *The Sociological Domain: The Durkheimians and the Founding of French Sociology*, Cambridge and New York: Cambridge University Press, 1983

Gane, Mike, *On Durkheim's Rules of Sociological Method*, London and New York: Routledge, 1988

Giddens, Anthony, *Durkheim*, London: Fontana, 1978

Hamilton, Peter (editor), *Emile Durkheim: Critical Assessments*, 8 vols, London: Routledge, 1990–95

Jones, Robert Alun, *Emile Durkheim: An Introduction to Four Major Works*, London and Beverly Hills, California: Sage, 1986

Lukes, Steven, *Emile Durkheim: His Life and Work, A Historical and Critical Study*, London: Allen and Unwin, and New York: Harper and Row, 1972

Morrison, Ken, *Marx, Durkheim, Weber: Formations of Modern Social Thought*, London and Thousand Oaks, California: Sage, 1995

Nisbet, Robert A., *Emile Durkheim*, Westport, Connecticut: Greenwood Press, 1976

Parkin, Frank, *Durkheim*, Oxford and New York: Oxford University Press, 1992

Parsons, Talcott, *The Structure of Social Action: A Study in Social Theory with Special Reference to a Group of Recent European Writers*, 2nd edition, Glencoe, Illinois: Free Press, 1949 (see especially chapters 8–12)

Pearce, Frank, *The Radical Durkheim*, London and Boston: Unwin Hyman, 1989

Pickering, W.S.F. and H. Martins (editors), *Debating Durkheim*, London: Routledge, 1994

Pope, Whitney, *Durkheim's Suicide: A Classic Analysed*, Chicago: University of Chicago Press, 1976

Thompson, Kenneth, *Emile Durkheim*, London and New York: Tavistock, 1982

Traugott, Mark (editor), *Emile Durkheim on Institutional Analysis*, Chicago: University of Chicago Press, 1978

Turner, Stephen (editor), *Emile Durkheim: Sociologist and Moralist*, London: Routledge, 1993

Emile Durkheim was born in Epinal, France in 1858 and died in 1917. He lectured in education and sociology at Bordeaux and then at the Sorbonne. Alongside Marx and Weber he is currently regarded as one of the three "founding fathers" of sociology. Of this trio, he was the most committed to the development of sociology as a separate discipline, and his influence was the earliest to be felt. On the other hand, his work is often now felt to be "difficult" and his influence is steadily waning, compared to that of Weber in particular. Durkheim's approach was to emphasize the collective, general, objective, and the importance of the moral order, and to establish the scientific status of sociology. His major four works are the *Division of Labour*, *Rules of the Sociological Method*, *Suicide*, and *Elementary Forms of the Religious Life*. However, he wrote extensively and a large number of further books have been published, sometimes from his own written lecture notes and sometimes from the notes of students. These include studies of education, socialism, civic politics and the state, professional organization, and pragmatism. Durkheim was very active, especially through his journal *Année Sociologique* and the collective that wrote for it, in the sustained intellectual development of French sociology.

All four of his major works were translated into English before the major advances of sociology in the post-World War II period, and this has helped their reception in English-speaking countries. Durkheim's influence was first of all on the work of his colleagues and successors in French sociology, although that tended to be limited to only a few heirs who survived World War I, especially Halbwachs and Mauss. He influenced structural-functional British anthropology – especially through the work of Radcliffe-Brown, and the thinking of the famous *Annales* school of French history, and later his work influenced the structural approach of Levi-Strauss. In the mid-1930s his work was taken up by Parsons and Merton, and was very influential in the development of empirically-orientated US sociological theory, partly because of the "scientific" way in which his work is written, as well as the array of concepts that he bequeathed for understanding society. Since Durkheim was elected into the trio of the founding fathers, discussion of his work has become *de rigeur* in much theoretical work in sociology, and as a result there is a huge literature (including standard theory texts) in which his work is discussed, sometimes in relation to that of Weber and Marx.

Apart from the continuing flow of translations, a variety of compilations (such as those of BELLAH, NISBET and TRAUGOTT), and the classic discussions by PARSONS, a series of introductory treatments have become available, especially since the 1970s: GIDDENS, THOMPSON and PARKIN. Such treatments are convenient and accessible. The close analysis of original material is particularly valuable in exegetical texts such as JONES and MORRISON. An interesting and innovative addition to the corpus of Durkheimian work has been POPE's reanalysis of Durkheim's theory and data in the research classic on suicide. Recent collections of essays on interpretation of Durkheim include ALEXANDER, PICKERING and TURNER. A massive four-volume collection of the secondary literature has been compiled by HAMILTON.

Of biographical studies only LUKES is definitive. This volume concentrates on Durkheim's ideas, and indeed on a sprightly critique of his ideas, but stitches together a reasonably detailed biographical account of his life. Other historical studies have illuminated aspects of the broader *Année* grouping, especially BRESNARD.

There are several issues that have been dealt with in detailed debates concerning the exegesis of Durkheimian concepts. A flurry of articles and several books have been written about each. One issue concerns the nature of the collective reality that Durkheim saw as central to sociology. It is now broadly agreed that, despite some excessive rhetorical flourishes,

Durkheim does commit the sin of reifying collectives. Nevertheless, more humanistically centred approaches are currently much more popular than the position Durkheim advocated. Whether there was a shift in his thinking over time has occasioned other debate: a "younger" Durkheim concerned particularly with social structural influences and a deterministic approach in terms of scientific method can be contrasted with an "older" Durkheim more concerned with cultural values and the collective conceptions held by societies, and broadly with the sociology of religion. ALEXANDER endeavours to build a renewed concern with cultural studies and especially with symbolic classifications on the base of what he sees as the "later Durkheimian" position. GANE actively defends Durkheim against charges that his work is fundamentally divided into two periods, and insists on a considerable degree of continuity in the development of his conceptual framework.

Another issue that has caused some debate is the extent to which Durkheim is seen as conservative (which has been the prevailing notion since the 1970s at least) or whether his work has a more radical edge. PEARCE argues for a radical Durkheim whose work often explores socialist solutions to social ills.

CHARLES CROTHERS

E

East Asian economies

Demetriades, Panicos O., Michael P. Devereux and Kul B.
Luintel, "Productivity and Financial Sector Policies:
Evidence from South East Asia", *Journal of Economic
Behaviour and Organization*, 35 (1998): 61–82

Krugman, Paul, "The Myth of Asia's Miracle", *Foreign
Affairs*, November/December (1994): 62–78

Krugman, Paul, *Pop Internationalism*, Cambridge,
Massachusetts: MIT Press, 1996; chapter 11

Morrissey, Oliver and Doug Nelson, "East Asian Economic
Performance: Miracle or Just a Pleasant Surprise?", *World
Economy*, 21/7 (September 1998): 851–54

Patrick, Hugh T. and Yung Chul Park (editors), *The Financial
Development of Japan, Korea and Taiwan: Growth,
Repression, and Liberalization*, Oxford and New York:
Oxford University Press, 1994

Rodrick, Danny, *King Kong meets Godzilla: The World Bank
and the East Asian Miracle*, London: Centre for Economic
Policy Research, 1994 (CEPR discussion paper no. 994)

Rodrick, Danny, "Globalisation, Social Conflict and
Economic Growth", *World Economy*, 21/2 (March 1998):
143–58

World Bank, *The East Asian Miracle: Economic Growth
and Public Policy*, New York: Oxford University Press,
1993

Young, Alwyn, "The Tyranny of Numbers: Confronting the
Statistical Realities of the East Asian Growth Experience",
Quarterly Journal of Economics, (August 1995): 641–80

Although the WORLD BANK book was written before the
Asian financial crisis erupted, it provides, possibly, the best available survey of the economic growth process in the East Asian
region spanning, broadly, the period from 1965–90. It contains
the results of a major piece of econometric research carried
out at the World Bank to estimate the contribution of different
factors in the growth process in the East Asian economies,
compared with other developed and developing countries. They
found that conventional factors, such as investment in education, population, growth, and capital accumulation, could not
explain a significant proportion of the differences in growth
between the high-performing East Asian economies and other
economies. Instead, their exceptional performance could only be
attributed to a faster rate of technical progress.

The rest of the book explores possible explanations for this
"miracle" factor. The World Bank rejects the two extreme
views concerning the miracle, namely, the neoclassical, which
emphasizes reliance on the market, and the revisionist view,
which points to the role played by the state in the growth
process. Instead, it adopts a middle position, which it defines
as a market-friendly approach. Government intervention did
help these economies to grow faster where it served to act as
a corrective for genuine market failure (for example imperfect
information). However, not all forms of intervention were
beneficial, as when governments tried to supplant the market
in areas where it worked well.

RODRICK (1994) challenges the analysis contained in the
World Bank's *East Asian Miracle* concerning the factors
explaining the growth performance of the East Asian newly
industrialising economies. Specifically, he argued that the World
Bank was too dismissive of policies of intervention, which
proved unsuccessful. Rodrick also argues that the World Bank
attached too much importance to export-push strategies. He
argues that the link between export performance and economic
growth has not yet been convincingly demonstrated. More
importance should be given to favourable initial conditions in
these countries, in particular higher levels of schooling and
educational attainment than in other developing countries and
an uncommonly low degree of inequality, as measured by the
distribution of income and land-ownership. Using cross-
country regressions, Rodrick shows that 90 per cent of the
growth enjoyed by these countries could be explained by these
factors. What is less clear is why, given these differences in
initial conditions, other developing countries (such as Argentina, India, and the Philippines) did so much worse.

MORRISSEY & NELSON's paper provides a useful overview of the debate about whether or not the growth performance of these economies was a "miracle". Their conclusion is
that the exceptional growth-rates enjoyed by these countries
were due to a combination of several factors, including strong
institutions, political will, and a concept of a social contract,
which provided the basis for growth with equity. The fact
that these factors should lead to relatively fast growth is not
itself surprising. However, it was the ability of the governments
of these countries to bring these factors together in a way that
generated exceptionally fast growth that was the supreme
achievement of these economies. However, Morrissey & Nelson
warn against the dangers of overgeneralization. Important
differences exist between the East Asian economies in the
factors that propelled rapid growth. Government policies
were important in all of these countries in contributing to
rapid growth, not least in ensuring macroeconomic stability.

However, insufficient evidence exists to demonstrate that micro-economic interventions had a positive or negative effect on performance.

RODRICK (1998) returns to a theme discussed in his earlier work, namely, the role of outward-oriented, export-promotion strategies in economic growth in developing economies. He remains unpersuaded by the conventional wisdom that differences in growth performance in developing countries can be attributed to differences in the extent to which trade polices promoted export growth as opposed to import substitution. He argues that the growth performance of certain developing countries worsened, significantly, in the wake of the oil crisis of the 1970s, not because these countries pursued import-substitution strategies or governments intervened too much. Rather, it was because these countries failed to make appropriate macroeconomic adjustments in response to the changed external environment. In particular, the East Asian economies grew faster because they adjusted more rapidly and so were able to get back on to a fast growth path quicker. Using an index of social conflict, Rodrick argues that those countries with deeper social divisions and weaker institutions of conflict management proved the least successful in adjusting quickly to external shocks. This suggests that social conflict and the institutions that exist to manage such conflict are more important than trade and industrial strategies in explaining growth differences between developing economies.

In what proved to be a prophetic anticipation of the growth crisis of the East Asian region, KRUGMAN (1994, 1996) argued that growth in the East Asian region must eventually taper off, as it was not the result of any exceptional factors. It was a myth to argue that there was anything miraculous about the performance of these economies, as it could be explained largely by conventional factors, such as increased investment in physical and human capital and population growth. In this respect, it was no different from the growth enjoyed by the Soviet Union in the 1950s, more the result of perspiration than inspiration. Krugman based his conclusions on the work of Alwyn Young (see below). East Asia's growth, Krugman declares, is the result of "deferred gratification, the willingness to sacrifice current satisfaction for future gain". Since this cannot last forever, it was inevitable that, before long, growth in the East Asian region would have to gravitate towards to those in other "less exceptional" regions of the world.

YOUNG examined aggregate data from 118 countries over the period from 1970–85 and measured the contribution of both increased inputs and technical progress, as measured by total factor productivity (TFP) growth. He found that factor accumulation, in the form of high investment rates, labour participation rates, and rising educational standards, was the major force behind the Asian growth experience. On the other hand, the growth of TFP was generally no higher in East Asia than in OECD or Latin American countries. Specifically, Young's estimates show that TFP growth ranged from almost zero in Singapore to 2.6 per cent per annum in Taiwan. This is a paper worth reading not only because it influenced subsequent literature so much but also because it provides an accessible account of technical issues.

DEMETRIADES, DEVEREUX & LUINTEL examines the influence of financial sector policies on the average produc-

tivity of capital in five Asian economies. The policies include interest rate controls, directed credit programmes, and reserve and liquidity requirements. These policies are found to have significant negative effects on productivity in most cases, except in South Korea, for which the policies had significant positive effects. The policy implication that emerges from this paper is that "repressionist" policies are not always bad, as predicted by the financial liberalization literature. The results are consistent with the presence of financial market imperfections, which in some cases may be addressed by appropriate policies. Korean policy makers, the authors argue, were effective in designing financial policies that promoted investment with high social returns.

PATRICK & PARK provides an excellent summary of the financial development of Japan, Korea, and Taiwan from the 1950s to the early 1990s. This period is divided into two phases: a "repressed" one and a "liberalized" one. In the first phase, interest rates were regulated to remain below market clearing levels, entry of financial institutions was restricted, and domestic finance was insulated from world markets. The second phase is characterized by gradual removal of restrictions that allowed the introduction of market forces alongside with prudential measures. When the book was written it was clearly thought that it would provide some lessons for less-developed and transition economies; however, in the aftermath of the Asian financial crisis the financial systems of these countries are hardly considered as models to follow.

NIGEL GRIMWADE AND PANICOS O. DEMETRIADES

See also Asian crisis, South Asian economies and economic record, Tiger economies

Eastern and Central European economies in transformation

Amsden, Alice H., Jacek Kochanowicz and Lance Taylor, *The Market Meets Its Match: Restructuring the Economies of Eastern Europe*, Cambridge, Massachusetts: Harvard University Press, 1994

Economic Policy: A European Forum, East Europe issue, 14 (April 1992)

Estrin, Saul (editor), *Privatization in Central and Eastern Europe*, Harlow, Essex: Longman, 1994

European Bank for Reconstruction and Development, *Transition Report Update 1998*, London: European Bank for Reconstruction and Development, 1998

Frydman, Roman and Andrzej Rapaczynski, *Privatization in Eastern Europe: Is the State Withering Away?*, Budapest and New York: Central European Press, 1994

Kornai, János, *The Socialist System: The Political Economy of Communism*, Oxford: Clarendon Press, and Princeton, New Jersey: Princeton University Press, 1992

Lipton, David and Jeffrey Sachs, "Creating a Market Economy in Poland", *Brookings Papers on Economic Activity*, 1 (1990)

Nove, Alec, *The Economics of Feasible Socialism Revisited*, 2nd edition, London and New York: HarperCollins, 1991

Pickles, John and Adrian Smith, *Theorising Transition: The Political Economy of Post-Communist Transformations*, London and New York: Routledge, 1998

Transformation is the term broadly applied to the transition of Central and Eastern European countries from planned economies to those that are more market-based. NOVE made a seminal contribution in 1980, revisited in 1991, in which he attempted to contrast the experience of Soviet-style economies with the legacy of Marx. He is highly critical of both liberal capitalism and the practices of Soviet-style planning, which he argues was neither efficient nor equitable. His agenda is to explore the possibility of a feasible socialism – a third way between the plan and the market. In so doing, rich insights are given into the workings of the planned economy. Furthermore, experiences of different reform models are discussed, contrasting the early and gradual reforms of Hungary with the disastrous attempts to reform the Polish economy in the 1970s and 1980s. The book concludes with an overview of the different paths of transformation.

KORNAI is another classic text. He provides an anatomy of the classical social system, taking a view more sympathetic to the market. The first part of the book gives an exhaustive account of the functioning of a planned economy, covering its coordinating mechanisms, employment, labour, and inflation. There are also chapters on politics, ideology, and power. In the second part of the book, the process of transition is discussed. The overriding argument is that a "third way" is not possible, and that successful change must be underpinned by a decisive move to the market and private property.

The mainstream approach to transformation is epitomized by LIPTON & SACHS, who were advisors to the Polish government in 1990. They identify the key tasks of transformation as comprising the stabilization of what were crisis-ridden economies, the liberalization of prices and foreign trade, and large-scale privatization. Furthermore, in terms of policy, they advocated what came to be termed "shock therapy" – an approach that emphasizes the need for the comprehensiveness, speed, and simultaneity of reforms. Another agenda-setting contribution is an edited collection in ECONOMIC POLICY: A EUROPEAN FORUM, which comprises five papers presented at an Economic Policy Panel meeting in 1991. The papers address a range of issues relating to appropriate economic aid from the West, the liberalization of trade, the problem of stabilization, and the debate concerning "big bang" approaches to transformation.

Privatization is viewed as a central task of the transformation process. FRYDMAN & RAPACZYNSKI is a book born from practical involvement in policy debates concerning privatization. They provide a taxonomy of privatization, discuss the structural interconnectedness of the various elements, and stress the importance of investor's choice, free entry of intermediaries, and the general competitiveness of the new institutional arrangements. In particular, the theme of potential conflict between the economic and political incentives of the main players in the privatization process – and the resulting dangers of bureaucracy – is pervasive throughout the book.

ESTRIN is also informed by a conventional approach to privatization, but contains interesting empirical material. The book provides an overview of the main themes of privatiza-

tion, and includes issues relating to justice and efficiency, the political dimensions of the process, and governance and mass privatization. There are also seven detailed country studies that give an empirical account of the contrasting experiences of privatization in East Germany, Poland, Hungary, the Czech and Slovak Republics, Russia, Romania, and Bulgaria.

The EUROPEAN BANK FOR RECONSTRUCTION AND DEVELOPMENT produces an annual report which provides an excellent and ongoing overview of economies undergoing transition. Reflecting on 1998, the authors point to a year of stresses and contrast with a crisis in confidence in emerging markets, seen at its most dramatic in the collapse of the Russian financial system. The report emphasizes the way in which transformation paths have differed widely between countries. Poland and Hungary have shown the greatest progress with institutional reforms in the financial sector and corporate governance, whereas other countries have backtracked and reintroduced government intervention. Vested interests have emerged to take further advantage of market distortions, preserving their gains at significant social cost. Although this volume focuses on reforms in the financial sector, it points to increases in poverty and inequality throughout all economies, with dramatic falls in life expectancy in some.

Other approaches have been critical of many of the assumptions unleashed by the euphoria of the apparent triumph of free-market capitalism. AMSDEN, KOCHANOWICZ & TAYLOR argues that the wrong sort of capitalism has been implemented, with serious social consequences. They look to the example of the East Asian economies for a more suitable growth model, suggesting that a degree of protection, with a greater emphasis on state intervention holds better prospects for growth and development. PICKLES & SMITH's edited book is informed by an approach that combines the insights of regulation theory with that of evolutionary and institutionalist economics. This approach suggests that the political economy of transformation is evolutionary and path dependent, in that it is based on broad institutional forms of learning, as well as struggles over pathways that emerge from the intersection of the old with the new. In addressing these issues, an interdisciplinary approach to transformation is taken. The book begins with a discussion of contrasting theoretical perspectives, and goes on to examine industrial and regional restructuring, the reform of state-owned enterprises, agrarian change, and decollectivization. The book draws on material relating to a wide variety of economies, including peripheral economies outside of Central and Eastern Europe. The book also includes chapters on gender and ethnicity – areas that have been neglected by more mainstream approaches to transformation.

JANE HARDY

Econometric methods, textbooks

Clements, Michael P. and David F. Hendry, *Forecasting Non-stationary Economic Time Series*, Cambridge, Massachusetts: MIT Press, 1999
Enders, Walter, *Applied Econometric Time Series*, New York and Chichester: Wiley, 1995

Hill, Carter, William E. Griffiths and George Judge, *Undergraduate Econometrics*, New York and Chichester: Wiley, 1997

Holden, K., D.A. Peel and J.L. Thompson, *Modelling the UK Economy: An Introduction*, Oxford: Martin Robertson, 1982

Maddala, G.S., *Introduction to Econometrics*, New York: Macmillan and London: Collier Macmillan, 1988; 2nd edition, 1992

Niemira, Michael P. and Philip A. Klein, *Forecasting Financial and Economic Cycles*, New York and Chichester: Wiley, 1994

Wallis, K.F., M.J. Andrews, D.N.F. Bell, P.G. Fisher and J.D. Whitley, *Models of the UK Economy: A Review by the ESRC Macroeconomic Modelling Bureau*, Oxford: Oxford University Press, 1984

Wallis, K.F., M.J. Andrews, D.N.F. Bell, P.G. Fisher and J.D. Whitley, *Models of the UK Economy: A Second Review by the ESRC Macroeconomic Modelling Bureau*, Oxford: Oxford University Press, 1985

Wallis, K.F., M.J. Andrews, P.G. Fisher, J.A. Longbottom and J.D. Whitley, *Models of the UK Economy: A Third Review by the ESRC Macroeconomic Modelling Bureau*, Oxford: Oxford University Press, 1986

Willenbockel, Dirk, *Applied General Equilibrium Modelling: Imperfect Competition and European Integration*, New York and Chichester: Wiley, 1994

There is a massive literature on econometric methods, including basic texts to suit all levels and interests. For texts (and articles) on specific aspects, see the other entries suggested at the end of this entry.

MADDALA is a standard textbook that deals with all the basic econometric methods, and incorporates developments in these methods up until the late 1980s. The book uses simple models to explain the various points rather than using more algebra than is necessary for exposition. Where proofs involve complicated expressions they tend to be omitted, but with appropriate references given. The more difficult sections are indicated so that students can skip them if necessary. Examples are used to illustrate the various techniques and where such illustrations are not given, data sets are provided so that students can compute the required results themselves.

HILL, GRIFFITHS & JUDGE is an elementary book, designed for a one-semester introduction to econometrics. It is intended for undergraduate students who have taken introductory courses in economics and elementary statistics, and an introduction to the idea of calculus. Chapters one to eight cover the core material on simple and multiple regression and provide a foundation for the remainder of the book. Chapters nine to seventeen are devoted to specific topics in econometrics. The book's chapters are generally structured as follows. First, a particular economic problem is identified. Second, an economic model consistent with the problem is formulated. Third, statistical assumptions describing the data generation process are introduced, thus defining the econometric model. Fourth, data consistent with the econometric model are introduced. Fifth, estimation and inference procedures appropriate for the econometric model are discussed. Sixth, empirical results are presented and their implications for the economic

model discussed. Finally, other models and situations in which the inference procedures discussed in the chapter might be inappropriate are suggested.

ENDERS is a textbook on time-series covering both macroeconometrics and microeconometrics, with examples drawn from different areas of economics, including agricultural economics and international finance. The book is intended for students with some background in multiple regression analysis, including the assumptions underlying the use of ordinary least squares, the concepts of correlation and covariation, and how to use t-tests and F-tests within a regression framework.

NIEMIRA & KLEIN presents the full spectrum of statistical techniques used to measure cycles, trends, seasonal patterns, and other changes in economic series. It offers step-by-step guidance on applying each method, detailing its uses and limitations. It shows the reader how particular techniques can be adapted to assess, track, and predict various cycles.

HOLDEN, PEEL & THOMPSON is a rather dated introduction to, and evaluation of, the major econometric models and forecasts in use in Britain in the early 1980s. It was overtaken by WALLIS *et al.* (1984, 1985, 1986), a series of books from the Macroeconomic Modelling Bureau at the University of Warwick. This Bureau was established by one of the UK's academic funding councils, the Economic and Social Research Council (ESRC) in 1983 with the main purpose of improving the accessibility of macroeconomic models, to promote general understanding of the properties of models of the UK economy, and to allow comparison between models to be made more easily. The seven models of the UK economy appraised in these books were the models of the Cambridge Growth Project, the City University Business School, Liverpool University, the London Business School, the National Institute of Economic and Social Research, Her Majesty's Treasury, and the Bank of England.

WILLENBOCKEL aims to contribute to the economic literature on imperfect competition and European integration, rather than simply providing a text on econometric methods. However, it goes about its task by providing an accessible step-by-step introduction to the state of the art in applied general equilibrium modelling, through the application of this to trade policy reforms and regional economic integration initiatives.

David Hendry has been a leading econometrician for some years now, and CLEMENTS & HENDRY is the second book on economic forecasting from these two authors. The book asks why some practices appear to work empirically despite a lack of formal support from theory. After reviewing the conventional approach to economic forecasting, they look at the implications for causal modelling, present a taxonomy of forecast errors, and delineate the sources of forecast failure. They show that forecast-period shifts in deterministic factors – interacting with model misspecification, collinearity, and inconsistent estimation – are the dominant source of systematic failure. They then consider various approaches for avoiding systematic forecasting errors, including intercept corrections, differencing, co-breaking, and modelling regime shifts. The authors emphasize the distinction between equilibrium correction (based on cointegration) and error correction (automatically offsetting past errors). Finally, they present three applications to test the implications of their framework. Their results on forecasting have wider implications for the conduct of empirical econometric research, model formulation, the testing of economic hypotheses, and model-based policy analysis. The book includes plenty of references although obviously these are to the research (journal article and monograph) literature rather than to texts on econometric methods.

JONATHAN MICHIE

See also Econometrics software packages, Economics and mathematics, Mathematization of economics, Multiple regression analysis, Nonlinear dynamics, Regression analysis, Time in economics

Econometric software packages

FRONTIER, Tim Coelli, Centre for Efficiency and Productivity Analysis, University of New England, Armidale, NSW 2351, Australia. Email: tcoelli@metz.une.edu.au, http://www.une.edu.au/econometrics/cepa.htm

GAUSS, Aptech Systems, Kent, Washington, US

LIMDEP, Econometric Software, Bellport, New York, US

MICROFIT, Electronic Publishing, Oxford University Press, Great Clarendon Street, Oxford OX2 6DP, UK

MicroTSP, Quantitative Micro Software, Irvine, California, US

PC-FIML, J. Doornik and D. Hendry, Institute of Economics and Statistics, Oxford University, St Cross Building, Manor Road, Oxford OX1 3UL, UK

PC-GIVE, J. Doornik and D. Hendry, Institute of Economics and Statistics, Oxford University, St Cross Building, Manor Road, Oxford OX1 3UL, UK

RATS, VAR Econometrics, Minneapolis, Minnesota, US

SPSS, SPSS Inc., Chicago, Illinois, US

STATA, Stata Corporation, 702 University Drive East, College Station, Texas 77840, USA, http://www.stata.com, E-mail stata@stata.com

TSP, TSP International, Palo Alto, California, US

FRONTIER is a DOS-based program catering for stochastic frontier estimation. It accommodates both cross-sectional and panel data, and gives the user two basic choices: a) stochastic frontier estimation with no efficiency effects (external variables that are not under the firm's control), and b) stochastic frontier estimation with a contemporaneous auxiliary regression of the efficiency error's mean on external efficiency effects. FRONTIER's main drawback is its inability to read data files from outside its home directory, as well as its need for a peculiar input data format (with special reference to panel data). On the other hand, it is quite user-friendly, and is expected to be available in a Windows version in the near future.

GAUSS is a programming facility that best suits expert users. It provides a very flexible language that allows the user to set up $x'x$ matrices, manipulate data, manually implement algorithms, and so on. Operations such as econometric estimation and testing are made possible, thanks to standardized routines, even though – by its nature – GAUSS is a step-by-step interactive program. It is essential that the user should have programming skills.

LIMDEP is probably the most suitable reference package for microeconometrics. It encompasses a wide range of estimation techniques, especially in the field of limited-dependent-variable estimation (logit, probit, tobit, multinomial probit, and so on). Its most recent version is a Windows-based program that provides the user with new options, making it almost complete, even for non-microeconometric work. Panel-data estimation has been particularly improved, and functions for dealing with time-series and stochastic production/cost frontiers have also been added. The Windows 95 version accepts both interactive commands and batch files, and is much more user-friendly than the older versions.

MICROFIT is a standard general econometric program that suits beginners and students. It is not very powerful in terms of data matrices, so it is not suitable for large data sets. It also comes in a new Windows version, which is much more convenient, in that it provides the user with a clear set of menu-driven options. The reading in of data has also been largely improved, and now makes MICROFIT compatible with a limited set of file formats. However, the main data format that still feeds Microfit is plain text/ASCII, which might not please all users.

MicroTSP stems from its parent package TSP, even though it has been separately programmed and administered. Like TSP, it was originally developed for time-series analysis, even though it actually caters for most simple kinds of econometric estimation. Its Windows version, also known as E-VIEWS (Econometric Views), is quite convenient for beginners, but is still very limited in terms of the size of data matrix which it can handle. For large (especially panel) data sets, use TSP (see below).

PC-GIVE and PC-FIML are traditional student packages that have gradually evolved towards a professional status, with the addition of new estimation options, and extra capacity in terms of data management. The acronyms GIVE (Generalized Instrumental Variables Estimation) and FIML (Full Information Maximum Likelihood) are not very consistent with the latest versions of these packages, which are now much more general and user-friendly than they were in the past. PC-GIVE, in particular, comes in a new Windows version, and still suits students and beginners. PC-FIML is slightly more sophisticated, and caters for functions such as macroeconometric work, system estimation, and co-integration. An advantage of these packages is that they can easily read data in spreadsheet (but not multi-sheet) format.

RATS is particularly useful for time-series analysis, with special reference to autoregressive processes. Vector auto-regression (VAR) is typically implemented by RATS. This software also deals with autoregressive conditional heteroskedasticity (ARCH) and generalized ARCH (GARCH) models. In general, RATS carries out sophisticated time-series analysis and co-integration, whereas it is less useful for microeconometric jobs. It requires strong familiarity with time-series econometrics, and is not as user-friendly as other general packages on offer. Beginners may find it difficult to use, but it is ideally suited to experienced econometricians.

SPSS is a comprehensive package doing virtually everything in terms of (even sophisticated) statistics, together with a limited selection of options that may also be used by econometricians. Its newest Windows version is particularly "fat", and should only be installed on very powerful machines. SPSS is particularly strong on statistical tests, both parametric and non-parametric. It also provides the user with a wide-ranging set of graphic options, and is particularly friendly in terms of data reading and importing. It is generally compatible with spreadsheet packages.

STATA is undoubtedly one of the more powerful statistical packages around. Even though it was originally conceived of as general statistical software, it actually caters for most econometric techniques, and also encompasses general biometric, medical statistic, and sociological techniques. Its Windows version is a multi-window package that shows the user virtually all aspects of the work that is being carried out (such as variables, batch files, results, and graphs). STATA has a menu-driven set of options and accepts very large data sets. It also caters for panel data analysis.

TSP is a traditional time-series analysis mainframe program, which has been adapted to microcomputers. It now comes in a (*démi*) Windows version named TLG. TSP/TLG is still basically a batch-file program, even though it now accepts interactive commands. It also caters for panel data estimation, very large data matrices, and forms of estimation not involving time-series. In fact, it is comprehensive for macroeconometrics, whereas it has only recently been extended to some microeconometric applications. TSP easily reads traditional spreadsheet (especially Lotus 123) data files, but does not accept newer multi-sheet, macro-inclusive files (such as files from Excel 5.0 and higher).

GIAN CARLO SCARSI

See also Econometric methods, textbooks

Economic analysis of law

Baird, Douglas G., Robert H. Gertner and Randal C. Picker, *Game Theory and the Law*, Cambridge, Massachusetts: Harvard University Press, 1994

Calabresi, Guido, *The Costs of Accidents: A Legal and Economic Analysis*, New Haven, Connecticut: Yale University Press, 1970

Coase, R.H., "The Problem of Social Cost", *Journal of Law and Economics*, 3 (1960): 1–44

Farber, Daniel A. and Philip P. Frickey, *Law and Public Choice: A Critical Introduction*, Chicago: University of Chicago Press, 1991

Hanson, Jon D. and Melissa R. Hart, "Law and Economics" in *A Companion to Philosophy of Law and Legal Theory*, edited by Dennis Patterson, Oxford and Cambridge, Massachusetts: Blackwell, 1996

Katz, Avery Wiener (editor), *Foundations of the Economic Approach to Law*, New York and Oxford: Oxford University Press, 1998

Newman, Peter (editor), *The New Palgrave Dictionary of Economics and the Law*, 3 vols, London: Macmillan, and New York: Stockton Press, 1998

Polinsky, A. Mitchell, *An Introduction to Law and Economics*, 2nd edition, Boston: Little Brown, 1989

Posner, Richard A., *The Economics of Justice*, Cambridge, Massachusetts: Harvard University Press, 1981

Posner, Richard A., *Economic Analysis of Law*, 5th edition, New York: Aspen, 1998

The origins of the modern law and economics movement are to be found in COASE and CALABRESI. Coase's work responded to a liberal theory of regulation: that (for example) polluters should be forced to pay the value of their pollution (through taxes, administrative fines, or tort liability) on the basis that *not* making them pay would constitute a kind of subsidy for that industry that would interfere with the efficient workings of the market. Coase's analysis showed that such costs are best attributed *not* to a single activity (affecting others nearby) but rather to the *interaction* of two or more activities. Within this larger context, a number of points became clearer: that whatever the initial distribution of entitlements (for example, to pollute a stream, or to prevent pollution of that stream), the parties might negotiate to transfer the entitlement in exchange for payment, if the party who does not have the right values it more than the party who does. In summary, Coase's theorem showed that, transaction costs aside, the amoral force of the market would override any policy-driven distribution of rights: rights would end up inevitably (through voluntary bargains) with the party who valued them the most. (However, Coase also noted that, because transaction costs were pervasive and non-trivial, the initial distribution of rights *might* have some consequences for which activities would occur.)

Calabresi was the first modern, comprehensive application of economic analysis to a whole area of legal doctrine, in this case, tort (accident) law. Calabresi's analysis used Coase's theorem, and developed an additional helpful analytical tool, the concept of the cheapest cost avoider (here, the cheapest accident avoider).

The most influential modern exponent of the movement is Richard Posner. Posner started from Coase's focus on voluntary (market) transactions in rights and duties. Where voluntary transactions were possible, a strong justification was needed (some sort of "market failure") for government intervention and regulation. Where voluntary transactions were not possible, legislatively or judicially imposed terms should, to the extent possible, mimic what parties would have agreed to, had they had the chance. POSNER (1998) is an influential textbook, now in its fifth edition, which ranges widely over law and human behaviour, offering an economic understanding for why people act the way they do, and why certain rules might be more "efficient" than alternative rules. However, because it covers so many topics in a single volume and because it is meant to be usable as a student text, there are some limits to its value as a reference work.

POSNER (1981) was an earlier work that contained a far more ambitious claim for law and economics: that economic analysis (in the form of a theory of "wealth maximization") could also work (a) as a historical explanation for the development of common law legal doctrines and (b) as a theory of justice. As to the first, Posner had argued that 19th-century judges had developed common law principles in line with "wealth maximization" as the result of intuition or a kind of "invisible hand" mechanism. As to the second, Posner had argued that wealth maximization, properly understood, combined the best elements of utilitarianism and Kantian moral theory by making decisions turn on the actual or hypothetical consent of parties (what they did agree to or would have agreed to had they been asked). Both the historical and normative claims were very controversial when offered, and they seem over time to have been largely abandoned, even by their author.

POLINSKY is a good introduction to the way in which economic analysis has been applied to a number of standard legal topics; however, this is now a decade old and a number of recent developments are not covered in the text. More detailed discussions of the claims, strengths, and weaknesses of the law and economics movement can be found both in HANSON & HART and in KATZ. Hanson & Hart is a sympathetic critique of a law and economics, including an interesting critical evaluation of the standard law and economics efficiency-based analysis of negligence cases. In particular, Hanson & Hart show how an economic analysis might depend on a determination of factors like the parties' activity levels, information that would probably *not* be available to the judge or other decision maker. Katz is a collection of excerpts from some of the most important articles written within the law and economics movement and in criticism of it, as well as excerpts from well-known articles applying economic analysis to a wide variety of doctrinal fields.

Some of the most interesting work now being done comes from the related areas of game theory and public choice theory. Game theory models interactions as though they were games: with different "players" using different "strategies" – each acting in a certain way based on an expectation of how the other player(s) might react. Public choice theory is the application of economic analysis, at least in terms of assuming that parties are always acting to maximize their self-interest (rather than, say, work for the public good), to the actions of officials. BAIRD, GERTNER & PICKER is an excellent and thorough introduction to game theory and its possible applications to law. Public choice theory is perhaps less well developed in its application to law; FARBER & FRICKEY is a competent, if occasionally unsatisfactory, introduction.

For those who want a deeper and wider-ranging introduction to the economic analysis of law, NEWMAN's reference work is likely to set the standard for some time to come. Its three volumes cover an enormous (and only occasionally idiosyncratic) range of topics; the quality of the entries inevitably is not uniform, but most of the pieces are very good discussions written by some of the most important contributors to the field.

BRIAN BIX

See also Law and economics

Economic anthropology

Bloch, Maurice (editor), *Marxist Analyses and Social Anthropology*, London: Malaby Press, and New York: Wiley, 1975

Dalton, George (editor), *Tribal and Peasant Economies: Readings in Economic Anthropology*, Garden City, New York: Natural History Press, 1967

Douglas, Mary and Baron Isherwood, *The World of Goods: Towards an Anthropology of Consumption*, revised edition, London and New York: Routledge, 1996

Firth, Raymond (editor), *Themes in Economic Anthropology*, London and New York: Tavistock, 1967

Gudeman, Steve, *Economics as Culture*, London and Boston: Routledge and Kegan Paul, 1986

Mauss, Marcel, *The Gift: The Form and Reason for Exchange in Archaic Societies*, New York: Norton, and London: Routledge, 1990 (French edition 1925)

Polanyi, Karl, Conrad M. Arensberg and Harry W. Pearson (editors), *Trade and Market in the Early Empires: Economies in History and Theory*, Glencoe, Illinois: Free Press, and London: Collier Macmillan, 1957

Sahlins, Marshall, *Stone Age Economics*, Chicago: Aldine Atherton, 1972; London: Tavistock, 1974

The main academic dispute in economic anthropology is between formalists and substantivists. The formalists emphasize similarities between primitive, peasant, aboriginal, tribal, ancient, and all other societies, analysing them from the perspective of modern economics. The substantivists, on the other hand, insist on the social and cultural specificity and embeddedness of economic relations. They use special categories of analysis, such as gift giving, reciprocity, redistribution, and special-purpose money, which have no counterparts in conventional economics.

MAUSS is the founding work in the substantivist tradition. For Mauss, the exchanges in primitive societies are total social phenomena. They are at the same time economic, legal, juridical, moral, aesthetic, religious, and mythological. Their meaning can only be grasped as a complex concrete reality needing ethnographic methods (especially knowledge of the relevant languages) rather than abstract models. This may be seen in the *potlatch* among Northwest American Indians, where excess goods are ceremonially and enthusiastically destroyed against all principles of self interest or utility. Thus, archaic societies are not just subsistence societies, but everywhere produce surplus that is exchanged because of obligations to give and return gifts. Indeed, for Mauss, the foundation of being human is reciprocity and the obligations related to giving and receiving. To receive something is to receive part of one's spirit (*hau*): "The thing given is not inert. It is alive and often personified, and strives to bring to its original clan and homeland some equivalent to take its place".

The substantivist discussion was a central element in the formation, by Karl Polanyi and Conrad Arensberg, of an interdisciplinary research project (on institutional aspects of economic growth), which became known as the "Columbia circle". POLANYI, ARENSBERG AND PEARSON compiled many of the related debates about trade and markets in early empires. DALTON added to these discussions, noting that among the reasons for a marked interest in the economic aspects of traditional communities are "the colonial revolutions in Africa, Asia, and Latin America". Many of the contributors are, again, connected to the Columbia circle, but there are several articles here that engage in the formalist debate (for example, by Mary Douglas, Paul Bohannan, and Richard Thurnwald on the nature and methodology of economics applied to social anthropology). It also includes articles on precapitalist Europe by Max Weber, M.I. Finlay, and Henri Pirenne; on South America by Eric R. Wolf, and Manning Nash; on Asia by Clifford Geertz, Matsuyo Takizawa, and

Martin C. Yang; on Oceania by Bronisław Malinowski; and on Africa by I. Shapera and Jacques Macquet.

SAHLINS provides one of the most scathing critiques of the formalist position. The opening article is a celebrated piece on "The Original Affluent Society". Sahlins contrasts the dismal economists' concept of subsistence economies with original affluence:

> the Galbraithian assumption that people's wants are great, not to say infinite, whereas means are limited, with a Zen assumption that human material wants are finite and few, and technical means unchanging but on the whole adequate.

Broadly speaking, says Sahlins, it is "a choice between business and culture". There are further essays on: "the domestic mode of production"; "the spirit of the gift"; and "exchange value and the diplomacy of trade".

The contributions in FIRTH, on the other hand, generally imply an acceptance of the formalist view that "the logic of scarcity is, in fact, operative over the whole range of economic phenomena, and that, however deep and complex may be the influence of social factors, the notions of economy and economizing are not basically separate". The opening article is a critique of Mauss and, by implication, substantivist perspectives. There are further discussions by Mary Douglas (on the Lele of the Kasai region in the Congo); Fredrik Barth (on the Mountain Fur economy, Dafur); Sutti Ortiz (on the structure of decision making among Indians of Colombia); Scarlett Epstein (on productive efficiency in the *jajmani* system in rural South India); and Lorraine Barić (on new economic opportunities in rural Yugoslav agriculture).

BLOCH represents the Marxist involvements in economic anthropology, influenced particularly by Levi-Strauss and Louis Althusser. Most of the essays are concerned with the relationships between kinship, systems of production, religion, culture, and representations of property. They are written by Maurice Godelier, Emmanuel Terray, Joel Kahn, Jonathan Friedman, and Maurice Bloch.

DOUGLAS & ISHERWOOD introduce a new perspective to economic anthropology, which examines consumer goods as a means through which culture is constituted. Commodities are said to be "good for thinking: treat them as a non-verbal medium for the human creative faculty". Thus, "the essential function of consumption is the capacity to make sense". Humans are said to be meaning-making animals more than they are profit-maximizing animals. Food is seen as not just good to eat, but good to think. Douglas shows how to decipher the social meaning of a meal, taking food as a system of cultural communication. The work investigates the communicative role of economic goods and the ways individuals confirm status through consumption, developing the idea that the flow of goods is part of a status etiquette.

GUDEMAN argues for a further approach beyond the formalist, neoclassical, Marxist, and substantivist, namely a cultural one which argues that all material life is itself a human construction. Gudeman combines positions (such as that of Mary Douglas) that think of exchange as linked to human classifications or thought, with those emphasizing the models that people construct of their material systems (in the same

ways as social scientists use models, metaphors and rhetoric in their constructions of markets or other phenomena). He notes that local economic models often explain material events by using human figures or images such as the body, family, or descent relationships. For example, in some societies land fertility may be linked to lineage. Keeping proper kinship relations may thus secure the ancestral benevolence that results in good harvests. Gudeman argues that such a perspective may avoid problems of misconstruing other peoples' actions more typical of abstract or ethnocentric methods and models.

ARTHUR E. McCULLOUGH

Economic crises

Armstrong, Philip, Andrew Glyn and John Harrison, *Capitalism since World War II: The Making and Breakup of the Great Boom*, London: Fontana, 1984

Baran, Paul A. and Paul M. Sweezy, *Monopoly Capital: An Essay on the American Economic and Social Order*, New York: Monthly Review Press, 1966

Bleaney, M.F., *Underconsumption Theories: A History and Critical Analysis*, London: Lawrence and Wishart, and New York: International Publishers, 1976

Cowling, Keith, *Monopoly Capitalism*, London: Macmillan, and New York: Wiley, 1982

Fine, Ben and Andy Murfin, *Macroeconomics and Monopoly Capitalism*, Brighton: Harvester, and New York: St Martin's Press, 1984

Gamble, Andrew and Paul Walton, *Capitalism in Crisis: Inflation and the State*, London: Macmillan, and Atlantic Highlands, New Jersey: Humanities Press, 1976

Luxemburg, Rosa, *The Accumulation of Capital*, London: Routledge and Kegan Paul, and New Haven, Connecticut: Yale University Press, 1951 (German edition 1921)

Strachey, John, *The Nature of Capitalist Crisis*, London: Gollancz, and New York: Covici Friede, 1935

The literature on economic crises is largely within Marxist economics, as non-Marxist economics tends not to use the term "crises" to describe the periodic downturns in economic activity within capitalist economies. Instead there are separate literatures within non-Marxist economics on the business cycle, and particularly acute crises such as the Great Depression of the 1930s. The literature on the Great Depression is covered in a separate entry, as is Marxist economics. This entry therefore reports some additional contributions, mostly still within the Marxist tradition and approach, that focus explicitly on the nature of economic crises within capitalism.

The starting point for Marx's own work on the topic is his three-volume work *Capital*, but this is discussed in the separate entry on Marxist economics, as are several other pieces of literature that report and discuss Marx's views. Marx saw numerous contradictions within the workings of the capitalist economy that could result in crises. Underlying these various contradictions is the fact that the capitalist economy is anarchic and unplanned. In addition, goods and services are only produced and provided so long as they can be sold at a profit to the individual capitalist. One of the major contradictions is that employers like the workers in all other firms to be well paid so they can afford to buy the goods that each capitalist is producing for sale, but at the same time want to pay their own workers as little as possible so as to maximise profits. The problem is that if workers collectively are paid less than the sum of what all wage goods are being sold for, there will be a lack of demand, or "underconsumption". This will leave profits "unrealised", output will be cut back, and workers laid off, exacerbating the original problem.

This strand of "underconsumption" theories – non-Marxist as well as Marxist – are reviewed and discussed by BLEANEY. Bleaney argues that Marx has often been misrepresented (by both followers and critics) as a crude type of "underconsumptionist", whereas in fact any such interpretation fails to appreciate the richness of Marx's analysis. Bleaney traces two distinct strands of "underconsumption" theory: one stemming from Malthus and emphasising the absolute level of savings, the other from Sismondi who emphasised the distribution of incomes as the cause of crises. He examines the connection of these theories with "classical" ideas of investment and revenues, and their influences in contemporary economic thinking.

Rosa LUXEMBURG was one of the early Marxists to analyse the nature of capitalist crises. The edition cited above includes an introduction by the late Professor Joan Robinson. Luxemburg's argument is usually reported as being essentially an underconsumptionist one, although Bleaney, in the book referred to above, argues that this is a misinterpretation of her analysis. Luxemburg's analysis is in any case a global, international one. Instead of focusing on the contradiction referred to above (of capitalists being unable to sell sufficient quantities to the domestic working class), she is concerned with the way that capital is continually attempting to expand globally, with the leading capitalist countries attempting to sell increasing quantities outside their domestic bases.

John STRACHEY produced several major works on the economic, social, and political nature of capitalist crises during the 1930s, including the one cited above. Although a member of the Labour Party, he wrote from a Marxist perspective; following World War II, however, he joined the Labour administration and moved to a firmly social democratic ideological position. In the above book, though, he describes the Marxist analysis of economic crisis, as well as non-Marxist approaches which, he argues, fail to give a satisfactory account of the phenomena to be explained. He also includes what at the time were contemporary discussions of the 1930s crisis, the role of fascism and of social democracy, and the causes of war.

BARAN & SWEEZY is an analysis of the US economy not in a time of crisis but rather during the long post-World War II boom. However, they argue that even then, the US economy had a tendency towards stagnation, largely for the sort of underconsumptionist reasons sketched above. They include a detailed discussion, though, of the various ways in which capitalist economies can avoid falling into underconsumptionist traps, although in the case of the US, they describe the powerful political and economic forces at work which may block these escape avenues. Their book also discusses price-fixing, the cartels, and the tendency towards monopoly within the US economic and social systems. The book analyses the implications of corporate monopoly and the dynamics of exploitation in the Third World.

The nature of monopoly capitalism is also analysed by COWLING, who argues that, in contrast to the US, European countries came later to the monopoly phase of capitalism, the implications of which he examines for the income of workers and also for the development of the economy as a whole. By dropping the unrealistic assumptions made in much mainstream economics about a competitive market, Cowling is able to be more realistic about the macroeconomy.

FINE & MURFIN is a critical appraisal not only of the monetarist and Keynesian approaches to modern economics, but also the Kaleckian, and includes a critique of the sort of approaches described above of Baran & Sweezy and of Cowling. The authors argue that the radical tradition associated with Baran & Sweezy, Kalecki, and the post-Keynesians has attempted to address the reality of monopolisation and economic crises but that, nevertheless, this tradition has also suffered from theoretical and empirical weaknesses.

A more explicit analysis of economic crisis is provided by GAMBLE & WALTON, which looks at Keynesian, monetarist, and Marxist theories of inflation, and dismisses what the authors see as the rather facile claim that trade unions are to blame. The book analyses how the post-war boom originated and why it petered out, emphasizing the contradictory but crucial role of the modern state in the past success as well as failure of the mixed economy.

A more detailed analysis of the "golden age" of capitalism, and subsequent demise of the long postwar boom, is provided by ARMSTRONG, GLYN & HARRISON. This starts with a very detailed discussion of how the global economy recovered from World War II and established the long post-war boom. The analysis is international, focussing on the US, Western Europe, and Japan. It looks in detail at how the European and Japanese employers had first to struggle to regain control of the shopfloor – a topic largely ignored in non-Marxist writing. The mechanisms that sustained the "golden years" and the forces that undermined them are then analysed, as are the subsequent responses of the new right and the left to the failure of conventional economic policies.

JONATHAN MICHIE

See also Great Depression, Marxist economics

Economic democracy

Adizes, Ichak, *Industrial Democracy, Yugoslav Style: The Effect of Decentralization on Organizational Behavior*, New York: Free Press, 1971

Blumberg, Paul, *Industrial Democracy: The Sociology of Participation*, London: Constable, 1968; New York: Schocken, 1969

Economic Analysis (and *Workers Management*), 1967–92; new series: *Journal of Enterprise and Participation*, 1998–

Economic and Industrial Democracy, 1979–

Greenberg, Edward S., *Workplace Democracy: The Political Effects of Participation*, Ithaca, New York: Cornell University Press, 1986

Horvat, Branko, Mihailo Marković and Rudi Supek (editors), *Self-Governing Socialism: A Reader*, 2 vols, White Plains, New York: International Arts and Sciences Press, 1975

Horvat, Branko, "Full Democracy – Socialism of 21st
    Century" in *Social Democracy in Europe Today*, edited by
    B. Marković, Belgrade: Institute of International Politics
    and Economics, 1996

Thomas, Henk and Chris Logan, *Mondragon: An Economic
    Analysis*, London and Boston: Allen and Unwin, 1982

Thomas Isaac, T.M., Richard W. Franke and Pyaralal
    Raghavan, *Democracy at Work in an Indian Industrial
    Cooperative*, Ithaca, New York: ILR Press, 1998

Vanek, Jaroslav, *The Participatory Economy: An
    Evolutionary Hypothesis and a Strategy for Development*,
    Ithaca, New York: Cornell University Press, 1971

ECONOMIC ANALYSIS and ECONOMIC AND INDUS-TRIAL DEMOCRACY are two international journals dealing with economic and industrial democracy. The former is dedicated to the economic analysis of labour-managed firms and national economies; the latter approaches the problem from the point of view of industrial relations and sociology. Economic democracy is an older term whose origin is to be found in social developments after the French Revolution, and was popularized by socialists, especially by Marxists. Political democracy, it is argued, cannot be genuine if economic opportunities are not equalized simultaneously – if political democracy is not complemented by economic democracy. The term "industrial democracy" is to be traced to the Webbs' book *Industrial Democracy* (1897). It has a narrower concept and denotes democracy within industrial plants. Related terms are "workers' self-management", "labour management", and "producer cooperatives".

HORVAT *et al.* collected all the most important writings on economic and industrial democracy since 1820 (Robert Owen). There are four clearly defined stages in the historical development of the idea and its implementation: the utopian stage in the 19th century, with isolated attempts at implementation that did not survive for long; joint consultation, pioneered in England after World War I; codetermination, introduced by Germany and other European countries after World War II; and labour management (self-management) as the highest stage, introduced in Yugoslavia in 1950 and also practised, in a more radical form, by Israeli *kibbutzim*.

ADIZES undertakes a detailed analysis of Yugoslav workers' management, its origins, aims, successes, and failures by studying effects of decentralization on organizational behaviour. Yugoslav workers' management was the first attempt to organize the entire national economy on self-management (decentralized) lines.

VANEK is interested in the efficiency of the participatory economy. He compares Western capitalism, the Eastern command economy, and the participatory economy as vehicles of economic development. He finds the participatory economy to be superior to the other two alternative systems.

GREENBERG analyses the experience of producer cooperatives. He is particularly interested in work alienation and class-consciousness. On the basis of his findings he draws conclusions about political effects of workplace democracy. He sees the drive towards political and economic equality and the dispersal of power as the most important.

THOMAS & LOGAN have written the first study on the Basque producer cooperative, which has become the best known case of industrial democracy that survived for decades. The Basque country is the most industrial part of Spain. The originator of the Mondragon producer cooperative was Catholic priest Don José María Arizmendi-Arrieta. The cooperative was founded in 1943, during the Franco dictatorship. The number of people it employed increased from 24 in 1956 to 15,672 in 1979. There are 70 cooperative factories. The shelter organization is a cooperative bank, Caja Laboral Popular, with 93 branches and 300,000 deposit accounts. Since then the Mondragon system has developed further and it is now the leading producer in Spain in its lines of production.

THOMAS ISAAC, FRANKE & RAGHAVAN present the history of an Indian producer cooperative, Kerala Dinesh Beedi Workers' Cooperative Society Ltd (KDB), which is likely to become an Indian Mondragon. Kerala is one of the poorest Indian states with a per capita annual income of $189. However, it achieved almost 100 per cent literacy and three-quarters of KDB workers have seven years' education or more. Kerala Dinesh Beedi Workers' Cooperative Society Ltd was created in 1969 by a directive of the socialist State Cabinet. In 1993, it consisted of 22 primary cooperatives employing 33,000 worker owners. From 1969 to 1992 the sales increased from 1,000,000 to 588,000,000 rupees. At first it was almost entirely financed by the government, which owned 93 per cent of capital. By 1994 the government share declined to 56 per cent. Although it is the majority owner, the government appoints only two members of the seven-member board of directors. Worker-owners elect the other five members. The 23rd cooperative, the central society, performs the role of a shelter organization.

BLUMBERG undertakes a sociological analysis of workers' participation. He reviews the literature on participation and tries to establish how much participation mitigates work alienation. Special attention is given to Yugoslav self-management. The traditional hierarchical setting in the factory, where directives flow from owners and managers down to operatives, is now complemented by a flow in the opposite direction so that the organizational pyramid is transformed into a sand-glass organization: managers issue technical directives (through the managerial structure of the firm's organization) and workers issue political directives (through the electoral structure), including the elections of managers.

HORVAT attempts to lay foundations for a theory of full democracy. Democracy, Horvat argues, as has been practised so far, is partial democracy. Full democracy has three components: political democracy, social democracy, and economic democracy. Political democracy, implying political and juridical equality, was developed after bourgeois revolutions in the 19th century, which generated economic liberalism. The awareness, generated by experience, that political democracy is not sufficient and cannot function properly if all citizens are not able to participate in public life on equal footing, led to the organization of social democratic parties in the second half of the last century. By the middle of the 20th century, the so-called welfare state came into existence as a result of the pressures of the numerous social-democratic parties that appeared in the meantime. It was again found that something was lacking. If all citizens are to be socially equal, the economic component of democracy must be added. That was an old request of early socialists, but it could not be satisfied in practice earlier.

Economic democracy completes the democratization of social life. Thus, full democracy represents the socialism of 21st century.

BRANKO HORVAT

Economic geography

Amin, Ash (editor), *Post-Fordism: A Reader*, Oxford and Cambridge, Massachusetts: Blackwell, 1994

Barnes, Trevor J., *Logics of Dislocation: Models, Metaphors, and Meanings of Economic Space*, New York: Guilford Press, 1996

Batty, Michael and Paul Longley, *Fractal Cities: A Geometry of Form and Function*, London and San Diego: Academic Press, 1994

Castells, Manuel, *Information Age: Economy, Society, and Culture*, 3 vols, *The Rise of the Network Society*, vol. 1, Oxford and Cambridge, Massachusetts: Blackwell, 1996–98

Dymski, Gary, "On Krugman's Model of Economic Geography", *Geoforum*, 27/4 (November 1996): 439–52

Economic Geography, 1992–

Gibson-Graham, J.K., *The End of Capitalism (as We Knew It): A Feminist Critique of Political Economy*, Oxford and Cambridge, Massachusetts: Blackwell, 1996

Harvey, David, *Explanation in Geography*, London: Arnold, 1969; New York: St Martin's Press, 1970

Harvey, David, *The Limits to Capital*, Oxford: Blackwell, and Chicago: University of Chicago Press, 1982

Harvey, David, *The Condition of Postmodernity: An Inquiry into the Origins of Cultural Change*, Oxford and Cambridge, Massachusetts: Blackwell, 1989

Krugman, Paul, *The Self-Organizing Economy*, Oxford and Cambridge, Massachusetts: Blackwell, 1996

Martin, Ron, "The New 'Geographical Turn' in Economics: Some Critical Reflections", *Cambridge Journal of Economics*, 23/1 (January 1999): 65–91

Massey, Doreen B., *Spatial Divisions of Labor: Social Structures and the Geography of Production*, 2nd edition, New York: Routledge, and London: Macmillan, 1995

Scott, Allen J. and Michael Storper, *Production, Work, Territory: The Geographical Anatomy of Industrial Capitalism*, London and Boston: Allen and Unwin, 1986

Sheppard, Eric and Trevor J. Barnes, *The Capitalist Space Economy: Geographical Analysis after Ricardo, Marx, and Sraffa*, London and Boston: Unwin Hyman, 1990

Soja, Edward W., *Thirdspace: Journeys to Los Angeles and Other Real-and-Imagined Places*, Oxford and Cambridge, Massachusetts: Blackwell, 1996

Straussfogel, Debra, "World-Systems Theory: Toward a Heuristic and Pedagogic Conceptual Tool", *Economic Geography*, 73/1 (January 1997): 118–30

Webber, Michael J. and David L. Rigby, *The Golden Age Illusion: Rethinking Postwar Capitalism*, New York: Guilford Press, 1996

In no area of social inquiry is multidisciplinary inquiry so advanced as in the field of geography. Drawing on diverse methods and bodies of evidence in their pursuit of spatial questions, geographers have created a synthetic approach that draws on sociology, economics, political science, and history. By contrast, economists working on spatial questions do not generally display this degree of methodological tolerance. In particular, economic theorists often insist that social relations are well conceptualized only when depicted mathematically in rational-choice models.

So the term "economic geography" itself is ambiguous: it represents an intersection point between two fields whose investigators often disagree about the appropriate languages of inquiry and representation. A reader's guide to this field can thus indicate this field's diversity, without the hope of being definitive.

One way of mapping this diverse field is to sample articles published in ECONOMIC GEOGRAPHY. A review of recent issues finds methods ranging from spatial equilibrium maps to empirical investigations to postmodern analyses; topics covered range from historical patterns of industrial development to world-systems theory and the contemporary spread of transnational corporations.

A second mapping traces the trajectory of some of the long-time contributors to the field of economic geography. The most intriguing intellectual odyssey is that of David Harvey. Harvey was originally an eminent analyst committed to technical tools of analysis rooted in linear programming and economic theory, a mastery eminently evidenced in HARVEY (1969). The opening of this field to diverse methodological approaches was boosted considerably by Harvey's exploration of Marxian theory, especially HARVEY (1982). This volume's spatial interpretation of Marx's economic theories remains among the best interpretations of Marx's opus. It powerfully portrays urban spatial growth as contradictory and uneven because it represents the embodiment of the class struggles and economic crises that accompany capitalist accumulation processes.

The acceptance of Marxian theory as a fundamental reference point has itself opened up multiple threads within economic geography. One thread explores the spatial implications of Marxian concepts. MASSEY's volume (first published in 1984), a progenitor of a huge literature on industrial restructuring within economic geography, was written partly in reaction to Harvey's extremely abstract treatment; her work emphasizes the importance of concrete depictions of place and context in understanding spatial relations.

A second thread in geographers' writings about industrial restructuring explores the spatial implications and logic of the French "regulation" school of Michel Aglietta, Alain Lipietz, and their co-thinkers (including many American and British political economists). In this approach, capitalist economic dynamics are modified profoundly by state and global institutions that enable and regulate market forces. AMIN reviews the application of regulationist ideas to geography, especially the notion that a mass-production "Fordist" regime of accumulation has been followed by a "post-Fordist" regime.

Sraffa's linear production model has also been profoundly influential within economic geography. This influence arises both because Sraffa's model formalizes some core Marxian ideas about value/price and wage/profit relationships, and because this model is formally identical to the input-output model of Leontief. The Leontief model *per se* provides the cornerstone of the literature on regional growth and impact analysis developed by theorists such as Isard and Stone.

The question of whether conclusions of abstract models must be contextualized, noted in the work of Harvey and of Massey, also arises in applications of Sraffian and Leontief models. For example, neo-Marxian geographers have used Sraffian models to develop rigorous models of capitalist crisis. SHEPPARD & BARNES showed how the capital–labour conflict inherent in Sraffa's framework, when combined with spatial interpretations of industrial cost and residential location decisions, can explain patterns of urban settlement, technical change and industrial restructuring, and monopoly power. WEBBER & RIGBY went further: they argued that, because the Sraffa-based spatial model already contains the potential for endogenous crises due to technological competition and productivity decline, regulationist ideas about the decline of capitalism's golden age are redundant.

For most economic geographers, purely formal analyses of phenomena such as capitalist crisis and urban dynamics cannot yield complete and sufficient explanations. BARNES himself has argued that because of the complex character of lived historical experiences, the insights derived from formal and other approaches, and from bodies of empirical evidence, are fundamentally discursive and narrative. No one formal approach, no matter how rigorous, can trump all others in explaining concrete reality. Consequently, many geographers work synthetically, combining insights from Marxian, neo-classical, and spatial-equilibrium theories to produce unique insights into industrialization and urbanization processes. SCOTT & STORPER is a representative synthetic work; these authors draw on locational equilibrium, network, and micro-economic theory, and on models of class processes, to write authoritatively about the growth and transformation of urban industrial clusters.

Barnes illustrates the growing importance within geography of the postmodern view that monolithic viewpoints are unsustainable and, ultimately, anti-intellectual (totalizing). Ironically, this appreciation of the need for methodological and theoretical multiplicity is derived from the Marxian reinterpretation of economic geography as a field; so Marxian logic remains at the centre even as it becomes one among many alternative perspectives for postmodernists. This brings us to the most recent stage in David Harvey's evolution – his efforts, including HARVEY (1989), to appreciate post-Modernism even while retaining the core insights of Marxian theory. Harvey's (1990) attempt at double vision has been controversial; some who embrace postmodernism would reject not only Harvey's suggested compromise, but also the possibility of an economic – as opposed to a social or human – geography.

For GIBSON-GRAHAM, the postmodernist rejection of the privileging of purely economic relations results in the virtual erasure of the line between lived individual perception and social analysis. Gibson-Graham argues, in particular, that discourse about both Fordism and post-Fordism is economistic and male centred; breaking free of this constraint means appreciating the presence of gender bias in geographers' choices of topics and in the very metaphors used to conceptualize social experience.

SOJA's appropriation of postmodern ideas leads in a different direction: for him, social complexity arises as much from the inescapability of space as from the inevitability of time and of struggles over social being. Following Lefebvre, Soja argues that space is not a terrain for playing out other social relations, but an independent dimension. "Trialectics" – non-reductive analytical attention to time, power, and space itself – is proposed as an open method that may permit the coexistence of diverse modernist and postmodernist methods and insights.

Sraffian models are not the only way to formalize spatial relations. Some of Paul Krugman's recent writings have given renewed impetus to spatial applications of formal choice-theoretic models. While Krugman has used microfoundational models to reinterpret classical problems in location theory, his work involves more broadly the application of nonlinear modelling–in his specific case, increasing returns to scale models–to spatial questions. KRUGMAN recognizes this link, in a volume marred less by gratuitous remarks about the field of geography than his previous books on spatial topics. MARTIN's penetrating response to this "geographical turn" by Krugman and other economic theorists argues that they model space too narrowly because they are interested in describing abstract space, not any specific place. DYMSKI, in turn, traces Krugman's lack of appreciation for geographers' synthetic approach to his equation of social-scientific modelling with rational-choice equilibrium theorizing.

Krugman's approach is only one way of incorporating nonlinearity and thus pathdependence in models of social processes. BATTY & LONGLEY present nonlinearity in the guise of fractal geometry; they adapt the chaotic dynamic approach of Mandelbrot to the problem of urban growth. They present a detailed depiction of urban dynamics, which incorporates a surprising amount of detail about micro-units' choices. These authors' models aptly demonstrate the power of formal nonlinear models in representing complex systems.

The problem that has most concerned economic geographers in recent years is globalization. CASTELLS' three-volume opus is especially adventurous. He argues that technological and social changes have created a new social context that revolutionizes social relations of production and reproduction. This perspective conflicts with the long-established world-systems perspective, according to which globalization has been an inherent feature of world social dynamics throughout the entire development of modern capitalism. The conceptual status of world-systems theory is uncertain in light of the emergence of possibly complementary frameworks such as complexity theory. STRAUSSFOGEL provides references to classic world-systems theoretical works, and argues that world-systems theory must be reconceptualized if it is to survive.

GARY A. DYMSKI

Economic history

Coleman, Donald C., *History and the Economic Past: An Account of the Rise and Decline of Economic History in Britain*, Oxford: Clarendon Press, and New York: Oxford University Press, 1987

Harte, Negley B., "Trends in Publications on Economics and Social History in Great Britain and Ireland, 1925–74", *Economic History Review*, 30/1 (1977): 20–39

Kadish, Alon, *Historians, Economists, and Economic History*, London and New York: Routledge, 1989

Lee, Clive H., *The Quantitative Approach to Economic History*, London: Martin Robertson, and New York: St Martin's Press, 1977

McCloskey, Donald N., *Econometric History*, Basingstoke: Macmillan, 1987

McCloskey, Donald N., George K. Hersh Jr and John Coatsworth, *A Bibliography of Historical Economics to 1980*, Cambridge and New York: Cambridge University Press, 1990

McDonald, John and G.D. Snooks, *Doomsday Economy: A New Approach to Anglo-Norman History*, Oxford: Clarendon Press, and New York: Oxford University Press, 1986

Middleton, Roger and Peter Wardley, "Annual Review of Information Technology Developments for Economic and Social Historians, 1990", *Economic History Review*, 44/2 (1991): 343–93

WebEc (http://www.helsinki.fi/WebEc/webecn.html)

This entry has selected publications that describe the origins of economic history, how the discipline evolved from the 1950s, the direction of research since the 1920s, and some of the sources available to economic historians on the internet.

There are numerous accounts of the evolution of the discipline of economic history in the UK. KADISH traces the disintegration of political economy in the second half of the 19th century and shows how economics and economic history emerged as separate disciplines. The book also discusses the contribution of some of the earliest economic historians such as W. J Ashley, John Clapham, Eileen Power and R H Tawney. The shortcoming of the book is that it deals more or less exclusively with the development of economic history at Oxford and Cambridge, and does not discuss developments beyond the foundation of the Economic History Society in 1926, and of the world's earliest economic history journal, the *Economic History Review* in 1927. COLEMAN offers a broader appeal than Kadish and discusses the challenge of historians, demographers, Annales and others from one side of economic history, and of economic development from the other. He also notes how economic history has remained relatively isolated throughout and while the discipline enjoyed a boom in schools and universities in the 1960s and 1970s, its popularity has since declined steadily.

To gain a flavour of what economic historians were writing about from the mid-1920s through to the mid-1970s, the reader is recommended to consult HARTE's article. He shows how the first twenty five years were characterized by a very slow growth in published output, with the annual number of articles exceeding 100 only three times during that period, and the annual number of books exceeding 50 only four times. Taking articles and books together, the biggest area of growth for publications before 1950 was in agriculture and agrarian society, followed by industry and internal trade. In the late 1950s, urban studies and local history displaced agriculture and industry, only to be replaced by agriculture in the early 1960s and by industry in the late 1960s. By the early 1970s, social conditions and policy had emerged as the biggest single category. Though Harte's article is a good indicator of how

the economic history literature has evolved in the UK, there are two limitations with his analysis. First, the survey is limited to published writings on Great Britain and Ireland. Second, Harte's article contains numerous sarcastic comments about the developments within economic history from the end of the 1950s.

During the last four decades economic history has been one of the most fortunate academic disciplines within the social sciences. Among others, LEE has shown that during this period economic history has been thrice blessed. First, with the stimuli of theoretical developments. These were inspired not only by the immediate and traditional concerns of the discipline but also by associated conceptual innovations in cognate disciplines. Naturally, economic theory and applied economics provided invaluable stimulants here but political science, sociology, and other branches of historical studies have also been influential. Second, with advances in quantitative techniques, including a number of variants of the basic regression model. Here the nature of historical enquiry has been sharpened as much by the necessary clarification of the historical question under investigation as by the application of statistical theory to test explicitly hypotheses concerning historical phenomena. Third, with the fruits of technological developments, that transformed machines that calculated, copied, and cached information. Of course, the most significant of these, which has been of ever increasing importance, was the computer, which allowed the mechanization of data collection, storage, representation and analysis.

It is the explicit combination of applied theory, quantification and IT, which has been the hallmark of scholars who have provided the most dynamic reshaping of economic history in the last forty years. As McCLOSKEY explains, a variety of labels have been used to describe the approach to economic history that achieved this synthesis; these include: the New Economic History, Econometric History, Quantitative Economic History, and the sobriquet Cliometric History. In spite of its jocular origin, and the not infrequent use of the term as a pejorative dismissal by critics of this approach, Cliometrics was incorporated in the title of the association of scholars which propounds this methodology. In her excellent pamphlet, McCloskey suggests that Historical Economics is not only a less misleading and less controversial designation, but also one which is more accurate.

The influence of this school is most apparent in the US and its success is demonstrated by the sheer volume of research output which has been achieved by scholars who have adopted this methodology. A recent bibliographic survey of historical economics by McCLOSKEY, HERSH & COATSWORTH cited 4,500 books and articles which encompass human history from the demise of the Roman empire to agricultural development in the tropics, via samurai income and the medieval monastic economy of the Cistercians. Despite the diversity of historical interest indicated here, it must be admitted that the greater proportion is comprised of nineteenth and twentieth century studies, and North American issues have a more than proportionate presence. However, it cannot be denied that the historical economists have ventured much further than is suggested by the usual delineation of their standard fare: railways, slavery and entrepreneurship.

As MIDDLETON & WARDLEY have illustrated, economic historians have been extraordinarily lucky in that many of the technical developments in IT have been prompted by the very activities which interest them most. Thus, for the economic historian, spreadsheets, econometric packages, and database management systems were literally made for the job. Despite the slow take-up rate of this technology – particularly as evidenced by its use as a research and teaching tool among economic historians – where it has been employed successfully the results can be very impressive. A good example is McDONALD & SNOOKS' investigation of the structure of manorial production in eleventh century Norman England. This work combines a historical and historiographic overview of the English economy in 1086 with an investigation of manorial income, production and taxation at the level of the region and locality, using models informed by neo-classical economic theory and the latest computer software.

Even the remaining IT sceptics would be foolish to ignore the importance of the internet for economic history. WEBEC, based at the Department of Economics at the University of Helsinki, hosts an excellent web page for the economic historian. From this page, it is possible to navigate to sites which contain working papers, book reviews, electronic journals, conference details, society listings and teaching materials. Within the next few years, it is hoped that both the student and professional economic historian will have full access to online teaching packages.

MICHAEL J. OLIVER AND PETER WARDLEY

See also Economics and history, Economic thought, history of

Economic psychology

Lea, Stephen E.G., Roger M. Tarpy and Paul Webley, *The Individual in the Economy: A Textbook of Economic Psychology*, Cambridge: Cambridge University Press, 1987

Lea, Stephen E.G. and Paul Webley, "Economic Psychology: An Introduction to a New Interdisciplinary Field" in *Elements of Applied Psychology*, edited by Peter Spurgeon, Roy Davies and Anthony J. Chapman, Chur, Switzerland: Harwood, 1994

Lewis, Alan, Paul Webley and Adrian Furnham, *The New Economic Mind: The Social Psychology of Economic Behaviour*, London and New York: Harvester Wheatsheaf, 1995

Lunt, Peter, "Rethinking the Relationship between Economics and Psychology", *Journal of Economic Psychology*, 17/2 (April 1996): 275–87

MacFadyen, Alan J. and Heather W. MacFadyen (editors), *Economic Psychology: Intersections in Theory and Application*, Amsterdam and New York: Elsevier, 1986

Poiesz, Theo B.C., "Introducing the Field of Economic Psychology" in *Handbook of Work and Organizational Psychology*, 2nd edition, edited by Pieter J.D. Drenth, Henk Thierry and Charles J. de Wolff, vol. 2, Hove: Psychology Press, 1998

Raaij, W. Fred van, Gery M. van Veldhoven and Karl-Erik Wärneryd, *Handbook of Economic Psychology*, Dordrecht and Boston: Kluwer, 1988

One of the problems for a reader new to this area is the disparate nature of the material described as "economic psychology". The term tends to be used loosely to cover a variety of related subjects such as experimental economics, the social psychology of economic behaviour, consumer psychology, and economic approaches to social behaviour. Most authors regard economic psychology as a branch of psychology and most texts concentrate on psychological approaches to various aspects of economic behaviour, but some texts contain a more eclectic mix of economics and psychology. A good starting point is the chapter by LEA & WEBLEY, which defines economic psychology in the context of related fields of enquiry such as occupational psychology and socio-economics. Most of the chapter is devoted to examples of psychological research on economic behaviour, but a short section discusses the assumptions of rationality in economics and economic psychology. This section provides a useful introduction to the question of whether or not people always act to maximize utility, which is at the heart of the paradigm difference between economics and psychology

LEA, TARPY & WEBLEY attempt to develop economic psychology as a genuine interdisciplinary effort between economics and psychology, at the same time as introducing the area to readers with no previous knowledge of either discipline. To this end they provide introductions to psychology, microeconomics, and macroeconomics and grapple with the question of whether or not human beings behave rationally. They go on to survey psychological research, and to a lesser extent economic research, on economic behaviour such as work, buying, saving, and giving. Several chapters address how the economy affects individual behaviour. The aims and achievements of the book are impressive. It is a rich source of material on individual economic behaviour, though it lacks a tight discursive structure.

The collection of papers in RAAIJ, VAN VELDHOVEN & WÄRNERYD also reflect a predominantly psychological approach to the study of economic behaviour. The opening chapter, by Wärneryd, defines economic psychology as the study of the psychological processes that underlie economic behaviour but argues that the boundaries of the discipline should remain open. Accordingly, most of the following chapters report psychological studies of economic behaviour but some, such as the chapter by March and Sevón on research relating to the behavioural theory of the firm, draw on economic theory as much as psychological theory. The organization of the rather eclectic chapters into sections on consumer behaviour, business behaviour and economic behaviour at the societal level reflects the design of the handbook as a text for marketing students, as well as psychology students.

One of the reasons why texts on economic psychology can seem confusing or chaotic is that economic psychologists draw on several subdisciplines in psychology. This "pick and mix" approach, drawing on such disparate theoretical fields as developmental, cognitive, social and biological psychology, is one of the reasons why non-psychologists, especially economists, find economic psychology cumbersome. The book by LEWIS, WEBLEY & FURNHAM achieves more theoretical consistency because it concentrates on social psychological research on economic behaviour. They concentrate on aspects of economic behaviour that are also quite social psychological because they relate to social problems or social issues, such as economic socialization, debt and gambling, poverty and wealth, unemployment, tax evasion, ethical investment and economic change. This may restrict interest in the text to social psychologists. LUNT argues that the only area of psychological theory and research in which economists have shown much interest is cognitive psychology, particularly the application of cognitive theories of reasoning to decision making. He points to problems in the concept of economic psychology as a unitary discipline and suggests ways in which social psychologists can engage more constructively with economics.

MACFADYEN & MACFADYEN is different in two ways from the texts described so far: it is North American rather than European in origin and most of the essays are written by economists. Indeed, MacFadyen & MacFadyen debate whether to describe the material as "economic psychology" or "behavioural economics", the latter being usually perceived as a branch of economics, but they conclude that the aims and interests are essentially the same. One strength of the book is that it includes essays by economists who have been influential in the development of cooperation between psychology and economics, such as Scitovsky and Maital. Another is that it manages to maintain some theoretical cohesion despite the usual disparate collection of topics by organizing the papers under two main themes – intersections in theory and intersections in application – and providing an editorial introduction to each paper. The book is useful and accessible to psychologists and economists alike.

Given that departments of management and organizational behaviour regularly employ both economists and psychologists, it is surprising that economic psychology is virtually never mentioned in texts on organizational behaviour or organizational psychology. POIESZ redresses that omission. He introduces the notion of economic behaviour with respect to allocation under conditions of scarcity, and concentrates on individual reactions to changing economic contexts, such as changes in income and taxation. He concludes by suggesting that the interests of economic and organizational psychologists coincide with respect to the question of rational decision making in organizations.

JULIE DICKINSON

Economic sociology

Becker, Gary S., *The Economic Approach to Human Behavior*, Chicago: University of Chicago Press, 1976

Etzioni, Amitai, *The Moral Dimension: Toward a New Economics*, New York: Free Press, and London: Collier Macmillan, 1988

Granovetter, Mark and Richard Swedberg (editors), *The Sociology of Economic Life*, Boulder, Colorado: Westview Press, 1990

Granovetter, Mark, "Economic Institutions as Social Constructions: A Framework for Analysis", Acta Sociologica, 35/1 (1992): 3–11

Ingham, G., "Some Recent Changes in the Relationship between Economics and Sociology", *Cambridge Journal of Economics*, 20/2 (1996): 243–75

McCloskey, Donald N., *The Rhetoric of Economics*, Madison: University of Wisconsin Press, 1985

Rowlinson, Michael, *Organizations and Institutions: Perspectives in Economics and Sociology*, Basingstoke: Macmillan, 1997

Smelser, Neil J. and Richard Swedberg (editors), *The Handbook of Economic Sociology*, Princeton, New Jersey: Princeton University Press, 1994

Swedberg, Richard, *Economics and Sociology, Redefining Their Boundaries: Conversations with Economists and Sociologists*, Princeton, New Jersey: Princeton University Press, 1990

Economic sociology (or the sociology of economic phenomena) is situated at the intersection between economics and sociology. Its intellectual origins can be traced back to the work of Marx, Weber, and Durkheim at the end of the 19th century. Between 1930 and 1980 interest in the field waned, but over the last two decades there has been a renaissance of both theoretical and empirical work in this area, centred especially around an intellectual movement known as the "new economic sociology".

GRANOVETTER provides a readable introduction to the subject area as he seeks to steer a middle path between "over- and under-socialized conceptions of human action". He does this by contending that behaviour is "embedded in concrete, ongoing systems of social relations" and therefore rejects the overly atomistic view that behavioural patterns can be explained simply by reference to the pursuit of narrow self-interest. Granovetter's socialized view of behaviour highlights the importance of the institutions within which actions takes place. Further, he notes that these institutions themselves are not inevitable but are socially constructed. They are "both facilitated and constrained by the structures and resources available in social networks in which they are embedded". Taking these contingencies into account is part of the distinctive contribution of new economic sociology.

The *Handbook of Economic Sociology* edited by SMELSER & SWEDBERG stands as a major testimony to the resurgence of interest in this area and represents the most comprehensive overview of the historical development and current challenges facing the discipline. The stated objectives of this collection of original essays are "to assemble, codify, systematise, and thereby advance knowledge about one of the most critical areas in the contemporary world-economy and society". This is a weighty tome of over 800 pages, and not the sort of book to be read from beginning to end in one sitting. It is best consulted selectively on specific topics of interest, or used as a reference guide.

The anthology edited by GRANOVETTER & SWEDBERG is a key text in drawing together many of the disparate strands of thought associated with new economic sociology (although not all the individual chapters are written from this perspective, as the book juxtaposes classic articles with more contemporary contributions). Interpretation of each chapter is enhanced with the use of extensive annotated references that locate each piece within an intellectual context. These annotations identify the follow up debates resulting from the work, and provide suggestions for further reading on the topic. Thus the book provides an excellent stepping-off point for newcomers to the discipline.

SWEDBERG is structured around the edited transcripts of interviews with 17 of the key academics associated with economic sociology since the late 1940s. The interviewees are grouped under three headings. The "contenders", including Gary Becker, James Colman, and Mark Granovetter, who "stand at the very centre of the current debate" about the changing boundary between economics and sociology; the "pioneers", including Kenneth Arrow and Albert Hirschmann, who have each produced seminal works in this area; and the "commentators", including Amartya Sen and Robert Solow, who stand largely outside the discipline but who have nevertheless reflected on the present interaction between economics and sociology. The interviews provide many rich insights into the development of the discipline and will particularly appeal to those with an interest in the evolution of thought within economics and sociology.

ETZIONI is a leading figure in the resurgence of interest in communitarian ideals – a resurgence seen on both sides of the Atlantic. In this influential text he develops the thesis that the neoclassical paradigm is inadequate for investigating complex economic phenomena, and asserts that a much broader interdisciplinary perspective is required. He advocates an approach, which he terms socioeconomics, drawing upon theories developed within sociology, psychology, and the political sciences. Socioeconomics uses deontological ethics to critique the neoclassical notion of "economic man" as a rational, calculative, monoutility maximizer. In its place Etzioni posits a new decision-making model, one that assumes people typically choose on the basis of emotions and value judgements, and only secondarily on the basis of logical-empirical observations. He thus places morality and ethics at centre stage in his analysis of economic behaviour.

In a major review essay commissioned by the *Cambridge Journal of Economics* as part of their "critical survey" series, INGHAM provides a comprehensive overview of recent changes in the relationship between economics and sociology. This work is well researched and meticulously documented. It is particularly useful for its insights into the sociological critique of transaction cost economics, and its account of the social construction of markets.

ROWLINSON explores the nature of the modern business organization from the contrasting perspectives of organizational economics and organizational theory. Topics covered include the economics of the firm, the historical transformation of work, issues of ownership and control, and the evolution of the multidivisional firm. The book provides a comprehensive overview of the major debates between sociologists and economists in these and related areas. Although it is very well organized and carefully referenced, in parts the text is dense and difficult to follow. The volume will perhaps be of most use as a textbook for researchers and postgraduate students.

McCLOSKEY provides the first sustained attempt to apply the sociological approaches of discourse theory and postmodernism to economics. By focusing on the rhetorical devices used by economists, including mathematical models, which are referred to as "non-ornamental metaphors", we are shown that when economists "do" economics they are engaged essentially in a process of persuasion. From a series of case studies of economists' dialogue, he shows that what persuades other economists is not empirical testing or successful prediction but things that no explicit methodology takes into account – such as mathematical virtuosity, arguments by analogy, or symmetrical reasoning. This is a groundbreaking book and will be of particular interest to those interested in the ontological and epistemological basis of economics.

BECKER is commonly associated with the so-called "economic imperialism" of the social sciences, and his ideas have influenced the current interest in rational choice sociology. In this classic book he develops the basic idea that the neoclassical model of human behaviour is capable of being extended to topics that have, by tradition, been the preserve of sociologists. This approach takes the "combined assumptions of maximizing behaviour, market equilibrium, and stable preferences, used relentlessly and unflinchingly". In this selection of essays, Becker shows how the neoclassical approach can be used to understand and predict a variety of human behaviours, including social interactions; crime and punishment; and marriage, fertility, and the family. To derive the most out of this work one requires some knowledge of algebra and at least an introductory knowledge of neoclassical economics.

Economic sociology acknowledges that people pursue economic goals alongside other objectives such as status, power, reputation, and moral obligations. In addition, it pays particular attention to the social contexts within which interactions are played out, and it recognizes that these contexts are themselves socially constructed and constrained. Thus economic sociology allows for a richer, contextualized, and holistic examination of human economic interactions and organizational constructions. The texts outlined above should help guide the reader through this emergent field.

RUSSELL MANNION AND HUW T.O. DAVIES

See also Economics and sociology

Economic theories of labour-managed and participatory firms

Abell, Peter, "The Economic Viability of Industrial Cooperatives", *International Yearbook of Organizational Democracy* (1981)

Alchian, Armen A. and Harold Demsetz, "Production, Information Costs and Economic Organization", *American Economic Review*, 62/5 (1972): 777–95

Balassa, Bela and T.J. Bertrand, "Growth Performance in Eastern European Economies and Comparative Western Economies", *American Economic Review, Proceedings*, 60 (1970): 314–20

Domar, Evsei D., "The Soviet Collective Farm as a Producer Co-operative", *American Economic Review*, 56/4 (1966): 734–57

Horvat, Branko, *The Political Economy of Socialism: A Marxist Social Theory*, Armonk, New York: Sharpe, 1982

Jensen, Michael C. and William H. Meckling, "Rights and Production Functions: An Application to Labour-Managed Firms and Co-determination", *Journal of Business*, 52/4 (1979): 469–506

Meade, James, "The Theory of Labour-managed Firms and Profit Sharing", *Economic Journal*, 82 (1972): 402–28

Prychitko, David L. and Jaroslav Vanek (editors), *Producer Cooperatives and Labor-Managed Systems*, Cheltenham, Gloucestershire: Elgar, 1996

Vanek, Jaroslav, *The General Theory of Labor-Managed Market Economies*, Ithaca, New York: Cornell University Press, 1970

Vanek, Jaroslav, *The Participatory Economy: An Evolutionary Hypothesis and a Strategy for Development*, Ithaca, New York: Cornell University Press, 1970b

Vanek, Jaroslav (editor), *The Labor-Managed Economy: Essays*, Ithaca, New York: Cornell University Press, 1977

Ward, Benjamin, "The Firm in Illyria: Market Syndicalism", *American Economic Review*, 48/4 (1958): 566–89

Economic theories on the labour-managed firm cover a wide range of alternative ownership and management structures that either have been operationalized within a market socialist system (workers' self-management) or have been functioning within a capitalist market system in competition with traditional firms. Branko Horvat has authored numerous books and articles on self-management socialism in former Yugoslavia. One important contribution is a multidisciplinary reader from 1975 (*Self-Governing Socialism*), co-edited with Mihailo Markovic and Rudy Supek. Most important is HORVAT which presents his Marxist social theory. Working in both a Marxist and a comparative economic systems context, Horvat considers the self-managed firm *socialist* and in essence different from either the *capitalist* firm in Western-type social settings or the *etatist* firm in the former central command systems of the USSR and Eastern Europe.

In his 1972 article, MEADE stressed that the labour-managed firm is characterized by a reversed relationship between capital and labour. The concept of labour hiring capital instead of the usual relationship of capital hiring labour suggests democratic decision making according to the democratic principle of one person, one vote. Furthermore, it presupposes profit sharing as well as participatory decision making. Several ownership structures can be combined with these principles, from pure rental of the socially owned assets and employee ownership to capital–labour partnerships.

Since WARD's market syndicalist "Firm in Illyria" and DOMAR's market socialist model for a Soviet *kholkoz* appeared, theorists have argued over the economic viability and efficiency of labour-managed firms. Typically, such analyses have not been grounded in real-world examples, but have argued from theoretical formulations modelled after either the Yugoslav system of workers' self-management or an idealized Rochdale cooperative, sometimes conflating the two, despite differences in ownership, relationship with the larger political system, and so forth. Theoretical criticisms of the labour-managed firm have included arguments that such firms would adjust employment levels to market signals too slowly or even "perversely". The income per head in the labour-managed firm consists of both an ordinary market wage and a profit share, and due to a maximization goal, the labour input is lower than in a conventional firm. Consequently, labour-managed systems react adversely to changes in prices (the negatively sloping

supply curve). The most comprehensive contribution in the field of the labour-managed economy is the path-breaking work of VANEK (1970a, 1970b, also PRYCHITKO & VANEK). In terms of mainstream economics, Vanek demonstrated that both a partial and a general equilibrium can be established, despite the short-term adverse adjustments.

In an information-cost framework, ALCHIAN & DEMSETZ argued that profit-sharing would dilute a residual claimant's income too to allow the employees to be efficiently monitored. A principal–agent argument was raised by JENSEN & MECKLING arguing that agency costs may be relative high to the firm, because employees need an economic incentive to join participatory arrangements or because the costs of exchange of information rise. In an opportunity-cost framework, ABELL has emphasized that cooperative firms with nonleveraged finance may face capital starvation if employees have expectations about higher future rates of return by investing earnings externally rather than by reinvesting in the firm. Excessive withdrawal of capital by employees would lead to a lower propensity to reinvest earnings. Nonleveraged employee-owned firms may then be less growth-oriented than their non-leveraged capitalist "twins"; on the other hand, employee-owned firms do not in all cases need to foresee a lack of finance, because the firm could adopt rules constraining the members not to withdraw capital. Vanek and Meade, both of whom support the concept of labour-managed firms, acknowledge the difficulties by suggesting that a financial leverage from a quasi capital market could assist free entry and exit in competitive markets in the long run, thus allowing for efficient adjustments of output by varying the number of firms instead of expanding existing firms. VANEK (1977) proposed external financing in the form of bonds as the solution to the danger of "self extinction".

Both Horvat and Vanek frequently argued that other, rarely discussed, competitive advantages of labour-managed firms more than compensate for potential weaknesses of the labour-managed economy. Such features as personal empowerment, job satisfaction, and a humanized work environment are not only beneficial in themselves, but can effect economic efficiency by motivating employees to increase labour productivity, act more creatively, and take more responsibility. What little evidence is available tends to favour the supporters, not the critics, of labour-managed firms. For instance, Horvat, using data compiled by BALASSA & BERTRAND, found that during the late 1950s and early 1960s, after Yugoslavia had instituted workers' self-management but had yet to lose control over investment policy, the Yugoslav economy grew faster than comparable capitalist and planned economies. Moreover, Horvat found that four Yugoslav industries grew faster during this period than during Yugoslavia's previous short history, which featured periods of both capitalism and a Soviet-style command economy.

GORM WINTHER

See also Democracy in the workplace, Employee ownership and cooperative societies, Producer cooperatives

Economic thought, history of

Backhouse, Roger E., "Economics Is a Historical Process" in *Foundations of Research in Economics: How Do Economists Do Economics?*, edited by Steven G. Medema and Warren J. Samuels, Cheltenham, Gloucestershire: Elgar, 1996

Blaug, Mark, *Economic Theory in Retrospect*, Homewood, Illinois: Irwin, 1962; 5th edition, Cambridge and New York: Cambridge University Press, 1996

Blaug, Mark (editor), *The Historiography of Economics*, vol. 1, Aldershot, Hampshire: Elgar, 1991

European Journal of the History of Economic Thought, 1993–

History of Political Economy, 1969–

Hutchison, T.W., *On Revolutions and Progress in Economic Knowledge*, Cambridge and New York: Cambridge University Press, 1978

Journal of the History of Economic Thought, 1990–

Medema, Steven G. and Warren J. Samuels, *Historians of Economics and Economic Thought: The Construction of a Disciplinary Memory*, London: Routledge, forthcoming 2001

O'Brien, D.P., *The Classical Economists*, Oxford: Clarendon Press, and New York: Oxford University Press, 1975

Perlman, Mark and Charles R. McCann Jr, *The Pillars of Economic Understanding: Ideas and Traditions*, Ann Arbor: University Press of Michigan, 1998

Research in the History of Economic Thought and Methodology, 1983–

Samuels, Warren J. (editor), *Research in the History of Economic Thought and Methodology*, vol. 1, *The Craft of the Historian of Economic Thought*, Greenwich, Connecticut: Jai Press, 1983

Schabas, Margaret, "Breaking Away: History of Economics as History of Science", *History of Political Economy*, 24/1 (Spring 1992): 187–203; followed by comments by 14 historians of economics

Schumpeter, Joseph A., *History of Economic Analysis*, edited by Elizabeth Boody Schumpeter, New York: Oxford University Press, and London: Allen and Unwin, 1954

Spiegel, Henry William, *The Growth of Economic Thought*, 3rd edition, Durham, North Carolina: Duke University Press, 1991 (1st edition 1971)

Winch, Donald, *Riches and Poverty: An Intellectual History of Political Economy in Britain, 1750–1834*, Cambridge and New York: Cambridge University Press, 1996

In contrast with political science and sociology, where familiarity with classic texts is considered by many practitioners to be an important part of a training in the discipline, economists have developed an indifference to the history of their subject. This raises questions concerning both how the subject should be studied and whether it is of any relevance to economics. Following on from this are questions about where coverage of the subject should begin and end. The classic attempt to defend the subject in the face of the disdain for it shown by contemporary economists was provided by BLAUG (1962). His book sought to justify the subject to graduate students by showing how it could contribute to an understanding of economics. The economic thought of the past was judged by the standards of present-day economic theory. This is an absolutist approach, which Blaug contrasted with the relativist approach in which economic ideas were explained in relation to the historical circumstances in which they arose. In the latest edition (1996) he reformulates the problem in terms of the distinction between "rational reconstructions" and "historical reconstructions". In writing his book he started with Adam Smith, and by the fifth edition had taken in key themes from post-1945 economics. This book is notable for its excellent bibliographies.

Another comprehensive textbook with excellent bibliographies is SPIEGEL. This differs from Blaug in focusing less on the analytical structure of past economic ideas, dispensing altogether with mathematical interpretations. It finds economic thought worth discussing as far back as the Old Testament and ancient Greece, in the early Church and in medieval scholastic writers. Its treatment of this early material is particularly good. The story is told in detail up to around the 1940s but offers only a cursory treatment of very recent developments.

This pattern of a history running from ancient times to the first half of the 20th century is followed by PERLMAN & McCANN. Their approach is distinguished by its focus on sources of authority, or what they term "patristic traditions". This takes them further into political and philosophical thought than either Blaug or Spiegel.

All three of these books are aimed at economists. The history of economic thought can also be studied as a branch of intellectual history. Here, we have to turn not to general histories of economic thought, for these almost by definition cannot delve very far into the historical context, but to studies of specific episodes or events. The book by WINCH, which considers the reception of Adam Smith in relation to political debates in Britain around the turn of the 19th century, is an excellent example. It would, however, be wrong to describe such work as "relativist". Its aim is not to establish whether the economic ideas of the past were justified as to understand how they arose and their role in the societies in which they emerged.

The conflict between history of economic thought as arising out of economics and arising out of intellectual history is confronted explicitly in the symposium based on the article by SCHABAS. She argued that historians of economics should break away from economics departments into philosophy and history departments. As well as being a rational response to the hostility shown by many economists towards the subject, this would foster greater historical sensitivity within the history of economic thought. Many of those commenting on this article argue that a separation of history of economic thought from economics would be damaging to both. A powerful defence of the need for history of economic thought is offered by HUTCHISON. He points out that economists frequently construct versions of the history of their discipline that serve their purposes and that these versions of history are often misleading. Traditional versions are used to support established economics, a notable example being the history constructed by J.R. McCulloch in the early 19th century to support classical economics. Revolutionary versions are designed to undermine orthodoxy, Hutchison's main example being those constructed by Joan Robinson and Maurice Dobb in the 20th century. Such histories are frequently misleading and need to be corrected. More recently, BACKHOUSE has illustrated this point using examples taken from contemporary economics textbooks that deny the importance of history. He has also argued that the way theories and theoretical concepts are used in contemporary economics cannot be understood without knowing something of their history.

Articles on the historiography of economic thought are collected in BLAUG (1991). These cover the issues discussed above and more. However, such discussions inevitably miss the variety of approaches that are to be found in the subject. This variety is revealed by the volume edited by SAMUELS, which contains essays on each of 14 historians of economic thought. The subjects of these appraisals range from Marshall and Pantaleoni, writing at the end of the 19th century, to Jaffé, Viner, and Hutchison, whose major work was completed after World War II, and include both heterodox economists (Commons and Mitchell) and orthodox ones (Stigler). The volume edited by MEDEMA & SAMUELS follows this up with appraisals of a more recent generation of historians of economic thought.

Mention should be made of two classics in the subject. SCHUMPETER's magnum opus is encyclopedic, unfinished (being published posthumously), idiosyncratic and contains judgements that have failed to stand up in the face of modern research. It remains, however, a formidable achievement. Its approach is absolutist, tracing the gradual emergence of economic analysis over several centuries. However, Schumpeter never keeps within such a framework, venturing into numerous related fields. Schumpeter's book is almost universally recognized as a classic in the field. The other is O'BRIEN. This is far more modest in that it covers only a limited period, albeit the one that, with the exception of Keynes, has probably received more attention from historians than any other. Its modest aims, however, conceal a depth of scholarship that has few rivals.

As with many fields in economics, journals have proliferated during the past few years. This has been particularly important for the history of economic thought, as general journals have increasingly excluded it from their pages. HISTORY OF POLITICAL ECONOMY is the longest-established specialist journal, dating back to 1969. The annual supplements, each of which focuses on a specific theme, are particularly valuable. RESEARCH IN THE HISTORY OF ECONOMIC THOUGHT AND METHODOLOGY goes back to 1983, and the JOURNAL OF THE HISTORY OF ECONOMIC THOUGHT (started 1990) and the EUROPEAN JOURNAL OF THE HISTORY OF ECONOMIC THOUGHT (started 1993) are amongst the newcomers.

ROGER E. BACKHOUSE

See also Economic thought, history of, Economics and history, Economics methodology

Economics and biology

Degler, Carl N., *In Search of Human Nature: The Decline and Revival of Darwinism in American Social Thought*, Oxford and New York: Oxford University Press, 1991

Hodgson, Geoffrey M. (editor), *Economics and Biology*, Aldershot, Hampshire: Elgar, 1995

Hodgson, Geoffrey M., *Economics and Evolution: Bringing Life back into Economics*, Cambridge: Polity Press, and Ann Arbor: University of Michigan Press, 1993

Hodgson, Geoffrey M., *Evolution and Institutions: On Evolutionary Economics and the Evolution of Economics*, Cheltenham, Gloucestershire: Elgar, 1999

Maasen, Sabine, Everett Mendelsohn and Peter Weingart (editors), *Biology as Society, Society as Biology: Metaphors*, Dordrecht and Boston: Kluwer, 1995

Mirowski, Philip (editor), *Natural Images in Economic Thought: "Markets Read in Tooth and Claw"*, Cambridge and New York: Cambridge University Press, 1994

Nelson, Richard R. and Sidney G. Winter, *An Evolutionary Theory of Economic Change*, Cambridge, Massachusetts: Harvard University Press, 1982

Tullock, Gordon, *The Economics of Non-Human Societies*, Tuscon, Arizona: Pallas, 1994

Weingart, Peter *et al.* (editors), *Human by Nature: Between Biology and the Social Sciences*, Mahwah, New Jersey: Erlbaum, 1997

Economics and biology have drawn inspiration from each other for centuries. Bernard Mandeville was inspired by the social organization of the bees and Charles Darwin drew stimulation from Thomas Robert Malthus' picture of competition for resources. Economics has used metaphors from biology, although physics has played a more prominent role.

The essays collected together in HODGSON (1995) touch on several of the key issues involved in the relationship between economics and biology. Topics covered in the volume include: biological and mechanical analogies, economics and sociobiology, classical economics and the Darwinian revolution, Alfred Marshall and economic biology, and optimization and rationality. Essays by prominent authors such as Armen Alchian, Gary Becker, Nicolai Foss, Nicholas Georgescu-Roegen, Jack Hirshleifer, John Maynard Smith, Edith Penrose, Gordon Tullock, Brinley Thomas, Ulrich Witt, and Robert Young are included.

Sociobiology has been seen as one means of linking biology and economics. The work of TULLOCK is an extreme case, similar in many ways to the approaches of Becker and Hirshleifer. Sociobiology has had a strong impact on these authors. According to the Becker–Hirshleifer–Tullock school of thought, common phenomena such as scarcity, competition, and rational behaviour are common to both human economies and the natural world. This approach is analytically controversial and is by no means the only way of conceiving the relationship between the two disciplines.

The WEINGART volume considers sociobiology as one of the options, and argues for a closer relationship between biology and the social sciences in general. Nevertheless, the essays in the volume show that the relationship is inevitably complex, and its subtleties are often obscured by reductionist approaches.

A specific form of the relationship involves transferring metaphors, from the biotic to the social world. According to modern arguments in the philosophy of science, metaphor is not merely a literary decoration: it is indispensable in scientific enquiry. The essays in the MAASEN volume provide an excellent overview and discussion of these issues. Not only is the transfer of metaphor between biology and the social sciences explored in detail, it provides one of the best general discussion of the role of metaphor in social science.

MIROWSKI complements the former volume in two ways: first by focusing more specifically on economics and second by raising some warnings about the use or misuse of naturalistic metaphors. There are some excellent essays here, including one by Michael Hutter on the notion of society as an organism in German economic thought, and another by James Murphy on the role of habit in linking the natural substratum of human society with conscious action and deliberation.

HODGSON (1993) is an account of different types of evolutionary thinking in economics. These days, terms such as "evolutionary economics" are common. Generally, however, there is inadequate discussion of the complexities of what "evolution" might mean, in biology or elsewhere. This volume attempts to fill this gap, without prescribing a single "correct" meaning of the word. Different notions of economic evolution in the works of economists such as Karl Marx, Carl Menger, Alfred Marshall, Thorstein Veblen, Joseph Schumpeter, and Friedrich Hayek are analysed and contrasted. In some cases, notably Schumpeter, the conception of evolution is shown to be explicitly non biological.

One of the foremost and most influential modern applications of evolutionary ideas from biology is NELSON & WINTER. They take the biological principles of natural selection, variation, mutation, and inheritance and show appropriate analogies in the evolution of firms and industries. This work is a modern classic in evolutionary economics.

However, in the 50 years before the appearance of the latter volume, biological analogies made only rare appearances in economics. (Some of these sparse exhibits are documented in Hodgson (1995).) As far as the relationship between economics and biology is concerned, these were the "dark ages". In contrast, in the late 19th and early 20th centuries, evolutionary and biological conceptions were widespread in economics. DEGLER gives a very useful overview of the history of ideas in this period, and explains why biology was written out of the social sciences for such a long time. HODGSON (1999) traces in more detail the exclusion of biology from economics, and raises some of the philosophical and conceptual problems involved in bringing it back in.

GEOFFREY HODGSON

See also Evolution, economic, Joseph Schumpeter, Sociobiology, Thorstein Veblen

Economics and history

Anderson, Philip W., Kenneth Arrow and David Pines (editors), *The Economy as an Evolving Complex System: The Proceedings of the Evolutionary Paths of the Global Economy Workshop*, Redwood City, California and Wokingham: Addison Wesley, 1988

Cairnes, John Elliott, *The Character and Logical Method of Political Economy*, London: Routledge/Thoemmes, 1997 (1st edition 1857, 2nd edition 1875)

Cairnes, John Elliott, *The Slave Power: Its Character, Career and Probable Designs: Being an Attempt to Explain the Real Issues Involved in the American Contest*, New York: Kelley, 1969 (originally published 1862)

David, Paul A., "Why are Institutions the 'Carriers' of History? Path Dependence and the Evolution of Conventions, Organizations and Institutions", *Structural Change and Economic Dynamics*, 5/2 (1994): 205–20

Georgescu-Roegen, Nicholas, "The Interplay between Institutional and Material Factors: The Problem and Its Status" in *Barriers to Full Employment*, edited by John Allen Kregel, Egon Matzner and Alessandro Roncaglia, London: Macmillan, and New York: St Martin's Press, 1988

Greif, Avner, "Cultural Beliefs and the Organization of Society: A Historical and Theoretical Reflection on Collectivist and Individualist Societies", *Journal of Political Economy*, 102/5 (1994): 912–50

Hicks, John, *Value and Capital: An Inquiry into Some Fundamental Principles of Economic Theory*, Oxford: Clarendon Press, 1939; 2nd edition 1946

Hicks, John, "Methods of Dynamic Analysis" in his *Collected Essays on Economic Theory*, vol. 2, Oxford: Blackwell, and Cambridge, Massachusetts: Harvard University Press, 1982 (originally published in Festschrift for Erik Lindahl, *Ekonomisk Tidskrift*, 1956)

Hicks, John, *A Theory of Economic History*, Oxford: Clarendon Press, 1969

Hill, Polly, *Dry Grain Farming Families: Hausaland (Nigeria) and Karnataka (India) Compared*, Cambridge and New York: Cambridge University Press, 1982

Keynes, John Neville, *The Scope and Method of Political Economy*, London: Routledge/Thoemmes, 1997 (1st edition 1891)

Marshall, Alfred, *Principles of Economics*, 9th edition, edited by C.W. Guillebaud, 2 vols, London and New York: Macmillan, 1961 (1st edition 1890)

Marshall, Alfred, "Distribution and Exchange", *Economic Journal*, 8/1 (1898): 37–59

Mayer, Hans, "Der Erkenntniswert der funktionellen Preistheorie" in *Die Wirtschaftstheorie der Gegenwart*, Wien: Springer, 1927–32

Menger, Carl, *Problems of Economics and Sociology*, edited by Louis Schneider, Urbana: University of Illinois Press, 1963 (originally published in German, 1883)

Mill, John Stuart, *Principles of Political Economy with Some of Their Applications to Social Philosophy*, edited by J.M. Robson, Toronto: University of Toronto Press, and London: Routledge and Kegan Paul, 1965 (originally published 1848)

North, Douglass Cecil, *Institutions, Institutional Change and Economic Performance*, Cambridge and New York: Cambridge University Press, 1991

Palomba, Giuseppe, *Introduzione allo studio della dinamica economica*, Naples: Jovene, 1939

Scazzieri, Roberto, "Economic Theory and Economic History: Perspectives on Hicksian Themes" in *The Legacy of Hicks: His Contributions to Economic Analysis*, edited by Harald Hagemann and Omar Hamouda, London and New York: Routledge, 1994

Schmoller, Gustav, "Zur Methodologie der Staats- und Sozialwissenschaften", *Jahrbuch für Gesetzgebund, Verwaltung und Volkswirtschaft*, 7 (1883): 975–94

Schumpeter, Joseph A., *The Theory of Economic Development: An Inquiry into Profits, Capital, Credit, Interest and the Business Cycle*, New Brunswick: Transaction, 1983 (German edition 1912)

Spiethoff, Arthur, "The 'Historical' Character of Economic Theories", *Journal of Economic History*, 12 (1952): 131–39

Spiethoff, Arthur, "Pure Theory and Economic Gestalt Theory: Ideal Types and Real Types" in *Enterprise and Secular Change: Readings in Economic History*, edited by Frederic C. Lane and Jelle C. Riemersma, Homewood, Illinois: Irwin, 1953

Steuart, James, *An Inquiry into the Principles of Political Oeconomy*, edited by Andrew S. Skinner, 4 vols, London: Pickering and Chatto, 1998 (originally published 1767)

The relationship between economics and history covers a wide field, encompassing both the history of economic facts and the history of economic theories (*See also* the entries on Economic history, and History of economic thought respectively). In either case, the role of history is ultimately due to certain structural features of economic processes, such as the mutable character of economic regularities, the role of intermediate generalization, and the "path dependence" of economic choices and behavioural patterns. STEUART, written in the second half of the 18th century, acknowledges the linkage between the emergence of economics as a body of knowledge primarily concerned with the structure and evolution of the exchange economy, and the historical formation of a "new system of political economy" characterized by a comprehensive economy of markets. Such a relationship is further explored by economists writing in the aftermath of classical political economy, such as John Stuart Mill, John Cairnes, and John Neville Keynes. MILL examines the logical structure of classical economic theory and maintains that some of its fundamental propositions critically depend upon behavioural assumptions (such as self-interested behaviour and profit maximization) whose validity is bound to specific historical circumstances.

CAIRNES (1857) outlines a theory of intermediate generalization that lends itself to a systematic treatment of the relationship between economics and history. In particular, Cairnes argues that economic analysis requires the formulation of "hypothetical cases framed with a view to the purpose of economic inquiry" (p.77 of 1875 edition). This method of intermediate generalization is used in CAIRNES (1862), an analysis of the slave economy of the US at the time of the Civil War. In this essay, the author outlines an interesting extension of classical economic theory beyond its traditional sphere. More recent variants of this approach are to be found in Spiethoff's analysis of "economic styles" (SPIETHOFF, 1952, 1953), and in HILL's reference to "modes" of economic organization (such as her "dry grain mode"), which may be used when examining a

relatively narrow range of different institutional set-ups. KEYNES considers the relationship between political economy and economic history, starting from a clear distinction of their respective roles: "[t]he propositions of economic history are . . . statements of particular concrete facts; economic theory, on the other hand, is concerned with the establishment of general laws" (p.268). He also argues for interaction and cross-fertilization between the two fields. In particular, this author maintains that economic theories can be illustrated, criticized, and established by history (pp.271–285); he also notes that "a knowledge of theory, i.e., of previously established general propositions relating to economic phenomena, teaches the historian what kinds of facts are likely to have an important economic bearing" (p.285). The mutual influence of economic theory and economic history is carefully examined by MARSHALL (1890, 1898). Marshall maintains that, as economic analysis moves away from the static investigation of "mechanical equilibrium", it is likely to become concerned with the interaction of different forces in determining patterns of growth and decay. In this case, economic theory becomes more similar to economic history in its use of inductive methods and biological analogies (see, for example, Marshall 1898, p. 43).

The relationship between economic theory and economic history has remained a significant focus of attention in subsequent developments of economic analysis, in spite of being partially overshadowed during the *Methodenstreit* (controversy of methods) between analytically and historically oriented economists (see, respectively, MENGER and SCHMOLLER). SCHUMPETER outlines a conceptual framework characterized by the coexistence of analytical reconstruction of static equilibrium (or "circular flow"), and historical investigation of the innovative processes by which static equilibrium might be disrupted and new patterns of behaviour and organization brought about. Other economists noted that the logical structure of general economic equilibrium involves a complex interplay of single-period and intertemporal relationships, and that economic linkages over time suggest a "genetic" approach to the analysis of economic equilibrium. In particular, MAYER outlines a possible way of combining Walrasian general equilibrium theory with an analysis of the historical process by which an equilibrium state may eventually be attained as a result of a sequence of intermediate steps. HICKS (1939) examines the relationship between time and economic choice, and highlights the respective roles of expectations (concerning future prices) and commodity stocks (carried over from one period to the next) in determining the structure of equilibrium and disequilibrium states over historical time. The distinction between equilibrium in a single period (temporary equilibrium) and equilibrium over a sequence of periods leads Hicks to argue that the economic system "is always in temporary equilibrium, always more or less out of equilibrium over time" (p.viii).

PALOMBA considers specific features of historical time by investigating the relationship between reversible and irreversible processes of production. He notes that the likelihood of any given process being reversed decreases as that particular process approaches its final state. An interesting implication is that, as we move from the microeconomic to the macroeconomic sphere, economic equilibrium takes a probabilistic rather than deterministic character, due to compensating influences among micro-processes. Subsequent literature has investigated the relationship between economic theory and economic history from a variety of points of view. In particular, HICKS (1982) introduces the historical dimension of economic dynamics by examining the "material heritage" that each accounting period may receive from previous periods if commodity stocks are carried over from one period to another. In this connection, Hicks calls attention to the need to overcome the "self-containedness" of each single period, if a dynamic investigation is to be undertaken. The implications of the above analytical perspective for the interpretation of economic history are explored in HICKS (1969). This essay finds the core of economic progress in the expansion of opportunities for freedom of choice, and in the greater availability of liquid funds, which allow the range and variety of fixed capital goods to be increased (*See also* SCAZZIERI 1994). GEORGESCU-ROEGEN tackles a different feature of the relationship between economics and history by addressing the logical distinction between analytical and historical reasoning. In this connection, he calls attention upon the role of analytical functions, which "can be determined over the entire range of variation by the values for an interval, however small" (p.302). Thus individual cases are not only "identified by numbers but also ordered meaningfully thereby" (ibid.). This ordering criterion is not normally available in cases of qualitative change, which make utilization of analytical functions impossible. Institutional change is a primary instance of a transformation that cannot be handled by using purely analytical tools: "institutions are not ruled by a general logic, although each situation has its own logic, an internal logic ... It is this logic that we must discover" (p.316).

Recent developments in economic theory have called attention to the multiplicity of possible equilibria, the far-reaching implications of small initial differences, and the role of complementarities over time (see ANDERSON, ARROW & PINES). This theoretical framework has been at the root of renewed analytical interest in historical paths and institutional evolution. In particular, NORTH calls attention to the distinction between institutions and organizations, and highlights the critical influence of formal and informal institutions in determining the costs of economic coordination through markets and division of labour (transaction costs). In North's view, rational economic choice is shaped by institutional constraints, and the evolution of constraints is a primary influence in determining the structure of economic behaviour. DAVID considers the evolving nature of institutions, and notes that the path dependence of institutional change is similar to the positive feedback dynamics characterizing path dependence in the technological sphere. Institutions may be considered to be "carriers of history" on condition that modes of communication and role types are durable, coordination benefits are compatible with multiple solutions, and complementarities are brought about from mutually adjusted procedures. GREIF examines the role of cultural beliefs as critical factors in determining the "evolution and persistence" of distinct social and institutional setups. The analysis of the different organizational devices adopted by Maghribi traders in the 11th century and Genoese traders in the 12th century leads Greif to highlight the importance of culture "in determining societal organization, in leading to path dependence of institutional frameworks, and in forestalling successful intersociety adoption of institutions"

(p.914). The prevailing patterns of economic behaviour are shaped by existing coordination rules, but the historical evolution of the latter reflects focal points associated with received cultural standards and communication paradigms.

ROBERTO SCAZZIERI

See also Economic history, Economic thought, history of

Economics and mathematics

Arrow, Kenneth J. and Michael D. Intriligator (editors), *Handbook of Mathematical Economics*, 4 vols (vol. 4 edited by Werner Hildenbrand and Hugo Sonnenschein), Amsterdam and New York: North Holland, 1981–91

Chiang, Alpha C., *Fundamental Methods of Mathematical Economics*, 3rd edition, New York: McGraw Hill, 1984

Debreu, Gerard, *Theory of Value: An Axiomatic Analysis of Economic Equilibrium*, New Haven, Connecticut: Yale University Press, 1986

Debreu, Gerard, "The Mathematization of Economic Theory", *American Economic Review*, 81/1 (1991): 1–7

Dixit, Avinash, *Optimization in Economic Theory*, 2nd edition, Oxford and New York: Oxford University Press, 1990

Duffie, Darryl, *Dynamic Asset Pricing Theory*, 2nd edition, Princeton, New Jersey: Princeton University Press, 1996

Grubel, Herbert G. and Lawrence A. Boland, "On the Efficient Use of Mathematics in Economics: Some Theory, Facts and Results of an Opinion Survey", *Kyklos*, 39/3 (1986): 419–22

Ingrao, Bruna and Giorgio Israel, *The Invisible Hand: Economic Equilibrium in the History of Science*, Cambridge, Massachusetts: MIT Press, 1990 (Italian edition 1987)

Mas-Colell, Andreu, *The Theory of General Economic Equilibrium: A Differentiable Approach*, Cambridge and New York: Cambridge University Press, 1985

Simon, Carl P. and Lawrence Blume, *Mathematics for Economists*, New York: Norton, 1994

Stokey, Nancy L. and Robert E. Lucas, *Recursive Methods in Economic Dynamics*, Cambridge, Massachusetts: Harvard University Press, 1989

Sundaram, Rangarajan K., *A First Course in Optimization Theory*, Cambridge and New York: Cambridge University Press, 1996

Takayama, Akira, *Mathematical Economics*, 2nd edition, Cambridge and New York: Cambridge University Press, 1985

Varian, Hal R. (editor), *Economic and Financial Modelling with Mathematica*, Berlin and New York: Springer, 1993

Varian, Hal R. (editor), *Computational Economics and Finance: Modeling and Analysis with Mathematica*, Berlin and New York: Springer, 1996

The use of mathematics in economic analysis has been extensive, fruitful, and controversial. Formal mathematical modelling in economics has two key advantages. First, formal modelling makes the assumptions explicit. It clarifies intuition and makes arguments transparent. More importantly, it uncovers the limitations of our intuition, delineating the boundaries and uncovering the occasional counterintuitive special case. Second, formal modelling aids communication. As the assumptions are explicit, participants spend less time arguing about what they really meant, leaving more time to explore conclusions, applications, and amendments.

DEBREU (1991), the presidential address of Gerard Debreu to the American Economic Association, is an eloquent justification for the mathematization of economics, by one of its leading exponents. GRUBEL & BOLAND ask whether the use of mathematics in economics has been overdone. They document the growth of mathematics in professional journals in the postwar years, and report a survey of economists concerning a number of issues in the use of mathematics in economics.

The mathematization of economics reached its zenith in general equilibrium theory. Initially, the object was to prove key results with the minimum of assumptions. DEBREU (1986) is an extremely elegant account of this theory, worth consulting as much for its style as for its content. It is a classic of economic writing, first published in 1959. In their efforts to minimize special assumptions, early practitioners eschewed familiar tools like differential calculus. More recently, these familiar tools have found renewed favour. MAS-COLELL is a coherent account of later developments, surveying some sophisticated tools and their application to general equilibrium theory.

INGRAO & ISRAEL trace the history of the mathematization of equilibrium analysis, and its interaction with the physical sciences. They argue that mathematization is not a secondary feature of the theory, but rather one of the basic reasons for its creation and development.

More recently, sophisticated mathematical analysis has become widespread in the field of macroeconomics, where dynamic models incorporating uncertainty are prevalent. These require somewhat different mathematical tools from the static constrained optimization predominant in microeconomics. STOKEY & LUCAS is a comprehensive account of the dynamic programming approach to economic modelling, which lucidly covers the mathematical foundations and outlines many applications, especially in the fields of macroeconomics and finance.

Finance is a field in which the application of mathematical analysis has proved especially potent. Formal models stimulated the innovation of new financial instruments, such as derivative securities, which have transformed financial markets. DUFFIE provides an authoritative account of mathematical finance in both discrete and continuous time, offering an informative illustration of the way in which sophisticated mathematical analysis has colonized Wall Street. Aimed primarily at doctoral students, it is not for the mathematically faint-hearted. However, specialized mathematical tools are reviewed in appendices, making the book accessible to those with a general mathematical background.

For an introduction to mathematical analysis, there is an abundance of "mathematics for economists" books, catering to a wide variety of tastes and abilities. For an elementary account, my favourite is CHIANG, which is outstanding for its clarity of exposition. He covers the basic topics of linear algebra, calculus, optimization and differential equations, and

their applications in economics. SIMON & BLUME cover essentially the same material, but at a slightly higher level of sophistication, incorporating some more modern developments. Careful study of this text would provide most of the mathematical knowledge required to beginning graduate level.

The next step up is TAKAYAMA, which covers both mathematics and mathematical economics. Although it is selective in its coverage, this book is careful, comprehensive, and authoritative. Not an easy read, it is an invaluable reference. A particular feature of this book is its informative footnotes, which highlight the context of some results and relate them to the literature.

Optimization theory is the basic tool of most economic analysis. DIXIT is a delightful and insightful account of this fundamental tool, which uses economics to explicate the mathematical ideas. SUNDARAM provides a more rigorous and extensive account of the same material, including some very recent applications of lattice theory.

ARROW & INTRILIGATOR is an indispensable source for graduate students and researchers, containing authoritative and comprehensive surveys on mathematical analysis and its application in all fields of economics. The advent of sophisticated mathematical software on personal computers has added a whole new dimension to mathematical modelling in economics. The two edited volumes VARIAN (1996) and VARIAN (1993) contain a host of economic models that readers can manipulate on their own computers, exploring, extending, and adapting to suit their own purposes.

MICHAEL CARTER

See also Mathematization of economics

Economics and politics

Alesina, A., "Macroeconomics and Politics" in *NBER Macroeconomics Annual*, Cambridge, Massachusetts: MIT Press, 1988

Alesina, A. and G. Tabellini, "Voting on the Budget Deficit", *American Economic Review*, 80 (1990): 37–49

Baron, D., "Service Induced Campaign Contributions and the Electoral Equilibrium", *Quarterly Journal of Economics*, 104 (1989): 45–72

Barro, Robert J. and David B. Gordon, "Rules, Discretion and Reputation in a Model of Monetary Policy", *Journal of Monetary Economics*, 12 (1983): 101–22

Becker, G., "A Theory of Competition Among Pressure Groups for Political Influence", *Quarterly Journal of Economics*, 98 (1983): 371–400

Besley, T. and S. Coate, "An Economic Model of Representative Democracy", *Quarterly Journal of Economics*, 112 (1997): 85–114

Black, D., "On the Rationale of Group Decision Making", *Journal of Political Economy*, 56 (1948): 23–34

Boycko, Martin, Andrei Shleifer and Robert Vishny, *Privatizing Russia*, Cambridge, Massachusetts: MIT Press, 1995

Brennan, Geoffrey and James M. Buchanan, *The Power to Tax: Analytical Foundations of a Fiscal Constitution*, Cambridge: Cambridge University Press, 1980

Buchanan, James M. and Gordon Tullock, *The Calculus of Consent: Logical Foundations of Constitutional Democracy*, Ann Arbor: University of Michigan Press, 1962

Cogan, John F., Timothy J. Muris and Allen Schick, *The Budget Puzzle: Understanding Federal Spending*, Stanford: Stanford University Press, 1994

Coughlin, Peter J., *Probabilistic Voting Theory*, Cambridge and New York: Cambridge University Press, 1992

Dhami, S., "The Political Economy of Tax Policy Under Asymmetric Information", mimeo University of Essex, 1997

Dixit, Avinash K., *The Making of Economic Policy: A Transaction-Cost Politics Perspective*, Cambridge, Massachusetts: MIT Press, 1996

Downs, Anthony, *An Economic Theory of Democracy*, New York: Harper and Row, 1957

Grossman, S. and O. Hart, "The Costs and Benefits of Ownership: A Theory of Vertical and Lateral Integration", *Journal of Political Economy*, 94 (1986): 691–719

Hettich, W. and S.L. Winer ,"Economic and Political Foundations of Tax Structure", *American Economic Review*, 78 (1988): 701–12

Kydland, F.E. and E.C. Prescott, "Rules Rather than Discretion: The Inconsistency of Optimal Plans", *Journal of Political Economy*, 87 (1977): 473–92

Laffont J.J. and Jean Tirole, "The Politics of Government Decision Making: A Theory of Regulatory Capture", *Quarterly Journal of Economics*, 106 (1991): 1089–127

Mueller, Dennis C., *Public Choice II*, Cambridge and New York: Cambridge University Press, 1989

Niskanen, William A., *Bureaucracy and Representative Government*, Chicago: Aldine Press, 1971

Osborne, M.J. and A. Slivinski, "A Model of Political Competition with Citizen Candidates", *Quarterly Journal of Economics*, 111 (1996): 65–95

Persson, T. and Lars E.O. Svensson, "Why a Stubborn Conservative Would Run a Deficit: Policy With Time-Inconsistent Preferences", *Quarterly Journal of Economics*, 104 (1989): 325–45

Roberts, K.W.S., "Voting Over Income Tax Schedules", *Journal of Public Economics*, 8 (1977): 329–40

Rogoff, K., "The Optimal Degree of Commitment to an Intermediate Monetary Target", *Quarterly Journal of Economics*, 100 (1985): 1169–89

Rogoff, K., "Equilibrium Political Budget Cycles", *American Economic Review*, 80 (1990): 21–36

Romer, T., "Individual Welfare, Majority Voting and the Properties of a Linear Income Tax", *Journal of Public Economics*, 4 (1975): 163–8

Schmidt, K.M., "The Costs and Benefits of Privatization: An Incomplete Contracts Approach", *Journal of Law Economics and Organization*, 12 (1996): 1–24

Shapiro, C. and R.D. Willig, "Economic Rationales for the Scope of Privatization" in *The Political Economy of Public Sector Reform and Privatization*, edited by Ezra N. Suleiman and John Waterbury, Boulder, Colorado: Westview Press, 1990

Shleifer, A. and R. Vishny, "Politicians and Firms", *Quarterly Journal of Economics*, 109 (1994): 995–1025

Spiller, P., "Politicians, Interest Groups and Regulators: A Multi-Principals Agency Theory of Regulation", *Journal of Law Economics and Organization*, 33 (1990): 65–101

Stigler, G., "The Economic Theory of Regulation", *Bell Journal of Economics*, 2 (1971): 3–21

Tollison, R.D., "Rent Seeking: A Survey", *Kyklos*, 35 (1982): 575–602

Economics was once known as political economy, however, politics gradually disappeared from mainstream economics. Since the 1980s, mainstream economics has seen a long overdue resurgence of interest in the intersection of economics and politics. This selective survey is restrictive in at least three respects. First, it looks mainly at the theoretical contributions. Second, it looks at the issues largely from an economist's perspective. Third, in a subject such as this, it is unavoidably coloured by the author's perceptions and views.

Democracies need rules and institutional mechanisms, for example majority voting, which translate society's preferences into collective social outcomes. In a majority vote, the alternative that wins against all others is known as a *Condorcet winner*.

BLACK showed that when preferences of all individuals are *single peaked* and voting takes place on a single issue, then a Condorcet winner always exists. Single peakedness implies that, on a graph with the alternatives on the horizontal axis and the individual preferences on the vertical, the ordering among alternatives should have only one peak. When all preferences are single peaked and voting takes place on a single issue there will exist a "median voter" with the characteristic that one half of the voters lie above him or her, and one half below him or her. So the outcome professed by the median voter is decisive. This is often referred to as the *median voter theorem*.

Majority voting runs into problems if voters are required to vote simultaneously on multiple issues. In this case, single peakedness of preferences (in each issue) is no longer a sufficient condition to guarantee a Condorcet winner.

The outcome produced by majority voting need not be unique; it need not be pareto-optimal and it performs poorly when several issues are to be simultaneously voted on: but alternative voting rules have their own associated problems – see MUELLER for a discussion on these issues.

Actual political outcomes are surprisingly stable, they rarely exhibit problems such as the non-existence of a Condorcet winner. It is conceivable that society might have devised clever rules and mechanisms to deal with these problems, such as *agenda-setting* powers. In the US Congress, for example, legislative committees have exclusive agenda-setting powers in bringing items of importance on the floor of the house for a vote. The committee could delete items from the original agenda in such a way that from among the remaining items on the agenda, a unique Condorcet winner emerges.

In median voter models, the median voter is decisive in choosing economic policy. Actual democracies, however, allow individual voters to vote only for political candidates who in turn choose an outcome. It is then pertinent to examine the incentives facing politicians subject to the re-election constraint.

In DOWNS, politicians are motivated purely by re-election. Among single peaked voters, any candidate who promised to implement the unique Condorcet winner would win the election, because a majority always prefers this outcome to all other alternatives. Since this outcome is also the outcome most preferred by the median voter, the Downsian outcome is identical to that predicted by the median voter model. Because all politicians in the Downsian model care only for re-election, they will then announce an identical economic policy, namely the Condorcet winner.

The Downsian model has been extended, but several shortcomings remain. First, candidates always implement their campaign promises; they never renege. Second, the prediction that all politicians announce an identical economic policy is not consistent with the empirical evidence. Third, the assumption of pure office-seeking behaviour is counterfactual; empirical studies show that politicians also care about ideology.

In BESLEY & COATE and OSBORNE & SLIVINSKI, candidates are determined endogenously within the model. Each citizen can decide to run for office. The elected citizen can implement his or her most desired economic policy and receive some spoils of office. However, there is a cost of running for the election, including the uncertainty that one might not be elected. One outcome, typical of two party systems, is that, under certain conditions, there will be only two candidates who will contest the election.

KYDLAND & PRESCOTT examine the possibility that politicians might renege on their promises made in the past. A policy announced at date t, for some future date, say $t + j$, $j > 0$, is *time consistent* if it is also optimal (for the government) when the date $t + j$ actually arrives; otherwise it is *time inconsistent*. To fix ideas, suppose that in order to encourage investment in the housing sector, the government announces an exemption from property tax for all new houses. Once the new houses have been built, the government can then renege and impose a property tax. However, being rational, the housing sector is well aware of the possibility that the government will renege and therefore, new investment in housing will not materialize. If the government can credibly commit not to use its *discretion* – for example through a constitutional *rule* that is effectively set in stone – then its announcement will have the desired effect.

The monetary policy literature has successfully exploited this "rules" versus "discretion" approach using a model with two essential ingredients. First, a simple model of how the economy works: the Lucas supply curve. This allows economy-wide output y to be written as $y = \bar{y} + [\pi - \pi^e]$, where $\bar{y}$ is full employment output, and, π and π^e are respectively the actual and expected inflation rates. Inflation is assumed to be fully under government control. Thus, government engineered deviations of actual inflation from expected inflation can boost output beyond $\bar{y}$. The second ingredient is a reduced form objective function for the government, $W = y^2 - \pi^2$. The government would like to achieve high output and low inflation.

The government dislikes inflation, so it ideally desires zero inflation, but an announcement of zero inflation is not trusted; it is not time inconsistent. For if it is trusted and hence $\pi^e = 0$, the government would renege later to produce unexpected inflation $\pi > 0$ and successfully increase output y, which it strongly desires. Thus, only announcements of strictly positive inflation by the government can be believed. The major contribution of this literature is to show why inflation might take place even when governments and society both dislike it.

These and extensions of such ideas really constitute the mainstream literature on the political economy of monetary policy. ROGOFF (1985) suggested that inflation could be avoided by installing a *conservative central banker*, whose objective function is $W = -\pi^2$. She cares only about inflation. Now, an announcement of zero inflation is immediately believed and is time consistent. There are at least two conditions for this model to work well. First, the central banker should have full control over monetary policy, without any political interference. Second, politicians cannot arbitrarily fire him or determine his salary once he is in office. There is empirical evidence that independent and conservative central bankers are indeed associated with lower rates of inflation.

BARRO & GORDON show that even in the absence of conservative bankers, it is possible to achieve low inflation if politicians and voters interact repeatedly. In a repeated setting, if the politician reneges on his promise of zero inflation she is never believed again. Thus, there is a cost and benefit to the politician if she reneges on her promise of zero inflation. The benefit occurs immediately; as actual inflation exceeds expected inflation, output increases (through the Lucas supply curve). However, voters never believe the politician's promise of zero inflation again and this lowers the politician's payoff for all times to come. If the politician cares sufficiently highly about the future, then she will never renege and inflation will continue to be at zero.

Barro & Gordon's model omits the possibility that politicians must face re-election if they are to remain in office. Fortunately, this does not change the conclusion. In ALESINA (1988), politicians who renege on a promise are not re-elected. The cost of reneging is now the possible loss of future office. If politicians care sufficiently about the future then they can be disciplined by elections to keep promises of low inflation. Alesina presents evidence from US presidential elections in support of his model.

In contrast to the traditional literature, modern political economy assumes sophisticated rational voters. In the older literature, voters are sometimes naive and are systematically fooled by the government. For instance, the government could engage in lowering taxes and increasing transfers to increase its re-election chances. A rational voter model conditions a politician's re-election chances only on his or her expected future behaviour.

There are two problems with the political economy of fiscal policy in comparison with the monetary policy literature. First, there is less agreement on the appropriate model that would adequately describe the affect of fiscal policy on the economy. Second, it is not clear just what the government is trying to maximize or achieve.

In HETTICH & WINER and COUGHLIN the government maximizes expected votes and in BRENNAN & BUCHANAN it is a leviathan that maximizes tax revenues. In ROMER (1975) and ROBERTS the median voter directly chooses over alternative tax schedules; governments are non-existent. The literature has shied away from postulating that political parties have *ideological differences*. This is counterfactual.

In ROGOFF (1990), the public does not know the incumbent politician's competence in providing a public good. Politicians who are more competent can provide public goods at a lower cost. In order to signal her competence, the more competent politician provides too high a level of public goods; a level that the less competent type is unable to provide given her lower competence. This distorts the provision of public goods.

In DHAMI, the incumbent politician prefers either a *moderate* amount of redistribution or prefers *extreme* redistribution, but voters do not know the incumbent's type. Redistribution affects voter's after-tax income. Suppose that the moderate type has a greater probability of re-election. The extreme type would now try to fool voters of his type and hence increase his re-election chances. However, this is costly because the extreme type does not really prefer a moderate amount of redistribution. In a separating equilibrium of this model, the moderate type ends up creating too moderate a level of redistribution, which would be prohibitively expensive for the extreme type to mimic. The Cho-Kreps intuitive criterion rules out all pooling equilibria.

The burgeoning budgetary deficits of the 1980s prompted interesting explanations. In PERSSON & SVENSSON the current government is strongly conservative; it fears that if it loses the elections, a liberal government might replace it, which would be unable to control its expenditures. The current conservative government can then influence the expenditure of the future liberal government by running a high level of debt. This debt must be repaid by the liberal government, and raising additional taxes is always costly (for example deadweight losses) so the latter's spending propensities are somewhat curbed.

In ALESINA & TABELLINI the median voter is decisive in choosing policy. In their two-period model, the current majority prefers education to health but another majority that prefers health to education might replace it in the future. The current majority might then engage in excessive debt financing of education. In the future, the new majority will slash education (which it would have done anyway), but will also have to slash health because tax revenues are limited. The current majority enjoys the full benefits of increased education but does not internalize the costs of the loss in future health expenditure; thereby issuing too much current debt.

The models of debt discussed above treat the government as a black box. In reality, the budget process is quite complex and the *micro-budgeting literature* has made a case for examining the practical aspects of the budgetary process. In the UK, individual ministries or government departments present budget estimates to the treasury, which then coordinates the division of scarce tax revenues among the various claimants. In the US, several house and senate budget committees have control of the appropriations decisions on distinct items.

COGAN, MURIS & SCHICK look into these issues for the US case. The different budget committees compete with each other for scarce tax revenues. Each committee cares only about its own budget; if it gets an extra dollar of tax revenues, it does not take account of the decrease in revenues available to other committees. The outcome is a *tragedy of the commons* situation; each committee asks for too large a budget. When budgetary powers are concentrated in a single authority, the problem of the tragedy of the commons disappears. Cogan, Muris & Schick. present empirical evidence to demonstrate that the explosion in the US budget has always been historically linked to the dispersal of spending authority.

Another interesting issue is the relation between income distribution and the size of the government. If the median voter is decisive in choosing policy, a more unequal distribution of income makes the median voter poorer, and this voter in turn chooses greater redistribution. In one variant of these models, education increases earnings (and bequests) but it is costly to obtain and borrowing/lending opportunities among individuals are limited. If the initial income distribution is skewed towards low incomes, then, because borrowing is ruled out, too many individuals are unable to afford an education. Their descendants remain poor because they do not inherit enough resources and, in turn, they are unable to get an education. So, poverty might be perpetuated across generations, depending on the income distribution. Empirically, however, the association between income distribution and the size of the government's redistributive activity is not a settled question.

A representative democracy approach to the association between income distribution and the size of the government is presented in Dhami. The outcome is more complex than that suggested by the median voter approach. It matters if an increase in income inequality is anticipated or unanticipated; the former creates changes in the size of the government in advance of the event. At a purely theoretical level, other important factors, which influence the results, are the party affiliation of the current policymaker (for example Democrat or Republican) and whether income inequality increases above or below average incomes.

The many diverse functions of governments are delegated to several distinct bureaux or ministries. How do bureaux behave? NISKANEN postulated that government-funded bureaux maximize the size of their budget and supply a public good directly to the government. One implication is that the bureau asks for too high a budget. There are several shortcomings of this model. First, although plausible, the objective of the bureau to maximize its budget does not have microfoundations. Second, it neglects the role of political institutions such as legislative oversight. Third, it does not explicitly model interest groups that might seek to influence the decisions of the bureau.

In the Chicago school approach, STIGLER identified several policy areas that interest groups might attempt to influence. These are government barriers to entry in the industry, subsidies for the industry, laws on related products, and legislation to fix a price ceiling above the market price.

BECKER extended Stigler's work to the case where there is competition among interest groups for political influence. Each interest group exerts political pressure, but exerting such pressure is costly, perhaps in terms of a contribution towards the campaign funds of politicians. Becker derives a Nash equilibrium in which all interest groups simultaneously decide on the level of political influence.

In other extensions, BARON looked at the case where interest groups do not know the politician-bureau's cost of supplying services and SPILLER has looked at a situation where a government agency is responsible to both, the Congress and to the interest groups. Since the objectives of the

Congress and the interest groups might be in conflict, they compete with each other for favourable decisions from the agency.

In the "Virginia school" tradition, politicians create artificial scarcities for public output/ services. This induces people to compete for the scarce output, maybe by offering a bribe to jump the queue. Politicians value bribes/rents, hence their original policy of creating artificial scarcities serves their ends. The early contributors were Buchanan, Tullock, and Tollison. See TOLLISON for a survey of the basic ideas.

LAFFONT & TIROLE use a three-tiered model in which Congress regulates a bureau that might be *captured* by private interest groups. The bureau observes some information on issues relevant to the interest groups, which Congress cannot observe. For instance, the bureau might be an environmental agency and the interest group might be an industry that discharges harmful pollutants into the atmosphere. In order to escape penalization for its actions, the industry might attempt to bribe the bureau to turn a blind eye. Congress now designs appropriate incentives for the bureau to reveal accurately information about the industry. One possibility is to pass regulation, which lowers industry output, and hence also lowers pollution and industry profits. Lower profits reduce the industry's ability to bribe the bureau; such regulation is *collusion-proof*.

The political economy approach may be applied to institutions. What accounts for the diverse forms of institutional arrangements, which facilitate exchange in a political as well as an economic setting? An important clue to the answer is the question of who has the *power* to make decisions.

Power is a nebulous concept but recently the incomplete contracts framework has been able to define and use it in a more precise way; for example see GROSSMAN & HART. Many real-world contractual situations are *incomplete* in the sense that the parties to a transaction cannot foresee all possible future contingencies, or even if they could, the costs of writing all the contingencies in a contract is infinite. A third possible reason for incompleteness is the inability to write the contract in a sufficiently clear way to enable an arbiter such as a court of law to decide if the terms of the contract have been violated. Therefore, many possible contingencies are not written down in the contract. However, the contract allocates *residual control rights*, or *power*, possibly but not necessarily to just one of the parties, to make binding decisions once a contingency, not specified in the original contract occurs. Many institutional features can be understood as the assignment of residual control rights, or power. For an enlightening and thought-provoking discussion, see DIXIT.

In the public choice approach to constitutions, exemplified in BUCHANAN & TULLOCK (1962), there are two stages. In the first, the constitution is formed and in the second, policy is announced, with the constitution acting as a reference point. The first stage is a "normative stage" in which the drafters of the constitution are placed behind a veil of ignorance and then choose a set of rules based on some criteria of fairness. Two problems arise with this approach. First the drafters of the constitution might not be acting behind a veil of ignorance; they could be protecting certain interests. Second, this framework does not deal with the vital issue of incomplete contracts.

What mix and level of public goods/ services should the government provide? The traditional literature argues that certain goods, and services, for example, insurance, pure public goods and so on will either not be provided in private markets or be provided in socially inefficient amounts. A newer literature has applied the *property rights approach* to this vexed question.

The basic problem is this: politicians or public enterprise managers have residual control rights over the operation of public enterprises, but they do not have rights to its cashflows, which belong to society. If the interests of politicians are not aligned with the social interest, they might act in socially inefficient manner. For instance, politicians might desire excess employment in public enterprises, because labour unions are important vote banks, or they might choose a location for the public enterprise that maximizes votes but is socially inefficient and so on. BOYCKO, SHLEIFER & VISHNY demonstrate how this led to inefficient Soviet enterprises. SHLEIFER & VISHNY use the Coase theorem to show that if bribes between politicians (who have control rights) and the treasury (which has the cashflow rights to public enterprises) are possible, the outcome is socially efficient. In the absence of such bribes however, the allocation of control and cashflow rights has serious efficiency consequences. *Privatization* might then be a good option under some circumstances.

In an interesting approach to privatization, the crucial difference between public firms and regulated private firms is the amount of information available to governments in each case. Clearly, if governments have access to identical information in both cases, regulation can be so designed that the outcomes under each case are identical. These issues are examined in SHAPIRO & WILLIG and in SCHMIDT (1996). Governments might have greater access to information when production takes place in a public enterprise (under government ownership). One reason is that ownership gives privileged access to a firm's accounting system. In the case of a regulated firm about which the government has less information, regulation involves leaving an informational rent to the firm, which is socially costly, so if the regulator is benevolent, all production should lie in the public sphere. However, if the regulator has objectives that are not congruent with the social interest, then privatization has a distinct advantage; the regulator's lack of information, will make it more difficult for him to pursue his private agenda.

SANJIT DHAMI

See also Contracts and competition, Political economy survey, Quasi-markets, Regulation and competition

Economics and sociology

Friedland, Roger and A.F. Robertson (editors), *Beyond the Marketplace: Rethinking Economy and Society*, New York: de Gruyter, 1990

Granovetter, Mark and Richard Swedberg (editors), *The Sociology of Economic Life*, Boulder, Colorado: Westview Press, 1992

Hirshleifer, Jack, "The Expanding Domain of Economics", *American Economic Review*, 75/6 (1985): 53–68

Ingham, Geoffrey, "Some Recent Changes in the Relationship between Economics and Sociology", *Cambridge Journal of Economics*, 20/2 (1996): 243–75

Lévy-Garboua, Luis (editor), *Sociological Economics*, London and Beverly Hills, California: Sage, 1979

Martinelli, Alberto and Neil J. Smelser (editors), *Economy and Society: Overviews in Economic Sociology*, London and Newbury Park, California: Sage, 1990

Smelser, Neil J. and Richard Swedberg (editors), *The Handbook of Economic Sociology*, Princeton, New Jersey: Princeton University Press, 1994

Steiner, Philippe, "Economic Sociology: A Historical Perspective", *European Journal of the History of Economic Thought*, 2/1 (1995): 175–95

Swedberg, Richard, *Economics and Sociology: Redefining Their Boundaries: Conversations with Economists and Sociologists*, Princeton, New Jersey: Princeton University Press, 1990

Swedberg, Richard (editor), *Explorations in Economic Sociology*, New York: Russell Sage Foundation, 1993

Swedberg, Richard (editor), *Economic Sociology*, Cheltenham: Elgar, 1996

Winship, Christopher and Sherwin Rosen (editors), *Organizations and Institutions: Sociological and Economic Approaches to the Analysis of Social Structure*, Chicago: University of Chicago Press, 1988

Zukin, Sharon and Paul DiMaggio (editors), *Structures of Capital: The Social Organization of the Economy*, Cambridge and New York: Cambridge University Press, 1990

INGHAM presents a survey of the relationship between economics and sociology as distinct academic disciplines. He contrasts the topics of methodological individualism, positivism, and functionalism as constitutive features of neoclassical economics with sociological notions such as the meaning of action, structural properties, and power-relations. Marginalism is identified as the most influential source of the intellectual separation of both disciplines, implying a reductionist notion of rationality, which was repeatedly criticized by Weber and Durkheim. Their arguments are mirrored by current debates between neoclassical economists and sociologists. It is concluded that an interdisciplinary perspective is only feasible for so-called heterodox schools of economic thought such as institutionalism and post-Keynesianism.

The account of conversations in SWEDBERG (1990) covers the life and works of major scholars who are engaged in the current dialogues among social scientists. The content of the volume supports the impression that the most relevant intellectual differences are those between certain cross-disciplinary strands of thought. A Becker–Coleman camp may be distinguished from the ideas of Akerlof or Granovetter. It follows, therefore, that a differentiation of economics and sociology according to rigid methodological or theoretical viewpoints may be an increasingly meaningless procedure.

LÉVY-GARBOUA brings together a broad range of economists with a common interest in the analysis of social phenomena. This means that the formal tools of economic theory are applied to the matter of individual choice. Becker's disputed approach to rational behaviour is accompanied by

Elster's elaboration of the limits of rationality. Tullock applies the public choice perspective to the matter of voting rights. An essay by Gintis and Katzner discusses the division of labour in the firm. It demonstrates once again that formal methods may be combined with astonishingly diverse political attitudes.

HIRSHLEIFER takes quite a controversial theoretical position, advocating an explicit economic imperialism. The expansion of economics to a universal social science, based upon the notions of scarcity, cost, and preferences, would help to establish a conceptual framework that fits the analytical concerns of the social sciences in general terms.

WINSHIP & ROSEN maintain in their introductory essay that the most decisive difference between sociology and economics is the inductive character of the former as compared with the deductive character of the latter. They conclude that the economist's strength lies in the provision of rigorous theories of individual behaviour whereas sociologists produce related empirical evidence. Further essays in their volume on the sociological and economic analysis of institutions do not necessarily follow that proposed division of labour. Coleman's essay on social capital, for instance, accentuates essential theoretical concerns of both disciplines.

The vast literature on economic sociology emphasizes the need for combining theoretical and empirical work. The editorial introduction in MARTINELLI & SMELSER discusses a continuum of concepts that range from the classical analyses of capitalism by Marx and Weber, via Schumpeter and Polanyi, to the more recent efforts of Parsons and his structural functionalism. The more empirically oriented essays of the volume cover quite diverse topics such as the cultural aspects of economic development and the ongoing internationalization of markets.

FRIEDLAND & ROBERTSON have edited together various approaches to the analysis of market processes. Regarding the demarcation of economics and sociology, Granovetter maintains that the embeddedness approach may contribute to an integration of theoretical and historical concerns in the analysis of economic dynamics.

Similar ideas may be found in ZUKIN & DIMAGGIO, who introduce their volume with a discussion of specific modes of embeddedness – that is, cognitive, cultural, structural, and political types as social-organizational concepts that counter the crisis in economic theorizing. Hirsch, Michaels and Friedman then address methodological issues. They point to the conflict between the modelling elegance of economics and the conceptual realism of sociology. Further essays are concerned with the topics of finance, entrepreneurship, and the state, for the volume attempts to highlight the variety of institutional and organizational forms within capitalism.

This approach is paralleled in the edited collection by SWEDBERG (1993). His own essay appraises the Schumpeterian heritage, while further chapters deal with the various modes of economic interaction.

GRANOVETTER & SWEDBERG introduce their volume with the thesis that economic action, as a form of social action, is socially situated and therefore embedded in socially constructed economic institutions. The collection of reprinted essays includes Granovetter's original elaboration of the embeddedness concept as well as classics like Gerschenkron and Polanyi. Further contributions point at the corresponding analysis of firms, markets, and institutions, including Granovetter's research on labour market networks. SWEDBERG (1996) is a similarly well-designed but even more exhaustive compilation of classics in economic sociology. Essays by Weber, Schumpeter, and Parsons shed light on the past controversies surrounding this school of thought, and current thinking is represented by scholars like Becker, Coleman, and Granovetter.

STEINER explores the intellectual development of economic sociology. He suggests that conceptual traces of that school of thought are even to be found in Jevons, and thus he rejects Swedberg's paradigmatic claims. Moreover, the notion of economic sociology as the general type of a unified social science is criticized, basically due to its all-embracing character. Instead the focused analyses of embeddedness and networks in Granovetter's terms may yield more useful results for future research.

The most comprehensive and indispensable account of the relationship between economic and sociological concerns is SMELSER & SWEDBERG. The first part of the book offers an all-inclusive perspective on its subject, which is well designed to illustrate the many facets of the ongoing discussions. Apart from the highly informative introductory essay by the editors, who review the essential concerns of economic sociology, there is a detailed presentation of institutional, evolutionary, and transaction cost economics as well as rational choice sociology. The application of sociological concepts to economic issues constitutes the second part of the volume, as various topics such as economic systems, market structures, consumption patterns, and business networks are taken to the fore. Finally, the intersections of the economic and social sphere are discussed, including gender and environmental issues. Obviously economic sociology will continue to reflect the indisputable relevance of interdisciplinary research in the social sciences.

ALEXANDER EBNER

See also Economic sociology

Economics methodology

Backhouse, Roger E. (editor), *New Directions in Economic Methodology*, London and New York: Routledge, 1994

Backhouse, Roger E., *Truth and Progress in Economic Knowledge*, Cheltenham, Gloucestershire: Elgar, 1997

Backhouse, Roger E., Daniel M. Hausman, Uskali Mäki and Andrea Salanti (editors), *Economics and Methododology: Crossing Boundaries*, Basingstoke: Macmillan, and New York: St Martin's Press, 1998

Blaug, Mark, *The Methodology of Economics: or, How Economists Explain*, London and New York: Cambridge University Press, 1980; 2nd edition, 1992

Caldwell, Bruce, *Beyond Positivism: Economic Methodology in the Twentieth Century*, revised edition, London and New York: Routledge, 1994 (originally published 1982)

Caldwell, Bruce J. (editor), *The Philosophy and Methodology of Economics*, 3 vols., Aldershot, Hampshire: Elgar, 1993

Davis, John B., D. Wade Hands and Uskali Mäki (editors), *Handbook of Economic Methodology*, Cheltenham, Gloucestershire: Elgar, 1998

De Marchi, Neil and Mark Blaug (editors), *Appraising Economic Theories: Studies in the Methodology of Research Programmes*, Aldershot, Hampshire: Elgar, 1991

Hands, D. Wade, *Testing, Rationality and Progress: Essays on the Popperian Tradition in Economic Methodology*, Lanham, Maryland: Rowman and Littlefield, 1992

Hausman, Daniel M., *The Inexact and Separate Science of Economics*, Cambridge and New York: Cambridge University Press, 1992

Hausman, Daniel M. (editor), *The Philosophy of Economics: An Anthology*, Cambridge and New York: Cambridge University Press, 1984; 2nd edition 1994

Hausman, Daniel M., "Problems with Realism in Economics", *Economics and Philosophy*, 14/2 (1998): 185[-]214

Hutchison, Terence, *Changing Aims in Economics*, Oxford and Cambridge, Massachusetts: Blackwell, 1992

Kincaid, Harold, *Philosophical Foundations of the Social Sciences: Analysing Controversies in Social Research*, Cambridge and New York: Cambridge University Press, 1996

Latsis, Spiro J. (editor), *Method and Appraisal in Economics*, Cambridge and New York: Cambridge University Press, 1976

Lawson, Tony, *Economics and Reality*, London and New York: Routledge, 1997

McCloskey, Donald N., *The Rhetoric of Economics*, Madison: University of Wisconsin Press, 1985; 2nd edition as Deirdre N. McCloskey, 1998

Mäki, Uskali, "Reclaiming relevant realism", *Journal of Economic Methodology*, 7/1 (2000): 109-25

Mayer, Thomas, *Truth versus Precision in Economics*, Aldershot, Hampshire: Elgar, 1993

Morgan, Mary and Margaret Morrison, *Models as Mediators*, Cambridge and New York: Cambridge University Press, 1999

Rappaport, Steven, *Models and Reality in Economics*, Cheltenham, Gloucestershire: Elgar, 1998

Rosenberg, Alexander, *Economics: Mathematical Politics or Science of Diminishing Returns*, Chicago: University of Chicago Press, 1992

The first attempt to define the field of economic methodology was by BLAUG. This provided three things: a survey of recent philosophy of science relevant to economics; a historical survey of economists writings on economic methodology, starting with Nassau Senior in 1836; and a series of case studies in economics. The book advocated a blend of Popperian and Lakatosian falsificationism, ending with the bold claim that economists did not practice falsificationism (their theories were often unfalsifiable and no serious attempt was made to falsify them) and that they should try harder to do so. Although it pays insufficient attention to themes that have come into the literature recently, it remains one of the best textbooks on the subject.

CALDWELL (1982) also surveyed the philosophy of science and economists' discussions of methodology, but drew a radically different conclusion. He was sceptical about whether it was plausible to argue convincingly that any one methodology was superior to others and advocated instead what he termed critical pluralism.

For much of the 1980s, the main focus of the literature on economic methodology was Imre Lakatos's "methodology of scientific research programmes". This could be seen as a more sophisticated version of Karl Popper's falsificationism, which, by introducing the concept of a research programme, provided a means to link methodological ideas to episodes in the history of economic thought. The book that placed Lakatosian methodology on the agenda in economics was LATSIS. The 8 chapters (including contributions by leading economists such as J.R. Hicks, A. Leijonhufvud, and H.A. Simon) explored different ways in which Lakatosian methodology could be applied. Two books perhaps stand out from the literature that followed. HANDS thoroughly explores the problems with Popperian/Lakatosian methodology. DE MARCHI & BLAUG is the outcome of a conference that sought to establish what progress had been made in applying Lakatosian methodology to economics. It shows clearly how opinion on Lakatos had changed during the preceding decade and, in doing so, it raises many critical questions about how we should understand economic theory. The range of contributions makes it essential reading on this subject.

During the 1990s the range of themes in economic methodology expanded. Although many of these themes were addressed in the earlier literature, they were developed much further. There are perhaps three reasons for this: growing awareness of the problems with traditional methodology; the challenge posed by McCLOSKEY and others who argued that rhetoric, not methodology, was the appropriate framework within which to view economics; and increased awareness, by methodologists, of developments in the sociology of scientific knowledge, discourse analysis, naturalized epistemology, and so on.

Perhaps the most important methodological issue in contemporary economics concerns the nature of economic theory. HAUSMAN (1992) sought to answer this question by reviving John Stuart Mill's (1844) notion of economics as an "inexact" science. Economics is inexact because it deals with only some of the causes operating in any real-world situation. Hausman sought to provide a version of Mill's method that more accurately described what contemporary economists do, and to defend it. However, the second major element in its thesis was that economists strive to achieve very general theories, with a wide scope, with the result that economics becomes separate from other sciences in the sense that it does not depend on them for their basic assumptions.

Another traditional methodological position is to emphasize the importance of prediction. ROSENBERG argued that the hallmark of any successful science was improved predictive power. This was not to be found in economics, and economists were pursuing a theoretical strategy that, he argued, could never achieve this. The reason is that actions, according to the "folk psychology" of economists, are determined by preferences and beliefs. This is a problem because beliefs and preferences can never be independently observed. Rosenberg thus suggested that economics made more sense if viewed as mathematical political philosophy: working out ways in which society can be ordered when decisions are decentralized.

Another economist to emphasize the importance of prediction was HUTCHISON, who focused on the deleterious effects of economists' having moved away from prediction as the goal of the subject. Unlike Rosenberg, however, Hutchison argued that economists' ability to predict *had* improved over the centuries but this was due not to progress in economic theory, but to quantitative and statistical work, such as improved methods of national income accounting.

The argument that economists cannot predict, and will never be able to do so, is one of the themes underlying LAWSON's critical realism. Prediction, he argues, is possible only in closed systems, such as those produced within a controlled experiment. Economic reality, in contrast, is structured in that behind the world of events is a deeper reality of causal powers and mechanisms. These two levels of reality are imperfectly synchronized, so even if there are regularities at the level of causal mechanisms, we can never expect to find regularities at the level of events. Prediction, which is based on the existence of event regularities, is thus doomed. A further reason why economies have to be modelled as open systems, ruling out both deductive theory and conventional econometrics, is the fact of human choice. If people have free choice, economic systems can never be predictable.

In marked contrast to this is the realism of Uskali Mäki (e.g. his contributions to the collection edited by BACKHOUSE (1994) and to the handbook edited by DAVIS, HAND & MÄKI). Where Lawson sees the task of methodology as that of providing a critique of a subject that has clearly failed, Mäki is more circumspect, offering tightly argued, logical analysis, from a realist perspective, of issues such as the role of assumptions in economic theories. MÄKI contains a nice summary of his approach to realism and lots of references to his own work. Against both Lawson and Mäki, HAUSMAN (1998) contends that the issue of realism is an irrelevance for economics, serving to distract from more important methodological differences.

Perhaps the main feature of contemporary economics is the importance of models. A historical approach underlies many of the papers in MORGAN & MORRISON. A key theme in this work is the similarities between mathematical or conceptual models and physical models. Amongst the approaches pursued in this book is that of seeing models as "instruments", analogous to scientific instruments such as a thermometer. Another is that the physical models that lie, often hidden, behind mathematical models, are important for the way economic models server to explain reality. A contrasting approach is the more traditionally philosophical approach of RAPPAPORT, who explores the idea that models (based on assumptions that are not true of reality) show us what the world would be like if certain conditions were satisfied. He links this to alternative notions of explanation and how models that do not predict might nonetheless provide explanations.

Econometrics is a field where methodological problems are regularly addressed in the sense that choices have to be made between a wide variety of techniques for data analysis. However, with the exception of Lawson, none of the works discussed above pays much attention to econometrics. One book that does is MAYER, which questions who uses the analogy of a chain, arguing that economists devote too much of their efforts to strengthening links that are already strong. He raises questions about whether, given the nature of the data facing economists, simpler techniques may be more appropriate.

BACKHOUSE (1997) is another book that considers econometrics in some depth. This focuses on the concept of progress, exploring different notions of what might constitute progress and how economists' practices, especially within econometrics, might contribute towards progress in the subject.

The literature on economic methodology has largely ignored many of the issues regarded as important in other social sciences. One reason for this is that, apart from heterodox minorities, economists largely agree on some of the issues on which other social scientists are more divided, notably individualism and the use of deductive modelling. A book that tried to bridge the gap, using examples from anthropology and sociology as well as economics, is KINCAID.

The diversity of themes found in the contemporary methodological literature is illustrated by BACKHOUSE *et al.* CALDWELL (1993) provides a guide to the extensive journal literature up to the start of the 1990s. The value of this collection is that, although there are better anthologies available, such as the one edited by HAUSMAN (1994), it lists their contents as well as its own.

ROGER E. BACKHOUSE

See also Economic thought, history of

Economics of information

Baron, D. and R. Myerson, "Regulating a Monopolist with Unknown Cost", *Econometrica*, 50 (1982): 911–30

Baron, D. and D. Besanko, "Regulation, Asymmetric Information and Auditing", *Rand Journal of Economics*, 15 (1984): 447–70

Bernheim, B. and M.D. Whinston, "Menu Auctions, Resource Allocation, and Economic Influence", *Quarterly Journal of Economics*, 101 (1986): 1–31

Blanchard, Olivier J. and Stanley Fischer, *Lectures on Macroeconomics*, Cambridge, Massachusetts: MIT Press, 1989

Cho, I.K. and D. Kreps, "Signaling Games and Stable Equilibria", *Quarterly Journal of Economics*, 102 (1988):179–202

Dhami, Sanjit, "Income Uncertainty, Measurement Problems and Optimal Multidimensional Income Taxation", University of Essex Discussion Paper no. 492, 1998a

Dhami, Sanjit., "A Multitask Agency Theory of Optimal Agrarian Labour Contracts", University of Essex Discussion Paper no. 490, 1998b

Dhami, Sanjit and Jack Mintz, "Risk, Moral Hazard and the Role of Capital Taxes", University of Essex Discussion Paper no. 475, 1997

Fudenberg, Drew and Jean Tirole, *Game Theory*, Cambridge, Massachusetts: MIT Press, 1991

Grossman, S. and Oliver Hart, "An Analysis of the Principal–Agent Problem", *Econometrica*, 51 (1983): 7–45

Hayami, Yujiro and Keijiro Otsuka, *The Economics of Contract Choice: An Agrarian Perspective*, Oxford: Clarendon Press, and New York: Oxford University Press, 1993

Hart, O. and J. Tirole, "Contract Renegotiation and Coasian Dynamics", *Review of Economic Studies*, 55 (1988): 509–40

Holmstrom, Bengt, "Moral Hazard and Observability" *Bell Journal of Economics*, 10 (1979): 74–91

Holmstrom, Bengt, "Moral Hazard in Teams", *Bell Journal of Economics*, 13 (1982): 324–40

Holmstrom, Bengt and Paul Milgrom, "Regulating Trade among Agents" *Journal of Institutional and Theoretical Economics*, 146/1 (1990): 85–105

Holmstrom, Bengt and Paul Milgrom, "Multitask Principal Agent Analysis: Incentive Contracts, Asset Ownership and Job Design", *Journal of Law Economics and Organization*, 7/2 (1991): 201–28

Holmstrom, Bengt and Paul Milgrom, "The Firm as an Incentive System", *American Economic Review*, 84 (1994): 972–91

Laffont, Jean-Jacques and Jean Tirole, *A Theory of Incentives in Procurement and Regulation*, Cambridge, Massachusetts: MIT Press, 1993

Mas-Colell, Andrea, Michael D. Whinston and Jerry R. Green, *Microeconomic Theory*, Oxford and New York: Oxford University Press, 1995

Mirrlees, J.A., "An Exploration in the Theory of Optimal Income Taxation", *Review of Economic Studies*, 38 (1971): 175–208

Mirrlees, J.A., "The Theory of Moral Hazard and Unobservable Behaviour: Part 1", *Review of Economic Studies*, 66/1 (1999): 3–22

Muthoo, A., "Renegotiation-Proof Tenurial Contracts as Screening Mechanisms", *Journal of Development Economics*, 56 (1998): 1–26

Myers, S. and N. Majluf, "Corporate Financing and Investment Decisions When Firms Have Information That Investors do Not Have", *Journal of Financial Economics*, 13 (1984): 187–221

Myerson, R. and M. Satterthwaite, "Efficient Mechanisms for Bilateral Trading", *Journal of Economic Theory*, 28 (1983): 265–81

Shapiro, Carl and Joseph E. Stiglitz, "Equilibrium Unemployment as a Worker Discipline Device", *American Economic Review*, 74 (1984): 433–44

Slade, Margaret E., "Multitask Agency and Contract Choice", *International Economic Review*, 37/2 (1996): 465–86

Spence, A. M., "Job Market Signaling", *Quarterly Journal of Economics*, 87 (1973): 355–74

Stiglitz, Joseph E. and Andrew Weiss, "Credit Rationing in Markets with Imperfect Information", *American Economic Review*, 71 (1981): 393–410

A situation of "asymmetric information" (AI) exists when of the two or more parties to a transaction, at least one of the parties has access to information that the other parties do not possess. Economists distinguish between two types of asymmetric information. In the first type, known as *adverse selection*, AI exists before the two parties enter into a relationship. The second type, which is known as *moral hazard*, occurs when AI arises after the parties enter into a relationship.

Problems involving adverse selection are generally addressed through one of the two methods, *signalling* or *screening*. In signalling models, the party that possesses the private information, offers the terms of exchange which the other party can either accept or reject. In screening models the uninformed party offers the terms of exchange, which the informed party can either reject or accept.

Suppose that the party, which possesses the private information, has one of N possible types. In the context of a signalling model, economists characterize two possible solutions to the problem. In a "separating equilibrium" all types take different actions thereby revealing their types, while in a "pooling equilibrium" different types take the same action so tat their types remain hidden. Rigorous treatments can be seen in FUDENBERG & TIROLE and MAS-COLELL, WHINSTON & GREEN.

SPENCE considered the problem of a worker seeking employment with a firm when the worker has private information on his ability, which is either high or low. If education is relatively harder for the low ability worker to acquire, the high ability worker, in order to signal his type, can attain a level of education, which the latter cannot possibly attain. When the firm looks at the curriculum vitae of the worker, it finds out his type. In the starkest version of the model, education does not enhance the worker's ability; hence, it is socially wasteful. Nevertheless, education performs a useful role in revealing information to the firm. The social cost in this case would be to acquire unproductive education. CHO & KREPS have shown that a pooling equilibrium can be ruled out in this model.

MYERS & MAJLUF use a signalling model to explain the debt to equity ratio (leverage) of companies. Suppose that investors are less informed about the firm's future profit prospects than the managers of the firm. Only a firm with good prospects can hope to repay a higher level of debt in the future, hence, a firm with good prospects can, by deciding on a high leverage, separate itself from a firm with bad prospects. Ex-post when investors observe a high leverage, they become informed of the firm's prospects.

Screening models make use of the "revelation principle" to "screen out" the different types. Suppose that an individual who has private information on his health seeks life insurance from an insurance company. Type A individuals face terminal illness and will certainly die this year, while type B clients are in good health. In order to solve the AI problem the insurance company offers two contracts. Contract 1 specifies reasonable benefits if the individual dies at any time. Contract 2 promises very limited benefits for the first year, but generous benefits in the following years. Type A clients would never accept contract 2; they are screened out. As in signalling models, information revelation imposes additional costs. The most visible cost is the distortion in exchange that results from lack of information. The revelation principle essentially states that it is possible, by using a set of cleverly designed contracts, to deal with the problems of AI when the uniformed party is required to move first. Treatments of the revelation principle can be found in Fudenberg & Tirole and in Mas-Colell, Whinston & Green.

Screening models have proved quite useful in the regulation literature (for a book-length treatment, that is both authorita-

tive and comprehensive, see LAFFONT & TIROLE). In the prototype model of BARON & MYERSON, a monopolist public firm has private information about its costs, which can either be high or low. The problem facing a regulator is to design an optimal regulatory scheme when he only observes the monopolist's output, but not his cost. They show that in order to induce the low cost type to separate from the high cost type, the latter is regulated to produce too low an output level that the former would not find profitable to imitate. There is therefore a distortion relative to the full information case. BARON & BESANKO extend this prototype model by allowing for occasional auditing of the monopolist's costs.

A literature in public economics looks at the issue of financing a public good through contributions from citizens when the citizens have private information on their willingness to pay for the public good. The revelation principle can now be used to screen among the different types of each citizens, so that in equilibrium, each citizen prefers to announce his true underlying type. See FUDENBERG & TIROLE (1992) for the solution to this problem under assumptions of varying complexity.

Another application of AI is in optimal tax theory (see MIRRLEES 1971). The problem here is to design the optimal income tax on individuals when they have private information on their abilities. One startling result of this literature is that the marginal tax on the richest individual is optimally zero.

In STIGLITZ & WEISS, each of several potential liquidity constrained investors has access to a project. The project's profitability is private information to the investor and projects having greater expected returns are also riskier. If the project succeeds, the loan is repaid to the bank; if it fails, the investor declares bankruptcy and the bank gets nothing. An increase in the bank's interest rate has two effects: (a) its profits increase in the event that the project is successful; (b) it attracts riskier investors at the margin because the greater amount that needs to be repaid can only be generated through riskier projects. Hence, the bank might be reluctant to raise the interest rates to a level that clears the loan market. Thus, credit might be rationed and investment curtailed. (See BLANCHARD & FISCHER for the macroeconomic implications of credit rationing for monetary policy.)

In the context of bargaining, suppose that a seller is bargaining with a buyer over the sale of one unit of an indivisible object. The buyer has private information on his valuation for the object, which can either be v_L or v_H dollars with respective probabilities λ and $1 - \lambda$ that are known to the seller. MYERSON & SATTERTHWAITE present a model in terms of two-sided AI; the buyer also has asymmetric information on the seller's cost of supplying the object. See Fudenberg & Tirole for a textbook treatment.

Screening models become quite complex when parties interact repeatedly. Consider a subsidiary of a parent firm that has private information on its profitability that can be either high or low. The parent firm is required to set profitability targets for the subsidiary in a two-period model. If in the first period the subsidiary achieves a high profit, it gives away its type and hence its second period profit target will be high. If producing higher profits requires greater effort, then the high profit type might want to hide its type in the first period by producing low profits. Therefore, the parent firm learns nothing in the first period and it does not set too stringent a second period profit target for the subsidiary, which is exactly what the subsidiary desired. This phenomenon is known as the ratchet effect. See chapters nine and ten in Laffont & Tirole for an introduction to models of repeated AI as well as for a good list of references.

There are two competing models of adverse selection that deal with repeated interaction. In the first, the parties interact through a series of *short-term contracts* (a new contract every period) and in the latter, through a *long-term contract* that is finalized at the beginning of the relationship. Long-term contracts can be renegotiated as information on types becomes available in subsequent periods. Parties can foresee this renegotiation in the future, so they might as well renegotiate now; the principle of renegotiation-proofness. See HART & TIROLE for the theory and for an application to the development literature see MUTHOO.

With regard to moral hazard, the issue is the appropriate design of incentive schemes for an agent who works for a principal but has private information on his effort level. For example, suppose that a manufacturer enters into a contract with a salesman to sell his product to the final customers. Subsequent to the signing of the contract, the salesman can either put in a high level of effort or he can shirk. The manufacturer only observes the final level of sales made by the salesman and not his effort. Notice that unlike adverse selection models, AI arises only after the contract has been signed. The principal only observes an imperfect indicator of the agent's effort, such as output, which could be influenced by factors beyond the agent's control. However, greater effort increases the probability of achieving higher output levels. The principal's offer of a wage to the agent must be based solely on the observable (and verifiable) output, for otherwise a court cannot enforce violations of the contract. If the agent is paid a fixed salary, he will shirk because he has no stake in output. Wage schemes based on output increase the agent's incentive to work by creating stakes in higher output levels. It is for this reason that salesmen are often paid on a commission basis.

Although a wage scheme based on output creates incentives for higher effort, it has one serious drawback. If output fluctuates too much (due to influences outside the agent's control) the agent faces too much of an income risk. The optimal wage scheme balances these opposing influences of incentives and risk. MIRRLEES (work written in 1975, reprinted in 1999) provided the initial framework that was extended by HOLMSTROM (1979) and GROSSMAN & HART.

Applications of the basic moral hazard model in economics are too numerous to list. Such models have been applied to agrarian contracts (HAYAMI & OTSUKA 1993), capital taxation on firms (DHAMI & MINTZ 1997), and the existence of unemployment (SHAPIRO & STIGLITZ) among the many diverse phenomena. For applications to political economy settings, see the entry on "'economics and politics'" in this volume.

HOLMSTROM (1982) deals with a moral hazard model when several agents work for the same principal. The basic idea is that one agent's output provides information on another agent's effort. An example is the practice of firms, especially retail firms, of declaring an "employee of the month"; this "yardstick competition" whereby one agent's reward is conditioned on the performance of all others creates incentives for all agents to work hard.

Common agency is another extension in which an agent works for several principals. NATO can be considered as an agent of several principals (the countries that comprise NATO). The aims of the principals can be in conflict, for example they might differ on the issue of sending ground troops into a troubled region. If there were a single principal, and he wanted to send in ground troops, NATO would do so. With common agency, some principals might create disincentives for NATO to send in ground troops, for example, by refusing to allow their countries to be used as launching pads for military action. Therefore, conflict among principals could result in very different incentives for NATO. BERNHEIM & WHINSTON provided the initial idea for this literature.

In the multitask agency literature – see HOLMSTROM & MILGROM (1990, 1991) – the agent performs several different tasks for the same principal. Consider the issue of performance-related pay for schoolteachers – for example, salaries that depend on student grades. Preparing students for examinations is only one of the many tasks that teachers perform. They might spend time in improving the reasoning capabilities of students, enhancing their critical abilities, making them more curious about the things around them and so on – tasks that are not necessarily well reflected in student grades. With performance-related pay, teachers might shift effort from tasks that are otherwise crucial in the development of their students to those that are well reflected in student grades. Thus, the multitask agency literature suggests that optimal incentives might well be "low powered". An example of this is fixed salaries.

The multitask agency literature has been applied to develop an incentive-based theory of the firm (HOLMSTROM & MILGROM 1994), to optimal multidimensional taxation (DHAMI 1998a) to agrarian labour contracts (DHAMI 1998b) and to an understanding of the optimal contractual forms in gasoline retailing (SLADE).

The economics of information is a very large and rapidly expanding field and even a semester-length course cannot do full justice to the theory and its rich applications in several distinct fields. Given the aims of this volume, this survey has been very selective and brief. It has striven only to offer a flavour of some of the issues.

SANJIT DHAMI

See also Adverse selection, Economics and politics, Moral hazard

Economics of the arts

Baumol, William J. and William G. Bowen, *Performing Arts: The Economic Dilemma: A Study of Problems Common to Theater, Opera, Music and Dance*, New York: Twentieth Century Fund, 1966

Blaug, Mark (editor), *The Economics of the Arts*, London: Martin Robertson, and Boulder, Colorado: Westview Press, 1976

Frey, Bruno S. and Werner W. Pommerehne, *Muses and Markets: Explorations in the Economics of the Arts*, Oxford and Cambridge, Massachusetts: Blackwell, 1989

Ginsburgh, Victor A. and Pierre-Michel Menger (editors), *Economics of the Arts: Selected Essays*, Contributions to Economic Analysis, vol. 237, Amsterdam and New York and Oxford: Elsevier, 1996

Hutter, Michael and Ilde Rizzo (editors), *Economic Perspectives on Cultural Heritage*, Basingstoke: Macmillan, and New York: St Martin's Press, 1997

Peacock, A.T., "Welfare Economics and Public Subsidies to the Arts, *Manchester School of Economics and Social Studies*, (December 1969); reprinted in *The Economics of the Arts*, edited by Mark Blaug, London: Martin Roberston, and Boulder, Colorado: Westview Press, 1976

Peacock, Alan and Ilde Rizzo, *Cultural Economics and Cultural Policies*, Dordrecht and Boston and London: Kluwer, 1994

Throsby, David, "The Production and Consumption of the Arts: A View of Cultural Economics", *Journal of Economic Literature*, 32/1 (1994): 1–29

Towse, Ruth and Abdul Khakee (editors), *Cultural Economics*, Berlin and New York: Springer, 1992

Towse, Ruth (editor), *Cultural Economics: The Arts, the Heritage, and the Media Industries*, 2 vols, Cheltenham and Lyme, New Hampshire: Elgar, 1997

The study of art and culture has always been part of the university curriculum. It is only comparatively recently that serious work has been undertaken on the economic dimension of the arts. Over the last decade "cultural economics" has emerged as a subdiscipline in its own right.

BAUMOL & BOWEN's study of the performing arts in the US was the first systematic analysis of a sector of the arts using economic tools. It is commonly seen as having "legitimized" the field. The book focuses on the determination of art prices – the factors affecting the supply and demand for works of art (in this case performed art) – and how rates of return on investment in theatres, opera production, dance training, and so on can be calculated and compared with returns in other sectors. The material – much of it pioneering – is a mix of the theoretical and the empirical and it has become a classic reference.

Two other books that have also earned their status as "classics" are PEACOCK and BLAUG. Peacock provides an insightful interpretation of arts funding, and, in particular, subsidy, using the instruments of conventional neoclassical microeconomics. Much of the emphasis is on the market failure implications of the status of many artistic good and services as public or quasipublic goods, and as such many of the results will be apparent to someone with a training in standard normative public economics. Blaug is an edited selection of articles published during this period and, as such, provides a useful account of the field's first decade.

Cultural economics has since established its position within the field. It has an International Association, hosting its own Annual Congress, an internationally-recognized refereed publication (the *Journal of Cultural Economics*), and a dedicated entry in the well-known "Classification of economics articles" published by the American Economic Association in the *Journal of Economic Literature*. The bulk of contributions are within the traditional boundary of conventional economies, but the current coverage also addresses a range of issues in philosophy, aesthetics, history, sociology, politics, cognitive psychology, and many other disciplines.

TOWSE & KHAKEE is a carefully edited collection of papers from the school that regards cultural economics as applied economics. It is a good, comparatively recent representation of the current research agenda. The contributors emphasize the applicability of much standard economic theory to the world of the arts. This includes risk theory, principal-agency theory, contract theory, and the valuation of intangibles. The papers can be categorized into those dealing with supply and demand for the end good (and pursuant policy issues, such as subsidy), trade, the operation of labour markets in the sectors (the training and employment of actors, sculptors, and so forth), and a particularly interesting section on country studies (overall the book represents 15 countries). The contributing authors are drawn from both inside and outside academia. The scope of FREY & POMMEREHNE is similar (although the level of presentation is less advanced), although with some additional political economy and with examples almost exclusively European.

HUTTER & RIZZO is a collective work on the specific subject of cultural heritage and emphasizes the empirical and policy aspects of work in the field. It includes a number of extremely interesting case studies examining the conception and operation of heritage policy in different countries. Although a variety of definitions of "cultural heritage" have been put forward in policy debate and in the drafting of laws, treaties, and conventions, the drawing of boundaries – deciding what exactly is culture or heritage, and what is not – remains difficult and controversial. The importance of how definitions are set and refereed is noted in a number of the contributions here, the repeated conclusion being that although economics has little to offer in determining what constitutes "heritage" it does have a role to play in determining the level and pattern within a class of artefacts, and it is able to make predictions about the effects of specific regulatory instruments. Much of the analysis here will be familiar to those with a background in regulatory economics or one of its other derivative fields. The book also touches upon some of the techniques available for the monetary valuation of intangibles, notably the contingent valuation method developed and routinely used for evaluating intangible environmental benefits by environmental economists, and the notion of non-use or existence values.

A book that focuses on the issues surrounding the financing and fiscal treatment of the arts is PEACOCK & RIZZO. Much of the material is standard public economics, but interesting nonetheless, and emphasizes the scope for market failure in cultural settings. The role that government can play in defining property rights for artistic and cultural "property" – and hence reducing the propensity for markets to fail – is repeatedly highlighted. This is a similar line of argument to that developed by Ronald Coase in the context of environmental externalities.

The definitive recent survey of the state of the art is provided by THROSBY in his influential and widely cited paper. Throsby, an important contributor to the field himself over a number of years, sets out to "assess how far economics has gone over the last thirty years and how far it might go in exposing and analysing the peculiar problems posed by production and consumption of the arts". The paper is not a conventional literature review (although its bibliography contains over 100 entries), but rather it draws together and interprets the principal themes that scholars have pursued. It analyses the role of tastes as a fundamental driving force in the demand for, and supply of art; how the markets for art and the performing arts "work"; labour markets in the arts; and industrial organization (firm structure and behaviour) in the supply of arts. He also looks ahead, identifying what 'needs to be done' in the field over the next two decades.

In terms of breadth of coverage one can do no better than TOWSE, whose two-volume set contains 82 previously published papers drawn from a wide variety of sources. The work can be regarded as a "reader" for students in the field. Volume one deals with the economics of art and culture; tastes and taste formation; studies of demand in various cultural markets; supply in the performing arts; supply in the museum and heritage industries; supply in the media industries; and the art market. Volume two contains contributions on the economic history of the arts; artists' labour markets; Baumol's cost disease; non-profit organizations in the arts; public subsidy for the arts; and the economic impact of the arts. GINSBURGH & MENGER is a similar (though much less comprehensive) volume.

Cultural economics has yet to develop its own distinctive programme of core research, borrowing, instead, from the established fields of public, labour, and industrial economics. Despite progress to date there are numerous non-trivial theoretical and empirical problems yet to be explored in this area – problems that are susceptible to the powerful tools of positive and normative economic analysis. The work cited here provides a broad introduction both to what has been done and to what needs doing. Several emphasize – correctly – that this is an area which cries out for good quality interdisciplinary work, and one in which economists must be willing to challenge traditional and ingrained disciplinary boundaries. This makes it a highly exciting area of intellectual pursuit.

CATHERINE LISTON-HEYES

Economies of scale and scope

Arthur, W. Brian, *Increasing Returns and Path Dependence in the Economy*, Ann Arbor: University of Michigan Press, 1994

Berndt, E.R, C.A. Morrison and G.C. Watkins, "Dynamic Models of Energy Demand: An Assessment and Comparison" in *Modeling and Measuring Natural Resource Substitution*, edited by Ernst R. Berndt and Barry C. Field, Cambridge, Masachusetts: MIT Press, 1981

Clark, Jeffrey A., "Economies of Scale and Scope at Depository Financial Institutions: A Review of the Literature", *Economic Review*, 73/8 (September/October 1988): 16–33

Economides, Nicholas, "The Economics of Networks", *International Journal of Industrial Organization*, 14/6 (1996): 673–99

Norsworthy, J.R. and S.L. Jang, *Empirical Measurement and Analysis of Productivity and Technological Change: Applications in High Technology and Service Industries*, New York and Amsterdam: North Holland, 1992

Norsworthy, J.R. and D.H. Tsai, "Performance Measurement for Price Cap Regulation of Telecommunications" in *Regulation under Increasing Competition*, edited by Michael A. Crew, Boston: Kluwer, 1999

Pindyck, R., "Adjustment Costs, Uncertainty and Behavior of the Firm", *American Economic Review*, 72/3 (1982): 415–27

Romer, P.M., "Increasing Returns and Long-Run Growth", *Journal of Political Economy*, 94/5 (1986): 1002–37

Treadway, A.B., "The Globally Optimal Flexible Accelerator", *Journal of Economic Theory*, 7 (February 1974): 7–39

The concept of economies of scale has always been important in economics. The entire apparatus of regulatory economics, for example, originates in the idea of natural monopoly, where economies of scale are significant over the whole range of production relevant to serving the market. The topic is more important now, in view of the theoretical and practical needs to analyse regulatory issues and transitions associated with deregulation and privatization; high technology, often network-based industries; product introduction and innovation; and human capital and network effects. The concept is used in economic growth theory, as well as related business disciplines such as accounting, finance, marketing, and tax analysis.

ROMER treats returns to scale in economic growth theory, while ARTHUR takes a broad look at the effects of increasing returns throughout the economy. In the recent burst of awareness of cost interdependencies in production, some intrepid social scientists have designated economies of scale and scope of almost every origin as *network externalities*. For example, ECONOMIDES provides a good treatment of network effects. This ferment does represent vigor in economics and the related business disciplines in addressing important technology- and network-related issues. CLARK reviews important contemporary issues concerning economies of scale and scope in banking regulation, and NORSWORTHY & TSAI look at these issues in telecommunications policy.

Economies of scale are short run effects. They result from spreading fixed costs across expanded output of goods or services. The fixed costs may result from a variety of causes, including research and development, fixed plant and equipment, training costs, patent license fees, etc. Scale effects resulting from delivery of goods or services on networks are short run effects. They result from *increased density of output* delivered on an existing network whose costs are fixed. Partly for this reason, it is necessary to set the conceptual model of production for analysing economies of scale in an explicit short run framework that recognizes short run effects. In other words, to the extent that there are fixed costs that the enterprise must recover during multiple time periods, there will be short run increasing returns to scale, other things being equal. *Economies of scope* arise when two or more outputs share inputs in such a way that expanding one output is less costly when the other is also produced.

True *long term economies of scale* are rare, and probably do not exist. In a classic textbook example, "external" economies of scale are said to result from economies of scale internal to another industry (presumably short run). So the distinction rests on a difference in the period of adjustment between the buying and supplying industries. *Learning effects* are one of the most common long run source of decreasing unit costs, but as NORSWORTHY & JANG (pp.139–44) consider, learning effects are not properly classified as scale effects, because they are not reversed by declining output, even when inputs are fully adjusted. *Communication protocols* are part of the technology that supports network transactions. These protocols may mediate economies of scale and scope, depending on demand responses to different protocols, but are not themselves sources of economies.

To define systematically the various sources of economies of scale it is necessary to use an implicit model of production: a cost function, which is the most commonly applied empirical representation of the technology of production. The cost function is the preferred stochastic specification. Norsworthy & Jang (chapter three) and Norsworthy & Tsai (chapter ten) consider the cost function in service industries and telecommunications respectively.

Adjustment costs result from changes in the technology of production that engender rearrangement of the factors of production. In the absence of adjustment costs, enterprises would adjust instantaneously to optimal levels of inputs, and there would be no economies of scale because there would be no fixed inputs. Consequently it is necessary to show how adjustment costs enter the cost model, and how they affect output elasticities. Dynamic cost functions of this general type are discussed in TREADWAY and further analysed and exemplified in BERNDT, MORRISON & WATKINS and PINDYCK. Recent literature on dynamic models is profuse, but it consists primarily of time series treatments that leave the technology of production implicit.

In summary, economies of scale and scope, while conceptually simple, are not easy to measure definitively because their empirical identification and quantification, to be reliable, must be adjusted for other potentially important confounding effects, especially adjustment costs. To do so is, however, important analytically, because both sources of cost reduction have accelerated with the information revolution, and have important implications for technology management and for regulatory policy.

RANDY NORSWORTHY

See also Network externalities, Regulation and competition

Efficiency analysis

Aigner, D.J., C.A. Knox Lovell, and P.J. Schmidt, "Formulation and Estimation of Stochastic Frontier Production Function Models", *Journal of Econometrics*, 6 (1977): 21–37

Banker, R.D., A. Charnes, and W.W. Cooper, "Models for Estimation of Technical and Scale Inefficiencies in Data Envelopment Analysis", *Management Science*, 30 (1984): 1078–92

Battese, G.E. and T.J. Coelli, "Prediction of Firm-Level Technical Efficiencies with a Generalised Frontier Production Function and Panel Data", *Journal of Econometrics*, 38/3 (1988): 387–99

Burns, P.J. and T. Weyman-Jones, *Regulatory Incentives, Privatisation, and Productivity Growth in UK Electricity Distribution*, London: Centre for the Study of Regulated Industries (CRI), 1994

Charnes, A., W.W. Cooper and E. Rhodes, "Measuring the Efficiency of Decision-Making Units", *European Journal of Operational Research*, 2 (1978): 429–44

Färe, Rolf, Shawna Grosskopf and C.A. Knox Lovell, *Production Frontiers*, Cambridge and New York: Cambridge University Press, 1994

Fried, Harold O., C.A. Knox Lovell and Shelton S. Schmidt (editors), *The Measurement of Productive Efficiency*, New York: Oxford University Press, 1993

Malmquist, S., "Index Numbers and Indifference Surfaces", *Trabajos de Estatistica*, 4 (1953): 209–42

Pollitt, Michael G., *Ownership and Performance in Electric Utilities: The International Evidence on Privatization and Efficiency*, Oxford: Oxford University Press, 1995

Varian, H.R., "The Nonparametric Approach to Production Analysis", *Econometrica*, 52/3 (1984): 579–97

AIGNER *et al.* first proposed the stochastic production frontier model. This is a seminal treatment of how to measure firm efficiency when the basic assumption of two-sided disturbance is dropped in favour of the more realistic hypothesis according to which the error term in production/cost analysis should be split up into two separate components, the first one accounting for inefficiency (one-sided), and the second one for statistical noise (two-sided, as under traditional "least squares" assumptions).

BANKER, CHARNES & COOPER proposed a variable returns to scale (VRS) data envelopment analysis (DEA) approach, which differentiates itself from CHARNES, COOPER & RHODES's (see below) proposal in that it investigates the possibility that decision-making units (DMUs) are not operating at a maximally efficient scale of production. By default, assuming that variable returns to scale is the short-run rule – whereas the long-run, steady-state hypothesis is constant returns (CRS) – the VRS DEA linear program measures how far the DMU is located from the DMU is located from the long-run (CRS) efficient frontier, thus capturing the concept of (short-run) "scale inefficiency". By looking at relative input ratios, the authors also provide a method for computing "technical" (input mix) inefficiency.

BATTESE & COELLI extend the idea of the "stochastic production frontier" to panel data analysis (the situation when a cross-section of observations is repeated over a relevant period of time) so that it can be viewed as an $n \times t$ matrix rather than as a simple series of stacked (or pooled) cross-sections. The authors also calculate an expected-value formula for the one-sided "efficiency error" (u), which characterizes stochastic frontier models, and they show that such a formula generally holds for both cross-sectional and panel data analyses.

BURNS & WEYMAN-JONES investigate productivity growth by means of DEA-based and Malmquist indices (see below) working on a panel of 12 regional electricity companies (RECs) running electricity distribution in England and Wales. They show that DEA can be used to build up both year-by-year and global productivity indices quite easily (as opposed to econometric computation of such measures). With special reference to the English and Welsh RECs, the authors discover that privatization did not boost productivity growth, which has simply followed a long-run expansion path starting at least in the early 1970s.

Charnes et al. introduced the DEA technique of efficiency measurement. Data envelopment analysis (DEA) is a linear-programming tool that minimizes the hyperspatial distance function (in input/output space) separating the firm (or DMU) under examination from its efficiency benchmark – or "best-practice peer" – lying on the efficient production isoquant, which the linear program automatically sets up. By measuring such a distance, DEA builds up a series of "efficiency ranks", which give a straightforward idea of the overall efficiency picture stemming from the data set. The main drawback of data envelopment analysis is that it does not cater for random effects, thus attributing every statistical noise to "inefficiency". Another major problem with DEA is that – by its nature – it is fairly sensitive to "extreme" data points in the sample (outliers) so that, depending on the presence of comparable units in the sample, it will tend to put non comparable observations automatically on the frontier. Such data points are often termed "efficient by default".

FÄRE, GROSSKOPF & LOVELL investigate efficiency measurement in depth. They recall standard production theory and build up links between microeconomics, econometrics, and linear programming. Several efficiency measures (which can generally be implemented with DEA) are examined, from simple radial measurement techniques to more complex non-radial (or "Russell") measures. The linear programs being proposed throughout the book belong to the DEA family. This is a technical book for the experienced reader.

FRIED, LOVELL & SCHMIDT provide the benchmark reference of this topic. Their book is a selection of very good papers concerning efficiency measurement. Both stochastic frontier estimation and data envelopment analysis are examined and compared. Other measurement techniques are also taken into account. The first part of the book mainly deals with theoretical issues, whereas the second part puts forward several empirical studies that apply both econometric and linear-programming techniques, and provide comparative outcomes. Utilities, banks, municipalities, non-profit organizations, and other sectors are analysed. This book even suits non-specialized readers and should be read first by those interested in the present entry.

MALMQUIST is the paper that first introduced productivity indices based upon hyperspatial distance functions. By constructing the ratio between two different efficiency measures relating to different time moments, the author shows that it is possible to obtain an overall measure of productivity growth (the "Malmquist index"), which can be easily compared – and can also converge – to more traditional productivity growth ratios. It may also be shown that the Malmquist index of productivity growth is – subject to some general assumptions – equivalent to a TFP (total factor productivity) measure.

POLLITT's contribution is a very interesting treatment of at least four different efficiency measurement techniques. Non parametric statistical tests are also performed to cross-check econometric results against linear programming ones. This contribution is described at length in the entry on Electricity industry.

Finally, VARIAN provides a general, yet technical, overview of nonparametric efficiency measurement methods, with special reference to DEA and "free disposability hull" techniques. The basic assumptions underlying common DEA programs (such as 100 per cent input disposability) are carefully assessed. This is a technical survey paper that would ideally suit the experienced reader with an interest in quantitative techniques.

GIAN CARLO SCARSI

See also Electricity industry

Efficient markets hypothesis

Boudoukh, Jacob, Matthew P. Richardson and Robert F. Whitelaw, "A Tale of Three Schools: Insights on Autocorrelations of Short-horizon Stock Returns", *Review of Financial Studies*, 7/3 (1994): 539–73

Cochrane, John H., "Volatility Tests and Efficient Markets: A Review Essay", *Journal of Monetary Economics*, 27/3 (1991): 463–85

Cuthbertson, Keith, *Quantitative Financial Economics: Stocks, Bonds, and Foreign Exchange*, New York and Chichester: Wiley, 1996

Fama, Eugene F., "Efficient Capital Markets: A Review of Theory and Empirical Work", *Journal of Finance*, 25/2 (1970): 383–417

Fama, Eugene F., "Efficient Capital Markets: 2", *Journal of Finance*, 46/5 (1991): 1575–1617

Kothari, S.P. and Jerold B. Warner, "Measuring Long-horizon Security Price Performance", *Journal of Financial Economics*, 43/3 (1997): 301–39

MacKinlay, A. Craig, "Event Studies in Economics and Finance", *Journal of Economic Literature*, 35/1 (1997): 13–39

McQueen, Grant R., "Long-horizon Mean-reverting Stock Prices Revisited", *Journal of Financial and Quantitative Analysis*, 27/1 (1992): 1–18

Richardson, Matthew, "Temporary Components of Stock Prices: A Skeptic's View", *Journal of Business and Economic Statistics*, 11/2 (1993): 199–207

Rozeff, Michael S. and Mir A. Zaman, "Overreaction and Insider Trading: Evidence from Growth and Value Portfolios", *Journal of Finance*, 53/2 (1998): 701–16

FAMA (1970) formalized the definition of informational efficiency. He points out that the theory of efficient markets is concerned with whether prices at any time fully reflect available information. He summarizes the early empirical work on the efficient market hypothesis into three types. He argues that the strong form efficient market, which requires all information to be reflected in prices, might not be practical. Evidence suggests that corporate insiders and financial specialists appear to possess superior information that can lead to superior returns. Tests on the semi-strong form market are more positive for the efficient market hypothesis. On average prices reflect information upon publicly announced news. A large volume of empirical research has been focused on testing the weak form markets. These tests appear to suggest that prices follow a random walk. Despite some evidence for dependence in successive price changes in certain cases, the results are largely consistent with the "fair-game" model. This paper shapes the way we look at market efficiency and the three forms of efficient markets defined by Fama are often included in finance textbooks.

Twenty years after his pioneer paper, FAMA (1991) re-addressed the efficient market hypothesis. He argued that a weak form efficient market implies that the market has no memory, and thus, returns should not be predictable. He provides a summary of empirical research on both the short-horizon and long-horizon predictability of stock returns. Possible explanations are given. This paper also includes a review of event studies as tests for semi-strong form efficiency and empirical findings of insider trading as evidence against strong form efficiency. The two Fama papers together lay an important step for the investigation of the efficient market hypothesis.

CUTHBERTSON is an excellent text book on financial economics. This book is written largely with a baseline paradigm throughout. It covers topics such as equilibrium asset pricing models and provides an overview of the theory on the efficient market hypothesis. It also reviews empirical work on efficiency in the stock market, the bond market, and the foreign exchange market.

BOUDOUKH, RICHARDSON & WHITELAW re-examine the autocorrelation patterns of short-horizon stock returns. They argue that the recent evidence for short-term predictability in returns can be explained by three schools of thought. First, markets rationally process information in an efficient manner, but autocorrelation can arise due to non-synchronous trading, bid–ask spreads, institutional structure, and systematic arrival of information. The second school suggests that correlation patterns are consistent with time-varying economic risk premia. Changing risk premia can induce variations in short-horizon risk premia. The final school argues that markets are essentially inefficient and, hence, profitable trading strategies exist.

BOUDOUKH, RICHARDSON & WHITELAW document empirical results that imply that these autocorrelations have been overstated in the existing literature. They provide evidence to support the market efficiency-based explanation and suggest that institutional factors are the probable source of the autocorrelation patterns.

A slowly mean-reverting component of stock prices tends to induce negative autocorrelation in returns. This autocorrelation pattern is particularly strong for long-horizon returns, which in turn casts doubt on the efficient market hypothesis. McQUEEN argues that much of the previous work suffers from two possible sources of errors: first, there is an undue weighting on the Depression and World War II observations in ordinary least-square tests, and, second, analyses based on multi-year stock returns have low power against other alternatives to the random walk. Using generalized least square to correct for heteroskedasticity and a large data set, McQueen

finds that the evidence of mean reversion has been overstated and, consequently, he does not reject the random walk for both the value- and equally-weighted real returns over the period 1926–87.

RICHARDSON demonstrates interesting behaviour in long-horizon stock returns. Based on a Monte Carlo simulation procedure, he shows that the U-shape autocorrelation pattern in long-horizon returns documented in previous work can be repeated in a sample of random walk data.

If the market is informationally efficient, a stock price should reflect the value of its fundamentals. This concept has led to a large amount of research on excess volatility in stock prices as evidence against the efficient market hypothesis. Cuthbertson provides a summary of the volatility tests.

COCHRANE argues that volatility tests are equivalent to return regressions. Both the volatility tests and return regressions are only discount-rate-model tests. As any model-based tests are indeed joint tests of market efficiency and the validity of the underlying models, the rejection of the efficient market hypothesis due to excess volatility is thus premature.

MACKINLAY provides a review of the methods usually employed in event studies, and points out the successes and limitations of those methods. He presents a new approach that focuses on measuring abnormal returns and making statistical inferences about those returns. He concludes that prices do respond to new information.

KOTHARI & WARNER look at the long-horizon stock returns around firm-specific events. Using simulation procedures, they find that parametric long-horizon tests often indicate abnormal performance when no event is present. The power of event studies using long-horizon stock return can be improved by using non-parametric and bootstrap tests.

To avoid using any underlying model to test the insider trading effect, ROZEFF & ZAMAN track the directions of insider trades along the growth/value stock path to see if they are consistent with attempts to profit from market over-reaction. They find that insider buying increases as stocks change from growth to value categories. Insider buying is also greater after low stock returns, and lower after high stock returns.

LIBON FUNG

See also Financial economics

Elections

Alford, Robert R., *Party and Society: The Anglo-American Democracies*, Chicago: Rand McNally, 1963; London: John Murray, 1964

Broughton, David, *Public Opinion Polling and Politics in Britain*, London: Prentice Hall, 1995

Butler, David and Donald Stokes, *Political Change in Britain: Forces Shaping Electoral Choice*, London: Macmillan, and New York: St Martin's Press, 1969; 2nd edition as *Political Change in Britain: The Evolution of Electoral Choice*, 1974

Butler, David and Austin Ranney (editors), *Referendums around the World: The Growing Use of Direct Democracy*, London: Macmillan, 1994

Butler, David and Dennis Kavanagh, *The British General Election of 1997*, London: Macmillan, 1997

Campbell, Angus *et al.*, *The American Voter*, New York: Wiley, 1960

Campbell, Angus *et al.*, *Elections and the Political Order*, New York: Wiley, 1966

Cox, Gary W., *Making Votes Count: Strategic Coordination in the World's Electoral Systems*, Cambridge and New York: Cambridge University Press, 1997

Crewe, Ivor and David Denver (editors), *Electoral Change in Western Democracies: Patterns and Sources of Electoral Volatility*, London: Croom Helm, 1985

Denver, David *et al.* (editors), *British Elections and Parties Review*, vol. 8: *The 1997 General Election*, London: Cass, 1998

Downs, Anthony, *An Economic Theory of Democracy*, New York: Harper, 1957

Dummett, Michael, *Principles of Electoral Reform*, Oxford and New York: Oxford University Press, 1997

Duverger, Maurice, *Political Parties: Their Organization and Activity in a Modern State*, 2nd edition, London: Methuen, and New York: Wiley, 1959

Enelow, James M. and Melvin J. Hinich, *The Spatial Theory of Voting: An Introduction*, Cambridge: Cambridge University Press, 1984

Evans, Geoffrey and Pippa Norris (editors), *Critical Elections: British Parties and Voters in Long-Term Perspective*, London and Thousand Oaks, California: Sage, 1999

Farrell, David M., *Comparing Electoral Systems*, London and New York: Prentice Hall / Harvester Wheatsheaf, 1997

Fiorina, Morris P., *Retrospective Voting in American National Elections*, New Haven, Connecticut: Yale University Press, 1981

Harrop, Martin and William L. Miller, *Elections and Voters: A Comparative Introduction*, London: Macmillan, 1987

Inglehart, Ronald, *The Silent Revolution: Changing Values and Political Styles Among Western Publics*, Princeton, New Jersey: Princeton University Press, 1977

Katz, Richard S., *Democracy and Elections*, New York and Oxford: Oxford University Press, 1997

King, Anthony (editor), *New Labour Triumphs: Britain at the Polls*, Chatham, New Jersey: Chatham House, 1998

Laver, Michael and Kenneth A. Shepsle, *Making and Breaking Governments: Cabinets and Legislatures in Parliamentary Democracies*, Cambridge and New York: Cambridge University Press, 1996

LeDuc, Lawrence, Richard G. Niemi and Pippa Norris (editors), *Comparing Democracies: Elections and Voting in Comparative Perspective*, Thousand Oaks, California and London: Sage, 1996

Lewis-Beck, Michael S., *Economics and Elections: The Major Western Democracies*, Ann Arbor: University of Michigan Press, 1988

Lijphart, Arend, *Electoral Systems and Party Systems: A Study of Twenty-Seven Democracies*, Oxford and New York: Oxford University Press, 1994

Lipset, Seymour Martin and Stein Rokkan, "Cleavage Structures, Party Systems, and Voter Alignments: An Introduction" in *Party Systems and Voter Alignments: Cross-national Perspectives*, edited by S.M. Lipset and S.E. Rokkan, New York: Free Press, 1967

Mair, Peter, *Party System Change: Approaches and Interpretations*, Oxford and New York: Oxford University Press, 1997

Moon, Nick, *Opinion Polls: History, Theory and Practice*, Manchester: Manchester University Press, 1999

Nie, Norman, Sidney Verba and John R. Petrocik, *The Changing American Voter*, Cambridge, Massachusetts: Harvard University Press, 1976

Pomper, Gerald M. (editor), *The Election of 1996: Reports and Interpretations*, Chatham, New Jersey: Chatham House, 1997

Rose, Richard and Ian McAllister, *The Loyalties of Voters: A Lifetime Learning Model*, London and Newbury Park, California: Sage, 1990

Särlvik, Bo and Ivor Crewe, *Decade of Dealignment: The Conservative Victory of 1979 and Electoral Trends in the 1970s*, Cambridge and New York: Cambridge University Press, 1983

Sartori, Giovanni, *Parties and Party Systems: A Framework for Analysis*, Cambridge and New York: Cambridge University Press, 1976

Scarbrough, Elinor, *Political Ideology and Voting: An Exploratory Study*, New York: Oxford University Press, and Oxford: Clarendon Press, 1984

Taagepera, Rein and Matthew Soberg Shugart, *Seats and Votes: The Effects and Determinants of Electoral Systems*, New Haven, Connecticut: Yale University Press, 1989

Elections are essential to the functioning of large-scale democracies in which some form of representation is necessary to allow all individual citizens to participate in their society's decision making processes. The study of elections is therefore an important component of political science, although other disciplines also have interests in various aspects of electoral study (as illustrated by the separate entries for Electoral law and Electoral geography).

The book edited by LEDUC, NIEMI & NORRIS covers the main topics in the study of elections in a comparative perspective. The chapters deal with: electoral systems; party systems; party organization and finance; interest groups and social movements; campaign strategies; legislative recruitment; electoral participation; polls and elections; the media; party leaders; the economy; and political cleavages. Only the more important of these are covered in this brief essay.

Among the large number of texts on democracy, KATZ focuses on the role and nature of elections within democracies. Two major sets of actors are involved in democratic elections – voters and political parties – and the interactions between them occur within the context set by the electoral system. Parties play two main roles – they provide a structure within which a legislature can be organized, thereby providing the continuity necessary for government; and externally they mobilize voters to provide continuity of support at and between elections.

The classic works on political parties include DUVERGER and SARTORI, both of whom classified party systems, the former very simply with regard to the number of parties and its relationship to the electoral system; Sartori included both number and size of parties as key criteria. Later work (such as KATZ) classifies parties differently, using criteria relating to their legislative performance, their grassroots structure and the degree of central control: the main types identified include elite, mass, catch-all and cartel parties. MAIR looks at recent changes in party systems in comparative perspective.

DOWNS developed a model of how parties would compete for electoral support (stimulated by Hotelling's work on competition between firms which also influenced work in location theory); his analyses have been generalized, extended and made technically much more sophisticated in work that goes under the heading of "spatial models of voting" (exemplified by ENELOW & HINICH) – in which the space is not geographical but rather abstract space whose dimensions are the various ideological and/or policy components along which parties locate themselves relative to the voters' positions.

Of the many texts that focus specifically on elections, HARROP & MILLER's reviews a large literature, concentrating on two types of model: *social cleavage* models, which relate voting behaviour to socio-demographic structures; and *responsive voter* models, which relate behaviour to short-term factors.

Early seminal studies of voters under the first heading were undertaken at the University of Michigan in the 1950s and 1960s. Two major books (CAMPBELL *et al.* 1960 and 1966) introduced *party identification theory*, whereby individual voters are socialized into identifying with a party, from which they get cues on how to respond to policy issues and which will normally retain their allegiance at elections – hence the normal vote model which argues that if people vote according to their party identification the election outcome is largely predictable.

This model was imported to the United Kingdom by David Butler in collaboration with Donald Stokes, whose surveys of the British electorate in the 1960s were reported in the two editions of their major book (BUTLER & STOKES). This explored the sociodemographic bases of party choice and how short-term issues at individual elections influenced these. Similar surveys have been conducted after every subsequent British general election, with major books covering the 1970s (SÄRLVIK & CREWE) and the 1980s/1990s (EVANS & NORRIS). Similar surveys have been conducted in other countries and have generated a large nationally based literature (reviewed in LEDUC *et al.*).

The party identification model is based on the American situation (pre-1980s) of relatively stable voter predispositions in a two-party system with few deep electoral cleavages within society. This was difficult to apply in many other countries, which had a range of cross-cutting cleavages producing a complex map of party support – even where that support was as consistent as the "normal vote" paradigm suggested. ALFORD's book shows that in the 1960s the British system was dominated by a single cleavage – class. Elsewhere in Europe, LIPSET & ROKKAN identified four major cleavages present to a greater or lesser extent in a range of countries. Two were based on divisions created after the *national revolution* from the 17th century onwards and the subsequent growth of nation-state building – between subject and dominant cultures (the *core–periphery cleavage*) and between churches and secular interest groups (the *church versus state cleavage*); the other two – between the primary and the secondary economy (the *urban–rural* or *town–country* cleav-

age) and employers and workers (the *class cleavage*) – were products of the *industrial revolution*. The class cleavage occurs in nearly all European countries but the relative strength of the others reflects local history and culture; understanding a country's geography of votes thus involves mapping its cleavage structures and exploring how parties mobilize support in different social milieux and places.

A second difficulty with the party identification model is its assumption of "normal voting" – once electors are socialized into supporting a particular party they remain loyal to it over most of their lifetime. This proved increasingly untenable from the 1970s on: as partisan links weakened so voters became more open to the campaigning of various parties and were less likely to identify strongly with any one – a process known as dealignment (on which NIE, VERBA and PETROCIK did important early work in the USA and CREWE & DENVER produced a set of comparative essays: Särlvik & Crewe's book focuses on dealignment in the UK during the 1970s). The class and other cleavages began to dissolve – though they have far from disappeared – and as many voters become less ideologically constrained so volatility in their party choices increased. Attempts have been made to forge new cleavages around new politics – such as those associated with post-materialism (INGLEHART), environmentalism and feminism, but there is little evidence that these have offered substantial replacements to the traditional mobilization focuses. Others have explored voters' values and attitudes, as a means of identifying their stable predispositions but, as SCARBROUGH has shown, have found the latter more easy to identify than the former: measured attitudes, derived from various scaling instruments applied in questionnaires, provide good predictors of party voted for, however (ROSE & McALLISTER).

One of the favoured models replacing party identification is economic voting, which focuses on short-term factors. FIORINA's book was one of the first to introduce the notion of *retrospective* voting, whereby people evaluate a governing party's economic performance either egocentrically (in terms of their own financial situation) or sociotropically (with reference to the national economic situation) and decide whether that justifies further support: in general, people vote to reward successful governments by returning them to office, and to punish, by voting against, those blamed for bad economic situations. The model has been extended to *prospective* evaluations, assessing the competing claims of various parties to deliver economic prosperity in the future. It has spawned a large literature, including studies of a "political business cycle" whereby governments manipulate their economies with electoral timetables in mind (LEWIS-BECK provides an overview of this literature): it has been exported to a range of other countries – in the UK, for example, voting among a dealigned electorate is related to what is termed the "feel-good factor", incorporating economic voting but also trust in political parties and their leaders.

As voters have become more volatile in their partisan preferences, so parties have needed information on trends in their support. This has stimulated growth in the opinion polling industry, which undertakes commissioned polls both for publication (notably in the media) and the parties' private use. BROUGHTON and MOON provide introductions to this important subject.

A major arena of party–voter interactions is the electoral system by which, in most countries, votes are translated into legislative seats. Electoral systems can be classified on three main criteria: the size of their constituencies (whether single- or multi-member); the method of voting (preferential or otherwise); and the means of translating votes into seats. FARRELL discusses the main features of various systems, and TAAGEPERA & SHUGART present a technical evaluation of the disproportionality and biases that characterize the various systems. DUMMETT is a more formal treatment of the various voting procedures in the context of pressures for electoral reform in the UK; COX looks in detail at strategic or tactical voting (the two terms are used in the USA and the UK respectively) in different electoral systems; and LIJPHART reports on a major comparative study of the inter-relationships between party and electoral systems.

Many elections create legislatures from which governments are formed. Where no party has a majority (which occurs in the most cases) coalitions are needed, and there are many studies of parties' power in the bargaining processes involved in the creation, maintenance and dissolution of coalitions based on the spatial models of voting discussed above – as illustrated by LAVER & SHEPSLE.

Alongside these theoretically driven studies of elections are academic works on individual elections – how they were won and lost. A major book has been produced on every British general election since 1945 (the latest is BUTLER & KAVANAGH) and there have been edited books on recent American and British elections (such as those by KING and by POMPER).

Referendums are being used in an increasing number of countries to canvass public opinion on a range of issues: their use is surveyed in BUTLER & RANNEY.

The continuing flow of material on elections can be tracked through the journal *Electoral Studies*, which carries listings of major book and journal publications. The Elections, Public Opinion and Parties Specialist Group of the British Political Studies Association also publishes an annual volume carrying a range of material in addition to academic papers (DENVER et al.).

RON JOHNSTON

See also Campaign, electoral, Electoral geography, Electoral law, Location theory

Electoral college

Adkinson, Danny M. and Christopher Elliott, "The Electoral College: A Misunderstood Institution", *PS, Political Science and Politics*, 30/1 (1997): 77–80

Best, Judith A., *The Choice of the People? Debating the Electoral College*, Lanham, Maryland: Rowman and Littlefield, 1996

Bickel, Alexander M., *Reform and Continuity: The Electoral College, the Convention, and the Party System*, revised edition, New York: Harper and Row, 1971

Glennon, Michael J., *When No Majority Rules: The Electoral College and Presidential Succession*, Washington, DC: Congressional Quarterly, 1992

Longley, Lawrence D. and Neal R. Peirce, *The Electoral College Primer*, New Haven, Connecticut: Yale University Press, 1996

Mann, I. and L.S. Shapley, "The A Priori Voting Strength of the Electoral College" in *Game Theory and Related Approaches to Social Behavior*, edited by Martin Shubik, New York: Wiley, 1964

Rabinowitz, George and Stuart Elaine MacDonald, "The Power of the States in US Presidential Elections", *American Political Science Review*, 80/1 (1986): 65–87

Szekely, Kalman S., *Electoral College: A Selective Annotated Bibliography*, Littleton, Colorado: Libraries Unlimited, 1970

Yunker, John H. and Lawrence D. Longley, *The Electoral College: Its Biases Newly Measured for the 1960s and 1970s*, Beverly Hills: Sage, 1976

Voters in the US do not, technically, elect the President or the Vice President. Rather, the Constitution provides for a "college of electors", chosen by each state in a manner decided by its legislature, every four years. Each state has a number of electors equal to its number of senators (two) and representatives (apportioned according to population). The District of Columbia receives three electors, bringing the total to 538. Currently all states choose by popular vote, with each political party running a slate of electors who are all but guaranteed to vote for that party's candidates. In all but two states – Maine and Nebraska – the party that receives a plurality of popular votes names all of the electors for that state.

The chosen electors meet in their state capitals and formally cast ballots for presidential and vice presidential candidates. To win the election, a candidate must receive a majority (270). Should this not occur, the House of Representatives chooses the President from among the top three finishers, by majority vote, with each state given one vote. The Senate chooses the Vice President from the top two votegetters, again by majority vote.

As Alexander Hamilton (writing as "Publius" in *Federalist No. 68*) points out, this peculiar design was intended to insulate the office from established political bodies such as the Congress, to preserve the federal principle in the selection of the president, and to dampen the ill effects of an uninformed populace. In his mind, "If the method of it be not perfect, it is at least excellent."

GLENNON provides an excellent summary of the current procedure, as well as a fine and detailed history of its development. He includes a thorough examination of the roles played by the House of Representatives and the federal courts, and an analysis of how the legal doctrines of "political questions", "standing", and "ripeness" may influence the selection process. Like most writers, he finds problems with the process, and proposes changes in how electors are selected and in procedures in the House of Representatives. Included are the US Constitution and excerpts from relevant legislation and Supreme Court cases.

Discussion about the electoral college has assumed two basic forms: theoretical and empirical. The former involves debate over the relative merits and disadvantages of the electoral system, and the basic arguments have changed little since its inception, with some authors disapproving of various "anti-democratic" features, and other praising it for nearly the very same reasons. The empirical approach is of more recent origin, extending not much farther back than the 1950s. Generally, such works avoid commenting on the desirability or fairness of the electoral college process, and instead analyse historical data or use game theory to determine actual influence that the structure and process may have on electoral outcomes.

MANN & SHAPLEY's seminal 1964 work found a bias in favour of large states as a result of the winner-take-all rule, although they did not seem to feel that it was particularly consequential.

YUNKER & LONGLEY expanded on this research with an excellent review of the empirical literature (up to 1976) and their own empirical analysis of various "systematic biases" inherent in the electoral procedure. As they note, the prior literature identified four major sources of such bias: (a) the "unit rule," or "winner-take-all" bias – the party with a plurality of the popular vote in a State gets all the State's electoral college votes (except in Maine and Nebraska); (b) the "constant two " bias – all states receive a minimum of two electors, irrespective of the size of their population; (c) the "population assignment" bias – remaining electors are assigned to states according to population rather than voter turnout; (d) the "census" bias – population assignments are made on a ten-year census cycle, whereas elections occur every four years. The authors found that these biases were offset somewhat by "countervailing biases", yet still lead to a "net advantage to large states, and a disadvantage to states with 4 to 14 electoral votes" (p.44). The college therefore "favours" states in the far west and east and those with large population centres, and "discriminates against" midwesterners, southerners, rural residents, and blacks.

RABINOWITZ & MACDONALD add to the game-theoretical and empirical analyses by developing a model that takes into account actual "electoral competitiveness" within individual states. They conclude that enormous disparities exist, both in the relative power of states to decide presidential elections, and in the relative impact of citizens of various states.

LONGLEY & PEIRCE have each written extensively on the electoral college, and present a summary of their historical research and arguments in the work cited here. Their work is an excellent example of what seems to be the prevailing viewpoint on the electoral college: through an analysis of a hypothetical election – in which the Speaker of the House of Representatives becomes President – they argue that the electoral college is a "system of disastrous failings" and is dangerously anti-democratic in its potential to thwart the choice of the people.

There are not as many works defending the current system as there are expressing opposition, but a few exist, and two in particular stand out.

BEST presents an impassioned argument that the electoral college is not only democratic – provided one does not identify democracy only with direct democracy – but also perfectly expresses and protects the federal principle that underlies the Constitution. If federalism is a good idea, she argues, then so is the electoral college. She is happy to take on all challengers (even Longley & Peirce) as she lays out their various arguments and picks them apart, one by one. Excellent historical background is provided, along with essential documents such as *Federalist* Nos. 39, 51, 68, and the 1997 report of the Senate Judiciary Committee on "Direct Popular Election of the President and Vice President of the United States".

BICKEL's 1968 work, is valuable as presenting a practically minded compromise proposal for a system, which, he believes, addresses the major concerns of its critics, yet eliminates the problems associated with a direct election. His opening chapter title summarizes his entire approach: "cautions for reformers".

Two other works deserve mention. SZEKELY's bibliography is divided into useful sections such as "historical background" and "arguments and proposals," and catalogues nearly 800 works, with brief annotations provided for many. The work was published nearly 30 years ago, so it presents very little empirical research, and many of the entries are no doubt now unavailable. However, the nature of the debate has changed little over time, and works cited here will remain relevant, provided they can be obtained.

ADKINSON & ELLIOTT is a straightforward examination of popular American government textbooks. As such, it is not a major empirical or theoretical work on the college itself. However, it performs a vital service pointing out several errors commonly made even by presumed experts discussing the system, and should therefore be read by anyone concerned with getting the details correct.

MICHAEL BERHEIDE

Electoral geography

Agnew, John A., *Place and Politics: The Geographical Mediation of State and Society*, London and Boston: Unwin Hyman, 1987

Agnew, J.A. "Mapping Politics: How Context Counts in Electoral Geography", *Political Geography*, 15 (1996): 129–46

Archer, J. Clark and Peter J. Taylor, *Section and Party: A Political Geography of American Presidential Elections from Andrew Jackson to Ronald Reagan*, Chichester and New York: Research Studios Press, 1981

Archer, J. Clark and Fred M. Shelley, *American Electoral Mosaics*, Washington, DC: Association of American Geographers, 1986

Cox, K.R., "The Voting Decision in a Spatial Context" in *Progress in Geography*, vol. 1, edited by Christopher Board *et al.*, London: Edward Arnold, 1969

Eagles, Munroe (editor), "Spatial and Contextual Models of Political Behaviour", special issue of *Political Geography*, 14/6–7 (1995)

Eagles, Munroe (editor), *Spatial and Contextual Models in Political Research*, London: Taylor and Francis, 1995

Gudgin, Graham and Peter J. Taylor, *Seats, Votes and the Spatial Organisation of Elections*, London: Pion, 1979

Johnston, R.J., *Political, Electoral and Spatial Systems: An Essay in Political Geography*, Oxford: Clarendon Press, 1979

Johnston, R.J., *Money and Votes: Constituency Campaign Spending and Election Results*, London: Croom Helm, 1987

Johnston, R.J., C.J. Pattie and J.G. Allsopp, *A Nation Dividing? The Electoral Map of Great Britain, 1979–1987*, London: Longman, 1988

Johnston, R.J., Fred M. Shelley and Peter J. Taylor (editors), *Developments in Electoral Geography*, London: Routledge, 1990

Key, V.O. Jr, "A Theory of Critical Elections", *Journal of Politics*, 17 (1955): 3–18

Key, V.O. Jr, *Southern Politics in State and Nation*, New York: Knopf, 1949

Lacoste, Yves (editor), *Géopolitiques des régions françaises*, 3 vols, Paris: Fayard, 1986

Morrill, Richard L., *Political Redistricting and Geographic Theory*, Washington, DC: Association of American Geographers, 1981

Rossiter, D.J., R.J. Johnston and C.J. Pattie, *The Boundary Commissions: Redrawing the UK's Map of Parliamentary Constituencies*, Manchester: Manchester University Press, 1999

Shelley, Fred M., J.C. Archer, F.M. Davidson and S.D. Brunn, *Political Geography of the United States*, New York: Guilford Press, 1996

Siegfried, André, *Géographie électorale de l'Ardèche sous la IIIème République*, Paris: Colin, 1949

Taylor, Peter J. and R.J. Johnston, *Geography of Elections*, London: Croom Helm, and New York: Holmes and Meier, 1979

Electoral geography is a small component of the subdiscipline of political geography, with few practitioners.

The classic statements that stimulated work by geographers included two 1949 books. KEY (1949) was seminal in portraying the importance of local influences on voting decisions – what became known as the *friends and neighbours effect* – identified through detailed mapping of voting patterns.

SIEGFRIED also mapped voting patterns, which he related to other aspects of the canton's physical, economic and social geography. His attempts to correlate aspects of the physical environment, human activities in that environment, and support for political parties involved careful analysis of aspects of the socioeconomic milieux in different parts of the Ardèche that were likely to generate support for different parties, and that he linked to variations in the physical environment. He found great continuity over time in the geography of voting, a situation also observed by KEY (1955) in his classic paper on *critical elections* in American history.

These separate strands were the foundations of much work on the geography of voting from the 1960s onward. COX formalized and generalized Key's work on the friends-and-neighbours effect by relating spatially biased information flows circulating within neighbourhood social networks to voter decisions (what he called an *acquaintance-circle process*). He suggested a process of "conversion by conversation" whereby the majority view in an area was accentuated, producing a polarized *neighbourhood effect*. This was later linked to the concept of an electoral cleavage, which identifies support for a party in socioeconomic terms: the operation of neighbourhood effect mechanisms would lead to greater polarization of party support than of the underlying factors, because people from the minority view in an area would be more attracted to the majority than vice versa. Cox also introduced the concept of a *forced-field process*, whereby a particular political culture is established in an area, continually refreshed by political parties and other interest groups, which leads to localized patterns of political activity and voting behaviour.

The book by JOHNSTON, PATTIE & ALLSOPP on the 1979, 1983 and 1987 general elections in Great Britain tested one aspect of the neighbourhood effect hypothesis, showing that people in the same class cleavage position voted differently in different areas, producing greater spatial polarization of support for the main political parties than the polarization in their support base in the country's class structure. These variations were closely related to differences in economic and social wellbeing, providing strong circumstantial evidence of spatial variations in voter response to government economic policies. The two volumes edited by EAGLES report on a range of other studies of the "conversion by conversation" process, whereas JOHNSTON (1987) presents detailed analyses of the impact of local campaigning by parties and its influence on election results.

Continuity in voting patterns over time is the focus of books by ARCHER & SHELLEY and by ARCHER & TAYLOR. They used multivariate statistical analyses to identify time periods with consistent geographies of support for the political parties in the US and also regions where those parties were weak and strong during each period. The book by SHELLEY *et al.* takes that work forward, relating the geography of support for presidential candidates and for parties at Congressional elections to local economic interests and to support by representatives for various policy proposals (such as the North American Free Trade Agreement).

Some interpretations of Cox's models are relatively mechanistic and pay little attention to the specific circumstances in individual places, the forced-field process. AGNEW (1987) is an exception, however, focusing on local political cultures and their electoral outcomes; he argues for the important role of places in the creation and maintenance of those cultures and associated voting behaviour, at various scales, substantially illustrated by examples from Italy and the US, and of Scottish nationalism. The processes involved are codified in his 1996 paper.

All electoral systems include procedures for translating votes into seats in a legislature; almost all involve the use of constituencies, blocks of territory that return their own members. Drawing constituency maps can have a significant influence on election results, depending on where the boundaries are located: two strategies – *malapportionment* and *gerrymandering* – have been used where political parties have control over the redistricting process, but GUDGIN & TAYLOR have shown that non-partisan redistricting procedures can produce outcomes consistent with those two partisan strategies. They developed a theory of redistricting that linked the process to the production of electoral biases, which are discussed in JOHNSTON's (1979) book. The book by ROSSITER, JOHNSTON & PATTIE deals with the UK's redistricting process, with detailed analyses of the procedures and their outcomes since 1944 and a historical treatment of redistricting there since the first Reform Act in 1832. MORRILL reviews geographical aspects of redistricting in the US.

TAYLOR & JOHNSTON is the only full-length study of the range of material normally considered within the orbit of electoral geography; it is unfortunately now both somewhat dated in its examples and out of print. They divide their material into three main parts covering the geography of voting (spatial variations in support for different parties and candidates); geographical influences on voting (geographical factors, such as the friends-and-neighbours and neighbourhood effects, which generate spatial variations in voting patterns, along with campaign effects); and geographical influences on representation (notably the translation of votes into seats in legislative contests). They also link the geography of support for a candidate or party to the geography of state activity. The essays in the book edited by JOHNSTON, SHELLEY & TAYLOR contain more recent material and overviews.

RON JOHNSTON

Electoral law

ACE Project, *Administration and Cost of Elections*, Washington, DC: IDEA/UN/IFES, 1999 (CD-ROM; the material is also available at http://www.aceproject.org)

Alexander, H.E., *Financing Politics: Money, Elections and Political Reform*, 4th edition, Washington, DC: Congressional Quarterly, 1992

Alexander, Herbert E. and Rei Shiratori (editors), *Comparative Political Finance Among the Democracies*, Boulder, Colorado: Westview Press, 1994

Blackburn, Robert, *The Electoral System in Britain*, London: Macmillan, and New York: St Martin's Press, 1995

Butler, David, *The Electoral System in Britain since 1918*, Oxford: Clarendon Press, 1963

Butler, David and Bruce Cain, *Congressional Redistricting: Comparative and Theoretical Perspectives*, New York: Macmillan, 1992

Clayton, R.J., *Parker's Conduct of Parliamentary Elections*, Croydon, Surrey: Knight, 1983

Committee on Standards in Public Life (Chair: Lord Neill of Bladen), *Standards in Public Life: The Funding of Political Parties in the United Kingdom*, 2 vols, London: HMSO, 1998 (Cm 4057)

Courtney, John C., Peter MacKinnon and David E. Smith (editors), *Drawing Boundaries: Legislatures, Courts and Electoral Values*, Saskatoon: Fifth House, 1992

Ewing, K.D., *The Funding of Political Parties in Britain*, Cambridge and New York: Cambridge University Press, 1987

Farrell, David M., *Comparing Electoral Systems*, London and New York: Prentice Hall / Harvester Wheatsheaf, 1997

Federal Election Commission, *Federal Election Campaign Laws*, Washington, DC: Federal Election Commission, 1997

Goodwin-Gill, Guy S., *Free and Fair Elections: International Law and Practice*, Geneva: Inter-Parliamentary Union, 1994

Grofman, Bernard and Arend Lijphart (editors), *Electoral Laws and Their Political Consequences*, New York: Agathon Press, 1986

Grofman, Bernard (editor), *Political Gerrymandering and the Courts*, New York: Agathon Press, 1990

Gunlicks, Arthur B. (editor), *Campaign and Party Finance in North America and Western Europe*, Boulder, Colorado: Westview Press, 1993

Home Affairs Select Committee, *Electoral Law and Administration: Fourth Report*, 2 vols, London: HMSO, 1998 (Cm 768)

IDEA, *Voter Turnout from 1945 to 1997: A Global Report on Political Participation*, 2nd edition, Stockholm: International Institute for Democracy and Electoral Assistance, 1997

Independent Commission on the Voting System, *The Report of the Independent Commission on the Voting System*, 2 vols, London: HMSO, 1998 (Cm 4090)

Inter-Parliamentary Union, *Electoral Systems: A World-Wide Comparative Study*, Geneva: Inter-Parliamentary Union, 1993

Jackson, Keith and Alan McRobie, *New Zealand Adopts Proportional Representation: Accident? Design? Evolution?*, Aldershot, Hampshire: Ashgate, 1998

Kavanagh, Dennis, *Election Campaigning: The New Marketing of Politics*, Oxford and Cambridge, Massachusetts: Blackwell, 1995

Lijphart, Arend and Bernard Grofman (editors), *Choosing an Electoral System: Issues and Alternatives*, New York: Praeger, 1984

Lijphart, Arend, *Electoral Systems and Party Systems: A Study of Twenty-Seven Democracies, 1945–1990*, Oxford and New York: Oxford University Press, 1994

McLean, Iain and David Butler (editors), *Fixing the Boundaries: Defining and Redefining Single-Member Electoral Districts*, Aldershot, Hampshire: Dartmouth, 1996

Mates, Rory and Andrew Scallan, *Schofield's Election Law*, 2nd edition, 3 vols, Crayford: Shaw, 1996

Rae, Douglas W., *The Political Consequences of Electoral Laws*, revised edition, New Haven, Connecticut: Yale University Press, 1971

Rawlings, H.F., *Law and the Electoral Process*, London: Sweet and Maxwell, 1988

Reeve, Andrew and Alan Ware, *Electoral Systems: A Comparative and Theoretical Introduction*, London: Routledge, 1992

Reynolds, Andrew and Ben Reilly, *The International IDEA Handbook of Electoral System Design*, Stockholm: International Institute for Democracy and Electoral Assistance, 1997

Rossiter, D.J., R.J. Johnston and C.J. Pattie, *The Boundary Commissions: Redrawing the UK's Map of Parliamentary Constituencies*, Manchester: Manchester University Press, 1999

Rush, Mark E. (editor), *Voting Rights and Redistricting in the United States*, Westport, Connecticut: Greenwood Press, 1998

Stanbury, W.T., *Money in Politics: Financing Federal Parties and Candidates in Canada*, Toronto: Dundurn Press, 1993

Taagepera, Rein and Matthew Soberg Shugart, *Seats and Votes: The Effects and Determinants of Electoral Systems*, New Haven, Connecticut: Yale University Press, 1989

Electoral law covers a number of subjects involved in the conduct of elections, with practices that vary considerably across the world. The ACE PROJECT is compiling a comprehensive data set about those practices, covering nine topics: electoral systems; legislative framework; electoral management; boundary delimitation; voter education; voter registration; voting operations; parties and candidates; and vote counting. Some of these have attracted much more interest from academic researchers than others.

A general survey of international variations is provided by GOODWIN-GILL. Changes in the development of the British electoral system during the first half of the 20th century are covered by BUTLER. More detailed surveys of the contemporary British situation are provided by two legal scholars: RAWLINGS treats a wide range of British Acts of Parliament and legal judgements regarding constituency delimitation, the franchise, candidature, campaigning and finance, and the role of the media; BLACKBURN covers similar ground plus the important issue (in the UK) of the timing of general elections. Regularly updated volumes on all aspects of electoral law in the UK are provided by CLAYTON and by MATES & SCALLAN.

Electoral systems are the focus of much attention. FARRELL's book is the most recent comprehensive discussion of the main systems used and how they operate. The book by REEVE & WARE is much less technical, setting the UK system in historical and theoretical context, together with comparative material.

REYNOLDS & REILLY provide a comprehensive coverage of electoral systems currently used in the great majority of countries: further material is available in the book produced by the INTER-PARLIAMENTARY UNION.

Although many countries rarely change their electoral system, some have done so recently (notably Italy, Japan, and New Zealand) and the issue of electoral reform is frequently on the agenda in many others. The book edited by LIJPHART & GROFMAN discusses the basic issues of proportionality and the nature of representation and evaluates the main systems available. JACKSON & McROBIE offer a detailed discussion of New Zealanders' decision to change their system, and a useful document for the UK is the report of an INDEPENDENT COMMISSION ON THE VOTING SYSTEM established by the British government to recommend a system more proportional than that currently used, while retaining the link between MPs and territorially delimited constituencies: its recommendation was a variant of the Mixed Multi-Member Proportional (MMP) system used in Germany and New Zealand.

Most electoral systems involve the delimitation of constituencies, territorially demarcated areas that return one or more members to a legislature or electoral college. The process of redefining constituencies – known in North America as redistricting and in the UK as redistribution – is a politically charged activity. It is open to abuse in certain circumstances, as in the USA where both *malapportionment* and *gerrymandering* strategies have commonly been employed by parties to promote their own electoral advantage. BUTLER & CAIN provide an overview of the current situation there, as does COURTNEY, MACKINNON & SMITH for Canada. The book edited by GROFMAN addresses the issue of gerrymandering as currently practised within the constraints of Supreme Court decisions and the Voting Rights Act, with that edited by RUSH providing more detail on the latter, which promotes representational equality for blacks and other minorities.

The changing procedure for defining constituencies in the UK since the Great Reform Act 1832 is set out in ROSSITER, JOHNSTON & PATTIE, which also provides a full analysis of the most recent (1991–95) redistribution. The book edited by McLEAN & BUTLER sets the British experience in wider context.

A major reason for research interest in electoral laws and systems is the way in which they translate votes into seats, and hence political power, which in turn means that electoral systems can influence the ways that party systems develop. RAE is a classic crossnational study of the political consequences of electoral laws: it has been updated in the volume edited by GROFMAN & LIJPHART and in LIJPHART's later analysis of 27 countries; TAAGEPERA & SHUGART provide technical analyses of the relationship between votes won and seats allocated in different electoral systems.

The funding of political parties, especially their election campaigns, is a topic of considerable interest and of frequent legislation in some countries. The books edited by GUNLICKS and by ALEXANDER & SHIRATORI provide comparative material, including coverage of the central issue in many countries – state funding for political parties. ALEXANDER has produced a number of books on political finance of US Congressional elections, for which the FEDERAL ELECTION COMMISSION has compiled the latest legal situation. Substantial work on the Canadian situation was reported in STANBURY's contribution to the Royal Commission on Electoral Reform and Party Finance there, and EWING's book covers the situation in the UK: the report of the Neill Committee (the UK House of Common's COMMITTEE ON STANDARDS IN PUBLIC LIFE) provides a comprehensive review of that situation, with many recommendations for reform. Modern campaigning methods are reviewed by KAVANAGH.

The issue of voter registration and turnout is covered in the report by IDEA and in the report of the British HOME AFFAIRS SELECT COMMITTEE on electoral law and administration.

Full bibliographies for all nine subjects are provided in the ACE PROJECT's CD-ROM and website.

RON JOHNSTON

See also Elections, Electoral geography

Electricity industry

Bohn, R., M.C. Caramanis and F. Schweppe, "Optimal Pricing in Electrical Networks over Space and Time", *Rand Journal of Economics*, 15 (1984): 360–75

Burns, P.J and T. Weyman-Jones, *Cost Drivers and Cost Efficiency in Electricity Distribution: A Stochastic Frontier Approach*, London: Centre for the Study of Regulated Industries (CRI), 1994

Christensen, L.R. and W.H. Greene, "Economies of Scale in US Electric Power Generation", *Journal of Political Economy*, 84 (1976): 655–76

Eden, Richard *et al.*, *Energy Economics: Growth, Resources, and Policies*, Cambridge and New York: Cambridge University Press, 1981

Foreman-Peck, J. and M. Waterson, "The Comparative Efficiency of Public and Private Enterprise in Britain: Electricity Generation between the World Wars", *Economic Journal*, 95 (1985): 83–95

Førsund, F.R. and S.A.C. Kittelsen, "Productivity Development of Norwegian Electricity Distribution Utilities", *Resource and Energy Economics*, 20/3 (1998): 207ff.

Lucas, Nigel, *Western European Energy Policy: A Comparative Study of the Influence of Institutional Structure on Technical Change*, Oxford: Clarendon Press, 1985

Nerlove, Marc, "Returns to Scale in Electricity Supply" in *Readings in Economic Statistics and Econometrics*, edited by Arnold Zellner, Boston: Little Brown, 1968

Neuberg, L.G., "Two Issues in the Municipal Ownership of Electric Power Distribution Systems", *Bell Journal of Economics*, 8 (1977): 303–23

Pollitt, Michael G., *Ownership and Performance in Electric Utilities: The International Evidence on Privatization and Efficiency*, Oxford: Oxford University Press, 1995

BOHN, CARAMANIS & SCHWEPPE examine electricity networks (for transmission and distribution) and the relationship between physical constraints (Kirchoff's and Ohm's laws) and economic requirements. Optimal pricing schedules are derived at different stages of the electricity chain (generation and dispatch, transmission, distribution, downstream transformation). Both spatial and seasonal constraints are accounted for, so that spatially-differentiated optimal tariffs are obtained – together with time-of-day and time-of-year prices (peak-load, off-peak, winter/summer). Sophisticated optimization techniques are used for both regional and time-of-day pricing on the vertical chain, which makes this paper complex and fairly technical.

BURNS & WEYMAN-JONES consider the twelve regional electricity companies (RECs) of England and Wales and apply panel-data stochastic frontier techniques (see the entry on Efficiency analysis) to show that efficiency gaps among different companies are mainly explained by such cost-drivers as the number of customers and maximum simultaneous demand. Several translog models are estimated before converging to the final one. Regional peculiarities or "exogenous" cost-drivers are also taken into account, in order to show that the policy-maker might implement "yardstick" regulation by comparing different efficiency records, after controlling for those regional peculiarities that may alter the efficiency picture even when lying outside of the firms' domain.

CHRISTENSEN & GREENE provide a thorough analysis of power generation in the US, following NERLOVE's seminal paper on this topic. They use a translog cost function and consider a cross-section of between 99 and 114 US power generators to show that economies of scale are decreasing as output rises. Moreover, they manage to show that, following several mergers that took place at the end of the 1960s, economies of scale in power generation have been exhausted since the early 1970s at the latest (this conflicts with Nerlove's outcomes).

Thus, the authors find that almost all of the utilities in their sample were working in the neighbourhood of Minimum Efficient Scale (MES), basically clustering around the flat bottom of the estimated Average Cost (AC) non linear relationship.

EDEN *et al.* provides a comprehensive review of electricity economics with reference to generation, despatch, transmission, distribution, and retail supply. Different kinds of plant mix in generation are assessed, and different types of transmission and distribution networks are also examined. Costs and prices are evaluated at different stages of the "electricity chain". This is a reference book catering for both economic and (light) engineering issues on electricity.

FOREMAN-PECK & WATERSON propose an historical analysis of electricity generation in the UK (during the interwar period), which is soundly based upon econometric estimation of dual-cost functions. By comparing publicly owned generators with privately owned ones, the authors find that ownership partially explains efficiency differentials between the two kinds of firm. However, different accounting policies and financial constraints across the two main categories probably distort the picture, especially given the fact that publicly owned UK utilities at the time were subject to a number of financial restraints. This has been true until at least the mid-1970s.

FØRSUND & KITTELSEN analyse local electricity distribution in Norway by Data Envelopment Analysis (DEA). A combination of stochastic frontier and DEA methods leads the authors to discover that optimal scale for electricity distributors is smaller than the average observed scale. Widespread inefficiency is found across decision-making units (DMUs), and the authors suggest the alteration of the current structure of local electricity distribution in Norway, as part of the reform programme that the Norwegian electricity supply industry has been undergoing over the last few years. Environmental (non-discretionary) variables are also considered, given their crucial importance for electricity distribution within the Norwegian territory, which couples very low population density with jagged coastlines (fjords), a mountain landscape, and some regions that are permanently covered in ice.

LUCAS examines the electricity supply industry in Germany, France, Italy, Sweden, and Denmark, using an institutional approach. His findings show that, in general, Denmark and Germany perform well whereas Italy does badly. It is useful to recall that, in Denmark and Germany, either privately owned or mixed enterprises produce most of the power, whereas in both Italy and France production is dominated by one large publicly owned monopolist (ENEL in Italy, EdF in France). However, publicly owned local distributors are present in Denmark and Germany, too, so the above results are not clear-cut – even though they suggest that competition (rather than ownership) is, whenever possible, the real efficiency-driver. It should also be noticed that, among the publicly owned firms, EdF has traditionally been run under heavy political pressure regarding nuclear power (irrespective of cost-efficiency considerations), whereas ENEL has been subject to delays in power station construction as a result of political interference (corruption) and concern for environmental factors in rural districts.

Nerlove examines a 1955 cross-section of 145 US electric-power generators. He fits a dual Cobb–Douglas cost function in input prices and output, which is normalized in terms of one of the input prices (fuel), so as to impose degree-one homogeneity. By examining regression residuals, Nerlove discovers *heteroskedasticity*, which, coupled with a U-shaped residuals pattern and a strangely low Durbin-Watson statistic for a cross-sectional analysis, suggests model re-specification. By fitting a corrected Cobb–Douglas cost function to include a quadratic element in output to the same data set, the author is able to detect that returns to scale are not constant in output. As a result, he concludes that the AC curve resulting from his data set is not monotonically increasing or decreasing; rather, it is a U-shaped curve, with minimum efficient scale (MES) occurring at quite a *high* output level. Compare this finding with that of Christensen & Greene (see above) which was on a later cross-section, using a translog cost relationship.

NEUBERG specifies a cost function that accommodates differences in factor prices. The author looks at two large samples of distribution companies in 1972 – consisting of both publicly owned and privately owned utilities – and runs separate regressions on both samples. The dependent variable is total distribution cost, and the regressors are the number of customers (a new measure of output that has been almost universally accepted by researchers in electricity distribution), number of MWh delivered to final customers, number of miles of distribution line, square miles of service territory, price of labour, and a dummy variable for ownership type. Although Neuberg's is the first "almost complete" cost function for electricity distribution, it still lacks some basic input components, such as capital and materials. Moreover, it does not take different customer and voltage types into account properly.

POLLITT specifies a total cost model for electricity distribution within a private and public ownership context. The number of customers is assumed as a proxy for output. The author basically develops a DEA specification for distribution, even though he refers to both econometric and linear programming articles in order to construct the model (regarding the choice of inputs and outputs). A 1990 cross-sectional sample of both US and UK public- and private-sector electricity distribution companies is analysed. By also looking at electricity transmission, the author concludes that it is not possible to reject the null hypothesis, according to which publicly owned and privately owned electricity transmission and distribution companies exhibit no significant difference in technical efficiency. DEA results are cross-checked against econometric ones. Dubious efficiency effects as a result of privatization (probably due to regulatory slackness) are confirmed by both econometric and DEA/Malmquist techniques. Finally, Pollitt outlines that, together, both the econometric and DEA results suggest no evidence for the belief that the British RECs were performing poorly – relatively to US distribution utilities – prior to privatization (1990).

GIAN CARLO SCARSI

See also Efficiency analysis

Emerging markets

Demirgüç-Kunt, Asli and Ross Levine, "Stock Markets, Corporate Finance, and
Economic Growth", *World Bank Economic Review*, 10/2 (1996): 223–39

Grabel, Ilene, "Assessing the Impact of Financial Liberalisation on Stock Market Volatility in Selected Developing Countries", *Journal of Development Studies*, 31/6 (1995): 903–17
Grabel, Ilene, "Financial Markets, the State and Economic Development: Controversies within Theory and Policy", *International Papers in Political Economy*, 3/1 (1996): 1–42
International Finance Corporation, *Emerging Stock Markets Factbook*, Washington, DC: International Finance Corporation, annual publication
Levine, Ross and Sara Zervos, "Stock Market Development and Long-Run Growth", *World Bank Economic Review*, 10/2 (1996): 323–39
Singh, Ajit, "The Stock-Market and Economic Development: Should Developing Countries Encourage Stock-Markets?", *United Nations Conference on Trade and Development Review*, 4 (1993): 1–28
Snowden, P.N., "Enterprise Ownership Constraints and the Role of Equity Markets in Financial Development", *Journal of Development Studies*, 34/1 (1997): 131–48
Stiglitz, Joseph E., "Banks versus Markets as Mechanisms for Allocating and Coordinating Investment" in *The Economics of Cooperation*, edited by James Roumasset and Susan Barr, Boulder, Colorado: Westview Press, 1992
World Bank, *Global Development Finance*, Washington, DC: World Bank, published biannually
World Bank, *Private Capital Flows to Developing Countries: The Road to Financial Integration*, New York and Oxford: Oxford University Press, 1997

The term "emerging markets" is used to refer to stock and bond markets in developing economies. These markets (and hence the literature dealing with them) are recent phenomena, as the growth and deepening of emerging markets is a result of the financial liberalization policies implemented by developing economies since the mid-1980s.

Data are becoming available on emerging markets, although coverage is incomplete. Two publications provide comprehensive information on the markets of individual countries, and analyses of regional trends. The INTERNATIONAL FINANCE CORPORATION's annual publication, *Emerging Stock Markets Factbook*, is the single best source of information on most aspects of emerging markets, especially their microeconomic features (concerning, for example, regulation, turnover, and market depth). The WORLD BANK's biannual two-volume publication, *Global Development Finance*, provides useful time-series data on the macroeconomic aspects of emerging markets, focusing on the forms of private capital flows to these markets (such as the types of debt flows, and the volume of portfolio equity versus foreign direct investment flows).

A number of studies of emerging markets seek to assess, theoretically and empirically, the factors that cause capital to enter and leave these markets. The debate over causality is framed in terms of "push" and "pull" factors. Push factors refer to global economic developments (such as the lack of promising investment opportunities in developed economies), whereas pull factors are internal to developing economies (such as the success of privatization programmes). A comprehensive study of emerging markets, published by the WORLD BANK

Policy Research Department, attempts to put to rest the push-pull debate. The empirical findings reported in the World Bank study show that pull factors matter more than push factors in determining the direction of capital flows to emerging markets. Moreover, the study finds that pull factors have become more important over time. Note that the World Bank study, although not breaking new ground analytically, is itself an important guide to the recent (neoclassical) academic and policy-oriented literature on emerging markets.

Neoclassical economic theory extols the virtues of emerging markets. From this perspective, the growth in emerging markets has been a boon to economic performance and investment activity in emerging economies. Written from the perspective of neoclassical theory, the study by LEVINE & ZERVOS provides a thorough econometric examination of the relationship between emerging market activity and growth in developing economies. The authors' cross-country regression results show that larger, more efficient emerging markets are positively associated with long-run economic growth. Stock markets are found to induce economic growth via five channels. They (a) enhance liquidity; (b) promote risk diversification through international financial integration; (c) promote the acquisition of information regarding firms; (d) influence corporate control by helping to mitigate the principal-agent problem (via the "threat of continual auction"); and (e) can ease the problem of savings mobilization (provided that markets are large and liquid). The Levine & Zervos article has an extensive bibliography of the literature on emerging markets (and related topics), and is one of a collection of useful articles in a symposium on emerging markets in the *World Bank Economic Review*.

Neoclassical theory reaches a uniformly sanguine conclusion on the role of emerging markets, but there is considerable tension within new-Keynesian economic theory on the subject. In a firm-level study in the new-Keynesian tradition, SNOWDEN argues that emerging markets are indeed beneficial for investment and economic growth in developing economies. Empirical studies of industrial organization in developing economies reveal that owner-controlled firms are a very common form of business organization. The gains to economic growth from emerging markets stem from the conclusion that equity issues are likely to facilitate borrowing by owner-controlled enterprises. So the ability to use equity has important implications for investment in developing economies where entrepreneurial wealth constrains firm scale. By relaxing the self-financing constraint, emerging markets have beneficial effects on investment and hence on overall economic performance.

Snowden's assessment of the developmental benefits of emerging markets is called into question in an important paper by STIGLITZ, a prominent new-Keynesian theorist. Stiglitz argues that, in the context of developing economies, emerging markets do not provide a significant volume of external finance for new investment. Moreover, to the extent that emerging markets do provide finance, it is relatively expensive, and its liquidity renders it a risky form of investment finance.

Post-Keynesian economic theory rejects the view that emerging markets present developing economies with unmitigated opportunities for increased growth and investment. Post-Keynesian writings on the subject, exemplified by the work of SINGH and GRABEL (1996), argue that emerging markets pose significant costs for developing economies. From a macroeconomic perspective these costs far outweigh the benefits. The expansion of emerging markets has often led to the creation of unsustainable speculative bubbles followed by financial crises. As a consequence of investor efforts to exploit available speculative opportunities, saving and investment can be misallocated, to the detriment of economic growth and stability.

From a post-Keynesian perspective, whether and to what degree expanded stock markets are a boon or an impediment to economic growth and stability in developing economies also depends on the level of volatility they exhibit. Markets with frequent and severe price swings might be much more likely to induce short-term speculative investment practices, and might also be more likely to induce broader macroeconomic instability. GRABEL (1995) therefore argues for the importance of measuring stock market volatility following financial liberalization in developing economies. Grabel develops three indices for measuring the volatility of emerging markets, and finds that following financial liberalization, the volatility of emerging markets increases significantly.

In view of the disputes among neoclassical, new-Keynesian and post-Keynesian economic theory on the potential contribution of emerging markets to the prospects of developing economies, it is not surprising that these approaches are associated with different policy recommendations. Neoclassical theory, exemplified by DEMIRGÜÇ-KUNT & LEVINE and Levine & Zervos, recommends that governments in developing economies should dismantle legal, regulatory, and tax obstacles to the promotion of emerging markets. New-Keynesian theorists, such as Snowden, who argue in favour of stock markets, propose analogous measures. New-Keynesian critics of stock markets, such as Stiglitz, and post-Keynesians, such as Singh and Grabel (in a 1996 paper), argue that policy makers in developing economies should approach emerging markets cautiously, and should not attempt to put into place markets that mirror their highly liberalized counterparts in developed economies. Singh also argues that developing economies should focus on improving the allocational and functional efficiency of their banking systems, prior to promoting the growth of emerging markets.

ILENE GRABEL

Emotion

Averill, James R., *Anger and Aggression: An Essay on Emotion*, New York: Springer, 1982

Ekman, Paul and Richard J. Davidson (editors), *The Nature of Emotion: Fundamental Questions*, New York: Oxford University Press, 1994

Frijda, Nico H., *The Emotions*, Cambridge and New York: Cambridge University Press, 1986

Jenkins, Jennifer M., Keith Oatley and Nancy L. Stein (editors), *Human Emotions: A Reader*, Oxford and Malden, Massachusetts: Blackwell, 1998

Lazarus, Richard S., *Emotion and Adaptation*, New York: Oxford University Press, 1991

Lewis, Michael and Jeanette M. Haviland (editors), *Handbook of Emotions*, New York: Guilford Press, 1993

Ortony, Andrew, Gerald L. Clore and Allan Collins, *The Cognitive Structure of Emotions*, Cambridge and New York: Cambridge University Press, 1988

Parkinson, Brian, *Ideas and Realities of Emotion*, London and New York: Routledge, 1995

Scherer, Klaus R. and Paul Ekman (editors), *Approaches to Emotion*, Hillsdale, New Jersey: Erlbaum, 1984

Strongman, Kenneth T., *The Psychology of Emotion: Theories of Emotion in Perspective*, 4th edition, Chichester and New York: Wiley, 1996

Emotion has been approached from a variety of angles within psychology, including neurophysiological, evolutionary, cognitive, developmental, and social perspectives. As an initial aid to assist readers in coming to terms with this diversity, the latest edition of STRONGMAN's popular textbook focuses exclusively on summarizing the most influential theories of emotion. About 150 such theories are described, categorized, and evaluated, although the brevity of presentation often means that critical analysis is minimal and some of the sophistication of the original accounts is necessarily simplified. Nevertheless, this volume continues to represent a valuable resource for sampling the range of available models.

SCHERER & EKMAN contains complete chapters on major theoretical approaches to emotions written by the theorists themselves and helps to flesh out some of the ideas covered in less detail by Strongman. Again, theories from across the whole spectrum of psychology are discussed, and the final section summarizes sociological and anthropological accounts. The inclusion of reprinted articles by Zajonc and Lazarus representing both sides of the recurrent "affective primacy" debate ("does emotion require prior cognition or not?") is also useful.

JENKINS, OATLEY & STEIN provides a helpful compendium of articles, including excerpts from early influential works by Darwin, James, and Freud, as well as sections on evolutionary considerations, emotional development, individual and social functions of emotion, and clinical affective disorders. Every section is preceded by a few pages of the editors' own introductory remarks, and each source article is accompanied by an instructive orienting paragraph and key references. The book was produced to be read alongside Oatley & Jenkins' introductory textbook, *Understanding Emotions* (1996), but also makes a very worthwhile volume on its own.

LEWIS & HAVILAND's 650-page edited handbook presents a broadly based survey of state-of-the-art thinking in the study of emotion. Its diverse contributions are arranged in five loosely defined sections, concerning different disciplines' approaches to emotion, neurophysiological, psychological, and social perspectives, and finally examinations of selected emotions such as anger, fear, embarrassment, and happiness. The contributors are all eminent and active researchers who generally attempt to provide an overview of current ideas concerning their assigned topic. The book is therefore a good place to start when the aim is to understand a specific area of emotion research in detail, and works best as an orienting frame and source of references for further reading.

EKMAN & DAVIDSON organize their edited volume around 12 key issues in emotion research and theory, including whether there are biologically basic emotions, how emotions should be contrasted with related psychological concepts such as mood and temperament, whether emotions can be distinguished from one another on the basis of their physiological accompaniments, and what degree of cognitive activity is necessary for the occurrence of emotion. Four or more theorists address each question and the editors summarize their contrasting or convergent views in concluding sections. Although the quality, style, and focus of the contributions are variable, the volume still manages to give a clear sense of the cut-and-thrust of emotion research and includes some outstanding contributions.

ORTONY, CLORE & COLLINS specifically adopts an artificial intelligence approach to questions of how emotion is distinguished from nonemotion and how different emotions are distinguished from each other. Based on a clear conceptual analysis of the domain, they conclude that emotions are "valenced reactions to events, agents, or objects, with their particular nature being determined by the way in which the eliciting situation is construed" (p.13). Most of the book is devoted to an attempt to articulate the specific cognitive interpretations underlying particular emotions and the determinants of their relative intensity.

LAZARUS' learned monograph represents the synthesis and culmination of an entire career in emotion and stress research. His influential appraisal approach, here recast as a "cognitive-motivational-relational" theory explaining how emotions are activated and differentiated by apprehension of the specific nature of a transaction's personal significance, is developed in detail and applied to a broad range of issues ranging from the cognitive basis of different emotions (cf. Ortony *et al.* above) to implications for health psychology. The analysis is partly inspired by systems theory principles and employs "contextualist" concepts that often cut across conventional distinctions between person and environment, cause and effect, or perception and cognition. This conceptual promiscuity also sometimes finds expression in an elaborate and potentially ambiguous prose style. Depending on the predilections of the reader, the results of such a combination may seem either frustratingly imprecise or appropriately subtle. Either way, a great deal can be learned from working through this book.

A related account is articulated in FRIJDA's weighty volume. According to his functionalist analysis, emotions are changes in modes of action readiness elicited by situational meaning structures. Rather than arising as a simple momentary feeling, the emotion process is said to unfold as a multilevel syndrome of interrelated cognitive, physiological, expressive, and behavioural events that is subject to various regulation mechanisms at all phases of its realtime development. Like Lazarus, Frijda considers that activation of emotion depends on events making contact with the individual's underlying concerns, which themselves may or may not be realistically or rationally derived, allowing for apparently dysfunctional responses. The book provides an integrative account of an impressively wide range of evidence and contains numerous telling insights. Although the text is again often dense and the digressions are many, the book repays careful reading and reveals a philosophically sophisticated and empirically grounded account of emotion that is prepared to acknowledge the complexity of the underlying set of phenomena.

The previous three monographs all address emotion from a mainly (although not exclusively) cognitive perspective. The final two give more emphasis to the role of social factors. PARKINSON critically reviews research into four aspects of emotional function: cognitive appraisals, action tendencies, bodily changes, and expressive displays, and presents an approach that attempts to place the phenomena into a broader interpersonal and cultural context. Interrelations between the ways in which emotions are represented and enacted comprise the recurrent theme of the volume. The basic argument is that emotions are embodied strategies for communicating evaluations and realigning identities over the course of real or imagined social interactions.

AVERILL's exemplary extended essay focuses on anger but also provides a thorough account of the author's pioneering social constructionist approach to emotion in general. Here emotional syndromes derive their organization mainly from sociocultural rather than cognitive or biological factors, opening up a space for intersocietal variation (as well as individual creativity). More specifically, many emotions are considered to be culturally provided strategies for dealing with conflicts between social norms, designed to allow the individual to disown responsibility for normally sanctioned actions (by treating them as passions). According to this account, adopting the socialized anger role potentially permits retaliation without retribution because the action is performed in the "heat of the moment" according to conventional interpretation. Part one of the book presents the theoretical analysis and contains informed reviews of anthropological, philosophical, and legal writings on anger coupled with an incisive and sustained critique of biological reductionism. Part two reports a series of empirical studies on the nature of anger and aggression from the perspective of both agent and target. Throughout, the chapters are characterized by a depth of insight and elegance of prose that remain unrivalled in the psychological literature on this topic. Despite being the oldest entry on the list of suggested readings, Averill's book is still in many ways the most definitive and relevant.

BRIAN PARKINSON

See also Affect regulation, Emotional labour

Emotional labour

Ashforth, Blake E. and Ronald H. Humphrey, "Emotional Labor in Service Roles: The Influence of Identity", *Academy of Management Review*, 18/1 (1993): 88–115

Fineman, Stephen (editor), *Emotion in Organizations*, London and Newbury Park, California: Sage, 1993

Goffman, Erving, *Strategic Interaction*, Philadelphia: University of Pennsylvania Press, 1969, and Oxford: Blackwell, 1970

Hochschild, Arlie Russell, *The Managed Heart: Commercialization of Human Feeling*, Berkeley: University of California Press, 1983

Morris, J. Andrew and Daniel C. Feldman, "The Dimensions, Antecedents, and Consequences of Emotional Labor", *Academy of Management Review*, 21/4 (1996): 986–1010

Parkinson, Brian, "Emotional Stylists: Strategies of Expressive Management among Trainee Hairdressers", *Cognition and Emotion*, 5/5–6 (1991): 419–34

Rafaeli, Anat and Robert I. Sutton, "Expression of Emotion as Part of the Work Role", *Academy of Management Review*, 12/1 (1987): 23–37

Van Maanen, John and Gideon Kunda, "'Real Feelings': Emotional Expression and Organizational Culture", *Research in Organizational Behavior*, 11 (1989): 43–103

Wharton, Amy S., "The Affective Consequences of Service Work: Managing Emotions on the Job", *Work and Occupations*, 20/2 (1993): 205–32

Wouters, Cas, "The Sociology of Emotions and Flight Attendants: Hochschild's *Managed Heart*", *Theory, Culture and Society*, 6 (1989): 95–123

Emotional labour occurs when people regulate feelings or their expression as part of paid employment. Inspired by C. Wright Mills' analysis (in *White Collar*) of how a salesforce culture had led to personality becoming a marketable but devaluing commodity and GOFFMAN's dramaturgical account of impression management, HOCHSCHILD developed this concept to cover encounters during which personnel either work up or play down their emotions in order to satisfy the needs of clients or employers. In particular, she investigated the emotional labour conducted by flight attendants encouraged to project an air of pleasant congeniality even when confronted with difficult passengers ("irates"), and by bill collectors whose job is to get tough with tardy debtors despite any residual sympathy they might feel ("the toe and the heel of capitalism").

According to Hochschild, emotional labour can be performed using either surface acting, wherein the employee feigns the expression or display of the required emotion, or by a Stanislavskian deep acting, which involves directly manipulating the affective experience itself. Central to this account is the notion that employees may become alienated from their true feelings when they have to work on them as institutional rather than personal reactions and attitudes. The book is written in an engaging style and contains a wealth of insights and telling observations. Its groundbreaking analysis has already made it a classic.

RAFAELI & SUTTON present a more formal and systematized model of the strategic use of emotional expression as part of the work role from an occupational psychology perspective. They consider possible organizational influences on this process including selective recruitment of appropriately expressive employees, training and modelling of correct emotional conduct, and monitoring of performance coupled with suitable reward structures. Thus, a salesperson who obtained the job partly because of her capacity for smiling may be taught to target and intensify this display for customers, and provided with incentives for keeping up the performance. Over the course of the service encounter, the employee's expressive displays are also influenced by the positive or negative reactions of customers.

Rafaeli and Sutton also emphasize the variety of possible outcomes of emotional labour, including enhanced or worsened performance of the employing organization, as well as material and psychological costs or benefits for the employees themselves. In cases where the required display is dissonant with experienced emotion, faking may be done either in good or bad faith, and the authors argue (*pace* Hochschild) that only the latter has necessarily negative psychological effects. As an example of adaptive faking in good faith, caring professionals may need to adopt an attitude of detached concern for their clients in order to avoid being overwhelmed by empathic distress.

In a related vein, the articles by ASHFORTH & HUMPHREY and PARKINSON both suggest that emotional labour is less likely to be experienced as negative if there is close identification with the work role and its associated prescriptions for expressive behaviour. For example, trainee hairdressers who expressed greater empathic concern for their clients reported greater rather than lower wellbeing in Parkinson's interview study. Ashforth and Humphrey also argue that work role identification may be increased as a *consequence* of engaging in emotional labour because the resultant emotion may provide self-relevant cues about involvement. Thus social identity not only moderates the psychological impact of emotional labour but is also itself influenced by its practice. Similarly, to the extent that the expressive performance is taken to be sincere by others, the actor may ultimately internalize it. The drawback of close identification with an occupational role is that failure in its performance will have more direct effects on wellbeing.

VAN MAANEN & KUNDA focus on the emotions managed as part of the transmission and maintenance of organizational culture, where the main addressees for affective communication are supervisors, colleagues, or subordinates, rather than customers. In two ethnographies – of ride operators at Disneyland, and engineers employed by a manufacturer of new technology – they demonstrate how emotional investment in work roles is encouraged and monitored during the performance of various institutional rituals and ceremonies. In the latter organization, for example, induction sessions, manuals, presentations, and team activities converge to sustain the image of a top-grade, no-nonsense, mutually respectful, and hardworking group of people. Employees experience a tension between accruing the emotional benefits of close identification with such a self-esteeming organization and preserving their personal identity in partial separation from the work role. Thus, corporate culture produces and is reproduced by the emotions of its members. The paper conveys a rich picture of the two work settings and makes many original points, but its central underlying theme is sometimes a little difficult to discern.

MORRIS & FELDMAN sketch out a preliminary analysis of some potential dimensions of the emotional labour demands made by different kinds of work, and argue that different consequences arise from variations along each of these dimensions. In particular, they distinguish frequency of required emotional display, attentiveness to display rules, variety of emotions to be expressed, and emotional dissonance (conceptualized as the discrepancy between experienced and required emotion, rather than the psychological consequence of this conflict as in Hochschild's original analysis). Although not definitive, their structural model makes a start at acknowledging the potential diversity of emotional labour phenomena.

WOUTERS provides a theoretical critique of Hochschild's analysis from an Eliasian figurational sociology perspective. Rather than emphasizing how organizations have tightened emotional controls on employees, this author argues that there has been an increasing "informalization" of emotion-regulation norms to allow flexible response in diverse interactional contexts. In Wouters's view, emotional labour can sometimes be a playful and enjoyable rather than a necessarily unpleasant or alienating experience. WHARTON also presents evidence that emotional labour (in banking and hospital employees) may have an upside as well as a downside.

FINEMAN's edited volume contains qualitative studies of organizations and theoretical analyses many of which are relevant to issues concerning emotional labour. There are two recurrent themes: that organizations impose structure and control on the emotional experiences of their members; and that emotional forces shape people's involvements and engagements in organizational life. On the one hand, emotions are handled, channelled, and reformulated by everyday organizational practices, such as traditional hospital procedures controlling when, how, and by whom traumatic news is broken to cancer patients and their relatives. On the other hand, our pre-existing feelings are thought to provide deeper motivations for what we do when fulfilling our organizational roles. The contributions are of variable quality but the collection still helps to give a flavour of how research into this important but still understudied topic is beginning to progress.

BRIAN PARKINSON

See also Affect regulation, Emotion

Empiricism

Alexander, Jeffrey C., *Positivism, Presuppositions and Current Controversies*, vol. 1, *Theoretical Logic in Sociology*, Berkeley: University of California Press, and London: Routledge and Kegan Paul, 1982

Barber, Bernard, "On the Relations Between Philosophy of Science and Sociology of Science" in *Social Studies of Science*, New Brunswick and London: Transaction, 1990

Becker, Howard S., *Tricks of the Trade: How to Think about Your Research While You're Doing It*, Chicago: University of Chicago Press, 1998

Brooke, John Hedley, *Science and Religion: Some Historical Perspectives*, Cambridge and New York: Cambridge University Press, 1991

Butterfield, Herbert, *The Origins of Modern Science 1300–1800*, revised edition, New York: Free Press, and London: Bell, 1957

Chalmers, A.F., *What is This Thing Called Science? An Assessment of the Nature and Status of Science and its Methods*, 3rd edition, Indianapolis: Hackett and Buckingham: Open University Press, 1999

Clouser, Roy A., *The Myth of Religious Neutrality: An Essay on the Hidden Role of Religious Belief in Theories*, Notre Dame: University of Notre Dame Press, 1991

Flax, Jane, "Postmodernism and Gender Relations in Feminist Theory", *Signs*, 12/4 (1987): 621–43

Gadamer, Hans-Georg, *Truth and Method*, 2nd revised edition, London: Sheed and Ward, and New York: Crossroad, 1989

Habermas, Jürgen, *Knowledge and Human Interests*, 2nd edition, London: Heinemann, 1978

Harding, Sandra, *Is Science Multicultural? Postcolonialisms, Feminisms, and Epistemologies*, Bloomington: Indiana University Press, 1998

Hecking, S.E. "Sociological Christianity and Christian Sociology: The Paradox of Early American Sociology", *Religion and American Culture*, 3/1 (1993): 49–67

Husserl, Edmund, *The Crisis of European Sciences and Transcendental Phenomenology: An Introduction to Phenomenological Philosophy*, Evanston: Northwestern University Press, 1970

Kuhn, Thomas S., *The Structure of Scientific Revolutions*, 2nd edition, Chicago: University of Chicago Press, 1970

Lyotard, Jean-François, *The Postmodern Condition: A Report on Knowledge* Minneapolis: University of Minnesota Press, and Manchester: Manchester University Press, 1984

Merton, Robert K., *Science, Technology and Society in Seventeenth Century England*, reprinted with a new introduction, Atlantic Highlands, New Jersey: Humanities, 1978 (originally published 1938)

Mills, C. Wright, *The Sociological Imagination*, New York: Oxford University Press, 1959

Mouzelis, Nicos, "Modernity: A Non-European Conceptualization", *British Journal of Sociology*, 50/1 (March 1999): 141–59

Outhwaite, William and Martin Bulmer, "Objective/Objectivism" in *The Macmillan Student Encyclopedia of Sociology*, edited by Michael Mann, London: Macmillan, 1983; as *The International Encyclopedia of Sociology*, New York: Continuum, 1984

Parsons, Talcott, *The Structure of Social Action: A Study in Social Theory with Special Reference to a Group of Recent European Writers*, New York: McGraw Hill, 1937; 2nd edition, New York: Free Press and London: Collier, 1968

Rorty, Richard, *Philosophy and the Mirror of Nature*, Princeton, New Jersey: Princeton University Press, and Oxford: Blackwell, 1980

Ross, Dorothy, *The Origins of American Social Science*, Cambridge and New York: Cambridge University Press, 1991

Shils, Edward A., *"Legitimating the Social Sciences: Meeting the Challenges to Objectivity and Integrity"* in *Controversies and Decisions: The Social Sciences and Public Policy*, edited by Charles Frankel, New York: Russell Sage Foundation, 1976

Skinner, Quentin (editor), *The Return of Grand Theory in the Human Sciences*, Cambridge: Cambridge University Press, 1985

Wallerstein, Immanuel, *Open the Social Sciences: Report of the Gulbenkian Commission on the Restructuring of the Social Sciences*, Stanford: Stanford University Press, 1996

Weber, Max "Author's Introduction" in *The Protestant Ethic and the Spirit of Capitalism*, London: Allen and Unwin, 1930

In social science the term "empiricism" has technical meaning as a scientific movement, but its use in evaluating scientific work can carry loaded implications. Scientists judge their own work and that of others by reference to some norm. An analysis of empirical credibility often decides the reliability of data-gathering methods and the strength of conclusions. BECKER and also PARSONS imply that appeal to the empirical involves the development of scientific confidence to not only explain, but also to understand, research.

For a range of definitions of the term, see the encylopedia or dictionary entries written for social sciences readership (e.g. *Collins Dictionary of Sociology*, 1995; *The Blackwell Dictionary of Sociology*, 1995; *Dictionary of Modern Sociology*, 1967; *The Penguin Dictionary of Sociology*, 1994, *The Concise Oxford Dictionary of Sociology*, 1994; *A New Dictionary of the Social Sciences*, 1979; *The Macmillan Student Encyclopedia of Sociology*, 1983; *Encyclopedia of Sociology*, 1992) or philosophical definitions of empiricism (e.g. *The Oxford Dictionary of Philosophy*, 1994; *The Encyclopedia of Philosophy*, 1987; *The Cambridge Dictionary of Philosophy*, 1985). These should be read carefully, as they give a good indication of how the term can be used, and illustrate the serious divergence in interpretations.

CLOUSER addresses the debate philosophically but also includes discussion of the scientific study of social structures. Clouser points out that "empiricism" can refer to a movement of scientific thinking, but, he argues, empirical openness should not hide the prescientific basis of this thinking. Scientific analysis always involves an appeal to reality and debates about the "truth", and as such the structure of social scientific reflection requires a scientific openness, directing the theorizing from the concrete results of scientific inquiry. Only such openness will short circuit dogmatic tendencies. It is this self-critical outlook that is the root for empirical openness. This is consistent with the historical studies of BROOKE, BUTTERFIELD, HECKING, KUHN, MERTON, ROSS, and WEBER, which remind late 20th-century secularized science about its historical and religious roots: debates over empiricism consistently bring worldviews, values, and religion onto the agenda. OUTHWAITE & BULMER specifically describe the empiricist view of the knowledge process as a pretender to an assumption-free account of reality.

Empiricism in philosophy and the social sciences also involves debate about the true value of trying to explain how an empirical attitude is possible. For example, Locke's explanation is at odds with Clouser. The empiricist view of experience is based on abstract sensory properties, and this raises the critical observation that we never in fact experience such abstract properties. Clouser builds on Whitehead's dissent from Hume's doctrine – "There is nothing in the mind not first in the senses" – in which Whitehead noted that the rule is not itself in the senses. An account of empiricism, therefore, must also explain this puzzle. It could be a "theory of theory" but then, on empiricist grounds, another theory of our "theory of theory", must result, *ad absurdum*.

Clouser's point is that "empiricism" in the sense of the word used by John Locke, and by those in the mainline empiricist tradition, involves an implicit assumption about science's religious neutrality, which itself prevents an open empirical attitude. In forms of "objectivism", emotion is excluded as the *a priori* polar opposite to reason. In "empiricism", religion is viewed as the opposite of science, and must likewise first be excluded before scientific thinking is possible. But is this view the result of empirical induction? Empiricists may sometimes resort to the historiographical record of science to derive empirical generalizations about science's historical relationship with religion. Such historical study will often bring about modifications to more strident forms of empiricism.

The historical and epistemological exposé of the myth of religious neutrality, appears, on the surface, consistent with a postmodern approach. The postmodernist perspectives, as put forward by LYOTARD, by HARDING, by FLAX, and by RORTY, are quite amenable to historicism, with radically empiricist approaches to history. But in much postmodern social science, the complexities of philosophical debate about empiricism no longer seem to hold any interest. Harding's discussion, for example, places science, as a powerful cultural institution, within the context of postcolonialism and feminism. But if her approach is to restore the empirical outlook, science is also subordinated to a pluralistic or postmodern ethic of liberation in which epistemologies of science are uncovered by a "borderlands epistemology". Harding's approach, with CHALMERS and with SHILS, who stress an ethic of scientific humility, could result in a modified postmodern empiricism.

There are many ideological collisions, including Chalmers's self-critical conclusion that discussion of science as a single "thing" is itself wrong headed and misleading. Science is disparate and fragmented, a view consistent with Lyotard's postmodernism. A scientist limited to empirical data within a particular disciplinary framework can no longer suggest an empiricist framework for science *per se*. Or rather, the empiricist approach is to refrain from making any such proscriptive overviews. One overarching method, or a view of an all-encompassing encyclopaedia, as Clouser intimates, is rejected as misconceived. Chalmers and Lyotard and WALLERSTEIN advocate empirical attitudes that reckon with the possibility that all possible data from all empirical investigation has no credible overall structure, even if science is now fired by a search, in Rorty's terms, for the strategy, or therapy, that works best. A new empiricism celebrates postmodernity, continuing scientific investigation of all the groups and subgroups of peoples of the earth with their cultures and their systems of knowledge, and encourages all peoples to do likewise. With no overall structure, all previous empiricisms have been undermined by their mutually alternative scientific "metanarratives", and in which each world-view now suffers from the postmodern incredulity to all world-views.

MOUZELIS reminds this new social scientific establishment that there is analytic and empirical value to be found in that modern sociological view of global society which now can be anchored in a non-European context.

The merging of sociology and social theory does not only mean a trend toward disparate theories but, as SKINNER indicates, a desire to recapture grand theory. The all-embracing interpretative frameworks of GADAMER, Kuhn, HABERMAS,

and HUSSERL also mean that for many this is the time to "revisit" earlier perspectives of Parsons, MERTON, and arch critic MILLS. The self-definition of "structural functionalism", as an empirical approach, is kept alive by ALEXANDER and BARBER.

BRUCE WEARNE

See also Objectivity

Employee ownership and cooperative societies: comparative performance studies

Berman, Katerina V., *Worker-Owned Plywood Firms: An Economic Analysis*, Pullman: Washington State University Press, 1967

Bradley, Keith and Allen Gelb, "Motivation and Control in the Mondragon Experiment", *British Journal of Industrial Relations*, 19/2 (1981): 221–31

Conte, Michael and Jan Svejnar, "Productivity Effects of Worker Participation in Management, Profit Sharing, Worker Ownership of Assets and Unionization in US Firms", *International Journal of Industrial Organization*, 6 (1988): 139–51

Defourney, Jacques, Saul Estrin and Derek Jones, "The Effects of Workers' Participation on Enterprise Performance: Empirical Evidence from French Cooperatives", *International Journal of Industrial Organization*, 3 (1985): 197–217

Jones, Derek and Jan Svejnar, "Participation, Profit Sharing, Worker Ownership and Efficiency in Italian Producer Co-operatives", *Economica*, 52 (1985): 449–65

Jones, Derek and Takao Kato, "The Scope, Nature, and Effects of Employee Stock Ownership in Japan", *Industrial and Labor Relations Review*, 46/2 (1993): 352–66

Kardas, Peter, Paul Sommers, Richard Marens, Katerina Gale and Gorm Winther, "Employment and Sales Growth in Washington State Employee Ownership Companies: A Comparative Analysis", *Journal of Employee Ownership Law and Finance*, 4/2 (1994): 83–135

Mygind, Niels, "Are Self-Managed Firms Efficient? The Experience of Danish Fully and Partly Self-managed Firms" in *Advances in Economic Analysis of Participatory and Labor-Managed Firms*, edited by Derek Jones and Jan Svejnar, Greenwich, Connecticut: Jai Press, 1987

Rosen, Corey and Michael Quarrey, *Employee Ownership and Corporate Performance*, Arlington, Virginia: National Center of Employee Ownership, 1986

Russell, Raymond, Patrick Grasso and Terry Hanford, "Employee Stock Ownership Plans: Consequences for Participation and Performance" in *Profit Sharing and Gain Sharing*, edited by Myron J. Roomkin, Metuchen, New Jersey: IMLR Press / Scarecrow Press, 1990

Thomas, Henk and Chris Logan, *Mondragon: An Economic Analysis*, London and Boston: Allen and Unwin, 1982

Thordarson, Bodil, "A Comparison of Worker-Owned and Conventionally Owned Firms in Sweden" in *Advances in the Economic Analysis of Participatory and Labor-Managed Firms*, edited by Derek Jones and Jan Svejnar, Greenwich, Connecticut: JAI Press, 1987

Winther, Gorm, *Employee Ownership: A Comparative Analysis of Growth Performance*, Aalborg: Aalborg University Press, 1995

Winther, Gorm and Richard Marens, "Participatory Democracy May Go a Long Way: Comparative Growth Performance of Employee Ownership Firms in New York and Washington States", *Economic and Industrial Democracy: An International Journal*, 18/3 (1997): 393–421

Surveying the literature on performance effects of employee ownership of firms, cooperative ownership, and participatory decision-making suggests a striking similar pattern in most studies. In a 1987 study for the Nordic Council of Government Secretaries, MYGIND analysed employee-owned firms in Scandinavian countries. His sample of 93 employee-owned firms had higher comparative labour and capital productivity than industry. BERMAN found American plywood cooperatives to be nearly 50 per cent more efficient than conventional firms in the same industry, and results from a study of Swedish employee-owned firms conducted by THORDARSON also demonstrated productivity advantages over conventional firms. The Mondragon group of cooperative enterprises in Euzkadi (the Basque country) in northern Spain is the most successful and famous of all modern worker cooperatives, and it follows this same pattern. THOMAS & LOGAN found that the Mondragon firms outperformed regional industry averages in terms of profitability and productivity, a result consistent with a near-contemporary analysis conducted by BRADLEY & GELB. Employee participation in decision making often appears to be a key explanatory variable in explaining competitive advantages. The results on participation appear both in conventional firms, in cooperatives, and in employee-ownership firms. In relation to European studies on cooperatives, effects were frequently found for ownership *per se*. For instance, JONES & SVEJNAR found the variable "negotiable co-op shares" in Italian manufacturing worker cooperatives to be positively related to productivity. DEFOURNEY, ESTRIN & JONES presented the same results for French cooperatives. JONES & KATO found that employee stock ownership plans (ESOPs) in seven Japanese industries had a positive impact on productivity.

Research in the US on ESOPs has tended to suggest positive economic benefits from worker participation in operational decisions. ROSEN & QUARREY reported in a 1986 National Center for Employee Ownership Study (NCEO) that firms with some form of employee ownership grew faster than control firms in both simple comparisons after the inception of employee ownership and in longitudinal comparisons. Moreover, sales totals grew even faster than employment, suggesting that both employment and a crude productivity proxy tended to increase with the introduction of an ESOP. The partial correlations run by the authors suggested that employee participation, as measured by managerial perceptions of employee influence, was an important variable. Participatory decisions mainly had positive strong and statistically discernible correlations with both Post-ESOP growth rates and positive differences between the relative post-ESOP and pre-ESOP rates. Simple correlations implied that the contribution to the ESOP, the degree of ownership, voting rights, or employees boards representation were not reliable predictors for the variance in growth leads to comparison firms.

However, in a 1987 General Accounting Office (GAO) study of the effects of ESOPs on productivity and profitability measures, RUSSELL, GRASSO & HANFORD reported that the only statistically discernible variable positively correlated with higher productivity was participation in decision making. In general the GAO found little evidence of strong employee ownership effects on productivity and profitability performance. CONTE & SVEJNAR later estimated the impact of employee ownership, profit sharing, participation, and unionization on value added in relation to production function analysis and found similar results to the NCEO and GAO. The results of Rosen and Quarrey's study were corroborated at the state level in two companion studies initiated by Gorm Winther for New York and Washington State in 1991 and 1992. In his 1995 book WINTHER reported on the New York findings and surveys the ESOP literature. The Washington findings are reported by KARDAS *et al.* and in a theoretical and comparative approach by WINTHER & MARENS.

GORM WINTHER

See also Democracy in the workplace, Economic theories of labour-managed and participatory firms, High performance work systems

Employee relations

Blyton, Paul and Peter Turnbull (editors), *Reassessing Human Resource Management*, London and Newbury Park, California: Sage, 1992

Davies, Paul and Mark Freedland, *Labour Legislation and Public Policy: A Contemporary History*, Oxford: Clarendon Press, and New York: Oxford University Press, 1993

Dunlop, John T., *Industrial Relations Systems*, New York: Holt, 1958; revised edition, Boston: Harvard Business School Press, 1993

Edwards, Mark R. and Ann J. Ewen, *360° Feedback: The Powerful New Model for Employee Assessment and Performance Improvement*, New York: Amacom, 1996

Fox, Alan, *Beyond Contract: Work, Power, and Trust Relations*, London: Faber, 1974

Kanigel, Robert, *The One Best Way: Frederick Winslow Taylor and the Enigma of Efficiency*, London and New York: Viking, 1997

Olson, Walter, *The Excuse Factory: How Employment Law Is Paralyzing the American Workplace*, New York: Free Press, 1997

Pfeffer, Jeffrey, *Competitive Advantage through People: Unleashing the Power of the Workforce*, Boston: Harvard Business School Press, 1994

Sisson, Keith, *Personnel Management: A Comprehensive Guide to Theory and Practice in Britain*, 2nd edition, Oxford and Cambridge, Massachusetts: Blackwell, 1994

DUNLOP's influential work has dominated the employment relations debate since its publication in 1958. This is largely due to the dominance of systems models in management, marketing, and the general literature on organizations. This model emphasizes the interdependencies and interactions between organizations and their environments. The organization is thought of as a system that draws upon certain inputs of labour, capital, energy and information from its environment and converts them, through a process of management, into the outputs of a product or service for sale or distribution to the consumer. The proceeds from this sale are then used to replenish the system. In the context of industrial relations Dunlop concluded that the major outputs of any industrial relations system are rules. These rules can be substantive (those that set out the terms and conditions of work) and procedural (those that govern how substantive rules are made and interpreted, such as legislation). What binds the system together is a common ideology about the interaction and roles of the respective actors. This is seen as its greatest weakness, although the general harmony between workers and management would throw this weakness into doubt. Like all systems models they are useful for understanding the whole picture of industrial relations, but not that useful in telling practitioners what they should do to keep the system alive, or what processes should be developed to ensure that the system is effective.

FOX has had by far the greatest influence on post-1974 industrial relations writing, and no doubt can bear a large amount of the blame for the inability of academics today to come to grasp with a more liberal economic environment in which harmony in the industrial relations system is left up to the parties involved, with the state taking a diminished role. Fox gave conflict the centre stage in industrial relations. He argued that ideologies of industrial relations fell into three camps: (a) unitary, (b) pluralist, and (c) radical or Marxist. This model did give recognition to the power and status of the actors within an industrial relations system, but by doing so unnecessarily elevated conflict between workers and management to an axiomatic level. Following this, academics have focused on methods to reduce the naturally occurring conflict between labour and capital. This model has little relevance for today's workplace where the focus is upon a "family", "team", or "culture" and everybody is working towards the same end. It is also of little use in an environment dominated by neoclassical models of economics that assume (correctly) a win-win situation between the aims of workers (higher wages and conditions) and management (improved productivity and profits).

It is reasonable to conclude that the most influential figure in employee relations – indeed in management thought – has been Frederick Winslow Taylor, the father of scientific management. Still a controversial figure, Taylor is revered and hated with equal passion by his followers and detractors alike. Despite this, rarely does one see a balanced approach to the life and ideas of the man who searched for the "one best way". In a detailed biography of Taylor, discussing his views on management, KANIGEL, runs through the influences on Taylor's later ideas, the experiments and results that came out of scientific management, and a detailed examination of Taylor's influence. For anyone seeking to understand today's employment relations system, this book is essential. Taylor laid the groundwork for what

was to become management by objectives, total quality management, pay for performance, job analysis, job design, and all the other key elements of human resource management.

PFEFFER's book makes a plea for managers to understand that people are the greatest source of competitive advantage. Writing at a time when US corporations were under attack from Japanese corporations, Pfeffer focuses on Japanese work methods and reward systems, and makes a plea for a more collective styled industrial relations system in the US. In particular, Pfeffer focuses on how the quality movement holds real promise for companies to create cultures were they can gain the most from their workers. Management must establish the right vision, and the right heroes and language, and keep with them over time if they are establish a culture that encourages new ideas, committed workers, and a sustainable competitive advantage. Despite its age, the current problems of the Japanese economy and its unsustainable employment practices, and a number of historical inaccuracies, the book is well worth a careful reading if one wants to understand the fundamental requirements of a human resource strategy to get the best out of people.

BLYTON & TURNBULL's edited collection of essays from top researchers in the field of human resource management is still relevant today. The key issues covered are, "what is the role of human resource management?" and, "what are the current issues confronting the profession today?" This book does not cover the legal issues around hiring and firing employees, but focuses on key organizational trends such as empowerment, organizational culture, just-in-time manufacturing systems, flexibility, decentralized decision making, and new technology. The book also covers some standard issues such as reward systems, management attitudes to human resource departments, supervisory management, and the link between human resources, strategy, and competitive advantage. The last two sections of the book are the weakest parts as they cover political and esoteric areas such as trade union views of human resource management and human resources as metaphor, myth, and morality. As a resource the book is useful for practitioners to familiarize themselves with some of the key debates and theoretical issues in the field. It is not a "how to" manual but does provide coverage of some important research studies that are still as relevant today as when they were written. It should not be seen as a stand-alone resource, but should be used in conjunction with some of the legal texts covered here and a few "how to" manuals such as Pfeffer or EDWARDS & EWEN.

SISSON's classic work in personnel management is one of the most comprehensive guides to personnel management today. The book is a blend of theory and practice, although it is based upon UK experiences and may not be as useful for non-British practitioners. The first four parts of the book are the best and the most universal. These cover a number of theoretical and practical issues such as recruitment, work design, appraisal, training, and equal opportunities. The strength of this book lies in the integration of employment relations into the overall strategy of the workplace. Much like Pfeffer's work, Sisson (and the authors of each chapter) seek to develop strategies to get the best out of people in the work environment. As such this book integrates general personnel management theories and practice into broader issues such as organizational culture, strategy, structure, and the general working environment. The weakest parts of the book are the last two sections covering more politicized issues like trade unions, worker participation, and the gender pay gap. These chapters could have been replaced with essays on reward systems and bargaining, resulting in a more rounded book. The final section, which covers worker participation, suffers from the general bias towards worker participation schemes that is found in academia, despite a large amount of evidence that illustrates that they neither work nor produce a more satisfied and productive workforce.

Edwards & Ewen's book on 360-degree feedback has become one of the most influential models for executive performance review. Following from Pfeffer's idea that the workforce is the organization's most important resource and source of competitive advantage, Edwards & Ewen argued that, as teamwork and empowerment have become more prevalent, organizations are now turning to "360-degree feedback" – a multi-perspective approach including feedback from peers, customers, supervisors, and those who work for the employee. This book is a useful "how to" guide based upon 20 years of field research. The book runs through the "dos" and "don'ts" of 360-degree feedback, and is useful for both unionized and non-unionized environments, and environments with a variety of team-based work structures and different ethnic backgrounds.

DAVIES & FREEDLAND's overview of the UK's legal environment reflects the other side of employment relations. With the deregulation of labour markets, a plethora of legal rules and procedures must be followed if one is to avoid running foul of the law when it comes to difficult employment relations issues like hiring, promotion, discipline, and dealing with trade unions. This book provides not only a detailed analysis of current legal trends but also provides a detailed historical background to the development of employment law in the UK. Given the nature of common law, this book will have some relevance for non-UK-based academics but the move to a more legalistic approach to employment relations worldwide will require the practitioner to supplement the "how to" best practice books with their own country-specific legal text.

OLSON provides a frightening glimpse into the world of American employment law – in particular the 1991 Civil Rights Act. Running through a number of case studies, Olson argues that the law is not only having unforeseen effects, but that it is crippling employment relations within the workplace. He documents how anti-discrimination law has actually worsened relations between men and women in the workplace. The fundamental issue is whether employers have the right to "hire at will". Olson concludes that employers do have this right, but that employers are constrained by law from removing non-performing (and in some cases dishonest) employees, and as a result he argues for the return of the "hire or fire at will" doctrine. This book highlights the unforeseen consequences of the law on the workplace and is worth having as it demonstrates the clear system principles highlighted by Dunlop in a way that Dunlop would have never foreseen.

MICHAEL BEVERLAND

See also High performance work systems, Human resource management, Organizational culture

Employee share-ownership plans

Blasi, Joseph R. and Douglas L. Kruse, "The New Owners", *Journal of Employee Ownership Law and Finance*, 3/3 (1991): 129–52
Chaplinsky, Susan and Greg Niehaus, "The Role of ESOPs in Takeover Contests", *Journal of Finance*, 49/4 (1994): 1451–70
Conte, Michael A. and Douglas Kruse, "ESOPs and Profit Sharing Plans: Do They Link Employee Pay to Company Performance", *Financial Management*, 20/4 (Winter 1991): 91–100
Klein, Katherine J. and Rosalie J. Hall, "Correlates of Employee Satisfaction with Stock Ownership: Who Likes an ESOP Most?", *Journal of Applied Psychology*, 73/4 (1988): 630–38
Kumbhakar, Subal C. and Amy E. Dunbar, "The Elusive ESOP-Productivity Link: Evidence from United States Firm-Level Data", *Journal of Public Economics*, 52/2 (1993): 273–83
McElrath, Roger G. and Richard L. Rowan, "The American Labor Movement and Employee Ownership: Objections to and Uses of Employee Stock Ownership Plans", *Journal of Labor Research*, 13/1 (1992): 99–119
Scholes, Myron S. and Mark A. Wolfson, "Employee Stock Ownership Plans and Corporate Restructuring: Myths and Realities", *Financial Management*, ESOP special issue, 19/1 (Spring 1990): 12–28
Swaine, Kieron, "Public Policy and Employee Ownership: Designing Economic Institutions for a Good Society", *Policy Sciences*, 26/4 (1993): 289–315

The references given here cover some of the different topics associated with employee share-ownership plans (ESOPs). All the references relate to the US, because the existing literature and debate has mainly focused on the US experience, although ESOPs also exist in other countries. Naturally, some of the issues covered are more pertinent than others when different legislative and institutional settings are considered.

SWAINE is a useful reference on the role of Louis Kelso and Russell Long in the appearance of ESOPs in the US legislative agenda until 1989. It contains an overall introduction to the several types of ESOPs and how they are used in practice, covering issues like dividends, voting rights and representation, inclusiveness, decision making, and economic performance. Moreover it lists some criticisms of ESOPs, namely that "the legal design of ESOPs entrenches and benefits managers at great risk and expense to the average employee". Finally, it has some good comments and suggestions for ESOPs redesign, "endorsing Blasi's proposal of tax credit provision for those companies that would use ESOPs as a 'serious' tool for labour-management cooperation".

How meaningful has the recent growth in employee ownership been? Using their list that gives the top 1000 companies by amount of employee ownership in all stock exchanges, BLASI & KRUSE provide evidence of the extent of employee ownership in publicly owned companies in the US. Here, they summarize their major findings and draw our attention to some dilemmas that employee ownership growth (about 50 per cent of which is imputed to ESOPs) presents to the actors involved.

Does this ownership have any corresponding representation rights and, given the employees' increased risk exposure, what will be the role of employees informed representatives? How will the existence of employee shareholders affect other shareholders behaviour? Will significant employee ownership make a difference in profits and productivity? What actions should the government take given the potential influence of employee ownership in several important areas?

Will unions still have a role in firms with democratically structured ESOPs? McELRATH & ROWAN acknowledge that ownership has rarely been accompanied by control and so unions remain the only reliable form of independent representation for workers. Union criticisms of ESOPs are given. These concern the elimination of important employee benefit plans and the subversion of the collective bargaining process. Although some unions have taken a more proactive stance concerning employee ownership, "in many instances they only react to management and employee initiatives in the face of imminent plant closures or demands for wage concessions". ESOPs can still be a useful tool for unions and "union involvement in the structuring of ESOPs can reduce the likelihood of their use to benefit management and outside investors to the detriment of nonmanagement employees".

The productivity gains expected from ESOPs and profit-sharing plans are based on the assumption that they provide positive feedback from company performance to nonmanagerial pay. CONTE & KRUSE argue that these compensation systems do this only weakly, if at all. Employees in most companies already benefit from good company performance through pay rises or increased availability of overtime work. So the relevant question is whether ESOPs relate nonmanagerial compensation to company performance more than already occurs with the traditional compensation system. They conclude that they raise the sensitivity of the overall compensation package, but only slightly. This link between pay and performance for ESOPs is uncertain.

Can firms with ESOPs expect to experience significant increases in productivity? The existing empirical evidence is mixed, although it emphasizes the importance of employee participation in decision making. Although KUMBHAKAR & DUNBAR do not control for the level of participation in decision making, their model specification separates ESOP effects, if any, from other factors that might mask the true ESOP effect. They control for firm- and time-specific effects, allow for factor shares to change over time, and finally they use the age of the ESOP as the relevant variable capturing the ESOP effect on productivity. These results suggest a positive relationship between the presence of an ESOP and firm's productivity. Despite allowing for the control of some important aspects, their work reveals that the production function approach does not account for the qualitative aspects of ESOPs: how, why, and by whom they are settled.

Are there some ESOPs characteristics that enhance employee motivation? Are all the employees equally satisfied with stock ownership? Without ignoring the evidence produced on the association between motivation/productivity and the existence of ESOPs KLEIN & HALL propose and test a model of individual employee satisfaction with employee ownership. Their results suggest that financial rewards are important but values and practices (both from employees and management) matter

too. Moreover, a close relation between an individual's general satisfaction with the company and satisfaction with the ESOP seems to exist, and company and individual-level variables contribute substantially to the prediction of ESOP satisfaction. In conclusion, ESOPs can influence employees' attitudes, either through their financial implications or through their influence on, or affinity with, management practices or cultural values.

SCHOLES & WOLFSON showed that tax provisions were not the primary motivation in ESOP establishment, especially in the case of large firms. Reviewing the tax and nontax motivations for adopting ESOPs, they took a closer look at the operational characteristics of ESOPs: contribution limits and risk-sharing considerations. The latter are emphasized and ESOPs are labelled as compensation arrangements adopted "at the expense of other more efficient forms (ignoring taxes), both for risk-sharing and incentive reasons". Taking a closer look at ESOPs' tax advantages, they conclude that "the differences between ESOPs and other compensation plans becomes restricted largely to the nontax dimensions". So the adoption of ESOPs ought to be related to their superiority as a takeover defence instrument.

ESOPs are believed to be effective deterrents of takeovers, and the Polaroid case has strengthened this belief. CHAPLINSKY & NIEHAUS explore the stock price reaction to ESOP announcements, but they go beyond it when they consider the possibility that the deterrent effect can be offset by the price effect (increase in the reservation price of the marginal shareholder) which will increase the probability of a bid. They therefore also compare the takeover incidence for targets with and without ESOPs. Their results show strong evidence of the important deterrent effect of ESOPs even after controlling for other defensive mechanisms.

LUIS MOURA RAMOS

Empowerment

Foster, Deborah and Paul Hoggett, "Change in the Benefits Agency: Empowering the Exhausted Worker", *Work, Employment and Society*, 13/1 (March 1999): 19–39

Harley, Bill, "The Myth of Empowerment: Work Organisation, Hierarchy and Employee Autonomy in Contemporary Australian Workplaces", *Work, Employment and Society*, 13/1 (March 1999): 41–66

Kerfoot, Deborah and David Knights, "Empowering the Quality Worker? The Seduction and Contradiction of the Total Quality Phenomenon" in *Making Quality Critical: New Perspectives on Organisational Change*, edited by Adrian Wilkinson and Hugh Willmott, London and New York: Routledge, 1995

Pickard, Jane, "The Real Meaning of Empowerment", *Personnel Management*, (November 1993): 28–33

Quinn, John J. and Peter W. Davies (editors), *Ethics and Empowerment*, Basingstoke: Macmillan, and West Lafayette, Indiana: Ichor Business Books, 1999

Sewell, Graham and Barry Wilkinson, "Empowerment or Emasculation? Shopfloor Surveillance in a Total Quality Organisation" in *Reassessing Human Resource Management*, edited by Paul Blyton and Peter Turnbull, London and Newbury Park, California: Sage, 1992

PICKARD is illustrative of how, by the early 1990s, there was growing interest in empowerment in the business community and among management theorists such as Tom Peters. This brief and introductory-level paper explores the meaning of empowerment via a series of case examples. Empowerment is identified as being embodied in an array of new management techniques representing the latest approach to employee involvement, and contributing to greater responsibility for employees. The author provides a sketch of empowering techniques, including movements to flatten organizational structures, more autonomous team working, and problem-solving groups. The author concludes that these moves have had a radical effect on the way people work and the analysis implicitly suggests that these moves have been beneficial for both employee job satisfaction and business performance.

Employee empowerment has been a prominent theme in contemporary, and inter-related, literatures on human resource management, total quality management (TQM), and just-in-time production systems. Using the financial services sector as an example, KERFOOT & KNIGHTS explores the contemporary pressure to devolve responsibility for quality to individuals. In so doing, they address empowerment as a tension and contradiction within quality programmes. Provocatively they identify a key tension in the lack of consultation of employees over the introduction of these practices, though "the employee is expected to submit unquestioningly to quality programmes as management policy, in terms of concepts of empowerment and continuous improvement, the demand is for an actively engaged subject".

The work of SEWELL & WILKINSON is illustrative of the radical critiques which present empowerment as domination and exploitation. Noting how employee self-management and responsibility for quality at the point of production within TQM systems are an essential feature of worker empowerment, they provide a critical exploration of mechanisms of individual control and surveillance. In a sophisticated and disturbing analysis they draw on Foucault's work on surveillance. Applying this to a detailed case study of an electronics company, they argue that new manufacturing and management techniques are underpinned by a substantial amount of personal surveillance of people at work. Empowerment is highly circumscribed by both electronic surveillance (vertical information and control systems) and peer group scrutiny (a horizontal disciplinary force). The reality of empowerment is the centralization of power and control, rather than the shift of the locus of power from management to the shopfloor ostensibly signalled by a growth in employee responsibility.

FOSTER & HOGGETT's findings on empowerment initiatives in the public sector are also sceptical of employee gains in highlighting on contemporary concerns about stress at work. Drawing on detailed case study material exploring the service quality framework in the UK benefits agency, their main contribution is in discussing how empowerment through the introduction of managerial job cuts, team working philosophies (accompanied by more individual performance-related reward and appraisal), and the devolution of responsibility has served only to increase levels of stress as workloads have grown. While employees reported improvements in the quality of life, they did so in a climate of heightened exploitation.

HARLEY goes some way in redressing the domination of case-study-based research in this area. He provides a succinct overview of the concept of empowerment from the perspective of both advocates and critics. Using data from the 1995 Australian Workplace Industrial Relations Survey he explores the extent to which empowering forms of work organization are present in Australian workplaces. While the empowerment thesis implies that the implementation of empowering practices renders workplace hierarchy no longer an important determinant of autonomy, Harley finds a growth in empowerment practices that is not correlated with autonomy. Rather there is a much stronger relationship between occupational status and self-reported autonomy; status providing more access to control and decision making. There is no major transformation taking place in workplaces. Drawing on the work of Warhurst and Thompson, Harley persuasively concludes that power is primarily exercised through organizational structures, which remain dominated by long-standing vertical divisions. Empowerment is therefore a modern myth and has little likelihood of becoming a reality as long as hierarchical structures remain a pervasive feature of contemporary organizations.

The 15 essays in QUINN & DAVIES collectively provide rich coverage of issues in the contemporary debate on empowerment. A focus on ethics is the route to wide-ranging discussions of power, control, and autonomy; the theory and practice of empowerment strategies; and broader issues of the role of business in society. Many of the essays consider the meaning and essence of empowerment, including a useful historical overview going back to the 1700s. In the section on business and society there is an exploration of the flaw in the assumption that business has a common purpose of generating shareholder value. Rather, it is business as a community of purpose, with moral and social aims as well as commercial ones, which is presented as embodying the prospect of real empowerment for employees. It is argued that there has been a rise in individuals' expectations of a more meaningful and empowered working life. Full membership of an organization requires a say in its purpose as mutual self-interest in pursuing improved business results will not develop the cooperation necessary to sustain a collective enterprise. There is a critical exploration of Foucauldian radical critiques. It is argued that empowerment is only partly exploitative and that virtue ethics provides a set of historically stable moral concepts against which the practice of empowerment, and indeed all business activities, may be judged. Virtue ethics requires that a number of questions be asked about social practices. That is, what is their contribution to the development of character and the identity of the community? What is the contribution of the firm to the common good? An underlying theme of this book is that empowerment practices need to be underpinned by an agenda of ethical standards if people at work are to take on new responsibilities as genuine stakeholders. Guidelines for this agenda are contributed to the ongoing debate. It is suggested that issues of employee voice and corporate governance should be centre stage in the sociopolitical discourse on rights and responsibilities which characterised the turn of the 20th century.

MARIA HUDSON

See also High performance work systems, Human resource management, Organizational learning, Stakeholder

End of ideology

Aron, Raymond, *The Opium of the Intellectuals*, London: Secker and Warburg, and New York: Doubleday, 1957

Bell, Daniel, *The End of Ideology: On the Exhaustion of Political Ideas in the Fifties*, Glencoe, Illinois: Free Press, 1960

Bell, Daniel, "The End of Ideology Revisited: Part 2", *Government and Opposition*, 23/3 (Summer 1988): 325–31

Brzezinski, Zbigniew and Samuel P. Huntington, *Political Power: USA/USSR*, New York: Viking, and London: Chatto and Windus, 1964

Crossman, R.H.S. (editor), *The God That Failed: Six Studies in Communism*, London: Hamish Hamilton, and New York: Harper, 1950

Lipset, Seymour Martin, *Political Man: The Social Bases of Politics*, revised edition, Baltimore: Johns Hopkins University Press, 1981; London: Heinemann, 1983

MacIntyre, Alasdair, "The End of the End of Ideology" in *Against the Self Images of the Age: Essays on Ideology and Philosophy*, New York: Schocken, and London: Duckworth, 1971

Mannheim, Karl, *Ideology and Utopia: An Introduction to the Sociology of Knowledge*, London: Routledge, and New York: Harcourt Brace, 1936; reprinted 1985

Rostow, W.W., *The Stages of Economic Growth: A Non-Communist Manifesto*, Cambridge: Cambridge University Press, 1960, New York: Cambridge University Press, 1965; 3rd edition 1990

Shils, Edward, "The End of Ideology?", *Encounter*, 5 (1955): 52–58

Waxman, Chaim I. (editor), *The End of Ideology Debate*, New York: Funk and Wagnalls, 1968

The "end of ideology" debate began in the mid-1950s with a provocative essay by SHILS. He thought it possible, perhaps even likely, that "ideology" – any system of ideas and beliefs that inspires and motivates people to act collectively – could become obsolete before the 20th century ended. Shils saw a coming consensus on political principles, especially in the West, centring on fundamental human rights and the economic protections afforded by the welfare state. It is important to note that the title of his essay ends with a question mark, for he raised it as a query and a possibility, not an assertion of fact.

So too did ARON, albeit in a somewhat different way. Aron viewed ideology – and the ideology of Marxism in particular – in much the same way that Marx viewed religion: as a drug ("opium") that distorted the vision and dulled the capacity for critical thinking of a particular social group. For Marx, the drugged group was the working class; for Aron, the intellectuals. Intellectuals in France and elsewhere have had an inordinate and unfounded faith in the power of reason and ideas to transform society for the better. This blinded them to facts that everyone else can see quite clearly: that the Soviet Union and other communist societies are repressive and retrograde; that they are ruled by bureaucrats and the secret police; that the ideology of Marxism-Leninism is a sham and a cover

for crimes committed in the name of "History" or "the People"; and so on. Still, Aron was not prepared to predict that ideology would end soon, and posed the end of ideology as a future possibility, not a present-day fact.

Matters were rather different with BELL (1960), who held that "political ideas" were already "exhausted" in the Western democracies in the 1950s and were becoming increasingly irrelevant in the Soviet Union and elsewhere. This was in part because the problems facing any affluent and advanced industrial society are essentially the same: the safety of the citizenry, economic prosperity, the protection of basic rights, providing a social safety net for the less fortunate members of the society, and so forth. To address such problems requires the sort of technical knowledge and expertise that ideology cannot supply; hence its increasing irrelevance. The social science disciplines – sociology, economics, psychology, political science, criminology, etc. – are, by contrast, concerned with producing the sort of knowledge needed to steer large and complex industrialized societies.

LIPSET largely agrees with Bell that in the Western democracies, at least, there has been a narrowing of differences between right and left, a tendency toward pragmatic accommodation and compromise, and a corresponding loss of interest in and allegiance to utopian visions of radical social and economic transformation as exemplified by revolutionary Marxism.

CROSSMAN is one of the early and admittedly anecdotal studies suggesting that Marxism was losing its appeal among intellectuals, many of whom had been disillusioned by Soviet purge trials in the 1930s, the Nazi-Soviet Pact, and the revelations about the crimes committed by Stalin. But this at most meant only that one ideology, not all ideologies, were in decline. As ideologies consist of ideas, they require people who deal in ideas – namely intellectuals – to create and sustain them. But because intellectuals are increasingly suspicious of, if not hostile to, Marxism, then that particular ideology is bound to lose its vitality and influence. Contributors to Crossman are distinguished and disillusioned former Marxists, including Ignazio Silone, Arthur Koestler, Andre Gide, Louis Fischer, Richard Wright, and Stephen Spender.

Drawing upon the distinction made by MANNHEIM, one might more plausibly argue that millenarian or messianic "utopia" could conceivably end, but not "ideology". The latter serves a legitimating function that any reasonably stable society requires to maintain the status quo and thus "ideology" cannot end.

Many other critics sounded similar themes. A good sampling of the arguments, pro and con, can be found in WAXMAN, which also includes a useful introduction and overview of the debate, along with Shils and portions of Lipset, Aron, Bell, and their critics.

Critics were quick to seize upon what they took to be the conceptual confusions and the shortcomings of arguments advanced in support of the end of ideology. MACINTYRE pointed out that for Bell and others, "ideology" was a synonym or stand-in for revolutionary Marxism and not for ideology as such. Thus what they took to be the end of ideology was really the end of the threat posed by revolutionary Marxism (which in the Soviet Union was rapidly ossifying into a cautious and even conservative force) and the triumph of a certain kind of rival ideology – namely, a liberalism that emphasized basic rights and welfare.

Claims about the ending of ideology were closely connected with what came to be called the "convergence" thesis, as advanced by ROSTOW, among others. All societies advance through several "stages of economic growth". As they modernize and become more affluent, they are subject to similar social and economic pressures. The demands or imperatives of modern societies, East and West, are making them increasingly similar. People everywhere are demanding more and better consumer goods, a modicum of prosperity, some degree of job security, and so on. In order to ensure their continuity and legitimacy, governments must adopt and pursue policies that promote these ends; hence the practical-political "convergence" of societies that are ostensibly ideologically opposed.

BRZEZINSKI & HUNTINGTON provide a sympathetic but critical evaluation of the "convergence" thesis. They concluded that full convergence of systems as different as the US and the Soviet Union was unlikely. They opted instead for the idea of parallel "evolution", in which the dominant ideology of each system would probably continue to play some legitimating role. Needless to say, neither champions nor critics of the convergence thesis foresaw the collapse and dissolution of the Soviet Union.

The late 1960s saw something like the revival of ideology – in the form of feminism, the New Left, the environmental or "green" movement, and other challenges to the status quo – and pretty much signalled the end of the debate. In the 1980s the resurgent conservatism of Mrs Thatcher in Britain and Ronald Reagan in America appeared to reconfirm the falsity of the claim that ideology was at an end. One noteworthy attempt to revisit – and revive – the end of ideology thesis is BELL (1988). The challenge has largely gone unheeded.

TERENCE BALL

See also Ideology

Endogenous growth theory

Denison, Edward F., *Why Growth Rates Differ: Postwar Experience in Nine Western Countries*, Washington, DC: Brookings Institution, 1967

Harrod, Roy, *An Essay in Dynamic Theory*, Oxford: Oxford University Press, 1939

Mankiw, Gregory, David Romer and David Weil, "A Contribution to the Empirics of Economic Growth", *Quarterly Journal of Economics*, 107/2 (1992): 407–38

Romer, Paul, "Increasing Returns and Long Run Growth", *Journal of Political Economy*, 94/5 (1986): 1002–37

Romer, Paul, "Capital Accumulation in the Theory of Long Run Growth" in *Modern Business Cycle Theory*, edited by Robert J. Barro, Cambridge, Massachusetts: Harvard University Press, 1989

Romer, Paul, "Endogenous Technical Change", *Journal of Political Economy*, 98 (supplement, part 2) (1990): S71–102

Romer, Paul, "The Origins of Endogenous Growth", *Journal of Economic Perspectives*, 8/1 (1994): 3–32

Scott, Maurice Fitzgerald, *A New View of Economic Growth*, Oxford: Clarendon Press, and New York: Oxford University Press, 1989

Solow, Robert, "A Contribution to the Theory of Economic Growth", *Quarterly Journal of Economics*, 70 (1956): 65–94

Solow, Robert, "Technical Change and the Aggregate Production Function", *Review of Economics and Statistics*, 39 (1957)

Solow, Robert, "Technological Progress, Capital Formation and Economic Growth", *American Economic Review*, 52 (1962): 76–86

Solow, Robert, *Growth Theory: An Exposition*, Oxford: Clarendon Press, and New York: Oxford University Press, 1970

Solow, Robert, "Perspectives on Growth Theory", *Journal of Economic Perspectives*, 8/1 (1994): 45–54

Swan, Thomas, "Economic Growth and Capital Accumulation", *Economic Record*, 32 (1956): 334–61

The theoretical progress that shaped contemporary debates on endogenous growth theory began with the work of HARROD in the late 1930s. He sought to discover whether a national economy could find a steady state growth path over time, without imbalances in the various sectors causing cyclical fluctuations. His quest for a clearer understanding of the dynamics of economic growth was replicated quite independently by Evsey Domar and their results became standard fare as the Harrod–Domar growth model in several generations of textbooks on economic principles.

The search for the principles underlying economic growth gathered momentum in the work of Robert Solow, who published a series of important papers in the 1950s (SOLOW 1956 and 1957). He retained, in his theoretical approach, important elements of the neoclassical one-sector model, such as a fixed savings coefficient and a labour force experiencing exponential growth. However, he went on to replace the conventional fixed-proportion production function with a much more flexible substitution between factors of production, capital, and labour. His theoretical approach was strongly influenced by his empirical studies of the growth of the US economy between 1909 and 1949, in which he discovered that the real output per worker had doubled with technological change accounting for 87.5 per cent of the growth rate and the balance attributable to capital growth.

The resultant model, demonstrated again independently by SWAN, allowed both the warranted rates of growth of the Harrod–Domar model and a natural rate of economic growth to coexist, through the modification of the proportions of capital to labour. This, he suggested, allowed for the existence of a long-run growth path, which resolved the Harrod–Domar problem that what they called an equilibrium rate of "warranted" growth could only be achieved if savings were equal to investment in any given time period, leaving the economy on a "knife edge" between success or market failure.

What became Solow's "baseline" theory was predicated on the assumption that economic growth took the form of a labour-augmented technological progress, in which technology is an exogenous factor. He went on to propose (SOLOW 1962, 1970 and 1994) that most growth is determined by extra-economic factors and is therefore not dependent on economic policy for the progress of science and technology. In essence technology was both an exogenous and a public good and he was pessimistic about the ability of any factor other than what he called raw improvements in technology to boost economic growth. It is now generally accepted that Solow's decision to so characterize technological progress was forced upon him by the technical limitations of the available econometric and computational tools.

The development of the infrastructure for a neoclassical, technology-based, economic growth model was accompanied by DENISON's parallel search for accounting identities that would explain why, when formal input–output analysis was applied to national accounts, a residual appeared that could not be explained through links to a given input. As a consequence the notion of technological progress came to the fore, together with the realization that the relationship between such progress and human capital, as exemplified by educational factors, might well be worth exploring.

More recent work, notably that of MANKIW, ROMER & WEIL, has extended and reformulated the original Solow–Swan model. Their work allocates a very important role to human capital and to education's share of national product. They treat human and physical capital as symmetrical. They also allow for the increasing importance of education as a factor that both adds to accumulation and slows down diminishing returns. Their parameter estimates for the production function also suggest a much larger return to physical capital than Solow's original findings.

The pathbreaking studies associated with ROMER (1986 and 1989) and SCOTT, which led in the 1990s to the development of endogenous growth theory, is the final link in the theoretical chain. Romer in particular admits that his work is grounded in the tradition that began with Solow, and that his earlier studies tracked the neoclassical approach. He took the argument a stage further, however, by attempting to model for both the exogenous residual and what he called "private provision", the fact that technological progress, by which is meant innovation-driven change, is also the result of a whole range of investment decisions taken by firms and private individuals.

By 1990 technological innovation had been identified by ROMER (1990 and 1994) as the more direct source of growth, dependent, in turn, on the available resources for research and development (R&D). Capital took the role of a set of intermediate goods, the sums of which increased as R&D efforts deepened. Drawing on the work of Lucas, his teacher at Chicago, Romer went on to argue that although physical capital might still be subject to diminishing returns, search and discovery actually add to knowledge capital.

The notion of proprietary capital and its effects upon the "social product of investment" also raises some serious problems. In Romer's view resultant externalities act as wedges between the social returns realized by the economy and the private returns accruing to private investors. Consequently, the advance of knowledge – an increasingly important increment in the growth of total factor productivity – depends very urgently on a widening flow of other forms of investment as a political strategy. The result sees contemporary endogenous growth theory located in two dimensions, with one concentrated upon direct returns to R&D and the other reflecting upon the wide range of channels whereby investment can influence total factor productivity.

ALAN WILLIAMS

See also Growth, Innovation

Energy politics

Baumgartner, Thomas and Atle Midttun (editors), *The Politics of Energy Forecasting*, Oxford: Clarendon Press, and New York: Oxford University Press, 1987

Cottrell, Fred, *Energy and Society: The Relation between Energy, Social Change, and Economic Development*, New York: McGraw Hill, 1955

Jahn, Detlef, *New Politics in Trade Unions: Applying Organization Theory to the Ecological Discourse on Nuclear Energy in Sweden and Germany*, Aldershot, Hampshire: Dartmouth, 1993

Jasper, James M., *Nuclear Politics: Energy and the State in the United States, Sweden, and France*, Princeton, New Jersey: Princeton University Press, 1990

Price, Terence, *Political Electricity: What Future for Nuclear Energy?*, Oxford and New York: Oxford University Press, 1990

Robinson, J.B., "Apples and Horned Toads: On the Framework-determined Nature of the Energy Debate", *Policy-Science*, 15 (1982): 23–45

Rudig, Wolfgang, *Anti-Nuclear Movements: A World Survey of Opposition to Nuclear Energy*, Harlow, Essex: Longman, 1990

Touraine, Alain *et al.*, *Anti-nuclear Protest: The Opposition to Nuclear Energy in France*, Cambridge and New York: Cambridge University Press, 1983

Useem, B. and M.N. Zald, "From Pressure Group to Social Movement: Organizational Dilemmas of the Effort to Promote Nuclear Power", *Social Problems*, 30/2 (1982): 144–56

JASPER is a comparison of energy politics and policies in the US, Sweden and France. It presents social movements, the political and economic elite, and unorganized citizens as actors in the field of energy politics. It is supported by extensive empirical data on the development of national energy politics (interviews with energy political decision makers and activists in the US, Sweden, and France) and argues that the direction and implementation of energy politics and policy resides in the hands of a small elite of experts in technology and politicians.

JAHN is a comparison of trade union politics in Sweden and Germany with a special emphasis on national energy politics. This is an empirical study based on content analysis of trade union newspapers and periodicals. It shows clear differences between Swedish and German labour organizations concerning energy politics and policies. It also contains a theoretical elaboration and a discussion of the place of occupational interests in political systems.

PRICE provides an analysis of energy politics from the point of view of the nuclear energy industry. It is an attempt to correct public perceptions of nuclear energy. It discusses the mechanisms of the antinuclear lobby, political campaigning, and decision making on national energy systems as well as the political consequences of public access to reliable information in countries that have engaged in nuclear energy projects. The book contains several examples of energy political controversies where there have been attempts to acquire political support from the public.

ROBINSON is an important text for understanding the energy political debate. The article analyses the public discussion that has occurred since the statement made by Amory Lovins about the two alternatives of future energy policies: the hard path and the soft path. It shows that public energy for political debate is constrained by conceptual and value-related frameworks, which explains why there is so little advancement in that debate.

RUDIG is an account of the energy political role of antinuclear movements based on empirical materials collected from 36 countries. It identifies the origins of opposition to nuclear power in expert dissent, from which it has spread widely in the form of grassroots activity. Rudig blends political analysis and theory with a detailed account of the growth and activities of individual antinuclear organizations.

TOURAINE reports on a study on the political, societal and cultural role of the antinuclear movement in France. It addresses extraparliamentary political forces in energy politics. Touraine applies the sociological intervention method developed in order to study social movements and conflict over the control of the historicity of entire nations. The method and its use are explained in detail in the book. The failure of the French antinuclear movement to develop into a national political force is discussed thoroughly.

USEEM & ZALD describes the metamorphosis of a powerful energy political actor into a social movement (with environmental concerns). The article exploits the theory of resource mobilization in its description of this movement.

COTTRELL provides an important insight into the social, cultural and political regulation of energy supply. It is a classic of social scientific theory on energy supply systems. It contains an historical account of the development of energy conversion technologies. Unlike the standard technological accounts of modernization in the energy sector, Cottrell does not view the extent of freedom from material constraints as directly proportional to the rate of energy available but instead sees social and material development to higher levels of energy consumption as a process of adopting new types of material constraints in the place of older ones.

BAUMGARTNER & MIDTTUN is a critical analysis of the promotion of the growth of energy supply and demand by political means. It is a collection of articles based on empirical studies of energy forecasting and its use in energy supply planning and politics in Western industrialized countries. It shows that (a) construction of detailed and reliable models for the need of unambiguous information of future development of the energy demand is impossible, and (b) as a rule, national

energy forecasts show a remarkably higher level of energy consumption than that of the realized consumption. The book contains a discussion about the relations between public energy forecasting, capacity construction, and actual level of energy consumption.

Ismo Kantola

See also Electricity industry, Energy supply

Energy supply

Baumgartner, Thomas and Atle Midttun (editors), *The Politics of Energy Forecasting: A Comparative Study of Energy Forecasting in Western Europe and North America*, Oxford: Clarendon Press, and New York: Oxford University Press, 1987

Cottrell, Fred, *Energy and Society: The Relation between Energy, Social Change, and Economic Development*, New York: McGraw Hill, 1955

Georgescu-Roegen, Nicholas, *The Entropy Law and the Economic Process*, Cambridge, Massachusetts: Harvard University Press, 1971

Hughes, Thomas, *Networks of Power: Electrification in Western Society, 1880–1930*, Baltimore: Johns Hopkins University Press, 1983

Martínez-Alier, Juan, *Ecological Economics: Energy, Environment, and Society*, Oxford and New York: Blackwell, 1987

Melosi, Martin V., *Coping with Abundance: Energy and Environment in Industrial America*, Philadelphia: Temple University Press, and New York: Knopf, 1985

Myllyntaus, Timo, *Electrifying Finland: The Transfer of Technology in to a Late Industrialising Economy*, Basingstoke: Macmillan, and Helsinki: ETLA, 1991

Wall, Göran, *Exergy: A Useful Concept*, Gothenburg: Physical Resource Theory Group, Chalmers University of Technology, 1986

HUGHES is a unique comparative history of the evolution of modern electric power systems. He stresses and demonstrates the importance of culture in the development of technology, and uses empirical material from North America, Europe, and, to some extent, China. Hughes demonstrates that the development of modern energy supply systems is an outcome of combinations of technical expertise, economic means, and political power by a relatively small elite whose intentions happen to merge with favourable social and cultural conditions.

GEORGESCU-ROEGEN is an insightful classic about the relations of physics to economics in the energy sector, and the social meanings of energy. The work is based on the concept of entropy and its relation to reproduction of value in socioeconomic systems. Physically, energy and matter can neither be consumed nor produced. From the point of view of economics, energy supply should be conceived as a qualitative change of energy capable of producing social value convertible further into a form that can be indicated by means available in economics.

COTTRELL is an early and important demarcation of the difference between technical and sociological views to energy supply. It is a classic of social scientific theorizing on energy supply systems. It contains an historical account of the development of energy conversion technologies. Contrary to the standard technological accounts of modernization in the energy sector, Cottrell does not view the extent of freedom from material constraints as directly proportional to the rate of energy available but sees, instead, the social and material development to higher levels of energy consumption as a process of adoption of new types of material constraints in the place of older ones.

BAUMGARTNER & MIDTTUN provides a critical analysis of the promotion of growth in energy supply. It is a collection of articles based on empirical studies of energy forecasting and its use in energy supply planning and politics in the Western industrialized countries. It shows that (a) construction of detailed and reliable models for the need of unambiguous information of future development of the energy demand is impossible, and (b) as a rule national energy forecasts show a remarkably higher level of energy consumption than that of the consumption that actually occurs. The book contains a discussion about the relations of public energy forecasting, capacity construction, and actual level of energy consumption.

MELOSI provides an analysis of the historical development of energy supply systems in the US, an environment of abundant energy sources. He states that rational and environmentally sound energy supply planning has been impeded in the US by the fact that the abundance of available energy has made it difficult to achieve political consensus about how to proceed to solve problems created by excessive and uncontrolled use of energy.

WALL defines energy supply as control of entropy. The useful energy – the part of energy that is not lost to entropy during energy conversions – is called exergy. The sociological point of the exergy approach is that success in meeting the demand for energy efficiency depends crucially on the structure and organization of the communities (local, national, or global) under evaluation. The book includes an extensive bibliography of studies on exergy and entropy in engineering, economics, and social science.

MYLLYNTAUS serves as an example of more objectivist than constructionist accounts on the history and meaning of electricity to a rapidly modernizing society. While constructionist approaches like Hughes and Baumgartner & Midttun explain technological development as a process initiated and controlled by powerful social agents, objectivists like Myllyntaus see technological development as a unique phenomenon and a part of the overall economic, cultural, and political development of the society. It is a success story of the transfer of a new technology to a small country without losing control of the national economy to the multinational companies providing that technology, which is, according to Myllyntaus, a challenge still unresolvable for many developing countries.

MARTÍNEZ-ALIER provides a vivid and thorough review of the classics of theoretical and visionary thought on how to organize energy supply for the whole society. He confines the timespan of the ideas presented from the establishment of thermodynamics in the 1860s to Hayek's critique of standard economics in the 1940s. The book not only familiarizes the reader with the classical ideas of energetics from Jevons to Amartiya Sen but it also exposes the ideas of Max Weber and Karl Marx and their followers on how to succeed in meeting with the demand of energy in future societies. Despite its title, the book can be regarded more as a sociological one than one of economics, because it assumes that economics lacks a theory of value, especially when dealing with problems of energy supply. Consequently, the writer holds that the economy is inseparable from politics. "Ecological economics" is in opposition to economics and close to human ecology. According to Martinez-Alier (taking the same line as Georgescu-Roegen) energy analysis and conventional economic analysis give contradictory judgements of the same process.

ISMO KANTOLA

See also Energy politics

Engels, Friedrich 1820–1895

German-born English sociologist, historian and philosopher

Arthur, Christopher J. (editor), *Engels Today: A Centenary Appreciation*, Basingstoke: Macmillan, and New York: St Martin's Press, 1996

Carver, Terrell, *Friedrich Engels: His Life and Thought*, London: Macmillan, 1989; New York: St Martin's Press, 1990

Henderson, W.O., *The Life of Friedrich Engels*, 2 vols, London: Cass, 1976

Henderson, W.O., *Marx and Engels and the English Workers and Other Essays*, London: Cass, 1989

Hunley, J.D., *The Life and Thought of Friedrich Engels: A Reinterpretation*, New Haven, Connecticut: Yale University Press, 1991

Kircz, Joost and Michael Loewy (editors), special issue on "Friedrich Engels: A Critical Centenary Appreciation", *Science and Society*, 62/1 (1998)

Levine, Norman, *The Tragic Deception: Marx contra Engels*, Santa Barbara, California: Clio, 1975

Marcus, Steven, *Engels, Manchester and the Working Class*, New York: Random House and London: Weidenfeld and Nicolson, 1974

Rigby, S.H., *Engels and the Formation of Marxism: History, Dialectics, and Revolution*, Manchester: Manchester University Press, 1992

Sayers, Janet, Mary Evans and Nanneke Redclift (editors), *Engels Revisited: New Feminist Essays*, London: Tavistock, 1987

Steger, Manfred B. and Terrell Carver (editors), *Engels after Marx*, Manchester: Manchester University Press, and University Park: Pennsylvania State University Press, 1999

The literature on Engels is divided in a complex way between those who read Engels against Marx, either as intellectual inferior and disciple or secret antagonist, and those who investigate Engels's own originality and individuality. If the literature of the last 25 years of the 20th century is examined, it is possible to say that there has been a considerable improvement of biographical knowledge at the same time as there have been changes in the focus of debate. In the 1970s the "dichotomous" thesis emerged with LEVINE: Engels was inferior to Marx and may have illegitimately replaced Marx's own ideas with "Engelsism", with perhaps devastating historical consequences. Around 1990, three new book-length studies of Engels appeared and took up the challenge of investigating and responding to Levine's thesis. There was no clear outcome to the debate, but there was general agreement that the individuality of Engels's work should be respected. The latter half of the 1990s was dominated by three major new collections on Engels – ARTHUR with eight contributions, KIRCZ & LOEWY with eleven, and STEGER & CARVER thirteen – and the focus of discussion is now clearly on Engels' own individual contribution. These studies are still, if in different ways, in the process of assessing the degree of independence of Engels from Marx, and what the consequences of this independence might have been.

Gustav Mayer's classic (1934) biography of Friedrich Engels (available in an abridged English edition of 1969) has been superseded by a number of works published over the last 25 years, especially HENDERSON (1976) (and, subsequently, HENDERSON (1989), which draws on material previously published in German and gives more detail on Engels' business life and Marx's visits to Manchester); also by the more recent CARVER, which also contains a still useful "Guide to Further Reading" (pp.261–264).

The revival of recent interest in Engels in English began, in the mid-1970s, with books which in their own ways looked for what distinguished Engels from Marx. MARCUS concentrates, with much literary flourish, on the experience of Engels as reflected in his account of the industrial revolution on the ground. Henderson (1976) provides a more empirically accurate biography, and shows the specific political involvement and effectiveness of Engels. LEVINE seeks to define the genuine and true humanistic theoretical Marxism (continued in Lukacs, Gramsci and Korsch) against the very crude evolutionist Engelian tradition which had usurped it and which had subsequently corrupted the communist movement.

The collection of seven contributions edited and introduced by SAYERS, EVANS & REDCLIFT reveals the continuing importance of Engels's writing, as opposed to Marx's, on feminism and gender theory for second wave feminism. Most of the essays acknowledge the significance of Engels's contribution, but some of them, particularly Evans', suggests that (as in the case of communism) his influence has not been a particularly valuable one.

CARVER was the first of three independent studies that debated the Levine thesis. Carver presents a detailed analysis of Engels's life and work which takes Engels to be a wayward disciple of Marx, and at important junctures fosters the impression that his work had Marx's approval when it did not. HUNLEY states in a dramatic way what he calls the "dichotomous portrait" (dealt with in chapter three) and then attempts to refute this systematically in the subsequent five chapters. He considers Engels's work to run parallel to, and enhance, that of Marx and believes that the two men had a genuine intellectual partnership. RIGBY begins by summing up the

dichotomy debate and proceeds to argue that both Marx and Engels were contradictory in their writings and open to various interpretations. Rigby attempts to refute Carver's analysis of Engels's supposedly systematic distortion of Marx by showing that Marx's ideas did not form a coherent whole in any case. He also makes the point that, in general, theorists are not good theorists about their own work (p.163).

The centenary of Engels's death, 1995, saw attempts to gather new assessments, but none were able to shed the constraints of the "dichotomy" debate. ARTHUR's edited collection, a centenary "appreciation", discusses democracy (Carver), realism (Collier), materialism (Sayers), nature (Benton), economics (Arthur), and gender (Vogel): issues which, the introduction argues, are still live. The essays are serious efforts at assessing Engels's individual contribution to Marxist theorising on the current problems posed in these domains.

KIRCZ & LOEWY, also a centenary "appreciation", includes three essays on gender (Trat, Haug, Pelz), and others on such topics as anti-semitism (Kessler), agriculture (Bergmann), religion (Lowy), philosophy (Labica). These essays were designed as conference papers, and tend to be critical and to the point.

Contributors to STEGER & CARVER revisit the theme of the "dichotomy" again in very many different spheres. The introduction notes that this controversy has even become the motor of interest in Engels. The collection is divided into two parts, the first on philosophy and theory (seven essays, of which those by Carver and Rigby discuss again in more sophisticated vein the Marx-Engels "question"), the second on politics and social science (six essays including one on the nation (Forman), and one on gender (Gould)).

Carver's essay in Steger & Carver ends by pointing to the limitations of the "dichotomy" debate and suggests that this should come to an end: "research on Marx and Engels has barely begun", he concludes (p.35). Rigby's essay, which draws substantially from his book (and announces in any case a preference for Weber), emphasises the futility of the "dichotomy" argument and hails, "by reading for the best not the worst", the arrival of Engels into "mainstream historiography" (p.137).

MIKE GANE

See also Marx and Marxism

Enterprise culture

Burrows, Roger (editor), *Deciphering the Enterprise Culture: Entrepreneurship, Petty Capitalism and the Restructuring of Britain*, London and New York: Routledge, 1991

Carr, Patricia, "The Cultural Production of Enterprise: Understanding Selectivity as Cultural Policy", *Economic and Social Review*, 29/2 (1998): 133–55

Curran, James and Robert A. Blackburn (editors), *Paths of Enterprise: The Future of Small Business*, London and New York: Routledge, 1991

du Gay, Paul, "Enterprise Culture and the Ideology of Excellence", *New Formations*, 13 (1991): 45–61

Gibb, Allan A., "Enterprise Culture: Its Meaning and Implications for Education and Training", *Journal of European Industrial Training*, 11/2 (1987): 3–38

Keat, Russell and Nicholas Abercrombie (editors), *Enterprise Culture*, London and New York: Routledge, 1990

Miller, Peter and Nikolas Rose, "Governing Economic Life", *Economy and Society*, 19/1 (1990): 1–31

Reed, Mike, "Managing Quality and Organizational Politics: TQM as a Governmental Technology" in *The Politics of Quality in the Public Sector: The Management of Change*, edited by Ian Kirkpatrick and Miguel Martinez Lucio, London and New York: Routledge, 1995

CURRAN & BLACKBURN's edited collection represents a major trend in writing in the areas of enterprise culture and entrepreneurship: a privileging of small business as an analytical category. Difficulties attached to trying to define the concept of enterprise culture have often meant it has been sidelined in favour of the more accessible concept of small business. This approach is reflected in the introductory chapter that argues that enterprise culture – and attempts to create it – had little or no material impact on the restructuring of the British economy, and the rebirth of small business over the past 20 years. Adopting this position, the rest of the book focuses solely on a range of small-business issues, including employment, policy, ethnicity, and gender.

BURROWS' edited collection is similar in orientation to that of Curran & Blackburn. The introductory chapter overlaps significantly with that of Curran & Blackburn's book, and most of the following chapters cover a range of small-business issues. However, chapter two presents an analysis of enterprise culture and its relationship with government and small business. The suggestion put forward is that a variety of positions on enterprise culture can be identified. This leads to the proposition that we should be talking about enterprise culture*s* as opposed to enterprise culture. The chapter argues that government and small business have a different relationship to enterprise culture, and that these two kinds of relationship stand in opposition to each other.

GIBB also adopts a strong small-business orientation, but does not dismiss the concept of enterprise culture. He associates enterprise culture with a range of enterprising traits and activities, including risk taking and leadership. He argues that, across a group of people, individuals are likely to have a different mix and strength of these traits. However, leaving this variety aside, the way in which these traits will develop largely depends on the organizational circumstances of individuals. Although such characteristics may be exercised within a range of organizations, large and small, they are more likely to be cultivated within the context of independent business ownership. Thus, from this perspective, Gibb defines enterprise culture as a culture that supports the exercise and development of enterprising traits within the context of independent business ownership.

Arguably KEAT & ABERCROMBIE is one of the first texts to separate consideration of the concept of enterprise culture from small business. It is a welcome relief that not one of the chapters in the book focuses on small business per se. Instead, this book provides one of the most comprehensive examinations to date of the notion of enterprise culture. It presents an excellent analysis of the phenomenon of enterprise, which highlights how it is both a central organizing principle of the contemporary social order, as well as acting as a highly significant government device used to restructure British society. The book, comprising three sections, examines the dimensions of enterprise culture, assesses enterprise culture across Europe, and examines the notion of the sovereign consumer.

MILLER & ROSE present an excellent analysis of state activity in advanced liberal democratic societies, which is extremely useful in helping us to understand the role of the state in producing an enterprise culture. Drawing on Foucault's concept of "governmentality", it is suggested that rather than understanding attempts at reforming the state in enterprise culture as a simple *withdrawal* of intervention in favour of market forces, such reformation should be understood as a *change* in the form of intervention. Current state intervention actively promotes an ethic of enterprise, making use of government technologies that restructure and align the relationship between the state and the individual in enterprise terms. A programme of government such as that of enterprise culture involves shaping people along enterprise lines, and relies upon specific notions of how individuals should behave and think of themselves.

Adopting a similar approach, REED argues that the introduction of quality management into the public sector should be understood within the wider ideological and political context of attempts to create an enterprise culture. From Reed's perspective, quality management is one of the means by which the public sector is restructured along enterprise lines. Such restructuring involves the introduction of a range of practices that shape, regulate, and instrumentalize the behaviour and attitudes of public-sector employees. However, Reed argues that such enterprise strategies are never entirely successful when applied to public-sector organizations; and that attempts to align the values and attitudes of public-sector employees with those of the overall project of enterprise culture are likely to be imperfect and contested.

CARR, making use of Foucault's concept of "governmentality", argues that if we are to understand the concept of enterprise culture, it is vitally important that we have an appreciation of the centrality of "enterprising" individuals, and how they are cultivated to ensure the optimal performance of a market economy. Incorporating a notion of government into enterprise culture allows us to focus on the norms and strategies which enable the self-actualizing capacities of individuals to become aligned with and provide the basis for success in a market economy. As an illustration of this conceptualization of enterprise culture, Carr presents an analysis of the Irish small-business policy of selectivity, demonstrating how it aims to shape and regulate the personal capacities of entrepreneurs, aligning their choices with those of state authorities.

DU GAY argues that literature in the 1980s highlighted the important role that culture played in structuring the way people think, act, and feel in organizations. A key question was how could people's values and aspirations be aligned with those of the organization they worked in, so that pursuit of their own goals meant pursuit of the organization's goals. Defining the latter as "the search for excellence", du Gay identifies a similarity between the pursuit of excellence within organizations, and the broader project of enterprise culture. Enterprise, understood as the privileging of the private-sector business and the promotion of enterprising qualities, is a central structural element in both projects. The use of the language of enterprise in the excellence project establishes linkages and symmetries between organizations, which are concerned to maximize their performance, and government, which is concerned to maximize the performance of the economy.

PATRICIA CARR

See also Entrepreneur

Entrepreneur

Carter, Sara and Tom Cannon, *Women as Entrepreneurs: A Study of Female Business Owners, Their Motivations, Experiences and Strategies for Success*, London and San Diego: Academic Press, 1992

Chell, Elizabeth, Jean Haworth and Sally Brearley, *The Entrepreneurial Personality: Concepts, Cases and Categories*, London and New York: Routledge, 1991

Hobbs, Dick, *Doing the Business*, Oxford: Clarendon Press, and New York: Oxford University Press, 1988

Musson, Gill and Laurie Cohen, "Making Sense of Enterprise: Identity, Power and the Enterprise Culture" in *Small Firms, Enterprising Futures*, edited by Ram Monder, David Deakins and David Smallbone, London: Paul Chapman, 1997

Reynolds, Paul D., "Sociology and Entrepreneurship: Concepts and Contributions", *Entrepreneurship: Theory and Practice*, 16/2 (1991): 47–70

Scase, Richard and Robert Goffee, *The Entrepreneurial Middle Class*, London: Croom Helm, 1982

Schumpeter, Joseph A., *History of Economic Analysis*, London: Allen and Unwin, 1954

CARTER & CANNON looks at the successes and failures of women entrepreneurs. Despite its business-school approach, it does acknowledge the influence of the researchers on the interviewees, and although statistical data are drawn from respondents, the sample of women interviewed for the research upon which the text is based is not viewed as representative (nor, indeed, is it viewed as failing for not being representative). Thus it is methodologically sensitive and cautious. The reader is directed, in particular, to the chapters in which the women respondents define failure and their attitudes towards it, which are refreshingly frankly documented.

CHELL, HAWORTH & BREARLEY examine what is meant by the entrepreneurial personality, starting with the problem of definition. The text examines economists' perspectives, sociological and organizational perspectives, and psychologists' perspectives. They describe attempts to distinguish the entrepreneur from a manager, and from other business owners, and proceed with a set of characteristics that they test against their own research. Although not a sociological text, it provides an accessible account of related disciplines' approaches to this complex concept, and as a widely cited text it is therefore a valuable contribution to the field.

HOBBS stands in complete contrast to those around it, and for this reason, if no other, is worth including here. The text is an ethnography of entrepreneurship in the East End of London. It explores the locality and the culture of the area,

bringing out the mixture of people who live cheek by jowl and practice their entrepreneurial skills in this part of London. Hobbs describes the culture of the entrepreneur and, with a schematic typology, describes the entrepreneurs in terms of their competencies for us. His typology ranges from the "Client" and the "Grafter" via the "Jump Up Merchant" to the "Holding Elite". The legality of the activities of these entrepreneurs can at best be described as borderline. The text provides a rich picture of the ways of being and doing of entrepreneurs.

MUSSON & COHEN wanted to gain a perspective on what is meant by an enterprise culture, and so they looked at the discourse of some of those in small business. They were interested both in how an enterprise discourse is mobilized and internalized, through the talk of individuals, and in how sense can be made of it. The groups they studied were general practitioners and women who had moved from what they describe as self-employed status to entrepreneurial status. This chapter is included here as an alternative way of understanding the "entrepreneur" embedded in a particular socioeconomic context through the use of language.

REYNOLDS gives a valuable overview of sociological perspectives on socioeconomic systems, with a pertinent critique that locates the entrepreneur as actor rather than merely an individual with particular personal attributes. He directs our attention to formal and informal actors as key players, and throughout reminds the reader of the incessantly dynamic characteristics of the socioeconomic world. This paper asserts the importance of a sociological perspective as a necessary complement to those of other disciplines as we seek to understand entrepreneurs.

SCASE & GOFFEE set out to examine the reproduction of the petit bourgeoisie through an examination of the construction industry. They describe the research on which the text is based as qualitative and exploratory. Their tentative findings find a divide within middle-class workers based upon production rather than consumption. This might be seen to date the work, and it is included here more as an example of concerns of the early 1980s, in which class perspectives were more dominant, as were means of production. If the variety in the texts cited here points to an unsettled idea of "entrepreneur", Scase & Goffee's text illustrates that the idea was no less settled at the time this text was produced.

SCHUMPETER is an early discussion of entrepreneurs and their economic role. The text is in four parts. It is comprehensive, well indexed, and accessible. The parts give a historical account of economic development from early history to his "mere sketch" of modern developments. The treatment of "entrepreneur" benefits from historical discussion, and we should read this to understand Schumpeter's treatment of the entrepreneur as a crucial economic actor.

JILLIAN DUTTON

See also Enterprise culture, Intrapreneurship

Environment, external

Christensen, C. Roland, Kenneth R. Andrews, Joseph L. Bower, Richard G. Hamermesh and Michael E. Porter, *Business Policy: Texts and Cases*, 6th edition, Homewood, Illinois: Irwin, 1987

Donaldson, Thomas and Lee E. Preston, "The Stakeholder Theory of the Corporation: Concepts, Evidence, and Implications", *Academy of Management Review*, 20 (January 1995): 65–91

Fahey, Liam and V.K. Narayanan, *Macroenvironmental Analysis for Strategic Management*, St Paul, Minnesota: West, 1986

Kotler, Philip, *Marketing Management: Analysis, Planning, Implementation, and Control*, 9th edition, Englewood Cliffs, New Jersey and London: Prentice Hall, 1996

Porter, Michael E., *On Competition*, Boston: Harvard Business School Publishing, 1998

If early management writings are characterized by a preoccupation with life inside organizations (for example, the scientific work methods or human relations considerations that affected how efficiently and effectively objectives were achieved), later writings are notable for the emphasis placed on understanding the external environment – in particular, how developments within organizations are conditioned by and affect it. Both the significance that contemporary management theorists attach to, and the approach they take to, analysing organizations' external environments have clear connections to the application of systems theory to management and organizational studies. A great deal of modern management literature aims, at least in part, to suggest how best organizations can assess and "manage" their external environmental relationships as strategic plans are formulated and implemented. A number of these topics are addressed elsewhere in this volume (see, for example, the entries on Change management, Competitive strategy, Corporate strategy, Organizational learning). The readings referred to here have been selected to illustrate how the management literature typically conceptualizes the external environment. Three of the readings are taken from the strategic management literature, where the most general (and exhaustive) discussions of external environmental relations are found. One reading comes from the marketing literature, where external environmental awareness and analysis are seen as critical to organizational success. Another considers the significance of the stakeholder conception of the corporation for organization–environment relations.

CHRISTENSEN *et al.* define "the environment of an organization in business, like that of any other organic entity" as comprised of "the pattern of all the external conditions and influences that affect its life and development" (p.227). Like many others who approach external environmental analysis from a strategic planning/strategic management/business policy perspective, they identify four key categories of (potential) "environmental influences"; "they are technological, economic, social, and political in kind" (p.227). They also remind the reader that mapping key influences within these four domains raises important questions regarding the appropriate level(s) of analysis, as "the environmental influences relevant to strategic decision operate in a company's industry, the total business community, its city, its country, and the world" (p.227). Christensen *et al.* is particularly valuable for readers interested in considering how such forces do, and should, affect strategic decisions; both the text (which comprises approximately 15 per cent of the book's 940 pages) and the cases are concerned less with the environment *per se*, and more with its relative significance to strategic planning. Christensen *et al.* are careful to emphasize the importance of subjective and situation-specific factors in what would otherwise appear to be a highly systematic and rational process. They also are quick to note that "the general manager is responsible to multiple constituencies with conflicting needs and goals" (pp.vii–viii), and to consider the impact of competing external environmental forces upon the managers and the policies that they help to develop for their organizations. Christensen *et al.* argue that "the combination of objective and subjective elements, of economic and personal purposes, and of complex ethical and social responsibilities makes automatic outcomes impossible" and that corporate strategies "reflect judgement, aspiration, desire, and determination in ways which no theoretical model can prescribe" (p.x). This is not the only text to underscore the nondeterministic nature of external environmental forces, but the clarity of the writing and the relative brevity of the text make this an ideal choice for readers interested in exploring the significance of subjective considerations – the personal, human, variable nature of managers – in determining how external forces are viewed and taken into consideration as business policies are formulated, implemented, and revised over time.

FAHEY & NARAYANAN is useful for readers primarily concerned with the first stage in the sort of strategic planning process Christensen *et al.* describe; their concern is with how organizations conceive and go about understanding the environments in which they operate – environmental analysis. As they describe it, environmental analysis "has three basic goals": to "provide an understanding of current and potential changes taking place in the environment", to "provide important intelligence for strategic decision makers", and to "facilitate and foster strategic thinking in organizations" (p.3). Written "with the macroenvironmental analyst in mind – that is, the person who must confront the task of analysing the macroenvironment and make use of the analysis in the process of strategic decision making", this text is intended to be used by "both practicing managers and business management students" (p.xv). The authors acknowledge four limitations. Fahey & Narayanan aim "to provide a comprehensive and systematic approach to macroenvironmental analysis that is applicable to any type of organization" (p.xv), yet they note that "the text is slanted toward practice in large organizations", an orientation that they justify with their claim that "although small organizations need some form of environmental analysis, only in large organizations is the analysis necessary in its full breadth" (p.8). A second "limitation" might now be viewed as a strength of the book, given that over a decade has already passed since its publication. Fahey & Narayanan devote seven chapters to a discussion of the potential impacts of key external environmental forces (specifically, demographics, lifestyles, social values, the economic environment, technology, the political milieu, and the regulatory milieu), yet these discussions are deliberately not exhaustive. Instead, the authors focus on "the key ideas that analysts need to keep in mind as they engage in analysis of particular segments" (p.8) with helpful hints for scanning to identify, and the monitoring, forecasting, and assessment of changes in each of these areas. In a related point, the authors acknowledge that the same seven chapters are "primarily oriented to the domestic US economy", as important "cross-country differences" are "beyond the scope of the text" (p.8). Finally, the authors acknowledge that their text "is oriented toward practice more than toward theory", although the 25-page "Conceptual Overview" (chapter 2) presents a useful theoretical review that, among other things, indicates "key areas of linkage between environmental analysis and strategic management" (p.10). This chapter alone may suffice to introduce readers to key issues regarding the significance of the macroenvironment, and environmental analysis, to the firm.

The information that such environmental analysis provides is typically portrayed as an input to a decision-making process in which managers match organizational "qualifications" (positive and negative) with the challenges posed by the various external environmental forces; the strategies that this process produces thus "position" organizations in the environment (see Christensen *et al.*, p.227). The notion that this positioning should be used to obtain or maintain an advantage over (to compete with) others in the industry is central to much contemporary management writing. Indeed, Christensen *et al.* argue that "the aspect of the environment that most tangibly affects a company is the competitive environment of the industry or industries in which it does business" (p.231). This is perhaps not surprising given that PORTER, whose work has been described as defining "our fundamental understanding of competition and competitive strategy" (flyleaf), is one of Christensen's co-authors. As described by Porter, his work on competition has "sought to capture the complexity of what actually happens in companies and industries in a way that both advances theory and brings that theory to life for practitioners" (pp.1–2). Eleven of Porter's (single and co-authored) contemporary classic *Harvard Business Review* articles, two new pieces, and an introduction in which he describes how the works that are the fruits of his two-decade study of competition have evolved and are related, are presented in a 1998 review volume. Included among the former are the 1979 "How Competitive Forces Shape Strategy", which presents the often-cited "five-forces framework" designed to describe the basic forces upon which the state of competition in an industry depends. This influential article is presented in the first part of the book, which "addresses competition and strategy for companies, first at the level of a single industry and then for multi-business or diversified companies" (p.2). The second and third parts of the book address "the role of location in competition" and draw "on the frameworks in Parts I and II to address some important societal issues" (pp.2–3). There are those who would question whether it is true that "no company, and no country, can afford to ignore the need to compete" (p.1). There is no question, however, that the literature is replete with references to the centrality of competitive considerations to (Western) management thinking, and that any attempt to describe and consider the potential impacts of external environmental forces would be incomplete if it did not consider Porter's work, key elements of which are so usefully combined in this volume.

The preceding texts are notable for their focus on a macro-environment (also referred to as the "mega" or "meta" environment), which arguably affects all organizations in a given geopolitical context (even if it does not affect all of them similarly). Of course, such external forces frequently have different types and magnitudes of effects on different organizational functions, activities, managers, and decisions. In addition, both these and a range of other external actors and events are more-or-less salient for individual firms, leading some to speak of "micro" or "task" environments, which also require careful consideration. KOTLER brings the concepts and norms of the strategic management literature to bear in discussing the significance of the organization's environment to the marketing function, and the significance of the marketing environment to the organization more generally. Like others, he finds it useful to distinguish a set of "external actors and forces" "close to" the organization from a set of "larger societal forces" (pp.135–6). The former microenvironmental forces include suppliers, marketing intermediaries, customers, competitors, and various "publics" (groups with "an actual or potential interest in or impact on a company's ability to achieve its objectives", for example, financial institutions, media organizations, governmental bodies, citizen-action groups, and the general public; see pp.141–3). As defined by Kotler, key macroenvironmental forces include not only the four forces described in so much of the business policy literature (political/legal, economic, socio/cultural, and technological) but also key demographic considerations (for example, the size, geographic and age distribution, density, racial, ethnic and religious structure of the world's population, as well as mobility trends and changes in birth, marriage, and death rates) and aspects of the physical or natural environment (including the availability and cost of raw materials and energy). Given Kotler's focus on marketing considerations, readers unfamiliar with external environmental analysis might be tempted to confine themselves to more general treatments of the subject. Such a choice would be regrettable. Kotler's enumeration of external environmental forces clearly underscores the complexity and variety of forces with which managers in the same and different organizations may have to contend. In addition, Kotler provides numerous examples to illustrate their potential (direct and indirect) impacts upon the organization. Finally, his discussion of the external environment from a marketing management perspective (as opposed to his own more general descriptions of the marketing environment, for example, in chapter three of Gary Armstrong and Philip Kotler's 1994 *Principles of Marketing*, 6th edition) highlights the instrumental arguments that underlie, and the practical implications for managers of, exhortations to establish environmental monitoring programmes as part of larger management information systems.

Stakeholder theory provides another way of conceptualizing the "external environment". As described by DONALDSON & PRESTON, stakeholder theory "describes the corporation as a constellation of cooperative and competitive interests possessing intrinsic value" (p.66). Stakeholder theory is concerned with "persons or groups with legitimate interests" (p.68) in organizational activities; in particular, it focuses on the nature of their relationships with the organization. With this emphasis, the distinction between the internal and the external blurs, or is at least less significant; the membrane that forms the boundary between, and thus separates, the organizational organism and its environment is less important than the activities that span it. Donaldson & Preston point out that the "large and evolving literature" (p.66) devoted to exploring the nature of stakeholder-corporation relationships is characterized by the "different purposes, and therefore different validity criteria and different implications" (p.70) employed and drawn by its authors. Donaldson & Preston "critique and integrate important contributions" (p.65) of this literature, which they describe as, in turns, essentially descriptive/empirical, instrumental, and normative in nature. Implicit in most strategic management literature is the notion that managers "should" monitor and take into account external environmental forces – a normative argument typically advanced (if not always won) on instrumental rather than "moral" grounds. The important questions that Donaldson & Preston raise, and which others have gone on to ponder (see, for instance, the April 1999 edition of *The Academy of Management Review*) concerning the links that may exist between how managers (and management functions) do and should conceptualize and address external stakeholder interests have important implications for our understanding of external environmental relations more generally.

SARAH-KATHRYN MCDONALD

See also Business plans, Change management, Competitive strategy, Corporate strategy

Environmental audit

Barton, Hugh and Noel Bruder (editors), *A Guide to Local Environmental Auditing*, London: Earthscan, 1995
Business in the Environment, *EC Eco-management and Audit Scheme (EMAS): Positioning Your Business*, London: Business in the Environment, 1995
Collison, David J. and Rob H. Gray, "Auditors' Responses to Emerging Issues: A UK Perspective on the Statutory Financial Auditor and the Environment", *International Journal of Auditing*, 1/2 (1997): 135–49
Elkington, John, *The Environmental Audit: A Green Filter for Company Policies, Plants, Processes and Products*, London: SustainAbility/World Wide Fund for Nature, 1989
Gray, Rob H. and Don Stone, "Environmental Accounting and Auditing in Europe: Shooting the Breeze and Missing the Point?", *European Accounting Review*, 3/3 (1994): 581–90
Grayson, Lesley, *Environmental Auditing: A Guide to Best Practice in the UK and Europe*, Oxford: British Library Science Reference and Information Service, 1992
Hillary, Ruth, "Environmental Auditing: Concepts, Methods and Developments", *International Journal of Auditing*, 2/1 (1998): 71–85
International Auditing Practices Committee, *The Auditing Profession and the Environment*, New York: International Federation of Accountants, 1995
Power, Michael, "Expertise and the Construction of Relevance: Accountants and Environmental Audit", *Accounting, Organizations and Society*, 22/2 (1997): 123–46

Renger, Michael, *Environmental Audit: The Background, Benefits and Financial Implications*, London: Institute of Chartered Accountants in England and Wales, 1992

An environmental audit is generally regarded as an environmental management tool employed by organizations to facilitate improvements in their environmental performance. HILLARY argues, in a comprehensive analysis of the development of the term, that a single and universally accepted definition of environmental auditing does not exist and that the term is not clearly defined because of its evolving nature. Nevertheless, she argues that an environmental audit has common features in that it is a systematic, documented, periodic, and objective checking process of an organization's environmental performance against preset standards and objectives. Hillary traces the origins of environmental auditing to the 1970s, with the first formal environmental audits being required of US companies by the Securities and Exchange Commission in 1977. She concludes that environmental auditing needs to be more clearly defined if it is to be an effective management tool that gains credibility with stakeholders. Further, she argues that auditor competence is the key to developing quality in environmental audits, and work is needed to define the key skills required by environmental auditors.

The issue of auditor competence and the potential role of the accountancy profession in environmental auditing have been examined in several studies. COLLISON & GRAY investigated the relevance of environmental issues for financial auditors by means of a large-scale postal survey of UK audit practitioners. The survey results revealed that the larger audit firms demonstrated a high level of environmental awareness, whereas smaller firms tended to be less concerned about environmental issues. However, the authors conclude that UK accountants are reluctant to take on the challenge of environmental auditing ahead of guidance from their professional bodies. They argue that a coordinated international response, based on legislation, is essential if the accountancy profession is to respond to the challenge of environmental auditing.

The role of UK accountants in environmental auditing is also examined by POWER in a very stimulating paper. He skilfully analyses the way in which environmental auditing is emerging, its managerial emphasis, and the way accountancy-based expertise has been promoted in the context of a developing market for audit skills. He argues that environmental auditing requires a multidisciplinary approach, and so audit teams could include personnel such as scientists, engineers, lawyers, and accountants. Although financial auditors have skills relevant to environmental auditing, Power argues that the field is a contested domain in which various experts seek to establish links between what they currently do and what they might do in an environmental audit. Thus, he concludes, the construction of relevant expertise in the environmental auditing field is an ongoing process.

GRAY & STONE provide a European perspective on the attempt to develop relevant expertise in environmental auditing. Their polemical review essay comments on the findings of the 1993 survey, by the European Federation of Accountants (FEE), of environmental accounting and auditing in Europe. The essay summarizes the FEE survey, which covered professional accountancy bodies in 18 countries, and highlights the disparity between what these accountancy bodies are doing and what the EC argues should be done. The EC Fifth Action Plan, for example, argued for moves towards sustainability and (very optimistically) anticipated that environmental accounting mechanisms would be adopted by the year 2000.

The INTERNATIONAL AUDITING PRACTICES COMMITTEE provides another valuable international perspective on environmental auditing. It produced a discussion paper that was intended to generate ideas on how the auditing profession should deal with environmental auditing and, in particular, how the auditing of environmental reports and management systems should be developed. The paper draws on the work of bodies such as the Canadian Institute of Chartered Accountants, and emphasizes the multidisciplinary nature of environmental auditing.

RENGER provides a well-written, concise guide to environmental audits and the benefits they can bring to companies. He reviews the growing pressures for environmental improvement, and examines UK and EC environmental legislation and standards. Renger includes details of recommended environmental audit procedures, and has useful appendices that provide further sources of information.

Another valuable guide to environmental audits is provided for companies by ELKINGTON. His pioneering study, informed by environmental consultancy work, aimed to establish the environmental audit as a business requirement in the 1990s. The book includes an analysis of the umbrella nature of environmental audit, which can include various types of work such as an environmental impact assessment and an independent attestation of environmental information. It also surveys the emerging trends in environmental auditing, and provides case studies of audits undertaken by UK companies.

A useful insight into the importance of environmental management and audit schemes to companies is gained from the BUSINESS IN THE ENVIRONMENT study. This EC-funded project involved 19 small and medium sized companies. The report details the positions adopted by the companies at the end of the project. One company registered for the EC Eco-Management and Audit Scheme (EMAS), an initiative to aid businesses to improve their environmental management performance, and seven companies were keeping EMAS registration under review. The study highlights the benefits of EMAS, but also quantifies the costs – a full registration, for example, is likely to require 40 person days of work for a small company.

GRAYSON provides a concise compilation of a range of environmental auditing publications. The guide is divided into five sections, covering areas such as environmental auditing in industry and environmental auditing in local government. Each section contains a critical commentary on the area, together with a comprehensive list of sources concentrating on the UK and other European countries.

The study of local environmental auditing by BARTON & BRUDER provides a comprehensive guide to the subject, which is divided into three sections. The first section introduces environmental auditing and the concept of sustainability, and the second section examines the auditing of key areas like energy and transport. The third section provides a reflective evaluation of current practices. There are useful appendices, which include an environmental auditing questionnaire, and an extensive bibliography. The editors have optimistic views on the prospects for local environmental auditing, concluding that its role is ultimately to bring about change through a process of raising awareness.

ROBERT JUPE

Environmental economics

Baumol, William J. and Wallace E. Oates, *The Theory of Environmental Policy*, 2nd edition, Cambridge and New York: Cambridge University Press, 1988

Brundtland Commission, *Our Common Future*, Oxford and New York: Oxford University Press, 1987

Coase, Ronald H., "The Problem of Social Cost", *Journal of Law and Economics*, 3 (1960): 1–44

Cropper, M.L. and Wallace E. Oates, "Environmental Economics: A Survey", *Journal of Economic Literature*, 30/2 (1992): 675–740

Environmental and Resource Economics, special issue on "Frontiers of Environmental and Resource Economics" 11/3&4 (1998)

Hanley, Nick and Clive L. Spash, *Cost-Benefit Analysis and the Environment*, Aldershot, Hampshire: Elgar, 1993

Hartwick, John M. and Nancy D. Olewiler, *The Economics of Natural Resource Use*, New York: Harper and Row, 1986

Kneese, Allen V. and James L. Sweeney, *Handbook of Natural Resource and Energy Economics*, 3 vols, Amsterdam and New York: Elsevier, 1985–93

Mitchell, Robert Cameron and Richard T. Carson, *Using Surveys to Value Public Goods: The Contingent Valuation Method*, Washington, DC: Resources for the Future, 1992

Oxford Review of Economic Policy, special issue on "Environmental Policy", 14/4 (December 1998)

Perman, Roger, Yue Ma and James McGilvray, *Natural Resource and Environmental Economics*, London and New York: Longman, 1996

Pigou, A.C., *The Economics of Welfare*, 4th edition, London: Macmillan, and New York: St Martin's Press, 1932

Xepapadeas, Anastasios, *Advanced Principles in Environmental Policy*, Cheltenham: Elgar, 1997

The economics of the natural environment is one of the most rapidly growing research fields in economics. The increased research interest in this field mirrors increasing public and political awareness of the significance of environmental quality in determining quality of life.

Environmental economics has its roots in early welfare economics and, in particular, in the theory of externality as expounded by PIGOU and COASE. An externality is said to exist when the actions of one agent affect (either positively or negatively) the wellbeing of another. Environmental economists concern themselves with the predominantly negative externalities associated with production, such as when a smoke-producing factory imposes air pollution upon people living nearby.

Both Pigou and Coase noted that when a negative externality exists, the efficiency characteristics generally attributed to free-market solutions no longer hold. In particular, in the absence of regulatory intervention, there is likely to be over-participation in the polluting activity, with the polluter having insufficient incentive to take into account the full social consequences of his actions. Pigou proved that, in certain circumstances, these incentive problems could be solved and efficiency restored, by appropriate use of fiscal instruments (in particular, the imposition of an appropriately calibrated "Pigouvian tax"). Coase, in contrast, contended that under certain conditions the social-cost problem could be mitigated by bargaining between the polluter and the victim of pollution, provided that there existed a well-defined set of property rights. The so-called "Coasian solution" remains hugely influential, is the foundation upon which laissez-faire environmental economics is built, and won Ronald Coase the Nobel Prize for Economics in 1996.

Most of modern environmental economics can be seen as the development, refinement, and application of the seminal ideas of Pigou and Coase. BAUMOL & OATES is an important intermediate textbook on the policy aspects of the control of externalities and, despite its age, it remains the best exposition of the foundations of the field – foundations to which both of the authors made their own substantial contributions in the 1960s and 1970s. It might usefully be read in conjunction with XEPAPADEAS, which deals with many of the same issues in a more mathematically rigorous way, and brings the analysis up to date. Much of the focus of the policy-oriented literature, which both of these books synthesize, is on the comparative properties of alternative regulatory instruments, and this is an area dealt with very well in CROPPER & OATES' excellent survey. A number of aspects of the implementation and practicalities of environmental policy design are surveyed in the OXFORD REVIEW OF ECONOMIC POLICY.

HANLEY & SPASH provide a thorough introduction to the state of the art in environmental valuation, including detailed treatments of the three techniques that are most often used: contingent valuation, the travel-cost method, and hedonic pricing. Although most neoclassical economists are comfortable with the theoretical development of environmental economics, much more contention surrounds its empirical part, and in particular, recent attempts to quantify the value of the natural environment and damage to it. Empirical evaluation is, of course, vital to policy prescription and appraisal. Theory allows us to define a desirable point in terms of marginal cost and marginal benefit curves, but empirical estimation of those curves is required for that theoretical point to be rendered operational. A particular strength of Hanley & Spash's book is the way in which it highlights the strengths and weaknesses of the respective methodologies. A particular strength of the intermediate textbook by PERMAN, MA & McGILVRAY. is its excellent treatment of the theory and practice of environmental monetization issues.

Contingent valuation involves the use of carefully designed questionnaires to elicit respondents' willingness to pay for hypothetical changes in the state of the natural environment. The technique has become the most widely applied in recent years, and it was adopted as the basis for the settling of damages following the Exxon-Valdez oil spill in the North Pacific. MITCHELL & CARSON provide a more or less definitive exposition of the technique and its application, with particularly thorough treatment of the econometric issues involved. High-quality applications of the contingent valuation technique to a variety of settings can be found in any issue of the *Journal of Environmental Economics and Management*, which is the pre-eminent journal in the field.

HARTWICK & OLEWILER provide an excellent and accessible treatment of the economic aspects of the use (and abuse) of natural resources. Analytically, the most important categorization of resources is between those that renew themselves at an economically meaningful rate (such as timber and fish) and those that do not (such as coal or oil). KNEESE & SWEENEY provide a three-volume set of handbooks that, together, constitute a comprehensive survey of knowledge in the field at the time of publication. The BRUNDTLAND COMMISSION show how the economics of "renewable" and "non-renewable" underpin the various concepts of "environmental sustainability" that have been such a focus of policy in this area over the past several years.

The special issue of ENVIRONMENTAL AND RESOURCE ECONOMICS, commissioned to mark the First World Congress of Environmental and Resource Economists, contains 26 papers. Each paper assesses the state of the art in a particular area of environmental economics, and provides some thoughts on the likely development of that area over the next decade. The volume as a whole provides a good starting point for anyone interested in finding their bearings in the current research agenda in environmental economics.

ANTHONY HEYES

See also Coase theorem

Environmental ethics

Callicott, J. Baird, *Earth's Insights: A Survey of Ecological Ethics from the Mediterranean Basin to the Australian Outback*, Berkeley: University of California Press, 1994

Fox, Warwick, *Towards a Transpersonal Ecology: Developing New Foundations for Environmentalism*, Boston: Shambhala, 1990

Leopold, Aldo, *A Sand County Almanac, and Sketches Here and There*, New York: Oxford University Press, 1949

Plumwood, Val, *Feminism and the Mastery of Nature*, London and New York: Routledge, 1993

Sagoff, Mark, *Economy of the Earth: Philosophy, Law, and the Environment*, Cambridge and New York: Cambridge University Press, 1988

Shiva, Vandana, *Staying Alive: Women, Ecology, and Development*, London: Zed, 1988

Stone, Christopher D., "Should Trees Have Standing? Towards Legal Rights for Natural Objects", *Southern California Law Review*, 45 (1972): 450

VanDeVeer, Donald and Christine Pierce, *The Environmental Ethics and Policy Book: Philosophy, Ecology, Economics*, 2nd edition, Belmont, California: Wadsworth, 1998

Zimmerman, Michael E., *Contesting Earth's Future: Radical Ecology and Postmodernity*, Berkeley: University of California Press, 1994

CALLICOTT takes the reader on a wonderful journey around the world of environmental ethics in its greatest diversity. The book offers a comprehensive global and synthetic view of the richness of the environmental ethics and values existing on this planet. Callicott's *tour du monde* builds bridges between old European attitudes, traditional Asian philosophies, the spirituality of the native people of Americas, the complex African reality, and the aboriginal Australian worldview. It looks into the past to build a better future with environmental wisdom for one shared and threatened Earth. To those readers who might believe that environmental ethics is a scholarly discipline restricted to Western universities, the book shows that ecological ethics is a real need and possibility in a secularized century.

FOX portrays the influential philosophy of deep ecology, detailing its origins, meaning, and content. He also sketches the careers and input of the main thinkers of the deep ecological movement and considers the theoretical objections against it. What makes this book outstanding is the author's own vision of ecophilosophy. Fox stresses the psychological elements of deep ecology without overlooking its philosophical basis. His concept of transpersonal ecology is an attempt to bridge science and philosophy; he argues that ecological awareness creates both solid knowledge and personal growth. A book that satisfies the appetite for holism embracing reason and spirituality alike.

LEOPOLD shares with us, in an intimate manner, the observations and reflections that the "natural, free and wild things" have inspired him. Beyond the naturalistic descriptions, the strength of this text lies in the deep-rooted conviction of the author that the individual belongs to a broader community than society; as members of the land community, humans do not only have rights but duties too. This underlying conception of the world, wrapped in beautiful prose, has made *A Sand County Almanac* one of the fundamental texts for the development of environmental ethics. It is certainly the most authentic text of non-anthropocentric ethics.

PLUMWOOD's uncompromising feminist and epistemological analysis offers a profound critique of the Western rationalist philosophy, which led to the "master model" of the relationship with the environment. Digging at the roots of our intellectual traditions Plumwood uncovers the several dualisms that formed and still frame the mechanistic view of the natural world. She argues that to conceive a balanced relationship with the environment, we need to recognize our difference with the non-human world as well as our continuity with it. This is one of the most enlightening books in the vast ecofeminist literature.

SAGOFF examines the role, the goals, and the limits of social regulation, a category in which he includes environmental legislation. He confronts economic concepts with social values and demonstrates how reductionist and inadequate the conceptual vocabulary of classical economics can be when applied to environmental problems. To respond to this inadequacy, Sagoff advocates an ethical and cultural interpretation of the goals underlying social regulation. Using common, explicit examples of daily life, he shows why ethical reflection is so essential. Ethical and cultural reasoning is the only way to reach a balance between social goals that define a nation and economic and technical constraints of society.

Based on her field experience, SHIVA has written a powerful text that demonstrates why the Western model of development is not the solution to the economic and ecological crisis experienced in Third World countries and the rest of the planet. Development has been repeating and reconstructing the structures of male domination over women and nature, omitting their life-sustaining role, and thus worsening their respective and inherently linked situations. Considering the particular role of women in rural India, Vandana Shiva argues that to liberate women and the nature, the revival of the feminine principle has to take place. The revival of a path where women and men join their efforts to create a non-violent, harmonious relationship with each other and with nature.

STONE's famous essay is a landmark in both environmental ethics and environmental law literature. Defending the case that nature should have legal rights, the author's reasoning aims to give a concrete sense to the rights of nature. He therefore explores not only the theoretical preliminary questions but also the practicalities of such a position (for example, the standing question). He demonstrates that sufficient elements exist in our legal culture to make natural objects holders of legal rights. First published in 1972, the text is still an inspiring piece of thinking for any environmentalist, whether lawyer or not.

VANDEVEER & PIERCE have edited what can be seen as *the* environmental ethics and policy book. This is the best primer for newcomers to the field of environmental ethics containing a very readable introduction to ethical theories and some 30 important, partly groundbreaking essays. The text casts a light on the many empirical and normative concepts underlying environmental policy. The contributions from leading biologists, ecologists, engineers, economists, lawyers, and philosophers give an account of the enormous range of disciplines relevant to the question of how we ought to live. The variety of disciplines and views is not only helpful for forming one's own view, but also demonstrates the interdisciplinary nature of environmental ethics. Some very useful learning and research tools add to the outstanding value of this book. There is a glossary of key terms, a time chart of evolutionary change, a bibliography, and a guide to Internet environmental resources.

ZIMMERMAN gives an excellent review of the three major theoretical branches of environmentalism. The philosophical concepts and features of deep ecology, social ecology, and ecofeminism are thoroughly examined. However, this book's greatest quality is the broadened scope of intellectual references confronting the currents of radical ecology. Linking them with attacks on modernity since Heidegger, Derrida, and Foucault, Zimmerman argues that radical ecology is still in search of its identity. The book provides grounding for environmentalists interested in a coherent postmodern intellectual framework. A signpost to the future.

KLAUS BOSSELMANN

Environmental law

Ball, Simon and Stuart Bell, *Environmental Law: The Law and Policy Relating to the Protection of the Environment*, 3rd edition, London: Blackstone Press, 1995

Bosselmann, Klaus and Benjamin J. Richardson (editors), *Environmental Justice and Market Mechanisms: Key Challenges for Environmental Law and Policy*, London and Cambridge, Massachusetts: Kluwer, 1999

Ebbesson, Jonas, *Compatibility of International and National Environmental Law*, London and Boston: Kluwer, 1996

Ginther, Konrad, Erik Denters and Paul J.I.M. de Waart (editors), *Sustainable Development and Good Governance*, Dordrecht and Boston, Massachusetts: Nijhoff, 1995

Gunningham, Neil and Peter Grabosky, *Smart Regulation: Designing Environmental Policy*, Oxford: Clarendon Press, and New York: Oxford University Press, 1998

Hughes, David, *Environmental Law*, London: Butterworths, 1986

Kiss, Alexandre and Dinah Shelton, *International Environmental Law*, 2nd edition, Ardsley, New York: Transnational, 2000

Kloepfer, Michael, *Umweltrecht* [Environmental Law], 2nd edition, Munich: Beck, 1998

Krämer, Ludwig, *Focus on European Environmental Law*, 2nd edition, London: Sweet and Maxwell, 1997

Winter, Gerd (editor), *European Environmental Law: A Comparative Perspective*, Aldershot, Hampshire: Dartmouth, 1996

BALL & BELL provide comprehensive coverage of British environmental law and discuss the issues emerging in this rapidly developing area in a precise and clear manner. The authors follow a sectorial coverage, emphasizing the effects of the Environmental Act 1995, and of aspects of environmental law such as integrated pollution control and environmental assessment. The reader is left with a strong sense that the British environmental legal system is undergoing a revolutionary modernization of its environmental law and management structures, propelled by the challenge of international and EU environmental law developments. The book does not emphasize the relationship between environmental and economic issues nor does it give comparative information on other countries.

BOSSELMANN & RICHARDSON examine tensions between environmental justice and the market in the context of international trade liberalization and deregulation. The book provides definitions and policy dimensions of environmental justice as a yardstick against which concepts of environmental law and policy are to be measured. The increased use of market-based tools of environmental law, such as voluntary agreements, tradeable permits, and ecotaxes is critically assessed. In an international comparative perspective, with contributions from 24 environmental law scholars, the book reports on experiences in European countries, the US, South Africa, Australia, and New Zealand. It concludes with a call for transcending the dichotomy between state intervention and market forces and suggests an overall framework of environmental justice guiding both the state and the market.

EBBESSON explores the compatibility of international law and national law arguing that environmental law consists of both international and national components. This idea is based on the fact that environmental problems are essentially transboundary, and thus need to be covered by transboundary concepts of environmental law. As the boundaries between national and international environmental law are, in fact, becoming transparent, the book is an excellent source for a future concept of transnational law. Ebbesson discusses measures that enable the legal environmental framework of states to become compatible with international developments. The book includes a discussion about how international law, through its treaty-based regimes, can act as a management tool for the incorporation of international legal principles into national law. This is illustrated by examples from the European Union. The reader is left with an appreciation of how the effectiveness of international environmental law depends on an understanding of issues such as the intention of states to acknowledge and apply international rules and the extent to which international law applies to the individual. These and other concepts explain the author's theory for effective compatibility of international and national environmental law.

GINTHER, DENTERS & DE WAART is based on challenging papers presented at an International Law Association conference. The overall theme is the use of legal principles for sustainable development and good governance. The emphasis on sustainable development has been interpreted in most papers as the concept of environmental sustainability. The authors also explain the interrelationship and compatibility and in some cases incompatibility of the economic, social, political, and ecological dimensions of sustainable development. The range of topics discussed is broad and includes global market economies, intergenerational equity, self determination, and environmental concerns in GATT/WTO rules. The authors of the papers represent several parts of the world including Europe, Africa, India, Japan, South America, and Australia. Such an international mix gives an interesting account of environmental developments and problems in the different social and political regions.

GUNNINGHAM & GRABOSKY, with Darren Sinclair, present theories to address the problems of costly and insensitive environmental regulation of business. One of the main theories is the redesign of environmental policy so it performs "optimally". The authors argue that this can be achieved by the use of integrated, as opposed to single, policy instruments. Single policy instruments are based on command-and-control regulations. The integrated approach uses permutations and combinations of a variety of regulatory instruments including information and education, voluntarism, self-regulation, broad based economic instruments, property rights, and performance standards. The book shows convincingly how the efficiency of environmental regulation increases when integrated environmental policy is tailor made for specific situations; helpful examples from the agricultural and chemical industries illustrate this. The book also presents an excellent overview of the main political and ecological arguments that have dominated the regulatory process in the 1990s.

HUGHES provides a valuable analysis of the overall structure and development of British environmental law. The book also contains a generous and helpful discussion of European Union law and policy, including its history. Included is a short discussion on the debate on ethics and the environment. A useful addition to this text is the reading list following each chapter; it contains general background and journal titles as well as references to official reports. The main emphasis is on the legal protection of the three environmental media: land, water, and air. An interesting aspect of the book is the discussion on controversial operations and hazardous uses of land such as regulation and enforcement of laws regarding genetically modified organisms.

KISS & SHELTON is the leading text on international environmental law, giving an in-depth and scholarly account of environmental law based on international developments in the field. The book discusses issues such as the object, ethics, evolution, sources, regulation, problems, and institution of international environmental law, and emphasizes the increasing interdisciplinary nature and internationalization of environmental problems, standards, and laws. The book also includes enlightening and concise chapters on the birth of international environmental law, biological diversity and biotechnology.

KLOEPFER is the leading text in German environmental law. It gives a thorough introduction to the philosophy, history, constitutional framework, and general principles of environmental law in Germany. The book covers all areas of federal environmental legislation including planning law, soil and water conservation law, clean air law, nuclear law, hazardous substances law, gene technology law, and waste management law. Each of these represents "state of the art" legislation, and thus needs to be studied closely. The book also includes European, international, and comparative aspects. One important aspect is how European civil law countries tend to differ from the British common law tradition in their approach to implementing European Union law.

KRÄMER offers a brilliant and thorough exploration of the main body of European environmental law and policy. The book is critical in its approach yet quick to realize the benefits of the European Union legal system. The emphasis tends towards an understanding of the reasons for continued general environmental degradation in Europe despite measures to counteract this at the international and national level. Kramer confronts the reader with soul-searching questions and sobering facts about the actual state of Europe's environment and in places offers his enthusiastic and professional opinion for improved environmental protection laws in Europe. The book covers an impressive range of environmental law issues including trade, liability, financial measures, and marine law. The discussion also contains an analysis of the structural problems encountered in the implementation process of EU law in member states.

WINTER provides an invaluable, well-presented European environmental law text containing contributions from 16 respected lawyers. The book offers an excellent overview of the development objectives and principles of EU environmental law, including case studies highlighting drafting and reform problems of Central and Eastern Europe where previously little environmental law existed. The case studies also highlight the tension between economic and environmental

development in countries emerging from communist domination into the arena of democracy and a free market economy. The authors provide a sophisticated study of a broad range of concepts central to the management and maintenance of environmental protection throughout Europe. The discussions include environmental impact assessment, public participation, judicial review, administrative and financial organization, regulation, and liability measures.

KLAUS BOSSELMAN

See also Tradeable pollution permits

Environmental politics

Dobson, Andrew, *Green Political Thought*, 3rd edition, London: Routledge, 2000

Goodin, Robert E., *Green Political Theory*, Cambridge: Polity Press, 1992

Meadows, Donella H. *et al.*, *The Limits to Growth: A Report for the Club of Rome's Project on the Predicament of Mankind*, New York: Universe Books, 1972; London: Pan, 1974

Kohák, Erazim, *The Embers and the Stars: A Philosophical Inquiry into the Moral Sense of Nature*, Chicago: University of Chicago Press, 1984

Lichterman, Paul, *The Search for Political Community: American Activists Reinventing Commitment*, Cambridge and New York: Cambridge University Press, 1996

Weale, Albert, *The New Politics of Pollution*, Manchester: Manchester University Press, 1992

MEADOWS *et al.* has become central to modern environmental politics for its argument that there are limits to industrial and associated types of growth. The book's conclusions derive from computer modelling four variables: population, resource use, available agricultural land, and pollution. The authors suggest that dealing with these problems in isolation from one another is inadequate, and they also argue that technological solutions alone cannot remove fundamental limits to growth. This conclusion has been used by the Green movement to argue that environmental problems are political, social, and economic, rather than simply technical and scientific. At this point, the environmental movement becomes a political movement, properly speaking.

DOBSON opened up and mapped a new field of inquiry in green normative thought, coming as it did just when "green consciousness" and public concern reached an all time high in Britain. In this book, Dobson popularized the deep/shallow ecology distinction (originally proposed by the deep ecologist Arne Naess), and introduced the main points and arguments within green politics – in particular, green visions of the sustainable society, arguments about agents of green political change, and the policy platform of greens. While the book could be argued to privilege a particular ideological account of green politics, based upon ecologism, it has been the main text for countless students and has done much to establish green political theory within the academic study of political theory.

LICHTERMAN analyses the cultural underpinnings of environmental activism. He shows how this produces different styles of commitment in different types of activist groups. Those committed to a radical green ideology tend to view their activism as motivated by individual experiences and so seek to make their political practice consistent with their ideals. Thus, for them the form of organization developed is an end in itself of their politics. Lichterman calls this style of activism personalism. This can be compared to groups whose traditions are more collective. For instance, African-American anti-toxics campaigners tended to give priority to community solidarity, deferred to community leaders and expected others in the community to accept political activism as an obligation. While personalists tended to be self-critical and perceive political activism as something unusual, anti-toxic campaigners saw politics as normal. Without an understanding of these cultural dimensions of activism, Lichterman suggests that environmentalists will continue to be puzzled about why attempts to build alliances between different types of environmental groups tend to fail.

GOODIN provides us with a "green theory of value", a "green theory of agency", and a discussion of the relationship between the two. For greens, argues Goodin, the value of something is a function of its history as a natural object, so the less it has been a part of the production and reproduction of human life, the more valuable it is. Goodin suggests that this is the "logical primitive" of green political theory, and that the greens' prime objective must be to get their theory of value into the policy-making process. For Goodin, there is no way of reading off a green theory of agency from the green theory of value; they are independent from one another.

WEALE has been very influential among those who analyse the policy process. He compares policy towards pollution control in Britain, Germany, and the Netherlands. He then explores how well four different explanatory models of public policy theory explain the nature of each national case. He finds that rational choice (individualist) approaches, social systems analysis, and analysis of institutions all work effectively to explain the context of policy formation, but they need to be supplemented by analysis of discourse. The various explanations can be integrated to explain particular policy outcomes. For instance, in Germany it was easier to justify the use of precautionary principles because the tradition of the Rechtstaat meant that policy required explicit justification on the basis of principles. In Britain, such principles have been harder to justify because scientific proof was required before action to avert risks that might affect economic interests could be justified. It is this interplay of discourse and other factors that makes the ideology of ecological modernization stronger in countries such as Germany and the Netherlands than in Britain.

It is odd that KOHÁK's beautiful, wonderfully written, highly original book has never received the attention it deserves. It is a wide-ranging, thought-provoking investigation into the relationship between the "order of nature" and the "human moral order". Kohák's starting point is that "The vital order of nature and the moral order of our humanity remain constant, but they grow overlaid with forgetting", and the aim of the book is to present a vision in which the two orders enter into a less distant, alienated, and destructive union.

Kohák ranges from the ancient Greeks, to modern phenomenology, existentialism, and psychoanalysis to present a unique position among environmental philosophers, developing what could be described as a spiritualized (but secular) vision of respectful human interaction and use of the natural world. Kohák places humanity at the centre of his concerns, but rightly sees that this is not be confused with an arrogance about our self-importance. For him, humans are "beings who are able to see the world in the order of its time, not only in the sterile atemporality of our man-made world". And as beings able to witness the intersection of time and eternity on our planet this is what justifies and gives meaning to our existence. As he puts it, "When humans surrender the arrogance of domination, they can reclaim the confidence of their humanity".

JOHN BARRY, ANDREW DOBSON,
AND BRIAN DOHERTY

See also Globalization, Globalization: critiques and alternatives, Risk society

Environmental science as a social science

Abram, David, *The Spell of the Sensuous: Perception and Language in a More-than-human World*, New York: Pantheon, 1996

Bateson, Gregory, *Steps to an Ecology of Mind*, New York: Ballantine, 1972; London: Paladin, 1973

Bateson, Gregory, *Mind and Nature: A Necessary Unity*, New York: Dutton, and London: Wildwood House, 1979

Berman, Morris, *The Reenchantment of the World*, Ithaca, New York: Cornell University Press, 1981

Blackburn, Thomas, "Sensuous-Intellectual Complimentarity in Science", *Science*, 172 (1971): 1003–07

Capitalism Nature Socialism: A Journal of Socialist Ecology, 1988–

Capra, Fritjof, *The Web of Life: A New Synthesis of Mind and Matter*, London: HarperCollins, and New York: Anchor, 1996

Csikszentmihalyi, Mihaly, *The Evolving Self: A Psychology for the Third Millennium*, New York, HarperCollins, 1993

Daly, Herman E. and John B. Cobb Jr, *For the Common Good: Redirecting the Economy towards Community, the Environment, and a Sustainable Future*, Boston: Beacon Press, 1989; 2nd edition, 1994

Damasio, Antonio R., *Descartes' Error: Emotion, Reason, and the Human Brain*, New York: Putnam, 1994; London: Picador, 1995

Diamond, Irene and Gloria Orenstein (editors), *Reweaving the World: The Emergence of Ecofeminism*, San Francisco: Sierra Club, 1990

Eckersley, Richard (editor), *Measuring Progress: Is Life Getting Better?*, Canberra: CSIRO, 1998

Environmental Ethics, 1979–

Etzioni-Halevy, Eva, *The Knowledge Elite and the Failure of Prophecy*, London and Boston: Allen and Unwin, 1985

Evernden, Neil, *The Social Creation of Nature*, Baltimore: Johns Hopkins University Press, 1992

Fisher, Frank, "Dissolving the Stranglehold of the Fix: A Role for Social Construction in Dealing with Environmental Dislocation", *Futures*, 25/10 (1993a): 1051–62

Fisher, Frank, "Emergence of a Circumspect Society: Introducing Reflexive Institutions", *Futures*, 25/10 (1993b): 1077–82

Hanson, F. Allan, *Testing, Testing: Social Consequences of the Examined Life*, Berkeley: University of California Press, 1993

Hardin, Garrett, "The Tragedy of the Commons", *Science*, 162 (1968): 1243–48

Harman, Willis, *Global Mind Change: The Promise of the Last Years of the Twentieth Century*, Indianapolis: Knowledge Systems, 1988

IEEE Technology and Society Magazine, 1982–

Krieger, Martin, "What's Wrong with Plastic Trees?", *Science*, 179 (1973): 446–55

Kuhn, Thomas, *The Structure of Scientific Revolutions*, 3rd edition, Chicago: University of Chicago Press, 1996

Lewis, C.S., *The Abolition of Man*, Oxford: Oxford University Press, 1943; New York: Macmillan, 1947

Maturana, Humberto R. and Francisco J. Varela, *The Tree of Knowledge: The Biological Roots of Human Understanding*, Boston: New Science Library, and London: Shambhala, 1987

Midgley, Mary, *Science as Salvation: A Modern Myth and Its Meaning*, New York and London: Routledge, 1992

Naess, Arne, "The Shallow and the Deep, Long-Range Ecology Movement: A Summary", *Inquiry*, 16 (1973): 95–100

Nelkin, Dorothy and Laurence Tancredi, *Dangerous Diagnostics: The Social Power of Biological Information*, New York: Basic Books, 1989

New Economics Magazine, 1986–; renamed as *News from the New Economy*, March 1999–

Polanyi, Michael, *Knowing and Being: Essays*, Chicago: University of Chicago Press, and London: Routledge and Kegan Paul, 1969

Report of the Institute for Philosophy and Public Policy, 1987–

Resurgence Magazine, 1966–

Sachs, Wolfgang, *Planet Dialectics: Explorations in Environment and Development*, London and New York: Zed, 1999

Sagoff, Mark, *The Economy of the Earth: Philosophy, Law, and the Environment*, Cambridge and New York: Cambridge University Press, 1988

Schumacher, E.F., *A Guide for the Perplexed*, London: Cape, and New York: Harper and Row, 1977

Science as Culture, 1991–

Science, Technology and Human Values, 1976–

Searle, John R., *Mind, Language and Society: Philosophy in the Real World*, New York: Basic Books, 1998, and London: Weidenfeld and Nicholson, 1999

Senge, Peter M., *The Fifth Discipline: The Art and Practice of the Learning Organization*, New York: Doubleday, 1990

Shepard, Paul, *Nature and Madness*, San Francisco: Sierra Club, 1982

Systems Research and Behavioral Science, 1984–

Thompson, M., M. Warburton and T. Hatley, *Uncertainty on a Himalayan Scale: An Institutional Theory of Environmental Perception and a Strategic Framework for the Sustainable Development of the Himalaya*, London: Milton Ash Editions/Ethnographica, 1986

Valaskakis, Kimon *et al.*, *The Conserver Society: A Workable Alternative for the Future*, New York: Harper and Row, 1979

Weizsäcker, Ernst von, *Earth Politics*, London: Zed, 1994

Wilber, Ken, *Sex, Ecology, Spirituality: The Spirit of Evolution*, Boston: Shambhala, 1995

Wilber, Ken, *A Brief History of Everything*, Boston: Shambahala, 1996

Wilden, Anthony, *System and Structure: Essays in Communication and Exchange*, 2nd edition, London and New York: Tavistock Press, 1980

Whole Earth Review, 1974–

Environmental science is quite a new intellectual domain – in a formal sense only some 30 years old. Environmental science as a social science is barely 20 years old and the majority of organizations that use the title to describe what they do would strenuously deny that what they do is a social science. This denial arises as a result of the legitimation game all disciplines must engage in and the relatively poor status enjoyed by disciplines unable to ground their work in the supposedly unambiguous quantities and relationships of science. Furthermore, it illustrates the need for the very concerns that occupy environmental science – the effort to engage humanity in recognizing that the essence of its (the human) project is: (a) to think, (b) to act on thought, and (c) to recognise that thinking and acting on thought are both socially derived phenomena and, therefore, that ours is the (d) responsibility for thought and thought-based action.

This entry therefore builds on a definition of environmental science as a science of context, in the most general meaning of context available, and beyond that, on a particular understanding of science itself. Moreover, environmental science is not a discipline but an inter- and trans- discipline. In that capacity it seeks to provide a rigorous intellectual context for disciplinary knowledge and the professional action based on it. An important part of such a rigorous intellectual framework is recognition that, although knowledge may be value free – to the extent that it is successfully tested and found to be coherent with pre-existing science – practice based on such knowledge is always value driven and therefore consideration of its sociopolitical contexts is always part of the "meta-science" (context of science) that the environmental scientist can be expected to expose and operationalize.

"Science itself" is understood as a uniquely rigorous, empirical-where-possible approach to knowledge wherein both knowledge and the notion of an approach to it are understood to be socially construed. Within this generalized definition the quantitative or "hard" sciences are a subset built upon and contributing to an internally coherent language of great clarity and specificity. In the latter part of the 20th century the domain of understanding of science as a social phenomenon has itself become a respected academic domain, for example in departments of history, philosophy, and sociology of science. It stems from the early work of social scientists such as philosopher Alfred North Whitehead (see *Science and the Modern World*, London: Free Association, 1985 (original 1926)) and is beautifully exemplified in the work of the late ecologist, Paul Shepard (for example, *The Subversive Science: Essays Toward an Ecology of Man*, edited with Daniel McKinley, 1969, and *The Tender Carnivore and the Sacred Game*, 1973).

Environmental science as the quintessential "science of context" aims to generate a new kind of "Renaissance man". Its graduates will be equipped with intellectual tools that enable them: (a) to recognise what context is; (b) to see context acting in the phenomena they and their societies perceive around them and to hypothesize, test, and isolate structures that render their contextual understanding useful; (c) to know how to act on what they see (to be familiar with the local social structures that enable action); and finally (d) to recognize that their own seeing and action are simultaneously a function of these structures and their ability to inform their actions from an understanding of them. It is a dialectically or reflexively built way of being-in-the-world.

The result is that the environmental scientists' action will necessarily be humble and that the mundane, will always be accorded a certain dignity.

A couple of such generalized intellectual structures will be useful here in understanding the current shape of the subject. Firstly, environmental science as a new "meta-analytical" science arose when it became apparent that "whistleblowing" about environmental dislocation (first generation action) produced no action, and political or second generation action on the whistleblowers' concerns led to "zero sum" action because existing political structures were causally related to the concerns. Third generation action involves social structural analyses and the generation of new, more circumspect frameworks for all action as outlined in THOMPSON, WARBURTON & HATLEY and FISHER (1993a, 1993b). The new frameworks are to be reflexive – able to recognise and act upon the enabling frameworks of both the concerns and the social-intellectual frameworks by which we strive to delineate the concerns. Secondly, the rise of so-called second generation systems' sciences, sensitive to their own subjectivities, has provided rudimentary intellectual tools to help us make a more rigorous sense of the behaviours we see around us. In turn, as these meta-sciences develop, they enable us to see phenomena that had hitherto been totally hidden from us. Prior to the advent of these new intellectual tools we were not able to see such things as so-called "chaotic" or "complex" behaviours.

Therefore, the readings offered here cover an eclectic array of analyses and priorities. It is not definitive. To some extent the selection is necessarily idiosyncratic because the domain is very much in gestation and intersects with other metadomains such as management and control theory or cybernetics.

Precisely because the domain is new, readers' insight into its breadth as well as its content is best assembled by reviewing the scope of its journals. That task is complicated by the fact that now many (disciplinary) journals incorporate regular inter- and trans-disciplinary sections such as "Science's Compass" in *Science*. The selection of journals offered range across the standard reviewed academic journals in the field of "metascience", such as SCIENCE AS CULTURE and SCIENCE, TECHNOLOGY & HUMAN VALUES, to institutional newsletters

such as the University of Maryland's outstanding Institute for Philosophy and Public Policy Report and the British New Economics Foundation's magazine NEW ECONOMICS to finally, the great "thoughtful" but non-peer-reviewed magazines in the domain, such as WHOLE EARTH REVIEW (formerly *Coevolution Quarterly*). Most notable among the academic journals are the early academic journal ENVIRONMENTAL ETHICS and RESURGENCE. Outstanding recent additions are CAPITALISM NATURE SOCIALISM and "outsiders" such as IEEE TECHNOLOGY & SOCIETY MAGAZINE from the Institute of Electrical and Electronic Engineers and SYSTEMS RESEARCH AND BEHAVIORAL SCIENCE.

Feminist concerns about man-nature dualisms and their consequences have made major contributions to the domain, and the anthology edited by DIAMOND & ORENSTEIN is accessible as an introductory reading. Similarly the work of futures' studies is represented by one of its most persistent and respected exponents, Willis HARMAN. The works by Richard ECKERSLEY (Australia), Ernst VON WEIZSÄCKER and Wolfgang SACHS (Germany) represent contributions from outside England and America. All three are well known in their respective countries and represent in their books, the work of substantial teams of respected researchers on practical environmental concerns. In the former, we touch upon the interesting and very revealing task of generating new indicators which are vital to the process of "creating new eyes" with which to "reweave" the world (see, for example, The New Economics Foundation's *New Economics Magazine* and in particular its newsletter, *Indicators Update*).

Analytical works illustrate one of the primary tasks environmental science addresses, namely, the nature of knowledge itself and how that nature manifests itself in institutions. The idea of meta-analysis is the intellectual effort by which inter- and transdisciplinarity are achieved. It is the capacity to stand outside the intellectual mechanisms or disciplines that enable action and, importantly, it includes the search for the frameworks by which we manage to do this.

Creating these categories within what is already a meta-analytical science says something about the nature of environmental science: it strives for reflexive context awareness and its practical implementation. It is, nevertheless, quite another thing to determine when precisely one is engaged in analysis and when in meta-analysis. Deciding which is which is a somewhat sterile exercise within a context concerned primarily with wider community recognition of the practice and legitimacy of meta-analysis. In a more general sense the analytical works would also be categorized as meta-analytical. They are not in that category here for reasons relating to their contexts rather than their contents – in the main, their historical contexts. The works by BATESON (1973, 1979), for example, were groundbreaking meta-analytical studies that set the scene for later analyses. Indeed most of the following works of analysis are classics of their kind; they established whole fields of meta-analysis and this "primacy" prompts their listing as analytical. On the other hand the meta-analytical works tend to be more recent (notably the works by Ken WILBER, 1995 and 1996) or explicitly or "knowingly" meta-analytical from the start such as those by POLANYI, SCHUMACHER, LEWIS, WILDEN and SHEPARD. Papers such as KRIEGER, NAESS and BLACKBURN are among the most famous ever written and offer radically divergent analyses. The HARDIN article, in particular, has spawned a whole literature, precisely because it was based on a breathtaking absence of meta-analytical understanding!

Other works on analysis and meta-analysis cover an extensive territory ranging from: (a) analyses of the social context of science itself (BERMAN, HANSON, KUHN, MIDGLEY), generalizations from scientific understandings (CAPRA, EVERNDEN, MATURANA & VARELA, and SHEPARD) to inferences from particular scientific understandings (DAMASIO); (b) meta-analyses of economics (DALY & COBB and SAGOFF); (c) a meta-analysis of management (SENGE); (d) a meta-analysis from psychology (CSIKSZENTMIHALI); (e) a meta-analysis of politics (ETZIONI-HALEVY); (f) meta-analyses of social structure itself, including the formally feminist, socialist, and spiritual (see ABRAM and SEARLE).

For works on practice, the title of NELKIN & TANCREDI makes its content obvious whereas THOMPSON, WARBURTON & HATLEY offers a quite remarkable insight into the social constructions associated with environmental analyses aimed at guiding institutional action. VALASKAKIS digests the most extensive single, government funded study ever conducted into sustainable national (Canadian) futures. It is worth noting in this context that throughout the 1970s and early 1980s, the Swedish Secretariat for Futures Studies published a series of English language synopses of the most remarkably insightful studies of directions in Swedish society. Finally, the two papers by Fisher (1993a, 1993b) present a range of practical applications of environmental science as a social science.

FRANK FISHER

Epistemology, feminist

Alcoff, Linda and Elizabeth Potter (editors), *Feminist Epistemologies*, New York and London: Routledge, 1993

Antony, Louise M. and Charlotte Witt (editors), *A Mind of One's Own: Feminist Essays on Reason and Objectivity*, Boulder, Colorado: Westview Press, 1993

Faber, M.D., *Culture and Consciousness: The Social Meaning of Altered Awareness*, New York and London: Human Sciences Press, 1981

Foucault, Michel, *The Archaeology of Knowledge*, New York: Pantheon, and London: Tavistock, 1972 (French edition 1969)

Harding, Sandra, (editor), *Can Theories Be Refuted? Essays on the Duhem-Quine Thesis*, Dordrecht and Boston: Reidel, 1976

Harding, Sandra, *Is Science Multicultural?: Postcolonialisms, Feminisms, and Epistemologies*, Bloomington: Indiana University Press, 1998

Lett, James, *Science, Reason, and Anthropology: The Principles of Rational Inquiry*, Lanham, Maryland: Rowman and Littlefield, 1997

Potter, Jonathan, *Representing Reality: Discourse, Rhetoric and Social Construction*, London and Thousand Oaks, California: Sage, 1996

Wertheim, Margaret, *Pythagoras' Trousers: God, Physics, and the Gender Wars*, New York: Random House, 1995; London: Fourth Estate, 1997

White, Alan R., *The Nature of Knowledge*, Totowa, New Jersey: Rowman and Littlefield, 1982

Explaining how we justify believing in the things we do is an important component of sociological methodology, and is particularly relevant in the move from quantitative to qualitative analysis. The nature of knowledge and claims to knowledge are considered in WHITE's philosophical treatise. He distinguishes between objects of knowledge, the extent of knowledge, and the necessary construction of criteria for knowing, supplying the initial basis for courses addressing the social construction of knowledge.

Feminist epistemology is a reaction to the implicit androcentrism of classical epistemology. ANTONY & WITT's edited collection of 13 essays seeks to demonstrate the ways in which classical methods of reason and empiricism are either inherently or historically sexist, and the ways in which objectivity is actually masculine subjectivity. They question both the possibility and desirability of objectivity through a selection of diverse essays that can be used alone or as a text in courses querying how knowledge is made, by whom, and for whom.

An extraordinary collaboration edited by ALCOFF & POTTER has produced a canonical text for feminist theoreticians. Each contributor analyses the notion that "feminist epistemology" is an oxymoron, combining feminism and philosophy to create a wary affiliation that benefits all sociocultural researchers. The 11 authors contribute to new perspectives proposing that reality is created through and by multitudes of knowledge-makers in great and small social worlds.

FABER presents a more psychosocial view of epistemology as conscious experience of the social world shaped by individual perception. In arguing that "reality" is made from an individual's active intellectual and physical evolution, rather than given, the author creates a different kind of epistemological theory to engage in the critique of culture.

FOUCAULT's innovative approach to the history of ideas has profoundly influenced sociological theory since its first publication and translation into English. He examines the continuities and discontinuities of historical moments and the ways in which these have shaped the ways of knowing of Europe's major philosophers. He traces the problems of division and limits, and of transformations as new foundations, to query categories of analysis that many theorists have perceived as immutable. This is a classic text for undergraduate and postgraduate students.

A great deal of recent feminist theory has addressed the universal validity of notions such as "objectivity", "rationality", and "good research methods". HARDING (1998) joins the recent academic and postcolonial challenge to Western masculinized theories of knowledge. Using accounts from postcolonial science and technology studies, she provides a unique and accessible overview and an excellent critique of the development of modern sciences in Europe. She proposes that all knowledge systems are local, and celebrates the potential for generating knowledge and increasingly democratic social relations.

In an earlier collection of 16 essays, HARDING (1976) edited a body of work that questions and explores the empirical aspects of scientific knowledge. Here some of the most celebrated European thinkers challenge Cartesian epistemology in order to consider the links between epistemology, ethics and political theory. The work provides an historical grounding to epistemological theory.

LETT's work about the epistemological foundations of anthropological theory is concerned primarily with the set of assumptions that underlie any acquisition of knowledge. He explains to the reader how to think critically, how to infer logically, and how to assess the validity of substantive evidence. Clear examples of philosophical constructions, as well as analyses of anecdotal evidence, provide a strong understanding of the ways that crosscultural research can be conducted as a social science.

POTTER's view of the social construction of science, and especially knowledge that is presented as scientific fact, is radically distinct from Lett's. Lett focuses on the empirical, but Potter is more concerned with the descriptions that interact with the social construction of facts to present a mirror of the world, and with how the "factuality of descriptions" is constructed through ideology and action. The author analyses the ways that fact is imbued within structuralist modes of thought, backed up with a reading of rhetoric to provide a pervasive feature of how people reach understanding. His engaging prose and accessible examples illustrate the value of diverse approaches to knowledge, and shows how theoretical and analytical tensions can be productive.

WERTHEIM, a physicist, discusses the intersection of gender, science, and knowledge. The book is a clear introduction to the issues of gender inequity in knowledge production and provides an astute social and cultural comment on the hard sciences. Her work asks what could have been achieved if women were acknowledged and accepted as co-producers of insight and intelligence.

HELEN JOHNSON

Equal opportunity, equal pay

Acker, Joan, *Doing Comparable Worth: Gender, Class, and Pay Equity*, Philadelphia: Temple University Press, 1989

Charnovitz, Steve, "Trade, Employment and Labor Standards: The OECD Study and Recent Developments in the Trade and Labor Standards Debate", *Temple International and Comparative Law Journal*, 11/1 (1997): 131–45

Duroska, Amelia K., "Comparable Work, Comparable Pay: Rethinking the Decision of the Ninth Circuit Court of Appeals in American Federation of State, County, and Municipal Employees v. Washington", *American University Law Review*, 36/3 (1986): 245–60

England, Paula, *Comparable Worth: Theories and Evidence*, New York: Aldine de Gruyter, 1992

Gunderson, Morley, *Comparable Worth and Gender Discrimination: An International Perspective*, Geneva: International Labour Office, 1994

Haveman, Robert H., *Earnings Inequality: The Influence of Changing Opportunities and Choices*, Washington, DC: American Enterprise Institute Press, 1996

Johansen, Elaine, *Comparable Worth: The Myth and the Movement*, Boulder, Colorado: Westview Press, 1984

Willborn, Steven L., *A Comparable Worth Primer*, Lexington, Massachusetts: Lexington Books, 1986

A variety of scholars and commissions have studied issues associated with equal opportunity/equal pay. As part of the US Civil Rights Act of 1991, the Glass Ceiling Commission issued a report containing recommendations to identify and remove barriers and promote employment opportunities for the advancement of minorities and women into positions of responsibility in the private sector. The following scholars present a variety of perspectives on this issue.

JOHANSEN views comparable worth as the convergence of two social movements: the pay equity movement as a spinoff of the women's rights movement of the 1960s and the civil service reform movement of the late 1970s. She then traces the diffusion of the comparable worth movement through interest-group strategies and calls for a legislative solution rather than seeking judicial or bargaining remedies. Ultimately objective job evaluations would be conducted by governmental agencies in separate technical units, insulated from political pressure. Her work is foundational to a study of this movement.

WILLBORN provided an overview of the economics, litigation, and legislation of comparable worth. Of special interest, he reviewed comparable worth in a number of countries including Sweden, Canada, and Australia. He discussed methods of comparing and evaluating jobs and a broad base of information and alternatives in order that the reader may make an informed personal decision about this social issue and gain an international perspective.

DUROSKA wrote in 1986 concerning the defeat in 1985 of comparable worth litigation in the US. The article is a helpful contemporary view of the relative positions of the parties to this landmark decision and the alternative legal theories under US law by which equal pay for men and women may be achieved.

ACKER attempts to link the work of practical feminist action with feminist theorizing. In particular she takes many lessons from the Oregon Comparable Worth Project. Issues of gender relations, organizational hierarchy, and marginalization are linked to the practical politics of union building and striking. The book documents a good "how to" case study.

ENGLAND's unique contribution to comparable worth scholarship is a series of policy debates constructed at the end of her book. They present the viewpoints of a number of stylized persons such as the "feminist advocate", "business critic", "neoclassical critic", and "social-psychological advocate", to name a few. The topics include "the sex gap in pay and discrimination", "is segregation and hiring discrimination the real problem", and "possible adverse effects on the economy, polity, and society", to list three of the total nine. Educators will find these debates of special help as they introduce students to these complex topics.

GUNDERSON's work is part of the Geneva-based International Labour Office's Project on Equality for Women in Employment. It discusses comparable worth in the international arena. Comparable worth is viewed as a remedy for occupational segregation. Comparable worth is limited, however, in that it is usually restricted to jobs within the same organization and does not address issues arising from differences in education, training, and work experience. This volume advocates a variety of approaches to the social issues surrounding the gender pay gap.

HAVEMAN's study was commissioned by the American Enterprise Institute and provides a "conservative" counterpoint to the "liberal" literature of comparable worth. While focusing on changes in men's earnings since the mid-1970s, he concludes that voluntary choice, such as full time versus part time work, accounts for more than half of the increase in earnings inequality that has taken place.

CHARNOVITZ reviews recent work of the Organization for Economic Co-operation and Development (OECD) in which a study was made of the International Labour Organization's (ILO's) convention regarding child labour, minimum age for admission to employment (no. 138). This is the first study conducted by the OECD secretariat on the linkage between labour standards and trade and Charnovitz's review is helpful in providing a context for understanding the multinational and global economic impacts of the equal opportunities/equal pay standards of nations.

BRAD REID

See also Glass ceiling

Equality

Arneson, Richard, "Equality" in *A Companion to Contemporary Political Philosophy*, edited by Robert E. Goodin and Philip Pettit, Oxford and Cambridge, Massachusetts: Blackwell, 1993

Dworkin, Ronald, "What Is Equality? Part 1: Equality of Welfare", *Philosophy and Public Affairs*, 10/3 (1981): 185–246

Dworkin, Ronald, "What Is Equality? Part 2: Equality of Resources", *Philosophy and Public Affairs*, 10/4 (1981): 283–345

Miller, David and Michael Walzer (editors), *Pluralism, Justice, and Equality*, Oxford and New York: Oxford University Press, 1995

Nagel, Thomas, "Equality" in his *Mortal Questions*, Cambridge and New York: Cambridge University Press, 1991

Nozick, Robert, "Equality, Envy, Exploitation, Etc." in his *Anarchy, State, and Utopia*, New York: Basic Books, and Oxford: Blackwell, 1974

Rawls, John, *A Theory of Justice*, Cambridge, Massachusetts: Harvard University Press, 1971, Oxford: Clarendon Press, 1972; revised edition, Cambridge, Massachusetts: Harvard University Press, and Oxford: Oxford University Press, 1999

Sen, Amartya, "Equality of What?" in *The Tanner Lectures on Human Values*, vol. 1, edited by Sterling M. McMurrin, Cambridge: Cambridge University Press, and Salt Lake City: University of Utah Press, 1980

Walzer, Michael, "Complex Equality" in *Spheres of Justice: A Defence of Pluralism and Equality*, edited by Michael Walzer, Oxford: Martin Robertson, and New York: Basic Books, 1983

Williams, Bernard, "The Idea of Equality" in *Problems of the Self: Philosophical Papers, 1956–1972*, edited by Bernard Williams, Cambridge: Cambridge University Press, 1973

The idea of equality occupies a central and controversial place in contemporary political philosophy. While most political philosophers agree upon the importance of this idea, there is a large amount of disagreement about what a substantive theory of equality requires. That people should be treated equally is a widely held view, but asking *how* one treats people equally elicits a wide range of conflicting responses. Are we to think of equality in terms of resources, welfare, capabilities, opportunity, or respect? Are these conceptions mutually exclusive or is an over-arching ideal of equality possible?

ARNESON provides a good survey of the major approaches to the issue. He argues that political egalitarianism goes beyond a notion of equality of democratic citizenship to encompass an ideal of equality of condition: that everyone should enjoy the same level of social and economic benefits. Acknowledging that this is an "amorphous ideal", Arneson investigates the arguments for equality of resources, of welfare, or desire satisfaction, and for functioning capabilities. He also situates these claims in relation to alternative views such as the doctrine of sufficiency and the Pareto norm.

RAWLS's seminal text retains a place at the heart of current debate. His theory of justice is a highly developed argument for liberal egalitarianism. Although it has come in for a lot of criticism over the years (Rawls has himself modified his arguments in the light of these criticisms), it remains essential reading for anyone trying to get to grips with equality. Of particular importance, here, is his concept of the difference principle, part (a) of his second principle of justice. This states that inequalities are justified only if they benefit the worst-off group in the society. It is argued that persons placed in the original position – a thought-experiment in which persons do not know their place in society or their socially significant characteristics – would rationally choose such a principle. However, it is not at all clear that rational choices *could* be made by such persons, given their lack of knowledge. Some have also considered there to be a tension between the difference principle and the first principle of justice, namely, the right to the greatest equal liberty compatible with a like liberty for all. Despite these and other criticisms Rawls's remains a persuasive argument for a form of liberal equality.

NOZICK challenges the claims of liberals such as Rawls and considers their attempts to secure equality as an infringement of individuals' rights and their liberty. His libertarian argument comprises probably the most influential critique of the ideal of equality in recent years. According to Nozick, unequal "distributional facts" are legitimate so long as they arose by a legitimate process. What he defines as legitimate cannot be investigated here; suffice to say that he grounds legitimacy in a theory of acquisition and property rights. Although Nozick makes some sophisticated criticisms of the ideal of equality, his conclusions are highly contestable.

NAGEL considers equality as a distributive principle: a way of addressing the conflicting needs and interests of individuals for resources. He evaluates this principle against the claims of utility and individual rights, by considering the quality of their respective justifications. Deciding that a "plausible social morality" should show the influence of equality, utility, and rights, Nagel nevertheless finds the idea of acceptability to each individual an appealing trait of equality *vis-à-vis* both utility and rights. He seeks to explain egalitarian values in terms of separate assessment from each person's point of view. This essay offers a clear exposition of equality's relation to utility and rights, and a powerful argument for the particular claims of the former.

DWORKIN considers two general theories of what he calls distributional equality, or ways of distributing resources equally: equality of welfare and equality of resources. The former "holds that a distributional scheme treats people as equals when it distributes or transfers resources among them until no further transfer would leave them more equal in welfare", whereas the latter "holds that it treats them as equals when it distributes or transfers so that no further transfer would leave their shares of the total resources more equal." The former takes account of tastes and ambitions whereas the latter does not. Dworkin skilfully argues through each, coming to the conclusion that a form of equality of resources is to be preferred. Indeed, he considers equality of welfare to be an undesirable political goal. He supports his conclusion with the hypothetical device of an auction, in which all bidders begin with an equal amount of purchasing power and bid for the resources they require to pursue their conception of the good. Although Dworkin's argument is complex, he writes with great clarity and his version of liberal egalitarianism has proven to be almost as influential as Rawls's. As such it is essential reading.

SEN investigates three particular types of equality – utilitarian, total utility, and Rawlsian – and argues that each has its limitations, and moreover that an adequate theory cannot be constructed even on the combined grounds of the three. Sen proposes an alternative, which he calls "basic capability equality". This focuses upon what persons are capable of *doing* with goods rather than their possession of them, and rejects a utilitarian appraisal of persons' mental reactions to their capabilities. This is an interesting argument but is only briefly sketched, with the bulk of the essay consisting of a critique of utility-based and Rawlsian forms of equality.

For WILLIAMS the idea of equality is composed of various elements that can pull in very different directions. In particular, he discusses equality of opportunity and equality of respect. Equality of opportunity holds that the equal distribution of goods amongst persons entails taking account of those persons' conditions, especially the fortuitous and changeable characteristics of their conditions. It seems to assume acceptance of the importance of the goods in question, and this can easily run into an acceptance of status or prestige based upon people's access to those goods. Equality of respect, on the other hand, gives less consideration to the structures in which people enjoy status or prestige and considers people independently of those goods. Although these two ideals are often in conflict, genuine political thought requires attention to both of them.

An important intervention in the debate over equality was made by WALZER. He rejects the idea that there are universal foundations of justice, and a crucial part of his argument is his claim that there is no single underlying principle behind the various distributive spheres operating in societies that could be used to argue for *simple equality*. Social goods – for example

welfare and medical care, money and commodities, education, kinship and love, and recognition – each have their own criteria of just distribution determined by the specific meanings intrinsic to those goods and their distributive spheres. Put simply, the nature of a specific social good rather than some abstract principle of equality dictates its just distribution. *Complex equality* obtains when the autonomy of each distributive sphere is maintained – when a person is unable to convert her or his advantages from one sphere into another. This constitutes a highly original approach to questions of equality, the ramifications of which Walzer explores in the chapters that follow. In invoking the idea of complex equality Walzer makes many controversial claims, and his work has occasioned both criticism and applause.

MILLER & WALZER includes 11 essays in which Walzer's idea of complex equality and his arguments about the spheres of justice are assessed, plus an introduction by Miller and a response from Walzer. Especially useful are the essays by Arneson, Miller, and Waldron. Arneson and Waldron both offer critiques of complex equality, the former considering it to be "a very weak brew" and the latter focusing on its mischaracterization of the role of money. Miller, on the other hand, develops and defends the idea of complex equality. This is an excellent volume with a range of contributions from some eminent figures.

JAMES HAMPSHIRE

Equity

Binmore, Ken, *Game Theory and the Social Contract*, vol. 1: *Playing Fair*, Cambridge, Massachusetts: MIT Press, 1994

Binmore, Ken, *Game Theory and the Social Contract*, vol. 2: *Just Playing*, Cambridge, Massachusetts: MIT Press, 1998

Kolm, Serge-Christophe, *Modern Theories of Justice*, Cambridge, Massachusetts: MIT Press, 1996

Le Grand, Julian, *Equity and Choice: An Essay in Economics and Applied Philosophy*, London and New York: HarperCollins, 1991

Rawls, John, *A Theory of Justice*, Cambridge, Massachusetts: Harvard University Press, 1971; revised edition, 1999

Roemer, John E., *Theories of Distributive Justice*, Cambridge, Massachusetts: Harvard University Press, 1996

Sen, Amartya, *Commodities and Capabilities*, Amsterdam: North Holland, 1985

Sen, Amartya, "Capability and Well-being" in *The Quality of Life*, edited by Martha C. Nussbaum and Amartya Sen, Oxford: Oxford University Press, 1993

While economics is supremely a moral science, there is no concept that is more misunderstood in economics than the concept of equity. Much of neoclassical economics maintains the fiction that economics is about *efficiency* and that *equity* is a question of the political values of decision makers and hence outside the scope of "positive economics". What is meant by efficiency is essentially non-wastefulness in exchange as well as in production. If a reallocation of given goods can make at least one person better off without making anyone else worse off, then the new allocation is said to be Pareto-superior to the original one, and such a move is said to be Pareto-improving. When all Pareto-improving moves in production and in exchange have been exhausted, the allocation is called Pareto-optimal. In welfare economics, there is a theorem that a general competitive equilibrium is Pareto-optimal (Theorem 1) and that decision makers can reach any desired Pareto optimum by a suitable redistribution of initial endowments (Theorem 2). This latter theorem guarantees the separability of equity from efficiency. It is also the foundation of cost–benefit analysis, in which a project is accepted if the total benefits of the gainers from the project could in principle compensate those who would suffer losses from the project. But this separability of efficiency and equity, based on Theorem 2, is patently false, because nobody would reveal their initial endowments if there were a threat of confiscation and redistribution. This supposed separability of efficiency and equity is well discussed in LEGRAND, who demonstrates the shortcomings of the neoclassical utilitarian approach. However, for a positive and nonutilitarian way out of the impasse the reader should turn to RAWLS, the most eminent 20th-century political philosopher.

Rawls argues that a just and equitable society could be achieved if two principles (in the order given here) were adopted: (1) guaranting certain basic liberties, of the sort stated in a typical bill of rights; and (2) ensuring that social and economic inequalities are arranged in a way that offers the greatest possible benefit to the worst-off in society, while upholding fair equality of opportunity.

These are the two principles that would be chosen by parties to a hypothetical contract in "the original position", when the parties do not know of their particular identities, talents, resources, and advantages. The first principle guarantees a set of "primary goods". The second principle is called the *maximin criterion*: only with this "veil of ignorance" would the parties accept a fair procedure, free from the biases resulting from the individuals' particular identities. This liberal theory of justice is based on the assumption that if reasonable people saw that they had a more or less equal chance of being in the shoes of the more disadvantaged members of the society, then in the absence of the knowledge of who each person will be, most people would agree to a social contract in which emphasis is placed on improving as much as possible the state of the least advantaged. Rawls' theory has had a profound impact on the question of equity in economics, and has directly or indirectly influenced several other researchers such as Binmore, Kolm, Roemer, and Sen.

BINMORE (1994, 1998) attempts to extend the work of Rawls by providing a vigorous reformulation. In Rawls' proposed society, the market mechanism would be fully utilized; but the allocative achievements of the market mechanism would be improved upon by judicious social intervention. Rawls' view is that, while the market assures efficiency, it is incapable of achieving equity, and often, achieving equity has resulted in some loss of efficiency. The main question tackled by Binmore is: in a liberal society, is it possible to choose among Pareto-efficient outcomes that enhance equity without sacrificing efficiency? He shows that while the Harsanyi utilitarian solution is possible, a nonutilitarian Rawls-

ian solution can also be rigorously determined. Furthermore, the Rawlsian solution is more equitable than the Harsanyi solution. His solution belongs to the same family as Rawls' maximin criterion, and requires the use of Nash bargaining theory, empathetic preferences, and results from evolutionary game theory.

While ROEMER's work was published after Binmore's, he makes no reference to the latter, although he is also concerned with the same issue – namely, how to aggregate individual preferences into social preferences. However, his focus is much narrower than Binmore's. Roemer is influenced principally by Walras, and consequently concentrates on the just distribution of existing initial endowments. He also offers a critique of the work on equity of other contemporaries, such as Kolm, Cohen, Nozick, Sen, and Dworkin. He proposes an organizing principle by suggesting that the different approaches arise from thinking of equity as attempts to *equalize* something, whether it be access to primary goods, opportunity, freedom to reach one's full potential and capabilities, or something else.

The capabilities approach is worthy of special mention. The restriction in welfare economics to utility information has been a straitjacket, which has excluded debate in economics on important issues of inequality – regarding income distribution, well-being, hunger, malnutrition, and gender inequality – and indeed, on all aspects of liberty, freedom, and the fulfilment of human potential. In the standard neoclassical theory, it is assumed that utility is derived from consuming commodities, which are limited only by the consumer's budgetary constraints. By contrast, SEN (1985, 1993) argues that commodities are desired because of their *characteristics*, whether it is to satisfy hunger, to meet a nutritional need, or to nourish the soul. The extent to which a person succeeds in utilizing the commodities at his or her command is called a *functioning*. A functioning is an achievement of a person – what he or she manages to do or to be. It is the part of the "state" of a person, and must be distinguished from the commodities which are used to achieve such functionings. *Capability* is the set of potential functionings that a person may reach. Sen's functioning and capabilities approach is a fruitful way to study many questions of equity.

A more wide-ranging and appealing approach to equity, justice, and fairness is offered by KOLM. He analyses the structure and methods of justice; the values and types of liberty; the principle of equal freedom; basic rights and basic needs; the measurement and alleviation of misery; the measurement of inequality and injustice; the principles of social and public choice and the ethical foundations of public economics. Kolm's treatment of equity and justice is multilayered and rich: he thinks of problems of global justice, including basic rights, as *macrojustice*; those of local justice, such as access to clean water, as *microjustice*; and other intermediate issues, of accessibility to healthcare and education, as *mesojustice*.

In the 1950s, equity issues were hamstrung by the old welfare economics, which did not permit interpersonal comparisons of "utility" and well-being, and which came to a dead end with the publication of the first and second theorems listed above. In the period 1970–80, economists thought of equity and fairness mostly in terms of allocations (of goods) that were "envy-free", itself a very limiting approach. However, after

Rawls, a much richer treatment of equity was possible. Writers like Binmore, LeGrand, Sen, and Kolm have opened up new vistas, and public economics may one day be transformed.

MOHAMMED DORE

See also Justice

Equity versus efficiency

Binswanger, Hans, Klaus Deininger and Gershon Feder, "Power, Distortions, Revolt and Reform in Agriculture Land Revolutions" in *Handbook of Development Economics*, vol. 3, edited by Jere Behrman and T.N. Srinivasan, Amsterdam: North Holland, and New York: Elsevier, 1995

Birdsall, Nancy, David Ross and Richard Sabot, "Inequality and Growth Reconsidered: Lessons from East-Asia", *World Bank Economic Review*, 9/3 (1995): 477–508

Bowles, Samuel and Herbert Gintis, "Efficient Redistribution: New Rules for Markets, States and Communities", *Politics and Society*, 24/4 (1996): 307–42

Creedy, John and Ian M. MacDonald, "A Tax Package to Reduce the Marginal Rate of Income Tax and the Wage Demands of Trade Unions", *Economic Review*, 66/194 (1990): 195–202

Eaton, B. Curtis and William White, "The Distribution of Wealth and the Efficiency of Institutions", *Economic Inquiry*, 29/2 (1991): 336–50

Grossman, Herschel I., "Production, Appropriation and Land Reform", *American Economic Review*, 84/3 (1994): 705–12

Hersoug, Tor, "Union Wage Responses to Tax Changes", *Oxford Economic Paper*, 36/1 (1984): 37–51

Hoff, Karla and Andrew B. Lyon, "Non-Leaky Buckets: Optimal Redistributive Taxation and Agency Costs", *Journal of Public Economics*, 58/3 (1995): 365–390

Lockwood, Ben and Alan Manning, "Wage Setting and the Tax System: Theory and Evidence for the United Kingdom", *Journal of Public Economics*, 52/1 (1993): 1–29

Ng, Yew-Kwang, "Towards a Theory of Third Best", *Public Finance*, 32 (1977): 1–15

Ng, Yew-Kwang, *Welfare Economics: Introduction and Development of Basic Concepts*, London: Macmillan, and New York: Wiley, 1979

Ng, Yew-Kwang, "Quasi-Pareto Social Improvements", *American Economic Review*, 74/5 December (1984): 1033–50

Okun, Arthur M., *Equality and Efficiency: The Big Tradeoff*, Washington, DC: Brookings Institution, 1975

Perotti, Roberto, "Growth, Income Distribution, and Democracy: What the Data Say", *Journal of Economics Growth*, 1 (1996): 149–87

Persson, Torsten and Guido Tabellini, "Is Inequality Harmful for Growth?", *American Economic Review*, 84/3 (1994): 600–21

Putterman, Louis, John E. Roemer and Joaquim Silvestre, "Does Egalitarianism Have a Future?", *Journal of Economic Literature*, 36/2 (1998): 861–902

Strauss, John and Duncan Thomas, "Human Resources: Empirical Modelling of Household and Family Decisions" in *Handbook of Development Economics*, vol. 3, edited by Jere Behrman and T.N. Srinivasan, Amsterdam and New York: Elsevier, 1995

As the title of OKUN proclaims, the issue of equality versus efficiency is *the* big tradeoff facing government economic policy. Personal differences in income and wealth levels in most economies are phenomenal and rose substantially during the 1980s and 1990s. Some of these differences are just due to different choices made; people also differ in native talents, inheritance, and luck. Large inequalities due to these factors are usually regarded as inequitable, especially if absolute poverty is also involved. However, attempts to redistribute income to increase equality typically lead to inefficiencies. Thus, liberal unemployment benefits may make people spend less time on job hunting and become choosier. Taxes to finance these benefits make people less willing to work, save, and take risks. There are also the substantial costs of administration, policing, and compliance in any system of redistribution.

This traditional concept of an equity versus efficiency tradeoff can be challenged. First, there are contributions emphasizing the complementarity between equality and efficiency/growth. STRAUSS & THOMAS consider the physiological effect of income on work effort, while others emphasize the principal-agent problems and imperfection in the credit market due to informational asymmetry, which may be lessened by the use of collaterals that the very poor lack (BINSWANGER, DEININGER & FEDER, HOFF & LYON). CREEDY & MACDONALD, HERSOUG, and LOCKWOOD & MANNING consider the moderation of tax progressivity on wage demands of unions. PERSSON & TABELLINI describe the discouragement of investment of high inequality which increases the difference between median and average incomes and hence the median voter demand for higher tax rate, but see PEROTTI on the negative empirical evidence for the mechanism, though the negative relationship between inequality and growth appears valid (see BIRDSALL, ROSS & SABOT). Both EATON & WHITE and GROSSMAN consider the crime-reduction effect of equality. *See also* BOWLES & GINTIS, and PUTTERMAN, ROEMER & SILVESTRE.

Second, the point that taxes are distortive may not be true. Since the production and consumption of most goods generates environmental disruption effects and relative-income effects, taxes may be more corrective than distortive. Also, taxes on "diamond goods" (goods valued for their values rather than their intrinsic consumption effects) generate not only no excess burden but no burden at all. (See the entry on public spending, optimal size for more details.)

The above means that more taxes/transfers may be undertaken to achieve equality without reducing efficiency significantly in the wider perspective. However, because the objective of equality is unlikely to be met fully, some conflicts remain. As equality and efficiency are both desirable, how do we sacrifice the least amount of one in trying to increase the other? In specific issues, how do we decide on the best policies taking into account their effects both on equality and efficiency? These difficult problems are made worse by the complication of second best. Economists know clearly the conditions that need to be satisfied for the economy to be efficient if all sectors can satisfy these first-best rules (for example, marginal benefits equal marginal costs). Due to monopolistic power, uncorrected pollution, and so forth, not all sectors can satisfy these rules. Then we are in a second-best situation where the efficient conditions are extremely complicated, requiring unavailable information regarding the interrelationships between the various sectors. Adding the equality consideration makes it well nigh impossible to prescribe an optimal policy in any specific situation. However, NG (1977, 1979, 1984) provides a theory of third best that makes policy formulation much simpler. In the absence of relevant information on the complicated interrelationships, following the simple first-best rules maximizes expected benefits. (See the entry on second and third best theories for details.) In specific issues, simply observe efficiency ("a dollar is a dollar"), leaving the objective of equality to be achieved through the general redistributive system of tax/transfer.

It is tempting for an economist to think that, because the substantial redistributive tax/transfer system has significant disincentive effects, it is better to shift some of the redistributive burden to specific items such as taxing/subsidizing goods consumed disproportionately by the rich/poor, using distributional weights in cost-benefit analysis, and using first-come-first-served in allocating car parking spaces. Although some *marginal* efficiency costs of distorting choice are created, they are generally thought to be smaller than the reduction in disincentive effects due to relying less on the progressive tax/transfer system. This belief is incorrect (as described by Ng 1979, 1984). The reason is that, assuming rational individuals, the disincentive effects are in accordance with the total system of tax/transfer, taxes/subsidies, plus all other redistributive and preferential measures, instead of having a separate and independent schedule of increasing marginal disincentive effects for each of the separate measures. Rational persons, in their work/leisure choices, do not just ask how much post-tax income they can earn, but they also have a rough idea of the utility of having the higher income. This utility is affected by whatever specific redistributive or preferential measures are in place. Thus, the preferential treatment against the rich will add on to the progressive tax/transfer system to determine the total disincentive effects. Hence, even if only marginal specific equality-oriented measures are used, the disincentive effects involved are not just marginal. Thus, for the same degree of equality in real income (utility) achieved, the same degree of disincentive occurs whether we use only the tax/transfer system or use a combination of it and some specific purely equality-oriented policies. But the latter alternative has the additional efficiency costs of distorting choice, and is thus inferior.

In NG (1979, 1984), the following proposition is proved:

Proposition A (A Dollar is a Dollar): For any alternative (designated *A*) using a system (designated *a*) of purely equality-oriented preferential treatment between the rich and the poor, there exists another alternative, *B*, which does not use preferential treatment, that makes no one worse off, achieves the same degree of equality (of real income, or utility) and raises more government revenue, which could be used to make everyone better off.

Under alternative *B*, a more (than alternative *A*) progressive tax/transfer system may have to be used. It is also argued that complications such as administrative costs, political constraints, and ignorance of benefits distribution either strengthen the proposition or do not affect the main thrust significantly.

YEW-KWANG NG

See also Optimal size, Public spending, Second and third best theories

Ergonomics

International Labour Office and International Ergonomics Association, *Ergonomic Checkpoints: Practical and Easy-to-Implement Solutions for Improving Safety, Health and Working Conditions*, Geneva: International Labour Office, 1996

Meister, David, *The History of Human Factors and Ergonomics*, Mahwah, New Jersey: Lawrence Erlbaum, 1999

Norman, Donald A., *The Psychology of Everyday Things*, New York: Basic Books, 1988

Osborne, David J., *Ergonomics at Work: Human Factors in Design and Development*, 3rd edition, New York and Chichester: Wiley, 1995

Salvendy, Gavriel (editor), *Handbook of Human Factors and Ergonomics*, 2nd edition, New York and Chichester: Wiley, 1997

Weimer, Jon (editor), *Research Techniques in Human Engineering*, Englewood Cliffs, New Jersey: Prentice Hall, 1995

Wilson, John R. and E. Nigel Corlett (editors), *Evaluation of Human Work: A Practical Ergonomics Methodology*, 2nd edition, London: Taylor and Francis, 1995

Woodson, Wesley E., Barry Tillman and Peggy Tillman, *Human Factors Design Handbook: Information and Guidelines for the Design of Systems, Facilities, Equipment, and Products for Human Use*, New York: McGraw Hill, 1991

Ergonomics is sometimes referred to as the "science of work"; it is also know as "human factors engineering", "human engineering", and "engineering psychology". It is the field that considers human capabilities and limitations in the design of machines and objects that people use in carrying on purposeful activity. It is an academic field that has developed in the 20th century and which began with the pioneering time-and-motion studies of Frederick W. Taylor and of Frank and Lillian Gilbreth. Taylor is sometimes called "the father of scientific management". His *Principles of Scientific Management*, which was first published in 1911, is a classic in industrial psychology. That same year Frank B. Gilbreth's classic study of bricklaying was also published. Frank B. Gilbreth and Lillian Gilbreth applied their studies to their home life as the parents of the family in the books *Cheaper by the Dozen* (1949) and *Belles on Their Toes* (1950), which were written by two of their 12 children. Ergonomics emerged as a recognized academic discipline during World War II, when engineers teamed together with psychologists and physiologists to design military equipment after it was discovered that the human operator was the weakest link in sophisticated military systems.

The early emphasis of the field was on human physiology and the increasing of human productivity in the workplace. However, as the discipline has matured, it has focused on the provision of safer and healthier work environments and improvement in the quality of working life. In recent years it has contributed to the development of industrial workplaces, office design, computer hardware, and consumer products. It has also contributed to the design of products to meet the needs of handicapped persons.

INTERNATIONAL LABOUR OFFICE (ILO) is a collection of practical, inexpensive, and easy-to-implement solutions to ergonomic problems that was prepared in collaboration with the International Ergonomics Association. The book is an illustrated manual of 128 ideas to improve conditions in the workplace and was compiled by an international panel of experts. Each one-page ergonomic checkpoint illustrates an action for improving the workplace environment and indicates both why it is necessary and how best to carry it out. The manual includes a complete list of all checkpoints to enable users to carry out surveys with ease.

MEISTER is a valuable addition to the literature in the field. It is a highly specialized but very readable disciplinary history that contains nine sections. The preface contains a list of common acronyms used in the field. Part I is a summary and introduction to human factors engineering (HFE). Part II discusses the conceptual structure of HFE. Part III discusses the nature of the human-machine system, the history of the system concept and tools, equipment and systems. Part IV is the formal history of HFE in America, the UK, and Russia. Part V is an informal history of HFE, methodology, results, and conclusions. Part VI focuses on characteristics of HFE research including HFE methodology. Part VII deals with special interests within HFE and compares HFE specialties. Part VIII discusses HFE in practice, the demographic context of HFE, and HFE employment. Part IX consists of the author's comments on the big issues as well as some concluding comments.

NORMAN is an enjoyable book that general readers rate very highly. It explains why things are designed the way they are; why some things work and why some things do not. It is recommended for anyone who designs or builds products used by the general public. It approaches the area from the perspective of a psychologist. OSBORNE is an excellent companion text to the Norman text. Its emphasis is on helping the reader develop an understanding of ergonomics through discussion of the flow of information between man and machine in the work system. It describes the extent to which diverse factors of the system may help or hinder the flow of information.

SALVENDY contains the invited contributions of more than 100 of the foremost authorities around the world. It contains 60 chapters, each of which was reviewed by an international advisory panel consisting of today's leading figures in human factors and ergonomics. The book's approach is primarily applications-oriented, containing case studies, examples, figures, and tables that optimize the usability of its

information. The text is recognized as a leading reference tool for industrial engineers and managers.

WEIMER is the only text on how to conduct research in the fields of ergonomics and human factors engineering. Each chapter is a primer on the issues, methods, and tools used when conducting research in a particular human factors subdiscipline, from aerospace to ageing to medical systems. Each chapter is written by a specialist in the field.

WILSON & CORLETT is a general text on ergonomics methodology that was first published in 1990 and is now in a revised edition. It is intended as a companion to a general textbook on ergonomics and human factors. It discusses human-machine interfaces for systems control and evaluating work conditions and risk of injury as well as techniques for field surveys and the practical measurement of psychophysiological functions for determining workloads.

WOODSON, TILLMAN & TILLMAN is recognized worldwide as a leading source of ergonomics data and guidelines that provides practical approaches to planning and designing products and facilities to be used by people. It contains facts and data on human body size, reach, strength, reaction time, and other factors useful to anyone who designs products or facilities. The latest edition contains information that reflects developments in computer and space technology.

GEORGIA HOLMES

See also Human-computer interaction

Essentialism

Bohan, Janis S., "Regarding Gender: Essentialism, Constructionism, and Feminist Psychology", *Psychology of Women Quarterly*, 17 (1993): 5–21

Cromby, John and Penny Standen, "Taking Our Selves Seriously" in *Social Constructionist Psychology: A Critical Analysis of Theory and Practice*, edited by David J. Nightingale and John Cromby, Buckingham: Open University Press, 1999

French, Sally, "Disability, Impairment or Something in Between" in *Disabling Barriers – Enabling Environments*, edited by John Swain *et al.*, London and Newbury Park, California: Sage, 1993

Fuss, Diana, *Essentially Speaking: Feminism, Nature, and Difference*, London and New York: Routledge, 1989

Glass, James M., "Multiplicity, Identity and the Horrors of Selfhood: Failures in the Postmodern Position", *Political Psychology*, 14/2 (1993): 255–78

Hughes, Bill and Kevin Paterson, "The Social Model of Disability and the Disappearing Body: Towards a Sociology of Impairment", *Disability and Society*, 12/3 (1997): 325–40

Levin, David M., "Psychology as a Discursive Formation: The Postmodern Crisis", *Humanistic Psychologist*, 19/3 (1991): 250–76

Oliver, Michael, "The Social Model in Context" in his *Understanding Disability: From Theory to Practice*, London: Macmillan, and New York: St Martin's Press, 1996

Sampson, Edward E., "The Deconstruction of the Self" in *Texts of Identity*, edited by John Shotter and Kenneth J. Gergen, London and Newbury Park, California: Sage, 1989

Young, Iris M., "Throwing Like a Girl: A Phenomenology of Feminine Body Comportment, Motility and Spatiality" in her *Throwing Like a Girl and Other Essays in Feminist Philosophy and Social Theory*, Bloomington: Indiana University Press, 1990

The *New Shorter Oxford English Dictionary* defines essentialism as "the belief that things have a set of characteristics which make them what they are, and that the task of science and philosophy is their discovery and expression; the doctrine that essence is prior to existence". The readings for this entry explore contemporary critiques of essentialism (a doctrine that underpins many approaches within the human sciences) in terms of three areas of research: the individual (or self), feminist theory, and disability politics.

SAMPSON provides a detailed analysis of essentialism as it applies to the study of the individual within psychology. He illustrates that Western essentialist notions of the individual, as a self-contained, autonomous, and unitary being, have been challenged by numerous approaches within the human sciences; cross-cultural investigations, feminist studies, social constructionism, systems theory, critical theory, and deconstructionism. He expands upon the latter two and demonstrates that Western notions regarding the individual (mirrored in traditional psychological inquiries) are deeply flawed in that they fail to acknowledge the fundamentally social nature of the individual.

At the heart of many contemporary accounts of the individual lies an (apparently) unquestioned acceptance of postmodern and poststructural critiques of essentialism. LEVIN, in a detailed analysis of what he terms "the narrative framework of postmodernism", explores the ontological, epistemological, and methodological implications of this acceptance for the discipline of psychology. His concern is that although postmodern deconstructions of the subject have successfully critiqued the implicit essentialism of many mainstream accounts, the only conclusion that seems to have been reached is that there is "no agreement on the description of our emptiness"; by which he means that anti-essentialist, postmodern accounts have seemingly failed to offer an adequate account of personhood.

GLASS further explores the limitations of postmodern accounts of the individual through an analysis of the postmodern notion of the multiplicity of the self in contrast to the lived experience of "multiple personality disorder". Although accepting that postmodernism has enabled many of the human sciences to challenge the rigid and often dogmatic essentialism of many contemporary accounts, he challenges its celebration of the multiplicity of the self in terms of its denial of meaning, coherence, structure, and continuity. He argues that it is precisely these characteristics (which postmodernism denies) that are at stake in the therapeutic reconstruction of the lives of people with multiple personality disorder. The remainder of the paper charts the progress of Molly's reconstructive journey from the horrors of multiplicity to the stability of a coherent self.

CROMBY & STANDEN argue that many contemporary constructionist accounts of the individual, in embracing a thorough going anti-essentialism, fail to offer an adequate account of the self. They begin by outlining and endorsing many of the critiques of mainstream psychology's essentialist conception of the self and consider some of the principal objections to notions of the self raised by such analyses. However, they go on to describe the costs and dangers for constructionism of theorizing without any notion of the self, and they explore the ways in which constructionist concerns regarding the reestablishment of the self might be addressed. They conclude by indicating some possible directions for the development of future constructionist work in this area.

BOHAN provides an accessible introduction to debates concerning essentialism within feminist psychology. She argues that recent essentialist construals of gender with cultural feminism are problematic in that they are grounded in universalizing assumptions (which fail to acknowledge diversity), that they fail to distinguish between qualities of gender and qualities that are produced by oppression, and that they offer a victim blaming model of individual and social change. In contrast, she suggests that constructionist (anti-essentialist) accounts of gender, grounded in the social, cultural, and political domain, provide a means whereby the problems that attend these essentialist accounts might be readily addressed.

Like Bohan, FUSS is concerned with issues of difference, essence, and social construction and she also begins with an analysis of the debates concerning essence versus construction. However, having identified the key issues that this debate raises, she goes on to question the (theoretical and political) utility of this oppositional, binary model. She demonstrates that although strict essentialism and constructionism may be incompatible, they nonetheless offer each other various possibilities that advance understanding of such notions as gender, race, and politics. In this sense, she seeks to blur the distinction between the two through demonstrating the ways in which these terms are "inextricably co-implicated with each other" (p.xii).

YOUNG approaches the notion of essentialism through an analysis of embodied practice and in so doing appears to side-step many of the theoretical difficulties associated with this debate. Drawing upon phenomenology, she demonstrates that "difference" can neither be explained as a consequence of a hidden essence(s) nor as a simple function of particular social and cultural arrangements. Through an analysis of feminine body comportment, motility, and spatiality, she demonstrates the fundamental ways in which the lived body exists within particular social and political contexts that determine its nature. In this sense, her analysis acknowledges difference as both real and constructed – as a common aspect of female existence in a particular culture at a particular time.

OLIVER demonstrates that the individual model of disability rests upon an implicit essentialism that conceptualizes disability as a necessary consequence or function of individual limitation or impairment. The social model of disability, in contrast, locates the problem of disability within society – specifically, its failure to provide adequate services and resources to ensure that the specific needs of disabled people are both recognized and provided for. Disability, then, is not an essential property of given individuals, but is all the ways in which society oppresses those whose needs depart from normalized and regularized expectations. To challenge and combat disability is to change society such that the needs and rights of people with impairments are addressed.

FRENCH, while acknowledging Oliver's distinction between impairment as "individual limitation" and disability as "socially imposed restriction", suggests that some profound problems that people may experience cannot always be easily solved in the ways he suggests, through changes to the physical and social environment. Using a range of examples, she discusses how some problems seem to occupy a middle ground between social oppression (disability as socially constructed) and individual limitation or impairment (essentialist notions of disability). She acknowledges the political and social gains that the social model of disability has made possible, but she suggests that it is now time to develop and deepen our understanding of these issues.

HUGHES & PATERSON discuss the ways in which the body (now a central topic within many of the human sciences) has been made "exile" within contemporary disability politics. In discussing the social model of disability they note that it has shifted "debates about disability from the biomedically dominated agendas to discourses about politics and citizenship" (p.325), but in so doing, it has relinquished the "body to medicine and understands impairment in terms of medical discourse" (p.326). Drawing upon poststructuralism and phenomenology they aim to develop a "sociology of impairment" that supersedes the disability (social construction)/impairment (essentialism) distinction and so allows for the future development of both disability theory and politics.

DAVID J. NIGHTINGALE

See also Constructionism

Estoppel

Baker, P.V. and P.St.J. Langan, *Snell's Equity*, 29th edition, London: Sweet and Maxwell, 1990

Coke, Edward, *The First Part of the Institutes of the Laws of England; or, a Commentary upon Littleton*, New York: Garland, 1979

Cross, Rupert and Colin Tapper, *Cross on Evidence*, London: Butterworths, 1990

Evans, P.T., "Choosing the Right Estoppel", *Conveyancer and Property Lawyer* (1988): 346–56

Feinman, Jay, "Promissory Estoppel and Judicial Method", *Harvard Law Review*, 97 (1984): 678–718

Lunney, Mark, "Towards a Unified Estoppel: The Long and Winding Road", *Conveyancer and Property Lawyer* (1992): 239–51

Smith, Roger, "How Proprietary is Proprietary Estoppel?" in *Consensus ad Idem: Essays in Honour of Guenter Treitel*, edited by Francis Rose, London: Sweet and Maxwell, 1996

Thompson, M.P., "From Representation to Expectation: Estoppel as a Cause of Action", *Cambridge Law Journal*, (1983): 257–78

Turner, Alexander Kingcome, *The Law Relating to Estoppel by Representation*, 3rd edition, London: Butterworths, 1977 (original text by George Spencer Bower, 1923)

A traditional starting point for the study of estoppel is still the account given by COKE, writing in 1628. He explains:

> '*Estoppe*', commeth of the French word *estoupe*, from whence the English word stopped: and it is called an estoppel or conclusion, because a man's owne act or acceptance stoppeth or closeth up his mouth to alleage or plead the truth ... [T]here be three kinde of estoppels, viz. by matter of record, by matter in writing, and by matter *in pais*.

What Coke calls "estoppel by matter of record" is often now called estoppel *per rem judicatam* (roughly, "estoppel because the court has already decided"). It is the rule that when a question has once been litigated, the parties cannot bring it back to court again. It differs from the rest of the law of estoppel in that it arises from judicial decision; it is not triggered by what the person who is estopped has said, or not said, or done, and is governed by rules quite different from those applicable to the rest of the law of estoppel. It forms part of the law of evidence, and is best approached through the medium of a work on evidence such as that by CROSS & TAPPER.

The rest of the law of estoppel can be described as a mechanism for enforcing consistency. It prescribes circumstances in which it is not permissible to go back on what one has said or done. Thus Coke's "estoppel by matter in writing" is known nowadays as estoppel by deed. It is the rule that one is not allowed to deny a statement of fact that one has made in a deed, nor to deny the validity of a property right that one has granted, by deed or, nowadays, otherwise (for example, a lease granted orally). These rather specialized areas are best regarded as rules of property law distinct from the bulk of the modern law of estoppel, which has grown out of Coke's third category, estoppel *in pais*.

The 19th-century courts developed estoppel as a rule of evidence of particular importance in commercial cases. The idea was that where a statement of fact had been made, and relied upon by the person to whom it was addressed, the maker of the statement could be prevented from going back on that statement. A simple example is where a consignor of goods on a ship confirms that they have been properly stowed by the carrier; if the goods are damaged and the consignor sues, he may be estopped from alleging that the damage was caused by improper storage. TURNER's work remains the classic exposition of this very traditional use of estoppel, and is still quoted judicially. Its weakness is that it does not give adequate recognition to the development of estoppel in the 20th century by the courts in their equity jurisdiction.

This development is seen in BAKER & LANGAN's discussion of the doctrines known as promissory and proprietary estoppel. The former is the idea that if one has promised not to exercise a right, one may be prevented from doing so, temporarily or permanently. The latter is a more powerful tool, arising where one person has given another the impression that his rights, particularly property rights, will not be exercised; proprietary estoppel will not merely give him a defence to the exercise of those rights (by, for example, enabling him to resist a claim for possession of property), but may be used as a cause of action, allowing him to apply to the court for the grant of a proprietary right (for example, full legal ownership of the property). The orthodox view has been that estoppel cannot be a cause of action outside the context of land; thus if one person promises to give another £1,000, and there is no contract between them, the promisee cannot claim the money on the basis that the other is estopped from withdrawing from his promise. To allow this would be to undermine the doctrine of consideration.

The view of estoppel as a doctrine comprising a number of distinct legal categories is further refined in EVANS, which explores the policy of the courts behind the maintenance of these separate doctrines. The opposite trend is seen in THOMPSON's discussion, which explores the idea of estoppel, at least in its equitable forms, as a unified doctrine based upon the principle of preventing unconscionable conduct, as seen in some significant decisions of the High Court and Court of Appeal in the early 1980s.

The vision of a unified estoppel has received further impetus from developments in Australia, which are discussed in LUNNEY's article. He argues, as did Thompson, for the use of estoppel as a cause of action outside the context of land. Thompson bases his argument on the established use of estoppel to support an action by, for example, blocking the use of a defence. Thus if the defendant has promised not to raise a defence of limitation he may be estopped from doing so. Lunney argues more directly from Australian developments. Despite these arguments, there is as yet no general acceptance by the courts in England and Wales of estoppel as a cause of action outside the context of land.

Recent discussion has covered more technical and detailed issues within proprietary estoppel, and in particular the question of how the courts respond to estoppel. Where one person has spent money on another's property in reliance upon the owner's promise to give it to him, the owner may be estopped from resiling from his promise. There has been some debate as to whether the court's response to this will be to satisfy the claimant's expectation by granting him ownership of the property, or merely to compensate him for his expenditure. Despite some argument for the latter option, drawing upon Australian developments, SMITH affirms the orthodox view that the courts will, in general, make an order that fulfils the claimant's expectation. He also discusses an issue that is of increasing importance, namely the proprietary nature of the rights created by estoppel. To take the example just given: suppose that, before the claimant brought his action, the owner had sold the property. Would the claimant be able to use estoppel as a cause of action against the purchaser, who of course was not involved in the parties' original dealings? Smith addresses this difficult question, which may be the subject of legislation in the future.

In the US, promissory estoppel has been developed as a mechanism for reliance-based promise enforcement, in marked contrast to the resistance to such development, outside the context of land, in England and Wales. FEINMAN recounts the evolution of promissory estoppel in the US, and then explores more recent cases in the context of the law of contract and of 20th-century legal thought.

ELIZABETH COOKE

Ethics in research

Advisory Committee on Human Radiation Experiments, "Research Ethics and the Medical Profession: Report of the Advisory Committee on Human Radiation Experiments", *Journal of the American Medical Association*, 276/5 (1996): 403–09

American Psychological Association, "Ethical Principles of Psychologists and Code of Conduct", *American Psychologist*, 47/12 (1992): 1597–1611

Brody, Janet L., John P. Gluck and Alfredo S. Aragon, "Participants' Understanding of the Process of Psychological Research: Informed Consent", *Ethics and Behavior*, 7/4 (1997): 285–98

Lehrman, Nathaniel S. and Vera H. Sharav, "Ethical Problems in Psychiatric Research", *Journal of Mental Health Administration*, 24/2 (1997): 227–50

Miller, Neil E., "The Value of Behavioral Research on Animals", *American Psychologist*, 40/4 (1985): 423–40

Plous, S., "Attitudes toward the Use of Animals in Psychological Research and Education", *American Psychologist*, 51/11 (1996): 1167–80

Sugarman, Jeremy, Nancy E. Kass, Steven N. Goodman, Patricia Perentesis, Praveen Fernandes and Ruth R. Faden, "What Patients Say about Medical Research", *IRB: A Review of Human Subjects Research*, 20/4 (1998): 1–7

The American Psychological Association (APA) has developed an extensive set of ethical principles and a code of ethics for psychologists engaged in a wide variety of activities, including research. These principles are consistent with federal laws, but involve details that are more specific than the legal code. The AMERICAN PSYCHOLOGICAL ASSOCIATION notes that ethical considerations begin with the planning process, asserting that a research must possess the competence and expertise for a planned study; further, researchers are responsible for those working under their supervision. During the conduct of research, psychologists must provide realistic informed consent or obtain it by proxy if a participant is not competent to make a decision; they should also inform participants about how the results of the research will be used. They must also refrain from deception unless justified by the potential beneficial outcome of the research. Subsequent to the research, psychologists must provide appropriate information about research outcomes to the participants and must honour any commitments made to the participants. The ethical code also provides guidelines regarding publishing the results of research and the sharing of data with other researchers. This set of guidelines is the latest revision of principles first enunciated in 1953.

Reports of possible violations of ethical codes in the scientific and medical community during the Cold War in the US spurred the federal government to investigate the nature and scope of the problem. The ADVISORY COMMITTEE ON HUMAN RADIATION EXPERIMENTS has reported on standards of ethical conduct in research and their evolution in the past half century. For example, the Committee cited documented cases of involuntary and unknowing participation involving exposure to radiation among developmentally disabled children and pregnant women. The Committee discovered that the federal government had initiated requirements for informed consent and voluntary participation beginning in the 1920s, but there is little consensus that such regulations had much effect on scientific practices. The Committee noted that researchers were required to inform healthy subjects about the research only if considerable risk existed. The stipulations regarding patient subjects were considerably looser, and patients were often unwitting participants in research that offered them little or no medical benefit. The Committee identified six basic ethical principles for research. These principles involve protecting subjects from deception and harm while promoting fair treatment, respect for individuals, and the rights of self-determination. The group concluded that most research with people today is ethically sound and poses little risk, but suggested changes in the system of guarantees of protection for human subjects.

One of the hallmarks of ethics in research is providing the subjects with sufficient information that they can make an informed judgement about whether to participate. BRODY, GLUCK AND ARAGON point out that researchers must provide information that would materially influence participation, that people must be able to comprehend this information and be competent to make voluntary decisions. Relevant information often comes from an informed consent form. The authors report that, although researchers may fulfil the requirements involving informed consent, participants may misunderstand the process of informed consent or may not feel comfortable withdrawing from a study even though they are told they may. The implications of BRODY, GLUCK & ARAGON's research include the possibility that subjects are not given enough information prior to appearing for an appointment with the researcher; that they do not realize that the stage of informed consent during research is meant to be a decision point for the participant; and that if people are uncomfortable with their participation, they may pretend to carry out the research task, generating invalid data. The authors provide suggestions for changes in the informed consent process. This research involved only college undergraduates who had previously participated as research subjects; at the same time, the vast majority of psychological studies involves this population.

SUGARMAN *et al.* queried medical patients about prior experience in medical research. Patients in waiting rooms of medical oncology, radiation oncology, and cardiology outpatient clinics responded to questions by the researchers regarding attitudes about and understanding of medical research. The authors note that patients may have participated in the research based on misunderstandings that could have limited them in their ability to make informed decisions. For instance, when learning about a prospective study, patients variously learned that they would participate in "medical research", in a "clinical trial", in a "clinical investigation", in a "medical study", or in a "medical experiment". These terms are often synonymous. Patients viewed "medical studies" as more benign, and "medical experiments" as riskier than "medical research". Patient participation is thus likely to be dependent on terminology, regardless of the nature of the actual research. The authors also report other factors associated with patient misunderstanding about their participation. For instance, a small proportion felt that they could not withdraw from the study without their physician's permission. Further, some patients mistook the research for treatment for their medical conditions and some participated because participation would help them pay for their treatment. A small percentage of respondents reported that they did not know they had participated in research; a roughly similar percentage claimed to have participated when they had not. The authors suggest strategies to overcome these problems, noting that such strategies will maintain the trust that most patients show regarding medical research.

LEHRMAN & SHARAV comment on the weaknesses they see in safeguarding psychiatric patients with compromised capacity for making informed judgments about research participation. They cite several cases in which patients sought treatment for psychiatric problems and were included in clinical research without their knowledge. The patients suffered relapses in their symptoms, sometimes involving irreversible damage. The authors point out the ethical lapses that they see in such research, failing to provide adequate description of experimental procedures, possible risks, and alternative treatments as required by federal law. Lehrman & Sharav assert that there is little real accountability in such research. They further state that not only are breaches of ethics tolerated – they are sanctioned by some groups. The authors cite one particular study in which an institution claimed that informing schizophrenic patient-subjects about the risk of a relapse would expose them to needless alarm, whereas exposing them to actual relapse would be less ethically problematic. They propose a set of safeguards to protect potential subjects.

Finally, in the past few decades, researchers (as well as the general public) have publicly discussed the desirability of using animals in research. MILLER has vigorously defended the use of animals in research, pointing out that such activity has actually benefited animals, has promoted human welfare, and involves more humane treatment of the animals than is generally reported in the popular media. Among psychologists, PLOUS reports, there is generally widespread support for the use of animals in research in studies that involve observation or confinement, but little support for studies that involve pain or death.

BERNARD C. BEINS

See also Informed consent

Ethnic cleansing: the debate on Yugoslavia

Bataković, Dušan, "Le Nettoyage ethnique sous la loupe de l'historien" [Ethnic Cleansing under the Magnifying Glass of the Historian"], *Raison garder*, 10–11 (1996): 11–25

Bell-Fialkoff, Andrew, "A Brief History of Ethnic Cleansing", *Foreign Affairs*, (Summer 1993)

Gorin, Julia, "'Never Again'? This Isn't Exactly What We Had in Mind", *Jewish World Review* (29 April 1999)

Grmek, Mirko, Marc Gjidara and Neven Simac, *Le Nettoyage ethnique: Documents historiques sur une idéologie serbe* [Ethnic Cleansing. Historic Documents on a Serb Ideology], Paris: Fayard, 1993

Haralambos, Michael and Martin Holborn, "'Race', Ethnicity and Nationality", (chapter 11) in their *Sociology: Themes and Perspectives*, 4th edition, London: HarperCollins, 1995

Judah, Tim, *The Serbs: History, Myth and the Destruction of Yugoslavia*, New Haven, Connecticut: Yale University Press, 1997

Landby, Kay, "NATO Maneuvers Risk Wider War in Balkans", *People's Weekly World* (11 July 1998)

Woodward, Susan, *Balkan Tragedy: Chaos and Dissolution after the Cold War*, Washington, DC: Brookings Institution, 1995

"Ethnic cleansing" represents a controversial subject in recent public discourse and social science research. There are different opinions concerning the meaning, boundaries, and causes of this category of violent collective practice. Emotions are aroused the most when different authors, directly affiliated to one of the groups in a conflict, attempt to present the affiliates of their own group as exclusive victims, or to accuse the affiliates of another social group as exclusive perpetrators.

The exact conjunction of the word "ethnic" (adjective derived from the noun designating human group whose members have – or believe they have – common genesis, mentality, culture or destiny) with the word "cleansing" (noun derived from the verb designating the action of purging or purifying) first became current in political debates and the mass media. Only subsequently did the phrase enter social science textbooks. The chronological content analysis of the relevant texts employing these key words suggests that this expression began its life as an element of the propaganda war that accompanied the violent breakup of the Socialist Federal Republic of Yugoslavia. In conditions of civil war and foreign intervention, only one party to the conflict was stigmatized as a "genocidal aggressor", while atrocities committed by the other parties during ethnic cleansing campaigns were either covered by a conspiracy of silence in the mainstream publications, or were minimized and justified as being isolated acts of revenge.

Although the term "ethnic cleansing" came into common usage only during the 1990s, the practice of forced migration, the violent expulsion of members of one group of people by members of another group in order to create an ethnically and religiously homogenous state territory, goes back to the earliest times on all continents, only under other names.

LANDBY's article sheds light on the process of the adoption of the expression "ethnic cleansing", from the initial approach of Croatian and Bosnian Muslim representatives paying $12,000 a month to the private public relations company Ruder Finn Global Affairs, based in Washington DC, to its final entry into the everyday speech. According to the article, James Harff, the director of Ruder Finn, bragged in an April 1993 interview to Jacques Merlino of French TV 2 that it was his firm that had given the impetus to the mass use of the expression "ethnic cleansing". He declared that he was most proud of the way in which the firm had managed to put Jewish opinion on the side of his clients.

The rather voluminous (340 pages) compilation of GRMEK, GJIDARA & SIMAC contains selected, abridged, translated, chronologically arranged and commented texts concerning the 19th- and 20th-century history of Serbian and other South Slav peoples. Reading it leaves the strong impression that the compilers did not and could not have realized the proclaimed theoretical aim of the compilation (to inform and understand, p.9), because they subordinated it to the political aim revealed in the title of their compilation. The need to prove that ethnic cleansing is an ideology peculiar to a specific ethnic group – the Serbs – thus became their *a priori* criterion for the selection of documents (or parts of documents) and omission of others. Their extrascientific aim induced the compilers to include in their compilation some documents whose authenticity, by their own admission, could not be proven (pp.296–300). They even had some difficulty distinguishing between satirical texts and authentic documents (pp.326–9). This provoked the protest of authors cited without authorization, against misuse of their texts for the "criminalization of Serbs as a people".

As could have been expected, one of the first well-documented reactions to the compilation of Grmek, Gjidara & Simac, three French intellectuals of Croat origin, was written by an intellectual of Serb origin, Dusan BATAKOVIC. As an historian by learning and profession, he focused on their violation of established principles of critical analysis of historical sources. Batakovic points out that Grmek, Gjidara & Simac were heavily influenced by another compilation published by a Croat publisher just before the secession of Croatia from Yugoslavia (Bozo Covic, Izvori velikosrpske agresije, *The Sources of Great Serbian Aggression*, Skolska Knjiga, 1991, Zagreb). Not only do they reuse the conceptual framework and borrow extensively from the documents for their own compilation, but they also, Batakovic argues, manifested the same tendency to interpret incomplete and unverified documents without taking into account the textual and sociohistoric context in which they originally appeared. Batakovic demonstrates how they extracted just those parts that called for the unification of Serbs or described acts of violence committed or propagated by Serbs against foreign occupiers, islamized Serbs, or members of other ethnic groups collaborating with occupiers. They suppressed the parts of the same sources that called for mutual cooperation and confidence building between different ethnic groups, not to mention sources written by members of other ethnic groups propagating different violent strategies for the elimination of Serbs, in the name of the creation of enlarged and ethnically pure nation states of Croats, Muslims, or Albanians. Batakovic's review specifies oversights and underestimation on the part of the compilers, notably with respect to the documented acts of forced conversion, mass killing, and the violent expulsion of the Serbian population that actually happened with the help of the Austro-Hungarian Empire in World War I and the Axis powers during World War II, in their *Drang nach Osten* (Push towards the East).

The content of JUDAH's book demonstrates advantages and limits associated with a foreigner researching an ethnic conflict without direct personal involvement. On the one hand, this status facilitates a greater degree of emotional detachment, and therefore less subjective perspective of events. This probably accounts for the fact that Judah mentions events that non-Serb authors from former Yugoslavia tend to suppress, like the violent resettlement of 5200 Serb families living in eastern Bosnia (Srebrenica region) in north-west Bosnia and the sending of 150,000 Serbs to concentration camps in Hungary during World War I, aiming at the transformation of the ethnic/religious structure of the region along the border with Serbia (pp.97–8).

On the other hand, the foreign researcher is disadvantaged to the extent to which he or she depends on interpreters and to which local sources expressing opposed views are inaccessible. When it came, for instance, to statistics about the changing ethnic structure of Kosovo and Metohija through time, Judah relied on figures and their interpretation by Hivzi Islami, published in English translation from the Albanian (*Demographic Reality in Kosova*, KIC, n.d.), but did not mention data and their presentation contained in a demographic study by Petrovic, Ruza, Blagojevic, Marina, *Seobe Srba i Crnogoraca sa Kosova i iz Metohije (Migrations of Serbs and Montenegrins from Kosovo and from Metohija)*, 1989, which were at the time available only in Serbian. Similarly, in the case of disputes concerning the ethnic/confessional structure of Croatia before the creation of Yugoslavia in 1918, Judah accepted the version of Ivo Banac (*The National Question in Yugoslavia: Origins, History, Politics*, 1984), but did not consult the contesting account by Psunjski, *Hrvati u svetlu istorijske istine (Croats in the light of historical truth)*, (1944) 1994.

BELL-FIALKOFF brings a deeper historical perspective to the theme of ethnic cleansing. Going back to Assyrian times, he demonstrates that campaigns to homogenize populations within inviolate borders have long been carried out in the name of God, nation, or ideology. In his historical review, however, conspicuously little is mentioned of the practice of ethnic cleansing by the white settlers in non-European continents and by the governments of the most powerful imperial states throughout history to our days. The label of ethnic cleansing is mostly reserved for practices of governments of less powerful states, especially when they are not compliant allies of the hegemonic power.

The fourth 1995 edition of HARALAMBOS's bestselling sociology textbook corroborates the thesis that the expression "ethnic cleansing" became a concept in sociological writings only in the 1990s, since the wars in Yugoslavia. Even the third edition of this textbook from 1990 does not contain the expression. The highly relevant eleventh chapter is a very good introductory text on the issues of race, ethnicity, and nationality. In an informative manner, it critically reviews major works on the subject written by authors that undertook research from different theoretical perspectives.

The term "ethnic cleansing" is only used in one short paragraph of the 1995 edition (p.650). The book begins by illustrating the point that racism and conflict between ethnic and national groups have long been a feature of human societies, citing the example of the maltreatment of African people during the slave trade and the gassing of Jews in World War II. The textbook authors mention the civil war in Yugoslavia as one of the examples showing that conflicts in which "whole ethnic groups were driven out of an area so that it might be claimed by another group", are not confined to past history.

WOODWARD was among the first social scientists who systematically introduced two important aspects previously ignored in the debate on forced expulsion of persons according to their ethnic and religious background, during the wars of independent nation state territory carving on the ruins of the former multi-ethnic and multi-faith Yugoslav Federation.

First, she goes beyond the rhetoric of "new Hitlers" and "centuries old ethnic hatreds". She reveals economic processes and interests leading to formation of independent national states out of former Yugoslav republics, within circumstances of the world oil and financial crisis, recession, reform and debt-repayment problems in the East and integration processes in the West (pp.47–145).

Second, Woodward places these processes within the wider context of international changes since the late 1980s, arguing that Western intervention in the Balkans not only failed to prevent the spread of violence or to negotiate peace, but actually exacerbated the conflict (p.146 ff.). She elucidates how the European Union's (EU) premature recognition of the secessionist republics, notably by Germany and Austria, disregarding the self-determination rights of Serbs as a people within those republics, as well as the later US threat of air strikes against the Serbs, undermined the interests of the Muslim and Croat leadership in a negotiated compromise settlement.

GORIN's article is a serious answer to the attempt to use accusations of an alleged "Serbian holocaust" to gain public support for an absurd and unjust war in which the oppressed are not so easily discerned from the oppressors. The author criticizes the identification of "ethnic rivalry" between Albanians and Serbs over the same land in Kosovo and Metohija with "genocide" as an unacceptable misuse of words.

VERA VRATUSA(-ZUNJIC)

See also Genocide

Ethnicity

Eriksen, Thomas Hylland, *Ethnicity and Nationalism: Anthropological Perspectives*, London: Pluto Press, 1993

Fenton, Steve, *Ethnicity: Racism, Class and Culture*, Basingstoke: Macmillan, and Lanham, Maryland: Rowman and Littlefield, 1999

Guibernau, Montserrat and John Rex (editors), *The Ethnicity Reader: Nationalism, Multiculturalism, and Migration*, Cambridge: Polity Press and Malden, Massachusetts: Blackwell, 1997

Hutchinson, John and Anthony D. Smith (editors), *Ethnicity*, Oxford and New York: Oxford University Press, 1996

Jenkins, Richard, *Rethinking Ethnicity: Arguments and Explorations*, London and Thousand Oaks, California: Sage, 1997

Jones, Siân, *The Archaeology of Ethnicity: Constructing Identities in the Past and Present*, London and New York: Routledge, 1997

McCrone, David, *The Sociology of Nationalism: Tomorrow's Ancestors*, London and New York: Routledge, 1998

Oommen, T.K., *Citizenship, Nationality, and Ethnicity: Reconciling Competing Identities*, Cambridge: Polity Press, and Cambridge, Massachusetts: Blackwell, 1997

For a term that appeared in social science discourse only in the mid-20th century, "ethnicity" had gained remarkable currency by the end of the century. HUTCHINSON & SMITH provide a collection of basic and essential readings on ethnicity. Though slightly dated, extracts and bibliographic references certainly make this a good place to begin for students as well as researchers. Readings are organized on themes dealing with theories of ethnicity, ethnicity in history, ethnicity in the modern world, race and ethnicity, future of ethnicity, and so forth. An extended introduction at the beginning and brief introductions preceding every section make it more accessible for the readers. Though slightly tilted in favour of "ethno-symbolic" approaches of people like Smith and Armstrong, the book on the whole is successful in introducing various point of views.

GUIBERNAU & REX provide another accessible reader on ethnicity and related concepts. This more recent book consists of 23 well-chosen extracts to familiarize students of social science with the ways in which the concept of ethnicity can be applied to the study of nationalism, and to the issues of migration and multiculturalism. The first part deals with basic but complex conceptual issues surrounding questions of nation state, nationalism and violence, and presents case studies of Catalonia, Scotland, Quebec and Native Americans. The second part deals with migration, transnational communities and multicultural societies. The last part shifts from focus on ethnicity to issues of racism, citizenship, diaspora, and globalization. Throughout, the issue of difference between the ethnicity claimed by the people themselves and that attributed to them by others is highlighted.

JENKINS re-emphasizes the importance of "cultural stuff" in any understanding of ethnicity. The rethinking advocated is to renew and elaborate on the basic social anthropological model of ethnicity summarized in terms of cultural differentiation, social interaction, malleability, and personal self-identification. He provides a contextual analysis of ethnic categorization across a range of informal and formal settings arranged in an 11-point sliding scale with primary socialization and official classification as the two extremes. He distinguishes between two analytically distinct processes of ascription: *group identification* and *social categorization*; the first occurs *inside* the ethnic boundary, the second *outside* and across it. Limits to the fluidity of ethnicity are drawn and limits to the fixity of ethnicity are established through the rejection of primordial arguments and further theorization of the instrumentalist position. He distinguishes between supposed arguments for "naturalness" and "givenness" of ethnicity and its ubiquity. Thus, he argues, although ethnicity *may* be a primary social identity, its salience, strength, and manipulability are situationally contingent. He also elaborates on the distinction between social identity as *nominal* – a name – and *virtual*, a practical meaning or an experience. The second half of the book concerns itself with provisional explorations of ethnicities in Wales, Northern Ireland, and Denmark. An intellectually stimulating work, the book is essential for those having more than a peripheral interest in the topic.

ERIKSEN draws insights from sociology as well as anthropology to examine the relationship between ethnicity, class, gender, and nationhood. Recognizing the controversies involved, he provides a broad overview of the main theoretical issues involved. Using a distinction between "emic" and "etic" categories, he argues for the strength of anthropological approaches to ethnicity. Particularly useful for readers with little initiation in the subject matter would be the first chapter on "What is ethnicity?"

FENTON insists on setting the study of ethnicity within the characteristic historical and present contexts of economy and polity. Some of the key themes underlying the book are: the distinction between the discourse of race and the discourse of ethnicity; the idea of ethnicity as socially constructed and as socially grounded; ethnicity as a global as well as local phenomenon; and ethnicity as simultaneously symbolic and materialist. Four case studies are taken to highlight differentials in three historical trajectories that have defined ethnicity in modern times. The trajectories specified are: that of slavery and postslavery; that of the world as colonial and postcolonial; and the formation of nation states in the capitalist West and beyond. The book is a strong contribution to the subject from the field of sociology.

OOMMEN warns against facile generalizations based on dichotomy of West/non-West and stresses the importance of differences between cultural baggage left behind by transplantive or replicative colonialism (New World) and intrusive and oppressive colonialism (Asia and Africa). Pointing out various types of "ethnification", a process through which the link between territory and culture is attenuated, he differentiates between nationalism and ethnicity. While he understands nationalism as a community in communication in its homeland, he argues that ethnicity is the product of disengagement between territory and culture as the community loses its homeland. These two concepts are therefore exclusive and could generate inequalities. His book argues that this problematic can be negotiated through the concept of citizenship and pluralism.

McCRONE's work, although primarily concerned with nationalism, also deals with its relationship with ethnicity. Arguing that the missing link between both concepts is "identity", he uses the work of Stuart Hall to highlight the power-laden symbolism lying behind these concepts.

JONES critically examines the history of the concept of ethnicity and contributes to a reevaluation of the way in which archaeological enquiry is intertwined with it. The comparative theoretical framework developed through the book argues for an ethnic identity based on shifting, situational, subjective identifications of self and others, which are rooted in ongoing daily practice and historical experience, but also subject to transformation and discontinuity. Though the book is academically situated in archaeology, its arguments are equally important for students of social sciences.

DIBYESH ANAND

See also Multiculturalism, Nationalism

Ethnicity, sociology

Barth, Fredrik (editor), *Ethnic Groups and Boundaries: The Social Organization of Culture Difference*, Boston: Little Brown, 1969
Cohen, Abner, *Custom and Politics in Urban Africa: A Study of Hausa Migrants in a Yoruba Town*, London: Routledge and Kegan Paul, and Berkeley: University of California Press, 1969
Epstein, A.L., *Ethos and Identity: Three Studies in Ethnicity*, London: Tavistock, and Chicago: Aldine, 1978

Glazer, Nathan and Daniel P. Moynihan (editors), *Ethnicity: Theory and Experience*, Cambridge, Massachusetts: Harvard University Press, 1975

Gluckman, Max, *Analysis of a Social Situation in Modern Zululand*, Manchester: Manchester University Press, 1958

Nash, Manning, *The Cauldron of Ethnicity in the Modern World*, Chicago: University of Chicago Press, 1989

Ethnicity is currently a major topic of interest to scholars in many disciplines, but it has actually made a relatively recent appearance on the academic landscape. BARTH did much to contribute to ethnicity's current popularity in his editing and introduction of a collection of essays presented to a Scandinavian anthropological conference. Contributors argued that the definition of human social groups rooted solely in previous arguments reliant on their social or geographical isolation was overly simplistic because social boundaries persisted even after isolation disappeared. Further, such group boundaries have never been impermeable anyway, and distinctions between individuals are constructed *from* interaction rather than being built from an absence of social interaction and acceptance. This dynamic view of ethnicity emphasized that there is little that is cross-culturally predictable about ethnicity; ethnicity may be writ large in many forms of social marker (from clothing through to less overt behaviour), or it may be highly subtle. Individuals have the power to claim membership from, and others have the power to ascribe individuals to, ethnic groups and so individuals become subject to the rules and expectations demanded, and anticipated, from such groups. Consequently, the analytical focus shifts to the "boundary" that defines the group rather than the "cultural stuff" that the boundary encloses.

The "Manchester School" of anthropological theorists comprised the next major moment in the elaboration of an even more sophisticated and fine-grained analysis of ethnicity. Anthropology has prided itself in basing itself on the products of long-term participant-observer fieldwork, and anthropologists such as Max Gluckman and Abner Cohen were pioneering in the richness of their ethnographic detail in colonial Africa. The work of this school is grounded in what came to be known as situational analysis – an approach that assumes that, from the close investigation of an event, broader lessons can be learned about the nature of a social phenomenon (such as ethnicity). In this regard, GLUCKMAN focused on the opening of a bridge in Zululand, and illustrated how wider social realities are expressed at individual events. The aim of such an approach was to make sense of the wider interrelatedness of social action by beginning with an appropriate starting point. Gluckman was quite unconventional by not couching analysis in terms of "tribes", but instead discussed the relationship between members of the categories of white colonial officials and Zulus, and paid attention to the separation between the categories *enforced* by the colonists, hence suggesting that boundaries did not necessarily exist outside the colonial context for the Zulus. Further, he had a considerable influence on the more recent humanistic turn in anthropology by describing the "multiplex" of relations between individuals, which did much to tie them together into networks of belonging, and which showed the people of the colonies to be individuals who

were capable of creativity and change in their social relations and, by extension, in social life as a whole.

COHEN addressed the ethnic and economic dimensions of Hausa traders in Ibadan. These traders deploy their ethnic belonging in a Yoruba-dominated society for good reason, concludes Cohen. Their economic and political survival depends on their ability to evolve a strategy that enables them to control trade in kola nuts and cattle. Nuts are traded to, and cattle from, Hausa in the north, and hence the Hausa in Ibadan just cooperate to ensure that their market monopoly is preserved, and also to enable them to collectively generate enough credit to keep trading consistently. In terms of politics, the Hausa increased their coherence as a response to the Islamicization of the majority Yoruba. Cohen emphasizes throughout the strategic, rational, pragmatic, and thoughtful adoption of ethnicity by the Hausa and notes that ethnic consciousness is created and maintained because of dimensions of competition between groups.

EPSTEIN notes that in ex-colonies in the Third World, as well as in highly industrialized countries like the US and UK, struggles have emerged between various groups witnessed by new assertions of distinctiveness and claims to autonomy, which had been précised under the catch-all term of "ethnicity". Epstein examines the attractiveness of the metaphor of the melting pot of ethnicity both to administrators and politicians, as well as social scientists who relied on the idea that people with competing identities instead subscribed to values of a dominant group. Epstein writes that the successful conclusion of such a process is still awaited in the US – in fact phenomena such as ethnic voting continue to prosper to date.

GLAZER & MOYNIHAN contend that there has been an upsurge of overtly "ethnic" identification and conflict, which is significantly different from old lines of division based on class and other factors. Conflicts that they gloss as "ethnic" encompass those where the disagreement is manifested around language, nationality, and religion. The increase in the conflictual prominence of "ethnicity" is more than the seeking of advantage, they claim, for it invokes more than interest alone. Ethnicity reflects a new social reality and is also a phenomenon that is not solely analytical.

NASH begins his survey of ethnicity with a cautionary declaration that while it appears to be both a word and an idea with clear, solid meaning that requires no further explanation, in fact issues surrounding ethnicity are some of the most complicated and volatile in social science. Nash addresses the primordial essentialist view of ethnicity, which presents it as the source of a deep, core, and fundamental identity, and tracks it as the collocation of body, language, shared history and origins, religion and nationality. However, ethnicity can only be understood in the context in which it exists at any moment, and one needs to be aware of its inherent malleability, and that there is a difference between choosing to be a member of an ethnic group, or being ascribed to one by others. Ethnic activity can also occur at both minor and major levels from songs and costumes used once a year, through to bloody wars. Nash concludes that, although the nationalist rhetoric of many countries call for their citizens to become amalgam products of a cultural melting pot, this process can be by no means smooth.

MILS HILLS

See also Multiculturalism, Nationalism

Ethnocentrism

Adleman, Jeanne and Gloria M. Enguídanos (editors), *Racism in the Lives of Women: Testimony, Theory, and Guides to Antiracist Practice*, New York: Haworth Press, 1995

Andereck, Mary, *Ethnic Awareness and the School: An Ethnographic Study*, London and Newbury Park, California: Sage, 1992

LeVine, Robert A. and Donald T. Campbell, *Ethnocentrism: Theories of Conflict, Ethnic Attitudes, and Group Behaviour*, New York and London: Wiley, 1972

Ramazanoglu, Caroline, *Feminism and the Contradictions of Oppression*, London and New York: Routledge, 1989

Rex, John, *Ethnic Minorities in the Modern Nation State: Working Papers in the Theory of Multiculturalism and Political Integration*, London: Macmillan, and New York: St Martin's Press, 1996

Reynolds, Vernon, Vincent Falger and Ian Vine, *The Sociobiology of Ethnocentrism: Evolutionary Dimensions of Xenophobia, Discrimination, Racism and Nationalism*, London: Croom Helm, and Athens: University of Georgia Press, 1987

Stack, John F. Jr (editor), *Ethnic Identities in a Transnational World*, Westport, Connecticut: Greenwood, 1981

Stasiulis, Daiva and Nira Yuval-Davis (editors), *Unsettling Settler Societies: Articulations of Gender, Race, Ethnicity, and Class*, London and Thousand Oaks, California: Sage, 1995

Young, Robert, *White Mythologies: Writing History and the West*, London and New York: Routledge, 1990

Inter-ethnic relations have been shaped by ethnocentrism, an attitude in which one's own cultural values are applied to other sociocultural contexts. Such an attitude often reflects the need for a singular point of view but, where multiple perspectives are acknowledged, those of other cultures may be judged as erroneous, inferior, or corrupt. LEVINE & CAMPBELL's classic text elaborates and clarifies the conceptual territory of ethnocentrism. The authors examine the contradictions and similarities within social science theories that seek to elucidate ethnocentrism, using social, psychological, and crosscultural theories to stimulate criticism and debate.

The testimonies collected by ADLEMAN & ENGUÍDANOS add powerful and persuasive substance to the authors' presentation of women's crosscultural oppression. Personal voices describe emotional and physical pain, then lead into theoretical and practical approaches for combating oppressive ethnocentric and racist practices. This handbook offers advice to enable students, teachers, and academics to changes modes of thinking and behaviour.

ANDERECK's work focuses on children's interactions in a small Catholic school in the southern US. While the book works well as a compelling ethnography, the author also explores the potential for ethnocentric action and reaction as the children of a small enclave of people called the Irish Travellers adapt to their host-dominated community. The work presents the social consequences of the children's presence, the author provides some modest recommendations for accommodating children from small cultural groupings into the formal education system.

While other scholars approach the issue of ethnocentrism from an ethnic or racial perspective, RAMAZANOGLU's work brings a welcome critical perspective to types of feminism as categories of thinking that exclude women who do not "fit" desired political stereotypes. She strives to clarify the differences that exist between women in order to expand theoretical approaches and political strategies that have the potential for liberation, and to challenge the bases of existing knowledge. An excellent work for all sociological courses engaging with feminist theory.

An investigation into the ways in which a democratic and egalitarian form of multiculturalism could be coupled with a recognition of cultural diversity informs the first three chapters of REX's work. Ensuing essays are concerned with a clarification of what is meant by the term "ethnicity". These are then linked to discussions about what constitutes the nation, nationalism, and the state, and whether these notions can be divorced from concepts of ethnicity. Although not directly addressing ethnocentrism as an issue, the book is a lucid theoretical treatise that details understandings of the concepts that can produce discriminatory practices, and links with recent scholarship about multiculturalism.

REYNOLDS, FALGER & VINE have edited a collection of 15 essays that examine the relevance of sociobiological and evolutionary concepts to an understanding of ethnocentrism. Examining prejudice, discrimination, and xenophobia, the authors propose that ethnocentrism is unconscious and can therefore direct a person's action in ways of which he or she may be oblivious.

STACK's collection of essays examines the ways in which the subdivisions of national or racial groups into ethnic groupings is reflected in the day-to-day experience of many within society. Theoretical work is encouraged here in order to understand how international integration can reinforce political hierarchies or can work to bypass established nation-state polities. Acknowledging ethnic groups as important transnational actors and agents can work not only against popular and academic perceptions that promote ethnocentric viewpoints, but can also foster recognition of the ways in which ethnic groupings have entered state, regional, and global political processes.

A diverse range of authors have contributed to STASIULIS & YUVAL-DAVIS' edited collection, which expands contemporary notions of ethnocentrism to include the dynamic interrelationship between race and ethnicity, adding the roles of women, people of colour, and indigenous peoples to the analyses of settler societies. This is an influential text that should be read by those examining the complex social organizations and historical realities of contemporary societies.

YOUNG's historical perspective questions the way in which Western history has been written, and elucidates the myths that European knowledge-producers have created about peoples from non-European societies. Anchored in a detailed reading of Western philosophy, the author argues against Western ethnocentrism through his proposal that the concept of history is collapsing under the onslaught of postmodernism, and that the West as a conceptual entity is dissolving as a consequence. This is an excellent theoretical text for later graduate and postgraduate students.

HELEN JOHNSON

Ethnography

Asad, Talal (editor), *Anthropology and the Colonial Encounter*, London: Ithaca Press, 1973

Bateson, Gregory, *Naven: A Survey of the Problems Suggested by a Composite Picture of the Culture of a New Guinea Tribe Drawn from Three Points of View*, 2nd edition, Stanford, California: Stanford University Press, 1958

Benedict, Ruth, *The Chrysanthemum and the Sword: Patterns of Japanese Culture*, Boston: Houghton Mifflin, 1946; London: Secker and Warburg, 1947

Best, Elsdon, *Tuhoe: The Children of the Mist*, 4th edition, 2 vols, Auckland: Reed, 1996 (1st edition, 1925)

Bremen, Jan van and Akitoshi Shimizu (editors), *Anthropology and Colonialism in Asia and Oceania*, Richmond, Surrey: Curzon, 1999

Brettell, Caroline B. (editor), *When They Read What We Write: The Politics of Ethnography*, Westport, Connecticut and London: Bergin and Garvey, 1993

Clendinnen, Inga, *Aztecs: An Interpretation*, Cambridge and New York: Cambridge University Press, 1991

Clifford, James and George E. Marcus (editors), *Writing Culture: The Poetics and Politics of Ethnography*, Berkeley: University of California Press, 1986

Crapanzano, Vincent, *Tuhami: Portrait of a Moroccan*, Chicago: University of Chicago Press, 1980

Evans-Pritchard, E.E., *The Nuer: A Description of the Modes of Livelihood and Political Institutions of a Nilotic People*, Oxford: Clarendon Press, 1940

Feld, Steven, *Sound and Sentiment: Birds, Weeping, Poetics, and Song in Kaluli Expression*, Philadelphia: University of Pennsylvania Press, 1982

Geertz, Clifford, *Works and Lives: The Anthropologist as Author*, Stanford, California: Stanford University Press, 1988

Griaule, Marcel, *Conversations with Ogotemmêli: An Introduction to Dogon Religious Ideas*, London: Oxford University Press, 1965 (French edition, 1948)

Labby, David, *The Demystification of Yap: Dialectics of Culture on a Micronesian Island*, Chicago: University of Chicago Press, 1976

Leach, E.R., *Political Systems of Highland Burma: A Study of Kachin Social Structure*, London: Bell, and Cambridge, Massachusetts: Harvard University Press, 1954

Lévi-Strauss, Claude, *Tristes Tropiques*, London: Cape, 1973; New York: Atheneum, 1974 (French edition 1955)

Malinowski, Bronisław, *Argonauts of the Western Pacific: An Account of Native Enterprise and Adventure in the Archipelagoes of Melanesian New Guinea*, London: Routledge, and New York: Dutton, 1922; reprinted London and New York: Routledge, 1992

Marcus, George E. and Michael M.J. Fischer, *Anthropology as Cultural Critique: An Experimental Moment in the Human Sciences*, Chicago: University of Chicago Press, 1986; 2nd edition 1999

Mead, Margaret, *Coming of Age in Samoa*, New York: Morrow, 1928; London: Cape, 1929

Mead, Margaret, *Sex and Temperament in Three Primitive Societies*, New York: Morrow, and London: Routledge, 1935

Rousseau, Jean-Jacques, "Discourse on the Origins and Foundations of Inequality among Men" in *Collected Writings of Rousseau*, edited by Roger D. Masters, vol. 3, Hanover, New Hampshire: University Press of New England, 1992 (first published 1755)

Sanjek, Roger (editor), *Fieldnotes: The Makings of Anthropology*, Ithaca, New York: Cornell University Press, 1990

Spencer, Baldwin and F. J. Gillen, *The Native Tribes of Central Australia*, London: Macmillan, 1899; reprinted New York: Dover, 1968

Stocking, George W. Jr, *The Ethnographer's Magic and Other Essays in the History of Anthropology*, Madison: University of Wisconsin Press, 1992

Tsing, Anna Lowenhaupt, *In the Realm of the Diamond Queen: Marginality in an Out-of-the-Way Place*, Princeton, New Jersey: Princeton University Press, 1993

Turnbull, Colin M., *The Mountain People*, New York: Simon and Schuster, 1972; London: Cape, 1973

An ethnography is an account based largely, but not necessarily exclusively, on participation in and observation of the life of a group of people which is self-consciously a group of people. Generally written by either an outsider or a person who seeks an intellectual and moral distance from their own people, any good ethnography contains elements of two moral orders. At its best, ethnography is necessarily both experimental and unsatisfactory in that minimally any attempt at illuminating two moral orders at once is thwarted by a requirement of fidelity to both orders. This is also ethnography's greatest strength, its source of renewal and continual interest.

Ethnographers have esteemed predecessors in commentators upon constitutions such as Aristotle, historians such as Polybius, and travellers such as Ibn Khaldun, but ROUSSEAU gave subsequent ethnographers a distinctly prescient vision of their activity in note eight to his second *Discourse*. He had "difficulty conceiving, how in a Century taking pride in splendid knowledge" men of money and genius could not come together "in order to study, not always stones and plants, but for once men and morals ...."

Rousseau contends:

> For the three or four hundred years since the inhabitants of Europe have inundated the other parts of the world, and continually published new collections of voyages and reports, I am persuaded that we know no other men except Europeans ... under the pompous name of the study of man everybody does hardly anything except study the men of his country.

He contemplates "a Montesquieu, Buffon, Diderot, Duclos, d'Alembert, Condillac, or men of that stamp travelling in order to inform their compatriots" who, returning from memorable expeditions, wrote the natural, moral, and political history of what they would have seen; we ourselves would see a new world come from their pens, and we would thus learn to know our own.

Accordingly, ethnography might repair moral parochialism by forcing what Lévi-Strauss has called "a view from afar", which illuminates both Europe and a world, new to Europeans, described in these writings. If ethnography was proposed as a kind of antidote to a broadly European malady, one tied to inequality and vanity (*amour propre*), ethnography now has many non-European practitioners, writers, readers, and purposes. Individual ethnographies have served as sources of cultural preservation. Ethnographers have gazed upon Europeans and the European diaspora. Nonetheless, ethnography remains tied to the liberal science of anthropology and the liberal colonial institutions with which anthropology was associated, a point brought forward by ASAD and modified somewhat by BREMEN & SHIMIZU's attention to ethnography's relation to Japanese imperialism.

One consequence has been ethnography's own version of the so-called crisis of representation. CLIFFORD & MARCUS attends to ethnographies as writings. Influenced by literary theory and historiography, the authors in this collection see ethnographies as neither transparent nor innocent, but rather as accounts enmeshed in encounters shaped by various changing political circumstances. They question the authority of ethnographic comment – see especially the essays by Crapanzano and Asad.

MARCUS & FISCHER sought to show how in what they call an experimental moment, when ostensibly new themes were introduced, ethnography could contribute to what some scholars called cultural critique. Their grasp of anthropology's history is occasionally shaky. Their reminder that symbolic anthropologists must approach the interests of their materialist colleagues is well placed. The work is, however, not so much an argument as an extended book report.

GEERTZ examines how a few ethnographers (Lévi-Strauss, Evans-Pritchard, Malinowski, and Benedict) attempt to show that they have been to the worlds they describe. For Geertz:

> [T]he problem ... is to represent the research process in the research product; to write ethnography in such a way as to bring one's interpretations of some society, culture, way of life, or whatever and one's encounters with some of its members, carriers, representatives, or whomever into an intelligible relationship. (p.84)

Geertz draws us, therefore, to the quotidian elements of encounter, the particularities of biography and situation, rather than the broad worries of a discipline uncomfortable with itself.

STOCKING has contributed much work of high quality, showing anthropology's emergence as a scholarly discipline and its place in the Anglo-American world. His early essays focus on the separation of so-called race and culture in the Boasians' work. Stocking has more recently studied British anthropology and edited the *History of Anthropology* series. Stocking's training as an historian underlies his repeated refusal to accept the appraisal of his work as an ethnography of ethnographers as well as his emphasis upon institutional developments. Stocking's discussions of the influence of the Rockefeller Foundations funding practices, the rise of the notion of the central importance of fieldwork, and the like are lucid explications of how anthropology came to its particular form of professionalism; any reasonably complete study of ethnography would include careful attention to Stocking. In addition, Bremen & Shimizu's volume provides good introductions to the comparable histories of Japanese and Dutch anthropology.

SANJEK's collection draws attention to the initial, raw products of ethnographic work: fieldnotes. These day-to-day records remain the best evidence of the human encounters underlying the edifice of published ethnographies. Some anthropologists have consulted other fieldworkers' notes. Fewer have treated other's notes as crucial evidence in their own accounts. Fewer still have taken fieldnotes as evidence of both the world examined ethnographically and the world of the ethnographer. The discussions of ethnographic writing referred to above have rarely taken up the collaborative encounters upon which ethnographies are based.

Most ethnographies have been written by academic specialists for other academic specialists; some have been intended for the intelligent reading public as well. Few have been written with much attention to an increasingly common but not solely recent phenomenon, i.e. that among an ethnography's readers may be its putative subjects. BRETTELL's volume takes up the responses of various ethnographers to their indigenous readers and those readers' criticisms.

A reasonable cross section of significant and always experimental ethnographies would include the following.

SPENCER & GILLEN describe ceremony and custom among the Arunta of Central Australia and their near neighbours. Their discussion stimulated examination of so-called totemism, serving as a basis for Durkheimian sociology.

BEST records the history, genealogies, and cosmogonic tales of the Tuhoe, a significant New Zealand Maori group living in the mountains of the central North Island. Present day Tuhoe refer to Best's records of *whakapapa* or genealogy as authoritative for current practice. Marcel Mauss' *The Gift* begins with a meditation upon Tuhoe thought as presented by Best; subsequent ethnohistorians equally follow Best's example.

MALINOWSKI describes the systematic exchange and counterprestation of two sorts of shell valuables circulating among members of several societies in the Masim, east of New Guinea. Like Spenser & Gillen and Best before him, Malinowski's account is based on his encounter with the people whose lives he records; unlike them, Malinowski claims fieldwork to be the indispensable tool of a scientific, in his case functionalist, anthropology. This claim inspired the myth of Malinowski as anthropology's first ethnographer (but see Stocking).

MEAD (1928 and 1935) is probably best known now for her early work on Samoa, if only because of Derek Freeman's misconceived assault on Boas through Mead. Mead never doubted biology's influences upon human life, but neither did she think human existence over determined by biology. Because the biological processes of human development are everywhere very nearly the same, these processes do not explain much about the regular variation of human life from society to society; rather, systematic differences in the ways adults raise children in various societies become systematic differences in those children's character as they become adults and hence underlie regular or patterned differences between societies. Undergirding her claim that three New Guinea peoples developed three distinct systems of adult male and female character are her implicit descriptions of three different kinship organizations, hence patterns of acceptable inter-personal relations, in a region of shared cult.

BATESON, working among Iatmul in the same region at the same time as Mead, examined the public, ceremonialized homosexual encounters between mother's brothers and sister's sons among Iatmul following upon any publicly significant event in the sister's sons life, such as the first time one of them killed another human being. These encounters intensified as one person's activity evoked a response, which itself evoked a counter response until the building tension dissipated in a final release. Bateson elaborates his analysis from a variety of vantage points, stressing how the violence of the ceremony organizes the emotional tone (*ethos*) of Iatmul society and the cognitive elements of Iatmul personalities (*eidos*). Together, Mead and Bateson foreshadow, if they did not develop, a truly morphological anthropology. BENEDICT continues this tradi-tion in her study of Japan.

EVANS-PRITCHARD shows how time as reflected in rela-tions between the Nuer, a Nilotic cattle herding people of southern Sudan, and their environment ("oecological time") and among Nuer ("structural time") alters as Nuer move their cattle away from the river, out to watering holes and back again as the seasons require.

GRIAULE recounts conversations in which he learned from Ogotemmêli, a Dogon elder from Mali, about Dogon meta-physics including the concrete expression of Dogon mythology in granaries, houses, courtyards, and the like. CRAPANZANO's later description of Tuhami, a Moroccan who considered him-self married to a camel-footed demon, shares much the same conversational style; Crapazano adds meditations upon his interpretation of Tuhami's mental life.

LEACH analyses an oscillation between two types of social organization, *gumsa* and *gumlao*, among the Kachin of high-land, northeast Burma. *Gumsa* consists in a network of related and ranked lineages; as the system presumes a consistent hierarchized distinction between wife givers (superior) and wife takers (inferior), it can only attain a temporary stability when the feudal lords marry outside their own society and into a society that conceives of hierarchy between affines in the opposite fashion. *Gumsa* feudalism begets *gumlao* revolt, but *gumlao* communities, which recognize no distinction of rank between affinal lines, nonetheless distinguish between wife givers and wife takers. This later distinction provides the possibility for those with aspirations to make claims to superiority. "[T]he two types are, in their practical application, always inter-related. Both systems are in a sense structurally defective" (p.204).

LABBY describes how among the Yapese of Micronesia sons live their lives out upon the same estates as their fathers; this fact, among others, led David Schneider to conclude Yapese society is organized patrilineally. The men who live upon the estates do not own them as they are the property of matri-clan(s) whose women's labour has brought them ownership; rather, these men guard their sister's interests in the estate. Those sisters move from their natal estate to the natal estate of their husbands. Thus, Yapese say "Our land belongs to someone else; someone else's land belongs to us" (p.35).

FELD takes up the interrelated domains of places, birds, and the dead, especially the recently dead, in the poetry and song of the Kaluli of the Great Papuan Plateau, Papua New Guinea.

Kaluli poetic grammar attempts to persuade those who hear songs and move them to tears. The recently dead become birds; bird song, like the insides of words in human song, reminds the living, both in general and specifically, that they have been abandoned.

CLENDINNEN writes of the Aztecs of the cities of Tenochtilan and Tlatelolco in the final years of the great system of tribute we call their empire. Based on the examination of "scattered, fragmentary and defective texts" (p.1), Clendinnen's account seeks the understanding of these often ordinary rather than exalted people who prepared and cared for the victims of human sacrifice, wore the skins of those sacrificed, and accepted themselves as proper victims. The section on the sacred is particularly stimulating.

TSING, in this justly praised account, focusing on the Meratus of the mountains of southeastern Kalimantan, Indonesia, seeks to shift attention from the supposedly internal dynamics of potentially separate societies. She takes up the interplay of processes such as the rule by a distant state, the interaction of smaller groups with more powerful ethni-cally different neighbours and gender differentiation. Tsing finds the discourse in which Meratus understand, engage, and situate the wider world of the more powerful and better connected crucial to the creation and maintenance of Meratus identities.

TURNBULL provides the more extreme case of the Ik of northern Kenya who, deprived of their livelihoods when the best hunting grounds in their seasonal round were turned into a national park, retreated to their inhospitable, almost food-less, yet sacred mountain. The Ik remained in some sense Ik although they lost or abandoned those mutual bonds called society. The veracity and morality of Turnbull's first person account of the brutalities he witnessed has been questioned; the account is both lucid and harrowing.

LÉVI-STRAUSS, part travel book, part ethnographic medi-tation, part philosophic rumination, returns finally to the themes established for ethnographers by Rousseau. Lévi-Strauss correctly reminds us that Diderot, not Rousseau, idealized the primitive wholeheartedly. He states most vividly the possible uses for the work done by people already separated from the moral imperatives of their own natal ways of living – uses that do not include the perfecting of mankind.

GERALD SULLIVAN

Ethnomethodology

Coulter, Jeff, *The Social Construction of Mind: Studies in Ethnomethodology and Linguistic Philosophy*, London: Macmillan, 1979

Garfinkel, Harold, *Studies in Ethnomethodology*, Englewood Cliffs, New Jersey: Prentice Hall, 1967

Garfinkel, Harold and Harvey Sacks, "On Formal Structures of Practical Actions" in *Theoretical Sociology: Perspectives and Developments*, edited by John C. McKinney and Edward A. Tiryakian, New York: Appleton Century Crofts, 1970

Heritage, John, *Garfinkel and Ethnomethodology*, Cambridge: Polity Press, 1984

Hester, Stephen and Peter Eglin (editors), *Culture in Action: Studies in Membership Categorization Analysis*, Washington, DC: International Institute for Ethnomethodology and Conversation Analysis, 1997

Hill, R.J. and K.S. Crittenden (editors), *Proceedings of the Purdue Symposium on Ethnomethodology*, Purdue, Indiana: Purdue Research Foundation, 1968

Lynch, Michael, *Art and Artifact in Laboratory Science: A Study of Shop Work and Shop Talk in a Research Laboratory*, London: Routledge and Kegan Paul, 1985

Sacks, Harvey, *Lectures on Conversation*, edited by Gail Jefferson, 2 vols, Oxford and Cambridge, Massachusetts: Blackwell, 1992

Sharrock, Wes and Robert Anderson, *The Ethnomethodologists*, London and New York: Tavistock, 1986

Turner, Roy (editor), *Ethnomethodology: Selected Readings*, Harmondsworth: Penguin, 1974

The essential early statement of ethnomethodology's programme is provided by GARFINKEL, who asserts the existence of commonsensical "members' methods" underlying both the organization of the social world and the interpretation of its possible meaning. A student of the grand theorist Talcott Parsons and a devotee of Alfred Schuetz, Garfinkel attempted to approach the Parsonian problem of order by respecifying the problem: rather than simply applying the neopositivist methods of conventional sociology so as to treat order as the outcome of social structure, Garfinkel successfully demonstrated social order's constitutive grounding in practical action. His book is exemplary for later ethnomethodological studies, offering richly detailed descriptions of such topics as the routine grounds of everyday activities, commonsense knowledge of social structures, methods of interpretation, members' decision-making rules, the performance of gender, and organizations as systems of practical action.

A specific and deeply influential ethnomethodological study of some constitutive language-based practices is offered by GARFINKEL & SACKS. The authors argue that natural language has as one of its properties that of indexicality, or context dependency. This feature renders all attempts at remedying indexicality – such as the ideal types or coding schemes used by sociologists – into phenomena worthy of study in their own right. Garfinkel and Sacks then demonstrate the social organization of indexical expressions by examining cases of practices such as "formulating" (i.e. providing an indexically bound characterization of some activity in question) and "glossing practices" (i.e. summarizing or defining some object or activity for practical purposes), as these practices appear in such contexts as that of ordinary conversation.

The tenuous relationship between ethnomethodology and conventional sociology, along with the basic questions of the definition and uniqueness of ethnomethodology, are the subject matters of HILL & CRITTENDEN's edited transcriptions of a two-day symposium, organized immediately after the publication of Garfinkel's book. Here Garfinkel, Sacks, Aaron Cicourel, and other ethnomethodologists offer a series of demonstrations of their studies with accompanying commentaries, yet the aim of mutual understanding by all parties is scarcely reached. The transcriptions offer useful insights into both the tenor of ethnomethodology's reciepiency by the sociology profession and the bewilderment surrounding its main claims.

TURNER's collection, containing both original essays and excerpted works, further demonstrates the flavour of the various studies being done during the period 1965–74. It contains works on such topics as knowledge and theorizing, the relationship between science and common sense, common-sense knowledge of social structures, practical conceptions of such sociological categories as ethnicity and organization, record keeping and the production of "facts", and group codes as representations of a local "moral order".

One particularly useful, though brief, overview and assessment of ethnomethodology is that of SHARROCK & ANDERSON, whose sympathetic treatment seeks to provide an explication of the underlying logic of the subject. The book begins with phenomenology as a precursor field, moves on to address the problemas of social theorizing, specifically considering Garfinkel's rethinking of Parsons, and ends with a discussion of various ethnomethodological studies. Sharrock and Anderson focus in particular on studies of ordinary conversation and of work, especially the work of scientists, although their main aim is to situate such studies in relation to mainstream sociology rather than to cover them in great detail.

HERITAGE's carefully written exigesis focuses on Garfinkel, placing his work within the "context of the traditional preoccupations of social theory", and concentrating on such central concerns as theories of action, the nature of intersubjectivity, and the social construction of knowledge. While arguing, similarly to Sharrock and Anderson, for an understanding of ethnomethodology's emergence from both sociological theory and phenomenology, Heritage's treatment is more fully wedded to the phenomenological/interpretivist tradition. Heritage also provides the conceptual linkages with conversation analysis, and offers much detail on this topic.

The collected work of SACKS, ranging from published articles and book chapters to transcribed lecture notes, offers a wide range of empirically based insights and logically rigorous analyses within the broad context of ethnomethodological concerns. In addition to studies which initiated conversation analysis, Sacks also provided the foundations for another analytic technique, that of membership categorization analysis. Sacks' influences were diverse, and included Garfinkel, Wittgenstein, and the work of linguistic anthropologists. Like Wittgenstein, Sacks can be read as offering something of a social logic, one with the potential of eventually revolutionizing the host discipline from which it emerged.

One of the later developments within ethnomethodology, the study of the conceptualization of mental phenomena, is provided by COULTER, who argues against the conventional, i.e. Cartesian, treatment of mentality as an internal reality. Coulter puts forth a Wittgensteinian argument, treating mentality as a conceptualization, tied to a variety of social practices (i.e. of avowal and ascription), and involving the use of various "grammars of cognition". Coulter's studies extend ethnomethodology into such areas as cognitive psychology, artificial intelligence, and the philosophy of mind, and offer an alternative framework for the understanding of human action.

HESTER & EGLIN's edited volume clarifies and elaborates on membership categorization analysis, which, as the authors indicate, focuses on "locally used, invoked and organized presumed commonsense knowledge of social structures which members are oriented to in the conduct of their everyday affairs". The book is a useful introduction to one of ethnomethodology's more enduring analytic programs.

Finally, an outstanding, and uniquely ethnomethodological treatment of the workplace practices, and work-based knowledge, of scientists is given in LYNCH's ethnographic study. Lynch's work, part of a larger pantheon of studies in the sociology of scientific knowledge, looks at such topics as the gaps between the glossing practices built into scientific texts, and how such texts compare and contrast with what scientists actually know and use in their studies.

THOMAS M. CONROY

Eurocommunism

Anderson, Perry and Patrick Camiller (editors), *Mapping the West European Left*, London: Verso, 1994

Boggs, Carl and David Plotke (editors), *The Politics of Eurocommunism: Socialism in Transition*, London: Macmillan, and Boston: South End Press, 1980

Brown, Bernard E. (editor), *Eurocommunism and Eurosocialism: The Left Confronts Modernity*, New York: Cyrco, 1979

Carrillo, Santiago, *"Eurocommunism" and the State*, London: Lawrence and Wishart, 1977

Filo della Torre, Paolo, Eward Mortimer and Jonathan Story (editors), *Eurocommunism: Myth or Reality?*, Harmondsworth and New York: Penguin, 1979

Godson, Roy and Stephen Haseler, *'Eurocommunism': Implications for East and West*, London: Macmillan, and New York: St Martin's Press, 1978

Kindersley, Richard (editor), *In Search of Eurocommunism*, London: Macmillan, and New York: St Martin's Press, 1981

Kriegel, Annie, *Eurocommunism: A New Kind of Communism?*, Stanford, California: Hoover Institution Press, 1978

Mandel, Ernest, *From Stalinism to Eurocommunism: The Bitter Fruits of "Socialism in One Country"*, 2nd edition, London: New Left Books, 1979

Sassoon, Donald, *One Hundred Years of Socialism: The West European Left in the Twentieth Century*, London and New York: Tauris, 1996

Eurocommunism became prominent in the 1970s and was the combined outcome of shifts in political strategies and in ideological positions by some of the foremost parties of the communist left in Western Europe. It was initiated by the Italian Communist Party (PCI) and the essays in KINDERSLEY provide an excellent overall account. The chapter on Italy (by Vacca) argues that Eurocommunism was an ambitious project pursued by the PCI in its efforts to define a new strategy that would take into account the particularities of Western Europe in the 1970s and would demonstrate a commitment to political democracy as a value in itself. He stresses the role of the PCI leader, Togliatti, and especially that of his successor, Berlinguer, in helping form a distinctively European approach.

The detailed political history of 20th-century socialism in Europe by SASSOON provides an important account of the general framework in which Eurocommunism evolved. He explores the shifts in the PCI's approach within the framework of relations between communist and socialist parties in Western Europe. Change was gradual. For example, the PCI abandoned its opposition to the European Community in the early 1960s, a decade before the birth of Eurocommunism. He shows that, for a limited period, Eurocommunism became an important chapter in the attempt to define a new path for European communism and it provided the PCI with "a platform from which it could speak to the entire European Left" (p.581).

Although initiated mainly by the PCI, Eurocommunism soon became a common approach shared by the communist parties of Italy, France (PCF), and Spain (PCE). CARRILLO, leader of the PCE at the time, provides a defence of Eurocommunism in terms of the need to get to grips with realities in Western Europe and achieve a degree of independence from the Soviet Communist Party. He grounds this analysis on a critical examination of the structures of power in the USSR. Defending Eurocommunism as a necessary European alternative, he acknowledges the role of the PCI and its leader, Togliatti, in encouraging a rethinking of communist strategy and ideology in the particular context of Western Europe.

Eurocommunism as a common project of the PCI, the PCF, and the PCE is examined from an analytical perspective by KRIEGEL. This is an analytical but also critical study, aiming to explore the "ambiguities and uncertainties" (p.103) involved in the Eurocommunist project. There is also a considerable (and influential) aspect in the book that deals with policy considerations, constructing scenarios about the possible development of Eurocommunism, and its effects for Western democracy. She is more concerned with divergence than common ground. For example, she notes that in some cases (notably the PCF) the bid for a degree of autonomy from Moscow was evident long before the launch of Eurocommunism. Examining the positions of the three parties on a number of issues, she shows that there are several lines of division between them, making it difficult to talk of a "regional strategy". She concludes that, as a result, while the Sino–Soviet split had important repercussions for international balances, Eurocommunism did not represent a similar development in terms of East-West relations.

The appeal of Eurocommunism was extremely limited when it came to the communist parties of Portugal (PCP) and Greece (KKE), both of which followed an unreconstructed Stalinist line. The essays in BROWN remain very useful as accounts of the differences between Italy and other Southern European countries. The chapters on Italy (by Sani) and Portugal (by Bruneau) are indispensable reading in this respect.

MANDEL provides a well-known polemical Marxist account of Eurocommunism as a political strategy that "marks a political and ideological regression by a section of the European workers' movement" in conditions of crisis and upheaval for capitalism (p.29). He argues that the Eurocommunist strategies of the Italian, French, and Spanish communist parties are "the bitter fruits of socialism in one country" in the USSR. Taking the PCI, the PCF, and the PCE in turn, he examines the development of Eurocommunist views in the three parties and concludes that what they have in common is mainly a reformist line that follows Kautsky's views in debates within the German Social Democratic Party (SPD).

BOGGS & PLOTKE provide analyses of the international dimensions of Eurocommunism, including the response of the USSR and the US. The essays in FILO DELLA TORRE, MORTIMER & STORY also include important accounts of the international dimensions. The book contains (as an appendix) the joint declarations of the Italian and Spanish Communist Parties (15 July 1975) and the Italian and French Communist Parties (15 November 1975). GODSON & HASELER take an international relations perspective and address in particular the interactions between Eurocommunism and East-West relations. They echo Atlanticist concerns that "the attitudes of the Eurocommunist parties to NATO are generally more hostile than those toward the European Community" (p.105) and seek to assess the implications for Cold War stability.

With the benefit of hindsight one can argue that Eurocommunism was an important chapter in the integration of communist parties in the changing political systems of their countries. The essays in ANDERSON & CAMILLER provide authoritative explorations of the national successes and failures of the West European left in the 1980s and 1990s. They are indispensable as accounts of the general picture of the left, aspects of which have been partly the result of the Eurocommunist attempts to redefine the relations between political democracy and communist party ideology.

KOSTAS A. LAVDAS

See also Communism, Communist party (US and UK), Social democracy

European Community and European Union, development of

Church, Clive and David Phinnemore, *European Union and European Community: A Handbook and Commentary on the Post-Maastricht Treaties*, London and New York: Harvester Wheatsheaf, 1994

Dinan, Desmond, *Ever Closer Union? An Introduction to the European Community*, London: Macmillan, and Boulder, Colorado: Rienner, 1994

Edward, David and Robert Lane, *European Community Law*, Edinburgh: Butterworths / Law Society of Scotland, 1995

McAllister, Richard, *From EC to EU: An Historical and Political Survey*, London and New York: Routledge, 1997

Middlemas, Keith, *Orchestrating Europe: The Informal Politics of European Union, 1973–1995*, London: Fontana Press, 1995

Pinder, John, *The Building of the European Union*, Oxford and New York: Oxford University Press, 1998

EDWARD & LANE attempt a presentation of the historical evolution of the Communities and the Union from a legal perspective. The authors follow the origins and development of the European Communities and the European Union and examine their institutions in detail. Reference is made to the role of the institutions throughout the history of the Communities and the Union, as well as to the basic substantive provisions of the Treaty of Rome and the Treaty of the European Union.

A detailed analysis of the post-Maastricht Treaty, article by article, is attempted by CHURCH & PHINNEMORE. The chapter entitled "On the road to Maastricht" provides an excellent insight into the legacy of European integration, the evolution of the European economy, and the political trends in member states, all of which were factors contributing to the passing of the Maastricht Treaty and the creation of the European Union. The chapter on the general axioms of the post-Maastricht Treaty is of particular interest for the purposes of understanding the end result of the journey between the European Communities and the European Union, and clearly defines issues such as citizenship and subsidiarity. The concluding chapter, entitled "The Union in Context", refers to the future of a wider Western Europe and to the relationships between the Union on the one hand and other European institutions and countries on the other hand.

An equally interesting in-depth historical examination of the Communities and the Union is offered by DINAN. In order to determine the political and historical European environment leading to the formation of the European Communities, the author provides a detailed analysis of reconstruction, reconciliation, and integration within Europe after the Second World War and before the Treaty of Rome. The history of the Communities is then examined in periods, starting with the Gaullist challenge between 1958 and 1969, and proceeding with the Community in flux between 1969 and 1979, the period of the second enlargement between 1979 and 1984, the transformation of the European Community between 1985 and 1988, and the New Europe of the Union until 1993. The author refers to all major events during this time, such as the Marshall and Schuman plans, the deepening and enlargement debate in the 1970s, the Single Market, and the Intergovernmental Conferences. The historical development of the role of the institutions is also presented, with specific reference to the history of the Commission, from its initial imperial presidency to the recent calls for democratic accountability. Similarly, the author demonstrates the evolution of the European Parliament to direct elections and discussions on the democratic deficit, and the change in the role and power of the European Court of Justice. A similar historical approach is used for the presentation of the policies and programmes of the EU, with specific reference to the external relations of the EU and the Common Foreign and Security Policy.

McALLISTER follows the same historical approach in his analysis of the evolution of the Communities and the Union, but chooses to interpret the relevant political phenomena in a much more indirect way. The author does not seek to present all the historical events leading to each step forward in the development of the Communities and the Union. Instead, he looks at selected events in order to assess their contribution to the evolution of the Communities and the Union, under the general framework of the political and economic environment within and outside Europe. Individual events are analysed with a focus on how they were perceived at the time, rather than with hindsight. Equally valuable is the analysis of the two years after the passing of the Maastricht Treaty, with specific reference to the Pleven Plan, GATT, the European Monetary Union, and the relationship of the Union with NATO.

MIDDLEMAS studies the Community from a historian's point of view, emphasizing the formal and informal links that have kept the whole system going, despite the fact that, in his eyes, the Community has no clearly defined aim. After examining the historical evolution, institutions, and policies of the Community, the author sees the Community system as a kind of proto-state or a state without a country or public, and casts doubts on the democratic legitimacy of such a system. His argument is that the Community system will continue in this vague manner as long as the interests of the main actors, especially the member states, continue to be satisfied. He suggests, though, that the strengthening of the Community indicates the inability of the nation state, in Europe, to provide its people with prosperity and happiness.

PINDER is one of the best-known European federalists. Through an examination of the Community's historical evolution, institutions, and some key policy areas, the author concludes that the Community is gradually moving towards a stable federal polity: a federal union. The author believes that a federal union is a desirable end, and postulates a new approach to federalism, called neo federalism, which he believes is best applicable to Europe. Neo federalism, or new federalism, is a mixture of federal and confederal approaches to statehood, with some areas of high politics, such as foreign policy, remaining at the intergovernmental or state level.

HELEN XANTHAKI

See also Treaty on European Union (Maastricht)

European Community, politics

Burley, Anne-Marie and Walter Mattli, "Europe before the Court: A Political Theory of Legal Integration", *International Organization*, 47/1 (1993): 41–76

Garrett, Geoffrey and George Tsebelis, "An Institutional Critique of Intergovernmentalism", *International Organization*, 50/2 (1996): 269–99

Grieco, Joseph M., "The Maastricht Treaty, Economic and Monetary Union and the Neorealist Research Programme", *Review of International Studies*, 21/1 (1995): 21–40

Haas, Ernst B., *The Uniting of Europe: Political, Social and Economic Forces 1950–1957*, Stanford, California: Stanford University Press, 1958

Hoffmann, Stanley, *The European Sisyphus: Essays on Europe, 1964–1994*, Boulder, Colorado: Westview Press, 1995

Marks, Gary, Liesbet Hooghe and Kermit Blank, "European Integration from the 1980s: State-Centric v. Multi-Level Governance", *Journal of Common Market Studies*, 34/3 (1996): 341–78

Moravcsik, Andrew, *The Choice for Europe: Social Purpose and State Power from Messina to Maastricht*, Ithaca, New York: Cornell University Press, 1998; London: UCL Press, 1999

Pierson, Paul, "The Path to European Integration: A Historical Institutionalist Analysis", *Comparative Political Studies*, 29/2 (1996): 123–63

Sandholtz, Wayne and Alec Sweet Stone, "European Integration and Supranational Governance", *Journal of European Public Policy*, 4/3 (1997): 297–317

HAAS pioneered the scientific study of European integration and governance. He presented an explanatory framework, neofunctionalism, which is still a point of reference and critique for most scholars working in this field today. The framework was substantially revised by Haas and others in the 1960s, buried by Haas himself in the 1970s, and resurrected in different forms since the late 1980s, following the Single European Act and the Maastricht Treaty. The 1958 book deals with the development of the European Steel and Coal Community during the 1950s, and its more substantive chapters have only an historical interest by now. The theoretical parts are still well worth reading, however, because they are the source of several concepts and hypotheses that still frame research on the European Community (EC), especially in those approaches holding that supranational institutions, once created, display an integrative logic of their own and can make a difference regarding the pace and direction of subsequent integration.

An alternative vision of European integration was given in the 1960s by HOFFMANN. He developed an intergovernmentalist interpretation of integration, which stressed the persistent primacy of the nation state and denied neofunctionalist expectations about the future of supranational governance. His book includes essays from three decades, and displays a gradual shift in his perception of the nature of the EC, due only in part to the institutional evolution of the EC itself. The early essays are a scholarly counterpart of the political ideal of the "Europe of Nations", but in the 1980s Hoffmann suggested that the EC could be thought of as an international regime, and in the 1990s he came to believe that the EC was a *sui generis* construction, mixing intergovernmental and federal elements and still moving towards a yet unclear destination. The essays are not very theoretically sophisticated, but provide insightful analyses, and are especially interesting on the relationship of the US to European integration.

MORAVCSIK is probably the best overall account of the evolution of the EC written so far. It combines a rigorous theoretical framework with detailed empirical research, and makes a powerful case for a specific intergovernmentalist interpretation of European integration. It argues that commercial interests, rather than geopolitics or ideology, explain national preferences for international economic policy coordination; that the asymmetries of interdependence, rather than supranational political entrepreneurship, explain the efficiency and the outcomes of interstate "great bargains"; and that the desire for credible commitments, rather than ideological outlooks or informational economies of scale, explains state decisions to delegate or pool sovereignty in international institutions. Moravcsik's theses, as expounded in his previous essays, are discussed by most recent theoretical works on integration, and this book is likely to frame the next round of the debate.

MARKS, HOOGHE & BLANK provide an excellent synthetic statement of the main contemporary theoretical adversary of intergovernmentalism – the "multi-level governance" approach. They explore why government leaders may wish to shift decision-making to the supranational level; and how the institutional structure, once established, limits individual and collective national executive control i.e. how the member states are individually and collectively constrained in their ability to control supranational institutions at the European level. They also analyse the various phases of policy-making (policy initiation, decision making, implementation, and adjudication) in order to assess the relative importance of national executives and supranational agencies, and conclude that the latter often decisively influence policy definition and outcomes.

GARRETT & TSEBELIS criticize intergovernmentalism on the grounds that it neglects the influence of supranational actors on EU policy-making. In particular, they examine the "power index" approach to EU decision making, and find it defective because it ignores the policy preferences of governments in the Council of Ministers, and it neglects the agenda-setting powers (the ability to make proposals that are difficult to amend) and the veto powers of supranational bodies. In addition, they provide rigorous analyses of decision making under the various legislative procedures provided for by the European Treaties. The objects of their compelling criticism are the intergovernmentalist accounts of EU decision making rather than the intergovernmentalist theories of integration, but they correctly stress that it is impossible to understand the process of treaty adoption without understanding the likely policy consequences of different possible treaties.

Another critic of intergovernmentalism is PIERSON, who employs historical institutionalism to explain why the member states' control over the integration process is constrained. Once member states reach an agreement on specific institutional and policy outcomes, microlevel adaptations, accumulated policy constraints and heavily discounted or unintended effects alter the context in which subsequent decisions are taken, affecting the national executives' preferences, their bargaining power, and the power of supranational actors. Pierson expounds the factors that contribute to generating gaps in member state control over policies, as well as the factors that prevent them from regaining control once these gaps become evident, so that the integration process appears as strongly path-dependent. Having provided a solid historical institutionalist foundation for the multi-level governance perspective, Pierson applies his very interesting approach to the case of EU social policy.

SANDHOLTZ & SWEET STONE advance a set of hypotheses the main aim of which is to explain the variation in institutionalization of supranational governance across issue areas and time. They hypothesize that the expansion of transnational activities has been the catalyst of European integration, and thus accounts for most of the variation. In turn, transnational exchanges stimulate the activity of supranational bodies. They discuss various dimensions and indicators of institutionalization, and cite empirical studies confirming their hypotheses. Sandholtz and Sweet Stone's alternative to intergovernmentalism builds heavily on neofunctionalism, but it discards the latter's expectation about an almost automatic "spillover" of supranational governance into new areas of activity. The stress on the sources of variation is the main strength of this valuable article.

BURLEY & MATTLI's seminal article focuses, from a political science perspective, on legal integration – the gradual penetration of EC law into the domestic law of its member states. It defines legal integration as formal and substantive penetration, and aims at providing microfoundation for this process. The authors argue that Haas's original neofunctionalist model correctly predicts the kind of actors, their motivations, the mechanisms involved in legal integration, and the context in which it occurs. In particular, they see legal integration as the outcome of the self-interested behaviour of supranational actors (the European Court of Justice) and subnational actors (lower national courts and individual litigants) and of spillover effects. This important study has stimulated a wide debate among political scientists on the origins of the EC legal system, finally recognized as a basic aspect of the European construction.

GRIECO advances an explanation of Economic and Monetary Union based on a revised realist model. It is widely held in EU studies that the realist approach to world politics, stressing the constant concern of states for self-preservation, is at best inadequate for understanding European integration and at worst undermined by it. Grieco's revision of the school's classic assumptions consists mainly of conceiving integration as a means by which weaker states can gain some influence on decisions affecting them and previously taken autonomously by more powerful states. Specifically, monetary integration gives a "voice opportunity" to states that otherwise would have to accept German policy preferences in this area. Grieco's approach is problematic because, in the end, it fails to explain why the powerful state should be willing to give up its autonomy, but the article is nevertheless a worthy and informative attempt to adapt a productive theoretical framework to new circumstances.

MATHIAS KOENIG-ARCHIBUGI

See also European Union (politics), Treaty on European Union

European Convention on Human Rights

Bratza, Nicolas and Michael O'Boyle, "Opinion: The Legacy of the Commission to the New Court under the Eleventh Protocol", *European Human Rights Law Review*, 3 (1997): 211–28

Dickson, Brice (editor), *Human Rights and the European Convention: The Effects of the Convention on the United Kingdom and Ireland*, London: Sweet and Maxwell, 1997

Gomien, Donna, David Harris and Leo Zwaak, *Law and Practice of the European Convention on Human Rights and the European Social Charter*, Strasbourg: Council of Europe Publishing, 1996

Harris, D.J., Michael O'Boyle and Colin Warbrick, *Law of the European Convention on Human Rights*, London: Butterworths, 1995

Harris, David and Sarah Joseph (editors), *The International Covenant on Civil and Political Rights and United Kingdom Law*, Oxford: Clarendon Press, and New York: Oxford University Press, 1995

Janis, Mark W., Richard S. Kay and Anthony W. Bradley, *European Human Rights Law: Text and Materials*, Oxford: Clarendon Press, and New York: Oxford University Press, 1995

Kruger, H.C. and C.A. Norgaard, "The Right of Application" in *The European System for the Protection of Human Rights*, edited by R. St J. Macdonald, F. Matscher and H. Petzold, Dordrecht: Nijhoff, 1993

Lavender, Nicholas, "The Problem of the Margin of Appreciation", *European Human Rights Law Review*, 4 (1997): 380–90

Robertson, A.H. and J.G. Merills, *Human Rights in Europe: A Study of the European Convention on Human Rights*, 3rd edition, Manchester: Manchester University Press, 1993

Steiner, Henry J. and Phillip Alston, *International Human Rights in Context: Law, Politics, Morals*, Oxford: Clarendon Press, and New York: Oxford University Press, 1996

Teitgen, P.H., "Introduction to the European Convention on Human Rights" in *The European System for the Protection of Human Rights*, edited by R. St J. Macdonald, F. Matscher and H. Petzold, Dordrecht: Nijhoff, 1993

The European Convention on Human Rights (ECHR) represents the convergence of two significant streams of postwar thought: the formation of ever-closer union between the European states, and the development of international human rights guarantees. The Convention has contributed to the development of domestic law within the signatories, and to the development of regional human rights guarantees elsewhere, as well as to the global regimes. At the same time, the Convention is a living document, capable of amendment by the signatories and, more tellingly, development by the Convention organs responsible for its application and interpretation. As a consequence of these characteristics, there is a very sizeable body of literature relevant to the Convention, both in English and other languages. The selected publications represent Anglophone contributions to the secondary literature on the Convention, and have been chosen for their value to potential readers who will have differing background knowledge of law in general, and international law in particular.

The Convention represents part of a more global movement to develop guarantees of fundamental rights against states. STEINER & ALSTON provides a solid introduction to this international human rights movement. Although primarily focused on international law, it succeeds in taking into account a variety of other perspectives, and has been written with a view to readers from other disciplines seeking to develop an understanding of the area. As well as collecting together tightly edited selections from key primary and secondary sources, the authors provide a useful commentary to these sources. Against these strengths, the text is inevitably selective in terms of the range of issues discussed, and necessarily deals with particular regimes, including the Convention, relatively briefly.

HARRIS & JOSEPH provides a strong collection of essays dealing with the International Covenant on Civil and Political Rights (ICCPR) and the law of the United Kingdom. The ICCPR and the Convention deal with many of the same issues, often in very similar terms. Commentators seeking to understand the Convention frequently have recourse to the ICCPR. Of narrower value to understanding the particular context of the Convention, TEITGEN provides a participant's account of the formation of the Convention. This account identifies a number of philosophical and strategic tensions present at the formation of the Convention, and still relevant today – particularly the tension between European union, and authority, and the independence of the nation states, which is discussed further below. Although informally written, and relatively poorly referenced, it provides a useful insight into the early formation of the Convention. In particular, there is a danger of retrospectively taking the ECHR guarantees as given, which this piece dispels.

As an introductory study of the Convention itself, ROBERTSON & MERILLS has many merits. The text is very clearly written, striking a fine balance between providing sufficient detail to support the arguments and overwhelming the reader, especially the reader new to the Convention. Unlike in many texts, the Convention is set out in a thematic way. The rights guaranteed under the Convention are discussed in clusters, and chapter five deals with overarching issues that affect the scope and application of these rights. The latter discussion is particularly strong. The text is not generally suitable as a basis for advanced study, however, due to the lack of fine detail and explicit engagement with the secondary literature, although key publications are mentioned. The current edition is now some years old, and obviously does not take account of recent developments, especially in relation to the procedure under the Convention. Supplementing this text with GOMIEN, HARRIS & ZWAAK may avoid these problems. The work represents a comprehensive, accessible, but relatively uncritical summary of the Convention and closely related human rights programs. Reporting of important primary sources is good, and there are no serious flaws in the discussion. Although there have been substantial developments since 1996, the text is relatively recent.

JANIS, KAY & BRADLEY is an introductory text, and guide to identification of issues for further research. As mentioned above, the Convention is a living document, which has been extensively developed by the European Commission on Human Rights, and the European Court of Human Rights. It is impossible to attain a proper understanding of the Convention without going to the reports, opinions, and decisions of these bodies. Janis, Kay & Bradley bring together excerpts from many of the key cases that have developed the Convention, supported by strong commentary. The careful editing of these excerpts is of especial value to the inexperienced reader of European case law. The choice of cases is particularly good, although inevitably highly selective. Although the book cannot be recommended for independent research into the Convention, it provides an excellent, well-thought-out introduction to Convention jurisprudence across a range of areas.

HARRIS, O'BOYLE & WARBRICK provides a very strong reference text for all aspects of the Convention, which is well on the way to becoming authoritative within the English jurisdiction. Coverage of the jurisprudence of the Convention is extremely good, with a high level of detail, and consistently strong analysis. Although ideal as a first point of reference for anyone with a background in the Convention, it is too complicated to serve as an introductory text. Nor, despite the consistently high level of argument, does it constitute an especially novel contribution to the field. It is, rather, an invaluable academic resource across a wide range of issues related to the Convention.

Moving to more specific issues, the Convention is an international document, which does not *per se* have direct application within all national legal systems. The DICKSON collection builds on a growing body of literature seeking to consider the impact of the Convention on national legal systems, in this case those of the United Kingdom and that of Ireland. In particular, the chapter by Burrows, which deals with the role of the Convention within the European Union, is a clear exposition of a difficult area. KRUGER & NORGAARD discusses the right of individual application, the most powerful internal enforcement mechanism for the Convention. This mechanism has recently been altered, to take account of the caseload now being submitted under the Convention, and the Commission on Human Rights has been abolished. BRATZA & O'BOYLE provides a retrospective on the role of this body, and a useful discussion of the recent changes.

Another key issue of general significance is the relationship between the Convention and the national governments of the states. This relationship is most clearly explored under the margin of appreciation doctrine, by which the Convention organs institutionalize a degree of deference to the judgement of the state. LAVENDER provides a timely, if brief, discussion of this issue.

PETER W. EDGE

See also Human rights

European Court of Justice

Bengoetxea, Joxerramon, *The Legal Reasoning of the European Court of Justice*, Oxford: Clarendon Press, and New York: Oxford University Press, 1993

British Institute of International and Comparative Law, *The Role and Future of the European Court of Justice: A Report by Members of the EC Section of the British Institute's Advisory Board*, London: British Institute of International and Comparative Law, 1996

Brown, Neville L. and Tom Kennedy, *The Court of Justice of the European Communities*, London: Sweet and Maxwell, 1994

Lasok, K.P.E., *The European Court of Justice: Practice and Procedure*, London: Butterworths, 1994

Mann, Clarence J., *The Function of Judicial Decision in European Economic Integration*, The Hague: Nijhoff, 1972

O'Neill, Aidan, *Decisions of the European Court of Justice and Their Constitutional Implications*, London: Butterworths, 1994

Schwarze, Jürgen, *The Role of the European Court of Justice (ECJ) in the Interpretation of Uniform Law among the Member States of the European Communities (EC)*, Baden-Baden: Nomos, 1988

Usher, John A., *European Court Practice*, London: Sweet and Maxwell, 1983

BROWN & KENNEDY have written an analytical review of the nature, function, and future of the European Court of Justice. Reference is made to the organization and composition of the Court, its jurisdiction, practice and procedure, and its role as a lawmaker. Without wishing to underestimate the work obviously put into the other chapters of the book, as well as into the statistical data presented in the annex, the last chapter, on the Court as a lawmaker, has proven to be an excellent analysis of the balance that the Court has been attempting to achieve between the need for further, specific legislation on matters brought before the judges, and the role of the Court as a judicial, rather than a legislative, organ. The ongoing debate in support of and against activism is magnificently presented here, and the roots of the problem, namely the methods of interpretation used by the Court, are examined in detail. Furthermore, the effects of the Maastricht Treaty on the remedies and general functioning of the Court are discussed, albeit briefly.

LASOK analyses the European Court of Justice in its function as a judicial organ, thus providing an excellent review of the procedural legal issues in relation to its functioning. A general outline of the procedure is followed by a unique analysis on intervention, admissibility, interim relief, pleading, evidence, costs, and forms of action. Equally detailed is the presentation of the appeals from the Court of First Instance. From the point of view of the British reader, specific reference is made to the availability of legal aid in relation to representation and assistance. USHER takes a similar approach to the subject.

MANN focuses on the theoretical debate concerning the legal basis of the Court's authority and the delimitation of its powers. In an attempt to assess the theoretical foundations of the Court's judicial decisions, the author discusses the challenge of legal positivism through the *Begriffsjurisprudenz*, the work of Kelsen and Hart, and the rationality of judicial decision, through persuasive and pragmatic reasoning. The institutional foundations of judicial decision are examined through the legacy of Montescieu and the illusion of judicial neutrality. The author analyses the nature and limits of judicial power, namely the power to legitimate and the institutional constraints. This leads to a presentation of the proper scope of judicial function, which is judicial creativity in the law as reflected in the rationality of judicial decision, defined in terms of three sometimes competing types of reasoning, namely self-critical search for purpose, persuasive search for authority, and pragmatic search for practicability in the law. For the purposes of the analysis of the European Court of Justice, this leads the author to the conclusion that the Court must initiate and press discussion on the enduring questions of constitutional law. In its search for purpose, the Court finds itself needing to frame a discussion among several EU institutions, a task which necessitates self-restraint. In its search for authority, the Court is found to have been active, emphasizing the integrity of EU procedures, while being aware of its leading but limited role in the formation of a general EU consensus. In its search for practicability, a search demanding large amounts of imaginative craftsmanship by the judges, the Court finds itself balancing between rule and discretion. The author concludes that the Court seems to have recognized the limits to its discretion.

This is not the conclusion reached by O'NEILL, who examines the constitutional decisions reached by the European Court in the first 35 years of its functioning, and discusses the direct and indirect reception of EU law by the legal order of the UK. O'Neill refers to the transformation of the Treaties by the Court through the introduction of the principles of direct effects, supremacy, effectiveness, and judicial review. Specific emphasis is given to *Factortame* and the consequent change of the British constitution. The author concludes that, after *Factortame*, the British legal order suffered a direct invasion of EU legislation, covering areas such as proportionality and its application to Sunday trading, sex discrimination, equal opportunities, and liability for damages. The author argues that this evident invasion was followed by an indirect flux of legislation, to which the UK has been especially vulnerable due to its lack of a written constitution. This indirect invasion is evident in areas such as the interim injunctive relief against Ministers of the Crown, and the restitution of charges and duties enacted under unlawful demand by a public authority.

BENGOETXEA's book refers to the issue of the legal justification of the European Court of Justice, and attempts to shed some light on the reasons behind the judgements of the Court. The author discusses the various factors leading to a judicial conclusion, such as motivation, social factors, idiosyncratic factors, and "factors of wide explanation" (namely institutional setting, the organization of the Court, conventions and rules of conflict resolution, legal tradition, and judicial style). These affect the European judges in their search for judicial rationality. The author follows the method of rational reconstruction in order to assess which is the doctrine of justification operative in the practice of the Court, as the theory of practical discourse is a necessarily ideal theory. The author concludes that the main feature of legal justification is that, in order to be legally justified, a judicial decision has to be connected with enacted law. In clear cases this suffices. In hard cases, however, reference to substantive laws is necessary. In these cases, the Court will try to justify its decisions on the basis of general principles of law that is values of a moral or philosophical nature, such as basic norms found in the Preamble or opening articles of the Treaties.

In his appraisal of the work of the Court, SCHWARZE examines the remedies available to the Court for the achievement of its institutional role, namely the procedures of infringement proceedings, preliminary references, actions for annulment, and action for failure to act. He argues that, through the use of these remedies, the Court has managed to interpret EU law in such way as to award it independence from the law of the member states. In fact, such has been the success of the judges of the Court that, through their judgements, they have managed to initiate a procedure of interaction between EU and national laws that will inevitably lead to the formation of a legal tradition common to the laws of the member states, based on the rules of EU law.

In its recent report on the future of the Court of Justice, the BRITISH INSTITUTE OF INTERNATIONAL AND COMPARATIVE LAW identifies the jurisdiction, procedure, and enforcement of judgements as the main problematic areas for the functioning of the Court. The measures adopted so far for the improvement of the efficiency of the Court of Justice include the establishment of the Court of First Instance, the reform of the procedure before the Court (amounting to the establishment of written procedure only if the Court wishes it, the possibility of dealing with preliminary references by reasoned opinion only and the increasingly adopted practice of sitting in chambers), and a reduction in the volume of reporting demanded by the officers of the Court. Possible solutions within the existing judicial structure include an increase in the use of technology, an increase in the number of judges and other staff, the use of chambers and plenum, the establishment of single-judge courts within the Court of First Instance, and the possibility of curtailing or even dispensing with some hearings. Other solutions include changes in the role of the Advocates General, the extension of the jurisdiction of the Court of First Instance, and modifications in the proceedings before the courts. Other options for reform involve a new judicial structure, namely the establishment of a federal court system along the lines of the US court system, the formation of Community Regional Courts and a European High Court of Justice, the creation of a two-tier Court of Justice, the creation of specialized tribunals or chambers, the introduction of a new distribution of jurisdiction between the Community courts and the national courts, and the introduction of a power allowing the European courts to refuse judgement.

HELEN XANTHAKI

European integration

Archer, Clive and Fiona Butler, *The European Community: Structure and Process*, London: Pinter, and New York: St Martin's Press, 1992

Barnes, Ian and Pamela M. Barnes, *The Enlarged European Union*, London and New York: Longman, 1995

Buckley, Peter J., *The Economics of Change in East and Central Europe*, London and San Diego: Academic Press, 1994

Cecchini, Paolo, *The European Challenge, 1992: The Benefits of the Single Market*, Aldershot, Hampshire: Wildwood House, 1988

Dearden, Steven and Frank McDonald (editors), *European Economic Integration*, 3rd edition, London and New York: Longman, 1997

Floyd, D., "UK Membership of the European Union: Establishing a Framework for Analysis", *European Business Review*, 97/2 (November 1997): 63–68

Maresceau, Marc, *Enlarging the European Union: Relating between the EU and Eastern and Central Europe*, London and New York: Addison Wesley Longman, 1997

Meyer, Klaus, *Direct Investment in Economies in Transition*, Cheltenham, Gloucestershire: Elgar, 1998

Randlesome, Collin *et al.*, *Business Cultures in Europe*, 2nd edition, Oxford and Boston: Butterworth Heinemann, 1993

Ravasio, Giovanni, "Economic Policy in EMU", *European Documentation*, 124 (1997); from Directorate General II,

Economic and Financial Affairs of the European
Commission
Welford, Richard and Kate Prescott, *European Business:
An Issue-Based Approach*, 3rd edition, London: Pitman,
1996

The main texts on European integration seem to focus strongly
on economic benefits of integration. ARCHER & BUTLER,
however, covers the politics of integration, as well as the main
institutions of the European Union (EU), and the decision-
making process. His text focuses on the external relations of
the EU, and gives sound coverage of the General Agreement
on Tariffs and Trade (GATT), the World Trade Organization
(WTO), the Lomé Convention, and trade with the US and
Commonwealth countries. However, more focus could have
been given to the relationship between the EU and other
nations in the triad including China and Japan. At present one
would have to rely on specific EU documentation and current
journals in the European integration field for discussion of
such areas.

BARNES & BARNES offers an innovative approach to
European integration in that it is concerned with politics,
economics, and social issues as well as with aspects of
European studies and European business. Specific chapters, for
example, focus on the social dimension of the European Union,
the promotion of new technology in Europe, and the free movement of people. The book also discusses many of the other
economic issues to be found in texts on European economic
integration. The interdisciplinary approach to the subject is to
be welcomed, although the material on monetary union would
benefit from being updated. Greater attention to other components associated with European integration, including analysis
of various cultural issues, might also have been beneficial.

BUCKLEY aims to contribute to the limited amount of literature available on issues surrounding future integration, and
it provides more specific updated information on the enlargement issue. It also provides key background information on
possible new entrants to the EU. The transition issue and the
problems associated with this process are well outlined. There
is also coverage of the main criteria that need to be met prior
to central and Eastern European countries achieving full
membership of the EU. However, as with many texts, this work
covers a number of other broad issues. For specific analyses
of particular countries, the reader should refer to articles in
The Economics of Transition Journal.

The literature on transition has been patchy in places, particularly in view of the recent origin of this subject. There are
several new texts focusing specifically on enlargement and
economic transition in Eastern Europe, for example MEYER,
although this text takes an "international business" approach
with little emphasis on the "integration" issue. It is likely that
the gaps in this literature will be filled gradually. Meyer's text
provides a start for this new exciting area of literature.

Another issue is the enlargement of the European Union.
Cyprus, the Czech Republic, Slovenia, Hungary, and Poland
could enter the EU early in the 21st century. Cyprus has
received little coverage in most texts on European integration,
and some further coverage would be most welcome.

CECCHINI, a work based on the report of a Commission-
appointed committee, is an essential work providing a more

quantitative analysis of the benefits of the single market. It has
good coverage of the various benefits arising from the removal
of non-tariff barriers. For example, opening up the public
procurement market is particularly relevant today. Since the
report came out, telecommunications throughout the EU have
been privatized and in the future we are likely to see further
contracting out to European tender of the health services as
well as other public services. Cecchini has limited analysis of
recent EU directives aimed at the completion of the single
market programme. For more detailed treatment, it would be
necessary to consult specific documentation published by EU
bodies. An update of the Cecchini Report would be desirable.
At present there is the opportunity to examine the EU White
Paper on *Growth, Employment and Competitiveness* and the
follow-up to this, which included the Bangermann Report of
1994. This examines future prospects for Europe and measures
put forward to create new jobs from the future Information
Society. Much reference is made to improving communications
and investing in communications and education. Investment is
to be channelled into high-speed rail links as well as encouraging teleworking and lifelong learning.

European integration is addressed across many disciplines
including economics, politics, and European studies, as well as
the new field of European business. The subject is dominated
by economists who have emphasized the main benefits to be
achieved from free trade and further deregulation of markets
arising from the single European market programme. DEAR-
DEN covers such issues with a useful theoretical analysis. The
updated text also includes an analysis of EU policy making. It
focuses specifically on regional policy, EU enlargement, and the
impact of a single currency. These latter issues, however, tend
to need updating very quickly, and for this reason, reference to
a regular journal focusing on European integration may be more
appropriate.

FLOYD tackles the issue of European integration from a
business perspective. This article provides useful, up-to-date
coverage on the completion of the single market and the future
cultural and political benefits from European integration.
Integration in the EU is evaluated within a broad framework
rather than from the perspective of any specific discipline. The
potential disadvantages and costs of European integration are
also assessed. There is scope to apply this framework to further
issues, including the issue of a single currency, and the issue
of enlargement.

MARESCEAU covers the political, economic, and legal
framework required for enlargement of the EU with respect to
Central and Eastern European countries. It covers European
agreements and pre-accession strategies, trade and competition,
and the cost–benefit analysis of enlargement. This text is very
welcome, given the somewhat limited information available on
such new and exciting issues. However, it is very specialized,
and is written by a number of authors. More information could
be provided on the prospects for each potential future EU
member country, and more could be made of the issues
surrounding the inclusion of countries such as Cyprus. The
specialized nature of the text might render it inaccessible to
some.

Meyer examines foreign direct investment into Eastern
Europe during the the period of transition towards EU
membership. It reviews the business environment in Eastern

Europe and the conditions facing foreign investors. There is much statistical data, which address both the theory and determinants of foreign investment, with a bias towards transition-cost economics. The text provides useful insights for firms wishing to invest, although it is constrained by an "international business" approach.

RAVASIO provides a sound current analysis of the single currency issue, which could be one of the main testing grounds for European integration over the next few years. Ravasio goes beyond the analysis of many of the European economic integration texts in providing analysis of what could happen after the implementation of a single currency. Many other texts focus solely on the main benefits of a single currency relating to transaction costs and optimum currency area theory. Ravasio gives an indication of how strong the currency may be in the long run, and the possibility of collapse, as well as the implications for, and constraints upon, the governments of countries that have joined. The controversy surrounding UK membership is also outlined.

RANDLESOME has now been reprinted in a number of editions. It takes a country-specific focus on the main countries of the EU and deals with business, government, economy, finance, training, and the labour market, identifying key differentials across member states. There is a great emphasis on business statistics and the policies of various EU member states. However, despite its broad and varied coverage, the book uses a concept of "culture" which is somewhat ill-defined, and which requires further analysis. Some of the materials would also require updating if the possible future enlargement of the European Union were to go ahead.

WELFORD & PRESCOTT provides good coverage of European integration, with a specific focus towards business. The text, now in its third edition, covers most of the key business functions, including marketing, culture, law strategy, and economic policy making. There are several recent sections, including one on Central and Eastern Europe. The implications of the Maastricht Treaty are explored thoroughly. The text is supported by useful case studies, focusing on issues such as social policy, the single currency, and industry-specific analyses. Most of the main aspects of European integration are covered, and the interdisciplinary approach is very much to be welcomed. There is a heavy emphasis on understanding the main issues that business has to face in the context of European integration.

DAVID FLOYD

European Monetary System (EMS), Exchange Rate Mechanism (ERM), and European Monetary Institute (EMI)

European Commission, *The EMS: Ten Years of Progress in European Monetary Co-operation*, Brussels: European Commission, 1989

European Commission, *Protocols of the Treaty on Economic and Monetary Union*, Brussels: European Commission, 1991

Fratianni, Michele and Jürgen von Hagen, *The European Monetary System and European Monetary Union*, Boulder, Colorado: Westview Press, 1992

Giordano, Francesco and Sharda Persaud, *The Political Economy of Monetary Union: Towards the Euro*, London and New York: Routledge, 1998

Kondonassis, A.J. and A.G. Malliaris, "Towards Monetary Union of the European Community: History and Experiences of the European Monetary System", *American Journal of Economics and Sociology*, 53/3 (1994): 291–301

Kuhn, W.E., "Settling for Less: European Monetary System vs European Monetary Union", *Journal of Economic Issues*, 18/2 (1984): 517–26

Mayes, David, "The European Monetary System" in *The European Union: History, Institutions, Economics, and Policies*, edited by Ali El-Agraa, 5th edition, London: Prentice Hall, 1998

Salvatore, Dominick, "The European Monetary System: Crisis and Future", *Open Economies Review*, 7 (1996): 601–23

KUHN reviewed early perspectives on the European Monetary System (EMS). Each view suggested contrasting prospects for its future. One school suggested that countries with high inflation would have to use restrictive policies to avoid the loss of reserves, which ultimately would not be beneficial to economic growth and employment. Another view suggested that countries intending to follow a stable growth path would be hindered by their obligation to intervene. When two currencies reached their agreed limits, both countries had to intervene in the strong currency to buy the weak currency, hence losing control of the domestic money supply. FRATIANNI & VON HAGEN discounted this option because central banks can sterilize their foreign exchange interventions. Yet another viewpoint suggested that countries with highly divergent economic performance needed policies to converge in order to maintain the EMS; however, if they followed this route it would result in frequent small and large realignments that would not help to create a zone of monetary stability. Circumstances at the time offered support for the latter view. Asymmetry remains within the EMS, despite efforts to reduce it, and no effective means exist to compel a country with a strong currency to weaken, but a weak currency is forced to strengthen.

EUROPEAN COMMISSION (1989) serves as a useful starting point for readers interested in the EMS and the exchange rate mechanism (ERM). It offers an account of the first ten years of the EMS, although one should treat the conclusions drawn by the authors as tentative given their perspective on the subject matter. Reasons for the establishment of the EMS are cited and one should pay particular attention to them because they are echoed in many commentaries on the subject. The EMS was established to pursue three main policy objectives: the creation of a "zone of monetary stability" involving both low inflation and stable exchange rates; the provision of a framework for improved economic policy cooperation between member states; and the easing of world monetary instability through the adoption of common policies in relation to third countries. The EMS is classified into three distinct phases:

(a) The learning phase (1979–83) when there was no convergence and frequent realignments.

(b) The transitory phase (1984–87) when only two realignments occurred and the rules of the EMS were changed, firstly, to improve the usability of the ECU and then, secondly, when in 1986 the European Union (EU) amended the Treaty of Rome with the Single European Act. The Basle/Nyborg Agreement was reached in 1987. This introduced a series of measures aimed at promoting the coordination of economic policies through the surveillance of economic indicators and the refinement of the EMS intervention mechanism to counter speculation after capital liberalization.

(c) The stability phase (1987 onward), when economic performance appeared to converge as signalled by reduced interest rate, lower inflation rate differentials, and smaller exchange rate differentials.

KONDONASSIS & MALLIARIS assessed the EMS in the wake of the 1992/1993 currency crisis that beset the EMS. They also placed the establishment of the EMS in the context of the general movement toward monetary integration in the European Community and the failure of the EU's attempt to complete monetary union by 1980. They identify the ERM as the main tool to realize the objectives of the EMS. It consisted of four components: the European currency unit (ECU), the parity grid, the divergence indicator, and credit financing. These are explained in some detail – especially the divergence indicator, which was an innovation introduced to overcome the asymmetry of the "snake". Fratiani & von Hagen also discussed this aspect in detail. The authors suggest that, although the EMS appeared to be successful in economic convergence, as was detailed by the European Commission (1989) this must be set in context. Inflation rates and interest rates were also falling in countries outside of the EMS. Although exchange rate variability became smaller, the events of 1992 (rejection of the Maastricht Treaty by Danes in June 1992 and the slender majority in favour of ratification of the Treaty in the French referendum) presaged attacks on the British, Spanish, and Italian currencies. These attacks ultimately led to the withdrawal of the pound and the lira, and the devaluation of the peseta in September 1992, and later, in 1993, the move to the wider band. In short, the European Commission assessment suggested that there was no conclusive proof of convergence at that time.

SALVATORE stated that when the Treaty of Rome was amended by the Single European Act, it required the removal of all remaining barriers to the free flow of goods, services, and resources by the end of 1992. Intra-EU capital controls were removed by July 1990; however, fixed exchange rates are not consistent with the free flow of capital and limited coordination of monetary policy. These inconsistencies were recognized and the Delors committee was established to study and propose concrete stages leading to economic and monetary union. The EMS appeared to realize its purpose. Among EMS members, there was convergence in inflation rates, interest rates, budget deficits, and government debt as a percentage of GDP between 1987–92. The belief still remained among some commentators that a large asymmetric shock would unsettle the EMS and place it under considerable strain. The EMS was tested to the point of destruction when the Bundesbank failed to lower the discount rate in May 1993. Germany was grappling with the cost of financing the restructuring of East Germany, and had historically high interest rates to curb inflationary pressure. Tight monetary policy in Germany acted as a trigger for the ERM crisis. However, pressures had been building up in the EMS since the signing of the Maastricht Treaty and the subsequent failure by Denmark to ratify it due to the "no" vote in their referendum. Financial market liberalization and unfettered capital flows coupled with the EMS required full monetary policy coordination. GIORDANO & PERSAUD suggested that, within the financial markets, there was a lack of sufficient credibility in the consistency and coordination of economic policy and a general feeling that the central bank power of strong currency countries would be used with discretion.

MAYES states unequivocally that the EMS was not designed as a device to achieve EMU. The creation of the EMS is set in historical context and provides a detailed description of its tools and improvements in its design in comparison with the "snake", which had problems due to German dominance and unilateral decision making. Mayes suggests that the EMS has achieved its primary objectives: stabilizing exchange rates, countering inflationary pressures, and preventing drastic changes in the real exchange rate. It has evolved to deal with the Single Market and the removal of exchange controls.

Giordano & Persaud provide a brief summary of the creation of the European Monetary Institute (EMI) as a transitional institution of EMU. After agreement at Maastricht on a new treaty to delegate responsibility for monetary policy to a new common institute, the second stage began on 1 January 1994. The EMI was created to assume a coordinating role. It was set up as a precursor to the European Central Bank (ECB) – the central institution of the third stage of monetary union. The EUROPEAN COMMISSION (1991) detailed the role of the Institute. The EMI's role is to strengthen cooperation between central banks and the coordination of monetary policies of member states, to monitor the functioning of the EMS, to take over the tasks of the European Monetary Cooperation Fund (EMCF), and to facilitate the use of the ECU and oversee its development. It also has general responsibility for making preparations for stage three of EMU, and to member states concerning the conduct of their monetary policy. In preparing for stage three it should draw up recommendations on the overall orientation of monetary policy and exchange rate policy – policies that might affect the internal or external monetary situation. Finally, in May 1998, the European Council met to announce the countries that met the necessary conditions for the adoption of a single currency. The third and final stage of EMU began on 1 January 1999, as planned. Participating states adopted "irrevocably fixed" exchange rates. The Euro would be substituted for national currencies, and the ECB would become the sole issuing authority for Euro notes, replacing the EMI.

PHILIP ARESTIS, KEVIN MCCAULEY
AND MALCOLM SAWYER

See also European single currency

European single currency

Arestis, Philip and Malcolm Sawyer, "Prospects for the Single European Currency" in *Full Employment and Price Stability in a Global Economy*, edited by Paul Davidson and Jan Kregel, Cheltenham, Gloucestershire: Elgar, 1999

Bovenberg, A.L. and A.H.M. de Jong, "The Road to Economic and Monetary Union", *Kyklos*, 50/1 (1997): 83–109

European Commission, *Report on Economic and Monetary Union in the European Community*, Luxembourg: Office for Official Publications of the European Communities, 1989

European Commission, *EURO 1999: Report on Progress towards Convergence and the Recommendation with a View to the Transition to the Third Stage of Economic and Monetary Union*, Luxembourg: Office for Official Publications of the European Communities, 1998

European Monetary Institute, *Convergence Report: Report Required by Article 109j of the Treaty Establishing the European Community*, Frankfurt: European Monetary Institute, 1998

Giordano, Francesco and Sharda Persaud, *The Political Economy of Monetary Union: Towards the Euro*, New York and London: Routledge, 1998

Klein, Michael W., "European Monetary Union", *New England Economic Review*, (March/April 1998): 3–12

Pinder, John, "Economic and Monetary Union: Pillar of a Federal Polity", *Publius: The Journal of Federalism*, 26/4 (1996): 123–40

The immediate ancestry of a European single currency and monetary union can be traced to the establishment of the European Economic Community (EEC) in 1957. Since then, there have been attempts to establish a European exchange rate system, but in recent years, according to PINDER, the attempt at monetary integration and, ultimately monetary union has assumed greater urgency for three main reasons. First, monetary union can be viewed as a response by European policy makers to the increases of intra-European trade, which has meant that different currencies and fluctuating exchange rates have become an increasing nuisance. Second, politically, there was a continual search for increased stability and security in Europe, which crucially hinged on anchoring Germany within Europe. And third, many economic interest groups perceived a single unified and integrated European economy as serving their interests.

The Delors report proposed a three-stage transition to economic and monetary union (EMU). The first stage was agreed by the European Council in June 1989, and at Maastricht in 1991 agreement on the final two stages was reached which included a set of strict criteria that would have to be met before a nation could join the final stage of monetary union:

(a) Average exchange rate not to deviate by more than 2.25 per cent from its central rate for the two years prior to membership.

(b) Inflation rate was not to exceed the average rate of inflation of the three community nations with the lowest inflation rate by 1.5 per cent.

(c) Long-term interest rates not to exceed the average interest rate of the three countries with the lowest inflation rate by two per cent.

(d) Budget deficit not to exceed three per cent of its GDP.

(e) Overall government debt not to exceed 60 per cent of its GDP.

In May 1998, the European Council selected the countries qualified to participate in Stage III of Economic and Monetary Union (EMU). Their decisions were based on reports, submitted by the European Monetary Institute (EMI) and European Commission (EC) in March 1998, which assessed how each country had complied with the convergence criteria. In June 1998, the European Central Bank (ECB) replaced the EMI and on January 1999, it took over responsibility for monetary policy within the euro zone and the euro was adopted as legal tender, albeit in a virtual form, by eleven countries of the European Union (namely Austria, Belgium, Finland, France, Germany, Ireland, Italy, Luxembourg, the Netherlands, Portugal, and Spain) on 1 January 1999. It is intended that this will lead into the full operation of the euro in 2002 with the introduction of notes and coins denominated in euros and the phasing out of national currencies during the first six months of that year. The institutional arrangements of monetary union involve the creation of an "independent" (of political control) European System of Central Banks (ESCB) with its operating arm, the ECB and the national central banks, which is given the sole policy objective of price stability. The complete separation of the monetary authorities (in the form of the central bank) and the fiscal authorities (in the shape of the national governments comprising the EMU) is mandated by the Maastricht Treaty, where the latter are constrained to keep their budget deficit below three per cent according to the Stability and Growth Pact.

EUROPEAN COMMISSION (1989) states that monetary union would necessitate a common monetary policy to be controlled by a central institution, although a single currency was not mandatory. Prerequisites for monetary union were identified as the total and irreversible convertibility of currencies, the complete liberalization of capital transactions, elimination of margins of fluctuation and the irrevocable fixing of exchange rate parities. The central institution overseeing the Community's monetary policy was an ESCB based on federal lines, which would formulate and implement policy. Its primary objective would be price stability while it would maintain total independence from member states. The report recommended a transition towards full monetary union in three stages. The first stage, defined as an initiation process towards EMU, advocated the convergence of economic performance and cooperation in monetary and fiscal polices. The common market was to be completed by the removal of all restrictions to intra-community capital movements. The second stage was a transitionary period where consolidation of procedures established in stage one would take place and an institutional framework would be created. Policy would still remain in the hands of national government, although policy guidelines would be mandated by majority voting. The third and final stage would begin with the irrevocable fixing of participating states' exchange rates, and national central banks would relinquish control of the domestic money supply to the EC institutions. Eventually national currencies would be replaced by a single currency. The ESCB would pursue a single monetary policy that would entail engaging in foreign exchange market interventions and union-wide open market operations, formulation and implementation of monetary policy, and the technical preparation necessary for a single currency.

GIORDANO & PERSAUD explore the economic and political reasons for monetary union (single currency). Monetary union is analysed drawing on the optimal currency area literature and prospects for the future are examined.

KLEIN charts the move towards a common European currency starting from the collapse of the Bretton Woods agreement. The EMS is identified as a "more comprehensive attempt" at forming a exchange rate system for Europe. Convergence of economic indicators among EMS countries post-1987 and the Single European Act (1986) lead to closer economic integration, strengthening the push towards monetary union. The author airs the arguments for and against a single currency. Criticism is made of the "one size fits all" monetary policy, which is a natural consequence of the introduction of the euro, yet, unlike the US, the safety net of fiscal transfers and labour mobility is not sufficient to offset the loss of monetary policy as an instrument.

BOVENBERG & DE JONG review the costs and benefits of EMU. They argue that the most important benefit of EMU is that it anchors the internal market by providing stable monetary and fiscal policies. They consider the uncertainty created at the transitional stage of EMU to be the most important cost. Overall they feel that the benefits may outweigh the costs, yet they stress that this view is entirely subjective. In an attempt to reduce the risks of a weak currency and to facilitate the ECB's primary task of price stability four rules were created: the ECB was granted independence from political influence; the no bail out rule was introduced; the monetary financing of government deficits was prohibited; and member states had to avoid excessive deficits. The convergence criteria are viewed as arbitrary yet essential to signal to the financial markets that the countries are willing to live with the fiscal discipline required by EMU.

EUROPEAN MONETARY INSTITUTE and EUROPEAN COMMISSION (1998) convergence reports submitted to the European Council indicate that France and Luxembourg were the only countries which, on a strict interpretation, satisfied all the convergence criteria. However, nine more countries have been deemed as meeting all the convergence criteria, even though they did not meet them on a literal interpretation. The decision on membership of the euro and whether the convergence criteria were met was based on data available in March 1998. In terms of the countries that will not participate from the birth of the EMU, Greece is the only country that meets none of the convergence criteria.

ARESTIS & SAWYER argue that the Maastricht criteria were confined to a narrow range of economic indicators. They argue that the transition to a single European currency entails essentially two serious problems. The first is that a number of countries that are not strictly able to meet the Maastricht criteria comfortably have been recommended to join the EMU.

As a result, the ECB is expected to be more deflationary than otherwise. The second is that the attempt to meet these criteria has been accompanied by higher unemployment rates throughout the EU. The problem of unemployment will persist for countries within the EMU and the single currency in view of the requirement not to deviate from the set criteria. It follows that individual EMU countries will face long periods of recession, with very few instruments to influence the outcome. In view of these problems they have suggested a new Stability and Growth Pact, the focus of which will be a common fiscal policy, along with the ECB monetary policy. They offer an alternative policy prescription to the "new monetarist" perspective in which the institution and policy framework of EMU is embedded. This new proposal would focus on full employment and economic growth.

PHILIP ARESTIS, KEVIN MCCAULEY,
AND MALCOLM SAWYER

See also European Monetary System, European Union, Optimum currency areas and currency unions, Treaty on European Union (Maastricht)

European Union development policy

Duran, Esperanza, *European Interests in Latin America*, London and Boston: Routledge and Kegan Paul, 1985

Gillespie, Richard (editor), *Mediterranean Politics*, vol. 1, London: Pinter, and Madison, New Jersey: Fairleigh Dickinson University Press, 1994; vol. 2, Pinter, 1996

Gillespie, Richard (editor), *The Euro-Mediterranean Partnership*, London: Cass, 1997

Grilli, Enzo R., *The European Community and the Developing Countries*, Cambridge and New York: Cambridge University Press, 1993

Grugel, Jean, *Politics and Development in the Caribbean Basin: Central America and the Caribbean in the New World Order*, London: Macmillan, 1995

Lister, Marjorie, *The European Union and the South: Relations with Developing Countries*, London and New York: Routledge, 1997

Lister, Marjorie (editor), *European Union Development Policy*, London: Routledge, and New York: St Martin's Press, 1998

Rein, Eberhard, "Europe and the Greater Middle East" in *Allies Divided: Transatlantic Policies for the Greater Middle East*, edited by Robert D. Blackwill and Michael Sturmer, Cambridge, Massachusetts: MIT Press, 1997

Sutton, Paul (editor), *Europe and the Caribbean*, London: Macmillan, 1991

The development, or development cooperation, policy of the European Union (EU) is one of the oldest of its common policies, with its origins in Part IV of the Treaty of Rome. From an initial focus on the colonies or former colonies of the member states, development cooperation has expanded to cover all regions of the developing world. Nevertheless, like the EU's nascent foreign policy, its development policy is rather disunited and amorphous, as evidenced by the failure of the

EU up to the present to publish an annual report covering all of its development activities. A substantial literature exists covering many aspects of EU development policy, with a greater concentration of publications, in terms of both depth and quantity, being devoted to the Lomé Convention, a comprehensive development treaty with the 71 countries of the African, Caribbean, and Pacific (ACP) group of states. At the opposite end of the spectrum, relations with the developing countries of Asia are particularly under-researched.

Two recent books critically examine the overall development efforts of the EU. GRILLI provides a useful, analytical overview of the EU's development policy, covering the Lomé Convention, Mediterranean policy, and relations with Latin America, Asia, and Eastern Europe. LISTER (1997) assesses the relationship between EU foreign and development policies, Europe's problems in dealing with societies defined as "other", and the broad spectrum of EU relations with countries of the South, especially in relation to the Mediterranean and Lomé policies.

The negotiations that began on 30 September 1998 for a successor agreement to the fourth Lomé Convention form the backdrop to the edited collection of essays by politicians, officials, and academics in LISTER (1998). These cover subjects ranging from the UK's view of its role in EU development policy (perhaps surprisingly positive) to the view from the African, Caribbean, and Pacific Group's side. The factors that keep Africa on Europe's agenda, the results of the first full-scale study of EU aid to one country (Ethiopia), and the state of EU–Pacific relations, are analysed. The final chapter investigates the EU's attempts to incorporate human rights and democracy issues into its foreign and development policies, finding that consistency in the application of these principles has yet to be achieved.

The increased interest of the EU in the developing countries of the Southern Mediterranean was a key element of EU policy up to the mid-1990s. GILLESPIE (1997) offers a concise introduction to the Euro–Mediterranean partnership process, which began at the Barcelona Conference of 1995, and was designed to create a free-trade area in the Mediterranean by 2010. However, REIN's critical analysis shows that, since 1995, the EU has somewhat lost interest in this project. One of the long-standing criticisms of EU initiatives towards the Mediterranean is their sporadic nature.

The resignation of the EU Commission in March 1999 was based inter alia on dissatisfaction with the Commission's poor administration of the Mediterranean and emergency aid policies. For a comprehensive discussion of many of the political and security issues relating to the Mediterranean, including both of its shores, see the edited collections by GILLESPIE (1994) and GILLESPIE (1996).

The mutual suspicion and disregard between the EU and Latin America through the mid-1980s is discussed in the classic study by DURAN. She argued that increasing European independence from the US and declining US hegemony in the region would allow for greater European influence. GRILLI takes a critical view of the EU's relations with the region, which he sees as lying in the outer periphery of the EU's development interests. He demonstrates how problems over trade and agriculture have affected the relationship particularly adversely. Lister (1997) observes that despite past problems and misunderstandings, there is considerable European interest in an enhanced relationship with MERCOSUR, the up-and-coming common market of the southern cone of South America.

The Caribbean region has, up to now, been treated by the EU as part of the ACP group of the Lomé Convention, not as part of Latin America. Themes including the roles of individual European states, the policies of the US and (former) Soviet Union, and of the EU, are skilfully addressed in the volume edited by SUTTON. GRUGEL's interesting study of the Caribbean basin delves further into its relations with the US, but also contains a useful, concise examination of Europe's role in the area.

MARJORIE LISTER

See also European Union, Lomé Convention

European Union, economic

Arestis, Philip, Kevin McCauley and Malcolm Sawyer, *From Common Market to EMU: A Historical Perspective of European Economic and Monetary Integration*, New York: Jerome Levy Institute, 1999 (working paper no. 263)

Dinan, Desmond, *Ever Closer Union? An Introduction to the European Community*, Basingstoke: Macmillan, and Boulder, Colorado: Rienner, 1994; 2nd edition 1999

Jovanovic, Miroslav, *European Economic Integration: Limits and Prospects*, London and New York: Routledge, 1997

Molle, Willem, *The Economics of European Integration: Theory, Practice, Policy*, Aldershot, Hampshire: Dartmouth, 1990

Tsoukalis, Loukas, *The New European Economy Revisited*, Oxford and New York: Oxford University Press, 1997

Urwin, Derek, *The Community of Europe: A History of European Integration since 1945*, London and New York: Longman, 1991

The European Union (EU) is a recent initiative (1990). It follows on from the European Economic Community (EEC), which was created in 1957 as part of the Treaty of Rome. The latter, in its turn, sprang from another initiative, this time from the Second World War as a result of the Marshall Plan that necessitated the establishment of the Committee of European Economic Cooperation (CEEC) in 1947 and later in 1951 the European Coal and Steel community (ECSC).

TSOUKALIS remarks that all European countries were hungry for reconstruction funds and America was the only country capable of providing much-needed financial resources. But American aid in the form of the European Recovery Programme (Marshall Plan) was conditional on cooperation among European governments and progressive liberalization of intra-European trade and payments. In order to comply with the conditions of the Marshall Plan, and to co-ordinate and realize its objectives, the European governments established the CEEC.

URWIN adds that, insofar as Western Europe had serious economic problems, they were related to foreign trade, currency convertibility, and cash reserves. The author reports that the range of bodies outside of governments and the established political parties, not content with the limited area of competence in the economic sphere given to the Organization for European Economic Cooperation, successor to the CEEC, continued to follow their alternative route to European integration. At the Hague, in May 1948, representatives from the European movement gathered to hold a Congress of Europe. After six months of deliberation, a compromise was reached that established a Council of Europe in 1949. The subsequent failure to extend the Council's powers and the slow progress towards European union frustrated the more federal-minded members who realized that quicker economic integration would have to be achieved outside the institutional framework provided by the Congress of Europe.

DINAN remarks that Jean Monnet had remained detached from the wrangling of the Congress of Europe. As early as 1943 Monnet, who was director of the French Modernization plan, suggested that the only way to prevent war in Europe was to replace national sovereignty by a "states of Europe" along federal lines. When the US pressed for economic growth in Germany to help European economic recovery, Monnet realized the moment had arrived to press for the implementation of his idea. France was faced with the need to reformulate its policy toward Germany. Monnet approached Robert Schuman, the French Foreign Minister, with his proposal for a supranational coal and steel community and, in May 1950, Schuman made a public statement proposing that German and French coal and steel production be "pooled" and placed under a common supranational authority. France, Germany, Italy, the Netherlands, Belgium, and Luxembourg signed the treaty creating the ECSC in Paris in April 1951. Other European countries did not join the ECSC because at the time they did not feel the political need or else argued that international co-operation should take place in the wider setting of the OEEC. For Britain, in particular, there was an unpalatable condition placed on participation at the negotiations: the acceptance of the principle of shared sovereignty.

As stated by Tsoukalis, the ECSC was unique in that it was the first time that institutional structures were established that had supranational powers. The Paris Treaty established an institutional structure for administering, controlling, and supervising the tasks defined in the Treaty. A free trade area was created in coal and steel, tariffs and quotas were removed. Free trade in these materials was promoted, so that no country could monopolize them for their own purposes and individuals could purchase the goods if they wished. In this way Germany became free to regenerate its economy while assuaging the fears of other European countries, which were concerned that it would use its revitalized economy to become a military power again.

The next phase of European integration was the Treaty of Rome in 1957, which created the EEC and the European Atomic Energy Community. JOVANOVIC states that the treaty established four main institutions to oversee the EEC: Council of Ministers, European Commission, European Assembly, and the Court of Justice. Two bodies fulfil the decision-making and executive functions: the Council of Ministers and the Commission. The institutional structure of the EEC was copied from the ECSC, yet in key aspects it differs. The Council is the primary decision-making body and the Commission is responsible for initiating decision making and fulfils an executive function. The EEC was based on the creation of a common market, which was achieved through specific measures outlined in Article 3 of the treaty: the elimination of custom duties and of quantitative restrictions on intra-EEC trade; the establishment of a common external tariff and of a commercial policy toward third countries; the free movement for goods, services, persons, and capital; common policies in agriculture and transport; the introduction of procedures to allow the co-ordination of economic policies, and the rectification of disequilibria in the balance of payments; the establishment of a system to ensure undistorted competition in the common market; the approximation of laws to enable the proper functioning of the common market; and the creation of the European Structural Fund and European Investment Bank to improve employment opportunities, support economic expansion, and raise the standard of living.

MOLLE remarks that despite these declared aspirations there were no specific provisions made in the treaty regarding co-ordination in the macroeconomic field. Article 2 refers to the "harmonious development of economic activities" and to "a continuous and balanced expansion" but there were not sufficient instruments created to realize these objectives. Regarding the lack of precise instruments for macroeconomic co-ordination, Tsoukalis offers several explanations. First, Keynesian ideas still held sway and governments wished to retain direct control over fiscal and monetary policies. Second, greater capital mobility across national boundaries would undermine the effectiveness of national monetary instruments. Third, the governments did not wish to push too far in case the whole enterprise was placed in jeopardy. In addition, exchange rate stability and a basic framework for policy co-ordination were provided externally by the Bretton Woods system. All tariffs for EC internal trade were eliminated on 1 July 1968, one-and-a-half years before the target date, and at the same time, the common external tariff came into force.

Dinan comments that the EC had emerged from the 1970s intact but considerably weakened. The decision-making process was paralysed, the cost of the Common Agricultural Policy (CAP) was spiralling out of control, the commission was impotent, and the Community's solidarity was strained by national politicians, who only seemed to have national interests at heart. The early years of the 1980s were characterized similarly. Slowly, however, things began to change. The accession of Greece and the pending accession of Spain and Portugal generated pressure for institutional reform. Direct elections had sent a new breed of vibrant and energetic politicians to the European Parliament who sought to broaden and strengthen the scope of the Parliament's powers. All these factors helped to create a new momentum in Europe for change. Early results were a resolution to the British budget question, and a renewed effort to implement the single market. The single market programme, in particular, was to herald a sea change in the fortunes of the EC. In the early 1980s, recession had hit the European economies hard. Europe's loss of competitiveness and the subsequent loss in jobs and rise in unemployment were linked, in part, to the fragmentation of the European market due to the existence of non-tariff barriers.

Jovanovic comments that the main aspects of the programme were the removal of non-tariff barriers for internal trade, increased competition, promotion of cooperation among firms in research and development, unification of factor markets through liberalization of factor mobility, monetary integration, and social protection. On its own the Single Market Programme was not sufficient to guarantee the completion of the single market, it would undoubtedly have become bogged down in procedural wrangling in the Council of Ministers. The Single Market Programme highlighted the need for institutional and constitutional reform of the Community. This provided the required impetus for reform resulting in the Intergovernmental Conference that lead to the Single European Act. The subsequent reform of the Treaty of Rome by the Single European Act (SEA, 1 July 1987) helped speed up the Single Market programme. The SEA extended the use of majority voting to most areas except for fiscal matters, rights of employees, and free movement of people, thereby sweeping aside the Luxembourg Compromise.

ARESTIS, McCAULEY & SAWYER discuss the historical perspective of the creation of the EEC along with the new institutional framework and the events leading to the establishment of the European Union. They argue that the reunification of Germany in 1990 and the disintegration of the Soviet Union in 1991 transformed the international political landscape and forced the pace of change in the European Community. These events eventually culminated in the Maastricht Treaty, which formally recognized the European Union as an entity; in addition it created new institutional structures and set out a timetable for further economic and monetary integration and, ultimately, a single currency.

Philip Arestis, Kevin McCauley,
and Malcolm Sawyer

See also European single currency, Treaty on European Union (Maastricht)

European Union law

Chalmers, Damien, *European Union Law*, 2 vols, Aldershot, Hampshire: Ashgate Dartmouth, 1998
Craig, Paul and Gráinne de Búrca, *EU Law: Text, Cases and Materials*, 2nd edition, Oxford and New York: Oxford University Press, 1998
Edward, David and Robert Lane, *European Community Law*, Edinburgh: Butterworths/Law Society of Scotland, 1995
Ellis, Evelyn and Takis Tridimas, *Public Law of the European Community: Text, Materials and Commentary*, London: Sweet and Maxwell, 1995
Evans, Andrew, *A Textbook on EU Law*, Oxford: Hart, 1998
Hanlon, James, *European Community Law*, London: Sweet and Maxwell, 1998
Hartley, Trevor C., *The Foundations of European Community Law*, 3rd edition, Oxford: Clarendon Press, 1994
Lasok, D. and K.P.E. Lasok, *Law and Institutions of the European Union*, 6th edition, New York: Oxford University Press, and London: Butterworths, 1994
Mathijsen, P.S.R.F., *A Guide to European Union Law*, London: Sweet and Maxwell, 1995
Steiner, Josephine and Lorna Woods, *Textbook on EC Law*, London: Blackstone Press, 1998
Tillotson, John, *European Community Law: Texts, Cases and Materials*, London: Cavendish, 1994
Weatherhill, Stephen and Paul Beaumont, *EC Law*, London: Penguin, 1993
Wyatt, Derrick and Alan Dashwood, *European Community Law*, 3rd edition, London: Sweet and Maxwell, 1993

HARTLEY views the European Union (EU) from a purely legal point of view. EU law is examined as a separate legal system, with its own sources of law and its own institutions or organs. The analysis of the sources of EU law is unique and quite exhaustive, with specific reference to the general principles of law, whereas the discussion on the institutions is concentrated on the powers and functions of each institution separately. Constitutional law is referred to in the form of direct effects and supremacy, but only in order to serve as an introduction to the remedies introduced by the Treaties for the effective enforcement of EU law within the member states. Although administrative law is examined, the review of the remedies is from the old-fashioned point of view of judicial review, with little reference to the rights awarded to individuals.

This point is clearly made by STEINER & WOODS, who in their detailed and exhaustive review of the case law of the European Court of Justice (ECJ) and the Court of First Instance (CFI), refer to supremacy, direct effects, and indirect effects, in order to introduce the main focus of their work, which is the issue of the effective protection of the individual. The main remedies introduced by the Treaties are examined with respect to their ability to provide effective judicial protection, mainly in order to assess whether the new and currently developing state-liability doctrine can solve the problem of the limited access of the individual to justice. In the second part of the book, the focus changes dramatically, and the main point of analysis becomes the much more commercial issue of competition law and the functioning of the internal market. Within this latter framework, some discussion takes place on the essence of the internal market, as expressed in the four freedoms introduced by the Treaties, namely the free movement of people, services, capital, and goods. The recent developments on sex discrimination are also briefly analysed.

A detailed presentation of most aspects of EU law is attempted in the books written by MATHIJSEN and by WEATHERHILL & BEAUMONT. In their analysis, the authors of the latter book attempt to cover the vast majority of legal topics, with reference to the institutions, the constitution, the procedural law of the EU, some aspects of the four freedoms, and their underlying policies. The book may serve as a good introduction to EU law, but it fails to present the topic in much depth or to introduce a new angle for analysis. What is worth noting, however, is the selection of relatively obscure topics, such as intellectual property or state intervention in the market.

The same aim, namely a detailed presentation of most aspects of EU law, seems to be the object of the books by TILLOTSON and by LASOK & LASOK. The latter is now in its sixth edition. Lasok & Lasok refer to many topics within EU law, such as the history of the EU, the legal nature of the Union and its predecessors (the Community and the Communities), the external relations of the Union, the sources of its law, its institutions, the position of the national legal systems in reference to the system of the EU, EU economic law, and the policies of the Union. In fact, the great virtue of this book is the theoretical legal approach that is applied to all aspects of the Union, from the purely legal constitutional matters to the undoubtedly political spheres of agriculture, transport, intellectual property, social policy, consumer protection, education, and the environment. The use of the case law of the European Courts is inevitable, but the relevant judgements are there in order to prove a point, rather than as a review of the relevant case law.

A similar approach is attempted by HANLON, whose excellent analysis on social policy merits a note. EVANS briefly refers to the institutions and the constitution of the EU, before quickly proceeding to an analysis of the free movements, taxation, and policies, whereas ELLIS & TRIDIMAS make a valuable comparison between the legislative process of the member states and that of the EU in order to make the issue of the democratic deficit easier to comprehend and assess. In their last chapter, the authors attempt an original review of the general principles of law. These are taken as a case study for the analysis of the current jurisprudential policy of the European Court of Justice, which is criticized as too activist and non-productive.

WYATT & DASHWOOD ignore the constitutional and procedural aspects of EU law, and concentrate on an excellent historical introduction of events, from the signing of the founding treaties until the Treaty on European Union. They provide an introductory presentation of the institutions, and an in-depth analysis of the substantive law of the EU, ranging from the four freedoms to the main policies of the EU. In their excellent analysis of the free movement of goods, the authors review the relevant case law of the European Courts, with particular reference to quantitative restrictions. The presentation of the freedom of establishment suffers from the total disregard of the freedom of establishment with reference to legal persons, a topic that is worth extensive analysis, especially in a book focusing on the substantive law of the EU. The original analysis of the legal basis for EU legislation on the internal market is truly exceptional, and indicative of the depth of legal argumentation in the book.

EDWARD & LANE is a mere presentation, rather than an in-depth analysis, of EU law. The authors aim to guide the reader through most issues of EU law, without attempting to present the case law of the European Courts, or the various theories on each issue. What makes this book different from the vast number of other works on the topic is its reference to currently evolving doctrines, which very few books have mentioned so far. Concepts such as variable geometry, EU citizenship, economic and monetary union, and the social charter are presented in the book in an interesting introduction to the relevant issues, which does make EU law easier to follow.

CRAIG & DE BÚRCA have written an exceptional book of texts and materials, which covers all aspects of EU law, from the history of the Union, to constitutional, institutional, procedural and substantive legal issues. The main strength of the book is the exceptional collection of materials on each and every topic, which reflects the vast majority of legal argumentation and debate on most of the current developments of EU legal thought. The authors do use the effective protection

of the individual as their focus, but do not limit themselves to issues related to that particular topic.

CHALMERS' recent two-volume work is an analytical reference to most areas of EU law, focusing on the underlying theories introduced and developed by the European Courts. His work is an excellent introduction to the topic, with exceptionally strong bibliographical references.

HELEN XANTHAK

European Union, politics

George, Stephen, *Politics and Policy of the European Union*, Oxford and New York: Oxford University Press, 1996

Marks, Gary et al., *Governance in the European Union*, London and Thousand Oaks, California: Sage, 1996

Marks, Gary, "The Third Lens: Comparing European Integration and State Building" in *European Integration in Social and Historical Perspective, 1850 to the Present*, edited by Jytte Klausen and Louise A. Tilly, Lanham, Maryland: Rowman and Littlefeld, 1997

Nugent, Neill (editor), *The European Union*, 2 vols, Aldershot, Hampshire: Dartmouth, 1996

O'Neill, Michael (editor), *The Politics of European Integration: A Reader*, London and New York: Routledge, 1996

Peterson, John, "Decision-Making in the European Union: Towards a Framework for Analysis", *Journal of European Public Policy*, 2/1 (1995): 69–93

Richardson, Jeremy J. (editor), *European Union: Power and Policy-Making*, London and New York: Routledge, 1996

Scharpf, Fritz W., "The Joint-Decision Trap: Lessons from German Federalism and European Integration", *Public Administration Review*, 66/3 (1988): 239–78

Wallace, Helen and William Wallace (editors), *Policy-Making in the European Union*, Oxford and New York: Oxford University Press, 1996

Among the introductory works on the European Union (EU), the reader edited by O'NEILL offers students a particularly useful guide through the theoretical debates that accompanied integration. It contains short excerpts from most important works written on this topic, ranging from the pioneers in the 1930s through to the early 1990s, but it lacks any contribution analysing the post-Maastricht situation. The editor provides a long and valuable introduction surveying the main "paradigms" that have dominated integration research since its inception.

GEORGE gives a good, concise introduction to both the politics and the policies of the EU. It outlines the history of integration, the institutional structure of the EU, and the debates among political scientists about the causes and consequences of integration. One chapter deals with the international context, and other chapters on national contexts deal with Germany, France, and Britain. Individual chapters then give clear overviews of specific policy areas, namely energy, agriculture, internal market policy, economic and monetary union, regional policy, social policy, and foreign policy cooperation.

The text edited by WALLACE & WALLACE is a very valuable general introduction to the policy-making process in the EU – its focus is thus on the effects rather than on the causes of integration. In addition to an introduction and a conclusion, the book includes 14 chapters, each devoted to a specific policy area. As a whole, the book shows that the EU is not merely a shell for intergovernmental negotiation, but a complex, multi-level policy-making structure, involving supranational, subnational, and national actors. It also shows that the specific policy style adopted may vary considerably, depending on the policy area concerned.

The excellent text edited by RICHARDSON covers the same ground as the Wallace & Wallace volume – policy-making in the EU – but is organized according to a different perspective. Instead of analysing the policy areas individually, the various chapters focus on the actors involved – the four EU institutions (European Parliament, European Commission, Council of Ministers and Court of Auditors), the national bureaucracies, the voters, the interest groups, and the regions. Other chapters are devoted to the history and the theory of integration, the enlargement question, the external relations of the EU, the EU as a regulatory state, and the problem of implementation. The editor's introduction usefully links European policy-making to concepts and insights drawn from several approaches to policy analysis.

In the book by MARKS et al., some of the most renowned scholars working on the EU present, in six essays, theoretically sophisticated accounts of various issues some more specific than others. Schmitter provides a brief but striking evaluation of neofunctionalist theory, to the development of which he contributed in the 1960s. Scharpf analyses insightfully the problems stemming from the fact that negative integration (the elimination of boundaries among the member states) is achieved more easily than positive integration (the creation of common economic and social policies), and considers possible solutions. Marks et al. examine the reasons behind the increasing efforts by regional governments to gain direct access to EU institutions. Streeck develops an impressive intergovernmentalist argument about the nature and the future evolution of social policies at the European level. Marks & McAdam explore the changing incentives and constraints which European integration is posing to social movements. In the concluding chapter, Schmitter boldly attempts, as he puts it, to "imagine the future of the Euro-Polity with the help of new concepts". Given the diverse outlooks of the authors, the chapters of this very valuable volume have little in common, apart from the high quality of their analyses.

PETERSON advances a useful framework for studying decision making in the EU, based on three levels of analysis, depending on whether the decisions taken are "history making", "policy setting", or "policy shaping". Since the actors and the rationale differ according to the type of decision, Peterson claims that, in order to be understood, any decisional level requires a particular theoretical approach, with specific explanatory variables. He then argues for a specific "policy network" approach as a tool to study the lower level of decision making, which is sometimes neglected, despite the fact that the peculiar institutional structure of the EU confers a special importance on that level.

Even though the institutional framework and the rules for decision-making have changed since the writing of SCHARPF's excellent article, it still provides valuable insights into the pathology of "multi-level" governance systems such as the EU. Considering the two main models of federalism – either power may be allocated to one or the other level of government in a zero-sum fashion, as in the US, or it may be shared by both levels, as in Germany – Scharpf stresses that the EU most resembles the latter model, and thus displays the same tendencies towards inefficiency, inflexibility, futility, and lack of democracy. He shows that the specific mechanisms involved in joint-decision systems are doubly vulnerable to disagreement – they may prevent agreement from being reached, and they may remove the ability of their member governments to act autonomously. He suggests the conditions under which the "joint-decision trap" could be avoided.

MARKS' insightful essay shows that, beyond the obvious differences between the EU and nation states, even federal ones, there are some fundamental similarities in the modalities of their emergence: their artificial rather than spontaneous character, the absence of a master plan specifying, *ex ante*, the features of the polity, the fact that they were erected not as ends in themselves but for the attainment of some other goal, and the importance of unintended side effects. But he also considers some important differences, such as the different role of democracy in state building as opposed to supranational integration, the "nested" character of citizens' identities in the EU, and above all the differences between state-building and European integration in relation to war and international conflict.

NUGENT's collection, two volumes in "The International Library of Politics and Comparative Government" series, comprises reprints of 39 articles, all but three originally published between 1991 and 1996. The articles appeared in scholarly journals and consist of theoretical analyses, or theoretically driven empirical analyses, of various aspects of the EU. As is inevitable in such cases, the quality of the articles is uneven, but the two volumes as a whole are certainly a useful reference work.

MATHIAS KOENIG-ARCHIBUGI

See also European Community (politics), Treaty on European Union (Maastricht)

Euthanasia

Angell, M., "Euthanasia in the Netherlands – Good News or Bad?", *New England Journal of Medicine*, 335 (1996): 1676–78

Billings, J.A. and S.D. Block, "Slow Euthanasia", *Journal of Palliative Care*, 12 (1996): 21–30

Davies, J., *Choice in Dying: The Facts about Voluntary Euthanasia*, London: Ward Lock, 1997

Donnison, D. and C. Bryson, "Matters of Life and Death: Attitudes to Euthanasia" in *British Social Attitudes: The 13th Report*, edited by Roger Jowell *et al.*, Aldershot, Hampshire: Dartmouth, 1996

Emanuel, E.J., "The History of Euthanasia Debates in the United States and Britain", *Annals of Internal Medicine*, 121 (1994): 793–802

Emanuel, E.J., D.L. Fairclough, E.R. Daniels and B.R. Clarridge, "Euthanasia and Physician-Assisted Suicide: Attitudes and Experiences of Oncology Patients, Oncologists, and the Public", *Lancet*, 347 (1996): 1805–10

Justice, C., "The 'Natural' Death While Not Eating: A Type of Palliative Care in Banaras, India", *Journal of Palliative Care*, 11/1 (1995): 38–42

Ryan, C.J., "Euthanasia in Australia: the Northern Territory Rights of the Terminally Ill Act", *New England Journal of Medicine*, 334 (1996): 326–28

Seale, C.F. and J. Addington-Hall, "Euthanasia: Why People Want to Die Earlier", 3 parts, *Social Science and Medicine*, 39/5 (1994): 647–54, and 40/5 (1995): 581–87 and 589–95

Seale, C.F., "Social and Ethical Aspects of Euthanasia: A Review", *Progress in Palliative Care*, 5/4 (1997): 141–45

Select Committee on Medical Ethics, *Select Committee on Medical Ethics: House of Lords Report*, London: HMSO, 1994

Ward, B.J. and P.A. Tate, "Attitudes Among NHS Doctors to Requests for Euthanasia", *British Medical Journal*, 308 (1994): 1332–34

Much of the literature on this topic is written as moral philosophy, or is a reflection on a single case, or outlines a particular position on the desirability of legalization of voluntary euthanasia. An example of the latter is DAVIES, written by an ex-president of the World Federation of Right-to-Die Societies, which puts the case for legalization. Davies reviews a number of case histories as well as the worldwide situation with regard to legislation on the subject. The book is written in a highly accessible style, but is of course from a particular point of view. Material of this sort is widely available; the present review concentrates largely on studies based on research.

Supplementary material on the legal position in various countries is available. RYAN, for example, presents a brief account of the thinking behind the Northern Territory Rights of the Terminally Ill Act, in Australia, which briefly came into force in 1995, allowing several individuals to receive voluntary euthanasia, before the Act was overturned a few months later. The SELECT COMMITTEE ON MEDICAL ETHICS, chaired by Lord Walton, heard evidence that together comprises an account of the chief arguments for and against legalization from a range of witnesses on all sides of the debate.

The best historical account of euthanasia debates in the UK and USA is EMANUEL. After a brief account of practices involving physician-assisted death in the ancient world, and discussion of the pro-euthanasia position taken by such philosophers as More, Bacon, Donne, Montesquieu, and Hume, Emanuel focused on the past 100 years. He argued that surges in public support have coincided with periods of economic depression, which leads to an acceptance of "social Darwinism" as a justification for social policies. Such periods are characterized by an intense individualism, where there is a premium on self-sufficiency and rational life planning, reflected in calls to legalize euthanasia. Whether one accepts this ambitious thesis or not, the article is a mine of information on historical trends in public opinion in the two countries.

DONNISON & BRYSON also review the public opinion literature, concentrating on what is known about differences of opinion in various subgroups of the British population. Their evidence suggests that support is stronger if people are young, better educated, less religious, white or disabled. SEALE's review of this and other literature across countries notes the same general trends in many countries where studies have been carried out, as well as some studies suggesting rising support for legalization.

The sequence of studies reported by SEALE & ADDINGTON-HALL, based on large-scale surveys of the views of relatives and friends of people who had died, elucidates the reasons for requests for euthanasia where they occur, as well as showing the extent of this desire in representative samples of the UK population in the last year of life. These studies show that the experience of dependency as well as pain influences many people to desire an earlier death. However, the evidence of these studies also provides some support for the "slippery slope" argument against legalization, whereby vulnerable elderly people (particularly elderly women) might experience undue pressure to choose death should legalization occur.

Studies of the opinions and, more recently, of the actual practices of healthcare professionals have begun to emerge in a variety of countries. In the UK, WARD & TATE caused considerable controversy when they reported that nine per cent of their sample of NHS doctors agreed that they had complied with a patient's request to hasten death (this being 36 per cent of those who reported being asked). EMANUEL et al., in a well-conducted study of US oncologists, reported nearly one in seven saying they had carried out euthanasia. This study is unusual in the literature in also reporting patients' views, showing that 12 per cent had seriously discussed the issue with a physician.

Perhaps the most detailed studies of the actual practice of euthanasia come from the Netherlands, where the practice has been quasi-legalized for some years. ANGELL summarizes the findings of two major studies of Dutch practice. In 1991 it was estimated that 1.8 per cent of all deaths in the Netherlands were by voluntary euthanasia with a further 0.3 per cent by assisted suicide. An additional 0.8 per cent of deaths were by "involuntary" euthanasia, perhaps an unfortunate choice of word given the outcry that this statistic produced. Half of this "involuntary" group had earlier expressed an interest in euthanasia but were unable to communicate at the time it was done. Most were judged "moribund" according to the doctors concerned. A 1995 Dutch study reviewed by Angell revealed little change beyond a slight decrease in the "involuntary" category, and a somewhat higher rate of notification by doctors, although the majority of cases still went unreported.

The literature contains many instances of dispute between representatives of the hospice movement and advocates of legalization. One particularly interesting example is the reaction that followed an initial article by BILLINGS & BLOCK on "slow euthanasia", a practice that these authors maintained was quite widespread, although rarely discussed openly, whereby patients are knowingly sedated to death. Reaction to this in several articles in the same issue centred on resistance to the introduction of such new linguistic terms as "slow euthanasia", as well as challenges to Billings & Block to support with evidence their claim that this was a widespread practice. The hospice case, which is partly motivated by religious principles, is generally predicated on the view that effective relief of suffering can help reduce the desire for euthanasia.

Finally, it is worth mentioning a piece by JUSTICE, who describes death by fasting in Banares, India. This is helpful in reminding us that the call for voluntary euthanasia depends on conditions that are quite specific to contemporary Western society, involving a paradoxical mixture of individualism (so that people feel they have a right to self-determination) and dependency on professional expertise (so that people also want a doctor to administer the lethal dose). Justice shows us that in another cultural climate it is possible for people to take control of the ending of their lives without involving professional assistance.

CLIVE SEALE

Evaluation

Alkin, Marvin (editor), *Debates on Evaluation*, Newbury Park, California: Sage, 1990

Chelimsky, Eleanor Shadish and William R. Shadish (editors), *Evaluation for the 21st Century*, Thousand Oaks, California: Sage, 1997

Chen, Huey-tsyh, *Theory-Driven Evaluations*, Newbury Park, California: Sage, 1990

Evaluation: The International Journal of Theory, Research and Practice, 1995–

Fetterman, David, Shake J. Kaftarian and Abraham Wandersman (editors), *Empowerment Evaluation*, Thousand Oaks, California: Sage, 1996

Newman, Dianna L. and Robert D. Brown, *Applied Ethics for Program Evaluation*, Thousand Oaks, California: Sage, 1996

Patton, Michael Q., *Utilization Focused Evaluation*, 3rd edition, Thousand Oaks, California: Sage, 1997

Rog, Debra and Deborah Fournier (editors), *Progress and Future Directions in Evaluation: Perspectives on Theory, Practice and Methods*, San Francisco: Jossey Bass, 1995

Rossi, Peter H., Howard E. Freeman and Mark W. Lipsey, *Evaluation: A Systematic Approach*, 6th edition, Newbury Park, California: Sage, 1998

Scriven, Michael, *Hard Won Lessons in Program Evaluation*, San Francisco: Jossey Bass, 1993

Shadish, William R. Jr, Thomas D. Cook and Laura C. Leviton, *Foundations of Program Evaluation*, Newbury Park, California: Sage, 1995

Stufflebeam, Daniel, "Empowerment Evaluation, Objectivist Evaluation, and Evaluation Standards: Where the Future of Evaluation Should Not Go and Where It Needs to Go", *Evaluation Practice*, 15/3 (1994): 321–38

Weiss, Carol H., *Evaluation: Methods for Studying Programs and Policies*, 2nd edition, Upper Saddle River, New Jersey: Prentice Hall, 1998

Evaluation commonly refers to the systematic collection of information about the operation and/or outcomes of social programmes for the purpose of assisting decision making about those programmes, although some would extend the list of evaluands to include others such as policies, products, and personnel. WEISS, in the second edition of her influential book, first published in 1972, provides a comprehensive overview of the current state of evaluation theory and methods, both quantitative and qualitative, and includes many practical examples. It includes an innovative chapter on the logic of analysis and interpretation of evaluation findings which focuses on the strategies available for interpreting findings and the questions which an evaluator might need to address.

Modern evaluation practice had its origins in the rapid expansion of social programmes in the 1960s, particularly in the US. Demands for accountability for government spending on health, education, and welfare programmes gave impetus to the development of evaluation methodology and theory.

SHADISH, COOK & LEVITON outline this development through a critical analysis of the contributions of seven theorists whose work has had a major influence on the development of evaluation theory and methodology. They use this analysis as a basis for identifying the key issues that need to be addressed by evaluation theorists and practitioners. These include evaluation practice and use, the nature of social programmes, the role of values, and what counts as knowledge about a programme.

Evaluation practice refers to methods used to conduct evaluations. Early evaluation methodology emphasized scientific rigour through the use of quantitative social research methods, often at the expense of failing to use findings to improve programmes. These quantitative methods, which include randomized experiments, quasi experiments, and cost-benefit analyses are described in ROSSI, FREEMAN & LIPSEY. They acknowledge, however, that evaluation is conducted in a political and social context and that this needs to be recognized in evaluation practice. Tailoring evaluations to a particular stage of programme development and to the purposes of the evaluation is a key feature of their approach to addressing this context, which they argue provides more direct and useful feedback on the operation and outcomes of the programme.

Maximizing use of evaluation findings by involving intended users in the planning and conduct of the evaluation is the central theme of PATTON's approach to evaluation. These users have become known as stakeholders, a term employed to describe those groups and individuals with a vested interest in the programme. This recognition of stakeholder input is a feature of most current approaches to evaluation. FETTERMAN, KAFTARIAN & WANDERSMAN make stakeholder involvement a central feature of their approach to evaluation by "empowering" them to take full control of the evaluation. They provide a theoretical framework and examples of applications of empowerment evaluation. These utilization-focused and stakeholder-based approaches tend to rely more heavily on qualitative research methods than on the quantitative methods that characterized more traditional approaches.

STUFFLEBEAM has expressed concern about what he sees as an overemphasis on stakeholder participation and has argued that there must be limits to its extent. He claims that evaluators should maintain a level of independence from stakeholders so as to ensure credibility and integrity, which are in danger of being compromised by handing over too much control of the evaluation to stakeholders. Eleanor Chelimsky, in CHELIMSKY & SHADISH, has also cautioned against an excessive preoccupation with use of evaluation findings as it may result in the stifling of important insights and a reiteration of the status quo.

Achieving a balance between scientific credibility of the evaluation and involving stakeholders in its design and conduct is currently a major source of division among evaluation practitioners and theorists.

Another source of disagreement in evaluation concerns the extent to which evaluators need to gain an understanding of the nature of social programmes in order to conduct useful evaluations. CHEN argues that treating the programme as if it were a "black box" can provide only limited information about programme outcomes. In order to understand how and why a programme works or fails to work an adequate understanding of the theoretical basis of the programme is necessary. The theory-driven approach to evaluation has been developed to provide a better understanding of how programmes work. This approach is outlined and developed by Chen.

SCRIVEN does not agree that an understanding of the theoretical basis of a programme is necessary for effective evaluation. He argues that evaluation involves making judgements of merit, worth or value, and claims that most approaches to evaluation neglect or avoid this key task and hence do not qualify as evaluation. These judgements are made on the basis of the extent to which a programme, or other evaluand, satisfies criteria of merit or worth that concern benefits to consumers and are not necessarily related to programme goals. He points out similarities between programme evaluation and product evaluation and sees the former as just one aspect of a broader field of evaluation. Scriven's approach to evaluation has generated controversy over the role of the evaluator and the nature of the evaluation task.

All modern approaches to evaluation acknowledge the centrality of values and the political context in which evaluations are conducted. Under these conditions, ethical considerations are particularly prominent and need to be addressed by evaluators. NEWMAN & BROWN discuss these considerations. They are also the subject of a debate by a group of prominent evaluation theorists and practitioners reported in ALKIN. The participants debate ethics along with other key evaluation issues including the use of evaluation findings, the role of the evaluator, and evaluation theory.

As evaluation theory and methodology have evolved, academic and professional journals have emerged to provide forums for communicating these developments. The American Evaluation Association publishes *New Directions in Evaluation*, a book series in which volumes focus on particular topics with contributions from evaluation practitioners and theorists. For example, the volume edited by ROG & FOURNIER focused on new developments in theory and practice including the use of meta-analysis to integrate evaluation findings from separate studies. The journal EVALUATION, launched in 1995, contains articles dealing with all aspects of evaluation.

RALPH HALL

See also Performance evaluation

Evaluation research

Campbell, Donald T., "Reforms as Experiments", *American Psychologist*, 24 (1969): 409–29

Chelimsky, Eleanor and William R. Shadish (editors), *Evaluation for the 21st Century: A Handbook*, Thousand Oaks, California and London: Sage, 1997

Fetterman, David M., Shakeh J. Kaftarian and Abraham Wandersman (editors), *Empowerment Evaluation: Knowledge and Tools for Self-Assessment and Accountability*, Thousand Oaks, California and London: Sage, 1996

Greene, Jennifer C. and Valerie J. Caracelli, "Defining and Describing the Paradigm Issue in Mixed-Method Evaluation" in *Advances in Mixed-Method Evaluation: The Challenges and Benefits of Integrating Diverse Paradigms*, edited by Jennifer C. Greene and Valerie J. Caracelli, San Francisco: Jossey Bass, 1997

Guba, Egon G. and Yvonna S. Lincoln, *Fourth Generation Evaluation*, Newbury Park, California and London: Sage, 1989

Patton, Michael Quinn, *Utilization – Focused Evaluation: The New Century Text*, 3rd edition, Thousand Oaks, California and London: Sage, 1997

Rossi, Peter H., "Advances in Quantitative Evaluation, 1987–1996" in *Progress and Future Directions in Evaluation: Perspectives on Theory, Practice and Methods*, edited by Deborah Fournier and Debra J. Rog, San Francisco: Jossey Bass, 1997

Scriven, Michael, "Beyond Formative and Summative Evaluation" in *Evaluation and Education: At Quarter Century*, edited by Milbrey W. McLaughlin and D.C. Phillips, Chicago: National Society for the Study of Education, 1991

The 33 essays in CHELIMSKY & SHADISH provide a comprehensive overview of evaluation research at the end of the 20th century. The essays reveal that evaluation research is moving from an emphasis on the evaluation of programmes, personnel, and products, toward the evaluation of human rights violations, environmental concerns, and nuclear power. Furthermore, there is an increasing use of multimethods such as case studies and survey research, in evaluation. The editors also include chapters on a wide variety of evaluation methods such as time series and cluster evaluations. The strength of the book is its inclusion of authors holding contradictory positions, a prime example being the juxtaposed chapters by Robert Stake and Michael Scriven. Stake argues that there is a place for advocacy in programme evaluation, whereas Scriven argues that evaluators should be objective, independent from the programme under review, and should avoid an advocacy role.

GUBA & LINCOLN trace the development of evaluation through three generations (technical, descriptive, and judgmental) to a fourth stage, which they identify as responsive. The fourth generation approach advances the value of constructivist inquiry, which serves as a critique of the positivist, scientific grip on evaluation research that characterized evaluation up until the 1980s. The authors hold that evaluators need to acknowledge the numerous human, political, social, and cultural dimensions of evaluation, and realize that evaluation affects all those involved and is affected by them. Because this fourth-generation approach necessitates collaboration between the evaluator and the evaluated, the stress is on negotiation. Guba & Lincoln clearly position themselves on the qualitative side of the evaluation paradigm debate, against those who prefer quantitative, scientific measurements. Their fourth-generation approach challenges the audit, fiscal responsibility approach to evaluation, and has become a touchstone for the evaluation debates.

CAMPBELL, a social psychologist, was one of the early advocates of experimental, scientific research in evaluation. This article is still worth reading as it served as a flashpoint for much of the debate in evaluation in the decades that followed. Campbell argued for continual testing and experimentation in evaluation research. He supported the use of technological advances and the improvement of methods to do scientific research.

GREENE & CARACELLI deals seriously with the problem of combining qualitative and quantitative data. The authors argue that the "either/or" perspective on the issue is misguided, and urge evaluators to move toward an acceptance of mixed methodologies. The debate, which has raged in evaluation research for several decades, positions constructivists such as Guba & Lincoln on one hand, against positivists, such as Campbell and Cook, on the other, and is sometimes referred to as the qualitative–quantitative debate. Greene & Caracelli argue that this debate is philosophical, whereas methods are merely ways of gathering data, and as such are far removed from the debate.

One of SCRIVEN's greatest contributions to evaluation was his classic 1967 distinction between summative and formative evaluations. In this 1991 article he clarifies some misconceptions about the terms. Whereas summative evaluation is primarily of interest to *decision makers* who need to make conclusions about a programme, formative evaluation is often of interest to *developers* who are focusing on making improvements to a programme. A philosopher of science, Scriven makes the point that he never intended to present summative and formative as types of evaluation but rather as *roles* of the evaluator. One of the main myths that Scriven addresses is that evaluators must be content experts. He holds that there are multiple advantages of using evaluation experts who consult content experts in the research process.

PATTON, the pragmatist of evaluation research, provides a comprehensive review of the literature on the use and practice of programme evaluation. He consciously avoids being caught in the evaluation paradigm debate (qualitative versus quantitative) and argues that applied or evaluation researchers ought to avoid this debate and leave it to academic researchers. Patton covers the gamut of both practical and theoretical issues in evaluation, and shows how to focus an evaluation, make methodological decisions, analyse data, and present findings. His focus is on utilization, or how to conduct evaluations that are useful, all the while being aware of the ethical and political dimensions of evaluation.

ROSSI describes advances in three main areas that have affected evaluation research: (a) changes that make the carrying out of research easier, such as the use of electronic mail for correspondence; (b) advances in measurement; and (c) advances

in statistical analysis. This article provides a useful compendium of information on methods that represent a strong, empirical basis for measurement in evaluation. The major weakness is that Rossi's work is primarily descriptive and does not raise ethical or political issues about a quantitative approach to evaluation.

FETTERMAN, KAFTARIAN & WANDERSMAN builds on ideas presented by Fetterman in his presidential address to the American Evaluation Association. His theory of empowerment evaluation stresses the management and assessment of programmes for the purpose of encouraging improvement and self-determination of participants. An effective empowerment evaluation engages the stakeholders and enables them to engage in a long-term internal process of evaluation, in order to renew their own organization continuously. Perhaps unintentionally, this type of evaluation raises the issue of whether internal or external evaluators are more effective. The main weakness of the book is the lack of clarification about how, and if, empowerment evaluation differs from its related forms, participatory and collaborative evaluation.

LEONA M. ENGLISH

See also Performance evaluation

Evidence

Anderson, Terence and William Twining, *Analysis of Evidence: How to Do Things with Facts, Based on Wigmore's Science of Judicial Proof*, Boston: Little Brown, 1991

Bentham, Jeremy, *Rationale of Judicial Evidence, Specially Applied to English Practice*, 5 vols, edited by John Stuart Mill, London: Hunt and Clarke, 1827; reprinted Littleton, Colorado: Rothman, 1995

"Boston University Law Review Symposium on Probability and Inference in the Law of Evidence", *Boston University Law Review*, 3–4 (1986): 377–952

"Cardozo Conference on Decision and Inference in Litigation", *Cardozo Law Review*, 2–3 (1991): 253–1075

Cohen, L. Jonathan, *The Probable and the Provable*, Oxford: Clarendon Press, 1977

Stephen, James Fitzjames, *A Digest of the Law of Evidence*, 7th edition, London: Macmillan, 1905 (originally published 1876); 12th edition by Harry Lushingston Stephen and Lewis Frederick Sturge, 1936

Thayer, James Bradley, *A Preliminary Treatise on Evidence at Common Law*, 2 vols, Boston: Little, Brown, 1896–98; reprinted New York: Kelley, 1969

Twining, William and Alex Stein (editors), *Evidence and Proof*, Aldershot, Hampshire: Dartmouth, and New York: New York University Press, 1992

Wigmore, John Henry, *The Science of Judicial Proof, as Given by Logic, Psychology and General Experience, and Illustrated in Judicial Trials*, Boston: Little Brown, 1913; 3rd edition 1937

Wigmore, John Henry, *Evidence in Trials at Common Law*, 4th edition, 13 vols, Boston: Little Brown, 1961–83, plus yearly supplement

Legal proof involves considering what it means to demonstrate the existence of those facts that justify a court making a particular order. This raises two recurring issues: what are valid ways for courts to reason about disputed facts, and what material should be excluded? Common-law adversarial trials traditionally used juries to determine facts. This shaped the development of the law on which the works selected focus.

BENTHAM shows how evidence law did not serve the greatest good of the greatest number but produced delay, vexation, and expense in a "fee gathering" system run by, and for, Judge & Co: the common law establishment. He explodes the old law of evidence with his caustic demands for more rational forms of proof. He opposes any rules that would restrict the admission of evidence. This follows from his "natural system of proof" based on family disputes where members give their account and are questioned in the presence of other members. He would admit all evidence except where it would produce delay, expense, or vexation. He reasons that, as the only cause for belief is a person's experience, the weight to be given to particular evidence should not be fixed by rules but should be subject to flexible standards to guide the triers of fact. The rectitude of decision making – the correct application of true laws to true facts – was all important. Bentham's writing is detailed and repetitive with a fatiguing anger that can tire a reader as much as the obsolete common law procedure he describes.

STEPHEN emphasizes Bentham's rationalist approach – the paramountcy of the integrity of the courts' determinations. Abandoning legislative reform, Stephen attempts what Bentham would regard as impossible, the simplification and rationalization of technical evidence law as part of procedural law, by recovering the principles concealed in the myriad cases. His first principle is a broad inclusionary one, that all relevant evidence – that evidence required for the rational determination of the existence of a material fact – should be admitted. He has none of Bentham's enthusiasm for masses of evidence and supports exclusionary rules. He seeks to justify them as excluding only irrelevant evidence. Thayer describes this as a "a splendid mistake".

THAYER also shares a belief in a rationalist process of proof. He owes much to Stephens. Thayer argues in chapter 12, "The present and future of the law of evidence", pp.508–38, that the admission of evidence is part of a system of free proof based on relevance. The exclusionary rules are a mixed group of exceptions justified by public policies. The role of juries in common law trials explains a number of them. His model underlies most subsequent codifications or restatements. McNamara, Philip, "The canons of evidence – rules as exclusion or rules of use", in TWINING, pp.291–314, distils and updates Thayer's theory.

WIGMORE (1983), *Evidence in Trials at Common Law*, was first published in 1905 as *A Treatise on the System of Evidence in Trials at Common Law*. A magisterial and encyclopedic statement of common law policies, principles and rules of evidence, including their historic development, it is admired as a great intellectual feat. Revised and edited by others, readers may find it like software redesigned by too many programmers. Wigmore's "science of proof", the source he argues of legal rules, and an evolutionary model of law underlying it are not made explicit and have not been equally appreciated by

all editors, yet there were contradictions in the original work. Editors continue to use clear cut expressions but are more willing to acknowledge argument and doubt and refrain from using scorn to encourage judges to do better.

WIGMORE (1937), a response to criticisms that the legal techniques of evidence are naive, makes Wigmore's "science of proof" clearer. He uses law, logic, psychology, and other sciences in a reductive and inductive theory of evidence and proof that purports to be comprehensive and integrating. Through charts and complex symbols he claims to show a process used by lawyers to argue from proof of a fact, through inferences from that fact, to the element that the law requires to be proved. Courts may not use these techniques. A simple case may have over 100 such chains and a complex case several thousands. His analysis suppresses the values of participants and attributes a consensus to the disciplines relied upon that does not exist. ANDERSON & TWINING is a more comprehensible simplification of Wigmore's system.

COHEN argues that a non-mathematical, inductive, or Baconian probability, different from mathematical or Pascalian probability, exists and is used in legal standards of proof, weighing evidence in the light of corroboration and assessing the convergence of the evidence as a whole. While he demonstrates the difficulty of applying mathematical probability in law this does not show that another form exists. This is further discussed by William Twining, "Debating probability", in Twining pp.157–70 and Richard Eggleston, "Focussing on the defendant" in Twining pp.171–17.

BOSTON UNIVERSITY LAW REVIEW SYMPOSIUM reveals the breakdown in consensus, called the "new evidence scholarship", over the use of common-sense empiricism in the rationalist approach to proof. It focuses on logic and mathematical probability in uncertainty and inference in legal proof. There is a comprehensive discussion of Bayes' theorem, or inverse probability – the increase in probability produced by the consideration of further evidence determined by the ratio between the probability of the event's existence in the face of further evidence and the probability of the event's nonexistence in the face of that same evidence. The articles ignore whether procedural law in varying litigious contexts, including the adversarial trial, impacts on fact finding, the practical obstacles to fact finding and the rationalist assumptions which underlie a number of other disciplines used.

CARDOZO CONFERENCE addresses criticisms that overreliance by the "new evidence scholarship" on theories misrepresents legal practice. Economic restraints on legal systems, the crossover between reasoning about law and reasoning about facts and the dynamic and contextualized character of litigation run through the articles. A number specifically consider the effect of procedural rules, adversarial processes, and burdens of proof.

TWINING & STEIN places a number of significant articles, drawing on epistemology, statistics, psychology and semiotics, in the context of debates over logic, probability theories, the relationship between facts and values, fact scepticism or the impossibility of recreating past events, the nature of the law of evidence and its basic concepts, such as burdens of proof, and its probative policies, including the protection of the accused. Issues include whether courts reason about facts in an atomistic way, following links in a single chain, as suggested by Wigmore, or in a holistic way, reviewing the number of strands in a rope, by comparing the coherence of varying accounts. Assumptions about law, requiring that findings by courts appear to be based on particular levels of probity, are also examined. Twining's article "The new evidence scholarship" in the Cardozo Conference, pp.295–305, questions the division between atomistic and holistic approaches. This, and the previous two collections, are unhelpful to readers looking for certainty. Proof is a complicated range of activities.

NEIL ANDREWS

Evolution, economic

Dawkins, Richard, The Extended Phenotype: The Long Reach of the Gene, revised edition, Oxford and New York: Oxford University Press, 1999 (1st edition 1982)

Goodwin, Brian, How the Leopard Changed Its Spots: The Evolution of Complexity, London: Weidenfeld and Nicolson, and New York: Scribner, 1994

Ho, Mae-Wan, Genetic Engineering – Dream or Nightmare? The Brave New World of Bad Science and Big Business, Bath: Gateway, 1998

Hodgson, Geoffrey M., Economics and Evolution: Bringing Life Back into Economics, Cambridge: Polity Press, and Ann Arbor: University of Michigan Press, 1993

Levins, Richard and Richard Lewontin, The Dialectical Biologist, Cambridge, Massachusetts: Harvard University Press, 1985

Maynard Smith, John, The Theory of Evolution, Cambridge and New York: Cambridge University Press, 1993

Nelson, Richard R. and Sidney G. Winter, An Evolutionary Theory of Economic Change, Cambridge, Massachusetts: Harvard University Press, 1982

Rose, Steven, Lifelines: Biology, Freedom and Determinism, London: Allen Lane, 1997; as Lifelines: Biology beyond Determinism, New York: Oxford University Press, 1998

Veblen, Thorstein, "Why is Economics Not an Evolutionary Science?", Quarterly Journal of Economics, 12/3 (1898): 373–97; edited version reprinted in Cambridge Journal of Economics, 22/4 (1998): 403–14

Attempts to include life processes in economic science go back to 1898, and the now-famous essay by the institutional economist VEBLEN. He argued that the political economy of the classical, historical, and Austrian schools needed bringing up to date, with developments in biology arising from the work of Darwin and Lamarck. Economists were criticized for appealing to natural laws and reducing all questions to answers in terms of causes and effects with absolute truth as the criterion for success. A theory of the development process was needed. Animistic and taxonomic accounts of economic behaviour were considered to be archaic habits of thinking in need of reformulation. In particular, the hedonistic utilitarian philosophy of Bentham and Mill was criticized: human beings, it was argued, were not individual passive "globules" of desire in equilibrium. Developments in anthropology and psychology led Veblen to argue that human beings and groups were involved in purposeful activities with coherent structures of propensities and habits.

HODGSON is at the forefront of modern critical research into the possibility of applying evolutionary ideas from biology to economics. He recognizes the importance of developments in the biological sciences to the social sciences research agenda, but rejects genetic and "nature red in tooth and claw" analogies, arguing that the idea of economic evolution has more to do with social culture. He develops this approach, after discussing the role of metaphor in science and economics, by taking the reader through the contributions of great thinkers in economics, and exploring the past and possible future relationships between economics and biology.

MAYNARD SMITH provides a straightforward introductory guide to Darwin's theory of evolution through natural selection. He explains the causes of the evolution of animals and plants in terms of variation, selection, and inheritance. The third and latest edition of his work includes discussion of recent advances in molecular biology and outlines its relevance to evolution theory.

NELSON & WINTER combine their talents to develop a general theory of economic change that focuses on firm and industry adaptations to their environments. The market determines, through a process analogous to natural selection in biology, which firms become successful. The evolutionary theory of Lamarck, in which characteristics acquired during the lifetime of an organism can be inherited, and variety appears as a result of struggle, provides their theoretical framework. The routines of firms play a role similar to genes in biological evolutionary theory, determining behaviour in conjunction with the environment. These routines are inheritable and selectable. The concept of search is introduced: this refers to the organizational activity of routine evaluation leading to stochastic change, and is similar to mutation in biology. The selection environment of the firm, consisting of both demand and supply conditions, and competitive pressures, leads to differential growth.

Analogies and metaphors are common tools of evolutionary biologists and economists. DAWKINS uses the Necker cube, a line drawing that can also be seen as a three-dimensional object, to argue that life can be viewed either in terms of genetic replicators, preserving themselves by means of extended phenotypes, or as separate organismic machines created by their genes. The predominant quality of a successful gene is a ruthless selfishness. Dawkins attempts to defend his theory against criticisms of genetic determinism and adaptationism. The evolutionary process of natural selection can be characterized in two equally feasible ways: as the differential survival of alternative replicators, the genes; or as vehicle (organism or group of organisms) selection, the process by which some vehicles are more successful than others in ensuring the survival of their replicators.

LEVINS & LEWONTIN, two Marxist biologists, argue in their selection of essays for a dialectical approach to questions of ontology. They suggest that an ideology of "evolutionism", the belief that systems were in a state of constant change, emerged out of the changing nature of social relations through history. The bourgeois revolution of the 17th and 18th centuries heralded an era in which individuals sell their labour power in competitive markets, and redefined the relation between the individual and the social. The atomism of Descartes, the Cartesian method, which was so successful in solving particular problems, was not applied to more difficult and important areas because of scientists' dislike of failure. Reassessing the nature of reality dialectically and holistically meant recognizing that parts and wholes evolve as a consequence of their relationship and that the whole relationship evolved as a consequence of this interpenetration. Materialism and evolutionism could be understood in dialectical terms, but the Darwinian metaphor of adaptation was essentially reductionist, alienating the organism from the environment.

HO's calculated polemic for a new genetics is a challenge to biologists and economists who wish to reduce phenomena to the simple gene or commodity. Climbing down from the ivory tower of an academic life to enter a life of political activism, Ho tackles head on the "central dogma" of biology, calling for a moratorium on further release of genetically engineered products. She argues that science has been corrupted through its involvement with monopolistic business. Governments, in their support for *laissez-faire* capitalism, were involved in misdirected policies of deregulation in the market for genetically modified organisms. Tampering with nature, Ho argues, leads to unexpected effects that impact on agriculture and biodiversity, creating the externality of genetic pollution. To Ho, science cannot be ethically neutral and no distinction can be made between science and technology. The analytic techniques of science determine the questions that can be asked and the range of answers given. Given that most molecular geneticists are involved in the business of biotechnology, this sets limits on the research agenda. Ho draws a parallel between the atomistic views of reductionist biologists and the views of orthodox economists, offering an alternative that transcends this determinism and involves recognizing that sustainable systems are organisms with anti-entropic tendencies. By minimizing dissipation, increasing energy storage capacities and utilization, increasing diversity, balancing flows of resources and energy, and encouraging cooperative reciprocity, she suggests, a sustainable future beyond genetic engineering is possible.

The thesis of ROSE, a neuroscientist, is that human beings are neither empty entities constrained by their environment nor reducible machines to replicate DNA; instead human beings exist because of a constant dialectic between the biological and social, which is responsible for life processes, history, and development. The book is a plea to place the organism as the central unit of life, taking into account the processes and paradoxes of development, and speaking in terms of the dialectic of specificity and plasticity during development. Essential to life is the capacity and necessity to build, maintain, and preserve itself, a process known as autopoeisis.

GOODWIN is interested in a paradox emerging from the work of Darwin, and particularly his method of inquiry. To Darwin, organisms were the basic elements of life. This focus on the organism has been replaced with a focus on the replicating gene. Organisms, interconnected wholes with lives and personalities, have become complicated molecular machines determined by their genes, which contain the history of their species. According to Goodwin, a modern theory of the organism is needed. A reductionist biology might explain the adaptive processes occurring within a species, but it fails to explain the problem of novelty and emergent order in evolution, and the great morphological differences between organisms. To explain the latter, insights from the new science of

complexity are necessary. Emergent order can be understood by describing living processes in terms of the computational capacity of interacting components. This approach results in a theory that sees the organism as the source of the emerging properties of life that have been revealed in evolution.

LYLE S. MITCHELL

See also Economics and biology

Exchange Rate Mechanism, *see* European Monetary System

Exchange rates

Branson, William, "Asset Markets and Relative Prices in Exchange Rate Determination", Seminar Paper no.66, Stockholm: Institute for International Economic Studies, 1976

Cassel, Gustav, *Money and Foreign Exchange after 1914*, London: Constable, 1922, New York: Macmillan, 1923; reprinted New York: Arno Press, 1972

Dornbusch, Rudiger, "Expectations and Exchange Rate Dynamics", *Journal of Political Economy*, 84/6 (1976): 1161–76

Eichengreen, Barry, *Golden Fetters: The Gold Standard and the Great Depression, 1919–1939*, Oxford and New York: Oxford University Press, 1992

Frenkel, Jacob, "A Monetary Approach to the Exchange Rate: Doctrinal Aspects and Empirical Evidence", *Scandinavian Journal of Economics*, 78 (1976): 200–24

Friedman, Milton, "The Case for Flexible Exchange Rates" in his *Essays in Positive Economics*, Chicago: University of Chicago Press, 1953

Krugman, Paul, "A Model of Balance of Payments Crises", *Journal of Money, Credit and Banking*, 11/3 (1979): 311–25

Mundell, Robert, "A Theory of Optimum Currency Areas", *American Economic Review*, 51 (1961): 657–65

Mundell, Robert, "Capital Mobility and Stabilization Policy under Fixed and Flexible Exchange Rates", *Canadian Journal of Economics and Political Science*, 29/4 (1963): 475–85

Nurkse, Ragnar, *International Currency Experience: Lessons of the Inter-War Period*, Geneva: League of Nations, 1944

Obstfeld, Maurice, "Rational and Self-Fulfilling Balance of Payments Crises", *American Economic Review*, 76 (1986): 72–81

CASSEL provides a classic early discussion of exchange rates in the wake of the dissolution of the gold standard regime in World War I. The main importance of the book today is that it introduced the concept of the purchasing power parity (PPP) approach to exchange rate determination, of which the essential premise is that a percentage change in exchange rates should offset the inflation differential between two countries. A basic problem of the approach was that it left open the question of which price indices are appropriate for use in these calculations. The book provides a lively, accessible, and interesting discussion of the instabilities inherent in the change of exchange rate regimes and should therefore be of interest to historians of the global monetary system.

EICHENGREEN presents a dense and detailed study of the late gold standard and its role in the global monetary instabilities of the 1920s and 1930s. He argues that the effective operation of the classical gold standard was based on a confluence of political, economic, and intellectual forces that disintegrated during World War I and its aftermath. The reintroduction of the gold standard in the absence of these conditions served to exacerbate the monetary imbalances and prevented the adoption of expansionary policies in the 1930s. Economic historians will find Eichengreen's exposition of international financial diplomacy in this period both clear and persuasively argued.

The instabilities of the interwar exchange rate regime described by Eichengreen led many economists and policymakers in the 1940s to support the introduction of a more stable order of fixed exchange rates that was later to find expression in the Bretton Woods system. NURKSE provides the most comprehensive critique of exchange rate volatility from this era. Essentially, Nurkse argued that the central lessons of the interwar period were that flexible exchange rates discouraged international trade by increasing risk; misallocated resources, increased costs, and increased frictional unemployment by continually shifting factors of production between the tradable and nontradable sectors; and often failed to promote adjustment because of destabilizing speculation that accentuated disequilibrium exchange rate movements. While Nurkse's empirical work was narrow in its range and subject to many criticisms, his work is still relevant in that exchange rates have been highly volatile under the flexible rate regime that has followed Bretton Woods whilst recurring currency crises have focused attention on the question of destabilizing speculation. Nurkse's study remains a valuable insight into the intellectual environment that fostered the creation of Bretton Woods and its clear presentation makes it accessible to a broad range of readers.

FRIEDMAN, writing at the beginning of the Bretton Woods era of fixed exchange rates, provides a classic defence of flexible exchange rates. He argues that flexible rates are efficient, in that they allow for the rapid and relatively smooth transition to a new equilibrium, and stabilizing, in that speculative flows moderate movements perceived as temporary but accelerate movements driven by more permanent, fundamental changes. Friedman also argues that alternative methods of external adjustment (direct controls, changes in internal prices and incomes, and the maintenance of fixed exchange rate regime by the monetary authorities) are either inefficient, difficult to administer and enforce, or prone to destabilizing speculation and crises. The essay remains a very good introduction to the free-market position regarding exchange rate regimes because of its clarity and accessibility to non-specialists.

Increasing international capital flows in the early 1960s spurred interest in developing models in which the balance of payments included endogenous capital flows in addition to merchandise trade. MUNDELL (1963) provides a seminal early discussion of stabilization policy with perfect capital mobility under both fixed and flexible exchange rate regimes. His analysis showed that under flexible exchange rates, monetary policy is highly effective in influencing the level of income and employment by inducing a capital outflow, depreciating the exchange rate, and causing an export surplus. In contrast, while expansionary fiscal policy initially raises income, it ultimately loses its effectiveness by attracting capital inflows and appreciating the exchange rate, which depresses income. Under fixed exchange rates, the conclusions are reversed – monetary policy is ineffective whereas fiscal policy has a strong effect on income and employment. Mundell's clear and penetrating analysis has been highly influential and has served as the basis for continual refinements.

MUNDELL (1961) is a pioneering discussion of the "optimum currency area" concept that seeks to analyse optimal exchange arrangements. While remaining critical of fixed exchange rate regimes for their inability to provide smooth adjustment in the terms of trade, Mundell criticizes the view, articulated most notably in Friedman's article, that flexible rates are appropriate in all circumstances. He therefore seeks to define the characteristics that make it optimal for two or more countries to fix the exchange rates between their currencies. Given that the central objective of policy is to reconcile external balance with full employment internally, Mundell argued that the central determinant of an optimal exchange rate regime was the degree of factor mobility. Economic integration was aided by fixed exchange rates that promoted relatively stable relative prices, while flexible rates aid smooth and rapid adjustment where factor mobility is low by altering the relative prices of home and foreign goods. Mundell's analysis remains influential in analyses of economic integration (particularly in Europe) and exchange rate regimes.

FRENKEL presents an analysis of exchange rate formation from a monetary perspective and applies it to the case of the German hyperinflation of the early 1920s. The two essential doctrinal pillars of this approach are PPP and an asset view of money (in which the supply and demand for money are the central determinants of exchange rates). The first pillar is formed by the assumption that PPP holds continuously while wages, prices, and exchange rates are perfectly flexible upwards and downwards in both the short and long run. The second pillar results in the postulate that relative stocks of money generate relative prices, which in turn determine the exchange rate. The article is technical in its presentation, but Frenkel provides a methodological discussion that traces the intellectual antecedents of the monetary perspective.

DORNBUSCH provides a highly influential model of exchange rate dynamics that significantly advanced the monetary theory of exchange rate formation. "Flexible-price" monetarist models (as presented, for example, by Frenkel) were constrained by their assumption that PPP held continuously and were thus not able to explain the sustained departures from PPP seen after the fall of Bretton Woods in 1973. The "sticky-price" Dornbusch model provided an explanation of these deviations within a monetary model. The model is based on the assumptions that wages in the labour market and prices in the goods market are relatively inflexible (especially in a downward direction) and slow changing, whereas exchange rates are flexible and respond rapidly to shocks. Thus, movements in the exchange rate are not accompanied by compensatory shifts in price movements, giving rise to recurring and sustained deviations from PPP. The greater realism of the model and its interesting dynamics (the Dornbusch model introduces the concept of exchange rate "overshooting") have made it a benchmark in the literature. The article is short, concise, and technical in its presentation.

Monetary models of exchange rate determination, as presented by both Frenkel and Dornbusch, assume that domestic and foreign bonds are perfect substitutes. BRANSON pioneered the portfolio balance model that allows for the differentiation of assets by characteristics other than just their currency of denomination. It represents an important addition to the literature because it provides for changes in the perceived risks of assets to influence the exchange rate. Branson's presentation is very technical and not readily accessible to non-economists.

KRUGMAN presents an early and influential analysis of exchange rate crises in fixed-exchange rate regimes. In the model, a government runs a persistent money-financed budget deficit while also using a limited stock of reserves to peg the exchange rate. This inconsistent policy stance leads speculators to anticipate the eventual abandonment of the peg by launching a speculative attack when reserves fall to a critical level. Krugman (reiterating Friedman) notes that a fixed exchange rate regime encourages such behaviour as the costs of speculating against the currency are minimal compared with the potential benefits if the government devalues the currency. While alternating crises and recovery may occur because of speculator uncertainty about the extent to which the government will commit reserves to the defence of the exchange rate, the policy inconsistency will eventually force a devaluation and a breakdown of the regime. Krugman's technical presentation spawned more detailed theoretical investigations of exchange rate crises and thus had a marked influence on the literature.

OBSTFELD presents an analysis of exchange rate crises that departs from the earlier Krugman-inspired models in that policy and speculator behaviour are less mechanical. In Obstfeld's model, the government faces a tradeoff in its defence of a fixed exchange rate between short-run macroeconomic flexibility and longer run credibility in the markets. Crises arise when the cost of defending the fixed rate is made prohibitive by high interest rates that reflect the market's assessment that a defence will fail. A speculative attack on the currency ensues from either a forecast deterioration in economic fundamentals in the economy or the self-fulfilling expectations of the market itself. Obstfeld's model is technical and not easily accessible to non-economists.

BRUCE A. WEISSE

See also Balance of payments, International economics

Exhaustion of rights

Cornish, W.R., "Trade Marks: Portcullis for the EEA?", *European Intellectual Property Review*, 20/5 (1998): 172–77

Garnett, Kevin, Jonathan Rayner James and Gillian Davies, *Copinger and Skone James on Copyright*, 14th edition, London: Sweet and Maxwell, 1999

Govaere, Inge, *The Use and Abuse of Intellectual Property Rights in EC Law: Including a Case Study of the EC Spare Parts Debate*, London: Sweet and Maxwell, 1996

Hays, Thomas, "The Silhouette Case: The European Union Moves to the Highest Common Denominator on the Gray Market Question", *Trademark Reporter*, 88/3 (1998): 234–49

Heath, Christopher, "Parallel Imports and International Trade", *International Review of Industrial Property and Copyright Law*, 28 (1997): 623–31

Korah, Valentine, "Intellectual Property Rights and the Free Movement of Goods" in *An Introductory Guide to EC Competition Law and Practice* (6th edition), Oxford: Hart, 1997

Oliver, Peter, *Free Movement of Goods in the European Community: Under Articles 30 to 36 of the Treaty of Rome*, 3rd edition, London: Sweet and Maxwell, 1996

Rothnie, Warwick A., *Parallel Imports*, London: Sweet and Maxwell, 1993

Verma, S.K., "Exhaustion of Intellectual Property Rights and Free Trade: Article 6 of the TRIPs Agreement", *International Review of Industrial Property and Copyright Law*, 29/5 (1998): 534–67

Zwaan, Marcel de and Wolter Wolfers Bettink, "Exhaustion of Rights: Recent Developments in Europe", *Copyright World*, 64 (1996): 26–30

The doctrine of exhaustion of rights is a response to the conflict between the exercise of intellectual property rights and the principle of free movement of goods. The rule, simply stated, is that the first release of a product into the market by or with the consent of the rights' owner, "exhausts" the intellectual property rights to the extent that the rights' owner is normally unable to use them to control further dealings in the product. In the United States, the concept is commonly known as the "first sale" doctrine. Depending on the context within which initial marketing and movement of goods occurs, exhaustion may be "regional", "national", or "international". The topic is usually treated within more comprehensive books on intellectual property rights and/or free movement of goods and several such works offer helpful introductions to the concept and its application.

KORAH, in her introduction to the wider topic of European competition law, offers a succinct statement of the problems. She discusses the development of the doctrine of Community-wide exhaustion by the European Court of Justice against the background of the principle of free movement of goods enshrined in Articles 30–36 of the Treaty of Rome and the adoption of Directives aimed at eliminating differences in the intellectual property laws of member states.

OLIVER's detailed work is required reading for anyone with a serious interest in the development by the European Court of doctrines dealing with the clash between intellectual property rights and free movement of goods. Chapter eight deals with exceptions to the free movement rules and includes analyses of European cases within the context of the exhaustion doctrine. Emphasizing that the "cornerstone of the exhaustion of rights is the proprietor's consent to marketing", Oliver discusses its application in respect of patents, trade marks, copyright, and plant breeders' rights.

GOVAERE's treatment of exhaustion is viewed in the context of "misuse" of intellectual property rights under the free movement of goods rules. She explains clearly how the doctrine was developed, in close parallel with the related concept of "specific subject matter", in order to curtail the effect of the principle of territoriality.

Strictly applied, the exhaustion doctrine favours the parallel importer and there is a considerable body of literature dealing specifically with the clash between intellectual property rights and parallel importation. ROTHNIE's comprehensive study of parallel imports (or "gray goods" as they are often termed in the United States) analyses the legal and economic theories underpinning the contradictory doctrines of "territoriality" and "exhaustion", and examines in detail the question whether power to block parallel imports can be found in rights resulting from different kinds of intellectual property. Rothnie's work is especially valuable for its analysis of the historical development of the exhaustion doctrine in numerous jurisdictions, including Australia, the United Kingdom, and other common law countries, the United States and the European Community.

Specific kinds of intellectual property rights give rise to particular problems in respect of parallel imports and there are numerous studies devoted to specific rights. HEATH looks at parallel imports of patented products in the context of international trade and the TRIPs (trade-related aspects of intellectual property rights) Agreement, contrasting the ways in which different jurisdictions have sought to deal with the problem, and illustrating the theoretical and practical difficulties of the exhaustion doctrine. Arguing that there is a need for worldwide harmonization, he concludes that there is no solution currently able to serve as a worldwide model of exhaustion. The most viable option is the classical theory of exhaustion whereby a patentee is given one opportunity to release patented goods under the monopolistic conditions of a patent right.

HAYS discusses the exhaustion of trade mark rights in the wake of the 1998 *Silhouette* case, in which the European Court of Justice ruled that individual member states were not permitted to adopt the principle of international exhaustion. This ruling, which was widely publicized in the media, will have a significant impact on the ability of retailers to sell parallel imports at discounted prices. Noting that the Court viewed internal market unity as more important than conclusively settling the parallel importation issue, Hays identifies several questions that remain to be answered, including the application of competition law.

CORNISH, writing before the European Court's ruling, argues that trade mark rights should not be used to form a barrier to entry into the European Economic Area (EEA). In the absence of unfair practice, the trade mark right should not extend to the distribution of goods marked by or with the consent of the proprietor. Parallel importation from outside the EEA may be objected to in certain cases, for example where there are serious quality differences in products, but the same rule should not be applied to goods that are exactly the same wherever first marketed. Cornish argues cogently that a rigidly applied non-exhaustion rule would not achieve the desired balance between the different interests of consumers, distributors, and producers.

VERMA begins his review of the principle and scope of exhaustion by noting that it developed out of 19th-century judicial practice in Germany and the US. He goes on to look at current state practice on exhaustion in Japan, the US, and the European Union. Territorial/national exhaustion is seen as protectionist and anti-competitive, whereas the principle of international exhaustion is consistent with free trade and commerce. He also considers the position of developing countries, arguing that international exhaustion is more likely to encourage local industry. Verma believes that resolution of the exhaustion issue (which was omitted from the TRIPs Agreement) is long overdue and that the problem must be settled in the context of the GATT/WTO multilateral trading system.

ZWAAN & BETTINK's article is a simple and clear explanation of the doctrine of exhaustion and its interplay with copyright and neighbouring rights. The article may usefully be read in conjunction with the more recent and scholarly chapter in *Copinger* (chapter 25 in GARNETT, RAYNER JAMES & DAVIES), which reviews the application of the doctrine by the European Court of Justice to copyright and related rights. Problems arising from the exhaustion doctrine are also identified, including the question of consent by the rights' owner, the absence of harmonization among the laws of member states, and the complex way in which copyright may be exploited in different countries.

ELLEN GREDLEY

See also Copyright, Intellectual property rights

Exhibitionism

Allen, David W., *The Fear of Looking, or Scopophilic-Exhibitionistic Conflicts*, Bristol: John Wright, and Charlottesville: University Press of Virginia, 1974

Blair, C. David and Richard J. Lanyon, "Exhibitionism: Etiology and Treatment", *Psychological Bulletin*, 89/3 (1981): 439–63

Blank, Leonard (editor), *Nudity and Nudism: Studies in Voyeurism and Exhibitionism*, Chicago: Aldine, 1966

Bonnet, Gérard, *Voir, être vu*, Paris: Presses Universitaires de France, 1981

Christoffel, Hans, "Exhibitionism and Exhibitionists", *International Journal of Psycho-Analysis*, 17 (1936): 321–45

Cox, Daniel J. and Reid J. Daitzman (editors), *Exhibitionism: Description, Assessment, and Treatment*, New York: Garland, 1980

Ellis, Havelock, "Erotic Symbolism" in *Studies in the Psychology of Sex*, vol. 2, part 1: *Erotic Symbolism, The Mechanism of Detumescence, The Psychic State of Pregnancy*, New York: Random House, 1937 (work first published in 7 vols, 1897–1928)

Hirschfeld, Magnus, *Sexual Anomalies and Perversions: Physical and Psychological Development and Treatment*, London: Torch, 1938

Hollender, Marc H., "Genital Exhibitionism in Men and Women" in *Sexual Dynamics of Anti-Social Behavior*, edited by Louis B. Schlesinger and Eugene Revitch, Springfield, Illinois: Thomas, 1983; 2nd edition 1997

MacDonald, John M., *Indecent Exposure*, Springfield, Illinois: Thomas, 1973

Maletzky, Barry M., "Exhibitionism: Assessment and Treatment" in *Sexual Deviance: Theory, Assessment and Treatment*, edited by D. Richard Laws and William T. O'Donohue , New York: Guilford Press, 1997

Rickles, Nathan King, *Exhibitionism*, Philadelphia: Lippincott, 1950

Sperling, Melitta, "The Analysis of an Exhibitionist", *International Journal of Psycho-Analysis*, 27/28 (1947): 32–45

Zavitzianos, George, "Fetishism and Exhibitionism in the Female and their Relationship to Psychopathy and Kleptomania", *International Journal of Psychoanalysis*, 52 (1971): 297–305

The term "exhibitionism" was coined by the French doctor Charles Lasègue in 1877 as a diagnostic label for men who repeatedly and intentionally offend other citizens, mostly women and children, through the public display of their genitals. Rapidly making its way into the French and German medico-legal catalogues of sexual perversion, the notion entered the Anglo-American psychiatric nomenclature around the turn of the 20th century, although many professionals still prefer to designate the behaviour in question as "indecent exposure" or "flashing".

The medical and psychological literature of the 20th century contains an overwhelming number of papers on exhibitionism, many of which include case-studies and discussions of treatment strategies. Until the 1960s, clinical and forensic evidence on exhibitionism was mainly viewed through a psychoanalytic lens, cognitive and behavioural paradigms gradually supplanting most of the alternative approaches from the 1970s onwards. Not surprisingly, most of these source materials refer to male subjects, the female exhibitionist remaining a sexual curiosity – at least in the professional literature if not in the social realm.

Unlike the specialist papers on exhibitionism, the monographs in English on the subject are easy to list, since a hundred years of research have generated no more than a handful of volumes that are exclusively devoted to the circumstances of genital exposure. RICKLES counts as the first general discussion of the nature, origin, and treatment of exhibitionism. Strongly inspired by psychoanalytic theory, Rickles defines exhibitionism as a male's compulsive behaviour of exposing his external genitalia publicly to another person, with both subjects being aware of the nature of the act. He distinguishes between depraved exhibitionists, who expose themselves with the intention of luring the other into a sexual act; neurotic exhibitionists, whose exposure is a sexual goal in itself; and normal exhibitionism, as occurring in children, nudists, and adults engaging in consensual sexual activity. In keeping with his psychoanalytic stance, Rickles attributes depraved and neurotic exhibitionism to unconscious infantile conflicts, especially *vis-à-vis* the mother.

Rickles' work remained a staple of the literature on exhibitionism for many years, and its prestige can for instance be inferred from John Macdonald's decision to expand his own book with a chapter by Rickles on "The Mothers of Exhibitionists" (pp.96–105 in MACDONALD). Macdonald

himself broadens Rickles' perspective by also considering the social-historical and sociological factors in the aetiology of indecent exposure. Both BLANK and ALLEN develop this sociocultural approach further on the basis of the idea that exhibitionism can only be understood when associated with its psychological counterpart voyeurism (scopophilia), and when situated within the larger dynamics of looking and being looked at. The significance of viewing and the gaze also underpins the two-volume treatise by BONNET, which is unfortunately only available in French, but which should not be absent from any bibliography on exhibitionism since it is the most comprehensive treatise on the issue available in any language. In each of these books, numerous case-studies underlie and exemplify the authors' theoretical propositions, which once again reflect a rigorous allegiance to psychoanalytic conceptions of the mind and sexuality.

A more recent collection of essays is COX & DAITZMAN, which relegates psychoanalytic theory to the background (there is one essay by D.W. Allen entitled "A Psychoanalytic View") and highlights behavioural viewpoints on the mainspring and clinical management of exhibitionism. This book is particularly informative in the realms of assessment and treatment, covering an extensive range of behavioural strategies from electrical aversion to covert sensitization, although the contemporary reader is likely to frown at the therapists' (lack of) ethical code in working with their clients. Some of the clinical interventions debated in Cox & Daitzman have been summarized in MALETZKY, which also discusses the use of specific questionnaires, psychological tests, and rating scales in the assessment of exhibitionistic individuals. Maletzky ends with a critical note pertaining to the lack of epidemiological research in this area and the difficulty of making general claims about the effectiveness of particular treatment approaches. Overall, this is a lucid and well-informed contribution to the clinical literature, which healthcare professionals will most certainly appreciate as a technical guide for orienting their practice.

Readers who wish to undertake a more in-depth study of the research on exhibitionism may start with BLAIR & LANYON, despite its being published some 20 years ago. Following an evaluation of the various explanations of exhibitionism, the authors critically discuss the most popular treatment strategies and the validity of the accompanying outcome studies. They also argue that more research is needed on the role of the fantasy in the aetiology of exhibitionism, and on the design of interventions that take account of individual differences. Equally valuable is HOLLENDER, which elucidates the personal profiles, behavioural patterns, and clinical prognosis of exhibitionists, in relation to a fourfold typology that distinguishes between compulsive, secondary, socially sanctioned, and attention-seeking individuals. Interestingly, Hollender also analyses case-studies of female exhibitionists, which constitute a rarity in the professional literature. Amongst the other authors who have challenged the idea that exhibitionism is a uniquely male phenomenon, ZAVITZIANOS is worth mentioning, although the reader needs to know that its frame of reference is strictly psychoanalytic.

Finally, even the non-historically minded reader may benefit from going to the trouble of reading some of the early sexological sources, such as ELLIS and HIRSCHFELD. These works are mainly descriptive and factual, yet they also contain welcome critical summaries of important German and French contributions that have not been translated into English. Despite the fact that they were written at the start of the 20th century, their account of the subject remains remarkably fresh and stimulating. The same is true for CHRISTOFFEL, which offers an astute commentary on early psychoanalytic materials and also integrates anthropological and sociohistorical data. Within the postwar psychoanalytic literature, SPERLING's case-study of a 29-year old man who enjoyed exhibiting himself on underground trains still deserves to be explored, whatever one's theoretical allegiance and professional practice.

DANY NOBUS

See also Perversion

Expectancy theory

Arnold, Hugh J., "A Test of the Validity of the Multiplicative Hypothesis of Expectancy-Valence Theories of Work Motivation", *Academy of Management Journal*, 24/1 (1981): 128–41

Arnold, J., Ivan T. Robertson and Cary L. Cooper, *Work Psychology: Understanding Human Behaviour in the Workplace*, London: Pitman, 1991

Eerde, Wendelien van and Henk Thierry, "Vroom's Expectancy Models and Work-Related Criteria: A Meta-Analysis", *Journal of Applied Psychology*, 81/5 (1996): 575–86

George, Jennifer M. and Gareth R. Jones, *Understanding and Managing Organizational Behavior*, Reading, Massachusetts: Addison Wesley, 1996; 2nd edition 1999

Muchinsky, P.M., "A Comparison of Within- and Across-Subjects Analyses of the Expectancy Valence Model for Predicting Effort", *Academy of Management Journal*, 20/1 (1977): 154–58

Shepperd, James A., "Productivity Loss in Performance Groups: A Motivation Analysis", *Psychological Bulletin*, 113/1 (1993): 67–81

Stahl, Michael J. and Adrian Harrell, "Modelling Effort Decisions with Behavioral Decision Theory: Toward an Individual Differences Model of Expectancy Theory", *Organization Behavior and Human Performance*, 27 (1981): 303–25

Taylor, K.F., "A 'Valence-Expectancy' Approach to Work Motivation", *Personnel Practice Bulletin*, 30/2 (1974): 142–48

Vroom, Victor H., *Work and Motivation*, New York: Wiley, 1964

Expectancy theory is among the more prominent theories of work motivation. Victor Vroom originally developed the theory in 1964. However the 1995 reprint of *Work and Motivation* may be of particular interest because the introduction includes Vroom's reflections, as at September 1994, on his theory and the subsequent research that it generated (VROOM). Although he acknowledges the unrealistic cognitive assumptions of the theory in that individuals are not always rational optimal decision makers, Vroom asserts that his model was intended to be of heuristic value by providing "a language for formulating questions" (p.xviii) about the work motivation process. In the introduction Vroom also acknowledges the importance of the extrinsic/intrinsic distinction in the work motivation process, and reasserts the significance of individual differences, as opposed to situational properties, in the motivation–job satisfaction relationship.

The introduction aside, the book contains Vroom's original work of which chapter 2 describes his expectancy theory of work motivation. Vroom specifies that motivation is the result of three different types of beliefs that individuals possess: (a) expectancy: the belief that one's effort will result in performance; (b) instrumentality: the belief that one's performance will be rewarded; and (c) valence: the perceived value of the rewards to the recipient. Importantly, Vroom posits that motivation is a multiplicative function of all three components. The remainder of the book is devoted to three closely related issues: (a) why people choose the jobs they do; (b) the factors that cause people to be satisfied with their work; and (c) the factors that influence individual's work performance. The literature relating to these three issues is very extensive and remains a useful reference for earlier works on work motivation.

Chapter 2 of Vroom's book, which describes expectancy theory, may not be easily understood by undergraduate psychology students or readers from a non-psychology background. Most organizational behaviour books generally contain a chapter on motivation theories, including expectancy theory. For example, GEORGE & JONES (pp.171–6) provides a clear and simple explanation of expectancy theory and its three major components: expectancy, instrumentality, and valence. The illustration of the model (Figure 6.1, p.175) is particularly useful in drawing the three elements together. The section concludes on a practical note offering advice to managers as to how to improve workers' performance using expectancy theory. Thus, entries in organizational behaviour books such as George & Jones may be particularly useful for business students and managers. ARNOLD, ROBERTSON & COOPER may also serve the same purpose as well as evaluating the research on the model.

TAYLOR writes in an accessible style, acknowledging the difficulty in understanding the theoretical chapters of Vroom's book and the "frightening formulae" within. Taking an applied personnel management approach, Taylor defines the key variables of expectancy theory followed by a brief discussion on the implications of the model for personnel management. The article concludes with a warning that the model is probably more useful in offering broad generalizations about work motivation rather than providing precise solutions. Taylor's main concern is that the assumption that people are motivated and are capable of making rational, logical choices may not adequately mirror reality, limiting the theory's practical value.

Considering the prominence of Vroom's expectancy theory and the numerous empirical studies it generated, EERDE & THIERRY undertook a meta-analytic study that integrated the correlations of 77 expectancy theory studies. The aim was to examine the relationship between single components of the model (valence, instrumentality, and expectancy) as well as the force model (expectancy-valence) and the valence model (valence-instrumentality), and five work-related criterion variables (performance, effort, intention, preference, and choice). The meta-analysis also distinguishes within-subject and between-subjects analyses. The authors note, however, that the between-subjects analyses are inconsistent with Vroom's conceptualization of the model.

The results of van Eerde & Thierry's analysis reveal somewhat lower correlations between Vroom's expectancy model and the work-related criterion variables than reported by previous researchers. Thus, the authors recommend using the components of the model rather than the model in its entirety. Their analysis also reveals that the criterion variables "intention" and "preference" are more strongly related to the models and components, compared with the criterion variables, performance, effort, and choice. Further, the within-subject correlations are significantly higher than the between-subjects correlations with respect to the criterion variables, effort, and preference. Eerde & Thierry's research is useful in highlighting that researchers place different interpretations on Vroom's model and apply different methodological techniques (not all of which are accurate) in testing the model and its components. The bibliography is extensive and provides a useful starting point for further research.

Differences in methodology and measurement of the key variables of the model have frustrated attempts to validate expectancy theory. As noted above, the theory as originally developed by Vroom proposes to explain different levels of effort from the same employee under different circumstances (a within-subject analysis), however, replication studies predominantly examine different people (a between-subject analysis). MUCHINSKY specifically addresses this issue and concludes that the validity of Vroom's expectancy model is enhanced using a within-subject analysis, which represents the appropriate conceptualization of the model.

Expectancy theory posits that motivation is a multiplicative function of all three components of the model: expectancy, instrumentality, and valence. This implies that, if any one component is zero, then the overall level of motivation will be zero.

STAHL & HARRELL adopt a behavioural decision theory approach to undertake four experiments with the aim of testing Vroom's multiplicative force model. The researchers find stronger support for an additive model compared with the multiplicative model. Stahl & Harrell link the differential processing of the expectancy model to individual differences, such as amount of statistical education, formal education, and age. ARNOLD also tested the multiplicative hypothesis implied by Vroom's expectancy theory model using an experimental research design. Arnold's results provide general support for the multiplicative hypothesis with respect to expectancy and valence. The work of Stahl & Harrell and Arnold is illustrative of the equivocal outcomes of research testing the multiplicative hypothesis. Methodology and measurement problems are cited as the cause for conflicting research outcomes in testing Vroom's multiplicative force model.

The article by SHEPPERD provides an example of an application of expectancy theory, in this case in the area of productivity loss (for example, social loafing) in groups. Shepperd limits his analysis to collective productivity loss that stems from reduced motivation (thus excluding non-motivational factors). Linking his ideas directly to the expect-

ancy theory model, Shepperd argues that lost collective productivity occurs when (a) individuals perceive no benefits to contributing, (b) perceive no link between their contributions and achieving a desired outcome, or (c) perceive the costs of contributing to be too high (p.79). Solutions are offered based on the source of productivity loss: (a) offer extrinsic/extrinsic rewards for contributing, (b) make individuals' contributions indispensable, and (c) eliminate barriers (costs) to contributing. Shepperd's article thus provides a framework derived from expectancy theory for organizing the research on productivity loss in groups. The article concludes with a real-world example where realistic strategies are offered (based on the theoretical framework) to improve group motivation and productivity in a factory assembly-line setting.

THERESE A. JOINER

See also Motivation

Expectations

Attfield, C.L.F., David Demery and N.W. Duck, *Rational Expectations in Macroeconomics: An Introduction to Theory and Evidence*, Oxford and New York: Blackwell, 1985

Cagan, P. "The Monetary Dynamics of Hyperinflation" in *Studies in the Quantity Theory of Money*, edited by Milton Friedman, Chicago: University of Chicago Press, 1956

Davidson, P. "Is Probability Theory Relevant for Uncertainty? A Post Keynesian Perspective", *Journal of Economic Perspectives*, 5/1 (1991): 129–43

Fisher, Irving, *The Theory of Interest as Determined by Impatience to Spend Income and Opportunity to Invest It*, New York: Macmillan, 1930; reprinted Fairfield, New Jersey: Kelley, 1986

Keynes, John Maynard, *The General Theory of Employment, Interest, and Money*, London: Macmillan, and New York: Harcourt Brace, 1936

Keynes, John Maynard, "The General Theory of Employment", *Quarterly Journal of Economics*, 51 (1937): 209–23

Muth, J.F. "Rational Expectations and the Theory of Price Movements", *Econometrica*, 29 (1961): 315–35

Simon, H.A. "Dynamic Programming under Uncertainty with a Quadratic Criterion Function", *Econometrica*, 24 (1956): 74–81

Von Neumann, John and Oskar Morgenstern, *Theory of Games and Economic Behavior*, Princeton, New Jersey: Princeton University Press 1944; 3rd edition 1953

Models of "expectations" are essential for accurate modelling of economic behaviour. Many decisions involve the formation of some form of expectation of economic variables in order to guide the choices made by economic agents. Various approaches to expectations have been used to attempt to capture such effects.

The expectation of changes in prices, or conversely the value of money, underly many of the areas in which expectations are applied. A basic model that does not incorporate an expectations mechanism effectively assumes static expectations. A common example of this is the Keynesian "money illusion", the case in which people mistake monetary values for real values. Under static expectations, all economic agents assume current variables will maintain their present values in all future periods. KEYNES (1936) does involve a more complex treatment of expectations in the analysis of particular, but not all, economic variables, particularly in the investment decisions of companies and the principle of "speculative" demand for money. His framework lacks a consistent expectations approach, but looks at the specific expectations conditions applying for certain types of activity.

Irving FISHER is possibly the earliest exponent of an expectations model of the type used by modern economists. Fisher followed his famous study of the *Quantity Theory of Money* (1911) with another highly empirical study in 1930, this time on the *Theory of Interest*. While it took a standard classical view of interest rates in many respects, such as their function being to balance supply of savings with the demand for investment, Fisher strongly emphasized throughout his work the importance of expectations of the future in determining interest rates. He states that the interest rate is a price like any other – the ratio of exchange between two things. It is distinctive in that it is the rate of exchange between present and future consumption, and therefore the level of the interest rate is extremely dependent upon people's expectations of, and attitudes towards, the future. In his statistical work, he tested the link between lagged price levels and interest rates to see how quickly people made the appropriate change, reflected by changes in market interest rates, after economic conditions altered. A lag of several periods was usually the best-correlated version of the model, compared to the appropriate change in interest rates. From this he concluded that people gradually incorporated past values into their formation of expectations, but that increasingly older values were seen as of decreasing significance over time. The outcome was an equation where previous years' values determined current expectations but the values were weighted, the weights declining linearly over time. For example

$$P^e = \alpha \left[4(P_{1990}) + 3(P_{1989}) + 2(P_{1988}) + 1(P_{1987}) \right]$$

The backward-looking mechanism created by Fisher is greatly similar to the "adaptive expectations" mechanism, which was later popularized for the overt use of expectations in economic models, in the hands of economists such as Milton Friedman and other monetarists.

Keynes' failure to incorporate expectations systematically into his models as Fisher had previously done is somewhat surprising as Keynes was an admirer of Fisher's work, providing a glowing review of the *Quantity Theory of Money* for the *Economic Journal* in September 1911 as well as basing some of his *Tract on Monetary Reform* (1923) on Fisher's views, and also following the Fisher approach to monetary business cycles. His failure is perhaps instructive – Fisher's work was tightly focused and suited to the incorporation of expectations, whilst Keynes' framework was broad and inclusive. It is perhaps not surprising that expectations modelling became popular in macroeconomics (and microeconomics)

after the monetarist economists began using much smaller models of the economy, and decision theorists began to use small scale scenarios in game theory after VON NEUMANN & MORGENSTERN (see below).

CAGAN made the first use of typical "adaptive expectations" modelling in his study of hyperinflation that accompanied Friedman's re-examination of the quantity theory of money, which launched the monetarist school into the modern policy debate. The obvious links between this group and the work of Irving Fisher make it highly probable that Cagan's model was a conscious adaptation of Fisher's simpler mechanism. Previous values of a variable are still used to predict its future value, but Cagan uses geometrically rather than linearly declining weights for the older values, so giving significantly greater strength to more recent observations. A simple version could be given:

$$P^e_t = P^e_{t-1} + \alpha(P_{t-1} - P^e_{t-1}) \text{ where } 1 \geq \alpha \geq 0$$

or

$$P^e_t = \alpha\, P_{t-1} + (1-\alpha)\, P^e_{t-1}$$

This second version will yield, by successive substitution for the lagged expectation term, a format where expectations are determined by geometrically declining lagged values of the price level. This implies that the present expectation is purely backward looking.

In its statistical sense, the term "expectation" is synonymous with the concept of the average or mean. This is simply because, if we are asked to predict something, choice of the mean as our forecast would provide us with the smallest total errors, which should cancel out over time. The mean is therefore referred to as the "expected value".

MUTH's form of "rational expectations" is a logical extension of this concept. It assumes that, rather than economic agents forming forecasts on the basis of past occurrences, and therefore leaving themselves open to (possibly avoidable) mistakes, economic agents would instead be forward looking. It is therefore anticipation of the future, rather than simple analysis of patterns revealed in the past, which leads to a forecast. Muth's reasoning is that it is irrational not to avoid avoidable mistakes when such mistakes can be extremely costly. Individuals' subjective assessments of economic variables' probability distributions will therefore coincide with the true distributions and their predictions will coincide with those of the underlying economic model of the economy. If they do make mistakes, these are used to improve future predictions so that they would then coincide with the true models. The mistakes will also be random, and so will cancel out over time. The advantage of this method is that, when expectations need to be incorporated into a model, we can assume that the true expected value (statistical mean) is an accurate and legitimate proxy for individual's expected values. For example, for some economic variable "X", the expectation can be stated:

$$E(X) = X + u_t$$

where E indicates an expectations operator, and u_t is a normally distributed random error term.

Muth's view of rational behaviour is more realistic than adaptive mechanisms as it allows for agents' ability to anticipate economic events. It delivers rather a strong conclusion, however: that agents' predictions are consistent with the true economic model. The extreme levels of information that agents, implicitly, would have to possess for their predictions to be this accurate are a serious shortcoming of Muth-rationality. The work of SIMON has led to a less extreme view of rational expectations, bounded rationality, which allows for the fact that costly information would be gathered incompletely, namely up to the point where the advantages of collecting further information disappeared. For a more general account of rational expectations, and an account of the empirical testing of the rational expectations hypothesis, see ATTFIELD, DEMERY & DUCK.

Expectations also form the basis of the most commonly used approach to uncertainty in economics, the Von Neumann Morgenstern utility theory, generally known as the expected-utility maximization approach. Following the statistical approach of using probabilities as weights attached to their associated possible outcomes, a simple method for predicting the expected outcome of a decision is produced, whether it be for utilities, or other types of outcome. For example if a farmer grows sunflowers they may succeed or fail depending on whether conditions are sunny or damp respectively. If sunny weather has a 60 per cent probability, and will yield 40 tons of seeds, and damp weather has a 40 per cent probability with a 20 ton yield, the expected yield will be:

$$(0.6).40 \text{ tons} + (0.4).20 \text{ tons} = 32 \text{ tons}$$

Such methods for dealing with choice under conditions of uncertainty bring us back to macroeconomic debates over expectations and uncertainty. KEYNES (1937) responded to criticisms of the *General Theory*'s lack of consistently incorporated expectations with a strong and influential defence. He noted that while some economic variables may have sufficiently well-defined probability distributions for expectations to provide dependable predictions, other economic variables were either not well enough defined, or were not sufficiently rationally determined, for a reliable prediction to be made. The latter case would be an example of a genuine and ineradicable uncertainty. DAVIDSON provides a good account of the post-Keynesian school's development of this principle in modern economics.

V.G. FITZSIMONS

See also Public choice theory and rational expectations

Experimental economics

Ball, Sheryl B., "Research, Teaching and Practice in Experimental Economics: A Progress Report and Review", *Southern Economic Journal*, 64/3 (1998): 772–79

Bergstrom, Theodore C. and John H. Miller, *Experiments with Economic Principles*, New York: McGraw Hill, 1997

Davis, Douglas D. and Charles A. Holt, *Experimental Economics*, Princeton, New Jersey: Princeton University Press, 1993

Friedman, Daniel and Shyam Sunder, *Experimental Methods: A Primer for Economists*, Cambridge and New York: Cambridge University Press, 1994

Hey, John D. and Graham Loomes (editors), *Recent Developments in Experimental Economics*, 2 vols, Aldershot, Hampshire: Elgar, 1993

Hey, John D. (editor), *Experimental Economics*, Heidelberg: Physica, 1994

Kagel, John H. and Alvin E. Roth (editors), *The Handbook of Experimental Economics*, Princeton, New Jersey: Princeton University Press, 1995

Loomes, Graham, "Experimental Economics" in *Current Issues in Microeconomics*, edited by John D. Hey, Basingstoke: Macmillan, 1989

Plott, Charles R., "Will Economics Become an Experimental Science?", *Southern Economic Journal*, 57/4 (1991): 901–19

Smith, Vernon L. (editor), *Research in Experimental Economics: A Research Annual*, vols 1–3, Greenwich: Jai Press, 1979–85

Experimental economics has seen tremendous growth in the past few decades and is now an established field with an economic science association, a journal, and a literature composed with much ingenuity and scholarship. The following texts are just a few indicators that point to an enormous literature on the topic.

An early collection edited by SMITH, who has written widely in the area, consists of three volumes of papers on experimental economics that are intended to reflect much of the spectrum of application of experimental economics. The first of these has papers is on public goods, animal behaviour, auctions and so on. One of the first published collection of works in experimental economics, it broke new ground. The second volume has specialist papers on similar topics including forms of market organization and rational expectations hypothesis. The third again has a wide selection, including preference reversal, winner's curse, and auctions. Together the papers are quite useful in their own specialist areas but can be best used for understanding the important and diverse applications of experimental methods.

The chapter by LOOMES in the text edited by Hey is essentially an attempt to convey the frontier issues in experimental theory to nonspecialists (and students) in a nonspecialist language. He illustrates the role of experiments in testing theories, gaining new information, and finding practical solutions, and he describes, with examples, experiments investigating individuals' dealings in an uncertain world, and the operation of markets and price mechanisms. An appraisal of the field is presented outlining criticisms concerning issues of realism, learning, and the potential in terms of promoting research, training, education, and better policy. The text is extremely readable, non-mathematical, interesting and interactive, entailing (for example in the auctions subsection) a constant sense of "what would you do under such a situation?"

HEY's collection professes to be more "forward looking than backward" and is not a comprehensive "state of the discipline" text. Its value arises from its innovative approach to questioning certain established truths of experimental economics. Essays by Bohm and by Harrison question the universal validity of preference reversals and the inapplicability of descriptive expected utility (EU) theory respectively. Some other essays are on the notion of fairness in bargaining problems and overlapping generations (OLG) models. It differs from other volumes in that it contains essays explicitly (even solely) considering methodological issues (which are usually often a small subsection in other publications) such as careful reporting of experimental results (even unsuccessful ones) and examining the notion of "ill-defined experiments". Thus, this is not a text from which to expect a narrative of the experimental technique in economics and its applications but one that raises some important theoretical issues enmeshed in the experimental procedure.

PLOTT looks at the transition of economics from a neoclassical to an experimental social science. He proposes several reasons for the increased use of experimentation by the economics profession. These include the learning of a questioning attitude, the making of important discoveries, the advancement of economic theory, increased laboratory data, and the appearance of paradoxes of all kinds. He ends by quaoting what he calls the Say's law of experimental methods: supply of experimental methods creating its own demand.

The 1990s have seen many attempts to classify, combine, and collate the experimental economics literature. KAGEL & ROTH in their excellent handbook provide an introduction to several fields that have been affected by the experimental method. These are: public goods, coordination problems, bargaining, industrial organization, asset markets, auctions, and individual decision making. The developments within these specialist fields are traced historically and for anyone seeking information on a sub-area of application, the essays are very self contained. Roth provides a lengthy (but conveniently subdivided) introduction to experimental economics. This is worth reading to know the subject area and its origins. It also gives useful material on history, uses, and a summary of experiments covered. The bibliography is very comprehensive and although the handbook does not (and cannot) cover all areas affected by the growing experimental trend, it is very useful and systematic for the ones it does.

DAVIS & HOLT aim their text towards the graduate curriculum and do not concentrate on new material. They focus on providing an organized introduction and evaluation of some of the key areas in experimental economics. These involve: decisions and games, double auction and posted offer markets, bargaining and auctions, public goods, externalities, voting, asymmetric information and individual decision making under risk. Also included is an introduction written for beginners, a summary at the end, and appendices at the end of most chapters elaborating on actual experimental instructions and so on. Although not as deep in its coverage of specialist issues, it is ideal for introductory curricula but may need supplementing for new and ongoing developments in the field.

The two-volume text by HEY & LOOMES is a collection of articles elaborating on developments in certain sub-areas of experimental economics. It has papers by most of the major names in the field today. The first volume has sections on methodology, preference reversals, willingness to pay and accept (WTP, WTA), the European Union and generalizations, and on games. There are some famous papers here including Harrison's on use of incentives, and one by Tversky and others

on the causes of preference reversal. The section on methodology is especially welcome as methodological concerns are generally insufficiently explored. The second volume deals with developments in the literature on bargaining (comparison of predictions of simple ultimatum games and more complicated ones), auctions (conditions and implications of the "winner's curse" phenomenon), public goods (including externalities, free riding, Coasian solutions) and markets (including variations of double auction settings and the role of information). Overall, the volume is a good reference for recent specialized literature in experimental economics, although one needs to remember that it is not a narrative handbook.

BALL's review article is an excellent source of information for those wanting an evaluation of experimental economics texts. A major advantage of the article is that Ball gives lots of Internet website references, which are extremely useful. She gives an account of the current acceptability of a discipline that was once regarded with suspicion, and directs attention at the resources for research devoting a section to undergraduate teaching. She also addresses some of the important questions in experimentation like the use of incentives, external validity, experimenter demand, and experimental design. One weakness is that the article omits some recent and very useful work, especially that by Hey and Loomes (1993) and that of Hey (1989, 1991). Moreover, only the literature from the 1990s is considered, and thus significant works in the decades before are omitted although they could have provided an historical background to the developments in the discipline. It is overall a very useful article for those involved in teaching and research.

Most of the texts above document the growing experimental trend in economics, but the book by FRIEDMAN & SUNDER is a backstage text in some ways. It is a primer for experimental economists (and very useful for students), providing a mine of information about the real-life considerations of conducting experiments. It covers all of the main areas of relevance including the principles behind experiments, their design, subject choice, laboratory facilities, the process of conducting them, and analysing and reporting the data. It even has a chapter at the end detailing the genealogy of the discipline, its emergence, influences, and applications. Further, an excellent appendix gives an exhaustive reading list, details of certain experimental economics courses and their prescribed texts, instructions used for actual experiments, guidelines for experimental articles, and a list of experimental economics laboratories all over the world. This book is an invaluable resource for anyone wanting to learn about the what, why, how and where of experimental methods. A very important text.

Finally, the experimental workbook by BERGSTROM & MILLER is a most effective teaching aid that can be used by economics teachers and students alike for classroom experiments to learn about economic principles in an innovative manner.

NITASHA KAUL

Exports and export-led growth

Cripps, Francis and Wynne Godley, "Control of Imports as a Means to Full Employment and the Expansion of World Trade: The UK's Case", *Cambridge Journal of Economics*, 2 (1978): 327–34

Harrod, Roy, *International Economics*, Cambridge: Cambridge University Press, 1933

Kaldor, Nicholas, "Employment Policies and the Problem of International Balance", *Review of Economic Studies*, 19 (1951): 42–49

Kaldor, Nicholas, "The Case for Regional Policies", *Scottish Journal of Political Economy*, 17 (1970): 337–48

Kaldor, Nicholas, "Conflicts in National Economic Objectives", *Economic Journal*, 81 (1971): 1–16

Kaldor, Nicholas, "Limitations of the *General Theory*", *Proceedings of the British Academy*, 68 (1982)

Kitson, Michael and Jonathan Michie, *The Political Economy of Competitiveness*, London and New York: Routledge, 2000

Mainstream neoclassical trade theory is based on a number of unrealistic and inappropriate assumptions, as described in the separate entry on New trade theory. New trade theory allows the assumption of constant or diminishing returns to be relaxed, but full employment is still assumed. This is why new trade theory is unable to concern itself with protectionism other than as an industrial policy – evaluating the benefits of protecting "strategic" sectors or industries – and failing to consider the possibility that protection could act as part of a macroeconomic or development strategy. This failure has led to a misrepresentation in the academic literature of the impact of protectionism. Although new trade theory can demonstrate welfare gains from protection, this approach argues that the benefits are small and that there are difficulties in devising and implementing effective trade policies. Within a neoclassical framework the gains from protectionism are reduced to rent shifting and externalities: the macroeconomic possibility of domestic demand and output increasing is ignored, as are the dynamic gains from such economic growth.

The contention that interventionist trade policies will necessarily encounter implementation problems also stems from evaluating protection as an industrial policy alone. Thus, it is difficult to identify "strategic sectors"; the gains from protectionism will be lost through retaliation; other industries will be harmed (the general equilibrium problem); interest groups will manipulate the policy framework; and the rules of the game would be complex. Where protection is devised as a demand management tool, under conditions of unemployment and slow growth, many of these implementation problems are circumvented. First, it is not necessary to identify strategic sectors, just competitive imports versus complementary imports. Second, as argued in detail in CRIPPS & GODLEY, protection need not lead to retaliation, as the expansion of domestic demand will stimulate the volume of trade. Third, the general equilibrium problem is not relevant under conditions of underemployed resources. Finally, the influence of interest groups is reduced when tariffs are used as a general rather than selective instrument.

KALDOR (1970, 1982), incorporating the Harrod foreign trade multiplier (HARROD), emphasizes that the trade cycle reflects fluctuations in export demand. Investment is an induced component of aggregate demand, being determined by the income changes that are in turn induced by the Harrod foreign trade multiplier. Given the importance of increasing returns in manufacturing industry, this relationship may help to explain virtuous circles of growth. Kaldor argues that the Ricardian rationale for free trade is dependent on the assumption of constant returns to scale. The existence of economies of scale in manufacturing, however, means that a nation that is successfully competing in foreign trade can expect that the advantage of an expanding market will increase its competitiveness. Similarly, a nation with a poor performance in international trade can expect a trend of deteriorating competitiveness and declining markets. Thus, while not explaining initial imbalances, the existence of economies of scale indicates why such imbalances may generate virtuous circles or vicious cycles of growth.

In analysing British post-war economic policies KALDOR (1971) argues that the poor economic performance was due to insufficient demand. This was not in the sense of an excessive propensity to save relative to the opportunities to invest, but an excessive propensity to import relative to the ability to export – a balance-of-payments constraint. The importance of the idea of export-led growth gave rise to a policy debate on the best means for securing full employment. While exchange rate adjustment seemed the most applicable method, its efficiency was called into question, particularly after the limited impact of the 1967 devaluation. This led Kaldor and others to argue for some form of protection of competitive manufacturers. Against this it has been argued that protection cannot promote export-led growth, since it acts solely on imports (whereas devaluation or depreciation acts on both sides of the trade account). However, by encouraging import substitutes, protection can expand the domestic traded goods sector. In terms of the Harrod foreign trade multiplier the means of expansion operates through reducing the propensity to import and thus reducing the leakages from the domestic economy. As KALDOR (1951) pointed out, the objective of protection in an underemployed economy should be to reduce the propensity to import competitive goods, not to reduce the actual volume of imports. If the policy was successful, the rise in domestic incomes should encourage more imports of complementary and subsequently competitive goods.

These issues regarding exports and export-led growth are analysed and discussed in detail in KITSON & MICHIE (chapter 3). The authors argue that the key policy point is not just that a high import propensity may constrain the growth of a domestic economy, but that variations in trade performance in an increasingly integrated world economy may lead to persistent divergences in growth. Success in international trade can become cumulative as increasing demand for net exports allows countries (or more specifically, the firms and industries within them) to exploit economies of scale and scope. This may improve their competitiveness and lead to further improvements in their trade performance, while weaker trading nations may fail to maintain balance-of-payments equilibrium at a high level of economic activity, with deflationary policies then pursued in an attempt to maintain external balance. The combined impact of poor trade performance and domestic deflation is then likely to lead to a cumulative deterioration in relative economic growth as countries fail to exploit the increasing returns associated with a high level of economic activity. Kitson & Michie also includes a discussion of how the UK economy achieved rapid growth from 1932–37 partly due to the stimulus to the economy of protecting domestic manufacturing (chapter 4), and an analysis of Britain's industrial performance since 1960 that confirms the dangers that under-investment in the traded goods sector represents, not only by leading to deindustrialization directly, with inadequate investment in the manufacturing sector, but also by exacerbating wider economic problems through the balance-of-payments effect (chapter 7).

JONATHAN MICHIE

See also New trade theory

Externalities

Baumol, William J. and Wallace E. Oates, *The Theory of Environmental Policy: Externalities, Public Outlays, and Quality of Life*, 2nd edition, Cambridge and New York: Cambridge University Press, 1988

Coase, R.H., *The Firm, the Market, and the Law*, Chicago: University of Chicago Press, 1988

Dasgupta, Partha, *The Control of Resources*, Oxford: Blackwell, and Cambridge, Massachusetts: Harvard University Press, 1982

Mishan, E.J., *Introduction to Normative Economics*, New York: Oxford University Press, 1981

Nichols, Albert L., *Targeting Economic Incentives for Environmental Protection*, Cambridge, Massachusetts: MIT Press, 1984

Pigou, A.C., *The Economics of Welfare*, London: Macmillan, 1920

Sandmo, A., "Optimal Taxation in the Presence of Externalities", *Swedish Journal of Economics*, 77 (1975): 86–98

Sandmo, A., "Direct vs Indirect Pigouvian Taxation", *European Economic Review*, 7 (1976): 337–49

Solow, R.M., "The Economist's Approach to Pollution and Its Control", *Science*, (6 August 1971): 498–503

Stiglitz, J.E., *Economics of the Public Sector*, 2nd edition, New York: Norton, 1988

BAUMOL & OATES' book on environmental policy tackles such crucial issues as corrective taxation, compensation payments, tradable permits, and other "Pigouvian" topics that are relevant to the environmental policy-making debate. Economists have started looking at environmental questions relatively recently. The fact that markets for clean air, water, and so on are very often missing leads economists to view environmental problems within an externality/public goods setting. Creating "markets for the environment" is then the aim of environmental economics. Apart from internalization – which simply implies integration between those who produce and those who suffer from the externality – the standard remedies to correct for under-provision of environmental care are "Pigouvian"

taxes (such as carbon taxes) and tradable (not "grandfathered") "pollution permits". These tools are discussed in depth by other papers in the above list.

COASE's nontechnical contribution is a mixture of law and microeconomics where the renowned Nobel Prize economist examines the very foundations upon which microeconomic theory is based. This volume collects some of Coase's classic articles such as "The Nature of the Firm" (1937) and "The Problem of Social Cost" (1960). The former work introduced the then-revolutionary concept of "transaction costs" and "missing markets" into economic theory, whereas the latter further developed this concept, emphasizing the effect of the law on microeconomic mechanisms (externality-corrective taxation, among other things). The remaining papers and a new introduction clarify and extend Coase's arguments and address criticisms from other social scientists. This "pure social science" collection of classic microeconomic papers will be of interest to economists, legal scholars, and sociologists.

DASGUPTA examines the problem of controlling resources from an economic point of view. Again, this implies that the externalities issue must be tackled properly. Keeping control of those resources for which markets are missing is a common policy-making problem today. Creating a market for valuable environmental resources also implies setting up a specific framework of taxes and subsidies and, wherever possible, of appropriate market-based mechanisms that minimize distortion and overcome the social problem of dead-weight losses.

MISHAN proposes a normative approach to economics. Different from a "positive" approach, this implies setting up a theoretical framework, from which applications and policy suggestions are derived. Even though this book does not provide the reader with a full descriptive microeconomic analysis of externalities, it advances an interesting discussion of resource scarcity, market failures, and hence the problem of externalities, public goods, and "merit" goods. Resource-saving devices are also analysed.

NICHOLS discusses environmental incentives stemming from economic theory. Principal–agent theory is a modern tool to analyse to what extent agents are correctly incentivized to pursue their principals' objectives, and still act in their own interest (incentive compatibility). There exist a number of market and non-market mechanisms, such as emissions tradable permits versus energy taxes. Examples of non-economic devices are regulations and bylaws. Incentive mechanisms generally take the form of a payment-and-reward scheme (as in the UK's railway industry). The author compares different incentive schemes in the presence of market failures, by focusing upon hidden information (adverse selection) problems *vis-à-vis* hidden action (moral hazard) issues.

PIGOU's classic book covers all microeconomic topics, but is rightly famous because of its *ante litteram* approach to externalities, and to their correction through market-based mechanisms. Typical "Pigouvian" topics are extensively treated. These include marginal and net social products (leading to the definition of externalities), price discrimination, monopoly, tariffs, and taxes. As well as expounding corrective or "Pigouvian" taxes in the presence of production externalities (what we now call "energy" or "carbon" taxes, for instance, are "Pigouvian" taxes in principle), the author also faces issues of imperfect information, monopoly regulation, cost and value of services ("public" and "merit" goods), state-owned enterprises, and Pareto efficiency.

SANDMO (1975, 1976) analyses issues of optimal taxation (inverse elasticity, or "Ramsey", rules), "Pigouvian" taxes in the presence of externalities, and – more specifically in the 1976 work – direct versus indirect Pigouvian taxes. This is a very interesting work in that it reckons that Pigouvian, or externality-corrective, taxation may take two forms. "Direct" Pigouvian taxes are those levied on the income directly stemming from the externality. For instance, an energy tax that is imposed upon the stream of revenues from a particular fuel is a "direct" Pigouvian tax. On the other hand, a carbon tax based upon the carbon contents of a given product, and levied upon the final good as a proportion of its carbon contents – or carbon-related compounds – is an "indirect" Pigouvian tax. An indirect Pigouvian tax works like a value-added tax, but hits the externality that is "built" into the product, rather than the value-added chain steps leading to the good as it is finally provided.

SOLOW provides a non-technical summary of how to face pollution problems using economic incentive mechanisms such as taxes and emissions permits. It is a very general discussion of externalities, lacking the mathematical sophistication that is generally encountered in the studies relating to this particular topic.

STIGLITZ is an intermediate public economics textbook. Without unduly complicating the analysis with sophisticated quantitative techniques, the author provides a full discussion of public choice topics. As regards externalities in particular, the author provides a useful treatment of the practical problems historically encountered by Western (and especially US) economies with consumption and production externalities. Whereas consumption externalities easily lead the discussion towards the examination of public goods, production externalities are more traditionally emphasized as externalities *tout court*, because they especially relate to industrial pollution and gas emissions (CO_2), as pointed out by the 1997 Kyoto Conference on Climate Change. Finally, Stiglitz's textbook is also a useful source of references on both externalities and public goods.

GIAN CARLO SCARSI

Eyewitness testimony

Cutler, Brian L. and Steven D. Penrod, *Mistaken Identification: The Eyewitness, Psychology, and Law*, Cambridge and New York: Cambridge University Press, 1995

Fisher, Ronald P. and R. Edward Geiselman, *Memory-Enhancing Techniques for Investigative Interviewing: The Cognitive Interview*, Springfield, Illinois: Thomas, 1992

Loftus, Elizabeth F. and Katherine Ketcham, *The Myth of Repressed Memory: False Memories and Allegations of Sexual Abuse*, New York: St Martin's Press, 1994

Loftus, Elizabeth F., *Eyewitness Testimony*, Cambridge, Massachusetts: Harvard University Press, 1996

Loftus, Elizabeth F. and James M. Doyle, *Eyewitness Testimony: Civil and Criminal* (3rd edition), Charlottesville, Virginia: Lexis, 1997

Penrod, Steven, Solomon Fulero and Brian Cutler, "Expert Psychological Testimony on Eyewitness Reliability before and after Daubert: The State of the Law and the Science", *Behavioral Sciences and the Law*, 13/1 (1995): 229–60

Pope, Kenneth, "Memory, Abuse, and Science: Questioning Claims about the False Memory Syndrome Epidemic", *American Psychologist*, 51/9 (1996): 957–74

Wells, Gary, "Applied Eyewitness Testimony Research: System Variables and Estimator Variables", *Journal of Personality and Social Psychology*, 36/5 (1978): 1546–57

Wells, Gary, Mark Small, Steven Penrod, Roy Malpass, Sol Fulero and Elizabeth Brimacombe, "Eyewitness Identification Procedures: Recommendations for Lineups and Photospreads", *Law and Human Behavior*, 22/6 (1998): 603–47

Although the legal system has long recognized the potential unreliability of eyewitness testimony as a form of evidence in criminal cases, social scientists did not seriously research this issue until the 1970s. Since that time, social and cognitive psychologists have brought principles and theories of memory to bear on the problem and have amassed considerable empirical evidence regarding the reliability of eyewitnesses. Most of this work involves the use of simulated crimes staged by the researchers for unsuspecting people. Control and systematic manipulation of the variables in these experiments allows the researchers to isolate cause-effect relations. The social science approach to eyewitness evidence has created a body of knowledge of considerable practical import to the legal system.

LOFTUS describes provocative evidence from psychological experiments showing how eyewitness testimony can be influenced by events that happen after the witnessed event. Although the theoretical interpretation that Loftus makes of these phenomena is not universally accepted, the phenomena themselves are replicable and relevant to understanding eyewitness testimony in criminal and civil cases. Hence, the book remains worth reading even if the precise interpretation of these phenomena is not fully understood. Legal practitioners might find LOFTUS & DOYLE more useful for the way it integrates scientific eyewitness research with case law, case preparation, and expert testimony issues. Social scientists will likely find CUTLER & PENROD to be the most useful single source covering the eyewitness literature broadly.

WELLS describes a research and application agenda for psychologists studying eyewitness testimony. Wells distinguishes between two types of variables affecting the accuracy of eyewitness testimony. Estimator variables are defined as random, uncontrollable factors in actual cases of witnesses to crime. Examples of estimator variables are lighting conditions, amount of attention paid by the witness, and stress from witnessing the event. System variables, on the other hand, are controllable in actual cases. Examples of system variables are the wording of questions asked of eyewitnesses and the structure of a lineup. This distinction has been useful in developing a body of research directed at system variables, which can be used to improve the accuracy of eyewitnesses. Attempts to increase the accuracy of eyewitness evidence are based on this system-variable approach.

FISHER & GEISELMAN uses the system-variable approach to develop techniques for interviewing eyewitnesses that work better than the standard police interview. Their work describes empirically tested interview techniques that were modelled on the best practices of crime investigators and the psychological literature on human memory.

WELLS *et al.* also uses the system-variable approach but their emphasis is on eyewitness identification evidence in which police use lineups and photo arrays to get witnesses to identify a perpetrator. They review research experiments showing that lineups and photo arrays can be conducted in such a way that they promote mistaken eyewitness identifications. They also review 40 actual cases in which juries convicted innocent persons and note that mistaken identification was at the heart of 90 per cent of these cases. They recommend four "rules" that the justice system should require for the collection and interpretation of eyewitness identification evidence.

PENROD, FULERO & CUTLER applies the body of empirical evidence on eyewitness memory to the current standard (Daubert) that most courts are using for deciding whether expert testimony by social scientists on eyewitness memory can be admitted. They conclude that expert testimony on eyewitness issues is likely to pass the Daubert standard.

Research and theory on the creation of false memories have been particularly controversial when applied to claims about the recovery of repressed memories. People who claim that they were sexually abused as children but, due to repression, did not recall the abuse until adulthood, are thought by many memory experts to be recalling false memories – a phenomenon dubbed in the popular press as the false-memory syndrome. LOFTUS & KETCHAM makes a provocative empirical and theoretical case that the phenomenon of repression, as defined in popular accounts of the recovery of repressed childhood memories of abuse, is a myth. Numerous memory experts agree with Loftus that false autobiographical memories can be created by suggestion, repeated imagination, and belief in the concepts of repression and recovery of repressed memories, and hypnosis or hypnotic-like interventions. Prominent psychological scientists of the 1990s note that there is little scientific support for the concept of repression, which has origins in the writings of Freud. The issue of a false-memory syndrome remains controversial, however. POPE describes some problems with making strong scientific claims on either side of the issue.

GARY L. WELLS

F

Fabianism

Bevir, Mark, "Fabianism, Permeation, and Independent Labour", *Historical Journal*, 39/1 (1996): 179–96

Britain, Ian, *Fabianism and Culture: A Study in British Socialism and the Arts, 1884–1918*, Cambridge and New York: Cambridge University Press, 1982

Cole, Margaret, *The Story of Fabian Socialism*, London: Heinemann, and Stanford, California: Stanford University Press, 1961

Hobsbawm, E.J., "The Fabians Reconsidered" in his *Labouring Men: Studies in the History of Labour*, London: Weidenfeld and Nicolson, 1964; New York: Basic Books, 1965

McBriar, A.M., *Fabian Socialism and English Politics, 1884–1918*, Cambridge: Cambridge University Press, 1962

McCarren, Margaret Patricia, *Fabianism in the Political Life of Britain, 1919–31*, 2nd edition, Chicago: Heritage Foundation, 1954

MacKenzie, Norman and Jeanne MacKenzie, *The First Fabians*, London: Weidenfeld and Nicholson, 1977; as *The Fabians*, New York: Simon and Schuster, 1977

Pease, Edward R., *The History of the Fabian Society*, London: Allen and Unwin, and New York: Dutton, 1916; 3rd edition, London: Cass, 1963

Pugh, Patricia, *Educate, Agitate, Organize: 100 Years of Fabian Socialism*, New York and London: Methuen, 1984

Wolfe, Willard, *From Radicalism to Socialism: Men and Ideas in the Formation of the Fabian Socialist Doctrines, 1881–1889*, New Haven, Connecticut: Yale University Press, 1975

Surprisingly, there is only one scholarly history, Patricia Pugh's (see below), that traces Fabianism from its origins to the 1980s. Most works deal with the Fabian Society's founding and early years, before 1919. The majority of works are complimentary and seek to trace Fabian origins, contributions, and influences in a favourable light. Although not listed here, there are numerous biographies of Sidney and Beatrice Webb, H.G. Wells, and other founders and framers that complement the broader texts cited. Outside of Great Britain, Fabianism made its greatest impact in Australia. For Fabianism in Australia see Race Mathews, *Australia's First Fabians: Middle-Class Radicals, Labour Activists, and the Early Labour Movement* (1993). To date, an authoritative, scholarly, and complete history of Fabianism from its origins until the present covering political, social, intellectual, and cultural issues remains to be written.

PEASE pioneered modern historical scholarship on Fabianism, and his remains the best and most authoritative account of the Fabian Society's early years, although it is somewhat too favourable. Pease was the Society's secretary for 30 years, and his book reflects this positively and negatively: factually accurate, its fascinating but flattering portraits of the early founders make the book informative. Yet, it is lacking in critical analysis and is surprisingly weak on Fabianism's internal policy conflicts, especially the issue of permeation – influencing all political parties rather than creating a new party or joining an already existing one. The chapter dealing with H.G. Wells' early 1900s attempt to reorganize the Society is particularly insightful. Pease's principal theme is that Fabianism broke the spell of Marxism in Britain.

McCARREN presents a largely political history of Fabianism, strong on Fabian Society permeation and on the Society's ultimate decision to join the Labour Party. She argues that Fabianism shaped the Labour Party and eventually assumed command of it. She is strong in discussing Fabianism's role in the first and second Labour governments. Weaknesses are numerous. Her political history is one dimensional, with hardly any discussion of personalities and little of ideas. Sister Margaret McCarren is influenced by her Catholicism and the Cold War, arguing that Fabianism and communism were equatable because they were both secular, statist, and averse to republicanism. She admires Fabian ideals; but without religion she finds theirs a false mind set.

An intimate and interesting history of Fabianism from one of its members is COLE's account spanning the 1880s to 1960. Cole, like Pease, was a Fabian Society secretary, and her book presents similar strengths and weaknesses. Her critical eye and historical perspective surpass Pease, especially her willingness to discuss the founders' intellectual arrogance and their character flaws. Her main concern is with demonstrating Fabian influence over British society, culture, and politics. The anecdotal nature of the book makes it diverting. Major weaknesses are found in the post-1950 period, where her personal involvement clouds her judgement.

The first major revision of Fabian historiography comes from McBRIAR, who challenges Fabian overall impact and influence. Well researched with few errors, this scholarly work provides one of the most balanced accounts of Fabianism ever produced. McBriar argues that Fabians were not original theorists as often claimed, nor was their influence on the Labour

Party as large as hitherto argued, especially in the pre-1919 era. Nonetheless, he argues that Fabianism did affect Britain politically, especially by challenging old established opinions, removing obstacles, and making socialism appealing to middle-class liberals as well as trade unionists. Like McCarren, however, McBriar fails to bring interesting Fabian personalities to life.

A more critical, but unbalanced, account of Fabianism is found in HOBSBAWM. He argues that Fabians stemmed from neither Marxist, radical, liberal, nor working-class traditions. They were opponents of late 19th-century *laissez-faire* capitalism who, suffering status anxiety, lashed out. Fabianism's impact, he argues, has been overblown, largely by the Fabians themselves who stridently blew their own horns. Fabians did not make the Labour Party by joining it, Hobsbawn maintains – rather the Labour Party made them more important.

There are a number of excellent more specialized studies of Fabianism. WOLFE provides the best intellectual history of the society. It is well researched and very scholarly, with a sophisticated analysis of how and why Victorian Radicalism evolved into Fabian socialism. Wolfe concentrates heavily on religious forces in Fabian origins, and he skilfully blends biographical sketches of early Fabians with their broader intellectual context. He also does a good job in tracing the Fabians' growing attachment to the Labour Party, especially the hitherto neglected role of Annie Besant.

MACKENZIE & MACKENZIE complements Pease and Cole in providing a study that concentrates on the Fabians as people and thinkers. This sympathetic and very readable history-through-biography excels in animating the Fabians, showing them as eclectic and colourful. It is thoroughly researched, but like so many Fabian studies, it concentrates on the pre-1918 Fabians. There is very little on Fabian political action or the permeation question. Equally absent is any institutional history.

BRITAIN provides the most unusual study of Fabianism, seeking to connect Fabians with larger British cultural issues, especially the arts. As the first to examine the Fabians from a cultural perspective, Britain complements their own critique of Victorian culture and their role as cultural reformers. Britain seeks to show that Fabians were neither philistine nor elitist and to vindicate them of their supposed narrow utilitarianism. The book is strongest in its discussion of Fabian origins and early cultural rebellion, but later grows repetitive and somewhat dull. It also seems excessively adulatory.

Though not a Fabian, PUGH was commissioned by the Fabian Society to write its centennial history. Neither an introductory text nor an anecdotal account, the work, based on Fabian archives, is a well-written institutional history. Its strength and value lay in its extended scope, particularly the never-before-covered post-1960 Fabianism. Its discussion of the Fabian Colonial Bureau is particularly good. It is also informative on internal quarrels and crises, the Society's relation with the Labour Party, and the institutional evolution of the movement. Yet, the book is too narrowly institutional, neglects to discuss Fabian historiography, and fails to analyse the numerous Fabian publications it mentions.

BEVIR provides the most recent and best synthesis of Fabian historiography, seeking to find middle ground between the traditionalists' uncritical account of Fabianism and the revi-

sionists' harsher critiques. Bevir's strength is in the complexity of his argument, noting that Fabianism defies simple categorization. For example, Webb and Shaw, the movement's two giants, held different and changing beliefs about permeation and about aligning with the Labour Party. This honest and relatively unbiased approach to Fabianism is refreshing.

KEN MILLEN-PENN

See also Labour party (UK)

Factor analysis

Bryant, Fred B. and Paul R. Yarnold, "Principal-Components Analysis and Exploratory and Confirmatory Factor Analysis" in *Reading and Understanding Multivariate Statistics*, edited by Laurence G. Grimm and Paul R. Yarnold, Washington, DC: American Psychological Association, 1995

Cattell, Raymond B., *The Scientific Use of Factor Analysis in Behavioral and Life Sciences*, New York and London: Plenum, 1978

Dillon, William R. and Matthew Goldstein, *Multivariate Analysis: Methods and Applications*, Chichester and New York: Wiley, 1984

Everitt, Brian S., *Making Sense of Statistics in Psychology: A Second-level Course*, Oxford and New York: Oxford University Press, 1996

Gorsuch, Richard L., *Factor Analysis*, 2nd edition, Hillsdale, New Jersey: Erlbaum, 1983

Grimm, Laurence G. and Paul R. Yarnold, "Introduction to Multivariate Statistics" in *Reading and Understanding Multivariate Statistics*, edited by Laurence G. Grimm and Paul R. Yarnold, Washington, DC: American Psychological Association, 1995

Kim, Jae-on and Charles W. Mueller, *Factor Analysis: Statistical Methods and Practical Issues*, London and Beverly Hills, California: Sage, 1978

Kline, Paul, *The Handbook of Psychological Testing*, London and New York: Routledge, 1993

Stevens, James, *Applied Multivariate Statistics for the Social Sciences*, 3rd edition, Mahwah, New Jersey: Erlbaum, 1996

Tabachnick, Barbara G. and Linda S. Fidell, *Using Multivariate Statistics*, 3rd edition, New York: HarperCollins, 1996

There are many basic and advanced texts that address the mathematics and applications of factor analysis, some of which require considerable sophistication in matrix algebra. Fortunately, there also exist a number of excellent texts that assume no technical knowledge and which are targeted at students and researchers. Good introductory texts cover two important aspects. The first aspect is to comprehend the rationale that lies behind factor analysis – what is it for? – and the second aspect is concerned with practical issues in computing and interpreting factor solutions. The following texts are sufficient to provide the social scientist, not expert in multivariate statistics, with the necessary knowledge and practical tools to understand and apply factor analytical techniques.

A very simple, yet informative, guide is provided by BRYANT & YARNOLD, who present factor analysis in the context of other multivariate statistics in the social sciences. In the same text, GRIMM & YARNOLD give an excellent general overview of multivariate techniques that should help the reader locate factor analysis in relation to alternative statistical procedures. All newcomers to multivariate analysis would appreciate this text.

One of the best introductions is DILLON & GOLDSTEIN. They provide a highly informative conceptual overview of the rationale and interpretation of factor analysis. They provide a clear distinction between principal components analysis (PCA) and common factor analysis (CFA) proper; and their discussion of the interpretation of components/factors is informative. They highlight the fact that in early stages of any investigation, the researcher is faced with the problem of which and how many variables to measure. As the approach at this stage is exploratory, and there is often little theory on which hypotheses may be based, it is common to collect a large amount of quantitative data. But then the researcher is faced with the problem of summarizing and understanding these data. Even with a relatively small number of variables this task is difficult. For example, with 20 variables, there are 190 correlations to be considered; with 40 variables there are 780 correlations, and so on. The family of statistical multivariate procedures that fall under the rubric of factor analysis allow solution to this problem. However, there is little guidance on running factor analyses on available statistical packages. This text is complemented by KIM & MUELLER, who provide a delightfully short account of the fundamentals of factor analyses from a practical point of view.

An excellent student text is TABACHNICK & FIDELL. In addition to good coverage of the main issues, there are clear and useful presentations of the kinds of research questions that can be addressed by factor analysis; the importance of initial screening of data (to identify missing variables, outliers, and to assess normality, linearity, and accuracy); the theoretical and practical issues of different procedures; and limitations and caveats concerning interpretation of components/factors. Extensive examples are taken from the most popular computer package (Statistical Package for the Social Sciences, SPSS). A major strength of this text is its comparison of the major statistical packages in common use in the social sciences (SPSS, BMDP, SAS, SYSAT). A data disk is provided that allows students to practise running statistical procedures. Factor analysis is explained in relation to other multivariate techniques (such as multiple regression), which promotes understanding of the interrelation of different types of multivariate statistics available to the social scientist. STEVENS is also illustrated with SPSS outputs and presents the main issues at a somewhat more technical level. It would be appropriate for advanced students, or those who are not intimidated by mathematical notation.

In the context of psychometrics, KLINE provides a very simple introduction to factor analysis, surveying the main topics with clarity and brevity. In addition, this text is useful for understanding the association of factor analysis and theories of intelligence. Factor analysis was developed, in the early part of this century, by Charles Spearman for the purpose of uncovering the structure of human cognitive abilities. On the basis of factor analysis, the notion of a general (g) factor of intelligence was postulated, which has since proved one of the most controversial, as well as one of the most validated, ideas in the behavioural sciences. Alternative theories of intelligence, based on a variety of factoring procedures, are discussed.

EVERITT provides a useful guide to factor analysis in the behavioural sciences with a focus on its applications in psychiatry and psychology. This text is appropriate for undergraduate and postgraduate students, including research students (the inclusion of data disk allows students to work through the examples given using their own statistical programs).

CATTELL is a somewhat more advanced text. It provides a masterly survey of the important conceptual and procedural issues in a way that promotes deep understanding of the philosophical and statistical bases of factor analysis. In particular, he illustrates the role of factor analysis in the "inductive-hypothetico-deductive spiral" in the behavioural sciences: factor analysis can be used to explore inductively new domains, suggest hypotheses, and then test operational predictions. The relation of different factoring procedures to scientific models is delineated. Plasmodes are also discussed: data sets based on objects of known dimensionality (for example the three dimensions of boxes) or artificial data sets with constrained (known) dimensionality. Plasmodes are important in checking the validity and robustness of different factor analytical procedures.

A more advanced, but still accessible, text that should also lead to a deeper understanding of the use of factor analysis in science is provided by GORSUCH. There is good use of examples to explain several important issues: selection of variables; choice of extraction procedure; number of factors to extract; different forms of rotation; and psychological interpretation of components/factors. The effects of noncontinuous data and transformations of raw data are also discussed.

The above texts cover the major issues in factor analysis in a reasonably accessible and informative fashion; but as Dillon & Goldstein adopt a conceptual approach, their text is most rewarding on first reading. They describe that the first function of factor analysis is a purely statistical/descriptive one: data reduction without psychological content. Principal components analysis (PCA) is used for this purpose: this procedure extracts the same number of components as there are variables in a descending order of statistical importance. The first factor explains a higher percentage of variance than the second, and so forth; usually only the first few components, which account for the majority of the variance in the data set, are extracted. Components are merely statistically convenient summaries of complex intercorrelations

Dillon & Goldstein then describe the second function of factor analysis, which is a psychological/inferential one: the revealing of underlying psychological factors (such as general intelligence, g) that give rise in a causal sense to the nature of the intercorrelations among the variables. Common factor analysis (CFA) is used for this purpose: this procedure begins with a theoretical model of data (a small number of latent variables is sufficient to account for the interrelations of observed variables). Unlike PCA, CFA makes a distinction between common variance (shared between the variables) and unique variance (not shared between variables). Only common variance is analysed in CFA. Common factor analysis may be broken down further into two categories: exploratory and confirmatory. Exploratory analysis proceeds without a theory concerning the final composition of the factors. In contrast, confirmatory analysis is designed to test the adequacy of an explicit theory – that is, the relationship between observed variables and latent (inferred) factors (a target matrix is specified and the structure of the observed correlation matrix is compared with this target matrix, as assessed with a goodness of fit index). Coupled with path analysis, CFA is a powerful tool with which to examine a wide range of questions in the social sciences.

PHILIP J. CORR

See also Multiple regression analysis

Factortame

Craig, Paul, "Sovereignty of the United Kingdom after *Factortame*", *Yearbook of European Law*, 11 (1991): 221–55

Duddington, John, "National Law and the Treaty of Rome", *Law Teacher*, 25/1 (1991): 170–73

O'Neill, Aidan, *Decisions of the European Court of Justice and Their Constitutional Implications*, London: Butterworths, 1994

Papadias, Lambros, "Interim Protection under Community Law before the National Courts: The Right to a Judge with Jurisdiction to Grant Interim Relief", *Legal Issues of European Integration*, 11/2 (1994): 153–93

Szyszczak, Erica, "Sovereignty: Crisis, Compliance, Confusion, Complacency?", *European Law Review*, 15 (1990): 480–88

Toth, A.G., "Case-note on *Factortame*", *Common Market Law Review*, 27/3 (1990): 573–87

O'NEILL presents the cluster of cases before the national and European courts that constitute the *Factortame* case within the framework of European judgements that have affected British constitutional law to a major degree. The factual background of *Factortame* begins with the passing by the UK Parliament of the Merchant Shipping Act 1988 as a means to implement the quota system imposed by the common fisheries policy. The Merchant Shipping (Registration of Fishing Vessels) Regulations 1988, brought in under this Act, included the introduction of a new regime under which fishing vessels could register within the UK, thus acquiring British nationality, and entitling them to fall within the British fishing quotas. The validity of the new Merchant Shipping Act was immediately challenged as being contrary to European law by owners of fishing vessels that could no longer be registered in the UK under the new regime. The Court of First Instance referred the issue to the European Court for a preliminary ruling, while in the meantime, the Divisional Court made an interim order "disapplying" the Act, and allowing the registration of these fishing vessels until a final judgement by the European Court. The Secretary of State appealed against the decision of the Divisional Court before the Court of Appeal, which reversed the interim relief order. The owners of the fishing vessels appealed against this reversal and the matter reached the House

of Lords. The House upheld the reversal by the Court of Appeal on two main grounds of British law, namely that the English courts have no power to grant injunctions against the Crown and that, in England, Acts of Parliament are considered valid and compatible with EC law unless the European Court of Justice declares otherwise in a final and authoritative judgement. However, the House felt that a preliminary ruling before the European Court would be necessary in order to clarify whether this legal position from the point of view of national law was incompatible with the principles of European law. In this request, which constitutes the second *Factortame* case, the Court held that, indeed, the principle of the effective judicial protection of individuals would prohibit the application of the well-established British constitutional principle concerning interim relief. Following this ruling, the House of Lords issued an order restraining the Secretary of State from withholding or withdrawing registration of vessels under the rules of the Merchant Shipping Act.

O'Neill argues that the strong negative feelings with which *Factortame* was received in the UK were almost inevitable. In fact, the effect of this judgement in the English legal order is equivalent to the effect of *Simmenthal* in German law. However, the author feels that these emotional reactions are not justified, as the judges of the Court proceeded with a logical judgement of a narrow legal point concerning the supremacy of EC law when in conflict with any type of national legislative text.

TOTH comments on the surprisingly dramatic headlines of the national press on the rewriting of the British constitution by Brussels, and argues that the judgement of the European judges on *Factortame* was legally valid on the basis of three principles of EC law. First, the principle of supremacy, as interpreted in *Simmenthal*, signifies that national laws – even constitutional rules – may be overruled when they clash with any type of EC legislative rule. Second, the principle of complete and effective judicial protection signifies that all persons have the right to obtain an effective remedy before a competent national court against national measures that are considered incompatible with European legislation. Third, an aspect of this principle refers to the obligation of all national courts to ensure the protection of rights that individuals derive from European law, in accordance with national remedies and procedures that must be no less favourable than those relating to similar disputes of a domestic nature, and must not be such as to render impossible the exercise of EC rights in practice. Thus *Factortame* does not purport to lay down substantive conditions for granting interim relief, or to define the measures that may be ordered. It merely requires of national courts to make an already existing national remedy available in order to protect rights deriving from EC law.

SZYSZCZAK argues that *Factortame* reflects four aspects of the issue of British sovereignty and its role within the framework of the EC. The first aspect of this issue, crisis, is reflected by the concern, expressed by British commentators, that the ultimate bastion of sovereignty, the supremacy of Parliament, has finally been breached; whereas the case law of the House of Lords prior to the judgement indicated that some of the "sea walls" of sovereignty remain intact, to the dismay of applicants wishing to enforce EC law before the British courts. The second aspect of the issue, compliance, is reflected in the final implementation of the judgement of the European Court of

Justice by the House of Lords. The third aspect, confusion, is present in the confused attitude of the House of Lords in relation to giving effect to Community obligations that do not give rise to direct effects in the national courts. Last but not least, complacency as a fourth aspect of sovereignty is evident in the good record of the UK in the implementation of EC law, despite the strong objections of Margaret Thatcher on the shape that the European Communities took at the time.

DUDDINGTON characterizes *Factortame* as a momentous decision. Community law was upheld not only where there was undoubtedly a conflict between UK and EC law, but where there was a strong possibility of one. The author makes a comparison between the drafting styles of *Factortame* and *Simmenthal*, and remarks that the grand style of the latter is not evident in the first, attributing this to the anxiousness of the judges of the case to avoid excessive controversy, and to pave the way for an easier reception of the decision into the British legal order. The author concludes that *Factortame* may eventually be seen as a great victory of Community law, which, had the frontiers of a somewhat obscure tort been slightly expanded, would never have been necessary.

CRAIG examines the issue of sovereignty, both from the point of view of constitutional law, and within the framework of the European Community. The author comments that the main future implication of *Factortame* for the United Kingdom is that its courts will continue to award primacy to European legal provisions, unless either the country departs from the Community or the government departs from Community law in a particular area, such as the field of human rights. The author finds both of these eventualities highly unlikely, especially if one takes into account that sovereignty as defined by Blackstone and Dicey was not a constitutional reality, even at the time when the authors wrote. In fact, in an attempt to rediscover the broader frame of constitutional discourse that characterized the work of classical writers, one could well discover that a system of government that is both balanced and normatively justifiable is one in which there are rights-based limits on the power of Parliament, which are to be policed by the courts. Any justification for parliamentary omnipotence must be based on arguments of principle. Once matters are perceived in such a way, there is no longer any principled justification for legally unconstrained parliamentary power. We are thus lead to the conclusion that some species of rights-based constraints may appear in any convincing, principled picture of 20th-century government.

PAPADIAS uses *Factortame* as an illustration of the second era in the relationship between national and Community law, in which national judges have acquired the power to enforce EC law before the national courts.

HELEN XANTHAKI

See also European Court of Justice

Fairness

Arvey, Richard D. and Paul R. Sackett, "Fairness in Selection: Current Developments and Perspectives" in *Personnel Selection in Organizations*, edited by Neal Schmitt *et al.*, San Francisco: Jossey Bass, 1993

Baron, Helen and Karen Janman, "Fairness in the Assessment Centre" in *International Review of Industrial and Organizational Psychology*, vol. 11, edited by Cary L. Cooper and Ivan T. Robertson, Chichester and New york: Wiley, 1996

Beugré, Constant D., *Managing Fairness in Organizations*, Westport, Connecticut: Quorum, 1998

Cawley, Brian D., Lisa M. Keeping and Paul E. Levy, "Participation in the Performance Appraisal Process and Employee Reactions: A Meta-Analytic Review of Field Investigations", *Journal of Applied Psychology*, 83/4 (1998): 615–33

Cropanzano, Russell (editor), *Justice in the Workplace: Approaching Fairness in Human Resource Management*, Hillsdale, New Jersey: Erlbaum, 1993

Cropanzano, Russell and Jerald Greenberg, "Progress in Organizational Justice: Tunneling through the Maze" in *International Review of Industrial and Organizational Psychology*, vol. 12, edited by Cary L. Cooper and Ivan T. Robertson, Chichester and New York: Wiley, 1997

Folger, Robert, Mary A. Konovsky and Russell Cropanzano, "A Due Process Metaphor for Performance Appraisal" in *Research in Organizational Behavior*, 14 (1992): 129–77

Folger, Robert and Russell Cropanzano, *Organizational Justice and Human Resource Management*, Thousand Oaks, California and London: Sage, 1998

Gilliland, Stephen W., "The Perceived Fairness of Selection Systems: An Organizational Justice Perspective", *Academy of Management Review*, 18/4 (1993): 694–734

Gilliland, Stephen W. and Jay C. Langdon, "Creating Performance Management Systems That Promote Perceptions of Fairness" in *Performance Appraisal: State of the Art in Practice*, edited by James W. Smither, San Francisco: Jossey Bass, 1998

Greenberg, Jerald, *The Quest for Justice on the Job: Essays and Experiments*, Thousand Oaks, California and London: Sage, 1996

Mitchell, Terence R., "Matching Motivational Strategies with Organizational Contexts" in *Research in Organizational Behavior*, 19 (1997): 57–149

Newell, Susan, *The Healthy Organization: Fairness, Ethics, and Effective Management*, London and New York: Routledge, 1995

Novelli, Luke, Bradley L. Kirkman and Debra L. Shapiro, "Effective Implementation of Organizational Change: An Organizational Justice Perspective" in *Trends in Organizational Behaviour*, vol. 2, edited by Cary L. Cooper and Denise M. Rousseau, Chichester: Wiley, 1995

Pinder, Craig C., *Work Motivation in Organizational Behavior*, Upper Saddle River, New Jersey: Prentice Hall, 1998

Sheppard, Blair H., Roy J. Lewicki and John W. Minton, *Organizational Justice: The Search for Fairness in the Workplace*, New York: Lexington Books, 1992

Fairness, or organizational justice, became one of the "hot" topics in the social sciences in the 1990s and consequently the body of literature has expanded. This entry will concentrate on justice concepts as applied in organizational (especially employment) settings, drawing on the organizational behaviour and human resource management literatures.

Probably the most useful starting point for gaining rapid access to the fairness literature is CROPANZANO & GREENBERG. This provides a relatively brief survey of the literature on organizational justice: as well as explaining the basic justice concepts, they provide an overview of research on fairness in organizational settings. As an alternative, consider the chapter on "Equity, Justice, and Fairness in the Workplace" in PINDER: this, too, covers the basic theory but has less wide-ranging coverage of relevant organizational research.

For fuller treatments than either of the above turn to one of the general texts on fairness at work. Though superseded in some respects by more recent volumes, two texts that appeared in the early 1990s merit consultation. SHEPPARD, LEWICKI & MINTON present a model of fairness in the workplace and review justice theory and research related to human resource management practices. The volume edited by CROPANZANO includes an historical overview and other general chapters on justice as well as ones dealing with fairness and particular human resource management practices such as appraisal, pay, managing layoffs, and grievances. GREENBERG is rather different as a general treatment of fairness. This is a volume of collected works and is important because the author has been one of the key theorists and researchers on fairness in organizations. This reproduces papers by the author that were published from the mid-1980s through to the mid-1990s: this volume is a convenient source for these often-cited papers.

However, readers looking for a comprehensive and up-to-date source should go to either BEUGRÉ or FOLGER & CROPANZANO. Both survey justice concepts and review research on fairness and various aspects of human resource management. Although largely academic in orientation, Beugré concludes with a chapter that has an applied focus: practical advice is offered, but this is not a "how to do it" text. Much that is practically useful also can be derived from Folger & Cropanzano; this, however, is predominantly a critical text mostly concerned with theory and research and directed towards the academic community. Because of their recency and comprehensiveness, these two are probably the most useful sources.

The pervasive nature of justice in the fields of organizational behaviour/human resource management is evident from these general overviews. So, for example, as Pinder indicates, there is a close association between theorizing on motivation and that on organizational justice; these linkages are also explored by MITCHELL. Increasingly, we have seen core topics in organizational behaviour examined from a justice perspective – organizational change, is one fairly recent example (NOVELLI, KIRKMAN & SHAPIRO). Similarly, the reading by FOLGER, KONOVSKY & CROPANZANO (see also Folger & Cropanzano) presented a reconceptualization of the nature of the performance appraisal process. Although some earlier research had examined justice concerns in performance appraisal (see, for example, Greenberg), Folger, Konovsky & Cropanzano offered a critical analysis that compared different perspectives on performance evaluation. Other researchers have taken justice concepts as an organizing framework, as in the case of the meta-analytic study of participation in appraisal by

CAWLEY, KEEPING & LEVY. More recently, and reflecting the shift in terminology from appraisal/evaluation to performance management, GILLILAND & LANGDON have provided a practitioner-orientated review of relevant research.

Thus, one trend that we have seen in the justice literature is the application of fairness concepts to more and more organizational phenomena. Another key trend has been the broadening of the fairness concept. This is well illustrated with reference to employee selection, one of the main domains in which fairness research has been conducted. Much of this research has been stimulated by the practical concern to ensure that selection procedures do not discriminate unfairly (and unlawfully) against those groups protected in law. NEWELL provides an examination of unfairness as unlawful discrimination, and sets her review in the broader, contemporary context of managing diversity. Readers looking for a review of the evidence about the fairness of selection procedures might start with BARON & JANMAN. This takes a more traditional and narrow perspective of fairness. Though about assessment centres, their component methods are considered separately. Their concern was originally primarily with the impact of selection methods on outcomes (for example is there bias such that women are discriminated against as compared to men?), but interest has broadened to include such matters as the content and operation of the procedures themselves. This shift reflects the broadening of our understanding of the concept of fairness, a theme that is taken up in the chapter by ARVEY & SACKETT and the paper by GILLILAND.

RICHARD WILLIAMS

See also Equal opportunity, equal pay, Human resource management, Organizational behaviour survey

Fairness and socialization

Allport, Floyd Henry, *Institutional Behavior: Essays Towards a Re-interpreting of Contemporary Social Organization*, Chapel Hill: University of North Carolina Press, 1933

Buss, David M., *Evolutionary Psychology: The New Science of the Mind*, Boston: Allyn and Bacon, 1999

Freud, Sigmund, *Civilization and Its Discontents*, London: Hogarth Press, and New York: Cape and Smith, 1930 (German edition 1930)

Gergen, K.J., "Social Psychology as History", *Journal of Personality and Social Psychology*, 26 (1973): 309–20

Hartshorne, Hugh and Mark A. May, *Studies in Deceit*, book 1: *General Methods and Results*, book 2: *Statistical Methods and Results*, New York: Macmillan, 1928

Heider, Fritz, *The Psychology of Interpersonal Relations*, New York: Wiley, 1958

Lewin, Kurt, *A Dynamic Theory of Personality: Selected Papers*, New York: McGraw Hill, 1935

McDougall, William, *An Introduction to Social Psychology*, 31st edition, London: Methuen, and New York: Barnes and Noble, 1960 (1st edition 1908)

Mead, George H., *Mind, Self, and Society: From the Standpoint of a Social Behaviorist*, Chicago: University Chicago Press, 1934

Sherman, Charles L., *The Moral Self: An Introduction to the Science of Ethics*, Boston: Ginn, 1927

Skinner, B.F., *Cumulative Record: A Selection of Papers*, 3rd edition, New York: Appleton Century Crofts, 1972

Wundt, Wilhelm Max, *Völkerpsychologie*, 10 vols, Leipzig: Englemann, 1900–20

There might be no conflict without notions of fairness and socialization. Or so might a naive phenomenological analysis of conflict suggest. Without notions of socialization – that people and cultural products of people affect people – conflict could not involve interpersonal and intrapersonal effects. Without notions of fairness – that there are more and less preferred modes in which people and their cultural products affect people and in which such effects are influenced – conflict could not involve motives to influence interpersonal and intrapersonal effects.

In the context of the vital linkages among socialization, fairness, and conflict, one might note that these constructs – as far as they have ontological validity – are the most crucial to the study and practice of political psychology. In fact, a reading of the history of social psychological theory and research as inferred from its major contributors – an important source for political psychology – could suggest that this history has ultimately been about fairness, socialization, and conflict.

The contemporary history of social psychology is usually viewed as beginning with Wilhelm WUNDT in the late 19th century. His *Volkerpsychologie* can be construed as describing national character(s) in a very comprehensive manner. Each national character denotes the structure, function, process, and content of socialization, and socialization's own self-reflexive properties. This self-reflexion leads to variants of fairness. In fact, one can infer from Wundt that conflict is unavoidable due to the self-reflexion of socialization and of fairness. Of course, this is also the case when different *Volkerpsychologies* come into contact.

In the early 20th century William McDOUGALL posited a number of socially defined instincts that seemed to imply a biological primacy engendering social behaviour – a bottom-up approach – over a sociological primacy or top-down approach. Fairness arose as a psychological superstructure from conflicts within, between, and among instincts of one person as well as the various combinations of conflict between and among people. Many scholars consider McDougall's work and much that came after him – until very recently – as a drawing back from Wundt's comprehensiveness.

SHERMAN's work on the moral self attributed socialization to a number of layers of analysis from the biological through to metaphysical. Unlike Wundt's work, however, Sherman's research focuses much more heavily on rationalism than empiricism. Notions of fairness and other elements of justice were deemed to be multidetermined. Sherman's construct of moral self was the product of, and was destined to navigate, continuous conflict.

In 1928, HARTSHORNE & MAY reported a series of studies carried on over several years by the Character Education Inquiry. The focus of this extensive web of empirical work was on the precursors and correlates of deception. The precursors and correlates studied were conceived as socialization variables. Deception was studied in the context of being "unfair."

Deception also was conceived as something placing the individual in conflict both with internal and external psychosocial standards. Finally, national character comparisons were made as to socialization, fairness, and conflict via the deception construct. Hartshorne & May's empirical foundation – while admirable – lacked theoretical breadth.

In 1930, Floyd ALLPORT examined socialization processes in an institutional setting. The most salient focus of this examination was on notions of fairness as it applied to institutional functioning. Notions of fairness were based on patterns of social stimulation and social consciousness. Allport also closely studied the interrelationships of the social self, social conflict, and social behaviour. Lastly, his work was intended to contain a significant applied significance.

FREUD delineated the sequelae of socialization, such as conceptions of fairness and varieties of intrapersonal and interpersonal conflict. The psychodynamic approach to social conflict also focused on the continuous compromise formations – within individuals through societies at large – leading to crests and troughs in the salience of various approaches to fairness, in social order, and even social progress.

MEAD analysed how the individual develops a sense of self – self-consciousness – through social interaction via language and symbol. This symbolic interactionist approach to socialization suggested that any social psychological interaction had the potential for conflict, because the fairness of the interaction would become salient. Mead has been read as both espousing a determinist bent to evolving conceptions of the self and fairness and a freedom of self-construction and social constructions of fairness. The latter has been congruent with existential philosophers' contention that consciousness is free to form the self and seems to be a forerunner of psychology's postmodernist dalliance.

LEWIN's topological studies integrated the dynamic approaches of Freud and his disciples with empirical and experimental activities soon to be labelled "action research". Here the individual was immersed in a dynamic field of continuous socialization, fairness was often conceived as a class of valence relationships between the social actors and social stimulus objects, and conflict was engendered by impediments to acting on the motive forces arising from these relationships.

HEIDER issued an extremely significant work that can be construed as an analysis of notions of fairness arising from socialization experiences. Heider virtually reified balance theories that, in retrospect, seem to be based on Lewin's valence construct and variants of social comparison theories. When the various elements between, within, and among a perceiver and social stimulus and social object configurations were not balanced, unfairness was perceived and the perceiver was in conflict or perceived conflict between and among configural elements. Conflict – as with Lewin – engendered a motive force seeking its own self dissolution.

By the time SKINNER's collection of papers in *Cumulative Record* was published, socialization, fairness, and conflict could be explicated by a number of researchers influenced by the variants of behaviourism. Skinner focused on behaviours and reinforcement histories per se, but other researchers attempted to integrate the behaviourist with the dynamic. These latter behaviourists have seemed to be less than successful in parsing fairness as the content of lay phenomenology, characteristics of a behavioural system, or covert responses labelling behavioural contingencies.

GERGEN's research from 1973 through the mid-1990s seemed at first to threaten the very constructs of fairness and socialization. While most previous work in the behavioural sciences intimated some immutable standard of fairness and adaptive socialization, Gergen's historical take on social psychology and his focus on the social construction and transformation of knowledge often was construed as a radical relativism without moral and ethical bearings. More recent interpretations suggest less radicalism and in fact a very strenuous moral and ethical engagement.

BUSS' evolutionary psychology textbook, published in 1999, in some surprising ways is a throwback to the work of Wundt with its biopsychosocial and empirical emphases. Both socialization and fairness are taken as evolved psychological mechanisms that help resolve conflict exemplified as impediments to survival and reproduction.

The huge mass of 20th-century social science theory and research bearing on fairness and socialization constitutes but varying combinations of the classical sources described above. Through social construction, social transformation, and psychocultural evolution, the future may see but the same and different combinations of these sources. This conclusion may be perceived by many in the field as conflictogenic, conflictopathic, and/or offered by a reviewer that has not been appropriately socialized and is not appropriately fair. Such a perception could only underline the fairness of social psychology as a source of enlightenment about fairness and socialization – as opposed to the humanities and other social sciences.

RICHARD BLOOM

False memory syndrome

Brenneis, C. Brooks, *Recovered Memories of Trauma: Transferring the Present to the Past*, Madison, Connecticut: International Universities Press, 1996

Hacking, Ian, *Rewriting the Soul: Multiple Personality and the Sciences of Memory*, Princeton, New Jersey: Princeton University Press, 1995

Herman, Judith Lewis, *Trauma and Recovery*, New York: Basic Books, 1992

Loftus, Elizabeth, "The Reality of Repressed Memories", *American Psychologist*, 48/5 (1993): 518–37

Loftus, Elizabeth and Katherine Ketcham, *The Myth of Repressed Memory: False Memories and Allegations of Sexual Abuse*, New York: St Martin's Press, 1994

Ofshe, Richard and Ethan Watters, *Making Monsters: False Memories, Psychotherapy, and Sexual Hysteria*, New York: Scribner, 1994

Pendergrast, Mark, *Victims of Memory: Incest Accusations and Shattered Lives*, 2nd edition, Hinesburg, Vermont: Upper Access, and London: HarperCollins, 1996

Pillemer, David B., *Momentous Events, Vivid Memories*, Cambridge, Massachusetts: Harvard University Press, 1998

Prager, Jeffrey, *Presenting the Past: Psychoanalysis and the Sociology of Misremembering*, Cambridge, Massachusetts: Harvard University Press, 1998

Rather than referring to a distinct psychiatric disorder, the false memory syndrome (FMS) epitomizes the stance of the sceptics, as opposed to the believers, on recovered memories of child abuse. This characterization expresses the polemic and ideological colour of the debate. In the 1980s, therapists in the US claimed that adult memories of infantile sexual abuse of which there was no prior conscious knowledge ("repressed memories") could be recovered during the course of psychotherapy (recovered memory therapy – RMT). By the 1990s, the debate polarized in the RMT Movement versus the FMS Foundation. From the mid 1990s, more scholarly and less polemical publications have been produced, discussing related topics of memory and trauma, the nature of psychotherapy, and the present culture of victimization. The selection of sources presented here not only highlights the major tenets of the debate, but also provides the necessary contextualization.

HACKING uses multiple personality and its link with child abuse to address the more general question as to why it has "been essential to organize so many of our present projects in terms of memory?" (p.3). He dissects the various aspects of the contemporary multiple personality epidemic (including the false versus recovered memories controversy), and traces its history back to the late 19th century, when the "sciences of memory" came into being. Gradually, he develops a convincing argument for interpreting the present wars over memory and forgetting in terms of "memoro-politics", power struggles built around "claims to knowledge" about memory. Scholarly, eloquent, and presented from the point of view of an outsider, Hacking is a philosopher of science, *Rewriting the Soul* offers a critical and comprehensive analysis of the present and the historical ramifications of the FMS debate.

The first part of *Trauma and Recovery* comprises an analysis of the history of the study of psychic "trauma" (and hence how society deals with trauma) in terms of the psychic mechanisms discernible in victims of (sexual) trauma (for example, amnesia, repression, denial, dissociation). Harvard psychiatrist HERMAN concludes that it takes a political movement to ensure serious research into trauma; in the case of (child) sexual abuse, this necessary political support is identified as the women's movement. The second part of the book addresses how adult women can "recover" from their past abuse through psychotherapy. Here, the political commitment is translated in the therapist's (necessary) involvement with the suffering of the patient. Herman's highly popular book presents a partisan yet well-documented argument for addressing the psychic effects of trauma, both on the level of society and in the consulting room. Hailed by the believers and criticized by the sceptics, if read in its own right, it presents a less ideological stance than is generally assumed.

LOFTUS, a cognitive psychologist, was drawn into the debate via her involvement as an expert witness on memory and eyewitness testimonies (the 1990 Franklin case). Her theory on the malleability of memory, based on experimental research, encompasses a conception of memory as a creative process. Her landmark article on repressed memories highlights the ways in which the RM/FM debate has affected the legal domain (for example, juror simulation studies), but is also a serious attempt at understanding the so-called reality of repressed memories through experimental memory research. The more popular *The Myth of Repressed Memory*, written with the help of a professional writer, documents the emotionally disruptive impact of the FMS debate by telling the stories of accusers and accused. Despite the dramatic tone of these stories, Loftus tries to keep her distance both from the sceptics and the believers, although she argues that research does not substantiate the existence of so-called repressed memories. LOFTUS & KETCHAM also draw attention to the influence of suggestive psychotherapeutic techniques and self-help literature (for example Bass, Ellen and Laura Davis, *The Courage to Heal*, 1988). They situate the debate within the larger cultural, moralizing climate about sexual abuse and its psychopathological sequels, but they mainly focus on how memories can be implanted.

OFSHE & WATTERS explicitly argue that "the practice of uncovering repressed memories, along with the attendant theories of multiple personality and satanic-cult abuse, are fads as widespread and as damaging as any the mental-health field has produced this century" (p.5). *Making Monsters* presents a well-founded critique of the RMT movement, taking into consideration theoretical as well as practical, individual as well as social aspects of the problem. The authors write with great clarity and conviction, with contributions from a personal involvement (Ofshe, a social psychologist, was involved as an expert in the Ingram case). They also rely on first-hand interview data, next to written sources. However, the limitations of their theses must be kept in mind. Their critique of RMT becomes an argument against psychotherapy in general – which is, according to the authors, strongly rooted in Freudian tradition – for being pseudoscientific and floating on suggestion. In this respect, *Making Monsters* represents a missed opportunity to deal with the delicate question of the role suggestion takes within all forms of therapy.

PENDERGRAST, journalist and author, is also personally involved in the debate as an accused father. The book is exposing the unbelievability and unscientific nature of the whole debate and provides an extensive overview of its stakes. It includes interviews with the various parties involved (therapists, survivors, retractors, accused parents), as well as an account of his own case. He also tries to reconstruct the essential contextual elements determining the debate (popular psychology, the media, feminism, and the fragmentation of the family), linking the phenomenon to earlier phenomena like hypnotism and mesmerism and putting the present debate into a historical perspective (drawing for instance on the Salem witch trials). His strongest and most effective assaults are reserved for *The Courage to Heal*, the bible of the repressed memory movement. The author makes a strong case for the argument that what began as a way to empower women has now victimized them, isolating them from their friends and families.

BRENNEIS is one of the first to take into account the clinical work of psychoanalytically oriented therapists. Combining the results of research conducted within various fields (cognitive research on memory, psychological research on suggestion and compliance, abuse and trauma, psychotherapeutic literature), he successfully bridges the gap between experimental research and psychoanalytic experience. Presented as a plea for informed scepticism rather than radical disbelief, he provides a well-informed and important synthesis of the clinical aspects of the debate. As such, he challenges the supposed links between clinical signs and trauma; the socially constructed nature of memory; and the interplay of memory, belief, and suggestion. Eventually arriving at the impossibility of eliminating the reciprocal unconscious influence (rather than suggestion) in the therapeutic context, he contends that (therapeutic) relationship dynamics are at the core of the recovered memories, especially in the context of so-called dissociative disorders. The book's title mirrors its central hypothesis that what cannot be directly worded in the present – therapeutic experience – is removed to the past. Recovered memories act as metaphors for present experience.

At the core of PRAGER's book is the case of a woman who began to recall scenes of her own childhood sexual abuse during the course of her analysis, but who subsequently came to believe that the trauma she remembered as a physical violation might have been an emotional one, the memory having been composed out of present and past relationships. Prager's analysis is particularly powerful on the point of the complex interaction of the individual and the collective. Trained as a sociologist and a psychoanalyst, he convincingly shows how memory is situated in interpersonal contexts. Independent of, but in the same vein as Brenneis, he illustrates how difficult it is, from a therapeutic point of view, to avoid the trap of becoming involved in the patient's system without alienating the patient. One of the major mechanisms he stipulates is that the widespread public dialogue about (sexual) abuse leads fragile individuals to seek and find external explanations for personal problems, whereby the external explanation objectifies the individual's unhappiness. Synthesizing research from social science, psychoanalysis, neuroscience, and cognitive psychology, he uses clinical examples to argue more generally that our memories are never simple records of events, but are constantly evolving constructions, affected by contemporary culture as well as by our own private lives. He demonstrates the need for sociology to rely on the insights of psychoanalysis, and the need for psychoanalysis to take account of the insights of sociology.

PILLEMER's book is in many ways similar to Prager's. He speaks in terms of scripts or schemas, which determine the way we view the world; events (such as traumas) can change these scripts and have a major impact on how we view and engage with the world.

He stresses the constructionist nature of memories, arguing in favour of a psychotherapy that helps to identify the holes in the patient's stories and which provides a coherent story through which the patient can carry on with his or her life. As such the truth of a memory is no longer a major criterion for psychotherapy.

KATRIEN LIBBRECHT

See also Mass hysteria

Family

Baber, Kristine M. and Katherine R. Allen, *Women and Families: Feminist Reconstructions*, New York and London: Guilford Press, 1992
Bilton, Tony, Kevin Bonnett, Pip Jones, David Skinner, Michelle Stanworth and Andrew Webster, "Theorising

Modern Family Life" in *Introductory Sociology*, edited by Tony Bilton *et al.*, 3rd edition, London: Macmillan, 1996

Cheal, David, *New Poverty: Families in Postmodern Society*, Westport, Connecticut: Greenwood Press, 1996

Cherlin, Andrew J., *Public and Private Families: A Reader*, Boston: McGraw Hill, 1996

Elliot, Faith Robertson, *Gender, Family and Society*, Basingstoke: Macmillan, and New York: St Martin's Press, 1996

Finch, Janet and Jennifer Mason, *Negotiating Family Responsibilities*, London and New York: Routledge, 1993

Hochschild, Arlie and Anne Machung, *The Second Shift: Working Parents and the Revolution at Home*, New York: Viking, 1989

James, Allison and Alan Prout (editors), *Constructing and Reconstructing Childhood: Contempory Issues in the Sociological Study of Childhood*, London and New York: Falmer Press, 1990

Morgan, David H.J., *Family Connections: An Introduction to Family Studies*, Cambridge: Polity Press, and Cambridge, Massachusetts: Blackwell, 1996

Stacey, Judith, *Brave New Families: Stories of Domestic Upheaval in Late Twentieth Century America*, New York: Basic Books, 1990

Understanding family life requires engaging with a wide range of conceptual debates including the relationship between the family and the State; the relationship between the paid labour market and the domestic labour market; and broader debates on gender relations, sexuality, and social change. This selection offers some introductory books, and some overviews, useful for undergraduate teaching or for those new to the field, and then some fine examples of studies that convey the complexity and fluidity of contemporary family life in Western societies.

The chapter on theorizing modern family life in the third edition of BILTON *et al.* is a good introduction to family sociology. The chapter clearly illustrates how family structures are culturally and historically specific. The major theoretical frameworks for understanding family life are outlined. There are sections on functionalist, Marxist, feminist, human agency, and poststructuralist approaches. For the most part, topics are dealt with in a concise but sophisticated manner. The specific section on postmodern theorizing is a little reactionary but at least an attempt is made to include this kind of material. By contrast, the sections on discourses on family life are useful and innovative for an introductory text. The chapter on the family in the second edition remains useful as a succinct introduction to changing sociological understandings of family life from the 1950s–1980s. In particular, the outline and critique of the "march of progress theories" is well done.

CHERLIN's introduction is a standard family studies textbook containing information, mainly from the US. It covers an impressive range of topics including broad themes such as families and race, ethnicity, class and the State, and topics on family interaction such as sexuality, family formation, partnerships, and marriage. There are chapters on power and conflict, links across the generations and demographic change. The strength of the book is that it pulls together a wide range of research and presents the material in an accessible way. The weakness is that sociological theory on the family is only briefly discussed.

ELLIOT provides more of an issues-based introduction to family sociology than one based around theoretical traditions. This is an accessible book with a focus on recent changes in family life. Much of the data and literature referred to are from the UK but there are some comparisons with other Western societies. There are chapters on ethnic differentiation, economic restructuring and unemployment, population ageing, violence and sexual abuse, and the AIDS epidemic.

MORGAN provides more of an overview for a reader with some knowledge of the field than an introduction in *Family Connections*. The book traces recent developments in family sociology, particularly in the British context. It describes the influence of Marxism and feminism on debates about the family and promotes more of a poststructural perspective. Topics discussed include the relationship between paid work and family life, the impact of class and stratification on families, and the importance of gender in understanding families. Morgan innovatively connects family practices to other current sociological topics such as sociology of the body, time and space, and food. He also provides useful ideas on where and how family sociology could develop.

For an overview of research on families from a feminist perspective, BABER & ALLEN's book is useful. They concentrate on research from the US and place "women as members of families" at the centre of their analysis. Their outline of postmodern theory is not particularly strong. In practice their "postmodern feminist" perspective means they just take diversity seriously. Nevertheless, their review chapters are a good way into a vast literature. There are chapters on the variety of women's adult relationships, sexualities, reproductive lives, caregiving, and work. Baber & Allen usefully highlight the gaps in research on families.

Children's issues are often neglected, even in family sociology. The interesting collection of articles edited by JAMES & PROUT corrects this tendency. Like family, childhood is not a single or universal phenomenon. Hendrick's chapter discusses historical changes in British understandings of childhood while Boyden points to the dominance and globalization of Western conceptions of childhood. The other articles provide good examples of research on childhood and critiques of dominant understandings of childhood.

For a detailed picture of contemporary family life STACEY's book is highly recommended. The contextualizing chapters of the study are very useful. The introduction is a concise outline of the making and breaking of the modern family, whereas the conclusion draws out the implications of the research to outline movement toward the postmodern family. The core of the book is a wonderfully rich ethnography of two families and post-industrial life in Silicon Valley in the US. Stacey found that a variety of new relationships not defined by blood ties and traditional gender roles are supplanting the traditional nuclear family. Stacey charts the contradictory influences of religion and feminism on the lives of these families.

HOCHSCHILD discusses the consequences of women moving into the paid labour market and men's reluctance to take responsibility for domestic labour. She labels this change in paid work but lack of change in unpaid work the "stalled revolution". Based on interviews with working parents living in California (US) she found that most men and women were "transitionals" holding a combination of traditional and egalitarian understandings of housework. Despite the diversity the women did much more domestic labour than their partners. The strength of Hochschild's work is in the powerful case studies she presents showing the diversity and contradictions in the way meanings are attached to domestic labour arrangements by individual women and men and the compromises made. This is a stimulating and insightful discussion of the topic.

For a discussion of kin relationships outside the nuclear family FINCH & MASON is recommended. The book draws on a quantitative survey and qualitative interviews on family responsibilities and reciprocity with people in Manchester (UK). They found that, in contrast with common understandings of the isolation of the nuclear family, relationships with wider kin remain an important part of most people's lives. Finch & Mason show how family support is negotiated over time rather than given automatically. They outline the material and moral dimensions of wider family responsibilities. They critique notions of duty and rules of obligation and instead discuss the construction and reconstruction of family commitments.

In more of a macrosociological vein, CHEAL argues that new types of family poverty have emerged with postmodernization. He compares government statistics from the United States and Canada to make his case. Cheal argues that "new poverty" is a conjunction of increased family instability and increased employment instability. One of his more provocative arguments is that the Welfare State in these countries actively creates inequality by supporting the elderly over children, particularly children in sole-parent female-headed families and large families. In sum, this is a useful account of recent developments and the relationship between families and the state.

JO LINDSAY

Family therapy

Ackerman, Nathan Ward, *The Psychodynamics of Family Life: Diagnosis and Treatment of Family Relationships*, New York: Basic Books, 1958

Bateson, Gregory, *Mind and Nature: A Necessary Unity*, New York: Dutton, 1978; London: Wildwood House, 1979

Broderick, Carlfred B. and Sandra S. Schrader, "The History of Professional Marriage and Family Therapy" in *Handbook of Family Therapy*, vol. 2, edited by Alan S. Gurman and David P. Kniskern, 1991

Family Therapy Networker, 1982–

Framo, James L., *Family-of-Origin Therapy: An Intergenerational Approach*, New York: Brunner/Mazel, 1992

Gladding, Samuel T., *Family Therapy: History, Theory, and Practice*, 2nd edition, Upper Saddle River, New Jersey: Merrill, 1998

Gurman, Alan S. and David P. Kniskern (editors), *Handbook of Family Therapy*, vol 2, New York: Brunner/Mazel, 1991

Haley, Jay, *The Power Tactics of Jesus Christ and Other Essays*, 2nd edition, Rockville, Maryland: Triangle Press, 1986

Kadis, Leslie B. and Ruth McClendon, *Concise Guide to Marital and Family Therapy*, Washington, DC: American Psychiatric Press, 1998

Minuchin, Salvador, *Families and Family Therapy*, Cambridge, Massachusetts: Harvard University Press, and London: Tavistock, 1974; new edition London: Routledge, 1991

Piercy, Fred P. *et al.*, *Family Therapy Sourcebook*, 2nd edition, New York: Guilford Press, 1996

Whitaker, Carl A. and William M. Bumberry, *Dancing with the Family: A Symbolic-Experiential Approach*, New York: Brunner/Mazel, 1988

White, Michael and David Epston, *Narrative Means to Therapeutic Ends*, New York: Norton, 1990

Zeig, Jeffrey K. (editor), *The Evolution of Psychotherapy: The Second Conference*, New York: Brunner/Mazel, 1992

From its origins in the post-World War II period, family therapy has enjoyed phenomenal growth, both in the number of its practitioners and in its inspiration of new theories concerning the development of psychological symptoms and new therapeutic techniques. GURMAN & KNISKERN is an excellent starting point for the reader seeking a thorough understanding of this field. The articles, written by leading family therapists, provide a clear exposition of the variety of therapeutic models and techniques. At this point in its development as a young profession, family therapy is characterized by the presence of numerous distinct schools and theoretical orientations. It is a challenge for the reader to reconcile the divergent approaches. BRODERICK & SCHRADER provides a concise history of this movement including a description of its origins in psychoanalytic and behavioural therapies as well as the major schools and theoretical frameworks that have emerged.

PIERCY *et al.* also provides a solid overview of the field, identifying the seminal works and ideas in each subfield within family therapy. Excellent summaries and definitions of key concepts help the reader deal with a field that has developed an often confusing array of concepts and accompanying jargon. Well-chosen annotated bibliographies help guide readers through the key published works, and direct them to the resources essential for more in-depth exploration of the field.

Not every reader will be interested in such comprehensive overviews, and KADIS & McCLENDON provides a concise and practical guide to the nuts and bolts of family therapy with the medical practitioner in mind.

It is sometimes difficult for the reader to clearly differentiate among competing theoretical approaches. GLADDING is suitable for senior undergraduate reading, and provides good summaries of each school of family therapy, comparing and contrasting it with other approaches.

Although each of the above works will provide a general grounding in the field, the richness and variety of family therapy can be found in the writings of family therapists themselves. These works are often personal and provocative; some are even visionary in the way they look at family or social problems in new ways. The differences among the following authors are rooted in some of the important social and philosophical ideas of our day and based upon differing notions of the nature of humanity, family, pathology, and change. ACKERMAN is by one of the early pioneers in the field, and describes the first tentative steps away from a purely psycho-dynamic model to one that explores how one person's pathology is affected by others'. A quarter of a century later, FRAMO describes family therapy in a more contemporary model. This model is based upon psychodynamic Object-Relations Theory, and is also intergenerational in its focus, looking at the historical roots of current problems. In contrast WHITAKER, written by a dynamic figure in family therapy, develops a therapeutic model that is atheoretical and experiential. This monograph presents the therapist's personal view of the therapy process through extensive commentary illustrating verbatim therapy sessions.

BATESON is a pioneering work on family communication. It includes the development of the popular concept of double bind, which arose in the course of the author's study of schizophrenia. The Mental Research Institute in Palo Alto continued work, not only on communication but also on brief and strategic interventions.

HALEY is a selection of essays on the therapeutic situation that both stirs controversy and provides insight into the special nature of therapeutic situations. It reflects the author's concerns with power and control in therapy. MINUCHIN's work with Black and Puerto Rican inner city children in New York gave rise to a family therapy model that focused on realigning family structures and roles. The author's key formulations in structural family therapy are clearly outlined with good use of annotated verbatim transcripts of therapy sessions.

WHITE & EPSTON presents a clear account and good introduction to the concepts of Narrative Therapy. This is a postmodern approach based upon Michael Foucault's theories, and is emerging as an influential movement within family therapy. It draws upon these ideas in order to overcome the disempowerment and objectification that clients have experienced. Clients rewrite their own personal stories or narratives in order to discover possible outcomes that differ from those to which their experience has constrained them.

New developments in the field can be followed in both the scientific and professional journals. While there are numerous scholarly journals in this field, one publication, *FAMILY THERAPY NETWORKER*, deserves special attention. This journal is written for professional marriage and family therapists in a readable and popular format, and is also appropriate for the informed lay reader. Topical issues and current controversies are discussed in an open dialogue.

Finally, ZEIG allows the reader to set the issues and controversies of family therapy approaches within the context of broader psychotherapeutic theory and practice. These conference proceedings provide an opportunity to read a dialogue between leading exponents of family therapy including Minuchin, Haley, Whitaker, Madanes, and Selvini-Palazzolli and those representing other psychotherapeutic orientations, including Ellis and Meichenbaum (cognitive-behavioural), Glasser (reality), and Rossi (mind-body work).

GEORGE LUCKI

See also Marital therapy

Famine

Arnold, David, *Famine: Social Crisis and Historical Change*, Oxford and New York: Blackwell, 1988

Boserup, Esther, *The Conditions of Agricultural Growth: The Economics of Agrarian Change under Population Pressure*, New York: Aldine, and London: Allen and Unwin, 1965

Castro, Josué de, *The Geopolitics of Hunger*, New York: Monthly Review Press, 1977

Dréze, Jean and Amartya Sen, *Hunger and Public Action*, Oxford: Clarendon Press, and New York: Oxford University Press, 1989

Malthus, Thomas, *An Essay on the Principle of Population*, enlarged edition, London: J. Johnson, 1803; edited by Patricia James, 2 vols, Cambridge and New York: Cambridge University Press, 1989

Raikes, Philip, *Modernising Hunger: Famine, Food Surplus, and Farm Policy in the EEC and Africa*, London: Currey, 1988

Sen, Amartya, *Poverty and Famines: An Essay on Entitlement and Deprivation*, Oxford: Clarendon Press, and New York: Oxford University Press, 1981

Watts, Michael and David Goodman, *Globalising Food: Agrarian Questions and Global Restructuring*, London and New York: Routledge, 1997

The problematic of famine is not easy to fathom, especially given that the literature on famine is now vast and growing rapidly. There have been disappointingly few books of a general interpretative nature as the subject has seemingly lent itself to more detailed monographs and papers than to broader or comparative discussion. The complexities of famines are also historically and geographically specific so such analyses may well be of limited value. In order to map a pathway through this literature it is advisable to begin with a selection of the seminal contributions to this subject such as MALTHUS or SEN. Such works should be read alongside a number of broader, comparative discussions of famine which review issues of definition and theories of causation. The geographical distribution of famines is constantly changing but sub-Saharan Africa has been particularly badly affected in recent years and so there is now a growing literature on food shortages in Africa. In order to move toward a nuanced and critical understanding of the literature on famine it is useful to consider a number of regional analyses of famine and starvation and to consult literature on the globalization of world food production and distribution.

Malthus is often associated with the beginnings of historical scholarship in theorizing the causation of famine. In outlining his vision of the dangers of "over-population", the fertility of man, and that of the soil are fused together as the limits of human reproduction were seen as directly linked to the earth's carrying capacity and available food supply. The thesis that some inevitable and inexorable tendency for the human population to outstrip subsistence had a profound influence on subsequent discussion of the topic. Concerned by a "great law of necessity, which prevents population from increasing in any country beyond the food it can produce or acquire" he saw food supply as relatively inelastic. An Anglican clergyman at the time he wrote the first version of the *Essay*, he wrote of "preventive checks" (abstinence, celibacy, and late marriages) but principally viewed war, pestilence, and famine as the key "positive" checks on human population. Little consideration was given to the issues of food distribution or how this might be subject to power relations and social or geographical variations.

BOSERUP gave perhaps one of the most influential responses to this perspective in her discussion of *The Conditions of Agricultural Growth* published in the mid-1960s when notions of a population "time-bomb" had resurfaced. In an attempted inversion of the Malthusian perspective she argued that population pressure, rather than being a cause of demographic catastrophe, has been the driving force behind agricultural innovation and the greatest incentive for increased agrarian production. Contesting the inelasticity of food production she urges that the transition from pastoralism and shifting cultivation to various forms of increasingly more intensive agriculture was not a random discovery but arose from the pressure of demographic necessity. Human relationships with the natural environment are seen as intrinsically harmonious, however, and human societies are accorded an almost unlimited freedom to adapt and to innovate.

DE CASTRO provides a powerful polemic against the "manmade" dimensions of famine and starvation. This is a stimulating contribution that includes the widely cited assertion that "The history of man from the beginning has been the history of his struggle for daily bread" (p.49). This book is full of interest and insights rather than simply providing a practical guide to the phenomenon of famine although some confusion could arise as a result of the author making little distinction between famine, malnutrition, and endemic hunger.

The idea that famines are caused by a "food availability decline" was fundamentally challenged by the Indian economist Sen at the beginning of the 1980s. The critical issue here was that food distribution and starvation were viewed as "the characteristic of some people not *having* enough to eat. It is not the characteristic of there not *being* enough to eat". The acknowledgement of his work with the Nobel Prize for Economics in 1998 shows that he has demonstrated both theoretically and through careful analysis of actual famines that a shock to food availability is never evenly distributed within a particular area or among the affected population. Instead he argued that access to food varies according to the individual's entitlement to food or the amount that can be commanded through production, the sale/exchange of assets, the sale of labour power, or through transfers from other people.

DRÉZE & SEN cemented the centrality of the entitlement approach to thinking on famine and food policy with the highly influential book *Hunger and Public Action*, which applied the approach to a range of famine and non-famine-related contexts. During the 1990s academics and policymakers have also attempted to extend and adapt the entitlement approach to other arenas of development discourse. Contemporary food security information systems and famine early warning systems now include indicators of access to food as the Food and Agriculture Organisation (FAO) was urged to move away from its tendency to view hunger entirely in food availability terms.

ARNOLD has since called for a "comparative phenomenology of famine" or comparative studies of the construction, understanding, and experience of famine. Reiterating the view that "famines are woven into the fabric of history" and that "food is power", this contribution provides a critical overview of definitions and theories of famine causation and explores the roles of states and peasantry. His work raises important questions about the historical importance of colonialism and about the roles of women in contemporary food production. Famine here forms part of a developing critique of state power although this is weakened by the liberal use of an essentialized "three worlds" schema and a limited discussion of the relevance of class analysis.

RAIKES also provides an interesting and accessible account of the social, political, and economic commonalties of famine in Africa, examining the neglected theme of African relationships with the European Community. This book looks at the conventional thinking on the food and economic crisis in Africa and raises questions about class, state, and policy formation. African food systems are viewed in relation to EEC policy formation since World War II and the case for and against food aid contributions is reviewed alongside a discussion of the implications for local production and distribution networks.

WATTS & GOODMAN also develop a critical interest in the global food system, bringing together a collection of case study chapters that illustrate the diversity and heterogeneity of agro-food systems while also raising theoretical questions about food restructuring and globalization at a variety of spatial scales. The chapters assembled in this volume attest to the new-found dynamism of agro-food studies, reinvigorated by the infusion of theoretical approaches and controversies from a variety of social sciences.

MARCUS POWER

See also Thomas Malthus

Fantasy

Adler, Alfred, *Understanding Human Nature*, New York: Greenberg, 1927; London: Allen and Unwin, 1928

Bettelheim, Bruno, *The Uses of Enchantment: The Meaning and Importance of Fairy Tales*, New York: Knopf, and London: Thames and Hudson, 1976

Freud, Sigmund, *Three Essays on the Theory of Sexuality*, edited and translated by James Strachey, London: Hogarth Press, and New York: Basic Books, 1962 (German edition 1905)

Isaacs, Susan, "The Nature and Function of Phantasy" in *The Freud–Klein Controversies 1941–45*, edited by Pearl King and Riccardo Steiner, London amd New York: Tavistock/Routledge, 1991 Isaacs, S. (1948) 'The Nature and Function of Phantasy', *International Journal of Psycho-Analysis* 29: 73–97.

Jung, C.G., *The Archetypes and the Collective Unconscious*, vol. 9, part 1 of *Collected Works*, New York: Pantheon, 1959; 2nd edition, Princeton, New Jersey: Princeton University Press, 1968

Klein, Melanie, "The Mutual Influences in the Development of Ego and Id" in *Envy and Gratitude and Other Works, 1946–1963*, London: Hogarth Press, 1975; New York: Free Press, 1984

Kolbenschlag, Madonna, *Kiss Sleeping Beauty Good-Bye: Breaking the Spell of Feminine Myths and Models*, New York: Doubleday, 1979; as *Goodbye Sleeping Beauty*, Dublin: Arlen House, 1983

Person, Ethel Spector, *By Force of Fantasy: How We Make Our Lives*, New York: Basic Books, 1995; London: HarperCollins, 1996

FREUD is probably the individual most often mentioned by other writers discussing fantasy. He explores the purpose of fantasies and the motives that instigate them, concluding that fantasy is compensation for what the fantasizer lacks in life, and that fantasies are most likely symptoms of neurosis. He further – erroneously – believed that motivating fantasies vary a great deal between the genders, with women fantasizing primarily about erotic desires and men about ambitions. Because Freud started the psychoanalytic movement and his ideas about fantasy were central to that movement, most literature on fantasy is psychoanalytic in nature. The Freudian definition of fantasy as a compensatory act is still strongly adhered to by both those in psychodynamic circles and by the individual with a passing interest in the meaning of fantasy. Unfortunately, this definition is not only narrow and simplistic – it casts fantasy in a negative and pathological light, failing to acknowledge that fantasy is an integral aspect of creativity.

ADLER states that considering a fantasy nothing more than a compensatory wish fulfilment is to ignore the importance of fantasy in problem solving. He cites the ability of fantasy to lift expectations, fuel productivity, and generally guide the fantasizer toward a superior goal. Finally, he remarks on the importance of fantasy in understanding the nature of the fantasizer's character and lifestyle.

KLEIN adds that our most basic drive is not libidinal or ambitious but relational. She says that the desire to relate in particular patterns with other humans is universal and innate, and that infants fantasize about these interactions even before they realize there are others in the world with whom they may relate. Her ideas of innate patterns of relating have been swept aside in favour of more modern theories by most clinicians, and her theory of a universal pattern of relating and wanting to relate is a typically narrow Western view that takes into account only observations of Western cultures.

Working from Klein's theory, ISAACS argues that a child's evolving fantasies are the basis for all motivation and behaviour. Human action, then, is conceptualized as an externalized attempt to satisfy instinctual urges, which are recognized by the individual only through fantasy. Like Klein, however, Isaacs focuses primarily on how internal representations influence perceptions of external reality and fails to consider how external experience shapes internal representations of people and things.

JUNG believed that all fantasy activity is directed by universal archetypes, producing amazing similarities in the fantasies of all people. He agrees that fantasy is a natural expression of unconscious life, but he distinguishes between two important categories of fantasy. First, there are fantasies of a personal character; these are based on personal experience. Second, there are those of an impersonal character that cannot be attributed to personal experience and must therefore be based in the collective human psyche shared by all people. He points to myths and fairytales as products of the impersonal collective human psyche. His investigations of myth and client cases in explaining the importance of the collective unconscious in the creation of human fantasies are both intriguing and convincing. He is often noted, however, for his interest in the occult and his pairing of psychology with parapsychological ideas, leaving some critics to dismiss his theories in favour of those more mundane and less radical.

BETTELHEIM dedicated an entire book to the manner in which fairytales help shape the preconscious and unconscious minds of children. Rather than seeing fairytales as evidence of archetypal collective fantasies born of generations of the human psyche, he believes that fairytales help shape the dreams and fantasies of our culture. Through fairytales, humans learn to structure their fantasies and use them to help them live better lives. He does an excellent job of addressing the Freudian criticisms that fantasy is unhealthy, creates an inability to appreciate reality, and leaves a person neurotically disconnected from the real world. Without fantasy, he explains, an individual is deprived of his or her ability to solve problems effectively. His work is, in some ways, an argument against Jung's theory, and Jung's is an argument against Bettelheim's. Perhaps because Bettelheim's ideas were less mystical, they have met much less criticism than Jung's. His ideas have, additionally, launched dialogues about how individuals, particularly those of minority groups, are socialized by fairy tales and the like to maintain their unequal positions in society.

One of the most notable works to come out of this movement is KOLBENSCHLAG, which attacks the societal values promoting fantasies of traditional feminine roles and continued sexism, and suggests new directions for both genders. She considers the difficulties of the traditional feminine roles that lead women in a compensatory search for what they do not – and often cannot – have in a world modelled on masculine ideals. She explores the confusion that women experience in view of the new egalitarian Western ideals and the ways in which culturally constructed and individual fantasies attempt to bridge that dissonance. Her book has the strong liberal tone of early feminism, but both feminism and other political movements have altered Western culture over the years, making some of the discussion seem simplistic in retrospect.

One of the most illustrative modern sources on fantasy is PERSON's study, which begins with acknowledgement of the Western belief that daydreaming and fantasy are wasteful, useless, and sometimes dangerous. Drawing on literature, art, research, and clinical experience, she tackles the major ideas that have evolved over the years regarding fantasy, demonstrates how collective fantasies are manifest in popular novels and films, and illustrates the import of fantasy on the everyday life of each individual. Her work reads more like a self-help book than a clinician's reference, but she does a wonderful job of tying abstract concepts posed by her predecessors to concrete examples. She also addresses the fears of discovery inherent in most individuals' fantasies. Although her work does not survey all or even most of the previous literature, it is a starting point for the interested, a source of case examples for clinicians, and a bridge from the abstract and academic studies to real comprehension of the nuances of fantasy.

CAROLYN KAUFMAN

Fascism

Berezin, Mabel, *Making the Fascist Self: The Political Culture of Interwar Italy*, Ithaca, New York: Cornell University Press, 1997

Cheles, Luciano, Ronnie Ferguson and Michalina Vaughan (editors), *Neo-Fascism in Europe*, London and New York: Longman, 1991

Delzell, Charles F. (editor), *Mediterranean Fascism, 1919–1945*, New York: Harper and Row, 1970

Gentile, Emilio, *The Sacralization of Politics in Fascist Italy*, Cambridge, Massachusetts: Harvard University Press, 1996

Gregor, James A., *The Ideology of Fascism: The Rational of Totalitarianism*, New York: Free Press, 1969

Mitcham, Samuel W. Jr, *Why Hitler? The Genesis of the Nazi Reich*, Westport, Connecticut: Praeger, 1996

Payne, Stanley G., *Fascism: Comparison and Definition*, Madison: University of Wisconsin Press, 1980

Reich, Wilhelm, *The Mass Psychology of Fascism*, New York: Orgone Institute Press, 1946 (from 3rd German edition); new translation, New York: Farrar Straus, 1970, London: Souvenir Press, 1972

Sturzo, Luigi, *Italy and Fascism*, New York: Fertig, 1967

Turner, Henry A. (editor), *Reappraisals of Fascism*, New York: New Viewpoints, 1975

BEREZIN scrutinizes the culture of Italian fascism, focusing upon the Mussolini regime's conscious construction of a widely based and highly politicized "state-civilization". She holds that the regime stressed form over content, and tried to build its political base through canny fabrication and manipulation of public spectacles and rituals such as parades, commemoration ceremonies, and state festivities. Berezin draws on an extensive knowledge and familiarity with social theory to lay the claim of the critical importance of fascist ritual, ritual which was constructed in the broadest sense to serve as the very core of the fascist experience for the individual. This experience was designed to replace, or at least shoulder aside, church and private conviction: it was to become "the town center", fusing the private self with the great public cause. The ever-permeable boundary between the public and the private is the book's central focus. When compounded with uniforms, music, youth movements, the arts, architecture, and pervading xenophobia, the fascist undertaking worked. How and why it worked, and to what degree, is the thrust of this study. It is a necessary element of the understanding of the powerful affective mystique of fascism as a political ideology, both then and now.

CHELES, FERGUSON & VAUGHAN have put together 12 contemporary studies of neofascism in Europe after the war to defeat fascism during the latter half of the twentieth century. Especially in the 1980s and 1990s, the re-emergence of self-styled "neofascist" movements and parties has been striking. They are no longer confined to the Iberian peninsula or to the lunatic fringes of parliamentary democracies. The neofascists have made significant electoral gains across all of Europe, East and West, and now win seats in national parliaments as well as in the European Parliament. These papers examine this contemporary phenomenon in Germany, Italy, France, Spain, Portugal, Greece, and Britain, as well as offering analyses of

left and right in contemporary Europe, the new propaganda of neofascism, and the role and place of women in the re-occurrence of an ideology mistakenly thought to have been defeated in Europe. The illustrations are outstanding, the bibliography complete and rewarding, and the notation and appendices worthy of the attention of any interested researcher.

DELZELL presents a comparative study of the historical development and ideologies of the fascist regimes in Italy (the corporate state), Spain (the *Falange Española*), and Portugal (the *estado novo*). The sections on the birth of the fascist ideology and the development of the fascist doctrine of the state are good, but not unique. The focus upon the three defining ideological fascisms in comparison with each other, however, is singular in the contemporary literature. The analysis is bolstered by extensive documentation from the three regimes, offering the reader a traverse prospect – a cross-view – of fascist ideology and policy in the three Mediterranean states. Of particular value is the study of Salazar's Portugal, perhaps the most successful of all the fascist regimes because of its moderation and its close integration of ideology with practicality. This was a singular achievement in Portugal, and an extraordinary failure in Mussolini's Italy. Old-style fascism of the Blackshirt variety is most unlikely to return to power in Europe, but the Mediterranean (including the French) political temperament is today still open to a moderate and practical fascism, as seen in this study.

GENTILE was originally published as *Il Culto del littorio: La Sacralizzazione della politica nell'Italia Fascista*. The work is a study of the search for and construction of a civil religion of the state (*Il Stato*), of the longing for a moral and thus a civil renewal of the Italian people. This serious, scholarly treatment deals with the piazzas of Italy, which for two decades were recast as a single huge stage upon which millions celebrated – as one celebrates the Mass – the national holidays, the anniversaries, the triumphs, the cult of the fallen, the consecration of symbols, and most importantly, the glory and glorification of the Duce. Italians became bound up in the politics of fantasy. They became enmeshed in a thick web of myths, symbols, rituals, and the uniformity (with uniforms) of a mass movement that made "sacred" all these elements of the national rebirth. The licter's fasces (a judicial symbol carried by the lictor in the presence of the Emperor, adopted by Mussolini as the party's symbol and ultimately used to name his entire movement) incorporated both meaning and sanctification: it became the very sacrament of both civil piety and moral ardour. It made the regime holy. It is this search for the holy in the fabric of the political that is the stuff of this leading work on the "religion" of Italian fascism. The primary focus is upon the formulation and institutionalization of this cult of the sacred, identifying and analysing the motivations, forms, and scope of the effort to baptize the political and make it spiritual, even divine, in the connotation of a new theology of the state.

GREGOR offers not just the historical background and development of fascism as an ideology, but an integrative examination of protofascism – the deeper social and cultural context underlying the ideology. From this he proceeds to the customary historical analysis of the doctrine, political philosophy, and definitive ideology of Italian fascism, but he includes elements not customary in other studies such as an analysis of racism and its doctrinal role. The explanation of "the totalitarian State" (Mussolini's term) in Italian fascism is detailed, and encompasses the major ideologues and thinkers of the fascist era. The work offers an historically accurate and strikingly objective account of the origins and rise of the ideology in the Italian peninsula, and suggests a general typology of revolutionary mass movements that reflects still contemporary thinking with respect to the describing and analysing of "totalitarian" movements in the particular sense of Italian Fascism. The role within the Italian fascist state of unions, youth groups, cooperatives, sport associations, and other such quasi-voluntary groups, is examined and analysed.

MITCHAM has as the central thrust of his study the question of why the Germans – a civilized and educated people – came to choose Adolf Hitler as their chancellor, unleashing upon the world one of the most barbaric regimes in history. It is a complex account, but one that Mitcham handles well. The research is current and comprehensive. The methodology is historical with significant documentary and factual data to support the conclusions. The focus is upon the Weimar era and its failures, leading to the elections of 1928, 1930, the two elections of 1932, and the Lippe Landtag election of January 1933. Each of these elections is intensively examined with statistical data. The role of the Freikorps, the impact of the world depression, and little-studied events such as the suicide of Geli Raubal are scrutinized and explained. Hitler's organizational abilities, and the willingness of the Nazis to engage in continuous electioneering and what they termed "cattle trading" are examined. The culminating street violence – as a tactic – and the Beer Hall Putsch (the failure that succeeded) are explained and evaluated not only historically but also in the context of the central focus: why did Germany empower Hitler? This is a contemporary and wide-ranging study that attempts to answer this question.

PAYNE presents a rewarding "definition and comparison" of fascism as a collection of separate, albeit related, phenomena. After an explication of the historical antecedents of European authoritarianism, separate chapters examine the Fascist and National Socialist Movements, the Mussolini and Hitler regimes, and other movements and regimes in Austria, Hungary, Romania, Greece, Bulgaria, Yugoslavia (particularly Croatia and Slovenia), Czechoslovakia, Poland, Finland, France, the Baltic States, and the Western European Lowlands. The examination of collaborationist administrations (in France, Norway, and the Netherlands) is detailed, as is the scrutiny of those regimes that survived World War II in Europe – in Spain and Portugal. Of particular note is the concluding chapter on "generic fascism", in which the analysis extends from Jacobin times to contemporary neo fascism in Europe. Payne offers a tour-de-force analysis of fascism that the serious researcher ignores at his peril.

REICH was originally published as *Die Massenpsychologie des Faschismus*, in 1942. Although it is now dated, this work is fundamental, and remains one of the most important – if out of the mainstream – perceptions of fascism. Reich advances a wide-ranging explanation based upon his "*sex-economic*" theory. Fascism is the expression of the irrational character structure of the average human being whose primary biological needs and impulses have been suppressed for millennia. His sharp focus is upon the ideology of fascism, which is seen as relieving this suppression, and which includes the racial content of German Nazism, symbolism in fascism, the role of sex-economic theory in the fight against what is termed "mysticism", and the biological function in the struggle for human freedom. By taking apart and examining the "organized mysticism" of what is termed "an international anti-sexual organization", Reich attempts to demonstrate the origins and roots of Nazism in particular, and fascism in general, in the "soil of mass psychology" as that soil is ploughed and turned by great institutions, including great sociopsychological forces such as the Church (widely Christian, and specifically Catholic) and the culture. Work, art, and communication with the masses are other significant foci of this unique work, a one-of-a-kind that is both eccentric and central in the literature.

STURZO was an Italian priest and a leader of the Partito Populare, a forerunner of the Partito Democrazia Cristiana. His single great book, originally published as *Italia e Fascismo* in 1926, is now a fundamental and even classic starting point for any study of the fascist phenomenon as seen from its own formative time by a perceptive contemporary opponent. Sturzo wrote a careful analysis of the process that led to the overthrow of the Italian constitution and the elevation of a virtual dictator who trampled "on the rotting corpse of Liberty". Prose of this sort, however, is not the work's standard: rather, Sturzo adopted a reasoned and even objective tone, without bitterness, even though he wrote from exile, having been forced to flee Italy to avoid the fate of Mateotti and Salvemini (both of whom were assassinated).

Only a few other sources – certainly few from that time – explain so well the ever-spreading, corrupting influence of violence. It is this pathology of violence – the fradulently, the lies, the obfuscation, the total moral degeneracy of fascism in its very origins and in its earliest activities – that Sturzo exposes so well. There was no "good time". Fascism was a tragedy for Italy from the first day of its existence, and this extraordinary work makes this reality clear in a literate and lucid manner.

TURNER offers a broad analysis of fascism, but one that is a reappraisal rather than a rehash of the older understanding. This collection of focused articles, by Turner and nine other scholars, is more current, and thus preferable to, Nolte's *Three Faces of Fascism* (1963), although Turner is humble in his statement that "without question, the single most important contribution to the reappraisal of fascism is Ernst Nolte's book". Turner's compilation is more current, more analytic, and simply more readable. It includes sections from Nolte and Epstein on recent (meaning post-World War II) studies of fascism. The analyses of Allen, Cassels, Sauer, and Turner himself allow for a recalibration of understanding of the phenomenon, a necessary readjustment of perception, given that the war is now well into past history. The case studies are tight and rewarding: Payne on Spanish fascism, Hans Rogger on Russian fascism, George Macklin Wilson on Japanese fascism, and Renee Winegarten on "The Fascist Mentality – Drieu la Rochelle". Breadth of coverage and depth of analysis recommend this work.

GERARD F. RUTAN

Fashion

Damhorst, Mary Lynn, Kimberly A. Miller and Susan O. Michelman (editors), *The Meanings of Dress*, New York: Fairchild, 1999

Horn, Marilyn J. and Lois M. Gurel, *The Second Skin: An Interdisciplinary Study of Clothing*, 3rd edition, Boston: Houghton Mifflin, 1981

Kaiser, Susan B., *The Social Psychology of Clothing: Symbolic Appearances in Context*, 2nd edition, New York: Macmillan, 1990; revised edition, New York: Fairchild, 1997

McDowell, Colin, *Dressed to Kill: Sex, Power and Clothes*, London: Hutchinson, 1992

Roach-Higgins, Mary Ellen, Joanne B. Eicher and Kim K.P. Johnson (editors), *Dress and Identity*, New York: Fairchild, 1995

Sproles, George, *Fashion: Consumer Behavior toward Dress*, Minneapolis: Burgess, 1979

Sproles, George, *Perspectives of Fashion*, Minneapolis: Burgess, 1981

Sproles, George B. and Leslie Davis Burns, *Changing Appearances: Understanding Dress in Contemporary Society*, New York: Fairchild, 1994

Storm, Penny, *Functions of Dress: Tool of Culture and the Individual*, Englewood Cliffs, New Jersey: Prentice Hall, 1987

The sociological study of fashion is most frequently presented within a larger, interdisciplinary framework that integrates psychology, sociology, and cultural aspects of dress. This viewpoint recognizes the complex individual and social contextual components of the relationship of people and clothing, and acknowledges the difficulty in teasing out any one aspect. Distinctions between dress and fashionable dress are often deliberately blurred. Reference to fashion sociology in particular can be found embedded in most treatments of the sociopsychological aspects of dress. It has also been recognized as an important business force in the realm of consumer behaviour. Costume history references are moving away from a recitation of detail of design features, to include broader treatments of the clothing with specific temporal and social contexts. The reader will find many books on the history of dress useful in the pursuit of information about fashion sociology for the time period covered.

Perhaps the most renowned and influential author in the field is KAISER, whose book is now in its third iteration. As a follower of the symbolic interaction perspective, she acknowledges cognitive and cultural perspectives, and emphasizes throughout the importance of a contextual framework for the study of clothing social psychology. She deals with a wide variety of subtopics, including symbolic appearances, the self, communication, and culture. This latest edition of 651 pages has an added chapter that incorporates late 20th-century thinking, as Kaiser tries to encourage reflection about changing appearance in relation to gender, sexuality, class, and ethnicity. As a reference, the book offers a tremendous bibliography with over 900 entries plus an author index. As a textbook, there are superior visual images and other suggested suitable readings with each chapter.

The last edition of HORN & GUREL presents the philosophy that dress should be studied as a multifaceted concept. Its treatment of fashion is woven through the text, in addition to a dedicated chapter. The book continues the thrust of earlier editions, when Horn was the single author. While now dated in its visual offerings and somewhat simplistic in its treatment, the book does offer a broad and simply written introduction to the subject.

STORM carried on the interdisciplinary theme with discussions of dress as a combination of individual, social, and cultural behaviour. The book's organization divides the subject into intrinsic, communicative, psychological, and sociological functions of dress. In the later section, she outlines the factors of social class, economics, government, and religion. While offering the basics of each, the book lacks any detailed treatment of meaning or interpretation. It is a useful introductory text, somewhat more complex than Horn & Gurel.

Despite being somewhat dated, SPROLES (1979 and 1981) continues to inform the student of fashion. In Sproles (1979), the perspective is that of consumer behaviour. The author describes fashion-oriented consumer behaviour as "among the most complex acts of consumer behavior" (p.iii). He examines various important components of fashion as a process, environmental influences on fashion and the relationship of the consumer to fashion, and makes good use of illustrative charts and tables. One can see the basis of much fashion research of the 1990s in the Sproles position.

Sproles (1981), written as a companion to Sproles (1979), presents an excellent book of fashion readings, including classical references from this century. Unfortunately the physical format of the book's pages – small print, very long lines and little white space – makes for difficult reading. The reader can revisit the early works of Simmel, Veblen, and Sapir, among others. Also included are the initial writings that established the now well known "trickle down", "trickle up", and "trickle across" movements. Additional pieces from the 1970s speculate on the development of fashion research.

SPROLES & BURNS update the consumer behaviour approach in a newer offering. Spanning the field from the evolution of fashion to fashion forecasting, the text is the latest to take up the banner of interdisciplinary study. It integrates research throughout, and is a textbook appropriate for post-secondary classes. While a little thin on text per se, it has a plethora of well-chosen images and explanatory graphs. It also offers a series of study/discussion questions at the end of each chapter, along with suggested supplementary readings.

In a deliberate attempt to examine the subject equally as fashion and as a social phenomenon, McDOWELL offers an insightful and visually effective view of fashion as a tool of sex and power. He highlights the dual nature of fashion as both a mask and conspicuous manifestation of social structures, as an artefact many think too familiar to be considered important, and one that others purposely manipulate for effect. His stated attempt is to move "intelligent interest in clothing" into the realm of recognized, intellectual discourse. Frequently controversial, McDowell generally succeeds in his goal.

The writings of several authors have been collected by ROACH-HIGGINS, EICHER & JOHNSON. *Dress and Identity* deals with several issues highlighted by McDowell, such as gender relationships and role enactment. The editors have not only chosen a wide variety of articles, but they have also offered a solid representation of different cultures. The message of the importance of dress and fashion in social settings is strong throughout the book. Examples include visual mechanisms of power reversals between Bedouin men and women, multiple social meanings in fashion images, and the declining perceived fashionability of the kimono.

One of the newest addition to the field of fashion and dress sociology is a collection of readings edited by DAMHORST, MILLER & MICHELMAN. Although the word "fashion" appears in only one of 14 chapter titles, the concept is constantly present. The editors have included readings on such topics as the fashionability of ecoclothing, several treatments of the debate of thinness versus plus-size desirability, and workplace dressing. The strength of the collection comes from its variety of well-documented sources: women's magazines, business and news publications, and academic research writings.

SUSAN TURNBULL CATON

Fear

Agras, Stewart, David Sylvester and Donald Oliveau, "The Epidemiology of Common Fears and Phobias", *Comprehensive Psychiatry*, 10/2 (1969): 151–56

Bandura, Albert, *The Principles of Behavior Modification*, New York: Holt Rinehart, 1969

Davey, Graham C.L. (editor), *Phobias: A Handbook of Theory, Research and Treatment*, Chichester and New York: Wiley, 1997

Marks, Isaac M., *Fears, Phobias and Rituals: Panic, Anxiety, and Their Disorders*, Oxford and New York: Oxford University Press, 1987

Rachman, S.J., "The Conditioning Theory of Fear-acquisition: A Critical Examination", *Behaviour Research and Therapy*, 15/5 (1977): 375–87

Rachman, S.J., *Fear and Courage*, 2nd edition, New York: Freeman, 1990

Reiss, Steven, "Pavlovian Conditioning and Human Fear: An Expectancy Model", *Behavior Therapy*, 11/4 (1980): 380–96

Seligman, Martin E., "Phobias and Preparedness", *Behavior Therapy*, 2/4 (1971): 307–20

Watson, John and Rosalie Raynor, "Conditioned Emotional Reactions", *Journal of Experimental Psychology*, 3/1 (1920): 1–22

Wolpe, Joseph, *Psychotherapy by Reciprocal Inhibition*, Stanford, California: Stanford University Press, 1958

Fear is an unpleasant emotional reaction to a perceived threat. It is such a common emotion, probably universally experienced, that a number of attempts have been made to ascertain the range, frequency, and severity of human fears.

The paper by AGRAS, SYLVESTER & OLIVEAU describes one of the first attempts to evaluate the types and degrees of fear experienced in a normal population. They classified fears reported into four types: mild, intense, phobias, and clinical

phobias. The most commonly reported intense fear was fear of snakes, followed by fear of heights. Fear and avoidance of public places and transport was the most commonly reported severe fear followed by fear of injury or illness. The typical pattern reported for example for fear of the dark and fear of animals, was for fear to reach peak incidence in early adulthood and then to decline in the following years. A second pattern, reported for example for fear of illness or injury, was for a gradual increase in fear reaching a peak in middle adulthood.

A number of theories have been advanced to account for the genesis of human fear. The most fundamental to both research and practice for more than half a century is the conditioning theory. WATSON & RAYNOR'S classic paper illustrated the basic principles with 11-month-old Albert. They presented Albert with an initially neutral, non-anxiety-provoking event (a white rat) which they then paired with an aversive experience (a loud sound produced by striking a metal bar) which caused Albert to jump, fall forward, and whimper (that is, to exhibit an anxiety response). After two such pairings of rat and loud sound Albert showed avoidance and cried when the rat was presented alone. In addition he showed such reactions when presented with similar stimuli (rabbit, dog, fur coat, cotton) which had not previously resulted in such reactions. Although subsequent attempts to replicate this study were unsuccessful conditioning theory has received much support. Indeed, a thoroughly revised version of the theory is incorporated into current cognitive theory and therapy.

RACHMAN (1977) presents a widely cited summary of six arguments against acceptance of a pure conditioning theory. He points out that people fail to acquire fears in what are theoretically fear-evoking situations; fear reactions are difficult to induce under laboratory conditions; the theory rests on the untenable equipotentiality premise (the idea that any stimulus can be transformed into a fear signal); the distribution of fear is not consistent with the theory; many phobic patients recount histories inconsistent with the theory; and fears can be acquired indirectly, contrary to the demands of conditioning theory. Rachman contended that fears could be acquired by conditioning, vicarious exposures, and by the transmission of information and instruction.

One revision to the basic conditioning paradigm centres on the notion that not all stimuli are likely to become cues for fear, but that evolution has predisposed organisms to learn easily those associations that facilitate species survival. While not originating this view, SELIGMAN elaborated on it, holding that human fears are best understood as instances of biologically prepared learning because they commonly involve objects and situations that have threatened the human species throughout its evolutionary history. Preparedness theory has since been tested in a number of experimental studies with both humans and animals and has itself undergone a number of revisions.

A further revision to the basic conditioning paradigm is the recognition that fears can be learned vicariously. Experimentation with human volunteers as well as research evidence from primate laboratories indicates that modelling, that is, observing another individual experiencing intense fear in a certain situation, can lead to the acquisition of fear in the observer. The converse of this, that fear reduction can be achieved by observing a model approaching a feared object or dealing with a feared situation, provides the basis for therapeutic modelling. The fundamental work relating to these issues was undertaken by BANDURA and is reported in his book.

As it became increasingly apparent that direct conditioning experiences were neither necessary nor sufficient to explain fear acquisition in humans, theories began to incorporate cognitive events into their explanations. Although primarily based upon learning principles, the central assumption of REISS's expectancy model was that some cognitive mediating process occurs between the occurrence of an initial stimulus and the resultant response. Reiss proposed that fear was initiated by danger or initiating expectancies that were evaluations of such factors as the perceived physical or social danger posed by an event. The likelihood that fear would occur in any given situation was heightened by anxiety expectancies, that is, an expectation that one will become anxious when a certain situation is encountered. Although viewed as important, cognitions were still only regarded as mediating events and it was only with the emergence of cognitive theories that cognitions were viewed as causal in relation to fear.

The 22 chapters in the second edition of RACHMAN's (1990) overview are organized into six sections dealing with the nature of fear, varieties of fear, acquisition of fear, modification of fear, courage, and a conclusion. Only half the material included in the first edition of this book remains, with several new chapters describing original research undertaken in the intervening twelve years leading to the publication of this second edition. Although not presenting an exhaustive account of the psychology of fear, Rachman's book provides an insightful commentary, which benefits from his own extensive research.

MARKS represents one of the most comprehensive overviews of the nature of fear. The 16 chapters in this extensive volume are organized into four sections dealing with normal fear, mechanisms for the genesis of fear, clinical syndromes, and treatment. As well as drawing upon his own extensive research Marks provides a synthesis of a vast array of research; the references section alone consists of 80 pages. The book brings together a widely scattered literature from fields as diverse as genetics, biochemistry, physiology, pharmacology, psychology, psychiatry, and ethology.

WOLPE's book is a landmark publication in relation to therapy aimed at fear reduction. Based upon learning theory he developed a technique that he called "systematic desensitization". This consists of two elements: the fearful person is given training in muscle relaxation and is then asked to imagine increasingly fearful scenes while remaining in a state of calm relaxation. The success of desensitization confirmed the value of applying findings from experimental psychology to clinical practice and heralded the dawning of a new era in clinical practice.

The handbook edited by DAVEY is divided into three sections. The first section discusses symptoms, prevalence rates, individual case histories, and etiological factors in the development of prevalent fears. The second section describes treatments with a discussion of outcome efficacy and comparisons between different therapeutic techniques. The final section discusses

theoretical and etiological factors that are general to a variety of human fears. Davey's text provides a comprehensive and up-to-date overview of developments and current knowledge in relation to theories of and therapies for human fears.

ROBERT J. EDELMANN

See also Agoraphobia

Fear of crime

Bannister, J., "Locating Fear: Environment and Ontological Security" in *Crime and the Urban Environment: The Scottish Experience*, edited by Huw Jones, Aldershot, Hampshire: Avebury, 1993

Ditton, J., J. Bannister, S. Farrall and E. Gilchrist, "Afraid or Angry?", *International Review of Victimology*, 6 (1999): 83–99

Ferraro, K.F. and R. LaGrange, "The Measurement of Fear of Crime", *Sociological Inquiry*, 57/1 (1987): 70–101

Hale, C., "Fear of Crime: A Review of the Literature", *International Review of Victimology*, 4 (1996): 79–150

Hough, Mike and Pat Mayhew, *The British Crime Survey: First Report*, London: HMSO, 1983

Hough, Mike and Pat Mayhew, *Taking Account of Crime: Key Findings from the Second British Crime Survey*, London: HMSO, 1985

Hough, Mike, *Anxiety about Crime: Findings from the 1994 British Crime Survey*, London: Home Office, 1995 (Research Study 147)

Mayhew, Pat, David Elliott and Lizanne Dowds, *The 1988 British Crime Survey*, London: HMSO, 1989

Sparkes, R., "Reason and Unreason in 'Left Realism': Some Problems in the Constitution of the Fear of Crime" in *Issues in Realist Criminology*, edited by Roger Matthews and Jock Young, London and Newbury Park, California: Sage, 1992

Van der Wurff, A., L. van Staaldunien and P. Stringer, "Fear of Crime in Residential Environments: Testing a Social Psychological Model", *Journal of Social Psychology*, 129/2 (1989): 141–60

Warr, M., "Fear of Victimisation: Why are Women and the Elderly More Afraid?", *Social Science Quarterly*, 65 (1984): 681–702

The literature on the fear of crime (or "anxiety about crime" as it has come to be known as more recently) is vast. It spans several decades of research and several continents, and various research methodologies have been employed to explore this topic. There is perhaps no better place to start than HALE's review (undertaken for the Metropolitan Police in the UK), which comprehensively covers most of the literature up until the mid 1990s. At the time of writing, Hale estimated that there were in the region of 200 publications on the fear of crime – by now this could well be nearer 300. Given the breadth of the review and the general ease of finding material on this topic, this entry will focus upon work that is truly seminal.

It must be said that some have raised serious doubts about the utility of the concept. For example, FERRARO &

LAGRANGE have critiqued (as have others) the research methodologies used to research the fear of crime. They suggest that there are serious problems resulting from the reliance upon poorly worded questions. One of the questions most commonly used to measure the fear of crime is "how safe do you, or would you, feel walking around in this area, on your own after dark?" They criticize the question for failing to mention the word "crime" anywhere; referring to a vaguely defined notion of "area"; mixing hypothetical and actual situations ("do you" and "would you") and asking respondents about something they may rarely do (walk alone in "this area"). Added to this is the observation that the question asks only about "safety" (rather than a wider range of emotions).

Question wording aside, the field of research has certainly uncovered a range of findings. Probably the most sustained investigation of the fear of crime in England and Wales has come from the Home Office, which has undertaken several rounds of the British Crime Survey (the Scottish Office has undertaken similar surveys in Scotland). The survey (HOUGH, HOUGH & MAYHEW (1983), HOUGH & MAYHEW (1985), MAYHEW, ELLIOTT & DOWDS) has produced a wealth of findings concerning the fear of crime and associated issues (such as victimization and risks of becoming a victim). The data is lodged with the ESRC data archive at Essex University for other academics to use.

One of the major areas of debate in relation to the fear of crime is the relationship between fear and risk. When it was found (from surveys such as the British Crime Survey) that some groups were very fearful, but had a relatively low chance of actually being victimized, it was argued that such groups were "irrationally fearful". These low risk/high fear groups consisted of women and the elderly. (Note that those groups who reported low fear levels but who had high rates of victimization – namely young males – were not cast as the "irrationally fearless".) This lead some to question what a rational level of fear actually was, and under which circumstances one should be fearful with good reason (see SPARKES).

Very few studies have relied upon qualitative data to investigate the fear of crime. BANNISTER reports one study that did. Bannister interpreted fear of crime as a response to fears about unknown areas and unknown people. Using data collected in Glasgow, Bannister demonstrated how people living in different areas of the same housing estate perceived each others' areas as being more dangerous than their own.

Those investigating the fear of crime from a sociological standpoint have largely dominated the field. As such, variables such as age, gender, economic status, and so on have dominated the explanatory models developed to account for the fear of crime. However, one article – that by VAN DER WURFF et al. – has employed social psychological variables to account for the fear of crime. This model has been supported by empirical data. The work is notable both for methodological innovation in the field (the researchers employed vignettes – short stories about a particular situation – in their measurement of the fear of crime) as well as its novel approach to this issue.

More recently, some researchers have started to treat the fear of crime as being made up not just of "fear", but other emotions too. As such, these efforts can be seen as attempts to deal with the some of the criticisms of Ferraro & Lagrange discussed previously. DITTON et al., building upon insights from in-depth interviewing, developed questions aimed to assess the range of emotions people felt about crime. They asked people about how much they thought about crime and how angry they were about crime as well as how afraid of it they were. Their results suggested that people were more angry about crime than they were afraid of it. Although the usefulness of this approach has yet to be fully assessed, it perhaps points to a new avenue of research in this field.

Another innovation in this field is referred to as "perceptually contemporaneous offences" (or "PCOs"). After it was found that, despite their relatively low risk of becoming victimized, women and the elderly were particularly fearful of crime (and in particular burglary), WARR proposed that they were fearful not of burglary as such, but of the implied risk of assault which they assumed would be associated with it. Thus when asked during a survey if they feared burglary, these groups reply that they did because of an underlying fear of assault (perhaps sexually motivated), which they assumed would accompany a burglary. This approach is not supported empirically (as yet), but it too breathes new life into research on the fear of crime.

STEPHEN FARRALL

Federalism

Beer, Samuel H., *To Make a Nation: The Rediscovery of American Federalism*, Cambridge, Massachusetts: Harvard University Press, 1993

Conlon, Timothy J., *From New Federalism to Devolution: Twenty-Five Years of Intergovernmental Reform*, Washington, DC: Brookings Institution Press, 1998

Dye, Thomas R., *American Federalism: Competition among Governments*, Lexington, Massachusetts: Lexington Books, 1990

Elazar, Daniel Judah, *The American Partnership: Intergovernmental Co-operation in the Nineteenth-Century United States*, Chicago: University of Chicago Press, 1962

Grodzins, Morton, "Centralization and Decentralization in the American Federal System" in *A Nation of States: Essays on the American Federal System*, edited by Robert A. Goldwin, Chicago: Rand McNally, 1963

Kincaid, John, "From Cooperative to Coercive Federalism", *Annals of the American Academy of Political and Social Science*, 509 (May 1990): 139–52

Oates, Wallace E., *Fiscal Federalism*, New York: Harcourt Brace, 1972

Peterson, Paul E., *The Price of Federalism*, Washington, DC: Brookings Institution, 1995

Rivlin, Alice M., *Reviving the American Dream: The Economy, the States, and the Federal Government*, Washington, DC: Brookings Institution, 1992

Walker, David B., *The Rebirth of Federalism: Slouching Toward Washington*, Chatham, New Jersey: Chatham House, 1995

Wheare, K.C., *Federal Government*, London: Oxford University Press, 1946

WHEARE began modern scholarship on federalism by characterizing the federalism principle as the mechanism of dividing powers so that general and regional governments are coordinated with each other while remaining autonomous within their prescribed spheres. This early characterization sets the tone for later research in the area. Written during the immediate post World War II era, he suggests that war, economic depression, the growth of social services, and the mechanical revolution have contributed to the strength of the general government. Nevertheless, he concludes that there is room under federalism for each regional government to govern itself and regulate its life in its own way.

GRODZINS asserts that the American federal system is principally characterized by a federal-state-local sharing of responsibilities for all functions. The federal system, according to him, should not be symbolized by a "layer cake form of governance structure with three distinct and separate spheres". Instead, he characterizes this form of governance sharing system as the "marble cake federalism" because there is "an inseparable mixture of differently coloured ingredients within the system". He further argues that efforts to decentralize government through the ordered separation of functions are contrary to the American political experience. He warns against any effort to sort out responsibilities between federal and subnational governments as it would undermine subnational governments. He concludes by stating that the American system is best conceived as "one government serving one people".

ELAZAR offers a similar characterization of federalism as cooperative throughout American history. In particular, he rejects the conventional interpretation of American federalism as dualistic during the 19th century. Drawing upon the major historical experiences during that period, he provides a rich description of how government officials at every level had to work cooperatively to solve problems associated with the continuing expansion of the nation. In particular, informal and cooperative relationships developed where officials exchanged information or cooperated to improve the nation's transportation and education systems.

OATES takes an economic perspective in characterizing federalism. This framework, known as "fiscal federalism", focuses on the characteristics of the public goods and services provided by governments in which a clear division of functions among levels of government would lead to the attainment of optimum welfare. In particular, he asserts that decentralization can result in a better fit between citizens' demands and public policy. He argues that it is always more efficient for local governments to provide the Pareto-efficient levels of output for their respective jurisdictions than for the central government to provide any specified and uniform level of output across all jurisdictions. His framework remains influential in public finance research.

KINCAID, in contrast to the earlier emphasis on cooperative federalism, suggests that America has entered a time of coercive federalism. Since 1978, the federal government has reduced its reliance on fiscal tools to stimulate intergovernmental policy cooperation and increased its reliance on regulatory tools to ensure the dominance of federal policy.

Similarly, DYE challenges the existing literature on American federalism by embracing a competitive federalism model that promotes opposite and rival interests among different units of governments. Rejecting the earlier models of federalism based on cooperation, partnerships, and sharing, he envisages a marketplace for governments where consumer-taxpayers can voluntarily choose the public goods and services they prefer. He believes this marketplace model would render more governmental responsiveness to citizen preferences, greater incentives for efficient service provision, lower taxes, and greater economic growth.

RIVLIN concentrates her efforts on linking the sagging economic performance during the 1980s with an overburdened government. To address these problems, Rivlin recommends allocating responsibilities according to the level of government that can most efficiently provide each service. States would carry out a productivity agenda in which they would be responsible for most domestic responsibilities such as education, housing, highways, social services, economic development, and job training. The federal government, on the other hand, should devote its efforts to the international arena, budget deficit reduction, and healthcare financing.

Like Rivlin, PETERSON advocates a major reassignment of responsibilities among levels of government. Through his empirical analysis, he shows that redistributive functions are more appropriately handled at the national level whereas developmental policies should be the responsibility of state and local government. He asserts that functional federalism can best characterize the relationship between all levels of government as each level of government has expanded in its area of competence and has contracted in the areas in which it is less effective. On the other hand, his analysis does not support the legislative model that posits the federal system as being shaped by the political needs of legislators responsible for its design.

In calling for a rebirth of an authentic federalism that would place greater confidence in the states and localities, WALKER criticizes the American federal system as overloaded, confused, and mistrusted. In contrast with previous scholars, Walker argues that the American system in the 1990s simultaneously reflects centralizing and decentralizing, cooperative and competitive, cooptive and collaborative, and activist as well as retrenching tendencies. In turn, Walker suggests distributing government responsibilities between national and state governments. He provides a vivid account of the political history of federalism from the founding era to 1994.

BEER contends that the Framers' conception of federalism was a unique response to the needs of national unity and the safeguarding of individual liberty, which eventually led them to build a coherent national federalism framework. Rather than a compact among the states, the basic tenets of American democratic nationhood are founded on two coordinated sets of institutions – federal and state. Beer's book offers a balanced account on the historical debate of the national idea in American federalist thought. Beer's discussion of the major political philosophers reaches back to the Middle Ages, beginning with Thomas Aquinas and moving to John Milton, and James Harrington. Then he examines the federal options, the discovery of the nation, and the constitutional movement from a confederate republic to a compound republic.

Drawing upon the experiences of the past three decades, CONLON details a refreshing account of American federalist reform efforts. He maintains that Nixon, Reagan, and Gingrich shared a belief that local decision making was generally preferable to national decision making, but he argues that they differed markedly in their beliefs about the ends of decentralization. He portrays Nixon's agenda as strongly rooted in management rationale whereas the primary focus of Reagan's initiative was to reduce the power and size of national bureaucracy. Advocates of the current federalism reform movement, however, favour wholesale elimination of federal domestic programmes with their anti-welfare state ideology. The earlier federalism reform was based on theories of public administration and public finance, but he finds few theoretical underpinnings for recent federalism reform efforts. Finally, he concludes that these reform initiatives have only produced small results as the federal system continues to reflect an increasing decentralization trend and a continuing federal preeminence.

SHAO-CHEE SIM

Feedback

Algera, Jen A., "Feedback Systems in Organizations" in *International Review of Industrial and Organizational Psychology*, vol. 5, edited by Cary Cooper and Ivan Robertson, Chichester and New York: Wiley, 1990

Borman, Walter C., "360 Degree Ratings: An Analysis of Assumptions and a Research Agenda for Evaluating their Validity", *Human Resource Management Review*, 7/3 (1997): 299–315

Farr, James L., "Informal Performance Feedback: Seeking and Giving" in *Personnel Selection and Assessment: Individual and Organizational Perspectives*, edited by Heinz Schuler, James L. Farr and Mike Smith, Hillsdale, New Jersey: Erlbaum, 1993

Fedor, Donald B., "Recipient Responses to Performance Feedback: A Proposed Model and its Implications" in *Research in Personnel and Human Resources Management*, 9 (1991): 73–120

Fletcher, Clive and Caroline Baldry, "Multi-Source Feedback Systems" in *International Review of Industrial and Organizational Psychology*, vol. 14, edited by Cary Cooper and Ivan Robertson, Chichester and New York: Wiley, 1999

Herold, David M. and Donald B. Fedor, "Individuals' Interaction with Their Feedback Environment: The Role of Domain-Specific Individual Differences" in *Research in Personnel and Human Resources Management*, 16 (1998): 215–54

Johnson, Jeff W., Andrea M. Olson and Carol Lynn Courtney, "Implementing Multiple Perspective Feedback: An Integrated Framework", *Human Resource Management Review*, 6/4 (1996): 253–77

Kluger, Avraham N. and Angelo DeNisi, "The Effects of Feedback Interventions on Performance: A Historical Review, a Meta-Analysis, and a Preliminary Feedback Intervention Theory", *Psychological Bulletin*, 119/2 (1996): 254–84

London, Manuel, *Job Feedback: Giving, Seeking, and Using Feedback for Performance Improvement*, Mahwah, New Jersey: Erlbaum, 1997

Waldman, David A., Leanne E. Atwater and David Antonioni, "Has 360 Degree Feedback Gone Amok?", *Academy of Management Executive*, 12/2 (1998): 86–94

Much of the writing on feedback is about individual employee performance feedback and is found in journal articles or as chapters in books on other related topics, such as feedback in the context of performance appraisal or performance management – see, for example, the discussions of Murphy & Cleveland and Williams in the entry on Appraisal. Against this background the book by LONDON is of particular interest. This is a substantial text, the scope of which is indicated clearly by the subtitle. It is not restricted to appraisal but also deals with feedback in the context of assessment centres. The section on giving feedback, although appropriately devoting much space to appraisal, ranges more widely than this and also deals with coaching. The whole volume is useful for practice (for designers of feedback systems, for deliverers of feedback, and for recipients) and is soundly based in theory and research.

Multi-source feedback (also known as 360° or multi-rater feedback) is popular today. Although anecdotal case-study reports may lead us to overestimate the extent of its popularity, there is no doubt that the use of multi-source feedback has increased. Much of the literature is of an uncritical practitioner-orientated kind. An important exception to this is the review chapter by FLETCHER & BALDRY. They take a research perspective and examine, amongst other things, the evidence on the psychometric properties of 360° ratings (often neglected in the practitioner literature), reactions to and impact of multi-rater feedback, and self-assessment.

Some other, shorter examinations of multi-source feedback, not included in the Fletcher & Baldry review, are noteworthy. BORMAN is of interest because he adopts a critical stance and challenges "the assumptions that different rating sources have relatively unique perspectives on performance and multiple rating sources provide incremental validity over the individual sources". JOHNSON, OLSON & COURTNEY note the relative absence of theory and propose a theoretical framework. This integrates contemporary theorizing on individual performance within the context of organizational development. Finally, as far as 360 degree feedback is concerned, the short paper by WALDMAN, ATWATER & ANTONIONI deserves to be mentioned as it offers a cautionary note on what might realistically be expected from a multi-source feedback system.

Much of the literature on feedback tends to be more about the delivery of feedback than about how it is received. London pays some attention to recipient perceptions and the impact of feedback and Fletcher & Baldry discuss theoretical frameworks. Important in this regard are the papers by FEDOR and HEROLD & FEDOR. Fedor "presents a model of how recipients perceive and respond to performance feedback". Herold & Fedor shift tack somewhat by dealing not just with the recipient of feedback and the influence of individual differences, but also considering the interaction with the feedback environment.

Feedback systems are implemented within organizations to serve various purposes – to control, to inform, to motivate, with an overall aim being to maintain (if not indeed improve) performance. One short review of the effects of feedback on performance is to be found in ALGERA who also reviews relevant theory (for example control theory and goal-setting). KLUGER & DENISI provide a meta-analytic review of the effects of feedback on performance. Although it is expected that feedback will increase performance, it does not always do so and sometimes leads to decreases. Kluger & Denisi present a theoretical model and offer possible explanations.

Finally, although much of the literature is about feedback that is formally provided as part of some organizational system, we need to recognize that feedback may be provided on an informal basis and solicited informally. This theme is explored by FARR who reviews the relevant literature and considers implications for practice.

RICHARD WILLIAMS

See also Appraisal, Goals, goal setting

Female employment, developing countries

Beneria, Lourdes, "Toward a Greater Integration of Gender in Economics", *World Development*, 23/11 (1995): 1839–50

Birdsall, Nancy and Richard Sabot, *Unfair Advantage: Labor Market Discrimination in Developing Countries*, Washington, DC: World Bank, 1991

Boserup, Ester, *Woman's Role in Economic Development*, London: Allen and Unwin, and New York: St Martin's Press, 1970

Horton, Susan, "Marginalization Revisited: Women's Market Work and Pay, and Economic Development", *World Development*, 27/3 (March 1999): 571–82

Schultz, T. Paul (editor), *Investment in Women's Human Capital*, Chicago: University of Chicago Press, 1995

Sparr, Pamela (editor), *Mortgaging Women's Lives: Feminist Critiques of Structural Adjustment*, London: Zed, 1994

Standing, Guy, "Global Feminization through Flexible Labor: A Theme Revisited", *World Development*, 27/3 (March 1999): 583–602

Tzannatos, Zafiris, "Women and Labor Market Changes in the Global Economy: Growth Helps, Inequalities Hurt and Public Policy Matters", *World Development*, 27/3 (March 1999), 551–69

The literature on female employment in developing countries can be broadly divided into two perspectives, namely feminist and neoclassical, the latter often using the "new household economics" approach and being more heavily empirical. Both strands are represented in two recent special issues of *World Development*, from 1995 and 1999, which contain the four articles by BENERIA, HORTON, STANDING, and TZANNATOS discussed below, as well as a number of other useful papers, along with many references. Of the four books discussed, BOSERUP's classic text predates the recent upsurge in interest in feminist economics; the books by BIRDSALL & SABOT and by SCHULTZ fall in the neoclassical tradition, and that edited by SPARR is an example of the feminist viewpoint.

Boserup describes broad patterns of female employment in the course of economic development. Women initially work as intensively as men in agriculture, but turn to work within the household as the advent of plough technology reduces the need for human labour. Urban migration initially reduces women's work in the market, because it is more difficult to combine non-agricultural work with childcare. Subsequently, as women's education catches up to men's in the course of development, and as family sizes shrink, more and more women work in the labour market. This makes the relationship between women's market employment and economic development U-shaped. Hence women's employment is recorded as high in Africa, where farming is not mechanized, low in south Asia (where population density has encouraged the adoption of plough technology), and generally increasing in the middle-income developing world.

Boserup also discusses the importance of cultural and historical factors that affect the broad pattern, for example in her extremely useful typology of migration. Migration tends to be by families in Arab countries (where women's participation in both agriculture and urban occupations is equally low) and in Southeast Asia (where women's participation in both rural and urban occupations is equally high). Towns and cities tend to be female-dominated in Latin America where women's participation in rural occupations is low but in urban occupations is high. By contrast urban areas are male-dominated in sub-Saharan Africa where women's participation rates are the reverse. Another key insight is her argument that women are disadvantaged when facing technological change relative to men, due to their lower levels of education in developing countries.

Beneria provides a recent brief description of the issues involved in measuring female employment. Time-use studies suggest that women with young children work longer hours than men in virtually all countries. However since much of their work occurs in the home, it is not counted in employment statistics. Employment statistics have been improved in that efforts are now made in household labour force surveys to include subsistence production and work in the informal sector, where women are often overrepresented. However the inclusion of domestic work and voluntary work (again, more often the preserve of women) requires conceptual changes in how GDP is defined. Although there are pilot efforts on this for industrialized countries, this has not been a focus of effort for developing country statistics. In the same article, Beneria provides a useful overview of the literature on gender and economics, and selected findings from feminist research relevant to employment.

One key area where the feminist and neoclassical literatures diverge concerns the degree to which they are optimistic about the benefits of economic development for women. The feminist literature has been extremely sceptical about the benefits of economic growth, and vociferously critical of the effects of structural adjustment on women. Chapters from seven countries in Sparr's book discuss these adverse effects. In Turkey, for example, under structural adjustment there was an increase in homeworking in manufacturing, which predominantly affected women. Female unemployment in the same country remained persistently higher than men's due to "added worker" effects, as women were impelled to supply more labour in the face of declining family income.

Standing's article discusses the phenomenon of globalization, which he argues has led to feminization of employment through the need for increasing flexibility of labour costs. Women's participation rates have been rising and men's falling in the majority of countries for which he has data, such that the labour force is being "feminized". The former effect often dominates the latter such that overall participation rates have risen. Moreover women's unemployment rates have been falling relative to men's since the 1980s, both in developed and developing countries.

Horton and Tzannatos see the same phenomenon of feminization in a more positive light, pointing to the increase in women's participation, the shift of women into better jobs in the course of development as female education catches up with that of males, and to the much more rapid catch-up of women's pay relative to men's in middle-income developing countries than occurred in the industrialized countries. Tzannatos discusses the important role of public policy in assisting women in the labour force.

A large number of studies examine women's pay relative to men's, and Birdsall & Sabot is one such collection. They find a wide variation in women's relative pay across developing countries and conclude that there is no universal relation between economic development and labour market discrimination.

Schultz's edited book discusses the investments in human capital that help to drive the patterns of female employment. His own chapter (chapter one) focuses on the more rapid increase in women's than men's education in the course of development, and the more rapid decline in mortality rates for women. Other chapters discuss labour force participation (Goldin's chapter on the US is particularly interesting).

SUSAN HORTON

See also Feminization of poverty, Labour market

Femininity

Buckley, Sandra (editor), *Broken Silence: Voices of Japanese Feminism*, Berkeley: University of California Press, 1997

Davis, Angela Y., *Women, Race, and Class*, New York: Random House, 1981; London: Women's Press, 1982

Frenier, Carol R., *Business and the Feminine Principle: The Untapped Resource*, Oxford and Boston: Butterworth Heinemann, 1997

Harris, Maxine, *Down from the Pedestal: Moving beyond Idealized Images of Womanhood*, New York: Doubleday, 1994

Jameson, Elizabeth and Susan Armitage (editors), *Writing the Range: Race, Class, and Culture in the Women's West*, Norman: University of Oklahoma Press, 1997

Karam, Azza M., *Women, Islamisms and the State: Contemporary Feminisms in Egypt*, Basingstoke: Macmillan, and New York: St Martin's Press, 1998

Kramer, Lawrence, *After the Lovedeath: Sexual Violence and the Making of Culture*, Berkeley: University of California Press, 1997

Lowe, Maria R., *Women of Steel: Female Bodybuilders and the Struggle for Self-Definition*, New York: New York University Press, 1998

Trioli, Virginia, *Generation f: Sex: Power and the Young Feminist*, Melbourne: Minerva, 1996

Whitford, Margaret (editor), *The Irigaray Reader*, Oxford and Cambridge, Massachusetts: Blackwell, 1991

The social construction and expression of femininity changes through time and within societies. The tensions of traditional definitions of the feminine have been necessarily and deservedly disclosed by recent feminist theory. BUCKLEY's volume brings together 10 Japanese women who explain why Japanese feminism's multiple voices operate through informal and non-mainstream channels. The women elucidate the variety of feminist practice and theory in Japan and the complex recent history of feminism. They write about the politics of language, the construction of the gendered body through dominant institutions, and the interrelationship of Japanese with "Western" feminisms, and they critique Japan's global role. This text is a significant contribution to Western understandings of the complexity of Japanese femininity and the importance of feminism to Japanese society.

DAVIS concentrates on the intersection of race and class in the construction of femininity, particularly that of black American women. She writes of the legacy of slavery and the ways in which class and race inscribed the women's rights campaign. She documents black women's irrepressible will to be educated and moves to the heart of derogatory stereotypes of black men to explode the myth of the black rapist. Her powerful work provides an intellectual foundation for understandings of black American women and their present sociopolitical needs.

Using the conceptual tool of the "archetypal feminine", FRENIER examines the notion of feminine leadership, charting a course through the rocky shoals of stereotypical notions of "masculinity" and "femininity" to suggest a productive, positive partnership that enhances life choices for both women and men. Her work questions acceptable consciousness in the social and commercial world, explores the notion of deep community, and presents different ways of thinking about work and leadership. This work can be linked with Mary Bateson's ideas about perceiving differently to offer students ways of thinking beyond their socialization.

Writing from a psychosocial perspective, HARRIS concentrates on the themes of living that resonate among women in the US, despite their different lives. She deconstructs the stereotypical images that may entrap women, then elaborates the shared life themes that can liberate and give meaning to women's daily existence. Using women's narrative to structure the work, she elucidates women's interior subjective dialogues in order to reconstruct a complex multifaceted concept of femininity.

JAMESON & ARMITAGE propose a view of US history that opposes the limited perspective of the urban east coast and of white male public power. Their inclusive perspective illustrates the diversity of the societies of the West; their differing cultures, races, and genders. The 29 contributors offer a rich array of experiences that illuminate the differing perspectives of women of colour, the gendered nature of history's frontiers, the ways in which women resisted many kinds of conquest, the lived realities of immigrant women, the ways in which women empowered themselves, and the changing cultures and identities generated by the new frontiers of the urban environment.

This is an exceptional work that adds detail and power to perceptions of femininity through time and space.

Understandings of Egyptian women after more than a century of feminism are limited amongst Western writers. KARAM's volume addresses this limitation and seeks to explain why women have attacked laws implemented through state power that have been designed to benefit them. She documents how a politicized "Islam" has become a key characteristic of debates involving political, social, cultural, and economic transformation. Her exploration of "Islamism" as a political ideology provides detail to analyses of the complex interplay of power and hegemony that constructs femininity in Egypt, and broadens ideas about what this term may mean in different societies.

According to KRAMER, femininity and masculinity are distinguished in ways that construct femininity as "the radically ambivalent polar opposite of a radically unambivalent masculinity". This binarism underlies his notion that normalized selfhood in modern Western culture promotes and rationalizes violence against women. He provides a series of reflections about how and why we imagine ourselves as gendered beings, the ways that imaginings can interplay with sexually violent actions, and how such interplays may be dismantled. His psychocultural approach provides an innovative model for analyses of social violence.

Through a sporting world where physical self-presentation confronts and (re)defines accepted notions of femininity, LOWE's focus on female body-building fills a gap in studies of the sociology of sport. By analysing the "look" that displays both musculature and femininity, the industry that supports the competitors, the hegemonic definitions and images, as well as the political and economic power wielded by the predominantly male gatekeepers, the author illuminates the tensions and contradictions that construct socially accepted notions of strength and femininity.

In a work that extends an analysis of the confusion and passion about women, sexism, feminism, and the law generated by the Ormond College sexual-harassment case and subsequent public discourse in Australia, TRIOLI identifies the anger expressed about a young woman's belief that she could publicly "identify as assault what others may choose to forgive". Although the author strikes a simplistic note with her dichotomy between old and young, she reviews interactions between older feminists and young women, illustrating the matronizing and exclusionary tactics of many senior women towards younger feminists.

In this selection of Luce Irigaray's writings, WHITFORD emphasizes her thoughts about femininity and feminism that are part of her project to introduce social and symbolic change. Irigaray's audacious and visionary work, her assertion that women are not symbolically self defined, and that there may be the potential for a different non-masculine discourse is presented so that the compelling and creative power of her imagination is revealed. The editor's glossary, introduction, and analysis enhance the work, making it accessible to later year tertiary students who wish to engage with Irigaray's fine intellect and accomplished philosophy.

HELEN JOHNSON

See also Gender ideology

Feminism, Eastern European

Berry, Ellen E. (editor), *Post-Communism and the Body Politic*, New York: New York University Press, 1995

Drakulić, Slavenka, *How We Survived Communism and Even Laughed*, London: Hutchinson, 1992

Einhorn, Barbara, *Cinderella Goes to Market: Citizenship, Gender and Women's Movements in East Central Europe*, London: Verso, 1993

Feminist Review, special issue: "Shifting Territories: Feminisms and Europe", 39 (Winter 1991)

Funk, Nanette and Magda Mueller (editors), *Gender Politics and Post-Communism: Reflections from Eastern Europe and the Former Soviet Union*, New York: Routledge, 1993

Mische, Ann, "Post-Communism's 'Lost Treasure': Subjectivity and Gender in a Shifting Public Sphere", *Praxis International*, 13/3 (1993): 242–67

Salecl, Renata, *The Spoils of Freedom: Psychoanalysis and Feminism after the Fall of Socialism*, London and New York: Routledge, 1994

BERRY's book contains articles by East European and US writers who address the situation for women in postcommunist Europe. Rather than being a strict examination of the sociological or political situation of women since 1989, the articles tend to be more theoretically adventurous, dealing with topics such as feminism and representation, the intersections of nationalism and gender, and some of the specificities of East European feminist perspectives. Some of the problems of cross-cultural feminisms are also addressed.

Based on the idea that the trivial is political, DRAKULIĆ examines the political and personal consequences of people's everyday lives under communism, from doing laundry to shopping at markets. These everyday experiences create a background for her discussion of misunderstandings within the West of the current events in postcommunist Europe. In particular she focuses on the war in the countries of former Yugoslavia. Her discussion of the conflict arising out of her contact with US feminist, Nanette Funk, provides a specific, practical instance of some of the problems involved in transnational feminist practice.

EINHORN examines the current situation for women during the transitional period in East Central Europe, specifically in the Czech Republic, Hungary, Poland, and former East Germany. She finds the decreasing visibility of women in the public sphere during the move to market capitalism quite perplexing, and looks to the specific combinations of Nationalist, Catholic, and Orthodox Christian, and right-wing libertarian discourses in search of reasons for this phenomenon. The book contains detailed examination of the various feminist initiatives that are reacting to the current changes. However, her examination of "feminist movements" based on a specific Western feminist model unnecessarily blinds her to other possible reasons for the rejection of "feminism" by many women in East Central Europe.

FUNK & MUELLER's collection of articles by Eastern European feminists aims to alleviate some of the tensions that have arisen between Eastern European and Western feminists since 1989. Feminist theorists from countries such as Czech

Republic, Bulgaria, Hungary, and the former German Democratic Republic address the problems for women and "feminism" in contemporary postcommunist Europe, predominantly with regard to education, welfare, and abortion issues. There are also a couple of articles that address the differences in theoretical heritage between postcommunist and Western Europe. These differences highlight some of the reasons Western feminisms, often deemed universally useable, are not appropriate for feminist practices in the aftermath of communism.

The collection of articles in issue 39 of FEMINIST REVIEW represent a range of perspectives on the changing situation for women in Europe since 1989. Both Eastern and Western European feminist writers are present and the topics of the articles cover areas such as gender and ethnicity, feminism and socialism, the implications of the European Union on postcommunist countries, and women's movements. The focus is primarily on social and political effects of the post-1989 period, although some articles also cover gender representations in postcommunist Europe. The article entitled "Between Hope and Hopelessness: Women in the GDR after the Turning Point", by Irene Dolling is particularly insightful as an introduction to postcommunist feminist perspectives.

MISCHE presents a unique perspective on the reasons for the general movement of women away from public sphere involvement in postcommunist Europe. She suggests that this phenomenon should be analysed in terms of the failure within current politics to institutionalize the reasons and motivations for the 1989 revolutions, rather than with the assumption that 1989 led to democratic pluralist societies on an idealized Western model. Rather than being a form of retraditionalization of women, Mische argues that the current period represents a "reconfiguration" of tradition in which new boundaries between public and private are set, and new attitudes to these boundaries prevail. Using Hannah Arendt's theory of action, she examines the concept of political agency in the light of an understanding of the notions of "private" and "privacy" in postcommunist cultural discourse. She suggests that the conception of privacy in postcommunist Europe differs significantly from Western understandings.

SALECL'S work begins by questioning the belief, often held by Western feminists, that feminists from Eastern Europe must write about the "situation for women in Eastern Europe". Rather than taking that approach, she examines how such signifiers as democracy, human rights, freedom, and capitalism have changed in the period since 1989 in both postcommunist countries and the West. She examines the ideological formation of these notions, the performance of ideology in culture in general, and what she perceives as the primary subjectivity of late capitalism in the West. Salecl proposes to examine ideology as something founded on fantasy in which structures of power are inherently fantasmatic. She draws connections between the political correctness movement in the US, the postsocialist moral majority, and what Etiene Balibar has described as "metaracism", suggesting that the current situation in Eastern Europe is the symptom that exposes the inherent contradictions of liberal democracy.

NICOLA NIXON

Feminism, political

Brooks, Ann, *Postfeminisms: Feminisms, Cultural Theory and Cultural Forms*, London and New York: Routledge, 1997

Butler, Judith and Joan W. Scott (editors), *Feminists Theorize the Political*, London and New York: Routledge, 1992

hooks, bell, *Ain't I a Woman: Black Women and Feminism*, Boston: South End Press, 1981; London: Pluto Press, 1986

Lovenduski, Joni and Pippa Norris (editors), *Gender and Party Politics*, London, Thousand Oaks, California: Sage, 1993

Lovenduski, Joni and Vicky Randall, *Contemporary Feminist Politics: Women and Power in Britain*, Oxford and New York: Oxford University Press, 1993

Mohanty, Chandra Talpade, Ann Russo and Lourdes Torres (editors), *Third World Women and the Politics of Feminism*, Bloomington: Indiana University Press, 1991

Nicholson, Linda (editor), *The Second Wave: A Reader in Feminist Theory*, London and New York: Routledge, 1997

Okin, Susan Moller, *Women in Western Political Thought*, Princeton, New Jersey: Princeton University Press, 1992

Phillips, Anne, *Engendering Democracy*, Cambridge: Polity Press, 1991

Ryan, Barbara, *Feminism and the Women's Movement: Dynamics of Change in Social Movement Ideology and Activism*, New York and London: Routledge, 1992

Schneir, Miriam (editor), *Feminism in Our Time: The Essential Writings, World War II to the Present*, New York: Vintage, 1994; as *The Vintage Book of Feminism: The Essential Writings of the Contemporary Women's Movement*, London: Vintage, 1995

This selection of works reflects the threefold relationship between feminism and politics. The first dimension is feminism's influence on political science research. Second is the actual politics of feminism and its movement. The third area concerns the relationship between feminism and political theory in terms of both feminist criticisms of traditional political thought and the development of separate feminist political theory.

The collection edited by LOVENDUSKI & NORRIS indicates feminism's place in traditional political science as gender becomes established as a viable research category. Its 13 essays collate the data for women's involvement in political parties throughout the Western world. As one of the few studies of its kind it is an invaluable source of information.

Some of these data are included in PHILLIPS. She successfully marries political science and political theory to present an analysis that compares women's actual involvement in politics with feminist dreams of a new, participatory political model. The latter permeated the second-wave feminist movement but Phillips considers it to have been largely unworkable and at times destructive.

These two studies reflect feminism's induction into the discipline of politics, but the specific nature of feminist politics is, itself, a separate area of interest. SCHNEIR is one of the most useful collections of essential feminist texts. It spans 50 years of feminist writing and numerous writers. Her book, however, does not address recent feminist debates in depth, and here NICHOLSON makes up the shortfall. Her anthology includes examples of feminist works on postmodernism and essentialism that are central to contemporary debates on feminist politics.

RYAN provides one of the most interesting studies of feminism's political development in terms of the movement's politics. She accepts that the second-wave movement had problems and was often divided but she argues that women can learn from these experiences to rejuvenate feminist political action. Given that Ryan is mainly concerned with the American movement, it is useful to supplement her work with LOVEN-DUSKI & RANDALL's British study. They also document the factionalism of the British movement but suggest that it had some success in penetrating British political life and institutions.

It is vital, though, that any study of feminist movement politics take account of non-white and non-Western women's experiences of it. In this regard, HOOKS is the classic text on black feminism and continues to influence scholarship, even though there are now many books on this subject. She outlines black women's exclusion from the feminist movement and the different historical basis of black feminism. According to hooks what makes black feminist experiences different from those of white feminists is that they suffer dual oppression: being oppressed by black men and white society. Similarly, the collection edited by MOHANTY, RUSSO & TORRES detail the different nature of Third World women's feminism and their criticisms of the Western movement. Again the essayists want to assert the specific nature of their oppression to avoid being excluded from, or subjected to, Western feminist interpretations of their situations.

Feminism's interactions with political theory and thought are also diverse. Feminist political theorists have always been keen to re-evaluate traditional Western political thought. OKIN takes the classical humanist approach, suggesting that most Western political thought has used seemingly gender-neutral concepts that, on closer inspection, exclude or ignore women's experiences. She wants, therefore, to theorize these concepts so that they are truly universal in their application. Okin, however, admits that in this work she was too hasty to link political thought to the actual social status of women, and readers must be wary of this conflation of theory and practice.

In terms of separate, feminist political theory, BUTLER & SCOTT's volume is an essential text. Its essayists provide interpretative pieces on the politics of the feminist movement and on their own feminist-inspired models of politics. Hence, it includes pieces ranging from the impact of postmodernism on feminist thought to details of new democratic models. The ethos underlining all these essays is that the marginal status of feminist scholarship enables it to approach political thought in a fresh manner.

Finally, BROOKS exemplifies recent developments in feminist political theory. This accessible book provides a general overview of the most up-to-date debates in feminist theory with particular reference to the contentious issue of whether there is now a "postfeminist" political landscape. Although she is sensitive to those who might see postfeminism as a further attempt to undermine feminism, she is convinced it marks a welcome "paradigm shift" to a new set of feminist questions.

Consequently, she provides a fascinating analysis of feminism's new postmodern and postcolonial concerns at a time when it is no longer possible to speak of a single body of oppressed "women".

FRANCES OLDALE

See also Postcolonial feminism

Feminism, sociology

Abbott, Pamela and Claire Wallace, *An Introduction to Sociology: Feminist Perspectives*, 2nd edition, London and New York: Routledge, 1997

Giddens, Anthony, David Held, Dan Hillman, Don Hubert, Debbie Seymour, Michelle Stanworth and John Thompson (editors), *The Polity Reader in Gender Studies*, Cambridge: Polity Press, 1994

Gottfried, Heidi (editor), *Feminism and Social Change: Bridging Theory and Practice*, Urbana: University of Illinois Press, 1996

hooks, bell, *Feminist Theory: From Margin to Center*, Boston: South End Press, 1984

Laslett, Barbara and Barrie Thorne (editors), *Feminist Sociology: Life Histories of a Movement*, New Brunswick, New Jersey: Rutgers University Press, 1997

Ramazanoglu, Caroline, *Feminism and the Contradictions of Oppression*, London and New York, Routledge, 1989

Shanley, Mary Lyndon and Uma Narayan (editors), *Reconstructing Political Theory: Feminist Perspectives*, University Park: Pennsylvania State University Press, 1997

Walby, Sylvia, *Gender Transformations*, London and New York: Routledge, 1997

Weedon, Chris, *Feminist Practice and Poststructuralist Theory*, Oxford and New York: Blackwell, 1987

Wolf, Naomi, *Promiscuities: The Secret Struggle for Womanhood*, New York: Random House, 1997; as *Promiscuities: A Secret History of Female Desire*, London: Chatto and Windus, 1997

ABBOTT & WALLACE divide their work (which has been updated to include contemporary debates within feminism and sociology) into 11 sections to encompass the more recent concerns of feminist sociological thinkers. Acknowledging the differences and commonalities that exist within the category "woman", the work moves from recent postmodern theorizations of "woman" and her concerns, to "traditional" sociological discussions about stratification, education, lifecycle events, the "family", women's health, and work, to the ways in which contentious feminist knowledges are produced. This is an excellent reader that may be used across sociology, women's studies, and gender relations courses.

A classic text from an intellectually stimulating black feminist scholar, HOOKS' work is as potent today as when first published. Launching modern scholarship about black women and feminism, the author contests the intellectual tyrannies of white feminism to argue for the situating of black women and their lived experiences firmly at the centre of feminist discourse. With gentle humour and biting acuity, she provides the reader with a mode of seeing that does not pander to the race-neutral ideologies of white feminists. Rather, she works to reshape feminist theory using concepts and examples of oppression that demand recognition and action. This is a required text for any course that examines racialized and sexualized relations of power.

GIDDENS *et al.* have drawn together an array of writings that provide a wide-ranging overview of the theorization of gender and sexual difference, gendered work and identity, and the interactions of social constructions of gender with the inscription of sexuality and the ideologies and practices of power. The 30 short pieces can be used in total or in part as a key text in undergraduate courses that debate feminist theories and gendered relations. They provide historical background to the development of discussion in these subject areas, and some essays address the important issue of the construction of masculinities in Western societies.

Although focused upon North American case studies, GOTTFRIED's anthology debates and demonstrates the range of methodologies that may assist in conducting feminist research. To bridge the impasse between theory and practice the essays discuss the need to give women a voice, the use of qualitative research methods and their potential for exploitation of informants, the necessity of cross-cultural understandings when researching in different social and ethnic contexts to one's own, and the use of differing strategies to build new kinds of participatory research. It is highly recommended for students in the later years of their undergraduate studies, or for courses focusing specifically upon the problematic nature of ethical research.

In a collection of 11 varied life histories, LASLETT & THORNE work to generate feminist insights into the discipline of sociology. The differing paths of each author's experience are used to illuminate the concurrences between a social political movement and an academic discipline. Linking life history as a genre to feminist theoretical agendas, the authors interrogate the resistance proffered by dominant discourses and ideologies to the perceptions generated by sociologically based feminisms. They examine gendered relations, emotions, and ways in which sexualities are socially inscribed, to enhance knowledge produced from considerations of the intersection of social structures with active agency.

In a text that astutely negotiates the difficulties of feminist social theory and feminist political strategy, RAMAZONOGLU contests WEEDON's perception of inexorable institutional oppression, to consider the political improvements that have been made for women, and to detail the ways in which oppressions may differ for different women in differing social contexts. She problematizes the concept of difference and recent feminist analyses of differences between women to explore the contradictions that arise in feminist discourse. This is a necessary text for undergraduates who wish to broaden their understanding of the complexities of contemporary feminisms.

SHANLEY & NARAYAN examine the multidisciplinary terrain of feminist political theory, linking philosophers, legal scholars, political scientists, and sociologists into an edited collection of 11 essays. They investigate the entwined yet polemical topics of independence and dependency, question the intellectual and social processes that constitute ideas about the public and the private, and evaluate how women and members of socially marginalized groups may be empowered as politically conscious citizens. The work engages with the issue of power and its many beneficial and coercive manifestations in order to understand better the ordering of society.

WALBY's text elucidates and analyses the patterns of convergence and polarization that shape contemporary gender relations in Britain, and the ways in which class, ethnicity, and region inscribe women's ways of being. Working from a detailed theorization of gendered power that she terms "patriarchy", the author takes an uncompromising look at patriarchal relations, and provides compelling examples to substantiate her contention that patriarchal relations run counter to a society in which women are equal and active shareholders. Using a sophisiticated feminist politics she focuses particularly on British and European Union labour markets in order to contextualize and theorize the gender politics generated by their integration.

In a classic work that blends poststructuralist theory with feminist politics in order to generate a powerful political practice, WEEDON theorises ways to change existing power relations between women and men in society. Her trenchant explanation of the social construction of subject positions, and their concomitant social inscription, breaks down the problematic relationship between experience and theory. Using the concept of discourse as a framework, she discusses how language shapes individual subjectivities that are multifaceted, fluid, and constantly changing. And she shows how they simultaneously reproduce and contest power relations in society. Her analysis of subjectivity, discourse, and power is used to argue that established meanings, values, and power relations may be contested as blatant self-interest rather than taken for granted as established sociopolitical practice.

In her ethnography of a particular kind of American woman's sexuality, WOLF uses a feminist perspective to celebrate young women's desire and, at the same time, promotes their need for a social framework that encourages their sense of self-esteem. She traces the explicit sexual awakening of many middle-class people during the 1960s and 1970s in the United States, casting a critical eye on the ramifications for their children and the ways in which that particular epoch continues to inscribe American women's ways of being at the end of the 20th century. Although focused narrowly on her own experiences and those of her friends, the work may generate useful discussion amongst undergraduates as they reflect upon contemporary sociocultural inscriptions of their subjectivities and bodies.

HELEN JOHNSON

Feminism and psychoanalysis

Burke, Carolyn, Naomi Schor and Margaret Whitford (editors), *Engaging with Irigaray: Feminist Philosophy and Modern European Thought*, New York: Columbia University Press, 1994

Butler, Judith, *The Psychic Life of Power: Theories in Subjection*, Stanford, California: Stanford University Press, 1997

Gallop, Jane, *The Daughter's Seduction: Feminism and*

Psychoanalysis, Ithaca, New York: Cornell University Press, 1982

Grosz, Elizabeth, *Jacques Lacan: A Feminist Introduction*, London and New York: Routledge, 1990

Mitchell, Juliet, *Psychoanalysis and Feminism*, London: Allen Lane, and New York: Pantheon, 1974

Moi, Toril (editor), *French Feminist Thought: A Reader*, Oxford and New York: Blackwell, 1987

Salecl, Renata, *The Spoils of Freedom: Psychoanalysis and Feminism after the Fall of Socialism*, London and New York: Routledge, 1994

Silverman, Kaja, *The Threshold of the Visible World*, New York and London: Routledge, 1996

Wright, Elizabeth (editor), *Feminism and Psychoanalysis: A Critical Dictionary*, Oxford and Cambridge, Massachusetts: Blackwell, 1992

The collection of 16 articles edited by BURKE, SCHOR & WHITFORD aims to dispel some myths and misunderstandings of Irigaray's theories in US feminism, which, according to the authors, have led to a premature rejection of her work there, based on the charge of "biological essentialism". The articles develop Irigaray's relationship to not only Lacan, but also Hegel, Derrida, and Heidegger in order to explore the complexity of her theoretical position, while remaining attuned to some of the problems it contains. They provide a useful introduction to the various ways of reading and interpreting Irigaray's work, which is also contextualized within the French post-1968 academic milieu.

BUTLER's relationship with psychoanalysis has always been tempered by the strength of Foucault's influence on her work. Her strategy in this book is to move beyond the assumed incompatibility between psychoanalysis and poststructuralism. Wishing to read Freud through Foucault and vice versa, Butler places specific emphasis on the tropological similarities between the depiction of subjectivity in both theories. She combines Foucault's notion of subjection – the process of both becoming a subject and becoming subordinated – with the psychoanalytic notion of the subject's inauguration through foreclosure. Her work represents an extremely insightful attempt to find ways in which poststructuralism and psychoanalysis may illuminate each other through their common belief that the subject is formed in an essential subordination.

GALLOP begins her writing by questioning the simple coupling of psychoanalysis and feminism to be found in many feminist psychoanalytic writings. Using Mitchell's rationalistic approach to Freud as her point of departure she explores some of the problems, as well as the potential, for feminist thought in psychoanalysis. She addresses the work of a number of seminal writers including Lacan, Freud, Irigaray, Kristeva, Cixous, and Clement. Structured as an ongoing fictional dialogue between various theorists, Gallop's book questions the power relations between feminism and psychoanalysis and the tendency of feminism to be seduced by master narrators. Through the use of wordplay and metaphors, which attempt to prevent authorial closure, the theatricality of her work provides insights into the potentials and limitations of current feminist psychoanalytic theory.

GROSZ's introductory work on psychoanalysis is one of the clearest available, succinctly working through Freud's theories as a precursor to understanding Lacan's work. She lucidly describes Lacan's concepts of the imaginary, the real, the symbolic order, language, and the unconscious as well as considering the relationship between feminism and Lacanian theory as it is manifested in the work of Irigaray and Kristeva. Grosz suggests that Lacanian psychoanalysis may be very useful for feminist theoretical pursuits for understanding sexual power relations, however she warns that a critical distance should be maintained by feminists towards psychoanalysis in the application of Lacan's theories for potential feminist ends.

In one of the earliest feminist psychoanalytic texts, MITCHELL examines the potential within Freud's theory for feminism. Differing from interpretations of Freud in which he is seen to advocate the forms of patriarchal sexuality he describes, in particular, in his formulation of the female Oedipus complex, Mitchell suggests that Freud's work be read as a complex and systematic analysis of patriarchy and, as such, is useful (even essential) to feminism. Although somewhat outdated, her book is still a highly successful refutation of various uncritical, anti-Freudian elements of Western feminist thought.

MOI brings together a variety of French feminist writings from De Beauvoir's to the present in order to avoid the traditional triad of French feminism – Irigaray, Kristeva, and Cixous – as well as including a personal account of the feminist movement in France. The close relationship between feminism, philosophy, and psychoanalysis to be found in France becomes apparent through the broad range of perspectives present in this collection. It is a relationship that differs significantly from feminism's relationships to these areas of knowledge in the US and Britain. Although some of the sections may be considered too short to be useful introductions to some French feminists, they provide a good overview of the diversity of views and styles within French feminist thought, congregating around the issue of sexual difference.

SALECL examines the ideological formations of such signifiers as democracy, human rights, freedom, and capitalism for the impact that the fall of communism has had on them, both in Eastern Europe and the West. She discusses the performance of ideology within culture in general, as well as the primary subjectivity of late capitalism in the West; the destabilized subject. From a Lacanian perspective, Salecl examines ideology as something founded on fantasy, arguing that structures of power are inherently fantasmatic. She suggests the postcommunist situation in Eastern Europe be read as the symptom through which the inherent contradictions of liberal democracy in the West become visible. Her work is emblematic of the move within feminism beyond "women's issues" to more complex notions of gender as they interact with ideology.

SILVERMAN examines various psychoanalytic theories in an endeavour to draw a specifically psychoanalytic theory of love from them. Coming from the area of feminist film theory, she extrapolates the Lacanian categories of "the screen" and "the gaze" in order to elaborate the sensational and visual elements of the ego. This bodily ego is examined as both raced and gendered and Silverman works to dispel certain cultural myths surrounding corporeal identifications. Traversing a wide range of theoretical perspectives, Silverman examines the meanings inherent to the valorization of particular bodily idealizations at the level of visualization. Her work is complex, so a prior familiarity with some of the work of Freud and Lacan would be beneficial.

As an invaluable companion to any feminist psychoanalytic study, WRIGHT's compilation contains a detailed explication of the ways in which key psychoanalytic terms are understood and have been used in feminist theory, as well as the work of many of the significant figures in the meeting of feminism and psychoanalysis. With contributions by many well-known theorists, the entries are succinct while still tending to retain the complexities of the relationship between feminist issues and psychoanalytic knowledge. The cross-disciplinary nature of the dictionary engenders a wide range of theoretical perspectives surrounding psychoanalysis.

NICOLA NIXON

See also Hysteria

Feminist anthropology

di Leonardo, Micaela (editor), *Gender at the Crossroads of Knowledge: Feminist Anthropology in the Postmodern Era*, Berkeley: University of California Press, 1991

Evans, Grant (editor), *Asia's Cultural Mosaic: An Anthropological Introduction*, New York and London: Prentice Hall, 1993

Fox, Richard (editor), *Recapturing Anthropology: Working in the Present*, Santa Fe, New Mexico: School of American Research Press, 1991

Keesing, Roger and Andrew Strathern, *Cultural Anthropology: A Contemporary Perspective*, 3rd edition, Fort Worth, Texas: Harcourt Brace, 1998

Kulick, Don and Margaret Willson (editors), *Taboo: Sex, Identity and Erotic Subjectivity in Anthropological Fieldwork*, London and New York: Routledge, 1995

Marcus, George E. and Michael M.J. Fischer, *Anthropology as Cultural Critique: An Experimental Moment in the Human Sciences*, Chicago: University of Chicago Press, 1986

Moore, Henrietta L., *Feminism and Anthropology*, Cambridge: Polity Press, and Minneapolis: University of Minnesota Press, 1988

Spradley, James and David W. McCurdy (editors), *Conformity and Conflict: Readings in Cultural Anthropology*, 9th edition, New York and Harlow, Essex: Longman, 1997

Visweswaran, Kamala, *Fictions of Feminist Ethnography*, Minneapolis: University of Minnesota Press, 1994

In this third edition of KEESING & STRATHERN, Strathern has updated Keesing's groundbreaking undergraduate text. The biases of the 1970s are retained in the new version, in that issues of gender receive cursory treatment and more recent postmodern theoretical developments are not included. However, the text provides a useful overview of many communities' different ways of being and thinking, as well as the many issues that should be understood as part of a sound base for later theoretical and empirical research.

DI LEONARDO's edited collection of 12 essays should be an integral text for undergraduates addressing issues of how knowledge is produced, and how gender relations act to enhance or limit academic and popular understandings of reality. This work is situated squarely in feminist anthropology and uses poststructuralist approaches to the construction of meaning.

EVANS' edited collection of essays examines the diverse societies that comprise Asia. The 15 chapters range from a treatise on anthropology and its traditional methodology to understandings of the social construction of language in Asian countries, kinship and family formations, and issues of power and governance including explorations of class, status, and caste. A classic chapter examines anthropology and the cross-cultural study of women, and the dilemmas of development and the increasing urbanization of many people's lives. This text places anthropological study in recent theoretical perspectives.

The authors of FOX's edited collection tackle contentious contemporary theoretical issues in anthropology, and discuss new understandings of fieldwork and of writing ethnography. Ranging from a critique of anthropology's invention of the "other", to a consideration of the political context in which all anthropologists work, an analysis of academic and scholarly constraints on knowledge production, an understanding of what kind of work has preceded the researcher's own, and a detailed and dazzling review of the concept of culture. Each author offers practical critiques of anthropology and its modes of production, in order to keep producing.

KULICK & WILLSON's clear presentation of researchers' experiences does not just join with the "confessional" stream of anthropological literature that has recently become popular in America but adds substance to discussions about the nature of fieldwork. Through its exploration of feeling, memory, and subjectivity, this text can be included in "how-to" courses that prepare students for field research.

Among the first authors to introduce the "crisis of representation" that has exercised the minds of most anthropological postgraduates since its publication, MARCUS & FISCHER provocatively dispute the theories that have shaped anthropological knowledge for most of this century. The authors combine the challenging notion of interpretation with empirical observation and faithful description in order to argue that contemporary anthropology should become a more incisive tool – that is, politically and historically sensitive and critical.

MOORE is a classic text for use in anthropological courses that address the issues implicit in theories about women's ways of being across cultures. This work examines the relationship between the development of a feminist approach to knowledge production and anthropology as two separate yet interconnected disciplines. Moore then evolves and complicates the debate with a lucid explanation of the difficulties inherent in defining what "women" and "gender" may mean in other societies, how women's work can be understood, and how women's lives are changing through local and global social transformations.

SPRADLEY & McCURDY's work is divided into ten sections. It spans 36 field research sites to give students who are new to the discipline a global and a local perspective across a diverse range of societies. Spradley & McCurdy have, however, remained faithful to the themes of earlier editions, with a focus on stability and change, language and communication, economic systems, cosmologies and worldviews, and applied anthropology.

VISWESWARAN makes explicit the implicit interactions between writing and reading in order to explore the relationship between the writing of ethnographies and literature. In querying how fact and fiction are constituted through the acts of reading and writing, she studies the ways in which disciplinary knowledge can form reality and the power relations inherent in acts of knowledge production.

HELEN JOHNSON

Feminist economics

Ferber, Marianne A. and Julie A. Nelson (editors), *Beyond Economic Man: Feminist Theory and Economics*, Chicago: University of Chicago Press, 1993

Folbre, Nancy, *Who Pays for the Kids? Gender and the Structures of Constraint*, London and New York: Routledge, 1994

Gardiner, Jean, *Gender, Care, and Economics*, Basingstoke: Macmillan, 1997

Grapard, Ulla, "Feminist Economics: Let Me Count the Ways" in *Beyond Neoclassical Economics: Heterodox Approaches to Economic Theory*, edited by Fred E. Foldvary, Cheltenham, Gloucestershire: Elgar, 1996

Hawkesworth, Mary, "Social Sciences" in *A Companion to Feminist Philosophy*, edited by Alison M. Jagger and Iris Marion Young, Malden, Massachusetts and Oxford: Blackwell, 1998

Hewitson , Gillian J., *Feminist Economics: Interrogating the Masculinity of Rational Economic Man*, Cheltenham, Gloucestershire: Elgar, 1999

Humphries, Jane (editor), *Gender and Economics*, Aldershot, Hampshire: Elgar, 1995

Kuiper, Edith and Jolande Sap (editors), *Out of the Margin: Feminist Perspectives on Economics*, London and New York: Routledge, 1995

Nelson, Julie A., *Feminism, Objectivity and Economics*, New York and London: Routledge, 1996

Waring, Marilyn, *If Women Counted: A New Feminist Economics*, New York: Harper and Row, 1988; London: Macmillan, 1989

Woolley, Frances R., "The Feminist Challenge to Neoclassical Economics", *Cambridge Journal of Economics*, 17/4 (1993): 485–500

Feminist theory and philosophy have informed the feminist concerns erupting across fields like economics in which gender has traditionally been a secondary concern. The formation of feminist economics as a defined field is a far cry from the early "add women and stir" approach and increasingly analyses have challenged neoclassical hegemony with varying degrees of success.

HAWKESWORTH provides an overview of the questions that feminist philosophers of social science have asked over the past three decades. These range from efforts to expose the persistence of androcentrism in allegedly "neutral" scientific claims to an expostulation of how positivism in all its manifestations and despite its claim to a factual, unified, objective knowledge, has been critiqued by the various postpositivist philosophies that have made gender the main focus of enquiry. Within the context of the emancipatory goal of feminism, the feminist researchers of social science are concerned with the questions of truth and reality interpreted variously. Hawkesworth outlines the challenge of unpacking the conception of knowledge in a way that places emancipatory interests of feminist cognitive practices at the heart of social relations.

WOOLLEY, as the title of her article suggests, examines these challenge(s) to neoclassical economics. She makes a progress report on the feminist economics agenda that involves documenting differences in the wellbeing of men and women, advocating policies to promote equity, and conducting research free from androcentric bias. The first aim is the closest to being achieved; the second is more problematic and its espousal leads feminist neoclassical economists to challenge their discipline. Overall, the article is interesting and thought provoking.

GRAPARD's article recognizes and appreciates the multiplicity of voices that constitute feminist economics and looks at how it differs from other heterodox approaches to questions about human nature, assumptions and methodologies of Western science, and definitions of the proper domain of economic inquiry. Feminist attempts to destabilize the essentialist *homo economicus* as the norm of human behaviour are rapidly developing to challenge the gendered lens of the "malestream" profession and its assumptions, methods, domain, and categories of analyses. The article also counts the ways in which this has happened, notably by the creation of the International Association for Feminist Economics (IAFFE) in 1992, and publication of the journal *Feminist Economics* (Routledge) since 1995. Such developments have fostered an interdisciplinary discourse on feminist perspectives towards economics and the economy.

FERBER & NELSON seems to be the first anthology of feminist economic writings and may claim the status of a discipline-defining textbook. The contributors provide the theoretical underpinnings of both a neoclassical critique and a reorientation of economic thinking toward a new paradigm. The essays deal with topics such as social construction of the discipline and gender (Ferber & Nelson), logical inconsistencies in the neoclassical paradigm (England), and the epistemology of economic theorizing and its androcentric nature (Strassmann, McCloskey, Jennings). The main critique embedded in some chapters (Nelson, Strassmann) concerns the failure of the definition of *economic* to even include the home production of necessities of life, thus rendering women's economic contributions invisible and ensuring that the consequences of economic policy at the household level are virtually ignored. Blank reflects on the main chapters from the perspective of a neoclassical economist; Williams evaluates them from a postmodernist perspective. Their aim of the criticism is reformulation and recreation of a more self-reflective economics.

KUIPER & SAP's *Out of the Margin* was the result of the first international conference at Amsterdam (June, 1993) that recognized and addressed the questions involving the impact of gender on economic theory and methodology. The book consists of 13 papers, plus comments reflecting the diverse interests, concerns, and approaches of feminist economics. These include studying the role of traditional Victorian values in shaping the neoclassical view of women and women's issues (Pujol), issues of growth and income distribution (Hutchinson), and human capital and gender earning gap (Polachek). Some interesting issues addressed in the other articles are economists' role as storytellers (Strassman & Polanyi), reading neoclassical economics (Feiner), empirical challenges facing feminist economics (MacDonald), feminist econometrics (Redmount), feminist redefinition of privatization and economic reform (Hopkins) and gender, property, and land rights (Bina Agarwal).

NELSON draws on feminist theories from many disciplines to produce the first full-length single-authored feminist critique of contemporary economics. She evaluates abstract core models of neoclassical economics by exploring their relationship with cultural conceptions of gender and value, and presents a tool called a "gender-value compass" for thinking about the relation of gender to value in a new way. Accusing neoclassical economics of pursuing the goal of spurious objectivity, she reformulates "objectivity" as something that, instead of denying culture altogether, recognizes that one is operating within a set of cultural parameters. She applies her suggested mode of analysis in some case studies on topics such as the theory of the family, income tax policy, and macroeconomics. Refraining from any instant solutions, the book does, however, provide some outlines for a less gender-biased discipline, which would be rendered richer and more objective by recognizing the role of the knower and the context.

WARING is a unique book developing the theme of sex discrimination in national income accounting and providing an inspired feminist critique of it. The book serves as a popular introduction to the assumptions and practices underlying national income accounting. There are detailed discussions from a feminist viewpoint on such topics as labour economics, statistical surveys, the history of national accounting, special problems of poverty in developing nations, and environmental issues among others. A prime concern throughout the book is the problem of lack of official measurement of household production services, and their production, consumption, and imputed labour income. Another theme permeating the book is the problem of measuring the value of (unpaid) volunteer labour services. Her unique and lasting contribution is her painstaking research into how all this erroneous theory has impacted on women, leading to their further impoverishment. She also suggests a sensible plan of action to begin with, zeroing in on how census taking must be changed, as the forms force women to declare themselves as "economically inactive" merely because their toil is unpaid or expropriated.

FOLBRE undertakes to provide a framework for explaining how the costs of caring for children and other dependants are distributed in different societies over time. She proposes a theory that combines aspects of neoclassical, institutional, and Marxist economics with insights from feminist thought. She contends that economists have paid little attention to social reproduction and ignore the fact of unequal distribution of cost of caring – between men and women, parents and non-parents. Traditional economic and feminist explanations of the relationships between economic development and social reproduction are integrated using comparative historical analysis of

situations in northwestern Europe, the US, and Latin America and the Caribbean. It is a refreshing attempt to integrate a sociobiological perspective on human action with the rather confining perspective of "economic man", historicizing its subject and thus making a creative use of economic concepts to crystallize important social policy issues.

Similarly, GARDINER explores the history of neglect of household as the basic unit of care and looks at household economic relations and gender divisions since the mid 1960s. An important chapter (Chapter 11) provides a critique of neoclassical, Marxist and feminist theories and looks at an alternative feminist economics. Another work in the tradition of feminist economics, but dealing more with women's labour, is *Sexual Economyths: Conceiving a Feminist Economics* (Chris Beasley, St Martin's Press, 1994).

HUMPHRIES is an edited collection of 27 articles divided into three parts. The first deals with articles by familiar names (Woolley, Nelson, England) on gender and mythology, the second is a look at gender and the history of economics (e.g. Pujol's reading of Marshall's *Principles of Economics*, Folbre on the housewife in 19th-century economic thought and a 1923 article on women's wages by F.Y. Edgeworth), and the third part has articles on the family, household production and market work (dealing with household production and allocation of time, gender and labour supply, and gender differences in occupations and earnings). There is an excellent, very comprehensive introduction to the work, and detailed discussion of some of the studies relating to labour supply, wage differentials etc. This volume attempts to provide the reasons why women and the "feminine" ways of knowing should not be absent from neoclassical economics, and an overview of the work that has attempted to write them in. The articles mostly adopt an empiricist or standpoint feminist perspective, which stresses broadening the scope of mainstream economics rather than challenging its basic foundations (which is a characteristic of feminist poststructuralist work). This is a good place to find some "classic" articles (Mincer, Becker, Bergmann, Hartmann amongst others) on the issues concerned.

HEWITSON is a rare, goundbreaking attempt at poststructuralist feminist economics. The author deals in detail with feminist economics, the term and its significance. In the first part of the book, she discusses the relationships between women and knowledge in economics. This involves an extensive survey of work done by feminist empiricists and standpoint theorists mostly within the mainstream economics framework. She points out the limits to what can be achieved in this way, and also provides a critique of Nelson's gender-value compass approach (see above). Her crucial argument is a rejection of the abstract individualism of neoclassical economics which relies on sexual indifference, and a call for treating neoclassical economics as a "productive" discourse which is implicated in the production of the economic, social, and symbolic positioning of women. Femininity is thus the "constructive other" of a discursive specific definition of masculinity. After, deconstructing the figure of Robinson Crusoe (the symbolic rational economic man), she looks at the issue of surrogate motherhood in detail, positing that its neoclassical analysis (within a model she puts forward) crucially needs to use the metaphor of "womb-as-capital" requiring and producing the one-sex world. Thus, women cannot be "included" in a neoclassical economics premised upon their exclusion. This book is extremely innovative theoretically, and has an extensive list of references. It sets the stage for the future agenda of feminist poststructural economics.

NITASHA KAUL

See also Household as an economic agent, Neoclassical economics

Feminist geographies

Gibson-Graham, J.-K., *The End of Capitalism (as We Knew It): A Feminist Critique of Political Economy*, Cambridge, Massachusetts and Oxford: Blackwell, 1996

Jones, John Paul III, Heidi J. Nast and Susan M. Roberts (editors), *Thresholds in Feminist Geography: Difference, Representation, Methodology*, Lanham, Maryland: Rowman and Littlefield, 1997

McDowell, Linda, "Space, Place and Gender Relations, Part 1: Feminist Empiricism and the Geography of Social Relations", *Progress in Human Geography*, 17/2 (1993a): 157–79

McDowell, Linda, "Space, Place and Gender Relations, Part 2: Identity, Difference, Feminist Geometries and Geographies", *Progress in Human Geography*, 17/3 (1993b): 305–18

McDowell, Linda, *Gender, Identity and Place: Understanding Feminist Geographies*, Cambridge: Polity Press, and Minneapolis: University of Minnesota Press, 1999

Mackenzie, Suzanne, *Visible Histories: Women and Environments in a Post-War British City*, Montréal: McGill-Queen's University Press, 1989

Massey, Doreen, *Spatial Divisions of Labour: Social Structures and the Geography of Production*, London: Macmillan, and New York: Methuen, 1984

Massey, Doreen, *Space, Place, and Gender*, Cambridge: Polity Press, and Minneapolis: University of Minnesota Press, 1994

Matrix, *Making Space: Women and the Man-Made Environment*, London: Pluto Press, 1984

Mattingly, Doreen and Karen Falconer Al-Hindi (editors), "Should Women Count? The Role of Quantitative Methodology in Feminist Geographic Research", *Professional Geographer*, 47/4 (1995): 427–66

Monk, Janice and Susan Hanson, "On Not Excluding Half of the Human in Human Geography", *Professional Geographer*, 34/1 (1982): 11–23

Moss, Pamela (editor), "Feminism as Method", *Canadian Geographer*, 37/1 (1993): 48–61

Moss, Pamela (editor), "Discussion and Debate: Symposium on Feminist Participatory Research", *Antipode*, 27 (1995): 71–101

Nast, Heidi J. (editor), "Women in the Field", *Professional Geographer*, 46/1 (1994): 54–102

Rose, Gillian, *Feminism and Geography: The Limits of Geographical Knowledge*, Cambridge: Polity Press, and Minneapolis: University of Minnesota Press, 1993

Spain, Daphne, *Gendered Spaces*, Chapel Hill: University of North Carolina Press, 1992

Women and Geography Study Group of the Institute of British Geographers (WGSG/IBG), *Gender and Geography: An Introduction to Feminist Geography*, London: Hutchinson, 1984

Women and Geography Study Group of the Royal Geographical Society with the Institute of British Geographers (WGSG/IBG), *Feminist Geographies: Explorations in Diversity and Difference*, Harlow, Essex: Longman, 1997

Zelinsky, Wilbur, "The Strange Case of the Missing Female Geographer", *Professional Geographer*, 25/2 (1973): 151–67

One of the central tenets of the feminism that informs our scholarship and political action as feminist geographers is the need to challenge the construction of authority. Putting into print a list of key works canonizes particular contributions, something that supports the construction of *a* feminist authority. However, a dilemma arises when feminist geographers must legitimate feminist geographies within the discipline of geography in order to establish them as acceptable fields of study. As a provisional resolution, we suggest the accompanying list of readings as an introductory survey of the range of feminist geographies in the English-language-based academy. We want to emphasize, though, that despite the history of struggle over establishing feminist geographies, the amount of literature available today compared to only a decade ago is remarkable. We encourage readers to review this list of readings and the bibliographies in these works to see for themselves the scope of feminist geographies today.

Like many of the social sciences in the English-language-based academy, feminism – as both scholarship and a political movement – has been influential in informing theories and practices in the discipline of geography. Yet feminist geography is not an integrated or cohesive academic subdiscipline itself. Although not singular in definition or practice, feminist geographies do place central sexual difference as a primary organizing element of society. For nearly three decades, feminists through their scholarship have been forging innovative analyses of spatial phenomena that frame both the understanding and explanation of themselves as scholars, their topics of study, the methods through which they collect and convey information, and their everyday politics. These analyses have drastically changed the way key traditional geographic constructs are conceptualized – space, place, home, community, city, environment, and work.

From early on, feminist geographers demonstrated that being a woman matters. ZELINSKY makes a persuasive argument that women are missing from the discipline of geography not only in topical terms, but also as geographers themselves. He argues that geography is diminished by their absence, intellectually and substantively. Although the specifics of his arguments may appear to be dated, the intention of his "outburst" (p.104) is much like a feminist call to political action today. In other words, geography needs more research with/by/for/on women. His piercing remarks sparked a rash of publications over the next decade to justify the existence of either a feminist perspective in geography or a feminist analysis of spatial phenomena. For example, MONK & HANSON suggest that building a geography that is feminist entails critically analysing issues involving women and sorting out sexist bias in geographic research. They usefully point out ways that feminism can inform a spatial analysis and list multiple ways that conventional research neglects and excludes women and women's interests.

Until the late 1980s, feminist geographers tended to focus on women's labour primarily because initial feminist approaches in geography were closely tied to the newly emerging Marxist analyses. MASSEY (1984) exemplifies this best with her work in locality studies. She details how global restructuring processes transformed the industrial organization of Britain. Using the concept of spatial division of labour, she demonstrates that the production process is concentrated in specific geographical areas according to sectors and tasks. She also shows that these spatial divisions of labour are *gendered*. MACKENZIE, working at the scales of the household and community, investigates the paid and unpaid labour of women in post-war Brighton. The scrutiny of these women's daily lives shows that these women, through engaging in the mundane, actively participate in the construction of their environments. Her work showcases the predominance of socialist analyses in feminist geography at the time while still taking seriously the notion that women shape and are shaped by their experiences of place. McDOWELL (1993a &1993b) provides a detailed review of the types of English-language-based feminist geographical studies throughout this period.

Feminism effected change by creating new analyses in a variety of geographical subdisciplines, including for example, political, cultural, social, urban, historical, and economic geography. For example, MASSEY's (1994) collection of essays, written over a period of two decades, illustrates how feminism transformed her own economic analysis. She begins in the late 1970s as a Marxist industrial geographer with no attention given to gender. By the mid 1990s, however, she uses gender relations as a central construct in explaining the impact of globalization.

As feminist analyses in geography in the English-language-based academy matured throughout the late 1980s and early 1990s, sexual difference and gender became merely two sets of power relations constituting social space. With the introduction of poststructuralist thought into feminist geography, issues of difference and representation became paramount. Drawing on these poststructuralist notions, JONES, NAST & ROBERTS edited a volume that demonstrates how some feminist geographers are elaborating the spatial aspects of these issues. One goal these articles collectively achieve is the recasting of "woman" – moving away from a monolithic ensemble acting and reacting in unison with all other women toward a complex being constituted by a multiplicity of power relations – a task that signifies the integration of diversity as an organizing theme for feminist geographies. Another example of the way poststructuralist thought is informing feminist critiques is GIBSON-GRAHAM's reworking of capitalism. They take to heart this notion of diversity and apply it to concepts in Marxist political economy. The result is an innovative look at how multiple capitalisms structure women's lives locally and globally and the ways in which they resist.

McDOWELL (1999), in her review of feminist geographies, systematically demonstrates how feminist geographers have critically assessed and extended notions of conventional geographic constructs such as home, workplace, community, city, public/private space, and nation state. She also includes more recent feminist work on new geographical terms such as identity, body, sexuality, and travel writing. Her work highlights the attention feminist geographers are giving to the multiple sets of power relations including, but not limited to, those arranged around ability, age, citizenship, class, ethnicity, nationality, race, and sexuality.

Another area that interests feminists is the construction of geographical knowledge. ROSE sets up a framework to explain how geographical thought and practice, including, for example, time geography, fieldwork, and humanistic, is "masculinist". Masculinism in a discipline means that men alone define what counts as knowledge, control the processes of creating knowledge, and deem men's experiences as the only worthwhile subject matter. Together, these epistemological claims support the notion that the existing (masculinist) geographical knowledge is exhaustive, and assumes there can be no other contributions. She goes on to demonstrate how masculinist thinking dominates several spheres of geographical thought and practice as, for example, time geography, fieldwork, and humanistic conceptions of home. In an attempt to reposition the subject of masculinism, she proposes "paradoxical space" as a way of thinking about how to access entry points into the construction of knowledge. In this way she is able to offer feminism as a new way of knowing geography – one that "refuses the exclusions of the old" (p.141).

Part of the rejection of a masculinist geography involved reworking approaches to research. The collection of articles edited by MOSS (1993) initiated a discussion about what makes research feminist. Although perspectives varied, contributors did agree that what makes research feminist is how research methods are used within and outside the academy. North American feminist geographers at that time held that researching with numbers had a dehumanizing effect on women's lives and many turned to qualitative methods of data collection. But the wholehearted acceptance of qualitative methods raised issues around experience, representation, critical reflection, and subjectivity. Feminists began recognizing the exploitation inherent in such interactive research methods. NAST introduced a collection of articles that addresses these specific issues in relation to being "women in the field". Each contributor problematizes the relationships among participants in research projects. Rather than promoting a set of ethical guidelines for undertaking feminist research (which would be a masculinist solution), these articles challenge feminist geographers to further reflect upon their roles as feminist researchers.

MATTINGLY & FALCONER AL-HINDI edit a set of essays wherein each contributor reflects on how numbers can or should be used in feminist research. Coming from a different location within debates over experience, representation, critical reflection, and subjectivity, these feminists assume that feminist geographers can undertake research without necessarily exploiting participants. The edited collection by MOSS (1995) takes up this issue of exploitation by offering sets of reflections on specific research projects. Each contributor discusses various sets of politics shaping their experiences of conducting academic research and their ways of coming to interim solutions to the dilemmas they encountered in the field.

Methodological concerns continue to be central in feminist geographies and remain open for critique, discussion, and debate.

There are few explicitly feminist geography courses in the English-language-based academy and even fewer required feminist courses (although there are some). Most books are pitched at graduate students and professional academics with only a few textbooks for undergraduates. WGSG/IBG (1984) was the only available text from its publication until the early 1990s. It includes the central theme of gendering spatial phenomena. This book is still useful because of its place in the history of feminist geographies. A more recent publication by the same group, WGSG/IBG (1997), attempts to capture the shifts in feminist geographies over the years. The group sought to produce a textbook for undergraduates that includes the "breadth, diversity, intellectual vibrancy, debate and difference currently to be found in feminist geography" (p.1). This is really the only textbook explicitly for undergraduate students in their second or third year of study.

ROSE's book would be useful as an upper level undergraduate text if the focus were feminist geography as a field of study. She provides an historical overview of the development of feminism in geography, a feminist critique of the construction of geographical knowledge, and a psychoanalytical conception of paradoxical space. Jones, Nast & Roberts, too, could serve as an upper-level text. It would be most useful if the course were oriented toward women in the city or toward the undertaking of feminist research in specific settings. The book is packed with concrete examples of how feminists conduct research and analyse data. SPAIN, who extends the concept of gendering to discursive spaces, and MATRIX, who exposes the masculinist assumptions underlying the construction of spaces, are examples of good companion texts for courses in urban studies. McDowell (1999) is probably the best text for an overview of feminist geography – inside the classroom and as background reading. It can be used as a resource manual, a survey text, or a primary discussion text for upper level courses. Depending on the organization of the course, it might also be used for second- and third-year students. All these books could be used in postgraduate studies.

Much feminist geographical scholarship is sandwiched between other critical or progressive analyses in mainstream journals or edited collections. Yet gaining some understanding or seeking an introduction to various feminist geographies is not a formidable task. Perusing the pages of journals such as *Gender, Place & Culture*, *Environment & Planning D: Society & Space*, and *Antipode*, is useful in finding current examples of feminist research and analysis. Reviews of the feminist literature in geography appear regularly in *Progress in Human Geography*. It might also be useful to look specifically for feminist geography links through, for example, GPOW.

PAMELA MOSS AND KATHLEEN GABELMANN

Feminization of poverty

Conroy, Pauline and Niahm Flanaghan, *Women and Poverty in the European Commission: Issues in the Current Debate*, European Commission, Employment, Industrial Relation and Social Affairs, Equal Opportunities Unit, 1993

Daly, Mary, "Europe's Poor Women? Gender in Research on Poverty", *European Sociological Review*, 8/1 (1992): 1–12

Gelpi, Barbara, Nancy C.M. Hartsock, Clare C. Novak and Myra H. Strober (editors), *Women and Poverty*, Chicago: University of Chicago Press, 1986

Glendinning, Caroline and Jane Millar (editors), *Women and Poverty in Britain: The 1990s*, London and New York: Harvester Wheatsheaf, 1992

Millar, Jane and Caroline Glendinning, "Gender and Poverty", *Journal of Social Policy*, 18/3 (1988): 363–81

Oppenheim, Carey and Lisa Harker, *Poverty: The Facts*, 3rd edition, London: Child Poverty Action Group, 1996

Payne, Sarah, *Women, Health and Poverty: An Introduction*, New York and London: Harvester Wheatsheaf, 1991

Ruspini, Elisabetta, "Women and Poverty Dynamics: The Case of Germany and Britain", *Journal of European Social Policy*, 8/4 (1998): 291–316

Schaffner Goldberg, Gertrude and Eleanor Kremen (editors), *The Feminization of Poverty: Only in America?*, New York: Greenwood Press, 1990

The issue of women's poverty has emerged under the concept of "feminization of poverty". Women's poverty is gradually becoming more visible through the growing numbers of women living without men as lone parents or in old age and through women's occupational segregation into the low-wage sector. However, the concept of "feminization of poverty" is ambiguous as it is not able to reveal the true nature of women's poverty. Focusing on the gender dimension of poverty is indeed far more than simply counting the number of poor women.

Within this context, SCHAFFNER GOLDBERG & KREMEN's cross-national study (of Canada, France, Japan, Sweden, the US, Poland, and the Soviet Union) contributes to a correct conceptualization of the feminization of poverty. The term has different meanings: in the stricter sense it refers to the fact that women who support themselves or their families are becoming the majority of the poor. None the less, the authors believe it is important to think of the feminization of poverty in broader terms because women's poverty stems from a complex set of circumstances: women's position in the labour market; demographic factors such as divorce, separation, and lone parenthood; and the adequacy of the social welfare system – a significant factor in determining whether the feminization of poverty will occur. The book assumes the context of an industrial society characterized by the increasing centrality of the service sector and the widespread absorption of women into the labour force. However, the inclusion of two socialist nations gives the reader an opportunity to examine the condition of women in contrasting economic systems.

The 12 essays in GELPI *et al.* illuminate the complex paradoxes of women's situation. Particularly, the contributions analyse the relationship between women's poverty and women's citizenship by examining the serious political consequences of women's poverty in the US. On the one hand, poor women seldom have the time or resources to participate in politics and, on the other hand, the nature of liberal political systems itself disempowers women as the liberal democratic state has traditionally failed to include women. The book focuses on the deteriorating economic situation that affects women in advanced industrial countries and in other parts of the world as well, such as Kenya, India, Cuba, where women experience a decreased labour force participation rate and an increasing literacy gap.

Another very useful overview of the relationship between women and poverty is provided by GLENDINNING & MILLAR. The collection of essays focus on women's experience of poverty by examining the interaction of economic disadvantages in the labour market, domestic circumstances, and welfare systems. Thus, it depicts the crucial role played by the inequalities in the distribution of resources within the family in shaping women's wellbeing. The book has two main aims: the first is to document the extent of poverty among British women in a variety of social roles (training schemes, employment, redundancy, retirement) and in a variety of contexts (as paid workers, lone parents, wives, mothers, carers). The second is to explore the causes of poverty for women that are the result of gendered division of labour and of the assumption of women's financial dependency on men.

Two clear overall accounts of the specific risk factors that affect women are given by CONROY & FLANAGHAN and OPPENHEIM & HARKER. Both contributions discuss different indicators of women's poverty: low income and low pay, unemployment, the lone parent factor, the social security factor, and the use of income support. Moreover, Oppenheim & Harker briefly take into account the importance of less quantifiable aspects to poverty, such as not being able to see friends and relatives. The non-monetary dimension of deprivation is very important if we want to capture the gender nature of poverty, because it gives us the possibility of understanding the consequences of economic hardship and the connections between low incomes and lack of resources.

The effects of the experience of poverty on women's lives are taken into consideration by PAYNE. In particular, her book explores the complex relationship between poverty, deprivation, and health. The effects of deprivation on health are cumulative as poverty makes demands on women's time and energy, both physical and emotional, and the draining effect of worry about meeting the needs of other members of the household leads to health costs for women.

Within this complex context, the gendered nature of poverty cannot be "captured" in the absence of a gender-sensitive methodological approach: the visibility of women's poverty crucially depends on the methodological choices made while trying to conceptualize and "measure" the phenomenon. This is the focus of two very interesting journal articles by MILLAR & GLENDINNING and DALY.

In the first article the two authors discuss why it is necessary to focus on the gender dimension of poverty by arguing that this involves far more than simply disaggregating data to produce statistics about the situation of women. Then the article considers some of the important conceptual and methodological issues that must be tackled if one is to find ways to investigate and measure poverty that are not gender blind: the unit of measurement, the issue of access to income and other material resources, the incorporation of a number of temporal dimensions.

The article by Daly sets out to identify the place of female poverty in research to date. The main purpose of her article is to review existing research on poverty for its capacity to reveal the true picture of female poverty in contemporary European society. The key sets of problems that weakens research on women's poverty are: shortcomings in the definition of poverty; specific measurement difficulties (the appropriate unit or level of measurement and the equivalence scale to be used); under-exploration of life-course changes; underuse of structural explanations.

Finally, RUSPINI's article shows that, in the case of women's poverty, the life-course perspective may be a very fruitful starting point. This work focuses on women's poverty in (West) Germany and Britain using household panel data. The panel approach allows understanding of the events or circumstances causing women and men to fall into and escape from poverty. The author explores poverty dynamics in terms of characteristics and duration of poverty spells; underlines the interaction between critical events and changes in the resource distribution (family, labour market, and welfare) in determining the gender characteristics of poverty trajectories; and verifies the different combination of beginning/ending events. Results show that women's greater vulnerability to economic poverty lies in two different elements: on the one hand, women's poverty spells are longer, and on the other hand women are particularly exposed to economic fluctuations. Moreover, specific risk factors affect women in particular.

ELISABETTA RUSPINI

See also Poverty

Financial accounting

Ball, R. and P. Brown, "An Empirical Evaluation of Accounting Numbers", *Journal of Accounting Research*, 6 (1968): 159–78

Beaver, William H., *Financial Reporting: An Accounting Revolution*, 3rd edition, Upper Saddle River, New Jersey: Prentice Hall, 1998

Burchell, S., C. Clubb, A. Hopwood, J. Hughes and J. Nahapiet, "The Roles of Accounting in Organisations and Society", *Accounting, Organisations and Society*, 5/1 (1980): 5–27

Feltham, G. and J. Ohlson, "Valuation and Clean Surplus Accounting for Operating and Financial Activities", *Contemporary Accounting Research*, 11 (Spring 1995): 689–731

Foster, George, *Financial Statement Analysis*, 2nd edition, Englewood Cliffs, New Jersey: Prentice Hall, 1986

Keasey, K. and M. Wright (editors), special issue on "Corporate Governance", *Accounting and Business Research*, 23 (1993)

Smith, Terry, *Accounting for Growth: Stripping the Camouflage from Company Accounts*, 2nd edition, London: Century, 1996

Watts, Ross L. and Jerold L. Zimmerman, *Positive Accounting Theory*, Englewood Cliffs, New Jersey: Prentice Hall, 1986

Whittington, Geoffrey, *Inflation Accounting: An Introduction to the Debate*, Cambridge and New York: Cambridge University Press, 1983

Much of the modern academic literature in financial accounting grew from a seminal study by BALL & BROWN of the impact of financial accounting data upon investors' beliefs. Focussing on the information content of financial accounting statements, they used econometric techniques to explore the relationship between unexpected changes in earnings disclosed in companies' annual reports and changes in share prices. A significant positive association emerged between the sign of the earnings change and the sign of the share price change; and within the framework of the efficient market hypothesis this was interpreted as an indicator of the value to investors of the accounting information.

The subsequent explosion of econometric work refining and extending the Ball & Brown approach is skilfully surveyed in FOSTER. Not only were more sensitive tests devised but also a whole array of further questions could be tackled. For example, did new disclosure requirements have an impact on the structure of share prices? Did the form as well as the substance of disclosure affect prices? Foster reports the new evidence, as well as providing an encyclopaedic and balanced review of the literature on the use of financial statements in many other contexts. These include, for example, predicting business failure and evaluating the effects of merger. Foster's book was out of date before it was published, so fast has this literature been growing; but it remains invaluable in providing a framework within which the new literature can be assessed.

FELTHAM & OHLSON provide an influential recent contribution to the literature on the link between accounting data and share values. They focus on the "clean surplus relation", where the book value of equity at the end of the year equals the opening book value plus earnings minus dividends. Armed with this relation they derive an expression for a company's market capitalization as a function of its book value and its expected "abnormal" future income (abnormal income arises when the return on equity deviates from the cost of capital). Their analysis has informed much subsequent empirical work.

BEAVER places the empirical innovation of Ball & Brown and his own contemporary pioneering work in a wider theoretical and institutional context. He charts the shift of emphasis in accounting from an *ex post* stewardship role (owners monitoring management) to an *ex ante* function: supplying data that inform decisions whether to invest in particular shares. He provides an authoritative account of the underlying theory drawn from information economics, followed by an even-handed discussion of the implications for, *inter alia*, accounting regulation.

A more polemical approach, building on the same foundations in empirical (or "positive") accounting, is offered by WATTS & ZIMMERMAN. Their book epitomizes the revival of *laissez faire* observed in accounting, as in other social sciences, in the late 1970s and 1980s. The targets of the *laissez faire* advocates were, in this case, on the policy side, the growing activity of accounting regulators, and, on the academic side,

the normative or prescriptive theorists who were seen as serving this extension of regulatory activity by supplying "excuses" for intervention couched as accounting theory.

The rapid shift in the focus of financial accounting charted by Beaver, from *ex post* stewardship to *ex ante* informing of investment decisions, has been checked in recent years. This is partly because of developments in principal–agent theory: shareholders look to financial accounting to relieve the problem of information asymmetry that underlies the principal–agent problem. Financial accounting also informs the market for corporate control with its disciplinary takeovers aimed at eliminating errant agents. And it is sometimes the basis for executive salary contracts designed to align the interests of manager agents with those of shareholder principals. Many of the relevant theoretical issues and empirical contributions are reviewed in KEASEY & WRIGHT.

Some of the fundamental accounting problems confronting practitioners grappling with the resulting measurement problems are explored in WHITTINGTON's lucid book. He reviews the main academic approaches to the recurrent accounting questions: how do/should we measure assets and income? And he uses that review to inform an analysis of a practical problem that has bedevilled the accounting profession and caused upheaval in accounting regulation: how do we make those measurements when there is inflation? As well as explaining the competing techniques, he demonstrates the more general link between, on the one hand, the economic question for which information is required and, on the other, the appropriate choice of accounting technique.

The sensitivity of the "bottom line" in financial accounts to the choice of accounting technique is well appreciated by sophisticated finance directors, some of whom have opportunistically exploited any discretion afforded by the accounting regulators. Their efforts have been directed either to misinform the capital market and the market for corporate control, or to ensure that contracts framed in terms of accounting numbers turn out favourably for the directors. SMITH illustrates such activity in the course of entertaining and revealing case studies from the accounts of major British companies.

The dominance of a framework drawn from economics or econometrics (which is common to all the above references) is challenged by BURCHELL *et al.* They bring instead a provocative sociological perspective to accounting, arguing that accounting is intertwined with social as well as organizational practice. They see social forces and political processes as influencing the development of accounting; and, in turn, accounting itself as performing an influential role in economic and social management. Their work has helped stimulate a considerable body of "critical" accounting.

GEOFF MEEKS

Financial deregulation

Barth, James R., R.D. Brumbaugh and Robert E. Litan, *The Banking Industry in Turmoil*, Washington, DC: US Government Printing Office, 1990

Colombatto, Enrico and Jonathan R. Macey, "A Public Choice Model of International Economic Cooperation and

the Decline of National State", *Cardozo Law Review*,
18/3 (1996): 925–56

Dewatripont, Mathias and Jean Tirole, *The Prudential
Regulation of Banks*, Cambridge, Massachusetts: MIT
Press, 1994

Federal Deposit Insurance Corporation, *An Examination of
the Banking Crises of the 1980s and Early 1990s*,
Washington, DC: Federal Deposit Insurance Corporation,
1997

Goodhart, C.A.E. (editor), *The Emerging Framework of
Financial Regulation*, London: Central Banking
Publications, 1998

Goodhart, C.A.E. *et al.*, *Financial Regulation: Why, How
and Where Now?*, London and New York: Routledge,
1998

Ostas, James R. and Frank Zahn, "Interest and Non-interest
Credit Rationing in the Mortgage Market", *Journal of
Monetary Economics*, 1/2 (1975): 187–201

Spong, Kenneth, *Banking Regulation: Its Purposes,
Implementation and Effects*, 3rd edition, Kansas City:
Federal Reserve Bank of Kansas City, Division of Bank
Supervision and Structure, 1990

A good account of regulatory change in the US banking and
finance industry is provided in a government-commissioned
paper by BARTH, BRUMBAUGH & LITAN, which describes
the past regulatory framework and the achievement of financial deregulation in the US. The authors also observe that
regulation might be the next step to reverse development. The
idea of regulation (and consequently that of deregulation)
appears to have arisen largely as a result of the US concept of
dealing with public utilities and the provision of public or
quasi-public goods. The authors are more interested in the
structural evolution of the banking industry than in giving a
brief of relevant financial legislation, such as The Depository
Institutions Deregulation and Monetary Control Act of 1980,
or later the Garn–St Germain Depository Institutions Act of
1982. They describe how bank regulators became increasingly
inert, and the timelag of their policy responses increasingly
longer, leading to a more fragile banking system.

COLOMBATTO & MACEY is a very important piece of
work. The authors argue for less intense regulation at the
national level, but for closer coordination at the international
level between the regulatory authorities of different countries.
Their article is a very good read, incorporating a theory of
banking and banking law with a theroy of public choice, and
at the same time drawing parallels with public interest regulatory theory, mainly adopted by political scientists. Interesting
and provocative, their work sheds new light on international
regulatory issues.

DEWATRIPONT & TIROLE gives a good account of the
state-of-the-art theory of prudential (preventive) banking regulation. It provides both positive and normative analysis. The
first part of the book is rather descriptive, and is suitable for
students new to banking regulation, but some later chapters
require previous knowledge of areas such as regulatory
economics, money and banking, and the economics of financial institutions. The authors offer a consistent theoretical
model of banking regulation, along with a rather general institutional framework for modern banking. The normative model

developed in the book is one of the classical "incentive" models
developed in regulatory economics.

The FEDERAL DEPOSIT INSURANCE CORPORATION
published a selection of analytical papers on the banking crises
in the 1980s and 1990s, focusing on different geographical
areas in the US, as well as on different aspects of the banking
and financial crises themselves. This work assumes that the
shortcomings of the regulatory arrangements undoubtedly
contributed to the spreading of the crisis, and that deregulation as such did not deliver the expected results. The book
gives a good account of the deregulation movement in the US,
beginning with the Hunt Commission and its findings
published in 1971, which first argued for the deregulation of
the banking market, by means of a gradual removal of interest-
rate ceilings on time and savings accounts, the addition of new
lending and investment powers for financial institutions, the
removal of restrictions on state-wide branching, and the elimination of differential reserve requirements for different types
of financial institutions. This is an invaluable work on the
history, pace, and dynamics of banking regulatory change in
the US.

GOODHART is a selection of papers prepared by leading
academics and professionals in the field of banking regulation
and deregulation. The topics covered range from general regulatory issues, to a case study analysis of German companies
that experienced severe problems due to trading in exotic financial instruments. Most of the papers are practically oriented
and provide a good overview of up-to-date regulatory experience. The editor's own contributions raise some burning regu-
latory-related issues, such as the separation of the regulatory
and supervisory powers of the central bank from its duty to
conduct monetary policy. Although to some extent cumbersome, this book proves valuable insights, especially for those
with good background knowledge of bank operating practices
and procedures, particularly in the international context.

GOODHART *et al.* is an edited selection of papers presented
at a conference held at the Bank of England, and is a very fine
mixture of works by academics and works by practitioners.
This book does not require prior knowledge of regulatory
economics and financial theory, as it gives a clear and straightforward introduction to the regulatory issues in both developed and developing economies. To a large extent, the book
takes a normative approach, is not highly technical, and is easy
to follow.

OSTAS & ZAHN makes a clear distinction between equilibrium and disequilibrium rationing. Disequilibrium rationing
appears when an institution maintains an evident and measurable excess demand for credit. Equilibrium rationing (often
called market clearing), by contrast, occurs when adjustments
to non-interest terms of lending or perceived risk induce a
shift in the demand for or supply of credit, and the market
for credit can clear on its own. This is a fairly mathematical
article that would require a good prior knowledge of neoclassical economic concepts (especially the concept of rational
expectations). As interest-rate regulation was most severe in
the US banking system, and was a main reason for banking
deregulation to be introduced, this work is essential reading
on financial deregulation matters.

SPONG is a classic example of an extremely useful reference book written by a practitioner for practitioners. It

provides a clear account of financial regulations in the US banking system, a good description of the main regulatory concepts, both theoretical and practically adopted in US federal units, and also includes issues such as consumer protection and the preservation of the financial stability and soundness of the national banking system. Although the book lacks academic rigour, it can satisfy the needs of anyone who is interested in how the US banking system has been regulated, especially in this century.

ŽELJKO ŠEVIĆ

See also Banking law

Financial economics

Bicksler, James L. (editor), *Handbook of Financial Economics*, Amsterdam and New York: North Holland, 1979

Blake, David, *Financial Market Analysis*, London: McGraw Hill, 1990; 2nd edition, Chichester: Wiley, 2000

Cuthbertson, Keith, *Quantitative Financial Economics: Stocks, Bonds and Foreign Exchange*, Chichester and New York: Wiley, 1996

Eatwell, John, Murray Milgate and Peter Newman (editors), *The New Palgrave: Finance*, London: Macmillan, 1989

Huang, Chi-fu and Robert H. Litzenberger, *Foundations for Financial Economics*, New York: North Holland, 1988

Markowitz, Harry M., *Portfolio Selection: Efficient Diversification of Investments*, 2nd edition, Cambridge, Massachusetts and Oxford: Blackwell, 1991

Neave, Edwin H., *Financial Systems: Principles and Organisation*, London and New York: Routledge, 1998

A voluminous collection of articles and entries edited by BICKSLER provides an insight into the field of financial economics, viewing the subject as a development of micro finance that tries to bridge the gulf between "institutionalists" on the one hand and "theoreticians" on the other. This book is not a primer on modern finance or financial economics, but rather, a collection of works that aim to familiarize the reader with "modern finance, its concepts, methodologies, and implications". However, the reader must have a good prior knowledge of economic and finance theory and methodologies in order to benefit fully from this book. It covers developments in the field of finance in the 1960s and 1970s, when most, if not all, dominant models in financial theory emerged. Like all books of similar scope, it covers capital markets, financial strategies, and portfolio choice, enough to analyse most of the financial theory. Although the book includes some previously published material, it provides a number of, at the time, newly written essays, which were widely quoted in the literature later.

In contrast, BLAKE is written for newcomers to the field of finance, targeting undergraduate students and those on professional courses. A well written and splendidly organized work, it introduces the reader to the basic principles of modern financial economics. Readers may learn more than they expect, and will master the terminology used by professionals in this field. A number of worked examples and graphics are provided to ease the learning process, making this book extremely user-friendly, but not oversimplified. It gives a good coverage of all the financial instruments (classical and derivatives) used in financial markets, explaining in detail the techniques for analysing their performance.

HUANG & LITZENBERGER can be considered as a primer on financial economics, but for graduate students. It is aimed at students beginning their doctoral studies at US universities, although the book can be of interest to professionals, or people with a good technical background who are interested in financial economics. The book focuses mainly on the foundations of asset pricing theory, which it presents with great clarity and elegance. However, readers must be familiar with multivariate calculus, linear algebra, and general equilibrium microeconomics, in order to follow the book. On the other hand, being primarily a textbook, it omits a number of disputed topics and technical proofs, and this may be seen as one of the book's few disadvantages. Many financial economics concepts are briefly introduced – sometimes too briefly – in order to offer a comprehensive account of an issue. For instance, Ito's calculus is used, but not explained in detail, and the discussion of the econometric properties of the capital asset pricing model (CAPM) lacks a thorough presentation of the techniques used. However, this is something that can be expected from a textbook that is limited by its scope and size. Overall, this is valuable reading for anyone with a basic knowledge in finance who wants to advance it further.

CUTHBERTSON provides a good and fairly lucid account of what he calls "quantitative financial economics" in a fairly lucid manner. His book covers major topics in empirical asset pricing, with reference to the relevant statistical issues involved, and also to the results in the empirical literature. However, there is essentially no material, for instance, on term structure models, market microstructure, or derivative securities. Instead, the book focuses on the testing of market efficiency, and on rational expectations in the stock, bond, and foreign exchange markets. Readers should be familiar with fields such as (stochastic) calculus, maximum likelihood, the generalized method of moments, and the effects of heteroskedasticity and serial correlation on standard errors. The book covers the main developments in the literature, and certainly provides a good review of the state-of-the-art literature in the field. Despite its relatively high technical level, it is still an accessible book, informative on many issues.

EATWELL, MILGATE & NEWMAN is a selection of entries previously published in the *New Palgrave Dictionary of Economics*, which was edited by the authors. A very good selection of papers explaining the basic concepts in modern finance, it includes all the important issues in the field. It does not require prior knowledge of finance, although this might be helpful for better understanding, especially for the more technical entries. This is useful reading for a beginner who wants to obtain a quick grasp of the main issues.

Harry Markowitz's works changed the outlook of modern finance. MARKOWITZ is a seminal work of modern financial theory. He dichotomizes the investment process into two stages: the formation of probability beliefs (security analysis), and portfolio choice. He argues that in choosing a portfolio, the objective of maximizing expected returns is not consistent with the widespread practice of diversification. He suggests that investor behaviour is consistent with minimizing expected utility, where utility is a function of the mean and variance, and points out that such an objective implies a concave utility function. He also analyses the utility implications of alternative selection rules, and in the case of the semi-variance criterion, he discusses the solution procedure. He includes a discussion of portfolio selection under logarithmic utility, and points out that the portfolio that maximizes the geometric mean return is approximately mean-variance efficient. He showed how, as the number of securities in the portfolio is increased, portfolio variance approaches the average covariance. Finally, he suggests that the covariance matrix might be simplified if the correlations between security returns result simply from the common influence of the market. As is usual for his work, he is very concerned in this book with the practical applicability of the solutions proposed, which is fairly rare for an academic researcher. However, unlike many academics, he has spent his life both in and out of academia. This is a very good, cult book that should be read, but probably after gaining a good grasp of modern finance theory and its main developments.

NEAVE gives an account of the institutionalist theory of finance and the financial system. In his book, he describes the functioning of the financial system, financial intermediation, and the trading of financial markets, in a lively and understandable way. Even an analysis of issues such as derivatives trading (where technicalities can hardly be avoided) is accessible, and does not require a great deal of prior knowledge. This book gives the reader a good grasp of finance and of the economics of financial systems, which now requires proficiency in advanced mathematics. It is highly rigorous and uses advanced formal logic. Overall it is a challenging work for a newcomer to the field of finance, and a challenge that will not disappoint.

ŽELJKO ŠEVIĆ

Financial fragility

Bernanke, Ben S., "Nonmonetary Effects of the Financial Crisis in the Propagation of the Great Depression", *American Economic Review*, 73/3 (1983): 257–76

Bernanke, Ben and Mark Gertler, "Financial Fragility and Economic Performance", *Quarterly Journal of Economics*, 105/1 (1990): 87–114

Calomiris, Charles W., "Financial Fragility: Issues and Policy Implications", *Journal of Financial Services Research*, 9 (1995): 241–57

Davis, E.P., *Debt, Financial Fragility, and Systemic Risk*, Oxford: Clarendon Press, and New York: Oxford University Press, 1992

Fisher, Irving, "The Debt Deflation Theory of Great Depressions", *Econometrica*, 1/1 (1933): 337–57

Kindleberger, Charles P., *Manias, Panics, and Crashes: A History of Financial Crises*, New York: Basic Books, 1978

Lagunoff, Roger D. and Stacey L. Schreft, "A Model of Financial Fragility", Kansas City: Federal Reserve Bank of Kansas City, 1998 (Research Working Paper 98/01)

Mankiw, G., "The Allocation of Credit and Financial Collapse", *Quarterly Journal of Economics*, 101/3 (1986): 455–70

Minsky, Hyman P., "The Financial-Instability Hypothesis: Capitalist Processes and the Behavior of the Economy" in *Financial Crises: Theory, History, and Policy*, edited by Charles P. Kindleberger and Jean-Pierre Laffargue, Cambridge and New York: Cambridge University Press, 1982

Rochet, J.C. and J. Tirole, "Interbank Lending and Systemic Risk", *Journal of Money, Credit and Banking*, 28/4 (1996): 275–84

BERNANKE assesses the relative contribution of financial and monetary factors in the downturn of economic activity during the Great Depression. He argues that the contraction of the money supply alone cannot explain the subsequent fall in output. Instead, he posits that the financial sector could not perform its functions efficiently, which resulted in a substantial increase in the costs of intermediation. This caused a credit squeeze that worsened the downturn of the business cycle by depressing aggregate demand. Although the article deals specifically with the Great Depression, its approach is general and the emphasis on the incomplete nature of financial markets has influenced the way economists look at the causes of financial fragility.

BERNANKE & GERTLER develop a theoretical model of financial fragility based on agency costs associated with outside finance. In this model, the individual wealth of the borrower determines the degree of fragility of the economic system. Bernanke & Gertler show that, in cases where entrepreneurs have low wealth relative to the size of their investment projects, investment and output would be low even when economic fundamentals are good. Bernanke & Gertler describe this state of the economy as financially fragile. In an extreme case when agency costs are very high due to very low net worth, no investment projects are undertaken and "financial collapse" could occur. One important implication that emerges from this model is that bailout policies or transfers to entrepreneurs with low net worth can reduce financial fragility. A "lender of last resort" policy aimed at protecting financial institutions from liquidity shocks can also be used by central banks to combat financial fragility. Even though the article is technical, it includes two very useful nontechnical sections on policy implications and the corporate debt debate.

A useful review of much of the theory and evidence on financial fragility is CALOMIRIS. He defines two broad sources of financial fragility: financial shocks and financial propagators. The former refer to real disturbances that originate in financial markets whereas the latter refer to mechanisms through which financial markets aggravate real shocks that originate elsewhere. Calomiris identifies several financial propagators but focuses mainly on regulatory distortions, arguing that government subsidies, by providing funds for optimists, increase macroeconomic instability by generating asset price bubbles and credit crunches. Although Calomiris recognizes that governments have the means to offset negative externalities, he emphasizes the costs embedded in government-imposed safety nets and argues for a cost-benefit type analysis of government interventions. Calomiris considers this policy recommendation as an important distinguishing feature between the new literature on financial fragility and earlier views, which recommend continuous and aggressive government intervention in financial markets. The article is clear and covers a wide range of issues relating to financial fragility.

A useful overall account is DAVIS. He provides an extensive review of the various theories of financial fragility and financial instability and tests the predictions of these theories against periods of financial instability. Davis also proposes a new way of looking at financial fragility using the insights of industrial economics. He argues that changes in the conditions of entry to financial markets, due to factors such as deregulation or innovation, can result in financial fragility and instability.

FISHER is still worth reading both for what he has to say about the roots of the depression and for his policy recommendations. Fisher argues that the severity of the economic downturn during the Great Depression was caused by a combination of overindebtedness and deflation – what is known as the debt deflation theory. The first stage of the debt deflation theory is a state of overindebtedness, which usually develops as a result of opportunities in new industries, inventions, or the opening up of new markets. Overindebtedness would ultimately result in debt liquidation and distress selling, which will cause a contraction in the deposit base and a general fall in the price level, reducing the net worth of borrowers and profits, which reduces investment, output, and employment. The fall in prices aggravates the real indebtedness of borrowers by increasing the value of each dollar owed, which may provoke a further series of bankruptcies. Thus, reflationary policies can significantly reduce the negative consequences of the economic downturn.

KINDLEBERGER provides a very useful account of the history of financial crises. The starting point of his analysis is a displacement or an exogenous shock to the system that causes an improvement in investment opportunities. The non-financial sector reacts to this displacement by increasing fixed investment and speculating in the stock market in prospects for higher capital gains. An important element in this approach is that banks mainly finance the boom. Kindleberger's approach rests on the assumption that the upturn of a cycle creates some type of "euphoria" both in the non-financial and the financial sector. "Euphoria" encourages banks not to provide sufficient cushion against liquidity shocks and causes investors to increase their speculative activity, which suggests that there exists an element of irrationality in the behaviour of both bankers and investors. At a certain stage, lenders realize that the debt cannot be paid, forcing debtors to liquidate their assets resulting in distress sale which causes a general deflation in the economy or may go as far as "door-shut- panic". Kindleberger emphasizes the role of the lender of last resort, both at domestic and international levels, in controlling the spread of panic.

LAGUNOFF & SCHREFT's usefulness lies in setting explicitly the major features of financial fragility models. These models usually have two key features: (a) some form of financial linkage between economic agents; and (b) investment projects are subject to shocks, which completely or partially break these linkages. Lagunoff & Schreft capture these features in a simple model in which a shock that causes some entrepreneurs to default leads to a series of failures through the financial system by breaking some of the existing linkages. The authors suggest two ways of measuring financial fragility depending on the assumption made about contagious effects. When agents cannot foresee contagious defaults, then financial fragility could be measured *ex post* – in terms of the severity of the crisis once it has occurred. When agents can foresee the contagious defaults, which will cause a simultaneous shift to risk-less assets and breakdown of financial linkages, the evaluation of financial fragility from an *ex ante* perspective is more useful – by asking "how soon an economy's financial structure would collapse completely from such a crisis if shocks were to hit at some date". The paper is narrow in focus but is a useful start for modelling financial fragility.

MANKIW's main contribution lies in showing how information asymmetry and the associated adverse selection problem could lead to a "collapsed credit market." His model shows that even small changes in the risk-free interest rate can greatly disrupt the workings of the credit market and in some cases can result in the collapse of the credit market driving out " socially profitable investment." The high costs associated with financial collapse justify the government's role as a lender of last resort. Another interesting conclusion that emerges from Mankiw's model is that restrictive monetary policy, by increasing interest rates, can be costly because such a policy can propagate a financial crisis. The article is very clear and concise and contains a useful section on government credit policy.

MINSKY paints a gloomy picture of capitalism by stating that the internal working of the capitalist system is conducive to financial fragility. Minsky's starting point is the distinction between the hedging firm and the speculative firm. While the hedging firm anticipates total revenues to exceed running expenses and cash payments in every period, a speculative firm's debt repayments exceed the income that its assets generate and as such the firm can meet its commitments only by running down its assets or securing new debt. Minsky defines a fragile financial system as one in which modest changes in cashflows, capitalization rates, or interest rates affect adversely the ability of private units to fulfil their financial commitments. The fragility of the financial system depends on the weight of speculative firms in the total financial structure. The larger the weight of these speculative firms in the total economy, the more fragile the system. Minsky claims that even if the system is dominated by hedge finance, there are enough incentives and inducements that will ultimately lead to the dominance of speculative finance. Hence, periods of stability are often a stage for future periods of instability or in his words, ". . . as long as the capitalist economy is capitalist, it will be financially unstable" (p.36). Minsky recognizes the importance of the lender of last resort function in reducing fragility and instability, but he argues that such operations would ultimately lead to inflationary recessions. The chapter is worth reading for its powerful conclusions, but lacks clarity while many concepts and ideas appear extraneous to the flow of the general argument.

ROCHET & TIROLE identify an important source of financial fragility: the interbank market. In so far as banks are linked to each other through interbank lending, a single bank's failure can trigger a series of failures and in some instances can lead to the closure of the entire banking system. Rochet & Tirole argue that the current system suffers from its "hybrid nature". On the one hand, the lending process in the interbank market is highly centralized. On the other hand, this market is characterized by implicit government insurance, which does not provide the proper incentives for peer monitoring among banks. This inconsistency can be addressed in two ways: through breaking the interbank linkages by centralizing banks' liquidity management with the central bank – an option that may not be desirable – or through creating an environment that provides banks with an incentive to monitor each other more effectively. Rochet & Tirole set the problem of systemic risk in terms of trade-off between peer monitoring and the risk of failure propagation. The article is very technical, which may detract the reader from its interesting thoughts.

BASSAM FATTOUH AND PANICOS O. DEMETRIADES

See also Economic crises, Instability

Financial globalization and financial integration

Baker, Dean, Gerald Epstein and Robert Pollin (editors), *Globalization and Progressive Economic Policy*, Cambridge and New York: Cambridge University Press, 1998

Bayoumi, Tamim, *Financial Integration and Real Activity*, Ann Arbor: University of Michigan Press, 1997

Bordo, Michael D., Barry Eichengreen and Jongwoo Kim, *Was There Really an Earlier Period of International Financial Integration Comparable to Today?*, Cambridge, Massachusetts: National Bureau of Economic Research, 1998

Braudel, Fernand, *Civilization and Capitalism, 15th–18th Century*, 3 vols, London: Collins, 1981–84; New York: Harper and Row, 1982–84

Cerny, Philip G., "The Dynamics of Financial Globalization: Technology, Market Structure, and Policy Response", *Policy Sciences*, 27/4 (1994): 319–42

Coleman, William D., *Financial Services, Globalization and Domestic Policy Change*, London: Macmillan, and New York: St Martin's Press, 1996

Dobson, Wendy and Pierre Jacquet, *Financial Services Liberalization in the World Trade Organization*, Washington, DC: Institute for International Economics, 1998

Knight, Malcolm, "Developing Countries and the Globalization of Financial Markets", *World Development*, 26/7 (July 1998): 1185–1200

Shepherd, William F., *International Financial Integration: History, Theory, and Applications in OECD Countries*, Aldershot, Hampshire: Avebury, 1994

World Bank, *Private Capital Flows to Developing Countries: The Road to Financial Integration*, Oxford and New York: Oxford University Press, 1997

World Bank, *Global Economic Prospects for Developing Countries, 1998/99: Beyond Financial Crisis*. Washington DC: World Bank, 1999

There is a large volume of literature dealing with financial integration and globalization. Economists test for financial integration by examining whether similar financial instruments in different countries have the same interest rates. They test for financial globalization by evaluating the correlation of national investment and savings levels. This last measure, the Feldstein–Horioka test, asserts that the more investment and savings diverge, the more pronounced is financial globalization.

BAYOUMI offers a comprehensive and up-to-date guide to the Feldstein–Horioka literature. He finds little evidence of financial globalization in studies using this test, and little support for the related hypothesis that global consumers use cross-border financial flows to smooth consumption. Bayoumi concludes that Feldstein–Horioka tests are better suited to measuring international business cycles.

BORDO, EICHENGREEN & KIM puts evidence on international capital flows together with the results of Feldstein–Horioka and interest-rate parity tests for different subperiods, ranging from the late 19th century to the 1990s. They argue that financial integration follows a U-shaped pattern: it was at very high levels until the early 20th century, collapsed between the wars, and then gradually returned to pre-1914 levels. They argue that the advances in information technology have reduced national market segmentation and permitted financial flows for a wider range of purposes.

SHEPHERD provides a useful complement to Bayoumi, and Bordo, Eichengreen & Kim by providing a clear technical exposition of the tests these authors employ. He also reviews the development of open-economy macroeconomic models, and builds some representative models incorporating financial assets and cross-border financial flows. Shepherd also includes extensive international data and reviews the origins of the IMF as an international monetary institution.

By interpreting financial prices and capital flows, the works discussed thus far measure financial globalization and integration only indirectly. CERNY takes a more direct approach. He argues that globalization consists above all else of organizational changes: the development of both integrated worldwide market structures and of firms with the organizational capacity to centre their activities on these markets. His work emphasizes the implications of integrated world markets and globally mobile firms for government behaviour.

The historical perspective in Bordo *et al.* is instructive; but a comprehensive historical grasp of financial integration and globalization requires an understanding of earlier history as well. Here the fundamental reference is BRAUDEL's monumental three-volume work on the rise of European capitalism in the 15th to 18th centuries. Authors such as Polanyi and Kindleberger have also examined the complex interrelations of states, economies, and financial systems over time.

Braudel discusses the evolution of money, credit, and banking institutions with unprecedented depth. He advances two historical propositions concerning international financial relations: first, that stable international financial arrangements are always organized by a dominant city state or nation state; and second, that it is international financial and trade flows that have permitted the rise of modern capitalist relations, and these predate the Industrial Revolution in England. The former theme, of course, is also advanced by Kindleberger.

One apparent casualty of the financial integration process

analysed by Cerny is national governments' control of the terms and conditions of activities in their financial systems. Two hypotheses about the link between national government power and finance have been explored by authors such as John Zysman, Michael Moran, Susan Strange, and Eric Helleiner. First, financial institutions' functions in any nation depend both on that nation's state of development and on its position within the world system. Second, global fixed exchange-rate systems such as Bretton Woods impose the authority of the reserve-currency country on the system as a whole. COLEMAN offers a good point of entry into this literature. In addition, his volume argues that the financial systems approach is increasingly by financial integration, which diminishes the power of nation-states to sustain distinct national financial systems.

DOBSON & JACQUET provides a comprehensive review of financial regulation and financial system liberalization in the world economy. Their volume centres on the December 1997 financial services agreement among the 102 member countries of the World Trade Organization, which, for the first time, included financial services in a multilateral framework. The agreement relies on the principle of reciprocity – that is, one country's financial firms can enter another's markets as long as that other country's financial firms have the same access in return. This volume also features a detailed discussion of financial regulation and liberalization in 15 nations with "emerging" financial systems (including Japan).

WORLD BANK (1997) offers an overview of the financial systems of the countries of the developing world taken as a whole. It also reviews the experience of the 1980s Latin American debt crisis and the 1994–95 Mexican currency crisis. World Bank (1997) admits that financial opening and cross-border financial flows entail the risks of financial instability and macroeconomic loss, but argues that these risks are manageable and are outweighed by prospective efficiency and output gains. This volume offers a version of the "there is no alternative" approach to financial liberalization, according to which developing nations' governments can monitor and police their financial systems' solvency and risk, but not control their behaviour.

The Asian financial crisis raises the spectre of the special vulnerability of developing countries to destabilizing global financial flows. KNIGHT argues that financial and banking-system instability during this crisis has primarily affected the developing countries because they lack a fully developed set of financial instruments and institutions. In consequence, information on the circumstances of borrowers is incomplete, and the prospect of financial instability due to uncertainty among overseas investors increases. The solution is tighter regulation, and further "deepening" and opening of financial systems.

Knight's view reflects the consensus of many economists, especially those at the IMF and World Bank. This view is not universally held. Some economists reject the idea that "there is no alternative" and that financial globalization renders national policy impotent and fosters the achievement of economic efficiency. The edited volume by BAKER, EPSTEIN & POLLIN presents an alternative view. The authors collected here argue that current global financial arrangements encourage increased inequality and financial instability. Further, they argue for national controls over financial flows, and for the use of national fiscal, monetary, and regulatory policy to

avoid global stagnation and unemployment. In the wake of the Asian crisis, official opinion on the effects of financial globalization and openness is more attuned to this sceptical view. WORLD BANK (1999) takes a very different view of financial integration from World Bank (1997). World Bank (1999) attributes the global financial crisis in the developing world not just to weaknesses and oversights in domestic financial systems, but also to imperfections in international capital markets, which can lead to contagion effects, liquidity crises, and panics. The report calls for a rethinking of the global financial architecture.

GARY A. DYMSKI

See also Globalization, International Monetary Fund, World Trade Organisation

Financial services

Alexander, Gordon J., Jonathan D. Jones and Peter J. Nigro, "Mutual Fund Shareholders: Characteristics, Investor Knowledge, and Sources of Information", *Economics Working Paper 97–13*, Washington, DC: Office of the Comptroller of the Currency, December 1997

Bassett, William F., Michael J. Fleming and Anthony P. Rodrigues, "How Workers Use 401(K) Plans: The Participation, Contribution, and Withdrawal Decisions", *Staff Report Number 38*, New York: Federal Reserve Bank of New York, 1998

Berger, Allen N., Rebecca S. Demsetz and Philip E. Strahan, "The Consolidation of the Financial Services Industry: Causes, Consequences, and Implications for the Future", *Staff Report Number 55*, New York: Federal Reserve Bank of New York, 1998; reprinted in *Journal of Banking and Finance*, 23/2–4 (1999): 135–94

Caskey, John P., *Fringe Banking: Check-Cashing Outlets, Pawnshops, and the Poor*, New York: Russell Sage Foundation, 1994

Dobson, Wendy and Pierre Jacquet, *Financial Services Liberalization in the WTO*, Washington, DC: Institute for International Economics, 1998

Ghilarducci, Teresa, *Labor's Capital: The Economics and Politics of Private Pensions*, Cambridge, Massachusetts: MIT Press, 1992

Greenbaum, Stuart I. and Anjan V. Thakor, *Contemporary Financial Intermediation*, Fort Worth, Texas: Dryden Press, 1995

Hudson, Michael (editor), *Merchants of Misery: How Corporate America Profits from Poverty*, Monroe, Maine: Common Courage, 1996

Kendall, Leon T. and Michael J. Fishman (editors), *A Primer on Securitization*, Cambridge, Massachusetts: MIT Press, 1996

Kirsch, Clifford E. (editor), *The Financial Services Revolution: Understanding the Changing Role of Banks, Mutual Funds, and Insurance Companies*, Chicago: Irwin, 1997

Kregel, Jan, "Derivatives and Global Capital Flows: Applications to Asia", Jerome Levy Economics Institute, Working Paper no. 246 (August 1998)

Leyshon, Andrew and Nigel Thrift, "Geographies of Financial Exclusion: Financial Abandonment in Britain and the United States", *Transactions of the Institute of British Geographers*, 20 (1995): 312–41

Litan, Robert E. and Anthony M. Santomero (editors), *Brookings-Wharton Papers on Financial Services, 1998*, Washington, DC: Brookings Institution Press, 1998

Mayer, Martin, *The Bankers: The Next Generation*, New York: Truman Talley, 1997

Until the 1980s, each specific financial need of households and businesses – for housing finance, deposits, insurance, retirement income, and so on – was met by distinctive specialist institutions, with different sets of practices evolving in different countries. In recent years, these institutions and practices have been the subject of rapid industrial change. The emergence of new information and communication technologies has permitted the standardization of many previously diverse financial practices; financial firms that previously specialized in meeting particular financial needs have evolved into suppliers of a growing range of "financial services" for a differentiated set of financial consumers. Among other trends, banks no longer simply engage in "banking" per se – that is, in loan making and deposit taking – but in a wide variety of financial practices.

Journalistic sources such as the *Economist* or *Financial Times* provide running coverage of trends in financial services; and analytical perspective on these institutional developments is to be found primarily in non-academic outlets. For example, KIRSCH presents an overview of the shifting line between the banking, insurance, and mutual fund industries. MAYER offers just one example of his extensive investigations of virtually every corner of the monetary world; this volume, like his others, both appreciates financial firms' competitive drive and registers scepticism about whether these struggles for turf and market share have anything to do with the attainment of efficiency.

The publications of economists at the official agencies and at think tanks that emphasize international economic issues also provide useful information. For example, DOBSON & JACQUET document that the growth and transformation of financial services is global in large part because of the liberalization of global trading rules under World Trade Organization guidelines.

Vigorous academic analyses of these institutional developments are hard to find. Theoretical economists generally lag far behind, and in many cases work with antiquated or institutionally misinformed models of what banking and financial firms do. Most of the well-established financial and economics journals pay only sporadic attention to institutional developments; and when they do cover these trends the focus often falls solely on how they might affect the efficiency of financial-market allocation. Fortunately, new scholarly venues tying financial-services issues to broader questions of financial and economic policy are emerging. The *Journal of Financial Services Research* has become an important outlet; and the first annual volume of the *Brookings-Wharton Papers on Financial Services*, edited by LITAN & SANTOMERO, is especially promising because of its broad coverage and intertwining of technical and policy issues.

Most current financial textbooks provide up-to-date but broad-brush treatments of these institutional trends. Among texts, GREENBAUM & THAKOR is uniquely useful. Its authors are among the few academic financial economists who have attempted to draw out the implications of current institutional developments for monetary and financial theory. The book reflects their years of investigations, and many articles, in this area of inquiry. Their text, while too dense for any but the most ambitious students, is especially invaluable for its attempts to conceptualize trends in financial practices by integrating features drawn from classical models of financial market efficiency and from the more recent crop of models featuring principal/agent tension and asymmetric information.

Writings about some key areas in financial services deserve mention. First, the financial services industry is engaged in a worldwide consolidation phase, with mergers and acquisitions occurring at a frantic pace. BERGER, DEMSETZ & STRAHAN offer a useful overview of financial services consolidation. Their paper first surveys recent institutional developments, and then reviews over 250 academic studies pertaining to the likely causes and effects of this trend.

A key trend in financial-service provision is the role of non-bank institutions in collecting savings and channelling them to investment vehicles. The most important non-bank vehicles for accomplishing this role are pension funds, individualized retirement accounts (IRAs), and mutual funds.

GHILARDUCCI's discussion of pension funds stands out because she discusses these funds in the context of the overall relationship of capital and labour: indeed, she shows how workers' vested rights in large-scale pension funds have eroded even as these funds' significance in financial markets has risen. Writing about IRAs is at a more elementary stage; the article by BASSETT, FLEMING & RODRIGUES collects basic information about these accounts, and makes the point that workers with low incomes generally do not have IRAs. Writing on mutual funds is also relatively underdeveloped. The survey by ALEXANDER, JONES & NIGRO shows that most participants in mutual funds have little knowledge of the composition of their portfolios.

Apart from new methods of transforming savings into investment, the financial-services arena has expanded to include new instruments for either insuring against or taking the risks associated with shifts in financial-market prices. These instruments encompass financial derivatives, created by bundling and recombining the cashflow commitments associated with underlying financial contracts, and options contracts, which allow contingent payments if certain price thresholds are passed. The literature on derivatives and options consists almost entirely either of very general or extremely specialized treatments. One of the few volumes that is analytical without requiring extensive prior knowledge of specialized jargon is KENDALL & FISHMAN. This volume has a useful overview of many of these new markets; however, like most writing in this field, the focus is solely on the problems these markets might solve, not the problems they might create. A useful corrective is KREGEL; his paper shows how financial derivatives and options contributed to the severity and scope of the Asian financial crisis.

The evolution of contemporary financial services has given rise to an increasingly dualistic financial system, wherein many lower income people lack accounts at, and access to, formalized financial institutions such as banks and investment firms. CASKEY has done the most systematic work on informal financial firms such as pawnbrokers and cheque cashers. He emphasizes that the informal financial sector has grown because the firms within it have tailored their services to the special needs of the lower income households that use them. The picture painted by Caskey cannot be called overly rosy; but it is incomplete. Investigators such as HUDSON have shown that many informal financial firms force lower income units to pay extortionate rates for loans and financial services. LEYSHON & THRIFT have led a movement among social geographers and urbanologists to investigate the implications and dynamics of financial exclusion. The growing literature on financial exclusion tries to identify the social and economic consequences of some households' and businesses' inadequate access to affordable financial services.

GARY A. DYMSKI

Financial services, law

Cremona, Marise, "A New European Passport for Investment Services", *Journal of Business Law* (1994): 195

Gilligan, George, "The Origin of UK Financial Services Regulation", *Company Law*, 18 (1997): 167ff.

Goodhart, C.A.E. (editor), *The Emerging Framework of Financial Regulation*, London: Central Banking Publications, 1998

Hall, Maximillian, *Financial Deregulation: A Comparative Study of Australia and the United Kingdom*, Basingstoke: Macmillan, 1987

McCrudden, Christopher (editor), *Regulation and Deregulation: Policy and Practice in the Financial Services Industries*, Oxford: Clarendon Press, and New York: Oxford University Press, 1998

Page, A.C. and R.B. Ferguson, *Investor Protection*, London: Weidenfeld and Nicolson, 1992

Financial services, as a separate topic within legal studies, is a creature of the last 20–30 years. Until then, insurance might have been studied as a topic by itself, and the other component parts of investment law would scarcely have been thought worthy of academic attention at all. At the present time, writing on the subject is split between the lawyers, who look at the legal rules and procedures, and the economists, who prefer to consider the structure of the system from the point of view of its economic effects. More recently, with the rise of business regulation as an academically respectable topic of study for lawyers, the regulation of the financial markets has attracted a certain degree of interest.

PAGE & FERGUSON view the regulatory environment of financial services as being essentially a matter of protecting the investors who deal in the market place. They draw on the tradition that sees the maintenance of an honest market place as essential if investors are to be persuaded to come into the market and stay in it. According to this view, that need is the only real justification for having any detailed regulatory structure at all. The authors look at the investor-protection aspects of the various different forms of savings and investments, contrasting the position of depositors in banks and building societies with that of stock market investors.

McCRUDDEN provides a much more modern example of the use of the financial services sector as a testing ground for more general theories about deregulation and, in particular, for approaches to the very modern phenomenon of so-called deregulation. The chapters directly relating to the financial services market look at efficient regulation of that market in the context of the increasing globalization of the market and the more-or-less complete colonization of the market place by various forms of electronic trading.

HALL writes from the perspective of an economist who has studied both the United Kingdom and the Australian systems of financial regulation. Like McCrudden, but at an earlier date, he was inspired by concerns about some of the likely consequences of the deregulatory agenda. However, he is also concerned about the fiscal and monetary effects of the possible deregulation of financial markets. He questions whether the enthusiasts for deregulation have done enough to quantify accurately the costs, both direct and indirect, of their proposals. From this perspective he seeks to undermine one of the major planks in the deregulationists' case, namely the assertion that avoidable compliance costs are having crippling effects on business.

The papers in GOODHART's collection address a number of themes. The first section is concerned mostly with the complexities of banking regulation, emphasizing the complexity of the market, and the sophistication of the players within it. The writers stress the need to devise structures that are both flexible and clear. The second section focuses on the problems of derivatives. The capacity of these instruments to destabilize the market is a commonplace of discussion in this area. The authors in this section appear to treat derivatives as something akin to nuclear energy – inescapable and potentially valuable, but also needing to be regulated with the utmost care and entrusted only to experts. The third section looks at regulation of financial services more generally, dealing with some of the well-known concerns about the failure of regulation because of underfunding and lack of expertise on the part of the regulators.

CREMONA develops the study of financial services as a UK phenomenon by introducing the EC regulatory dimension. Her article is inspired by the final adoption of the Directive on Investment Services in the Securities Field, and she traces the history of the Directive, showing that the European Commission has chosen to adopt a minimalist approach to this area of regulation, evidently believing in the power of the market to produce optimal practical solutions. At the same time she shows that there are considerable technological and cultural problems to be overcome before a genuine single market in this sphere can be achieved. The question of a single market in investment services is, in any event, to be seen as part of a broader picture involving the whole single market programme.

GILLIGAN brings an unusual historical perspective to the study of financial services regulation. He concentrates on regulation in the UK, which he traces back to the Middle Ages. He shows the influence of the City of London over the centuries and identifies the skilful process of lobbying of politicians and others through which it has achieved its ambitions. He shows that the chief of these ambitions has been to secure the freedom to regulate itself, ostensibly for the good of the market as a whole, but in practice also because this solution safeguarded the vested interests of those being regulated. Thus he suggests that regulatory capture is a phenomenon that has existed for centuries.

ANDREW McGEE

See also Banking law

Flexible specialization

Asheim, Björn, "Flexible Specialization, Industrial Districts and Small Firms: A Critical Appraisal" in *Regional Development and Contemporary Industrial Response: Extending Flexible Specialisation*, edited by Huib Ernste and Verena Meier, London and New York: Belhaven, 1992

Benko, Georges and Michael Dunford (editors), *Industrial Change and Regional Development: The Transformation of New Industrial Spaces*, London and New York: Belhaven, 1991

Blyton, Paul and Jonathan Morris (editors), *A Flexible Future: Prospects for Employment and Organization*, Berlin and New York: de Gruyter, 1991

Christopherson, Susan and Michael Storper, "The Effects of Flexible Specialization on Industrial Politics and the Labour Market: The Motion Picture Industry", *Industrial and Labour Relations Review*, 42/3 (1989): 331–47

Dore, Ronald, *Flexible Rigidities: Industrial Policy and Structural Adjustment in the Japanese Economy, 1970–1980*, London: Athlone Press, and Stanford, California: Stanford University Press, 1986

Ernste, Huib and Verena Meier (editors), *Regional Development and Contemporary Industrial Response: Extending Flexible Specialisation*, London and New York: Belhaven, 1992

Florida, Richard, "Regional Creative Destruction: Production Organization, Globalization, and the Economic Transformation of the Midwest", *Economic Geography*, 72/3 (1996): 314–34

Florida, Richard and Martin Kenney, "High Technology Restructuring in the USA and Japan", *Environment and Planning A*, 22/2 (1990): 233–52

Gertler, Meric S., "Flexibility Revisited: Districts, Nation-States, and the Forces of Production", *Transactions of the Institute of British Geographers*, 17/3 (1992): 259–78

Hirst, Paul and Jonathan Zeitler (editors), *Reversing Industrial Decline? Industrial Structure and Policy in Britain and Her Competitors*, Oxford and New York: Berg, 1989

Isaksen, Arne, "New Industrial Spaces and Industrial Districts in Norway: Productive Concepts in Explaining Regional Development?", *European Urban and Regional Studies*, 1/1 (1994): 31–48

Jessop, Bob, "Post-Fordism and Flexible Specialization: Incommensurable, Contradictory, or Just Plain Different Perspectives" in *Regional Development and Contemporary Industrial Response*, edited by Huib Ernste and Verena Meier, 1992

Leslie, D., "Flexibly Specialized Agencies? Reflexivity, Identity and the Advertising Industry", *Environment and Planning A*, 29/6 (1997): 1017–38

Mair, Andrew, Richard Florida and Martin Kenney, "The New Geography of Automobile Production: Japanese Transplants in North America", *Economic Geography*, 64/4 (1988): 352–73

Markusen, Ann, "Sticky Places in Slippery Space: A Typology of Industrial Districts", *Economic Geography*, 72/3 (1996): 293–313

Oliver, Nick and Barry Wilkinson, *The Japanization of British Industry: New Developments in the 1990s*, 2nd edition, Oxford and Cambridge, Massachusetts: Blackwell, 1992

Pedersen, Poul Ove, Arni Sverrisson and Meine Pieter van Dijk (editors), *Flexible Specialization: The Dynamics of Small Scale Industries in the South*, London: Intermediate Technology Publications, 1994

Piore, Michael J. and Charles F. Sabel, *The Second Industrial Divide: Possibilities for Prosperity*, New York: Basic Books, 1984

Pollard, Jane and Michael Storper, "A Tale of Twelve Cities: Metropolitan Employment Change in Dynamic Industries in the 1980s", *Economic Geography*, 72/1 (1996): 1–22

Potter, Jonathan, "Branch Plant Economies and Flexible Specialization: Evidence from Devon and Cornwall", *Tijdschrift voor Economische en Sociale Geografie*, 86/2 (1995): 162–76

Pyke, F., G. Becattini and W. Sengenberger (editors), *Industrial Disricts and Local Economic Regeneration*, Geneva: International Institute for Labour Studies, 1990

Sabel, Charles F., "Flexible Specialization and the Re-emergence of Regional Economies" in *Reversing Industrial Decline?*, edited by Paul Hirst and Jonathan Zeitlin, Berg, 1989

Sadler, David, "The Geographies of Just-in-Time: Japanese Investment and Automotive Components Industry in Western Europe", *Economic Geography*, 70/1 (1994): 41–59

Scott, Allen J., "Flexible Production Systems and Regional Development: The Rise of New Industrial Spaces in North America and Western Europe", *International Journal of Urban and Regional Research*, 12/2 (1988): 171–86

Scott, A.J., *New Industrial Spaces: Flexible Production Organization and Regional Development in North American and Western Europe*, London: Pion, 1988

Sengenberger, Werner and Frank Pyke, "Small Firm Industrial Districts and Local Economic Development: Research and Policy Issues", *Labour and Society*, 16/1 (1991): 1–24

Sheard, P., "Auto Production Systems in Japan: Organizational and Locational Features", *Australian Geographical Studies*, 21/1 (1983): 49–68

Smith, Adrian, "Contemporary Capitalism? Small and Medium Enterprises, Industrial Districts and Regional Policy in Slovakia", *European Urban and Regional Studies*, 4 (1997)

Storper, Michael and Susan Christopherson, "*Flexible Specialization and Regional Agglomeration: The Case of*

the US Motion Picture Industry", Annals of the
Association of American Geographers, 77 (1987): 104–17

Storper, Michael and Allen J. Scott (editors), *Pathways to Industrialization and Regional Development*, London and New York: Routledge, 1992

Wolch, Jennifer and Michael Dear (editors), *The Power of Geography: How Territory Shapes Social Life*, Boston and London: Unwin Hyman, 1989

The flexible specialization theory arises from a model proposed by PIORE & SABEL, two US sociologists at MIT, who demonstrated the difficulty that specialized industrial districts experienced in surviving after the evaporation of the trust and mutual cooperation characteristic of more traditional craft-oriented communities. Their identification of a simple dichotomous contrast between two opposing industrial paradigms (craft production and mass production) suggested the rise of the assembly line as an "industrial divide" determined not by technological advances but by social and political conflict. Idealistically, they forecast a future Proudhonian democratic republic of craft workers as a "second divide" in which flexible specialization would be restored for craft workers. In the context of post-Fordist debate of the 1980s, some writers contended that the "second divide" had arrived in such forms as the "third Italy" of Emilia Romagna and Tuscany, the hyper-entrepreneurial "Silicon Valley" and Orange County of California, England's "Cambridge phenomenon", Japanese subcontracting networks and technopoles, and the decentralization of the giant German Konzerne. Papers assembled by PYKE, BECATTINI & SENGENBERGER. and STORPER & SCOTT cover this viewpoint (see also entry on Post-Fordism).

SABEL applied flexible specialization theory to explain the re-emergence of regional economies, and HIRST & ZEITLER contend that this theory is superior to post-Fordism as a concept because of its ideal-type "techno-economic paradigm". JESSOP challenges all this in a critique that extends the analysis to include flexible restructuring within banking, commerce, the liberal professions, and government. He suggests that a richer typology would result from replacement of the simple dichotomy to account for new forms of the technical division of labour and the benefits derived from computer automation of various production processes, changes in the nature and use of human labour, changes in the means of production (including materials consumed in the production process), and new methods for allocating capital investment in marketing, research, and development. Jessop's essay is just one of 16 compiled by ERNSTE & MEIER, which is a primary reference for this subject and offers a diverse range of case studies.

Apart from Jessop, the Ernste & Meier collection includes a valuable paper by ASHEIM, who provides a sharper level of theoretical conceptualization by restricting the interpretation of Fordism to denote "assembly-line based mass production" rather than as a more inclusive mode of regulation. Noting that flexibility is not a new industrial phenomenon and is not restricted to small or medium-sized enterprises, Asheim lists four flexible elements of "industrial production" (not to be confused with industrial specialization), namely:

flexible technology – including such innovations as flexible manufacturing systems (FMS), computer numerically controlled technology (CNC), computer- integrated manufacturing (CIM), computer-aided design (CAD) and computer- aided manufacture (CAM)

flexible labour – functional flexibility and numerical flexibility

organizational flexibility – often in association with technological innovation and internal restructuring of labour management

network flexibility – including the vertical and/or horizontal integration of co- operative arrangements between SMEs, the external division of labour, technology transfers, joint ventures, common R&D projects, and territorial agglomeration or deglomeration

Overall, Asheim considers the fundamental value of the flexible specialization model to be a "combination" of flexibility and efficiency, accessible to small firms in industrial districts as only one of several forms of production flexibility discussed in sets of papers assembled by the geographers WOLCH & DEAR and by Storper & Scott. Asheim explains that flexible specialization "could be regarded as a new form of manufacture using advanced technology to produce relative surplus value with an efficiency which was traditionally maintained only by large firms". Asheim draws upon contemporary theory promoted by SENGENBERGER & PYKE concerning the revival of Marshall's 1919 socioeconomic concept of the "industrial district" as the "most important micro-regulatory institutional framework" of the flexible specialization model. Such a district possesses a quantitative dimension of "external economies" and a qualitative dimension of "agglomeration economies".

Examples of new industrial districts constructed since the 1970s as networks of flexible specialization are provided in papers collected by BENKO & DUNFORD and by ISAKSEN, by POTTER and by SMITH. However, Jessop and SCOTT both make the point that such districts do not necessarily exclude the operation of large transnational corporations. MARKUSEN, supported by a useful bibliography, reviews the interpretation of "new industrial districts" as "sticky places" that sustain economic development through the role of small innovative firms "embedded with a regionally co-operative system of industrial governance" and she identifies three additional types of industrial districts. POLLARD & STORPER, however, shift the debate from industrial districts to suggest a typology of "intellectual capital industries", "innovation-based industries" and "variety-based industries" for their analysis of different forms of metropolitan restructuring.

One distinction between flexible production and flexible specialization is that the former focuses upon the regulatory mechanisms and organizational structures of transnational corporations (TNCs), including "merger mania" trends to capture larger global markets, whereas the latter term gives preference to a variety of small and medium-sized enterprises, which provide either consumer or producer goods and services. Both types of activity can lead to the restructuring of national, regional, and local space economies. Analysis of the Japanese TNC model of regional subcontracting networks stems from work by SHEARD, and predates the Piore–Sabel paradigm. DORE interprets "flexible rigidities" in such structural adjustments, and a range of US and British case studies of

"Japanization" as transplanted forms of flexible management responsible for new industrial regions is given by CHRISTO-PHERSON & STORPER, BLYTON & MORRIS, MAIR, FLORIDA & KENNEY, FLORIDA & KENNEY, SADLER, and OLIVER & WILKINSON. Two important papers offset the neglect of geographical research into the flexible role of service industries: STORPER & CHRISTOPHERSON, and LESLIE.

Various flexible globalization-localization strategies common to many transnational corporations are covered by references listed in the previous paragraph but these studies fit Asheim's framework only if large firms disintegrate to provide alliances with small specialist firms. "Vertical disintegration", however, has been a frequent form of Japanese industrial territorial organization and in Europe and North America has created new industrial spaces through what Scott describes as "the organization of firms". A collection of essays assembled by PEDERSEN, SVERRISSON & VAN DIJK is valuable for its attention to the dynamics of small and medium-sized enterprises in Africa, Asia, and Mexico.

GERTLER has written a valuable critique of 121 publications relevant to the debate about flexible practices and "true" industrial districts, and he highlights dilemmas in translating the theory of flexible industrialization into practice. In similar fashion, FLORIDA provides an important examination of the role of new forms of production organization in the process of regional economic transformation, to question much of the theory propounded by Piore & Sabel, Scott, and others, that older manufacturing regions remain trapped in outmoded forms. Florida stresses the role of "hub firms" of larger manufacturing enterprises responsible for the transfer and diffusion of new technologies and organizational practices–a form of revitalization described as "creative destruction". Both studies suggest that geographical theory can only consider flexible specialization as one of several possible outcomes.

TERRY G. BIRTLES

See also Globalization, Industrial districts, Post-Fordism

Folklore

Aarne, Anti and Stith Thompson, *The Type of the Folktale: A Classification and Bibliography*, Helsinki: Folklore Fellows Communications 184, 1961

Dorson, Richard M. (editor), *Folklore and Folklife: An Introduction*, Chicago: University of Chicago Press, 1972

Dundes, Alan, *The Study of Folklore*, Englewood Cliffs, New Jersey: Prentice Hall, 1965

Finnegan, Ruth, *Oral Literature in Africa*, Oxford: Clarendon Press, and New York: Oxford University Press, 1970

Grimm, Jakob and W.K. Grimm, *Grimm's Household Tales*, translated and edited by Margaret Hunt, 2 vols, London: Bell, 1884; reprinted as *The Complete Grimm's Fairy Tales*, New York: Pantheon, 1972, London: Routledge, 1975 (German edition 1812–15 and later revisions)

Propp, V., *The Morphology of the Folktale*, 2nd edition, revised by Louise A. Wagner, Austin: University of Texas Press, 1968

Sebeok, Thomas Albert (editor), *Myth: A Symposium* vol. 5: *Bibliographical and Special Series of the American Folklore Society*, Philadelphia: American Folklore Society, 1955

Taylor, Archer, *English Riddles from Oral Tradition*, Berkeley: University of California Press, 1951

Taylor, Archer, *The Proverb, and An Index to "The Proverb"*, Hatboro, Pennsylvania: Folklore Associates, 1962; reprinted Bern and New York: Peter Lang, 1985

Thompson, Stith, *The Folktale*, New York: Dryden Press, 1946; reprinted New York: AMS Press, 1979

Thompson, Stith, *Motif-Index of Folk-Literature: A Classification of Narrative Elements in Folk-tales, Ballads, Myths, Fables, Mediaeval Romances, Exempla, Fabliaux, Jest-books, and Local Legends*, 6 vols, Bloomington, Indiana: Indiana University Press, 1966 (originally published 1932)

Any professional study of the folktale requires AARNE & THOMPSON's seminal work on classificatory systems of folktales. Translated and enlarged by Thompson it is useful for bringing a great mass of folktales from various European countries into a single classification. The tale index differs from the motif index in its concern with whole tales with independent traditions limited to a specific area. It affords a common base of reference for collectors and scholars. It is a pioneer work that has spawned other regional tale types.

DORSON is a two part anthology in the scope and methods of folklore and folklife studies. The Editor's introduction is a *tour de force* on folklore theories and studies by a historian by training and a prolific folklore teacher and scholar. Eminent folklore scholars deliver lean masterpieces in inimitable styles on various genres of folklore including narrative, poetry, and folksay. Further essays on folklife covers behavioural materials like custom, arts, crafts, and cookery. Each contribution includes a valuable selected annotated bibliography. The second part addresses methodology with an equally masterful coverage of archiving, mapping, and other rarely treated topics of fieldwork. This is an essential work in folklore studies.

A near-perfect introduction to the study of folklore (folkloristics) is the anthology by DUNDES. Multidisciplinary in approach, the collection of 34 essays covers definition, origins, form, transmission, function, and selected studies in folklore. The scope is universal because materials from all over the world are used to delineate method and theory in the study of folklore. The collection is also valuable because it includes several hard-to-come-by classic studies and the perspectives include historical, psychological, structural-functional, and conflict approaches. His work stands out for an introductory text because of its humanistic and scientific approach, its wide coverage, its discerning selection of, papers and masterful editorial comments and footnotes.

FINNEGAN provides a panoramic survey of African oral poetry, prose and special forms including drum language and literature, and drama from puppet shows and masquerades. She succeeds in her aim of putting together vast variegated materials into a readily available systematic form that would also serve as a guide to further research. She offers a balanced presentation of materials between general discussion and actual instance. More detailed description and quotation are included for accessibility and less abstraction. Intricate and artistic conventions are skilfully presented against social backgrounds of purely artistic and stylistic features. Of exceptional value is the introduction, which provides a historical, social, linguistic, and literary grounding to the study.

The brothers GRIMM mark the beginning of the collection and publication of Germanic folk narratives and myths. Their work is of historical significance. It marks the beginning of folktale scholarship and is central to the origin and development of the collection and study of folktales. It is valuable reference for any study of 19th century folkloristics. The folktales are ageless.

PROPP is an important classical tool in the structural study of folklore. It is a pioneer work laying the groundwork for structuralism, which continues to be an influential theory in folklore studies, especially in the US. The work marks a turning point from typology by content to typology by structure. It bridges the typology of Aarne-Thompson with Dundes and younger folklore scholars who consider structruralism a superior methodology.

SEBEOK offers a collection of essays on myth from nine different points of view by distinguished folklorists and anthropologists. Each essay is an outstanding contribution to the study of myth in structure, symbolism, metaphor, actual, and semantics. All of the essays still maintain a freshness and topicality. It is an important benchmark in the study of myth.

TAYLOR's (1962) foremost study of the proverb primarily surveys the different types of English-language proverbs and proverbial phrases from literature rather than fieldwork, which is the only flaw in an otherwise flawless research and presentation. This work is considered the most valuable study of the proverb genre in English. Four sections discuss etiology, composition, composition, mode, and kind of proverbs. There is a final section devoted to proverbial phrases, comparisons, and wellerism. The index section categorizes all proverbs and proverbial expressions according to language. There are references to sources in this altogether scholarly introduction to the proverb genre in English by an outstanding authority.

He is also noted authority on the riddle. TAYLOR's (1951) superb collection of riddles is considered one of the finest in any language. His focus is on the enigma of the question, not the answer. His collection is a researcher's dream employing a massive classification system, a full index, and bibliography.

THOMPSON's (1946) general survey is a useful introduction to basic problems and approaches in folk narrative study. He outlines forms of folk narratives and traces their distribution using the historic-geographic method. His work is valuable for the review of folktale scholarship from its beginning to the time of writing and the long, separate section on North American Indian tales is an additional pleasure. This work contains a bibliography and both motif and type indexes. His six-volume index of folk literature (THOMPSON 1932) is a classic.

AYODOLE OGUNDIPE

Football, *see* Soccer, economics of

Force field analysis

Bargal, David, Martin Gold and Miriam Lewin, "Introduction: The Heritage of Kurt Lewin", *Journal of Social Issues*, 48/2 (1992): 3–13

Brager, George and Stephen Holloway, "Assessing Prospects for Organizational Change: The Uses of Force Field Analysis", *Administration in Social Work*, 16/3–4 (1992): 15–28

Cartwright, Dorwin, "Lewinian Theory as a Contemporary Systematic Framework" in *Psychology: A Study of a Science*, vol. 2, edited by Sigmund Koch, New York: McGraw Hill, 1959

Deutsch, Morton, "Field Theory in Social Psychology" in *The Handbook of Social Psychology*, 4th edition, edited by Gardner Lindzey and Elliot Aronson, Boston: McGraw Hill, 1998

French, Wendell L. and Cecil H. Bell Jr, *Organization Development: Behavioral Science Interventions for Organization Improvement*, 6th edition, Upper Saddle River, New Jersey and London: Prentice Hall, 1999

Grundy, Tony, *Implementing Strategic Change: A Practical Guide for Business*, London: Kogan Page, 1993

Harrison, Michael I. and Arie Shirom, *Organizational Diagnosis and Assessment: Bridging Theory and Practice*, Thousand Oaks, California and London: Sage, 1999

Hawkinshire, Frank B. and William A. Liggett, "Lewin's Paradigm of Planned Change: Theory and Application" in *Advances in Field Theory*, edited by Susan A. Wheelan, Emmy A. Pepitone and Vicki Abt, Newbury Park, California and London: Sage, 1990

Hellriegel, Don, John W. Slocum and Richard W. Woodman, *Organizational Behavior*, 8th edition, Cincinnati, Ohio: South-Western College Publishing, 1998

Hersey, Paul and Kenneth H. Blanchard, "The Management of Change", *Training and Development Journal*, 34/6 (June 1980): 80–98

Huse, Edgar F. and Thomas G. Cummings, *Organization Development and Change*, 4th edition, St Paul, Minnesota: West, 1989

Kahn, Robert L., "Organizational Development: Some Problems and Proposals", *Journal of Applied Behavioral Science*, 10/4 (October/November/December 1974): 485–502

Lewin, Kurt, "Frontiers in Group Dynamics: Concept, Method and Reality in Social Science; Social Equilibria and Social Change", *Human Relations*, 1/1 (June 1947): 5–41

Lewin, Kurt, *Field Theory in Social Science: Selected Theoretical Papers*, edited by Dorwin Cartwright, New York: Harper, 1951

Nicholas, John M., "Successful Project Management: A Force-Field Analysis", *Journal of Systems Management*, 40/1 (January 1989): 24–30

Rickards, Tudor, *Creativity and Problem Solving at Work*, new edition, Aldershot: Gower, 1997; originally published as *Creativity at Work*, Aldershot: Gower, 1988

Rummel, Rudolph J., *Field Theory Evolving*, Beverly Hills, California and London: Sage, 1977

Sprott, Walter J.H., *Social Psychology*, London: Methuen, 1952

Wheelan, Susan A., "New Frontiers in Group and Organizational Dynamics: Introduction to the Special Issue", *Systems Practice*, 9/1 (February 1996): 5–6

White, Ralph K., "Has Field Theory Been Tried and Found Wanting?", *Journal of the History of the Behavioral Sciences*, 14/3 (July 1978): 242–246

Zand, Dale E., "Force Field Analysis" in *The Blackwell Encyclopedic Dictionary of Organizational Behavior*, edited by Nigel Nicholson, Randall S. Schuler and Andrew H. Van de Ven, Oxford: Blackwell Business, 1995; revised edition 1998

In the challenging global environment in which today's successful organizations exist, one common denominator stands out: continual change is an inevitable fact of operational life. A central issue is how well organizations achieve success in implementing specific changes, which are often deemed important in keeping an enterprise viable, current, and sustainable.

Supported by a coherent body of literature, both GRUNDY and HARRISON & SHIROM provide useful discussions regarding several social science-based techniques and decision-making tools designed primarily to assist managers in analysing change, diagnosing various interrelationships, predicting the likely consequences of change processes, and identifying motivators and barriers along the way. FRENCH & BELL is a good introduction to one of the early and often-used techniques, *force field analysis* (FFA), which was developed by Kurt Lewin, a German-educated experimental social psychologist whose pioneering work was largely carried out during World War II.

HAWKINSHIRE & LIGGETT guides the reader through a beneficial explanation of Lewin's research activities involving FFA. These centered primarily around *planned change* – a systematic, purposeful, and deliberate type of change that serves to alter the way an individual, group, or organization functions. In work which had an important influence on subsequent thinking, Lewin argued that the study of various circumstances for change begins appropriately with an analysis of the conditions for "no change". That is, as succinctly discussed in HUSE & CUMMINGS, a state of *quasi-stationary equilibrium* or the status quo.

The contributions of both DEUTSCH and CARTWRIGHT offer a thorough examination of how Lewin conceived of human beings existing in a dynamic "field" of various, coexisting, and interdependent "forces", which determine the behaviours and actions of individuals within a particular setting, thereby generating a movement toward desirable solutions or away from them. Hawkinshire & Liggett go on to explain that with influence from Sir Isaac Newton's Laws of Motion, Lewin postulated that forces tend to work in opposing directions – representing a kind of tug-of-war – with a desired outcome or optimal situation achieved by "rebalancing" those factors for and against a particular action or change initiative. French & Bell, for instance, help to illustrate that one can think of current production levels within a manufacturing plant as a quasi-stationary equilibrium point in a field of forces. Some forces pushing toward higher levels of production (e.g. *driving forces*) and some forces pushing toward lower levels of production (e.g. *restraining forces*).

In his often-cited pieces of work, published posthumously in 1947 and 1951, LEWIN recommends against intensifying or adding driving forces for change because such an approach may actually *increase* resistance, tension, and conflict in the situation, thereby causing the formation of immediate countervailing forces and a "state of blockage" or "inhibited action". However, Harrison & Shirom contribute to this debate by cautioning that organizational and situational contingencies, along with specific change targets or goals, may determine which emphasis is more appropriate within a particular setting.

On the subject of driving and restraining forces within the context of FFA, the well-developed text of Huse & Cummings reminds the reader that it is imperative to concentrate on whether an intended change initiative is itself worth undertaking from the start. This view is embraced by Grundy, who also expounds upon the importance of determining whether those forces identified by an organization are actual or largely imagined, whether they are weak or strong, and whether the forces are within a firm's capacity to influence. HELLRIEGEL, SLOCUM & WOODMAN offers the insight that all too often managers waste a great deal of time and energy considering actions related to forces over which they have little or no control. When managers direct their attention and resources to those forces over which they do have some control, they increase the likelihood that the action plans they develop will be effective.

In an attempt to help organizations decide where best to concentrate efforts in seeking to bring about change, RICKARDS has developed several useful questions that should be considered when carrying out FFA, including: (a) has a general statement been developed which outlines the desired condition in terms of moving from one state to another?; (b) have any of the important variables been overlooked?; (c) has reasonably accurate information been developed regarding the strength of various forces?; (d) how can additional data be obtained if needed?; and (e) how do the various identified forces interrelate?

The seminal research of Lewin helps to illustrate that an effective way of evaluating a decision situation – where some change is seen as necessary – is to do so pictorially. For example, Hellriegel, Slocum & Woodman along with Hersey & Blanchard, each use a clear diagram that visualizes the plateaux of the present state (or status quo) and the desired future state (or goal/target position), and the gap between the two, which implies organizational change. They illustrate the restraining and driving forces as arrows, with the length of each vertical arrow corresponding to the relative strength of a particular force and the arrowheads pointing toward the equilibrium line.

HERSEY & BLANCHARD develops a useful discussion regarding the specific steps involved in carrying out the FFA process. They summarize the key steps as: (1) clearly define the present state or situation (current performance level) and the desired future state (goal or target position); (2) identify and prioritize the restraining forces; (3) identify and prioritize the driving forces; (4) examine both the restraining and driving forces critically for their specificity, importance, amenability to change, and note any interrelationships between forces; (5) represent both restraining and driving forces diagrammatically on a rating-type scale, from say 1 (Low) to 5 (Very High), portraying the relative strength of each force and the degree to which it is possible to influence each force; and (6) devise a strategy and manageable action plan for reducing restraining forces with the highest weighted score, increase those forces which can best facilitate implementation success or alter the status quo, assess the feasibility, priority, resources and timing necessary for each action specified or considered, and identify the level of management best suited to carry out the developed strategy and action plan.

Grundy emphasizes to the reader that a key benefit that flows from the FFA technique is management's enhanced ability to highlight and make transparent the motivators or enablers for a desired change, and focus attention on those barriers or inhibitors working against a change initiative. With its relative simplicity and clarity of visual display, both driving and restraining forces can be brought into sharper focus and a more effective strategy for implementing change can emerge.

NICHOLAS shows that in project management, for instance, the FFA technique can be used to investigate forces that act on a current project or that might influence an upcoming project, and to determine where emphasis is needed to increase a project's likelihood for success. Similarly, SPROTT provides useful examples whereby FFA has been applied to relatively long-term or short-term social phenomena (i.e. organizational changes which operate over months, or situations lasting for a matter of hours or days).

When following up a FFA for purposes of action planning, Rickards helps to articulate several matters worth careful managerial attention, such as: (1) what is the relative importance or significance of the forces identified?; (2) to which individuals or groups and about which forces does a manager have access – what is the point of entry?; (3) where does management have leverage or influence?; (4) what is the state of readiness for change?; (5) what are the linkages between individuals or groups that are now important or could be important for implementing change?; and (6) what are the consequences of failing to move from the present state to the desired future state?

WHEELAN observes in her discerning introduction to a special issue of *Systems Practice* that Lewinian field theory, and subsequent variations thereof, continue to figure prominently in the work of social scientists and practitioners alike. This view is also shared by BARGAL, GOLD & LEWIN in their thought-provoking guest editorial that appeared in a 1992 special issue of *Journal of Social Issues* commemorating the life and work of Lewin.

While FFA represents an effective problem-solving tool and starting point for action relating to desired change, it does not, however, address the actual costs of implementing change or the resources necessary to carry out the change process. Grundy, for example, helps to emphasize that FFA is not a form of cost–benefit analysis; it does not purport to assess whether the content of a specific change, particularly the outputs, is of greater value or not.

Additionally, KAHN provides a constructive contribution that the Lewinian concept of quasi-stationary equilibrium, while frequently mentioned by various authors, often suffers from a lack of systematic conceptualization or measurement of the alleged opposing forces. Furthermore, WHITE reveals

that some critics of the FFA technique hold to the view that it is inherently limited, since an organization's operating environment cannot be easily divided into two distinct fields, those forces in favor and those against an implementation effort or proposed change. It is asserted that there exists a large grey area or third force factor that must be dealt with – referred to by some as the "rainbow effect" because it represents a combination of both restraining and driving forces.

Harrison & Shirom explain, as does Grundy, that no one simple prescription exists that will solve every organization's problem with regard to diagnosing and implementing change. The thorough treatise by RUMMEL argues that the function of field theory is not to describe what exists in all its complexity and profusion. Instead, as White helps to discern, FFA attempts to parsimoniously relate and integrate the similarities and interdependencies of data on and concepts of diverse phenomena in a consistent and explicit structure.

To summarize, the fundamental nature of FFA embraces a combination of defining the problem or situation carefully, followed by reviewing driving and restraining forces, assessing the relative strength of each force in order to identify key barriers and pathways to change, and developing of an appropriate strategy and action plan. Importantly, as BRAGER & HOLLOWAY conveys, FFA offers a useful mechanism to direct attention on, and systematize the assessment and analysis of, forces advancing or impeding implementation efforts, and focus managerial energy on those steps necessary to facilitate desired change.

ZAND's useful synopsis helps to emphasize that the FFA technique, going well beyond the traditional brainstorming process, can aid management in organizing information in terms of its relevance for change, incorporating diverse classes of data and individual, group, and firm-level variables. As such, FFA has been shown to be a beneficial technique that offers a visual mechanism for structural, behavioural, or technical intervention appraisal.

DANIEL B. WAGGONER

See also Change management, Organizational behaviour, Organizational change, Organizational learning, Power, Stakeholder, Stakeholder analysis

Fordism

Aglietta, Michael, *A Theory of Capitalist Regulation: The US Experience*, London: New Left Books, 1979 (French edition 1976)

Chandler, Alfred D. Jr, *The Visible Hand: The Managerial Revolution in American Business*, Cambridge, Massachusetts: Harvard University Press, 1977

Ford, Henry, *My Life and Work*, Garden City, New York: Garden City Publishing, 1922; London: Heinemann, 1923

Hounshell, David A., *From the American System to Mass Production, 1800–1932: The Development of Manufacturing Technology in the United States*, Baltimore: John Hopkins University Press, 1984

Meyer, Stephen, *The Five Dollar Day: Labor Management and Social Control in the Ford Motor Company,*

1908–1921, Albany: State University of New York Press, 1981

Nevins, Allan and Frank Ernest Hill, *Ford: The Times, the Man, the Company, 1865–1915*, New York: Scribner, 1954

Nevins, Allan and Frank E. Hill, *Ford: Expansion and Challenge, 1915–1933*, New York: Scribner, 1957

Piore, Michael J. and Charles F. Sabel, *The Second Industrial Divide: Possibilities for Prosperity*, New York: Basic Books, 1984

Tolliday, Steven and Jonathan Zeitlin (editors), *Between Fordism and Flexibility: The Automobile Industry and Its Workers*, Cambridge: Polity Press, 1986; 2nd edition Oxford: Berg, 1992

Womack, James P., Daniel T. Jones and Daniel Roos, *The Machine That Changed the World*, New York: Rawson, 1990

Fordism, in its narrowest sense, refers to the system of production that Henry Ford and the Ford Motor Company developed to manufacture the Model T automobile. FORD's autobiography, therefore, is a good starting point for a general discussion of his 'recipe' for success, mass production, high wages, and low product prices. Ford explains how the Ford Motor Company was able to apply modern production methods in "a big way" – he describes his system without explicit reference to mass production – and produce a lower priced automobile while still improving on its quality. Of special interest is his highly charged discussion of the increased deskilling of most workers in his plants and their loss of autonomy as the division of labour became more extreme.

In a still unrivalled series of books on Ford and his company, NEVINS gives a thorough but generally uncritical narrative of Henry Ford's life and the rise of the Ford Motor Company. In the first volume, Nevins discusses the anatomy of Ford's success, his adoption of a simple standardized product, the Model T, with precision-made interchangeable parts, and assembled by workers using a continuous or moving assembly line. This production system enabled Ford to achieve impressive economies of scale. Nevins then tackles the motives behind the introduction of the five-dollar day at Ford's Highland plant in 1914. His conclusion that it was the result of Ford's genuine desire to better the lives of his workers seems naive. MEYER provides a good counterpoint to Nevins as his discussion of the five-dollar day is placed within the larger context of the Ford Motor Company's ominous sounding Department of Sociology, its overbearing corporate paternalism, and its attempt to Americanize an increasingly immigrant labour force. Moreover, Meyer is quite convincing in his claim that the five-dollar day was introduced in an attempt to increase productivity and deal with the high labour turnover and poor morale that followed the introduction of the assembly line.

In the second volume of the series, NEVINS & HILL go on to detail the revolution in mass production taking place in Ford's Highland Park factory and explain how it came to be seen as the exemplar of mass production in America. They follow the company's increasing vertical integration as it acquired forests and mines, foundries and steel mills, as well as railroads and shipping fleets, all in an attempt to bypass the instability of purchasing inputs in the market. CHANDLER complements the Nevins & Hill narrative. Although he does not deal with the Ford Motor Company in any great detail, his work places the developments at Ford within a larger movement in American business history. The essays contained in TOLLIDAY & ZEITLIN offer a much-needed view of Fordism beyond America, and detail its diffusion and modification in different countries.

HOUNSHELL is essential reading for anyone who wants to understand the cluster of developments that helped bring about mass production in America. His discussion of the American system of manufactures and the evolution in machine-made or precision-made interchangeable parts, and how this set the stage for Ford's production system with its reliance on dedicated, or single-purpose machine tools, is invaluable. The reader can now fully understand just how timely the Ford Motor Company's adoption of the assembly line was in dealing with the assembly bottlenecks generated by these new machines. The limits to Ford's system, however, became apparent when his competitor, General Motors, introduced annual model changes and pioneered flexible mass production. Houndshell also discusses and tends to minimize the influence Taylorism or scientific management may have had on Fordism. The connection is one that Nevins & Hill and Meyer have chosen to highlight.

The inherent simplicity and economy of attaching consistently interchangeable parts is, for WOMACK, JONES & ROOS, the key to Ford's high-volume mass production. This development, more so than the assembly line with its semiskilled worker, they argue, accounts for higher increases in productivity per worker. This book is prescriptive and it is clear that the authors abhor the Fordist assembly line. They find it to be an anathema both in the production of good cars and a good society. While the consistent interchangeability of parts is fundamentally important and ought to be emulated, they have no use for Fordism with its heavy bureaucracy, highly inflexible dedicated machines, and conflict-ridden plants, where workers struggle against the pace and monotony of the assembly line. With a seemingly religious fervour, which is, at times, very offputting, the authors walk the reader through their alternative, a flexible system of production they call lean production, or the Toyota Production system, with its leaderless work groups, total quality management, and just-in-time-inventory control. For the best accounting of the history and possibility of flexible production, however, the reader should look to PIORE & SABEL.

AGLIETTA and his views of Fordism have been very influential in a number of disciplines and are worth reading. He redefines Fordism as the system of mass production and mass consumption that characterized industrialized capitalist economies, particularly the United States, in the 1945–70 period. This system, despite its paced assembly lines, which promoted absenteeism and labour conflict, also produced sustained economic growth, employment stability, and a rising standard of living for most workers. By the late 1960s, however, economic growth was beginning to stall and workers, wages, and unions were under attack. The economic stagnation that followed in the 1970s, for Aglietta and his followers in the regulation school, constitute a major crisis in capitalist development.

LOUISE LAMONTAGNE

See also Antonio Gramsci, Post-Fordism

Foreign aid

Bauer, P.T., *Dissent on Development*, London: Weidenfeld and Nicolson, 1971; revised edition, Cambridge, Massachusetts: Harvard University Press, 1976

Development Assistance Commission, *Development Cooperation, 1997*, Paris: OECD, 1997

Feyzioglu, Tarhan *et al.*, "A Panel Data Analysis of the Fungibility of Foreign Aid", *World Bank Economic Review*, 12/1 (January 1998): 28–58

Independent Commission on International Development Issues, *North–South, A Programme for Survival: Report of the Independent Commission on International Development Issues*, Cambridge, Massachusetts: MIT Press, and London: Pan, 1980 (known as the Brandt Report)

Johnson, Harry, "The Crisis of Aid and the Pearson Report" in *Foreign Resources and Economic Development: A Symposium on the Report of the Pearson Commission* edited by T. J. Byres, London: Cass, 1972

Rix, Alan, *Japan's Foreign Aid Challenge: Policy Reform and Aid Leadership*, London and New York: Routledge, 1993

Thapa, G.B. *et al.*, *Banking with the Poor: Report and Recommendations Adopted by the Second Regional Workshop, Kuala Lumpur*, Brisbane: Foundation for Development Cooperation, 1992

Todaro, Michael P., *Economic Development*, 7th edition, London: Longman, and Reading, Massachusetts: Addison Wesley, 2000

White, Howard, "The Macroeconomic Impact of Development Aid: A Critical Survey", *Journal of Development Studies*, 28/2 (January 1992) 163–240

World Bank, *World Development Report 1998/99*, Oxford and New York: Oxford University Press, 1999

TODARO notes that foreign aid encompasses grants and concessional loans made to developing countries in the interests of promoting their development. Official development assistance (ODA) has grown from an annual rate of $4.6 billion in 1960 to $55 billion in 1996. As a percentage of developed country GNP, however, ODA has steadily declined from 0.51 per cent in 1960 to 0.25 per cent in 1996, reflecting a mood of "aid weariness". Moreover, it can scarcely be argued that the allocation of foreign aid is determined by the relative needs of developing countries. South Asia, for example, is home to nearly 50 per cent of the world's poorest people but receives only $4 per person in aid, whereas the Middle East, with more than five times South Asia's per capita income, receives six times the per capita aid. The richest 40% of the Third World's people receive more than twice as much per capita aid as the poorest 40 per cent. Todaro adds that donor countries give aid primarily because it is in their political or economic self-interest to do so, rather than because of moral or humanitarian reasons.

WORLD BANK tables for 1996 further show that in terms of ODA per capita China and India both received only $2, while Nicaragua received $212 and Israel $389. Recalling the "debt crisis" of the 1980s they also show that as a percentage of GNP in 1996, external debt varied widely from 17 per cent in China, to 45 per cent in Niger – which received virtually no foreign direct investment, to 310 per cent in Angola.

Although the advantage of aid in principle is that it accelerates growth in recipient countries by easing savings and foreign exchange constraints, the result in practice depends on how effectively aid is implemented. Largely because of the way bilateral government aid expands the size of government BAUER has long objected that in practice aid has been a transfer of resources from poor people in rich countries to rich people in poor countries. He rejected any notion of moral obligation to provide aid and opposed the disbursement of aid through multilateral agencies such as the World Bank, because that was likely to result in even less careful scrutiny of expenditures by donors. As a Chicago school writer, Bauer argues that the main determinants of development lie in domestic attitudes and values. He argued emphatically that aid is plainly not indispensable for development "and is indeed likely to obstruct it". In 1970 JOHNSON likewise argued that the Pearson Report – commissioned by the World Bank in response to a perceived "crisis in aid" – amounted to no more than a "set of pious but self contradictory platitudes".

FEYZIOGLU *et al.* conclude that the rate of return on a specific donor-funded project tells little about the impact of that assistance because most aid appears to be fungible. As developing countries receiving aid earmarked for agriculture, education and energy divert their own resources elsewhere, a better approach may be to tie aid to an overall public expenditure programme that provides adequate resources to crucial sectors.

WHITE reviews recent attempts to measure the empirical effectiveness of aid flows. He focuses on two questions: (a) does empirical evidence in fact show a relationship between aid receipts and economic growth? and (b) given that US$1.4 trillion was disbursed in the three decades to 1988, what did aid achieve?

In this context, White notes that by and large microlevel evaluations of aid have been positive, whereas evaluations of macro-level impact are ambiguous at best since they have failed to find a significant aid/growth relationship. Possible explanations of this apparent micro/macro paradox include measurement problems, fungibility, and the fact that microevaluations use social data relevant to benefit-cost analyses whereas macroevaluations use financial data from the national accounts. White concludes that there is no basis for saying whether there is a micro/macro paradox since we are not in a position to say what aid does at the macro level.

Whatever the impact of aid at the macroeconomic level, one increasing concern of developing countries is poverty alleviation. The Foundation for Development Cooperation's *Banking with the Poor* project (THAPA *et al.*) has successfully sponsored micro-finance facilities, in recognition that even very small loans can have a significant impact on the lives of the very poor. This non-government organization (NGO) project stresses the importance to the poor of access to credit – as against the cost of credit – and set about linking banks with NGOs in eight Asian developing countries. Non-government organizations have become increasingly significant in efforts to ensure that those most in need benefit from both aid in particular and economic growth in general.

All too little research has been done on the donor side of the aid relationship. RIX provides an alternative line of enquiry and focuses on administrative issues affecting Japanese aid. While the empirical impact of aid on recipient country growth or savings is one measure of aid's worth, Rix argues that Japan has been more interested in the political leverage gained for itself. He notes that whereas Japan reached the position of a top world donor in 1989, it remains well known in the aid community for its relatively poor aid quality. Amongst the criticisms of Japanese aid are that aid is more concerned with Japan's goals than with its impact on recipients, that Japanese aid is just a business tied to exports, that it is a foreign policy tool, that its aid tying is notoriously tight and that too little aid is directed towards the least developed countries. Japan's aid priorities are less concerned with the improvement of its aid quality than with lessening its own vulnerabilities. New guidelines issued in 1991 at least state the intention of giving increased attention to recipients' general stance towards weapons, human rights, and market forces.

The Brandt Report (INDEPENDENT COMMISSION ON INTERNATIONAL DEVELOPMENT ISSUES) argued that the gulf between the world's "haves" and "have nots" is a threat to world peace so that, despite past failings and criticisms of aid, it may be that there is "one future for all or no future at all". The OECD DEVELOPMENT ASSISTANCE COMMISSION (DAC) likewise continues to argue that poor people and poor countries need to be better integrated in a new paradigm of "people centred participatory development". Accordingly, the DAC seeks donor policy change and seeks progress regarding gender equality, environmental sustainability, peace, and participatory development. In recent years, however, it has seemed apparent that the future of international aid efforts is most likely to be linked to trade liberalization.

L.A. DUHS

See also Development economics

Foreign direct investment

Archibugi, Daniele, Jeremy Howells and Jonathan Michie (editors), *Innovation Policy in a Global Economy*, Cambridge and New York: Cambridge University Press, 1999

Buckley, Peter J. (editor), *New Directions in International Business: Research Priorities for the 1990s*, Aldershot, Hampshire: Elgar, 1992

Buckley, Peter J. and Mark Casson (editors), *Multinational Enterprises in the World Economy: Essays in Honour of John Dunning*, Aldershot: Elgar, 1992

Buckley, Peter J. and Jean-Louis Mucchielli (editors), *Multinational Firms and International Relocation*, Cheltenham: Elgar, 1997

International Journal of the Economics of Business, special issue on "The Internationalisation of the Innovation Process", 5/3 (November 1998)

Levy-Livermore, Ammon (editor), *Handbook on the Globalization of the World Economy*, Cheltenham: Elgar, 1998

Michie, Jonathan and John Grieve Smith (editors), *Global Instability: The Political Economy of World Economic Governance*, London: Routledge, 1999

Safarian, A.E., *Multinational Enterprise and Public Policy: A Study of the Industrial Countries*, Aldershot, Hampshire: Elgar, 1993

Strange, Roger, *Japanese Manufacturing Investment in Europe: Its Impact on the UK Economy*, London and New York: Routledge, 1993

Tolentino, P.E., *Multinational Corporations: Emergence and Evolution*, London: Routledge, 2000

United Nations Conference on Trade and Development, *World Investment Report 1997: Transnational Corporations, Market Structure and Competition Policy*, New York: United Nations, 1997

As its title suggests, LEVY-LIVERMORE aims to serve as a handbook. It provides documentation and analysis of the key issues relating to the globalization of the international economy, including of course foreign direct investment (FDI). There are chapters on "Foreign Direct Investment and Economic Growth in Selected LDCs" by Akorlie A. Nyatepe-Coo and "The Role of Multinational Corporations in Globalizing the World Economy: Evidence from Affiliates of US Multinational Companies" by Bijit Bora; while most of the other 24 chapters include some reference to FDI.

Edward Elgar publish a series edited by Peter Buckley on "New Horizons in International Business". BUCKLEY aims to survey internationalization theory, international trade theory, and the role of the firm in strategic management. A number of the chapters discuss the role of FDI, and in particular the chapter by Donald J. Lecraw on "Multinational Enterprises and Developing Countries". BUCKLEY & CASSON was published as a tribute to John Dunning on his retirement from the University of Reading and thus reflects the contribution of Dunning's work to the academic study of the multinational enterprise and international business. Again, most of the chapters discuss FDI, with some focussing on this explicitly, such as Jeremy Clegg's "Explaining Foreign Direct Investment Flows". SAFARIAN analyses the relations between multinational corporations and the governments of the industrialized states. BUCKLEY & MUCCHIELLI focuses on the impact of inward foreign direct investment on the host country and the extent to which this displaces jobs in the FDI's "home" country.

Japanese manufacturing investment in Europe, and its impact on the UK economy, is analysed in STRANGE. This book includes a discussion of the theoretical framework for analysing such issues, background on the Japanese economy, discussion of FDI in the UK, and several case studies, firstly of industries and then of firms.

The UNITED NATIONS CONFERENCE ON TRADE AND DEVELOPMENT (UNCTAD) *World Investment Report* provides a useful source of data and analysis regarding FDI. UNCTAD serves as the focal point within the UN for all matters related to FDI and transnational corporations. The *World Investment Report* is an annual series. The 1997 issue referenced above focuses on the interrelationship between transnational corporations, market structure, and competition policy, and in particular on global and regional trends as regards FDI, including its interlinkages with foreign portfolio equity investment; the impact of FDI on market structure and competition in host economies, as well as globally; and the implications of the interaction between FDI, market structure, and competition for investment and competition policies at the national, regional, and global levels.

Various aspects of FDI are analysed and discussed by the contributors to the INTERNATIONAL JOURNAL OF THE ECONOMICS OF BUSINESS special issue, and also by several of the contributors to ARCHIBUGI, HOWELLS & MICHIE. This book has a particular focus on innovation, but the operation of multinationals and the role of FDI is discussed explicitly in the chapters by Daniele Archibugi, Jeremy Howells, and Jonathan Michie on "Innovation systems and policy in a global economy"; Paolo Guerrieri on "Patterns of national specialisation in the global competitive environment"; John H. Dunning and Clifford Wymbs on "The geographical sourcing of technology-based assets by multinational enterprises"; and by Daniele Archibugi and Simona Iammarino on "The policy implications of the globalisation of innovation". In their introductory chapter the editors argue that there are location-specific advantages which have not lost their importance, and that FDI is increasingly sensitive to exploiting the locality-specific advantages associated with certain areas or regions.

MICHIE & GRIEVE SMITH is an edited collection analysing the key problems besetting today's global economy in the era of globalization. There is a particular emphasis on possible national and international policy responses. Several of the authors discuss FDI explicitly, including Elissa Braunstein and Gerry Eplstein, "Creating international credit rules and the Multilateral Agreement on Investment: What are the alternatives?" and Paz Estrella Tolentino, "Transnational rules for transnational coporations: What next?". In his introductory chapter, Michie argues that the fact that the economy is becoming increasingly internationalized does not dictate the form that this process must take. The free market, *laissez faire* agenda is one being pursued by those who benefit from such a deregulated, winner-take-all environment. But it is not the only choice, and for the majority of the world's population, it is an inappropriate one.

TOLENTINO examines the emergence and evolution of multinational corporations from a broad range of both developed and developing countries. The book analyses the pattern of the early stages of outward FDI from a range of countries including Brazil, Germany, Hong Kong, Japan, Singapore, South Korea, Sweden, Switzerland, Taiwan, the UK, and the US. The contribution of this book to the literature is set out in an excellent foreword by John Cantwell which itself constitutes a useful discussion of the determinants of FDI.

JONATHAN MICHIE

Forensic linguistics

American Speech, special issue on "Forensic Linguistics", 65/4 (1990)

Baldwin, John and Peter French, *Forensic Phonetics*, London: Pinter, 1990

Berk-Seligson, Susan, *The Bilingual Courtroom: Court Interpreters in the Judicial Process*, Chicago: University of Chicago Press, 1990

Cushing, Steven, *Fatal Words: Communication Clashes and Aircraft Crashes*, Chicago: University of Chicago Press, 1994

Dumas, Bethany K., "An Analysis of the Adequacy of Federally Mandated Cigarette Package Warnings" in *Language in the Judicial Process*, edited by Judith N. Levi and Anne Graffan Walker, New York and London: Plenum, 1990

Gibbons, John (editor), *Language and the Law*, London and New York: Longman, 1994

Hollien, Harry, *The Acoustics of Crime: The New Science of Forensic Phonetics*, New York and London: Plenum, 1990

Kurzon, Dennis, *It Is Hereby Performed: Explorations in Legal Speech Acts*, Amsterdam and Philadelphia: Benjamins, 1986

Labov, William, "The Judicial Testing of Linguistic Theory" in *Linguistics in Context: Connecting Observation and Understanding*, edited by Deborah Tannen, Norwood, New Jersey: Ablex, 1988

Levi, Judith N. and Anne Graffan Walker (editors), *Language in the Judicial Process*, New York and London: Plenum, 1990

Levi, Judith N., *Language and Law: A Bibliographic Guide to Social Science Research in the U.S.A.*, Chicago: American Bar Association, 1994

Mellinkoff, David, *The Language of the Law*, Boston: Little Brown, 1963

O'Barr, William M., *Linguistic Evidence: Language, Power, and Strategy in the Courtroom*, New York and London: Academic Press, 1982

O'Barr, William M. and John M. Conley, *Rules versus Relationships: The Ethnography of Legal Discourse*, Chicago: University of Chicago Press, 1990

O'Barr, William M. and John M. Conley, *Just Words: Law, Language, and Power*, Chicago: University of Chicago Press, 1998

Rieber, Robert W. and William A. Stewart (editors), *The Language Scientist as Expert in the Legal Setting: Issues in Forensic Linguistics*, New York: New York Academy of Sciences, 1990

Shuy, Roger W., *Language Crimes: The Use and Abuse of Language Evidence in the Courtroom*, Oxford and Cambridge, Massachusetts: Blackwell, 1993

Solan, Lawrence M., *The Language of Judges*, Chicago: University of Chicago Press, 1993

Solan, Lawrence M., "Can the Legal System Use Experts on Meaning?", *Tennessee Law Review*, 66 (1999): 1167ff.

Tiersma, Peter M., *Legal Language*, Chicago: University of Chicago Press, 1999

The term "forensic linguistics" is relatively recent. It has been heard in presentations by linguists since at least the1980s, and it was being used in print by 1990. Its precise sense is still under development, for it is used both broadly and narrowly: broadly, in the sense of the application of linguistics principles of analysis to language used in judicial proceedings; and narrowly, in the sense of the use of linguistic expertise by a linguist in a judicial proceeding, particularly expert testimony by a linguist at trial. The latter sense is preferred in the journal begun in 1994, *Forensic Linguistics: The International Journal of Speech, Language and the Law*. This is the official publication of the International Association of Forensic Linguists

(IAFL), an organization that has met biannually since 1992. The highly international nature of IAFL is indicated by the meeting sites to date: Birmingham, UK; Bonn, Germany; Armidale, Australia, and Durham, North Carolina, in the US. The International Association of Forensic Phonetics (IAFP) was founded in 1991; it hosts conferences and seminars and also serves as a registered professional body for phoneticians involved in forensic work. Beginning in 1990, the Law and Society Association, another international organization, began scheduling fairly regular sessions on "language and law", and both the Linguistic Society of America and the American Dialect Society have had scheduled sessions on language and law since 1990. *American Speech*, the journal of the American Dialect Society, has published a number of important articles (see below).

Linguists have testified in legal cases implicating a wide range of linguistic levels, e.g. phonetics, phonology, morphology, syntax, semantics, pragmatics, and variation. Legal issues have included the following: statutory and contract language ambiguity; comprehensibility of jury instructions (see entry on Jury instructions); problems with "verbatim" transcripts; spoken language as evidence of intent; adequacy of warning labels on consumer products; verbal offences (libel, slander); compliance with plain language requirements; trademark and copyright infringement; informed consent; and the regulation of advertising language by the Federal Trade Commission in the US. The best-known and most experienced forensic linguist in North America is Roger W. Shuy, Emeritus Professor at Georgetown University, whose name was for a number of years synonymous with forensic linguistics in the sense of trial consultant/expert. SHUY, his first book on the topic, remains an excellent introduction to the work he has done as a consultant and expert witness in many cases. He has published two additional books, *The Language of Confession, Interrogation, and Deception* (1998) and *Bureaucratic Language in Government & Business* (1998).

The first comprehensive book on forensic linguistics was LEVI & WALKER. While some of the content is dated, the collection remains a useful overview of the range of activities of forensic linguists. The collection of eleven chapters, many of them based on the pioneering 1985 Conference on Language in the Judicial Process at Georgetown University, presents an overview by Levi, then sections on the following topics: "Analyzing Language in Legal Settings" (cross-examination, plea bargaining, issues of litigant satisfaction, and lawyer-client communication); "Transforming Language in Legal Proceedings" (bilingual court proceedings and court reporting); and "Construing Language for Legal Purposes" (conversational analysis, social conversation as evidence, language and cognition in products liability law, and the adequacy of cigarette package warnings).

Another book published the same year, RIEBER & STEWART, grew out of a Spring 1988 workshop entitled "The Use of the Language Scientist as Expert in the Legal Setting". It also reports experiences of linguists as consultants/expert witnesses. Shuy's article "Evidence of Cooperation in Conversation: Topic-Type in a Solicitation to Murder Case" is particularly recommended.

Other books that have appeared since 1990 focus on the nature of legal language, phonetics, speech act theory, the ethnography of legal discourse, and miscommunication (including bilingualism in the courtroom). One good general introduction to these topics is GIBBONS; it has a useful, if brief, section on forensic linguistics. The classic book on the nature of legal language is MELLINKOFF. A later book that examines some of the same topics, and also looks at the role of hierarchy and power, is O'BARR. Some of the contents of the books by Mellinkoff and O'Barr have been updated and supplemented in TIERSMA, which is being widely used as a textbook in language and law courses in the US. SOLAN (1993) examines the relationship between jurisprudential goals and linguistic principles.

Work in forensic phonetics is reflected in two 1990 books, BALDWIN & FRENCH and HOLLIEN, though both are somewhat hard to find.

Research in speech act theory is best reflected in KURZON, while O'BARR & CONLEY (1990 and 1998) are the work of the dominant researchers in the ethnography of legal discourse. The authors show how the dynamics of legal process can be explored through linguistic analysis by analysing such judicial processes as the cross-examinations of victims, and divorce mediation. The more recent book analyses the dynamics of power in everyday judicial process and alternative dispute resolution.

BERK-SELIGSON is an excellent introduction to issues involving languages other than English. CUSHING is an invaluable contribution to the literature of miscommunication. The author presents an overview of the crucial role of language in aircraft crashes and near-crashes caused by communication failures. Cushing looks at both individual and social cognitive factors and suggests encoding options that would provide potential solutions for the airline industry.

Two articles illustrate the analysis of issues in criminal and civil cases. LABOV attempts to establish practical importance as a criterion of theory validity, based on a discussion of three judicial cases in which testimony of linguistic experts was used. A similar approach is used in DUMAS.

A collection of articles in a special issue of AMERICAN SPEECH provides a more recent overview of topics being addressed by forensic linguistics. Finally, SOLAN (2000) explores the notion of the linguist as tour guide in judicial process.

Judith Levi first published a bibliography of language and law in 1982 (*Linguistics, Language and the Law: A Topical Bibliography*). Between 1982 and 1994, she enlarged and expanded the work, drawing widely upon social science research on language in the judicial process. Particularly helpful is LEVI'S inclusion of two outlines, one of pertinent legal topics (Spoken Language in Legal Settings, Language as a Subject of the Law, The Written Language of the Law, Other Categories, Overviews and Collections, and Forensic Linguistics), the other of linguistics subfields (Phonetics and Phonology, Morphology and Syntax, Semantics and Pragmatics, Discourse Analysis (Including Conversational Analysis), Sociolinguistics, and Psycholinguistics). Each section or subsection begins with a brief overview, then lists bibliographical items, with key items in bold type. The bibliography is somewhat dated, but remains an excellent resource, particularly for those just entering the field.

BETHANY K. DUMAS

Forensic psychology

Cleckley, Hervey M., *The Mask of Sanity: An Attempt to Re-interpret Some Issues about the So-Called Psychopathic Personality*, St Louis: Mosby, 1941

Hanson, Karl R. and Monique T. Bussiere, "Predicting Relapse: A Meta-Analysis of Sexual Offender Recidivism Studies", *Journal of Consulting and Clinical Psychology*, 66/2 (1998): 348–62

Hare, Robert D., "A Research Scale for the Assessment of Psychopathy in Criminal Populations", *Personality and Individual Differences*, 1 (1980): 111–19

Loftus, Elizabeth F., *Eyewitness Testimony*, Cambridge, Massachusetts: Harvard University Press, 1979

Quinsey, Vernon L., Grant T. Harris, Marnie E. Rice and Catherine Cormier, *Violent Offenders: Appraising and Managing Risk*, Washington, DC: American Psychological Association, 1998

Wrightsman, Lawrence S., Michael T. Wietzel and William H. Fortune, *Psychology and the Legal System*, 4tg edition, Pacific Grove, California: Brooks Cole, 1998

Yochelson, Samuel and Stanton E. Samenow, *The Criminal Personality*, 3 vols, Northvale, New Jersey: Aronson, 1976–86

A comprehensive overview of the interaction of psychology and the legal system is provided by WRIGHTSMAN, WIETZEL & FORTUNE. The many arenas in which the two intersect are addressed: legality and justice, theories of crime, crime investigation, evaluation of offenders, trial process, juries, profiling, and insanity. Arguments for and against psychology's participation are examined and examples are abundant. This book is of an introductory nature in that the discussions encompass a broad range, however enough specifics are included to give the reader an adequate understanding of the material.

LOFTUS is well known for her research in the area of memory. In this book she examines the way memories are encoded and the various ways they can be altered. Forensic psychologists are frequently called upon to assess the veracity of an eyewitness testimony. Loftus makes a strong argument against the eyewitness with a multitude of studies that have demonstrated the unreliability of their reports. New memories can be implanted and old memories altered with ease and this renders memories susceptible to tampering. The manner in which a question is posed can alter or implant a memory. The multiple-choice style versus the open-ended style of questions are examples of this. The latter allows the witness to respond with "I don't know" whereas the former demands a response. Loftus has found that people unknowingly convince themselves of an answer when forced to give an answer. With numerous real-life examples that address how we retain and retrieve memories to the differences in eyewitness ability, this book is vital to the understanding of forensic psychology.

QUINSEY et al. provide an exhaustive examination of risk factors and the field of violence prediction. Risk factors have been identified as the key to violence prediction and the use of them in the various actuarial risk appraisal guides is the focus here. The Violence Risk Appraisal Guide (VRAG) is the most recent instrument in assessing violence risk. It is scored on the basis of 12 risk factors that include developmental variables, substance abuse history, psychiatric and criminal history, marital status, age, and victim data. The longitudinal studies – where risk factors are identified – using mentally disordered offenders, fire setters, and sex offenders, comprise a substantial portion of the book and include the history, characteristics, and treatment of not only these classifications but the history and treatment of violent offenders over the past 300 years.

HARE's research scale for the assessment of psychopathy has made a significant impact in psychopathy research. With this scale, researchers and clinicians can identify the severity of the disorder rather than identifying only whether it is present or not. Since its publication in 1980, the psychopathy checklist, as it is known, has been revised and is known as the PCL-R. The revised version consists of 20 items scored on a three-point scale. A score of zero indicates that there is no fit between the item and the individual and a score of two indicates that the individual fits the description of the item well. The 20 items are then divided among two factors. Factor one is considered to be the interpersonal, affective traits of glibness/superficial charm, grandiose sense of self worth, pathological lying, conning/manipulative, lack of remorse/guilt, shallow affect, callous/lack of empathy, and a failure to accept responsibility for one's actions. Factor two consists of socially deviant behaviours and is comprised of the following: need for stimulation/proneness to boredom, parasitic lifestyle, poor behavioural controls, early behavioural problems, lack of realistic long-term goals, impulsivity, irresponsibility, juvenile delinquency, and revocation of conditional release. Scores range from zero to 40 and are divided into categories. Hare considers the individual who scores 30 and above to have severe psychopathy and essentially to be incapable of rehabilitation, while below 22 psychopathy is considered low or not present. The Hare PCL-R correlates highly with antisocial personality disorder and reoffence rates.

HANSON & BUSSIERE analysed 61 previous studies on sex offender recidivism in this meta-analysis in order to identify the factors most strongly related to recidivism among sex offenders. They found the average recidivism rate to be lower than expected (13.4 per cent), however more important than this, it was found that certain sub-groups recidivated at a higher rate. Those with prior sex-offences and deviant sexual preferences were found to be most at risk. Age (young), and marital status (single) also predicted recidivism. Failure to complete treatment was also found to be a significant risk factor. This article is the first of its kind and is considered to be a substantial contribution to the arena of risk assessment as well as one of the primary sources that forensic psychologists, judges, and lawyers refer to when assessing the likelihood of reoffence.

CLECKLEY, in this oft-cited work that is the first book of its kind, has described the psychopathic personality. The psychopath is portrayed as a person with a severe disability – a social disability. The description "a biological organism, outwardly intact however centrally deficient and disabled" is an apt one. Cleckley supports statements like this with numerous descriptive case examples, comparisons with other disorders, and an attempt to identify the disorder's origins. The psychopath fails to grasp social expectations because of this deficit, which encompasses a wide range of behaviours/characteristics: lack of empathy, failure to experience the most basic of feelings, an ability to disregard others, absence of nervousness/anxiety, untruthfulness, lack of remorse, lack of insight, and a general unresponsiveness in interpersonal relations. The psychopath's behaviour is as damaging as any other severe mental disorders, however the psychopath appears to be in control of his behaviour and only follows society's rules when he deems it appropriate. Cleckley is somewhat of a challenge to read and tends toward overusing metaphors. Despite this, the book is valuable in both an historical context and in trying to understand the psychopathic personality.

YOCHELSON & SAMENOW in this three-volume series, examine the criminal personality. The series starts at the first encounter with the offender and continues through to the process of change. It includes the issue of drug use in this population. The authors have detailed their research with what they term the "criminal mind". Their definition of the criminal strongly resembles the description of antisocial personality disorder and psychopathy. During the early stages of their research, Yochelson & Samenow limited their work to observation without the intent of doing treatment. They detailed 52 features of criminal thinking that needed to be changed for rehabilitation to be a possibility. Patterns of deception are established early in this population and others' rights are characteristically disregarded, and when arrested, this population tends to see themselves as victims and believe they were good people despite their lengthy criminal records.

Over time a treatment plan, or "process of change" was defined. It was found that change was most likely to occur in this population when the individual was vulnerable and desirous of change. The desire for change must be accompanied by an in-depth knowledge of what needs to be changed. Finally, change is only possible when the long-term benefits of change outweigh the benefits of maintaining a criminal lifestyle. Overall, change is considered a possibility, although not a common one. These three volumes comprise the most detailed, long-term examination of the criminal mind documented.

CHANTAL DEINES

See also Eyewitness testimony, Psychopathy

Foucault, Michel 1926–1984

French social theorist

Ball, Stephen J. (editor), *Foucault and Education: Disciplines and Knowledge*, London and New York: Routledge, 1990

Dreyfus, Hubert L. and Paul Rabinow, *Michel Foucault: Beyond Structuralism and Hermeneutics*, Chicago: University of Chicago Press, 1982

Foucault, Michel, *Madness and Civilization: A History of Insanity in the Age of Reason*, New York: Pantheon, 1965; London: Tavistock, 1967 (French edition 1961)

Foucault, Michel, *The Order of Things: An Archaeology of the Human Sciences*, New York: Pantheon, and London: Tavistock, 1970 (French edition 1966)

Foucault, Michel, *Discipline and Punish: The Birth of the Prison*, New York: Pantheon, and London: Allen Lane, 1977 (French edition 1975)

Foucault, Michel, *The History of Sexuality*, vol. 1: *An Introduction*, New York: Pantheon, 1978; London: Allen Lane, 1979 (French edition 1976)

Foucault, Michel, *Power/Knowledge: Selected Interviews and Other Writings 1972–1977*, edited by Colin Gordon, New York: Pantheon, and Brighton: Harvester Press, 1980

Miller, James, *The Passion of Michel Foucault*, New York: Simon and Schuster, and London: HarperCollins, 1993

Sawicki, Jana, *Disciplining Foucault: Feminism, Power, and the Body*, New York and London: Routledge, 1991

Michel Foucault was considered one of the most influential French thinkers since Jean-Paul Sartre. His work, which offered both a method for the study of human beings and a critical insight to modern society, has permanently altered our understanding of many institutions of Western society. He worked in a psychiatric hospital during the 1950s and lectured in many universities throughout the world. In 1970, he was elected to the chair of History of Systems of Thought at the College de France.

Foucault's first major book was *Madness and Civilization* (FOUCAULT, 1965). Foucault examines the archaeology of madness in the West from 1500 to 1800 and argues that madness is an invention, a product of historical process, rather than a universal objective category. Before 1600, the mad person was not confined in any institution and insanity was considered part of everyday life. Then in the 17th century, madness became a shame and a threat which thus had to be hidden and confined. Not only did the conception of madness change, but so too did society's strategies for dealing with it. Until the 19th century, madness was more a police matter than a medical matter. As Foucault demonstrated, historical discontinuities predominate in the history of madness – first, between the Renaissance and the Classical Age, where madness was reduced to silence and unreason; and, second, between the Classical Age and the 19th century where madness was medicalized through the language of psychiatry as "mental illness".

The Order of Things: An Archaeology of Human Sciences, FOUCAULT (1970) appeared during the rise of structuralism. It represents an attempt to further the structuralist paradigm's search for "a philosophical foundation for the possibility of knowledge" (p.335). With the archaeological method, Foucault examines the history of human sciences as a whole and shows how the classical system of knowledge – science of life, language, and economics – in the Renaissance gave way to the modern sciences of biology, philology, and political economy.

In his next book, *Discipline and Punish*, FOUCAULT (1977) shifts his focus onto the history of power relations and oppression by examining the development of disciplinary technology within the broader historical grid of biopower. Like madness, legal punishment has a varied and unstable history: from sovereign torture to humanist reform, and finally to normalized detention and surveillance in the era of modern technology of disciplinary power. Foucault's analysis suggests that modern human sciences had taken over the role of Christianity in disciplining the body, substituting for the soul, subject to indefinite supervision and discipline. Foucault picks out Jeremy Bentham's Panopticon as the paradigmatic example of a disciplinary technology. It would have allowed for the invisible surveillance of a large number of people by a single person.

This new power is continuous, disciplinary, anonymous, and highly efficient.

In the first volume of the *History of Sexuality*, FOUCAULT (1978) argues against the repressive hypothesis that holds that truth is intrinsically opposed to power and therefore inevitably plays a liberating role. He offers an alternative view to the standard historical chronology, which sees a change in the 18th and especially the 19th century, from a sexuality that is relatively free to one that is controlled and guarded. Rather than seeing the last several centuries as a history of increasing repression of sexuality, Foucault suggests an increasing channelling of sexuality. Sex was posed as such a powerful drive that dramatic forms of individual self as well as collective control were imperative in order to keep these forces leashed. According to Foucault, sexuality was invented at the beginning of the 18th century, as an instrument effect in the spread of biopower, an administrative concern for the welfare of the population. Scientific classifications of sexual activity were carried out, police control over prostitution and disease was administrated, and intervention in the sexual life of the population was instituted. Starting from political-economic concerns, sex became both an individual and a state issue. A major shift occurred at the beginning of the 19th century when the discourse about sexuality was recast into medical terms. Through "scientific discoveries", sexuality was linked to a powerful form of knowledge. It was this change that triggered an explosion in discourses about sexuality throughout bourgeois society. Here, Foucault presents a genealogy of the modern subject and analyses the construction of a particular technology of the subject, confession, through which the body, knowledge, discourse, and power are brought into a common location.

Power / Knowledge (FOUCAULT 1980), which consists of sets of essays and interviews with Foucault, provides readers with a guide to grasp the consistent purposes that lay behind Foucault's individual studies and the broad social vision and political aims that unified his work. As Foucault shows, what holds together his wide field of study is the interest and concern with power and knowledge and how they work together. Foucault describes the nature of power in society not through the conventional definition that concentrates on powerful individuals and repressive institutions, but the much more pervasive and insidious mechanisms by which our bodies, minds, and everyday lives are disciplined and controlled. By bringing into clearer focus the political and intellectual environment in which this work was carried out, this volume also helps to clarify some confusion around Foucault's work produced by the use of some vague and polemical labels such as "structuralism" and "post-Marxism".

DREYFUS & RABINOW represents an effort to resolve some of the misunderstandings around Foucault's work. It situates Foucault's thought in phenomenology, structuralism, and hermeneutics, and uses his work as an aid to examine the most influential contemporary attempts to study human beings. It discusses Foucault's work chronologically to show the movement of his tools of analysis of human beings and his diagnosis of human society. This volume also contains the interview with Foucault, "On the genealogy of ethics: an overview of work in progress", which shows clearly how the project of the history of sexuality was constructed.

BALL's collection is the first effort to explore Foucault's key ideas and concepts in relation to educational issues. It argues that schools, like prisons and asylums, are one form of modern institution that is fundamentally concerned with moral and social regulation and in which complex technologies of disciplinary control take place. In different ways the essays in this collection assess the relevance of Foucault's work to educational practice. Some apply a genealogical approach to explore aspects of the constitution of modern educational practice, and others examine the role of discourse about education in the contemporary politics of education restructure. Together they demonstrate how the application of Foucauldian analysis to education unmasks the politics that underlie some of the apparent neutrality of educational reform.

SAWICKI represents an important effort to appropriate Foucault for feminism. Her essays lay out the basic features of a Foucauldian feminism that is compatible with feminism as a pluralistic and emancipatory radical politics. Arguing against prevailing assumptions, her analysis demonstrates how Foucault's discourse can be used to support, rather than completely reject, specific liberatory political struggles, namely, struggles for sexual and reproductive freedom.

MILLER explores the wider context of Foucault's work and provides a bold reinterpretation of the philosopher's life and his texts. His work chronicles every stage of Foucault's personal and professional odyssey, from his early interest in dreams, his enthusiasm in politics, to his final preoccupation with sexuality and the nature of personal identity.

PEI-YAO CHEN

Franchise, *see* Suffrage

Free trade

American Economic Association (AEA), *Readings in International Economics*, Homewood, Illinois: Irwin, 1968

Cook, Gary (editor), *The Economics and Politics of International Trade: Freedom and Trade*: vol. 2, London and New York: Routledge, 1998

Harley, C. Knick (editor), *The Integration of the World Economy, 1850–1914*, 2 vols, Cheltenham: Elgar, 1996

Irwin, Douglas A., *Against the Tide: An Intellectual History of Free Trade*, Princeton, New Jersey: Princeton University Press, 1996

Larudee, Mehrene, "Trade Policy: Who Wins? Who Loses?" in *Creating a New World Economy: Forces of Change and Plans for Action*, edited by Gerald Epstein, Julie Graham and Jessica Nembhard, Philadelphia: Temple University Press, 1993

List, Frederich, *National System of Political Economy*, Fairfield: Kelley, 1977 (originally published 1856)

Mander, Jerry and Edward Goldsmith, *The Case against the Global Economy, and for a Turn toward the Local*, San Francisco: Sierra Club, 1996

Marrison, Andrew (editor), *Free Trade and Its Reception, 1815–1960*, vol. 1: *Freedom and Trade*, London: Routledge, 1998

Mill, John Stuart, "The Corn Laws", *Westminster Review*, 3
    (April 1825): 394–420

Organisation for Economic Cooperation and Development
    (OECD), *Open Markets Matter: The Benefits of Trade and
    Investment Liberalisation*, Paris: OECD, 1998

Ricardo, David, "On the Principles of Political Economy and
    Taxation" in *The Works and Correspondence of David
    Ricardo*, edited by Piero Sraffa and M.H. Dobb, vol. 1,
    Cambridge: Cambridge University Press, 1951 (1st edition
    1817; 3rd edition 1821)

Rodrik, Dani, *Has Globalization Gone Too Far?*,
    Washington, DC: Institute for International Economics,
    1997

Semmel, Bernard, *The Rise of Free Trade Imperialism:
    Classical Political Economy, the Empire of Free Trade
    and Imperialism, 1750–1850*, Cambridge: Cambridge
    University Press, 1970

Smith, Adam, *An Inquiry into the Nature and Causes of the
    Wealth of Nations*, edited by Kathryn Sutherland,
    Oxford and New York: Oxford University Press, 1993
    (first published 1776)

The development of the Classical Theory of trade – and its implicit defence of free trade – was a collaborative effort. The most essential elements of the case for free trade had been presented before Smith and Ricardo, but the contributions of these and a few other classical political economists deserve particular attention. SMITH's great contribution is a clear, coherent case for free trade that was, at the time of its publication, unprecedented. The power of Smith's argument is enhanced by the fact that it flows so easily from his lucid, systematic vision of markets, the division of labour, and the creation of wealth that is at the core of this profoundly important book. According to Douglas A. Irwin, "Smith created such a compelling and complete case for free trade that commercial policy could no longer be seriously discussed without contending with his views" (Irwin, p.75; see Irwin).

Chapter seven of RICARDO includes the author's illustration of the principle of comparative advantage, perhaps the single most important idea in trade theory. The few paragraphs that Ricardo devotes to comparative advantage could be clearer and more comprehensive, but this passage is nonetheless an enormously important moment in the history of economic thought. MILL's argument for free trade, and his discussion of the principle of comparative advantage, are clearer and more persuasive than that of Ricardo. The author, like many of his classical contemporaries, emphasizes that the benefits of trade are not shared by everyone and that these victims of free trade ought to be compensated.

LIST, a popular and influential book first published in 1841, challenged the classical consensus on free trade, and was both popular and influential. List argues that the best commercial policy for a particular country cannot be determined in the abstract. It depends, rather, on a nation's history, its industrial mix, and its stage of economic development. The author's most enduring and persuasive critique of the free trade doctrine is his argument that the protection of infant industries can improve a nation's economic wellbeing, especially in manufacturing, which has a "powerful influence on the increase in the national wealth". A country "must sacri-

fice some present advantages in order to insure to itself future ones" (pp.144–145).

The origins and development of the theoretical case for free trade are presented skillfully by IRWIN. This "intellectual history of free trade" includes a survey of preclassical theories of foreign trade (including the Greeks, Aquinas, mercantilism, and physiocracy); a detailed discussion of the development of the classical "free trade doctrine"; and a careful and serious consideration of many critical and sceptical views of free trade, including those focusing on infant industries, international wage differentials, and Keynesian concerns about the macroeconomic consequences of trade. The central theme in Irwin is that the case for free trade has endured, despite a long history of energetic dissent, because the case is intellectually sound.

The theory, history, and politics of free trade raise a wide range of issues, some of them grand and some of them quite specific. Harley, Cook, and Marrison are rich collections of papers that shed light on many of these issues. HARLEY is a two-volume collection of 48 papers (all reprints) which chronicle and analyse the "integration of the world economy" during the 19th and early 20th centuries. The seven papers on the repeal of the corn laws and the "emergence of free trade" are particularly interesting. Other papers assess the extent to which the benefits of free trade have been borne out in reality. The two volumes also include a number of case studies of the liberalization/protection of specific commodities. Most contributions are written by economists, some by historians. The volume includes Kindleberger's classic "The Rise of Free Trade in Western Europe, 1820–1875."

MARRISON and COOK are companion volumes commemorating the 150th anniversary of the repeal of the corn laws. Collectively, they present a series of 30 papers (plus comments on some papers), offering a variety of perspectives on the feasibility, history, and politics of free trade. Contributors include Richard Caves, Frank Hahn, Paul Krugman, and many other important trade economists and economic historians.

The AMERICAN ECONOMIC ASSOCIATION book is a collection of 33 papers in international economics, many of them classics. The volume presents several important papers on trade (by the likes of Samuelson, Johnson, Bhagwati, Leontief, and Friedman), and it conveys well the strong consensus on trade theory and policy that prevailed in the decades following World War II. This consensus has provided a rigorously derived and widely accepted defence of free trade, and it continues to frame discussions of trade policy.

RODRIK is a short, readable, carefully crafted book that argues that the case for free trade, while unquestionably sound, is more ambiguous than many economists allow. Along with its widely recognized benefits, economic openness has important distributional effects and it creates tensions within, between, and among nations over domestic norms (on, for example, environment, social insurance, and labour rights) and the institutions that embody these norms. "Economists' standard approach to globalization," Rodrik writes, "is to emphasize the benefits of the free flow of goods, capital, and ideas and to overlook the social tensions that may result" (p.3). Economists and policy makers, Rodrik concludes, would do well to acknowledge and address these tensions rather than dismissing them as "protectionism". The book's greatest strength is its careful, rigorous, and serious presentation of the most substantial criticisms of free trade.

LARUDEE argues in a clear, non-technical manner that trade theorists and policy makers have paid too little attention to the distribution of trade's costs and benefits and, further, that the classical theory of trade has been used inappropriately to justify the liberalization of capital flows. Larudee warns that unmanaged trade liberalization tends to undermine the bargaining power of workers, communities, and nation states *vis a vis* large, mobile corporations, leaving the typical citizen with less job security, less income, and less political power than they might have under a more thoughtful and more egalitarian trade regime.

MANDER & GOLDSMITH is a provocative collection of 43 essays, each of which views globalization with deep scepticism. Some authors echo the concerns articulated in Larudee and Rodrik, while many others focus on the effects of globalization on cultural diversity, the spread of disease, the environment, democracy, and other "non-economic" issues. Ralph Nader, Herman Daley, William Greider, and Richard Barnet are among the book's contributors. Some of this volume's essays are quite good, others are weak.

SEMMEL looks at the emergence and consolidation of the theory and policy of free trade, from the middle of the 18th century to the end of the 19th century. The author, an intellectual historian, argues that influential arguments for free trade – including Ricardo's – depended to a considerable extent on neo-mercantilist ideas rather than a rejection of them. Free trade, he argues, was seen by many participants in the debate over trade policy as an effective way of extending British power. It makes sense to speak of "free trade imperialism".

The ORGANISATION FOR ECONOMIC COOPERATION AND DEVELOPMENT report is a self-conscious effort to make an accessible case for free trade. Its argument is rooted in classical trade theory and a more general belief that liberalization improves welfare. Like many works that advocate trade liberalization, its claims go beyond the static gains from trade. OECD argues that liberalization promotes dynamic gains, transfer of technology, and employment. OECD is included here because it is a typical (and very credible) example of the sort of argument that dominates debates over trade policy: a mix of trade theory, suggestive empirics, and an underlying urgency about making the case.

TIM KOECHLIN

See also International trade policy, New trade theory, Trade theory, development of

Free will and moral responsibility

Honderich, Ted, *A Theory of Determinism: The Mind, Neuroscience, and Life-Hopes*, Oxford: Clarendon Press, and New York: Oxford University Press, 1988; reprinted in 2 vols as *Mind and Brain* and *The Consequences of Determinism*, Oxford: Clarendon Press, 1990
Kane, Robert, *The Significance of Free Will*, Oxford and New York: Oxford University Press, 1996
Magill, Kevin, *Freedom and Experience: Self-Determination without Illusions*, Basingstoke: Macmillan, and New York: St Martin's Press, 1997
Strawson, Galen, *Freedom and Belief*, Oxford: Clarendon Press, and New York: Oxford University Press, 1986
Strawson, Peter F., "Freedom and Resentment" in *Free Will*, edited by Gary Watson, 1982
Watson, Gary (editor), *Free Will*, Oxford and New York: Oxford University Press, 1982
Watson, Gary, "Free Action and Free Will", *Mind*, 96/382 (1987): 145–72

Free will is one of philosophy's oldest and hardest problems and a classic example, as far as many natural and social scientists are concerned, of its exasperating preoccupation with perennially irresolvable *a priori* puzzles. By contrast, philosophers are apt to regard declarations by sociologists that *free will* is an illusion, or claims by psychologists to have established by experimental means either that we do or do not have it, as dodging the crucial issue of what it is that they are claiming to be illusory or to have established. Although the concept of *free will* can be distinguished from that of *moral responsibility*, the two often go hand in hand in philosophical discussions. The most commonly discussed philosophical problem about free will is whether it can exist if determinism, or something probabilistically close to it, should be true. (Note that when social scientists refer to determinism, often enough what they have in mind is *reductionism*. Determinism, in philosophy, is, roughly, the doctrine that all events, including the choices and actions of human beings, have sufficient causes, in virtue of which they cannot fail to happen as they do.) Among the other major problems about free will is that of whether the concept is coherent and also its relationship to other key concepts such as agency and free action.

In the *locus classicus* of postwar discussion about free will and moral responsibility, Peter STRAWSON argues that the concepts are grounded in a "complicated web of attitudes and feelings which form an essential part of the moral life as we know it". Like sentiments and practices such as resentment, love, gratitude, moral indignation, (and approbation) and asking and giving forgiveness, holding people responsible for their actions is an interpersonal "reactive attitude" and, as such, a natural expression of human desires that the conduct of others should reflect respect and goodwill, as well as the disappointment felt when instead it manifests indifference or malice. Strawson contrasts the reactive attitudes with the "objective attitude", in which interpersonal engagement is withdrawn or modified for the purposes of analysis, understanding or treatment, or even for relief from "the strains of involvement". Unwavering objectivity of attitude in our dealings with others, according to Strawson, is something of which we are simply incapable. Therefore, the idea that we might be led, on the grounds of its inconsistency with determinism, or some other theoretical perspective about human behaviour, to cease to hold others responsible for their actions involves the mistaken assumption that this is something we have a general choice about.

HONDERICH presents a magisterial attempt to work out a defensible account of determinism and what our responses should be to it. The first part sets out a general account of causation and determinism, which is then applied to mind, actions, and choices, drawing on neuroscientific research. The second part argues that the opposing camps in the dispute about determinism and free will and moral responsibility share a mistaken assumption that the key terms have single unified meanings. Rather, it is argued, we each have two opposing sets of attitudes about the initiation of actions in relation to hopes for the future, feelings towards others, the status of knowledge claims, various modes of moral judgement and evaluation, and the standing of social institutions such as punishment. One set of attitudes is at home with the idea of deterministic causation of actions, while the other is opposed to it. The two sets of attitudes issue in the characteristic responses to determinism of intransigence (determinism does not matter) and dismay. Honderich offers a third response of affirmation, in which we recognize the fact and irreconcilability of our opposing attitudes and set about adapting ourselves to the truth of determinism by attempting to relinquish, as best we can, those feelings and attitudes that are opposed to it and by recognizing the value of those that are consistent with it.

Galen STRAWSON argues that there is a fundamental sense in which there is no such thing as free will or "true moral responsibility". Much of the book is devoted to attempting to explain why, despite this, most of us continue firmly to believe both that we have free will and that we are truly morally responsible for what we do. It examines various aspects of the "cognitive phenomenology" of freedom: the nature, causes, and consequences of our deep commitment to belief in freedom. This is a lucid and entertaining book, which is probably the freshest and most unusual treatment of free will in recent years.

KANE surveys recent philosophical work on free will and explores its significance for contemporary concerns in ethics, politics, science, religion, and the social sciences. It defends a "libertarian" conception of free will, according to which free will is both incompatible with determinism and true of human beings, in consequence of which determinism is false. Kane attempts to show that this kind of free will is compatible with recent developments in the physical, biological, neurological, cognitive, and behavioural sciences.

WATSON (1987) was and continues to be a state-of-the art account of contemporary philosophical discussions of free will and related problems. It begins by locating contemporary arguments about free will and determinism in relation to the old problem about two opposing conceptions of freedom: *the liberty of spontaneity* (that freedom consists in a self-determining ability to do what we want) and the *liberty of indifference* (that freedom consists in an ability categorically to choose between alternatives, without reference to what we want). Watson clearly sets out the various philosophical difficulties in providing a coherent account of what is required for free will, considered as the capacity to be truly self determining, where this calls in turn for a self-reflective ability to evaluate one's goals and values and not to be bound by past habit and societal convention or to be open to external control or manipulation. It is a systematic and illuminating overview of contemporary philosophical debate in the area.

MAGILL begins with a survey of attempts by analytical philosophers in the 20th century to resolve disagreements about free will, moral responsibility, and agency through analysis of key terms (for example "necessity" and "could have done otherwise"), concluding that they have resulted in failure. He goes on to argue, nevertheless, that (contra Honderich and Galen Strawson) free will can be shown to be compatible with determinism and that the philosophical stalemate about free will and related problems has arisen through lack of attention to the content of the experiences that shape our understanding of free will and agency and through a mistaken belief that the concept of moral responsibility requires a moral, metaphysical, or theoretical justification. His treatment of moral responsibility therefore follows Peter Strawson's naturalistic rejection of the idea that holding agents responsible for their actions is something we could give up, but goes on to argue that this still leaves us with practical dilemmas about whether to blame or try to understand particular instances of wrongdoing. Such dilemmas can be resolved, however, according to the particular cares and interests we have in others, rather than according to universal principles. Magill argues that free will consists in "being able to do what you really want because it is what you really want", thus effectively incorporating the notion of causation into that of free will, and argues that the supposed "liberty of indifference" (see WATSON 1987) is actually a concept of action rather than freedom. Magill sets out original accounts of the various ways we experience choosing, deciding, and acting (and their causal bases), which reconcile the apparently opposing intuitions that have fuelled the traditional dispute. The book concludes with an investigation of what is required for fully human agency of the kind we take ourselves to have in being able to judge between competing motives for action and in being able to act on such judgements.

WATSON (1982) is probably the best of the many published collections on free will and moral responsibility, bringing together a diverse set of seminal contributions to the post-war philosophical debate about free will, including Peter Strawson's "Freedom and resentment", Harry Frankfurt's highly influential "Freedom of the will and the concept of a person", and A.J. Ayer's "Freedom and Necessity", as well as pieces by Charles Taylor, Thomas Nagel, Daniel Dennett, and Peter van Inwagen. It also contains a useful (although by now somewhat dated) selected bibliography.

KEVIN MAGILL

Freedom

Benn, Stanley I., *A Theory of Freedom*, Cambridge and New York: Cambridge University Press, 1988

Berlin, Isaiah, "Introduction" and "Two Concepts of Liberty" in his *Four Essays on Liberty*, Oxford and New York: Oxford University Press, 1969

Bird, Colin, *The Myth of Liberal Individualism*, Cambridge and New York: Cambridge University Press, 1999

Christman, John, *The Inner Citadel: Essays on Individual Autonomy*, Oxford and New York: Oxford University Press, 1989

Dworkin, Gerald, *The Theory and Practice of Autonomy*, Cambridge and New York: Cambridge University Press, 1988

Geuss, Raymond, *The Idea of a Critical Theory: Habermas and the Frankfurt School*, Cambridge and New York: Cambridge University Press, 1981

MacCallum, Gerald, "Positive and Negative Liberty" in *Philosophy, Politics and Society: Fourth Series*, edited by Peter Laslett, W.G. Runciman and Quentin Skinner, Oxford: Blackwell, 1972

Skinner, Quentin, "The Republican Idea of Political Liberty" in *Machiavelli and Republicanism*, edited by Gisela Bock, Quentin Skinner and Maurizio Viroli, Cambridge and New York: Cambridge University Press, 1990

Skinner, Quentin, *Liberty before Liberalism*, Cambridge and New York: Cambridge University Press, 1998

Steiner, Hillel, *An Essay on Rights*, Oxford and Cambridge, Massachusetts: Blackwell, 1994

Taylor, Charles, "What's Wrong with Negative Liberty" in his *Philosophy and the Human Sciences: Philosophical Papers 2*, Cambridge and New York: Cambridge University Press, 1985

BERLIN remains the best starting point for recent discussions of freedom and liberty (these two terms are used interchangeably). Berlin distinguishes between negative and positive liberty. The negative conception of liberty defines freedom as the *absence* of impediments to agents' actions: in this sense liberty is always "freedom *from*". The positive conception defines it in terms of the *presence* of a certain kind of rational self-direction: in this sense liberty is "freedom *to*". Berlin's main concern in this essay was to chart the divergent historical careers of these two concepts within European political culture during the 19th and 20th centuries, but his analytical distinction itself has in fact proved far more influential than these historical claims.

MACCALLUM is an important early criticism of Berlin that is still worth reading. MacCallum suggests that the attempt to distinguish sharply between negative and positive liberty overlooks the essentially "triadic" nature of the concept of liberty. On this view *any* conception of freedom always refers to three things: (a) the freedom *of* a person, (b) *from* obstacles that interfere with (c) their ability *to* do something. Whereas MacCallum highlights the rather elusive nature of Berlin's original distinction, later writers have continued to make use of it.

Much of the controversy aroused by Berlin's distinction stems from the connection (to which he drew attention himself) between negative liberty and liberalism. But liberals have sometimes also deployed positive conceptions of liberty. Readers seeking to clarify the relationships between the liberal tradition and Berlin's two concepts are directed to BIRD's fourth chapter for guidance. Here Bird argues for a revision of some common assumptions about the liberal credentials of positive and negative liberty. In the process of this discussion, Bird identifies some of the main issues in the ongoing debate about liberty and liberal values.

Critics of liberalism, who frequently perceive a strong affinity between liberalism and negative liberty, have often suggested that a strictly negative view of freedom is unattractive and possibly untenable. TAYLOR makes an effective, if not wholly convincing, argument along these lines, claiming that the extent to which individuals are free must depend in part on the significance or worth of the activities in which they choose to engage. According to Taylor, the fatal defect of negative conceptions is that they sever this connection between freedom and significance.

Whether or not criticisms like Taylor's succeed, few now defend a strictly negative concept of liberty. STEINER is a notable exception. Starting from the claim that to be free to act in a certain way requires that no one prevent you from so acting, Steiner elaborates a full-scale, if idiosyncratic, theory of rights and justice. The first three chapters, however, offer as rigorous account of the negative concept of liberty as we are likely to see. Perhaps the most striking (and controversial) claim made by Steiner is that the overall amount of negative liberty cannot be increased: the distribution of negative liberties is zero-sum. The implication of this view is that the only relevant question concerning liberty as a political value is how it is to be distributed or dispersed. On this view, it makes no sense to demand that liberty be *maximized*.

In series of important articles, Quentin Skinner has provided indispensable historical background to 20th-century debates about freedom. SKINNER (1998) and SKINNER (1990) are brilliant representative samples. Although their focus is slightly different, they are united by the attempt to excavate forgotten understandings of liberty that cut across more familiar contemporary conceptions. Skinner (1990) applies this sort of procedure to Berlin's two concepts, claiming that the classical republican notion of liberty implicit in Machiavelli's work entails a concept of freedom that is neither fully negative nor fully positive.

Much recent thinking about freedom within Anglo-American political theory and philosophy has focused on the notion of autonomy and has thus implicitly or explicitly turned its back on a strictly negative concept of liberty. CHRISTMAN is an excellent collection of essays dealing with themes relating to the idea of autonomy. Many of these essays discuss the relationship between autonomy and more philosophical questions about free will and the conditions of responsible agency. In particular, Christman reprints Frankfurt's classic article, "Freedom of the Will and the Concept of a Person" (1971). In this Frankfurt develops a "hierarchical" model of agency, according to which self-determination involves subjecting one's desires and motivations to a higher order review by so-called "second order volitions". Although Frankfurt does not put it in these terms, his account can be thought of as revamping Berlin's positive conception of liberty as self-direction in a contemporary idiom.

A similar hierarchical model of autonomy is developed in DWORKIN. This useful book not only explores some of the moral and philosophical aspects of freedom as autonomy – it also contains helpful discussion of some of the practical political and social issues in which individuals' autonomy is at stake. For example, Dworkin's arguments significantly clarify the issues surrounding informed consent and privacy in medical contexts and the problem of paternalism.

BENN stands out among recent contributions as a serious and largely successful attempt to develop a systematic and comprehensive account of freedom, autonomy, and politics. Benn explicitly draws on both positive and negative conceptions of freedom. The chief merit of this work lies in its attempt to leave behind purely verbal or conceptual aspects of the definition of freedom and to focus on its role within ethical and evaluative discourse about (for example) respect for persons, ideals of self-realization, self-development, and social commitment. Although much of the book deals with related issues about the nature of practical reasons and moral objectivity, the central chapters on freedom of action, freedom as "autarchy", and autonomy provide much-needed clarity. The book also has a final chapter that summarizes Benn's major claims and serves as a useful guide to the often intimidatingly complex arguments pursued in the body of the book.

Anglo-American discussions of freedom often overlook the persistence of neoMarxist views about freedom within continental political theory. GEUSS is the best and most lucid introduction to what has been the most influential of these neoMarxist traditions, that of the Frankfurt School in general and of the work of Jürgen Habermas in particular. The Frankfurt School theorists try to develop a form of critical analysis of society that would enable agents to become aware of their own complicity in social practices that oppress them in one way or another. The chief merit of Geuss lies in its rigorous and jargon-free exploration of the claim that through exposure to critical theory of the right kind, agents can free themselves from alienating and oppressive social structures and practices.

COLIN BIRD

See also Autonomy, Liberalism, Liberty

French economy and economic record

Balassa, Bela, "The French Economy under the Fifth Republic, 1958–1978" in *The Impact of the Fifth Republic on France*, edited by William G. Andrews and Stanley Hoffman, Albany: State University of New York Press, 1981

Caron, François, *An Economic History of Modern France*, New York: Columbia University Press, 1979

Cohen, Stephen S., *Modern Capitalist Planning: The French Model*, Berkeley: University of California Press, 1977

Eichengreen, Barry and Charles Wyplosz, "The Economic Consequences of the Franc Poincaré" in *Economic Effects of the Government Budget*, edited by Elhanan Helpman, Assaf Razin and Efraim Sadka, Cambridge, Massachusetts: MIT Press, 1988

Estrin, Saul and Peter Holmes, *French Planning in Theory and Practice*, London and Boston: Allen and Unwin, 1983

Landes, David, "French Entrepreneurship and Industrial Growth in the Nineteenth Century", *Journal of Economic History*, 9/1 (1949): 45–61

Muet, Pierre-Alain and Alain Fonteneau, *Reflation and Austerity: Economic Policy under Mitterand*, New York: Berg, 1990

O'Brien, Patrick and Caglar Keyder, *Economic Growth in Britain and France, 1780–1914: Two Paths to the Twentieth Century*, London and Boston: Allen and Unwin, 1978

Roehl, Richard, "French Industrialization: A Reconsideration", *Explorations in Economic History*, 13 (1976): 233–81

Schmidt, Vivien A., *From State to Market? The Transformation of French Business and Government*, Cambridge and New York: Cambridge University Press, 1996

CARON provides a fine general introduction to French economic history from 1815 to 1973. The study is divided into two parts which address the 19th and 20th centuries respectively. Caron discusses a wide range of issues from the structure of economic growth across time and the process of industrialization to the development of trade and agriculture. In his analysis of 19th-century growth, Caron emphasizes four elements: the very slow growth in population (in contrast to Great Britain); the particular nature of technical progress in industry and agriculture; the structures of production and finance; and the institutions of the agricultural sector. Caron's analysis of French economic growth in the 20th century highlights its continuities with France's 19th-century experience and analyses are presented of the relationship of the state to business and the evolving structure of French capitalism. The analysis is sophisticated but accessible to non-specialist readers.

LANDES presents a concise and classic analysis of entrepreneurs in the French economy, society, and culture of the 19th century. Landes argues that a complex of organizational, attitudinal, and cultural factors surrounding business is important in explaining what he views as the "retarded status" of the French economy. Among these factors he includes the conservative outlook of small, family-based entrepreneurs who sought to preserve wealth as much as to augment it; the "fundamentally infantile" position of entrepreneurs *vis-à-vis* the state; the shortage of risk capital for new entrepreneurs who lacked connections; and the low social status of businessmen and the anti-capitalist values of the aristocracy and intellectual classes. The study therefore fits into a stream of primarily Anglo-American analysis that views French economic history in terms of industrial "backwardness" and "retardation". Despite its lack of quantitative and empirical analysis, the Landes analysis is an early and seminal contribution to this school of thought and usefully initiated a debate on the effect of the French cultural and social *milieu* on industrial development.

ROEHL offers a classic analysis of the process of French industrialization. In contrast to earlier analyses, such as that of Landes, which argue that France was a late industrializer that suffered from "retarded" growth, Roehl argues that France was instead a successful early industrializer whose emergence coincided with that of Great Britain. Using criteria employed by Alexander Gerschenkron to characterize late industrialization, Roehl argues that France experienced a different form of early industrialization that differed from the British one in both its pace and structure. Previous writers, in Roehl's view, had been too quick to accept the British model of early industrialization as the only model, which led them to classify France, because of her different experience, as relatively backward and stunted (particularly with regard to the agricultural sector). Roehl's thesis, and earlier writings with a similar orientation, fuelled an intense and ongoing debate among economic historians of France and has led to more detailed investigations of the nature of the industrialization process.

O'BRIEN & KEYDER offer the most sophisticated and complete exposition of the "revisionist" position on French industrialization. The subtitle of their book, "two paths to the twentieth century", encapsulates their conclusion that France experienced a process of industrialization that was different from Britain's rather than one that was retarded and incomplete. The study employs a sophisticated analysis of income and real wages, labour productivity, and capital resources in *per capita* terms. Like Roehl, they conclude that French performance along these dimensions was comparable or even superior to that of Britain. O'Brien & Keyder also compare French social and economic structures with those of Britain and conclude that they were widely divergent. Thus, O'Brien & Keyder's analysis suggests that French development must be viewed as an alternative model of economic transformation, rather than as a continental "follower country" as in the standard analysis.

EICHENGREEN & WYPLOSZ offer a concise reinterpretation of the comparatively buoyant French economic performance in the 1920s and France's initial immunity to the world depression of the 1930s. The standard analysis of the period argues that the depreciation of the franc by 80 per cent between 1919 and 1926 and its subsequent stabilization at an undervalued parity enhanced the competitiveness of French exports and thus stimulated export industries and the macroeconomy. This period of export-led growth, it is argued, shielded France from the onset of the depression until successive devaluations of other major currencies beginning in 1931 led to an overvaluation of the franc, which exacerbated and prolonged the French depression. Eichengreen & Wyplosz find little support for this explanation and instead contend that robust investment rates resulting from fiscal stabilization were the primary engines behind the high French growth rate. In challenging the standard analysis of a key period in modern French economic history, Eichengreen & Wyplosz provide a classic analysis that affords an accessible blend of discursive economic history and theoretical modelling that has stimulated further reassessments of this period.

COHEN offers an accessible and detailed study of the mechanisms of French planning during the 1950s and 1960s. The study adopts a political economy approach that traces a complex five-stage process by which a plan is formulated and executed by the bureaucracy. The construction, implementation, and results of the first two post-war plans, the Monnet Plan (1946–52) and the Second Plan (1953–7), are examined in detail. The study also includes discussions of the relationship of economic planning to the political process and to France's membership in the Common Market. Cohen presents an essentially favourable view of French postwar planning and, in the context of a then-current debate on economic planning, views it as a possible model for the US and other advanced capitalist economies.

ESTRIN & HOLMES present a fine study of French planning that complements Cohen's earlier study. While Cohen's study concentrates on the political and administrative aspects of the planning process, Estrin & Holmes' study focuses more on the economic rationale for "indicative" planning and the results obtained by planning in France. Based on these consid-

erations, the authors argue that a capitalist market economy and a traditional administrative system can benefit from the operations of an economic agency that promotes both consultation and coordination. The analysis is wide ranging, including discussions on planning in relation to macroeconomic policy, public sector management, and industrial policy.

BALASSA presents a clear and lucid mainstream economic analysis of French economic policy and performance during the Fifth Republic (1958–78). Balassa argues that the integration of France into the Common Market and the increased openness of the economy rendered the more intrusive and ambitious planning system (the *économie concertée* described by Cohen) untenable and led instead to the acceptance of more general planning that sought to promote investment and industrial upgrading across the whole economy. The study argues that a more liberal government policy stance, greater competition and concentration in industry, stable monetary and economic conditions, and an undervalued franc, enabled France to transform and revitalize its industrial structure.

MUET & FONTENEAU provide a detailed macroeconomic assessment of French economic performance and policy in the first half of the 1980s. Mitterand's Socialists came to power in 1981 with the goal of reflating the economy but by 1983 they had been compelled to adopt austerity policies in the face of external constraints. There was also an acceptance that the mixed economy was beneficial and that consequently the nationalization campaign inaugurated by the Socialists had to be curtailed and even rolled back. Just as Balassa argues that planning became circumscribed over the course of the 1960s and 1970s, Muet and Fonteneau argue that the experience of the early 1980s led both the French Left and Right to realize the severe limitations of national economic policy in the context of an increasingly integrated European and global economy. The study includes enlightening discussions of the attempt at reflation in 1981; the external constraints that derailed reflation; unemployment policy; and the consequences of the shift to austerity.

SCHMIDT offers an exhaustive and accessible analysis of the evolving relationship between the French state and business, particularly in the 1980s and 1990s. The study argues that the conflict between the post-war *dirigiste* model that viewed the state as the promoter of industry and the essentially market-based liberalism promoted by the EU was resolved in the early 1980s, after the failed attempt at reflation, in favour of liberalization. Schmidt's study complements Muet and Fonteneau's technical economic analysis of this period by examining the administrative and political changes that accompanied the shift in economic policy. As well as analysing the evolution of policy towards business and the process of policymaking, Schmidt also carefully examines the players engaged in forming policy and the elite recruitment system that dominates the highest positions of the French state and business.

BRUCE A. WEISSE

French regulation school

Aglietta, Michel, *A Theory of Capitalist Regulation: The US Experience*, London: NLB, 1979; 2nd edition, London: Verso, 1999 (French edition 1976)

Aglietta, Michel, "Capitalism at the Turn of the Century: Regulation Theory and the Challenge of Social Change", *New Left Review*, 232 (1998): 41–90

Bowles, Samuel, David M. Gordon and Thomas E. Weisskopf, *Beyond the Wasteland: A Democratic Alternative to Economic Decline*, London: Verso, and New York: Doubleday, 1983

Boyer, Robert, *The Regulation School: A Critical Introduction*, New York: Columbia University Press, 1990 (French edition 1986)

Clarke, Simon, "Overaccumulation, Class Struggle and the Regulation Approach", *Capital and Class*, 36 (1988): 59–92

Howard, M.C. and J.E. King, *A History of Marxian Economics*: vol. 2: *1929–1990*, Basingstoke: Macmillan, and Princeton, New Jersey: Princeton University Press, 1992

Jessop, Bob, "Regulation Theories in Retrospect and Prospect", *Economy and Society*, 19/2 (1990): 153–216

Kotz, David M., "The Regulation Theory and the Social Structure of Accumulation Approach" in *Social Structures of Accumulation: The Political Economy of Growth and Crisis*, edited by David M. Kotz, Terrence McDonough and Michael Reich, Cambridge and New York: Cambridge University Press, 1994

Lipietz, Alain, *Mirages and Miracles: The Crisis in Global Fordism*, London: Verso, 1987 (French edition 1985)

Lipietz, Alain, *Towards a New Economic Order: Post-Fordism, Ecology, and Democracy*, Cambridge: Polity Press, 1992 (French edition 1989)

The French regulation school offers an idiosyncratic and highly original approach to Marxian political economy. The movement began in several centres in France, but soon extended internationally; JESSOP provides a substantial bibliography in three languages.

The school emerged from the debates in Marxian political economy over the causes of the long boom after 1945 and the onset of renewed crisis in the 1970s that are summarized in HOWARD & KING (chapter 16). It displays a particular concern with periodization, and with the need to escape from the mechanistic, deterministic, and narrowly economic theorizing of more conventional Marxism. Although most of its leading figures are economists, the regulation school has also been influential among social, political, and even cultural theorists. Much academic work on industrial relations, to take one example, has drawn heavily on the characteristic regulation school concepts of "Fordism" and "post-Fordism".

In English, the first important book to appear was that by AGLIETTA (1976), who starts from the concept of surplus value but proceeds with a comprehensive critique of the Marxian theory of production, distribution, and exchange. He distinguishes two "regimes of accumulation", the extensive and intensive. The latter, which corresponds to Fordism, emerged from the great crisis of 1929. It was characterized by mass production, the intensification of labour according to Taylorist principles, rapid productivity growth, and the equally rapid growth of mass purchasing power through rising wages and higher social welfare expenditures. The crisis of Fordism began in the mid-1960s with a sustained rise in the social cost of reproduction of labour power. It could only be resolved, Aglietta concluded, by a new mode of regulation based on the "massive socialization of the conditions of life" which would "destroy free enterprise as the pillar of liberal ideology" (p.385).

Aglietta's book is very heavy going. Much more accessible is the work of Lipietz, who also pays more attention to policy questions. LIPIETZ (1987) takes a global view of the crisis of Fordism, from the perspective first of the core capitalist economies and then of the periphery. In *Towards a New Economic Order* (LIPIETZ 1992) Lipietz attacks the paradigm of "liberal-productivism", which fragments social existence, undermines solidarity, and causes great environmental damage but is unable to solve the Fordist labour management problems or to avoid severe macroeconomic difficulties at both the national and international levels. He proposes a new wages pact with greater worker control of production and increased leisure time, and calls for the establishment of a self-managed community work sector. Lipietz also argues for the introduction of a new world order with international credit money, debt relief for poor countries, and social restrictions on free trade and capital movements. He envisages a much greater ecological focus in development choices, both locally and globally.

Arguments broadly similar to those of the regulation school were advanced in the US by BOWLES, GORDON & WEIS-SKOPF, using the concept of "the social structure of accumulation". They explain the economic success of US capitalism after 1945 by reference to three important social institutions. The "capital-labour accord" generated industrial peace, fast productivity growth, and wage rises that did not threaten profits. US hegemony supplied cheap raw materials and access to overseas markets and investment outlets. The "capitalist-citizen accord" contributed to the maintenance of aggregate demand through both military and civilian welfare expenditures by the state. The crisis of the 1970s resulted from the undermining of these accords by pressure from militant workers and citizens' groups at home and resistance from foreign competitors and national liberation movements overseas. Bowles, Gordon, and Weisskopf also set out detailed plans for the increased economic and industrial democracy that they believe to be necessary to overcome the crisis.

KOTZ compares the regulation and social structure of accumulation approaches. Both regard capitalism as moving through a series of stages, separated by periods of crisis that serve as the prelude for a transition from one stage to another. There are also significant differences. The regulation school has a more traditionally Marxist conception of accumulation, focusing on the determinants of the rate of profit, while the social structure of accumulation is more Keynesian and places more stress on the role of institutions and class struggles as sources of regime change. Kotz concludes that the French school is too structuralist and the US theorists too voluntarist. Each school would benefit from moving towards the position of the other.

A good critical assessment of the regulation school, from the viewpoint of a relatively orthodox Marxist, is that of CLARKE, who attacks it on both theoretical and historical grounds. He argues that the regulation theorists rely on a deeply flawed structuralist-functionalist method that cannot deal adequately with class struggle, and fail to present a coherent analysis of the overaccumulation of capital. Nor is there convincing evidence that the 1929 crisis marked the transition from one regime of accumulation to another, as all the crucial features of the "intensive" regime were already present in 19th-century capitalism. Equally, the postwar boom had little or nothing to do with the introduction of Fordist modes of regulation.

JESSOP's critique is the work of a sociologist, and concentrates on methodological problems. He identifies seven regulation schools (Grenoble, Paris, PCF-CME, Amsterdam, West German, Nordic, and US), and four types of theory, along the twin axes of "national-international focus" and "economic-societal focus". Jessop analyses the ontological assumptions underpinning regulation theory, its relation to Althusserian structuralism, and the extent to which it has been able to avoid teleology and functionalism. He concludes by discussing regulationist theories of the state.

BOYER regards the regulation approach as a method of analysis rather than a complete theory that is capable of replacing neoclassical or Marxian economics, and the concept of Fordism as just one product of this line of thought. He defends the regulation school from some common objections, denying that it is untheoretical, functionalist, or technologically reductionist. Boyer admits, however, that the regulationist analysis of the state is underdeveloped and that its policy proposals fall short of providing a coherent strategy for overcoming the crisis. He suggests that future research should concentrate on historical case studies, formal modelling of the wage relation and the role of credit and money, and more thorough analysis of institutions and organizational forms.

In the new introduction to the second English edition of his book, AGLIETTA (1998) admits that regulation theory requires substantial revision in face of the changes that have occurred in the capitalist system since 1979, including the growing power of financial markets, more pronounced labour market segmentation, and the establishment of European monetary union. He proposes a comprehensive but far from radical programme that combines macroeconomic policy to stimulate growth and structural policies to improve the quality and flexibility of the labour force. To defend social cohesion and protect those excluded from the benefits of globalization, Aglietta calls for a guaranteed minimum income to replace the existing welfare system.

Thus the regulation school continues to thrive, although it has become more diffuse and much less clearly Marxian in orientation than it was at the beginning.

JOHN E. KING

See also Regulation and competition

French revolution

Baczko, Bronisław, *Ending the Terror: The French Revolution after Robespierre*, Cambridge and New York: Cambridge University Press, 1994 (French edition 1989)

Baker, Keith, *Inventing the French Revolution: Essays on French Political Culture in the Eighteenth Century*, Cambridge and New York: Cambridge University Press, 1990

Chartier, Roger, *The Cultural Origins of the French Revolution*, Durham, North Carolina: Duke University Press, 1991 (French edition 1990)

Cobban, Alfred, *The Social Interpretation of the French Revolution*, Cambridge: Cambridge University Press, 1964; 2nd edition, with introduction by Gwynne Lewis, 1999

Doyle, William, *Origins of the French Revolution*, Oxford and New York: Oxford University Press, 1980; 3rd edition 1999

Furet, François, *Interpreting the French Revolution*, Cambridge and New York: Cambridge University Press, 1981 (French edition 1978)

Furet, François and Mona Ozouf (editors), *A Critical Dictionary of the French Revolution*, Cambridge, Massachusetts: Harvard University Press, 1989 (French edition 1988)

Hunt, Lynn, *Politics, Culture, and Class in the French Revolution*, Berkeley: University of California Press, 1984; London: Methuen, 1986

Jones, Colin, "Bourgeois Revolution Revivified: 1789 and Social Change" in *Rewriting the French Revolution*, edited by Colin Lucas, Oxford: Clarendon Press, and New York: Oxford University Press, 1991

Landes, Joan B., *Women and the Public Sphere in the Age of the French Revolution*, Ithaca, New York: Cornell University Press, 1988

Markoff, John, *The Abolition of Feudalism: Peasants, Lords, and Legislators in the French Revolution*, University Park: Pennsylvania State University Press, 1996

Tackett, Timothy, *Becoming a Revolutionary: The Deputies of the French National Assembly and the Emergence of a Revolutionary Culture, 1789–1790*, Princeton, New Jersey: Princeton University Press, 1996

Woloch, Isser, *The New Regime: Transformations of the French Civic Order, 1789–1820s*, New York and London: Norton, 1994

Late 20th-century historiography of the French revolution begins with COBBAN and FURET. The former provided the empirical critique of French Marxist orthodoxy on the revolution, which was to power an entire school of Anglo-American "revisionists" through the 1970s and 1980s, whereas the latter seized the intellectual agenda within France from Marxism with a devastating critique of its qualities as an unthinking "catechism" of revolutionary faith. Cobban's work, while slim, highlighted the fatal flaws in the model of a rising, anti-feudal bourgeoisie seizing power in 1789, and left the way open for this message to be reinforced by waves of further studies, documented approvingly in DOYLE, which also offers an overview of late Old-Regime society as seen through the "revisionist" lens.

Furet challenged the whole conceptual basis of the revolution as an event in the structural transformation of society. Instead, he posited the revolution as an event in politics, in which it was the control of concepts, and the unleashing of new ways of thinking, which marked its true dynamic, and significance. This line of argument has been pursued most notably in the detailed study of prerevolutionary shifts in political culture by BAKER, in which fundamental changes in the conception of public life are shown to have been occurring, and critiques of monarchical sovereignty emerge from a variety of philosophical and administrative avenues.

CHARTIER's survey takes on board this perspective, and adds to it a closer reading of general political and cultural attitudes in the late Old Regime. Together, these works indicate something of the tectonic shifts under way as a society of rank and privilege fought against a multitude of forces threatening its stability. The hierarchical nature of society was being challenged by many of its constituent groups, which offered critiques of the wider system, and of those "above" them, while scorning simultaneous criticism from further down the corporate order. The story of the origins of the French revolution increasingly appears to be an ironic narrative, in which the inability of a wide variety of elites to foresee the implications of their own patterns of behaviour and attitudes led to the collapse of those same groups' legitimacy, and power. In FURET & OZOUF, the panoply of "revisionist" attitudes to the political narrative of the revolution is displayed.

The groundbreaking work of HUNT also enters these cultural dimensions, shaping a vision of the revolution as a constantly rewritten "script", in which participants grope for meaning, assembling a sense of the purpose and direction of revolutionary events through a newly coined or consciously reinvented symbolic repertoire. In the first half of this text, Hunt illustrates the rich diversity of symbolic forms and interpretations taken up by the revolutionaries, at the same time as pointing out the intensely gendered nature of the political identifications that were created. The publicly oriented, self-controlled, rational male citizen was unquestionably one of the revolution's key ideals, and was continually lauded in comparison to effete aristocrats and irrational women. LANDES has generalized further from this point, positing the revolution as a central point in the removal of women from European public life for the following century, its actions and rhetoric playing a key role in the exclusive masculinization of political activity that she contends is visible from the 1790s.

While gender has become a key determinant of many analyses of the revolution, attention to the dynamics of social class has not entirely waned. The second part of Hunt is a sociological analysis of local office-holders during the revolution, which demonstrates the continued relevance of thinking about this period as a transformation in the relations of society and state power. WOLOCH explores this issue from several directions, beginning with the investment of power in local communities through the establishment of new municipal organizations early in the revolution, and moving on to examine education, welfare, justice, police, and conscription. Each of these dimensions involved local communities and power structures in different relations with the state, as that latter structure came to claim back ever more of the power that the revolution had initially seemed to seize from it for the people.

Although this text argues for the centrality of the state/society relationship, JONES has made an eloquent case for reviving the bourgeoisie as a category in the analysis of the revolution. If Hunt's work shows clearly the dominance of a sociologically defined middle class in the ranks of revolutionary office-holders, Jones is concerned to articulate a new version of the cultural and political importance of bourgeois thinking in the coming of the revolution. Civic identities, egalitarian patterns of sociability, market-driven economic strategies, and popular consumerism permeate this vision of an Old Regime in which only the structures of the state stand between society and modernity.

MARKOFF, however, demonstrates the intense presence of the older, "feudal" model of social relations in the life of the rural majority. Feudal rights may have been a commodity to be exchanged at the level of those who owned them in the 1780s, but they remained an oppressive burden for those subjected to them. When the Estates-General were summoned in 1789, and communities recorded their grievances to lay before the king, these *cahiers de doléances* contained a massive outpouring of anger and resentment, at the feudal order, and at state taxation. Often scorned by revisionist historians, these records, under computer analysis, reveal the social volcano on which Louis XVI sat, and Markoff goes on to document the endemic rural protest and violence that erupted through the early years of the revolution.

Two works on revolutionary politics stand as testimony to the enormous transformations that took place within the revolutionary decade itself, as well as highlighting the complexities of analysis that have replaced any simple political narrative of the revolution. TACKETT illustrates the massive difference in background and attitudes that divided the noble and Third Estate deputies to the Estates-General in 1789, but is also able to show how a variety of common assumptions helped to shape a new political landscape in the first year of the revolution. BACZKO writes eloquently about the remarkably different political world confronted by those who had disposed of Robespierre in the summer of 1794, and the struggle of these "Thermidorians" to stabilize a public realm that had changed almost beyond recognition from that of 1789.

DAVID ANDRESS

Freud, Sigmund 1856–1939

Austrian psychoanalyst

Brunner, José, "Oedipus Politicus: Freud's Paradigm of Social Relations" in *Freud: Conflict and Culture*, edited by Michael S. Roth, 1998

Forrester, John, "Portrait of a Dream Reader" in *Freud: Conflict and Culture*, edited by Michael S. Roth, 1998

Jones, Ernest, "Psycho-analysis and Biology" in *Proceedings of the Second International Congress for Sex Research, London 1930*, edited by A.W. Greenwood, London: Oliver and Boyd, 1930

Jones, Ernest, *The Life and Work of Sigmund Freud*, 3 vols, London: Hogarth Press, and New York: Basic Books, 1953–57

Marcuse, Herbert, *Eros and Civilization: A Philosophical Inquiry into Freud*, Boston: Beacon Press, 1955, London: Routledge and Kegan Paul, 1956; reprinted with a new preface, 1966

Ricoeur, Paul, *Freud and Philosophy: An Essay on Interpretation*, New Haven, Connecticut: Yale University Press, 1970 (French edition 1965)

Roth, Michael S. (editor), *Freud: Conflict and Culture*, New York: Knopf, 1998

Sacks, Oliver, "The Other Road: Freud as Neurologist" in *Freud: Conflict and Culture*, edited by Michael S. Roth, 1998

Sulloway, Frank J., *Freud, Biologist of the Mind: Beyond the Psychoanalytic Legend*, New York: Basic Books, 1979

Wollheim, Richard, *Sigmund Freud*, Cambridge and New York: Cambridge University Press, 1981

Since Sigmund Freud's death in 1939, a genre has developed in literary and psychological circles devoted to analyses of his life, his work, and his ideas. Indeed, though "Freud studies" thrives as an intellectual forum, much of the work completed in this area is a critique of Freud's ideas – whether the body of his theory or particular aspects – rather than an endorsement. This entry is separated into two parts which serve to locate the perspectives of the authors of books about Freud and his work: the first perspective describes him as a biologist constructing a theory that makes a biological contribution, while the second perspective describes his theory as sociological in nature.

Theorists representing Freud primarily as a biologist may reflect different backgrounds and approaches, and may support or critique Freud's work, though they are all agreed on the central role that biologically inspired ideas played in Freud's theory.

Ernest JONES (1953–57) wrote over the course of several years the definitive biography of Freud, which evolved into a three-volume set. Jones was perhaps the first to notice the psychobiological emphasis in Freud's work and conferred upon him the title, the "Darwin of the mind" in 1913. Later, in 1930, Jones wrote: "If psychology is regarded as part of biology, and surely it must be, then it is possible to maintain that Freud's work, that is, the creation of psycho-analysis, signifies a contribution to biology comparable in importance only with that of Darwin's" (JONES 1930, p.601). The esteem that Jones felt for Freud and his work is obvious in this statement, and it appears throughout all three volumes of his biography of Freud. His perspective, or lack of perspective, when writing about Freud has led reviewers to claim that his biography, "reveals to its readers everything about Freud that Anna Freud thought fit to print" (Richard Wollheim in "The Mighty Father", *The New York Times Book Review*, 1988). Embedded in the biography by Jones is a flattering portrait of Freud as a hero, courageously fighting critiques by others, the ultimate betrayal of numerous friends and students, the disbelief of the larger society, and, inevitably, the cancer that killed him.

The representation of Freud as a hero of his times is also reflected in the biography by SULLOWAY. However, rather than embrace this representation, Sulloway challenges it as a historical myth. Based on the conceptual framework articulated by Ellenberger in *The Discovery of the Unconscious: The History and Evolution of Dynamic Psychiatry* (1970), Sulloway proposes that the legend of Freud has two aspects:

> The first is the theme of the solitary hero struggling against a host of enemies, suffering 'the slings and arrows of outrageous fortune' but triumphing in the end ... The second feature of the Freudian legend is the blotting out of the greatest part of the scientific and cultural context in which psychoanalysis developed, hence the hero is credited with the achievements of his predecessors, associates, disciples, rivals, and contemporaries (Ellenberger, p.547; in Sulloway, p.6).

Ultimately, Sulloway argues that many of Freud's fundamental conceptions were not only *implications* of biological theory, but *inspired* by biology to begin with; and that this emphasis is hidden by a historical misunderstanding of Freud given his mythical, heroic status. He notes, "After more than half a century since publication of the first biography of Freud (Wittels, 1924a), the mythical bubble surrounding Freud's life and achievements is finally beginning to show signs of rupture and gradual deflation" (Sulloway, p.5). In chapter 13, "The Myth of the Hero in the Psychoanalytic Movement," Sulloway directly addresses 26 myths about Freud and his work, of which the last two attempt to uncover the deep underlying biological inspiration to psychoanalytic theory.

From the perspective of WOLLHEIM, Freud's influence was immediate, broad, and deep. Taking perhaps a more supportive tone, Wollheim's focus – representative of the biological perspective – was to chart the development of Freud's ideas around the *instincts*. Freud never believed that instincts were solely sexual, beginning instead with hunger and thirst, then moving to sexuality, love (*Eros*), and ego instincts, and finally to the death instinct, *Thanatos*. According to Wollheim, after proposing the death instinct as characteristic of the human psyche, Freud extended this characteristic to all of human society and argued that society is the setting for the warring instincts of *Eros* and *Thanatos*: "In abandoning the traditional dichotomy between love and hunger, Freud now divided the instincts of man along the no less familiar lines of love and hate" (p.205). Though Freud articulated in interesting position on society, according to Wollheim, his ideas do not add up to a social theory or a social ethic.

SACKS notes in the beginning of his chapter that

> Everyone knows Freud as the father of psychoanalysis, but most people know little about the twenty years (1876–96) when he was primarily a neurologist and anatomist; Freud himself rarely referred to them in later life. Yet, his "other," neurological life was the precursor to his psychoanalytic one, and perhaps an essential key to it (p.221).

Largely working from Freud's *Project for a Scientific Psychology* – published in *The Standard Edition of the Complete Psychological Works of Sigmund Freud*, edited and translated by James Strachey (1953–74) – Sacks notes that the *Project* merges domains like memory, attention, and dreams with primary and secondary thought processes into a unified view of the mind, with a foundation of all these psychological processes in a physiological frame. That frame, according to Freud, consisted of systems of neurons, their interactions and possible modifications, and states of excitation which were free or bound. The potential for treatment, and ultimately change, for patients lies in the ability of patients – through psychoanalysis – to dig up old "disabling" connections and interpretations and *retranscribe* them in the present, in order to allow the individual to begin growing again. *Retranscription* provides a mechanism that links the outcome of psychological transformation with a biological or neural modification.

There is a great deal of evidence supporting the view that Freud's early experiences in neurology had a lasting impression on his later theory, and that his ideas – biologically inspired – have at the core a biological foundation. Some current sociologists have emphasized Freud's ideas, however, in a slightly different fashion, choosing instead to focus on their implications for social theory, and in particular, sociolinguistics. It is to this group of theorists that we now turn.

Another group of theorists have placed Freud's theory within the realm of civilization and society. As sociologists, social theorists, and sociolinguists, the ideas exemplified here show the influence of Freud's ideas on social theory and human social organization. This perspective of Freud emphasizes his role as a social commentator contributing to the understanding of societies.

MARCUSE articulates the sociological position, when he argues that "In contrast to the revisionists, I believe that Freud's theory is in its very substance 'sociological,' and that no new cultural or sociological orientation is needed to reveal this substance" (p.5). Marcuse draws parallels between Freud's work with individuals, given the tensions between the id, ego, and superego, and his claims about society's recurrent cycle of "domination-rebellion-domination" (p.89). Over time, as the child moves toward adulthood and the rational understanding of the ways in which his or her past has *transcribed* certain behaviors, attitudes, and interpretations, society also emerges as a hierarchy of useful functions and relations that assumes the form of rationally and objectively sound practices. According to Marcuse,

> The development of a hierarchical system of social labor not only rationalizes domination but also "contains" the rebellion against domination. At the individual level, the primal revolt is contained within the framework of the normal Oedipus conflict. At the societal level, recurrent rebellions and revolutions have been followed by counterrevolutions and restorations (p.90).

Marcuse ends by critiquing the neo-Freudian accounts of Freud's position as "revisionist" and states that they devalue the sphere of the material world by deemphasizing the influence of the social conditions and social relations which position people within a particular society or social context. For Marcuse, "individual" pathologies like repression and neurosis have a sociological component and are a function of the dialectical relationship that a person has with his or her social context.

In many respects RICOEUR fits within the framework set out by Marcuse, although Ricoeur's primary foci is on language and discourse, symbolism and interpretation, and meaning as social constructions. The role of psychoanalytic discourse, as well as its structure, is the focus of study here, and psychoanalysis is located in dialectical relation to the total sphere of language. The area of symbols or double meanings is confronted by manners of interpretation and this *hermeneutic field* reflects both the narrowness of psychoanalysis and the depth of language theory as a whole. For Ricoeur, dreams are a kind of language that can be "told, analyzed, and interpreted" (p.15). Therefore, the work of Freud was to explore symbols in the patient's telling of events, memories, and dreams – all of which are representational and can be read like a text – and to create an interpretation of meaning through meaning making with the patient.

ROTH's edited volume reflects several chapters which emphasize Freud's speculations on the origins of human social organization. Freud proposed that society created and operated with mechanisms analogous to psychological mechanisms that operate to inhibit the satisfaction of desires in individuals. Again, as in Ricoeur's work, we have society constructed through forms of social regulation and repression. Socially constructed artifacts, reflecting social history, remain vital to us on both an individual and a social level: "The emphasis on the archaic as active, on a history that is alive in us, is as important in the psychoanalytic approach to social life as it was in its approach to the individual" (Roth, p.12). One of the central questions for Roth is as follows: "Given his [Freud's] understanding of symptoms as expressions of conflict and his speculations on the violent origins of society in male sexual competition, how did Freud view the development of the elaborate cultural constructions that societies would eventually produce?" (p.12). Work by the following two authors attempts to address this question.

FORRESTER positions Freud in historical context and provides an analysis of *The Interpretation of Dreams* as a book that is at once an advancement of theory, and again an autobiographical account of Freud's own life as a physician. This tension between autobiography and scientific theory was recognized by Freud who told of his own experiences and dreams as "material" to be used for dream analysis. Indeed, Forrester commends Freud's layering of autobiography and theory as "exemplary and originary of psychoanalysis itself: the first self-analysis in history, and the epitome of all analyses" (p.52). Method, theory, and the inner life of the author are bound together in this work, which in many respects reflects the hand of Wilhelm Fliess, as analyst and censor, friend, and, ultimately, critic. For Fliess, Freud's excessive candor and self-exposure became a point of criticism, though perhaps for Freud, this was the very point that would allow readers to engage with, to *transfer* onto, the dreamer and his dreams presented in the book.

Perhaps the most interesting aspect of Forrester's analysis is his emphasis on Freud's argument, made explicit in *The Interpretation of Dreams*, regarding a critique of his claim that that all dreams are fulfilments of wishes. Here Freud created a dialogue between himself and his patients, as interpreters of the "material" laid out before them, to engage with their obvious question: How does this interpretation fit with the theory presented? Forrester argues that "every contradiction is not only a refutation of his theory but embodies the *wish* that he might be wrong. In this way, every possible criticism of the theory is undercut" (italics in the original, p.59). In fact one of the time-honored critiques of Freud's work is this aspect of being "beyond critique," conceptualized in a way that disallows scrutiny.

BRUNNER highlights the way in which Freud maps his notion of the Oedipus complex, in all people, to the hierarchical nature of society. Reflecting love and aggression, and from love both security and anxiety, and leading to a desire universally extant for all people, according to Freud, boys desire their mother as a sexual object and fear their father as an obstacle to achieving satisfaction with the sexually desired object, while girls dissociate from their mothers feeling that they've already been castrated. The power in this conception, as noted by Brunner, is the idea that social relations have a basis in the relationships constructed within families, such that though the Oedipus complex may be successfully resolved in familial relations, it is the basis upon which societal relations are constructed as well. Resolution occurs when we incorporate the father's rules against incest, and become autonomous members of society.

With the superego established, the rules of "societal fathers" are recognized and adhered to, including laws, moral standards, and religious principles and rules. Moving from family into the larger society, the rules of the father and the obedience required are reflected in social laws and legal principles which require obedience as well. Brunner adds

Nowhere in Freud's writings can one find an instance where people rebel against despots because their lives and property, rights and interests have been threatened or violated by autocratic leaders. In Freud's discourse, rebellions invariably appear as the deed of masses/sons who refuse obedience to the leaders/fathers because they cannot tolerate the restrictions that the latter impose on them (p.92).

Brunner continues to further note that this approach is the outcome of the relationships embedded in the Oedipus complex "which presents submission and obedience to father figures as necessary for social existence and which discounts the dangers of authoritarianism" (p.92), and one would have to add an obvious patriarchal bias.

Perspectives on Freud's ideas continue to grow and change. In addition, his ideas foster new thinking based on challenges to his theory. There are, however, two basic positions on his work: one locating its relevance as a theory with biological roots, and the other arguing for its sociological import and applications. Two points must be made at this time in order to conclude this entry. First, though perspectives on Freud are certainly helpful and illuminating treatises in their own right, his reflection on his own work is crucially important to an understanding of his theory. For example, *The Origins of Psycho-Analysis, Letters to Wilhelm Fliess, Drafts and Notes: 1887–1902*, edited by Marie Bonaparte, Anna Freud, and Ernst Kris (1954), provides Freud's perspectives on his work shared in letters to Fliess which is helpful to the reader coming to understand Freud's ideas. Second, and consistent with the

sociological perspective, it is impossible to separate Freud, the man, from his ideas, and from his social and historical context. His ideas and theories surfaced from his own relationships and the context of 19th-century Vienna, as well as from the work of philosophers before him and contemporaries. There is no question, as exemplified in Brunner's chapter, that embedded within his theory are cultural assumptions, socially constructed gender specific roles, and, more generally, biased perspectives that were reflected in his social context. While Freud saw his work as universal, over time it becomes more and more obvious how culturally specific it was.

JENNIFER A. VADEBONCOEUR

See also Dreams, Oedipus complex, Psychoanalysis

Frontal lobe impairments

Feinberg, Todd E. and Martha J. Farah, *Behavioral Neurology and Neuropsychology*, New York: McGraw Hill, 1997

Harlow, John M., "Recovery from the Passage of an Iron Bar through the Head", with introduction by Edgar Miller, *History of Psychiatry*, 4 (1993): 271–82

Lishman, William Alwyn, *Organic Psychiatry: The Psychological Consequences of Cerebral Disorder*, Oxford: Blackwell, 1998

Roberts, A.C., T.W. Robbins and Lawrence Weiskrantz (editors), *The Prefrontal Cortex: Executive and Cognitive Functions*, Oxford and New York: Oxford University Press, 1998

Valenstein, Elliot S., *Great and Desperate Cures: The Rise and Decline of Psychosurgery and Other Radical Treatments for Mental Illness*, New York: Basic Books, 1986

Walsh, Kevin W. and David Darby, *Neuropsychology: A Clinical Approach*, 4th edition, Edinburgh: Churchill Livingstone, 1999

Watson, Stanley J., *Biology of Schizophrenia and Affective Disease*, Washington, DC: American Psychiatric Press, 1996

The frontal lobes are large structures within the brain whose roles in the control of psychological functioning are diverse and have not always been easy to determine. The motor strip and Broca's area (linked to aphasia) both lie within the more posterior parts of the frontal lobes and the psychological interest described in this entry has focused on the prefrontal regions that exclude these areas. Both FEINBERG & FARAH and ROBERTS, ROBBINS & WEISKRANTZ provide basic anatomical descriptions of the frontal lobes and their main connections within the brain. The latter also gives a recent discussion of some psychological issues of more recent concern.

Many accounts start by mentioning the case of Phineas Gage, the foreman of a railroad construction gang in Vermont, who in 1848 had a metal rod blown through his head and damaging the frontal regions of his brain. According to HARLOW, the physician who attended Gage after this accident and who followed his subsequent career up to his death 12 years later, this injury resulted in a marked personality change. Having been reliable and industrious, Gage became irreverent, profane, unwilling to accept advice, and unable to make consistent plans for the future. (The citation above is to a more recent reprint of Harlow's account, which was originally published in 1868.)

Personality changes like those reported in Gage continue to be regarded as a common feature in those who have suffered frontal lobe lesions. A more contemporary description is that of LISHMAN (p.187) who states that these consist of "lack of foresight and concern, inability to plan ahead, and a facile euphoric disposition . . . disinhibition is often marked . . . the patient typically has little insight into the changes which occur."

The frontal lobes were the focus of psychosurgical procedures (prefrontal leucotomy or lobotomy), originally developed in the 1930s but now largely abandoned. These involved lesions in the prefrontal regions and were used in an attempt to relieve certain psychiatric disorders. Present neuropsychological understanding of the roles of the frontal lobes owes little to the research that was carried out in these operations. However, they are important from an historical point of view and VALENSTEIN provides a good account of their rise to popularity and subsequent decline.

A number of more cognitive impairments have been linked to frontal lobe damage and, by implication, relate to the loss of abilities or functions subserved by the prefrontal regions of the brain. One commonly cited example of these is indicated by performance on the Wisconsin Card Sorting Test and described in greater detail by WALSH & DARBY. A deck of cards has to be sorted into four piles to correspond with exemplars. The cards can be sorted in three possible ways according to the colour of the shapes shown on the cards, the nature of the shapes (circles, triangles, etc.), or the number of shapes on the card. Participants have to learn to sort in one way (for example, by shape) and when this has been learned to a set criterion, in another way (for example, by colour), and so on.

The key finding is that those with frontal lobe damage can learn to sort in the first way (for example by shape) with normal facility. However, when the requirement changes arbitrarily and it is necessary to learn to sort by another characteristic, say, colour, they have undue difficulty in learning to sort in the new way. They tend to perseverate and unduly persist in sorting by the previously correct characteristic shape. Roberts, Robbins & Weiskrantz argue that this inability to inhibit preestablished responses when they become inappropriate is a well-established feature of those with prefrontal lesions.

Another feature of those with frontal lesions is a difficulty in planning. Again Walsh & Darby describes some relevant investigations. One of these involves the use of Shallice's "Tower of London" test. This has three vertical rods in a line onto which can be placed different coloured beads, each of which has a hole drilled through the middle so as to fit on the rods. From a starting point in which the beads are placed on the rods according to a set pattern, the participant is then required to move the beads from one rod to another, one at a time, in order to achieve a given goal position within a stated number of moves. Those with frontal lesions, especially of the left frontal lobes, are impaired on this task.

The previous two paragraphs illustrate the kinds of impairment that are now being revealed in patients with pathology of the frontal lobes. Further examples can be found, especially in Roberts, Robbins & Weiskrantz and Walsh & Darby. As a final comment, it is interesting that the relationship between the frontal lobes and mental disorder is now being re-explored. The frontal lobes, once a focus of a treatment in the form of psychosurgery, have now returned as an interesting means of understanding schizophrenia. Roberts, Robbins & Weiskrantz and WATSON consider various aspects of evidence including the fact that studies using appropriate brain scanning methods show a decreased level of activity in schizophrenic patients as compared to normal controls when carrying out certain tasks sensitive to frontal lobe lesions.

Overall, the frontal lobes are no longer such enigmatic structures as was once the case. Advances in understanding of the highly complex and varied functions served by these structures are being made and it may be that these will have some wider practical gains in the enhanced understanding of some mental disorders.

EDGAR MILLER

See also Neuropsychology

Full employment

Arestis, Philip and Mike Marshall (editors), *The Political Economy of Full Employment: Conservatism, Corporatism, and Institutional Change*, Aldershot, Hampshire: Elgar, 1995

Beveridge, William Henry, *Full Employment in a Free Society*, London: Allen and Unwin, 1944

Chang, Roberto, "Is Low Unemployment Inflationary?", *Economic Review – Federal Reserve Bank of Atlanta*, 82/1 (1997): 4–13

Cross, Rod (editor), *The Natural Rate of Unemployment: Reflections on 25 Years of the Hypothesis*, Cambridge and New York: Cambridge University Press, 1995

Friedman, Milton, "The Role of Monetary Policy", *American Economic Review*, 58/1 (1968): 1–17

Keynes, John Maynard, *The General Theory of Employment, Interest and Money*, London: Macmillan, and New York: Harcourt Brace, 1936; as vol. 7 of *The Collected Writings of John Maynard Keynes*, London: Macmillan, and New York: Cambridge University Press, 1973

Krueger, Alan B. (editor), "Symposium: The Natural Rate of Unemployment", *Journal of Economic Perspectives*, 11/1 (1997): 3–108

Neubourg, Chris de (editor), *The Art of Full Employment: Unemployment Policy in Open Economies*, Amsterdam: North Holland, 1991

Phillips, A. William, "The Relation between Unemployment and the Rate of Change of Money Wage Rates in the United Kingdom, 1861–1957", *Economica*, 25/100 (1958): 283–99

Solow, Robert M., "On Theories of Unemployment", *American Economic Review*, 70/1 (1980): 1–11

Summers, Lawrence H., *Understanding Unemployment*, Cambridge, Massachusetts: MIT Press, 1990

While "full employment" may more generally refer to the full utilization of all available factors of production in an economy, the term in popular usage nearly always refers exclusively to labour. This convention begins with Keynes.

In his landmark work, KEYNES seeks to explain the high levels of unemployment associated with the Great Depression. Unconvinced that classical macroeconomic models can account for the phenomenon of persistent unemployment, Keynes offers his own competing story. According to Keynes, if nominal wages are "sticky" then it is indeed possible for labour markets to move away from their market-clearing levels. Hence, involuntary unemployment may be observed in the presence of such nominal wage stickiness. For Keynes, then, full employment is the level of employment at which only frictional and structural unemployment exist. In order to keep the economy at the full employment level, Keynes advocates the use of fiscal policy.

As Keynes indicates, there is no reason to think that there must necessarily be zero unemployment at the full employment level. However, economists disagree considerably concerning what level of unemployment constitutes full employment. Such disagreement occurs along both theoretical and empirical lines: theorists want to know how to model full employment and empiricists want to know how to ascertain what that level is for a given economy.

Beveridge, Phillips, and Friedman give three early – and still very frequently cited – assertions of what constitutes full employment. BEVERIDGE contends that, at full employment, the number of unemployed persons exactly equals the number of available job openings. PHILLIPS, a New Zealand economist, examines the empirical relationship between unemployment and wage inflation in the United Kingdom over a 100-year span ending in 1957. Discovering an inverse relationship between the two variables, Phillips concludes that full employment lies at the level corresponding to zero wage inflation.

FRIEDMAN is the first to ascribe a name to the rate of unemployment corresponding to the situation of full employment. He refers to the full-employment unemployment rate as the natural rate of unemployment. In articulating his own definition of what constitutes full employment, Friedman simultaneously points out flaws in the definitions of Beveridge and Phillips. First, Friedman holds that there is no reason to believe that the number of job seekers is equal to the number of job vacancies at the natural rate of unemployment. Second, Friedman contends that Phillips's analysis is flawed because it focuses upon nominal rather than real wage inflation.

For Friedman, tradeoffs between inflation and unemployment are possible in the short run but not in the long run. Since, in Friedman's view, the short-run tradeoffs are due to unanticipated inflation, then the natural rate of unemployment is the rate of unemployment that would be observed if inflation were perfectly foreseen.

Many economists use the terms "natural rate of unemployment" and "NAIRU" (non-accelerating inflation rate of unemployment) interchangeably. The possibility exists that these rates may numerically be identical, but they are theoretically quite different concepts. CHANG provides a reasonably clear articulation of this often misunderstood or overlooked distinction.

Solow and Summers attempt to give insight into the unemployment experience of the 1970s and 1980s. SOLOW catalogues six possible explanations for movements of the economy away from the full employment level; his focus, unsurprisingly, is upon explaining unemployment greater than the full employment level. His most inventive explanation is a sociological one. Solow holds that currently unemployed workers will not attempt to underbid currently employed workers due to the behavioural constraints of society. Further, employers would not accept such offers anyway due to the possibility of antagonizing the current workforce. Hence, the labour market is not as easily cleared as other markets can be. Having listed his explanations, Solow concludes by describing the necessary features that a labour market must have in order for his explanations to be viable. Such features include a stable labour pool and the presence of unemployment compensation.

The book by SUMMERS is a collection of nine previously published papers and one new paper dealing with unemployment. All of the articles except the new paper are either descriptive or empirical studies of the phenomenon of unemployment. The text is divided into three sections: describing and measuring unemployment, cyclical unemployment, and structural unemployment. Of particular interest is his paper, "Why is the unemployment rate so very high near full employment?", which appears in the structural section of the book. Summers examines how the nature of unemployment evolved during the period 1955–85, and speculates which structural changes during the period may be most responsible for changes in the level of full employment. Summers recommends that many of the structural changes of the period be reversed in order to reduce the rate of unemployment corresponding to the full employment level.

Both the theoretical and empirical states of the art are given in the collections edited by CROSS and by KRUEGER. Cross consists of three major parts. The first is a theoretical assessment both of the theory underlying the notion of full employment and of the evolution of the natural rate of employment over time. Of particular relevance to the concept of full employment are the essays by James Tobin and Huw Dixon. As Tobin continues to be a celebrated critic of the natural rate concept, his indictment here makes very interesting reading. Dixon provides a well-balanced accounting of the evolution of the natural rate story. The book's second part consists of empirical studies, and the final part considers issues of policy.

Krueger features articles that debate the existence of a natural rate of unemployment. Those authors who subscribe to the notion of the natural rate of unemployment assess whether or not it may be estimated and, if so, whether such estimates are useful for policy purposes. Contributors include such notable authors as Olivier Blanchard, Robert J. Gordon, and Joseph Stiglitz.

Finally, the edited volumes of De Neubourg and Arestis & Marshall concern policy approaches to achieving full employment. DE NEUBOURG collects previously unpublished papers that discuss unemployment and full employment policies within the context of open economies. Eleven of the contributions focus upon the policy experiences of Belgium and the Netherlands. The remaining 12 papers consider the experiences of such nations as Australia, Austria, France, Germany, Sweden, the UK, and the US.

ARESTIS & MARSHALL also possesses a strong policy orientation, but does not explicitly consider an open economy perspective. The first two chapters are especially good, and discuss the obstacles to achieving full employment, as well as strategies for overcoming those obstacles. Nations specifically considered in the remainder of the book include Australia, Sweden, the UK, and the US.

VICTOR V. CLAAR

See also Natural rate of unemployment and NAIRU

Functionalism in sociology

Alexander, Jeffrey C. (editor), *Neofunctionalism*, Beverly Hills, California: Sage, 1985

Colomy, Paul (editor), *Neofunctionalist Sociology: Contemporary Statements*, Aldershot, Hampshire: Elgar, 1990

Durkheim, Emile, *The Division of Labor in Society*, New York: Free Press, and London: Macmillan, 1984 (French edition 1893, 1st English edition 1933)

Luhmann, Niklas, *The Differentiation of Society*, New York: Columbia University Press, 1982

Malinowski, Bronisław, *A Scientific Theory of Culture and Other Essays*, Chapel Hill: University of North Carolina Press, 1944

Parsons, Talcott, *Action Theory and the Human Condition*, New York: Free Press, and London: Collier Macmillan, 1978

Radcliffe-Brown, A.R., *Structure and Function in Primitive Society*, New York: Free Press, and London: Cohen and West, 1952

Spencer, Herbert, *The Principles of Sociology*, 3 vols, New York: Appleton, 1896–97

Turner, Jonathan H., *Macrodynamics: Toward a Theory on the Organization of Human Populations*, New Brunswick, New Jersey: Rutgers University Press, 1995

Although, as the founder of sociology, Auguste Comte had used a crude form of functionalism, it was SPENCER who established functionalism in sociology. For Spencer, functional analysis was based on an analogy to organisms in which the parts of the organism are analysed for their contribution to its survival. This analogy, which later became recessive, is nonetheless the core of all functional approaches. Spencer also developed another key feature of functionalism: the analysis of how system parts meet or fail to meet a few fundamental *requisites* or *needs* for survival. In Spencer's eye, all *super-organic* systems, composed of relations among organisms, must meet needs for (a) operation or production of life-sustaining substances and reproduction of new system members; (b) regulation or coordination of relations among system parts; and (c) distribution of information, resources, and organisms around the system. In addition to these features, Spencer was interested in long-term evolutionary change – as would all sociological functionalists after him. Such change was viewed as the result of differentiation with and between structures meeting needs for operation, regulation, and distribution. Spencer saw population growth and size as one of the key forces behind differentiation, since a larger social mass requires a more complex structure to support it. Moreover, distinct stages along the path of differentiation

could be established: simple (hunting and gathering), compound (horticulture), double compound (agrarian), and treble compound (industrial). Spencer saw war as an important force in this evolution, because the better organized society usually wins a war, thereby ratcheting up the level of complexity of society. Spencer's famous phrase "survival of the fittest" captures some of the sense of his ecological view of social systems as competing for resources, with increasing complexity making a society more fit.

The next significant functional theorist was DURKHEIM who posited one master functional requisite – the need for integration and then analysed all sociocultural phenomena with respect to their effects on societal integration. Like all functionalists, Durkheim was concerned with the long-term process of differentiation and the integrative problems that it posed; like Spencer, he proposed an ecological model to explain such differentiation. For Durkheim, population growth increases the density – both social and physical – of actors who then begin to compete for resources; out of such competition, some are able to sustain themselves within the niche where they began, whereas less-successful actors must find or create new niches for survival, thereby increasing the level of differentiation among members of a population. Differentiation increases problems of integration, since actors live in different spheres and are guided by distinctive norms and beliefs; and as differentiation occurs, the common culture (core values, history, traditions, and other symbol systems, or what he termed *the collective conscious*) must become abstract and general so as to reach across the barriers of differentiation, but in so doing, the collective conscious is weakened and, in his words, "enfeebled." What force, then, is to maintain integration? For Durkheim, the structural interdependence (sustained by exchange relations) that comes with differentiation and the reattachment of the generalized tenets of the collective conscience to the diverse beliefs and norms of each differentiated sphere would be sufficient to maintain integration.

Functionalism might well have died with Durkheim had it not proven useful to the first generation of anthropologists writing ethnographies on preliterate societies. At a time when evolutionary analysis was fast fading in the early 20th century, and when diffusionist theory was increasingly called into question, functionalism provided an analytical tool for conducting research on societies that had no written history. Anthropologists could make sense of preliterate societies by analysing how each practice, belief, and structure contributes to the survival of the population. RADCLIFFE-BROWN adopted the approach pursued earlier by Durkheim, assessing rituals, beliefs, kinship structures, and other phenomena in terms of their contribution to the integration of the population. In contrast, MALINOWSKI pursued a strategy more in tune with Spencer's approach, but he added new features. For Malinowski, varying functional requisites exist for different system levels. At the biological, social structural, and cultural levels, diverse sets of system needs could be isolated, with analysis then proceeding to assess the effects of various parts in meeting these needs. For example, at the cultural or symbolic level, there exist needs for symbols to provide a communal rhythm, an ability to control destiny, and a store of information necessary to adjust to the environment; or at the structural level, needs for production and distribution, for social control, for education, and for execution of authority relations were postulated (in a manner that follows Spencer's emphasis).

It was within anthropology, then, that functionalism was carried to the mid-20th century. In the 1950s, however, sociologists began to use functional approaches once again. The most important figure in this resurgence of functionalism was PARSONS who posited that the social universe consists of four *action systems* – cultural, social, personality, and behavioral (originally termed organismic) – and that each of these systems must meet the same four basic requisites – adaptation, goal attainment, integration, and latency. Adaptation denotes the problem of securing necessary resources, converting these resources into useable commodities, and distributing them; goal attainment concerns the problem of establishing goals, while mobilizing and allocating system resources to meet these goals; integration is the problem of coordination of relations among system parts; and latency includes the dual problems of reproducing new system units (pattern maintenance) and managing tensions within system units (tension management). At the level of the social system (the subject matter of sociology), Parsons argued that the actors and structures meeting each of the four functional requisites utilize a distinctive symbolic media to regulate relations. For example, money is the dominant medium of exchange in the adaptive sphere where the economy is the key structure; power is the medium in the goal attainment sphere where polity is the central structure; commitment is the medium in the latency sphere where family and education are important structures; and influence is the medium in the integrative sphere where law is the key institutional system. Thus, Parsons introduced a new element into functional analysis, seeing social systems as differentiated within and between the spheres created by the four functional requisites, with distinctive media of exchange organizing relations within and between actors and structures in these different spheres. Parsons also reintroduced the concern of early sociological functionalist with long-term evolutionary change. Like Spencer and Durkheim before him, Parsons saw evolution as revolving around differentiation; and in his scheme, such differentiation moves first to create distinctive structures for each of the four functional spheres, and then, to differentiate further the structures within these spheres. Thus, for example, economies (adaptation), governments (goal attainment), legal systems (integration), and family-education systems (pattern maintenance) become ever more complex and differentiated with societal evolution; and like his predecessors, Parsons felt that distinctive stages of evolution associated with profiles of differentiation within and between functional spheres could be demarcated. As is evident, elements of all previous functional approaches could be found in Parsons' scheme; and for nearly a decade, it was the most dominant theoretical approach in American sociology.

By the late 1950s criticisms of all functional approaches mounted, accelerating with the 1960s, with particular attention to Parsons' scheme. These criticisms took several forms: (a) functional explanations are tautologies in which the existence of a system need and parts to meet this need explain each other; (b) functional explanations, especially in Parsons' hands, assume that by finding the category to which a phenomenon belongs is sufficient to explain why it existed in the first place and why it operates the way it does; (c) functional explanation can easily become tools for legitimating the status quo by emphasizing that existing structures meet important needs and, therefore, must be retained. These criticisms mounted through the 1960s and, by the late 1970s, pushed functional explanations to the sidelines. It appeared that functional sociology was indeed dead.

In the 1980s, however, a neofunctionalist movement was initiated. ALEXANDER and COLOMY proposed that the basic subject matter of functional theory could be retained – that is, an emphasis on social change revolving around differentiation among system levels (i.e. personality, culture, and structure). In many ways, this neofunctionalist movement was not functional, because the notions of system needs or requisites was abandoned.

Another contemporary theorist retained the notion of requisites, but only implicitly. LUHMANN presents his approach as a general systems scheme, emphasizing the relationship of systems to their environments. The environment is, in turn, conceived as existing along three fundamental dimensions: temporal, symbolic, and material. These environments present the problem of complexity for any system's adaptation to its environment. Time can project onto the horizons of the future or focus on the distant past; material relations among actors can involve all possible connections as well as limitless physical space; and symbols and their recombination can pose vast numbers of potential alternatives to actors. Thus, for Luhmann, the master functional requisite is the need to reduce environmental complexity along the material, temporal, and symbolic dimensions of the environment. Social structures and culture can be analysed in terms of how they operate to reduce this complexity. Like all functionalists, Luhmann is concerned with patterns of differentiation and long-term change, but he emphasizes that analogies should not be to the organism but to the processes delineated in the theory of evolution – that is, variation, selection, and stabilization of traits that increase adaptation in the temporal, symbolic, and material environments. In some ways, Luhmann is reintroducing the ecological reasoning of Spencer and Durkheim back into a muted mode of functional analysis. For Luhmann, evolution involves the increasing differentiation among interaction, organizational, and societal systems, the internal differentiation of these systems, the differentiation of the societal system into functional domains such as economy, family, polity, law, education, science, or religion, the development of distinctive media of communication within each of these functional domains, the differentiation among persons, roles, programs, and values, the movement of societies through three distinctive stages (segmentation, stratification, and functional differentiation), and the increasing complexity of systems and their relationships to environments. Although Luhmann has argued against the organismic analogy, he has none the less retained many of the distinctive features of all functional approaches.

A final form of analysis that draws inspiration from functionalism is TURNER's analysis of macrodynamics. From Spencer, Turner takes the idea that the differentiation of institutional spheres reflects the size of the population, the level of production, the degree to which power is consolidated and centralized, and the technologies and infrastructures for distribution of resources, people, and information. Turner also introduces another way to conceptualize the ecological dynamics that are a key mechanism of differentiation. For Turner, there is not only the kind of selection that Durkheim and Luhmann emphasized (that is, niche density, competition, selection, and differentiation), but there is what he terms *Spencerian selection* in deference to the first sociologist to use the idea. Spencerian selection occurs when there is an absence of structures to meet crises of adaptation. Under these conditions, goal seeking actors attempt to create new structures to manage the problem (sometimes successfully, and at other times not). When successful, differentiation and complexity increase, as does the level of adaptation to the environment.

In sum, functional sociology has thus retained certain consistent themes: the emphasis on differentiation as the hallmark of long-term evolutionary change and modernity, the stress on ecological dynamics as a key mechanism for such change, the concern with institutional differentiation in particular, and the distinctive cultural symbols as well as media of discourse and exchange used by actors in diverse spheres. The notion of functional requisites has, however, receded or become more implicit because of the kinds of criticisms that are level against analysis in which functional requisites remain a central analytical tool. But it is clear that the near death experience of functionalism is over because new, less problematic schemes employing the themes of functionalism have emerged at the close of the 20th century.

JONATHAN H. TURNER

Futures markets

Bakken, H. H., "Futures Trading: Origin, Development and Economic Status" in *Futures Trading Seminar*, vol. 3, Madison: Mimir, 1966

Cargill, Thomas F. and Gordon C. Rausser, "Temporal Price Behavior in Commodity Futures Markets", *Journal of Finance*, 30/4 (1975): 1043–53

Chance, D.M., "The Reaction of the Chicago Board of Trade GNMA Futures Contract to the Announcement of Inflation Rates: A Study of Market Efficiency", *Review of Research in Futures Markets*, 4/1 (1985): 132–54

Edwards, Franklin R. and Hugh T. Patrick (editors), *Regulating International Financial Markets: Issues and Policies*, Boston and London: Kluwer, 1992

Goss, B.A. and B.S. Yamey (editors), *The Economics of Futures Trading*, 2nd edition, London: Macmillan, and New York: Wiley, 1978

Hansen, Lars Peter and Robert J. Hodrick, "Forward Exchange Rates as Optimal Predictors of Future Spot Rates: An Econometric Analysis", *Journal of Political Economy*, 88/5 (1980): 829–53

Harris, Lawrence, "Transaction Data Tests of the Mixture of Distributions Hypothesis", *Journal of Financial and Quantitative Analysis*, 22/2 (1987): 127–41

Hodrick, Robert J., *The Empirical Evidence on the Efficiency of Forward and Futures Foreign Exchange Markets*, Chur, Switzerland: Harwood, 1987

Johnson, L.L., "The Theory of Hedging and Speculation in Commodity Futures", *Review of Economic Studies*, 27/3 (1960): 139–51

Keynes, John Maynard, *A Treatise on Money*, vol. 2: *The Applied Theory of Money*, London: Macmillan, and New York: Harcourt Brace, 1930

Leuthold, Raymond M. and Peter A. Hartmann, "A Semi-strong Form Evaluation of the Efficiency of the Hog Futures Market", *American Journal of Agricultural Economics*, 61/3 (1979): 482–89

Stein, Jerome L., *The Economics of Futures Markets*, Oxford and New York: Blackwell, 1986

Working, H., "Futures Trading and Hedging", *American Economic Review*, 43 (1953): 314–43

Futures contracts are contracts for delivery (or settlement) of a specified quantity of a commodity or financial instrument, at a specified future date. These contracts, which are also standardized with respect to quality and delivery location, are traded on organized futures exchanges, on which a clearing house interposes itself between buyer and seller, and guarantees all contracts. Historically, futures trading evolved from forward trading arrangements (BAKKEN), and modern futures exchanges, with leading centres in Chicago and London, deal in a wide range of commodities from grains, through livestock and fibres, to precious and non-ferrous metals and energy products, as well as financial instruments. Since the mid 1970s there has been near exponential growth in trading on world futures markets, following the introduction of financial futures contracts (especially in interest rates, foreign exchange and share price indices).

A classic early statement of price determination in futures markets was KEYNES's theory of "normal backwardation", in which hedgers paid a risk premium to speculators in return for risk reduction. It was predicted that spot prices would exceed futures prices under "normal conditions" so that a spot premium (or backwardation) would prevail. This theory, which has had little empirical support, assumed that hedgers pursued the sole aim of risk reduction. A rival view of hedger behaviour, which also has become a classic, is that hedgers pursue the joint objectives of risk reduction and profit (WORKING), an idea that was analysed further within the framework of portfolio theory (JOHNSON; GOSS & YAMEY, pp.1–59 provide surveys of these developments).

Futures markets perform several important functions. First, they facilitate risk management through hedging (which may be defined as holding a futures market position, in conjunction with a spot market position of opposite sign, in pursuit of expected gain and risk reduction). Second, futures markets act as centres for the collection and dissemination of information, which aids the price-formation process. If this information is reflected in prices as fully as possible, the price-formation process is said to be efficient. Third, futures markets perform a forward pricing function in the sense that they determine prices for subsequent delivery.

Transactions on futures markets employ leverage: when a transaction is initiated, both buyer and seller must pay a deposit, typically between 10 and 30 per cent of the value of the contract, as a performance bond. All transactors must also pay a margin, equal to any reduction in value of their market positions, due to adverse price movements, as demanded by the clearing house. Such margin calls are usually made daily: this process is called "marking to market".

The performance of futures markets has been analysed against a variety of criteria. First, because futures markets form prices for subsequent delivery dates, the hypothesis has been tested that futures prices are unbiased anticipations of these delivery date spot prices. While the evidence on this issue is mixed, there has been a predominance of findings rejecting the hypothesis. Unbiasedness is a joint hypothesis, embodying the branches of full utilization of information and risk neutrality, so that the reason for any rejection is not immediately apparent (see HODRICK for a discussion of this problem in the context of foreign exchange). The informational efficiency of futures markets has been studied also by tests that seek to establish whether there is statistical dependence in past prices (see CARGILL & RAUSSER), and by tests that investigate whether futures prices reflect public information as fully as possible. In studies of this latter issue three different approaches have been used, including an event studies approach, adapted from research on equities, and a forecast error approach (see CHANCE; HANSEN & HODRICK; LEUTHOLD & HARTMANN). Again the evidence is mixed.

The welfare implications of futures trading have been studied, mainly using partial equilibrium analysis (which focus on individual markets, see STEIN, chapter 6), although general equilibrium analyses of this question are beginning to appear. Generally, however, this issue has received inadequate attention.

Futures markets facilitate speculation, partly because there is no restriction on short selling as in spot markets, partly because of specialized resources devoted to collection and dissemination of information, and also because of their generally lower transaction costs than spot markets, a characteristic enhanced by contract standardization. Indeed, futures markets require speculation to take up the balance of hedging positions, and to implement the price formation process. Questions have been addressed about the effects of speculation, in particular whether futures markets increase spot price volatility, whether informed speculators cause price fluctuations, and whether asset prices generally fluctuate more than can be justified by market fundamentals. Evidence tends to suggest negative answers to the first two questions, but economic theories, if not hard futures market evidence, suggests a positive answer to the third question.

The statistical distribution of price changes in futures markets has also received attention. Researchers had assumed that these price changes were normally distributed, although now it is generally recognized that daily price changes in security markets, including futures markets, are leptokurtic (with relatively more observations in the tails and around the central value than the normal distribution). Two of the main rival hypotheses to explain this phenomenon are the stable Paretian distribution (which has infinite variance) and mixture of normals (normal distribution with changing mean and variance); evidence tends to favour the latter (HARRIS).

Finally, the regulation of futures markets is a matter of concern to business, government and academia. The first group wants to ensure that the facilities for risk management operate efficiently, whereas government wants to protect users and avoid crises. Academics are interested in all these issues, as well as the quality of the price formation process (EDWARDS & PATRICK, chapters 11–13). Futures markets are subject to both internal and external regulation. Internal regulation is provided by the clearing house, which makes decisions on matters such as deposits and margins, and a clearing house may increase deposits if it believes there is excessive speculation. Internal regulation is also provided by the rules and regulations of the exchange, which are concerned *inter alia* with the constitution and conduct of members of the exchange. Some exchanges recently have addressed the issues whether to change from open outcry to screen trading, and whether to merge with other exchanges. External regulation is normally provided by a government agency, such as the Commodity Futures Trading Commission in the US, whose concerns include the public interest and the conduct of the futures industry. Both internal and external regulations usually include measures to prevent manipulation and fraud.

BARRY GOSS

Futurism

Aburdene, Patricia and John Naisbitt, *Megatrends for Women*, New York: Villard, 1992

Anderson, Walter Truett, *Evolution Isn't What It Used to Be: The Augmented Animal and the Whole Wired World*, New York: Freeman, 1996

Bell, Daniel and Stephen R. Graubard (editors), *Toward the Year 2000: Work in Progress*, Cambridge, Massachusetts: MIT Press, 1997

Bell, Wendell, *Foundations of Futures Studies: Human Science for a New Era*, vols 1–2, New Brunswick, New Jersey: Transaction, 1996–97

Callenbach, Ernest, *Ecotopia: The Notebooks and Reports of William Weston*, Berkeley, California: Banyan Tree, 1975

Cetron, Marvin and Owen Davies, *Probable Tomorrows: How Science and Technology Will Transform Our Lives in the Next 20 Years*, New York: St Martin's Press, 1997

Coates, Joseph F., John B. Mahaffie and Andy Hines, *2025: Scenarious of US and Global Society Reshaped by Science and Technology*, Akron, Ohio: Oakhill Press, 1996

Dator, Jim (editor), *Advancing Futures: Futures Studies in Higher Education*, London: Adamantine Press, 1999

Dertouzos, Michael L., *What Will Be: How the New World of Information Will Change Our Lives*, San Francisco: HarperEdge, 1997

Didsbury, Howard F. (editor), *Futurevision: Ideas, Insights, and Strategies*, Bethesda, Maryland: World Future Society, 1996

Drexler, K. Eric and Chris Peterson, *Unbounding the Future: The Nanotechnology Revolution*, New York: Morrow, 1991

Dublin, Max, *Futurehype: The Tyranny of Prophecy*, New York: Viking, 1989

Elliott, Elton (editor), *Nanodreams*, Riverdale, New York: Baen, 1995

Gelbspan, Ross, *The Heat Is On: The High Stakes Battle over Earth's Threatened Climate*, Reading, Massachusetts: Addison Wesley, 1997

Gibson, William, *Neuromancer*, New York: Ace, and London: Gollancz, 1984

Igbaria, Magid and Margaret Tan (editors), *The Virtual Workplace*, Hershey, Pennsylvania: Idea Group, 1998

Kaku, Michio, *Visions: How Science Will Revolutionize the 21st Century*, New York: Anchor, 1997; Oxford: Oxford University Press, 1998

Kitcher, Philip, *The Lives to Come: The Genetic Revolution and Human Possibilities*, New York: Simon and Schuster, and London: Allen Lane, 1996

Kroker, Arthur and Marilouise Kroker (editors), *Digital Delirium*, New York: St Martin's Press, 1997

Kurzweil, Ray, *The Age of Spiritual Machines: When Computers Exceed Human Intelligence*, New York: Viking, 1999

Loader, Brian D. (editor), *The Governance of Cyberspace: Politics, Technology and Global Restructuring*, London and New York: Routledge, 1997

Meadows, Donella H. *et al.* (editors), *Beyond the Limits: Confronting Global Collapse, Envisioning a Sustainable Future*, Post Mills, Vermont: Chelsea Green, 1992

Mills, Stephanie (editor), *Turning Away from Technology: A New Vision for the 21st Century*, San Francisco: Sierra Club, 1997

Molitor, Graham T.T. and George Thomas Kurian (editors), *Encyclopedia of the Future*, 2 vols, New York: Macmillan, and London: Simon and Schuster, 1996

Moorcroft, Sheila M. (editor), *Visions for the 21st Century*, Westport, Connecticut: Praeger, 1993

Moravec, Hans, *Mind Children: The Future of Robot and Human Intelligence*, Cambridge, Massachusetts: Harvard University Press, 1988

Negroponte, Nicholas, *Being Digital*, New York: Knopf, 1995

Ogden, Frank, *Navigating in Cyberspace: A Guide to the Next Millennium*, Toronto: Macfarlane Walter and Ross, 1995

Paul, Gregory S. and Earl Cox (editors), *Beyond Humanity: CyberEvolution and Future Minds*, Rockland, Massachusetts: Charles River Media, 1996

Rawlins, Gregory J.E., *Slaves of the Machine: The Quickening of Computer Technology*, Cambridge, Massachusetts: MIT Press, 1997

Rifkin, Jeremy, *The End of Work: The Decline of the Global Labor Force and the Dawn of the Post-market Era*, New York: Tarcher/Putnam, 1995

Shostak, Arthur B., *CyberUnion: Empowering Labor through Computer Technology*, Armonk, New York: Sharpe, 1999

Slaughter, Richard A., *The Foresight Principle: Cultural Recovery in the 21st Century*, London: Adamantine Press, and Westport, Connecticut: Praeger, 1995

Stephenson, Neal, *The Diamond Age; or, A Young Lady's Illustrated Primer*, New York: Bantam, 1995; London: Penguin, 1996

Strozier, Charles B. and Michael Flynn (editors), *The Year 2000: Essays on the End*, New York: New York University Press, 1997

Tracing its lineage back to shamans in prehistoric times, futurism today is a cutting-age art form that draws on every field of knowledge, especially the arts, computer sciences, economics, history, and literature, in a systematic effort to illuminate policy options for shaping a finer future. With humility and an open mind, it struggles to unravel linkages, uncover possibilities, and highlight perils and preferences beyond the obvious. Methods include scenario writing, trend analysis and extrapolation, computer modelling, brainstorming, simulation and gaming, expert genius forecasting, polling, intuition, and the search for lessons in history, science-fiction, and the environmental sciences.

Without doubt, one of the best introductions is a seminal two-volume work by W. BELL, a 1997 publication that raised the bar for all such books. A sociologist and applied futurist, he reviews the history of forecasting, its purposes, and its strengths and weaknesses. Leaving forecasts to other authors, he tackles instead the fundamental question of how a futurist might determine whether one future is more-or-less desirable than another. As this question of validating value judgements is a critical one, Bell's contribution is substantial.

For specific forecasts, the 1998 encyclopedia edited by MOLITOR & KURIAN is a treasure trove. With over 450 articles on nearly every imaginable topic, it has no peer. Invaluable is a remarkable chronology of futurism and the future, the first part of which covers the field from 47,000 BC to AD 1995, while the second dares to go many millions of years out ahead to a breathtaking close. Attention is also owed to a unique list of "One hundred most influential futurists" – thinkers like Daniel Bell, Arthur C. Clarke, Hazel Henderson, Herman Kahn, Marshall McLuhan, and Alvin Toffler, as selected by the book's contributors. (DUBLIN's fervent insistence that futurism distracts from present-day opportunities warrants attention.)

Sweeping monographs, such as those by KAKU or DERTOUZOS, commonly go into greater depth than do "brushstroke" essay collections, such as those edited for the World Future Society by DIDSBURY. Exceptions include an essay collection offered by STROZIER & FLYNN, which focuses in depth on only one topic – the dread and hope stirred by millennialism. Similarly, the MOORCROFT essay collection emphasizes only the preferable futures we can work to create, thereby making it an especially hope-stirring volume.

"Alarm bell" volumes are a mainstay, such as GELBSPAN's vexing forecast of major climate change problems (global warming, food shortages, and so on), RAWLIN's misgivings about our forthcoming relations with artificial intelligence, RIFKIN's forebodings about the possible loss of jobs to "smart" equipment, and the environmental anxieties of MEADOWS *et al.*

Helpful rebuttals are offered by COATES, MAHAFFIE & HINES and CETRON & DAVIES. Special attention is owed to SLAUGHTER's book, complete with an exceptional annotated bibliography, which emphasizes how our pursuit of wisdom remains one of our major defences against dystopian perils.

Naturally, ever greater attention is being paid to a time soon when an intelligence (us) may have created another intelligence more intelligent than itself. KURZWEIL's book is outstanding here, as he dares to explore what "life" might resemble if and when humans merge with "spiritual machines", and human life expectancy becomes infinite. MORAVEC thinks this prospect attractive, as do PAUL & COX. Novelists like GIBSON are far less certain.

All the more important, therefore, are volumes by sceptics, such as ANDERSON and also MILLS. Similarly, fictional versions of lifestyles that shun reliance on "high tech", as by CALLENBACH, offer much to usefully ponder. A related set of forecasts extrapolates from the anticipated rise to power and influence of women with a humanistic agenda, a scenario well developed in ABURDENE & NAISBITT.

Nanotechnology, or the science of building at the sub-atomic level (one billionth of a meter), is being hailed by some futurists at the next Great Revolution, on a level with the Agricultural, the Industrial, and the Information Age Revolutions. It is well introduced in DREXLER & PETERSON and this factual acccount is handsomely supplemented by a brilliant novel (STEPHENSON) and a short story collection edited by ELLIOTT. Other futurists nominate biotechnology as the next frontier, and KITCHER is very helpful in understanding why. The synergy between these two topics recommends attention to both.

Finally, futurism at present is understandably preoccupied with the Information Age and its pressing impacts, especially as Internet use is doubling every 12 months and computer power is doubling every 18 months. This subject is well explored by NEGROPONTE and also by OGDEN. Both experts focus on possibilities, while others, such as the essayists gathered by the KROKERS, underline the perils involved. Studies of the related ongoing transformation of major institutions, such as the labour movement (SHOSTAK), the virtual workplace (IGBARIA & TAN), or governance (LOADER), lend specificity and depth to the Information Age discussion.

All of this material, when taken in combination with retrospective evaluative studies, such as a review in 1997 of forecasts first offered in 1965 (BELL & GRAUBARD), can make a sound contribution to the future-shaping efforts of us all. To explore how higher education is taking up this challenge and using futurism, a new volume edited by DATOR could not be more timely.

ARTHUR B. SHOSTAK

See also Cyberspace revolution

G

Galbraith, J.K. 1908–

US economist

Breit, William, "Galbraith and Friedman: Two Versions of Economic Reality", *Journal of Post Keynesian Economics* (Galbraith Symposium), 7/1 (Fall 1984): 18–29

Friedman, Milton, *From Galbraith to Economic Freedom*, London: Institute of Economic Affairs, 1977 (Occasional Papers 49)

Galbraith, J.K., *The Affluent Society*, Boston: Houghton Mifflin, and London: Hamish Hamilton, 1958

Galbraith, J.K., *The New Industrial State*, Boston: Houghton Mifflin, and London: Hamish Hamilton, 1967

Galbraith, J.K., *Economics and the Public Purpose*, Boston: Houghton Mifflin, 1973; London: Deutsch, 1974

Galbraith, J.K., "The Defence of the Multinational Company", *Harvard Business Review*, 56/2 (1978)

Galbraith, J.K., *The Good Society: The Humane Agenda*, Boston: Houghton Mifflin, and London: Sinclair Stevenson, 1996

Gruchy, Allan G., *Contemporary Economic Thought: The Contribution Of Neo-Institutional Economics*, Clifton, New York: Kelley, 1972

Krugman, Paul, *Peddling Prosperity*, New York: Norton, 1994

Meade, James, "Is 'The New Industrial State' Inevitable?", *Economic Journal*, 78/310 (June 1968): 372–92

Samuels, Warren, "Galbraith on Economics as a System of Professional Belief", *Journal of Post-Keynesian Economics* (Galbraith Symposium), 7/1 (Fall 1984): 61–76

Sharpe, Myron, *John Kenneth Galbraith and the Lower Economics*, White Plains, New York: International Arts and Sciences Press, and London: Macmillan, 1973

Galbraith rose to prominence in 1958 with the publication of *The Affluent Society* (GALBRAITH 1958), in which he argued that American society had come to see an imbalance between its private and public sectors: an imbalance between "private opulence and public squalor". He accordingly argued that American society was being distorted by corporate power, via advertising, and by the nexus thereby established between goods (or materialism) and happiness. Galbraith objected that orthodox economics failed to deal adequately with what he saw as the self-evident power of the corporate sector and its advertising.

BREIT acknowledges that *The Affluent Society* influenced an entire generation on the question of sectoral imbalance.

Galbraith pushed his theme further in his *New Industrial State* (GALBRAITH 1967), in which he argued that the cornerstones of orthodox economic theory were more myth than reality. Thus Galbraith made famous his heterodox claim that corporate power had now grown to the point where producer sovereignty had replaced consumer sovereignty. He similarly argued that the divorce between corporate ownership and control meant that it was no longer reasonable to assume that profit maximisation was the goal of the firm, since the technostructure actually controlling the firm had an interest in pursuing other goals as well, including size, growth, and the quiet life. A third orthodox assumption lampooned by Galbraith was the assumption that the State acted as an independent arbiter. For Galbraith, the State acted as executive arm of the producer corporations by virtue of interconnections between corporate and State hierarchies. While corporate planning was well designed to serve corporate goals, Galbraith argued that society as a whole was nonetheless left with significant planning lacunae, which helped undermine the quality of life and left American cities with excessive problems of crime and environmental degradation.

Galbraith completed his principal trilogy of critiques of economic theory and practice with the publication of *Economics and the Public Purpose* (GALBRAITH 1974), in which he further developed his theme that economics was not value-neutral science, but a set of beliefs which produces conclusions convenient to the big corporations. As distinct from Friedman, Galbraith's argument was that market forces don't work for the best, *except* for the powerful. Accordingly Galbraith continued to press the view that orthodox economics is obsolete, that it omits to consider the role of power, and that it omits to consider the *sources* of both government policy and consumer tastes. By implication significant reforms were needed in government policy formation, including reduced reliance on monetary policy, nationalisation of weapons corporations and the major oil companies (which had unwelcome influence over US foreign policy, not just over the economy), and wage/price controls to stem the inflationary spiral. Also needed was what Galbraith called "the emancipation of belief" from the misconceptions of orthodoxy, along with recognition that the anti-trust laws are "admirably innocuous". Galbraith's emphatic theme was that the competitive model and modern technology are simply incompatible. He therefore argued that although Friedman's theory is consistent with Friedman's ideal world, Friedman's ideal world no longer exists. In defending the multinational company – despite his earlier objections to the problematic power of the corporate sector – GALBRAITH (1978) accordingly accepted the reality of economies of scale and argued that the exercise of such power is simply inevitable, and can be socially useful if properly guided. Multinational companies have led to reduced tariff barriers, for example, and enhanced global efficiency.

MEADE provided an early, balanced review of *The New Industrial State*. Meade conceded points of truth in Galbraith – regarding corporate planning, producer sovereignty, corporate links with government, and a less direct concern for profit – while arguing that Galbraith is too much of a technological determinist in arguing that technical progress underpins the whole tone of society. Government action is *not* always a response to the technostructure. It is after all possible to tax advertising, if the power of advertising is felt to be excessive. Moreover, Galbraith overlooked the relevance of general equilibrium.

FRIEDMAN and subsequent critics have caustically dismissed Galbraith's work as unrealistic, oversimplified and overgeneralised. They object that he simply makes sweeping generalisations, much repeated, without adducing much empirical support for them. They dismiss Galbraith as *nonscientific* in that he rarely formulates specific, refutable hypotheses. To Friedman, Galbraith was not an economist but a missionary seeking converts.

SAMUELS takes Galbraith's message to be that "economics is a system of belief, not a body of truth", causing Galbraith to affirm that "within a considerable range [the economist] is permitted to believe what he pleases". Professional pursuit of the technically esoteric – what SHARPE calls "the higher economics"– is what Galbraith condemns as an attempt to establish the credentials of "a priestly circle", whereby to exclude the inconvenient and disturbing. Samuels commends Galbraith for his interest in the sociology of professional belief and concludes that Galbraith's analysis warrants the attention of others.

GRUCHY notes that Galbraith and other neo-institutionalists distinguished themselves from conventional economists by disagreeing as to what should be included within the province of economics. Galbraith's position of prominence – of controversial but respected gadfly – has now faded.

KRUGMAN is utterly dismissive of Galbraith as but a "policy entrepreneur", as distinct from an economic scientist. While the general public thinks of Galbraith as an important economist "he has never been taken seriously by his academic colleagues". Krugman notes that history has not been kind to *The New Industrial State* and that Galbraith was not even remotely on target in arguing his case about the increasing dominance of giant corporations, technocratic managers increasingly independent of shareholders, and corporate immunity to market forces.

Unbowed by such criticism, Galbraith's own views have continued to evolve. In his *The Good Society: The Humane Agenda* GALBRAITH (1996) effectively recurs to *The Affluent Society* in arguing that Western societies continue to pay a high price for the view that the public sector is harmful and a burden. He likewise argues that we pay a high price for the increasingly prevalent views that balanced budgets are necessary and important; that unemployment must be tolerated for fear that faster growth will lead to the greater evil of inflation; and that certain market mechanisms have gained the status of unassailable wisdom. He continues to object that markets produce "bads" as well as "goods", thus necessitating regulation to keep the bads to a minimum. Externalities remain a real problem in Galbraith's view of markets, as do employer–employee power imbalances. Many social economists continue to adopt similar views.

L.A. DUHS

Gambling

Abt, Vicki, James F. Smith and Eugene Martin Christiansen, *The Business of Risk: Commercial Gambling in Mainstream America*, Kansas: University Press of Kansas, 1985

Chinn, Carl, *Better Betting with a Decent Feller: Bookmaking, Betting and the British Working Class, 1750–1990*, Hemel Hempstead, Hertfordshire and New York: Harvester Wheatsheaf, 1991

Clapson, Mark, *A Bit of a Flutter: Popular Gambling and English Society, 1823–1961*, Manchester: Manchester University Press, 1992

Devereux, Edward C., *Gambling and the Social Structure: A Sociological Study of Lotteries and Horse Racing in Contemporary America*, Cambridge, Masachusetts: Harvard University Press, 1949

Dickerson, Mark, "The Characteristics of the Compulsive Gambler: A Rejection of a Typology" in *Gambling in Australia*, edited by Geoffrey Caldwell *et al.*, London: Croom Helm, 1985

Dixey, Rachel, "It's a Great Feeling When You Win: Women and Bingo", *Leisure Studies*, 6 (1987): 199–214

Dixon, David, *From Prohibition to Regulation: Bookmaking, Anti-Gambling and the Law*, Oxford: Clarendon Press, and New York: Oxford University Press, 1991

Downes, D.M. *et al.*, *Gambling, Work and Leisure: A Study Across Three Areas*, London and Boston: Routledge and Kegan Paul, 1976

Eadington, William R. (editor), *Gambling Research: Proceedings of the Seventh International Conference on Gambling and Risk-Taking*, Reno: University of Nevada, 1988

Fisher, Sue, "The Pull of the Fruit Machine: A Sociological Typology of Young Players", *Sociological Review*, 41/3 (1993): 446–74

Freud, Sigmund, "Dostoevsky and Parricide" in his *Collected Papers*, edited by James Strachey, vol. 5, London: Hogarth Press, 1950

Griffiths, Mark, *Adolescent Gambling*, London and New York: Routledge, 1995

Halliday, Jon and Peter Fuller (editors), *The Psychology of Gambling*, London: Allen Lane, 1974; New York: Harper and Row, 1975

Herman, Robert D. (editor), *Gambling*, New York: Harper and Row, 1967

Kaplan, H. Roy, *Lottery Winners: How They Won and How Winning Changed Their Lives*, New York: Harper and Row, 1978

McMillen, Jan (editor), *Gambling Cultures: Studies in History and Interpretation*, London and New York: Routledge, 1996

Munting, Roger, *An Economic and Social History of Gambling in Britain and the USA*, Manchester: Manchester University Press, 1996

Reith, Gerda, *The Age of Chance: Gambling in Western Culture*, London: Routledge, 1999

Rosecrance, John D., *The Degenerates of Lake Tahoe: A Study of Persistence in the Social World of Horse Race Gambling*, New York: Peter Lang, 1985

FREUD's short essay on *Dostoevsky and Parricide* established the framework for the discussion of gambling in the social sciences for the first half of the 20th century. In it he explained the activity with reference to the Oedipus complex of the player's youth – the desire to kill the father and possess the mother – and referred specifically to Dostoevsky's ambivalent relations with his father and his subsequent "mania" for gambling to illustrate his argument. The guilt the former felt for his hatred of his father was assuaged in gambling, where in exposing himself to fate he symbolically confronted his father, so that gambling became "a symbolic means of self-punishment".

This psychoanalytic type of analysis was continued by writers such as HALLIDAY & FULLER who described gamblers as masochists, who, because of various unresolved conflicts in their past, were compelled to repeat an endless cycle of punishment by continually losing the games they played. Such approaches inevitably regarded gambling as evidence of pathology, with the emphasis on its symbolic nature precluding examination of its social and experiential dimensions for participants.

In sociology, DEVEREAUX's classic study rationalized gambling in terms of its latent social function. According to Devereaux, the tensions and conflicts in the capitalist economic system produce ambivalent feelings of anxiety and hostility, and these disrupt individual as well as social wellbeing. Certain activities such as gambling that work to resolve, or at least accommodate, this disequilibrium are therefore vital in advanced society, and tend to become institutionalized. In this, they function as "shock absorbers" or "safety valves" that allow the psychological consequences of economic strain to be worked out and cathartically discharged in a socially acceptable manner.

HERMAN has collected together works on this theme of displacement and catharsis, which ran as a *leitmotif* through much of the sociology of gambling of the 1950s, 1960s, and 1970s. It was argued that gambling acted as a social safety valve for frustrated (mainly working class) citizens, providing a context in which the deprivations of the outside world could be compensated for by symbolic activity. For those denied access to socially legitimate modes of the pursuit of wealth, gambling provided an alternative economy, with its own set of rules and its own measures of success. Although endowed with positive features, in such analyses gambling was still regarded essentially as a substitute for social deprivation.

DOWNES *et al.* took a slightly different approach, studying various forms of gambling as positive features of cultural life, and examining their social constitution according to class, age, and gender. Although comprehensive at the time, their study suffered from a rather over-formal approach to its subject: despite methodical description of the structure and organization of games, there is little accompanying investigation into the actual experiences or attitudes of gamblers themselves.

More recently, a number of studies have begun to focus on gambling as a form of leisure that is imbued with social and cultural meaning for participants. These have tended to develop along the lines of specialist research into specific types of gambling. For example, DIXEY has studied the social and gendered nature of bingo, and the dynamics of fruit machine playing has been thoroughly examined, in Britain by FISHER and by GRIFFITHS and in Australia, by DICKERSON. Meanwhile the political and social aspects of American lotteries have been analysed by KAPLAN and by ABT, SMITH & CHRISTIANSEN. Horse racing has been the subject of a number of studies, the most important of which have been conducted by ROSECRANCE. A useful compendium of ongoing research into all these areas is to be found in the collected papers of the *International Conference on Gambling and Risk Taking*, which publishes its regular conference proceedings and is edited by EADINGTON.

More detailed studies into the history of gambling in general and horseracing in particular have also flourished. CHINN and CLAPSON have examined the development of racing, paying particular attention to its place in 19th-century working-class culture. They describe how commercial developments turned betting from an elite hobby into a widespread spectator sport, tracing the criticisms that grew up around such expansion and the legislation that attempted to halt it. Chinn's analysis is informed by extensive use of first-hand interviews with veteran bettors, bookies, and agents, and lends an air of authenticity and colour to his subsequent discussion.

DIXON and MUNTING share an interest in the historical regulation of gambling – in the former in Britain and in the latter, in comparison with the United States. Dixon analyses the social and political context of the anti-gambling arguments of late Victorian society, as well as the reasons for their decline and for the gradual commercialization of gambling in the early 20th century. Munting's subject matter is wider: after a general survey of the history of gambling in Britain and the US he moves on to look at the organization of the main commercial types, the social basis of participation, and the problems generated by its expansion. Although ostensibly a comparison of Britain and the US, the focus of the book is slanted more to the British case, with aspects of American gambling frequently receiving no more than a perfunctory mention. As such, it is more useful to regard it as a study of British gambling that makes illuminating reference to the US than as a fully fledged comparative analysis. In this more limited context, it is a valuable contribution to understanding the complex relation of gambling with political and commercial interests.

A more comparative, international perspective is to be found in McMILLEN's edited collection, which contains contributions on the economic, political, and legal as well as the cultural and social aspects of gambling. The role of government in the spread of commercial gambling ventures and, more recently, in the globalization of gambling markets, is discussed, as is the historical regulation and also the contemporary medicalization of the activity. Social diversity is considered in chapters on the cross-cultural appeal of the slot machine, the gendered nature of bingo, and the existence of specific types of gambling in Cameroon and Senegal. Cultural variation is also examined, in essays that focus on representations of gambling in both American and Australian culture.

This interdisciplinary approach is continued by REITH, who analyses the philosophical, sociological, and cultural dimensions of gambling in Western society in both historical and contemporary perspective. In the first part of the book, the development of the notion of chance, the commercialization of various gambling games and their dynamic relation to socioeconomic institutions are examined. From this, a typology of modern gambling is established, in which the formal properties of games and the social characteristics of their participants are delineated. In the second part, the focus moves from the social to the individual: to the experiences and beliefs of gamblers themselves. In an attempt to explain the unique appeal of games of chance, a phenomenological investigation of the inner world of the gambler is made. This covers an analysis of the experiences of temporality and causation, the disregard for money, the deliberate seeking out of risk and uncertainty, and the adoption of a range of superstitious notions such as the belief in luck and fate.

GERDA REITH

Game theory

Aumann, Robert J. and Sergiu Hart (editors), *Handbook of Game Theory with Economic Applications*, Amsterdam: North Holland, 1992

Baird, Douglas G., Robert H. Gertner and Randal C. Picker, *Game Theory and the Law*, Cambridge, Massachusetts: Harvard University Press, 1994

Binmore, Ken, *Game Theory and the Social Contract*, 2 vols, Cambridge, Massachusetts: MIT Press, 1994–98

Dixit, Avinash K. and Barry J. Nalebuff, *Thinking Strategically: The Competitive Edge in Business, Politics, and Everyday Life*, New York: Norton, 1991

Fudenberg, Drew and David K. Levine, *The Theory of Learning in Games*, Cambridge, Massachusetts: MIT Press, 1998

Fudenberg, Drew and Jean Tirole, *Game Theory*, Cambridge, Massachusetts: MIT Press, 1991

Gibbons, Robert, *Game Theory for Applied Economists*, Princeton, New Jersey: Princeton University Press, 1992; as *A Primer in Game Theory*, Hemel Hempstead, Hertfordshire: Harvester Wheatsheaf, 1992

Heap, Shaun P. Hargreaves and Yanis Varoufakis, *Game Theory: A Critical Introduction*, London and New York: Routledge, 1995

Kreps, David M., *Game Theory and Economic Modelling*, Oxford: Clarendon Press, and New York: Oxford University Press, 1990

Luce, R. Duncan and Howard Raiffa, *Games and Decisions: Introduction and Critical Survey*, New York: Wiley, 1957

McMillan, John, *Games, Strategies and Managers*, New York: Oxford University Press, 1992

Maynard Smith, John, *Evolution and the Theory of Games*, Cambridge and New York: Cambridge University Press, 1982

Morrow, James D., *Game Theory for Political Scientists*, Princeton, New Jersey: Princeton University Press, 1994

Osborne, Martin J. and Ariel Rubinstein, *Bargaining and Markets*, San Diego: Academic Press, 1990

Osborne, Martin J. and Ariel Rubinstein, *A Course in Game Theory*, Cambridge, Massachusetts: MIT Press, 1994

Phlips, Louis, *Competition Policy: A Game-Theoretic Perspective*, Cambridge and New York: Cambridge University Press, 1995

Schelling, Thomas C., *The Strategy of Conflict*, London and New York: Oxford University Press, 1960

Tirole, Jean, *The Theory of Industrial Organization*, Cambridge, Massachusetts: MIT Press, 1989

Von Neumann, John and Oskar Morgenstern, *Theory of Games and Economic Behavior*, Princeton, New Jersey: Princeton University Press 1944; 3rd edition 1953

Walker, Paul, *A Chronology of Game Theory*, http://www.econ.canterbury/history.htm

VON NEUMANN & MORGENSTERN initiated the formal study of game theory with the publication of their *Theory of Games and Economic Behaviour* in 1944, which laid the conceptual foundations for all subsequent work. Although it was enormously influential in its time, this work is often cited but seldom read today. It is technically demanding and some of its major foci have been superseded by subsequent developments. One enduring contribution is expected utility theory, which remains the accepted paradigm for incorporating uncertainty into economic analysis.

Following the lead of von Neumann & Morgenstern, the bulk of early research focused on cooperative games. LUCE & RAIFFA is an elegant survey of this early work, which gives a feel for the history and tradition of the subject. Written primarily for social scientists, it is an exceptionally clear and lucid account of elementary game theory, which is still well worth reading today. In particular, the appendices contain excellent expositions of some more technical material.

The literature on game theory has grown dramatically in recent years, and this review must therefore necessarily be superficial. It is organized below as follows. First, some standard texts are listed in decreasing order of difficulty. Then, important contributions in applied game theory are considered. Finally, a major source of survey papers and a detailed chronology of results are discussed.

In the last two decades, the main thrust of game theory has shifted from cooperative to noncooperative games. In a static game, players play simultaneously, whereas a dynamic game is played over time. Another fundamental distinction depends upon whether it is assumed that the players have complete information about the game. In a careful logical progression, FUDENBERG & TIROLE provide an authoritative textbook account of modern game theory, from the simplest static games to the more challenging dynamic games of incomplete information. A final part deals with advanced topics such as common knowledge, Markov equilibria, and differential games. A major strength of this text lies in its wealth of applications, the authors being very successful in integrating different contributions into a common framework and exposing the underlying structure. However, this source requires careful study: although the coverage is encyclopedic, the treatment of some topics is brief and rather spartan.

At a similar level of sophistication, the text by OSBORNE & RUBINSTEIN (1994) places somewhat different demands on the reader, rigorously developing a consistent theory from first principles. Their text is more coherent than Fudenberg & Tirole, but devotes less attention to applications. Compared to the latter, Osborne & Rubinstein are more successful in laying a secure foundation for the theory, but less successful in describing its place in the world. Unusually in modern texts, they cover cooperative as well as non cooperative games.

Both of the preceding texts are pitched at the level of the graduate student or practitioner. Of the myriad of lower-level texts, GIBBONS stands out for its clarity and range of applications. It covers similar material to Fudenberg & Tirole, but at a lower level of sophistication, and should be readily accessible to the senior undergraduate or beginning graduate student. Selected applications, drawn from a range of fields in economics, are treated in some depth.

MORROW performs a similar task for political scientists. He covers the standard fare of non-cooperative game theory and its applications in political science, especially the role of legislative voting rules, deterrence in international crises, voting in elections, and bargaining. Similarly, BAIRD, GERTNER & PICKER outline the basic concepts of game theory from a legal perspective. Aimed at the general reader as well as the legal scholar, their book provides not only a new domain of application for game theory, but also new insights into the way in which laws affect the way people behave. A glossary of legal and economic terms makes the book accessible to a wider audience.

SCHELLING is the classic non-technical introduction to strategic behaviour. Although it is dated, it still merits reading for its powerful and important insights, such as the value of commitment and the role of focal points in selecting equilibria. In the same tradition, DIXIT & NALEBUFF, and McMILLAN are accessible introductions to the fruits of recent research, stripped of sophisticated mathematics and much of the jargon. Dixit & Nalebuff is a popular introduction to the core ideas of game theory, leavened with a host of entertaining examples from sports, personal life, business, and politics. McMillan, aimed at practising managers, is narrower in focus, attempting to distil from the research literature a few general principles of widespread applicability in business decision-making. Successive sections are devoted to negotiation, contracting, and bidding. They are illustrated by real-life examples, ranging from the social behaviour of pigs and the salaries of baseball players, through politics and the Iran–Iraq war, to bidding for Olympic games broadcast rights, and a comparison of the use of subcontracting in Japanese and US industry.

One of the earliest applications of game theory was to the study of market behaviour. OSBORNE & RUBINSTEIN (1990) present the theory of bargaining and its application to behaviour in markets. Bargaining games are a special class of games, the simplified structure of which makes them more tractable for formal analysis. Recent research has seen a convergence in the cooperative and non cooperative approaches

to these games. The first half of this book is an authoritative account of this work, in which a small number of models are explored in depth. The second half of the book applies bargaining theory to the study of market behaviour.

Probably the most potent and influential application of game theory has been in industrial organization, where game theory has come to influence the competition policy and legal decisions in antitrust cases. The theoretical contribution is incisively surveyed by TIROLE, who displays a masterly ability to strip away irrelevant details and integrate divergent models by different authors into a coherent account. In a more applied vein, PHLIPS uses game theory to analyse anticompetitive behaviour among firms and to consider its implications for competition policy, using actual antitrust cases and empirical studies for illustration.

Adapting theory to explain some puzzles in evolutionary biology, MAYNARD SMITH introduced game theory to biology. Not only did he revolutionize the study of evolution – he initiated a new field of game theory, evolutionary games. This has shed some light on one of the most intriguing questions in game theory: how do players arrive at an equilibrium? FUDENBERG & LEVINE address this issue of learning in games, collating the state of knowledge in this fast-developing field. They present and compare a wide range of models of learning and evolution in both static and dynamic games.

BINMORE explores the implications of game theory for political philosophy. The first volume restates the classical problems of moral and political philosophy within a game-theoretic framework, while the second volume outlines the author's own theory of the social contract. Intended both for economists interested in ethics and fairness and philosophers interested in formal analysis, the book provides a provocative tour of classical wisdom and modern scholarship.

Following in the tradition of Luce & Raiffa, HEAP & VAROUFAKIS is a modern critical review, which offers an accessible overview of modern game theory for the social scientist. Aiming to locate game theory in the wider debates within social science, the authors pay more than usual attention to fundamental assumptions and examine links with other social sciences. A final chapter outlines some experimental evidence on how people actually play games. KREPS addresses similar fundamental issues from the viewpoint of an economist, highlighting both the strengths and the weaknesses of game theory in economic modelling.

For researchers, AUMANN & HART is a convenient source of comprehensive and authoritative surveys covering most aspects of game theory. The innovative chronology by WALKER lists all the significant contributions to game theory, together with a brief comment on their contents. Serious students will find this an invaluable resource to obtain an outline of the history of game theory as well as a convenient bibliography to guide their further study.

MICHAEL CARTER

Gardens, urban use and value

Cook, J.A., "Gardens on Housing Estates: A Survey of User Attitudes and Behaviour on Seven Layouts", *Town Planning Review*, 39 (1968): 217–34

Dunnett, N.P. and M. Qasim, "Perceived Values of Urban Gardens", *Hort-technology* 10/1 (2000): 40–45

Francis, Mark and Randolph T. Hester (editors), *The Meaning of Gardens: Idea, Place, and Action*, Cambridge, Massachusetts: MIT Press, 1990

Francis, M., "Childhood's Garden: Memory and Meaning of Gardens", *Children's Environments*, 12 (1995): 183–91

Grampp, C., "Social Meaning of Residential Gardens" in *The Meaning of Gardens: Idea, Place, and Action*, edited by Mark Francis and Randolph T. Hester Jr, Cambridge, Massachusetts: MIT Press, 1990

Halkett, I.P.B., "The Recreational Use of Gardens", *Journal of Leisure Research*, 10 (1978): 13–20

Kaplan, R., "Some Psychological Benefits of Gardening", *Environment and Behaviour*, 5 (1973): 145–62

Kellet, J.E., "The Private Garden in England and Wales", *Landscape Planning*, 9 (1982): 105–23

Lewis, C.A., "Gardening as Healing Process" in *The Meaning of Gardens: Idea, Place, and Action*, edited by Mark Francis and Randolph T. Hester, Cambridge, Massachusetts: MIT Press, 1990

Roberts, J., "Researching the Vernacular Garden", *Landscape Research*, 21 (1996): 175–87

Despite the very high proportion of households that own garden space and the large area of land that they cover, the role of these private open spaces has been the subject of very little research. In particular, the functions they perform beyond the purely utilitarian have been little studied.

HALKETT contains a concise and clearly argued discussion of the value of urban gardens to their owners. The focus of the work is on the various practical and recreational functions that gardens perform. This is an Australian study, carried out in the context of pressure from planners to reduce the density of urban development, and by implication, garden sizes, and it is particularly relevant to the current debate over sustainable urban development and compact cities. Gardens are described as "the smallest and most ubiquitous elements in the hierarchy of urban spaces that offer residents a unique range of recreational opportunities". It was found that suburban households make more intensive and flexible use of their gardens than they do of any other type of outdoor space, and that reductions in garden space may significantly alter recreational patterns.

COOK carried out an intensive survey of user attitudes and behaviour with regard to gardens on new housing estates. This study concentrates mainly on the utilitarian uses of gardens and pays particular attention to privacy needs, optimum garden sizes, and the value of social contact. These factors are related to age, economic status, and the nature of the household. There is some interesting discussion of how public open space can accommodate some of the functions of gardens. Although over 30 years old, this study remains one of the few detailed pieces of work that considers housing layout from the viewpoint of garden provision and is fascinating for being carried out at a time of social change, represented by increasing affluence and car ownership.

KELLET contains a valuable summary of the development of the private garden in England and Wales and attempts to explain why gardens are considered to be such a vital attribute of housing in Britain as compared with the rest of Europe. Kellet contends that this is partly linked with the high degree of owner-occupied housing in the UK. The role of gardens in projecting an image to the outside world, their role as a status symbol and their value in defining personal defensible space are discussed.

KAPLAN undertook a pioneering study into the environmental psychology of gardening. Three groups of gardeners were sampled: community gardeners (where gardening was carried out by individuals at a specific location), plot gardeners (who had their own parcel of land, also away from home), and home gardeners. The benefits of gardening were grouped into three categories: Primary garden experiences (such as working with the soil and being outside), tangible benefits (food production), and sustained interest (relaxation and aesthetic experiences). Overall satisfaction and sustained interest scored highest with home gardeners. This is an important introduction that includes particularly valuable discussion on the role of gardening in stress-relief and relaxation. The samples used were very small, however, and were non random, consisting of self-selecting keen gardeners.

DUNNETT & QASIM carried out a large, wide-ranging, and random sample of urban private garden owners, and related the results to social, personal and economic variables. They included a wide-ranging discussion of the various functional, environmental, and psychological roles of gardens. The perceived benefits of gardens and gardening agreed with those of Kaplan, but it was suggested that Kaplan's classification of benefits was too simplistic. The importance of creativity and self-expression is explored. The perceived benefits of gardens are discussed not only in relation to the individual household, but also collectively as a contribution to the wider environment.

ROBERTS discusses an important aspect of "popular" gardens: the way in which gardens can represent local character, through use of materials or their type of layout or style. The work moves the focus away from the designed garden to that which has evolved as a reflection of local culture. Gardens are seen as being important contributors to distinctive landscape patterning, both urban and rural. A number of case studies are given and a theoretical framework for research is outlined.

FRANCIS & HESTER bring together a range of short essays on the theme of the meaning of gardens, grouped under the headings of faith, power, ordering, cultural expression, personal expression, and healing, of which the last three are of most relevance. This is the most wide-ranging statement on the artistic, social, psychological, and human well-being aspects of gardens, although many of the contributions are rather anecdotal. There are, however, some accessible introductions to particular topics. For example GRAMP reports on a study of Californian gardens, which again lays emphasis on the importance of the image of the owner a garden can convey to the world in general. LEWIS successfully discusses the therapeutic value of gardening.

FRANCIS introduces an important aspect of why particular aspects of the garden have value and why meanings are attached to specific landscapes. It is suggested that childhood memories of gardens are important in determining adult relationships with the garden. Based on common preferences for natural vegetation, wildness, shelter, and privacy, recommendations are made for the design and planning of present gardens – the future gardens of childhood.

NIGEL DUNNETT

GATT, *see* General Agreement on Tariffs and Trade

Gay and lesbian politics

Abelove, Henry, Michèle Aina Barale and David M. Halperin (editors), *The Lesbian and Gay Studies Reader*, London and New York: Routledge, 1993

Adam, Barry D., Jan Willem Duyvendak and André Krouwel (editors), *The Global Emergence of Gay and Lesbian Politics: National Imprints of a Worldwide Movement*, Philadelphia: Temple University Press, 1999

Blasius, Mark, *Gay and Lesbian Politics: Sexuality and the Emergence of a New Ethic*, Philadelphia: Temple University Press, 1994

Blasius, Mark and Shane Phelan (editors), *We Are Everywhere: A Historical Sourcebook of Gay and Lesbian Politics*, London and New York: Routledge, 1997

Edwards, Tim, *Erotics and Politics: Gay Male Sexuality, Masculinity, and Feminism*, London and New York: Routledge, 1994

Medhurst, Andy and Sally R. Munt (editors), *Lesbian and Gay Studies: A Critical Introduction*, London and Washington, DC: Cassell, 1997

Nardi, Peter M. and Beth E. Schneider (editors), *Social Perspectives in Lesbian and Gay Studies: A Reader*, London and New York: Routledge, 1998

Seidman, Steven, *Difference Troubles: Queering Social Theory and Sexual Politics*, Cambridge and New York: Cambridge University Press, 1997

Wilson, Angelia R. (editor), *A Simple Matter of Justice? Theorizing Lesbian and Gay Politics*, London and New York: Cassell, 1995

MEDHURST & MUNT recognize the centrality of politics in defining the evolving field of lesbian and gay studies. They argue for retention of the name "lesbian and gay studies" despite the trend towards renaming to "queer studies". The essays in the reader perform two main tasks: examining the interventions of lesbian and gay perspectives in traditional academic disciplines such as geography, history, film studies; and, charting the developments within the lesbian and gay studies on defining themes including identity and subculture, race, class, bisexuality, heterosexuality, transgender, and gender performativity. Promoting dialogue remains one of the main tasks of the reader, in which it is largely successful.

For those interested in "what", "why", and "how" questions related to gay and lesbian movements in various parts of the world, ADAM, DUYVENDAK & KROUWEL is an important book. Using observations from social movement theories and various analyses of relationship between movements and modernity/postmodernity, valuable insights are offered into gay and lesbian movements in various countries (16 to be precise). Various essays show how differences and complementarities exist among the national gay and lesbian movements as well as between them and the international gay and lesbian movement. Any presumption of existence of the gay and lesbian movement in the singular at the global level is rendered problematic. The concluding section discusses some social, political, and international prerequisites for the existence of lesbian and gay movements. Interestingly, the authors believe the capitalist system to be an essential prerequisite. This work certainly deserves to be a source book on the subject.

An essential reading for gaining historical background of the contemporary politics of homosexuality is the collection of historically and theoretically important statements representing the evolving lesbian and gay politics by BLASIUS & PHELAN. Recognizing the inadequacy of the term "homosexuality" in comprehending diversity of sexuality and identities, the editors argue that, nevertheless, it has helped those involved in "same-sex love" to forge a common understanding of themselves and come together to constitute "lesbian and gay politics". Arguing that the modern gay or lesbian identity is a Western invention, it is recognized that international struggles for homosexual rights are no mere replication of Euro-American understandings of sexuality. The book treats the subject matter in chronological order, starting with the "Enlightenment" period and the French Revolution, and going on to chart the beginning of a distinctively homosexual political concerns, re-emergence of the "homophile movement" after the Second World War, followed by the "gay liberation and lesbian feminism". There is a separate part dealing with the politics of AIDS and its significance for lesbian and gay politics. The last part deals with contemporary debates marked by, apart from other things, queer theories, and issues of race and difference. Short introductory notes before each chapter and each document put the readings in a proper perspective. Uninitiated students to the field of lesbian and gay politics may, however, begin with some other book before reading this one.

EDWARDS' work addresses an issue which has come under increased attention in last two decades–the relationship between sexuality (politics of sexuality) and gender (sexual politics), particularly with reference to male homosexuality and masculinity. Combining personal experiences with theoretical insights from gay men's studies as well as the feminist critique of masculinity he reveals interfaces of conflict or consensus on certain issues as they occur historically. He suggests the need to move to "erotic politics", which is a politics of sexuality recognizing racism, sexism, and ageism as a part of sexuality and also recognizing rights of sexual minorities. The ultimate aim of the book remains to produce a perspective that is "neither gay affirmative nor pro–feminist, but gay affirmative *and* pro–feminist".

ABELOVE, BARALE & HALPERIN provide one of the best guides to lesbian and gay studies. Recognizing the contested and unsettled nature of the field, the essays drawn from various disciplines argue in their own different ways the oppositional character of lesbian and gay studies. They reveal how the political and academic pursuit of attempting to understand lesbian and gay experiences is necessarily informed by resistance politics of sexuality. The reader is essential for anyone interested in the history of sexuality, sexual politics, and gender studies.

SEIDMAN's vital contribution lies in linking together of sexual politics with social theory in terms of implication "difference" has on both. The "problem of difference" continues to affect even the postmodernist social theories as well as new identity-based politics. He argues how even the queer theory that emerged to expose the normalizing role of sexual identity politics suffers from difference troubles. Deconstructive stance is combined with a pragmatic approach to questions of knowledge and power. There are different parts dealing with human sciences – especially sociology – recent gay and lesbian studies, especially queer theory, and, political aspects of the debates about knowledge, identity, and social difference, including AIDS as politics of knowledge. Despite containing some concepts that are difficult for beginners to grasp, the strength of the book lies in the attempts at bridging lesbian and gay issues with social theory in general.

BLASIUS' work is an accessible reading on the theme of intermingling and inseparability of homoerotic desires, sexual politics, and ethics. He argues how an individual's act of coming "out" as a gay/lesbian is inherently political. This politics of sexuality challenges the dominant "regimes of truth" and makes possible a new kind of politics based on an ethics that is encompassing without subsuming differences.

Contributors to WILSON's book question the belief that the ending of discrimination against gay/lesbian/bisexual is "a simple matter of justice". The discourse of equality, rights, and justice, which is used by activists, often ignores inherent heterosexist hegemony of these terms. Contributors from different backgrounds explore various dimensions of the problematic and explore possibilities for a new reimagined justice, which they argue is not a simple matter.

Sociology is one of the disciplines that concerns itself with study of human life, and how it looks at lesbian and gay issues is important. NARDI & SCHNEIDER performs this task. The articles range from the earliest research into the underground marginal worlds of gay men to feminist perspectives on lesbian and gay lives, from social constructionist debates on identity to emerging queer theories of transgression and postmodern identities. For those who do not want to go into detail, the introductory section might be helpful in giving a feel of what lies ahead.

DIBYESH ANAND

Gemeinschaft and Gesellschaft

Etzioni, Amitai, *The Spirit of Community: Rights, Responsibilities, and the Communitarian Agenda*, New York: Crown, 1993; London: Fontana, 1995

Heberle, Rudolf, "The Sociological System of Ferdinand Tönnies: 'Community' and 'Society'" in *An Introduction to the History of Sociology*, edited by Harry Elmer Barnes, Chicago: University of Chicago Press, 1948

Kemmis, Daniel, *Community and Politics of Place*, Chicago: University of Chicago Press, 1990

Loomis, Charles P. and Cohn C. McKinney, "Systematic Differences between Latin-American Communities of Family Farms and Large Estates", *American Journal of Sociology*, 61 (1956): 404–12

Lynd, Robert S. and Helen Merrell Lynd, *Middletown: A Study in American Culture*, New York: Harcourt Brace, and London: Constable, 1929

Lyon, Larry, *The Community in Urban Society*, Philadelphia: Temple University Press, 1987

Martindale, Don, *The Nature and Types of Sociological Theory*, Boston: Houghton Mifflin, 1960; London: Routledge and Kegan Paul, 1961

Nisbet, Robert A., *The Quest for Community: A Study in the Ethics and Order of Freedom*, London and New York: Oxford University Press, 1953

Tönnies, Ferdinand, *Community and Association: Gemeinschaft und Gesellschaft*, London: Routledge and Kegan Paul, 1955; as *Community and Society: Gemeinschaft und Gesellschaft*, translated and edited by Charles P. Loomis, East Lansing: Michigan State University Press, 1957 (German edition 1887)

Vidich, Arthur J. and Joseph Bensman, *Small Town in Mass Society: Class, Power and Religion in a Rural Community*, Princeton, New Jersey: Princeton University Press, 1958

TÖNNIES developed the ideas of Gemeinschaft and Gesellschaft (generally translated as "community" and "society") to explain two different types of human relations: those based on "natural will", and those based on "rational will". Tönnies observed a shift from the natural will-based Gemeinschaft type of relationship to the rational will-based Gesellschaft type of relationship that roughly paralleled the growth of capitalism and urbanization. Gemeinschaft relationships emerge naturally in the sense that they are ends in themselves. Individuals enter into Gemeinschaft relationships, which include family, friendship, neighbourhood, and community relationships, because they are inherently fulfilling. Gesellschaft relationships, on the other hand, are means to particular ends. According to Tönnies, "when one is not receiving something in a Gemeinschaft-like relationship, such as from within the family, one must earn or buy it by labor, service, or money which has been earned previously as payment for labor or service" (p.251). Gesellschaft relationships, then, are primarily entered into as rational means of acquiring a need unmet in Gemeinschaft relationships.

Gesellschaft relationships, examples of which include citizen–state, employer–employee, and consumer-producer relationships, can be thought of as exchange relationships that lack the emotional attachment of a Gemeinschaft relationship. Tönnies own accounts of Gemeinschaft and Gesellschaft are quite readable thanks to a translation by Loomis. Part V of *Community and Society*, "The Summing Up", is a good place to begin for an overview, in Tönnies' own words, of the Gemeinschaft /Gesellschaft concepts. For a lengthier and more detailed description of the concepts, see Part I of *Community and Society*.

A good source for a description of Tönnies' Gemeinschaft / Gesellschaft concepts, as well as the rest of his sociological ideas, is HEBERLE's chapter in *An Introduction to the History of Sociology*. In this frequently cited review of Tönnies and the Gemeinschaft/Gesellschaft concepts, Heberle explains how Tönnies linked the Gemeinschaft and Gesellschaft concepts to an account of social norms and values. Heberle also compares Tönnies with Marx, and provides an analysis of the historical context shaping Tönnies' ideas, and a bibliography separated into works by Tönnies, and criticisms and expositions of Tönnies' works.

MARTINDALE's description of the Gemeinschaft and Gesellschaft concepts is also very useful. He employs a table to demonstrate how the emphasis on Gemeinschaft or Gesellschaft varies according to factors such as the dominant type of social relationship; central institutions; the place of the individual in the social order; the characteristic forms of wealth; the type of legal framework; ordering of institutions; and the type of social control. Martindale also provides useful comparisons of Tönnies' concepts with Durkheim's "mechanical" and "organic" forms of solidarity, Maine's status- versus contract-based societies, and Redfield's folk society and secular society.

Although Tönnies' Gemeinschaft / Gesellschaft concepts are a central part of almost every course on sociological theory, only a small number of social scientists have elaborated on the concepts or attempted to investigate them empirically. One use of Tönnies' concepts in empirical work is LOOMIS & McKINNEY's study of the differences in Latin American communities formed around small family farms versus communities formed around large estates. Loomis & McKinney compared two Costa Rican towns in terms of how power is employed in each. In the town comprised of small family farms, it was found that the employment of power was characterized by traits consistent with Gemeinschaft. In the town comprised of large estates, Loomis & McKinney found that the employment of power was more characteristic of Gesellschaft. A summary of their findings can be found in the introduction to the 1957 edition of *Community and Society*.

The application of the Gemeinschaft / Gesellschaft concepts has been most frequent in the field of community research. The concepts are employed regularly by those attempting to suggest that there has been a fundamental change in sense of community resulting from industrialization and modernization. For example, NISBET furthers Tönnies' assertion that modern industrial society is characterized by a breakdown in traditional communities. Nisbet does not identify Tönnies' ideas as instrumental in his own intellectual development, but the influence is apparent when Nisbet writes "capitalism . . . has substituted quantity for quality, process for function, bigness for smallness, impersonality for personality, competitive tensions for the psychological harmonies of co-operation. It has transformed intense communities of purpose into the sprawling relationships of the marketplace" (p.87). Along with capitalism, Nisbet suggests that the centralized state, with its sole claim to legitimate power and authority, is to blame for the increasing individualism that leads to the breakdown of society.

The influence of Tönnies, though not always explicitly acknowledged, can be seen in the flood of community research in the 1950s and 1960s. VIDICH & BENSMAN's study of a small American town concludes that small towns are affected by mass society in economic, political and cultural manners. LYND & LYND's study of Middletown, a small city in the

US Midwest, suggests that external forces lead to changes in some cases, but in other instances are resisted by the community institutions of Middletown.

The intellectual legacy of Tönnies can be seen in the 1980s and 1990s as well. KEMMIS relates his experiences of rural Montana, in the US Northwest, to suggest that increasingly mobile citizens fail to develop a sense of community. Consequently, according to Kemmis, because there is no vested interest in a particular community and the place it inhabits, attachments to fellow citizens do not develop. LYON provides an overview of the study of communities by beginning with the claim that Tönnies' concepts of Gemeinschaft and Gesellschaft serve as the foundation of community theory. He compares Tönnies' use of a continuum with that of other theorists who have described community as existing along a rural–urban continuum. Finally, ETZIONI describes a new movement known as communitarianism, which emphasizes the need to establish shared values and responsibilities among community members, in a society that is increasingly dominated by attention to individual rights and privileges.

The studies by Vidich & Bensman, Lynd & Lynd, Kemmis, Lyon, and Etzioni do not make extensive use of the Gemeinschaft and Gesellschaft concepts. However, each is worth examining as an example of the intellectual legacy left by Tönnies. Although there are some critics who now point to the re-emergence of examples of Gemeinschaft in otherwise Gesellschaft-dominated Western nations, the theoretical developments and vast body of research in the field of community studies suggests that Tönnies' concepts of Geminschaft and Gesellschaft continue to play a significant role in our understanding of the social world.

STEVE ZAVESTOSKI

Gender, constructions of

Belenky, Mary Field, Blythe McVicker Clinchy, Nancy Rule Goldberger and Jill Mattuck Tarule, *Women's Ways of Knowing: The Development of Self, Voice, and Mind*, New York: Basic Books, 1986

Bly, Robert, *Iron John: A Book about Men*, Reading, Massachusetts: Addison Wesley, 1990; Shaftesbury, Dorset: Element, 1991

Chodorow, Nancy, *The Reproduction of Mothering: Psychoanalysis and the Sociology of Gender*, Berkeley: University of California Press, 1978

Clatterbaugh, Kenneth, *Contemporary Perspectives on Masculinity: Men, Women and Politics in Modern Society*, 2nd edition, Boulder, Colorado: Westview Press, 1997

Culbertson, Philip, *New Adam: The Future of Male Spirituality*, Minneapolis: Fortress Press, 1992

Gergen, Mary M. and Sara N. Davis, *Toward a New Psychology of Gender*, New York and London: Routledge, 1997

Gilligan, Carol, *In a Different Voice: Psychological Theory and Women's Development*, Cambridge, Massachusetts: Harvard University Press, 1982

Gilmore, David D., *Manhood in the Making: Cultural Concepts of Masculinity*, New Haven, Connecticut and London: Yale University Press, 1990

Gray, John, *Men Are from Mars, Women Are from Venus: A Practical Guide for Improving Communication and Getting What You Want in Your Relationships*, New York: HarperCollins, 1992; London: Thorsons, 1993

hooks, bell, *Yearning: Race, Gender, and Cultural Politics*, Boston: South End Press, 1990; London: Turnaround, 1991

Ortner, Sherry B., *Making Gender: The Politics and Erotics of Culture*, Boston: Beacon Press, 1996

Tavris, Carol, *The Mismeasure of Woman*, New York: Simon and Schuster, 1992

Walsh, Mary Roth (editor), *Women, Men, and Gender: Ongoing Debates*, New Haven, Connecticut: Yale University Press, 1997

Gender is a controversial topic. Older literature did not use the term "gender" with precision, but today we make a sharp distinction between biological sex (male, female) and gender (masculine, feminine). Previously much of the published work on gender emerged from the women's movement or feminism, and subsequently from the men's movement. Today there is virtually no field of knowledge in which the impact of gender is not being explored, producing an explosion of books and articles.

Approaches to gender may be divided into three basic categories: essentialist, mythopoetic, and constructionist. Essentialist often implies nature ("biology is destiny") whereas constructionist may imply nurture ("the personal is political").

The essentialist position is well illustrated in the popular works of GRAY. He speaks of male instinct and female intuition as though these were part of a genetic code, making gender biological and essentialist rather than conditioned and constructionist. For Gray, biology *is* destiny, and the best that men and women can hope for is to develop a way of communicating crossculturally with each other. Gray's work is very culture bound by an American point of view, and shows complete ignorance of those many cultures throughout the world that sustain three or four genders, rather than just two (see below, Ortner).

The mythopoetic stream within the men's movement is founded on the neo-Jungian conviction that masculinities derive from deep unconscious patterns or archetypes. These patterns are best revealed through a tradition of stories, myths, and rituals. In this sense, the writers of men's mythopoesis are also essentialists. The best-known writer within mythopoetics is the poet BLY, whose *Iron John* became in international best seller. Adapting a fairy tale by the Grimm brothers, Bly argues that masculine identity is available only to men who travel a specific developmental path: bonding with and then separating from mother and again from father, locating a mentor, becoming apprenticed to a "hurricane energy", and marrying the archetypal Holy Woman or Queen. Bly's work has been highly controversial among women and other streams of the men's movement. Among those who have set out to rebut Bly is CULBERTSON, who claims that violence, irresponsibility, and misogyny are endemic to Bly's mythopoesis.

Essentialism and mythopoesis are not the only influences in the contemporary movement among men to find a healthy gender identity. CLATTERBAUGH identifies eight "perspectives" within the men's movement. The moral perspective is essentialist, seeking to protect institutions and practices grounded in traditional society. The profeminist perspective understands masculinity as a set of limitations imposed upon men, often reflecting misogyny and violence against women. The men's rights perspective argues that men are discriminated against in an increasingly profeminist world, particularly in issues of child custody. The mythopoetic perspective has been explained above. The socialist perspective holds the workplace accountable as the primary site of sexism and gender inequality. The gay male perspective challenges the authority of heterosexism, the privileging of the worldview of powerful white heterosexual men. The African-American men's perspective argues that hegemonic masculinities are racist in their construction, ignoring the uniqueness of the Black experience. The evangelical Christian men's movement returns to essentialism, primarily through Promise Keepers, assuring its followers that men are to women as Christ is to the church.

Standing between essentialism and constructionism in men's studies is GILMORE. Manhood is defined as "the approved way of being an adult male in any given society". He explores the way that all masculinities are structured around three basic roles: protector, provider, impregnator. The specific manifestation of these roles, however, is worked out differently from one culture to the next.

It will be noted that the above writers are men. It could be claimed in fact that Gray's and Bly's writings are expressions of "backlash," a term made popular by Susan Faludi (*Backlash: The Undeclared War against American Women*, New York: Crown, 1991). Women writers are much less likely to write from the point of view of essentialism, but rather employ social, historical, or narrative constructionism.

CHODOROW is a social constructionist, arguing that motherhood reproduces itself because women are programmed to see children as replacements for their own loss, and because capitalist society needs new generations of children to perpetuate itself. In this sense, Chodorow builds her argument upon classical Freudian Oedipal theory and Winnicottian object relations theory, both of which she feels explain women's drive to reproduce motherhood better than either biology or role socialization. Yet within the socially constructed expectation of women's mothering are inbuilt tensions that produced overmothered daughters and emotionally shutdown sons. In her epilogue she calls for a deconstruction of this gender asymmetry to yield new forms of equal parenting.

GILLIGAN begins her work with a critical response to Chodorow, but then asks: if the mothering role is so important, why are women not more valued in our societies, and why are we unable to hear their voice? To answer her own question, she critiques Piaget's and Kohlberg's arguments on moral development, and Erikson's schema of developmental tasks. Gilligan points out that these, as well as most other schema in developmental psychology, are based on research samples or clinical experience of males only. As long as this is so, women will be measured as deficient. The gender stereotype of male identity is forged in relation to the world and measured by individuation and separation; female identity is forged in relationships of intimacy with others. Not every developmental "voice" is a voice of justice, rules, and power; there is another voice, common but not exclusive to women, that is the voice of care, contextuality, and relationality. The different voice – the ethic of care – is necessary to bring balance to the ethic of justice, and hence to bring cultures to a mature balance.

Developmental psychologists BELENKY *et al.* argue that Gilligan's "different voice" is systematically buried by methods of education that ignore the ways of knowing that women have cultivated and learned to value. They identify five non-stagelike epistemological perspectives common to women, conceptions of knowledge and truth that are often devalued both at school and in home life. The five are silence (mindless and voiceless), received knowledge (from higher authorities), subjective knowledge (personal, private, and intuitive), procedural knowledge (ways of acquiring and communicating), and constructed knowledge (contextual and narrative, both subjective and objective). Family systems that are built on narrative structures of empowerment and disempowerment, and educational systems that privilege epistemologies devised by men and intended for men, leave women feeling voiceless and "stupid". What is needed are educational methods that help women develop their own authentic voices by emphasizing connection over separation and competition.

TAVRIS represents the ultimate constructionist. She argues that there is nothing essential or universal in the natures of men and women. What women and men do at a moment in time tells us nothing about who women and men are, or what they can be. Most gender research is based on false polarities, including that of Gilligan, who studied what happened when girls played with girls, or boys with boys, but not when girls play with boys. By failing to take context into account, Gilligan fell victim to the same false polarities that plague almost all conversations about gender. Rather, says Tavris, gender discourse must take context seriously, recognizing that what seem to be gender inequalities are really inequitably distributed power. At the heart of all gender discourse lies narrative: our gender identity is a product of the way we each tell our own story and, as such, is always open to reframing.

Gender issues have not been as widely received in other cultures as they have been in Caucasian cultures. African-American women often find middle-class American feminism to be out of touch with their needs, and some have consequently adopted the term "womanist" to cover an approach to gender studies which includes issues of race, poverty, and social disempowerment. Ethnologist HOOKS has written repeatedly of how black men and women are gendered in contemporary media. She speaks of "homeplace" as the locus in which black women's gender identity is forged, but which is also a site of resistance. In general the construction of gender is markedly different in non-White cultures. ORTNER, a feminist anthropologist, draws heavily on the work of French theorists Derrida and Foucault in her exploration of gender issues in 19th-century Hawaii, contemporary Polynesia, and among the Tibetan Sherpas. Ortner argues that gender is a game, not unlike chess, in which people make predictable and unpredictable moves and countermoves. Her work also highlights the identity dislocation when the gender narratives of colonizing cultures are overlaid upon indigenous gender narratives.

There are a number of readers or collections of essays exist in this rapidly expanding field. Both GERGEN & DAVIS and WALSH are good places to begin a more detailed exploration of gender construction.

PHILIP L. CULBERTSON

Gender and social relations

Baden, Sally and Anne Marie Goetz, "Who Needs [Sex] When You Can Have [Gender]? Conflicting Discourses on Gender at Beijing" in *Feminist Visions of Development: Gender Analysis and Policy*, edited by Cecile Jackson and Ruth Pearson, London and New York: Routledge, 1998

Collins, Patricia Hill, *Black Feminist Thought: Knowledge, Consciousness, and the Politics of Empowerment*, Boston: Unwin Hyman, and London: HarperCollins, 1990

Connell, R.W., *Gender and Power: Society, the Person, and Sexual Politics*, Stanford, California: Stanford University Press, and Cambridge: Polity Press, 1987

Ferree, Myra Marx, "Beyond Separate Spheres", *Journal of Marriage and the Family*, 52 (1990): 866–84

Ferree, Myra Marx, Beth B. Hess and Judith Lorber (editors), *Revisioning Gender*, London and Thousand Oaks, California: Sage, 1999

Hess, Beth B. and Myra Marx Ferree (editors), *Analyzing Gender: A Handbook of Social Science Research*, Newbury Park, California, and London: Sage, 1987

Lorber, Judith, *Paradoxes of Gender*, New Haven, Connecticut: Yale University Press, 1994

Nicholson, Linda, "Interpreting Gender", *Signs: Journal of Women in Culture and Society*, 20/1 (1994): 79–105

Scott, Joan, "Gender: A Useful Category of Historical Analysis", *American Historical Review*, 91 (December 1986): 1053–75

West, Candace and Don Zimmerman, "Doing Gender", *Gender and Society* 1/2 (1987): 125–51

Social science academics in this field have debated whether to focus primarily on "women" or on "gender". This debate has encompassed both intellectual and political arguments and raises more complex issues than might at first appear. Those advocating a focus on "women" have argued that a book about gender will inevitably be predominantly about women rather than gender as an analytic category, and that a reluctance to make this explicit is due to a desire to sound academic, that is more respectable, less political and therefore more acceptable within the academy.

BADEN & GOETZ discuss this debate in the context of the Fourth World Conference on Women in Beijing in 1994. The understanding of gender as a social construct has grounded feminist cross-cultural work on women's status in the sense that all women are assumed to share sufficient psychological givens to generate a common range of social constructions. The changeability of these social reactions across culture – the important exceptions – rescues this approach from complete biological essentialism, in stressing the mutability of sex identities. The cost of this approach has been a central dilemma and political schism within feminism, stemming from the underplaying of differences between women, across culture and race in particular, in the interests of maintaining a notion of universality in the crosscultural feminine; a universality, moreover, which disguised its roots in the experiences of white Western women. As northern feminists, Baden & Goetz call for a dialogue with feminist activists and researchers from the south and take on board their perspectives and priorities.

Focusing on the family, FERREE argues for moving away from the emphasis on dichotomies such as public or private, tradition or modern, and towards "recognition of the diverse and contested nature of gender convention both today and in the past". The article provides a critical analysis of the concept of sex roles and elaborates on the gender theory. Gender theory focuses upon how specific behaviours and roles are given gendered meanings, how labour is divided to express gender differences symbolically and how diverse social structures – rather than just families – incorporate gender values and convey gender advantages.

Using several analytical strands, SCOTT argues for the adoption of gender as an analytic category. In the past, she claims, there has been a tendency for gender to be used either descriptively, as a substitute for women, or causally, in the quest for origins of women's subordination. Scott proposes a two-part (interrelated) definition of gender, which she claims must remain analytically distinct. First, gender is a constitutive element of social relationships based on perceived differences between the sexes, for example through the representation of cultural symbols and their interpretation; subjective identities and the construction of gender not just in the kinship system but also in the polity and economy. Second, gender is a primary way of signifying relations of power. This article is significant in its attempt to define gender.

WEST & ZIMMERMAN advocate an approach to understanding gendered relationships they describe as "doing gender":

Doing gender involves a complex of socially guided perceptual interactions and micropolitical activities that cast particular pursuits as expressive of masculine and feminine "natures". [Gender is] an emergent feature of social institutions: both as an outcome of and a rationale for various social arrangements and as a means of legitimating [those arrangements].

The proposition that gender is continuously being constructed and used to further a variety of individual and group goals is central to what they conceptualized as "doing gender", the interactional processes in which individuals claim a gender identity for themselves and convey it to others. To the degree that a society is organized in terms of what it understands as essential differences between men and women, "doing gender" seems unavoidable.

CONNELL outlines a formal social theory of gender focusing mainly on an understanding of how gender relations are organized as a social concern. He proposes that gender relations are historically composed and are an ongoing composition of relationships among the structures of production, power, and sexuality. Connell's model recognizes that gender permeates every social arrangement: the schools, the street, and the government. Theories of gender, with few exceptions, usually focus either on one-to-one relationships between people or on the society as a whole. Particular social institutions like the family and kinship are singled out for analysis, which allows analysis of gender in other institutions to marginalized or not addressed at all. Thus discussions have centred around the family, ignoring the intermediate level of social organization. Connell proposes that this may be the most important

level to understand. Using the conclusions from earlier research, Connell asserts that gender relations are present in all types of institutions, and the "place of gender in social process" cannot be understood by "drawing a line around a set of 'gender institutions'". Connell, however, pays little attention to the impacts of race and class or the experiences of women in the developing world.

LORBER offers a new paradigm of gender – gender as a social institution. Its focus is the analysis of gender as a social structure that has its origins in the development of human culture, not in biology or procreation. Lorber sees gender as "a more general term encompassing all social relations that separate people into differentiated gendered statuses". Gender is not seen as located in individuals but as "an institution that establishes patterns of expectations for individuals, orders the social processes of everyday life, is built into the major social organizations of society, such as the economy, ideology, the family, and politics, and is also an entity in and of itself". The concept of gender as an institution is then used to explain work patterns, family patterns, norms of sexuality, the micropolitics of authority, and symbolic cultural representations.

NICHOLSON points out that understanding of the implications of the gender argument has come unevenly to feminists. She shows that there have been two trends in the way feminists currently think of gender. First, there is the more familiar use of the term to stress the social construct in contrast to the biological given. Second, gender is increasingly used to refer to any social construction having to do with the male/female, as opposed to the masculine/feminine distinction. Nicholson argues that the problem with the first definition is that it is self-contradictory and risks biological essentialism, because biological sex has to be invoked at the very moment that the influence of the biological is being challenged – in other words, "woman" remains a given upon which characteristics are imposed through social reactions to the body. The extreme postmodern unravelling of both "woman" and "women" is disconcerting enough to many feminists, whether academics or activists – it has often been pointed out that it may lead to a nihilistic conception of women. As Nicholson observes, "If those who call themselves feminists cannot even decide upon who women are, how can political demands be enacted in the name of women?"

Explaining that gender is a central way of organizing society, and adopting a structural perspective, HESS & FERREE attempt to provide an overview of feminist perspectives in the social sciences today. In the structural perspective, attention is directed outward from the individual to the social structures that shape experience and meaning, give people a location in the social world, and define and allocate economic and social rewards. The volume traces the experiences of people within a gendered social structure. Nineteen review essays address gender relations in the family, the state, the economy, sexuality, knowledge, law, and militarism. These essays, although primarily North American, would be of use to anyone seeking an introduction to recent work on gender. This volume has been reprinted as FERREE, HESS & LORBER.

COLLINS, a well-researched and comprehensive book, captures the interconnections of race, gender, and social class in black women's lives and examines their impact on black feminist thought. Placing black women's experiences at the centre of the analysis, she includes numerous quotations from a range of African–American women thinkers – blues singers, poets and artists, everyday workers, and political luminaries – and the issues discussed relate to the interdependence of experience and consciousness. Collins, in this book, accomplishes what gender scholars have urgently called for over the last decade – the reconceptualization of race, class, and gender as interlocking systems of oppression.

MANGALA SUBRAMANIAM

See also Patriarchy

Gender ideology

Alexander, M. Jacqui and Chandra Mohanty (editors), *Feminist Genealogies, Colonial Legacies, Democratic Futures*, New York and London: Routledge, 1997

Eickelman, Dale, *The Middle East: An Anthropological Approach*, 2nd edition, Englewood Cliffs, New Jersey: Prentice Hall, 1989

Eisenstein, Sarah, *Give Us Bread but Give Us Roses: Working Women's Consciousness in the United States, 1890 to the First World War*, London: Routledge and Kegan Paul, 1983

Kondo, Dorinne K., *Crafting Selves: Power, Gender, and Discourses of Identity in a Japanese Workplace*, Chicago: University of Chicago Press, 1990

Lancaster, Roger N. and Micaela di Leonardo (editors), *The Gender/Sexuality Reader: Culture, History, Political Economy*, New York and London: Routledge, 1997

Ortner, Sherry B., *Making Gender: The Politics and Erotics of Culture*, Boston: Beacon Press, 1996

Rofel, Lisa, *Other Modernities: Gendered Yearnings in China after Socialism*, Berkeley, California: University of California Press, 1999

Sacks, Karen Brodkin, "Toward a Unified Theory of Class, Race, and Gender", *American Ethnologist*, 16/3 (1989): 534–46

There are several ways to approach the analysis of gender ideology. A classical Marxist approach would envision gender ideology as a form of *false consciousness:* a worldview that is created and maintained by the dominant class, and does not allow people to see beyond it. A second approach continues this discussion of a *dominant gender ideology*, but does not conceptualize people unable to envision an alternative way of life. There may be *critical ideologies* at work within a society, competing with the dominant ideology. A third approach recognizes that a person's identity is influenced not just by the prevalent gender ideologies, but also by other parameters such as race and class. A recent approach shifts the focus from how culture *makes* men and women by means of gender ideologies, to how men and women both manipulate the gender ideology and actually defeat it. Other scholars assert that a person's *multiple selves*, including gendered self definitions, are constructed by the person herself, by others, and by multiple ideologies.

EISENSTEIN's discussion of the consciousness of working women in the US prior to World War I demonstrates the futil-

ity of envisioning ideology (which she calls a dominant value system) as coherent and exclusive, that is, a seamless whole with all of society responding to it in identical ways. Eisenstein explores the development of critical gender (or oppositional) ideologies in response to the dominant gender ideology and the way in which women (and men) respond to and modify these competing ways of envisioning and enacting men's and women's roles. In doing so, she deepens our ability to understand the often slow, incomplete, and intermittent transformation of gender ideologies that takes place while cultures are experiencing the fast pace of modernization and Westernization.

In a chapter on "constructed meanings", EICKELMAN has a very useful discussion of *practical ideologies* and sociocultural change in which he examines ideologies of self, gender, and ethnicity. By practical ideologies, Eickelman refers to those implicit beliefs and notions put into practice by social actors, rather than the formal ideological frameworks promoted by institutions or states. His exploration of ideologies that have a quotidian existence in the Middle East enhances our ability to move beyond envisioning gender *ideology* as a hegemonic construct that is slow to change, to viewing a plethora of gender *ideologies*, both practical and formal, dominant and critical, all vying for space in the actions and beliefs of people.

ORTNER's work involves the linking of practice theory with gender theory, and provides a dynamic model of gender ideologies. In changing the focus from acculturation to empowerment, Ortner's compilation of articles reinserts the intentional subject and the concept of agency into the discussion of gender ideology. Ortner shifts the discussion from "how culture makes women and men" to "how women and men conquer culture". Ortner rejects theorizing gender ideology in a purely constructivist manner, but also rejects any depiction of gender roles and behaviour utilizing a purely volunteerism departure point. Agency and practice provide the link between the cultural construction of gender ideology and the complete free agent approach to gender roles. Her answer to the debate between constructivism and volunteerism is the concept of *gender hegemonies*, rather than gender ideologies. For Ortner, hegemony implies a concept that is related to culture and ideology, yet contains within it *practice* and *agency*. Although each culture may have a multiplicity of gender ideologies, according to Ortner, one set of beliefs about men and women will have a hegemonic presence among the others. In such a situation, the hegemonic gender beliefs inform and mould people's experience and action, but not every facet of life is determined by them.

KONDO's experimental ethnography on Japanese work life also rests on the concept of *multiplicity*, but beyond multiple ideologies, Kondo asserts there exist a *multiplicity of selves* for each person. Rather than speaking of *the self*, Kondo dissects the making and remaking of a plurality of selves. To Kondo, identity (including gender identity) is ever-changing and shifting – influenced by what she calls *culturally available meanings* (ideology) and the everyday *enactment* (or practice) of those meanings. Identity is crafted, selves are crafted, and the crafting takes place in particular contexts. Identities are not fixed and cannot be essentialized – they are relational and contextual. In this way, Kondo envisions gender as something that is performed and enacted; people constitute their gendered identities. At the same time, however, others are also involved in constituting one's gendered identity. Kondo's approach, then, moves us even further from a static, one-dimensional exploration of gender ideology, beyond a recognition of a multiplicity of gender ideologies, to an appreciation of the multiple ways in which gender ideologies are performed, enacted and used to constitute multiple selves.

SACKS examines men's and women's identities in all their complexity and depth, moving beyond a simple analysis of *gender* ideology to a broader discussion of identity formation through the interlocking components of gender, class, and race. In questioning whether race and gender can be reduced to class, as postulated within the Marxist paradigm, Sacks concludes that although race and gender can *not* be reduced to class, neither can a society's gender ideology be properly analysed *separately* from its systems of class and racial divisions. In other words, a person's gender identity is intimately enmeshed with, and understood within, particular economic and racial/ethnic realities.

ROFEL's challenging ethnography envisions gender ideologies as fluid and unstable, and open to negotiation, conflict and change. For Rofel, gender is "compelled through" other aspects of human existence such as class and race, rather than running in parallel to these other ways of differentiating and defining persons. Using the narratives of workers from a silk-weaving factory to discuss the constitution and imagery of *modernity* in China, she dissects the ways in which both the drive for modernity and the content of gender ideologies have been configured differently in different historical periods, leading to the development of very distinct individuals and creating what she calls the "heterogeneity of Chinese women".

ALEXANDER & MOHANTY is a challenging examination of the ways in which postmodernism, liberal feminism, and liberal-pluralist multiculturalism have provided a limited view of gender identity and ideology, in that the theoretical frameworks of women of colour have been largely absent. The articles in this volume examine the way in which gender identity and ideology, and constructions of self, are affected by the processes of globalization and transnationalization. Of particular importance is the development and manipulation of gender identity during the intersection of postcolonialism and transnationalism. The articles demonstrate the way in which gender ideologies, inherited from colonial pasts, are intersecting with the current period of transnationalism.

Using a political economy approach, LANCASTER & DI LEONARDO move beyond one-dimensional considerations of gender ideology, to enlarge the discussion to include sexuality and the body. Highlighting the necessity of including an analysis of the influence of inequality, domination and power, this anthology explores issues of sexual identity and cultural representations of bodies, and their linkages to the construction and manipulation of gender ideologies. Lancaster & Di Leonardo also demonstrate the need for a more profound approach to gender in this postcolonial period of transnationalism.

SUZANNE BAKER

Gender politics, *see* Feminism, politics and Gay and lesbian politics

Gender roles

di Leonardo, Micaela (editor), *Gender at the Crossroads of Knowledge: Feminist Anthropology in the Postmodern Era*, Berkeley: University of California Press, 1991

Herdt, Gilbert (editor), *Third Sex, Third Gender: Beyond Sexual Dimorphism in Culture and History*, New York: Zone, 1994

Lancaster, Roger N., *Life Is Hard: Machismo, Danger, and the Intimacy of Power in Nicaragua*, Berkeley: University of California Press, 1992

Lepowsky, Maria, *Fruit of the Motherland: Gender in an Egalitarian Society*, New York: Columbia University Press, 1993

Mead, Margaret, *Sex and Temperament in Three Primitive Societies*, New York: Morrow, and London: Routledge, 1935

Nanda, Serena, *Neither Man nor Woman: The Hijras of India*, 2nd edition, Belmont, California: Wadsworth, 1990

Rosaldo, Michelle Zimbalist and Louise Lamphere (editors), *Women, Culture, and Society*, Stanford, California: Stanford University Press, 1974

Sanday, Peggy Reeves and Ruth Gallagher Goodenough (editors), *Beyond the Second Sex: New Directions in the Anthropology of Gender*, Philadelphia: University of Pennsylvania Press, 1990

Weiner, Annette, *Women of Value, Men of Renown: New Perspectives in Trobriand Exchange*, Austin: University of Texas Press, 1976

While most social scientists of the late 1800s and early 1900s asserted a biological basis for gender roles (or sex roles, as they were then called), anthropologists since at least the 1960s have used the term *sex* to refer to the biological differences between the males and females of any species, and *gender* to refer to the sociocultural meanings attached to those biological differences (what it is to be a man or a woman). Within this framework, gender is viewed as socially and culturally constructed, and *gender roles* are the tasks and activities that a culture assigns to each sex, based on those perceived differences. Although this framework is still considered useful, contemporary scholars have begun to question, and even refute, the absolute and essentialist dichotomy of two genders based on two biological sexes.

One of the first anthropologists to explore the way in which gender roles are socially and culturally constructed was MEAD. Prior to this, most anthropological research focused very little on gender roles, assuming them to be biologically based and fairly uniform across all cultures. Indeed, if women were mentioned at all in an ethnography, it was in the limited contexts of birth, marriage, and child-rearing. In *Sex and Temperament*, Mead examines the way in which three distinct societies in New Guinea: the Mundugumor, Arapesh, and Tchambuli construct social personalities and gender roles in very different ways, leading her to conclude that gender roles are assigned by society, not by biology.

Despite Mead's early contributions, scant attention was paid to women's activities, and thus to gender roles in general, until the publication of ROSALDO & LAMPHERE's reader on gender and gender roles in 1974. With the women's movement of the 1970s came an increased interest in the way in which gender roles were seen to vary crossculturally and a desire to turn the anthropological lens to women's activities. However, underlying Rosaldo & Lamphere's groundbreaking collection of articles is a universalist view. Contributors to the collection strive to demonstrate that women's subordination is universal across time (throughout history) and space (in all cultures). Gender roles may vary cross-culturally, but the value assigned to women's roles is universally less than that of men's. This view was to have primacy until the mid-1980s.

Not all anthropologists at this time, however, subscribed to the view of women's universal subordination. WEINER, for example, in her study of Trobriand Island society, discusses the vital role women play in the Trobriand's elaborate system of exchange and value, and its impact on the society's configuration of gender roles, practices, and concepts. Weiner's study is a re-examination of the society described by Bronislaw Malinowski in his classic monograph *Argonauts of the Western Pacific* (1922), an ethnography that did little to acknowledge the role of Trobriand women in exchange and systems of value.

In the mid-1980s, the theoretical focus turned from one of universal male dominance in the social and cultural valuation of gender roles, to one in which terms such as *equality*, *inequality*, *dominance*, and *subordination* were called into question, refined, and redefined. The articles in SANDAY & GOODENOUGH, for example, demonstrate the variable ways in which gender roles may be constructed, distributed, and evaluated crossculturally. Several selections provide ethnographic evidence to refute the theory of universal male dominance, while other selections question anthropology's interpretation of ethnographic "facts" in a way that denies the existence of female authority, influence, prestige, and power.

LEPOWSKY's ethnography of the people of Vanatinai provides a compelling argument against women's universal subordination. Controversial when first published in 1993, it describes a society in which the roles of men and women are equally valued, and many roles are shared. Lepowsky convincingly demonstrates the equality men and women enjoy in horticultural, gathering, ceremonial, magical, exchange, political, sexual, and burial activities in this New Guinea island society.

Recent research on gender roles has focused on how this discussion has been framed entirely within Western models of gender. Highlighting the need to include history, class, ethnicity, and race in examining women and men crossculturally, anthropologists such as DI LEONARDO formulate a postmodernist approach to examine gender and gender roles. Underlying her text is the question, "*whose* gender roles are we examining?" In order to understand the diversity of gender roles fully both *among* societies and *within* societies, Di Leonardo recognizes that one must also take into account the significance of race, ethnicity, class, and political economy.

LANCASTER's work on the intersection of power, political economy, war, ideology, and gender in revolutionary Nicaragua is another example of a postmodernist approach to gender roles. By giving voice to his informants, Lancaster allows them to demonstrate to us the complexity of gender relations, particularly at a time in which all of society's blueprints for behaviour and belief are in flux. By relating gender roles to a myriad of sociocultural, political, and economic factors, Lancaster's

work provides a rich and multilayered assessment of gender roles in Nicaragua in the 1980s.

HERDT and others take this question of "*whose* gender roles?" even further by questioning the binary oppositions assumed to exist between male and female, and man and woman, as culture-bound perspectives obscuring the deeper complexity that exists in biological and sociocultural constructions of sex, sexuality, and gender. Herdt and his contributors argue that previous discussions of gender identity and gender roles – while firmly based in a social constructionist framework – have strongly assumed that there are only *two* types of gender identity in which to be socialized, and only *two* sets of gender roles to learn. The research presented in this volume, however, demonstrates the crosscultural existence of a wider range of possibilities: third sexes and third genders. These individuals, whether hermaphrodite, eunuch, *hijra*, or two spirit, are not simply "exceptions to the norm" nor examples of people "born in the wrong body", but people embodying a gender identity and enacting gender roles that are *neither* male *nor* female.

NANDA's in-depth account of *hijras* is a compelling ethnography that clearly demonstrates the inadequacy of models that limit both gender and sex to two opposing entities. One of several recent texts on *third genders* or the *intersexed*, Nanda provides a rich account of the lives of ritually emasculated men (eunuchs) and hermaphrodites who dress and act as women in India, and places her discussion firmly within the larger framework of the cross-cultural examination of alternative gender roles.

SUZANNE BAKER

Gender schema

Bem, Sandra Lipsitz, "Gender Schema Theory: A Cognitive Account of Sex-Typing", *Psychological Review*, 88/4 (1981): 354–64

Bem, Sandra Lipsitz, "Gender Schema Theory and Its Implications for Child Development: Raising Gender-Aschematic Children in a Gender-Schematic Society" in *The Psychology of Women: Ongoing Debates*, edited by Mary Roth Walsh, New Haven, Connecticut: Yale University Press, 1987

Deaux, Kay, Mary Kite and Laurie Lewis, "Clustering and Gender Schemata: An Uncertain Link", *Personality and Social Psychology Bulletin*, 11/4 (1987): 387–97

Deaux, Kay and Brenda Major, "Putting Gender into Context: An Interactive Model of Gender-Related Behavior", *Psychological Review*, 94/3 (1987): 369–89

Fagot, Beverly and Mary Leinbach, "Gender-Role Development in Young Children: From Discrimination to Labeling", *Developmental Review*, 13/2 (1993): 205–24

Freedman, Susan and Hilary Lips, "A Response Latency Investigation of the Gender Schema", *Journal of Social Behavior and Personality*, 11/5 (1996): 41–53

Hudak, Mary, "Gender Schema Theory Revisited: Men's Stereotypes of American Women", *Sex Roles*, 28/5–6 (1993): 279–93

Larsen, Randy and Edward Seidman, "Gender Schema Theory and Sex Role Inventories: Some Conceptual and

Psychometric Considerations", *Journal of Personality and Social Psychology*, 50/1 (1986): 205–11

Levy, Gary and Robyn Fivush, "Scripts and Gender: A New Approach for Examining Gender-Role Development", *Developmental Review*, 13/2 (1993): 126–46

Schmitt, Bernd and Robert Millard, "Construct Validity of the Bem Sex Role Inventory (BSRI): Does the BSRI Distinguish Between Gender-Schematic and Gender-Aschematic Individuals?", *Sex Roles*, 19/9–10 (1989): 581–88

Spence, Janet, "Do the BSRI and PAQ Measure the Same or Different Concepts?", *Psychology of Women Quarterly*, 15/1 (1991): 141–65

The original author of gender schema theory is Sandra Bem, and probably the most frequently cited of her works is her publication on gender schema theory and sex typing (BEM 1981). Bem's article thoroughly describes the concept of gender schema and gender-based schematic processing, and contains three studies supporting her notion that sex-typed individuals' self- and social perceptions are organized in terms of gender schema. One study supports a relationship between sex typing (versus androgyny and undifferentiation) and the clustering of gender-related words during free recall. A response-latency study demonstrates that sex-typed individuals make gender schema-consistent judgements about themselves faster than do androgynous and undifferentiated individuals. The tendency to possess and use gender schema, Bem offers, arises from a pernicious social insistence to evaluate and promote appropriate behaviour in a manner that accentuates a difference in the attributes of men and women. This article is valuable not only because it contains one of Bem's best articulated descriptions of gender schema theory, but also because it includes a nice discussion on the philosophical and political implications of society's subtle creation and reinforcement of gender schema, beginning with childhood.

Bem's 1981 *Psychological Review* piece has stimulated a good deal of empirical research and conceptual elaboration on her work; included here is additional work in the area of child development, emphasizing children's conceptions of gender roles. A special issue of *Developmental Review*, titled "Early Gender-Role Development", provides excellent examples of research in this area, with several articles investigating and/or incorporating the concept of gender schema. Particularly good articles from this issue include FAGOT & LEINBACH, with an examination of very young children's gender-related categorical discrimination. These authors argue that gender schema may develop as early as one year of age. LEVY & FIVUSH combine the concept of gender schema with the concept of gender scripts and report an investigation demonstrating that children have better organized knowledge of scripts associated with their own sex than they do for the other. Although her empirical studies primarily investigate sex-typing and gender-schematicity among adults and college students, BEM (1987) has also published work relating gender schema theory to child development, the best of which is probably her chapter in *The Psychology of Women: Ongoing Debates*.

In addition to inspiring work in the area of child development, gender schema theory has been incorporated into theories explaining sex differences in behaviour. A prominent example of this is DEAUX & MAJOR's interactive model of gender-related behaviour. According to the authors, gender-related behaviour during interaction is a product of the actor's and/or the perceiver's expectations for gender-related behaviour and features of the situation, some of which may make salient gender characteristics of the interactants. Expectations for gender-related behaviour arise with the activation of interactant's gender schema, which may occur if gender schema are chronically high in the perceiver's schema hierarchy, if gender schema have been primed by thoughts or events immediately preceding the interaction, if sex attributes of the actor are immediately observable, if gender is a central component of the self-concept, if the perceiver's behaviour makes gender salient, and/or if the situation makes gender-related activities salient. Deaux & Major's interactive model is comprehensive in that it not only incorporates the concept of gender schema, but it also includes other theoretical concepts pertaining to gender differences, and it is much lauded by scholars investigating gender differences in behaviour.

Some scholars have conducted work to empirically test, extend, and/or modify premises of gender schema theory. Examples of this type of research include a study by DEAUX, KITE & LEWIS, replicating Bem's 1981 recall study investigating the relationship between sex typing and the clustering of gender-related words. Although participants in the study demonstrated comparable levels of clustering, this study failed to replicate Bem's results: there was no relationship between masculinity and femininity and clustering of gender-related words. HUDAK's examination of masculine, androgynous, or undifferentiated men's stereotypes of American women, in contrast, is more supportive of gender schema theory. Masculine and gender-schematic men in this study tended to stereotype women as high in femininity and low in masculinity, while androgynous men were more likely to see women as having androgynous characteristics. FREEDMAN & LIPS propose a modification to Bem's initially proposed relationship between sex typing and the tendency to use gender schema. Results of their response latency study, indicating that gender-schematic processing does not occur exclusively in women sex-typed as either feminine or masculine, suggest that gender-related schematic processing is not a sufficient condition for sex typing; sex-typed individuals must not only organize information according to gender but also value gender stereotypes.

A number of articles and studies debate methodological issues surrounding, primarily, the use of the Bem Sex-Role Inventory (BSRI) as a measure of gender-schematicity. An outstanding example of these works is SPENCE's comparison of the BSRI and the Personal Attributes Questionnaire (PAQ), an attempt to examine the construct validity of the BSRI. Spence finds that the scales, including the male and female subscales, are similar, and that both are measures of instrumental and expressive characteristics. Both measures, however, have a very low to nonsignificant relationship with sex-role attitudes, suggesting that both the BSRI and PAQ are not good indicators of gender schematicity. Spence adds that very few studies of gender-schematic processing using the BSRI have produced replicable results. In contrast, SCHMITT & MILLARD's test of the BSRI's construct validity is more favourable than is Spence's. These authors' purpose in investigating the measure was to determine if it adequately distinguished gender-schematics from gender-aschematics. Both schematic items (masculine and feminine) and "neutral" items (androgynous, undifferentiated) were factor analysed and the factors of each suggest that schematicity and aschematicity are substantially different, as measured by the BSRI. Gender-schematic factors tended to be bipolar in nature, while aschematic factors were unipolar.

LARSEN & SEIDMAN's comparison of the BSRI with the Personality Research Form, ANDRO, also tends to favour the construct validity of the BSRI, finding that both the BSRI and the PFR ANDRO are adequate measure of gender schematicity. Like Schmitt & Millard, the authors found that gender-schematic items tended to produce bipolar factors.

A. ELIZABETH LINDSEY

See also Gender roles

General Agreement on Tariffs and Trade (GATT) and World Trade Organisation (WTO)

Croome, John, *Reshaping the World Trading System: A History of the Uruguay Round*, Geneva: World Trade Organisation, 1995

Dam, Kenneth W., *The GATT: The Law and International Economic Organization*, Chicago: University of Chicago Press, 1970

Evans, John W., *The Kennedy Round in American Trade Policy: The Twilight of the GATT?*, Cambridge, Massachusetts: Harvard University Press, 1971

Hoekman, Bernard M. and Michael M. Kostecki, *The Political Economy of the World Trading System: From GATT to WTO*, Oxford and New York: Oxford University Press, 1995

Hudec, Robert E., *The GATT Legal System and World Trade Diplomacy*, New York: Praeger, 1975; 2nd edition, London: Butterworths, 1990

Jackson, John H., "Managing the Trading System: The World Trade Organisation and the Post-Uruguay Round GATT Agenda" in *Managing the World Economy: Fifty Years after Bretton Woods*, edited by Peter B. Kenen, Washington, DC: Institute for International Economics, 1994

Jackson, John H., *The World Trading System: Law and Policy of International Economic Relations*, 2nd edition, Cambridge, Massachusetts: MIT Press, 1997

Krueger, Anne O. (editor), *The WTO as an International Organisation*, Chicago: University of Chicago Press, 1998

Trebilcock, Michael J. and Robert Howse, *The Regulation of International Trade*, London and New York: Routledge, 1995

WTO Secretariat, *Guide to the Uruguay Round Agreements*, Boston: Kluwer, 1999

The International Monetary Fund (IMF) and the World Bank, the sister institutions responsible for managing post World War II international financial affairs, were conceived during the 1944 Bretton Woods summit, but wartime plans for an International Trade Organization (ITO) foundered when the US Congress failed to approve the Havana Agreement. The General Agreement on Tariffs and Trade (GATT) then became the focus for trade negotiations. As a loosely knit organization, effectively an agreement between contracting parties, GATT worked through a series of negotiating rounds, in which member countries agreed to tariff reductions. The movement towards freer trade was given substance in the eight GATT negotiating rounds held since World War II.

TREBILCOCK & HOWSE focus on the role of rules and institutions in regulating world trade in the post-1945 era. *The Regulation of International Trade* is notable for its effective integration of trade theory and trade policy and for its clearly written, policy-oriented chapters, especially Chapter 3 "Trade exchange rates, and the balance of payments", and Chapter 4, "Tariffs, The MFN Principle, and Regional Trading Blocs". Trebilcock & Howse examine the functioning of international trade agreements and trade blocs, and examine barriers to trade including antidumping laws, subsidies, countervailing duties, and government procurement practices. In later chapters, the authors examine issues relating to trade in agricultural products, trade in services, and trade in investment. The concluding chapter raises questions concerning the future of the global trading system. A useful guide to the issues for students of economics, international relations, and law, and a book that is accessible to that mythical beast the "intelligent layman".

HOEKMAN & KOSTECKI have also written a comprehensive and non-technical introduction to the world trading system. Although the subtitle of their book "from GATT to WTO" is misleading, in so far as it suggests that the book contains an extended chronological account of the GATT and WTO (the "historical overview" is limited to a single chapter), the authors' coverage of the WTO, including the agreements relating to trade in services and intellectual property, is excellent. This is a valuable study of the economics and politics of the world trading system as well as of the WTO, the primary organization through which member states manage their trade relations. Those wanting to understand the evolution and nature of GATT should look to DAM or HUDEC rather than Hoekman & Kostecki.

Written in 1968 and published in 1970, Dam's study of GATT has become a standard reference to GATT rules and procedures. This is the source to consult if you wish to understand what is meant by the "most-favoured-nation" principle, technical aspects of the GATT tariff system, the ramifications of Article XXIV (regional economic arrangements), or the GATT rules relating to antidumping or countervailing duties. Dam's book is more than a simple handbook, for it contains excellent chapters relating GATT to broader trade and development problems. It is essential reading for any student of GATT.

The first edition of Hudec's study was published in 1975 when the GATT was under severe criticism, especially in the USA. The book is written from a legal rather than an economic perspective. The author argues that the distinctive character of the GATT legal system can only be understood by looking at the organization in historical context and that GATT "law" has evolved as a result of a unique blend of legal and diplomatic strategies. Hudec asserts that, contrary to appearances,

GATT's early success was a fragile creation, based on particularly favourable circumstances that allowed GATT to use its limited armoury of legal and diplomatic tools to the maximum effect. The author attributes the perceived failings of GATT in the 1970s to the emergence of a new, and much less GATT-friendly international environment.

The international institutions created during and after World War II helped create the trade expansion and income growth of the 1950–71 period, but problems (actual or potential) developed in both international finance and international trade. On the trade side, problems arose as a result of: the dissatisfaction of developing countries with the GATT system; the failure to include agriculture and textiles in successive GATT rounds; as well as a revival of protectionism in the 1970s and 1980s. EVANS focuses on the campaign launched by the incoming administration of John F. Kennedy which culminated in the passage of the Trade Expansion Act of 1962, giving the President unprecedented authority to reduce tariffs, as well as the subsequent and much vaunted Kennedy round (1962–67) of GATT negotiations. The author concludes that, despite much backsliding, the Kennedy round made modest progress in introducing multilateralism into tariff negotiations. The problem was that, measured against expectations, the results appear modest.

As CROOME notes, the most recent GATT negotiating round, the Uruguay Round, was held in a difficult international environment, taking almost eight years (1986–93) to conclude. Negotiations broke down on several occasions, the inclusion of agriculture, textiles and trade-related investment measures (TRIMS) proving highly contentious, and success proved elusive until the midnight hour. Many of the problems encountered during the Uruguay Round stemmed from an ambitious agenda, which sought to extend GATT disciplines to areas such as trade in agricultural products, trade in services, and intellectual property. Croome's study is rather dry, but it chronicles the progress (or lack of progress) of the Uruguay round effectively. It is a useful reference.

Given the sheer volume of the Uruguay Round's agreements and decisions (the joint undertakings and decisions alone add up to well over 500 pages of printed text, with the individual undertakings, or schedules, bringing the page count up to no less than 30,000) the WTO SECRETARIAT have performed a valuable public service in producing their *Guide to the Uruguay Round Agreements*. This is a volume to consult as and when necessary: it is most definitely not bedtime reading.

Several valuable studies of the evolution and nature of the WTO are available, including those by JACKSON and by KRUEGER. The first edition of Jackson's *The World Trading System* was published in 1989, prior to the conclusion of the Uruguay Round. The second edition, published in 1997, has been substantially rewritten to reflect the successful conclusion of the Round and the creation of the WTO. Jackson has published extensively in this area and is one of the foremost authorities on the international trading system. His concern is, above all, with the legal rules and constraints that shape both institutions and trade policy. His writing highlights the tension between a "rules-based" trade system, designed to bring predictability and stability into trade relations, and the tendency of sovereign governments to move to a "results-based" system when making exceptions to "solve" short-run problems.

The useful volume edited by Krueger contains papers given to a 1996 Conference on the WTO. The papers are of particular value to the economist specializing in international trade, but they will appeal also to political scientists and policy makers and they are written in a manner that makes them accessible to the noneconomist. The first part of the volume focuses on the institutional capabilities of the WTO, including the capacity to fulfil its mandate (Blackhurst) and the relationship between the WTO and the IMF/World Bank (Vines). Krueger's second section deals with substantive issues and challenges, including Sampson's chapter on the role of the WTO in promoting greater coherence in global policy making, Snape's brief but insightful remarks on the extension of the GATT disciplines to trade in services, and Baldwin's examination of the anti-dumping and countervailing-duty rules of the GATT/WTO. The two papers in the third section focus on the WTO's relationship to economies in transition (Pietras) and developing countries (Finger & Winters). This is a valuable collection that should be on the bookshelf of anyone with an interest in the area.

KEITH TRACE

See also International Monetary Fund, World Trade Organisation

General equilibrium theory

Debreu, Gerard, "Existence of Competitive Equilibrium" in *Handbook of Mathematical Economics*, vol. 2, edited by Kenneth J. Arrow and Michael D. Intriligator, Amsterdam: North Holland, and New York: Elsevier, 1982

Ellickson, Bryan, *Competitive Equilibrium: Theory and Applications*, Cambridge and New York: Cambridge University Press, 1993

Grandmont, Jean-Michel (editor), *Temporary Equilibrium: Selected Readings*, Boston: Academic Press, 1988

Hahn, Frank, "Stability" in *Handbook of Mathematical Economics*, vol. 2, edited by Kenneth J. Arrow and Michael D. Intriligator, Amsterdam: North Holland, and New York: Elsevier, 1982

Hildenbrand, Werner, "Core of an Economy" in *Handbook of Mathematical Economics*, vol. 2, edited by Kenneth J. Arrow and Michael D. Intriligator, Amsterdam: North Holland, and New York: Elsevier, 1982

Kehoe, Timothy J., "Computation and Multiplicity of Equilibria" in *Handbook of Mathematical Economics*, vol. 4, edited by Werner Hildenbrand and Hugo Sonnenschein, Amsterdam: North Holland, 1991

Mas-Collel, Andreu, *The Theory of General Economic Equilibrium: A Differentiable Approach*, Cambridge and New York: Cambridge University Press, 1985

Scarf, Herbert, "The Computation of Equilibrium Prices: An Exposition" in *Handbook of Mathematical Economics*, vol. 2, edited by Kenneth J. Arrow and Michael D. Intriligator, Amsterdam: North Holland, and New York: Elsevier, 1982

Shoven, John B. and John Whalley, *Applying General Equilibrium*, Cambridge and New York: Cambridge University Press, 1992

Unlike partial equilibrium theory which concentrates on one market at a time, general equilibrium theory looks at the entire economy as a whole with individual components such as consumers, producers, markets, government interacting with each other giving rise to the fundamental notion of interdependence where "everything depends on everything else." The subject is quite technically demanding and highly mathematical. ELLICKSON provides a good rigorous textbook treatment at the first-year graduate level.

One key issue of the theory is to ascertain the existence of an equilibrium price vector such that consumers, producers, and markets are all in equilibrium at the same time in a perfectly competitive economy. This question was one of the key developments of mathematical economics during the postwar period. Early mathematical proofs were usually based on a fixed-point theorem by Brouwer or Kakutani and more modern approaches were developed in the last few decades. DEBREU summarizes the vast literature of existence proofs including many of his path-breaking works.

An existence proof only assures the existence of an equilibrium price vector that is consistent with equilibrium states of all individual components of the economy. It does not, however, address the dynamic issue of stability of whether a small perturbation of prices can move the economy away from its original equilibrium position or not. The traditional law of demand and supply is an example of the so-called Walrasian "tâtonnement" (groping) process of price adjustment where prices increase in case of shortages and decrease in case of surpluses. HAHN reviews various conditions required of market excess demand functions in order to ensure the dynamic stability of equilibrium in the economy.

The concept of the "core" of an economy refers to optimal allocations which no group of agents can further improve upon, i.e. by making their own members better off, regardless of actions of the remaining agents. Recent developments in general equilibrium theory have been devoted to the inter-relationship between these two concepts of equilibrium and core. For an economy with a finite number of agents, the core is a bigger set than the set of competitive equilibria. However, if we make a sequence of "replica economies" where the number of agents grows larger and larger towards infinity then each individual agent becomes more and more negligible, and the discrepancy between the core and the set of competitive equilibria becomes increasingly small. In other words, the core is shrinking in the limit until it coincides with the set of competitive equilibria. The proof of this core convergence result requires the advanced mathematical tool of measure theory. Details can be found in HILDENBRAND.

The concept of a "regular economy" refers to an economy having a finite number of equilibria, each of which corresponds smoothly to small parametric price changes. This idea of regularity is particularly relevant to various dynamic issues of general equilibrium theory such as local uniqueness of equilibria, continuity of equilibrium price correspondence, the traditional technique of comparative static analysis, and core allocations in a large economy. Developments in the area of regular economies also lead to a revival of calculus methods in general equilibrium theory using advanced techniques of differentiable topology. Details can be found in MAS-COLLEL.

Temporary general equilibrium theory extends the traditional general equilibrium framework of a static competitive economy with additional features such as quantity rationing, self-fulfilling expectations, and money. By allowing "disequilibrium" phenomena such as Keynesian unemployment in the model, temporary general equilibrium theory can provide a theoretical bridge between the price-centered paradigm of Walrasian general equilibrium theory and the quantity-centered paradigm of modern Keynesian macroeconomics. GRAND-MONT provides an extended survey of the fast growing literature on the subject as well as a nice collection of key papers on the subject.

So far, the literature of general equilibrium theory is highly theoretical with mathematical theorems and proofs. SCARF provides the first algorithm to actually calculate the equilibrium price vector. Subsequent authors refine Scarf's seminal work in various directions including multiplicity and index number of equilibria (see KEHOE). This burgeoning area of research has grown into a specialized subfield often known as Computable General Equilibrium (CGE) or Applied General Equilibrium (AGE) with various applications in public policy, trade, taxation, development, and environment. SHOVEN & WHALLEY provide an excellent survey of this applied area of general equilibrium theory.

TRIEN T. NGUYEN

General will

Barry, Brian, "The Public Interest" in *Proceedings of the Aristotelian Society*, supplementary vol. 38 (1964): 1–18

Bosanquet, Bernard, *The Philosophical Theory of the State*, 4th edition, London and New York: Macmillan, 1951 (1st edition 1899)

Dent, N.J.H., *Rousseau: An Introduction to His Psychological, Social, and Political Theory*, Oxford and New York: Blackwell, 1988

Held, Virginia, *The Public Interest and Individual Interests*, New York and London: Basic Books, 1970

Jones, W.T., "Rousseau's General Will and the Problem of Consent", *Journal of the History of Philosophy*, 25/1 (1987): 105–30

Masters, Roger D., *The Political Philosophy of Rousseau*, Princeton, New Jersey: Princeton University Press, 1968

Riley, Patrick, *The General Will before Rousseau: The Transformation of the Divine into the Civic*, Princeton, New Jersey: Princeton University Press, 1986

Runciman, W.G. and A.K. Sen, "Games, Justice and the General Will", *Mind*, 74 (1965): 554–62

Shklar, Judith N., General Will entry in *Dictionary of the History of Ideas: Studies of Selected Pivotal Ideas*, edited by Philip P. Wiener, New York: Scribner, 1973–74: vol. 2

Talmon, J.L., *The Origins of Totalitarian Democracy*, London: Secker and Warburg, 1952; New York: Praeger, 1960

Trachtenberg, Zev M., *Making Citizens: Rousseau's Political Theory of Culture*, London and New York: Routledge, 1993

Although he was hardly the first to employ it, the concept of the general will is inextricably linked to Jean-Jacques Rousseau. In *Du Contrat Social* (*The Social Contract*, 1762) Rousseau draws a fundamental distinction between *man* and *citizen*. That is, we may think of every person as a unique individual with a particular set of interests *and* as a member of the public who shares a common interest in the welfare of the body politic. As a *man*, everyone has a *private will* that aims at his particular good or personal interests; as a *citizen*, everyone has a *general will* that aims at the common good or public interest. This general will, Rousseau insists, is different from "the will of all"; it is always right; it is to be found on the side of the majority when votes are cast (presuming that "the characteristics of the general will are still in the majority"); and those who refuse to follow it must be "forced to be free".

Rousseau's enigmatic account of the general will has provoked a remarkable range of reactions. As SHKLAR's useful survey indicates, philosophers such as G.W.F. Hegel, T.H. Green, and Bernard Bosanquet followed Immanuel Kant in regarding the general will as a "higher will" that is somehow more real than the actual wills of individual men and women. On BOSANQUET's interpretation, the "indestructible impulse towards the Good, which is necessarily a common good, the substantial unity and filling of life by the interests through which man is human, is what Rousseau plainly has before him in his account of the General Will" (p.103). The general will is thus a "Real Will", according to Bosanquet, and this Real Will is the foundation and justification of all "State" action.

Such "metaphysical" readings of Rousseau, however, seem to have given many of Rousseau's 20th-century critics additional reason to dismiss the general will as either vacuous or incoherent nonsense. Other critics have deemed it downright dangerous. TALMON, writing shortly after World War II, combined both views when he charged Rousseau with "dangerous ambiguity" (p.40). The general will is ambiguous because it points toward both democracy, in its attention to the will of the people, and totalitarianism, for it "gives those who claim to know and to represent the real and ultimate will of the nation . . . a blank cheque to act on behalf of the people, without reference to the people's actual will" (p.48). Rousseau's ambiguity thus contributes to the danger of "totalitarian democracy".

More sympathetic readings have predominated in recent years as scholars have looked for ways to make sense of Rousseau's discussion of the general will. One way to do this is to try to recapture Rousseau's intentions by examining his use of the term in light of its use by his predecessors and contemporaries. Thus MASTERS (pp.323–34) and Shklar explain what the term meant for such thinkers as Montesquieu, Diderot, and Pufendorf in order to establish the problems Rousseau was addressing and to highlight the distinctiveness of his conception of the general will. RILEY takes this approach further and deeper by tracing the concept to a theological debate in the 17th century that centred on the question, does God "have a *general will* that produces universal salvation? And if he does not, why does he will *particularly* that some men not be saved?" (pp.4–5). By way of Pascal, Malebranche, and others, these questions entered social and political thought in the form of an opposition between the general, or the impartial, and the particular, or the selfish.

Understanding how this opposition developed and how it informed Rousseau's thinking thus enables us to see how Rousseau could be both an advocate of the general will and a champion of individuality: "Generality rules out *particularism*, not individualism; in Rousseau, an individual can and should have a general will" (p.249).

Other scholars have turned to philosophical analysis rather than history to make sense of the general will. The two approaches are not mutually exclusive, as Masters demonstrates, but the commentators who take the analytical path typically prefer a close scrutiny of Rousseau's texts to the investigation of the context in which he wrote. For these commentators, the task is to show how those aspects of the general will that seem paradoxical, contradictory, or nonsensical are really insightful and coherent, if not necessarily complete or persuasive. DENT, for instance, provides an analysis of Rousseau's claim that the general will "must 'both come from all and apply to all'" (p.175) that meticulously sets out the relationship between individual volition and the public interest in Rousseau's compressed argument.

This philosophical analysis of the general will often has proceeded by way of concepts drawn from economics and game theory. Thus BARRY draws on Condorcet's jury theorem to defend Rousseau's insistence that majority-rule voting is, in the right circumstances, the best way to declare or express the general will. In similar fashion RUNCIMAN & SEN explain the general will in terms of game theory's "prisoners' dilemma", in which individuals would do better, individually as well as collectively, to pursue their common interest than their self-interests. The Pareto principle, which holds that a policy is in the common interest if it makes some member of a group better off without worsening the condition of any other member, provides the basis for a rival explanation in HELD.

JONES also believes that Rousseau's general will is similar to the Pareto principle, but he argues, with particular reference to Runciman & Sen, that "such readings of *The Social Contract* go astray if they also read Rousseau as a rational-choice theorist" (p.118). His essay includes a brief response to "metaphysical" or "Hegelian" readings of Rousseau and a helpful explication of the five procedures Rousseau relies on "to permit the general will of the assembly to emerge" (pp.110–12).

Despite their differences, commentators sympathetic to Rousseau typically agree that the general will is not simply the sum of individual wills. If it were, why would Rousseau distinguish "citizen" from "man" and "the general will" from "the will of all"? According to TRACHTENBERG, however, the general will *is* the aggregation of individual wills: "the 'ingredients' of the general will . . . are the individual members of society's conceptions of their own welfare" (p.9). His defence of this claim may not be persuasive, but it is subtle, sophisticated, and an original contribution to the continuing effort to make sense of the general will.

RICHARD DAGGER

See also Jean-Jacques Rousseau

Generalizability theory

Brennan, Robert L., *Elements of Generalizability Theory*, Iowa City: American College Testing Program, 1983

Cronbach, Lee J., Goldine C. Gleser, Harinder Nanda and Nageswari Rajaratnam, *The Dependability of Behavioral Measurements: Theory of Generalizability for Scores and Profiles*, New York and London: Wiley, 1972

Shavelson, Richard J. and Noreen M. Webb, "Generalizability Theory: 1973–1980", *British Journal of Mathematical and Statistical Psychology*, 34 (November 1981): 133–66

Shavelson, Richard J. and Noreen M. Webb, *Generalizability Theory: A Primer*, Newbury Park, California and London: Sage, 1991

CRONBACH *et al.* presented the first substantial account of how the traditional psychometric concepts of reliability and validity, derived within the context of statistical correlation, could be subsumed within a single framework based on univariate and multivariate analyses of variance. Their book concerns both conceptual and statistical matters. Conceptually, the notion that variability in test scores might be broken down according to its various sources (known as *facets* in generalizability theory, a term directly paralleling the term *factors* in the analysis of variance) provided a means of subsuming reliability and validity under a single notion of *generalizability*. The basic argument runs roughly as follows: reliability is typically considered in terms of the extent to which a test result obtained under one set of conditions (for example, one form of a test, or at a specific time) might be closely approximated by a result obtained when these conditions change (for example, by using a different form of a test, or testing at a later point in time). Looked at another way, the measure could be seen to have reliability to the extent that the scores could be generalized across these facets, a procedure that would be admissible if the facets did not constitute a major source of variance. A similar argument applies with validity – typically seen as a reflection of the extent to which a test result measures that dimension in which the investigator is interested, it could be assessed by methods such as discerning how well the test distinguished between different groups (for example, individuals with and without some form of disorder). From the viewpoint of generalizability theory, this reduces to noting that a successful test would be one in which it would not be possible to generalize the results from one group to the other – that is to say, where this particular facet (having or not having the disorder) constituted a major source of variance in the data, generalizability theory reduced the two classical notions of reliability and validity to a single one of generalizability.

The book outlines not only the ways in which an approach based on (especially multivariate) analyses of variance might be advantageous, but also provides a detailed statistical account of both the development and the application of the theory. In addition, some of the problems and limitations are outlined, especially as regards such statistical anomalies as negative estimates of variance, which might arise in some circumstances. The statistical content, however, requires a reasonable degree of sophistication on the part of the reader, probably making this section of the book inappropriate for most undergraduate, and indeed many graduate students.

SHAVELSON & WEBB's review article is usefully read in conjunction with the Cronbach *et al.* book. It gives a (necessarily brief) outline of the theory, cites a number of references where examples of the use of generalizability theory can be found, and considers a number of theoretical developments that followed the original publication of the theory (including the problem of negative variance estimates, and the possibility of Bayesian approaches to variance estimation). Although the paper as a whole demands a fair degree of mathematical and statistical sophistication on the part of the reader, useful elements can still be understood by those of relatively modest ability who are willing to consider the more accessible sections of the paper in isolation.

A much simpler, although inevitably less deep, introduction to the theory is given in the book by SHAVELSON & WEBB (1991). Restricting themselves to the univariate case, they provide an excellent account of the reasoning behind generalizability theory. The statistical content is accessible to any reader with a good grasp of the principles of the analysis of variance, and indeed it is likely that those whose understanding is at times uncertain would not only be able to follow the text but might even find that it enhances their comprehension both of generalizability theory and of the analysis of variance itself. As always, however, there is something of a price to pay for the increased accessibility, most evident in the omission of some of the most crucial elements of the fully developed theory (especially the multivariate cases), as well as areas such as the application to random-effects models.

BRENNAN's monograph provides a text at a level somewhat intermediate between that of the previous two texts, not as deep or advanced as the Cronbach *et al.* book, but discussing a number of topics excluded from consideration in the book by Shavelson & Webb, such as random-effects models and an outline, at least, of multivariate methods in generalizability theory. To illustrate calculations and methods as the text proceeds, the author uses both fictitious and real data, the former typically being used in the early chapters, and the latter and somewhat more difficult data only brought in later, once the reader has had the opportunity to become familiar with the basic concepts.

R.G. OWENS

See also Reliability, Validity

Genocide, politics

Adelman, Howard and Astri Suhrke (editors), *The Path of a Genocide: The Rwanda Crisis from Uganda to Zaire*, New Brunswick, New Jersey: Transaction, 1999

Andreopoulos, George J. (editor), *Genocide: Conceptual and Historical Dimensions*, Philadelphia: University of Pennsylvania Press, 1994

Chalk, Frank and Kurt Jonassohn (editors), *The History and Sociology of Genocide: Analyses and Case Studies*, New Haven, Connecticut: Yale University Press, 1990

Drost, Pieter Nicolaas, *The Crime of State*, vol. 2: *Genocide*, Leiden: Sythoff, 1959

Horowitz, Irving Louis, *Taking Lives: Genocide and State Power*, 4th edition, New Brunswick, New Jersey: Transaction, 1997

Kuper, Leo, *Genocide: Its Political Use in the Twentieth Century*, New Haven, Connecticut: Yale University Press, 1981

Lemkin, Raphael, *Axis Rule in Occupied Europe: Laws of Occupation, Analysis of Government, Proposals for Redress*, Washington, DC: Carnegie Endowment for International Peace, 1944

Robinson, Nehemiah, *The Genocide Convention: A Commentary*, New York: Institute of Jewish Affairs, 1960

Ruhashyankiko, Nicodème, *Study of the Question of the Prevention and Punishment of the Crime of Genocide*, New York: United Nations Economic and Social Council, 1978 (U.N. Doc. E/CN.4/Sub.2/416)

Whitaker, Ben, *Revised and Updated Report on the Question of the Prevention and Punishment of the Crime of Genocide*, New York: United Nations Economic and Social Council, 1985 (U.N. Doc. E/CN.4/Sub.2/1985/6)

Genocide draws on specialists in history, sociology, and law, and the literature is accordingly multidisciplinary. The legal definition of genocide is found in article II of the United Nations 1948 *Convention for the Prevention and Punishment of the Crime of Genocide*. Much writing on the subject reflects a frustration with the narrowness of the definition and the difficulties in extending its scope to human rights atrocities since World War II. Starting from a core of genocides on which there is really no debate – those against the Armenians, the Jews, and the Tutsi – writers debate the term's application to massacres in Cambodia, East Timor, Central Africa, Sudan, Vietnam, and the Ukraine. Although the definition in the 1948 Convention has often been criticized, international lawmakers reaffirmed its validity by repeating it unchanged in the 1998 *Rome Statute of the International Criminal Court*.

LEMKIN coined the term "genocide" in his 1944 book, and for this reason alone it retains its relevance. Lemkin underlines the link between the prohibition of genocide and earlier approaches to the protection of ethnic minorities, including the interwar treaties. The author's proposals on the definition of the crime were only partially incorporated into international law. Lemkin strongly believed in the importance of opposing cultural genocide, but this concept cut too close to the bone of many states that had attempted to assimilate national minorities and indigenous peoples. Thus, the 1948 Convention retained the concepts of physical and biological genocide but dropped that of cultural genocide.

ROBINSON was the first detailed examination of the 1948 Convention. It is based essentially on an analysis of its drafting history, relying on the debates in the General Assembly of the United Nations and its subordinate bodies. The original documents can be obtained in UN depository libraries, but their volume is considerable and Robinson's useful digest obviates such a task except for the most fastidious. The volume also contains, as an appendix, the three principal drafts of the Convention.

DROST is contemporary to Robinson. Neither refers to the other; publication seems to have gone completely in parallel. Drost takes a more critical perspective than Robinson, and finds shortcomings in the definition of the crime; specifically, because it limits the scope of genocide to national, racial, ethnic, and religious groups. Drost believed the Convention should be applicable to all mass killing. Like Robinson, Drost had nothing in the way of judicial interpretation and virtually no academic literature on the subject to enrich his analysis.

RUHASHYANKIKO's study for the Sub-Commission on human rights of the United Nations is the most recent monograph on legal aspects of genocide. Building on the work of Robinson and Drost, the author conducted surveys of state practice as well as examining the first genocide case law, such as the Eichmann decisions. The work was presented in a cloud of controversy because Ruhashyankiko refused to qualify the Armenian massacres during World War I as genocide. In 1985, the Sub-Commission issued a "revised and updated" report, by WHITAKER. This amended Ruhashyankiko's historical judgment but added little else to his study, which remains a rich and important source. Ruhashyankiko is more comfortable with the Convention definitions, whereas Whitaker's study is full of proposals for reform.

Leo Kuper was one of the most prolific writers on genocide, and KUPER is very much the seminal study. It examines the major genocides of the 20th century, then turns to the perceived shortcomings of the Convention and to the hesitant and inadequate initiatives of the UN. Kuper situates the debate within the development of human rights monitoring, considering the application of the concept to contemporary issues such as apartheid in South Africa and religious strife in Northern Ireland. Kuper launches the tradition of sociologists and historians who are troubled by the limits of the legal definition, and propose the enlargement of the Convention to address a broader range of human rights atrocities.

The first edition of HOROWITZ (it is now in a fourth edition) appeared in 1976. It is a profoundly disturbing attempt to understand the mechanics of genocide and its intimate and inescapable relationship with the state. Horowitz rejects a variety of determinist explanations, as well as what he calls "vulgar economism", i.e. the frequently advanced suggestion that genocide is the result of problems in economic development. The insights into state involvement in genocide are enriching. Horowitz takes into account and reviews in detail the literature on the subject.

ANDREOPOULOS and CHALK & JONASSOHN are two collections that stand out for the quality of the essays and the scope of the coverage. The Andreopoulos volume consists of papers by the leaders in the field, including Kuper, Chalk, Charny, Fein, Hovannisian, and Kiernan. It has specific chapters focusing on Turkey, East Timor, and Cambodia, as well as more conceptual pieces that look at the definitional questions. The CHALK & JONASSOHN volume consists of a general presentation by the editors in which they set out their theses on the definition and scope of genocide, followed by relatively short excerpts from a variety of sources. These demonstrate the perpetration of genocide well before the 20th century and the development of the term itself.

A reassessment of the law, history, and sociology of genocide in light of the Rwandan genocide of 1994 is essential. ADELMAN & SUHRKE constitutes a very useful beginning, presenting a series of essays describing the build-up to the massacres and the factors that might have contributed, including the role of hate radio and the position taken by neighbouring powers. Much of this volume is not strictly speaking addressed to genocide, but deals with broader issues such as preventive diplomacy and peacekeeping which are applicable to all human rights crises.

WILLIAM SCHABAS

See also Ethnic cleansing: the debate on Yugoslavia

Genocide, sociology

Chalk, Frank and Kurt Jonassohn (editors), *The History and Sociology of Genocide: Analyses and Case Studies*, New Haven, Connecticut: Yale University Press, 1990

Horowitz, Irving Louis, *Genocide: State Power and Mass Murder*, New Brunswick, New Jersey: Transaction, 1976; 4th edition as *Taking Lives: Genocide and State Power*, 1997

Kuper, Leo, *Genocide: Its Political Use in the Twentieth Century*, New Haven, Connecticut: Yale University Press, 1981

Lemkin, Raphael, *Axis Rule in Occupied Europe: Laws of Occupation, Analysis of Government, Proposals for Redress*, Washington, DC: Carnegie Endowment for International Peace, 1944

Mayer, Arno J., *Why Did the Heavens Not Darken: The "Final Solution" in History*, New York: Pantheon, 1988; London: Verso, 1990

Melson, Robert F., *Revolution and Genocide: On the Origins of the Armenian Genocide and the Holocaust*, Chicago: University of Chicago Press, 1992

Rummel, R.J., *Death by Government: Genocide and Mass Murder since 1900*, New Brunswick, New Jersey: Transaction, 1994

Totten, Samuel, William S. Parsons and Israel W. Charny (editors), *Century of Genocide: Eyewitness Accounts and Critical Views*, New York: Garland, 1997

Genocide has occurred through conquest, punishment, and religious conflict, but the major attention today is drawn from the postwar 20th-century concerns of human rights and international law, even though neither of these have exerted much influence. Although the literature focuses substantially on Europe, genocide has been most prevalent in new authoritarian states in Asia, Africa and Central and Latin America. A particular focus on the Holocaust can be seen in journals such as *Holocaust and Genocide Studies*, *History and Memory*, and *Dimensions: A Journal of Holocaust Studies*.

RUMMEL's statistical investigations show that governments have been directly responsible for the deaths of 120 million people of their own states in this century, whereas war (both civil and international) accounts for 35 million. In the former category 95 million were killed in communist states and 20 million in non-communist authoritarian ones. Rummel's work is concerned with the forms of democracy and of the ways in which systems sustain themselves without destroying oppositions.

The essays and accounts in TOTTEN, PARSONS & CHARNEY relate to the major genocidal acts committed in the 20th century, including: the 1904 genocide of the Hereros in South West Africa; the Armenian genocide (1915–19); the man-made famine in the Ukraine (1932–33); the Holocaust; the Bangladesh genocide (1971); the Burundi genocide (1972); the East Timor genocide (1975–79); the Cambodian genocide (1975–79); the genocidal massacres in Bosnia; and the Rwandan genocide (1994). Each contributor asks questions about who committed the genocide, how and why was it committed, who were the victims, what were the responses and outcomes, and what are the interpretations and conclusions today? Much of this work has the imprint of the social psychological work of Israel Charney and his associates in the Institute on the Holocaust and Genocide.

LEMKIN provides the first social scientific analysis of the coercive laws imposed on European countries occupied by the Axis powers, as evidence of violations against humanity and international law. He defines genocide as several factors: destroying peoples' self-government and imposing colonization or administration on them; disrupting social cohesion or removing national leadership groups; destroying cultural or educational institutions, substituting vocational for humanistic thinking. There are also disruptions and debasements in the fields of economic distribution, biology, physical existence, religion, and morality. As a jurist, Lemkin lobbied United Nations officials and representatives to secure a resolution by the General Assembly, and his analyses are reflected in the 1948 United Nations Convention on Genocide. However, the United Nations has contributed little to the eradication of genocide, and no states have been willing to bring complaints of genocide to the International Court of Justice.

CHALK & JONASSOHN argue that genocide is, "a form of one sided mass killing in which a state or other authority intends to destroy a group, as that group and membership in it are defined by the perpetrator" (p.23). Their comprehensive survey presents over two dozen examples from antiquity to the present. They provide a typology of the motives for genocide: a) To eliminate a real or potential threat; b) to spread terror among real or potential enemies; c) to acquire economic wealth; d) to implement a belief, a theory, or an ideology" (pp.29–30). The first three motives have played a role in the establishment and maintenance of empires. Ideologically motivated genocides have become the most important type of genocide in the twentieth century.

KUPER considers genocides that are domestic to societies in the 20th century and do not follow from wars. Examples are Algeria, Burundi, Rwanda, northern Nigeria, the Sudan, the Ukraine, Zanzibar, and German South West Africa. Kuper's detailed cases represent the different contexts, conditions and groups that relate to genocide. These include: colonization or decolonization; struggles for power or secession by racial, ethnic, or religious groups; scapegoats and defenceless groups; hunters and gatherers; urban populations; political groups; and bureaucratically managed or mechanized genocide. Domestic genocides are thus mostly phenomena of plural societies, which superimpose order on different racial, ethnic or religious groups, and generate polarizations and reverberations of conflict.

MELSON presents an historical comparison of the Armenians in the Ottoman empire and Jews in imperial Germany, and proposes that revolutions in such regimes make it possible to implement ideological ideas, including total genocide. Both Jews and Armenians survived as ethnic and religious minorities until the two old regimes were engulfed by revolution and war.

HOROWITZ argues that genocide is an advanced form of state terrorism, a premeditated use of force by elites within a society to maintain or extend their power, and he argues against both extreme statism and those social scientists who further it with schemes of development and system building. Horowitz writes about "the essential issues of death-making and life-giving forces in the structure of societies and states" (p.5). He defines genocide as a structural and systematic destruction of innocent people by a state bureaucratic apparatus: "The question of genocide is once again returned to the nation-state, to competition between sovereigns as much as to efforts to prevent opposition to a sovereign from within" (p.25). Hence the German genocide against the Jewish people rested on a national model of state power unencumbered by considerations of class, ethnicity, gender, or any other social factors affecting Nazi responses to non Jewish groups.

MAYER's view is that the Holocaust was "part and parcel of a syncretistic ideology combining key tenets of conservatism, reaction and fascism" (p.449). Following his general interest in the survival into the 20th century of the old order in Central and Eastern Europe, and what he sees as the disastrous consequences of that survival, the argument in this book is typically, controversially, that fascism prevailed because the old elites resorted to it to preserve their superannuated positions of class, status, and power.

ARTHUR E. McCULLOUGH

See also Ethnic cleansing

Geographical education

Bailey, Patrick and Peter Fox (editors), *Geography Teachers' Handbook*, Sheffield: Geographical Association, 1996

Biddle, Donald S., *Translating Curriculum Theory into Practice in Geographical Education: A Systems Approach*, Melbourne: Australian Geography Teachers Association, 1976

Boardman, David, *Graphicacy and Geography Teaching*, London: Croom Helm, 1983

Boden, Philip, *Developments in Geography Teaching*, London: Open Books, 1976

Chorley, Richard J. and Peter Haggett, (editors), *Frontiers in Geography Teaching*, London: Methuen, 1965

Downs, Roger M. and David Stea, *Maps in Minds: Reflections on Cognitive Mapping*, New York: Harper and Row, 1977

Fairgrieve, James, *Geography in School*, London: University of London Press, 1926

Gold, John R. *et al.*, *Teaching Geography in Higher Education: A Manual of Good Practice*, Oxford and Cambridge, Massachusetts: Blackwell, 1991

Graves, Norman J., *Geography in Education*, 3rd edition, London: Heinemann, 1984

Gunn, A.M. (editor), *High School Geography Project: Legacy for the Seventies*, Montreal: Centre Educatif et Culturel, 1972

Huckle, John (editor), *Geographical Education: Reflection and Action*, Oxford and New York: Oxford University Press, 1983

Kent, Ashley, David Lambert, Michael Naish and Frances Slater (editors), *Geography in Education: Viewpoints on Teaching and Learning*, Cambridge and New York: Cambridge University Press, 1996

Kurfman, Dana G. (editor), *Evaluation in Geographical Education*, Belmont, California: Fearon, 1970

Marsden, W.E., *Evaluating the Geography Curriculum*, Edinburgh: Oliver and Boyd, and New York: Longman, 1976

Naish, Michael (editor), *Geography and Education: National and International Perspectives*, London: Institute of Education, University of London, 1992

Slater, Frances A., *Learning through Geography: An Introduction to Activity Planning*, London: Heinemann, 1982

Williams, Michael (editor), *Understanding Geographical and Environmental Education: The Role of Research*, London and New York: Cassell, 1996

Geographical education is an applied field of study in which practical advice to teachers at all levels of education has always been mixed, sometimes uncomfortably, with the theoretical basis on which the advice is based. The subject began in the latter part of the 19th century but did not become well established until after World War II. The practical and the empirical tended to dominate in the early stages of the field's development, whereas later, the theoretical underpinnings loomed larger. This guide will review the field historically.

FAIRGRIEVE, an early British writer, attempted to integrate useful advice to teachers with a study of the theoretical issues involved. He was conscious of the need to provide a justification for including the subject in the curriculum, to argue a rationale for a syllabus structured not only on content, but on pedagogical considerations. Inductive processes based on "reality" were more appropriate than deductive ones, hence his advocacy of regional geography syllabuses. He influenced many teachers at the Institute of Education in the University of London. His immediate successors at the Institute of Education – Scarfe, Long, Honeybone, and Robertson, had been trained by him.

The 1950s and 1960s were a period of turmoil in the discipline: descriptive regional geography and environmental determinism came under attack from those wishing to make geography a nomothetic discipline rather than an idiographic one. In geographical education this was reflected in the High School Geography Project in the US, analysed by GUNN. In Britain, CHORLEY & HAGGETT's *Frontiers in Geography Teaching* was a milestone marking the development of the "new geography", which was largely positivistic. The Schools Council in England and Wales made it possible to finance a number of curriculum development projects in geography that made use of the new insights. These projects are described in BODEN.

In the field of education the development of curriculum theory led to its application to the planning of the geography curriculum. A pioneer here was the Australian BIDDLE, whose monograph uses a systems approach to guide teachers through the process of developing their own curriculum. He raises the question of which paradigm of geography is the most suitable for use in education. Curriculum theory integrates evaluation (curriculum evaluation, and the evaluation of student learning), because it is evaluation that activates the whole process. Evaluation in the US is reviewed by KURFMAN who gathered expert views on the topic, and introduced geography educators to the concept of formative evaluation. A British view is provided by MARSDEN, who illustrated evaluation theory with practical examples. His book has a wider scope, and discusses issues relating to aims, objectives, and the nature of geography.

Developments in educational psychology, in knowledge about spatial behaviour – for example by DOWNS & STEA, and later by BOARDMAN – threw new light on perception and cognitive development. Epistemological discussions deliberated on the nature of geographical knowledge. GRAVES attempted to put the whole field of geographical education into perspective using the insights of the educational disciplines, and those of geography in particular. He covered the development of the discipline and of the subject in school, its aims and objectives, curriculum development, evaluation, and perceptual and conceptual problems in learning geography. For him, the ecosystem paradigm of geography is the most suitable for the subject in schools.

SLATER was concerned with the very practical task of planning classroom activities, but dealt with the process at a high intellectual level. In her book, she raises the kinds of questions and problems that may be used to plan learning activities; questions about the processing and interpretation of data, about the analysis of attitudes and values, and their influence on the kind of generalizations that students will make. Each discussion is illustrated by case studies of questions and problems to be solved. The role of language in geographical learning is adumbrated. Throughout she recognized that teaching is a personal activity and that there is no single teaching strategy that works for everybody.

Philosophical positions among geographers multiplied in the 1980s, with behavioural, humanistic, radical, and postmodern geographies. Concern by geographers over environmental, urban, and Third World problems resulted in teachers reflecting these in their classroom practice. HUCKLE's book illustrates these concerns and has a radical slant.

Four books of readings best represent the 1990s. The first is edited by NAISH; its international authors carry the debate further with respect to curriculum, ideology, paradigms and values, and the use of various learning resources. The second, edited by KENT et al., addresses experienced teachers who wish to reflect more deeply on issues of curriculum practice and research. The third, edited by WILLIAMS, focuses on research in geographical and environmental education. The different approaches to research are elaborated: positivistic, interpretative, critical, and eclectic. Particular techniques are outlined: interviews, questionnaire surveys, case studies, action research, discourse analysis. Certain topics are illustrated, such as the history of geographical education, feminist perspectives, postmodernism and geographical education, and teacher education. It is the best contemporary account of research in this field. The fourth book of readings, written by GOLD et al., marks the establishment of geographical education as a

respectable field of study in higher education, an area pioneered by the authors through their *Journal of Geography in Higher Education*.

It may be noted that the era of the practical handbook for teachers is not over. Someone requiring a fund of information on teaching techniques, teaching aids, sources of information, examinations and tests, and so forth, could not do worse than consult BAILEY & FOX, although he or she should be warned that it is orientated to the British educational system.

NORMAN GRAVES

Geographic information systems (GIS)

Bernhardsen, Tor, *Geographic Information Systems: An Introduction*, 2nd edition, New York: Wiley, 1999

Cho, George, *Geographic Information Systems and the Law: Mapping the Legal Frontiers*, Chichester and New York: Wiley, 1998

Craglia, Massimo and Helen Couclelis, *Geographic Information Research: Bridging the Atlantic*, London: Taylor and Francis, 1997

Foresman, Timothy W. (editor), *The History of Geographic Information Systems: Perspectives from the Pioneers*, Upper Saddle River, New Jersey: Prentice Hall, 1998

Grimshaw, David J., *Bringing Geographic Information Systems into Business*, 2nd edition, New York: Wiley, 2000

Hanna, Karen C. and R. Brian Culpepper, *GIS and Site Design: New Tools for Design Professionals*, New York: Wiley, 1998

Healey, R., S. Dowers, B. Gittings and M. Mineter (editors), *Parallel Processing Algorithms for GIS*, London: Taylor and Francis, 1997

Heuvelink, Gerard B.M., *Error Propagation in Environmental Modelling with GIS*, London: Taylor and Francis, 1998

Heywood, I., S. Cornelius and S. Carver, *An Introduction to Geographic Information Systems*, New York: Addison Wesley, 1999

João, Elsa M., *Causes and Consequences of Map Generalisation*, London: Taylor and Francis, 1998

Johnston, Carol A., *Geographic Information Systems in Ecology*, Oxford and Malden, Massachusetts: Blackwell, 1998

Jones, Christopher B. (editor), *Geographica; Information Systems and Computer Cartography*, New York: Addison Wesley, 1996; Harlow, Essex: Longman, 1997

Kreveld, Marc van, *Algorithmic Foundations of Geographic Information Systems*, Berlin and New York: Springer, 1997

Longley, P., M. Goodchild, D. Maguire and D. Rhind (editors), *Geographical Information Systems: Principles, Techniques, Applications and Management*, 2nd edition, London: Longman, 1999

Masser, Ian, *Governments and Geographic Information*, London: Taylor and Francis, 1998

Morain, Stan (editor), *GIS Solutions in Natural Resource Management: Balancing the Technical-Political Equation*, Santa Fe, New Mexico: OnWord Press, 1999

Openshaw, Stan and Christine Openshaw, *Artificial Intelligence in Geography*, Chichester and New York: Wiley, 1997

Plewe, Brandon, *GIS Online: Information Retrieval, Mapping and the Internet*, Santa Fe, New Mexico: OnWord Press, 1998

Savitsky, Basil G. and Thomas E. Lacher, *GIS Methodologies for Developing Conservation Strategies*, New York: Columbia University Press, 1998

Vckovski, Andrej, *Interoperable and Distributed Processing in GIS*, London: Taylor and Francis, 1998

Geographic information systems (GIS) are a science, a technology, a database, a technique and methodology, as well as an application in spatial science. The term defies strict definition. This review focuses on texts detailing a history, pedagogic aids, theoretical underpinnings, research, and applications.

In the 1980s it would be difficult to find books specifically on GIS technology and its applications. However, that has all changed. FORESMAN's collection of essays of its history is written by key contributors and pioneers who both shaped and continue to shape the GIS industry. That many of the pioneers and authors of the chapters in the book are still active practitioners also attests to the industry's youth. This book is a primer that takes the reader through key projects that defined the industry's evolution through to present-day applications and technical analyses. Readers should however not be misled that this book gives *the* history of the technology. It is perhaps *a* history of the technology with a bias towards US developments.

Many users of GIS will have used the "bible" published in 1991 by Maquire, Goodchild & Rhind. That publication gave an unambiguous definition and clear documentation of underlying principles of GIS. It has become a major reference work. Now a completely revised second edition by LONGLEY *et al.* is available. There are 72 chapters in two volumes (1296 pages) with nearly 90 per cent of the authors being new. Volume one deals with principles and methodology and volume two addresses management issues and operational applications. It remains a primary reference. There are, of course, other less intimidating and ambitious books such as BERNHARDSEN's second edition. It is an intermediate introductory text that defines GIS and its historical development. In two major parts he discusses the principles and methodology of GIS. There is a conscious endeavour to give more "depth" of treatment and user-friendliness as a teaching text. Apart from more and shorter chapters it is supplemented by additional material on new technological developments such as the Internet and multimedia. HEYWOOD, CORNELIUS & CARVER is authoritative, up-to-date, and will appeal to students at all levels from the undergraduate to the professional. It focuses on practical applications of GIS and explains how the technology works. Each of the chapters addresses a specific theme from concepts of space to project design. There are recommended readings, suggestions for further study, and review questions to help the reader. Sidebars cover specific topics and case studies in depth.

KREVELD's edited book is a text on the technology that brings together two lines of research and development that have a significant impact on spatial information processing: GIS and geometric computation. The various authors provide a unique survey ranging from the history and basic characteristics of geometric algorithms and spatial data structures through to current issues of precision and robustness of geometric computation. Similarly, the edited book by HEALEY *et al.* deals with parallel processing algorithms for GIS. The benefits of parallel processing of large data sets requiring high performance is self evident. The authors focus on how this technology can be applied to GIS with an emphasis on software and data standards. Hardware requirements are also discussed including the overall process of algorithm design especially vector data processing. The growing sophistication of computation technology has led scientists to address issues of interoperability and distributed processing in GIS. VCKOVSKI posits that the principles and technology of object-oriented programming, distributed processing, and Internet protocols can be used to improve reliability and interoperability of GIS data sets. The book describes the central concept of the interface specification between the data consumer and producer. The book also looks at implementation, how Java and other object oriented distributed computing environments may be applied in GIS. More generally PLEWE's book is for those planning to incorporate GIS and mapping technologies into a Web site. It is not a "how to" book but rather a guide for various stages of Web site implementation.

The theory of geographic information science has also been addressed. OPENSHAW & OPENSHAW provide a complete and in-depth view of a variety of artificial intelligence based methods to solve problems of interest to geographers and GIS. The book gives a good review of different forms of artificial intelligence including expert systems, neural networks, fuzzy logic, artificial life, and genetic algorithms. In each of these there is a simple introduction to the technique or technology. Sophisticated mathematics and statistical skills are not required to understand the concepts and applications within the book. However a basic understanding of algebra and geographic concepts may be necessary. HEUVELINK's book re-emphasizes the idea that accuracy of GIS results cannot be naively based on the quality of the graphical output. All data are collected, measured, classified, generalized, interpreted, and estimated. Each step in this process provides opportunities for introducing error. GIS users need to understand how these errors originate so that they may build more accurate systems. This book is an authoritative account for developing, applying, and implementing error detecting techniques for use in environmental modelling using GIS. JOÃO's text is more specific because it addresses the causes and consequences of map generalization. The loss of information from generalization is dependent on the source scale, a problem inherent in all digital maps. This may be the first book to focus on a precise measurement of generalization. Local maps of Europe are used for illustrative purposes and a new method to counter the effects of generalization inherent in maps is uncovered.

The application of GIS has become the *raison d'être* of much work. CRAGLIA & COUCLELIS reports on cutting-edge research in Europe and the US. The chapters in this book have been peer reviewed and selected from the European Science Foundation (ESR) and National Centre for Geographic Information and Analysis (NCGIA) first International Summer Institute in Geographic Information held at the University of Southern Maine in 1995. The book includes most of the papers and incorporates feedback from colleagues both during and after the meeting. Applications of GIS in contemporary cartography are found in JONES – an edited text that emphasizes management, analysis, and graphical display of spatial information. In five parts various authors review the development and application of GIS, coordinate systems and map projections, data storage and database management, spatial modelling and analytical techniques for decision-making and graphical representations that emphasize the technology, cartographic design, and map generalization. Applications of GIS in conservation are found in SAVITSKY & LACHER who use Costa Rica's tropical environment as an equatorial laboratory in biodiversity. They suggest state-of-the-art digital mapping technology that is sophisticated but relatively inexpensive and accessible to all. They describe powerful tools available for those involved in decision making about the natural environment particularly in developing countries. The specialist areas include geography, conservation biology, wildlife, and natural resource management. HANNA & CULPEPPER discuss GIS and site design and how the technology is redefining the way landscape architects and planners work. It is perhaps the only guidebook to GIS written expressly for landscape architects. A CD ROM of GIS data is included. MASSER discusses how GIS technology has transformed spatial data-handling capabilities and has caused governments to rethink their roles in the supply of geographic information. The book describes experiences in Britain, the Netherlands, Australia, and the US and the development of national geographic information strategies. It also examines the roles played directly through policy initiatives and indirectly through broad institutional contexts within which these strategies have been developed and maintained. GRIMSHAW provides a unique contribution to business-based GIS. In three parts he discusses the management of geographic information, the organizational challenge, and the use of geographic information in business. There are numerous case studies that demonstrate problems and their solutions as well as implementation issues. JOHNSTON uses ecology as the discipline area and GIS as the technique to solve purely ecological problems. While there is a breadth of treatment it is at the expense of depth. CHO's text suggests that there are legal issues to be addressed with the use of GIS. These issues are stretching the limits of legal systems around the world. The book clarifies the issues of the rights, limitations, and responsibilities of GIS users and providers. It addresses the legal relations between those who provide data and those who use data. This text serves to illustrate the increasing awareness of the significant interrelatedness between disciplines and applications of GIS technology. MORAIN outlines the multiple uses of GIS in natural resource management. It explores how diverse data sets are applied to specific areas of study. The case studies illustrate social and life sciences and the combined efforts to respond to and solve sociopolitical challenges. Some of these include the protection of endangered species, the prevention of famine, the management of water and land usage, the transport of toxic materials, and the preservation of local scenic trails through diverse public and private lands.

GEORGE CHO

See also Business geography, Spatial analysis

Geography of money

Agnew, John and Stuart Corbridge, *Mastering Space: Hegemony, Territory and International Political Economy*, London and New York: Routledge, 1995

Black, Iain, "Geography, Political Economy and the Circulation of Finance Capital in Early Industrial England", *Journal of Historical Geography*, 15/4 (1989): 366–84

Budd, Leslie and Sam Whimster (editors), *Global Finance and Urban Living: A Study of Metropolitan Change*, London and New York: Routledge, 1992

Clark, Gordon L., *Pensions and Corporate Restructuring in American Industry: A Crisis of Regulation*, Baltimore: Johns Hopkins University Press, 1993

Clark, Gordon L., "Pension Funds and Urban Investment: Four Models of Financial Intermediation", *Environment and Planning, A*, 29/7 (July 1997) 1297–1316

Clark, Gordon L. and Kevin O'Connor, "The Informational Content of Financial Products and the Spatial Logic of the Financial Industry" in *Spaces of Globalization: Reasserting the Power of the Local*, edited by Kevin R. Cox, New York: Guilford Press, 1997

Clark, Gordon L., "Why Convention Dominates Pension Fund Trustee Investment Decision-Making", *Environment and Planning, A*, 30/6 (June 1998): 997–1015

Corbridge, Stuart, *Debt and Development*, Oxford and Cambridge, Massachusetts: Blackwell, 1993

Corbridge, Stuart, Nigel Thrift and Ron Martin (editors), *Money, Power, and Space*, Oxford and Cambridge, Massachusetts: Blackwell, 1994

Harvey, David, *The Limits to Capital*, Oxford: Blackwell, and Chicago: University of Chicago Press, 1982

Harvey, David, "The Geopolitics of Capitalism" in *Social Relations and Spatial Structures*, edited by Derek Gregory and John Urry, Basingstoke: Macmillan, and New York: St Martin's Press, 1985

Laulajainen, Risto, *Financial Geography: A Banker's View*, Gothenburg: School of Economics and Commercial Law, 1998

Lee, R., "Moral Money? LETS and the Social Construction of Local Economic Geographies in Southeast England", *Environment and Planning, A*, 28/8 (August 1996): 1377–94

Leyshon, Andrew, "Geographies of Money and Finance 1", *Progress in Human Geography*, 19/4 (1995): 531–43

Leyshon, Andrew and Nigel Thrift, "Geographies of Financial Exclusion: Financial Abandonment in Britain and the United States", *Transactions of the Institute of British Geographers*, 20/3 (1995): 312–41

Leyshon, Andrew, "Geographies of Money and Finance 2", *Progress in Human Geography*, 21/3 (1997): 381–92

Leyshon, Andrew and Nigel Thrift, *Money/Space: Geographies of Monetary Transformation*, London and New York: Routledge, 1997

Leyshon, Andrew, "Geographies of Money and Finance 3", *Progress in Human Geography*, 22/3 (1998): 433–46

McDowell, Linda and Gillian Court, "Missing Subjects: Gender, Power and Sexuality in Merchant Banking", *Economic Geography*, 70/3 (July 1994) 229–51

McDowell, Linda, *Capital Culture: Gender at Work in the City*, Oxford and Malden, Massachusetts: Blackwell, 1997

Martin, Ron (editor), *Money and the Space Economy*, Chichester and New York: Wiley, 1999

Mitchell, Katharyne, "Flexibility Circulation in the Pacific Rim: Capitalisms in Cultural Context", *Economic Geography*, 71/4 (1995): 364–82

Peck, J. and Adam Tickell, "The Social Regulation of Uneven Development: 'Regulatory Deficit', England's South East and the Collapse of Thatcherism", *Environment and Planning A*, 27/1 (1995): 15–40

Popke, E.J., "Recasting Geopolitics: The Discursive Scripting of the International Monetary Fund", *Political Geography*, 13/3 (1994): 255–69

Porteous, David J., *The Geography of Finance: Spatial Dimensions of Intermediary Behaviour*, Aldershot, Hampshire: Avebury, 1995

Thrift, Nigel and Andrew Leyshon, *Making Money: The City of London and Social Power in Britain*, London: Routledge, 1992

Tickell, Adam, *Rogues, Regulation and the Culture of Finance*, New York: Guilford Press, 1999

Williams, Colin C., "Local Exchange Trading Systems: A New Source of Work and Credit for the Poor and Unemployed?", *Environment and Planning, A*, 28 (1996): 1395–415

Reading on this theme should begin with 13 essays assembled by MARTIN. Most publications on monetary issues by a geographer or regional economist until 1997 are placed in perspective through the introductory essay. Here, Martin claims the emergence of an economic geography of money and finance as a subdiscipline, with four identifiable lines of enquiry: (a) Marxist theorization of the geographically uneven and crisis-prone tendencies of the capitalist space economy; (b) specific studies of spatial organization and the operation of particular financial institutions, services and markets; (c) studies of the dynamics through which the world's major financial centres are moulding global geographies of money (especially London, New York and Tokyo); and (d) studies of services to link regional financial flows and regional industrial development. Within this discussion, Martin demonstrates that financial systems are inherently spatial in terms of "location structure" and "institutional geographies" that influence the way money moves between locations and communities, as well as "regulatory spaces" and the "public financial space of the state" (including cooperation and competition within the international monetary system). He notes that money "has a habit of seeking out geographical discontinuities and gaps" to reinforce, rather than reduce, uneven regional patterns. In addition to its functions as an economic store of value and a means of exchange, money is a "social relation" that Martin suggests can be linked to "time-space distanciation" and that provides a mechanism for "the simultaneous 'stretching' and 'compression' of social interaction across time and space". The other essays in the volume cover aspects of the changing geography of banking, the rise of global financial centres, functions of money in the local economy, and research into the retreat of

government intervention. The volume is supported by a comprehensive bibliography.

Many contributors to Martin's volume have established their credentials previously. PORTEOUS, a South African development banker, offers a theoretical viewpoint that highlights the significance of "information externalities" and "an information hinterland" to account for urban agglomeration of financial activities. He also explains "spatial switching" as a reversal of the rank order of importance of rival financial centres within national economies (for example Montreal/Toronto and Melbourne/Sydney). CLARK's work about the importance of US and British geography of pension funds reveals why this source of capital has such high influence upon the global economy and CLARK & O'CONNOR have attempted an analysis of the "spatial logic" of the financial industry. Research into the operation of alternative forms of non-official or "local money" through LETS (local exchanges and trading systems) has been reviewed by LEE, with further comment by WILLIAMS.

Pioneer geographical work in Canada and France, as Martin explains, has been overlooked and he also acknowledges Marxist theoretical leadership by David Harvey. HARVEY is still worth reading as a classic study that stresses the importance of time and geographical space to argue that contradictions in the primary or productive circuit of capital could be dampened down by foreign direct investment to secondary and tertiary circuits. These circuits export wider financial instability in new forms through the creation of fictitious credit money in advance of actual production and consumption–thereby producing "systems instability". On this platform, Harvey identifies different types of crises, including "sectoral switching crises" (where fixed capital formation is switched to another sphere, such as education), "geographical switching crises" relating to different geographical scales (for example, urban, regional, national and international configurations) and "global crises". Harvey considers the further dimension of "geopolitics" at each scale to suggest that crisis tendencies are not resolved in an orderly manner but involve competitive struggles influenced by discriminatory institutional practices, circuits of money, and cost reduction according to financial, economic, political, and military power.

CORBRIDGE recognizes Harvey's view, but balances this with an outline of other "system-instability", "system-stability" and "system-correction" perspectives by different theorists. Whereas Corbridge's book does not constitute empirical analysis, it was one of the first to suggest, with narrative examples, limitations to Keynesian measures of financial debt in the consideration of the geography of commercial bank lending in Latin America, the Caribbean, eastern Europe, and "Third World" African countries. MITCHELL examines the cultural context of capitalism in the Pacific Rim nations. AGNEW & CORBRIDGE and LAULAJEINAN give additional examples.

A collection of 17 essays assembled by CORBRIDGE, THRIFT & MARTIN is grouped according to three themes: "the geopolitics of money", "money, states and markets" and "money politics and the community of money". Case studies include the geography of offshore financial flows, the impacts of Keynesian and monetarist theory on the geography of inflation, the rise and fall of Japan's postwar economy, global and

European financial integration (and access to credit in peripheral regions), shifting structures (and levels of public confidence) in housing and commercial finance, the role of oil as money in developing countries, and the locational relevance of Wall Street and the City of London in an era of sophisticated electronic communication.

LEYSHON & THRIFT (1997), who have collaborated since the mid-1980s, provide empirical research that is influenced by Harvey. In *Money/Space* they explore the "world of paper and money" with four aims: to describe the economy of international money, to link this economy with the distribution of social power, to show some of the ways in which the world of money is discursively constituted through social-cultural practices, and to show how the world of money is constructed out of and through geography. The authors follow neo-Gramscian regulatory theory (see entry on Post-Fordism) and operate within four spatial frames: the global monetary economy, the national space of Britain, the regional space of the south of England, and the concentrated urban space of the City of London. The book is a critique of the rise and fall of "Thatcherism and Reaganomics", which marked unprecedented growth of the financial services industry, followed by the rise of disintermediation, a wave of financial innovation and then more sophisticated forms of risk management. One chapter gives attention to "geographies of financial exclusion" in Britain and the US (including sub-branch bank closures) and recaptures LEYSHON & THRIFT's (1993) suggestion that "financial citizenship" is needed as a means of exerting pressure on state governments to reform their financial systems. The theme of financial exclusion is also the subject of a 1996 issue of *Environment and Planning A* (volume 28/1).

The impact of changing geopolitics upon the circulation of capital is enlarged by POPKE and PECK & TICKELL. BLACK has reconstructed highly fluid spatial mobility of finance within a London-centred political economy during the industrial revolution and a more contemporary analysis of metropolitan London responses to the financial revolution of the 1980s is given through a collection of 14 interdisciplinary papers, most contributed from the City of London Polytechnic (BUDD & WHIMSTER), with some wider international parallels drawn. THRIFT & LEYSHON examine London's money accumulation in the context of national power relationships and McDOWELL has researched the socioeconomic effects of boom and recession on the lifestyles, career paths, and gender segregation of men and women employed in London's merchant banks. TICKELL comments on the "culture of finance" with reference to fraud and regulatory controls.

LEYSHON's three progress reports keep abreast of the growth of geographical treatments of money and finance. His first report links such contributions to the concept of a "geopolitical economy", explores the "geoeconomics of finance" and reflects upon wide unease over the geographies of financial exclusion. The second report draws upon Viviana Zelizer's theory of the social meaning of money and Nigel Dodd's critique of existing theories of money, then reviews geographical analysis of the social and cultural construction of financial centres. The third report links together widening geographical interpretations beyond economic explanation of money, and draws in studies of built-environmental iconography, media representations of financial crises and the roles of gender, embodiment and corporeality in the constitution of financial labour markets.

TERRY G. BIRTLES

See also Economic geography, Post-Fordism

Geopolitics

Dalby, Simon, *Creating the Second Cold War: The Discourse of Politics*, London: Pinter, and New York: Guilford Press, 1990

Hepple, Leslie W., "The Revival of Geopolitics", *Political Geography Quarterly*, supplement 5 (1986): 21–36

Kjellén, Rudolph, *Der Staat als Lebenform*, Leipzig: Hirzel, 1917

Livingstone, David N., *The Geographical Tradition*, Oxford and Cambridge, Massachusetts: Blackwell, 1993

Mackinder, Halford J., *Democratic Ideals and Reality: A Study in the Politics of Reconstruction*, London: Constable, and New York: Holt, 1919

O'Tuathail, Gearoid, *Critical Geopolitics*, London and New York: Routledge, 1996

O'Tuathail, Gearoid and Simon Dalby (editors), *Rethinking Geopolitics*, London and New York: Routledge, 1998

O'Tuathail, Gearoid, Simon Dalby and Paul Routledge (editors), *The Geopolitics Reader*, London and New York: Routledge, 1998

Parker, Geoffrey, *Western Geopolitical Thought in the Twentieth Century*, London: Croom Helm, and New York: St Martin's Press, 1985

Taylor, Peter J., *Political Geography: World-Economy, Nation-State, and Locality*, 3rd edition, Harlow, Essex: Longman, and New York: Wiley, 1993

Weigert, Hans W., *Generals and Geographers: The Twilight of Geopolitics*, London and New York: Oxford University Press, 1942

KJELLÉN is widely credited with inventing the term "geopolitics" at the end of the 19th century and, although his work has never been translated into English, there are useful English-language summaries provided by PARKER and by LIVINGSTONE. Kjellen's original interest in geopolitics was provoked by a recognition that the condition of states and their citizens was changing rapidly towards the end of the 19th century. He argued that "geopolitics" was a useful term because it highlighted the importance of territorial factors in shaping the political life of the state. In doing so, Kjellen provoked a major European debate in the first half of the 20th century, as his work was translated into German and French.

MACKINDER provided another entry point into European geopolitical discussions. As a former Member of Parliament and Professor of Geography at Oxford University, his analysis of the world political map paid considerable attention to the relationship of military power to the physical environment. It was argued that Britain, as a sea-power, had to contribute to a Euro-American strategy designed to contain the expansionist ambitions of Germany and Russia in the aftermath of World

War I. O'TUATHAIL, DALBY & ROUTLEDGE provides an excellent and well-annotated guide to some of the most significant geopolitical articles and books published in the 20th century. Their work is an excellent teaching resource, and their commentaries on particular writers, such as Mackinder, are invaluable.

PARKER provides a very readable summary of how geopolitical ideas began to circulate in various parts of Western Europe. British, French, German, and Italian scholars exchanged ideas and thoughts on the role of territorial factors in the shaping of inter war European politics. In Germany, Karl Haushofer emerged as a key figure in the development of a particular German school of geopolitics called *Geopolitik*, which stressed the significance for Germany of retaining key territories in Central and Eastern Europe. It was later alleged that Haushofer's ideas about geopolitics influenced Hitler's policies of territorial conquest and *lebensraum*.

WEIGERT details how subsequent American and European geographers reacted to the allegations concerning *Geopolitik's* links with Nazism. Most contributors to his important volume condemned geopolitics more generally as an expansionist ideology and an insult to the respectable scientific discipline of geography. Geopolitics in the 1940s received unprecedented popular coverage in journals such as the *Reader's Digest* and *Life* in the midst of this hysteria about German geopolitical writers and the Munich-based School of Geopolitics.

HEPPLE provides a very helpful survey of this period and the subsequent effect on geopolitics as a study area. He noted that many geographers in America and Europe abandoned the term in the 1950s and 1960s because they were concerned that they would be tainted with the stain of Nazism. The allegations about geopolitics' links to Hitler's Germany were exaggerated, but it was only when Henry Kissinger began using the term "geopolitics" in the 1970s that it was possible to see a reversal in this decline.

TAYLOR offered further details on this revival of geopolitics and made an important contribution to the theoretical reconstruction of the term. Using a world-systems framework, he argues that geopolitics should be concerned with exploring how the world is geographically divided into a core, a semi-periphery, and a periphery. His work is explicitly concerned with locating geopolitics within the cycles of global capitalism. With the ending of the Cold War and the implosion of the "Second World" of socialist states, he has modified his theories.

DALBY charts a new stage in the development of Anglo-American geopolitics, which has been labelled "critical geopolitics". With a detailed study of the American Committee on Present Danger, a product of the Cold War, he shows how geopolitics can be used to examine the geographical assumptions behind the Carter administration's Cold War rhetoric. He demonstrates how the Soviet Union's history and geography was consistently represented as unbendingly expansionist and threatening to other states and as a consequence these representations were used to justify America's hawkish approach to the USSR. Using poststructuralist theories on discourse and representation, he illustrated a theoretical sophistication previously missing from the field.

O'TUATHAIL is the definitive guide to the field of Anglo-American critical geopolitics. He charts, in some detail, the construction of the field of geopolitics, and showed convincingly that geopolitics can be reconstituted as an approach that examines the interrelationships between power, knowledge, space, and politics. Case studies from the humanitarian crisis in Bosnia and the ending of the Cold War are used to illustrate how American policy-makers and the media have attempted to represent the varied cartographies of the new world order. One of the most important contributions of this book is that it argued that geopolitics should not just be concerned with the activities of states and political leaders, but that it should also be attentive to how a range of popular sources, from the media to education, perpetuate particular geographical representations of places and peoples.

The various essays in O'TUATHAIL & DALBY provide an excellent overview of recent scholarship in critical geopolitics. The essays demonstrate that critical geopolitics is pursuing a number of research agendas, ranging from the role of the media in reporting global politics, to the analysis of the politico-economic condition of the world at the end of the 20th century. The methods, concepts, and sources of critical geopolitics are clearly illustrated in this collection, which is likely to play a significant role in shaping future research directions.

KLAUS DODDS

German economy and economic record

Abelshauser, Werner, *Wirtschaftsgeschichte der Bundesrepublik Deutschland, 1945–1980* [Economic History of the Federal Republic of Germany (1945–1980)], Frankfurt am Main: Suhrkamp, 1983

Braun, Hans-Joachim, *The German Economy in the Twentieth Century*, London and New York: Routledge, 1990

Deutsches Institut für Wirtschaftsforschung *et al.*, *Die Lage der Weltwirtschaft und der deutschen Wirtschaft im Herbst 1999* [The State of the World Economy and of the German Economy in Autumn 1999] Hamburg: HWWA-Institut für Wirtschaftsforschung, 1999 (Assessment of the Economic Situation by the Members of the Working Group of German Economic Research Institutes Comprising DIW, HWWA, ifo, IWH, IfW, RWI)

Giersch, Herbert, Karl-Heinz Paqué and Holger Schmieding, *The Fading Miracle: Four Decades of Market Economy in Germany*, Cambridge and New York: Cambridge University Press, 1992

International Monetary Fund, *Germany: Staff Report for the 1999 Article IV Consultation*, Washington, DC: International Monetary Fund, 1999

OECD, *OECD Economic Surveys 1998–1999: Germany*, Paris: OECD, 1999

Owen Smith, Eric, *The German Economy*, London and New York: Routledge, 1994

Peacock, Alan and Hans Willgerodt (editors), *Germany's Social Market Economy: Origins and Evolution*, Basingstoke: Macmillan, 1989

This selection of publications tries to capture the current state and outlook of the economy, sources for up-to-date statistics, policy evaluation, historical background including German unification, and the dominant economic philosophy relevant for an understanding of Germany's economy today.

The particular value of ABELSHAUSER lies in its discussion and refutation of a number of myths relating to the origins of West Germany's postwar growth and the subsequent slowdown. In the section on the foundations of West Germany's economy, based on considerable archival research, the author has moved forward the debate on issues like the so-called "economic miracle" and the actual relevance of the Marshall Plan for recovery. The author contests the suggestion that the successes of the 1950s were the consequence of consistent economic policy. The study demonstrates how the basic institutional framework was shaped before 1953 and how formal corporatist features crept back into the West German political economy against the will of the Federal Republic's first minister of economics, Ludwig Erhard, at an early stage, owing partly to the impact of external shocks. Abelshauser also examines Germany's postwar growth performance in a longer term perspective and discusses the Keynesian policy approach of the late 1960s and 1970s, income distribution, and the comparatively slow structural change.

BRAUN provides an overview of the German economy since 1871 with an exclusive focus on West Germany from 1949 to 1985. In its first part (1871 to 1948) the narrative is structured according to subperiods, while the second part analyses the economy of the Federal Republic along the lines of issues such as growth, foreign trade, or structural change. Braun does not present new research on existing debates, but provides accurate accounts and insightful discussions on the major contentious points in the relevant literature. Given that the work is both comprehensive and concise, it will serve as a useful introduction for the student aiming to become acquainted with the subject in its historical context.

GIERSCH, PAQUÉ & SCHMIEDING is an essay in applied economics that describes, evaluates, and draws lessons from Germany's postwar economic development. This is interpreted as the fading of Germany's "economic miracle" due to corporatist rigidities and an excess of regulation. In the authors' view, these factors have, over time, impaired the scope for spontaneity and flexible adjustment, which are regarded as prerequisites for economic "miracles". While the term "miracle" appears to be of little interpretative value to the overall essay, the self-contained chapters on the liberal order, spontaneous growth, managed growth, and the slowdown provide lucid analyses of the conditions for growth set by the institutional framework and economic policy in each of the periods discussed. The chapter on unification illustrates the economic shortcomings of the process and assesses the outlook. The firm link between theoretical reasoning and institutional description throughout the book, and its solid analysis of relevant statistics, make this valuable reading for any economist interested in the subject.

The INTERNATIONAL MONETARY FUND Staff Report is the product of annual discussions between IMF staff and the representatives of the governments and central banks of the institution's member states: in the case of Germany, these were the Federal Government and the Bundesbank. The 1999 report – which includes an IMF staff analysis of German economic and financial policies, as well as the IMF's Executive Board's assessment – is the first one to be made public as part of a pilot project. Its regular publication in future is likely but not certain. The report subjects the German economy to a thorough examination and focuses particularly on Germany's poor labour market performance in recent years. Comments and concrete policy recommendations are made by the IMF on all areas of economic performance. The 1999 report links the historical evolution of the institutional framework to the present weaknesses of the German economy. It provides a direct insight into the thinking of an international institution and of the German authorities on concrete economic policy issues.

The OECD's economic survey gives an annual assessment of economic policies and performance, and contains core macroeconomic and fiscal statistics, as well as forecasts for the most important of these variables. The assessment is accompanied by policy recommendations whose observance is reviewed in the survey published the following year. The surveys for 1990 to 1993 still provide good analyses of the effects of German unification on both the East and West German economies, whose convergence is yet to be achieved. The main issues addressed in the most recent survey are structural unemployment and the reforms of pension and health systems, as well as tax reform. The series for Germany covers the period from 1961 to the present.

OWEN SMITH provides an in-depth analysis of the German economy, East and West, in the mid-1990s. His work is firmly grounded in economic theory. It focuses on the current state of the main economic policy areas, the labour market, financial markets, and industry. The study explores the historical and regional dimension reflected in the institutions that determine economic policy making in Germany. Owen Smith discusses and evaluates the existing literature on the subject and engages in the relevant debates on issues like the role of the concept of "Social Market Economy" in Germany's postwar performance. He provides thorough descriptive accounts of relevant laws and regulations governing economic policy. The reader gains a detailed understanding of the major economic issues confronting Germany after unification as well as the virtues and weaknesses of the institutions which have to address them.

The articles in PEACOCK & WILLGERODT portray the concept of the Social Market Economy (SME) from the perspectives of the major proponents of the Freiburg school of Ordoliberalism; some of whom, like Alfred Müller-Armack and Franz Böhm, were involved in economic policy making after World War II, while others are economists who represent or write on German economic liberalism. The SME is defined by the free market as its core, effective competition as its principle of coordination, and a fully-fledged social security system made possible through the proper functioning of the free market itself. The collection provides a deep profile of the economic philosophy behind the SME concept, as it covers various issues like international interdependence, the role of trade unions, unemployment, and monetary policy from an SME viewpoint. The debatable contention is that without the influence of SME on economic policy, the development of the West German economy would have been dramatically different from the actual course of events. The editors also contend that, given the influence of SME on West Germany's economic policy, the success of that policy was by no means a miracle.

The report by DEUTSCHES INSTITUT FUR WIRT-SCHAFTSFORSCHUNG ET AL. assesses the state and outlook of the German economy in the context of the world economy. The report is published every six months by Germany's six leading economic research institutes and receives considerable public attention. It represents a consensus view and contains forecasts for the main macroeconomic variables and public finances. The report also passes a verdict on all areas of economic policy and makes concrete recommendations to the political leadership and sometimes to the social partners. The assessment of the stance of fiscal and monetary policies as well as most other sections of the report are recurring features. Particular attention is paid to recent policy measures, such as the 2000 austerity program, and areas such as the catching up process of the East German economy since unification.

MARKUS SCHULTE

Gerontology

Bernard, M., J. Phillips, C. Phillipson and J. Ogg, "Continuity and Change: The Family and Community Life of Older People in the 1990s" in *The Myth of Generational Conflict*, edited by Sara Arber and Claudine Attias-Donfut, London: Routledge, 2000

Featherstone, Mike and Mike Hepworth, "Images of Ageing" in *Ageing in Society*, 2nd edition, edited by John Bond, Peter Coleman and Sheila Peace, London: Sage, 1993

Grundy, Emily, "Ageing: Age-Related Change in Later Life", *Population Studies*, 45 (1991): 133–56

Hazan, Haim, *Old Age: Constructions and Deconstructions*, Cambridge: Cambridge University Press, 1994

Laslett, Peter, *A Fresh Map of Life*, 2nd edition, Basingstoke: Macmillan, 1996

Riley, Matilda, Robert L. Kahn and Anne Foner (editors), *Age and Structural Lag*, New York: Wiley, 1994

Thompson, Paul, Catherine Itzen and Michelle Abendstern, *I Don't Feel Old*, Oxford and New York: Oxford University Press, 1990

Turner, Bryan S., "Ageing, Dying and Death" in *Medical Power and Social Knowledge*, edited by Bryan S. Turner, London and Beverly Hills, California: Sage, 1987

Walker, Alan and Tony Maltby, *Ageing Europe*, Buckingham: Open University Press, 1997

There is a distinction within social gerontology between studies of ageing as a social process extending over the life course and studies that focus on the social conditions of life of the elderly. These two orientations are not mutually exclusive and there has been much interesting work bringing ageing, life course, and structural conditions together. For example, RILEY, KAHN & FONER argue that social structures lag behind the changing realities of people's lives. There is a paradox in developed societies whereby people are living longer and healthier lives and yet, at the same time, they are increasingly encouraged to take early retirement. Riley, Kahn & Foner emphasize that, throughout the life course, people move along multiple pathways that include education, work, leisure, and family life. However social structures do little to facilitate such age integration.

TURNER argues that we can theorize the stigma of both youth and the aged with reference to a disengagement from the community expressed as a relative absence of reciprocity. Turner posits a "reciprocity-maturation curve" to demonstrate an increase in social prestige as one moves into mid-life and reciprocity and social integration increase. In line with disengagement theory, as people become elderly and unable to reciprocate and perform responsibilities they are forced to withdraw from powerful social roles and this, in part, explains their loss of prestige.

Disengagement theory has been challenged in a fascinating book reviewing the cultural construction of representations of ageing, HAZAN claims how disengagement theory and its opposite, activity theory, reveal two complementary aspects of contemporary Western society. On the one hand, once people cease to be "productive" and to "contribute" to society they are expected to be put out to graze. On the other, they are expected to maintain a constant quest for a sense of achievement. Hazim also criticizes social exchange theory as inconsistent with the prevalence of dependency and powerlessness among the aged and the limited resources available to them. Drawing on a variety of detailed ethnographic accounts of the old and representations of older people in the media, Hazim suggests that there is a gulf between the world of the elderly and societal conceptions of old age.

FEATHERSTONE & HEPWORTH reflect on the significance of public images of ageing and old age for understanding the position of elderly people in British society. They highlight the tension between public images and personal perceptions and question the way public images are used in everyday life and how this differs by gender, ethnicity, and social class. Adopting a broad historical viewpoint, they explore images of the pre-industrial period and those that emerged out of the process of modernization. They also examine the tensions within current images of the elderly, especially with respect to conceptions of the ageing body.

Where Featherstone and Hepworth are concerned with the cultural representations of micro-level processes, LASLETT is concerned with the population level changes of ageing societies. However he, like the authors of the previous two studies, sees a gap between societal conceptions and experiences of the elderly. In the developed world more people can confidently expect to live for a considerable time in reasonable health, after the period of retirement. However, Laslett sees society's response to this ageing revolution as one of concern, even panic, because societal attitudes to the old are informed by perceptions belonging to the past. Laslett argues that the Third Age – the years beyond the breadwinning and childrearing years – can be a time of great personal fulfilment. Combining social history, demography, sociology, and ethics, Laslett tackles subjects as diverse as the secular shift in ageing, the preponderance of hostile and demeaning stereotypes of the elderly, kinship, and changing family structures and responsible citizenship in later life.

Laslett has been criticized for not taking sufficient account of class differences and for drawing attention away from the desperate plight that older people who lack the necessary social and economic support can experience. The study by THOMPSON, ITZEN & ABENDSTERN, however, provides support for Laslett's optimistic portrayal of the Third Age.

Drawing on life-story interviews with members of three generations of families, and hundreds of printed and recorded autobiographical recollections, Thompson, Itzen & Abendstern provide forceful confirmation that many people from their sixties to their eighties do not *feel* old. For many, later life is an active challenge and meaning and fulfilment are found in different and often strikingly creative ways. But, as the authors freely admit, this study is biased towards those who survive and even thrive in old age.

It has been argued that, at the start of the third millennium, European societies are facing generational conflicts that focus upon the sharing of pubic resources between different cohorts, before, during, and after the working life. The generational contract is seen as becoming increasingly fragile, as pensions stretch the public purse to the limit. In an interesting study that revisits three classic community studies undertaken in the1940s and 1950s, BERNARD *et al.* explore the changes and continuities in the life of the elderly over the past half century. Despite all the changes that the postwar period has witnessed in terms of family structures and social relationships, kinship remains of central importance and intergenerational help is usually reciprocal. However, it is not clear whether this evidence really questions the "myth of generational conflict". Even if there is little conflict within families, there may be generational conflict at the societal level.

GRUNDY highlights how the ageing of the elderly population is a topic of great concern, in part, because the very old make far greater use of health and social services than any other age group. Understanding the cohort differences in survival and the heterogeneity of the elderly population is challenging because the processes affecting ageing are so complex. One of the most distinctive demographic features of the elderly population is the preponderance of women. There has been a widening of sex differences in age-specific mortality rates and this gender difference is evident among even the oldest old. Yet suicide rates peak in the seventies for women and in the eighties for men. Why? We don't know, but investigation would require interdisciplinary research crossing the social and medical divide.

The WALKER & MALTBY report is part of the European Observatory on Ageing and Older People. Although predominantly concerned with social policy, it also contributes to the understanding of the role that senior citizens had in European societies in the late 20th century. Comparative research is important not only for understanding what trends are common throughout the European Union, but also for how individual cultures and welfare regimes differ in the opportunities and constraints they impose on the elderly. Walker and Maltby demonstrate that social integration is still an elusive goal and they identify four main barriers: economic hardship, age-discrimination practice in the labour force, inadequate health and social care, and personal vulnerability. The book ends on an optimistic note and suggests that, in ageing societies, it is in everyone's interest to promote the full citizenship of older people. Unfortunately, this optimism would require a rather selective reading of the studies included in this review.

JACQUELINE L. SCOTT

See also Ageism, Age stratification, Disengagement theory, Human longevity

Gestalt psychology, *see* Psychology, major entry

Glass ceiling

Catalyst, *Women in Corporate Leadership: Progress and Prospects*, New York: Catalyst, 1996

Heilman, Madeleine E., "Sex Discrimination and the Affirmative Action Remedy: The Role of Sex Stereotypes", *Journal of Business Ethics*, 16/9 (1997), 877–89

International Labour Organization, *Breaking through the Glass Ceiling: Women in Management*, Geneva: International Labour Office, 1997

Korn Ferry International and UCLA Anderson Graduate School of Management, *Decade of the Executive Woman: A Joint Study*, Los Angeles: Korn Ferry International, 1993

Morrison, Ann M., Randall P. White and Ellen Van Velsor, *Breaking the Glass Ceiling: Can Women Reach the Top of America's Largest Corporations?*, Reading, Massachusetts: Addison Wesley, 1987; 2nd edition, 1992

Ragins, Belle R., Bickley Townsend and Mary Mattis, "Gender Gap in the Executive Suite: CEOs and Female Executives Report on Breaking the Glass Ceiling", *Academy of Management Executive*, 12/1 (1998): 28–42

Tharenou, Phyllis, "Gender Differences in Advancing to the Top" in *International Journal of Management Reviews*, edited by Cary Cooper and Alan Pearson, Oxford: Blackwell, 1999

US Department of Labor, *A Report on the Glass Ceiling Initiative*, Washington, DC: Office of Information and Public Affairs, 1991

MORRISON, WHITE & VAN VELSOR presented the seminal empirical work on executive women "breaking the glass ceiling". They examine the causes of women entering executive ranks, the factors that propel women upwards, and those that derail them; they compare the factors for men and women, and discuss whether women need the same development as men. A limitation is that the empirical study from which the conclusions are drawn has weaknesses in research design relating to its sample, measures, source of ratings, and type of data. The findings do, however, provide the first in-depth analysis of, and much insight into, what helps and hinders women's advancement to the top.

The US DEPARTMENT OF LABOR's report on the "glass ceiling" provides a useful introduction to this topic including its definition and major causes. The report is valuable in focusing on the "glass ceiling" as it affects both women and minorities, and it provides useful information on the causes of the "glass ceiling" from both perspectives, albeit one based on a small sample of companies. The analysis is thoughtful; for example, it was one of the first to show that the "glass ceiling" operates at lower levels than first believed, especially at lower management, and that the focus for change needs to start at low levels.

KORN FERRY INTERNATIONAL has conducted regular surveys to determine what assists, or deters, women from advancing to the very top executive levels. Although the survey on which this report is based uses simple items and analyses, they provide a wealth of useful quantitative information on, and interpretations of, possible causes of women advancing or not advancing to the top, using a large sample of women top executives. The results of this survey are also given in comparison with earlier surveys of women, and surveys of men. Hence, the data are a valuable, comprehensive, and comparative source of information. The weakness is that the research design is not rigorous, and the results are thus open at times to other interpretations.

This is one of the regular CATALYST surveys of women who have reached top executive levels assessing the barriers and facilitators to their advancement and covering a comprehensive range of factors. A strength of the approach taken is that both top women executives and the male chief executive officers (CEOs) of the women are surveyed, allowing comparison of the factors that women and their bosses say explain why women do not break the "glass ceiling". The interview data provided from the women are valuable in providing illustrations of the factors helping or hindering women's advancement to the top. The contrast with CEOs is particularly enlightening, indicating that differing perceptions are a part of the problem. The interpretation of the impact of interpersonal factors (for example, lack of networks) is particularly helpful. The nature of the retrospective research design means that there are still other interpretations to these findings, although they are in agreement with those from more rigorous studies.

RAGINS, TOWNSEND & MATTIS present an interpretation of the 1996 Catalyst data incorporating theory and relevant empirical evidence to explain why the "glass ceiling" arises. They particularly discuss the differences in the perceptions of the women and their CEOs, and their importance. The strength of the article is in the theoretical underpinning it provides for the results. The conclusions are compelling and thought provoking and help advance understanding of the problem. However, they are limited by the research design underlying the data.

The INTERNATIONAL LABOUR ORGANIZATION provides a rare comparative report on the "glass ceiling" across many countries, including relevant statistics. The report also covers a comprehensive range of causes and barriers to women's advancement to the top, from various theoretical and disciplinary perspectives, and examines women's advancement to all levels in management. It also examines not getting to the top. It provides statistics comparing women's representation in management across countries, and incorporates illuminating results from other studies. The report provides an insightful analysis into why women do not break the "glass ceiling", and, throughout, it provides examples from practice of what has helped in different countries. However, there are too few statistical data on women in upper management and executive positions, the group being discussed, although there is much material on lower levels.

HEILMAN provides an analysis of why women do not gain top management jobs based on her theory of sex stereotypes. She extends her "lack of fit" theory in regard to sex-stereotyped attributes about women and the characteristics of the management job from women's general representation in management, to explain why women do not advance to top management. Her analysis, including the contingent factors that trigger sex discrimination and bias, is one of the strongest theoretical frameworks developed in an area lacking in theory, and is helpful in explaining why the "glass ceiling" exists. The strength of her article is its strong theoretical framework. The limitation is in the lack of empirical evidence from the field, a general weakness in this area.

THARENOU reviews recent empirical evidence on why women do not break the "glass ceiling", using studies of upper managers and executives, and of stages or transitions for advancement. She provides a summary of the findings from the most rigorous studies conducted, classifying them into human capital, social capital, and developmental resource-based approaches, the latter two classifications rarely covered in this area. She reviews only studies using strong research designs, but also builds in the results of the other kinds of studies, and concludes that they are congruent in their conclusions. She arrives at several general principles to explain why women do not break the "glass ceiling", and provides integrative summaries throughout with an extensive set of future research questions for investigation.

PHYLLIS THARENOU

See also Equal opportunity, Women in management

Globalization, economic

Castells, Manuel, *The Information Age: Economy, Society and Culture*, 3 vols: vol. 1: *The Rise of the Network Society*, Oxford and Cambridge, Massachusetts: Blackwell, 1996; vol 2: *The Power of Identity*, Oxford, and Malden, Massachusetts: Blackwell, 1997; vol. 3: *End of Millennium*, Oxford and Malden, Masachusetts: Blackwell, 1998

Dicken, Peter, *Global Shift: Transforming the World Economy*, 3rd edition, London: Paul Chapman, and New York: Guilford Press, 1998

Dunning, John H., *The Globalization of Business: The Challenge of the 1990s*, London and New York: Routledge, 1993

Hirst, Paul and Grahame Thompson, "The Problem of 'Globalization': International Economic Relations, National Economic Management and the Formation of Trading Blocs", *Economy and Society*, 1/4 (1992): 357–96

Humbert, Marc (editor), *The Impact of Globalisation on Europe's Firms and Industries*, London: Pinter, 1993

Lash, Scott and John Urry, *Economies of Signs and Space*, London and Thousand Oaks, California: Sage, 1994

O'Brien, Richard, *Global Financial Integration: The End of Geography*, London: The Royal Institute of International Affairs, and New York: Council on Foreign Relations Press, 1992

Ohmae, Kenichi, *The Borderless World: Power and Strategy in the Interlinked Economy*, London: Collins, and New York: Harper Business, 1991

Porter, Michael E., *The Competitive Advantage of Nations*, New York: Free Press, 1990

Sassen, Saskia, *The Global City: New York, London, Tokyo*, Princeton, New Jersey: Princeton University Press, 1991

Strange, Susan, *States and Markets*, 2nd edition, London: Pinter, 1994

Thrift, Nigel and Andrew Leyshon, "A Phantom State? The De-traditionalisation of Money, the International Financial System and International Financial Centers", *Political Geography*, 13/4 (1994): 299–327

The literature on economic globalization is now vast, with a growing body of opinion solidifying around the view that economic activity is no longer based on cross border exchanges (international trade) but on a high "degree of functional integration between internationally dispersed economic activities" (DICKEN).

A key proponent of the view that economic globalization has produced a world economy that is no longer characterized by international trade but by global and transnational economic exchanges operating in a "borderless world" is OHMAE. He suggests that an increasingly global economy exists in which a free exchange of capital, knowledge, individuals, and industry has begun to produce an organically interlinked economy that has brought with it the erosion of the nation as the primary economic unit and laid the seeds for "boundless prosperity" (p.269). In pointing to the decline of the national territories as the building blocks of contemporary economic functioning he emphasizes the dominance of consumer spending patterns in determining the prospects of companies and countries. In such a situation, it is suggested that regionally interlinked economic areas as well as city-focused economies may become prominent.

SASSEN takes as her starting point the often observed phenomenon that, despite the decentralization and globalization of economic processes, the importance of certain key regions and urban areas in the world economy has perversely become ever more accentuated. Sassen suggests that the global cities of New York, London, and Tokyo are key sites for the production of specialist services upon which the operation of world markets and processes rely. In order to understand the productive relations and control of economic globalization, then, the role of economic units other than nations, such as global cities, must be understood. THRIFT & LEYSHON's analysis of contemporary financial markets and trading similarly stresses the role of global cities in the production and control of globalized markets. With the deregulation of important forms of finance and the interconnected nature of computerized markets they suggest the international financial system is co-ordinated and negotiated in key centres. This approach is in contrast to O'BRIEN's argument that location is of no consequence to the international financial system. In his interesting book he suggests that money is now hypermobile and that a single global financial system exists in such a way that no one place, group, or sector can control it.

Dicken paints a picture of a major shift towards a globalized economy driven by rapid technological change within which the interaction of nation states and transnational corporations work to effect the nature of economic activity and outcomes. He also draws critical attention to new forms of firms' overseas operations such as international subcontracting and strategic alliances. This is an empirically abundant and far-reaching text that is extremely useful for focusing on the crucial role transnational corporations have played in global-ization. However, the roles of multinational companies and small to medium sized enterprises are not fully emphasized.

DUNNING stresses the role of the multinational enterprise as one of the key instruments in the increasing globalization of business. This is a thorough and balanced approach that appreciates the interaction of national, regional, and multinational economic forces and actors in determining the opportunities and tensions brought with the globalization of business. Equally, PORTER asks important questions about the competitive position of national economies within globalization. By presenting arguments that suggest that the death of the national economic scale may be overexaggerated or need not necessarily occur in such a straightforward way, he is useful in countering the often unquestioned assumption that globalization is a pervasive force over which nation states and economies have little or no control. Offering a similarly critical approach to the claims made by the strongest believers in the globalized economy HIRST & THOMPSON argue that there are few firms that are operational in more than a few countries. Furthermore they suggest that it remains true that, for the majority of firms, it is the competitive position of their home base that most strongly determines their profits and performance.

An excellent volume edited by HUMBERT presents interesting and detailed accounts of the effects of globalization on the European economy and its firms. Many of the findings have been outdated in the time since its publication, but some important historical detail is treated and crucial questions about the meaning of globalization for industry and firms are asked.

LASH & URRY suggest that there has been an "end of organized capitalism" resulting in a set of capitalistic relations based on the reflexivity of organizations and actors. On the basis of an analysis of Germany, Japan, UK, and the US they suggest the world's advanced economies are economies of "signs" (images, symbols, brands, information) and spaces in which "subjects" (labour) and signs are ever more mobile. As an account of economic globalization it stresses a transition to a postindustrial and postmodern era.

CASTELLS' trilogy *The Information Age* also stresses a break with previous modes of international economic functioning. This is a very important work for anyone interested in the contemporary world economy. He skilfully portrays the existence of a dynamic global economy in which trade, production, and consumption rely on information that itself is undergoing a revolution. Seamless markets operate in "spaces of flows" rather than in bounded space. The final volume is perhaps most pertinent and includes analysis of the collapse of USSR, the global criminal economy, the Asia-Pacific region, and European integration.

In an entertaining and well-theorized textbook, STRANGE emphasizes the essential link between the power states and the wealth of nations. By emphasizing the role of structures of power in the world economy the book is useful for helping readers think through the dynamic relations of power – economic and political – that have had determinate effects on the patterns and processes of economic globalization.

DOMINIC POWER

See also Financial globalization, Globalization: critiques and alternatives

Globalization, human geography

Appadurai, Arjun, *Modernity at Large: Cultural Dimensions of Globalization*, Minneapolis: University of Minnesota Press, 1996

Barber, Benjamin R., *Jihad vs McWorld*, New York: Times Books, 1995

Brown, David, "Globalisation, Ethnicity, and the Nation-State: The Case of Singapore", *Australian Journal of International Affairs*, 52/1 (1998): 35–47

Elteren, Mel van, "Conceptualizing the Impact of US Popular Culture Globally", *Journal of Popular Culture*, 30/1 (1996): 47–90

Giddens, Anthony, *The Consequences of Modernity*, Stanford, California: Stanford University Press, and Cambridge: Polity Press, 1990

Goldsmith, William, "The Metropolis and Globalization", *American Behavioral Scientist*, 41/3 (1997): 299–311

Lehmann, David, "Fundamentalism and Globalism", *Third World Quarterly*, 19/4 (1998): 607–35

Lin, Jan, "Globalization and the Revalorizing of Ethnic Places in Immigration Gateway Cities", *Urban Affairs Review*, 34/2 (1998): 313–40

Globalization is frequently discussed and infrequently defined. Although globalization has strong political and economic dimensions, this essay focuses on the dimensions of globalization that affect human geography, namely the impacts on culture and place. The study of globalization is emergent, so I have included works that provide basic guiding principles to its study, as well as some that are provocative, even if they are less than conclusive.

Although ostensibly about modernity, GIDDENS provides an excellent starting point for considering issues of globalization. This book allows us to understand the flows of images, values, and people that characterize globalization in the context of the institutions of late capitalism: the world capitalist economy, the nation-state system, the world military order, and the international division of labour. Capitalism is seen as a driving force in globalization because it is primarily an economic order. Politics, migration, and the dissemination of images are secondary.

To discuss the flow of images and commodities, BARBER uses "McWorld" as a gloss for the spread of American popular culture. McWorld will inevitably destroy all local culture and remake it into a Disneyesque theme park of shopping malls. A common response to the homogenization of McWorld are searches for local identity that often end up as bloody struggles for group sovereignty, which he calls "Jihad." Barber sees both McWorld and "Jihad" as threats to democracy, to which he clings dogmatically. Nonetheless, this book provides a thought-provoking base from which to explore the issues of identity and globalization further.

APPADURAI argues cogently and succinctly against theorists like Barber and firmly states that globalization does not necessarily entail the Americanization of local cultures across the globe. However, it examines how the movement of media and images can sometimes challenge local values. This book characterizes globalization as involving a high degree of mobility of people, technology, finances, media, and images. By proposing a number of global landscapes (ethnoscapes, technoscapes, financescapes, mediascapes, and ideoscapes, respectively), Appaduri suggests that the five dimensions of cultural flows are best understood as fluid and irregular. The greatest contribution of this book is that it sets out a broad theoretical outline for exploring how globalization is manifested differently in various local settings.

ELTEREN explores the impact of US culture on globalization. Those who equate globalization with "Americanization" ignore the historical sources, US culture, and the transnational nature of US media. Cultures are not clearly demarcated bounded wholes and therefore positing antagonism between local and global cultural processes may be somewhat misguided. It is more useful to think of new articulation between the local and the global rather that the replacement of the local by the global. The strongest contribution of this piece is that it shows the importance of seeing how the elements of US popular culture are given new symbolic meanings in each new setting. Overlooking this process has lead to a distorted view of globalization.

LEHMANN suggests that globalization has two modes of interacting with local cultures. The first is homogenizing – it either eliminates local elements or incorporates them without acknowledging their source. This is the mode commonly associated with the expansion of global consumerism – or "McWorld", to use Barber's term. In a surprising but provocative way, this work shows that religious fundamentalisms also operate in this mode. The majority of the article focuses on how this mode manifests itself in fundamentalism, using mostly Latin American examples. The second mode in which globalization interacts with local cultures is "cosmopolitanism", which incorporates and celebrates local elements.

BROWN explores the common scholarly assumption that globalization necessarily weakens nation states and thereby encourages the development of ethnic nationalisms. By examining the case of Singapore, Brown shows that interactions between the global, the national, and the ethnic are far more complicated. He shows that the place of the state in the global order must be evaluated on a case-by-case basis. It shows that it is not international capital that threatens the nation state as much as the cultural absorption rising from the flow of migrants and media. Singapore made economic globalization a primary nation-building strategy. As part of this it emphasized its Chineseness to gain economic ties with China. However, it emphasized this Chineseness as embodying "Asian values" that all Singaporeans share.

LIN takes up the theme that globalization must be understood in both political-economic and cultural-semiotic terms. It examines the role of ethnic places, including enclaves, in two linked processes in 15 immigration gateway cities. The first process is the recovery of US cities from deindustrialization and urban decline. The second process is the creation, in the city centres, of ethnic places that are hubs of transnational commerce as well as cultural flows. The main contribution of this piece is its depiction of the ways in which flows of people, commodities, and culture interact to globalize US cities. Another significant contribution is its examination of the pitfalls of the revalorization of ethnic places, namely the unwitting creation of quaint tourist attractions ("honeypots") and the difficulties faced by some ethnic groups in (re)claiming land to develop.

GOLDSMITH delineates a provocative theory that links urban form and globalization. Conventional wisdom holds that globalization changes the shape of cities, much as suggested by Lin. This piece suggests that the reverse may also be true by examining how the racially segregated nature of US cities shaped the nature of international markets, through US economic dominance, and thereby created in Europe racially segregated sectors in the urban landscape where none had previously existed. Although not entirely convincing, this work is important because it challenges us to think about how global processes may be affected by human landscapes as well as affecting them.

RON LUKENS-BULL

See also Foreign direct investment, Globalization: critiques and alternatives

Globalization, management and business

Barnet, Richard J. and John Cavanagh, *Global Dreams: Imperial Corporations and the New World Order*, New York: Simon and Schuster, 1994

Barry-Jones, R.J., *Globalisation and Interdependence in the International Political Economy: Rhetoric and Reality*, London: Pinter, 1995

Bergsten, C. Fred, *Competitive Liberalization and Global Free Trade: A Vision for the Early 21st Century*, Washington, DC: Institute for International Economics, 1997

Dunning, John H., "Reappraising the Eclectic Paradigm in an Age of Alliance Capitalism", *Journal of International Business Studies*, 26/3 (1995): 461–91

Guisinger, Stephen and Thomas L. Brewer, "Symposium on Multinational Enterprise and Economic Analysis", *Journal of International Business Studies*, 29/1 (1998): 1–115

Hirst, Paul and Grahame Thompson, *Globalization in Question: The International Economy and the Possibilities of Governance*, Cambridge: Polity Press, and Cambridge, Massachusetts: Blackwell, 1996

Michie, Jonathan and John Grieve Smith (editors), *Managing the Global Economy*, Oxford and New York: Oxford University Press, 1995

Moore, James F., *The Death of Competition: Leadership and Strategy in the Age of Business Ecosystems*, Chichester: Wiley, and New York: Harper, 1996

Ohmae, Kenichi, *The End of the Nation State: The Rise of Regional Economies*, New York: Free Press, and London: HarperCollins, 1995

Ohmae, Kenichi, *The Borderless World: Power and Strategy in the Interlinked Economy*, revised edition, New York: Harper, 1999

Pieper, Ute and Lance Taylor, "The Revival of the Liberal Creed: The IMF, the World Bank and Inequality in a Globalized Economy", New School of Social Research, Center for Economic Policy Analysis, *Working Paper*, 1/4 (1998): 1–47

Sachs, Jeffrey D., "Ten Trends in Global Competitiveness in 1998", *World Economic Forum: Global Competitiveness Report*, 3 (February 1999): 1–17

Snow, Charles C., John A. Mathews and Raymond E. Miles, "The Concept of the Corporation in the Twenty First Century", Carnegie Bosch Institute for Applied Studies in International Management, *Working Paper*, 99/1 (1999): 1–24

Stiglitz, Joseph E., "More Instruments and Broader Goals: Moving toward the Post Washington Consensus", United Nations University, World Institute for Development Economics Research, Second WIDER Annual Lecture (7 January 1998): 1–47

Tapscott Don, *The Digital Economy: Promise and Peril in the Age of Networked Intelligence*, New York: McGraw Hill, 1996

Globalization has created an enormous multidisciplinary literature in both the scholarly and the popular domains, particularly during the 1990s. Despite continuing and strong international interest in its various themes and topics, as BARRY-JONES has noted, major problems of definition, and confusion over ambiguous terminology as well as heroic myths remain to confront any attempts at objective inquiry.

There is, however, a reasonable degree of consensus that the economic activities of national economies are following a path of increasing global integration. The primary drivers as suggested by OHMAE's (1995, 1999) initial perception of the forces that are shaping these changes are: the new information technologies and knowledge-based industries; the global movement of financial capital of which over 75 per cent is in private hands; the development of strategic alliances and joint ventures by transnational firms, which now dominate their various markets (DUNNING; BARNET & CAVANAGH; GUISINGER & BREWER; and SNOW, MATHEWS & MILES) and major shifts within the international division of labour.

BERGSTEN suggests that one of the primary debates that creates much current controversy involves the notion of a neo-liberal market order driven by the quest for multinational free trade. According to Ohmae the reality is somewhat more complex given the growth of highly regionalized free trade and the tendency for subnational trading links to emerge activated by communication networks. These assumptions either overarch in the first case or subsume in the second, the concept of the national economy as a sovereign entity. They also raise important issues with regard to the ability of national governments to exercise their own sovereignty. This has led a number of critics to question whether national governments will retain any real role as global integration continues to gain momentum.

The prevailing notion of a global shift toward market liberalization has also attracted strong support from international agencies such as the World Bank and the IMF, which with the US Treasury, constitute the "Washington consensus". They have viewed the less developed part of the world as best served by the same reformist notions based on deregulative principles that were associated with the return of neoliberalism as a force for macro policy change in the West, in the era of Thatcher, Reagan, and Kohl.

More recently growing awareness that the consequences of such policies have resulted in manifest inequalities between the developed and the undeveloped nations, as noted by PIEPER & TAYLOR, has created serious cracks within the Washington consensus. The public reaffirmation of the need for a strong state by STIGLITZ in 1998 is reflective of the World Bank's attempt to reshape its role. SACHS suggests that the problem lies in what he calls the "profound democratic deficit" of international institutions, which reflect an often total lack of transparency as demonstrated in the way in which the International Monetary Fund acted during the East Asian financial crisis. From his perspective globalization is exerting strong pressures on decision making in two different directions. One pulls toward the local and parochial view of change, while the other places decision making at a significant distance from the people it is intended to serve. He sees a manifest danger in both the extreme form of national parochialism on the one hand and the considerable distance between the major international agencies and the constituencies they are reputed to serve on the other.

The belief that there is a need for the clearer identification and consensus management of the profound institutional changes being shaped by globalization is reflected in the critical scholarship of writers such as HIRST & THOMPSON and MICHIE & GRIEVE SMITH. They raise numerous questions in regard to the hard realities as opposed to the rhetoric and mythologies that surrounds globalization as a major issue that may require new forms of institutional regulation and maintenance on an international scale.

The popular view of globalization presents the transnational firm as the key driving force behind the integrative process, but oversimplifies the fact that in keeping with all the other institutional players, such firms have their own structural problems. According to TAPSCOTT, in the emerging world of digital commerce transnational corporations will have to struggle with an entirely new set of functional roles in which much broader concepts of existence and purpose will be needed to replace the present and traditional assumption that firms are in business solely to obtain a profit.

From a strategic perspective MOORE's use of biological metaphor to present the future globalized firm as an organizational entity within an integrated business ecosystem also spells the end of the traditional concept of market competition as we have known it. The prize, it seems, would be a form of strategic leadership that transcends industry, location, and even corporate rivalry. Such matters remain surrounded by a considerable amount of both scholarly as well as popular speculation with only the reality of ever increasing industrial and market integration as a truly stable variable in the debate.

ALAN WILLIAMS

Globalization, politics

Baylis, John and Steve Smith (editors), *The Globalization of World Politics: An Introduction to International Relations*, Oxford and New York: Oxford University Press, 1997

Boyer, Robert and Daniel Drache (editors), *States against Markets: The Limits of Globalization*, London and New York: Routledge, 1997

Diehl, Paul F., *The Politics of Global Governance: International Organizations in an Interdependent World*, Boulder, Colorado: Rienner, 1997

Hirst, Paul and Grahame Thompson, *Globalization in Question: The International Economy and the Possibilities of Governance*, Cambridge: Polity Press, and Cambridge, Massachusetts: Blackwell, 1996

Hurrell, Andrew and Ngaire Woods, "Globalization and Inequality", *Millennium*, 24/3 (1995): 447–70

McGrew, Anthony G. and Paul G. Lewis (editors), *Global Politics: Globalization and the Nation-state*, Cambridge: Polity Press, and Cambridge, Massachusetts: Blackwell, 1992

Ohmae, Kenichi, *The End of the Nation State: The Rise of Regional Economies*, New York: Free Press, 1995; London: HarperCollins, 1996

Reich, Robert B., *The Work of Nations: Preparing Ourselves for 21st-Century Capitalism*, London: Simon and Schuster, and New York: Knopf, 1991

Thomas, Caroline and Peter Wilkin (editors), *Globalization and the South*, London: Macmillan, and New York: St Martin's Press, 1997

Waters, Malcolm, *Globalization*, London and New York: Routledge, 1995

Weiss, Linda, *The Myth of the Powerless State: Governing the Economy in a Global Era*, Cambridge: Polity Press, and Ithaca, New York: Cornell University Press, 1998

World Bank, *The State in a Changing World: The World Development Report 1997*, Oxford and New York: Oxford University Press, 1997

The introduction to McGREW & LEWIS explores how the three principal paradigms of international relations theory have conceptualized global politics. This work is the ideal introduction to the globalization of politics because it analyses the nature and extent of globalization, the degree to which there is greater global political fragmentation or integration, and whether globalization is undermining the power and autonomy of the modern nation state. These are important themes addressed in an expert but approachable style. DIEHL's exploration of global governance provides an ideal accompaniment to this broad canvas by providing a detailed introduction to the politics of international organizations.

BAYLIS & SMITH have furnished an eclectic collection of 25 essays on international relations, which provides an informative introduction to the politics of globalization. Scholte's concise analysis of the definition and implications of globalization is an ideal starting point, and Willetts' exploration of actors in global politics demonstrates the limitations of a state-centric approach to globalization.

WATERS explores globalization by analysing its impact not only upon the polity, but also on the economy and culture. His questionable thesis is that globalization of the polity and economy depends on the degree to which culture is also globalized.

HIRST & THOMPSON have shown how globalization, as portrayed by the more extreme globalizers, is predominantly a myth. Identifying the political impact of globalization as "the pathology of over-diminished expectations", their work convincingly demonstrates that the loss of state sovereignty to global actors has been exaggerated and that, consequently, national governments retain the capacity for implementing radical domestic agendas. The continuing role of the state in the governance of the global polity and economy is attributed to the importance of states as sources of the rule of law. States are the prerequisites for regulation through international law of the market, environment, and polity. This work provides a welcome antedote to those who have overdosed on the hyperbole of globalization and assumed that all was lost.

WEISS has also tellingly exposed the extent to which globalization is a big idea resting on slim foundations. Three hypotheses about globalization are identified in the existing literature, namely strong globalization (with state power either eroded or unchanged) and weak globalization (strong internationalization) with the state power reduced. Weiss advances a fourth hypothesis that posits weak globalization (strong internationalization), with the role of the state capable of adaptation and assuming different forms. Political impotence as a justification for inaction is thus eliminated from international relations and political economy. The limits of globalization are further explored in BOYER & DRACHE. This text serves as a reminder that political intervention and bargaining at the global level are likely to deliver a better settlement than merely allowing market forces to deliver an international order that suits their interests.

The polar opposite perspective on globalization is provided in OHMAE's analysis, which attempts to convince the reader that nation states have already lost their role as significant actors in the global polity and economy. His contention is that the rapid cross-border migration of investment, industry, information technology, and individual consumers has rendered the nation state "a nostalgic fiction". In this borderless world, the stark and sole political option is for the state to cede operational autonomy to the region states, which are held to have supplanted their national predecessors. This is a splendid example of the overstatement of the globalization of politics, economics, and governance.

In a similar vein, REICH's opening contention is that globalization will so transform the politics and economics of the next century to the extent that only people will remain rooted within national boundaries. In responding to globalization, Reich asserts that the choice need not be between zero-sum nationalism and impassive cosmopolitanism. There is a third, superior, position that locates a positive economic nationalism where citizens assume responsibility for enhancing their own and others' capacity to live full and productive lives, but also cooperate with other nations to ensure that progress is not at the expense of rival populations. An optimistic if perhaps overly utopian vision.

The WORLD BANK's perspective on globalization suggests that the task confronting the state is to redefine its role so that it is matched to its capability to undertake and promote collective actions efficiently. To ensure sustainable, shared, poverty-reducing development, the state should respond to globalization by establishing a foundation of law, maintaining a non-discretionary policy environment, investing in basic services and infrastructure, and protecting the vulnerable and the environment. The advocacy of greater predictability in rule-making, reliability in judicial enforcement and freedom from corruption is a thinly disguised device for further limiting the role of the political and accentuating the role of the market in

a response to globalization intended to reinforce the Bank's neoclassical orthodoxy.

In sharp contrast, HURRELL & WOODS' analysis of the relationship between globalization and inequality usefully reminds the reader of how globalization is profoundly affected by inequalities among states, regions, and non-state actors, principally transnational corporations. This theme is more extensively developed in the edited collection from THOMAS & WILKIN, which contends that globalization is compounding the political, economic, and social inequalities between the industrialized north and the underdeveloped south. Growing global divisions are held to be developing because of the universal privileging by liberal ideology of the private over the public sphere and through the marginalization of the actual, as well as the potential, role of the commons. A sobering reminder that the number of losers may exceed the winners arising from globalization.

SIMON LEE

See also Globalization: critiques and alternatives, International relations theory, Nation state

Globalization, sociology

Belay, Getinet, "The (Re)construction and Negotiation of Cultural Identities in the Age of Globalization" in *Interaction and Identity: Information and Behavior*, vol. 5, edited by Hartmut B. Mokros, New Brunswick, New Jersey: Transaction, 1996
Hannerz, Ulf, *Transnational Connections: Culture, People, Places*, London and New York: Routledge, 1996
Mokros, Hartmut B. (editor), *Interaction and Identity: Information and Behavior*, vol. 5, New Brunswick, New Jersey: Transaction, 1996
Werbner, Pnina, "Introduction: The Dialectics of Cultural Hybridity" in *Debating Cultural Hybridity: Multi-Cultural Identities and the Politics of Anti-Racism*, edited by Pnina Werbner and Tariq Modood, London: Zed, 1997
Wicker, Hans-Rudolf, "From Complex Culture to Cultural Complexity" in *Debating Cultural Hybridity: Multi-Cultural Identities and the Politics of Anti-Racism*, edited by Pnina Werbner and Tariq Modood, London: Zed, 1997

In a key chapter in MOKROS' edited volume, BELAY re-examines identity in a globalized world. Belay takes issue with the random attribution of classifications to human groups. More than ever before, he argues, we should be aware of the inherent diversity of social groups, where "cultural communities such as Asian-Americans display significant internal heterogeneity, depending on whether they are of Vietnamese, Japanese, or Indian origin". In turn, he argues, by simply defining individuals in terms of one category, there is no system for classifying further difference. Belay critiques those who continue to analyse identity in terms of a perspective focusing on nation states. Within the globalized world, trans-societal processes of identity construction and negotiation demand that researchers adopt an interdisciplinary approach. Belay tackles the taken-for-granted assumption that the planet is evolving into a single "global village" by stating that the world displays none of the qualities of a village, where there is intimacy, shared meanings and symbols, and norms/rules of conduct. Difference is as predominant as ever. Although theorists of cultural imperialism see globalization as a form of electronic colonialism perpetrated on the poorer nations of the world, Belay cautions that this view relies on the recipients of this colonialism being passive rather than active, and concludes that this outcome is far from guaranteed. Instead, Belay sees globalization as an historically unique condition for the reconstruction of cultural identities. Rigid views of self and other may be fragmented in the best interests of all; individuals' identities may be more self-made than ever before.

HANNERZ is a key text by a major theorist of globalization. It observes that distances and boundaries are not what they used to be. Hannerz notes that globalization is reacted to with either cheering (from business people) or booing (cultural imperialists), and adds that as global interconnectedness is such a complicated and diverse event, both reactions are rather too hasty. Also criticizing the notion of the "global village", Hannerz finds little sense of a greater togetherness and of immediacy and reciprocity in social relationships. Globalization increases long-distance interconnectedness across national and continental boundaries, which takes many forms (global warming through to the trade in human organs), and has changed the way many people think of other people and other places. Although, in the social sciences, globalization challenges intellectual traditions of cultural mosaics, there has been some deglobalization as well, which receives much less attention. Hannerz notes that countries such as Burma and Hoxha's Albania actively deglobalized. Hannerz vitally adds that whereas globalization argues that national boundaries, states, and rigidly defined social groupings have passed their time as analytical constructs, it may well be that they were never very useful. People have always moved around (between groups, between geographical areas), even though this has not always been very widespread or quick. Hannerz asks whether there are transnational modes of understanding that allow individuals to appreciate each others' social practices (song, dance) regardless of the languages in which they are made manifest: "if this is the case, the notion of the boundaries of 'a culture,' as a self-evident package deal, with a definite spatial location, becomes suspect". There is also a likelihood of a large dimension of resistance to cultural homogenization, Hannerz predicts, and so globalization leads to cultural gain, as some items are taken up by new social groups, and others are not.

MOKROS' edited volume, in an interesting series, is much under-read. Beginning with the supposition that contemporary academic research accepts that identity is not given, but instead constituted through interaction, contributors discuss individual identity in an exciting range of globalized contexts and cast some doubt on the validity of conventional approaches to the study of human behaviour. In a spirit informed by globalization, contributors take aspects of social theory from a range of disciplines, and apply them in novel ways. Rather than seeing globalization as a phenomenon that transforms human diversity into solid homogeneity, Mokros and contributors emphasize the range of individual meaning making pursued in selected social contexts.

WICKER, in a chapter in Werbner & Modood's edited volume, notes the disarming attractiveness of ideas that seem to solve complex problems with ease. In a globalized world, he claims, easy and exhaustive solutions to problems of social complexity (difference, diversity, change) will not be sustainable. The globalized world is a creolized world, and in such a set of social systems, "culture as an invariable and homogeneous whole makes no sense at all".

WERBNER grounds the useful Werbner & Modood edited volume in a postmodern ethos, an approach that has lent much weight to the analysis of the globalized world. Essentializing ideological movements that reduce the significance of diversity must be countered, she notes. What is presently required is scholarly efforts to theorize the problems surrounding intercultural translation. Werbner deploys Bakhtin's metaphor that an "ocean of heteroglossia" surrounds monological national languages. Difference is all pervasive. Globalization is a theme that must be tackled with care, though, continues Werbner, as reality is increasingly produced in and by the media: real difference can be commoditized and transformed into something that is simply an aspect of our reality with a small hint of difference. Within globalization, a right to be different needs to be transmitted. Picking up on a theme explored by Belay, Werbner highlights the "constructedness" of all categorizations of human beings.

MILS HILLS

See also Globalization: critiques and alternatives

Globalization: critiques and alternatives

Balanyá, Belén, *et al.*, *Europe Inc.: Regional and Global Restructuring and the Rise of Corporate Power*, London: Pluto Press, 2000

Barnet, Richard J. and John Cavanagh, *Global Dreams: Imperial Corporations and the New World Order*, New York: Simon and Schuster, 1994

Gray, John, *False Dawn: The Delusions of Global Capitalism*, London: Granta, and New York: New Press, 1998

Greider, William, *One World Ready or Not: The Manic Logic of Global Capitalism*, New York: Simon and Schuster, 1997

Hines, Colin, *Localization: A Global Manifesto*, London: Earthscan, 2000

Korten, David C., *When Corporations Rule the World*, London: Earthscan, and San Francisco: Berrett Koehler, 1995

Mander, Jerry and Edward Goldsmith (editors), *The Case Against the Global Economy and for a Turn Towards the Local*, San Francisco: Sierra Club, 1996; London: Earthscan, 2000

Shuman, Michael H., *Going Local: Creating Self-Reliant Communities in a Global Age*, New York: Free Press, 1998

Wallach, Lori and Michelle Sforza, *Whose Trade Organization? Corporate Globalization and the Erosion of Democracy*, Washington, DC: Public Citizen, 1999

GRAY argues that attempts to impose the Anglo-American-style free market on the world will create a disaster on the scale of Soviet Communism. He predicts wars, worsening ethnic conflicts, and millions impoverished. America will experience moral and social disintegration as it loses ground to other cultures that understand that the market works best when embedded in society. Gray, a former supporter of the New Right, believes that the free market is undermining the values of bourgeois civilization in the heartland of capitalism. The book offers no answers, but is a powerful antidote to those who regard the free market as the solution, compared with Gray's view that, as practised, it is the problem.

BARNET & CAVANAGH describes the evolution of corporations over the last 20 years and how they are replacing national power, controlling the flow of money, goods, and information across the world. The novelty of the book is that it divides up the way the global economy shapes people's lives; changing politics, patterns, and location of work and family life. It considers Global Images, the Global Shopping Mall, the Global Workplace, and Global Money. It argues that the interaction of technology and globalization allows corporations to control an increasingly pervasive global commercial culture, become less accountable to public authorities and the adverse implications of this for culture, the rise of fundamentalism, the environment, and the economic future. It ends by briefly discussing the local backlash that is occurring, and calls for a globalization from below.

SHUMAN details how most communities globally are losing control of their economies, but how a range of them are regaining it by employing three new kinds of strategies: investing in locally owned businesses; focusing on import-replacing rather than export-led development by reducing dependence on distant sources of energy, water, food, and basic materials; and demanding more local political power from governments, rather than dubious politically motivated handouts and subsidies. It also calls for changes in tax and trade laws that disempower communities. This is a very detailed, but optimistic, "can do" response to the adverse effects of globalization on localities.

GREIDER is a journalist's look at the dynamics of the global economy in terms of its opportunities and dangers for diverse peoples and nations, and the rich and poor within them. His travels take him from Boeing in Seattle, to China, Germany, Sweden, and Japan. From these case studies he concludes that as the global economy's contradictions multiply and its instabilities deepen, there is a choice. This is one between possible world depression and the rise of the extreme right or the reassertion by national governments of their right to regulate the global market and protect communities and the rights of workers everywhere.

KORTEN details how the convergence of ideological, political, and technological forces is leading to an ever greater concentration of economic and political power in the hands of a few corporations. He shows how these entities have restructured values and institutions everywhere to serve narrow financial ends and the central role this plays in creating contemporary social, economic, environmental, and political problems. The book ends with a call for the establishment of the legal principle that corporations are public bodies created to serve public needs. He calls for more stakeholder control, a

cut in tax breaks, and stronger antitrust enforcement. He ends with the need to transform the global system to create a bias towards the local via more local control of the economy, constraining exports, and encouraging cooperation by localities in the search for solutions to shared problems.

WALLACH & SFORZA explains how the World Trade Organisation (WTO) works, its priorities and results. Using numerous case studies it shows how the WTO's rulings have adversely affected the environment, food safety standards and public health, medicines for the poor and labour rights. To reverse these trends it calls for a halt to further trade liberalization and a review and revision of world trade rules, such that they ensure people's access to essential goods and services while safeguarding product, food and workplace safety, and a healthy environment. It also calls for controls on transnational corporations (TNCs), their mergers and market concentration, and the imposition of investment rules.

BALANYÁ et al. details the role of that little known entity of European TNCs "The European Roundtable of Industrialists" and similar groupings that have shaped European policy from the Single Market to the Single Currency in their own interest. Their research gives the lie to the idea that all that is wrong with the European Union is just the result of poor decisions by national politicians, or the actions of faceless unaccountable Eurocrats. It shines the light on the central, if off stage role that big business in Europe has played and continues to play in shaping developments in the continent.

MANDER & GOLDSMITH is a collection of over 40 essays that outlines the adverse effects of free trade and its rules on the wilderness and the rest of the environment, local culture, unemployment, mass migration, increased inequality worldwide, and what it terms a "new corporate colonialism". It then documents ideas for reversing course away from the global towards a revisitation of local political and economic control, self-sufficiency, and ecological health.

HINES concentrates on alternatives. After a debunking of the theories behind free trade, it details a comprehensive set of self-reinforcing policies that can allow local economies to rediversify and take back control of their future. These internationalist "Protect the Local, Globally" policies for "Localization" consist of a goal of regional self reliance and sustainability achieved by reintroducing import controls, a "site here to sell here" policy for industry, grounding most finance locally, resource taxes for sustainability, local competition laws and a change in the end goal of trade, and aid policies to ensure such policies globally. Hines ends by proposing Localization as a route for consideration by the politically active to solving their campaign goals of dealing with inadequate social provision, community renewal, jobs, environmental protection, and the meeting of poorer countries' basic needs.

COLIN HINES

See also Globalization, economic

Globalization of technology

Archibugi, Daniele and Jonathan Michie, "The Globalisation of Technology: A New Taxonomy", *Cambridge Journal of Economics*, 19/1 (1995): 121–40

Archibugi, Daniele, Jeremy Howells and Jonathan Michie (editors), *Innovation Policy in a Global Economy*, Cambridge and New York: Cambridge University Press, 1999

Bartlett, C.A. and S. Ghoshal, "Managing Innovation in Transnational Corporations" in *Managing the Global Firm*, edited by Christopher A. Bartlett, Yves Doz and Gunnar Hedlund, London and New York: Routledge, 1990

Cantwell, John, "The Globalisation of Technology: What Remains of the Product Cycle Model?", *Cambridge Journal of Economics*, 19/1 (1995): 155–74

Commission of the European Communities: Directorate-General for Science, Research and Development, *Second European Report on Science and Technology Indicators*, Luxembourg: Office for Official Publications of the European Communities, 1997

Dosi, Giovanni, Keith Pavitt and Luc Soete, *The Economics of Technical Change and International Trade*, London: Harvester Wheatsheaf, and New York: New York University Press, 1990

Dunning, John H., *Multinational Enterprises and the Global Economy*, Reading, Massachusetts: Addison Wesley, 1993

Guerrieri, Paolo, "Patterns of National Specialisation in the Global Competitive Environment" in *Innovation Policy in a Global Economy*, edited by Daniele Archibugi, Jeremy Howells and Jonathan Michie, 1999

Hagedoorn, John, "Trends and Patterns in Strategic Technology Partnering since the Early Seventies", *Review of Industrial Organization*, 11/5 (1996): 601–16

Krugman, Paul, "Technological Change in International Trade" in *Handbook of the Economics of Innovation and Technological Change*, edited by Paul Stoneman, Oxford and Cambridge, Massachusetts: Blackwell, 1995

Pavitt, Keith and Pari Patel, "Global Corporations and National Systems of Innovation: Who Dominates Whom?" in *Innovation Policy in a Global Economy*, edited by Daniele Archibugi, Jeremy Howells and Jonathan Michie, 1999

New technologies have been a fundamental vehicle for contemporary economic and social globalization. Without aeroplanes, media, satellites, and the internet, it would not be possible to transfer information, knowhow, and expertise across different parts of the world. Globalization in areas as different as production, culture, news, finance, and fashion relies on the technologies which have allowed new operations in terms of accuracy and timeliness at negligible costs.

The generation and transmission of technological innovation has in turn been affected by the processes of globalization. ARCHIBUGI & MICHIE identifies three main categories of this process: the international *exploitation* of technologies, the global *generation* of innovations by multinational corporations, and global scientific and technological *collaborations*. The first category includes the oldest attempts made by profit-seeking firms to exploit innovations overseas via exports, licenses, or even by establishing production facilities in host countries. The second category is devoted to exploring the ways in which multinational corporations develop technological assets in host countries as well as in their home country. The

third category reports on the scientific and technological collaborations between organizations that are based in different countries but continue to preserve their institutional autonomy. While the academic community has always been international in scope, in the last decades there has been an increasing amount of strategic joint ventures related to technology that involve business firms.

KRUGMAN reviews the standard literature on the impact of technological change on international trade and the new critical departures. DOSI, PAVITT & SOETE argues that technological change has become more and more a key component for international competitiveness. The authors show that countries' export patterns in each product group, especially in those with a greater technological component, are associated with national innovative strengths. The share of technology-intensive products in world trade has more than doubled in a quarter of a century, as indicated by GUERRIERI. This essay also quantifies how Japan and other East Asian economies have progressively eroded the market shares of Europe and the US in technology-intensive industries.

DUNNING reviews the literature on the determinants and impact of multinational corporations' investment in R&D and innovative activities. More than 50 per cent of world expenditure on R&D by business enterprises is contributed by the top 500 multinational corporations. Multinational firms may locate R&D facilities abroad for various reasons: to serve their local plants; to respond better to the host market needs; to keep a window open on the technological developments of other countries; to benefit from the lower wages of scientists and engineers in developing countries; or to exploit the expertise of a nation in its field of comparative advantage.

The quantitative significance of R&D-related foreign direct investment is controversial. Using patent-based indicators, CANTWELL indicates that a significant growth has occurred in the last decades. PAVITT & PATEL, on the contrary, shows that in large firms, only a small share of technological activities originate from subsidiaries in host countries. According to this study, the so-called "global" corporations continue to keep the bulk of their technological activities in their home country. And, against expectations, the firms which are more "global" in the distribution of their technological activities are operating in traditional industries. US-based firms have for many years located around 10 per cent of their R&D investment overseas with little variation over time. The greatest part of US firms' foreign R&D has been performed in European subsidiaries. The Japanese economy continues to have limited inward and outward flows of direct R&D investment. Europe has been significantly affected by this form of globalization: European firms have substantially increased their R&D investment abroad, both in other European countries and in North America.

BARTLETT & GHOSHAL identifies three principal strategies followed by multinational corporations to develop their own technological base: (a) centre-for-global when the bulk of the product design and knowhow is produced in the corporation's headquarters and it is subsequently disseminated to subsidiaries; (b) local-for-local when each subsidiary of the firm develops its own technological knowhow to serve local needs; (c) local-for-global when the corporate technological strategy is built with ingredients coming from the various subsidiaries.

The COMMISSION OF THE EUROPEAN COMMUNITIES shows that academic collaborations across borders have been constantly increasing. Sabbatical years, exchanges of students, conferences, and projects have become more and more international in scope, allowing the transmission of knowhow across borders. This also generates a growing number of internationally coauthored articles published in academic journals.

While the academic community has traditionally been open to international collaboration, HAGEDOORN shows that a new trend has emerged in inter-firm technological collaborations since the 1970s. Firms are willing to share their knowledge base with potential competitors, if this helps them to acquire additional information and to lower the costs and risks associated with innovative projects. Strategic technology partnering seems to have opened a new form of organization where inter-firm cooperation goes alongside competition. More than 60 per cent of these agreements involve firms based in different countries. US corporations report the highest share of international agreements, both with Japanese and European counterparts.

The controversy about the impact of the globalization of technology on national economies is reported in ARCHIBUGI, HOWELLS & MICHIE. Some argue that national policies to enhance technological capabilities have been made ineffective by globalization. Others support national self-sufficiency and advocate policies to restrict the inward flow of foreign R&D, or even access for foreign students to national universities. Others, on the contrary, argue convincingly that it is in the interest of a nation to become a junction of scientific and technological exchange, especially if this is associated with endogenous learning. Governments should therefore design targeted policies that would allow the national economy to assimilate the available knowhow. The globalization of technology requires a more active government role if it is to allow nations to exploit the innovative frontier.

DANIELE ARCHIBUGI

See also Innovation (economic), Technology

Goals, goal setting

Austin, James T. and Howard J. Klein, "Work Motivation and Goal Striving" in *Individual Differences and Behavior in Organizations*, edited by Kevin R. Murphy, San Francisco: Jossey Bass, 1996
Austin, James T. and Jeffrey B. Vancouver, "Goal Constructs in Psychology: Structure, Process, and Content", *Psychological Bulletin*, 120/3 (1996): 338–75
Earley, P. Christopher and Christina E. Shalley, "New Perspectives on Goals and Performance: Merging Motivation and Cognition", *Research in Personnel and Human Resources Management*, 9 (1991): 121–57
Farr, James L., David A. Hoffman and Kathleen L. Ringenbach, "Goal Orientation and Action Control Theory: Implications for Industrial and Organizational Psychology" in *International Review of Industrial and Organizational Psychology*, vol. 8, edited by Cary Cooper and Ivan Robertson, Chichester and New York: Wiley, 1993

Latham, Gary P. and Edwin A. Locke, "Self-Regulation through Goal Setting", *Organizational Behaviour and Human Decision Processes*, 60 (1991): 212–47
Locke, Edwin A. and Gary P. Latham, *A Theory of Goal Setting and Task Performance*, Englewood Cliffs, New Jersey: Prentice Hall, 1990
Mitchell, Terence R., "Matching Motivational Strategies with Organizational Contexts", *Research in Organizational Behaviour*, 19 (1997): 57–149
Rodgers, Robert and John E. Hunter, "Impact of Management by Objectives on Organizational Productivity", *Journal of Applied Psychology*, 76/2 (1991): 322–36
Thierry, Henk, "Motivation and Satisfaction" in *Handbook of Work and Organizational Psychology*, 2nd edition, vol. 4: *Organizational Psychology*, edited by Pieter J.D. Drenth, Henk Thierry and Charles J. de Wolff, Hove, Sussex: Psychology Press, 1998
Williams, Richard S., *Performance Management: Perspectives on Employee Performance*, London and Boston: International Thomson Business Press, 1998

Much of the literature on goals and goal setting is about the nature of individual employees' work goals and the process of setting those goals. One class of writing is very much of a prescriptive, practitioner-orientated kind, offering practical guidance on how to set goals/targets/objectives. Such goal setting commonly takes place within the framework of a formal management system, for example performance appraisal or performance management. An introduction to this body of literature is found in WILLIAMS. Although it is orientated towards practitioners, this also draws on relevant theory and research. Williams's treatment of goals is mostly at the individual level of analysis but some material is also included about organizational goals. Moreover, it is clear from Williams's account that goal setting does not sensibly stand alone as a management practice and its effects may be enhanced when used in combination with other practices – feedback in particular. RODGERS & HUNTER summarize evidence that bears on this issue. Their meta-analytic study considers the combined effects of goal setting, employee participation, and feedback. They also investigated the role of top management commitment as a moderator variable.

Goal setting has been the subject of considerable research over the years and although Rodgers & Hunter provide an introduction to this, a much better source is the volume by LOCKE & LATHAM, with whom the theory of goal setting is most closely associated. This is a substantial work and is essential reading for anyone looking for an in-depth treatment of goal setting theory and research.

LATHAM & LOCKE provide a briefer introduction. This paper presents their theory, summarizes key research, and updates slightly their 1990 text.

As well as the accounts of goal-setting theory that have been presented by these two leading proponents, there are several other reviews. Some of these form parts of wider-ranging examinations of motivation theory, whereas others are more concerned with exploring the interrelationship of goal-setting theory with other psychological theory. One example of the latter is the essay by EARLEY & SHALLEY who discuss goal-setting theory in relation to cognitive processes. FARR, HOFFMAN & RINGENBACH pursue a somewhat similar theme but also consider the orientation that individuals take towards goals. They review practical implications, not just for goal setting, but also for performance feedback and for training and development. AUSTIN & KLEIN pursue the theme of interconnections among different bodies of theory and go further in that they explore linkages not just with the cognitive domain but also with the fields of personality and affect. Readers interested in the interconnectedness of theories should consult these sources, but those looking for more of a straightforward summary and assessment of goal-setting theory are likely to be better served by one of the more general reviews.

THIERRY, for example, offers a brief description of goal setting theory as part of a broad overview of theories of motivation and satisfaction. MITCHELL provides a rather more critical essay, and gives a fuller account of recent research. In this regard, Mitchell is a helpful update of Latham & Locke. Mitchell also identifies some unanswered theoretical and research questions and notes some of the continuing difficulties that surround the use of goal setting in practice. This is all set within the context of a broader assessment of motivational processes from which Mitchell draws some general principles.

Finally, there is a more general body of literature about people's goals that needs to be noted. The review paper by AUSTIN & VANCOUVER provides an accessible introduction. They identify some 30 theories in psychology that have posited goal-like constructs that they review within the framework of three categories: structure, process, and content.

RICHARD WILLIAMS

See also Appraisal, Feedback, Motivation

Gold standard

Bloomfield, Arthur I., *Monetary Policy under the International Gold Standard 1880–1914*, New York: Federal Reserve Bank of New York, 1959

Bloomfield, Arthur I., *Short-Term Capital Movements under the pre-1914 Gold Standard*, Princeton: Department of Economics, Princeton University, 1963

Bordo, Michael D. and Anna J. Schwartz (editors), *A Retrospective on the Classical Gold Standard, 1821–1931*, Chicago: University of Chicago Press, 1984

de Cecco, Marcello, *The International Gold Standard: Money and Empire*, 2nd edition, London: Pinter, and New York: St Martin's Press, 1984

Eichengreen, Barry, *Golden Fetters: The Gold Standard and the Great Depression, 1919–1939*, New York: Oxford University Press, 1992

Eichengreen, Barry and Marc Flandreau (editors), *The Gold Standard in Theory and History*, 2nd edition, London and New York: Routledge, 1997

Ford, Alec George, "International Financial Policy and the Gold Standard, 1870–1914" in *The Cambridge Economic History of Europe*, vol. 8: *The Industrial Economies: The Development of Economic and Social Policies*, edited by Peter Mathias and Sidney Pollard, Cambridge and New York: Cambridge University Press, 1989

Nurkse, Ragnar, *International Currency Experience: Lessons of the Interwar Period*, Geneva: League of Nations, 1944

Panić, Mića, *European Monetary Union: Lessons from the Classical Gold Standard*, London: Macmillan, and New York: St Martin's Press, 1992

Triffin, Robert, *The Evolution of the International Monetary System: Historical Reappraisal and Future Perspectives*, Princeton, New Jersey: Department of Economics, Princeton University, 1964

DE CECCO provides a useful introduction to the subject, with a survey of the ideas, policies, and developments that shaped the classical gold standard that operated between 1880 and 1914. It is written very much from a British perspective. This can be justified by the key role that the country, backed by the resources of its vast empire, played in sustaining the system; and the fact that the standard became increasingly unstable with Britain's relative economic decline in the years leading to the First World War. However, the author does not ignore the important supporting roles played by France and Germany.

BLOOMFIELD's (1959) comparative study of the monetary policies pursued by the leading central banks under the gold standard before 1914 has had a major influence on subsequent research in the field. Based on careful empirical analysis, it challenged a number of widely held beliefs by demonstrating (a) that the standard was managed rather than quasi-automatic; and (b) that the central banks were neither unaware of, nor indifferent to, the effect that their policies, imposed by the rules of the standard, might have on business confidence and economic activity. This led many of them to resort to various monetary devices in order to promote monetary and economic stability. Nor did the standard work as "smoothly" as it is supposed to have done. The study remains a classic.

BLOOMFIELD's (1963) analysis of short-term capital movements before 1914 represents an important contribution to our understanding of how the system worked. He assembled statistical data for a number of countries and, as a result, was able to present clear evidence that the standard was much more complex and unstable than generally believed. Short-term capital flows during the period were influenced by factors other than interest and exchange rate differentials, although the two did play a dominant role. There were also, then as later, "capital flights", which contributed to balance of payments problems. As these tendencies increased over time, there was growing concern in the 1900s about long-term viability of the gold standard.

FORD's article, which draws heavily on his earlier contributions to the subject, casts further doubts on the grossly simplified and idealised picture of the "gold standard behaviour stereotypes" painted by many monetary specialists. He makes the important distinction between institutions, policies, and experience of the countries at the centre and those at the periphery of the system. The adjustment burdens and costs were unequally distributed between the two groups. Given these differences, his analysis points to dangers of treating British monetary behaviour and experience before 1914 as being representative of the way that the countries whose currencies were tied to gold behaved.

TRIFFIN analyses some of the most important features of the gold standard since the early 19th century in the context of the evolution of the international financial system. He starts with a critical review of some of " the myths", perpetuated in "academic literature", about the way that the classical gold standard is supposed to have operated. This is followed by a brief and highly relevant account of "the vast changes in economic and political environment" that made a revival of the system in the interwar period unworkable and, therefore, short lived. This is developed in much more detail in NURKSE's justly famous report for the League of Nations, published 20 years earlier, which provides what is still the most influential analysis of the collapse, in 1931, of the interwar gold standard and, with it, of the international financial system.

EICHENGREEN's analysis of the interwar gold standard demonstrates in greater detail than previous studies the dangers inherent in attempts to revive an international financial system, judged to have worked successfully in the past, when conditions required to make it viable and sustainable no longer exist. The great economic, social and political changes after 1918, plus a better understanding of the link between monetary policy and unemployment, meant that governments could not ignore adverse effects of "monetary discipline" demanded by the gold standard. The drying up of international capital flows increased the adjustment cost of external imbalances. Preoccupied with their own problems, countries became less able and willing to help one another in times of crises. The interwar gold standard, which lasted only six years, was therefore doomed from the start. There are important lessons here for those who dream of reviving past financial systems – analysed and highlighted well by the author.

The 16 chapters in EICHENGREEN & FLANDREAU consist of a collection of extracts from and abridged versions of already published works on the gold standard. They deal almost exclusively with the monetary issues, treated not so much as the means to an economic (and thus social and political) end as an end in themselves. Together, the works selected provide, therefore, only a partial view of the classical and interwar gold standards. Nevertheless, the book includes a number of important contributions in this area, such as: David Hume's famous price-specie model of the adjustment process, written in the 18th century; Whales' analysis of the adjustment process, which emphasizes the importance of interest rates and short-term capital flows; and relevant extracts from the influential Cunliffe and Macmillan Reports produced in Britain between the wars.

The 15 essays in BORDO & SCHWARTZ, together with comments that accompany each, provide a valuable survey of monetary and economic developments under the gold standard, and political considerations that influenced them: both before 1914 and between the two world wars. Written specially for a conference held in 1982 by a number of leading monetary economists, they cover a wide range of important issues, as well as the policies and experience of several countries whose currencies were linked to gold during the two periods. The issues covered include, among others: technical aspects of "the rules of the game" that the countries were expected to observe, operations of two of the world's leading central banks before 1914 (the Bank of England and the Reichsbank), the growth

of real output, the transmission of business cycles, and "the image of the gold standard".

PANIĆ provides a systematic and detailed analysis of the adjustment process under the classical gold standard, integrating into the analysis many of the issues raised by previous studies in the field. The book, based on statistical data covering a number of economies, makes it clear why only some countries stayed on the standard throughout its long existence while others either never tied their currencies to gold or did so for a short time only. It shows that factor movements and levels of protection were of critical importance in influencing individual decisions as well as the success of the whole system. These lessons are then used as a guide to the nature and scale of national cooperation and common policies needed for long-term viability and success of the European Monetary Union. In other words, the study shows how history can be used in this context to improve understanding of contemporary problems and, in this way, act as a guide to policy.

MIĆA PANIĆ

Golden age of capitalism

Abramovitz, Moses, *Thinking about Growth and Other Essays on Economic Growth and Welfare*, Cambridge and New York: Cambridge University Press, 1989

Armstrong, Philip, Andrew Glyn and John Harrison, *Capitalism since 1945*, Oxford and Cambridge, Massachusetts: Blackwell, 1991

Boltho, Andrea (editor), *The European Economy: Growth and Crisis*, Oxford and New York: Oxford University Press, 1982

Crafts, Nicholas and Gianni Toniolo (editors), *Economic Growth in Europe since 1945*, Cambridge and New York: Cambridge University Press, 1996

Eichengreen, Barry (editor), *Europe's Post-War Recovery*, Cambridge and New York: Cambridge University Press, 1995

Maddison, Angus, *Dynamic Forces in Capitalist Development: A Long-run Comparative View*, Oxford and New York: Oxford University Press, 1991

Marglin, Stephen A. and Juliet B. Schor (editors), *The Golden Age of Capitalism: Reinterpreting the Postwar Experience*, Oxford: Clarendon Press, and New York: Oxford University Press, 1990

Olson, Mancur, *The Rise and Decline of Nations: Economic Growth, Stagflation, and Social Rigidities*, New Haven, Connecticut: Yale University Press, 1982

Webber, Michael J. and David L. Rigby, *The Golden Age Illusion: Rethinking Postwar Capitalism*, New York: Guilford Press, 1996

Between 1950 and 1973 the advanced capitalist countries enjoyed high rates of economic growth, with mild cyclical fluctuations, and low and stable rates of unemployment and inflation. At least in retrospect, this period appears to have been a golden age. Scholarly debate has examined the range of factors that brought the golden age into being, variations in growth between countries during the period, and why the golden age came to an end.

BOLTHO is an early attempt by a group of economists to assess the golden age and its aftermath. It consists of a set of more than 20 papers that examine the development of key variables such as growth and the balance of payments, survey aspects of policy, and also provide studies of individual European economies. In explaining the success of the golden age, the role of the demand side is emphasized, and policy is seen as having beneficial effects on the progress of the postwar economies. The development of a Keynesian consensus committed governments to active demand management, and the Bretton Woods exchange rate system guaranteed stability during the 1950s and 1960s.

OLSON is a highly original contribution that explains cross-country variations in growth with an elegant political economy model. Stable democratic countries accumulate special interest groups, which act as a drag on growth. War or revolution can break up the special interest groups, but, in some countries, encompassing groups may develop that promote, rather than inhibit, growth. This model appears to explain the stylized facts of postwar growth well. Countries such as West Germany and Japan, which had been defeated in war and where, it was argued, special interest groups had been broken up, grew much faster in the postwar period than did countries such as Britain, which had a long history of democratic stability in which interest groups could develop unhindered. Countries with encompassing groups, such as Sweden, also performed well.

ABRAMOVITZ is a collection of essays on growth economics. The most important is entitled "catching up, forging ahead and falling behind", in which the potential for convergence of per capita incomes as follower countries catch up with the technological leader is perceptively analysed. It is argued that the potential for catching up is not automatic but depends on the social capability of a nation. This social capability is partly determined by the educational attainments of the workforce but also by a range of political and institutional factors. These ideas of catching up and convergence have been the starting point for a huge empirical effort in the growth economics literature.

The most thorough and up-to-date study in the growth accounting tradition is provided by MADDISON. Growth accounting involves estimating a conventional production function weighted by factor shares. This enables the proportions of growth in each country to be estimated according to the extent of factor accumulation and total factor productivity growth. It emerges that Total Factor Productivity (TFP) growth was the most important source of fast growth during the golden age, but increases in physical capital were also significant. Human capital plays only a small role. These proximate sources of growth find their ultimate explanation in the unique characteristics of the golden age, notably the backlog of opportunities for catching up, the liberalization of trade, and demand management.

Taken together, the four works described above have largely defined the research agenda on the golden age. CRAFTS & TONIOLO is an assessment of the results of that research effort by a group of leading economic historians. In many ways, it is an updated version of the earlier work edited by Boltho, and consists of a similar blend of wide-ranging surveys of major themes, along with in-depth studies of particular countries. In the course of the work, growth accounting, "catch

up" and convergence, and Olson's theory are all assessed, and the emphasis is on the valuable insights provided by new growth theory. In contrast with earlier work, supply-side factors are seen as more important than those on the demand side, and the role of education in contributing to growth is given much more prominence than in conventional growth accounting models. The empirical limitations of the Olson model are also analysed.

Recent work stressing the importance of supply-side factors during the golden age has tended, at least implicitly, to downplay the role of institutions. The essays collected in EICHEN-GREEN represent an attempt to restore a more active part for institutions. The editorial introduction is a valuable survey of the existing literature. The conceptual framework draws on recent developments in the theory of institutions, which sees institutions as solutions to commitment problems. Individual essays examine the Marshall Plan, IMF, GATT, and the European Payments Union in this light.

MARGLIN & SCHOR's edited volume focuses on the institutional arrangements in place to support sustained growth and high employment in the postwar period. A major concern is the nature and importance of the interlocking institutions, and the interactions between those institutions. The book is an important contribution to the literature, and emphasizes the lessons that can be learned from golden age experiences for shaping contemporary economic policy in capitalist countries.

ARMSTRONG, GLYN & HARRISON develop a Marxist perspective on the golden age. In a very readable narrative, they focus on capitalism in general rather than the experience of individual countries. The fragility of the factors that brought the golden age into being is emphasized and it is argued that the golden age came to an end because of accumulating pressures within the capitalist system rather than because of exogenous factors such as oil price shocks, which tend to be emphasized in other historical accounts.

WEBBER & RIGBY challenge the notion that there was a sudden change in the early 1970s from long boom to crisis. Cyclical variations and differences between countries are stressed instead. Both mainstream and Marxist economic theories are criticized. All this is highly controversial, but an undoubted strength of the book is that it offers a very thorough and interesting account of the rise of the newly industrialized countries since the 1950s. In particular, the role played by the state in the growth of these economies is convincingly analysed.

ANDREW JENKINS

Governance

Charkham, Jonathan P., *Keeping Good Company: A Study of Corporate Governance in Five Countries*, Oxford: Clarendon Press, and New York: Oxford University Press, 1994

Gann, Nigel, *Improving School Governance: How Better Governors Make Better Schools*, London: Falmer Press, 1998

Humes, Samuel IV, *Local Government and National Power: A Worldwide Comparison of Tradition and Change in Local Government*, London: Harvester Wheatsheaf, 1991

Kooiman, Jan (editor), *Modern Governance: New Government–Society Interactions*, London and Newbury Park, California: Sage, 1993

Prentice, D.D. and P.R.J. Holland (editors), *Contemporary Issues in Corporate Governance*, Oxford: Clarendon Press, and New York: Oxford University Press, 1993

Rhodes, R.A.W., "The New Governance: Governing without Government", *Political Studies*, 44 (1996): 652–67

Sayer, John, *The Future Governance of Education*, London: Cassell, 1992; New York: Cassell, 1993

Stoker, Gerry and Robert Pyper, "Editorial: Understanding Governance", *Public Policy and Administration*, 12/2 (Summer 1997): 1–3

Tricker, Robert Ian, *International Corporate Governance: Text, Readings, and Cases*, New York and London: Prentice Hall, 1994

Traditionally the term "governance" has been taken to mean government, control, or direction. More recently, however, its association with government has been extended to relate specifically to *change* within government procedures and practices. As we shall see, the word has also been used to describe activities within specific branches of government and the arrangement of affairs within private sector organizations.

RHODES summarizes the situation well when he states that the term is popular but imprecise. In an essay examining the different uses of the term he argues that current usage treats governance as a descriptor for a new process of governing, or a changed condition of the ordered rule, or a new method by which society is governed. Rhodes' favoured use of the word emphasizes the growth of self-organizing, interorganizational networks in an era of new public management. He develops the view that such networks are a pervasive feature of service delivery in Britain, providing a challenge to governability because their increasing autonomy enables them to resist central guidance. The article articulates the author's reading of the situation based on a preferred definition and its discussion of six different uses of the term provides a valuable overview of the practice of governance within Britain.

STOKER & PYPER, in a special issue of *Public Policy and Administration* devoted to governance, also emphasize the current dichotomy faced by governments. In their editorial they refer to the tensions felt by government when it seeks to encourage individual enterprise on the one hand while keeping control of key facets of society and the economy. The breadth and complexity of the topic is underscored by the variety of articles that form the content of this issue of the journal. Harrison, Barnes & Mort consider the consequences of user involvement in the field of mental health, and Mackintosh focuses on changes to the economic culture of local government. An article by Lowndes also discusses management change in local government, and separate offerings by Rhodes and by Peters concentrate on issues for central governance. Richards & Smith consider change within government departments, and Judge, Hogwood & McVicar analyse the work of executive agencies.

The volume edited by KOOIMAN provides an excellent overview of governance in the modern sense. Writers from a number of European countries share their thoughts on the changes occurring within their own country, or within some aspect or service in their country. Its content is arranged in sections entitled "conceptualizations" (the theory of governance), "predicaments" (problematic issues in governance), "prospects for reform", and "evaluations" (both of which are self explanatory). The theme of change runs throughout the book, as does an emphasis on the development of new patterns of interaction between society and government.

Contributions relating to governance at a level below central government are examined in HUMES' work. Building upon other work in the local government area, the first part of his work is devoted to the development of a framework that can be employed to compare different systems of local governance. A major focus in the work is its description of the systems employed in France, Germany, the Soviet Union, and Britain and an enumeration of the differences between them. The book concludes with a valuable examination of traditions and trends within local governance and some proposals for reform.

Two very different views of governance within education can be examined through the works of SAYER and of GANN. Sayer's approach is a visionary, holistic one, which examines the total system and provides an outline for the future shape of the education service within Britain. In a succinct analysis he begins by cataloguing a series of changes that he sees occurring within society, and then carefully builds an argument on the demands that such changes may make upon the education service. In the development of such a service he foresees a need for educators "to find new systems and sets of relationships" that will include (*inter alia*) participative models of organization, the formation of task groups, the development of teamwork skills, and inter-team cooperative activity in education and all related services. The book discusses community-wide, lifelong learning, and covers all aspects of education and its management. Chapters are also devoted to regional governance and the future of school management in Europe. In contrast Gann concentrates on governance at the level of the school. While some attention is paid to the changing role of national government in education, the focus of the book is about how "a governing body made up of 'ordinary' people with no professional educational experience can make a positive contribution to the management of schools". With chapters devoted to context (the history of school governership), a strategic model of governance, and how individual governors can contribute to the task the book provides an excellent summary of the work of school governors and how they can bring about improvements to their own task and to their school. The sections examining the governors' relationships with relevant others (the headteacher, inspectors, local education authorities, and local communities) provide a practical and realistic assessment of the complex nature of the governors' work.

The field of *corporate* governance must also be considered. Previously, the area was seen merely as a branch of company law but, as TRICKER indicates, corporate governance "is concerned with the way corporate entities are governed, as distinct from the way businesses within those companies are managed". Company law may relate to the statutory arrangements of the host country, but Tricker sees the broad issues of corporate governance to be universal. Hence his volume focuses on text, readings, and case studies from an international perspective. The first chapter contains a valuable review of the literature on corporate governance. CHARKHAM's text also has an international theme in that the systems of five countries (Germany, Japan, France, the US, and the UK) are examined. Each chapter begins with a brief account of the focal society's features, followed by a description of its corporate governance framework, and concludes with a statement of the current issues of importance within the country. A final chapter considers which of the systems is best in terms of the principles of freedom and accountability. Finally, attention can be drawn to the volume edited by PRENTICE & HOLLAND, which examines contemporary issues in corporate governance and includes contributions on a wide range of related topics from an impressive list of academics and practitioners.

RAY McCHESNEY

See also Corporate governance

Governance and human geography

Ashenden, Samantha, "Reflexive Governance and Child Sexual Abuse: Liberal Welfare Rationality and the Cleveland Inquiry", *Economy and Society*, 25/1 (1996): 64–88

Bulmer, Simon, "The Governance of the European Union: A New Institutional Approach", *Journal of Public Policy*, 13 (1993): 351–80

Campbell, John L., J. Rogers Hollingworth and Leon N. Lindberg (editors), *Governance and the American Economy*, Cambridge and New York: Cambridge University Press, 1991

Clarke, M. and J. Stewart, "The Local Authority and the New Community Governance", *Local Government Studies*, 20/2 (1994): 163–76

Cochrane, Allan, *Whatever Happened to Local Government?*, Buckingham: Open University Press, 1993

Commission on Global Governance, *Issues in Global Governance: Papers Written for the Commission on Global Governance*, London and Boston: Kluwer, 1995a

Commission on Global Governance, *Our Global Neighborhood: The Report of the Commission on Global Governance*, Oxford and New York: Oxford University Press, 1995b

Cox, Kevin R. and A. Mair, "Locality and Community in the Politics of Local Economic Development", *Annals of the Association of American Geographers*, 78/2 (1988): 307–25

Cox, Kevin R., "Governance, Urban Regime Analysis and the Politics of Local Economic Development" in *Reconstructing Urban Regime Theory: Regulating Urban Politics in a World Economy*, edited by Mickey Lauria, London and Thousand Oaks, California: Sage, 1997

Goodwin, Mark and Joe Painter, "Local Governance, the Crises of Fordism and the Changing Geographies of Regulation", *Transactions of the Institute of British Geographers*, 21/4 (1996): 635–48

Hammond, Thomas H., "Formal Theory and the Institutions of Governance", *Governance: An International Journal of Policy and Administration*, 9/2 (1996): 107–85

Hay, Colin, "Re-stating the Problem of Regulation and Re-regulating the Local State", *Economy and Society*, 24/3 (1995): 387–407

Hirst, Paul and Graham Thompson, "Globalization, Foreign Direct Investment and International Economic Governance", *Organization*, 1 (1994): 277–303

Holland, Stuart, *The European Imperative: Economic and Social Cohesion in the 1990s: A Report to the Commission of the European Communities*, Nottingham: Russell Press, 1993

Hunt, Alan, "The Governance of Consumption: Sumptuary Laws and Shifting Forms of Regulation", *Economy and Society*, 25/3 (1996): 410–27

Imrie, Rob and Huw Thomas (editors), *British Urban Policy and Urban Development Corporations*, London: Chapman, 1993

Jessop, Bob, "The Regulation Approach, Governance and Post-Fordism: Alternative Perspectives on Economic and Political Change", *Economy and Society*, 24/3 (1995): 307–33

Kinsman, Gary, "'Responsibility' as a Strategy of Governance: Regulating People Living with AIDS and Lesbians and Gay Men in Ontario", *Economy and Society*, 25/3 (1996): 393–409

MacLeod, Gordon, "Globalizing Parisian Thought-waves: Recent Advances in the Study of Social Regulation, Politics, Discourse and Space", *Progress in Human Geography*, 21/4 (1997): 530–53

O'Malley, Pat, "Indigenous Governance", *Economy and Society*, 25/3 (1996): 310–26

Painter, Joe and Mark Goodwin, "Local Governance and Concrete Research: Investigating the Uneven Development of Regulation", *Economy and Society*, 24/3 (1995): 334–56

Pearce, Frank and Steve Tombs, "Hegemony, Risk and Governance: 'Social Regulation' and the American Chemical Industry", *Economy and Society*, 25/3 (1996): 428–54

Peck, Jamie, "Moving and Shaking: Business Elites, State Localism and Urban Privatism", *Progress in Human Geography*, 19/1 (1995): 16–46

Peck, Jamie and M. Jones, "Training and Enterprise Councils: Schumpeterian Workfare State, or What?", *Environment and Planning A*, 27/9 (1995): 1361–96

Pickvance, Christopher, "Spatial Policy in Territorial Politics: The Role of Spatial Coalitions in the Articulation of 'Spatial' Interests and in the Demand for Spatial Policy" in *Political Action and Social Identity: Class, Locality and Ideology*, edited by Gareth Rees et al., Basingstoke: Macmillan, 1985

Pollack, Mark A., "The New Institutionalism and EC Governance: The Promise and Limits of Institutional Analysis", *Governance: An International Journal of Policy and Administration*, 9/4 (1996): 429–58

Stoker, G. and K. Mossberger, "Urban Regime Theory in Comparative Perspective", *Environment and Planning C: Government and Policy*, 12/2 (1996): 195–212

Thomas, Huw and Rob Imrie, "Urban Development Corporations and Local Governance in the UK", *Tijdschrift voor Economische en Sociale Geografie*, 88/1 (1997): 53–64

Valverde, Mariana, "'Despotism' and Ethical Liberal
    Governance", *Economy and Society*, 25/3 (1996): 357–72
Ward, K.G., "Coalitions in Urban Regeneration: A Regime
    Approach", *Environment and Planning A*, 29/8 (1997):
    1493–1506

"Governance" has entered 20th-century literature as a restatement of a belief in democratic processes and values as a basis
for economic and social security. Governance is defined by the
COMMISSION ON GLOBAL GOVERNANCE (1995b) as
"the sum of the many ways individuals and institutions, public
and private, manage their common affairs", according to a
principle of the United Nations Charter "to live in peace with
one another as good neighbours". The Commission's proposal
for "global governance" built upon the structures of international law, multilateralism, and global economic interdependence has been motivated by the transformation of
"citizenship" as a concept rooted in territoriality (i.e. as individuals who belong to a polity, local or national, within specified regional boundaries) towards citizenship as membership
of a wider world conveyed by the electronic media, education,
travel and migration. This sense of governance has been translated by HOLLAND into a European Union context to imply
"strengthening of democratic institutions and procedures of the
Community and intergovernmental decision-making", to
defend and reinforce individual rights, to allow members of
the Committee of the Regions to represent regional interests,
and to "extend accountability at each level of government".
BULMER, and also POLLACK, have developed administrative
theory in the form of a "new institutional" approach to
analysis of the transformation of the governance of the EU.
HAMMOND presents detailed mathematical examination of
the political institutions of governance.

Governance has been reinterpreted by HIRST & THOMP-
SON as "economic governance", possible at five geographical
levels ranging from global to local, through regulatory
agencies that respond to the globalization of the world economy
and changing properties of nation states. Sociological authors
have explored a "sociology of governance" and the "governance
of consumption" (HUNT), "ethical 'liberal' governance" (VAL-
VERDE), "responsibility" as a strategy of governance (KINS-
MAN), "reflexive governance" and "governance of crisis"
(ASHENDEN), a "hegemonic mode of governance" (PEARCE
& TOMBS) and "indigenous governance" of Australian
Aborigines (O'MALLEY).

A more limited meaning of "local" or "community" governance is peculiar to British geographical analysis of the transformation of central government and local relationships as part
of the restructuring of the British welfare state. COCHRANE
and CLARKE & STEWART expand upon this thesis. They
suggest that a new form of "local governance" emerged with
the reduction of national spending and local government
powers by the Thatcher government, leading to fragmentation
of service providers and the creation of a diverse range of quasi
markets, institutions and agencies responsible for the distribution of goods and services. Products such as privatized utilities, Training and Enterprise Councils (TECs), and Urban
Development Corporations (UDCs) have required informal
collective social action in what PICKVANCE terms "spatial
coalitions". This concept of a geographical framework has been

advanced further by STOKER & MOSSBERGER and by
WARD as urban regime theory. PECK has examined the roles
of TECs in the geographies of governance and IMRIE &
THOMAS review British UDCs within local governance
context. Each is worth reading.

Much of the work on British local governance is locked into
post-Fordist or "Parisian" regulation theory as JESSOP, and
PAINTER & GOODWIN, and also HAY demonstrate.
Elsewhere, GOODWIN & PAINTER view local governance as
being broader than local government because of a wider "range
of actors" within the social and political processes, including
voluntary organizations, the mass media and even supranational institutions such as the European Union (EU). This
concept of governance focuses upon the "relations between
these various actors". Moreover, "local areas" are neither
autonomous nor isolated from wider state structures.

Several geographers have acknowledged the leadership of
Bob Jessop (Lancaster University) and his social thesis of reorganization of the national state, with three identifiable
shifts–"denationalization of statehood" with structural "hol-
lowing out" as territorial and functional reorganization, a shift
from government to governance ("destatization of politics"),
and "internationalization of policy" in the form of a shift from
Keynesian theory to a Schumpeterian "workfare regime" (a
model scrutinized by PECK & JONES). MACLEOD summarizes Jessop's work. Both references contain extensive bibliographies relevant to regulation theory.

TERRY G. BIRTLES

See also Post-Fordism

Governmentality

Barry, Andrew, Thomas Osborne and Nikolas Rose (editors),
    *Foucault and Political Reason: Liberalism, Neo-liberalism,
    and Rationalities of Government*, Chicago: University of
    Chicago Press, and London: UCL Press, 1996
Burchell, Graham, Colin Gordon and Peter Miller (editors),
    The Foucault Effect: Studies in Governmentality, London:
    Harvester Wheatsheaf, and Chicago: University of Chicago
    Press, 1991
Foucault, Michel, "Omnes et Singulatim: Towards a Criticism
    of Political Reason" in *The Tanner Lectures on Human
    Values 2*, edited by Sterling M. McMurrin, Salt Lake City:
    University of Utah Press, and Cambridge: Cambridge
    University Press, 1980a
Foucault, Michel, *Power/Knowledge: Selected Interviews and
    Other Writings*, edited by Colin Gordon, Brighton:
    Harvester, and New York: Pantheon, 1980b
Foucault, Michel, "Governmentality" in *The Foucault Effect:
    Studies in Governmentality*, edited by Graham Burchell *et
    al.*, 1991
Hindess, Barry, *Discourses of Power: From Hobbes to
    Foucault*, Oxford and Cambridge, Massachusetts:
    Blackwell, 1996

The term "governmentality" is most closely associated with
the name of Michel Foucault. It arises in connection to his
work on the critique of political reason (FOUCAULT 1980a)

and the nature of governmental power (FOUCAULT 1980b, 1991). These two aspects can to be examined separately although, as we shall see, they are closely interlinked.

In the case of the critique of political reason, Foucault argues that the study of politics and power needs to move away from its traditional concerns with sovereignty, legitimacy, and consent. Ever since Bodin and Hobbes the issue of sovereignty has been at the forefront of political discourse. Sovereignty implies that there is a certain centre of power either from which authority and legitimacy are derived or to which people owe their allegiance and consent. From this point power can be possessed or denied. Foucault calls this the domination approach to power. Broadly speaking it means that power is hierarchically determined and that sovereignty is located either in a person (the "King"), in an institution (the "Parliament"), in a group (the "ruling class", the "people"), and has a clear spatial dimension (as in "national" sovereignty). From this centre of authority radiates an essentially repressive and negative conception of power: the power to control, to deny, to order, and to coerce.

As HINDESS demonstrates with a careful analysis of Foucault's political thought, there is also another conception of power from which Foucault wants to distance himself (although at the same time he is more sympathetic to this and incorporates some of its features into his own conception). This can be termed the "strategic games of power" approach. In this case power is always fluid and in play. It rests upon the essentially free will of liberties that are unconstrained by anything other than the moves and positions of the other parties. In the fields of reciprocity set up by these interactions, power is always ambiguous, unstable, and potentially reversible.

Between these conceptions of power as domination and power as pure gaming, Foucault inserts his own conception of power as an instance of governmentality. This governmental power concerns those modalities, rationalities, mechanisms, and techniques that seek to act on the conduct of conduct. Here power is exercised through "technologies" that are in no way held in a single place or by an individual or entity, but are rather dispersed throughout the interstices and fabric of social, political, and economic life. Thus from the perspective of governmentality, there is nothing analytically privileged about a sovereign power that rules by either coercion or consent. Indeed, the state is itself subject to the same processes of governmentalization as are other elements and parts of the social fabric. Thus in principle the attempt to act on the conduct of conduct or on the actions of others – to act at a distance so to speak – not only involves what is usually understood as the domain of government (the enactment of laws, the promulgation of rules and administrative edicts, the organization of juridical review, and so on), but can be an attribute of any social actor. Thus companies, churches, families, populations, or whatever, and indeed, individuals themselves, are all equally both made "available" to the practices of governmentality – subject to its powers – and are parties to its initiation. In as much, for instance, as persons are the subjects of the processes of governmentality, their personal conduct is already politically charged. It operates to regulate their own behaviours though a process of self-regulation – the organization of the self in terms of the way that self conducts its behaviours. The governance of the self is thus in a certain

continuity with the operation of "the government", or the household, or the firm, and so on, in respect to their capacities to govern. Governmentality aims to affect conduct, whether that is at the level of the individual, the household, the firm, or the state.

There are a number of further consequences of this approach that are worth mentioning. Trying to affect how others conduct their own conduct always implies that there is a certain freedom enacted through this conception of power. Power is not the denial of a freedom. Liberties are always presupposed as a part of power. Governmentality invokes its own regulatory freedoms. This means that power is productive and enabling, it is a positive attribute of conduct. In addition, then, this also means that there is a possibility of resistance to, and an evasion of, power (possibly even, as a limit case, an ultimate guarantee of its failure). Once again, however, this should not be read in the form of a denial. Resistance and evasion are part of the constitution of power, not something that happens as a subsequent reaction to it.

The question is, then, through what political processes is this conduct of conduct organized? Here we have both Foucault's own preliminary presentations and a current intense debate amongst a Foucauldian scholarship (BURCHELL, GORDON & MILLER; BARRY, OSBORNE & ROSE). Foucault outlined three such broad programmes of governmentality, which he labelled "the shepherd and his flock", "disciplinarity", and "liberalism". Each of these has a particular meaning and provenance. The shepherd and his flock refers to the way that populations are constituted as the objects of governance, to be organized into entities that are not mere aggregations of their members, who have a certain freedom to devise their own behaviours but who are nevertheless "husbanded" and nurtured by a kind of pastoral power that has the population's health and welfare foremost in mind. Disciplinarity is that form of governmentality designed to provide agents with the capacity for self-control, to promote their abilities to act in concert, and to render them amenable to instruction. It proliferated during the 17th and 18th centuries in Europe and came to characterize such institutions as the school, the military, manufacturing, the administration and regulation of prisons, hospitals, and other institutions of confinement. Finally, liberalism is seen by Foucault as neither a political philosophy or ideology, nor a space for the untrammelled operation of a natural order, but rather as another kind of power promoting the operation of free decisions by individuals as the best way to secure the operation of government. It requires a degree of freedom to operationalize "security" of populations through interdependency and self restraint arranged around a series of "norms" of acceptable behaviour. The current debate within Foucauldian scholarship involves a refinement and development of these initial suggestions, to bring them up to date, and to extend the notion of liberalism in particular so as to accommodate contemporary changes in governmental regimes of regulation.

GRAHAME F. THOMPSON

Gramsci, Antonio 1891–1937

Italian political philosopher

Anderson, Perry, "The Antinomies of Antonio Gramsci",
    New Left Review, 100 (1976–77): 5–78
Bellamy, Richard and Schecter, Darrow, *Gramsci and the
    Italian State*, Manchester: Manchester University Press,
    1993
Clark, Martin, *Antonio Gramsci and the Revolution that
    Failed*, New Haven, Connecticut: Yale University Press,
    1977
Davidson, Alastair, *Antonio Gramsci: Towards an Intellectual
    Biography*, London: Merlin Press, and Atlantic Highlands,
    New Jersey: Humanities Press, 1977
Femia, Joseph V., *Gramsci's Political Thought: Hegemony,
    Consciousness, and the Revolutionary Process*, Oxford:
    Clarendon Press, 1981
Hall, Stuart, "Gramsci and Us" in *The Hard Road to
    Renewal: Thatcherism and the Crisis of the Left*, London:
    Verso, 1988
Martin, James, *Gramsci's Political Analysis: A Critical
    Introduction*, Basingstoke: Macmillan, and New York: St
    Martin's Press, 1998
Sassoon, Anne Showstack, *Gramsci's Politics*, 2nd edition,
    London: Hutchinson, and Minneapolis: University of
    Minnesota Press, 1987

Gramsci was a Sardinian-born intellectual and political activist on the militant left in Italy. After relinquishing his university studies in Turin in 1915, due to ill health, he became a full-time journalist and cultural critic. Aligning politically with the revolutionary wing of the Italian Socialist Party and intellectually with idealist anti-positivism, he promoted a revolutionary socialism based on the idea of the working class as a cultural vanguard. During the industrial conflicts that followed World War I in 1919–20, Gramsci outlined a theory of factory council democracy to replace the bourgeois state. When the workers' struggles were eventually defeated and Italy was enthralled by Mussolini's fascists, he assisted in the formation of the Italian Communist Party, of which he became leader in 1923. Arrested by Mussolini's police in 1926 he was eventually sentenced to 20 years imprisonment. While incarcerated he managed to obtain reading and writing materials and succeeded in producing a series of notebooks filled with theoretical essays: these texts are known collectively as the "Prison Notebooks" (*Quaderni del carcere*). The Notebooks were smuggled out of prison by his sister-in-law and, along with his numerous letters, they were published in Italy in the 1940s and 1950s. However, prison conditions destroyed Gramsci's already poor health and he died soon after being granted a conditional release.

DAVIDSON's sympathetic biographical account of Gramsci's intellectual development and political activity prior to his incarceration is written with the express intention of releasing its subject from the narrow interpretative frame established by the Italian Communist Party (PCI) after his death. Davidson traces the growth and ongoing revision of Gramsci's views as he grew up in underdeveloped Sardinia, studied in industrial Turin, and worked as a revolutionary socialist during and after the war. In addition, he underlines the profound psychological isolation Gramsci felt, both as a result of his disability (he was a hunchback) and as a "southerner" in northern Italy. Davidson traces Gramsci's movement through Sard nationalism, radical idealism and, eventually, as a mature political activist, to a form of Leninism. His account supports the view that Gramsci developed his own, independent position on revolutionary strategy: namely, a Leninism informed by a deep concern for the self-emancipation of the working class.

CLARK provides an excellent historical analysis of the factory council struggles in 1919–20 during which Gramsci came to prominence as a political thinker. Tracing the origins of the factory council (*consiglio di fabbrica*) to the early part of the century, he sketches in detail the emergence of the councils as sites of political antagonism between workers and industrialists after the war.

In a full and analytical treatment of Gramsci's political theory, FEMIA gives possibly the most balanced and accessible commentary on the Prison Notebooks. He concentrates his analysis on the implications of the concept of hegemony for a Marxist theory of capitalism and revolution. Crude interpretations are corrected by highlighting the distinctively humanist Marxism of Gramsci's "later" thoughts. Gramsci draws a balance between a materialist theory of society and an emphasis on the decisive importance of subjectivity and consciousness in social change. The concept of "hegemony" is treated as the fundamental key to his Marxism: it denotes the "intellectual and moral leadership" that the ruling class achieves over subordinate classes. Hegemony functions as an explanation for the persistence of capitalism despite its crises: Gramsci's analysis displaces the "conflict model" of capitalism with one focused on the struggle for consent, and it functions as the basis for a revolutionary strategy in which subordinate classes are persuaded to consent to an alternative social order by a revolutionary party.

The revolutionary party is the central theme of SASSOON's interpretation of Gramsci's thought. She argues that Gramsci's novelty lies in developing a concept of "the party" appropriate to the conditions of advanced capitalism. Sassoon argues that the concepts and categories in the Prison Notebooks support a theory of the party as the protagonist of a new hegemony. The integrative processes of monopoly capitalism – in which the workforce is progressively incorporated into an organized system of production, and intellectual knowledge and the apparatuses of the State are subordinated to this system – demands a political strategy appropriate to its form. Generating hegemony requires that the party offer an alternative form of integration: one that is based on the democratic inclusion of the masses rather than their pacification.

ANDERSON traces the development of the concept of hegemony in Russian Marxist debates and offers a critical account of Gramsci's version of it. The central weakness of Gramsci's theory, he argues, is a persistent "slippage" between different accounts of how hegemony operates. Sometimes consent is treated as part of civil society alone, sometimes of the state, and sometimes both. For Anderson, this obscures the distinctive role of the state in capitalism, which functions as the legitimate source of violence. Gramsci's emphasis on the building of consent misunderstands the nature of class political domination in capitalism.

By contrast, HALL reads Gramsci as a theorist of ideology and politics and employs his ideas to comprehend the emergence of "Thatcherism" in Britain in the 1970s and 1980s. Gramsci's contribution to political analysis lies in his subtle awareness of the role of ideology and "discourse" in cementing the power of economic classes. Hall points to Gramsci's term "common sense" as the discursive form through which political power negotiates its domination over the masses. Unlike other political thinkers on the left, Gramsci was aware of the tentative, ever-contested nature of power in contemporary capitalism, the way in which popular experiences are constantly (re-)articulated into political programmes. Thus Gramsci's thought illuminates the rise of the New Right in Britain as Margaret Thatcher sought to develop a hegemonic common sense joining together elements of traditional conservatism and neoliberalism.

BELLAMY & SCHECTER seek to redress the bias in favour of Gramsci as a theorist of contemporary Western society by placing his thought in a specifically Italian context. Gramsci, they argue, was preoccupied with questions concerning the Italian State and its failure to secure full cultural and political unity. Consequently, the normative dimension of his thought is permeated by a concern for a cultural homogeneity lacking in modern Italy, and this leaves strong traces of authoritarianism in his prescriptions. Both in his early theory of factory-based democracy and his later suggestions concerning the party, Gramsci is argued to place unity and discipline before pluralism and liberty.

MARTIN steers between the "contextual" and the "contemporary" interpretations of Gramsci. Focusing on the notion of "crisis" as the key to Gramsci's political analysis, he argues that the theoretical apparatus constructed in the Prison Notebooks is undoubtedly engaged with the quite unique conditions of Italy's social and political environment after World War I. It is this attention to crisis, when political and theoretical boundaries are put in doubt, that makes Gramsci's analyses so insightful. Yet, his prescriptions remain within a "modernist" theoretical frame that promotes the integration of state and civil society, cultural and ethical unity, and looks to the working class as the foundation for a new political order.

JAMES MARTIN

See also Civil society, Hegemony

Gramsci and Fordism

Boothman, Derek (editor and translator), *Further Selections from the Prison Notebooks*, by Gramsci, London: Lawrence and Wishart, and Minneapolis: University of Minneapolis Press, 1995

Buttigieg, Joseph A. (editor), *Prison Notebooks*, by Gramsci, 2 vols, New York: Columbia University Press, 1992–96

Davidson, Alastair, *Antonio Gramsci: Towards an Intellectual Biography*, London: Merlin Press, and Atlantic Highlands, New Jersey: Humanities Press, 1977

Davis, John A. (editor), *Gramsci and Italy's Passive Revolution*, London: Croom Helm and New York: Barnes and Noble, 1979

Fiori, Giuseppe, *Antonio Gramsci: Life of a Revolutionary*, London: NLB, 1970; New York: Dutton, 1971

Ford, Henry, in collaboration with Samuel Crowther, *My Life and Work*, New York: Doubleday Page, 1922, London: Heinemann, 1923; translated into French 1926

Ford, Henry, in collaboration with Samuel Crowther, *Today and Tomorrow*, New York: Doubleday Page, and London: Heinemann, 1926; translated into French 1926

Hoare, Quintin and Geoffrey Nowell Smith (editors and translators), *Selections from the Prison Notebooks of Antonio Gramsci*, London: Lawrence and Wishart, 1971; New York: International Publishers, 1972

Jessop, Bob, "Accumulation Strategies, State Forms, and Hegemonic Projects", *Kapitalstate*, 10 (1983): 61–81

Lawner, Lynne (editor and translator), *Letters from Prison*, by Gramsci, New York: Harper and Row, 1973; London: Jonathan Cape, 1975

Morera, Esteve, *Gramsci's Historicism: A Realist Interpretation*, London and New York: Routledge, 1990

Mouffe, Chantal (editor), *Gramsci and Marxist Theory*, London and Boston: Routledge and Kegan Paul, 1979

Poulantzas, Nicos, *Fascism and Dictatorship: The Third International and the Problem of Fascism*, London: New Left Books, 1974

Sassoon, Anne Showstack, *Gramsci's Politics*, 2nd edition, London: Hutchinson, and Minneapolis: University of Minnesota Press, 1987

Simon, Roger, *Gramsci's Political Thought: An Introduction*, revised edition, London: Lawrence and Wishart, 1991

It is perhaps remarkable that "Fordism" as a theory can be traced to handwritten notes from an Italian prison cell. Produced as thirty-four notebooks between 1926 and 1933, the tightly condensed words of Antonio Gramsci were not published until 1947 and only slowly entered Marxist political philosophy. Since 1968, Gramsci's outlook has replaced the popularity of Louis Althusser's philosophy, and ranks amongst Marxists and non-Marxists as one of the most incisive critiques of 20th-century political and economic organization.

Several events in Gramsci's life proved important to his interpretation of political power. Born in Sardinia in 1891, he witnessed his father's arrest then six years of imprisonment for no other reason than his support of the losing candidate in the 1897 elections. This placed the family in extreme poverty. Plagued by malnutrition and persistent ill-health, Gramsci struggled for an education and studied intermittently at the University of Turin where he identified closely with socialist ideas during the political upheavals of post-Risorgimento Italy after 1910. He became conversant with the anti-positivist views of Benedetto Croce, the anti-extremist speeches by Lenin, and the principles of the Third International. Italy's entry into World War I, the Torinese factory uprising of 1917, and the Russian Revolution inspired him as a popular newspaper writer. One of the founders of the Communist Party of Italy (CPI) in 1920, Gramsci developed close links with the Russian Central Committee and, in 1924, was elected deputy president of the CPI as an outspoken opponent of Fascism. His parliamentary address of that year attacked Mussolini's proposed law to abolish secret associations and the liquidation of all political opposition. Gramsci was incarcerated under this law from 1926, to be released in extreme ill-health, only because of international intervention by the Soviet Union. Gramsci never recovered, and died in April 1937. More complete biographical accounts are given by FIORI, by DAVIDSON, by LAWNER and by Levy (*Gramsci and the Anarchists*, 1999).

While in prison, Gramsci received French editions of two works written by Henry FORD. These assisted his interpretation of the Wall Street Crash of 1929, as well his reflection on the Italian political crises from 1910 to 1921, the 1917 Russian Revolution, and Hitler's *Mein Kampf*. Gramsci's Notebook 22, entitled "Americanism and Fordism", is one of a selection translated by HOARE & SMITH as the first English text of Gramsci's writing. This notebook provides only a portion of his broader reinterpretation of Marxist doctrine. More recent translation of other notebooks by BOOTHMAN expands Gramsci's reference to "Fordism", but a new English translation by BUTTIGIEG, directly from the notebooks, suggests that the 1947 source used by Hoare and Smith might have contained pro-American embellishment.

The uniqueness of Notebook 22 is Gramsci's analysis of contemporary philosophical problems, especially the global depression, the first Soviet Five-Year Plan, and Soviet interest in applying US ideas, notably Frederick Taylor's concept of "scientific management", to socialist assembly-line factory production. Suggesting that "Americanism" and "Fordism" derived from "an inherent necessity to achieve an organization of a planned economy" as an evolutionary process which had never experienced European feudalism, Gramsci presumed US Prohibition and its authoritarian rules to be a necessary condition for developing a new type of worker suited to "Fordized" industry. Gramsci prepared a catalogue of the most important issues raised by Fordism:

(a) replacement of the "present plutocratic stratum" by a new mechanism of accumulation and distribution of finance capital, based directly on industrial production;
(b) the "question of sex" and the formation of a new feminist personality, in which women achieved a genuine independence in relation to men;
(c) the prospect that Americanism might constitute an "epoch", either as a *passive revolution* or mass movement, similar to the rise of Gandhism in India, and reminiscent of Tolstoy's theory of nonresistance to evil, or as an *explosive upheaval* comparable to the French Revolution;
(d) the question of whether "rationalization of the demographic composition" of Europe would follow the American example, and discard as functionless to a production economy the purely parasitic classes retained only as burdens of heritage, namely the fossilization of civil service personnel and intellectuals, of clergy and landowners, of piratical commerce and professionals;
(e) the question of whether this evolution would have its starting point within industrial production activity, or whether this would occur through massive construction of a formal juridical arm to guide production;
(f) the question of whether "high wages" paid by Fordized and rational industry would persist;
(g) whether Fordism constituted the "ultimate" stage in the process of progressive attempts by industry to over-

come the Marxist "law of the tendency" for the rate of profits to fall as the rate of exploitation rises;
(h) the enormous diffusion of psychoanalysis since the war and in response to a "pathological crisis" resulting from increased moral coercion exercised by the apparatus of the state and society upon individuals;
(i) whether Rotary Clubs and the YMCA as forms of Freemasonry "without the petits bourgeois and without the petits bourgeois mentality" constituted an element of American rationalist ideology representative of a new type of civilization.

Much of Gramsci's analysis of Fordism cannot be taken out of context of the ideas presented in his other notebooks as overlapping monographs. An important pervading theme is his development of the concept of *hegemony*. He observed that Lenin adopted hegemony as a strategy for revolution, but was restricted by his own definition. Gramsci drew upon the older foundations provided by Russian Marxists during the 1880s, especially Plekhanov, and he argued that a class and its representatives exercise power over a subordinate class through a combination of coercion and power. Gramsci's interpretation also re-examined Machiavelli's *Prince* to identify "hegemony as a relation, not determined by force," but through political and ideological leadership as "the organization of consent". For Gramsci, the merits of Fordism included the fluidity gained as the affirmation of capitalism in a form acceptable by the working class as a means of decreasing costs. However, he wrote that the "puritanical" initiatives espoused by Ford held no other purpose than the preservation, outside work, of a certain "psycho-physical equilibrium" that prevented the physiological collapse of workers exhausted by the new method of production. To Gramsci, the Italy of the early 1930s showed the beginnings of a "Fordist fanfare" in the form of "exaltation by cities" and the overall planning of the Milan conurbation. Gramsci prophesied that these tendencies might affect the political structures of Fascism.

The timing of the Hoare–Smith translation of Gramsci's notes coincided with the demise of US global financial hegemony and the collapse of the Bretton Woods agreement. It was an environment particularly receptive to any new philosophy to interpret the sense of economic and political crisis. Gramsci's work has stimulated a range of studies of hegemony. These include a set of papers, edited by MOUFFE, which evaluate the Marxist implications of Gramsci's work, and two important works about Gramsci's political ideas by SIMON and by SASSOON. DAVIS has edited a volume by historians who have endeavoured to apply Gramsci's interpretation to case studies of the Italian "passive revolution" or the Second International as a shift from liberalism to corporatism. MORERA provides a study of Gramsci's humanistic but anti-democratic form of historicism.

Gramsci's writings have since assisted with interpretations of the internationalization of capital, initially through the work of POULANTZAS and other French Marxists. In Britain, JESSOP, a sociologist at Lancaster University, was the first to introduce Gramsci. Overall, Jessop suggests the primary, most defensible meaning of Fordism to be a distinctive mode of social regulation.

Boothman's translation of Gramsci adds information that would not have been available to Jessop and others. Boothman notes Gramsci's clear distinction between the Taylorist emphasis on assembly-line labour skills and the wider meaning of Fordism.

TERRY G. BIRTLES

See also Fordism, Antonio Gramsci

Great Depression

Beenstock, M., F. Capie and B. Griffiths, "Economic Recovery in the United Kingdom in the 1930s" in *The UK Recovery in the 1930s*, Bank of England Panel Paper no.23 (1984): 57–85

Cooper, R.N., "Fettered to Gold? Economic Policy in the Interwar Period", *Journal of Economic Literature*, 30 (1992): 2120–28

Eichengreen, Barry and T.J. Hatton (editor), *Interwar Unemployment in International Perspective*, Dordrecht: Kluwer, 1988

Eichengreen, Barry, *Golden Fetters; The Gold Standard and the Great Depression, 1919–1939*, New York: Oxford University Press, 1992

Friedman, Milton and Anna Jacobson Schwartz, *A Monetary History of the United States, 1867–1960*, Princeton, New Jersey: Princeton University Press, 1963

ILO, *Year Book of Labour Statistics, 1940*, Geneva: International Labour Office, 1940

Kindleberger, Charles Poor, *The World in Depression, 1929–1939*, Berkeley: University of California Press, and London: Allen Lane, 1973; revised edition 1986

Kitson, Michael and Solomos Solomou, *Protectionism and Economic Revival: The British Interwar Economy*, Cambridge and New York: Cambridge University Press, 1990

Kitson, Michael and Jonathan Michie, "Depression and Recovery: Lessons from the Interwar Period" in *Unemployment in Europe*, edited by Jonathan Michie and John Grieve Smith, London and San Diego: Academic Press, 1994; revised version in their *The Political Economy of Competitiveness*, London and New York: Routledge, 2000

Lewis, W. Arthur, *Economic Survey, 1919–1939*, London: Allen and Unwin, 1949

Ransom, R.L., "Great Depression" in *Encyclopaedia of Economics*, edited by Douglas Greenwald, New York: McGraw Hill, 1982

Romer, C., "The Great Crash and the Onset of the Great Depression", *Quarterly Journal of Economics*, 105 (1990): 597–624

Temin, Peter, *Lessons from the Great Depression*, Cambridge, Massachsetts: MIT Press, 1989

The "Great Depression" is the term used to describe the economic recession that hit the capitalist world economy following the Wall Street crash of 1929, and lasted through to the mid-1930s. As good a starting point as any into the literature is probably the encyclopaedia entries on the topic, such as RANSOM, although this discussion concentrates on the US economy. Ransom reports the facts and figures and key dates, and includes discussions of the collapse of asset prices, bank failures and the decline in the supply of money, the decline in spending, structural weaknesses in the American economy, institutional reform, economic philosophy in the US, and the new economics that emerged in response to the Great Depression.

Apart from historical description of the events around the Great Depression, the main focus of the literature is on the causes, firstly of the recession and secondly of the subsequent recovery. Under the impact of recession, world unemployment increased to nearly 25 per cent in 1932 before falling during the 1930s (although the level remained high – unemployment averaged 17.5 per cent during 1930–32 compared with 15 per cent during 1932–37). For contemporary estimates of unemployment figures, see ILO. Modern estimates of output and unemployment levels and growth rates internationally over this period are given in EICHENGREEN & HATTON. Such levels of unemployment were a major economic and social problem during the interwar period. Unemployment was a major cause of poverty, driving families below the most basic of subsistence levels and leading to deteriorating health, as documented for example by Harris in the chapter on "Unemployment, Insurance and Health in Interwar Britain".

BEENSTOCK, CAPIE & GRIFFITHS argues that it was wage movements that accounted for the cyclical fluctuations in output, both for the Great Depression and the subsequent recovery. It is true that real wages (adjusted for price changes) did move countercyclically over the 1929–37 cycle in Britain (rising relative to trend in the recession and then falling relative to trend during the recovery). But the causes of the output fluctuations lay elsewhere, and the timing of the wage fluctuations does not actually fit the claim that recession was caused by wage rises and recovery caused by wage cuts. This wage-output correlation itself does not in any case hold outside those particular years (on which, see J. Michie, *Wages in the Business Cycle*, 1987), a finding which reinforces the argument that the output and wage series are independently generated, with output influenced crucially by the level of demand for output, and wages by factors such as productivity levels and bargaining strength.

FRIEDMAN & SCHWARTZ emphasizes the role of tight monetary policy in causing the Great Depression. This of course is in line with Milton Friedman's monetarist interpretation of economics, history, society, and politics. COOPER observes that Friedman & Schwartz, "having never met a central bank they liked, of course attributed the severity of the depression to the perverse behaviour of the Federal Reserve Board" (p.2125). KINDLEBERGER stresses the fall in consumption due to a redistribution of income from the agricultural sector, where prices were falling. ROMER points to the decline in the consumption of durables, due to increased uncertainty created by the Wall Street Crash. LEWIS blames the collapse of American capital exports. Other possible factors include the alleged failure of fiscal policy to provide automatic stabilisers, and the Smoot-Hawley tariff of 1930, which is said to have initiated a mutually destructive trade war. Other studies have focused on the Great Depression as being caused by structural problems in the international economy. An explanation which embraces the cumulative impact of structural problems, adverse demand shocks, and policy mistakes would seem to be a more realistic approach than any of the above mono-causal views. One such policy mistake was certainly the adherence to the gold standard.

The role of trade in the interwar years, in the run-up to the Great Depression, during the international transmission of the Depression itself, and in the subsequent recovery, is analysed and discussed by KITSON & SOLOMOU. The role of the gold standard itself in the Great Depression is discussed in both EICHENGREEN and TEMIN.

KITSON & MICHIE argues that the extent of the Great Depression can be attributed to the operation of the gold standard: the impact of adverse shocks, such as the recession in the US and the collapse in capital exports, were transmitted to the rest of the world through the exchange rate regime. As foreign loans were called in due to developments in the domestic economy, the gold flows to the US increased. The draining of reserves in the debtor countries accelerated and monetary policy was tightened to ensure gold convertibility. Thus the deflationary bias of the gold standard system resulted in a perverse reaction to adverse demand shocks. Rather than facilitating an expansion of demand to ameliorate the depression, the system magnified the problem, leading to a collapse in world trade. As countries moved into recession they needed the capacity to initiate domestic policies in order to insulate themselves from the collapse in the world economy. The structure, characteristics, and paths of development of the major economies were different, and thus the timing and the composition of the policy mix required was also different. Yet during this period economic policy was constrained by the gold standard, leaving little flexibility to deal quickly with domestic problems. The authors argue that the Great Depression was caused by a number of self-reinforcing mechanisms and would most probably have occurred in the absence of the gold standard regime, but that its severity was almost certainly exacerbated by that regime.

JONATHAN MICHIE

See also Economic crises

Greece (ancient), political economy

Baeck, Louis, *The Mediterranean Tradition in Economic Thought*, London and New York: Routledge, 1994
Blaug, Mark (editor), *Aristotle, 384–322 BC*, Aldershot, Hampshire: Elgar, 1991
Finley, Moses I., *The Ancient Economy*, Berkeley: University of California Press, and updated edition, 1999
Gordon, Barry, *Economic Analysis before Adam Smith: Hesiod to Lessius*, London: Macmillan, and New York: Barnes and Noble, 1975
Langholm, Odd, *Price and Value in the Aristotelian Tradition: A Study in Scholastic Economic Sources*, Bergen: Universitetsforlaget, 1979
Lowry, S. Todd, *The Archaeology of Economic Ideas: The Classical Greek Tradition*, Durham, North Carolina: Duke University Press, 1987
McCarthy, George E. (editor), *Marx and Aristotle: Nineteenth-Century German Social Theory and Classical Antiquity*, Savage, Maryland: Rowman and Littlefield, 1992
Meikle, Scott, *Aristotle's Economic Thought*, Oxford: Clarendon Press, and New York: Oxford University Press, 1995
Petrochilos, George, "The Hellenic Contribution to Economic Thought", *Global Business and Economics Review*, 1/2 (1999): 215–46
Polanyi, Karl, Conrad M. Arensberg and Harry W. Pearson (editors), *Trade and Market in the Early Empires: Economies in History and Theory*, Glencoe, Illinois: Free Press, 1957
Schumpeter, Joseph A., *History of Economic Analysis*, edited by Elizabeth Boody Schumpeter, New York: Oxford University Press, and London: Allen and Unwin, 1954

Since the 1970s we have witnessed a renewed interest in, and a re-evaluation of, the economic thinking of ancient Greek philosophers, sophists, and writers, particularly, in the relationship between ethics and economics, where old doctrines are rediscovered and studied. The ideas of Democritus, Protagoras, and, most importantly, those of Plato (*The Republic, The Laws*), Xenophon (*Oikonomikos, Poroi, Cyropaedia*), and Aristotle (*Nicomachian Ethics, Politics*) on atomistic behaviour and private ownership of property, division of labour, free foreign trade, value, money, interest, as well as the efficient and effective estate management, leading to wealth creation and growth, compare favourably with our present views on these matters. However, the Greeks did not develop economics as a separate discipline but considered economic questions as part of their general inquiry on ethics and politics and the wider study of the best social organization of the city state. One could argue that they were more concerned with political economy than economics. This may have also contributed to the great dispute that has existed for at least a hundred years as to whether or not the economic ideas of the Greeks contributed anything of significance to the corpus of economic science. Writers such as Schumpeter, Finley, and Polanyi have dismissed ancient Greek economic thought, whereas others have argued forcefully for the relevance of such ideas for the development of modern economics. Indeed, the classical Hellenic teachings have influenced subsequent thinkers including Adam Smith and Karl Marx, and have been instrumental in the development of German social theory.

BAECK considers Hellenic economic thought within the context of the Mediterranean tradition. The book covers a time span of five millennia and shows that the premodern or Mediterranean tradition of economic thought perceived the economy as embedded in a web of social and political institutions, regulated by religious and ethical norms. Its understanding becomes important, as the genesis and flourishing of Western ideas and conceptual roots can be traced to the successive civilizations of the Mediterranean. The author explores the evolution of the Mediterranean tradition through biblical, classical Hellenic, Iranian and Arabic economic ideas, and the influence they exercised on the West through the Arab conquest of Spain and the role of schoolmen. What emerges is an economic tradition with a strong underpinning of ethical values, which in Hellenic economic thought is crystallized in the concept of *kalokagathia*.

BLAUG has collected, in a neat volume, fourteen influential articles of scholarship and debate on Hellenic economic thought, spanning almost a century of research on the Ancient Greeks (the first having appeared in 1895 and the last in 1985). Twelve of the articles deal, almost exclusively, with the economic contribution of Aristotle and two on the beginnings of economic thought and language and a review of recent literature (up to 1979) of Ancient Greek economic thought. They consider the debate as to the importance or not of Hellenic economic thought (for example Finley, Lowry, Kauder), Aristotle's contribution to the theory of value and to utility theory (Soudek, Kauder), thus, both neoclassical economics and Marxist economics can claim to trace their lineage from Aristotle, on barter, exchange, money, and so on. In all, they provide a useful picture of the role of Hellenic economics.

FINLEY has approached Hellenic economics from the standpoint of a classicist and ancient historian rather than an economist, although he claims that *The Ancient Economy* is not a book of "economic history". Nevertheless, the book is of considerable value both because of its meticulous scholarship and detailed research on the nature of ancient economic life and also because of its controversial nature, because together with his 1970 article, contained in Blaug above, it is very dismissive of Hellenic economic thought. Plato, Xenophon, and Aristotle are criticized as not having contributed anything to economics. Following Schumpeter (of which more below), Finley argues that in the absence of the mass of exchange value phenomena, required for proper economic theorizing, it was impossible for the Greeks to engage in economic thought. He thus agrees with the Polanyi group (see below), of which he was a member, about the non-market features of the Greek economy. However, their criticisms seem to be based on the misconception that the role of economics is the study of the market economy and, in particular, its self-regulating mechanism.

GORDON looks at early economic analysis and his book deals with Hellenic economic thought; biblical and patristic assessments of economic activity; rabbinical, roman, and canonical legal traditions; Aristotle's influence on the economic thinking of St Thomas Aquinas and the scholastics; scholastic economic thought on money, price, and value between 1300–1600 AD culminating in the ideas of Lessius on loans, exchanges, interest, prices and markets, wage determination, monopoly, and so on. In his treatment of Hellenic economic thought, which covers a quarter of the book, Gordon examines in considerable detail the economic relevance of the work of Hesiod and that of the Ionian and other pre-Socratic philosophers and the Sophists (who are likened to present day technocratic economists, able to argue both sides of an argument), before discussing in great detail the Platonic, Xenofontian, and Aristotelian economic contributions. He finds that their observations on economic matters have genuine analytical content and interest and are very useful for present day economics, as utility theory and Marx's labour theory of value and his commodity theory can be traced back to the Greeks. He also demonstrates why the strong ethical foundation of Hellenic economic thought made the acceptance by the Greeks of an unfettered market mechanism and the pursuit of growth, wealth, and, generally, riches simply incompatible.

LANGHOLM offers a meticulous and detailed examination of the accumulated knowledge of scholastic analysis and the role in economic analysis played by chapter five, book V of Aristotle's *Nicomachian Ethics*, dealing with economic exchange, price, and money. The author finds this part of *Ethics* of exceptional suggestiveness and analytical potential, and considers it as a forerunner to the theory of value and the basis of what is best and relevant in scholastic economics. He then proceeds to survey the Latin Aristotelian economics, by tracing the various interpretations/commentaries of Aristotle's work from 1240 AD, when he was introduced to the West by the Arabian philosopher Averroes. In the next century or so the following commentaries were formulated with their main exponents given in parentheses: context (Robert Grosseteste); labour and expenses (Albertus Magnus); human wants (Thomas Aquinas); aggregation and scarcity (Hernicus de Frimaria); effective demand (Johaness Buridanus), and synthesis (Geraldus Odonis). It is this Latin Aristotle, through the above commentaries, who came to dominate scholastic economic thinking and who was also introduced into the great Western universities in mediaeval times. While the main thrust of the book is easy to follow, the details do require linguistic competence, particularly, Latin.

LOWRY adopts a modernist approach to the debate between the substantivists or primitivists versus the modernists or formalists (of which more below under Polanyi). He builds a compelling case that the Greeks did do economics by emphasizing the administrative nature of their economics, which could be used to avoid the market. He argues that the control mechanism of ancient economies was not the market but administrative procedures, which were influenced by ethical considerations. Thus, ancient writings framed in administrative terms do bear an appropriate analytical superstructure and indeed the administrative superstructure is the only context in which ancient economic statements could be expected to be framed.

McCARTHY has introduced and edited twelve essays, most of which were written after the end of the Cold War and the collapse of the Iron Curtain, dealing with the influence of classical Greek philosophy, mainly Aristotelian and Epicurean, on the shaping and formation of German social theory in general and Karl Marx in particular. They demonstrate that the strong ethical underpinning of ancient Greek economics, which is not value free, is echoed not only in the writings of Marx, but also in the German historical school of economic thought. Nowadays this influence still survives in the form of the social market model, as distinct from the Anglo-American approach of the free and unfettered market.

MEIKLE, shifting through the conflicting evidence of the primitivists versus modernists debate, finds that Aristotle does develop a coherent theory of economic value, wealth, exchange, and money. However, this theory cannot be assimilated to what we call "economics" because its metaphysical foundation is incompatible with the Humean metaphysics on which our economics is built. From an Aristotelian standpoint, ethics and economics are competitors over the same ground, as rival sources of reasons for decision-making in the public realm, and they cannot be reconciled.

PETROCHILOS argues that the Hellenic economic contribution on private ownership of property, atomistic behaviour, division of labour, free foreign trade, exchange, value, money, interest, as well as the efficient, and effective estate management compare favourably with our present ideas on these matters. However, the main concern of Plato, Xenophon, and Aristotle is the best organization of society and, thus, their economics has a strong ethical underpinning, in the form of *kalokagathia,* which provides an effective constraint to the excesses of the market. Their economics is not value free, as neoclassical economics is, but it is rather akin to what we call today political economy.

POLANYI, ARENSBERG & PEARSON reports the results of an interdisciplinary project on the nonmarket ancient economies, which has split economic anthropologists and classicists between the substantivists or primitivists, who, like Polanyi, think that economic theory applies only to price-oriented market economies, and the formalists or modernists, who hold that economic theory can be applied to primitive or ancient economies. Polanyi in his own contribution, "Aristotle Discovers the Economy", finds that economic theory cannot expect to benefit from either Aristotle's *Politics* or his *Ethics,* because economic analysis aims at elucidating the functions of the market mechanism, an institution that was still unknown.

SCHUMPETER, in his monumental treatise, dismisses the economic writings of the Greeks at best as modest and feels that those classic scholars and economists who thought more highly of it were confusing it with general philosophy rather than technical economics. He thinks that in economics most statements of fundamental facts acquire importance only by the superstructures they are made to bear and are commonplace in the absence of such superstructures. He treats Xenophon in a footnote as not necessary to discuss; Plato's discussion of the division of labour is considered as commonplace; and in Aristotle he finds decorous, pedestrian, slightly mediocre, and more than slightly pompous common sense, despite conceding that there is an analytic intention in Aristotle, not found in Plato.

GEORGE A. PETROCHILOS

Greek economy and economic record

Alogoskoufis, George and Nicos Christodoulakis, "Fiscal Deficits, Seigniorage, and External Debt: The Case of Greece" in *External Constraints on Macroeconomic Policy: The European Experience,* edited by George Alogoskoufis, Lucas Papademos and Richard Portes, New York and Cambridge: Cambridge University Press, 1991

Alogoskoufis, George and Apostolis Philippopoulos, "Inflationary Expectations, Political Parties and the Exchange Rate Regime: Greece 1958–1989", *European Journal of Political Economy,* 8 (1992): 375–99

Alogoskoufis, George, "The Two Faces of Janus: Institutions, Policy Regimes and Macroeconomic Performance in Greece", *Economic Policy,* 20 (1994): 147–92

Christodoulakis, Nicos, Sophia Dimelis and Tryphon Kollintzas, "Comparisons of Business Cycles in Greece and the EC: Idiosyncrasies and Regularities", CEPR Discussion Paper, 809, 1993

OECD, *Economic Surveys,* Greece, Paris: OECD Publications, 1998

Papadopoulos, Athanasios, "An Interpretation of Post-War Stabilization Policies in the Greek Economy: 1953–1981", *Journal of European Economic History,* 20/1 (1991): 187–205

Pirounakis, Nicholas G., *The Greek Economy: Past, Present and Future,* Basingstoke: Macmillan, and New York: St Martin's Press, 1997

Skouras, Thanos S. (editor), *Issues in Contemporary Economics,* vol. 5: *The Greek Economy: Economic Policy for the 1990s,* Basingstoke: Macmillan, 1992

ALOGOSKOUFIS analyses the causes of changes in macroeconomic policy regimes in the postwar Greek economy. His inclusive study focuses on the fact that, until 1974, the economic performance of Greece was one of the most impressive in postwar Europe. After the second oil shock and admission to the European Union (EU), Greece then went into a period of persistent stagflation from which it has yet to recover.

Alogoskoufis argues that postwar Greece has exhibited two faces. During 1954–73, average annual growth was 7 per cent and annual inflation only 4 per cent. In the 20 years after 1974, these figures reversed completely. Growth slowed in the late 1980s and collapsed after 1980. Inflation exploded and remained consistently high. Alogoskoufis stresses that the this picture of the Greek economy is due to both external causes, like the collapse of Bretton Woods and the two oil shocks, and internal causes like the failure of labour market reform, the loss of credibility of the tax authorities vis-à-vis investors and firms, and the large increase in public sector expenditure.

The 16 papers edited by SKOURAS provide a comprehensive overview of the present state of the Greek economy, and its development in the future. Specifically, they focus on the following subjects: (a) fiscal problems and the role of the state, (b) monetary policy issues and banking developments, (c) balance of payments and external economic relations and, (d) structural issues and industrial policy. With regard to (a), there is a consensus among the majority of researchers that budget deficits are the prime cause of the macroeconomic imbalances in the Greek economy. A widely accepted solution is that a cost-benefit analysis should be conducted in order to determine which kinds of service should be left to the state and which should be transferred to the private sector. The need for monetary stability, combined with the deregulation and liberalization of the financial markets, which is considered to be essential for participation of drachma in the exchange rate mechanism (ERM), is the main conclusion with regard to (b). A comparison of the Greek and Italian banking systems also reveals a need for major changes to make Greek banks competitive in an integrated European financial system. The last two papers examine the prospects of the Greek public and private sector in the forthcoming European single market.

PIROUNAKIS offers an integrated picture of the modern Greek economy by examining its past performance and analysing the present state of Greece and its future economic prospects. A brief review of the Greek economic record between the years 1204 and 1990 is followed by an instructive examination of the fundamental elements of the Greek economy. These elements include (a) the public sector and public finances and taxes, (b) monetary policy, (c) the financial markets and institutions, (d) the social security system,

(e) the "real" economy, (f) the building sector, and (g) tourism and environmental issues. The strong point of this book, besides its important economic policy suggestions, is its analysis of the future prospects of the Greek economy both in a sociopolitical and international framework. A minor disadvantage is the lack of more sophisticated econometric analysis and the very short discussion about the prospects of Greece as a member of the European Union.

The OECD economic surveys, which are published annually for every member country, provide the most reliable and objective assessments of current Greek economic activity. These surveys each have three sections: "recent trends and short-prospects", "macroeconomic and structural policies", and a third section devoted to special economical issues. The first section focuses on microeconomic activity (such as labour market) in contrast with the second one, which analyses the success and socioeconomic consequences of fiscal, monetary, and structural policy. The special topics in the last two issues, for example, were the public healthcare system and the progress of the structural reforms implemented in the financial and health sectors.

CHRISTODOULAKIS, DIMELIS & KOLLINTZAS examine the cyclical behaviour of the Greek economy compared to that of the other EU economies using annual data from 1960 to 1990. Following the methodology of Kydland and Prescott and the real business cycles analytical framework, they find that variables that are not directly controlled by government, such as consumption, inventories, net exports, and prices, behave in similar way in Greece and the EU. On the other hand, variables that are directly controlled by institutions, like government spending and money, behave very differently across European countries. This conclusion implies that, if shocks in EU economies are asymmetrical, common institutional policies will tend to disappear as common European institutions and policies begin to emerge.

PAPADOPOULOS offers a survey of stabilization policies in the Greek economy for the period 1953–81. The paper is separated into four parts: (a) trends in major macroeconomic variables, (b) policies applied since 1953, (c) the implications of the chosen policies, and (d) general conclusions concerning the structure of the Greek economy.

ALOGOSKOUFIS & PHILIPPOPOULOS investigate the compatibility of the "rational partisan" and "exchange rate regime" models of inflation for the Greek economy in the period 1958–89. Due to a polarized political system they conclude that the differences in the policy preferences of political parties are taken into account by wage setters, thus influencing inflation outcomes.

ALOGOSKOUFIS & CHRISTODOULAKIS analyse fiscal debts, seigniorage, and Greece's external debt by implementing the Yaari–Blanchard dynamic model. Their main conclusion is that Greece's external indebtedness in the 1980s can be ascribed to the rapid growth of public expenditure and persistently high budget deficits.

MICHALIS VAFOPOULOS

Green, Thomas Hill 1836–1882

British philosopher

Cacoullos, Ann R., *Thomas Hill Green: A Philosopher of Rights*, New York: Twayne, 1974

Greengarten, I.M., *Thomas Hill Green and the Development of Liberal-Democratic Thought*, Toronto and Buffalo: University of Toronto Press, 1981

Milne, A.J.M., *The Social Philosophy of English Idealism*, London: George Allen and Unwin, 1962: chapters 3–7

Nicholson, Peter P., *The Political Philosophy of the British Idealists: Selected Studies*, Cambridge and New York: Cambridge University Press, 1990: studies 2–5

Richter, Melvin, *The Politics of Conscience: T.H. Green and His Age*, London: Weidenfeld and Nicolson, and Cambridge, Massachusetts: Harvard University Press, 1964

Sidgwick, Henry, *Lectures on the Ethics of T.H. Green, Mr. Herbert Spencer, and J. Martineau*, edited by E.E. Constance Jones, London and New York: Macmillan, 1902; reprinted New York: Kraus, 1968

Simhony, Avital, "On Forcing Individuals to be Free: T.H. Green's Liberal Theory of Positive Freedom", *Political Studies*, 39/2 (1991): 303–20

Simhony, Avital, "Beyond Negative and Positive Freedom: T.H. Green's View of Freedom", *Political Theory*, 21/1 (1993): 28–54

Thomas, Geoffrey, *The Moral Philosophy of T.H. Green*, Oxford: Clarendon Press, and New York: Oxford University Press, 1987

Vincent, Andrew (editor), *The Philosophy of T.H. Green*, Aldershot, Hampshire and Brookfield, Vermont: Gower, 1986

Political philosopher and social reformer T.H. Green sought to transform liberalism, from within a liberal framework, by ridding it of its association with self-centred competitive individualism and connecting it with the idea of the common good, rightly understood as a community of mutually developing individuals. The result was an expanded version of liberalism that may be adequately described as positive or communitarian liberalism, and which sought to reconcile individuality with community while extending liberal concerns with individual rights and freedom. Positive liberalism grew out of criticism of the empiricism, utilitarianism, *laissez-faire* practices, natural rights doctrines, and the conception of negative liberty of earlier liberals.

SIDGWICK is the most consistent and severe critic of Green. In particular, Sidgwick is critical of the idea of the common good, which Green forged as a solution to the tension in practical reason between egoism and benevolence. Sidgwick thought that this tension posed the "profoundest problem of ethics" – how to reconcile the claims of oneself with the claims of others – and he admittedly failed to solve it. His critical study of Green was propelled by his belief that Green offered the most credible alternative to his own ethics. However, it is possible to say that Sidgwick consistently misinterprets Green because he radically disagrees with him; indeed, Sidgwick is predisposed to misinterpret Green because he interprets the latter from a dualist framework – the self versus others – which is not Green's own and which Green seeks to replace as the foundation of liberalism.

RICHTER studies the man, his thought, and his influence in the intellectual milieu of his time. Although Green owed a great deal to Kant and Hegel, his idealism was very much bound up with a "mid-Victorian style of politics". Recasting liberalism in terms of idealist philosophy, Green's achievement was twofold: his idealist-based liberalism expanded liberal thought beyond merely negative liberty and narrow individualism. Further, Green's philosophy had an avowed religious purpose. Political liberalism realized the true meaning of Christianity via activities of citizenship and reform, thereby resolving the crisis of faith and conscience, precipitated by science and biblical scholarship, that educated people at the time experienced, but MILNE, THOMAS, and GREEN-GARTEN claim that religion and metaphysics have been given too large a role in interpreting Green's thought.

Milne holds that there is much value in the idealism of Green, but it has to be disentangled from his dubious idealist metaphysics. In his ethics Green develops a theory of morality, an important part of which is the idea of citizenship. Understood as a sphere of rational activity that embodies genuine human achievement in a certain way of living and acting, citizenship can only be attained on a noncompetitive basis, for it is interdependent with the achievements of others. Green's political theory is not so much an application of his moral theory, but a further development of it, since to understand fully the theory of citizenship is to follow its development in the context of his political theory and especially in the context of his notions of state and of rights.

THOMAS provides the most comprehensive and invaluable study of Green's moral philosophy, which, he claims, is shaped neither by metaphysical concerns nor by his religious interests. Rather, at the heart of his moral philosophy lies the moral psychology of the rational agent. This agent seeks abiding self-satisfaction, which he can ultimately find by "self-intervention" to revise his life plans which, in turn, can only be realized through fulfilling social roles and membership in a good society. Thomas claims that Green's moral philosophy possesses contemporary relevance because it is neither an act-ethic nor an agent-ethic, but allows for a more comprehensive view of agents as persons than is available in the mainstream of contemporary ethics.

Contrary to Richter, Greengarten contends that it is not religion but concern with social and economic problems that propelled Green's thought. Greengarten claims that Green defends two contradictory ethical and economic conceptions of the individual: as a developer and exerciser of capacities and as a possessor or infinite appropriator, respectively. This dichotomous conception of the person reveals an inherent contradiction, characteristic of liberal-democratic theory, at the heart of Green's liberalism: a capitalist market economy (which is required by the possessor view of the person) produces inequalities that thwart the development of human capacities (which is required by the ethical view of the person). The main problem with this interpretation is its tendency to read into Green a preconceived framework of "possessive individualism" borrowed from C.B. Macpherson's work.

In a perceptive and careful study CACOULLOS concentrates on Green's political philosophy and especially on his theory of rights. Particularly valuable is her discussion of the relationship between the common good and interests (chapter six) and the common good and rights (chapter seven), not least because of the (misconceived) tendency of the of the recent liberal-communitarian debate to view rights and the common good as representing rival and irreconcilable perspectives.

In an excellent study of Green's political philosophy, NICHOLSON offers a thorough and sympathetic defence of Green against major criticisms, chief among them criticisms of his conceptions of the common good, rights, property, and freedom. He also explores extensively Green's common good-based view of state action – including its application to the issues of liquor legislation and education – which he locates between Mill's and Spencer's views of state action. Nicholson firmly situates Green in the tradition of Greek and German philosophy, emphasizing the distinctive nature of his political philosophy by contrast with the social contract and natural rights traditions.

In two complementary articles on the idea of freedom, SIMHONY (1991 and 1993) makes two claims. First, regarding Isaiah Berlin's claim – in his essay "Two Concepts of Liberty" (in Four Essays on Liberty, 1969) – that positive freedom is hostile to liberalism because it justifies an oppressive society, Simhony maintains that Green's positive freedom is immune to Berlin's criticism, and indeed is essential to his expanded liberalism. Second, she argues that Green's freedom ought to be understood not in terms of the negative/positive distinction, but in terms of the intertwining of internality (capacities) and externality (opportunities), a complex view that embraces the former distinction and places ability at the heart of freedom.

The seven essays in VINCENT, including an excellent introduction, provide a valuable insight into important aspects of Green's thought: criticism of Hume, theological views, citizenship, common good and rights, liquor legislation, natural rights, and political obligation. Three essays are of special interest because of their unique topics and their treatment: Harris's claim that Green's position on political obligation is ambivalent; Martin's discussion of Green's notion of rights as an outgrowth of the natural rights that he was criticizing; and Walsh's sympathetic examination of Green's criticism of Hume.

AVITAL SIMHONY

Grounded theory

Bartlett, Dean and Sheila Payne, "Grounded Theory: Its Basis, Rationale and Procedures" in Understanding Social Research: Perspectives on Methodology and Practice, edited by George McKenzie, Jackie Powell and Robin Usher, Lewes: Falmer Press, 1997

Corbin, Juliet and Anselm Strauss, "Grounded Theory Research: Procedures, Canons and Evaluative Criteria", Qualitative Sociology, 13/1 (1990): 3–21

Dey, Ian, Grounding Grounded Theory: Guidelines for Qualitative Inquiry, San Diego: Academic Press, 1999

Glaser, Barney G. and Anselm L. Strauss, *The Discovery of Grounded Theory: Strategies for Qualitative Research*, London: Weidenfield and Nicolson, and Chicago: Aldine, 1967

Glaser, Barney G., *Theoretical Sensitivity: Advances in the Methodology of Grounded Theory*, Mill Valley, California: Sociology Press, 1978

Glaser, Barney G., *Emergence vs Forcing: Basics of Grounded Theory Analysis*, Mill Valley, California: Sociology Press, 1992

Strauss, Anselm L., *Qualitative Analysis for Social Scientists*, Cambridge and New York: Cambridge University Press, 1987

Strauss, Anselm and Juliet Corbin, *Basics of Qualitative Research: Grounded Theory Procedures and Techniques*, London and Newbury Park, California: Sage, 1990

Strauss, Anselm and Juliet Corbin, "Grounded Theory Methodology: An Overview" in *Handbook of Qualitative Research*, edited by Norman K. Denzin and Yvonna S. Lincoln, London and Thousand Oaks, California: Sage, 1994

Strauss, Anselm and Juliet Corbin (editors), *Grounded Theory in Practice*, London and Thousand Oaks, California: Sage, 1997

BARTLETT & PAYNE provide a comprehensive but concise introduction to grounded theory, which covers three main areas: the empirical rationale behind grounded theory, its historical development, and the practical procedures embodied in the method. The chapter describes how grounded theory adds to the toolkit of the social scientist by explaining in some depth how it fits into the research process as a whole. In particular, the chapter discusses how the inductive logic of grounded theory relates to the deductive logic underlying the hypothetico-deductive experimental research paradigm and this discussion is located within a broad overview of the philosophy of science. The chapter then goes on to describe the discovery and development of grounded theory, providing a review of the key texts and events that have shaped its evolution, and discussing some of the issues and controversies that have arisen during its development. Finally, the chapter provides a summary of the main stages of a grounded theory research project and a detailed account of the practical coding procedures associated with the technique. This includes both the methodological procedures and particular analysis techniques of grounded theory, and also contains some practical tips on actually carrying out grounded theory research.

DEY provides a scholarly analysis of the methodological principles underlying grounded theory. It considers what guidelines grounded theory has to offer qualitative inquiry in general and provides an essential supplement to some of the more practically focused "how to" guides such as STRAUSS & CORBIN (1990), directly addressing some of the controversial issues raised in other key texts mentioned here. This excellent book covers a number of key areas of inquiry in qualitative research including the use of categorization, the coding of data, the analysis of process and causality, and the role of theory as well as considering the essential process of validation in qualitative inquiry.

CORBIN & STRAUSS discuss in this article perhaps the single most important issue in qualitative research – that of how to judge the quality of a piece of research that uses qualitative methods. In quantitative research, this is achieved primarily by appeal to the notions of validity and reliability; however, Corbin & Strauss do not frame this methodological issue in those conventional terms. The article considers three specific and related methodological issues: how the usual scientific canons should be reinterpreted for qualitative research in general (and for grounded theory in particular) how researchers should report, or write-up, the procedures they have used; and, finally, what evaluative criteria should be used in judging the quality of a grounded theory study. Unfortunately, Corbin & Strauss do not pay equal attention to each of these three endeavours. Following a lengthy description of the principal canons of grounded theory, the article goes on to provide a brief description of each of the main types of coding which lie at the heart of the technique. Buried towards the end of this section is a short discussion of the issue of generalizability. This leads on to the development of 14 evaluative criteria, seven of which cover the research process itself, and therefore relate to the issue of how to write-up methodological procedures, while the remaining seven relate to the substantial issue of how well the research findings are empirically grounded in the data. A particular strength of this article lies in its accessibility in dealing with potentially complex methodological issues and the use of numerous examples certainly aids clarity in this respect. While the article raises the important issue of quality evaluation in grounded theory, the downside to its strengths is that it falls somewhat short of providing definitive, detailed, and convincing guidelines for exactly how this can be achieved.

GLASER & STRAUSS is the first book ever written on grounded theory and is the original text that presented grounded theory to the research community. In it the two authors and inventors of grounded theory explain the background and main thrust of the grounded theory method, that is the generation of theory from data by the use of comparative analysis. Although subsequent publications by both authors have elucidated and refined the technique, this original publication is useful in two respects. Firstly, it illuminates our understanding of exactly where grounded theory is located epistemologically – that is somewhere in between the "grand theory" (which so often remains largely empirically unsubstantiated) and the empirically rigorous (but more often than not theoretically impoverished) research that is published in many contemporary social science research journals. Secondly, the book remains the single definitive text on grounded theory, owing to a subsequent split between the two researchers (described in more detail in Bartlett & Payne), who each developed their own particular ideas about grounded theory methodology and published their own refinements to the analytic methods described in this seminal text.

GLASER (1978) is the first of a series of books following the publication of Glaser & Strauss in which Glaser details what he sees as the main developments in grounded theory methodology. In particular, the book focuses upon the social psychology and creativeness of the analyst, describing in detail the concept of theoretical sensitivity. Also covered are the processes of memoing, theoretical coding, sampling and sorting, and the write-up and generation of formal grounded theory.

GLASER (1992) sets out to correct what Glaser sees as basic errors in the work of Strauss and Strauss & Corbin (see later). The book is highly critical of both of these publications, the main criticism being that the procedures set out in each of them lead to forced, as opposed to emergent, theorizing. The main value of this volume may well lie in its questioning of some of the basic procedures and underlying rationale set out in the more popular texts of Strauss and Strauss & Corbin. Such questioning is potentially valuable to the grounded theorist as it leads to a reflexive self-consciousness with respect to the analytic procedures that are being adopted when carrying out grounded theory. This is conducive to the development of theoretical sensitivity in the analyst. Furthermore, the alternative perspective it offers on grounded theory itself may tend to enrich the treatments offered by Strauss and Strauss & Corbin.

STRAUSS is the first solo volume by the other inventor of grounded theory. It sets out in detail what Strauss sees as the main principles and analysis methods of grounded theory. The volume is essentially a practical guide to the analytic procedures of grounded theory and is, in this sense, a forerunner or earlier version of Strauss & Corbin (1990).

STRAUSS & CORBIN (1990) is considered by many researchers to be the definitive standard text on grounded theory. Similar in coverage to Strauss, it updates that volume and acts as a practical handbook of grounded theory, focusing on how to actually conduct a grounded theory analysis and describing in detail the analytic procedures it employs. The book offers a thorough treatment of the coding techniques that lie at the heart of grounded theory and it also covers the writing-up process and evaluation of grounded theory. While there remain some basic differences between this treatment and those of Glaser, this text is the most popular, comprehensive and widely accessible book about grounded theory that is currently available.

STRAUSS & CORBIN (1994) offers an overview of the origins of and subsequent developments in grounded theory methodology. Unlike Strauss & Corbin (1990) it is not a practical handbook and does not cover the coding procedures involved in carrying out grounded theory analysis or the logic underlying these procedures. The chapter compares and contrasts grounded theory with other modes of qualitative research and includes a discussion of the theoretical diffusion of grounded theory. The chapter also covers the style in which grounded theory is written up, how it relates to the interpretative process, and the ontological status of theories developed using grounded theory. While this chapter covers some rather complex issues, it does remain clear and relatively easy to understand. As with the earlier works on grounded theory with which Strauss has been associated, however, this accessibility must be balanced against the inevitably reduced depth to which some of these theoretical and philosophical issues are taken.

STRAUSS & CORBIN (1997) provide a collection of previously published articles that have used grounded theory as their primary method of analysis. The text therefore provides a useful book of readings that demonstrate exactly how grounded theory has been used by previous researchers and the additional commentary that the editors provide to accompany each of the articles offers the reader additional insight into the use of grounded theory in qualitative research.

DEAN BARTLETT

Group socialization theory

Collins, W.A., E.E. Maccoty, L. Steinberg, E.M. Hetherington and M.H. Bornstein, "Contemporary Research on Parenting: The Case for Nature and Nurture", *Merican Psychologist*, 55 (2000): 1–15
Harris, J.R., "Where Is the Child's Environment? A Group Socialisation Theory of Development", *Psychological Review*, 102 (1995): 458–89
Harris, Judith Rich, *The Nurture Assumption: Why Children Turn out the Way They Do*, New York: Free Press, and London: Bloomsbury, 1998
Rutter, M., "Blame It on Their Peers?", *Times Higher Educational Supplement*, (22 January 1999): 29

Many developmental psychologists have assumed that parents have a formative and even decisive influence on the development of children. Important theoretical views have buttressed this assumption. These include the psychoanalytic tradition of Freud, carried forward into more modern views of attachment theory by Bowlby; and the learning theory views of Watson and Skinner. The last three decades have seen very many studies of parenting styles and parenting influences on children's development, which have largely looked at the nature of such effects rather than querying whether such effects exist.

An influential article and book by Judith Rich Harris have provided a vigorous challenge to this view. Her "group socialisation" theory of development is described in HARRIS (1995), and is taken further in her book (HARRIS 1998).

There are undoubtedly similarities between parents and children; but Harris suggests two main reasons for this, which do not involve children learning from parents; these are firstly, genetic effects, and secondly, community effects mediated by the peer groups children are in.

Parents and children share genes in common. From recent behaviour genetic work, Harris argues that some commonalities of temperament, personality, and intelligence can be expected from genetic factors. This behaviour genetic research, while suggesting some influence of genes, also leaves plenty of scope for environmental effects. However, it also suggests that the major environmental effects are due to non-shared rather than shared environment. What this means is that the shared environment of a household, with particular parents, has not made siblings substantially more alike than if they were not in the same household with the same parents. The major environmental effects seem to come from outside the shared home environment. These conclusions come from research on identical and non-identical twins, and on natural and adoptive children.

Harris suggests that the major environmental factor is the child's peer group. She believes that, at least after infancy, the peer group provides the major important reference group for children. They adapt to peer group norms and compare themselves to their peers.

Of course, there is – at a cultural and subcultural level – some correspondence between peer group values and parental values. Depending on ethnicity and social class, there are likely to be some shared values and assumptions held widely in a community. These will be shared in the peer group of children, and also in the older generation "peer group" of parents. Thus, some similarity of parents and children will just reflect this general community similarity of values. Harris, however, argues that this similarity comes via the peers rather than directly via the parents.

The situation of immigrant children provides what Harris sees as a compelling argument for her view. She takes as an exemplar a family coming to a country such as the US from a quite different country – say, for example, Poland. The parents speak Polish, and although they learn English they speak it with a strong accent, and they keep many Polish traditions. Their children, however, once they enter school, very rapidly learn English and learn an American way of life; the strong influence of the peer group produces assimilation in a generation or at most two.

Harris argues for the importance of code switching, or the context dependency of learning. Here, code can refer to a language, or to values, ways of behaving. Even if children learn one code for the home context, they learn another code for the peer context. Harris invokes ideas from social psychology and evolutionary psychology to suggest the importance of group processes, especially the peer group, such as group affiliation, hostility to strangers, improving one's status in the group, and forming close dyadic relationships from within the group.

On these bases, Harris argues that what children learn from parents specifically (rather than peers, and others generally) is transient to the infancy period and/or limited to the home context. Empirical data showing parent-child effects – which are often quite low, she claims – are explained by genetic similarities with the parent, and general cultural similarities mediated via the peer group. Argued thoroughly in her 1995 article, her 1998 book presents similar views in a more accessible form for a wider audience.

As reviews such as those by COLLINS *et al.* and by RUTTER point out, Harris' theory has occasioned considerable controversy, and some hostility from those committed to the view that the behaviour of parents can have strong positive or negative effects on their children's development. Rutter suggests that the challenge of Harris' theory is to be welcomed, but that it is premature to accept all her conclusions. He believes that even if parents have rather little effect within the normal range of parenting, there is good evidence for specific effects at the extremes (for example, in cases of child abuse). He suggests that Harris also neglects the more complex effects of parents on children's development, via their choice of neighbourhoods, schools, and peer groups for their children. In general, although her 1995 article is seen as a valid theoretical argument within the academic tradition, her 1998 book is viewed more as a one-sided work of advocacy. Powerful counterviews, such as recent developments in attachment theory, receive limited consideration in her work. However, there is little doubt that her ideas have had a timely impact and will result in a refocus and more critical thinking in writings on socialization.

PETER K. SMITH

Group therapy

Agazarian, Yvonne M., *Systems-Centered Therapy for Groups*, New York: Guilford Press, 1997

Berne, Eric, *Principles of Group Treatment*, New York: Oxford University Press, 1966

Bion, Wilfred R., *Experiences in Groups*, London: Tavistock, and New York: Basic Books, 1961

Group Analysis: The Journal of Group Analytic Psychotherapy, 1967–

Group Dynamics: Theory, Research and Practice, 1997–

International Journal of Group Psychotherapy, 1954–

Kaplan, H.I. and B.J. Sadock, *Synopsis of Psychiatry: Behavioral Sciences, Clinical Psychiatry*, 6th edition, Baltimore: Williams and Wilkins, 1991

Yalom, Irvin D., *Inpatient Group Psychotherapy: A Psychodynamic Perspective*, New York: Basic Books, 1983

Yalom, Irvin D., *The Theory and Practice of Group Psychotherapy*, 4th edition, New York: Basic Books, 1995

BION, an analyst whose work was heavily influenced by the work of Melanie Klein, expanded on her concept of projective identification to include an interpersonal process whereby a therapist contains what the patient projects onto him by the patient, while the patient processes it and it is later returned to the patient in a healthier, modified form. Bion is best known for his application of psychoanalytic ideas to group therapy. He believed that when a group becomes derailed from its task, it deteriorates into one of three basic states: dependency, pairing, or flight-fight. Bion's book is a collection of papers he wrote during the years when he conducted group therapy, mostly in the 1940s. The book is a good starting point for those interested in reading the beginnings of psychoanalytic group therapy and previous references.

GROUP ANALYSIS derives concepts from psychoanalytic psychology, social psychology, group dynamics, sociology, and anthropology. It is considered to provide an international interdisciplinary forum for dialogue among practitioners, theoreticians, and researchers. It includes sections devoted to particular themes, and book reviews are a regular feature. The journal is an excellent resource for information on group treatments and can be read on the Internet as well as in hardcopy.

BERNE is still considered by many practising group therapists to be an important resource. He bases his group therapy on his well-known book *Games People Play*, which uses transactional analysis as the underlying principle. The book presents chapters on group dynamics, teaching, research and writing, and the literature of group therapy from the viewpoint of the therapist. A glossary and several diagrams are provided to assist the explanations of the therapy. All group therapists should read this classic book, whether or not they embrace the concepts and interventions.

GROUP DYNAMICS: THEORY, RESEARCH AND PRACTICE is a journal that discusses basic and applied topics in the field of group research and application. The journal covers several types of groups in addition to group psychotherapy, including friendship groups and cliques, organizational units, self-help groups, and learning groups. Recent editions have presented articles regarding the roles that emerge in groups, which are thought to be based on early family–child interactions. The importance of these roles and the necessity of identifying such roles so as to reduce polarized positions that people find themselves in are discussed. The journal is interesting and the articles are useful for clinical application.

Although the INTERNATIONAL JOURNAL OF GROUP PSYCHOTHERAPY has been in existence for more than half a century, the current focus is on informing therapists about the impact of managed care on three critical domains: the treatment of everyday, low-severity concerns, the creation of group alternatives to hospital care; and the psychosocial treatment of severe and persistent disorders. The journal is important as a forum for the exchange of ideas and experiences. Each issue covers the diverse work of noted researchers in the field of group therapy. For example, recent issues have covered the effect of managed care on group therapy, group therapy for cancer patients and their families, Jungian group therapy, and dream analysis in a group setting. This journal is probably the most important of all current journals on group psychotherapy.

YALOM (1995) is his most well-known work, the usual textbook for classes on group therapy. The most recent (fourth) edition changes his earlier use of the term "curative" factors to "therapeutic" factors to reflect that the goal is change or growth rather than cure. These therapeutic factors are the central organizing principle of the book. After a detailed discussion of each of the eleven therapeutic factors, a discussion of a psychotherapeutic approach utilizing these factors is undertaken. Yalom discusses what he terms "a prototypic type of group therapy" and then offers a set of principles that he believes will enable the student to modify this fundamental group model to fit any specialized clinical situation. The prototypic model he uses is the intensive, heterogeneously composed, outpatient group, with the goals of both symptom relief and characterological change. Excellent clinical illustrations are given throughout the book. Yalom applies current research to his work, while at the same time noting that therapy is both an art and a science, and as such will always be a "deeply subjective, non-quantifiable experience". Yalom believes that interpersonal interaction is "crucial" in group therapy, and that it allows patients to identify maladaptive patterns and correct them. He cautions that managed care could thwart this most important aspect, rendering group therapy ineffective as an alternative to individual therapy. This book is probably the major reference on the topic and is definitely recommended for any student or therapist conducting group therapy.

YALOM (1983) is a book on inpatient group therapy, in which he argues that an acute psychiatric ward is quite different from the conventional outpatient group setting, and thus a different clinical approach must be taken. He states that hospital treatment is now shorter, the psychopathologies more varied, some wards are locked and some are not, the staff come from many disciplines including students, and the insurance companies play a major role in admission and discharge. All of these factors result in rapid turnover of patients and staff, high tension and dissension, and fragmented psychotherapy. The implications of these factors as they apply to the therapist are addressed at length. The author points out that, with the shorter time frame, the therapist needs to be active and efficient, and he elaborates on the need for therapists to provide structure and to work in the here-and-now, with

support, cohesiveness, and self-validation. Yalom states that the "central, indispensable ingredient" of inpatient therapy is the daily "talking" therapy group. The book is a must-read primer for inpatient caregivers who provide group therapy.

KAPLAN & SADOCK, in their synopsis of psychiatry, provide an eclectic, multidisciplinary approach that includes biological, psychological, and sociological factors. The textbook is written to facilitate the teaching of psychiatry and the behavioural sciences. It briefly reviews all approaches to group therapy. The authors discuss when to use group therapy, and the different roles of the therapist depending on their therapeutic orientation. The book discusses indications for group therapy and the benefits of each type of therapy. Several group situations are briefly covered, including special populations such as bereavement and eating disorder groups. With these more focused groups, actual tasks may be practised during the group meetings.

Kaplan & Sadock include a chapter that reviews the definition of group therapy and, in agreement with Yalom, states that the purpose of group therapy is to effect personality change in the emotionally ill. The authors compare the benefits of group therapy to individual therapy. The chapter reviews the many approaches to group therapy, including psychoanalytic, behavioural, transactional, Gestalt, and client-centred. The authors include a wonderful chart that compares each type of therapy on such topics as frequency, durations, and therapeutic goals. The relevance of diagnosis in determining the best therapeutic approach, motivation for treatment, and estimated capacity for change are covered. The basic tasks of the therapist and twenty therapeutic factors in group therapy are described. Comparison of inpatient and outpatient groups is included. The positive benefits of combined individual and group therapy are discussed.

AGAZARIAN presents a here-and-now approach using a systems-centred therapy. The book is useful for its different approach from other authors and its in-depth coverage of the here-and-now topic. The author presents her viewpoint of the three phases of group therapy. The theory, method, and techniques used to deal with the approach are delineated. The format can be adapted for short or long-term group therapy.

PATTY FERGUSON

Growth

Aghion, Philippe and Peter Howitt, *Endogenous Growth Theory*, Cambridge, Massachusetts: MIT Press, 1998

Barro, Robert J. and Xavier Sala-i-Martin, *Economic Growth*, New York: McGraw Hill, 1995

Foley, Duncan K. and Thomas R. Michl, *Growth and Distribution*, Cambridge, Massachusetts: Harvard University Press, 1999

Hahn, F.H. (editor), *Readings in the Theory of Growth: A Selection of Papers from the "Review of Economic Studies"*, London: Macmillan, and New York: St Martin's Press, 1971

Harcourt, G.C. and N.F. Laing (editors), *Capital and Growth: Selected Readings*, Harmondsworth: Penguin, 1971

Marglin, Stephen A., *Growth, Distribution, and Prices*, Cambridge, Massachusetts: Harvard University Press, 1984

Morgenstern, Oskar and G.L. Thompson, *Mathematical Theory of Expanding and Contracting Economies*, Lexington: Lexington Books, 1976

Morishima, Michio, *Theory of Economic Growth*, Oxford: Clarendon Press, 1969

Panico, Carlo and Neri Salvadori (editors), *Post Keynesian Theory of Growth and Distribution*, Aldershot, Hampshire: Elgar, 1993

Solow, R.M., *Growth Theory: An Exposition*, Oxford: Clarendon Press, and New York: Oxford University Press, 1970

AGHION & HOWITT are known for their revival of "Schumpeterian" ideas in modern growth theory. Unlike many of the equilibrium growth models in the endogenous growth literature, they stress the fact that economic growth need not be beneficial to all agents. This is epitomized in Schumpeter's concept of "creative destruction". In the book they present a large number of models designed to clarify various aspects pertinent to the problem under consideration. Fundamental to the development of research-and-development-based models of growth was the observation that the characteristics of physical capital goods and technology differ profoundly. While technology is non rival, which means that its use in one employment does not necessarily preclude its use in another, capital goods are rival. Technology, as opposed to capital goods, may also be to some degree non-excludable, which reflects the fact that competitors often cannot be prevented from using the technology protected by a patent. The main idea underlying much of this literature is that knowledge is not an exhaustible resource and thus does not face the same limitations to accumulation as physical capital goods. While earlier models by Romer and Grossman and Helpman focused attention mainly on increasing product varieties, Aghion & Howitt put forward quality ladder models, in which new technology improvements generate productivity growth. Both kinds of models rely on technology spillovers to generate permanent growth. The notion of a quality ladder starts from the hypothesis that every product can be improved an infinite number of times and that each improvement involves a discrete jump in the level of productive services provided. Often new technologies appear together with new firms, who crowd out old firms. This is the meaning of creative destruction. Obviously, in these kinds of models the assumption of perfect competition is no longer acceptable. The book contains many insights into the process of economic growth and discusses also in some detail economic policy issues.

BARRO & SALA-I-MARTIN takes stock of the outburst of contributions to what is known as "new" or "endogenous" growth theory since the mid 1980s. After a discussion of the traditional neoclassical growth model of Robert Solow and Trevor Swan, they investigate a number of "new" growth models, whose characteristic feature is that the rate of profit need not fall as capital accumulates. The problems dealt with include positive externalities associated with human capital formation and investment in research and development, product diversification, and quality ladders. In addition, the book displays the empirical evidence contained in the Penn World Table (Mark 5) put together by Summers and Heston and discusses inter alia the question of convergence of growth rates between countries and regions.

FOLEY & MICHL deal with the problem of growth and distribution essentially in a one-sector model. Their main tool of the analysis is the relationship between the real wage rate and the rate of profit or wage frontier. Technical progress shifts that relationship over time. Different forms of technical progress can be distinguished according to how they affect the wage frontier. The analytical work, which derives its main inspiration from modern classical economics, is complemented by empirical studies. The authors also confront the classical approach to the theory of growth and distribution with the traditional neoclassical (Solow) one on the one hand and the endogenous growth literature on the other. The book is particularly useful as an intermediate textbook in the theory of growth and distribution.

HAHN contains important contributions to the theory of economic growth as they were published in the *Review of Economic Studies* over the years. Among these there is J. von Neumann's influential paper on "A model of general equilibrium" (first published in German in 1937) and D. Champernowne's commentary; the well-known papers by H. Uzawa, R.M. Solow, and K. Inada on the two-sector model; the paper by K.J. Arrow on learning by doing and the extension by D. Levhari; the paper by L.L. Pasinetti on growth and distribution.

HARCOURT & LAING contains some selected readings in the theory of growth, placing special emphasis on the problem of capital discussed in the so-called Cambridge controversy in the theory of capital.

MARGLIN's book counterposes three different approaches to the theory of economic growth and income distribution: the classical-Marxian, the neoclassical, and the post Keynesian approaches. The differences concern what is taken as a given or independently variable magnitude within an analytical framework characterized by the duality of the relationship between the rate of growth and consumption per capita on the one hand and the rate of profit and the real wage rate on the other. What is at stake is best explained in the case in which technical progress is set aside. The classical-Marxian approach takes the real wage as given. The corresponding rate of profit then translates into the rate of growth, given the propensity to accumulate out of profits. The neoclassical approach of Solow takes the rate of population growth as given and assumes continuous substitutability between labour and capital. The rate of capital accumulation is then shown to adjust to the rate of population growth, thereby bringing about steady-state growth. The wage rate and the profit rate are equal to the marginal products of the respective factors of production. The post Keynesian model takes the rate of accumulation as given, reflecting the "animal spirits" of entrepreneurs. For a given savings propensity out of profits, the distribution of income is taken to adjust. The mechanism under consideration is epitomized in the famous Cambridge equation, according to which the rate of profit equals the ratio of the rate of accumulation and the savings propensity out of profits. In addition, the book contains an extensive discussion of saving behaviour, including some empirical work.

MORGENSTERN & THOMPSON deal with linear models of production and growth, starting from von Neumann's contribution.

MORISHIMA's book contains a thorough attempt at generalizing the von Neumann model, including a combination of the model with the conventional theory of demand. The assumptions of the original model that all wages are consumed and all interest is saved and invested are abandoned. A large part of the book is concerned with steady states, but there are also discussions of adjustment processes, of the problem of stability, and of turnpike theorems.

PANICO & SALVADORI have collected a useful set of major contributions to the post-Keynesian theory of growth and distribution, starting with contributions by Nicholas Kaldor and Joan Robinson. Amongst the authors included there are L.Pasinetti, F. Modigliani, P. Samuelson, and I. Steedman.

SOLOW expounds his 1956 growth model with and without exogenous technical progress and discusses the impact of a change in the propensity to save on the economic performance of the system. (The entire argument is couched in terms satisfying Say's law: there is no problem of effective demand – that is, any act of saving is taken to lead instantaneously to an act of investment of equal size.) Obviously, a rise in the savings rate can increase the rate of growth only temporarily, but not permanently: the steady-state rate of growth is exogenously fixed. In addition the role of money in the process of growth and the role of economic policy to foster growth are discussed.

HEINZ D. KURZ AND NERI SALVADORI

See also Endogenous growth theory

Growth accounting

Aziz, Jahangir, *Growth Accounting and Growth Processes*, Washington, DC: International Monetary Fund, 1996 (working paper no. 96/116)

Barro, Robert J., *Notes on Growth Accounting*, Cambridge, Massachusetts: National Bureau of Economic Research, 1998 (working paper no. W6654)

Bartelmus, Peter, *Environment, Growth, and Development: The Concepts and Strategies of Sustainability*, London and New York: Routledge, 1994

Benhabib, Jess and Boyan Jovanovic, "Externalities and Growth Accounting", *American Economic Review*, 81/1 (1991): 82–113

Gort, Michael and Richard A. Wall, "Obsolescence, Input Augmentation, and Growth Accounting", *European Economic Review*, 42/9 (1998): 1653–65

Greenwood, Jeremy and Boyan Jovanovic, *Accounting for Growth*, Cambridge, Massachusetts: National Bureau of Economic Research, 1998 (working paper no. W6647)

Miller, Edward M., "The Definition of Capital for Solow's Growth Accounting Formula", *Southern Economic Journal*, 56/1 (1989): 157–65

The paper from BARRO provides an introduction to the growth accounting model, explaining how it breaks down economic growth into components associated with changes in factor inputs, and the "Solow residual" that reflect techno-logical progress, and other elements. The author then considers dual approaches to growth accounting – considering changes in factor prices rather than quantities – as well as spillover effects and increasing returns, taxes, and multiple types of factor inputs. The paper then positions the growth accounting process within the context of two recent strands of endogenous growth theory, namely varieties-of-products models, and quality-ladders models. In these situations, the author believes that the "Solow residual" may be interpreted in terms of measures of the endogenously changing level of technology that corresponds, in one case, to a number of types of intermediate products that have been invented and, in the other case, to an index of the aggregate quality of intermediate inputs.

MILLER suggests that one detail of Solow's growth formula for ascertaining the contribution factor growth to total growth in output still needs explaining: that is, the definition of capital quantity that should be used for growth accounting. He believes the answer lies in the dependence of Solow's formula on the law of one price, which states that the price for a unit of capital services is the same regardless of the type or age of capital rendering the services. The author proposes that the quality of capital services must be a weighted sum of the service provided by the different goods. Furthermore, he suggests the weights should be proportional to the prices of the services of the different capital goods, with this proportionality applying to goods of different ages as well as to goods of different types. Using this definition of capital, the author argues that Solow's results may be obtained without assuming the existence of an aggregate production function. He concludes that the applicability of the law of one price is a necessary condition in growth accounting.

GORT & WALL present an argument along similar lines by identifying a serious conceptual inconsistency in conventional measures of capital used in most empirical work on economic growth. They contend that this inconsistency arises as a result of a failure to decompose depreciation into its obsolescence and physical decay components. The authors report that, when appropriate, corrections are made, plausible alternatives for the relative magnitude of obsolescence and physical decay suggest very different rates of growth in capital. They conclude by arguing that this will result in large variances in the fraction of growth in output attributed to input augmenting technical changes from the "Solow residual".

In yet another critique of the growth accounting model, AZIZ suggests that using aggregate data in the model will fail to distinguish different processes of development. His proposition is that the standard growth accounting framework, which weights various inputs by their factor shares to measure their contribution to output growth, underestimates the contribution of inputs in the presence of externalities, and increasing returns. The author provides an alternative model in which, in the absence of such departures from the standard neoclassical framework, growth may occur through either embodied technological progress or replication of existing technology.

GREENWOOD & JOVANOVIC use Solow's growth accounting model to explain the impact since the 1970s of a slow-down in productivity growth, the steady fall in the price of new equipment, and an increasing skill premium on the growth experience of the US. Their analysis concludes that first, productivity slowed down because the implementation of information technologies was both costly and slow. Second, technological advances in the capital goods sector have led to a decline in equipment prices. Third, skill premiums have risen because the new, more efficient capital is complementary with skilled labour and/or because the use of skilled labour facilitates the adoption of new technologies.

The question of how to explain the variation in the levels and rates of growth of output across countries is addressed by BENHABIB & JOVANOVIC. Their investigation focuses on the question of whether this cross-border variation supports the proposition that there are increasing aggregate returns to capital and labour as a result of either the external effects associated with capital investment or a secular increase in the variety of intermediate inputs. The authors revisit earlier evidence and conclude there is no support for the assertion that capital-related externalities are present. They go on to demonstrate that the variations in countries' growth rates are consistent with each country having the same constant-returns-to-scale production function, and with a stochastic process for technological change that is the same for different countries but has a different initial starting point.

BARTELMUS offers a unique analysis of sustainable economic growth and development based on operational variables derived from the new systems of "green accounting". His volume provides a new focus on macroeconomic concepts, comparing the positives of economic production with the negatives of the loss of natural resources, and the reduction in the quality of the environment. Beyond economics, ways of evaluating social, cultural, aesthetic, and ethical issues are proposed. Focusing on operational, quantifiable concepts and, methods, the author systematically links the different policies, strategies, and programmes of growth and development to advance an integrated policy framework for sustainable development at local, national, and international levels in both developing and industrialized countries. In his examination of some of the thorny problems, such as accounting for environmental costs, the author provides a new slant on the traditional growth accounting model.

GEOFF TURNER

Guardianship

Bell, H.E., *An Introduction to the History and Records of the Court of Wards and Liveries*, Cambridge: Cambridge University Press, 1953

Bromley, P.M., *Family Law*, 5th edition, London: Butterworths, 1976

Carlton, Charles, *The Court of Orphans*, Leicester: Leicester University Press, 1974

Dershowitz, Alan, "The Origins of Preventive Confinement in Anglo-American Law, part 2: The American Experience", *University of Cincinnati Law Review*, 43 (1974): 781–846

Forsyth, William, *A Treatise on the Law Relating to the Custody of Infants, in Cases of Difference between Parents or Guardians*, London: Benning, and Philadelphia: Johnson, 1850

Hartog, Hendrik, "The Law and Mrs Packard", *Yale Journal of Law and Humanities*, 1 (1988): 79–103

Helmholz, Richard, "The Roman Law of Guardianship in England, 1300–1600", *Tulane Law Review*, 52 (1978): 223–57

Hurstfield, Joel, *The Queen's Wards: Wardship and Marriage under Elizabeth I*, Cambridge, Massachusetts: Harvard University Press, 1958; 2nd edition, London: Cass, 1973

Johns, Frank, "Guardianship Folly: The Misgovernment of Parens Patriae and the Forecast of Its Crumbling Linkage to Unprotected Older Americans in the Twenty-First Century: A March of Folly? or Just a Mask of Virtual Reality?", *Stetson Law Review*, 27 (1997): 1–90

Rozmus, Kelly C., "Representing Families Affected by HIV/AIDS: How the Proposed Federal Standby Guardianship Act Facilitates Future Planning in the Best Interests of the Child and Family", *American University Journal of Gender and the Law*, 6 (1998): 299–332

Tyler, Ransom H., *Commentaries on the Law of Infancy, Including Guardianship and Custody of Infants, and the Law of Coverture*, 2nd edition, Albany, New York: Gould, 1882

Viner, Charles, "Guardian and Ward" in *A General Abridgment of Law and Equity*, 2nd edition, vol. 14, 1793 (pp.160–205, and supplement, 17–27)

Wright, Danaya, "DeManneville v. DeManneville: Rethinking the Birth of Custody Law under Patriarchy", *Law and History Review*, 17 (1999): 247–307

Very little recent scholarship has been done on the law of guardianship because interspousal custody disputes have played a more prominent role in the courts and in the legislatures of both the US and England in the last two hundred years. In the medieval period, guardianship law in England was closely linked to feudal landholding practices and probate matters so heirs to certain types of property would be treated differently from heirs to other types of property. Pollock & Maitland wrote that the law of guardianship "was more disjointed and incomplete" than any other part of the law. In 1600 English law recognized ten different kinds of guardians for heirs to property. Younger children, daughters, and incapacitated adults did not fall under any legal category that would guarantee protection of their body or property. In 1646 the feudal practice of wardship was abolished and land held of the crown in military service was converted to socage tenure, thus unifying the type of most freehold lands owned by potential heirs and simplifying guardianship practices. In the 18th century, changing attitudes toward the patriarchal right of custody and control over children led to a series of attacks on paternal dominance in this area. At the same time, the equity courts took over ecclesiastical court jurisdiction in wardships and announced that they had what was termed *parens patriae* jurisdiction over lunatics, idiots, and *miserabiles personae*, which at times included infants and married women, all who were deemed non-persons under the law. (*Coke on Littleton*, edited by Hargrave and Butler, 88b n.16; 8th edition 1831).

The law of medieval guardianship is best outlined in the works by HELMHOLZ and by CARLTON who explain the multiple jurisdiction of the royal, ecclesiastical, borough, and equity courts in guardianship matters. Helmholz focuses on the role of the church courts in providing guardians for children who otherwise were unprotected in the royal courts and their reliance on the Roman law categories of the curator and tutor, distinctions based on the age of the ward. Carlton's book is a thorough analysis of the borough courts and their jurisdiction over orphans from the 1200s to the 1600s. But as with most work of this period, it acknowledges the scarcity of written records and the haphazard nature of the court structures in medieval England.

From 1540–1646, the Court of Wards and Liveries exercised jurisdiction over the feudal wardships that netted the crown significant revenues when an underage heir was orphaned who held land in military tenure. BELL's and HURSTFIELD's books on the court are excellent studies of the inner workings of the court, the ways in which the court interacted with other courts and Parliament, and the black market that arose in the sales of wardships to landowners who sought control over the ward's land until the ward reached majority. If he were lucky, a guardian could marry the ward into his own family and thus insure the addition of the ward's land to his own, but doing so sometimes brought criminal penalties for guardians who abused their custodial duties.

For the 18th and 19th century, WRIGHT's study of the rising inter-spousal custody law grows out of a study of guardianship categories and their inadequacy for dealing with disputes between two living parents. Because guardianship was seen at that time as an issue of control over property and care of the child upon death of the father, it was wholly inadequate for the exploding interspousal custody disputes that raised issues of which parent should be entitled to custody when both were living and ostensibly fit.

In the 20th century, guardianship is frequently viewed as applying only when a child has lost both parents and thus requires a non-parent to stand *in loco parentis*. So long as at least one parent remains living, that parent is the legal guardian, and if both parents are living but separated, both have the legal power of guardians, although one or the other might have legal custody of the child. Although not entirely accurate, the best way to think of the difference between guardianship and custody of children is that the guardian has all legal powers of the parent to make educational, medical, and religious decisions for a child, whereas custody may refer only to the *de facto* care and control of a child. Hence, a child might have multiple guardians, including one parent, but be in the custody of only one of the guardians, and perhaps not the parent. For detailed treatises on the law of guardianship and the primary cases see VINER for the medieval period, FORSYTH for the 18th and 19th centuries, and BROMLEY for the 20th century.

Because the US rejected primogeniture and the feudal land-holding practices of England, US guardianship law was adopted primarily from the English law of the 18th century, with equity courts deciding custody and guardianship of children either under the paternal rights preference or under a fledgling best interests standard. A detailed treatise on the US law of guardianship as applied to children is TYLER's work on infancy and coverture. Guardianship of minor children in the 20th century follows the requisite best interests standard and thus is often subsumed in the scholarship on child custody.

Of course, we cannot forget that guardianship issues may arise at both the beginning and end of one's life. Guardianship of the elderly and incapacitated has received a fair amount of attention. For histories of guardianship law for the incapacitated, see DERSHOWITZ and also HARTOG. Dershowitz's article examines the rising trend of confinement in nineteenth-century criminal and mental deviance cases. Hartog's article on Mrs Packard is a gender-sensitive study of one woman's quest to change the lunacy laws that allowed a married woman to be confined merely on the signature of her husband.

An exceptionally thorough history of guardianship laws affecting the elderly and contemporary issues surrounding reform of court procedures in the US is JOHNS. Johns suggests a bifurcated procedure that would help avoid adversarial procedures and paternalistic intervention for parties in which incapacity is not clear. He suggests that an administrative hearing is better when the question of incapacity is clear and there are no objections by third parties to the guardianship, and an adversarial hearing is better when incapacity is not clear and the interested party needs a day in court. He then suggests a way to accommodate both procedures under the umbrella of a single law.

Finally, little has been done on two areas of adult guardianship that have become especially prominent in the past few years: the AIDS patient suffering dementia whose family may have different ideas about guardianship from the patient, and the Alzheimer's patient whose mental capacity waxes and wanes for a long period as it slowly deteriorates. ROZMUS discusses a few issues relating to AIDS and guardianships, although it is primarily focused on guardianship of minor children when the parent has HIV/AIDS. Nothing satisfactory has been done on Alzheimer's disease and incapacity in the legal arena.

DANAYA C. WRIGHT

Guilt

Fenichel, Otto, *The Psychoanalytic Theory of Neurosis*, New York: Norton, 1945; London: Routledge, 1946

Freud, Sigmund, "The Ego and the Id" (published in German 1923) in *The Ego and the Id, and Other Works*, London: Hogarth Press, 1961 (*The Standard Edition of the Complete Psychological Works*, vol. 19)

Gilbert, P., J. Pehl and S. Allan, "The Phenomenology of Shame and Guilt: An Empirical Investigation", *British Journal of Medical Psychology*, 67 (1994): 23–36

Greenspan, P.S., *Practical Guilt: Moral Dilemmas, Emotions, and Social Norms*, Oxford and New York: Oxford University Press, 1995

Lewis, Helen B., *Shame and Guilt in Neurosis*, New York: International Universities Press, 1971

Sandywell, Barry, *Logological Investigations*, vol. 1: *Reflexivity and the Crisis of Western Reason*, London and New York: Routledge, 1996

Tangney, June Price and Kurt W. Fischer (editors), *Self-Conscious Emotions: The Psychology of Shame, Guilt, Embarrassment, and Pride*, New York: Guilford Press, 1995

Tangney, J.P., "The Self-conscious Emotions: Shame, Guilt, Embarrassment, and Pride" in *Handbook of Cognition and Emotion*, edited by Tim Dalgleish and Mick J. Power, Chichester and New York: Wiley, 1999

Tomkins, Silvan S., *Affect, Imagery, Consciousness*, vol. 2: *The Negative Affects*, London: Tavistock, and New York: Springer, 1963

Guilt (its origins are associated with Latin *debitum* and German *schuld*) generally implies responsibility for some violation of moral standards. It is regarded as a powerful self-conscious emotion and feelings of guilt are often associated with mental disorders (for example depression). Much recent empirical research into guilt has focused on differentiating guilt from shame as both emotions often occur together and one may be subsumed under the other. However, attempts to differentiate between the two concepts have not been totally successful and evidence for the existence of two separate emotions (guilt and shame) remains equivocal.

FENICHEL is a classic text on the psychoanalytical theory of neurosis wherein guilt represents the anxiety of the *ego* to the "severe" *superego* ("you ought to do . . ."). Fenichel describes guilt as a combination of trauma, danger (of annihilation), and panic where the *superego* can work either on the side of the *ego* or the *id* depending on whether guilt feelings motivate the defence or whether the *ego* is defending itself. There are several chapters on guilt and numerous references to guilt feelings over a wide range of behaviours: sex, addictions, aggressiveness, and so on. This is an authoritative and standard text for the psychoanalytically orientated.

FREUD is a landmark text in the field of Freudian theory. It describes the psychoanalytical anatomy of the mind (the *id*, *ego*, and *superego*) and outlines the unconscious mechanisms (for example the Oedipus complex) responsible for guilt feelings. Freud, probably the inventor of the modern sense of guilt, viewed the concept as a "moral factor" and suggested that a sense of guilt arises when the *ego* fails to satisfy the needs of the *superego*. Readers already familiar with distinctions between guilt and shame may notice how shame appears to be subsumed under guilt.

GILBERT, PEHL & ALLAN describe the concepts of guilt and shame with reference to sociobiological mechanisms and take the view that guilt has its basis in cooperative behaviour whereas shame has its basis in ranking behaviour (ethnological/evolutionary theory). Statistical analyses of data from questionnaires are carried out to examine the relationships of shame and guilt to different personal and emotional experiences (submissive behaviour, social anxiety, depression). One criticism of this study might be that a student population is assessed rather than a clinical population; the latter might have been more appropriate considering the nature of mood disorders. This article provides an historical overview of guilt and shame and serves as a useful introduction to social ranking theory.

GREENSPAN focuses on the social bases of guilt: moral dilemmas may result in emotional guilt although no one is to blame except perhaps the societal moral code that condemns all the alternative responses as being wrong. A good distinction is made between moral and nonmoral guilt and several case examples are used to illustrate situations of moral dilemmas. This is a detailed and well-argued philosophical text – although the actual content is sociological and psychological in nature – which offers an interesting sociomoral perspective on the concept of guilt.

LEWIS is a landmark and pioneering text in the field of affect. Lewis, a psychoanalyst, studies the phenomenologies of guilt and shame and defines the characteristics of each. Transcripts of psychotherapy sessions are used to examine individuals' perceptual styles and susceptibility to guilt and shame. Results indicate that guilt is more readily expressed whereas shame is silent; it is also shame that appears to shape symptoms of psychopathology. This book (now out of print) is mentioned in nearly every paper that I have read on the concepts of guilt and shame.

TANGNEY, a clinical psychologist, looks at the selfconscious emotions of shame, guilt, embarrassment, and pride and argues that there is enough empirical support to distinguish between shame and guilt: shame motivates an avoidance response whereas guilt motivates reparative behaviour (see also Klein, M., *Love, Guilt and Reparation and Other Works, 1921–1945*, 1975). It is suggested that some of the guilt reactions often reported in cases of mental disorders may actually be feelings of "shame-fused guilt" (see also TOMKINS). This text provides a good overview on recent research on the links between shame and guilt and the handbook in which it is published includes much more on self-conscious emotions.

The 20 chapters in TANGNEY & FISCHER cover the whole range of self-conscious emotions. The major theories on guilt and shame are outlined (for example K.C. Barrett,: "A Functionalist Approach to Shame and Guilt", chapter two) and the early development of guilt is examined (for example C. Zahn-Wechsler& J. Robinson: "Empathy and guilt: early origins of feelings of responsibility', chapter five). There is an excellent review of validation studies involving many of the current scales used to measure shame proneness and guilt proneness (D.W. Harder: "Shame and guilt assessment and relationships of shame- and guilt-proneness to psycho pathology", chapter 15) and a complete section (chapters 18, 19, and 20) is given to crosscultural perspectives. This academic and well-referenced text points the reader to probably every relevant published paper in the field at that time. No one who is serious about studying the concept of guilt can be without this book.

Tomkins proposes a physiological affect theory that identifies shame/humiliation as an innate affect (each of Tomkins' nine affects is a two-worded grouping that describes the nature and range of the affect) of which guilt is simply a variant: a combination of *shame* plus *fear of reprisal*. Guilt is shame about moral issues and thus the concept of morality has to be formed before guilt can be experienced. Links have been made between psychoanalytical theory and affect theory (M.F. Basch, "The concept of affect: a re-examination", *Journal of the American Psychoanalytic Association*, 24, (1976) 759–78) and shame is now acknowledged as a major affect in psychopathology. This dense and complex work cannot be ignored when studying affect.

Chapter nine on phonetic reflexivity (pp.318–43) in this first volume of logological investigations, although not a key text on guilt, offers a short and interesting perspective on the concept. SANDYWELL argues that self-reflection, resulting in feelings such as guilt and shame, is a form of social control that cannot be divorced from our social and political institutions; religion, for example, defines the moral self through such concepts as guilt and shame. A detailed, scholarly work on the historical, traditional, and sociological development of self-identity, self-examination, and interpersonal conduct with numerous references to more detailed texts on guilt (for example Rousseau's *Confessions* and Augustine's *The City of God*).

JOHN P. DONNELLY

See also Shame

H

Habeas corpus

Barnett, Hilaire, *Constitutional and Administrative Law*, 2nd edition, London: Cavendish, 1998

Bradley, A.W. and K.D. Ewing, *Constitutional and Administrative Law*, 12th edition, London and New York: Longman, 1997

de Smith, Stanley and Rodney Brazier, *Constitutional and Administrative Law*, 7th edition, London and New York: Penguin, 1994

Dicey, A.V., *Introduction to the Study of the Law of the Constitution*, London: Macmillan, 1885; 10th edition, with introduction by E.C.S. Wade, London: Macmillan, and New York: St Martin's Press, 1959

Jennings, W. Ivor, *The Law and the Constitution*, London: University of London Press, 1933; 5th edition 1959

Keir, D.L., *The Constitutional History of Modern Britain, 1485–1937*, London: A. & C. Black, 1938; 9th edition 1969

Le Sueur, Andrew and Maurice Sunkin, *Public Law*, London and New York: Longman, 1997

McEldowney, John, *Public Law*, 2nd edition, London: Sweet and Maxwell, 1998

Marsh, Henry, *Documents of Liberty: From Earliest Times to Universal Suffrage*, Newton Abbot, Devon: David and Charles, 1971

Habeas corpus – the right to have a restriction on liberty reviewed by a court of law – is regarded as a touchstone of the liberty of the subject. BARNETT emphasizes this symbolism, and DE SMITH & BRAZIER record that habeas corpus is emotionally entrenched: it would be "easier . . . to abolish the House of Lords or the hereditary peerage or the Privy Council than, say, to abolish the remedy of habeas corpus".

MARSH sketches over the common law origins of habeas corpus. This is to be expected in a book focusing on documents. He provides historical background in respect to the Petition of Right 1628, which was based in part on the denial of habeas corpus, and sets out in full the central Habeas Corpus Act of 1679. The detail in Marsh is invaluable.

DICEY famously records that habeas corpus has "done for the liberty of Englishmen more than could have been achieved by any declaration of rights" (a reference to achieving more than "a hundred constitutions" is also often quoted). A thorough reading of his text, though, demonstrates that the prac-

tice does not necessarily match this claim. It is significant that he moves from a discussion of habeas corpus to an analysis of the effects of Acts of Indemnity on, among others, those who have been denied habeas corpus.

KEIR sounds a cracked note concerning the value of habeas corpus from the mid-16th century to the mid 17th century. He refers to the judges having "demonstrated their dependability" concerning the protection of liberty through habeas corpus. This dependability was shown not to the people but to the holders of power, first the Crown and then Parliament after 1688. Indeed, as late as 1704 the courts were prepared to hold that a writ of habeas corpus would not lie to release anyone committed for contempt by the House of Commons. This was so even if the cause of committal stated in the return to the writ was insufficient in law (*Paty's Case* (1704) 1 Sm LC 281). Keir notes that in the early 20th century the judges would, under normal conditions, throw their protection over "such rights as those of personal liberty, vindicated by habeas corpus". However, he detected "a new bias in favour of authority."

JENNINGS mentions habeas corpus only in passing. He even seeks to excuse the outrageous decision in *Liversidge (alias Perlzweig) v. Anderson* (1942) AC 206 HL. In Liversidge, the House of Lords ruled that that imprisonment by executive discretion was not justiciable by writ of habeas corpus, nor were the facts upon which such imprisonment was based. This decision shows habeas corpus at its lowest ebb.

LE SUEUR & SUNKIN place no significance on habeas corpus at all. Perhaps this is no surprise, given that Le Sueur also wrote "Should We Abolish the Writ of Habeas Corpus" (1992) PL 13. The omission is also in keeping with the current tendency towards constitutional vandalism.

De Smith & Brazier give a much more lawyerly, serious treatment to habeas corpus. They record that it is central to any discussion of civil rights and freedoms, and write that, in their view, Dicey could have claimed that it was worth "a thousand Universal Declarations of Human Rights" in addition to a hundred constitutions.

They also identify a convincing explanation of the outcome of *Paty's Case* (above). Technically, Parliament is properly referred to as the "High Court of Parliament," and is on an equal footing with the judicial High Court. To allow the latter to review the former would have been to recognize a form of horizontal appeal that was alien to UK usage. Even now, the High Court is not allowed to judicially review the Crown Court conducting a trial on indictment. In such circumstances the Crown Court is on an equal footing with the High Court.

Barnett does what is needed in terms of an historical overview, coupled with a brief description of modern practice regarding habeas corpus. Useful contrasts are also drawn between habeas corpus and the European Convention on Human Rights, and between habeas corpus and judicial review.

This latter contrast is also drawn by McELDOWNEY, who also floats a possible future role for habeas corpus – as interim relief at the leave stage of a judicial review. There are hints in the judgement of Lord Justice Simon Brown in *Regina v. Oldham Justices ex parte Cawley* (1996) 1 All ER 464 that the judges might favour such a clarification of the modern role of habeas corpus.

It would not be possible to complete this review without mentioning BRADLEY & EWING, whose masterful work underlines that habeas corpus is unconnected with Magna Carta. They set out the procedure for pursuing habeas corpus in some detail, and make several passing references to it throughout their text. They note that there are unresolved current issues concerning habeas corpus, and provide pointers to the discussion in *ex parte Cawley* (above) as to the status of habeas corpus as a flexible remedy capable of development to meet modern needs.

DAVE RADLETT

See also Constitutional law, Magna Carta

Habituation effect

Gleitman, Henry, *Psychology*, 4th edition, New York: Norton, 1995

Gray, J.A., *Elements of a Two-Process Theory of Learning*, London and New York: Academic Press, 1975

Kalat, James W., *Biological Psychology*, 6th edition, London and Pacific Grove, California: Brooks/Cole, 1998

Lynn, R., *Attention, Arousal and the Orientation Reaction*, Oxford and New York: Pergamon Press, 1966

O'Gorman, J.G., "Individual Differences in Habituation of Human Physiological Responses: A Review of Theory, Method, and Findings in the Study of Personality Correlates in Non-Clinical Populations", *Biological Psychology*, 5 (1977): 257–318

Zuckerman, Marvin, *Psychobiology of Personality*, Cambridge and New York: Cambridge University Press, 1991

The habituation effect consists of the waning of a response as a consequence of the stimulus that elicits the response being repeatedly presented – reduced responding due to fatigue or receptor adaptation does not count as habituation. It has been studied extensively because it seems to represent a simple form of behavioural plasticity. This effect may be contrasted with the opposite behavioural process: *sensitization*, which refers to the broadening of the range of effective stimuli to which the organism is sensitive following repeated presentation of a stimulus. The habituation effect has been studied from a number of perspectives, and has been used for a number of different research purposes. References have been chosen to reflect these

perspectives, and to illustrate how this effect has been used to probe different physiological and psychological processes.

GRAY discusses the habituation effect within the context of the orienting reflex and learning theory. He provides an insightful exposition of the important components of this effect. He notes that habituation is used only for stimuli that elicit a response in an innate manner (the ability of the stimulus to elicit the response does not depend upon learning, such as Pavlovian conditioning). In standard conditioning terms, this stimulus is an *unconditioned stimulus* and the habituated response is an *unconditioned response*. The waning of a learned (*conditioned*) response falls under other headings in behavioural psychology (such as extinction and conditioned inhibition). Although habituation is a relatively simple and primitive behavioural phenomenon, it has proved influential in studying higher order processes.

For instance, as Gray discusses, expectancies are important in habituation. For example, a rat presented with 200 startle stimuli within a five-minute period will show rapid habituation, but when the stimulus is presented once again the next day the startle response will be reinstated (spontaneous recovery). However, if the 200 startle stimuli are distributed over time, then long-term habituation will be achieved: in this instance, the rat has a memory of the startle stimuli distributed across time. Therefore, in addition to the known neurophysiological bases of habituation, this effect is also under partial psychological control.

In relation to orienting responses (ORs) (responses elicited by novel stimuli, presented in any sensory modality, which decline in strength upon repeated presentation; for example, turning of the head towards an auditory stimulus), Gray notes that reinstatement of habituated ORs occurs with: (a) changes along any of the sensory dimensions (such as pitch or loudness); (b) a period of time elapsing after habituation and before presentation of the stimulus again; and (c) presentation of an extra novel stimulus just before presentation of the habituated stimulus (this effect persists on a few subsequent trials where the habituated stimulus is presented alone).

The psychological basis of habituation and its implications for understanding ORs in relation to arousal and attention is discussed in detail by LYNN. In particular, much of the early Russian literature on the OR is discussed, starting with the work of the physiologist Ivan Pavlov. The chapter on "The habituation of the orientation reaction" summarizes, in a few pages, the essential elements; and the one on "neurological models for habituation of the orientation reaction" provides a succinct introduction to the historical background to accounting for this effect.

Habituation is a ubiquitous phenomenon across the phylogenetic scale. Extensive physiological research has been conducted on *Aplysia* (a marine invertebrate related to the common slug). If its siphon, mantle, or gill is touched, the animal withdraws vigorously; but if touched repeatedly the gill-withdrawal reflex becomes progressively less vigorous, and finally disappears. This habituation effect lasts two to three hours following a single stimulus habituation session. The neurophysiology of habituation has been delineated in *Aplysia* (chosen as the object of study because it has fewer neurons than any vertebrate; its neurons are large; and there are few inter-individual differences in neuronal pathways). A simple introduction to this research in relation to the neurophysiology of information storage (memory) is given by KALAT.

The habituation effect is of theoretical importance in its own right, but it has also served as a simple, robust behavioural measure of a number of other psychological processes. That is, habituation is used also to probe psychological processes (commonly referred to as the habituation method). For example, a researcher may be interested in whether neonates can make a perceptual discrimination between two types of stimuli: one stimulus may be repeatedly presented with the result that, after several presentations, the neonate loses interest and looks away (loss of orienting response); then the second stimulus is presented: the degree of interest in the new stimulus is taken as an indication of the degree of perceptual discrimination. A brief, but very useful introduction to the habituation method as it is applied in psychology is provided by GLEITMAN.

ZUCKERMAN provides an accessible, yet detailed, account of its applications in personality research and psychiatry. Impaired habituation is deficient in a number of psychopathological disorders involving cognitive dysfunction (for example, acute schizophrenia). For example, a failure to habituate to everyday common sounds (such as road traffic and voices) would lead to inattention to important stimuli, lack of concentration, and the assignment of undue importance to irrelevant stimuli (for example delusions).

Although the habituation effect is of fundamental importance in physiology and psychology, there are a number of problems with its operational definition that limits its value in the behavioural sciences. Zuckerman summarizes this literature. He lists the common measures of habituation: trials to criterion (the number of presentation trials required for a response to meet the criterion of habituation; for example, 50 per cent reduction in response strength); difference scores (subtracting response scores obtained after repeated presentation from those obtained at the beginning of the experiment); and amplitude trial slope (using linear regression to calculate, for each individual subject, the decline in response strength expressed as a slope coefficient). Many habituation measures are contaminated by initial response strength: if strength is weak at the start of the experiment then there is a "floor effect" below which responses never fall, leading to the spurious conclusion that habituation has not occurred (as sometimes found in anxious patients); in contrast, if an individual starts with a strong response, then there is more response space in which the response strength can fall, leading to a high rate of habituation. Thus, habituation effects may be the result of initial values, not a decline in response strength *per se*. Such data point to the complex nature of habituation and its dependency upon other physiological processes. O'GORMAN covers these issues in much greater detail.

In addition, O'Gorman provides a highly detailed and informative review of the human habituation literature. Both theoretical and methodological issues are discussed, including the strengths and weakness of the different operational definitions; experimental conditions conducive to habituation are also well reviewed. In relation to personality studies, to which the habituation effect has been extensively applied, 46 studies were surveyed. Twenty studies investigated the construct of extraversion, which is known to be related to psychophysiological responses: eight found the expected effect of faster habituation in extraverts (due to their putative underarousal), as compared with introverts, who showed resistance to habituation (due to their putative overarousal); however, 12 studies failed to find a significant relationship between extraversion and habituation. It is clear that the apparent simplicity of the habituation effect conceals a reality of considerable complexity.

PHILIP J. CORR

See also Learning

Hate speech

Butler, Judith, *Excitable Speech: A Politics of the Performative*, London and New York: Routledge, 1997

Cover, Robert M., "Violence and the Word", *Yale Law Journal*, 95/8 (1986): 1601–29

Fiss, Owen M., *The Irony of Free Speech*, Cambridge, Massachusetts: Harvard University Press, 1996

Gates, Henry Louis Jr *et al.*, *Speaking of Race, Speaking of Sex: Hate Speech, Civil Rights and Civil Liberties*, New York: New York University Press, 1994

Langton, Rae, "Speech Acts and Unspeakable Acts", *Philosophy and Public Affairs*, 22/4 (1993): 293–330

Matsuda, Mari *et al.*, *Words That Wound: Critical Race Theory, Assaultive Speech, and the First Amendment*, Boulder, Colorado: Westview Press, 1993

Scarry, Elaine, *The Body in Pain: The Making and Unmaking of the World*, New York: Oxford University Press, 1985

Shapiro, Michael J. (editor), *Language and Politics*, New York: New York University Press, and Oxford: Blackwell, 1984

Walker, Samuel, *Hate Speech: The History of an American Controversy*, Lincoln: University of Nebraska Press, 1994

BUTLER moves beyond the polarity of the "free speech versus restricted speech" debate in the US, into the realm of the philosophy of language. She complicates the understanding of language to be found in that debate using the writings of J.L. Austin and Althusser's theory of interpellation and she effectively questions the notion that the injurious quality of a word is inherent to the word itself. She examines the theory of language underlying the work of the critical race theorists, together with Catherine MacKinnon, suggesting the need for a more complex understanding of the relationship between language and materiality. In order to decide which words wound, and how they do so, Butler proposes that it is not sufficient to examine merely the words themselves but rather the tone with which they are said. Developing further her theory of performativity, Butler proposes that the power of specific words to cause pain may be diffused through reiteration rather than through restriction.

COVER's analysis provides a significantly different focus from the debate around the First Amendment within the US. Moving laterally from this debate he examines judicial discourse as an enactment of violence through the speech of the judge's sentence. The supposed neutrality of the judiciary, encompassing judges as well as prison officers, and security police, is examined and exposed as a systemic form of violence that achieves the image of neutrality through complex systems of spatial and temporal rituals. Cover suggests that the violence of the judiciary is left unexamined when the fairness and efficacy of the courts is presumed in advance.

FISS concentrates his analysis of the US freedom of speech debate on specific controversial court cases. He situates the current controversy over campus hate speech regulations in the history of the American civil rights movement, identifying the nexus of the debate as the polarization of libertarian and democratic tendencies within the liberalist discourse. Advocating a democratic understanding of free speech, which he perceives as emphasizing the rights of collective freedoms over individual ones, Fiss suggests that state regulations may actually be seen to further free speech. The discussion covers pornography and racial vilification debates as well as the restriction of political parties' access to media advertising in the US. However the depth of analysis is limited by its brevity.

The articles in GATES et al. constitute a reaction to the arguments put forward by the critical race theorists. According to Gates, the general aim of the book is to create a more careful analysis, and thus disputation, of the arguments for restricting instances of hate speech on US university campuses. Existing firmly within the bounds of American liberal thought, the legitimacy of the First Amendment is deemed to be guaranteed on the basis of a certain historical perspective of the civil rights movement in the US. Although the book is useful for its examination of the tendencies towards totalitarianism inherent in forms of state speech restrictions, the limitations of the analysis lie in an inadequate theorization of the relationship between language and power.

LANGTON's article addresses the critique of the proposal, predominantly associated with Catherine MacKinnon, that pornography constitutes a speech act; that it both depicts and causes the subordination of women. Using J.L Austin's distinction between locutionary, perlocutionary and illocutionary speech acts, she explores the idea that pornography may be better conceptualized as unprotected action rather than protected speech. Her work contextualizes the speech act in the conventions in which it exists in order to elucidate the ways in which "silencing" may be understood as the silencing of the force or power of a statement even when it is actually made. Langton explores the less-apparent qualities of language, as it relates to societal rituals and norms. Although she offers no overall conclusions with regard to the problems of censorship and pornography, she adeptly shows how the bases of the antipornography arguments of MacKinnon are, at least, philosophically coherent.

MATSUDA et al., calling themselves critical race theorists, attempt to use versions of speech act theory to create a distance between the belief in speech restrictions and a position of simple censorship. The blurring of a strict boundary between speech and action, these theorists suggest, moves violent speech acts away from the realm of protection by First Amendment "freedoms", and opens the possibility for state-sanctioned restrictions. Focusing on instances of racial hatred, these writers believe that the emphasis needs to be placed on the feelings and experiences of the victims of hate speech rather than always on the rights of the assailant. Although quite insightful, the arguments inadequately address systemic racism, remaining within the territory of individual acts.

SCARRY destabilizes the polarization of the "free speech versus hate speech" debate with a quite unique examination of the relationship of words to violence and pain. She looks at what it is that happens, both to the victim and to the words, when speech injures. In order to understand why language is so inadequate for expressing pain, she analyses speech as a bodily act in which she suggests violence is a threat to language itself, to its "sense-making possibilities". In the light of this destructive power of language, Scarry pursues the question of how to account for the specific kinds of injuries performed by language.

Although not specifically addressing the hate speech debate, the collection of articles edited by SHAPIRO brings to light current trends in the philosophy of language through the work of a number of theorists, such as De Man, Jameson, and Foucault. Authorship and subjectivity are examined as a function of language rather than its initiating moment. Language is understood not as a relationship between thought and things but as a domain of human practices. The writers advocate various discursive practices based on the interrogation of the text for its political commitments, evident through the various conventions, tropes and metaphors used. This works to dispel the distinction between realist and nonrealist genres of writing. Shapiro's own contribution elaborates, clearly and succinctly, the philosophical issues involved in contemporary poststructuralist thought.

WALKER examines the quite unique understanding of free speech to be found in the US, pointing out that many other countries place restrictions on offensive or hurtful speech. He wishes to explain why the US has such an extreme commitment to this understanding through a survey of the various manifestations of hate speech controversies from the 1920s–1990s. The period is analysed through the various criminal law debates that occurred. However, Walker leaves many terms, including both "freedom" and "speech", unexamined, and his unquestioned belief in the US's "triumph" over speech restrictions tends to create something of a critical vacuum.

NICOLA NIXON

Hawthorne effect

Adair, John G., "The Hawthorne Effect: A Reconsideration of the Methodological Artifact", *Journal of Applied Psychology*, 69/2 (1984): 334–45

Carey, Alex, "The Hawthorne Studies: A Radical Criticism", *American Sociological Review*, 32/3 (1967): 403–16

Gottfredson, Gary D., "The Hawthorne Misunderstanding (and How to Get the Hawthorne Effect in Action Research)", *Journal of Research in Crime and Delinquency*, 33/1 (1996): 28–48

Mayo, Elton, *The Social Problems of an Industrial Civilization*, Boston: Harvard University, 1945; London: Routledge, 1949

Roethlisberger, F.J. and William J. Dickson, *Management and the Worker*, Cambridge, Massachusetts: Harvard University Press, 1939

Silver, Jim, "The Ideology of Excellence: Management and Neo-Conservatism", *Studies in Political Economy*, 24 (1987): 105–29

Whitehead, T.N., *The Industrial Worker*, vols 1–2, Cambridge, Massachusetts: Harvard University Press, 1938

Whyte, William Foote, review of Fritz J. Roethlisberger's *The Elusive Phenomenon*, in *Human Organization*, 37/4 (1978): 412–20

ADAIR provides a useful introduction to the somewhat confusing concept of the Hawthorne effect. Any student of this topic will quickly discover that while most textbook writers give references to the Hawthorne studies (see entry on Hawthorne research), and less often to the effect, it is clear they have rarely even consulted the works they cite, let alone carefully studied them. Adair did research into texts that described Hawthorne and what he found "was appalling". Not one text described the Hawthorne studies accurately. Definitions of the "effect" varied, but he found that the majority defined it as roughly equivalent to "some behaviour change as a result of awareness of being a subject in an experiment". Adair finds this meaningless as it "gives no indication of why the change occurs or what mediates the effect". However, it does encourage better research design so that the control group is identical to the subject group, with the phenomenon that is being researched the only difference. Adair discusses 40 studies that had employed controls for three Hawthorne effects: special attention, awareness of experiment participation, and novelty. The paper makes it clear that without understanding the Hawthorne *studies*, any consideration of the Hawthorne *effect* will almost certainly be flawed.

ROETHLISBERGER & DICKSON is frequently cited, although in all probability very infrequently studied. Their work has been widely heralded as the major contribution to the human relations movement, but also strongly criticized. Early attacks were primarily concerned with the work's ideology: the book showed pro-management bias, was anti-union (or ignored unions), and was concerned with manipulating workers. Later attacks were more devastating, pointing out the scientific ineptitude of the research and the way conclusions were reached that contradicted the evidence. The book details what went on in the Hawthorne research, and readers can reach their own conclusions from the descriptions and evidence. Proper study enables the later distorted, and indeed dishonest accounts to be revealed in their true colours.

WHITEHEAD, in his two-volume work examines in detail the relay assembly test room experiment. Although it was only part of the Hawthorne research, the relay assembly room has been given the most attention, being credited as the "source" of the Hawthorne effect. Whitehead provides details of output from each of the "five girls" and extracts from reports of their conversation and their relationship with supervisors. As an example: "almost daily the latter (operator 2a) is on record as having been reproved for her 'low output and behaviour'," and also: "Ops 1a and 2a were removed for a lack of cooperation."

MAYO should be read to gain an understanding as to how the misconceptions over Hawthorne arose. His few brief chapters proved to be a popular source for lazy textbook writers who wholeheartedly accepted this version of events from the "leader" of the Hawthorne research. Thus, they read about "the retirement of the original first and second workers" with no mention of the almost daily reprovals and their dismissals

from the experiment. Conforming to Mayo's vision, they also read that "what actually happened was that six individuals became a team and the team gave itself wholeheartedly and spontaneously to cooperation in the experiment".

CAREY is not the only critic both of the Hawthorne studies, and the conclusions made by the major authors quoted above. However, his is possibly the most devastating critique and it is essential reading. He argues that Mayo's work is dishonest, and that the conclusions reached by Roethlisberger and Dickson are based on a "scientifically illiterate procedure", which basically rejected any explanations other than the preferred ones, that social factors were more significant than financial factors. In fact a more logical explanation is that the relay assembly results "are surprisingly consistent with a rather old-world view about the value of monetary incentives, driving leadership, and discipline".

The book review by WHYTE is basically an article concerning the Hawthorne research and the Hawthorne effect, with a primary focus on Roethlisberger. Although Whyte was not personally involved in the Hawthorne studies, he was quite close to the major actors so it is highly significant that he writes:

> It is indeed extraordinary that a phenomenon with so many possible explanations should have achieved popular recognition and even some scientific standing under the name of the Hawthorne Effect. To be sure, Roethlisberger did not name the phenomenon, but he adopted the term and used it frequently in his writings, as if the words "Hawthorne Effect" actually explained something.

SILVER relates the Hawthorne studies and the Hawthorne effect to later management "theories" such as those expressed in Peters & Waterman's *In Search of Excellence* (1982). Silver claims "ISOE is, in fact, merely the most recent in a long line of similarly flawed management techniques whose origins are in the Hawthorne experiments". He provides interesting insights into Hawthorne, quoting the operators who were interviewed 50 years later. What they liked about the test room was: "We made more money". Silver considers that Hawthorne, rather than showing the merits of good human relations, could be taken to confirm the value of hard traditional management: "sack troublemakers; replace them with more ambitious and cooperative workers". In Silver's view, Hawthorne was simply the first of a line of management techniques characterized by methodological flaws and misinterpretations, "whose intentions are to win the hearts and minds of workers in order to lure from them harder work without higher pay".

GOTTFREDSON accepts that the traditional interpretations of the Hawthorne research are incorrect, and rejects the idea that the Hawthorne effect came from interest in the employees' wellbeing. He suggests a simple explanation is that there was feedback on performance, opportunities for goal setting followed by improvement and contingent reinforcement. That is, financial reward was dependent on output.

ALAN JAMES GEARE

See also Hawthorne research

Hawthorne research

Altenbaugh, Richard J., "The Children and the Instruments of a Militant Labor Progressivism: Brookwood Labor College and the American Labor College Movement of the 1920s and 1930s", *History of Education Quarterly*, 23/4 (1983): 395–411

Baritz, Loren, *The Servants of Power: A History of the Use of Social Science in American Industry*, New York: Wiley, 1965

Bernstein, Irving, *The Lean Years: A History of the American Worker, 1920–1933*, Boston: Houghton Mifflin, 1960

Bramel, Dana and Ronald Friend, "Hawthorne, the Myth of the Docile Worker, and Class Bias in Psychology", *American Psychologist*, 36/8 (1981): 867–78

Dickson, William J. and F.J. Roethlisberger, *Counseling in an Organization: A Sequel to the Hawthorne Researches*, Boston: Graduate School of Business Administration, Harvard University, 1966

Gillespie, Richard, *Manufacturing Knowledge: A History of the Hawthorne Experiments*, Cambridge and New York: Cambridge University Press, 1991

Gilson, Mary, "Review of *Management and the Worker*", *American Journal of Sociology*, 46 (1940): 98–101

Hogan, David, "Education and the Making of the Chicago Working Class, 1880–1930", *History Education Quarterly*, 18 (1978): 227–70

Landsberger, Henry A., *Hawthorne Revisited: Management and the Worker: Its Critics, and Developments in Human Relations in Industry*, Ithaca, New York: Cornell University Press, 1958

Lynd, Robert, "Review of Whitehead's *Leadership in a Free Society*", *Political Science Quarterly*, 52 (1937): 590–92

Mayo, Elton, *The Human Problems of an Industrial Civilization*, New York: Macmillan, 1933; reprinted Salem, New Hampshire: Ayer, 1992

Mills, C. Wright, *The Power Elite*, New York: Oxford University Press, 1956; London: Oxford University Press, 1959

Nelson-Rowe, Shan, "Corporation Schooling and the Labor Market at General Electric", *History of Education Quarterly*, 31/1 (1991): 27–46

Roethlisberger, F.J. and William J. Dickson, *Management and the Worker: An Account of a Research Program Conducted by the Western Electric Company, Hawthorne Works, Chicago*, Cambridge, Massachusetts: Harvard University Press, 1939

Susman, Warren I., *Culture as History: The Transformation of American Society in the Twentieth Century*, New York: Pantheon, 1983

Weiss, Bernard J., *American Education and the European Immigrant*, Urbana: University of Illinois Press, 1982

Whitehead, T.N., *The Industrial Worker: A Statistical Study of Human Relations in a Group of Manual Workers*, 2 vols, Cambridge, Massachusetts: Harvard University Press, 1938

From 1924 to 1932, an innovative series of research studies was funded by the Western Electric Company at its Hawthorne plant in Chicago, then a manufacturing division of AT&T. The plant was one of the oldest in operation and employed approximately 25,000 of Western Electric's 45,000 workers. The research proceeded through five phases: (a) The initial *illumination studies* (1924–7) aimed at evaluating the effect of lighting conditions on productivity; (b) *the relay-assembly room studies* (August 1928–March 1929) assessed the effects of pay incentives, rest periods, and active job input on the productivity of five selected woman workers; (c) *the Mica-Splitting Test group* (October 1928–September 1930) in which a group of piece workers were used to corroborate the relative importance of work-group dynamics versus pay incentives; (d) *the Bank Wiring Observation group* (November 1931–May 1932) a covert observational design in which the dynamics of control in a work-group of 14 male employees on the regular factory floor were observed; and (e) *the plantwide interviewing programme* (September 1928–early 1931) essentially an attempt by the company to categorize concerns, mitigate grievances, and manipulate employee morale according to the principles of social control learned in the previous phases). The latter two phases were interrupted by the detrimental effects of the Great Depression on company production orders, but the interviewing phase was later reinstated as a "personnel counselling" programme, and was even expanded throughout the Western Electric company system between 1936–55.

The Hawthorne effect, defined as the tendency under conditions of observation for worker productivity to steadily increase, was discovered during the earliest "scientific management" phases of the research. It was suggested that when human work relations (supervision and worker camaraderie) were appropriate, adverse physical conditions had little negative effect upon worker productivity. If the company could only learn more about the human relations aspects of the workplace, they might soon be able to utilize them to increase overall plant production. The latter phases of research, therefore, become more sociopsychological in design.

MAYO was the most prominent early popularizer of these studies. His previous industrial psychology work included reducing turnover in a Philadelphia area textile mill by establishing a system of rest periods for workers but he now stressed a social relations interpretation of the ongoing Hawthorne research. This portrayal had the eventual disciplinary effect of extending the purview of industrial testing beyond the previous individualized placement of workers toward the wider realm of manipulation of workplace relationships. Mayo's account is altogether more programmatic than the guarded comments of WHITEHEAD or of ROETHLISBERGER & DICKSON in their official company research report (where more of the messy empirical details of the early phases of research were presented). All three sources, however, intentionally portray the Harvard Business School researchers as equally benevolent toward worker and company interests.

The standard portrayal of wholehearted cooperation between the workers and supervisors in the latter phases of research came under sharp attack from industrial sociologists from 1937 onward, including: GILSON; LYND; MILLS; LANDSBERGER. It was BARITZ, however, who popularized the notion that industrial researchers were inevitably "servants of power". The counselling phase of research in particular was designed to apply the listening techniques of the "Catholic confessional" and the "psychiatric couch" (p.116) with the aim of adjusting people to situations (rather than alleviating those situations from the workplace). An attempt at disciplinary damage control was then published by DICKSON & ROETH-LISBERGER. A more convincing counterargument can be gained from other sources. Baritz clearly overstated his argument. Early 20th-century immigrant workers were not simply hapless victims of capitalism. They used the limited opportunities presented by the industrial workplace to create their own conditions for the further development of their subcultures. ALTENBAUGH; BERNSTEIN; SUSMAN; NELSON-ROWE all indicate that these self-made conditions included such features as parochial schools, organized labour unions, and even labour colleges.

GILLESPIE follows up this line of historical reasoning by placing the Hawthorne research into the context of the rise of labour unions. The Hawthorne subject pool did not mindlessly *react* to industrial management techniques nor did they simply *adjust* or *adapt* to the less than subtle contingencies of social relations experiments. They recognized these contingencies for what they were: new company attempts to increase overall production and control union sentiment. Both HOGAN and also WEISS indicate that transplanted peasant culture, which emphasized family collectivism, religious devotion, and attitudes toward the value of work and formal education, probably affected workplace relations as much as any company-based programme.

Whereas scientific management *decorticated* workers, and the mental testing tradition *individualized* workers, social relations research portrayed workers as ruled by a *sentiment of interpersonal irrationality*. This was, of course, an improvement; but not much of an improvement. BRAMEL & FRIEND caution modern researchers to bear in mind that the results of industrial research can not be fully understood by mere appeal to subject expectancy effects, nor even to contextualized social work group relations. They must be understood in the wider, shifting, societal-historical context of management–union relations.

PAUL F. BALLANTYNE

See also Hawthorne effect

Hayek, F.A. 1899–1992

British (Austrian-born) economist

Caldwell, Bruce J. and Stephan Boehm (editors), *Austrian Economics: Tensions and New Directions*, Boston: Kluwer, 1992

Hayek, F.A., *Prices and Production*, London, Routledge, 1931; New York: Macmillan, 1932

Hayek, F.A., *Monetary Theory and the Trade Cycle*, London: Jonathan Cape, and New York: Harcourt Brace, 1933

Hayek, F.A., *The Road to Serfdom*, Chicago: University of Chicago Press, and London: Routledge, 1944

Hayek, F.A., *The Constitution of Liberty*, Chicago: University of Chicago Press, and London: Routledge, 1960

Hayek, F.A., *The Fortunes of Liberalism: Essays on Austrian Economics and the Idea of Freedom*, edited by Peter G.

Klein, London: Routledge, and Chicago: University of Chicago Press, 1992 (Collected Works, vol. 4)

Kirzner, Israel M., *The Meaning of Market Process: Essays in the Development of Modern Austrian Economics*, London and New York: Routledge, 1992

Michie, Jonathan and Renée Prendergast, "Government Intervention in a Dynamic Economy", *New Political Economy*, 3/3 (1998): 391–406

Born in 1899, Hayek gained two doctorates from the University of Vienna. From 1927 until 1931 he was the Director of the Austrian Institute for Economic Research. In 1931 he became a lecturer at the London School of Economics, where he delivered a series of lectures that were published as *Prices and Production*. This publication brought him to prominence in the academic debate concerning the causes of the Great Depression. Later in 1931 he was appointed Took Professor of Economic Science and Statistics at the University of London. In 1950, he joined the University of Chicago as Professor of Social and Moral Science. In 1962 he accepted the position of Professor of Economic Policy at the University of Freiburg. In 1974 he was awarded the Nobel Prize.

Throughout his long academic career Hayek applied his formidable intellect to a broad range of issues across a number of disciplines. His most substantial and original contribution was to economics. His most influential and widely read work was, however, in the field of political philosophy, and his most famous book *The Road to Serfdom* played a significant role in strengthening the intellectual credentials of the forces that would coalesce into the "New Right" in the 1970s, as well as providing inspiration to democrats seeking to dismantle the communist regimes in Eastern Europe. He was to live to see the reunification of Germany, an event that marked the start of the collapse of the socialist experiment in Eastern Europe.

Hayek's first major contribution was his highly original account of the nature of the trade cycle that appeared as *Prices and Production* (HAYEK 1931, see also HAYEK 1933), which was later revised as a long essay in *Profits, Interest and Investment* (1939). In this work he brought to the attention of the world what was later to become known as the "Austrian trade cycle theory". Hayek, in *Profits, Interest and Investment*, set out to dissolve the confusion between "rate of interest" and "rate of profit", this was important since Hayek ascribes the trade cycle's fluctuations to the natural action of the banking system. Hayek's business cycle theory is a mixture of the Austrian theories of capital, prices, and money. In essence, if a monetary disturbance (such as an increase in the money stock) causes a fall in interest rates below an equilibrium level, which encourages investment in capital, this results in the diversion of production away from consumer goods towards the production of capital goods. As a result, the prices of capital goods rise and the prices of consumption goods fall. This modification in relative prices alters the structure of production. Such an alteration in the structure of production, because of the longer time element involved in producing capital, leads to overinvestment in these methods of production. This causes a disruption in the co-ordination of plans between consumers and producers, and between savers and investors, which in turn Hayek felt explained the cyclical alterations in the pace of economic growth. The policy conclusion advocated by

Hayek, to "do nothing", must in part answer the question as to why he lost out to Keynes in the debate concerning macro-economic theory. This sort of conclusion proved politically unacceptable amidst the widespread suffering caused by the Great Depression.

Hayek next turned his attention to a subject that became a continual theme in his later work, namely the futility of human attempts to adapt or abolish the price mechanism. This was developed in a pithy essay, "Economics and Knowledge", in *Economica* in 1937. In this Hayek argued that the price mechanism is so sophisticated an antenna of peoples' needs that its existence reduces the economic task of government due to its innately superior ability to handle information.

During World War II, Hayek developed the ideas that would appear in his most widely read and influential publication, *The Road to Serfdom* (HAYEK 1944). It must be remembered that this classic critique of the dangers of "creeping socialism" was written in the time when the UK, for the purposes of the war effort, was virtually a planned economy and when Keynesian ideas were gaining a powerful ascendancy within both academic and government economic circles. Hayek was not advancing a viewpoint that was in step with majority intellectual opinion at that time, however by the time he lecture-toured the US in the late 1940s the ideas of *The Road to Serfdom* were absolutely in step with the deepening mood of anticommunism arising from the West's fear of the USSR.

The main thesis put forward in the *The Road to Serfdom* is that there is little to distinguish the essential characteristics of either fascism or communism, as both creeds were collectivist and anti-individualist in character. More controversially, Hayek cast doubts on whether social democracy and extreme collectivism differed significantly from each other, and suggested that even moderate planning such as Keynesian demand management, or a welfare state, could produce outcomes that were not foreseen by the planners. A "road to serfdom" could be embarked upon because intervention in the spontaneous evolution of the economy could initiate developments that would stifle spontaneity. Creeping totalitarianism was a likely outcome of economic intervention. Hayek knew that the case that he had to argue in *The Road to Serfdom* would never find a hearing among the intelligentsia to whom it was really addressed, so he took his case to the people, which explains why the *The Road to Serfdom* is his most accessible publication. In 1945 the book made the bestseller list in the UK, a remarkable achievement for a book concerned with political philosophy. It was even more successful in the US, provoking an enormous amount of media and popular interest. Ironically it was this very success that possibly led to a decline in Hayek's credibility among his peers in the world of economics, as some believed that he was a scholar turned propagandist.

His major publication in the US was *The Constitution of Liberty* (HAYEK 1960). In this work he developed his ideas on liberty and justice. What is unique about Hayek's approach to the concept of liberty is his insistence on the priority of freedom over other ideals, and his intellectual unease at the appeal of other values, especially those of equality and social equity. Freedom was at the very centre of his social thought, and informed his perspective on the welfare state. For Hayek, welfare had done much to undermine peoples personal respon-

sibility, which in itself is essential for liberty. Furthermore the "welfare" extended to the needy was not genuine altruism as it was carried forward in a framework of compulsion – for example, we have no right *not* to pay the taxes that go towards welfare expenditure. Furthermore, the social responsibility that collectivists believe individuals ought to possess, has in the end been imposed by the state.

Receiving the Nobel Prize marked a revival in his fortunes. By the early 1970s the fiscal burden of maintaining the welfare state was beginning to cause severe economic difficulties, and Hayek's warnings of the economic and social dangers of creeping socialism were looking increasingly credible. Many right-wing thinkers turned to Hayek's pure and logical defence of the free market in an attempt to find a new intellectual framework, as an alternative to the failed model that had arisen from the years of postwar "consensus". In the UK a number of intellectuals on the Right were influenced by Hayek's insights, notably the late Sir Keith Joseph, who in turn was a major influence upon Margaret Thatcher.

Hayek offered a cogent defence of a free market as a foundation for a free society. He insisted that the market will prevail, no matter how far underground it goes. In Hayek's view life in all its multitudinous forms is far too complex for the human mind to regulate and control. In comprehending this, Hayek attacked the constructivist ideal of controlling society by demonstrating the impossibility of ever achieving this goal without restricting human liberty, and therefore human development. He argued that the evolution of spontaneous systems such as a free market is the only way to ensure that flexible adaptation to change occurs. HAYEK (1992) contains some of his later essays.

CALDWELL & BOEHM's edited work discusses Hayek's work within the context of "Austrian" economics more generally, and also provides a thoughtful discussion and analysis of that school of thought. The various authors discuss a range of issues from the historical and methodological basis of Austrian economics, and the various methodological weaknesses of this school of thought, through to the key implications of Austrian theory, and Hayek's specific arguments on the nature of market coordination, and the role of institutions in the economy.

The role of the market and market processes within Austrian economics, and Hayek's writings, are analysed in detail by KIRZNER who argues that "equilibrium" economics is inadequate to explain the real functioning of markets and that instead a theory of market process is required which emphasizes the role of the entrepreneur and of ignorance, uncertainty and the passage of time.

A critique of Hayek's views of economic development, as well as Kirzner's arguments, is provided by MICHIE & PRENDERGAST, who argue that there is simply no theoretical basis for Kirzner's assumption that the competitive process tends to be an equilibrating process. On the contrary, against both Hayek and Kirzner, they argue that there is nothing perfect about the spontaneous order in the sense of selection order, and that the formation, revelation, and interpretation of the emerging selection profiles depend on subjective interpretations, expectations, and decisions. Consequently, this process is prone to error and can be characterized by a high level of uncertainty. Market participants may therefore look for institutions to reduce uncertainty, thereby improving the performance of the market order. Far from supporting a non-interventionist programme as Hayek would have it, the logic of Austrian economics can sanction all kinds of intervention.

Hayek's ideas have undoubtedly been influential, and his status as one of the great thinkers of the 20th century is widely acknowledged. Ultimately every economy and society is forced to prioritize its key values. For Hayek the choice had to be liberty above all else. Many critics of this view express the fear that this unlimited and unregulated society would display such vast inequalities of opportunity and wealth that "freedom" would only be achieved by the "winners", and that the fate of the majority of "losers" would in fact merely be the "freedom" to remain poor, exploited, and powerless.

JOHN CORCORAN

See also Austrian school of economics

Health and illness

Barbour, Allen B., *Caring for Patients: A Critique of the Medical Model*, Stanford, California: Stanford University Press, 1995

Baum, Andrew and Donna Posluszny, "Health Psychology: Mapping Biobehavioral Contributions to Health and Illness", *Annual Review of Psychology*, 50 (1999): 137–63

Davey, Basiro, Alastair Gray and Clive Seale (editors), *Health and Disease: A Reader*, 2nd edition, Buckingham: Open University Press, 1995

Davis, Lennard J. (editor), *The Disability Studies Reader*, New York and London: Routledge, 1997

Gabe, Jonathan (editor), *Medicine, Health, and Risk: Sociological Approaches*, Oxford and Cambridge, Massachusetts: Blackwell, 1995

Oliver, Michael, *Understanding Disability: From Theory to Practice*, New York: St Martin's Press, and Basingstoke: Macmillan, 1996

Schwartz, Harvey J. and Ann-Louise S. Silver (editors), *Illness in the Analyst: Implications for the Treatment Relationship*, Madison, Connecticut: International Universities Press, 1990

Shakespeare, Tom (editor), *The Disability Reader: Social Science Perspectives*, London and New York: Cassell, 1998

Taylor, Shelley, Rena Repetti and Teresa Seeman, "Health Psychology: What Is an Unhealthy Environment and How Does It Get under the Skin?", *Annual Review of Psychology*, 48 (1997): 411–47

Wendell, Susan, *The Rejected Body: Feminist Philosophical Reflections on Disability*, New York and London: Routledge, 1996

DAVEY, GRAY & SEALE includes 62 articles addressing a broad spectrum of issues related to definitions, perspectives, and experiences of health and illness. Many are abridged versions of the original papers, which allows great diversity to be covered although at the expense of depth on any particular topic. This introductory text provides a good overview of changes in approaches to and perceptions about health and illness over time, as well as a range of current issues. Categories included are: concepts of health, disease, and healing; experiencing health and disease; influences on health and disease; the role of medicine; the social context of healthcare; health work; and prospects and speculations. Articles related to illness as a metaphor, malingering, holistic medicine, alternative therapies, gender, cultural, and ethnic differences are included. The experiences and perceptions both of healthcare workers and recipients of health services are addressed.

GABE was the first in a series of monographs on the sociology of health and illness that focused on health and risk and included articles by academics and researchers primarily associated with universities in the UK. Topics covered include public and individual health risks, social construction, regulation, and medical interventions. The second volume in this series was edited by Veronica James and Jonathan Gabe (*Health and the Sociology of Emotions*, 1996) and addressed the sociology of emotions and effects relationships between researchers and those researched.

The *Annual Review of Psychology* is a compilation of literature reviews on current issues in psychology, and in most years includes a paper related to health and illness. The 1999 edition article is by BAUM & POSLUSZNY and discusses the influence of psychological processes and emotional states on etiology, vulnerability, resistance, and progression of disease. The effects of stress and coping on cardiovascular risk, cancer, and the immune system are addressed. Risk factors associated with health and illness, as either health-enhancing or health-impairing behaviours are identified, as are the ways in which people behave when they believe they are ill or at risk of serious illness. The 1997 edition review by TAYLOR, REPETTI & SEEMAN was on the role of geographic, social, developmental, and economic environments on health and illness. It includes discussion of aspects of socioeconomic status, race, community, family, peers, and work, arguing that psychosocial predictors of health outcomes across the lifespan should include consideration of environmental influences on psychological, behavioural, and physiological functioning. For an overview of the influence of psychological factors on health and illness see the 1994 review by Alder & Matthews, which summarized findings from research in health psychology between 1989–94. The *Annual Review of Public Health* is also a useful source of reviews of current issues related to health and illness.

BARBOUR presents a critique of aspects of the medical model and the limitations of treating organic disease without consideration of the effects of illness on patients' lives. He describes "getting to know" his patients and argues for collaboration and understanding between physicians and patients. WENDELL offers a feminist perspective on illness and physical disability and the social and cultural factors that interact with biological differences. She puts forward a thorough critique of the "mind over body" argument with discussion of the "myth of control", idealization, and objectification of the body and the perceived authority of Western scientific medicine.

OLIVER connects personal and political views while linking theory and practice. He discusses the usefulness of distinguishing between illness and disability. While illness can have disabling consequences that may be able to be treated, disability is a long-term social state that is not medically treatable. He provides a framework for discussion of models of disability in particular aspects of a social model that describes the medicalization of the individual. The social model rejects the "personal tragedy" theory of disability and locates it as a problem within society. As prejudice and discrimination are imposed on top of impairments there may be no causal relationship between illness, impairment, and disability. DAVIS is a collection of writings, some of which were previously difficult to access because of difficulties in how these were categorized, but they can now be related to the field of disability studies. It includes historical perspectives, politics, stigma, gender and disability, education, culture, as well as fiction, and poetry.

SHAKESPEARE is a reader for those new to the field of disability studies. It includes articles by disabled writers, researchers, and academics on activism, academia, and the establishment of the discipline of disability studies and has a comprehensive bibliography.

The work of Elisabeth Kubler-Ross, *On Death and Dying* (1970), has proved to be enduring in the field of health and illness. Her model, which includes stages of "shock, denial, anger, depression, bargaining, acceptance and decanthexis", threaded through with "hope", experienced by the person who is dying has also been applied to other situations involving grief and loss. SCHWARTZ & SILVER is a collection of papers that discuss aspects of the effect on the relationship between healthcare practitioners and patients when the analyst has a catastrophic acute or life-threatening illness, as well as the impact of the death of an analyst on patients. The chapter by Schwartz includes a literature review and case studies from his own practice. Silver discusses resuming work with a life-threatening illness and others offer perspectives on the death of an analyst.

ROSALIE HOLIAN

See also Medicalization

Health and safety at work

Aldrich, Mark, *Safety First: Technology, Labor, and Business in the Building of American Work Safety, 1870–1939*, Baltimore: Johns Hopkins University Press, 1997

Annals of Occupational Hygiene, Derby: British Occupational Hygiene Society, 1958

Boissevain, Andrea L., Eric A. George, David J. Claybaugh and Robert E. Henderson (editors), *Managing Environmental Issues in the Workplace*, Southampton, Pennsylvania: Ergonomics, 1997

Clayton, George D., Florence E. Clayton, Lewis J. Cralley, James Bus, Robert Harris and Lester V. Cralley (editors), *Patty's Industrial Hygiene and Toxicology*, CD-Rom Version 2.0, New York: Wiley, 1998

DiBerardinis, Louis J. (editor), *Handbook of Occupational Safety and Health*, New York: Wiley, 1998

Dinardi, Salvatore R. (editor), *The Occupational Environment: Its Evaluation and Control*, Fairfax, Virginia: American Industrial Hygiene Association Press, 1997

Lack, Richard W. (editor), *Essentials of Safety and Health Management*, Boca Raton, Florida: Lewis, 1996

Stellman, Jeanne Mager (editor), *Encyclopaedia of Occupational Health and Safety*, 4th edition Geneva: International Labour Organization, 1998 (print and CD)

Vincoli, Jeffrey W., *Basic Guide to Industrial Hygiene*, New York: Wiley, 1997

As an academic discipline, the area of workplace health and safety is frequently referred to as "occupational hygiene" or "industrial hygiene". Occupational hygiene includes the identification, evaluation, and control of health-and-safety hazards in the workplace environment. Industrial hygiene focuses on these issues in the manufacturing environment. The area is multidisciplinary and draws upon the disciplines of chemistry, engineering, medicine, law, and management.

ALDRICH, an economist who once worked as an investigator for the US Occupational Health and Safety Administration (OSHA), offers the first full account of why the American workplace became so dangerous in the 1800s and why it is now much safer. He first describes the increasing dangers of industrial work in late 19th-century America as a result of factors such as technological change, careless work practices, and a legal system that minimized the employer's responsibility for industrial accidents. He then discusses the developments that led to improved safety. These include government regulation, corporate publicizing of safety measures, and the emergence of worker's compensation – a factor that raised the costs of accidents by requiring employers to pay injured workers. Aldrich contends that the emergence of a safety ideology that stressed both worker and management responsibility for work accidents was a reversal of earlier attitudes.

The British Occupational Hygiene Society (BOHS) was founded in 1952 and now has members in over 30 countries. The aim of the society is to promote the science of occupational hygiene by raising awareness through education, information exchange, research, and professional networking. Since 1958 it has published a peer-reviewed journal entitled *The Annals of Occupational Hygiene*, which is commonly referred to as the "Annals". It also publishes other professional guides and educational videos.

The BOISSEVAIN *et al.* guide contains seven chapters, each of which is an essay by an expert in the field. Each of these essays addresses broad issues that should be of concern to managers. The book is a comprehensive compilation of information on the most important environmental considerations facing the business community. The authors represent a broad range of knowledge and expertise, and each chapter offers a thoughtful overview of the state of knowledge and technology.

The Patty's industrial hygiene series is the most reliable and complete source reference available on the principles and practice of industrial hygiene. CLAYTON *et al.*'s 1998 CD-Rom update incorporates the National Institute for Occupational Safety and Health (NIOSH) *Manual of Analytical Methods*. The National Institute for Occupational Safety and Health is part of the US Centers for Disease Control and Prevention (CDC) and is responsible for conducting research and making recommendations for the prevention of work-related illness and injuries.

Although DIBERARDINIS is directed toward non-health-and-safety people, it was written by over 30 health-and-safety professionals for the purpose of providing one reference source on health and safety. It uses techniques and methods from various disciplines applicable to occupational safety and health. Written with the presumption that its reader is mature and intelligent but not necessarily a full-time practitioner, the book provides a basic understanding of the important concepts of workplace health and safety. It contains 30 chapters and includes checklists, charts, and figures to aid the reader. LACK is also a comprehensive handbook that can be used by managers and supervisors as well as by students of workplace safety and health management. It details safety and health programme management, regulatory compliance, legal issues, risk management, training issues, and international developments. It also includes numerous checklists and sample forms.

DINARDI is the director of the Industrial Hygiene Program at the University of Massachusetts, Amherst. Working with experts in the field and with the involvement of the American Industrial Hygiene Association technical committees, he has designed an invaluable tool for both practice and instruction. The book contains more than 1300 pages and is organized into six parts: (a) introduction and background; (b) hazard recognition and evaluation; (c) physical agents; (d) the human environment at work; (e) controlling the occupational environment; and (f) programme management. It contains chapters on subjects such as ergonomics, computers, psychology, and worker education and training. An instructor's guide is available for lecturers who adopt the book for classroom use.

STELLMAN's encyclopedia is available in both print and CD formats. It was developed through an extensive process of consultation with leading professionals worldwide. This well-respected reference work provides comprehensive, timely, and accurate coverage of occupational health and safety and allied fields. It is directed at the specialist and non-specialist alike and would be useful for lawyers, industrial hygienists, safety professionals, managers, and regulators. It contains more than 1000 illustrations, has an attractive layout, and provides up-to-date literature reviews.

In contrast with Stellman's comprehensive encyclopedia, VINCOLI is a one-volume guide that presents the history and fundamentals of environmental regulation in a pragmatic, applied fashion. It offers a complete survey of compliance protocols in a single source that is directed toward compliance with US regulatory laws. It discusses a number of US regulatory statutes including the Clean Air Act, the Clean Water Act and Comprehensive Environmental Response, Compensation, and Liability Act (CERCLA). It also includes an appendix that defines various acronyms by which US environmental laws have become known.

GEORGIA HOLMES

Health economics

Arrow, Kenneth J., "Uncertainty and the Welfare Economics of Medical Care", *American Economic Review*, 53/5 (1963): 941–73
Feldman, Roger and Bryan Dowd, "A New Estimate of the Welfare Loss of Excess Health Insurance", *American Economic Review*, 81/10 (1991): 297–301
Fuchs, Victor R., *Who Shall Live? Health, Economics, and Social Choice*, New York: Basic Books, 1974; revised edition, River Edge, New Jersey: World Scientific, 1998
Gold, Marthe R., Joanna Siegel, Louise Russell and Milton Weinstein (editors), *Cost-Effectiveness in Health and Medicine*, New York and Oxford: Oxford University Press, 1996
Grossman, Michael, "On the Concept of Health Capital and the Demand for Health", *Journal of Political Economy*, 80/5 (1972): 223–55
Luft, Harold S., *Health Maintenance Organizations: Dimensions of Performance*, New York: Wiley, 1981
Miller, Robert and Harold Luft, "Managed Care Plan Performance since 1980", *Journal of the American Medical Association*, 271/19 (1994): 1512–19
Newhouse, Joseph P. and the Insurance Experiment Group, *Free for All? Lessons from the RAND Health Insurance Experiment*, Cambridge, Massachusetts: Harvard University Press, 1993
Pauly, Mark, "The Economics of Moral Hazard: Comment", *American Economic Review*, 58/10 (1968): 531–37
Pauly, Mark, "Taxation, Health Insurance, and Market Failure in the Medical Economy", *Journal of Economic Literature*, 26 (1986): 629–75
Rothschild, Michael and Joseph E. Stiglitz, "Equilibrium in Competitive Insurance Markets: An Essay on the Economics of Imperfect Information", *Quarterly Journal of Economics*, 80 (1976): 629–49
Starr, Paul, *The Social Transformation of American Medicine*, New York: Basic Books, 1982

Health economics analyses the production and provision of healthcare services and the impact of the healthcare sector on the economy. The healthcare sector of the economy is characterized by a multitude of unique institutional arrangements. In his landmark 1963 article, Kenneth ARROW provided an economic rational for the structure of the health industry and helped establish health economics as a field of research. Arrow pointed out five special characteristics of the medical care market. First, demand for healthcare is irregular and stochastic. Second, physicians (and other healthcare providers) have different expectations regarding their professional behaviour than members of other professions. Physicians are expected to act as an agent for their patients and to put the patient's welfare ahead of the physician's interests. Third, the effectiveness of treatment is often uncertain, the outcomes of care are unpredictable, and the quality of treatment is unmeasurable by the patient. This combination of uncertainty and asymmetric information is relatively unique. Fourth, the supply of providers (physicians) is simultaneously subsidized by the government and rationed by the medical profession (through limiting enrolment in medical schools). Fifth, common pricing schemes are not consistent with competition.

Arrow then explained the structure of the medical care industry as a rational response to the unique nature of illness and medical care. Arrow's discussion not only established the foundation for health economics, but the five special characteristics he described have each been the focal point of extensive research. In a sense, Arrow elucidated the research agenda for health economics for the next two decades.

STARR provides a context for Arrow's work. This book, which won the 1984 Pulitzer Prize for non-fiction works, documents the history of medicine and the medical profession in America from 1760 through 1974. The book explores the historical origins of many of the institutional structures of today, including the rise of private insurance and reasons behind the failure to nationalize the healthcare industry. As documented by Starr, the development of the medical care industry has been strongly influenced by changes in technology, wars, government financing and regulation, macroeconomic fluctuations, and varying social standards.

PAULY (1968) pointed out the major shortcoming of insurance: that the change in price caused by the contract may lead directly to increased utilization of healthcare services (moral hazard) and substantial welfare losses. The work of Pauly suggested that the price of healthcare strongly influenced the quantity of healthcare consumed. Nevertheless, seemingly unanswerable questions about the degree of influence remained. In the United States, the creation of publicly funded health insurance for the elderly ("Medicare") and poor ("Medicaid") renewed interest in establishing the relationship. As a result, the RAND Health Insurance Experiment (HIE) was launched. As summarized by NEWHOUSE, the HIE was one of the longest and costliest social experiments ever. The HIE randomized 2000 non-elderly families from six regions of the US into 15 health insurance plans. The insurance plans varied in coinsurance rates and maximum dollar expenditures. The randomization allowed separation of the price effect ("moral hazard") from the individual choice decision ("adverse selection"). The actual RAND experiment took place from 1974–82. Families were enrolled for between three and five years. Use of healthcare services and health status were both tracked. Despite its limitations, RAND remains the definitive authority on the impact of cost sharing, and its conclusions – that increasing cost sharing has significant effects on use of services but minimal effects on health – are widely accepted. Following RAND, FELDMAN & DOWD used the results of the HIE to estimate that the welfare loss associated with health insurance is between $33 billion and $109 billion, in 1984 dollars.

A somewhat different stream of research has focused on the individual. GROSSMAN adapted theories of human capital to develop the standard theory of individual demand for healthcare. Grossman hypothesized that demand for healthcare is a derived demand from the demand for health. Consumers are viewed as both purchasers of healthcare and producers of health, and health is viewed as a capital good. Health itself is desired both for pure consumption reasons and because it facilitates economic production. FUCHS, in an update of his classic 1974 text, argues that health is the outcome of a complex series of decisions by individuals and healthcare professionals. Healthcare professionals control expenditures, but individual decisions ranging from whether to wear a seatbelt to whether to get a physical have more impact on health status.

Finally, the topic of adverse selection has been the subject of extensive research. ROTHSCHILD & STIGLITZ developed a theoretical model that showed how adverse selection into insurance plans could prevent the development of optimal insurance contracts. The Rothschild & Stiglitz article is the classic theoretical exposition on the topic. Subsequently, there has been much effort put into the identification and empirical estimation of adverse selection in the purchase of individual, group, and supplemental insurance, as well as individual choice of plans from insurance "menus". Much of the discussion of premium "death" spirals and separating equilibriums stems from the Rothschild & Stiglitz article.

In the US, healthcare has been purchased by the government, employers and individuals from a myriad of private and public, for profit and non-profit entities. The insurance contract has changed from a simple cost-plus reimbursement to a fee-for-service versus health maintenance organization dichotomy, to a veritable alphabet soup of contractual arrangements. Comparing and contrasting the options has provided fertile ground for health economists. Harold Luft has twice reviewed the literature on health maintenance organizations (HMOs), in 1981 and in 1994 with Robert Miller. Health maintenance organizations are the most significant innovation in health financing for many years, and became widespread during the 1980s in commercial markets. Both reviews concluded that they reduce costs, mostly through reductions in use of hospital services, with mixed results on health outcomes. PAULY (1986) evaluated the impact of the various subsidies and distortions placed on the health insurance market by the government. Pauly discusses the arguments for and against the subsidization of insurance, and concludes that lowering the tax subsidy would lead to greater efficiency. Although the article is now quite old, the arguments regarding public subsidization of healthcare have not changed, and the summary remains relevant.

Research in the US has focused on issues of insurance contracting, but health economics in Europe, where health insurance is generally provided by the government, has been directed toward issues of production efficiency. Measuring the output of healthcare has proven challenging, and much effort has been devoted to that end. Cost effectiveness analysis has had widespread applications in Europe, where resource allocation choices are made directly, and limited application in the US, where resource allocation choices are made indirectly. In an effort to standardize practices, the United States Public Health Service sponsored a multidisciplinary panel to develop the "gold standard". The result was *Cost-Effectiveness in Health and Medicine*, with Marthe GOLD as the chief editor. This text may not be as clear as some others on the topic, but it provides a broad brush of critical issues and accepted practices in cost-effectiveness analysis.

ADAM ATHERLY

Health services research

Baker, Mark and Simon Kirk, *Research and Development for the NHS: Evidence, Evaluation and Effectiveness*, Oxford: Radcliffe Medical Press, 1996; 2nd edition, 1998

Cochrane A.L., *Effectiveness and Efficiency: Random Reflections on Health Services*, London: Nuffield Provincial Hospitals Trust, 1972

Department of Health, *Research for Health: A Research and Development Strategy for the NHS*, London: Department of Health, 1991

Department of Health, *Supporting Research and Development in the NHS: A Report to the Minister for*

Health by a Research and Development Task Force Chaired by Professor Anthony Culyer, London: HMSO, 1994

Dunn, Earl V. *et al.* (editors), *Disseminating Research / Changing Practice*, London and Thousand Oaks, California: Sage, 1994

Jenkinson, Crispin (editor), *Assessment and Evaluation of Health and Medical Care: A Methods Text*, Buckingham: Open University Press, 1997

Muir Gray, J.A., *Evidence-Based Healthcare: How to Make Health Policy and Management Decisions*, Edinburgh and New York: Churchill Livingstone, 1997

National Health Service Management Executive, *Research for Health: A Research and Development Strategy for the NHS*, London: HMSO, 1991

Ong, Bie Nio, *The Practice of Health Services Research*, London and New York: Chapman and Hall, 1993

Research involves systematic investigation into phenomena in order to generate new knowledge and establish new facts. Health services research involves primary investigation but also incorporates the distinct, but related, concepts of development and dissemination. In the UK health services research is defined in the context of the National Health Service (NHS) Research and Development (R&D) Strategy.

A strategic declaration, setting out for the first time an explicit statement of the purpose and the organization of health services research within the NHS, is of considerable historical importance (DEPARTMENT OF HEALTH, 1991). The strategy recognizes the collective responsibilities and opportunities for researchers, clinicians, managers, and other health sector staff, which extend well beyond the conduct of primary research. Specific objectives are set out, which include the facilitation and the development of a knowledge-based NHS and an evaluative culture within it, harnessing the capacity of R&D, from basic science through to applied research, to address problems of national concern in health and social care and to ensure that the benefits of research are systematically and effectively translated into practice. Principal features are also introduced, including a national and regional infrastructure for identifying research priorities, the initiation of major programmes of research and development on NHS priority topics and a structure for disseminating R&D information to users and for establishing research-based practice. Two substantive conceptual and pragmatic issues are raised by this strategy. The first relates to precise definitions of health services research and its various dimensions (research, dissemination, and development) and the second relates to the relationship between these dimensions. The assumed relationship between research, development, and dissemination, represented by a linear and logical progression from the precise activity of research to the direct and uncomplicated implementation of the findings of research into practice is an idealistic and unsophisticated expression and one that is increasingly challenged.

Considerable uncertainty about the boundary between health services research and development was found to exist by a task force chaired by Professor Anthony Culyer (DEPARTMENT OF HEALTH, 1994). The report offered a formal definition of R&D, which is reproduced below:

All Research and Development whose direct costs are met with NHS funds should: be designed to provide **new knowledge** needed to improve the performance of the NHS in improving the health of the nation; be designed so that findings will be of value to those in the NHS facing similar problems outside the particular locality or context of the project i.e. be **generalisable**; follow a clear, well-defined **protocol**; have had the protocol **peer reviewed**; have obtained the approval, where needed, of the **Local Research Ethics Committee** and any other appropriate body; have clearly defined arrangements for **project management**; plan to report findings so that they are open to critical examination and accessible to all who could benefit from them – this will normally involve **publication**. (N.B. emphasis in the original)

This definition is particularly useful because of the distinction made between two types of development. Development designed to produce generalizable models for service organization and development designed to adopt these general models to local circumstances.

COCHRANE's classic monograph provides an illuminating historical perspective on the nature of the relationship between health services research and practice, as well being a major influential text in health policy, the development of evidence-based practice, and the emergence of the randomized control trial (RCT) as the "gold standard" for the evaluation of clinical interventions. Cochrane recalls the period immediately preceding the introduction of the NHS and the traditional distinction between basic (pure, scientific) research and applied (operational) research (now termed health services research), which resulted in bias towards the former and opposition to the latter, to the extent that pressing practical issues were largely ignored. Cochrane's account is a personal and persuasive appeal for useful research and a reminder of the radical changes that have occurred in the field of health services research in the past 50 years.

The 13 chapters in BAKER & KIRK reflect contributions from social scientists, healthcare managers, and professionals. Some contributions are more descriptive than analytical but taken together this collection offers a comprehensive, accessible and thorough description and analysis of the interface between research and development policy and its implementation within the NHS. Of particular interest are the contributions made by representatives of those sectors and professional groups that have traditionally been marginalized or underdeveloped in health services research. Dedicated chapters to research and development in nursing and professions allied to medicine and primary care, although relatively short, make timely and interesting contributions to current debates.

Health services researchers from a range of disciplines and specialities contribute to JENKINSON's comprehensive research designs and methods textbook. The book focuses on methodologies for the assessment and evaluation of health and medical care. The chapters reflect the variety of approaches that are used in health services research including RCTs, case control and cohort studies, surveys, and qualitative methods. It is not simply a descriptive list of advantages and disadvantages. Although the book is biased towards quantitative biomedical research methods, at the expense of quantitative methods, which are incorporated into one chapter, its strength lies in the consideration given to the principles and theoretical perspectives that underpin particular methods, combined with detailed examples and comprehensive reading lists at the end of each chapter.

MUIR GRAY's book provides a framework with the specific aim to increase the application of health services research findings to decision making. The framework covers three main topics: finding and appraising research evidence; developing the capacity of individuals and organizations to use research evidence, and putting research into practice. The book provides a well-structured and thorough practical guide to accessing, critiquing and applying research findings as well as short but informed and informative, introductions to key policy themes or issues such as equity, effectiveness, and quality. A brief section is also provided on the limits of evidence-based medicine. A limitation of Muir Gray's text is its emphasis on research that evaluates specific clinical interventions and which often relies on RCTs. The socioeconomic and sociopolitical contexts are important determinants of the experience of health, illness and disease, as well as the allocation of resources and indeed the construction of the research agenda. As such qualitative research exploring these issues and consideration of how this kind of research can be applied to healthcare decision making is worthy of more attention.

The relationship between social science research, strategic planning and health services management is a theme explored throughout ONG's book. Ong's distinctive contribution to the field of health services research is her examination of how the research agenda is defined and research is practised within an evolving sociopolitical context, in the developed world and specifically in the UK NHS. She does not lose sight of the responsibilities that healthcare managers and professionals have in their respective roles, but argues and demonstrates with detailed and illuminating examples (including lay involvement and needs assessment) how health services research can provide the underpinnings for managerial decision making. The normally invisible process of formulating research questions and identifying appropriate study designs is explored in the context of problems facing health services. The purpose and the practice of surveys and evaluations are introduced. Of particular interest is the attention paid to demonstrating the relevance of ethnographic research for managerial decision making. Cultural differences and the need to develop effective communication between researchers, clinicians, and managers are alluded to but not explored in any depth. Ong successfully illustrates a key feature of health services research – its capacity to examine social structures, behaviours and ways of thinking by employing varied and flexible research designs and methods.

DUNN's book brings together Canadian scientists, social scientists, medics, nurses, and managers in an exploration of various aspects of dissemination and changing practice, including methodological issues and issues around changing the behaviour of individual practitioners, from a range of perspectives. Of particular value is the consideration given to those aspects of dissemination that are rarely scrutinized and yet are of considerable relevance to practising health-service researchers. In this context the chapters dedicated to the ethics of dissemination and relationships between health services researchers and the media are of particular interest.

ANN MAHON

Hegemony, politics

Bennett, Tony, "Popular Culture and the 'Turn to Gramsci'" in *Cultural Theory and Popular Culture: A Reader*, edited by John Storey, 2nd edition, London: Prentice Hall, and Athens: University of Georgia Press, 1998

Gill, Stephen (editor), *Gramsci: Historical Materialism and International Relations*, Cambridge and New York: Cambridge University Press, 1993

Gramsci, Antonio, "State and Civil Society" in his *Selections from the Prison Notebooks*, edited by Geoffrey Nowell Smith and Quintin Hoare, London: Lawrence and Wishart, 1971; New York: International Publishers, 1972

Hoffman, John, *The Gramscian Challenge: Coercion and Consent in Marxist Political Theory*, Oxford and New York: Blackwell, 1984

Jessop, Bob, "Accumulation Strategies, State Forms and Hegemonic Projects" in *State Theory: Putting the Capitalist State in Its Place*, Cambridge: Polity Press, and University Park: Pennsylvania State University Press, 1990

Laclau, Ernesto and Chantal Mouffe, *Hegemony and Socialist Strategy: Towards a Radical Democratic Politics*, London: Verso, 1985

Poulantzas, Nicos, *Political Power and Social Classes*, London: NLB–Sheed and Ward, 1973 (French edition 1968)

GRAMSCI provides the theoretical basis for most contemporary uses of this term: "hegemony" denotes the cultural and ideological dominance of one social group or economic class over others. For Gramsci the term describes a form of leadership by which subordinate classes were incorporated by their own consent into the supporting "bloc" of the economically dominant class. Hegemony is therefore a form of power manifested through discourse and ideology, rather than through violence and coercion, and is the predominant form of social control exercised in developed Western capitalism. The dominant class survives the tendency of capitalism to fall into crisis by establishing hegemony over "civil society" in such a way that its own values and aspirations are shared by the wider public. Any attempt at the direct revolutionary overthrow of the State, Gramsci suggests, will fail unless the ruling class's hegemony over civil society is first dismantled. His rather unstructured and undeveloped formulation of the concept, written while in prison in the 1930s, was aimed at combating the economic determinism and reductionism inherited from Second International Marxism. It implies that classes do not automatically generate their own ideologies and that the State is not simply an instrument of the dominant class.

POULANTZAS incorporates Gramsci's concept into a more rigorous Marxist theory of the capitalist State. He draws upon the structuralist Marxism of Louis Althusser to support his claim that hegemony does not require the dominant class to be the hegemonic class. For instance, in the 18th century the British bourgeoisie was the dominant economic class and yet hegemony was exercised through the ideological leadership of the aristocracy. Hegemony denotes a form of social cohesion achieved through the State. By means of its various apparatuses, the capitalist State's function is to ensure the unity of a "power bloc" made up of numerous economic classes. As long as this unity is secured – and the extended reproduction of capital ensured – the ideological cast of hegemony may take numerous, perhaps even contradictory, forms. However, Poulantzas's attempt to incorporate the concept of hegemony into a formal theory of the State is hampered by the obscurity of his language and the functionalist implications of his structuralism.

A rather more accessible theory of the State that builds upon Poulantzas's interpretation of hegemony can be found in JESSOP. For him, the State is configured by both economic structures and political strategies. The "form" of the State is structured by its relation to capitalism over which it must act as a neutral regulator and as a unifier of the various branches of capital. However, the substantive organization of the State is given in the "hegemonic project" through which an "accumulation strategy" is realized.

LACLAU & MOUFFE take the anti-deterministic thrust of Gramsci's theory a stage further and develop a "post-Marxist" interpretation of hegemony. Drawing on postmodernist themes and poststructuralist philosophy, they argue that the hegemonic political agent need not be an economic class at all. A variety of discourses may function as the unifying core of a political movement. They thus dispense with the assumption that hegemony must ultimately be grounded in the interests of an economic class. Stripped of its class connotations, hegemony denotes the logic of "articulation", that is, the contingent assembling of distinct discourses and values around certain unifying themes such as "the people" or "nation". The fundamentally arbitrary nature of these articulations, they argue, allows for a socialist politics that validates the demands of new social movements.

HOFFMAN rejects the so-called "Gramscian" thesis that capitalism is sustained in the West by a form of consensual domination. The general compliance of the working population with the interests of the capitalist class, he claims, can adequately be explained by reference to Marx's own analyses in *Capital*. The "illusion" that capitalist society is fair and just is maintained by the contractual nature of exchange. Commodities, such as labour power, are bought and sold at a seemingly fair price by apparently free individuals. This "commodity fetishism" obscures the inequality of the process of production, in which the worker is exploited by creating more value than is actually received in wages. For Hoffman it is contractual exchange, rather than ideological hegemony, which dominates civil society, and which perpetuates the view that society is essentially just.

The essays in GILL approach hegemony from the perspective of international relations and international political economy. Working within a neo-Marxist frame, the various authors share a rejection of the "neorealist" approach in international relations theory. That approach is argued to "reify" the nation state as a self-interested agent. Hegemony is employed to denote the dominance by one state, such as the US, over others in a system of states. A Gramscian approach to hegemony, however, draws attention to the combination of economic, political, and cultural factors in the international environment. The various essays consider the uses of Gramsci's concept in comprehending the changing global order. In particular, the authors acknowledge the role of transnational businesses and agencies in securing the consent of various national civil societies to the dominance of capital.

BENNETT helpfully demonstrates the significance of hegemony for the discipline of cultural studies. Marxist and non-Marxist approaches to the study of culture have, in the past, derided popular culture as inferior, shallow and possibly even socially damaging. However, viewed within the context of the struggle for hegemony, popular culture can be critically appreciated, not as the instrument of the bourgeoisie over a passive working class, nor as part of the deformation of cultural tastes, but as the site of a power struggle fought through contested meanings. Forms of popular culture represent a process of "negotiation" between dominant values and the experiences of potentially oppositional groups such as the working class. The latter are incorporated into the hegemony of the ruling class through the symbolic fusion of dissident values with dominant ideologies. Gramsci's theory of hegemony, therefore, permits an understanding of popular culture that is neither class-reductionist nor uncritically populist. It points to the way in which seemingly apolitical cultural forms such as pop music and TV viewing are linked into wider questions of social power.

JAMES MARTIN

See also Civil society, Antonio Gramsci

Hegemony, sociology

Anderson, Perry, "The Antinomies of Antonio Gramsci", *New Left Review*, 100 (1976/77): 5–78

Bennett, Tony, Colin Mercer and Janet Woollacott (editors), *Popular Culture and Social Relations*, Milton Keynes: Open University Press, 1986

Buci-Glucksmann, Christine, *Gramsci and the State*, London: Lawrence and Wishart, 1980 (French edition 1975)

Gramsci, Antonio, *Selections from the Prison Notebooks*, edited by Geoffrey Nowell Smith and Quintin Hoare, London: Lawrence and Wishart, 1971; New York: International Publishers, 1972

Hall, Stuart *et al.*, *Policing the Crisis: Mugging, the State and Law and Order*, London: Macmillan, and New York: Holmes and Meier, 1978

Laclau, Ernesto and Chantal Mouffe, *Hegemony and Socialist Strategy: Towards a Radical Democratic Politics*, London: Verso, 1985

Mouffe, Chantal (editor), *Gramsci and Marxist Theory*, London and Boston: Routledge and Kegan Paul, 1979

Simon, Roger, *Gramsci's Political Thought: An Introduction*, London: Lawrence and Wishart, 1982

Togliatti, Palmiro, *On Gramsci and Other Writings*, London: Lawrence and Wishart, 1979

The concept of "hegemony" arrived on the stage of Western thought with the writings of GRAMSCI, one-time leader and co-founder of the Italian Communist party, who was imprisoned under Benito Mussolini's fascist rule in 1926. For Gramsci, hegemony refers to intellectual, moral, and educational leadership. Unlike the notion of "domination", which is predicated on coercion and force, the notion of hegemony highlights consent. In this sense, for Gramsci, ideological struggle and the formation of alliances across classes and class factions become central issues for politics. Whereas, for Marx, the dominant ideology of a society is the dominant set of ideas of the ruling class, for Gramsci, a dominant ideology can never simply be imposed on the people. Rather, for example, the ideas of the dominant class are articulated and negotiated with those of a subordinate class, in order that consent can be granted and the structural relations of capitalism reproduced.

ANDERSON argues that, although Gramsci extends and develops the notion of hegemony in his prison writings, much of the foundational work was laid by Lenin, who, in turn, drew upon the work of Plekhanov and other Russian activists in the late 19th century. These earlier writers argued that the working class needed to construct an alliance with the peasants in order to bring down the Tsarist regime. Only if the working class developed an intellectual and moral leadership of the majority classes in Russia could the old regime be toppled. The concept of hegemony was used to theorize the role of the working class in a bourgeois revolution. Although Gramsci's understanding of hegemony is clearly derived from these earlier writings, Anderson argues that its was unlikely that Gramsci would have had direct knowledge of many of these writings, but would have come into contact with the idea of hegemony through the resolutions of the Comintern (during Gramsci's brief visit to Moscow in 1922).

The concept of hegemony and the translation of Gramsci's writings were of central importance to left of centre postwar politics, particularly in Europe. Taking their lead from TOGLIATTI's reconstruction of the Italian Communist Party in the 1940s, a number of European communist parties (including the French, Spanish, and British) adopted the path of Eurocommunism. This meant a change in political strategy from a revolutionary position to one that realised the necessity of an engagement with liberal parliamentary democracy. In this sense, a communist party, it was argued, should shift from a party of opposition to a party of government and one in which the "national-popular" was the central ideological motivation.

SIMON provides a clear introduction to the concept of hegemony and its attendant concepts, such as the national-popular, locates the development of these concepts within their historical and social contexts, and also provides an interesting example, in its own right, of one of the educational texts of the Communist Party of Great Britain. Similarly, BUCI-GLUCKSMANN provides a detailed analysis of the concept of hegemony and relates this to both Lenin's and Bukharin's work. MOUFFE in her edited collection locates the importance of the concept of hegemony for Marxist thinking and for contemporary social and political analysis.

Outside of political theory, the notion of hegemony became an important conceptual tool for thinking about social and cultural relations and political power. HALL et al, in their detailed analysis of the moral panic surrounding the construction of the "black mugger" in the 1970s, used the notion of hegemony to show how the dominant ideology of "law and order" gained popular consent. They show how the postwar social democratic consensus in the UK began to fracture in the 1970s under the strain of a revivified political militancy and the increasingly visible contradictions of global capitalism. As the signs of crisis began to show, the Conservative government of the day (under the premiership of Edward Heath) moved closer to neoliberal politics at the same time as it embraced an increasing authoritarianism. An ideological consensus was constructed through an increasing fear of crime and racism directed at the UK's black population. The "black mugger" formed a condensation of these concerns and enabled the development of an "authoritarian populism", which, in 1979, provided the platform for the onset of Thatcherism.

In a series of articles edited by BENNETT, MERCER & WOOLLACOTT, a number of writers broadly within the field of cultural studies show how the notion of hegemony is able to inform the analysis of culture, and particularly how it is able to elucidate the relations between popular culture and the state. Instead of adopting the argument of the Frankfurt School, such that a dominating culture industry is involved in the deception of the masses, these writers point to the complex relations and negotiations through which popular culture is produced and lived. A number of case studies are developed in the book, from wartime radio broadcasting, to the working-class pleasures of Blackpool, to television police series. The book initiated a number of similar studies within the field of cultural studies.

LACLAU & MOUFFE radically rethink the Gramscian notion of hegemony within the context of poststructuralist theory and a radical democratic politics. They provide a genealogy of the concept and argue that the notion of hegemony introduces a logic of the social that is incompatible with the basic categories of Marxist theory. For them, hegemony introduces a contingency of the social that deconstructs a hegemonic formation's foundation (even in the last instance) in the economic and in relations of class. In this sense, they move well beyond the Gramscian notion of strategic alliances and the importance of ideology in the cementing of such negotiated blocs. For Laclau & Mouffe there is nothing more than the hegemonic articulation of social elements. Moreover, they show how these hegemonic formations never foreclose the contingency of the social. The social is never completely sutured and fixed, either at the level of the totality or at the level of individual atomization. All social relations are necessarily overdetermined. Their work has had a profound impact on left-of-centre thinking, on poststructural analysis within political theory, and on other disciplines.

DAVID OSWELL

See also Antonio Gramsci

Hicks, John R. 1904–1989

British economist

Amendola, Mario and Jean-Luc Gaffard, *Out of Equilibrium*, Oxford: Clarendon Press, and New York: Oxford University Press, 1998

Baumol, William J., "John versus the Hicksians; or, Theorist Malgré Lui", *Journal of Economic Literature*, 28/4 (1990): 1708–15

Hicks, John R., *Capital and Growth*, Oxford: Clarendon Press, and New York: Oxford University Press, 1965

Hicks, John R., *Critical Essays in Monetary Theory*, Oxford: Clarendon Press, 1967

Hicks, John R., *A Theory of Economic History*, Oxford: Clarendon Press, 1969

Hicks, John R., *Capital and Time: A Neo-Austrian Theory*, Oxford: Clarendon Press, 1973

Hicks, John R., *The Crisis in Keynesian Economics*, Oxford: Blackwell, 1974

Hicks, John R., *Causality in Economics*, Oxford: Blackwell, and New York: Basic Books, 1979

Hicks, John R., *Methods of Dynamic Economics*, Oxford: Clarendon Press, and New York: Oxford University Press, 1985

Hicks, John R., *A Market Theory of Money*, Oxford: Clarendon Press, and New York: Oxford University Press, 1989

Hicks, John R., "The Unification of Macroeconomics", *Economic Journal*, 100/40 (1990): 528–38

Laidler, David, "Hicks's Later Monetary Thought" in *The Legacy of Hicks: His Contribution to Economic Analysis*, edited by Harald Hagemann and O. F. Hamouda, London and New York: Routledge, 1994

Samuels, Warren J., "John R. Hicks and the History of Economics", *History of Political Economy*, 25/2 (1993): 351–74

J.R. Hicks is well known mainly for his contributions to general equilibrium, welfare economics, and monetary theory, which constitute the basis of modern economic analysis. His later contributions on dynamic economics, to which Hicks himself attributed great importance, are less well known. They should be read further, though, as they represent interesting steps forward, and a key for a deeper and more coherent understanding of the whole of his thought.

From the time of his earliest writings Hicks was concerned with change, and was aware that this cannot be reduced to a steady state, that is, to a static equilibrium continuously blown up by multiplication by a scalar. In his perspective, change implies a structural modification, which can only be brought about through a process in real irreversible time. Innovation, which follows what he names an "impulse" (HICKS 1973), is the foremost example of change. When change does take place, the previously existing productive structure is disturbed, and its way of functioning is affected. Problems of "intertemporal complementarity" of production then arise, which call for coordination of economic activity over time. The world should be approached from several angles, with different methods (SAMUELS) to deal with the different aspects of the

coordination problems associated with change. In Hick's mind theorizing proceeded in multiple directions in pursuit of various problems. In particular, Hicks argued in HICKS (1990) that dealing with production, capital, market, and monetary aspects of any economic change should require "a coherent system of thought", making the teaching of Keynes compatible with that of the classical economists.

Hicks always considered an adequate theory of capital to be necessary in order to develop a truly dynamic analysis. His "neo-Austrian" model (described in HICKS (1973) and HICKS (1985)) allows the concept of capital assimilated to a wage fund to be reconciled with the consideration of capital goods that belong to the process within which they are produced and cannot be transferred. It makes it possible to exhibit the intertemporal complementarity and the unilateral dependence of the successive events on their predecessors that characterize the phenomenon of production. The explicit consideration of the temporal structure of the production process throws light on the fact that a change of the technique in use necessarily implies a change in the age structure of productive capacity, and hence a dissociation of inputs from output, and of costs from proceeds. This makes it possible to demonstrate Ricardo's machinery effect, according to which the introduction of machinery has an adverse effect on employment. This is only a first step of the analysis, though. It is also possible to understand under what conditions and to what extent productivity temporarily decreases despite the introduction of a superior technique (as discussed by AMENDOLA & GAFFARD). More generally Hicks's neo-Austrian framework allows the analysis of growth paths as out-of-equilibrium processes of change by introducing a decision-generating process into this framework. This shows that coordination problems arise in the production side of the economy and hence draws attention to the relation between the coordination of economic activity over time and the intertemporal complementarity of the production process.

As discussed in HICKS (1969), the rise of markets is one of the key events in economic history. The working of markets plays a crucial role in Hicks's dynamic economics. His market theory (expounded in HICKS (1965), HICKS (1985) and HICKS (1989)) lays emphasis on stock-flow relations. This emphasis goes hand-in-hand with his concern with out-of-equilibrium processes, although he warned of the analytical limitations of dynamic adjustment models. In fact, one of the main implications of focusing on sequentially articulated decisions in an out-of-equilibrium context is that markets can no longer be represented as auctions or bidding games in the sense that instantaneous price adjustments allow the markets to clear systematically. Their functioning obeys stock-flow mechanisms, which mediate transactions among agents using periodic price-adjustment rules. In Hicks' terminology, markets are fix-price. Price rigidity – as rendered by the fix-price method – on the one hand allows disequilibria to come to the surface through the appearance of stocks, and on the other hand, is the expression of a behaviour, which, through the management of these stocks, facilitates the correct the sheer working of price adjustment mechanisms. In this perspective, price rigidity is no longer seen as the cause of persistent unemployment. Instead, it appears as a means for making viable a process of change (as discussed by Amendola & Gaffard).

LAIDLER argues that Hicks treated money as a part of "the institutional framework within which goods and services are traded" (p.163). The later developments of Hicks' monetary theory (described in HICKS (1967) and HICKS (1974)) focus on the sequential nature of liquidity and the flexibility that this provides, in a context where successive choices are not independent, because of dynamic transaction costs. The production process provides the essential analytical background. Because of their incomplete knowledge, rational economic agents may need to hold liquid assets, in order to be able to realize appropriate real (and irreversible) investments at the right moment. In this context, Hicks argues, "liquidity is not a property of a single choice; it is a matter of a sequence of choices" (Hicks 1974, p.38). However, Hicks' analysis goes beyond that. From simple substitution not only among financial assets but also between these and real assets, it goes on to consider complementary relations, with the focus always on production. For this purpose, financial and real assets are further classified as running, reserve, or investment assets. What characterizes running assets is that they are complementary with each other. Money is thus complementary with real running assets in the sense that there cannot be production of commodities unless the required money balances exist. It is called to play a crucial role when the time structure of production processes comes back to the surface, and when costs are dissociated from proceeds (see the discussion by Amendola & Gaffard). Constraints on investment due to a lack of liquidity result in distortions in the structure of productive capacity, and appear as one of the main causes of instability in an economy facing structural changes.

BAUMOL describes Hicks as "a theorist malgré lui". In so far as he was concerned with economic history, he adopted the target of searching for approximate uniformities that account for the major economic developments. As an economist, he did not believe that economics could produce general propositions about classes of phenomena. On the contrary, as he put it in HICKS (1979), "As economics pushes on beyond 'statics', it becomes less like sciences, and more like history".

JEAN-LUC GAFFARD

Hidden economy

Aigner, Dennis J., Friedrich Schneider and Damayanti Ghosh, "Me and My Shadow: Estimating the Size of the U.S. Hidden Economy from Time Series Data" in *Dynamic Econometric Modeling*, edited by William A. Barnett, Ernst R. Berndt and Halbert White, Cambridge and New York: Cambridge University Press, 1988

Cagan, Philip, "The Demand for Currency Relative to the Total Money Supply", *Journal of Political Economy*, 66/3 (1958): 302–28

Feige, Edgar L., "How Big Is the Irregular Economy?", *Challenge*, 22/1 (1979): 5–13

Feige, Edgar L., *The Underground Economies: Tax Evasion and Information Distortion*, Cambridge and New York: Cambridge University Press, 1989

Frey, Bruno S. and Hannelore Weck-Hannemann, "The Hidden Economy as an 'Unobserved' Variable", *European Economic Review*, 26 (October–November 1984): 33–53

Gaertner, Wulf and Alois Wenig (editors), *The Economics of the Shadow Economy*, Berlin and New York: Springer, 1985

Giles, David, "The Hidden Economy and the Tax-Gap in New Zealand: A Latent Variable Approach", *Empirical Economics*, 24/4 (1999): 621–40

Giles, David and Lindsay Tedds, *Taxes and the Canadian Underground Economy*, Toronto: Canadian Tax Foundation, 2000

Gutmann, P.M., "The Subterranean Economy", *Financial Analysts Journal*, 34 (1977): 24–27

Kaufmann, Daniel, "The Missing Pillar of a Growth Strategy for Ukraine" in *Ukraine Accelerating the Transition to Market: Proceedings of an IMF/World Bank Seminar*, edited by Peter K. Cornelius and Patrick Lenain, Washington, DC: International Monetary Fund, 1997

Lippert, Owen and Michael Walker (editors), *The Underground Economy: Global Evidence of its Size and Impact*, Vancouver: Fraser Institute, 1997

MacAfee, Kerrick, "A Glimpse of the Hidden Economy in the National Accounts", *Economic Trends*, 136 (1980): 81–87

Schneider, Friedrich and Dominik H. Enste, "Shadow Economies: Size, Causes and Consequences", *Journal of Economic Literature*, 38/1 (2000): 77–

Tanzi, Vito, "The Underground Economy in the United States: Estimates and Implications", *Banca Nazionale del Lavoro*, 135/4 (1980): 427–53

Tanzi, Vito (editor), *The Underground Economy in the United States and Abroad*, Lexington, Massachusetts: Lexington Books, 1982

The hidden economy is also known as the underground economy, the irregular economy, the black economy, the subterranean economy, or the shadow economy. It involves economic transactions that go unreported to the authorities and that therefore generally form the basis for tax evasion. The transactions themselves may be either legal or illegal, but in each case the intent is avoid the burden of regulation. Examples include smuggling, extortion, money laundering, the preparation and distribution of drugs, "cash" jobs, and the underreporting of legitimate income.

CAGAN pioneered empirical investigations into the hidden economy by suggesting the "currency ratio" approach. He compared the ratio of currency to M2 in 1940 and 1945 in the US, and found a large amount of excess currency in 1945 (compared to that in circulation in 1940). He credited this increase with unreported income that seems to produce an abnormal demand for currency to hoard.

This approach was taken up by several authors, including GUTMANN. Based on the assumption that currency is the sole medium of exchange in the underground economy, Gutmann estimated the size of this entity by examining the composition of the stock of money where its two components are currency held outside of banks and demand deposits. Any increase in the amount of currency to demand deposits, Gutmann argued, reflects a growth in the hidden economy. This method is now referred to as the simple "currency/demand deposit ratio" approach. Prior to calculating an estimate of the size of the hidden economy in this way, a number of assumptions must be satisfied, and this can be problematic. Accordingly, this simple approach was refined by other authors.

FEIGE (1979) argued that the assumption of equal income velocity is likely to lead to an underestimation of the underground economy. This was based on the suspicion that the underground economy is more integrated than the regular sector, in that it takes a smaller number of financial and intermediate transactions to produce a dollar of final output.

TANZI (1980) questioned the primary assumption in Gutmann's method, namely that any changes in the circulation of money are influenced only by changes in taxes and government restrictions. Tanzi argued that the demand for currency depends on several variables, including the interest rate of time deposits, the share of wages and salaries in personal income, per capita income, and the tax level. In measuring the sensitivity of currency demand to taxes, an estimate of currency held for illegal activities can be derived and this can lead to estimates of the hidden economy and tax evasion.

Other authors, however, have raised conceptual and econometric objections to Tanzi's procedure. In response to some of the criticisms of the currency ratio approach, Feige (1979) developed what has become known as the monetary transactions approach. This challenges Gutmann's cash assumption but is still based on the assumption that the total value of monetary transactions in the economy is a good measure of aggregate economic activity. Feige also relies heavily on currency and demand deposit data, but he believes that information concerning the volume of transactions supported both by currency and demand deposits will lead to more accurate estimates of the black economy. The conceptual basis for Feige's approach is that if a constant relationship between money and transactions is assumed, the total stock of money gives an indication of total transactions in both the official and black economies. Then, by relating total nominal GNP to total transactions, the black economy's GNP can be derived residually by subtracting officially measured GNP from total GNP.

The "national income accounts method" was popularized by MACAFEE, and is based on the fact that in most OECD countries gross domestic product is measured in two ways: an expenditure-based measure and an income-based measure. The income-based measure is usually the sum total of factor incomes arising from productive activity, while the expenditure measure is the sum total of final expenditures on production. They are, therefore, essentially two completely independent methods of estimation. The two measures should, therefore, be equal to each other since the value of each final transaction can be measured by the sum of money spent on goods and services by the final purchaser or by the independent sum of incomes of individuals in producing it. It is often revealed that the expenditure side of the national accounts is larger than the income side and this is conventionally held to reflect the fact that while some incomes may be unreported or unrecorded, much of the expenditure will show up in the official statistics.

KAUFMANN proposed a method taking the measured electricity/GDP ratio in some base period, extrapolating this value to the period of interest, and comparing it with actual recorded use. Any discrepancy would reflect changes in the hidden economy. This "physical output approach" has its own shortcomings. For instance, not all underground activities involve the (direct) use of electricity – activities in the personal services sector are a case in point. The effects of technological change will have a bearing on the accuracy of Kaufmann's method.

Several authors have attempted to overcome the many weaknesses of these various approaches to measuring the size of the hidden economy by adopting a totally different methodology. FREY & WECK-HANNEMANN used structural latent variable models to estimate the size of the hidden economy in OECD countries. Various "causal" and "indicator" variables were used. Such models are often called "multiple indicators, multiple causes", or "MIMIC", models. AIGNER, SCHNEIDER & GHOSH used this approach for the US underground economy.

Recently, such structural modelling has been refined and extended in several ways by authors such as GILES, in the case of New Zealand, and GILES & TEDDS for Canada. The latter authors also provide an overview of research into the Canadian hidden economy, and the related taxation policy issues. This more recent work emphasizes a proper treatment of non-stationary time-series data, and uses more sophisticated econometric techniques to calibrate the index generated by a "MIMIC" model.

SCHNEIDER & ENSTE provides a remarkably comprehensive and thorough coverage of international trends in the hidden economy, with recent estimates for both developed and developing countries. The authors employ several different techniques to obtain these estimates.

Useful collections of readings on the topic of the hidden economy, with an emphasis on empirical issues, appear in volumes edited by FEIGE (1989), by GAERTNER & WENIG, by TANZI (1982), and by LIPPERT & WALKER.

DAVID E.A. GILES

Hierarchies, economic

Carroll, Glenn R. and David J. Teece (editors), *Firms, Markets, and Hierarchies: The Transaction Cost Economics Perspective*, Oxford and New York: Oxford University Press, 1999

Casson, Mark (editor), *The Theory of the Firm*, Cheltenham: Elgar, 1996

Chandler, Alfred D. Jr and Herman Daems (editors), *Managerial Hierarchies: Comparative Perspectives on the Rise of the Modern Industrial Enterprise*, Cambridge, Massachusetts: Harvard University Press, 1980

Francis, Arthur, Jeremy Turk and Paul Willman (editors), *Power, Efficiency and Institutions: A Critical Appraisal of the "Markets and Hierarchies" Paradigm*, London: Heinemann, 1983

Hamilton, Gary G. and Robert C. Feenstra, "Varieties of Hierarchies and Markets: An Introduction", *Industrial and Corporate Change*, 4/1 (1995): 51–91

Marglin, Stephen A., "What Do Bosses Do? The Origins and Functions of Hierarchy in Capitalist Production", *Review of Radical Political Economics*, 6/2 (1974): 60–112

Naschold, Frieder and Casten von Otter, *Public Sector Transformation: Rethinking Markets and Hierarchies in Government*, Amsterdam: Benjamins, 1996

Pitelis, Christos (editor), *Transaction Costs, Markets and Hierarchies*, Oxford and Cambridge, Massachusetts: Blackwell, 1993

Putterman, Louis, "Some Behavioral Perspectives on the Dominance of Hierarchical over Democratic Forms of Enterprise", *Journal of Economic Behavior and Organization*, 3/2 (1982): 139–60

Scott, W. Richard, *Organizations: Rational, Natural, and Open Systems*, 3rd edition, Englewood Cliffs, New Jersey: Prentice Hall, 1992

Simon, Herbert A., "The Architecture of Complexity", *Proceedings of the American Philosophical Society*, 106/6 (1962): 467–82

Stone, Katherine, "The Origins of Job Structures in the Steel Industry", *Review of Radical Political Economics*, 6/2 (1974): 113–73

Thompson, Grahame *et al.* (editors), *Markets, Hierarchies, and Networks: The Coordination of Social Life*, London and Newbury Park, California: Sage, 1991

Tullock, Gordon, *Economic Hierarchies, Organization, and the Structure of Production*, Dordrecht and Boston: Kluwer, 1991

Van de Ven, Andrew H. and William F. Joyce (editors), *Perspectives on Organization Design and Behavior*, New York and Chichester: Wiley, 1981

Williamson, Oliver E., "Hierarchical Control and Optimum Firm Size", *Journal of Political Economy*, 75/2 (1967): 123–38

Williamson, Oliver E., "Markets and Hierarchies: Some Elementary Considerations", *American Economic Review*, 63/2 (1973): 316–25

Williamson, Oliver E., *Markets and Hierarchies: Analysis and Antitrust Implications: A Study of the Economics of Internal Organization*, New York and London: Free Press, 1975

The beginnings of scholarly work on hierarchies may be found in the writings of Coase (included in CASSON) and Barnard, *The Functions of the Executive*, 1938. It is Williamson, however, who may be credited with the revitalization, propagation, and advancement of hierarchies as an area of study.

WILLIAMSON's (1967) supposition is that there exist diminishing returns to scale owing to the limitations of hierarchy. Impediments arise concerning accurate transmission of "images" among administrative levels. Hierarchical organization distances top executives from the "locus of productive activity". Loss in detail is due to error in the process of relaying information up the chain of command as well as in human cognitive ability – the bounds of rationality allow for knowledge breadth at the expense of knowledge depth. Span of control is proportional to control loss and thus provides a limit to the size of an efficient firm.

WILLIAMSON (1973) outlines the tenets whereby hierarchy may displace the market. These factors are divided into human and transactional. Human factors encompass bounded rationality, opportunism, and preferences for atmosphere – an individual's values and non-pecuniary satisfactions. Transactional factors comprise uncertainty, small numbers, and information impactedness.

WILLIAMSON (1975) elucidates the human and transactional factors of economic organization and asserts that the "powers and limits" of these modes (market and hierarchy) are best understood alongside one another. He delivers on this claim through depth of analysis and clarity of implications drawn. This text is considered the landmark study of hierarchies and provides the genesis for intellectual grist on the subject. CARROLL & TEECE pay homage to this work and note the pressure it has exerted throughout the social sciences. Their collection of essays by economists, sociologists, and political scientists draws on the transaction costs perspective to explore theoretical propositions, policy applications, and systematic empirical research.

CASSON's volume of 36 previously published works on the theory of the firm allots space to early and recent views. This evolution incorporates discussions on information/communication structure and the allocation of decision rights. Notable among the classic articles by economics laureates are works by Aoki, Ouchi, Radner, Winter, and Casson himself.

Chandler, author of *Strategy and Structure*, 1962, and *The Visible Hand*, 1977 – both works that provide historical perspective and detail on hierarchies not seen since Barnard – teams with Daems to produce a collection of original papers (CHANDLER & DAEMS). Similarities and differences are documented in the rise of managerial hierarchies in the US, UK, Germany, and France. Variance among the four nations in development of large industrial enterprises and in underlying institutional arrangements – a reflection of underlying economic idiosyncrasies – resulted in variations in the "capitalist mode of operation" in these countries.

FRANCIS, TURK & WILLMAN's collection of essays promises a critical and constructive appraisal of Ouchi and Williamson's markets and hierarchies perspective. Born out of the observed "tendency of economics to engulf less hardy disciplines", these papers counteract strict efficiency arguments by incorporating power and structure into the dialogue. Ultimately there is admission that polarization in the debate has much to do with disciplinary training. In terms of public policy, Daem's insight is that understanding the development of hierarchical organization is as important as discerning its societal impact.

HAMILTON & FEENSTRA marry the worlds of institutional economics and industrial sociology. Both of these subdisciplines recognize a continuum from market forces to authoritative organization. Difficulties arise when an explanation of the spectrum is generated from the rigid adherence to one of the perspectives (markets or hierarchies) at the exclusion of an alternative interpretation. In an effort to avoid an impasse in dialogue, Hamilton and Feenstra enter this pernicious fray with a discussion of networks – the balance point between the poles. Their discussion of vertically and horizontally controlled networks as well as the contexts of South Korea and Taiwan – a complement to the Chandler & Daems treatment – enriches a debate for which closure is not pending.

MARGLIN questions whether hierarchical authority displaces self-expression and choice. PUTTERMAN, too, notes that "participatory" modes of organization may be unavailable in capitalist market economies. The explanation offered is that political forces may override demand for workplace democracy. That hierarchies materialize has been predicated on the exogenous influence of technology. Marglin questions why this need necessarily be so. He posits that hierarchical authority may not be the only means of arriving at high levels of production and that nonhierarchical organization may be compatible with achieving material prosperity. STONE corroborates that technology is credited as a precondition to the emergence of hierarchy, but holds neoclassical economics liable for the view that action within the firm is an "economically efficient adaptation to market conditions". She sees division of labour as a significant social issue concerning the struggle between labour and capital over control of the production process and allocation of the rents that obtain.

NASCHOLD & VON OTTER apply the markets and hierarchies dichotomy to government operations. They chronicle the shift from hierarchy ("domination") to "more facilitating, encouraging, and supportive regimes". Their ambition is to instruct the public sector in lessons learned in other settings. Economic and social conditions have placed public-sector responsibilities in a position to be questioned and redefined. A fundamental change is observed in the interface and exchange relationships between public and private provision of goods and services.

PITELIS provides a collection of 12 original essays that extend and pointedly consider limitations of Williamson (1975). Basic assumptions and specific applications are poured over in directed detail. Kay's chapter runs the gamut, inadequacies at several levels are noted, and well-reasoned amendments are offered.

SCOTT "attempts to provide a coherent introduction to the sociological study of organizations". While this text is certainly as coherent as any writing on the subject, its strength lies in its comprehensiveness. Weber's theory of bureaucracy is distilled; hierarchy is considered from the systems vantagepoint; Fayol's theory of administration is reviewed; and recent studies of the limitations and strengths of hierarchies are synthesized.

SIMON finds hierarchic systems or hierarchies analogous to those found in the biological or physical realm. Issues such as: span of control, symbolic hierarchies, decomposition, complexity, and evolution – including selection-are explored.

Among VAN DE VEN & JOYCE's collection of 23 original essays from organization theorists of diverse backgrounds is a piece by Williamson and Ouchi that engenders a response from Perrow, which in turn draws Chandler into a rhetorical battle already underway. Several rounds of lively argumentation are exchanged.

THOMPSON *et al.* have assembled 24 existing writings into sections on markets, hierarchies, networks, and comparison between models. This collection provides a thorough basis to study the organization of social behaviour. Powell's article – "Neither Market nor Hierarchy" – in the final section is particularly compelling.

In an enlightening and entertaining treatment, TULLOCK delves into the structure and interior of the corporation. Although he acknowledges that questions outnumber solutions, they are an important basis for resolving perplexing matters. He provocatively considers the mixture of different-sized hierarchies; non-firm hierarchies; coordination in insect societies; nonhierarchical relationships; and disorganization.

PRESCOTT C. ENSIGN

See also Contracts and competition

Hierarchies, organizational

Arrow, Kenneth J., *The Limits of Organization*, New York: Norton, 1974

Beckmann, Martin J., "Some Aspects of Returns to Scale in Business Administration", *Quarterly Journal of Economics*, 74 (1960): 464–71

Beckmann, Martin J., *Rank in Organizations*, Berlin and New York: Springer, 1978

Chandler, Alfred D. Jr, *Strategy and Structure: Chapters in the History of the Industrial Enterprise*, Cambridge, Massachusetts: MIT Press, 1962

Chandler, Alfred D. Jr and Stephen Salsbury, *Pierre S. Du Pont and the Making of the Modern Corporation*, New York: Harper and Row, 1971

Coase, R.H., "The Nature of the Firm", *Economica*, 4 (1937): 386–405

Hess, James D., *The Economics of Organization*, Amsterdam and New York: North Holland, 1983

Keren, Michael and David Levhari, "The Optimum Span of Control in a Pure Hierarchy", *Management Science*, 25 (1979): 1162–72

Keren, Michael and David Levhari, "The Internal Organization of the Firm and the Shape of Average Costs", *Bell Journal of Economics*, 14/2 (1983): 474–86

Marglin, Stephen A., "What Do Bosses Do? The Origins and Functions of Hierarchy in Capitalist Production", *Review of Radical Political Economics*, 6/2 (1974): 60–112

Marschak, Jacob, "Efficient Organizational Design" in *Theory for Economic Efficiency: Essays in Honor of Abba P. Lerner*, edited by Harry I. Greenfield *et al.*, Cambridge, Massachusetts: MIT Press, 1979

Marschak, Thomas, "Organization Design" in *Handbook of Mathematical Economics*, edited by Kenneth J. Arrow and Michael D. Intriligator, vol. 3, Amsterdam and New York: North Holland, 1986

Milgrom, Paul and John Roberts, *Economics, Organization and Management*, Englewood Cliffs, New Jersey: Prentice Hall, 1992

Sah, Raaj Kumar and Joseph E. Stiglitz, "The Architecture of Economic Systems: Hierarchies and Polyarchies", *American Economic Review*, 76/4 (1986): 716–27

Sah, Raaj Kumar and Joseph E. Stiglitz, "Committees, Hierarchies and Polyarchies", *Economic Journal*, 98/391 (1988): 451–70

Simon, Herbert A., "A Formal Theory of the Employment Relationship", *Econometrica*, 19 (1951): 293–305; reprinted in his *Models of Bounded Rationality*, vol. 2: *Behavioral Economics and Business Organization*, Cambridge, Massachusetts: MIT Press, 1982

Spence, Michael (editor), "Symposium on the Economics of Internal Organization", *Bell Journal of Economics*, 6/1 (1975): 163–278

Williamson, Oliver E., "Hierarchical Control and Optimum Firm Size", *Journal of Political Economy*, 75/2 (1967): 123–38

Williamson, Oliver E., *Markets and Hierarchies: Analysis and Antitrust Implications: A Study in the Economics of Internal Organization*, New York and London: Free Press, 1975

Williamson, Oliver E., *The Economic Institutions of Capitalism*, New York and London: Free Press, 1985

Williamson, Oliver E., "Transaction Cost Economics: How it Works; Where it is Headed", *De Economist, Quarterly Review of the Royal Netherlands Economic Association*, 146/1 (1988): 23–58

A non-formal treatment of hierarchy was first developed by the renowned sociologist Max Weber in his pioneering writings on the nature of bureaucracy. As firms responded to the market imperative for greater efficiency, innovations in organizational structure preceded by many decades the formal analysis of organizations. One of the earliest example of such organizational innovation was the Hudson's Bay Company's response to the competitive challenges posed by its 18th-century arch rival, The Northwest Company, described in MILGROM & ROBERTS. Other noteworthy examples were the emergence of multidivisional firms in the early 20th century, under the leadership of Pierre du Pont at the DuPont Company (CHANDLER) and Alfred Sloan, Jr. at General Motors (CHANDLER & SALSBURY).

A seminal paper by COASE poses the basic questions "why are there firms?" and "why is not all activity organized in one large firm?" (WILLIAMSON 1988, p.32). The Coase article proved to be an important precursor of the formal analysis of organizations. It identified *transaction costs* as the key to understanding the very existence and limitations of the firm as an organizational form. While Coase considers the advantages to an employer of quasi-permanent employees, SIMON examines the "peculiarities" of the employment relationship, identifying the circumstances in which workers as well as employers would prefer an employment contract to a "sales" contract. The organizational form of the production unit depends on the choice made between contracting out various tasks and using inhouse services.

Similar in spirit to Coase is the book by ARROW, which argues that "organizations are a means of achieving the benefits of collective action in situations in which the price system fails" (p.32). An organization functions by processing information, where information is viewed *qualitatively*. Arrow emphasizes that two *quantitatively* identical "units" of information, such as "the truth value of statement A" and "the truth value of statement B" could differ markedly in their cost of acquisition and in their value to an organization. Many models of information transmission within organizations ignore this fundamental observation. Arrow extends his range of inquiry to address the issues of authority and control within organizations. Although a formal analysis of incentive structures is not carried out, the issues are addressed in a systematic but non-formal way.

Technical efficiency is almost universally regarded as the fundamental driver of decisions about organizational structure. An exception to this viewpoint is MARGLIN (p.61) whose inquiry into the rationale for the historical emergence of "the capitalist hierarchy" leads him to conclude that preservation of its class structure and the imperative of capital accumulation, rather than *technical efficiency*, can best explain the hierarchical structure of the production process under capitalism.

HESS is a treatise that is ambitious in the scope of its framework. It undertakes a formal analysis of organizations within the framework elucidated by Coase, Simon, Marglin, and Arrow. This book is an excellent survey and synthesis of much of the relevant literature to 1981. Topics range from the "market versus non-market debate", the nature and limitations of the employment relation, transaction costs, asymmetric information as an impediment to efficient market allocation (as in the case of adverse selection), communication and coordination in organizations, the valuation of qualitatively differentiated information, the acceptability to employees of an authority structure within organizations, transfer pricing within organizations, and incentive structures to overcome agency problems. Unfortunately, the Hess contribution is rarely cited and appears to have escaped the attention of most researchers in the field.

Under the editorship of SPENCE, a very interesting symposium on the internal organization of the firm included contributions from, among others, such celebrated scholars as K. Arrow, R. Radner, R. Wilson, and O. Williamson. The papers have a common theme summarized by Spence (p.164): "The papers . . . can be viewed as an exploration into a variety of informationally constrained resource allocation problems and institutional responses that characterize firms, organizations, and groups."

Despite the hazards inherent in all classification schemes, the formal analysis of hierarchies might usefully be classified into two broad categories: the *structuralist* approach and the *agency* approach. The ultimate goal in the formal modelling of organizations in general and hierarchies in particular is a grand synthesis of both the structuralist approach and the agency approach. The pioneer in the formal modelling of organizations, Jacob Marschak, made some progress in this direction. MARSCHAK (1979) is representative of his approach and models an organization "by a network of tasks performed by its individual members or groups of members (agencies, conferences, and so forth)." Although Marschak assembles the elements of a general approach to the formal modelling of efficient organizational design, his work does not fully integrate the structuralist aspects and the incentive issues.

The structuralist approach focuses on an organization's general shape, examining variables such as the number of levels in its chain of command (from president or chief executive officer at the top to the factory worker at the bottom), the ratio of superiors to subordinates at each level in the chain (the organization's "span of control"), the loss of information transmitted between various levels in the chain of command, and the degree of compliance by subordinates executing the instructions of superiors.

Perhaps the simplest structuralist approach can be found in the series of papers of SAH & STIGLITZ (1986) in which the performance of hierarchical (centralized), polyarchical (decentralized) decision processes are compared with respect to their impact on the aggregation of individual errors and their ultimate effectiveness (their relative probabilities of committing type I and type II errors, rejecting good projects and accepting bad projects, respectively) in screening prospective projects. In polyarchies, several decision makers can undertake projects independently, while in a hierarchy, only a few decision makers, or possibly one, can undertake projects, with others providing support. Denoting by p the probability that an individual judges a good project to be good, the authors assume that p is a function of candidate project's quality, denoted x. Perfect screening would render the "architecture" of the organization inconsequential in terms of projects. Among many interesting results is the proposition that screening in a polyarchy is more conservative than that in a hierarchy. In SAH & STIGLITZ (1988), the authors extend their comparison of decision processes involving exogenous errors in individual judgements to include consensus-based committees.

The contributions by WILLIAMSON (1975, 1985) have played a central role in developing this stream of literature. In contrast to an earlier stage of capitalistic development for which "the central problem of economic organization is one of defining and enforcing property rights", in a later stage of capitalism, "the principal problem of organization is that of aligning transactions with governance structures so as to support high performance results" (WILLIAMSON 1988, p.32). Williamson's latter characterization of the central problem of organizations suggests the need to formally synthesize the structuralist and the agency approaches.

The shape of an organization chart depicts its chain of command and, to a considerable extent, its authority structure. *Ceteris paribus*, a steep and narrow organizational tree suggests a more "top-down" style of management, with the upper administrative echelons more removed from the operational levels than one that is shallow and of greater breadth. Organizations have been formally analysed in a purely "structuralist" manner by WILLIAMSON (1967), KEREN & LEVHARI (1979, 1983), and BECKMANN (1960, 1978). The structuralist approach typically parameterizes all but one of these variables and then solves an optimization problem where the remaining variable is the control variable. A number of contributions appear to fit this category reasonably well; for example Williamson (1967), Keren & Levhari, and Beckmann (1960, 1978).

Both the useful insights and limitations of the structuralist approach can be seen in Williamson (1967). Williamson develops a formal model that embeds "the control loss features of hierarchical organization ... advanced in the bureaucratic-theory literature" in order to account for a static limitation to firm size. Williamson cites psychological experiments wherein the successive oral transmission of messages through a chain of serially linked individuals, analogous to the transmission of instructions or information across successive hierarchical levels generally results in serious distortions of the original message. To grapple with this issue, Williamson (1967) presents a model in which a subordinate performs only a fraction α ($0 < \alpha < 1$) of the intentions of a superior; α is thus the subordinate's degree of compliance. The actual production occurs only at the lowest level in a hierarchical organization; those at all higher levels do purely administrative work, such as planning, forecasting, accounting, and supervising. The span of control, defined as the number of employees that a supervisor can handle effectively, is assumed to be constant at all levels in the hierarchy and is assumed to be greater than one. Control loss is assumed to be strictly cumulative. Finally, each superior is assumed to earn β ($\beta > 1$) times as much as each subordinate. Williamson determines the optimal number of hierarchical levels, n, in an organization, given its objective of maximizing net revenue. Williamson's model demonstrates that *n increases with increases in α or s and decreases with decreases in β*. The

exogenous parameterization of the degree of compliance α, earnings differentials β between contiguous levels in the hierarchy, and the span of control s at all levels in the organization ignores many issues. In particular, the degree of compliance in this model is attributed entirely to information degradation at each stage of its transmission. As, at each level within an organization, there is a principal-agent problem between a superior and the immediate subordinate within his or her span of control, an obvious limitation of structuralist models is their failure to address agency problems within organizations and their impact on the structure of the organization.

In the past few decades, the strategic interaction between superiors and subordinates, possessing asymmetric information, has been the subject of intense research. A subordinate's degree of compliance or intensity of effort has subsequently been treated as an *endogenous* variable. Because a superior cannot, in general, observe (or indirectly infer with reasonable precision) an agent's degree of compliance or effort level, the problem confronting the superior has been to design an optimal reward system that will induce a subordinate to comply with the superior's instructions or to exert more effort than would otherwise be the case. Milgrom & Roberts have produced a highly lucid and accessible textbook that surveys the relevant modern literature on the design of optimal incentive structures in firms against a rich empirical backdrop. What renders this task quite challenging is that the firm's shareholders, managers, and workers possess asymmetric information whereas the firm generally operates in a stochastic environment

In a masterful survey and unification of the field of organization design, Thomas MARSCHAK (1986) builds on the foundation laid by Jacob Marschak. Marschak argues that at this stage in the development of the field, the task treating both the efficiency of designs and the incentive issues simultaneously is unmanageable. Nonetheless, he maintains (p.1360) that

> one *can* usefully study the efficiency of designs, separately from incentive issues ... [by assuming] that members *are* programmable robots. A design which has been found to be promising from the efficiency point of view can then be studied further to see if its incentive properties are acceptable – to see whether some system of rewards can induce humans to behave as the design's robots behave.

Having noted that "Designing an organization is perhaps the most complex decision making that one can study", Marschak proceeds to render the task more tractable by adopting a "one-step design" process. Although the elusive grand synthesis is still beyond the horizon, the Marschak survey is an encouraging indicator of the significant progress that has been made to date in the formal modelling of organizations and hierarchies.

IRWIN LIPNOWSKI

See also Organizational structure

High Court

Civil Justice Review: Report of the Review Body on Civil Justice, London: HMSO, 1988 (Cm 394)

Civil Procedure Rules, 3 vols, London: HMSO, 1999

Glasser, Cyril and Simon Roberts (editors), special issue on "Dispute Resolution: Civil Justice and Its Alternatives", *Modern Law Review*, 56/3 (1993): 452–

Heilbron, Hilary and Henry Hodge, *Civil Justice on Trial: The Case for Change*, London: Bar Council/Law Society, 1993

Jacob, Jack I.H., *The Reform of Civil Procedural Law and Other Essays in Civil Procedure*, London: Sweet and Maxwell, 1982

Jacob, Jack I.H., *The Fabric of English Civil Justice*, London: Stevens, 1987

Plant, Charles (editor in chief), *Blackstone's Guide to the Civil Procedure Rules*, London: Blackstone Press, 1999

Rosenbaum, Samuel, *The Rule-Making Authority in the English Supreme Court*, Boston: Boston Book Company, 1917; reprinted Littleton, Colorado: Rothman, 1993

Scott, I.R. *et al.* (editors), *The Supreme Court Practice*, London: Sweet and Maxwell, 1999a

Scott, Richard *et al.* (editors), *Civil Procedure: The Civil Procedure Rules*, London: Sweet and Maxwell, 1999b (with updates "Civil Procedure News")

Woolf, Harry (Lord Woolf), *Access to Justice: Interim Report [and Final Report] to the Lord Chancellor on the Civil Justice System in England and Wales*, 2 vols, London: HMSO, 1995–96

Zander, Michael, *Cases and Materials on the English Legal System*, 5th edition, London: Weidenfeld and Nicolson, 1988

Zuckerman, A.A.S. and Ross Cranston (editors), *Reform of Civil Procedure: Essays on "Access to Justice"*, Oxford: Clarendon Press, and New York: Oxford University Press, 1995

Texts on the English High Court divide into a handful of materials on the Court as an institution, putting it in its historical context and critiquing its performance, and a much larger number of books and guides on how to bring a case in the High Court. Readers approaching either category must keep in mind that there is a proposal to abolish the High Court and merge it with the County Court. No date has yet been set, nor any name given for the new court, but the first step towards it was taken with the introduction of the new CIVIL PROCEDURE RULES on 26 April 1999 (part of what is known as the "Woolf reforms" of civil justice, after the law lord who drafted them).

The Civil Procedure Rules replace SCOTT *et al.* (1999a) (also known as "the White Book") and the equivalent County Court Rules. The "Supreme Court" describes both the High Court and the Court of Appeal. A number of texts that describe the new rules are coming onto the market, including PLANT and Scott *et al.* (1999b). All have their advantages and disadvantages. The rules themselves – produced in three loose-leaf volumes – have the advantage of being updated as frequently as the rules change. Scott (1999b) is perhaps the most overall user-friendly volume in that it is only slightly less frequently updated, is considerably smaller and cheaper, and yet combines the rules themselves with a detailed commentary, case law, and other precedents, that draw upon the editors' experience of writing the notes to the *The Supreme Court Practice*.

In order to understand the High Court's function, its relationship with other courts and tribunals, how it developed, and the pressures that led to the introduction of the Woolf reforms, the best starting point is probably ZANDER. Zander is the key text on many degree programmes on the English legal system, and its benefits include its author's 35 years or so experience in writing about the subject. Zander is a cases and materials book, and so the reader can use it as an introduction to a much wider range of material, including case law, government consultation papers, and articles.

In addition to describing the Court's jurisdiction, appellate function, and some of its history, Zander also touches upon the key issue in the reform of the High Court: the conflict between the need to reduce cost and delay on the one hand, and the interest in producing the best procedure and the best (or most just) possible outcome on the other. This issue has never satisfactorily been resolved, although the Woolf reforms mark the most significant attempt to do so, at least this century.

The Woolf reforms might properly be said to be founded in the proposals made over a decade earlier in the CIVIL JUSTICE REVIEW. Many of the procedural changes that the High Court eventually adopted were floated there. Some were floated again in the HEILBRON & HODGE report of 1993. Lord WOOLF himself produced two reports, both entitled *Access to Justice*, in 1995 and 1996. All these reports rehearse the problems of cost and delay in High Court proceedings, and contain useful statistics that will interest the comparative researcher. Comparisons with Australian, American, and Canadian court systems are particularly relevant, but there is also some useful German material in the appendices to the 1996 report.

This series of reports and reform proposals also spawned a huge amount of academic comment. The best of it is contained in two volumes: GLASSER & ROBERTS, a special edition of the *Modern Law Review* from May 1993, and ZUCKERMAN & CRANSTON, published in late 1995. All of these essays impact upon the High Court, and in particular, its relationship with mediation and other alternatives to litigation. Much of it, however, is addressed more towards broader policy concerns about the civil justice reforms, including the move away from the traditional adversarial and oral method of resolving civil disputes towards more inquisitorial, judicially managed, and document-based methods. Both volumes also contain a number of useful foreign and comparative perspectives, and Zuckerman & Cranston has some economic analyses.

For readers with a more historical interest in the High Court, pickings are considerably less rich, but JACOB is by far the best source, both in his Hamlyn Lecture from 1987 (also probably the best overview of the fundamentals of English civil procedure) and his essays from 1982. The latter contain the excellent "Civil Procedure Since 1800" and "The Judicature Acts 1873–1875: Vision and Reality". The reader who wants to go beyond these essays should trawl the main texts on English legal history, including Holdsworth's *History of English Law* (17 volumes, 1903–72) and Pollock & Maitland's *History* of English Law, Volume 2 (2nd edition 1898). However, any reader sufficiently interested to get to this stage should really go back to the original source material, including the legislation and committee papers.

Another work, recently republished in the US, which is also worth looking at from the historical perspective, is ROSENBAUM.

NICK ARMSTRONG

High culture

Adorno, Theodor W., *The Culture Industry: Selected Essays on Mass Culture*, edited by J.M. Bernstein, London: Routledge, 1991

Bakhtin, Mikhail, *Rabelais and His World*, Cambridge, Massachusetts: MIT Press, 1968 (written 1940)

Billington, Rosamund, Sheelagh Strawbridge, Lenore Greensides and Annette Fitzsimmons, *Culture and Society: A Sociology of Culture*, London: Macmillan, 1991

Bourdieu, Pierre, *Distinction: A Social Critique of the Judgement of Taste*, London: Routledge and Kegan Paul, and Cambridge, Massachusetts: Harvard University Press, 1984 (French edition 1979)

DiMaggio, Paul, "Cultural Entrepreneurship in Nineteenth-Century Boston: The Creation of an Organizational Base for High Culture in America" in *Media, Culture and Society: A Reader*, edited by Richard Collins et al., Beverly Hills, California and London: Sage, 1986

Gans, Herbert J., *Popular Culture and High Culture: An Analysis and Evaluation of Taste*, New York: Basic Books, 1974

Gripsrud, Jostein, "'High Culture' Revisited", *Cultural Studies*, 3/2 (1989): 194–207

Mulgan, Geoff and Ken Worpole, *Saturday Night or Sunday Morning? From Arts to Industry – New Forms of Cultural Policy*, London: CoMedia, 1986

Williams, Raymond, *Culture*, London: Fontana, 1981; as *The Sociology of Culture*, New York: Schocken, 1982

Wolff, Janet, *The Social Production of Art*, 2nd edition, New York: New York University Press, 1993

High culture, as a term, has little conceptual force, emerging in the 19th century to indicate a troubled awareness of differences between valued and (on various grounds) less valued or stigmatized cultural forms and interests. For many intellectuals (including, for example, Matthew Arnold, Ortega y Gasset, and F.R. Leavis) culture without an adjective denoted the most significant (if mainly artistic) works of human achievement. However amid the slowly accelerating advent of democracy, education, commercial forms of entertainment, and modern media, the meaning of culture was brought into question. New terms such as mass culture (often with a hostile connotation of debasement) or popular culture (with its implicit celebration of the broader interests of the people or popular classes) began to problematize high culture as a particular form of culture, open to analysis and debate. Its investigation took place within very different intellectual traditions and political circumstances in various countries.

BAKHTIN and his associates worked in the highly charged and, for intellectuals, dangerous circumstances of the post-revolutionary Soviet Union. They were concerned to study issues of language, culture, and ideology in what they took to be always and necessarily contested social settings. The dissertation on Rabelais, only published decades later, explores the writer within the contexts of folk culture, such popular forms as laughter (which liberates "from the great interior censor") and carnival. Writing under Stalin, Bakhtin explores the dialectical interplay between popular customs with their "consciousness of freedom" that "could be only limited and utopian" and, by contrast, an "official culture" of seriousness that "terrorized, demanded and forbade". Into this world the earthy, the humorous, the grotesque, and the bodily intermittently erupt as a carnival. He concludes a wide-ranging and remarkable study by suggesting that the cultural life of the past (and implicitly the present) cannot be understood through the "ideologists" of "official culture" who seek to deny the breadth of contemporary cultural activities.

If Bakhtin's views were implicitly optimistic and joyous, situating the work of a great writer dialectically within the popular culture of his time, the German writers of the interwar Frankfurt School were austerely pessimistic. Drawing on their dense and complex formation as intellectuals, and confronting the rise of Fascism and its dissemination through powerful new forms of media, they produced troubled analyses of the fate of culture as a capitalist commodity form. ADORNO's scathing polemics on Hollywood film, popular music, and the seductions of the "culture industry" are shot through by repeated (if cryptic) affirmations of non-commercial culture as a realm of freedom. An awareness of Utopian possibilities (found more strongly in the work of Adorno's contemporary Walter Benjamin) is undercut by commentary on the contradictions and fissures within culture: "Schoenberg and Hollywood represent twin halves of a divided freedom to which however they do not add up". A reading of Bakhtin next to Adorno shows writers influenced by, yet innovating within, Marxist traditions of thought who struggle in remarkable but entirely different ways (the Russian densely referential to popular culture and its circumstances, the German bleakly sardonic and abstract) with relationships between popular and learned culture, in feudal and industrial capitalist conditions respectively.

In the postwar West, culture for some time received only intermittent attention from sociologists. An exception is the American Herbert GANS in his sympathetic exploration of forms of taste. The work shows his own and characteristically American strengths. At about the same time in France, BOURDIEU and his colleagues were producing a remarkable and for the first time ambitiously theorized series of studies concerned with education, museums, photography, and the operations of "legitimate culture". Bourdieu's major text, very widely cited and the most significant and extended study to date of cultural institutions, affinities, and tastes, is prolific in its conceptual reach. High or "legitimated" culture is argued to require specific cultural competences that are developed through the family "habitus" of particular social groups (professionals and others within the "dominated fraction of the dominant class"). They are validated and reproduced through the curricula of formal education, which delivers its products to positions in the field of culture characterized by social "distinction" from other groups. In this way there develop–invisibly– forms of "cultural capital" that can be used to strategic effect. The argument is backed up by elaborated and singular field research attempting to quantify the "distribution of preferences" in relation, for example, to forms of music or of photography. Contentious though Bourdieu's work may be–arguably tinged by the pessimism of a deterministic functionalism, quite without attention to gender or ethnicity–it compels attention and response.

The leading British (in fact Welsh) contributor to this field is Raymond Williams, whose long and distinguished body of publications (including *Culture and Society*, 1958; *The Long Revolution*, 1961; *Keywords*, 1976; and many others) has reflected on and significantly contributed to debates about culture and its meanings, from his starting point that "culture is ordinary". WILLIAMS is an example of Williams' development of a "cultural materialism", studying the arts as social forms including the ways in which they are produced and re-produced. This project finds an English feminist parallel through WOLFF's study, which in her ironic description "fails to provide a Marxist-feminist sociology of art" but in fact successfully analyses how artists evolve through institutional structures involving class, gender, and race.

Many of the most revealing studies of the institutional and social operations of high culture are found in particular case studies, of which there are several rather than a great many good examples. Thus DiMAGGIO analyses the organization of culture in 19th-century Boston, while MULGAN & WORPOLE show how the British state intervened to develop and protect high culture after the World War II.

Among recent work, which is surprisingly scanty perhaps for reasons that would interest Bourdieu, GRIPSRUD's discussion is lively and helpful. He contests a postmodern assumption that the distinction between high and low culture has collapsed (which "may serve as an ideological veiling of the social positions of researchers"), argues it to be "alive as a social fact throughout the western world", and assesses the relevance of issues and questions including those of aesthetic value. By comparison BILLINGTON *et al.*, in a concise and lucid chapter of their book, review positions and arguments in a succinct and interesting way, and offer useful leads to other reading.

MICHAEL GREEN

See also Culture, Popular culture

High performance work systems

Black, Sandra E. and Lisa M. Lynch, *How to Compete: The Impact of Workplace Practices and Information Technology on Productivity*, Cambridge, Massachusetts: National Bureau of Economic Research, and London: Centre for Economic Performance, 1997

Cuomo Commission on Trade and Competitiveness, *The Cuomo Commission Report: A New American Formula for a Strong Economy*, New York: Simon and Schuster, 1988

Dertouzos, Michael L., R. Lester and R. Solow, *Made in America: Regaining the Productive Edge*, Cambridge, Massachusetts: MIT Press, 1989

Huselid, Mark A., "The Impact of Human Resource Management Practices on Turnover, Productivity, and Corporate Financial Performance", *Academy of Management Journal*, 38/3 (1995): 635–72

Ichniowski, Casey, Kathryn Shaw and Giovanna Prennushi, "The Effects of Human Resource Management on Productivity: A Study of Steel Finishing Lines", *American Economic Review*, 87/3 (1997): 291–313

Keep, E. and K. Mayhew, "Evaluating Assumptions that Underlie Training Policy" in *Acquiring Skills: Market Failures, Their Symptoms and Policy Responses*, edited by Alison L. Booth and Dennis J. Snower, Cambridge and New York: Cambridge University Press, 1996

Lam, A., "Engineers, Management and Work Organisation: A Comparative Analysis of Engineers' Work Roles in British and Japanese Electronics Firms", *Journal of Management Studies*, 33/2 (1996): 183–212

Lynch, Lisa M. and Sandra E. Black, *Beyond the Incidence of Training*, Washington, DC: US Department of Education, 1996; London: Centre for Economic Performance, 1997

Michie, Jonathan and Maura Sheehan, "HRM Practices, R & D Expenditure and Innovative Investment: Evidence from the UK's 1990 Workplace Industrial Relations Survey (WIRS)", *Industrial and Corporate Change*, 8/2 (1999): 211–34

Osterman, P., "How Common Is Workplace Transformation and Who Adopts It?", *Industrial and Labour Relations Review*, 47/2 (1994): 173–88

Storey, John (editor), *Human Resource Management: A Critical Text*, London and New York: Routledge, 1995

A considerable body of literature, based primarily on US data, examines how human resources, industrial relations practices, and the organization of work influence productivity and product quality. Much of this appears in the "human resource management" (HRM) literature, with the empirical evidence suggesting that the presence of high performance work systems increases the likelihood of a firm also being a "high performer" in terms of productivity and profitability. This has been reported in a number of statistical studies, for example HUSELID.

Training is found to have an important role in many of these "high performance" work systems, with increased hours of training being associated with higher productivity and lower scrap rates (see LYNCH & BLACK for evidence and discussion).

According to STOREY, the central tenet of HRM theory is that, of the various "factors of production", it is the human resource – that is, human capability and commitment – that distinguishes successful organizations from the rest. The view has emerged among HRM analysts in both the UK and US that gains in productivity depend crucially on adopting new models of work organization that entail the use of "innovative work practices". Such practices include the use of work teams, job rotation, quality circles, total quality management (TQM), high levels of training, and innovative pay systems. A variety of terms describe such systems: "transformed" systems, "salaried" systems, "flexible specialization", "high commitment" organization and "high performance" work organization. There are several surveys of this literature – see for example OSTERMAN.

Perhaps the most significant recent empirical finding in the HRM literature is that, while groups or clusters of "complementary" HRM practices have large effects on productivity, changes in individual work practices have only a minimal effect. Thus:

> These theories also identify complementarities among specific practices which span seven different HRM areas: incentive compensation plans, extensive recruitment and selection, work teams, employment security, flexible job assignment, skill training, and labour-management communication. Taken as a whole, these theories also predict that adopting this entire complement of practices across all seven HRM policy areas will produce the highest level of productivity. (ICHNIOWSKI, SHAW & PRENNUSHI p.295)

BLACK & LYNCH emphasize the importance of complementarities in work practices and the extent of workers' voice associated with such practices:

> simply introducing high performance workplace practices is not enough to increase establishment productivity. The increased employee voice that is associated with these practices seems to be a necessary condition to making the practices effective. For example, although almost three-quarters of all the establishments in our sample have some form of Total Quality Management (TQM) system in place, TQM is not itself associated with higher productivity. Instead the percentage of workers involved in regular decision making meetings is positively related to labour productivity. (p.22)

Factors associated with a firm's adoption of innovative work practices include: producing in an internationally competitive product market, having a technology that requires high levels of skill, and following a "high road" strategy that emphasises variety, service, and quality rather than low cost. KEEP & MAYHEW argues that there is also evidence of a link between high levels of investment in training and the use of innovative work practices:

> those companies that have invested heavily in training . . . have normally done so as simply one part of a broader shift to very different models of industrial relations and personnel management, which stress commitment, trust, good communication between management and employees, and the breakdown of status that divides. (p.322)

Influential US reports such as DERTOUZOS, LESTER & SOLOW and the CUOMO COMMISSION emphasize the importance of adopting new work practices to improve productivity and competitiveness. In 1993 the Secretaries of Commerce and Labor hosted a conference on workplace innovation, providing a forum for top government officials to learn from managers, labour leaders, and workers who had direct experience in implementing various innovative work practices.

As noted by Osterman, in the US, "A common policy prescription is for state, local and federal governments to intervene with training or incentives [for firms] to adopt new work systems" (p.173).

In contrast, while the UK government has intervened in the area of training and skills, there has been less focus on issues of work organization, job design, employee participation, and involvement and reward systems. Work and organizational systems are treated within the confines of "managerial prerogative"; as Keep & Mayhew notes, "For the state, or other outside parties to intervene in these crucial areas has generally been regarded as fruitless or as anathema" (p.329). Rather, government strategy has focused on promoting measures aimed at improving an often very broadly defined concept of "competitiveness". In terms of the labour market, such measures have included the creation of training markets, the introduction of Training and Enterprise Councils, and legislation and policies targeted at deregulating the market. A growing body of research (see for example LAM) indicates that the value of skill acquisition by employees and managers can only be fully realized if training is accompanied by organizational restructuring and changes in work practices.

MICHIE & SHEEHAN uses evidence from the UK's Workplace Industrial Relations Survey to investigate the relationship between firms' human resource management practices on the one hand, and their tendency to innovate (or not) on the other. The results from their econometric analysis suggest that what the authors characterize as "low road" HRM practices – for example short-term contracts – are *negatively* correlated with investment in R&D and new technology. In addition, they find that "high road" work practices such as "high commitment" organization and other such systems are *positively* correlated with investment in R&D and new technology.

JONATHAN MICHIE

See also Human resource management, Total quality management, Training

Historical school (German and British)

Backhaus, Jürgen (editor), "Essays on Gustav Schmoller", special issue *History of Economic Ideas*, 1/3 (1993) and 2/1 (1994)
Backhaus, Jürgen (editor), *Werner Sombart (1863–1941), Social Scientist*, 3 vols, Marburg: Metropolis, 1996
Betz, Horst K., "How Does the German Historical School Fit?", *History of Political Economy*, 20/3 (1988): 409–30
Coats, A.W., "The Historist Reaction in English Political Economy, 1870–1890", *Economica*, 21/82 (1954): 143–53
Koot, Gerard M., *English Historical Economics, 1870–1926: The Rise of Economic History and Neomercantilism*, Cambridge and New York: Cambridge University Press, 1987
Koslowski, Peter (editor), *The Theory of Ethical Economy in the Historical School: Wilhelm Roscher, Lorenz von Stein, Gustav Schmoller, Wilhem Dilthey and Contemporary Theory*, Berlin and New York: Springer, 1995
Koslowski, Peter (editor), *Methodology of the Social Sciences, Ethics and Economics in the Newer Historical School:*

From Max Weber and Rickert to Sombart and Rothacker, Berlin and New York: Springer, 1997

Moore, Gregory C.G., "T.E. Cliffe Leslie and the English Methodenstreit", *Journal of the History of Economic Thought*, 17/1 (1995): 57–77

Richter, Rudolf (editor), "Views and Comments on Gustav Schmoller", special issue on *Journal of Institutional and Theoretical Economics*, 144/3 (1988)

Schefold, Bertram, "The German Historical School and the Belief in Ethical Progress" in *Ethical Universals in International Business*, edited by F. Neil Brady, Berlin and New York: Springer, 1996

BETZ provides a general survey of the German historical school as he summarizes the ideas of major scholars such as Roscher, Hildebrand, Knies, Schmoller, Sombart, and Spiethoff. Characteristic motives of historism include the interpretation of economic life as an organic, developmental, and historically conditioned process. Betz's essay points at the philosophical roots of German historism and highlights its specific social and political context.

SCHEFOLD combines his account of the German historical school with an analysis of its ethical concerns and normative implications. Belief in ethical progress has been typical for German historism from Roscher to Schmoller onwards, rooted in the traditions of an Aristotelian moral philosophy. It is held that World War I caused an intellectual break, for that developmental optimism was replaced by the critically distanced attitude of scholars such as Sombart. Moreover, the influence of historism on the further development of economic reasoning in Germany is exposed with a focus on Eucken's concept of ordoliberalism.

The essays in KOSLOWSKI (1995) mirror the historist programme of reconciling history, economics, and ethical affairs. The volume includes a critical assessment of Roscher by Priddat, who criticizes the notion of developmental laws. Shionoya interprets the Schmollerian research agenda from a Schumpeterian point of view as an evolutionary programme. Schefold's essay on the historical approach to a comparison of economic systems maintains that the analytical concepts of economic systems and economic order are compatible with the historist notion of economic styles, which integrates cultural aspects in the analysis of economic phenomena.

A second compilation of essays on the German historical school has been edited by KOSLOWSKI (1997), this time dealing with the impact of the youngest German historical school on Austrian economics, institutionalism, and Marshallian economics, among others. The volume also studies the relationship between the historical school and neo-Kantian philosophy and related lines of methodological reasoning during the early years of German sociology. An essay by Lenger reconsiders the conceptual breaks and continuities in the intellectual development of Sombart, and Gioia presents an account of Spiethoff's methodology and his notion of economic styles. The character of German historism as a comprehensive intellectual movement with a strong affinity for the human sciences is exposed accordingly.

RICHTER has devoted an issue of the *Journal of Institutional and Theoretical Economics* to the appraisal of Schmoller's works, concentrating on methodological topics. Häuser's essay analyses the *Methodenstreit* among Schmoller and Menger on the relationship between theory and history regarding its impact on the course of modern economics, as that debate prepared the ground for discussions on methodological individualism. Dopfer maintains that Schmoller was indeed a theoretical economist, but that he did not formulate a workable historical economics due to methodological shortcomings with respect to his empiricist attitudes.

The most complete account of Schmoller's research programme has been edited by BACKHAUS (1993, 1994) as a special issue of the *History of Economic Ideas*. Balabkins' essay on Schmoller's approach to social topics specifies the theoretical relevance and policy implications of Schmollerian ideas. Streissler and Milford elaborate on an exposition of German economics in the 19th century. Their survey of the methodological positions in Roscher, Knies, and Schmoller concludes that the shift from subjectivism to historism resulted in an intellectual degeneration of German economics as compared with Menger's Austrian school. An essay by Senn reviews Schmoller's reception by the English-speaking public, underlining his influence on major British and American economists.

To assess Sombart's approach to the analysis of capitalist development, BACKHAUS (1996) edited a compilation of essays on Sombart's life and works in three volumes. The first volume covers a broad range of biographical, theoretical, and methodological aspects, including a complex discussion of Sombart's position on nationalism and anti-Semitism. An extensive contribution is provided by vom Brocke's reconstruction of Sombart's intellectual development from a sympathizer of Marxism and social democracy to a proponent of social conservatism with an ambiguous attitude towards the Nazi movement. The second volume reviews Sombart's historical-theoretical approach to the analysis of modern capitalism by presenting his point of view on topics such as entrepreneurship, technological change, and market dynamics, among others. The third volume then deals with the intellectual heritage of that approach. Senn's essay on the English-speaking reception indicates that Sombart remains a controversial but important figure in the history of economic thought.

KOOT has written the most comprehensive and authoritative analysis of the related British historical school, which is described as an intellectual tradition biased towards neomercantilist policy conclusions. Introducing all the major scholars of British historism the book opens with Leslie's and Ingram's propagation of a historical economics in the context of the crisis of Ricardian orthodoxy since the 1870s. Rogers' statistical-historical approach is debated as well as Toynbee and Price's attempts of integrating history and economics. Ashley's historical economics are examined concerning their Schmollerian influences. Foxwell and Cunningham are portrayed as major Cambridge economic historians, the latter being engaged in fierce struggles against Marshall's ideas on economic theory. While Marshall succeeded, the London School of Economics still provided intellectual space for historist ideas, as the review of Hewins and the Webbs reveals. The volume concludes that Keynes continued implicitly with some aspects of the British historist critique of neoclassical economics, at least concerning the policy conclusions.

With regard to the Irish strand of British historism, the essay by COATS is still useful. It reviews the Comtist influence on

Ingram and Leslie who emphasized the need for a unified social science. Their historical method was directed against the abstractions and generalizations of Ricardian dogmatism. Still it should uncover the historical laws of social evolution. The essay concludes that despite their academic failure, historist ideas were responsible for Marshall's caution regarding the application of pure theory to actual policy issues.

MOORE discusses Leslie's role in the English battle of methods. He portrays Leslie as an advocate of Baconian methodology and anti-realist positions. The essay points at Leslie's beliefs concerning the historical specificity of economic theories as well as the normative and activist elements of his works, both rooted in the matter of social reform in Ireland. Policy concerns are thus identified as an essential motive of Leslie's approach to a historical economics.

ALEXANDER EBNER

Homelessness

Avramov, Dragana (editor), *Coping with Homelessness: Issues to Be Tackled and Best Practices in Europe*, Aldershot, Hampshire: Ashgate, 1999

Baum, Alice S. and Donald W. Burnes, *A Nation in Denial: The Truth about Homelessness*, Boulder, Colorado: Westview Press, 1993

Baumohl, Jim (editor), *Homelessness in America*, Phoenix, Arizona: Oryx, 1996

da Costa Nunez, Ralph, *The New Poverty: Homeless Families in America*, New York: Insight, 1996

Helvie, Carl O. and Wilfried Kunstmann, *Homelessness in the United States, Europe, and Russia: A Comparative Perspective*, Westport, Connecticut: Bergin and Garvey, 1999

Jencks, Christopher, *The Homeless*, Cambridge, Massachusetts: Harvard University Press, 1994

Kozol, Jonathan, *Rachel and Her Children: Homeless Families in America*, New York: Crown, 1988

Rossi, Peter H., *Down and Out in America: The Origins of Homelessness*, Chicago: University of Chicago Press, 1989

Van Whitlock, Rod, Bernard Lubin and Jean R. Sailors, *Homelessness in America, 1893–1992: An Annotated Bibliography*, Westport, Connecticut: Greenwood Press, 1994

Vissing, Yvonne M., *Out of Sight, Out of Mind: Homeless Children and Families in Small-Town America*, Lexington: University Press of Kentucky, 1996

Yeich, Susan, *The Politics of Ending Homelessness*, Lanham, Maryland: University Press of America, 1994

One should begin one's study of homelessness with JENCKS; this small volume started as a review of Peter Rossi's *Down and Out in America* and was expanded into a 120-page narrative exploring the causes of homelessness as well as several possible solutions. Christopher Jencks begins with a discussion of the "numbering" of the homeless, noting that in the US the official census counts households and not people, and, as the homeless have no house to hold, they are often uncounted.

This diminishes the numbers so necessary to persuade policy makers and funding resources that a problem really exists and resulted in advocates for the homeless creating their own numbers, solely as a means of attracting attention to the problem.

Jencks then pursues the possible causes of increased homelessness in the US, and finds, among others, that the *deinstitutionalization* of the mentally ill was a significant factor. Here liberals joined conservatives to empty publicly operated hospitals, the liberal in the cause of liberty and human rights, and the conservative in pursuit of less government and balanced budgets. The theory was to discharge mental patients from centralized, high-cost institutions and to relocate them to community-based, low-cost residences. However, while the discharges were completed in a timely and cost-effective fashion, the relocation was stalled for lack of available resources. The result was upwards of 100,000 former mental patients on the streets.

The book advocates specific reforms based on the author's balanced rationale. His is not the approach of the zealot but of the pragmatist recognizing that, although all problems associated with the homeless may not be resolved, this should not keep us from trying.

Christopher Jencks was influenced by the work of Peter H. Rossi. Although ten years old, ROSSI remains a definitive work in this field, combining the best of objective scholarship with a compassion for the real people behind the statistics. Rossi is particularly notable for making the necessary correlation between "homelessness" and "extreme poverty", a correlation that becomes obvious only upon reflection. Homelessness, Rossi relates, is not really a new and unique social problem but rather the consequence of unremedied poverty. Where many of the poor have been invisible, homelessness has made them visible.

BAUMOHL would be an excellent debater's ready-reference. It is neither sociology nor journalism – it is advocacy and while the information and documentation can pass any test of veracity and substance it is, in the main, a book authored by true believers. Jim Baumohl edited the book on behalf of the leading homeless advocacy group in the US, the National Coalition for the Homeless. The book best serves activists wishing to become involved in their communities and seeking a compendium of useful facts and proposals to support their efforts. The bibliography and appendix listing of advocacy groups will be helpful for further study.

BAUM & BURNES deals with a psychological condition known as *denial*. Most often used in conjunction with an individual's inability to face particular facts in their life, a disease or disorder, pending death or a loved one's addiction, nevertheless it is a condition that must be overcome before healing or coping is possible. The authors, with a track record in programming of direct service to the homeless, find that the US is in denial over the existence of the problem of homelessness, even denying that the homeless exist. Where many of those who advocate policies to end homelessness point to the lack of housing as the key cause and hence the prime need of the homeless, Baum & Burnes suggest that homeless persons have varied needs and require varied responses. Homeless people who are mentally ill need mental health treatment. Homeless people who are chemically dependent require dependency counselling. This is at the core of the "truth about homelessness" that forms the subtitle of the book.

The stereotypical homeless person is an alcoholic male of advanced years. However, children are the fastest growing segment of the homeless population in the US. It is probably the most shocking finding in current research that reports on the ever-increasing numbers of homeless families to be distinguished from homeless individuals. KOZOL, DA COSTA NUNEZ and VISSING provide accounts that part from the stereotype.

Kozol is a classic. One of the greatest myths involving homelessness is that it is the consequence of the free choice of individuals. Kozol undermines this myth with a factual and yet moving account as to how homelessness is a systemic defect rather than personal choice. Well written and easily read, the book is suitable for an introductory class.

Da Costa Nunez links the increase in homeless families to the increase in the numbers of households headed by young single mothers and proposes a systemic policy that focuses on the family with a goal of self-sufficiency. This is less a "what-is-the-problem" book and more of a "this-is-a-solution" work. It is best used in public policy and administration courses.

VISSING is the product of a study of homelessness in small town communities in Maine and New Hampshire, states and towns far from the big cities where homelessness is commonplace. Indeed, in communities where, according to tradition and culture, extreme poverty is mitigated by close family and neighbourly ties. VISSING may be unique in a field that has documented the problem in metropolitan areas, among the chemically dependent, in racial and ethnic enclaves, within the migrant communities and among the mentally ill. This volume explores homelessness and children in rural communities.

YEICH offers an approach quite different from the rest considered in this brief essay, in fact, most different from the general references available on homelessness. Where the standard treatise addresses the problem and proposes solutions to an unidentified problem-resolver (society, government, or policy makers in general), this work begins by expressing the belief that any such proposals would be futile. The author relates that

> Government has catered to the interests of elite groups not only by implementing conservative policies, but by propagating conservative ideology which has served to justify inequality and keep impoverished people docile and self-blaming. The response to homelessness is an example of these efforts. (p.26)

The "problem" is not lack of housing, deinstitutionalization or family breakup but organized oppression. The solution is organized protest. This would be a useful tonic for those students or scholars who have, by diligent study, come up with their own grand solutions for the problems of other people. It would also be a welcome supporting text in courses devoted to other victims of oppression: Third World peoples, feminism, labour studies and the like.

The postgraduate or specialist seeking a detailed academic approach within a multidisciplinary format would be advised to pursue AVRAMOV and HELVIE. These works are definitely not for the beginner nor for the social work practitioner but can reward the serious policy scholar with a comparative analysis of the problem and the resources being made available in nations other than Britain and the US.

As one delves further into the subject, a useful guide to the available literature can be found in VAN WHITLOCK, a comprehensive bibliography of 1703 citations including books, articles, and dissertations encompassing 11 subject classifications and covering a hundred years of exposition and research. Unfortunately, the work has not been continued through the 1990s.

LAWRENCE A. WINANS

Homogamy

Becker, Gary S., *A Treatise on the Family*, Cambridge, Massachusetts: Harvard University Press, 1981; enlarged edition 1991

Blau, Peter M., Carolyn Beeker and Kevin M. Fitzpatrick, "Intersecting Social Affiliations and Intermarriage", *Social Forces*, 62/3 (1984): 585–606

Bozon, Michel and François Héran, "Finding A Spouse: A Survey of How French Couples Meet", *Population*, English Selection 44/1 (1989): 91–121 (published in French 1987–99)

Dean, Gillian and Douglas T. Gurak, "Marital Homogamy the Second Time Around", *Journal of Marriage and the Family*, 40/3 (1978): 559–70

Glenn, Norval D., Sue Keir Hoppe and David Weiner, "Social Class Heterogamy and Marital Success: A Study of the Empirical Adequacy of a Textbook Generalization", *Social Problems*, 21/4 (1974): 539–50

Kalmijn, Matthijs, "Intermarriage and Homogamy: Causes, Patterns, Trends", *Annual Review of Sociology*, 24 (1998): 395–421

Lampard, Richard James, "Party Political Homogamy in Great Britain", *European Sociological Review*, 13/1 (1997): 79–99

Smits, Jeroen, Wout Ultee and Jan Lammers, "Educational Homogamy in 65 Countries: An Explanation of Differences in Openness Using Country-Level Explanatory Variables", *American Sociological Review*, 63/2 (1998): 264–85

Tzeng, Meei-Shenn, "The Effects of Socio-economic Heterogamy and Changes on Marital Dissolution for First Marriages", *Journal of Marriage and the Family*, 54/3 (1992): 609–19

Uunk, Wilfred J.G., Harry B.G. Ganzeboom and Péter Róbert, "Bivariate and Multivariate Scaled Association Models: An Application to Homogamy of Social Origin and Education in Hungary between 1930 and 1979", *Quality and Quantity*, 30/3 (1996): 323–43

Homogamy exists when marriage partners are in some sense similar to each other; it is thus a rather more general term than endogamy, which occurs when marriage partners belong to the same social group. Conversely, a couple is heterogamous if the partners are in some way different from each other. KALMIJN, who has himself carried out a great deal of valuable homogamy-related research, provides a wide-ranging empirical and theoretical overview of research on intermarriage and homogamy. He suggests that past research in this area has most often focused on race/ethnicity, religion, and socioeconomic status, although this arguably underemphasizes the attention that has been paid to the similarity of spouses' ages. His article draws a useful distinction between three different approaches to the explanation of homogamy: the first approach emphasizes the role of individuals' preferences, the second highlights the role of "third parties", and the third stresses the importance of constraints within the "marriage market".

Other commentators have examined what is sometimes referred to as "assortative marriage" (or "assortative mating") from within narrower explanatory frameworks. For example, the work of the economist BECKER, who has used a rational choice framework for his analyses of marriage and the family, prioritizes preferences over cultural and demographic factors. Socioeconomic homogamy at the aggregate level is thus viewed as a consequence of each individual's attempt to obtain a partner with the greatest possible socioeconomic status.

However, other authors have suggested that homogamy is induced by geographical propinquity. BOZON & HÉRAN expand on the idea that spatial segregation underpins homogamy by examining social segregation with respect to the places where marriage partners meet each other. Their account acknowledges that both social structure and human agency are significant within the marital formation process. Similar research, although with a more macrosociological slant, is discussed by BLAU, BEEKER & FITZPATRICK. Drawing upon Simmel's concepts of "crosscutting social circles" and "the web of group affiliations", the article provides evidence in support of the theory that intersecting social affiliations promote intermarriage. As in Blau's earlier work, the idea that population distributions within social environments influence marriage choices is central, although the salience of cultural values in marital selection is also recognized.

It has often been suggested that heterogamy leads to marital instability and dissolution. However, as noted some decades ago by GLENN, HOPPE & WEINER (with reference to homogamy of class background), this suggestion is usually an unsupported hypothesis rather than an empirically grounded finding. The hypothesis often reflects two assumptions: (a) observed differences between spouses' socioeconomic characteristics inevitably map onto conflict-generating differences in cultural values, and (b) differences between spouses do not offer benefits, and thus cannot reflect positive, conscious marital choices. However, empirical research has, in fact, indicated that some forms of heterogamy are associated with an increased risk of marital dissolution. Work by TZENG suggests that educational heterogamy increases the risk, and Tzeng also uses longitudinal data to demonstrate that shifts from homogamy to heterogamy (or vice versa) during marriage can increase (or reduce) the risk. This research also focuses on partners' joint employment situations, highlighting the fact that asymmetries between spouses' characteristics (as in the traditional, gendered division of labour) sometimes constitute a norm rather than deviations from a norm.

Research has often examined variations in the extent of homogamy, for example between different societies, over time within a society, or between different groups of marriages within a single society. DEAN & GURAK compared the levels of homogamy of women in first marriages and women in second marriages, focusing on age, education, and religious identification. The marriages of the latter group of women were found to be less homogamous than those of the former group. Dean and Gurak suggest that this may reflect the existence of a category of "divorce-prone" individuals, who are also disproportionately inclined to marry heterogamously. Embedded within this suggestion is the standard assumption that heterogamous marriages are less stable than homogamous marriages. Two alternative explanations for the greater heterogamy found among remarriages suggest that when women remarry they are less orientated towards finding a partner who is similar to them, and that the "second marriage market" induces heterogamy via a smaller but more diverse range of potential partners. However, the first marriages of the remarried women in Dean and Gurak's study were also found to be more heterogamous than average, which is not accounted for by these alternative explanations.

The study of party political homogamy by LAMPARD also attempts to evaluate different explanations of an observed pattern of homogamy. Many forms of social relationship are characterized by party political similarity, and there are significant levels of party political homogamy among people whose party political identifications are not very strong. Lampard therefore concludes that demographic constraints of the sort discussed by Bozon and Héran, and by Blau, Beeker & Fitzpatrick are more significant than has usually been recognized. However, the high level of party political homogamy observed among individuals with very strong party political identifications suggests that preferences also play a role in generating homogamy. Lampard also notes that most members of heterogamous partnerships are not against their partners' parties, and hence there seems little reason to assume that heterogamy will generate conflict in these cases. However, his findings suggest that it is possible that a minority of couples who are heterogamous with respect to party political identification are disproportionately prone to conflict and marital dissolution.

Examinations of trends in homogamy, and crossnational homogamy comparisons, have generally viewed the extent of socioeconomic homogamy as an indicator of societal openness. A between-country comparison of levels of educational homogamy by SMITS, ULTEE & LAMMERS, attempts to explain international variations in homogamy in terms of factors such as industrial and technological development, and political democracy. Smits, Ultee & Lammers, like other authors such as Kalmijn and Lampard, use loglinear models in their analyses. Advances in statistical techniques have facilitated analyses with a greater level of sophistication and hence methodological superiority. For example, different forms of homogamy frequently overlap, and UUNK et al. use log-multiplicative models of the type introduced by Goodman (quasi-association models) to disentangle educational homogamy and social origin homogamy. However, as noted by Kalmijn, the use of cutting-edge statistical modelling approaches may unfortunately render research findings less accessible to general readers.

RICHARD LAMPARD

Homosexuality, law

Bray, Alan, *Homosexuality in Renaissance England*, 2nd edition, London: Gay Men's Press, 1988

Eskridge, William N., *Gay Law*, Cambridge, Massachusetts: Harvard University Press, 1999

Herman, Didi and Carl Stychin, *Legal Inversions: Lesbians, Gay Men, and the Politics of Law*, Philadelphia: Temple University Press, 1995

Moran, Leslie J., *The Homosexual(ity) of Law*, New York and London: Routledge, 1996

Moran, Leslie J., Daniel Monk and Sarah Beresford (editors), *Legal Queeries: Lesbian, Gay and Transgender Legal Studies*, London and New York: Cassell, 1998

Norton, Rictor, *Mother Clap's Molly House: The Gay Subculture in England, 1700–1830*, London: Gay Men's Press, 1992

Richards, David A.J., *Identity and the Case for Gay Rights: Race, Gender, Religion as Analogies*, Chicago: University of Chicago Press, 1999

Rimmerman, Craig A. (editor), *Gay Rights, Military Wrongs: Political Perspectives on Lesbians and Gays in the Military*, New York: Garland, 1996

Rubenstein, William B. (editor), *Lesbians, Gay Men, and the Law*, New York: New Press, 1993

Strasser, Mark, *Legally Wed: Same-Sex Marriage and the Constitution*, Ithaca, New York: Cornell University Press, 1997

Stychin, Carl F., *Law's Desire: Sexuality and the Limits of Justice*, New York and London: Routledge, 1995

Tatchell, Peter, *Europe in the Pink: Lesbian and Gay Equality in the New Europe*, London: Gay Men's Press, 1992

Wintemute, Robert, *Sexual Orientation and Human Rights: The United States Constitution, the European Convention, and the Canadian Charter*, Oxford and New York: Oxford University Press, 1995

In order to understand the relationship of the law with the homosexual, a historical overview is essential. BRAY examines the image of the sodomite in 16th- and 17th-century literature, and demonstrates how widely that image differed from the everyday occurrences of male homosexual behaviour in ordinary households and communities. NORTON chronicles the growth of a distinctive male homosexual urban subculture in the 18th and early 19th centuries, and describes the origins of the modern gay community. Bray and Norton are not writing about the law as such, but throughout their books they give a clear account of the relationship between the law and homosexuality at that time, and the origins of the modern involvement of the law with gay men.

There are many commentaries on the legal situation of homosexual and lesbian people in the early 20th century, both before and after the Wolfenden report and the 1967 Sexual Offences Act. TATCHELL, however, gives a late 20th-century overview of the law throughout Europe. He not only produces a great deal of useful empirical data as regards legislation, ages of consent, and partnership rights, but also gives an incisive account of the inequalities and discrimination that exist. In the US, RUBENSTEIN's book was a major breakthrough in the study of lesbians, gay men, and the law. The many contributors

examine the history of the legal treatment of both lesbians and gay men in the US. Coming from a variety of disciplines, they discuss the ways in which the law attempts to regulate people's sexuality. The book is both comprehensive and creative in the way it requires scholars to look at the law not just through cases but also through academic and social commentary.

HERMAN & STYCHIN examines the law reform struggles of lesbians and gay men over the last 30 years of the 20th century. The text scrutinizes the politics of the engagement of the homosexual lobby with the legislature and courts in America. The book is broad in its overview, including topics such as the legal definitions of homosexuality through to the AIDS activism movement. STYCHIN follows this with a critical examination of the relationship of law and sexual orientation in the US, the UK, and Canada. He sees law as one of the primary means through which lesbian and gay male sexuality is not only monitored and controlled but also constructed. He uncovers this connection through an exploration of key questions of current interest and controversy such as: homoerotic art; the regulation of safe sex educational materials; gay pornography and feminist theory; lesbians and gay men in the US military; sadomasochism and the law; and legal restrictions on the "promotion" of homosexuality. He examines the social discourses behind legal restriction and their impact both upon sexual subcultures and society at large. Stychin concludes with an examination of the challenges posed by the newly emerging queer identities that are superseding the gay liberation movement. MORAN complements Stychin by offering an understanding of the histories of the contemporary legal tradition and their current operation. The author uses specific examples to look at how the legal discourse around homosexuality is constructed. He focuses on gay and civil rights, equality under the law, and social attitudes towards homosexuals by looking closely at the means and methods of social regulation.

WINTEMUTE tackles the question of whether lesbian and gay rights are human rights. He argues that this is not just a political slogan; rather, there are legal arguments to support the claim that the right to be free from sexual orientation discrimination is a human right. In particular he asks the question: can national constitutions or international human rights treaties be interpreted as prohibiting discrimination against same-sex activity, gay, lesbian and bisexual individuals, and same-sex couples? Wintemute attempts to answer the questions by examining three of the most commonly used arguments in favour of such an interpretation: sexual orientation is an "immutable status"; sexual orientation is a "fundamental choice"(or part of "privacy"); and sexual orientation discrimination is sex discrimination. To assess the merits of these arguments he examines their relative success and failure in cases brought under three of the world's most influential human rights instruments: the US Constitution, the European Convention on Human Rights, and the Canadian Charter of Rights and Freedoms.

RICHARDS continues on from Wintemute by charting a course toward legal recognition of gay rights as basic human rights. The author explores the connections between gay rights and three successful civil rights movements: black civil rights, feminism, and religious toleration. He explores how these might serve as analogies for the gay rights movement. Richards argues that racial and gender struggles are informative but partial models, for example achieving gay rights also requires doing away with prejudiced stereotypes. However, Richards argues that gay identity is an ethical choice based on gender equality, thus the right to religious freedom offers the most compelling analogy for a gay rights movement. He concludes that gay identity should be protected legally as an ethical decision of conscience.

RIMMERMAN provides a good in-depth overview of one of the most controversial areas that legislatures have had to address in recent years: gays in the military. He places the issue of homosexual military service in its historical, theoretical, and political context and looks at the legal validity of policies in this domain. STRASSER looks at another controversial area: same-sex marriage. He sets forth many legal and moral arguments for opposing the organised right-wing anti-gay, anti-same sex marriage campaign that have grown up in the light of the *Baehr v Lewin* case in Hawaii.

ESKRIDGE provides a comprehensive analysis of the legal issues concerning gender and sexual nonconformity in the US. Part One covers the years from the post-Civil War to the 1980s, and is a comprehensive history of state efforts to discipline and punish the behaviour of homosexuals and other people considered to be deviant. Part Two addresses contemporary issues. The author demonstrates that, despite it being no longer illegal to be gay in America, gay men and lesbians still suffer from state discrimination in many aspects of life, and private discrimination and violence against gays is rife. Eskridge presents a persuasive case for the "sexualization" of the First Amendment: showing why, for example, same-sex ceremonies and intimacy should be considered "expressive conduct" deserving the protection of the courts. Furthermore he draws on legal reasoning, sociological studies, and history to develop an effective answer to the arguments made in defence of the "don't ask, don't tell" policy of the military. He places his legal arguments in contemporary liberal theory and combines them within the prevailing stance toward freedom, gender equality, and religious pluralism.

Another question is whether law reform should move beyond the traditional confines of decriminalization, partnership rights, and social equality. MORAN, MONK & BERESFORD explores issues in sexuality, gender and the law in a broad framework using examples ranging from continental Europe to Australia. The book presents a new set of perspectives on the way lesbians, gays, and transsexual people are represented in society and dealt with by the law, and the legal areas of commonality between these different interest groups.

STEPHEN WHITTLE

See also Human rights, Queer theory in law

Hoshin kanri

Akao, Yoji (editor), *Hoshin Kanri: Policy Deployment for Successful TQM*, Cambridge, Massachusetts: Productivity Press, 1991

AT&T Quality Steering Committee, *Policy Deployment: Setting the Direction for Change*, Indianapolis: AT&T, 1992

Babich, P., *Hoshin Handbook*, Poway, California: Total Quality Engineering, 1996

Bechtell, Michelle L., *The Management Compass: Steering the Corporation Using Hoshin Planning*, New York: American Management Association, 1995

Colletti, J., *A Field Guide to Focused Planning: Hoshin Kanri American Style*, Granby, Colorado: Woodledge, 1995

Cowley, Michael and Ellen Domb, *Beyond Strategic Vision: Effective Corporate Action with Hoshin Planning*, Boston: Butterworth Heinemann, 1997

Eureka, William E. and N.E. Ryan, *The Process-Driven Business: Managerial Perspectives on Policy Management*, Dearborn, Michigan: American Supplier Institute Press, 1990

King, B., *Hoshin Planning: The Developmental Approach*, Methuen, Massachusetts: GOAL/QPC, 1989

Melum, M.A. and C. Collett, *Breakthrough Leadership: Achieving Organizational Alignment through Hoshin Planning*, Methuen, Massachusetts: American Hospital Publishing, 1995

QPC Research Committee and MBP/Hoshin Planning Team, *Hoshin Planning: A Planning System for Implementing Total Quality Management (TQM)*, Methuen, Massachusetts: GOAL/QPC, 1990

Sheridan, Bruce M., *Policy Deployment: The TQM Approach to Long-range Planning*, Milwaukee: American Society for Quality Control Quality Press, 1993

Smith, S., *Plan to Win: Turning Strategy into Success*, Godalming, Surrey: Quest Worldwide, 1997

Hoshin kanri translates as "policy management" or "deployment". It is about the implementation of corporate strategy. The emphasis is not so much on the "what" of strategy as on the "how". It is a form of strategic management that has four stages: focus, alignment, integration, and review.

It includes several tasks. Top management specifies a few vital annual strategic priorities (focus). Local management teams will then clarify, reconcile, and agree annual objectives (alignment). Everybody then manages annual objectives in their daily work (integration). Top managers audit the whole strategic management process (review).

All but two of the following texts take a United States perspective. The influence of Hewlett Packard is very strong throughout. All the texts are based on "total quality management" (TQM), although many stress the importance of strategic management. *Hoshin kanri* is really strategic management by TQM principles and the Deming (plan–do–check–act) cycle is central.

AKAO is the original and seminal text but was translated from the Japanese after the publication of KING's book (see below). The Western edition of Akao contains a chapter from Greg Watson (ex-Xerox). Akao is a Japanese academic; the text has case studies from practitioners as well as discussions involving all the contributory authors apart from Watson. There is a good account of *hoshin kanri's* history. The book is wide ranging and deals with a Japanese TQM-based context. It has a preoccupation with quality control and is targeted at TQM readers. This is a difficult text to read as its edited nature makes the structure obtuse and Western managers may find it too hard going. However it is the only text that places *hoshin kanri* very firmly in daily management.

The AT&T text is an AT&T Quality Office publication and so it is internally focused; it is very much an early TQM publication and it has a very limited availability. However it is probably the best text for prospective practitioners. AT&T have produced one of the best concise overviews of how to do *hoshin kanri*, and it has proved a favourite with practitioners. There is an example from AT&T's operations systems business unit.

BABICH is ex-Hewlett Packard and this is a consultant's publication. It includes examples of documentation including ones used by Rockford International. It presents a very simple conceptualization of *hoshin kanri* as a breakthrough (as opposed to a *kaizen*) methodology – which in practice may be misleading as *hoshin kanri* is an integrative and very organic approach to general management. It has limited availability but is available through TQE's web pages. There is also reference to *hoshin* planning software.

BECHTELL is a consultant's management briefing. It includes information from Hewlett Packard, Procter & Gamble, and Zytec, among others. The uniqueness of *hoshin kanri* is lost in explanations of strategic management and quality management. This text is not widely available but it can be readily obtained through the AMA in the USA. It is fairly recent and a useful introduction.

COLLETTI is another US consultant's publication, but this time presented as a manual. The author visited six Japanese companies in 1991 with Bob King, as part of a GOAL/QPC study team. His examples, however, include Ford Motor Company material.

COWLEY & DOMB is an American text written fairly recently by consultants. It is based largely on the American influence of Hewlett Packard. There is an emphasis, however, on strategic vision and an example of practice at North Island Federal Credit Union.

EUREKA & RYAN is an early text but very easy to read. It is based too much on the early example of (the now unsuccessful) Florida Power & Light. It has a very short but friendly style, but it is dated and in some respects misleading about what *hoshin kanri* is. However, it manages to convey a good sense of what is involved.

The publication authored by the QPC RESEARCH COMMITTEE AND MBP/HOSHIN PLANNING TEAM is described as a research report, but in fact is really no more than an outline without any statements of issues or illustrative practice. However some notable names are listed as collaborators: Yoji Akao, Noriake Kano, Hewlett Packard, Florida Power & Light, Procter & Gamble, and Bob King are all named as consultants.

KING is the first English-language text. It is presented as a manual. There is a strong influence from Hewlett Packard. A pioneering work, put together when *hoshin kanri* was confused with quality function deployment.

The MELUM & COLLETT text includes various authors with case studies of the following: Bethesda Incorporated, Our Lady of Lourdes Medical Centre, Sisters of the Sorrowful Mother Ministry Corporation, Southwest Texas Methodist Hospital, AT&T Transmission Systems, and Hewlett Packard's Medical Products Group. There are good samples of *hoshin*

plans though the influence of Hewlett Packard is perhaps overly strong. Despite this, this text remains the only one to give detailed service examples although perhaps they are rather prescriptive in tone.

SHERIDAN is very short and mostly about Florida Light & Power. It contrasts a large and small company case, and illustrates the Japanese approach to TQM.

SMITH is a UK TQM consultant's publication. It has a populist and checklist style of presentation that obscures the substance of *hoshin kanri*. The text tries to put across its ideas without directly using the Japanese term.

BARRY WITCHER

See also Japanese management, Total quality management

Hours of work, working hours

CATALYST, *A New Approach to Flexibility: Managing the Work/Time Equation*, New York: Catalyst, 1998

Hamermesh, Daniel S., *Workdays, Workhours and Work Schedules: Evidence for the United States and Germany*, Kalamazoo, Michigan: Upjohn Institute for Employment Research, 1996

Hochschild, Arlie Russell, *The Time Bind: When Work Becomes Home and Home Becomes Work*, New York: Metropolitan, 1997

LaJeunesse, Robert, "Toward an Efficiency Week", *Challenge*, 42/1 (1998): 92–109

Perlow, Leslie A., *Finding Time: How Corporations, Individuals, and Families Can Benefit from New Work Practices*, Ithaca, New York: ILR Press, 1997

Perlow, Leslie A., "The Time Famine: Toward a Sociology of Work Time", *Administrative Science Quarterly*, 44/1 (1999): 57–81

Robinson, John P. and Geoffrey Godbey, *Time for Life: The Surprising Ways Americans Use Their Time*, University Park: Pennsylvania State University, 1997

Schor, Juliet B., *The Overworked American: The Unexpected Decline of Leisure*, New York: Basic Books, 1991

Stredwick, John and Steve Ellis, *Flexible Working Practices: Techniques and Innovations*, London: Institute of Personnel and Development, 1998

Taddei, D., *Reduction in Working Time: A Literature Review*, Luxembourg: Office of Official Publications of the European Community, 1998

This entry does not focus on the legal aspects of working hours and hours of work because there is so much variation from one country to another.

SCHOR argues that Americans are working longer hours. This book received an enormous amount of attention in both academic circles and in the popular press. Clearly, it stimulated interest in the topic of working hours. Schor, an economist, contends that in the US, longer working hours and less leisure time result in time poverty. One of the major causes of this time poverty is the consumer culture, which puts workers into a time squeeze, or a work-spend cycle that is never ending. There are very large amounts of data in this book, including the fact that US manufacturing employees work 320 more hours per year than their German or French counterparts.

A recent book that complements Schor's work is HOCHSCHILD. This author is a sociologist with an interest in the interaction between work and home. Her research, which was conducted in a Fortune 500 firm, found that, despite family-friendly work schedules running the gamut from part-time to flexible hours, employees are not cutting back their hours. Rather than escaping to their homes, they are escaping by going to work.

ROBINSON & GODBEY reaches quite different conclusions than either Schor or Hochschild. These time-use experts found that Americans have almost five hours more free time per week than they did in the 1960s. So where do they find that this time has gone? Television. Their unique perspective is shaped by the use of time diaries. They are involved in the Americans' Use of Time Project, where every ten years (since 1965) thousands of subjects are asked to report their daily activities on an hour-by-hour basis. Other controversial or unexpected findings include that parents are not spending less time with their children and that those with less education (the working class) have more free time than their college-educated counterparts. The cross-cultural chapter is especially thought provoking. For example, the Japanese work longer hours, yet generally feel less time pressured than Americans. Their final chapter is appropriately titled: "brother, can you spare some time?" In summary, Robinson & Godbey is the definitive and comprehensive review of how Americans spend their time.

Whereas, in the US, marketplace solutions rather than government intervention are the primary mechanism for regulating the length of the work week, in European countries, such as in France, the legal work week is being reduced from 39 to 35 hours for all but senior executives. And top executives can be held accountable for infractions by fines and even jail sentences. TADDEI is not a literature review in the traditional sense, but a summary of case studies on five different countries, Belgium, Germany, France, Sweden, and the Netherlands.

For a discussion and literature review of the advantages of a shorter work week, LAJEUNESSE has written a readable article. LaJeunesse is clearly an advocate of a shorter workweek. But rather than using the conventional argument of ameliorating unemployment, he argues that a shorter work week will lead to higher productivity. Whereas Taddei only profiled specific countries, LaJeunesse provides several pages of citations for those who want to do further reading on the shorter work week.

For a comparative study of Germany and the US by a labour economist, HAMERMESH uses what he terms an instantaneous approach to the study of time use. This approach analyses workers' and employers' choices of workdays and working hours per day. It addresses questions such as how these decisions are affected by issues such as childcare or government policy. However, this book is not as accessible or readable for non-academics as, for instance, Robinson & Godbey or Schor.

PERLOW is an interesting account of how engineers, spouses, and managers struggle to meet the competing demands of work and home. This book is rich with stories and is quite accessible to non-academics. Another more scholarly version of work/home issues by the same author is "The Time Famine: Towards a Sociology of Work Time" (*Administrative Science Quarterly* 44/1, 1999). Both versions are well done and both deal qualitatively with how people use their time at work in a Fortune 500 firm. Perlow's nine-month field study of software engineers found that the group's collective use of time created an environment of too much to do and too little time to do it. Hence, a time famine. Perlow's work has both theoretical and practical implications.

A study focussing on part-time work arrangements was sponsored by CATALYST, an organization in the US that works for the advancement of women. *A New Approach to Flexibility* was funded by the Alfred P. Sloan Foundation and it documents and evaluates the effectiveness of part-time work arrangements. A limitation is that it focuses on professionals only and it confines itself to part-time schedules and not other non-traditional schedules such as flextime or compressed workweeks. Nevertheless, the report is well written and organized, and it is undoubtedly useful for organizations concerned with alternative work schedules.

STREDWICK & ELLIS is a more comprehensive approach to non-traditional work schedules. This book is based on experiences in the UK, and the topics it covers include annual hours, job sharing, shiftwork, outsourcing, telecommuting, and a range of other issues related to flexible work schedules. It is filled with relevant case studies. Its UK legal context does not detract from its readability and it is not filled with legalese. Each topical chapter concludes with a list of useful references.

DANIEL J. GALLAGHER

See also Part-time employment, Work–leisure interaction

House of Lords as a judicial body

Blom-Cooper, Louis and Gavin Drewry, *Final Appeal: A Study of the House of Lords in Its Judicial Capacity*, Oxford: Clarendon Press, 1972

Halsbury, H.S.G., *Halsbury's Laws of England*, edited by Lord Hailsham of Marylebone, 4th edition, London: Butterworths, 1973–; vol. 10, 338ff.

Heuston, R.V.F., *The Lives of the Lord Chancellors, 1940–1970*, Oxford: Clarendon Press, and New York: Oxford University Press, 1987a

Heuston, R.V.F., *The Lives of the Lord Chancellors, 1885–1940*, revised edition, Oxford: Clarendon Press, and New York: Oxford University Press, 1987b

Murphy, T.F. and R.T. Rawlings, "After the Ancien Régime: The Writing of Judgments in the House of Lords 1979/1980", parts 1 and 2, *Modern Law Review*, 44 (1981): 617; and 45 (1982): 34ff.

Paterson, Alan, *The Law Lords*, London: Macmillan, 1982

Robertson, David, *Judicial Discretion in the House of Lords*, Oxford: Clarendon Press, and New York: Oxford University Press, 1998

Stevens, Robert, "The Final Appeal: Reform of the House of Lords and Privy Council, 1867–1876", *Law Quarterly Review*, 80 (1964): 34ff.

Stevens, Robert, *Law and Politics: The House of Lords as a Judicial Body, 1800–1976*, Chapel Hill: University of North Carolina Press, 1978; London: Weidenfeld and Nicolson, 1979

A useful summary of the applicable law is to be found in HALSBURY. In its judicial capacity the current jurisdiction of the House of Lords was established by the Appellate Jurisdiction Act 1875, creating a further appellate layer beyond the newly established Supreme Court, and establishing it as the highest Court of appeal in England and Wales and Northern Ireland in all cases, and in Scotland on questions of civil law. The history surrounding the jurisdiction and the transition period is set out in STEVENS (1979). The foundation of the statutory jurisdiction is laid out in STEVENS (1964). Highly readable accounts of judicial behaviour and selection are to be found in the short biographies of Lord Chancellors in HEUSTON (1987a) and HEUSTON (1987b).

MURPHY & RAWLINGS concentrated upon the texts that were generated by the Lords, and established that, far from adducing arguments of principle, it was much more usual for the judges to indulge in rhetorical forms of a sort that might very easily be adduced for either side. There are now several significant accounts of the ways in which the House operates. PATERSON had a good deal of access to the judges in the House of Lords in the late 1970s. BLOM-COOPER & DREWRY were less privileged but excised greater analytical power *ab extra*. Far more modern is ROBERTSON, a political scientist who has produced the kind of jurimetric analysis which is more familiar when dealing with the US Supreme Court. It is clear that the behaviour of a given judge, in terms of whether or not he or she will give a judgement or simply concur, whether or not he or she will dissent, and so on, can be determined by the presence or absence of other judges.

The kinds of decisions that will be forced upon the House (and the lower judiciary, of course) by the Human Rights Act 1998 and the devolution legislation will serve to concentrate greater attention upon the relationship of the House to the legislature. For the first time the Courts will be undertaking a serious review function typical of constitutional courts elsewhere. The Pinochet saga (*R. v Bartle and the Commissioner of Police for the Metropolis, ex parte Pinochet* [No 1: 1998 3 WLR 1456; 1998 4 All ER 897]; *R. v Bartle and the Commissioner of Police for the Metropolis, ex parte Pinochet* [No 2: 1999 1 All ER 577; 1999 2 WLR 272]; *In re Pinochet* [1999 2 WLR 272; 1999 1 All ER 77]) brought to a head a series of concerns as to the way in which the House could divorce its discharge of its judicial function in cases of great political sensitivity. (The case concerned an application to extradite the former head of state of Chile; Lord Hoffman was held to have acted inappropriately by holding decisively against Pinochet whilst having links to Amnesty International which was joined as a party to the case. A fresh chamber of seven judges was convened, which decided the case along the same lines but for different reasons.)

The different results arising in the second from the first hearing has explicated the fact that the decision in the case depended upon the choice of judges allocated to it. The reformers argue for a constitutional court in which appointments are more openly scrutinized, and in which all judges sit on all hearings.

PETER ALLDRIDGE

Household as an economic agent

Anderson, Michael, Frank Bechhofer and Jonathan Gershuny (editors), *The Social and Political Economy of the Household*, Oxford and New York: Oxford University Press, 1994

Becker, Gary S., *A Treatise on the Family*, revised edition, Cambridge, Massachusetts: Harvard University Press, 1991

Bryant, W. Keith, *The Economic Organisation of the Household*, Cambridge and New York: Cambridge University Press, 1990

Fraad, Harriet, Stephen Resnick and Richard Wolff, *Bringing It All back Home: Class, Gender, and Power in the Modern Household*, London: Pluto Press, 1994

Grossbard-Shechtman, Shoshana, "Home Economics, New" in *Encyclopedia of Political Economy*, edited by Phillip Anthony O'Hara, vol. 1, London and New York: Routledge, 1999

Hudson, Pat and W.R. Lee (editors), *Women's Work and the Family Economy in Historical Perspective*, Manchester: Manchester University Press, 1990

Kooreman, Peter and Sophia Wunderink, *The Economics of Household Behaviour*, Basingstoke: Macmillan, and New York: St Martin's Press, 1996

Menchik, Paul L. (editor), *Household and Family Economics*, Boston: Kluwer, 1996

Nerlove, Marc, Assaf Razin and Efraim Sadka, *Household and Economy: Welfare Economics of Endogenous Fertility*, London and Boston: Academic Press, 1987

Saradamoni, K. (editor), *Finding the Household: Conceptual and Methodological Issues*, London and Newbury Park, California: Sage, 1992

This topic transcends the strict boundaries of economics and hence the texts suggested here are from the wider field of political economy. Some prominent themes that come under this umbrella term of "household as an economic agent" are "new home economics", "feminist political economy", "household labour", and "household production and national income".

Most of BECKER's works are relevant to the study of household economics, but it is *A Treatise on the Family* that is an essential reading. He provides a systematic analysis of the family based on a rational choice approach and tries to explain not only the determinants of divorce, family size and the like, but also the effects of changes in family composition and structure on inequality and economic growth. The enlarged edition of 1991, following the early edition of 1981, includes replies to earlier criticisms and some general comments in supplementary chapters. The work is open to criticisms on account of its neoclassical assumptions, but Becker certainly applies "rigorous economic reasoning to understanding the family" quite productively. thereby making it imperative for students and scholars to read it.

MENCHIK is a collection of essays and discussions by prominent economists in the area of household and family economics. While Taubman looks at both "altruistic" and "strategic" models in his explanation of intergenerational human capital transfers, Davies emphasizes "nonhuman" wealth transfers. Macunovich writes a comprehensive essay examining the theories and recent evidence on economic determinants of fertility. Her support for "relative income theory" resonates with the views of Easterlin, whose discussion follows her essay. In contrast, the next set of essays and discussions represent differing viewpoints on interpretation of trends in female labour market experience – while Polachek and Sibert focus on choice, Wolfe criticizes their lack of focus on constraints. Gravelle's essay and its discussion by Rosen tackle the issue of tax treatment of the family. Stafford discusses the "efficiency" approach and the "equity" approach in studying the early education of children. Hamermesh provides the third, mixed-model approach. The essays do not cover the entire area of household and family economics, but the strength of the volume lies in its comprehensive treatment of female earnings, education and human capital formation, births, deaths, and taxes.

An interest in household as an economic agent entails having some idea about the field of "new home economics" (NHE). GROSSBARD-SHECHTMAN's entry on this branch of economics is a good place for beginners. Apart from suggesting some essential readings in the field, it is a lucid, readable and concise description of the field. While accepting criticisms of some dubious assumptions made even by the prominent proponents (such as that of "constant preferences" and "decisions made by families"), the author appreciates the historical role and future potential of NHE in promoting research based on household economic dynamics. The entries on "household labour" by Rhoda Adelaide O'Hara & Philip Anthony O'Hara and on "household production and national income" by Therese Jefferson, in the same volume, are also helpful. An important work in the area of household production and national income accounting is Waring's *If Women Counted* (discussed fully in entry on Feminist economics).

Focusing upon the microeconomic behaviour of members of private households and their place in macroeconomic environment, the book by KOOREMAN & WUNDERINK is also important. It is similar to other works in the field in its use of the utility theory, but differs in its emphasis on the interaction among the household members. Rather than provide a comprehensive treatment of issues, the text chooses to provide introductions, deal with key concepts, and offer further guidance to reading. The text not only concerns itself with theoretical enterprises but applies them in empirical work, often using international comparative data. The introduction sketches out a general model of economic behaviour and defines concepts such as income, price, wage, and so on, used in the modelling. The first half of the book considers static models only, but the second half uses dynamic models. Some aspects of household economic behaviour studied are intra-household allocation of resources, institutional and social setting, effects of uncertainty, household production and consumption, its formation and dissolution, and investment in human capital. Wide coverage, interesting tables, insightful exercises, and a comprehensive bibliography make the work seem like a textbook.

In contrast, BRYANT explicitly writes a textbook on the neoclassical economics of family and the household. Its short introduction is strong in its discussion of the meaning of the most basic of terms – household and its economic organization. The book also deals with issues such as household

consumption and saving, work and leisure activities, human capital, fertility behaviour, and the economics of marriage and divorce. The analysis is in the form of formalized models of economic behaviour. Although limited by its exclusion of asymmetry of gender power relations within the household, the book is nevertheless an essential reading in the field.

Drawing insights from Marxism, feminism and psychoanalysis, the book by FRAAD, RESNICK & WOLFF offers an excellent examination of relationships between class, gender, and power grounding these in the arena of household. The "Marxist-feminist analysis of the household" given by the authors is later debated by some prominent feminist theorists. The book also has separate essays on a gendered description of economic reality in the Reagan–Bush years, and on anorexia. This stimulating and thought-provoking collection of essays is recommended to those with multidisciplinary interests.

The volume edited by ANDERSON, BECHHOFER & GERSHUNY is geographically limited in its coverage, but it might be useful for those interested in the study of "the social and political economy of the household" in the UK. Giving adequate attention to power differentials within the household, the contributors stress a sociologically informed understanding of its economic behaviour, and on the importance of integrating various research methods.

For those interested in studying the history of women's work and the family economy, avoiding the dominant masculine perspective, the edited volume by HUDSON & LEE is important. It is limited by its exclusive consideration of modern European situations, but the persistent striving of the contributors to appreciate the role of myriad dynamics including gender, class, race, the construction of knowledge, and the functioning of local, national and international economies in their study is commendable.

NERLOVE, RAZIN & SADKA draw inspiration from Becker in their discussion about the welfare economics of endogenous fertility. The book largely deals with the general equilibrium implications of endogenous fertility for many social issues of population policy. Particularly relevant for our purpose are the fourth and fifth chapters, dealing with the traditional theory of household behaviour and its extension to decisions about fertility. However, a high level of formalization makes it more accessible to those with a penchant for mathematics.

All the works cited above are concerned with the developed areas of the world. SARADAMONI is a good collection for someone interested in the issue of women and household in developing countries. It argues how a crosscultural perspective is required to study the relationship between household and the condition of women in Asian countries. The papers engage conceptual and methodological issues involved in the notion of "household" in research and data collections. It is a good starting point for those studying household as an economic agent in developing world.

Nitasha Kaul

See also Female employment, developing countries, Feminist economics

Human capital

Angrist, Joshua and Alan Krueger, "Does Compulsory School Attendance Affect Schooling and Earnings", *Quarterly Journal of Economics*, 106/4 (1991): 979–1014

Barro, Robert J. and Xavier Sala-i-Martin, *Economic Growth*, New York: McGraw Hill, 1995

Becker, Gary S., "A Theory of the Allocation of Time", *Economic Journal*, 75/299 (1965): 493–517

Becker, Gary S., *Human Capital: A Theoretical and Empirical Analysis with Special Reference to Education*, 3rd edition, Chicago: University of Chicago Press, 1993

Ben-Porath, Yoram, "The Production of Human Capital and the Life Cycle of Earnings", *Journal of Political Economy*, 75/4 part 1 (1967): 352–65

Betts, Julian, "Is There a Link between School Inputs and Earnings? Fresh Scrutiny of an Old Literature" in *Does Money Matter?*, edited by Gary Burtless, Washington, DC: Brookings Institution Press, 1996

Card, David and Alan B. Krueger, "Does School Quality Matter? Returns to Education and the Characteristics of Public Schools in the United States", *Journal of Political Economy*, 100/1 (1992): 1–40

Card, David, "Earnings, Schooling and Ability Revisited" in *Research in Labor Economics*, edited by Ronald Ehrenberg, Greenwich, Connecticut: Jai Press, 1995

Denison, Edward F., "Education, Economic Growth and Gaps in Information", *Journal of Political Economy*, 70/5, part 2 (1962): 124–28

Griliches, Zvi, "Estimating the Returns to Schooling: Some Econometric Problems", *Econometrica*, 45/1 (1977): 1–22

Grossman, Michael, "On the Concept of Health Capital and the Demand for Health", *Journal of Political Economy*, 80/2 (1972): 223–55

Haveman, Robert and Barbara Wolfe, "Schooling and Economic Well-Being: The Role of Nonmarket Effects", *Journal of Human Resources*, 19/3 (1984): 377–407

Juhn, Chinhui, Kevin M. Murphy and Brooks Pierce, "Wage Inequality and the Rise in Returns to Skill", *Journal of Political Economy*, 101/3 (1993): 410–42

Mincer, Jacob, *Schooling, Experience and Earnings*, New York: National Bureau of Economic Research, 1974

Schultz, Theodore W., "Investment in Human Capital", *American Economic Review*, 5/1 (1961): 1–17

Spence, Michael, "Job Market Signaling", *Quarterly Journal of Economics*, 87/3 (1973): 353–64

Strauss, John and Duncan Thomas, "Health, Nutrition and Economic Development", *Journal of Economic Literature*, 36/2 (1998): 766–817

Willis, Robert, "Wage Determinants: A Survey and Reinterpretation of Human Capital Earnings Functions" in *Handbook of Labor Economics* vol. 1, edited by Orley Ashenfelter and Richard Layard, Amsterdam: North Holland, 1986

Human capital may be defined as any investment that increases the market or nonmarket productivity of human beings. While this is a rather broad definition, this entry focuses on three of the most important dimensions of human capital. These include investments in education, on-the-job training, and health. An associated reason for this restricted focus is that almost all the theoretical and empirical literature deals primarily with these three investments. In fact, as human capital issues have traditionally been scrutinized by labour economists, the bulk of the work concentrates on investments in education and-on-the job training. The factors motivating human capital investments and the effects of these investments may be examined from a macro or a micro perspective. This entry provides a flavour of the work from both perspectives.

A fundamental issue that motivates the economic analysis of human capital is the extent to which it contributes to economic growth and output. DENISON lays out an analytical framework and uses it to identify the contribution of education to economic growth and national output. His efforts provided the catalyst for the study of investment in human beings.

However, rather than approaching the issue from a growth-theoretic perspective, subsequent work investigated investments in human capital from the perspective of the individual and the family. SCHULTZ's pioneering work introduces and discusses the concept of human capital and its role as an investment that raises the productivity of human beings, while BECKER (1965) provides the most comprehensive initial theoretical treatment of human capital issues. He examines the motivation for individual investments in education and on-the-job training and derives implications for labour supply, wage determination, and age-earnings profiles.

One of the most important elements that does not show up in this basic model is the role that may be played by the family in producing human capital. However, in subsequent work, BECKER (1993) clarifies and incorporates the role of the family in determining human capital investments.

BEN-PORATH provides an important extension of the Becker framework. Incremental investments in human capital are based on the marginal benefits and costs associated with these investments. His paper focuses on the changes in marginal benefits and marginal costs as individuals age in order to derive implications for the pattern of human capital investments over the lifecycle.

GROSSMAN extends the application of the human capital model to investments in health. Grossman views health as a capital stock that depends on individual investments in health improvement, time allocation, and exogenously determined health status. The benefits include increased productivity and increased time availability for productive activities and direct benefits due to reduced pain and suffering.

The papers discussed above argue that investments in human capital increase market and nonmarket productivity. SPENCE's signalling model provides a theoretical challenge to this conception and suggests that investments in human capital increase earnings not because of any productivity increases but because these investments signal the ability of workers to handle more complex tasks. Discriminating between the two approaches leads us to a consideration of the empirical literature.

MINCER's book is the pioneering empirical work in the human capital area. Mincer develops a simple empirical framework that captures the key ingredients of the human capital model. This empirical framework, widely termed the human capital earnings function, allows convenient estimation of the returns to education and on-the-job training. Mincer uses his framework to conduct a detailed analysis of how post school training affects the shape of earnings functions and the variance of earnings by age. This study has been extremely influential in producing numerous replica studies.

WILLIS provides a comprehensive review of the literature generated by Mincer's empirical framework. While Mincer's model represents a blend of theory and pragmatism, it has several shortcomings. In an important and widely cited paper GRILICHES identifies the major problems associated with the use of the Mincer framework. Foremost among these is the inability to distinguish between the role of human capital and ability in determining earnings. In recent years several ingenious methods have been used to examine this issue. These papers estimate the rate of return to human capital investments on the basis of the effect of an exogenous event on earnings and human capital. For example, ANGRIST & KRUEGER measure the effect of compulsory schooling laws on educational attainment and earnings, and then use the earnings–educational attainment ratio as a measure of returns to schooling that is not contaminated by ability bias.

A second problem with the Mincer framework is that it takes the level of human capital attained by an individual as exogenous, whereas the theory of human capital treats investments in human capital as endogenous. CARD provides a discussion of the issues and a review of empirical estimates that account for the bias that may be generated by this inconsistency.

The human capital earnings function is designed to estimate the effect of the quantity of human capital investments on earnings. CARD & KRUEGER extend the framework to examine the role of educational quality and report that there are substantial returns to investments in quality. However, their findings have been challenged. BETTS provides a comprehensive flavour of the debate and attempts to resolve the contentious issues raised by different authors.

A slew of recent research work in this area has focused on the temporal patterns in returns to human capital skills. JUHN, MURPHY & PIERCE provide a framework to analyse these changes and suggest that the increases in returns to human capital skills are driven by the increasing demand for skilled workers.

So far the discussion of the empirical work has focused on human capital investments in the form of education and on-the-job training. Although health is also viewed as a human capital investment, its link to labour market success has received considerably less attention. STRAUSS & THOMAS review the literature in this area and note that in recent years a small number of studies have documented the existence of a causal impact of health on wages and productivity, especially in low-income countries.

The empirical literature on returns to human capital investments focuses largely on market returns. The paper by HAVEMAN & WOLFE is one of the few that tries to calculate the nonmarket benefits associated with these investments. The authors identify a catalogue of nonmarket effects and then propose a procedure that may be used to estimate the returns associated with these effects.

In the early years of the human capital debate, Denison, Schultz, and other economists emphasized the contribution of human capital investments to economic growth. However, soon after, the link between human capital and growth was ignored as economists grew increasingly pessimistic about the insights offered by available growth theory. One of the benefits identified by Haveman & Wolfe is the effect that human capital investments may have in sparking technological change and hence contributing to economic growth. This insight has been incorporated in several new growth models. BARRO & SALA-I-MARTIN provide a comprehensive review of the theoretical and empirical contributions to this new growth theory that have once again brought human capital to the forefront of discussions on economic growth.

ARJUN SINGH BEDI

See also High performance work systems, Intellectual capital, Labour economics, Labour market, Wages

Human geography survey

Abler, Ronald, John S. Adams and Peter R. Gould, *Spatial Organization: The Geographer's View of the World*, Englewood Cliffs, New Jersey: Prentice Hall, 1971

Abler, Ronald, Melvin G. Marcus and Judy Olson (editors), *Geography's Inner Worlds: Pervasive Themes in Contemporary American Geography*, New Brunswick, New Jersey: Rutgers University Press, 1992

Ackerman, Edward A., *Geography as a Fundamental Research Discipline*, Chicago: Department of Geography, University of Chicago, 1958 (Research Paper 53)

Agnew, J.A., "The Territorial Trap: The Geographical Assumptions of International Relations Theory", *Review of International Political Economy*, 1 (1994): 53–80

Agnew, John, David N. Livingstone and Alisdair Rogers (editors), *Human Geography: An Essential Anthology*, Oxford and Cambridge, Massachusetts: Blackwell, 1996

Barnes, Trevor J. and James S. Duncan (editors), *Writing Worlds: Discourse, Text and Metaphor in the Representation of Landscape*, London and New York: Routledge, 1992

Barnes, Trevor J., *Logics of Dislocation: Models, Metaphor and Meanings of Economic Space*, New York and London: Guilford Press, 1996

Bell, Morag, Robin A. Butlin and Michael Heffernan (editors), *Geography and Imperialism, 1820–1940*, Manchester: Manchester University Press, 1995

Berry, Brian J.L. and Duane F. Marble (editors) *Spatial Analysis: A Reader in Statistical Geography*, Englewood Cliffs, New Jersey: Prentice Hall, 1968

Berry, Brian J.L. and John B. Parr, *Market Centers and Retail Location: Theory and Applications*, Englewood Cliffs, New Jersey: Prentice Hall, 1988

Blaikie, P.M., *The Political Economy of Soil Erosion*, London: Longman, 1985

Blaikie, Piers and Harold Brookfield (editors), *Land Degradation and Society*, London and New York: Methuen, 1987

Braun, Bruce and Noel Castree (editors), *Remaking Reality: Nature at the Millennium*, London and New York: Routledge, 1998

Brown, E. H. (editor), *Geography, Yesterday and Tomorrow*, Oxford and New York: Oxford University Press, 1980

Bunge, William, *Theoretical Geography*, Lund: Gleerup, 1962; 2nd edition 1966

Burton, I., "The Quantitative Revolution and Theoretical Geography", *Canadian Geographer*, 7 (1962): 151–62

Buttimer, Anne, *Geography and the Human Spirit*, Baltimore: Johns Hopkins University Press, 1993

Chisholm, Michael, *Human Geography: Evolution or Revolution?*, Harmondsworth and Baltimore: Penguin, 1975

Chisholm, Michael, *Rural Settlement and Land Use: An Essay in Location*, 3rd edition, London: Hutchinson, 1979

Chorley, Richard J. and Peter Haggett (editors), *Models in Geography*, London: Methuen, 1967

Chorley, Richard J. and Peter Haggett (editors), *Frontiers in Geographical Teaching*, 2nd edition, London: Methuen, 1970

Christaller, Walter, *Die zentralen Orte in Suddeutschland*, 1933; as *Central Places in Southern Germany*, Englewood Cliffs, New Jersey: Prentice Hall, 1966

Cliff, A.D. and J.K. Ord, *Spatial Autocorrelation*, London: Pion, 1973

Cliff, A.D. and J.K. Ord, *Spatial Processes: Models and Applications*, London: Pion, 1981

Cloke, Paul, Chris Philo and David Sadler, *Approaching Human Geography: An Introduction to Contemporary Theoretical Debates*, London: Chapman, and New York: Guilford Press, 1991

Cloke, Paul, Philip Crang and Mark Goodwin (editors), *Introducing Human Geographies*, London: Arnold, 1999

Cormack, Lesley, *Charting an Empire: Geography at the English Universities, 1580–1620*, Chicago: University of Chicago Press, 1997

Cox, Kevin R. and Reginald G. Golledge (editors), *Behavioral Problems in Geography: A Symposium*, Evanston, Illinois: Northwestern University, 1969; 2nd edition as *Behavioral Problems in Geography Revisited*, New York and London: Methuen, 1981

Darby, H. C., *Domesday England*, Cambridge and New York: Cambridge University Press, 1977

Davies, Wayne K.D. (editor), *The Conceptual Revolution in Geography*, London: University of London Press, and Totowa, New Jersey: Rowman and Littlefield, 1972

Dear, M., "The Postmodern Challenge: Reconstructing Human Geography", *Transactions of the Institute of British Geographers*, 13/3 (1988): 262–74

Dicken, Peter, *Global Shift: Transforming the World Economy*, 3rd edition, London: Chapman, and New York: Guilford Press, 1998

Dickinson, Robert E., *City Region and Regionalism: A Geographical Contribution to Human Ecology*, London: Routledge and Kegan Paul, and New York: Oxford University Press, 1947

Doel, Marens, *Poststructuralist Geographies: The Diabolical Art of Spatial Science*, Edinburgh: Edinburgh University Press, 1999

Dorling, Daniel, *A New Social Atlas of Britain*, Chichester and New York: Wiley, 1995

Dorling, Daniel and David Fairbairn, *Mapping: Ways of Representing the World*, Harlow: Longman, 1997

Duncan, James S. and David Ley (editors), *Place/Culture/Representation*, London and New York: Routledge, 1993

Duncan, James S. and Derek Gregory (editors), *Writes of Passage: Reading Travel Writing*, London and New York: Routledge, 1999

Freeman, T.W., *A Hundred Years of Geography*, London: Duckworth, 1961; Chicago: Aldine, 1963

Freeman, T.W., *A History of Modern British Geography*, London and New York: Longman, 1980

Gaile, Gary L. and Cort J. Willmott (editors), *Geography in America*, Columbus, Ohio: Merrill, 1989

Gaile, G. L. and Cort J. Willmott (editors), *American Geography at the Millennium*, New York: Oxford University Press, 2000

Giddens, Anthony, *Studies in Social and Political Theory*, London: Hutchinson, and New York: Basic Books, 1977

Giddens, Anthony, *The Constitution of Society: Outline of the Theory of Structuration*, Cambridge: Polity Press, and Berkeley: University of California Press, 1984

Glacken, Clarence J., *Traces on the Rhodian Shore: Nature and Culture in Western Thought from Ancient Times until the End of the Eighteenth Century*, Berkeley: University of California Press, 1967

Gregory, Derek, *Ideology, Science and Human Geography*, London: Hutchinson, 1978; New York: St Martin's Press, 1979

Gregory, Derek and John Urry (editors), *Social Relations and Spatial Structures*, Basingstoke: Macmillan, and New York: St Martin's Press, 1985

Gregory, Derek, *Geographical Imaginations*, Oxford and Cambridge, Massachusetts: Blackwell, 1994

Guelke, Leonard, *Historical Understanding in Geography: An Idealist Approach*, Cambridge and New York: Cambridge University Press, 1982

Hägerstrand, Torsten, *Innovation Diffusion as a Spatial Process*, Chicago: University of Chicago Press, 1967

Hägerstrand, T., "Diorama, Path and Project", *Tijdschrift voor Economische en Sociale Geografie*, 73/6 (1982): 323–39

Haggett, Peter, *Locational Analysis in Human Geography*, London: Arnold, and New York: St Martin's, 1965; 2nd edition, with Andrew D. Cliff and Allan Frey, New York: Wiley, 1977

Haggett, Peter, *Geography: A Modern Synthesis*, 3rd edition, New York: Harper and Row, 1983

Haining, R.P. *Spatial Data Analysis in the Social and Environmental Sciences*, Cambridge and New York: Cambridge University Press, 1990

Hanson, S. "Isms and Schisms: Healing the Rift Between the Nature-society and Space-society Traditions in Human Geography", *Annals of the Association of American Geographers*, 89/1 (1999): 133–43

Harley, J.B., "Deconstructing the Map", *Cartographica*, 26 (1989): 1–20

Hart, J.F., "The Highest Form of the Geographer's Art", *Annals of the Association of American Geographers*, 72 (1982): 1–29

Hartshorne, Richard, *The Nature of Geography: A Critical Survey of Current Thought in the Light of the Past*, Lancaster, Pennsylvania: Association of American Geographers, 1939

Harvey, David, *Explanation in Geography*, London: Arnold, 1969; New York: St Martin's Press, 1970

Harvey, David, *Social Justice and the City*, London: Arnold, and Baltimore: Johns Hopkins University Press, 1973

Harvey, David, *The Limits to Capital*, Oxford: Blackwell, and Chicago: University of Chicago Press, 1982

Harvey, David, *Consciousness and the Urban Experience: Studies in the History and Theory of Capitalist Urbanization*, Oxford: Blackwell, and Baltimore: Johns Hopkins University Press, 1985

Harvey, David, *The Urbanization of Capital: Studies in the History and Theory of Capitalist Urbanization*, Oxford: Blackwell, 1985

Harvey, David, *The Condition of Postmodernity: An Enquiry into the Origins of Cultural Change*, Oxford and Cambridge, Massachusetts: Blackwell, 1989

Harvey, David, *Justice, Nature and the Geography of Difference*, Oxford and Cambridge, Massachusetts: Blackwell, 1996

Holt-Jensen, Arild, *Geography: History and Concepts: A Student's Guide*, 3rd edition, London: Sage, 1999

Humboldt, Alexander von, *Cosmos: A Sketch of a Physical Description of the Universe*, introduction by Michael Dettelbach, Baltimore: Johns Hopkins University Press, 1997– (German edition, 5 vols, 1845–62)

James, P.E. and C.F. Jones (editors), *American Geography: Inventory and Prospect*, Syracuse, New York: Syracuse University Press, 1954

Johnston, R.J., *Urban Residential Patterns: An Introductory Review*, London: Bell, 1971; New York: Praeger, 1972

Johnston R.J. and P. Claval (editors), *Geography since the Second World War: An International Survey*, London: Croom Helm, and Totowa, New Jersey: Barnes and Noble, 1984

Johnston, R.J. (editor), *The Future of Geography*, London and New York: Methuen, 1985

Johnston, R.J., *Nature, State and Economy: A Political Economy of the Environment*, Chichester and New York: Wiley, 1996

Johnston, R.J., Peter J. Taylor and Michael J. Watts (editors), *Geographies of Global Change: Remapping the World in the Late Twentieth Century*, Oxford and Cambridge, Massachusetts: Blackwell, 1995

Johnston, R.J., *Geography and Geographers: Anglo-American Human Geography since 1945*, 5th edition, London and New York: Arnold, 1997

Johnston, R.J., D. Gregory, G. Pratt and M. J. Watts (editors), *The Dictionary of Human Geography*, 4th edition, Oxford: Blackwell, 2000

King, Gary, *A Solution to the Ecological Inference Problem: Reconstructing Individual Behavior from Aggregate Data*, Princeton, New Jersey: Princeton University Press, 1997

Kobayashi, Audrey and Suzanne MacKenzie (editors), *Remaking Human Geography*, Boston: Unwin Hyman, 1989

Kuhn, Thomas S., *The Structure of Scientific Revolutions*, 2nd edition, Chicago: University of Chicago Press, 1970

Lee, Roger and Jane Wills (editors), *Geographies of Economies*, London and New York: Arnold, 1997

Lewis, G. M., "The Origins of Cartography" in *The History of Cartography*, vol 1: *Cartography in Prehistoric, Ancient and Medieval Europe and the Mediterranean*, edited by J.B. Harley and David Woodward, Chicago: University of Chicago Press, 1987

Ley, David and Marwyn S. Samuels (editors), *Humanistic Geography: Prospects and Problems*, Chicago: Maaroufa Press, and London: Croom Helm, 1978

Liverman, D.M., "Geography and the Global Environment", *Annals of the Association of American Geographers*, 89/1 (1999): 107–20

Livingstone, David N., *The Geographical Tradition: Episodes in the History of a Contested Enterprise*, Oxford and Cambridge, Massachusetts: Blackwell, 1993

Longley, Paul A. and Michael Batty (editors), *Spatial Analysis: Modelling in a GIS Environment*, Cambridge: GeoInformation International, 1996

Longley, Paul A., S.M. Brooks, R. McDonnell and B. Macmillan (editors), *Geocomputation: A Primer*, Chichester and New York: Wiley, 1998

Longley, Paul A. and Graham Clarke (editors), *GIS for Business and Service Planning*, Cambridge: GeoInformation International, and New York: Wiley, 1995

Longley, Paul A., M.F. Goodchild, D.J. Maguire, and D.W. Rhind (editors), *Geographical Information Systems*, 2 vols, New York: Wiley, 1999

McDowell, L., "Space, Place and Gender Relations, Part 1: Feminist Empiricism and the Geography of Social Relations", *Progress in Human Geography*, 17/2 (1993a): 157–79

McDowell, L., "Space, Place and Gender Relations, Part 2: Identity, Difference, Feminist Geometries and Geographies", *Progress in Human Geography*, 17/3 (1993b): 305–18

McDowell, L., "Understanding Diversity: The Problem of/for 'Theory'" in *Geographies of Global Change: Remapping the World in the Late Twentieth Century*, edited by R.J. Johnston, Peter J. Taylor and Michael J. Watts, Oxford and Cambridge, Massachusetts: Blackwell, 1995

Macmillan, Bill (editor), *Remodelling Geography*, Oxford: Blackwell, 1989

Martin, Geoffrey J. and Preston E. James, *All Possible Worlds: A History of Geographical Ideas*, 3rd edition, New York and Chichester: Wiley, 1993

Martin, R., "The New 'Geographical Turn' in Economics: Some Critical Reflections", *Cambridge Journal of Economics*, 23/1 (1999): 65–91

Massey, Doreen and Richard Meegan, *The Anatomy of Job Loss*, London and New York: Methuen, 1982

Massey, Doreen, *Spatial Divisions of Labour: Social Structures and the Geography of Production*, London: Macmillan, and New York: Methuen, 1984

Massey, Doreen, John Allen and Philip Sarre (editors), *Human Geography Today*, Cambridge: Polity Press, and Malden, Massachusetts: Blackwell, 1999

National Research Council, *Rediscovering Geography: New Relevance for Science and Society*, Washington, DC: National Research Council, 1999

Olsson, Gunnar, *Birds in Egg*, London: Pion, 1980

Openshaw, S., *The Modifiable Areal Unit Problem*, Norwich: Geo, 1984

Openshaw, Stan and Christine Openshaw, *Artificial Intelligence in Geography*, Chichester: Wiley, 1997

O'Riordan, T., *Perspectives on Resource Management*, London: Pion, 1971

O'Riordan, T., *Environmentalism*, 2nd edition, London: Pion, 1981

Ó Tuathail, Gearóid, *Critical Geopolitics: The Politics of Writing Global Space*, London: Routledge, and Minneapolis: University of Minnesota Press, 1996

Peet, Richard (editor), *Radical Geography: Alternative Viewpoints on Contemporary Social Issues*, London: Methuen, and Chicago: Maaroufa, 1977

Peet, Richard, *Modern Geographical Thought*, Oxford and Malden, Massachusetts: Blackwell, 1998

Pickles, John (editor), *Ground Truth: The Social Implications of Geographic Information Systems*, New York: Guilford Press, 1995

Pile, Steve, *The Body and the City: Psychoanalysis, Space and Subjectivity*, London and New York: Routledge, 1996

Pred, Allan, *Making Histories and Constructing Human Geographies: The Local Transformation of Practice, Power Relations and Consciousness*, Boulder, Colorado: Westview Press, 1990

Rhoads, Bruce L. and Colin E. Thorn (editors), *The Scientific Nature of Geomorphology*, New York and Chichester: Wiley, 1996

Ritter, Carl, *Die Erdkunde*, 20 vols, Berlin: Reimer, 1832–59

Rose, Gillian, *Feminism and Geography: The Limits of Geographical Knowledge*, Cambridge: Polity Press, and Minneapolis: University of Minnesota Press, 1993

Sack, Robert David, *Human Territoriality: Its Theory and History*, Cambridge and New York: Cambridge University Press, 1986

Sack, Robert David, *Homo Geographicus: A Framework for Action, Awareness, and Moral Concern*, Baltimore: Johns Hopkins University Press, 1997

Said, Edward W., *Orientalism*, New York: Pantheon, and London: Routledge, 1978; with new afterword, New York: Vintage, 1994, Harmondsworth: Penguin, 1995

Sauer, Carl Ortwin, *Agricultural Origins and Dispersals*, New York: American Geographical Society, 1952

Sayer, Andrew, *Method in Social Science: A Realist Approach*, London: Hutchinson, 1984; 2nd edition, London: Routledge, 1992

Schaefer, F.K., "Exceptionalism in Geography: A Methodological Examination", *Annals of the Association of American Geographers*, 43 (1953): 226–49

Schuurman, N., "An Interview with Michael Goodchild", *Environment and Planning D: Society and Space*, 17/1 (1999): 3–16

Sheppard, E., "Dissenting from Spatial Analysis", *Urban Geography* 16/4 (1995): 283–303

Simmons, I.G., *Humanity and Environment: A Cultural Ecology*, Harlow: Addison Wesley Longman, 1997

Smith, David M., *Industrial Location: An Economic Geographical Analysis*, 2nd edition, New York and Chichester: Wiley, 1981

Smith, David M., *Geography and Social Justice*, Oxford and Cambridge: Massachusetts: Blackwell, 1994

Soja, Edward W., *Postmodern Geographies: The Reassertion of Space in Critical Social Theory*, London: Verso, 1989

Stamp, L.D., *Applied Geography*, Harmondsworth: Penguin, 1960

Stoddart, D.R., *On Geography and its History*, Oxford and New York: Blackwell, 1986

Taylor, P.J., "A Materialist Framework for Political Geography", *Transactions of the Institute of British Geographers*, 7/1 (1982): 15–34

Taylor, P.J., "Places, Spaces and Macy's: Place-space Tensions in the Political Geography of Modernities", *Progress in Human Geography*, 23/1 (1999), 7–26

Taylor, Thomas Griffith (editor), *Geography in the Twentieth Century: A Study of Growth, Fields, Techniques, Aims and Trends*, 3rd edition, New York: Philosophical Library, 1957

Thrift, N.J., "On the Determination of Social Action in Space and Time", *Environment and Planning D: Society and Space*, 1/1 (1983): 23–67

Thrift, Nigel J., *Spatial Formations*, London and Thousand Oaks, California: Sage, 1996

Thünen, Johann Heinrich von, *Isolated State*, edited by Peter Hall, Oxford and New York: Pergamon Press, 1966 (German edition 1926)

Turner, B.L. *et al.* (editors), *The Earth as Transformed by Human Action: Global and Regional Changes in the Biosphere over the Last 300 Years*, Cambridge and New York: Cambridge University Press, 1990

Unwin, Tim, *The Place of Geography*, Harlow: Longman, 1992

Whatmore, S., "Hybrid Geographies: Rethinking the 'Human' in Human Geography" in *Human Geography Today*, edited by Doreen Massey, John Allen and Philip Sarre, Cambridge: Polity Press, and Malden, Massachusetts: Blackwell, 1999

Women and Geography Study Group of the Institute of British Geographers, *Geography and Gender: An Introduction to Feminist Geography*, London: Hutchinson, 1984

Wooldridge, S.W., *The Geographer as Scientist: Essays on the Scope and Nature of Geography*, London and New York: Nelson, 1956

Geography as an academic discipline focuses on analysing and providing explanatory accounts for the nature and implications of the material character of the earth's surface and its use by people and societies. Its key concepts are space, place, and environment, each studied at a variety of scales.

Histories of geography

A number of histories of geography are available – including those by HOLT-JENSEN, MARTIN & JAMES, and UNWIN. All trace the discipline back well beyond its academic institutionalization in the late 19th century, identifying its roots in classical Greece, although concentrating upon the 20th century. HOLT-JENSEN, for example, discusses the writings of Herodotus, Eratosthenes, Ptolemy, and Strabo, which covered three main types of work – what is now known as *cartography* (although covering issues such as the dimensions of the earth as well as map-making); what some call *chorology*, the provision of detailed descriptions of particular areas, their environments and peoples; and *the inter-relationships among peoples and environments*. All remain within the core of the modern discipline, although cartography is now practised as a separate science.

During the Middle Ages geography was practised and studied at various universities, although there were no specific degree programmes in the subject, as CORMACK indicates for Cambridge and Oxford during the period 1580–1620. Its main themes, as in classical times, included cartography (seen as part of applied mathematics) and chorology, and the skills and knowledge provided by these two were crucial to the development of England as an emergent world power: geography had clearly defined commercial, diplomatic and military functions. The development of cartography is covered in the major multi-volume history of cartography project (LEWIS).

GLACKEN produced the most detailed study of writing about people-environment interactions, from classical times until the eighteenth century. He identified three main questions addressed in such writings: (a) "Was the earth purposefully created for human habitation?"; (b) "Has the nature of the earth influenced the moulding of individual characteristics and of human cultures?", and (c) "In what manner have people changed the environment during their long tenure of the earth?". He identified three main themes: that the earth was designed for human occupation, as the highest species; that all life adapts to its environments; and that humans worked together with God to improve the earth for their own use.

During the 19th century the third of these classical traditions – the interrelationships among peoples and environments – was developed and promoted as a foundation for a separate academic discipline, largely through the stimulation of two German scholars. HUMBOLDT assembled a great deal of material from his Latin American and other travels, and drew on a wide range of what are now known as separate sciences, to portray the nature of different areas in terms of the connections between organic life and its environment. RITTER similarly collated information about different places, relying much more on secondary sources than on his own field experience, unlike Humboldt; his writings were teleological, identifying an underlying purpose to the "laws of nature". These views were later challenged by Darwinism, which had a considerable effect on the emerging field of geography, as described by STODDART.

The case for geography as an academic discipline was promoted by National Geographical Societies, most of them founded during the early 19th century as STODDART and BELL, BUTLIN & HEFFERNAN illustrate. These societies attracted the interest of a range of people, both lay and scientific. Instruction in geography was needed, they argued, because of the need for knowledge about various parts of the world by those involved in the imperialism project (such as traders, diplomats, and military strategists), and such knowledge should also be imparted in the schools, as part of the creation of an aware citizenry. Universal education required teachers trained in university geography departments. (On the role of the societies in the UK, see BROWN and FREEMAN.)

As the discipline became established in the universities, its practitioners sought a scientific rationale for themselves within the academic division of labour. Various options were explored around the people-environment symbiosis, including *environmental determinism*, which in its extreme forms implied that human characteristics and behavioural traits were the creatures of their environments, and *possibilism*, which argued that individuals controlled their own destinies through mastery of their environments. Neither was widely accepted for long, and by the end of the 1930s geographers had settled for a definition of their discipline, adumbrated in particular by HARTSHORNE and based on a wide reading of continental European literature, which focused on the identification, description and accounts of the nature of *regions*, separate areas on the earth's surface with unique characteristics based on the interactions among people and environments. Hartshorne defined geography's task as to "provide accurate, orderly and rational description and interpretation of the variable character of the Earth surface" by bringing together the findings from a wide range of systematic studies (by geographers and others). Geography was thus an integrating discipline, akin to history: history integrated material by time periods whereas geography integrated by area.

Many histories of geography are organized chronologically, with the implication that the discipline has evolved in a linear sequence towards its present condition. Others argue that the practice of geography, like most other disciplines, is strongly influenced by external circumstances, which vary over time and from place to place. This is the main theme of LIVINGSTONE's book. For him, geography has no "essential core . . . independent of historical circumstances"; instead it means different things to different people in different places, and what geographers do is continually being renegotiated, both among themselves and with influential external bodies – both through the flow of ideas and through the provision of resources and other support. His eight chapters deal with "episodes in the history of a contested tradition" from the age of discovery to the present, illustrating his argument that the best way to understand what geographers have done in particular places and periods is through appreciation of the "social and intellectual environments" within which they were practising.

Livingstone's argument does not imply an absence of continuity in the discipline, with no common threads to its studies. Throughout its history, both before and after its institutionalization as an academic discipline, certain concepts have remained central to geographers' concerns – environment, space, place, region, and scale, for example: geographers have always explored the understanding of spatial variations, of the human and environmental mosaics that comprise the great diversity of the earth and its peoples. BUTTIMER suggests that they have employed four major metaphors in this, with their relative popularity waxing and waning: the *mosaic* metaphor emphasizes difference and how it is portrayed; the *machine* metaphor focuses on explanation of that mosaic through general processes; the *organism* metaphor, which presents the world and its parts as unified wholes; and the *arena* metaphor, which stresses contextual accounts.

These common threads reflect interaction among geographers – much of the development of geography in the UK and North America during the early 20th century was built on foundations laid down in Germany and France, for example. But there were considerable local variations. In Britain, for instance, a strong tradition of *historical geography* was established from the 1930s on, led by DARBY (himself much influenced by contemporary historians), and whose main task was the reconstruction of past geographies – as in his multivolume work on the *Domesday Book* – from which changes could be inferred. Contemporaneously, in the US there was a strong tradition in *cultural geography*, led by SAUER at the University of California, Berkeley; he was influenced by anthropologists and focused on responses to the physical environment that lead to the production of cultural landscapes, notably in Latin America.

As the discipline slowly expanded, largely in response to student demand for its courses, so geographers branched out into a range of specialisms, both topical (systematic geographies) and synthetic (regional geographies). Reviews produced in the middle of the 20th century – notably those edited by TAYLOR and by JAMES and JONES – illustrate the range of concerns. But the continuing focus was the definition and description of regions: regional geography was promoted, in the UK (as by WOOLDRIDGE) as well as in North America, as what a later author (HART) termed "the highest form of the geographer's art".

This hegemony of the region began to decline during the 1950s, although the term and concept remain in common use – in part to claim continuity between the "old" and the "new", so that those promoting change in disciplinary practices could argue that what was occurring was evolution not revolution (as discussed in CHISHOLM's 1975 book). Geography in the various language domains began to follow separate, somewhat isolated, paths at about that time, as the essays in JOHNSTON & CLAVAL illustrate. Anglo-American human geography became a very vibrant discipline, with a rapid increase in its number of practitioners and the exploration of a great variety of approaches to studying the discipline's basic subject matter, as well as many additional ones too – as illustrated by the five editions of JOHNSTON's (1997) comprehensive survey published over a 20-year period.

Science and planning

The origins of the changes that gathered pace in the 1950s and 1960s, were in part, as FREEMAN argued in his 1961 book, disillusion – especially among recent recruits to the discipline – with its established practices, but also, and importantly so, responses to changes in the milieux within which geography was practised. *Science* and *planning* were keywords of the times: scientific methods were promoted as the model for geographers to follow (and also to their contemporaries in the burgeoning social sciences – notably economics, political science, and sociology) and research results were to be used for the improvement of society – indeed some argued that the conduct of research should be restructured to focus on its relevance. The case for change was carried to geographers in a variety of ways: in the US, for example, ACKERMAN argued that geographers had not been very effective during World War II and that they needed to adopt the more rigorous approaches and methods of the sciences if they were to be influential; in

the UK, DICKINSON argued for use of the regional concept as a fundamental tool in the conduct of the emerging field of urban and regional (town and country) planning. Geography was to be scientific and useful – although some emphasized one of those roles much more than the other (as in STAMP's case for an *applied geography*).

The argument for a "scientific approach" to geography had two main strands. The first was that geography should abandon its concern with describing and accounting for the unique, for the characteristics of individual regions, and instead focus attention on the search for laws, particularly spatial laws. This was a *conceptual revolution*, in DAVIES's terms, requiring geographers to develop an acquaintance with the philosophy of science as a foundation for a rigorous approach to law making: SCHAEFER's paper is seen by many as an early seminal contribution to this shift, which was carried forward by BUNGE's arguments for *Theoretical Geography*; HARVEY (1969) presented the philosophical case in detail. The second was a concern with measurement, as part of the precision associated with science: the inexactitudes of language were to be replaced by the certainties of numbers and equations. This was a *quantitative revolution*, as described by BURTON, and involved geographers developing methods for spatial analysis, on which BERRY & MARBLE produced the first compilation of methods for analysing point, line, area and flow patterns.

As geographers explored the philosophies and methods of other disciplines so they also came into contact with their subject matter and identified the potential for a "spatial approach" to a wide range of topics previously not considered by geographers. Human geography was repackaged as "spatial science" or "locational analysis". At the same time, while interest in both theory and methods (especially quantitative methods) provided the links among geographers (including physical geographers) the discipline fragmented into an increasingly wide range of subdisciplinary specialisms such as urban geography, which was the focus of much of the innovative work at the time.

The combination of methodological commonality and systemic separateness was well illustrated by two seminal collections of essays edited by CHORLEY and HAGGETT, which synthesized and stimulated interest in the new work: *Models in Geography*, in particular, was extremely influential, being repackaged in a number of ways for use as a teaching texts. It had five main parts, covering the role of models, models of physical systems, models of socioeconomic systems, models of mixed systems, and information models.

Location theory

Although the widespread adoption of quantitative methods attracted much attention at the time, and became the focus of debate among those for and against the changes, in the longer term the concern with theory had most impact. *Location theory* became the focus, with geographers concerned to identify the major factors that determine the spatial distributions of economic (and later social) activities. Several separate areas of interest were explored, most getting their major stimuli from outside the discipline. Regarding agricultural land use, for example, CHISHOLM and others developed the ideas of a 19th-century German landowner (VON THÜNEN) regarding the best location for different agricultural activities relative to a market centre; studies of the location of manufacturing industries were influenced by a range of works by economists (synthesized by SMITH). The locations of market centres and shopping facilities were investigated in the context of the innovative work by a German geographer, CHRISTALLER, on central place theory (the large corpus of studies is reviewed in BERRY & PARR), and residential patterns within cities were pursued in the light of the ideas derived from American sociologists (as reviewed in JOHNSTON's 1971 book). Flow patterns were studied in the context of theories based on the Newtonian gravity model (on which see OLSSON 1965) and the diffusion of ideas and people through models developed by a Swedish geographer (HÄGERSTRAND) in his 1968 book. In all of this work, distance was presented as the key influence – as the variable which, because of the time and costs involved in movement, determined what was done where; *human geography's role within the social sciences was as a "discipline in distance" and its rationale was the search for spatial order.*

Whereas various systematic specialisms grew and adopted their own paradigms (in industrial geography and urban geography, for example), some authors sought to integrate their work in overarching statements about the nature of the "new geography". HAGGETT's (1965) *Locational Analysis in Human Geography* was one of the most influential: he suggested that the structure of a functional region could be decomposed into five (six in the second edition) key elements: flows; networks (along which the flows moved); nodes; hierarchies (of nodes); surfaces (the areas between the networks and nodes); and diffusion of changes (along the networks, down the hierarchies, and across the surfaces). He summarized knowledge on each of these, following those chapters with a section on methods – moving from what we know to how we find out. A contemporary volume – ABLER, ADAMS & GOULD's *Spatial Organization* – took the opposite path, presenting methods first as the key to appreciating what geographers do. HAGGETT (1983) later sought a wider synthesis of both human and physical geography, in a widely used, innovative introductory text.

Much of the early work in the locational analysis/spatial science mould was based on economic models of behaviour: people make least-cost decisions, which, given the priority that geographers accorded to the spatial variable, mean "least travel-cost decisions". This relatively myopic view was extended later by more widely based analyses of decision making (on where to site a factory, where to move home to, where to attend university, and so forth), which used data on the decision-making processes themselves rather than just mapping and analysing the results of those decisions. This work, which became known as behavioural geography, was heralded in a book of original essays edited by COX & GOLLEDGE. Its overall rationale remained that of seeking spatial order, but it was less restricted in the factors that it considered as potential contributors to that order and so less concerned to test models that suggested relatively simple spatial arrangements.

Humanistic geography

Despite the common interests in methods and in spatial order, and some successful syntheses of wide-ranging materials,

human geography fragmented very much at this time into a number of separate subfields, most of them defined by what they studied – such as economic geography (with further subdivisions such as agricultural geography and industrial geography), transport geography, social geography (alongside which there were separate concerns with population geography and medical geography), political geography (which was largely separate from electoral geography), urban geography, rural geography, historical geography, and development geography. These divisions were institutionalized within the leading academic bodies such as the Institute of British Geographers (IBG) and the Association of American Geographers (AAG), both of which created specialist subgroups that held their own conferences as well as sessions within the larger bodies' main conferences: those in the AAG, for example, were used as the chapter structure for GAILE & WILLMOTT's two compendia surveying the contemporary discipline. Most of these fields (not all of which were based on systematic specialisms: the largest group within the IBG for several years was the Quantitative Methods Study Group) are associated with separate academic journals for the publication of research papers. As the discipline expanded, so it fragmented into many areas of specialized knowledge, with few human geographers treating the discipline as a whole.

Despite the very substantial volume of work undertaken in the locational analysis/spatial science mould, and the claims of its protagonists that this represented "the future" for geography, this broad approach never achieved hegemony over the discipline that its protagonists sought and there was no "revolution" in the sense portrayed by KUHN for the physical sciences, and whose model several geographers adopted at the time. It soon became the focus of critiques, from two main sources. The first was largely based within the discipline's continuing stream of work in historical and cultural geography, whose practitioners declined to join the bandwagon of the "quantitative and theoretical revolutions". They argued, as did GUELKE for example, that the models adopted by location theorists reduced all decision making to a financial calculus and took no account of the role of culture, values and other criteria in the conduct of human life: spatial science was based on a pallid model of human nature. The case was made for the exploration of alternative philosophies to the *positivism* advanced by Harvey and others, and these became bracketed under the umbrella term of *humanistic geography* (exemplified by the book edited by LEY and SAMUELS), whose goal was to explore the roles of human agency, consciousness and creativity in landscape creation and which emphasised the particular rather than the general.

A major difference between spatial science and humanistic geography was in their goals. For most spatial scientists, the ambition was to uncover general laws of spatial behaviour that could be incorporated in location theories that had strong predictive powers and so could be applied in creating a better society through more efficient spatial structures. Their scientific goal was *explanation*, causal statements of the form "if A then B". Humanistic geographers denied that such statements could be produced with regard to human behaviour: the best that could be achieved was *understanding*, an appreciation of spatial structures and the events involved in their production, but no more, because people have "free will" and are not subject to deterministic laws of behaviour – hence preventing prediction.

Radical geography

Whereas the roots for humanistic geography lay in what had been some of the discipline's traditional practices, those for the second critique were mainly outside it, in other social sciences and in contemporary developments outside academia, to which it responded. The late 1960s were a period of considerable social unrest, with concerns about inequalities and discrimination and conflicts generated by the Cold War (notably in Vietnam). There was a growing feeling that capitalism was failing and should be replaced. Theoretical justifications for this view were based on a "rediscovery" of Marxism among Western intellectuals, offering both a diagnosis of the current condition and a way forward to a better society. By the early 1970s some geographers were actively exploring this, led by HARVEY's 1973 book *Social Justice and the City*, which mounted a sustained attack on spatial science and its perceived failings. A Marxist or *radical geography* was heralded, which had an applied goal very different from that advanced by location theorists (as described in PEET's 1977 book). Marx's ideas were adapted for the study of spatial structures, of patterns of development and underdevelopment at a variety of scales – in which HARVEY's 1982 book was at the fore.

These two critiques sought to take geography in very different directions, towards a form of voluntarism in the first case and structural determinism in the second. Although many sympathized with their identification of the shortcomings of the locational analysis approach, the articulation of "new paradigms" based on the offered alternatives was not straightforward: the atheoretical nature of some humanistic geography was unattractive, for example, as was the derogation of human agency (and the political programme) associated with the Marxian enterprise (its explanations allowed for no more variation in human decision-making than did those of some location theories). The need for a "middle way", which took into account both the constraints of socioeconomic structures (general and local) and the degrees of freedom for individual decision-making ("free will") of human agency, was the focus of GREGORY's (1978) book. His later work built on that, much influenced by the work of GIDDENS on *structuration theory*. This identifies a dialectic relationship between human agency and social structures, with each involved in the continual reproduction of the other: people are "made" by their societies, which both constrain and enable their actions, and at the same time are involved in remaking their societies.

This dialectic process involved in structuration is necessarily spatially constrained, an argument accepted by Giddens in the context of HÄGERSTRAND's ideas regarding *time geography* (as in his 1982 paper). Individuals pursue projects that involve movement between places, with most journeys starting and ending at the same point – their homes. The paths followed are constrained in three ways. First, there are capability constraints: there are physical limits to journeys based on resources and available transport modes, for example, so that only certain places are accessible. Secondly, there are coupling constraints: some places can only be visited at particular times (a shop's opening hours, for example). Finally there are authority constraints: some places are "off-limits" for certain

people, as with the rigid territorialization under *apartheid* in South Africa. Together these limit where people can go, what they can do, who they will meet, and so forth: their face-to-face contacts are constrained by their time geography, which influences the dialectic process involved in ongoing structuration processes. To the extent that interaction is constrained by co-presence, so people's contacts with, and their contributions to, social structures are limited by the spatial horizons imposed by their time geographies.

This insertion of a geographical component to structuration theory led THRIFT to identify two separate (though far from independent) influences on individuals. *Compositional approaches* associate particular traits and behaviour patterns with people's positions within a social structure – such as their class position, which Marxist theory identifies as key. *Contextual approaches*, on the other hand, associate those traits and patterns not with what people are but rather with where they are and where they come from. If, as time geography argues, people do not interact with an entire social structure but rather with one or a few local components of it only, then there may be significant differences in how the structuration processes proceed: slight variations between places – in interpretations of class positions and how they should be represented in voting for different political parties, for example – may become deeply ingrained in local cultures (what GREGORY in 1978 called regional social formations), and indeed exaggerated over time.

These various strands of work sought to move geographers away from the search for spatial order based on universally-applicable laws of behaviour and back towards appreciation of local (regional) variation and difference, albeit within the context of "general forces". The humanistic geography movement waned somewhat, but the Marxist strand remained strong – with HARVEY a leading figure, as in his two 1985 books exploring the potential for a Marxist-based theory of urbanization. Other geographers sought alternative formulations that embraced the dialectic interaction of structure and agency without necessarily embracing Marxism. SAYER's exploration of the potential of *realist* philosophies (within which some were able to locate Marxist approaches) was very influential. This separates out three levels: the deepest is that of the invariant structures or processes; at the intermediate level there are the mechanisms that make those processes operate; and at the highest level there are the outcomes of those mechanisms – these form the *domain of the real*, the *domain of the actual* and the *domain of the empirical* respectively. In the physical sciences, for example, the gravity model is located in the domain of the real – it is an invariant law; it comes into effect in the domain of the actual, when a relevant event occurs (as with an item being dropped); and the consequence of that event is observed in the domain of the empirical – we can never see the gravity model; we can only observe outcomes that are consistent with its operation. In a capitalist economy, the laws of supply and demand are in the domain of the real; they are acted upon in the domain of the actual, when a decision is made (whether to close a factory because it is unprofitable and move its operations to where labour is cheaper, for example, or to change the nature of its operations – and perhaps that of its workforce: such strategies were discussed in an influential book by MASSEY & MEEGAN); and the outcome is observed in the domain of the empirical – the factory closure and its impact on the people directly and indirectly affected.

Central to Sayer's arguments for a realist approach was the use of the term explanation: an event could be explained (i.e. its cause could be identified) through the processes and the mechanisms involved in its production. But the realist search for an explanation differed from the positivist: the latter identified an explanation through repeated observation whereas in realism an explanation may be singular – the conditions that brought it about need never recur. In some situations there may be *constant conjunctions*, with the same circumstances recurring and producing the same outcomes. (The paradigm case is the laboratory experiment, which replicates the circumstances many times over, with consistent results.) Such constant conjunctions may be typical of some of the physical sciences, but not the social sciences. In the latter, circumstances are always changing, as structuration proceeds and people learn and alter their behaviour: if the circumstances within which people act change, different events and outcomes will occur, even if the underlying processes remain invariant. (Some argue that this is the case in environmental sciences too; because of the complexity of environmental systems, the same circumstances are never replicated in "reality" rather than the laboratory – as essays in RHOADS & THORN illustrate.) The absence of constant conjunctions – in both time and space, because places differ as well as periods – means that explanations can only be identified through the study of individual cases – what Sayer terms *intensive research*. Studies of aggregates – of population groups, for example, as in much statistical analysis in the behavioural geography mould: *extensive research* in Sayer's terminology – can suggest potential explanations, but no more.

The way forward offered by realism alongside other approaches was debated during the early 1980s (as in the volumes edited by JOHNSTON in 1985 and by KOBAYASHI & MACKENZIE); the importance of space in these developments of social theory was discussed in several of the essays in a major collection edited by GREGORY & URRY. These sought accommodations among the various strands promoting intensive research, and largely ignored extensive work in the spatial analysis field.

Feminist geography
This range of arguments was significantly extended by other approaches that identified a wider range of cleavages in society than that based on class, which is the foundation of Marxist work. Feminist geography was launched within the relatively very small number of women academic geographers in the early 1980s, with its initial focus on discrimination against women in academic life, their absence from the more senior positions there, and the lack of treatment given to gender issues in mainstream geographical work. A WOMEN AND GEOGRAPHY STUDY GROUP was established within the Institute of British Geographers, for example, which published the first book-length exposition of these arguments. A later book by ROSE extended the case that geography is a masculine-dominated discipline, in every sense.

The interests of feminist geographers expanded through their interactions with contemporary writings in other disciplines, addressing wider issues of discrimination, representation, iden-

tity-formation and politics (as reviewed in McDOWELL's two papers). This stimulated a realization among geographers generally that societies are divided in a number of significant ways, that people's interpretations of the world are significantly influenced by their positions within them, that power structures reflect these divisions, and that politics are based on place-based self-identities (views of "us") and representations of "others" (views of "them").

Postmodernism and poststructuralism
Developments in associated disciplines – in the humanities as much as the social sciences – influenced this evolving concern with *difference* (as set out in McDOWELL's 1995 essay). Debates about *postmodernism* were introduced by DEAR, SOJA and others, with its emphasis on "multiple truths" rather than all-embracing grand theories (such as Marxism): people view the world from different perspectives among which there is no criterion for judging ultimate truth. This approach was linked to changes in economic organization then under way, with a switch from the Fordist regime of accumulation, characterized by mass production of uniform commodities for mass consumption, to post-Fordism, with its emphasis on niche markets and consumption for status. HARVEY argued in his 1989 critique that this switch merely reflected a further strategy for capitalist survival, with changes in the cultural superstructure (the domain of the empirical in realist terminology) promoted to sustain accumulation, but he was criticized in turn for continuing to emphasize a class-based model.

Alongside, and more influential than, postmodernism were the various strands of *poststructural* thinking on which geographers drew and to which they contributed. These emphasize human subjectivity as created rather than given, with the creative processes operating in locales, the term for interaction settings introduced in GIDDENS's 1984 book. Places are important contexts in identity-creation – and are in turn being continually recreated (in processes akin to those described in structuration theory). The stress is on contingency: human subjectivity and identity are produced and reproduced in places, so that truth and knowledge are contingent too. They vary over time and space as mosaics of situated and local knowledge which provide the resources on which individuals and groups draw in their social conduct, and to whose maintenance they contribute through their social actions. Representation of these local knowledges is central to their use and survival, and post-structuralist literature stresses the important role of *language* in this, not only as a mode of communication and hence an instrument in the creation of identities but also as a social construction itself. Arguments along these lines had been developed for several decades, notably by OLSSON (1980), but geographers became increasingly aware of the role of language in the creation and transmission of meanings (as exemplified in a number of edited volumes – by BARNES & DUNCAN, by DUNCAN & GREGORY and by DUNCAN & LEY – as well as in DOEL's overview, and in BARNES's deconstruction of the language of economic geography, specifically its use of metaphors).

Although most poststructural work focuses on the role of language in the creation and representation of situated knowledges, geographers have explored other "textual strategies" such as landscapes, various art forms, and maps. Seminal works included HARLEY's essays on deconstructing maps, showing that far from being "objective and neutral" representations of the world, these are important documents (in what they show and omit as well as how they depict things) in the portrayal of power relationships.

One of the most influential works for geographers interested in the creation, representation and transmission of identities and meanings has been SAID's *Orientalism*, which demonstrates how Western intellectuals and others had created a "mythical East", a view of part of the world and its inhabitants that structured attitudes towards it and them. Alongside this the wider field of *postcolonial* studies developed, challenging not only the economic and political geographies of colonialism and imperialism but also their roles in creating imaginative geographies at variance from those of the people who experienced those power relations and whose own literatures were central to the creation of alternative geographies, knowledges, and identities. These geographical imaginations are dealt with in GREGORY's (1994) book.

Much of this emerging work was located within the subdiscipline of cultural geography, but has not been confined to it. Indeed, there was something of a "cultural turn" in much of human geography throughout the 1990s, which was instrumental in breaking down some of the intradisciplinary fragmentation. The interdependence of cultural and economic processes, for example, was explored in a major book of essays edited by LEE & WILLS. Similarly, poststructural and associated ideas have been central to the creation of a critical geopolitics – illustrated by Ó TUATHAIL's book – which explores how representations of the world, and of the significant "others" within it, are central to the "us and them" depictions on which so much geopolitical strategy and tactics are based, and in which both identities and language are crucial underpinnings to the geography of conflict.

Cultural studies, globalization and environmentalism

A substantial number of geographers locate their work within the broader interdisciplinary grouping known as cultural studies, within which some (such as MASSEY, ALLEN & SARRE) identify a "spatial turn", an increased use of spatial metaphors and a growing realization of the importance of situated and local knowledges. The goal of geographers within that enterprise is to demonstrate how space and place are deeply implicated in the processes involved in the creation of identities and in the power relationships that follow – not just as the arenas within which those processes take place but rather as constituent components of the processes themselves. Places and spaces are not unchanging "givens"; they are created by people, fought over in a great variety of ways, and continually reshaped. Indeed, spatial strategies are fundamental to many power relationships, as argued in SACK's book on *territoriality*, on the use of bounded spaces for the exercise of power.

This work on local knowledges is set within an appreciation of the increasing intensity of globalization processes, especially, though not only, in economic organization (as portrayed in DICKEN's text and the volume of essays edited by JOHNSTON, TAYLOR & WATTS). The integration of the global and the local has stimulated renewed interest in the concept of scale, not just as a cartographic ratio for representing the world but rather as an aspect of the making and remaking of places and spaces. TAYLOR, for example, argued in his 1982 essay that three scales are crucial: although economic processes now operate globally, they are experienced, and thus acted on, locally; furthermore, they are mediated and regulated regionally, by state apparatus – together these comprise the trilogy of world economy, nation state and community as the three crucial scales, each of which is responding to changes in the others (as argued by AGNEW with regard to the changing role of the territorially defined nation state). Within these approaches there is what TAYLOR refers to in his 1999 essay as place–space tensions: places are discontinuous segments of the earth's surface, containers within which local knowledges and self identifies are created and recreated, some bounded others not, whereas space is continuous. Both are continually being manipulated in the restructuring of spatial structures.

Interaction with cultural studies has involved geographers exploring an ever-wider range of topics and approaches. This has involved, for example, work at smaller spatial scales, exploring – as does PILE – the body as a site of identity formation (on which *See also* some of the essays in MASSEY, ALLEN & SARRE). Other work – as in THRIFT's using nonrepresentational theory – focuses on the transitory "performances" that characterize everyday life but which are never recorded in the source materials traditionally used in geographical scholarship.

The interrelationships between people and nature, so characteristic of geography prior to the 1960s, were relatively ignored for some decades – reflecting both the clear cleavage of human from physical geography and human geographers' concern for spatial structures conceived of as occupying isotropic planes with no topographic or other variations (on which see HANSON). There was a continuing stream of studies on various aspects of environmentalism, on which O'RIORDAN's books have been important stimuli, and on a political economy approach to environmental problems and issues – as illustrated by books by BLAIKIE and by JOHNSTON and the volume edited by BLAIKIE & BROOKFIELD. Much of the former focused on environmental policy – with some arguing that studies of environmental management integrated physical and human geography, presented a major opportunity for geographers to undertake relevant research in the context of increased awareness of impending "ecological disasters" (on which see LIVERMAN); others have continued to develop the theme of the human transformation of the earth, as in the major volume edited by TURNER *et al.* Poststructuralist work has argued that nature too is a social construction and – as illustrated by the essays in the book edited by BRAUN and CASTREE – the interrelationships of nature and culture must take account of the cultural constructions of nature: indeed some, such as WHATMORE, argue that the binary division between nature and culture is unsustainable. This has stimulated attempts at reintegrating aspects of human and physical geography (as by SIMMONS) but the two remain almost totally separate and distinct approaches to knowledge, while cohabiting in the same intellectual space in many universities.

Spatial analysis and social theorists

Contemporary human geography contains a major cleavage, characterized by SHEPPARD as spatial analysts on the one hand

and social theorists on the other. The two operate very separately (although HANSON identifies some evidence of convergence), with relatively little debate between the protagonists of very different approaches to research, explanation, and understanding. One of the few edited volumes to contain elements of such a debate is that edited by MACMILLAN, where several authors make the case for spatial analysis. Most of the other volumes concerned with contemporary debates within human geography concentrate virtually exclusively on the social theory branch of the discipline – as in MASSEY, ALLEN & SARRE. Some texts on "contemporary geographic thought" – such as PEET's and that by CLOKE, PHILO & SADLER – similarly ignore the approaches introduced before the 1970s, treating spatial analysis as part of human geography's past rather than a substantial continuing stream of work.

That spatial analysis stream has become technically much more sophisticated during the last three decades. Quantitative workers within geography initially assumed that the statistical methods employed in other social sciences could readily be applied to geographical data. They only later realized that there is a major problem of *spatial autocorrelation*, which can lead to inefficient and/or biased results from statistical analyses because spatial data frequently violate the independence criterion of the widely used general linear model: observations of a variable at one point in space may be influenced by values at adjacent points. CLIFF & ORD explored means of tackling this problem, which current work in spatial analysis – as in HAINING's presentation – takes fully into account.

Other technical issues that human geographers (among others) have tackled include the *modifiable areal unit problem* (maup), clarified by OPENSHAW. Much geographical work involves analysing the characteristics of groups of people classified by where they live – such as the enumeration districts and other areas used for collating and reporting census data. There is an extremely large number of ways to create such areal classifications – as, for example, with the grouping of electoral wards to form parliamentary constituencies in the UK. Each aggregation will produce its own result for a particular analytical question – such as the relationship between an area's ethnic composition and level of illiteracy – because of two separate components to the problem. The *scale effect* involves using classes of different sizes, which may produce different results; the *aggregation effect* refers to the various ways of grouping areas of the same size, each of which may also produce a unique answer. The problem is to evaluate the validity of the particular result obtained. Much of the work in this mould uses areal data on population aggregates to make statements about individuals: if there is a positive relationship between the percentage of blacks in an area and the percentage who are illiterate, does this mean that more blacks than non-blacks are illiterate? A variety of means of tackling this ecological fallacy have been explored, as illustrated in the book edited by LONGLEY & BATTY and in KING's proposed solution.

The greater analytical sophistication now undertaken in spatial analysis has been facilitated by the major developments in computing power in recent decades. These allow analysts to handle very large data sets and modelling strategies, in an area known as geocomputation (set out in LONGLEY, BROOKS, McDONNELL & MACMILLAN), and to use computer methods based on artificial intelligence to search for relationships and order (OPENSHAW & OPENSHAW).

Geographical information systems

These expanded technical facilities include the development of *geographical information systems (GIS)*, combined computer software and hardware for the organization, integration, display and analysis of spatial data. These facilities not only make it much easier to undertake traditional forms of analysis but have also substantially widened the scope of spatial analysis in a great variety of ways: the display facilities, for example, have spawned a sub-field of *visualization* studies, enabling investigators to experiment with different ways of mapping (DORLING & FAIRBAIRN) and portraying relationships – as in DORLING's innovative *A New Social Atlas of Britain*. The use of GIS is now central to much spatial analysis, well beyond the traditional academic discipline of geography, as illustrated by the state-of-the-art reviews in LONGLEY, GOODCHILD, MAGUIRE & RHIND. It has been the focus of some critique by social theorists (as in the volume edited by PICKLES), interested in GIS not only as a technical apparatus used in a range of commercial and military applications but also as a new means of representing the world – some of which has stimulated a sympathetic response within the GIS community (for example, SCHUURMAN).

Geographical information systems are widely used for commercial applications and are a major component of applied geographical work that employs spatial analyses of various types – illustrated by the essays in LONGLEY & CLARKE. Although many of these continue to search for order, including spatial order, they are no longer founded on the location theories that characterized geography in the 1970s, although some of the models applied to identify, say, the best locations for new retail outlets, are based on them. (It is intriguing that, as MARTIN points out, economists are now exploring – as the "new economic geography" – just such restricted models that geographers have abandoned in their adoption of the "cultural turn" in their searches for explanations of what is where, a stream of work for which MASSEY's study of economic restructuring in 1970s/1980s provided a major stimulus.) Work in areas such as *geodemographics*, whereby classifications of areas according to their populations' characteristics are used in a wide range of marketing strategies, from new products to political parties, builds on geographers' expertise and is the source of contract work for university departments seeking external income in their institutions' straitened financial circumstances.

Conclusions

The focus on applications is currently strong throughout geography because of the situation in universities, especially in the US where, unlike the UK, geography is not a strong subject in the secondary schools and university departments have to recruit potential students based on the value that they can expect to gain from geography courses and degrees. A report to the country's NATIONAL RESEARCH COUNCIL stresses this aspect of the discipline within the overall research enterprise, selling geography through its technical skills (in physical as well as human geography), showing that these areas are very much in demand, and substantially underplaying the social theory side of the discipline.

Those who work on the social theory side do not, however, accept that their work has no applied value – only that it cannot be "sold" commercially in the way much spatial analysis can. They argue that the value of a *critical human geography* lies in its emancipatory role, disclosing to people (and, perhaps even more importantly, assisting them to discover for themselves) how places and spaces are manipulated in the creation and maintenance not only of differences but also of inequalities, including unequal power relationships: there is no necessary equation between the "is" and the "ought". Such work has a strong ethical/moral component, as addressed in recent books by HARVEY, by SACK and by SMITH (1996, 1997 and 1994 respectively).

Human geography is a large and very diverse discipline, therefore. It is fragmented along a variety of cleavages, with a plethora of subgroups identified by either or both what they study and how they study – a diversity illustrated in the two volumes edited by GAILE & WILLMOTT, who solicited review chapters from each of the subdisciplinary specialty groups operating within the Association of American Geographers. Others have sought to integrate these separate specialisms and identify the major substantive themes in contemporary geographical work, as in the volume edited by ABLER, MARCUS & OLSON, which concentrates more on the spatial analysis stream of work than on that in social theory. Some of the fragmentation that characterized most of the later decades of the 20th century has been removed, however, as human geographers have realized the interdependence of political, economic, social and cultural processes. But the divide between the "spatial analysts" and the "social theorists" is wide and few authors or editors cover both: a recent excellent introduction for students, for example (CLOKE, CRANG & GOODWIN), contains nothing on the spatial analysis stream, and anthologies of selections from "classic works" such as that compiled by AGNEW, LIVINGSTONE & ROGERS similarly favour the social theory approach.

The breadth of material and approaches now covered within geography is set out in the *Dictionary of Human Geography* (JOHNSTON, GREGORY, PRATT & WATTS) and its evolution can be traced in the quarterly journal *Progress in Human Geography*, notably its annual reviews of developments in various areas of the discipline.

RON JOHNSTON

See also Economic geography, Environmental science as a social science, Feminist geographies, Geographical education, Geographical information systems, Geography of money, Geopolitics, Globalization, Governance, Region and regional geography, Social geography, Spatial analysis

Human longevity

Friedman, Meyer and Ray H. Rosenman, *Type A Behavior and Your Heart*, New York: Knopf, and London: Wildwood House, 1974
Samuelsson, S.M., B. Nordbeck, B. Bauer Alfredson, A. Brun, B. Hagberg, L. Gustafson, G. Samuelsson and J. Risberg,

"The Swedish Centenarian Study: A Multidisciplinary Study of Five Consecutive Cohorts at the Age of 100", *International Journal of Aging and Human Development*, 45/3 (1997): 223–53
Savage, R.D., P.G. Britton, N. Bolton and E.H. Hall, *Intellectual Functioning in the Aged*, London: Methuen, 1973
Smith, David W.E., *Human Longevity*, Oxford and New York: Oxford University Press, 1993
Stokes, Graham, *On Being Old: The Psychology of Later Life*, London: Falmer Press, 1992
Temoshok, Lydia and Henry Dreher, *The Type C Connection: The Behavioral Links to Cancer and Your Health*, New York: Random House, 1992

SMITH provides a general overview of the topic of human longevity, drawing on a number of different disciplines including biology, medicine, psychology, and sociology. Pointing out that humans have, in general, the longest lifespan by far of mammals (at least as far as data are available) he also draws useful attention to parametric aspects of changes, and the shift in shape of survival curves over the years (and particularly the 20th century). Chapters discuss the biological, behavioural, and social determinants of longevity, and the observation, common in most societies, that women live longer than men. As a general introduction to the topic, and a reference for basic information, Smith provides a useful text whilst remaining easily readable.

Psychological interest in longevity originally centred around the kinds of intellectual and related changes that might be associated with increasing age. The limitations of cross-sectional studies, especially where the subjects' lives have covered periods of substantial social change, led psychologists to attempt longitudinal studies over relatively long periods. The book by SAVAGE *et al.* is typical of the studies of the time, assessing changes in intelligence of elderly people in Newcastle, England, over an eight-year period. The book is in the form of a research report, providing a wealth of data including comparisons of intelligence test scores (both full-scale and subtest) as well as analyses of broader interest, for example into the factor structure of the measures, the latter supporting the notion that intelligence has "crystallized" and "fluid" components.

Subsequent to these early studies, the interest of psychologists expanded beyond the assessment of intellectual change to the consideration of a wider range of psychological and social changes associated with ageing. More recent books have therefore concerned themselves with a host of topics including personality changes, creativity, and sexuality. STOKES is typical of more recent introductory texts on the psychology of ageing, addressing a range of topics at a level suitable for those with no prior knowledge of the field.

With increasing amounts of research on psychological aspects of ageing, it started to become apparent that the relationship between longevity and psychological functioning might operate in both causal directions. Besides ageing affecting psychological processes, it appeared that psychological processes might directly influence longevity. The potential influence of psychology on longevity appears to go beyond obvious links such as smoking, diet, and exercise, all of which can be affected by psychological stressors and all of which affect longevity. Increasingly the suggestion has been made that certain psychological factors might impact directly on major killers such as heart disease and cancer. TEMOSHOK & DREHER describe their concept of the "Type C" personality; their book is aimed at a general audience and is highly readable while providing initial directions for further reading to those interested in pursuing the subject. It is impossible to determine whether the kind of personality they describe is in any sense itself predisposing to cancer or simply an indicator of some other (for example genetic) predisposition thereto.

Temoshok's own work was itself inspired, at least in part, by the earlier work of FRIEDMAN & ROSENMAN into the so-called "Type A/Type B" behaviour pattern. Their notion that the Type A lifestyle – driven, impatient, time pressured, and so forth – was a significant risk factor for coronary heart disease has by now entered popular folklore. Their 1974 book no doubt did much to generate this widespread awareness, being written as a guide for the public at large and especially those who may consider themselves, for one reason or another, to be at risk of heart attack. The detailed research that has taken place in the subsequent 25 years has questioned a great deal of the early model, in particular highlighting the particular importance of the "hostility" component of the Type A pattern relative to the remaining components, and those interested in the current status of the Type A concept will need to read the current research journals and more recent texts. Nevertheless, Friedman and Rosenman's book remains worth reading as one of the best ways to obtain the "feel" of what they had in mind when first describing the Type A pattern.

Finally it is important to remember that the elderly are not a homogeneous group, and there is now increasing recognition that a subgroup (often called the "old old") of very elderly people can be identified and is of interest. In particular, there have been several studies of the large number of individuals who live to or beyond the age of 100. Detailed studies of such individuals have now been conducted in a number of countries, including the US, Japan, and Sweden. SAMUELSSON *et al.*'s study from Sweden typifies such research, investigating medical, social, and psychological characteristics of 100 centenarians. Notable amongst the psychological findings were that the majority rated their quality of life as "rather" or "very" good, and that although Alzheimer-like changes were found in most of the brains that were available post mortem, these were not associated with clinical signs of dementia. Slightly over half managed activities of daily living with minimal or no assistance. It appears, therefore, that in principle at least, living to an extreme age need not be associated with an unacceptable degree of physical or mental degeneration.

R.G. OWENS

See also Gerontology

Human nature

Gove, Walter R., "Why We Do What We Do: A Biopsychosocial Theory of Human Motivation", *Social Forces*, 73/2 (1994): 363–94

Kemper, Theodore D., *Social Structure and Testosterone: Explorations of the Socio-bio-social Chain*, New Brunswick, New Jersey: Rutgers University Press, 1990

Maryanski, Alexandra, "The Last Common Ancestor: An Ecological Network Model on the Origins of Human Sociality" in *Advances in Human Ecology*, edited by Lee Freese, Greenwich, Connecticut and London: Jai Press, 1992

Turner, Jonathan, *On the Origins of Emotions: A Sociological Inquiry into the Evolution of Human Affect*, Stanford, California: Stanford University Press, 2000

Udry, J. Richard, "The Nature of Gender", *Demography*, 31/4 (1994): 561–73

Interest in human nature has long intrigued scholars in philosophy and many more specialized disciplines. Some postulated a natural state for humans that was truly basic to human nature. Within the social sciences, as they began to emerge in the 19th and early 20th centuries, scholars focused on the basic needs driving human behaviour and organization. The introduction of Darwin's ideas on the nature of evolution, and later, the discovery or rediscovery of Mendel's ideas about genetics added complications to simple notions of fundamental need states in humans. Coupled with social Darwinism and highly ethnocentric views of evolutionary theory, there was a general rejection of biological explanations of human behaviour in all the social sciences. In sociology, a heavy emphasis was placed on the nurture side of the nature–nurture debate as characteristics of humans were increasingly viewed as the sole products of socialization, of location in social structures, and of exposure to cultural expectations and opportunities. Quietly, however, biological ideas are making their way back into sociology; and Darwinian theory informs these ideas.

UDRY has been one of the most persistent advocates of bringing biology back into sociology. Human nature, or the common behavioural predispositions of humans that give them a distinctive character, must once again be a topic of inquiry. These proclivities – or what Udry terms "persistent motivation states" – can be divided into two categories: those that are panhuman, and those that vary across individuals and between the sexes. A goal of sociology, Udry contends, should be to see how genetically determined motivation states interface with sociological and psychological processes.

To illustrate the importance of motivation states and their interrelations with sociocultural processes, Udry has proposed a theory of gender that explores the interplay between "gendered behaviours" and the biology of sex. Although most sociologists view all sex roles as purely human inventions, Udry argues that the sexual dimorphism between males and females and the distinctive ratios of sex hormones characteristic of each sex indicate that gender roles must have some biological basis. To convey just how gendered behaviours interface with human proclivities, Udry devised a "thought experiment" in which a hypothetical society adopts over time three distinctive gendered ideologies: first, a traditional sex-segregated ideology in which strict male and female sex-typed roles are required; second, a single-sex ideology in which males and females are expected to behave virtually the same in unisex roles; and third, a permissive society in which males and females are free to follow their predispositions. As this society moves across these three phases, what would the distribution of gendered roles look like over time?

Udry's gender theory predicts the following pattern. In the first or sex-segregated stage, normative sanctions would drive out or repress any predispositions that conflict with gender norms. Similarly, at the single-sex stage, dispositional differences between males and females would be driven out to conform to unisex norms. At the permissive stage, however, the biologically based predispositions within and between males and females, would be allowed free expression; and as a result, a diversity of gender roles would be evident. Thus, in all three phases a "gendered structure" would exist although only the first two would be culturally invented gender norms. Yet, the time-travelling sociologist would conclude that all three ideologies – even the gender-permissive one generated purely on biological predispositions – were all socially constructed because most sociologists still think it is impossible for any behaviours to have a biological foundation. Udry maintains that it is unrealistic to assume that humans are exempt from sex influenced genes because they have virtually the same hormonal foundation as other primates whose gendered behaviours are linked to sex hormones.

Udry acknowledges that biologically driven variations in human gender roles would never express themselves fully in a real society, since it is inconceivable that any society would suspend all socially invented social roles, but he does submit that when individual choices are broad (as they are in industrialized societies) natural human affinities will surface and gain expression. As Udry's thought experiment emphasizes, however, it is time for sociologists to examine natural human affinities, as these interact with cultural norms and ideologies as well as the sanctioned roles in social structures that these cultural systems define.

KEMPER also explores the interplay between biological and sociological processes by introducing the notion of socio-bio-social chains in which many biological conditions are themselves nested in social processes that shape them; and, in turn, these transformed biological conditions then feed forward to reproduce or change social arrangements. He also views sexuality as a complex amalgam of hormonal, psychological, and social processes. For example, in his research on the male hormone, testosterone, Kemper found a relationship between male dominance or eminence attainment in social encounters and elevations or surges of testosterone. A small but growing number of studies confirm that hormonal responses to victory and defeat for human males parallel those in other animals.

Kemper has also examined the biology of human emotions and argues that modern humans have four physiologically grounded primary emotions – fear, anger, depression, and satisfaction – which he thinks are common to all humans and linked to the outcomes of many social encounters. In contrast, such emotions as guilt, shame, pride, gratitude, love, and nostalgia are secondary emotions that are sociologically grafted onto the primary ones through processes of socialization. For Kemper, humans are animals and endowed with innate predispositions but these proclivities only predispose humans toward particular behaviours; they do not, by themselves, determine the outcome. Instead, social structure and culture can override these natural tendencies and thereby determine whether they will be expressed or repressed depending upon societal norms and values.

In seeking to develop a more biologically-grounded theory of motivation, GOVE argues against the *antibiological bias* in sociology and the idea that variation in human capacities is determined solely by the society in which an individual lives, his or her location in that society, and socialization experiences. These are important but, unless sociology wishes to portray humans as genetic clones, it is also necessary to acknowledge the genetic variation in human capacities and attributes. For example, recent quantitative research on large-scale samples of identical and nonidentical twins, both adopted and reared apart, has revealed heritability components for such basic personality traits as extroversion, neuroticism, consciousness, agreeableness, and openness. Until sociologists stop viewing human biology as irrelevant and human behaviour infinitely flexible, the door will remain closed on the interactional effects among culture, genes and the environment.

Another line of sociological inquiry into human nature compares humans with their closest living relatives, the great apes (chimpanzees, gorillas, and orangutans). Humans and chimpanzees are especially close, sharing nearly 99% of their DNA – the result of belonging to the same species less than 6 million years ago. In pursuing human nature, MARYANSKI used comparative historical reconstruction, which in biology is called cladistic analysis, and social network methods to compare the social structural patterns of living apes, who like humans are the evolutionary products of the hominid lineage, a super-family that flourished about 20 million years ago. Comparative historical reconstruction is a widely accepted methodology and is used in a variety of fields as well as biology – for example, linguistics and literature (when reconstructing a mother language or an original text). Maryanski's goal was to reconstruct *ultimate history* through a social network analysis of the *last common ancestor* (LCA) population of all living hominids (apes and humans). To accomplish this task, she focused on the strength of ties among living apes and their associated dispersal patterns. These relational traits were then systematically coded into social network patterns to provide a kind of ancestral "looking glass" on which to glimpse the hominid portion of humans' basic social nature. In particular, Maryanski compared both the social ties of apes as they create social structures with those of a control group of representative monkeys (who differentiated from apes some 30 million years ago). By plotting these relations among age and sex classes into social network ties, Maryanski was able to construct social networks of monkey and ape societies in terms of the strength of ties (non-existent/weak, moderate, and strong). These data were then used to reconstruct relational blueprints of their respective last common ancestor populations. These data supported the following: (a) the adaptive ability of all living hominids (apes and humans) was constrained by phyletically based social affinities that operated to shape organizational structures; (b) the population of the last common ancestor of apes and humans was organized into a social network predisposed towards many weak, fluid ties and low sociality compared to the *collectivist* networks of monkeys where dominance/subordinate relationships among adult males along with matrifocal lineages among females serve to provide tight-knit networks and intergenerational continuity over time; (3) the key adaptive trend in later hominid social evolution was the building of social network ties, a trend that culminated in humans.

Maryanski put the nearly solitary orangutans at the lower end of this sociality trend since their organizational structure (or near lack of adult social bonds) closely parallels the last common ancestor population, whereas chimpanzees were put at the higher end. What emerges from a cladistic analysis is a startling fact of ape life: they all reveal relatively few strong ties, many weak ties, and a lack of group continuity over time (save for the sense of a larger community or regional population in which members freely move about from group to group). If this is the defining characteristic of present-day ape networks, then by the reasoning of cladistic analysis, the last common ancestor (LCA) of apes and humans is very likely to have had propensities for autonomy, individualism, mobility, and weak ties. Maryanski concludes that humans retain, to some degree, these propensities for weak ties and for autonomy, individualism, and mobility, despite later modifications to the human line. She argues that humans are much more social than other hominids, in part because selection favoured greater sociality when human ancestors made an ecological shift from forest to more open environments.

Yet the primate data also suggest that the collectivist touchstone often used to characterize the natural state of humans is misguided. Instead the *collectivistic* nature of humans is primarily generated culturally and transmitted through socialization processes when selection favoured the elaboration of culture (for example, speech, religious rituals) as a means to build social solidarity and override humans' basic ape behavioural tendencies. Indeed, if the bands of recent hunter-gatherers are examined (this is the basic structural unit in which the ancestors of humans and subsequently humans themselves evolved), they also reveal relatively fluid ties among members, with considerable individualism and mobility. These data also help to explain the apparent conflicts between collectivism and individualism so evident in many human spheres as a clash between cultural constructions and our ape legacy. The comparative study of primates, Maryanski contends, offers one of the most fertile grounds for ascertaining what human nature is, once the complexity of modern culture and social structure is stripped away and once we begin to visualize humans as primates who share an evolutionary history in common with the great apes.

Another approach borrows from Maryanski's data the basic conclusion that humans have strong genetic behavioural propensities for individualism, autonomy, mobility, and weak ties, and that these characteristics may help explain the long decline of the ape species and the surprising success of the human species. Today, apes and the human species make up only five per cent of primate species and only humans are not in danger of extinction. What, then, allowed the ancestors of humans (or hominids) to survive as their ape-like cousins continued to decline over the last 15 million years?

TURNER has argued that the propensities that enabled most apes to survive in the forests were maladaptive once the forests began to recede some 15 million years ago; and that, as a result, apes and eventually hominids were forced to live in woodlands, secondary forests, bush lands, and open savanna. Loose and fluid social structures are not well-suited to more open country habitats where predators abound; instead more

organization is adaptive to allow animals to hunt for food collectively and to engage in defence against predators. There were, then, intense selection pressures for apes in open country niches to become better organized; and as the long decline of ape species attests, most could not make the transition to more tight-knit patterns of cohesive social organization. Turner argues that natural selection worked on the ancestors of humans to forge a unique way around the low sociality propensities of apes: the elaboration of emotional capacities so that the ancestors of humans could build stronger but still flexible emotional ties creating enhanced patterns of social solidarity. Selection pressures worked, first, to give hominids greater neocortical control of emotions that are generated in subcortical areas of the brain (since a loud primate is soon a dead one in open-country niches) and once this control was in place, selection could work to expand the complexity and subtlety of emotional responses. By using emotions and emotional languages (syntaxes of emotional cues carrying meaning), Turner contends, cohesive group structures could be built without the collectivist monkey networks organized around male dominance hierarchies or female matrilines; and these structures would be more flexible than those among monkeys.

Turner believes that selection worked along several paths to produce enhanced emotional capacities among hominids. One was the mobilization of emotional energy along a broader spectrum of emotions that could forge more complex ties. Another was the attunement of responses so that hominids could read this wider spectrum of emotions through their dominant visual senses to create increased responsiveness to the internal states of others, thereby increasing sympathy and empathy as well as facilitating coordination of responses among individuals. A third path was sanctioning, elaborating less severe variants of anger and fear as the emotions behind negative sanctions and expanding variants of satisfaction and happiness to create arrays of positive sanctions that are more likely than negative ones to promote social solidarity. A related path was to create the moral codes that are subject to sanctioning. These codes cannot exist without the charge of emotions that give them their moral character. A fourth involved creating new ways to mobilize values that could be subject to solidarity-enhancing exchange relations, for without a spectrum of emotional valences to give differing levels of value to resources, exchange relations cannot be very complex or flexible. A final path was to elaborate the emotions so that more complex and rational decision making could occur; for without the emotional valences attached to alternatives, decision making cannot occur, with the range of emotional valences determining how complex decision making can be. From Turner's perspective, then, human nature revolves around an interplay between phyletic propensities for weak ties and low sociality inherited from the last common ancestor of apes and humans, mitigated by the expanded emotional abilities of hominids that were used to overcome these low sociality propensities. Without humans' enhanced emotional abilities, sociocultural evolution could not have occurred, for the unique features of human organization and culture are ultimately built from the control of a wide array of emotions, attunement of interpersonal responses, development of moral codes, use of mixes of positive and negative sanctions, and from the forging of exchange relations that expanded the capacity for complex decision making.

Human nature is thus a delicate compromise between the force of collective relations powered by our emotional abilities fighting against our ape ancestry for weak ties and low sociality. It is no coincidence, Turner argues, that human ideologies and social structural arrangements constantly fluctuate between collectivism and individualism. This conflict is built into human nature as it evolved along the hominid line.

A.R. MARYANSKI

See also Nature vs nurture

Human resource management

Beaumont, P.B., "Trade Unions and HRM", *Industrial Relations Journal*, 22/4 (1991): 300–08

Boxall, Peter F., "The Significance of Human Resource Management: A Reconsideration of the Evidence", *International Journal of Human Resource Management*, 4/3 (1993): 645–64

Fombrun, Charles J., Noel M. Tichy and Mary Anne Devanna (editors), *Strategic Human Resource Management*, New York: Wiley, 1984

Guest, David E., "Personnel Management: The End of Orthodoxy?", *British Journal of Industrial Relations*, 29/2 (1991): 149–75

Hart, Tim J., "Human Resource Management: Time to Exorcize the Militant Tendency", *Employee Relations*, 15/3 (1993): 29–36

Lengnick-Hall, Cynthia A. and Mark L. Lengnick-Hall, "Strategic Human Resources Management: A Review of the Literature and a Proposed Typology", *Academy of Management Review*, 13/3 (1988): 454–70

Moore, Larry F. and P. Devereaux Jennings (editors), *Human Resource Management on the Pacific Rim*, Berlin and New York: de Gruyter, 1995

Rousseau, Denise M. and Kimberly A. Wade-Benzoni, "Linking Strategy and Human Resource Practices: How Employee and Customer Contracts are Created", *Human Resource Management*, 33/3 (1994): 463–89

Schuler, Randall S. and Susan E. Jackson, "Linking Competitive Strategies with Human Resource Management Practices", *Academy of Management Executive*, 1/3 (1987): 207–19

Schuler, Randall S., *Personnel and Human Resource Management*, 3rd edition, St. Paul: West Publishing, 1987

Storey, John (editor), *Human Resource Management: A Critical Text*, London and New York: Routledge, 1995

Welch, Denice, "Determinants of International Human Resource Management Approaches and Activities: A Suggested Framework", *Journal of Management Studies*, 31/2 (1994): 139–64

SCHULER'S 1987 edition of one of his many texts is a useful starting point for a study of Human Resource Management (HRM) as it illustrates how, in the 1980s, the term began to gain domination in the United States over the term "personnel management" – without any real change in substance. (In 1986 Schuler co-authored a text with Stuart Youngblood entitled *Effective Personnel Management*. Although the two texts are not identical, there are huge similarities.) Both texts covered planning, job analysis, recruitment, selection and placement, performance appraisal, compensation, indirect compensation, training and development, quality of work life, occupational safety and health, employee rights, unionization, and collective bargaining. As with most personnel management texts and HRM texts of this type, the book is more prescriptive than analytical.

FOMBRUN, TICHY & DEVANNA is one of the first HRM texts that is not simply a retitled personnel management offering. It comprises 25 chapters, 18 of which are by contributors other than the editors. The text heavily emphasizes the strategic role of HRM, and strategic issues in HRM. The editors propose a framework for strategic HRM, stressing that the "critical managerial task is to align the formal structure and the human resource systems so they drive the strategic objectives of the organization". This book sets the scene for practitioner-based articles offering solutions on how to link HR planning and strategic planning.

SCHULER & JACKSON provide a good example of a prescriptive article aimed at practitioners. They suggest three competitive strategies: innovation, quality enhancement, and cost reduction, and the employee role behaviours needed to carry out these strategies successfully. Human resource management practices are considered in the areas of planning, staffing, appraising, compensating, training, and development and they discuss the range of decisions that has to be made within each area. There are also a number of brief HRM "success stories" of United States firms who pursued competitive strategies "to gain competitive advantage and beat the competition".

LENGNICK-HALL & LENGNICK-HALL provide a more academic and analytical consideration relating HRM to business strategy. They give a good review of the early literature of strategic HRM – that is, HRM linked to organizational strategy – and they provide a "growth readiness" matrix that, in fairly simple form, captures the basic features of their typology for the strategic management of human resources.

ROUSSEAU & WADE-BENZONI also consider the relationship between HRM and business strategy but take a novel approach and consider the impact that HRM practices have on employees' psychological contracts where the timespan is short term or open ended, and where the performance terms are specific or not. They claim their research shows most organizations contain one or more variants of these four contracts, and they provide cases to support that claim. They stress the importance of employee psychological contracts and how they shape performance, motivation, cooperation, and customer responsiveness.

As well as the link between HRM and business strategy, a second development has been the growing interest in international HRM. WELCH provides a useful review of the fairly limited literature in this area, and claims to contribute to theory building by examining how four Australian companies managed expatriates with regard to selection, pre-departure training, compensation, and repatriation. The study shows that, in terms of selection, no consideration was given to the international aspect. Some pre-departure training did take place, but "in some cases as a result of hindsight rather than careful forethought". The paper is worth reading as it reflects research into an aspect of HRM as employed by organizations rather than the selection of "best practice" examples designed to bolster support for HRM.

BEAUMONT considers the impact of HRM on unions, the major emphasis being on British unions, but with some discussion of Canadian and US experiences. The paper discusses the view, widely held by British trade unions, that HRM is "in essence the development of a set of policies, practices and arrangements designed essentially to 'individualize' industrial relations, and thus circumvent the unions". Although some British unions and the Trade Union Congress are seeking to become more proactive, the paper discusses a lack of proactive behaviour, with most unions simply reacting to management-led initiatives in HRM.

HART deserves to be read for its very different view of HRM – the paper is not only sceptical about the supposed advantages of HRM: it is openly hostile to the concept, claiming that HRM is "amoral and anti-social, unprofessional reactive, uneconomic, and ecologically destructive". Hart's extreme views ensure this text is unlikely to become mainstream, but it gives a valuable perspective to those prepared to read this "unapologetically polemic article".

GUEST is one of the more prolific British writers on theoretical aspects of HRM. This paper references eight of his earlier works on HRM topics. It gives valuable insights into the relationships between HRM, personnel management, and industrial relations. The tone ranges from sceptical to critical and argues that only modest innovation has occurred in human resource management, with little evidence of positive outcomes. The paper questions the sustainability of the "new orthodoxy" built around HRM.

BOXALL is a much more enthusiastic proponent of HRM. His paper reviews the early literature, and categorizes it into two main streams. The first stream is that which sees HRM as "a particular management strategy emphasizing employee commitment, and rendering unions unnecessary". This is predominantly the British approach, and it sees HRM as replacing unions (unitarist), as opposed to the pluralist style that works alongside trade unions. The second stream is primarily the US approach, which is concerned with "building links between the business disciplines of HRM and strategic management". Boxall discusses how HRM may prove to be of genuine academic significance through its potential to provide a better theory of management behaviour in employment relations, an area in which HRM literature has already made a greater contribution than that to personnel management.

MOORE & JENNINGS provide a significant contribution to the literature on the practice of HRM in 11 Pacific Rim countries: Australia, Canada, Hong Kong, Japan, New Zealand, Peoples Republic of China, South Korea, Singapore, Taiwan, Thailand, and the work also covers the US. Each chapter provides a valuable and detailed analysis covering the HRM practices of each country and a prediction of future developments. The two theoretical chapters describe concepts used elsewhere in the book.

The 15 contributions in STOREY encompass most arguments relating to the HRM debate. The introductory section assesses HRM, examining the "rhetoric, reality and hidden agendas", there is a section devoted to the two key current issues in HRM – the degree to which it can be considered

strategic, and the degree to which it can be considered international – both of which include papers by leading writers. One section is devoted to "key practice areas" – the traditional ground of personnel studies. The text is predominantly British, containing only one chapter by American authors, but it is probably the most useful single reference work.

ALAN JAMES GEARE

Human rights, law

Alston, Philip (editor), *Human Rights Law*, Aldershot, Hampshire: Dartmouth, and New York: New York University Press, 1996

Ghandhi, P.R. (editor), *Blackstone's International Human Rights Documents*, London: Blackstone Press, 1995

Green, L.C., *The Contemporary Law of Armed Conflict*, Manchester: Manchester University Press, 1993

Human Rights Quarterly, 1979–

Human Rights Watch, *Human Rights Watch World Report*, New York: Human Rights Watch, published annually from 1991 and on the Internet at http://www.hrw.org/

Janis, Mark W., Richard S. Kay and Anthony W. Bradley (editors), *European Human Rights Law: Text and Materials*, Oxford: Clarendon Press, and New York: Oxford University Press, 1995

Mahoney, Kathleen E. and Paul Mahoney, *Human Rights in the Twenty-first Century*, Dordrecht: Nijhoff, 1993

Roberts, Adam and Richard Guelff (editors), *Documents on the Laws of War*, 3rd edition, Oxford: Clarendon Press, 2000

Robertson, A.H. and J.G. Merrills, *Human Rights in the World: An Introduction to the Study of the International Protection of Human Rights*, 4th edition, Manchester: Manchester University Press, 1996

Steiner, Henry J. and Philip Alston, *International Human Rights in Context: Law, Politics, Morals: Text and Materials*, Oxford: Clarendon Press, and New York: Oxford University Press, 1996

Tobin, Jack and Jennifer Green, *Guide to Human Rights Research*, Cambridge, Massachusetts: Harvard Law School, Human Rights Program, 1994

Veenhoven, Willem A. (editor), *Case Studies on Human Rights and Fundamental Freedoms: A World Survey*, 5 vols, The Hague: Nijhoff, 1975–76

The evolution of human rights from an idea to the basis of codified domestic, regional, and international law has been a rapid one. ROBERTSON & MERRILLS offer a good basic introduction to the actors and issues associated with human rights law, in addition to providing an assessment of the development of the idea of human rights and transitions into positive international law. The text explores progress made by the United Nations in promoting human rights and their protection through law. It also covers regional developments before addressing questions on economic, social and cultural rights, and the issue of humanitarian law. A concluding chapter considers the current position and the potential for progress in the protection and promotion of human rights through the use of positive law.

A more detailed exploration is found in STEINER & ALSTON. This work examines the philosophical development of human rights in conjunction with the evolution of international law in general, in addition to assessing the work of NGOs, regional institutions and processes, and the role of the state in the protection and enforcement of human rights. There is analysis on various topics, including development and women's rights. This text also provides a wide selection of readings chosen by the authors to illustrate their discussion. In addition, GREEN's work is a useful text for those with a specific interest in humanitarian law, perhaps the first area in which human rights law developed.

GHANDHI is an accessible source text for the main statutes and conventions on human rights law. The majority of international instruments that have been adopted are included, providing an overview of the level of global agreement that has been reached. Regional instruments are also included, which indicate the areas of interest and extent of legislative development at a subglobal level. The main area of omission is in the field of humanitarian law. ROBERTS & GUELFF fill this gap, providing a collection of the relevant documents relating to codified humanitarian law since the mid-1850s.

JANIS, KAY & BRADLEY provide a combination of analysis and instruments in considering the situation in Europe. In addition to providing a discussion on the institutions and procedures, the chapters on substantive adjudication examine specific cases and draw parallels between developments in the European Court of Human Rights and the legal context of other states, including the US and Canada, providing a useful tool for comparative research.

ALSTON provides a collection of 22 essays assessing the maturity of human rights law, arguing that "international human rights law is in its early adolescence". The works selected also examine the relationship between this specific field and other areas of more established international law. There are a number of essays that consider the idea of human rights from a variety of philosophical perspectives in contrast to the Western liberal tradition. In contrast to this assessment of the evolution of human rights law, the 75 papers found in the collection edited by MAHONEY & MAHONEY consider alternative paths for the future, offering a critical approach to the Western liberal philosophy that underpins the concept of human rights. The various authors suggest new approaches to the concept, focusing on interdependence rather than individualism, and considering the difficulties of overcoming inherent gender, race, and class bias found in societies and their legal, political and economic structures.

Vast amounts of material and case studies, although somewhat dated, are found in VEENHOVEN. Most of the subjects covered are from specific countries or geographical areas but there are also sections relating to human rights for groups that cannot be classified on purely territorially based grounds, such as women, religious adherents, and members of ethnic groups.

For updates on recent developments in the field of human rights as a whole, there are two excellent sources. HUMAN RIGHTS WATCH publish an annual report on the status of human rights around the world, which is useful both for case study material and for observing wider trends. The annual report is split into two sections, the first covering a country-by-country analysis of adherence to human rights law, violations, and developments in enforcement mechanisms and practice, and the second section examining specific issues. In the 1999 edition, this included a section on the use of child soldiers and a discussion of the establishment of the International Criminal Court. In addition to the annual report, various other publications are produced from time to time and details of all publications can be found on the Internet at http://www.hrw.org/. A cross-disciplinary approach is taken in the HUMAN RIGHTS QUARTERLY, with articles covering research and also policy development at the global level of the United Nations and at regional levels in both governmental and nongovernmental organizations. It also carries occasional philosophical essays on the concept of human rights and reviews of the latest books. It is regarded as essential reading for those with an interest in human rights seeking to be informed on contemporary developments.

Finally, TOBIN & GREEN provide a detailed guide to further research in the field of human rights law. Gathering together sources from a multitude of publications, this guide provides an excellent "map" to help the reader locate works from the United Nations and regional organizations together with academic texts and journals and material published through the work of various nongovernmental organizations.

CLARE MILLS

See also Bill of Rights, European Convention on Human Rights, Human rights, politics

Human rights, politics

Brownlie, Ian (editor), *Basic Documents on Human Rights*, 3rd edition, Oxford: Clarendon Press, and New York: Oxford University Press, 1992

Davidson, Scott, *Human Rights*, Buckingham: Open University Press, 1993

Eide, Asbjørn, "The Historical Significance of the Universal Declaration", *International Social Science Journal*, L/4 (1998): 475–98

Falk, Richard, "A Half-Century of Human Rights", *Australian Journal of International Affairs*, 52/3 (1998): 255–72

Hadjor, Kofi B., "Whose Human Rights?", *Journal of African and Asian Studies*, 33/4 (1998): 359–68

Peters, Julie and Andrea Wolper (editors), *Women's Rights, Human Rights: International Feminist Perspectives*, London and New York: Routledge, 1995

Shute, Stephen and Susan Hurley (editors), *On Human Rights*, New York: Basic Books, 1993

Smith, Jackie, Ron Pagnucco and George Lopez, "Globalizing Human Rights: The Work of Transnational Human Rights NGOs in the 1990s", *Human Rights Quarterly*, 20 (1998): 379–412

Vincent, R.J., *Human Rights and International Relations*, Cambridge and New York: Cambridge University Press, 1986

Waldron, Jeremy (editor), *Theories of Rights*, Oxford and New York: Oxford University Press, 1984

This eclectic series of readings mirrors the huge and wide-ranging impact that the development of human rights has had across the social sciences since World War II. Human rights issues are the focus for lawyers, philosophers, the "new social movements" such as feminism and environmentalism, for scholars of international and constitutional politics, development studies, human geography, sociology, and economics. The items presented here offer an introduction to the scope and substance of the issues at stake. The first readings focus on the development of the instruments of human rights. The second series of readings focuses on two key objections to the direction of current developments in human rights discourse and practice. The third set of texts offers a comprehensive introduction to the ideas and ideals that motivate social scientists and practitioners to defend or criticize human rights.

The primary literature of human rights is huge and complex. Nevertheless it is invaluable for those who wish to obtain an insight into the aspirations and achievements of the human rights movements. BROWNLIE's book succeeds in its stated aim of providing "a useful collection of sources on human rights in the form of a handbook". It offers brief, but helpful, notes to the principal documents that chart the development of the contemporary human rights culture. The book contains the United Nations (UN) charter, the universal Declaration of Human Rights, the European Convention on Human Rights and its protocols, as well as documents covering Latin American and African developments. A useful complement to Brownlie's book is DAVIDSON's comprehensive yet accessible introduction to human rights. This book charts the development of human rights theory and practice and offers some important introductory insights into the place of human rights as part of public international law. As well as covering the development of the instruments of human rights law and politics in the European system, the inter-American system, and the African system, Davidson presents the philosophical debates as an integral part of this process. The book includes useful guides to further reading and an interesting comparative table of rights and freedoms protected by the major human rights instruments.

EIDE's article, situated in an issue celebrating 50 years of the UN Declaration of Human Rights, offers a broad-ranging yet detailed introduction to the role that the Declaration of Human Rights has played since 1948. Eide offers a concise and lucid introduction to the historical, normative, and political implications of the articles of the declaration. The article ranges from the philosophical roots of conflicting conceptions of human rights (found in the political theories of Locke and Rousseau), to the complexities of upholding cultural rights (ascribed by article 26), and incorporates the development of non-European human rights concerns (such as the African Charter on Human and People's Rights of 1981). The article also argues that the declaration and associated conventions have become the foundations upon which the current world order is founded and upon which any future world order must build.

Human rights are often thought of as solely a political concern but no overview would be complete without an examination of the ever-increasing role of nongovernmental organizations (NGOs). SMITH, PAGNUCCO & LOPEZ offer a survey-based article that introduces the reader to the complex ways in which NGOs relate to the issues and actors associated with human rights activities. The data presented and the observations drawn from the returned survey offers the reader a fact-based account of the scope of NGO activity that will offer the context for further and more specific reading.

The progress of the development of a human rights culture is controversial. Two of the key concerns with this process come from quite different sources. HADJOR's article presents clearly, if somewhat rhetorically, the claims that the Western world's concern "to save the south from itself" is simply cultural arrogance bordering on cultural imperialism. He concludes that "the field of human rights is therefore a battle ground for the projection of power politics". FALK examines in scholarly detail the issues raised by the anti-hegemonic discourses generated in the post-colonial global south and situates these concerns within a wider-ranging and thoughtful survey of the main concerns with the political development of human rights since 1948. Falk deals concisely with the charge that the phrase "human rights" simply masks the preferences of the developed liberal democracies.

The second key set of objections stem from a quite different series of concerns. Feminist criticisms of the prevailing human rights culture are both widely discussed within the social sciences and clearly of crossdisciplinary concern. The collection of 32 essays edited by PETERS & WOLPER offers a comprehensive introduction to the variety of concerns that constitute the divergent feminist perspectives. Concerns range from the claim that many vital women's issues are left out of what is basically a sound framework to the more radical claim that the concerns of human rights are necessarily gendered. The book also details the many ways in which "universal" human rights can be seen to systematically ignore the basic freedoms of women throughout the world.

SHUTE & HURLEY present a series of essays by a number of the most important contemporary political theorists. All these essays have generated a wealth of literature and debate and they inform a huge section of the response of social scientists to the issues surrounding human rights. For example, this collection includes the essay in which Rawls extends his "political liberalism" to the international sphere along with Rorty's essay arguing that postmodern thinkers can still adopt human rights as the ethical basis for political action. In similar vein, WALDRON's much-cited collection of essays offers a series of insights into the political philosophy of human rights. The principal advantage of this collection is that it contains seminal examples of a wide range of theoretical responses to the ontological, epistemological, and political questions associated with the UN's "faith" in human rights. For example, the opposing views of R. Dworkin and H.L.A Hart are represented in a collection that also includes M. MacDonald, G. Vlastos, A. Gewirth, D. Lyons, T.M. Scanlon, J.L. Mackie and J. Raz. Waldron's wide-ranging yet detailed introduction shows the need for a discussion of the political theory of rights.

VINCENT offers the staple text on human rights for students of international relations. Vincent explores the issues from three classical perspectives (the "egg box" or "morality of states" theory, the "realist" position, and the "cosmopolitan" view). The book ranges from an understanding of the theory and practice of human rights in international politics to a policy prescription for the role of human rights in international society. This book still serves as an important introduction to the issues of human rights and international politics and acts as a necessary forerunner to one of the most hotly contested debates in international relations theory today.

PETER SUTCH

See also Civil rights, European Convention on Human Rights

Human-computer interaction

Card, Stuart K., Thomas P. Moran and Allen Newell, *The Psychology of Human–Computer Interaction*, Hillsdale, New Jersey: Erlbaum, 1983

Finn, Kathleen E., Abigail J. Sellen and Sylvia B. Wilbur, *Video-mediated Communication*, Mahwah, New Jersey: Erlbaum, 1997

Greenberg, Saul (editor), *Computer-supported Cooperative Work and Groupware*, London and San Diego: Academic Press, 1991

Kraut, R., T. Mukhopadyay, J. Szczpula, S. Kiesler and W. Scherlis, "Communication and Information: Alternative Uses of the Internet in Households" in CHI'98: Human Factors in Computer Systems, edited by Claire-Marie Karat, New York: ACM Press, 1998

Microsoft Corporation, *The Windows Interface Guidelines for Software Design*, Redmond, California: Microsoft Press, 1995

Monk, Andrew F. and Nigel Gilbert, *Perspectives on HCI: Diverse Approaches*, London and New York: Academic Press, 1995

Preece, Jenny, Yvonne Rogers, Helen Sharp, David Benyon, Simon Holland and Tom Carey, *Human–Computer Interaction*, Reading, Massachusetts: Addison Wesley, 1994

Williams, Marian G., M.W. Altom, K. Ehrlich and W. Newman, *CHI'99: Human Factors in Computing Systems*, New York: ACM Press, 1999

MONK & GILBERT is a collection of articles describing how different scientific disciplines, from computer science to ethnomethodology, have contributed to the study of human-computer interaction (HCI). HCI research is concerned with providing theories, concepts, and tools for designers who wish to create technological artefacts that are effective, efficient, and satisfying to use. In short, HCI takes a user-centred approach to design. Its beginnings in the late 1970s and early 1980s came about through an alliance between computer scientists and psychologists. Since then ethnography, ergonomics, and activity theory have been recruited to the cause. What is clear from the articles in this collection is that the original methods and concepts get subtly modified when adapted to this practical task of designing more usable technology. For this reason HCI may be best thought of as a discipline in its own right rather than an interdisciplinary activity.

PREECE *et al.* is a substantial text book (770 pages) for teaching HCI, and illustrates the maturity of the topic. Topics covered include theories for understanding human behaviour with technology, a framework for understanding the technology itself, design methods, and techniques for evaluating and improving a prototype.

MICROSOFT CORPORATION is a "style guide". This rather misleading term is taken to mean a set of guidelines and principles describing how a graphical user interface (GUI) should work: for example, what a menu should look like, how it should behave when the user interacts with it, and when it should be used rather than some other device such as a dialogue box. Apple produced the first style guide in 1987. It encapsulated a great deal of empirical and analytic work carried out by HCI researchers to find out what actually was the best way of doing things. Style guides are supported by software tools that make it much easier for software developers to obey the style guide than to ignore it. By enforcing a degree of consistency in this way, style guides ensure that when a user learns to do something in one context that knowledge will transfer to new contexts in a sensible way. There are now style guides for all the commonly used graphical user interfaces and also more generally framed international standards that do a similar job.

WILLIAMS *et al.* is part of the CHI conference series. This is the premier platform for work in HCI, and its proceedings have served to define the nature of the discipline. ACM is the major computing society in the US, and ACM SIGCHI is the Specialist Interest Group concerned with HCI. The conference is truly international: CHI2000, for example, is in Holland. The topic has evolved rapidly and the phrase "Human-Computer Interaction" no longer gives a very good picture of what HCI researchers are concerned with. For example, in the proceedings listed here there are as many articles on technology for human-human communication as human-computer communication *per se* (though there may be a computer in there somewhere). If you want an up-to-the minute picture of the concerns of HCI researchers, this conference series is where to go first.

GREENBERG is a landmark set of papers considering the HCI research area concerned with human-to-human communication. Research on Computer-Supported Cooperative Work (CSCW) includes all sorts of technologies for communication including: electronic meeting rooms; video conferencing; and text-based systems such as email and "chat". Sociologists have had a large influence on this area and CSCW research is concerned with the whole work context, i.e. how these technologies may influence personal and organisational relationships through their effects on the way work is done.

FINN, SELLEN & WILBUR is another useful set of papers on electronically mediated communication from a more psychological point of view. These papers are all concerned with the use of video to support communication when people are working together but cannot be together in the same place at the same time. They report various empirical studies of people using views of the other person, the context they are in, or some aspect of the work. This research draws heavily on theories of communication based in linguistics and psychology.

CARD, MORAN & NEWELL is included lest the reader should assume that HCI has no theory. This book presented the first coherent attempt to provide a unified account of how people interact with computers, e.g. what information processing goes on in the head of a user when they edit some text in a word processor. Since this book was published, the models of information processing have got very much more sophisticated and make use of specialised computer languages built for this purpose.

Finally KRAUT *et al.* is included as a pointer to where HCI is going next. All the key companies supplying information and communications technology are betting heavily that the next big development is to take this technology into the home. Media, communication, and computing technologies are said to be "fusing". Computers are now used for communication (e.g. email) and entertainment (e.g. DVD films). Communication devices are used to store data (e.g. the address book on a mobile phone) and media for home entertainment now rely on considerable computing power (e.g. the "set top box"). Kraut *et al.* report some findings from a large scale experiment that involved giving 110 households a PC with an internet connection and then monitoring their behaviour over a period of several months. The particular question asked in this paper is whether people get most value from communication (email) or information access (the world wide web). The answer is that interpersonal communication may be a more important use and determinant of a participant's commitment to the Internet than is information acquisition and entertainment. The technology for this next step is there, what the consumer will want to do with these technological opportunities is anybody's guess. What is certain is that usability is an even more sensitive issue in the home than it is in the office and that HCI researchers are having, and will continue to have, a large part to play in the development of this exciting new area.

ANDREW MONK

Humanism and world politics

Bullock, Alan, *The Humanist Tradition in the West*, London: Thames and Hudson, and New York: Norton, 1985

Davies, Tony, *Humanism*, London and New York: Routledge, 1997

Fromm, Erich (editor), *Socialist Humanism: An International Symposium*, Garden City, New York: Doubleday, 1965; London: Allen Lane, 1967

Hebblethwaite, Peter, *The Christian–Marxist Dialogue: Beginnings, Present Status and Beyond*, London: Darton Longman and Todd, and New York: Paulist Press, 1977

Keohane, Robert O. and Joseph S. Nye, *Transnational Relations and World Politics*, Cambridge, Massachussetts: Harvard University Press, 1972

Levi, Albert William, *Humanism and Politics: Studies in the Relationship of Power and Value in the Western Tradition*, Bloomington: Indiana University Press, 1969

Mathew, George (editor), *Towards Christian Humanism: An Indian Perspective*, New Delhi: Juhanon Mar Thoma Memorial Committee, 1983

Petrosyan, Mariya, *Humanism: Its Philosophical, Ethical and Sociological Aspects*, Moscow: Progress Publishers, 1972 (Russian edition, 1964)

Schiller, F.C.S., *Humanism: Philosophical Essays*, Westport, Connecticut: Greenwood Press, 1970 (1st edition 1903; 2nd edition 1912)

Soper, Kate, *Humanism and Anti-Humanism*, London: Hutchinson, and La Salle, Illinois: Open Court, 1986

In the absence of any definitive treatment of its subject, this entry will seek merely to explain why humanism can be seen as a relevant category from a world politics perspective, and to indicate to the reader some relevant sources that discuss two particular varieties of humanism that have enjoyed an international reputation since World War II: "socialist humanism" and "Christian humanism". For, as DAVIES has recently explained, the term "humanism" can be deployed in an extraordinarily large number of ways: "The seven distinct sub-definitions of humanism rather conservatively offered by the *Oxford English Dictionary* . . . represent only a fraction of the senses and contexts in which the word has been used, and a drastic oversimplification of those" (Davies, p.3).

Unfortunately, Davies is aimed primarily at the student of world literature, and the student of world politics has no readily usable "source book", mainly because the particularly vague connotations of the word humanism have not endeared it to political scientists of a positivist hue, who aspire to linguistic clarity as well as to quantifiable, testable hypotheses about political life. As LEVI argued as long ago as 1969, "the concepts of politics" associated with what has become known as the humanist tradition "are difficult to contain within the narrow limits of a pragmatic political science concerned exclusively with the exercise of power as a fragmented section of the total human enterprise" (Levi, p.6).

The phrase "world politics perspective" is associated with KEOHANE & NYE, who have sought to move traditional international relations scholarship away from a state-centred viewpoint towards a more pluralistic assessment of the relationships between global actors. In practice (according to Keohane & Nye) this meant giving special consideration to economic corporations – rather than other forms of human association – but it did at least indicate that political scientists could view human agents from other perspectives than those of "the subject" or "the citizen". Perhaps this was in keeping with Ferdinand Schiller's axiom that a "humanist philosopher is sure to be interested in the *rich variety* of human thought and sentiment" (SCHILLER, pp.xxi-xxii, my emphasis), but even periodic references to Thucydides may not save Keohane & Nye from the full force of Levi's critical observation.

A good case can be made to the effect that "the humanist tradition" is a retrospective invention of certain 19th-century German-speaking intellectuals; one that limits any culturally specific understanding of such "humanists" as Chaucer, Petrarch, or Erasmus that we might be able to reconstruct today (cf. Davies, pp.9–11, 15–17). But it can also be seen as a useful heuristic device. The "tail end" of history is contemporary life, and the closing pages of Levi (pp.298–445) and BULLOCK (pp.133–197) offer significant discussions of the (alleged) continuity of a Renaissance humanist/individualist tradition into the late-twentieth century. Levi is a recognisable work of intellectual history (history of political thought), while Bullock's perspective is more eclectic, taking note of developments in art history and social history. Thus the author states that "symbols and myths express a society's beliefs and values as one can see from the customs and conventions concerned with the universal experiences of birth, marriage and death"; but the visual arts possess a special power to "communicate across the barriers of separate languages" (Bullock, p.158). Consequently, a world politics perspective that took account of cultural as well as governmental and economic associations/communications would need to be aware of the *possibility* of the "existence"/relevance of a *European* humanist tradition, albeit one now widely disseminated by trade and conquest.

Clearly the concept of political "myth" has had important ramifications in the 20th century. According to some authorities, the increasingly widespread recognition among intellectuals that human imperfections cannot be superseded as a result of profound social change or spiritual restoration has demonstrated the centrality of "myth" to both Marxism and Christianity. One possible corollary of this argument is that many of the writers who have recognized this problem (and sought to reorder the connections between their own "myth" and the "myths" of others) are those who have been labelled "socialist humanists" or "Christian humanists".

In the immediate aftermath of Stalin's death, officially sanctioned Soviet humanism was merely one dimension of a policy of "coexistence" with capitalist ideology/ "myth", rather than a positive engagement with "the enemy". PETROSYAN's rather turgid discussions of "the general fate of mankind" indicate that an army marches at the pace of its slowest member, but Levi (pp.347–445) and Davies (pp.57–69) suggest that Sartre, Merleau-Ponty, Lukacs, Thompson, and the Yugoslavian *Praxis* group were all scouts on a mission to construct a pluralistic theory of communism. Hence, the socialist humanist debate was "deliberately" constructed to engage with "the other", and FROMM includes interesting texts written by "Catholics, independent liberals and non-Marxist labour party members" alongside essays by "socialists" and "Marxists" (Fromm, p.xiii).

The 1960s and 1970s were also the decades of the "Marxist-Christian dialogue" and while it is somewhat descriptive (rather than analytical) in character, HEBBLETHWAITE gives a broad outline of the debate, of the political content of liberation theology and Sino-Christianity, and of the religious aspect of Eurocommunism. Many of the participants in the "dialogue" described themselves as "liberal Christians" or "Christian humanists" and sought to promote conversation between Protestants and Catholics (as well as with Marxists) through organizations such as the World Council of Churches. MATHEW is a useful collection of Christian humanist essays, with a "Third World", rather than a Eurocentric, perspective.

The absence of a large number of generally recognised "secondary sources" in this field of political study has meant that this entry has only sought to furnish the reader with a limited agenda for their own research. (Davies is the best resource for further bibliography.) Political theorists may see opportunities to treat socialist and Christian humanist texts as resources for their own debates on freedom, rights, and justice, while political scientists might perceive explorable connections between the socialist and Christian humanist movements of the 1960s and 1970s and contemporary "civic" movements in Eastern Europe and the Third World. Moreover, the fact that "political" debates about socialist humanism triggered Althusser's famous anti-humanist polemics of the 1960s (which had profound significance for all the social sciences) should not be forgotten (see SOPER).

CLIVE E. HILL

Humour

Bergson, Henri, *Laughter: An Essay on the Meaning of the Comic*, New York: Macmillan, 1911

Bryant, John, *Melville and Repose: The American Renaissance*, New York: Oxford University Press, 1993

Boskin, Joseph, *Rebellious Laughter: People's Humor in American Culture*, Syracuse, New York: Syracuse University Press, 1997

Davies, Christie, *Jokes and their Relation to Society*, Berlin and New York: Mouton de Gruyter, 1998

Eastman, Max, *Enjoyment of Laughter*, New York: Simon and Schuster, 1936; London: Hamish Hamilton, 1937

Freud, Sigmund, *Jokes and their Relation to the Unconscious*, London: Hogarth Press, 1960

Goldstein, Jeffrey H. and Paul E. McGhee (editors), *The Psychology of Humor: Theoretical Perspectives and Empirical Issues*, New York and London: Academic Press, 1972

Gutwirth, Marcel, *Laughing Matter: An Essay on the Comic*, Ithaca, New York: Cornell University Press, 1993

Lent, John A., *Animation, Caricature, and Gag and Political Cartoons in the United States and Canada: An International Bibliography*, Westport, Connecticut: Greenwood Press, 1994a

Lent, John A., *Comic Books and Comic Strips in the United States: An International Bibliography*, Westport, Connecticut: Greenwood Press, 1994b

Morreall, John, *Taking Laughter Seriously*, Albany, New York: State University of New York, 1983

Morriss, Linda A. (editor), *Americana Women Humorists: Critical Essays*, New York: Garland, 1994

Nilsen, Donald L.F., *Humor Scholarship: A Research Bibliography*, Westport, Connecticut: Greenwood Press, 1993

Powell, Chris and George E.C. Paton (editors), *Humour in Society: Resistance and Control*, London: Macmillan and New York: St Martin's Press, 1988

Ruch, Willibald (editor), *The Sense of Humor: Explorations of a Personality Characteristic*, Berlin and New York: Mouton de Gruyter, 1998

Weisenburger, Steven, *Fables of Subversion: Satire and the American Novel 1930–1980*, Athens: University of Georgia Press, 1995

FREUD is the first significant study about the nature of humour in the modern world. Painstakingly, Freud outlines the power of humour to underscore the depth of human feelings and thoughts. Freud traces the growth of a psychological profile through the careful study of the use of humour to envelop the emotional and physical well-being of an individual. Humour, Freud contends, is an individual's attempt to "make sense of their spirit in the face of the universe".

BERGSON is considered the seminal work on why people laugh, and the significance of their laughter. It attempts to rationalize the apparently ephemeral and subjective feeling evoked by humour. Bergson's thesis is that laughter is an instrument of social correction that allows individuals to see themselves from afar and thereby improve themselves inwardly. The book clearly draws upon the early years of European modernism, and the author's emphasis on physical humour seems to be inspired by the works of film comics like Charlie Chaplin, Buster Keaton, and Harold Lloyd. Although this is a scholarly treatise, it is also a bracing read that will make you think twice about laughing the next time someone stumbles into a lamppost. EASTMAN also discusses why people laugh. Careful observations about human behavior in precarious everyday dilemmas are underscored by philosophical thought.

NILSEN provides the most complete synthesis of modern humour scholarship. More than a bibliography, this state of the art reference book underscores the abundance and importance of the interdisciplinary subject matter of humour studies. Documenting its output in careful detail, the author organizes his mammoth work into ten chapters reflecting various types of humour and topics of humour research. Extensive bibliographies on 45 fields of humour study – including humour by nationality, ethnicity, and by religious affiliation – are each introduced by a perceptive and absorbing essay outlining trends and major findings. Also included is an exhaustive bibliography of humour research institutes, journals, scholars, and academic programmes. Nilsen's influence on humour scholarship is profound because he is one of the first academics to include so much varied and distinguished scholarly work in one unique reference book.

MORRISS covers women's humour from 1840 to the present, with a wide variety of essays drawn from many academic sources. Social issues and gender roles figure heavily in these essays, particularly in Naomi Weinstein's "Why We Aren't Laughing . . . Any More", which underlines the terms in which feminist interpreters see humour. There are also exceptionally fine essays on 19th-century humour and how women's humour has changed in the years since. This book lays down criteria for what is becoming an increasingly interesting field of feminist studies. The select bibliography is short, but a fine start for anyone wishing to begin their studies of women's humour in relationship to American history.

LENT (1994a) provides a wide collection of American contemporary comic art, satire, animation, comic books, and related material. The author provides the necessary working bibliography for any thorough research of animation and comic art. The focus is largely on the modern, but mention is given to significant comic artists and work prior to 1920. Popular cartoonists like Zim, Art Young, VIP, and Oliphant are covered. Also included is a valuable section entitled Julie Sullivan's "Another Voice: The Black Cartoonists". Lent should be applauded for amassing so much material, and indexing it in appropriate subsections for the ready discovery of topical information. LENT (1994b) is a massive compilation of national and international resources for the study and analysis of cartoon strips. The author's list of sources, reviewed in the preface, is stunning in its detail.

BRYANT provides a definitive inquiry into the 19th-century form of American "amiable humour". Bryant's exploration of 19th-century writing, from Washington Irving to Herman Melville, gives a good discussion of sexuality, social ambivalence, and other concerns in American literature. It analyses attempts by 19th-century authors to come to grips with authorial experience in America. Thoughtful inquirers into pre-Civil War American humour will enjoy this book's attention to an American literary genre.

DAVIES is a comparative and historical study of jokes and other forms of humour. The focus is international, as she explores the idea that in ethnic jokes, the butt of the humour must always appear either stupid or crafty. There are strong essays about the sociology of humour as a weapon to explore the underbelly of modern society – alcoholism, sexuality, bestiality, and death. The collection concludes with an interesting study of the humorous writings of H.G. Wells. MORREALL argues for an equally serious approach to learning about humour and its relevant and contemporary ramifications in the development of social and political action.

GUTWIRTH reviews three approaches to explaining laughter – social, emotional, and intellectual – and presents a new analysis that considers the full range of funny events, from childish pranks and scatological jokes to comedies of mistaken identity. This is an excellent reference to explain contemporary events as seen through a funny lens.

BOSKIN offers a social record of people's humour in operation, while at the same time highlighting the extent to which humour is at the centre of social change and conflict. It explores how humour in the second half of the 20th century has defined and defused world events. During America's unprecedented social upheaval, humour reaffirmed communal realities and empowerment, while enlarging personal and historical perspectives.

POWELL & PATON brings together a revealing collection of essays on political, religious, and ethnic jokes. The essays describe how the use of humour can reinforce the social control of deviance from shared standards.

RUCH presents the latest thinking on the concept of "sense of humour" and how it applies to the understanding of human personality. A complete source book for the study of personality and humour, it distinguishes the characteristics that define the facets of humorous and humourless personalities. It also contains sections on history of humour, different aspects of sense of humour, developmental changes, cultural differences, and existing assessment tools for the study of personality characteristics. GOLDSTEIN & McGHEE gathers psychologists to discuss the ramifications of a sense of humour on personal development. The result is illuminating, exhaustive, and provocative.

WEISENBURGER's thesis is that postmodern satire (1930–80) is not conventionally corrective, but, rather, a form of black humour that is subversive of all value hierarchies. Modern authors Nathaniel West, Kurt Vonnegut, Thomas Pynchon, Flannery O'Connor, and Ishamel Reed are at the centre of this study. Weisenberger demonstrates how their humour is really a discourse of violence and a break from the modern tradition. This study shows how radically different humour has become in recent literary offerings.

JEFFREY S. KAPLAN

Hunting and gathering

Burbank, Victoria, *Fighting Women: Anger and Aggression in Aboriginal Australia*, Berkeley: University of California Press, 1994

Burch, Ernest S. and Linda J. Ellanna (editors), *Key Issues in Hunter-Gatherer Research*, Oxford: Berg, 1994

Gowdy, John M. (editor), *Limited Wants, Unlimited Means: A Reader on Hunter-Gatherer Economics and the Environment*, Washington, DC: Island Press, 1998

Grinker, Roy Richard, *Houses in the Rain Forest: Ethnicity and Inequality among Farmers and Foragers in Central Africa*, Berkeley: University of California Press, 1994

Kent, Susan (editor), *Cultural Diversity among Twentieth-Century Foragers: An African Perspective*, Cambridge and New York: Cambridge University Press, 1996

Kratz, Corinne Ann, *Affecting Performance: Meaning, Movement, and Experience in Okiek Women's Initiation*, Washington, DC: Smithsonian Institution Press, 1994

Ngaté-Grosz, Maria and Omari Kokole (editors), *Gendered Encounters: Challenging Cultural Boundaries and Social Hierarchies in Africa*, New York and London: Routledge, 1997

Silberbauer, George B., *Hunter and Habitat in the Central Kalahari Desert*, Cambridge and New York: Cambridge University Press, 1981

Turnbull, Colin, *The Forest People*, New York: Simon and Schuster, and London: Chatto and Windus, 1961

BURBANK is a confronting and detailed scholarly study of the meaning of gender relations amongst a Northern Australian Aboriginal group, thematically anchored in "aggression" as a key activity among women. The author, in a potent cross-cultural analysis, uses the concepts, categories, connections, and rules that are provided by her Aboriginal female protagonists to investigate the notion of "victim" constructed by Western feminists and to further sociological understanding of women.

BURCH & ELLANNA deftly edited a compelling collection of 19 essays. It is thematically divided into sections focusing on territories, hunter affluence, social stratification, cultural contact, gender, government intervention, native perspectives, and the future of field research. The section discussing gender begins a necessary deconstruction of the hunter-gatherer binary, to highlight the important contribution of gathering to people's daily food supply, thereby making women's work visible. It is refreshing to note that the collection also constructs yet contests the binary of simple and complex societies, to question the notion of "complex societies". For these reasons the book is useful as an early undergraduate text for contesting common-sense notions about "primitive" peoples.

GOWDY's edited collection of 12 classic articles examines a sampling of "original affluent societies" to analyse the ways in which they are adapting to processes of accelerating social change. The authors are particularly concerned with considerations of environmental sustainability and issues of social equality and justice. Its broad theoretical base ensures that the work can be used across a variety of sociological courses, in particular those focusing upon conceptual issues and methodological processes.

GRINKER works in dialogue with, and in contrast with, Turnbull's pioneering work with the Mbuti peoples. Focusing upon the Lese, a group of farmers in the Ituri forest, the author argues that the Efe foragers and Lese farmers are integral parts of the same ethnically-differentiated social system. In working with the relations between groups rather than focusing on a particular group, he construes the labels "farmer" and "forager" to be markers of ethnicity rather than of ecological adaptation, thereby adding complexity to sociological debates about hunting and gathering peoples.

The intrinsic similarity that can be constructed between hunter-gatherers' reliance on wild plants and animals is deconstructed in KENT, an edited collection of 12 essays that displays the tapestry of possibilities of human social organization. Each essay works to portray the extraordinary diversity of the modern world, and the cultural and behavioural diversity between groups labelled "hunter-gatherers". The different theoretical and band informants' locations collected by Kent generate greater understanding and knowledge about social interaction and behaviour.

KRATZ's detailed work traces the social and economic adaptations of several small tribal groupings in Kenya, including their interactions with pastoral and agricultural neighbours. The author employs a regional perspective that anchors her thematic concern with initiation ceremonies. Ceremonial styles and performances are incorporated into a study of the changing nature of peoples who were hunters and gatherers, and the ways in which they undertake social and economic diversification in an environment of accelerating change.

NGATÉ-GROSZ & KOKOLE edit, introduce, and provide a postscript to a dynamic collection of 11 essays that contest the identification of Africa with distinct tribes, many of whom are reified as "hunter-gatherers". Using gender as an analytic tool they work from a historical and sociocultural perspective to destabilize the concept of homogeneous and bounded social wholes and to examine the intersection of global historical forces with local social relations. This is a commanding and erudite edition that adds recent theoretical complexity and global analysis to debates generated by studies focused on "simple" societies.

Written with the compassion of a writer who wishes to promote a clear understanding of the nature of sociocultural systems so that members of powerful industrial societies may do minimal harm when encountering members of less powerful societies, SILBERBAUER executes a socioecological perspective to create an astute, lively, and detailed illumination of life among the G/wi peoples. His observations of congenial social intercourse and imaginative actions to counter stressful environmental living conditions provide poetic insights that are useful to provoke and stimulate early undergraduate students.

TURNBULL's classic text examines the hunting and gathering lives of the Mbuti (pygmy) peoples. He perceives the hunter-gatherers as socially and culturally independent from their Bila neighbours. The Mbuti are portrayed as viewing the farmers and their villages as simply one of several hunting grounds, and their interaction with the farmers as a luxury that complements their daily exploitation of forest products.

The compelling text provides a lucid description of lived experience among people who perceive their benevolent forest to be a provider of joy.

HELEN JOHNSON

See also Traditional society

Hypnosis

Bongartz, Walter (editor), *Hypnosis: 175 Years after Mesmer*, Konstanz: Universitätsverlag Konstanz, 1992

Crasilneck, Harold B. and James A. Hall, *Clinical Hypnosis: Principles and Applications*, 2nd edition, Orlando, Florida: Grune and Stratton, 1985

Fromm, Erika and Ronald E. Shor (editors), *Hypnosis: Developments in Research and New Perspectives*, 2nd edition, New York: Aldine, 1979

Fromm, Erika and Michael R. Nash, *Contemporary Hypnosis Research*, New York: Guilford Press, 1992

Gardner, G. Gail and Karen Olness, *Hypnosis and Hypnotherapy with Children*, New York: Grune and Stratton, 1981

Hammond, D. Corydon, *Handbook of Hypnotic Suggestions and Metaphors*, New York: Norton, 1990

Laurence, Jean-Roch and Campbell Perry, *Hypnosis, Will and Memory: A Psycho-legal History*, New York: Guilford Press, 1988

Lynn, Steven Jay and Judith W. Rhue, *Theories of Hypnosis: Current Models and Perspectives*, New York: Guilford Press, 1991

Spiegel, Herbert and David Spiegel, *Trance and Treatment: Clinical Uses of Hypnosis*, New York: Basic Books, 1978

Udolf, Roy, *Handbook of Hypnosis for Professionals*, 2nd edition, New York: Van Nostrand Reinhold, 1987

Weitzenhoffer, André M., *General Techniques of Hypnotism*, New York: Grune and Stratton, 1957

Any exploration of hypnosis must begin with the classic work by WEITZENHOFFER. He brings the novice from a thorough understanding of the nature and dynamics of hypnosis to a carefully laid out description of hypnotic inductions. It can easily serve as *the* book for teaching introductory and advanced courses in hypnosis. Weitzenhoffer builds the book in such a way as to permit the reader to understand the basics of trance before beginning the actual work of teaching inductions. Simple inductions are taught first (with illustrations when relevant) followed, in a progressive fashion, by the more difficult or complicated inductions. This book completes its in-depth analysis with a discussion of special problems and applications of hypnosis.

Another classic is the work by FROMM & SHOR. Erika Fromm is one of the masters of the field. The book, while not recent, remains one of the classic works. It is not written so much for the novice as for the expert who wishes to delve more deeply into the field. Some of the research it refers to is now dated but the book has certainly not lost its value due to its age. In fact, many later works refer to much of the research and many of the theories first mentioned in this work.

LYNN & RHUE provide an excellent overview of the various theories concerning hypnosis. Each chapter is written by one of the recognized masters in his or her particular field. The major headings are historical perspective, single-factor theories, clinical perspectives, sociocognitive perspective, and interactive-phenomenological models. As mentioned in the preface, the book is intended "to appeal to students, instructors, researchers, and clinicians who desire an insider's view of major hypnosis theories." This is indeed the case. Most chapters are very well written and are in depth. Lynne & Rhue include a conclusions chapter, where there is a synthesis of the earlier chapters, and a general discussion of the direction of the field.

FROMM & NASH's work is a continuation of Fromm's previous work. It differs from Lynne & Rhue in that the latter tends to be more clinical whereas Fromm & Nash is more research oriented. As the two authors are considered among the five or so top experts in the field, they had no trouble convincing the other masters to contribute. This book is not for the light reader. Only the serious student or expert should attempt it. However, one cannot hope to master the field of hypnosis without reading it.

BONGARTZ successfully combines the best in various aspects of hypnosis to give the reader a thorough understanding of the different issues and uses of hypnosis. Major subject headings are: *History; Experimental Hypnosis; Theoretical Aspects; Hypnosis in Psychotherapy; Hypnosis in the Medical Setting; Hypnosis in Dentistry;* and *Hypnosis in Sports.* Particularly enjoyable is the section on history where the life of Anton Mesmer is described at depth. The one drawback is the difficulty in obtaining the book.

LAURENCE & PERRY has a very different focus. Their book attempts to explore the viability of hypnosis in the courtroom setting. This very readable and fascinating book traces the history of modern-day hypnosis from Mesmer. It slowly and carefully considers the case for including hypnosis in the courts. It is very careful not to take sides but simply explores the nature of hypnosis and how it was regarded over the generations.

For a more clinical view, UDOLF is recommended. His book is appropriate for those who are beginning to learn how to use hypnotic suggestions in clinical practice. He describes hypnotic phenomena at depth in an understandable manner, explains how to measure for hypnotic susceptibility, and addresses clinical and ethical issues as well as potential dangers.

GARDNER & OLNESS is a clinical work that focuses on hypnosis with children. The book focuses on practical suggestions rather than theory. It includes scripts of inductions as well as some normative data on the hypnotic treatment of children. However, it essentially includes and discusses aspects of the hypnotherapeutic treatment of children.

CRASILNECK & HALL is also a clinical text. This is perhaps the most clinical of the texts listed above in the sense that it provides both examples of suggestions as well as a description of when to use them. There are some markers in relation to differential diagnosis and a thorough listing of references so the reader can go to the original sources.

HAMMOND's 600-page book provides the budding hypnotist with a massive number of hypnotic inductions, metaphors, and hypnotic suggestions. Most are written in a script fashion that the hypnotist could read directly to the patient (although this is not recommended – individual "fitting" of the suggestions or metaphors is more appropriate). The chapter titles reflect the diversity of content. They vary from psychological disorders to almost every aspect of medical disorders (non-psychological, physical). There is also a section on time reorientation; a subject not frequently explored.

Superficially SPIEGEL & SPIEGEL resembles yet another book where clinical and theoretical aspects of hypnosis is presented, but in reality it is not. The authors are considered among the masters of the field. Theirs is a different theory where dissociation plays a major part. This book is not so much for the researcher or the clinician who makes use of behavioural techniques as for the more psychodynamic clinician.

RICHARD KRAMER

Hysteria

Breuer, Josef and Sigmund Freud, *Studies on Hysteria*, London: Hogarth Press, and New York: Macmillan, 1955 (Freud's *The Standard Edition of the Complete Psychological Works*, vol. 2)

Charcot, J.-M., *Leçons du mardi à la Salpêtrière: policlinique 1887–1888*, 2nd edition, Paris: Louis Battaille, 1892

Didi-Huberman, Georges, *Invention de l'hystérie: Charcot et l'iconographie photographique de la Salpêtrière*, Paris: Macula, 1982

Freud, Sigmund, "The Defence Neuro-Psychoses" (published in German 1894) in *Early Psycho-analytic Publications*, London: Hogarth Press, 1962 (*The Standard Edition of the Complete Psychological Works*, vol. 3)

Freud, Sigmund, "Further Remarks on the Neuro-Psychoses of Defence" in *The Standard Edition of the Complete Psychological Works*, vol. 3, London: Hogarth Press, and New York: Macmillan, 1957 (published in German 1896a)

Freud, Sigmund, "The Aetiology of Hysteria" in *The Standard Edition of the Complete Psychological Works*, vol. 3, London: Hogarth Press, and New York: Macmillan, 1957 (published in German 1896b)

Herman, Judith Lewis, *Trauma and Recovery*, New York: Basic Books, 1992; revised edition 1997

Lacan, Jacques, "Variantes de la cure type" in his *Écrits: A Selection*, London: Tavistock, and New York: Norton, 1977 (essay published in French, 1955)

Lacan, Jacques, *Le Séminaire, Livre 20: Encore (1972–1973)*, edited by Jacques-Alain Miller, Paris: Seuil, 1975; as *On Feminine Sexuality: The Limits of Love and Knowledge: Encore 1972–1973*, New York: Norton, 1998

Lacan, Jacques, "Comptes rendus d'enseignement: la logique du fantasme", *Ornicar*, 29 (1984): 7–25

Lacan, Jacques, *Le Séminaire, Livre 17: L'Envers de la psychanalyse (1969–1970)*, edited by Jacques-Alain Miller, Paris: Seuil, 1991

Micale, Mark S., *Approaching Hysteria: Disease and its Interpretations*, Princeton, New Jersey: Princeton University Press, 1995

Miller, J.-A., "Symptôme et fantasme", *Actes de l'Ecole de la Cause Freudienne*, 2 (1982)

Mitchell, Juliet, *Psychoanalysis and Feminism*, Harmondsworth: Penguin, and New York: Vintage, 1975

Ortner, Sherry B. and Harriet Whitehead, *Sexual Meanings: The Cultural Construction of Gender and Sexuality*, Cambridge and New York: Cambridge University Press, 1981

Papyrus Ebers: Oldest Medical Book in the World, Chesapeake, New York: ECA Associates, 1990

Ragland-Sullivan, E., "Dora and the Name-of-the-Father: The Structure of Hysteria" in *Discontented Discourses: Feminism/Textual Intervention/Pyschoanalysis*, edited by Marleen Barr and Richard Feldstein, Urbana: University of Illinois Press, 1989

Ragland-Sullivan, E., "The Sexual Masquerade: A Lacanian Theory of Sexual Difference" in *Lacan and the Subject of Language*, edited by Ellie Ragland-Sullivan and Mark Bracher, New York and London: Routledge, 1991

Rose, Jacqueline, "Femininity and its Discontents" in *Sexuality in the Field of Vision*, London: Verso, 1986

Soler, Colette, "Hysteria and Obsession" in *Reading Seminars I and II: Lacan's Return to Freud*, edited by Richard Feldstein, Bruce Fink and Maire Jaanus, Albany: State University of New York Press, 1996

Veith, Ilse, *Hysteria: The History of a Disease*, Chicago: University of Chicago Press, 1965

Verhaeghe, Paul, *Does the Woman Exist? From Freud's Hysteric to Lacan's Feminine*, New York: Other Press, 1999a

Verhaeghe, Paul, "Subject and Body: Lacan's Struggle with the Real", *The Letter: Lacanian Perspectives on Psychoanalysis*, 17 (1999b): 79–119

The first known theory of hysteria appears in a 4000-year old papyrus found in Kahun in Egypt (PAPYRUS EBERS). It explains hysteria as being caused by the migration of the uterus (Greek *hyster* = "uterus"), which was considered to be an independent, autonomous organism. Since the treatment of hysteria aimed to pin down this organ to the right place, the standard therapy prescribed in those days by the physician-priests consisted, logically, of marriage. Like most grotesque theories, it contains a kernel, or better, two kernels of truth. With its conception of a sexual organ as heterogeneous to the rest of the body, this theory implied the idea of a split within the human being, thus anticipating Freud's discovery of the unconscious as a kind of intimate stranger within ourselves: part of us and yet unknown. Second, this link between hysteria and womanhood persisted systematically through history, although in a very particular way (since hysteria has a pre-eminently subversive character). From the Middle Ages to today, hysteria has manifested itself as undermining and destabilizing the reigning authority, be it religious or scientific, by uncovering or incarnating the gaps in that authority's knowledge (see VEITH and MICALE). Hysteria denounces the failure of symbolic (phallic) logic to grasp the essence of femininity. It can be seen as an oscillation in matters of sexual identity, pointing to the ever-impossible relation between the real and the symbolic. As a result, all of language and knowledge comes down to a masquerade around a sexual harmony that is not one (RAGLAND-SULLIVAN 1991).

Charcot was the first man to study hysteria in a scientific way, through observation and objective classification (see CHARCOT). In his work at the Salpêtrière in Paris, a hospital, insane asylum, and shelter for women, he focussed on the hysterical attack, trying to differentiate it from epilepsy. His drawings and photographs of different stages in the hysterical attack are still noteworthy (see DIDI-HUBERMAN). Through the use of hypnosis, Charcot discovered the traumatic aetiology. Nevertheless, he remained with observation and failed to formulate the link between this aetiology and an eventual treatment.

Freud broke away from the scientific tradition of observation and description, i.e. from the spell hysteria puts on the male gaze. In the wake of Breuer's experience with "Anna O" and the talking cure, he listened to his hysterical patients in order to understand and to treat them. Soon, Freud found that the aetiology of hysteria wasn't biological but strictly psychological. More precisely, he discovered that traumatic experiences or ideas become split off from consciousness and form a separate psychical group, inaccessible to consciousness (BREUER & FREUD). A few years later, he was more precise about the particular nature of the trauma: it concerns sexual experiences that occurred in early childhood. The fantasy of seduction by the father is a defensive effect of the Oedipus Complex, containing and hiding a ground of reality through the mother's pre-Oedipal bodily ministrations (see FREUD 1894, 1896a, 1896b; also "Female Sexuality" in volume 21 and "Femininity" in volume 22 of the Standard Edition of his Collected Works). In order to remove any misunderstanding and avoid the post-Freudian controversy on the issue of "fantasy or real trauma?", it is necessary to emphasise that if Freud abandoned his trauma theory in matters of hysteria, he never denied the psychopathological consequences of trauma as such. Indeed, Freud created a separate clinical category for it, known today as "post traumatic stress disorder" (see HERMAN).

In his later work, Freud shifted his attention from hysteria to femininity and the preOedipal stage without really solving the problem. MITCHELL explains Freud's delay and failure to get to the bottom of the female Oedipus complex as follows: as a man, he could not have ears for what was really important for a woman. His discovery was nothing but a further development of what he had received as a gift from women analysts. Lacan presented us with a further elaboration, by making a differentiation between hysteria and femininity. According to Lacan, the imaginary order in general and desire in particular are two coping strategies of the hysterical subject to defend itself against the traumatic real of the drive (LACAN 1984). Hysteria can be characterized by its basic fantasy (*fantasme fondamental*), i.e. the way in which the hysterical subject defines itself in relation to the Other and his or her desire. This basic fantasy can be analysed as a Symbolico-Imaginary montage that tries but fails to translate the real *jouissance* into phallic pleasure (MILLER, VERHAEGHE 1999a). The fundamentally unsatisfiable nature of desire that characterizes hysteria is also a coping strategy with respect to *jouissance*, since it comes down to the refusal (*dérobade*) to be reduced to the passive object of *jouissance* of the other/Other (LACAN 1977, SOLER). In this way, hysteria is a failed attempt to solve the problem of femininity, i.e. the relation of the female subject to the not-all of her body, the part that lies beyond the phallic signifier (LACAN 1998).

The idea of passivity brings us to the question of gender identity. The link between hysteria and femininity led the feminists to study Freud. Their main conclusion (ORTNER & WHITEHEAD, ROSE) comes down to the differentiation between sex (the biological) and gender (the psychosexual identity). Further development privileged the gender part, thus answering the basic question of hysteria ("What am I as a sexual being ?") from a sociocultural point of view. Ragland-Sullivan's thesis was far more profound. Sex/gender and the privileging of one of the two is not the issue, but rather the issue concerned the effort of others pinning woman down as a sexual body in terms of an identity for which she precisely lacks a signifying base (RAGLAND-SULLIVAN 1989). For VERHAEGHE (1999b), combining Freud's terms of activity and passivity with Lacan's theory on the drive, gender identity is even less important. The basic opposition is not male/female, nor gender/sex, but the active versus the passive position of the subject, in relation to the primal asexual, genderless drive. It is this internal relationship that will determine the later intersubjective relationship, be it a heterosexual or a homosexual one.

Since hysteria concerns the lack of the symbolic order, making sexuality and gender identity structurally problematic, hysteria is neither a disease nor a dysfunction, but the essence of the human condition. Hence, LACAN (1991) raised hysteria to the level of a discourse structure, i.e. hysterical discourse. As a discourse, it endorses the discourse of the master by questioning it, which explains its ever-failing subversive character (Lacan 1991). This is one of the reasons why therapy, and even analysis, often fails in a predictable structural way (see Verhaege 1999b).

FRÉDÉRIC DECLERCK

See also Feminism and psychoanalysis

I

Idealism

Allison, Henry E., *Kant's Transcendental Idealism: An Interpretation and Defense*, New Haven, Connecticut: Yale University Press, 1983

Coates, Paul and Daniel D. Hutto (editors), *Current Issues in Idealism*, Bristol: Thoemmes Press, 1996

Ewing, A.C. (editor), *The Idealist Tradition: From Berkeley to Blanshard*, Glencoe, Illinois: Free Press, 1957

Foster, John, *The Case for Idealism*, London and Boston: Routledge and Kegan Paul, 1982

Kant, Immanuel, *Critique of Pure Reason*, unified edition, Indianapolis: Hackett, 1996 (original edition 1781)

Rescher, Nicholas, "Conceptual Idealism Revisited", *Review of Metaphysics*, 44/3 (1991): 495–523

Solomon, Robert C. and Kathleen M. Higgins (editors), *The Age of German Idealism*, London and New York: Routledge, 1993 (vol. 6 of Routledge History of Philosophy)

Sprigge, T.L.S., *The Vindication of Absolute Idealism*, Edinburgh: Edinburgh University Press, 1983

Sprigge, Timothy L.S., entry on Idealism in *Routledge Encyclopedia of Philosophy*, edited by Edward Craig, vol. 4, London and New York: Routledge, 1998

Vesey, Godfrey (editor), *Idealism: Past and Present*, Cambridge and New York: Cambridge University Press, 1982

The ideas and viewpoints termed as "idealism" (used generally in juxtaposition to "realism") permeate most of the social sciences, but as a doctrine idealism is first and foremost a philosophical concept. In the modern Western philosophical tradition it is usually understood as the view that mind is the most basic reality and that the physical is derived from the mind. The area is vast and complex and the literature on it is enormous. The best place to start with may be SPRIGGE (1998). He charts the evolution of the idealist tradition in the modern West, summarizing the main arguments of prominent proponents. He first advocates a general case for idealism, and then goes on to distinguish between Berkeleian ontological idealism and Kantian transcendental idealism. He ends up with short notes on Anglo-American absolute idealism, Panpsychism, and personal idealism. The entry also includes suggestions on further reading. The entry may prove to be an easy introduction and therefore the best place to start.

"Idealism in its philosophical sense is idea-lism": this is what

VESEY discusses in the insightful foreword to the collection of Royal Institute of Philosophy lectures on the theme of idealism. Among other things, the contributors address themselves to issues such as Descartes's influence on Berkeley, comparison between Berkeley's immaterialism and Kant's transcendental idealism, differences and similarity between Kant's "subjective" idealism and Hegel's "absolute" idealism, compatibility of idealist as well as materialist aspects within Marxism, and so on. The articles do not provide a comprehensive survey of the philosophical concept, they do give an in-depth analysis of some of the areas within it.

In contrast, the Routledge *History of Philosophy*, volume six, by SOLOMON & HIGGINS, is a comprehensive treatment of German idealism. It traces the emergence of German idealism from Kant and his predecessors through the first half of the 19th century, ending with the irrationalism of Kierkegaard. It provides a broad, scholarly introduction to this period for students of philosophy and related disciplines, as well as some original interpretations of these authors. The chapters have many points of contact and contrast – for instance, between the logical analyses of concepts in Kant, Fichte, and Hegel, and the political philosophies of Kant, Hegel, and Marx. A glossary of technical terms is provided, together with a chronological table of philosophical, scientific and other important cultural events. An accessible and useful collection of articles on individual thinkers, the book is important reading for beginners.

For a classic statement on transcendental idealism one has to go for one of the greatest philosophical works of all time: KANT's *Critique of Pure Reason*. Numerous editions and translations exist of the same work, but the unified edition mentioned in the list is a safe bet for its accuracy and readability. The translator's footnotes may assist readers by providing explanatory comments of various kinds. It is worth reading the whole book to understand the finer points of Kant's arguments, but it is the first part dealing with the "transcendental aesthetic" and the section "on transcendental ideas" that are more relevant.

ALLISON aims to provide "a more or less comprehensive study of Kant's theoretical philosophy, organised around the theme of transcendental idealism". For the most part the text consists of a series of painstaking analyses of crucial Kantian arguments. He also provides a polemic against "the standard picture" of Kantian idealism as an unstable combination of phenomenalistic subjectivism and the postulation of transcendental entities for which there is no evidence. Although Allison himself essentializes Kantian arguments in some places, overall his work is superbly organized and lucidly written. For those interested in his works, another book worth examining is his more recent collection of essays, *Idealism and Freedom: Essays on Kant's Theoretical and Practical Philosophy* (1996).

SPRIGGE (1983) shows the richness of the tradition of "absolute idealism" as different from ontological idealism and transcendental idealism. He argues in three progressive stages for the existence of "psychical realities", "panpsychism", and "absolute idealism". The book has important discussions of issues such as space, time, causality, and memory. It is a book only for those are familiar with the basic concepts of idealism.

EWING's book may be quite old, but it does prove to be a readable and comprehensive work on idealism. It not only contains selections from important representatives of the school, but also has a good introduction by the editor, setting out the main doctrines and some of the criticisms to which they have been subjected. This volume has works by British, American, and Italian idealists like Bradley, Bosanquet, Royce, Rashdall, Howison, Croce, and Blanshard, which may not be found in the other works mentioned in the bibliography. The volume may also be helpful as it has views of prominent critics of idealism such as Moore, Russell, Nagel, and Wilson.

FOSTER's primary aim is to refute realism about the physical world and to develop, in its place, a version of phenomenalism. He defends the claims made by earlier proponents of idealism – that ultimate contingent reality is wholly non-physical, and that physical world is the logical product of facts about human sense experience. The book introduces some technical concepts including different versions of realism, antirealism, mentalism, and physicalism; provides a "topic neutrality thesis" followed by a "full anti-realism", and makes a case for phenomenalism. However, beginners may find the book slightly inaccessible on account of its complex and technical formulations.

RESCHER's article is a result of his endeavour to restate more clearly the position he had adopted in his earlier book *Conceptual Idealism* (1973). He provides a lucid elaboration of his central thesis that the mind is responsible for nature as we understand it. In the process he contests several common objections to idealism, including the most common one centred on the issue of the mind, independence of the real. Throughout he stresses the hermeneutic rather than the causal role of mind. The article contains strong arguments and is worth reading.

COATES & HUTTO provide one of the rare current anthologies on 20th-century idealism. The contributions by scholars such as Sorell, Wilson, Marsonet, and Armour show how the debate between idealism and realism is as important now as it was at the beginning of the 19th century. Each individual paper contains a list of references at the end, which may act as guide for further readings on specific themes.

DIBYESH ANAND

See also Critical realism

Identification

Abrams, Dominic and Michael A. Hogg (editors), *Social Identity and Social Cognition*, Oxford and Malden, Massachusetts: Blackwell, 1999

Antaki, Charles and Sue Widdicombe (editors), *Identities in Talk*, London and Thousand Oaks, California: Sage, 1998

Hogg, Michael A. and Dominic Abrams, *Social Identifications: A Social Psychology of Intergroup Relations and Group Processes*, London and New York: Routledge, 1988

Robinson, W.P. (editors), *Social Groups and Identities: Developing the Legacy of Henri Tajfel*, Oxford and Boston: Butterworth Heinemann, 1996

Tajfel, Henri, C. Flamment, M. Billig and R.P. Bundy, "Social Categorization and Intergroup Behaviour", *European Journal of Social Psychology*, 1 (1971): 149–78

Tajfel, Henri, *Human Groups and Social Categories: Studies in Social Psychology*, Cambridge and New York: Cambridge University Press, 1981

Turner, John C. *et al.* (editors), *Rediscovering the Social Group: A Self-Categorization Theory*, Oxford and New York: Blackwell, 1987

Wetherell, Margaret (editor), *Identities, Groups and Social Issues*, London: Sage, 1996

Worchel, Stephen *et al.* (editors), *Social Identity: International Perspectives*, London and Thousand Oaks, California: Sage, 1998

It is often acknowledged that Henri Tajfel provides the starting point for any examination of identification within modern social psychology. TAJFEL's *Human Groups and Social Categories: their Social Psychology* contains all of his major theoretical and empirical writing, from his early research on the categorization of physical stimuli to his later work on social identity. Tajfel introduced the notions of personal identity and social identity into social psychology in an attempt to resolve the individual–group dilemma. He stated that a person can either act according to his personal identity or social identity, depending on how the situation is understood and which identity is made salient. Personal identity refers to those qualities and characteristics we see in ourselves that are strictly individual. Social identity is that part of individuals' self-concepts that derives from their knowledge of their membership of a social group (or groups) together with the value and emotional significance of that membership.

This distinction grew from the "minimal group" experiments conducted by TAJFEL *et al.* Tajfel wished to investigate the "minimal" necessary conditions for intergroup discrimination and ethnocentrism. He experimentally created two artificial groups outside any real or meaningful context and where no intergroup conflict existed. Participants were told their group membership and put in separate cubicles and then requested to allocate money to two recipients (one ingroup and one outgroup) using a prepared booklet containing decision matrices. Participants tended to allocate more rewards to members of their own group than members of other group, while still maximizing the profit of their group. They were not just concerned with sheer profit, but with "beating" the outgroup. Tajfel *et al.* conducted numerous studies that replicated the findings of this experiment, and Tajfel's social identity theory was created to explain these unexpected results. Central to this explanation was the notion that people have a powerful and perhaps universal motive to think well of themselves (to increase their self-esteem). One way to enhance self-esteem is to create a positive sense of social identity by favouring members of one's own group.

HOGG & ABRAMS provide a very accessible account of social identification, and probably still have the most comprehensive overview of social identity theory. They look at the way people derive their identity from social groups to which they belong, and the consequences for their feelings, thoughts, and behaviour of psychologically belonging to a group. In chapter two they discuss social identity theory in detail, highlighting its various assumptions and its specific theoretical propositions. Hogg & Abrams also spend some time locating the social identity perspective in the broader framework of social psychology and the social sciences. They state that social identity theory does take a distinctive structuralist perspective (which has its roots in the ideas of Marx and Weber) because it maintains that society consists of social categories that stand in power and status relations to one another. Furthermore, social identity theory states that social categories are often in conflict with each other due to their different power relationships. These social categories give a society its distinctive social structure and an individual is born into this social structure, and enters a dynamic relationship with it. Hogg & Abrams also state that social identity theory has a functionalist strand as the psychological processes involved in social identification and group behaviour are considered universal and transhistorical, because they are functional for the human organism.

TURNER et al. present an extension of social identity theory, namely self-categorization theory. Unlike social identity theory, this theory did not develop from a desire to explain intergroup bias. Rather, it developed because of a need to understand further how a collection of individuals become a social and psychological group, perceiving, defining themselves and acting as a single unit, feeling, thinking, and self-aware as a collective entity. The book contains a detailed description of self-categorization theory, including the central assumptions and hypotheses of the theory. Essentially Turner et al. argue that psychological identification takes place to the degree that two or more people come to perceive and define themselves in terms of some shared ingroup–outgroup categorization. Self-categorization theory is founded on the assumption that identification reflects self-categorization – the cognitive grouping of the self as identical to some class of stimuli in contrast to some other class of stimuli.

ROBINSON presents an interesting collection of chapters from the numerous authors who were closely associated with Tajfel's far-reaching insights into social identity, including Turner, Hogg, Oakes, Eiser, Abrams, Brown, Giles, Milner, Wetherell, Condor, Reicher, and Billig. Although social identity and self-categorization theory (Brown, Abrams, Turner) are, of course, well represented, there is also intriguing diversity and breadth in these chapters. The contributions range from Eiser's reappraisal of Tajfel's accentuation principle in terms of recent developments in cognitive science, to the critical social psychology of authors like Billig, Reicher, Condor, and Wetherell who argue that social identity theory must avoid reification of the social context.

The edited book by WORCHEL et al. provides an up-to-date insight into current researchers working within the frameworks of social identity theory and self-categorization theory. The book brings together an international cast of social psychologists (including Bar-Tal, Doise, Deschamps, Oakes, Haslam, Turner, Marques, Hinkle, and Mugny). The first section of the book examines the relationship between the self or personal identity and the group; the second examines social or group identity explicitly; the third examines the relationship between social identity and intergroup relations; and the final section investigates the influence of cultural values on identification.

ABRAMS & HOGG have managed to produce a milestone in the progress of social psychology. The very up-to-date edited book brings together key researchers in the social identity and social cognition traditions to address the interface between the two traditionally opposing approaches. The chapters represent an excellent sample of the range of areas across which social identity and social cognition researchers are integrating aspects of each other's research (for example the self, stereotyping, intergroup discrimination, group identification, and social influence). The book is aimed at researchers and upper-level students and includes contributions from some of the leading figures in the field of social psychology (for example Fiske, Oakes, Haslam, Sherman, Hamilton, Hewstone, Brown, Walker, Smith, and Mackie).

The chapters in WETHERELL provide a very accessible, authoritative, and engaging overview of social psychological research on social identity, group life, and intergroup relations. The focus of the book is broad, with a representative mix of European and North American research drawing from a range of theoretical backgrounds: psychoanalysis, social theory, discourse analysis, and feminism. The book includes a chapter each from Potter and from Wetherell who adopt a discourse analytic approach, which is predominately concerned with how people socially construct their identities in everyday interaction, particularly in talk and discourse. Discourse analysis does not attempt to explain identity in terms of cognitive process (social categorization) but, rather, focuses upon how certain identity constructions enable particular actions.

A similar approach is taken among the contributors to the edited book by ANTAKI & WIDDICOMBE. In a collection of chapters drawing on ethnomethodology and conversation analysis, this book gathers together authors who contend that identities are constructed "live" in the exchange of talk. Real social interactions from tapes and transcripts are examined throughout the book to show how social identities are often contested, negotiated, and sometimes resisted.

ADAM RUTLAND

See also Bias

Identity

Bauman, Zygmunt, *Intimations of Postmodernity*, London and New York: Routledge, 1992

Brah, Avtar, *Cartographies of Diaspora: Contesting Identities*, London and New York: Routledge, 1996

Davis, Fred, *Fashion, Culture and Identity*, Chicago: University of Chicago Press, 1992

Erikson, Erik H., *Identity and the Life Cycle: Selected Papers*, New York: International Universities Press, 1959

Freud, Sigmund, "Group Psychology and the Analysis of the Ego" (1921) and "The Ego and the Id" (1923) in *A General Selection from the Works of Sigmund Freud*, edited by John Rickman, London: Hogarth Press, 1937

Giddens, Anthony, *Modernity and Self Identity: Self and Society in the Late Modern Age*, Cambridge: Polity Press, and Stanford, California: Stanford University Press, 1991

Goffman, Erving, *The Presentation of Self in Everyday Life*, New York: Doubleday, 1959; London: Allen Lane, 1969

Goffman, Erving, *Stigma: Notes on the Management of Spoiled Identity*, Englewood Cliffs, New Jersey: Prentice Hall, 1963; London: Penguin, 1968

Lash, Scott and Jonathan Friedman (editors), *Modernity and Identity*, Oxford and Cambridge, Massachusetts: Blackwell, 1992

Lunt, Peter K. and Sonia M. Livingstone, *Mass Consumption and Personal Identity: Everyday Economic Experience*, Buckingham: Open University Press, 1992

Mead, George H., *Mind, Self and Society from the Standpoint of a Social Behaviorist*, Chicago: University of Chicago Press, 1934

Rattansi, Ali and Sallie Westwood (editors), *Racism, Modernity and Identity: On the Western Front*, Cambridge and Cambridge, Massachusetts: Polity Press, 1994

Skevington, Suzanne and Deborah Baker (editors), *The Social Identity of Women*, London: Sage, 1989

Weeks, Jeffrey and Janet Holland (editors), *Sexual Cultures: Communities, Values and Intimacy*, London: Macmillan, 1996

Personal and social identity has been studied from a variety of academic angles, resulting in a highly differentiated literature that often appears to cover almost as many different *types* of identity as there are social groups. A range of some of the most influential of these studies has been selected in the review that follows.

Although he did not explicitly use the term "identity", FREUD formulated an overarching theory of consciousness and the self that had a profound influence on the understanding of concepts that were later to be grouped around the notion of "identity", and particularly on the formation of the American "ego psychology" movement. He divided mental life into a three-tiered mechanism involving the id, ego and superego. In this schema the id represents the individual's most basic, instinctual drives, the superego is broadly associated with the conscience and with qualities such as self-reflection, and the ego is the unifying force that holds them all together. As the representative of reason and the constraints of the external world, it ensures the consistency and continuity of the self by uniting the various aspects of the personality into "a coherent organization of mental processes".

ERIKSON developed these ideas into a theory in which the specific concept of identity was paramount. For him, identity is a multifaceted notion formed by the interrelations of individuals with their social surroundings and refers to "a persistent sameness within oneself (self-sameness) and a persistent sharing of some kind of essential character with others". Ultimately, the continuity of this sense of self ensures that whatever happens to individuals during their lifetime, and however traumatic the transition from one phase to another, they always

retain a fundamental sense of who they are and do not consider themselves to have substantially changed. For Erikson, the development of self-identity meets a catalyst – an "identity-crisis" – around adolescence or early adulthood that must be successfully resolved in order for the individual to establish this coherent sense of self. At this point, social interaction is crucial. Individuals attempt to attach themselves to a social group or niche, and this they do by experimenting with different roles, lifestyles, and friendships and by formulating a longer term "life plan" for themselves. Success in these pursuits leads to a stable sense of identity, whereas failure in them (for example, through unemployment or ethnic differences) leads to alienation and "acute identity confusion".

As opposed to the individualistic nature of identity proposed in the psychoanalytic movement, in the symbolic interactionism of MEAD the self emerges out of dynamic social interaction with others. In this process, individuals "take the role of the other"; in other words, they see themselves reflected through the attitudes and perceptions of others. This process is a gradual development, and Mead postulated a dichotomy between the concepts of "I" and "me" to explain its emergence. The "I" represents the individual's most basic inner being, whereas the "me" refers to the individual as seen by others – "the generalized other". These two aspects are involved in constant interaction as the individual engages with the larger social group and self-consciously reflects on such interaction. The display of social symbols such as gestures, language, and role playing are crucial in this process, as it is through them that individuals negotiate a dialogue between "me" and "I" and so formulate and present their self image to others.

In the same broad tradition, GOFFMAN (1959 and 1963) demonstrates the construction of identity through face-to-face social interaction. Using various methodologies, including ethnomethodology, conversation analysis, and participant observation, he analyses forms of social interaction and the manner in which they influence – and are influenced by – the interrelations and role playing of their individual members. In GOFFMAN (1959), he examines the minutiae of everyday life, focusing on the frequently arbitrary nature of forms of social intercourse such as "encounters", small groups and gatherings. In GOFFMAN (1963), his subject is the creation of deviant identities through the breakdown of such standardized, conventional forms of interaction. Goffman likens all forms of social interaction to ritual and drama, in which the individual adopts various roles and techniques whose ultimate aim is the "maintenance of the self" – the creation and presentation of a coherent self image to others. Although not generally interested in larger social forces or the existence of wider structures of power, symbolic interactionism demonstrates the active, social nature of the construction of identity through the actions and meanings held by those individuals engaged in it.

Recently, identity – or rather, the fragmentation of identity – has become a central issue in the study of modernity and postmodernity, or "posttraditional" society. A range of authors, such as LASH & FRIEDMAN, have described the breakdown of traditional social structures and the emergence of pluralism and uncertainty as defining features of modern life. In contrast to the momentary "identity crisis" depicted by Erikson, here the state of crisis is ongoing and endemic throughout the individual's life, involving the constant creation and recreation of identities that no longer possess a "core" or "essential" nature.

The practice of consumption is often regarded as central to this process. For example, DAVIS and LUNT & LIVINGSTONE, in various ways, argue that, in the modern world, commodities are invested with symbolic and cultural significance as well as with utilitarian value. These properties are appropriated by individuals in such areas as fashion, leisure, and lifestyle, both to differentiate themselves from others as well as to demonstrate solidarity and membership of particular social groups. For BAUMAN, the converse of the freedom to "choose" an identity in this way is the responsibility of thereby having to choose an appropriate or acceptable one. The anxiety that this provokes is, for him, the main problem faced by the modern individual in the quest for self-identity.

GIDDENS is also aware of the problematic nature of apparently "free" choice, stressing that, despite being free, the individual has "no choice but to choose". For him, the individual is engaged in "the reflexive project of the self": the self-conscious examination of how to live in the modern world, out of which emerges their sense of self or, as he puts it, their "narrative of identity". Such a narrative is created by individuals interacting with their surroundings and integrating their relationships and experiences into an ongoing "story" of the self. Although constantly subject to revision, this narrative is coherent and continuous across time and space, linking the self in the past with the self in the present and the future. These conditions are vital for a stable sense of identity, and when they are not met a sense of "ontological insecurity" prevails.

Within the context of pluralism and postmodernity, the debate about identity has opened up to focus on distinctive forms of *social* identity, examining those that have traditionally been marginalized and that are based on ethnicity, gender, sexuality, youth, and nationality. For example, writers like RATTANSI & WESTWOOD have argued that some identities are more prescribed than others and are not so amenable to free choice and self creation. Hence they suggest that the so-called old modernist categories of class, gender, and ethnicity are still relevant for the understanding of identity in the postmodern world. At the same time, they chart the emergence of identities organized around specific political and "lifestyle" issues such as gay and lesbian rights, vegetarianism, and environmentalism. These new affiliations can be seen as indicative of the increasing pluralization and politicization of identity in the modern world.

On a similar theme, other writers have focused on the complex intersections and negotiations of identities within individuals and across social groups. For instance, BRAH explores the implications of the overlaps between issues of race, class, gender, ethnicity, nationalism, and sexuality for both the creation of various types of discourse and for the understanding of the construction of identities. In their edited collection, WEEKS & HOLLAND examine the importance of sexuality for personal identity and political action, highlighting the distinctive "commonalities of identity" that grow up around specific expressions of sexuality. Again, the intersections of sexuality with other forms of identity, such as those based on gender and ethnicity, are emphasized. In SKEVINGTON & BAKER's compendium, the focus is also on the

multifaceted nature of "female identity" and the diverse range of factors (such as the impact of feminism, domestic relations, and interactions with other social groups) that exist to shape it. In all of these works the focus is on contested identities, which are defined as much through exclusion and opposition to mainstream culture as with interaction and assimilation with it.

GERDA REITH

Ideology, political

Bell, Daniel, *The End of Ideology: On the Exhaustion of Political Ideas in the Fifties*, revised edition, New York: Free Press, 1962

Campbell, Angus *et al.*, *The American Voter*, New York and London: Wiley, 1960

Conover, Pamela Johnston and Stanley Feldman, "How People Organize the Political World: A Schematic Model", *American Journal of Political Science*, 28/1 (1984): 95–126

Converse, Philip E., "The Nature of Belief Systems in Mass Publics" in *Ideology and Discontent*, edited by David Ernest Apter, New York: Free Press, 1964

Geertz, Clifford, "Ideology as a Cultural System" in *Ideology and Discontent*, edited by David E. Apter, New York: Free Press, 1964

Gerring, John, "Ideology: A Definitional Analysis", *Political Research Quarterly*, 50/4 (1997): 957–94

Hamilton, Malcolm B., "The Elements of the Concept of Ideology", *Political Studies*, 35/1 (1987): 18–38

Mannheim, Karl, *Ideology and Utopia: An Introduction to the Sociology of Knowledge*, New York: Harcourt Brace, and London: Routledge and Kegan Paul, 1936 (German edition 1929)

Nie, Norman H., Sidney Verba and John R. Petrocik, *The Changing American Voter*, Cambridge, Massachusetts: Harvard University Press, 1976; enlarged edition 1979

Smith, Eric R.A.N., "The Levels of Conceptualization: False Measures of Ideological Sophistication", *American Political Science Review*, 74 (1980): 685–96

Tomkins, Silvan S., "Affect and the Psychology of Knowledge" in *Affect, Cognition and Personality*, edited by Silvan S. Tomkins and Carroll E. Izard, New York: Springer, 1965; London: Tavistock, 1966

Ideology is such a multifaceted term that one may wish to become familiar with the range of definitions in use by scholars who have written on the topic. Definitional analyses by GERRING and by HAMILTON cover most, if not all, of the major works in the field. Hamilton examines 85 publications on ideology and finds "27 different elements or definitional criteria" in use (p.18). From these a minimal definition is fashioned using some variant or synthesis of eight of the most common criteria. Hamilton's final definition is:

> a system of collectively held normative and reputedly factual ideas and beliefs and attitudes advocating a particular pattern of social relationships and arrange-

ments, and/or aimed at justifying a particular pattern of conduct, which its proponents seek to promote, realise, pursue or maintain. (p.38)

Gerring's field essay also provides a core definition of ideology after establishing a "comprehensive framework" that catalogues the attributes commonly used in defining the term. Citing over 150 works, Gerring is more comprehensive than Hamilton. He outlines seven major attributes of the definitions that he examined and details 35 parts of those attributes. In the end, the definitional attribute he finds common to virtually all accounts of ideology is coherence (meaning internal consistency or constraint among one's values and beliefs; p.974). Gerring's definition, then, is far more minimal than Hamilton's.

The literature on ideology may crudely be divided into those works that are theoretical, perhaps informed by historical perspectives, and those that are empirical. Karl Marx's writings on the topic are among the former, although his concept of ideology is scattered throughout his work and never clearly formulated. Also among the theoretical works is that of MANNHEIM, who emphasizes the "historical situations" and "social conditions" within which an individual or group adopts and expresses an ideology (p.56). Though his work has been influential, many (including Hamilton) have criticized it for being of limited use for empirical studies of ideology.

GEERTZ, too, is theoretical and perhaps of limited empirical use. Furthermore, some (like Raymond Boudon) have argued that his conceptualization of ideology is less clear than Mannheim's. Nevertheless, Geertz's work is valuable, at least to the extent that it reminds us of the symbolic nature of ideology. For him, ideologies are "systems of interacting symbols [and] patterns of interworking meanings" (p.56). According to Geertz, ideology makes sense of a complex world, especially one that is shedding tradition.

Many scholars have suggested that this century has witnessed the "end of ideology". Perhaps the most debated version of this thesis is BELL's; it is also, according to its author, the most misunderstood. Bell's argument is that ideologies proffering socially engineered "blueprints" for society are incompatible with the economic, social, and political realities of the 20th century. In the West, furthermore, "a rough consensus among intellectuals on political issues", including support for welfare programmes and free (if regulated) markets, has occurred (p.402). Misreadings of Bell's point stem largely from the fact that Bell's use of "ideology" is ambiguous. Indeed, he maintained at the time his book was written that "new ideologies", premised on economic development and national power, were forming in Asia and Africa. Thus, it was not so much the end of ideology that Bell anticipated, but the end of "19th-century ideologies", particularly socialism.

A considerable amount of the empirical work in this field has focused on the link between personality and ideology. Some, like Adorno et al. (*The Authoritarian Personality* 1950) on the authoritarian personality, seek to explain one ideology. TOMKINS, however, offers a theory that explains the connection between different personality types (or "scripts") and ideologies along a left–right spectrum. According to his "polarity theory", personalities can either be humanistic or normative. The former are linked to left-wing ideologies (not only in

politics but in art, educational theory, metaphysics, and virtually all areas of life) and the latter have a right-wing orientation. One of the most interesting, and controversial, aspects of the theory accounts for people's scripts by the way they were reared as a child.

In a classic study of electoral behaviour, CAMPBELL et al. explored the American voter's "level of conceptualization" of politics. They established four categories within which each person in the study could be placed. The most "sophisticated" voters, which Campbell et al. called ideologues, evaluated parties and candidates using "any suggestion of the abstract conception one would associate with ideology" (p.222). Only 2.5% of the total sample were classified as ideologues (with another nine per cent qualifying as near ideologues; p.249). Thus, Campbell et al.'s study portrayed the American electorate in a rather unfavourable light. Unlike much of the theoretical work on ideology, however, Campbell et al. view ideology as a positive concept; the more ideological one's thinking, the more sophisticated it was considered to be.

CONVERSE provided additional evidence that the American voter was ideologically unsophisticated, although he preferred the phrase "belief system" to ideology. Among his most important findings was his suggestion that voters often had no position on the key policy issues of the day, that their attitudes were not constrained (by which he meant that various attitudes in a person's belief system were not necessarily correlated in the way we would expect if that person were ideological), and that the attitudes of many voters displayed a great deal of instability over time, as if they were randomly choosing responses to questions. Such findings lead Converse to argue that many Americans' belief systems are composed of "nonattitudes".

Critics of the Campbell et al. and Converse conclusions come from a number of perspectives. NIE, VERBA & PETROCIK, for example, argued that the American electorate became significantly more sophisticated in the 1960s and 1970s than it had been in the 1950s. Using a different measure of the levels of conceptualization from the one used in *The American Voter*, although "parallel" to it, the authors showed that the number of ideologues and near-ideologues in the electorate grew from 18 per cent in 1956 to 49 per cent in 1972 (p.115). From a methodological perspective, SMITH questioned the reliability and validity of all measures of the levels of conceptualization in use at the time. He also criticized Nie et al.'s findings specifically. Rather than becoming more sophisticated in terms of ideological evaluation, Smith suggests that the American voter became more adept at using the *rhetoric* of ideological evaluation.

Recent work on political information processing, often referred to as "schema theory" research, suggests that people organize the political world in a coherent, systematic way, although the organization may not be structured along the traditional liberal–conservative dimension. Indeed, CONOVER & FELDMAN find that the political schemas of most people cannot be described in bipolar terms but imply a "single, distinct perspective" (p.108). Besides an ideological domain, which contains "neoconservative", "free-market conservative", and "democratic socialist" schemas, the authors find schemas for economic, racial, social, and foreign affairs domains as well as four schemas for a "basic human philosophy" domain (which was considered a "superordinate" level of abstraction). Q methodology was used to "load" people's responses onto various factors, which were then interpreted as schemas. This methodology, as well as the theory's conceptualization, has led many to criticize this school of thought for producing statistical constructs rather than uncovering real cognitive structures.

STEPHEN K. MEDVIC

See also End of ideology

Ideology, sociology

Comte, Auguste, *Cours de philosophie positive* [Course of Positive Philosophy], in *Oeuvres d'Auguste Comte*, 12 vols, Paris: Anthropos, 1968–71 (originally published 6 vols, 1830–42); selections in English in *The Essential Comte*, edited by Stanislav Andreski, London: Croom Helm, and New York: Barnes and Noble, 1974

Destutt de Tracy, Antoine Louis Claude, *Les Eléments d'idéologie* [Elements of Ideology], 2 vols, Paris: Vrin, 1970 (originally published 5 vols, 1801–05)

Durkheim, Emile, *The Rules of Sociological Method*, edited by Steven Lukes, London: Macmillan, and New York: Free Press, 1982 (French edition 1895)

Engels, Friedrich, *Herr Eugen Dühring's Revolution in Science* [*Anti-Dühring*], New York: International Publishers, 1894; London: Lawrence and Wishart, 1931 (German edition 1894)

Engels, Friedrich, *Dialectics of Nature*, translated and edited by Clemens Dutt, London: Lawrence and Wishart, 1941; New York: International Publishers, 1960 (German edition 1878)

Mannheim, Karl, *Ideology and Utopia*, London: Routledge, and New York: Harcourt Brace, 1936 (German edition 1929)

Marx, Karl, *A Contribution to the Critique of Political Economy*, New York: International Publishers, and London: Kegan Paul and Trench Trübner, 1904; in German in Marx and Engels, *Gesamtausgabe* (MEGA), vol. 13, Berlin: Dietz, 1972 (1st German edition 1859)

Marx, Karl and Friedrich Engels, *The German Ideology*, Moscow: Progress, 1964; London: Lawrence and Wishart, 1970; also vol. 5 in Marx and Engels *Collected Works*, New York: International Publishers, 1975– (original German edition 1845–46)

Marx, Karl, *Grundrisse: Foundations of the Critique of Political Economy*, New York: Random House, and Harmondsworth: Penguin, 1973 (written in German, 1857–58)

Picavet, François Joseph, *Les Idéologues: essai sur l'histoire des idées et des théories scientifiques, philosophiques, et religieuses, en France depuis 1789*, Paris: Olms, 1985 (1st edition 1891)

The debates and dilemmas surrounding the concept of ideology in sociology are rooted in distinct philosophical traditions of the ontological and epistemological study of ideas from classical times, through the Middle Ages to the modern era. From a vast literature, this entry will review only the works in which the term ideology is explicitly construed by some of the "founding fathers" of modern social sciences, in the period when secular belief was progressively replacing religious faith. The teaching on ideals by Francis Bacon, the critique of collective prejudices by Holbach and Helvétius, Niccolò Machiavelli's immoralist handbook for rulers ready to apply terror in the name of a republican ideal, Locke's treatises on the right of rebellion against absolutism in the name of the ideal of liberty, Hegel's philosophy of history in which entire peoples are conceptualized as falsely conscious instruments of the dialectical development of the idea of freedom, and many other works that contributed important elements to the philosophical prehistory of the modern concept of ideology in the social sciences, are omitted. The same holds true for later heirs, developers, and critics of the founders' interpretations of ideology.

Destutt de Tracy, the French philosopher, politician, and economist, deliberately introduced the neologism "ideology" in a 1796 lecture on the capacity of thinking, to give a short name to the new "science of ideas". He installed the foundations of the new science in DESTUTT DE TRACY, a collection of five volumes. Apart from ideology in the strict sense, they deal with grammar, for expressing and sharing ideas, logic, for combining ideas, and the moral will that formulates the rules for social action, based upon knowledge arrived at by ideology. This collection is characteristic of the modern shift in the study of ideas from the ontological and theological approach to the epistemological, psychological, and semantic one. In these works one can detect traces of Aristotelian nominalism and Stoicist materialism, revived through the Enlightenment's double interest in the enlargement of human scientific knowledge and its implementation with the aim of improving social and political life – all reformulated in Locke's empiricist and sensualistic conviction that humans can mentally conceive through ideas only that which had been previously perceived through the senses. Ideology itself is understood as an exact natural science, part of zoology and the first science in the genealogical order.

Destutt de Tracy's work presents the archetype for the neutral and scientific interpretation of the meaning of the term ideology – as an explanatory theory of human knowledge of the real world, and for linking ideology with notions of "good" social organization and political conduct.

PICAVET's study presents the classic exposition of the new science of ideas, as it was conceptualized by Destutt de Tracy and those like-minded French theoreticians from the National Institute of Sciences and Arts who called themselves "idéologues" (P.-J.-G. Cabanis, J.-D. Garat, P.C.F. Daunou, M.-J. Chenier, J.-B. Say, and others). Picavet asserts that for all idéologues, ideology is the science that analyses human ideas in order to differentiate in them elements of true, certain, and clear knowledge, ridding them of error, prejudice, and obfuscation. Thus ideology can, for example, provide a scientific basis for the deduction of practical rules for a national system of education in the spirit of the sovereignty of reason and individual liberty. The idéologues saw the realm for the practical implementation of ideology in the spheres of law, state planning, and political action in general.

Picavet's study contains elements important for the investigation of the shift in the relationship between the ideologues and Napoleon, who was himself originally a partisan of the new science and attended their meetings in the salon of Madame Helvétius in Auteuil. During the Directory (1795–99) of the French Republic, ideology became the official doctrine, with great influence on an atheist and empiricist reform of the educational system. After the 18th Brumaire, however, Napoleon realized that criticism by republican-minded ideologists of his monarchist tendencies and his changed attitudes toward the church might undermine the legitimacy of his authoritarian power politics, and he turned against their teaching.

Ideology became the object of scorn, while ideologues were branded as idealistic "metaphysicians and fanatics", deducing from pure reason (as they interpreted it) unrealistic plans concerning the liberal reform and improvement of the state and society. These abstract and ridiculous speculations could not, according to Napoleon, have practical political effect, as they were not based on the historical experience and knowledge of human character. Napoleon thus gave a new negative meaning to the concept of ideology, and used it to denigrate his political opponents.

COMTE, author of the neologism "sociology" (science of society) in his 47th lecture, continued the Enlightenment endeavour to create a scientific or positive knowledge of the invariable natural laws underlying all phenomena. Knowledge should be based on the empirical observation of facts and be liberated from irrational factors (imagination), false notions (idols), and speculative concepts (final cause, force). In contrast to Destutt de Tracy, and implicitly following the Platonist tradition of the idealistic and realistic understanding of ideas, Comte does not reduce ideas to individual empirical facts. In fact, the idea of humanity as the phenomenon *sui generis* is, according to Comte, the starting point of the scientific investigation of society. In his 51st lecture Comte elaborates the fundamental laws of social dynamics – the theory of the natural progress of human society's functions in general, and of cognitive ideas in particular – through the theological, metaphysical, and positive stages. Only in the last stage is imagination subordinated to observation, focusing research on the discovery of regularity in the connections between observable social phenomena. The task of science is to answer the question "how", ignoring the extra-scientific, and therefore ideological, question "why". In Comte's work the term ideology is associated not only with the neutral meaning of the scientific study of any set of ideas, but with negative and critical connotations as well, i.e., misleading, illusory theological, and metaphysical ideas.

By accepting the idea of humanity as a "collective organism" in abstract opposition to the human individual, Comte himself breached the self-proclaimed tenets of positivist methodology and remained on the terrain of metaphysics. In his later works he professed the idea of the "religion of humanity", returning to ideology and theology, albeit labelled as "positive politics".

Continuing Comte's theoretical and methodological orientation, DURKHEIM systematized the positivist approach to the study of society. The accent is on breaking away from "metaphysical speculation" and "ideological" approaches that make "ideas" about society the object of research, rather than "social facts".

The presence of just such an approach, however, is recognizable in Durkheim's work. He defines a "social fact" as a fundamental reality, something that is general over the whole of a given society, and having an existence outside of and entirely independent of its individual manifestations. "Social facts" are, according to Durkheim, modes of believing, behaving, and feeling, instituted by the collectivity, that regulate an individual's way of thinking and acting. This regulation is achieved by the exercise of external coercion over individuals, primarily through the power of sanctioning deviations from "normality" as it is defined in laws, morals, customs, fashions, and other institutionalized forms of "collective representations" or "collective conscience".

Durkheim's positivist and functionalist perspective attributes a mainly positive connotation to the spiritual content of social conscience, especially religion. His perspective stresses almost exclusively the function of social conscience as a spiritual bond and as the generator of the indispensable cohesion in society. Durkheim was at the same time enough of a scientist to note the repressive and divisive potential of these "social facts".

MARX & ENGELS is the first use of the term ideology by these writers, and they ascribe to it principally negative and critical meanings. They denote by it various forms of seemingly independent – but in fact societally dependent – forms of false or "inverted" consciousness, vividly comparing these with the upside-down picture in a *camera obscura*. Central to their negative conception of ideology is the insistence that the inverted perception of the world is not mere illusion or error, but the necessary distortion and concealment of the real contradictions of the "inverted world". Social contradictions are, according to Marx and Engels, anchored in the alienated and alienating class divisions of human labour. The divisions between the producers and the private owners of productive forces, as well as between the particular and common interests of isolated producers, constitute the real basis of different ideological standpoints. Marx and Engels suggest that those individuals and groups who monopolize spiritual activity in bourgeois society are structurally disposed to overlook and conceal the fact that the "ruling thoughts" or ideas of an epoch are expressions of the interests of the social bearers of these ideas – the "ruling class". These thoughts contribute to the defence, justification, and perpetuation of the privileged social position of the ruling class, idealizing its particular interests and presenting them as universal and eternal. On the other hand, those social groups limited to the execution of material production tend to invent imaginary, action-oriented, or passive-compensatory solutions to real social contradictions for as long as they are unable to solve them in practice.

Through this double criticism of inverted consciousness and inverted world, Marx and Engels elaborate general premises of their own, "new" – both "historical" and "materialist" – approaches to the study of people, society, and history. They propose a dialectical conception of human essence as the totality of social relations. Social relations determine human material and spiritual activity. However, social relations can be and are being changed through human revolutionary praxis. Marx and Engels explicitly state that their aim is not only to understand and explain the world but also to revolutionize it from the standpoint of "human society or social humanity". Not the theoretical critique, as the Young

Hegelians thought, but the revolutionary practice based on real possibilities, is the propelling force of history and forms of consciousness.

The German Ideology contains in embryonic form the central point of the later and still ongoing debate concerning the status of historical materialism – is it a class ideology connected with the interests of the proletariat opposing the ideology of the ruling class, or is it a science? The first assertion, answering the practical political need for the development of the action-oriented theory of the class struggle, leads to the displacement of the original negative connotation of the term ideology by a positive one. An unintended consequence is the resurgence of a relativistic epistemological position. The second claim reanimates an unhistorical and unreflective positivist epistemology.

The treatment of ideology in Marx's later works (MARX 1904 and 1973), notably in *A Contribution to the Critique of Political Economy* (published eight years before the first volume of *Das Kapital*), and in those posthumously assembled under the common title *Grundrisse*, is distinguished in two ways. First, Marx uses the term ideology less often or not at all. Second, when he uses it, he tends to attribute to it a more neutral and general meaning than in his earlier works. In the autobiographical introduction to *A Contribution to the Critique of Political Economy* he identifies ideology with all forms of social consciousness, "corresponding" to the totality of material relations in "bourgeois society".

Marx analyses the "anatomy" of "bourgeois society" in these later works in terms of political economy. "Forms of communication and exchange" are now defined more precisely than in the earlier philosophical works as *necessary*, independent of human consciousness and will. They are "relations of production" or "ownership relations" that correspond to the historically determined development level of social productive forces. Their historical combination he portrays metaphorically as the "economic structure" of society, or the "real basis" upon which arises a legal and political "superstructure", and corresponding ideological forms of consciousness. In the chapter on capital in *Grundrisse*, Marx demonstrates that double aspects of reality exist in capitalist modes of production. Market competition mediates the circulation and exchange of merchandise and gives birth to the sphere of reified "phenomenal forms". This surface sphere of apparently "equal" and "free" exchange of "exchange values" between autonomous individuals in fact expresses in reverse the inner and concealed underlying sphere of the "real relations" of inequality and unfreedom in the modern capitalist form of hired labour slavery. These surface appearances strongly influence the conceptions through which social relations are understood.

The grip of ideological "phenomenal forms" on the psychological consciousness of capitalist producers is undermined in periods of social revolution, when material productive forces come into conflict with the existing relations of production that begin to block their further development.

To the extent that Marx in his later works uses the term ideology as a shorthand label for the totality of the spiritual life of a historical period, and interprets ideology as the constitutive objective layer of capitalist society's immediate reality, he prepares the way for the neutralization and generalization of the ideology concept.

Engels is an important reference point for the study of ideology in the works of Marx and himself at different periods of their lives, and even more so in the works of their followers and critics. In contrast to the dialectical formulations concerning the role of ideas in history used in earlier works, Engels in numerous passages, especially in the preparatory works for ENGELS (1894), encourages the interpretation of ideology as an all-encompassing superstructural sphere. He empirically reduces the genesis of ideas within ideological superstructures to sensual experience and defines them as correct or distorted subjective "reflections" of objective reality. His furthest development of this dualistic separation of subject from object is ENGELS (1941; in German c.1878). This prepared the ground for the return, among many social-democrat and communist theoreticians, to an undialectical materialist and positivist conceptualization of ideas as mere passive extracts from experience.

If the approach of historical materialism was applied to an analysis of the work of Marx and Engels, this shift in their conceptualization of ideology could be interpreted as related to the changing phases of economic crisis and stabilization at the time they had been writing a particular piece.

MANNHEIM is considered to be the classic founding work of the sociology of knowledge. He discards the psychologist's use of the term ideology that relates contested views of the opponent to his/her particular interests, and qualifies these views as erroneous or even deliberate lies. He introduces the total concept of ideology, meaning that all historical thinking is possible only from the standpoint of the concrete social position of the thinker (Seinsverbundenheit des Denkers). Through a functional analysis devoid of motivational considerations, all unconscious or subconscious but objective structural differences in the world-views (Weltanschauung) of different social groups are related to the structural differences in the real social existence of these groups, notably their class.

Both ideology (in the specific sense of the conservative world-view of the ruling class) and utopia (the radical world-view of the dominated class) are, according to Mannheim, ideologies in the sense of being societally related "perspectives". They should both be subordinated to an evaluation of the existential congruence between them and a concrete historic time and place (Standortsgebundenheit der Denkens). The relationist assertion that every idea is conditioned by the corresponding social situation of a given social group or class implies that all social thinking is ideologically coloured. Even a proposition with scientific pretensions is no more than a disguised statement of class. A scientific critique of ideology is impossible. No ideology can be objective, and no ideology can be more objective than any other. Not wanting to endorse some of these relativist implications, Mannheim attempted to identify the potential social bearer of the scientific study of ideas. He found that agent in a "free-floating" intelligentsia. Embracing a totalizing orientation and attempting to detach itself from subjective points of view and biases, this group successively synthesizes varieties of truth – themselves each a function of different social situations – into dynamic images of an ever-changing social reality. Mannheim contributed to the search for the scientific foundation of the study of ideas in specific research and communicative procedures. The weakest point of his attempt to avoid the extreme relativist implications of the total concept of ideology is his conceptualization of a creative intelligentsia in social terms as a classless social group, as if it did not have an identifiable place in the hierarchical class division of labour and a corresponding particular interest.

VERA VRATUSA(-ZUNJIC)

See also End of ideology

Imitation

Bandura, Albert, Dorothea Ross and Sheila A. Ross, "Transmission of Aggression through Imitation of Aggressive Models", *Journal of Abnormal and Social Psychology*, 63/3 (1961): 575–82

Bandura, Albert, Dorothea Ross and Sheila A. Ross, "Imitation of Film-Mediated Aggressive Models", *Journal of Abnormal and Social Psychology*, 66/1 (1963): 3–11

Braten, Stein (editor), *Intersubjective Communication and Emotion in Early Ontogeny*, Cambridge and New York: Cambridge University Press, 1998

Byrne, Richard W. and Anne E. Russon, "Learning by Imitation: A Hierarchical Approach", *Behavioral and Brain Sciences*, 21/5 (1998): 667–721

Eckerman, Carol O. and Mark R. Stein, "How Imitation Begets Imitation and Toddlers' Generation of Games", *Developmental Psychology*, 26/3 (1990): 370–78

Eckerman, Carol O. and Sharon M. Didow, "Nonverbal Imitation and Toddlers' Mastery of Verbal Means of Achieving Coordinated Action", *Developmental Psychology*, 32/1 (1996): 141–52

Masur, Elise Frank, "Infants' Early Verbal Imitation and Their Later Lexical Development", *Merrill-Palmer Quarterly*, 41/3 (1995): 286–306

Meltzoff, Andrew N. and M. Keith Moore, "Imitation of Facial and Manual Gestures by Human Neonates", *Science*, 198/4312 (1977): 75–78

Meltzoff, Andrew N., "Understanding the Intentions of Others: Re-enactment of Intended Acts by 18-Month-Old Children", *Developmental Psychology*, 31/5 (1995): 838–50

Meltzoff, Andrew N. and M. Keith Moore, "Explaining Facial Imitation: A Theoretical Model", *Early Development and Parenting*, 6 (1997): 179–92

Nadel, Jacqueline and George Butterworth (editors), *Imitation in Infancy*, Cambridge and New York: Cambridge University Press, 1999

Tomasello, Michael, Sue Savage-Rumbaugh and Ann Cale Kruger, "Imitative Learning of Actions on Objects by Children, Chimpanzees, and Enculturated Chimpanzees", *Child Development*, 64/6 (1993): 1688–1705

BANDURA, ROSS & ROSS (1961, 1963) provide the seminal experiments of the effects of modelling aggressive behaviours to children. Aggression is modelled by real-life models, these same models on film, and a film depicting an aggressive cartoon character. The authors interpreted the results to indicate that aggression was transmitted via modelling, whether from adult or televised demonstration. These researchers have demonstrated how models can influence many behaviours, thus allowing for a better appreciation of how the social environment affects behaviour. Unfortunately, this research is based in laboratory settings, making it difficult to extrapolate to real life situations.

The modern investigation of imitation began with MELTZOFF & MOORE (1977), a seminal laboratory study of the ability of 12 to 21-day-old infants to imitate adults' facial and manual gestures. The results of this study demonstrated that infants could imitate at a much earlier age than was previously thought. The authors argue that the infant's replication of the adult's gesture is true imitation (and not merely arousal of oral activity) through the use of differential imitation of three facial gestures and one manual gesture. They also assert that the ability to use intermodal equivalencies is an innate ability of humans.

MELTZOFF & MOORE (1997) later went on to discover that six-week-old and two to three-month-old infants could imitate strangers just as well as they could imitate their mothers. There was no variation in imitation due to familiarity. The infants could also imitate both static and dynamic facial gestures. Contrary to findings by other researchers, they did not find any decrease in imitative behaviour in infants between the ages of two and three months. These investigators theorized that imitation serves to enrich the infant's understanding of others, as well as their communicative abilities.

ECKERMAN & STEIN reports the authors' observations of the play of 24-month-old toddlers when they are either imitated by an adult partner or engaged in parallel play with an adult partner. Toddlers who were imitated engaged in twice as many play actions and more often looked at the face of the adult. Being imitated led to continuous action on the same play material and repetition of the same act. In addition, imitated toddlers engaged in more prolonged episodes of coordinated activity. It was found that adults and toddlers used reciprocal imitation as an interactive device. Eckerman & Stein concludes that being imitated leads to reciprocal imitation and the generation of sustained imitative games.

ECKERMAN & DIDOW describes how six types of speech associated with the facilitation of coordinated activity all increased following the emergence of nonverbal imitative behaviour. These types of speech occurred more often during games that were constructed through nonverbal imitation. The authors theorize that "nonverbal imitative acts create social understanding of what the toddlers are doing together and facilitation of the use of verbal means of achieving coordinated actions".

MASUR is a study of the relationship between imitation and lexical development longitudinally across ages 10, 13, 17, and 21 months. The children who imitated the most words developed larger noun and non-noun lexicons by the end of the second year. The author also examined children's abilities to imitate words outside of their usual repertoire. He discovered that children who did this developed significantly larger lexicons at later ages, and inferred from this data that such children are using imitation as a cognitive strategy for mastering vocabulary.

MELTZOFF also uses imitation as a way of exploring what infants know about the intentions of other people. As part of the experiment, adults performed an action, but they slipped or made a mistake in the process. Instead of imitating what the adult did, the children imitated what the adult intended to do. This paper implicates imitation in not only the development of understanding of intention, but also the development of theory of mind and social cognition.

TOMASELLO, SAVAGE-RUMBAUGH & KRUGER compare and contrast imitative abilities in children, mother-reared chimpanzees, and enculturated chimpanzees. Results demonstrated that mother-reared chimpanzees demonstrated poorer performance during immediate imitation paradigms than either the enculturated chimpanzees or the children. The latter two groups did not differ significantly from one another. Unexpectedly, on the delay trials, the enculturated chimpanzees outperformed the other two groups. The authors conclude from these results that a human-like sociocultural environment is an essential component in the development of human-like social-cognitive and imitative learning skills for chimpanzees, and possibly even human beings.

In research investigations, imitation has traditionally been viewed as an all-or-nothing phenomenon. BYRNE & RUSSON proposes a hierarchical approach to imitative learning, of which two levels are highlighted: the programme level (great apes can imitate at this level) and the action level (at which great apes seldom imitate). Programme-level imitation implies an ability to notice the organization of another's behaviour, and is thus closely related to planning and thought. These authors speculate that action-level imitation might have a largely social role in both humans and apes. Unfortunately, there is no mention or examination of motivation, especially considering the arbitrary nature of the tasks to be imitated.

MELTZOFF & MOORE (1997) provides a comprehensive theory of early facial imitation, extending their previous work by including a computational account of the mechanism involved and how infants map from self to other.

BRATEN examines the role of intersubjectivity in early ontogeny. Various subjects within the study of imitation are discussed, ranging from its development in non-human primates, neonates, and atypical children to its subcomponent processes and its importance for developing a theory of mind.

NADEL & BUTTERWORTH is a timely volume devoted to the evidence for innate imitation in newborns. This compilation of leading researchers' work reiterates this notion by stressing the importance of this natural activity for the later development of communication and learning. Primarily, imitation is discussed in terms of its appearance in typical and atypical development, its proficiency in a range of primate species and its importance as a foundation for communication, symbolic processes, and social cognition.

GREG WALLACE AND DONNA MARINO

Imperialism, economic

Brewer, Anthony, *Marxist Theories of Imperialism: A Critical Survey*, 2nd edition, London and New York: Routledge, 1990

Cain, P.J. and A.G. Hopkins, *British Imperialism: Crisis and Deconstruction, 1914–1990*, London and New York: Longman, 1993

Cain, P.J. and A.G. Hopkins, *British Imperialism: Innovation and Expansion, 1688–1914*, London and New York: Longman, 1993

Chaudhuri, Nupur and Margaret Strobel (editors), *Western Women and Imperialism: Complicity and Resistance*, Bloomington: Indiana University Press, 1992

Etherington, Norman, *Theories of Imperialism: War, Conquest and Capital*, London: Croom Helm, and Totowa, New Jersey: Barnes and Noble, 1984

Kiernan, V.G., *Imperialism and Its Contradictions*, edited and introduced by Harvey J. Kaye, London and New York: Routledge, 1995

Midgley, Clare (editor), *Gender and Imperialism*, Manchester: Manchester University Press, 1998

Porter, Andrew, *European Imperialism, 1860–1914*, Basingstoke: Macmillan, 1994

Said, Edward W., *Culture and Imperialism*, London: Chatto and Windus, and New York: Knopf, 1993

Smith, Simon C., *British Imperialism, 1750–1970*, Cambridge and New York: Cambridge University Press, 1998

Tomlinson, John, *Cultural Imperialism: A Critical Introduction*, London: Pinter, and Baltimore: Johns Hopkins University Press, 1991

For an easy beginner's guide to the history of British Empire one may chose to read SMITH. Informed by chronological history of the Empire since the end of 18th century, the book, in a very short space, deals with various dimensions of British imperialism. Document case studies make the readings more fruitful. However, students already initiated in the field may find treatment of subjects too sweeping.

PORTER provides an accessible analysis of European imperialism between 1860 and 1914. It is the best place to gain information about historiographical trends within the study of imperialism. Porter puts various definitions and theories and approaches within their proper perspective and critically examines them. The bibliography serves as a useful guide for those interested in further details. It is difficult to find any other survey of the subject that is so concise and yet so brilliant.

Although slightly older than most of the books suggested in this section, ETHERINGTON's work may be helpful for those interested in various theories of imperialism–both Marxist and non-Marxist. He combines his survey with discussion in which he raises some noteworthy points. His main thesis about earlier theories like those of Hobson, Lenin, Wilshire and others is that the theories that originated as policy recommendations of capitalists were turned into accounts of history by these later writers who assumed that what capitalists wished to happen did happen. Particularly fascinating is his concise exposition of classic theories in a separate chapter, which may help those who require only a broad outline of these theories. He also maintains that there is a need to differentiate between theories of imperialism and theories of empire – something that has often been lost. His suggestions regarding the study of historical problems of imperialism are for teachers and students alike.

BREWER provides one of the best surveys of the Marxist tradition's understandings of capitalist imperialism. His typology of Marxist thinkers based on their analyses of imperialism uses three categories. Lenin and Rosa Luxemburg's views may be considered to be "classical Marxist theories of capitalist expansion". Bukharin, Hilferding and others expounded "classical Marxist theories of imperialism and inter–imperialist rivalry". Ideas of Baran, Frank, Wallerstein, Amin and others are classified as "modern Marxist theories of development and underdevelopment". He critically examines all these theories. He also discusses debates between the Frank–Wallerstein position and the revived classical Marxist approach over the concept of a mode of production and its application in contemporary underdeveloped world, as well as over the trends in the relative standing of different capitalist states.

KIERNAN is one of the brilliant historians of imperialism. This work is a collection of essays edited and introduced by Kaye. Kiernan, writing in a critical Marxist style and spirit, provides a historical narrative of the development of world capitalism by way of the respective national capitalisms. He also takes up the issue of relationship between imperialism and Third World economic development, and addresses the balance sheet of imperialism and colonialism. In one of the essays, he discusses the implications of works of Gramsci for the study of imperialism.

Unlike the majority of works suggested here, the two-volume work of CAIN & HOPKINS is not in a Marxist tradition. Instead, drawing upon revisionism within imperial historiography, the authors use the key concept of "gentlemanly capitalism" to explain the "innovation, expansion, crisis, and deconstruction" of British imperialism. Their "gentility" thesis attempts the gargantuan task of explaining something that persisted for almost three centuries. They argue for recasting the periodization of British imperialism pushing it back to cover the rise of financial revolution and the rise of "moneyed interest" at the close of the 18th century. The imperial mission was the export version of the gentlemanly order. It was the gentlemanly elites, and not the manufacturing interests, which played a leading role in imperial expansion because they saw in empire a means of generating income flows in ways that were compatible with their high ideals of honour and duty. Another of their controversial arguments is that decolonization was not an inevitable culmination of a long process of decay, but came about largely because the empire had served its purpose. "Gentlemen of the city headed towards the new horizon of global opportunities." Though tedious and contradictory at times, the book may be read by those with more than peripheral interest in the subject of imperialism.

SAID has singularly made vital contributions in highlighting the worldliness of imperial culture. Carrying on from his earlier books like *Orientalism*, he reveals how scholarships as well as cultural productions in the metropolitans were not only informed but largely shaped by their nexus with imperialism. In this work, he offers a new strategy of reading the metropolitan cultural texts–contrapuntal reading–to reveal the power-knowledge nexus in cultural productions and appreciate hybridity of experiences. The link between European literature and imperial ideology is illustrated through contrapuntal discussion of several Victorian and French novels such as Conrad's *Heart of Darkness*, Verdi's *Aida*, and Austen's *Mansfield Park*. Anti-imperialist resistance discourses arising out of peripheries (colonies) are also discussed.

CHAUDHURI & STROBEL's collection is concerned with examining the diversity of British women's writings and inter-

ventions within British colonialism. Their position was of constant negotiation between the limits of complicity and resistance to the dominant cultural values. Essays are on themes such as women travel writers, gender and race issues, and relations between white women and indigenous men and women. A particularly interesting essay is by Burton regarding the use of representation of "other" women by British women as attempts to bolster the sense of their own liberation. A common theme underlying all is the heterogeneity of women's experiences as participants in colonial power. Though lack of attention to working class women is noteworthy, overall it goes a significant step forward in highlighting multiplicity of role played by British women in British imperialism.

A more specific book, which undertakes the task of mapping the connections between gender and imperialism, is the collection of essays edited by MIDGLEY. Drawing upon insights from postcolonial theories, the book takes gender as its central concept. It discusses both colonizing men and women, as well as women and men in Britain affected by empire. The essays perform the significant task of highlighting the need to study colonized and colonizers as gendered subjects, recognize the importance of female agency, interrogating the questions of empire and masculinity, and exploring interrelationship between feminisms and imperialism as well as anti colonial nationalisms.

Inspired by Foucauldian discourse theory, TOMLINSON gives valuable insights into the concept of "cultural imperialism", which today is talked of in similar terms, as "imperialism" was during the peak of decolonization. He sees "cultural imperialism" basically as a critical discourse that paradoxically defends the autonomy of other cultures by representing them in its own Western terms. Disposing of the idea of cultural imperialism as cultural domination, he discusses four ways in which to talk about it: as "media imperialism"; as a discourse of nationality; as the critique of global capitalism; and lastly, as the critique of modernity. It is the last that may encompass all the other critiques. He ends up by pointing out that in the critical discourses of cultural imperialism the sense of cultural agency and assertiveness is implicit.

DIBYESH ANAND

Imperialism, sociology

Etherington, Norman, *Theories of Imperialism: War, Conquest and Capital*, London: Croom Helm, and Totowa, New Jersey: Barnes and Noble, 1984

Hobsbawm, Eric, *The Age of Empire, 1875–1914*, London: Weidenfeld and Nicolson, and New York: Pantheon, 1987

Hobson, J.A., *Imperialism: A Study*, 3rd edition, London: Allen and Unwin, 1938 (1st edition 1902)

Kiernan, V.G., *America, The New Imperialism: From White Settlement to World Hegemony*, London: Zed, 1978

Kiernan, V.G., *Imperialism and Its Contradictions*, New York and London: Routledge, 1995

Owen, Roger and Bob Sutcliffe (editors), *Studies in the Theory of Imperialism*, London: Longman, 1972

Porter, Andrew, *European Imperialism, 1860–1914*, Basingstoke: Macmillan, 1994

Said, Edward W., *Orientalism*, New York: Pantheon, and London: Routledge, 1978; with new afterword, New York: Vintage, 1994, Harmondsworth: Penguin, 1995

Said, Edward W., *Culture and Imperialism*, New York: Knopf, and London: Chatto and Windus, 1993

Scammell, G.V., *The First Imperial Age: European Overseas Expansion, c.1400–1715*, London and Boston: Unwin Hyman, 1989

The classic work on imperialism, almost universally invoked by other authors on the subject, is that by HOBSON. Originally published in 1902, Hobson expounds his theory of imperialism building on material elucidated in earlier publications, most notably his idea of "the economic taproot of imperialism". Hobson suggests that although the desire to expand markets may have played a role, the prime motivating factor in European imperial expansion was the creation of new opportunities for capital. While the core of Hobson's theory is economic, he also explores, moral, scientific, and political dimensions of imperialism in language that reflects prevailing views on the ability of the so-called "lower races" to govern themselves. Hobson's work is important in itself but has acquired added significance in that it shaped Lenin's view of imperialism as the last stage of capitalism. Hobson's liberal critique of imperialism as "a depraved choice of national life, imposed by self-seeking interests" (p.368) prefigures many later debates.

A good overview of a range of theories and approaches to imperialism is that by ETHERINGTON. He adopts a broadly chronological approach beginning with the "classical" theories, such as those of Wilshire, Hobson, Angel, and Brailsford, before moving on to the "socialist" theories of Luxembourg, Bukharin, and Lenin. The "capitalist" ideas of Veblen and Schumpeter are explored, followed by a discussion of "informal imperialism". He deals with the ideas of Woolf, who separated imperialism out from broader militaristic considerations, and casts some light on the Round Table movement of imperial patriots such as Cecil Rhodes. He looks at the work of Sweezy and Baran and explores dependency theory. Etherington provides a careful reading of the work under discussion. For example, Hobson's view is sometimes portrayed in "enlightened" terms, yet Hobson, as Etherington reminds us, concurred with the prevalent racist notions of the day, for example regarding Africans in the same light as children. Of particular value in Etherington's book are the snippets of biographical detail provided in respect of the chief protagonists. Through this, and through a discussion of their work, we can see how each theorist built on earlier work sometimes developing their own theories on the basis of inaccurate interpretations of those of others.

PORTER provides a concise and highly readable overview of the major theories of imperialism. Noting the view promulgated by some historians that the term should not be used in scholarly discourse, he proceeds to discuss in readily accessible language the key perspectives that exist on the issue. He deals with what he terms both "metropolitan" theories and "peripheral" theories. He dissects the older theories of Hobson, Lenin, Hobsbawm, Schumpeter, and others before dealing with the more recent work of Wallerstein and Said, which he locates under the umbrella of "alternative" approaches. His treatment ranges over political theories associated with diplomatic, strategic, or prestige considerations, touching upon the connections between overseas conquest and nationalism within Europe, before dealing with social and economic theories of imperialism. The latter, related to the search for markets and investment opportunities, are scrutinized closely and Porter rejects what he sees as simplistic connections between the evolution of the modern capitalist system and imperialism. Porter also devotes attention to those theorists who have emphasized the complex interactions between colonial powers and local elites. The pattern of imperialism was often subject to local factors. Thus, a concern with "peripheral" explanations is seen as offering some light. Under the umbrella of "alternative" theories he pays some limited attention to the work of Said and to Wallerstein's world systems theory, as well as to ideas of imperialism in terms of scientific endeavour and the advancement of knowledge.

An older, but still useful, compilation of approaches to imperialism is that provided by OWEN & SUTCLIFFE. This edited volume draws together a range of theoretical positions and case studies. It is noteworthy in including essays from theorists with quite different perspectives on imperialism, thereby serving to highlight areas of confusion and ambiguity and the importance of ideological position. The theoretical chapters include Tom Kemp's discussion of Marxist theories of imperialism followed by a critique of such theories by Michael Barratt Brown. He argues against the importance attached by Lenin to the export of European capital and stresses the importance of the competition between European states for the creation of new export markets. Hans-Ulrich Wehler's view of imperialism as a means of maintaining social order domestically is followed by Thomas Hodgkin's stress on the viewpoint of those being colonized and the contribution that non-European theorists can make to the study of the phenomenon. Robinson's chapter follows his earlier work in stressing the accommodation and collaboration between imperial powers and local elites. Two subsequent chapters, by Magdoff and Sutcliffe, explore Marxist interpretations of contemporary imperialism. This is followed by six case studies drawn from Asia, Africa, and Latin America. The book concludes with a well-argued discussion by Sutcliffe on the ambiguities concerning the definition and the historical origins of imperialism.

As a historian, SCAMMELL provides an account of what he and others identify as "the first imperial age". He provides a history of early European overseas expansion, explores the early origins and the complex motivations underlying exploration, and he addresses the ways in which the European powers exploited their overseas territories. He examines the nature of colonial societies and explores both the impact of colonial acquisition on the colonies and its impact on Europe. Through reference to the "civilising" role of imperialism, Scammell points to the evolution of an ideology whereby Europeans generally saw themselves as superior, thus marking the way towards Europe's rise to global hegemony.

HOBSBAWM's *The Age of Empire* is part of his four-volume series on modern European history. This volume explores developments in Europe leading up to World War I and set against the backdrop of colonial expansion. He begins with a personal 'overture' in which he tells us his mother, a native of Vienna, met his father, of Polish parentage but raised in

London, while in Egypt. He asserts that such a meeting was only likely to occur in a world of European colonial expansion. While the volume is an erudite and highly readable account, the main section of relevance here is chapter three (from which the volume takes its title). While not denying the importance of other factors, Hobsbawm emphasizes the economic dimension to imperial expansion. He points to the fact that the word imperialism only began to appear in the latter part of the nineteenth century. His essential argument is that imperialism cannot be separated out from the growth of capitalism – the creation of a truly global economy. This is not to deny the existence of strategic or prestige factors in the acquisition of particular territories, but the underlying logic was, in Hobsbawm's view, intrinsically bound up with economic considerations.

KIERNAN (1995) is a collection of essays spanning the time period from 1975 to 1990. The eight pieces capture the essence of his thoughts on imperialism and are very wide ranging. They cover the links between imperialism and the development of a global economy where he points to the brutality inflicted on Europeans by other Europeans before such behaviour was "exported". In the second essay Kiernan critiques dependency theory. He points to the exploitation of periphery by core within Europe (linked to industrialization) prior to overseas territorial expansion. The third essay discusses the imperial practice of recruiting "native" armies often used to fight in their own country, as well as in others. In the fourth and fifth essays Kiernan addresses assumptions of European superiority and the "progressiveness" of anti-colonial struggles, in the process raising questions over restitution and the undemocratic nature of many post-independence regimes. In the succeeding chapter, Kiernan addresses the issue of how European identity has been shaped by the colonial experience examining the impact of imperialism on European culture and Europe's self image. He also deals with Gramsci's idea of cultural hegemony as it relates to imperialism. The final chapter offers a slightly quirky look at a postcolonial and multicultural Britain.

KIERNAN (1978) takes as its starting point the idea that imperialism is manifested through a coercive overseas policy designed to extract profits greater than might be gained through normal processes of trade. In this way he portrays the US as a neocolonialist entity. Not everyone would agree with his view of the US, or his characterisation of its overseas policy in imperialist terms, but this book provides a highly readable overview of the history of the US from its own colonial origins leading up to its position of global hegemony. It might be argued that Kiernan's book is more a study of geopolitics than of imperialism *per se*, but it does provide a trenchant analysis of various dimensions of US foreign policy, most notably in relation to Vietnam.

The importance of the cultural legacy and implications of imperialism are the subject matter of SAID's hugely influential book *Orientalism* and his subsequent *Culture and Imperialism*. Said's concern is with how the West's interaction with its colonial world (in the case of Orientalism, Said is primarily concerned with the "Arab world") produced a way of thinking that essentialized the West's view of the East rendering it either exotic or threatening. He sees three meanings to the term "orientalism". Firstly, it is a description for a field of academic enquiry. Secondly, it is a style of thought that

separates "orient" from "occident", thirdly it is a discourse integrally linked to Western domination; a discourse of power in which the West is normal, the East is "other". Central to Said's work is the sense in which Western culture was (invisibly, in many respects) shaped by the colonial project. Through novels, paintings, and other art forms, the non-Western world was depicted in particular ways that rendered it subordinate to the dominant West. Said's highly readable volumes explore the traces of colonialism through the writings of Joseph Conrad, Jane Austen, and many more.

DAVID STOREY

See also Colonialism

Imperialism and feminism

Aldrich, Robert, *Greater France: A History of French Overseas Expansion*, London: Macmillan and New York: St Martin's Press, 1996

Alexander, M. Jaqui and Chandra T. Mohanty, *Feminist Genealogies, Colonial Legacies, Democratic Futures*, New York and London: Routledge, 1997

Barrington, Brook, *Empires, Imperialism and Southeast Asia*, Clayton, Victoria: Monash Asia Institute, 1997

Kabbani, Rana, *Imperial Fictions: Europe's Myths of Orient*, London: Macmillan, 1994

Midgley, Clare (editor), *Gender and Imperialism*, Manchester: Manchester University Press, 1998

Rutherford, Jonathan, *Forever England: Reflections on Race, Masculinity and Empire*, London: Lawrence and Wishart, 1997

Said, Edward, *Culture and Imperialism*, New York: Knopf, and London: Chatto and Windus, 1993

Sinha, Mrinalini, *Colonial Masculinity: The "Manly Englishman" and the "Effeminate Bengali" in the Late Nineteenth Century*, Manchester: Manchester University Press, 1995

Williams, Patrick and Laura Chrisman (editors), *Colonial Discourse and Post-colonial Theory: A Reader*, New York: Columbia University Press, 1994

Yegenoglu, Meyda, *Colonial Fantasies: Towards a Feminist Reading of Orientalism*, Cambridge and New York: Cambridge University Press, 1998

ALEXANDER & MOHANTY have edited a collaborative enterprise that engages in globalized feminist analyses of the residue of imperialist ideologies, the potentialities of postcolonialism, and the depredations of the advanced capitalist nation state. Anchored in the challenge of personal negotiation of the politics of racial fragmentation, the essays contest the recolonization that operates through structural, institutional, and psychic ways of being, particularly those initiated by nation states produced through, or in contrast to, imperialist practices.

French imperialism provides the basis for ALDRICH's work. He details the ideas and uses of empire, the ways in which colonies and colonized populations were treated and mistreated, and how imperialist ideologies shaped French pride and commitment in the metropolitan consciousness. Aimed at undergraduate students, the study successfully describes the social and historical complexity of the French imperial experience.

Various issues relating to the different kinds of imperial practice are examined in BARRINGTON's edited collection of 12 essays. They explore the concepts of order and influence that often accompanied or replaced early imperial ideas about territorial possession or sovereignty. Rather than focusing upon one individual imperial power, the essays present the interwoven complexities that were constituted between empires, including those of southeast Asia that were displaced or used as allies. More recent trading of colonies between empires (as in the case of Hong Kong) is linked with the rise of nationalisms and the increase in self-determination to present a book that gives chronological depth to the geopolitical breadth of contemporary societies.

In an elegantly written exploration of the ways in which Western imagination has projected evil onto others in order to protect its self-created dogmas, KABBANI provides a lively and comprehensive examination of travellers' tales, contemporary texts, and artistic production from the colonial "West" to construct a sociopolitical analysis of European imperialist penetration of Muslim societies. Written from the perspective of a Muslim feminist, her work is a useful addition to that of many Muslim writers who labour to evaluate the burdens of persistent colonialisms that interweave with present ideological and actual restrictions upon female autonomy.

MIDGLEY's edited work adds useful detail to elucidations of the social and cultural encounters of empire in colonial contexts and in Britain. An edited collection of nine essays that explores the ways in which imperialism is a highly gendered phenomenon, this work ranges from the late 18th century to the present and across a variety of colonial and metropolitan societies. The essays examine the insights provided by postcolonial theory; that dominant forms of knowledge production assisted imperial enterprise, and that a singular normative concept of imperialism has maintained popular perceptions of colonialism.

A linkage of the sociopolitical complexity of imperialism to the construction of masculinity forms the thematic structure of RUTHERFORD's work. He examines the relationship of British imperial masculinity to English ethnicity and the rise of a particular kind of family in the late 19th century. The social construction of narcissistic, emotionally immature, and self-sacrificing men is linked to contemporary political and cultural production that reflects on "Britain" as an imperial creation.

SAID's classic study of the relationship between imperialism and culture investigates the mutual implication of power and knowledge, arguing that imperialism did not vanish with empire. It examines and critiques the power of "Western" nation states to penetrate other societies physically and intellectually, and the concomitant production of knowledge that accompanies such encounters. He elucidates how nations may be viewed as narrative constructions with the material power to obstruct the formation and development of other nations. His interrogation of the link between imperialism and metropolitan cultural production is an effective counter to geopolitical works.

SINHA addresses the strength of orientalism and the romanticization of people as "other", the feminization of the colonized, and the enshrining of predominantly European and male power via the structures of law and social custom. She challenges the assumption that the contours of colonial masculinity were shaped in the context of an imperial formation that included both Britain and India. Rather, she argues, the imposition of a constructed dualism of the "manly Englishman" and the "effeminate Bengali" should be studied in relation to colonial Indian society and some aspects of late 19th-century British society. She interlinks her analysis with the world system that was fashioned by imperialism and the social, economic, political, and ideological aspects of colonial processes and practices.

WILLIAMS & CHRISMAN have edited an intellectually and politically invaluable array of writers' work for their collection of 31 essays. It is recognized academically as a contemporary classic addressing theoretical aspects of present sociological and political encounters generated by imperial practices. In acknowledging the persistence of imperialist and neocolonial practices the authors work through the contentions and the generative capabilities of theorizing "postcolonialism". The essays are prefaced by a theoretically concentrated discussion of imperialism, colonial discourse, and postcolonial practice, ensuring this work remains significant for tertiary students and educators.

Anchored in discourse theory, YEGENOGLU's work examines the discursive dynamics that propose and protect the West as a sovereign subject and the ways in which Westerners will use perceptions of people as "other" to maintain a stable and potent self-representation. She focuses specifically upon the gendered categories and significations that inscribe perceptions of orientalism, so her work is more useful as a sociocultural analysis of "otherness" rather than as an ethnographic study of "the other".

HELEN JOHNSON

See also Postcolonial feminism

Import substitution

Balassa, Bela, *The Newly-Industrializing Countries in the World Economy*, New York: Pergamon Press, 1981

Brohman, John, "Postwar Development in the Asian NICs: Does the Neoliberal Model Fit Reality?", *Economic Geography*, 72 (1996): 107–30

Dell, Sidney, *A Latin American Common Market?*, Oxford and New York: Oxford University Press, 1966

Douglass, M., "The Developmental State and the Newly Industrialised Economies of Asia", *Environment and Planning A*, 26 (1994): 543–66

Gereffi, Gary and Donald L. Wyman (editors), *Manufacturing Miracles: Paths of Industrialization in Latin America and East Asia*, Princeton, New Jersey: Princeton University Press, 1990

Gereffi, Gary, "Global Production Systems and Third World Development" in *Global Change, Regional Response: The New International Context of Development*, edited by Barbara Stallings, Cambridge and New York: Cambridge University Press, 1995

Kaplinsky, Rafael, "The International Context for Industrialisation in the Coming Decade", *Journal of Development Studies*, 21 (1984): 75–95

Kemp, Tom, *Industrialization in the Non-western World*, London and New York: Longman, 1989

Lewis, W. Arthur, "Economic Development with Unlimited Supplies of Labour", *Manchester School of Economic and Social Studies*, 22/2 (1954): 139–92

Little, Ian, Tibor Scitovsky and Maurice Scott, *Industry and Trade in Some Developing Countries*, Oxford and New York: Oxford University Press, 1970

Moseley, K.P., "West African Industry and the Debt Crisis", *Journal of International Development*, 4 (1992): 1–27

Prebisch, Raúl, *The Economic Development of Latin America and its Principal Problems*, Santiago: United Nations Economic Commission for Latin America, 1950 (Spanish edition 1949)

UN, "Fifty Years of the Economic Survey" in *Economic Survey of Latin America, 1997–98*, New York: United Nations Economic Commission for Latin America and the Caribbean, 1998

UN, Centre for Industrial Development, Research and Evaluation Division, *A Study of Industrial Growth*, New York: United Nations, 1963

Wade, Robert, *Governing the Market: Economic Theory and the Role of Government in East Asian Industrialization*, Princeton, New Jersey: Princeton University Press, 1990

Wade, Robert, "Lessons from East Asia" in *Development Studies: A Reader*, edited by Stuart Corbridge, London and New York: Arnold, 1995

Britain developed because it industrialized. France, Germany, and the US all industrialized and so improved their level of development. Thereafter every country that wished to develop felt that it needed to industrialize. Studies of labour productivity and the income elasticity of demand supported the belief that countries would only succeed if they reduced the labour force in agriculture and raised that in higher productivity industrial enterprise (LEWIS). The United Nations (1963, p.1) claimed in 1963 that "Rapid industrial growth constitutes in the majority of cases the most potent dynamic factor in the process of accelerated economic growth."

In the less-developed world, belief in industrialization was underlined by the work of PREBISCH at the Economic Commission for Latin America, (ECLA). He demonstrated that the terms of trade had shifted against primary products over the period 1870–1930. For every ton of copper or pound of coffee produced in 1870, poor countries received much less in terms of manufactured products in 1930. Moreover, as it was clear that a poor country's demand for industrial imports would increase much more rapidly than foreign demand for its exports, the clear lesson was that less-developed countries should industrialize.

According to ECLA, the most plausible way in which less-developed countries should industrialize was in stages. The first industries to be established were those that had the largest internal market. In general, these were consumer-goods industries. Later, industries should be established that would provide the new industries with the parts needed to produce the consumer goods. Finally, factories producing capital goods like machinery would be set up.

There was an alternative approach to industrialization, which was based on the Soviet model. This was followed subsequently to some degree by China, Egypt, India, and initially by Cuba (KEMP). Here demand for consumer goods would be depressed and industrial expansion would concentrate on the production of capital goods. Plants to produce the steel, railway goods, glass, and cement required to build infrastructure and services would receive priority in investment allocations. Only later should investment go into consumer goods production.

There can be little doubt that a great deal was achieved through import substituting industrialization. In the larger countries, this form of development attracted foreign investment and created jobs. By definition, it was also replacing foreign manufactures with local production. In hindsight, the growth rates in most countries were quite respectable. In Latin America, growth during the 1950s, 1960s, and 1970s was superior to that for later decades (UN 1998).

However, it was increasingly apparent that import-substituting industrialization created numerous problems. First, it did not resolve the problem of employment since much of the new industry was capital intensive and fertility rates in many less-developed countries were still very high. Second, it did not overcome the problem of dependency because the vast bulk of the investment and technology came from developed countries. Third, it did not actually help the balance of payments because in order to establish the new factories imports of capital goods were required and later intermediate goods and raw materials were needed to create the new consumer products. Fourth, import-substituting industrialization often created inefficient industries in part because the size of the local market was often very limited. Fifth, import substituting industrialization involved the state and frequently the ways in which the state intervened helped to distort the development process, it favoured industry against agriculture, formal workers against informal workers, and favoured interest groups against the rest of society. Finally, import-substituting industrialization had the problem that it was bound to slow down. This was a particular problem in the smaller economies with limited markets. In most of Africa, the Caribbean, and Asia, the amount of industrial development that was achieved was extremely limited (Kemp, LITTLE, SCITOVSKY & SCOTT, MOSELEY). But sooner or later even large countries such as Brazil or India would find that there was a limit to the degree to which import-substituting industrialization would function.

What to do when import-substituting industrialization slowed down involved a choice between three alternatives. The first was to try to produce industrial goods for export; a route that was regarded by most less-developed countries' governments in the 1960s and 1970s as virtually impossible. The second route was the second-best solution of exporting industrial goods to poor neighbours, a route that could be encouraged by setting up some kind of trade agreement, customs union, or common market (DELL). The final route was to redistribute income in society to increase the demand for basic consumer goods among the poor and to reduce demand for expensive consumer durables such as automobiles.

Of the three routes, the most popular was the second and, by the 1980s, most Third World governments were involved, or had been involved, in some kind of customs union. Unfortunately, it is very difficult to encourage trade relationships between poor countries and few of these agreements were very successful (see Dell, WADE).

However, the onset of the debt crisis, the revival of neoliberal economic thinking in the developed world, and the experience of the Asian "tigers" all conspired to change conventional wisdom. During the 1980s, the advice being given to most less-developed countries was to reduce protection and to attempt to produce manufactured exports. The critique of import substituting industrialization became widespread with BALASSA, pushing the argument for export-orientated industrialization very hard. Balassa argued that the economic records of countries such as Korea and Taiwan, which had pushed export production very hard, was greatly superior to those of countries such as Argentina or India that had stuck to import substitution. According to Balassa the reason was simple:

> The discrimination in favour of import substitution and against exports did not permit the development of manufactured exports in countries engaging in second-stage import substitution behind high protection. There were also adverse developments in primary exports as low prices for producers and for consumers reduced the exportable surplus by discouraging production and encouraging consumption. (p.16)

In short, import-substituting industrialization sucked in imports and discouraged the emergence of exports.

Trade liberalization and sometimes devaluation were needed to make exports more competitive. This did not necessarily mean free trade and discrimination in favour of industries producing for export. According to Balassa, "Rather, it is characterized by providing similar incentives to production for domestic and for export markets."

Today, the conventional wisdom has it that every country should strive to replicate the experience of the "tiger economies" and "newly industrializing economies". However there are defenders of import substituting industrialization as an initial stage that must be gone through. WADE (1995: p.320) wrote that:

> Protection has to be seen as a part of longer-term measures to gain experience of industry and large-scale organization. In its absence resources may remain largely unemployed or confined to very small-scale production. The trick is to use such longer-term protection in a way which does not eliminate all competitive pressures.

Authors such as Wade and DOUGLASS also question whether we really understand the real reasons behind the success of the "tiger" economies, and, increasingly, many authors (for example, BROHMAN, GEREFFI, and KAPLINSKY) are asking whether world conditions are any longer favourable to export expansion and whether the poorer economies will ever develop the kind of infrastructure and human capital required to produce manufactured exports. Nevertheless, export-oriented industrialization is now as fashionable today as import-substituting industrialization was in the 1960s.

ALAN GILBERT

See also Tiger economies, Newly industrializing countries, economics

Impulsivity

American Psychiatric Association, *Diagnostic and Statistical Manual of Mental Disorders*, 4th edition (DSM-IV), Washington, DC: American Psychiatric Association, 1994

Barratt, Ernest S., "Impulsiveness and Anxiety: Information Processing and Electroencephalograph Topography", *Journal of Research in Psychology*, 21 (1987): 453–63

Davison, Gerald C. and John M. Neale, *Abnormal Psychology*, 7th edition, Chichester and New York: Wiley, 1998

Gray, Jeffrey Alan, *The Psychology of Fear and Stress*, Cambridge and New York: Cambridge University Press, 1987

Matthews, Gerald and Kirby Gilliland, "The Personality Theories of H.J. Eysenck and J.A Gray: A Comparative Review", *Personality and Individual Differences*, 26 (1999): 583–626

Newman, Joseph, "Reaction to Punishment in Extraverts and Psychopaths: Implications for the Impulsive Behaviour of Disinhibited Individuals", *Journal of Research in Personality*, 21 (1987): 464–80

Raine, Adrian, "Classical Conditioning, Arousal, and Crime: A Biosocial Perspective" in *The Scientific Study of Human Nature: Tribute to Hans J. Eysenck at Eighty*, edited by Helmuth Nyborg, Oxford: Pergamon Press, and New York: Elsevier, 1997

Revelle, William, "Extraversion and Impulsivity: The Lost Dimension?" in *The Scientific Study of Human Nature: Tribute to Hans J. Eysenck at Eighty*, edited by Helmuth Nyborg, Oxford: Pergamon Press, and New York: Elsevier, 1997

Rosenhan, David L. and Martin E.P. Seligman, *Abnormal Psychology*, 3rd edition, New York: Norton, 1995

Zuckerman, Marvin, *Psychobiology of Personality*, Cambridge and New York: Cambridge University Press, 1991

Impulsivity refers to a number of interrelated psychological concepts and processes: specific psychiatric (symptomatic) conditions (such as lack of behavioural constraint, psychopathy); certain forms of (overt) behaviour (such as rapid responding, delay of gratification deficit); and a stable (inferred) trait of personality (as measured by personality questionnaire). The references reflect these different aspects.

DAVISON & NEALE provide a good introduction to the concept of *impulse control disorder*, as defined in psychiatry (by the American Psychiatric Association – APA). These disorders encompass: *excessive gambling*, that is out of control and results in personal and family distress; *intermittent explosive disorder*, involving episodes of violence and the destruction of property; *kleptomania*, in which the individual cannot resist the urge to steal objects that are not needed for personal use or monetary value; *pyromania*, in which the individual cannot resist setting fires; and *trichotillomania*, in which individuals cannot resist the urge to pull at their hair. These authors also provide a very informative discussion of the role of impulsivity in psychopathy (now classified by the APA as *antisocial personality disorder* – APD).

ROSENHAN & SELIGMAN and Davison & Neale provide excellent introductions to impulsive personality disorders, which include *conduct disorder* (CD) and *oppositional defiant disorder* (ODD), which, in many cases, serve as precursor to a later diagnosis of APD. These conditions are also related to *attention-deficit/hyperactivity disorder* (ADHD): many children diagnosed as having ADHD later go on to receive a diagnosis of CD, ODD, and APD. ADHD refers to developmentally inappropriate degrees of inattention, impulsiveness, and hyperactivity; impulsivity is often demonstrated by blurting out answers to questions before they are completed, making comments out of turn, failing to wait one's turn in group tasks, failing to follow directions, interrupting the teacher, along with an inability to delay gratification, low frustration tolerance, and temper outbursts. The diagnostic criteria for these impulse control disorders are delineated by the AMERICAN PSYCHIATRIC ASSOCIATION.

In order to advance the empirical study of impulsivity, various psychometric measures have been developed. One well-validated measure of impulsivity was developed by BARRATT, which is composed of five traits: (a) motor impulsiveness (for example, reckless responding); (b) cognitive impulsiveness (for example, rapid decision making); (c) nonplanning impulsiveness (for example, lack of delay of gratification); (d) inhibitory control; and (e) decision time. Other impulsivity measures focus on monotony avoidance, sensation seeking, and boredom vulnerability.

One of the best reviews of the factorial nature of impulsivity is REVELLE, who delineates the psychometric development of the construct and its role in biological models of personality. Although impulsivity is known to be statistically related to the broad traits of extraversion, neuroticism, and psychoticism, there is still a debate concerning its proper position within the hierarchy of personality traits as well as its relation to biological processes. Revelle sees impulsivity as a lost dimension in current descriptive models of personality. On the basis of experimental research relating to cortical arousal, Revelle argues for the importance of impulsivity over sociability in accounting for the relationship of extraversion to arousal-mediated performance. The role of impulsivity in biological personality research is important because personality and arousal effects are implicated in the psychological processes that contribute to the development and maintenance of a number of psychiatric disorders. RAINE provides an excellent review of the evidence for a link between personality, arousal, conditioning, and crime. ZUCKERMAN relates impulsivity and other personality measures to anxiety disorders.

The relationship between stable traits of temperament/personality and psychopathology has long intrigued behavioural scientists, and has been the subject of extensive research. Zuckerman provides the most accessible and detailed exposition of this important relationship. He discusses the biological basis of personality and its relation to anxiety and impulsivity disorders. In relation to the impulsivity disorders, he includes the literature on the *disinhibitory syndrome*, which encompasses a range of impulsive and antisocial behaviours that, taken together, point to a single underlying neurophysiological basis of a major dimension of personality ranging from the highly socialized to the impulsive, addictive, aggressive, antisocial type.

A number of important theoretical models of impulsivity have been proposed in recent years. The best-developed model is offered by GRAY, who proposes a neuropsychological theory based upon a *behavioural approach system* (BAS). The BAS forms a positive feedback loop, activated by the presentation of stimuli associated with reward and the termination/omission of signals of punishment. The positive feedback loop initiates approach behaviour towards appetitive stimuli (such as food, or a sexual partner). The BAS/impulsivity is linked to a second system, *behavioural inhibition system* (BIS), which is responsible for the temperament/personality of fear and anxiety. The BIS forms a negative feedback loop, mediating responses to secondary aversive stimuli (punishment and the omission/termination of reward), extreme novelty, high intensity stimuli, and innate fear stimuli (such as snakes or blood). The BIS imposes a brake on impulsive behaviour.

In relation to the BIS and BAS, MATTHEWS & GILLILAND provide an impressive survey of Gray's biological model of personality, evaluating the major evidence for and against this model, as well as comparing and contrasting it with Hans Eysenck's personality model, which is based upon arousal (extraversion) and emotional activation (neuroticism). The effects of impulsivity and sociability on different forms of laboratory behaviour (such as conditioning and psychophysiological effects) are also evaluated. The authors argue for a cognitive account of personality traits, including impulsivity, to replace more reductionistic models based upon biological processes.

NEWMAN (1987) argues that impulsivity is a key feature behind many psychopathological conditions involving disinhibition (for example, drug abuse, criminality, psychopathy). Building on Gray's reinforcement-sensitivity theory, he postulates that impulsive individuals are sensitive to rewarding stimuli and, as a consequence of this sensitivity, have difficulty switching behaviour when required in order to avoid punishment. That is, impulsive people suffer from a "response modulation deficit", which results in a secondary effect of inadequate attention being directed to punishing stimuli, leading to impaired learning of aversive environmental stimuli/events. Impulsive people thus do not learn to avoid aversive situations, engage in self-destructive behaviour (such as drug abuse), and antisocial behaviour (such as criminal acts). A neurophysiological account of this deficit is proposed, based on the septal syndrome (the behavioural effects evident in the rat following ablation of the septum in the brain).

Impulsivity is a multifaceted construct with important social and psychiatric consequences; however, both its factorial and neuropsychological nature have yet to be clarified. Nonetheless, significant advances in knowledge have already been accomplished, as comprehensively summarized by Zuckerman.

PHILIP J. CORR

See also Learning, Psychopathy

Incest

Briere, John *et al.* (editors), *The APSAC Handbook on Child Maltreatment*, Thousand Oaks, California and London: Sage, 1996

Butler, Sandra, *Conspiracy of Silence: The Trauma of Incest*, San Francisco: Volcano Press, 1985

Courtois, Christine A., "Healing the Incest Wound: A Treatment Update with Attention to Recovered-Memory Issues", *American Journal of Psychotherapy*, 51/4 (1997): 464–96

Courtois, Christine A., *Healing the Incest Wound: Adult Survivors in Therapy*, New York: Norton, 1988

Fischer, Donald G. and Wendy L. McDonald, "Characteristics of Intrafamilial and Extrafamilial Child Sexual Abuse", *Child Abuse and Neglect*, 22/9 (1998): 915–29

Horton, Anne L. *et al.* (editors), *The Incest Perpetrator: A Family Member No One Wants to Treat*, Newbury Park, California and London: Sage, 1990

Marshall, W.L., D.R. Laws and H.E. Barbaree (editors), *Handbook of Sexual Assaukt: Issues, Theories and Treatment of the Offender*, New York: Plenum Press, 1989

Myers, John E.B., *A Mother's Nightmare – Incest: A Practical Legal Guide for Parents and Professionals*, Thousand Oaks, California and London: Sage, 1997

Russell, Diana E. H., *The Secret Trauma: Incest in the Lives of Girls and Women*, New York: Basic Books, 1986

Trepper, Terry S. and Mary Jo Barrett, *Systemic Treatment of Incest: A Therapeutic Handbook*, New York: Brunner Mazel, 1989

Wurtele, Sandy K. and Cindy L. Miller-Perrin, *Preventing Child Sexual Abuse: Sharing the Responsibility*, Lincoln: University of Nebraska Press, 1992

Incest, or the sexual abuse of a child by a family member, accounts for approximately 25 per cent of all cases of child sexual abuse. For an overview of the research comparing outcomes for children abused by family members with those of children abused by nonfamily members, see FISCHER & McDONALD. Despite work indicating significant differences between the two forms of abuse, the literature often fails to differentiate between the two. Except where otherwise noted, this entry is limited to literature specific to incest. For a more general review, see the *APSAC Handbook on Child Maltreatment*, edited by BRIERE *et al.* This handbook includes a compilation of essays on all aspects of child abuse (including incest) by the leading professionals in the field.

The social problem of incest broke into public awareness in the late 1970s, in large part due to the publication in 1978 of BUTLER (updated in 1985 with a new forward and afterward). Written from a decidedly feminist perspective, this work presents an overview of the dynamics of incest, including sections on victims, offenders, and families. However, the author focuses on the most common pattern of incest: an adult male perpetrator and female child. In researching this book, Butler interviewed over 130 families. She uses case studies of these families, rather than scientific studies, to illustrate her main points. This makes for a compelling account of incest,

but is unlikely to satisfy the social scientist looking for well-documented conclusions.

In the same year that Butler first published her book, RUSSELL began the first large-scale study of incest, the results of which were published in 1986. This book presents an excellent overview of the problem of incest in women's lives and includes both results from Russell's own study as well as other scientific studies. In the introduction, Russell provides a brief history of the study of incest and discusses the differences between exploitative, interfamilial sexual abuse and normal sexual exploration. Latter chapters are devoted to the results of Russell's study, including discussions of incestuous acts, victims, perpetrators, and other family members' reactions to discovering the incestuous relationship.

Responding to a case of incest typically involves psychosocial assessment and treatment, medical attention, and legal intervention. TREPPER & BARRETT focus on treatment of not only the victim, but the entire family. In the two opening chapters, they review some of the common models of child sexual abuse and then go on to outline a multiple systems model that encompasses many of these factors. The remainder of their book focuses on the treatment of incest families, with the three main sections of the book mirroring the three phases of treatment: creating a context for change, challenging behaviours and exploring alternatives, and consolidating changes. Within the second section, each of four chapters is devoted to a different treatment modality (for example, family therapy, subsystem therapy, individual therapy, and group therapy).

COURTOIS (1988) provides similar information as Trepper & Barrett, but focuses on adult survivors (rather than children). She discusses the symptoms and after effects of incest from four different theoretical perspectives before turning her attention to treatment issues. In addition to discussing goals and strategies for treatment, Courtois devotes several chapters on issues unique to adult survivors, such as unique transference issues, dissociation, and repressed memory. Another chapter is devoted to special populations, including male victims and members of religious communities. Vignettes are presented throughout the book to illustrate key points. COURTOIS (1997) updated her treatment model. Although much of the treatment model remains the same, the updated version draws more heavily on object relations/attachment and self-psychology perspectives.

The treatment of perpetrators has been much slower to evolve than treatment of victims for a variety of reasons (for example, social stigma and legal consequences). In fact, in previous years treatment for perpetrators was considered the greatest unmet need in incest cases. MARSHALL, LAWS & BARBAREE provide an abundance of information related to sexual offenders. Several chapters discuss treatment for a specific behaviour or characteristic (for example, his social skills or cognitive distortions), whereas others address various forms of treatment, including hormonal treatment and cognitive-behavioural treatment. However, the majority of the chapters are not limited to the incest perpetrator.

All of the 16 essays in HORTON *et al.* specifically address the incest perpetrator, with a heavy emphasis on treatment. Also included are discussions of some of the unique aspects of working with perpetrators, such as overcoming one's own biases about perpetrators and balancing the need to treat with the duty to report.

Sexual abuse of all types, including incest, may also necessitate medical treatment for a variety of medical conditions, including pregnancy, injury, and sexually transmitted diseases. For a review of medical issues in child sexual abuse, see Briere *et al.*

Because the victims are young and the abuse happens within the family, law enforcement is often uninvolved in incest cases. As a result, there is very little information available about legal responses to incest. Briere *et al.* contains chapters on legal responses to child sexual abuse, including both investigation and legal proceedings but, as previously mentioned, is not limited to incest. For information specific to incest cases, MYERS is one of the few resources available. Myers provides an overview of the American court system, focusing on the three courts likely to be involved in incest cases, and follows an incest case through each of these three courts. He presents advice for mothers who suspect that their children have been the victims of incest. Although primarily written for mothers, professionals will also benefit from the important information contained here.

Recent attention has begun to turn from investigation and treatment of child abuse toward prevention of it. Unfortunately, the evidence on the efficacy of child sexual abuse prevention programmes has been inconclusive. WURTELE & MILLER-PERRIN review many of these prevention programmes and the evidence for their efficacy. Unlike other reviews, however, they do not limit themselves to child-focused programmes. Instead, they argue that preventing child sexual abuse (including incest) necessitates involvement by a variety of individuals and groups. As a result, they include a review of prevention programmes aimed at parents and professionals and include recommendations for researchers and policy makers.

MARCIA J. MCKINLEY-PACE

See also Child abuse, Domestic violence, Rape, Sexual offenders

Income

Edgeworth, Francis Y., Income entry in *Palgrave's Dictionary of Political Economy*, edited by Henry Higgs, 3 vols, London: Macmillan, 1925–26; reprinted New York: Kelley, 1963

Fisher, Irving, *The Nature of Capital and Income*, London and New York: Macmillan, 1906

Gossling, W.F., *Productivity Trends in a Sectoral Macroeconomic Model: A Study of American Agriculture and Supporting Industries, 1919–1964*, London: Input-Output, 1972

Hicks, John R., *Value and Capital: An Inquiry into Some Fundamental Principles of Economic Theory*, Oxford: Clarendon Press, 1939; 2nd edition 1946

Hicks, John R., *Capital and Time: A Neo-Austrian Theory*, Oxford: Clarendon Press, 1973

Keynes, John Maynard, *The General Theory of Employment, Interest and Money*, London: Macmillan, and New York: Harcourt Brace, 1936; as vol. 7 of *The Collected Writings of John Maynard Keynes*, London: Macmillan, and New York: Cambridge University Press, 1973

Marshall, Alfred, *Principles of Economics*, 9th edition, edited by C.W. Guillebaud, 2 vols, London and New York: Macmillan, 1961 (1st edition 1890)

Meacci, Ferdinando, "Irving Fisher and the Classics on the Notion of Capital: Upheaval and Continuity in Economic Thought", *History of Political Economy*, 21/3 (1989): 409–24

Meade, James Edward and John Richard Stone, "The Construction of Tables of National Income, Expenditure, Saving and Investment", *Economic Journal*, 51 (1941): 216–33

Mun, Thomas, *England's Treasure by Forraign Trade*, Oxford: Blackwell, 1933 (originally published 1664)

Nordhaus, William D., "Reflections on the Concept of Sustainable Economic Growth" in *Economic Growth and the Structure of Long-Term Development*, edited by Luigi L. Pasinetti and Robert M. Solow, Basingstoke: Macmillan, and New York: St Martin's Press, 1994

Pasinetti, Luigi Lodovico, "The Notion of Vertical Integration in Economic Analysis", *Metroeconomica*, 25 (1973): 1–29

Pigou, Arthur Cecil, *The Economics of Welfare*, 3rd edition, London: Macmillan, 1929

Scazzieri, Roberto, "Vertical Integration in Economic Theory", *Journal of Post Keynesian Economics*, 13/1 (1990): 20–46

Scott, Maurice Fitzgerald, *A New View of Economic Growth*, Oxford: Clarendon Press, and New York: Oxford University Press, 1989

Seton, Francis, *The Economics of Cost, Use and Value: The Evaluation of Performance, Structure and Prices across Time, Space, and Economic System*, Oxford: Clarendon Press, and New York: Oxford University Press, 1992

Stone, Richard, *Input-Output and National Accounts*, Paris: OECD, 1961

Studenski, Paul, *The Income of Nations*, New York: New York University Press, 1961

The concept of income entails a measure of purchasing power, either at the level of individuals or at the level of the economic system as a whole. HICKS (1939) calls attention to the distinction between income and wealth by maintaining that, unlike the measurement of wealth, "[t]he purpose of income calculations in practical affairs is to give people an indication of the amount which they can consume without impoverishing themselves" (p.172). This approach to the definition of income suggests an ex post measurement of income, such that income coincides with "the value of the individual's consumption plus the increment in the money value of his prospect . . . [I]t equals Consumption plus Capital accumulation" (p.178). Following the perspective originally outlined in this book, individual (and social) income becomes associated with the concept of "take out", that is, with that amount of purchasing power that can be freely used without diminishing the over-all capacity to sustain a new consumption flow (*See also* HICKS 1973).

The distinction between a flow measure of purchasing power (income) and a fund measure of it (wealth) goes back to the transition from pre-classical economic thought to classical political economy. Pre-classical writers (such as MUN) lay their emphasis upon the relationship between revenue and treasure (that is, accumulated wealth), and examine the conditions under which treasure can be increased by means of yearly additions to the purchasing power existing in the economic system. STUDENSKI (part one, chapter one) reconstructs the process by which the pre-classical point of view (as expressed in the Mercantilist literature) is reversed by the classical economists and other "dissenters from mercantilism". He describes the way in which a "comprehensive production concept of national income" came to be established with contributions by William Petty, Gregory King, and Pierre de Boisguillebert (pp.13–15). The subsequent work of Francois Quesnay and other Physiocrats, as well as of Italian economists such as Ferdinando Galiani and Pietro Verri, led to the formation of a conception of national income rooted in the analysis of production activity and in the consideration of human labour as the ultimate source of purchasing power. Adam Smith and the other classical economists outline a conception of national income that combines attention to labour with the Physiocratic theory of net product. In this way, income formation comes to be associated with the flow of material resources that an economic system can generate over and above the yearly amounts necessary to maintain a stationary state (net output or surplus). FISHER outlines an approach to individual and social income that is sharply different from the classical framework and suggests a revival of the pre-classical attention for the accountancy of stored and disposable wealth (see above). However, Fisher shifts the concentration of attention from the ex post (or historical) measurement of (stored) purchasing power to its ex ante (or prospective) evaluation, and maintains that the value of a capital fund at any given time can be derived from the discounted value of the future income flows that such a capital fund is expected to generate. (*See also* MEACCI for a detailed investigation of the relationship between Fisher's conception and classical income theory.)

Recent theoretical and applied income analysis is rooted in a reformulation of the classical approach originally suggested by MARSHALL, EDGEWORTH, and PIGOU, and subsequently developed by KEYNES, and MEADE & STONE. In particular, Marshall introduces a comprehensive notion of income "as including all the benefits which mankind derive at any time from their efforts, in the present and in the past, to turn nature's resources to their best account" (p.76). Marshall also argues that aggregate income ("social income") can be "estimated by adding together the incomes of the individuals in the society in question" (p.79), and that "[l]abour together with capital and land ... are the sources of all that income of which account is commonly taken in reckoning up the National Income" (p.79). Edgeworth highlights the need to identify net income (from an individual or a social point of view) after deducing replacement expenses, which would include the expenses needed to maintain worker's efficiency constant. Pigou discusses the concept of "national dividend" (national income) and introduces a distinction between the conception of income suitable in the analysis of a stationary economy and the conception of income to be used when considering an expanding economy. In the former case, national income coincides with the amount of "national dividend" compatible with the maintenance of the existing national capital (p.35). In the latter case, new materials entering the

production process may exceed materials embodied in finished products, and new machinery may lead to increased productive capacity (p.36). In a non-stationary expanding economy, total income is normally different from the "national income of consumption goods", also called by Pigou "consumption income" (p.37), and a certain (net) investment income has to be reckoned.

Keynes takes up Pigou's revised classical approach and calls attention to the nature of national income as the net output of a non-stationary economy, or "the net addition ... to the resources of the community available for consumption or for retention as capital stock" (p.38). In particular, Keynes defines aggregate income as the sum of entrepreneurial income and the amounts paid out "to the other factors of production in return for their services" (p.53). Following this approach, aggregate income is equal to the value of finished output minus the cost of using existing capital equipment (user cost).

Meade and Stone undertake the construction from statistical data of national income and related variables (such as national expenditure, saving, and investment) by making use of a classificatory framework close to Keynes' analysis. In this connection, Stone notes that the general interdependence between national accounting magnitudes, which entails that expenditure cannot be identified independently of saving and income (total income being the sum of expenditure and saving), and that consumption cannot be identified independently of production and accumulation (total output of any given commodity being the sum of consumption and accumulation) (p.25). The interdependence of national accounting magnitudes suggests to Stone the consideration of intersectoral relationships as a way to connect "final demand for the outputs of different industries with the primary inputs into those industries through the whole network of intermediate demand by each industry for the products of the others" (p.15).

GOSSLING calls attention to the distinction between "gross output sub-systems" and "final output sub-systems", and notes that, in general, gross output subsystems cannot be added up due to the existence of overlaps (except in the case of zero interindustry flows). On the other hand, final output (net product) subsystems are additive as overlaps are excluded by definition.

PASINETTI discusses the vertical integration of interindustry production flows as an analytical tool that may be used to derive national accounting magnitudes from a set of "circular" input-output relationships. In particular, Pasinetti introduces the vertical integration algorithm, and shows how statistical information relative to interindustry transactions may become the basis of a set of vertically integrated sectors (or net product subsystems). Each vertically integrated sector includes the amounts of produced inputs directly and indirectly necessary to the production of one particular commodity as a component of the economic system's net output. As a result, the total output of any given commodity used as an intermediate input is split between non-overlapping subsystems, and the double counting of the same magnitudes can be avoided. SCAZZIERI further explores the implications of vertical integration in the construction of national income totals. He notes that, in each vertically integrated sector, no magnitude can appear both as value added and as production cost. This property makes it possible to derive national income and its elements (such as total wages, profits, and rents) from the consideration of net product subsystems. The value added of any given subsystem can be expressed as a sum of wages, profits, and rents, and the overall value added (national income) may be obtained by summing up the quantities of value added across the different subsystems.

Recent theoretical and applied work has considered social income from the point of view of its long-run persistence (sustainability). In this connection, NORDHAUS examines Hicks' definition of income (see above) and argues that intangible assets are the source of a major difference between individual and social income. In particular, Nordhaus argues that, under conditions of technological change, a community should include in its capital accounting "the growth of its "knowledge capital", which is improving over time and is understated in the value of physical capital in conventional output measures" (p.318). The importance of knowledge capital makes the Hicksian measures of social income inadequate in so far as they do not fully acknowledge the increasing stock of human capabilities. The economic role of embedded skills is also examined by SCOTT in his contribution to the capital and income accounts of an expanding economy. In particular, Scott highlights that a suitable measure of income requires the consideration of human capital, but also notes that net investment in human capital may be difficult to identify, due to the need of measuring the level of education necessary to maintain human capital constant. A way to overcome the above difficulty (that is especially serious in the case of economic systems subject to intense structural dynamics) is found in the definition of (net) investment as consumption foregone if structural change is to be possible.

Both classical and recent contributions to (net) income analysis call attention to the relationship between primary (nonproduced) inputs and final use. Such a relationship is investigated by SETON, who examines the simultaneous determination of cost-prices for commodities and use-prices for factors. In this way, social income and social cost can be seen as complementary results of the same set of fundamental structural properties, and alternative ways to distribute social income or social cost may be associated with differences in ethical judgement or policy attitude.

ROBERTO SCAZZIERI

Incomplete contracting, *see* Contracts and competition

Increasing returns

Aghion, Philippe and Peter Howitt, "A Model of Growth through Creative Destruction", *Econometrica*, 60/2 (1992): 323–51

Arthur, Bryan, "Competing Technologies, Increasing Returns and Lock-in by Historical Events", *Economic Journal*, 99/394 (1989): 116–31

Chamberlin, Edward H., *The Theory of Monopolistic Competition*, Cambridge, Massachusetts: Harvard University Press, 1933

David, Paul, "Clio and the Economics of QWERTY", *American Economic Review*, 75/2 (1985): 332–37

Georgescu-Roegen, Nicholas, "Measure, Quality and Optimum Scale" in *Energy and Economic Myths: Institutional and Analytical Economic Essays*, New York: Pergamon Press, 1976

Hicks, John R., *Capital and Time: A Neo-Austrian Theory*, Oxford: Clarendon Press, 1973

Kaldor, Nicholas, "The Irrelevance of Equilibrium Economics", *Economic Journal*, 82 (1972): 1237–55

Krugman, Paul R., "Increasing Returns, Monopolistic Competition and International Trade", *Journal of International Economics*, 9 (1979): 469–79

Krugman, Paul R., "Increasing Returns and Economic Geography", *Journal of Political Economy*, 99 (1991): 483–99

Lucas, Robert E., "On the Mechanics of Economic Development", *Journal of Monetary Economics*, 22/1 (1988): 3–42

Lucas, Robert E., "Making a Miracle", *Econometrica*, 61/2 (1993): 251–72

Richardson, Georges B., *The Economics of Imperfect Knowledge*, Cheltenham, Gloucestershire: Elgar, 1998

Romer, Paul M., "Increasing Returns and Long Run Growth", *Journal of Political Economy*, 94 (1986): 1002–37

Romer, Paul M., "Endogenous Technical Change", *Journal of Political Economy*, 98 (1990): 426–57

Stokey, Nancy, "Learning by Doing and the Introduction of New Goods", *Journal of Political Economy*, 96 (1988): 701–17

Weitzman, M., "Increasing Returns and the Foundations of Unemployment Theory", *Economic Journal*, 92 (1982): 787–804

Young, Allyn, "Increasing Returns and Economic Progress", *Economic Journal*, 38 (1928): 527–42

Young, Alwyn, "Learning by Doing and the Dynamic Effects of International Trade", *Quarterly Journal of Economics*, 106/2 (1991): 369–405

Although pervasive increasing returns are an important feature in industry generally, traditional economic theory maintained that in order for competition to be preserved, firms should not operate under increasing returns. Incompatibility between competition and increasing returns was made to appear inevitable by the nature of the models in terms of which economic reality was described. The question gives rise to new considerations, both in the field of industrial organization, and in the field of macrodynamics.

Increasing returns prevail as long as the firm can increase its output of a given product with a less-than-proportionate increase in total costs. It is clear, then, that as long as any of the firms making identical products experiences increasing returns, competition will produce concentration and, eventually, monopoly. A simple solution consists in supposing that each firm has its own market, because its product is a little bit different from those of its competitors. Thus it will operate under increasing returns, but will be subject to competition from rivals offering close but not perfect substitute products (see the discussion of this issue in CHAMBERLIN).

RICHARDSON maintains that, when firms enjoy increasing returns in the presence of a high rate of innovation, competition may obtain due to the continuous changes in demand and cost conditions, even when there is no differentiation, and the products of competing firms are essentially homogeneous. As stressed by GEORGESCU-ROEGEN, increasing returns, far from being a property of a standard production function, can only emerge as a consequence of an innovative choice which implies carrying out new production processes bringing about new products. Richardson argues that, in industries where there is continuous development and innovation, existing products are subject to displacement by new ones, and that the result of this process will be to leave several producers in the market, "not only because they cater to different needs, but because it takes time for new products to gain ground and for old ones to be driven from the field " (p.174). As Richardson says:

> In general, manufactured products will gain market share only gradually, as their merits become apparent and as the capacity to produce them is built up. During this period, rival offerings will still be on the market, and their life may be prolonged somewhat by price reductions that go some way to offset their disadvantages. Meanwhile, a new product, ready to challenge the one gaining ground, will be under development. (p.172)

In such a context, competition may be consistent with increasing returns. It appears that a process of discovery of the relevant information that would not exist if information were complete and production processes timeless. As Richardson further argues:

> without imperfect knowledge, it might be said, all demand would switch to the best product within the particular market, and without imperfect mobility of resources, the supply of that product would appropriately respond. They would exist only one producer of each product variety as in the equilibrium associated with monopolistic competition. (p.173)

Until recently, in growth models, the assumption of perfect competition dictated the assumptions that there were no increasing returns, and that technological change was exogenous. The introduction of the notion of externality in an appropriate technical framework made it possible to reconcile increasing returns with competition in models of endogenous growth (as described by ROMER (1986) and LUCAS (1988)).

Developing an original contribution by YOUNG (1928), according to which the introduction of new goods is the crucial driving force in economic growth, KALDOR considered that every reorganization of production activities created the opportunity for further change, and gave rise to dynamic increasing returns. The appearance of different types of intermediate inputs provides the technical device for modelling this process, which focuses on the division of labour. Along the same lines, increasing returns resulting from an enlargement of the range of capital goods imply monopolistic competition between firms producing these goods (see the discussion in ROMER (1990)).

Also focusing on the role of capital goods, AGHION & HOWITT manage to give an analytical content to the Schumpeterian notion of a creative destruction process. Innovations are seen to consist of the invention of a new intermediate good which replaces the old one, and the use of which raises the efficiency parameter in the production function. Current innovations have positive externalities for future research and development, and negative externalities for incumbent producers.

Following STOKEY and YOUNG (1991), LUCAS (1993) introduced the concept of learning from spillover technology as a form of dynamic increasing returns. Such learning requires that the labour force systematically shift towards the most productive activities. This results in a catching-up process, and explains some so-called economic miracles provided that the goods produced can be exported.

KRUGMAN (1979) developed the tools that implemented the view according to which increasing returns are a cause of international trade. The scale economies associated with increasing returns are seen as internal to firms, but sufficiently moderate to ensure the survival of a large number of firms in the free-entry equilibrium of a group of firms producing goods that are not perfect substitutes for each other. Then between two countries with identical factor endowments, under increasing returns, a Chamberlinian monopolistic competition emerges, through a combination of an increase in the variety of products and in the size of each firm, which generates an intra-industry trade.

WEITZMAN (1982) showed that, under increasing returns, at every unemployment level, there is no incentive for a firm to hire more workers. In this context, cutting real wages actually increases unemployment in the equilibrium state.

Path dependence and lock in are phenomena associated with the increasing returns arising from learning effects. They emerge with reference to problems of competitive diffusion of alternative technologies (as noted by ARTHUR and DAVID). The focus is on the fact that small events, occurring early on the path of economic evolution, have great importance in selecting one or another among the set of stable equilibria. An interesting implication is the relative importance of "history" as opposed to "expectations" in determining the location of economic activities (see KRUGMAN 1991).

However, a steady state is representative of an economy in which the productive capacity is fully adjusted to the production required at each moment. Any change that would imply increasing returns makes it necessary for the economy to adjust itself to a new production technique. Adjustment of this sort brings about traverse problems. Instead of focusing on the exploitation of increasing returns, the "traverse model", described by HICKS, addresses the question of how these returns obtain. In this perspective, increasing returns are a source of both growth and fluctuations.

JEAN-LUC GAFFARD

Independence

Akehurst, Michael, *A Modern Introduction to International Law*, 5th edition, London and Boston: Allen and Unwin, 1984

Brown, Chris, "Back to Normal? Some Reflections on Sovereignty and Self-determination after the Cold War", *Global Society*, 10/1 (1996)

Deutsch, Karl W. and William J. Foltz (editors), *Nation-Building*, 3rd edition, New York: Atherton Press, 1969

French, Patrick, *Liberty or Death: India's Journey to Independence and Division*, London: HarperCollins, 1997

Gray, Alasdair, *Why Scots Should Rule Scotland*, Edinburgh: Canongate Press, 1992

Halliday, Fred, "Nationalism" in *The Globalization of World Politics: An Introduction to International Relations*, edited by John Baylis and Steve Smith, Oxford and New York: Oxford University Press, 1997

Pinto, Constancio and Matthew Jardine, *East Timor's Unfinished Struggle: Inside the Timorese Resistance*, Boston: South End Press, 1997

Roy Chowdhury, Subrata, *The Genesis of Bangladesh: A Study in International Legal Norms and Permissive Conscience*, New York and Bombay: Asia Publishing House, 1972

Skidmore, Max J. (editor), *The Future of Hong Kong*, Thousand Oaks, California: Sage, 1996

AKEHURST's modern introduction to international law, first published in 1970, must be considered the most widely used introductory text in international law available. Besides dealing with the standard questions of international law this text draws the reader's attention to the legal aspects of acquisition of territory and the notion of independent, sovereign states. The book contains a wealth of information presented in a style that is easy to read. This stimulating introduction includes material on the legal consequences of state succession, self-determination, and civil wars. In addition to a table of cases, the appendix outlines the Falkland Islands dispute and the 1982 Convention of the Law of the Sea.

Hong Kong's future now lies in the hand of the Chinese government. SKIDMORE's collection of essays debating Hong Kong's new life as a special administrative region provides a good introduction to the practical aspects of decolonization and territorial acquisition. Hong Kong's success as a cosmopolitan city-state with one of Asia's highest standards of living would arguably make a good example for the positive influences colonialism promises colonized. The 13 essays cover a wide range of topics concerning the return of Hong Kong to the Chinese government. In addition, the majority of the contributions provide a list of current reference sources. As this was only the first retrocession, with Macau having been the next territory to be returned to China, further research must be undertaken. The Annals opened this process with an excellent treatment of the Hong Kong retrocession.

In BROWN's short but poignant article on the end of the Cold War and the future of self determination, he takes an analytical detour through the historical events of the last 400 years and arrives at the less-than-rhetorical question of how to proceed. The puzzling events of ten years under the new world order have done their best to demonstrate that independent states are prepared to exercise their power within the international community. Brown suggests that states no longer need to put up with the outrages sanctioned by sovereignty. This essay presents a tightly woven treatment of the concept of independence and statehood as it developed over the course of time. It is easy to read, and clear in its analysis and argumentation.

ROY CHOWDHURY's account of Bangladesh's struggle for liberation focuses on the question of international moral and legal responsibility. Carefully researched and documented, the author presents the first major study of the political and constitutional history of Pakistan in his attempt to describe the liberation movement that lead to an independent Bangladesh. He examines the principle of international recognition of newly formed states by debating India's application of the Jeffersonian norm in international law. The book is rich in its attention to detail, and incorporates an excellent reference section. It is the first and still best treatment of Bangladesh's journey on the road to independence observed through the lens of international law.

DEUTSCH & FOLTZ created a classic work with their analysis of the formation and rise of nation-states. Written at a time when the decline of colonialism gave rise to the independent state, the words have not lost their power. The book was the result of a panel discussion in 1962 that sought to examine the birth of nations in various parts of the world and at various historical periods. The first part of the book focuses on the philosophical aspects of nation building. The middle section provides a number of essays on colonial Africa, Latin America, and colonial America. At the end, Foltz addresses short-term and long-term problems of nation building. The large section on reading material is a reflection of the period when the book was written and has only limited use for today's readers. However, the essays in this collection mirror the thoughts and opinions of social scientists who had the opportunity to observe first hand the revolutionary processes that facilitated the change from colonial territory to sovereign state.

Perhaps the greatest mass migration in history was put in motion when Britain's 350-year-old hold on India ceased. Many books have been published describing the rise of India's freedom movement and the struggle for independence that lead to the end of Britain's presence on the Indian subcontinent. FRENCH's journey into India's history offers a radical reinterpretation of the events based on newly declassified intelligence documents. Exploring the powerful relationships between the major political players Winston Churchill and Rear-Admiral Viscount Mountbatten, Nehru, Ghandi, and Jinnah, French uncovers disastrous mistakes committed by these politicians that arguably still influence India's political developments today. A good index and reference section is provided, as well as maps and photographs.

Theory can provide insight, real life experiences help to improve understanding. The struggle for independence has been won by many nations, and was lost by uncountable cultures and societies. The renewed call for independence for the Scottish people has recently been heard and resulted in a new Scottish Parliament. GRAY outlines this struggle beginning with an account of Scottish heritage, the birth of the Scottish nation, the loss of its government, and the search for a modern identity. This essay stands on its own, for it is sincere in its appeal to understand what drives a nation to follow through with the desire to govern its own people. The narrative makes for a quick read without undermining the seriousness of the topic. A new edition is already being prepared.

HALLIDAY's chapter on nationalism provides a wealth of information on self determination, nation states, and nation building. The text is divided up into sections addressing the historical development of nation states, the ideology of nationalism, and the paradox of nationalism as a product of globalization. This last point in particular deserves attention as it deals with the argument that, in a highly unified world, the state will play a lesser role. Yet, an increase in the number of states has been observed giving rise to a growth rate that affects greater disorder, disharmony, and war. The chapter finishes with an outline of the major points addressed, and a guide to further reading material. Halliday succeeds in presenting this complex topic in a way that is neither simplistic nor one sided.

Jose Antonio Ramos Horta, the co-winner of the 1996 Nobel Peace Prize, played a crucial role in East Timor's slow transformation from a colony to an autonomous island nation. His thoughts on the people's struggle for independence of East Timor fill the opening pages of PINTO & JARDINE's topical monograph on this subject. Horta offers a thoughtful political analysis of the long history of East Timor's suppression by colonial powers. However, it is Pinto & Jardine's own experience with the underground movement in Dili and the constant threat of arrest and torture that turns this historical analysis into an insightful and captivating account of the dangers of political activism. In part this book perhaps does not differ greatly from other stories told by victims of state suppression. In light of Suharto's resignation in May 1998, however, the argument of the authors has gained even more momentum that the writing of history is too important to be left only to those in power. Those who risk their lives for the sake of change deserve a voice, and this comprehensive study of the life cycle of states succeeds in including them. East Timor's peace plan concludes the book and serves as a reminder that the global community must work toward global political structures that promote an understanding of human determination, instead of merely capturing the official steps toward state independence.

SABINA W. LAUTENSACH

See also Decolonization, Devolution, Nationalism

Indian law and legal system

Basham, A.L., *The Wonder That Was India: A Survey of the Culture of the Indian Sub-continent before the Coming of the Muslims*, 3rd edition, London: Sidgwick and Jackson, 1967; New York: Taplinger, 1968

Jain, M.P., *Outlines of Indian Legal History*, 4th edition, London: Sweet and Maxwell, 1987

Jois, M. Rama, *Legal and Constitutional History of India*, vol. 1: *Ancient Legal, Judicial and Constitutional System*, vol. 2: *Modern Legal, Judicial and Constitutional System*, London: Sweet and Maxwell, 1984

Kulshreshtha, V.D., *Landmarks in Indian Legal and Constitutional History*, 2nd edition, Lucknow: Eastern Book Company, 1995

Mittal, J.K., *Indian Legal and Constitutional History*, Allahabad: Allahabad Law Agency, 1990

Pylee, M.V., *Constitutional History of India, 1600–1950*, 2nd edition, Bombay and New York: Asia Publishing House, 1980

Sternbach, L., *Juridical Studies in Ancient Indian Law*, 2 vols, Delhi: Motilal Banarsidass, 1965–67

BASHAM has provided not only an account of Indian legal system but also written on ancient Indian civilization. He has made an attempt to cover aspects of Indian life, thought, and the legal system. The book opens with an account of Indian culture, beginning with the ancient Indian Harappa culture, and medieval empires. Though the king was supreme, there were checks on his powers. According to Kautilya's Arthasastra, a Sanskrit work of *c.*4th century BC, the royal ordinance could override any source of law. But this led to much criticism. The caste system and economic position influenced the legal system and judiciary.

Jain published his first book dealing with the Indian legal system in 1952, and has been teaching the subject ever since. JAIN begins with a study of early charters and the establishment of a factory at Surat by the East India Company. The early administration of justice in Madras, Bombay, and Calcutta since 1639 is discussed. The reorganization of the legal system, judicial measures by the British and the judicial system, and the development and codification of law is highlighted. An account of the present law commission, law reporting in India, and the growth of the legal profession in modern India is also discussed. On 5 August 1955, the government decided to appoint a Law Commission to review the system of judicial administration, to examine the Central Acts, and to review the legal system.

A very useful account of Indian law and the legal system is provided by volume I of JOIS. The work begins with the sources of law and the place of a King as God in ancient India. A discussion of legal literature is useful for beginners and the origin and development of law, aspects of civil law, criminal law, evidence, and the importance of interpretation are highlighted. The administration of justice was considered to be the most important function of a king. Ancient jurists in India paid great attention to the laws governing administration of justice. There are good descriptions of the highest court located at the capital city and of lower courts established under royal authority, and the work contains a detailed survey of the Indian legal, and judicial system. The supremacy of Dharma, where judiciary and legal systems were tested in the hall of justice and other courts, and the role of learned scholars and sanctions or punishments provided and the origin of state are discussed. Judgement was mostly based on evidence. Different types of ordeal, like ordeal by balance, water, fire, poison, and so forth, were widely accepted.

In the second volume, Jois covers the legal, judicial and constitutional history of India under Muslim and British rule. The legal system in colonial India is discussed, and the salient features of the constitution of India and its impact on the legal and judicial system are highlighted. The role of law commissions in shaping the Indian legal system is elaborated. The evolution of modern legal and judicial systems and the introduction of English laws in presidency towns, the role of the judiciary under the constitution, the history, development, salient features of the constitution, and its impact on the legal system are discussed. The uncertain and confused state of the criminal law led to the intervention by the Law Commission, which prepared the Indian Penal Code of 1860. The process of codification began with the First Law Commission in 1833, headed by Macaulay.

KULSHRESHTHA is a handy and concise book on the legal

system in India. This book has 21 chapters dealing with the history of judicial systems in ancient and mediaeval India; the early administration of justice in the presidency towns; the history of courts, the Adalat system in Bengal; the reforms of Warren Hastings, Lord Cornwallis, Bentinck, and others; the evolution of the High Courts; the role of Federal Court; the importance of the Supreme Court – the highest court in the land; the evolution of writs; and the constitutional history of India, along with the 59th Constitutional amendment. The very purpose of establishing the High Courts was to effect a fusion of the Company's Courts and the Supreme Courts. These Courts were expected to improve the administration of justice in India. Efforts to unite these two sets of courts began as early as 1861. The Charter Act of 1833 empowered the Governor-General in Council to legislate for all provinces. The Charter Act of 1833 was passed by the British Parliament to deal with the defective state of legislation.

MITTAL gives an account of the Indian legal system from 1600 until 1990. His book on the Indian legal and constitutional history begins with the Charter of 1600 and the East India Company. English settlements at Madras, Bombay, and Calcutta provide a view of the company's early settlement, the administration of justice, and the various courts such as the Mayor's Court, Choultry Courts, Courts of Judicature, the Court of Conscience, and other inferior Courts. A brief account of the rule and judicial plan of Warren Hastings and Lord Bentinck is also provided. The establishment of High Courts and the Federal Court is also highlighted. In addition to a discussion of Indian legal history and the legal system, the book also examines constitutional history and its impact on the Indian legal system. It also deals with the assumption of government by the British Crown and the growth of representative institutions, major Acts like the Indian Councils Act 1909, the Government of India Act 1919, the Government of India Act 1935, the Indian Independence Act 1947, and the present constitution.

PYLEE begins by outlining the importance of the British Indian Empire and concludes with a description of the Indian constitution and the Republic of India. The incorporation of the East India Company in England in 1600 and the transformation of the company into a great ruling power are discussed with ease. The East India Company ruled India with direct control exercised by the Royal family and later by the British Parliament. An assessment of the Indian Government under the Crown from 1784 to 1858 proved the success of the British rule. In the year 1858, the Company's rule came to an end and the British Government took over the responsibility of ruling India. The Government of India Act of 1919 and the Constitution Act of 1935 greatly influenced the administration in India. For two centuries, the British administration influenced Indian life and culture. It was only in 1947 that India became independent. There was a transfer of power from the British government to the Indian government due to mutual agreement. Hence, India inherited the British system of law, government, and administration.

STERNBACH has published 40 comprehensive studies on ancient Indian law since 1937, which have now been compiled in two volumes. The first volume contains a discussion of ancient Indian law, based on Dharma and Arthashastras. It also deals with the theory and practice of the law of deposit,

labour, debts and marriage, and with the legal position of women, prostitutes, physicians, infanticide, the protection of plants, and other aspects of life peculiar to Indian society. The second volume deals with the application of the law, sources of law, and the technicalities of the legal system. The book also provides an interesting outline of infanticide and exposure of newborn children in ancient and modern India. There is interesting material on the harmonization of law with the requirements of economic conditions.

ASHRAF KAZI

Individualism and economics

Collard, David, *Altruism and Economy: A Study in Non-Selfish Economics*, Oxford: Martin Robertson, and New York: Oxford University Press, 1978

Hayek, F.A., *Individualism and Economic Order*, Chicago: University of Chicago Press, 1948; London: Routledge, 1949

Hindess, Barry, *Political Choice and Social Structure: An Analysis of Actors, Interests and Rationality*, Aldershot: Elgar, 1989

Hodgson, Geoffrey M., *Economics and Institutions: A Manifesto for a Modern Institutional Economics*, Cambridge: Polity Press, and Philadelphia: University of Pennsylvania Press, 1988

Lachmann, Ludwig M., *Capital, Expectations and the Market Process: Essays on the Theory of the Market Economy*, edited by Walter E. Grinder, Kansas City: Sheed Andrews and McMeel, 1977

Lukes, Steven, *Individualism*, Oxford: Blackwell, and New York: Harper and Row, 1973

Mises, Ludwig von, *Human Action: A Treatise on Economics*, London: Hodge, and New Haven, Connecticut: Yale University Press, 1949; 4th edition, New York: Foundation for Economic Education, 1996

Rizvi, S. Abu Turab, "The Microfoundations Project in General Equilibrium Theory", *Cambridge Journal of Economics*, 18/4 (August 1994): 357–77

Roemer, John (editor), *Analytical Marxism*, Cambridge and New York: Cambridge University Press, 1986

Mainstream economics is often associated – by advocates and critics alike – with versions of both methodological and political individualism. However, these categories and ideas are typically used with insufficient clarity and reflection. A large number of quite different doctrines can be grouped together under the label "individualism", and the use of the I-word should never be taken for granted. Ontological individualism can amount to statements such as "society consists of individuals" or "only individuals have intentions". Methodological individualism is generally, but not universally, defined as the view that all explanations of social phenomena must solely be in terms of individuals. Political individualism is typically taken to mean some version of libertarian or pro-market politics. Historically, economists have flirted with both of these doctrines.

Although it is written by a social theorist rather than an economist, LUKES is an ideal starting point from which to begin to untangle the confusion. The author carefully distinguishes between various versions of ontological, methodological, and political individualism. The book is also noted for its powerful critique of the type of methodological individualism advocated by economists. As a whole, this work is a brilliant and penetrating overview. It is highly recommended.

HINDESS, which provides astute and philosophically sophisticated discussions of the problems of individualism and rational choice theory in politics and sociology, usefully supplements the latter work. His arguments apply directly to economics. Particularly notable are his criticisms of rational choice theory in general, and of the methodological individualism of Jon Elster and others.

COLLARD is the work of a mainstream economist. The author shows clearly that the commonplace assumption that individuals maximise their utility does not rule out the possibility of altruism, as long as individuals gain utility by helping others. As a result, selfish and non-selfish versions of the utility-maximising individual are possible. In sum, this book is an antidote to the view that individualism or utilitarianism must always involve self-seeking behaviour.

In general, however, the major discussions of methodological individualism have been produced outside the mainstream of economics. For example, a group of "analytical Marxists", represented here by ROEMER, have been at the forefront in the promotion and clarification of methodological individualism. The essay by Jon Elster in this collection is particularly revealing in this respect.

Another non-mainstream group involved with these issues is the Austrian School, including the works cited here by HAYEK, LACHMANN, and VON MISES. The works of Hayek and von Mises are acknowledged classics and essential reading for any social scientist. However, the problem in Hayek's case is that his advocacy of methodological individualism – despite the political individualism of the Austrian School viewpoint – is surprising limited and somewhat opaque. Several interpreters of Hayek's work, for instance, have argued that his methodological individualism is subdued, and was eventually overshadowed by later developments in his thinking. On closer inspection, many authors associated with methodological individualism do not turn out to be the true advocates portrayed in the hagiography of their converts.

The critique of methodological individualism in HODGSON focuses on the problem of using the individual as the ultimate unit of analysis, especially when social institutions and conditions mould individual preferences and purposes. Hodgson argues that the individualist view, that the explanations of all social phenomena must be based on individuals, cannot work if the purposes and preferences of individuals themselves are continuously affected by socioeconomic circumstances.

A particular theme is pursued brilliantly by RIZVI, which charts the acknowledged failure of mainstream economists to develop substantive propositions from the individualistic foundations of Walrasian general equilibrium theory. This microfoundations project is widely acknowledged, even by mainstream economists, to be a failure. Rizvi is the best and most informative discussion of this topic known to the writer of this entry.

Methodological individualism is very much a mantra of mainstream economics. What is remarkable, however, is that economists themselves have engaged in very little discussion of its meaning and implications. In general, the best discussions of the issue are found in the works of philosophers and social theorists. Individualism, it seems, is too important to be left to the economists.

GEOFFREY HODGSON

See also Neoclassical economics

Industrial democracy

Bernstein, Paul, *Workplace Democratization: Its Internal Dynamics*, Kent, Ohio: Kent State University Press, 1976

Blumberg, Paul, *Industrial Democracy: The Sociology of Participation*, London: Constable, 1968

Bolle de Bal, Marcel, *The Double Games of Participation: Pay, Performance, and Culture*, New York: de Gruyter, 1993

Espinosa, Juan G. and Andrew S. Zimbalist, *Economic Democracy: Workers' Participation in Chilean Industry, 1970–1973*, New York: Academic Press, 1978

Fox, Alan, *Beyond Contract: Work, Power and Trust Relations*, London: Faber, 1974

Kester, Gérard and Henri Pinaud (editors), *Trade Unions and Democratic Participation in Europe: A Scenario for the 21st Century*, Aldershot, Hampshire: Avebury, 1996

Mellor, Mary, Jane Hannah and John Stirling, *Worker Cooperatives in Theory and Practice*, Milton Keynes: Open University Press, 1988

Obradović Josip and William N. Dunn (editors), *Worker's Self-Management and Organizational Power in Yugoslavia*, Pittsburgh: University of Pittsburgh Center for International Studies, 1978

Poole, Michael, *Towards a New Industrial Democracy: Workers' Participation in Industry*, London and New York: Routledge and Kegan Paul, 1986

Vanek, Jaroslav (editor), *Self-management: Economic Liberation of Man: Selected Readings*, Harmondsworth and Baltimore, Penguin, 1975

Participation relates to fundamental processes involved in the exercise of power at the place of work and in society. In a unitary model of a work organization, FOX argues, there is a unified structure of authority, leadership, and loyalty, with full managerial prerogative legitimized by all members of the organization. Once that legitimacy is withdrawn, a "pluralist model" characterized by power relations, arises. Fox deals extensively and deeply with the nature and exercise of power, and its formal and institutional shape, but also with its cultural underpinnings, including the role of social values and ideologies. Fox's book is a necessary introduction to a deeper understanding of industrial democracy.

VANEK's reader is a multidisciplinary presentation of industrial democracy in its broadest sense. In the introduction, Vanek describes the historical development of the idea of worker participation and presents a clear conceptual introduction, with an emphasis on the underlying operational principle of industrial democracy, which is that of a fully democratic rule on the basis of equality of vote. He introduces the distinction between a purely self-managed firm and a purely capital-controlled one, and reviews a broad spectrum of "participatory" variants in between. Apart from the excellent introductory chapter, the book is highly valuable because of its ten brief chapters containing summaries and excerpts from classical texts of the past 200 years on working men's production associations, collectivism, syndicalism, guilds, workers' control, and Yugoslav self-management.

A more sociologically focused introduction to industrial democracy may be found in POOLE. He defines industrial democracy as the exercise of power by workers or their representatives over decisions within their places of employment, coupled with a modification of the locus and distribution of authority within the workforce itself. Poole focuses his classification of the main types of industrial democracy (workers' self-management, production cooperatives, codetermination, works councils, trade-union initiatives and shopfloor programmes) not only on their distinctive defining characteristics and internal structural properties, but also on the initiating agents. In Fox's tradition, he draws special attention to cultural dimensions and evaluates the different forms of participation in terms of the power position of their originators (management, workers, government, and so on), and in terms of the values that those in power hold.

An attractive supplement to Poole's classification is that of BERNSTEIN, who offers a longitudinal and dynamic perspective of industrial democracy, based on broad comparative research (including a secondary analysis of some 100 research studies in places including the US, Western Europe, Yugoslavia, and China). Bernstein formulates a number of propositions about critical thresholds that have to be crossed to enable work organizations to move towards greater democratization and humanization. His model consists of six components (participation in decision making, sharing in economic results, information, guaranteed individual rights, independent right of appeal, and "participatory consciousness"). For each of these components he defines the criteria for crossing thresholds to more effective participation.

An outstanding and still very relevant contribution to the sociology of industrial democracy is BLUMBERG's analytical comparison between collective bargaining and participation (in chapter seven of his book). He demonstrates that collective bargaining is not industrial democracy comparable to political democracy, as democracy is appropriately defined as accountability of leadership to an electorate that has the power to remove that leadership. Since bargaining and participation systems often coexist it is important – as Blumberg fully elaborates – that the different roles of trade unions are clearly assigned and specified, so that the autonomy of each can be protected and unions can remain effectively accountable to their members.

The development of workers' self-management in Yugoslavia marks the first serious effort to introduce "ultimate" industrial democracy on a national scale. Self-management as an institutional model has, from the beginning, envisioned a radical distribution of power to workers. The editors OBRADOVIĆ & DUNN provide a brilliant multidisciplinary introductory chapter on the history and theory of self-management. This is followed by six thematic parts, addressed by 19 Yugoslav researchers, who test the assumptions underlying the theory and practice of self-management. The book includes many independent empirical studies on participation and power, and, fascinatingly, shows the struggle of the many representative self-management structures against an authoritarian management. Despite the later demise of the Yugoslav system, the book remains an important contribution to the sociology of industrial democracy.

ESPINOSA & ZIMBALIST argue that capitalism in Latin America and in other parts of the developing world has meant both underdevelopment and extreme inequality for the overwhelming majority of people. They describe how, in Chile under the Allende regime (1970–3), an attempt was made to realize industrial democracy within the existing constitutional framework. Even though Chile's experiment was short-lived, this study shows that historic change is a process open to human action and to aspirations for freedom, self-determination, and self-realization. The authors also make an important contribution to general participation theory by showing that participation at higher levels within the enterprise is more effective when accompanied by active participation at the base or lower levels – especially through workers' assemblies at the shopfloor level and in general assemblies of the whole enterprise.

MELLOR, HANNAH & STIRLING consider the theory and practice of the cooperative idea from the perspective of current sociological theory of labour relations and industrial democracy. A major asset of their book is that it addresses the issue of equality between the sexes, a subject long ignored in studies of industrial democracy. The authors review how gender balance operates in cooperatives, and offer clues for generalizations on feminism in labour relations. They argue that the sphere of production and the sphere of reproduction, the public and the private, and the personal and the political, must be integrated.

Where mainstream sociological analysis of industrial democracy concentrates on power and human relations, BOLLE DE BAL defines it as essentially financial. In a highly original fashion he contributes to the theoretical foundations of the sociology of remuneration. He holds that the triangular game of pay, performance, and culture fosters the "double games" of participation: participation is at the same time distribution and reward. His book puts pay systems, in particular payment by results, into social and cultural perspective. Bolle de Bal's analysis, broadly based on a comparative study of both market economies and planned economies, leads him to describe "the theatre of participation", providing sociological groundwork for participation strategies. Thus his book contributes significantly to the futurology of industrial democracy.

The book edited by KESTER & PINAUD also considers industrial democracy and the future. In 12 chapters, researchers trace major trends in the evolution of participation in Europe and in other parts of the world, paying special attention to the role of trade unions. On the basis of these longitudinal studies, a scenario for the growth of democratic participation in the 21st century is presented. In this scenario, five different forms of workplace level participation (collective bargaining, comanagement, codetermination, organizational and financial participation) are brought into synergy and under democratic control, with active trade-union involvement. A more coherent trade-union policy and strategy for participation is spelt out. The book also contains two chapters on the history of European Union policy on democratic participation and on European works councils.

GÉRARD KESTER

See also Democracy in the workplace, Organizational participation, Participatory democracy in organizations

Industrial districts

Bagnasco, Arnaldo, *Tre Italie: la problematica territoriale dello sviluppo italiano*, Bologna: Il Mulino, 1977

Becattini, G., "The Marshallian Industrial District as a Socio-economic Notion" in *Industrial Districts and Inter-firm Cooperation in Italy*, edited by F. Pyke *et al.*, 1990

Brusco, S., "The Idea of the Industrial District: Its Genesis" in *Industrial Districts and Inter-firm Co-operation in Italy*, edited by F. Pyke *et al.*, 1990

Cossentino, F. *et al.* (editors), *Local and Regional Response to Global Pressure: The Case of Italy and Its Industrial Districts*, Geneva: International Institute for Labour Studies, 1996

Garofoli, Gioacchino (editor), *Endogenous Development and Southern Europe*, Aldershot, Hampshire: Avebury, 1992

Marshall, Alfred, *Industry and Trade*, 3rd edition, London: Macmillan, 1921

Marshall, Alfred, *Principles of Economics*, 9th edition, edited by C.W. Guillebaud, 2 vols, London and New York: Macmillan, 1961 (1st edition 1890)

Piore, Michael J. and Charles F. Sabel, *The Second Industrial Divide: Possibilities for Prosperity*, New York: Basic Books, 1984

Putnam, Robert D., *Making Democracy Work: Civic Traditions in Modern Italy*, Princeton, New Jersey: Princeton University Press, 1993

Pyke, F., G. Becattini and W. Senegenberger (editors), *Industrial Districts and Inter-firm Co-operation in Italy*, Geneva: International Institute for Labour Studies, 1990

Storper, Michael, *The Regional World: Territorial Development in a Global Economy*, New York: Guilford Press, 1997

UNCTAD, *Technological Dynamism in Industrial Districts: An Alternative Approach to Industrialization in Developing Countries?*, New York and Geneva: United Nations, 1994

In MARSHALL's (1921, 1961) writings on industrial districts and related themes, as they appear in *Principles of Economics* and *Industry and Trade*, the original rationale for industrial districts rests on the creation of "external economies of scale" (economies that are external to the firm but internal to the area), "which can often be secured by the concentration of many small businesses of a similar character in particular localities: or, as is commonly said, by the localisation of industry" (Marshall 1930: p.266) as a competitive alternative to the "internal economies of scale" of big companies.

In contrast to traditional regional economics, Marshall attaches a more independent role to agglomeration economies as the specific *territorial* aspects of a geographical agglomera-

tion of industrial production. Marshall focuses on traditional sociocultural factors, which concern the quality of the social milieu of industrial districts, and that only indirectly affect the profits of firms. Among such factors Marshall emphasizes in particular the "mutual knowledge and trust" that reduces transaction costs in the local production system; the "industrial atmosphere" that facilitates the generation of skills and qualifications of the workforce required by local industry; and the effect of both these aspects in promoting (incremental) innovations and innovation diffusion among small firms in industrial districts.

An important factor in the reinterpretation of the concept of the industrial district has undoubtedly been the contextualization of the concept brought about by the sociological analysis by BAGNASCO, identifying that the "Third Italy" (the central and north-eastern regions) represented a specific path of modernization based on clusters of small and medium enterprises, which was qualitatively different from the developed north-west as well as from the underdeveloped southern parts of Italy.

The main new theoretical achievement of Marshall's Italian followers in their formulation of the neo-Marshallian approach to industrial districts, was to strengthen the noneconomic, socioterritorial dimension of the concept when changing the focus from the cluster of small firms as such to the broader perspective of the merger of community and firms. BECATTINI, perhaps the most well-known of these Italian economists, has termed the Marshallian industrial district a *socioeconomic notion*, and has defined the industrial district as a socio-territorial entity which is characterised by the active presence of both a community of people and a population of firms in one naturally and historically bounded area. In the district, unlike in other environments, such as manufacturing towns, community and firms tend to merge. (Becattini, p.38) Becattini maintains that "the firm become rooted in the territory, and this result cannot be conceptualised independently of its historical development. (Becattini 1990: p.40)

Looking more systematically at the structural characteristics of industrial districts, they have been summarized in the following way by Garofoli: a) an extensive division of labour between firms in the local production system; b) a strong product specialization at the firm and company level; c) the existence of an effective information network at the district level; d) the high competence level of the working force.

GAROFOLI has presented a typology of Italian industrial districts representing a redynamization of the concept. This implies that industrial districts can pass through a possible development process from "areas of productive specialization" via "local productive systems" to "system areas" as the most advanced form. In this view, industrial districts do not represent a stable (or static) organizational model of industrial production. On the contrary, development and change should be looked upon as a "natural" part of the history of industrial districts (Garofoli 1992).

BRUSCO has also developed a typology of development paths of industrial districts in his advocacy for a transition from the original "industrial district Mark I" (districts without local government intervention) to "industrial district Mark II" (districts with considerable government intervention). Brusco points out that "industrial districts eventually face the problem of how to acquire the new technological capabilities which are necessary to revive the process of creative growth. It is here that the need for intervention appears" (Brusco, p.17), in order to support organizational innovations such as "centers of real services" in the industrial districts of Emilia-Romagna.

The seminal book by PIORE & SABEL represents the starting point of the contemporary process of international diffusion of "industrial districts". They use the Italian industrial districts as the main example in their global, macro-historical analysis of the transformation from Fordist standardized mass production to the flexible specialization of the post-Fordist model of organizing the world of production.

This diffusion process has been followed up by the International Institute For Labour Studies in Geneva, which during the 1990s published three books from a program of research on small firms, of which two of them had a strong focus on the industrial districts of the Third Italy (PYKE, BECATTINI & SENEGENBERGER; COSSENTINO et al.). The titles and themes of the books describe the development of theoretical perspectives as well as empirical trends with respect to the change and growth of industrial districts. UNCTAD in New York and Geneva published a similar book in 1994, which focused on the relevance of the experience of industrial districts in the developed countries as an alternative approach to industrialisation in developing countries. In all these books we find, in addition to contributions from well-known Italian scholars on industrial districts and their disciples, chapters written by researchers mainly within economic geography, such as Ash Amin, Bjørn Asheim, and Michael Storper, which reflects the huge impact research on industrial districts has had on the development of economic geography and its contribution to the new heterodoxy in economics (see STORPER).

In the literature on industrial districts from Piore & Sabel and until today, it has been underlined that one central characteristic of the "industrial district" is the balance between competition and cooperation within networks of firms. This ambivalence regarding the relationship between, and the relative importance of, competition and co-operation is basically caused by a traditional, Marshallian focus on the locational efficiency of industrial districts and of the achievement of external economies through vertical cooperation with subcontractors along the value chain. This limits the potential for horizontal technological cooperation between principal firms and suppliers, which could promote radical innovations, thus hindering the transformation of local industrial districts into technological districts, being capable of taking on international competition through making dynamic use of new technologies (see Storper).

Consequently, not every industrial district is doing equally well, which basically concerns the competitiveness of the small firms in the districts. The problems of reduced competitive advantage in certain districts have to be considered as a challenge to every district, which has resulted in structural changes in many of the districts, such as growing concentration among small and medium enterprises in the form of group formations, problems, and potentials connected to the entrance of multinational companies and a decentralization of certain production stages to areas outside the region, for example to East European countries or countries in the Third World. The outcome of these changes, and not least their effect on the innovativeness and competitiveness of the firms, will play a decisive role in determining the future economic prospects of the districts (see Cossentino et al.).

Learning from the Emilia-Romagna model of policy making it is important to understand that the economic development of the region has not simply been the result of a "spontaneous" development, where non-economic factors, such as social capital (such as trust and institutional thickness), have been of great importance for the economic performance of the districts (see PUTNAM). Rather, it has been a process of organizational building and institutional learning, which based on private-public partnerships succeeded in establishing intermediate governance structures aiming at creating a supportive environment for innovation and firm formation (see Cossentino et al.).

BJØRN T. ASHEIM

See also Clusters, Location theory

Industrial dynamics

Andersen, B., J.S. Metcalfe and B.S. Tether, "Distributed Innovation Systems and Instituted Economic Processes" in *Innovation Systems in the Service Economy: Measurement and Case Study Analysis*, edited by J.S. Metcalfe et al., Dordrecht: Kluwer, 2000

Carlsson, Bo, "Reflections on Industrial Dynamics: The Challenges Ahead", *International Journal of Industrial Organisation*, 5 (1987): 135–48

Carlsson, Bo (editor), *Technological Systems and Industrial Dynamics*, Boston: Kluwer, 1997

Eliasson, Gunnar, "Modelling the Experimentally Organized Economy", *Journal of Economic Behavior and Organization*, 16/1–2 (1991): 153–82

Eliasson, Gunnar, "Competence Blocs and Industrial Policy in the Knowledge-Based Economy", *Science, Technology, Industry Review*, 22 (1997)

Forrester, Jay, *Industrial Dynamics*, Cambridge, Massachusetts: MIT Press, 1961

Foss, Nicolai, "Theories of the Firm: Contractual and Competence Perspectives", *Journal of Evolutionary Economics*, 3/2 (1993): 127–44

Lundvall, Bengt-Åke (editor), *National Systems of Innovation: Towards a Theory of Innovation and Interactive Learning*, London and New York: Pinter, 1992

Nelson, Richard R., "Why Do Firms Differ, and How Does It Matter?", *Strategic Management Journal*, 12 (1991): 61–74

Penrose, Edith Tilton, *The Theory of the Growth of the Firm*, 3rd edition, Oxford and New York: Oxford University Press, 1995

Richardson, G.B., "The Organisation of Industry", *Economic Journal*, 2 (1972): 883–96

Schumpeter, Joseph A., *Capitalism, Socialism, and Democracy*, New York: Harper, 1941, London: Allen and Unwin, 1943; 6th edition London and Boston: Unwin, 1987

Industrial dynamics is a "problem oriented" approach to a particular set of questions, rather than a subfield within a discipline. The three principal questions relate to investment in productive capacity, changes in technique, and product innovation. The approach is mainly about understanding the causes and effects of the open-ended transformation processes of industry structures (i.e. the rules for changes). The pioneering works of Nathan Rosenberg (*Perspectives on Technology*, 1976, *Inside the Black Box: Technology and Economics*, 1982) and Richard Nelson and Sidney Winter (*An Evolutionary Theory of Economic Change*, 1982) have led to an emphasis on how technologies, organizations, and the dynamic capabilities of firms change incrementally, and are accumulated along specific paths or trajectories. NELSON reviews how the boundaries to firms' technological trajectories also explains why firms differ in their behaviour, in their knowledge base, in their capability to innovate, and in their ability to appropriate from the innovations they make. Hence, the mainstream model of the representative firm does not apply.

Selection or competition is not constrained to product markets. In the industrial dynamics approach, long-term competitiveness is as much located within the firm's dynamic supply capabilities (for example technological capabilities, adjustment capabilities, and local networks), or distributed in cooperative arrangements among firms and other institutions. Hence, industrial dynamics is compatible with the resource-based theories of the firm (see PENROSE, RICHARDSON, FOSS). In the management literature, similar issues have been addressed with respect to learning organizations. ELIASSON (1991) defines the "competence bloc" as a critical component within industrial dynamics concerned with selection and choices, and explaining the path dependency. His analysis is set in the context of the experimentally organized economy.

In this framework, firms only optimize locally, if at all (i.e. there is no generally applicable best corporate practice), since they are constrained in the choices they make and by the resources and capabilities that they control (everything is context-specific). Hence, the production function of mainstream economics cannot be taken for granted.

Obviously, competitive advantage in markets as well as in the corporate endowments and resource bases (technology, organization, and capabilities) are causes and effects of one another. There are interaction processes (or cumulative causation processes), as opposed to linear development processes, between supply and demand factors. The ideas of Joseph Schumpeter have been influential. This includes both his early work (*The Theory of Economic Development: An Inquiry Into Profits, Capital, Credit, Interest and The Business Cycle*, 1934) in which he focuses on the "individual" entrepreneur, as well as his later work (SCHUMPETER) focusing on the "collective work" in R&D laboratories. These ideas have been integrated with the notion of "science push–demand pull" by evolutionary economists, who argue that the structures and institutional set-up of a society form the framework for a process of interactive learning that sometimes results in innovation and progress. LUNDVALL refers to "national systems of innovation" in which he points to the existence of national specificities in "collective entrepreneurship" as well as in user-producer interaction. CARLSSON (1997) illustrates how innovative activity and industrial development coevolve in relation to specific sectors and technologies. Others, for example ANDERSEN, METCALFE & TETHER, suggest how the emergence and shaping of innovative activity may be distributed across a wider matrix of structures, interrelationships, constraints, and tradeoffs throughout the economic system. Hence, it is a general assumption within industrial dynamics that technologies and firms are not transformed in isolation but rather in systemic contexts.

When addressing the effects of industrial transformations, a major aim is to use the above information to gain an understanding of the processes and performances of a specific socioeconomic system, including its sustainability and its inherent contradictions. It raises questions with respect to the varieties of capitalism and the evolution of such systems (e.g. what are the industrial consequences of change?). As the nature of such "problems" follows neither disciplines nor political boundaries, it is possible to find Schumpeterian, Marxian, as well as Hayekian ideas strongly represented within industrial dynamics.

Hence, the questions industrial dynamics raises are very different to those posed within standard industrial economics. The methodology of industrial dynamics might be considered as a field within evolutionary economics, while drawing upon perspectives broader than "economics" implies.

The product cycle literature (for example Simon Kuznets, *Secular Movements in Production and Prices* 1930, Raymond Vernon, *International Investment and International Trade in the Product Cycle*, 1966, James Utterback, *Mastering the Dynamics of Innovation*, 1966) has helped us to understand changes in the characteristics of markets, technology, and products along associated lifecycles within specific industries. The industrial dynamics literature typically involves a more interactive and multisectoral focus on change, in order to identify the industrial dynamic structures at a given time. In this context the macro socioeconomy is not simply the aggregate of various micro units, but is instead regarded as a complex outcome of micro relationships or interactions. CARLSSON (1987) and ELIASSON (1997) emphasize the micro to macro (or the "micro-based macro") perspective as characteristic for industrial dynamics. The basic mechanism is one where, as entities grow at different rates, the associated structures change (due to new sorting). This transforms the overall configuration of systems of development, so that the parameters which determine (i.e. select) the directions of change and development processes, facilitate the emergence of new structures, and so forth. The role of innovation in interactive development and selection processes (i.e. the structural dimensions of the transformations of entities) are central areas examined within industrial dynamics.

The industrial dynamics literature is not concerned with industries in relation to their product markets. Rather, it focuses on the underlying technological capabilities of firms relative to their major industrial competitors, or distributed capabilities of cooperative arrangements among firms and other institutions. The level of analysis is therefore flexible, being distributed across meso, macro, and "micro-based macro" factors that contribute to the development and transformation of a common knowledge base. Viewing industries from a capability perspective takes into account "untraded interdependencies" (i.e. knowledge interchange and interactive learning in parallel with, and often independently from, market transactions). The boundaries of industrial dynamics have especially been conceptualized in relation to system approaches (innovation systems, technological systems, or distributed innovation systems) or "micro-based macro" models of the economy. Hence, the units, levels, and boundaries within industrial dynamics are determined by the particular problem of investigation.

The industrial dynamics approach has been successful in challenging mainstream theoretical, conceptual, and measurement issues, and it has opened an interesting research agenda. The explicit recognition of path-dependency and cumulativeness in competence building, as well as selection and development processes, makes industrial dynamics a potential supporter of historical studies of industrial development, and vice versa. In general it is open to interdisciplinary collaboration around industrial transformation.

However, the empirical work has been rather restricted, being focused mainly on manufacturing industries and technical innovations (important as they may be). It tends to overlook services and non-technical innovations (for example within organization or management). Studies have also been partial, focused mainly on the behaviour of firms within individual industries rather than the interplay between industries or industrial behaviour. More understanding is also needed with respect to the interactive role and the dynamics of the demand side. On the supply side, industrial dynamics has not made important contributions to the analysis of strategy or other related factors at the micro-firm level. That is, corporate strategy (in common with many technological phenomena) has been treated as events transpiring inside a black box (cf. Rosenberg's "black box" notion: Rosenberg, *Inside the Black Box: Technology and Economics*, 1982). Theoretical modelling has to date been somewhat narrow, in so far it has mainly taken the form of simulation models (see FORRESTER). Some policy implications of the industrial dynamics approach are also worth exploring.

Finally, because most approaches address industrial dynamics in a very indirect or informal way, and given the great diversity within the field, a number of journals that comes closest to covering the range of issues addressed within industrial dynamics are recommended: *Economics of Innovation and New Technology, Industrial and Corporate Change, Journal of Economics and Management Strategy, Journal of Evolutionary Economics, Journal of Industry Studies* (relaunched as *Industry and Innovation* in 1997), *Small Business Economics,* and *Structural Change and Economic Dynamics.*

BIRGITTE ANDERSEN AND BENGT-ÅKE LUNDVALL

See also Resource-based economics, Edith Penrose, Theory of the firm

Industrial organization

Bresnahan, T.F. and R.L. Schmalensee, *The Empirical Renaissance in Industrial Economics*, Oxford and New York: Blackwell, 1987

Geroski, Paul, Richard J. Gilbert, Alexis Jacquemin, *Barriers to Entry and Strategic Competition*, Chur, Switzerland and New York: Harwood, 1990

Geroski, Paul and Paul Gregg, *Coping with Recession: UK Company Performance in Adversity*, Cambridge and New York: Cambridge University Press, 1997

Kwoka, John E., Jr, *Power Structure: Ownership, Integration, and Competition in the US Electricity Industry*, Boston: Kluwer, 1996

Laffont, Jean-Jacques and Michel Moreaux (editors), *Dynamics, Incomplete Information and Industrial Economics*, Oxford and Cambridge, Massachusetts: Blackwell, 1991

Martin, Stephen, *Advanced Industrial Economics*, Oxford and Cambridge, Massachusetts: Blackwell, 1993

Schmalensee, Richard and Robert D. Willig (editors), *Handbook of Industrial Organization*, Amsterdam and New York: North Holland, 1989

Tirole, Jean, *The Theory of Industrial Organization*, Cambridge, Massachusetts: MIT Press, 1988

BRESNAHAN & SCHMALENSEE are the editors of a comprehensive monograph on the empirical study of industrial organization (IO). The purpose of their book is to show that, during the 1980s, several IO theories were finally tested by empirical researchers, with the help of quantitative techniques of varying degrees of sophistication, especially in the fields of econometrics, economic statistics, and applied game theory. Empirical contributions include market tests of profitability differentials among industrial sectors, oligopoly pricing, competition in the long run, and excess capacity as a tool for deterring strategic entry. The papers on oligopoly supergames, tacit collusion, research-and-development (R&D) intensity, and strategic entry deterrence in game theory terms are of particular interest because they illustrate some of the central discussion themes in American IO over the last 15 years.

GEROSKI, GILBERT & JACQUEMIN review the extensive theoretical and empirical literature on entry and strategic competition in markets. Their analysis first focuses on barriers to entry, and on the role of incumbent behaviour in affecting entry conditions. In particular, they pay attention to the ability of incumbents to maintain supernormal profits in the long run. The book then examines the relation between entry and exit conditions, before moving onto an analysis of dynamic limit pricing. Finally, a number of empirical models of entry and strategic behaviour are surveyed. This book is a thorough treatment of entry and exit barriers and of dynamic market games from three world-class experts in IO.

GEROSKI & GREGG examine how companies cope with the pressures that are unleashed by recession. Their work is based upon a large-scale survey undertaken in 1993 that elicited the participation of more than 600 leading UK companies. The data, coming from questionnaires, were combined with a long time-series on the financial performance of most of the participating companies, starting from the early 1980s. The four main issues being examined are vulnerability to recessionary pressures, the companies' reactions to such pressures, the impact of recessionary pressures upon labour markets, and the relationship between recessionary pressures and innovative activity. This is a very recent empirical treatment of recession and markets, providing an impressive contribution in terms of data analysis. It is particularly useful to the general reader who does not want to wade into theoretical IO models.

KWOKA's book is a powerful contribution concerning the limited amount of competition in electricity distribution in the US. With respect to the US case, the author finds that competition in electricity distribution does reduce costs. The relevance of this monograph to general IO readers is to be found in the survey approach taken by Kwoka, which suggests how empirical IO studies should be conducted. The American experience with public utilities is a long-term tradition of private ownership and federal/state regulation (through Public Utility Commissions). In particular, some states (California, Massachusetts, Pennsylvania, Illinois, and Rhode Island) are now undergoing massive restructuring of their energy sectors, as is surveyed by Kwoka's work.

LAFFONT & MOREAUX investigate dynamic issues in IO when informational constraints are present. Theirs is a somewhat technical book, consisting of three sections. Part I covers strategies and non-cooperative behaviour (Nash equilibrium, subgame perfect and Bayesian equilibria, supergames). Part II presents models under complete information (spatial competition, product differentiation, quality, R&D, and patents). Finally, Part III illustrates models under incomplete information, and is probably the most interesting section of the work. It includes contributions on limit pricing (Laffont), deterrence and reputation (Belloc), and bargaining (Cresta). This book is a benchmark in IO, but requires trained readers who are adequately prepared to face the technicalities.

MARTIN provides a thorough analysis of IO, with special reference to empirical issues. Each theoretical chapter has an interesting applied section dealing with real-world issues, particularly those relating to Europe and the US. Competition policy and anti-trust policy are the strongest points of this book – which, on the other hand, is not as comprehensive in terms of game theory and principal-agent models.

SCHMALENSEE & WILLIG address virtually every IO question in their handbook. The most recent edition is particularly strong on modern IO topics, including strategic entry deterrence, repeated oligopoly (super)games, principal-agent theory, "new" market dominance economics, vertical integration issues, reputation, signalling, IO-applied econometrics, and many more. The handbook is intended for advanced users, however, and does not particularly suit beginners. It is a comprehensive reference book for graduate students in IO.

TIROLE is arguably the benchmark book for intermediate IO students and readers. It is particularly strong on game theory and strategic issues. Its approach to IO is very modern and stimulating. The reader faces a challenging and mathematical approach to the topic (a number of exercises are also provided), but the empirical applications enliven the discussion and are a fine complement to the technicalities. The book comes in an unusual "square" format, and also features an original (non-MIT) French version, plus a vast number of other foreign translations.

GIAN CARLO SCARSI

Industrial policy

Baumol, William J., "Contestable Markets: An Uprising in the Theory of Industry Structure", *American Economic Review*, 72/1 (1982): 1–15

Best, Michael H., *The New Competition: Institutions for Industrial Restructuring*, Cambridge: Polity Press, and Cambridge, Massachusetts: Harvard University Press, 1990

Coase, Ronald H., "The Problem of Social Cost", *Journal of Law and Economics*, 3/1 (1960): 1–44

Cowling, K. and R. Sugden, "Industrial Strategy: A Missing Link in British Economic Policy", *Oxford Review of Economic Policy*, 9/3 (1993): 83–100

Modigliani, F., "New Developments on the Oligopoly Front", *Journal of Political Economy*, 66 (1958): 215–32

Pitelis, C.N., "Industrial Strategy: For Britain, in Europe and the World", *Journal of Economic Studies*, 21/5 (1994): 2–92

Pitelis, C.N., "Productivity, Competitiveness and Convergence in the European Economy", *Contributions to Political Economy*, 17 (November 1998): 1–20

Porter, Michael E., *The Competitive Advantage of Nations*, Basingstoke: Macmillan, 1990

Porter, Michael E., "Clusters and the New Economics of Competition", *Harvard Business Review* (November/December 1998)

Scherer, Frederic M. and David Ross, *Industrial Market Structure and Economic Performance*, 3rd edition, Boston: Houghton Mifflin, 1990

Spence, A.M., "Entry, Capacity, Investment and Oligopolistic Pricing", *Bell Journal of Economics*, 8/2 (1977): 534–44

Varian, Hal R., *Intermediate Microeconomics: A Modern Approach*, 5th edition, London and New York: Norton, 1999

The term "industrial policy" (IP) refers to a set of measures taken by a government and aimed at influencing a country's industrial performance towards a desired objective. Industry refers in the main to manufacturing. This focus on manufacturing tends to recede, however, given an emerging fuzziness between manufacturing and services. As all government measures and policies affect industry one way or the other, boundaries between IP and other policies, notably those concerning competition, technology, the regions, competitiveness, structure, and macroeconomics, are not always clear. This is particularly true for the case of competition policy, for reasons to become clear later. Perhaps the nearest we can get to a demarcation line is to combine the government's own perception of what they aim IP to be with an underlying body of theoretical knowledge that informs such perceptions. The government's objective, it may be argued, is to improve the welfare of its citizens, and this is assumed to happen when resources are allocated efficiently and wealth creation is taking place, preferably at a faster pace than in other countries (to improve international competitiveness). Industry is supposed to be an important contributor to the wealth creation process for numerous reasons, notably the tradability of its products, its positive link with technology and innovation, and even its close links with services. It follows that a government wishing to improve welfare will be well advised to design measures that support industry's wealth creation process. The billion-dollar question is "how?" There is no easy answer, and certainly not a generally accepted or adopted one.

The dominant approach to IP stems from mainstream (neoclassical) economic theory. There is a legion of important contributors here, notably Kenneth Arrow, but the main body of this theory is summarized in any good microeconomics text-book, see, for example VARIAN. The focus here is on efficient allocation of scarce resources. It is shown that under certain rather restrictive assumptions, this can be achieved through perfectly competitive markets, i.e. markets characterized by the absence of market power in the form of oligopoly or monopoly. When market power is present, there exists misallocation of resources, and a reduction in consumer welfare, which takes the form of a reduction in "consumer surplus" (a measure of consumer welfare). This is characterised as "market failure". As COASE argues, such failure can also exist for transaction costs-related reasons. In such cases, the government can inter-vene to restore the conditions for perfect competition. For "first best" optimum, this needs to apply in all markets. If not, restoring competitive conditions in one market may not improve welfare.

Theoretical models, like "limit pricing" (MODIGLIANI) or "contestable markets" (BAUMOL), have been proposed, with differing implications on the impact of monopoly and resource allocation. For example, according to contestable markets theory, monopoly need not imply a consumer surplus reduc-tion, if there exists free entry and costless exit of firms. In contrast to this, if there are barriers to entry, prices that are above perfectly competitive levels will emerge, leading to consumer surplus losses. Barriers might include economies of scale (as proposed by Modigliani); or there could be "strategic" barriers, i.e. conscious attempts by established firms to deter entrants (see, for example, SPENCE). Many industrial econo-mists have tried to estimate such losses, and SCHERER & ROSS provides a survey of this literature. In general it was found that there exist static welfare losses due to monopoly power in most countries. In such cases, the government should take steps to guard against the emergence and abuse of monopoly power by monitoring mergers, breaking up domi-nant firms, etc.

PITELIS (1994) summarizes much of the literature and claims that the neoclassical approach is very restrictive in its assumptions, its focus, its objectives, and its concept of compe-tition and IP. Competition is seen as a static concept, or a type of market structure, not as a dynamic process. Its role is limited to achieving allocative efficiency, not in dynamic wealth creation. Despite such limitations, it has dominated industrial policy thinking in the Western world for decades. For example, antitrust legislation in the US, as well as Articles 85 and 86 of the Treaty of Rome in Europe, seem to be directly informed and influenced by the aforementioned perspective. However, the "national champions" or "picking winners" policy, which various European countries pursued in the 1960s and 1970s', involved identifying potentially successful firms or industries and using a number of measures like subsidies, tax breaks etc. to promote them. It also involved a lenient and even encour-aging attitude towards mergers, and in some cases (often in pursuit of considerations of fairness and distribution) nation-alizations of utilities and other "strategic" industries, such as the car industry. Underlying this policy was the hope that such firms could compete successfully with foreign rivals, thus raising export surpluses and the country's competitiveness. But

it tended to exacerbate structural market failures, and was inconsistent with the theoretical pursuit of "perfect competi-tion". The policy was also pursued at a pan-European level, in search of a pan-European company, which could outcom-pete large American multinationals.

The IP of Japan and the so-called "tigers" of the Far East was different. Japanese policy, led by the Ministry of International Trade and Industry (MITI), was not informed by neoclassical economics (see summaries in BEST and Pitelis 1994). It involved a strongly interventionist approach by the government, aimed at creating dynamic advantages in sectors of the future. Such sectors were chosen on the basis of being high value-added, with high income elasticity of demand, and gradually knowledge-intensive. In such sectors, MITI provided financial and other support and guidance. It regulated the degree of competition (neither too little, nor too fierce) by aiming at an "optimum" number of firms in each sector, and at the same time protected these sectors from foreign compe-tition. The approach of the "tigers" was similar, though some of them, especially Singapore, extended the art of "technology transfer" (practised by the Japanese) through an aggressive inward investment policy. The success of the Japanese economy and that of the "tigers" has been in part to its industrial policy (as well as to other characteristics of the Far Eastern economies, like education, equitable distribution of incomes, high saving ratios, etc). The Japanese focus on wealth creation, not just efficient allocation, may well be the *differentia specifica* of the Far Eastern approach. It has been associated with major inno-vations, such as total quality, "just-in-time", lifetime employ-ment, the coexistence of competition with cooperation ("coopetition"), and others.

There have been numerous developments in economics and management in recent years (the knowledge-based perspective, the new international trade theory, endogenous growth theory, new location economics, "new competition", etc.) that arguably offer support to the Japanese perspective and policies. Partly because of this, recent approaches to IP in the Western world have tended to move away from the neoclassical perspec-tive, to an approach and policies aiming at improving compet-itiveness at the firm and macro levels. There are various versions of this new approach. The "new industrial policy" approach, for example, retains its neoclassical flavour but emphasizes input, linkages, and technology policies as incen-tive-compatible means of improving firm and industry compet-itiveness. More general competitiveness models, such as Porter's, focus on the determinants of national competitiveness (factor and demand conditions, firm strategy and structure, related and supporting industries), and claim that the govern-ment can and should influence all of these (see PORTER 1990).

PITELIS (1998) moves away from industrial policy to com-petitiveness policy. The author proposes four major determi-nants of productivity and competitiveness (infrastructure, human resources, innovation, unit cost economies), all operat-ing within the macroeconomic and institutional context. He claims that government can influence all of these positively, and attributes an important role to firm clusters. Porter (1998) focuses on clusters, and claims them to be the new industrial policy, as they improve productivity and competitiveness. COWLING & SUGDEN suggests a role for industrial policy that guards against the overarching power of transnational corporations by establishing a "level playing field". Clusters are seen as crucial in this context. Recent focus by the European Union on education, (soft) infrastructure, technology and innovation, and (clusters of) small firms moves in the right direction. It still lacks any well developed or adhered to theoretical model linking firm competitiveness to national competitiveness. We have moved on from the narrow confines of the neoclassical perspective, but there is still scope for improvement.

CHRISTOS PITELIS

See also Competitiveness, Contracts and competition, Regulation and competition

Industrial relations

Braverman, Harry, A., *Labor and Monopoly Capital: The Degradation of Work in the Twentieth Century*, New York: Monthly Review Press, 1974

Clegg, Hugh Armstrong, *Trade Unionism under Collective Bargaining*, Oxford: Blackwell, 1976

Dunlop, John Thomas, *Industrial Relations Systems*, New York: Holt, 1958

Fox, Alan, *Beyond Contract: Work, Power and Trust Relations*, London: Faber, 1974

Kerr, Clark, J.T. Dunlop, F. Harbison and C.A. Myers, *Industrialism and Industrial Man: The Problems of Labor and Management in Economic Growth*, Cambridge, Massachusetts: Harvard University Press, 1960

Kochan, Thomas A., *Collective Bargaining and Industrial Relations*, Homewood, Illinois: Irwin, 1980

Perlman, Selig, *A Theory of the Labor Movement*, New York: Macmillan, 1928

Strauss, George, "Collective Bargaining" in *Handbook of Human Resource Management*, edited by Michael Poole and Malcolm Warner, London: International Thomson Business Press, 1998

Webb, Sidney and Beatrice Webb, *The History of Trade Unionism*, London: Longman, 1894; revised edition 1920

Webb, Sidney and Beatrice Webb, *Industrial Democracy*, 2 vols, London: Longman, 1897; revised edition 1920

BRAVERMAN, although not a teacher of industrial relations, had an important influence on the field. His work is associated with the study of "labour process", which Marx wrote about, and the "deskilling thesis", which this American neoMarxist author developed in the postwar years. He was mainly concerned with how work was routinized and how "the bosses" substituted unskilled labour for skilled labour to maximize management control in the later stages of "monopoly capitalism". Braverman's work has had a wide impact on radical writers in the industrial relations and sociology literature amongst others since the late 1970s.

CLEGG is a British author who was the doyen of the subject in his prime years. He wrote an authoritative history of British trade unionism and many other studies on collective bargaining, industrial democracy and incomes policy, among other subjects. His book on trade unionism under collective bargaining, for example – one of several important contributions

in his substantial publications list – is a model of clarity and comparative studies. As an author and scholar, he was not only concerned with theoretical analysis but also public policy: he was the drafter of the report of the Royal Commission that dealt with reform of industrial relations and trade unions in the late 1960s in Britain. As a pluralist, he was a rebel against both Christianity and Marxism. He did not believe, however, that by pursuing his own line of pragmatic reformism he was serving the interests of management or capital.

The role of DUNLOP in the study of industrial and labour relations cannot be underestimated. His book shaped the way most contemporary scholars in the field think about industrial relations systems. Following Talcott Parsons, he helped to establish industrial relations as a discipline in its own right through his work on dispute resolution as well as wage determination, among other topics. His work was pathbreaking and helped to create his reputation as one of the major industrial relations theorists of his time, as did his role as an advisor on public policy in the area in the US.

The work of FOX centres on the analysis of "unitary", "pluralist" and "radical" approaches to the field. He was a defender of "pluralism" against its Marxist critics. He emphasized "trust" as a critical factor in good industrial relations. Fox's work is often associated with the "Oxford School" as it was known, and his colleagues, Clegg and Flanders. Fox was an able social scientist and his work made a substantial impact on industrial sociology.

The theme of "convergence" was central to KERR's writings. Kerr and colleagues argued that industrial relations across the globe would eventually converge because of the exigencies of technology and industrialization. Their work became very influential not only in the US but also in Europe and further afield amongst scholars in this area of study, in the 1960s and 1970s. In spite of so-called "globalization", many crucial national differences still prevail, however, to a greater extent than they anticipated, even between economies at the same stage of development such as within the European Union.

KOCHAN is probably the most influential writer in the field of industrial and labour relations at the present time, not only in the US but also across the profession worldwide. He has taught at the Sloan School of Management at the Massachusetts Insititute of Technology for most of his career and has been responsible for the integration of industrial relations with human resource management. He aimed to achieve a more analytical approach to the study of the field. By emphasizing the role of "strategic choice", he has provided a useful interdisciplinary tool both for scholars and practitioners.

Perlman's books are now mostly cited in the historical analysis of the field but they remain most important analytically. He emphasized the "homegrown" ideology of American labour, attacking the Marxist approach. PERLMAN, published in 1928, has been seen as promoting business unionism against class conscious unionism. He thought workers should look after their immediate economic interests rather than pursue wider political goals.

STRAUSS has made an important contribution to the study of collective bargaining. He also contributed to the study of union government and leadership as well as worker participation. Strauss believed that participation was not possible if unions opposed it. Trade unions often saw the former as a threat. Representative participation and collective bargaining, he argued, have much in common. He similarly had a major impact on the evolution of personnel relations and human resource management concepts and practices through his textbooks.

WEBB & WEBB ("the Webbs", as they are collectively known in the literature) in many ways "invented" collective bargaining, industrial relations, and trade unions around the turn of the century in Britain (WEBB & WEBB 1897), although they were not the very first to write on these emerging institutions. They wrote the initial and "classic" history of unions (WEBB & WEBB 1894), as they had emerged in the industrial revolution and its aftermath. The Webbs conceptualized the "common rule" in their analysis of unions. They also wrote seminally on cooperatives. They believed that the final end of society was the citizen, as both consumer and producer. They were among the main founders of the British welfare state and were responsible for setting up the London School of Economics.

MALCOLM WARNER

See also Human resource management, Trade unions

Industrial revolution

Berg, Maxine, *The Age of Manufactures, 1700–1820: Industry, Innovation and Work in Britain*, 2nd edition, London and New York: Routledge, 1994

Crafts, N.F.R., *British Economic Growth during the Industrial Revolution*, Oxford: Clarendon Press, and New York: Oxford University Press, 1985

Feinstein, Charles H., "Pessimism Perpetuated: Real Wages and the Standard of Living in Britain during and after the Industrial Revolution", *Journal of Economic History*, 58/3 (1998): 625–58

Floud, Roderick and Donald McCloskey (editors), *The Economic History of Britain since 1700*, vol. 1: *1700–1860*, 2nd edition, Cambridge and New York: Cambridge University Press, 1994

Hudson, Pat, *The Industrial Revolution*, London: Arnold, 1992

Mokyr, Joel (editor), *The British Industrial Revolution: An Economic Perspective*, Boulder, Colorado: Westview Press, 1993

O'Brien, Patrick K. and Roland Quinault (editors), *The Industrial Revolution and British Society*, Cambridge and New York: Cambridge University Press, 1993

Polanyi, Karl, *The Great Transformation: The Political and Economic Origins of Our Time*, New York: Farrar and Rinehart, 1944

Teich, Mikuláš and Roy Porter (editors), *The Industrial Revolution in National Context: Europe and the USA*, Cambridge and New York: Cambridge University Press, 1996

The "Industrial Revolution" is generally understood to refer to the spurt of industrialization in the UK from the mid-18th to the mid-19th century. Modern macroeconomic treatments however tend to play down the notion of a "spurt", measured

in economic terms, while not denying the change in nature of industry and society. A key issue is the extent to which change spread across the country. The most enduring debate over the Industrial Revolution is the extent to which it brought about an improvement in workers' living standards – the so-called "standard of living debate". An underlying issue is whether the Industrial Revolution should be equated with the rise of modern industry or with the rise of capitalism.

The volume edited by MOKYR begins with a survey article by the editor running to about 130 pages, which is arguably the best such survey in recent times. The author covers both macro and micro, both technological and organizational perspectives on the Industrial Revolution. His view that technology and growth developed faster in the UK than elsewhere because of less worker resistance seems less plausible, but in most respects the essay displays careful judgement. This long essay is followed by two on macro growth by Landes (which includes a brief account of the terminology linked to the "Industrial Revolution") and by Harley, ostensibly opposing each other but in reality quite easy to reconcile; then two more specific but still survey like, on agriculture and on education.

The volume edited by FLOUD & McCLOSKEY is a substantially rewritten first volume of a three-volume economic history of Britain. It and its predecessor are widely regarded as the high tide of the "new economic history" – the application of formal economic and statistical techniques to economic history (sometimes playfully termed "cliometrics"). However both editions also give considerable emphasis to non-economic considerations. In the second edition especially, the contributions aim at accessibility to students with a wide range of expertise. Both editions contain (different) surveys by the second editor of the Industrial Revolution period itself, that have achieved a strong reputation for their felicity of style as well as their content. The second edition provides comprehensive and up-to-date surveys of the particular topics attended to in the specific chapters, which cover many fields. Some of the chapters in the first edition of 1981 remain worth reading as well.

The relatively short textbook by HUDSON gives potted summaries of many aspects of the Industrial Revolution that are often glossed over, and is pitched at the undergraduate market. However there is little study of industry itself. The author emphasizes regional diversity and social changes. In many places she argues for the slowness of change, but at other points contends that transformation was faster than implied by the macroeconomic viewpoint, including the effects transmitted to regions well away from the centres of industrial expansion.

The monograph by CRAFTS provides the evidence for his view that, on the basis of macroeconomic data, Britain experienced only slow growth during the classic period of the Industrial Revolution. Moreover, the growth in productivity was restricted to a small number of sectors, notably cotton textiles. An unusual aspect of Crafts' approach is that British achievements are put in an international context, highlighting the relative differences from other countries about to industrialize. The author queries, but does not reject, the possibility of greater change at the micro level.

The text by BERG takes a very different view from that of Crafts. Her focus is primarily on the micro level, and takes social and political as well as economic factors into account. One of the greatest strengths of her book is the attention paid to work practices, in looking at both different industries and different types of workplace environment. The more micro focus leads to a standpoint that sees more conflict and social problems in the industrialization effort than is handled from a macro position.

The reappraisal by FEINSTEIN provides the most up-to-date quantitative assessment of the course of real wages in British industrialization – the classic "standard of living debate", presenting the studied reflections of one of today's most senior economic historians. As his title suggests, the evidence comes down in favour of a very slow, almost imperceptible, rise during the orthodox Industrial Revolution period down to the 1950s. Feinstein makes corrections for such factors as unemployment, but does not venture into the more political domain of the impact of capitalism itself.

The collection edited by O'BRIEN & QUINAULT covers social, political, and organizational issues, and contributions are mostly written as survey pieces. The fields covered include some that lie well off the beaten track of social history, including Laqueur's very readable study of sex and desire. More traditional surveys of the period's economic history, by Hawke, and social history, by Stevenson, are also included.

While most studies focus on the UK, there are a number of comparative histories of industrial revolutions. The essays collected by TEICH & PORTER allow each of the authors a country to examine for industrialization, though disappointingly (in view of the subtitle) there is only one non-European chapter. The contributions come mainly from an older generation of historians and tend to the staid, though a brief summary chapter by the late Sidney Pollard updates with the more modern interpretations of Crafts and others. To a degree, this volume replaces the earlier and invaluable Fontana series of booklets on industrialization in particular European countries.

The remarkable work of POLANYI, though over half a century old, is arguably still the finest treatment of the emergence of markets under modern capitalism and liberalism. The subjects are analysed in thematic rather than chronological fashion. Polanyi's emphasis on carefully weighting the importance of market liberalization with the role of states and other agencies in forming markets has been taken up in modern times by the historical "neo-institutionalists", led by Nobel Laureate Douglass North, and while these studies have undoubtedly recovered the issue and advanced the debate, they have not supplanted it. A more historical and less analytical treatment of these issues is given in the works of Fernand Braudel.

G.N. VON TUNZELMANN

Inequality

Béteille, André, *The Idea of Natural Inequality and Other Essays*, Delhi: Oxford University Press, 1983

De Vos, George A. and Marcelo Suárez-Orozco, *Status Inequality: The Self in Culture*, Newbury Park, California and London: Sage, 1990

Frizzell, Alan and Jon H. Pammett, *Social Inequality in Canada*, Ottawa: Carleton University Press, 1996

Glyn, Andrew and David Miliband (editors), *Paying for Inequality: The Economic Cost of Social Injustice*, London: IPPR / Rivers Oram Press, and Concord, Massachusetts: Paul, 1994

Hagell, Ann and Catherine Shaw, *Opportunity and Disadvantage at Age 16*, London: Policy Studies Institute, 1996

Hamilton, Malcolm and Maria Hirszowicz, *Class and Inequality: Comparative Perspectives*, New York and London: Harvester Wheatsheaf, 1993

Laslett, Peter and James Fishkin (editors), *Philosophy, Politics and Society: Justice between Age Groups and Generations*, New Haven, Connecticut: Yale University Press, 1992

O'Leary, Jan and Rachel Sharp (editors), *Inequality in Australia: Slicing the Cake*, Port Melbourne: Heinemann, 1991

Robbins, David *et al.* (editors), *Rethinking Social Inequality*, Aldershot, Hampshire: Gower, 1982

Thompson, Leonard, *The Political Mythology of Apartheid*, New Haven, Connecticut: Yale University Press, 1985

The study of inequality has been a key undertaking within sociological inquiry, forming an essential mode of thinking about and addressing social issues.

BÉTEILLE's classic study of ideas about "natural" inequality begins with a review of Rousseau's celebrated discourse on inequality. Although his work is anchored in an analysis of the ranking traditions and hierarchic order of contemporary India, the author uses a comparative perspective to reflect upon Western systems of inequality that are generated by market and nation-state relations.

DE VOS & SUÁREZ-OROZCO have collaborated to produce a work that comprehensively examines the structure and experience of social inequality, blending sociological, anthropological, and psychoanalytic understandings of human behaviour. They argue that it is important to differentiate self and social attitudes from the structuring of social roles in sociology, in order to theorize the developmental experience of the self in greater detail. This text is informative for later-year students in a variety of social science disciplines.

Using a comparative dimension that incorporates Canadian attitudes and values into questions about identity, FRIZZELL & PAMMETT provide "ladders to understanding" Canadian identity for sociologists and policy makers. The seven contributors examine notions of social inequality through the various prisms of language, region, race, gender, and earnings to portray Canada as an advanced industrial pluralistic society with comprehensive class divisions, yet low class consciousness. The work is helpful for researchers engaging in international and comparative studies.

The relationship between equality and efficiency in Britain is examined by the contributors to GLYN & MILIBAND's edited collection. They argue against inequality as a necessity to spur prosperity, documenting the inefficiency of maintaining inequality amongst human capital rather than skilling people as an economic resource, the inequalities in access to training with resultant economic inefficiencies, and the rise in criminality that can be allied with minimal investment in people. They deconstruct the notion of the "labour market", and examine the difficulties of unemployment to undermine efficiency arguments and to promote the benefits of egalitarian policies.

HAGELL & SHAW survey over 3,000 inner-city 16 year olds from 34 schools within six urban areas of England in order to illuminate the social inequalities facing young people from disadvantaged groups – in particular those from the inner cities, ethnic minorities, and with low examination results. They propose that viable alternatives to education and training as "holding" devices must be sought, and that financial support be considered to ease the burden of limited opportunity for income generation. The work is significant in tracking how social inequality can mark lives at an early age.

Thematically linking with Hagell and Shaw's work, HAMIL-TON & HIRSZOWICZ show that education is not merely a means of establishing membership in a society's dominant status group, but is also crucial for the acquisition of qualifications that are required to secure positions in business and legal elites. The work uses a sound theoretical basis to examine the rise of the middle and working classes, the potential for social mobility, and increasing inequalities in postcommunist societies. Its comparative perspective and extraordinary social range demand that this text reach as many undergraduates as possible through a broad sweep of courses.

In LASLETT & FISHKIN's edited collection of 10 essays, contributors considered the substantive effects of policies across generations and the conceptual framework that would be required to rethink the social contract to take into consideration changing population size and moral values. They focus on issues that pertain to common principles across generational boundaries, variations in population and birth cohort size, and problems of personal identity. Through lively debates this group of political philosophers generate theories about justice, property rights, liberty, equality, and utility, and consider the potential for social and political justice over time.

A work to be read more for its historical and comparative social perspectives, O'LEARY & SHARP's collection examines a range of policy areas focusing on inequality in the 1980s in Australia, and the possibilities for the future. Many chapters examine the role of the Accord; an agreement between government, trade unions, and employers about the equality of sacrifice required to produce the necessary economic and social restructuring that was claimed to produce benefits for all and special attention to the needs of the low-paid. The authors offer insights into the ways that inequalities can exist and intensify.

ROBBINS et al. review the British tradition of studies about social inequality, targeting the political contexts of class conflict and compromise in which the tradition emerged. They argue that conceptualizing inequality in distributional terms masks the experience of inequality as relational, "the deprivation and powerlessness of one group following as the necessary consequence of the endowment and power of another". Hence, the thematic unity of the papers is an exploration of unequal social relations and their manifestations in a variety of forms, through the intersection of class with race, gender, and age.

THOMPSON's deeply political work elucidates how the South African white minority has exploited history for political ends. The author uses this specific case to exemplify how powerful people at all historical moments use historical images as tools within relations of power. His detailed exploration of

a particular nation state's mythologies, the dynamic nature of mythology, and the ruling class' use of "race" as a marker of uncivilized inferiority stimulate thinking about how inequalities are constructed and perpetuated for the benefit of self-constituted authorities. The work is a lucid exposition that can be used in late secondary and early tertiary courses.

HELEN JOHNSON

Infantile sexuality

Abraham, Karl, *On Character and Libido Development*, New York: Norton, 1966

Freud, Anna, *Normality and Pathology in Childhood: Assessments of Development*, New York: International Universities Press, 1965; London: Hogarth Press, 1966

Freud, Sigmund, "Three Essays on the Theory of Sexuality" (published in German 1905) in *A Case of Hysteria, Three Essays on Sexuality, and Other Works*, London: Hogarth Press, 1953 (*The Standard Edition of the Complete Psychological Works*, vol. 7)

Freud, Sigmund, "Analysis of a Phobia in a Five Year Old Boy" (published in German 1909) in *Two Case Histories: "Little Hans" and the "Rat Man"*, London: Hogarth Press, 1955 (*The Standard Edition of the Complete Psychological Works*, vol. 10)

Holt, Robert R., *Freud Reappraised: A Fresh Look at Psychoanalytic Theory*, New York: Guilford Press, 1989

Horney, Karen, "Feminine Psychology" in *An Outline of Psychoanalysis*, edited by Clara Thompson, Milton Mazer and Earl Witenberg, revised edition, New York: Modern Library, 1955

Klein, George S., *Psychoanalytic Theory: An Exploration of Essentials*, New York: International Universities Press, 1976

Watson, James B. and Rosemary Raynor, "Conditioned Emotional Reactions", *Journal of Experimental Psychology*, 3/1 (1924): 1–14

This topic is among the most controversial in psychology and the social sciences. Accepted as a truism by most psychoanalysts, and by many in the arts and in literature, the concept of child sexuality has not been accepted by the large majority of academics. Freud, who wrote the seminal works, and whose thinking remains most important, continues to dominate the literature on infantile sexuality.

FREUD (1905) introduced the psychoanalytic concept of infantile sexuality, and remains the most influential work on this topic. His discovery that children are active sexual beings was introduced in this work, and was met with extraordinary acrimony by many critics. There continues to be much contentious debate about the validity and existence of infantile sexuality, both within the domain of psychoanalysis and in the broader range of the social sciences. This volume is the source of concepts that have influenced and outraged scholars and laypersons for over 90 years. These notions include the finding that the sexual instinct arises and is experienced in children between the ages of two and five. This instinct moves through an invariant developmental sequence of erotogenic zones, each of which was defined by the organ of instinctual arousal, and by the aim or activity through which excitation was discharged. Herein we find the initial discussion of the oral, sadistic-anal and genital stages of childhood sexuality, and of the Oedipus complex, which, in Freudian theory, is the most important event in psychological life. The universal psychosexual drama of childhood is identified for the first time as that in which each child must put aside her or his incestuous longing for the opposite-sexed parent, and murderous rivalry for the parent of the same sex, in order to become an acceptable member of society.

Also originating in this work is the key psychoanalytic notion that adult sexual perversions and neuroses result from infantile sexual desires that had been inadequately repressed and upon which the person remained unconsciously preoccupied, or "fixated". The clinical path of Freudian psychoanalysis was laid out with this formulation: it became an enterprise in which the unconscious childhood sexual roots of psychopathology are sought out and made accessible to the patient's awareness.

The most famous clinical demonstration of Freud's theory of infantile sexuality with a psychologically troubled child (rather than through psychoanalytic reconstruction of childhood in the analyses of adults) introduced the world to "Little Hans" (FREUD 1909), who suffered from a severe phobia of being bitten by horses. This child underwent psychoanalytic treatment that was conducted by Hans' father under Freud's supervision. This case study indicated that this fear of being bitten was a disguised expression of the child's sexual desire for his mother, his hostile rivalry with his father for his mother's affection, and his fear of retaliation in the form of castration by his father. Freud's discussion of this case described the unconscious mechanisms of displacement and projection through which these sexual dynamics were transformed into the conscious content of the phobia.

Freud's conclusion that such phobias were explainable in this way was severely, and to many successfully, challenged, by WATSON & RAYNOR, in their study of Hans' American counterpart, Little Albert, in whom they created a phobia of fluffy animals through the application of principles of Pavlovian conditioning. This critique took root in the highly behavioural academic psychology of the 1920s, causing an almost complete exclusion of psychoanalytic thinking from university departments of psychology.

Freud's prevailing philosophy that "anatomy is destiny" in psychological life was elucidated most vividly in his discussion of the impact of children's discovery of the anatomical differences between girls and boys on subsequent mental development. The thesis herein was that girls perceive their genitals as lacking in comparison to a penis, and consider themselves as having been maimed. Girls and women thus are left with an enduring sense of inferiority, shame, humiliation, and resentful envy towards males. The discovery by the boy that some children do not possess a penis is the origin of lifelong castration anxiety, but without the permanent damage to self esteem suffered by females. These critical differences in emotional experience and perception of the self are further explored with regard to their mature ramifications in the spheres of identity, morality, interpersonal relationships, and psychopathology.

Among the many and horrified rebuttals of Freud's view of feminine psychology one of the most significant came from within the psychoanalytic community. HORNEY argued convincingly that the inferiority and envy experienced by many women were appropriate responses to the sociocultural conditions in which they lived, and were not reflections of childhood disappointments in their genitals. The psychodynamics that Freud misinterpreted from his anatomically deterministic (and, some said, misogynistic) position might better be understood as reflecting a real imbalance of power between the sexes.

ABRAHAM contributed the foundation of the psychoanalytic study of the role of infantile sexuality in the formation of the adult personality. He found that traits such as sarcasm, passivity, sadism, envy, parsimony, and submissiveness were derived from unconscious sexual desires that were repressed during the oral and the sadistic-anal stages. Abraham was concerned with tracing the ways in which character traits symbolically reflected conflict over renouncing oral and anal pleasures and the consequent progression to the genital stage. This collection offers an in-depth introduction to the specific interrelationships among the anxieties, sexual wishes, and defence mechanisms that coalesce to produce adult character structure.

Critics of the psychoanalytic literature have correctly pointed out that most discussions of infantile sexuality fail to place these experiences within the broader context of developmental and social psychology. Anna FREUD (1965) answered these critics by exploring the interactions of children's sexual development with an extensive number of other psychological, social, and biological variables such as cognition, perception, intelligence, motor development, and evolving relationships with parents, adult authorities, and peers. This book described the ways in which idiosyncratic progression by a child in any of these non-sexual "developmental lines" could mould, and at the same time, be moulded by, that child's predominant sexual concerns, conflicts, and points of fixation.

KLEIN wrote a contemporary critique of the psychoanalytic view of infantile sexuality that reflected his training in both academic, experimental psychology, and in Freudian psychoanalysis. He divided the theory of infantile sexuality into two theories. The speculative, "meta-psychological" theory that describes quasi-physiological sexual instincts is unsubstantiated and does not inform clinical practice. The more important but neglected clinical theory is close to the data of clinical psychoanalysis and describes the experience and meaning of sensuality in childhood. Clinical theory separates infantile sensual experience from overt behaviour, although childhood sensual experiences are compellingly craved, existing in memory as the developmental organizing factors of adult sensual wishes and behaviours. Sexual development is a complex, conflicted progression during which sensuality is imbued with meaning and moves towards integration with sexual behaviour and relationships. The child learns which sensual pleasures and persons he or she is permitted to crave or forbidden to seek. The specific meanings of sexuality are the outcome of the interaction of the child's psychology, familial values, and societal norms.

HOLT, who was a colleague of Klein, and who also straddled the worlds of academic psychology and psychoanalysis, offered a research-based critique of many central psychoanalytic tenets, including infantile sexuality, and found these constructs lacking in empirical support. This critique was especially provocative and powerful because, as Holt himself noted ruefully, he had been an arch defender of traditional psychoanalytic theory, but had come to the position that the future of psychoanalysis depended on jettisoning its canon if that body of knowledge was unsupported by current data.

He challenged the notion of a preformed, biologically determined sexual instinct, noting that most recent studies have found sexual desire and behaviour to be highly context dependent. He concluded that the child's experiences of sensual pleasure in bodily functions are the repressed precursors of adult sexual experiences.

JEROLD R. GOLD

See also Oedipus complex

Inferential statistics

American Psychologist, 53/7 (1998): 796–803

Deshpande, J.V., A.P. Gore and E.A. Shanubhogue, *Statistical Analysis of Nonnormal Data*, New York: Wiley, 1995

Feingold, Alan, "The Additive Effects of Differences in Central Tendency and Variability Are Important in Comparisons between Groups", *American Psychologist*, 50/1 (1995): 5–13

Hagen, Richard L., "In Praise of the Null Hypothesis Statistical Test", *American Psychologist*, 52/1 (1997): 15–25

Iversen, Gudmund R. and Helmut Norpoth, *Analysis of Variance*, 2nd edition, Newbury Park, California and London: Sage, 1987

Rosnow, Ralph L. and Robert Rosenthal, "Statistical Procedures and the Justification of Knowledge in Psychological Science", *American Psychologist*, 44/10 (1989): 1276–84

Siegel, Sidney and John Castellan Jr, *Nonparametric Statistics for the Behavioral Sciences*, 2nd edition, New York and London: McGraw Hill, 1988

Wilcox, Rand R., "How Many Discoveries Have Been Lost by Ignoring Modern Statistics?", *American Psychologist*, 53/3 (1998): 300–14

Winer, B.J., Donald R. Brown and Kenneth M. Michels, *Statistical Principles in Experimental Design*, 3rd edition, New York and London: McGraw Hill, 1991

The most common inferential statistic used by psychologists is the analysis of variance (ANOVA). IVERSEN & NORPOTH provide a useful introduction to the topic. They explain the basic concepts associated with this approach and link it to regression analysis, both of which are subsumed under a broader category called the general linear model. This small volume is relatively nontechnical, requiring only an understanding of basic algebra. The authors do a good job in introducing this statistical approach, but the applications of the ANOVA are complex and multifaceted; readers who need information about the controversies and subtleties of the ANOVA should consult any of the widely used sources of information, such as the updated classic by WINER, BROWN & MICHELS

Soon after Ronald Fisher developed and popularized null hypothesis statistical test (NHST) in general and ANOVA in particular in the 1920s, criticisms arose; they have increased recently. HAGEN reviews some of the criticisms of this approach to inferential statistics over the past several decades and attempts to counter the arguments against the use of NHST. Hagen discusses the relationships among NHST, the likelihood that a null hypothesis is true, and subjective levels of confidence in one's research findings. He also defends the use of NHST on logical grounds, which have come under attack. Hagen's commentary drew responses published in the AMERICAN PSYCHOLOGIST from a number of others who provide additional useful perspective regarding this controversy.

Despite the growing concerns about the typical use of inferential statistics in behavioural research, the approaches to hypothesis testing with inferential statistics seem resistant to change. Standard statistical and methodological textbooks vary minimally in their presentations of techniques for data analysis. At the same time, researchers continue to refine the use of statistical tests. For example, WILCOX identifies the most common inferential statistics like analysis of variance, Student's t-test, and regression methods and discusses some of their limitations. He comments that apparently minor departures from normality result in low power during data analysis. That is, there is a lower likelihood of spotting true relationships among variables. He provides examples that reflect the problems associated with the presence of outliers, unequal variances among groups, and skewed distributions. As Wilcox points out, problems with hypothesis testing using the standard inferential statistics can be overcome with appropriate use of modern statistical techniques. Unfortunately, as is usually the case with complex probabilistic analyses, one cannot identify a single, universal, statistical approach that ameliorates the situation.

FEINGOLD further extends the discussion of refinements to the use of inferential statistics. In analysis of research results, it is sometimes helpful to examine the differences between groups in the tails of distributions. He points out that the traditional approach of identifying mean differences can produce misleading results when variances across groups are heterogeneous. He illustrates this effect by examining gender differences on the Differential Aptitude Tests (DAT). Feingold reports that sex differences in variability were the norm on the DAT in this study as well in some of his previous work. He suggests that researchers test for differences both for measures of central tendency and for variability.

Although most behavioural researchers prefer to use parametric statistics like the analysis of variance, Student's t-test, and Pearson product-moment correlation, these tests may not be appropriate for data that are not normally distributed. As such, SIEGEL & CASTELLAN provide a compendium of distribution-free inferential statistics. This second edition of Siegel's classic work provides an overview of statistical use in research and guidelines for the appropriate selection of tests. One of the helpful concepts the authors discuss involves how well the nonparametric statistics compare to their parametric counterparts, a concept known as power efficiency. Siegal & Castellan also provide a useful discussion of the different scales of measurement, a relevant concept for nonparametric measurements.

DESHPANDE, GORE & SHANUBHOGUE have also contributed to the discussion of appropriate statistical tests when research data are not normally distributed, a prerequisite for the standard parametric techniques. This book overlaps, to a degree, with Siegel & Castellan's work, but it includes useful statistical tests that are probably unfamiliar to most psychologists.

Even if one accepts the legitimacy of testing the null hypothesis in behavioural research, ROSNOW & ROSENTHAL caution that researchers should use inferential statistics with knowledge of their limitations. The authors comment that the use of a dichotomy in deciding whether a research finding is significant is fraught with difficulty, especially because many behavioural studies involve low power. As such, failing to attend to a nearly significant result may cause one to ignore a potentially interesting finding. Further, they note that the use of effect sizes to replace significance levels may obscure important and useful phenomena. Finally, Rosnow & Rosenthal note the limitations of the traditional analysis of variance and illustrate the use of contrast analysis as an alternative approach. This accessible article is fairly nontechnical and presents a useful depiction of some philosophical elements of using inferential statistics.

BERNARD C. BEINS

See also Meta-analysis, Significance

Infertility

Abbey, Antonia, Frank M. Andrews and L. Jill Halman, "Gender's Role in Responses to Infertility", *Psychology of Women Quarterly*, 15/4 (1991): 295–316

Berg, Barbara J. and John F. Wilson, "Psychiatric Morbidity in the Infertile Population: A Reconceptualization", *Fertility and Sterility*, 53/4 (1990): 654–61

Connolly, Kevin J., Robert J. Edelmann, Ian D. Cooke and Jill Robson, "The Impact of Infertility on Psychological Functioning", *Journal of Psychosomatic Research*, 36/5 (1992): 459–68

Edelmann, Robert J. and Kevin J. Connolly, "Psychological Aspects of Infertility", *British Journal of Medical Psychology*, 59/4 (1986): 209–19

Greil, Arthur A., "Infertility and Psychological Distress: A Critical Review of the Literature", *Social Science and Medicine*, 45/11 (1997): 1679–1704

Kedem, Peri, Mario Mikulincer, Yvonne E. Nathansson and Benjamin Bartov, "Psychological Aspects of Male Infertility", *British Journal of Medical Psychology*, 63/2 (1990): 73–80

Leiblum, Sandra R. (editor), *Infertility: Psychological Issues and Counseling Strategies*, New York: Wiley, 1997

McEwan, K.L., C.G. Costello and P.J. Taylor, "Adjustment to Infertility", *Journal of Abnormal Psychology*, 96/2 (1987): 108–16

Stanton, Annette L. and Christine Dunkel-Schetter (editors), *Infertility: Perspectives from Stress and Coping Research*, New York: Plenum Press, 1991

Stanton, Annette L., Howard Tennen, Glenn Affleck and Richard Mendola, "Coping and Adjustment to Infertility", *Journal of Social and Clinical Psychology*, 11/1 (1992): 1–13

The 13 chapters in LEIBLUM provide an excellent up-to-date review of the psychological stresses and strains imposed by infertility. Chapters review immediate and long-term reactions to infertility, focusing both upon the individual and the couple. Differential gender effects are also examined. This book provides a good overview but there is a tendency for chapters to focus on the stress of infertility on women to the neglect of psychological distress caused by male infertility.

Although the review by EDELMANN & CONNOLLY was written over a decade ago, it served as a watershed between "old" and "new" research themes in the area. Much early psychological research in relation to infertility focused primarily upon seeking to determine whether psychological factors were a primary cause of infertility. Research in the past decade has focused upon the stresses and strains imposed by infertility and associated medical investigations and their implications for counselling. It has been grounded rather more clearly within key psychological theories.

GREIL's review presents an up-to-date analysis of the literature examining the psychological impact of infertility. The review pays particular attention to gender differences in the social and emotional consequences of infertility. Although the methodological rigour of research studies evaluating psychological aspects of infertility has improved considerably in the past decade, much of research undertaken is of questionable value. This no doubt explains many of the equivocal results reported in the literature. This review pays particular attention not only to methodological flaws in much research undertaken but also to theoretical shortcomings of the literature.

The article by ABBEY, ANDREWS & HALMAN presents both a brief review of the literature relating to differences in women's and men's responses to infertility and an empirical evaluation of such differences derived from a sample of 185 couples. Unlike much research in this area the study benefited from the inclusion of a fertile comparison group. Both the review and the study itself suggest that infertile women, when compared with their male partners, perceive their infertility problem as more stressful and feel more responsible for it whereas infertile men experience more general home life stress than their partners. However, many of the gender differences found in the study were not unique to infertility problems; instead they reflect more general gender differences in response to stress, hence placing gender differences in infertility within a broader context.

Evidence suggests that men consistently demonstrate less disturbance than women on various indices of emotional functioning, but whether this is due to a general tendency for men to under report emotional responses is less clear. However, the few studies that have examined the effect of a gender-specific diagnosis indicate that a fertility problem that lies solely with the male inflicts a particular psychosocial burden. The paper by KEDEM *et al.* was one of the first studies to systematically compare infertile and fertile males on a range of psychological variables. Infertile men were found to have lower self-esteem, higher anxiety and showed more somatic symptoms than fertile men. This finding that male infertility provokes particular distress has subsequently been replicated in more recent research.

BERG & WILSON draw an important distinction between psychiatric morbidity and infertility strain; the latter representing "normative or commonly occurring distress experienced by patients in medical settings". Numerous clinical and anecdotal reports suggest that infertility is a major life stress resulting in anxiety, depression, and loss of self-esteem. In seeming contrast to this almost wholly negative view, research studies present a rather different picture. Many such studies report few, if any, differences between infertile individuals and fertile controls on measures of psychopathology. Berg & Wilson argue that examining patterns of psychological strain reactions in relation to infertility may be more useful than merely applying conventional measures of psychopathology.

The paper by CONNOLLY et al. was one of the first longitudinal studies published examining the impact of infertility on psychological functioning. One hundred and sixteen couples were assessed at their initial visit to an infertility clinic and on a second occasion some seven to nine months later. There was little evidence for psychopathology in the sample and, interestingly, scores on measures of anxiety and psychiatric morbidity declined between the first and second assessment except in the case of men who were diagnosed with a fertility problem. The study highlighted the possibility that male infertility may be associated with particular psychological difficulties.

The paper by McEWAN, COSTELLO & TAYLOR. was the first to evaluate the relative risk of emotional problems of infertile men and women. Demographic, medical, and cognitive variables in addition to life events and social support were examined as potential mediators of reactions to infertility. The findings indicated that younger women and women who had not received a diagnosis were more distressed than patients who had received a diagnosis, and women who felt responsible for their infertility showed poorer adjustment. Although a handful of similar studies have since been undertaken, predicting who is likely to be distressed by their failure to conceive is an important theoretical and practical issue.

The ten chapters in the book edited by STANTON & DUNKEL-SCHETTER focus specifically upon the application of theoretical suppositions in the field of stress and coping to investigation of the infertility process. Chapters evaluate the role of causal explanations, coping processes, social relationships, childbearing motives, and perceptions of control in relation to adjustment to infertility. Much of the research investigating psychological aspects of infertility that predated this volume was atheoretical in nature. In grounding research on infertility within a broader stress and coping framework this volume thus changed the research agenda.

The paper by STANTON et al. is one of a number over the last decade that have investigated coping in relation to infertility. The large sample, use of standard measures, and gender comparison makes this one of the better such pieces of research. The general finding from this research, in line with the general literature on coping with threatening events, is that escape-avoidance methods are associated with more distress for men and women and mobilizing support associated with less distress.

ROBERT J. EDELMANN

Inflation

Dawson, Graham, *Inflation and Unemployment: Causes, Consequences and Cures*, Aldershot, Hampshire: Elgar, 1992

Desai, Meghnad, *Testing Monetarism*, London: Pinter, and New York: St Martin's Press, 1981

Fine, Ben, "World Economic Crisis and Inflation" in *Economic Theory and Ideology*, London: Arnold, 1980; New York: Holmes and Meier, 1981

Foley, Patrick (editor), *Why Inflation?*, London: Pinter, 1992

Friedman, Milton and Anna J Schwartz, *Monetary Trends in the United States and the United Kingdom: Their Relation to Income, Prices, and Interest Rates, 1867–1975*, Chicago: University of Chicago Press, 1982

IEA, *Inflation: Causes, Consequences, Cures: Discourses on the Debate between the Monetary and Trade Unions Interpretations*, London: Institute of Economic Affairs, 1974

Jackson, Dudley, H.A. Turner and Frank Wilkinson, *Do Trade Unions Cause Inflation? Two Studies: With a Theoretical Introduction and Policy Conclusion*, 2nd edition, London and New York: Cambridge University Press, 1975

Jones, Aubrey, *The New Inflation: The Politics of Prices and Incomes*, Harmondsworth and Baltimore: Penguin, 1973

Parkin, Michael and Michael T. Sumner (editors), *Incomes Policy and Inflation*, Manchester: Manchester University Press, and Toronto: University of Toronto Press, 1973

The literature on inflation reflects the period when this was seen as *the* major economic issue, problem, and policy challenge, namely the 1970s. This period saw the end of the long postwar boom and a rise in inflation levels, as commodity prices rose and governments attempted to keep down rising unemployment. Thus all the above references are from the 1970s or early 1980s (plus two from 1992). Milton Friedman had of course been propounding his monetarist theories of inflation (and other economic phenomena, such as the Great Depression – see separate entry) for years before the rise in inflation levels began in the late 1960s. FRIEDMAN & SCHWARTZ was published at a fortuitous time for the policy debates around inflation, with the first Thatcher Government having been elected in 1979 with a pledge to eliminate inflation once and for all. This was to be done by simply cutting the growth in the money supply, which would – it was argued – feed through to a concomitant fall in the rate of price inflation. The Friedman & Schwartz book claimed to provide weighty academic rigour to such a policy agenda, being presented as it was as the culmination of more than 25 years of research by the authors on money and its effects. It claimed to be the first study that provided statistical and theoretical analysis of such a long period of time, and so allowed the authors to purge the data of cyclical fluctuations and examine long-term trends. It also claimed to be the first to provide a cross-country comparison. The authors argue that a single demand function for money is applicable to the whole century the book covers, in both the US and UK. Their findings are in favour of the (monetarist) quantity theory approach to inflation, with prices being driven by growth of the money supply.

This monetarist theory of inflation is discussed and rigorously tested by DESAI. The book considers monetarism from the Quantity Theory of Money through to its current academic form. Desai looks at the major predictions from the theory and in each case examines the claims made in the literature. The book includes a consideration of how one can decide whether a theory has been validated by the data or not, and what the criteria for choosing between rival formulations should be. Desai then applies these criteria for each of the monetarist claims, bringing the econometric evidence to bear, including original econometric work by Desai himself. He concludes that the empirical support for monetarism is much weaker than is claimed, and that these claims are in fact invalid. Much of the work in this book is at a fairly technical level, but it is an extremely rigorous discussion of the theory, evidence, and policy implications.

The Institute of Economic Affairs (IEA) is a free-market think tank in the UK, and their study presents a debate between the "monetary and trade union interpretations" of inflation – i.e. whether "excessive" monetary growth is to blame or "excessive" wages. The main contributors are Lord Robbins, A.W. Coats, David Laidler, Milton Friedman, Samuel Brittan, F.A. Hayek, and Peter Jay (who famously wrote the monetarist speech for the then Labour Party Prime Minister – who happened to be his father-in-law – in 1976).

The theory and practice of Governments controlling inflation through the use of prices and incomes policies is discussed by JONES, and by the various contributors to PARKIN & SUMNER. Both books reflect the policy concerns of the day, with Jones' book being published in 1973 to analyse what was then seen as a new inflationary problem. Jones headed the UK's National Board for Prices and Incomes from 1965 until its dissolution in 1970. He argues explicitly that inflation is a social and political issue rather than an economic or monetary one, and that the answer to the problem does need to be through a prices and incomes policy. Parkin & Sumner sets itself the question of whether such prices and incomes policies actually do affect the rate of inflation. The broad answer which emerges from the studies presented in this book is that, on the average, prices and incomes policies do *not* seem to be a useful means of reducing the inflation rate: they may delay inflation but are powerless to prevent it.

A rather more sophisticated analysis of the problem than most of the above work is presented by JACKSON, TURNER & WILKINSON. They argue that "Economists . . . have largely ignored the importance of social conflict and adjustment in economic processes, but to the mechanics of inflation these things appear vital". The empirical work reported in the book was based on a worldwide analysis of post-World War II price and wage movements, and of "strato-inflation" as an observable and continuous condition. This condition is intermediate between moderate inflation (experienced by most capitalist economies during the 1950s and 1960s), and the hyperinflation which, in the few cases it has occurred, has always led to political and economic upheaval. The authors argue that the forces keeping the industrial countries on a moderately inflationary path were weakening at the time of writing, and their analysis of the process – economic, social, and political – of "strato-inflation" soon became clearly relevant to the state of Britain and many other countries at that time. The book also concludes that governments themselves had materially contributed to accelerating inflation by greatly increasing taxation on wage-earners at a critical time, and thus directly stimulating intensified wage-pressures.

A Marxist approach to the causes of inflation is developed by FINE. He points out, among other things, that the monetarist idea that an increase in the money supply will lead to an increase in prices completely ignores the key intermediaries between increased industrial credit on the one hand (which will boost broad measures of money) and increased levels of output on the other. Without knowing the relative size of these two magnitudes there is no way of knowing whether we have "too much money chasing too few goods" or whether, on the contrary, the increase in credit (and money) has actually led to a relatively greater amount of goods. How great an increase in output will actually follow from any boost to credit will depend on what happens at the point of production, and this in turn is influenced by the outcome of class struggles at the point of production.

DAWSON discusses inflation in the context of unemployment and government policies that aim to target both variables, possibly trading one off against the other. He argues that the economic and social costs of unemployment are far greater than even double-digit inflation, not to mention single-digit inflation. For Dawson, there is something very wrong with the economic policies generally being pursued by governments, for they seem to put much more emphasis on achieving low inflation than reducing unemployment.

FOLEY is a collection of articles on inflation, from Douglas McWilliams and Andrew Sentence; Bill Robinson and Tom Skinner; N.D. Kondratieff; Nicholas Kaldor and James Trevithick; James Meade; Wilfred Beckerman; Christopher Dow; Robin Marris; and S. Hall, S.G.B. Henry, A. Markandya, and M. Penderton. The collection is presented as finding that inflation persistence is linked to rigidities in labour and product markets, and that if labour and product markets were fully competitive, inflation reduction could be achieved with minimal cost in terms of lost output or unemployment. This begs rather a lot of questions, though, including whether this "fully competitive" outcome can ever be reached outside of a textbook, and also how such an economy would actually operate (given that many of the other textbook assumptions are also unrealistic, so it cannot be assumed that the textbook "fully competitive" model would actually behave as it is modelled).

JONATHAN MICHIE

See also Great Depression, Economic crises

Informal and feminist organizations

Clemens, Elisabeth S., "Organizational Repertoires and Institutional Change: Women's Groups and the Transformation of U.S. Politics, 1890–1920", *American Journal of Sociology*, 98/4 (1993): 755–98

Ferree, Myra Marx and Patricia Yancey Martin (editors), *Feminist Organizations: Harvest of the New Women's Movement*, Philadelphia: Temple University Press, 1995

Martin, Patricia Y., "Rethinking Feminist Organizations",
Gender and Society, 4/2 (1990): 182–206

Rothschild-Whitt, Joyce, "The Collectivist Organization:
An Alternative to Rational-Bureaucratic Models",
American Sociological Review, 44 (August 1979): 509–27

Staggenborg, Suzanne, "The Consequences of
Professionalization and Formalization in the Pro-Choice
Movement", *American Sociological Review*, 53 (August
1988): 585–606

CLEMENS provides a basis for examining what shapes organizational structures. Stating that structure may be associated with type of action, Clemens explains that "Models of organization comprise both templates for arranging relationships within an organization and sets of scripts for action culturally associated with that type of organization". Models can refer to "organizations of that type" or to "organizations that do that type of thing". Mention of either an attribute or an action may invoke a shared model or form of organizing. The set of organizational models that are culturally or experientially available may be thought of as an "organizational repertoire". Organizations, then, can serve as "living" repertoires that can be drawn upon, possibly in the cultural context. Consequently, the effects of organization may vary with the social identity of those who are organized. Structures of organizations have often been affected or transformed based on the source of funding. Analyses of funding stress the danger posed by a reliance on outside funding or patronage, while noting the limitations of resources within various communities marginalized by political institutions. Clemens argues that the form of organization mediates the impact of these resource constraints. This is extremely important for organizations that do not have a specific source of funding, or rely on the state for resources. Thus, organization has consequences beyond the process of mobilization itself. As a group organizes in a particular way, it signals its identity both to its own members and to others. Models of organization are part of the cultural tool kit of any society and serve expressive or communicative as well as instrumental functions. In addition, the adoption of a particular organizational form influences the ties that an organized group forms with other organizations. The chosen model of collective action shapes alliances with other groups and relations with political institutions. Thus, the informal structure may be associated with particular types of organizations – women's organizations or feminist organizations.

Arguing that theories of organization have focused mainly on large corporations, state bureaucracies, and labour unions that presume men to be the primary members and that relegate women and women's experiences to the periphery, FERREE & MARTIN feel that feminist groups have largely been ignored by organization scholars. Most sociologists of organizations are unlikely to perceive small, grassroots, social movement organizations founded by feminists as interesting or important. If the dominant models and norms that guide organizational theory, research, and publication view such low-budget, huge-commitment, women-run organizations as uninteresting, women scholars (who have low status within the discipline, the academy, and the subspecialty of organizational research) may be reluctant or unable to challenge them. Ferree & Martin argue that, to change this situation, a critical mass of feminist scholars in many disciplines must cooperatively develop new theory and discourse about feminist organizations. Such theory should have practical value for feminist activists who work in organizations to produce social transformations that benefit women. Feminist organizations are defined as the places in which, and the means through which, the work of the women's movement is done. This volume concerns feminist organizations in the US, with some references to Canada and Australia that serve as examples for comparing organizing across societies. Ferree & Martin have collected 25 essays that vividly document the organizational creativity of the women's movement of the past three decades. The movement's capacity for organizational innovation persisted not only despite but often because of the discomfort of many feminists with formal organization structures.

MARTIN sets an agenda within sociology for research on feminist organizations that focuses on their concrete forms and practices and on the dilemmas and effects that their participants experience. Several popular claims are questioned, including the assumption that bureaucracy is inherently antithetical to feminism, and its corollary, that institutionalized feminist organizations cannot be agents of change. Martin calls for a more open-ended approach to the study of feminist organizations and a focus on what they do, how they work, and their transformative impact on members, other women, and all of society. She explains that an organization is feminist if it meets any one of the following criteria: (a) has feminist ideology, (b) has feminist guiding values, (c) has feminist goals, (d) produces feminist outcomes, and (e) was founded during the women's movement as part of the women's movement. Martin lays out 10 dimensions that characterize a feminist organization. An informal organization may be a feminist organization.

ROTHSCHILD-WHITT argues that, under specific conditions, social movement organizations "militate" against the all "too common transformational patterns". Movement organizations can preserve their decentralized communal structures by adopting restrictions on size, using mutual criticism to restrain core activists, remaining economically marginal, relying strictly on internal financing, and attempting to reduce knowledge differentials among participants. Although there is a "process" involved in organizing, the structure that emerges may be typical or atypical. Social movement organizations are of diverse types and may be bureaucratic or collectivist, or some combination of these types. In contrasting collectivist democracy and rational bureaucracy along eight continuous dimensions, Rothschild-Whitt emphasizes the differences between the two extreme kinds – the collectivist organization and the rational-bureaucratic model. The term "collectivist" refers to a specific type of decision-making structure that is distinguished from "bureaucratic" organizations; not all informal social movement organizations are collectivist.

STAGGENBORG examines organizations in the pro-choice (abortion rights) movement and explores the consequences of professional leadership and formal structure in social movements using the resource-mobilization perspective as the basic framework. Although not directly addressing issues related to feminist organizations, Staggenborg provides an alternative characterization of structural differences in social movement organizations based on differences in operating procedure. Formalized social movement organizations have established procedures or structures that enable them to perform certain tasks routinely and to continue to function with changes in leadership. Formalized social movement organizations have bureaucratic procedures for decision-making, a developed division of labour with positions for various functions, explicit criteria for membership, and rules governing subunits. In contrast, informal social movement organizations have few established procedures, loose membership requirements, and minimal division of labour. The organizational structure of an informal social movement organization is frequently adjusted and because they lack established procedures, individual leaders can exert an important influence on the organization. The term "informal" is used to describe social movement organizations that do not adopt a more "corporate" form. The term "classical" is used in some social movement literature but it does not describe the structure of the organization. The more descriptive term "grassroots" implies a mass membership base that may or may not be present in either "formalized" or "informal" social movement organizations. The term "collectivist" used by Rothschild-Whitt refers to a specific type of decision-making structure, which is distinguished from "bureaucratic" organizations, but not all informal social movement organizations are collectivist.

MANGALA SUBRAMANIAM

See also Organizational structure

Informal economy, *see* Work

Information and communication technologies

Allen, Thomas J. and Michael S. Scott Morton (editors), *Information Technology and the Corporation of the 1990s: Research Studies*, New York and Oxford: Oxford University Press, 1994

Babe, Robert E. (editor), *Information and Communication in Economics*, Boston: Kluwer, 1994

Cairncross, Frances, *The Death of Distance: How the Communications Revolution Will Change Our Lives*, Boston: Harvard Business School, and London: Orion, 1997

Castells, Manuel, *The Information Age: Economy, Society and Culture*; vol. 1: *The Rise of the Network Society*; vol. 2: *The Power of Identity*; vol. 3: *End of Millennium*, Oxford and Cambridge, Massachusetts: Blackwell, 1996

Dutton, William H. (editor), *Information and Communication Technologies: Visions and Realities*, Oxford and New York: Oxford University Press, 1996

Katz, Harry C. (editor), *Telecommunications: Restructuring Work and Employment Relations Worldwide*, Ithaca, New York: ILR Press, 1997

Mansell, Robin, *The New Telecommunications: A Political Economy of Network Evolution*, London and Thousand Oaks, California: Sage, 1993

Mansell, Robin and Uta Wehn (editors), *Knowledge Societies: Information Technology for Sustainable Development*, Oxford and New York: Oxford University Press, 1998

Miles, Ian (editor), *Mapping and Measuring the Information Economy*, London: British Library Research and Development Department, 1990

Sapolsky, Harvey M., Rhonda J. Crane, W. Russell Neuman and Eli M. Noam (editors), *The Telecommunications Revolution: Past, Present and Future*, London and New York: Routledge, 1992

Thomas, Graham and Sally Wyatt, "Shaping Cyberspace: Interpreting and Transforming the Internet", *Research Policy*, 28/7 (1999): 681–98

In recent years, the notion of "information technology" (IT) has tended to be supplanted by that of "information and communication technologies" (ICTs). This reflects what is generally understood to be a "convergence" between the two formerly distinct areas of technology, each with long separate histories of their own. This convergence arises from the common reliance on digital technologies in recent times. However the exact nature and extent of such convergence remains in dispute. Few doubt that the rise of ICTs represents a major departure in industrial development, though whether we are turning into an "information society" is more debatable.

The three large tomes written by CASTELLS are an attempt to cover the entire field of socioeconomic aspects of the "information society". The author draws the boundaries of ICTs much more widely than most, for example including genetic engineering. The result is something of a catch all. The author is not as well read on many of the huge variety of subjects included as he would like us to think. Views of other academics differ widely on the merits of the trilogy. Some respected sociologists regard this as the key treatise of the "information society" and intensely inspiring, others see it as intensely exasperating. Volume one deals with the internet, volume two with the self, and volume three with current transformations.

The collection of essays edited by DUTTON is based on a research programme of the UK Economic and Social Research Council (ESRC), known as the PICT Programme, which ran from the late 1980s to the mid 1990s. The essays examine the social and economic implications of ICTs. There is a strong bias towards approaches emanating from the social sciences (political science, sociology, gender studies, geography, and so forth). The authors of the essays adopt supportive but somewhat critical attitudes towards received opinions about the emergence of an "information society" and "information superhighway". Most of the essays appear to have been written specifically as surveys for this collection, so they cover a wider range of subject matter than is usual in collected essays.

The collection edited by BABE is much broader in scope than its title suggests, as the essays reflect a wide range of social sciences and not just economics, for example through semiotics. The opening essay by Lamberton is optimistic about economists taking information seriously, but other contributions are more pessimistic, and generally adopt an antineoclassical stance, which is associated with the treatment of information as a commodity.

By contrast, the collection edited by KATZ is much more specific in orientation, with the focus directed fairly exclusively at the impact of ICTs on work practices. This includes such issues as employment security, work organization, training, compensation, and governance. Though these issues have been described in many articles and books, the collection in question is particularly valuable for its crosscountry perspective. There are ten country studies (US, UK, Australia, Canada, Germany, Japan, Norway, Italy, Mexico, and Korea).

The progress towards computerization and absorption of ICTs has perhaps been slower than generally anticipated, though possibly speeding up with the Internet in the 1990s. The essays collected by ALLEN & SCOTT MORTON present expectations for the impact on the corporation and management in the US. Most take a rather upbeat tone, suggesting imminent radical change.

The analysis conducted by CAIRNCROSS is an attempt to use recent developments to advance a range of predictions about social futures consequent on the rise of ICTs. The author is a highly respected economic journalist, well aware of balancing popular needs with academic caution. The predictions advanced in the introduction err on the side of optimism, ending with "global peace". The chapters to follow, however, point out as many problems as possibilities with the achievement of desirable social and economic outcomes.

The collection on telecommunications edited by SAPOLSKY and colleagues contains a large number of essays by well-respected authorities, though the bulk of the essays are quite short, and essentially résumés of what they have said elsewhere. For noviciates in the subject this can of course be very helpful. The emphasis throughout is on policy and politics, though largely written by academics rather than practising politicians. Most of the chapters focus on the US though several look at other countries (Germany, France, Japan).

The monograph by MANSELL appraises the technically difficult area of the emergence and evolution of the "intelligent network", from a political economy standpoint. The author's underlying objective is to contrast the typically uncritical "idealist" model with a more accurate and sophisticated "strategic" model. She therefore stresses problems such as new disparities, market imperfections, monopolization, and so forth. This helps unravel the tensions that remain in, for instance, Cairncross' book. Mansell concentrates mostly on European experience, including individual country studies for the UK, France, Germany, and Sweden. Inevitably parts of the study have dated rapidly, but the elucidation of key issues is still well worth reading.

The paper by THOMAS & WYATT is a welcome "crash course" on the evolution of the Internet. The authors eschew gung-ho futurism for a cool assessment of the problems that have arisen in this evolution. They highlight the conflict between individual access on the one side and attempts at corporate control on the other. However they balance negative with positive aspects. This is an excellent introduction for any social scientist wanting a non-"techie" evaluation of the history of the Internet.

The contribution of ICTs is awkward to assess from conventional statistics, because it cuts across conventional categories. The book edited by MILES is a brave attempt to reconstruct this contribution from existing datasets, for the case of the UK. A wide range of statistical sources is used. There is considerable emphasis on applications and on workplaces, as well as

social implications. The results are not definitive but indicate the kinds of problems involved in establishing any assessment. Naturally the precise results have dated considerably, but the issues are still poorly dealt with in official statistics.

The UN Commission on Science and Technology for Development commissioned the study edited by MANSELL & WEHN. It is a comprehensive and up-to-date survey of the implications of modern developments in ICTs for developing countries. The main issue is whether ICTs will draw developing countries closer into the development net or instead further polarize world society. The editors have compressed the findings of the many original authors utilized into a fluent and well illustrated text.

G.N. VON TUNZELMANN

See also Communication and new media: economics, policy and regulation, Cyberspace revolution, Information society

Information processing

Anderson, John R. (editor), *Rules of the Mind*, Hillsdale, New Jersey: Erlbaum, 1993

Anderson, John R., *Cognitive Psychology and Its Implications*, New York: Worth, 2000

Atkinson, Richard and Richard Shiffrin, "Human Memory: A Proposed System and Its Control Procedures" in *The Psychology of Learning and Motivation: Advances in Research and Theory*, edited by Kenneth W. Spence and Janet Taylor Spence, New York: Academic Press, 1968

Markman, Arthur B., *Knowledge Representation*, Mahwah, New Jersey: Lawrence Erlbaum, 1999

Miller, George A., "The Magical Number Seven, Plus or Minus Two: Some Limits on Our Capacity for Processing Information", *Psychological Review*, 63 (1956): 81–97

Newell, Allen, *Unified Theories of Cognition*, Cambridge, Massachusetts: Harvard University Press, 1990

Schneider, Walter and Richard M. Shiffrin, "Controlled and Automatic Human Information Processing, 1: Detection, Search, and Attention", *Psychological Review*, 84/1 (1977): 1–66

Shiffrin, Richard M. and Walter Schneider, "Controlled and Automatic Human Information Processing, 2: Perceptual Learning, Automatic Attending, and a General Theory", *Psychological Review*, 84/2 (1977): 127–90

Sternberg, Robert J. (editor), *The Nature of Cognition*, Cambridge, Massachusetts: MIT Press, 1999

Information processing is a term denoting a broad array of theory related to learning and memory. Specifically, information processing examines the processes or components of cognition responsible for the acquisition, retention, and retrieval of information or knowledge. Information processing began in the 1950s with a methodology that examined human cognition through the use of discrete tasks that required finite mental activity.

MILLER provides classic examples of the use of discrete tasks involving finite mental activity. The author examined a series of experiments that explored individuals' memory for tones, monosyllabic words, dots on a page, and numbers. He did not himself conduct the research in his article, but rather he used previously published experiments to provide a rationale for determining the magnitude of "absolute judgements of unidimensional stimuli" and the "span of immediate memory". Miller concluded that there was a limit to the number of stimuli that one could receive, process, and remember simultaneously, and that limit was seven items. He further demonstrated that the amount of information conveyed by these seven items could be extended by chunking groups of knowledge within each item. Miller's article highlights the reductionistic nature of the early work in information processing and provided psychologists with the groundwork for decades of research into determining the nuances of his "magical number seven".

ATKINSON & SHIFFRIN is the result of two decades of research into discrete tasks involving finite mental activity. It is the first systematic development of an overall model of the human memory system to try to account for the myriad of individual experiments on memory, such as those analysed by Miller. This model is based on sensory input and two modes of memory storage, the short-term store and the long-term store. Each memory store is described in detail and is followed by several experiments designed to assess the validity of the stated model. Atkinson & Shiffrin is involved and detailed, but a complete understanding of the roots of information processing must include this work. While the Atkinson & Shiffrin model has been modified over the years as a result of new research, it still forms the basis of most information processing theory.

The Atkinson & Shiffrin memory model provided a theoretical framework for the examination of cognitive processing. SCHNEIDER & SHIFFRIN, together with SHIFFRIN & SCHNEIDER, extend the Atkinson & Shiffrin basic model. These two articles investigate cognitive processing as both automatic (automatic detection) and under the individual's conscious control (controlled search). These two processing modes were constructed as involving qualitatively different mechanisms and responding to qualitatively different stimuli. The articles provide detailed explanations and sound empirical support for the proposed adjustments to the basic Atkinson & Shiffrin model. The three articles, Atkinson & Shiffrin, Schneider & Shiffrin, and Shiffrin & Schneider, comprise the foundational triumvirate of information processing.

Information processing theory and the Atkinson & Shiffrin model were further developed, analysed, and synthesized during the 1980s and 1990s. ANDERSON (2000) provides a thorough and empirically based synopsis of the current state of information processing and cognition. The essential information processing components (e.g. sensation, perception, attention, encoding, retention, and retrieval) emerge from a lucid discussion of empirical research spanning the last five decades. In addition, Anderson aptly relates the abstract principles of information processing to human functioning (e.g. problem solving, decision making, development of expertise, and language). Finally, Anderson attempts to integrate the basics of cognitive neuroscience with the findings of information processing. Unfortunately, cognitive neuroscience is currently underdeveloped, resulting in a somewhat awkward information processing/cognitive neuroscience synthesis. Ultimately,

however, those in search of a single source concerning modern information processing should start here.

While Anderson provides a broad look at modern information processing, the 20 essays in STERNBERG provide a deeper and narrower view of specific topics related to information processing. These essays span five main themes: general issues, representation, methodology, kinds of cognition, and individual differences in cognition. All of the essays use a dialectic approach, examining and analysing opposing viewpoints relative to a specific topic, with a subsequent synthesis of the viewpoints. For a reader that addresses advanced issues not normally found in a foundational text, such as Anderson's, Sternberg has provided an excellent repository of information. These essays, written by respected leaders in their fields, provide concise delineations of advanced information processing topics such as domain-generality versus domain-specificity, prototype versus exemplar model, laboratory versus field approaches, and culture-free versus culture-based cognition. A caveat, that is typical of information processing, is that most of the essays examine cognition from the perspective of the individual. There is little discussion of social processes.

A core issue that underlies all of information processing is knowledge representation. While Sternberg briefly addresses this concept, it is worth a deeper look. MARKMAN deftly negotiates the multiple interpretations of this controversial topic. It examines broad types of representation, based on the assumptions of those who conduct research into knowledge representation. The strength of this text lies in its balance of representational types (e.g., spatial, featural, structured, perceptual, networked, and conceptual representations).

Taken together, Anderson, Sternberg, and Markman provide a clear picture of the components of modern information processing. However, the mere understanding of the components of cognition is not the ultimate goal of information processing. Rather, as stated by NEWELL, the ultimate goal is a unified theory of cognition. Newell proposes such a theory, based on a production system architecture. Newell first describes the essential elements of human cognitive architecture, and then provides a detailed account of a model of a unified theory of cognition which he calls "Soar". Newell's Soar model is based on a production system that acts as a universal problem solver motivating responses. Newell provides a rich description of the Soar model, an explanation of the rationale that underlies its creation, and concrete implementations. The Soar model has been sufficiently developed to the point that it is now being implemented as a software simulation.

The primary competitor to the Soar model, as a model of a unified theory of cognition, is ANDERSON's (1993) ACT-R model. Anderson's ACT-R model is comprised of both a declarative and a production system architecture. Anderson provides a coherent explanation of the rationale underlying the theory as well as the specifics of its implementation. Anderson provides an excellent introduction to ACT-R theory, although the author's description of its implementation using LISP can be daunting for those not familiar with computer programming. Overall, however, Anderson's ACT-R model is the most parsimonious and easiest architecture to understand.

Information processing is a well-developed theory of human memory and cognition. It has developed from a series of reductionistic experiments (Miller), to a basic model of how information is processed in the mind (Atkinson & Shiffrin), to a highly evolved model of both general and specific processes (Anderson and Sternberg) that is capable of being implemented as a computer simulation (Newell and Anderson).

PETER E. DOOLITTLE

Information society

Bell, Daniel, *The Coming of Post-Industrial Society: A Venture in Social Forecasting*, New York: Basic Books, 1973; London: Heinemann, 1974

Beniger, James R., *The Control Revolution: Technological and Economic Origins of the Information Society*, Cambridge, Massachusetts: Harvard University Press, 1986

Castells, Manuel, *The Rise of the Network Society*, vol. 1: *The Information Age: Economy, Society and Culture*, Oxford and Cambridge, Massachusetts: Blackwell, 1996

Lash, Scott and John Urry, *Economies of Signs and Space*, London and Thousand Oaks, California: Sage, 1994

Lyon, David, *The Information Society: Issues and Illusions*, Cambridge: Polity Press, and New York: Blackwell, 1988

Masuda, Yoneji, *The Information Society as Post-Industrial Society*, Washington, DC: World Future Society, 1981

Mulgan, Geoff J., *Communication and Control: Networks and the New Economics of Communication*, Cambridge: Polity Press, and New York: Guilford Press, 1991

Piore, Michael J. and Charles F. Sabel, *The Second Industrial Divide: Possibilities for Prosperity*, New York: Basic Books, 1984

Porat, Marc U., *The Information Economy*, Washington, DC: Office of Telecommunications, 1977

Toffler, Alvin, *Powershift: Knowledge, Wealth, and Violence at the Edge of the 21st Century*, New York: Bantam, 1991

BELL effectively initiated discussion of the information society when he wrote his "venture in social forecasting" in the mid-1970s. In this book he predicted the demise of industrial society and the emergence of an information age, and he discussed the ways in which the proliferating role of information in society might change the structures of control in government and within business organizations. He predicted that codified knowledge would become the key resource of the information economy. In his vision of the future he argued that the old industrial-based class antagonisms discussed by the Marxists would disappear. This is a rather utopian book (and many of Bell's predictions have not come to pass), but it is a good place to start exploring the information society because it is a seminal text on the topic. It is also useful for exploring the relationship between the emergence of an information society and the growth of the service sector.

BENIGER's approach to the information society is especially useful. He asks a fundamental question – why did an information society arise? His answer is that the information revolution has its roots in a series of crises growing out of the industrial mode of production. He examines these crises,

starting in the late 19th century. The book explores how information technologies emerge from attempts to solve the problems of organizing and controlling the highly complex processes of industrial society. His thesis, in short, is that a need for control is behind the new society that is emerging out of proliferating information technologies.

CASTELLS has produced an extraordinarily comprehensive examination of the information society in a book that synthesizes a huge array of previously published material on the topic together with a wealth of empirical data. The result is something of a magnum opus on the emergent information economy and on the social and cultural changes being wrought by this new economic order. Castells examines these changes through exploring emergent information technologies, globalization, organizational forms, work practices, cultural forms, and urban planning. If it were only possible to read one book on the information society, then it would have to be this one.

LASH & URRY do an excellent job in examining the social changes being wrought by the proliferation of the new information technologies. Theirs is a comparative analysis of how capitalism is reorganizing itself in the US, the UK, and Japan, into what they call an economy of signs (information, symbols, and images). Among other things, they look at the way in which work practices are changing, the emergence of a new underclass, and the cultural shifts being produced by the restructuring of global capitalism.

LYON does a great deal to help move discussion of the information society out of the realms of utopian dreaming and hypothesizing, and into the realms of a considered debate. He systematically works his way through the main themes found in the literature and critically examines the validity of the claims and proposals postulated by others. In the process he adds a great deal to our understanding of the phenomenon and places the study of the information society onto more solid ground.

MASUDA picked up on the ideas of Bell and Porat in arguing that a post-industrial society was necessarily going to emerge from the new communication technologies. He argued that information and computing technologies had become central to building a new desirable (and utopian?) civilization. Mental labour and knowledge are seen to be the new key resources for creating wealth and growth. This is an important book to read given the importance of Masuda's work in generating governmental promotion of an information economy in both Japan and the USA.

MULGAN looks at communication as a mechanism of social control and at how technologies are developed to service the needs of control. His is a study of the communication networks built in the late 20th century, with a view to ascertaining what role these serve within the emerging matrix of production, distribution, exchange, and governance. He also looks at the tensions between the old (industrial) mechanisms of control and the emerging (post-industrial) ones. The result is a useful book on the information society from the perspective of how information technology is likely to be configured in such a way as to service the needs of the emerging post-industrial elite.

PIORE & SABEL focus on how work practices and organizational structures are shifting in response to the penetration of information technology into the workplace. The result is a useful analysis of the crisis of industrial mass production methods (or what some have called Fordism) and its replacement by what they call "flexible specialization" (or what some have called post-Fordism).

PORAT's work did much to popularize the notion of an information society within the US's corridors of power. In fact, together with Bell and Masuda, Porat's work was central in generating the notion of a coming information society. This report, commissioned by the US Department of Commerce, presented an array of empirical data that showed how the US economy was changing into an information economy. It is a very useful document from the early days of discussing the information society and it has the advantage of being less utopian than Bell's and Masuda's work.

TOFFLER has, over the years, written a number of high-quality, futurology-type books. His 1991 book *Powershift* hypothesizes about the ways in which the shift into an information economy looks set to radically reshape society. The central focus of this book is a discussion of how power relationships between people and organizations seem set to be completely restructured by the "information" revolution. Toffler's key argument is that hierarchical social structures are set to decay as a result of the new information revolution. This is an insightful book, written by a generalist, which contains much food for thought, although it is perhaps marred by Toffler's tendency to become too much of an advocate for an information-age utopia.

ERIC LOUW

See also Cyberspace revolution

Information technology law, *see* Cyberlaw

Informed consent

American Psychological Association, "Ethical Principles of Psychologists and Code of Conduct", *American Psychologist*, 47/12 (1992): 1597–1611

Applebaum, Binyamin C., Paul S. Applebaum and Thomas Grisso, "Competence to Consent to Voluntary Psychiatric Hospitalization: A Test of a Standard Proposed by APA", *Psychiatric Services*, 49/9 (1998): 1193–96

Braaten, Ellen B. and Mitchell M. Handelsman, "Client Preferences for Informed Consent Information", *Ethics and Behavior*, 7/4 (1997): 311–28

Brody, Janet L., John P. Gluck and Alfredo S. Aragon, "Participants' Understanding of the Process of Psychological Research: Informed Consent", *Ethics and Behavior*, 7/4 (1997): 285–98

Lehrman, Nathaniel S. and Vera H. Sharav, "Ethical Problems in Psychiatric Research", *Journal of Mental Health Administration*, 24/2 (1997): 228–50

Reynolds, Paul D., *Ethics and Social Science Research*, Englewood Cliffs, New Jersey: Prentice Hall, 1982

Psychologists deal with the principles of informed consent from two different perspectives – clinical practice and scientific research. The AMERICAN PSYCHOLOGICAL ASSOCIATION provides guidelines to mental health providers regarding informed consent, noting that prior to therapy, patients or clients must learn what the therapy involves, be able to give consent for treatment (either directly or by proxy), and give explicit consent that they agree to the treatment. Informed consent has implications beyond this, however. For example, in therapy with couples or with families, the therapist must indicate which individuals are patients or clients and the relationship among all parties involved. Further, psychologists are bound to inform those they serve about issues of privacy and confidentiality. In research, psychologists must inform participants about the nature of the research in which they will engage, including potential risks, discomfort, or other negative aspects. Before or during a research session, participants must be accorded the right to terminate their participation with no negative consequences. In the event that deception is a necessary component of the research, researchers must inform participants of the nature of the deception as soon as practical. Informed consent is generally deemed unnecessary in some cases, as with some anonymous questionnaires, naturalistic and public observations, or some archival research.

Most of the published literature regarding informed consent relates to research on psychiatric (and other medical) populations. LEHRMAN & SHARAV have presented a thought-provoking discussion on a variety of ethical problems in psychiatric research. The authors introduce several cases in which the welfare of individual patients was compromised as they participated in research, often with poorly conceived attempts at informed consent. Lehrman & Sharav also suggest that such victimization is common because hospital patients are often feeling physically unwell, are frightened, and are concerned about their health. Minimal attempts at informed consent may not lead to truly voluntary participation. The authors also report that much research of this nature involves drug treatment, the effectiveness of which is often vastly overstated; the result is the approval of what is hoped to be even more successful treatment that often does not really materialize. Finally, they discuss the implications of such problems for mental health policies and for researchers.

BRAATEN & HANDELSMAN note that, by law, informed consent for patients or clients in the United States is mandated to be patient based. This means that information of material concern to the individual drives what a psychologist or physician communicates to the individual about a course of treatment. Braaten & Handelsman assert that, unfortunately, practitioners have not reached consensus about the type of information that should reasonably be disclosed to a patient. Using questionnaire data from current and former counselling clients, the researchers discovered that college students with a history of therapy rated as most important the information about therapeutic techniques, risks of alternative treatments, and aspects of the benefits of counselling. Clients differed during the course of therapy as to what elements of informed consent are most important. This article presents useful information about client or patient perspectives and how the desire for information evolves through the course of therapy. The results are limited in that the participants constituted a small, relatively homogeneous sample.

Although a population like college students seeking counselling for remedy of often relatively minor problems may have no difficulty dealing with informed consent issues, psychological professionals have pondered whether patients in a psychiatric hospital can made competent decisions about their treatment. APPLEBAUM, APPLEBAUM & GRISSO investigated whether voluntarily admitted patients can understand enough about their treatment to be able to grant or withhold consent regarding treatment. The researchers created a two-paragraph informed consent instrument dealing with diagnosis, treatment, and harm to self or others, and with the fact that even with voluntary hospitalization, discharge is not automatic. They discovered that the patients who were voluntarily committed were generally able to understand that their liberty could be abridged, although they were less able to remember information about diagnosis and treatment. Patients who had been involuntarily committed fared worse in their ability to understand, suggesting that practitioners must take even greater care than usual to ensure true informed consent.

In a consideration of research with nonclinical populations, BRODY, GLUCK & ARAGON discuss the status of informed consent as it is actually practised. They point out that a prime consideration when a person consents to participate in research is that the person must be accorded personal autonomy. This autonomy requires a) full disclosure of material that would affect willingness to participate, b) adequate comprehension of the information presented by researchers, c) a voluntary decision to participate, and d) competence to make that decision. In research conducted in psychology with college students, the first three considerations may be most relevant. These authors interviewed students to assess their responses to research projects in which the students had participated. When the students characterized studies positively, it was because participation was interesting or fun, or had provided some self-insight; negative characteristics related to boredom and apparently pointless activity. Approximately 80 per cent characterized informed consent positively; negativity arose when informed consent information was vague, incomplete, or inaccurate. In a few cases, students asserted that they would have opted out of the study had they been more fully informed of the procedures. The students also felt uncomfortable with the idea of withdrawing from the study, especially in group-testing sessions; some claimed to have faked participation (leading to invalid responses). The authors point out that students frequently do not understand the purpose of the informed consent procedure, rendering it less effective in helping them make a decision about participation. They suggest ways to ameliorate the situation.

REYNOLDS provides a number of interesting situations in which informed consent may not be easily implemented. For example, a researcher must inform a participant about possible negative consequences of the research. Unfortunately, the outcome of the research is not entirely predictable, so it may not be possible to inform an individual of an eventuality that may be surprising, even when the researcher is acting with complete integrity. Reynolds also discusses alternatives to informed consent that may be appropriate in certain circumstances. He notes that, even when participants provide informed consent, such action does not diminish the legal liability of the researcher for negligent behaviour. Reynolds presents some controversial ideas that can lead to fruitful discussion of the principles and applications of informed consent.

BERNARD C. BEINS

Ingroup and outgroup

Allport, Gordon W., *The Nature of Prejudice*, Reading, Massachusetts: Addison Wesley, 1954

Brewer, Marilynn B., "Ingroup Bias in the Minimal Intergroup Situation: A Cognitive-Motivational Analysis", *Psychological Bulletin*, 86/2 (1979): 307–24

Dovidio, John F. and Samuel L. Gaertner, "Stereotypes and Evaluative Bias" in *Affect, Cognition and Stereotyping*, edited by Diane M. Mackie and David L. Hamilton, San Diego: Academic Press, 1993

LeVine, Robert A. and Donald T. Campbell, *Ethnocentrism: Theories of Conflict, Ethnic Attitudes and Group Behavior*, New York: Wiley, 1972

Mullen, Brian and Li-tze Hu, "Perceptions of Ingroup and Outgroup Variability: A Meta-analytic Integration", *Basic and Applied Social Psychology*, 10 (1989): 233–52

Sherif, Muzafer *et al.*, *Intergroup Conflict and Cooperation: The Robbers Cave Experiment*, Norman, Oklahoma: University Book Exchange, 1961

Sumner, William G., *Folkways*, New York: Ginn, 1907

Tajfel, Henri and A.L. Wilkes, "Classification and Quantitative Judgment", *British Journal of Psychology*, 54 (1963): 101–14

Tajfel, Henri, "Experiments in Intergroup Discrimination", *Scientific American*, 223/2 (1970): 96–102

Tajfel, Henri and John C. Turner, "An Integrative Theory of Intergroup Conflict" in *The Social Psychology of Intergroup Relations*, edited by William G. Austin and Stephen Worchel, Monterey, California: Brooks Cole, 1979

SUMNER first introduced the terms "ingroup" and "outgroup" in his theory of ethnocentrism, to refer to social groups to which an individual did or did not belong respectively. Ingroups could be of varying types and sizes ranging from small face-to-face groups, such as families, to large social categories such as nationality, religion or sex. Ingroups were seen as more than a cognitive categorization. They were viewed as also involving emotional significance for the group members. Sumner saw the differentiation of people into distinct ethnic groups as both reflecting and sustaining a basic state of conflict between ingroups and outgroups for survival. This differentiation was said to lead to loyalty and preference for ingroups over outgroups, hence maintaining ingroup solidarity and justifying the exploitation of outgroups. LEVINE & CAMPBELL elaborated on this theory in regard to ethnocentrism, arguing that the greater the competitive interdependence between groups the more attraction there would be to the ingroup and the greater the corresponding hostility to outgroups.

ALLPORT provided an interesting early discussion of the nature and formation of ingroups, differentiating between achieved and ascribed ingroup membership. He also differentiated between ingroups and reference groups – groups in which an individual wishes to be, but may not be, included. Allport considered the flexible nature of ingroup membership as a function of context and salience and considered whether ingroups can exist independent of outgroups. Finally, Allport foreshadowed the notion of esteem as a key feature in ingroup identification.

A classic example of the conceptualization of intergroup relations as ingroup–outgroup hostility is seen in the "robbers cave boys' summer camp" studies by SHERIF *et al.* Groups of boys showed strong ingroup favouritism and outgroup hostility. The behaviour of groups of strangers could be transformed by dividing them into subgroups that then competed for valued limited resources.

TAJFEL & TURNER articulated the premises and implications of social identity theory (SIT), which has been enormously influential in research on intergroup relations. The notion that ingroup identification is linked to a striving for positive self and social identity or esteem is a fundamental tenet of SIT. Ingroup favouritism is, then, a way of feeling good about oneself. There is evidence both of a striving for positive identity leading to intergroup discrimination and for intergroup differentiation leading to positive social identity. Social identity theory predicts greater ingroup favouritism and outgroup derogation when identification with the ingroup is strong or when one's identity or esteem had been threatened.

Ingroup favouritism occurs even when there is no competition for resources. Much research has investigated the minimal conditions necessary to generate ingroup–outgroup discrimination. TAJFEL and colleagues introduced two important methodological paradigms, which have been hugely influential in research on intergroup relations. The first, the minimal group paradigm, was to create ingroups and outgroups in which individuals were told their group membership but there was no face-to-face interaction within or between groups, there was anonymity of group membership, there was an absence of any link between the basis for intergroup categorization and the response measure, and the response measure had no direct utility to participants. The response measures used were the second innovation of Tajfel and colleagues. Participants were presented with a series of payoff matrices in which they choose between a number of alternative allocations of points or money to two anonymous participants in the same experiment, one an ingroup member and one and outgroup member. Even under such conditions, ingroup favouritism was reliably demonstrated: participants allocated more rewards to ingroup members than to outgroup members. Any salient and situationally meaningful ingroup/outgroup differentiation is sufficient to bring about discrimination. Such discrimination has been demonstrated on evaluative, affective, and behavioural measures. The minimal group and payoff matrices have been hugely influential in intergroup research in both the laboratory and real-life settings.

BREWER provided a comprehensive review of research in which ingroup favouritism has been demonstrated. She identified those factors that enhance ingroup favouritism, including features of the group members such as similarity and status differentials and features of the response dimensions employed. Outgroup favouritism, although rare, is also considered. Brewer considered the differentiation of three processes of ingroup/outgroup discrimination – ingroup favouritism, outgroup derogation, and intergroup differentiation – and how each is an independent aspect of intergroup relations. She discussed research on ingroup favouritism in terms of its implications for positive applications of group identification. Brewer also revisited the debate on whether outgroups are necessary for ingroup identification to occur.

Ingroup/outgroup differentiation has a number of cognitive and affective consequences. TAJFEL & WILKES demonstrated that differentiation into distinct groups results in an attenuation of within-group differences and an exaggeration of between-group differences. This is related to the outgroup homogeneity effect, which is the tendency of perceivers to see less variability among members of an outgroup than among members of an ingroup. MULLEN & HU provided an integrative review of research that has considered perceptions of ingroup and outgroup variability. The role of features such as familiarity and future interaction was considered. They also considered conditions under which an ingroup homogeneity effect occurs. DOVIDIO & GAERTNER described a series of experiments that demonstrated that ingroup and outgroup labels spontaneously, and without conscious awareness, elicit different evaluative associations, which are then conveyed on to new stimuli. These evaluative responses can bias the nature of subsequent interactions.

LUCY JOHNSTON

Innovation, diffusion of

Acs, Zoltan J. and David B. Audretsch, *Innovation and Small Firms*, Cambridge, Massachusetts: MIT Press, 1990

Brown, Lawrence A., *Innovation Diffusion: A New Perspective*, London and New York: Methuen, 1981

Freeman, Christopher and Luc Soete, *The Economics of Industrial Innovation*, 3rd edition, Cambridge, Massachusetts: MIT Press, 1997

Mahajan, Vijay and Robert A. Peterson, *Models for Innovation Diffusion*, Beverly Hills, California and London: Sage, 1985

Rogers, Everett M., *Diffusion of Innovations*, 4th edition, New York: Free Press, 1995 (1st edition 1962; 2nd edition, with F. Floyd Shoemaker, as *Communication of Innovations*)

Rosenberg, Nathan, *Perspectives on Technology*, Cambridge and New York: Cambridge University Press, 1976

Sahal, Devendra, *Patterns of Technological Innovation*, Reading, Massachusetts: Addison Wesley, 1981

Stoneman, Paul (editor), *Handbook of the Economics of Innovations and Technological Change*, Oxford and Cambridge, Massachusetts: Blackwell, 1995

Zaltman, Gerald, Robert Duncan and Jonny Holbek, *Innovations and Organizations*, New York: Wiley, 1973; reprinted Malabar, Florida: Krieger, 1984

ROGERS' classic text is the best introduction available to the study of technology transfer. He provides a solid theoretical treatment, well grounded in communication theory, and identifies the four key elements of diffusion as being the innovation, the channels of communication, time, and a social system. He elaborates on each of these elements and their interrelationships, and provides clear definitions and explanations of the key concepts. The book also explores the history and, indeed, the criticisms of diffusion research, while pinpointing areas for further research. It includes an extensive bibliography and is interspersed throughout with illustrative case studies drawn from a wide selection of fields.

The differential equation, $dN(t)/dt = g(t)[M - N(t)]$ in which $N(t)$ is the cumulative number of adopters at time t, M is the total number of potential adopters, and $g(t)$ is the coefficient of diffusion, has dominated much of the diffusion modelling literature. MAHAJAN & PETERSON refer to this model as the "fundamental diffusion model" and they provide an informative discussion of its mathematical underpinnings, as well as considering the full range of possible variations and extensions. Their strength is also their weakness for, although they raise most of the important issues in diffusion modelling, they sometimes fail to explore them in sufficient depth. The book is intended for an interdisciplinary audience, but has a tendency to fall back on marketing terminology. Overall the book is well written and informative with a good mix between mathematical material and descriptive text.

BROWN not only provides a worthwhile discussion of diffusion from a spatial perspective but goes a long way in integrating the geographical work on diffusion with that of marketing, sociology, and other disciplines. However, more importantly, he develops a supply-side perspective on innovation diffusion to complement rather than replace the more conventional demand-side perspective that has perhaps been overemphasized in previous research. His concern with supply-side effects leads to a useful discussion of innovation diffusion in a developmental context, with examples taken almost exclusively from the developing countries. Overall the theoretical perspective is sometimes weak and the criticism of the standard quantitative methods and concepts would have more impact if counterbalanced with well-developed alternatives.

In a framework grounded in economics and forecasting, SAHAL explores the factors that determine why organizations innovate. He concentrates on modelling technological evolution rather than diffusion. He stresses the importance of taking into account the continuity of development that accompanies new innovations. Importantly, he provides a link between the concepts of innovation and diffusion, while concentrating mainly on the process of innovation and technical substitution. Unfortunately he ignores most of the demand-side effects associated with the adopter and this is a major weakness. The references are limited mainly to industrial engineering.

ROSENBERG's collection of essays represents an insightful examination of the conceptual approach used by economists in the study of technology transfer. Based on thorough examination of technology transfer from historical perspectives he is able to reveal the complexities and difficulties of the subject, while questioning some of the basic concepts and stressing the need to step outside narrow disciplinary boundaries. He explores the determinants of the speed and extent of technology transfer, as well as the two-way relationship between technology and the environment. The book also includes an examination of the Schumpeterian heritage and some discussion of the determinants of invention. As the author himself admits, the book is more explorative than definitive.

ACS and AUDRETSCH offers the best discussion of the relationships between innovation, firm size and market structure. The role of the small firm within the economy is well highlighted. They suggest that small firms have an important part to play in the generation of innovations and that innovation activity can influence market structures. They also include an extensive bibliography.

In the context of business and management, ZALTMAN, DUNCAN & HOLBEK provide the most cohesive treatment of innovation adoption in organizations. They focus on the innovation-adoption process as it takes place within multi-member units of adoption, and explore how the characteristics and structures of organizations, and indeed their environments, influence innovation. They include a review of the existing theories of innovation in organizations.

The essays in STONEMAN provide an up-to-date treatment of the central issues in the economics of technological change and diffusion. There is coverage of the concepts, measurement and importance of technological change, as well as discussion of technology policy issues. New approaches to modelling technical change are outlined. The performance of technology markets is explored and technology change is discussed in relation to finance, employment, and international trade. However, as with many other texts in this area, the role of technology change in developing countries is omitted.

FREEMAN makes a major contribution to the study of the economics of innovation. The first section is a study of technical change in the 20th century, which highlights the evolution of innovation and the consequent evolution of industry structure within three different industries. The second section addresses firm innovation strategies, risk assessment and success and failure in innovation, as well as discussing the relationship between firm size and innovative ability. The final section includes a substantial treatment of policy issues. Within the wider context of economic growth, plausible explanations of booms and slumps, stagflation and depression are put forward. The book attempts to explain how innovation and diffusion lead to fluctuations in employment and growth rates. In parts the book is too general, but is an excellent introduction to many key issues.

SEAMUS MCERLEAN

See also Systems of innovation, Technology transfer

Innovation, economic

Arrow, Kenneth J., "Economic Welfare and the Allocation of Resources for Invention" in *The Rate and Direction of Inventive Activity*, edited by Richard R. Nelson, Princeton, New Jersey: Princeton University Press, 1962

Dosi, Giovanni, Chris Freeman, Richard R. Nelson, Gerry Silverberg and Luc Soete (editors), *Technical Change and Economic Theory*, London: Pinter, 1988

Freeman, Christopher and Luc Soete, *The Economics of Industrial Innovation*, 3rd edition, London: Pinter, 1997

Gort, Michael and Steven Klepper, "Time Paths in the Diffusion of Product Innovations", *Economic Journal*, 92/367 (1982): 630–53

Granstrand, Ove (editor), *Economics of Technology*, Amsterdam: North Holland, 1994

Griliches, Zvi, "The Search for Research-and-Development Spillovers", *Scandinavian Journal of Economics*, 94/55 (1992): 29–47

Hippel, Eric von, *The Sources of Innovation*, Oxford and New York: Oxford University Press, 1988

Levin, Richard C., Alvin K. Klevorick, Richard R. Nelson and Sidney G. Winter, "Appropriating the Returns from Industrial Research and Development", *Brookings Papers on Economic Activity*, 3 (1987): 783–831

Mansfield, Edwin, *Industrial Research and Technological Innovation: An Econometric Analysis*, New York: Norton, 1968

Nelson, Richard R. and Sidney G. Winter, *An Evolutionary Theory of Economic Change*, Cambridge, Massachusetts: Harvard University Press, 1982

Pavitt, Keith, Michael Robson and Joe Townsend, "The Size Distribution of Innovating Firms in the UK: 1945–1983", *Journal of Industrial Economics*, 35/3 (1987): 297–316

Rosenberg, Nathan, *Inside the Black Box: Technology and Economics*, Cambridge and New York: Cambridge University Press, 1982

Schumpeter, Joseph A., *Capitalism, Socialism and Democracy*, London: Allen and Unwin, 1943

Stoneman, Paul (editor), *Handbook of the Economics of Innovations and Technological Change*, Oxford and Cambridge, Massachusetts: Blackwell, 1995

Innovation was a curiously neglected field of economics until the late 1950s and early 1960s. Technological change entered into the aggregate production function as a residual, but most economists did not consider that the provenance of technological change was a matter for economic analysis. From time to time new products and processes would emerge, would be codified in "blueprints" or technical manuals, and would then diffuse throughout competitive markets. However, the central economic questions were to do with how well a market would supply the new goods, and not whether enough resources were being devoted to the creation of innovations. Since then, innovation has grown to become one of the largest literatures within industrial economics.

Possibly the single most influential work on the economics of innovation is chapter 7 of SCHUMPETER's *Capitalism, Socialism and Democracy*. In this, Schumpeter argues that innovation in the form of new products, new processes, new organizational forms, new sources of supply, or new methods of selling, is a far more potent competitive force than price competition, which did – at that time – dominate most formal economic analysis. Schumpeter argues that, because of this, economists should be less preoccupied with the risk that market power may prevent prices from being driven down to their competitive levels, and more concerned about the dynamic capacity of the economy to sustain a stream of innovation.

Three of the most influential contributions to the economics of innovation from the 1960s and 1970s have been essentially empirical. One is the empirical tradition started by Freeman and continued by his colleagues at the Science Policy Research Unit (SPRU), University of Sussex. In a most valuable textbook, FREEMAN & SOETE describe the rise of science-based technologies, including the industrial revolution, electricity, steel, oil and chemicals, synthetics, autos, and computers. They offer an analysis of the microeconomics of innovation, including the determinants of success and failure, and of the determinants of innovation strategies. They also analyse the macroeconomics of innovation, including the implications for diffusion, growth, globalization, and trade. Finally, they

study public policy towards innovation, and the emergence of the information society and the environment. The text contains valuable literature surveys. SPRU created a major database of innovations across all sectors of the economy, and this has been the basis for many influential studies of innovation. PAVITT, ROBSON & TOWNSEND show that the incidence of innovation in the small firms is higher than would be expected from the low share of formal research and development or patenting that is carried out in small firms. This finding reinforced the view that, although much innovation is based on science and technology, drawing on the work of research and development departments, a substantial share of innovation happens elsewhere. It also underlines the fact that, although inventions are commonly patented in some industries, not all patents lead to an innovation, and neither are all innovations preceded by a patent.

A second stream of work in a historical tradition is that by ROSENBERG and co-authors. In this collection of 12 essays, Rosenberg tries to open up what he calls the "black box" of the economics of innovation. He offers a historical view of technical progress, describes some of the main characteristics of technologies, analyses some of the determinants of innovation, and takes an international perspective on technology transfer and technological leadership. Three of these essays are especially important. One examines the vital role of technological expectations for company behaviour. A second asks "how exogenous is science?" and concludes that technological concerns do shape the development of science. A third examines the impact of demand on innovation, and concludes that neither a pure "technology push" nor a pure "demand pull" explanation of innovation can satisfactorily account for observed patterns of innovation.

A third stream of work, again in an essentially empirical tradition but closer to the economic mainstream, is that of MANSFIELD and colleagues. Mansfield looks at the determinants of research and development and at its effects on inventive output. He examines the characteristics of companies' research and development portfolios and the returns to research and development. He also offers a broader perspective of the relationship between market structure and innovation, and of the implications of innovation for investment and growth. Mansfield was also one of the pioneers of diffusion studies, and the final part of this book focuses on inter-firm diffusion, imitation, and intra-firm diffusion. The work of VON HIPPEL is an important complement to this. He focuses on the determinants of innovation – in particular, the role of customers as sources of innovative ideas.

ARROW's classic paper explained why inventive and innovative activity is prone to market failure. To the extent that technological knowledge is codified, non-rival, and non-excludable, then innovative activity by one company will generate externalities of spillovers to others. LEVIN *et al.* offer one of the classic studies of the appropriating of returns from industrial research and development. A more recent paper by GRILICHES surveys a wide range of evidence to assess the actual importance of spillovers.

An important methodological advance arising from the activity of economists who have studied innovation has been the rise of evolutionary economics. NELSON & WINTER made the pioneering contribution to this. Their book develops an evolutionary theory of the business firm, its capabilities, and its behaviour in markets. They use that to analyse a wide range of issues in economic change, including shifts in demand, changes in factor supply conditions, growth, and innovation on the part of firms. Their analysis rests on two premises: first, that economic change is important and interesting, and deserves greater attention than neoclassical theory has given it; and second, that a major reconstruction of the theoretical foundations of economics is a precondition for the understanding of economic change.

Drawing on the foundations provided by Nelson & Winter's work, DOSI *et al.* develop a sustained critique of the appropriateness of neoclassical economic analysis for understanding innovation, and take some steps to make evolutionary economics operational. Their massive book, with 28 papers in all, sets out a wider framework for economic analysis of evolution, innovation, and institutions. Four key themes are: innovation and the evolution of firms; national systems of innovation; the international diffusion of technology and international trade; and the formal modelling of evolutionary economic change.

The papers in GRANSTRAND follow on this tradition, and provide a useful perspective on the development of the economics of innovation. Some of these could, perhaps, be said to emanate from an evolutionary–mainstream synthesis. Themes discussed include: micro-to-macro analysis, positive feedback and research productivity; technology, competencies and the theory of the firm; technology and economic dynamics; innovation, competitive advantage and trade; technological forecasting; and technology and development.

Many of the pioneering studies have examined the factors determining the diffusion of new technologies, but the work of David, Stoneman, and others has made significant advances in our understanding of the diffusion process. The chapter on diffusion in STONEMAN gives a valuable survey of this literature to the mid-1990s. Other chapters in Stoneman's invaluable handbook summarise the state of the literature on: research and development and productivity; markets for technology; game-theoretical analysis of technological change; finance and technological change; technological change and international trade; technological change and employment; and technology policy. GORT & KLEPPER provide an especially interesting empirical study of time-paths in diffusion.

G.M. PETER SWANN

See also Globalization of technology, Patents, Technology, economics

Innovation, organizational

Agrell, Anders and Roland Gustafson, "Innovation and Creativity in Work Groups" in *Handbook of Workgroup Psychology*, edited by Michael A. West, Chichester and New York: Wiley, 1996
Bower, Joseph I., *Managing the Resource Allocation Process: A Study of Corporate Planning and Investment*, revised edition, Boston: Harvard Business School Press, 1986
Burns, Tom and George M. Stalker, *The Management of Innovation*, 3rd edition, Oxford and New York: Oxford University Press, 1994
Kanter, Rosabeth Moss, *The Change Masters: Innovations and Productivity in the American Corporation*, London: Allen and Unwin, and New York: Simon and Schuster, 1984
Leonard-Barton, Dorothy, *Wellsprings of Knowledge: Building and Sustaining the Sources of Innovation*, Boston: Harvard Business School Press, 1995
Martinelli, Alberto, "Entrepreneurship and Management" in *The Handbook of Economic Sociology*, edited by Neil J. Smelser and Richard Swedberg, Princeton, New Jersey: Princeton University Press, 1994
Roberts, Edward B., *Entrepreneurs in High Technology: Lessons from MIT and Beyond*, Oxford and New York: Oxford University Press, 1991
Schön, Donald A., *Technology and Change: The New Heraclitus*, New York: Delacorte Press, 1967
Tushman, Michael L. and Philip Anderson (editors), *Managing Strategic Innovation and Change: A Collection of Readings*, Oxford and New York: Oxford University Press, 1997
West, Michael A. and James L. Farr (editors), *Innovation and Creativity at Work: Psychological and Organizational Strategies*, Chichester and New York: Wiley, 1990
Woodward, Joan, *Industrial Organization: Theory and Practice*, 2nd edition, Oxford and New York: Oxford University Press, 1980

In selecting the texts listed here, three criteria have been used to sift works from this still modest area of research. First, the works have been chosen for their clarity of writing and novelty of presentation, exposition, or analysis, in whatever genre the authors chose to express themselves. Second, the texts offer the reader different gateways in which to explore this field further, as shown in the extensive bibliographies of each text. Last, the authors attempt a rigorous approach to research as substantiated by whatever kind of evidence they find necessary to advance their insights and ideas.

For those who are not familiar with the field of research underpinning innovation, my working definition of innovation is primarily concerned with the creation and commercialization of outputs that have economic value. This definition is in contrast to much of the research literature referred to here, which often implicitly adopts a definition where innovation is synonymous with any kind or type of social action inside organizations in general. Furthermore, this area of research can be traced to work of the economist Joseph A. Schumpeter and the sociologist Max Weber. For a review of this field see Richard Swedberg, "The tradition of economic sociology, 1800s-1960s", *Current Sociology*, 35/1 (1987).

AGRELL & GUSTAFSON offer a review of research on the psychology of innovation. The review is up to date and comprehensive in the range of organizational issues that the authors consider relevant. An evaluation of the research literature is combined with a psychoanalytic perspective, which adds up to a novel approach to the review. It does not, however, consider the economic or technical conditions under which innovation may take place.

LEONARD-BARTON presents a model that is a synthesis of research on the management of innovation, organizational behaviour, and organizational learning. Her model focuses on creating and managing distinctive core technological capabilities by understanding behavioural interactions during innovation. This is one of the first management texts on the emerging issue of knowledge management. Barton's model is illustrated with reference to an exemplary case study in the steel industry, integrated with numerous vignettes from other manufacturing firms. This book is a good example of an expository management text from the stable of the Harvard Business School. However, it requires more consistency and depth in relation to the social psychology of innovation.

BOWER's work lies firmly within the domain of management research and analyses the sociopolitical side of innovation. Bower presents a detailed model of how new capital investment projects are contrived, defended, and planned, and of who becomes involved in the decision making. Bower's approach is analytically rigorous and combines a case-study approach with a form of ethnography. This special later edition contains a helpful preface, which throws light on the background to the research, and particularly on the way in which Bower argues for the importance of combining economics with the study of human behaviour in understanding corporate strategy. Bower's approach and model have been extended and developed by Robert A. Burgelman and Leonard R. Sayles in *Inside Corporate Innovation: Strategy, Structure, and Managerial Skills* (1986) in relation to the management of research and development.

BURNS & STALKER is a classic sociological dissertation on the study of innovation inside a number of British manufacturing companies. The analysis shows how changes in the competitive environment of companies influence changes in the search for new technologies, and looks at the consequences for changes in organizational structure. A psychological dimension enters the account, in the form of the contradiction between the competition for status and the cooperation required for innovation. The case studies are described in great detail, with clarity and rigour, all of which adds to creating a persuasive argument and a model for others' research. The background chapters and bibliography also provide an important link to a much earlier literature, much of which has been forgotten, but which still influences research today. Even more enlightening is the preface to the third edition, which traces, in a critical way, the lines of sociological research on the nature, structure, and processes of industrial organization since the 1950s. Mariann Jelinek & Claudia B. Schoonhaven's *The Innovation Marathon: Lessons from High-Tech Firms* (1990) is an example of recent research that has built on the analysis of Burns & Stalker.

KANTER presents a sociological account of the sources and barriers to innovation in the case studies of ten large US manufacturing companies. Switching to a management exposition, Kanter argues that there are a number of key success factors. These factors include the development of new sets of skills, freedom of movement across functions, and rearticulation of a corporate vision for the future direction of the company. At the root of this capacity for change is the release of the spirit of the entrepreneur from the culture of the organization. Although this is a highly accessible account of innovation, it is not always clear to what extent the line of argument can be sustained with case studies which are mainly retrospective and which focus on managers.

MARTINELLI delivers a review of theoretical and empirical studies on the history, sociology, psychology, and social psychology of the role of the entrepreneur (and manager) in business, a role first propounded in economics by the French physiocrat Cantillon, and subsequently given a central position in an expository essay on innovation by the Austrian economist Schumpeter in *The Theory of Economic Development: An Inquiry into Profits, Capital, Credit, Interest, and the Business Cycle* (1934). Martinelli does not, however, consider the specific technical or economic conditions under which entrepreneurs may have to perform in different industries.

ROBERTS provides a compendium of mainly management research on the nature of high-tech business start-ups and their entrepreneurs, including social and psychological aspects. His principal concern is to examine what conditions the success of the individual entrepreneur. Not only is this work a compendium of research on innovation; it is also a manual for budding entrepreneurs, although it is placed in a US context. Furthermore, it is a useful introduction to the extensive research by Roberts and other researchers at the Massachusetts Institute of Technology on the management of high-technology businesses and innovation.

SCHÖN's thesis takes a sociological perspective on the nature of technology development, its management, and its relationship to changes in organizational structure. It is here that the role of the "product champion" in supporting the emergence of new ideas and in overcoming resistance to change is introduced and given its full exposition. This role has entered management thought and practice, as well as ramifying into research on innovation but, as Schön accepts, the concept of identity has yet to be addressed in his analysis. Schön's text is a useful gateway into his other work, which extended into developing a model of public policy.

TUSHMAN & ANDERSON present a compilation of reprinted classic papers from various well-established authors, many of whom include an organizational behaviour perspective in their research on the practicalities of managing innovation and change. There is a difference of emphasis compared to an earlier compilation of papers edited by Tushman & Moore, *Readings in the Management of Innovation* (1988). This earlier compilation is still well worth a visit for a further introduction into this field of research literature. Tushman's own work is worth investigating in its own right. It emphasizes the sociology of innovation.

WEST & FARR have prepared an exemplary compilation of authors contributing to analyses of innovation at various levels, including mining of earlier research, reviews of the psychology research literature, and cases studies of innovation. Many of these contributions put the reader in touch with much earlier research that addressed themes and issues still being pursued today, although there is room for a greater awareness of the research on the economics of technology and innovation, with which it could usefully be integrated, such as, in particular, case studies with a sociological slant of innovation inside firms and companies.

WOODWARD's sociological account of manufacturing practices inside British firms is explained in the form of a taxonomy relating organizational structure to technical complexity. The account is more intuitive than analytical, but convincing none the less. Attempts have been made to be replicate these studies, with little success. Together with Burns & Stalker, this text heralded the emergence of what is now known as "contingency theory". The second edition contains a useful review of developments in the field since 1965.

JONATHAN E. ALLTIMES

See also Enterprise culture, Entrepreneur, Innovation, economic

Input-output analysis

Carter, A.P. and A. Brody (editors), *Proceedings of the Fourth International Conference on Input-Output Techniques, Geneva, 8–12 January 1968*, vol. 1: *Contributions to Input-Output Analysis*; vol. 2: *Applications of Input-Output Analysis*, Amsterdam: North Holland, 1970

Johansen, Leif, *A Multi-Sectoral Study of Economic Growth*, Amsterdam: North Holland, 1960; 2nd edition 1974

Koopmans, Tjalling C. (editor), *Activity Analysis of Production and Allocation*, New York: Wiley, 1951

Kurz, Heinz D., Erik Dietzenbacher and Christian Lager (editors), *Input-Output Analysis*, 3 vols, Cheltenham: Elgar, 1998

Leontief, Wassily et al., *Studies in the Structure of the American Economy: Theoretical and Empirical Explorations in Input-Output Analysis*, New York: Oxford University Press, 1953

Leontief, Wassily, *Input-Output Economics*, Oxford: Oxford University Press, 1986

Miller, Ronald E. and Peter D. Blair, *Input-Output Analysis: Foundations and Extensions*, Englewood Cliffs, New Jersey: Prentice Hall, 1985

Miller, Ronald E., Karen R. Polenske and Adam Z. Rose, *Frontiers of Input-Output Analysis*, New York: Oxford University Press, 1989

Stone, Richard, *Mathematical Models of the Economy and Other Essays*, London: Chapman and Hall, 1970

Input-output analysis is an empirical tool introduced by Wassily Leontief in the late 1930s, and is designed to take account of the interdependencies of industries in the economy. Actually, the underlying idea of circular flow is much older and can be traced back to the old physiocrats and the classical economists.

The state of the art in input-output has always been presented at the occasion of national and international input-output conferences. Many volumes that collect some or all of the contributions to these conferences exist. CARTER & BRODY is a two-volume edition of selected contributions presented at the Fourth International Conference on Input-Output Techniques. Volume one contains chapters on dynamic analysis, structural change, interregional analysis, price analysis, and demographic accounting and modelling. Highlights of the volume are Leontief's article on the dynamic inverse, Carter's analysis of embodied technical change, Polenske's essay on multiregional analysis, Gigantes' reflections on input and output tables, and Stone's extension of the input-output method to the analysis of demographic structures. Volume two is devoted to accounting

and data processing: it deals with regional and interregional analysis, the stability of input-output coefficients, and forecasting methods.

One branch of input-output analysis that has already become a subject in itself is Computable General Equilibrium (CGE) analysis. Its foundation and starting point is JOHANSEN, a multisectoral study of economic growth whose statistical basis is an input-output table. The theoretical foundation of the CGE-model is the concept of short-term general equilibrium. The analysis assumes full employment of labour and capital equipment, and the two kinds of factors are taken to be perfectly mobile between sectors. Production possibilities of each sector are defined by a set of Cobb-Douglas production functions, and the distribution of income is governed by the marginal productivity principle. Consumer demand depends on disposable income and prices, while total investment is taken to be regulated by economic policy and is given from outside. The CGE model determines sectoral shares of employment of capital and labour, relative prices, and changes in production.

The input-output approach is primarily designed for empirical applicability and is therefore based on some restrictive assumptions. One of these assumptions is that a sector uses inputs in fixed proportions (given technical input-output coefficients); this defines away the problem of the choice of technique. KOOPMANS contains several articles that demonstrate that the input-output model has a greater generality than its assumptions concerning fixed coefficients might at first suggest. Given the rate of interest or the rate of profit, constant returns, a single primary factor (homogeneous labour), and no joint production, the Non-substitution Theorem holds, i.e. the (optimal) coefficients of production will, in the long-run, assume a constant value and, consequently, relative prices are independent of demand. Samuelson proves the Non-substitution Theorem using differentiable production functions. Koopmans, Arrow, and Georgescu-Roegen restate Samuelson's results within the more general framework of activity analysis.

KURZ, DIETZENBACHER & LAGER consists of three volumes containing selected articles on input-output analysis. Part I of volume one is devoted to historical roots and the foundation of input-output analysis. In Part II some important contributions to the theory and the application of dynamic input-output analysis are reprinted. Part III consists of selected articles on multiplier analysis, demographic accounting and modelling, and extended input-output models that take account of the demand for labour, the generation of income, and consumers' expenditure. Volume two contains four parts. Part I is concerned with input-output studies of energy demand and environmental models. Part II is devoted to the analysis of foreign trade and international models. Part III deals with regional and interregional input-output tables and models. Part IV is concerned with methods that recast make and use matrices into the usual form of square sector by sector matrices used in input-output analysis. Volume III contains three parts. The first of them contains papers on "structural analysis". The second part deals with price models. Part III takes account of the labour-intensive process and the various methods used in compiling, projecting, and forecasting input-output data.

LEONTIEF et al. is a comprehensive report that contains the results elaborated by the Harvard Research Project on the

Structure of the American Economy. This was established in 1948 and closed in 1972. Leontieff *et al.* deals with some important aspects of input-output analysis, with chapters on static and dynamic theory, extension of input-output techniques to interregional analysis, problems of classification and aggregation, and some more applied studies, such as analyses of the cotton textile industry or commercial air transportation in the US.

LEONTIEF is a collection of essays published by the author over a period of forty years. It contains early publications such as an essay on wages, profits, prices, and taxes published in 1947 as well as articles on multiregional and environmental input-output analysis and on dynamic modelling. It contains also some results of Leontief's investigations into the structure of American foreign trade, which found that US exports are less capital-intensive than US imports. Thus, following the Heckscher-Ohlin-Theorem, one would have to conclude that, compared to the rest of the world, the US economy is characterized by a relatively high labour (rather than capital) endowment. This finding, which contradicts the empirical fact that the US possessed, at that time, more capital per worker than any other country, was later labelled "the Leontief paradox".

MILLER & BLAIR is one of the most comprehensive English textbooks on input-output analysis. It contains chapters on the theoretical foundation of the input-output method, multiplier analysis, extensions to regional, interregional, and multiregional input-output analysis. It also discusses energy and environmental modelling, and deals with such data-related topics as the temporal stability of input-output coefficients and methods to update or project these coefficients. Two appendices, one devoted to the basics of matrix algebra and the other presenting some input-output tables for the US, complete the volume.

MILLER, POLENSKE & ROSE includes 22 essays, selected from about 200 papers given at three conferences in honour of Wassily Leontief and Walter Isard. One of the most interesting extensions of Leontief's basic model concerns the combination of large-scale macro models based on econometric estimates, and the multisectoral approach to production provided by the input-output method. Some papers that attempt to join the two methods are included in Part I of the volume. Alternative accounting frameworks are discussed in Part II. Part III is concerned with input-output multiplier analysis that does also include the generation of income and the expenditure of private households. Regional, interregional, and international models are discussed in Part IV. Input-output is always concerned with data issues such as measurement errors, data availability, sensitivity analysis, or forecasting procedures. This is accounted for in Part V of the volume. Finally, Part VI is devoted to the measurement and analysis of technological change.

STONE is a collection of the author's essays that reflects his broad interests and comprehensive contributions. Sixteen out of nineteen papers are devoted to economics and economic statistics. Not all of them deal with either one or another aspect of input-output. The first paper gives a highly simplified and condensed summary of the Cambridge Growth Model. The next two papers deal with foreign trade and the balance of payments. Reflections on consistent forecasting in multisector models and input-output projections, with special reference to price and quantity structures, are dealt with in papers IV and V. The great importance given to national accounting – six papers deal with the subject – reflect Stone's interest in these issues. The origin, development, and analytical use of national accounts are discussed in some detail. The last three papers are concerned with sociodemographic issues, and demonstrate that the input-output method also provides a useful instrument to deal with these issues.

HEINZ D. KURZ AND CHRISTIAN LAGER

Insolvency

Bailey, Edward, Hugo Groves and Cormac Smith, *Corporate Insolvency: Law and Practice*, London and Boston: Butterworth, 1992

Bhandari, J. S. and L.A. Weiss (editors), *Corporate Bankruptcy: Economic and Legal Perspectives*, Cambridge and New York: Cambridge University Press, 1996

Cooke, T.E. and Andrew Hicks, "Wrongful Trading – Predicting Insolvency", *Journal of Business Law* (July 1993): 338

McCormack, G., "Proprietary Claims and Insolvency in the Wake of Westdeutsche", *Journal of Business Law* (1997): 338

Pennington, R.R., *Pennington's Corporate Insolvency Law*, London: Butterworth, 1997

Rajak, Harry (editor), *Insolvency Law: Theory and Practice*, London: Sweet and Maxwell, 1993

Snaith, Ian, *The Law of Corporate Insolvency*, London: Waterlow, 1990

Wheeler, Sally, "Swelling the Assets for Distribution in Corporate Insolvency", *Journal of Business Law* (May 1993): 256–338

Williams, Christina and Andrew McGee, *A Company Director's Liability for Wrongful Trading*, London: Certified Accountants Educational Trust, 1992

Insolvency is a subject within legal study, which impacts significantly on many other areas of law as well as having important economic and social aspects. Historically it was regarded as no more than a part of company law, but modern scholarship has focused on two important points, namely the way in which insolvency situations bring to the fore more general legal questions, especially property rights, and the broader social consequences of business failure, of which insolvency and its procedures are merely the formal legal manifestation.

The collection of essays edited by RAJAK covers a wide range of aspects of the theory and practice of insolvency, ranging across the differing approaches of accountants, lawyers, and insolvency practitioners, and including contributions from lawyers in a number of different jurisdictions, both common law and civil law. Given the international nature of much corporate insolvency, this broad perspective makes a valuable contribution to the literature of the subject. Taken collectively, the papers emphasize the commonality of problems across many jurisdictions, coupled with a remarkable similarity in approaches to those problems. They also show

how uniformly unsuccessful have been the various attempts to impart any effective rescue culture to this area of the law. The possible weakness of the collection is that, being based on a conference, it offers no synthesis of the differing points of view. Although the collection is now some years old, the discussion of principles contained in many of the essays remains a very valuable resource.

BHANDARI & WEISS have put together a collection of essays that spans a variety of approaches to insolvency law. Some are concerned with technical legal questions, whereas others look at insolvency in a broader economic and social context.

PENNINGTON seeks to provide a thorough exposition of the principles underlying the law of corporate insolvency. For him insolvency is as much as anything a part of company law, the task of the liquidator and the court being simply to bury the corpse of the dead company as decently and as equitably as possible. In carrying out this process due regard must be had to the law of personal and real property, as filtered through the mesh of the *pari passu* principle. He is rather inclined to see recent developments, which impose potential personal liabilities on directors of failed companies, as at best a diversion from the real work of insolvency law and at worst an unjustified allocation of necessarily scarce resources.

SNAITH sets out to expound the relevant legal principles, giving less attention to procedural issues than do some other writers in this area. He primarily conceives the legal issues in terms of the enforcement or attempted enforcement of security rights, recognizing that, in practice, by the time this is done there is usually little or nothing left for unsecured creditors. He does not give significant attention to the questions of corporate rescue, preferring to start his examination at the point where rescue attempts are seen to have failed.

BAILEY, GROVES & SMITH provide another early evaluation of the 1986 legislation from the point of view of practitioners active in this area. They show the complexity of the legislation as well as the underlying conceptual clarity of the new rules.

McCORMACK's article is a response to an important judicial decision in another area – unjust enrichment. He examines the implication of this decision in relation to the passing of property in *ultra vires* contracts made by local authorities, mistaken payments and void contracts more generally, tracing claims, the *scintilla temporis* doctrine in relation to the passing of property, and the use of the remedial constructive trust as a way of enabling creditors to jump the queue in insolvency situations. All these proprietary issues are of importance in insolvency situations, and the author demonstrates the ways in which the decision may affect the development of the law of insolvency.

COOKE & HICKS look at one of the most contentious features of modern insolvency law – the use of the wrongful trading doctrine as a way of making directors of failed companies personally liable. They examine the ways in which directors of struggling companies can become more accurate in predicting whether their company will survive and thus can decide whether or not to continue trading.

WHEELER is also concerned with issues of wrongful trading, but her focus is on the difficulties of making the wrongful trading legislation work properly.

WILLIAMS McGEE were among the first to conduct empirical research on the effects of the new wrongful trading legislation after it came into force in 1988. Their work with lawyers, accountants, insolvency practitioners, and bankers identified the major practical difficulties – lack of funding to bring the action, lack of incentive for creditors to support the action, the reluctance of the courts to impose liability, and the relative unlikelihood of defendants having worthwhile funds against which recovery could be pursued.

ANDREW McGEE

See also Bankruptcy law

Instability

Alba, Pedro, Amar Bhattacharya, Stijn Claessens, Swati Ghosh and Leonardo Hernandez, "Volatility and Contagion in a Financially-Integrated World: Lessons from East Asia's Recent Experience", World Bank Working Paper, 2008 (December 1998)

Corbridge, Stuart, Ron Martin and Nigel Thrift (editors), *Money, Power, and Space*, Oxford and Cambridge, Massachusetts: Blackwell, 1994

Dymski, Gary and Robert Pollin (editors), *New Perspectives in Monetary Macroeconomics: Explorations in the Tradition of Hyman P. Minsky*, Ann Arbor: University of Michigan Press, 1994

Fisher, Irving, "The Debt-Deflation Theory of Great Depressions", *Econometrica*, 1 (1933): 337–57

Grabel, Ilene, *Rejecting Exceptionalism: Reinterpreting the Asian Financial Crisis*, Sydney: Centre for Japanese Economic Studies, Macquarie University, 1999 (CJES Research Papers no. 99–1)

Hubbard, R. Glenn (editor), *Financial Markets and Financial Crises*, Chicago: University of Chicago Press, 1991

Kaminsky, Graciela L. and Serio L. Schmukler, "What Triggers Market Jitters: A Chronicle of the Asian Crisis", Washington, DC: Board of Governors of the Federal Reserve System, 1999 (International Finance Discussion Paper no.1999–634)

Koop, Gary and Simon M. Potter, "Are Apparent Findings of Nonlinearity Due to Structural Instability in Economic Time Series?", New York: Federal Reserve Bank of New York, 1999 (Staff Report Number 59)

Kregel, Jan, "Yes, 'It' Did Happen Again: A Minsky Crisis Happened in Asia", Jerome Levy Economics Institute, 1998 (Working Paper no. 234)

Mankiw, N. Gregory, "The Allocation of Credit and Financial Collapse" in *New Keynesian Economics*, vol. 1, edited by N. Gregory Mankiw and David Romer, Cambridge, Massachusetts: MIT Press, 1991

Minsky, Hyman P., *Stabilizing the Unstable Economy*, New Haven, Connecticut: Yale University Press, 1986

Mishkin, Frederic, "The Causes and Propagation of Financial Instability: Lessons for Policymakers" in *Maintaining Financial Stability in a Global Economy: A Symposium*, Kansas City: Federal Reserve Bank, 1997

Rosser, J. Barkley, "On the Complexities of Complex Economic Dynamics", *Journal of Economic Perspectives*, 13/4 (Fall 1999): 169–92

The pervasive and plastic term "instability" might describe anything in economic theory from market entry and exit in individual industries to fluctuations in financial markets and macroeconomic indicators. This entry reviews the literature on financial and macroeconomic instability and ignores microeconomic instability.

FISHER's landmark paper on the interaction of real-sector and financial collapse in the Great Depression due to contagion effects and market interlinkages defined literally the entire scope of inquiry in this field. It remains a crucial paper because of its careful descriptive analysis of debt-deflation processes.

Descriptive analysis of the sort Fisher embodied has been set aside in much contemporary research in favour of a focus on the root analytical causes of instability. Many contemporary theorists have taken on the challenge of explaining how financial-market and macroeconomic instability can arise when agents are rational. Typical papers here are MISHKIN and the edited volume by HUBBARD. Mishkin, for example, blames interest-rate increases, deteriorating bank balance sheets, stock-market declines, and increases in uncertainty for the foreign-exchange and banking crises observed in recent years. In his view, as in the papers in Hubbard, the fundamental task of lenders in financial markets is to reduce moral hazard and adverse selection problems in their borrower pool. MANKIW is the most celebrated rational-agent paper interpreting financial crisis in an asymmetric-information context; this article describes how a financial market "collapses" – in the sense that lenders cease to extend credit – due to an exogenous interest-rate shift that substantially increases repayment risk.

In these theorists' approach, macroeconomic and structural stability is a precondition for financial stability; but financial-market processes are not inherently unstable. Exogenous shocks of the sort listed by Mishkin reduce lenders' capacity to overcome information asymmetries and to induce good borrower behaviour, leading to a higher incidence of bad loans and ultimately to banking crises. The focus is on how credit markets propagate shocks, not how they might generate shocks. The emergence of financial crisis under sound structural conditions then constitutes a paradox in this framework: how would rational agents knowingly put themselves into a situation so detrimental to their own welfare?

MINSKY takes a very different approach to financial-market processes: he regards them as inherently unstable. Minsky argues that financial instability emerges endogenously in the macroeconomic cycle, due to the transformation of economic units' balance sheets from robust to fragile and overextended balance sheets. Minsky does not assume that agents are irrational; rather, he assumes that they become increasingly reckless and forgetful of past disasters as an expansionary period lengthens. Minsky has spurred an outpouring of research, especially by post-Keynesian economists; DYMSKI & POLLIN contains a number of significant theoretical and empirical papers extending Minsky's ideas. The papers collected here suggest some additional sources of apparently "irrational"

individual behaviour, including coercive competitive processes in financial markets and the fundamentally uncertain nature of the economic environment.

While Minsky emphasizes microeconomic behavioural factors over the cycle as the source of instability, other theorists have explored the possibility that instability is rooted in the structural features of the economy as it develops over time or in space. Some researchers have used mathematical complexity theory to formalize this idea. ROSSER presents a cogent overview of this sprawling literature, comparing and contrasting the various permutations of complexity theory, including chaos theory and catastrophe theory. Rosser's wide-ranging essay also demonstrates the large number of microeconomic and macroeconomic problems to which complexity theoretic models have been, and can be, applied.

The idea that structural complexity endogenously generates instability is hardly the proprietary domain of mathematically oriented social scientists. Political economists, geographers, and others have rooted their investigations of complexity in dense institutional and historical investigations. CORBRIDGE, MARTIN & THRIFT offer work in this tradition, with an emphasis on how power differentials permeate and define contemporary financial structures.

The vastly different approaches to the analytical causes of instability are paralleled by a variety of different empirical approaches. KOOP & POTTER show that empirical findings of structural breaks in macroeconomic time-series data could be due instead to nonlinear generating functions, and vice versa. Empirical issues such as these are difficult or impossible to resolve because of the low frequency of many time series. Econometricians have developed methods for resolving these ambiguities using high-frequency (for example, daily stock-market) data; but lower frequency data series are often too short to permit the use of these methods.

The Asian financial crisis of the late 1990s has forced economists using the rational-agent approach to broaden their thinking, as this crisis affected some economies with sound and stable structural conditions. These economists have now allowed for contagion effects and for difficulty in recognizing or reacting to fundamentals; KAMINSKY & SCHMUKLER provide a cogent discussion of these new trends. Still, the basic posture of rational-agent-oriented economists remains that the market mechanisms in question must be somehow flawed: Kaminsky & Schmukler conclude that the Asian crisis must be due in part to how markets receive and process "news". In another representative rational-agent explanation, ALBA *et al.* attribute the depth and breadth of the Asian crisis to both flawed government policies and banking regulations in the affected countries, and to spillovers from other countries. That is, process news better or regulate better and avoid another Asian crisis.

This line of research has drawn strong challenges from economists working in the Minskian and post-Keynesian traditions. GRABEL, for example, argues that far from being anomalous, the Asian crisis constitutes yet another illustration of how instability arises endogenously in the contemporary global economy, in which underregulated cross-border lending flows often generate higher repayment obligations than developing-country borrowers can afford (either economically or politically). KREGEL has applied Minsky's framework most directly and effectively to the Asian crisis. His papers, the research of his colleagues at the United Nations Commission for Trade and Development (UNCTAD), and the work of other post-Keynesians, taken together, marshal substantial empirical and institutional evidence for the importance of endogenous instability in the contemporary world.

GARY A. DYMSKI

See also Asian crisis, Economic crises, Financial fragility

Institutional economics

Furubotn, Eirik G. and Rudolf Richter, *Institutions in Economic Theory: The Contribution of the New Institutional Economics*, Ann Arbor: University of Michigan Press, 1997

Hodgson, Geoffrey M., *Economics and Institutions: A Manifesto for a Modern Institutional Economics*, Cambridge: Polity Press, and Philadelphia: University of Pennsylvania Press, 1988

Hodgson, Geoffrey M. (editors), *The Economics of Institutions*, Aldershot, Hampshire: Elgar, 1993

Hodgson, Geoffrey M., Warren J. Samuels and Marc R. Tool (editors), *Elgar Companion to Institutional and Evolutionary Economics*, Aldershot, Hampshire: Elgar, 1994

North, Douglass C., *Institutions, Institutional Change and Economic Performance*, Cambridge and New York: Cambridge University Press, 1990

Rutherford, Malcolm, *Institutions in Economics: The Old and the New Institutionalism*, Cambridge and New York: Cambridge University Press, 1994

Samuels, Warren J. (editor), *Institutional Economics*, 3 vols, Aldershot, Hampshire: Elgar, 1988

Searle, John R., *The Construction of Social Reality*, London: Allen Lane, and New York: Free Press, 1995

Williamson, Oliver E., *Markets and Hierarchies, Analysis and Anti-Trust Implications: A Study in the Economics of Internal Organization*, New York: Free Press, 1975

The term "institutional economics" includes both the "old" institutional economics of Thorstein Veblen, John Commons, Wesley Mitchell, and others, and the "new" institutional economics of Ronald Coase, Douglass North, Mancur Olson, Oliver Williamson, and many more.

RUTHERFORD gives a good and relatively extensive summary of some of the most important ideas involved in both of these traditions, and explores the similarities and differences between the "old" and "new" institutionalism. The thrust of his argument is to suggest the existence of much common ground. However, Rutherford does not examine the philosophical underpinnings in sufficient depth and, as a result, the essence of the distinction between the "old" and "new" institutionalism is not made sufficiently clear. He fails to identify the adoption of ontological and methodological individualism – involving the assumption that the individual can be taken as given – as the key defining characteristic of the "new" institutionalism. The "old" institutionalists all agreed that individuals are partly formed by institutions just as institutions result from individual behaviour. Nevertheless, Rutherford's work is the nearest thing to a modern conceptual overview of both types of institutional economics.

Other attempts to compile ideas found in both institutional approaches include the anthology of influential articles on the subject, edited by HODGSON (1993). This collection includes works by Robert Axelrod, Paul Bush, Giovanni Dosi, Jon Elster, Alexander Field, Walton Hamilton, Philip Mirowski, Ugo Pagano, Viktor Vanberg, William Waller, Ulrich Witt, and others. This book attempts to introduce the reader to the key concepts and problems, and concentrates on the more recent contributions.

The three-volume anthology edited by SAMUELS fulfils a complementary role but differs in some respects. First, it concentrates on the "old" institutionalism. Second, it brings in earlier as well as recent key articles written within the intellectual tradition of the "old" institutionalists. It includes works by Clarence Ayres, John Commons, Morris Copeland, Robert Gordon, Allan Gruchy, Walton Hamilton, K.W. Kapp, Philip Mirowski, Wesley Mitchell, Yngve Ramstad, Malcolm Rutherford, Warren Samuels, Marc Tool, Donald Walker, Edwin Witte, and others. It is a very good introduction to the ideas and controversies within the "old" institutional economics.

HODGSON, SAMUELS & TOOL is a two-volume, encyclopaedic treatment of both the "old" and the "new" institutional economics, and it contains works by many authors. It provides the reader with a fairly comprehensive reference work. It also explores the links between institutional economics and various "evolutionary" approaches to economics, promoted by, for example Thorstein Veblen, Joseph Schumpeter, Richard Nelson, and Sidney Winter.

FURUBOTN & RICHTER provide an overview of the "new" institutional economics, but without much attention to the "old" variety. The work includes lucid discussions of property rights theory and transaction cost economics. The exposition is generally clear and helpful, and the book is an excellent introduction to this literature. Each chapter ends with useful recommendations for further reading. A flaw of the book – in addition to its neglect of the "old" institutional economics – is that the authors do not spend much time considering modern, alternative explanations of institutional phenomena, outside the transaction cost paradigm. Furthermore, some of its key definitions are questionable or inadequate.

WILLIAMSON is a pioneering monograph. It is written from the perspective of the "new institutional economics" and within this volume that phrase is coined for the first time. Williamson's primary achievement is to develop the transaction cost theory of the firm as originally formulated by Ronald Coase. The main argument is that different types of organization, including the firm, emerge and survive as a result of their capacity to reduce the cost of formulating, negotiating, and policing contracts between economic actors. Williamson's work has been criticized for its claim that competition always tends to select the most efficient form of economic organization. In modern scholarship the transaction cost approach is now rivalled by the "capabilities" or "competence-based" theory of the firm, as developed by Edith Penrose, David Teece, and others.

NORTH is an interesting and widely cited book. In contrast with the earlier works of this Nobel-prizewinning economic historian, this book incorporates an understanding of path dependence. North thus recognizes that institutional outcomes depend on their past evolution and only partly on competitive selection. Accordingly, competitive selection does not always lead to optimal outcomes. The recognition that what exists, even in a competitive economy, may not be the most efficient, is an important point of contrast with the work of Williamson and others working within the framework of the "new" institutional economics. Furthermore, in this and other works, North explores in some depth the ideological influences on the purposes and attitudes of individuals. Unlike many "new" institutionalists, North does not always take the individual as given. In some respects his work is a bridge between the "new" and the "old" institutional economics.

HODGSON (1988) is an attempt to update the "old" institutional economics in a modern setting. It not only includes a critique of the individualistic and rationalistic assumptions of mainstream economics and of the "new" institutionalism, but also a discussion of the key institutions of the firm and the market. However, it does not attempt to provide a comprehensive and systematic theory for the "old" institutionalism. It is more of a ground-clearing exercise.

The philosophical foundations of a developing institutionalist perspective might usefully build on SEARLE's extremely clear and well-written volume. This is one of the best conceptual analyses of the nature of institutions and of how they function in a socioeconomic context. The main problem with this work is that it fails to make links with the literature in either the "new" or the "old" institutional economics, despite extensive discussions of particular economic phenomena such as money.

Overall, the literature on institutional economics is fascinating and extensive. Yet in vital places it is patchy and incomplete. No adequate history of the "old" or the "new" institutional economics has yet been written. The "old" institutionalism is often wrongly charged as being antitheoretical. However, despite the falseness of this accusation, there is no systematic outline of its approach to social theory or economic science.

GEOFFREY HODGSON

See also Institutions, New institutionalism, Thorstein Veblen

Institutionalism in international relations theory

Brown, Michael E. *et al.* (editors), *Theories of War and Peace: An International Security Reader*, Cambridge, Massachusetts: MIT Press, 1998

Duffield, John S., *Power Rules: The Evolution of NATO's Conventional Force Posture*, Stanford, California: Stanford University Press, 1995

Haas, Peter M., Robert O. Keohane and Marc A. Levy (editors), *Institutions for the Earth: Sources of Effective International Environmental Protection*, Cambridge, Massachusetts: MIT Press, 1993

Keohane, Robert O., *International Institutions and State Power: Essays in International Relations Theory*, Boulder, Colorado: Westview Press, 1989

Keohane, Robert O., Joseph S. Nye and Stanley Hoffmann (editors), *After the Cold War: International Institutions and State Strategies in Europe, 1989–1991*, Cambridge, Massachusetts: Harvard University Press, 1993

March, James G. and Johan P. Olsen, "The Institutional Dynamics of International Political Orders", *International Organization*, 52/4 (1998): 943–70

Martin, Lisa L., *Coercive Cooperation: Explaining Multilateral Economic Sanctions*, Princeton, New Jersey: Princeton University Press, 1992

Mitchell, Ronald B., *Intentional Oil Pollution at Sea: Environmental Policy and Treaty Compliance*, Cambridge, Massachusetts: MIT Press, 1994

In international relations theory, scholars adopting an institutionalist perspective hold that international institutions – formal organizations, regimes, and conventions – can affect state behaviour and can have a significant independent effect on international outcomes. Thus they reject realism's view of institutions as epiphenomenal. On the other hand, different strands of institutionalism lay emphasis on different mechanism through which institutions are supposed to be effective. Recent work has attempted to elaborate and test systematically this old approach to international politics.

MARCH & OLSEN's article provides a good introduction to recent theoretical debates on international institutions. They develop a fourfold division of perspectives on the character of international institutions, based on the intersection of two criteria. The first issue concerns the basic logic by which human action is interpreted. Human action can be seen as driven by expectations of consequences, and politics is accordingly seen as aggregating individual preferences into collective actions by some procedure of bargaining, coalition formation, and exchange; or it can be seen as following rules that associate particular identities to particular situations, and politics is about identity rather than just about interests. The second issue concerns historical efficiency. History can be seen as leading to a unique equilibrium dictated by exogeneously determined interests and resources; or it can be seen as inefficient and characterized by path dependencies, multiple equilibria, and endogenous transformations of interests and resources. These divisions produce an interesting typology of approaches to international institutions: functional rationality; functional institutionalism; history-dependent rationality; and history-dependent institutionalism.

KEOHANE's collection includes essays elaborating his own extremely influential version of institutionalism. Among them is his International Studies Association presidential address, entitled "international institutions: two approaches". He contrasts two research programmes concerned with international institutions, which he calls "rationalistic" and "reflective". Rationalistic theories see institutions as affecting pattern of costs of state actors with given preferences, for example, by reducing uncertainty and altering transaction costs. Reflective theories see institutions as shaping the identities, preferences, and resources of the actors that created them in the first place. Keohane defends the rationalistic research programme from the charge that it ignores the endogenous dynamic of preference formation by pointing out that no theory is complete and that by reducing complexity rationalistic theories have reached important results.

The contributors to the outstanding volume edited by HAAS, KEOHANE & LEVY, on environmental institutions, ask whether and how international institutions can be effective in protecting the environment. Seven environmental problems are examined: stratospheric ozone depletion, acid rain, pollution of the Baltic and North Seas, intentional oil pollution from tankers, management of fisheries, misuse of farm chemicals, and overpopulation. The detailed case studies focus on the impact of international institutions on the three requirements for effective problem solving: the stimulation of governmental concern (agenda setting), the provision of a favourable environment for agreements (international policy formulation), and the improvement of national political and administrative capacities for implementing the international norms (national policy responses). The cumulative findings are strengthened by the fact that all studies employ the same analytical framework, and each author attempts a hypothetical counterfactual analysis: what would have happened to the problem in absence of the international institution? The overall finding is that institutions can also be successful without enforcement powers, and a remarkable final chapter offers recommendations for improving the effectiveness of international environmental institutions.

Another strong empirical case for the institutionalist perspective in the economic/environmental domain is provided by MITCHELL. He carefully evaluates the international regime controlling intentional oil pollution, which aims at reducing the discharges of waste oil by tankers after they deliver their cargoes. He examines two different compliance systems established by international treaties since the late 1970s, and finds that one of them has been considerably more effective than the other. Since the two "subregimes" regulated similar behaviour of the same nations over the same time period, this case study supports the institutionalist contention that power and interest alone cannot explain behaviour in international relations. More specifically, Mitchell's insightful analysis shows that one "subregime" was successful because it allowed for greater transparency, increased the likelihood of responding forcefully to violations, built on existing institutions, and prevented actors from violating regulations rather than merely deterring them from doing so.

Critics sometimes concede that institutionalism may have some relevance for "low politics" issues like environmental protection, but that it lacks explanatory power in "high politics" domains such as military security. The volume edited by KEOHANE, NYE & HOFFMANN takes up this challenge and examines how, during the crucial years 1989–91, European institutional configurations affected the strategies of state leaders and vice versa in a variety of domains. Perceptive case studies deal with the constraints and policies of the major powers (Germany, the Soviet Union, the US, France, and Britain) and with developments in specific issue areas (trade, financial assistance, foreign direct investment, environmental policies, and military security). The overall picture emerging from the case studies is that the existence of international institutions had a strong effect on the governments' reactions to the end of the Cold War in Europe. Specifically, international institutions allowed powerful states to exercise influence, constrained bargaining strategies, helped in balancing against other institutions, facilitated the signalling of governments' intentions, specified obligations allowing anticipatory adaptation, and sometimes influenced the fundamental preferences of state leaders.

The effect of international institutions on security affairs is also the subject of DUFFIELD's study. In this rich historical overview of NATO's conventional force posture from 1949 to 1989, he aims at explaining why that posture was remarkably stable form the early 1960s to the late 1980s. Duffield shows that structural factors, such as the evolving balance of power vis-à-vis the Soviet bloc and the divergences among the major members of the alliance, are not sufficient to explain the evolution of NATO's conventional force posture, and in particular its stability over time. These factors must be supplemented by a third perspective, which emphasizes the development of institutional norms and rules that prevent changes unless a very strong change in the structural environment occurs. Duffield argues that each of the three perspectives (balance of power politics, intra-alliance politics, and institutionalism) is necessary to explain some specific aspect of the evolution of NATO's force posture, and explores the conditions under which the factors emphasized by each of the theories were particularly influential.

MARTIN employs an interesting multi-method approach in order to show that the involvement of international organizations in the imposition of economic sanctions produces high levels of cooperation among states. Drawing on game theory, she develops a typology of "cooperation problems" that may arise in situations involving economic sanctions. A statistical analysis on 99 cases of economic sanctions shows a robust correlation between the involvement of international organizations and level of cooperation attained. In addition, Martin examines four cases in depth: US sanctions against Latin American countries over human rights in the 1970s, UK sanctions against Argentina during the Falklands War, Western controls on high-technology exports to the Soviet Union, and 1982 sanctions against the Soviet Union and Poland. The case studies support the results of statistical analysis and show the operation of causal mechanisms: international organizations foster cooperation mainly by reducing fears of cheating and by facilitating tactical issue linkages.

The collection edited by BROWN et al. includes the contributions to an important debate on international institutions that appeared in the journal International Security. John Mearsheimer mounts a comprehensive attack against what he considers the three main contemporary variants of institutionalism (liberal institutionalism, collective security, and critical theory), showing their alleged theoretical flaws and the lack of empirical support for the proposition that international institutions affect state behaviour. Prominent exponents of the three perspectives respond to the criticisms.

MATHIAS KOENIG-ARCHIBUGI

See also International relations theory, Liberalism in International relations theory

Institutions

Chandler, Alfred Dupont, *Scale and Scope: The Dynamics of Industrial Capitalism*, Cambridge, Massachusetts: Harvard University Press, 1990

Chataway, Joanna and Alan Thomas et al., *TU872 Institutional Development: Conflicts, Values and Meanings*, Milton Keynes: Open University, 1998

Commons, John R., *Institutional Economics: Its Place in Political Economy*, New Brunswick, New Jersey: Transaction, 1990 (original edition 1934)

Hodgson, Geoffrey M., *Economics and Institutions: A Manifesto for a Modern Institutional Economics*, Cambridge: Polity Press, 1988

March, James G., and Johan P. Olsen, *Rediscovering Institutions: The Organizational Basis of Politics*, New York: Free Press, 1989

North, Douglass C., *Institutions, Institutional Change and Economic Performance*, Cambridge and New York: Cambridge University Press, 1990

Ostrom, Elinor, *Governing the Commons: The Evolution of Institutions for Collective Action*, Cambridge: Cambridge University Press, 1990

Rutherford, Malcolm, *Institutions and Economics: The Old and the New Institutionalism*, Cambridge and New York: Cambridge University Press, 1994

There is increasing interest, in the social science literature, in the role of institutions in capitalist economies. This has lead to a reassessment of the work of COMMONS. The contemporary relevance of his work is considerable. The introduction to the Transactions edition of this work, by Malcolm Rutherford, correctly dispels two myths about the founder of institutional economics, namely that his approach was descriptive and lacked theory, and that the book was obscure and unintelligible. This is a book that requires close reading but is worth struggling with for the enormous insight it offers the reader into the workings of modern capitalist economies. Commons recognized the multiplicity of meanings attributable to the word "institution". An institution can be seen metaphorically as a framework of laws and natural rights with individuals constrained in action, the behaviour of these individuals, a dynamic, a process, an activity, a mass action, managing change or control. To find a universal approach to institutional behaviour, Commons suggested defining an institution as: "Collective action in control, liberation and expansion of individual action".

The units of individual action that brought together law, economics, and ethics and involved conflict, dependence, and order were the transaction, the alienation, and acquisition of rights. Three interdependent types of transactions – bargaining, managerial, and rationing – constituted the going concern that was considered analogous to an organism in biology. This going concern was kept together by working rules, enforced by collective action.

An intelligent comparison of two traditions, the "old" and the "new", in institutionalist thought, is undertaken by RUTHERFORD. The strengths and weaknesses of both traditions are outlined, and more fruitful lines of enquiry suggested. This is a full treatment of the problems associated with incorporating institutions, here broadly defined, into economic theory. The most important lesson to be learned, after reading this work, is that it is unhelpful to draw sharp distinctions between schools of economic thought. The issues and problems presented for analysis are far too complex and challenging for any one theory to provide satisfactory answers to them, and an interdisciplinary approach is thus preferable.

HODGSON has written an excellent work of modern scholarship providing a sophisticated contribution to the study of institutions. He recognizes the cracks in the theoretical framework and assumptions of orthodox economics, and argues for the inclusion of a theory of cognition and culture. By taking individual preferences as given, economic theorists have ignored both cognitive processes and the social and institutional forces operating through and interacting with these processes. These forces govern individual desires and actions. Distinctions have, he suggests, to be made between sense data, information, and knowledge: these concepts are not independent of the beliefs, concepts, or theories of the observer. Institutions are not simply organizational structures but, as the sociologist Talcott Parsons emphasized, normative patterns defining actions and relationships. The writer thus dissents from orthodoxy, stressing inertia, routines and habits, and the emancipatory possibilities for institutional change through deliberative purposeful action.

A clear and readable introduction about how to integrate institutions into economic theory and history is offered by NORTH, who provides an outline theory of institutions and institutional change. An explanation is offered as to why some economies stagnate and others grow in terms of the evolution of their institutional frameworks. The focus is on the problem of human cooperation and how this allows or prevents economies from realizing the gains from trade. Institutions are social constructions reducing uncertainty, structuring incentives, and moulding human interaction. A theoretical framework is applied to the interrelationship between institutional evolution and political and economic organization, using examples from history.

In OSTROM, institutional analysis is applied in an examination of the different ways of governing common resources. Ostrom reflects on three models: the tragedy of the commons, the prisoner's dilemma game, and the logic of collective action, in order to assess whether and how common resources can be organized to avoid overconsumption and excessive costs. Case studies of communal tenure in meadows and forests, irrigation, and fisheries, support her argument that neither privatization nor enforcement by external authorities are solutions to the problem. If answers to problems of supply, credibility, and monitoring can be found, institutions of self-government offer the best solution.

CHANDLER provides a rich and thorough empirical contribution to the literature on institutional change. The emergence of a new economic institution, the managerial business enterprise, is the focus of this extensive study. To build and run the railway and telegraph systems in the late 19th century, huge investments were necessary. This encouraged the separation of control from ownership. Operational decisions came to be made by salaried managers, and this new type of capitalist institution provided a core dynamic, the result of increasing organizational abilities, for economic growth and transformation. The collective histories of the largest 200 industrial enterprises in the US, where a system of competitive managerial capitalism came to predominate, the UK, where personal capitalism persisted, and Germany, where a cooperative managerial capitalism evolved, are compared and analysed, and general conclusions are derived. A review is undertaken of the impact of the financial, educational, and legal institutions on these enterprises. The role of economies of scale and the importance of three types of interrelated investments, production, distribution, and management are analysed, and there is a focus on how internal decision-making processes produced patterns of institutional change. Although this study does not attempt to look at the wider impact of the managerial enterprise on the polity or society, it does provide the reader with an internal history of the important institution of managerial capitalism.

In CHATAWAY et al., a postgraduate course on institutional development, the importance for development practitioners of questioning concepts and arriving at a working definition of the terms "institution" and "institutional development" are emphasized. The course explores the major areas of debate concerning institutions of "good governance" and institutions "designed" to reduce poverty and promote growth. In development management, as in economic theory, institutions matter. They are the hubs around which development revolves. To carry out development interventions the complexity of multi-actor institutional environments needs to be understood, and one of the three institutional forms – competition, coordination, or cooperation – adopted.

MARCH & OLSEN, in a plea for the reintroduction of institutions into political theory, argue that ideas that embedded morality in institutions emphasizing citizenship and community have been replaced by a moral individualism that concentrates on bargaining between conflicting interests. This replacement theory, emerging in the 1950s, was contextual, reductionist, utilitarian, instrumentalist, and functionalist. They argue that a political theory focusing on institutions is preferable. The focus of this book is on the ways political institutions operate, order life processes and influence change. Political actors are seen not to be making self-interested calculated choices, but to be affected by institutional duties and roles. Routines, roles, and institutional forms evolve in a dynamic process that is dependent on an historical context. The writers reject conventional political theory, claiming that it describes reality poorly. Institutions, seen as interrelated rules and routines defining appropriate behaviour in relation to roles and situations, are found to be essential to any realistic political theory.

H. LYLE MITCHELL

See also Institutional economics, New institutionalism

Insurance

Arnould, Joseph, *Arnould's Law of Marine Insurance and Average*, 17th edition, edited by Jonathan C.B. Gilman and Michael J. Mustill, London: Stevens, 1997 (original edition 1848)
Bennett, Howard N., *The Law of Marine Insurance*, Oxford: Clarendon Press, 1996

Birds, John, *Modern Insurance Law*, 4th edition, London: Sweet and Maxwell, 1997
Clarke, Malcolm A., *The Law of Insurance Contracts*, 3rd edition, London: Lloyd's of London Press, 1997a
Clarke, Malcolm A., *Policies and Perceptions of Insurance: An Introduction to Insurance Law*, Oxford: Clarendon Press, and New York: Oxford University Press, 1997b
Hodgin, R.W., *Insurance Law: Text and Materials*, London: Cavendish, 1998
Legh-Jones, Nicholas (editor), *MacGillivray on Insurance Law: Relating to All Risks Other than Marine*, 9th edition, London: Sweet and Maxwell, 1997
McGee, Andrew, *The Law and Practice of Life Assurance Contracts*, London: Sweet and Maxwell, 1995
McGee, Andrew, *The Single Market in Insurance: Breaking down the Barriers*, Aldershot, Hampshire: Ashgate, 1998
Surridge, Robert J. et al., *Houseman and Davies Law of Life Assurance*, 11th edition, London: Butterworths, 1994

MacGillivray on Insurance Law (LEGH-JONES) is well established as the leading text in insurance law. It is voluminous and detailed and is regularly updated. Its emphasis is on insurance contract law as a technical subject, and within this it concentrates primarily on the decisions of the English courts – other Commonwealth authorities and the decisions of US courts being given no more than a secondary role. It scarcely touches on the regulation of insurance and does not deal at all with the broader social issues in relation to insurance. The book draws additional strength from being edited largely by practising lawyers and can be recommended to those concerned with the detailed practice of insurance law.

CLARKE's (1997a) *The Law of Insurance Contracts* is a monumental work of scholarship, taking the major areas of insurance contract law and reviewing them from the point of view of all the principal case law in the common-law world. This approach gives it a broader scope than, for example, *MacGillivray*, and leads to the discussion of many issues that are ignored elsewhere in the English literature. The author does not feel himself obliged to come to any conclusions on the many questions that he discusses, which allows more room for interesting speculation, while possibly reducing the value of the book from the point of view of the practising insurance lawyer.

McGEE (1995) has written a book that deals with an important area of insurance, namely life business. This is an area where traditional principles of insurance are now overlaid with significant statutory regulation, and the interrelationship between the two is fully analysed. The book also derives strength by addressing issues arising from the increasing relevance to personal life assurance policies of the various Ombudsman schemes that have been set up in recent years.

SURRIDGE et al. is a well-established text in the law of life assurance. It was originally written for use by those working in the legal departments of insurance companies, and traces of this can still be seen in the most recent edition. The book is especially good in its treatment of the use of life assurance policies as tax planning devices, but is less strong in its discussion of difficult points of law, where it tends to eschew detailed analysis of the difficulties in favour of forthright statements of the answer to the question.

BIRDS is well regarded as the leading student text. It offers a very clear exposition of the major aspects of the subject, including some attention to the regulatory questions. Within the constraints of length and pitch dictated by its intended market, it does a good job of introducing the student to the principal difficulties and controversies within insurance law.

CLARKE's (1997b) *Policies and Principles of Insurance* is an attempt to approach the writing of a student text from a different point of view. Clarke, as is usual in his work, tries to look at the legal rules in a broader context than merely that of English law. He also tries to go beyond the traditional taxonomy of the subject and to relate different parts of it in unusual ways. Clarke's work is always interesting and erudite, but it may be doubted whether the average student will find the book as accessible as Birds'.

HODGIN has produced the first attempt in modern times at a collection of text and materials in relation to insurance. The great advantage of such works is that they make some primary materials readily available to students. The usual disadvantage is that the materials are extracted rather than reproduced in full, with the result that readers are subject to the author's views about which are the important parts of the material. The work also suffers from the inevitable tendency of such collections to be reactive to case law rather than having any coherent approach to the theoretical issues. Within these limitations, however, this book provides a clear account of the traditional view of the subject.

Marine insurance has traditionally been treated as a discrete aspect of insurance contract law, principally because of the existence of the Marine Insurance Act 1906. This classification is increasingly suspect in view of the growing tendency of the courts to treat that Act, which formally applies only to marine insurance, as at least a powerful guide in resolving issues of general principle in non-marine insurance. Despite this, both ARNOULD and BENNETT are restricted in their coverage to marine risks. There is, of course, no doubt that marine policies do raise a number of specialized issues which are not encountered in other branches of insurance, and both books tend to concentrate on these aspects of their subject. Arnould is well established as the leading practitioner text on marine insurance. It is detailed, meticulous, and authoritative but, as with many such works, it concentrates on detail rather than on principle. Bennett's work is intended as a student text, and is lucidly written, though perhaps with a slight tendency to become bogged down in detail.

The European dimension of both insurance contract law and insurance regulation has only recently begun to receive significant attention, despite the growing importance of this area as an aspect of the single European market. McGEE (1998) concentrates on the regulatory aspects of the single market, the contractual side being still no more than embryonic. The author demonstrates the importance of financial services in the single market, and makes a powerful case for much closer legislative and political integration as an essential element in the completion of the single market.

ANDREW McGEE

Insurance, economics

Akerlof, G., "The Market for Lemons: Quality Uncertainty and the Market Mechanism", *Quarterly Journal of Economics*, 89 (1970): 488–500

Anscombe F. and R. Aumann, "A Definition of Subjective Probability", *Annals of Mathematical Statistics*, 34 (1963): 199–205

Arrow, Kenneth J., *Essays in the Theory of Risk-Bearing*, Amsterdam: North Holland, 1970; Chicago: Markham, 1971

Gravelle, Hugh and Ray Rees, *Microeconomics*, 2nd edition, London and New York: Longman, 1992

Herstein, I. and J. Milnor, "An Axiomatic Approach to Measurable Utility", *Econometrica*, 21 (1953): 291–97

Machina, M., "Expected Utility Analysis without the Independence Axiom", *Econometrica*, 50 (1982): 77–323

Pratt, J., "Risk Aversion in the Small and in the Large", *Econometrica*, 32 (1964): 122–36

Rothschild, M. and J. Stiglitz, "Equilibrium in Competitive Insurance Markets: An Essay on the Economics of Imperfect Information", *Quarterly Journal of Economics*, 80 (1976): 629–49

Spence A. Michael, *Market Signaling: Informational Transfer in Hiring and Related Screening Processes*, Cambridge, Massachusetts: Harvard University Press, 1974

Von Neumann, John and Oskar Morgenstern, *Theory of Games and Economic Behavior*, Princeton, New Jersey: Princeton University Press 1944; 3rd edition 1953

AKERLOF analyses the problem that most insurers face when they propose uniform contracts to all customers. When the customer is not perfectly informed about the characteristics of the good she is going to buy, her natural reaction will just be to drive her reservation price down in response to doubts about the good's quality. Similarly, an insurance company (or a bank) might raise its premium in response to imperfect knowledge about the riskiness of its customers. Sadly, rather than leading to quality (or riskiness) being correctly revealed in the final market, this problem will typically lead to low-quality (high-risk) deals being incorrectly selected by the company. "Adverse selection" then takes place because low reservation prices (or high premiums) will attract low-quality sellers (or high-risk customers) – exactly the ones who should have been ruled out in the first place. It is not only "adverse selection" of bad deals that takes place as a result of asymmetric information. "Hidden action" (leading to "moral hazard") might well happen, because the insurance company is not able to monitor the behaviour of insured people at all times. Since the most natural *ex post* strategy of insured people is to reasonably take higher risks than those they have declared they would have taken at the time of signing the contract, the insurance company will face a "moral hazard" problem as a consequence.

ANSCOMBE & AUMANN provide an interesting contribution on probability theory, which is at the core of insurance theory in economics. From statistical theory, we know that probability may be viewed from several different standpoints. For instance, a classical definition of probability follows the so-called "frequentist" approach, according to which probability asymptotically tends to the frequency with which a given event takes place (as opposed to alternative events). However, modern statistical theory has sometimes rejected frequentist probability on the grounds that subjective factors should also be allowed for, and these are not always consistent with the frequency distribution of a given event. For instance, the probability attached to tomorrow being a sunny day depends on genuinely subjective expectations, as well as on the time series of already observed weather figures and on the weather forecast for tomorrow. The "subjective" component of probability processes is obviously the most difficult one to capture (and model) for statisticians, actuarial mathematicians, and insurers.

ARROW discusses the basic features of the theory of risk bearing. When an individual prefers the expected value of a lottery to actually "playing" the lottery *ex post*, she is said to be "risk averse". A consumer may also be "risk loving", in which case she prefers a lottery (to be actually played) to its *ex ante* expected value in cash (with 100 per cent attached probability). It is very convenient to have a quantitative measure of risk aversion. Mathematically, the more "concave" the expected utility function, the more risk averse is the consumer. In terms of calculus, risk aversion may be measured by computing the second derivative of the expected utility function. The absolute-value ratio of the second to the first derivative of the expected utility function gives an idea of the "shape" of the expected-utility contour, and thus of the individual's (absolute) attitude towards risk. Risk-aversion measures have been developed along the seminal path of Arrow and Pratt. There is also a difference between absolute and relative risk aversion. Attitudes towards risk are obviously crucial to insurance theory, in that insurance contracts will depend upon them. In fact, insurance contracts exist simply because the vast majority of people are characterized by risk aversion. Risk is therefore hedged via insurance contracts, which pass through risk on to the insurer versus payment of a certain sum (premium). By so doing, risk-averse parties trade an uncertain expenditure for a certain one, and prefer paying premiums in order to buy cover against random losses.

GRAVELLE & REES put forward a comprehensive treatment of expected utility and insurance economics in their microeconomics textbook. Insurance theory is treated according to different viewpoints, from pure expected utility theory to applied topics such as optimal cover purchase, "fair" versus "unfair" premiums, insurance policies as opposed to financial types of risk hedging, and so on. Among graduate microeconomics textbooks, the one by Gravelle & Rees is undoubtedly the most useful reference when it comes to the treatment of uncertainty. For instance, a detailed analysis of the demand for optimal cover is carried out. The authors show that the "optimal cover" equilibrium outcome crucially depends on the assumption that the individual seeking coverage cannot influence the probability of the "covered loss" taking place. Suppose event X gives rise to a financial loss, which is the matter of the insurance contract. If the individual's actions do affect the probability of financial loss, the insurance firm might only offer partial (less than 100 per cent) cover, so that the individual will still have a minimal incentive to take reasonable risks. This microeconomics textbook also discusses

advanced models of "adverse selection" and "moral hazard", which represent typical problems faced by ill-informed insurance companies *vis-à-vis* insured parties (an "asymmetric information" issue).

HERSTEIN & MILNOR discuss expected utility in depth, starting from the seminal contribution of VON NEUMANN & MORGENSTERN. Many choices made by individuals take place under states of uncertainty. The authors discuss how to derive a unique expected utility function from a set of theoretically infinite monotonic transformations of a probability-weighted utility relationship. Under some hypotheses it is possible to find a particular monotonic transformation of the utility function that has the properties of both (a) uniqueness and (b) additive separability. Uniqueness is required for the expected utility function to reflect preferences and probability univocally. Additive separability is required in order to clearly distinguish across different states of the world, and comes as a direct consequence of linearity in probabilities. Once again, it is worth emphasizing the theory of expected utility in an economic treatment of insurance, since the rationale for insurance originates from the existence of uncertainty in individual utility functions. Actually "realised" utility depends on different states of the world and attached (subjective) probabilities of each state taking place *ex post* (so-called "state-contingent" utility).

MACHINA provides a discussion of recent work on generalizations of expected utility theory, with applications to subjective probability and insurance theory. An aspect of expected utility theory – and uncertainty more generally – that is crucial to insurance theory is the dependence of payoffs upon different states of the world. The usefulness of a good often depends on the circumstances, or "states of nature", in which it becomes available (and is used). An umbrella on a rainy day is literally not the same good – from a microeconomic point of view – as an umbrella on a sunny day (in which case, it can even be a "bad"). By the same token, insuring a good for an insurance company may not be the same thing under different states of the world. Insuring an individual depends on how, where, and when she lives and works, who she is, and so on. Insuring the same good belonging to the same person under different states of nature need not appear to be the same business from the insurer's point of view. The author discusses advanced topics in expected utility theory, including limit cases, paradoxes, and inter-related (or statistically inter-dependent) events. Expected utility with inter-related states of nature is a complex matter that defines the "state of the art" in uncertainty economics.

Von Neumann & Morgenstern made a pioneering contribution to mathematical economics first, and then to its application to utility and game theory. By setting up a structure of preferences and payoffs, the two authors introduce the possibility of varying payoff levels in response to changes in external scenarios. Thus, *ex ante* randomization across a set of possible outcomes takes place. It is worth noticing that introducing the concept of "expected utility" also led the authors to define a set of possible strategies in response to alternative "realised" events. This is consistent with the concept of "non-cooperative" games. In fact, von Neumann & Morgenstern are today renowned not only for their seminal contribution to uncertainty and expected utility in economics, but also for their pioneering treatment of game theory. The relevance of this to insurance theory rests with the use of game theory in modelling insurance decisions. The insurance game may be viewed as a principal–agent relationship in which the insurer and the insured play under asymmetric information circumstances, thus implying more complex equilibria than standard, full-information Nash equilibria.

PRATT is one of the main contributors to the theory of risk. Pratt and Arrow's risk aversion coefficients are the ones most commonly used in microeconomic uncertainty theory. Pratt's contributions on risk aversion are crucial to insurance theory because he rightly emphasizes the variability of risk aversion according to the peculiar features of each economic agent. For instance, it might be assumed that large organizations are globally less risk-averse than individuals, as the former are able to hedge and/or diversify risk more effectively as a result of size-related advantages. It might also be claimed that particular categories of organizations (for example, publicly versus privately owned firms) react to the same amount of risk in a different fashion. Pratt discusses different degrees of risk aversion in depth.

ROTHSCHILD & STIGLITZ discuss the close relationship between insurance markets and imperfect information. Equilibrium in insurance markets is affected by the presence of asymmetric information jamming the signals that an efficient market should send and receive (through prices). The variables that convey signals to an insurance market are (a) price of policies (premium) and (b) probability of loss. The two variables are obviously interrelated. Under a zero-profit condition for the insurance firm, a "fair" insurance premium would exactly equal the monetary value of the probability of loss. However, policy premiums do not usually appear to be actuarially "fair" even when the insurance company is not allowed to make supernormal profits. This happens because insurers react to imperfect information by trying to select the best deals via higher insurance premiums. Sadly, in the presence of hidden action (moral hazard), this is often counterproductive in that higher premiums select riskier individuals, similarly to the way in which banks react to hidden action by increasing interest rates on loans (as pointed out by Stiglitz and Weiss in a famous paper on credit rationing). The outcome is generally a suboptimal supply of insurance coupled with higher-than-optimal premiums and lower-than-optimal quality/quantity of insured people (high-quality demand "quits the game").

SPENCE is a seminal paper on signalling. Under asymmetric information circumstances, people will try to "signal" their true nature by undertaking particular courses of action that may "distinguish" them from the "average tendency". The job market suffers from asymmetric information because, *ex ante*, firms do not know the level of effort and ability that an individual is likely to be putting into the business once hired. However, individuals may "signal" their ability and willingness to work prior to being hired by embarking on demanding training courses, postgraduate programmes, and the like. In a similar fashion, insured people may "signal" their degree of riskiness (in order to be granted a fair insurance contract) by committing to binding courses of action that reduce their exposure to risk (for example giving up dangerous jobs, risky trips, and the like). Signalling in insurance markets is crucial

because it can modify equilibrium strategies, hopefully by pushing the market towards Pareto-improving price-quantity combinations.

GIAN CARLO SCARSI

See also Game theory

Intellectual capital

Bassi, Laurie J. and Mark E. van Buren, "Sharpening the Edge: The 1999 ASTD State of Industry Report", *Training and Development*, 1/53 (January 1999): 23

Brooking, Annie, *Intellectual Capital*, London and New York: International Thomson Business Press, 1996

Edvinsson, Leif and Michael S. Malone, *Intellectual Capital: Realizing Your Company's True Value by Finding Its Hidden Brainpower*, New York: Harper, 1997

Fruin, W. Mark, *Knowledge Works: Managing Intellectual Capital at Toshiba*, Oxford and New York: Oxford University Press, 1997

Greco, JoAnn, "Knowledge Is Power", *Journal of Business Strategy*, 20/2 (March/April 1999): 18–22

Imparato, Nicholas, *Capital in Our Time: The Economic, Legal and Management Challenges of Intellectual Capital*, Stanford, California: Hoover Institution Press, 1999

Knight, Daniel J., "Performance Measures for Increasing Intellectual Capital", *Strategy and Leadership*, 2/27, (March 1999): 22ff.

Kwiatkowski, Stefan and Leif Edvinsson (editors), *Knowledge Café for Intellectual Entrepreneurship*, Warsaw: Leon Kozminski Academy of Entrepreneurship and Management, 1999

Miller, Marlane, "Leveraging Your Hardwired Intellectual Capital", *Strategy and Leadership*, 2/27 (March 1999): 28

Skyrme, David J. and Debra M. Amidon, "New Measures of Success", *Journal of Business Strategy*, 19/1 (January/February 1998): 20–24

Stewart, Thomas A., "Brainpower: How Intellectual Capital is Becoming America's Most Valuable Asset", *Fortune*, (June 1991): 44

Stewart, Thomas A., *Intellectual Capital: The New Wealth of Organizations*, New York: Doubleday, 1997

GRECO's short article raises the issue of how companies acquire, store, and retrieve "knowledge". Greco suggests that recent downsizing of middle managers had the result of propelling organizations toward a better understanding and appreciation of middle management roles particularly their role as information or knowledge repositories. Greco describes Dow Chemical's effort to mine their 30,000 patents, Sears' strategy of questioning customers, and Hewlett-Packard's intranet to manage knowledge.

MILLER describes a system developed to describe how people think. The article briefly describes a new tool, the BrainStyle Inventory Center for Creative Leadership based in Greensboro NC. A key principle in the BrainStyles approach is that people tend to have one core strength (of four defined) that does not change. However, by knowing one's BrainStyle one can leverage one's strength. The article presents a case study of Research Polymers International and how David Cherry implemented a strategy to save the firm from bankruptcy using the BrainStyles approach to create a team-based, intellectual capital-generating organization.

KNIGHT, a management consultant, offers an article that attempts to present a new framework for measuring performance. Some of his declarations are not new: that "intellectual capital is the sum of a company's intangible assets" and that goodwill is the recognition of a firm's future extraordinary profit potential that arises from the growth of intellectual capital. However, his article is useful in suggesting three levels of a framework for building knowledge-based organization. Level one is market value. Level two involves creating a "virtuous cycle" in which investments in human capital result in more competent and capable people to develop better structural capital for an organization. Level three is performance measurement, which Knight explains involves performance indicators that are generic and can be used by almost any organization.

BASSI & VAN BUREN summarizes a report on an annual survey conducted by the American Society for Training and Development. Eight hundred and one organizations, both profit and non-profit, participated in the survey in 1998. Interesting results included the finding that firms are spending as much as ten times more per employee on information technologies as they are on training! Among other findings was that, compared with previous surveys, firms are increasing the amount of spending on training, and the proportion of employees receiving training increased. The selection of the sample – those firms that voluntarily join the organization's benchmarking service – precludes making conclusions on the extent or nature of training among industries or something missing within the US. However, the study does give useful insights into the amount of money spent on training, and types of training offered that should be useful to those in the training industry.

KWIATKOWSKI & EDVINSSON is a collection of commentaries on intellectual capital related to entrepreneurship. This collection of provocative articles should be regarded as a pioneering discussion of intellectual capital and entrepreneurship. Contributors include management scholars and entrepreneurs. The book was prepared in advance of the first world conference on Intellectual Entrepreneurship held at Nieborow Palace in Poland in March 1999. The short essays explore various aspects of intellectual capital as they relate to the creation of new enterprises and new wealth. One of Kwiatkowski's articles traces the history of the development of the term "intellectual entrepreneurship" and the struggle towards an operational definition. Kwiatkowski's other article provides short case studies of "intellectual entrepreneurs". In separate articles, Renuta Gut and Tadeusz Jacewicz share their experience as entrepreneurs who created businesses from intellectual capital. Charles R.B. Stowe looks at implications of intellectual capital for venture capitalists. His other article offers ideas on how business schools should adopt pedagogy to create "intellectual capitalists" – those capable of creating and managing in an information age.

Thomas Stewart, an American, who is on the board of editors of *Fortune* magazine, was one of the first American journalists to popularize the term "intellectual capital" in the US. STEWART (1997) is directed at corporate managers. He offers very specific advice on how to discover and map the human capital, structural capital, and customer capital that embody the knowledge assets of a corporation, and how intellectual capital can free up financial resources to dramatically increase a firm's profitability. Written in a pleasant journalistic style, the book offers hundreds of specific examples of innovative strategies used to enhance both personal and corporate intellectual assets. This book draws on Leif Edvinsson's work at Skandia for its theoretical basis and for specific examples of how that firm implemented its management strategy to enhance the firm's intellectual capital and profitability. Though less poetic than Edvinsson, Stewart thoroughly explores practical aspects of intellectual capital including the impact of the information age on corporate hierarchy – "how technology destroyed the hierarchy . . . expertise not position determines power . . .", the new economics of information, the role of knowledge managers, and the impact of the information age on careers. Stewart's book and the Edvinsson book are the major works on intellectual capital.

In EDVINSSON & MALONE, Leif Edvinsson as Corporate Director of Intellectual Capital at Skandia AFS is clearly the subject matter expert on intellectual capital while Malone is a professional journalist/writer. This book reveals Skandia's approach to intellectual capital and includes a detailed discussion of the Skandia "navigator" – their management tool to measure and improve the firm's intellectual capital. Some readers will find the treatment highly theoretical and mentally tiring to read, but this book is not meant to amuse but to explore a work in progress. They discuss Skandia's intellectual capital financial report, which reveals their early attempts at measurement of intellectual capital. The system is far from perfected, but the discussion of its implications on the firm has profound implications for corporate managers.

BROOKING, written from a management consultant and artificial intelligence perspective, defines components of intellectual capital as market assets, human-centred assets, intellectual property assets, and infrastructure assets. Each subsequent chapter provides an "audit" system that includes a discussion of methods for evaluating such assets and suggestions on strategies to enhance a firm's intellectual capital assets. The text offers a very pragmatic approach with its checklists, flowcharts, and sets of questions. Chapter nine, "intellectual capital management" presents a flowchart outlining the process of managing intellectual capital, which includes identification, development, audit, documentation, protection, growth, and dissemination elaborated more fully in later chapters. A very useful text on conducting management audits of intellectual capital.

SKYRME & AMIDON's article describes several methods for measuring intellectual capital including the Skandia navigator, economic value added (EVA), and the inclusive valuation methodology (trade mark by Philip M'Pherson emeritus professor of systems engineering and management at the City University in London).

FRUIN's book is drawn on a five year study plus one year of personal observation of the 60-year-old Tokyo-based Yanagicho Works (one of Toshiba's 27 domestic Japanese factories) and the author's extensive experience in studying Japanese business. This is an exploration of intellectual capital from direct observation of one Japanese manufacturing firm. While the detailed description of intellectual capital and knowledge management strategies within one Japanese company offers useful insight on one company's approach, it is uncertain that all Japanese companies practice "knowledge works". Nor is it possible to conclude that non-Japanese manufacturing companies do not use similar strategies. The value of this work lies not in drawing conclusions about the nature of Japanese management or culture, but in describing the strategies the author observed at Toshiba.

Nicholas Imparto is a professor of marketing and management at the University of San Francisco's McLaren School of Business and a research fellow at the Hoover Institution at Stanford University. One of the more interesting perspectives IMPARATO offers is the question of how much change can customers absorb? Is there a threat from change overload?

STEWART's (1991) front page feature article in *Fortune* was the precursor of his book (STEWART 1997) but also inspired many American scholars and business writers to address the issue of intellectual capital. What makes this article so convincing is Stewart's ample use of examples and quotes drawn from many interviews of American firms and executives who applied innovative ideas to their products, services, manufacturing, or procedures to gain market share and increase profitability. This article is absolutely critical for any researcher tracing the development of intellectual capital as a concept in the American context.

Charles R. Stowe

Intellectual property rights

Aoki, Keith, "Authors, Inventors and Trademark Owners: Private Intellectual Property and the Public Domain", *Columbia–VLA Journal of Law and the Arts*, parts 1–2, 18/1–2 (1993/94): 1–74 and 18/3–4 (1993/94): 191–267

Bainbridge, David I., *Intellectual Property*, 4th edition, London: Financial Times Management, 1999

Cornish, W.R., *Intellectual Property: Patents, Copyright, Trade Marks, and Allied Rights*, 4th edition, London: Sweet and Maxwell, 1999

D'Amato, Anthony and Doris Estelle Long (editors), *International Intellectual Property Law*, London and Boston: Kluwer, 1997

Drahos, Peter, *A Philosophy of Intellectual Property*, Aldershot, Hampshire: Dartmouth, 1996

Drahos, Peter (editor), *Intellectual Property*, Aldershot, Hampshire: Dartmouth, 1999

Firth, Alison, Shelley Lane and Yvonne Smyth (editors), *Readings in Intellectual Property*, London: Sweet and Maxwell, 1998

International Chamber of Commerce, *Intellectual Property and International Trade: A Guide to the Uruguay Round TRIPs Agreement*, Paris: ICC Publishing, 1996

Phillips, Jeremy and Alison Firth, *Introduction to Intellectual Property Law*, 3rd edition, London: Butterworths, 1995

World Intellectual Property Organization, *Intellectual Property Reading Material*, revised edition, Geneva: WIPO, 1998

Intellectual property law includes the core areas of copyright, designs, patents, confidential information, and trademarks. Often described as "intangible property rights", intellectual property rights differ from rights in tangible property, such as land or goods, in that they exist to protect the manifestations of human creativity. From the substantial body of literature dealing with intellectual property in general and with specific types of intellectual property, this list (a) focuses mainly on general accounts and works that represent the diversity of the subject and (b) aims to offer something of interest to readers at different levels of experience.

There are a number of undergraduate textbooks that provide a useful starting point. PHILLIPS & FIRTH is an entertainingly written and engaging introduction to intellectual property and is ideal for those new to the subject. Basic concepts are clearly explained and illustrated and the book is an effective blend of academic analysis and practical information. A revised edition is forthcoming. BAINBRIDGE covers the core areas of intellectual property in more detail and gives particular attention to the interplay between intellectual property rights and new technology, including the Internet. There is an introduction that addresses basic principles of intellectual property and attempts to draw together common elements underlying individual rights.

The WORLD INTELLECTUAL PROPERTY ORGANIZATION (WIPO) is one of the United Nations' specialized agencies and deals with intellectual property on a global scale. Its publication is essentially an introduction to the subject with suggested readings. The book explains the major types of intellectual property rights and their enforcement and introduces the reader to the multifaceted role of intellectual property in international development. There are useful sections on the administration and teaching of intellectual property, technological developments affecting intellectual property, and international treaties and conventions. The work is limited in that readings are confined to WIPO documents, but this is nevertheless an extremely informative overview of the field. A slightly expanded version of this work is also available under the title *Introduction to Intellectual Property: Theory and Practice*, published in 1997.

CORNISH is widely regarded as the authoritative account of intellectual property rights and the historical and socioeconomic factors that have influenced their development. The book is scholarly and closely argued and may present some difficulties for nonlawyers, being best suited to academics and students already familiar with the law. Cornish offers a comprehensive discussion of the nature of specific intellectual property rights as well as an analysis of common themes and principles.

FIRTH, LANE & SMYTH is a selection of key articles from two major European intellectual property journals: *European Intellectual Property Review* and *Entertainment Law Review*. The work covers copyright and designs, passing off, trademarks, patents, and confidential information. General aspects of intellectual property and remedies are also represented. For those without easy access to these journals, the work is an invaluable resource.

DRAHOS (1996) takes an interdisciplinary approach to intellectual property rights and for this reason his work will appeal to philosophers, political scientists, economists, and sociologists, as well as lawyers. He argues for a rejection of the proprietarian approach to intellectual property and its replacement by an instrumentalist approach, exchanging the traditional language of property rights for the language of monopoly privileges, whose grant would be tied to the notion of duty. The book assumes some prior theoretical knowledge and is in this sense not for the inexperienced; at the same time it is an intellectually stimulating and groundbreaking work.

AOKI's two-part article explores the controversial view that the advent of intellectual property rights has brought about the withdrawal of increasing amounts of material from the public domain. Drawing on the earlier work of writers such as Boyle and Jaszi, he analyses the concepts of authorship, originality, creativity, and invention as evidenced in US copyright, patent, and trademark law. Aoki argues that the pervasive notion of "author" has been employed to confer private proprietary rights, which exclude other valuable forms of cultural production, curb the free flow of socially beneficial information, and are at odds with the stated goals of the intellectual property system.

DRAHOS (1999) brings together a collection of previously published articles by different authors on economic, political, and philosophical aspects of intellectual property rights. The collection is grouped by discipline and is a useful compilation of major critical articles on various theoretical aspects of intellectual property. There is a substantial introduction that analyses the state of theory in intellectual property.

Intellectual property rights are assuming an increasingly significant role in the international market place. The INTERNATIONAL CHAMBER OF COMMERCE's (ICC's) publication is a guide to the Agreement on Trade Related Aspects of Intellectual Property Rights (TRIPs), written for the business and legal community. As well as outlining the background to the negotiations and the structure and content of TRIPs, the work includes separate chapters by authors from the corporate and legal sectors on specific intellectual property rights and their protection under TRIPs. The text of the agreement is also included. More detailed analysis can be found in Michael Blakeney's *Trade Related Aspects of Intellectual Property Rights* (1996) and Daniel Gervais's *The TRIPs Agreement: Drafting and Analysis* (1998).

D'AMATO & LONG assembles contributions from various authors on the theory of international intellectual property law. Overall the work constitutes a thought-provoking analysis of the nature of intellectual property rights and the theories underpinning their protection. The book is particularly useful for its treatment of issues such as the interrelationship between intellectual property and the protection of cultural patrimony and the protection of authorship as a cultural value. A substantial appendix includes the text of major international treaties and conventions.

ELLEN GREDLEY

See also Chinese intellectual property law, Copyright

Intelligence

Ceci, Stephen J., *On Intelligence – More or Less: A Bio-ecological Treatise on Intellectual Development*, Englewood Cliffs, New Jersey: Prentice Hall, 1990; expanded edition, Cambridge, Massachusetts: Harvard University Press, 1996

Gardner, Howard, *Frames of Mind: The Theory of Multiple Intelligences*, London: Heinemann, 1984; New York: Basic Books, 1985; 2nd edition, London: Fontana, and New York: Basic Books, 1993

Gould, Stephen Jay, *The Mismeasure of Man*, New York: Norton, 1981; revised edition, New York: Norton, 1996; London: Penguin, 1997

Herrnstein, Richard J. and Charles Murray, *The Bell Curve: Intelligence and Class Structure in American Life*, New York: Free Press, 1994; London: Simon and Schuster, 1996

Howe, Michael J.A., *IQ in Question: The Truth about Intelligence*, London and Thousand Oaks, California: Sage, 1997

Jensen, Arthur R., *The g Factor: The Science of Mental Ability*, Westport, Connecticut: Praeger, 1998

Mackintosh, N.J., *IQ and Human Intelligence*, Oxford and New York: Oxford University Press, 1998

Nash, Roy, *Intelligence and Realism: A Materialist Critique of IQ*, London: Macmillan, and New York: St Martin's Press, 1990

Sternberg, Robert J., *Beyond IQ: A Triarchic Theory of Human Intelligence*, Cambridge and New York: Cambridge University Press, 1985

The traditional approach to intelligence and its assessment was initiated by psychologists such as Alfred Binet and Charles Spearman at the beginning of the 20th century. That approach is kept alive by JENSEN. He agrees with Spearman that the outcome of applying factor analysis to indicators of individuals' performance at mental feats is to identify a common factor that can be regarded as a kind of core intelligence.

HERRNSTEIN & MURRAY also favour the traditional approach. They claim that intelligence is a largely fixed and unchangeable quality. Consequently, they believe, attempts to increase intelligence in people with low mental abilities are unlikely to be successful. These authors are concerned about the possible future burgeoning of an underclass made up of people whose restricted abilities make them ill-equipped for success in a complex modern society.

GOULD is severely critical of much early research into intelligence, arguing that the belief that intelligence is largely fixed is ill founded. He identifies numerous defects in the research studies and many abuses of mental testing. Gould demonstrates that researchers' biases and prejudices, particularly in relation to racial differences, have contaminated a number of investigations.

GARDNER argues that the concept of a single general intelligence is unhelpful. He claims that it makes better sense to regard individuals as possessing a number of relatively separate intelligences. These relate to various spheres of activity, including language, spatial control and awareness, social competence, science and mathematics, and music. Gardner believes that his insights have strong implications for education. He urges that children should be encouraged to excel at tasks based upon those varieties of intelligence with which they are innately (in his view) most strongly endowed.

STERNBERG, in common with Gardner, sees intelligence as taking a number of distinct forms. This perspective helps to account for the fact that people differ not only in their overall level of intelligence but in the kinds of mental challenges at which they are most likely to succeed. Sternberg considers that the extent to which a person can act intelligently depends to a considerable degree upon the knowledge that individual has acquired, as a consequence of that person's experiences.

CECI, like Sternberg, regards knowledge and mental skills as being interdependent. He points to evidence demonstrating that intelligence levels are far from being the fixed or unchanging quantities that the traditional approach assumes them to be. Ceci also shows that performance at tasks that depend on mental skills can be strongly affected by the particular context in which a task is presented. He cites findings indicating that the apparently superior thinking and reasoning displayed by people in advanced nations compared with "primitive" men and women may be largely a product of differences between societies in the cultural knowledge they instil.

HOWE regards the concept of intelligence as one that is useful for describing the differences between people in their accomplishments, but less helpful for accounting for how those differences arise. He disputes the common belief that the presence of a distinct quality of intelligence is what makes people intelligent, arguing that the actual reasons for some people being more intelligent than others are numerous and complex. Howe is also critical of intelligence testing. He suggests that the extent to which intelligence test scores provide predictors of individuals' future success is rarely sufficient to justify their use as practical selection devices.

NASH raises fundamental queries about intelligence, and even takes issue with the rarely challenged assumption that a psychological construct such as intelligence is actually measurable. He points out that true measurement is only possible in conjunction with variables that, unlike intelligence, have been clearly and unambiguously defined.

MACKINTOSH provides a thoughtful and balanced survey of the contrasting views and perspectives on intelligence. His book gives the reader a clear and well-informed introduction to most of the important issues.

MIKE HOWE

Interest rates

Alexander, Gordon J., William F. Sharpe and Jeffery V. Bailey, *Fundamentals of Investments*, 2nd edition, Englewood Cliffs, New Jersey: Prentice Hall, 1993

Anderson, Nicola, Francis Breedon, Mark Deacon, Andrew Derry and Gareth Murphy, *Estimating and Interpreting the Yield Curve*, Chichester and New York: Wiley, 1996

Bakshi, Gurdip and Zhiwu Chen, "Inflation, Asset Prices and the Term Structure of Interest Rates in Monetary Economies", *Review of Financial Studies*, 9/1 (1996): 241–75

Cox, John, Jonathan Ingersoll and Stephen Ross, "A Theory of the Term Structure of Interest Rates", *Econometrica*, 53 (1985): 385–407

Fisher, Irving, *The Rate of Interest: Its Nature, Determination, and Relation to Economic Phenomena*, New York: Macmillan, 1907

Fisher, Irving, *The Theory of Interest as Determined by Impatience to Spend Income and Opportunity to Invest It*, New York: Macmillan, 1930; reprinted Fairfield, New Jersey: Kelley, 1986

Heath, David, Robert Jarrow and Andrew Morton, "Bond Pricing and the Term Structure of Interest Rates: A New Methodology for Contingent Claims Evaluation", *Econometrica*, 60 (1992): 77–105

Homer, Sidney and Richard Sylla, *A History of Interest Rates*, 3rd edition, New Brunswick, New Jersey: Rutgers University Press, 1991

Lutz, Friedrich A., *The Theory of Interest*, Dordrecht: Reidel, and Chicago: Aldine, 1967

Schaefer, Stephen, "Taxes and Security Market Equilibrium" in *Financial Economics: Essays in Honor of Paul Cootner*, edited by William F. Sharpe, Englewood Cliffs, New Jersey: Prentice Hall, 1982

Vasicek, Oldrich, "An Equilibrium Characterization of the Term Structure", *Journal of Financial Economics*, 5 (1977): 177–88

HOMER & SYLLA provide a comprehensive history of interest rates from 3000 bc to 1989. They chart the parallel geographical and financial history of money, loans, and interest rates from prehistoric times, through Mesopotamia, Greece, and Rome, to Eastern Europe in medieval times and to Europe and America in modern times. Almost one half of the study is devoted to the 20th century and to the Western economies, and includes many useful tables of annual data on interest rates applying to a wide variety of loans.

FISHER (1930) is the classic reference on the determination of interest rates and continues to reward newcomers to the literature. His theory is based upon the fundamental concept of "time preference", which refers to the inclination that individuals naturally possess to receive a certain cash sum now rather than wait until some future date. To induce saving, an appropriate rate of exchange between cash now and cash in the future has to be offered, and that rate of exchange determines the interest rate on the savings. LUTZ provides a critical survey of the major contributors to the literature up to that date on the determination of interest rates within real (that is, without money) economies.

Using Fisher's (1930) formalization of a dynamic economy and interest compounding, Lutz provides a tour of the literature on the "term structure" of interest rates. This seeks to explain the relationship between default-free loans that differ in only their time to maturity. What has become known as the "expectations theory" views interest rates for long-term loans as (geometric) averages of interest rates for short-term loans. With perfect foresight the rate of return over two years must equal the rate of return from rolling over two one-year loans. Under uncertainty, the theory maintains that the two-year rate of return equals the expected return from rolling over two one-year loans, as the one-year rate in one-year's time is unknown today. Interest-rate data continue to provide competing evidence regarding the expectations information embedded in the term structure, and Lutz reviews early, largely behavioural, theories offered to explain this.

COX, INGERSOLL & ROSS present the first general economic equilibrium model of (real) term structure of interest rate determination under uncertainty. Unlike models that preceded it, this model provides a formal treatment of both the risk and the (expected) return from interest rate based investments. Although the expectations theory recognizes the uncertainty involved in rolling over two one-year investments, it does not provide the investor with any compensation for taking on that risk, and foregoing the safe two-year investment that generates the same return. The Cox, Ingersoll & Ross model explicitly recognizes that the difference between longer and shorter term interest rates will contain both an expectations component and compensation for risk. ANDERSON et al. provide an excellent review of this model and other more recent contributions to this area of the literature.

FISHER (1907) drew attention to the difference between nominal and real interest rates: the former being intertemporal rates of exchange in money terms, the latter being intertemporal rates of exchange in terms of goods and services (real terms). The "Fisher relation", as it has become known, states that nominal rates of return must equal real rates of return plus the inflation rate expected over the same time period. As the construction of monetary economic models is far more complex than that required for models of the real economy alone, the development of these models has taken small and gradual steps. Thus, in many monetary economic models of the determination of asset prices, inflation, and (short) interest rates, the term structure is often not included. By contrast, those financial economic models that consider the difference between the real and nominal term structures have tended to do so in a partial equilibrium setting.

BAKSHI & CHEN draw contrasts between these two approaches to interest-rate determination and provide the first attempt to integrate them. They develop a complete monetary model of asset prices, inflation and the term structure of interest rates where there are both monetary and real (productive market uncertainties). An implication of the Fisher (1907) relation is that nominal interest rates are influenced by both real uncertainties and inflation uncertainties, such that the nominal and real interest rate term structures can never be independent of each other. Bakshi & Chen demonstrate that it is also possible for real (productive) uncertainties to have offsetting effects in the real term structure and inflation, so generating a nominal term structure that is completely unaffected by shock in the real economy.

In addition to the general equilibrium models of the term structure of interest rates, there is another branch of literature, starting with VASICEK, considering partial equilibrium models. These models, surveyed in Anderson et al., begin within an assumed model of interest-rate behaviour, such as the changes in a short-term interest rate, and derive the term structure of interest rates using no-arbitrage requirements. The advantage of this class of models over the general equilibrium models is that they can be used to model either the term structure of nominal or real interest rates, although some of the models, including that of Vasicek, which do not exclude

negative interest rates, are naturally suited to real interest rates.

A disadvantage of both the general and partial equilibrium models is that the term structure is an output rather than an input of the model. In well-functioning capital markets, it is possible to observe the term structure of interest rates, in addition to the behaviour of short-term interest rates and other, economic, variables. HEATH, JARROW & MORTON have developed a model of the behaviour of the term structure that takes the current term structure as the starting point and uses no-arbitrage conditions to determine its potential future course as a whole. This kind of model is particularly important for pricing complicated financial products, such as interest-rate options and futures contracts, whose value depends on both the currently observed interest-rate term structure and its future path. These models are not, however, equilibrium models of the determination of the current term structure, although it may be possible to embed them within one.

The term structure of interest rates may be observed directly in the markets for interest-rate-based financial products, or may be derived from them using mathematical approximation techniques. A critical survey of the competing methods for estimating the term structure of interest rates can be found in Anderson et al.

In addition to the maturity of the loan, interest rates may also reflect the risk that the borrower may default on the payments of interest or principal (the repayment of the loaned amount), and the tax treatment of these payments. SCHAEFER provides a thorough analysis of the distortions within the term structure that can be introduced if investors face differential tax rates, and ALEXANDER et al., provide extensive treatment of the impact of default on interest rates.

JAMES STEELEY

International debt crisis

Aggarwal, Vinod, Debt Games: Strategic Interaction in International Debt Rescheduling, Cambridge and New York: Cambridge University Press, 1996

Calvo, Guillermo, Morris Goldstein and Eduard Hochreiter, Private Capital Flows to Emerging Markets after the Mexican Crisis, Washington, DC: Institute for International Economics, 1996

Cline, William, International Debt and the Stability of the World Economy, Washington, DC: Institute for International Economics, 1984

Cline, William, International Debt Reexamined, Washington, DC: Institute for International Economics, 1996

Darity, William Jr and Bobbie L. Horn, The Loan Pushers: The Role of Commercial Banks in the International Debt Crisis, Cambridge, Massachusetts: Ballinger, 1988

Eaton, Jonathan and Lance Taylor, "Developing Country Finance and Debt," Journal of Development Economics, 22/1 (1986): 209–65

Goldstein, Morris and Carmen Reinhart, Forecasting Financial Crises: Early Warning Signals for Emerging Markets, Washington, DC: Institute for International Economics, 1996

Kindleberger, Charles P., *Manias, Panics, and Crashes: A History of Financial Crises*, 3rd edition, New York: Wiley, 1996

Kregel, Jan, "Yes, 'It' Did Happen Again: A Minsky Crisis Happened in Asia", *Jerome Levy Economics Institute Working Paper*, 234 (April 1998)

Sachs, Jeffrey (editor), *Developing Country Debt and the World Economy*, Chicago: University of Chicago Press, 1989

Sachs, Jeffrey and Steven C. Radelet, "The Onset of the East Asian Financial Crisis", Cambridge, Massachusetts: National Bureau of Economic Research, 1998 (Working Paper 6680)

United Nations Conference on Trade and Development (UNCTAD), *Trade and Development Report*, Geneva: United Nations, 1998

KINDLEBERGER is the indispensable book on the last several centuries of financial crises in the global economy. His volume introduces the two distinct dimensions of any international debt crisis: on one hand, a precipitous stoppage in the flow of cross-border loans and repayments; on the other, a crisis of debt deflation and loan repayment that is experienced simultaneously in numerous countries. Everything Kindleberger has written on international capital flows is worth reading and rereading. Some may prefer the richer historical detail of his later work, but this volume offers an unparalleled combination of historical sweep and analytical backbone.

Four years after Kindleberger first appeared, Mexico's August 1982 debt moratorium triggered the first international debt crisis in 50 years. This event also launched a contemporary literature on international debt. This literature is demanding because it mixes microeconomic, macroeconomic, and political economy interpretations, and because it assumes the reader's familiarity with contemporary models of international finance and open-economy macroeconomics. The writings of CLINE (1984, 1996) provide an accessible introduction to this contemporary literature and policy debate. His 1984 volume was the first systematic book-length treatment of the Latin American debt crisis; his 1996 volume, published on the heels of the 1994–5 Mexican financial crisis, provides a thorough overview of the gains and risks associated with private-sector international financial flows. Cline, like all participants in this literature, has his own view on where the blame lies for the intermittent crises associated with these private-sector flows; but his books are indispensable for their analysis of trends over time and their comprehensive coverage.

The Latin American debt crisis of the early 1980s occurred just as principal-agent theory and the microfoundational explanation of macroeconomic phenomena were coming into fashion in economics. Not surprisingly, this crisis inspired many economists to suggest game-theoretic models of debt crisis; generally, these view sovereign debt default as the outcome of a one-shot game in which penalties for non-payment are set too low. These articles and many other contributions to the literature on the causes of the Latin American debt crisis are surveyed in the review essay by EATON & TAYLOR. This essay does not rank among either of its authors' best work, perhaps due to their decidedly different approaches to modelling. None the less, it warrants inclusion here because it covers the work on the causes of the debt crisis very broadly, whereas other review essays largely restrict attention to game-theoretic models. Of particular interest outside the penalty-cost framework is some economists' characterization of the debt crisis as a Kindleberger lending mania. The best work here is by DARITY & HORN. These authors develop a segmented-market view of international debt crisis, in which global macroeconomic fallacies of composition interacted perversely with uneven development. In their view, the problem is not greedy borrowers intent on cheating lenders, but over-eager lenders whose credit flows are collectively irrational.

The literature on the causes of the Latin American debt crisis eventually gave way to work on the pricing of securitized debt and on sovereign debt renegotiation. AGGARWAL summarizes this vast literature and interprets it using game-theoretic models of bargaining – especially the repeated prisoner's dilemma model. This book stands out from the many other game-theoretic interpretations of international debt repayments problems because of its historical depth and institutional richness: Aggarwal treats the cases of Argentinian and Brazilian debt in the 1980s and 1990s in depth, and also examines the cases of Mexican and Peruvian debt problems from the 1820s to the present. The author's broad scope is aimed at demonstrating the necessity for multicausal, not unicausal, understandings of international debt crisis.

Some subsequent works also explored more debt crises thoroughly in the context of global financial flows and the macroeconomic structures of debtor and creditor nations. Among these, SACHS is authoritative and comprehensive in coverage. The contributors to Sachs generally share the view that international capital and credit flows can enhance growth prospects in the developing world; avoiding renewed instances of debt crisis then depends on adopting proper macroeconomic structures. In effect, the Sachs volume participates in the re-evaluation of the Latin American debt crisis, which was firmly entrenched by the early 1990s, when large-scale financial flows resumed to many economies in Eastern Europe and East Asia.

The Mexican crisis of 1994–5 then came as a rude shock. The essays in CALVO, GOLDSTEIN & HOCHREITER explore the origins of this new crisis and its lessons for emerging economies receiving large capital-market inflows. The papers in this volume reflect a renewed appreciation for the reversibility of capital flows and the vulnerability of economies with systematic capital inflows. These chapters emphasize the need for policies protecting borrower countries – especially the maintenance of adequate reserves and provisions for orderly workouts; stronger measures, such as exchange and capital controls, are rejected.

The recurrence of financial crises emphasized the importance of information in ascertaining which borrower nations might face future repayment problems. Reinhart has been at the forefront of efforts to develop such "early warning systems". GOLDSTEIN & REINHART describe these techniques, which have attracted increasing attention in the wake of the 1997 Asian financial crisis.

The East Asian crisis (and the Russian and Brazilian crises) has, like its predecessors, unleashed vigorous economic debate. The view propounded by the International Monetary Fund (IMF) is that although borrower nations caught in this crisis may have had sound macroeconomic strategies, they were vulnerable because of their improperly supervised banking systems. This view is summarized in UNCTAD, which also puts forth the contrary interpretation that slow global macro-economic growth combined with unstable "hot money" flows are at the root of the East Asian crisis. SACHS & RADELET argue that this crisis involves a contagion effect among creditors and banks. UNCTAD and Sachs & Radelet provide detailed institutional information on the context and outbreak of the 1997 crisis. Unstable expectations, bandwagon effects, and asset-price collapses – all elements that have accompanied this continuing episode – are among the central elements in the work of Hyman Minsky, who originated the financial instability hypothesis. Minsky died a year before this crisis broke out: however, KREGEL provides a vigorous application of Minsky's ideas to this most recent international debt crisis.

GARY A. DYMSKI

International economics

Caves, Richard E. and Harry G. Johnson (editors), *Readings in International Economics*, Homewood, Illinois: Irwin, 1968

Dornbusch, Rudiger and Jacob A. Frenkel (editors), *International Economic Policy: Theory and Evidence*, Baltimore: Johns Hopkins University Press, 1979

Ellis, Howard S. and Lloyd A. Metzler (editors), *Readings in the Theory of International Trade*, Philadelphia: Blakiston, 1949

Ellsworth, P.T., *The International Economy: Its Structure and Operation*, New York: Macmillan, 1950

Grossman, Gene M. and Kenneth Rogoff (editors), *Handbook of International Economics*, vol. 3, Amsterdam and New York: Elsevier, 1995

Haberler, Gottfried, *The Theory of International Trade with Its Applications to Commercial Policy*, London: Hodge, 1936 (revision of 1933 German edition)

Haberler, Gottfried, *A Survey of International Trade Theory*, revised edition, Princeton, New Jersey: International Finance Section, Princeton University, 1961

Jones, Ronald W. and Peter B. Kenen (editors), *Handbook of International Economics*, vols 1–2, Amsterdam and New York: North Holland, 1984–95

Kenen, Peter B. (editor), *International Trade and Finance: Frontiers for Research*, Cambridge and New York: Cambridge University Press, 1975

Meade, J.E., *The Theory of International Economic Policy*, 2 vols, London and New York: Oxford University Press, 1951–55

Metzler, Lloyd A., "The Theory of International Trade" in *A Survey of Contemporary Economics*, edited by Howard S. Ellis, Philadelphia: Blakiston, 1948

Officer, Lawrence H. (editor), *International Economics*, Boston: Kluwer, 1987

Ohlin, Bertil, *Interregional and International Trade*, Cambridge, Massachusetts: Harvard University Press, 1935

Vanek, Jaroslav, *International Trade: Theory and Economic Policy*, Homewood, Illinois: Irwin, 1962

Viner, Jacob, *Studies in the Theory of International Trade*, New York: Harper, 1937

International economics (also named "international trade" when that term is used in a general sense) has both a real and a monetary side: international trade (in the strict sense of that term) and international monetary economics (or "international finance"). Pertinent studies combine the two manifestations of the field. These studies take four forms, in rough order of chronological dominance: textbook treatises, self-contained surveys, collections of readings, and collections of commissioned surveys.

Until the early 1960s it was deemed possible to cover international economics in its entirety in a treatise textbook. HABERLER (1936) is the first great work of that nature. The approach is theoretical, with empirical and history-of-doctrine references only to illustrate the theory. The logical organization of the field and the quality of exposition constitute a standard for future authors. Haberler completely presents the international economic theory of his time–and goes beyond it. His innovations, which revolutionized the field, include giving equal attention to the monetary theory and the pure theory, unification of all the elements of the pure theory, discussion of trade policy as an application of theory, analysis of monetary systems that existed between the extremes of a gold standard and an inconvertible paper currency, introduction of the production-possibilities curve and of specific factors in the pure theory, and a superb reformulation of classical comparative-cost theory in terms of opportunity cost.

HABERLER (1961) classifies arguments for protection into valid/invalid, revenue/protective, economic/noneconomic, short-run/long-run, and equilibrium/disequilibrium – which was as good a taxonomy as that of any future author, if not better. In fact, the modernity of the book is striking. Much of the discussion of trade policy is relevant today. Even Haberler's acknowledged omissions of topics (both from the book and from the state of the discipline at that time)–application of business-cycle theory and imperfect/monopolistic competitive theory to international trade–were harbingers of things to come.

Acknowledging the same omissions as Haberler, future Nobel-Prize winner OHLIN wrote a treatise rather than a textbook. This work is famous for development of the factor-proportions theory of international trade and for the viewpoint (anticipating geographic economics) that international trade theory is a branch of location theory. Even though the mathematics is in an appendix, the book is difficult – but nevertheless rewarding – reading. Most of the volume is concerned with the real side, and is distinguished by general-equilibrium modelling, attention to the history of thought, presentation of factor-price (and commodity-price) equalization as tendencies, emphasis on qualitative differences in factors of production, focus on locational considerations, and substantial resort to real-world phenomena to illustrate and qualify the general equilibrium system. Original contributions on the monetary side include the incorporation of Keynesian-type income effects into the adjustment mechanism, and the recognition that private short-term capital movements and changes in official reserves can substitute for gold movements in effecting changes in the money supply and income.

VINER's treatise is a masterpiece, still consulted by scholars today. The book has five themes: a history of thought evolving into modern theory, an examination of controversies in the theoretical literature, Viner's own analysis of the major theoretical topics in international economics, an economic history as relevant to theoretical issues, and empirical evidence. Viner weaves these themes into an integrated pattern that has never been equalled. The history of doctrine is superb, with comprehensive coverage of the literature–including even the most obscure authors.

Substantive topics are: mercantilist doctrine, bullionism (mercantilist policies), the bullionist controversy associated with the Bank Restriction Period, the currency versus banking-school controversy, balance-of-payments adjustment mechanisms (both under a simple specie currency and under modern banking), free trade, comparative cost theory (including the factor-proportions theory, for which Viner finds predecessors among the classical economists), and gains from trade. The discussion of non constant costs is excellent, and the synthesis of terms-of-trade concepts superb. Viner has been criticized for his adherence to the real-cost (extension of the classical labour-cost) theory in opposition to Haberler's (and later the profession's) adoption of opportunity cost as underlying comparative cost.

ELLSWORTH provides perhaps the last great comprehensive textbook, with over 900 pages (including a 21-page bibliography). The approach is an integration of historical, institutional, and theoretical material. The parts of the book dealing with mercantilism, the transition to liberalism, and the decline of the international economy (including protectionism and the abandonment of the gold standard) are entirely or mainly historical. The pure theory section is analytical, whereas the gold standard section is both historical and theoretical. The synthesis of the various strands of the balance-of-payments adjustment process is particularly good. Exchange-rate flexibility is discussed in historical-theoretical fashion under the rubrics of a "disorganized trading system" and postwar reconstruction. The topics are logical given the time of writing, but placing fluctuating exchange rates in the same context as direct controls is unusual. The author can also be criticized for postponing balance-of-payments accounting until chapter 10, for the overly strong statement that Ohlin's factor-proportions theory made classical theory obsolete, and for the omission of advanced material (for example, the Edgeworth-Bowley box diagram).

In two volumes, future Nobel Prize winner MEADE completely (but separately) synthesizes the monetary and pure theories of international economics, and develops them significantly further, all from a policy orientation. Amazingly, this is done at an advanced level without the use of mathematics (mathematical supplements are published separately) or even graphs, but with adroit use of arithmetical examples. Meade's innovations include the theory of economic policy (independent of Jan Tinbergen), the absorption approach (prior to Sidney S. Alexander), the theory of the second best, operational welfare economics, and incorporation of non tradable commodities in balance-of-payments adjustment. Discussions of interregional versus international economics, the gold standard, direct controls, and international factor movements are superb. The sections on multilateral trade and multilateral payments mechanism are works of genius. Meade has been criticized for his taxonomic approach. His orientation is also Keynesian rather than monetarist, defining monetary policy in terms of interest-rate rather than money-supply change.

VANEK is comprehensive in theory, but without attention to institutions, economic history, or history of doctrine. There is considerable focus on policy, again from a purely theoretical standpoint. The book is balanced about equally between the real and monetary sides. Much of the work remains pedagogically useful today. Among the innovations are derivation of the balance of payments as a consolidation of sectoral income statements and balance-sheet changes, and the demonstration that community indifference curves are unnecessary for the incorporation of demand in the pure theory. The chapters on trade policy and customs unions (the latter an original contribution) remain relevant today. Theories are presented as coherent wholes, but little is said about qualifications to, and deviations from, them.

METZLER presents a self-contained survey that focuses on changes in theory during the interwar period (and somewhat beyond). The exposition is at an advanced level, with no diagrams and almost no mathematics, but is eminently readable. Measured reference is made to doctrinal history. Topics discussed are employment and the balance of payments, fluctuating exchange rates, the pure theory, and tariffs. Metzler can be criticized for minimizing the applicability of the classical monetary mechanism, which was a harbinger of the monetary approach to the balance of payments. He also understates the case for free trade, and shows no appreciation of the practical difficulties in applying the terms-of-trade argument for protection.

Haberler's 1961 book, mentioned earlier, is primarily a synthesis, but the exposition (verbal without mathematics or graphs) is masterful. The work is a theoretical survey, with a minimum of institutional detail or empirical data. The pure theory is divided into the classical and modern phases. Taussig and Viner are criticized for adoption of a real-cost theory, because of its foundation on artificial assumptions; whereas opportunity-cost theory merges into general-equilibrium theory. Haberler does not recognize that Ricardian theory can also be placed in this framework. Ohlin is praised for expositing his theory not only in an abstract static framework, but also from a historical and dynamic viewpoint; however, he is criticized for obscurity, inconsistencies, and contradictions. Haberler's discussion of the terms of trade is still applicable today, and he rightly praises Viner in this respect. The exposition of price and income effects in the balance-of-payments mechanism is beautifully done. The value judgement in discussing trade policy is made explicit, and the relationships of import and export duties and subsidies are made unusually clear. Much of what Haberler writes is exposited mathematically or graphically in Vanek.

ELLIS & METZLER is the first of two volumes of reprinted essays and articles chosen by a selection committee (the editors) under the auspices of the American Economic Association. About 25 specialists in international economics were asked for recommendations on the included articles. The readings were published in the period 1919–47 and are uniformly theoretical, with empirical studies excluded by design. Included are many classic works on such topics as (in the pure theory) indifference curves, gains from trade, factor-proportions theory, critiques of classical theory, and tariffs; and (in the monetary theory) beggar-my-neighbour policies, the foreign-exchange market, and the transfer problem. Much of the book remains good reading for the serious scholar.

CAVES & JOHNSON is the second volume of readings from the American Economic Association. The editors consulted not only experts in the field, but also university reading lists to decide on contents. There are 33 selections (all but one having been published since the first volume) versus 23 in the previous volume. Unlike the first volume, this volume has no bibliography; but the editors provide honourable mention of specific excluded items. Included are empirical studies on testing the pure theory, estimating elasticities, and measuring tariffs. Classic theoretical articles in the pure theory involve the factor-proportions theory, changing factor supplies, factor mobility, the transfer problem, gains from trade, deviations from ideal conditions, immiserizing growth, and tariffs. In the monetary theory the topics covered include the absorption approach, exchange rates, and stabilization policy. Almost every article in the book remains rewarding reading.

KENEN is the first collection of commissioned surveys. With nine papers under the rubric of trade and protection, econometric models of trade and payments, and payments adjustment and the monetary system, balance between the real and monetary sides is maintained. The entire book manifests the quantification of international economics. The papers mainly survey empirical research, sometimes with an overview of theory. There are discussions of the papers, and the book closes with a valuable overview. A defect is the omission of a comparison of research methods across the subfields of international economics.

DORNBUSCH & FRENKEL also presents nine essays, with discussions, encompassing both trade and payments. Attention to theory, even with some original modelling, is greater than in KENEN, and there is emphasis on policy as well as empirical research. Traditional pure and monetary theory has less space in favour of new developments, with the paper on the efficient markets hypothesis particularly valuable. The round table on problems and prospects for the world economy is not at all related to the essays. In fact, the volume exhibits a lack of unity, with no attempt to treat international economics as a coherent whole. There is divergence among the papers in their coverage of theory relative to empirical research, and in terms of survey content relative to originality.

OFFICER consists of four essays, with discussions, on the pure theory, protection, international linkages under alternative exchange-rate regimes (an optimizing-model framework), and national policies in relation to the international monetary system. The surveys address the theoretical rather than empirical state of the art. Each chapter has a short, but useful, bibliography. Again there is no synthesis of the papers, and no unification of the entire field of international economics.

JONES & KENEN is a *tour de force*. In 1200 pages virtually the entirety of international economics is surveyed at an advanced level; insufficient coverage only of multinational firms, Euromarkets, and international bank lending is acknowledged by the editors. Volume 1 (12 essays) is concerned with the real side, and volume 2 (11 essays) the monetary side, now termed open-economy macroeconomics. The quality of the

authors, organization of the material, and thoroughness of the treatment eclipse all previous work. In volume 1, chapters 1–9 together constitute a complete survey of the theoretical state of the real side. Chapter 10 surveys econometric techniques and studies, and chapters 11–12 address trade policies in developing and developed countries. Volume 2 consists of theoretical surveys (chapters 13–18), empirical studies (chapters 19–21) and essays on international monetary arrangements and policy coordination (chapters 22–23). Each chapter has a useful bibliography, but no discussion is attached. Although the editors provide an overview in the preface, no attempt is made to unify the field.

GROSSMAN & ROGOFF is a worthy successor to Jones & Kenen, and in fact it is a continuation of volumes 1–2 of the *Handbook*, carrying the total number of pages to 2100. There is recognition that the real and monetary sides of international economics are becoming intertwined; but again the organization is dichotomous, with trade theory and policy (chapters 24–31) followed by open-economy macroeconomics and international finance (chapters 32–39). Acknowledged omissions are direct foreign investment, computable equilibrium models, and the institutional/historical aspects of European Monetary Union. Theoretical, policy, and empirical studies and techniques receive varying attention in the essays. A criticism of the *Handbook*, and in fact of the entire survey literature, is the neglect of economic history and the omission of empirical evidence gleaned from that source.

LAWRENCE H. OFFICER

See also International trade policy

International law

Amerasinghe, C.F., *Principles of the International Law of International Organizations*, Cambridge and New York: Cambridge University Press, 1996

Brownlie, Ian, *Principles of Public International Law*, 5th edition, Oxford: Clarendon Press, and New York: Oxford University Press, 1998

Evans, Malcolm D. (editor), *Remedies in International Law: The Institutional Dilemma*, Oxford: Hart, 1998

Falk, Richard, *Law in an Emerging Global Village: A Post-Westphalian Perspective*, Ardsley, New York: Transnational, 1998

Franck, Thomas M., *Fairness in International Law and Institutions*, Oxford: Clarendon Press, and New York: Oxford University Press, 1995

Higgins, Rosalyn, *Problems and Process: International Law and How We Use It*, Oxford: Clarendon Press, and New York: Oxford University Press, 1994

Koskenniemi, Martti (editor), *International Law*, Aldershot, Hampshire: Dartmouth, and New York: New York University Press, 1992

Malanczuk, Peter, *Akehurst's Modern Introduction to International Law*, 7th edition, London and New York: Routledge, 1997

Merrills, J.G., *International Dispute Settlement*, 3rd edition, Cambridge and New York: Cambridge University Press, 1998

Taylor, Prue, *An Ecological Approach to International Law: Responding to Challenges of Climate Change*, London and New York: Routledge, 1998

AMERASINGHE examines the institutional aspects of the law on international organizations. Multilateral relations between States are the classic arena of international law, but the establishment of public international organizations since the late 19th century has created a new and increasingly important dimension. This dimension includes the functional aspects of international law alongside its material aspects. Today's international law is, in fact, largely administered, and sometimes created, by well-known bodies such as the UN, the WTO, the IMF, the World Bank, the EU, and numerous others. Amerasinghe does not describe the workings of specific international organizations, but rather the principles, legal, and administrative features governing them. Starting with a brief history of international organizations, the 14 substantive chapters deal with subjects such as interpretations of texts, the concept of legal personality, the legal nature of organs and their acts, forms of responsibility and liability, financing, and the various means of dispute settlement. The book gives an insight into the practice of international law and international decision making.

BROWNLIE is a classic and one of the leading textbooks on public international law. Now in its fifth edition, the book revises and updates developments since 1990, and a new chapter on international environmental law has been added. However, it still retains its original strengths: clear exposition, rigorous analysis, detailed referencing, and comprehensive coverage. For a researcher new to the field of international law, Brownlie provides a thorough grounding; for the expert it remains an invaluable reference. Covered are all the key features including sources of the law, the relation between municipal and international law, personality and recognition, territorial sovereignty, the law of the sea, co-operation in the use and protection of resources, state jurisdiction and responsibility, human rights, self-determination, international organizations, and the judicial settlement of international disputes. The book's great strength is its comprehensiveness and accuracy; a weakness is its descriptive approach. While critical, it lacks discussion of philosophical, political, and economic issues underpinning so much of today's international law.

EVANS examines the system of justice provided by international law. There is a wide and growing spectrum of remedies available in international fora for breaches of international obligations. This collection of essays by judges, practitioners, and academics gives a useful overview and identifies some shortcomings in the use of remedies. Although remedies sought by individuals against states are not dealt with, the various aspects of the quest for a remedy by a state give an insight into the "institutional dilemma" under which the current system operates. On the one hand, the International Court of Justice, the International Tribunal for the Law of the Sea, and numerous mechanisms of dispute settlement, for example within GATT/WTO, provide for a comprehensive system. On the other hand, the actual success of remedies is still determined by the sovereignty of states, in particular the powerful. Unfortunately, there is no supremacy of law, but of states and their competing preferences.

Richard FALK is one of the pioneers of global governance and world order. Among his many inspiring books this recent text gives an up-to-date account of the "law in an emerging global village". Falk first considers the prevailing historical circumstances to see whether the time is right now for an innovative synthesis of the past, present, and future of international law. He then describes how states are losing their normative high ground to humanity giving way to a "global civil society". A series of substantive chapters looks at more specific, mostly environmental issue-areas, and the concluding chapters give a vision of a transformed world referred to as "humane governance". The book is best summed up by Falk's own words:

> Whether humane governance is a viable political project or mere utopianism, only time will tell. But let us not forget the rapidity with which such utopian undertakings as self-determination for the countries of East Europe and racial equality in South Africa became transformative experiences.

FRANCK attempts to link contemporary international law to the idea of fairness. Is it possible to identify a universal concept of fairness and assess developments of international law accordingly? If so, we would have a yardstick to measure progress towards a world of peace and justice. In his careful, well-written analysis of material law and international institutions Franck concludes that fairness is, essentially, a fair selection of participants. Since the "global discourse" is not just a conversation between states, but a hubbub of voices of multinational corporations, professional networks, non-governmental organizations, indigenous peoples, and many others, the question arises how to channel the discourse. There is a need for new structures of international law based on common values, and this book gives a clue how such values could be found. The challenge is to transform current state-centred international law to a global law based on fairness and solidarity.

HIGGINS gives a solid introduction into some key features of international law, but goes considerably beyond a mere textbook. The book's main thesis is that international law does not exist per se, but only through its perception. Higgins distinguishes between the perception of international law as a system of neutral rules, and a system of decision-making informed by certain declared values. She rejects the idea of a pre-defined "correct rule" to be applied in a given case and describes international law as a dynamic process of (changeable) opinions and values. As a consequence, there is little point in identifying sources of law or using 'buzz-words' (such as self-determination or rights and duties, *erga omnes*) as long as the context remains unclear. What is one's legal philosophy underpinning one's choice of terms? Higgins is a brilliant example of feminist jurisprudence questioning the merit of static rules and abstract ideas.

Martti KOSKENNIEMI is known as a provocative and innovative international lawyer. The introduction to this collection of essays by leading scholars in the field is an excellent account of problems and controversies surrounding the study of international law. Noting that international law participates in the struggle for economic and spiritual values, Koskenniemi's starting-point is a social conception of international law embedded in Europe's history since the Enlightenment. International law, therefore, follows the prevailing social and political controversies, for example, natural law versus positivism, idealism versus realism, or theory versus pragmatism. The essays selected to describe what constitutes "international law" reflect these controversies and invite readers to think for themselves. In some ways Koskenniemi is the counterpart to Brownlie as it raises the relevant questions rather than trying to give all the answers. Certainly not a bad approach to effective learning.

MALANCZUK is the seventh and substantially revised edition of Michael Akehurst's widely used textbook. The merit of this book is its clarity, precision, and accessibility, making it very useful for students with a background in social sciences (outside jurisprudence). It covers all the areas readers would expect: history and theory, sources, treaties, international law and municipal law, role of states, companies, non-governmental organizations and other groups, law of the sea and air space, human rights, economy, environment, state responsibility, peaceful settlement of disputes between states, criminal responsibility, and the United Nations. Taking a conceptual approach with a historical perspective, the book shows the transition of international law from its narrow European origins to a universal system of rules, procedures, and institutions. The reader also benefits from an excellent system of easy-to-find references, tables, and indexing.

MERRILLS gives a comprehensive, up-to-date account of one of the key issues in international law and international relations, the peaceful settlement of disputes between states. The mechanisms of negotiation, mediation, inquiry, conciliation, arbitration, and judicial review are clearly explained. Further chapters cover the dispute settlement provisions of the International Court of Justice, the International Tribunal for the Law of the Sea, the World Trade Organization, and the United Nations. The concluding chapter, "trends and prospects", critically discusses gaps and shortcomings of what the author emphatically calls "the most critical issue of our time". This is a useful and informative book with a good selection of recent documents (in appendices) and case law.

TAYLOR provides the reader with an ecological vision of international law. Using the example of global climate change, the book shows in an impressive manner how ill defined international law is to meet the challenges of the future. There is, at present, no sufficiently accepted ethic upon which states could act. Traditional doctrines of state sovereignty and state responsibility appear as major obstacles for the essential task of international law – creating and maintaining a world order based on peace and solidarity. Taylor argues for a radical shift in how the world should be perceived, a world of commonality (rather than competition) and shared responsibility (rather than individual state responsibility). The book takes an interdisciplinary approach linking international law with ecology and ethics. A good read that also introduces environmental ethics.

KLAUS BOSSELMANN

See also Environmental law, Human rights (law)

International Monetary Fund (IMF)

Bordo, Michael D., "The Bretton Woods International Monetary System: A Historical Overview" in A Retrospective on the Bretton Woods System: Lessons for International Monetary Reform, edited by Bordo and Barry Eichengreen, Chicago: University of Chicago Press, 1993a

Bordo, Michael D., "The Gold Standard, Bretton Woods and Other Monetary Regimes: A Historical Appraisal", Federal Reserve Bank of St Louis Review (March-April 1993b): 123–91

Bretton Woods Commission, Bretton Woods: Looking to the Future, Washington, DC: Bretton Woods Commission, 1994

Broughton, James M. and K. Sarwar Lateef (editors), Fifty Years after Bretton Woods: The Future of the IMF and the World Bank, Washington, DC: International Monetary Fund, 1995

Danaher, Kevin (editor), Fifty Years Is Enough: The Case against the World Bank and the IMF, Boston: South End Press, 1994

Eichengreen, Barry and Peter B. Kenen, "Managing the World Economy under the Bretton Woods System: An Overview" in Managing the World Economy: Fifty Years after Bretton Woods, edited by Peter B. Kenen, Washington, DC: Institute for International Economics, 1994

Goldstein, Morris, The Asian Financial Crisis: Causes, Cures, and Systemic Implications, Washington, DC: Institute for International Economics, 1998

James, Harold, International Monetary Cooperation since Bretton Woods, Oxford and New York: Oxford University Press, 1996

Kenen, Peter B., Financing, Adjustment, and the International Monetary Fund, Washington, DC: Brookings Institution, 1986

Williamson, John and C. Randall Henning, "Managing the Monetary System" in Managing the World Economy: Fifty Years after Bretton Woods, edited by Peter B. Kenen, Washington, DC: Institute for International Economics, 1994

Following the dramatic collapse of the international economy in the 1930s, representatives of the allied nations met at Bretton Woods (New Hampshire) in 1944 to plan the future of the post-World War II international monetary system. Delegates recognized the desire for full employment and rising income levels. They also recognized the need for the postwar international financial system to combine exchange rate stability (thus avoiding competitive devaluations) and national independence in macroeconomic policy making.

A fixed exchange rate system requires central banks to intervene in foreign exchange markets to maintain balance-of-payments equilibrium at the chosen exchange rate. A country experiencing balance-of-payments problems, arising from a reduction in exports or an increase in imports, might have to take (politically unacceptable) corrective action leading to unemployment and falling income levels. If an international institution, such as the IMF, lent reserves to countries experiencing temporary balance-of-payments problems, member countries could maintain their chosen exchange rate without the need to change the level of activity in their domestic economies.

JAMES offers a comprehensive, readable, and perceptive historical account of international monetary cooperation since the end of World War II, emphasizing several recurring themes: the close link between developments in international money markets and the performance of the world economy; the effects of misguided national policy responses on economic growth; and the continuing need for the Fund to adapt in the face of changes in the global economy. James begins with an account of the monetary problems of the 1930s and the events leading to Bretton Woods (see especially Chapter 5, "Development and Bretton Woods"). Later chapters deal with the "classic" era of the Bretton Woods system (1950–71), the events leading to the breakdown of the fixed exchange rate system (1971–3), the era of floating exchange rates (post 1973), and proposals for reform of the international monetary system.

The IMF has been the target of vocal criticism, not only from some economists who have argued that the conditions imposed on borrowers are too harsh and/or likely to add to, rather than ameliorate, the problems faced by the Fund's clients, but also from supporters of developing countries who argue that the Bretton Woods system favours the interests of industrial at the expense of developing countries, and from environmentalists, who accuse both the Fund and the World Bank of pursuing policies aimed at economic growth with detrimental consequences to the global environment. DANAHER is one of a number of critics who argue that IMF actions have been counterproductive and who have called for fundamental reforms. In general, such critics have failed to develop a convincing alternative model of the international monetary system.

Problems with the international financial system led to the breakdown of the Bretton Woods fixed exchange rate system in the period 1971–73. A hybrid exchange rate regime, in which some countries pegged their currencies to the American dollar, some pegged to a basket of currencies, and others "floated" their currencies (allowed the value of their currencies to be determined by market forces) now emerged. KENEN focuses on the international economic crises of the 1970s and 1980s (the OPEC oil price increases of 1973–74 and 1979–80, the deep and relative long-lasting recession of 1981–83, and the Third World debt crisis), noting the heavy demands made on the IMF's limited resources. In examining the evolution of the Fund over the period 1973–86, Kenen argues that the pressures it faced altered its fundamental character. Thus, when it began to borrow to provide additional funding to Third World countries experiencing debt crises, the balance between the rights and obligations of members changed: each member had clear-cut rights of access to the Fund, but none had an obligation to contribute on a scale sufficient to meet its expanded obligations. Kenen is also preoccupied with the concept of "conditionality", whether or not it is wise for the IMF to act *in loco parentis*, substituting its judgements about the nature of its members' problems for the judgements of the members themselves. Finally, the author proposes reforms of the financial structure of the Fund to give more weight to its role as a reserve-creating institution and provide for an orderly expansion of its own activities.

John Williamson has published prolifically on issues such as exchange rate management, equilibrium exchange rates, and the international coordination of economic policy. The WILLIAMSON & HENNING chapter begins by asking what postwar experience has taught us about the form that an international monetary regime should take. They argue that, of all the international monetary regimes developed to date, the Bretton Woods system (in its heyday from 1959–68) performed the best. However, the system did not prove robust in the face of the instability of the early 1970s. Williamson & Henning offer a blueprint for a more robust international financial system.

The Asian financial meltdown clearly posed a threat to the international economy. The IMF put together packages to rescue Thailand ($17 billion), Indonesia ($40 billion) and South Korea, following their 1997 currency and stockmarket crashes. However, the IMF's remedies have been criticized, raising questions as to how best to help a country in financial trouble and how to avoid contagion (stopping a crisis in one country spreading to others). Not only did the Fund come under fire for giving "inappropriate advice" to Asian countries, but it lacked funds to inject credit into further Asian or Latin American countries that might find themselves in situations similar to those experienced by Thailand or South Korea. In one of the earliest analyses of the Asian financial crisis, GOLDSTEIN focuses on both causes and cures for the crisis as well as its implications for the international financial system. He does not subscribe to the "fashionable" view that the Fund got it all wrong; rather, he argues that much more has been right than wrong about the overall design of these official rescue packages. Those that favour the abolition of the IMF, Goldstein argues, have forgotten the lessons of the 1920s and 1930s.

BORDO (1993a, b), together with EICHENGREEN & KENEN, offers perceptive evaluations of the 50-year history of the Bretton Woods system. Eichengren & Kenen's overview of the management of the world economy under the Bretton Woods system is especially valuable. Not only does it provide a sound introduction for a student wishing to obtain a basic grasp of the evolving system, but it is worth reading a second time when the student has a developed understanding of the role of the IMF. For many, a second reading will reveal a series of insights that have been missed the first time around.

Two recent studies focus on the future of the IMF and the Bretton Woods system. The BRETTON WOODS COMMISSION, an independent group of senior businessmen, civil servants and academics, convened by Paul Volcker, reviews and reports on the state of the international financial system, development finance and the IMF and World Bank. Reaffirming the importance of multilateral economic cooperation, the Report argues that governments of major industrial countries should give a high priority to international monetary reforms aimed a reducing exchange rate fluctuations and serious currency misalignments. More specifically, the Report argues that governments should strengthen their macroeconomic policies and achieve greater economic convergence, and establish a more formal system of coordination and avoid excessive exchange rate misalignments and volatility. The Report rejects criticism that the IMF imposed harsh and/or inappropriate conditions in its financing packages and argues that the Fund should be given a central role in coordinating macroeconomic policies and in developing and implementing monetary reforms.

BROUGHTON & LATEEF are also impressed by the flexibility shown by IMF/World Bank in response to the challenges of the 1970s and 1980s. However, they argue for the further reform of Bretton Woods institutions in the light of: the need to adapt to a global economy characterized by an increasingly open trade system; the need for improved monetary coordination and greater exchange rate stability; the need to reduce poverty in Africa and southern Asia; the need to protect the environment; and the need to encourage the flow of private capital to developing countries. Contributors argue that the IMF should focus on short-term macro policy, leaving the problem of "long-term structural transformation" to the World Bank.

KEITH TRACE

See also Bretton Woods, Financial globalization, Gold standard

International regimes

Hasenclever, Andreas, Peter Mayer and Volker Rittberger, *Theories of International Regimes*, Cambridge and New York: Cambridge University Press, 1997

Keohane, Robert O., *After Hegemony: Cooperation and Discord in the World Political Economy*, Princeton, New Jersey: Princeton University Press, 1984

Krasner, Stephen D. (editor), *International Regimes*, Ithaca, New York: Cornell University Press, 1983

Levy, Marc A., Oran R. Young and Michael Zürn, "The Study of International Regimes", *European Journal of International Relations*, 1/3 (1995): 267–330

Rittberger, Volker (editor), *Regime Theory in International Relations*, Oxford: Clarendon Press, and New York: Oxford University Press, 1993

Young, Oran R., *International Cooperation: Building Regimes for the Natural Resources and the Environment*, Ithaca, New York: Cornell University Press, 1989

In his editor's introduction to a path-breaking collection of essays, KRASNER provides the most widely accepted definition of international regimes: they are "sets of principles, norms, rules, and decision-making procedures around which actor expectations converge in a given issue area" of international relations. He distinguishes three approaches to their study: conventional realism, which denies that regimes have any independent causal impact on international relations, because they are just reflections of deeper structural variables (power and interests); modified structural realism, which allows for the possibility of regimes having a significant impact under certain restrictive conditions; and Grotianism, which considers regimes as a normal and omnipresent feature of world politics. He discusses also the basic causal variables that have been proposed to explain the development of regimes. Krasner's conclusion to the same volume discusses how regimes may assume a life of their own and feed back on these basic causal variables, by changing assessments of interest and the distrib-

ution of power. The volume, in addition to general theoretical discussions about international regimes, includes case studies of regimes in security affairs, trade, and money since World War II.

LEVY, YOUNG & ZÜRN provide a very valuable survey of the literature on international regimes, which advances the debate as well. They record a recent shift in research efforts from the issue of regime formation to the issue of regime effectiveness. They discuss the questions of definition and classification, as well as of regime formation. But the issue of regime consequences receives special attention. Levy, Young & Zürn report various answers to the question of whether regimes are able to influence behaviour when the underlying power relationships change, and the question of the mechanisms through which regimes are effective (capable of solving the problems that motivate actors to create them). The authors conclude by suggesting an agenda for future research.

Another useful survey of the literature on international regimes is presented by HASENCLEVER, MAYER & RITTBERGER. They distinguish three schools of thought within regime analysis, each emphasizing different explanatory variables: constellations of interests, power relationships, or knowledge dynamics. Interest-based theories rely mainly, but not exclusively, on functional arguments about the contribution regimes can offer to states that have common interests but face transaction costs and collective action problems. Power-based theories focus on the issues of hegemonic stability, conflict over the distribution of the benefits from cooperation, and concern about relative rather than absolute gains. Knowledge-based theories, on the contrary, emphasize the importance of ideas, learning, and the role of epistemic communities, and the existence of international normative structures constraining state behaviour and affecting identity formation. Hasenclever, Mayer & Rittberger conclude by discussing how the three perspectives could be fruitfully synthesized.

KEOHANE has developed the most systematic and influential framework for studying the formation and the functions of international regimes from a rationalistic perspective. He accepts one major proposition of hegemonic stability theory – the high level of economic cooperation among the advanced capitalist countries after World War II has been a consequence of US hegemony – but argues that the decline of this hegemony since the late 1960s did not make cooperation necessarily much more difficult. To explain how international cooperation can occur in the absence of hegemony, Keohane develops a functional theory of regimes, borrowing insights from game theory and economic theories of collective goods and market failure. States that have common interests but exist in a world where rules cannot be authoritatively enforced can build institutions that facilitate cooperation by improving the quality and quantity of information available to them or reduce other transaction costs. Keohane illustrates his arguments by assessing the period of American hegemony after World War II and by examining the evolution of international regimes for international finance, trade, and oil between the mid-1960s and the early 1980s. He concludes that the realist perspective on international politics has not to be abandoned, but revised by bringing in elements from the institutionalist tradition.

The collection edited by RITTBERGER includes several outstanding contributions on the topic. In the first part, Rittberger and Robert Keohane report on the development of regime analysis in Germany and the US, respectively. In the second part, a number of conceptual and theoretical problems are discussed, such as the relationship between regime analysis and Grotian conceptions of international society, and the contribution of game theory for understanding regimes. In the third part, the question of the origins of regimes is explored, with individual chapters testing specific causal hypotheses on cases of regime formation in the human rights field, in environmental protection in the Mediterranean, in the management of the Arctic, and in East–West relations. Michael Zürn examines the domestic sources of regime formation. In the fourth part, several authors discuss the conceptual and methodological problems associated with assessing whether and how different regimes have a causal impact on international politics. In particular, Thomas Biersteker argues that causal statements about regimes must rely on historical counterfactual arguments, and provides suggestions on the difficult task of constructing valid counterfactuals. A final chapter by Peter Mayer, Rittberger, and Zürn usefully reviews the state of the art in regime analysis.

YOUNG provides both a thorough discussion of the theoretical issues associated with regime analysis and an application of the concept to cases of natural resources management and environmental protection. By placing regime analysis firmly in the tradition of studies about social institutions, Young explores the meaning of rights and rules in international politics, and stresses the importance of the distinction between international institutions and international organizations. He argues that institutions can constrain effectively the behaviour of individual actors and thus determine a substantial part of the variance in international outcomes, and discusses how regimes form in the first place and how they continuously change in response to their own internal dynamics as well as to changes in their political and economic environments. The analytical framework is illustrated by means of case studies: the regulation of marine fisheries and of deep-seabed mining, the handling of nuclear accidents, and conflicts over transit rights in the Arctic seas. Stressing the practical relevance of regime analysis, Young spells out its implications for actual institutional design and construction.

MATHIAS KOENIG-ARCHIBUGI

International relations theory

Baldwin, David A. (editor), *Neorealism and Neoliberalism: The Contemporary Debate*, New York: Columbia University Press, 1993

Booth, Ken and Steve Smith (editors), *International Relations Theory Today*, Cambridge: Polity Press, and University Park: Pennsylvania State University Press, 1995

Doyle, Michael W., *Ways of War and Peace: Realism, Liberalism, and Socialism*, New York: Norton, 1997

Dyer, Hugh C. and Leon Mangasarian (editors), *The Study of International Relations: The State of the Art*, Basingstoke: Macmillan, and New York: St Martin's Press, 1989

Katzenstein, Peter J., Robert O. Keohane and Stephen D. Krasner (editors), "*International Organization* at Fifty: Exploration and Contestation in the Study of World Politics", special issue of *International Organization*, 52/4 (1998)

Kegley, Charles W. Jr (editor), *Controversies in International Relations Theory: Realism and the Neo-Liberal Challenge*, New York: St Martin's Press, and Basingstoke: Macmillan, 1995

Viotti, Paul R. and Mark V. Kauppi, *International Relations Theory: Realism, Pluralism, Globalism*, New York: Macmillan, and London: Collier Macmillan, 1987; revised edition 1993

Waltz, Kenneth N., *Man, the State, and War: A Theoretical Analysis*, New York: Columbia University Press, 1959

Wight, Martin, *International Theory: The Three Traditions*, edited by Gabriele Wight and Brian Porter, Leicester: Leicester University Press, 1991

WALTZ's very influential work is an extensive exploration into the classical literature on the causes of war. He finds that thinkers on this topic have located the source of war in one of three possible factors: some writers explain war by human nature, others by the social and political features of states, and others by the anarchic character of the international system – the absence of any supreme power that would prevent war from happening. His "three images" scheme inaugurated a debate on the appropriate "level of analysis" that to some extent still frames international relations theory up to the present day. Waltz argues for the superiority of the "third image" over the other perspectives, on grounds of logical, empirical, and normative considerations.

WIGHT consists of the edited notes prepared for the lectures he gave at the London School of Economics in the 1950s and which were very influential on subsequent British theorizing on international relations. Like Waltz, Wight advances a broad categorization of classical international relations theorists, but he does not consider the level of analysis a significant criterion for differentiation. On the contrary, he shows that the three main "traditions" of international relations theory offer a relatively coherent set of views about each level: human nature, national power and interest, international society, diplomacy, and war. The three groups of thinkers are the realists, the rationalists, and the revolutionists (also called Machiavellians, Grotians, and Kantians). Wight's tour across centuries of debate on international politics is undoubtedly very fascinating and informative, but many people interested in international relations theory will find the tight intermingling of normative and descriptive assumptions and statements quite confusing, or even misleading, and indeed the three traditions should be handled with care as sources of inspiration for contemporary international relations theory.

Waltz's categorization of authors according to the level criterion is also rejected by DOYLE, but Wight's three traditions are substituted by a different tripartite division: realists, liberals, and socialists, which in turn are divided into various subcategories. Doyle reconstructs the thought on the sources of war and peace of the main representatives of these perspectives; that is of the realists, Thucydides, Machiavelli, Hobbes, and Rousseau; of the liberals, Locke, Bentham, Smith, Schumpeter, and Kant; and of the socialists, Marx and Lenin. He then considers more closely the implications and recommendations of each of these perspectives for the moral questions relating to military intervention abroad and the duties of people in rich countries towards people in poor countries. Surprisingly, in Doyle's account, what differentiates the traditions and subtraditions is not always as clear as it should be, but this does not prevent this book from being an impressive and very informative overview of the sources of contemporary thinking about international politics.

Even though already a little outdated, DYER & MANGASARIAN still offers a useful and well-balanced survey of international relations as an academic field. In the first part a range of theoretical issues are explored, such as paradigmatic shifts, state–society relations, critical theory, and historical approaches. The second part comprises of short chapters on both the content and the academic organization of international relations studies in the UK, France, Germany, Italy, the USSR, Israel, the US, Hispanic America, Brazil, Nigeria, South Africa, China, and Japan. The third part covers specific subject areas – strategic studies, peace research, foreign policy analysis, international political economy, and international law.

VIOTTI & KAUPPI is one of the most utilized and valuable textbooks on international relations theory. The authors divide the literature in this field into three broad "images" that frame the research and provide the building blocks for more specific theories: realism, pluralism, and globalism (this categorization is similar to Doyle's, but Viotti & Kauppi's focus is on contemporary scholarship). For each of these images, the authors discuss the main actors and basic assumptions, the intellectual precursors and influences, the central concepts, some representative theoretical works, and the main criticisms that have been directed against it. A special chapter is devoted to normative questions. The volume includes selected readings (comprising about half of it) and provides extensive suggestions for further reading.

BALDWIN collects the main contributions to what was probably the central debate in international relations theory during the 1980s – the controversy between neorealism and neoliberal institutionalism on the feasibility and the conditions of international cooperation. The collection includes some early neoliberal institutionalist articles criticizing the realists' scepticism about the possibility of cooperation in a world of rational egoistic states. Joseph Grieco's neorealist countercritique based essentially on the absolute/relative gain distinction, and the subsequent contributions by other authors, represents a considerable advance in the theoretical understanding of world politics. The concluding essays by Keohane and Grieco are especially important because they show how much the two perspectives become similar if their propositions are intended as conditional rather than absolute.

KEGLEY's helpful anthology similarly covers current theoretical controversies but its scope is broader than Baldwin's collection, as it purports to explore the traditional realist/liberal debate from many points of view and to take into account several versions of the two perspectives. Among the more theoretical essays there is a comparison between realism and neorealist theory and a survey of the varieties of liberalism. Other contributions apply the two theoretical perspectives to specific questions, namely the proposition that democracies do not fight each other, the role of the United Nations, the

evolution of the European Union, disarmament, international trade, and international law.

The volume edited by BOOTH & SMITH covers many aspects of international relations theory, but is especially useful for those interested in recent applications of critical theory and postmodern approaches to this field. Notably, it includes chapters on the idea of a world community, on postpositivism, on the problem of identity in international relations theory, and on the concept of the political in relation to international politics. Booth's chapter provides a "genealogical" account of the main debates in international relations theory since its establishment as an academic field.

KATZENSTEIN, KEOHANE & KRASNER assembled an excellent collection of essays written by some of the most outstanding scholars in the field. Individual chapters offer updated accounts of the study of institutions, domestic factors in international politics, national responses to interdependence, the relationship between economics and security, and the role of norms and of rationality in interstate relations. A chapter by Ole Waever discusses the relationship between American and European scholarship in international relations theory.

MATHIAS KOENIG-ARCHIBUGI

See also Politics survey

International trade policy, political economy

Caves, Richard, "Economic Models of Political Choice: Canada's Tariff Structure", Canadian Journal of Economics, 9/2 (1976): 279–99

Magee, Stephen P., William A. Brock and Leslie Young, Black Hole Tariffs and Endogenous Policy Theory: Political Economy in General Equilibrium, Cambridge and New York: Cambridge University Press, 1989

Mayer, Wolfgang, "Endogenous Tariff Formation", American Economic Review, 74/5 (1984): 970–85

Ray, Edward John, "Tariff and Nontariff Barriers to Trade in the United States and Abroad", Review of Economics and Statistics, 63/2 (1981): 161–68

Tullock, Gordon, "The Welfare Costs of Tariffs, Monopolies and Theft", Western Economic Journal, 5 (1967): 224–32

Vousden, Neil, The Economics of Trade Protection, Cambridge and New York: Cambridge University Press, 1990

TULLOCK laid the scene for the study of the contemporary "dynamics" in trade policy formation. This classic contribution is an excellent introduction to the political economy dimensions of trade policy formation. On the one hand, it represents an eloquent and succinct analysis of the incentives of domestic producers of import-competing commodities to lobby policymakers for trade barriers, and, on the other, it provides a comprehensive analysis of the welfare losses that ensue from restricting trade. These losses are normally expected to motivate consumers to object to the implementation of trade-restricting policies.

As early as 1978, MAGEE developed the first genuinely formalized model of the political economy of international trade policy formation. Magee, who coined the term "endogenous policy formation", proposed a framework of analysis that incorporated politico-economic agents who, in the context of economic process and a probabilistic voting model, interact strategically to produce trade policy that advances their narrow self interests. The importance of this framework is that it explicitly identified plausible parameters within which trade policy, previously treated as exogenous, can be treated endogenously.

Unlike Magee's model, MAYER's model of trade-policy formation reconciles the theory of endogenous protection with the standard orthodox models of international trade without entirely relinquishing the intricacies of contemporary political systems present in Magee. His model assumes a "direct majority voting" regime, which is intended to approximate the decision-making process in contemporary democracies, and is formulated in the context of two prominent theorems of international trade designed to "explain" the flow of commodities in the global economy: the Hecksher–Ohlin–Samuelson–Vanek (HOSV) and the specific factors model. In the context of the analysis consistent with the latter model, Mayer finds that although trade impediments may decrease economy-wide social welfare, they may still be implemented in democratic regimes. This is so because even though the "losers" of trade policy outweigh those who gain, the per capita benefit of the "gainers" is disproportionately large to the per capita loss of the "losers". In this context the existence of transaction cost associated with registering votes may remove the majority of the "losers" from the political process if it outweighs their loss from the implementation of trade restricting policies. Hence, Mayer's model explains the paradox that, although trade policy benefits a minority of the population and hurts everyone else, it may still be implemented simply because the average loser's loss is sufficiently small not to warrant costly involvement in the political process to obstruct unpalatable policies.

Although it is not the first empirical study of the political economy dimensions of international trade policy formation, CAVES is an excellent starting point as it is the most innovative and comprehensive study of its time. Caves employs conventional regression analysis techniques to examine three models of trade-policy formation. These models assume that tariffs are adopted by policymakers in response to various politico-economic pressures. The first is an interest group model, the second assumes that the government's objective function entails maximizing its chances of re-election, and the third represents a "national policy" model. These models receive statistical support of varying degrees.

RAY provides the first empirical model in which both trade impediments and imports are treated endogenously by adopting simultaneous equation regression techniques. This approach is undertaken in an effort to capture the bidirectional causal relationship between trade impediments and imports. This relationship derives from the fact that lobbying for trade restrictions is likely to be more intense the larger the import penetration, and therefore damage to domestic producers of import-competing commodities. At the same time, trade impediments that result from such lobbying activities will restrict the magnitude of import penetration. The added sophistication of

this framework of analysis produces substantially more accurate estimates of trade policy determinants.

VOUSDEN provides an excellent review of the evolution of research in the area of international trade policy formation. He extends the discussion by providing a summary of studies that incorporate the fundamentals of endogenous trade policy in the context of imperfectly competitive, or otherwise "distorted", markets.

CHRISTIS G. TOMBAZOS

See also Trade theory, development of

Internet law, *see* Cyberlaw

Interview

Atkinson, Robert, *The Life History Interview*, Thousand Oaks, California: Sage, 1998

Bailey, Kenneth D., *Methods of Social Research*, 3rd edition, New York: Free Press, and London: Collier Macmillan, 1987

Foddy, William, *Constructing Questions for Interviews and Questionnaires: Theory and Practice in Social Research*, Cambridge and New York: Cambridge University Press, 1994

Fowler, Floyd J. Jr and Thomas W. Mangione, *Standardized Survey Interviewing: Minimizing Interviewer-related Error*, Newbury Park, California: Sage, 1990

Frey, James H. and Sabine Mertens Oishi, *The Survey Kit*, vol. 4: *How to Conduct Interviews by Telephone and in Person*, Thousand Oaks, California: Sage, 1995

McCracken, Grant, *The Long Interview*, Newbury Park, California: Sage, 1988

Rubin, Herbert J. and Irene S. Rubin, *Qualitative Interviewing: The Art of Hearing Data*, Thousand Oaks, California: Sage, 1995

Saris, William E., *Computer-Assisted Interviewing*, Newbury Park, California: Sage, 1991

Interviewing is a complex and demanding task. It is a direct conversation the purpose of which is to gather information by administering a set of questions. The interview is a key data-collection tool for conducting surveys.

Two useful general introductions to the basic principles of interviewing are provided by BAILEY and by FREY & OISHI.

In his introductory textbook, Bailey offers an overview of the ways in which survey data can be gathered. He discusses questionnaire design and interview techniques, and analyses in detail the fundamental characteristics of the interview as a structured method of obtaining information in a target population, evaluating its relative advantages and disadvantages.

Frey & Oishi's aim is to guide the reader in the preparation and administration of survey interviews both by telephone and in person. This guide explains in great detail how to write interview questions with structured interviewer instructions, how to write questions that are most effective for telephone and personal interviews, and how to write preletters and scripts for a precall as well as organize a flowing interview script that considers possible question order effects. The volume also deals with the key issue of interviewer selection and training. One of its specific objectives is to prepare the reader to write a job for an interviewer, develop an interviewer training manual, design an interviewer training session, and describe the role of a supervision.

FOWLER & MANGIONE discuss the standardized survey interviewing process in detail. The goal of the practical guide is to provide the reader with a concise summary of the key elements necessary to produce standardized, and reliable, interviews. In meeting this goal, the authors consider different key aspects of standardized interview development: interviewer-related error, standardized interviewing techniques, the role of question design in the standardized interview, interviewer selection and training, and interviewer supervision. The authors draw from their own extensive research on interview-related error and research evidence from other prominent methodologists to illustrate the practical advice offered. Thus, the volume represents a blend of social science theories of interviewing dynamics.

Recent technological developments have made interviewing more feasible and more reliable. The integration of the computer into data gathering has improved the level of data quality for both telephone and in-person interviewing. Computer-assisted interviewing makes it possible for the interview to be completed with fewer problems of interviewer error. The well-organized monograph by SARIS aims to aid researchers to improve their data's quality, and to help the reader identify the possibilities and difficulties that arise in computer-assisted interviewing. Examples of actual research questionnaires are given so that the reader can compare the usual paper questionnaire against the extra statements needed for clear computer-assisted interviewing. The chapters cover different issues such as the definition of computer-assisted interviewing, its various applications, questionnaire construction, a description of computer programs, and an overview of the important features to consider if one wants to purchase a computer-assisted data collection (CADAC) program.

FODDY closely examines the issue of constructing questions for interviews (and questionnaires). The success of any interview or questionnaire depends upon good question design: this practical book provides a coherent, theoretical basis for the construction of valid and reliable questions. The book describes in detail methods for formulating intelligible requests for information: the theoretical framework used provides a set of principles that will increase the validity and reliability of verbal data collected for the social sciences.

Interviewing is an essential tool in qualitative research: through qualitative interviews one can understand experiences and reconstruct events. Qualitative interviewing requires intense listening, a respect for and curiosity about what people say, and a systematic effort to really hear and understand what people tell. Qualitative interviewing encompasses a variety of ways of questioning: interviews differ in style and in the relative emphasis on understanding culture as the main object of study. The scope of the research arena also varies from one type of interview to another.

Two useful contributions focus on qualitative interviewing. RUBIN & RUBIN is an introduction to the theory and practice of qualitative interviewing. It describes the philosophy of qualitative research and provides the underpinning for the more technical skills of interviewing. The authors help readers to develop their own style and confidence as qualitative interviewers. First, the book explores the theories that underlie qualitative interviewing. It also shows researchers how to design research based on interview data, how to form and maintain conversational relationships, how to encourage people to talk, how to guide the flow of conversation, and how to analyse and present an informed description of the data. It also describes how to conduct the two major types of interviews: cultural and topical.

The volume by McCRACKEN provides a systematic guide to the theory and methods for use in the long qualitative interview or in intensive interviewing. It gives a clear explanation of the qualitative interview process by outlining both the theoretical underpinnings and the practical aspects of the process. The volume begins with a general overview of the character and purpose of qualitative inquiry and a review of key issues. The author then introduces important theoretical and methodological issues, various research strategies, and a four-stage model of inquiry, from the design of an open-ended questionnaire to writing up the results. He also offers practical advice for those who commission and administer this research, including sample questionnaires and budgets to help readers design their own.

ATKINSON's interesting book provides an altogether practical and broad introduction to the sensitive collection of first person narratives. Life histories focus on the experiences of an individual and what he or she felt as he or she passed through the different stages of life: a life story is the essence of what has happened to a person. Thus, life histories can tell us about life's passages; they can also provide a window on social change. A specific life story is the best illustration for studying the ways in which culture has shaped and influences that one life. Within this context, the book offers suggestions and guidelines for the process of preparing for and carrying out a life story interview. The text discusses how to plan the interview, how to do the interview, and how to interpret it. The last chapter addresses a specific transcription approach, interpretation issues, and how to make meaning from first-person narratives.

ELISABETTA RUSPINI

See also Questionnaire design

Interview, the selection interview

Anderson, Neil R., "Eight Decades of Employment Interview Research: A Retrospective Meta-review and Prospective Commentary", *European Work and Organizational Psychologist*, 2/1 (1992): 1–32

Arvey, Richard A. and James E. Campion, "The Employment Interview: A Summary and Review of Recent Research", *Personnel Psychology*, 35 (1982): 281–322

Campion, Michael A., David K. Palmer and James E. Campion, "A Review of Structure in the Selection Interview", *Personnel Psychology*, 50/3 (1997): 653–702

Cawley, Brian D., Lisa M. Keeping and Paul E. Levy, "Participation in the Performance Appraisal Process and Employee Reactions: A Meta-Analytic Review of Field Investigations", *Journal of Applied Psychology*, 83/4 (1998): 615–33

Cederblom, Douglas, "The Performance Appraisal Interview: A Review, Implications, and Suggestions", *Academy of Management Review*, 7/2 (1982): 219–27

Dipboye, Robert L., "Structured and Unstructured Selection Interviews: Beyond the Job-Fit Model", *Research in Personnel and Human Resources Management*, 12 (1994): 79–123

Dipboye, Robert L., "Structured Selection Interviews: Why Do They Work? Why Are They Underutilized?" in *International Handbook of Selection and Assessment*, edited by Neil Anderson and Peter Herriot, Chichester and New York: Wiley, 1997

Eder, Robert W. and Michael M. Harris, *The Employment Interview Handbook*, 2nd edition, Thousand Oaks, California: Sage, 1999

Huffcutt, Allen I. and Winfred Arthur, "Hunter and Hunter (1984) Revisited: Interview Validity for Entry-Level Jobs", *Journal of Applied Psychology*, 79/2 (1994): 184–90

Hunter, John E. and R.F. Hunter, "Validity and Utility of Alternative Predictors of Job Performance", *Psychological Bulletin*, 96 (1984): 72–98

London, Manuel, *Job Feedback: Giving, Seeking, and Using Feedback for Performance Improvement*, Mahwah, New Jersey: Erlbaum, 1997

McDaniel, Michael A., Deborah L. Whetzel, Frank L. Schmidt and Steven D. Maurer, "The Validity of Employment Interviews: A Comprehensive Review and Meta-Analysis", *Journal of Applied Psychology*, 79/4 (1994): 599–616

Maurer, Steven D., "The Potential of the Situational Interview: Existing Research and Unresolved Issues", *Human Resource Management Review*, 7/2 (1997): 185–201

Murphy, Kevin R. and Jeanette N. Cleveland, *Understanding Performance Appraisal: Social, Organizational, and Goal-Based Perspectives*, Thousand Oaks, California and London: Sage, 1995

Salgado, Jésus F., "Personnel Selection Methods" in *International Review of Industrial and Organizational Psychology*, vol. 14, edited by Cary L. Cooper and Ivan T. Robertson, Chichester and New York: Wiley, 1999

Smither, James W. (editor), *Performance Appraisal: State of the Art in Practice*, San Francisco: Jossey Bass, 1998

There are many kinds of interview, each having its own literature. This entry will be primarily about selection interviews but some brief attention will be paid to the appraisal interview as a complement to the entries on appraisal and feedback. Other types of interview (such as counselling at work) are covered elsewhere in this guide. The emphasis will be on more academic treatments, rather than "how to interview" or "how to be interviewed" (although many of the items reviewed also consider implications for practice).

Surveys of practice continue to point to the near-universal use of interviews for selecting staff. Although they are widely used, selection interviews have not always received favourable assessments from academic researchers. For example, a review paper by ARVEY & CAMPION summarized earlier reviews of the selection interview before going on to more recent research. The Arvey & Campion paper is important as a source for the earlier literature. One theme that is evident is the relatively low reliability and validity of employment interviews. This was most strikingly demonstrated in the meta-analytic study carried out by HUNTER & HUNTER. Not exclusively about interviews, this work compared the relative effectiveness (defined in terms of predictive validity) of various selection tools: the employment interview fared rather poorly. Being a comparative study the Hunter & Hunter paper is more generally relevant to those interested in personnel selection methods.

Despite these unenthusiastic assessments, interviews continue to be widely used for selection purposes (as noted above). One theme that appears in the literature has to do with why interviews are still so widely used in the face of the evidence that casts doubt on their predictive effectiveness. A related theme that emerges points out that psychometric properties are not the only criteria of effectiveness. But even if one takes a narrow measurement perspective on the selection interview then we find that some reappraisal is underway.

With respect to this last point, a number of meta-analytic studies have been of particular significance. There is little to be gained by summarizing all of these here: it will be sufficient to cover two of the more recent ones, especially as they refer to earlier meta-analyses. A feature of the later meta-analytic studies of the employment interview is that they have become more sophisticated, and they have sought to determine the effect of various moderator variables. McDANIEL *et al.*, for example, considered such features as the content and structure of the interview and the nature of the criterion being predicted. HUFFCUTT & ARTHUR take what is probably the most detailed look to date at structure, defining this in terms of standardization of questioning and standardization of response scoring. One general conclusion that emerges is that structure enhances the psychometric properties of the interview: predictive validity coefficients generally are higher for structured than unstructured interviews.

This, of course, merely begs the question as to what is meant by structure. There are now several papers that examine aspects of this question. One, by CAMPION, PALMER & CAMPION, identifies different components of structure and reviews relevant research. The two readings by DIPBOYE (1994, 1997) offer less full treatments of what is meant by "structure" but none the less overview much of the pertinent evidence. Prominent, however, in these two papers is the first of the themes mentioned above – more specifically, the continued use of unstructured forms of interview and the apparent reluctance (on the part of line managers, for example) to use more structured approaches to interviewing. This theme also is examined by Arvey & Campion. It also is worth noting at this point that the term "structure" is often used in a loose way (to denote any one or more of the 15 properties identified by Campion, Palmer & Campion) and sometimes it is used as an alternative for a particular (almost proprietary) approach to structuring the interview. One example of a particular structured approach is the situational interview – see MAURER.

Much of the literature, particularly the meta-analytic studies, continues to take a measurement perspective on the selection interview, placing special emphasis on such matters as reliability and validity. Some writers, however, have challenged undue emphasis on these psychometric issues. Of interest here is the review paper by ANDERSON. He compares and contrasts two main traditions – an objectivist-psychometric perspective and a subjectivist-social perception perspective. These apply not only to the employment interview but to selection more generally and reflect one of the contemporary debates in the literature on employee selection.

Much of the literature on selection interviews is in journals: books tend to be of a "how to" kind. One important exception to this is the volume edited by EDER & HARRIS. Following an historical overview, the volume has five sections: interview outcomes (validity, fairness, and applicant reaction); constructs assessed – five chapters dealing with what is being measured in the interview; the interviewer's decision-making process; interviewer-applicant dynamics; and finally a commentary on the state of theory, research, and practice. Readers seeking a comprehensive academic treatment of the many aspects of the employment interview should look here first.

Finally, for the selection interview, readers wanting quick access to research published in the early to mid-1990s should refer to SALGADO. This review paper deals not only with the interview but also with other selection methods, as well as touching on other issues in selection practice.

Moving on to the appraisal interview, it would appear that this has become less of a topic of interest in recent years with the "hot" topic of the 1990s having become 360° appraisal/feedback. The two texts (referred to in the entry on Appraisal) by MURPHY & CLEVELAND and by SMITHER do not, for example, include specific chapters on the appraisal interview nor, indeed, is the term indexed in either. Both, however, contain relevant material. The review by CEDERBLOM is helpful as an introduction to the earlier literature. Access to more recent material is gained by referring to sources on feedback (see the separate entry on Feedback) and participation. For the former consult the text by LONDON, which includes chapters on the appraisal interview. For the latter, CAWLEY, KEEPING & LEVY provide a recent meta-analytic review of participation in the appraisal interview. One problem noted by the authors has been the tendency to operationalize participation in several different ways: as an organizing framework for their meta-analysis they adopt an organizational justice perspective (see also the entry on fairness).

RICHARD WILLIAMS

See also Appraisal, Assessment

Intrapreneurship

Block, Zenas and Ian C. MacMillan, *Corporate Venturing: Creating New Business Within the Firm*, Boston: Harvard Business School Press, 1993

Carrier, Camille, "Intrapreneurship in Small Businesses: An Exploratory Study", *Entrepreneurship Theory and Practice*, 21/1 (Fall 1996): 5–20

Kanter, Rosabeth Moss, *The Change Masters: Innovation for Productivity in the American Corporation*, New York: Simon and Schuster, 1983

Kanter, Rosabeth Moss, *When Giants Learn to Dance: Mastering the Challenge of Strategy, Management, and Careers in the 1990s*, New York: Simon and Schuster, 1989

Pinchot, Gifford, *Intrapreneuring: Why You Don't Have to Leave the Corporation to Become an Entrepreneur*, New York: Harper and Row, 1985

Schumpeter, Joseph A., *Capitalism, Socialism, and Democracy*, New York: Harper, 1941, London: Allen and Unwin, 1943; 6th edition London and Boston: Unwin, 1987

Zucker, Lynne G., "Where Do Institutional Patterns Come From: Organizations as Actors in Social Systems" in *Institutional Patterns and Organizations: Culture and Environment*, edited by Lynne Zucker, Cambridge, Massachusetts: Ballinger, 1988

Although KANTER (1983) was not the first to write about internal or corporate entrepreneurship (the phrase "intrapreneurship" had yet to be coined at the time this work was being written), her book is influential. She suggested that collectives do not spark innovation; rather it is the ability of individuals working within given constraints that lead to innovative solutions. The work discusses how the corporate or internal entrepreneur acts as an individual reformer, gaining support from, and operating within, the political environment of the corporation by building networks, and power blocks. In order to do so the individual actor needs to "champion" the cause. In this respect she laid the path for others to follow with the idea that internal entrepreneurship is motivated by a desire to innovate. However this emphasis on the individual ignores the importance of institutional forces. Institutional theory is raised in the book, but this concept and its effect on the "champion" is discussed only as a constraining element and not as an initiating or enabling force.

PINCHOT is one of the first in a long line of "how to" books. This book is important for introducing the word "intrapreneur". This is first introduced to the reader in the following passage:

> These corporate risk takers are very much like entrepreneurs. They take personal risks to make new ideas happen. The difference is they work within large organisations instead of outside them. I call them the intrapreneurs – my shorthand for intracorporate entrepreneur.

This book is light on substance, preferring to highlight how the embattled executive marshals resources by begging, borrowing, and cajoling those within the organization to allow funds, development time, and equipment to fall into his or her hands. The book suggests that internal entrepreneurship is necessary for future development of the organization. However, there is little attempt to describe the preconditions necessary for this to happen. Overall, the book is a basic introduction aimed at those who wish to actively participate in intrapreneurial activity.

The short article by CARRIER, although focused on the small business, provides a good literature review concerning the development of intrapreneurship as a discipline within the conceptual framework of entrepreneurship. Carrier outlines the debate concerning the definitions of entrepreneurship, which leads into a discussion regarding the internal entrepreneur within large firms and how the practice of intrapreneurship differs within the small or emerging firm. In addressing the subject she does not offer a list of "how to" explanations; rather, she identifies trends and discusses the relevance of both the individual and environment in setting the scene for successful internal entrepreneurial acts. The approach Carrier uses in addressing innovation is important in that she does not limit her discussion of innovation to technology. Rather, innovation is seen as a process that has different flavours depending upon the size and complexity of the firm in which the individual internal entrepreneur is placed.

At first glance, *Capitalism, Democracy and Socialism* is not a title that would suggest intrapreneurship. This book contributes to the underlying philosophy that eventually manifests in the appearance of the internal entrepreneur. SCHUMPETER saw capitalism as the goal of successful society, not only because of the technological advances this brought but also because of the potential pacifying nature of capitalism. Schumpeter believed that the driving force of the capitalist economy was the entrepreneur. To him, the entrepreneur was a person who reformed or revolutionized production through the use of innovation. Of particular importance is the concept of "creative destruction". It is this process – one of continuous improvement and renewal – that results in an improvement in business process and an improvement in the product or service offering of a firm. Again it is the role of the entrepreneur to initiate and push through such acts of creative destruction. At no time does Schumpeter suggest that only founders of firms carry out this activity; rather. the tone of the work suggests that this activity is best carried out by those within the firm. His work is considered here, as there was no distinction made between the internal and external entrepreneur. The important aspect is the function of entrepreneurship.

KANTER (1989) envisaged *When Giants Learn to Dance* as the third instalment of a trilogy she started with *Men and Women of the Corporation*. This book is one of the few published in recent times that address the external and internal economic and political reasons for engaging in internal entrepreneurship. Kanter does not call the activity of the innovator within the organization "intrapreneurship". Instead, she sees internally driven innovation as a necessity and therefore an essential part of the overall management function. Entrepreneurship therefore is the role of a modern manager, and should not be confined only to the self-employed or to new-venture start-ups. Following on from *The Change Masters*, this book outlines some successful organizations and why they have been successful. Kanter seems to following in the footsteps of

Schumpeter in the suggestion that continuous improvement can only been found through continuous innovation – a different way of saying "creative destruction". This book uses example organizations along with example individuals to illustrate the point that internal entrepreneurship is essential and that "intrapreneurship" is a modern business buzzword.

BLOCK & MACMILLAN have produced one of the better examples of the genre. As the title suggests, the text moves away from describing how individuals can benefit from internal entrepreneurship and examines the corporate and organizational benefits obtained through corporate venturing. The authors rest the concept of internal entrepreneurship firmly within the overall paradigm of entrepreneurship, preferring to see the activity as a process rather than a function within the organization. As a management "how to" guide, the book includes many examples of best practice. These examples are discussed in context of existing trends and future directions through the use of appropriate academic and industrial references. The book comprises organized, logical, easy to follow sections, with justifications for the assertions made. It gives the feeling of an authoritative, well-researched guide to internal entrepreneurship for both practitioners and academic researchers.

ZUCKER argues that collective actors – especially those organized along formal lines – are the primary source for change within organizations. In saying this, Zucker provides a philosophical base in which to rest the concept of internal entrepreneurship. She argues that when an institution or organization is placed under threat or stress, then collectively the individuals will form networks or collaborations. These networks will, in turn, actively seek opportunities for innovative solutions to overcome the perceived threat.

Zucker therefore argues that change within organizations is as a result of externally perceived threats to the longevity of the collective and the organization. She further argues that self-interest acts in harmony with the collective in ensuring power acquisition and position within the organization. Overall, this article gives us a base from which to form future theory regarding the sociological aspects relating to the emergence of internal entrepreneurship within organizations.

ANDREW CARDOW

See also Enterprise culture, Entrepreneur, Innovation, organizational

Investments, business

Griffiths, Howard, *Financial Investments*, London: McGraw Hill, 1990

Haugen, Robert A., *Modern Investment Theory*, 4th edition, London and Upper Saddle River, New Jersey: Prentice Hall, 1997

Levy, Haim and Marshall Sarnat, *Capital Investment and Financial Decisions*, 5th edition, New York and London: Prentice Hall, 1994

Lumby, Steve and Chris Jones, *Investment Appraisal and Financial Decisions*, 6th edition, London: International Thomson Business Press, 1999

Markowitz, Harry M., *Portfolio Selection: Efficient Diversification of Investments*, 2nd edition, Oxford and Cambridge, Massachusetts: Blackwell, 1991

Pike, Richard and Bill Neale, *Corporate Finance and Investment: Decisions and Strategies*, 3rd edition, London and New York: Prentice Hall, 1999

Sharpe, William F., G.J. Alexander and Jeffery V. Bailey, *Investments*, 6th edition, Upper Saddle River, New Jersey: Prentice Hall, 1999

GRIFFITHS is a classical textbook for second year undergraduates in British further and higher education. It covers most of the expected material in the books of this kind (risk and returns, operation of the market, Markowitz's portfolio theory, the capital asset pricing model (CAPM), options and futures, financial corporate restructuring, and so on). The book has a clear British note in a market dominated by the textbooks produced by American scholars. Particularly useful is the last chapter on the crash of 1987 and its implications for the British financial system. The book also gives a good exposure to basic quantitative skills and therefore can be read by a person with very little or no prior knowledge of mathematical tools.

In contrast, HAUGEN is a textbook aimed at postgraduate and advanced undergraduate students. It is intended for a more advanced readership, so prior knowledge of introductory finance and accounting is therefore assumed, although profound knowledge of mathematical methods is not required. A reader with basic algebra and calculus should be able to follow this book without many difficulties. The book covers extensively portfolio theory and capital assets pricing, besides futures and options, and other issues that are generally included in classical investment texts. An introductory section contains an exposure to the development of modern investment theory (Markowitz, Sharpe, Roll, Fama, Ross, Black-Scholes), allowing a reader to have a good grasp of major developments.

LEVY & SARNAT is a good textbook that can be used equally successfully at undergraduate and postgraduate levels. The material is separated under three main groupings: capital budgeting, risk and uncertainty, and long-term financial decisions. It looks at the viability of the proposed projects and lists different methods of evaluation (net present value, internal rate of return) developing further a very good exposure of CAPM and arbitrage pricing theory (APT) models. The book was written with clear aspirations to address complex issues of financial policy, with a special emphasis on a firm's long-term capital resources and commitments. It does not require significant knowledge of mathematical and econometric techniques. Graphical presentations are often used in places where in other books authors would opt for clear mathematical expressions. It is an interesting and overall user-friendly textbook that can be used for the range of courses.

LUMBY & JONES is another seminal textbook in modern investment theory, written with a British exposure. The book covers regular material expected to be taught on courses in investment, financial decision making, or financial strategy. The book particularly focuses on corporate financial decision making, especially when it comes to committing to the financing of long-term capital expenditures. The book gives a fairly good balance between theory and practice. Theoretical

underpinnings (CAPM, APT, portfolio selection, and portfolio choice) are presented in a very accessible way, while some practical applications may require the somewhat profound knowledge of mathematical techniques. A classical but interesting and accessible textbook aimed at beginners and intermediate undergraduate students. However, it may also be successfully used as a textbook for the first course in finance (financial management, financial decision making) and for masters, particularly MBA students.

MARKOWITZ changed the outlook of modern finance. Its portfolio selection is a seminal work of modern investment (portfolio) theory. He dichotomized the investment process into two stages, the formation of probability beliefs (security analysis) and the portfolio choice. He argued that, in choosing a portfolio, the objective of maximizing expected return is not consistent with the widespread practice of diversification, suggesting that investor behaviour was consistent with minimizing expected utility, where utility was a function of the mean and variance, and pointed out that such an objective implied a concave utility function. He also analysed the utility implications of alternative selection rules, and in the case of semi-variance criterion, he discusses the solution procedure. Markowitz's theory includes a discussion of portfolio selection under logarithmic utility and points out that the portfolio that maximizes the geometric mean return is approximately mean-variance efficient, showing how as the number of securities in the portfolio is increased, portfolio variance approaches the average covariance. This is a very important book with which any serious study of investment theory and policy must both start and finish. Although it is a book primarily intended for advanced postgraduate students and professionals, surprisingly it can be followed by a beginner as well. It is always advisable to refer to it, when a reader acquires more profound knowledge of modern finance. He or she may be surprised how some things may have a couple of different perspectives.

PIKE & NEALE is another textbook on investment that was written with a British (European) perspective in mind, for both undergraduate and postgraduate students. It covers the usual material in some depth and allows a student to extend his/her knowledge according to their interests. It gives a strategic and practical focus to the financial decision-making process. The main topics are approached in a classical manner, starting with cashflow analysis, and moving on to different techniques of project appraisal (internal rate of return and net present value). It incorporates very well modern methods of investment risk analysis and portfolio theory. Two dominant models (CAPM and APT) are covered in significant depth, with many critical notes. Students are given a number of worked examples, which should help them to develop the skills of technical analysis and at the same time enable them to see how theory works in practice. This is a text that students may find interesting and user friendly. Although it is written for university level studies, it can also be used by those who are attending professional courses in accounting, as it covers much of the material taught at the professional stages.

SHARPE, ALEXANDER & BAILEY is a classic American intermediate/advanced undergraduate and first-year postgraduate textbook. It can be also used by professionals to refresh basic principles of investments. The book gives a first account of the development of investment theory from Markowitz

(Sharpe's former professor), and then exposes Sharpe's improvement of portfolio theory. Answering the question as to how prices of securities would be affected if every portfolio manager would manage their investments using portfolio theory, and investing at the frontier, Sharpe developed the CAPM in 1964, almost in parallel with Litner and Mossin. This was a model that dominated the field of finance for some 15 years. However, this textbook gives a very good account of other developments in this field of finance, such as Ross' APT, the Black–Scholes option pricing model, and so on. This textbook has probably influenced the development of a large number of current portfolio managers. It is fairly user friendly, but sometimes inconsistent as the second author has updated the text in places, so the book may lose the internal harmony that characterizes one-author textbooks. However, despite these shortcomings, it is still recommended.

ŽELJKO ŠEVIĆ

Irish economy and record: Northern Ireland

Bradley, John, *An Island Economy: Exploring Long-Term Consequences of Peace and Reconciliation in the Island of Ireland*, Dublin: Forum for Peace and Reconciliation, 1996

Bradley, John (editor), *Regional Economic and Policy Impacts of EMU: The Case of Northern Ireland*, Belfast: Northern Ireland Economic Council, 1998

Dunford, Mick and Ray Hudson, *Successful European Regions: Northern Ireland Learning from Others*, Belfast: Northern Ireland Economic Council, 1996

Hutton, Will, *Britain and Northern Ireland, The State We're In: Failure and Opportunity*, Belfast: Northern Ireland Economic Council, 1994

Munck, Ronnie, *The Irish Economy: Results and Prospects*, London: Pluto Press, 1993

Munck, Ronnie and Douglas Hamilton, "Politics, the Economy and Peace in Northern Ireland" in *Rethinking Northern Ireland: Culture, Identity and Colonialism*, edited by David Miller, London and New York: Addison Wesley Longman, 1998

O'Dowd, Liam, "Development or Dependency? State, Economy and Society in Northern Ireland" in *Irish Society: Sociological Perspectives*, edited by Patrick Clancy *et al.*, Dublin: Institute of Public Administration, 1995

Rowthorn, Bob and Naomi Wayne, *Northern Ireland: The Political Economy of Conflict*, Cambridge: Polity Press, 1988

Sheehan, Maura, Douglas Hamilton and Ronnie Munck, "Political Conflict, Partition and the Underdevelopment of the Irish Economy", *Review of Radical Political Economics*, 30/1 (1998): 1–31

Teague, Paul (editor), *The Economy of Northern Ireland: Perspectives for Structural Change*, London: Lawrence and Wishart, 1993

The Northern Ireland economy has received extensive and detailed analysis over the past few decades, with particular discussion of the economy in terms of performance, explanation, and prospects over the period of political and violent conflict.

Although now rather dated, the analysis by ROWTHORN & WAYNE remains useful in highlighting key economic issues that continue today in changed political circumstances. In a detailed but accessible account, they present a political and economic explanation of the industrial crisis that Northern Ireland has experienced since the early 1970s. The crisis is accounted for by a combination of factors: events in the world economy, dependence of the regional economy on exports to Britain, the branch-plant nature of the industrial base and its dependence on outside firms, and armed conflict and political instability. A key aspect of the analysis is its focus on the excessive level of public subsidization of the economy through what has become known as the British subvention. This insightful analysis, especially at the time of publication, describes Northern Ireland as a "workhouse economy", which imports a great deal from outside while providing few exports in return. The gap between imports and exports is seen to be funded out of taxes levied in mainland Britain, which allows a standard of living in Northern Ireland to be maintained well in excess of its productive capacity.

MUNCK takes a longer historical perspective and, at the time of publication, was the first to understand the experience and record of both the North and South of Ireland in the context of an island economy. Using the theoretical framework of dependent development, the book usefully presents the record of the Northern Ireland economy from the time of the industrial revolution and its dependence on shipbuilding and linen, through the long-term decline in the postwar period, and more recently the deep problems of the 1970s and 1980s, with the onset of political violence, conflict, and instability. Useful chapters examine the effects on workers of these economic changes and the key questions and issues raised by an increasingly integrated European economy. The book ends by looking forward to five possible development scenarios: "more of the same", devolution in the North, economic harmonization on the island, a capitalist united Ireland, and a "democratic economy". This discussion considers the crucial relationship between possible constitutional change and economic development.

TEAGUE presents a range of essays on various aspects of the Northern Ireland economy, such as the dominant public sector, religious discrimination in the labour market, foreign investment, and North–South cooperation. An important chapter by the editor discusses the relationship between governance and economic performance, and argues that the three components of the governance structure – the role of institutions, commercial connections, and the form of enterprise calculation – are all deeply faulty.

O'DOWD, in a comprehensive analysis, also starts with a historical perspective and argues that the North's economy needs to be understood in the context of the particular kinds of political conditions and social relationships that have sustained it. In particular, he places emphasis on the colonial nature of the economy. He clearly shows the important links between the weak nature of the productive base of the economy and the issue of inequality, which permeates every aspect of Northern Ireland in terms of class, gender, religion, and locality.

The excessive, but nondevelopmental state dependency of the economy is highlighted.

HUTTON, in a trenchant essay, argues that the Northern Ireland economy is unsustainable in its present form and that it suffers from a particularly acute version of the "British disease". A suitable framework for economic development will only emerge with the radical overhaul of the governance system in the UK as a whole. Foreseeing recent political developments, he argues that the way forward is devolution within a reformed UK, and the creation of consensual political and economic institutions within Northern Ireland, and between the North and South.

In one of the few studies that places Northern Ireland in an explicitly European comparative context, DUNFORD & HUDSON provide a pathbreaking multidisciplinary analysis, drawing on insights from economic and social geography, politics, history, cultural studies, and orthodox economics. By looking in some detail at "successful" regions in Europe, they identify key policy directions that would need to be followed in Northern Ireland if success were to be replicated there. In particular, they highlight: the difficulties in transferring success from one specific political, economic, social, and cultural space to another; the continuing importance of natural resource endowment and location; social cohesion; the key aspects of cooperation, trust, and networking; the nature of inward investment; industrial relations; government, institutions and culture; cross-border activity and internationalization; technology and innovation; and institutional performance.

BRADLEY's (1996) study of the island economy provides a wealth of statistical and other information and places the performance of the Northern economy explicitly alongside that of the South. Taking a long historical perspective, dating back to 1750, he presents a highly comprehensive analysis of the Northern Ireland economy, focusing on changing demography, the evolving sectoral mix of the economy, labour market failure in terms of unemployment and religious segmentation, public expenditure and the humiliating effect of the British subvention, competitiveness, and the costs of the "troubles". Looking forward, he discusses possible development paths for the economy. Discounting separate development of North and South, he places emphasis on the key North–South axis on the island and looks at coordinated development and the idea of a single island economy.

BRADLEY (1998) presents an even more detailed statistical analysis of the Northern Ireland economy, and looks specifically at the implications for Northern Ireland of Economic and Monetary Union (EMU) in Europe. In particular, it examines the asymmetrical nature and consequences, especially for the creation of an island economy, of the North being outside EMU and the South an active partner within.

SHEEHAN, HAMILTON & MUNCK provide an eclectic mix of radical and orthodox approaches to analysis of the Northern Ireland economy. They argue that the partition of Ireland not only contributed to over 70 years of conflict and instability, but also to the underdevelopment of the Irish economy, North and South. The historical development of the economy is examined, with particular reference to models of dependent development and the economic costs of partition.

MUNCK & HAMILTON extend their earlier work by usefully expanding on their analysis of possible future path-ways for the Northern and all-Ireland economy. They dismiss those who assume that there will be "more of the same" with regard to separate economic development on the island, coupled with failed policy; they critically assess the limited benefits of economic integration; and they present an ambitious and radical scenario of democratic development for Ireland. They stress the adoption of developmentalist perspectives in Ireland and, in so doing, they touch on some of the important debates around globalization, the "third sector", and the need to move away from overly economistic approaches.

DOUGLAS HAMILTON

Irish economy and record: Republic of Ireland

Bradley, John, *An Island Economy: Exploring Long-Term Consequences of Peace and Reconciliation in the Island of Ireland*, Dublin: Forum for Peace and Reconciliation, 1996

Bradley, John, John FitzGerald, Patrick Honohan and Ita Kearney, "Interpreting the Irish Growth Experience" in *Medium-Term Review: 1997–2003*, Dublin: Economic and Social Research Institute, 1997

Crotty, Raymond, *Ireland in Crisis: A Study in Capitalist Undevelopment*, Dingle: Brandon, 1986

Kennedy, Kieran A., Thomas Giblin and Deirdre McHugh, *The Economic Development of Ireland in the Twentieth Century*, London: Croom Helm, 1988

Lee, Joe, *Ireland, 1912–1985: Politics and Society*, Cambridge: Cambridge University Press, 1989

Mjøset, Lars, *The Irish Economy in a Comparative Institutional Perspective*, Dublin: Stationery Office, 1992

O'Hagan, John W. (editor), *Policy and Performance of a Small European Country*, Basingstoke: Macmillan, 1995

O'Hearn, Denis, *Inside the Celtic Tiger: The Irish Economy and the Asian Model*, London: Pluto Press, 1998

O'Malley, Eoin, *Industry and Economic Development: The Challenge for the Latecomer*, Dublin: Gill and Macmillan, 1989

Recent years have witnessed a fundamental turnaround in the fortunes of the Southern Irish economy. From a situation of low growth, high unemployment, and excessive national debt, the economy has been dubbed the "Celtic Tiger" because of its extraordinarily high rates of growth during the 1990s.

Although primarily a history book, LEE presents a wide-ranging account of the many changes that the South of Ireland has experienced this century, in particular the period of protectionism in the postwar period, the opening up of the economy to free trade and foreign investment in the late 1950s and early 1960s, and the crippling economic problems of the 1980s. His main thesis is that Irish society has a "possession" ethic rather than a "performance" ethic, and that this has suppressed entrepreneurship, to the detriment of more positive economic development.

KENNEDY, GIBLIN & McHUGH provide a more orthodox account of the Southern Irish economy this century and provide a useful assessment of its performance since independence. The key issues of demography, capital investment, trade, agriculture, and manufacturing are all examined in detail, with copious statistics presented. In conclusion, the book argues that the South of Ireland experienced economic problems up until the 1990s because of the implications of its smallness, a lack of a long-term perspective, and inadequate attention to human resources.

Although it is now dated, CROTTY provides a fascinating and eclectic account of Irish economic development, arguing that the South has been a unique example in Europe of "capitalist post-colonial undevelopment". Drawing on both dependency analysis and neoclassical theory, Crotty sees the economic structure as having been oriented towards the profitability and advantage of British colonial capital, which is reflected in conditions on the land and in the actions of local comprador elites who benefited from colonialism.

O'MALLEY also draws on more general development theory to explain Southern Irish performance, arguing that as a latecomer to industrialization, the South was greatly inhibited by barriers to entry into international markets. This means that it has been unable to develop firms and industries to a size sufficient to overcome the high development costs of first entering markets and then subsequently competing successfully against international firms without substantial and specific public assistance. Such barriers to entry include economies of scale, large capital requirements, product differentiation, advanced technology, specialized skills, and the external economies inherent in large advanced industrial centres. The important policy conclusion of this thinking is that the conventionally understood constraints on industrial development, such as lack of entrepreneurship, lack of capital, an insufficient physical infrastructure, and a low-quality labour force, are misguided. A more appropriate policy response is one that is highly interventionist, long-term and strategic, which tackles the deep-rooted structural problems of a late-industrializing economy and which often goes against the short-term dictates of the market.

MJØSET's study continues the application of development theory to the Southern Irish experience. He makes a number of insightful comparisons with other small and peripheral economies, arguing that the South of Ireland has a strange combination of both advanced and retarded economic and social characteristics, which mean that it falls between the First and Third Worlds. He uses the framework of autocentric and peripheral development to show that the economy suffers from a number of factors: a weak national system of innovation; a unique demographic pattern of population decline through emigration; an agrarian-based society with paternalist family structures; and the negative impact of British colonialism. As a result of the interaction of these factors, the economy has suffered a sequence of vicious rather than virtuous circles of development.

The edited volume by O'HAGAN provides a broad and comprehensive coverage of the main economic issues in the South from a largely orthodox point of view. Sixteen contributors make a brave attempt at the difficult task of linking economic theory with analysis of actual experience. The issues range from fiscal and monetary policy, through economic growth, the labour market and European integration, to sectoral analysis of agriculture, manufacturing, and services.

The study by BRADLEY provides a wealth of statistical information on te Southern economy and places it explicitly alongside that of the North. Taking a long historical perspective, dating back to 1750, he presents a highly comprehensive analysis of the Southern Ireland economy, with focus on changing demography, the evolving sectoral mix of the economy, labour market failure in terms of unemployment, and public expenditure. Unusually from a Southern perspective, he places an important focus on the need to develop an island economy in Ireland.

The edited volume by BRADLEY et al. provides an important study of the exceptional economic performance of the South of Ireland in the 1990s, arguing that a range of mutually supportive factors help to provide an explanation: fiscal restructuring in the mid-to-late 1980s; a huge inflow of high-quality foreign investment; the sequence of national pay agreements from 1987 onwards; the two major devaluations of the Irish pound in 1986 and 1993; the convergence of Irish interest rates towards German rates; the increasing level of average educational qualifications; the inflow of aid from the EU; and widely based improvements in competitiveness.

In a far more critical assessment of the "Celtic Tiger", O'HEARN provides a radical and insightful account that argues that many of the fundamental changes taking place were partly illusory, often had a negative side, and were unlikely to be sustainable. Southern Irish performance has been characterized by a strange set of contradictory results: high growth of transnational production and exports without correspondingly high investment or job creation in manufacturing; concentration of employment growth in services without correspondingly rapid growth in service provision; and rapid overall economic growth with stagnant investment, sluggish consumption growth, and rising inequality and social exclusion.

DOUGLAS HAMILTON

Islamic economics

Ahmad, Khurshid (editor), Studies in Islamic Economics, Jeddah: International Centre for Research in Islamic Economics, King Abdul Aziz University, and Leicester: Islamic Foundation, 1980

Al-Sadr, M.B., Iqtisaduna: Our Economics, 4 vols, Tehran: World Organization for Islamic Services, 1982–84 (original Arabic edition 1961)

Anwar, M., Modelling Interest-free Economy: A Study in Microeconomics and Development, London and Herndon, Virginia: International Institute of Islamic Thought, 1987

Chapra, M. Umer, Islam and the Economic Challenge, Leicester: Islamic Foundation, and Herndon, Virginia: International Institute of Islamic Thought, 1992

Choudhury, Masudul Alam, Contributions to Islamic Economic Theory: A Study in Social Economics, New York: St Martin's Press, and Basingstoke: Macmillan, 1986

Essid, Yassine, A Critique of the Origins of Islamic Economic Thought, Leiden and New York: Brill, 1995

Faridi, F.R. (editor), Aspects of Islamic Economics and the Economy of Indian Muslims, New Delhi: Institute of Objective Studies, 1993

Jomo, K.S. (editor), *Islamic Economic Alternatives: Critical Perspectives and New Directions*, Basingstoke: Macmillan, 1992

Rodinson, Maxime, *Islam and Capitalism*, London: Allen Lane, and New York: Pantheon, 1974

AHMAD contains a selection of papers presented by professional economists to the first International Conference on Islamic Economics held at Mekka in 1976. It regroups nine specialized papers and two surveys. The areas of studies specifically explored in this volume include: theory of consumption and consumer behaviour; money, interest, and profit sharing; interest-free banking; efficiency of an interest-free economy; fiscal policy and *Zakat*; the Islamic welfare state, and economic development in an Islamic framework. An article also surveys the literature on Islamic economics written in Arabic, Urdu, and English up to 1976. A second survey paper explores the Turkish literature on Islamic economics during the republican era. Despite being slightly outdated, this selection of articles covers the most important aspects of Islamic economics.

AL-SADR is one of the first Arab scholars who wrote on Islamic economics. Being a Shiite jurist, his analysis draws heavily on Islamic jurisprudence. His fierce attack on Marxism and capitalism and his comparison of the two systems with Islam throughout the book appears to have set an example for later books on Islamic economics. His concentration on Marxism and capitalism makes his work more apologetic than positive. However, Islamic economics being a discipline strongly intermingled with Islamic jurisprudence, the book is a good reference for those who are interested in the juristic sources of Islamic economics. The philosophical bases of property, the economic problem, pre- and post-production distribution, production, and the role of the state in economics are thoroughly discussed. At every possible opportunity, he reminds the reader of the superiority and soundness of Islamic economics over Marxism and capitalism. The book is a good introduction to the philosophical side of Islamic economics.

ANWAR develops a theoretical, interest-free general equilibrium model that reflects the intent of Islam in the area of finance. In this technical study, only the "interest free" principle has been considered. Other principles of Islamic economics are not included to obtain a complete Islamic macroeconomic model. Chapter one of the study is a general introduction to interest-bearing and interest-free economies. Chapter two deals with Islamic economics and in particular economies with interest-free banking systems. Chapter three is concerned with methodological questions on how to construct a general equilibrium model for interest-free economies. Chapter four is concerned with the building of macroeconomic model with an interest-free financial sector. The following chapter covers policy analysis in interest-free economies. Chapter six analyses how development is financed in interest-free economies. The last chapter is a comparative analysis of mainstream and Islamic economic systems. The book is of interest to macroeconomists interested in interest-free economies.

In a similar but more refined style to Al-Sadr, CHAPRA criticizes both socialism and capitalism. He argues that the fall of socialism does not necessarily mean that capitalism has overcome its own problems, and that Islamic economics may be the answer to many economic questions of our time. His main contribution appears to be his emphasis on the morality factor in economics: according to capitalism, socialism and the welfare state are irrelevant to the solution of economic problems. Chapra contends that concepts of efficiency and equity can only become operational if they are linked to moral values. He suggests an Islamic economic system based on the goals of Islam (*Maqasid al-Shari`ah*). These goals are to be fulfilled on the basis of a moral filter that scrutinizes all production, distribution, and consumption decisions. The book is a serious attempt to provide a comprehensive view of an Islamic economic system, and how it would be implemented in today's world. *Tawhid* (Divine unity), *Khilafa* (vicegerency) and justice are the three fundamental sources of Islamic economic strategy. Some of his suggestions include activating *Zakat* (Islamic tax), changing consumer behaviour through moral filters, and replacing the interest-based financial system by Islamic alternatives.

CHOUDHOURY is a rigorous and comprehensive contribution to Islamic economic theory. It is a work in normative economics as it develops and systematically presents the theory of Islamic economics based on its fundamental sources, the Quran, the Sunnah, and Ijtihad. The author exposes the theory of Islamic economics within the framework of mainstream economics. However, he advocates the formulation of a political economy of social policy that includes philosophy, religion, and value judgement. Hence, he suggests that Islamic economics can be considered as a special case of social economics. The methodology used combines discursive, geometric, and mathematical approaches. The book contains four parts: principles of Islamic economics, microeconomics, macroeconomics, and a postscript. The postscript develops a rigorous exposition of Islamic economics as a special study in social economics where ethical problems are included. This book is essential for a study of Islamic economics, and is also useful in studying social economics, the history of economic thought and comparative economic systems.

ESSID is a discursive exposition of the origin of Arabic–Islamic economic thought. It examines and evaluates the validity of economic ideas in Islam through three models: *Tadbir Al-Khilafa* (government of the state), *Hisba* (administration of the city), and *Tadbir Al-Manzil* (management of the household). The book is divided into three parts and a general conclusion. Part one is concerned with the optimal, ideal, and rational political organization of the state. Part two deals with the administration of the economic and social relations in the city. This is carried out by institutions that make sure that these relationships are in conformity with Islamic precepts. The third part, is concerned with *Tadbir Al-Manzil* (administration of the household), and *Tadbir Al-Mal* (the art of managing one's fortune). The author contends that most ideas have been borrowed from the Greeks. Finally, the general conclusion asserts that the general principle of Arab–Islamic economics is to avoid both excess and deficiency (middle course). The author affirms that Greek thinkers also inspired this. The book may be useful for historians of economic thought.

FARIDI contains a collection of 10 essays discussing a number of aspects of Islamic economics. Although the majority of essays deal with Islamic banking, other microeconomic, macroeconomic, and accounting topics are also discussed. The essays are most suitable for introductory purposes. The essays include some attempts to lay down a theory of consumer behaviour and macroeconomic models under an interest-free regime. The methodology of Islamic economics is outlined, with particular emphasis on the role of *Ijtihad* in deriving the Islamic economic corpus. Financial accounting is also touched upon, using a comparison between the American accounting system and Islamic law. Two essays are dedicated to empirical findings on interest-free banking. The first reveals that there have been many difficulties in implementing an Islamic banking system in Pakistan. The second, using time-series financial data from Tunisia, suggests that the Islamic interest-free system would perform better than an interest-based system.

The eight essays in JOMO provide an excellent critical view of Islamic economics both from a theoretical and a practical perspective. The principles upon which Islamic economics is based (behavioural norms, *Zakat*, interest prohibition, justice, and equality) are shown to be fraught with inconsistencies. One major point made is that Islamic economists have so far relied upon outdated religious opinions and interpretations of the *Quran* and the *Sunnah* (the Prophet's sayings). Islamic economists are criticized on the grounds that they attempt to justify existing economic relationships and the status quo rather than dealing with the immediate socioeconomic problems of the masses. Instead, a progressive approach to Islamic economics is suggested. The collection also includes a critical review of RODINSON's book, an assessment of the Islamization of the economy in Pakistan, and a summary of the major features of an Islamic economic system.

Criticism of both the doctrine and practice of Islamic economics is rare and Rodinson is a very useful source for those who are looking for the alternative view on Islamic economics. He reveals a number of ambiguities and contradictions within the Islamic economic doctrine and finds that there is a divergence between the doctrine and economic practice in the Islamic world. He also argues that the Islamic ideology has nothing to do with the economic path followed by Muslims. This, according to him, has been the result of social forces of production. Conflict between Islamic ideals and Muslim practices involves the use of ruses to get around the prohibition of interest, unequal distribution of income in favour of a small minority, and exploitation of the poor.

CHERIF GUERMAT AND KADDOUR HADRI

Islamic fundamentalism

Barber, Benjamin, *Jihad vs McWorld*, New York: Times Books, 1995

Davis, Joyce M., *Between Jihad and Salaam: Profiles in Islam*, New York: St Martin's Press, 1997

Eickelman, Dale F. and James Piscatori, *Muslim Politics*, Princeton, New Jersey: Princeton University Press, 1996

Huntington, Samuel P., "The Clash of Civilizations", *Foreign Affairs* 72 /3 (1993): 22–49

Huntington, Samuel P., *The Clash of Civilizations and the Remaking of the World Order*, New York and London: Simon and Schuster, 1996

Lawrence, Bruce, *Defenders of God: The Fundamentalist Revolt against the Modern Age*, San Francisco: Harper and Row, 1989

Miller, Judith, *God has Ninety-Nine Names: Reporting from a Militant Middle East*, New York: Simon and Schuster, 1996

Sayyid, Bobby S., *A Fundamental Fear: Eurocentrism and the Emergence of Islam*, London: Zed, 1997

Tibi, Bassam, *The Challenge of Fundamentalism: Political Islam and the New World Disorder*, Berkeley: University of California Press, 1998

HUNTINGTON (1993, 1996) suggests the controversial idea that, in the post-Cold War era, conflicts will be civilizational in character. Although he explores other possible threats to Western democracy, he concentrates on the threat of Islam. His depiction of Islam as violent and bloody indicates that his view of Islam is shaped by media presentations of Islamic extremists. His article and book are important to the study of Islamic fundamentalism because they allow us to engage common misconceptions about Islam that have become well established in the works of otherwise well-respected scholars.

BARBER likewise establishes a general frame for considering globalization and fundamentalist responses to it. Despite the book's unfortunate title, it is a fairly sophisticated macrolevel analysis of these processes. It does not explore the nitty-gritty of Islamic fundamentalism and is therefore considered here as a supplementary text.

LAWRENCE is the key text in the study of fundamentalism as a general category. He examines how certain Jewish, Christian, and Islamic movements can all be considered fundamentalist. He responds to critics who wish to assert that fundamentalism can be neither crosscultural nor multicreedal. He argues that fundamentalists are moderns and that fundamentalism is a form of modernism. By this he means that fundamentalists are not merely defending tradition in the face of modernity, but are defining a particular way to be modern. Fundamentalists engage the technological, philosophical, and political dimensions of modernity. The bulk of the book is a general treatment of the category of fundamentalism and a comparative consideration of the common ways fundamentalists respond to modernity. Lawrence includes chapters discussing the details of Jewish, Muslim, and Christian fundamentalism. The chapter on Islamic fundamentalism highlights the fundamentalist movements of Egypt, Malaysia, and Pakistan.

SAYYID rejects any attempt to understand "Islamic fundamentalism" in any comparative manner. Arguing that the label "Islamic fundamentalism" does violence by forcing dissimilar movements into a single category, Sayyid proposes an alternative label, "Islamism". He defines an Islamist as anyone who places his or her Muslim identity at the centre of his or her political practice. He divides the Islamic world into two basic camps: Kemalists and Islamists. By dividing the Muslim world into those who reject Islam in public discourse (Kemalists) and those who use Islamic metaphors to narrate their political projects (Islamists), Sayyid puts both the Palestinian *Hamas* and the Indonesian *Nahdlatul Ulama* in the same category. Apart from the fact that both movements use Islamic metaphors in their politics, they have very little in common. This work does not use any case examples, textual or ethnographic, or even any survey data.

DAVIS and MILLER each base their works on journalistic interviews with members of various Islamic fundamentalist movements. In this way, both of these works are important contributions in that they give us detailed case material. Davis, like Sayyid, rejects the term Islamic "fundamentalist" in favour of two terms: Islamist (a politically active Muslim scholar or intellectual) and Islamic militant (those who advocate violence to establish an Islamic state). She provides captivating case studies of 17 Islamist leaders from Algeria to Indonesia. The perspectives portrayed range from peaceful, moderate positions of those committed to democracy to the extreme positions of people regularly involved in terrorist activities. This book portrays even the extremists in a very human manner.

So far, many of the works considered wish to move from the study of Islamic fundamentalism to the study of Islamism or Muslim politics. EICKELMAN & PISCATORI move beyond nomenclatural sleight of hand to discuss the dynamics and processes of Muslim politics. They demonstrate clearly that the symbols used by those called fundamentalists or Islamists by other authors are contested and subject to debate. There is no single Islamic political vision. They examine the range of symbols used in Muslim politics, and examine the invented nature of these symbols and Islamic tradition in many societies. They turn to a discussion of sacred authority and the role of *ulama* in modern Muslim societies. The volume concludes by examining the place of family and ethnicity in Muslim politics.

One of the most sophisticated recent works on fundamentalism by far is TIBI. This particular work is just one selection of the author's substantial contribution to the study of fundamentalism and global politics. As a self-professed "liberal Muslim", Tibi explores the dimensions of the "clash of civilizations" that he acknowledges without attributing to it Huntington's sense of inevitability. In fact, he argues that it is fundamentalism of all sorts that is driving the new world disorder and preventing emergence of a peaceful global order. This book deals with Islamic fundamentalism on a philosophical and global political level and does not examine case material. None the less, Tibi's personal take on the issues demonstrates a rational, liberal Muslim position, which contrasts with the fundamentalists about whom he writes.

RONALD LUKENS-BULL

See also Nation of Islam

Islamic law

Al-Zwaini, Laila and Rudolph Peters, *A Bibliography of Islamic Law, 1980–1993*, Leiden and New York: Brill, 1994

David, René and John Brierly, *Major Legal Systems in the World Today: An Introduction to the Comparative Study of Law*, 3rd edition, London: Stevens, 1985

Kamali, Mohammad Hashim, "Methodological Issues in Islamic Jurisprudence", *Arab Law Quarterly*, 11 (1996): 3–33

Makdisi, John, "Islamic Law Bibliography", *Law Library Journal*, 78 (1986): 103–89

Modarressi Tabātabā'i, Hossein, *An Introduction to Shī'ī Law: A Bibliographical Study*, London: Ithaca Press, 1984a

Modarressi Tabātabā'i, Hossein, "Rationalism and Traditionalism in Shī'ī Juriprudence", *Alserat*, 10/2 (1984b): 30–42

Omar, Mohamed Abdel-Khalek, "Reasoning in Islamic Law", *Arab Law Quarterly*, 12 (1997): 148–96 and 353–99

Schacht, Joseph, *An Introduction to Islamic Law*, London: Oxford University Press, 1964

The work of MODARRESSI TABĀTABĀ'I (1984a) constitutes an outstanding introduction to Shī'ī law, which is one of the two major divisions of Islamic law. The Shī'ī legal system is a developed integrated system of law with a traditional openness to new ideas and legal concepts. This is basically due to the dual capacity of the Shī'ī jurists, many of which were philosophers whose main contribution to legal thought was in the reception of Islamic philosophy and logic into the Shī'ī law and jurisprudence. This is reflected in the characteristic evaluation of legal concepts and criticism of certain traditions in Shī'ī jurisprudence. The main focus of this work is to put forward the innovative legal thinking of Shī'ī culture, as reflected in the work of Shī'ī jurists published both in Islamic countries and in the West. Of particular value are the detailed analyses of the general structure of the Shī'ī legal system, the presentation of its sources, the examination of its basic concepts, and the description of the evolution of Shī'ī law centuries, starting with the period of the presence of the Imāms to the first century of the occultation, to the rationalists, the schools of Shaykh Al-tā' Ifa, Al-Shahīd Al-Awwal, the law of the Safavid period, and the schools of Al-Wahīd Al-Bihbahānī and Shaykh Al-Ansārī. The main advantage of this work lies in the emphasis given by the authors to clarity, a quality much appreciated by legal scholars unfamiliar with the structure and concepts of Islamic law. An equally important disadvantage of this publication is its compilation of materials published almost exclusively in Arabic.

AL-ZWAINI & PETERS, on the other hand, have managed to produce a complete compilation of articles, books, and monographs on Islamic law produced mainly in English by Western publishers. The main advantage of this publication lies in the approachability of the material presented there. In fact before this work was published, collections of listings referring to Islamic law were only found in the short article of MAKDISI or the now old compilation by SCHACHT. Another quality of the publication concerns the classification of the material included in the second part of its compilation according to the country of reference. Thus, materials included refer to 35 geographical regions, starting with Afghanistan and Africa and ending with the United Arab Emirates and Yemen. It is a shame that the book really is just a compilation with no commentary on the listings other than its classification in clearly defined classes on the basis of the country of reference in part two and the particular fields of law to which it refers in part one. For those Islamic counties where both Islamic and Western type law are used in parallel only Islamic law material is included.

The deep, mainly philosophical, clash between the traditionalists and the rationalists is presented in the article by

MODARRESSI TABĀTABĀ'I (1984b). The author presents the traditionalist school as a reflection, or continuation, of the conservative legal tendency in the period of the Presence, devoting its efforts to the collection and religious presentation of the work of the Imams. From a legal point of view the author draws parallels between the Ahl al-hadīth and the Sunnī school of traditionalists, where Ahmad b. Hanbal rejected the *kalām* even when used in the defence of Islam. The author then contrasts this legal methodology to the work of Ibn Abī 'Aqīl and Ibn al-Junayd, who came to disagree with the traditionalist legal method and began to discover the rationale of a precept. This method establishes general principles in legal matters without the need to rely on the specific texts in traditions in each case.

The issue of the methodology of Islamic jurisprudence is analysed in some detail in the work of KAMALI. The author suggests that many of the rational doctrines of *usul* have become burdened with technicality or unrealistic stipulations that often frustrate the original purpose and undermine their capacity to be used as effective formulas for legal reconstruction. The problem over technicality and empirical weakness of the *usul al-fiqh* seems to be exacerbated by the fact that prevailing practice in the area of statutory legislation has departed from the operational premises of the conventional methodology of *usul*. The authors suggests that a new scheme for *usul al-fiqh* should incorporate the proposed approach, which is the use of the best potential of that methodology and the parallel reform of it through the identification of the problems in regard to each of its particular doctrines. However, the need to depart from some of the structures of the conventional methodology and its unfeasible propositions may not be taken to signify the need for the total abolition of the whole concept. The basic approach must be one of continuity and imaginative reform, which might well entail taking bold steps along the way as well as adding new dimensions to the existing methodology of *usul al-fiqh*. This seems to be the answer to the doubts of Muslim masses, which are desirous of harmony and cohesion between their cultural heritage and the applied laws of their lands.

A detailed and clear analysis of the different aspects of the process of reasoning to form legal and judicial opinions and rulings according to the principles and rules of Islamic law is offered by the excellent work of OMAR. The author places his analysis in the framework of the core of Islamic legal science, which consists of legal opinions supported by one or more of the primary and subsidiary sources of proofs of the Shari'ah. Although there is an almost unanimous agreement among the scholars of different schools of jurisprudence that the Qu'aran and the Sunnah are the only primary sources, there is no consensus on the subsidiary sources. The most commonly adopted subsidiary sources can be found in consensus of opinion, reasoning by analogy, equitable discretion and interests. In this article (divided into two parts) the author examines the theoretical and practical aspects of the process of reasoning and forming legal opinions within the framework of the Shari'ah, the Quar'an, and the Sunnah under the prism of the necessity for scientific understanding of these texts and the secondary sources that complement them.

Islamic law from a non-Muslim perspective is analysed by the masters of comparative work, DAVID & BRIERLY. In one

of the fullest presentations of legal culture in contemporary world, the authors refer to the close link between law and religion, the sources of Islamic law, and the recent adaptation of Islamic law to the modern world. One of the noteworthy observations included in their work is the attempt of the authors to explain the archaic nature of some of the institutions of Islamic law, its casuistic outlook, and its lack of systematization by reference to its development and stabilization during the Middle Ages.

HELEN XANTHAKI

Italian economy and economic record

Acs, Zoltan J. and David B. Audretsch (editors), *Small Firms and Entrepreneurship: An East–West Perspective*, Cambridge and New York: Cambridge University Press, 1993

Baldassarri, Mario (editor), *The Italian Economy: Heaven or Hell?*, London: Macmillan, and New York: St Martin's Press, 1994

Baldassarri, Mario and Franco Modigliani (editors), *The Italian Economy: What Next?*, London: Macmillan, and New York: St Martin's Press, 1995

Baltensperger, Ernst and Hans-Werner Sinn (editors), *Exchange-rate Regimes and Currency Unions*, London: Macmillan, and New York: St Martin's Press, 1992

Brunetta, Renato and Leonello Tronti (editors), *Report '89: Labour and Employment Policies in Italy*, Rome: Ministry of Labour and Social Security, 1989

Carello, Adrian Nicola, *The Northern Question: Italy's Participation in the European Economic Community and the Mezzogiorno's Underdevelopment*, Newark: University of Delaware Press, 1989

Locke, Richard M., *Remaking the Italian Economy*, Ithaca, New York: Cornell University Press, 1995

Padoa-Schioppa, Fiorella, *The Sheltered Economy: Structural Problems in the Italian Economy*, Oxford: Clarendon Press, and New York: Oxford University Press, 1993

Pyke, Frank, Giacomo Becattini and Werner Sengenberger (editors), *Industrial Districts and Inter-firm Co-operation in Italy*, Geneva: International Institute for Labour Studies, 1990

Scobie, H.M. *et al.*, *The Italian Economy in the 1990s*, London and New York: Routledge, 1996

An in-depth analysis of Italy is among the case studies in the investigation of West European industrial districts by ACS *et al.* A prominent feature of the Italian economy is the predominance of medium and small enterprises. Moreover, firms belonging to the same sector tend to concentrate within particular areas in order to exploit positive network effects and take advantage of public goods (infrastructure) provided nearby. Italian industries – especially those located in the north and centre of the country – include metal products, textiles, food processing, leather, pottery, furniture, and general houseware.

BALDASSARRI tackles some of the basic problems faced by the Italian economy today. The private sector is represented as the strength of the economy, especially family-owned, non-listed companies performing well on both internal and foreign markets. The weakness in the economy is companies that are either publicly owned or that prosper under the government's shelter, and are generally protected from the stimulus of competition (statutory monopolies). Another aspect of Italy's economy is the north–south divide, which has long persisted since unification (1861) took place.

The north–south problem is analysed more in depth by CARELLO. The author takes a slightly different approach to the topic, by viewing the issue from a "northern" perspective. During recent years, Italy has experienced a wave of protest coming from the northern regions, demanding that subsidies (and other kinds of state aid) to the south should be phased out. A folkloristic political movement (*Lega Nord*) has supported these demands. There are also fears the Mezzogiorno's backwardness could jeopardize full integration into the European Union (EU) and the adoption of the euro as the national currency. Proposed remedies include privatization, encouragement of private enterprise, and the promotion of tourism. A more sensible use of EU funds should also be made. Finally, proposals for fiscal federalism across Italy's regions have also been made.

BALDASSARRI & MODIGLIANI outline future perspectives for the Italian economy as a whole. Again, the crucial issue of European integration is tackled. Other worrying features of Italy's economic record in the medium to long term are: persistent instability; the thinness of financial markets; the pending reform of welfare state arrangements; the slowing down of privatization; the small number of enterprises and banks that are functioning well and, finally, the north–south and public–private dilemmas again. Although the government has taken decisive steps to reform the public sector, to speed up privatization, to allow bank mergers (1999), and to boost the stock market, the remaining problems are far from being solved. The authors discuss the above issues in a fairly comprehensive manner from an international – and especially EU – standpoint.

BRUNETTA's report on labour and employment policies is a mainly statistical review of Italy's (micro) data on the topic. Labour policies are surveyed, with some useful insights on the different treatment of Italian civil servants *vis-à-vis* their private-sector counterparts. Detailed statistics are provided on unemployment, social security contributions and the like, by region, gender, and age. Even though one does not find much economic analysis in this publication, it gives an overall idea of the actual numbers behind different levels of employment and real wages across the country in Italy's labour market.

PADOA-SCHIOPPA's book on the "sheltered economy" is a comprehensive treatment of Italy's peculiar economic system. Many Italian firms, irrespective of their ownership structure, enjoy statutory protection from competition, which is unusual for an industrial economy. Regardless of any underlying economic reason for "natural" monopoly, the Italian government has traditionally protected the domestic industry from internal – and sometimes also foreign – competition. Rather than creating "national champions", however, the government has just allowed inefficient monoliths to survive and prosper, and now faces the problem of divesting itself of them at a fair price. Statutory protection in Italy ranged from utilities to the car-making, iron and steel, and chemical sectors, before the retreat of the state from centralized industrial policymaking began to take place a few years ago.

PYKE, BECATTINI & SENGENBERGER again analyse Italy's regional industrial districts, with a special focus upon interfirm agreements. In view of the forthcoming EU integration, Italian firms are well positioned to compete, but lack critical mass. They are generally too small (on average) in comparison with their European counterparts. In order to avoid being taken over by foreign groups, some of Italy's small and medium enterprises are now either merging, or creating non-equity networks that are intended to counteract foreign competition. One of the most important problems that Italy's well-functioning private enterprises have to face is to reach the necessary "critical mass".

A related issue is family ownership, which often constrains expansion and might facilitate takeovers. Boosting the underdeveloped and erratic Milan Stock Exchange (MSE) is consistent with providing family-owned firms with a larger and far more robust capital base. Floating these concerns in Milan is a policy decision that could have an effect far into the future.

BALTENSPERGER & SINN analyse several Europe-wide issues, which are also relevant to the Italian economy. Questions relating to monetary union, inflation, public debt, interest rates, the Maastricht Treaty, financial market reforms, and inter-country arbitrage are tackled. Italy's high public debt and old-fashioned, expensive welfare schemes are now central issues in the country's EU integration process. With inflation and interest rates at their lowest levels since the 1960s, Italy has now the chance to boost the thin MSE, and simultaneously reduce its public debt exposure. Social security reforms, and north–south cross-subsidization issues appear now to be pivotal for the country.

LOCKE also tackles the fundamental questions of market liberalization, privatization (with contextual regulation), fiscal federalism, stock exchange and financial market reforms, EU integration, social security expenditure cuts, and public debt. Italy's "microeconomic" problems are centred upon the fact that the Italian economic system has long been recognized as one of the most public-sector dominated in the Western world. Command-and-control techniques have long been applied to several economic sectors, and statutory monopoly rights have long been granted to firms, irrespective of their underlying cost and demand conditions. However, privatization programmes have now started, and the issues of promoting competition (when feasible) and/or devising adequate regulatory schemes (when needed) are finally appearing as absolute priorities in the Italian policymaking agenda.

SCOBIE *et al.* focuses upon Italy's economy in the 1990s. This book can be regarded as a summary of all of the publications mentioned above. Italy's structural economic problems (inherited from the 1970s and 1980s) are linked to the country's endemic political instability. Italy underwent a huge political crisis in the early 1990s, following the discovery of bribes and kickbacks in Milan and other cities. This led to the resignation of eminent party leaders, as well as to an overall restructuring of the political system in the country. Economic recession also hit Italy at the very end of the 1980s, which contributed to the lira's departure from the European Monetary System (EMS) in the early 1990s. The crucial issue today is Italy's participation in European monetary union, which took its first step on 1 January 1999.

GIAN CARLO SCARSI

J

Japanese economy and economic record

Aoki, Masahiko (editor), *The Economic Analysis of the Japanese Firm*, Amsterdam: North Holland, 1984

Aoki, Masahiko and Ronald Dore (editors), *The Japanese Firm: Sources of Competitive Strength*, Oxford: Clarendon Press, and New York: Oxford University Press, 1994

Dore, Ronald, *Flexible Rigidities: Industrial Policy and Structural Adjustment in the Japanese Economy, 1970–80*, London: Athlone Press, and Stanford, California: Stanford University Press, 1986

Ito, Takatoshi, *The Japanese Economy*, Cambridge, Massachusetts: MIT Press, 1992

Johnson, Chalmers, *MITI and the Japanese Miracle: The Growth of Industrial Policy, 1925–1975*, Stanford, California: Stanford University Press, 1982

Komiya, Ryutaro, *The Japanese Economy: Trade, Industry, and Government*, Tokyo: University of Tokyo Press, 1990

Murakami, Yasuske and Hugh T. Patrick (general editors), *The Political Economy of Japan*, Stanford, California: Stanford University Press, 1987–92

Pempel, T.J., *Regime Shift: Comparative Dynamics of the Japanese Political Economy*, Ithaca, New York: Cornell University Press, 1998

Yamamura, Kozo, "The Japanese Political Economy after the 'Bubble': Plus ça Change?", *Journal of Japanese Studies*, 23/2 (1997): 291–331

The three-volume collection of essays edited by MURAKAMI & PATRICK forms a wide-ranging analysis of the postwar Japanese economy by leading academics. Volume one focuses on the domestic economy, with sections on macroeconomic issues, the Japanese firm, and the role of government in the economy. The focus of volume 2 shifts to the international dimension, featuring articles on international finance, trade policy (especially relations with the US), and the role of Japan regionally and globally. The views put forward in these volumes reflect differing explanations of Japan's postwar economic achievements, and also contribute to the debate on whether there is a distinctively Japanese model of economic system that can be contrasted in key respects with other models, mainly the American. Volume 1 sets the scene thematically with an article, "The Japanese Model of Political Economy", by Murakami. This ambitious but carefully constructed overview argues that there are two major lines of thought: models that emphasize economic factors and those that emphasize cultural factors, such as a tradition of group-orientedness. Murakami contends that the two schools of thought present a false dichotomy, and that the organizational interfaces – mainly informal – contain the key to a Japanese model that is both complex and dynamic. The view that economic, social, and cultural factors must all be taken into account reappears in volume 3, entitled, *Cultural and Social Dynamics*. Imai's article, "Japan's Corporate Networks", is noteworthy as an examination of the interaction between market processes and the organizational linkages traditional to, and distinctive of, Japan.

The economist AOKI argues that each school of thought has limitations. In his preface to the collection of essays entitled *The Economic Analysis of the Japanese Firm*, he warns that the cultural uniqueness theories risk losing sight of economic rationality as a factor, but he also says that the neoclassical paradigm is too simplistic. The neoclassical concept of the firm and of internal efficiency must be broadened to encompass the complexities of associational ties both within and between Japanese firms, which he himself formulates in terms of cooperative game theory. The articles in this book focus in turn on key elements that make up the Japanese system, including firm-specific employment structures, enterprise unionism, and corporate finance based on the system of interlocking institutional shareholdings (*keiretsu*). Although unfortunately not up to date, this volume is still useful for its approach, which aims to encompass cultural and organizational factors within economic analysis.

The first, and still the most often cited, analysis of Japan's postwar economic "miracle" is that of JOHNSON. This is an impressive piece of scholarship, tracing the rise of industrial policy and workings of the economic bureaucracy from the prewar years, and, indeed, going back to the powerful 19th-century bureaucrats who orchestrated Japan's first industrial policy. However, Johnson's influence rests primarily on his lucid exposition of the Japanese model of the capitalist developmental state, or state-led economic development, which is contrasted with both the market-oriented system and the communist system. In Johnson's analysis, the economic "miracle" owes more to economic necessity than to a cultural bias towards consensus: Japan's postwar economic situation necessitated high growth as a national priority, for which MITI was the key institution, and administrative guidance was its key tool. Although Johnson's approach has been criticized as oversimplifying institutional decision-making structures and overestimating bureaucratic power, his model has become a useful tool for analysts of government–business relations in late-industrializing economies generally.

DORE gives an account of the economic restructuring necessitated by the decline, in the 1970s, of traditional manufacturing industries, encumbered by high energy costs and labour-intensive production. Dore argues that the successful shift towards more technologically advanced – and internationally competitive – industries involved structural changes in output, employment, trade, and industrial organization. In contrast to Johnson's top-down view of industrial policy, Dore maintains that Japan's "adjustment capacity" stems from a cultural legacy of consensus-building and cooperation, which characterizes enterprises, labour unions, and government–business relations. Dore's praise of "organized capitalism", which he sees as based in cultural values, over Western individualistic enterprise structures, indicates his own normative position. Nonetheless, he offers a valuable analysis of the ways in which Japan went about successful structural readjustment in a period that reveals obvious parallels with the current difficulties faced by Japanese industry.

AOKI & DORE revisited the theme of the Japanese firm in their jointly edited collection of articles in 1994. In an opening chapter, Aoki expands on his earlier economic analysis of the Japanese firm, this time venturing into comparative institutional analysis and convergence theories. Aoki suggests that the dynamic paths of Japanese and Western corporate systems will interact, with institutional consequences for both systems. He eschews any definite predictions, but does foresee a breaking down of the closed institutional framework as it becomes enmeshed in the global system. Other scholarly contributions in this book are in the fields of labour economics, information economics, financial economics, and organization theory. Dore's final chapter focuses on the cultural debate, examining equality–efficiency tradeoffs.

KOMIYA, which is a collection of his own essays and lectures, focuses on the Japanese economy in the 1980s, with a particularly strong section on international economic relations. This section examines Japan's trade history with the USA and Japanese foreign direct investment, both historically and in terms of strategy. The chapter, "Structural and Behavioral Characteristics of Japanese Firms", provides a good introduction and expands on standard microeconomic analysis. With the express aim of refraining from normative evaluation, the author provides clear explanations of basic principles, and also many comparative points of analysis with other systems, including the American and Chinese.

YAMAMURA examines Japan's economic downturn in the 1990s, looking at a range of recent socioeconomic and institutional changes. He analyses the evidence in terms of the theoretical debate between the convergence view, based on neoclassical economics, and the nonconvergence view, based on a nation-specific view of Japanese capitalism. He sees evidence for both views, and opts for a hybrid interpretation, tending towards the nonconvergence view. On the one hand, economic data show the increasing importance of market forces, deregulation, and loosening of institutional ties, all in a context of growing global competition. On the other hand, he argues, deregulation is less significant than it appears, and

Japan's "embedded rent-seeking institutions" are resistant to fundamental change.

PEMPEL, too, interprets the events of the 1990s and indicates possible directions of the Japanese economy in the future. He uses the concept of "regime shift" to describe the current institutional upheaval in a historical perspective. "Regime shift" refers to economic, social and political changes, all interlinked, which make the Japan of the 1990s radically different from the Japan of the 1960s. Pempel sees pressures in the global economy as the major challenge confronting Japan, and the country's conservative, inward-looking institutions as the main obstacle to economic rejuvenation. The book's conclusion – that tension between the internationalists and the protectionists will probably continue for the foreseeable future – might seem disappointingly noncommittal, but the enduring value of this scholarly work is the author's use of the analytic tool of regime shift for understanding the Japanese political economy.

Finally, ITO provides a useful introductory textbook, the core of which is macroeconomic analysis, with chapters devoted to each sector. Historical background and some current issues are also included.

JANET MORRISON

See also Keiretsu

Japanese law and legal systems

Baum, Harald and Luke R. Nottage, *Japanese Business Law in Western Languages: An Annotated Selective Bibliography*, Littleton, Colorado: Rothman, 1998

Beer, Lawrence Ward, *Freedom of Expression in Japan: A Study in Comparative Law, Politics, and Society*, Tokyo and New York: Kodansha, 1984

Gresser, Julian, Koichiro Fujikura and Akio Morishima, *Environmental Law in Japan*, Cambridge, Massachusetts: MIT Press, 1981

Haley, John O., "The Myth of the Reluctant Litigant", *Journal of Japanese Studies*, 4/2 (1978): 359–90

Haley, John Owen, *Authority without Power: Law and the Japanese Paradox*, Oxford and New York: Oxford University Press, 1991

Henderson, Dan Fenno, *Conciliation and Japanese Law: Tokugawa and Modern*, 2 vols, Seattle: University of Washington Press, 1964

Iwasawa, Yuji, *International Law, Human Rights, and Japanese Law: The Impact of International Law on Japanese Law*, Oxford: Clarendon Press, and New York: Oxford University Press, 1998

Ramseyer, J. Mark and Minoru Nakazoto, *Japanese Law: An Economic Approach*, Chicago: University of Chicago Press, 1999

Steenstrup, Carl, *A History of Law in Japan until 1868*, Leiden and New York: Brill, 1991

Tanase, Takao, "The Management of Disputes: Automobile Accident Compensation in Japan", *Law and Society Review*, 24/3 (1990): 651–91

Upham, Frank K., *Law and Social Change in Postwar Japan*, Cambridge, Massachusetts: Harvard University Press, 1987

von Mehren, Arthur Taylor, *Law in Japan: The Legal Order in a Changing Society*, Cambridge, Massachusetts: Harvard University Press, 1963

The period since 1868 has seen a succession of changes in the area of law every bit as sweeping and profound as in any area of Japanese society. There is not as yet, however, any comprehensive legal history of modern Japan available in Western languages. STEENSTRUP provides a cohesive, streamlined, and well-written account of Japanese law and legal institutions from earliest times to 1868. The book treats law within the context of social and political institutions, enhancing its value for non-legal specialists as well.

HENDERSON describes and analyses the development of state-sponsored dispute-resolution mechanisms during the Tokugawa period (1603–1868) (in volume one) and the continuing use of informal or alternate dispute resolution methods to channel disputes away from litigation in the modern period (volume two). Henderson says that Tokugawa procedures were characterized by the use of what he calls "didactic conciliation", in which the authorities exerted pressure upon litigants to settle their dispute "voluntarily", without formal reference to externally adjudicated legal norms. Henderson finds parallels in the modern use of court-sponsored *chôtei*, referral of disputes to a panel of lay conciliators, more likely to bring social, rather than strictly legal norms to bear in assisting the parties to reach a solution. While viewing such approaches in part as a hindrance to the development of a system where the law grows through adjudication, Henderson stresses the importance of continuity in understanding certain aspects of Japan's legal system.

Continuity, and breaks, in legal tradition also figure prominently in VON MEHREN. This collection of essays on most of the important categories of law in Japan remains indispensable as a starting point for study or research. The contributors are Japanese legal scholars or professionals who were, or would become, noted experts in their fields. The first essay by Kenzo Takayanagi gives a brief history of the development of Japanese law from 1868–1961, a period that saw the end of the feudal Tokugawa institutions, the reception and adaptation of continental-style laws and institutions from roughly 1875 onwards, and then the integration of American democratic and individualistic models after World War II. Most of the essays trace developments in the authors' particular areas of specialty over the same span, with an emphasis on the postwar period and the absorption, once again, of foreign ideas. No essay became better known than Takeyoshi Kawashima's "Dispute Resolution in Contemporary Japan", in which he asserted that the Japanese have a traditional *cultural* resistance to litigation, the final adjudication of disputes by courts applying objectively determined legal norms.

HALEY (1978) was the first to challenge Kawashima's *cultural* thesis, mustering empirical evidence, particularly from the first three decades of the 20th century, to argue that Japanese litigated quite frequently and enthusiastically and that it was the political elite, regarding this trend as subversive to traditional values, who acted to stem the tide. Haley posits an *institutional* explanation for Japan's relatively low litigation rates in the postwar period, pointing to the low number of judges and lawyers and the relatively weak enforcement powers of the courts, factors controlled by conservative policy makers, as the prime disincentives to litigation.

TANASE puts forth a *management* model to explain the relatively minor social and political role that litigation is said to play in Japan. He presents a detailed and illuminating case study of the system under which almost all claims for injuries sustained in motor vehicle accidents are resolved through negotiations between the parties themselves, without the use of lawyers or courts. Tanase shows how the cooperation of the courts, insurance companies, and administrative authorities achieved this result, which, as Haley suggests, was engineered from above, but which, in line with Kawashima's theory, works because it is consonant with deep-seated cultural assumptions, satisfies individual interests, and is seen as furthering the collective good.

UPHAM explores the relationship between litigation and social change in Japan in the postwar period. Upham presents carefully documented case studies of legal and governmental responses to social conflict in the following four areas: pollution (particularly the famous Minamata case), the struggle of burakumin (a traditional untouchable caste) against discrimination, the campaign for equal employment opportunities for women, and the use of informal means of governance ("administrative guidance") by the central bureaucracy in fashioning and implementing industrial policy. He concludes that although litigation has been an important factor in the furtherance of some social causes (especially in the pollution and equal opportunity areas) "the Japanese government has attempted to prevent the development of litigation into an effective and ongoing vehicle for social change" (p.18) propelled by an active judiciary that could threaten the interests of Japan's dominant triumvirate (the ruling Liberal Democratic Party, big business, and the bureaucracy).

HALEY (1991) posits a grand theory for understanding law and governance in Japan, a theory applied to the specific areas of litigious behaviour, criminal justice, and administrative regulation. Haley asserts that although imposing administrative and judicial structures are vested with considerable formal authority, they lack the sort and degree of coercive legal power observable in other industrial democracies. Because law is thus constrained, says Haley, informal social mechanisms serve to produce a mode of consensual governance in which power is shared in a framework parallel to Japan's traditional *mura* (village) community structure.

RAMSEYER & NAKAZOTO is the first monograph that applies a single theoretical approach (law and economics) to a broad palette of basic areas of Japan's substantive law. Ramseyer (sometimes with co-authors) was one of the first to flesh out, in a series of articles, Haley's critique of Kawashima's assertion of cultural uniqueness in the Japanese approach to law. In this book, the authors emphasize the similarities rather than the differences between law in Japan and the US. Using case-based storytelling, straightforward exposition of law, and economic and institutional analysis, the authors succeed in depicting a legal system that provides the certainty needed for economic decision making and within which actors make rational choices.

Among the large and increasing number of works that focus on particular areas of Japanese law, the following are included here because of their attention to law and society issues. BEER provides a wide-ranging account illuminating what he calls the ecology of freedom of expression in Japan, as well as specific legal issues that have been treated in the courts and elsewhere. GRESSER, FUJIKURA & MORISHIMA is a comprehensive account of judicial and legislative responses to pollution. IWASAWA is the first monograph to explore, both in theoretical and specific contexts, the relationship between international human rights norms and Japanese domestic law.

BAUM & NOTTAGE is an indispensable bibliographical work. Despite its title, its scope is by no means restricted to business law in a narrow sense, extending to areas such as legal history and public law and embracing in a carefully selective way the social science literature as well. Truly comprehensive, it is especially valuable for its annotated guide to introductory sources, its extended listing and discussion of pertinent Internet websites, and its inclusion in the main bibliographical listings of the large body of work written in German and French.

STEPHAN M. SALZBERG

Japanese management

Abegglen, James C. and George Stalk Jr, *Kaisha: The Japanese Corporation*, New York: Basic Books, 1985

Doeringer, Peter B., Christine Evans-Klock and David G. Terkla, "Hybrids or Hodgepodges? Workplace Practices of Japanese and Domestic Startups in the United States", *Industrial and Labor Relations Review*, 51/2 (1998): 171–86

Gannon, Martin J. *et al.*, "The Japanese Garden" in *Understanding Global Cultures: Metaphorical Journeys through 17 Countries*, Thousand Oaks, California and London: Sage, 1994

Keys, J. Bernard and Thomas R. Miller, "The Japanese Management Theory Jungle", *Academy of Management Review*, 9/2 (1984): 342–53

Keys, J. Bernard, Luther Trey Denton and Thomas R. Miller, "The Japanese Management Theory Jungle: Revisited", *Journal of Management*, 20/2 (1994): 373–402

Lincoln, James R., Christina L. Ahmadjian and Eliot Mason, "Organizational Learning and Purchase-supply Relations in Japan: Hitachi, Matsushita, and Toyota Compared", *California Management Review*, 40/3 (1998): 241–65

Meek, Christopher B., "Ganbatte: Understanding the Japanese Employee", *Business Horizons*, 42/1 (1999): 27–35

Monden, Yasuhiro, *Toyota Production System: An Integrated Approach to Just-in-Time*, 3rd edition, Norcross, Georgia: Engineering and Management Press, 1998

Nonaka, Ikujiro and Hirotaka Takeuchi, *The Knowledge-creating Company: How Japanese Companies Create the Dynamics of Innovation*, New York and Oxford: Oxford University Press, 1995

Ornatowski, George K., "The End of Japanese-style Human Resource Management?", *Sloan Management Review*, 38/3 (1998): 73–84

During the early 1980s, William Ouchi's *Theory Z* (1981) and *The Art of Japanese Management* (1981) by R. Pascale and A. Athos were best-selling books. These two books were important in shaping popular and much academic opinion during this time period. KEYS & MILLER provides a comprehensive overview of Japanese management, beginning with the early years of its popular recognition in the West. The authors plough through the developing literature in the popular and academic press in an attempt to classify the plethora of conflicting theories purported to explain the apparent superiority of Japanese management practices.

KEYS, DENTON & MILLER extend and update Keys and Miller. Whereas in the latter, there were a total of 37 references, Keys, Denton & Miller has 162 references, reflecting the growing interest in Japanese management. In summary, these two articles document the deluge of books and articles that have been written primarily since 1980. Among the issues addressed are culture, *keiretsu* (a form of industrial organization), long-term planning, consensus decision making, human resource management practices such as lifetime employment, and quality. The 1994 article also documents the tremendous ongoing change that Japanese management had experienced within the span of the previous decade.

GANNON examines how Japanese management practice is influenced by national culture. He describes a number of cultural underpinnings of Japanese organizational life such as *wa*. *Wa* is typified by the strong emphasis Japanese managers place on group cohesion and conformity. Gannon also explains how variations in management practices across nations are influenced by more general variations in national cultures.

For those with an interest in manufacturing management and lean productions systems, MONDEN is required reading. This book has been extraordinarily influential with both academics and managers and this classic work, originally published in 1983, is available in a recently updated third edition. This book describes Toyota's just-in-time manufacturing system, which links production schedules to demand changes while meeting the goals of low cost, high quality, timely delivery, and improved worker morale. This latest edition includes strategic information systems and computer integrated manufacturing technology.

NONAKA & TAKEUCHI challenges many of the simplistic stereotypes regarding Japanese organizations in that they maintain that Japanese firms are successful because they are innovative and not just what might be termed copycats. Instead they claim that Japanese firms have been successful because of their skill and expertise in creating "organizational knowledge". Whereas Western management is familiar with "explicit knowledge", the Japanese firms add a second type of knowledge, "tacit knowledge". The book is filled with case studies from firms such as NEC and Matsushita and how these firms create knowledge and transfer it from individuals to groups to organizations.

No discussion of Japanese management would be complete without reference to *keiretsu*, by which is meant a network of independently managed firms with long-term business ties such as interlocking directorates or partial cross-ownership. LINCOLN, AHMADJIAN & MASON examines the recent experiences of three large firms, Hitachi, Matsushita, and Toyota, and how their interfirm purchase-supply networks shape and are shaped by the process of organizational knowledge creation, learning, and innovation. The Toyota, Hitachi, and Matsushita cases are especially interesting in examining whether *keiretsu*-style partnerships are being strengthened or weakened. This article dovetails nicely with Nonaka & Takeuchi's book described in the preceding paragraph.

Whereas many of the works on Japanese management have emphasized the soft side of management (human resources, consensus decision making, and so on), ABEGGLEN & STALK emphasize the financial and marketing strategies of Japanese firms. This 1985 book examining Japanese corporations (*kaisha*) was quite influential vis-à-vis American managers and consultants. The authors shed a good deal of light on key Japanese business practices.

Do Japanese management theories and practices apply abroad? The management literature has characterized many of the Japanese human resource management practices as being apparently superior. This being the case, can these Japanese management practices be adapted to, for instance, the US? DOERINGER, EVANS-KLOCK & TERKLA found that Japanese transplants in the US were likely to adopt "hybrid" Japanese management practices in contrast to domestic startups, which used Japanese-style practices less frequently.

Japanese human resource management practices such as lifetime-employment and company unions have received much attention in the West and are often perceived as cornerstones of Japanese management. Despite these unique human resource management practices, there is a puzzling aspect in that studies have consistently pointed out that Japanese workers have among the lowest levels of job satisfaction of workers around the world. MEEK summarizes and analyses this data on job satisfaction in Japan and provides insight into how changes in the Japanese economy and society may influence job satisfaction in the future.

Clearly Japanese business firms are facing fundamental challenges brought about by factors such as global competition and changes in technology. Will Japanese firms change their practice of lifetime employment and seniority-based pay? ORNATOWSKI describes a process of incremental or evolutionary change rather than abrupt revolutionary change. Lifetime employment seems rather secure whereas a new job performance-based system is taking root. In short, Ornatowski challenges the view that Japanese companies are becoming clones of Western firms in terms of their human resource management practices.

DANIEL J. GALLAGHER AND JOHN C. PALMER

See also Hoshin kanri, Keiretsu

Job design

Buchanan, David A., *The Development of Job Design Theories and Techniques*, London and New York: Praeger, 1979

Frei, Felix, Margrit Hugentobler, Susan Schurman, Werner Duell and Andreas Alioth, *Work Design for the Competent Organization*, Westport, Connecticut: Quorum, 1993

Ketchum, Lyman D. and Eric Trist, *All Teams Are Not Created Equal: How Employee Empowerment Really Works*, London and Newbury Park, California: Sage, 1992

Kompier, Michiel, "Job Design and Well-being" in *Handbook of Work and Health Psychology*, edited by Marc Schabracq, Jacques A.M. Winnubst and Cary L. Cooper, Chichester and New York: Wiley, 1996

Parker, Sharon and Toby Wall, *Job and Work Design: Organizing Work to Promote Well-being and Effectiveness*, London and Thousand Oaks, California: Sage, 1998

Pruijt, Hans D., *Job Design and Technology: Taylorism vs Anti-Taylorism*, London and New York: Routledge, 1997

Robertson, Ivan T. and Mike Smith, *Motivation and Job Design: Theory, Research, and Practice*, London: Institute of Personnel Management, 1985

An important topic within the field of organizational behaviour is the design of jobs. Job design involves not only creating the structure of the job but also identifying the mission and methods associated with the job and placing the job within the broader context of the organization as a whole. PARKER & WALL provide an extensive look at both the history and current use of job design in organizations. The authors stress that the environment in which organizations exist today is substantially different from that in which job design theory evolved. Parker & Wall provide numerous examples of job design in organizations and discuss topics such as the job characteristics model, the demand-control model, and action theory. An emphasis is placed on the diverse options available when designing jobs. They point out that such seemingly contradictory approaches as job enrichment and job simplification can both be viable options in job design. This book adequately portrays the current state of job design theory in organizations and stresses that there is no one best approach to job design.

BUCHANAN provides an excellent historical analysis of job design theory. His discussion traces job design from its origin in scientific management during the late 19th century to the relatively modern concepts of expectancy and systems theory. Buchanan reviews and integrates much of the research literature on job design and presents a discussion that manages to be both academic and easily understood. Although now somewhat dated, Buchanan is an excellent complement to later works dealing with job design and is useful in gaining an understanding of the evolution of job design theory and practice.

ROBERTSON & SMITH discuss the design of jobs within the context of employee motivation. They argue that simply designing jobs for efficiency does not always result in improved job performance. Concepts such as job satisfaction and employee perceptions of the organization must also be taken into account. In order to motivate, jobs should be designed to interest and inspire employees. Robertson & Smith discuss the theoretical and practical implications of motivation and how these concepts can be applied to work design. Real-world examples are provided, which illustrate many of the motivational issues that must be taken into account during job design.

Of increasing importance is the role of technology in today's workplace. Accordingly a number of texts have been written that deal with the influence of technology on work and job design. One of these texts is PRUIJT. Pruijt discusses technology and job design within the context of scientific management or "Taylorism". One of the central themes of Taylorism is the division of labour. Under a strict division of labour managers plan and strategize while line employees simply execute orders. Pruijt contends that while this approach does not make sense in today's dynamic, technology-oriented workplace it is still stringently practised by many organizations. By analysing over 100 "anti-Taylorist" initiatives in Europe, Pruijt demonstrates how concepts such as job enrichment and worker empowerment can be used to successful compete in today's marketplace.

KOMPIER discusses the relationship between job design and employee health. For both legal and ethical reasons it is in the best interest of employers to promote good employee health and wellbeing. Kompier provides a well thought out and organized discussion of the theoretical models, empirical research, and legislation dealing with designing jobs to promote health. Stress prevention is suggested as an integral part of job design, and a general systematic, stepwise approach to job design is proposed to help employees and employers successfully design jobs to promote employee health and reduce injury.

KETCHUM & TRIST approach job design from a productivity standpoint. Absenteeism, turnover, lack of commitment, and decreased productivity are common problems in today's workplace. Often, however, managers become so involved in treating the symptoms of these problems that the cause is overlooked. Ketchum & Trist contend that the lack of fit between workers and the job is often the cause of problems in organizations and it is possible to design jobs to promote employee satisfaction and improve performance. Concepts such as team structuring, communication, and employee empowerment are discussed, and case studies are presented that demonstrate job design in real-world organizations.

Job design cannot be understood without considering its place within the broader topic of organization change. FREI et al. present a macro-level discussion that incorporates both the design of work activities and organizational change. An emphasis is placed on the importance of properly training and using employees. For readers that wish to broaden their understanding of job design and fit it within the broader context of the organization as a whole, Frei et al. is a thorough, complete, and interesting reference. Work is presented as a learning tool, which, when designed properly, can motivate and educate employees.

BART WEATHINGTON

Job enrichment

Appelbaum, Eileen and Peter Berg, "Work Reorganization and Flexibility in Job Design" in *The Human Resource Management Handbook*, edited by David Lewin, Daniel J.B. Mitchell and Mahmood A. Zaidi, Greenwich, Connecticut and London: Jai Press, 1997
Berlinger, Lisa R., William H. Glick and Robert C. Rodgers, "Job Enrichment and Performance Improvement" in *Productivity in Organizations: New Perspectives from Industrial and Organizational Psychology*, edited by John P. Campbell and Richard J. Campbell, San Francisco: Jossey Bass, 1988
Hackman, J. Richard, "On the Coming Demise of Job Enrichment" in *Man and Work in Society*, edited by Eugene Louis Cass and Fredrick G. Zimmer, New York: Van Nostrand Reinhold, 1975
Miller, Richard B., *Participative Management: Quality of Worklife, and Job Enrichment*, Park Ridge, New Jersey: Noyes, 1977
Parker, Sharon and Toby Wall, *Job and Work Design: Organizing Work to Promote Well-being and Effectiveness*, London and Thousand Oaks, California: Sage, 1998
Savall, Henri, *Work and People: An Economic Evaluation of Job-Enrichment*, Oxford: Clarendon Press, and New York: Oxford University Press, 1981
Wall, Toby and Robin Martin, "Job and Work Design" in *International Review of Industrial and Organizational Psychology*, edited by Cary L. Cooper and Ivan T. Robertson, Chichester and New York: Wiley, 1989
Yorks, Lyle, *Job Enrichment Revisited*, New York: Amacom, 1979

Job enrichment is the process of increasing job depth or the degree of control employees have over their work. The goal of job enrichment is to make work more interesting, challenging, and rewarding for employees, while improving productivity. This is typically accomplished by giving workers greater freedom, independence, and responsibility in the accomplishment of work objectives. WALL & MARTIN provide an excellent historical analysis of the origin of job enrichment and other work-change methods. Early work in the design of jobs focused on simplifying work processes. Job enrichment was developed as a solution to the negative attitudes towards work that were often exhibited by employees working in simplified jobs. Wall and Martin discuss influential theories such as Herzberg's two-factor theory and the job characteristics model as well as current issues and deficiencies in the research literature dealing with job enrichment and the design of work.

SAVALL provides an analysis of job enrichment from an economics perspective. He stresses that job enrichment must be analysed from the perspective of both the organization and the individual employee. Without taking into account both perspectives a fair assessment of effectiveness cannot be made. Savall was originally written in French and then translated into English. The major problem with this book is the stilted and sometimes awkward language that exists due to this translation. All in all, however, the book is well written and organized and is worth reading to gain a broader perspective of job enrichment beyond that available through the management and psychological literature.

Much of the research on the effectiveness of job enrichment has resulted in mixed findings. Accordingly, several books have been written that attempt to explain these mixed results and provide guidelines for successful implementation of job enrichment programmes. HACKMAN reviews job enrichment in terms of both its successes and failures. Management often makes the mistake of looking for a quick solution to organizational problems. Job enrichment, however, does not and should not be expected to improve work performance in every situation. Hackman provides an analysis of why it works in some situations and fails in others. The benefits and drawbacks of job enrichment are discussed, and advice is given for the implementation of a successful job enrichment programme. Hackman argues that job enrichment is more than just a management fad and can be a valuable and effective way in which to improve employee performance if used properly.

BERLINGER, GLICK & RODGERS also analyse job enrichment in terms of its mixed empirical findings. A brief, but thorough, review of the research literature on job enrichment is presented, and a meta-analysis is conducted that examines the relationship between job characteristics and on-the-job performance. Results of the meta-analysis generally support the positive influence of job enrichment on employee performance. The implications of the study and suggestions for future research are also presented.

A brief yet practical guide to job enrichment is presented by YORKS. The discussion is targeted towards the practitioner who is interested in the applied uses of job enrichment. Yorks avoids becoming bogged down in theory and instead focuses on the information managers need in order to make an informed decision about applying job enrichment practices in organizations. While it does not provide an exhaustive coverage of job enrichment, Yorks' applied focus is an excellent complement to some of the more theoretical research-oriented works on job enrichment.

Job enrichment cannot be discussed without considering the issues of employee motivation and the quality of work life. MILLER considers these aspects. Understanding and properly rewarding employees is presented as the key to successfully improving productivity. By understanding what motivates employees, jobs can be designed to fulfil the needs and desires of workers. Worker participation in management decisions is discussed in detail, and several case histories are presented that demonstrate the principles suggested in the book.

In studying job enrichment it is important to keep in mind that it is just one of many approaches organizations use to change jobs and promote productivity. APPELBAUM & BERG present a historical overview of job change methods and how they have been successfully (and unsuccessfully) implemented in many organizations. The benefits of work change and flexibility in the design of jobs are presented, and the obstacles to implementing approaches, such as job enrichment, are discussed. PARKER & WALL also provide an excellent discussion of job enrichment in terms of other types of job change. Parker & Wall stress that theories of work change have themselves changed over time and organizations today are not the same as they were when concepts such job design and job enrichment were first developed. Taken together, both Appelbaum & Berg and Parker & Wall provide a thorough review of the history and current status of job-change techniques and allow the reader to gain an understanding of the role of job enrichment in organizations.

BART WEATHINGTON

See also Motivation

Job loss, redundancy, downsizing

Arroba, Tanya, "The Social and Psychological Aspects of Redundancy: To What Extent a Problem?", *Personnel Review*, 8/3 (1979): 26–29

Gowing, Marilyn K., John D. Kraft and James Campbell Quick (editors), *The New Organizational Reality: Downsizing, Restructuring, and Revitalization*, Washington, DC: American Psychological Association, 1997

Hartley, Jean, Dan Jacobson, Bert Klandermans and Tinka van Vuuren (editors), *Job Insecurity: Coping with Jobs at Risk*, London and Newbury Park, California: Sage, 1991

Holbeche, Linda, *Motivating People in Lean Organizations*, Oxford: Butterworth Heinemann, 1998

Kets de Vries, Manfred and Katharina Balazs, "The Downside of Downsizing", *Human Relations*, 50/1 (1997): 11–50

Kozlowski, Steve, Georgia Chao, Eleanor Smith and Jennifer Hedlund, "Organizational Downsizing: Strategies, Interventions, and Research Implications", *International Review of Industrial and Organizational Psychology*, 8 (1993): 263–332

Leana, Carrie R. and Daniel C. Feldman, *Coping with Job Loss: How Individuals, Organizations, and Communities Respond to Layoffs*, New York: Lexington Books, 1992

Noer, David M., *Healing the Wounds: Overcoming the Trauma of Layoffs and Revitalizing Downsized Organizations*, San Francisco: Jossey Bass, 1993

Tetrick, Lois E. and Julian Barling (editors), *Changing Employment Relations: Behavioral and Social Perspectives*, Washington, DC: American Psychological Association, 1995

In selecting the articles and texts to be included in this literature review, an attempt has been made to choose empirical and theoretical writings that contribute to both the understanding of job loss, redundancy, and downsizing and also to the breadth of theory that surrounds this topic.

One of the early studies that explored aspects of redundancy was written by ARROBA. Her paper discusses the lack of research into redundancy as a phenomenon from both an individual and social perspective. Although the basis of the discussion is narrow, the paper highlights some interesting questions in relation to the further study of redundancy, whether it is treated as a psychological or social problem. Arroba illustrates the lack of objectivity and assumptions of previous studies of redundancy and calls for future research to clarify definitions of the problematic nature of redundancy from both a psychological and social level before embarking on research into its negative implications.

To some extent HARTLEY *et al.* confronts this proposition by drawing together key research regarding job insecurity and coping with a changing economy and employment relationship. The articles include studies from the UK, Europe, and the US, each making a contribution to the understanding of redundancy, restructuring, and job insecurity. These articles tackle the issues of job insecurity from three perspectives:

individual level, organizational level, and industrial relations. Hartley *et al.* offer a starting point for many of the sociological and psychological discussions of insecurity and job loss in an era of organizational restructuring and change. The numerous authors explore experiences and coping strategies of individuals faced with job insecurity and uncertainty. They also examine the effect of job insecurity on collective behaviour in terms of union activities and relations. Hartley *et al.* develop both theory and conceptual frameworks through the presentation of research findings from the individual, organizational, and environmental perspectives.

LEANA & FELDMAN proposes an expansion of the psychological understanding of unemployment through an empirical examination of how individuals, organizations and communities cope with job loss. Their basic model suggests that contextual factors and individual perceptions of these factors influence whether a person reacts positively or negatively to job loss, taking into account personality and organizational intervention programmes. Thus the interaction between individual behaviour and external factors produce the ultimate effects of job loss. Their basic finding is that negative perceptions of redundancy lead a person to select more symptom-focused strategies, to be less well adjusted to the layoff, and to perceive little chance of re-employment. However, although their study is filled with rich comments, the impact of their research on unemployment theory is fairly limited. Leana & Feldman tend to focus on the individuals coping with job loss so the effect on organizations and communities is lost, which may be seen as a shortcoming.

From a slightly different perspective NOER describes experiential and empirical evidence of the effects of layoffs on those who remain, the survivors. The research is American and offers insights into the experience of downsizing for those directly involved. Although written in the style of a management self-help book, the contents provides numerous insights onto the effects of downsizing for individuals remaining in the organization, and for the management of the downsizing process. Noer draws comparisons with other research in the field and builds a four-level intervention model on coping with organizational change and developing a new employment relationship with survivors. In effect Noer offers some practical advice for managers implementing and coping with breaking the co-dependency chain between the employee and the organization.

In contrast, KOZLOWSKI *et al.* critically examines the concept of downsizing as an evolving phenomenon. Their paper outlines clear definitions of downsizing and separates the associated organizational process from the individual level processes. Kowlozki *et al.* propose a number of reasons why organizational downsizing does not achieve its projected aims and objectives, in particular, the mismanagement of the downsizing process. This article successfully draws together the majority of researchers from this broad and varied field using organizational theory, psychology, and management theory to cement their discussion. Their paper offers future directions for research and creates a framework for downsizing theory upon which the research might be based.

The implications of continued downsizing and redundancy for organizations today are far reaching, in particular the changing organizational structures and changing career dynamics. From this perspective, HOLBECHE provides a conceptual framework. Holbeche draws on her research studies in discussion of the effects of flatter structures on working life and changing career patterns. The research focuses on the implementation of motivational strategies, internal communications, and new career development structures following downsizing. Although the audience appears to be managerial, Holbeche offers insight into many of the challenges facing flatter and leaner organizations of the 1990s, which might be used as a platform for further research.

From a more holistic viewpoint a compendium of articles are bought together by TETRICK & BARLING to illustrate the effects of the changing economic, political, and social structures on the employment relationship. The numerous authors focus on how the shifts caused by downsizing and restructuring are moving towards a more part-time, contingent, and female workforce and a decrease in unionized employees. The articles are divided into two parts; the first explores recent changes and discusses implications for specific populations of workers (blue collar/professional) and the second part discusses changes in union membership, commitment, and relations. The articles included by Tetrick & Barling offer an international perspective as they cover work from the US, UK, and Europe.

More recently, following the sharp increase in research into downsizing and stress at work in the mid to late 1990s, GOWING, KRAFT & QUICK draws from some of the leading researchers in the field of downsizing, stress, and managing change. A number of articles have been bought together to discuss both the changing nature of work, the reasons behind the changes, such as technological change, the impact of the information age, and increasing knowledge intensity. The selection of articles successfully draws from interdisciplinary empirical research from economics, social psychology, and psychology and provides a framework for coping with the new organizational reality.

Research conducted by KETS DE VRIES & BALAZS provides a more in-depth view of downsizing and job loss from three different perspectives. Based on qualitative research, open-ended interviews were conducted with "victims", "survivors", and "executioners". The results show a number of coping strategies for those made redundant, those who survived, and those who were implementing the change. The analysis of the results leads to a discussion of change management and key tactics for effective downsizing. Kets de Vries & Balazs combine practical suggestions for executives faced with planning and implementing organizational downsizing with an attempt to further understanding of the effects of downsizing on the individual. Although, thorough in their examination of individual responses, Kets de Vries & Balazs do little to suggest how research could progress in this field, although the results do imply that further research in the field of downsizing, redundancy, and job loss is needed.

FIONA K. CAMPBELL

Job satisfaction

Aryee, Samuel and Yue Wah Chay, "An Examination of the Impact of Career-Oriented Mentoring on Work Commitment Attitudes and Career Satisfaction among Professional and Managerial Employees", *British Journal of Management*, 5 (1994): 241–49

Cranny, C.J., Patricia Cain Smith and Eugene F. Stone (editors), *Job Satisfaction: How People Feel about Their Jobs and How It Affects Their Performance*, New York: Lexington Books, 1992

Fletcher, Clive and Richard Williams, "Performance Management, Job Satisfaction and Organizational Commitment", *British Journal of Management*, 7 (1996): 169–79

Geare, A.J., "Job Stress: Boon as Well as Bane", *Employee Relations*, 11/1 (1989): 21–26

Herzberg, Frederick, Bernard Mausner and Barbara Bloch Snyderman, *The Motivation to Work*, New York: Wiley, 1959

House, Robert J. and Lawrence A. Wigdor, "Herzberg's Dual Factor Theory of Job Satisfaction and Motivation: A Review of the Evidence and a Criticism", *Personnel Psychology*, 20 (1967): 369–89

Podsakoff, Philip M. and Larry J. Williams, "The Relationship between Job Performance and Job Satisfaction" in *Generalizing from Laboratory to Field Settings*, edited by Edwin A. Locke, Lexington, Massachusetts: Lexington Books, 1986

Smith, Patricia Cain, Lorne M. Kendall and Charles L. Hulin, *The Measurement of Satisfaction in Work and Retirement: A Strategy for the Study of Attitudes*, Chicago: Rand McNally, 1969

Vroom, Victor H., *Work and Motivation*, New York: Wiley, 1964

Given the degree of influence of their job satisfaction theory, and the level of criticism it has generated, HERZBERG, MAUSNER & SNYDERMAN deserves to be read in the original, rather than in summary. Their monograph details how they interviewed some 200 accountants and engineers about their jobs using the critical incident technique. They concluded that job factors extrinsic to the work (pay, conditions, supervision, job security, company policy) – which they termed "hygienes" – caused job dissatisfaction if they deteriorated below an acceptable level. If they were good, dissatisfaction disappeared but there was "not much in the way of positive attitudes". Job satisfaction itself came from factors intrinsic to the work (work itself, recognition, achievement, advancement), which they termed "motivators".

HOUSE & WIGDOR provide a comprehensive review of the studies that are critical of Herzberg's "motivator-hygiene" theory and also provide a critique of Herzberg's later work. Using Herzberg's own data, they provide a secondary analysis that contradicts the proposition that satisfiers and dissatisfiers are unidimensional and independent. Ironically, Herzberg's own data reveal that two motivators (achievement and recognition) are cited more frequently as dissatisfiers, than are hygienes such as working conditions and relations with the superior.

Although VROOM is dated, it is a comprehensive and perceptive review of motivation and job-satisfaction theories. It also provides useful insights into the relationship between job satisfaction and job behaviour, and between motivation and job performance.

SMITH, KENDALL & HULIN should be read in order to understand how they developed the Job Descriptive Index (JDI) – one of the most frequently used measures of job satisfaction. Less well known is the Retirement Descriptive Index (RDI), for which they also provide norms. Given the increase in research into the aged, the RDI may become more significant. The book also provides a useful discussion of the research that the authors undertook into job satisfaction.

PODSAKOFF & WILLIAMS examine the similarities and differences in the relationships between job satisfaction and job performance as observed in laboratory and field settings. They consider any conclusion of an inherent relationship between satisfaction and performance to be questionable at best, with reward contingencies playing a crucial role in the pattern of relationships.

GEARE discusses a further aspect of job satisfaction, namely its relations with job stress. Many studies reveal that managers perceive themselves to be working under quite high levels of job stress – as confirmed in this study across two countries – but little information is available as to how much stress is wanted, both for maximum performance and maximum enjoyment. This paper shows that quite high levels of job stress are actually wanted in order to give job satisfaction.

A related, and currently more popular, area of research than job satisfaction is that of work commitment. ARYEE & CHAY look at mentoring and how it impacts on both job commitment and job satisfaction. FLETCHER & WILLIAMS's paper is similar, looking at job satisfaction, performance management, and organizational commitment. Their findings suggest that most elements of performance management, accounted for a substantial proportion of the variance in job satisfaction in particular, but also commitment. Both papers are useful for the insights they give into job satisfaction, and into other interrelated subjects.

CRANNY, SMITH & STONE have edited an excellent collection of papers covering most aspects of job satisfaction. The papers examine the relationships between job satisfaction and general life satisfaction, job withdrawal, job performance, and job stress. This recent publication is a very useful reference as the chapters provide both insightful analysis and extensive literature reviews.

ALAN JAMES GEARE

See also Motivation

Johnson, Lyndon Baines 1908–73

US president

Barrett, David M., *Uncertain Warriors: Lyndon Johnson and His Vietnam Advisers*, Lawrence: University Press of Kansas, 1993

Brands, H.W., *The Wages of Globalism: Lyndon Johnson and the Limits of American Power*, New York and Oxford: Oxford University Press, 1995

Caro, Robert A., *The Years of Lyndon Johnson*, 2 vols, New York: Knopf, 1982–90; vol. 1 London: Collins, 1983; vol. 2 London: Bodley Head, 1990

Dallek, Robert, *Lone Star Rising: Lyndon Johnson and His Times, 1908–1960*, New York and Oxford : Oxford University Press, 1991

Dallek, Robert, *Flawed Giant: Lyndon Johnson and His Times, 1961–1973*, New York and Oxford: Oxford University Press, 1998

Divine, Robert A. (editor), *The Johnson Years*, vol. 2: *Vietnam, the Environment, and Science*, Lawrence: University Press of Kansas, 1987

Divine, Robert A. (editor), *The Johnson Years*, vol. 3: *LBJ at Home and Abroad*, Lawrence: University Press of Kansas, 1994

Graham, Hugh Davis, *The Civil Rights Era: Origins and Development of National Policy, 1960–1972*, New York and Oxford: Oxford University Press, 1990

Herring, George C., *LBJ and Vietnam: A Different Kind of War*, Austin: University of Texas Press, 1994

Johnson, Lyndon Baines, *The Vantage Point: Perspectives of the Presidency, 1963–1969*, New York: Holt Rinehart, 1971

Jordan, Barbara C. and Elspeth Rostow (editors), *The Great Society: A Twenty-Year Critique*, Austin, Texas: Lyndon Baines Johnson Library, 1986

Schulman, Bruce J., *From Cotton Belt to Sun-Belt: Federal Policy, Economic Development, and the Transformation of the South, 1938–1980*, New York and Oxford: Oxford University Press, 1991

Lyndon Baines Johnson was a controversial president, and opinions of historians on his character and achievements are deeply divided. This bibliography deals with Johnson's personality and background, his policies on civil rights and the "Great Society", and his foreign policy – especially his involvement in the Vietnam War.

JOHNSON's memoirs on his presidency were published in 1971. At the time these were not highly regarded by reviewers. Johnson found writing hard and left most of the final composition to others. He therefore appears remote within the narrative. However, in recent years the book has gained a greater respect as a starting point for a study of Johnson. It provides a sense of his views on civil rights, the aims of his domestic reforms, and a strong defence of his Vietnam policies. The book, despite its age, is much more useful than many biographies of this period.

DALLEK has provided the best biography of Johnson's entire career. In his first volume he argues that Johnson developed a genuine commitment to social reform, born of the harsh experiences of Texas in the 1930s and of his admiration for Roosevelt and the New Deal. He also traces Johnson's career as Majority Leader in the Senate in the 1950s, arguing that he effectively supported reform whenever possible as well as embracing the assumptions of the Cold War. In his second volume he covers the successes and failures of the "Great Society", Johnson's important commitment to civil rights legislation, and his problems in trying to deal with the Vietnam War. The war destroyed his presidency and brought Johnson close to a psychological breakdown. This work replaces the previous best biography, namely Paul Conkin's *Big Daddy from the Pedernales* (1986), which was well written but did not do justice to the period of Johnson's presidency.

CARO was more critical of Johnson's early career in his two volumes, which end with the election to the Senate in 1948. There is little that is admirable in Johnson's character – a character that, he argues, hid a dark secret: the need to dominate and exercise power over others. Brief references in his second volume to Johnson's later support for the Civil Rights Act view this as commendable in its own right (given Johnson's earlier opposition to such legislation). This, however, is juxtaposed against his disastrous Vietnam policies (pp.xiv–xxvi), which again reveal his dark side. These volumes should be read with caution, although they are very thoroughly researched in terms of Texas and New Deal politics.

DIVINE has edited three volumes on Johnson, although other works have superseded the first volume (published in 1981). In both his 1987 and 1994 volumes he has provided introductory critical essays (written by himself) on all the writings on Johnson between each published volume. These are very useful guides on Johnson historiography.

JORDAN & ROSTOW edited a collection of essays evaluating the "Great Society" on its twentieth anniversary. These are a relatively uneven collection but capture some of the enthusiasm of the reformers. Divine's later two volumes contain better articles on certain aspects of Johnson's domestic policies. In volume two, Martin V. Melossi argued that Johnson took an active interest in environmental issues and policies, which should have received more recognition. Clarence G. Lasby chronicled Johnson's encouragement of medical research, particularly into heart disease and cancer. In volume three, Susan M. Hartmann noted Johnson's relatively progressive policies towards women's issues, despite his privately held sexist attitudes. More research is still needed on these domestic policies, although DALLEK'S overview of domestic policies in his biography provided the best-balanced account of Johnson's successes and failures.

SCHULMAN has given a regional but important study on the effects of federal aid in the South. He argues that the modern South was virtually a product of this funding and that Johnson was a major figure in supporting such policies. Yet, this aid was often used in ways never intended by Washington. The local Southern leaders were able to direct monies to create highways and other infrastructure to attract new industry, but showed little interest in alleviating poverty. Despite Johnson's intentions, the region gained economically for some without solving the problems of poverty and low wages.

GRAHAM has examined the issue of civil rights during the 1960s and the important contributions of the Johnson administration in this area. The account is probably too detailed in parts and does not easily reveal the role of Johnson in the struggle. However, it is a comprehensive study and reveals how liberals like Johnson moved from the position of denying any individual differences between races to acceptance of the need for affirmative action programmes to assist disadvantaged minority groups.

BARRETT considers Johnson's decision to send American combat troops to South Vietnam in 1965. He disagrees with a common criticism that the president directed the war in isolation from within the White House. Instead he argues that

Johnson was not in any way irrational or isolated and actively sought information and advice from all points of view. Although the study is limited to the workings within the White House, it is a useful corrective to the view of an isolated Johnson.

HERRING builds upon Larry Berman's *Lyndon Johnson's War: The Road to Stalemate in Vietnam* (1989) and examines the problems of Johnson in managing the war. Anxious to avoid a Korean-type conflict and also a breakdown in civilian–military relations, Johnson was committed to fighting a limited war in Vietnam under his personal control. This however left military strategy unclear and Johnson failed to provide any coordinated planning to the war whereas his consensus-building made it unlikely that the Joint Chiefs of Staff would adopt military policies that would challenge the President. Despite his personal political skills, Johnson also failed to unite the country behind him in fighting the war.

BRANDS dealt with Johnson's foreign policy in areas other than Vietnam. He argued that Johnson was very much trapped by the previous worldwide commitments of Truman, Eisenhower, and Kennedy, which, by the mid-1960s, had over-stretched US power, especially in the light of the Vietnam War. Despite these commitments, the problems of Vietnam, and his own domestic reform interests, Johnson still performed reasonably well in this complex area. He applied himself to trying to defend the status quo. Brands argues for a President who might have proven to be quite competent in foreign policy if he had not been faced with the problems of Vietnam.

PETER E. BASTIAN

Jurisprudence, *see* Law survey

Jury instructions

Abbott, Walter F. and John Batt (editors), *A Handbook of Jury Research*, Philadelphia: American Law Institute, 1999

Charrow, Robert P. and Veda R. Charrow, "Making Legal Language Understandable: A Psycholinguistic Study of Jury Instructions", *Columbia Law Review*, 79 (1979): 1306–74

Dann, Michael B., "'Learning Lessons' and 'Speaking Rights': Creating Educated and Democratic Juries", *Indiana Law Journal*, 68/4 (1993): 1229–77

Dumas, Bethany K., "US Pattern Jury Instructions: Problems and Proposals", *Forensic Linguistics*, 7/1 (2000): 49–71

Dumas, Bethany K., "Jury Trials: Lay Jurors, Pattern Jury Instructions, and Comprehension Issues", *Tennessee Law Review*, 67 (2000): 701–742

Lieberman, Joel D. and Bruce C. Sales, "What Social Science Teaches Us about Jury Instructions", *Psychology, Public Policy, and Law*, 3/4 (1997): 589–644; a modified version is also a chapter in Abbott and Batt, 1999

Munsterman, G. Thomas, Paula L. Hannaford and G. Marc Whitehead (editors), *Jury Trial Innovations*, Williamsburg, Virginia: National Center for State Courts, 1997

National Jury Trial Innovation Project, *Order in the Classroom*, Chicago: IADC Foundation, 1998 (video)

Schwarzer, William W., "Communicating with Juries: Problems and Remedies", *California Law Review*, 10 (1981): 731–69

Steele, Walter W. Jr. and Elizabeth G. Thornburg, "Jury Instructions: A Persistent Failure to Communicate", *North Carolina Law Review*, 67 (1988): 77–119

Tennessee Bar Association Jury Reform Commission, *Report of the Tennessee Bar Association Commission on Jury Reform*, 1999 http://www.tba.org/news/juryreform.html

Tiersma, Peter Meijes, "Reforming the Language of Jury Instructions", *Hofstra Law Review*, 22/1 (1993): 37–78

ABBOTT & BATT is a splendid recent handbook on jury process. The chapters on "Jury Research: An Inventory of Findings" and "The Effectiveness of Jury Instructions" provide contemporary overviews of issues and perspectives.

Robert and Veda Charrow (he is a lawyer, she is a linguist) are well known for their important pioneering research. CHARROW & CHARROW shows empirically that jurors do not understand the law they are given, often performing at no better than chance level on objective tests of legal comprehension. They demonstrated that the problem lies not so much in basic conceptual barriers to understanding as in the arcane concepts and abstruse syntax that characterize many instructions. They also demonstrated that rewritten instructions improved comprehension.

DANN, written by a trial judge of the Superior Court of Arizona and recent chair of the Arizona Jury Trial Reform Committee, suggests that issues of context, control, and democracy may be as important as those of sentence structure and terminology if improved communication is the goal. The author led a reform movement in Arizona with his conviction that juror comprehension will improve as jurors become fuller participants in the trial process. In particular, he has been an advocate of jurors' "speaking rights" – the right to talk with each other about what they hear and see as the trial progresses.

DUMAS, written by a linguist and lawyer, suggests reasons for the current inertia with regard to jury reform, identifies chinks in the wall of resistance (notably in Arizona), and suggests a model for reform that draws upon the recognition that the role of the jury as finder of fact has to compete with the judicial perception that the jury must be highly constrained and controlled. She suggests that jurors must be empowered as the domain experts that they are.

LIEBERMAN & SALES critically examines the social science research relevant to evaluating the effectiveness of judicial instructions, examining in particular the factors that contribute to instruction ineffectiveness. It reviews limitations associated with a variety of specific types of instructions and discuss the implications of their findings for public policy.

MUNSTERMAN, HANNAFORD & WHITEHEAD summarizes social science research on how jurors process information and then states why innovations in jury trial procedures are necessary. Subsequent chapters describe techniques for reform.

The video from the NATIONAL JURY TRIAL INNOVATION PROJECT depicts current jury instruction practice by a demonstration of what the first day of a university class would be like if students were treated the way jurors typically are treated. SCHWARZER, written by a senior judge in San Francisco, has been influential in urging the revision of procedures that restrict the extent to which jurors may look to their colleagues for help and mutual support by discussing a case as it progresses. STEELE & THORNBURG shows that jurors conscientiously try to follow their instructions, but that most of those instructions cannot be understood by most jurors. They then show that jury instructions can be written to greatly enhance the jurors' level of comprehension. Finally, the authors analyse the forces inherent in the American judicial system that inhibit any individual efforts to improve the comprehensibility of jury instructions. They conclude that improvement is unlikely unless institutional changes are made that will create incentives for lawyers and judges to write instructions that juries can understand.

The TENNESSEE BAR ASSOCIATION JURY REFORM COMMISSION REPORT is based on a study of: (a) jury administration and management, pretrial management, and post-verdict issues; (b) jury selection and trial procedures; and (c) jury instructions. It gives the conclusions of the Commission, including recommendations for change, and has been accepted by The Board of Governors of the Tennessee Bar Association. Steps are underway to begin implementation of all recommendations of the Committee, including the rewriting of all Tennessee pattern instructions.

TIERSMA reviews the California civil jury instructions criticized by Charrow & Charrow and analyses the progress that has been made since then, concluding that the California Committee has made definite progress toward its goal of making jury instructions understandable to the average juror.

BETHANY K. DUMAS

See also Trial

Just-in-time production

Goldratt, Eliyahu M. and Jeff Cox, *The Goal: A Process of Ongoing Improvement*, 2nd edition, Great Barrington, Massachusetts: North River Press, 1992; Aldershot, Hampshire: Gower, 1993

Goldratt, Eliyahu, "What Is the Theory of Constraints", *APICS: The Performance Advantage*, 3/6 (June 1993): 18–20

Hall, Robert W., *Attaining Manufacturing Excellence: Just-in-Time, Total Quality, Total People Involvement*, Homewood, Illinois: Dow Jones Irwin, 1987

Jones, Robert L., "TQC: Required Tools for JIT Success" in *CPIM Just-in-Time Reprints*, edited by the Just-in-Time Committee of the APICS Curricula and Certification Council, Falls Church, Virginia: APICS, 1994

Monden, Yasuhiro, *Toyota Production System: An Integrated Approach to Just-in-Time*, 2nd edition, Norcross, Georgia: Industrial Engineering and Management Press, 1993

Sandras, William A. Jr, *Just-in-Time: Making It Happen: Unleashing the Power of Continuous Improvement*, Essex Junction, Utah: Wight, 1989

Schniederjans, Marc J., *Topics in Just-in-Time Management*, Boston: Allyn and Bacon, 1993

Schonberger, Richard J., *Japanese Manufacturing Techniques: Nine Hidden Lessons in Simplicity*, New York: Free Press, 1982

Wantuck, Kenneth A., *Just-in-Time for America: A Common Sense Production Strategy*, Milwaukee: Forum, 1989

Womack, James P., Daniel T. Jones and Daniel Roos, *The Machine That Changed the World*, New York: Rawson, 1990

Vollmann, Thomas E., William L. Berry and D. Clay Whybark, *Manufacturing Planning and Control Systems*, Homewood, Illinois: Dow Jones Irwin, 1984

GOLDRATT reintroduces the reader to the *theory of constraints*, found in his book *The Goal* (GOLDRATT & COX). This article summarizes the steps and diagrams used to find root causes and core problems for process improvement. Process improvement is one of the key elements toward eliminating waste in a production system. He outlines a current reality tree, which is more of a thought process to better pinpoint the core problem. He also discusses the "evaporating cloud" concept, which focuses on any conflict occurring with the core problem. Goldratt summarizes the important points of Goldratt & Cox, which is a business-textbook, written as a novel. This book is not for the novice in just-in-time principles and philosophy. It focuses on the life and work of a manufacturing manager who must improve his factory's process, decrease cost, and become more competitive in order to keep the factory open. The manager struggles to analyse his troubled production process through the help of the mentor named Jonah. The book illustrates the concepts of problem identification, material flow, and worker training and empowerment.

Total quality management and control concepts are an integral part of a successful just-in-time system. When a company begins producing only what it needs, no buffer stock for replacing defects and mistakes is available. Therefore, quality control must be implemented. JONES looks at total quality control tools needed in a just-in-time system. He discusses how these tools and concepts can enhance the objectives of a just-in-time system at the team level.

MONDEN discusses Toyota's production system, which started the just-in-time phenomenon in industry and how integration with information systems has improved it. A central evil in other production systems is waste. The Toyota production system regards overproduction, time spent at the machine, use of transport, processing, taking inventory, motion, and defective units as waste. These are important principles of a just-in-time philosophy. The Toyota production system requires each stage of production to go the previous stage to pick up the exact number of units needed. This concept was a reversal of previous production processes. Monden presents the various components and concepts in a broad and balanced manner for practitioners and academics alike.

Another practical approach to presenting just-in-time principles is SANDRAS' discussion of the need of quality/just-in-time partnership. Instead of just focusing on the production floor alone, the author discusses how quality/just-in-time philosophy affects various functional areas in a company and what are the responsibilities of each area to make a successful implementation. Sandras discusses accounting, supplier partnerships, customers, and empowerment of the worker, as well as performance measurements, Kanban cards, and decision-making techniques. The book is a comprehensive guide for a successful just-in-time implementation.

HALL discusses the topic from a leadership viewpoint. He writes about the need to move from outmoded to leading-edge practices for a company to be competitive. Like other authors, he feels that total quality issues are interconnected with just-in-time practices and principles.

SCHNIEDERJANS's book addresses various advanced topics in just-in-time management. It is more of an academic approach to just-in-time than any of the other books discussed here. Several diagrams and example problems illustrate just-in-time principles and techniques in general, rather than for a specific industry. A just-in-time simulation game is included.

SCHONBERGER demonstrates how Japanese techniques can be applied in American industries with their different cultures. The author includes examples of successful implementations in America and describes in depth the just-in-time techniques that were used. This classic book on just-in-time techniques was published only two years after Western industry began to wake up to the success of Japan.

WANTUCK approaches just-in-time principles from a strategic viewpoint. The author discusses how business strategy, production strategy, and the seven key principles of just-in-time strategy tie together. As with other books, he covers the importance of total quality to the just-in-time principles. He covers similar topics to those covered by Sandras but in a less "hands-on" manner. He provides a very comprehensive list of just-in-time concepts and techniques.

WOMACK, JONES, & ROOS look at how just-in-time principles have changed the automobile industry, taking an historical perspective. They reveal specific manufacturing approaches behind Japanese techniques and consider ways in which the Western automobile industry can implement these techniques. Besides being very entertaining, the book comprehensively describes the supplier partnership and tier system used in just-in-time better then most books. It also discusses the complete supply chain system from the conception of the car, through suppliers, to the arrival of the car at the customer.

VOLLMAN, BERRY & WHYBARK is a standard reference for certification in production and inventory management through the American Production and Inventory Control Society. The various chapters examine many principles, linkages, and theoretical considerations associated with the topic of just-in-time. The book stresses that it is more than a control system: it is a system-wide philosophy.

KIMBERLEE SNYDER

See also Total quality management

Justice

Avineri, Shlomo and Avner de-Shalit (editors), *Communitarianism and Individualism*, Oxford and New York: Oxford University Press, 1992

Cohen, G.A., "Where the Action Is: On the Site of Distributive Justice", *Philosophy and Public Affairs*, 26/1 (1997): 3–30

Crisp, Roger, *Routledge Philosophy Guidebook to Mill on Utilitarianism*, London and New York: Routledge, 1997

Elster, Jon, *An Introduction to Karl Marx*, Cambridge and New York: Cambridge University Press, 1986

Forsyth, Murray and Maurice Keens-Soper (editors), *A Guide to the Political Classics: Plato to Rousseau*, Oxford and New York: Oxford University Press, 1988

Goodin, Robert E. and Philip Pettit (editors), *A Companion to Contemporary Political Philosophy*, Oxford and Cambridge, Massachusetts: Blackwell, 1993

Goodin, Robert E. and Philip Pettit (editors), *Contemporary Political Philosophy: An Anthology*, Oxford and Cambridge, Massachusetts: Blackwell, 1997

Kymlicka, Will, *Contemporary Political Philosophy: An Introduction*, Oxford: Clarendon Press, and New York: Oxford University Press, 1990

Nozick, Robert, *Anarchy, State, and Utopia*, New York: Basic Books, and Oxford: Blackwell, 1974

Okin, Susan Moller, *Justice, Gender, and the Family*, New York: Basic Books, 1989

Phillips, Anne (editor), *Feminism and Politics*, Oxford and New York: Oxford University Press, 1998

Rawls, John, *A Theory of Justice*, Cambridge, Massachusetts: Harvard University Press, 1971, Oxford: Clarendon Press, 1972; revised edition, Cambridge, Massachusetts: Harvard University Press, and Oxford: Oxford University Press, 1999

Wolff, Jonathan, *An Introduction to Political Philosophy*, Oxford and New York: Oxford University Press, 1996

The subject matter of justice is diverse. So are the approaches to understanding it. An excellent starting point for inquiry into this variety of subjects and methods is GOODIN & PETTIT (1993). This exceptional collection is divided into three parts. The first part contains essays on the distinct contributions that different contemporary disciplines (analytic philosophy, continental philosophy, history, sociology, economics, political science, and legal studies) have made to the study of justice, politics, and law. The second part canvasses a number of normative theories of justice (such as conservatism, liberalism, feminism). The third part contains 28 pieces on specialized topics in political theory, such as autonomy, democracy, equality, power, rights, and welfare. Each essay is written at the introductory level and includes extensive references. Many of the essays are followed by helpful lists for further reading. GOODIN & PETTIT (1997) is another helpful anthology. It includes 38 previously published works in recent political theory, including many well-known and influential articles on a variety of debates. It is a good place to turn for a state-of-the-art introduction to professional theorizing about justice.

KYMLICKA provides critical analyses of contemporary theories of justice. It is an introductory book, but it does not shy away from rigorous consideration of the virtues and defects of each theory. In that sense, it is not merely an introduction to the content of contemporary political philosophy, but also to its style of analysis. Kymlicka argues that each of the theories he discusses (utilitarianism, liberalism, libertarianism, Marxism, communitarianism, and feminism) relies on treating persons, in some sense or another, as equals. He assesses the theories in light of how well they realize this egalitarian ideal. Though Kymlicka could have chosen another political ideal (such as autonomy) by which to evaluate these theories, his general approach works well, and should not alienate those who are less concerned with equality. The book–the best of its kind–is a sophisticated and penetrating introduction to some of today's most important debates in political theory.

A more historically informed introduction to topics concerning theories of justice is provided by WOLFF. In the course of answering questions about democracy, liberty, property, community, feminism, and the need and justification for a state, he takes care to show how major historical figures fit into these contemporary debates. His highly accessible book includes discussions of the views of Plato, Hobbes, Locke, Rousseau, Mill, Marx, and others.

For those who wish to study primary materials in the history of theories about justice, some important works include Plato's *Republic*, Aristotle's *Politics*, Hobbes' *Leviathan*, Locke's *Second Treatise of Government*, and Rousseau's *Social Contract*. One might add to the list Saint Augustine's *City of God* and Machiavelli's *The Prince*. But before taking up these works, one might want to begin with FORSYTH & KEENS-SOPER, a collection of nontechnical, introductory essays on each of the texts. Each essay provides historical setting, an exposition of the texts' main points, and a bibliographic note recommending certain editions, translations (where applicable), and secondary literature.

Further historical study should also include John Stuart Mill's *On Liberty* and *Utilitarianism*. The former work is known for its vigorous defence of thoroughgoing individualism and its arguments for liberty of conscience and speech, and against paternalism. The latter is an exposition and defence of the view that the right individual, social, or political action is the one that maximizes happiness. CRISP is a helpful and comprehensive introduction to Mill's utilitarianism – a very influential theory. Crisp clearly explains Mill's theory, covers important distinctions crucial to understanding it, and addresses contemporary criticisms of utilitarianism. Importantly, Crisp also defends the consistency between the apparently competing positions Mill advances in "Utilitarianism" and "On Liberty".

No historical study of political thought would be complete without consideration of Karl Marx. Marx's criticisms of capitalism, based on ideas of alienation, exploitation, power relations, ideology, and class, have had profound influence on ideas about justice beyond the relatively small group of thinkers who today consider themselves Marxists. Even so, there is considerable debate amongst Marxists about whether Marx ever considered himself to be presenting a theory of justice, or whether communism was in some way "beyond justice". ELSTER presents a balanced and well-written introduction to these and other issues in Marx. Each chapter is followed by a note suggesting further readings. But what makes this introduction to Marx stand out is Elster's candid parsing of what is insightful in Marx from what is outdated or false.

Far and away the most significant work of political philosophy in the 20th century was written by RAWLS, and his *A Theory of Justice* remains at the centre of political philosophy today (though Rawls has subsequently revised some aspects of his position). In *A Theory of Justice*, Rawls presents both a method for arriving at principles of justice for a society's basic institutions, and also his own view about what principles that method yields. The method, a hypothetical social contract, strives to capture a sense of moral equality by denying the contractors knowledge of their own morally arbitrary features (sex, race, wealth, talents, and so on). Rawls argues that such a method would yield principles that grant each citizen the right to the greatest equal liberty compatible with a like liberty for all, require that offices and positions be open to all under conditions of fair equality of opportunity, and allow inequalities only insofar as they benefit the worst-off in society. Apart from its defence of liberal egalitarianism, *A Theory of Justice* is also known for, among other things, its criticisms of utilitarianism and libertarianism. It is often credited with breathing new life into the now flourishing field of political philosophy.

NOZICK criticizes Rawls' theory from a libertarian, or classical liberal view. Nozick, unlike many of his contemporaries, takes anarchism seriously, and spends the first part of the book arguing against it. But Nozick also argues, in the second part of his book, that the legitimate functions of the state are extremely limited to protection against force, theft, and fraud, and the enforcement of contracts and other features of a *laissez-faire* market economy. These arguments involve an analysis of opposing approaches to the issue of distributive justice, and an extensive discussion of Rawls' arguments.

The revival of liberal debate in the 1970s led to a variety of criticisms, the "communitarian" aspect of which is well chronicled in AVINERI & DE-SHALIT. Thinkers such as Michael Sandel, Charles Taylor, and Alasdair MacIntyre are among the more prominent representatives of the communitarian view. Communitarianism arose in response to certain implausible assumptions about the self on which, it is argued, liberal theories (such as Rawls' and Nozick's) rely. Communitarians emphasize the social nature of the self and its connections to communally-given norms and roles, and take this essential sociality as the basis for a criticism of, among other things, the characteristically liberal view that the state should (or could) be neutral between competing conceptions of the good life. Avineri & de-Shalit provide the best collection of primary materials from this debate.

There are affinities between communitarian and some feminist views about justice, including a critical position on the liberal conception of the self and the liberal emphasis on justice. But feminist political theory also tends to be critical of communitarianism because of its insensitivity to potentially oppressive power relations and gender stereotypes embedded in the norms of communities. The diversity and sophistication of recent feminist scholarship is well represented in PHILLIPS, a collection of previously published essays by noted feminist authors that variously feature criticisms of the public/private dichotomy; arguments against traditional understandings of sexual relations and the role of the family; an emphasis on the importance of caring and the emotions; and inquiries into group membership, identity, and difference, to name a few salient issues.

For the most part, theories of justice have primarily concerned themselves with the "basic structure" of society. The trend has been to argue for certain political and economic institutions and policies within which people would be free to live their lives more or less as they see fit. This is Rawls' view, yet it has recently come under some criticism. OKIN targets the kinds of institutions Rawls thinks are appropriate arenas for considerations of justice. She argues that Rawls' theory can be modified so that the family is taken as a subject of justice. Her book is also valuable for its feminist-informed critiques of the major competing contemporary political theories. COHEN also criticizes what he sees as the limited scope Rawls envisions for justice, claiming that a society's principles of justice should not apply merely to evaluations of features of the basic structure (laws, institutions, policies, rights, and the like) but also to people's legally free choices within that structure. Beyond institutions, he argues, justice requires a social ethos.

JUSTIN WEINBERG

See also Anarchism, Communitarianism, Feminism, Liberalism, Libertarianism, Marx and Marxism, Utilitarianism

K

Kaldor, Nicholas 1908–86

British (Hungarian-born) economist

Dixon, Robert and Anthony P. Thirlwall, "A Model of Regional Growth-Rate Differences on Kaldorian Lines", *Oxford Economic Papers*, 27/2 (1975): 201–14 (reprinted in King)

Harcourt, Geoffrey C., "Nicholas Kaldor, 12 May 1908–30 September 1986", *Economica*, 55/218 (1988): 159–70 (reprinted in King)

Kaldor, Nicholas, "Prof. Pigou on Money Wages in Relation to Unemployment", *Economic Journal*, 47/188 (1937): 745–53 (reprinted in Targetti and Thirlwall)

Kaldor, Nicholas, *An Expenditure Tax*, London: Allen and Unwin, 1955

Kaldor, Nicholas, "Alternative Theories of Distribution", *Review of Economic Studies*, 23/2 (1955–56): 83–100 (reprinted in Targetti and Thirlwall)

Kaldor, Nicholas, "A Model of Economic Growth", *Economic Journal*, 67/268 (1957): 591–624

Kaldor, Nicholas, "Capital Accumulation and Economic Growth" in *The Theory of Capital*, edited by F.A. Lutz and D.C. Hague, London: Macmillan, and New York: St Martin's Press, 1961 (reprinted in Targetti and Thirlwall)

Kaldor, Nicholas, *Causes of the Slow Rate of Economic Growth of the United Kingdom: An Inaugural Lecture*, London: Cambridge University Press, 1966 (reprinted in King, and Targetti and Thirlwall)

Kaldor, Nicholas, "The Case for Regional Policies", *Scottish Journal of Political Economy* (17 November 1970): 337–48 (reprinted in King and Targetti and Thirlwall)

Kaldor, Nicholas, "The Irrelevance of Equilibrium Economics", *Economic Journal*, 82/328 (1972): 1237–55 (reprinted in Targetti and Thirlwall)

Kaldor, Nicholas, "What is Wrong with Economic Theory", *Quarterly Journal of Economics*, 89/3 (1975): 347–57 (reprinted in Targetti and Thirlwall)

Kaldor, Nicholas, "The Role of Increasing Returns, Technical Progress and Cumulative Causation Theory in International Trade", *Economie Appliqué*, 34/4 (1981): 593–618 (reprinted in Targetti and Thirlwall)

Kaldor, Nicholas, *The Scourge of Monetarism*, Oxford and New York: Oxford University Press, 1982

Kaldor, Nicholas, *The Economic Consequences of Mrs Thatcher: Speeches in the House of Lords, 1979–82*, London: Duckworth, 1983

Kaldor, Nicholas, "Reflections of an Economist", *Banca Nazionale del Lavoro Quarterly Review*, 39/156 (1986): 3–26 (reprinted in King)

King, John E., *Economic Growth in Theory and Practice: A Kaldorian Perspective*, Aldershot, Hampshire: Elgar, 1994

Pasinetti, Luigi L., "Nicholas Kaldor: A Few Personal Notes", *Journal of Post Keynesian Economics*, 5/3 (1983): 333–40 (reprinted in King)

Targetti, Ferdinando and Anthony P. Thirlwall, *The Essential Kaldor*, London: Duckworth, and New York: Holmes and Meier, 1989

Targetti, Ferdinando, *Nicholas Kaldor: The Economics and Politics of Capitalism as a Dynamic System*, Oxford: Clarendon Press, and New York: Oxford University Press, 1992

Thirlwall, Anthony P., *Nicholas Kaldor*, Brighton: Wheatsheaf, 1987

Nicholas Kaldor was one of the most innovative and influential postwar economists, although his influence was much greater in the UK than in the US. In 1969, the *Financial Times* reported that he was one of 10 economists shortlisted for the first Nobel Prize in economics, but he was never to receive it (see THIRLWALL). Born in Budapest, Kaldor went to the London School of Economics to study in 1927, graduated in 1930, and then spent the next 15 years there, first as a lecturer and then as a reader. After a two-year sojourn at the Economic Commission for Europe, he moved to the University of Cambridge in 1949, was promoted to Reader in 1952, and then to Professor of Economics in 1966. Kaldor combined his academic writings with a distinguished career as a policy advisor. He advised a number of developing countries on taxation, and made the convincing case that an expenditure tax was preferable to an income tax, which penalized savings twice (KALDOR, 1955). He was also special advisor to three Labour Chancellors of the Exchequer between 1964 and 1976. In 1974 he was made a life peer. He used the House of Lords to launch a series of brilliant polemics on the economic policies (especially monetarism) of the Conservative government of Mrs Thatcher (KALDOR, 1983). In the course of his career, he published over 160 articles, plus 39 books, pamphlets, and official publications.

Brief overviews of his life and works can be found in PASINETTI and in HARCOURT. An autobiographical note is KALDOR (1986). The most comprehensive and definitive account is his biography written by THIRLWALL. This traces Kaldor's life, career, and the development of his academic ideas, together with the forces that shaped them. The book provides a masterly exposition of Kaldor's contributions to economics in a non-technical way, and thus provides an excellent introduction to, and assessment of, his theories. The book also includes a bibliography of Kaldor's complete works. A more technical and excellent comprehensive discussion of Kaldor's work is TARGETTI.

Kaldor never published a major book encompassing his worldview of economics, possibly because it changed so much. A very useful collection of his papers is TARGETTI & THIRL-WALL, which contains 23 of his most influential articles, grouped thematically as follows – (I) "The Firm, Equilibrium and Welfare"; (II) "Contributions to Keynesian Economics"; (III) Distribution, Growth and Cumulative Causation"; (IV)"The Challenge to Equilibrium Theory"; and (V) "Domestic and International Economic Policy". There is also a concise introduction to these papers. A more extensive collection of his papers has been published by Duckworth in a set of eight volumes, namely, *Essays on Value and Distribution* (1960); *Essays on Economic Stability and Growth* (1960); *Essays on Economic Policy I* (1964); *Essays on Economic Policy II* (1964); *Further Essays on Economic Theory* (1978); *Further Essays on Applied Economics* (1978); *Reports on Taxation I* (1980); and *Reports on Taxation II* (1980). KING is also a very useful collection of papers, as it includes not only a number of Kaldor's important papers on economic growth, but also both theoretical and applied articles by other authors extending and testing Kaldor's work on economic growth.

It is difficult to give more than a flavour of Kaldor's contributions here. As Harcourt has noted, there are three stages to Kaldor's career. First, there was the brilliant young orthodox economist at the London School of Economics. Second, there was the "enthusiastic Keynesian" who contributed to the early Keynesian revolution. Third, there was the Kaldor of the postwar period, whose main concern was with distribution, accumulation, and growth. It was during this time that he became increasingly disenchanted with neoclassical economics, especially with what he saw as its irrelevant assumptions and, in particular, its neglect of increasing returns to scale. It is also noticeable that from the late 1960s, he became more interested in broad themes, leaving it to others to formalize his ideas in mathematical models or to test his conclusions. Indeed, many of his most influential papers were presented as lectures to various august audiences.

Kaldor's early work included a paper on the stability of equilibrium – Kaldor coined the term "cobweb theorem". He wrote a number of papers on the theory of the firm at a time when Joan Robinson's *Economics of Imperfect Competition* (1936) was causing a great deal of interest. He also proposed his well-known compensation tests in welfare economics in an attempt to avoid the limitations inherent in the Pareto criterion (see Targetti & Thirlwall, Part I).

Kaldor became an early convert to Keynesian economics. He was 28 when the *General Theory* was published. It was his paper "Prof. Pigou on Money Wages in Relation to Unemployment" (KALDOR, 1937) which finally convinced Pigou he was wrong in arguing that a cut in money wages was a necessary and sufficient condition to reduce unemployment. He also made a notable contribution to the theory of the trade cycle. (His early contributions are discussed in chapter 2 of Thirlwall. *See also* Targetti & Thirlwall, Part II.)

However, it was in the 1950s when he published papers that have had a lasting effect on the profession, and have helped to establish the post-Keynesian school of thought (see Thirlwall, chapter 6). Kaldor rejected the neoclassical notion of the marginal productivity theory of distribution. His famous alternative macroeconomic model of distribution was first articulated in the last section of a very lucid exposition of the various theories of distribution in his "Alternative Theories of Distribution" (see KALDOR (1955–6)). By this time, he had moved away from short-run Keynesian problems, and had become interested in trying to explain the long-run economic dynamics of capitalist economies. Long before the advent of endogenous growth theory, he had concluded that it made no sense to distinguish between shifts *of* the production function and shifts *along* the production function (or in other words, that the assumption that technical change could be modelled as an exogenous shift of the production function was unsound). In his "Model of Economic Growth" (KALDOR, 1957), he first used his technical progress function, which attempted to remove this dichotomy, together with his distribution theory, in an attempt to build a growth model without relying on neoclassical assumptions. The model went through a number of transformations – see, for example, his paper "Capital Accumulation and Economic Growth" (KALDOR, 1961).

From the mid-1960s Kaldor lost interest in formal growth models. He began to paint on a much broader canvas and launched his attack on what he saw as the sterility of Walrasian equilibrium theory. His two papers "The Irrelevance of Equilibrium Economics" (KALDOR, 1972) and "What is Wrong with Economic Theory" (KALDOR, 1975) should still be required reading today. In the first he considers what he regards as the devastating implications of increasing returns to scale for equilibrium theory. If returns to scale are large relative to the scale of the economy, the notions of equilibrium and the Pareto optimal allocation of resources lose all meaning. Here we find one of the first discussions of what has come to be known as path dependency in economic growth. Increasing returns to scale, broadly defined, have profound implications for economic growth, which proceeds in a "cumulative causation" manner. Countries can become locked into virtuous or vicious circles of growth. He outlined such a model in his paper KALDOR (1970), but it was left to DIXON & THIRLWALL to provide a formalization of the model. In KALDOR (1981), he showed how international trade may not be to the benefit of both trading partners. He stressed the importance of export-led growth and the Harrod foreign trade multiplier in accounting for international growth rate differences. In "What's Wrong with Economic Theory" (Kaldor, 1975) he outlines his two-sector model of economic growth for a closed economy – such as the world economy – stressing the complementary nature of growth between agriculture and industry. He had lectured on this model at Cambridge, but had never published a formal model. This, once again, he left to others

– see the papers by Targetti, Thirlwall, Molana &Vines, and Canning, in Part IV of King.

Kaldor was also interested in the applied aspects of growth and his inaugural lecture KALDOR (1966) initiated a whole spate of papers concerned with the empirical regularities of economic growth. These became known generically as Kaldor's laws (see Thirlwall, chapter 7). They included the famous Verdoorn law, which is the relationship between the growth of manufacturing (or industrial) productivity and output growth. Its importance is that it provides empirical evidence of substantial increasing returns to scale of both the static and dynamic variety. There is now a substantial literature on this topic (see King, Part III, "The Romance with Verdoorn").

Kaldor made many contributions to the policy debates of his day, and his *Scourge of Monetarism* remains a powerful critique of those macroeconomic policies that, for a time, held sway in the United Kingdom. Like Keynes before him, Kaldor was not only a noted theoretician, but also a brilliant advocate of his ideas in the policy arena, and a ruthless critic of those with whom he disagreed.

JOHN S.L. McCOMBIE

Kaldor's laws

(including the Verdoorn law)

Bairam, Erkin I., "The Verdoorn Law, Returns to Scale and Industrial Growth: A Review of the Literature", *Australian Economic Papers*, 26/48 (1987): 20–42

Bernat, G. Andrew, "Does Manufacturing Matter? A Spatial Econometric View of Kaldor's Laws", *Journal of Regional Science*, 36/3 (1996): 463–77

Cripps, Francis and Roger J. Tarling, *Growth in Advanced Capitalist Economies, 1950–70*, Cambridge: Cambridge University Press, 1973

Fingleton, Bernard and John S.L. McCombie, "Increasing Returns and Economic Growth: Some Evidence for Manufacturing from the European Union Regions", *Oxford Economic Papers*, 50/1 (1998): 89–105

Harris, Richard I.D. and Eunice Lau, "Verdoorn's Law and Increasing Returns to Scale in the UK Regions, 1968–91: Some New Estimates Based on the Cointegration Approach", *Oxford Economic Papers*, 50/2 (1998): 201–19

Kaldor, Nicholas, *Causes of the Slow Rate of Economic Growth of the United Kingdom: An Inaugural Lecture*, London: Cambridge University Press, 1966

Kaldor, Nicholas, "Economic Growth and the Verdoorn Law: A Comment on Mr Rowthorn's Article", *Economic Journal*, 85/340 (1975): 891–96

King, John E., *Economic Growth in Theory and Practice: A Kaldorian Perspective*, Aldershot, Hampshire: Elgar, 1994

McCombie, John S.L., "What Still Remains of Kaldor's Laws?", *Economic Journal*, 91/361 (1981): 206–16

McCombie, John S.L., "Economic Growth, Kaldor's Laws and the Static-Dynamic Verdoorn Law Paradox", *Applied Economics*, 14/3 (1982): 295–304

McCombie, John S.L. and John R. de Ridder, "The Verdoorn Law Controversy: Some New Empirical Evidence Using US State Data", *Oxford Economic Papers*, 36/2 (1984): 268–84

McCombie, John S.L. and Anthony P. Thirlwall, *Economic Growth and the Balance-of-Payments Constraint*, Basingstoke: Macmillan, and New York: St Martin's Press, 1994

Rowthorn, Robert, E., "What Remains of Kaldor's Law?", *Economic Journal*, 85/337 (1975a): 10–19

Rowthorn, Robert E., "A Reply to Lord Kaldor's Comment", *Economic Journal*, 85/340 (1975b): 897–901

Thirlwall, Anthony P. (editor), "Symposium on Kaldor's Laws", *Journal of Post Keynesian Economics*, 5/3 (1983a): 341–429

Thirlwall, Anthony P., "A Plain Man's Guide to Kaldor's Growth Laws", *Journal of Post Keynesian Economics*, 5/3 (1983b): 345–58

Verdoorn, P.J., "Fattori che regolano lo sviluppo della produttivita del lavoro", *L'Industria*, 1 (1949): 3–10

The Golden Age from 1950–73 saw the advanced countries experiencing a rate of output and productivity growth that was, for each country, on average over twice its historic norm. (After 1973 there was a return to the previous rates of growth.) However, there were substantial disparities between countries in their productivity and output growth rates with, especially, the UK and the US lagging behind the continental European countries and Japan. In his seminal inaugural address, KALDOR (1966) addressed the question of why the UK had performed so relatively badly in the early postwar period.

Notwithstanding his notable contributions to growth theory, Kaldor had by this time become more interested in establishing empirical regularities that could explain differences in international and interregional growth rates. He was also concerned (long before the advent of endogenous growth theory) with the question of why growth rate differences seemed to persist between countries. In Kaldor (1966), he adduced the first two of his three "laws of economic growth" (see THIRLWALL (1983a and b) and McCOMBIE & THIRLWALL, chapter 2, for surveys). The first law was the observation that manufacturing could be regarded as the "engine of growth", in that there is a positive correlation between the growth of GDP and the excess of the growth of the manufacturing sector over the growth of the non manufacturing sector.

The second law, or the Verdoorn law (see VERDOORN), has attracted more attention. (See BAIRAM for a survey.) When the growth of manufacturing productivity was regressed on the growth of manufacturing output, using cross-sectional data for the advanced countries for the period 1953/54–1963/64, a close correlation was found, with a slope coefficient (the Verdoorn coefficient) of about one-half. Kaldor attributes this statistically significant Verdoorn coefficient to the existence of substantial increasing returns to scale, of both the dynamic and the static variety.

ROWTHORN (1975a) criticized Kaldor's specification of the Verdoorn law. It was Kaldor's thesis that the slow rate of productivity growth of the UK was due to its "premature maturity" in that a labour shortage constrained the growth of manufacturing. This prevented the UK from reaping the full benefits of productivity growth induced by increasing returns to scale. Consequently, employment growth and not output growth, should be the regressor. This was the specification adopted by CRIPPS & TARLING. When Japan was excluded as an outlier from the advanced countries, however, Rowthorn (1975a) found no evidence of increasing returns to scale.

KALDOR'S (1975) rejoinder was that, although it was true that he had argued that UK manufacturing did face a labour constraint, he never argued that this was true of the other countries. Moreover, he now believed, on the basis of subsequent evidence, that even the UK did not face a labour shortage. Output growth, and not employment growth should be the regressor. ROWTHORN (1975b) pointed out that if there were a process of cumulative causation, with a faster growth of productivity feeding back into a faster growth of output growth, the estimate of the Verdoorn coefficient would be subject to simultaneous equation bias. McCOMBIE (1981), using an instrumental variable technique, instead of ordinary least squares, was not able to resolve the issue.

McCOMBIE & DE RIDDER estimated the Verdoorn law using regional data from the US. This avoided a number of objections that had been levelled against Kaldor's original results. These included the fact that international differences in socioeconomic factors might bias the results, the possibility of productivity growth being due to the diffusion of technology from the more advanced to the less advanced industrialized countries, and the omission of the growth of capital stock. McCombie & De Ridder found strong returns to scale for both the Verdoorn law and Rowthorn's specification.

BERNAT, using later data for the US and an estimating technique that allowed for spatial autocorrelation, confirmed McCombie & De Ridder's findings. FINGLETON & McCOMBIE used a similar estimating technique and found a Verdoorn coefficient of one-half for the European Union regions. HARRIS & LAU, using time-series data for the UK regions, found similar support for the Verdoorn law.

McCOMBIE (1982) discovered what he termed the static–dynamic paradox. When the same data are used to estimate the Verdoorn law in logarithms of the levels rather than growth rates, both Kaldor's and Rowthorn's specifications suggest constant returns to scale. McCombie & De Ridder and Fingleton & McCombie found similar results. McCombie (1982) considers some possible explanations for this paradox.

Kaldor (1975) argued that the growth of manufacturing output had a dual effect, on the growth of GDP per worker, and this led him to postulate his third law. First, a faster growth of manufacturing leads to a faster growth of manufacturing productivity growth through the Verdoorn effect and, second, to a faster growth of non-manufacturing productivity. The latter occurs as a result of the manufacturing sector drawing off surplus labour from the remainder of the economy. However, McCombie (1981) showed that the regression of GDP per worker on manufacturing output growth and the growth of non manufacturing employment, which Kaldor (1975) had argued support this contention, conveyed no more information than the first and second laws, because of an underlying identity. Thus, the third law cannot really be considered a law in its own right.

KING is a useful reader, which contains many of the theoretical and applied articles on growth from a Kaldorian perspective. (See especially Part III, "The Romance with Verdoorn", which contains a number of other papers on Verdoorn's law.)

JOHN S.L. McCOMBIE

Kalecki, Michał 1899–1970

Polish economist

Kalecki, Michal, *Works*, edited by Jerzy Osiatynski, 7 vols, Oxford: Clarendon Press, 1990–1997

King, J.E. (editor), *An Alternative Macroeconomic Theory: The Kaleckian Model and Post-Keynesian Economics*, London and Boston: Kluwer, 1996

Sawyer, Malcolm, *The Economics of Michal Kalecki*, Basingstoke: Macmillan, 1985

Sawyer, Malcolm (editor), *The Intellectual Legacy of Michal Kalecki*, 2 vols, Aldershot, Hampshire: Elgar, 2000

The first two volumes of KALECKI's collected works are devoted to his papers and books on capitalism, covering business cycles and full employment in volume one (contains one book, 33 articles, – many previously unpublished in English – and five annexes) and economic dynamics in volume two (two books, 17 articles, and five annexes). A number of the papers in volume one written in the first half of the 1930s form the basis of the case that Kalecki discovered the role of effective demand in setting the level of economic activity and the significance of fluctuations in investment expenditure. Kalecki's articles from the early 1940s expressing scepticism about the prospects for sustained full employment in capitalist economies are also included.

Kalecki saw the relationship between price and unit costs as determined by market power, which he summarized in the phrase "degree of monopoly". In the first paper in volume two he showed how the distribution of income between wages and profits is influenced by the "degree of monopoly", and in a further paper how the struggle between labour and capital can influence the "degree of monopoly".

Kalecki's writings on socialism are covered in volumes three (27 papers and seven annexes) and four (one book, 13 papers, and eight annexes) encompassing, first, the functioning of socialism and long-run planning and, second, economic growth and the efficiency of investment. The papers in volume three range from remarks on rationing, through comments on specific plans developed in Poland to the role of workers' councils in the context of central planning. Volume four opens with a reprint of *Introduction to the Theory of Growth in a Socialist Economy*. The first paper compares growth under capitalism (viewed as demand constrained) with growth under socialism (viewed as resource constrained). Other papers focus on issues of the efficiency of investment under central planning.

Volume five covers Kalecki's writings on developing countries with (ten papers and three annexes). A number of papers introduce and then apply the notion of an "intermediate regime", in which government represents the interests of the lower middle-class and rich peasants. There are further papers on the problems of financing economic development, which also identify the constraints that developing countries generally face.

The final two volumes are entitled "studies in applied economics 1927–1941" (volume six) and "studies in applied economics 1940–1967 and miscellanea" (volume seven). The papers in volume six, with a few exceptions, have not previously been available in English, and the majority refer to economic conditions in prewar Poland; most of the papers in volume seven have been previously available in English, and the first half of the book reproduces papers written by Kalecki during his time at the Oxford Institute during World War II, which are mainly commentaries on the economic conditions of the wartime economy.

After an introductory chapter, SAWYER (1985) provides six chapters, each of which deals with a major element in Kalecki's analysis of industrialized capitalist economies. These elements are prices, profits, and the degree of monopoly; investment, business cycles, and growth; differential savings, the degree of monopoly, and the level of economic activity; money, finance, and interest rates; wages, employment, and inflation; and finally the political economy of full employment. The writings of Marx were important influences on Kalecki's thinking, and chapter eight considers those influences, discusses the similarities in their analyses, but concludes with five groups of major differences. Kalecki and Keynes are often seen as both being discovers of the principle of effective demand during the 1930s. Chapter nine provides some comparisons and some contrasts in their approaches. Kalecki's writings on development in mixed economies are discussed in chapter ten, and his writings on the socialist economies and the growth process are considered in chapter 11. The book is completed by a chapter speculating on future developments in Kaleckian macroeconomics.

The edited volume by KING provides evaluations of Kalecki's work and the relationship of his work with the post-Keynesian tradition. Arestis presents an overview of Kalecki's role in post-Keynesian economics and considers the main elements of Kalecki's analysis. The question of the relationship between the analyses of Kalecki and Keynes, both of whom are considered to have discovered the principle of effective demand, is considered by Chapple. He argues that the balance of probabilities suggest that Kalecki anticipated both the theory of effective demand and the IS-LM/AS-AD model in his pre-1936 work. Kriesler discusses a Kaleckian perspective on the microfoundation of macroeconomics. He argues that micro and macro theories are interrelated in Kalecki's analysis in a way such that further information is gained that is not available from either in isolation. Kalecki's theory of prices and distribution is considered by Reynolds. He identifies three main areas (real wages determined in the product market rather than the labour market, the theory of income distribution, and the degree of monopoly in the long run) where he believes post-Keynesian economists have misunderstood or misrepresented Kalecki's work. Sawyer, in an elaboration of Kalecki's analyses of the trade cycle and economic growth, points to the central feature of such analysis and the continuous search by Kalecki for improved understanding of those issues. Dymski argues, in an essay on Kalecki's monetary economics, that Kalecki's approach to firms' behaviour "sheds new light on the contemporary debate over the importance of financial constraints". Further, the conceptions of Kalecki on the links between microeconomic and macroeconomic analysis, and between finance and power, are seen as important in the context of recent debates. King's essay begins by outlining Kalecki's work in the decade beginning in 1945, which he spent in North America. This is followed by asking how Kalecki affected the work of some notably post-Keynesian economists. The writings of Kalecki on socialism and the influence of Marx are considered by Toporowski. He argues that Kalecki's starting point "was a clear appraisal, in the marxist tradition, of the fundamental problems of capitalism and the limits of Keynesianism, which could only be overcome by central planning in a socialist economy". McFarlane states that Kalecki's writings on the Third World are policy oriented though informed by an "incisive theoretical scaffolding". Kalecki's aim was to give advice to improve the rate and structure of growth with an identification of the constraints on growth.

The two volumes edited by SAWYER (2000) contain editorial introductions on the life and work of Kalecki and reprint some articles by Kalecki and many others which discuss and extend the work of Kalecki.

MALCOLM SAWYER

See also Planned economy

Kant, Immanuel 1724–1804

German philosopher

Beck, Lewis White, *Early German Philosophy: Kant and his Predecessors*, Cambridge, Massachusetts: Harvard University Press, 1969

Cassirer, Ernst, *Kant's Life and Thought*, New Haven, Connecticut: Yale University Press, 1981 (original German edition 1918)

Caygill, Howard, *A Kant Dictionary*, Oxford and Cambridge, Massachusetts: Blackwell, 1995

Chadwick, Ruth F. and Clive Cazeaux (editors), *Immanuel Kant: Critical Assessments*, 4 vols, London and New York: Routledge, 1992

Gardner, Sebastian, *Kant and the Critique of Pure Reason*, London and New York: Routledge, 1999

Guyer, Paul (editor), *The Cambridge Companion to Kant*, Cambridge and New York, Cambridge University Press, 1992

Scruton, Roger, *Kant*, Oxford and New York: Oxford University Press, 1982

Stuckenberg, J.H.W., *The Life of Immanuel Kant*, facsimile reprint, Bristol: Thoemmes, 1990 (originally published 1882)

Sullivan, Roger J., *Immanuel Kant's Moral Theory*, Cambridge and New York: Cambridge University Press, 1989

STUCKENBERG provides an old but tolerably accurate account of Kant's life. Though detailed, this study is very accessible to readers of all levels of familiarity with Kant's life. Written in a dramatic style, it details Kant's life from his heavily religious childhood to a heartfelt account of his old age, weak health, and death.

Although dated, CASSIRER's *Life and Thought* remains a classic. It places Kant's thought in the context of his life, and his life in the context of his social and intellectual society. What emerges is a personal picture of Kant the man. Cassirer also draws out many contrasts and affinities between Kant's thought and those of his prominent contemporaries and near contemporaries. He does all this while producing an influential, important, and committed interpretation of the broad sweep of Kant's philosophy.

BECK constitutes an invaluable aid to those who wish to place Kant's work more specifically in relation to its philosophical context. A clear and comprehensive account of pre-Kantian German philosophy, this work provides useful background on such topics as the Pietist, Leibnizian, and especially Wolffian influences on Kant's early intellectual environment and development. It also contains a very helpful and wide-ranging bibliography.

SCRUTON is a good introduction designed for the newcomer to Kant's philosophical edifice, and does not sacrifice solid scholarship in the search for simplification. It is difficult to adequately cover the breadth of Kant's thought in such a short book but Scruton does so admirably. There are two chapters on the *Critique of Pure Reason*, one on his moral philosophy, and one on his aesthetics. Each can be read with benefit.

For a more detailed, but still broad, introduction to Kant the reader should turn to GUYER. The collection of essays is of the highest quality. Each is written by one of the leading commentators in the relevant area: it is hard to envisage a list of more notable contemporary Kant scholars. Again, the full range of Kant's interests is covered although, as is fitting, emphasis is placed on the *First Critique*.

The four volumes of CHADWICK & CAZEAUX give the opportunity for more in-depth study. The first volume contains historically and theoretically important critical pieces from contemporaries such as Fichte, Hegel, and Schopenhauer. These are supplemented with criticisms from the 19th-century work of Mill, Green, and Marx to the early 20th-century work of Heidegger, Paton, and Strawson. The remaining three volumes consist of sets of free-standing essays by prominent modern commentators. The second volume is focused on Kant's *Critique of Pure Reason* and deals with the basis of his critical philosophy and critique of traditional metaphysics. The third volume deals with his moral and political philosophy and covers concerns raised in *Critique of Practical Reason*, the *Groundwork*, and the *Metaphysics of Morals*. The fourth volume concentrates on the *Critique of Judgement*, on Kant's aesthetics and its relationship to the rest of Kant's work. Overall this is a fine selection of important accounts and criticisms of major aspects of the Kantian project but in manageable chunks. The set will be useful for the scholar aiming to become further immersed in the general arguments and issues surrounding particular areas of Kant's thought.

Kant's *Critique of Pure Reason* is one of the most challenging, but at the same time one of the most influential, texts in philosophy. GARDNER, in what is ostensibly a student guidebook, does an excellent job of making this difficult work accessible and as such this is an invaluable book even for more experienced Kant scholars. Gardner provides detailed commentary and examination of the argument of the *First Critique*, concentrating on Kant's transcendental idealism. In discussion he draws on the recent flood of strong scholarship in the area.

As such he treats Kant's idealism not only as a part of the history of philosophy but also as a lively and ongoing philosophical project. Gardner also includes short chapters relating the *First Critique* to the rest of Kant's "critical system" and on its reception and influence.

Kant's critical philosophy is also importantly a practical philosophy. The practical is to the fore in his political and his moral philosophy and here his influence is difficult to overestimate. Kant is one of the most important forerunners of contemporary moral and political theory. SULLIVAN'S work is an ideal starting point for a detailed understanding of the power of Kantian practical thought. He does not shirk detail but achieves comprehensive coverage of the important aspects of Kant's position. Sullivan, unlike many commentators, also deserves credit for drawing on, and doing justice to, the full range of Kant's writings on the subject. More impressively, he manages to do this with a largely non-technical vocabulary. This work gives the reader a good sense of Kant's importance in this field.

A dictionary may seem like an unlikely inclusion but CAYGILL is a superb piece of scholarship. Kant's work would be difficult enough to understand in the best of circumstances, most notably due to his tendency to draw a bewildering number of distinctions and sub-distinctions in the analysis of any concept. Furthermore, Kant has a notorious propensity for redefining key terms and concepts in philosophical debate, often without informing the reader. As such, Caygill's attempt to facilitate (but not usurp) interpretation is a welcome aid to understanding. Coverage of terms is both detailed and comprehensive and each entry is accompanied by extensive cross references. This cross referencing is supplemented by an excellent index of concepts. This is an invaluable reference work for both student and scholar. The dictionary is prefaced by an essay on "Kant and the 'age of criticism'".

PERI ROBERTS

Keiretsu

Fruin, Mark, *The Japanese Enterprise System: Competitive Strategies and Cooperative Structures*, Oxford: Clarendon Press, and New York: Oxford University Press, 1992

Gerlach, Michael L., *Alliance Capitalism: The Social Organization of Japanese Business*, Berkeley: University of California Press, 1992a

Gerlach, Michael L., "Twilight of the Keiretsu: A Critical Assessment", *Journal of Japanese Studies*, 18/1 (1992b): 79–118

Gilson, Ronald J. and Mark J. Roe, "Understanding Japanese Keiretsu: Overlaps between Corporate Governance and Industrial Organization", *Yale Law Journal*, 102 (1993): 871–906

Morikawa, Hidemasa, *Zaibatsu: The Rise and Fall of Family Enterprise Groups in Japan*, Tokyo: University of Tokyo Press, 1992

Nakatani, Iwao, "The Economic Role of Financial Corporate Grouping" in *The Economic Analysis of the Japanese Firm*, edited by Masahiko Aoki, Amsterdam: North Holland, 1984

Scher, Mark J., *Japanese Interfirm Networks and Their Main Banks*, New York: St Martin's Press, and Basingstoke: Macmillan, 1997

Sheard, Paul, "Interlocking Shareholdings and Corporate Governance" in *The Japanese Firm: Sources of Competitive Strength*, edited by Masahiko Aoki and Ronald Dore, Oxford: Clarendon Press, and New York: Oxford University Press, 1994

The *Keiretsu*, broadly defined as a loose, diversified business grouping, is a uniquely Japanese phenomenon that, although instrumental in Japan's postwar economic development, has much deeper historical roots. MORIKAWA is not, strictly speaking, about *keiretsu* at all, but about its institutional predecessor, *zaibatsu*. Dating from Japan's first industrialization in the late 1880s, *zaibatsu* were essentially family-owned enterprises that evolved into holding companies with multiple subsidiaries. Morikawa demonstrates that *zaibatsu* were not the monolithic structures they have often been made out to be. The families relied heavily on salaried managers, to whom considerable strategic decision making was delegated. Although the families maintained overall ownership, their role was more one of coordination of policy than tight control of the subsidiaries. Morikawa's book is thus an illuminating analysis of the origins of Japan's managerial capitalism. The *zaibatsu* were formally dismantled after World War II, but their influence is evident in successor groupings.

A major feature of postwar corporate groupings is cross-shareholding, whereby companies hold shares in each other. This subject is explored by SHEARD, who looks at the effects of these ties on corporate governance. Interlocking shares are typically between companies in the same group and between a company and its "main bank". The result is stable shareholding arrangements involving long-term commitment, which, importantly, acts as a barrier to hostile takeovers, and as protection for incumbent management. As Western notions of corporate governance traditionally rest on the existence of a competitive market for corporate control, are there substitute mechanisms in Japan's more closed system? Sheard finds that the main bank, both as lender and shareholder, plays the key monitoring role, which can extend to direct intervention in cases of management deficiencies or financial hardship in linked firms.

GILSON & ROE also explores the corporate governance conundrum, but are more concerned with US–Japan comparisons. Their well-organized and clearly written article begins with the theoretical background of the corporate governance debate, highlighting the increasingly activist role of shareholders in monitoring management in corporate America. They then describe the Japanese system as a "hybrid between contract and organization", explaining how long-term relation-specific investment reduces opportunism. They agree with Sheard's view that the main bank is the chief monitor, serving as an agent for the other factors, but they question how effective a monitor it is, and doubt that the internalized market for corporate control is a substitute for a takeover market. They also pose the question of the banks' changing – and diminishing – role, as companies shift from debt financing to equity financing.

NAKATANI, although not up to date, is nonetheless relevant for its comparison of group-affiliated firms with independent firms. His research findings show a tendency to lower profits and lower growth rates in the group firms studied, but also that there is less variability and therefore more stable economic performance over time in group-affiliated firms. He attributes these findings, first, to the risk attitudes of management, which seek to stabilize performance at the cost of lowering the level of performance; and, second, to the need to maximize benefit to the company's many constituents, including employees, financial institutions, shareholders, and management. Significantly, the average income of an employee in a group firm is higher than in an independent firm. Nakatani sees the system of reciprocal shareholding as insulating group firms from the vicissitudes of a capital market, as the major shareholders are effectively insiders who support management. He concludes that the group is primarily aimed at ensuring stable corporate performance through risk-sharing arrangements among member firms and the banks, and, moreover, that this attitude is vital to an understanding of the Japanese economy as a whole.

GERLACH (1992a) is probably the most comprehensive piece of research devoted to *keiretsu*. Taking an interdisciplinary approach, he presents a theory of intercorporate alliances as the essence of the Japanese economic system. He sees the alliance as a dynamic form, comprising direct and indirect linkages among industrial firms, banks and commercial enterprises, forming networks of enduring business relationships. *Keiretsu* may be vertical, as between suppliers and customers, or intermarket *keiretsu*, horizontal interfirm groupings, but Gerlach argues that, whatever the organizational form, *keiretsu* is more of "a metaphor for general patterns of interfirm organizations in Japan" than a reflection of specific structures. He sees the growing impact of global trading as the greatest challenge to these alliance forms, and it is this issue that he addresses in his article, "Twilight of the Keiretsu?" (GERLACH, 1992b) In it he reviews the evidence, looking in particular at the apparent breakdown in bank-led groupings, and the growing internationalization of the Japanese economy. He concludes that, although structures may change and become more diffuse, the relational contracting that is the essence of *keiretsu* remains an enduring characteristic which pervades Japanese industry.

FRUIN offers an engaging historical study of the development of industrial corporations in Japan in the 20th century, from which emerges a theory of Japanese organizational development. His central theme is that of organizational interdependence. He develops an interorganizational model based on three levels– factory, firm, and interfirm network – and provides helpful, detailed accounts of the development of particular enterprises and enterprise groupings. He sees the conditions of late economic development and resource constraints as crucial to the shaping of Japan's dynamic, interdependent enterprise structures. The appendix contains detailed lists of Japan's 200 largest industrial firms in 1918, 1930, 1973, and 1987.

SCHER starts from a view of *keiretsu* as networks of relational contracts, but Scher is concerned to develop his own "holistic" model, based largely on Japan's unique historical and cultural legacies, which predate even the *zaibatsu*. Having outlined a number of possible models, derived from agency and transaction cost theories, he settles on the concept of "relational access" as the key to Japanese industrial groups. He traces this concept back to the *ie* (household) system of the Tokugawa era (1606–1868), during the formative years of the household or family firm. His overall model is perhaps less original than he apparently imagines it to be, but he does make some telling analytical points. First, he draws the reader's attention to the distinction between the vertical *keiretsu*, which are descendants of the *zaibatsu*, and the intermarket groupings, usually centred around banks, which – although he acknowledges that they are often called "intermarket *keiretsu*" – should not, in his view, be termed *keiretsu* at all, but *kigyo shudan*. Second, he revisits the modern role of the main bank in corporate governance, demonstrating from his research findings that behind the alleged monitoring role lurks what he terms "anti-governance", in that the banks he studied viewed cross-shareholding arrangements from a self-interested point of view as a source of profits, with only token monitoring in the agency sense. This last point, although possibly not fully substantiated by his research, does ring true in the light of the unfolding financial and banking troubles of the 1990s, which are altering the main role of the bank in traditional *keiretsu* relational ties.

JANET MORRISON

See also Japanese economy and economic record, Japanese management

Kennedy, John F. 1917–1963

US political leader

Bernstein, Irving, *Promises Kept: John F. Kennedy's New Frontier*, New York and Oxford: Oxford University Press, 1991

Branch, Taylor, *Parting the Waters: America in the King Years, 1954–63*, New York: Simon and Schuster, and London: Macmillan, 1988

Hilty, James W., *Robert Kennedy: Brother Protector*, Philadelphia: Temple University Press, 1997

Paterson, Thomas G. (editor), *Kennedy's Quest for Victory: American Foreign Policy, 1961–1963*, New York and Oxford: Oxford University Press, 1989

Posner, Gerald, *Case Closed: Lee Harvey Oswald and the Assassination of JFK*, New York: Random House, 1993; London: Warner, 1994

Reeves, Thomas C., *A Question of Character: A Life of John F. Kennedy*, New York: Free Press, and London: Bloomsbury, 1991

Reeves, Richard, *President Kennedy: Profile of Power*, New York: Simon and Schuster, and Oxford: Maxwell Macmillan, 1993

Schlesinger, Arthur M., *A Thousand Days: John F. Kennedy in the White House*, Boston: Houghton Mifflin, and London: Deutsch, 1965

Watson, Mary Ann, *The Expanding Vista: American Television in the Kennedy Years*, New York and Oxford: Oxford University Press, 1990

White, Mark J., *The Cuban Missile Crisis*, Basingstoke: Macmillan, 1996

SCHLESINGER's account, despite its age, is still an important memoir and history of the Kennedy administration. Although occasionally critical of his subject, Schlesinger portrayed Kennedy as a glamorous, reforming President. His "New Frontier" successes in the arts, education, and economics, and his space programmes, were cited as evidence of a reformist presidency. Kennedy is portrayed sympathetically in defending civil rights, despite problems with a hostile Congress. However the real focus of this study is foreign policy. Kennedy's firm and decisive leadership over Berlin and during the Cuban missile crisis were his greatest successes. His policies in South Vietnam were also successful in 1961–2 but ran into difficulty in 1963 because of internal problems among the South Vietnamese. The account implies that Kennedy might have pulled out of that country after the 1964 election. This study set the standard for all subsequent biographies of JFK.

REEVES (Richard) has provided perhaps the best study of Kennedy among the plethora of biographies since 1965. He portrays a more flawed Kennedy than earlier accounts. Although generally supportive of liberal domestic reforms, Kennedy's administration was long on style but rather short on achievements. He dragged his feet on civil rights until 1963. He was a Cold War warrior whose Cuban policies were dubious, although he did show sound leadership during the missile crisis. In South Vietnam his policies were ill-advised and often chaotic. He was also a poor administrator, and his chronic ill health and his womanizing created additional problems for his administration. Yet, for all of his flaws, Kennedy seemed to personify the hopes of the American people and his assassination shocked the nation.

REEVES (Thomas) is one of the more critical biographies of Kennedy. It deals with Kennedy's fundamental character flaws. His personality, family influences, and general behaviour meant that Kennedy could rarely provide real moral leadership for the nation. The President is depicted as a purely pragmatic, rather than liberal, idealist. Despite these arguments, the author is forced to concede that Kennedy displayed strong leadership over Berlin and Cuba and even a degree of moral leadership by 1963 over civil rights.

HILTY has dealt with the important relationship between John and his younger brother Robert. The latter subsumed his own career to that of his older brother, and played a crucial role in the 1960 election campaign. As his brother's Attorney General, Robert effectively became the junior partner of the presidency. He protected John from the worst of his sexual indiscretions, covered up his poor health, and took the blame for failings in the early civil rights policies. In many ways Robert was more mature and less self-absorbed than his brother, although he shared the same sense of political opportunism and avoided hard decisions that were politically inconvenient.

BERNSTEIN has defended the "New Frontier" policies, much maligned by critics in the past two decades – critics such as Herbert S. Parmet (*JFK: The Presidency of John F. Kennedy*, 1984) who argued that Kennedy's domestic programmes were characterized by limited achievements. His study provides a good history of areas such as price policies, taxation, and education, and highlights the achievements of the administration. However Kennedy remains a relatively remote figure in the book and the study of his civil rights policies is too limited in the light of other writings on this topic.

BRANCH provides some excellent insights into the sometimes ambiguous and always difficult relationship between the Kennedy administration and the civil rights movement. Kennedy believed that segregation was an anachronism but also felt that modernity would prevail in the South. He therefore stressed calm over activism, especially given his own difficulties with the Southern Democrats. However the grass-roots activism of the civil rights movement pushed Kennedy, often quite unwillingly, along the road towards active reform by 1963. Ironically, after his death he was given credit for many of the achievements of King and others who had led the President forward in this area.

WATSON deals with another important domestic aspect of how Kennedy used television not only in his election campaign but to project positive views of his work in the space race and even civil rights. At the same time he was active in attempting to influence television content and format, including news, documentaries, drama, and children's television. Ironically, television coverage of events surrounding Kennedy's assassination and funeral produced images and legacies that were as profound as any actively sought by Kennedy in his lifetime.

PATERSON's edited collection of 11 essays reviewed all of the main areas of Kennedy's foreign policy and suggested that it had few positive results. Despite his criticism of Eisenhower's performance, Kennedy was rigid in his own approach to foreign policy. This was due to his personality, his inherited military commitments, and his deep-seated views on conducting foreign policy within a Cold War setting. In the important area of Vietnam, the article by Stephen E. Pelz and Laurence J. Bassett argued that Kennedy ignored advice on becoming deeply involved in South Vietnam, preferring to believe that the nationalist elite of that country was caught between French colonialism and communist insurgents. Since the US was not a colonialist power it could assist them to create a pro-Western state. This type of thinking pushed Kennedy into deeper commitments and there is no evidence to suggest that he would have withdrawn US forces if he had lived to win the 1964 election. Paterson has long been a critic of Kennedy's foreign policy, especially over Cuba, and these essays should be read with caution. Nevertheless they provide a comprehensive critique of the Kennedy administration's dealings with the world.

WHITE is the most recent of a series of works over nearly a decade that have re-examined the Cuban missile crisis by making use of declassified documents and discussions with Soviet historians and other surviving participants. These include Robert Divine, *The Cuban Missile Crisis* (1988) and Robert Smith Thompson, *The Missiles of October* (1992). White argues that Kennedy's policies towards Cuba from 1960 onwards were misguided and only exacerbated the Soviet decisions to assist Castro. On the other hand, his handling of the crisis itself, especially by the second week, highlighted his leadership qualities. Although several other central participants, including Robert Kennedy, performed well, the author also reveals the important and balanced role played by Adlai Stevenson who had crafted the solution very early in the crisis. These recent studies have added to our knowledge of the events and motives surrounding the crisis, but have not undermined the performance of Kennedy's leadership that Schlesinger presented in 1965.

POSNER provides a thorough examination of the evidence surrounding the assassination of Kennedy. Despite problems with some of the investigative methods and findings of the Warren Commission, he argues that its conclusions were essentially correct. Recent technology indicates that Lee Harvey Oswald fired three bullets with the last two hitting the president and the third being the fatal shot. The book is also valuable in discussing the various conspiracy theories that have abounded since 1963. However it will probably not satisfy those who do not want to believe that Oswald acted alone.

PETER E. BASTIAN

Keynes, John Maynard 1883–1946

British economist

Bensusan-Butt, D.M., *On Economic Knowledge: A Sceptical Miscellany*, Canberra: Research School of Pacific Studies, Australian National University, 1980

Carabelli, Anna M., *On Keynes's Method*, Basingstoke: Macmillan, and New York: St Martin's Press, 1988

Cate, Thomas (editor), *An Encyclopedia of Keynesian Economics*, Cheltenham, Gloucestershire: Elgar, 1997

Clarke, Peter, *The Keynesian Revolution in the Making, 1924–1936*, Oxford: Clarendon Press, and New York: Oxford University Press, 1988

Coates, John, *The Claims of Common Sense: Moore, Wittgenstein, Keynes and the Social Sciences*, Cambridge and New York: Cambridge University Press, 1996

Davis, John B., *Keynes's Philosophical Development*, Cambridge and New York: Cambridge University Press, 1994

Harrod, Roy, *The Life of John Maynard Keynes*, London: Macmillan, and New York: Harcourt Brace, 1951; 2nd edition 1963

Keynes, John Maynard, *The Economic Consequences of the Peace*, London: Macmillan, 1919, New York: Harcourt Brace, 1920; in *The Collected Writings of John Maynard Keynes*, vol. 2, London: Macmillan, and New York: Cambridge University Press, 1971

Keynes, John Maynard, *A Treatise on Probability*, London: Macmillan, 1921; as vol. 8 of *The Collected Writings of John Maynard Keynes*, London: Macmillan, and New York: Cambridge University Press, 1973

Keynes, John Maynard, *The General Theory of Employment, Interest and Money*, London: Macmillan, and New York: Harcourt Brace, 1936; as vol. 7 of *The Collected Writings of John Maynard Keynes*, London: Macmillan, and New York: Cambridge University Press, 1973

Mantoux, Etienne, *The Carthaginian Peace: or, The Economic Consequences of Mr Keynes*, London and New York: Oxford University Press, 1946

Moggridge, D.E., *Keynes*, London: Macmillan, 1976; 3rd edition, 1993

Moggridge, D.E., *Maynard Keynes, An Economist's Biography*, London and New York: Routledge, 1992

O'Donnell, R.M., *Keynes: Philosophy, Economics and Politics: The Philisophical Foundations of Keynes's*

Thought and Their Influence on His Economics and Politics, Basingstoke: Macmillan, 1989

Robinson, Austin, "John Maynard Keynes, 1883–1946", *Economic Journal*, 57/1 (1947): 1–68

Schumpeter, Joseph A., "John Maynard Keynes, 1883–1946", *American Economic Review*, 36 (1946): 495–518

Skidelsky, Robert, *John Maynard Keynes: A Biography*, vol. 1: *Hopes Betrayed, 1883–1920*, London: Macmillan, 1983; New York: Viking, 1986

Skidelsky, Robert, *John Maynard Keynes: A Biography*, vol. 2: *The Economist as Saviour, 1920–1937*, London: Macmillan, 1992; New York: Viking Penguin, 1994

Where best to go in order to understand John Maynard Keynes – man, economist, philosopher, man of action, bibliophile, loving friend, devoted son, happy husband? Undoubtedly SKIDELSKY's two volumes (1983, 1992) dominate all else because of their insights, depth of economic, historical, and philosophical analyses, and overall erudition. Especially masterly is Skidelsky's account of the making and the significance of *The General Theory*. It is to be hoped that the third and final volume will be published soon and be as good as its companion volumes. For the detailed authoritative account of Keynes's history and contributions, MOGGRIDGE's economist's biography (1992) cannot be bettered. His discussion of Keynes's roles in the two world wars is especially masterly. From his discussion of Keynes's activities at the Treasury and then the Treaty of Versailles, we may see clearly why and how Keynes changed from being an extremely clever, gifted, but often flippant and unserious, even immature person – similar to many of his Bloomsbury friends – to a mature, courageous, passionate defender of what he saw as right values, and just outcomes and procedures.

The upshot of this was his resignation from the UK delegation at Versailles and the writing of *The Economic Consequences of the Peace*, KEYNES (1919). Whatever its lasting merits as an accurate account of the likely consequences of the clauses of the Treaty, (see MANTOUX for doubts), it must surely always survive as a courageous and noble statement of a good man's reaction to events and people, and to what he saw as foolish and evil.

In World War II, through Moggridge's account we witness Keynes literally killing himself by overwork for his country and for a wider world. The account of the consequences of his death on Easter morning 1946 as immediately perceived are described with crystal clarity by ROBINSON in his superb *Economic Journal* obituary of Keynes in 1947.

HARROD, although fascinating, is flawed by the biographer not referring to crucial aspects of Keynes's personal life – that he was bisexual certainly before his extremely happy marriage to Lydia Lopokova in 1925 and probably after, and by an intrusion of Harrod's views and roles into the story.

For the making of *The General Theory* and the so-called Keynesian revolution and the historical events accompanying them, CLARKE stands alone. Since the 1980s, an important literature on the relationship between Keynes's economics and his philosophy has arisen. (His Fellowship Dissertation for King's in the first decade of the 20th century was published in 1921 as *A Treatise on Probability*.) Three philosophical emphases of Keynes are crucial for his economic thinking,

especially in *The General Theory* (KEYNES 1936). First, his realization that the whole need not be the sum of its parts. Second, his systematic pondering on the principles of reasonable behaviour in an uncertain environment. Third, his discernment of the existence of the spectrum of appropriate languages with which to discuss different theoretical issues in a discipline such as economics. The outstanding books in this literature are: O'DONNELL; CARABELLI; DAVIS; and COATES.

A shorter essay that may be read with great profit and pleasure is SCHUMPETER. Schumpeter so managed to suppress his jealousy of Keynes as to make this an absorbing read. BENSUSAN-BUTT wrote a delightful essay about Keynes's unique impact on the idealistic and searching young in the interwar period. Finally, to obtain a quick feel of what Keynes the man and his writings were about, MOGGRIDGE (1976) and the entry on Keynes in CATE provide appreciative and succinct accounts.

G.C. HARCOURT

Keynes' General Theory

Amadeo, Edward J., *Keynes's Principle of Effective Demand*, Aldershot, Hampshire: Elgar, 1989

Asimakopulos, A., *Keynes's General Theory and Accumulation*, Cambridge and New York: Cambridge University Press, 1991

Chick, Victoria, *Macroeconomics after Keynes: A Reconsideration of The General Theory*, Cambridge, Massachusetts: MIT Press, and Oxford: Philip Allan, 1983

Chick, Victoria, *On Money, Method and Keynes: Selected Essays*, edited by Philip Arestis and Sheila C. Dow, Basingstoke: Macmillan, and New York: St Martin's Press, 1992

Clarke, Peter, *The Keynesian Revolution in the Making, 1924–36*, Oxford: Clarendon Press, and New York: Oxford University Press, 1988

Clower, R.W., "The Keynesian Counter-revolution: A Theoretical Appraisal" in *The Theory of Interest Rates*, edited by F.H. Hahn and F.P.R. Brechling, London: Macmillan, and New York: St Martin's Press, 1965

Davidson, Paul, *Money and the Real World*, London: Macmillan, and New York: Wiley, 1972; 2nd edition 1978

Hahn, Frank and Robert Solow, *A Critical Essay on Modern Macroeconomic Theory*, Oxford: Blackwell, and Cambridge, Massachusetts: MIT Press, 1995

Harcourt, G.C. and P.A. Riach (editors), *A 'Second Edition' of The General Theory*, 2 vols, London and New York: Routledge, 1997

Harrod, R.F., "Mr Keynes and Traditional Theory", *Econometrica*, 5 (1937): 74–146

Harrod, R.F., *The Life of John Maynard Keynes*, London: Macmillan, and New York: Harcourt Brace, 1951; 2nd edition 1963

Hicks, J.R., "Mr Keynes and the 'Classics': A Suggested Interpretation", *Econometrica*, 5 (1937): 147–59

Kahn, Richard F., "Some Aspects of the Development of Keynes's Thought", *Journal of Economic Literature*, 16/2 (June 1978): 545–59

Kahn, Richard F., *The Making of Keynes' General Theory*, Cambridge and New York: Cambridge University Press, 1984

Keynes, John Maynard, *A Treatise on Money*, 2 vols, London: Macmillan, and New York: Harcourt Brace, 1930; in *The Collected Writings of John Maynard Keynes*, vols 5–6, London: Macmillan, and New York: Cambridge University Press, 1971

Keynes, John Maynard, *The General Theory of Employment, Interest and Money*, London: Macmillan, and New York: Harcourt Brace, 1936; as vol. 7 of *The Collected Writings of John Maynard Keynes*, London: Macmillan, and New York: Cambridge University Press, 1973

Keynes, John Maynard, "The General Theory of Employment", *Quarterly Journal of Economics*, 51/2 (1937): 209–23; in *The Collected Writings of John Maynard Keynes*, vol. 14, London: Macmillan, and New York: Cambridge University Press, 1973

Leijonhufvud, Axel, *On Keynesian Economics and the Economics of Keynes: A Study in Monetary Theory*, London and New York: Oxford University Press, 1968

Lekachman, Robert, *Keynes' General Theory: Reports of Three Decades*, London: Macmillan, and New York: St Martin's Press, 1964

Meade, J.E., "A Simplified Model of Mr Keynes' System", *Review of Economic Studies*, 4 (1937): 98–107

Meade, J.E., "The Keynesian Revolution" in *Essays on John Maynard Keynes*, edited by Milo Keynes, London and New York: Cambridge University Press, 1975

Moggridge, D.E., *Maynard Keynes: An Economist's Biography*, London and New York: Routledge, 1992

Patinkin, Don, *Keynes' Monetary Thought: A Study of Its Development*, Durham, North Carolina: Duke University Press, 1976

Reddaway, W.B., "The General Theory of Employment, Interest and Money [review]", *Economic Record*, 12 (1936): 28–36; reprinted in Lekachman, 1964

Robinson, Joan, *Introduction to the Theory of Employment*, London: Macmillan, 1937; 2nd edition, London: Macmillan, and New York: St Martin's Press, 1969

Skidelsky, Robert, *John Maynard Keynes: A Biography*, vol. 2: *The Economist as Saviour, 1920–1937*, London: Macmillan, 1992; New York: Viking Penguin, 1994

Tarshis, Lorie, *The Elements of Economics: An Introduction to the Theory of Price and Employment*, Boston: Houghton Mifflin, 1947

Trevithick, J.A., *Involuntary Unemployment: Macroeconomics from a Keynesian Perspective*, London: Harvester Wheatsheaf, and New York: St Martin's Press, 1992

Young, Warren, *Interpreting Mr Keynes: The IS-LM Enigma*, Cambridge: Polity Press, and Boulder, Colorado: Westview Press, 1987

KEYNES' magnum opus (1936) was published at a subsidised price in order to encourage as many people as possible to read it; even though Keynes warned that, as it was addressed principally to his fellow economists, the general public, while welcome to eavesdrop, could not expect fully to understand. For Keynes, writing the book represented his final escape from old ideas that he had been taught and that he, in turn, had taught to others. It required scrapping the quantity theory of money and shifting the focus of analysis of the system as a whole (itself a new emphasis) from the long period to the short period, and from preoccupation with the determination of the general price level to concern with the overall levels of employment and income.

Moreover, it required the acceptance of the revolutionary idea that the ultimate resting place of the economic system – its equilibrium – was not necessarily one of full employment but one that exhibited sustained unemployment of labour and capital goods in both the short and the long period. It also required, as MEADE (1975) told us, that we change from viewing the world as a dog called "saving" wagging an investment tail to viewing it as a dog called "investment" wagging a saving tail.

Associated with the shift of vision was the scrapping of the dichotomy between the real sector, where relative prices and quantities were determined, and the monetary sector, where, given the long-period equilibrium level of the economy (a Say's Law position of long-period full employment) and prevailing habits and institutions, the quantity of money served to determine the general price level. Under the dichotomy, money itself was but a veil and the money rate of interest was dominated by the natural rate of interest in the real sector – the latter ruled the roost and all else had to conform to its level.

All this was replaced by the theory of a monetary production economy in which the real and the monetary factors intermingled indissolubly from the start of the analysis, the money rate of interest ruled the roost, and the concept of aggregate demand had equal status with that of aggregate supply in the determination of the rest state point of effective demand. The determination of the general price level itself was presented as a natural extension of Marshall's short-period supply curve analysis at the level of the industry to the level of the economy as a whole. KAHN (1984) gave the most authoritative account of this process, in the later stages of which he played a fundamental role. *See also* KAHN (1978). KEYNES (1937) gives its author's own evaluation and further thoughts, which put his book into perspective. This article is the definitive account in which he replied to the criticisms of Dennis Robertson and Jacob Viner and spelt out the roles of expectations and uncertainty in the new system.

There are a number of other excellent accounts of this process – AMADEO, CLARKE and an ultimately flawed one, PATINKIN – flawed, because he tried to fit Keynes'analysis into a Walrasian general equilibrium framework (see Harcourt's review of Patinkin, *Economic Record* December 1977). The story is also, of course, the highlight of all the three great biographies of Keynes: HARROD (1951), MOGGRIDGE, and SKIDELSKY. For a modern understanding of the process and where we are now, pride of place in the 1980s must be given to CHICK (1983), together with her selected essays (CHICK 1992). The most comprehensive evaluations of Keynes and his influence, by scholars coming from many different directions, is to be found in the two volumes edited by HARCOURT & RIACH. The volumes may have a jokey title but they have a serious purpose. In the framework of modern economic analysis (a framework that involves an approach that is alien to Keynes's own views on the nature of theory in a subject such as economics), there is no better derivation of Keynes's results than HAHN & SOLOW. For thoughts 30 years on by those who were originally bitten by the *General Theory* bug, LEKACHMAN's collection is absorbing reading. Especially so is REDDAWAY's review of the book, reprinted in Lekachman's volume. (Reddaway was Keynes' pupil when Keynes was writing *The General Theory*.) His review even contains a clear (but unconscious) account of the essentials of IS and LM analysis. The best early introduction to the essential ideas, an introduction that is still relevant today, is ROBINSON's "told to the children" introduction. DAVIDSON is an authoritative postwar account and extension of KEYNES's (1930) ideas as well as his ideas in Keynes (1936)

How Keynes' ideas came to us through textbooks requires, first, that we read HICKS, together with the complementary articles of HARROD (1937) and MEADE (1937). The history of this process has been written by YOUNG. Finally, for an attempt to tease out what Keynes must really have meant within the postwar developments of the Walrasian general equilibrium system, CLOWER's paper on the dual decision hypothesis and LEIJONHUFVUD are essential reading. For a critical account of the ideas of Keynes and his principal followers, which nevertheless accepts the essential correctness of their contributions, ASIMAKOPULOS is a priceless book for teachers and students alike. The best textbook accounts that are true to Keynes's vision are TARSHIS and also TREVITHICK. Both are as critically faithful to their mentor as they are crucially relevant for their respective times.

G.C. HARCOURT

See also John Maynard Keynes, Keynesian economics

Keynesian economics

Cate, Thomas, Geoff Harcourt and David C. Colander (editors), *An Encyclopedia of Keynesian Economics*, Cheltenham: Elgar, 1997

Clower, Robert W., *Money and Markets: Essays by Robert W. Clower*, edited by Donald A. Walker, Cambridge: Cambridge University Press, 1984

Coddington, Alan, *Keynesian Economics: The Search for First Principles*, London and Boston: Allen and Unwin, 1983

Hall, Peter A. (editor), *The Political Power of Economic Ideas: Keynesianism across Nations*, Princeton, New Jersey: Princeton University Press, 1989

Harcourt, G.C. and P.A. Riach (editors), *A 'Second Edition' of The General Theory*, 2 volumes, London and New York: Routledge, 1997

Keynes, John Maynard, *The General Theory of Employment, Interest and Money*, London: Macmillan, and New York: Harcourt Brace, 1936; as vol. 7 of *The Collected Writings of John Maynard Keynes*, London: Macmillan, and New York: Cambridge University Press, 1973

Leijonhufvud, Axel, *On Keynesian Economics and the Economics of Keynes: A Study in Monetary Theory*, New York and London: Oxford University Press, 1968

Malinvaud, E., *The Theory of Unemployment Reconsidered*, Oxford: Blackwell, and New York: Wiley, 1977

Mankiw, N. Gregory, and David Romer (editors), *New Keynesian Economics*, 2 vols, Cambridge, Massachusetts: MIT Press, 1991

Mankiw, N. Gregory, David Romer, Bruce Greenwald, Joseph E. Stiglitz, James Tobin and Robert G. King, "Symposium: Keynesian Economics Today", *Journal of Economic Perspectives*, 7/1 (1993): 3–82

Minsky, Hyman P., *John Maynard Keynes*, New York: Columbia University Press, 1975

Tobin, James, *Asset Accumulation and Economic Activity: Reflections on Contemporary Macroeconomic Theory*, Chicago: University of Chicago Press, and Oxford: Blackwell, 1980

KEYNES argued that a monetary economy may not automatically return to full employment after a demand shock, so that there is a need for government management of aggregate demand to stabilize the economy. His book remains well worth reading, as its richness is not fully captured by any of the later attempts at formalization of Keynesian economics.

The 39 essays in HARCOURT & RIACH reconsider the many aspects of Keynes' *General Theory* after 60 years, in most (but not all) instances from a post-Keynesian perspective. Some of the contributors adopt the suggestion of the editors to write in the persona of J.M. Keynes reflecting on particular chapters of *The General Theory* a decade after its 1936 publication.

The essays in the volume edited by HALL document the worldwide spread of a simplified form of Keynesian economics, and the influence of such ideas on economic policymaking and on econometric modelling in the quarter-century following World War II. This version of Keynesian economics emphasized the multiplier and the IS-LM model of the determination of aggregate demand, with a fixed money wage (augmented in the 1960s by the Phillips Curve relating money wage changes to unemployment).

CLOWER and LEIJONHUFVUD argue that such simplified, mechanical models of "Keynesian economics" misrepresented the original "economics of Keynes". If all that Keynes had to offer was an assumption of a rigid money wage, then Keynes would not have made any fundamental innovation in economic theory. Clower and Leijonhufvud urge that economists take seriously Keynes' rejection of what he thought the classical economists had propounded as Say's law of markets ("supply creates its own demand", in Keynes' formulation). They stress the distinction between effective demand (taking quantity constraints in other markets into account) and notional demand, and focus attention on asset prices that induce a level of investment inconsistent with full employment.

CODDINGTON's stimulating essays on the reappraisal of Keynes' economics identified three varieties of Keynesianism: hydraulic (the mechanical multiplier and IS-LM models), fundamentalist (the post-Keynesian economics of fundamental uncertainty, attributing volatile investment to the impossibility of knowing the future), and "reconstituted reductionist" Keynesianism. This last variety, exemplified by Clower and Leijonhufvud and subsequently by the flourishing new Keynesian school, attempts to ground Keynesian macroeconomics upon microeconomic foundations of individual rational choice.

MANKIW & ROMER collect the most important new Keynesian journal articles. New Keynesian economics seeks microeconomic foundations in rational choice by optimizing individuals, at a level of rigor equal to New Classical economics, but with unemployment as a possible outcome. Several of the articles in Mankiw & Romer advance theories explaining sticky adjustment of nominal wages and prices as the result of individual optimization (such as the "menu costs" of changing nominal prices, or "efficiency wage" theories that wage cuts impair morale and thus productivity). An important article by Russell Cooper and Andrew John provide a game-theoretic explanation of coordination failure as the result of strategic complementarity: an economy can be stuck in an undesirable equilibrium because each agent will switch to a high-output strategy only if other agents switch to high-output strategies.

MALINVAUD's Yrjö Jahnsson lectures were the first of four sets of invited lectures he has published on the microeconomic foundations of Keynesian unemployment due to deficient demand for goods. They are the most accessible introduction to the work of the French and Belgian fixed-price equilibrium theorists (including most notably Jean-Pascal Benassy, Jacques Drèze, and Jean-Michel Grandmont in addition to Malinvaud), a diverse group of mathematically sophisticated unemployment theorists who are better known in continental Europe than in North America. Like the new Keynesians (but unlike the post Keynesians), these economists pursue their concern with Keynesian issues of demand deficiency and persistent unemployment without any close attention to Keynes' own writings and contributions.

MINSKY, drawing inspiration from Irving Fisher as well as from Keynes, emphasized the fragility of the financial system. His book on Keynes succeeded in bringing a fresh point of view to a well-worn subject, and remains a landmark of the post-Keynesian literature on how a monetary economy differs from a barter economy. The *Journal of Post Keynesian Economics* is the best venue for further exploration of this literature.

The symposium by MANKIW *et al.* (four papers, plus Mankiw's introduction) debates the status of new Keynesian economics as an advance over traditional Keynesian economics, and whether Keynesian economics continues to be relevant (but does not consider Post Keynesian economics). David Romer provides a New Keynesian account of how even small barriers to nominal price flexibility ("menu costs") by imperfectly competitive firms can have large macroeconomic consequences, while Bruce Greenwald and Joseph Stiglitz emphasize costly and imperfect information as a source of market failure in labour and capital markets. In contrast, a new classical critic, Robert King, denies that Keynesian models, whether new or old, adequately incorporate expectations and dynamics. James Tobin, writing on "price flexibility and output stability: an old Keynesian view", argues that the new Keynesian emphasis on rational choice explanations of nominal rigidity is misplaced, because (as previously noted by Keynes, chapter 19) faster adjustment of nominal wages and prices might exacerbate economic fluctuations (through effects on expectations and on the demand for real-money balances). The concise and argumentative essays in the Mankiw *et al.* symposium provide a very readable introduction to the ideas and literature of the controversy over new Keynesian economics.

TOBIN's Yrjö Jahnsson Lectures demonstrate the continuing intellectual vigour of "old Keynesian" economics. Drawing on Irving Fisher's debt-deflation theory of depressions, as well as on Keynes' chapter 19, Tobin questions whether increased price flexibility is stabilizing. Aggregate spending is affected by the redistribution of wealth between borrowers and lenders due to unanticipated changes in the real value of nominal debts, an effect on spending that can swamp the Pigou real balance effect that is crucial to the classical case for macroeconomic stability. Tobin also engages in a sharp critique of new classical macroeconomics (to which Robert Lucas replied in a review article in the *Journal of Economic Literature*).

CATE, HARCOURT & COLANDER, a comprehensive *Encyclopedia of Keynesian Economics*, is an indispensable reference work on the history of Keynesian economics, combining subject articles and biographical entries, including coverage of alternative approaches and of critics of Keynesian economics. Such a large work, written by scores of authors, is necessarily uneven in quality, but the editors have succeeded in their goal of making a large body of information conveniently accessible. The articles are written at an accessible level, and the bibliographies are especially valuable.

ROBERT DIMAND

See also John Maynard Keynes, New Keynesian economics, Say's Law

Khrushchev, Nikita 1894–1971

Soviet political leader

Beschloss, Michael R., *The Crisis Years: Kennedy and Khrushchev, 1960–1963*, New York: Burlingame, 1991

Burlatsky, Fedor, *Khrushchev and the First Russian Spring: The Era of Khrushchev through the Eyes of His Advisor*, New York: Scribner, and London: Weidenfeld and Nicolson, 1991

Conquest, Robert, *Russia after Khrushchev*, New York: Praeger, 1965

Kemp-Welch, Tony, "Khrushchev's 'Secret Speech' and Polish Politics: The Spring of 1956", *Europe-Asia Studies*, 48/2 (1996): 181–206

Khrushchev, Nikita, *Khrushchev Remembers*, Boston: Little Brown, 1970; London: Deutsch, 1971

Khrushchev, Nikita, *Khrushchev Remembers: The Last Testament*, Boston: Little Brown, and London: Deutsch, 1974

Khrushchev, Nikita, *Khrushchev Remembers: The Glasnost Tapes*, Boston: Little Brown, 1990

Khrushchev, Sergei, *Khrushchev on Khrushchev: An Inside Account of the Man and His Era*, Boston: Little Brown, 1990

Linden, Carl A., *Khrushchev and the Soviet Leadership, 1957–1964*, updated edition, Baltimore: Johns Hopkins Press, 1966

Medvedev, Roy and Zhores A. Medvedev, *Khrushchev: The Years in Power*, New York: Columbia University Press, 1976

Medvedev, Roy, *Khrushchev*, Oxford: Blackwell, 1982; New York: Doubleday, 1983

Thompson, William J., *Khrushchev: A Political Life*, New York: St Martin's Press, and London: Macmillan, 1995

Nikita Khrushchev remains a source of controversy nearly three decades after his death. Stalin may have made the Soviet Union strong, but Khrushchev used that strength to make the nation a force of international change. In East and West Germany and Cuba he was responsible for some of the most dangerous moments of the Cold War. In Africa and Asia he supported communist regimes and guerrilla movements and advocated the Soviet economic system as a model of quick industrial development. Khrushchev's rule also marked the perception of the Soviet Union as the leader in technology by the launching of Sputnik and the first man into space. Nowhere is Khrushchev's legacy more evident than in terms of the 1956 "secret speech", in which he denounced Joseph Stalin and the purges, forever breaking the myth of the infallibility of the Communist Party. At the same time his policies were often gambles, as seen with the Virgin Lands agricultural programme and the Cuban missile crisis. Scholars continue to debate whether his policies were dedicated to improving the position of the Soviet people or his own position of power.

BESCHLOSS is a comprehensive account of the relationship between Kennedy and Khrushchev during the Cuban missile crisis as well as the limited détente which followed. Examples are provided showing the dependency of Kennedy and Khrushchev on their advisers and how those advisers used their positions to advance personal and political goals over the head of state. Beschloss' use of Soviet sources is limited considering the fact that it was published in 1991, but the study allows for an excellent examination of the relationship between the two world leaders. It is particularly interesting to observe how, when one was assassinated and the other was removed from power, national leaders in the other country speculated on the implications for American–Soviet relations.

BURLATSKY produces a work of the Khrushchev period from the vantage point of a Soviet speechwriter who served under every Soviet leader from Khrushchev to Gorbachev. The most startling of the reminiscences is that the decision to oust Khrushchev was made over a period of months to ensure that the First Secretary would be isolated from all sources of power. Burlatsky also goes beyond the traditional assessment, questioning whether the lack of popular knowledge about the West and the existence of cunning leaders did not doom Kruschchev's ouster. Yet Khrushchev's policies are credited as arousing the Soviet people by ending the Stalinist terror, and exposing them to Western democracy and a higher standard of living, thus making possible the rise of Mikhail Gorbachev.

CONQUEST focuses on the constraints on reform. Although the title of his work suggests that it has little to do with the Khrushchev period, the focus is in fact on the political system created by Stalin and challenged by Khrushchev. Starting from the premise that a ruling elite controlled the *apparatchiks* controls Soviet politics by their dominance of ideology and institutions, he argues that change could occur only when they were disorganized. Thus Stalinism led to the concentration of power in their hands, whereas in the aftermath of the "secret speech" they were disoriented, thereby allowing Khrushchev

to engage in "ill-considered schemes" (p.4). Conquest's work represents an early attempt to explain the fall of Khrushchev, at a time when Western access to Soviet materials was virtually nonexistent.

KEMP-WELCH is a comprehensive examination of the impact of Khrushchev's "secret speech" on Polish politics and society. In rejecting Stalinism, Khrushchev opened the way for a more critical Polish examination of their Stalinist leaders as well as of Poland's relationship with the Soviet Union. Kemp-Welch concludes that the revelations of the "secret speech" set off a chain reaction in Poland against those who had created their own cults of personality at the national and local levels. In this way, the basis of Poland's allegiance to the Soviet bloc was undermined, prompting demands that Poland's needs should be placed on a par with those of the Soviet Union. Original Polish sources are used for this valuable study of client relations with the Soviet Union – especially once Stalinism was removed as the primary link.

The three books by KHRUSHCHEV (1970, 1974, and 1990) represent a unique primary source as they are the only memoirs of any Soviet leader to be published prior to those of Gorbachev. They offer glimpses of communist leaders like Stalin, Beria, Mao, and Tito, as well as crucial events from the purges, the Winter War with Finland, the "secret speech", and the Cuban missile crisis. They also include historical notes about Khrushchev, discussing his early involvement in the Communist Party and his rise to power. Clearly the goal of these works was for Khrushchev to demonstrate his Marxist–Leninist correctness even after being ousted. His personal involvement in carrying out the purges is avoided, as is the decision by Brezhnev to invade Czechoslovakia. Scholars may also find inaccuracies, because Khrushchev was forced to rely on his memory in creating these works, yet they remain a crucial first step for the student or scholar seeking to penetrate the official veil of Soviet secrecy.

Sergei KHRUSHCHEV offers an intimate portrait of his father, beginning just prior to his forced retirement, and ending with an account of the family's long struggle to have a memorial erected over his grave. Although there is little new information on Khrushchev as a national leader on his humble beginnings, a keen insight is offered into the attempts by the new leadership to banish Khrushchev from public sight, even in death. Sergei reveals the chain of plans and warnings of the coming removal of Khrushchev in 1964 and how Khrushchev came to write his memoirs, and offers personal memories of key Soviet leaders, including Leonid Brezhnev and Yuri Andropov. Most moving is the final chapter, which describes the death of the Khrushchev, the refusal of the Communist Party to honour him, the efforts of the Soviet state to prevent any demonstration of support, and the transformation of artists from critics to admirers. The work offers insights, but one should not forget that the author is the son of the subject, and other than a few footnotes, there is no bibliography on which the reader can draw.

LINDEN's central concern is why Khrushchev was removed from power. Linden uses a conflict model of analysis. Soviet politics is seen as a constant battleground between vested interest groups who were held in check by terror during Stalin's time, but released from tight official control by Kruschchev's "secret speech". Thus, although Khrushchev was able to crush the opposition to his rule in the Presidium in 1957, he was never totally in charge. Khrushchev's destalinization programme served to open the existing policy fractures, and in the end made possible the attacks that led to his removal. Although dated, Linden contains solid Soviet and American references, and exemplifies the conflict model in operation.

The twin issues of why Khrushchev would be victorious and why he sought the liberalization of Soviet life are central to MEDVEDEV. Khrushchev's working-class background, which taught him the fine art of power politics, but failed to prepare him to deal with the implications of destalinization in the areas of the East European satellites and Soviet art, is heavily emphasized. The 15-point indictment of Khrushchev's rule is especially interesting. Despite the memorial quality attached to much of the work in terms of destalinization, Medvedev shows a Khrushchev caught up both caring for his nation and chastizing fellow Soviet leaders for perceived incompetence.

Soviet agricultural policies and their eventual failure were the source of Khrushchev's rise to power and of his eventual downfall, according to MEDVEDEV & MEDVEDEV. Their examination of the Stalinist system, Khrushchev's rise in it, and the "secret speech", are all standard. Likewise, his foreign affairs successes are seen as important for the legitimatization they brought from the Soviet people. The thesis is that Khrushchev's rise to political power was predicated on winning a series of agricultural policy debates, beginning in 1947. Khrushchev's mistakes in agricultural policy, such as his support for Lysenko and the belief that chemical fertilizers were not required for increasing harvest yields, are examined. Only with the removal of the anti-Party group in 1957 do the authors see Khrushchev as emerging supreme. With this came a stronger tendency toward economic reforms, which necessitated political reforms, thereby threatening the position of the national leadership. This is important reading for those seeking an explanation of Khrushchev's rise and decline in power and of collectivization under his rule.

THOMPSON is a political biography of Khrushchev. Beginning with his birth in 1894, it traces Khrushchev's career, from his early days as a Party activist in the Donbass region, through his leadership in Kiev and Moscow, and his eventual triumph in the post-Stalin period, to his final forced retirement. Khrushchev's relationship with Kaganovich – whom Thompson sees as Khrushchev's patron – and the anti-Party affair, which resulted in Kaganovich's removal, are fascinating. Several popular myths about Khrushchev, such as his lack of involvement in the purges, are traced and dispelled. Thompson portrays Khrushchev as deeply committed to communism, including Stalinist institutions like collectivization and heavy industry, but also as a leader who sought to deliver peaceful coexistence with the West and the long-promised rewards of communism to the consumer. Khrushchev's "harebrained schemes" are delineated. The nine pages of bibliography are well balanced between Soviet, Russian, Ukrainian, and Western sources, and for this reason alone, warrant reading by those seeking to research the life and political career of Khrushchev.

JEFFREY L. PREWITT

See also Cold War, Collectivization

King, Martin Luther, Jr 1929–1968

US civil rights leader

Branch, Taylor, *Parting the Waters: America in the King Years, 1954–63*, New York: Simon and Schuster, and London: Macmillan, 1988

Branch, Taylor, *Pillar of Fire: America in the King Years, 1963–65*, New York and London: Simon and Schuster, 1998

Fairclough, Adam, *To Redeem the Soul of America: The Southern Christian Leadership Conference and Martin Luther King, Jr*, Athens: University of Georgia Press, 1987

Garrow, David J., *Bearing the Cross: Martin Luther King, Jr, and the Southern Christian Leadership Conference*, New York: Morrow, 1986; London: Cape, 1988

Garrow, David J. (editor), *Martin Luther King, Jr, and the Civil Rights Movement*, 18 vols, New York: Carlson, 1989

Lischer, Richard, *The Preacher King: Martin Luther King, Jr, and the Word That Moved America*, New York and Oxford: Oxford University Press, 1995

McKnight, Gerald, *The Last Crusade: Martin Luther King, Jr, the FBI, and the Poor People's Campaign*, Boulder, Colorado: Westview Press, 1998

Oates, Stephen B., *Let the Trumpet Sound: The Life of Martin Luther King, Jr*, New York: Harper and Row, 1982

As the most prominent black activist of the US Civil Rights Movement, Revd Martin Luther King, Jr embodies both the successes and the failures of America's struggle with race relations. His early career was marked by optimism and success, just as the US seemed ready to dissolve an abiding and embarrassing racial caste system. He grabbed the public spotlight with a successful boycott of the bus system in Montgomery, Alabama. He captured the country's conscience with moving sermons, essays, and speeches. He helped lead a march on Washington DC, which solidified the central role of racial issues on the nation's political agenda. Both King's career, and America's stunning experiment in self-improvement, culminated in unprecedented civil rights legislation: the 1964 Civil Rights Act and the 1965 Voting Rights Act.

Yet rising expectations soon outpaced both what King could accomplish and what the US was willing to countenance. King and his white allies faded in prominence, as a result of a combination of changing times and their own limitations, to be replaced by radical young blacks who possessed little of their predecessors' moral authority. Urban riots and militant threats replaced non-violent protests and appeals to conscience. King himself, isolated and (by most accounts) bitter, lost control of the movement he had led just as American race relations fell into their own bitter spiral of recriminations and white backlash. He fell to an assassin's bullet the same year segregationist George Wallace's presidential campaign helped tear apart the racially liberal Democratic Party.

The congruence of King's career with America's racial struggles makes him a fascinating study, and the intellectual depth with which he pursued his goals make him a worthwhile one. The historical literature is therefore voluminous, including both biographies and broader works assessing King's place in the movement. Indeed, multi-volume collections are, or shortly will be, available giving a full picture of this expansive body of research; the collection compiled by GARROW (1989) includes both prominent articles and whole dissertations. The remainder of this entry, however, focuses on the individual works that either are or probably will be most valuable to readers outside the research area.

OATES serves as a good starting point. Written with the cooperation of King's family, the book has been criticized as practically an "authorized biography". Yet such an apologia is valuable, compiled as it was a decade after the subject's assassination. Oates is able to rebut the posthumous criticisms that had begun to mar King's legacy, yet he does so with the authoritative voice of a respected historian (known for his earlier work on Abraham Lincoln). The King who dominates these pages is an unambiguous hero. LISCHER's volume, similarly, communicates King's rhetorical skills and religious vision – and therefore provides a clear picture of why this one astounding man was able to "move America". King's rhetoric and approach was shaped in part by his previous training as a Protestant minister, a background that lent weight to his message.

GARROW (1988) completed a trilogy on King, with the publication of what is still probably the most influential biography available – a Pulitzer Prize winner. It is a hefty book, one that walks through every major civil rights confrontation in which King participated, comprehensively describing the stratagems that led up to each event. Garrow manages to communicate a deep respect for King, spending rather excessive effort describing the man's emotional fluctuations. At the same time, Garrow sees King as "bearing a cross", taking on a sacrificial chore that defined him much more than he defined it. The thesis is not particularly persuasive. Just because King suffered his burden noisily does not mean he did not choose it and did not shape it. Indeed, Garrow's book itself documents how actively King pursued influence, pushing his way into the media spotlight (sometimes to the resentment of local black leadership), and building up a civil-rights bureaucracy to promote himself. It is clear that, among King and his associates, the man often superseded the message – something that younger activists eventually came to despise. Garrow also downplays, yet nevertheless reveals, how King's sexism put off talented female activists and created strife in his own home. Matters of interpretation aside, however, the research is invaluable.

FAIRCLOUGH, a British historian, had the misfortune to release his book within a year of Garrow's. That the early volume overshadowed his, however, does not mean that the two are redundant. Their emphases are quite different. Just as Garrow's subtitle puts King himself before the Southern Christian Leadership Conference (SCLC), while Fairclough's subtitle reverses the billing, the presentation of the books follows this reversal. Fairclough neglects the emotional ups and downs that rocked King and instead focuses on the organization that King constructed. The SCLC does not appear as a mere satellite of its founder, but as a force that had a strength and potential of its own, with internal rivalries that helped shape the movement just as King's internal struggles did.

The two volumes by BRANCH (1988, 1998) offer a broader sweep, a treatment of the civil rights movement during the period King found himself "at its heart". Branch's first volume

won a Pulitzer Prize. It follows the civil-rights movement from the Montgomery bus boycott of 1954, where King was first thrust onto the national stage, to the time just before the movement's greatest victories. The book is a major addition to scholarship on King precisely because Branch's lens offers a wider picture than the biographies. He gives frequent side glances at the Eisenhower and Kennedy administrations, as well as civil rights leaders outside the SCLC. The National Association for the Advancement of Colored People (NAACP) and NAACP leader Roy Wilkins, for example, fought fiercely against King and therefore play a more prominent role in Branch's work. These external forces formed the context in which King operated, and are a fundamental part of the historical figure he became. The second Branch volume has not received such close attention, but continues the tradition of "narrative biographical history" begun by the first. Branch is particularly successful at illustrating how factional rivalries and petty political concerns directly shaped historical events.

King's legacy has many claimants-not only the preacher's wife, descendants, and former associates, but also racial conservatives who consider themselves the true heirs of his colour-blind rhetoric. For American conservatives, King is frozen at his 1963 stage of development, when he led the March on Washington and delivered his famous "I have a dream" oratory. Many civil rights supporters resent this appropriation of King's message, shaped as it was to attract white supporters and ensure passage of practical legislation. The recent volume by McKNIGHT is therefore a valuable corrective, because it explores King's growing radicalism as he moved the civil rights movement northward. King was frustrated with what rights rhetoric alone could accomplish for African Americans, when they were still held back by poverty from north to south.

D. STEPHEN VOSS

See also Civil rights (US)

Kondratieff cycles

Garvy, G., "Kondratieff's Theory of Long Cycles", *Review of Economics and Statistics*, 25 (1943): 203–23

Gelderen, J. van (pseudonym: J. Fedder), "*Springvloed*", (parts 1–3), in *De Nieuwe Tijd*, 18 (1913): 253–77; 369–84; 445–64

Kleinknecht, Alfred, "Are there Schumpeterian Waves of Innovations?", *Cambridge Journal of Economics*, 14/1 (1990): 81–92

Kleinknecht, Alfred, Ernest Mandel and Immanuel Wallerstein (editors), *New Findings in Long-Wave Research*, London: Macmillan, and New York: St Martin's Press, 1992

Kondratieff, Nikolai, D., "Die langen Wellen der Konjunktur, *Archiv für Sozialwissenschaften und Sozialpolitik*, vol. 56, 1926; abridged English translation as "The Long Waves in Economic Life", *Review of Economics and Statistics*, 17 (1935): 105–24

Rosenberg, Nathan and Claudio Frischtak, "Technological Innovation and Long Waves", *Cambridge Journal of Economics*, 8/1 (1984): 7–24

Solomou, Solomos, "Innovation Clusters and Kondratieff Long Waves in Economic Growth", *Cambridge Journal of Economics*, 10/2 (1986): 101–12

Spree, Reinhard, "Lange Wellen wirtschaftlicher Entwicklung in der Neuzeit", *Historical Social Research / Historische Sozialforschung*, 4 (1991): 3–138

Wolff, S. de, "Prosperiteits- en depressieperioden", *De Socialistische Gids*, 6: 19–40; in German as "Prosperitäts- und Depressionsperioden" in *Der lebendige Marxismus, Festgabe zum 70. Geburtstage von Karl Kautsky*, edited by Otto Jenssen, Jena: Thüringer, 1924, reprinted: Glashütten im Taunus: Auvermann, 1973

The term "Kondratieff cycles" (sometimes also transcribed from Russian as Kondratiev cycles) was coined by Schumpeter in his *History of Economics Analysis*. KONDRATIEFF became famous mainly due to a German translation of his 1926 article, and an English translation published in 1935. One can argue, however, that two Dutch economists (VAN GELDEREN, alias Fedder, and DE WOLFF) published similar work earlier (from 1913 onwards). However, owing to the language barrier, their publications (in Dutch) remained relatively unknown outside the Netherlands. The early work on long cycles concentrated on identifying long-run movements in price indices, interest rates, and, to a limited extent, in "real" economic variables such as production.

Early in the 20th century, periods of rising prices were generally identified as "good" times whereas declining prices indicated "bad" periods. Hence, when authors like van Gelderen, de Wolff and Kondratieff identified a long-wave pattern in price indices and interest rates, they tended to interpret this as an indication of ups and downs in *general* economic activity. Only later was this called into question. GARVY was among the first of a number of authors who doubted the existence of a long-cycle pattern in "real" series such as industrial production (see the thorough survey by SPREE). During the 1980s, there was a renaissance of research into long waves, including econometric work on time series. Authors like SOLOMOU remained sceptical about the existence of long cycles. However, others argued that Kondratieff-type fluctuations could indeed be identified, not only in price and interest rate series, but also in *world* industrial production, and in the GNP of a number of core countries (see several chapters in the work edited by KLEINKNECHT, MANDEL & WALLERSTEIN).

The following table gives a sketch of rising and declining long cycle periods as they emerged from the early works by van Gelderen, de Wolff and Kondratieff for the first, second, and third Kondratieff cycle; a fourth and possibly fifth cycle is added, judging from recent time series analyses.

Kondratieff cycles:	Periods of rise:	Periods of decline:
First cycle	end 1780s–early 1790s to 1810–17	1810–17 to 1844–51
Second cycle	1844–51 to 1870–5	1870–5 to 1890–6
Third cycle	1890–96 to 1914–20	1914–20 to 1939–48
Fourth cycle	1939–48 to 1974–5	1974–5 to early 1990s
Fifth cycle	early 1990s to ?	

Much discussion focused on the question of causation of the alleged Kondratieff cycles. If such long-term fluctuations exist, can they be conceived as endogenous (self-reproducing) cycles, or are they historically unique fluctuations that happened by historical accident (and do not necessarily need to be reproduced in the future)? Only in the former case, can these fluctuations be regarded as true "cycles". In the latter case, it is appropriate to speak of historically unique (exogenously caused) long-run fluctuations that happened to resemble the time schemes proposed by Kondratieff and others (see ROSENBERG & FRISCHTAK for a thorough discussion of this point).

From the latter viewpoint one can argue that, during the last 200 years, capitalism has undergone dramatic structural change (including, for example, the rise of trade unions and welfare states, internationalization, and concentration of capital). It would therefore appear plausible to argue that subdivision by historically unique periods is more adequate than assuming that one causal mechanism will repeatedly cause identical cycles. Against this, adherents of the cycle approach will argue that there are certain basic "laws" of development of capitalism that will apply (with minor modifications) in all periods and under different structural regimes.

The early authors offered a number of explanations of long cycles. These included theories about periodic over- and under-investment of capital, credit expansion and financial instability, scarcity and abundance of basic materials, the opening up of new territories and migration waves, or periodic expansion and contraction of gold production. One hypothesis was formulated by van Gelderen and received much attention in later research. According to this hypothesis, each upswing of the long cycle is driven by the rapid expansion of one or several leading sectors. As examples, van Gelderen names railways during 1850–73, and the electricity and car industries after 1996. In each cycle, these leading industries have powerful side effects on upstream and downstream industries. As far as the emergence of leading sectors is linked to breakthroughs in technological innovation, van Gelderen's position is consistent with the way Kondratieff put the problem: "During the recession of the long waves, an especially large number of important discoveries and inventions . . . are made, which, however, are usually applied on a large scale only at the beginning of the next long upswing" (p.118).

This is an early formulation of the Schumpeterian hypothesis that major innovations occur discontinuously in time. This hypothesis has been discussed in the literature during the 1980s, and has caused some controversy. A sceptical argument has been made by Solomou, whereas a defence of Schumpeter's hypothesis is presented by KLEINKNECHT, who also gives a brief survey of the debate.

ALFRED KLEINKNECHT

See also Long swings in economic activity

L

Labelling theory

Becker, Howard Saul, *Outsiders: Studies in the Sociology of Deviance*, Glencoe, Illinois: Free Press, 1963; reprinted with a new chapter, "Labelling Theory Revisited", New York: Free Press, 1973

Cohen, Stanley, *Folk Devils and Moral Panics: The Creation of the Mods and Rockers*, London: MacGibbon and Kee, 1972; new edition, Oxford: Martin Robertson, and New York: St Martin's Press, 1980

Goode, Erich and Nachman Ben-Yehuda, *Moral Panics: The Social Construction of Deviance*, Oxford and Cambridge, Massachusetts: Blackwell, 1994

Kitsuse, John I. and Aaron V. Cicourel, "A Note on the Uses of Official Statistics", *Social Problems*, 11 (1963): 131–39

Lemert, Edwin M., *Human Deviance, Social Problems, and Social Control*, Englewood Cliffs, New Jersey: Prentice Hall, 1967; 2nd edition, 1972

Matza, David, *Becoming Deviant*, Englewood Cliffs, New Jersey: Prentice Hall, 1969

Spector, Malcolm and John I. Kitsuse, *Constructing Social Problems*, Menlo Park, California: Cummings, 1977

Sumner, Colin, *The Sociology of Deviance: An Obituary*, Buckingham: Open University Press, and New York: Continuum, 1994

Taylor, Ian, Paul Walton and Jock Young, *The New Criminology: For a Social Theory of Deviance*, London: Routledge and Kegan Paul, 1973; New York: Harper and Row, 1984

Labelling theory is not a theory in the narrow sense but a sociological perspective for investigating deviant phenomena. It rests upon the idea that deviance is not a characteristic of persons (like psychopathic personality features or genetic composition) or particular forms of conduct (taking property, killing people) but is best understood as an interaction in which perceived rule breakers are labelled as deviant by significant others (notably staff of agencies of social control). In the oft-quoted words of BECKER, "deviance is *not* a quality of the act a person commits, but rather a consequence of the application by others of rules and sanctions to an 'offender'" (1963, p.9). Becker's account of the origins of the Marihuana Tax Act highlighted the importance of moral crusaders whose activities led to the outlawing of marihuana use. Labelling theory also encouraged the close investigation of the (often-arbitrary) workings of social control.

Labelling theory originated in the merger of symbolic inter-actionism (see entry on symbolic interactionism) and social control theory found in LEMERT's writings of the 1940s and 1950s (a selection of which are included in his 1967/1972 book). Lemert emphasized that social control can impact on deviant identity through his distinction between "primary deviation", which had only marginal consequences for the person's psychic structure, and "secondary deviation", where significant reorganization of self-regarding attitudes occurs in order to deal with the problems associated with the societal reaction to the person's deviant conduct.

MATZA's synthesis consolidates and develops many of the latent themes of labelling theory. His book reinstates the importance of the state as well as will, association, and the local circumstances leading up to engagement in deviant actions. In restoring the volitional element Matza counteracts crude "give a dog a bad name" readings of the theory.

A methodological critique of official statistics as a source of sociological data about deviance is associated with labelling theory. KITSUSE & CICOUREL suggest that the collection of statistics on deviance by organizations such as psychiatric hospitals or juvenile agencies is framed by their administrative and political concerns that may well not coincide with those of the sociologist. At the extreme, this argument proposes that, for example, crime statistics bear an unknown relation to the amount of "real" crime in the society.

COHEN's study of the exaggerated public response ("moral panic") in the UK to the Mods and Rockers youth subcultures of the mid-1960s places societal reaction centre stage. Cohen defines a moral panic descriptively. At certain times

a condition, episode, person or group of persons emerges to become defined as a threat to societal values and interests; its nature is depicted in a stylized and stereotypical fashion by the mass media; the moral barricades are manned by editors, bishops, politicians and other right-thinking people; socially accredited experts pronounce their diagnoses and solutions; ways of coping are evolved . . . (Cohen p.9)

Cohen's book details the responses of the press, public, police, courts, and local action groups that served to cast Mods and Rockers as "folk devils", visible reminders of attitudes and conduct deplored by the wider society. Cohen also examines "deviance amplification": the tendency for the identification produced by labelling actually to intensify the original deviation. Cohen shows how misperception of the threat posed by Mods and Rockers resulted in a sensitization to the menace they represented that was then confirmed by subsequent deviant acts. Cohen's study adopted a consistent labelling theory focus on the societal reaction, the processes of social control, rather than on the actors, the mods and rockers themselves.

GOODE & BEN-YEHUDA seeks to systematize the moral panic concept by identifying its characteristic features: (1) concern: there must be a heightened degree of concern about the behaviour of a group or segment within the society (the putative folk devils); (2) hostility: there must be an increased level of hostility towards the folk devil group; (3) consensus: there must be wide agreement that the folk devil group and their behaviour represent a real and serious threat; (4) disproportionality: the degree of concern over the threat is beyond that which could be sustained by a realistic appraisal; (5) volatility: moral panics erupt suddenly and may subside just as quickly. While moral panics often have an objective basis, their defining feature is that claims about their seriousness are out of step with what the empirical evidence can warrant.

TAYLOR, WALTON & YOUNG presents a politically radical critique of labelling theory. They complain that it focuses on the underdog instead of the crimes of the powerful; it carries an unwelcome relativism; it exaggerates the difficulty of identifying deviant acts (the meaning of which is seen to reside in the acts themselves).

SUMNER places labelling theory as a late stage in the history of the sociology of deviance (a specialism whose life force, he believes, has now expired). Sumner is especially good on Goffman's and Lemert's contributions. But by regarding labelling theory as a creature of its times (the 1960s), his analysis loses sight of the real issues it placed on the sociological agenda.

Becker's reconsideration of labelling theory deals with many of the more common criticisms. He argues that it underscores how deviant phenomena are the products of collective action, people doing things together; it encourages a demystification of deviance by stressing the importance of first-hand observation in research; and it raises questions about the moral implications of deviance theory that are more difficult to resolve than some of the easy formulations offered by self-styled radicals.

Labelling theory has also influenced thinking about social problems. In SPECTOR & KITSUSE's formulation, social problems are conditions of society that groups of activists make claims about – claims about the unsatisfactoriness of the condition and the need for remedial action. The only adequate criterion of the social problems of a society is the activities of "claimsmaking" groups: the social scientist cannot offer any better-informed or more privileged authority. This raises the vexatious issue of relativism: to what extent are sociologists' conceptions beholden to those of society members? On the one hand there are those who insist that any attempt to lend the sociologist greater authority on account of a more privileged knowledge amounts to "ontological gerrymandering". On the other there are those who champion the position of the sociologist as a strategic fact finder who is in a position to adjudicate the validity of claims that are being made. At stake are differing conceptions of the social role of the sociologist and the balance of power between experts and citizenry.

GREG SMITH

Labour economics

Abowd, John M. and Orley Ashenfelter, "Anticipated Unemployment, Temporary Layoffs, and Compensating Wage Differentials" in *Studies in Labor Markets*, edited by Sherwin Rosen, Chicago: University of Chicago Press, 1981

Aigner, Dennis J. and Glen G. Cain, "Statistical Theories of Discrimination in Labor Markets", *Industrial and Labor Relations Review*, 30/2 (1977): 175–87

Angrist, Joshua D. and Alan B. Krueger, "Does Compulsory School Attendance Affect Schooling and Earnings", *Quarterly Journal of Economics*, 106/4 (1991): 979–1014

Ashenfelter, Orley and James J. Heckman, "The Estimation of Income and Substitution Effects in a Model of Family Labor Supply", *Econometrica*, 42/1 (1974): 73–85

Becker, Gary S., *The Economics of Discrimination*, 2nd edition, Chicago: University of Chicago Press, 1971

Becker, Gary S., *Human Capital: A Theoretical and Empirical Analysis with Special Reference to Education*, 3rd edition, Chicago: University of Chicago Press, 1993

Ben-Porath, Yoram, "The Production of Human Capital and the Life Cycle of Earnings", *Journal of Political Economy*, 75/4 part I (1967): 352–65

Bergmann, Barbara R., "The Effect on White Incomes of Discrimination in Employment", *Journal of Political Economy*, 79/2 (1971): 294–313

Berman, Eli, John Bound and Zvi Griliches, "Changes in the Demand for Skilled Labor Within U.S. Manufacturing Industries: Evidence from the Annual Survey of Manufacturers", *Quarterly Journal of Economics*, 109/2 (1994): 367–97

Betts, Julian, "Is There a Link Between School Inputs and Earnings? Fresh Scrutiny of an Old Literature" in *Does Money Matter?*, edited by Gary Burtless, Washington, DC: Brookings Institution Press, 1996

Borjas, George J., "Self-Selection and the Earnings of Immigrants", *American Economic Review*, 77/4 (1987): 531–53

Borjas, George J., Richard Freeman and Lawrence Katz, "Searching for the Effect of Immigration on the Labor Market", *American Economic Review*, 86/2 (1996): 246–51

Brown, Charles, Curtis Gilroy and Andrew Kohen, "The Effect of the Minimum Wage on Employment and Unemployment", *Journal of Economic Literature*, 20/2 (1982): 487–528

Burdett, Kenneth, "A Theory of Employee Job Search and Quit Rates", *American Economic Review*, 68/1 (1978): 212–20

Card, David and Alan B. Krueger, *Myth and Measurement: The New Economics of the Minimum Wage*, Princeton, New Jersey: Princeton University Press, 1995

Card, David, "Earnings, Schooling and Ability Revisited" in *Research in Labor Economics*, edited by Ronald G. Ehrenberg, Greenwich, Connecticut: Jai Press, 1995

Griliches, Zvi, "Estimating the Returns to Schooling: Some Econometric Problems", *Econometrica*, 45/1 (1977): 1–22

Gronau, Reuben, "Leisure, Home Production, and Work:
The Theory of the Allocation of Time Revisited", *Journal
of Political Economy*, 85/6 (1977): 1099–123

Ham, John C., "Testing Whether Unemployment Represents
Intertemporal Labor Supply Behaviour", *Review of
Economic Studies*, 53/4 (1986): 559–78

Hamermesh, Daniel S., "Labor Demand and the Structure of
Adjustment Costs", *American Economic Review*, 79/4
(1989): 674–89

Hamermesh, Daniel S., *Labor Demand*, Princeton: Princeton
University Press, 1993

Hutchens, Robert M., "A Test of Lazear's Theory of Delayed
Payment Contracts", *Journal of Labor Economics*, 5/4
Part 2 (1987): S153–70

Hwang, Hae-shin, W. Robert Reed and Carlton Hubbard,
"Compensating Wage Differentials and Unobserved
Productivity", *Journal of Political Economy*, 100/4 (1992):
835–58

Juhn, Chinhui, Kevin M. Murphy and Brooks Pierce, "Wage
Inequality and the Rise in Returns to Skill", *Journal of
Political Economy*, 101/3 (1993): 410–42

Katz, Lawrence F. and Kevin M. Murphy, "Changes in
Relative Wages, 1963–1987: Supply and Demand
Factors", *Quarterly Journal of Economics*, 107/1 (1992):
35–78

Kiefer, Nicholas M. and George R. Neumann, "An Empirical
Job-Search Model with a Test of the Constant Reservation
Wage Hypothesis", *Journal of Political Economy*, 87/1
(1979): 89–107

Kiefer, Nicholas M., "Economic Duration Data and Hazard
Functions", *Journal of Economic Literature*, 26/2 (1988):
646–79

Killingsworth, Mark R. and James J. Heckman, "Female
Labor Supply: A Survey" in *Handbook of Labor
Economics*, edited by Orley Ashenfelter and Richard
Layard, vol. 1, Amsterdam: North Holland, 1986

Krueger, Alan and Jörn-Steffen Pischke, "The Effect of Social
Security on Labor Supply: A Cohort Analysis of the Notch
Generation", *Journal of Labor Economics*, 10/4 (1992):
412–37

Lancaster, Tony, "Econometric Methods for the Duration
of Unemployment", *Econometrica*, 47/4 (1979):
939–56

Lazear, Edward P., "Why Is there Mandatory Retirement?"
Journal of Political Economy, 87/6 (1979): 1261–84

Lazear, Edward P. and Sherwin Rosen, "Rank-Order
Tournaments as Optimum Labor Contracts", *Journal of
Political Economy*, 89/5 (1981): 841–64

McElroy, Marjorie B. and Mary-Jean Horney, "Nash-
Bargained Household Decisions: Towards a Generalization
of the Theory of Demand", *International Economic
Review*, 22/2 (1981): 333–49

Meyer, Bruce D., "Unemployment Insurance and
Unemployment Spells", *Econometrica*, 58/4 (1990):
757–82

Mincer, Jacob, *Schooling, Experience and Earnings*, New
York: National Bureau of Economic Research, 1974;
Aldershot: Gregg Revivals, 1993

Mincer, Jacob, "Family Migration Decisions", *Journal of
Political Economy*, 86/5 (1978): 749–73

Mortensen, Dale T., "Job Search, the Duration of
Unemployment and the Phillips Curve", *American
Economic Review*, 60/5 (1970): 847–62

Mortensen, Dale T., "Unemployment Insurance and Job
Search Decisions", *Industrial and Labor Relations Review*,
30/4 (1977): 505–17

Mroz, Thomas A., "The Sensitivity of an Empirical Model
of Married Women's Hours of Work to Economic and
Statistical Assumptions", *Econometrica*, 55/4 (1987):
765–99

Murphy, Kevin J., "Corporate Performance and
Managerial Remuneration: An Empirical Analysis,
Journal of Accounting and Economics, 7/1–3 (1985):
11–42

Murphy, Kevin M. and Robert H. Topel, "Efficiency Wages
Reconsidered: Theory and Evidence" in *Advances in
Theory and Measurement of Unemployment*, edited by
Yoram Weiss and Gideon Fishelson, London: Macmillan,
and New York: St Martin's Press, 1990

Oaxaca, Ronald, "Male-Female Wage Differentials in Urban
Labor Markets", *International Economic Review*, 14/3
(1973): 693–709

Oi, Walter Y., "Labor as a Quasi-Fixed Factor", *Journal of
Political Economy*, 70/6 (1962): 538–55

Pencavel, John H., "Labor Supply of Men: A Survey" in
Handbook of Labor Economics, edited by Orley
Ashenfelter and Richard Layard, vol. 1, Amsterdam:
North Holland, 1986

Rosen, Sherwin, "Short-Run Employment Variation on Class-
I Railroads in the U.S., 1947–1963", *Econometrica*,
36/3–4 (1968): 511–29

Rosen, Sherwin, "Hedonic Prices and Implicit Markets:
Product Differentiation in Pure Competition", *Journal of
Political Economy*, 82/1 (1974): 34–55

Smith, Robert S., "Compensating Wage Differentials and
Public Policy: A Review", *Industrial and Labor Relations
Review*, 32/3 (1979): 339–52

Spence, Michael A., "Job Market Signaling", *Quarterly
Journal of Economics*, 87/3 (1973): 355–74

Triest, Robert, "The Effect of Income Taxation on Labor
Supply in the United States", *Journal of Human
Resources*, 25/3 (1990): 491–516

This entry focuses on analytical labour economics and does
not delve into institutional labour market issues. The various
topics that fall under the rubric of modern labour economics
are discussed sequentially, and key theoretical and empirical
contributions in each area are referenced.

PENCAVEL deals with the labour supply of men. The author
traces the roots of the modern analysis of labour supply to the
work of Hicks and presents static and dynamic models of
labour supply. KILLINGSWORTH & HECKMAN provides a
survey of female labour supply. It provides a review of the
theoretical literature focusing on the paper by ASHENFELTER
& HECKMAN and additional work by GRONAU, which
explicitly allows for the role of marriage and the family
in determining the labour supply of household members.
McELROY & HORNEY presents a model based on the notion
that family labour supply decisions may be treated as a result
of bargaining between household members.

Pencavel and Killingsworth & Heckman provide surveys of the empirical literature on, respectively, male and female labour supply. MROZ carefully examines the statistical and economic assumptions underlying various estimates of female labour supply. His work tends to conclude that the empirical results are not very robust. TRIEST's work examines labour supply responses to changes in income tax, while KRUEGER & PISCHKE examines the link between labour supply and the provision of social security. Labour supply is usually treated as a decision made by employees; however, partly due to the poor empirical results, HAM's empirical specification allows the employer to play a greater role in determining labour supply.

HAMERMESH (1993) provides an authoritative and comprehensive survey of the field of labour demand. Chapter two deals with the static theory of labour demand and elasticity of demand, while chapter six surveys dynamic models of labour demand. Traditional analyses of labour demand treat labour as a variable factor of production. OI points out that several labour costs, such as hiring and training costs, are fixed, and labour might be viewed more appropriately as a quasi-fixed factor of production. Oi's model provides testable predictions of the manner in which firms may adjust the composition of their work force to changes in the business cycles or to other exogenous shocks.

Chapter two in Hamermesh 1993 reviews static empirical studies. ROSEN (1968) deals with dynamic issues, and examines whether the variation in the skill composition of a firm's workforce over the business cycle may be attributed to quasi-fixed costs. HAMERMESH (1989) is a more recent empirical work that examines the costs faced by firms in adjusting labour demand due to exogenous shocks. The evidence suggests that fixed costs lead to a discrete pattern of labour adjustment, i.e. changes in employment do not respond to small shocks, but do respond sharply to large shocks.

Two important and topical policy issues pertaining to this topic are the effect of minimum wage legislation on employment, and the role of demand factors in fuelling increases in wage inequality. BROWN, GILROY & KOHEN is an important survey of several empirical studies on the effects of minimum wages. Their paper suggests that minimum wages adversely effect the employment of less skilled workers. More recent and controversial work has challenged these findings. CARD & KRUEGER find no evidence for any negative employment effects associated with minimum wage legislation. Turning to the second policy issue, KATZ & MURPHY consider the various demand and supply factors that might be responsible for recent increases in wage inequality.

BECKER (1993) provides the most comprehensive initial theoretical treatment of human capital. He examines the motivation for individual investments in education and on-the-job training, and derives implications for labour supply, wage determination, and age-earnings profiles. In an important extension of the Becker framework, BEN-PORATH adds a dynamic dimension by examining the pattern of human capital investments over the life cycle. The human capital approach argues that investments in human capital increase market and non-market productivity. However, the signalling model found in SPENCE provides a challenge to this conception. It suggests that investments in human capital might increase earnings, not because of any productivity increases, but because workers who have acquired more education signal their abilities and employers reward them with higher earnings and better job opportunities.

Turning to empirical and policy issues, the pioneering empirical work in the human capital area is MINCER (1974), which develops a simple empirical framework that captures the key ingredients of the human capital model. Although Mincer's model represents a blend of theory and pragmatism, it has several shortcomings. GRILICHES is an important and widely cited paper that identifies the major pitfalls and problems associated with the use of the Mincer framework. The main concern is whether the estimated impact of a human capital investment on earnings is a true causal effect, or rather a spurious effect due to lack of controls for ability. In recent years, several ingenious methods have been used to examine this issue. For example, ANGRIST & KRUEGER measures the effect of compulsory schooling laws on educational attainment and earnings, and then use the earnings-educational attainment ratio as a measure of returns to schooling that are not contaminated by ability bias. The consequences of other shortcomings of the Mincer framework, such as ignoring the role of school quality and treating schooling as an exogenous variable, are considered by BETTS and CARD respectively.

The change in returns to human capital over time is an important topic of current research in this area. JUHN, MURPHY & PIERCE examine the pattern of increased wage inequality in the US. Their paper provides a convenient and comprehensive framework for decomposing temporal changes in the wage distribution into various components. It is widely regarded that a major cause of the rise in the returns to skills is the diffusion of information technology in all sectors of the economy. BERMAN, BOUND & GRILICHES considers the effect of technological changes on earnings and employment patterns.

The topic of compensating wage differentials considers the role of intersectoral and interoccupational differences in job characteristics in determining wages and employment. The notion that differences in working conditions influence labour market outcomes was first posited by Adam Smith. ROSEN (1974) provides a modern statement of this insight. ABOWD & ASHENFELTER construct a theoretical framework that treats the level and variability of unemployment as an undesirable job characteristic that should be compensated.

SMITH reviews early empirical work in this area and appears to conclude that workers in risky jobs are compensated with higher wages. HWANG, REED & HUBBARD provides some recent evidence on this issue. However, it has been argued that evidence on compensating wage differentials is not convincing as most of the existing work has been unable to isolate the impact of unobserved productive characteristics from the role of job characteristics in influencing wage determination.

The major theme explored in the area of the employment relationship is the manner in which employment contracts may be designed so as to align employees' interests with those of employers. LAZEAR examines the manner in which the sequencing of pay may be used to motivate workers over their working life, while LAZEAR & ROSEN considers the role of job promotion possibilities in inducing work effort. MURPHY & TOPEL reviews another set of arguments based on efficiency wage theories which suggest that workers may be paid wages above market levels in order to increase work effort.

HUTCHENS examines the empirical validity of the argument that delayed pay is a worker motivation device. MURPHY considers the effect of managerial compensation schemes on corporate performance.

The search approach is a relatively recent development in labour economics and concentrates on the mobility of workers between jobs and/or between unemployment and employment. MORTENSEN (1970, 1977) are pioneering papers in this area that consider two issues: first, the link between search efforts and the duration of unemployment; and second, the effect of unemployment insurance on the motivation to search for work and to exit from unemployment. While Mortensen's work concentrates on the transition to employment, BURDETT examines worker mobility between jobs. KIEFER & NEUMANN develops a search model for the transition to employment and point out several testable predictions of the model.

The development of the search approach with its focus on the temporal element requires the development and the application of a new set of econometric tools. LANCASTER discusses the appropriate econometric tools to analyse duration data with a special focus on the duration of unemployment. KIEFER provides a survey of duration models and a discussion of the econometric problems that arise while using duration data. MEYER applies some of these techniques to examine the influence of unemployment insurance on the duration of unemployment.

BECKER (1971) lays out the foundation for the economic theory of discrimination. It puts forward the theory that labour market discrimination arises from the tastes or preferences that employers might have for certain groups of workers, and in attempting to indulge these tastes, employers are willing to incur additional costs. AIGNER & CAIN provides an alternative conception of discrimination. They argue that in the absence of perfect information individuals might be judged by the characteristics of the group to which they belong. This evaluation strategy can lead to discrimination (often called statistical discrimination) even in the absence of any prejudice. Still another view of discrimination is provided by BERGMANN, which examines discrimination arising from the sorting of certain groups of workers into particular occupations.

OAXACA lays out an empirical framework that can be used to analyse wage discrimination. The framework allows the decomposition of mean wages into a component that may be attributed to differences in the productive characteristics among individuals, and differences in returns to the same characteristics. Although questionable, this latter difference is usually attributed to discrimination. Oaxaca has sparked a number of replica studies, and is still widely used to examine wage discrimination.

BORJAS and MINCER (1978) are two important papers that set out a theoretical framework for analysing migration decisions. Borjas considers the migration decisions of individuals, while Mincer emphasizes the role of the family as the basic decision making unit. Borjas' work emphasizes that migration decisions and the pattern of migration, that is whether migrants are more skilled (positively selected) or less skilled (negatively selected) depends on a comparison of the wage distribution in the two locations. This analysis has led to controversial discussions on whether migrants are less skilled or more skilled as compared to domestic workers, and whether the net contribution of migrants to the host region is positive. BORJAS, FREEMAN & KATZ provide empirical evidence on this issue.

ARJUN SINGH BEDI

See also Human capital, Labour market, Unemployment, Wages

Labour market

Borooah, V.K. and M. Hart (guest editors), special issue on "Labour Market Outcomes and Economic Exclusion", *Regional Studies*, 29/5 (1995): 433–87

Freedman, M., "The Search for Shelters" in *Work, Employment and Unemployment: Perspectives on Work and Society*, edited by Kenneth Thompson, Milton Keynes: Open University Press, 1984

Green, A.E., M.G. Coombes and D.W. Owen, "Gender-specific Local Labour Market Areas in England and Wales", *Geoforum*, 17/3 (1986): 339–51

Green, A.E. and D.W. Owen, "Ethnic Minority Groups in Regional and Local Labour Markets in Britain: A Review of Data Sources and Associated Issues", *Regional Studies*, 29/8 (1995): 729–35

Haughton, G. and J. Peck (guest editors), special issue on "Geographies of Labour Market Governance", *Regional Studies*, 30/4 (1996): 319–441

Lee, R., Labour Market entry in *The Dictionary of Human Geography*, 3rd edition, edited by R.J. Johnston, Derek Gregory and David M. Smith, Oxford and Cambridge, Massachusetts: Blackwell, 1994

Layard, Richard, Stephen Nickell and Richard Jackman, *Unemployment: Macroeconomic Performance, and the Labour Market*, Oxford and New York: Oxford University Press, 1991

Pahl, R.E., *Divisions of Labour*, Oxford and New York: Blackwell, 1984

Rifkin, Jeremy, *The End of Work: The Decline of the Global Labor Force and the Dawn of the Post-Market Era*, New York: Putnam, 1995

Storper, M. and A.J. Scott, "Work Organization and Local Labour Markets in an Era of Flexible Production", *International Labour Review*, 129/5 (1990): 573–91

Thompson, Kenneth, (editor), *Work, Employment and Unemployment: Perspectives on Work and Society*, Milton Keynes: Open University Press, 1984

Thompson, P., "The Labour Process and Deskilling" in *Work, Employment and Unemployment: Perspectives on Work and Society*, edited by Kenneth Thompson, Milton Keynes: Open University Press, 1984

LEE defines a labour market as "a mechanism whereby labour power is exchanged for the material conditions of its reproduction". This inclusive definition links labour markets directly to the study of work, employment, and unemployment. More exclusively, labour markets refer to discrete spatially bounded areas within which the workforce is located. These areas may be considered at a variety of levels but are discussed most frequently in a regional or metropolitan context. A number of distinct subgroups within the wider labour market have been identified and much research focuses on specific issues related to the operation and performance of these distinct submarkets.

PAHL's historical account distinguishes between different forms of work and different categories of worker by tracing the emergence of a division of labour based on gender back to the 17th-century household. This probably ranks as the earliest formal recognition of labour markets. The emphasis on households continues to the contemporary era, where he notices a process of polarization between households that have an increasing proportion of multiple wage and salary earners and those that have no work. This identification of an underclass, or socially excluded group, has added a new dimension to the recent study of labour markets. Pahl concludes that capitalism, through uneven development and a shift to consumption, plays an important role in shaping households and thus the labour markets of the future.

A volume of contributions edited by K. THOMPSON illustrates the broadening focus in the sociology of work to take account of relations between work, economic processes, and class division. Two contributors in particular highlight key elements in relation to labour markets. FREEDMAN introduces the concept of distinctions within the labour market based on occupational and industrial differentiation. Noticing the rapid growth of employment in the service sector she distinguishes growing occupational groups from each other and demonstrates that a segmentation, rather than a duality, of the labour market might emerge. Linked to this is a chapter by P. THOMPSON that highlights a potential struggle in the labour process where the labour force becomes deskilled as a result of external shifts in the size and nature of labour markets. He views deskilling as an attempt by capital to dominate labour but asserts that this can never completely occur.

One of the recurring themes in labour market research is unemployment. LAYARD, NICKELL & JACKMAN provide an economist's view of this phenomenon. Their book is quite accessible to non-specialists, at least in the lengthy and useful overview section. To fully understand unemployment they propose a detailed microanalysis of labour markets in combination with a macroeconomic perspective. They develop a single integrated model of the labour market that explains both the stock and flows of unemployed people as well as the processes of wage and price inflation.

If one accepts that the global economy is one large labour market then one must consider the views put forward by RIFKIN who, in a most thought-provoking contribution, identifies the influence of technology on the labour force, past, present, and future. The impact of the new information society, increasing automation and post-Fordism are portrayed as the third Industrial Revolution. Exploring the potential demise of farmers, blue-collar and service workers as a direct result of the revolution described above, he identifies the unequal impacts these changes will have on the global labour market. The labour market of the future may find itself in what Rifkin terms the postmarket era, where working weeks are shorter, relations with government are changed, and a new third sector based on community bonds will emerge.

The gender specificity of individual labour markets is uncovered by GREEN, COOMBES & OWEN who explore the concept of local labour market areas (LLMA) and differentials in journeys to work by gender in England and Wales. Defining boundaries for labour markets is a primary concern and the issue of self containment within travel-to-work areas (TTWA) is considered, with evidence for increasing differentiation of the male and female TTWAs described. Another aspect of labour markets considered by GREEN & OWEN is that of ethnicity. In a review of data sources and issues related to ethnic minority groups in British labour markets they identify the Labour Force Survey (LFS) as the richest source of labour market information available on British minorities and highlight the diverse range of labour market subjects covered by the survey. The authors also identify weaknesses with the available data in their current form.

STORPER & SCOTT analyse labour market changes resulting from the shift from Fordist mass production systems to the more flexible forms of production found in the post-Fordist era. They focus on labour relations, labour flexibility, and the security of labour within local labour markets. Key aspects of labour market research linked to changes in the limits of local labour market flexibility and changes in the location of flexible production are examined. The authors continue by identifying three types of flexible production complex in North America and Europe: flexible specialization, high-technology production complexes, and business and financial service complexes. They conclude by investigating the problems that these new forms of production generate and the policy responses to those problems.

BOROOAH & HART edited a special issue of the journal *Regional Studies* on labour market outcomes and social exclusion. The editors emphasize the fact that the analysis of issues associated with exclusion is increasingly defining the research agenda of social scientists. The special issue also contains valuable contributions by Kennedy, Forsythe, Perrons and Borooah, McGregor & McKee. These examine three themes within contemporary labour market analysis: unemployment, male joblessness, and women and the labour market. The various papers examine subgroups within the labour market, focusing on the economic exclusion of each group with particular reference to regional differentiation.

Another special issue of *Regional Studies*, edited by HAUGHTON & PECK is concerned with forms of labour market governance and is based on "a conviction that the analysis of labour markets is inseparable from a consideration of the complex of institutional forms, patterns of governance and processes of social regulation that together constitute its underpinning" (p.319). The volume contains a series of eight papers written by a variety of researchers, all well known and respected in the field. Examples are drawn from labour markets in places as geographically diverse as Australia, Canada, South Africa, and the European Union. The themes cover a spectrum of topics related to the governance of labour markets in contemporary society. As such the collection makes for an excellent starting point for anybody interested in learning more about the complex operation and dynamism of labour markets.

DAN O'DONOGHUE

See also High performance work systems, Natural rate of unemployment and NAIRU, Unemployment

Labour market flexibility

Atkinson, John A. and N. Meagher, *Changing Work Patterns*, London: NEDO, 1986

Beaumont, Peter B., "The United States HRM Literature: A Review" in *Human Resource Strategies*, edited by Graeme Salaman *et al.*, London and Newbury Park, California: Sage, 1992

Beer, Michael, Russell A. Eisenstat and Bert Spector, *The Critical Path to Corporate Renewal*, Boston: Harvard Business School Press, 1990

Blank, Rebecca M., "The Misdiagnosis of Eurosclerosis", *American Prospect*, 30 (1997): 81–85

Blyton, Paul and Jonathan Morris (editors), *A Flexible Future? Prospects for Employment and Organization*, Berlin and New York: de Gruyter, 1991

Boyer, Robert (editor), *The Search for Labour-market Flexibility: The European Economies in Transition*, Oxford: Clarendon Press, and New York: Oxford University Press, 1988 (French edition 1986)

Dastmalchian, Ali and Paul Blyton, "Organizational Flexibility in Cross-national Perspective: An Introduction", *International Journal of Human Resource Management*, 9/3 (1998): 437–44

Keenoy, Tom, "Human Resource Management: Rhetoric, Reality and Contradiction", *International Journal of Human Resource Management*, 1/3 (1990): 363–84

Mayne, Lesley, Mireia Valverde, Chris Brewster and Rudiger Kabst (editors), special issue on "New Developments in Labour Flexibility", *Employee Relations*, 19/6 (1997): 503–608

Piore, Michael and Charles F. Sabel, *The Second Industrial Divide: Possibilities for Prosperity*, New York: Basic Books, 1984

Pollert, Anna, *Farewell to Flexibility*, Oxford and Cambridge, Massachusetts: Blackwell, 1991

Rojot, Jean and Paul Tergeist, *New Directions in Work Organizations*, Paris: OECD, 1992

Solow, Robert, "What Is Labour Market Flexibility? What Is it Good For?", Keynes Lecture in Economics, *Proceedings of the British Academy*, 97 (1997): 189–211

Williams, Alan, *Human Resource Management and Labour Market Flexibility: Some Current Theories and Controversies*, Aldershot: Avebury, 1993

WILLIAMS suggests that the concept of labour market flexibility (LMF) has defied attempts dating back to the 1980s to give it a single and all-embracing definition. While it now stands part of the rhetoric of management and is continuously identified as a central component of human resource management (HRM) by commentators. DASTMALCHIAN & BLYTON argue that considerable conceptual imprecision still surrounds the term often compounded by an element of contradiction.

At the level of practice, according to ROJOT & TERGEIST, labour market flexibility is a variety of functional techniques that employers use to maximize the increased efficiency of the labour contribution to the strategic purposes of the organization. It is a view that would find a significant level of concurrence with BEER, EISENSTAT & SPECTOR, within the qualifying assumption that the modern industrial organization

is really a network of stakeholders, who have a common interest in change. In the American case, BEAUMONT suggests, LMF is thus a natural consequence of the structural shifts described in the US literature, in which firms moved from traditional personnel management practices toward HRM models strongly influenced by notions of incremental change and the identification of common goals and congruent organizational values.

In turn ATKINSON & MEAGHER writing from the British perspective adapted the notion of LMF as an internalization process in which the firm sought a flexible balance of interests linked by common needs as the first step toward a competitive response to the structural changes taking place in the world of business.

Such arguments carry a strongly deterministic tone and it is the idea of LMF as a logical response to organizational needs for increased market competitiveness within the firm in particular that aroused a considerable and countervailing responses from KEENOY, POLLERT, and the authors in BLYTON & MORRIS and other scholars working in the UK. They reflect very considerable cultural differences with regard to the central notion of conjoint and common interest, which emerge from quite different historical traditions of labour market regulation.

The notion of LMF as a reaction to organizational change takes on a deeper dimension in the work of PIORE & SABEL, they see serious discontinuities in not only the organization but the nature of industrial processes. The notion of discontinuity implies a sharp break in the conventional evolutionary development of industrial progress. They propose an industrial world where small high-technology operations stand cheek-by-jowl with large ones. More importantly and from an LMF perspective, all operational labour market practices are found to be radically different from mainstream and standardized divisions of labour. What emerges in the final analysis is a pattern of largely decentralized economies that house a number of highly regionalized production systems, all of which have a balance of both industrial continuity and discontinuity.

The concept of discontinuity finds further modification in the approach of the French regulationist school of which BOYER is an exemplar. The Marxist assumption that capitalist regimes of accumulation are unable to sustain themselves in the long run is given emblematic identity in the notion of "Fordism" as the most developed form of mass production for mass consumption.

The focus of further analysis has become the social and economic dynamics of "post-Fordist" accumulation, which implies the need to accommodate individual autonomy over the control of work processes. Regulationist scholars thus face a problematic agenda on which they try to discover whether changes imply a response to organizational needs imposed by technological imperatives, or a genuine attempt to redefine the employer–employee relationship?

In a recent introduction to a special issue of *Employee Relations*, MAYNE *et al.* suggest that while there have been considerable changes involving LMF in Europe, traditional practices remain in many countries. They go on to argue that the nature, extent, and motivation for LMF vary from country to country, and that the national context, rather than organizational size or location of sector has more predictive power. There is also little evidence of the impact of legislation as a shaping force. Both highly regulated as well as less-regulated countries reveal similar patterns of levels of adoption as well as rates of increase.

SOLOW in turn notes the lack of correlation between the introduction of LMF and the level of employment. He argues that the introduction of LMF, in the neoliberal policy sense, has done little to resolve one of the original problems that LMF was intended to address. The significant and negative employment effects of excessive and regulative forms of wage and condition settlements leading to the production of high cost rigidities and insider-outsider problems for employers.

Using the growing income inequalities being experienced by the US labour markets as background evidence, BLANK observes that where wage inequality has grown it has been to the advantage of the skilled and the disadvantage of the unskilled. By contrast the US has experienced an actual decline in real wages for all workers. She concludes that the presumption of a diametrical conflict between LMF and labour market regulation in terms of positive employment outcomes does not hold in all cases.

It is clear that the question of the strategic and operational validity of LMF remains highly problematic, and questions of definition, universality of application, and the impact of particular national experiences as qualifiers offering exceptions to any attempt at normative rules will remain subjects of lively debate in the future.

ALAN WILLIAMS

See also High performance work systems

Labour parties

Beer, Samuel H., *Modern British Politics: A Study of Parties and Pressure Groups*, London: Faber, 1965; 3rd edition 1982

Braunthal, Julius, *History of the International*, 3 vols, New York: Praeger, and London: Gollancz, 1967–80

Cole, G.D.H., *A History of Socialist Thought*, vol. 3: *The Second International*, London: Macmillan, and New York, St Martin's Press, 1960

Esping-Andersen, Gøsta, *Politics against Markets: The Social Democratic Road to Power*, Princeton, New Jersey: Princeton University Press, 1985

Fox Piven, Frances (editor), *Labor Parties in Post-Industrial Societies*, Cambridge: Polity Press, 1991; New York: Oxford University Press, 1992

Joll, James, *The Second International, 1889–1914*, 2nd edition, London and Boston: Routledge and Kegan Paul, 1974

Korpi, Walter, *The Working Class in Welfare Capitalism: Work, Unions and Politics in Sweden*, London and Boston: Routledge and Kegan Paul, 1978

Michels, Robert, *Political Parties: A Sociological Study of the Oligarchical Tendencies of Modern Democracy*, New Brunswick, New Jersey: Transaction, 1999 (originally published 1915)

Sassoon, Donald, *One Hundred Years of Socialism: The West European Left in the Twentieth Century*, London and New York: Tauris, 1996

Scase, Richard, *Social Democracy in Capitalist Society: Working-class Politics in Britain and Sweden*, London: Croom Helm, and Totowa, New Jersey: Rowman and Littlefield, 1977

JOLL provides a concise account of the Second International, the loose federation of socialist and labour parties founded in 1889. It focuses on the ideological milieu salient to its foundation and the subsequent controversies that divided its affiliates from and within each other with respect to revisionism, nationalism, and war. The author also devotes one of his longest chapters to the struggle with the anarchists. His account ends with the disintegration of the Second International in 1914. COLE is part of the author's multi-volume history of socialist thought. Despite its title it provides much more than a guide to the doctrinal development of the International and its affiliated parties. The origins and seminal experiences of the labour and socialist parties receive detailed attention and the range of Cole's coverage is truly international, with separate chapters on many of the parties of North and South America, Australasia, Japan, and Asia, as well as the European continent. BRAUNTHAL is also an indispensable handbook for students of labour parties. It provides a summary of the activities of all the principal parties of world socialism up to 1968, including the communists, and covers all the main attempts to give international coordination to the work of the Left. SASSOON is the most recent of these comprehensive source books, contributing an immensely detailed narrative focused on the West European Left. It is the best reference work for the student of labour and socialist governments in Western Europe since 1945.

Robert Michels produced a classic of political analysis in his study of the pre-1914 Social Democratic Party of Germany (SPD), the Marxist party that dominated the Second International and stood as a role model for revolutionaries and reformists alike. In MICHELS he formulates and seeks to justify his iron law of oligarchy, which maintains that democracy and large-scale organisation are incompatible. Michels focuses on the socialists, partly because of the author's own personal experience of membership of the SPD; but also because he knew that his thesis would acquire additional force if it could be shown that the parties most committed to the extension of democracy were themselves subject to irresistible oligarchical tendencies. This work has been the model for many subsequent analyses of party organisation.

BEER is a minor classic. It concerns the transformations in British political parties that created the two-party system, which prevailed in the twenty years following World War II. The section on the Labour Party begins with the decisions and issues that affected its origins, but Beer is especially stimulating when explaining the effects and consequences of the party's later decision to embrace socialism. In the author's view, the party's commitment to gradualist revolution ruled out the old cooperative relationship with the Liberal Party. Beer also emphasizes the immense growth of trade unionism in the years 1910–20 in influencing this sense of independent power, and the strong sense of class that propelled the "movement" to seek its conquest in the form of governmental office. The embrace of "socialism" is seen as an effect of this "thrust for power". While Michels gives reasons to doubt the feasibility of anything other than a very bureaucratic form of socialism, Beer sees socialism as an ideology of labour parties that loses its utility, at least for leaders, once power has been won. Hence the crisis of identity which, according to Beer, afflicted the Labour Party in Britain immediately following its greatest triumph of 1945–51.

The Swedish Social Democratic Party (SAP) was widely regarded as the most successful labour party by the 1960s and consequently attracted enormous attention as a model for others. SCASE draws on empirical survey research to examine the impact of the organized labour movements in Britain and Sweden in shaping the sociopolitical orientations of manual workers in the two countries. While the author found no evidence that Sweden had less class inequality than Britain, he concluded that the institutions of the labour movement enjoyed greater legitimacy and exerted a bigger cultural influence than their counterparts in Britain. He also argued that the explicit and concerted egalitarian aims of the SAP and the Swedish manual unions were stronger than those of British labour and had evoked a correspondingly explicit commitment to equality among Swedish workers. Scase also argued that the power of capital had been considerably moderated in Sweden by the organized power of labour, not least because of 34 years of continuous social democratic government since 1932.

Chief among the reforms of this period was the "welfare state", something that was associated with labour and social democratic parties throughout Western Europe, but especially in Scandinavia where the system was more comprehensive and generous than elsewhere. ESPING-ANDERSEN and KORPI provide imaginative analyses of these institutions, linking them to goals of social solidarity, equality, and rights of social citizenship (goals that were long advocated by labour parties), while showing that movement towards these objectives strengthened the parties in question by providing them with certain "power resources". By the late 1970s many commentators perceived the Scandianvian democracies as the best examples of countries in which full employment, high levels of trade union density, ever-present social democratic government, and the institutions of the welfare state had provided cumulative assets for labour in its contest with capital. Korpi and Esping-Andersen reflect a widespread view of the period that, at least in Sweden, further movement towards a socialist society was a distinct possibility.

The collection of essays edited by FOX PIVEN – covering England, France, Germany, Sweden, Israel, Canada, and the United States – is representative of the very different view of labour politics that came to prevail in the 1990s after the collapse of communism and ten years of renascent neoliberalism. The century-old focus on capturing the power of the nation state as citizens, and exerting power in industry as trade unionists, is now seen as problematic. The contemporary world no longers fits the old strategy as capitalism restructures and disperses globally. Labour parties now grapple with the decay of their class and occupational strongholds, their policy instruments, and belief systems in the face of postindustrialism.

JOHN CALLAGHAN

See also Centre-left, Parliamentary socialism, Revisionism

Labour Party (UK)

Coates, David, *The Labour Party and the Struggle for Socialism*, Cambridge: Cambridge University Press, 1975

Drucker, H.M., *Doctrine and Ethos in the Labour Party*, London and Boston: Allen and Unwin, 1979

Harmar, H.J.P., *The Longman Companion to the Labour Party, 1900–1998*, Harlow, Essex: Longman, 1999

Howell, David, *British Social Democracy: A Study in Development and Decay*, 2nd edition, London: Croom Helm, and New York: St Martin's Press, 1980

Kavanagh, Dennis, *The Politics of the Labour Party*, London and Boston: Allen and Unwin, 1982

McHenry, Dean E., *The Labour Party in Transition, 1931–1938*, London: Routledge, 1938

McKibbin, Ross, *The Evolution of the Labour Party 1910–1924*, Oxford: Oxford University Press, 1974

Miliband, Ralph, *Parliamentary Socialism: A Study in the Politics of Labour*, London: Allen and Unwin, 1961; New York: Monthly Review Press, 1964

Minkin, Lewis, *The Labour Party Conference*, 2nd edition, Manchester: Manchester University Press, 1980

Minkin, Lewis, *The Contentious Alliance: Trades Unions and the Labour Party*, Edinburgh: Edinburgh University Press, 1991

Morgan, Kenneth O., *Labour in Power, 1945–51*, Oxford: Clarendon Press, 1984

Morgan, Kenneth O., *Labour People: Leaders and Lieutenants, Hardie to Kinnock*, Oxford and New York: Oxford University Press, 1987

Pelling, Henry and Alastair J. Reid, *A Short History of the Labour Party*, 11th edition, Basingstoke and New York: Macmillan, 1996

Pimlott, Ben, *Labour and the Left in the 1930s*, Cambridge and New York: Cambridge University Press, 1977

Shaw, Eric, *The Labour Party since 1979: Crisis and Transformation*, London and New York: Routledge, 1994

Tanner, Duncan, *Political Change and the Labour Party, 1900–1918*, Cambridge and New York: Cambridge University Press, 1990

Thorpe, Andrew, *A History of the British Labour Party*, Basingstoke: Macmillan, and New York: St Martin's Press, 1997

The British Labour Party has been the subject of numerous books. Any survey of the literature on this particular topic is necessarily superficial and partial. PELLING & REID is perhaps the most famous of the general historical surveys into the origins, development, and life of the organization. A more recent addition to the literature is THORPE. Both detail how the Party was formally launched in the early 20th century as an at times uneasy alliance between the burgeoning trades union movement, socialist activists, and an assortment of radical progressives. The books also provide an assessment of how the Party has fared in terms of its often-fluctuating electoral and governmental fortunes. Both studies end in the 1990s.

In addition to the titles above and the many other introductory texts, HARMER offers a comprehensive and fact-filled guide to many aspects of the Party's history, policies, organization, and performance. Leading Labour politicians have been the subject of many biographical accounts. In his useful overview MORGAN (1987) offers a useful introduction to some of the most important personalities as well as some of the lesser known but nevertheless influential actors.

In his important study of how Labour emerged to challenge for governmental office McKIBBIN places emphasis on the role of the trades union movement in facilitating this process both in terms of organization and through the promotion of the Party as a vehicle for working-class political aspirations. This thesis provided an influential rejoinder to the view that Labour's emergence can be explained by the negative impact of World War I on the fortunes of the once electorally dominant Liberal Party. Rather than concentrating on any particular theory to explain the growth of Labour as a political force TANNER offers a comprehensive and multifaceted account of how the Party emerged, not least as a force at the level of localized politics.

PIMLOTT assesses the fallout from the party's two brief periods of government that ended in the defection of leader and Prime Minister Ramsay MacDonald and the serious electoral setback that was the landslide defeat of 1931. The book offers an insight into the various strands of thought both within and around the party. The organization is situated as a largely marginalized force during a decade of profound social and economic change. Nonetheless the study identifies actors like Hugh Dalton, who would come to exert such an influence over the groundbreaking Labour governments of the immediate postwar era. Less a study of the party's intellectual development during the same period, American observer McHENRY offers a useful and painstaking analysis of Labour as a political and bureaucratic organization.

The impact and legacy of the 1945–51 Labour governments underpin most postwar analyses of the Party either implicitly or explicitly. MORGAN (1984) offers a sympathetic appraisal of the achievements of Prime Minister Clement Attlee and his colleagues who, in a politically difficult and economically austere environment, significantly transformed and extended the British state's remit in the arenas of industrial and social policy. By contrast Marxist scholars like MILIBAND have offered a sustained critique of what he identified as the timidity and 'sickness of labourism'. In his famous attack the author pinpointed the party's deferential attitude to the established order, its "parliamentary socialism", as a serious barrier to it effecting radical change. The approach of the author influenced successive academics such as COATES and HOWELL in their respective works on later Labour governments, most notably those led by Harold Wilson in the 1960s and 1970s.

The fractious nature of the Party, which became so apparent during the Wilson leadership, is discussed by MINKIN (1980) in his thorough and painstaking account of how the Party conference, what Attlee once called the "parliament of the movement", works. The study discusses how the myriad of trade union affiliates, supporting socialist societies, ordinary local members, and parliamentarians coalesce to discuss and debate issues at the Party's annual meeting. The book demonstrates how the federal organization of the Party, embodied in the conference and its National Executive Committee, can and does enable challenges to the will of even the most determined Labour leadership.

DRUCKER accounts for the way in which the Party, born of extra-parliamentary struggle, historically differed from its main rivals. In doing so the author identifies what he terms Labour's own "doctrine and ethos", a disposition that attaches particular importance to the retention of democracy and accountability within the organization. The explosion of debate within the party that characterized the uncomfortable and fraught years of the Callaghan government forms the backdrop to the collection of essays edited by KAVANAGH. Contributors offer analysis on the Party's declining fortunes. In his final published work McKenzie, a leading student of British political parties, revisits an earlier discussion of Labour to attack what he believes to be the incompatibility between the Party's commitment to internal as well parliamentary democracy.

Labour's prolonged spell in opposition to the Thatcher and Major governments provoked a serious and wide-ranging reassessment of political strategy within the Party. Central to this process were those influential allies within the affiliate trades union movement. MINKIN (1991) explores the evolving and changing Party–union relationship, taking care to show how the simplistic view of the unions as a bloc vote controlling the Party misunderstands the very real political differences which exist between different affiliates. SHAW provides a thorough assessment of how the Kinnock leadership sought to reinvent the party during the 1980s and early 1990s. Consideration is given to the restructuring of the bureaucracy as well as the reformulation of policy, changes that culminated in providing the conditions that facilitated the election of Tony Blair as leader in 1994.

DOMINIC WRING

See also New Labour

Labour process

Braverman, Harry, *Labor and Monopoly Capital: The Degradation of Work in the Twentieth Century*, New York: Monthly Review Press, 1974

Burawoy, Michael, *Manufacturing Consent: Changes in the Labor Market under Monopoly Capitalism*, Chicago: Chicago University Press, 1979

Edwards, Richard, *Contested Terrain: The Transformation of the Workplace in the Twentieth Century*, London: Heinemann, and New York: Basic Books, 1979

Felstead, Alan and Nick Jewson, *Global Trends in Flexible Labour*, Basingstoke: Macmillan, 1999

Friedman, Andrew L., *Industry and Labour: Class Struggle at Work and Monopoly Capitalism*, London: Macmillan, 1977

Jermier, John M., David Knights and Walter R. Nord (editors), *Resistance and Power in Organisations*, London and New York: Routledge, 1994

Knights, David and Hugh Willmott (editors), *Labour Process Theory*, Basingstoke: Macmillan, 1990

Littler, Craig R., *The Development of the Labour Process in Capitalist Societies*, London: Heinemann, 1982

Littler, Craig R., "The Labour Process Debate: A Theoretical Overview, 1974–1988" in *Labour Process Theory*, edited by David Knights and Hugh Willmott, Basingstoke: Macmillan, 1990

Marx, Karl, *Capital*, vol. 1: *A Critical Analysis of Capitalist Production*, London and New York: Penguin, 1976 (German edition 1867)

Meiksins, Peter, "Labor and Monopoly Capital for the 1990s", *Monthly Review*, 46/6 (1994): 45–59

Smith, Chris and Paul Thompson "Re-Evaluating the Labour Process Debate", *Economic and Industrial Democracy*, 19/4 (1998): 551–77

Taylor, Frederick Winslow, *Scientific Management: Comprising Shop Management, The Principles of Scientific Management, and Testimony before the Special House Committee*, New York: Harper, 1947

Teulings, A.W.M., "Managerial Labour Processes in Organised Capitalism: The Power of Corporate Management and the Powerlessness of the Manager" in *Managing the Labour Process*, edited by David Knights and Hugh Willmott, Aldershot, Hampshire: Gower, 1986

Thompson, Paul and Chris Warhurst, *Workplaces of the Future*, Basingstoke: Macmillan, 1998

Thompson, Paul, *The Nature of Work: An Introduction to Debates on the Labour Process*, 2nd edition, Basingstoke: Macmillan, 1989

Thompson, Paul and David McHugh, *Work Organizations: A Critical Introduction*, 3rd edition, Basingstoke: Macmillan, 2000

Warhurst, Chris, "Recognising the Possible: The Organisation and Control of a Socialist Labour Process", *Administrative Science Quarterly*, 43/2 (1998): 470–97

Warhurst, Christopher, *Between Market, State and Kibbutz: The Management and Transformation of Socialist Industry*, London: Mansell, 1999

Williams, Karel, John Williams and Colin Haslam, "Do Labour Costs Really Matter?", *Work, Employment and Society*, 3/3 (1989): 281–305

Zimbalist, Andrew (editor), *Case Studies on the Labor Process*, New York: Monthly Review Press, 1979

The labour process is sometimes loosely termed "work organization". The starting point for discussion of the labour process is MARX. It is defined by Marx as consisting of three elements: the act of working, a predefined subject being worked upon (a good or service), and the physical instruments by which the first element creates the second: "In the labour process, therefore, man's activity, with the help of the instruments of labour, effects an alteration, designed from the commencement, in the material worked upon" (p.160). That which is produced can either be useful in supporting human existence and so have a "use value" or it can be traded and attain an "exchange value". The latter value, of course, presupposes the former. As a consequence of humans wanting to improve their material condition, a surplus is generated within the labour processes, that is an enhancement of the value between inputs and outputs. Labour processes exist in all societies, capitalist or socialist, and it is argued that the organization and control of a labour process is indicative of the type of society within which it exists. Analysing the labour process therefore creates an under-standing of that society – or mode of production. (A mode of production reflects political economy and thus the logic governing the production, exchange, and distribution of goods and services.) It is within the labour process that surplus is generated and, moreover, appropriated, thereafter to be distributed according to the form of ownership and control of the means of production. The labour process is thus important for two reasons; it ensures the material and ideological reproduction of a mode of production. Control of the labour process ensures that reproduction.

WARHURST (1999) describes the organization and control of labour processes within socialism. Most writers focus on labour processes within capitalism. Within capitalism, control is manifest in a managerial prerogative (however moderated) to direct, evaluate, discipline, and reward labour, and is codified in an employment relationship based on an "effort-reward" bargain. Here labour is subordinated and exploited; controlled to yield the desired output and deprived of the full exchange value of that output. THOMPSON offers a core theory of the labour process within capitalism. The practical reasons for management's inordinate concern with the labour process can be found in WILLIAMS, WILLIAMS & HASLAM and TEULINGS.

Although Marx was writing in the 19th century about the labour process, debate about the importance of the labour process arose from the mid-1970s. With the publication in 1974 of *Labor and Monopoly Capital* by BRAVERMAN accounts of paid work began to be discussed in relation to capitalism as a mode of production. The book's appeal, suggests LITTLER (1990, p.47), was the provision of an easy-to-understand, apparently coherent theoretical framework that linked "a range of issues and problem areas within and beyond the workplace, which had previously been seen as unrelated." In so doing, labour process analysis provided a paradigmatic shift from analyses of the social relations *in* production (or relations among organizational actors) that generally characterized post-war (what was then termed "industrial") sociology in the UK and US to the explicit recognition of a relationship between the organization and control of the labour process and the social relations *of* production (or class relations). That is, subordinating and exploitative, managerial organization and control of the labour process was necessary and indicative of capitalist production, and reproduction as a mode of production.

Analysis of the labour process quickly became a cross-disciplinary concern of the sociology of work and employment, organization studies, industrial relations (latterly, human resource management), and management and business studies. A UK-based conference drawing together radical academics from these disciplines from around the world was then organized, with the *18th Annual International Labour Process Conference* hosted in 2000. Many of the empirical case studies presented at this conference later appear as articles in the UK journal *Work Employment and Society*. Published in turn by Gower, Routledge, and Macmillan, a series of edited books (on, for example, white-collar work, job redesign, total quality management, and Japanization) have appeared after these conferences, the latest and complementary pair being those of FELSTEAD & JEWSON, which analyses new labour markets, and THOMPSON & WARHURST, which assesses new forms of work organization. A textbook-type publication on the labour process (Thompson's *The Nature of Work*) – has a complement in THOMPSON & McHUGH.

It is the case studies that have mainly driven labour process analysis subsequent to Braverman however. Braverman focused on TAYLOR's promotion of deskilling through scientific management which "represented the explicit verbalization" (p.86) of capitalism everywhere. The first significant case study evidence to support Braverman's claim appeared in the edited case studies of ZIMBALIST and represents a good starting point for understanding how deskilling effected paid work at that time. Subsequent case studies challenged this argument and are likewise still important for their conceptual points. This evidence, provided by FRIEDMAN, BURAWOY, EDWARDS, and LITTLER (1982), basically demonstrated that other forms of organization and control exist and that these forms can vary across both time and countries. A first systematic attempt to engage the range of omissions and weaknesses occurred with *Labour Process Theory* edited by KNIGHTS & WILLMOTT. This book provides chapters on such labour process issues as technology, gender, and the state. One of the more forceful criticisms made here of Braverman is his failure to articulate workers' subjective experience of control by the managerial agents of capital, and it is this issue that has dominated labour process conference and debate in recent years. One of the post-conference books was explicitly dedicated to this issue (JERMIER, KNIGHT & NORD). However, the insertion of subjectivity by these authors has reduced the analysis to a situationalism that resonates with pre-labour process analysis industrial sociology and its concern with the social relations in production, though now disguised as an examination of individual identity. It also obviates the radical project for the collective emancipation or at least amelioration of the condition of labour advanced by Braverman.

Although few do it, Braverman and Taylor should be read as primary sources; certainly the latter provides wonderful quotations from his conversations with workers at the beginning of the 20th century that today both amuse and shock students. The US journal *Monthly Review*, of which Braverman was the editor before his death, published a "twenty years after" edition in 1994, which outlines *Labor and Monopoly Capital's* contribution to understanding past and current trends in the labour process. Among others here MEIKSINS' contribution is particularly useful as an update. Short reviews of the conceptual development of labour process analysis, its omissions, and weaknesses, can be found across WARHURST (1998 and 1999). Responding to suggested conceptual shifts away from labour process analysis and the recent restructuring of the labour process itself, SMITH & THOMPSON continue to assert the importance of labour process analysis. A synthesis of this recent literature suggests that analysing the labour process requires an awareness of the dynamic and interactive relationship of political economy representative of modes of production, national business systems, sectoral best practices and firm-specific organization, and that the labour process itself remains an important analytical focus in understanding the nature and development of capitalist (and any) society.

CHRIS WARHURST

Labour theory of value

Bortkiewicz, A. von, "On the Correction of Marx's Fundamental Theoretical Construction in the Third Volume of *Capital*" in *Karl Marx and the Close of His System*, by Eugen Böhm-Bawerk, New York: Kelley, 1949 (article first published 1907)

Krause, Ulrich, *Money and Abstract Labour: On the Analytical Foundations of Political Economy*, London: NLB, 1982

Marx, Karl, *Capital: A Critique of Political Economy*, vols 1 and 3, London and New York: Penguin, 1976–81 (German edition 1867–94)

Ricardo, David, "On the Principles of Political Economy and Taxation" in *The Works and Correspondence of David Ricardo*, edited by Piero Sraffa and M.H. Dobb, vol. 1, Cambridge: Cambridge University Press, 1951 (1st edition 1817; 3rd edition 1821) 6/diminishing returns

Sen, Amartya, "On the Labour Theory of Value: Some Methodological Issues", *Cambridge Journal of Economics*, 2 (1978): 175–90

Sinha, Ajit, "A Critique of Part One of *Capital* vol. 1: The Value Controversy Revisited" in *Latest Developments in Marxist Theory*, a special issue of *Research in Political Economy* (1996): 195–222

Sraffa, Piero, Introduction in *The Works and Correspondence of David Ricardo*, edited by Piero Sraffa and M.H. Dobb, vol. 1, Cambridge: Cambridge University Press, 1951

Steedman, Ian, *Marx after Sraffa*, London: NLB, 1977

Steedman, Ian (editor), *The Value Controversy*, London: NLB, 1981

The labour theory of value (LTV) was first developed by David RICARDO in his classic work the *Principles*. Before Ricardo, Adam Smith in the *Wealth of Nations* (1776) had argued that the exchange ratio of commodities would be equal to the ratio of labour time needed to produce the commodities in a classless society of labourers only. In a society divided into landlords, capitalists, and labourers, this rule of exchange would not remain valid because labourers will have to share the total produce with the other two classes. Ricardo argued that Smith was wrong in abandoning the LTV in the context of capitalist society. The rule of exchange, according to the LTV, is not violated due to the division of net income into wages, profits, and rents. It, however, needs to be "modified" due to differences in the "time structure" of capitals. Ricardo argued that, in a capitalist economy, competitive forces would require a tendency for the rate of profits on capitals to be equalized. Thus, even if two commodities x and y are produced by the same amount of labour time, if it takes more time for the capital of x to circulate then 1x must exchange for more than 1y to ensure an equal rate of profits in both the sectors. Such deviations of exchange ratios from the total labour time ratios are not violation of the theory itself because the theory only claims to identify the sole cause of the variations in the exchange ratios or the "natural prices". But Ricardo had to confront the fact that once it is admitted that the exchange ratios deviate from the labour ratios, it cannot be denied that a change in the real wages would have an independent impact on the exchange ratios to ensure equal rate of profits in all sectors. This meant that the cause of change in the "natural prices" is not only the technology of production but also the changes in the distribution of the net output itself. Ricardo tried to overcome this difficulty by arguing that the changes in the natural prices due to changes in the real wages are very small, and can be safely ignored. This, of course, is not a satisfactory solution to a theoretical problem, and Ricardo shows full awareness of this.

SRAFFA, in collaboration with Maurice Dobb, gave a coherent and authoritative interpretation of Ricardo's LTV. He argued that Ricardo's concern was to establish that division of income is independent of prices. The effect of changes in distribution on the prices and thus the size of the net money income are due to the arbitrary nature of the measuring rod, as the value of the money commodity itself changes due to changes in the distribution of income. Thus, to prove the correctness of his proposition, Ricardo needed to discover the condition of production of a commodity or a composite commodity whose value will not be affected by changes in distribution. In his later work, *Production of Commodities by Means of Commodities* (1960), Sraffa constructed the Standard commodity, which remains invariant in the face of changes in distribution. This helped him to show that Ricardo's proposition that distribution of income is independent of prices is sound.

The unsatisfactory manner in which Ricardo had left his LTV was one important reason for the decline of this theory over the years. MARX saw this development as a movement away from scientific inquiry to superficiality. In *Capital* Marx tries to rehabilitate and develop the LTV much further than Ricardo had done. In part one of *Capital* volume 1 he argued that exchange ratios of commodities represent the alienated form of social labour. Every society must distribute its total labour in various activities to satisfy its needs. In a commodity-producing society, the distribution of total labour is regulated by the market. Hence the exchange ratios of commodities are reflections of the real relations of different kinds of labours with one another. In volume 3 of *Capital* (chapters ix–x), he concentrated on Ricardo's "first modification" of LTV, and tried to establish that the exchange ratio of commodities, although in general differ from the labour-value ratio, are nevertheless derived from and depend on the labour values of commodities. This he could do by deriving the uniform rate of profits as total surplus value divided by total constant and variable capital. These concepts are Marx's innovation to economic theory. On the basis of such concepts, and his uniform rate of profits, Marx was able to argue that profits represent nothing but exploitation of labour – it is an economic form of labour time extracted by the capitalists for which nothing in return was paid to the labourers. Furthermore, Marx could also argue that competition, which is responsible for the divergence of exchange ratios from their labour-value ratios, only effects a redistribution of the total surplus value among the capitalists but leaves the exploitative relation between capital and labour untouched.

BORTKIEWICZ later showed that Marx's solution to Ricardo's "first modification" was unsatisfactory because he measured capital in terms of labour-values and not prices of production. If prices diverge from values, then capital must be accounted in terms of prices and not values. Once the accounting of capital is made consistent in Marx's scheme, then it can no longer be guaranteed that total profits in the system will equal total surplus value (see entry on Transformation problem).

Following Bortkiewicz and Sraffa, STEEDMAN (1977) argued that Marx's uniform rate of profits was incorrect as it was derived on the basis of labour-value accounting, and so could not be applied to a system of accounting in terms of prices. He went on to argue that Sraffa's physical input-output system should be used to derive the correct uniform rate of profits and prices. As both labour values and Sraffa's prices and profits are derived from the same given physical input-output system, there is no point in deriving profits and prices via the route of labour values. Furthermore, there is no open avenue from labour values to profits and prices.

In STEEDMAN (1981), Gerald Cohen adds a punch to Steedman's thesis by claiming that Marx's notion of exploitation is quite independent of his concept of labour values. He argues that the mistake stems from the notion that "labour alone creates value". In the strict sense, value is not "created" by labour, since Marx defines "value" of a commodity as socially necessary labour time needed to reproduce the commodity at the time when valuation is made. Thus in the cases of technological change, as well as labours of more or less efficiency than the socially necessary level, there is no one-to-one relationship between actual labour spent in production and the value of the commodity. The correct proposition, according to Cohen, would be "The Labourer is the only person who creates the product, that which has value". As capitalists take a share of the products created by labourers, it is exploitation because it is taking something for which nothing is given in return, but this proposition does not require any so-called labour theory of value. In the same book, Anwar Shaikh defends Marx's labour values from the perspective of arguments put forward in *Capital*, volume 1. On the issue of the relation of Marx's labour values and the uniform rate of profits, Shaikh argues that although the price rate of profits diverges from value rate of profits, it can be shown that there is a monotonic relationship between the two. This, however, does not solve the basic problem of not needing labour-values to derive the price rate of profits. In separate contributions to the book, Michel De Vroey, and Himmelweit and Mohun defend Marx's labour values by arguing that value appears for a fleeting moment at the interface of production and exchange. Its relation to labour is due to production; however, it is at the point of exchange that value takes its quantitative dimension *vis-à-vis* another commodity or money. This approach obliterates the theoretical distinction between value and prices or "prices of production". Their argument is unconvincing and it leaves us with neither a theory of value nor a theory of prices of production.

Ulrich KRAUSE, in his highly mathematical book, argues that the relationship of "abstract labour" to money is the essential aspect of Marx's theory of value. He asserts that exchange between two commodities facilitated by money can be represented by an equation of two sets of concrete labours of different proportions, where these proportions are determined by both input-output structures as well as their prices. From here on Krause picks up one form of concrete labour and reduces all other forms of concrete labours in its term. This is what Krause calls "abstract labour" and he develops the value-structure of production from it. The work is of high quality, but it fails to solve any of the problems with LTV as, here, the "abstract labour" is derived from given prices rather than the other way round. One wonders what is the point of deriving "values" from given prices?

Amartya SEN argues that a theory may be developed from three different viewpoints: (a) predictive, (b) evaluative, and (c) descriptive. The LTV may not be a strong theory from the first two viewpoints. However, it is a strong theory from the descriptive point of view since it selects to focus on the most essential aspect of production – labour is the only human aspect in the (re)production of the material conditions of life.

Ajit SINHA (1996) argues that there is a break in the logic of *Capital*. Part one of *Capital*, volume 1, situates the problem of value in the context of allocation of given total labour; whereas the rest of *Capital* deals with the problem of surplus production and thus the determination of the total labour itself. He argues that Marx's strategy of uniting the two problematics through the concept of labour power being a commodity did not succeed. In this context he suggests that the defence of LTV on the basis of labour as the *cause* of value should be given up; however, labour as the *measure* of value should be entertained to capture Marx's notion of exploitation.

AJIT SINHA

See also Transformation problem

Lateral thinking

Burt, Ronald S., *Structural Holes: The Social Structure of Competition*, Cambridge, Massachusetts: Harvard University Press, 1992

Butler, Joseph, *The Analogy of Religion, Natural and Revealed, to the Constitution and Course of Nature: To Which are Added Two Brief Dissertations: 1. Of Personal Identity, 2. Of the Nature of Virtue*, New York: Ungar, 1961 (originally published 1736)

de Bono, Edward, *Lateral Thinking: A Textbook of Creativity*, London: Ward Lock, and New York: Harper and Row, 1970

Keynes, John Maynard, *A Treatise on Probability*, London: Macmillan, 1921; as vol. 8 of *The Collected Writings of John Maynard Keynes*, London: Macmillan, and New York: Cambridge University Press, 1973

Merton, Robert, *Social Theory and Social Structure*, New York: Free Press, 1968

Poni, Carlo, "Fashion as Flexible Production: The Strategies of the Lyons Silk Merchants in the Eighteenth Century" in *A World of Possibilities: Flexibility and Mass Production in Western Industrialization*, edited by Charles F. Sabel and Jonathan Zeitlin, Cambridge and New York: Cambridge University Press, 1997

Roberts, Royston M., *Serendipity: Accidental Discoveries in Science*, New York and Chichester: Wiley, 1989

Rosenberg, Nathan, "Technological Change in the Machine Tool Industry, 1840–1910", *Journal of Economic History*, 23/3 (1963): 414–43

Shackle, George Lennox Sharman, *Imagination and the Nature of Choice*, Edinburgh: Edinburgh University Press, 1979

Walpole, Horace, *Letters to Sir Horace Mann, British Envoy at the Court of Tuscany*, edited by Lord Dover, 3 vols, London: Bentley, 1833; in *The Yale Edition of Horace Walpole's Correspondence*, edited by W.S. Lewis, 48 vols, New Haven, Connecticut: Yale University Press, 1937–83

Lateral thinking is a thought process by which the discovery of a certain degree of likeness breeds the expectation of more extensive likeness. As a consequence, lateral thinking is associated with analogical reasoning and stems from a peculiar combination of similarity and variety: similarity makes identification of likeness possible, variety extends the scope of (partial) likeness and turns it into a powerful cognitive procedure.

Some anticipation of a philosophical theory of likeness may be found in BUTLER, who considered it to be at the root of analogical and probabilistic statements. KEYNES, in his *Treatise on Probability*, discussed the distinction between induction by enumeration and induction by analogy, and associated the latter with a logical procedure in which an abstract concept is "decomposed" into an essential core and a contingent cluster of characteristics. According to Keynes, this "open" structure of empirical concepts is at the root of the lateral transfer of information from one empirical context to another: the likelihood of a general proposition is greater, the greater is the variety between the different cases to which that proposition applies. Induction by enumeration presupposes complete likeness of cases and constrains any given argument to the limited field in which complete likeness may be found. On the other hand, induction by analogy presupposes, at the same time, partial likeness and variety: formation of indirect knowledge is more effective if similar characteristics are limited and empirical cases are far apart from each other.

Induction by analogy (as described by Keynes) is independent of the existence of a prior probability distribution of outcomes: indeed, the strength of a causal hypothesis reflects precisely the likelihood that improbable (and unexpected) cases be explained by the "lateral extension" of propositions concerning a limited set of essential characteristics. In this way, induction by analogy and lateral thinking comes to be associated with the measurement of novelty and the formal analysis of surprise.

More recently, the relationship between analogy, discovery, and creative thinking has been considered by DE BONO. This author has introduced a distinction between vertical and lateral thinking. Vertical thinking is a thought process by which a conclusion may be reached by a series of steps. In this case, the conclusion is acceptable if each step is justified, and a general appraisal of its informational content may be avoided. Lateral thinking is a thought process by which a new cognitive pattern is generated and new ideas are introduced. In this case, a "correct solution" may eventually be reached by steps that may be partially wrong or misguided, provided the final step generates a new and successful restructuring of information.

Lateral thinking is associated with the restructuring of cognitive patterns and creative intellectual activity. However, De Bono distinguishes lateral thinking as "the description of a process", from creativity as "too often only the description of a result" (p.11). He also argues that "[v]ertical thinking selects a pathway by excluding other pathways" (p.37), whereas "[w]ith lateral thinking one generates as many alternative approaches as one can", even "after one has found a promising [approach]" (p.37).

An important route of lateral thinking is the selection and utilization of analogies (see above). In lateral thinking, analogies are used as routes by which new ideas (pattern restructuring) may be brought about, rather than as means by which a particular causal structure may be identified.

Lateral thinking is associated with imagination, discoveries, unexpected encounters. SHACKLE maintains that imagination exerts a critical influence upon human choice since the process of "choosing" presupposes the consideration of rival options. Such options

> are the products of [the chooser's] original thought, his re-assembly, in configurations never realized in the field in its past, of the elements into which he resolves his basic scheme of that field. These re-assemblies can be rivals for the same stretch of time-to-come, but they must conform to the scheme of Nature and of human nature which he has evolved, ... they must be possible in his judgement. (p.13)

But, in Shackle's view, the relationship between imagination and choice also works the other way round. For choice reveals a "structure of intentions", and allows the chooser "to envisage as possible some desired variants of history-to-come" (p.15). In this way, choice shapes imagination and implicitly denies possibility to "imagined histories conflicting with the one in question" (p.15).

Discoveries are related with the identification of new cognitive patterns, which may lead to the restructuring of available information, and to the generation of new empirical data. In this connection, lateral thinking may be associated with serendipity, which was defined by WALPOLE as a capability or an attitude by which human beings can be "making discoveries, by accidents and sagacity, of things they were not in quest of" (letter to Mann, 28 January 1754).

Serendipity (as defined above) may be considered an important condition for discoveries in science, as well as in the generation of technical innovation and in the utilization of business opportunities. In scientific investigation, discoveries often result from successful restructuring of available information (MERTON, ROBERTS); in the diffusion of new technical practices, novelties are often associated with the "lateral" transfer of knowledge from one production process to another (or from one service activity to another) (see ROSENBERG and also PONI); in business organization, joint ventures and spinoffs may be encouraged by unexpected encounters and from the existence of "open spaces" in which social actors can meet under unusual circumstances and new proximity relationships can be detected (BURT).

Lateral thinking may be essential to the successful governance of the competitive process. In this connection, Burt has recently argued that the existence of open spaces in which the outcome of social interaction is not fully determined (structural holes) may be essential to the working of competition as a creative (rather than destructive) activity. In particular, Burt has noted that structural holes may extend the scope of possible action by enhancing the relational capabilities of social actors and reducing the degree to which competitors have to "share" the same pool of fixed resources. The criterion of the *tertius gaudens* calls attention to an important route by which competitive advantage may be derived from the ability to make effective use of external resources.

ROBERTO SCAZZIERI

See also Creativity, Innovation

Latin America: economy and economic record

Brundenius, Claes, *Revolutionary Cuba: The Challenge of Economic Growth with Equity*, Boulder, Colorado: Westview Press, 1984

Bulmer-Thomas, Victor (editor), *The New Economic Model in Latin America and Its Impact on Income Distribution and Poverty*, Basingstoke: Macmillan, and New York: St Martin's Press, 1996

Corbridge, Stuart, *Debt and Development*, Oxford and Cambridge, Massachusetts: Blackwell, 1993

Edwards, Sebastian, *Crisis and Reform in Latin America: From Despair to Hope*, Oxford and New York: Oxford University Press, 1995

Frank, Andre Gunder, *Capitalism and Underdevelopment in Latin America: Historical Studies of Chile and Brazil*, New York: Monthly Review Press, 1967

Frank, Andre Gunder, *Latin America: Underdevelopment or Revolution? Essays on the Development of Underdevelopment and the Immediate Enemy*, New York: Monthly Review Press, 1969

Furtado, Celso, *Economic Development of Latin America: A Survey from Colonial Times to the Cuban Revolution*, Cambridge: Cambridge University Press, 1970

George, Susan, *A Fate Worse than Debt*, London and New York: Penguin, 1988

Hofman, André A., *The Economic Development of Latin America in the Twentieth Century*, Aldershot, Hampshire: Elgar, 2000

Hojman, David E., *Chile: The Political Economy of Development and Democracy in the 1990s*, London: Macmillan, 1992; Pittsburgh: University of Pittsburgh Press, 1993

Iglesias, Enrique V., *Reflections on Economic Development: Toward a New Latin American Consensus*, Washington, DC: Inter-American Development Bank, 1992

Kay, Cristóbal, *Latin American Theories of Development and Underdevelopment*, London and New York: Routledge, 1989

Meller, Patricio, "Adjustment and Social Costs in Chile during the 1980s", *World Development*, 19 (1991): 1545–61

Morley, Samuel A., *Poverty and Inequality in Latin America: The Impact of Adjustment and Recovery*, Baltimore: Johns Hopkins University Press, 1995

Prebisch, Raúl, *The Development of Latin America and Its Principal Problems*, Santiago: United Nations Economic Commission for Latin America, 1950 (Spanish edition 1949)

Quijano, Aníbal, "The Marginal Pole of the Economy and the Marginalized Labour Force", *Economy and Society*, 3 (1974): 393–428

Rostow, W.W., *The Stages of Economic Growth: A Non-communist Manifesto*, Cambridge: Cambridge University Press, 1960; 3rd edition, 1990

Santos, Theotonio dos, "The Structure of Dependence" in *The Political Economy of Development and Underdevelopment*, edited by Charles Wilber, New York: Random House, 1973; 2nd edition, 1979

Thorp, Rosemary, *Progress, Poverty and Exclusion: An Economic History of Latin America in the 20th Century*, Baltimore: Johns Hopkins University Press, 1998

UN, "Fifty Years of the Economic Survey" in *Economic Survey of Latin America, 1997–98*, New York: United Nations Economic Commission for Latin America and the Caribbean, 1998

UN, *Debt: A Crisis for Development*, New York: United Nations, 1990

Williamson, J., "The Progress of Policy Reform in Latin America", *Policy Analyses in International Economics* 28, Washington, DC: Institute for International Economics, 1990

Basic accounts of the economic history of Latin America during the 20th century are provided by BULMER-THOMAS, FURTADO, HOFMAN and THORP. A good brief summary of basic trends illustrated with plenty of figures is provided by the UN (1990).

During the 20th century Latin America did relatively well compared to most of Africa and large areas of Asia but it performed disappointingly when compared with the US, Western Europe, and more recently East Asia. For years, the perceived failure of Latin America to replicate the success of the developed countries has been subject to debate.

During the 19th century, Latin America relied heavily on the export of primary goods, agricultural, and mineral, to generate economic growth. Furtado shows how certain of these products, particularly coffee and cereals, were successful in generating economic and social development. By the turn of the century Argentina, Uruguay, and southern Brazil were expanding rapidly and attracting large-scale immigration from southern Europe. By contrast, most tropical agricultural exports and mineral exports were producing very limited economic growth and little trickle-down in terms of benefits for the poor. It was the nature of export production that explained the differences in prosperity within Latin America.

Furtado's explanation was typical of Latin American explanations of the region's problems insofar as they gave greatest emphasis to the external constraints to growth. This differed from modernization theory and traditional economic analysis, which emphasized the internal constraints to growth. The classic example of this traditional form of thinking is ROSTOW. The tricks of economic growth are simple. Essentially a country needs to raise its savings rate and to invest heavily in education, industry, and infrastructure and it will replicate the

experiences of Western Europe and the US. Latin American economists, sociologists, and historians tended to reject that view and to argue that Latin America remained poor because of its relationship with the world economy. Broadly, this argument is termed dependency theory and the development of this school of thinking is described well by KAY.

Perhaps the key text on economic development in Latin America during the 20th century is that provided by PREBISCH. As head of the Economic Commission for Latin America he provided a critique of established conventional wisdom by arguing that free trade was damaging Latin America's economic prospects.

Prebisch's prescription for Latin America was import substitution (see separate entry) and protection against imported manufactures formed the basis of Latin American economic policy in most countries through to the 1980s. Latin American economies could benefit from a partial and selective cutting off from the world economy. They would encourage foreign capital to help construct the industrialization process within the region. In that way, the negative consequences of relying excessively on primary exports and manufactured imports would be overcome.

Furtado and Prebisch form part of the dependency school but are on the reformist end of the spectrum of dependency writers. The radical end of the spectrum consisted of writers like SANTOS and QUIJANO. The best known interpreter of dependency theory in English is FRANK (1967, 1969), a Chicago-trained economist who adopted a highly effective if polemical argument against modernization theory. His historical explanation of the poverty of Latin America blames the combination of capitalism and colonialism for Latin America's poverty. He uses the case of the northeast of Brazil to argue that the greater the links between Latin America and the rest of the world, the poorer Latin America became. This argument has been largely rejected, both from the right and the left, but during the 1970s it was hugely influential in intellectual circles. The argument was essentially that Latin America needed to cut off from the world community in a similar way to that adopted by China under Mao. In order to do this, social revolution was required to overthrow the elites of Latin America. The nearest example of such a strategy in Latin America is Cuba and much of that country's experience with socialism and partial autarky is explained by BRUNDENIUS.

In practice, most of Latin America accepted Prebisch's recipe and followed import-substituting industrialization policies. These were relatively successful in generating economic growth (see UN 1998) but brought major problems in their train. According to the most critical observers, they created uncompetitive industrial structures, worsened income inequality, raised levels of debt, and increased dependence on advanced capitalist countries.

The demise of import-substituting industrialization came with the debt crisis of the 1980s, which is well-described in a series of works including CORBRIDGE, GEORGE, and UN (1990). This period saw capital flowing out of Latin America and the region suffering from a severe economic recession. It also induced hyperinflation in a number of countries. The remedies to the economic ills of the region were strongly contested but a new economic strategy became common in most of the region. This consisted of a period of stabilization following rules laid down by neoliberal economists operating in the IMF and subsequent structural adjustment. The latter consisted broadly of reducing levels of trade protection, encouraging foreign capital inflows, reducing government budget deficits, reducing government controls on the economy, and freeing employers from labour controls. This approach became known as the Washington Consensus, identified by WILLIAMSON as ten areas where policy makers and scholars in Washington "could arguably muster a fairly wide consensus as to the character of the policy reforms that debtor countries should pursue." These were: fiscal discipline, public expenditure priorities, tax reform, financial liberalization, exchange rates, trade liberalization, foreign direct investment, deregulation, and property rights.

The new broadly export-oriented approach to development is commonly known as the new economic model (NEM) and its strengths and weaknesses are described in BULMER-THOMAS, EDWARDS, and MORLEY. The best exemplar of the NEM's strength is Chile, whose development of export markets and rapid economic growth is widely admired. Unfortunately, the model is associated with military government, human rights abuses, and widespread inequality. A good defence of Chile's record is provided by HOJMAN, a good critique is provided by MELLER. Like Cuba, Chile is a highly contentious model for the future.

Edwards (p.6) provides an energetic defence of the new economic model but recognizes the limits to progress:

> The Latin American reforms of the 1980s and early 1990s are impressive. Most countries opened up their economies to international competition, implemented major stabilization programs, and privatized a large number of state-owned firms. . . . By 1992, the reforms were beginning to bear fruit, as more and more countries began to recover and to experience higher rates of growth. Also, macroeconomic equilibrium had been achieved in most countries, exports were expanding, and productivity had grown substantially. Additionally, starting in 1991 private foreign capital entered the region at a pace that surprised even the most optimistic observers.

In spite of this progress, a decade after the crisis a number of problems persisted. Physical infrastructure had deteriorated severely, and in many countries the extent of poverty had increased. Despite spectacular progress, inflation continued to be high, refusing, even in some of the best cases, to drop back to single digits. Moreover, in some countries, the economic reforms were not accompanied by the modernization of political institutions. This created economic tensions, and in some cases political unrest, including serious crises in Brazil, Guatemala, Haiti, Peru, and Venezuela.

The current orthodoxy in Latin America is again in dispute. On the right, the answer is clear. Latin American problems lie in the region's failure to reform itself. As ROBERTS & LAFOLLETTE (p.97) put it:

> Latin Americans spent the twentieth century building the blocked society. They never managed to develop the institutions conducive to progress, such as efficient capital

markets, legal systems that protect private property rights, or banking institutions that serve the public. Theirs was a poverty of policy, not of people or natural resources.

The left, and even the centre, fear that liberalization of trade and labour markets will lead to growing poverty and inequality. IGLESIAS and MORLEY demonstrate how economic restructuring aggravated income inequality during the 1980s and the Inter American Development Bank has argued that until inequality is reduced within the region, the benefits of development are unlikely to benefit most Latin Americans. In 1993, Iglesias (p.74) wrote:

> we have learned that without adjustment, social problems can become insoluble and more devastating. But we have also learned that there is a limit to how much society will tolerate and that adjustment programs must therefore be accompanied by emergency social compensation measures and a clear vision of a different future for disadvantaged social groups.

The jury is still out on the new development model and given the wide fluctuations in thinking that have occurred over the last 50 years, the possibility that some revised form of dependency theory will soon return is likely.

ALAN GILBERT

Law survey

Allen, Carleton Kemp, *Law in the Making*, Oxford: Clarendon Press, and New York: Oxford University Press, 1927; 7th edition, 1964

Austin, John, *The Province of Jurisprudence Determined*, edited by Wilfred E. Rumble, Cambridge and New York: Cambridge University Press, 1995 (1st edition 1832)

Bacon, Francis, *The Elements of the Common Lawes of England*, New York: Legal Classics Library, 1997 (originally published 1630)

Bellomo, Manlio, *The Common Legal Past of Europe*, Washington, DC: Catholic University of America Press, 1995

Bentham, Jeremy, *An Introduction to the Principles of Morals and Legislation*, edited by J.H. Burns and H.L.A. Hart, Oxford: Clarendon Press, and New York: Oxford University Press, 1996 (originally published 1789)

Berle, Adolf A., Jr and Gardiner C. Means, *The Modern Corporation and Private Property*, New York: Commerce Clearing House, 1932; revised edition, New York: Harcourt Brace, 1968

Berman, Harold J., *Law and Revolution: The Formation of the Western Legal Tradition*, Cambridge, Massachusetts: Harvard University Press, 1983

Bigelow, Melville (editor), *Centralization and the Law: Scientific Legal Education, An Illustration*, Boston: Little Brown, 1906; reprinted South Hackensack, New Jersey: Rothman Reprints, 1972

Blackstone, William, *An Analysis of the Laws of England*, reprint of 3rd edition, New York: Hein, 1997 (1st edition 1756; 6th edition 1771)

Blackstone, William, *Commentaries on the Laws of England*, 4 vols, New York: Legal Classics Library, 1983 (originally published 1765–69)

Brooks, Peter and Paul Gewirtz, *Law's Stories: Narrative and Rhetoric in the Law*, New Haven, Connecticut: Yale University Press, 1996

Calabresi, Guido, *A Common Law for the Age of Statutes*, Cambridge, Massachusetts: Harvard University Press, 1982

Calabresi, Guido, *The Cost of Accidents: A Legal and Economic Analysis*, New Haven, Connecticut: Yale University Press, 1970

Cambridge Law Journal, 1921–

Cardozo, Benjamin N., *The Nature of the Judicial Process*, Holmes Beach, Florida: Gaunt, 1998 (originally published 1921a)

Cardozo, Benjamin N., *Cardozo on the Law*, New Haven: Yale University Press, 1921b

Cardozo, Benjamin N., *The Paradoxes of Legal Science*, Westport, Connecticut: Greenwood Press, 1970 (originally published 1928)

Carter, James Coolidge, *Law: Its Origin, Growth and Function*, New York: Legal Classics Library, 1996 (originally published 1907)

Coke, Edward, *The First Part of the Institutes of the Laws of England*, reprint of 19th edition, Abingdon: Professional Books, 1985 (19th edition originally published 1832)

Craig, Thomas, *Jus Feudale tribus libris comprehensum*, 2 vols, Edinburgh: Hodge, 1934 (originally published 1655)

Current Legal Problems, 1948–

David, René and John E.C. Brierley, *Major Legal Systems in the World Today: An Introduction to the Comparative Study of Law*, 3rd edition, London: Stevens, 1985

Dugdale, William, *Origines Juridiciales; or Historical Memorials of the English Laws*, 2nd edition, London: Thomas Newcomb, 1671

Dworkin, Ronald, *Taking Rights Seriously*, Cambridge, Massachusetts: Harvard University Press, and London: Duckworth, 1977

Dworkin, Ronald, *Law's Empire*, Cambridge, Massachusetts: Harvard University Press, 1986

Finch, Henrie, *Nomotechnia*, London: Societie of Stationers, 1613

Finnis, John, *Natural Law and Natural Rights*, Oxford: Clarendon Press, and New York: Oxford University Press, 1980

Frank, Jerome, *Law and the Modern Mind*, Birmingham, Alabama: Legal Classics Library, 1985 (originally published 1930)

Fuller, Lon L., *Legal Fictions*, Stanford, California: Stanford University Press, 1967

Fuller, Lon L., *The Morality of Law*, New Haven, Connecticut: Yale University Press, 1964; revised edition, 1969

Garner, Bryan A, (editor), *Black's Dictionary of Law*, 7th edition, St Paul, Minnesota: West, 1999 (1st edition as

A Dictionary of Law, edited by Henry Campbell Black, 1891)

Gray, John Chipman, *The Nature and Sources of the Law*, 2nd edition, New York: Macmillan, 1921

Grotius, Hugo, *The Law of War and Peace*, Indianapolis: Bobbs Merrill, 1962 (published in Latin 1625)

Hart, H.L.A., *The Concept of Law*, Oxford: Clarendon Press, 1961; 2nd edition, 1994

Harvard Law Review, 1887–

Hoeflich, M.H., *Roman and Civil Law and the Development of Anglo-American Jurisprudence in the Nineteenth Century*, Athens: University of Georgia Press, 1997

Holdsworth, W.S., *A History of English Law*, 17 vols, London: Methuen, 1903–72 (5 revised editions)

Holland, Thomas Erskine, *The Elements of Jurisprudence*, 13th edition, Oxford: Clarendon Press, 1924

Holmes, Oliver Wendell, Jr, *The Common Law*, with a new introduction by Sheldon M. Novick, New York: Dover, and London: Constable, 1991 (1st edition 1881)

Hurst, James Willard, *The Growth of American Law: The Law Makers*, Boston: Little Brown, 1950

The Irish Jurist, 1966–

Jhering, Rudolph von, *The Struggle for Law*, 2nd edition, Westport, Connecticut: Hyperion Press, 1979 (German edition 1870; 1st English edition 1879)

The Journal of Legal Studies, 1972–

Judicial Review, 1889–

Katsh, Ethan M., *Law in a Digital World*, New York and Oxford: Oxford University Press, 1995

Kelsen, Hans, *General Theory of Law and State*, Cambridge, Massachusetts: Harvard University Press, 1945

Kent, James, *Commentaries on American Law*, vol. 1, New York: Halsted, 1826; 14th edition, 1896

Kocourek, Albert and John H. Wigmore, *Sources of Ancient and Primitive Law*, Littleton, Colorado: Rothman, 1979 (originally published 1915)

Langdell, C.C., *A Selection of Cases on the Law of Contracts*, Boston: Little Brown, 1871

The Law Quarterly Review, 1885–

Lieber, Francis, *Legal and Political Hermeneutics*, Buffalo, New York: Hein, 1970 (originally published 1839)

Llewellyn, K.N. and E. Adamson Hoebel, *The Cheyenne Way: Conflict and Case Law in Primitive Jurisprudence*, Norman: University of Oklahoma Press, 1941

Llewellyn, Karl N., *The Common Law Tradition: Deciding Appeals*, Boston: Little Brown, 1960

Maine, Henry Sumner, *Ancient Law*, London: Dent, and New York: Dutton, 1960 (originally published 1917)

Miller, Perry, *The Legal Mind in America: From Independence to the Civil War*, New York: Doubleday, 1962

Miller, Perry, *The Life of the Mind in America from the Revolution to the Civil War*, New York: Harcourt Brace, 1965

Oxford Journal of Legal Studies, 1981–

Pannick, David, *Judges*, Oxford and New York: Oxford University Press, 1987

Pannick, David, *Advocates*, Oxford and New York: Oxford University Press, 1992

Pencak, William and Wythe W. Holt, Jr (editors), *The Law in America, 1607–1861*, New York: New York Historical Society, 1989

Plato, *The Republic*, translated and edited by F.M Cornford, London and New York: Oxford University Press, 1945 (written *c.*360 BC)

Posner, Richard A., *Economic Analysis of Law*, Boston: Little Brown, 1972; 5th edition 1998

Rawls, John, *A Theory of Justice*, Cambridge, Massachusetts: Harvard University Press, 1971, Oxford: Clarendon Press, 1972; revised edition, Cambridge, Massachusetts: Harvard University Press, and Oxford: Oxford University Press, 1999

Rawls, John, *Collected Papers*, edited by Samuel Freeman, Cambridge, Massachusetts: Harvard University Press, 1999

Savigny, Frederick Charles von, *Of the Vocation of Our Age for Legislation and Jurisprudence*, Birmingham, Alabama: Legal Classics Library, 1986 (originally published 1831)

Sloss, Peter F., *Alice's Adventures in Jurisprudencia*, Belvedere, California: Borogove Press, 1982

Stair, James, *The Institutions of the Law of Scotland*, Edinburgh: Edinburgh University Press, 1981 (originally published 1681)

Susskind, Richard, *The Future of Law: Facing the Challenges of Information Technology*, Oxford: Clarendon Press, and New York: Oxford University Press, 1996

The University of Kansas Law Review, 1952–

The University of Toronto Law Journal, Toronto: University of Toronto Press, 1935–

Watson, Alan, *Sources of Law, Legal Change, and Ambiguity*, Philadelphia: University of Pennsylvania Press, 1984; Edinburgh: Clark, 1985

White, G. Edward, *Patterns of American Legal Thought*, Indianapolis: Bobbs Merrill, 1978

Wigmore, John Henry, *A Panorama of the World's Legal Systems*, Washington, DC: Washington Law Book Company, 1936

Wormser, René A., *The Law: The Story of Lawmakers, and the Law We Have Lived By, from the Earliest Times to the Present Day*, New York: Simon and Schuster, 1949

Development of Western law

WORMSER provides a very readable and popularized version of Western legal history. It is excellent for beginners, but too unreliable for serious scholars. ALLEN, a basic historical approach to the development of Western Law, is designed for the beginning student or layperson with some general knowledge of European and British history but without any specialized knowledge of law or legal history. While somewhat dated, it retains value as a general introduction to law. CARTER, like Allen, is an early 20th-century attempt to provide an introduction to Anglo-American law for beginners. Like Allen, it is somewhat dated but still a useful starting point for the beginner.

BERMAN is a modern scholarly attempt to understand the development of law in the West in terms of major "revolutions" in the law such as the Gregorian Reform, the "rediscovery" of Roman law, and the impact of various other social and historical movements on law. Berman is a good introduction for the advanced student or for a layperson with some knowledge of legal history.

BACON is one of the first and greatest of the attempts to systematize English Common Law. The author was one of the most brilliant polymaths of the early modern period and combined an innovative mind and a broad interest in philosophy with a scholarly interest in the law. This is an important source for the history of English law.

BELLOMO is a work of European legal history designed to introduce the reader to those aspects of the European legal tradition that derive primarily from the Roman and Canonical traditions as opposed to national customs. Bellomo is an important introduction to the history of European Law that underlies contemporary attempts to find "one law" for Europe. It is most suitable for advanced students and specialists.

HOEFLICH explores the little known influence of Roman and civil law ideas on the development of Anglo-American legal theory in its formative years. The author focuses his attention on the work of the principal legal theorists in Britain and the US during this period.

BIGELOW presents a series of related essays on the development of law particularly in England and the United States. It is especially good for the relationship between law and government. The scholarship is dated, but retains importance as the work of a prominent American legal scholar at the turn of the 20th century

BLACKSTONE (1765) is, without question, the most important work on law and legal history produced in Great Britain during the past three centuries. The work is derived from a series of lectures delivered by the author at Oxford University and designed to acquaint students not destined for legal careers with the basics of English law. While a study of English law, Blackstone also provides comparative notes on civil law. Blackstone was the principal text used to study law until well into the 19th century in both Britain and the US. While no longer up-to-date, it remains one of the classics of Anglo-American jurisprudence. BLACKSTONE (1756) is an attempt to provide a systematic arrangement of the common law of England so as to render it more useable by students. It is the basis for the *Commentaries* (Blackstone 1765) and is often appended to editions of that work. It is based upon earlier works by Wood (*An Institute of the Laws of England, A New Institute of the Imperial or Civil Law*) and Finch (see below) and remains an essential starting point for research into systematizing efforts by jurists.

FINCH was the first modern attempt to provide some systematic arrangement of the common law, then perceived to be chaotic and without an analytic framework. This volume was succeeded by the works of Blackstone and Wood, neither of which could have been written without it.

COKE is one of the greatest early modern British treatises on the law by an author who was one of the most important jurists of its day. Although nominally a commentary on an earlier text, Littleton's *Tenures*, Coke is one of the fundamental treatises on property law. Additional parts covering other areas of the law were also published. While no longer useful as a source of law, Coke is a crucial text for those who wish to understand the development of English law during the early modern period.

HOLDSWORTH is the great multivolume history of English law from its origins to the 20th century. Like all such works it is a work of synthesis. Especially strong are its sections on the period from the 16th to the 19th century. This volume must be consulted by anyone interested in the history of English law.

DUGDALE is one of the best guides to the history of the legal profession and the Inns of Court written during the early modern period. The volume is a rich source for information in 16th and 17th century legal usages. KOCOUREK & WIGMORE provides a convenient set of materials on early law and legal development put together by two of the greatest legal historians of the early 20th century.

HOLMES began life as a series of lectures to working men in Boston and was first published to universal acclaim in 1881. The author of the volume served as a justice of both the Massachusetts Supreme Judicial Court and of the Supreme Court of the United States. In this volume he presents his theoretical and historical analysis of the development of the common law in Britain and the US and championed what has come to be known as the "formalist" approach to private law. Along with Blackstone this is one of the great classics of Anglo-American law.

KENT is known as the "American Blackstone". These volumes are the most important American attempt to create a set of commentaries on the Blackstonian model for American students.

HURST presents an episodical history of American law by one of the first legal scholars to use a social science approach to the law and legal history. This volume, along with others published by the author, moved legal history away from dry histories of doctrinal development and focused instead on the relationship between social and legal history. The volume is an important source both for the legal history of the US as well as legal historiography in the 20th century.

WHITE is an episodic history of the law in the US. The volume focuses on the major legal figures of the past two centuries in American law. The author is a professor of law at the University of Virginia and one of the leading historians of American law. PENCAK & HOLT presents a series of useful essays on the development of law in the United States.

CALABRESI (1982) is the work of a former dean of the Yale Law School who became a United States Appellate Judge and is one of the most important commentators on modern American law. In this work the author chronicles the changes in American law in the latter half of the 20th century and shows the shift in the law from being based primarily upon case law decisions to a system based, in large part, on legislative enactments.

CALABRESI (1970) is one of the first attempts to utilize economic analysis for the study of Anglo-American private law. In this volume, the author demonstrates how the use of economic concepts has affected the development of the American law of torts and changed the course of liability law in both the US and Britain.

MILLER (1965) presents a brilliant history of American intellectual life with a focus on the development of law and its impact on American culture. The author was a professor of literature at Harvard University and one of the most cogent commentators on the intellectual traditions of American law. MILLER (1962) is the companion volume. This volume provides in extract form some of the most important writings on American law from the 19th century.

Comparative and international law

DAVID & BRIERLEY has been the leading treatise on comparative law studies for more than four decades. The volume presents a survey of the highlights of the major legal systems in use in the world today, and is as useful for the practitioner as for the student.

WATSON is by one of the greatest comparative lawyers of the later 20th century. In this volume he attempts to explain how laws and legal traditions move across national, cultural, and linguistic borders. This is a "must read" for anyone interested in transnational law.

WIGMORE provides a grand survey of the various legal systems of the world. The volume is extremely useful for those who want to read one book that will introduce them to all of the world's legal systems. A good book for beginners and dilettantes. Experts should consult David & Brierly.

The publication of GROTIUS marked a milestone in the history of international law and the law of nations. This volume is the best modern translation of this classic work originally published in Latin. Grotius stands as the first and most important text on international law and is still an important source of international legal rules even today, three centuries after its first appearance in print.

National systems of law

The UNIVERSITY OF KANSAS LAW REVIEW, edited by students at the University of Kansas Law School, represents the many student-edited American law reviews published by regional schools. It is an excellent source for understanding the legal concerns of the vast majority of the practicing Bar in the US.

The UNIVERSITY OF TORONTO LAW JOURNAL is one of the leading Canadian legal periodicals important for its articles on Canadian law and practice.

CRAIG is one of the primary sources for Scottish law and the best compilation of the law of medieval Scotland. STAIR, too, is a major early modern source of Scots law. Along with *The Laws of Scotland: Stair Memorial Encyclopaedia* they are essential reading for anyone interested in Scottish law. JUDICIAL REVIEW is one of the leading legal periodicals published in Scotland. It is useful both for its articles and notes on current Scottish law, but also for its historical articles as well.

THE IRISH JURIST is one of the leading law reviews published in contemporary Eire. It is especially good not only for articles about contemporary Irish law, but is also very strong on Irish legal history.

LLEWELLYN & HOEBEL is the first serious study of Native American law by a lawyer and a sociologist, although the conclusions of the authors have since been challenged by a new generation of Native American legal scholars.

Jurisprudence and philosophy of law

SAVIGNY is an English translation of one of the most important modern German tracts on jurisprudence. In this work the author set forth the basis for what came to be known as the "historical school" of jurisprudence. One of the fundamental texts of this school is MAINE, one of the first great works of comparative law written by an English jurist. It is one of the basic texts of 19th-century legal philosophy and should be read by anyone interested in the development of law and legal thinking in Britain.

AUSTIN is, without doubt, the most important work of systematic jurisprudence written in English in the first half of the 19th century. The author was the first Professor of Jurisprudence at the University of London. The theories expounded in this volume represent an important instance of the introduction of German jurisprudential ideas to the English-speaking world. This volume, along with Kelsen (see below), was one of the most significant influences on Hart.

When first published, HART caused a revolution in the way English-speaking scholars approach law and jurisprudence. The volume brings to the study of law and legal philosophy the insights developed by the Oxford School of analytic jurisprudence. Hart is a perfect introduction to the analytic and linguistic approach to understanding law and should be read by every student interested in the subject. Though the author's approach has recently been modified by scholars such as Raz and Dworkin (see below), it remains of great importance.

KELSEN represents the high point of German 20th-century analytic jurisprudence, in an English translation understandable by the nonspecialist reader. Hart based much of his jurisprudence upon, and in response to, Kelsen. Thus, anyone wishing to pursue Hart must also study Kelsen.

DWORKIN (1986) is one of a series of major works on jurisprudence produced by its author, an American scholar who succeeded Hart in the Chair in Jurisprudence at Oxford. In this volume, and others he has produced, the author has established himself as the leading liberal theorist of law. Along with the work of Rawls this and others of the author's works should be read by every legal philosopher.

LLEWELLYN presents the substance of the jurisprudential work of one of the greatest 20th-century commercial lawyers and legal scholars. The author, a law professor at Columbia and Yale Law Schools, was the leading exponent of the "realist" approach to jurisprudence, an approach developed in this book.

GRAY is a classic exposition of the Anglo-American positivist tradition in jurisprudence and legal philosophy. Gray was a leading professor at Harvard Law School whose tenure straddled the late 19th and early 20th centuries. He was also a practising lawyer and his approach to jurisprudence shows a marked practical bent. HOLLAND is a British counterpart to Gray. This volume presents a positivist approach to the law representative of the thought of leading theorists of the 19th century.

THE JOURNAL OF LEGAL STUDIES is one of the oldest and most eminent journals produced by and for the jurisprudential school of law and economics. This periodical has published some of the most important works in this field.

SLOSS is an amusing – and somewhat idiosyncratic – attempt to make jurisprudence enjoyable for non-lawyers. It is a literary trifle worth noting.

In DWORKIN (1977) the Oxford legal philosopher sets forth his theories on the role of law in the liberal democratic state. This is one of the finest expositions of the legal nature of rights ever written.

BENTHAM sets forth the legal and legislative theories of one of the most important British political philosophers, who is best known for developing the theory of utilitarianism. The work is still of vital importance to understand modern legislation.

FINNIS, by one of the leading Catholic jurists of the 20th century, provides an important exposition of natural law theory in the tradition of the medieval jurists. The book has been extremely influential in both Britain and the US in conservative legal circles.

FRANK is one of the best written accounts of the thinking of the "realist" circle of legal philosophers. The author, along with Llewellyn, helped to establish realist jurisprudence in the US during the 1930s.

FULLER (1967) is a brilliant exposition of the important legal concept of the legal fiction and of how legal fictions have been used to develop the law. This is an excellent volume for beginners and advanced students alike.

FULLER (1969) provides an important modern account of the ways in which law and morality intermix and intercept. This volume was an important part of the development of a morality-influenced legal philosophy during the 20th century.

JHERING presents in an English translation one of the most important tracts published by one of the leading German jurists of the 19th century concerned with the nature of law. It is not for beginners, rather it is a hugely complex work most suitable for advanced students and legal scholars.

Analysis of law/theory

Many would argue that PLATO is the most important theoretical treatment of the idea of government and public law in the Western tradition. After more than two thousand years, *The Republic* retains its importance and should be read by anyone interested in either law or government. This edition, one of many translations into English, is by a noted British classicist.

POSNER was the start of the "law and economics" movement, which came to be one of the principal approaches to legal analysis of the late 20th century. The fundamental thesis of this text – and its many progeny – is that economic efficiency should be and is a principal goal of the law. The author was a professor at the University of Chicago Law School and is now a United States Appellate Judge.

RAWLS (1972) is, perhaps, the most important American treatise of the latter part of the 20th century dealing with law and rights. The author here attempts to set forth a broad view of the nature of law and individual rights. The work has been the subject of intense commentary and debate since its publication. The author is a professor at Harvard University. RAWLS (1999) is a companion volume. It presents a series of papers written by the author over more than two decades in which he attempts to refute critics of his earlier work and refine the theories he first set out there.

LIEBER was one of the first modern attempts to establish a basis for the hermeneutical analysis of law. The author was a German emigre to the US, and was influenced by German research into Biblical hermeneutics. He ended his career as a professor at Columbia Law School.

BROOKS & GEWIRTZ collects a number of essays first delivered at a conference at the Yale Law School by leading exponents of the school of "law and literature". The authors of these essays attempt to show the ways in which law is used in literary contexts, and how literary works can be used to further an understanding of the nature of law.

BERLE was one of the first to recognize the importance of the rise of the modern corporation and its impact on modern law. This work can truly be called the "Bible" of modern corporate law theory.

Practice of law

GARNER is now the standard law dictionary used in the US and in the English-speaking world. It has gone through countless editions. This is the best place to find definitions for legal terms.

PANNICK (1992) is one of the best accounts of the modern British legal profession. The author has been both an Oxford academic and a practicing lawyer and provides a unique insight into the law as it is practised in Britain today. PANNICK (1987) is a companion volume focusing on the British judiciary. It provides one of the best and most balanced views of today's judiciary in Britain.

CARDOZO (1928) is a collection of essays by one of the greatest progressive jurists and judges of the 20th century. The author was a champion of the expansion of liability in a long series of cases involving torts, contracts, property law, and corporate law when he sat as a judge of the New York State Court of Appeals and Justice of the United States Supreme Court. CARDOZO (1921a) is a selection of essays on the nature of judicial decision-making in the Anglo-American legal tradition. This is a "must read" for anyone interested in common law judging. Finally, CARDOZO (1921b) provides a selection from the author's legal and juristic writings. It is perfect for beginning readers and students.

CURRENT LEGAL PROBLEMS provides a selection of articles each year dealing with the most recent legal issues of the day. It is indispensable.

LANGDELL was the first "casebook" to be published and, as such, is the precursor of all modern casebooks in use in law schools in Britain and the US. The author was the dean of the Harvard Law School and an important innovator in legal education.

General law reviews

CAMBRIDGE LAW JOURNAL is one of the most important law reviews published in Great Britain today. It is edited by the Law Faculty at Cambridge University.

HARVARD LAW REVIEW is unquestionably the leading law review in the US. It features some of the best legal scholarship published in the US and reflects the current thinking of America's legal elite.

THE LAW QUARTERLY REVIEW is arguably the leading law review published in Britain. It is extremely useful for its notes on current cases as well as its scholarly articles. OXFORD JOURNAL OF LEGAL STUDIES is one of the most recent of the leading British law reviews. It is published by the Oxford Law Faculty and features articles written by them and other top legal scholars.

Law and new technologies

KATSH is a brilliant analysis of the ways in which new technologies, including the Internet are affecting the nature and practice of law. This volume will prove useful both to beginners as well as to experts. SUSSKIND is one of the most acute analyses of the problems the rapid changes in information technology will cause for the development of law and suggests ways in which the law must adapt to these technologies. It should be read in conjunction with Katsch.

M.H. Hoeflich

See also Administrative law, Ancient law, Canon law, Constitutional law, Consumer law, Criminal law, Cyberlaw, Law and history, Legal realism, and the various entries on national systems of law

Law and anthropology

Bentzon, Agnete Weis *et al.* (editors), *Pursuing Grounded Theory in Law: South-North Experiences in Developing Women's Law*, Oslo: Aschehoug, and Harare: Mond, 1998

Bohannan, Paul, "Ethnography and Comparison in Legal Anthropology" in *Law in Culture and Society*, edited by Laura Nader, Chicago: Aldine, 1969

Chanock, Martin, *Law, Custom and Social Order: Tthe Colonial Experience in Malawi and Zambia*, Cambridge and New York: Cambridge University Press, 1985

Comaroff, John L. and Simon Roberts, *Rules and Processes: The Cultural Logic of Disputes in an African Context*, Chicago: University of Chicago Press, 1981

Griffiths, John, "What Is Legal Pluralism?", *Journal of Legal Pluralism and Unofficial Law*, 24/1 (1986): 1–56

Lazarus-Black, Mindie and Susan F. Hirsch (editors), *Contested States: Law, Hegemony, and Resistance*, New York and London: Routledge, 1994

Llewellyn, Karl N. and E. Adamson Hoebel, *The Cheyenne Way: Conflict and Case Law in Primitive Jurisprudence*, Norman: University of Oklahoma Press, 1941

Maine, Henry Sumner, *Ancient Law: Its Connection with the Early History of Society, and its Relation to Modern Ideas*, London: John Murray, 1861; many subsequent editions

Malinowski, Bronisław, *Crime and Custom in Savage Society*, London: Kegan Paul, and New York: Harcourt Brace, 1926

Snyder, Francis G., *Capitalism and Legal Change: An African Transformation*, London and New York: Academic Press, 1981

The association of law and anthropology began towards the end of the 19th century, when European colonial powers decided to recognize the indigenous laws of their colonies. The legal profession had an obvious need for information – a need that anthropologists were best qualified to provide. Although both disciplines would have profited from close collaboration, two separate theoretical traditions persisted until recently.

MAINE is generally taken to be the founder of legal anthropology. Using an analogy with the natural science theory of evolution, he argued that, as political systems progressed through clearly marked stages from a lower, primitive state to a higher, more civilized state, so did legal systems. By comparing various archaic laws, he claimed a universal pattern of evolution for key legal institutions, the most famous being the movement from status to contract. Maine's evolutionist theorizing has been attacked for being conjectural and implicitly ethnocentric, but his work is still a provocative source of ideas about the sociopolitical forces shaping law.

The break with evolutionism came with MALINOWSKI, who pioneered the functionalist method, namely, actual observation in the field and an evaluation of modes of social control in terms of the culture in question, without reference to notionally more civilized standards. Because Malinowski's work provided the methodological basis for most ethnolegal texts until the 1960s, it continues to merit attention.

At the time Malinowski was writing, jurisprudence in the US turned from a positivist quest of defining what law *is* to the concrete question of what it *does*. By expanding the scope of jurisprudence to include the social context in which law was applied, "American realism" presented an opportunity for merging law and anthropology.

LLEWELLYN & HOEBEL used realist thinking to recover the almost extinct system of Cheyenne law and, by doing so, set legal anthropology on a new course. They identified three possible ways of investigating preliterate legal systems. An "ideological" method implied asking those who dispense justice in a community for an account of the rules they considered appropriate for controlling behaviour. Lawyers usually favour this method – which has latterly come to be called "rule-centred" or "legal centralist" – because it endorses certain typically positivist assumptions about law, notably, a strict distinction between law and other forms of social control, the courts' monopoly of power and the timeless validity of abstract rules. However, an ideological method will not necessarily give an accurate representation of how people behave, because it does not take into account the latitude allowed for deviance and it ignores the interactive processes underlying the creation and application of rules.

The second method, one traditionally preferred by anthropologists, is to observe how people behave and, from consistent patterns, to infer the rules that regulate behaviour. This approach is also fraught with difficulties, mainly the possibility that certain patterns will escape detection. Llewellyn & Hoebel championed a third, "case study" method that concentrated on what was done in the event of breaches of the law. By analysing how courts applied rules to disputes, a field worker could gauge what rules were deemed "proper to prevail in the pinch". Although Llewellyn & Hoebel's method immediately entered the canons of legal anthropology, its concern with court trials was unduly restrictive. Today, therefore, the range of inquiry is normally extended from the beginnings of a grievance in its social matrix to the effect of a settlement on the disputants' subsequent relationship.

Interest in disputes has generally broadened into a "processual" (in contrast with a "rule-centred") paradigm. This perspective of law regards conflict as nonpathological and application of rules as dependent on the relative power of the disputants. COMAROFF & ROBERTS produced a classic text in the processual paradigm. Through a detailed study of cases heard by traditional courts in a Botswana community, the authors demonstrate how the nature of a claim, the parties'

social relationship and their rhetorical abilities determine the role and application of rules in disputes.

The article by GRIFFITHS is another milestone in legal anthropology, for it defines legal pluralism, a concept that has been responsible for a large (and still growing) body of literature. Legal pluralism, in Griffiths's sense, opposed the central tenets of the established paradigm of legal centralism by contending that social action always occurs in the context of multiple, overlapping, semiautonomous social fields. These fields have their own normative orders that may work to support, ignore, or frustrate the designs of the central state. The pluralist model now informs all thinking in law and anthropology, in particular, of course, research directed at discovering relationships between official and unofficial laws.

BOHANNAN addresses a constant epistemological problem: whether to treat legal institutions as universal or unique to particular cultures. His discussion turns on the linguistic question of how best to present data from what he terms "folk" cultures. Bohannan contests the claim that it is appropriate to use English terminology on the ground that a term, such as "ownership", cannot reliably translate culturally specific concepts. He argues that to disregard folk terms would be to miss significant clues about the workings of a foreign thought system.

Fuctionalist anthropology studied each culture as if it were a changeless, self-contained unit, an understanding that operated ideologically to suggest racial segregation and the safeguarding of native traditions against subversive western influences. From the 1960s onwards, Marxist anthropology began an attack on this view of culture and the empiricist methods of functionalism.

Through his study of the Casamance region of Senegal, SNYDER is one of the few writers to transpose these ideas to the study of customary law. He shows how a precapitalist way of life, together with its system of indigenous law, articulated with the dominant mode of production. Snyder rejects any simplistic proposition that capitalism destroyed indigenous institutions. Instead, he argues that customary law was transformed, a process whereby the same legal form (such as bridewealth) could serve different socioeconomic functions or new legal forms (such as commercial contracts) were fashioned on capitalist models.

CHANOCK represents the start of a distinctive trend in legal anthropology, one concerned less with field work and more with the ideological implications of states recognizing subordinate legal systems. This development has involved collaboration between anthropologists and revisionist historians to expose the manipulation of tradition for ulterior political ends. Chanock produces a detailed exposition of how chiefs and colonial authorities in central Africa either deliberately excluded or simply overlooked contemporary social practices in their endeavour to create a customary tradition in line with the broader purposes of colonialism.

LAZARUS-BLACK & HIRSCH draw together a collection of essays by authors interested in legal pluralism and the ideological implications of law. Mainly through analysis of legal discourses, ranging from 16th-century Turkey to postcolonial Kenya, these papers show law being used as a resource to be contested and exploited in the competition between dominant and subordinate groups. The authors take a common standpoint on the position of law in relation to ideology and hegemony. These two concepts are conceived to be in an opposing and dynamic tension so that the more successful the dominant group, the more of its ideology disappears into hegemony (which has the effect of representing the dominant worldview as "natural"). Law is paradoxically both a maker of ideology and hegemony and a means of resistance. Hence, far from being an impartial arbiter of conflict, it is subject to continual negotiation and transformation.

The essays in Lazarus-Black & Hirsch disclose many of the preoccupations of modern legal anthropology. The first is a concern to break down traditional disciplinary boundaries. Secondly, there is a marked shift from purely descriptive accounts of the domestic laws of indigenous peoples to critical reflections about historically and culturally specific disputes. Thirdly, in reaction to earlier Marxist theory, the authors avoid committing themselves to any particular dogma on social causation.

The grand theory and scholastic style of the previous text reveal its links with cultural studies and the critical legal studies movement. BENTZON et al., which represents another major trend in current legal anthropology, stands in marked contrast. This clear and simply written book is aimed at university teachers or students, in fact anyone who has the prosaic task of gathering information about law. The authors bring research experiences from Scandinavia and Africa to bear on a specific project about women and the law in southern and eastern Africa. To counteract the distorting influences of legal centralism and a traditionally male-dominated perspective, the ordinary woman's perception of law is taken as the starting point. The book pays careful attention to the conflicts and overlaps between structures of gender, generation, law, culture, and semiautonomous social fields and how these intersections affect individuals. The theories within which findings are placed are as eclectic as the data-gathering methods.

THOMAS W. BENNETT

See also Customary law

Law and economics

Backhaus, Jürgen G. (editor), *The Elgar Companion to Law and Economics*, Cheltenham, Gloucestershire: Elgar, 1999

Bouckaert, Boudewijn and Gerrit de Geest (editors), *Bibliography of Law and Economics*, Dordrecht and Boston: Kluwer, 1992

Bouckaert, Boudewijn and Gerrit de Geest (editors), *Encyclopaedia of Law and Economics*, 5 vols, Cheltenham, Gloucestershire: Elgar, 2000

Coase, R.H., "The Problem of Social Costs", *Journal of Law and Economics*, 3 (1960): 1–44

Dnes, Anthony W., *The Economics of Law*, London: International Thomson Business Press, 1996

Geest, Gerrit de, *Economic Methodology and the Economic Analysis of Law*, Antwerp: MAKLU, 1994

Posner, Richard A., *Economic Analysis of Law*, 4th edition, Boston: Little Brown, 1992

Veljanovski, Cento, *The Economics of Law: An Introductory Text*, London: Institute of Economic Affairs, 1990 (Hobart Paper 114)

BACKHAUS provides a selection of papers by leading, mainly Europe-based, scholars on the various issues in law and economics. The topics are grouped according to discipline, and the authors provide an overview of up-to-date work and their own assessment of the work done and of prospective future research directions. The book may prove very valuable for those new to the field of law and economics, wishing to gain a good grasp of the discipline, but fairly quickly. A project that was carefully prepared and patiently guided over a number of years has resulted in a high-quality publication that attracts the attention, both of new students, and of more experienced researchers and professionals interested in the interplay between law and economics. Interestingly, the book has a dominant "European flavour", which is fairly unusual in a field "invented" – and for a long time dominated by – American, or American-based, scholars and the Anglo-Saxon (Anglo-American) legal system, with its associated legal thinking.

BOUCKAERT & GEEST's (1992) bibliography provides a list of publications in the field of law and economics, which was fairly comprehensive at the time of publication, especially as regards work relating to Europe. This was an interesting attempt to provide an overview of work done by Europe-based scholars and practising lawyers. The five-volume work by BOUCKAERT & GEEST (1999) is a natural continuation of their earlier efforts, and an attempt to provide an overview of the modern theory of law and economics. This work is less dominated by European scholars, and many fine scholars have contributed to it. It is a good selection of carefully scrutinized essays that describe up-to-date results on various economic, legal, and social problems, from a law and economics perspective. Each essay is followed by an ostensibly complete and exhaustive list of all publications on the issue, published in English and in other, particularly European, languages. In this book, "Europe" includes Western, Central, and Eastern European countries. This voluminous work demonstrates the state-of-the-art knowledge in the field, and will be suitable for those who wish to acquire general but also fairly profound knowledge of the classical and modern law and economics literature.

COASE's now already seminal paper set the foundations for the development of law and economics as a separate school of economic thought. In economic literature, which began to be dominated largely by the neoclassical school, his paper was both refreshing, and a brave attempt to give a different account of social structure and of the institutions of economic life. The paper established assumptions that would later be labelled as the Coase theorem.

The theorem states that, in a world of zero transaction costs, any initial definition of rights will lead to an efficient outcome. It is important not because we live in such a world, but because it shows us a different way of looking at a large range of problems, those resulting from the transaction costs that prevent the parties affected from bargaining their way to an efficient outcome. The Coase theorem addresses the question as to which bundling of rights would lead, under various circumstances, to an efficient outcome, and if a particular initial bundling of rights leads to an inefficient outcome, how easy it would be for the parties to negotiate a change, with the party who has a greater value for one of the rights in a bundle purchasing it from its initial owner.

GEEST is an important contribution to the methodology of law and economics, and to the discipline's interrelations with other schools of economic thought. The book encompasses different methodological approaches to law and economics, such as the philosophical, legal, economic, and sociological. It includes a critical survey of works by leading philosophers of science – such as Popper, Kuhn, Lakatos, and Friedman – covering Friedman's instrumentalism, the defence of Kaldor-Hicks efficiency analysis, and so on. The author is not satisfied with the Austrian economics approach as an alternative to mainstream law and economics. The work is written in fairly difficult language, and a full understanding of it requires a good background knowledge of legal and economic philosophy, along with a good grasp of economic methodology and of comparative economic thought.

DNES is a very good introductory textbook in law and economics. The book encompasses the results of both subschools, the American and the European. Although the book is based on an analysis of common law, the basis of the Anglo-Saxon legal system, it provides a unique European perspective on law and economics. The book does not require any prior knowledge of either economics or law: reading it is sufficient to provide an understanding of the main concepts of law and economics. The author analyses the main areas of law, such as property, contracts, and torts. He also includes the rare topic of the economics of crime, which is his own speciality. This gives a particular strength to this book. In the manner of Tullock, the author analyses the litigation process, and the social costs associated with law enforcement. The book, in itself, is a new concise introduction to the interface between legal and economic ways of reasoning. The text explains all economic analyses as they are introduced. The book raises the question of the economic efficiency of law, which makes it even more valuable, especially for the beginners without prior knowledge of either law or economics. – certainly a valuable read, with few shortcomings.

POSNER is the best-known textbook on the economic analysis of law. It covers classical material, like other similar texts. However, its distinctive features are that it includes a practice-oriented approach, and that it is a predominantly economic work written by a prominent lawyer. The author incorporates a number of issues not usually included in textbooks, such as sections on banking and financial regulation, which make this a text that should not be missed by any serious student of law and economics.

A basic British equivalent is VELJANOVSKI, a short pamphlet that describes the main lines of development of thought in law and economics. In contrast to other books, this draws heavily upon some related disciplines, such as public choice and institutional economics. A very interesting essay, which should be read by any new student of law and economics, especially if based or educated in Europe. The author analyses the early development of law and economics, applied to a couple of burning economic issues, in which the law and economics approach is applied. He also provides a good account of the different theoretical economic concepts underpinning modern law and economics, focusing on regulatory issues, and on an analysis of law as a specific incentive system. To a great extent, this book covers a much wider scope of topics than one would expect given its format and size. And is invaluable reading for anyone genuinely interested in (European) law and economics and non-mainstream concepts in law and economics.

Željko Šević

See also Economic analysis of law

Law and geography

Bassett, Thomas J. and Donald E. Crummey (editors), *Land in African Agrarian Systems*, Madison: University of Wisconsin Press, 1993

Blomley, N., "Text and Context: Rethinking the Law–Geography Nexus", *Progress in Human Geography*, 13 (1989): 512–34

Blomley, N. and G.L. Clark (editors), "Law, Regulation and Geography" special issues of *Urban Geography*, 11/5–6 (1990)

Blomley, Nicholas K., *Law, Space and the Geographies of Power*, New York: Guilford Press, 1994

Clark, Gordon L., *Judges and the Cities: Interpreting Local Autonomy*, Chicago: University of Chicago Press, 1985

Clark, G.L., "The Geography of Law" in *New Models in Geography*, vol. 1, edited by Richard Peet and Nigel Thrift, London and Boston: Unwin Hyman, 1989

Clark, W.A.V., "Geography in Court: Expertise in Adversarial Settings", *Transactions, Institute of British Geographers*, new series 16 (1991): 5–20

Evans, David J., Nicholas R. Fyfe and David T. Herbert (editors), *Crime, Policing and Place: Essays in Environmental Criminology*, London and New York: Routledge, 1992

Fyfe, N.R., "The Police, Space and Society: The Geography of Policing", *Progress in Human Geography*, 15 (1991): 249–67

Glassner, Martin Ira, *Neptune's Domain: A Political Geography of the Sea*, Boston: Unwin Hyman, 1990

Herbert, Steve, *Policing Space: Territoriality and the Los Angeles Police Department*, Minneapolis: University of Minnesota Press, 1997

Johnston, R.J., *Residential Segregation, the State and Constitutional Conflict in American Urban Areas*, London: Academic Press, 1984

Johnston, R.J., *Nature, State, and Economy: A Political Economy of the Environment*, Chichester and New York: Wiley, 1996

Prescott, J.R.V., *The Maritime Political Boundaries of the World*, London and New York: Methuen, 1985

Rossiter, D.J., R.J. Johnston and C.J. Pattie, *The Boundary Commissions: Redrawing the UK's Map of Parliamentary Constituencies*, Manchester: Manchester University Press, 1999

Wigmore, John Henry, *A Panorama of the World's Legal Systems*, 3 vols, St Paul, Minnesota: West, 1928

The interface between geography and law did not attract much attention until the 1980s and the research that has been undertaken does not (as yet) form a coherent whole. Early work, such as WIGMORE's, recognized spatial variability in legal systems but little more and, similarly, research in political geography did not explore the legal bases of state power.

Interest in law, as a significant component of any society's superstructure, developed during the 1980s through specific pieces of research that addressed issues concerning the application and/or interpretation of laws in the production of space, in the creation of spatial variations that lie at the heart of geography's rationale. JOHNSTON (1984), for example, explored legal interpretations of the Fourteenth Amendment to the United States' constitution in conflicts over urban residential segregation and Gordon CLARK (1985) addressed similar issues in his book on local autonomy in the US – both for local governments and for the judiciary in their interpretations of the concept. William CLARK used his geographical expertise gained through many years studying residential segregation and migration in American urban areas when acting as an expert witness in a number of desegregation cases, on which basis he drew certain conclusions regarding the role of academic research in the adversarial setting of the courtroom.

Further work on the interface between law and geography was initiated by two scholars, Nick Blomley and Gordon Clark, who explored the literature of critical legal studies and suggested the development of a *critical legal geography*. In this, law is not seen as a "given", applied by the state apparatus, but rather as an arena of conflict between various interest groups, both in its creation and in its interpretation through legal judgements. These judgements are based on key individuals' interpretations of the law as it is applied to specific cases and, because of the importance of precedent, are fundamental to the continued evolution of law. Such interpretations are "situated" in space and place, hence the conflicts over and interpretations of laws have a geographical component: space and place are integral to the creation and recreation of laws and not just arenas in which they are applied.

These arguments were developed in Gordon CLARK's (1989) essay, which identified three main components to geographers' work on law: the spatial impacts of law; the geography of the judiciary; and (in the US) issues relating to federalism. He asked whether law was "just a framework for social decision-making" and argued that such decision making varied through time and space because of judicial incapacity and the incoherence of the principles they had to apply. BLOMLEY (1989) advanced the argument that legal knowledge is both contextual and continually contested as it is created and interpreted, like all other forms of knowledge: law and space are necessarily interrelated and law cannot be "closed off" from economic, social, and political life. BLOMLEY (1994) extended his argument that contests over laws and their interpretations are both spatially located and implicated in the production of spaces. This is illustrated by four case studies: of the systemization of common law in 16th-century England; of cases relating to worker safety in the USA; of the restrictions on personal mobility during the 1980s miners' strike in the UK; and of the closure of a factory in a small British Columbia town. All illustrate conflicts over laws

and power involving space as an active component and not simply as the arena in which they are played out.

BLOMLEY & CLARK edited a series of papers on "legal geographies" in *Urban Geography* and have since sponsored a continuing series of articles on "legal geographies" in that journal. They argued that studies of the law must be theoretically located, and that its applications have to be set in their local contexts. ROSSITER, JOHNSTON & PATTIE, a detailed case study of the laws relating to the redistribution of Parliamentary constituencies in the UK, exemplifies such work on variations over time and space in their interpretation, as well as conflicts over their meaning and rewriting.

The implementation of laws involves policing, and a number of geographers have investigated aspects of the geography of crime, as in EVANS, FYFE & HERBERT. The critical legal geography approach is relevant to this, as illustrated by FYFE's essay on the nature of the police and policing, and HERBERT's detailed study of the Los Angeles Police Department. The police interpret laws in the context of their local situations, and their operational policies create both spaces and places.

Other geographical work operates on the boundary of the interface between law and geography, as illustrated by the essays on land rights in BASSETT & CRUMMEY. Geographical interest in environmental issues and problems and the laws involved in regulating environmental use is a further example, as are the discussions of international law in JOHNSTON's (1996) book and PRESCOTT's work on maritime boundaries. As yet the field has only generated a small amount of literature.

RON JOHNSTON

Law and history

American Journal of Legal History, 1957–

Baker, J.H., *An Introduction to English Legal History*, 3rd edition, London and Boston: Butterworths, 1990

Friedman, Lawrence M., *A History of American Law*, 2nd edition, New York: Simon and Schuster, 1985

Hall, Kermit L., William M. Wiecek and Paul Finkelman, *American Legal History: Cases and Materials*, 2nd edition, New York: Oxford University Press, 1996

Holdsworth, W.S., *A History of English Law*, 16 vols, London: Methuen, and Boston: Little Brown, 1903–1966 (5 revised editions)

Journal of Legal History, 1980–

Law and History Review, 1983–

Pollock, Frederick and F.W. Maitland, *The History of English Law before the Time of Edward I*, 2nd edition reissued, Cambridge: Cambridge University Press, 1968 (originally published 1898)

Pound, Roscoe, *The Formative Era of American Law*, Boston: Little Brown, 1938

The AMERICAN JOURNAL OF LEGAL HISTORY is the oldest journal dedicated solely to legal history published in the US. It publishes a wide range of articles on both Anglo-American legal history and continental legal history. On occasion, it also publishes articles on legal history from the non-Western world. The articles are generally of high quality and the authors come from both the US and the UK.

BAKER is an introductory text by the Downing Professor at Cambridge who is one of the leading English legal historians of the 20th century. Professor Baker is particularly known for his use of primary source materials and this introductory textbook reflects this expertise. It is clearly written and provides a thorough exposition of current views on English legal history. The notes are particularly helpful as guides to further study.

FRIEDMAN is the leading introductory textbook to American legal history by the best known of American legal historians. Its approach is noteworthy for the attention paid not only to traditionally used sources such as treatises and textbooks, but because the author also uses statistical and economic evidence and attempts to view law both as a phenomenon of low culture (that is, from a popular perspective) as well as of high culture.

HALL, WIECEK & FINKELMAN is the joint work of three leading 19th- and 20th-century American legal historians. It is a collection of primary and secondary source materials rather than a textbook. As such it is extremely useful for the reader who wants to be exposed to the sources used by legal historians in writing the history of American law. It is particularly rich in 19th-century sources, including those on slavery.

HOLDSWORTH is still the standard multi-volume source for English legal history. Sweeping in scope, it covers English law from its Anglo-Saxon beginnings to the 19th century. While it has not been updated to take into account more modern research, it still remains an indispensable source for both beginning and advanced students. Many of its chapters remain of value and its notes are an inexhaustible source for further reading. It should be used in conjunction with Baker and other more recent texts.

The JOURNAL OF LEGAL HISTORY is the leading English periodical on legal history. While the majority of the articles published in the journal concern English legal history, it does print important articles on other legal history topics, particularly Roman law.

LAW AND HISTORY REVIEW is published by the American Society of Legal History. Its articles are primarily in the fields of American and British legal history. It is particularly useful because it prints articles by many younger American and Canadian scholars and often prints articles using new methodologies and perspectives on traditional legal history.

POLLOCK & MAITLAND is thought by many legal historians to be the greatest work of legal history ever published in the English language. Maitland was the Downing Professor of Law in the University of Cambridge and Pollock was the Corpus Professor at Oxford. Maitland wrote most of the work. Pollock & Maitland, while old, still must be the starting point for anyone interested in the history of English law. Professor Maitland was the first great modern legal historian of England and his knowledge of the sources remains unmatched today. While the serious reader must also use more modern works, Pollock & Maitland remains a masterpiece.

POUND is one of the many works written by the greatest dean of the Harvard Law School in the 20th century. The

volume is an excellent starting point for those interested in the early period of American law. It is beautifully written and excellent as a text for the non-specialist. For the specialist, the sections on foreign influences on American law continue to be indispensable.

M.H. HOEFLICH

See also Law and the legal profession, history of, Law survey

Law and history through textbooks

Beale, Joseph Henry, supplemented by Robert Bowie Anderson, *A Bibliography of Early English Law Books*, Buffalo, New York: Hein, 1994 (originally published 1926)
Fidler, Ann, "'Till You Understand Them in Their Principal Features': Observations on Form and Function in Nineteenth-Century American Law Books", *Papers of the Bibliographical Society of America*, 92/4 (1998): 427–42
Hoeflich, M.H., "Legal History and the History of the Book: Variations on a Theme", *University of Kansas Law Review*, 46/3 (1998): 415–31
Holdsworth, W.S., *Sources and Literature of English Law*, Buffalo, New York: Hein, 1983 (originally published 1925)
Johnson, Herbert A., *Imported Eighteenth-Century Law Treatises in American Libraries, 1700–1799*, Knoxville: University of Tennessee Press, 1978
Mason, Alexandra (editor), *Civil, Canon and Common: Aspects of Legal History*, Lawrence: Kenneth Spencer Research Library, University of Kansas, 1996
Parrish, Jenni, "Law Books and Legal Publishing in America, 1760–1840", *Law Library Journal*, 72 (1979): 355–452
Roeber, A.G., "The Scrutiny of the Ill-Natured Ignorant Vulgar: Lawyers and Print Culture in Virginia, 1716 to 1774", *Virginia Magazine of History and Biography*, 91/4 (1983): 387–417
Simpson, A.W.B., "The Rise and Fall of Legal Treatise: Legal Principles and the Forms of Legal Literature", *University of Chicago Law Review*, 48 (1981): 632–79
Surrency, Erwin C., *A History of American Law Publishing*, New York: Oceana, 1990
Wolf, Edwin II, *The Book Culture of a Colonial American City: Philadelphia Books, Bookmen, and Book Sellers*, Oxford: Clarendon Press, and New York: Oxford University Press, 1988

HOEFLICH is an introduction to the importance of textbooks in understanding the history of law and the legal profession. Ranging over two millennia, he examines the importance of books to the reinvigoration of legal studies in the Middle Ages, looks at the importance of indices and other aspects of book production to the development of law, and looks at the importance of booksellers in the distribution of law books in the 19th century.

BEALE is one of the standard bibliographies of early common law textbooks. It provides a useful starting point for a study of textbooks used by lawyers in England (and subsequently in the US) prior to the modern period.

MASON is a catalogue of an exhibition mounted by the Spencer Research Library at the University of Kansas in 1996. The Spencer Research Library has one of the richest collections of antiquarian legal materials in the US. The exhibition catalogue provides detailed bibliographical material for a large number of early legal textbooks unavailable elsewhere.

FIDLER is a superb introduction to the study of legal textbooks as objects and how lawyers, particularly in the US, used their books not only for research, but also as symbols of their status as members of a learned profession.

HOLDSWORTH is, along with Beale, the traditional starting point for studying common law legal literature. Unlike Beale, Holdsworth examines both printed and manuscript material. Because of its age, Holdsworth should be read in conjunction with the more recent works of Professor John Baker on early sources of English law.

JOHNSON is the classic study outlining the foreign books that were used by lawyers during the early years of the US. As such, it is an indispensable source for any study of early American legal history as well as for the transatlantic book trade prior to the modern period.

PARRISH provides an introduction and detailed bibliography of law books published in the US prior to 1840. Particularly useful is the section of the introduction that discusses early American law booksellers and printers. A particularly helpful aspect of the bibliography is the inclusion of crossreferences to the *National Union Catalogue of Pre-1956 Imprints* and other general bibliographical aids.

ROEBER is a brilliant and path-breaking study of the ways in which lawyers in colonial Virginia used law books. Roeber explores the intersections of law and literacy in the Virginia colony and also studies the importance of law printing during this period.

SIMPSON is, perhaps, the best account of the "rise and fall" of treatise literature in the Anglo-American legal world. Simpson provides a guided tour of the first legal treatises and traces their history and the history of their successors into the 19th and 20th centuries. It is the starting point for any reader interested in the ways in which 19th- and 20th-century lawyers in England and the US utilized legal treatises.

SURRENCY is the standard history of legal publishing in the US. It is broader in scope than in profundity. Many subjects are covered only briefly, but, in many cases, Surrency is the only place to find any discussion at all. It is a good starting point for the reader who is new to this subject.

WOLF is a general history of the importation, sale, and use of books in colonial Philadelphia. However, while it treats more than law books, law books play a central role in the history told by Wolf. Indeed, Wolf remains as the best-detailed study of how law books were distributed and used in any city in England or the US during this period. It is suitable for both the beginner and the advanced reader.

M.H. HOEFLICH

See also Law and history, Law and the legal profession, history of

Law and multiculturalism

Bozeman, Adda B., *The Future of Law in a Multicultural World*, Princeton, New Jersey: Princeton University Press, 1971

Dimauro, Julie, "Toward a More Effective Guarantee of Women's Human Rights: A Multicultural Dialogue in International Law", *Women's Rights Law Reporter*, 17 (1996): 333–44

Dupuy, Rene-Jean (editor), *The Future of International Law in a Multicultural World* The Hague: Nijhoff, 1984

Schlesinger, Arthur M. Jr, *The Disuniting of America: Reflections on a Multicultural Society*, New York: Norton, 1998

Shusta, Robert M. *et al.*, *Multicultural Law Enforcement: Strategies for Peacekeeping in a Diverse Society*, Englewood Cliffs, New Jersey and London: Prentice Hall, 1995

Soifer, Aviam, *Law and the Company We Keep*, Cambridge, Massachusetts: Harvard University Press, 1995

Stanford Law Review, "Symposium: Race and Remedy in a Multicultural Society", 47/5 (1995): 819–1097

Williams, Robert A. Jr, "Large Binocular Telescopes, Red Squirrel Piñatas, and Apache Sacred Mountains: Decolonizing Environmental Law in a Multicultural World", *West Virginia Law Review*, 96 (1994): 1133–64

The broad theme of law and multiculturalism encompasses many components, each of which highlights a different set of problems that emerge out of the intersection of law with the fact of multiculturalism. The works described below address distinct aspects of this problematic relationship, each drawing attention to a new set of normative and/or practical concerns about law.

BOZEMAN is an insightful and provocative treatise that calls attention to the uncertain future of Western concepts of international and constitutional law in a multicultural world. Any attempt to create and/or utilize international legal regimes as a solution to world problems must grapple with the fact, discussed and illustrated in this book, that the particular connotations attached to law in the West cannot be presumed to exist in other, non-Western systems of public order. Bozeman analyses the various meanings carried by law in the political systems of the West, the Islamic Middle East, Africa south of Sahara, Indianized Asia, and China, and argues that because Western vocabularies, norms, values, and beliefs relating to the sphere of politically significant behaviour do not carry over to their non-Western counterparts, reliable intercultural accords are difficult to reach. The comparative analysis of the various systems of law and meaning contained in this book is not comprehensive, however it provides a clear overview of the precariousness of Western-centred legal discourse in a multicultural world.

DUPUY provides a thorough examination of the challenges facing international law in a multicultural world. This collection of papers presented at The Hague contains works by approximately fifty writers, in both French and English, from a variety of disciplinary fields. The primary question addressed in this book pertains to the future of international law. Dupuy asks: in conditions of multiculturalism, "towards which future is community law oriented, since it no longer always functions in the same manner as formerly, and since vast finalities are assigned to it in a universe belabored by socio-cultural systems clashing or co-operating?" Contributors' responses to this question are divided into three primary categories. The first encompasses writings by political economists, philosophers, sociologists, and jurists, who engage a global approach to this question. The second group of articles is devoted to a thematic and comparatist approach similar to that embraced by Bozeman, which "examines the variable content of juridical concepts through various cultural systems." The third set of writings deals with the search for solutions for the future. While the three sections are clearly complementary, they can also be read independently of one another and in this respect the book is valuable to readers who are interested in only one type of issue raised by the intersection of multiculturalism with international law.

DIMAURO focuses on one particular aspect of international law that suffers at the hands of multiculturalism, namely enforcement of the human rights recognized in international legal instruments such as the Universal Declaration of Human Rights (1948). Discussing the phenomenon of female genital mutilation practised in many countries today, this piece points to the difficulty inherent in determining the proper balance between deference to the cultural traditions of autonomous groups whose practices violate the human rights principles set forth in international instruments, and desire to enforce those (Western) rights. While the doctrines of cultural relativism and universalism, two possible approaches to striking this balance, are discussed only briefly in this article, their practical implications in a radically diverse and multicultural world are clearly illuminated.

WILLIAMS addresses the types of uncertainties that multiculturalism creates for environmental law and legal policy. He illustrates the vast differences between the concept of environmental justice embraced by the Apache Indians and that embraced by US law, and points to the disparate outcomes that each concept would produce in actual cases. This article suggests that a healthy and viable approach to environmental law in a multicultural world would accord environmental concerns the same status as enjoyed by legally protected interests such as freedom of speech, religion, or bodily integrity. While the discussion in this piece is restricted to the specific problems that emerge out of one particular legal skirmish, and in this sense is limited, the biases Williams identifies in approaches to environmental law are a valuable starting point to any multicultural critique of this field of law.

One of the pressing problems that many legal regimes face today is how to address inter-minority group conflict in a multicultural society. The paradigms typically used to address such conflicts centre around a two-faceted model of race relations, usually focusing on the majority group and on a single minority group. Legislation intended to alleviate group conflicts also draws on the same paradigms. The various works included in STANFORD LAW REVIEW's May 1995 Symposium on "Race and Remedy in a Multicultural Society" tries to suggest innovative ways of conceptualizing the problems that contribute to inter-minority group conflict in a society that contains more than one minority. Most of the articles focus on general problems of race relations, racial classifications, race consciousness,

and racial identity. The papers by Wilkinson, Brest and Oshige, and Ramirez extend the debate over the morality, legality, and political efficacy of affirmative action. Hing's article proposes a rule requiring attorneys working on cases involving racial tension to initially pursue non-adversarial approaches. Dong discusses the case of a specific high school in California that limits the number of enrollees from a given racial or ethnic group to 40 per cent of the student body, and illuminates the types of claim that can be made in such cases when they reach the judicial system. Natapoff analyses a number of United States Supreme Court decisions in order to challenge the traditional bipolar black-white model that dominates American equal protection decisions. Habermas illuminates the philosophical aspects of the relationship of minority cultures and political identities to the majority culture within a constitutional democracy. The first article in the collection, by Charles R. Lawrence III, is especially instructive both in its organization of the different types of writing on this topic and in its explanation of why law's prevailing paradigm for achieving racial equality has failed.

SCHLESINGER represents a school of thought that maintains that legally entrenched multiculturalism is destructive of the unity required to maintain national cohesion, and that law therefore ought not to be used in support of multiculturalism. For this reason he argues against policies such as state-sponsored bilingual education and for immigration policies that will "lead newcomers to an acceptance of the language, the institutions, and the political ideals that hold the nation together". He maintains that while multiculturalism in the sense of freedom is a laudable goal, law should be employed in the service of unifying ideals and a common culture rather than in what he views as divisive sustenance of competing subgroups. Although this treatise deals specifically with US history, society, and policy, its arguments apply to other multicultural societies as well.

Readers interested in devising legal bases for a system of rights capable of defending multicultures of association will find SOIFER extremely valuable and enlightening. Unlike the main bulk of writing on multiculturalism which focuses on religious, cultural, and/or ethnic groups, Soifer focuses instead on the boundaries between secular groups and governments. He proposes legal recognition of a strong constitutional right to association, on a par with freedom of speech and religion. Soifer's analysis is limited to US law, however the ideas he proposes are easily applicable to other constitutional democracies as well as to countries that do not have constitutions. While the work incorporates some case analysis and discussion of legal doctrine, no formal legal background is required in order to understand the analysis.

SHUSTA et al. addresses an interesting and important facet of law and multiculturalism that has generally been neglected. This textbook highlights the pervasive influences of culture, race, and ethnicity on law enforcement. The book is premised on the notion, explained well in Part 1, that a multicultural society has implications for law enforcement both within and outside the police agency, and that these implications can and should be addressed through heightened awareness, cross-cultural knowledge, sensitivity, and tolerance. Because the work is intended as a guide to assist law enforcement officials in structuring their workplaces and developing their work methods, it also contains material that is practical in nature in Parts 2–5. Readers interested in the practical concerns that stem from multiculturalism on a day-to-day basis will find this book very instructive.

ZEHAVA ZEVIT

See also Cultural relativism, International law

Law and society

Abel, Richard L. and Philip S.C. Lewis, *Lawyers in Society*, 3 vols, Berkeley: University of California Press, 1988–89

Black, Donald, *The Social Structure of Right and Wrong*, San Diego and London: Academic Press, 1993

Bonsignore, John J. *et al.* (editors), *Before the Law: An Introduction to the Legal Process*, 6th edition, Boston: Houghton Mifflin, 1998

Cotterrell, Roger, *The Sociology of Law: An Introduction*, 2nd edition, London: Butterworths, 1992

Macaulay, Stewart, Lawrence M. Friedman and John Stookey (editors), *Law and Society: Readings on the Social Study of Law*, New York: Norton, 1995

Merryman, John Henry, David S. Clark and John O. Haley (editors), *The Civil Law Tradition: Europe, Latin America and East Asia*, Charlottesville, Virginia: Michie, 1994

Nelken, David (editor), *Comparing Legal Cultures*, Aldershot, Hampshire: Dartmouth, 1997

Rheinstein, Max (editor), *Max Weber on Law in Economy and Society*, Cambridge, Massachusetts: Harvard University Press, and New York: Simon and Schuster, 1954

Roberts, Simon, *Order and Dispute: An Introduction to Legal Anthropology*, Oxford: Martin Robertson, and New York: St Martin's Press, 1979

Weisberg, D. Kelly (editor), *Women and the Law: A Social Historical Perspective*, 2 vols, Cambridge, Massachusetts: Schenkman, 1982

Zweigert, Konrad and Hein Kotz, *An Introduction to Comparative Law*, 3rd edition, Oxford: Clarendon Press, and New York: Oxford University Press, 1998

BLACK offers his original conception of the "behaviour of law" in which he classifies law according to style (whether penal, compensatory, conciliatory, or therapeutic), quantity (amount of punishment or sanctions), and form (unilateral, bilateral, or involving third persons). Important chapters deal with Black's view of crime as social control in which disputes are settled by self-help including violence; the structural conditions underlying compensation in legal disputes; and types of conflict management (besides self-help he includes avoidance, negotiation, settlement, and toleration). Three chapters present original treatments of partisanship, looking at taking sides, making enemies, and (with Baumgartner) a theory of the third party. Black also applies his approach to the self, examining how individuals invite the imposition of social control on themselves by pleas of guilt, the seeking out of therapists, or the extreme measure of committing suicide. The author ranges widely among European, American, and cross-cultural sources to support his theoretical claims.

The field of feminist jurisprudence has received increasing attention from both scholarly and ideological sources. The two volumes edited by WEISBERG provide a superb historical treatment not of feminist approaches, strictly speaking, but of encounters of women with the law and the legal institutions. Volume 1 focuses on female deviance and crime, inluding papers dealing with the punishment of female felons in colonial Massachusetts in the hundred-year period from the 1670s onwards, and with the paternalistic treatment of women in 18th century Rhode Island. The differential treatment of women in decisions on commitment to mental institutions in the 19th century highlights many of the themes taken up by writers in recent years. Other pieces deal with female criminality in 14th- and 18th-century England. Volume 2 turns to civil law, with articles on women as property in the early Roman empire and on women's property rights in medieval England. Other articles report on rape in 13th-century England (one of the few actions allowed women before the royal courts), and raise contemporary issues with a study of the special problems presented by American social security for women who secure benefits secondary to those of their husbands. The volume concludes with the shifting role of women in the legal profession. Each section of the two volumes concludes with suggested readings for further elucidation of themes discussed in the articles. The two volumes testify to the extent to which modern concerns have been anticipated, and often dealt with, in earlier periods, as well as correcting the simplistic picture of women in historical times as simply adjuncts to their husbands.

Although there are many texts on the sociology of law, COTTERRELL is both comprehensive and judicious in his selection of research materials. His basic point is that law, considered as a body of normative principles, is inadequate on its own for an appreciation of the impact of law on society or of society on law (assuming they can be separated at all). He focuses on the various approaches to law and society (whether law integrates society, changes society, or represents a set of instruments with which power elites may dominate social institutions). Particularly useful is his treatment of legal professionals (lawyers, judges, courts) and of the acceptance and legitimacy of law, however conceived. The book concludes with an excellent set of notes for further reading.

ABEL & LEWIS' three-volume work on lawyers is among the most comprehensive comparative review of lawyers in society yet available. Volume one reviews the roles of lawyers in England and Wales, Scotland, Canada, Australia, and New Zealand. Volume two does the same for civil law countries, with separate chapters for Norway, Germany, Japan, Holland, Belgium, France, Italy, Switzerland (Geneva), Spain, Venezuela, and Brazil. Volume three presents analyses of changes in the legal profession, the feminization of the profession, new class approaches, the impact of revolutions, and other general topics. Although the first two volumes are encyclopaedic in the sense that readers will dip into them for particulars of various countries, the third volume offers analytic depth and a global view of the basic social processes forming and changing the character of the legal profession. Although there are obvious gaps, as the editors note (such as lawyers in Third World countries) and many countries are not included (for example, in Asia and Africa), the coverage is still impressive, and mostly in-depth as well.

In his brief but intensive crosscultural work, ROBERTS argues that the identification of law with centralized government, as assumed in most classic studies of law (such as Hart's) sheds little light on law in tribal society, where formal government may be missing or much attenuated. Therefore Roberts begins not with law, but with the basic means whereby societies preserve order and handle disputes as they arise. Although, as he notes, some societies assume order, regarding conflict as a rarity to be avoided or dealt with quickly to restore harmony, other societies convert even minor disturbances into occasions for seeking redress of justice. Even then, most conflicts may still be settled out of court by self-help, vengeance, feuds, or by ritualized methods of conflict resolution such as song contests, head-butting, or in other ways. The contrast with organized, bureaucratic society may be somewhat overdrawn (the use of self-help for example, is very common in Western urban society, and most disputes are settled outside of court there also), but Roberts ranges over a vast body of materials on dispute settlement, both, in interpersonal relations and in property issues.

ZWEIGERT & KOTZ compare legal systems in order to illuminate the interaction between culture and the world's major legal systems. Volume 1 presents analyses of what they call the "romanistic" legal family (using France and Italy as majors exemplars), the Germanic family (including Germany, Austria, and Switzerland), the Anglo-American family (with special attention to trusts), the Scandinavian family, and socialist law (with special attention to the problems of contract and ownership). Volume 2, dealing with private law, is unusual, because private law is only sparsely covered in most comparative discussions. The focus is on contracts, torts, and an excellent treatment of unjustified enrichment. In each case, the authors are at pains to try to catch the spirit of these systems. For example, the French courts are reluctant to allow contract negotiators to escape contractual requirements in case of impossibility, as in war, forcing businesspersons to make allowance for risk. By contrast, German and American law allows courts greater discretion in such instances. The discussion is heavily laced with actual cases, as well as extensive citation to the relevant research literature.

NELKEN's edited series of analytical and substantive papers suggests that the task of studying legal cultures has hardly begun. Several authors express despair that the legal culture concept itself is so riddled with confusion and inconsistencies that its usefulness is reduced. Yet others find the concept can, in some respects, be quantified, for example describing some countries (Austria, Belgium, and West Germany) as litigation-prone, in comparison with others that avoid litigation (Italy, Denmark, Netherlands, and Japan). Mediation and other "filtering" institutions play major roles in the latter countries. Other writers take up more limited questions, such as accounting for the prevalence of plea-bargaining, or why there is devaluation of gender in some industrial countries. One author explores the peculiarity of American law, not in terms of the overworked reduction of that law to "individualism", but in terms of entrepreneurial drives and the instrumental value of law in keeping Coasian transaction costs down. Other substantive chapters deal with the enigma of Japan, with its extremely low official crime rate; and with copyright law, a kind of law that, by definition, cannot be limited to one country, in a world where national borders are routinely crossed, if not by caravans of goods, then by transactions on the World Wide Web. However vague, the idea of legal culture turns out to stimulate significant research.

RHEINSTEIN's edited version of Weber's classic treatment of law and society grows even more useful as critiques and evaluations continue to pour out. Weber's ideal typical categories of formal/substantive and rational/irrational, and their cross-classifications, are still central to societal comparison. Although abstract, Weber's work continually provides detailed examples, drawn from dozens of countries and cultures, particularly of substantive law. His accounts of the role of legal honoratiores, as he calls them, of sacred law, of the contrasts between natural and revolutionary law, and of the impact of types of authority on the structure and content of law, are original, and show the limited value of discussing law without reference to the social setting in which law operates.

The edited book by BONSIGNORE et al. offers a vast and judicious selection of discussions, court cases, and literary treatments that cover the major areas of formal and substantive law. The topics include lawmaking by judges and lawyers, the limits on official discretion, the relationships between law and values and between values and interests, class differences in legal power, and feminist perspectives on the legal order. Law enforcement and the jury are given detailed treatment, as well as lawyers. Conflict resolution, both in court settings and in extralegal contexts, is evaluated and summarized. The book offers a special section on the legal issues raised by computerization and on the problems raised by the fact that "cyberspace" crosses national boundaries. The selections emphasize US situations, but the problems addressed are generic and generalizable.

MACAULAY, FRIEDMAN & STOOKEY have brought together a wide-ranging collection of the leading studies and discussions concerning law and society. Although the selections are largely drawn from US sources, the range of issues is broad. Particular issues examined include the role of sanctions, the effect of law on society, the structure of legal institutions, and the key legal actors, particularly judges and lawyers. Classic articles are included, such as Blumberg's view of the practice of law as a confidence game, Macaulay's demonstration that businesspersons tend to ignore the details of legal contracts that are so dear to lawyers, Ross' data on how insurance adjusters settle claims by formula and by mutual understanding rather than by resorting to litigation, Friedman's treatment of legal culture, Gusfield's study of the symbolic designation of deviance, and Weitzman's data on the unintended consequences of the divorce problem.

MERRYMAN, CLARK & HAKEY's case book presents detailed theoretical and substantive treatment of the civil law in Europe, Latin America, and Japan. The editors include articles on the history of the civil law tradition, on methods of studying comparative law, and on such practical problems as litigating cases with foreign defendants, the Hague convention on evidence, and as other evidence issues on appeal. Particularly useful are the treatment of the basis of civil law in Roman and canon law, and of the impact of revolutions in modern times in giving rise to codes and legal science paradigms. The discussion in compressed form of the legal systems of Latin America, as well as that of Japan and of countries in

Asia influenced by Japanese law and methodology, is especially useful. Although strong on substance, the editors also give extensive coverage of the legal process and appeals systems, civil and criminal procedure, and the legal professions. Intended for use in university classes, the book is an essential reference for scholars and practitioners alike.

EDWARD GROSS

Lawyers and the legal profession, history of

Baker, J.H., *The Legal Profession and the Common Law: Historical Essays*, London: Hambledon Press, 1986

Brand, Paul, *The Origins of the English Legal Profession*, Oxford: Blackwell, 1992

Bloomfield, Maxwell, *American Lawyers in a Changing Society, 1776–1876*, Cambridge, Massachusetts: Harvard University Press, 1976

Cocks, Raymond, *Foundations of the Modern Bar*, London: Sweet and Maxwell, 1983

Cohen, Herman, *History of the English Bar and Attornatus to 1450*, London: Sweet and Maxwell, 1929

Lemmings, David, *Gentlemen and Barristers: The Inns of Court and the English Bar, 1680–1730*, Oxford: Clarendon Press, 1990

Pound, Roscoe, *The Lawyer from Antiquity to Modern Times, with Particular Reference to the Development of Bar Associations in the United States*, St Paul, Minnesota: West, 1953

Prest, Wilfrid R., *The Rise of the Barristers: A Social History of the English Bar, 1590–1640*, Oxford: Clarendon Press, 1986

Prest, Wilfrid R., *Lawyers in Early Modern Europe and America*, London: Croom Helm, 1981

Warren, Charles, *History of the Harvard Law School and of Early Legal Conditions in America*, 3 vols, New York: Lewis, 1908; reprinted 2 vols, New York: Da Capo Press, 1970

Warren, Charles, *History of the American Bar*, Boston: Little Brown, 1911

BAKER collects 23 essays by the Downing Professor of the Laws of England at Cambridge. Of these, the vast majority deal with the history of the legal profession in England during the Middle Ages and the early modern period. The essays on "The English Legal Profession, 1450–1550" and "Learning Exercises in the Medieval Inns of Court and Chancery" are particularly important.

BRAND is the most recent attempt to trace the earliest origins of the English legal profession in medieval England. The volume analyses the origins of the legal profession in Anglo-Norman England and places this development within its social and political context. Although some of the book's conclusions remain controversial, it is fully annotated and will be of great value to both the beginner and the advanced reader.

BLOOMFIELD is a brilliant history of the American legal profession in its formative period. The author ranges widely through literary and historical sources to paint a picture of the profession that will be of immense value to historians, lawyers, and those interested in the ways in which the profession was portrayed and understood in popular services. It is particularly important in tracing the history of how American lawyers came to view themselves as a profession rather than a trade.

COCKS is a brief account of the development of the English Bar during the Victorian period in England. It focuses particularly upon the development of ideas of professionalism and self-regulation and places the history of the Bar squarely within the Victorian intellectual tradition. The volume presents both a chronological history of the Bar during this period as well as short biographical accounts of the leading lawyers who helped to shape the Bar. It contains a very useful bibliography.

COHEN is a classic account of the origins of the English profession going back as far as Anglo-Saxon England. Although it is now somewhat dated, it provides the reader with the traditional account of the English legal profession during the Middle Ages and as such is still quite useful. It should be read in conjunction with more modern works such as Brand. The appendix contains a selection of original documents relating to the early history of the Bar, which are quite useful and otherwise difficult for the average reader to locate.

LEMMINGS is a superb monographic history of the Inns of Court and the barristers who lived and worked there from 1680–1730. It should be read in conjunction with Prest's study of the immediately preceding era (see below). The chapters on legal education at the Bar and the role of barristers in politics are especially useful. Throughout the study, the author uses quantitative methods to provide a detailed picture of the legal profession. The volume contains an extremely useful bibliography.

POUND is a popular and brief survey of the history of the legal profession in both Britain and the United States by the most famous dean of the Harvard Law School. Although it is now outdated in some respects, it has still not been fully replaced by more modern works. Its account of the rise of Bar Associations is particularly useful. A good book for beginners.

PREST (1981) is a collection of nine essays by leading scholars of the American, British, and European legal professions. Of particular note are the essays by C.W. Brooks, "The Common Lawyers in England, c.1558–1642"; Brian P. Levack, "The English Civilians, 1500–1750"; and Alexander Murdoch, "The Advocates, the Law and the Nation in Early Modern Scotland". Each of the essays is annotated but the volume does not contain a bibliography.

Prest is a comprehensive treatment of the history of the English Bar during the 50-year period 1590–1640. The author is the leading historian of the English legal profession during the early modern period and this is his greatest work. It presents a wide-ranging study of the social context of the English Bar during the period as well as details the lives at work of barristers. The chapters dealing with the business of the Bar and the supply and demand for barristers' services during this period are especially important. An appendix contains useful biographical data on the barristers studied, organized in alphabetical order.

WARREN (1911) is a useful, short book on the history of the legal profession in America. Like Pound, it is now somewhat out of date, but is still a useful starting point for beginners.

WARREN (1908) is a detailed – and still yet to be replaced – history of the Harvard Law School by one of its greatest professors. Because the history of Harvard Law School so dominates traditional histories of the American Bar in the late 18th and early 19th centuries, Warren provides a superb traditional history of the American Bar during this period. At the same time, because of the strong Harvard / northeastern US bias of the volume, it tends to ignore or underplay the significance of developments in other parts of the US.

M.H. HOEFLICH

Leadership

Bass, Bernard M., *Leadership and Performance beyond Expectations*, New York: Free Press, and London: Collier Macmillan, 1985

Bass, Bernard M., *Bass and Stogdill's Handbook of Leadership*, 3rd edition, New York: Free Press, and London: Collier Macmillan, 1990

Fiedler, Fred E., *A Theory of Leadership Effectiveness*, New York: McGraw Hill, 1967

Fiedler, Fred E. and Joseph E. Garcia, *New Approaches to Effective Leadership: Cognitive Resources and Organizational Performance*, New York: Wiley, 1987

House, Robert J., "A Path-Goal Theory of Leader Effectiveness", *Administrative Science Quarterly*, 16 (1971): 321–39

House, Robert J. and Ram N. Aditya, "The Social Scientific Study of Leadership: Quo Vadis?", *Journal of Management*, 23/3 (1997): 409–73

Kerr, Steve and John M. Jermier, "Substitutes for Leadership: Their Meaning and Measurement", *Organizational Behavior and Human Performance*, 22 (1978): 375–403

Yukl, Gary, "Managerial Leadership: A Review of Theory and Research", *Journal of Management*, 15/2 (1989): 251–89

Leadership studies have been conducted in a variety of disciplines, such as management science, psychology, and political science. There has been an incredible number of studies done on leadership, so it is helpful to begin with some reviews and guides to the field. BASS (1990) provides the most comprehensive review and cites over 7000 studies. He begins with an introduction to the basic concepts and theories of leadership, which is of use to either a novice or an expert in the field. The introduction also provides an overview of the multitude of definitions of leadership that researchers have used. The remainder of the book provides a well-organized categorization of the studies. Bass attempts to avoid overlap by grouping studies together based on their specific focus. He also includes a glossary of terms used in the book to benefit readers from all disciplines. Overall, this book has extreme depth but is also very accessible.

YUKL provides a concise and easy-to-read review and evaluation of the major theories and empirical findings in leadership studies up to 1989. He divides the field into four categories based on whether the study's primary focus is on power and influence, leader behaviour, the leader's personal traits, or situational factors that interact with any of the other categories. This article also contains short summaries of the nine main theories of situational leader effectiveness (including path-goal theory, leader substitutes theory, and cognitive resource theory), and the main theories of transformational and charismatic leadership (including those of House, Burns, and Bass). Yukl concludes the article with a detailed integrating conceptual framework that attempts to identify the interrelationships between the many studies cited.

HOUSE & ADITYA is a more recent review of leadership theory and empirical research than Bass and Yukl. Their article provides the reader with a succinct overview of the field and complements Yukl's article well by tracing how the early theories of leadership have evolved into the current theories. In addition, this article concludes with a discussion of areas where there is a need for future research, including the distinction between leadership and supervision, focusing on the organizational context, the management of diversity, cross-cultural leadership, and other matters.

HOUSE is one of the "classic" readings in leadership theory discussed below. House's path-goal theory of leadership focuses on the relationship between the superior and the subordinate. He specifies the leader's motivational function of providing valued outcomes to the subordinate for achieving a goal and by making the path to that goal attainment easier. For path-goal theory, and the others discussed below, the review articles listed above discuss how these theories have been empirically tested, refined, and (sometimes) reformulated.

BASS (1985) developed the Multifactor Leadership Questionnaire (MLQ) to test the ideas of transformational and transactional leadership, and their relationship. The MLQ has received considerable attention. For example, House and Aditya report that the MLQ is the most widely used measure of charismatic leadership.

FIEDLER presents his contingency theory, which was one of the first theories to analyse the relationship between the situation and the leader's behaviour. His theory focuses on the relationship between the leader's style (either relationship-motivated or task-motivated) and the "favourableness" of the situation. FIEDLER & GARCIA present a situational leadership theory termed cognitive resources theory. This theory considers the interaction between the situation (including the stress experienced by leaders and the group) and the cognitive resources of the leader (such as the leader's intelligence and experience), and how that interaction affects the performance of the group. Fiedler and Garcia also discuss the empirical studies of the theory and its counterintuitive results.

KERR & JERMIER provide a different perspective on leadership by focusing on what can substitute for leadership or neutralize it. These potential substitutes include organizational characteristics, the task, and the specific subordinate. By being aware of these substitutes (or neutralizers), we can gain a better understanding of how and when certain leader behaviours may not affect subordinate performance.

DAVID HESS

League of Nations

Burton, Margaret E., *The Assembly of the League of Nations*, Chicago: University of Chicago Press, 1941

Gill, George, *The League of Nations from 1929 to 1946*, New York: Avery, 1996

Henig, Ruth B., *The League of Nations*, New York: Barnes and Noble, and Edinburgh: Oliver and Boyd, 1973

Knock, Thomas J., *To End All Wars: Woodrow Wilson and the Quest for a New World Order*, New York and Oxford: Oxford University Press, 1992

Kuehl, Warren F. and Lynne K. Dunn, *Keeping the Covenant: American Internationalists and the League of Nations, 1920–1939*, Kent, Ohio: Kent State University Press, 1997

Miller, David Hunter, *The Drafting of the Covenant*, New York and London: Putnam, 1928

Ostrower, Gary B., *The League of Nations from 1919 to 1929*, Garden City Park, New York: Avery, 1995

Rovine, Arthur W., *The First Fifty Years: The Secretary-General in World Politics, 1920–1970*, Leiden: Sijthoff, 1970

Scott, George, *The Rise and Fall of the League of Nations*, London: Hutchinson, 1973; New York: Macmillan, 1974

Walters, F.P., *A History of the League of Nations*, vols 1–2, London and New York: Oxford University Press, 1952

The League of Nations was the world's first universal, intergovernmental organization (IGO) that was designed to "promote international cooperation and to achieve international peace and security." The Covenant of the League of Nations comprised the first 26 articles of the Treaty of Versailles, which was signed on 28 June 1919, formally ending World War I. Some 63 countries were members of the organization for at least part of its existence from 15 November 1920 to 8 April 1946, when it was replaced by the United Nations (UN). The US was one of a few countries, and certainly the most significant country, which never joined the League of Nations. The Soviet Union was a member of the League of Nations from 1934 until its expulsion from the organization in 1939.

MILLER provides a historical analysis of the drafting of the Covenant of the League of Nations from the submission of the first draft by Lord Phillimore's Committee on the League of Nations to the British government on 20 March 1918 to the signing of the Treaty of Versailles on 28 June 1919. Writing his book eight years after the formation of the League of Nations, Miller suggested that the "Covenant since it went into force in 1920 has been weighed in the balance of the happenings in world affairs; and it has not been found wanting." While he could not have anticipated the failure of the League to prevent World War II, Miller correctly points out the significant impact that the Covenant of the League of Nations had on world politics in the interwar period and the impact that it would have on the drafting of the Charter of the United Nations some 25 years later.

WALTERS' two-volume book remains one of the most comprehensive historical reviews of the origins and activities of the League of Nations. Walters, a former deputy secretary-general of the League of Nations, begins in the first volume with the historical roots of the League in the Concert of Europe in the 19th century and the Hague Conferences of 1899 and 1907. He then discusses the origins and drafting of the charter of the League during World War I. The rest of the first volume focuses on the activities of the League during its first decade. In the second volume, Walters examines the activities of the League through the beginning of World War II, including the League's efforts to deal with conflicts in Manchuria, South America, Ethiopia, and Spain.

OSTROWER provides a less comprehensive history of the League of Nations from its creation in 1919 through its first decade in existence. He focuses on some of the notable successes of the League during this period, including the resolution of the Greco–Bulgarian territorial dispute, the Franco–German dispute regarding the Saar region, and the Finnish–Swedish dispute over the Aaland islands. Ostrower concludes by suggesting that "the twenties did not reveal enough failure – did not confront enough crisis – for the League to learn just how weak it really was." GILL picks up where Ostrower leaves off with a history of the League of Nations from the start of the Great Depression to the end of World War II. He focuses on several of the important events of this period that led to the demise of the League and the start of World War II, including the Manchurian crisis, the Italian–Ethiopian crisis, and the Spanish civil war. Gill also devotes considerable attention to the controversial tenure of Joseph Avenol as secretary-general of the League from 1 July 1933 to 31 August 1940.

ROVINE analyses the role and accomplishments of the secretary-general of the League of Nations (and the UN) from 1920 to 1970. The first three chapters of the book are devoted to the three secretaries-general of the League of Nations: Sir Eric Drummond (1920–33), Joseph Avenol (1933–40), and Sean Lester (1940–6). Rovine's unique contribution to the literature on the League of Nations is his focus on the change in the resources and functions of the secretary-general across a 50-year period and two different international organizations. BURTON's emphasis is on the character, composition, and organization of the Assembly of the League of Nations and on the role of the Assembly in the management and resolution of international disputes. Although she wrote the book in the early months of World War II when the League of Nations had largely ceased to exist as a functioning international organization, Burton correctly concluded that "whether or not the Assembly of the League of Nations is ever again convened to meet in the Palais des Nations at Geneva, it has done much to lay down the lines for the representative body of the international organization of the future."

HENIG uses hundreds of historical documents related to the League of Nations – including British Foreign Office memoranda and speeches by delegates to the Assembly of the League of Nations – to examine the circumstances in which the League was established and the events that resulted in the successes and failures of the League in the 1920s and 1930s. Henig's book is particularly useful for scholars interested in the activities of the League of Nations in the area of disarmament. In another well-written account of the League of Nations, SCOTT offers an analysis of the "rise and fall" of the League during the 1916–46 period. He devotes considerable attention to the factors that influenced the establishment and eventual collapse of the League, including the idealism of Woodrow Wilson, the Great Depression, and the Manchurian crisis. Scott concludes with a quote by one of the founders of the League of Nations,

Lord Robert Cecil of Britain, who spoke before the last session of the League of Nations Assembly on April 18, 1946: "The League is dead. Long live the United Nations."

KNOCK provides an excellent assessment of President Woodrow Wilson's quest for a "new world order" during and after World War I. The book is an especially significant contribution to the literature on the League of Nations in that it describes in detail the unique American origins of the organization in the half decade or so prior to its formal establishment in 1920. Knock concludes with an account of the failure of the US Senate to ratify the Treaty of Versailles on 19 March 1920 and the failure of the US to join the League of Nations that had partly been created by President Woodrow Wilson. KUEHL & DUNN focus on the activities of American internationalists following the Senate rejection of American membership of the League of Nations through the beginning of World War II in Europe in September 1939. Specifically, the authors examine in detail the political efforts of some individuals and organizations to change American public opinion regarding membership in the League of Nations, as well as membership in the Permanent Court of International Justice (PCIJ).

MARK MULLENBACH

Learning

Gleitman, Henry, *Psychology*, 4th edition, London and New York: Norton, 1995

Gray, J.A., *Elements of a Two-Process Theory of Learning*, London and New York: Academic Press, 1975

Matute, Helena, "Learning and Conditioning" in *Psychology: An Integrated Approach*, edited by Michael Eysenck, Harlow, Essex: Longman, 1998

Miller, George A., *Psychology: The Science of Mental Life*, New York: Harper and Row, 1962; Harmondsworth: Penguin, 1982

Patrick, J., *Training: Research and Practice*, London: Academic Press, 1992

Pavlov, Ivan P., *Conditioned Reflexes: An Investigation of the Physiological Activity of the Cerebral Cortex*, London: Oxford University Press, 1927; New York: Dover, 1960

Skinner, B.F., *Science and Human Behavior*, New York: Free Press, and London: Collier Macmillan, 1953

Stadler, Michael A. and Peter A. Frensch (editors), *Handbook of Implicit Learning*, London and Thousand Oaks, California: Sage, 1998

Stammers, Rob, "Training and Acquisition of Knowledge and Skill" in *Psychology at Work*, 4th edition, edited by Peter Warr, London: Penguin, 1996

Learning refers to a change in behaviour as a direct result of experience (changes in behaviour that are due to maturation are not defined as learning, and nor are changes due to transient influences, such as mood fluctuations or drug intake). Learning is inferred from measures of performance (however, learning may not always be manifest in performance – for example, latent learning, in which learning is revealed in performance only when motivated by reward). The concept of learning, as used in the social sciences, relates to a number of rather distinct theories and applications. References have been selected to encompass these diverse areas, providing the reader with accessible introductions that point the way to more advanced texts.

Much of what counts as learning falls under the general heading of inculcation. This approach is largely concerned with practical ends, with the focus of interest on the events (for example, methods of instruction) and conditions (for example, distributed versus spaced practice) of learning. This instructional view (commonly referred to as training) is concerned with the acquisition of skills sufficient to reach a criterion level of performance, typically in occupational contexts. PATRICK provides a detailed account of the psychology of training, discussing needs assessment analysis, training programme design, and evaluation of training. In the field of education, events and conditions of learning are also of importance, but there is greater emphasis on understanding and appreciation of information. STAMMERS provides a brief but informative account of some of the technical processes operating in training and learning.

In academic psychology, an important theoretical problem concerns the psychological mechanisms of learning: this research literature is known as *learning theory*. A number of prominent theories have been developed to account for the psychological mechanisms of learning. Excellent basic introductions are provided by both MATUTE and GLEITMAN. Gleitman also provides an historical survey of learning and conditioning theory. There are two main types of learning: associative learning (also known as Pavlovian, or classical, conditioning), and instrumental learning (also known as operant, or Skinnerian, learning). MILLER, in a classic text on the major branches of psychology, provides insightful chapters on Pavlovian conditioning, the experimental methodology of Ivan Pavlov, and the search for fundamental behavioural laws reflected in instrumental conditioning.

Both Mutate and Gleitman discuss how associative learning consists in the observation that if two stimuli are paired systematically, so that they are related both temporally and spatially, then each stimulus will take on the properties of the other stimulus. Associative theories are concerned with explaining the processes involved in the association of two stimuli. The well-known Pavlovian version of associative learning involves two stimuli. The first stimulus is the *unconditioned stimulus* (UCS), which is an innate stimulus capable of eliciting an *unconditioned response* (UCR) – for example, a foot shock leading to pain, or the sight of juicy meat leading to salivation. The second stimulus is the *conditioned stimulus* (CS), which is initially neutral, that is unable to elicit the UCR before learning. After CS-UCS pairings (the CS usually precedes the UCS for a few seconds), the CS takes on the power of the UCS to elicit a response that resembles, although it is not identical to, the UCR: this is the *conditioned response* (CR). Reading PAVLOV's original work provides a fascinating first-hand account of classical conditioning theory, and the types of experimental and philosophical reasoning that lie behind his approach.

Instrumental learning is a form of trial-and-error learning where responses are shaped by reinforcement (the delivery and termination/omission of reward and punishment). Reinforcement provides information concerning the appropriateness of responses (knowledge of results) as well as assigning emotional significance to responses. Through progressively rewarding and punishing behaviour (schedules of reinforcement), the organism learns which responses lead to desirable outcomes and which do not: this is known as shaping of behaviour. Unlike associative learning, in which the subject has no control over the presentation of stimuli, in instrumental learning the presentation of stimuli (reinforcement) is contingent upon responses. Matute provides a useful comparison of a number of current associative learning theories.

SKINNER argues in favour of a strong form of instrumental learning (called "radical behaviourism"), which holds important implications for the management of society (for example education and the control of crime). In everyday society, instrumental learning is widespread (for instance, the shaping of children to acquire numerical proficiency; incentives at work to motivate performance, where reward, pay, is spaced out over days and weeks, rather than minutes or hours – a schedule of reinforcement that has been experimentally shown to promote high work rates). However, Skinner's form of radical behaviourism is not representative of the vast majority of work in conditioning theory, which is concerned with highly detailed analysis of the elements of learning. Only in psychiatry has Skinnerian principles had an direct and obvious impact (for example, in the token economy); however, many of the operant principles studied experimentally by Skinner in the pigeon are already part of the fabric of human society. Skinner's argument is that these operant principles, which all human societies endorse, could be improved upon by the application of behavioural technologies (for example, rewarding criminals for good socially desirable behaviour, not simply punishing bad behaviour – the latter is known from learning experiments to be relatively ineffective in shaping behaviour).

GRAY, in a rather technical but highly insightful presentation, discusses the empirical and theoretical arguments for a two-process model of learning: associative and instrumental learning working together. This text is important in that it provides an excellent example of the uses to which learning theory may be put. It is argued that behavioural data, and theoretical models of learning based upon these data, may be used to construct a "conceptual nervous system" (cns), which delineates the behavioural components of the central nervous system (CNS). For instance, the delivery of reward and punishment (cns) can only work if there are corresponding CNS neurological processes. By careful delineation of the structure of the cns (learning theory) inferences may be made concerning the structure of the actual CNS. This research tradition was first articulated by Pavlov, who postulated that inhibitory and excitatory neuronal processes underlie conditioning and, furthermore, that the functioning of these processes underlies personality and psychiatric disorder. Following this tradition, GRAY argues that learning theory provides the conceptual foundations, as well as the scaffolding necessary to construct the structure upon which a physiological model of personality and emotion may be built.

Matute covers other forms of learning that are also important: concept, or category, learning that involves learning to categorize items into families (for example, animal, furniture,

social); and imitation, or vicarious learning, which involves observing other people behaving and receiving reinforcement. There is also discussion as to whether these forms of learning differ fundamentally from associative processes.

In recent years, there has been increasing interest in the distinction between explicit and implicit learning. Where explicit learning refers to knowledge and skills that are available to awareness and can be verbalized, implicit learning refers to knowledge and skills that are acquired without the involvement of conscious awareness (for example, sequence and artificial grammar learning). A related concept is implicit memory, which refers to the performance of learned material (such as completion of word stems or fragments) without conscious awareness of using such material. STADLER & FRENSCH's edited handbook presents the major findings and controversies in this important area of research. One limitation of this field, which is reflected in this text, is the neglect of temperamental and emotional influences in implicit learning. It is also not clear whether implicit learning is just a more complex form of associative learning. However, this line of research poses new and interesting questions in the rapidly developing science of consciousness.

PHILIP J. CORR

See also Habituation effect

Learning economy

Antonelli, Cristiano, *The Economics of Localized Technological Change and Industrial Dynamics*, Boston: Kluwer, 1995

Archibugi, Daniele, Jeremy Howells and Jonathan Michie, "Innovation Systems and Policy in a Global Economy" in *Innovation Policy in a Global Economy*, edited by Daniele Archibugi, Jeremy Howells and Jonathan Michie, Cambridge and New York: Cambridge University Press, 1999

Freeman, Chris, "The Economics of Technical Change", *Cambridge Journal of Economics*, 18/5 (1994): 463–514; reprinted in *Trade, Growth and Technical Change*, edited by Daniele Archibugi and Jonathan Michie, Cambridge and New York: Cambridge University Press, 1998

Hodgson, Geoffrey M., *Economics and Institutions: A Manifesto for a Modern Institutional Economics*, Cambridge, Massachusetts: Polity Press, and Oxford: Blackwell, 1988

Kitson, Michael and Jonathan Michie, "Markets, Competition and Innovation" in *The Political Economy of Competitiveness*, edited by Michael Kitson and Jonathan Michie, London and New York: Routledge, 2000

Lundvall, Bengt-Åke, "Innovation as an Interactive Process: From User–Producer Interaction to National Systems of Innovation" in *Technical Change and Economic Theory*, edited by Giovanni Dosi et al., London: Pinter, 1988

Lundvall, Bengt-Åke (editor), *National Systems of Innovation: Towards a Theory of Innovation and Interactive Learning*, London and New York: Pinter, 1992

Lundvall, Bengt-Åke and Bjorn Johnson, "The Learning Economy", *Journal of Industry Studies*, 1 (1994): 23–42

Lundvall, Bengt-Åke, "The Global Unemployment Problem and National Systems of Innovation" in *Globalisation, Networking and Small Firm Innovation*, edited by Dermot P. O'Doherty, London and Boston: Graham and Trotman, 1995

Lundvall, Bengt-Åke, "Technology Policy in the Learning Economy" in *Innovation Policy in a Global Economy*, edited by Daniele Archibugi, Jeremy Howells and Jonathan Michie, Cambridge and New York: Cambridge University Press, 1999

Michie, Jonathan and Maura Sheehan, "HRM Practices, R & D Expenditure and Innovative Investment: Evidence from the UK's 1990 Workplace Industrial Relations Survey (WIRS)", *Industrial and Corporate Change*, 8/2 (1999): 211–34

LUNDVALL (1988) stresses the role that learning plays in binding together production and innovation. It places these processes within the operation of national systems of innovation, while making it clear that learning also plays an important role within the economy more generally. LUNDVALL (1992) further emphasizes the importance of learning, again with particular emphasis on the notion of national systems of innovation. This is an important edited collection, and Lundvall himself brings out the particular importance of learning in the economy within his introductory chapter. Building on this work, Lundvall has sought to develop a theory about the role of learning in the economy, and to put this at the core of national systems of innovation construct. This project has been pursued through a number of publications, but see in particular LUNDVALL & JOHNSON. In these latter works, Lundvall has stressed the role of learning in new and competitive national systems of innovation and has discussed in particular the process of interactive learning.

Learning is important in Lundvall's conception of systems of innovation because it is both a key element in the *dynamic* of the system and a key agent in *binding* the whole system together. Thus, "many different sectors and segments of the economy contribute to the overall process of interactive learning and the specificity of the elements, as well as the linkages and modes of interaction between them, are crucial for the rate and direction of technical change" (LUNDVALL 1995, p. 39).

Learning thus plays a major role in the development of the system, while forming the key element in its connectivity. In this framework, learning takes place at all levels: not just from the individual to the organization, but beyond this, to inter-firm and inter-organizational learning, institutional learning, cross-institutional learning, and, ultimately, to the whole system of the "learning economy". Obviously, the learning process involves a clear interactive and collective dimension. There are also inter-firm and more general institutional routines that can be set up through this interactive learning process, as detailed by HODGSON.

However, it is much harder to ascribe a single, clear cognitive process, involving both a decision-making and memory function, to collections of firms, organizations, or institutions. The notion that what is learned will be exactly the same for each individual, firm, organization, and institution is difficult to accept: on which, see the discussion in ANTONELLI.

The literature on the learning economy is discussed and put into context within the more general issues of economic policy, globalization, and innovation by ARCHIBUGI, HOWELLS & MICHIE. This is the introductory and overview chapter in the final volume of a series by the same editorial team. This particular volume argues that the opportunities offered by globalization will only be fully realised by organizations which have developed institutions that allow for the transfer, absorption, and use of knowledge. In the introductory chapter, the editors tie the literature on the learning economy to the broader literature on technology and innovation, and to such topics as knowledge flows, linkages and networks, and to systems of innovation as "task environments" for firms.

This edited book also includes several other relevant contributions, including one from LUNDVALL (1999), in which he discusses the theoretical and policy issues not only in relation to his previous contributions as mentioned above, but also in relation to the policy agendas of the OECD and other bodies. He stresses that part of the reason for speaking about the learning economy is that changes in the structure of the labour market and production show how the economy is to an increasing extent becoming knowledge based, and that this means that knowledge building and learning are becoming increasingly important for economic growth and competitiveness.

The contributions of Lundvall and others are reported in FREEMAN, a comprehensive survey article on the economics of technical change. Chris Freeman, the founder of the Science Policy Research Unit (SPRU) at the University of Sussex in the UK, is without doubt one of the world's leading authorities on issues of technical change and innovation. This survey article covers the theory, evidence, and policy implications of the key issues within the economics of technical change, including learning and the learning economy.

KITSON & MICHIE investigate how firms cooperate in practice, both between themselves and with outside organizations such as universities, research institutes, and other public bodies. The authors argue that deregulatory policies aimed at "freeing-up" the labour market are often based on a picture of economic processes whereby firms compete in markets with large numbers of customers and competitors, with keen prices and low costs as the key determinants of success. However, this misrepresents or at least dangerously oversimplifies the real character of the competitive process in most sectors in advanced economies. Using evidence from an innovation survey carried out by Cambridge University's Economic and Social Research Council (ESRC) Centre for Business Research, they show that factors such as trust and cooperation can play an important role in competitive success, and might actually be undermined by a policy approach that prioritizes deregulation. They report that innovating firms – in contrast to non-innovating ones – stress the importance of higher-order qualitative factors, which require investment in skill and technical capability. One of the important ingredients for achieving competitive success appears to be the need to establish effective collaboration with others – customers, suppliers, higher education establishments, and so on. Such collaboration allows firms to expand their range of expertise and to develop specialist products and processes.

What makes firms – and workers – innovative is analysed by MICHIE & SHEEHAN with particular reference to human resource management and other policies pursued by companies. Recognizing that labour "flexibility" is often portrayed as necessary for a learning and innovative economy, they use evidence from the UK's Workplace Industrial Relations Survey to investigate the relationship between firms' human resource management practices and innovation. Their results suggest that "low road" HRM practices – for example short-term contracts – are *negatively* correlated with investment in R&D and new technology. "High road" work practices on the other hand – "high commitment" organization and other systems – are *positively* correlated with investment in R&D and new technology.

JONATHAN MICHIE

See also Innovation, National systems of innovation

Learning organization

Easterby-Smith, Mark, "Creating a Learning Organization", *Personnel Review*, 19/5 (1990): 24–28

Gardiner, Penny and Peter Whiting, "Success Factors in Learning Organizations: An Empirical Study", *Industrial and Commercial Training*, 29/2 (1997): 41–48

Garratt, Bob, *The Learning Organization, and the Need for Directors Who Think*, London: Fontana, 1987

Garvin, David A., "Building a Learning Organization", *Harvard Business Review*, 71/4 (July–August 1993): 78–91

Iles, Paul, "Developing Learning Environments: Challenges for Theory, Research and Practice", *Journal of European Industrial Training*, 18/3 (1994): 3–9

Marquardt, Michael J. and Angus Reynolds, *The Global Learning Organization*, Burr Ridge, Illinois: Irwin, 1994

Pedler, Mike, John Burgoyne and Tom Boydell, *The Learning Company: A Strategy for Sustainable Development*, 2nd edition, London and New York: McGraw Hill, 1997

Senge, Peter, *The Fifth Discipline: The Art and Practice of the Learning Organization*, New York: Doubleday, 1990

Slater, Stanley F. and John C. Narver, "Market Orientation and the Learning Organization", *Journal of Marketing*, 59/3 (July 1995): 63–74

Tsang, Eric W.K., "Organizational Learning and the Learning Organization: A Dichotomy between Descriptive and Prescriptive Research", *Human Relations*, 50/1 (1997): 73–89

One of the earliest descriptions of the learning organization is provided by GARRATT, who considers organizations from the perspective of directors. This book analyses problems that arise from ineffective leadership and suggests the development of learning organizations as the solution to this problem, with the directors providing the central, integrating role – the "business brain". Garratt describes the process of becoming a learning organization through establishing a climate where technical aspects are integrated with socioemotional factors, where people work together in carefully designed teams, and where learning is the central focus of the organization.

SENGE examines the learning organization from a US perspective. This account provides a comprehensive, if highly idealistic, look at learning in an easy-to-read format, illustrated by many examples and case studies. It begins by considering how barriers to learning develop in many organizations and describes the shift of mind, or *metanoia*, needed to overcome such obstacles. Senge suggests that there are five disciplines of the learning organization, of which the fifth, systems thinking, is the key, and the one on which the other five components depend. Systems thinking takes a holistic view of organizations that are described as a series of interconnected actions and effects, related to other patterns within the wider world. A useful insight is provided into the changing roles of leaders as designers, stewards, and teachers rather than directors and manipulators.

A more critical consideration is provided by GARVIN, who notes that there are few clear definitions of the concept. Garvin suggests that learning organizations excel at five activities: systematic problem solving, experimentation, learning from their own and others' experiences, and effective knowledge transfer. Several case studies demonstrate interesting examples of these skills. The importance of measuring learning in organizations is emphasized; it is pointed out that developing a learning organization is a long-term process and that many measures to date have focused solely on results, which may fail to show short-term learning gains. The removal of organizational boundaries and the development of an environment conducive to learning are advocated in order to foster idea sharing and establish learning goals.

Many discussions of learning organizations focus on designing appropriate conditions for learning. EASTERBY-SMITH describes a number of ways of creating a learning climate through structural reorganization, cultural change, and modification of the systems that control behaviour and performance. The author recommends the development of flexibility and experimentation in organizations and maintains that employees should be rewarded for risk taking and proactive behaviour. He concludes that organizational learning, and by implication the learning organization, are difficult concepts to understand and suggests that the way forward may be through the development of competence in dealing with uncertainty.

The learning organization is frequently perceived as a response to environmental pressure, rapid technological development, and worldwide competition. The emphasis in MARQUARDT & REYNOLDS is on the development of *global* learning organizations. The authors draw on a number of existing models and present their own model of the global learning organization. A useful metaphor is suggested for the learning organization as an orchestra, where the end product (for example. a symphony) results from the embedded knowledge of the whole group working together. Eleven essential elements of learning organizations are identified from research into companies worldwide, although no European organizations are included in the sample. Some learning barriers and disabilities in organizations are described, together with practical means of surmounting these to create global learning organizations.

Perhaps the best known work in this field is PEDLER, BURGOYNE & BOYDELL. This revised edition comprises probably the most up-to-date and comprehensive account of the learning organization from a British perspective. It also contains the most widely used definition of such an organization, referred to throughout as the "learning company". This is a very readable description, with much practical advice on how to develop a learning company. The authors admit the concept is aspirational and probably no company measures up to the ideal completely. They have also identified 11 characteristics of learning organizations, although these mostly differ from those of Marqardt & Reynolds, and supply a number of practical insights into organizations that illustrate the importance of these 11 aspects.

ILES discusses the development and promotion of learning environments with the aim of designing learning organizations. He emphasizes the need to integrate work and learning activities, particularly at a strategic level, so that different organizational aspects are aligned with overall learning goals. Organizations need to recognize and value individual diversity in background, experience, and learning style, and utilize the full potential of employees to develop learning communities where people are capable of effectively using all the resources available to them.

Much of the recent literature has confused organizational learning with the learning organization; TSANG supplies a clear differentiation between the two. A clear association is indicated between learning capability and performance, and the value of learning in all organizations is underlined. He notes that two streams of research in this area currently exist: descriptive and prescriptive, much of the latter having no empirical basis and largely ignoring the influence of national culture. Tsang disputes that there is "one best way" to achieve the learning organization and recommends a contingency approach, which takes into account organizational size, sector, and learning style.

A useful descriptive account is GARDINER & WHITING. This assesses learning organization characteristics in one department of a large engineering company and presents research findings, using eight conceptual groups. This study found that although the company had developed capabilities in empowerment of the workforce and individual learning, there was little involvement of employees at strategic level. The achievement of learning organization status in this department was impeded by organization-wide factors, which included a lack of information sharing, low levels of trust, and a deeply entrenched culture that was resistant to change.

The development of a learning organization may not necessarily be beneficial *per se*, but only when the knowledge and learning acquired can help to improve its performance. SLATER & NARVER highlight the value of a market orientation in conjunction with a learning climate and a spirit of entrepreneurship. They explain how competence in learning creates and sustains competitive advantage, particularly during periods of environmental change. Five components of learning organizations are proposed, which include both climate and cultural factors; a market orientation is considered the key cultural foundation. The authors suggest the scope of market orientation in a learning organization needs to incorporate all information and stakeholders that may improve outputs or warn of potential threats. Future research should focus on validating the link between learning and competitive advantage.

PENNY GARDINER

See also Organizational learning

Legal aid

Hudson, Alastair, *Law, Labour and Legal Aid*, London: Pinter, 1999

Legal Action Group, *A Strategy for Justice: Publicly Funded Legal Services in the 1990s*, London: Legal Action Group, 1992

Legal Services Commission, *The Legal Services Commission Manual*, London: Sweet and Maxwell, 2000

Napier, Michael and Fiona Bawdon, *Conditional Fees: A Survival Guide*, London: Law Society, 1996

Regan, Francis, Alan Paterson, Tamara Goriely and Don Fleming (editors), *The Transformation of Legal Aid: Comparative and Historical Studies*, Oxford and New York: Oxford University Press, 1999

Sachs, Eric, *Legal Aid*, London: Eyre and Spottiswoode, 1951

Smith, Roger (editor), *Achieving Civil Justice: Appropriate Dispute Resolution for the 1990s*, London: Legal Action Group, 1996

Underwood, Kerry, *No Win, No Fee, No Worries*, Sutton Coldfield: CLT Professional, 1998

Young, Richard and David Wall (editors), *Access to Criminal Justice*, London: Blackstone Press, 1996

REGAN *et al.* brings together the leading scholars in the field to provide a definitive set of essays on historical and comparative themes. It ranges over the history of legal aid in a number of countries during the last century, and makes observations on the reasons for the turn away from state funding that has characterized the last two decades, particularly in the UK, North America, Australia, Sweden, and the Netherlands. It is not however primarily a narrative, since the authors employ both legal and social science techniques to develop a coherent theoretical appraisal of legal aid. A valuable feature of a number of the essays is that they range over global and comparative themes and do not simply give an account of a single jurisdiction. Thus, for example, Frederick Zemans reviews "Law Centres in Australia, Ontario, and England" and sees a general tendency to bureaucratize and centrally manage their operations. His study of the responses in the separate jurisdictions draws out common lessons, especially the need for local networks of supporters within their communities. In a well-researched historical review, "Making the Welfare State Work", Tamara Goriely stresses the need for legal aid to move beyond the model of individual casework to provide a voice for the citizen to confront state bureaucracies. Erhard Blankenberg, who has pioneered comparative studies of legal aid, provides one of the most innovative of the essays in comparing the political economy of legal aid in several countries. He traces a diversity of institutional infrastructures, derived from the differing levels of expenditures in the welfare states and the diverse sociology of the legal profession. Overall the book is a distillation of international legal aid scholarship over recent decades.

LEGAL SERVICES COMMISSION provides the definitive practitioners' guide. It covers extracts from the relevant statutory material, and gives guidance on rates, applications, and schemes such as the work of duty solicitors. Formerly called the *Legal Aid Handbook*, it comes in four loose-leaf volumes. As of 2001 there will be three updates a year.

LEGAL ACTION GROUP reviews the development of legal aid since World War II, and compares the provision of civil legal aid in Britain with that in other jurisdictions including Holland, Canada, and Australia. The book emphasizes the gaps in legal aid provision, particularly in the areas of family law, personal injury, debt, and employment. It demonstrates that legal aid in England and Wales remains dominated by the narrow framework in which it was originally conceived. The Legal Aid Group aims to achieve equal access to justice, shifting the emphasis from the means by which publicly funded legal services are delivered to their intended result. In the group's view, the ultimate policy aim must be to give anyone with a legal problem equal access to its just conclusion, so that disputes are determined on their intrinsic merits and not by inequalities of wealth or power. The final part of the book is a manifesto for development of civil legal aid through a "legal services approach". The appendices include performance evaluation criteria for the legal clinics and centres in Ontario and Australia.

SACHS, first published in 1951, is an exhaustive account of the original Legal Aid and Advice Act 1949, which the author rightly describes as an important landmark in British legal history. In accordance with the shape of the original act, the book is divided into three parts: legal aid in civil courts; legal advice and preliminary legal aid; and legal aid in criminal courts. This book is of great interest to the historian, but of little use to the present day practitioner, since the scope of legal aid and most of the details of its administration have changed radically in the last half century. But those interested in what Sir Hartley Shawcross called "the charter of the little man to the British courts of justice" will still find interesting material here.

YOUNG & WALL is a collection of essays and research papers about criminal legal aid, covering the topic from a large number of different standpoints: constitutional, legal, economic, and historical. It critically examines the way in which the present system operates, bringing to bear a variety of professional disciplines and research techniques. There are particularly interesting chapters on the likely impact of the European Convention on Human Rights, the effect of the concentration of legal aid work in particular nominated firms of solicitors, and on access to justice in the police station. A major theme of the book is that without legal aid the current system of justice cannot achieve legitimacy. The English system is contrasted with the operation of the court system in Scotland. There are chapters on the way in which court clerks exercise their discretion to determine whether defendants should be legally aided, and on the operation of the Legal Aid Board's case workers and area committees. If nothing else, the book demonstrates the extent to which legal aid has become an academic discipline in its own right.

NAPIER & BAWDON describes itself as a practical guide to using conditional fees in personal injury work. It sets out the new legal framework, which permits solicitors in certain cases to enter into "no win, no fee" arrangements. It clearly indicates what is and what is not permitted under the rules. Sensibly, it warns firms contemplating conditional fee work to think first whether they should undertake it at all. But it also shows how the potential pitfalls can be minimized or in some cases completely eliminated. There are extensive extracts from the relevant statutes and regulations, and chapters dealing with insurance and marketing.

UNDERWOOD is a must for any solicitor who wants to take advantage of conditional or contingent fees. It is a very practical guide that demolishes many of the myths surrounding this topic. The book shows that much of the fear of conditional and contingent fees is misplaced and based on ignorance. It contains a comprehensive survey of recent case law, includes extensive appendices setting out the statutes and rules governing solicitors' conduct on conditional fee cases, and deals in depth with each of the areas in which such fees are now allowed. Underwood does not trouble to hide his passion for conditional fees and some might find his enthusiasm irritating. But anyone in search of a clear account of "no win, no fee" business should read this book.

HUDSON is a wide ranging critique of Blairite legal affairs policy. It highlights the conflict between the government's cost-cutting objective and its stated aims of social inclusion and greater social justice. The author believes that constitutional affairs and the reform of the legal system will become major political issues. His preoccupation is with citizens' access to dispute resolution. Hudson, himself a barrister, is well aware of the defects of the existing legal system. But he believes that only a comprehensive approach to its reform can deliver the objectives that New Labour claims to be pursuing. Legal aid is important but it is not coterminous with the availability of justice. As Hudson points out, it is a payment of money from central taxation directly into lawyers' pockets. He asks why voluntary agencies and advice agencies should not be able to provide some of the services that are currently paid for by legal aid and provided exclusively by lawyers. The primary goal of legal aid, in Hudson's view, is to serve the citizen.

SMITH is an Anglo-American collection of essays. Its theme is summed up by the editor: "The problems of civil justice cannot be narrowly defined as 'cost, complexity and delay' and solved by reform of court procedure". It draws on American and South African as well as British experience to undertake a critical examination of Lord Woolf's reforms of civil procedure. It includes proposals for changes in legal aid provision designed to deliver the original objectives of the legal aid scheme in a modern context.

MAUREEN SPENCER

Legal positivism

Austin, John, *Lectures on Jurisprudence; or, The Philosophy of Positive Law*, 5th edition, revised by Robert Campbell, London: John Murray, 1885

Bentham, Jeremy, *Of Laws in General*, edited by H.L.A. Hart, London: Athlone Press, 1970

George, Robert P. (editor), *The Autonomy of Law: Essays on Legal Positivism*, Oxford: Clarendon Press, and New York: Oxford University Press, 1996

Guest, Stephen (editor), *Positivism Today*, Aldershot, Hampshire: Dartmouth, 1996

Hart, H.L.A., *The Concept of Law*, 2nd edition, Oxford: Clarendon Press, and New York: Oxford University Press, 1994

Jori, Mario (editor), *Legal Positivism*, New York: New York University Press, 1992

Kelsen, Hans, *Introduction to the Problems of Legal Theory: A Translation of the First Edition of Reine Rechslehre or Pure Theory of Law*, Oxford: Clarendon Press, and New York: Oxford University Press, 1992 (published in German 1934)

Legal theory, like law itself, tends to be local and monocultural. The code tradition of civil law systems, derived from Roman law, has led to different positivist models less likely to fit judge-made law on which writing in English has concentrated. Legal positivism takes a number of forms and the discussion of it has been long and complex.

BENTHAM shows his contempt for the irrational disorder of the common law, for example in his attack on common law case reports in chapter 15. His remedy is legislative codification. This avoids a problem with positivist descriptions of the law as "laid down". Based in customs and reasonable social practices the common law has arguably "sprung up". Chapter one succinctly summarizes Bentham's theory. He reversed the concept of the sovereign in the political theories of Hobbes (*Leviathan*, 1651) and Bodin (*Six Livres de la république*, 1577). They are defined by their natural law rights to command. Based on this authority their commands are law. Bentham developed command positivism from this, what the political sovereign commands is law. He sheared any natural law foundation from it by noting the habitual obedience of the people in a community to such commands. He did not exclude limits on the power of the sovereign to make law but never resolved what they were. As the sovereign's power to legislate was not conferred by law it was difficult to describe any commands as illegal. Bentham's combative prose may attract some readers and repel others.

AUSTIN, Bentham's disciple, in Lectures I, V, and VI, develops command positivism. He seeks to exclude from the concept of law all things that are not commands of a sovereign or political superior. Also excluded are commands that are not rules – those requiring the performance of a specific act and not capable of general application. Common-law judges in making law are delegates of the sovereign. Austin did not avoid the problem inherent in Bentham. Habitual obedience to a political sovereign is a fact but also involves issues of law. As a sovereign could not be subject to any obligation to obey Austin is even more difficult to apply in states with fixed constitutions. His search for precision in writing tormented him and resulted in dreary prose relieved only by the unintended jokes of further qualification of qualifications. Consequently he is known from secondary accounts that suppress nuances. The best edition is the fifth by his wife, Elizabeth Austin, and further revised by Robert Campbell from John Stuart Mill's notes of Austin's lectures. Philip Schofield's essay "Utilitarian politics and legel positivism: the rejection of contractarianism in early utilitarian thought" in GUEST re-evaluates Bentham and Austin.

KELSEN argues that whether a law is a law can only be determined by the legal system. When the validity of a law cannot be further traced the basic or fundamental norm or *grundnorm* is reached. The validity of this *grundnorm* lies outside the legal system and cannot be adjudicated within it.

This *grundnorm* can limit the laws derived from it by allocating to particular institutions law-making powers, regulating the process for law making and the content of laws made, for example where a constitution prohibits the making of particular laws. Kelsen does not specifically deal with the common law but he accepts custom as a source of law. He fits it into his theory by arguing that customs are human acts. He ignores the possibility that non-legal impurities in the *grundnorm* might be traced into the laws based on it and the convergence that does occur between what the law is and what it "ought" to be. His theory underwent substantial revisions in the course of his long life. Some argue that he departs from the purity of the model he described in 1934.

HART marks a turn to empiricism in which law is represented as a social phenomenon. Based on a linguistic analogy law and legal systems are analysed as if they are sets of sentences and meanings. Hart argues that the legal system consists of primary rules supplemented by secondary rules. In a "primitive" society law consists only of primary rules which impose obligations on people. They rest on the uncertainty of the social structure, are static and dependent on inefficient social pressures to enforce them. Hart argues that secondary rules are needed to supplement them. These rules confer power. They include the rule of recognition used by law officials to determine whether a primary rule is valid. Two additional secondary rules, the rule of change and the rule of adjudication, permit institutions to change the primary rules and to authoritatively determine disputes over them. While breaching primary rules may carry sanctions, Hart finds that the rules are largely internalized by people living under them so that the sanctions are not as significant as they might appear. Contemporary legal systems are built of rules and not commands. Hart understates the significance of the "intelligence" of the sovereign and the "habitual" obedience of the community in Austin's theory. His "primitive" society may not exist.

Norberto Bobbio's essay "'Sein' and 'Sollen' in legal science" in JORI, influenced by scientific positivism, analyses legal codes as translations into tight, integrated, and exhaustive language. He argues that while there is conflict over the meaning of "normative science", legal science is normative as its contents are norms, it examines social reality from the viewpoint of such norms, and it makes and proposes norms. Difficult to apply to common law, it emphasizes the significance of scientific models in the civil law.

Most recent developments in positivist common law legal theory have been responses to the criticisms of Hart's student and critic, Ronald Dworkin. Dworkin claims that law is based on principles that are weighed by judges rather than rules generated from these principles, which are applied in an all or nothing way. Hart addresses Dworkin's criticisms in his postscript. Other answers to Dworkin are suggested in Neil MacCormick's essays "Dworkin as pre-Benthamite" and "Law and institutional fact", in Jori's edited collection.

Jori collects significant articles on legal positivism with an introduction giving an overview of the theories. GEORGE and Guest are more recent collections. Jori and George reflect the collapse of boundaries that is taking place within disciplines as well as between disciplines, sometimes described as postmodernism, in the 1980s and 1990s. Jori notes that legal positivists have failed to identify any argument that marks off legal positivism distinctively from various theories that are alternatives to it. George proclaims that "the legal positivist is mainly concerned to produce a rich and accurate description of law and legal systems as they function in human societies", p.vi. Other essays query to what extent can law be autonomous or be separated from morality and suggest that it is possible to reconcile natural law and positive law theories. Guest includes essays considering the problems of objectivity and truth in positivism and the implications of globalization for positivist theory. The varied perspectives and divergent opinions in these collections give wide perspectives as well as some close-up details but this also means that they are fragmented.

NEIL ANDREWS

Legal realism

Frank, Jerome, *Law and the Modern Mind*, New York: Brentano, 1930

Holmes, Oliver Wendell, "The Path of the Law" in his *Collected Legal Papers*, New York: Harcourt Brace, and London: Constable, 1920

Horwitz, Morton J., *The Transformation of American Law, 1870–1960: The Crisis of Legal Orthodoxy*, New York and Oxford: Oxford University Press, 1992

Kalman, Laura, *Legal Realism at Yale, 1927–1960*, Chapel Hill: University of North Carolina Press, 1986

Llewellyn, Karl N., "A Realistic Jurisprudence: The Next Step", *Columbia Law Review*, 30/4 (1930): 431–65

Llewellyn, Karl N., "Some Realism about Realism: Responding to Dean Pound", *Harvard Law Review*, 44/8 (1931): 1222–64

Purcell, Edward A. Jr, "American Jurisprudence between the Wars: Legal Realism and the Critics of Democratic Theory", *American Historical Review*, 75/2 (1969): 424–46

Singer, Joseph W., "Legal Realism Now", *California Law Review*, 76/2 (1988): 465–544

Legal realism is a school of thought concerning law and legal institutions that emerged in the 1920s and 1930s in response to the dominant 19th-century theory of law, or what might be called orthodox jurisprudence. To the legal luminaries of the 19th century, a legal system was premised upon a small number of core principles from which lawyers and judges deduce specific legal rules and categories. They stressed the importance of logic, analogy, and deduction in explaining how judges reach decisions. In their minds, judges methodically use these modes of reasoning to find and apply the appropriate legal rule or precedent. Thus, law was understood as certain, neutral, and apolitical.

The significant social and economic changes preceding World War I, including industrialization and urbanization, led many to challenge this orthodox jurisprudence. Legal realists, for instance, saw law and the legal system as neither predictable, neutral, nor apolitical. They questioned the importance of reason in explaining judicial decision making and stressed instead the influence of human idiosyncrasies. In an effort to better understand how judges reach decisions, realists called for greater use of social science in the study of law. Realists also argued that the orthodox jurisprudence provided a false sense of neutrality; in fact, it belied a conservative ideology in law.

The works summarized below divide into two groups. The first four works provide histories of legal realism and assess its legacy and importance. The latter four represent some of the best-known examples of legal realist writings.

HORWITZ does an admirable, easily accessible job of tracing the struggle at the turn of the century between the orthodox jurisprudence and progressive legal thought. The author concludes that legal realism is best understood as "a continuation of the reform agenda of pre-World War I Progressivism." Chapters six and seven focus exclusively on legal realism. Chapter six traces the emergence of legal realism, beginning with the famous exchange between Columbia University's Karl Llewellyn and Harvard Law School's Dean Roscoe Pound. Horwitz also describes contributions of other legal realists, including Jerome Frank and Benjamin Cardozo. Perhaps most intriguing are the parallels drawn between Llewellyn's personal life and his jurisprudential outlook.

Horwitz assesses the legacy of legal realism in chapter seven. Using key articles and court cases, he explores the realist critique of the naturalness of the economic market, its response to orthodox legal reasoning, and its challenge to the legal division between public and private spheres. In its early years, legal realism was primarily about the task of impugning the orthodox legal model. Not until after the New Deal did realists become more reform minded, calling for a turn toward positive social science in legal study. These two chapters are particularly helpful in introducing the key contributors, works, and ideas of legal realism.

PURCELL's article does an excellent job describing the philosophical and cultural context in which legal realism emerged. The early part of the 20th century witnessed several academic disciplines turning increasingly to the scientific method and empirical research. This trend eventually evidenced itself in law via the legal realists. This article does an impressive job presenting the perspectives of several legal realists and raising important considerations that distinguish each thinker. Purcell also considers how legal realists understood democratic theory. To them, the abstractions, formalism, reliance on reason, and other aspects of the orthodox approach were impediments to a truly democratic society. The writings of several critics of legal realism are also explored, including Lon Fuller, Roscoe Pound, and various Catholic legal scholars.

What is legal realism's legacy? A recent work by KALMAN concludes that realism failed to bring significant change in legal education. Realists criticized the case method for removing law from its social context and called for greater use of social science, but the first generation of legal realists (those writing in the 1920s and 1930s) failed to implement this pedagogy. Contributions from realists to legal education were inconsequential until the 1950s. Focusing on the law schools at Yale and Harvard, this book provides a fascinating look at how institutional constraints thwarted the advancement of realism in legal education.

SINGER takes issue with Kalman's thesis that legal realism failed as a movement. He demonstrates how many of today's legal theories are reactions to or permutations of legal realism. Realists, according to Singer, fundamentally changed our understanding of legal reasoning and the relationship between law and society. For the reader who seeks an organized, systematic analysis of how legal realism operates in current legal theories, this article is an excellent starting point.

The remaining works exemplify legal realist writing. To many observers, Justice Oliver Wendell HOLMES, Jr is rightfully understood as the father of legal realism. His speech delivered in 1897, "The Path of the Law", is selected here because it presages many realist arguments from the 1920s and 1930s. Holmes argued that law is a social creation and that the role of lawyers is to predict court decisions. Law involves prophecy, so Holmes rejected the power of reasoning, writing that "the logical method and form flatter that longing for certainty and for repose. But certainty generally is an illusion and repose is not the destiny of man." He likewise discounted the role of history in decision making.

Jerome FRANK is attributed with first using the term "legal realism" in this occasionally irreverent work. Frank essentially employed a psychoanalytic approach to criticize the formalism of 19th-century jurisprudence, in particular its emphasis on predictability and certainty in law. In short, he concluded that the desire for certainty and predictability in law stems from an individual's tendency to replace law for the father-as-infallible-judge. Frank wrote that law represents a "rediscovery of a father, a childish, completely controllable universe . . . That childish longing is an important element in the explanation of the absurdly unrealistic notion that law is, or can be made, entirely certain and definitely predictable." Ironically, Frank started writing this work while undergoing his own psychoanalysis.

Columbia University's Karl Llewellyn was a key advocate of legal realism. In the early 1930s, he published a series of articles challenging the veracity of the orthodox jurisprudence. The first (LLEWELLYN 1930) was "A Realistic Jurisprudence – The Next Step", where one sees many of Llewellyn's ideas in their formative state. The article criticized the emphasis placed on legal rules and categories. Such verbalisms led to unnecessary rigidity in law, forcing new facts and situations to fit within the established rules and categories. Thus, Llewellyn called for legal scholarship that focused on judicial behaviour, not legal rules.

LLEWELLYN's (1931) article "Some Realism about Realism" is a rejoinder to a critique that Roscoe Pound lodged against legal realism. Analysing the writing of 20 legal realists, Llewellyn concluded that many of Pound's sweeping attacks were unfounded. This article is valuable in that it demonstrates Llewellyn's own take on legal realism. He insisted that one is justified in speaking of "legal realists" as a group only in that its members share common points of departure from the orthodox jurisprudence. In short, all legal realists agree that there is less predictability in what courts will do than the orthodox approach claims.

JASON L. PIERCE

Legislative drafting

Dickerson, Reed, *The Fundamentals of Legal Drafting*, 2nd edition, Boston: Little Brown, 1986

Doonan, Elmer, *Drafting*, London: Cavendish Press, 1995

Fraser, Bruce, *The Complete Plain Words*, 2nd edition, London: HMSO, 1973; 3rd edition revised by Sidney Greenbaum and Janet Whitcut, London: HMSO, 1986 and Boston: Godine, 1988

Fung, Spring Yuen Ching and Anthony Watson-Brown, *The Template: A Guide for the Analysis of Complex Legislation*, London: Institute of Advanced Legal Studies, 1994

Hansard Society Commission, *Making the Law: The Report of the Hansard Society Commission on the Legislative Process*, London: Hansard Society for Parliamentary Government, 1993

Kellermann, Alfred E., Giuseppe Ciavarini Azzi, Scot H. Jacobs and Rex Deighton-Smith, *Improving the Quality of Legislation in Europe*, The Hague and Boston: Kluwer, 1998

Thornton, G.C., *Legislative Drafting*, 4th edition, London: Butterworths, and Charlottesville, Virginia: Michie, 1996

DOONAN examines legal drafting in general. The author argues that the general considerations to be taken into account when any legal document is being compiled include the objectives of the document, accuracy, the client's instructions, the use of the chosen language, the use of the chosen presentation and division of the document, the relevant legal knowledge, and the relevant precedents. In the compilation of any legal text, the drafting process includes the comprehension of the topic and the requested result, the thinking stage, the collection of the relevant documents and papers, the legal research, and the composing stage. The latter involves the structuring of the document into divisions, schedules, paragraphs, and – if necessary – annexes, the use of definitions, and the choice of language with its implications concerning ambiguity, consistency, certainty and precision, and the drafting pleadings. The legal author must be particularly careful to use the passive voice and gender-reflecting terms sparingly, to use the present tense as a rule, to include one provision per sentence, to use "shall" and "may", "and" and "or", and to use simple English, which will allow the use of the legal document by legalists and laypersons alike.

In discussing legislative drafting in particular, THORNTON achieves a classic review of the problems involved in the composition of legislative texts. The author uses the Ullmanian and Potterian definition of language as a system of vocal or linguistic symbols used in a particular society as a means of communication, and follows the Aristotelian definition of words as the smallest significant units of speech, as interpreted and modified by modern linguists. Language is the only weapon available to drafters in their task to delimit and establish the law and to communicate the law from the law-making authority to society. In order to fulfil their duties, drafters must be intelligible. Intelligibility comprises simplicity and precision. Simplicity can be achieved through economy, directness, and familiarity of language and orderliness. Precision requires that the words chosen express accurately and unequivocally the meaning intended to be communicated. In the search for precision, definitions – albeit delimiting, extending, or narrowing – may be used as the means to avoid ambiguity and tedious repetition. Deviations from common style by use of words such as "aforesaid", "aforementioned" and "abovementioned" are to be avoided, and clear expressions of time must be used. The author distinguishes amongst five stages of drafting, namely understanding, analysis, design, composition, and scrutiny.

FRASER is another advocate of the Plain English movement, which he attributes to Sir Ernest Gowers. The author suggests that legislative drafters must know their subject, the reason for their writing, and the reader, to whose needs the style and content of the legal text is to be adapted. Any legal document must in principle be clear, simple and brief, accurate and complete, polite and human, and prompt. In order to achieve this task, the author of legal texts must ensure that the language used is easily understood, is free from useless legal jargon, has a clear structure, gives only the essential facts, includes only the essential words and phrases, contains correct information that conforms with policy and rules, is free from grammatical errors, and is tactful, frank, forceful, and sympathetic. The author concludes that "legalese" must give way to plain English, so that English officials can think as wise men do and speak as common people do.

DICKERSON examines the process of legal drafting and concludes that a good drafter must avoid ambiguity in its syntactic, semantic, and contextual forms. In order to combat syntactic ambiguity, the drafter must avoid any uncertainty of modification or reference. Semantic ambiguity can be eluded through certainty in the use of specific terms, such as "and" and "or", tabulation, active voice, clear temporal provisions, and lack of provisos. Contextual ambiguity can be evaded by lack of adjectives, lack of incorporations by reference, and by refraining from stating as a command what is a condition precedent. In general, consistency, good arrangement, and adherence to established usage, perfect the substance of a legal message. In the quest for a readable legal style of drafting, the drafter must take into account the need for brevity, the use of the present tense as a rule, the preferred employment of active voice and the utilization of examples, diagrams, marginal headings and – less frequently – cross-references as acceptable aids.

FUNG & WATSON-BROWN discuss the complicated problems of legislative drafting faced by drafters in multilingual jurisdictions, such as Hong Kong. The authors suggest the use of present tense as a reflection of the "speaking nature" of the law and the use of active voice as a solution to the very real problem of identifying the legal subject of each verb for the purposes of the translation. Equally avoidable is the use of negative forms, since negation is not necessarily attached to nouns, at least in many languages. The authors note that the traditional use of "shall" as the preferred form of the imperative must be questioned in the case of multilingual jurisdictions, because in some languages, like Chinese, it merely signifies "must" or "required to". Such problems can be addressed in the interpretation ordinance of each jurisdiction, which, however, is not always as short, accurate, and precise as the drafters wish. With reference to style, the template advocates simplicity; one legislative clause per sentence expressed in the active voice; the omission of internal cross-referencing,

because sections are read as a whole; the use of verbs in the present tense, indicative mode, and active voice; and the avoidance of legal jargon, provisos, long sentences, negation, and couplets and triplets of mixed origin. With reference to substance, the template follows Coode's analysis of legislative sentence into the components of legal subject, legal action, case and condition, but adds a final element of condition precedent.

HANSARD SOCIETY COMMISSION refers to the issue of legislative process and the challenge of lack of accuracy, intelligibility, effective and efficient format, and communicability of the current legislation in Britain. The committee, chaired by the Rt. Hon Lord Rippon of Hexham, suggests that one of the ways under which the present situation may be improved is through the modification of legislative process, which must be governed primarily by the needs of the users, rather than the needs of those who pass the legislation. Although the volume of contemporary legislation is identified as an aspect of the current confusion, the key to resolving it is to improve the procedures for passing legislation, rather than merely to reduce the volume of legislation produced in the near future. These procedural improvements must be governed by the following principles. Laws are made for the benefit of the citizens of the state. Statute law should be certain, intelligible, and clear. Statute law must be rooted in the authority of the Parliament and thoroughly exposed to democratic scrutiny. Ignorance of the law is no excuse, therefore the law must be accessible to all. The government must be able to secure the passage of its legislation, but making the law intelligible is as important as passing it quickly. In order to comply with these principles, parliamentary counsel must decide who are to be regarded as the main users of the legislation concerned, so that the drafters can choose a drafting style appropriate to these users. Drafters must always seek clarity, simplicity, and brevity, but certainty is paramount. Parliamentary counsel and departmental lawyers must take into account the criticisms of their style of drafting and review their styles accordingly. Complicated and unnecessary detail is to be abolished in legislative texts. Some means of communicating the intention of the statute must be found. Delegated legislation, although a method with distinct disadvantages, is still a good method of passing legislation, if the main provisions of statute law are clearly set out in Acts of Parliament.

KELLERMANN *et al.* tackle the complicated issue of improving legislation in Europe. The authors suggest that the simplification of existing legislation will improve the quality of European legislative texts, as will the introduction of a consultation procedure for the evaluation of draft legislation before it is actually passed.

HELEN XANTHAKI

Legitimacy

Confucius, *Analects*, translated by D.C. Lau, Harmondsworth and New York: Penguin, 1979

Dogan, Mattei (editor), *Comparing Pluralist Democracies: Strains on Legitimacy*, Boulder, Colorado: Westview Press, 1988

Ferrero, Guglielmo, *The Principles of Power: The Great Political Crises of History*, New York: Putnam, 1942

Lipset, Seymour Martin, *Political Man: The Social Bases of Politics*, 2nd edition, Baltimore: Johns Hopkins University Press, 1981; London: Heinemann, 1983

Locke, John, *The Second Treatise of Government*, edited by C.B. Macpherson, Indianapolis: Hackett, 1980

Mencius, *Mencius*, translated by D.C. Lau, Harmondsworth and New York: Penguin 1970

Plato, *The Republic of Plato*, edited by Allen Bloom, New York: Basic Books, 1991

Tocqueville, Alexis de, *Democracy in America*, edited by J.P. Mayer and Max Lerner, translated by George Lawrence, 2 vols, New York: Harper, 1966

Weber, Max, *From Max Weber: Essays in Sociology*, edited by H.H. Gerth and C. Wright Mills, New York: Oxford University Press, 1946, London: Kegan Paul Trench Trubner, 1948; new edition, London: Routledge, 1991

The study of political legitimacy must begin with the classic account of the subject by PLATO in Ancient Greece. In his *Republic*, Plato defines legitimacy in terms of justice. Justice, according to Plato, is the recognition of each individual's unique role in society. Justice requires that everyone perform duties that he or she is by nature best fit to do. A state becomes just only when philosophers are given the authority to govern. As reason and knowledge constitute the basis for claims to political legitimacy, a king must be a philosopher, because only philosophers are capable of discovering and understanding divine value – an eternal form of the heaven. In Plato's world, justice is the highest goal of political life; the ability of the wise ruler to offer just order is the foundation of the government. To Plato, the legitimate right of a ruler to political power is absolute, because they know the good and evil, and can apply this knowledge to their decision making. They can do so because they have rationally to know good, which enables them to control their appetites and govern justly.

The Chinese philosopher CONFUCIUS shares the same moral tone in his discussion of political legitimacy. Although Chinese rulers traditionally claimed to be the "son of heaven" and justify their rule by "mandate of heaven", a phrase that is synonymous with the Western concept of "divine right", Confucius emphasizes the need for moral authority. He states that the ruler's virtue and the contentment of the people, rather than power, should be the true measures of political success. MENCIUS further develops the Confucian version of virtue-based political legitimacy. He believes that government is primarily an exercise of ethics. The rule of a truly moral king, according to him, is characterized by his benevolence towards his people. He transforms the divine legitimacy as is symbolized by the "mandate of heaven" to the acceptance of rule by his people. He goes even further by saying that people have a right to overthrow a ruler who has forfeited his mandate.

LOCKE continues this civil tradition and develops a theory of civil society and civil legitimacy. He first invalidates the age-old theory of divine right based on the theory of popular sovereignty. He believes that government is a human creation based on voluntary consent. He goes on to point out that a government's power to govern is derived from the consent of the people in an agreement that he called the social contract. The purpose of the civil government is to preserve the natural rights of the contracting parties.

German sociologist WEBER provides another classical account of political legitimacy. He classifies three types of legitimacy, namely, traditional, charismatic, and rational and legal. Traditional authority is based on the claim of godly origin – for example, the claim that the ruler is a god-king or son of God. Charismatic authority is based on the leader's personal charisma, heroism, and other extraordinary individual qualities. Rational-legal authority is based on popular belief in the validity of legal statue and functional competence based on rationally created rules.

TOCQUEVILLE points out the dangers of the consensus model of democracy. According to him, the accepted right to govern by the majority should not be achieved by sacrificing the rights of the minority, otherwise majority tyranny may force the minority to challenge the legitimacy of majority rule. FERRERO's answer to the same concern is that legitimacy must be based on the consent of both majority and minority.

In his study of social conditions for democracy, LIPSET considers the effectiveness and legitimacy of the political system to be of crucial importance. Effectiveness refers to the extent to which the system satisfies the needs of the people, and legitimacy is defined as the capacity of the system to maintain the belief that the existing political institutions are the most appropriate ones for the society. Since legitimacy is derived from shared beliefs, crises of legitimacy can occur when a traditional institution such as a monarchy is challenged by democratic forces, or when a major social group is denied access to the political system – all resulted in the breakdown of the common belief systems.

DOGAN's volume further broadens our understanding of the strains on legitimacy. Authors in this book analyse the phenomenon of crises of legitimacy. Although it focuses primarily on pluralist democracies, it shows the dialectic, multifaceted nature of political legitimacy. According to the authors, there are five types of crises that all pluralist democracies have to face: crisis of national independence, crisis of religious institution, crisis of popular suffrage, crisis of economic redistribution, and crisis of the welfare state.

BAOGANG GUO

Lenin, V.I. 1870–1924

Soviet economic theorist and political leader

Ball, Alan M., *Russia's Last Capitalists: The Nepmen, 1921–29*, Berkeley: University of California Press, 1987

Bukharin, Nikolai I., *Economics of the Transformation Period, with Lenin's Critical Remarks*, New York: Bergman, 1971 (Russian edition 1920)

Desai, Meghnad (editor), *Lenin's Economic Writings*, Atlantic Highlands, New Jersey: Humanities Press, and London: Lawrence and Wishart, 1989

Grosskopf, Sigrid, *L'Alliance ouvrière et paysanne en U.R.S.S, 1921–1928: le problème du blé*, Paris: Maspero, 1976

Harding, Neil, *Lenin's Political Thought: Theory and Practice in the Democratic and Socialist Revolutions*, 2 vols, London: Macmillan, and New York: St Martin's Press, 1977–81

Lawler, James, "Lenin and the Socialist Transition in Russia" in *Research in Political Economy*, edited by Paul Zarembka, Greenwich, Connecticut: Jai Press, 1996

Lenin, Vladimir Ilich, *The Development of Capitalism in Russia*, Moscow: Progress, 1956 (original Russian edition 1899)

Lenin, Vladimir Ilich, *The Agrarian Program of Social-Democracy in the First Russian Revolution, 1905–1907* in *Collected Works*, vol. 13, Moscow: Progress, 1962 (original Russian edition confiscated by police, 1908, republished 1917)

Lenin, Vladimir Ilich, *Imperialism: The Highest Stage of Capitalism*, Moscow: Progress, 1956 (original Russian edition 1917)

Linhart, Robert, *Lenine, les paysans, Taylor: essai d'analyse matérialiste historique de la naissance du système productif soviétique*, Paris: Seuil, 1976

Lenin's economics contains two main strands, a theoretical one and a practical one. The theoretical strand persists until 1907, concluding by analysing the failed 1905 revolution. There is sporadic theoretical work later, most notably LENIN (1917) and his annotated reading of BUKHARIN. The practical strand begins in 1917 with the October revolution and represents the first Marxist confrontation with the task of actually building a socialist society. A useful introduction to Lenin's economic writings appears in DESAI, which also reprints 14 of them and provides the full list of 133. HARDING provides a thorough survey of Lenin's entire political life and discusses Lenin's political economy in context. Generally, Lenin as an economist is underappreciated, as his political genius has dominated discussion.

LENIN (1899) represents a culmination of research over a period of six years. The work is divided into sections: an introductory theoretical chapter, followed by three long chapters on the agrarian economy, three on the development of industry, and a concluding chapter on the formation of a market economy within Russia (in all, representing almost 700 pages in English). The theoretical chapter summarizes his interpretation of Marxist economics versus that of "Narodnik" economists. Narodniks had argued that the poverty of the Russian peasantry prevented capitalism from finding a sufficient internal, or "home", market for capitalism to be a viable system, particularly given that the international market was dominated by stronger powers. Lenin's interpretation was already in place in 1893 when he wrote "On the So-called Market Question" (reprinted in DESAI) and seems to have remained unchanged in his lifetime (much later, he criticized Rosa Luxemburg for Narodnism with regard to the viability of capitalism). His position was that the conversion of peasant production into production for the market, as well as the development of production of constant capital (machinery, particularly), would provide the expanding home market.

The chapters discussing the agrarian and industrial sectors of the economy are detailed examinations of the pattern of changing economic structures, including changing social relations of production. Lenin was fortunate, in being from a country that, at the time, collected reliable statistics and thus provided him the opportunity for analysis. He made great use of it, and the book still represents a classic of Marxist economics. Harding (p.107), after surveying its contribution and the work that went into it, concludes that "the book is arguably the most important" that Lenin wrote and "remains the fullest, best documented and best-argued examination of the crucial period of the evolution of capitalism out of feudalism in the literature of Marxism".

Lenin learned from new events, and the failed revolution in 1905 confronted the necessity to rethink his understanding of the Russian economy. Thus, LENIN (1908) concludes that he had earlier overestimated the degree of penetration of the Russian economy by capitalism. Furthermore, he connects his reinterpretation to the range of political forces existing in Russian society.

Lenin (1917) represents one of his most famous works. It hardly qualifies as theory – Lenin's own prefatory statement notwithstanding, nor, as one example among others, HARDING's (1981, Chapter 3) discussion. It rather has much more the character of a descriptive work. The work has been used as an explanation for the origins of interimperialist wars, World War I in particular. Some thought-provoking ideas are introduced, such as the idea of a "labour aristocracy" in more "advanced" countries, which is bribed by higher wages to support imperial interests (see particularly Section VIII).

The very first public statement Lenin made after the October Revolution is purported to be, "we shall now proceed to construct the socialist order". We cannot pretend that what Lenin said, others did; nevertheless, there were economic policies adopted by the Soviet government that Lenin proposed and for which he argued. They may be categorized into nationalizations of land and workers' control initially, then war communism during the Civil War, followed by the New Economic Policy.

A decree, issued by Lenin as Premier on the day after the October Revolution, abolished private ownership of land and offered no compensation. All citizens of either sex could use the land as long as they actually cultivated it without using wage labour. Three weeks later, workers' control was decreed throughout the economy, although this did not include nationalization of industry. After the Brest-Litovsk peace treaty with Germany on 3 March 1918 (signed after much controversy within the Bolshevik party), Lenin argued that the principal economic difficulty lay in "the introduction of the strictest and universal accounting and control of production and distribution of goods, raising the productivity of labour and *socializing* production *in practice*" ("The Immediate Tasks of the Soviet Government", April 1918, reprinted in Desai, p.223, italics in original.) Lenin articulated what workers' control was to mean in that immediate context (before the Civil War) – capitalist private property in industry, but with a state under workers' control and workers' committees in factories. This "state capitalism" included the open admission of using capitalistic methods in the factory, for example adapting "Taylorism" to promote Soviet industrial development (see LINHART, Part 2).

Civil war began toward the end of May 1918 and dramatic economic changes took place. Nationalizations, which had been sporadic before, became widespread – locally, more often than not, rather than from "above". Lenin's slow approach evaporated. Industry declined precipitously as raw material supplies fell into enemy hands. Forced requisitioning of food became absolutely necessary to avoid total starvation in the cities and towns and of soldiers. Markets and use of money became atrophied. Policies based upon these developments were called "war communism", and some thought there was a form of communism in it. It was in place until early 1921 as famine ravaged the countryside and millions starved from a bad harvest.

GROSSKOPF surveys the conditions underlying the struggle to maintain an alliance between workers and peasants in that context. Drastic steps were needed and Lenin abruptly proposed the New Economic Policy to the Tenth Party Congress in March 1921 (see BALL). It substituted a tax in kind on the peasantry (fixed early each Spring, although later changed to money) for the confiscatory food requisitioning which had been used before; it legalized trade by peasants of any of their surpluses, and permitted a money economy. Land remained nationalized. Lenin surveyed some of the issues involved in "The Tax in Kind" (reprinted in Desai). This policy did stabilize the economy in that, by 1927, Russia returned to pre-War World I production levels in both industry and agriculture. However, it also led to increased class differentiation in the countryside, including a proliferation of merchant intermediaries, "Nepmen", and was associated with deepening bureaucratization. Some, such as LAWLER, now argue that markets along with promotion of agricultural cooperatives on nationalized land, form a basis for socialism Lenin could recognize as such, particularly taking account of one of his last writings ("On Cooperation", reprinted in Desai). If so, the prior war communism would represent a retreat from initial development of such market socialism of early 1918; the New Economic Policy would represent its re-establishment. Others are far less sanguine, and instead view the New Economic Policy as the "retreat" back to elements of capitalism as Lenin explicitly described it. But a retreat from what exactly? This remains a much debated question.

PAUL ZAREMBKA

Leninism

Besançon, Alain, *The Rise of the Gulag: Intellectual Origins of Leninism*, New York: Continuum, and Oxford: Blackwell, 1981

Chirot, Daniel (editor), *The Crisis of Leninism and the Decline of the Left: The Revolutions of 1989*, Seattle: University of Washington Press, 1991

Dovring, Folke, *Leninism: Political Economy as Pseudoscience*, Westport, Connecticut and London: Praeger, 1996

Egan, David R., Melinda A. Egan and Julie Anne Genthner, *V.I. Lenin: An Annotated Bibliography of English-Language Sources to 1980*, Metuchen, New Jersey: Scarecrow Press, 1982

Evans, Alfred B., *Soviet Marxism-Leninism: The Decline of an Ideology*, Westport, Connecticut and London: Praeger, 1994

Harding, Neil, *Leninism*, Durham, North Carolina: Duke University Press, and Basingstoke: Macmillan, 1996

Kautsky, John H., *Marxism and Leninism, Not Marxism-Leninism: An Essay in the Sociology of Knowledge*, Westport, Connecticut: Greenwood Press, 1994

DOVRING provides an in-depth analysis of the economic and political doctrines of Lenin, creator of the Communist Party that came to power in Russia in 1917. Based upon the author's comprehensive reading of Lenin's *Collected Works*, the study dissects Lenin's political economy, and shows it to be pseudo-science, based on simple, arbitrary, and unrealistic assumptions. According to Dovring, Lenin was a politician, not a scientist, and his aim was power, not truth. The work begins by providing a brief sketch of Lenin's life and an overview of his career as a writer. Four substantive chapters analyse Lenin's treatment of the peasant problem, science, the proletariat, and democracy. Closing chapters deal with Lenin's personality, which is shown to be pathological in its inability to make concessions to intellectual argument, and the prevalence of pseudoscience in his doctrines. Lenin's doctrines became the groundwork of the Soviet system, and he is responsible for creating its absurdities. The subsequent collapse of the Soviet system, therefore, must be seen in this light.

EGAN & EGAN is an indispensable contribution not only for the study of Lenin but for the study of early 20th-century Russian political science and history as well. Most of the entries (total of 2926) have annotations which are short, to the point, stimulating, and written in an objective style. Especially valuable is the coverage of the 1920s and 1930s, a period of rapid growth in Communism which is frequently documented in publications that are not always easily accessible. Book reviews are listed along with the work they review and the most important publications have been marked by an asterisk, a much-appreciated help for the beginning student. The importance of the subject and the care and expertise with which the authors did their work make the book absolutely essential for all those interested in the topic.

BESANÇON represents a well-researched source on the ideas that have made a difference in history and on the personalities and movements that have served as their messengers. According to the author, the essential feature of the Soviet regime was not the bureaucracy, the new class, a particular socioeconomic or political structure, not even the party, but a certain belief or a way of thinking: in other words, an "ideology". By ideology, the author means:

> a systematic doctrine which offers salvation by means of conversion; which presents itself as being at one with a cosmic order, whose development is open to our understanding; which declares that it is based on scientific certainty; and which imposes a system of practical politics aimed at totally transforming society to fit with the immanent model which had lain concealed and which the true doctrine had lain bare (p.52).

The author provides a fascinating analysis of the ideological roots of Leninism, and the explanations as well as his interpretations are extremely insightful.

The essays in CHIROT are more interesting, often more provocative, and form a more coherent collection than is the case with other collections about recent events in Eastern Europe. While addressing such general questions as how countries in the East and in the West must adjust to a rapidly changing world in an economy dominated by information technology, most of the authors also take care to consider these countries' specific historical, institutional, and cultural contexts. Most, though not all, also maintain that the retreat of Socialism does not introduce the triumph of liberalism, that liberalism's own moral contradictions will continue to provoke challenges from more communitarian traditions and ideologies all over the globe. In the book, nine scholars discuss one of the most critical questions posed by the events of 1989. They focus on the political and military role of the US in the 21st century; the worldwide decline of the left; Gorbachev's search for Socialist renewal; the loss of moral legitimacy in Communist systems; the failure of student demonstrations in China; and the need for a comprehensive plan to promote economic development in formerly communist countries.

EVANS examines the development of Marxist-Leninist ideology in the USSR from its origins to the collapse of the Soviet regime. Evans argues that Soviet Marxism-Leninism was subject to significant adaptation under various leaders, contrary to the widespread impression that official Soviet ideology remained static after Stalin. While taking account of scholarly literature on each of the periods covered, the work is significant for being based principally on an analysis of primary (Soviet) sources. Evans' integrated analysis of changes in ideology during the post-Stalin decades is an important contribution to the literature in political science, political economy, and Soviet studies.

HARDING presents a comprehensive reinterpretation of Leninism. Challenging much of the conventional wisdom regarding Leninism's effectiveness as a mobilizing body of ideas, its substance, and its origins and evolution, Harding offers both a controversial exposition of this ideology and a critical engagement with its consequences for the politics of contemporary Communism. Rather than tracing the roots of Leninism to the details of Lenin's biography, Harding shows how it emerged as a revolutionary Marxist response to World War I, and to the perceived treachery of social democratic leaders in supporting that war. The economics, politics, and philosophy of Leninism, he argues, were rapidly theorized between 1914 and 1918 and deeply imprinted with the peculiarities of the wartime experience. Its complementary metaphysics of history and science was as intrinsic to its confidence and sureness of purpose as it was to its contempt for democratic practice and tolerance. But, as Harding also shows, although Leninism articulated a complex and coherent critique of capitalist civilization and held a powerful appeal to a variety of constituencies, it was itself caught in a time bias that fatally limited its capacity to adapt. This book will engage not only Russian and Soviet specialists, but also readers concerned with the varieties of 20th-century Socialism.

KAUTSKY challenges the pervasive view, responsible for much confusion in both politics and scholarship, that there is such a thing as Marxism-Leninism – that Marxism and Leninism are one ideology, or that Leninism is merely reinterpreted Marxism. Kautsky argues that the two have always been quite distinct ideologies, and by distinguishing between the words and substance of ideology, he shows how the employment of a single vocabulary by Marx and Lenin has confused Marxists, Leninists, and outside observers. This study analyses the two ideologies in terms of the sociology of knowledge. It explains the differences between Marxism and Leninism with reference to their respective relationships to certain labour movements in industrialized countries, and revolutionary movements in underdeveloped countries. Following the generation of Marx and Engels, Kautsky was the leading theorist, interpreter, and popularizer of Marxism, and as such, this book can serve as an important source for studying the topic.

CARMELA LUTMAR

See also Communism, V.I Lenin, Marx and Marxism

Lesbianism, psychology

Boston Lesbian Psychologies Collective (editors), *Lesbian Psychologies: Explorations and Challenges*, Urbana: University of Illinois Press, 1987

Bradford, Judith, Caitlin Ryan and Esther D. Rothblum, "National Lesbian Health Care Survey: Implications for Mental Health Care", *Journal of Consulting and Clinical Psychology*, 62/2 (1994): 228–42

Cabaj, Robert P. and Terry S. Stein, *Textbook of Homosexuality and Mental Health*, Washington, DC: American Psychiatric Press, 1996

D'Augelli, Anthony R. and Charlotte J. Patterson (editors), *Lesbian, Gay, and Bisexual Identities over the Lifespan: Psychological Perspectives*, New York and Oxford: Oxford University Press, 1995

Glassgold, Judith M. and Suzanne Iasenza (editors), *Lesbians and Psychoanalysis: Revolutions in Theory and Practice*, New York and London: Free Press, 1995

Greene, Beverly, "Lesbian Women of Color: Triple Jeopardy" in *Women of Color: Integrating Ethnic and Gender Identities in Psychotherapy*, edited by Lilian Comas-Diaz and Beverly Greene, New York: Guilford Press, 1994

Kitzinger, Celia and Rachel Perkins, *Changing our Minds: Lesbian Feminism and Psychology*, New York: New York University Press, 1993

Perez, Ruperto M., Kurt A. DeBord and Kathleen J. Bieschke (editors), *Handbook of Counseling and Psychotherapy with Lesbian, Gay, and Bisexual Clients*, Washington, DC: American Psychological Association, 2000

Renzetti, Claire M., *Violent Betrayal: Partner Abuse in Lesbian Relationships*, Newbury Park, California: Sage, 1992

Rothblum, Esther, "'I Only Read about Myself on Bathroom Walls': The Need for Research on the Mental Health of Lesbians and Gay Men", *Journal of Consulting and Clinical Psychology*, 62/2 (1994): 213–20

The BOSTON LESBIAN PSYCHOLOGIES COLLECTIVE's anthology may be considered a classic text on the topic. Published over a decade ago, it was one of the first comprehensive books to examine lesbian experience from a feminist, non-pathologizing stance. Despite its age, it still provides a valuable overview of many of the psychological issues central to lesbian experience. It is an anthology written primarily by clinicians who work with lesbian clients. Its five sections include Identity, Relationships, Family, Therapies, and Community. One weakness of this text is its lack of empirical backing; at the time of its publication, little solid empirical research on lesbian psychology had been published. Since its publication, some of the topics discussed in this text have been empirically examined; others await the attention of researchers.

BRADFORD, RYAN & ROTHBLUM presents the results from the first large national survey of lesbians conducted in the US. This article is especially significant because of its empirical basis; much of the literature published prior to this article was based on theory or clinical observation. Previous research on lesbians was hampered by small, homogeneous, geographically circumscribed samples. In contrast, this article provides data from a large sample and includes questions on a variety of mental health topics including depression and anxiety, suicide, interpersonal victimization, substance abuse, and use of mental health services.

ROTHBLUM examines the current state of mental health research on lesbians and gay men and places it in historical and social context. The author describes a reluctance among researchers to focus on the mental health of lesbians and gay men and attributes this to the fact that it was not until the 1970s that homosexuality itself was considered a mental health issue. She highlights important methodological considerations in studying this population, including operational definitions of sexual orientation, recruitment of subjects, and selection of appropriate control groups. Rothblum identifies the many areas in which empirical data is inadequate or lacking. She argues for the importance of conducting this research; for, rather than further stigmatizing lesbians and gay men, it might help understand the unique mental health risks and protective factors in their lives. This article should serve as a useful guide in planning and designing future studies of lesbians.

The 18 essays in GLASSGOLD & IASENZA constitute a reinterpretation of traditional psychoanalytic theory and practice. It adds to the growing body of feminist psychoanalytic texts by emphasizing and affirming lesbian experience. Unlike traditional psychoanalytic texts, the authors in this volume pay careful attention to the impact of the broader cultural context on both the client's intrapersonal dynamics as well as on the therapeutic relationship and process. This book will be particularly useful to psychoanalytically oriented clinicians, with its abundance of clinical case examples illustrating the application of theory. It may be less relevant to researchers or to clinicians who are more behaviourally oriented.

GREENE is a clear and concise introduction to the psychological issues unique to lesbians of colour. Most theory and research on lesbians has focused on white middle class women and/or have not paid adequate attention to the role of ethnicity and race in women's individual and collective experiences. Greene argues that the intersection of racism, sexism, and homophobia creates unique challenges and strengths for lesbians of colour and describes some of the general themes to consider in understanding their lives. Issues specific to lesbians from different ethnic minority groups in the US are explored in the dual cultural contexts of their ethnic communities and of the US lesbian community. Implications for clinical practice are also included.

The literature on domestic violence within the lesbian community has been sparse and limited by methodological difficulties, stereotypes, and assumptions. RENZETTI is a sociological account of one of the first comprehensive studies of partner abuse among lesbians. The author examines the correlates and dynamics of the abuse and places it in its social context, looking at the responses of social service agencies, law enforcement, and the lesbian community to the victims' requests for help. While this book does not directly address the prevalence of partner abuse among lesbians, it makes a significant contribution to our understanding of this phenomenon and the ways that it is both similar to and different from domestic violence in heterosexual relationships.

KITZINGER & PERKINS provides an engaging yet provocative argument against lesbian feminist psychology and psychotherapy. According to these authors, psychology has depoliticized the lesbian community by relegating problems to the private, individual realm and removing them from the political realm. Kitzinger & Perkins argues that the individualism and moral relativism of psychology are fundamentally incompatible with radical lesbian political goals. This book is important in its willingness to challenge assumptions and take a controversial stance. Its value lies in its potential to provoke the reader to examine more carefully the relationship between personal growth and political change.

Much of the current literature on lesbian psychology can be found in anthologies that also cover gay male and bisexual psychology. One such anthology, which provides a useful overview, is D'AUGELLI & PATTERSON. This text approaches the topic from a developmental perspective, highlighting issues of particular relevance in adolescence, midlife, and late life. Throughout the text, social context variables are considered as they impact and interact with individuals' life experiences. A strength of this text is that it reviews and critiques theoretical approaches to sexual identity; Laura Brown's chapter "Lesbian Identities: Concepts and Issues" is particularly useful in this regard. Additionally, the book provides a solid review of the empirical research in many areas, including lesbian couples and families and the psychology of heterosexism.

Broader in scope than the above anthology is CABAJ & STEIN. This text also reviews theoretical approaches and examines lifespan development issues for lesbian, gay, and bisexual populations. However, its emphasis is more clinical and it examines therapy issues in greater depth and breadth, covering such topics as the sexual orientation of the therapist: ethical concerns in therapy; and therapy with lesbian, gay, and bisexual families. Particularly valuable in this volume is the section on differences and diversity, which addresses mental health issues of specific relevance to several ethnic minority populations. Klinger and Stein's chapter on the impact of violence and abuse on lesbians, bisexuals, and gay men is another unique feature of this book, providing a useful review of an often neglected topic.

PEREZ, DEBORD & BIESCHKE is more recently published and consequently provides a useful look at the most up-to-date developments in theory and research. This book is clinically focused, and many chapters will be particularly useful to clinicians in conceptualizing and working with the specific needs of lesbians, gay men, and bisexuals who present themselves for therapy. It is particularly strong in providing historical and sociological perspectives on lesbian, gay, and bisexual experience in a way that clearly illustrates their relevance to psychological practice and research. Similarly, this book is solidly grounded in the growing body of empirical research and synthesizes findings in a way that highlights implications for ethical, informed clinical practice with this population.

KIMBERLY F. BALSAM

Leverage, leveraged buy-outs

Barclay, Michael J., Clifford W. Smith and Ross L. Watts, "The Determinants of Corporate Leverage and Dividend Policies", *Journal of Applied Corporate Finance*, 7/4 (1995): 4–19

DeAngelo, Harry and Ronald W. Masulis, "Optimal Capital Structure under Corporate Taxation", *Journal of Financial Economics*, 8/1 (1980): 5–29

Harris, Milton and Artur Raviv, "The Theory of Optimal Capital Structure", *Journal of Finance*, 46/1 (1991): 297–356

Jensen, Michael C. and William H. Meckling, "Theory of the Firm: Managerial Behavior, Agency Costs and Ownership Structure", *Journal of Financial Economics*, 3/4 (1976): 305–60

Jensen, Michael C., "The Eclipse of the Public Corporation", *Harvard Business Review*, 67 (September–October, 1989): 61–74

Kaplan, Steven, "The Effects of Management Buyouts on Operating Performance and Value", *Journal of Financial Economics*, 24/2 (1989): 217–54

Long, William F. and David J. Ravenscraft, "Decade of Debt: Lessons from LBOs in the 1980s" in *The Deal Decade: What Takeovers and Leveraged Buyouts Mean for Corporate Governance*, edited by Margaret M. Blair, Washington, DC: Brookings Institution, 1993

Miller, Merton H., "Debt and Taxes", *Journal of Finance*, 32/2 (1977): 261–76

Modigliani, Franco and Merton H. Miller, "The Cost of Capital, Corporation Finance and the Theory of Investment", *American Economic Review*, 48/3 (1958): 261–97

Leverage refers to the situation where an investor finances an investment with debt (or some other fixed-charge security). The advantage this provides to the investor is attained when that investor can receive a higher return on the investment of the borrowed funds than the fixed charge on those funds. Here, we are concerned with a business firm. For a firm, management must choose the appropriate mix of debt and equity to finance the firm (choose its capital structure). When the firm's earnings on the borrowed funds exceed the cost of those funds, the return to the contributed capital is higher than if the firm was financed entirely by equity. The more debt financing used by the firm (the higher it is leveraged), however, the higher the risk to the firm's equity investors (the stockholders). In times of high earnings, the stockholders will receive higher returns due to the leverage, but in times of low earnings, the stockholders will receive lower returns. So what is the optimal use of leverage to maximize the firm's market value? Except where noted, these articles are fairly abstract and require a basic knowledge of economic theory.

MODIGLIANI & MILLER lays out the theory behind their famous "proposition I" and is the starting point for any discussion on choosing the appropriate mix of debt and equity. "Proposition I" states that, assuming perfect capital markets and no taxes, a firm's total value cannot be changed by changing its mix of debt and equity. Essentially, an investor is not concerned about the firm's leverage because that investor always has the option of borrowing on his or her own account, rather than relying on the firm to obtain debt financing. Moreover, although leverage can increase the expected return to a firm, that increase is exactly balanced out by the extra risk caused by that degree of leverage. Thus, Modigliani and Miller claim that financial leverage is irrelevant to the value of the firm.

MILLER extends the Modigliani and Miller proposition to include the costs of personal and corporate taxes. Corporate taxes are important because interest payments on debt are deducted from taxable income, and therefore raise the value of the firm. Miller also shows how the personal tax rate on equity income and interest affects the optimal capital structure. DEANGELO & MASULIS argues that other tax shields, such as from accounting depreciation and investment tax credits, should reduce the amount of funds the firm will borrow. The reader should be aware, however, that both discussions may be affected by the significant changes to the US tax rates for corporations, capital gains, and personal interest and dividend income, that have occurred since these publications.

JENSEN & MECKLING advances the discussion of capital structure by recognizing the importance of agency costs (the costs associated with an agent not always acting in the best interests of the principal). There are different agency costs associated with use of debt (bondholders) and equity (shareholders), which affect the optimal mix of debt and equity. Jensen & Meckling also show that we must pay attention to the amount of equity held by the managers of the firm (inside equity).

HARRIS & RAVIV provides a review of the variety of theories and the empirical studies on capital structure. This article does not review theories based on tax considerations, but it includes theories divided into the following categories: agency costs, asymmetric information, corporate control considerations, and product and input market interactions. BARCLAY, SMITH & ROSS provides a less technical discussion of the leverage choice than the other readings. In the process of presenting a study of over 6700 industrial corporations, this article provides a clear discussion of the factors that may affect a corporation's choice of leverage. This discussion includes the traditional explanations of capital structure: taxes and financial distress costs (including bankruptcy costs).

Leveraged buyouts (LBOs) involve the purchase of the outstanding shares of a publicly held corporation by an outside investor or management (a management buyout or MBO), with the purchase being primarily debt-financed. This purchase changes the corporation from a publicly held corporation to a privately held corporation. JENSEN argues, in non-technical language, that there is a conflict between owners and managers over what to do with the firm's "free cashflow", and that LBOs can help solve this problem. "Free cashflow" refers to the cash-flow in excess of that required to fund all investments with a positive net present value. Jensen argues that management does not have an incentive to distribute this cashflow to shareholders, and instead will tend to waste it. With more debt, however, management will be forced to pay out this cashflow in the form of interest payments. This use of debt also creates a crisis situation and gives management the incentive to create a more efficient and competitive corporation.

KAPLAN is an empirical study of MBOs in the US in the early 1980s. The article finds that, in the years following an MBO, these firms achieved increases in market value, operating income, and net cashflow, and decreases in capital expenditure. Kaplan argues that these changes were due to improved managerial incentives. LONG & RAVENSCRAFT provides evidence from a sample of LBOs that contradict some of Kaplan's findings. The authors also find that LBOs can have negative effects on capital spending and spending on research and development.

DAVID HESS

Libel and slander

Bosmajian, Haig A., "Freedom of Speech and the Language of Oppression", *Western Journal of Speech Communication*, 42 (1978): 202–21

Dumas, Bethany K., "'Put Me on the Program or I'll Kill You!': Establishing the Existence of Verbal Crimes", *Ninth Annual Practical Conference on Communication Proceedings*, Knoxville: Society for Technical Communication, East Tennessee Chapter, 1986

Jones, W.R., "'Actions for Slaunder': Defamation in English Law, Language, and History", *Quarterly Journal of Speech*, 57/3 (1971): 274–83

Labunski, Richard, *Libel and the First Amendment: Legal History and Practice in Print and Broadcasting*, New Brunswick, New Jersey: Transaction, 1987

Pullum, Geoffrey K., "The Linguistics of Defamation" in *The Great Eskimo Vocabulary Hoax and Other Irreverent Essays on the Study of Language*, Chicago: University of Chicago Press, 1991

Rosenberg, Norman L., *Protecting the Best Men: An Interpretive History of the Law of Libel*, Chapel Hill: University of North Carolina Press, 1986

Sack, Robert D., *Sack on Defamation: Libel, Slander, and Related Problems*, 3rd edition, New York: Practising Law Institute, 1999 (2 vols loose-leaf for updating)

Tiersma, Peter Meijes, "The Language of Defamation", *Texas Law Review*, 66/2 (1987): 303–50

Tousignant, C., "L'Ambiguïté lexicale et le milieu juridique" [Lexical Ambiguity in the Courtroom], *Cahiers de Lexicologie*, 59 (1991–92): 29–38

In a brief survey of legal cases in the US charging defamatory language, BOSMAJIAN examines the problems raised when "the commitment to fight those elements and practices that contribute to the dehumanization of human beings meets head on with the commitment to give preferred position to the First Amendment, especially freedom of speech" (p.220). He suggests that the answer cannot be state censorship that reduces adults to reading or hearing only what is fit for children.

DUMAS draws upon one of the first cases in which the author testified as an expert. It suggests the usefulness of linguistic testimony by reporting the author's method of analysis in a libel case involving a county coroner in Kentucky and the president of the local division of the American Heart Association. At issue was whether a letter written by the coroner could reasonably be construed as saying what the defendant's press release claimed it did. Dumas concludes that certain statements in the plaintiff's letter had been grossly misrepresented in the defendant's press release, partly by reporting the original statements to have had a communicative purpose other than the actual purpose, partly by referring too alleged directives in the original letter that simply did not exist.

JONES traces the development of defamation law in England from Anglo-Saxon days, pointing out that the English law of libel or published defamation developed independently of the common law of spoken libel or defamation.

LABUNSKI explores issues that have increasingly faced journalists since the 1980s, particularly the complicated and potentially damaging effect of libel suits on their First Amendment rights. Labunski suggests that there are indications that the number of lawsuits against media organizations began increasing in the 1980s. He argues that many newspapers and broadcast stations base some decisions on the recognition that a single successful lawsuit could put them out of business, partly because of the cost of defending a libel suit.

PULLUM examines the nature of libel with reference to cases involving General W. Westmoreland. He demonstrates that under current interpretation, libel need not involve written or spoken language, but may involve an act or gesture. Further, a libelous statement need not be a declarative statement, but may involve a presupposition. Pullum suggests that

> almost anything anybody says can be construed as defamatory. One consequence is that the rich and influential have curbed the freedom of the news media in England through exploiting the law. American state libel laws are less easy to characterize, but libel suits are far less common and less successful than in England. As a consequence, the American media have been able to uncover and publicize the mendacity and criminal misdeeds of top US public figures.

ROSENBERG traces the history of libel law, focusing on the significant difference between the doctrine and practice of libel law.

TIERSMA offers an analysis of defamation, encompassing both libel and slander, that is based on speech act theory. Speech act theory holds that every utterance comprises both an illocutionary act, one related to its intended force, and a perlocutionary act, one related to its effect on the hearer. Defamation law has traditionally focused on the effect of a speaker's (or writer's) utterance and has imposed liability for utterances that harm the reputation of the target. Tiersma argues that a more precise analysis involves defining defamation in terms of an utterance's illocutionary force and, more specifically, as the illocutionary act of accusing. An accusation is a successfully communicated utterance that intentionally attributes responsibility to someone for a blameworthy act.

A speaker defames if he or she accuses without a privilege to do so or if he or she accuses in violation of the norms of the speech community that regulate accusations. Defining defamation as accusation would allow courts to distinguish between an accusation and a report, which is intended merely to inform the hearer of an actual state of affairs, and between an accusation and an opinion, which is a report of the speaker's state of mind. The development in defamation law of such doctrines as the actual malice standard, the fair report privilege, and the fact-opinion distinction indicates an implicit understanding of defamation as the illocutionary act of accusing.

TOUSIGNANT suggests that when vocabulary items used in contracts, wills, murder threats, and criminal libels is examined, it is clear that lexicology offers an invaluable tool to the jurist, all the more so since lexical ambiguity is often at issue in a lawsuit.

The third edition of SACK is widely regarded in the US as an essential resource on defamation law, the standard against which other texts should be judged. It reflects many recent developments in such areas as: nonactionable opinion; application of the fair report privilege to foreign government statements; liability for statements on the Internet; punitive damage awards and due process; protection for employers making job evaluations and references; protection of reporters' confidential sources; compliance with retraction statutes; compelled self-publication; and intracorporate publication.

BETHANY K. DUMAS

See also Forensic linguistics

Liberal democracy

Duncan, Graeme and Steven Lukes, "The New Democracy", *Political Studies*, 11/2 (1963): 156–79

Holden, Barry, *Understanding Liberal Democracy*, Oxford: Philip Allan, 1988; 2nd edition, New York and London: Harvester Wheatsheaf, 1993

Locke, John, *Two Treatises of Government*, edited by Peter Laslett, 2nd edition, London: Cambridge University Press, 1967 (originally published 1690)

Macpherson, C.B., *The Life and Times of Liberal Democracy*, Oxford and New York: Oxford University Press, 1977

Mill, John Stuart, *Considerations on Representative Government*, Buffalo, New York: Prometheus, 1991 (originally published 1861)

Miller, David, "The Competitive Model of Democracy" in *Democratic Theory and Practice*, edited by Graeme Duncan, Cambridge and New York: Cambridge University Press, 1983

Schumpeter, Joseph A., *Capitalism, Socialism, and Democracy*, New York: Harper, 1941, London: Allen and Unwin, 1943; 6th edition London and Boston: Unwin, 1987

Wintrop, Norman (editor), *Liberal Democratic Theory and Its Critics*, London: Croom Helm, 1983

One of the earliest advocates – some might argue *the* earliest advocate – of what subsequently became known as liberal democracy is LOCKE, who originally propounded his ideas concerning the relationship between government and the governed in the latter half of the 17th century. His concern was to establish the functions and the limits of government and the state, thereby establishing a balance between authority and liberty. The primary function, he maintained, was to protect "life, liberty and property", thereby guaranteeing a framework of law (the rule of law) within which individuals could pursue their interests. Government was accountable and representative, however, because if it failed to provide this protection, then it would forfeit its legitimacy and authority, whereupon the people would be entitled to seek a replacement. Herein lie the origins and rudiments of liberal democracy.

MILL subsequently developed these ideas of representation and accountability during the 19th century, when he explicitly recommended a system of regular elections whereby citizens could endorse or replace the government. Mill saw such a political system as a vital means of elevating the moral calibre of the citizenry, for periodic elections would inculcate individuals with democratic principles, respect for the views of others, and generate an interest in current affairs. However, Mill had a somewhat narrow definition of who constituted a citizen (and thus of who was entitled to participate in political matters), and also feared the ignorance of the working classes. He thus recommended "weighted voting", whereby the votes of educated citizens would effectively be worth more than the votes of the lower orders, at least until such time that the working classes had been sufficiently "educated" and morally enriched via their (limited) participation in the democratic process.

During the 20th century, the concern of several political scientists *vis-à-vis* liberal democracy turned towards the potential tension between democratic participation and political stability. Thus SCHUMPETER sought to consolidate liberal democracy, rather than encourage even wider political involvement by the electorate. The stability of the political system, rather than increasing and extending the involvement of the masses, became the primary objective. He sought to define democracy merely as a political method whereby the citizens selected which group of politicians would govern them for the next four or five years, whereupon the electorate should largely leave the government alone to perform the tasks for which it had been elected. If the citizenry were not satisfied with the government's performance, they would have the opportunity to remove it at the next election, but in the meantime, constant "interference" and lobbying would inhibit responsible and effective political rule by elected leaders. Meanwhile, the realization that it might be voted out of office and replaced by one of its rivals at the next election was deemed likely to ensure that the government would seek faithfully to serve the interests of the electorate, thereby preventing its degeneration into despotism. Self-interest would ensure self-restraint.

This perspective is critically evaluated by MILLER, who notes the extent to which this competitive model of democracy, whereby voters merely choose between a range of prospective political leaders, corresponds significantly with the operation of a market economy, in which the role of consumers is to select from whichever products are on offer. This approach also likens political leadership contenders to entrepreneurs, whose livelihood depends upon maximizing their market share by offering the most attractive or popular commodities, or by innovating to exploit newly recognized gaps in the market. However, whilst "sovereignty" is deemed ultimately to reside with the voters and consumers, the reality is that they are vulnerable to manipulation by political leaders and entrepreneurs, whereby their choices and preferences are effectively shaped from above. Miller believes that this problem could at least partly be overcome by developing more participatory modes of democracy, particularly at local level.

This perspective echoes a number of observations and criticisms about the limits of liberal democracy previously advanced by DUNCAN & LUKES. They note how many defenders of extant liberal democracies have come to share a pessimistic view of the masses' commitment to democratic values and the liberties of others. This revival of John Stuart Mill's original concern about the potential "tyranny of the majority", they explain, has led a number of writers to argue that apathy amongst citizens is actually a positive feature, rather than an indication of systemic dysfunction and electoral deficiency, for it enables leaders to govern effectively, rather than be "overloaded" by the inchoate demands of the voters on a regular basis. For Duncan and Lukes, however, such a defence of liberal democracy is too complacent, conservative, and cynical. Meanwhile, the collection of essays edited by WINTROP provides an eclectic and extensive range of philosophical and ideological approaches examining the problems and prospects of liberal democracy.

An intelligent and well-organized overview of liberal democracy is provided by HOLDEN, whose comprehensive exposition of its defining characteristics and historical development is followed by an examination of the critiques advanced by Marxists and "radical democrats". The former focus on the incompatibility of political equality with the massive socioeconomic inequalities intrinsic to capitalism, whereby liberal democracy is rendered little more than a sham that nonetheless serves to promote a false consciousness by persuading the masses that they (rather than capital or the bourgeoisie) actually wield political power. The radical critique, meanwhile, argues that simply voting in a general election once every four or five years, and choosing between a handful of parties or leaders, is an unduly narrow form of democracy – one that discourages or denies the possibility of more regular and active involvement in political affairs, whereupon liberal democracy could be transformed into a much more meaningful and invigorating participatory democracy. Yet Holden responds by offering a robust defence of liberal democracy, irrespective of its alleged deficiencies and inadequacies.

MACPHERSON, meanwhile, skilfully periodizes liberal democracy into four historically sequential "models", namely protective democracy, developmental democracy, equilibrium democracy, and participatory democracy. Protective democracy sought to provide individuals with a defence against an autocratic or aristocratic minority at a time when the establishment of capitalism was accompanied by the advocacy of liberty (albeit not yet for everyone). Developmental democracy viewed regular elections as a means of inculcating democratic values amongst the wider population, whereas equilibrium democracy was primarily concerned to strike a balance between stable political leadership and accountability to the voters via regular elections. Macpherson himself makes clear his preference for participatory democracy, desiring to see much wider and more regular involvement in politics by ordinary citizens, although he readily acknowledges that the gross inequalities of capitalism militate against the establishment of this particular model.

PETER DOREY

See also Democracy, John Locke

Liberalism

Arblaster, Anthony, *The Rise and Decline of Western Liberalism*, Oxford and New York: Blackwell, 1984

Bellamy, Richard, *Liberalism and Modern Society: A Historical Argument*, University Park: Pennsylvania State University Press, and Cambridge: Polity Press, 1992

Dworkin, Ronald, "Liberalism" in his *A Matter of Principle*, Cambridge, Massachusetts: Harvard University Press, 1985

Feinberg, Joel, *The Moral Limits of the Criminal Law*, 4 vols, Oxford and New York: Oxford University Press, 1984–88

Kymlicka, Will, *Liberalism, Community, and Culture*, Oxford: Clarendon Press, and New York: Oxford University Press, 1989

Kymlicka, Will, *Multicultural Citizenship: A Liberal Theory of Minority Rights*, Oxford: Clarendon Press, and New York: Oxford University Press, 1995

Larmore, Charles E., *Patterns of Moral Complexity*, Cambridge and New York: Cambridge University Press, 1987

Nozick, Robert, *Anarchy, State, and Utopia*, New York: Basic Books, and Oxford: Blackwell, 1974

Rawls, John, *A Theory of Justice*, Cambridge, Massachusetts: Harvard University Press, 1971; Oxford: Oxford University Press, 1973

Rawls, John, *Political Liberalism*, New York: Columbia University Press, 1993

Raz, Joseph, *The Morality of Freedom*, Oxford and New York: Oxford University Press, 1986

Sandel, Michael J., *Liberalism and the Limits of Justice*, 2nd edition, Cambridge and New York: Cambridge University Press, 1998

Wall, Steven, *Liberalism, Perfectionism, and Restraint*, Cambridge and New York: Cambridge University Press, 1998

Liberalism is not easy to define, and readers encountering the literature for the first time will need some orientation as to the historical and conceptual extension of the term. ARBLASTER is a helpful point of departure. The first and second parts of the book, devoted respectively to the analysis of liberalism as a body of doctrine and to its evolution as a social and political movement, supply comprehensive and reliable guidance. The third section, however, devoted to explaining the "decline" of liberalism, now seems dated in light of intervening events, which seem, if anything, to imply the triumph and reassertion of liberal hegemony in both East and West.

BELLAMY provides a further perspective on the intellectual heritage of liberalism. This work is especially valuable for its coverage of the thought of Italian, French, and German liberals. These aspects of the tradition are often ignored, thanks to a pervasive tendency to focus on the litany of familiar Anglo-American figures. The book effectively relates the historical context of liberal ideas to more general philosophical questions raised by liberalism, although Bellamy's final chapter on recent liberal philosophy is too brief to do justice to the richness of the contemporary debate. It is this contemporary debate about the merits and demerits of liberal ideas that has dominated political theory in the last quarter of the 20th century. All the remaining works discussed here are either by commentators on, or participants in, this debate.

The best point of entry into the contemporary discussion of liberal theory is DWORKIN. This brief essay captures the essential spirit of the liberal theoretical project as it has been conceived by such figures as John Rawls. Dworkin argues that the core idea of liberalism is the demand that individuals be treated with "equal concern and respect". But this liberal principle of equality does not, in Dworkin's view, compete with the value of freedom; rather, it expresses a claim about the status of free and independent individuals. Dworkin insists, moreover, that liberals can defend this norm of equal concern and respect without relying on a controversial theory of the good life. On this view, liberalism aspires to a kind of *neutrality* about disputed conceptions of the good life. Much of the subsequent debate about the viability of liberal principles has centred on the coherence of this apparently paradoxical proviso.

RAWLS (1971) is best understood as an attempt to construct a complete, integrated, self-consistent, liberal theory of justice around something like Dworkin's principle of equal concern and respect. The theory of justice that results is a magnificent intellectual edifice that has dominated all subsequent debate. The book's many achievements include: (a) a provocative and attractive description of the just society, one that justifies a liberal welfare state; (b) a novel hypothetical contractual method of political justification; and (c) an argument against utilitarian moral theory that has largely succeeded in putting utilitarian political theory on the defensive.

Some of the most telling criticism of Rawls came from within, rather than outside, the liberal tradition. NOZICK, for example, accepts many of Rawls's assumptions, but asserts forcefully that they argue not for a welfare state but rather for the classical liberal view that the only legitimate functions of the state are the protection of individuals' rights to personal and proprietary security. Nozick's elaboration of his rival "entitlement theory" of justice gave new impetus to libertarian versions of liberal doctrine.

Much of the critical literature charges that liberalism is unattractively individualistic. This criticism has been made with particular force in recent years by a group of theorists who have come be known as "communitarians". SANDEL offers an influential communitarian criticism of Rawls. Sandel's main complaint is that Rawls presupposes a view of the self as essentially disconnected from social and communal attachments. But Sandel argues that this abstract picture of the self as radically independent of society is implausible and fails to account for the ways in which individuals' moral identity and sense of

purpose are bound up with membership in particular cultural and political communities.

The first part of KYMLICKA (1989) is a brilliant defence of liberalism against the criticisms of communitarians and others. Along the way, Kymlicka (1989) provides an invaluable survey of the major critical challenges to liberal theory since Rawls (1971). The book concludes with an excellent discussion of how liberals ought to deal with the rights of cultural and ethnic groups, a topic to which KYMLICKA (1995) returns. These two works are largely responsible for placing the issue of cultural rights at the forefront of contemporary discussion of liberalism.

FEINBERG is a work that deserves to be ranked with Rawls (1971) as one of the major intellectual accomplishments of recent liberal theory. This four-volume masterpiece is a comprehensive and unfailingly resourceful exploration of liberal arguments about the proper reach of the criminal law. The work develops the position defended by John Stuart Mill in his classic 1859 essay, *On Liberty*. However, its discussion of the fine grain of such issues as paternalism, the legal enforcement of morality, and so-called "victimless crimes" deepens and clarifies the liberal position far beyond what Mill, or indeed any other liberal, has yet been able to provide.

In recent years, liberal theorists have tended to divide into two camps. One has remained loyal to, and sought to extend, Dworkin's principle of neutrality. The other has abandoned it in the name of a "perfectionist" form of liberalism. Chapters 5 and 6 of LARMORE provide a clear account of the motivation behind, and aspiration of, liberal neutrality. The basic aspiration is to justify liberal principles and institutions on terms that agents with radically different conceptions of the good life could all endorse in that they would see no conflict between liberalism and their own conceptions of the good. The centrepiece of Larmore's attempt to realize this aspiration is the imperative to show equal respect to participants in a rational dialogue. Adapting some of Habermas's recent views about dialogue, Larmore claims that this norm of equal respect qualifies as an appropriately neutral basis for political compromise on a range of divisive issues.

Although RAWLS (1993) dispenses with Larmore's argument about rational dialogue, the book arrives (by a different route) at a similarly neutralist liberal position. Rawls (1993) is conceived as an amendment to the theory presented in Rawls (1971). The amendment is allegedly necessary because Rawls now believes that his earlier presentation failed to provide an appropriately neutral justification for liberal principles of justice. On the older version of the theory, citizens might have to choose between their personal moral, religious and philosophical convictions and allegiance to liberal principles; as a result, we cannot guarantee the stability of a just society. Rawls (1993) conceives of a liberal "overlapping consensus" as a way of securing this sort of stability under conditions of radical pluralism and moral disagreement.

Liberal perfectionists have offered powerful criticisms of this kind of neutrality. RAZ is the best and most sophisticated articulation of a perfectionist liberal position, although it predates Larmore and Rawls (1993). Perfectionists argue that a liberal state can, and must, promote sound ideals of human flourishing, or valid "conceptions of the good life". Chapters 5 and 6 of Raz develop a powerful criticism of liberal neutrality, while chapters 12, 14 and 16 lay out an alternative perfectionist view centred on the value of individual autonomy.

Although Raz remains the central and pioneering work of perfectionist theory, its arguments will intimidate first-time readers. They may turn to WALL for an admirably lucid defence of liberal perfectionism. Moreover, Wall responds directly to the more recent neutralist arguments of Rawls (1993) and Larmore. In the second half of the book, Wall clarifies and extends the perfectionist commitment to individual autonomy, and (unlike Raz) suggestively explores the public policy applications of perfectionist liberal principles.

COLIN BIRD

See also Freedom

Liberalism in international relations theory

Evans, Peter B., Harold K. Jacobson and Robert D. Putnam (editors), *Double-Edged Diplomacy: International Bargaining and Domestic Politics*, Berkeley: University of California Press, 1993

Keohane, Robert O. and Joseph S. Nye, *Power and Interdependence*, 2nd edition, Glenview, Illinois: Scott Foresman, 1989

Milner, Helen V., *Interests, Institutions, and Information: Domestic Politics and International Relations*, Princeton, New Jersey: Princeton University Press, 1997

Moravcsik, Andrew, "Taking Preferences Seriously: A Liberal Theory of International Politics", *International Organization*, 51/4 (1997): 513–53

Moravcsik, Andrew, *The Choice for Europe: Social Purpose and State Power from Messina to Maastricht*, Ithaca, New York: Cornell University Press, and London: UCL Press, 1998

Risse-Kappen, Thomas, *Cooperation among Democracies: The European Influence on U.S. Foreign Policy*, Princeton, New Jersey: Princeton University Press, 1995

Russett, Bruce, *Grasping the Democratic Peace: Principles for a Post Cold-War World*, Princeton, New Jersey: Princeton University Press, 1993

Zacher, Mark W. and Richard A. Matthew, "Liberal International Theory: Common Threads, Divergent Strands" in *Controversies in International Relations Theory: Realism and the Neoliberal Challenge*, edited by Charles W. Kegley Jr, New York: St Martin's Press, 1995

Even more than realism and institutionalism, its main competitors in international relations theory, liberalism is far from being a coherent theory, but rather a family of assumptions, hypotheses, and theories on the nature and dynamics of world politics. The essay by ZACHER & MATTHEW is particularly useful in showing the diversity of liberalism. The authors trace the historical roots of the liberal tradition in international thinking back to the early modern era, highlight some common themes in the variants that emerged, and propose a typology of the contemporary strands of contemporary liberalism (republican, commercial, military, cognitive, sociological, and institutional), discussing exemplary works in those traditions.

MORAVCSIK's 1997 article is probably the best statement of liberal international relations theory that has appeared to date. For him, liberalism "elaborates the insight that state-society relations – the relationship of states to the domestic and transnational social context in which they are embedded – have a fundamental impact on state behaviour in world politics. Societal ideas, interests, and institutions influence state behaviour by shaping state preferences". Moravcsik proposes a set of core assumptions, elaborates three major variants of liberalism (ideational, commercial, and republican), and shows that liberalism has analytical priority over realism and institutionalism since it defines the conditions under which their respective assumptions about state preferences hold.

In their influential book, KEOHANE & NYE construct an ideal–typical liberal international system, which they call "complex interdependence", by reversing the basic assumptions of political realism. Complex interdependence has three basic features: (a) societies are connected by multiple channels of contact, with no state monopoly; (b) different state policy goals are not arranged in a hierarchy, but are subject to trade-offs; (c) military force is largely irrelevant. They assume that any real situation in world politics falls somewhere on a continuum between the liberal and the realist ideal types, and locate on this continuum two issue areas (oceans and international finance) and two bilateral relationships (US–Canada and US–Australia), which they examine thoroughly. The second edition contains an Afterword which critically reconsiders the framework and proposes avenues for future research.

A basic tenet of liberalism, going back at least to Immanuel Kant, is that the foreign policy of liberal democracies is fundamentally different from the foreign policy of other polities – specifically, that democracies are inherently more pacific regimes or that democracies almost never wage war against each other. RUSSETT is an outstanding contemporary exponent of this "republican liberalism". Here, he provides a thorough exploration of the "democratic peace thesis", presenting relevant quantitative data on militarized disputes, laying out possible explanations of the phenomenon, presenting evidence from Ancient Greece, the post-World War II era, and pre-industrial societies, and discusses the implications of democratic peace for international relations after the Cold War.

The idea that relations among democratic states do not conform to the rules of power politics is central also to RISSE-KAPPEN's important book on the European NATO partners' influence on US foreign policy. The book is designed as an empirical test of three alternative theories of alliance interaction: structural realism, traditional realism, and liberalism. He confronts these theories with the results of four detailed case studies (the Korean War, the Suez crisis, the 1958–63 test ban negotiations, and Cuban missile crisis) and an overview of NATO decisions concerning nuclear strategy and deployments from the 1960s to the 1980s. Highlighting both the outcomes of those episodes and the processes leading to the outcomes, Risse-Kappen finds that structural realism yields wrong predictions concerning most of the outcomes, traditional realism predicts correctly most outcomes but the processes do not conform to its expectations, and that liberalism can account for both the outcomes and the processes. In summary, he finds that democratic allies form democratic alliances. Risse-Kappen's book provides a powerful empirical support for the contention that Western states have formed a community of liberal democracies, in which interactions are governed more by a sense of collective identity and shared norms than by power-based bargaining.

The volume edited by EVANS, JACOBSON & PUTNAM includes the path-breaking article by Robert Putnam on "Diplomacy and Domestic Politics: The Logic of Two-Level Games" (1988). Putnam develops a very fruitful framework for studying systematically the interaction of domestic and international constraints on decision makers involved in inter-governmental negotiations, suggesting seminal concepts and hypotheses. In the other essays in the volume, a set of outstanding scholars employ, enhance, and modify this frame-work in order to shed light on a broad range of issues, from security relations to economic disputes and North–South tensions. The volume has given a strong impulse to the use and development of one of the most interesting innovations in recent international relations theory.

MILNER's study is a remarkable attempt at providing rigorous foundations for the study of the impact of domestic politics on international cooperation and developing further the two-level game approach. She develops a framework of analysis where the dependent variable, the probability of inter-national cooperation and its terms, is influenced by three inde-pendent variables: the structure of domestic preferences (of national political leaders as well as societal groups), the distri-bution of information among internal actors, and the type of domestic political institutions. She constructs a two-level bargaining model and tests it by examining eight cases of successful or failed international cooperation, from 1940–93.

MORAVCSIK's book (1998) is an impressive account of the evolution of the European Community, which combines a liberal theory of state preference formation with an inter-governmentalist account of international institution-building. He shows that the main force propelling European integration in successive interstate "great bargains" was not concern for the geopolitical situation or federalist ideology, but rather concrete economic interests of specific social groups within nation-states, which prompted national governments to pursue international economic policy coordination in certain issue areas.

MATHIAS KOENIG-ARCHIBUGI

See also Constructivism in international relations theory, International relations theory, Realism in international relations theory

Libertarianism

Bergland, David, *Libertarianism in One Lesson*, 7th edition, Costa Mesa, California: Orpheus, 1997

Boaz, David, *Libertarianism: A Primer*, New York and London: Free Press, 1997a

Boaz, David (editor), *The Libertarian Reader: Classic and Contemporary Writings from Lao-tzu to Milton Friedman*, New York and London: Free Press, 1997b

Haworth, Alan, *Anti-libertarianism: Markets, Philosophy, and Myth*, London and New York: Routledge, 1994

Macey, Jonathan R., "On the Failure of Libertarianism to Capture the Popular Imagination", *Social Philosophy and Policy*, 15/2 (1998): 372–411

Machan, Tibor R. and Douglas B. Rasmussen (editors), *Liberty for the Twenty-First Century: Contemporary Libertarian Thought*, Lanham, Maryland, and London: Rowman and Littlefield, 1995

Narveson, Jan, *The Libertarian Idea*, Philadelphia: Temple University Press, 1988

Newman, Stephen L., *Liberalism at Wit's End: The Libertarian Revolt against the Modern State*, Ithaca, New York: Cornell University Press, 1984

Raimondo, Justin, *Reclaiming the American Right: The Lost Legacy of the Conservative Movement*, Burlingame, California: Center for Libertarian Studies, 1993

Rand, Ayn, *Atlas Shrugged*, New York: Random House, 1957; London: Muller, 1959

Rothbard, Murray N., *For a New Liberty: The Libertarian Manifesto*, New York: Macmillan, 1973; revised edition, New York: Collier, 1978

The basic tenets of libertarianism are attributed to RAND, whose novel depicts an American society weakened by many years of welfare. The society has made selfishness and pro-ductiveness into an evil. Instead of working for a life, the characters in this novel believe that government owes them lives. Although the book is long (over 1,000 pages), the message is clear: selfishness is good. This message is a pithy introduction to the basis of libertarianism, a philosophy that holds that people should work to benefit themselves and not the government or the larger community.

ROTHBARD presents a theoretical outline of libertarianism. The state is inherently aggressive and exploitative. Libertarian-ism combines Lockean rights to life, liberty, and property, with an appeal to the free market as the most efficient mech-anism for the allocation of resources. The author applies his theory to various political issues of the day including public education, welfare, economic regulation, and foreign affairs, and finds that the free market is better able to solve societal problems than is the state.

NEWMAN presents a relatively neutral assessment of liber-tarianism. He examines the basic tenets of the philosophy without becoming an uncritical supporter. The major figures associated with the movement are identified and the positions analysed. As the title suggests, the author finds that libertari-anism in the United States is at "wit's end" because it is diffi-cult to convince Americans on the value of privatizing many of the functions performed by government.

NARVESON provides a defence of libertarianism against almost all of its critics. His argument is not based on a grand theory of freedom but on the view that "to be free is to do what you want". The government is the adversary. The primary contribution of this work is its application of libertarian theory to "concrete social policy". His comparison of liber-tarianism with the tenets and shortcomings of welfare state liberalism is particularly interesting.

RAIMONDO examines the development of the libertarian movement in the broader context of the history of the conservative movement in the US. He provides sketches of the intellectual founders of libertarianism including Rand and Rothbard. The conflict with other parts of the American right over such things as hatred of the Soviet Union is described in detail. The development of the Libertarian Party as a participant in national politics forms the conclusion of the analysis and illustrates the tension within libertarianism on the proper role of libertarians in American politics. This work is a careful analysis of how libertarianism fits in the broader American conservative movement.

HAWORTH is highly critical of libertarianism. He frames his argument by questioning whether or not the free market is the only economic mechanism capable of respecting and furthering human freedom. The analysis offers the view that libertarianism is nothing little more than an unfounded, quasi-religious statement of faith: "a market romance". This criticism of libertarianism offers the best discussions of the philosophy by a non-libertarian.

The 19 essays in MACHAN & RASMUSSEN together provide an excellent overview of libertarianism and its application to "real" political issues. Several of the essays also address the many critics of libertarianism. Taken as a whole, this collection offers an academic introduction to the philosophy.

A thoroughly modern overview of libertarianism is found in BOAZ (1997a). The author summarizes much of the thought on liberty in an accessible way. The reader will find that libertarianism challenges modern social conservative thought as well as the liberal supporters of the "welfare state". Unfortunately, although clearly defining libertarianism, the author dedicates almost no space to defending it against its critics. One significant contribution of the book is the brief, but complete, historical summary of the development of the philosophy. The appendix "Are You a Libertarian?" allows for a revealing self-examination.

A brief introduction to libertarianism and its application to practical politics can be found in BERGLAND. Written by the Libertarian Party's candidate for President in 1984, this book was originally published as a political manifesto for his campaign. As such, it is limited by appearing to be solely an exposition of the party's platform. One advantage of this political campaign document, updated in seven editions, is that it is concise while being comprehensive. It also provides comparisons of liberal, conservative, and libertarian positions on current issues.

The essays presented in BOAZ (1997b) provide an excellent introduction to the works that serve as the building blocks of libertarianism. The writings come from a number of historical eras and across various cultures, illustrating the fact that the ideas of libertarianism are not new. Of course, each work explores the common theme of intrusive government and its threat to individual liberty while propounding the virtues of the free market.

MACEY identifies why libertarianism has not become a widely accepted ideology in the United States. In part, he finds that libertarians are unable to convince potential adherents that this philosophy of life can be adapted to the "real world". Libertarianism is too utopian a concept for most people, in part because libertarians do not understand people. This essay

incorporates much libertarian thought and concludes with a call for a "kinder, gentler libertarianism" (p.411).

JOHN DAVID RAUSCH, JR

Liberty

Benn, Stanley I., *A Theory of Freedom*, Cambridge and New York: Cambridge University Press, 1988

Berlin, Isaiah, "Two Concepts of Liberty" in his *Four Essays on Liberty*, London and New York: Oxford University Press, 1969

Cohen, G.A., *History, Labour, and Freedom: Themes from Marx*, Oxford: Clarendon Press, and New York: Oxford University Press, 1988

Connolly, William E., *The Terms of Political Discourse*, revised edition, Princeton, New Jersey: Princeton University Press, 1983

Green, T.H., "Liberal Legislation and Freedom of Contract" in *Works of T.H. Green*, 5 vols, Bristol: Thoemmes, 1997 (originally published 1888)

Long, Douglas G., *Bentham on Liberty: Jeremy Bentham's Idea of Liberty in Relation to His Utilitarianism*, Toronto: University of Toronto Press, 1977

MacCallum, Gerald Jr, "Negative and Positive Freedom", *Philosophical Review*, 76 (1967): 312–24; reprinted in *Liberty*, edited by David Miller, 1991

Mill, John Stuart, *On Liberty*, London: Parker, 1859; with *The Subjection of Women, and Chapters on Socialism*, edited by Stefan Collini, Cambridge and New York: Cambridge University Press, 1989

Miller, David (editor), *Liberty*, Oxford: Oxford University Press, 1991

Oppenheim, Felix E., *Dimensions of Freedom: An Analysis*, New York: St Martin's Press, and London: Macmillan, 1961

Pitkin, Hanna Fenichel, "Are Freedom and Liberty Twins?", *Political Theory*, 16/4 (November 1988): 523–52

Plamenatz, John, "On le Forcera d'être libre" in *Hobbes and Rousseau: A Collection of Critical Essays*, edited by Maurice Cranston and Richard S. Peters, Garden City, New York: Doubleday, 1972

Rees, John C., *John Stuart Mill's On Liberty*, constructed from published and unpublished sources by G.L. Williams, Oxford: Clarendon Press, and New York: Oxford University Press, 1985

Skinner, Quentin, *Liberty before Liberalism*, Cambridge and New York: Cambridge University Press, 1998

Stephen, James Fitzjames, *Liberty, Equality, Fraternity*, London: Cambridge University Press, 1967 (originally published 1873)

Taylor, Charles, "What's Wrong with Negative Liberty" in *Liberty*, edited by David Miller, 1991

In English, "liberty" and "freedom" are for the most part used interchangeably. PITKIN suggests that such linguistic parochialism blinds us to differences in the origin and development of the two terms. Liberty derives from the Latin term *libertas*; freedom is from the old Saxon word *freo*. The former has, or originally had, political connotations that the latter largely lacks. Here, however, we shall use the two terms interchangeably. Scholarly analyses of liberty (or freedom) tend to take one of three forms. The first consist of conceptual analyses: what do we mean when we use the term "liberty"? The second approach is historical: what did the concept mean in earlier times and how has its meaning altered over time? And thirdly, how did a specific thinker – Hobbes or Bentham or Mill, say – understand the concept of liberty?

CONNOLLY (chapter 4) claims that freedom is an "essentially contested concept". People of different ideological and political persuasions mean different things by the term: a traditional conservative understands it in one way, a libertarian in another, and a Marxist in yet another. Each wishes to claim that their conception of liberty is the "real" or "correct" one and that competing conceptions are incorrect. Nor should this surprise us, because "liberty" carries strong commendatory force, and no ideology or political movement would dare to claim to be "against" or "opposed" to liberty (though of course not all ideologies favour liberty for all). Connolly advances his own view of liberty, according to which an individual "X is free with respect to z if (or to the extent that) he is unconstrained from conceiving or choosing z and if (to the extent that), were he to choose z, he would not be constrained from doing or becoming z" (p.157).

As BERLIN notes, understandings of liberty are conventionally classified according to whether they are (more or less) "negative" or "positive". These are not terms of condemnation or commendation but refer, rather, to two quite different concepts, each with opposing views of liberty. A "negative" view of liberty (which Berlin favours) holds that liberty signifies the absence of humanly imposed external obstacles or impediments to someone's achieving his or her aims or desires. A "positive" view claims that liberty is (or involves) freedom from false aims or unworthy desires and, correspondingly, freedom to achieve true or worthy aims. Champions of the negative view include Hobbes, Bentham, and Berlin, who is among the most ardent critics of the positive view. Defenders of one or another version of the positive view include Plato, Rousseau, and Marx, T.H. Green, and Charles Taylor.

MACCALLUM calls into question the negative/positive distinction and attempts to refute the claim that these represent two distinct "concepts" of liberty. He argues, rather, that liberty (or freedom) is a "triadic" relation involving (a) an agent who confronts (b) barriers or obstacles to (c) his aims or desires. The chief differences between the positive and negative views consist of their different ways of identifying (a), (b), and (c). Negative libertarians like Berlin identify (a) as individuals, (b) as humanly imposed external obstacles, and (c) as the desires or aims of (a). Positive libertarians like Marx identify (a) as a class, (b) as the "false consciousness" from which (a) suffers, and (c) as the full and free development of all in a classless society.

GREEN maintained that parties to a contract cannot be equally free unless they have roughly equal power. Thus a poor labourer who enters into a contract to sell his labour to a wealthy industrialist is not free in the same sense, or to the same degree, as his wealthy employer. The state should therefore act as a "powerful friend" to the relatively powerless employee. This is not an infringement on freedom but an extension of it to those who are not free (or are less free) to develop their talents and capacities to their fullest, for their own and for the common benefit.

TAYLOR argues, against Berlin and other defenders of negative liberty, that the positive view has no necessary connection or affinity with totalitarian ideologies. Indeed, it recognizes (as the negative view does not) that obstacles or impediments to one's actions may be internal or psychological as well as external or physical. Moreover, our desires to act in certain ways or to be a certain sort of person may be inauthentic or counterproductive. Therefore liberty cannot be understood simply as the absence of obstacles to achieving what we desire.

COHEN defends a somewhat subtle and sophisticated version of Marx's view of freedom. Against libertarians who hold that an unfettered free-market society maximizes freedom, Cohen argues that while it does indeed promote a certain sort of freedom for those who benefit most from the institution of private property, the kind of "unfreedom" for the propertyless goes unrecognized.

MacCallum and Taylor and abridged versions of Berlin, Cohen, and Green, are reprinted in MILLER, which includes a very useful introduction.

OPPENHEIM offers a philosophical analysis and reconstruction of freedom, trying to free it from the muddles and confusions that have long attended that concept. His overriding aim is to reconstruct that concept so as to make it useful for social scientific inquiry. And this requires, among other things, making it a non-normative or value-free concept. His conception of liberty thus clashes with Connolly who views liberty as an irreducibly normative notion.

BENN is among the most noteworthy attempts to devise a systematic or general theory of liberty. His theory links liberty to autonomy, the latter being a characterological ideal involving the individual's having an internally consistent system of beliefs that he or she holds self-critically and is prepared to readjust in response to criticism and evidence. The ideal of autonomy is contrasted with the condition of "autarchy", understood as the power or capacity to control one's own life.

Different theories, ideologies, or traditions of discourse typically advance and defend quite different views of liberty, not all of which can be conveniently classified as negative or positive. Histories of the concept of liberty include SKINNER, who reconstructs a "republican" or "neo-Roman" view of liberty as requiring service to the community of which one is a member and citizen.

MILL is a famous defence of a particular view (in this instance a liberal view) of liberty, and STEPHEN is a prominent critique of that view. Mill argues that individuals ought to be free to say what and do as they wish, so long as their doing so does not cause harm to others (this is the so-called "harm principle"). Stephen counters that this gives individuals too much latitude and does not take into account the wider interests of the community in maintaining order and respecting authority.

Significant studies of earlier thinkers' conceptions of liberty include PLAMENATZ on Rousseau, LONG on Bentham, and REES on J.S. Mill.

TERENCE BALL

See also Autonomy, Freedom, Power

Life expectancy, *see* Human longevity

Life history

Bertaux, Daniel (editor), *Biography and Society: The Life History Approach in the Social Sciences*, London and Beverly Hills, California: Sage, 1981

Bertaux, Daniel, *Les Recits de vie: Perspectives ethnosociologique*, Paris: Nathan, 1996

Chamberlayne, Prue, Tom Wengraf and Joanna Bornat (editors), *The Turn to Biographical Methods in Social Science: Comparative Issues and Examples*, London: Routledge, 1999

Chanfrault-Duchet, Marie-Françoise, "Biographical Research in Former West Germany", *Current Sociology*, 43/2–3 (1995): 209–19

Garz, Detlef and Klaus Kraimer (editors), *Die Welt als Text: Theorie, Kritik und Praxis der objektiven Hermeneutik* [The World as Text: The Theory, Criticism and Practice of Objective Hermeneutics], Frankfurt: Suhrkamp, 1994

Jung, Thomas and Stefan Müller-Dohm (editors), *"Wirklichkeit" im Deutungsprozess: Verstehen und Methoden in den Kultur- und Sozialwissenschaften* ["Reality" in Interpretive Processes: Understanding and Methods in Cultural and Social Science], Frankfurt: Suhrkamp, 1993

Miller, Robert L., *Researching Life Stories and Family Histories*, London, and Thousand Oaks, California: Sage, 2000

Plummer, Ken, *Documents of Life: An Introduction to the Problems and Literature of a Humanistic Method*, London: Allen and Unwin, 1983

Simeoni, Daniel and Marco Diani (editors), special issue on biographical research, *Current Sociology*, 43/2–3 (1995)

The use of life histories, or "the biographical perspective", as a method of sociological research has a long pedigree, going back to Thomas and Znanicki's highly influential *The Polish Peasant in Europe and America* – which devoted a whole volume to the life history of a Polish immigrant – and the collection of life histories by the Chicago School in the 1920s. The rise of quantitative sociology in the United States caused the method to go into a precipitate decline in the 1940s, which was only reversed as part of the general blooming of qualitative methods of research in the 1970s. PLUMMER provides an excellent overview of the early stages of life-history research and places the method in the context of the broad spectrum of qualitative research techniques, in particular those that use personal documents as a primary source.

The current revival of the biographical perspective and the use of life histories was sparked largely by Daniel Bertaux, a French sociologist who set up an international working group on life histories in the late 1970s, which quickly developed into the "Biography and Society" Research Committee 38 of the International Sociological Association (ISA). This ISA Research Committee acts as the main contact point for socio-logists carrying out life-history and biographical research. Its meetings during and between ISA World Congresses are important forums for the development of the method.

BERTAUX's (1981) edited book is an influential early statement of the work of the Biography and Society Research Committee. The chapters in the book give an overview of the attempts of the proponents of the life-history method to define the technique's parameters as distinct from a conventional approach to interviewing. Rather than concentrating upon a "snapshot" of an individual's present situation, the life-history approach emphasizes the placement of the individual within a nexus of social connections, historical events, and life experiences. The book can still reward the reader with insights into the method's potential.

Recent methodological debate in the area has centred upon a division between: a) "realists", who emphasize the development of sociological concepts through the use of grounded theory techniques and/or neo-positivist theory testing; and b) "narrativists", who emphasize the essentially fluid nature of the interplay that takes place when a narrator constructs their life story for a listener. As well as disseminating Research Committee information, the Biography & Society Newsletter has provided a forum for this methodological debate.

Much of the current development of the biographical perspective is taking place outside anglophone sociology, particularly among German-speaking sociologists. A recent international review was presented in a special double issue of *Current Sociology* edited by SIMEONI & DIANI. The contributions, which can be recommended generally, range across an international spectrum of approaches to the biographical perspective, from textual analyses that border on literary criticism to methods of collecting and presenting family history data. CHANFRAULT-DUCHET provides the best overview of German approaches to life-history research that is available in English. Her article is particularly useful in its succinct but informative survey of hermeneutic approaches to biographical research. German-language sources that provide an introduction to the hermeneutic approach are GARZ & KRAIMER and JUNG & MÜLLER-DOHM.

Until now there have been no texts explicitly designed to teach life history or biographical research but this gap is currently being filled. BERTAUX (1996) has produced a French-language text about collecting life stories. CHAMBER-LAYNE, WENGRAF & BORNAT have produced an edited text of readings on "biographical methods in the social sciences". Methodological issues feature prominently in this volume, including discussion of: "biographical work" (structuring narrative accounts of lives); hermeneutics and subjectivity; comparison across cultures; the interplay between structure and agency; and generalizing or theorizing in biographical analysis. Strong points of this text are the participation of prominent German and English practitioners and the illustration of methodological issues through practical case studies. MILLER is the first English-language textbook directly about conducting life history research. This text contrasts the so-called "realist" approach to life-history research with the "narrative" approach to collecting life stories. The interplay between historical events and time periods, ageing and life course, and generations and cohorts is discussed. Practical advice is given on interviewing and analysis within different methodological approaches to biographical research. The text makes links to closely aligned methods for collecting family histories.

ROBERT L. MILLER

Likert scale

Albaum, Gerald, "The Likert Scale Revisited: An Alternate Version", *Journal of the Market Research Society*, 39/2 (1997): 331–48

Maurer, Todd J. and Heather R. Pierce, "A Comparison of Likert Scale and Traditional Measures of Self-Efficacy", *Journal of Applied Psychology*, 83/2 (1998): 324–29

Nanna, Michael J. and Shlomo S. Sawilowsky, "Analysis of Likert Scale Data in Disability and Medical Rehabilitation Research", *Psychological Methods*, 3/1 (1998): 55–57

Royeen, Charlotte B., "Adaptation of Likert Scaling for Use with Children", *Occupational Therapy Journal of Research*, 5/1 (1985): 59–69

Schwartz, Norbert, "Self-Reports: How the Questions Shape the Answers", *American Psychologist*, 54/2 (1999): 93–105

Rensis Likert developed in the 1930s the now familiar technique of measuring attitudes with a five-point scale ranging from "strongly disagree" to "strongly agree". This scale and other Likert-type scales (which may have more than five points on the continuum) have become standard research tools in the social sciences. Researchers who use such scales realize that a variety of social, cognitive, and linguistic factors affect the way respondents answer. SCHWARTZ has identified some of the pitfalls associated with measurement on a Likert scale. He points out that the choice of rating scales leads to different types of answers because respondents systematically interpret questions differently based on the scale (for example, an eleven-point scale from -5 to +5 versus 0 to 10). Schwartz suggests that when a scale involves both negative and positive numbers, respondents see the endpoints on the continuum as being opposite to one another (for example, failure versus success). On the other hand, if the scale involves only positive numbers, respondents see a continuum reflecting different degrees of a single attribute (for example, the degree of success). The author also points out that when a respondent uses a Likert-type scale to indicate the frequency of some behaviour, different scales of numbers from which the respondent chooses lead to different results. Schwartz also comments on some of the problems associated with context effects, such as the order of questions. He notes that psychologists have begun to understand the cognitive, linguistic, and social frameworks of respondents that affect their interpretations of questions and replies to them. This very readable article presents useful information on construction of surveys and questionnaires that rely on Likert scales.

One advantage of Likert scales is their simplicity. A possible drawback is that they may generate data that do not capture the complexity of attitudes or beliefs that they measure. MAURER & PIERCE compare the traditional measurement of self-efficacy on the two dimensions of strength and magnitude with measurement using a unidimensional Likert scale. Self-efficacy relates to a person's judgement about what he or she is able to accomplish, given current skill levels. The researchers correlated the traditional and Likert measurements with final grades, grade point averages, expected grades, and scores on the Scholastic Aptitude Test. Maurer & Pierce report that, even with its simple and unidimensional nature, the Likert scale was as useful in assessing self-efficacy as the traditional approach. Although this research involved only a single latent construct (self-efficacy) in relation to academic performance, the implication is that complex concepts can be captured adequately through the use of a simple Likert scale.

Although a simple Likert scale may represent attitudes accurately, ALBAUM points out that attitudes involve two separate dimensions: direction (positive or negative) and strength or intensity. As such, a two-stage questioning process may be useful. He compares the standard format for a Likert scale with a two-stage questioning process in which a respondent provides input on the direction of an attitude, followed by the intensity with which the person holds the attitude. Albaum reports that the one-stage process seems to result in an error of central tendency, that is, a predisposition to report moderate values on the response scale. A two-stage question results in greater incidence of reporting of extreme positions on the questions. He notes several implications of his findings for conducting research. This research reflects some of the hidden complexity associated with using an ostensibly simple procedure.

Most research using Likert scales has involved adults. It is not clear whether such scales generate valid or reliable data when used with children. ROYEEN reports that, with some modification, researchers can satisfactorily use Likert scales with children. She tested children who were six years of age and discovered that using pictures to illustrate behaviours associated with a question tended to distract children and make it more difficult for them to respond. Children preferred verbal choices instead. Further, Royeen notes that a three-choice scale (for example, "no", "a little", and "a lot") was better than the standard five-choice scale. Finally, she found that children were better able to comprehend an item and respond to it when the tester phrases it in a question format rather than as a statement. The combination of verbal presentation of a question and a three-point response scale with children generated useful data. This brief and readable article provides practical tips about studying children with Likert scales. One drawback is that the number of children who participated in this research was quite small and the sample came from a small, private school; the sample was not representative of six-year-old children. Hence, it is uncertain whether their responses resemble those of typical children of that age.

As psychometricians began to study the properties of Likert-type responses, there has been disagreement about the statistical treatment of data generated from this approach. NANNA & SAWILOWSKY note that, strictly speaking, Likert-type data exist on an ordinal scale of measurement. As such, some researchers have argued that traditional parametric statistics requiring interval or ratio data are inappropriate with Likert scales. Nanna & Sawilowsky tested this thesis. They used a seven-point Likert scale to collect data on level of functioning at the beginning and at the end of rehabilitation for 714 patients. They created subsamples of patient scores and compared the results of data analysis using either the parametric t-test or its nonparametric counterpart, the Wilcoxon rank-sum test. They concluded that, for their data, the Wilcoxon rank-sum test outperforms the t-test, showing greater power for sample sizes ranging from ten to sixty per group. The researchers state that for non-normal data sets like theirs, the Wilcoxon test shows notably greater power; for a given effect size, fewer participants are needed to achieve statistical significance. The authors conclude that there are significant practical implications of the choice of statistical tests for research on patient outcomes in particular, and on behaviours and attitudes in general.

BERNARD C. BEINS

See also Questionnaire design

Lincoln, Abraham, 1809–1865

US political leader

Boritt, Gabor S., *Abraham Lincoln and the Economics of the American Dream*, 2nd edition, Urbana: University of Illinois Press, 1994

Cox, LaWanda, *Lincoln and Black Freedom: A Study in Presidential Leadership*, 2nd edition, Charleston: University of South Carolina Press, 1994

Davis, William C., *Lincoln's Men: How President Lincoln Became Father to an Army and a Nation*, New York: Free Press, 1999

Donald, David Herbert, *Lincoln*, New York: Simon and Schuster, and London: Cape, 1995

Neely, Mark E. Jr, *The Fate of Liberty: Abraham Lincoln and Civil Liberties*, New York: Oxford University Press, 1991

Paludan, Phillip S., *The Presidency of Abraham Lincoln*, Lawrence: University Press of Kansas, 1994

Peterson, Merrill D., *Lincoln in American Memory*, New York: Oxford University Press, 1994

Wills, Garry, *Lincoln at Gettysburg: The Words That Remade America*, New York: Simon and Schuster, 1992

Wilson, Douglas L., *Honor's Voice: The Transformation of Abraham Lincoln*, New York: Knopf, 1998

DONALD is the new standard biography of Lincoln. It is a very good, well-written narrative account of Lincoln's life, thoroughly grounded in the available primary and secondary source materials. The author informs the reader from the outset that he has tried to write his biography entirely through Lincoln's eyes, writing only of what Lincoln himself would have seen and experienced. This is an excellent narrative approach, but it does make the book a bit thin in the way of serious analysis of Lincoln's career.

PALUDAN is a comprehensive overview of Lincoln's political leadership during the American Civil War. It stresses Lincoln's respect for law and order as well as his expansive reading of the Declaration of Independence's guarantee of human equality. Thus, Paludan argues, Lincoln pursued the idealistic, liberal end of emancipation and freedom through the largely conservative means of wartime politics and constitutionalism. Paludan and Donald together offer a very thorough overview of Lincoln's overall life and career.

Readers interested in Lincoln's early life would do well to begin with WILSON. This examines Lincoln's early career as store clerk, labourer, attorney, and local Illinois politician, stressing Lincoln's private doubts and insecurities during this time.

BORITT provides a useful study of Lincoln's economic thought, covering his entire career but offering a particularly fine analysis of the role economics played in Lincoln's antebellum political career. Boritt convincingly demonstrates that the economics of a free market economy, not slavery, dominated Lincoln's early thinking, and continued to play a key role in his political thought during the war.

COX, though a bit dated, is still the best book-length study of Lincoln's approach to issues of emancipation and racial equality. This classic work convincingly refutes the arguments of Lincoln critics who have sometimes suggested that he really cared little about racial equality or the plight of African-Americans. On the contrary, Cox argues, Lincoln's pursuit of emancipation and early reconstruction policies were quite sensitive to issues of racial equality and harmony.

WILLS is an exhaustive analysis of the history of Lincoln's most renowned speech, the Gettysburg Address. Offering a thorough description of the events surrounding the speech, Wills also provides a detailed intellectual history for it, placing the Address within a larger tradition of classical and American political rhetoric. Though guilty at times of hyperbole (he argues at one point that Lincoln's address forever altered American politics), Wills provides the definitive account of the Gettysburg Address and its implications for American democracy.

DAVIS examines Lincoln's rapport with ordinary Union soldiers, illustrating his success in assuming a fatherly role for the thousands of young men. This study is well written, and useful as a detailed catalogue of the impressions Lincoln left in the minds of ordinary American soldiers.

NEELY won its author the 1992 Pulitzer Prize for its study of Lincoln's record in the area of wartime civil liberties. Lincoln labored under the reputation of being something of a tyrant in this regard, a president who used military power to suppress criticism of his administration. Neely tests this reputation by minutely examining the arrest records of thousands of civilian prisoners in the North, and shows that Lincoln was in fact a pragmatic and fair-minded practitioner of civil liberties. He did not engage in a wholesale suppression of political dissent, but rather used his presidential powers in this area carefully.

PETERSON is the definitive study of how Lincoln has fared in the minds and hearts of Americans from the time of his death until the present day. The book does not offer much in the way of interpretation or analysis; it is, rather, a very thorough description of Lincoln's image in books, poems, fiction, art, music, and film.

BRIAN DIRCK

Linear programming

Beasley, J.E. (editor), *Advances in Linear and Integer Programming*, Oxford: Clarendon Press, and New York: Oxford University Press, 1996

Carter, Michael, "Linear Programming with *Mathematica*" in *Computational Economics and Finance: Modeling and Analysis with Mathematica*, edited by Hal R. Varian, New York: Springer, 1996

Chvátal, Vašek, *Linear Programming*, New York: Freeman, 1983

Dantzig, George B., *Linear Programming and Extensions*, Princeton, New Jersey: Princeton University Press, 1963

Dantzig, George B. and Mukund N. Thapa, *Linear Programming*, vol. 1: *Introduction*, New York: Springer, 1997

Dorfman, Robert, Paul A. Samuelson and Robert M. Solow, *Linear Programming and Economic Analysis*, New York: McGraw Hill, 1958

Garfinkel, Robert S. and George L. Nemhauser, *Integer Programming*, New York: Wiley, 1972

Nemhauser, G.L., A.H.G. Rinnooy Kan and M.J. Todd (editors), *Optimization*, Amsterdam: North Holland, 1989

Roos, C., T. Terlaky and J.-Ph. Vial, *Theory and Algorithms for Linear Optimization: An Interior Point Approach*, Chichester and New York: Wiley, 1997

Williams, H.P., *Model Building in Mathematical Programming*, 3rd edition, Chichester and New York: Wiley, 1990

The formulation, in 1947, of the simplex algorithm for solving linear programs ranks as one of the most significant discoveries of the 20th century. Fortuitously, the algorithm was conceived at the same time as the development of electronic computers. For the first time, it became practical to pose and solve large-scale optimization problems. The demand for optimization originated with defence forces in the aftermath of World War II. The potential of this new tool was soon recognized by business, which rapidly and profitably adopted it in the oil, food-processing, and steel industries for production and distribution planning. It also sparked whole new fields of study, such as mathematical programming and operations research.

DANTZIG is the classic exposition of linear programming by its inventor, George Dantzig. He covers the nature of linear programming and its history, presents the theory underlying the simplex algorithm, and outlines some of the variants. He provides applications to a variety of specific problems, such as transportation and assignment problems, and network flows. Dantzig is authoritative and comprehensive, and has probably been more widely read than any subsequent book on the subject. However, it was published in 1963 and hence does not address subsequent developments.

The recent text by DANTZIG & THAPA is significant in that it is one of the first to include appropriate software on an accompanying CD-ROM, so that the reader can actually solve the problems discussed in the text. This book is the first of a planned multi-volume series by these authors. This first volume covers standard theory, techniques, and applications at the undergraduate level. Subsequent volumes are aimed at graduate students. Volume 2 will cover "theory and implementation" and volume three "structured LPs and planning under uncertainty". This series promises to become an authoritative and modern replacement for Dantzig.

There are literally scores of texts on linear programming. My personal favourite is CHVÁTAL, who covers the standard theory, techniques, and applications of linear programming in an innovative fashion. In motivating and explaining the simplex algorithm, he rejects the conventional use of tableaux, preferring to write out in full the system of linear equations expressing the problem at hand. "These 'dictionaries' reveal all information they carry at first glance, and updating is a natural procedure impossible to forget" (p.xi). Chvátal's second chapter "how the simplex method works" is as concise and insightful an introduction to the basics of the simplex algorithm as I have encountered. CARTER implements the dictionary approach in the symbolic programming language *Mathematica*. This allows the reader to explore the mechanics of the simplex algorithm and sensitivity analysis in a straightforward manner. This implementation is not meant to supplant special purpose packages in solving real-life problems, but to provide a more natural vehicle than the traditional tableaux for the student to experiment with the solution of simple examples.

In many practical problems of interest (such as the assignment problem), some or all of the variables are constrained to take only integer values. Efficient solution of such problems requires supplementation of the basic simplex algorithm. GARFINKEL & NEMHAUSER provide a clear and unified presentation of integer programming, covering both enumeration and cutting-plane methods.

Publication in 1984 of the interior point algorithm, a practical alternative to the simplex method, triggered a flood of new research in linear optimization. The collection edited by BEASLEY provides an accessible overview of these recent developments, covering computational refinements of the simplex method, as well as interior point methods in both linear and integer programming. ROOS, TERLAKY and VIAL provide a more comprehensive account of the interior point approach, aimed at both researchers and students. The chapter on "Implementing interior point methods" contains a succinct summary of the essential elements of interior point methods, together with a useful list of available software and its sources.

For an appreciation of the place of linear programming in the broader field of optimization, NEMHAUSER, RINNOOY KAN & TODD contains comprehensive and authoritative surveys by leading researchers. In addition to separate chapters covering the various classes of problem, unconstrained, linear, nonlinear, and integer, there are chapters on stochastic programming, network flows, polyhedral combinatorics, nondifferentiable, and global and multicriterion optimization. The book provides a coherent overview of the state of the art in optimization theory, emphasizing the important unifying ideas.

Given the enormous computational power of modern computers, calculation of the optimal solution is perhaps the easiest part of optimization. Formulation of the problem and interpretation of the optimal solution are just as important, requiring judgment, skill, and experience. WILLIAMS focuses on the principles of model building, and the practical aspects of model solution and interpretation. He presents 20 practical optimization problems, drawn from different contexts. Sufficient data are given to enable the reader to build a mathematical programming model using the numerical data given. The idea is that the reader should attempt to solve each problem before proceeding to the subsequent parts of the book, where the problems are discussed in detail, including a possible formulation and an optimal solution. Students and practising managers will find this book an invaluable resource for honing the subtle skills of model formulation and interpretation.

DORFMAN, SAMUELSON & SOLOW emphasizes the economic interpretation of linear programming, exploring applications in input–output analysis, general equilibrium theory, welfare economics, capital accumulation, and the theory of zero-sum games. Although linear models no longer lie at the forefront of economic theory, linear programming had a significant influence on the development of modern economic and game theory. This book summarizes this heritage.

MICHAEL CARTER

Literacy

Arnove, Robert F. and Harvey J. Graff, *National Literacy Campaigns: Historical and Comparative Perspectives*, New York: Plenum, 1987

Beder, Hal, *Adult Literacy: Issues for Policy and Practice*, Malabar, Florida: Kreiger, 1991

Fingeret, Arlene, *Adult Literacy Education: Current and Future Directions*, Columbus: Ohio State University, ERIC Clearinghouse on Adult, Career, and Vocational Education, 1984

Fingeret, Arlene and Paul Jurmo, *Participatory Literacy Education*, San Francisco: Jossey Bass, 1989

Lankshear, Colin and Peter L. McLaren, *Critical Literacy: Politics, Praxis, and the Postmodern*, Albany: State University of New York Press, 1993

Mace, Jane, *Talking about Literacy: Principles and Practice of Adult Literacy Education*, London and New York: Routledge, 1992

Quigley, B. Allan, *Rethinking Literacy Education: The Critical Need for Practice-Based Change*, San Francisco: Jossey Bass, 1997

Stuckey, J. Elspeth, *The Violence of Literacy*, Portsmouth, New Hampshire: Boynton Cook, 1991

ARNOVE & GRAFF provide a landmark collection of 12 critically analytical chapters on literacy campaigns which have occurred throughout history in Germany, Scotland, Sweden, the US, Russia, China, Cuba, Tanzania, India, Nicaragua, and in a variety of developing countries under the UNESCO-sponsored Experimental World Literacy Programme. The editors' opening chapter introduces the argument that literacy campaigns throughout history have had little to do with providing adult reading and writing skills, and a great deal to do with establishing "a more moral society or a more politically stable political order" (p.2). This book is significant because it provides historical data that clearly indicate the social engineering purposes that have so often been the unstated motivation for state- and Church-initiated national

literacy movements. It is a valuable, astutely critical, history of how adult literacy has been used to achieve state rather than personal goals.

BEDER gives a thorough review of the research around key adult literacy issues in American adult literacy policy and practice. His description of the literacy target population and his overview of motivation theory as applied to literacy is helpful; however, the real strength of this book is that it compiles and critiques the participation and non-participation research for the adult literacy field for the first time. Together with his concluding discussion on implications for policy and practice, this book provides a research baseline for understanding how policymakers and practitioners might seek to improve adult literacy education in the US.

Although Beder compiles and synthesizes research on adult literacy around *key issues*, they are the key issues as he defines them. FINGERET, by contrast, provides the most complete review and analysis available on the entire range of literature on adult literacy in America irrespective of issues. This macro-study takes the literature only to 1984, however. Nevertheless, this covers the halcyon days of adult literacy in America and most of the significant literature published to the mid-1980s. Here is an excellent analysis and review of the US literature when the field came of age in both practice and research. Her conclusion is that adult literacy needs more theoretical and philosophical articles. Formal and informal studies have proliferated, as have how-to-do guides, according to Fingeret. All of the areas arising are reviewed and discussed.

The field of adult literacy is challenged to reconsider the way it views and teaches low-literate adults by FINGERET & JURMO. Traditionally, approaches to teaching adult literacy have tended to reproduce the schooling methods and pedagogical assumptions proven ineffective for this population. Chapters by the editors and by active literacy practitioners (non-academics), describe how more adult-centred participatory approaches can be used successfully to treat adults as adults, not as children.

LANKSHEAR & McLAREN's book locates literacy in the discourse of postmodernity as critical literacy. It challenges traditional understandings of the conceptualization of literacy as a functional tool. The frame of reference here is often school-based pedagogy: From a chapter by Michael Apple on the cultural contradictions of school-based texts, to critical literacy for urban school reform by Dennis Carlson, to the issues of critical literacy in English studies through to higher education by James Berlin. However, other authors, such as James Paul Gee, raise issues inherent in literacy when understood in postmodern terms. David Sholle and Stan Denski examine critical literacy in reference to the media. Jeanne Brady and Adriana Hernanández discuss feminist literacies from a critical perspective. This may be considered one of the most significant works for those interested in critical literacy in relation to postmodernity.

MACE bases her book on her 20 years as an adult literacy practitioner in Britain. Like Quigley, Fingeret, and Jurmo on the other side of the Atlantic, she challenges traditional understandings of what low literacy is and how educators and the public should perceive it. Rather than viewing illiteracy as a problem, an educational view that takes other people's solutions and tries to solve others' perceived problems, she argues that literacy education is an opportunity for collective inquiry with literacy learners themselves. She argues that literacy programmes should have open-ended syllabi and teachers should understand that their job is not to teach students to write but to allow them to find out what they need to say and how to say it (p.xviii). Mace discusses trends in Britain since the mid-1970s at the programme and policy level and argues that policy and practice trends have gradually worked to remove the learner from participating in his or her own education. This book gives practical approaches to literacy teaching that would compliment the North American authors listed here.

QUIGLEY is grounded – as he says North American adult literacy itself is grounded – in the myths and stereotypes of illiterate adults. He gives the first historical overview of how the popular press and political policy documents have helped shape and reinforce public notions of who adult illiterates "are", and "best" ways to both control and remediate them at a societal level. He then analyses traditional teaching programmes and a number of the textbook readers used in literacy classrooms, showing how myths can be insidiously reinforced in classroom. A discussion follows on how to improve both the teaching and the recruitment of low-literate adults using programme-grounded knowledge. Besides being the first book to examine literacy's place in popular history, it is the first to provide ways that practitioners can recreate their field using practitioner action research at the classroom level while advocating accurate public information on low-literate adults at the public level.

STUCKEY deals with many of the schooling issues raised by the authors in Lankshear & MacLaren's book and echoes a number of the themes found in the adult literacy books listed here. One of the clearest critiques of the schooling system in the literature, this book argues that literacy is a class-based issue. Stuckey indicts many teachers–English teachers in particular–for not recognizing the nature of literacy in this postmodern age. Literacy remains a "prepackaged product" (p.12) for human capital formation, she says, and does not well reflect the current discourse around the nature of literacy from cultural, class, and work perspectives. Here is a valuable perspective on education as part of the problem, not part of the solution, for literacy.

ALLAN QUIGLEY

Local government finance

Bailey, Stephen J., *Local Government Economics: Principles and Practice*, Basingstoke: Macmillan, 1999

Barnett, R.R., R. Levaggi and P. Smith, "Does the Flypaper Model Stick? A Test of the Relative Performance of the Flypaper and Conventional Models of Local Government Budgetary Behaviour", *Public Choice*, 69/1 (1991): 1–18

Bramley, Glen, *Equalisation Grants and Local Expenditure Needs: The Price of Equality*, Aldershot: Avebury, 1990

Buchanan, James M. and R.A. Musgrave, *Public Finance and Public Choice: Two Contrasting Visions of the State*, Cambridge, Massachusetts: MIT Press, 1999

Butler, David, Andrew Adonis and Tony Travers, *Failure in British Government: The Politics of the Poll Tax*, Oxford and New York: Oxford University Press, 1994

Department of the Environment, *Paying for Local Government*, presented to Parliament by the Secretary of State for the Environment, the Secretary of State for Scotland and the Secretary of State for Wales, London: HMSO, 1986 (Cmnd. 9714)

Department of the Environment, Transport and the Regions (DETR), *A Plain English Guide to the Local Government Finance Settlement*, 3rd edition, London: Department of the Environment, Transport and the Regions, 2000, http://www.local.detr.gov.uk/finance/ssa/0001/data/plaineng.doc

Foster, C.D, R.A. Jackman and M. Perlman, *Local Government Finance in a Unitary State*, London and Boston: Allen and Unwin, 1980

Gibson, John, *The Politics and Economics of the Poll Tax: Mrs Thatcher's Downfall*, Warley: EMAS, 1990

Gramlich, E.M., "Intergovernmental Grants: A Review of the Empirical Literature" in *The Political Economy of Fiscal Federalism*, edited by W.E. Oates, Lexington, Massachusetts: Lexington Books, 1977

House of Commons, Environment, Transport and Regional Affairs Committee, Environment Sub-Committee: *Eighth Report: Local Government Finance*, London: Stationery Office, 1999

House of Lords, Select Committee on Relations between Central and Local Government, *Rebuilding Trust*, London: HMSO, 1996

Inman, R.P., "The Economics of Fiscal Federalism and Local Finance", *National Tax Journal*, 52/4 (December 1999): 843–53

King, David N., *Fiscal Tiers: The Economics of Multi-Level Government*, London and Boston: Allen and Unwin, 1984

Layfield, F., *Local Government Finance*, Report of the Committee of Inquiry, London: HMSO, 1976 (Cmnd. 6453)

Musgrave, Richard A., *The Theory of Public Finance: A Study in Public Economy*, New York and London: McGraw Hill, 1959

Oates, Wallace E., *Fiscal Federalism*, New York: Harcourt Brace, 1972

Oates, Wallace E., "An Essay on Fiscal Federalism", *Journal of Economic Literature*, 37 (September 1999): 1120–49

Ostrom, Vincent, Charles M. Tiebout and Robert Warren, "The Organization of Government in Metropolitan Areas: A Theoretical Inquiry", *American Political Science Review*, 55 (1961): 831–42

Qian, Yingyi and Barry R. Weingast, "Federalism as a Commitment to Preserving Market Incentives", *Journal of Economic Perspectives*, 11/4 (Fall 1997): 83–92

Tiebout, Charles M., "A Pure Theory of Local Expenditures", *Journal of Political Economy*, 64 (1956): 416–24

Tullock, Gordon, "Federalism: Problems of Scale", *Public Choice*, 6 (1969): 19–29

Watt, P.A. and J. Fender, "Feasible Changes in the UK Controls on Local Government Expenditure", *Public Money and Management*, 19/3 (July–September 1999): 17–22

MUSGRAVE's pathbreaking public finance text established the convention of separating the public budget into three branches: allocation, distribution, and stabilisation. This approach is generally extended to local government finance.

OATES (1972) is the classic statement of the economic basis for the organization of local government. He argues in his *decentralization theorem* that, on allocational efficiency grounds, local public goods should be provided by local governments rather than in a standardised form by central governments.

For a public good – the consumption of which is defined over geographical subsets of the total population [and for which there are not cost advantages to central provision] – it will always be more efficient (or at least as efficient) for local government to provide the [locally preferred] levels of output for their respective jurisdictions than for central government to provide any specified and uniform level of output across all jurisdictions (Oates, p.35).

An important early development in the discussion of allocational efficiency in the theory of local government finance was provided by TIEBOUT. This argues that, under certain assumptions, efficient provision of local government services can be achieved in a system where residents "vote with their feet" by migrating to the local authority that provided the goods and services that most closely matched their preferences. TULLOCK provided an early discussion of the considerations determining the optimal scale of local government (more recently analysed in KING and BAILEY). He pointed out, with OSTROM, TIEBOUT & WARREN, that the importance of economies of scale to considerations of organizing local government production is largely removed where provision can be by private contractors.

A major element of local government finance is the analysis of intergovernmental grants. King provides a full account of the theory of inter governmental grants and other useful references are BRAMLEY and Bailey. The so called "flypaper effect" has been much discussed in the local government finance literature. This is the effect whereby a grant has a much stronger effect on raising local expenditure than an equivalent increase in local incomes – hence "money sticks where it hits" – and the puzzle is that this does not accord with basic economic theory (see GRAMLICH and BARNETT, LEVAGGI & SMITH).

OATES (1999) sets out the generally accepted case that redistribution is best carried out at the central rather than local government level, as any significant level of redistribution carried out at the local level is likely to lead to inefficient migration. Stabilization is also considered to be generally a function for central rather than local government finance (see Bailey).

In Britain, the principal grant to local government is the Revenue Support Grant. This grant has three objectives: to compensate local authorities for differences in local spending needs, to compensate for differences in local taxable resources, and to pay for a substantial proportion of local expenditure out of national taxation (see DEPARTMENT OF THE ENVIRONMENT). The government's view on local authorities' need to spend is set out in its annually produced Standard Spending Assessments (SSAs), and the Revenue Support Grant broadly has the effect that if each local authority spent at its SSA, the level of local taxes would be equalized (see DETR).

The British system of local government finance was the subject of extensive analysis in the Layfield enquiry (see LAYFIELD), and also in the comprehensive study of FOSTER, JACKMAN & PERLMAN. A Green Paper (HMSO) led to the introduction of the poll tax, which placed the British system of local government finance strongly in the public eye for a brief period and led to Mrs Thatcher's downfall. This episode is discussed in GIBSON and in BUTLER, ADONIS & TRAVERS. The current system of council tax and revenue support grant is described in DETR, and discussed in HOUSE OF LORDS and HOUSE OF COMMONS, while recent policy changes and options are discussed in WATT & FENDER.

Recent general surveys and discussion are provided by INMAN and BUCHANAN & MUSGRAVE and QIAN & WEINGAST and, with a more British focus, Bailey.

PETER A. WATT

Local government management

Aristotle, *The Politics*, translated by T.A. Sinclair, Harmondsworth and New York: Penguin, 1981 (written 4th century BC)

Considine, Mark and Martin Painter (editors), *Managerialism: The Great Debate*, Carlton South: Melbourne University Press, 1997

Enteman, Willard F., *Managerialism: The Emergence of a New Ideology*, Madison: University of Wisconsin Press, 1993

Hughes, Owen E., *Public Management and Administration: An Introduction*, Basingstoke: Macmillan, and New York: St Martin's Press, 1994

Kafka, Franz, *The Castle*, translated by J.A. Underwood, London: Penguin, 1997 (German edition 1925)

Mill, John Stuart, *Utilitarianism, On Liberty, Considerations on Representative Government*, edited by Geraint Williams, London: Dent, and Rutland, Vermont: Tuttle, 1993

Osborne, David and Ted Gaebler, *Reinventing Government: How the Entrepreneurial Spirit Is Transforming the Public Sector*, Reading, Massachusetts: Addison Wesley, 1992

Policy Studies Journal, 1992–

Political Quarterly, 1930–

Public Administration, 1963–

Public Administration Review, 1940–

Public Management, 1968–

Weber, Max, *The City*, translated and edited by Don Martindale and Gertrude Neuwirth, Glencoe, Illinois: Free Press, 1958; London: Heinemann, 1960

The historiography of local government is vast, in terms of both scope and depth. The works referred to below only scratch the surface of a very rich vein in terms of the political organisation of local government. The works on the whole contain a thread – that thread is one of corporatization and internal entrepreneurship within local government business operations. The growing trend within the Western world is for management control, regardless of the eventual owner of the business. Selected below are works that will aid the reader in understanding the history and development of local government management.

WEBER is a bedrock thesis detailing the emergence and justification for a modern city. *The City* is not the first thesis in local government administration, MILL and, before him, ARISTOTLE also described the city. Aristotle had much to say on the city as a functional entity; however, he wrote from the basis of a city *state*. Weber, on the other hand, addresses the organization and function of a local government entity. For Weber the purpose of a city is to engage in commerce. In this respect he shares Aristotle's views. To achieve the level of commerce necessary, a city must have a regular market, its citizenry must be sovereign, with their rights being upheld as part of an overall urban economic policy. Weber, when read in tandem with Aristotle and Mill, provides a good general background for understanding the context of a modern city.

Popular opinion would have us believe that local government is bureaucratic and staffed by petty politicians. KAFKA is not a textbook but a warning against bureaucratic management set within the political context of local government. The story itself concerns K and his frustrating attempts to gain an audience with his employer. However to do so he must go through a number of gatekeepers. Their job is to hinder not expedite his progress. In his attempt to enter the Castle, K encounters many well-known obstacles, such as the politicians' extravagant spending, and their inability to utilise new technology and new ways of thinking. Throughout his attempts to meet his employer K encounters townspeople who are compliant and put their trust in the government officials without question. The book provides both a satirical and cynical comment upon the excesses that can befall unwary local government officials. Also by inference, is the suggestion that the population get the leaders they deserve, a comment to which both Aristotle and Mill would subscribe.

CONSIDINE & PAINTER attempt to shed light on a growing trend in Western local and central government. This volume addresses the topic of managerialism, a phrase first given meaning by ENTEMAN. Considine & Painter have collected a number of works that attempt to show the differences and conflicts involved in local government management as opposed to private sector management. Much is made of the need to reconcile public sector management with the distinct political, constitutional, and social dimensions involved in management with local and central government. An associated theme within the chapters is the extent to which the political masters or the centre has in being able to influence the day-to-day duties of a local or central government manager. In general the individual chapters discuss the modern drive towards entrepreneurism within local and central government and question the methods being employed to achieve internal entrepreneurship within local government.

Enteman is included in this review as it provides an ideological base from which to view managerialism. The term "managerialism" is gaining ground within the literature of local government. Enteman describes ideology, democracy, and socialism, and shows how managerialism borrows from all three political concepts, describing managerialism as a collec-tive ideology that expresses itself through management transactions between internal and external managers of an organization. Managerialism works in a nondemocratic way to ensure the longevity of the business unit. The attraction of managerialism for local government managers lies in the belief that corporatization, as currently practised, stifles organizational development in that the city has the final say in management decisions not the managers.

HUGHES is a general textbook that addresses the recent developments in the organisation of Western local government. Hughes takes the reader through a critical and brief history of local government, before getting into the real purpose, that is the development, and criticism of, a commercial model of management within a local government framework. Hughes constantly compares the practice of management in private and public business operations. For example in the chapter "Headed Strategic Management", Hughes describes private sector strategy and public sector strategy, and finally offers a criticism of the application of private sector practices to local government business. Just over two thirds of the book is devoted to the emergence of commercial models. The book wraps up with a brief description of managerialism and criticizes the tendency of local government managers to embrace the concept of managerialism. In general the book is a good introduction to the Western trend in local government management.

OSBORNE & GAEBLER, while not strictly a book describing local government, recognizes that a great deal of time is devoted to how local government businesses are becoming entrepreneurial. This book is essentially a "how to" book, aimed at the local and central government business manager. The book describes specific case studies of local government entrepreneurship, and in particular shows how the public business can be structured to take advantage of non-tax dollars. Osborne & Gaebler are writing from a US perspective and in some cases the examples do not translate well into a European context. *Reinventing Government* has, as a central theme, the concept of allowing public managers to share financially in some of the political and financial risks involved in setting up commercial enterprises using public money.

There are a large variety of journals devoted to the examination and development of public policy, with specific reference to local government. To gain a general overview of the local government political landscape readers could first turn to *Public Administration*, *Public Administration Review*, *Policy Studies Journal*, *The Political Quarterly*, and *Public Management*. The contributors to these five journals are active in the debates surrounding public versus private goods, and the emergent trend of corporatization and the associated theme of managerialism within local government enterprises. The five journals all have different flavours, with *Public Management* being the most accessible due to its primary focus on practitioners rather than academics. The next most accessible journal out of these five would be the *Public Administration Review*, which attempts to cross the boundary between academia and informing practitioners. Overall, all five journals will bring the first time reader in local government up to speed on issues that are currently being debated within the practice and study of local government management and politics.

ANDREW CARDOW

Locale

Cooke, Philip (editor), *Localities: The Changing Face of Urban Britain*, London and Boston: Unwin Hyman, 1989

Duncan, S. "What Is Locality?" in *New Models in Geography: The Political Economy Perspective*, edited by Richard Peet and Nigel Thrift, vol. 2, Boston and London: Unwin Hyman, 1989

Environment and Planning A, special issue on "New Perspectives on the Locality Debate", 23, part 2 (1991)

Giddens, Anthony, *The Constitution of Society: Outline of the Theory of Structuration*, Cambridge: Polity Press, and Berkeley: University of California Press, 1984

Hägerstrand, T., "Diorama, Path and Project", *Tijdschrift voor Economische en Sociale Geografie*, 73 (1982): 323–56

Massey, Doreen, *Spatial Divisions of Labour: Social Structures and the Geography of Production*, 2nd edition, London: Macmillan, 1995

Schatzki, T., "Spatial Ontology and Explanation", *Annals of the Association of American Geographers*, 81 (1991): 650–70

Thrift, N.J., "On the Determination of Social Action in Space and Time", *Environment and Planning D: Society and Space*, 1 (1983): 23–57

Urry, J., "Society, Space and Locality", *Environment and Planning D: Society and Space*, 5 (1987): 435–44

The concept of locale was introduced by the British sociologist Anthony GIDDENS as part of his project to develop a *structuration theory* that would dissolve the opposition between structure and agency that characterizes much social theory. His theory portrays individuals and the societies to which they belong as involved in a continuous dialectical process, whereby society is continually being reconstituted by the actions of its individual members and they in turn are changing as a consequence of that interaction. Each both constrains and enables change in the other.

The interactions between people and their societies – in other words, with (some of) its other members – occur in locales, settings for social interaction among individuals who are "co-present"; these "social spaces" constitute the geographical reality of social action and interaction, according to SCHATZKI. Giddens argues that all collectivities within a society have their own locales – characteristic areas within which interaction occurs – such as school classrooms. Many are fixed, some are transient, and their geography is the mosaic of milieux within which structuration occurs.

Giddens is one of the few social theorists to have been influenced by geographical work, specifically that of HÄGER-STRAND on *time-geography*. According to this formulation, individual projects, both long- and short-term, involve them following paths through time and across space. The contours of those paths are constrained in three ways: (a) by capability constraints: the physical capacities of individuals to be in particular places given where they are starting from, where they have to get to, the time at their disposal, the availability of transport and other resources, and the speed at which they can move; (b) by coupling constraints, which determine who they can meet and when – such as a shop's opening hours; and (c) by authority constraints, which limit access to certain areas and places. Geography, then, is deeply implicated in the creation of locales and thus the entire process of structuration.

Giddens argued strongly for the term "locale" rather than others already widely used, such as "place", "locality", and "location", because he wanted to stress the importance of the setting having characteristics that facilitate the form of interaction being undertaken. He also stressed the importance of co-presence, of the interaction being face-to-face, and yet at the same time used examples, such as cities and nation states, which are large in scale, leading THRIFT, in an important essay developing the notion of a locale as a context for interaction, to note that "a locale does not have to be local". In this context, Giddens referred to a further concept – that of *time-space distanciation*. As societies, in Marx's phrase, "annihilate space by time" through the development of transport and communications systems, so they are increasingly stretched over time and space, extending the potential space within a locale.

Although Giddens's ideas were widely discussed in the 1980s, relatively little empirical work has been undertaken that explicitly employs the locale concept. It has informed the growing body of research and writing on places as socially constructed settings for interaction, but little more.

Despite Giddens's insistence on the distinction between locales and other spatially-defined settings, there has been some debate over whether the terms should be used interchangeably, notably in the context of the *localities research programme* undertaken in Britain in the 1980s as an outcome of MASSEY's seminal work on spatial variations in labour market characteristics and their relationships with the processes of economic restructuring. This programme, summarized by COOKE, stimulated its own debates (see URRY, DUNCAN and the special issue of ENVIRONMENT AND PLANNING A), very little of which related to terminological specifics. Locale did not become a central concept in geographical analysis.

RON JOHNSTON

See also Structuration theory

Location theory

Alonso, William, *Location and Land Use: Toward a General Theory of Land Rent*, Cambridge, Massachusetts: Harvard University Press, 1964

Beavon, Keith S.O., *Central Place Theory: A Reinterpretation*, London and New York: Longman, 1977

Berry, Brian J.L. and John B. Parr *et al.*, *The Geography of Market Centers and Retail Distribution*, 2nd edition, Englewood Cliffs, New Jersey: Prentice Hall, 1989

Chisholm, Michael, *Rural Settlement and Land Use: An Essay in Location*, 3rd edition, London: Hutchinson, 1979

Christaller, Walter, *Central Places in Southern Germany*, Englewood Cliffs, New Jersey: Prentice Hall, 1966 (German edition 1933)

Dunn, Edgar Streeter, *The Location of Agricultural Production*, Gainesville: University of Florida Press, 1954

Garrison, W.L., "Spatial Structure of the Economy", *Annals of the Association of American Geographers*, 49 (1959): 238–49 and 471–82; and 50 (1960): 357–73

Greenhut, Melvin L., *Plant Location in Theory and Practice: The Economics of Space*, Chapel Hill: University of North Carolina Press, 1956

Haggett, Peter, Andrew D. Cliff and Alan Frey, *Locational Analysis in Human Geography*, 2nd edition, London: Edward Arnold, and New York: Wiley, 1977

Harvey, David, *The Limits to Capital*, Oxford: Blackwell, and Chicago: University of Chicago Press, 1982

Hoover, Edgar Malone, *The Location of Economic Activity*, New York: McGraw Hill, 1948

Hotelling, Harold, "Stability in Competition", *Economic Journal*, 39 (1929): 40–57

Isard, Walter, *Location and Space Economy: A General Theory Relating to Industrial Location, Market Areas, Land Use, Trade, and Urban Structure*, Cambridge, Massachusetts: MIT Press / Wiley, 1956

Johnston, R.J., *A Question of Place: Exploring the Practice of Human Geography*, Oxford and Cambridge, Massachusetts: Blackwell, 1991

Krugman, Paul R., *Geography and Trade*, Cambridge, Massachusetts: MIT Press, 1991

Krugman, Paul R., *Development, Geography and Economic Theory*, Cambridge, Massachusetts: MIT Press, 1995

Lösch, August, *The Economics of Location*, New Haven, Connecticut: Yale University Press, 1954 (German edition 1940)

Martin, R.L., "The New 'Geographical Turn' in Economics: Some Critical Reflections", *Cambridge Journal of Economics*, 23 (1999): 65–91

Massey, Doreen, *Spatial Divisions of Labour: Social Structures and the Geography of Production*, London: Macmillan, 1984

Pred, Allan, *Behavior and Location: Foundations for a Geographic and Dynamic Location Theory*, 2 vols, Lund: Gleerup, 1967–69

Schoenberger, Erica J., *The Cultural Crisis of the Firm*, Oxford and Cambridge, Massachusetts: Blackwell, 1997

Scott, A.J., *New Industrial Spaces: Flexible Production Organization and Regional Development in North American and Western Europe*, London: Pion, 1988

Sheppard, Eric and Trevor J. Barnes, *The Capitalist Space Economy: Analysis after Ricardo, Marx and Sraffa*, London and Boston: Unwin Hyman, 1990

Smith, David M., *Industrial Location: An Economic Geographical Analysis*, 2nd edition, New York and Chichester: Wiley, 1981

Storper, Michael and Richard Walker, *The Capitalist Imperative: Territory, Technology, and Industrial Growth*, Oxford and New York: Blackwell, 1989

Thünen, J.H. von, *Isolated State*, edited by Peter Hall, Oxford and New York: Pergamon Press, 1966 (Dutch edition 1926)

Webber, Michael J., *The Impact of Uncertainty on Location*, Cambridge, Massachusetts: MIT Press, 1972

Weber, Alfred, *Alfred Weber's Theory of the Location of Industries*, Chicago: University of Chicago Press, 1929 (German edition 1909)

Location theory offers accounts for the spatial ordering of economic activities. It originated in works by economists operating on the margins of their own discipline, which has only recently adopted what is termed the "new economic geography" (in which KRUGMAN's books have been very influential). That normative approach is now largely discredited within geography, however, as MARTIN's essay indicates. It dominated the intellectual landscape of human geography in the 1960s and 1970s, when it had strong links with regional science.

The oldest location theory classic is VON THÜNEN's consideration of agricultural land use patterns around a central market, which suggested a zonal structure with the more extensive uses furthest from the market. DUNN reworked this from a modern economist's perspective, and CHISHOLM introduced it to the geographic literature. ALONSO adapted Von Thünen's method to the study of land values and residential location decisions within urban areas.

Most work has been done on industrial location theory at the level of the individual plant. Transport costs were presented as key to the decision-making process, as suggested in the title of GREENHUT's book. WEBER's work was extremely influential: his locational triangle was a simple device for integrating the location of raw materials and market places with transport costs to identify both the least-cost location for a production facility and the increased costs of locating away from that point. HOOVER, ISARD and LÖSCH, all of whose approaches are detailed in SMITH's text, extended it.

The third main area in "classic" location theory concerned the spatial patterning of market centres. The key stimulus was CHRISTALLER's work on central places in southern Germany, which argued that market systems would be structured hierarchically and ordered spatially in a series of nested hexagonal hinterlands. LÖSCH's work generalized this model of settlement patterns, incorporating secondary as well as tertiary economic functions, and BEAVON integrated the two approaches. A large literature on central place theory is reviewed by BERRY & PARR.

A further classic, widely influential in the social sciences, was HOTELLING's paper on the importance of agglomeration economies when firms are competing. They should be spatially more concentrated than other models imply because of the benefits – externalities – they reap from spatial proximity, as argued in SCOTT's book.

These theories were presented as the basis for a formal approach to spatial theory by GARRISON, and were integrated with others relating to networks, flows and surfaces to provide an overall picture of a space economy, most notably in the book by HAGGETT. Others explored alternative foundations to those provided by neo-classical economics: SHEPPARD & BARNES draw on Sraffa, for example; HARVEY introduces space to Marxist theory; and STORPER & WALKER explore a wider range of theories within political economy.

By the mid-1970s many of the normative location theories (setting out what spatial patterns should emerge if decision makers act in prescribed ways) were being rejected by geographers as overly simplistic in emphasizing the centrality of transport costs in location decision making and for their unrealistic reliance on static patterns in what was a dynamic process. MASSEY presented one of the strongest arguments. She set her appreciation of changing locational patterns within the wider context of the operations of capitalism and the search for profits, especially during periods of crisis when substantial restructuring involving locational shifts takes place. The characteristics of localities – both their relative accessibility to materials and markets and the nature of their labour markets (including the power of trades unions) and the cultures of their civil societies (explored at various scales by JOHNSTON) – are crucial influences on whether firms either stay or move there.

Others introduced behavioural perspectives to locational decision making. WEBBER, for example, stressed the importance of uncertainty, which can lead to conservative decisions and greater agglomeration of firms than would occur with complete information. PRED added the ability to use information in an attempted dynamic, behavioural theory. SCHOENBERGER's work argues for the importance of social as well as economic influences on executives' choices.

RON JOHNSTON

Locke, John 1632–1704

English philosopher

Cranston, Maurice, *John Locke: A Biography*, New York: Macmillan, and London: Longman, 1957

Creppell, Ingrid, "Locke on Toleration: The Transformation of Constraint," *Political Theory*, 24/2 (1996): 200–40

Dunn, John, *The Political Thought of John Locke: An Historical Account of the "Two Treaties of Government"*, Cambridge: Cambridge University Press, 1969

Harrison, John and Peter Laslett, *The Library of John Locke*, 2nd edition, Oxford: Oxford Bibliographical Society, 1971

Locke, John, *An Essay Concerning Human Understanding*, edited by A.D. Woozley, London: Collins, 1964; New York: American Library, 1974 (1st edition 1689)

Macpherson, C.B., *The Political Theory of Possessive Individualism: Hobbes to Locke*, Oxford: Oxford University Press, 1962

Strauss, Leo, *Natural Right and History*, Chicago: University of Chicago Press, 1953.

Tully, James, *An Approach to Political Philosophy: Locke in Contexts*, Cambridge and New York: Cambridge University Press, 1993

John Locke was born in Somerset on 29 August 1632, the son of an attorney and clerk to a Justice of the Peace. CRANSTON's authoritative biography notes that, although his family was comfortable, Locke was not born wealthy; his father was a small landowner who had not bettered his social station by marrying a tanner's daughter.

Locke attended Westminster, then Christ Church, Oxford, and studied the sciences, taking a particular interest in botany, and achieving a bachelor's degree in medicine. After the Stuart Crown removed him from his research position for his close friendship with Anthony Ashley Cooper, first Earl of Shaftesbury, Locke twice fled to Holland for fear of arrest for his pro-exclusionary politics. After the Glorious Revolution, in

1689, he returned from hiding in Holland and became well known and active in public affairs until his death on 28 October 1704.

HARRISON & LASLETT's exhaustive study indicates that Locke read and wrote widely, his topics ranging from the growing of olives to the education of youth to economics. Although authored years earlier, Locke's three best known texts, *The Essay Concerning Human Understanding*, *Epistola de Tolerantia*, and the famed *Two Treatises of Government* were all published in 1689, when their contrarian positions were not going to imperil Locke's safety. Even then, however, the latter two were published anonymously.

Perhaps the least influential of the three, the *Essay Concerning Human Understanding*, was Locke's longest meditation on epistemology. As Woozley indicates in his lengthy introduction to his abridgement of LOCKE's *Essay Concerning Human Understanding*, Locke was a rationalist like Descartes, although he vigorously disputed Descartes' formulation of the long-standing doctrine of innate ideas, and denied the Cartesian claim that extension is the essence of body and thought that of mind. Locke argued that the mind was a *tabula rasa*, that the brain was born blank, and that all knowledge was derived from the senses and the actions of the mind thereupon. Although Locke's empiricism was later demolished by thinkers like Kant, his sceptical position regarding the limits of man's knowledge remains, and the *Essay Concerning Human Understanding* is an elegant expression thereof.

There have been various views of the basis of the argument of Locke's *Epistola de Tolerantia*. CREPPELL's superlative essay recounts the scholarship on Locke's justification for religious toleration into three viewpoints: that such toleration is based upon his conception of the natural rights of man; that it was politically attractive to Locke because it urged his audience to avoid a return to internecine religious strife; and that it was an expression of Locke's belief that government power did not extend to man's relationship with God.

Creppell bases her interpretation on Locke's belief in the limited power of reason and Man's fallen nature. As Man can never have certain knowledge, he therefore cannot know whether his way of worship is the correct one, thus he must tolerate different modes of worship. Also, those who practise tolerance keep man's cruel side from manifesting itself in religious persecution. The salubrious result, according to Creppell, is that should Locke's doctrine be followed, each man will let his neighbour alone while tending only to his own soul, which Locke described as Man's "principal care".

By far the most famous of his texts, Locke's *Two Treatises of Government*, was enormously influential in the history of English and American politics. The first of the *Two Treatises* directly assails Filmer's argument in *De Patriarcha* for unlimited paternal monarchy, exposing it as a reactionary misconstrual of both the Scriptures and English history.

The *Second Treatise*, by far the more widely read of the two, argues for limited, constitutional government, created by the consent of the governed, accountable to its citizens, and kept stable by the separation of powers. In the beginning, says Locke, there was a state of nature, where each man cared for his own good. This peace was occasionally disrupted by quarrels among men, so they gathered and agreed to found government to uphold the law of nature – that each man has property in his person and in the materials with which he mixes his work.

Both STRAUSS and MACPHERSON assert that this formulation of the origin of political power is an esoteric argument masking Locke's true view. From the right, Strauss declared that although Locke made many references to a law of nature by which man was to guide his actions, in fact this was a ruse, Locke was not a believer in "natural right", and Locke was an immoralist and a hedonist. MacPherson, on the other hand, interpreted Locke as endeavouring to justify capitalism and making a paragon of the "possessive individualist" whose entire being is devoted to material self-satisfaction.

DUNN's scholarship emphasizes the political and social context in which Locke wrote, arguing that Locke wrote in commonsensical terms that Englishmen of the time would have understood, and that he offered a political and a personal theology. The political theology asks men to remember that government is their creation, and that it exists to uphold the personal moral order as prescribed by God. Further, man ought not forget the distinction between living a life of liberty and an immoral life of license, for in doing so he dishonours his station and falls to the level of beasts and may be so treated.

TULLY further contextualizes Locke's arguments as responding to the religious strife and patriarchialists like Filmer. Tully's research indicates that Locke derived much of his thought from medieval juristic philosophy, which emphasizes transcendent law and man's prepolitical obligations as a rational creation of God. Tully gives extensive evidence that Locke was a mercantilist not a protocapitalist and that he did not think individual freedom a matter of material self-indulgence. Rather, a free man needs property so that his survival is not dependent on the will of another or government. Good government serves to protect man's property and person, so he may worship freely and follow the law of nature, which the *Second Treatise* declares to be to preserve oneself and mankind as best he can.

KEVIN R. KOSAR

Locus of control

Burger, Jerry M., "Personality and Control" in *Personality: Contemporary Theory and Research*, edited by Valerian J. Derlega, Barbara A. Winstead and Warren H. Jones, Chicago: Nelson Hall, 1991

Joe, Victor C., "Review of the Internal-External Control Construct as a Personality Variable", *Psychological Reports*, 28 (1971): 619–40

Klandermans, P.G., "Rotter's I.E.-Scale and Socio-Political Action-Taking: The Balance of 20 Years of Research", *European Journal of Social Psychology*, 13 (1983): 399–415

Lefcourt, Herbert M., "Locus of Control" in *Measures of Personality and Social Psychological Attitudes*, edited by John P. Robinson, Phillip R. Shaver and Lawrence S. Wrightsman, San Diego: Academic Press, 1991

Lefcourt, Herbert M. and Karina Davidson-Katz, "Locus of Control and Health" in *Handbook of Social and Clinical Psychology: The Health Perspective*, edited by C.R. Snyder

and Donelson R. Forsyth, New York: Pergamon Press, 1991

Phares, E. Jerry, *Locus of Control in Personality*, Morristown, New Jersey: General Learning Press, 1976

Skinner, Ellen A., *Perceived Control, Motivation, and Coping*, Thousand Oaks, California and London: Sage, 1995

Spector, Paul E., "Behavior in Organizations as a Function of Employee's Locus of Control", *Psychological Bulletin*, 91/3 (1982): 482–97

Steitz, Jean A., "Locus of Control as a Life-Span Developmental Process: Revision of the Construct", *International Journal of Behavioral Development*, 5 (1982): 299–316

Wallston, Kenneth A. and Barbara Strudler Wallston (editors), "Health Locus of Control", *Health Education Monographs*, 6/2 (1978): 101–72

PHARES provides a basic and useful overview of Rotter's 1966 theory of internal–external locus of control. Locus of control is a construct that refers to how individuals perceive reinforcing events and the causal attributions they make concerning that event (resultant from their own actions or from external causes). Phares states that, while locus of control is an important determinant of human behaviour, its effects may be moderated by other personality and environmental factors. The bulk of the book is devoted to examining both the antecedents and consequences of locus of control. Some of the antecedents include parental nurturance, consistency of experience, and socio-economic status, while consequences include academic achievement, anxiety, adjustment, and reaction to threat.

BURGER provides the most recent discussion on locus of control. This chapter explores both control and personality within the context of peoples' reactions to perceived personal control. Burger examines this context in light of two individual difference variables; locus of control and desire for control. Locus of control is portrayed as a control belief, while desire for control is discussed as a motivational concept.

SKINNER provides a comprehensive examination of the concept of perceived control. Perceptions of control are proposed to be a system of beliefs that an individual possesses that affects the way that individual interacts with the environment and makes assessments of causality. Although easily mistaken as a stable, cross-situational trait-like predisposition, perceived control is both shaped by development and guides development as well. Thus, these perceptions comprise a constructed belief set that can be subsequently altered. Skinner proposes a model of a competence system that regulates and interprets goal-directed interactions with the environment. This model encompasses previous control theories, with locus of control depicted primarily as a regulative function. As such, the competence system provides an excellent framework from which to view locus of control.

As a personality variable, locus of control has generated a tremendous amount of research. JOE provides an informative five-year review of locus of control beginning with its 1966 inception. He describes research on internal-external control of reinforcement in 12 areas (such as achievement motivation, reaction to social stimuli, and strategy preferences/learning). Locus of control is presented as a robust construct, although not completely consistent across studies. Joe discusses some of the less expected findings within the theory, such as the role sex differences play in influencing beliefs of control.

STEITZ reviews the locus of control construct from a lifespan developmental perspective. She argues that the construct has failed to reflect this perspective due to incongruence with the basic principles of developmental interactionism. Locus of control theory downplays the interactional relationship between the person and the environment, with the person having little effect on the environment. Additionally, Steitz states that within locus of control theory individuals change across time in a quantitative manner additive from past experience. This fails to account for substantial *qualitative* differences that occur with age. Finally, she posits that locus of control theory is deficient in its assessment what interaction means, as the theory only describes a unidirectional effect of environment on individual. The solution to these suggested deficiencies lies in (a) adopting a lifespan concept of situations, (b) investigation of qualitative changes in perceived control, and (c) incorporating a transactional meaning to interactionism.

One implication of the internal–external (IE) control of reinforcement construct is that individuals who are more internal are more likely to take action than individuals who are external. KLANDERMANS proposes that under certain circumstances, externals are just as likely to take action. He investigates the tenability of this proposal by examining 31 separate locus-of-control and action-taking studies. Of these, five studies support the implication that internal locus of control is positively related to action taking, while four studies support Klandermans' hypothesis of the relationship between externals and action taking. However, the remaining studies showed no relationship between locus of control (either internal or external) and sociopolitical action taking. As explanation for these findings, the IE scale is suggested to be inappropriate for disadvantaged groups, as well as being too general of a scale. Klandermans also suggests that the change in social conditions between the 1960s and 1980s may have lead to changes in the relationship between locus of control and action taking.

Locus of control is theorized to be a powerful determinant of behaviour within an organizational setting as well. SPECTOR provides a discussion on the validity of the construct, as well as its relationship to organizational variables within the workplace. There is some degree of empirical evidence to support these relationships, though Spector provides cautions about the cross-sectional and correlational nature of such studies. Higher internal perception of control has been found to be positively related to work motivation as well as higher expectancies that effort will lead to positive outcomes. On the other hand, people with external locus of control were found to be more satisfied with direct supervision and to comply more with demands (both supervisory and social) than people with internal control beliefs. On a final note, Spector discusses the inconsistent findings concerning the relationship between perceived job characteristics, role strain, and locus of control.

Internal–external control of reinforcement has shown great promise in explaining health-related behaviours. WALLSTON & WALLSTON is a series of monographs that discuss the relationship between health and locus of control. Wallston & Wallston themselves provide a very brief overview of studies that have examined the relationship that smoking, birth control, weight loss, and sick-role behaviours each have with locus of control. Other monographs within this special edition include the effects that health locus of control has on compliance, the development of a children's health locus-of-control measure, and the development of a multidimensional health locus-of-control scale.

In a more recent review of health locus of control, LEFCOURT & DAVIDSON-KATZ conduct an in-depth discussion of this construct. They focus on the impact locus of control has as a stress moderator, how this construct may be used to predict the onset of illness and finally, how people cope with illness. There is some degree of evidence that people who have an internal locus of control are more likely to attend to and perceive potential threats to their health than people with an external locus. Internals also appear to deal better with the stress induced by these threats by seeing them as a challenge to be solved as opposed to despairing or feeling helpless. The affective states generated by these differing responses to stress have then been associated with vulnerability and recovery.

LEFCOURT reviews 16 attitude scales that measure varying aspects of locus of control or internal–external control of reinforcement. He provides an overview of how the measures were developed and then individually describes each one. Information is provided on the specific variable with an accompanying description. The psychometric properties are presented in the form of reliability (internal consistency and test–retest) and validity (convergent and discriminant). Finally, Lefcourt provides comments and analyses of each scale as well as source location for the reported information. This provides an excellent resource for the selection of appropriate measurement instruments of locus of control.

MICHAEL W. GROJEAN AND D. BRENT SMITH

Lomé Convention

Cosgrove Twitchett, Carol A., *Europe and Africa: From Association to Partnership*, Farnborough, Hampshire: Saxon House, 1978

Davenport, Michael, Adrian Hewitt and Antonique Koning, *Europe's Preferred Partners? The Lomé Countries in World Trade*, London: Overseas Development Institute, 1995

Grilli, Enzo R., *The European Community and Developing Countries*, Cambridge and New York: Cambridge University Press, 1993

Harrop, Jeffrey, *The Political Economy of Integration in the European Union*, 2nd edition, Aldershot, Hampshire: Elgar, 1992

Lister, Marjorie R., *The European Union and the South: Relations with Developing Countries*, London and New York: Routledge, 1997

Long, Frank (editor), *The Political Economy of EEC Relations with African, Caribbean and Pacific States: Contributions to the Understanding of the Lomé Convention on North–South Relations*, Oxford and New York: Pergamon Press, 1980

Stevens, Christopher (editor), *EEC and the Third World:
    A Survey*, no. 4: *Renegotiating Lomé*, London: Hodder
    and Stoughton, 1984
Whiteman, Kaye, "After Lomé, What Next?", *West Africa*,
    4193 (9–22 November 1998): 798–803

COSGROVE TWITCHETT has provided one of the best
sources for the early background material that laid the foundations of association between the EU and the Lomé countries
in the Treaty of Rome. The book covers this association from
1958 to 1963, its renewal, and the Yaoundé Conventions. It
contains important historical information for those wishing
to know more about the inception of this association, but its
limitation is that it only covers the move towards Lomé itself
in the final 23 pages of the book.

The book by LONG has seven contributors, who together
provide a strong and useful coverage of Lomé I – agreement
for Lomé II was only being reached at the time the book was
being edited. The introductory chapter covers the road to
Lomé, and chapter two covers asymmetrical interdependence
and the renegotiation of the Lomé Convention. Chapter 3 is
concerned with indexation and chapter four with the European
Union's export revenue stabilization scheme (STABEX).
Chapter five, by Long himself, relates to transnational corporations, technology transfer and Lomé. Chapter six is again by
Cosgrove Twitchett and deals with patterns of trade between
the African, Caribbean, and Pacific (ACP) countries and the
European Economic Community (EEC), whereas the final
chapter concludes by considering Lomé and market access.

Chapter one of STEVENS is concerned with analysis of past
stagnation in Lomé I 1975–80 and the negotiation of Lomé II
1980–85, plus the pathway to Lomé III. The second chapter
examines whether Lomé helped trade diversification. Chapter
three deals with the interpretation of mutual interest and
non-fuel minerals. Other chapters have plenty on aid, and there
are also two useful country studies: of Malawi and Sierra
Leone.

HARROP devotes one of his chapters to setting the
European Union's (EU's) preferential relations with the ACP
countries in the context of the EU's worldwide trading links.
He covers both trade and aid (illustrating the volume of aid
for the first five years of Lomé IV in comparison with Lomé
III). The strengths and weaknesses of STABEX and the Système
Minérais (SYSMIN) for mineral products are also covered.
Finally, the book confirms that association with the ACP
provided very limited trade gains.

The starting point of the book by GRILLI is the EU's association with the African countries. Chapters two and three deal
with aid, and chapter four with trade. However, the author's
purpose is to show that the EU Commission has created a bias
in its development policy with plentiful material and overemphasis on the ACP at the expense of cooperation between the
EU and other parts of the world. Only readers interested in
going beyond the ACP will find chapters on the Mediterranean,
Latin America, Asia, and eastern Europe of interest in
providing a broader and more balanced coverage of total EU
development policies and challenges.

DAVENPORT, HEWITT & KONING prepared a special
report for Britain's Overseas Development Administration for
the medium-term review of Lomé in 1995. It addresses the
problem that the ACP under the Lomé convention only
accounted for 3.9 per cent of EU imports in 1995, despite
decades of preferences. The report provides plenty of trade
statistics for the ACP countries and their many products, with
a good explanation for the poor performance of most countries. For example, preferences only offer opportunities, and
if, unlike Mauritius, countries lack entrepreneurial dynamism,
then they will fail. The report argues that new policies are
needed to revitalize the Lomé relationship in the new multilateral trade liberalization, post-Uruguay situation. For
example, the phasing out of the multi-fibre arrangement (MFA)
will further hit ACP textile producers. One strength of the
report is that it looks to a future in which Lomé-type preferences seem likely to be downgraded in a global world of multilateralism and trade liberalism.

LISTER covers the less-developed countries (LDCs) in the
South, with particular focus on Africa, although other areas
are included, such as the Mediterranean. The most relevant
chapters, after chapter two on Europe's colonial history, are
chapters four and five on the Fourth Lomé Convention and
finally chapter six, which argues the case for Europe to have
a mission exemplified by positive attempts to construct a
stronger European–African relationship. The strength of this
book is that it is an up-to-date coverage written by a specialist
in the field.

WHITEMAN's very short journalistic article brings the
Lomé situation up to date and also has the strength that it
focuses primarily on key areas, especially West Africa. The
Lomé IV Convention expires in the year 2000, and Whiteman
explores what is likely to replace it for the 71 ACP states. The
key change that it concentrates upon is the establishment in
1995 of the World Trade Organization (WTO), and how its
globalizing, liberalizing aspirations will shift the emphasis away
from the preferential and non-reciprocal Lomé system. The EU
is likely to promote free-trade areas (FTAs), although there are
few groupings in the ACP with their own FTAs that might
qualify. The ACP will be reluctant to provide full reciprocity
as it feels that trade is not fair. In addition, the ACP is also
worried about being fragmented into groups by the EU. The
WTO ruling against the discriminatory, preferential EU banana
policy (as part of Lomé) opens up competition. As a result of
the Chiquita Company enlisting American support, there is
likely to be an adverse effect, particularly on the Caribbean
producers in Lomé. Overall, the article concludes that there is
likely to be some transitional continuity for the bulk of Lomé
arrangements until at least 2005 (and perhaps for ten years
beyond that).

JEFFREY HARROP

Long swings in economic activity

Freeman, Christopher and Carlota Perez, "Structural Crises
    of Adjustment, Business Cycles and Investment Behaviour"
    in *Technical Change and Economic Theory*, edited by
    Giovanni Dosi *et al.*, London and New York: Pinter,
    1988
Freeman, Christopher (editor), *Long Wave Theory*,
    Cheltenham, Gloucestershire: Elgar, 1996

Kleinknecht, Alfred, *Innovation Patterns in Crisis and Prosperity: Schumpeter's Long Cycles Reconsidered*, London: Macmillan, and New York: St Martin's Press, 1987

Kleinknecht, Alfred, Ernest Mandel and Immanuel Wallerstein (editors), *New Findings in Long Wave Research*, New York: St Martin's Press, 1992

Kondratiev, Nikolai, "Long Cycles of Economic Conjuncture" in *The Works of Nikolai D. Kondratiev*, edited by Natalia Makasheva, Warren Samuels and Vincent Barnett, vol. 1, London: Pickering and Chatto, 1998: 25–63 and 122–47; tables 159–254

Kuznets, Simon S., *Secular Movements in Production and Prices: Their Nature and Their Bearing upon Cyclical Fluctuations*, Boston: Houghton Mifflin, 1930 ; reprinted New York: Kelley, 1967

Louçã, Francisco and Jan Reijnders (editors), *The Foundations of Long Wave Theory: Models and Methodology*, 2 vols, Cheltenham, Gloucestershire: Elgar, 1999

Mandel, Ernest, *Long Waves of Capitalist Development: A Marxist Interpretation*, London: Verso, 1995

Perez, Carlota, "Structural Change and Assimilation of New Technologies in the Economic and Social Systems", *Futures*, 15/5 (1983): 357–75

Reati, Angelo, *Taux de profit et accumulation du capital dans l'onde longue de l'après guerre: le cas de l'industrie au Royaume-Uni, en France, en Italie et en Allemagne*, Brussels: Editions de l'Université de Bruxelles, 1990

Reijnders, Jan, *Long Waves in Economic Development*, Aldershot, Hampshire: Elgar, 1990

Solomou, Solomos, *Phases of Economic Growth 1850–1973: Kondratieff Waves and Kuznets Swings*, Cambridge and New York: Cambridge University Press, 1987

Tylecote, Andrew, *The Long Wave in the World Economy: The Present Crisis in Historical Perspective*, London and New York: Routledge, 1993

The discussion on the existence or otherwise of long periods of oscillation in economic series dates from the 19th century. MacKenzie detected these long periods in climateric data, and Hyde Clarke extended his findings to an interpretation of agricultural cycles and the evolution of economic conjuncture. Hyde Clarke corresponded with and influenced Jevons, who accepted the idea and referred to it in a book, and this hypothesis became more widely known. Other scientists, such as John Bates Clark, apparently quite independently claimed that a 50-year cycle was obvious in data. It may be argued that the macroeconomic experience of the developed economies of this century provided some evidence for the long fluctuations and sharp periods of transition. Until KONDRATIEV, however, no one provided a detailed statistical discussion or sketched a theory to explain these phenomena. His 1926 paper was prepared for a discussion at the Conjuncture Institute in Moscow and was contradicted by his colleagues: the counterargument and the debate were recently published in English and are important documents for the history of applied statistical analysis of long-term evolution.

Two large collections of papers were also recently published on this topic. FREEMAN (editor) includes papers that antici-pated Kondratiev's conjecture – although Kondratiev did not know about them – such as the work by Van Gelderen, a Dutch economist who wrote about this in 1913. Tinbergen and Kuznets are also represented in this collection, although its main concern is the presentation of recent discussions on the topic. LOUÇÃ & REIJNDERS edited two companion volumes including larger sections on the history of the topic, and publishing or even translating into English some previously inaccessible papers by Hyde Clark, Parvus and De Wolff, forerunners of long cycles analysis. Their book is dedicated to the main families of methods, time series methods, chaos and nonlinear modelling, historical analyses, and some overviews. The different interpretations of these long periods – and the discussion of whether they really represent the evolution of the economies or are statistical artefacts – are represented in the collection.

One of the scientists who could read this discussion as early as the late 1920s was Simon KUZNETS, as he knew Russian; furthermore, he was interested in statistical analysis of macro-economic variables. His 1930 book on "secular movements" gives credit to Kondratiev and his fellow researchers, but argues for another interpretation: Kuznets detected shorter movements of 23 to 25 years, which were later explained by migratory movements and their implications for the building industry. Kuznets was much more careful about this conjecture than his own disciples, but the concept of the "Kuznets cycle" was born.

SOLOMOU studied data from developed countries for the period 1850–1973 and supported Kuznets's theses but not those of Kondratiev, although acknowledging that the statistical conclusion is highly dependent on technical choices, such as the form of detrending and whether or not attempts are made to avoid the impact of the world wars that marked economic evolution in the 20th century.

FREEMAN & PEREZ follow Kondratiev and combine his insights with the later contribution by Schumpeter, who stressed the importance of waves of infrastructural investment due to replacement of capital goods in the framework of systemic changes in industry and society. Their model builds on this and presents a new taxonomy of innovations, discussing the role of changes in the technoeconomic paradigm and insti-tutional changes for the dynamics of the economies as a whole.

KLEINKNECHT studied the dynamics of innovation and, in a book with a preface by Jan Tinbergen, argued for a Schumpeterian approach, explaining long waves by the intro-duction and diffusion of major innovations. The author uses some statistical tests to show the differences of rates of growth at the aggregate levels for variables representing the evolution of the economies, under the assumption that these rates tend to be larger when the economies moves in a long-term expan-sionary wave, in spite of the business cycle fluctuation.

PEREZ suggests that long periods of depression are gener-ated by the contraction of innovation opportunities and by the mismatch between the technological and economic subsys-tems and the institutional setting. If and when this mismatch is overcome, a new long period of expansion is propelled by the diffusion of radical innovations and a new "technological style".

TYLECOTE develops Perez's model in a broad historical explanation of long waves. Different technological styles are discussed in relation to Britain in the 19th century and in relation to the industrially developed countries in the 20th century. Variables such as population growth and movements, innovation, capital accumulation, and political institutions are included in the scheme.

Another theory of long waves of capitalist development was presented by MANDEL. His Marxist analysis takes into account the contributions of the previous authors and relates them to the study of the movements in capital accumulation and profitability. Mandel was one of the first to revive long-wave analysis, based on an early – and verified – prediction of the end of the "'thirty golden years" of the postwar expansion. His detailed empirical and theoretical analysis is still one of the coherent building blocks of this corpus of interpretation.

In 1990, REIJNDERS published a dissertation on the statistical identification of long waves. A review of previous work identifies some of the shortcomings of the current techniques, and the author carefully discusses the effect of the "perspectivistic distortion" for time series methods – the distortion imposed by the fact that the available temporal window of data is too short for the correct analysis of the long cycles. Using spectral analysis, Reijnders was able to present new evidence for the long-wave hypothesis, although this was conditional on the treatment of the statistical outliers.

KLEINKNECHT, MANDEL & WALLERSTEIN edited the proceedings of a conference dedicated to new evidence and new explanations of the Kondratievian conjecture. The collection of essays includes different statistical treatments of data, theoretical explanations and conclusions. In general, the authors share some scepticism about the strict cyclical regularity but accept that economic history develops through structural arrangements accounting for the periods of dominance of expansion (1945–75) and periods of dominance of depression (1975 onward).

Many empirical studies have been developed in order to check these hypotheses. REATI conducted one such piece of research on capital accumulation in postwar Britain, France, Italy and Germany, and related these expansionary and depressive movements to the schedule of the rate of profit. A mass of information is used and detailed econometric procedures were employed. These are explained in this book, one of the best empirical confirmations of the long-term dynamics of the modern economies.

FRANCISCO LOUÇÃ

See also Business cycles, Kondratiev cycles, Real business cycles

Longitudinal research in psychology

Bergman, Lars R., Gunnar Eklund and David Magnusson, "Studying Individual Development: Problems and Methods" in *Problems and Methods in Longitudinal Research: Stability and Change*, edited by David Magnusson *et al.*, Cambridge and New York: Cambridge University Press, 1991

Bergman, Lars R., "Some Methodological Issues in Longitudinal Research: Looking Ahead" in *Longitudinal Research on Individual Development*, edited by David Magnusson and Paul Casaer, Cambridge and New York: Cambridge University Press, 1993

Brown, George W., Tirril O. Harris and Louise Lemyre, "Now You See It, Now You Don't: Some Considerations on Multiple Regression" in *Problems and Methods in Longitudinal Research: Stability and Change*, edited by David Magnusson *et al.*, Cambridge and New York: Cambridge University Press, 1991

Duncan, Susan S., Terry E. Duncan and Hyman Hops, "Analysis of Longitudinal Data within Accelerated Longitudinal Designs", *Psychological Methods* 1/3 (1996): 236–48

Goodman, Jodi S. and Terry C. Blum, "Assessing the Non-Random Sampling Effects of Subject Attrition in Longitudinal Research", *Journal of Management*, 22/4 (1996): 627–52

Helson, Ravenna, "Comparing Longitudinal Studies of Adult Development: Toward a Paradigm of Tension between Stability of Change" in *Studying Lives through Time: Personality and Development*, edited by David C. Funder *et al.*, Washington, DC: American Psychological Association, 1993

Janus, Magdalena and Susan Goldberg, "Factors Influencing Family Participation in a Longitudinal Study: Comparison of Pediatric and Healthy Samples", *Journal of Pediatric Psychology*, 22/2 (1997): 245–62

BERGMAN, EKLUND & MAGNUSSON discuss the three critical elements of longitudinal research: the nature of the problem under consideration, the data that reflect underlying structures and processes, and the statistical methods used to evaluate the data. They point out that, too often, researchers adopt more sophisticated statistics than are necessary or even appropriate for the research questions they address. Such inappropriate approaches lead to meaningless data and poor theories. As they note, "no sophisticated methods for data analysis can save bad data or contribute to better knowledge". Nonetheless, sound longitudinal research strategies can provide useful information. Researchers must make choices, such as whether to use prospective or retrospective approaches. Another decision involves using variable-oriented methods or profile-oriented methods. In the former, the focus is on the variable to be predicted or measured, leading to quantitative data analysis; in the latter, an information profile may be the basic unit of analysis, often leading to descriptive analyses. In all cases, the researcher must start with careful analysis of the phenomena involved. The authors have provided an excellent overview of the different models that undergird longitudinal approaches.

BERGMAN asserts that longitudinal research is the most direct way of studying an individual's development over time. He points out that, optimally, researchers will spend considerable time constructing appropriate measurements and obtaining good samples; he says that too little time is spent on these, however. Once data are collected, he recommends that researchers observe raw data for interesting relationships initially, then rely on more complex statistical models to test theory. In the end, longitudinal research will be most productive when the overlap increases between the methods that experts use in asking questions and the methods developed for answering them.

In considering statistical approaches, BROWN, HARRIS & LEMYRE argue that complex multivariate statistics pose as many dangers to successful longitudinal research as they provide benefits. They assert that

> in our own field of social psychiatry we know of no important findings whose dissemination required such statistics; we suspect that most discoveries have not owed their origin to such statistics, and the statistics may at times actually have prevented important insights. (p.67)

Further, complex statistical approaches may deter some researchers with less quantitatively oriented approaches from benefiting from research. They cite research on depression to support their arguments. Specifically, if a researcher were to use multiple regression to detect the interaction between vulnerability to depression and the existence of some provoking agent as predictor of depression, the regression analysis could fail to detect such a relationship; this finding could emerge despite the fact that when depression is measured categorically (rather than continuously), such an interaction clearly exists. The authors suggest that the standard multiple regression approach using continuous variables includes the effects of too many noncausal variables. Such analysis may very well be inappropriate in research designed to open a field of inquiry. In this article, the authors have provided some compelling arguments about the need to approach longitudinal research with more varied statistical methodologies and not to forego "eyeballing" the data for obvious patterns. The authors provide a useful perspective regarding the perils of blind acceptance of what may be inappropriate statistical approaches.

As researchers have studied change over a lifespan, they have stressed the stability of personality, according to HELSON. This has meant that little attention is paid to the nature and degree of change that occurs in adulthood. Part of the problem is that some have equated the lack of maturational change across time with a lack of change altogether. The author notes that considerable stability exists in the adult personality, but that change may occur in individuals with different personality types and with different experiences. The author stresses that one of the difficulties in assessing empirical results of different research projects is the variability in measurement tools; she also stresses the importance of obtaining good samples and provides suggestions for doing so. This chapter provides a useful comparison of different perspectives regarding the study of stability and change.

One of the obvious difficulties of longitudinal research is that the research takes place over a timespan that may pose problems, such as attrition among participants, cost of continued measurement, and time commitment. Nonetheless, DUNCAN, DUNCAN & HOPS pointed out that one of the advantages of longitudinal approaches over cross-sectional approaches is that longitudinal designs permit analysis of intraindividual changes. They investigated whether an accelerated design using several short-term longitudinal studies would reduce problems associated with true longitudinal designs. They compared data from four overlapping cohorts, the cohort-sequential design, with the data from a true longi-

tudinal study spanning six years. Studying alcohol use in adolescents with both accelerated and longitudinal approaches, they found that the two approaches led to very similar results. The authors noted that the longitudinal approach might not be universally valid, but they provide helpful ideas regarding its suitability in different situations.

JANUS & GOLDBERG looked at attrition, also known as "subject mortality". They noted some of the factors that affect continued participation in longitudinal research. Over four years, they discovered that, with respect to research involving children, attrition related to parental age and socioeconomic status, health factors associated with the child, level of parental feelings of wellbeing, and degree of mother-infant attachment. They also pointed out that failure to complete the four-year study often resulted from factors beyond the control of the family.

GOODMAN & BLUM described procedures for assessing the effects of attrition. They proposed that researchers use four steps for assessing the effects of attrition. The researchers should assess a) the presence of nonrandom sampling, b) effects of non-random sampling on means, and c) on variances, and d) on relationships among variables. They proposed statistical tests for this assessment. The article introduces useful interventions when attrition may affect different components of the statistical relationship.

BERNARD C. BEINS

Longitudinal research with offenders

Farrington, D. et al., "Minimising Attrition in Longitudinal Research" in Data Quality in Longitudinal Research, edited by David Magnusson and Lars R. Bergman, Cambridge and New York: Cambridge University Press, 1990

Farrington, D., "The Development of Offending and Antisocial Behaviour from Childhood to Adulthood" in Readings in Contemporary Criminological Theory, edited by Peter Cordella and Larry Siegel, Boston: Northeastern University Press, 1996

Glueck, Sheldon and Eleanor Glueck, Juvenile Delinquents Grown Up, New York: Commonwealth Fund, 1940

Gottfredson, M. and T. Hirschi, "The True Value of Lambda Would Appear to Be Zero", Criminology, 24/2 (1986): 213–34

Menard, Scott, Longitudinal Research, London and Newbury Park, California: Sage, 1991

Sampson, Robert J. and Laub, John H., Crime in the Making: Pathways and Turning Points through Life, Cambridge, Massachusetts: Harvard University Press, 1993

Longitudinal research refers to a group of methodologies and techniques of analysis rather than to a particular methodology. It essentially means following the same respondents over a period of time, collecting data at two or more points. Usually this period of time lasts years, if not decades. This usually means that the same people are repeatedly interviewed about, amongst other things, their offending, current life style, and associated factors. This entry focuses upon longitudinal research on offending, it should be noted that the use of this technique is widespread in other fields too.

The advantages of longitudinal research, it has been claimed, are that the causal direction of relationships can be addressed (does X cause Y, or does Y cause X) and that the magnitude of such relationships can be assessed (causality is much harder to assess fully in "one-off" surveys). Possibly the best single volume introduction to longitudinal research methods is that by MENARD–but readers should be warned that this is a highly technical, professional, text and readers new to such methodologies should familiarize themselves with the key issues before approaching this text.

Longitudinal research on offending has had a long, and sometimes controversial, history in criminology. The early pioneers were Sheldon and Eleanor Glueck in the USA during the interwar years. GLUECK & GLUECK has contributed greatly to the current agenda for longitudinal research on patterns of offending. Although the Gluecks' own work is of interest, by far the most interesting analysis of their data set is that by SAMPSON & LAUB. In *Crime in the Making* (1993), Sampson & Laub argue that people's engagement in offending is mediated by structural contexts (such as family background) and by informal social bonds and social control (to friends, teachers or marriage partners). This book is an excellent place to get to grips with longitudinal research, desistance, current theoretical debates in criminology, and statistical analyses. In addition it is very well written and makes for an interesting read.

In the UK, the best-known longitudinal study of offending is that initiated by Donald West and now co-ordinated by David Farrington at Cambridge University. The Cambridge Study in Delinquent Development has followed the progress of over 400 boys from 1961 (when they were eight years old) to the present and has been exhaustively analysed and written about by Farrington and his co-workers (FARRINGTON *et al.*; FARRINGTON). The data set is one of the best examples of this style of research outside of the US and has played a key part in the development of both knowledge about patterns of offending over the life course and the theoretical debates that surround this area.

The data generated by longitudinal research have led to a number of important observations. Two, however, stand out. First, that those people who start to offend earliest are also those who continue to offend longest. Second, that whereas a large number of people (especially males) engage in criminal activities at an early age, this behaviour ceases in the late teens to early 20s and tails off significantly there after. This observation, known as the "age-crime curve", has formed the basis of a lively debate among criminologists.

In a provocative article published in 1986, GOTTFREDSON & HIRSCHI argued that the reliance upon longitudinal research methodologies in the study of patterns of offending was "unjustified" because of flawed theorizing about the relationship between age and crime and poor data analysis. The debate that this one article has stimulated has been tremendous, and it is still being argued and discussed. The full nature of the argument is too weighty to summarize here, but for those interested in a full understanding of longitudinal research the Gottfredson & Hirschi article remains essential reading.

Other problems exist with longitudinal research methodologies too. Attrition (the loss of cases over time) presents the most obvious of problems. People die, refuse further involvement in the research, become untraceable, and so on. Although techniques exist for coping with this issue, attrition still represents the biggest worry of all those undertaking longitudinal research. FARRINGTON *et al.* (1990) offer several approaches to minimizing attrition using examples drawn from their own research using the Cambridge Study in Delinquent Development. A further problem is "conditioning", which refers to the extent to which respondents learn that certain responses to certain questions lengthen the interview–and hence bias can creep into the data through respondents wishing to get the interview over. Recall represents yet a further problem: if the phases of interviewing are years apart, respondents may fail to remember salient details, or forget events altogether, leading to an undercounting of important events. On the other hand, if the phases are too close respondents may report the same event in more than one interview phase leading to over-counting. Finally, longitudinal research is costly both in terms of the money needed to fund such an exercise and the time taken to collect the data. Often answers are needed quickly in order to aid policy formation – longitudinal research may take years to generate sufficient data to deal with such concerns.

However, when undertaken with good resources and with sufficient cases to reduce the problem of attrition, longitudinal research offers researchers the opportunity to examine causal theories, chart changes in offending careers, and refine and improve questioning styles with several "chances" to ask questions about particular topics. Despite the debate started by Gottfredson & Hirschi, it is hard to imagine criminological research without longitudinal research.

STEPHEN FARRALL

See also Criminology

Looking-glass self

Cooley, Charles Horton, *Human Nature and the Social Order*, New York: Schocken, 1964 (originally published 1902)

Franks, David D. and Viktor Gecas, "Autonomy and Conformity in Cooley's Self-Theory: The Looking-Glass Self and Beyond", *Symbolic Interaction*, 15/1 (1992): 49–68

Gecas, Viktor and Michael L. Schwalbe, "Beyond the Looking-Glass Self: Social Structure and Efficacy-Based Self-Esteem", *Social Psychology Quarterly*, 46/2 (1983): 77–88

Mead, George Herbert, "Cooley's Contribution to American Social Thought" (written 1930) in *On Social Psychology: Selected Papers*, edited by Anselm Strauss, Chicago: University of Chicago Press, 1964; revised edition 1977

Petryszak, Nicholas G.L., "Human Nature and the Social Self", *Sociologia Internationalis*, 14/1–2 (1976): 23–36

Reitzes, Donald C. and William E. Hall, "Cooley Revisited: The Treatment of Cooley's Sociological Orientation in Introductory Textbooks", *Sociological Spectrum*, 2/2 (1982): 133–56

Winterer, Caroline, "A Happy Medium: The Sociology of Charles Horton Cooley", *Journal of the History of Behavioral Sciences*, 30 (1994): 19–27

The influence of the notion of looking-glass self in social psychology and sociology has been vast: the phrase has been freely used for nearly a century, and is still mentioned in social psychology and sociology textbooks. However, it can also be said that the meaning of this impact is illusory because the looking-glass self has never been extensively studied with reference to its introducer's – Charles Horton Cooley – overall ideas on society and the social. The selected sources represent the fragmentary nature of the discussions of the looking-glass self as well as its often uninformed use, but also include a general presentation of Cooley's sociology.

The "reflected" or "looking-glass" self was introduced by the American sociologist COOLEY in *Human Nature and the Social Order*, to denote the self as being structured through the process of social interaction. "A self-idea of this sort seems to have three principal elements: the imagination of our appearance to the other person; the imagination of his judgment of that appearance, and some sort of self-feeling, such as pride or mortification" (p.184). Cooley did not particularly stress the looking-glass self as a concept, but his name remains strongly associated with it, probably because it exemplifies his social psychological vantage point. According to Cooley, the ideas that we human beings have of one another are the solid facts of society. In considering self and society as twin-born and inseparable phases of a common whole, he took an organic view of the social process – the social being psychological and vice versa. However, he also emphasized the subjective element of interpretation or imagination. As WINTERER argues, it is not so much the subject of the self's genesis – a subject inspired by William James – but the conception of science and methodology, for example his use of introspection, that differentiates Cooley from his contemporaries such as George Herbert Mead.

MEAD, the founding father of social interactionism, was highly appreciative of Cooley's "establishment of self and others on the same plane of reality" (p.307) but criticized him for being too psychological, i.e. taking only the mental conception of the social into account. He argued that Cooley failed to acknowledge the necessary distinction between the possible objective and direct experience of the other and the social on the one hand, and the psychical, subjective aspects of self and other on the other hand, thus closing the door to a scientific (objective) conception of society. Mead also pointed out that Cooley's method of introspection restricted the validity of his analysis to the social reality of the American community of which he was a part.

Several authors have remarked that whereas Cooley's looking-glass self served as a major reference within social psychology, his understanding of society and social processes in general – based on the idea of organic growth and social relativity – received less serious attention. REITZES & HALL demonstrated that Cooley's name is foremost associated with catchphrases and the single concepts of the looking-glass self and primary group. This can possibly explain the circulation of distorted interpretations of these concepts and of fragmented presentations of Cooley's theoretical orientation.

The social conception of self, attributed to Cooley, was especially powerful in sociology until the 1980s. Viktor Gecas has co-authored several articles that are critical to this overall emphasis on the social determination of self to the detriment of the more active role of human beings. In their 1983 article, GECAS & SCHWALBE attributed the passive and oversocialized view of human beings in sociology to the overemphasis on the looking-glass self as a general metaphor for the construction of self, and argued for more attention to the active part played by self-efficacy in the construction of self. In 1992, FRANKS & GECAS rephrased that criticism by stating that because so much attention had been lavished on Cooley's notion of the looking-glass self and the passive view of the actor that this entails, his view of an active and assertive self, so evident in his general social psychology, has largely been neglected.

In his discussion of the pragmatists and symbolic interactionists, PETRYSZAK argues in favour of including the element of human nature in the sociological analysis of personality and behaviour. Petryszak considers that the pervasive social conception of self is not necessarily antagonistic to the sociobiological viewpoint, the rising star of the 1970s. With respect to Cooley, he posits that most critics of the looking-glass self turned a blind eye to his ideas on innate human nature, i.e. socially-oriented instincts. His discussion, though tendentious, is nevertheless interesting because it addresses and assesses Cooley's notion of social self as part of a "social generation of the social self" (p.27).

KATRIEN LIBBRECHT

See also Self, Symbolic interactionism

Love

Berscheid, Ellen, "Interpersonal Relationships", *Annual Review of Psychology*, 45 (1994): 79–129

Brehm, Sharon S., *Intimate Relationships*, 2nd edition, New York and London: McGraw Hill, 1992

Buss, David M., *The Evolution of Desire: Strategies of Human Mating*, New York: Basic Books, 1994

Hatfield, Elaine and G.W. Walster, *A New Look at Love*, Reading, Massachusetts: Addison Wesley, 1978

Hazan, Cindy and Phillip Shaver, "Attachment as an Organizational Framework for Research on Close Relationships", *Psychological Inquiry*, 5/1 (1994): 1–22

Lee, John Alan, *The Colors of Love*, Englewood Cliffs, New Jersey: Prentice Hall, 1976

Rubin, Zick, *Liking and Loving: An Invitation to Social Psychology*, New York: Holt Rinehart, 1973

Rusbult, Caryl, "Commitment and Satisfaction in Romantic Associations: A Test of the Investment Model", *Journal of Experimental Social Psychology*, 16 (1980): 101–17

Simpson, Jeffry A. and W. Steven Rholes (editors), *Attachment Theory and Close Relationships*, New York: Guilford Press, 1998

Sternberg, Robert J. and Michael L. Barnes, *The Psychology of Love*, New Haven, Connecticut: Yale University Press, 1988

Sternberg, Robert, "A Triangular Theory of Love", *Psychological Review*, 93 (1986): 119–35

Once considered the realm of philosophy and mysticism, love and associated concepts have become areas of burgeoning interest and empirical research in the social sciences. While no one conceptualization has proven superior, many theories and taxonomies of types of love have been offered with differing levels of empirical support. Investigators have employed a variety of approaches in the study of love, including approaches that are psychometric, evolutionary, cognitive, and qualitative. Consequently, there is a wide range of available literature on love. The following citations are intended to serve as a starting point for the interested reader and represent those sources that provide either comprehensive reviews or key advances in the study of love.

RUBIN's influential text served as the catalyst for later typologies of love by differentiating between two types of affectionate attachments. In a cardinal study, Rubin presented college students with a series of statements indicative of interpersonal relationships and asked them to endorse those that applied to their friends and those that applied to their romantic partners. On the basis of students' differential responsiveness to these statements, Rubin proposed that liking and loving are distinct and mutually exclusive to an intimate relationship and developed one of the first psychometric instruments for their assessment.

HATFIELD & WALSTER made a distinction between two types of love: passionate and companionate. Passionate love is defined as "a state of intense longing for union with another". Companionate love is defined as "the affection we feel for those with whom our lives are deeply entwined". Drawing on theories of emotion, Hatfield and Walster propose that a central difference between passionate and companionate love is arousal. Passionate love is characterized as a state of intense physiological arousal accompanied by the attribution of that arousal to the beloved. In contrast, companionate love is characterized as involving friendship, trust, understanding, and concern for the welfare of another.

LEE presents a typology of love styles using colour as a metaphor. Just as there are three primary colours, Lee maintains that there are three primary love styles that form the basis for myriad combinations. These primary love styles include eros (love based on physical attraction and passion), storge (love based on long-term involvement and friendship), and ludus (a noncommittal style of loving). Further, Lee emphasizes three secondary love styles: mania, agape, and pragma. These six love styles differ in the intensity of the loving experience, desired characteristics of the beloved, expectations about being loved in return, and commitment to the beloved. Lee contends that relationship satisfaction is a function of the congruence between partner's love styles.

STERNBERG takes a psychometric approach to love, attempting to identify the dimensions that underlie heterosexual love relationships. He proposes a triangular theory of love that consists of three primary dimensions that can combine to produce a range of loving experiences. Sternberg predicts that many proposed subtypes of love can be accounted for by different combinations of intimacy, passion, and decision/ commitment. Intimacy is the emotional component of love, which involves feelings of closeness, bondedness, and attachment. Passion is the motivational component of love, which describes romantic sexual attraction. Decision/commitment is the cognitive component of love, which includes the decision that one is "in love" and intentions to continue the relationship. Sternberg describes eight major types of relationships ranging from non-love to consummate love. Further, the triangular theory provides an account of the temporal course of love and the predictors of relationship satisfaction.

In contrast to the triangular theory of love, RUSBULT considered love one feature of commitment and the most important predictor of relationship satisfaction. Drawing on interdependence theory, Rusbult proposed an investment model of commitment. Commitment is defined as "the tendency to maintain a relationship and to feel psychologically attached to it." The investment model contends that commitment results from three factors: satisfaction, investments, and quality of alternatives. Rusbult's model extends previous typologies of love by offering a conceptual explanation for relationship stability and duration. That is, the investment model offers a process-oriented approach to the study of love and romantic relationships.

Other psychologists have taken an evolutionary approach to the study of heterosexual love. BUSS has spearheaded this evolutionary conceptualization and associated research, focusing primarily on mate selection preferences. The evolutionary model contends that individuals are biologically motivated to act in ways that promote reproductive success. Accordingly, Buss views love as a "category of naturally occurring actions" that have had proximate goals in the generation and reproductive success of offspring. Buss proposes that love, or love acts, have four primary goals: to attract a mate, to retain a mate, to reproduce with the mate, and to invest parentally in the resulting offspring. The evolutionary approach to love offers a conceptual explanation for gender differences in relational behaviour, as well as for parenting versus partnering love. Consequently, the evolutionary approach has generated a tremendous amount of interest and empirical research.

HAZAN & SHAVER approach the study of love using attachment theory as an organizational framework. This article provides an extensive review of the empirical literature on close relationships and love in an attempt to demonstrate that attachment theory can incorporate a broad range of findings on adult relationships. They also demonstrate how attachment theory addresses a wide array of research questions concerning the functions, emotional dynamics, evolutionary origins, and developmental pathways of human affectional bonds. Overall, this article presents one of the most comprehensive theories of love and close relationships.

In their new book SIMPSON & RHOLES provide a scholarly and integrative review of the major theoretical and empirical issues in adult attachment theory. This text addresses measurement issues, affect regulation processes, clinical applications, and conceptual and empirical extensions of adult attachment theory in an attempt to integrate and consolidate important theoretical and empirical advances. Over the last decade, no single area of research in personality or social psychology has attracted more attention or more interest than the application of attachment theory to adult romantic relationships. Simpson & Rholes provides the most comprehensive text available on this issue, a must read for individuals interested in the study of love or close relationships.

BERSCHEID presents a comprehensive review of the empirical research and theory on love and close relationships. This article addresses the current state of the field with regard to relationship cognition, the representation of self and others, relationship schemas, attributional processes in relationships, love, jealousy, social support, and relationship dissolution. As a result of its breadth of coverage, this article represents a good starting point for individuals interested in theory, methodology, and empirical research on love and close relationships.

Two comprehensive texts on love and close relationships are currently available. BREHM provides a good overall account of the available empirical research and theory on interpersonal attraction, love and romance, sexuality, relationship development, reciprocity, communication, social power, jealousy, conflict and dissolution, loneliness, and therapeutic interventions. This work could serve as a textbook for undergraduate courses on romantic relationships and, because of its breadth of focus, provides a good general text for the interested reader.

STERNBERG & BARNES provide a comprehensive, more in-depth account of the major theories of love. This text addresses global theories of love, theories of romantic love, and theories of relationship maintenance, with sections written by the major theorists in each area. It is an outstanding resource for both scholars and students in the social sciences interested in love and close relationships.

NATHAN L. WILLIAMS

Lucas critique, *see* Public choice theory and rational expectations